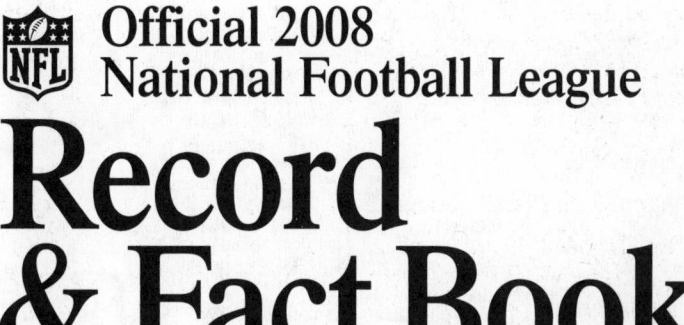

Official 2008
National Football League
Record
& Fact Book

NATIONAL FOOTBALL LEAGUE
280 Park Avenue, New York, N.Y. 10017 (212) 450-2000. NFL Internet Address: http://www.NFL.com

Printed in the United States of America.

A National Football League Book.

Compiled by the NFL Communications Department and Seymour Siwoff, Elias Sports Bureau.
Statistics by Elias Sports Bureau.

Edited by Jon Zimmer, NFL Co⬚ ⬚, and Matt Marini. Layout by Will⬚ ⬚ NFL Creative.
Produced by NFL Communicatio⬚

Cover photograph of Eli Manning ⬚ ⬚pion New York Giants by Andy Ly⬚

HOME ENTERTAINMENT

Time Inc. Home Entertainment
1271 Avenue of the Americas, Ne⬚
Manufactured in the United States
First printing, July 2008.
10 9 8 7 6 5 4 3 2 1

TABLE OF CONTENTS

All times local. Dates and times subject to change.
Nationally televised games indicated by network in parentheses.

PRESEASON 2008	**Sunday, August 3**	Hall of Fame Game at Canton, Ohio	
		Washington _____ vs. Indianapolis _____	(NBC) 8:00
PRESEASON/WEEK 1	**Thursday, August 7**	New Orleans _____ at Arizona _____	(ESPN) 5:00
		N.Y. Giants _____ at Detroit _____	7:00
		Baltimore _____ at New England _____	7:30
		N.Y. Jets _____ at Cleveland _____	7:30
		Kansas City _____ at Chicago _____	7:00
	Friday, August 8	Philadelphia _____ at Pittsburgh _____	7:30
		Seattle _____ at Minnesota _____	7:00
		San Francisco _____ at Oakland _____	7:00
	Saturday, August 9	Buffalo _____ at Washington _____	7:00
		Atlanta _____ at Jacksonville _____	7:30
		Indianapolis _____ at Carolina _____	7:30
		Tampa Bay _____ at Miami _____	7:30
		Denver _____ at Houston _____	7:00
		St. Louis _____ at Tennessee _____	7:00
		Dallas _____ at San Diego _____	7:00
	Monday, August 11	Cincinnati _____ at Green Bay _____	(ESPN) 7:00
PRESEASON/WEEK 2	**Thursday, August 14**	Pittsburgh _____ at Buffalo (Toronto) _____	7:30
		Carolina _____ at Philadelphia _____	(FOX) 8:00
	Friday, August 15	Oakland _____ at Tennessee _____	(FOX) 7:00
	Saturday, August 16	Washington _____ at N.Y. Jets _____	7:00
		Indianapolis _____ at Atlanta _____	7:30
		Miami _____ at Jacksonville _____	7:30
		Minnesota _____ at Baltimore _____	7:30
		Arizona _____ at Kansas City _____	7:00
		Houston _____ at New Orleans _____	7:00
		San Diego _____ at St. Louis _____	7:00
		Chicago _____ at Seattle _____	6:00
		Dallas _____ at Denver _____	7:00
		Green Bay _____ at San Francisco _____	6:00
	Sunday, August 17	Detroit _____ at Cincinnati _____	7:35
		New England _____ at Tampa Bay _____	(NFLN) 8:00
	Monday, August 18	Cleveland _____ at N.Y. Giants _____	(ESPN) 8:00
PRESEASON/WEEK 3	**Thursday, August 21**	San Francisco _____ at Chicago _____	(FOX) 7:00
	Friday, August 22	Tennessee _____ at Atlanta _____	7:30
		Philadelphia _____ at New England _____	7:30
		Houston _____ at Dallas _____	7:00
		Green Bay _____ at Denver _____	7:00
	Saturday, August 23	Cleveland _____ at Detroit _____	4:00
		N.Y. Giants _____ at N.Y. Jets _____	7:00
		Jacksonville _____ at Tampa Bay _____	7:30
		Kansas City _____ at Miami _____	7:30
		Washington _____ at Carolina _____	7:30
		New Orleans _____ at Cincinnati _____	7:35
		Pittsburgh _____ at Minnesota _____	(CBS) 7:00
		Baltimore _____ at St. Louis _____	7:00
		Arizona _____ at Oakland _____	6:00
	Sunday, August 24	Buffalo _____ at Indianapolis _____	(NFLN) 8:00
	Monday, August 25	Seattle _____ at San Diego _____	(ESPN) 5:00

2008 NFL Record & Fact Book

PRESEASON/WEEK 4

Thursday, August 28	Detroit _____ at Buffalo _____	6:30
	N.Y. Jets _____ at Philadelphia _____	6:30
	Atlanta _____ at Baltimore _____	7:00
	Cincinnati _____ at Indianapolis _____	7:00
	Jacksonville _____ at Washington _____	(NBC) 7:00
	New England _____ at N.Y. Giants _____	7:00
	Carolina _____ at Pittsburgh _____	7:30
	Chicago _____ at Cleveland _____	7:30
	Miami _____ at New Orleans _____	7:00
	Minnesota _____ at Dallas _____	7:00
	St. Louis _____ at Kansas City _____	7:00
	Tampa Bay _____ at Houston _____	7:00
	Tennessee _____ at Green Bay _____	7:00
Friday, August 29	Denver _____ at Arizona _____	7:00
	Oakland _____ at Seattle _____	7:00
	San Diego _____ at San Francisco _____	7:00

KICKOFF WEEKEND

Thursday, September 4	Washington _____ at N.Y. Giants _____	(NBC) 7:00
Sunday, September 7	Detroit _____ at Atlanta _____	1:00
FOX-TV National Weekend	Cincinnati _____ at Baltimore _____	1:00
	Seattle _____ at Buffalo _____	1:00
	N.Y. Jets _____ at Miami _____	1:00
	Kansas City _____ at New England _____	1:00
	Tampa Bay _____ at New Orleans _____	12:00
	St. Louis _____ at Philadelphia _____	1:00
	Houston _____ at Pittsburgh _____	1:00
	Jacksonville _____ at Tennessee _____	12:00
	Dallas _____ at Cleveland _____	4:15
	Carolina _____ at San Diego _____	1:15
	Arizona _____ at San Francisco _____	1:15
	Chicago _____ at Indianapolis _____	(NBC) 8:15
Monday, September 8	Minnesota _____ at Green Bay _____	(ESPN) 6:00
	Denver _____ at Oakland _____	(ESPN) 7:15

SECOND WEEKEND

Sunday, September 14	Chicago _____ at Carolina _____	1:00
CBS-TV National Weekend	Tennessee _____ at Cincinnati _____	1:00
	Green Bay _____ at Detroit _____	1:00
	Buffalo _____ at Jacksonville _____	1:00
	Oakland _____ at Kansas City _____	12:00
	Indianapolis _____ at Minnesota _____	12:00
	N.Y. Giants _____ at St. Louis _____	12:00
	New Orleans _____ at Washington _____	1:00
	San Francisco _____ at Seattle _____	1:05
	Atlanta _____ at Tampa Bay _____	4:05
	Miami _____ at Arizona _____	1:15
	San Diego _____ at Denver _____	2:15
	Baltimore _____ at Houston _____	3:15
	New England _____ at N.Y. Jets _____	4:15
	Pittsburgh _____ at Cleveland _____	(NBC) 8:15
Monday, September 15	Philadelphia _____ at Dallas _____	(ESPN) 7:30

THIRD WEEKEND

Sunday, September 21	Kansas City _____ at Atlanta _____	1:00
CBS-TV National Weekend	Oakland _____ at Buffalo _____	1:00
	Tampa Bay _____ at Chicago _____	12:00
	Carolina _____ at Minnesota _____	12:00
	Miami _____ at New England _____	1:00
	Cincinnati _____ at N.Y. Giants _____	1:00
	Houston _____ at Tennessee _____	12:00
	Arizona _____ at Washington _____	1:00
	New Orleans _____ at Denver _____	2:05
	Detroit _____ at San Francisco _____	1:05
	St. Louis _____ at Seattle _____	1:05
	Cleveland _____ at Baltimore _____	4:15
	Jacksonville _____ at Indianapolis _____	4:15
	Pittsburgh _____ at Philadelphia _____	4:15
	Dallas _____ at Green Bay _____	(NBC) 7:15
Monday, September 22	N.Y. Jets _____ at San Diego _____	(ESPN) 5:30

FOURTH WEEKEND
Open Dates:
Detroit, Indianapolis, Miami,
New England, N.Y. Giants, Seattle

Sunday, September 28
FOX-TV National Weekend

Atlanta _____ at Carolina _____	1:00
Cleveland _____ at Cincinnati _____	1:00
Houston _____ at Jacksonville _____	1:00
Denver _____ at Kansas City _____	12:00
San Francisco _____ at New Orleans _____	12:00
Arizona _____ at N.Y. Jets _____	1:00
Green Bay _____ at Tampa Bay _____	1:00
Minnesota _____ at Tennessee _____	12:00
San Diego _____ at Oakland _____	1:05
Buffalo _____ at St. Louis _____	3:05
Washington _____ at Dallas _____	3:15
Philadelphia _____ at Chicago _____	(NBC) 7:15

Monday, September 29

Baltimore _____ at Pittsburgh _____	(ESPN) 8:30

FIFTH WEEKEND
Open Dates:
Cleveland, N.Y. Jets, St. Louis, Oakland

Sunday, October 5
CBS-TV National Weekend

Tennessee _____ at Baltimore _____	1:00
Kansas City _____ at Carolina _____	1:00
Chicago _____ at Detroit _____	1:00
Atlanta _____ at Green Bay _____	12:00
Indianapolis _____ at Houston _____	12:00
San Diego _____ at Miami _____	1:00
Seattle _____ at N.Y. Giants _____	1:00
Washington _____ at Philadelphia _____	1:00
Tampa Bay _____ at Denver _____	2:05
Buffalo _____ at Arizona _____	1:15
Cincinnati _____ at Dallas _____	3:15
New England _____ at San Francisco _____	1:15
Pittsburgh _____ at Jacksonville _____	(NBC) 8:15

Monday, October 6

Minnesota _____ at New Orleans _____	(ESPN) 7:30

SIXTH WEEKEND
Open Dates:
Buffalo, Kansas City, Pittsburgh, Tennessee

Sunday, October 12
FOX-TV National Weekend

Chicago _____ at Atlanta _____	1:00
Miami _____ at Houston _____	12:00
Baltimore _____ at Indianapolis _____	1:00
Detroit _____ at Minnesota _____	12:00
Oakland _____ at New Orleans _____	12:00
Cincinnati _____ at N.Y. Jets _____	1:00
Carolina _____ at Tampa Bay _____	1:00
St. Louis _____ at Washington _____	1:00
Jacksonville _____ at Denver _____	2:05
Dallas _____ at Arizona _____	1:15
Philadelphia _____ at San Francisco _____	1:15
Green Bay _____ at Seattle _____	1:15
New England _____ at San Diego _____	(NBC) 5:15

Monday, October 13

N.Y. Giants _____ at Cleveland _____	(ESPN) 8:30

SEVENTH WEEKEND
Open Dates:
Arizona, Atlanta, Jacksonville, Philadelphia

Sunday, October 19
CBS-TV National Weekend

San Diego _____ at Buffalo _____	1:00
New Orleans _____ at Carolina _____	1:00
Minnesota _____ at Chicago _____	12:00
Pittsburgh _____ at Cincinnati _____	1:00
Tennessee _____ at Kansas City _____	12:00
Baltimore _____ at Miami _____	1:00
San Francisco _____ at N.Y. Giants _____	1:00
Dallas _____ at St. Louis _____	12:00
Detroit _____ at Houston _____	3:05
Indianapolis _____ at Green Bay _____	3:15
N.Y. Jets _____ at Oakland _____	1:15
Cleveland _____ at Washington _____	4:15
Seattle _____ at Tampa Bay _____	(NBC) 8:15

Monday, October 20

Denver _____ at New England _____	(ESPN) 8:30

EIGHTH WEEKEND
Open Dates:
Chicago, Cincinnati, Denver, Green Bay, Houston, Minnesota

INTERNATIONAL SERIES

Sunday, October 26	Oakland _____ at Baltimore _____	1:00
FOX-TV National Weekend	Arizona _____ at Carolina _____	1:00
	Tampa Bay _____ at Dallas _____	12:00
	Washington _____ at Detroit _____	1:00
	Buffalo _____ at Miami _____	1:00
	St. Louis _____ at New England _____	1:00
	San Diego _____ at New Orleans (London) _____	5:00
	Kansas City _____ at N.Y. Jets _____	1:00
	Atlanta _____ at Philadelphia _____	1:00
	Cleveland _____ at Jacksonville _____	4:05
	N.Y. Giants _____ at Pittsburgh _____	4:15
	Seattle _____ at San Francisco _____	1:15
Monday, October 27	Indianapolis _____ at Tennessee _____	(ESPN) 7:30

NINTH WEEKEND
Open Dates:
Carolina, New Orleans, San Diego, San Francisco

Sunday, November 2	N.Y. Jets _____ at Buffalo _____	1:00
FOX-TV National Weekend	Detroit _____ at Chicago _____	12:00
	Jacksonville _____ at Cincinnati _____	1:00
	Baltimore _____ at Cleveland _____	1:00
	Tampa Bay _____ at Kansas City _____	12:00
	Houston _____ at Minnesota _____	12:00
	Arizona _____ at St. Louis _____	12:00
	Green Bay _____ at Tennessee _____	12:00
	Miami _____ at Denver _____	2:05
	Dallas _____ at N.Y. Giants _____	4:15
	Atlanta _____ at Oakland _____	1:15
	Philadelphia _____ at Seattle _____	1:15
	New England _____ at Indianapolis _____	(NBC) 8:15
Monday, November 3	Pittsburgh _____ at Washington _____	(ESPN) 8:30

TENTH WEEKEND
Open Dates:
Baltimore, Dallas,
Tampa Bay, Washington

Thursday, November 6	Denver _____ at Cleveland _____	(NFLN) 8:15
Sunday, November 9	New Orleans _____ at Atlanta _____	1:00
CBS-TV National Weekend	Tennessee _____ at Chicago _____	12:00
	Jacksonville _____ at Detroit _____	1:00
	Cincinnati _____ at Houston _____	12:00
	Seattle _____ at Miami _____	1:00
	Green Bay _____ at Minnesota _____	12:00
	Buffalo _____ at New England _____	1:00
	St. Louis _____ at N.Y. Jets _____	1:00
	Carolina _____ at Oakland _____	1:05
	Indianapolis _____ at Pittsburgh _____	4:15
	Kansas City _____ at San Diego _____	1:15
	N.Y. Giants _____ at Philadelphia _____	(NBC) 8:15
Monday, November 10	San Francisco _____ at Arizona _____	(ESPN) 6:30

ELEVENTH WEEKEND

Thursday, November 13	N.Y. Jets _____ at New England _____	(NFLN) 8:15
Sunday, November 16	Denver _____ at Atlanta _____	1:00
CBS-TV National Weekend	Detroit _____ at Carolina _____	1:00
	Philadelphia _____ at Cincinnati _____	1:00
	Chicago _____ at Green Bay _____	12:00
	Houston _____ at Indianapolis _____	1:00
	Tennessee _____ at Jacksonville _____	1:00
	New Orleans _____ at Kansas City _____	12:00
	Oakland _____ at Miami _____	1:00
	Baltimore _____ at N.Y. Giants _____	1:00
	Minnesota _____ at Tampa Bay _____	1:00
	St. Louis _____ at San Francisco _____	1:05
	Arizona _____ at Seattle _____	1:05
	San Diego _____ at Pittsburgh _____	4:15
	Dallas _____ at Washington _____	(NBC) *8:15
Monday, November 17	Cleveland _____ at Buffalo _____	(ESPN) 8:30

*-Sunday Night Games In Weeks 11-16 Subject To Change

TWELFTH WEEKEND

Thursday, November 20	Cincinnati _____ at Pittsburgh _____	(NFLN) 8:15
Sunday, November 23	Carolina _____ at Atlanta _____	1:00
FOX-TV National Weekend	Philadelphia _____ at Baltimore _____	1:00
	Houston _____ at Cleveland _____	1:00
	San Francisco _____ at Dallas _____	12:00
	Tampa Bay _____ at Detroit _____	1:00
	Minnesota _____ at Jacksonville _____	1:00
	Buffalo _____ at Kansas City _____	12:00
	New England _____ at Miami _____	1:00
	Chicago _____ at St. Louis _____	12:00
	N.Y. Jets _____ at Tennessee _____	12:00
	Oakland _____ at Denver _____	2:05
	N.Y. Giants _____ at Arizona _____	2:15
	Washington _____ at Seattle _____	1:15
	Indianapolis _____ at San Diego _____	(NBC) *5:15
Monday, November 24	Green Bay _____ at New Orleans _____	(ESPN) 7:30

*-Sunday Night Games In Weeks 11-16 Subject To Change

THIRTEENTH WEEKEND

NFL THANKSGIVING 2008

Thursday, November 27	Tennessee _____ at Detroit _____	(CBS) 12:30
	Seattle _____ at Dallas _____	(FOX) 3:15
	Arizona _____ at Philadelphia _____	(NFLN) 8:15
Sunday, November 30	San Francisco _____ at Buffalo _____	1:00
CBS-TV National Weekend	Baltimore _____ at Cincinnati _____	1:00
	Indianapolis _____ at Cleveland _____	1:00
	Carolina _____ at Green Bay _____	12:00
	Denver _____ at N.Y. Jets _____	1:00
	Miami _____ at St. Louis _____	12:00
	New Orleans _____ at Tampa Bay _____	1:00
	N.Y. Giants _____ at Washington _____	1:00
	Atlanta _____ at San Diego _____	1:05
	Pittsburgh _____ at New England _____	4:15
	Kansas City _____ at Oakland _____	1:15
	Chicago _____ at Minnesota * _____	(NBC) *7:15
Monday, December 1	Jacksonville _____ at Houston _____	(ESPN) 7:30

*-Sunday Night Games In Weeks 11-16 Subject To Change

FOURTEENTH WEEKEND

Thursday, December 4	Oakland _____ at San Diego _____	(NFLN) 5:15
Sunday, December 7	Washington _____ at Baltimore _____	1:00
FOX-TV National Weekend	Jacksonville _____ at Chicago _____	12:00
	Minnesota _____ at Detroit _____	1:00
	Houston _____ at Green Bay _____	12:00
	Cincinnati _____ at Indianapolis _____	1:00
	Atlanta _____ at New Orleans _____	12:00
	Philadelphia _____ at N.Y. Giants _____	1:00
	Cleveland _____ at Tennessee _____	12:00
	Miami _____ at Buffalo (Toronto) _____	4:05
	Kansas City _____ at Denver _____	2:05
	N.Y. Jets _____ at San Francisco _____	1:05
	St. Louis _____ at Arizona _____	2:15
	Dallas _____ at Pittsburgh _____	4:15
	New England _____ at Seattle _____	(NBC) *5:15
Monday, December 8	Tampa Bay _____ at Carolina _____	(ESPN) 8:30

*-Sunday Night Games In Weeks 11-16 Subject To Change

FIFTEENTH WEEKEND

Thursday, December 11	New Orleans _____ at Chicago _____	(NFLN) 7:15
Sunday, December 14	Tampa Bay _____ at Atlanta _____	1:00
CBS-TV National Weekend	Pittsburgh _____ at Baltimore _____	1:00
	Denver _____ at Carolina _____	1:00
	Washington _____ at Cincinnati _____	1:00
	Tennessee _____ at Houston _____	12:00
	Detroit _____ at Indianapolis _____	1:00
	Green Bay _____ at Jacksonville _____	1:00
	San Diego _____ at Kansas City _____	12:00
	San Francisco _____ at Miami _____	1:00
	Buffalo _____ at N.Y. Jets _____	1:00
	Seattle _____ at St. Louis _____	12:00
	Minnesota _____ at Arizona _____	2:05
	New England _____ at Oakland _____	1:15
	N.Y. Giants _____ at Dallas _____	(NBC) *7:15
Monday, December 15	Cleveland _____ at Philadelphia _____	(ESPN) 8:30

*-Sunday Night Games In Weeks 11-16 Subject To Change

SIXTEENTH WEEKEND

Thursday, December 18	Indianapolis _____ at Jacksonville _____	(NFLN) 8:15
Saturday, December 20	Baltimore _____ at Dallas _____	(NFLN) 7:15
Sunday, December 21	Cincinnati _____ at Cleveland _____	1:00
FOX-TV National Weekend	New Orleans _____ at Detroit _____	1:00
	Miami _____ at Kansas City _____	12:00
	Atlanta _____ at Minnesota _____	12:00
	Arizona _____ at New England _____	1:00
	Carolina _____ at N.Y. Giants _____	1:00
	San Francisco _____ at St. Louis _____	12:00
	Pittsburgh _____ at Tennessee _____	12:00
	Philadelphia _____ at Washington _____	1:00
	Buffalo _____ at Denver _____	2:05
	Houston _____ at Oakland _____	1:05
	N.Y. Jets _____ at Seattle _____	1:05
	San Diego _____ at Tampa Bay _____	(NBC) *8:15
Monday, December 22	Green Bay _____ at Chicago _____	(ESPN) 7:30

*-Sunday Night Games In Weeks 11-16 Subject To Change

SEVENTEENTH WEEKEND

Sunday, December 28	St. Louis _____ at Atlanta _____	1:00
CBS-TV and FOX-TV National Weekend	Jacksonville _____ at Baltimore _____	1:00
	New England _____ at Buffalo _____	1:00
	Kansas City _____ at Cincinnati _____	1:00
	Detroit _____ at Green Bay _____	12:00
	Chicago _____ at Houston _____	12:00
	Tennessee _____ at Indianapolis _____	1:00
	N.Y. Giants _____ at Minnesota _____	12:00
	Carolina _____ at New Orleans _____	12:00
	Miami _____ at N.Y. Jets _____	1:00
	Dallas _____ at Philadelphia _____	1:00
	Cleveland _____ at Pittsburgh _____	1:00
	Oakland _____ at Tampa Bay _____	1:00
	Seattle _____ at Arizona _____	2:15
	Denver _____ at San Diego _____	1:15
	Washington _____ at San Francisco _____	1:15

*-Sunday Night Game In Week 17 TBD

PLAYOFFS

Wild Card Playoff Games
Site Priorities
Two Wild Card teams (division non-champions with best two records) from each conference and the division champions with the third and fourth-best record in each conference will enter the first round of the playoffs. The division champion with the third-best record will play host to the Wild Card team with the second-best record. The division champion with the fourth-best record will play host to the Wild Card team with the best record. There are no restrictions on intra-division games.

Saturday, January 3, 2009 American Football Conference

_____ at _____ (NBC)

National Football Conference

_____ at _____ (NBC)

Sunday, January 4, 2009 American Football Conference

_____ at _____ (CBS)

National Football Conference

_____ at _____ (FOX)

Divisional Playoff Games
Site Priorities
In each conference, the two division champions with the highest won-lost-tied percentage during the regular season will play host to the Wild Card winners. The division champion with the best record in each conference is assured of playing the lowest seeded Wild Card survivor. There are no restrictions on intra-division games.

Saturday, January 10, 2009 American Football Conference

_____ at _____ (CBS)

National Football Conference

_____ at _____ (FOX)

Sunday, January 11, 2009 American Football Conference

_____ at _____ (CBS)

National Football Conference

_____ at _____ (FOX)

Championship Games
Site Priorities for
Championship Games
The home teams will be the surviving playoff winners with the highest seeds. A Wild Card team cannot play host unless two Wild Card teams are in the game, in which case the Wild Card team that was seeded highest in the first round of the playoffs will be the home team.

Sunday, January 18, 2009 American Football Conference

_____ at _____ (CBS)

National Football Conference

_____ at _____ (FOX)

Super Bowl XLIII

Sunday, February 1, 2009 Super Bowl XLIII at Raymond James Stadium, Tampa, Florida

_____ vs. _____ (NBC)

AFC-NFC Pro Bowl

Sunday, February 8, 2009 AFC-NFC Pro Bowl at Aloha Stadium, Honolulu, Hawaii

AFC_____ vs. NFC _____ (NBC)

2008 NATIONALLY TELEVISED PRIME-TIME GAMES
All times ET.

Thursday, Sept. 4	Washington at N.Y. Giants (NBC)	7:00
Sunday, Sept. 7	Chicago at Indianapolis (NBC)	8:15
Monday, Sept. 8	Minnesota at Green Bay (ESPN)	7:00
	Denver at Oakland (ESPN)	10:15
Sunday, Sept. 14	Pittsburgh at Cleveland (NBC)	8:15
Monday, Sept. 15	Philadelphia at Dallas (ESPN)	8:30
Sunday, Sept. 21	Dallas at Green Bay (NBC)	8:15
Monday, Sept. 22	N.Y. Jets at San Diego (ESPN)	8:30
Sunday, Sept. 28	Philadelphia at Chicago (NBC)	8:15
Monday, Sept. 29	Baltimore at Pittsburgh (ESPN)	8:30
Sunday, Oct. 5	Pittsburgh at Jacksonville (NBC)	8:15
Monday, Oct. 6	Minnesota at New Orleans (ESPN)	8:30
Sunday, Oct. 12	New England at San Diego (NBC)	8:15
Monday, Oct. 13	N.Y. Giants at Cleveland (ESPN)	8:30
Sunday, Oct. 19	Seattle at Tampa Bay (NBC)	8:15
Monday, Oct. 20	Denver at New England (ESPN)	8:30
Monday, Oct. 27	Indianapolis at Tennessee (ESPN)	8:30
Sunday, Nov. 2	New England at Indianapolis (NBC)	8:15
Monday, Nov. 3	Pittsburgh at Washington (ESPN)	8:30
Thursday, Nov. 6	Denver at Cleveland (NFL Network)	8:15
Sunday, Nov. 9	N.Y. Giants at Philadelphia (NBC)	8:15
Monday, Nov. 10	San Francisco at Arizona (ESPN)	8:30
Thursday, Nov. 13	N.Y. Jets at New England (NFL Network)	8:15
Sunday, Nov. 16	Dallas at Washington (NBC)*	8:15
Monday, Nov. 17	Cleveland at Buffalo (ESPN)	8:30
Thursday, Nov. 20	Cincinnati at Pittsburgh (NFL Network)	8:15
Sunday, Nov. 23	Indianapolis at San Diego (NBC)*	8:15
Monday, Nov. 26	Green Bay at New Orleans (ESPN)	8:30
Thursday, Nov. 27	Tennessee at Detroit (CBS)	12:30
	Seattle at Dallas (FOX)	4:15
	Arizona at Philadelphia (NFL Network)	8:15
Sunday, Nov. 30	Chicago at Minnesota (NBC)*	8:15
Monday, Dec. 1	Jacksonville at Houston (ESPN)	8:30
Thursday, Dec. 4	Oakland at San Diego (NFL Network)	8:15
Sunday, Dec. 7	New England at Seattle (NBC)*	8:15
Monday, Dec. 8	Tampa Bay at Carolina (ESPN)	8:30
Thursday, Dec. 11	New Orleans at Chicago (NFL Network)	8:15
Sunday, Dec. 14	N.Y. Giants at Dallas (NBC)*	8:15
Monday, Dec. 15	Cleveland at Philadelphia (ESPN)	8:30
Thursday, Dec. 18	Indianapolis at Jacksonville (NFL Network)	8:15
Saturday, Dec. 20	Baltimore at Dallas (NFL Network)	8:15
Sunday, Dec. 21	San Diego at Tampa Bay (NBC)*	8:15
Monday, Dec. 22	Green Bay at Chicago (ESPN)	8:00
Sunday, Dec. 28	To be determined (NBC)*	8:15

POSTSEASON GAMES

Saturday, January 3	AFC and NFC Wild Card Playoffs (NBC)
Sunday, January 4	AFC and NFC Wild Card Playoffs (CBS and FOX)
Saturday, January 10	AFC and NFC Divisional Playoffs (CBS and FOX)
Sunday, January 11	AFC and NFC Divisional Playoffs (CBS and FOX)
Sunday, January 18	AFC and NFC Championship Games (CBS and FOX)
Sunday, February 1	Super Bowl XLIII in Tampa, Florida (NBC)
Sunday, February 8	AFC-NFC Pro Bowl in Honolulu, Hawaii (NBC)

*The NFL again will utilize "flexible scheduling" in 2008.

Flexible scheduling moves will be announced at least 12 days before games in Weeks 11-16. In Week 17, the flexible scheduling move will be announced at least six days before the game. Flexible scheduling will ensure quality matchups on Sunday night in those weeks and give "surprise" teams a chance to play their way on to primetime.

2008

July 7 — Claiming period of 24 hours begins in waiver system.

Mid-July — Preseason training camps open. Clubs not permitted to open official preseason camp earlier than July 5. Veteran players cannot be required to report earlier than 15 days prior to club's first preseason game.

July 15 — Deadline at 4 P.M., New York time, for any club that designated a Franchise Player to sign such player to a multi-year contract or extension. After this date, the player may sign only a one-year contract with the designating club for the 2008 season, and such contract cannot be extended until after the Club's last regular season game.

July 22 — Signing period ends at 4 P.M., New York time, for Transition Players with outstanding tenders. After this date and through 4 P.M., New York time, on the Tuesday after the 10th regular season weekend, Old Club has exclusive negotiating rights to these players.

July 22# — Signing period ends at 4 P.M., New York time, for Unrestricted Free Agents to whom a June 1 tender was made by Old Club. After this date and through 4 P.M., New York time, on the Tuesday after the 10th regular season weekend, Old Club has exclusive negotiating rights to these players.
#or the first scheduled day of the first NFL training camp, whichever is later.

August 1-3 — Hall of Fame Weekend.

August 3 — Pro Football Hall of Fame Game, Canton, Ohio: Indianapolis vs. Washington

August 5 — Deadline for players under contract to report to earn a season of free-agency credit.

August 8 — If a Drafted Rookie has not signed with his club by this date, he may not be traded to any other club in 2008.

August 7-11 — First Preseason Weekend.

August 9-13 — Deadline for club to provide written notice to certain unsigned players and the NFLPA of its intent to place them on the Exempt List if they fail to report no later than one day prior to the club's second preseason game. Any player who fails to report prior to the deadline will be ineligible to play or receive compensation for at least three games (preseason or regular season) from the time that he reports.

August 26 — Roster cut-down to maximum of 75 players on Active List by 4 P.M., New York time.

August 27 — All tryouts on this date and for the remainder of the season must be reported to the League office.

August 30 — Roster cut-down to maximum of 53 players on Active/Inactive List by 4 P.M., New York time. Clubs may dress minimum of 42 and maximum of 45 players and Third Quarterback for each regular-season and postseason game.

August 30 — Simultaneously with the cut-down to 53, clubs that have players in the categories of Active/Physically Unable to Perform or Active/Non-Football Injury or Illness must take one of the following options: place player on Reserve/Physically Unable to Perform or Reserve/Non-Football Injury or Illness, whichever is applicable; ask waivers; terminate; trade; or continue to count him on Active List.

August 31 — After 12 noon, New York time, clubs may establish a Practice Squad of eight players by signing free agents who do not have an accrued season of free-agency credit or who were on the 45-player Active List for less than nine regular-season games during their only Accrued Season(s). A player cannot participate on the Practice Squad for more than three seasons.

September 3 — All clubs are required to file a personnel (injury) report with their conference information manager by 4:00 p.m., New York time. Reports are to be filed every Wednesday, Thursday and Friday before a regular-season game by 4:00 p.m., New York time (or as soon as possible after the completion of practice). An update must also be reported if there is any change in a player's condition after Friday.

September 3 — Beginning at 4 P.M., New York time, Team Salary includes all players receiving compensation under their 2008 contracts. Top 51 rule is no longer in effect.

September 4-8 — Regular Season opens.

September 4-8 — Beginning on these dates vested veterans terminated from the Active List or Inactive List (and from Reserve/Injured if the player is placed on Reserve/Injured after the beginning of the regular season) are entitled to receive, after the end of the regular-season schedule, Termination Pay pursuant to the terms of the CBA.

September 23 — Priority on multiple waiver claims is now based on the current season's standing.

October 14 — Beginning the day after the conclusion of the sixth regular-season weekend and continuing through the day after the conclusion of the ninth regular-season weekend, clubs are permitted to begin practicing players on Reserve/Physically Unable to Perform and Reserve/Non-Football Injury or Illness for a period not to exceed 21 days. Players may be activated during the 21-day practice period or until 4 P.M., New York time, on the day after the conclusion of the 21-day period.

October 14 — All trading ends at 4 P.M., New York time.

October 15 — Players with at least four previous pension-credited seasons are subject to the waiver system for the remainder of the regular season and postseason.

November 3	Deadline at 4 P.M., New York time, for an increase in a player's 2008 Salary to be counted as Salary for the current year. Any notice of an increase in a player's 2008 Salary received by the NFLMC after this deadline will be treated as a Signing Bonus.
November 11	Signing period ends at 4 P.M., New York time, for Franchise Players who are eligible to receive Offer Sheets.
November 11	Deadline for clubs to sign by 4 P.M., New York time, their unsigned Franchise and Transition Players, including Franchise Players who were eligible to receive Offer Sheets until this date. If still unsigned after this date, such players are prohibited from playing in NFL in 2008.
November 11	Deadline for clubs to sign by 4 P.M., New York time, their Unrestricted Free Agents to whom June 1 tender was made. If still unsigned after this date, such players are prohibited from playing in NFL in 2008.
November 11	Deadline for clubs to sign by 4 P.M., New York time, their Restricted Free Agents to whom June 1 tender was made. If such players remain unsigned, they are prohibited from playing in NFL in 2008.
November 11	Deadline for clubs to sign Drafted players by 4 P.M., New York time. If such players remain unsigned, they are prohibited from playing in NFL in 2008.
November 29	Deadline for reinstatement of players in Reserve List categories of Retired, Did Not Report, and Exclusive Rights, and of players who were placed on Reserve/Left Squad in a previous season.
December 26	Deadline for waiver requests in 2008, except for "special waiver requests," which have a 10-day claiming period, with termination or assignment delayed until after the Super Bowl.
December 29	Clubs may begin signing free-agent players for the 2009 season.

2009

January 3-4	Wild Card Playoff Games.
January 10-11	Divisional Playoff Games.
January 18	AFC and NFC Championship Games.
February 1	Super Bowl XLIII, Raymond James Stadium, Tampa, Florida.
February 8	AFC-NFC Pro Bowl, Honolulu, Hawaii.

2010

February 7	Super Bowl XLIV, Dolphin Stadium, South Florida.

2011

February 6	Super Bowl XLV, Dallas Cowboys New Stadium, North Texas.

2012

February 5	Super Bowl XLVI, Lucas Oil Stadium, Indianapolis, Indiana

The NFL is online to provide fans and media quick and easy access to all the latest professional football information.

NFL.COM—(http://NFL.com or AOL Keyword: NFL.com)
NFL.com, the league's year-round home page on the Internet, enters its 12th season in cyberspace. The site provides NFL information during the regular season, postseason, and offseason, including:

NEWS/STATS: Up-to-the-minute news from around the league, plus game previews, injury reports, and player and team stats.

GAMEDAY COVERAGE: The site showcases NFL Films video highlights of the previous week's games as well as upcoming matchups. Video also supports feature stories and team highlight clips from every game last season. In addition, exclusive NFL Network programming is featured.

VIDEO HIGHLIGHTS: The site showcases NFL Films video highlights of the previous week's games as well as upcoming matchups. Video also supports feature stories and team highlight clips from every game last season. In addition, exclusive NFL Network programming is featured.

TEAM AREAS: Customized areas for all 32 clubs, featuring updated rosters, depth carts, and all the latest news from the teams.

SUPERBOWL.COM—(http://SuperBowl.com)
Look for SuperBowl.com in late December for complete coverage of the playoffs and Super Bowl XLIII. The multimedia site follows all postseason action and features audio and video clips of past Super Bowls.

During the week leading up to Super Bowl XLIII, the site will go "live" from Tampa Bay, providing coverage of events, press conferences, and chats with Super Bowl players and coaches. On Super Bowl Sunday, SuperBowl.com will showcase a live Internet cybercast, complete with online commentators calling the action. The site also features digital photos from the game, live public address audio and press box announcements, and live audio from foreign broadcasts.

NFLATINO.COM POWERED BY UNIVISION.COM—(http://NFLatino.com)
The official U.S. Spanish-language site of the NFL provides in-depth information on teams and players, and is the only destination online for NFL video highlights in Spanish. In addition, the site includes Hispanic player diaries, live radio broadcasts, up-to-date stats, as well as fantasy football.

NFLYOUTHFOOTBALL.COM—(http://nflyouthfootball.com)
NFLyouthfootball.com is the NFL's official youth football website. Boys and girls ages 6-18 can be a part of something big by getting involved nationwide with one of the NFL's Youth Football programs. Coaches, parents, and youth organizations can learn how to host their own local NFL Punt, Pass, and Kick event and can learn how to get children involved with an NFL FLAG league in their local community. Our website is also a resource for coaches and parents to help them promote a positive experience for all youth participants.

NFLRUSH.COM—(http://www.NFLRUSH.com)
NFLRUSH.com is the official kids' website of the National Football League. The site offers an NFL experience solely for kids, with unique customizable content, games, contests, fun daily features on NFL players and information on the NFL's Youth Football programs. NFLRUSH.com also features fun and interactive fitness information as part of the NFL PLAY 60 campaign, which encourages kids to be active for 60 minutes a day. The NFLRUSH ZONE, a role playing game on NFLRUSH.com, was launched in December 2007. The NFLRUSH ZONE is an immersive virtual world where kids are able to create avatars, play games, chat, watch cartoons and compete with friends all in a safe and fun environment. NFLRUSH.com, which is targeted to kids 6-15, provides an environment where kids can share their interest in their NFL and delivers the NFL experience they want to have – as a fan or player or both.

USAFOOTBALL.COM—(http://usafootball.com)
USA Football, America's independent national governing body of the sport on youth and amateur levels, provides resources for players, coaches, game officials, league administrators and youth players' parents. The site encompasses all things football, teaching the game's fundamentals and emphasizing its qualities of leadership, responsibility and teamwork. The non-profit provides coaching and officiating education through more than 100 football-specific training events annually as well as through its nationally-recognized coaching and officiating training curriculum at usafootball.com. Based near Washington, D.C., USA Football was endowed by the NFL and NFLPA in 2002.

JOINTHETEAM.COM—(http://JoinTheTeam.com)
JoinTheTeam.com is the official website dedicated to the off-the-field community work of the NFL and the member clubs. The site provides news and information regarding how the NFL gives back and serves as a useful tool for individuals who are looking for a way to make a difference in their communities. As part of the NFL's Join The Team platform, the site encourages people to unite with NFL teams, players and partners to give back to communities across America. The site also serves as the online home for NFL Charities, and provides opportunities to learn about and apply for funding. JoinTheTeam.com highlights the ways the league, our teams and our fans come together to make a difference through community involvement.

PROFOOTBALLHOF.COM—(http://profootballhof.com)
Profootballhof.com is the official site of the Pro Football Hall of Fame in Canton, Ohio. In addition to a complete visitor's guide to the Hall, the site features bios, stories and Q & A's with Hall of Fame inductees, a detailed archive of football history, and information on appearances by members of the Hall.

OFFICIAL NFL TEAM SITES
In addition to a dedicated area on NFL.com, all 32 teams have their own Websites, which have separate URLs, and are linked from NFL.com.

Arizona Cardinals (www.azcardinals.com)
Atlanta Falcons (www.atlantafalcons.com)
Baltimore Ravens (www.baltimoreravens.com)
Buffalo Bills (www.buffalobills.com)
Carolina Panthers (www.panthers.com)
Chicago Bears (www.chicagobears.com)
Cincinnati Bengals (www.bengals.com)
Cleveland Browns (www.clevelandbrowns.com)
Dallas Cowboys (www.dallascowboys.com)
Denver Broncos (www.denverbroncos.com)
Detroit Lions (www.detroitlions.com)
Green Bay Packers (www.packers.com)
Houston Texans (www.houstontexans.com)
Indianapolis Colts (www.colts.com)
Jacksonville Jaguars (www.jaguars.com)
Kansas City Chiefs (www.kcchiefs.com)
Miami Dolphins (www.miamidolphins.com)
Minnesota Vikings (www.vikings.com)
New England Patriots (www.patriots.com)
New Orleans Saints (www.neworleanssaints.com)
New York Giants (www.giants.com)
New York Jets (www.newyorkjets.com)
Oakland Raiders (www.raiders.com)
Philadelphia Eagles (www.philadelphiaeagles.com)
Pittsburgh Steelers (www.steelers.com)
St. Louis Rams (www.stlouisrams.com)
San Diego Chargers (www.chargers.com)
San Francisco 49ers (www.sf49ers.com)
Seattle Seahawks (www.seahawks.com)
Tampa Bay Buccaneers (www.buccaneers.com)
Tennessee Titans (www.titansonline.com)
Washington Redskins (www.redskins.com)

NFL Network provides fans with a network to call their own. Seven days a week, 24 hours a day, 365 days a year, fans turn to NFL Network to receive information and insight straight from the field, team headquarters, league offices and wherever else the NFL is making news.

NFL Network gives fans unprecedented year-round access to all NFL events, including the Super Bowl, Playoffs, regular season, preseason, Pro Bowl, Pro Football Hall of Fame induction weekend, NFL Draft, Scouting Combine, Senior Bowl, Insight Bowl, Texas Bowl, league meetings, minicamps and training camps.

In addition, NFL Network is the only place on television for fans to view NFL games outside their initial live airings. From original broadcast versions of past Super Bowls, in-week replays of current games, original network telecasts of classic NFL regular season and postseason games, to live telecasts of preseason games, regular season NFL games and college bowl games— NFL Network is truly the year-round destination for football fans.

NFL Network is available on cable, telcos and satellite television through your local service provider. If your provider doesn't currently offer NFL Network, please call (866) NFL-NETWORK to make them aware of your interest in receiving it.

KEY PROGRAMMING

EXCLUSIVE LIVE PRIMETIME GAMES
NFL Network's eight-game, regular-season Thursday Night primetime schedule kicks off in high definition on November 6. Each game, at 8:00 PM ET, will be preceded by a two-hour onsite pregame show and followed by a live post-game show from the field.

NFL TOTAL ACCESS
NFL Network's signature show is the football show of record. *NFL Total Access* is uniquely structured to see the game through the participants' eyes, airing at 6:00 PM ET every Monday and 7:00 PM ET each Tuesday through Saturday and hosted by Rich Eisen.

Covering all 32 teams, *NFL Total Access* features interviews with players, coaches and other key league personnel. Using the most advanced technology, *NFL Total Access* has the ability to go live to any NFL team headquarters at any time.

NFL GAMEDAY
After each Sunday's final game, the 90-minute *NFL GameDay* delivers comprehensive coverage of the day's action. Host Rich Eisen is joined by Steve Mariucci and Deion Sanders. *NFL GameDay* kicks off at 11:30 PM ET and features highlights, post-game press conferences, on-field interviews, analysis and more in wrapping up each NFL Sunday. *GameDay* runs in a continuous loop until 6:00 PM ET each Monday.

NFL REPLAY
NFL games will be re-aired with the original television announcers and cameras. This offering features the five most exciting games each week in a 90-minute format (eliminating halftime and other non-critical elements) at 7:00 PM ET on Mondays and 8:00 PM ET and 9:30 PM ET each Tuesday and Wednesday. Enhancements to each broadcast include additional camera angles, sideline sound and post-game interviews.

PLAYBOOK
NFL Network uses the "all 22" game film watched each week by coaches and players to present football's ultimate chalkboard show. Twice each week – at 8:00 PM ET Thursday and Friday.

Playbook offers 60-minute strategy sessions with Brian Baldinger, Sterling Sharpe and Solomon Wilcots, who analyze each week's key matchups and discuss technique and game planning with coaches and players.

AMERICA'S GAME
This Sports Emmy-winning original series continues its profiles of Super Bowl champions with the 2007 New York Giants. In addition, a new group of shows in the series—*America's Game: The Missing Rings*—debuts on NFL Network in September on Thursdays at 10:00 PM ET. *Missing Rings* chronicles some of the greatest teams which did not win the Super Bowl.

NFL's TOP 10
Putting a fresh twist on the countdown genre, *NFL's Top 10* is a fast-paced series airing Saturdays at 9:00 PM ET. *NFL's Top 10* provides an irreverent look at some of the most intriguing subjects in the NFL, creating and debating a top ten list for each category. Each 60-minute episode counts down from No. 10 to the top ranking in each category.

COLLEGE FOOTBALL NOW
Join college football experts Mike Mayock, Charles Davis and Paul Burmeister at 6:30 PM ET from Tuesday through Friday for a daily dose of college football highlights, news and analysis. The *College Football Now* trio analyzes the college game's top players, teams, rivalries and traditions in each 30-minute episode.

NFL CLASSICS
The only place on television to catch the complete network broadcasts of classic NFL regular season and playoff games is on NFL Network every Friday at 9:00 PM ET. Each *NFL Classics* telecast features the original network announcers and graphics.

NFL SCOREBOARD
After Sunday's early games conclude, *NFL Scoreboard* takes viewers around the league for post-game press conferences and game highlights. *NFL Scoreboard* airs at 4:00 PM ET on Sundays and continues through the Sunday evening game.

RED ZONE
NFL Network provides the best place on television to get up-to-the-minute scores, statistics and news each game day during the season. Airing at 1:00 PM ET on Sundays, *Red Zone* features continuously scrolling real-time game statistics with audio from Sirius NFL Radio's *Around the League* program.

PRESEASON GAMES
NFL Network is the only place on television where fans can view the majority of NFL preseason games. This summer, NFL Network televises 54 preseason games—every game that does not appear on the four NFL broadcast partners (CBS, FOX, NBC, and ESPN).

SCHEDULING FORMULA

The NFL expanded to 32 teams in 2002 with the addition of the Houston Texans. In addition, the NFL realigned for the first time since 1970—into eight divisions of four teams each—and the scheduling formula that was introduced guarantees for the first time that all teams play each other on a regular, rotating basis. Although the number of teams has increased to 32, the number of playoff teams remains the same at 12.

Under the NFL scheduling formula, every team within a division plays 16 games as follows:

- Home and away against its three division opponents (6 games).
- The four teams from another division within its conference on a rotating three-year cycle (4 games).
- The four teams from a division in the other conference on a rotating four-year cycle (4 games).
- Two intraconference games based on the prior year's standings (2 games). These games will match a first-place team against the first-place teams in the two same-conference divisions the team is not scheduled to play that season. The second-place, third-place, and fourth-place teams in a conference will be matched in the same way each year.

The schedule format takes each team through a cycle of games—home and away—against every other team in the league. From 2002-2009, every team will play every other team at least twice—once home and once away. After the 2009 season, a decision will be made on whether to continue with the same rotation or modify it.

In determining how to begin the divisional rotation in 2002, the displacement of teams from their old divisions in the new alignment was taken into account. Preference was given to scheduling games with former division rivals and other regional opponents for clubs realigned from otherwise intact divisions.

FUTURE SCHEDULING ROTATION

		2008	2009
AFC EAST	Intraconference	AFCW	AFCS
	Interconference	NFCW	NFCS
AFC NORTH	Intraconference	AFCS	AFCW
	Interconference	NFCE	NFCN
AFC SOUTH	Intraconference	AFCN	AFCE
	Interconference	NFCN	NFCW
AFC WEST	Intraconference	AFCE	AFCN
	Interconference	NFCS	NFCE
NFC EAST	Intraconference	NFCW	NFCS
	Interconference	AFCN	AFCW
NFC NORTH	Intraconference	NFCS	NFCW
	Interconference	AFCS	AFCN
NFC SOUTH	Intraconference	NFCN	NFCE
	Interconference	AFCW	AFCE
NFC WEST	Intraconference	NFCE	NFCN
	Interconference	AFCE	AFCS

AFC EAST NON-DIVISIONAL OPPONENTS 2008-2009

BUFFALO BILLS

	2008 Home	Away	2009 Home	Away
	2008		**2009**	
	Home	**Away**	**Home**	**Away**
Intraconference by Division	OAK	DEN	HOU	JAX
	SD	KC	IND	TENN
Interconference by Division	SF	ARIZ	NO	ATL
	SEA	STL	TB	CAR
Intraconference by Position	AFCN	AFCS	AFCN	AFCW

MIAMI DOLPHINS

	2008		**2009**	
	Home	**Away**	**Home**	**Away**
Intraconference by Division	OAK	DEN	HOU	JAX
	SD	KC	IND	TENN
Interconference by Division	SF	ARIZ	NO	ATL
	SEA	STL	TB	CAR
Intraconference by Position	AFCN	AFCS	AFCN	AFCW

NEW ENGLAND PATRIOTS

	2008		**2009**	
	Home	**Away**	**Home**	**Away**
Intraconference by Division	DEN	OAK	JAX	HOU
	KC	SD	TENN	IND
Interconference by Division	ARIZ	SF	ATL	NO
	STL	SEA	CAR	TB
Intraconference by Position	AFCN	AFCS	AFCN	AFCW

NEW YORK JETS

	2008		**2009**	
	Home	**Away**	**Home**	**Away**
Intraconference by Division	DEN	OAK	JAX	HOU
	KC	SD	TENN	IND
Interconference by Division	ARIZ	SF	ATL	NO
	STL	SEA	CAR	TB
Intraconference by Position	AFCN	AFCS	AFCN	AFCW

AFC NORTH NON-DIVISIONAL OPPONENTS 2008-2009

BALTIMORE RAVENS

	2008		**2009**	
	Home	**Away**	**Home**	**Away**
Intraconference by Division	JAX	HOU	DEN	OAK
	TENN	IND	KC	SD
Interconference by Division	PHIL	DALL	CHI	GB
	WASH	NYG	DET	MINN
Intraconference by Position	AFCW	AFCE	AFCS	AFCE

CINCINNATI BENGALS

	2008		**2009**	
	Home	**Away**	**Home**	**Away**
Intraconference by Division	JAX	HOU	DEN	OAK
	TENN	IND	KC	SD
Interconference by Division	PHIL	DALL	CHI	GB
	WASH	NYG	DET	MINN
Intraconference by Position	AFCW	AFCE	AFCS	AFCE

CLEVELAND BROWNS

	2008		**2009**	
	Home	**Away**	**Home**	**Away**
Intraconference by Division	HOU	JAX	OAK	DEN
	IND	TENN	SD	KC
Interconference by Division	DALL	PHIL	GB	CHI
	NYG	WASH	MINN	DET
Intraconference by Position	AFCW	AFCE	AFCS	AFCE

PITTSBURGH STEELERS

	2008		**2009**	
	Home	**Away**	**Home**	**Away**
Intraconference by Division	HOU	JAX	OAK	DEN
	IND	TENN	SD	KC
Interconference by Division	DALL	PHIL	GB	CHI
	NYG	WASH	MINN	DET
Intraconference by Position	AFCW	AFCE	AFCS	AFCE

AFC SOUTH NON-DIVISIONAL OPPONENTS 2008-2009

HOUSTON TEXANS

	2008 Home	Away	2009 Home	Away
Intraconference by Division	BALT	CLE	NE	BUFF
	CIN	PITT	NYJ	MIA
Interconference by Division	CHI	GB	SF	ARIZ
	DET	MINN	SEA	STL
Intraconference by Position	AFCE	AFCW	AFCW	AFCN

INDIANAPOLIS COLTS

	2008 Home	Away	2009 Home	Away
Intraconference by Division	BALT	CLE	NE	BUFF
	CIN	PITT	NYJ	MIA
Interconference by Division	CHI	GB	SF	ARIZ
	DET	MINN	SEA	STL
Intraconference by Position	AFCE	AFCW	AFCW	AFCN

JACKSONVILLE JAGUARS

	2008 Home	Away	2009 Home	Away
Intraconference by Division	CLE	BALT	BUFF	NE
	PITT	CIN	MIA	NYJ
Interconference by Division	GB	CHI	ARIZ	SF
	MINN	DET	STL	SEA
Intraconference by Position	AFCE	AFCW	AFCW	AFCN

TENNESSEE TITANS

	2008 Home	Away	2009 Home	Away
Intraconference by Division	CLE	BALT	BUFF	NE
	PITT	CIN	MIA	NYJ
Interconference by Division	GB	CHI	ARIZ	SF
	MINN	DET	STL	SEA
Intraconference by Position	AFCE	AFCW	AFCW	AFCN

AFC WEST NON-DIVISIONAL OPPONENTS 2008-2009

DENVER BRONCOS

	2008 Home	Away	2009 Home	Away
Intraconference by Division	BUFF	NE	CLE	BALT
	MIA	NYJ	PITT	CIN
Interconference by Division	NO	ATL	DALL	PHIL
	TB	CAR	NYG	WASH
Intraconference by Position	AFCS	AFCN	AFCE	AFCS

KANSAS CITY CHIEFS

	2008 Home	Away	2009 Home	Away
Intraconference by Division	BUFF	NE	CLE	BALT
	MIA	NYJ	PITT	CIN
Interconference by Division	NO	ATL	DALL	PHIL
	TB	CAR	NYG	WASH
Intraconference by Position	AFCS	AFCN	AFCE	AFCS

OAKLAND RAIDERS

	2008 Home	Away	2009 Home	Away
Intraconference by Division	NE	BUFF	BALT	CLE
	NYJ	MIA	CIN	PITT
Interconference by Division	ATL	NO	PHIL	DALL
	CAR	TB	WASH	NYG
Intraconference by Position	AFCS	AFCN	AFCE	AFCS

SAN DIEGO CHARGERS

	2008 Home	Away	2009 Home	Away
Intraconference by Division	NE	BUFF	BALT	CLE
	NYJ	MIA	CIN	PITT
Interconference by Division	ATL	NO	PHIL	DALL
	CAR	TB	WASH	NYG
Intraconference by Position	AFCS	AFCN	AFCE	AFCS

NFC EAST NON-DIVISIONAL OPPONENTS 2008-2009

DALLAS COWBOYS

	2008 Home	2008 Away	2009 Home	2009 Away
Intraconference by Division	SF	ARIZ	ATL	NO
	SEA	STL	CAR	TB
Interconference by Division	BALT	CLE	OAK	DEN
	CIN	PITT	SD	KC
Intraconference by Position	NFCS	NFCN	NFCW	NFCN

NEW YORK GIANTS

	2008 Home	2008 Away	2009 Home	2009 Away
Intraconference by Division	SF	ARIZ	ATL	NO
	SEA	STL	CAR	TB
Interconference by Division	BALT	CLE	OAK	DEN
	CIN	PITT	SD	KC
Intraconference by Position	NFCS	NFCN	NFCW	NFCN

PHILADELPHIA EAGLES

	2008 Home	2008 Away	2009 Home	2009 Away
Intraconference by Division	ARIZ	SF	NO	ATL
	STL	SEA	TB	CAR
Interconference by Division	CLE	BALT	DEN	OAK
	PITT	CIN	KC	SD
Intraconference by Position	NFCS	NFCN	NFCW	NFCN

WASHINGTON REDSKINS

	2008 Home	2008 Away	2009 Home	2009 Away
Intraconference by Division	ARIZ	SF	NO	ATL
	STL	SEA	TB	CAR
Interconference by Division	CLE	BALT	DEN	OAK
	PITT	CIN	KC	SD
Intraconference by Position	NFCS	NFCN	NFCW	NFCN

NFC NORTH NON-DIVISIONAL OPPONENTS 2008-2009

CHICAGO BEARS

	2008 Home	2008 Away	2009 Home	2009 Away
Intraconference by Division	NO	ATL	ARIZ	SF
	TB	CAR	STL	SEA
Interconference by Division	JAX	HOU	CLE	BALT
	TENN	IND	PITT	CIN
Intraconference by Position	NFCE	NFCW	NFCE	NFCS

DETROIT LIONS

	2008 Home	2008 Away	2009 Home	2009 Away
Intraconference by Division	NO	ATL	ARIZ	SF
	TB	CAR	STL	SEA
Interconference by Division	JAX	HOU	CLE	BALT
	TENN	IND	PITT	CIN
Intraconference by Position	NFCE	NFCW	NFCE	NFCS

GREEN BAY PACKERS

	2008 Home	2008 Away	2009 Home	2009 Away
Intraconference by Division	ATL	NO	SF	ARIZ
	CAR	TB	SEA	STL
Interconference by Division	HOU	JAX	BALT	CLE
	IND	TENN	CIN	PITT
Intraconference by Position	NFCE	NFCW	NFCE	NFCS

MINNESOTA VIKINGS

	2008 Home	2008 Away	2009 Home	2009 Away
Intraconference by Division	ATL	NO	SF	ARIZ
	CAR	TB	SEA	STL
Interconference by Division	HOU	JAX	BALT	CLE
	IND	TENN	CIN	PITT
Intraconference by Position	NFCE	NFCW	NFCE	NFCS

NFC SOUTH NON-DIVISIONAL OPPONENTS 2008-2009

ATLANTA FALCONS

	2008 Home	Away	2009 Home	Away
Intraconference by Division	CHI	GB	PHIL	DALL
	DET	MINN	WASH	NYG
Interconference by Division	DEN	OAK	BUFF	NE
	KC	SD	MIA	NYJ
Intraconference by Position	NFCW	NFCE	NFCN	NFCW

CAROLINA PANTHERS

	2008 Home	Away	2009 Home	Away
Intraconference by Division	CHI	GB	PHIL	DALL
	DET	MINN	WASH	NYG
Interconference by Division	DEN	OAK	BUFF	NE
	IKC	SD	MIA	NYJ
Intraconference by Position	NFCW	NFCE	NFCN	NFCW

NEW ORLEANS SAINTS

	2008 Home	Away	2009 Home	Away
Intraconference by Division	GB	CHI	DALL	PHIL
	MINN	DET	NYG	WASH
Interconference by Division	OAK	DEN	NE	BUFF
	SD	KC	NYJ	MIA
Intraconference by Position	NFCW	NFCE	NFCN	NFCW

TAMPA BAY BUCCANEERS

	2008 Home	Away	2009 Home	Away
Intraconference by Division	GB	CHI	DALL	PHIL
	MINN	DET	NYG	WASH
Interconference by Division	OAK	DEN	NE	BUFF
	SD	KC	NYJ	MIA
Intraconference by Position	NFCW	NFCE	NFCN	NFCW

NFC WEST NON-DIVISIONAL OPPONENTS 2008-2009

ARIZONA CARDINALS

	2008 Home	Away	2009 Home	Away
Intraconference by Division	DALL	PHIL	GB	CHI
	NYG	WASH	MINN	DET
Interconference by Division	BUFF	NE	HOU	JAX
	MIA	NYJ	IND	TENN
Intraconference by Position	NFCN	NFCS	NFCS	NFCE

ST. LOUIS RAMS

	2008 Home	Away	2009 Home	Away
Intraconference by Division	DALL	PHIL	GB	CHI
	NYG	WASH	MINN	DET
Interconference by Division	BUFF	NE	HOU	JAX
	MIA	NYJ	IND	TENN
Intraconference by Position	NFCN	NFCS	NFCS	NFCE

SAN FRANCISCO 49ERS

	2008 Home	Away	2009 Home	Away
Intraconference by Division	PHIL	DALL	CHI	GB
	WASH	NYG	DET	MINN
Interconference by Division	NE	BUFF	JAX	HOU
	NYJ	MIA	TENN	IND
Intraconference by Position	NFCN	NFCS	NFCS	NFCE

SEATTLE SEAHAWKS

	2008 Home	Away	2009 Home	Away
Intraconference by Division	PHIL	DALL	CHI	GB
	WASH	NYG	DET	MINN
Interconference by Division	NE	BUFF	JAX	HOU
	NYJ	MIA	TENN	IND
Intraconference by Position	NFCN	NFCS	NFCS	NFCE

TOP ACTIVE PASSERS
1,000 or more attempts

		Yrs.	Att.	Comp.	Pct. Comp.	Yards	TD	Pct. TD	Had Int.	Pct. Int.	Ratings Pts.
1.	Peyton Manning, Ind.	10	5,405	3,468	64.2	41,626	306	5.7	153	2.8	94.7
2.	Kurt Warner, Ari.	10	2,959	1,926	65.1	24,008	152	5.1	100	3.4	93.2
3.	Tom Brady, N.E.	8	3,642	2,294	63.0	26,370	197	5.4	86	2.4	92.9
4.	Ben Roethlisberger, Pit.	4	1,436	908	63.2	11,673	84	5.8	54	3.8	92.5
5.	Carson Palmer, Cin.	4	2,036	1,305	64.1	14,899	104	5.1	63	3.1	90.1
6.	Daunte Culpepper, *	9	2,927	1,867	63.8	22,422	142	4.9	94	3.2	89.9
7.	Chad Pennington, NYJ	8	1,919	1,259	65.6	13,738	82	4.3	55	2.9	88.9
8.	Marc Bulger, St.L.	6	2,484	1,578	63.5	18,625	106	4.3	74	3.0	88.1
9.	Drew Brees, N.O.	7	3,015	1,921	63.7	21,189	134	4.4	82	2.7	87.9
10.	Jeff Garcia, T.B.	9	3,300	2,020	61.2	22,825	149	4.5	77	2.3	87.2
11.	Trent Green, St.L.	10	3,668	2,228	60.7	27,950	162	4.4	108	2.9	86.9
12.	Matt Hasselbeck, Sea.	9	3,138	1,904	60.7	22,333	142	4.5	84	2.7	86.2
13.	Donovan McNabb, Phi.	9	3,732	2,189	58.7	25,404	171	4.6	79	2.1	85.8
14.	Jake Delhomme, Car.	7	2,020	1,206	59.7	14,589	100	5.0	64	3.2	85.2
15.	Mark Brunell, N.O.	14	4,594	2,738	59.6	31,826	182	4.0	106	2.3	84.2
16.	Brian Griese, T.B.	10	2,612	1,642	62.9	18,367	114	4.4	92	3.5	83.6
17.	Brad Johnson, Dal.	14	4,248	2,627	61.8	28,627	164	3.9	117	2.8	83.1
18.	Byron Leftwich, *	5	1,402	821	58.6	9,321	52	3.7	38	2.7	79.7
19.	Charlie Batch, Pit.	10	1,459	818	56.1	10,033	57	3.9	44	3.0	77.9
20.	Jon Kitna , Det.	11	3,994	2,394	59.9	26,535	147	3.7	146	3.7	76.8
21.	Vinny Testaverde, *	21	6,701	3,787	56.5	46,233	275	4.1	267	4.0	75.0
22.	David Carr, NYG	6	2,206	1,316	59.7	14,026	62	2.8	70	3.2	74.4
23.	Gus Frerotte, Min.	14	2,805	1,521	54.2	19,134	102	3.6	91	3.2	74.3
24.	Eli Manning, NYG	4	1,805	987	54.7	11,385	77	4.3	64	3.5	73.4
25.	Kerry Collins, Ten.	14	5,254	2,918	55.5	34,717	174	3.3	172	3.3	73.3

TOP ACTIVE SCORERS
(number in parentheses represents 2-point conversions scored)

		Yrs.	TD	FG	PAT	TP
1.	Morten Andersen, *	25	0	565	849	2,544
2.	Matt Stover, Bal.	17	0	435	517	1,822
3.	John Carney, *	20	0	425	537	1,812
4.	Jason Elam, Atl.	15	0	395	601	1,786
5.	Jason Hanson, Det.	16	0	385	504	1,659
6.	John Kasay, Car.	17	0	358	430	1,504
7.	Adam Vinatieri, Ind.	12	0	311	454(1)	1,389
8.	Ryan Longwell, Min.	11	0	267	442	1,243
9.	Olindo Mare, Sea.	11	0	255	347	1,112
10.	David Akers, Phi.	10	0	197	308	899
11.	Kris Brown, Hou.	9	0	202	267	873
12.	Joe Nedney, S.F.	12	0	199	261	858
13.	Sebastian Janikowski, Oak.	8	0	179	271	808
14.	Terrell Owens, Dal.	12	131	0	0(3)	792
15.	Phil Dawson, Cle.	9	1	182	237	789
16.	Jay Feely, Mia.	7	0	177	249	780
17.	LaDainian Tomlinson, S.D.	7	129	0	0	774
18.	Rian Lindell, Buf.	8	0	175	248	773
19.	Randy Moss, N.E.	10	125	0	0(3)	756
20.	Marvin Harrison, Ind.	12	123	0	0(5)	748
21.	Neil Rackers, Ari.	8	0	164	209	701
22.	Shayne Graham, Cin.	7	0	152	233	689
23.	Shaun Alexander, *	8	112	0	0	672
24.	Martin Gramatica, N.O.	8	0	149	212	659
25.	Jeff Reed, Pit.	6	0	135	211	616

TOP ACTIVE RUSHERS

		Yrs.	Att.	Yards	TD
1.	Edgerrin James, Ari.	9	2,849	11,607	77
2.	Fred Taylor, Jac.	10	2,285	10,715	61
3.	LaDainian Tomlinson, S.D.	7	2,365	10,650	115
4.	Warrick Dunn, T.B.	11	2,483	10,181	47
5.	Shaun Alexander, *	8	2,176	9,429	100
6.	Jamal Lewis, Cle.	7	2,120	9,105	54
7.	Ahman Green, Hou.	10	1,941	8,751	56
8.	Clinton Portis, Was.	6	1,710	7,715	63
9.	Ricky Williams, Mia.	7	1,763	7,112	47
10.	Thomas Jones, NYJ	8	1,659	6,503	35
11.	Travis Henry, Den.	7	1,488	6,086	38
12.	Rudi Johnson, Cin.	7	1,441	5,742	48
13.	Deuce McAllister, N.O.	7	1,322	5,678	44
14.	Michael Pittman, T.B.	10	1,316	5,307	21
15.	Brian Westbrook, Phi.	6	1,014	4,785	27
16.	Larry Johnson, K.C.	5	1,050	4,764	50
17.	Willis McGahee, Bal.	4	1,162	4,572	31
18.	Steven Jackson, St.L.	4	971	4,249	30
19.	Willie Parker, Pit.	4	945	4,198	19
20.	Mike Anderson, *	7	919	4,067	37
21.	Anthony Thomas, *	7	1,044	3,891	23
22.	Ron Dayne, *	7	983	3,722	28
23.	Chester Taylor, Min.	6	833	3,659	17
24.	Michael Bennett, *	7	810	3,615	13
25.	Reuben Droughns, NYG	7	929	3,602	19

*Free agent; subject to developments.

TOP ACTIVE PASS RECEIVERS

	Yrs.	No.	Yards	TD
1. Marvin Harrison, Ind.	12	1,042	13,944	123
2. Isaac Bruce, S.F.	14	942	14,109	84
3. Keenan McCardell, *	16	883	11,373	63
4. Terrell Owens, Dal.	12	882	13,070	129
5. Tony Gonzalez, K.C.	11	820	9,882	66
6. Torry Holt, St.L.	9	805	11,864	71
7. Randy Moss, N.E.	10	774	12,193	124
8. Eric Moulds, *	11	764	9,995	49
9. Muhsin Muhammad, Car.	12	742	9,934	56
10. Hines Ward, Pit.	10	719	8,737	65
11. Derrick Mason, Bal.	11	710	9,024	47
12. Joey Galloway, T.B.	13	669	10,572	77
13. Amani Toomer, NYG	12	620	8,917	50
14. Joe Horn, Atl.	12	603	8,744	58
15. Bobby Engram, Sea.	12	598	7,201	35
16. Terry Glenn, Dal.	12	593	8,823	44
17. Laveranues Coles, NYJ	8	561	7,245	37
18. Chad Johnson, Cin.	7	559	8,365	49
19. Troy Brown, *	15	557	6,366	31
20. Eddie Kennison, *	12	548	8,345	42
21. Marty Booker, Chi.	9	509	6,311	34
22. Donald Driver, G.B.	9	503	6,977	38
23. Ike Hilliard, T.B.	11	499	5,973	31
24. Reggie Wayne, Ind.	7	494	6,984	47
25. Darrell Jackson, *	8	487	6,942	50

TOP ACTIVE PUNT RETURNERS
40 or more punt returns

	Yrs.	No.	Yards	Avg.	TD
1. Devin Hester, Chi.	2	89	1,251	14.1	7
2. Roscoe Parrish, Buf.	3	73	990	13.6	2
3. Santana Moss, Was.	7	95	1,092	11.5	2
4. Pacman Jones, Dal.	2	63	712	11.3	4
5. B.J. Sams, *	4	121	1,320	10.9	2
6. Dennis Northcutt, Jac.	8	228	2,389	10.5	3
7. Dante Hall, St.L.	8	207	2,168	10.5	6
8. Bobby Engram, Sea.	12	101	1,053	10.4	2
9. Troy Brown, *	15	252	2,625	10.4	3
10. Mewelde Moore, Pit.	4	74	768	10.4	2
11. Hank Poteat, *	7	77	788	10.2	1
12. Nate Clements, S.F.	7	72	732	10.2	2
13. Deltha O'Neal, Cin.	8	136	1,368	10.1	2
14. Eddie Kennison, *	12	153	1,528	10.0	3
15. James Thrash, Was.	11	42	418	10.0	0
16. Nate Burleson, Sea.	5	123	1,215	9.9	3
17. Allen Rossum, S.F.	10	280	2,749	9.8	3
18. Michael Lewis, *	7	186	1,818	9.8	1
19. Wes Welker, N.E.	4	152	1,481	9.7	0
20. Amani Toomer, NYG	12	109	1,060	9.7	3
21. Tim Dwight, *	10	185	1,773	9.6	3
22. Joey Galloway, T.B.	13	141	1,349	9.6	5
23. Steve Breaston, Ari.	1	42	395	9.4	1
24. Steve Smith, Car.	7	171	1,596	9.3	4
25. Justin McCareins, Ten.	7	56	519	9.3	1

TOP ACTIVE INTERCEPTORS

	Yrs.	No.	Yards	TD
1. Darren Sharper, Min.	11	53	1,024	8
2. Ty Law, *	13	52	791	7
3. Champ Bailey, Den.	9	42	428	4
Sammy Knight, NYG	11	42	664	4
5. Aaron Glenn, N.O.	14	41	560	6
6. Dre' Bly, Den.	9	38	581	5
7. Sam Madison, NYG	11	37	574	2
8. Patrick Surtain, K.C.	10	36	380	2
9. Ed Reed, Bal.	6	34	880	3
10. Ronde Barber, T.B.	11	33	584	6
Brian Dawkins, Phi.	12	33	490	2
Rodney Harrison, N.E.	14	33	361	2
13. Walt Harris, S.F.	12	32	307	4
14. Deltha O'Neal, Cin.	8	31	403	3
Shawn Springs, Was.	11	31	421	2
16. Greg Wesley, K.C.	8	29	542	0
Charles Woodson, G.B.	10	29	437	4
18. Donnie Edwards, K.C.	12	28	347	4
Anthony Henry, Dal.	7	28	507	3
Samari Rolle, Bal.	10	28	420	1
21. Nate Clements, S.F.	7	27	415	5
22. John Lynch, Den.	15	26	204	0
Mike McKenzie, N.O.	9	26	411	4
24. Ray Lewis, Bal.	12	25	421	2
25. Three tied	—	24		

TOP ACTIVE KICKOFF RETURNERS
40 or more kickoff returns

	Yrs.	No.	Yards	Avg.	TD
1. Jerome Mathis, Was.	3	72	2,054	28.5	3
2. Ellis Hobbs, N.E.	3	60	1,632	27.2	2
3. Justin Miller, NYJ	3	108	2,929	27.1	3
4. Maurice Jones-Drew, Jac.	2	62	1,671	27.0	2
5. Josh Cribbs, Cle.	3	165	4,397	26.6	4
6. Terrence McGee, Buf.	5	203	5,358	26.4	5
7. Pacman Jones, Dal.	2	63	1,648	26.2	0
8. Leon Washington, NYJ	2	53	1,370	25.8	3
9. Miles Austin, Dal.	2	53	1,365	25.8	0
10. Darren Sproles, S.D.	3	100	2,536	25.4	0
11. Michael Turner, Atl.	4	44	1,111	25.3	0
12. Jerious Norwood, Atl.	2	65	1,637	25.2	0
13. Yamon Figurs, Bal.	1	46	1,138	24.7	1
14. Tyson Thompson, Dal.	3	98	2,416	24.7	0
15. Koren Robinson, *	7	84	2,070	24.6	1
16. Glenn Holt, Cin.	2	76	1,851	24.4	1
17. Kevin Kasper, Cle.	7	77	1,869	24.3	0
18. Deuce McAllister, N.O.	7	45	1,091	24.2	0
19. Steve Smith, Car.	7	98	2,371	24.2	2
20. Michael Lewis, *	7	248	5,989	24.1	3
21. Dante Hall, St.L.	8	389	9,373	24.1	6
22. Chris Carr, Ten.	3	201	4,841	24.1	0
23. Reuben Droughns, NYG	7	71	1,709	24.1	0
24. Ladell Betts, Was.	6	85	2,033	23.9	1
25. Rock Cartwright, Was.	6	132	3,157	23.9	1

TOP ACTIVE PUNTERS
50 or more punts

		Yrs.	No.	Avg.	LG
1.	Shane Lechler, Oak.	8	592	46.5	73
2.	Mat McBriar, Dal.	4	275	44.7	75
3.	Jon Ryan, G.B.	2	144	44.5	72
4.	Donnie Jones, St.L.	4	277	43.8	80
5.	Mike Scifres, S.D.	5	290	43.8	71
6.	Andy Lee, S.F.	4	389	43.8	81
7.	Steven Weatherford, N.O.	2	140	43.8	61
8.	Ben Graham, NYJ	3	212	43.7	69
9.	Chris Kluwe, Min.	3	245	43.6	70
10.	Dustin Colquitt, K.C.	3	231	43.4	81
11.	Hunter Smith, Ind.	9	524	43.3	69
12.	Sam Koch, Bal.	2	164	43.2	64
13.	Brandon Fields, Mia.	1	77	43.2	61
14.	Mitch Berger, *	13	730	43.1	75
15.	Brian Moorman, Buf.	7	552	43.1	84
16.	Kyle Larson, Cin.	4	279	42.8	75
17.	Craig Hentrich, Ten.	14	1,054	42.8	78
18.	Chris Hanson, N.E.	8	472	42.7	74
19.	Michael Koenen, Atl.	3	242	42.7	67
20.	Josh Bidwell, T.B.	8	650	42.6	68
21.	Ryan Plackemeier, Sea.	2	170	42.4	72
22.	Matt Turk, Hou.	12	917	42.4	77
23.	Daniel Sepulveda, Pit.	1	68	42.4	59
24.	Jason Baker, Car.	7	488	42.2	70
25.	Brad Maynard, Chi.	11	1,002	42.2	75

TOP ACTIVE QUARTERBACK SACKERS

		Yrs.	No.
1.	Michael Strahan, NYG	15	141.5
2.	Jason Taylor, Mia.	11	117.0
3.	Kevin Carter, T.B.	13	100.5
4.	Bryant Young, *	14	89.5
5.	Willie McGinest, Cle.	14	85.0
6.	La'Roi Glover, St.L.	12	83.0
7.	Trevor Pryce, Bal.	11	79.0
8.	Leonard Little, St.L.	10	75.0
9.	Kabeer Gbaja-Biamila, G.B.	8	74.0
10.	Patrick Kerney, Sea.	9	72.5
11.	Jevon Kearse, Ten.	9	69.5
12.	Greg Ellis, Dal.	10	69.0
13.	John Abraham, Atl.	8	67.5
14.	Aaron Schobel, Buf.	7	67.0
15.	Joey Porter, *	9	65.5
16.	Dwight Freeney, Ind.	6	60.0
17.	Phillip Daniels, Was.	12	59.0
18.	Rod Coleman, *	9	58.5
19.	Junior Seau, *	18	56.5
20.	Julius Peppers, Car.	6	56.0
21.	Adewale Ogunleye, Chi.	7	55.5
	Mike Rucker, *	9	55.5
23.	Bertrand Berry, Ari.	10	54.0
24.	Shaun Ellis, NYJ	8	53.5
25.	Rosevelt Colvin, *	9	52.5

ACTIVE COACHES' CAREER RECORDS (Order Based on Career Victories)
Start of 2008 Season

Coach	Team(s)	Regular Season					Postseason			Career			
		Yrs.	Won	Lost	Tied	Pct.	Won	Lost	Pct.	Won	Lost	Tied	Pct.
Mike Holmgren	Green Bay Packers, Seattle Seahawks	16	157	99	0	.613	13	11	.542	170	110	0	.607
Mike Shanahan	Los Angeles Raiders, Denver Broncos	15	138	90	0	.605	8	5	.615	146	95	0	.606
Bill Belichick	Cleveland Browns, New England Patriots	13	127	81	0	.611	15	4	.789	142	85	0	.626
Tony Dungy	Tampa Bay Buccaneers, Indianapolis Colts	12	127	65	0	.661	9	9	.500	136	74	0	.648
Jeff Fisher	Tennessee Titans	13	115	99	0	.537	5	5	.500	120	104	0	.536
Tom Coughlin	Jacksonville Jaguars, New York Giants	12	103	89	0	.536	8	6	.571	111	95	0	.539
Andy Reid	Philadelphia Eagles	9	88	56	0	.611	8	6	.571	96	62	0	.608
Jon Gruden	Oakland Raiders, Tampa Bay Buccaneers	10	86	74	0	.538	5	4	.556	91	78	0	.538
Norv Turner	Washington Redskins, Oakland Raiders, San Diego Chargers	10	69	87	1	.443	3	2	.600	72	89	1	.448
Wade Phillips	New Orleans Saints, Denver Broncos, Buffalo Bills, Atlanta Falcons, Dallas Cowboys	8	61	42	0	.592	0	4	.000	61	46	0	.570
John Fox	Carolina Panthers	6	51	45	0	.531	5	2	.714	56	47	0	.544
Herm Edwards	New York Jets, Kansas City Chiefs	7	52	60	0	.464	2	4	.333	54	64	0	.458
Dick Jauron	Chicago Bears, Detroit Lions, Buffalo Bills	8	50	67	0	.427	0	1	.000	50	68	0	.424
Jack Del Rio	Jacksonville Jaguars	5	45	35	0	.563	1	2	.333	46	37	0	.554
Marvin Lewis	Cincinnati Bengals	5	42	38	0	.525	0	1	.000	42	39	0	.519
Lovie Smith	Chicago Bears	4	36	28	0	.563	2	2	.500	38	30	0	.559
Mike McCarthy	Green Bay Packers	2	21	11	0	.656	1	1	.500	22	12	0	.647
Romeo Crennel	Cleveland Browns	3	20	28	0	.417	0	0	—	20	28	0	.417
Sean Payton	New Orleans Saints	2	17	15	0	.531	1	1	.500	18	16	0	.529
Mike Nolan	San Francisco 49ers	3	16	32	0	.333	0	0	—	16	32	0	.333
Brad Childress	Minnesota Vikings	2	14	18	0	.438	0	0	—	14	18	0	.438
Eric Mangini	New York Jets	2	14	18	0	.438	0	1	.000	14	19	0	.424
Gary Kubiak	Houston Texans	2	14	18	0	.438	0	0	—	14	18	0	.438
Scott Linehan	St. Louis Rams	2	11	21	0	.344	0	0	—	11	21	0	.344
Mike Tomlin	Pittsburgh Steelers	1	10	6	0	.625	0	1	.000	10	7	0	.588
Rod Marinelli	Detroit Lions	2	10	22	0	.313	0	0	—	10	22	0	.313
Ken Whisenhunt	Arizona Cardinals	1	8	8	0	.500	0	0	—	8	8	0	.500
Lane Kiffin	Oakland Raiders	1	4	12	0	.250	0	0	—	4	12	0	.250
John Harbaugh	Baltimore Ravens	0	0	0	0	—	0	0	—	0	0	0	—
Mike Smith	Atlanta Falcons	0	0	0	0	—	0	0	—	0	0	0	—
Tony Sparano	Miami Dolphins	0	0	0	0	—	0	0	—	0	0	0	—
Jim Zorn	Washington Redskins	0	0	0	0	—	0	0	—	0	0	0	—

COACHES WITH 100 CAREER VICTORIES (Order Based on Career Victories)
Start of 2008 Season

Coach	Team(s)		Regular Season				Postseason			Career			
		Yrs.	Won	Lost	Tied	Pct.	Won	Lost	Pct.	Won	Lost	Tied	Pct.
Don Shula	Baltimore Colts, Miami Dolphins	33	328	156	6	.677	19	17	.528	347	173	6	.666
George Halas	Chicago Bears	40	318	148	31	.682	6	3	.667	324	151	31	.682
Tom Landry	Dallas Cowboys	29	250	162	6	.607	20	16	.556	270	178	6	.603
Earl (Curly) Lambeau	Green Bay Packers, Chicago Cardinals, Washington Redskins	33	226	132	22	.631	3	2	.600	229	134	22	.631
Chuck Noll	Pittsburgh Steelers	23	193	148	1	.566	16	8	.667	209	156	1	.572
Marty Schottenheimer	Cleveland Browns, Kansas City Chiefs, Washington Redskins, San Diego Chargers	21	200	126	1	.613	5	13	.278	205	139	1	.596
Dan Reeves	Denver Broncos, New York Giants, Atlanta Falcons	23	190	165	2	.535	11	9	.550	201	174	2	.536
Chuck Knox	Los Angeles Rams, Buffalo Bills, Seattle Seahawks	22	186	147	1	.558	7	11	.389	193	158	1	.550
Bill Parcells	New York Giants, New England Patriots, New York Jets, Dallas Cowboys	19	172	130	1	.569	11	8	.579	183	138	1	.570
Joe Gibbs	Washington Redskins	16	154	94	0	.621	17	7	.708	171	101	0	.629
Paul Brown	Cleveland Browns, Cincinnati Bengals	21	166	100	6	.624	4	8	.333	170	108	6	.612
Mike Holmgren	Green Bay Packers, Seattle Seahawks	16	157	99	0	.613	13	11	.542	170	110	0	.607
Bud Grant	Minnesota Vikings	18	158	96	5	.621	10	12	.455	168	108	5	.608
Bill Cowher	Pittsburgh Steelers	15	149	90	1	.598	12	9	.571	161	99	1	.619
Marv Levy	Kansas City Chiefs, Buffalo Bills	17	143	112	0	.561	11	8	.579	154	120	0	.562
Steve Owen	New York Giants	23	151	100	17	.602	2	8	.200	153	108	17	.586
Mike Shanahan	Los Angeles Raiders, Denver Broncos	15	138	90	0	.605	8	5	.615	146	95	0	.606
Bill Belichick	Cleveland Browns, New England Patriots	13	127	81	0	.611	15	4	.789	142	85	0	.626
Tony Dungy	Tampa Bay Buccaneers, Indianapolis Colts	12	127	65	0	.661	9	9	.500	136	74	0	.648
Hank Stram	Kansas City Chiefs, New Orleans Saints	17	131	97	10	.574	5	3	.625	136	100	10	.576
Weeb Ewbank	Baltimore Colts, New York Jets	20	130	129	7	.502	4	1	.800	134	130	7	.508
Mike Ditka	Chicago Bears, New Orleans Saints	14	121	95	0	.560	6	6	.500	127	101	0	.557
Dick Vermeil	Philadelphia Eagles, St. Louis Rams, Kansas City Chiefs	15	120	109	0	.524	6	5	.545	126	114	0	.525
Jim Mora	New Orleans Saints, Indianapolis Colts	15	125	106	0	.541	0	6	.000	125	112	0	.527
George Seifert	San Francisco 49ers, Carolina Panthers	11	114	62	0	.648	10	5	.667	124	67	0	.649
Sid Gillman	Los Angeles Rams, Los Angeles-San Diego Chargers, Houston Oilers	18	122	99	7	.552	1	5	.167	123	104	7	.542
Jeff Fisher	Tennessee Titans	13	115	99	0	.537	5	5	.500	120	104	0	.536
George Allen	Los Angeles Rams, Washington Redskins	12	116	47	5	.712	2	7	.222	118	54	5	.686
Dennis Green	Minnesota Vikings, Arizona Cardinals	13	113	94	0	.546	4	8	.333	117	102	0	.534
Don Coryell	St. Louis Cardinals, San Diego Chargers	14	111	83	1	.572	3	6	.333	114	89	1	.561
John Madden	Oakland Raiders	10	103	32	7	.759	9	7	.563	112	39	7	.739
Tom Coughlin	Jacksonville Jaguars, New York Giants	12	103	89	0	.536	8	6	.571	111	95	0	.539
Ray (Buddy) Parker	Chicago Cardinals, Detroit Lions, Pittsburgh Steelers	15	104	75	9	.581	3	1	.750	107	76	9	.585
Vince Lombardi	Green Bay Packers, Washington Redskins	10	96	34	6	.739	9	1	.900	105	35	6	.750
Tom Flores	Oakland-Los Angeles Raiders, Seattle Seahawks	12	97	87	0	.527	8	3	.727	105	90	0	.538
Bill Walsh	San Francisco 49ers	10	92	59	1	.609	10	4	.714	102	63	1	.617

Active coaches in bold.
From 1920-71, tie games were not included in winning percentage.

The **Chicago Bears** need seven victories to become the first team in NFL history with 700 total victories. Chicago's all-time record is 693-508-42.

The **Pittsburgh Steelers** need nine victories to become the first AFC team to reach 550 total victories. Pittsburgh's all-time record is 541-517-21.

The **Philadelphia Eagles** need four victories to reach 500 total victories. Philadelphia's all-time record is 496-541-25.

The **Detroit Lions** need five victories to reach 500 total victories. Detroit's all-time record is 495-563-32.

The **Dallas Cowboys** need four victories to reach 450 total victories. Dallas' all-time record is 446-326-6.

The **Denver Broncos** need five victories to reach 400 total victories. Denver's all-time record is 395-351-10.

The **Buffalo Bills** need nine regular-season wins to reach 350 regular-season victories. Buffalo's all-time regular-season record is 341-375-8.

The **Seattle Seahawks** need four regular-season wins to reach 250 regular-season victories. Seattle's all-time regular-season record is 246-254-0.

The **Tampa Bay Buccaneers** need four regular-season wins to reach 200 regular-season victories. Tampa Bay's all-time regular-season record is 196-303-1.

The **Carolina Panthers** need three regular-season wins to reach 100 regular-season victories. Carolina's all-time regular-season record is 97-111-0.

The **Baltimore Ravens** need four regular-season wins to reach 100 regular-season victories. Baltimore's all-time regular-season record is 96-95-1.

The **New England Patriots** can become the first team in NFL history to win 20 consecutive regular-season games. New England's current 19-game regular-season win streak dates back to 2006 and is the longest in NFL history.

The **Indianapolis Colts** need 12 regular-season wins to become the first team in NFL history with six consecutive 12-win seasons. Indianapolis and Dallas (1992-95) are the only two teams with at least four consecutive seasons with 12 regular-season wins.

Mike Holmgren, Seattle, needs 14 victories to pass Joe Gibbs (171) and Bill Parcells (183) for tenth place all-time in career victories. In 16 seasons, Holmgren has 170 career victories.

Mike Shanahan, Denver, needs four victories to reach 150 total victories. In 15 seasons, Shanahan has 146 career victories.

Bill Belichick, New England, needs eight victories to reach 150 total victories. In 13 seasons, Belichick has 142 career victories.

Andy Reid, Philadelphia, needs four victories to reach 100 total victories. In nine seasons, Reid has 96 career victories.

Jon Gruden, Tampa Bay, needs nine victories to reach 100 total victories. In 10 seasons, Gruden has 91 career victories.

Peyton Manning, Indianapolis, needs 4,000 passing yards to become the first quarterback in NFL history with nine 4,000-yard seasons. Manning is the only quarterback to accomplish the feat in eight seasons.

Manning needs 25 touchdown passes to become the first player in NFL history to throw 25 touchdown passes in 11 consecutive seasons. Manning is the only player to have 10 consecutive seasons with 25 touchdown passes.

Manning has passed for 3,000 yards in each of the past 10 seasons and owns the second-longest streak of consecutive 3,000-yard seasons (Brett Favre, 16). Manning is the only player in NFL history to start a career with 10 consecutive 3,000-yard seasons.

Manning has led the league in touchdown passes three times in his 10-year career and can tie Brett Favre, Johnny Unitas, Len Dawson and Steve Young (4) for the most seasons leading the league in touchdown passes.

Manning has passed for 400 yards in a game seven times in his 10-year NFL career. Manning needs one 400-yard passing game to surpass Joe Montana and Warren Moon (7) for the second-most games with 400 yards passing in NFL history (Dan Marino, 13).

Manning needs 37 touchdown passes to surpass Fran Tarkenton (342) to move into third place all-time. In 10 seasons, Manning has thrown 306 touchdown passes.

Manning needs 2,986 passing yards to surpass Dan Fouts (43,040) and Drew Bledsoe (44,611) to move into seventh place all-time. In 10 seasons, Manning has passed for 41,626 yards.

Manning needs 32 completions to become the eighth player in NFL history with 3,500 passes completed. In 10 seasons, Manning has completed 3,468 passes.

LaDainian Tomlinson, San Diego, needs 10 rushing touchdowns to extend his NFL-record streak of consecutive seasons to begin a career with 10 rushing touchdowns to eight.

Tomlinson needs 1,200 rushing yards to become the first player in NFL history to begin a career with eight consecutive 1,200-yard rushing seasons. Tomlinson and Eric Dickerson (1983-89) are the only players to begin a career with seven such seasons.

Tomlinson needs nine rushing touchdowns to pass Marcus Allen (123) to move into second place all-time. In seven seasons, Tomlinson has scored 115 rushing touchdowns.

Tomlinson needs 17 touchdowns to surpass Terrell Owens (131), Cris Carter (131), Marshall Faulk (136) and Marcus Allen (145) to move into third place all-time (see Owens note). In seven seasons, Tomlinson has scored 129 touchdowns.

Tomlinson has gained 2,000 scrimmage yards three times in his seven-year career. With one more 2,000-scrimmage yard season, Tomlinson will tie Eric Dickerson, Marshall Faulk and Walter Payton (4) for the most all-time (see James note).

Tomlinson has gained 2,000 combined yards three times in his career. Tomlinson needs one more season with 2,000 combined yards to tie Tiki Barber, Eric Dickerson, Marshall Faulk, Dante Hall, Brian Mitchell and Walter Payton (4) for the most all-time (see Hall and James notes).

Tomlinson has four 200-yard rushing games in his career. Tomlinson needs two to surpass Tiki Barber (5) and tie O.J. Simpson (6) for the most all-time.

Edgerrin James, Arizona, has gained 2,000 scrimmage yards three times in his nine-year career. With one more 2,000-scrimmage yard season, James will tie Eric Dickerson, Marshall Faulk and Walter Payton (4) for the most all-time (see Tomlinson note).

James has gained 2,000 combined yards three times in his career. James needs one more season with 2,000 combined yards to tie Tiki Barber, Eric Dickerson, Marshall Faulk, Dante Hall, Brian Mitchell and Walter Payton (4) for the most all-time (see Hall and Tomlinson notes).

James needs 1,133 rushing yards to surpass Thurman Thomas (12,074), Franco Harris (12,120), Marcus Allen (12,243), Marshall Faulk (12,279), Jim Brown (12,312) and Tony Dorsett (12,739) to move into seventh place all-time. In nine seasons, James has 11,607 rushing yards.

James needs 133 scrimmage yards to become the 14th player in NFL history with 15,000 scrimmage yards (see Dunn and Bruce notes). In nine seasons, James has 14,867 scrimmage yards.

Warrick Dunn, Tampa Bay, needs 810 scrimmage yards to become the 14th player in NFL history with 15,000 scrimmage yards (see Bruce and James notes). In 11 seasons, Dunn has 14,190 scrimmage yards.

Marvin Harrison, Indianapolis, needs 100 receptions to pass Jerry Rice (4) to become the first player in NFL history with five 100-catch seasons. In 12 seasons, Harrison has four seasons with 100 receptions.

Harrison needs 991 yards to surpass James Lofton (14,004), Isaac Bruce (14,109) and Tim Brown (14,934) to move into second place all-time (see Bruce note). In 12 seasons, Harrison has 13,944 receiving yards.

Harrison needs 60 receptions to surpass Tim Brown (1,094) and Cris Carter (1,101) to move into second place all-time. In 12 seasons, Harrison has 1,042 receptions.

Harrison needs eight receiving touchdowns to surpass Randy Moss (124), Terrell Owens (129) and Cris Carter (130) for second place all-time (see Moss and Owens notes). In 12 seasons, Harrison has 123 touchdown receptions.

Harrison has recorded 1,000 receiving yards in a season eight times in his 12-year NFL career. Moss can join Jerry Rice (14), Tim Brown (9) and Jimmy Smith (9) as the only players in NFL history with nine seasons with 1,000 receiving yards (see Bruce, Holt, Moss and Owens notes).

Isaac Bruce, San Francisco, needs 826 receiving yards to surpass Tim Brown (14,934) to move into second place all-time (see Harrison note). In 14 seasons, Bruce has 14,109 receiving yards.

Bruce needs 58 receptions to become the fifth player in NFL history with 1,000 career receptions. In 14 seasons, Bruce has 942 receptions.

Bruce needs 741 scrimmage yards to become the 14th player in NFL history with 15,000 scrimmage yards (see Dunn and James notes). In 14 seasons, Bruce has 14,259 scrimmage yards.

Bruce has recorded 1,000 receiving yards in a season eight times in his 14-year NFL career. Bruce can join Jerry Rice (14), Tim Brown (9) and Jimmy Smith (9) as the only players in NFL history with nine seasons with 1,000 receiving yards (see Harrison, Holt, Moss and Owens notes).

Terrell Owens, Dallas, needs two receiving touchdowns to surpass Cris Carter (130) for second place all-time (see Harrison and Moss notes). In 12 seasons, Owens has 129 touchdown receptions.

Owens needs 15 touchdowns to surpass Cris Carter (131), Marshall Faulk (136) and Marcus Allen (145) to move into third place all-time (see Tomlinson note). In 12 seasons, Owens has scored 131 touchdowns.

Owens has recorded 1,000 receiving yards in a season eight times in his 12-year NFL career. Owens can join Jerry Rice (14), Tim Brown (9) and Jimmy Smith (9) as the only players in NFL history with nine seasons with 1,000 receiving yards (see Bruce, Harrison, Holt and Moss notes).

Owens needs 18 receptions to become the ninth player in NFL history with 900 receptions (see McCardell note). In 12 seasons, Owens has 882 receptions.

Randy Moss, New England, needs seven receiving touchdowns to surpass Terrell Owens (129) and Cris Carter (130) for second place all-time (see Harrison and Owens notes). In 10 seasons, Moss has 124 touchdown receptions.

Moss has recorded 100 receptions in a season two times in his 10-year NFL career. Moss can join Marvin Harrison and Jerry Rice (4) as the only players in NFL history with three seasons with 100 receptions (see Boldin, Fitzgerald and Holt notes).

Moss has recorded 1,000 receiving yards in a season eight times in his 10-year NFL career. Moss can join Jerry Rice (14), Tim Brown (9) and Jimmy Smith (9) as the only players in NFL history with nine seasons with 1,000 receiving yards (see Bruce, Harrison, Moss and Owens notes).

Torry Holt, St. Louis, has recorded 100 receptions in a season two times in his nine-year NFL career. Holt can join Marvin Harrison and Jerry Rice (4) as the only players in NFL history with three seasons with 100 receptions (see Boldin, Fitzgerald and Moss notes).

Holt has recorded 1,000 receiving yards in a season eight times in his nine-year NFL career. Holt can join Jerry Rice (14), Tim Brown (9) and Jimmy Smith (9) as the only players in NFL history with nine seasons with 1,000 receiving yards (see Bruce, Harrison, Moss and Owens notes).

Anquan Boldin, Arizona, has recorded 100 receptions in a season two times in his five-year NFL career. Boldin can join Marvin Harrison and Jerry Rice (4) as the only players in NFL history with three seasons with 100 receptions (see Fitzgerald, Holt and Moss notes).

Larry Fitzgerald, Arizona, has recorded 100 receptions in a season two times in his four-year NFL career. Boldin can join Marvin Harrison and Jerry Rice (4) as the only players in NFL history with three seasons with 100 receptions (see Boldin, Holt, and Moss notes).

Keenan McCardell, needs 18 receptions to become the ninth player in NFL history with 900 receptions (see Owens note). In 17 seasons, McCardell has 883 receptions.

Dante Hall, St. Louis, has six kickoff-return touchdowns in his eight-year career, tied for the most all-time. Hall needs one kickoff-return touchdown to pass Mel Gray, Ollie Matson, Gale Sayers and Travis Williams (6) for sole possession of first place in NFL history.

Hall has 12 combined kick-return touchdowns (six kickoff, six punt) in his eight-year career, tied for the second-most all-time. Hall needs two combined kick-return touchdowns to pass Brian Mitchell (13) for first place in NFL history (see Hester note).

Hall has gained 2,000 combined yards four times in his eight-year career, tied for the most in NFL history. Hall needs one more season with 2,000 combined yards to pass Tiki Barber, Eric Dickerson, Marshall Faulk, Brian Mitchell and Walter Payton (4) for the most all-time.

Devin Hester, Chicago, has 11 combined kick-return touchdowns (seven punt, four kickoff) in his two-year career, the third-most all-time. Hester needs three combined kick-return touchdowns to pass Dante Hall, Eric Metcalf (12) and Brian Mitchell (13) for first place in NFL history (see Hall note).

Tony Gonzalez, Kansas City, needs 80 receptions to become the first tight end in NFL history with 900 receptions. In 11 seasons, Gonzalez has 820 receptions – the most ever by a tight end.

Gonzalez needs 50 receptions to become the first tight end in NFL history with 11 consecutive 50-reception seasons. Gonzalez is the only tight end in NFL history with 10 consecutive 50-reception seasons.

Michael Strahan, New York Giants, needs 8.5 sacks to become the fifth player in NFL history with 150.0 sacks. In 15 seasons, Strahan has 141.5 sacks.

Darren Sharper, Minnesota, needs six interceptions to pass Eric Allen, Willie Brown, Darrell Green (54), Aeneas Williams (55), Lem Barney, Pat Fischer (56), Mel Blount, Bobby Boyd, Eugene Robinson, Johnny Robinson, Everson Walls (57) and Emmitt Thomas (58) to move into ninth place all-time. In 11 seasons, Sharper has 53 interceptions.

Jason Elam, Atlanta, has scored 100 points in each of his first 15 seasons and needs 100 points to extend his NFL record streak for consecutive 100-point seasons to 16. Elam is the only player in NFL history to score 100 points in 15 seasons.

Adam Vinatieri, Indianapolis, has scored 100 points in each of his first 12 seasons and needs 100 points to become the second player (Jason Elam, 15) in NFL history with 100 points in each of his first 13 seasons.

Matt Stover, Baltimore, has successfully kicked 348 consecutive points after touchdowns, the third-longest streak in NFL history. Stover needs to convert 24 in a row to pass Jason Elam and Jeff Wilkins (371) for the longest streak all-time.

73rd Annual NFL Draft, April 26-27, 2008
+Denotes Compensatory Selection
#Denotes Underclassman Selection

ARIZONA CARDINALS
1. Dominique Rodgers-Cromartie—16, DB, Tennessee State
2.#Calais Campbell—50, DE, Miami
3. Early Doucet—81, WR, Louisiana State
4. Kenny Iwebema—116, DE, Iowa
5. Tim Hightower—149, RB, Richmond
6. Chris Harrington—185, DE, Texas A&M
7. Brandon Keith—225, G, Northern Iowa

ATLANTA FALCONS
1. Matt Ryan—3, QB, Boston College
   Sam Baker—21, T, Southern California, from Washington
2.#Curtis Lofton—37, LB, Oklahoma
3. Chevis Jackson—68, DB, Louisiana State
   Harry Douglas—84, WR, Louisville, from Washington
 + Thomas DeCoud—98, DB, California
5. Robert James—138, LB, Arizona State
   Kroy Biermann—154, DE, Montana, from Washington
6. Thomas Brown—172, RB, Georgia
7. Wilrey Fontenot—212, DB, Arizona
   Keith Zinger—232, TE, Louisiana State, from Pittsburgh

BALTIMORE RAVENS
1. Joe Flacco—18, QB, Delaware, from Houston
2.#Ray Rice—55, RB, Rutgers, from Seattle
3. Tavares Gooden—71, LB, Miami, reacquired through
   Buffalo and Jacksonville
   Tom Zbikowski—86, DB, Notre Dame, from Seattle
 + Oniel Cousins—99, T, Texas-El Paso
4. Marcus Smith—106, WR, New Mexico
 + David Hale—133, T, Weber State
5. Exercised in 2007 Supplemental Draft for
   Jared Gaither, T, Maryland
6.+Haruki Nakamura—206, DB, Cincinnati
7. Justin Harper—215, WR, Virginia Tech
 + Allen Patrick—240, RB, Oklahoma

BUFFALO BILLS
1. Leodis McKelvin—11, DB, Troy
2.#James Hardy—41, WR, Indiana
3. Chris Ellis—72, LB, Virginia Tech
4. Reggie Corner—114, DB, Akron
 + Derek Fine—132, TE, Kansas
5. Alvin Bowen—147, LB, Iowa State
6. Xavier Omon—179, RB, Northwest Missouri State
7. Demetrius Bell—219, T, Northwestern State (La.)
   Steve Johnson—224, WR, Kentucky, from Philadelphia
 + Kennard Cox—251, DB, Pittsburgh

CAROLINA PANTHERS
1.#Jonathan Stewart—13,RB, Oregon
   Jeff Otah—19, T, Pittsburgh, from Philadelphia
3. Charles Godfrey—67, DB, Iowa, from New York Jets
   Dan Connor—74, LB, Penn State
5. Gary Barnidge—141, TE, Louisville, from New York Jets
6. Nick Hayden—181, DT, Wisconsin
7. Hilee Taylor—221, DE, North Carolina
 + Geoff Schwartz—241, T, Oregon
 + Mackenzy Bernadeau—250, G, Bentley

CHICAGO BEARS
1. Chris Williams—14, T, Vanderbilt
2. Matt Forté—44, RB, Tulane
3.#Earl Bennett—70, WR, Vanderbilt, from San Francisco
   Marcus Harrison—90, DT, Arkansas, from San Diego
4. Craig Steltz—120, DB, Louisiana State, from Tampa Bay
5. Zackary Bowman—142, DB, Nebraska, from Carolina
   Kellen Davis—158, TE, Michigan State, from
   Seattle through Jacksonville and Tampa Bay
7. Ervin Baldwin—208, DE, Michigan State, from Miami
   Chester Adams—222, G, Georgia
 + Joey LaRocque—243, LB, Oregon State
 + Kirk Barton—247, T, Ohio State
 + Marcus Monk—248, WR, Arkansas

CINCINNATI BENGALS
1. Keith Rivers—9, LB, Southern California
2. Jerome Simpson—46, WR, Coastal Carolina
3.#Pat Sims—77, DT, Auburn
 + Andre Caldwell—97, WR, Florida
4.#Anthony Collins—112, T, Kansas
5. Jason Shirley—145, DT, Fresno State
6. Corey Lynch—177, DB, Appalachian State
 + Matt Sherry—207, TE, Villanova
7.+Angelo Craig—244, DE, Cincinnati
#+Mario Urrutia—246, WR, Louisville

CLEVELAND BROWNS
4. Beau Bell—104, LB, Nevada-Las Vegas, from
   Oakland through Dallas
   Martin Rucker—111, TE, Missouri, from
   Detroit through Dallas
6. Ahtyba Rubin—190, NT, Iowa State, from Seattle
   Paul Hubbard—191, WR, Wisconsin, reacquired
   through Philadelphia
7. Alex Hall—231, LB, St. Augustine's (NC)

DALLAS COWBOYS
1.#Felix Jones—22, RB, Arkansas, from Cleveland
   Mike Jenkins—25, DB, South Florida, from Seattle
2.#Martellus Bennett—61, TE, Texas A&M
4. Tashard Choice—122, RB, Georgia Tech, from Cleveland
5.#Orlando Scandrick—143, DB, Boise State, from
   Chicago through Buffalo and Jacksonville
6. Erik Walden—167, LB, Middle Tennessee State, from Miami

DENVER BRONCOS
1.#Ryan Clady—12, T, Boise State
2. Eddie Royal—42, WR, Virginia Tech
4. Kory Lichtensteiger—108, G, Bowling Green
   Jack Williams—119, DB, Kent State, from Washington
5. Ryan Torain—139, RB, Arizona State, from Oakland
   Carlton Powell—148, DT, Virginia Tech
6. Spencer Larsen—183, LB, Arizona, from Houston
7. Josh Barrett—220, DB, Arizona State
   Peyton Hillis—227, RB, Arkansas, from Tampa Bay

DETROIT LIONS
1. Gosder Cherilus—17, T, Boston College, from Minnesota through Kansas City
2. Jordon Dizon—45, LB, Colorado
3. # Kevin Smith—64, RB, Central Florida, from Miami
   Andre Fluellen—87, DT, Florida State, from Cleveland
   Cliff Avril—92, DE, Purdue, from Dallas
5. Kenneth Moore—136, WR, Wake Forest, from Miami through Kansas City
   Jerome Felton—146, RB, Furman, from New Orleans
7. Landon Cohen—216, DT, Ohio
   Caleb Campbell—218, DB, Army, from New Orleans

GREEN BAY PACKERS
2. Jordy Nelson—36, WR, Kansas State, from New York Jets
   Brian Brohm—56, QB, Louisville, from Cleveland
   Pat Lee—60, DB, Auburn
3. # Jermichael Finley—91, TE, Texas
4. Jeremy Thompson—102, DE, Wake Forest, from New York Jets
   + Josh Sitton—135, G, Central Florida
5. Breno Giacomini—150, T, Louisville, from Minnesota
7. Matt Flynn—209, QB, Louisiana State, from St. Louis through Minnesota
   Brett Swain—217, WR, San Diego State, from Cincinnati through St. Louis

HOUSTON TEXANS
1. Duane Brown—26, T, Virginia Tech, from Jacksonville through Baltimore
3. Antwaun Molden—79, DB, Eastern Kentucky
   # Steve Slaton—89, RB, West Virginia, from Jacksonville through Baltimore
4. Xavier Adibi—118, LB, Virginia Tech
5. Frank Okam—151, DT, Texas
6. Dominique Barber—173, DB, Minnesota, from Baltimore
7. Alex Brink—223, QB, Washington State

INDIANAPOLIS COLTS
2. Mike Pollak—59, G, Arizona State
3. Philip Wheeler—93, LB, Georgia Tech
4. Jacob Tamme—127, TE, Kentucky
5. Marcus Howard—161, DE, Georgia
6. Tom Santi—196, TE, Virginia
   + Steve Justice—201, C, Wake Forest
   + Mike Hart—202, RB, Michigan
   + Pierre Garcon—205, WR, Mount Union
7. Jamey Richard—236, G, Buffalo

JACKSONVILLE JAGUARS
1. # Derrick Harvey—8, DE, Florida, from Baltimore
2. Quentin Groves—52, DE, Auburn, from Tampa Bay
5. Thomas Williams—155, LB, Southern California, from Cleveland through Dallas
   Trae Williams—159, DB, South Florida
7. Chauncey Washington—213, RB, Southern California, from Oakland through Dallas

KANSAS CITY CHIEFS
1. Glenn Dorsey—5, DT, Louisiana State
   # Branden Albert—15, T, Virginia, from Detroit
2. # Brandon Flowers—35, DB, Virginia Tech
3. # Jamaal Charles—73, RB, Texas, from Denver through Minnesota
   Brad Cottam—76, TE, Tennessee, from Detroit
   # DaJuan Morgan—82, DB, North Carolina State, from Minnesota
4. William Franklin—105, WR, Missouri
5. Brandon Carr—140, DB, Grand Valley State
6. Barry Richardson—170, T, Clemson
   Kevin Robinson—182, WR, Utah State, from Minnesota
7. Brian Johnston—210, DE, Gardner-Webb
   Mike Merritt—239, TE, Central Florida, from New York Giants

MIAMI DOLPHINS
1. Jake Long—1, T, Michigan
2. # Phillip Merling—32, DE, Clemson
   Chad Henne—57, QB, Michigan, from San Diego
3. Kendall Langford—66, DE, Hampton, from Kansas City through Detroit
4. Shawn Murphy—110, G, Utah State, from Chicago
6. Jalen Parmele—176, RB, Toledo, from Detroit
   Donald Thomas—195, G, Connecticut, from Dallas
   + Lex Hilliard—204, RB, Montana
7. + Lionel Dotson—245, NT, Arizona

MINNESOTA VIKINGS
2. Tyrell Johnson—43, DB, Arkansas State, from Carolina through Philadelphia
5. John David Booty—137, QB, Southern California, from St. Louis through Green Bay
   # Letroy Guion—152, DT, Florida State, from Philadelphia
6. John Sullivan—187, C, Notre Dame, from Tampa Bay through Kansas City
   Jaymar Johnson—193, WR, Jackson State, from Jacksonville

NEW ENGLAND PATRIOTS
1. # Jerod Mayo—10, LB, Tennessee, from New Orleans
2. Terrence Wheatley—62, DB, Colorado
3. Shawn Crable—78, LB, Michigan, from New Orleans
   Kevin O'Connell—94, QB, San Diego State
4. Jonathan Wilhite—129, DB, Auburn
5. Matt Slater—153, WR, UCLA, from Tampa Bay
6. Bo Ruud—197, LB, Nebraska

NEW ORLEANS SAINTS
1. Sedrick Ellis—7, DT, Southern California, from San Francisco through New England
2. Tracy Porter—40, DB, Indiana
5. DeMario Pressley—144, DT, North Carolina State, from Detroit
   Carl Nicks—164, T, Nebraska, from New England
6. Taylor Mehlhaff—178, K, Wisconsin
7. # Adrian Arrington—237, WR, Michigan, from Green Bay

NEW YORK GIANTS
1. # Kenny Phillips—31, DB, Miami
2. Terrell Thomas—63, DB, Southern California
3. # Mario Manningham—95, WR, Michigan
4. Bryan Kehl—123, LB, Brigham Young, from Pittsburgh
5. Jonathan Goff—165, LB, Vanderbilt
6. Andre' Woodson—198, QB, Kentucky
   + Robert Henderson—199, DE, Southern Mississippi

NEW YORK JETS
1.#Vernon Gholston—6, LB, Ohio State
   Dustin Keller—30, TE, Purdue, from Green Bay
4. Dwight Lowery—113, DB, San Jose State, from
   New Orleans through New York Jets and Green Bay
5. Erik Ainge—162, QB, Tennessee, from Green Bay
6. Marcus Henry—171, WR, Kansas
7. Nate Garner—211, T, Arkansas

OAKLAND RAIDERS
1.#Darren McFadden—4, RB, Arkansas
4. Tyvon Branch—100, DB, Connecticut
   Arman Shields—125, WR, Richmond
6. Trevor Scott—169, DE, Buffalo
7. Chaz Schilens—226, WR, San Diego State

PHILADELPHIA EAGLES
2. Trevor Laws—47, DT, Notre Dame, from Minnesota
  # DeSean Jackson—49, WR, California
3. Bryan Smith—80, DE, McNeese State
4. Mike McGlynn—109, G, Pittsburgh, from Carolina
   Quintin Demps—117, DB, Texas-El Paso, from Minnesota
+ +#Jack Ikegwuonu—131, DB, Wisconsin
6. Mike Gibson—184, G, California
 + Joe Mays—200, LB, North Dakota State
 + Andy Studebaker—203, DE, Wheaton
7. King Dunlap—230, T, Auburn, from Seattle

PITTSBURGH STEELERS
1.#Rashard Mendenhall—23, RB, Illinois
2. Limas Sweed—53, WR, Texas
3. Bruce Davis—88, LB, UCLA
4. Tony Hills—130, T, Texas, from New York Giants
5. Dennis Dixon—156, QB, Oregon
6. Mike Humpal—188, LB, Iowa
   Ryan Mundy—194, DB, West Virginia, from
   Green Bay through New York Giants

ST. LOUIS RAMS
1. Chris Long—2, DE, Virginia
2. Donnie Avery—33, WR, Houston
3. John Greco—65, T, Toledo
4.#Justin King—101, DB, Penn State
   Keenan Burton—128, WR, Kentucky, from Green Bay
5. Roy Schuening—157, G, Oregon State, from
   Tennessee through Washington
7. Chris Chamberlain—228, LB, Tulsa, from Washington
 + David Vobora—252, LB, Idaho

SAN DIEGO CHARGERS
1. Antoine Cason—27, DB, Arizona
3. Jacob Hester—69, RB, Louisiana State, from
   Oakland through New England
4. Exercised in 2007 Supplemental Draft for
   Paul Oliver, DB, Georgia
5.+Marcus Thomas—166, RB, Texas-El Paso
6. DeJuan Tribble—192, DB, Boston College
7. Corey Clark—234, T, Texas A&M

SAN FRANCISCO 49ERS
1. Kentwan Balmer—29, DT, North Carolina, from Indianapolis
2.#Chilo Rachal—39, G, Southern California
3.#Reggie Smith—75, DB, Oklahoma, from Chicago
4. Cody Wallace—107, C, Texas A&M
6. Josh Morgan—174, WR, Virginia Tech
7. Larry Grant—214, LB, Ohio State

SEATTLE SEAHAWKS
1. Lawrence Jackson—28, DE, Southern California
   from Dallas
2. John Carlson—38, TE, Notre Dame, from Baltimore
4. Red Bryant—121, DT, Texas A&M
5. Owen Schmitt—163, RB, West Virginia, from Dallas
6. Tyler Schmitt—189, LS, San Diego State, from Tennessee
7. Justin Forsett—233, RB, California, from Jacksonville
   Brandon Coutu—235, K, Georgia

TAMPA BAY BUCCANEERS
1.#Aqib Talib—20, DB, Kansas
2. Dexter Jackson—58, WR, Appalachian State,
   from Jacksonville
3. Jeremy Zuttah—83, G, Rutgers
4. Dre Moore—115, DT, Maryland, from
   Philadelphia through Miami and Chicago
5. Josh Johnson—160, QB, San Diego, from
   San Diego through New England
6.#Geno Hayes—175, LB, Florida State, from Chicago
7. Cory Boyd—238, RB, South Carolina, from New England

TENNESSEE TITANS
1. Chris Johnson—24, RB, East Carolina
2. Jason Jones—54, DT, Eastern Michigan
3. Craig Stevens—85, TE, California
4. William Hayes—103, DE, Winston-Salem, from
   Atlanta through Washington
   Lavelle Hawkins—126, WR, California
 + Stanford Keglar—134, LB, Purdue
7. Cary Williams—229, DB, Washburn

WASHINGTON REDSKINS
2.#Devin Thomas—34, WR, Michigan State, from
   Oakland through Atlanta
   Fred Davis—48, TE, Southern California, from
   Houston through Atlanta
  # Malcolm Kelly—51, WR, Oklahoma
3.+Chad Rinehart—96, T, Northern Iowa
4. Justin Tryon—124, DB, Arizona State, from Tennessee
6. Durant Brooks—168, P, Georgia Tech, from St. Louis
   Kareem Moore—180, DB, Nicholls State, from
   Denver through St. Louis
   Colt Brennan—186, QB, Hawaii
7.+Rob Jackson—242, DE, Kansas State
 + Chris Horton—249, DB, UCLA

NUMBER OF PLAYERS DRAFTED— 2008

BY POSITION:
Defensive Backs	45
Wide Receivers	35
Linebackers	30
Running Backs	27
Defensive Ends	23
Tackles	23
Defensive Tackles	17
Tight Ends	16
Guards	14
Quarterbacks	13
Centers	3
Kickers	2
Nose Tackles	2
Punters	1
Long Snapper	1

BY COLLEGE:
Southern California	10
Virginia Tech	8
Louisiana State	7
Arkansas	6
California	6
Michigan	6
Arizona State	5
Auburn	5
Louisville	5
Texas	5
Texas A&M	5
Arizona	4
Georgia	4
Kentucky	4
Kansas	4
Notre Dame	4
Oklahoma	4
San Diego State	4
Wisconsin	4
Boston College	3
Central Florida	3
Florida State	3
Georgia Tech	3
Iowa	3
Miami	3
Michigan State	3
Nebraska	3
Ohio State	3
Oregon	3
Pittsburgh	3
Purdue	3
Tennessee	3
Texas-El Paso	3
UCLA	3
Vanderbilt	3
Virginia	3
Wake Forest	3
West Virginia	3
Appalachian State	2
Boise State	2
Buffalo	2
Cincinnati	2
Clemson	2
Colorado	2
Connecticut	2
Florida	2
Indiana	2
Iowa State	2
Kansas State	2
Missouri	2
Montana	2
North Carolina	2
North Carolina State	2
Northern Iowa	2
Oregon State	2
Penn State	2
Richmond	2
Rutgers	2
South Florida	2
Toledo	2
Utah State	2
Akron	1
Arkansas State	1
Army	1
Bentley	1
Bowling Green	1
Brigham Young	1
Coastal Carolina	1
Delaware	1
East Carolina	1
Eastern Kentucky	1
Eastern Michigan	1
Fresno State	1
Furman	1
Gardner-Webb	1
Grand Valley State	1
Hampton	1
Hawaii	1
Houston	1
Idaho	1
Illinois	1
Jackson State	1
Kent State	1
Maryland	1
McNeese State	1
Middle Tennessee	1
Minnesota	1
Mount Union	1
Nevada-Las Vegas	1
New Mexico	1
Nicholls State	1
North Dakota State	1
Northwest Missouri	1
Northwestern State (La.)	1
Ohio	1
St. Augustine's (NC)	1
San Diego	1
San Jose State	1
South Carolina	1
Southern Mississippi	1
Tennessee State	1
Troy	1
Tulane	1
Tulsa	1
Villanova	1
Washburn	1
Washington State	1
Weber State	1
Wheaton	1
Winston-Salem	1

BY CONFERENCE:
Southeastern	35
Pacific 10	34
Atlantic Coast	33
Big 12	29
Big Ten	28
Big East	19
Conference USA	11
Mid-American	9
Western Athletic	8
Mountain West	7
Independent	6
Atlantic 10	4
Big Sky	3
Southern	3
Southland	3
Sun Belt	3
Big South	2
Gateway Football	2
Mid-America Intercollegiate Athletic	2
Ohio Valley	2
Central Intercollegiate Athletic	1
College Conference of Illinois and Wisc.	1
Great Lakes Intercollegiate Athletic	1
Great West Football	1
Mid-Eastern Athletic	1
Northeast-10	1
Pioneer	1
Ohio Athletic	1
Southwestern Athletic	1

UNDERCLASSMEN IN THE DRAFT
Year	Entered	Drafted	In Top 10
1989	25	12	3
1990	38	18	5
1991	33	22	2
1992	48	25	5
1993	46	24	5
1994	43	26	6
1995	42	22	2
1996	46	21	4
1997	44	27	7
1998	41	20	3
1999	42	27	5
2000	31	20	4
2001	54	31	5
2002	43	26	5
2003	54	32	5
2004	44	35	5
2005	57	38	4
2006	62	34	6
2007	40	29	4
2008	53	39	4

WAIVERS

The waiver system is a procedure by which player contracts or NFL rights to players are made available by a club to other clubs in the League. During the procedure, the 31 other clubs either file claims to obtain the players or waive the opportunity to do so—thus the term "waiver." Claiming clubs are assigned players on a priority based on the inverse of won-and-lost standing. The claiming period is 24 hours from the first business day after the Pro Bowl through the last business day prior to June 1. From June 1 through the last business day prior to July 4, the claiming period is three days. From the first business day after July 4 through the conclusion of the regular season, the claiming period is 24 hours. If a player passes through waivers unclaimed, he becomes a free agent. All waivers are no recall and no withdrawal. Under the Collective Bargaining Agreement, from the beginning of the waiver system each year through the trading deadline (October 14, 2008), any veteran who has acquired four years of pension credit is not subject to the waiver system if the club desires to release him. After the trading deadline, such players are subject to the waiver system.

ACTIVE/INACTIVE LIST

The Active/Inactive List is the principal status for players participating for a club. It consists of all players under contract who are eligible for preseason, regular-season, and postseason games. Teams are permitted to open training camp with no more than 80 players under contract and thereafter must meet two mandatory roster reductions prior to the season opener. Teams will be permitted an Active List of 45 players and an Inactive List of eight players for each regular-season and postseason game. Provided that a club has two quarterbacks on its 45-player Active List, a third quarterback from its Inactive List is permitted to dress for the game, but if he enters the game during the first three quarters, the other two quarterbacks are thereafter prohibited from playing. Teams also are permitted to establish Practice Squads of up to eight players who are eligible to participate in practice, but these players remain free agents and are eligible to sign with any other team in the league.

August 26	Roster reduction to 75 players
August 30	Roster reduction to 53 players
August 31	Teams establish a Practice Squad of up to eight players

In addition to the squad limits described above, the overall roster limit of 80 players remains in effect throughout the regular season and postseason. The overall limit is applicable to players on a team's Active, Inactive, and certain Exempt Lists, players on the Practice Squad, and players on the Reserve List as Injured, Physically Unable to Perform, Non-Football Illness/Injury, and Suspended by Club.

RESERVE LIST

The Reserve List is a status for players who, for reasons of injury, retirement, military service, or other circumstances, are not immediately available for participation with a club. Players on Reserve/Injured are not eligible to practice or return to the Active/Inactive List in the same season that they are placed on Reserve. Players in the category of Reserve/Retired, Reserve/Did Not Report, Reserve/Exclusive Rights, and players who were placed in the category of Reserve/Left Squad in a previous season may not be reinstated during the period from 30 days before the end of the regular season through the postseason.

TRADES

Unrestricted trading between the AFC and NFC is allowed in 2008 through October 14, after which trading will end until 2009.

ANNUAL ACTIVE PLAYER LIMITS

NFL

Year(s)	Limit
1991-2008	45**
1985-90	45
1983-84	49
1982	45†-49
1978-81	45
1975-77	43
1974	47
1964-73	40
1963	37
1961-62	36
1960	38
1959	36
1957-58	35
1951-56	33
1949-50	32
1948	35
1947	35*-34
1945-46	33
1943-44	28
1940-42	33
1938-39	30
1936-37	25
1935	24
1930-34	20
1926-29	18
1925	16

** 45 plus a third quarterback
† 45 for first two games
* 35 for first three games

AFL

Year(s)	Limit
1966-69	40
1965	38
1964	34
1962-63	33
1960-61	35

NFL FREE AGENCY MOVEMENT

The following chart details veteran free agents who signed with new teams:

	Unrestricted	Restricted	Transition	Franchise	TOTALS
1993	108	8	4	1	121
1994	121	7	4	0	132
1995	171	6	2	0	179
1996	100	4	2	0	106
1997	86	2	2	0	90
1998	112	4	1	2	119
1999	115	2	1	0	118
2000	107	4	0	0	111
2001	93	4	0	0	97
2002	130	1	0	0	131
2003	111	5	1	0	117
2004	124	1	1	0	126
2005	104	3	0	0	107
2006	149	4	1	0	154
2007	126	4	0	0	130

The following procedures will be used to break standings ties for postseason playoffs and to determine regular-season schedules.

Note: Tie games count as one-half win and one-half loss for both clubs.

TO BREAK A TIE WITHIN A DIVISION

If, at the end of the regular season, two or more clubs in the same division finish with the best won-lost-tied percentage, the following steps will be taken until a champion is determined:

TWO CLUBS

1. Head-to-head (best won-lost-tied percentage in games between the clubs.)
2. Best won-lost-tied percentage in games played within the division.
3. Best won-lost-tied percentage in common games.
4. Best won-lost-tied percentage in games played within the conference.
5. Strength of victory.
6. Strength of schedule.
7. Best combined ranking among conference teams in points scored and points allowed.
8. Best combined ranking among all teams in points scored and points allowed.
9. Best net points in common games.
10. Best net points in all games.
11. Best net touchdowns in all games.
12. Coin toss.

THREE OR MORE CLUBS

(Note: If two clubs remain tied after a third club is eliminated during any step, tie-breaker reverts to Step 1 of the two-club format.)

1. Head-to-head (best won-lost-tied percentage in games among the clubs.)
2. Best won-lost-tied percentage in games played within the division.
3. Best won-lost-tied percentage in common games.
4. Best won-lost-tied percentage in games played within the conference.
5. Strength of victory.
6. Strength of schedule.
7. Best combined ranking among conference teams in points scored and points allowed.
8. Best combined ranking among all teams in points scored and points allowed.
9. Best net points in common games.
10. Best net points in all games.
11. Best net touchdowns in all games.
12. Coin toss.

TO BREAK A TIE FOR THE WILD-CARD TEAM

If it is necessary to break ties to determine the two Wild Card clubs from each conference, the following steps will be taken:

A. If all the tied clubs are from the same division, apply division tie-breaker.

B. If the tied clubs are from different divisions, apply the following steps:

TWO CLUBS

1. Head-to-head, if applicable.
2. Best won-lost-tied percentage in the games played within the conference.
3. Best won-lost-tied percentage in common games, minimum of four.
4. Strength of victory.
5. Strength of schedule.
6. Best combined ranking among conference teams in points scored and points allowed.
7. Best combined ranking among all teams in points scored and points allowed.
8. Best net points in conference games.
9. Best net points in all games.
10. Best net touchdowns in all games.
11. Coin toss.

THREE OR MORE CLUBS

1. Apply division tie-breaker to eliminate all but highest ranked club in each division prior to proceeding to Step 2. The original seeding within a division upon application of the division tie-breaker remains the same for all subsequent applications of the procedure that are necessary to identify the Wild Card participants.
2. Head-to-head sweep (apply only if one club has defeated each of the others or one club has lost to each of the others).
3. Best won-lost-tied percentage in games played within the conference.
4. Best won-lost-tied percentage in common games, minimum of four.
5. Strength of victory.
6. Strength of schedule.
7. Best combined ranking among conference teams in points scored and points allowed.
8. Best combined ranking among all teams in points scored and points allowed.
9. Best net points in conference games.
10. Best net points in all games.
11. Best net touchdowns in all games.
12. Coin toss.

When the first Wild Card team has been identified, the procedure is repeated to name the second Wild Card (i.e., eliminate all but the highest ranked club in each division prior to proceeding to Step 2.) In situations where three teams from the same division are involved in the procedure, the original seeding of the teams remains the same for subsequent applications of the tie-breaker if the top-ranked team in that division qualifies for a Wild Card berth.

OTHER TIE-BREAKING PROCEDURES

1. Only one club advances to the playoffs in any tie-breaking step. Remaining tied clubs revert to the first step of the applicable division or Wild Card tie-breakers. As an example, if two clubs remain tied in any tie-breaker step after all other clubs have been eliminated, the procedure reverts to Step 1 of the two-club format to determine the winner. When one club wins the tie-breaker, all other clubs revert to Step 1 of the applicable two-club or three-club format.
2. In comparing records against common opponents among tied teams, the best won-lost-tied percentage is the deciding factor since teams may have played an unequal number of games.
3. To determine home-field priority among division-titlists, apply Wild Card tie-breakers.
4. To determine home-field priority for Wild Card qualifiers, apply division tie-breakers (if teams are from the same division) or Wild Card tie-breakers (if teams are from different divisions).

TIE-BREAKING PROCEDURE FOR SELECTION MEETING

If two or more clubs are tied in the selection order, the strength-of-schedule tie-breaker is applied, subject to the following exceptions for playoff clubs:

1. The Super Bowl winner is last and the Super Bowl loser next-to-last.
2. Any non-Super Bowl playoff club involved in a tie shall be assigned priority within its segment below that of non-playoff clubs and in the order that the playoff club exited from the playoffs. Thus, within a tied segment a playoff club that loses in the Wild Card game will have priority over a playoff club that loses in the Divisional playoff game, which in turn will have priority over a club that loses in the Conference Championship game. If two tied clubs exited the playoffs in the same round, the tie is broken by strength of schedule.

If any ties cannot be broken by strength of schedule, the divisional or conference tie-breakers, whichever are applicable, are applied. Any ties that still exist are broken by a coin flip.

The NFL utilizes a system of Referee Replay Review to aid officiating.

Prior to the two-minute warning of each half, a Coaches' Challenge System will be in effect. After the two-minute warning, and throughout any overtime period, a Referee Review will be initiated by a Replay Assistant from a Replay Booth.

The following procedures will be used:

Reviews by Referee: All Replay Reviews will be conducted by the Referee on a field-level monitor after consultation with the other covering official(s), prior to review. A decision will be reversed only when the Referee has *indisputable visual evidence* available to him that warrants the change.

Coaches' Challenge: In each game, a team will be permitted two challenges that will initiate Referee Replay reviews. Each challenge will require the use of a team time out. If a challenge is upheld, the time out will be restored to the challenging team. If both challenges are upheld, a third challenge will be awarded to the challenging team. No challenges will be recognized from a team that has exhausted its time outs.

Replay Assistant's Request for Review: After the two-minute warning of each half, and throughout any overtime period, any review will be initiated by a Replay Assistant. There is no limit to the number of reviews that may be initiated by the Replay Assistant. His ability to initiate a review will be unrelated to the number of time outs that either team has remaining, and no time out will be charged for any review initiated by the Replay Assistant.

Time Limit: Each review will be a maximum of 60 seconds in length, timed from when the Referee begins his review of the replay at the field-level monitor.

Reviewable Plays: The Replay System will cover the following play situations only:

A) **Plays Governed by Sideline, Goal Line, End Zone, End Line, and Goal Posts:**
1. Scoring plays, including a runner breaking the plane of the goal line.
2. Pass complete/incomplete/intercepted at sideline, goal line, end zone, and end line.
3. Runner/receiver in or out of bounds.
4. Recovery of loose ball in or out of bounds.
5. A field goal or try attempt when it is lower than the top of the uprights.

B) **Passing Plays:**
1. Pass ruled complete/incomplete/intercepted in the field of play.
2. Touching of a forward pass by an ineligible receiver.
3. Touching of a forward pass by a defensive player.

4. Quarterback (Passer) forward pass or fumble.
5. Illegal forward pass beyond line of scrimmage.
6. Illegal forward pass after change of possession.
7. Forward or backward pass thrown from behind line of scrimmage.

C) **Other Detectable Infractions:**
1. Runner ruled not down by defensive contact.
2. Runner ruled down by defensive contact and there is a recovery by defense.
3. Forward progress with respect to first down.
4. Touching of a kick.
5. Number of players on the field.
6. Recovery of loose ball in the field of play.

INSTANT REPLAY HISTORY

From 1986-1991, a limited system of Instant Replay was used on a year-by-year basis. Replay also was experimented with during the 1996 and 1998 preseasons. For the 1999 season, the NFL introduced a system of Referee Replay Review to aid officiating. That system was extended on a one-year basis for the 2000 season and then approved for the next three years through 2003. The system was extended on a five-year basis in March 2004 and was later installed permanently in March 2007.

Following are the results of the different systems:

REGULAR SEASON, 1986-1991

Year	Games	Plays Closely Reviewed	Reversals
1986	224	374	38
1987	210	490	57
1988	224	537	53
1989	224	492	65
1990	224	504	73
1991	224	570	90
TOTAL	1,330	2,967	376

PRESEASON, 1996, 1998

Year	Games	Challenges	Reversals
1996	10	13	3
1998	10	10	3
TOTAL	20	23	6

REGULAR SEASON, 1999-2007

Year	Games	Total Replay Reviews	Challenges	Reversals
1999	248	195	133	57
2000	248	247	179	84
2001	248	258	191	89
2002	256	294	208	94
2003	256	255	184	66
2004	256	283	233	88
2005	256	295	223	92
2006	256	311	237	107
2007	256	327	250	122
TOTAL	2,280	2,465	1,838	799

The AFC

American Football Conference
North Division
Team Colors: Black, Purple, and Metallic
  Gold
1 Winning Drive
Owings Mills, Maryland 21117
Telephone: (410) 701-4000

2008 SCHEDULE
PRESEASON
Aug. 7   at New England 7:30
Aug. 16 **Minnesota** 7:30
Aug. 23 at St. Louis.........................7:00
Aug. 28 **Atlanta**..............................7:30

REGULAR SEASON
Sep. 7   **Cincinnati** 1:00
Sep. 14 at Houston 3:15
Sep. 21 **Cleveland** 4:15
Sep. 29 at Pittsburgh (Mon.) 8:30
Oct. 5   **Tennessee** 1:00
Oct. 12 at Indianapolis 1:00
Oct. 19 at Miami 1:00
Oct. 26 **Oakland** 1:00
Nov. 2   at Cleveland 1:00
Nov. 9   BYE
Nov. 16 at N.Y. Giants.....................1:00
Nov. 23 **Philadelphia** 1:00
Nov. 30 at Cincinnati 1:00
Dec. 7   **Washington** 1:00
Dec. 14 **Pittsburgh** 1:00
Dec. 20 at Dallas (Sat.) 7:15
Dec. 28 **Jacksonville** 1:00

Stadium: M&T Bank Stadium
  (opened in 1998)
  • **Capacity:** 71,008
  1101 Russell Street
  Baltimore, Maryland 21230
Playing Surface: Sportexe Momentum
Training Camp: McDaniel College
  2 College Hill
  Westminster, MD 21157

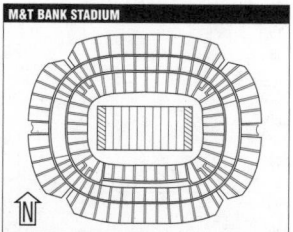

M&T BANK STADIUM

CLUB OFFICIALS
Owner: Steve Bisciotti
President: Dick Cass
Executive Vice President/General
  Manager: Ozzie Newsome
Senior Vice President/Public and
  Community Relations: Kevin Byrne
Vice President of Football Administration:
  Pat Moriarty
Vice President of Medical Services/
  Head Certified Athletic Trainer:
  Bill Tessendorf
Vice President, Corporate Sales:
  Mark Burdett
Vice President and Chief Financial
  Officer: Jeff Goering
Vice President, Regional Partnerships
  and Sales: Ed Burchell
Vice President, Marketing:
  Gabrielle Dow
Vice President, Operations: Bob Eller
Vice President, Ticket Sales and
  Operations: Baker Koppelman
Vice President, National Partnerships and
  Sales: Kevin Rochlitz
Vice President, Broadcasting:
  Larry Rosen
Vice President, Stadium Operations:
  Roy Sommerhof
Senior Director of Publishing/Game
  Credential Management:
  Francine Lubera
Director of Pro Personnel: George Kokinis
Director of College Scouting:
  Eric DeCosta
Director of Player Development:
  O.J. Brigance
Director of Media Relations:
  Chad Steele
Assistant Director of Pro Personnel:
  Vincent Newsome
Assistant Director of Player Development:
  Harry Swayne
Scouts: Chad Alexander, Joe Douglas,
  Milt Hendrickson, Joe Hortiz,
  Lionel Vital, Jeremiah Washburn,
  Andrew Weidl
Equipment Manager: Ed Carroll
Director of Football Video Operations:
  Jon Dubé
Assistant Director of Football Video
  Operations: Mark Bienvenu
Senior Director, Fields & Grounds/Head
  Groundskeeper: Don Follett
Senior Director, Information Technology:
  Bill Jankowski
Director of Premium Services/Suites:
  Theresa Abato
Director, Community Relations:
  Kenny Abrams
Director, New Media: Michelle Andres
Controller: Jim Coller
Director, Broadcasting Administration:
  Don DiRaddo
Director, Information Technology:
  Nick Fusee
Director, Human Resources:
  Elizabeth Jackson
Director, Security: Darren Sanders

COACHING HISTORY
(101-98-1)
Records include postseason games
1996-98   Ted Marchibroda 16-31-1
1999-2007 Brian Billick................85-67-0

PAID ATTENDANCE
Home 556,938   Away 540,720
Total 1,097,658
Single-game home record,
  71,382 (12/03/07)
Single-season home record, 557,707
  (2006)

2008 DRAFT CHOICES

Round	Name	Pos.	College
1	Joe Flacco	QB	Delaware
2	Ray Rice	RB	Rutgers
3	Tavares Gooden	LB	Miami
	Tom Zbikowski	DB	Notre Dame
	Oniel Cousins	T	Texas-El Paso
4	Marcus Smith	WR	New Mexico
	David Hale	T	Weber State
5	Choice Exercised in 2007		
	Supplemental Draft for		
	Jared Gaither	T	Maryland
6	Haruki Nakamura	DB	Cincinnati
7	Justin Harper	WR	Virginia Tech
	Allen Patrick	RB	Oklahoma

2007 TEAM RECORD

PRESEASON (1-3)

Date	Result		Opponent
8/13	W	29-3	Philadelphia
8/19	L	12-13	New York Giants
8/25	L	7-13	at Washington
8/31	L	10-13	at Atlanta

REGULAR SEASON (5-11)

Date	Result		Opponent	Att.
9/10	L	20-27	at Cincinnati	66,093
9/16	W	20-13	New York Jets	71,246
9/23	W	26-23	Arizona	71,372
9/30	L	13-27	at Cleveland	73,024
10/7	W	9-7	at San Francisco	67,885
10/14	W	22-3	St. Louis	71,175
10/21	L	14-19	at Buffalo	70,727
11/5	L	7-38	at Pittsburgh	63,457
11/11	L	7-21	Cincinnati	71,130
11/18	L	30-33	Cleveland (OT)	71,055
11/25	L	14-32	at San Diego	63,337
12/3	L	24-27	New England	71,382
12/9	L	20-44	Indianapolis	70,513
12/16	L	16-22	at Miami (OT)	70,287
12/23	L	6-27	at Seattle	68,164
12/30	W	27-21	Pittsburgh	71,353

(OT) Overtime

SCORE BY PERIODS

Ravens	33	110	44	88	0 —	275
Opponents	69	136	87	83	9 —	384

2007 TEAM STATISTICS

	Ravens	Opp.
Total First Downs	291	258
Rushing	96	69
Passing	175	162
Penalty	20	27
3rd Down: Made/Att	90/234	82/224
3rd Down Pct.	38.5	36.6
4th Down: Made/Att	11/21	7/13
4th Down Pct.	52.4	53.8
Possession Avg.	30:46	29:14
Total Net Yards	4832	4825
Avg. Per Game	302.0	301.6
Total Plays	1042	968
Avg. Per Play	4.6	5.0
Net Yards Rushing	1797	1268
Avg. Per Game	112.3	79.3
Total Rushes	446	446
Net Yards Passing	3035	3557
Avg. Per Game	189.7	222.3
Sacked/Yards Lost	39/273	32/183
Gross Yards	3308	3740
Att./Completions	557/341	490/293
Completion Pct.	61.2	59.8
Had Intercepted	14	17
Punts/Average	79/43.0	76/43.1
Net Punting Avg.	79/36.0	76/37.4
Penalties/Yards	107/873	84/728
Fumbles/Ball Lost	35/26	12/6
Touchdowns	28	39
Rushing	11	9
Passing	13	27
Returns	4	3

2007 INDIVIDUAL STATISTICS

PASSING	Att.	Comp.	Yds.	Pct.	TD	Int.	Tkld.	Rate
Boller	275	168	1743	61.1	9	10	24/159	75.2
McNair	205	133	1113	64.9	2	4	11/85	73.9
T. Smith	76	40	452	52.6	2	0	4/29	79.5
Clayton	1	0	0	0.0	0	0	0/0	39.6
Ravens	557	341	3308	61.2	13	14	39/273	75.2
Opponents	490	293	3740	59.8	27	17	32/183	87.6

SCORING	TD R	TD P	TD Rt	PAT	FG	Saf	PTS
Stover	0	0	0	26/26	27/32	0	107
McGahee	7	1	0	0/0	0/0	0	48
Mason	0	5	0	0/0	0/0	0	30
Darling	0	3	0	0/0	0/0	0	18
Figurs	0	0	2	0/0	0/0	0	12
Mu. Smith	2	0	0	0/0	0/0	0	12
Heap	0	1	0	0/0	0/0	0	6
Lewis	0	0	1	0/0	0/0	0	6
McClain	0	1	0	0/0	0/0	0	6
Reed	0	0	1	0/0	0/0	0	6
Ross	1	0	0	0/0	0/0	0	6
T. Smith	1	0	0	0/0	0/0	0	6
Sypniewski	0	1	0	0/0	0/0	0	6
Wilcox	0	1	0	0/0	0/0	0	6
Ravens	11	13	4	26/26	27/32	0	275
Opponents	9	27	3	35/36	37/43	1	384

2-Pt. Conversions: Ravens 0-2, Opponents 1-2

RUSHING	No.	Yds	Avg	LG	TD
McGahee	294	1207	4.1	46t	7
Mu. Smith	75	264	3.5	24	2
Boller	19	89	4.7	15	0
Ross	12	72	6.0	32t	1
Anderson	15	62	4.1	16	0
T. Smith	12	54	4.5	14	1
McNair	10	32	3.2	13	0
McClain	8	18	2.3	4	0
Figurs	1	-1	-1.0	-1	0
Ravens	446	1797	4.0	46t	11
Opponents	446	1268	2.8	36	9

RECEIVING	No.	Yds	Avg	LG	TD
Mason	103	1087	10.6	79t	5
Clayton	48	531	11.1	52	0
McGahee	43	231	5.4	30	1
Sypniewski	34	246	7.2	13	1
Mu. Smith	27	192	7.1	29	0
Heap	23	239	10.4	37	1
Williams	20	290	14.5	34	0
Darling	18	326	18.1	53	3
McClain	9	55	6.1	13t	1
Wilcox	6	18	3.0	7	1
Anderson	4	26	6.5	10	0
Green	2	16	8.0	10	0
Vickers	2	4	2.0	5	0
Figurs	1	36	36.0	36	0
Willis	1	11	11.0	11	0
Ravens	341	3308	9.7	79t	13
Opponents	293	3740	12.8	78t	27

INTERCEPTIONS	No.	Yds	Avg	LG	TD
Reed	7	130	18.6	32	0
Lewis	2	35	17.5	35t	1
Pittman	2	21	10.5	29	0
Martin	2	3	1.5	3	0
Ivy	1	22	22.0	22	0
Edwards	1	1	1.0	1	0
McAlister	1	0	0.0	0	0
Rolle	1	0	0.0	0	0
Ravens	17	212	12.5	35t	1
Opponents	14	293	20.9	100t	1

PUNTING	No.	Yds.	Avg.	In 20	LG
Koch	78	3397	43.6	20	64
Ravens	79	3397	43.0	20	64
Opponents	76	3277	43.1	26	74

PUNT RETURNS	Ret	FC	Yds	Avg	LG	TD
Figurs	16	9	171	10.7	75t	1
Reed	10	3	94	9.4	63t	1
Ross	5	0	36	7.2	15	0
Sams	4	0	37	9.3	16	0
Ravens	35	12	338	9.7	75t	2
Opponents	38	16	375	9.9	49	0

KICKOFF RETURNS	No.	Yds	Avg	LG	TD
Figurs	46	1138	24.7	94t	1
Ross	9	148	16.4	25	0
Sams	5	140	28.0	47	0
Mu. Smith	3	89	29.7	52	0
Anderson	2	10	5.0	10	0
Ravens	65	1525	23.5	94t	1
Opponents	61	1444	23.7	50	0

FIELD GOALS	1-19	20-29	30-39	40-49	50+
Stover	1/1	11/11	7/7	8/12	0/1
Ravens	1/1	11/11	7/7	8/12	0/1
Opponents	1/1	14/14	10/12	10/11	2/5

SACKS	No.
Suggs	5.0
Gregg	3.0
Ivy	3.0
Ngata	3.0
Bannan	2.0
Barnes	2.0
Johnson	2.0
Lewis	2.0
Pryce	2.0
Sapp	2.0
Edwards	1.0
Jones	1.0
Landry	1.0
Scott	1.0
Stills	1.0
(group)	1.0
Ravens	32.0
Opponents	39.0

RECORD HOLDERS
INDIVIDUAL RECORDS—CAREER

Category	Name	Performance
Rushing (Yds.)	Jamal Lewis, 2000-06	7,801
Passing (Yds.)	Kyle Boller, 2003-07	7,846
Passing (TDs)	Vinny Testaverde, 1996-97	51
Receiving (No.)	Todd Heap, 2001-07	339
Receiving (Yds.)	Todd Heap, 2001-07	3,897
Interceptions	Ed Reed, 2002-07	34
Punting (Avg.)	Sam Koch, 2006-07	43.2
Punt Return (Avg.)	Jermaine Lewis, 1996-2001	11.8
Kickoff Return (Avg.)	Yamon Figurs, 2007	24.7
Field Goals	Matt Stover, 1996-2007	327
Touchdowns (Tot.)	Jamal Lewis, 2000-06	47
Points	Matt Stover, 1996-2007	1,342

INDIVIDUAL RECORDS—SINGLE SEASON

Category	Name	Performance
Rushing (Yds.)	Jamal Lewis, 2003	2,066
Passing (Yds.)	Vinny Testaverde, 1996	4,177
Passing (TDs)	Vinny Testaverde, 1996	33
Receiving (No.)	Derrick Mason, 2007	103
Receiving (Yds.)	Michael Jackson, 1996	1,201
Interceptions	Ed Reed, 2004	9
Punting (Avg.)	Kyle Richardson, 1998	43.9
Punt Return (Avg.)	Jermaine Lewis, 2000	16.1
Kickoff Return (Avg.)	Corey Harris, 1998	27.6
Field Goals	Matt Stover, 2000	35
Touchdowns (Tot.)	Michael Jackson, 1996	14
	Jamal Lewis, 2003	14
Points	Matt Stover, 2000	135

INDIVIDUAL RECORDS—SINGLE GAME

Category	Name	Performance
Rushing (Yds.)	Jamal Lewis, 9-14-03	295
Passing (Yds.)	Vinny Testaverde, 10-27-96	429
Passing (TDs)	Tony Banks, 9-10-00	5
Receiving (No.)	Priest Holmes, 10-11-98	13
Receiving (Yds.)	Qadry Ismail, 12-12-99	268
Interceptions	Many times	2
	Last time by David Pittman, 12-30-07	
Field Goals	Matt Stover, 9-21-97, 12-26-99, 10-28-00, 10-14-07	5
Touchdowns (Tot.)	Marcus Robinson, 11-23-03	4
Points	Marcus Robinson, 11-23-03	24

2008 VETERAN ROSTER

No.	Name	Pos.	Ht.	Wt.	Age	NFL Exp.	College	Hometown	How Acq.	'07 Games/ Starts
96	Ayanbadejo, Brendon	LB	6-1	228	31	6	UCLA	Santa Cruz, Calif.	UFA(Chi)-'08	16/0*
94	Bannan, Justin	DT	6-3	310	29	7	Colorado	Orangevale, Calif.	UFA(Buff)-'06	15/1
50	Barnes, Antwan	LB	6-1	240	23	2	Florida International	Miami, Fla.	D4a-'07	14/0
7	Boller, Kyle	QB	6-3	220	27	6	California	Newhall, Calif.	D1b-'03	12/8
60	Brown, Jason	G/C	6-3	320	25	4	North Carolina	Henderson, N.C.	D4-'05	16/16
54	Burgess, Prescott	LB	6-3	240	24	2	Michigan	Warren, Ohio	D6-'07	8/0
65	Chester, Chris	G/C	6-3	305	25	3	Oklahoma	Tustin, Calif.	D2-'06	16/5
89	Clayton, Mark	WR	5-10	195	26	4	Oklahoma	Arlington, Texas	D1-'05	16/12
53	Cody, Dan	LB	6-5	255	26	4	Oklahoma	Ada, Okla.	D2a-'05	0*
30	Daniels, P.J.	RB	5-10	214	25	3	Georgia Tech	Houston, Texas	D4b-'06	0*
93	Edwards, Dwan	DT	6-3	315	27	5	Oregon State	Columbus, Mont.	D2-'04	16/13
16	Figurs, Yamon	WR/RS	5-11	175	26	2	Kansas State	Fort Pierce, Fla.	D3a-'07	14/0
71	Gaither, Jared	T	6-9	350	22	2	Maryland	White Plains, Md.	SD5-'07	6/2
63	Gordon, Amon	DT	6-2	305	26	3	Stanford	San Diego, Calif.	FA-'07	1/0
33	Green, Justin	FB	5-11	251	26	4	Montana	San Diego, Calif.	D5-'05	15/0
97	Gregg, Kelly	DT	6-0	310	31	9	Oklahoma	Edmond, Okla.	FA-'00	16/16
59	Greisen, Nick	LB	6-1	244	29	7	Wisconsin	Berlin, Wisc.	FA-'07	14/2
66	Grubbs, Ben	G	6-3	315	24	2	Auburn	Eclectic, Ala.	D1-'07	16/12
86	Heap, Todd	TE	6-5	252	28	8	Arizona State	Mesa, Ariz.	D1-'01	6/6
35	Ivy, Corey	CB	5-9	188	31	8	Oklahoma	Moore, Okla.	UFA(StL)-'06	16/13
95	Johnson, Jarret	DE	6-3	270	27	6	Alabama	Cedar Key, Fla.	D4a-'03	16/16
91	Jones, Edgar	LB	6-3	263	23	2	Southeast Missouri	Rayville, La.	FA-'07	4/0
70	Katula, Matt	LS	6-6	272	26	4	Wisconsin	Brookfield, Wisc.	FA-'05	16/0
4	Koch, Sam	P	6-1	230	26	3	Nebraska	Seward, Neb.	D6a-'06	16/0
26	Landry, Dawan	S	6-0	220	25	3	Georgia Tech	Ama, La.	D5a-'06	16/16
36	Leonhard, Jim	S	5-8	185	25	4	Wisconsin	Tony, Wisc.	FA-'08	13/6*
52	Lewis, Ray	LB	6-1	250	33	13	Miami	Lakeland, Fla.	D1b-'96	14/14
29	Martin, Derrick	CB	5-10	202	23	3	Wyoming	Denver, Colo.	D6b-'06	16/3
85	Mason, Derrick	WR	5-10	192	34	12	Michigan State	Detroit, Mich.	FA-'05	16/16
21	McAlister, Chris	CB	6-1	206	31	10	Arizona	Pasadena, Calif.	D1-'99	8/8
37	McClain, Le'Ron	FB	6-0	260	23	2	Alabama	Northport, Ala.	D4b-'07	16/11
58	McCune, Robert	LB	6-0	240	29	2	Louisville	Mobile, Ala.	FA-'07	2/0
23	McGahee, Willis	RB	6-0	232	26	6	Miami	Miami, Fla.	T(Buff)-'07	15/15
92	Ngata, Haloti	NT	6-4	340	24	3	Oregon	Salt Lake City, Utah	D1-'06	16/16
75	Ogden, Jonathan	T	6-9	345	34	13	UCLA	Washington, D.C.	D1a-'96	11/10
69	Parker, J'Vonne	DT	6-4	325	26	2	Rutgers	Newark, N.J.	FA-'07	0*
24	Pittman, David	CB	5-11	182	24	3	Northwestern St.	Gramercy, La.	D3-'06	8/1
27	Prude, Ronnie	CB	5-11	178	26	3	Louisiana State	Shreveport, La.	FA-'06	15/0
90	Pryce, Trevor	DT	6-5	286	33	12	Clemson	Winter Park, Fla.	FA-'06	5/2
20	Reed, Ed	S	5-11	200	29	7	Miami	St. Rose, La.	D1-'02	16/16
22	Rolle, Samari	CB	6-0	175	32	11	Florida State	Miami, Fla.	FA-'05	6/5
34	Ross, Cory	RB	5-6	201	25	3	Nebraska	Denver, Colo.	FA-'06	6/0
57	Scott, Bart	LB	6-2	240	28	7	Southern Illinois	Detroit, Mich.	FA-'02	16/16
51	Smith, Mike	LB	6-1	235	27	4	Texas Tech	Lubbock, Texas	D7-'05	0*
10	Smith, Troy	QB	6-0	225	24	2	Ohio State	Cleveland, Ohio	D5-'07	4/2
56	Stills, Gary	LB	6-2	250	34	10	West Virginia	Trenton, N.J.	FA-'06	16/0
3	Stover, Matt	K	5-11	178	40	19	Louisiana Tech	Dallas, Texas	PB(NYG)-'91	16/0
55	Suggs, Terrell	LB	6-3	260	25	6	Arizona State	Chandler, Ariz.	D1a-'03	16/16
88	Sypniewski, Quinn	TE	6-6	270	26	3	Colorado	Johnston, Iowa	D5b-'06	15/9
78	Terry, Adam	T	6-8	330	26	4	Syracuse	Queensbury, N.Y.	D2b-'05	13/9
80	Vickers, Lee	TE	6-6	275	27	2	North Alabama	Athens, Ala.	FA-'07	8/2
41	Walker, Frank	CB	5-11	196	27	6	Tuskegee	Tuskegee, Ala.	UFA(GB)-'08	12/0*
31 t-	Washington, Fabian	CB	5-11	185	25	4	Nebraska	Bradenton, Fla.	T(Oak)-'08	15/3*
83	Wilcox, Daniel	TE	6-1	245	31	6	Appalachian State	Atlanta, Ga.	FA-'04	5/1
87	Williams, Demetrius	WR	6-2	197	25	3	Oregon	Concord, Calif.	D4a-'06	9/4
17	Willis, Matt	WR	5-11	185	24	2	UCLA	La Palma, Calif.	FA-'07	5/0
28	Winborne, Jamaine	DB	5-10	202	27	4	Virginia	Chesapeake, Va.	FA-'05	16/0
73	Yanda, Marshal	G/T	6-3	310	23	2	Iowa	Anamosa, Iowa	D3b-'07	16/12

* Ayanbadejo played 16 games with Chicago in '07; Cody missed '07 season because of injury; Daniels missed '07 season because of injury; Leonhard played 13 games with Buffalo; Parker did not play in 1 game; M. Smith missed '07 season because of injury; Walker played 12 games with Green Bay; Washington played 15 games with Oakland.

t- Ravens traded for Washington (Oak).

Retired—Steve McNair, 13-year quarterback, 6 games in '07.

Players lost through free agency (2): WR Devard Darling (KC; 16 games in '07), CB B.J. Sams (KC; 1).

Also played with Ravens in '07—RB Mike Anderson (8 games), C Mike Flynn (15), CB Willie Gaston (4), LB Dennis Haley (2), K Ryhs Lloyd (2).

2008 FIRST-YEAR ROSTER

Name	Pos.	Ht.	Wt.	Age	College	Hometown	How Acq.
Barnes, Brandon	G	6-2	315	23	Grand Valley State	Detroit, Mich.	FA
Carter, Patrick	WR	6-3	200	23	Louisville	St. Petersburg, Fla.	FA
Cousins, Oniel	T	6-4	310	24	Texas-El Paso	Fullerton, Calif.	D3c
Czech, Piotr	K	6-5	210	22	Wagner	Keyport, N.J.	FA
Dato, Ben	P	6-2	205	22	Fordham	Wyomissing, Pa.	FA
Dumford, Sean	T	6-5	293	23	Eastern Kentucky	Washington Court House, Ohio	FA
Fitch, Zarnell (1)	DT	6-3	320	25	TCU	Spencer, Okla.	FA-'07
Flacco, Joe	QB	6-6	235	23	Delaware	Audubon, N.J.	D1
Gooden, Tavares	LB	6-1	235	23	Miami	Fort Lauderdale, Fla.	D3a
Hale, David	G/T	6-6	315	25	Weber State	Plain City, Utah	D4b
Harper, Justin	WR	6-3	215	23	Virginia Tech	Catawba, N.C.	D7a
Kracalik, Mike (1)	T	6-8	337	25	San Diego State	San Diego, Calif.	FA-'05
Kraus, Adam	G	6-6	295	23	Michigan	New Orleans, La.	FA
Kuhn, Scott	TE	6-6	257	22	Louisville	Hebron, Ky.	FA
McClain, Jameel	LB	6-1	256	23	Syracuse	Philadelphia, Pa.	FA
Nakamura, Haruki	S	5-10	205	22	Cincinnati	Cleveland, Ohio	D6
Nordin, Jake (1)	FB	6-3	255	24	Northern Illinois	Lake Lillian, Minn.	FA-'07
Patrick, Allen	RB	6-1	200	24	Oklahoma	Conway, S.C.	D7b
Reed, Kerry (1)	WR	6-1	201	23	Michigan State	Homestead, Fla.	FA
Reitz, Joe	TE	6-7	256	23	Western Michigan	Fishers, Ind.	FA
Rice, Ray	RB	5-8	200	21	Rutgers	New Rochelle, N.Y.	D2
Roach, Brad	QB	6-6	245	23	Catawba	Williamston, N.C.	FA
Smith, Marcus	WR	6-1	220	23	New Mexico	San Diego, Calif.	D4a
Wheelwright, Ernie	WR	6-5	215	24	Minnesota	Columbus, Ohio	FA
Wiggins, Isaiah	G	6-4	290	23	Illinois State	Chicago, Ill.	FA
Williams, Lorenzo	DL	6-0	304	23	Missouri	Midwest City, Okla.	FA
Zbikowski, Tom	S	5-11	215	23	Notre Dame	Arlington Heights, Ill.	D3b

The term NFL Rookie is defined as a player who is in his first season of professional football and has not been on the roster of another professional football team for any regular-season or postseason games. A Rookie is designated by an "R" on NFL rosters. Players who have been active in another professional football league or players who have NFL experience, including either preseason training camp or being on an Active List or Inactive List, or on Reserve/Injured or Reserve/Physically Unable to Perform for fewer than six regular-season games, are termed NFL First-Year Players. An NFL First-Year Player is designated by a "1" on NFL rosters. Thereafter, a player is credited with an additional year of experience for each season in which he accumulates six games on the Active List or Inactive List, or on Reserve/Injured or Reserve/Physically Unable to Perform.

Log on to www.baltimoreravens.com for an up-to-date roster; Age listed is as of September 4, 2008.

COACHING STAFF
Head Coach,
John Harbaugh

Pro Career: John Harbaugh became the third head coach in Baltimore Ravens history on January 19, 2008. Harbaugh spent the previous 10 seasons (1998-2007) with the Philadelphia Eagles. He was the team's secondary coach in 2007, after 9 seasons as its special teams coordinator. Under his leadership, Harbaugh's special teams units were consistently ranked among the NFL's best. From 2000-04, Philadelphia was the only team to rank in the top 10 in the comprehensive annual special teams report created by The Dallas Morning News' Rick Gosselin. (Gosselin's report is recognized by NFL teams as the special teams measuring stick.) In 2001 and 2003, the Eagles were ranked 1st by Gosselin, who compiles his report based on 22 kicking-game categories. Following the 2001 season, Harbaugh was voted the NFL's Special Teams Coach of the Year by his coaching peers. He was also named The Dallas Morning News Special Teams Coach of the Year that season. Career record: 0-0.
Background: Harbaugh played defensive back for 4 years at Miami (Ohio) from 1980-83, while earning his degree in political science. He coached on the collegiate level at Western Michigan (1984-86), Pittsburgh (1987), Morehead State (1988), Cincinnati (1989-1996), and Indiana (1997).
Personal: Age 45, born in Perrysburg, Ohio, Harbaugh and his wife, Ingrid, have a daughter, Alison. He is the son of longtime college coach Jack Harbaugh, and his brother, Jim, the current Stanford head coach, played quarterback in the NFL for 14 years, including a season in Baltimore (1998). John's brother-in-law, Tom Crean, Indiana University's head basketball coach, is married to his sister, Joani.

ASSISTANT COACHES
Clarence Brooks, defensive line; born New York, N.Y. Guard Massachusetts 1970-73. No pro playing experience. College coach: Massachusetts 1976-1980, Syracuse 1981-89, Arizona 1990-92. Pro coach: Chicago Bears 1993-98, Cleveland Browns 1999, Miami Dolphins 2000-04, joined Ravens in 2005.
Cam Cameron, offensive coordinator; born Chapel Hill, N.C. Quarterback Indiana 1980-83. No pro playing experience. College coach: Michigan 1984-1993, Indiana 1997-2001 (head coach). Pro coach: Washington Redskins 1994-96, San Diego Chargers 2002-06, Miami Dolphins 2007 (head coach), joined Ravens in 2008.
Mark Carrier, defensive backs; born Lake Charles, La. Cornerback Southern California 1987-89. Pro cornerback Chicago Bears 1990-96, Detroit Lions 1997-99, Washington Redskins 2000.

College coach: Arizona State 2004-05. Pro coach: Joined Ravens in 2006.
John Dunn, asst. strength and conditioning; born Great Barrington, Mass. Guard Penn State 1974-77. No pro playing experience. College coach: Penn State 1978. Pro coach: Washington Redskins 1984-86, Los Angeles Raiders 1987-89, San Diego Chargers 1990-96, New York Giants 1997-2003, Washington Redskins 2004-05, joined Ravens in 2008.
Vic Fangio, special asst. to the head coach; born Dunmore, Pa. Attended East Stroudsburg State. No pro playing experience. College coach: North Carolina 1983. Pro coach: Philadelphia/Baltimore Stars (USFL) 1984-85, New Orleans Saints 1986-1994, Carolina Panthers 1995-98, Indianapolis Colts 1999-2001, Houston Texans 2002-2005, joined Ravens in 2006.
Wade Harman, tight ends; born Corydon, Iowa. Linebacker Drake 1985, Utah State 1986. No pro playing experience. College coach: Utah State 1987-1991, Pacific 1992-95, Morningside 1996. Pro coach: Minnesota Vikings 1997-98, joined Ravens in 1999.
Jim Hostler, wide receivers; born Pittsburgh. Defensive back Indiana (Pa.) 1986-89. College coach: Indiana (Pa.) 1990-92, 1994-99, Juniata (Pa.) 1993. Pro coach: Kansas City Chiefs 2000, New Orleans Saints 2001-02, New York Jets 2003-04, San Francisco 49ers 2005-07, joined Ravens in 2008.
Hue Jackson, quarterbacks; born Los Angeles. Quarterback Pacific 1985-86. No pro playing experience. College coach: Pacific 1987-89, Cal State-Fullerton 1990, Arizona State 1992-95, California 1996, Southern California 1997-2000. Pro coach: London Monarchs (WFL) 1991, Washington Redskins 2001-03, Cincinnati Bengals 2004-06, Atlanta Falcons 2007, joined Ravens in 2008.
Marwan Maalouf, asst. special teams; born Beirut, Lebanon. Guard Baldwin-Wallace 1997-99. No pro playing experience. College coach: Baldwin-Wallace 2000, Fordham 2001, Rutgers 2002-03. Pro coach: Cleveland Browns 2004-06, joined Ravens in 2008.
John Matsko, offensive line; born Cleveland. Fullback Kent State 1970-73. No pro playing experience. College coach: Kent State 1973, Miami (Ohio) 1974-75, 1977, North Carolina 1978-1984, Navy 1985, Arizona 1986, Southern California 1987-1991. Pro coach: Phoenix Cardinals 1992-93, New Orleans Saints 1994-96, N.Y. Giants 1997-98, St. Louis Rams 1999-2005, Kansas City Chiefs 2006-07, joined Ravens in 2008.
Greg Mattison, linebackers; born Madison, Wisc. Guard Wisconsin-LaCrosse 1967-1970. No pro playing experience. College coach: Illinois 1976, Cornell 1977, Northwestern 1978-1980, Western Michigan 1981-86, Navy 1987-

88, Texas A&M 1989-1991, Michigan 1992-96, Notre Dame 1997-2004, Florida 2005-07. Pro coach: Joined Ravens in 2008.
Andy Moeller, asst. offensive line; born Grand Rapids, Mich. Linebacker Michigan 1983-86. No pro playing experience. College coach: Indiana 1987, Army 1988-1993, Missouri 1994-99, Michigan 2000-07. Pro coach: Joined Ravens in 2008.
Wilbert Montgomery, running backs; born Greenville, Miss. Running back Abilene Christian 1973-76. Pro running back Philadelphia Eagles 1977-1984, Detroit Lions 1985. Pro Coach: St. Louis Rams 1997-2005, Detroit Lions 2006-07, joined Ravens in 2008.
Chuck Pagano, secondary; born Boulder, Colo. Safety Wyoming 1980-83. No pro playing experience. College coach: Southern California 1984-85, Miami 1986, Boise State 1987-88, East Carolina 1989, Nevada-Las Vegas 1990-91, East Carolina 1992-94, Miami 1995-2000, North Carolina 2007. Pro coach: Cleveland Browns 2001-04, Oakland Raiders 2005-06, joined Ravens in 2008.
Mike Pettine, outside linebackers; born Doylestown, Pa. Safety Virginia 1984-87. No pro playing experience. College coach: Pittsburgh 1993-94. Pro coach: Joined Ravens in 2002.
Bob Rogucki, strength and conditioning; born Clarksburg, W.Va. No college or pro playing experience. College coach: Penn State 1981, Weber State 1982, Army 1983-89. Pro coach: Arizona Cardinals 1990-2003, Jacksonville Jaguars 2004, Philadelphia Eagles 2006-07, joined Ravens in 2008.
Jerry Rosburg, special teams coordinator; born Fairmont, Minn. Linebacker North Dakota State 1974-77. No pro playing experience. College coach: Northern Michigan 1981-86, Western Michigan 1987-1991, Cincinnati 1992-95, Minnesota 1996, Boston College 1997-98, Notre Dame 1999-2000. Pro coach: Cleveland Browns 2001-06, Atlanta Falcons 2007, joined Ravens in 2008.
Rex Ryan, defensive coordinator/asst. head coach; born Ardmore, Okla. Defensive end Southwest Oklahoma State 1983-86. No pro playing experience. College coach: Eastern Kentucky 1987-88, New Mexico Highlands 1989, Morehead State 1990-93, Cincinnati 1996-97, Oklahoma 1998. Pro coach: Arizona Cardinals 1994-95, joined Ravens in 1999.
Craig Ver Steeg, offensive assistant; born Inglewood, Calif. No college or pro playing experience. College coach: Southern California 1984-85, Utah 1986-89, Cincinnati 1990-93, Harvard 1994-95, Illinois 1998-2000, Utah 2001-02, Rutgers 2003-07. Pro coach: Chicago Bears 1996-97, joined Ravens in 2008.

**American Football Conference
East Division**
Team Colors: Dark Navy, Red, Royal,
and Nickel
One Bills Drive
Orchard Park, New York 14127-2296
Telephone: (716) 648-1800

2008 SCHEDULE
PRESEASON
Aug. 9   at Washington 7:00
Aug. 14 **Pittsburgh** (Toronto)...........7:30
Aug. 24 at Indianapolis 8:00
Aug. 28 **Detroit** 6:30

REGULAR SEASON
Sep. 7   **Seattle** 1:00
Sep. 14 at Jacksonville 1:00
Sep. 21 **Oakland** 1:00
Sep. 28 at St. Louis 3:05
Oct. 5   at Arizona 1:15
Oct. 12 BYE
Oct. 19 **San Diego** 1:00
Oct. 26 at Miami 1:00
Nov. 2   **N.Y. Jets** 1:00
Nov. 9   at New England 1:00
Nov. 17 **Cleveland** (Mon.) 8:30
Nov. 23 at Kansas City 12:00
Nov. 30 **San Francisco** 1:00
Dec. 7   **Miami** (Toronto) 4:05
Dec. 14 at N.Y. Jets 1:00
Dec. 21 at Denver 2:05
Dec. 28 **New England** 1:00

Stadium: Ralph Wilson Stadium
(opened in 1973)
• **Capacity:** 73,967
One Bills Drive
Orchard Park, New York
14127-2296
Playing Surface: AstroPlay
Training Camp: St. John Fisher College
Rochester, New York
14618

RALPH WILSON STADIUM

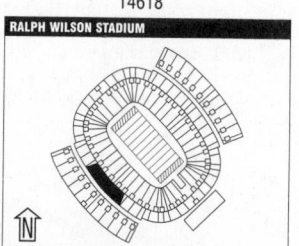

CLUB OFFICIALS
Owner and President:
Ralph C. Wilson, Jr.
Chief Operating Officer: Russ Brandon
Treasurer: Jeffrey C. Littmann
Senior Vice President of Business
Development: Pete Guelli
Senior Vice President of Marketing and
Broadcasting: Marc Honan
Senior Vice President of Football
Administration: Jim Overdorf
Senior Vice President of Business
Operations and Ticketing: Dave Wheat
Vice President/Assistant Director of
College and Pro Scouting:
Linda Bogdan
Vice President of Communications:
Scott Berchtold
Vice President of Stadium Operations:
Joe Frandina
Vice President of Community Relations:
Gretchen Geitter
Vice President of Pro Personnel:
John Guy
Vice President of College Scouting:
Tom Modrak
Vice President of Government
Relations/External Affairs: Bill Munson
Vice President of Strategic Planning:
Mary Owen
Consultant: Christy Wilson Hofmann
Executive Director of Information
Technology: Dan Evans
Director of Security: Chris Clark
Director of Stadium Operations: Perry Dix
Director of Merchandise: Tim Kehoe
Director of Player Programs:
Paul Lancaster
Controller: Frank Wojnicki
Strength and Conditioning Assistant:
Kenne Pitts
Equipment Manager: Dave Hojnowski
Assistant Equipment Managers:
Randy Ribbeck, Jeff Mazurek
Head Athletic Trainer: Bud Carpenter
Athletic Trainers: Chris Fischetti,
Shone Gipson, Greg McMillen
Video Director: Henry Kunttu
Assistant Video Director: Greg Estes
Video Assistant: Wes Burnard
Scouts: Brian Fisher, Brad Forsyth,
Joe Haering, Matt Hand (BLESTO),
Shawn Heilen, Doug Majeski,
Tom Roth, (emeritus) Bob Ryan,
(emeritus) David G. Smith,
(emeritus) David W. Smith

COACHING HISTORY
(355-390-8)
Records include postseason games
1960-61	Buster Ramsey	11-16-1
1962-65	Lou Saban	38-18-3
1966-68	Joe Collier*	13-17-1
1968	Harvey Johnson	1-10-1
1969-1970	John Rauch	7-20-1
1971	Harvey Johnson	1-13-0
1972-76	Lou Saban**	32-29-1
1976-77	Jim Ringo	3-20-0
1978-1982	Chuck Knox	38-38-0
1983-85	Kay Stephenson***	10-26-0
1985-86	Hank Bullough****	4-17-0
1986-1997	Marv Levy	123-78-0
1998-2000	Wade Phillips	29-21-0
2001-03	Gregg Williams	17-31-0
2004-05	Mike Mularkey	14-18-0
2006-07	Dick Jauron	14-18-0

*Released after two games in 1968
**Resigned after five games in 1976
***Released after four games in 1985
****Released after nine games in 1986

PAID ATTENDANCE
Home 557,058   Away 571,994
Total 1,129,052
Single-game home record,
80,368 (10/4/92)
Single-season home record,
635,889 (1991)

2008 DRAFT CHOICES
Round	Name	Pos.	College
1	Leodis McKelvin	DB	Troy
2	James Hardy	WR	Indiana
3	Chris Ellis	LB	Virginia Tech
4	Reggie Corner	DB	Akron
	Derek Fine	TE	Kansas
5	Alvin Bowen	LB	Iowa State
6	Xavier Omon	RB	N.W. Missouri
7	Demetrius Bell	T	Northwestern St. (LA)
	Steve Johnson	WR	Kentucky
	Kennard Cox	DB	Pittsburgh

2007 TEAM RECORD
PRESEASON (2-2)

Date	Result	Opponent
8/10	W 13-10	at New Orleans
8/17	L 10-13	Atlanta
8/24	L 17-28	Tennessee
8/30	W 16-13	at Detroit

REGULAR SEASON (7-9)

Date	Result	Opponent	Att.
9/9	L 14-15	Denver	71,132
9/16	L 3-26	at Pittsburgh	64,307
9/23	L 7-38	at New England	68,756
9/30	W 17-14	New York Jets	70,600
10/8	L 24-25	Dallas	71,575
10/21	W 19-14	Baltimore	70,727
10/28	W 13-3	at New York Jets	76,688
11/4	W 33-21	Cincinnati	70,745
11/11	W 13-10	at Miami	70,615
11/18	L 10-56	New England	71,338
11/25	L 14-36	at Jacksonville	64,546
12/2	W 17-16	at Washington	85,831
12/9	W 38-17	Miami	71,018
12/16	L 0-8	at Cleveland	73,196
12/23	L 21-38	New York Giants	71,302
12/30	L 9-17	at Philadelphia	68,594

SCORE BY PERIODS

Bills	79	41	68	64	0	—	252
Opponents	63	104	92	95	0	—	354

2007 TEAM STATISTICS

	Bills	Opp.
Total First Downs	248	322
Rushing	91	104
Passing	141	203
Penalty	16	15
3rd Down: Made/Att	65/195	101/224
3rd Down Pct.	33.3	45.1
4th Down: Made/Att	8/18	10/22
4th Down Pct.	44.4	45.5
Possession Avg.	28:51	31:09
Total Net Yards	4434	5807
Avg. Per Game	277.1	362.9
Total Plays	919	1047
Avg. Per Play	4.8	5.5
Net Yards Rushing	1800	1993
Avg. Per Game	112.5	124.6
Total Rushes	448	454
Net Yards Passing	2634	3814
Avg. Per Game	164.6	238.4
Sacked/Yards Lost	26/208	26/144
Gross Yards	2842	3958
Att./Completions	445/263	567/354
Completion Pct.	59.1	62.4
Had Intercepted	14	18
Punts/Average	81/40.8	61/42.6
Net Punting Avg.	81/37.6	61/31.8
Penalties/Yards	78/633	73/567
Fumbles/Ball Lost	20/7	29/12
Touchdowns	25	39
Rushing	8	15
Passing	12	19
Returns	5	5

2007 INDIVIDUAL STATISTICS

PASSING

PASSING	Att.	Comp.	Yds.	Pct.	TD	Int.	Tkld.	Rate
Edwards	269	151	1630	56.1	7	8	12/105	70.4
Losman	175	111	1204	63.4	4	6	14/103	76.9
Lynch	1	1	8	100.0	1	0	0/0	139.6
Bills	445	263	2842	59.1	12	14	26/208	73.8
Opponents	567	354	3958	62.4	19	18	26/144	81.1

SCORING

SCORING	TD R	TD P	TD Rt	PAT	FG	Saf	PTS
Lindell	0	0	0	24/24	24/27	0	96
Lynch	7	0	0	0/0	0/0	0	44
L. Evans	0	5	0	0/0	0/0	0	30
Parrish	1	1	1	0/0	0/0	0	18
Royal	0	3	0	0/0	0/0	0	18
Gaines	0	2	0	0/0	0/0	0	12
Wilson	0	0	2	0/0	0/0	0	12
Kelsay	0	0	1	0/0	0/0	1	8
McGee	0	0	1	0/0	0/0	0	6
A. Thomas	0	1	0	0/0	0/0	0	6
Crowell	0	0	0	0/0	0/0	1	2
Bills	8	12	5	24/24	24/27	2	252
Opponents	15	19	5	37/37	27/30	1	354

2-Pt. Conversions: Lynch, Bills 1-1, Opponents 0-2

RUSHING

RUSHING	No.	Yds	Avg	LG	TD
Lynch	280	1115	4.0	56t	7
Jackson	58	300	5.2	27	0
Losman	20	110	5.5	17	0
Wright	29	94	3.2	15	0
A. Thomas	36	89	2.5	9	0
Edwards	14	49	3.5	14	0
Parrish	3	19	6.3	24t	1
Moorman	4	14	3.5	10	0
Reed	4	10	2.5	12	0
Bills	448	1800	4.0	56t	8
Opponents	454	1993	4.4	88t	15

RECEIVING

RECEIVING	No.	Yds	Avg	LG	TD
L. Evans	55	849	15.4	85t	5
Reed	51	578	11.3	30	0
Parrish	35	352	10.1	47t	1
Royal	25	248	9.9	28t	3
Gaines	25	215	8.6	20	2
Jackson	22	190	8.6	54	0
Lynch	18	184	10.2	30	0
A. Thomas	15	95	6.3	11	1
Price	7	68	9.7	22	0
Schouman	3	19	6.3	10	0
Wright	3	17	5.7	8	0
Neufeld	2	14	7.0	8	0
Aiken	1	10	10.0	10	0
Everett	1	3	3.0	3	0
Bills	263	2842	10.8	85t	12
Opponents	354	3958	11.2	59t	19

INTERCEPTIONS

INTERCEPTIONS	No.	Yds	Avg	LG	TD
McGee	4	4	1.0	2	0
Leonhard	2	60	30.0	36	0
Wilson	2	25	12.5	25t	1
Greer	2	1	0.5	2	0
DiGiorgio	1	38	38.0	38	0
Whitner	1	29	29.0	29	0
Youboty	1	19	19.0	19	0
K. Thomas	1	8	8.0	8	0
Crowell	1	5	5.0	5	0
Ellison	1	4	4.0	4	0
Kelsay	1	0	0.0	0t	1
Tripplett	1	0	0.0	0	0
Bills	18	193	10.7	38	2
Opponents	14	291	20.8	70	2

PUNTING

PUNTING	No.	Yds.	Avg.	In 20	LG
Moorman	81	3302	40.8	30	75
Bills	81	3302	40.8	30	75
Opponents	61	2598	42.6	15	62

PUNT RETURNS

PUNT RETURNS	Ret	FC	Yds	Avg	LG	TD
Parrish	27	2	440	16.3	74t	1
Leonhard	4	2	36	9.0	13	0
Bills	31	4	476	15.4	74t	1
Opponents	37	16	196	5.3	29	0

KICKOFF RETURNS

KICKOFF RETURNS	No.	Yds	Avg	LG	TD
McGee	45	1082	24.0	103t	1
Parrish	6	126	21.0	24	0
Scobey	5	112	22.4	29	0
Jackson	3	46	15.3	19	0
Neufeld	3	6	2.0	7	0
Leonhard	2	32	16.0	17	0
A. Thomas	2	26	13.0	15	0
Chambers	1	6	6.0	6	0
Preston	1	12	12.0	12	0
Wilson	1	0	0.0	0	0
Wright	1	0	0.0	0	0
Bills	70	1448	20.7	103t	1
Opponents	56	1150	20.5	100t	1

FIELD GOALS

FIELD GOALS	1-19	20-29	30-39	40-49	50+
Lindell	0/0	11/11	7/7	4/6	2/3
Bills	0/0	11/11	7/7	4/6	2/3
Opponents	0/0	10/10	9/10	7/8	1/2

SACKS

SACKS	No.
Schobel	6.5
Kelsay	2.5
McCargo	2.5
Crowell	2.0
DiGiorgio	2.0
K. Williams	2.0
(group)	2.0
Hargrove	1.5
R. Denney	1.0
Ellison	1.0
Haggan	1.0
Tripplett	1.0
Youboty	1.0
Bills	26.0
Opponents	26.0

RECORD HOLDERS
INDIVIDUAL RECORDS—CAREER

Category	Name	Performance
Rushing (Yds.)	Thurman Thomas, 1988-1999	11,938
Passing (Yds.)	Jim Kelly, 1986-1996	35,467
Passing (TDs)	Jim Kelly, 1986-1996	237
Receiving (No.)	Andre Reed, 1985-1999	941
Receiving (Yds.)	Andre Reed, 1985-1999	13,095
Interceptions	George (Butch) Byrd, 1964-1970	40
Punting (Avg.)	Brian Moorman, 2001-07	43.1
Punt Return (Avg.)	Roscoe Parrish, 2005-07	13.6
Kickoff Return (Avg.)	O.J. Simpson, 1969-1977	30.0
Field Goals	Steve Christie, 1992-2000	234
Touchdowns (Tot.)	Andre Reed, 1985-1999	87
	Thurman Thomas, 1988-1999	87
Points	Steve Christie, 1992-2000	1,011

INDIVIDUAL RECORDS—SINGLE SEASON

Category	Name	Performance
Rushing (Yds.)	O.J. Simpson, 1973	2,003
Passing (Yds.)	Drew Bledsoe, 2002	4,359
Passing (TDs)	Jim Kelly, 1991	33
Receiving (No.)	Eric Moulds, 2002	100
Receiving (Yds.)	Eric Moulds, 1998	1,368
Interceptions	Billy Atkins, 1961	10
	Tom Janik, 1967	10
Punting (Avg.)	Brian Moorman, 2005	45.7
Punt Return (Avg.)	Roscoe Parrish, 2007	16.3
Kickoff Return (Avg.)	Terrence McGee, 2005	30.24
Field Goals	Steve Christie, 1998	33
Touchdowns (Tot.)	O.J. Simpson, 1975	23
Points	Steve Christie, 1998	140

INDIVIDUAL RECORDS—SINGLE GAME

Category	Name	Performance
Rushing (Yds.)	O.J. Simpson, 11-25-76	273
Passing (Yds.)	Drew Bledsoe, 9-15-02	463
Passing (TDs)	Jim Kelly, 9-8-91	6
Receiving (No.)	Andre Reed, 11-20-94	15
Receiving (Yds.)	Lee Evans, 11-19-06	265
Interceptions	Many times	3
	Last time by Nate Clements, 10-20-02	
Field Goals	Steve Christie, 10-20-96	6
Touchdowns (Tot.)	Cookie Gilchrist, 12-8-63	5
Points	Cookie Gilchrist, 12-8-63	30

2008 VETERAN ROSTER

No.	Name	Pos.	Ht.	Wt.	Age	NFL Exp.	College	Hometown	How Acq.	'07 Games/ Starts
89	Anderson, Courtney	TE	6-6	270	27	5	San Jose State	Richmond, Calif.	UFA(Atl)-'08	4/0*
36	Barnes, Darian	FB	6-2	240	28	7	Hampton	Toms River, N.J.	FA-'08	5/3*
96	Bryan, Copeland	DE	6-4	253	25	2	Arizona	San Jose, Calif.	FA-'07	2/0
60	Butler, Brad	OL	6-7	315	24	3	Virginia	Lynchburg, Va.	D5b-'06	16/16
73	Chambers, Kirk	OL	6-7	315	29	4	Stanford	Provo, Utah	FA-'07	16/1
54	Costanzo, Blake	LB	6-2	235	24	2	Lafayette	Franklin Lakes, N.J.	FA-'07	3/0
55	Crowell, Angelo	LB	6-1	246	27	6	Virginia	Winston-Salem, N.C.	D3-'03	16/16
92	Denney, Ryan	DE	6-7	264	31	7	Brigham Young	Thornton, Colo.	D2b-'02	7/2
52	DiGiorgio, John	LB	6-2	229	26	3	Saginaw Valley State	Shelby Township, Mich.	FA-'06	16/14
66	Dockery, Derrick	OL	6-6	330	27	6	Texas	Lakeview, Texas	FA-'07	16/16
5	Edwards, Trent	QB	6-4	231	24	2	Stanford	Los Gatos, Calif.	D3-'07	10/9
56	Ellison, Keith	LB	6-0	229	24	3	Oregon State	Redondo Beach, Calif.	D6-'06	12/9
79	Estes, Patrick	T	6-7	310	25	4	Virginia	Richmond, Va,	FA-'07	0*
83	Evans, Lee	WR	5-10	197	27	5	Wisconsin	Bedford, Ohio	D1a-'04	16/16
67	Fowler, Melvin	OL	6-3	310	29	7	Maryland	Wheatley Heights, N.Y.	FA-'06	16/16
35	Fox, Dustin	DB	5-11	200	25	4	Ohio State	Canton, Ohio	FA-'07	5/0
63	Gaddis, Christian	OL	6-1	300	23	2	Villanova	North Miami Beach, Fla.	FA-'07	1/0
33	Greer, Jabari	CB	5-11	180	26	5	Tennessee	Jackson, Tenn.	FA-'04	16/13
10	Hamdan, Gibran	QB	6-4	220	27	2	Indiana	San Diego, Calif.	FA-'07	0*
22	Jackson, Fred	RB	6-1	215	27	2	Coe College	Fort Worth, Texas	FA-'06	8/1
21	James, William	CB	6-0	200	29	8	Western Illinois	Brownsville, Pa.	UFA(Phil)-'08	14/6*
98	Jefferson, Jason	DT	6-1	295	26	4	Wisconsin	Chicago, Ill.	FA-'05	11/0
17	Jenkins, Justin	WR	6-0	207	27	2	Mississippi State	Pearl, Miss.	FA-'07	11/0
91	Johnson, Spencer	DT	6-3	286	26	5	Auburn	Waynesboro, Miss.	UFA(Minn)-'08	16/0*
87	Johnson, Teyo	TE	6-6	260	26	4	Stanford	White Rock, B.C., Canada	FA-'08	0*
90	Kelsay, Chris	DE	6-4	261	28	6	Nebraska	Auburn, Neb.	D2-'03	14/14
9	Lindell, Rian	K	6-3	233	31	9	Washington St.	Vancouver, Wash.	FA-'03	16/0
7	Losman, J.P.	QB	6-2	212	27	5	Tulane	Venice, Calif.	D1b-'04	8/7
23	Lynch, Marshawn	RB	5-11	215	22	2	California	Oakland, Calif.	D1-'07	13/13
88	Massaquoi, Tim	TE	6-5	255	26	3	Michigan	New York City, N.Y.	FA-'07	4/0
97	McCargo, John	DT	6-2	307	25	3	North Carolina State	Drakes Branch, Va.	D1b-'06	16/0
24	McGee, Terrence	CB	5-9	198	27	6	Northwestern State	Athens, Texas	D4a-'03	15/15
59	Mitchell, Kawika	LB	6-1	253	28	6	South Florida	Winter Springs, Fla.	UFA(NYG)-'08	16/16*
8	Moorman, Brian	P	6-0	172	32	8	Pittsburg State	Sedgwick, Kan.	FA-'01	16/0
70	Murphy, Matt	OL	6-5	277	28	8	Maryland	New Haven, Mich.	FA-'06	2/0
72	Neill, Ryan	DL	6-3	253	25	2	Rutgers	Wayne Hills, N.J.	FA-'06	16/0
76	Nua, Shaun	DE	6-5	280	27	4	Brigham Young	Pago Pago, American Samoa	FA-'07	0*
11	Parrish, Roscoe	WR	5-9	171	26	4	Miami	Miami, Fla.	D2-'05	16/5
71	Peters, Jason	OL	6-4	340	26	5	Arkansas	Queen City, Texas	FA-'04	15/15
51	Posluszny, Paul	LB	6-1	238	23	2	Penn State	Aliquippa, Pa.	D2-'07	3/3
75	Preston, Duke	OL	6-5	326	26	4	Illinois	San Diego, Calif.	D4-'05	12/0
82	Reed, Josh	WR	5-10	210	28	7	Louisiana State	Rayne, La.	D2a-'02	15/9
84	Royal, Robert	TE	6-4	255	30	7	Louisiana State	New Orleans, La.	FA-'06	16/15
94	Schobel, Aaron	DE	6-4	243	31	8	TCU	Columbus, Texas	D2a-'01	16/16
80	Schouman, Derek	TE	6-2	223	23	2	Boise State	Eagle, Idaho	D7a-'07	3/1
43	Scott, Bryan	S	6-1	219	27	6	Penn State	Doylestown, Pa.	FA-'07	15/2
30	Simpson, Ko	S	6-1	202	24	3	South Carolina	Rock Hill, S.C.	D4-'06	1/1
99	t- Stroud, Marcus	DT	6-6	310	30	8	Georgia	Thomasville, Ga.	T(Jax)-'08	9/9*
68	Walker, Langston	OL	6-8	366	29	7	California	Oakland, Calif.	FA-'07	16/16
29	Wendling, John	S	6-1	222	25	2	Wyoming	Cody, Wyo.	D6-'07	14/0
20	Whitner, Donte	S	5-10	208	23	3	Ohio State	Cleveland, Ohio	D1a-'06	15/15
65	Whittle, Jason	OL	6-4	297	33	10	Missouri State	Camdenton, Mo.	FA-'07	3/0
95	Williams, Kyle	DT	6-1	306	25	3	Louisiana State	Ruston, La.	D5a-'06	16/16
37	Wilson, George	S	6-0	212	27	3	Arkansas	Paducah, Kent.	FA-'04	12/9
31	Wright, Dwayne	RB	5-11	228	25	2	Fresno State	San Diego, Calif.	D4-'07	14/0
26	Youboty, Ashton	CB	5-11	189	24	3	Ohio State	Klein, Texas	D3-'06	11/3

* Anderson played 2 games with Detroit and 2 games with Atlanta in '07; Barnes played 5 games with N.Y. Jets; Estes inactive for 2 games; Hamdan did not play in 1 game; James played 14 games with Philadelphia; S. Johnson played 16 games with Minnesota; T. Johnson last active with Arizona in '05; Mitchell played 16 games with N.Y. Giants; Nall did not play in 2 games; Stroud played 9 games with Jacksonville.

t- Bills traded for Stroud (Jax).

Players lost through free agency (5): WR Sam Aiken (NE; 12 games in '07), TE Michael Gaines (Det; 15), LB Leon Joe (TB; 8), LB Josh Stamer (Tenn; 16), CB Jason Webster (NE; 1).

Also played with Bills in '07—DT Tim Anderson (4 games), DB Jerametrius Butler (7), TE Brad Cieslak (2), TE Kevin Everett (1), LB Mario Haggan (16), DE Anthony Hargrove (12), LB Kevin Harrison (1), S Jim Leonard (13), TE Ryan Neufeld (9), DE Eric Powell (1), WR Peerless Price (4), RB Josh Scobey (3), RB Anthony Thomas (10), DB Kiwaukee Thomas (9), DT Larry Tripplett (16), LB Coy Wire (7).

2008 FIRST-YEAR ROSTER

Name	Pos.	Ht.	Wt.	Age	College	Hometown	How Acq.
Baker, Matt (1)	QB	6-2	217	25	North Carolina	East Lansing, Mich.	FA
Banks, Jon	LB	6-2	232	24	Iowa State	East Moline, Ill.	FA
Bell, Demetrius	OL	6-5	307	24	Northwestern State	Summerfield, La.	D7a
Bowen, Alvin	LB	6-1	222	24	Iowa State	East Orange, N.J.	D5
Buggs, Marcus	LB	5-11	223	22	Vanderbilt	Madison, Tenn.	FA
Corner, Reggie	CB	5-9	175	24	Akron	Canton, Ohio	D4a
Corto, Jon (1)	DB	6-0	208	24	Sacred Heart	Orchard Park, N.Y.	FA
Cox, Kennard	DB	6-0	192	23	Pittsburgh	Miami, Fla.	D7c
Drone, Luke	QB	6-1	217	23	Illinois State	Mt. Carmel, Ill.	FA
Ellis, Chris	DE	6-4	261	23	Virginia Tech	Hampton, Va.	D3
Felton, Robert	OL	6-4	324	23	Arkansas	Houston, Texas	FA
Fine, Derek	TE	6-3	247	25	Kansas	Sallisaw, Okla.	D4b
Hall, Bruce	RB	5-11	205	23	Mississippi	Milton, Fla.	FA
Hardy, James	WR	6-5	212	22	Indiana	Fort Wayne, Ind.	D2
Huggins, Felton (1)	WR	6-2	186	25	Southeastern Louisiana	Zachary, La.	FA-'07
Johnson, Steve	WR	6-2	202	22	Kentucky	San Francisco, Calif.	D7b
Jones, Jason	WR	6-1	182	25	Arkansas-Pine Bluff	Forrest City, Ark.	FA
Mace, Corey (1)	DE	6-3	287	22	Wyoming	Port Moody, B.C., Canada	FA-'07
Mayle, Scott (1)	WR	6-1	175	24	Ohio	Philippi, W. Va.	FA-'07
McCray, Teraz	DT	6-1	286	24	Miami	Pompano Beach, Fla.	FA
McKelvin, Leodis	CB	5-10	184	23	Troy	Waycross, Ga.	D1
Omon, Xavier	RB	5-11	227	23	Northwest Missouri State	Beatrice, Neb.	D6
Viti, Michael	FB	5-9	236	22	Army	Berwick, Pa.	FA

The term NFL Rookie is defined as a player who is in his first season of professional football and has not been on the roster of another professional football team for any regular-season or postseason games. A Rookie is designated by an "R" on NFL rosters. Players who have been active in another professional football league or players who have NFL experience, including either preseason training camp or being on an Active List or Inactive List, or on Reserve/Injured or Reserve/Physically Unable to Perform for fewer than six regular-season games, are termed NFL First-Year Players. An NFL First-Year Player is designated by a "1" on NFL rosters. Thereafter, a player is credited with an additional year of experience for each season in which he accumulates six games on the Active List or Inactive List, or on Reserve/Injured or Reserve/Physically Unable to Perform.

Log on to www.buffalobills.com for an up-to-date roster; Age listed is as of September 4, 2008.

BUFFALO BILLS

COACHING STAFF
Head Coach,
Dick Jauron

Pro Career: Now in his third season, Jauron was named Buffalo's fourteenth head coach on January 23, 2006. He enters 2008 with a 14-18 record over his first two seasons. He earned a tremendous amount of respect for his coaching in 2007 as the Bills overcame the loss of 17 players to season-ending injured reserve. Jauron is in his third stint as an NFL head coach after serving as the head coach of the Chicago Bears (1999-2003) and as interim head coach of the Detroit Lions for the final five games of 2005. The highlight of his Bears' tenure career came in 2001 when Chicago finished 13-3 and claimed its first division championship since 1990. Under Jauron's leadership, the 2001 Bears were 8-0 in games decided by seven points or less, and engineered five second half, come-from-behind victories. The Bears defense ranked first in the NFL in yards allowed and second in rushing yards allowed. For his efforts, Jauron was selected as the *Associated Press* NFL Coach of the Year. He was just the third coach in team history to win 13 games in a season. The 2001 season marked the greatest single-season turnaround in team history improving from 5-11 in 2000 to 13-3. In his five seasons in Chicago, Jauron posted a 35-46 record. He began his coaching career with the Buffalo Bills (1985, defensive backs), Green Bay Packers (1986-1994, defensive backs), and Jacksonville Jaguars (1995-98, defensive coordinator). As Jacksonville's inaugural defensive coordinator, the Jaguars made three playoff berths. He served as the Lions' defensive coordinator from 2004-05. Career record: 50-68.

Background: A three-sport (football, basketball, and baseball) standout at Swampscott (Mass.) High School. Named one of the top 10 prep athletes of the 20th Century in the state of Massachusetts by the *Boston Globe*. Played running back at Yale (1970-72) where, for 27 years, he held the school's career rushing mark with 2,947 yards. Drafted by the Detroit Lions in the fourth round of the 1973 draft. Played defensive back for Detroit (1973-77) and was named to the Pro Bowl following the 1974 season after leading the NFC in punt return average (16.8). He finished his career with the Cincinnati Bengals (1978-1980).

Personal: Age 57, born in Peoria, Ill. Dick and his wife Gail have two daughters—Kacy and Amy.

ASSISTANT COACHES

John Allaire, strength and conditioning; born Woonsocket, R.I. Attended Springfield College. No college or pro playing experience. College coach: Boston College 1992, Clemson 1993-95, Tulsa 1996-2001. Pro coach: Joined Bills in 2002.

Bobby April, asst. head coach/special teams; born New Orleans. Linebacker/defensive end Nicholls State 1972-75. No pro playing experience. College coach: Southern Mississippi 1978, Tulane 1979, Arizona 1980-86, Southern California 1987-1990. Pro coach: Atlanta Falcons 1991-93, Pittsburgh Steelers 1994-95, New Orleans Saints 1996-99, St. Louis Rams 2001-02, joined Bills in 2004.

Ray Brown, asst. offensive line; born Marion, Ark. Offensive lineman Arkansas State 1982-85. Pro offensive lineman St. Louis/Phoenix Cardinals 1986-88, Washington Redskins 1989-1995, 2004-05, San Francisco 49ers 1996-2001, Detroit Lions 2002-03. Pro coach: Washington Redskins 2006, joined Bills in 2008.

George Catavolos, defensive backs; born Chicago. Defensive back Purdue 1964-67. No pro playing experience. College coach: Purdue 1967-68, 1971-76, Middle Tennessee State 1969, Louisville 1970, Kentucky 1977-1981, Tennessee 1982-83. Pro coach: Indianapolis Colts 1984-1994, 1998-2001, Carolina Panthers 1995-97, Washington Redskins 2002-03, Detroit Lions 2004-05, joined Bills in 2006.

Charlie Coiner, tight ends; born Wayensboro, Va. Attended Catawba College, Appalachian State. No college or pro playing experience. College coach: Appalachian State 1983-86, Minnesota 1987, Louisville 1995-97, Tennessee-Chattanooga 1998, Louisiana State 1999, Texas Southern 2000. Pro coach: Chicago Bears 2001-05, joined Bills in 2006.

DeMontie Cross, asst. linebackers/special teams; born St. Louis, Mo. Free safety Missouri 1994-96. No pro playing experience. College coach: Missouri 1998-99, Sam Houston State 2000, Iowa State 2001-05. Pro coach: Joined Bills in 2006.

Perry Fewell, defensive coordinator; born Gastonia, N.C. Defensive back Lenoir-Rhyne 1981-84. No pro playing experience. College coach: North Carolina 1985-86, Army 1987, 1992-94, Kent State 1988-1991, Vanderbilt 1995-97. Pro coach: Jacksonville Jaguars 1998-2002, St. Louis Rams 2003-04, Chicago Bears 2005, joined Bills in 2006.

Nathaniel Hackett, offensive quality control; born Fullerton, Calif. Linebacker/long snapper U.C. Davis 1999-2002. No pro playing experience. College coach: U.C. Davis 2003, Stanford 2003-05. Pro coach: Tampa Bay Buccaneers 2006-07, joined Bills in 2006.

Sean Hayes, asst. strength and conditioning; born Peabody, Mass. No college or pro playing experience. College coach: Springfield College 1997-98, Tulsa 1999-2000, Harvard 2001-03, Clemson 2004-05. Pro coach: Joined Bills in 2006.

Bill Kollar, defensive line; born Warren, Ohio. Defensive end Montana State 1971-74. Pro defensive end Cincinnati Bengals 1974-76, Tampa Bay Buccanneers 1977-1981. College coach: Illinois: 1985-87, Purdue 1988-89. Pro coach: Tampa Bay Buccaneers 1984, Atlanta Falcons 1990-2000, St. Louis Rams 2001-2005, joined Bills in 2006.

Sean Kugler, offensive line; born Lockport, N.Y. Offensive line Texas-El Paso 1985-89. No pro playing experience. College coach: Texas-El Paso 1993-2000, Boise State 2006. Pro coach: Detroit Lions 2001-05, joined Bills in 2007.

Chuck Lester, defensive assistant/coaching operations; born Chicago. Linebacker Oklahoma 1974. No pro playing experience. College coach: Iowa State 1980-81, Oklahoma 1982-84. Pro coach: Kansas City Chiefs 1984-86 (scout), joined Bills in 1987.

Turk Schonert, offensive coordinator; born Torrance, Calif. Quarterback Stanford 1975-79. Pro quarterback Cincinnati Bengals 1980-85, 1987-89, Atlanta Falcons 1986. Pro coach: Tampa Bay Buccaneers 1992-95, Buffalo Bills 1998-2000, Carolina Panthers 2001, New York Giants 2003, New Orleans Saints 2005, rejoined Bills in 2006.

Matt Sheldon, linebackers; born Berwyn, Ill. Cornerback Minnesota 1987-1991. No pro playing experience. College coach: Wisconsin 1997-99. Pro coach: St. Louis Rams 2001-05, joined Bills in 2006.

Eric Studesville, running game coordinator/running backs; born Madison, Wis. Defensive back Wisconsin-Whitewater 1985-88. No pro playing experience. College coach: Wingate 1994, Kent State 1995-96. Pro coach: Chicago Bears 1997-2000, New York Giants 2001-03, joined Bills in 2004.

Tyke Tolbert, wide receivers; born Conroe, Texas. Wide receiver Louisiana State 1988-1990. No pro playing experience. College coach: Louisiana-Monroe 1994-97, Auburn 1998, Louisiana-Lafayette 1999-2001, Florida 2002. Pro coach: Arizona Cardinals 2003, joined Bills in 2004.

Alex Van Pelt, quarterbacks; born Pittsburgh. Quarterback Pittsburgh 1990-94. Pro quarterback Buffalo Bills 1995-2003. College coach: Buffalo 2005. Pro coach: Frankfurt Galaxy (NFLE) 2005, joined Bills in 2006.

Adrian White, defensive quality control; born Orange Park, Fla. Defensive back Southern Illinois 1983, Florida 1985-86. Pro defensive back: New York Giants 1987-1991, Green Bay Packers 1992, New England Patriots 1993. No college coaching experience. Pro coach: Rhein Fire (NFLE) 2001-07, joined Bills in 2008.

American Football Conference
North Division
Team Colors: Black, Orange, and White
One Paul Brown Stadium
Cincinnati, Ohio 45202-3492
Telephone: (513) 621-3550
Ticket Office (513) 621-TDTD (8383)

2008 SCHEDULE
PRESEASON
Aug. 11	at Green Bay	7:00
Aug. 17	**Detroit**	7:35
Aug. 23	**New Orleans**	7:35
Aug. 28	at Indianapolis	7:00

REGULAR SEASON
Sep. 7	at Baltimore	1:00
Sep. 14	**Tennessee**	1:00
Sep. 21	at N.Y. Giants	1:00
Sep. 28	**Cleveland**	1:00
Oct. 5	at Dallas	3:15
Oct. 12	at N.Y. Jets	1:00
Oct. 19	**Pittsburgh**	1:00
Oct. 26	BYE	
Nov. 2	**Jacksonville**	1:00
Nov. 9	at Houston	12:00
Nov. 16	**Philadelphia**	1:00
Nov. 20	at Pittsburgh (Thu.)	8:15
Nov. 30	**Baltimore**	1:00
Dec. 7	at Indianapolis	1:00
Dec. 14	**Washington**	1:00
Dec. 21	at Cleveland	1:00
Dec. 28	**Kansas City**	1:00

Stadium: Paul Brown Stadium
(opened in 2000)
•**Capacity:** 65,515
One Paul Brown Stadium
Cincinnati, Ohio 45202-3492
Playing Surface: Synthetic
Training Camp: Georgetown College
Georgetown, KY 40324

PAUL BROWN STADIUM

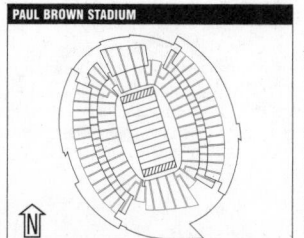

CLUB OFFICIALS
President: Mike Brown
Senior Vice President: Pete Brown
Executive Vice President: Katie Blackburn
Vice President: Paul Brown
Vice President: John Sawyer
Vice President: Troy Blackburn
Business Manager: Bill Connelly
Chief Financial Officer: Bill Scanlon
Director of Development—Paul Brown
Stadium: Bob Bedinghaus
Managing Director of Paul Brown
Stadium: Eric Brown
Directors of Technology: Michael Kayes,
Jo Ann Ralstin
Bengals.com Editor: Geoff Hobson
Director of Security: Rusty Guy
Director of Sales and Public Affairs:
Jeff Berding
Director of Corporate Sales and
Marketing: Vince Cicero
Ticket Manager: Tim Kelly
Director of Ticket Sales: Kevin Lane
Director of Player Relations: Eric Ball
Director of Football Operations:
Jim Lippincott
Director of Player Personnel: Duke Tobin
Public Relations Director: Jack Brennan
Athletic Trainer: Paul Sparling
Equipment Manager: Jeff Brickner
Video Director: Travis Brammer

COACHING HISTORY
(273-351-1)
Records include postseason games
1968-1975	Paul Brown	55-59-1
1976-78	Bill Johnson*	18-15-0
1978-79	Homer Rice	8-19-0
1980-83	Forrest Gregg	34-27-0
1984-1991	Sam Wyche	64-68-0
1992-96	Dave Shula**	19-52-0
1996-2000	Bruce Coslet***	21-39-0
2000-02	Dick LeBeau	12-33-0
2003-07	Marvin Lewis	42-39-0

* Resigned after five games in 1978
** Released after seven games in 1996
*** Resigned after three games in 2000

PAID ATTENDANCE
Home 514,083   Away 555,488
Total 1,069,571
Single-game home record,
65,362 (12/28/03)
Single-season home record, 516,154
(2006)

2008 DRAFT CHOICES
Round	Name	Pos.	College
1	Keith Rivers	LB	Southern California
2	Jerome Simpson	WR	Coastal Carolina
3	Pat Sims	DT	Auburn
	Andre Caldwell	WR	Florida
4	Anthony Collins	T/G	Kansas
5	Jason Shirley	DT	Fresno State
6	Corey Lynch	DB	Appalachian St.
	Matt Sherry	TE	Villanova
7	Angelo Craig	DE	Cincinnati
	Mario Urrutia	WR	Louisville

CINCINNATI BENGALS

2007 TEAM RECORD
PRESEASON (1-3)

Date	Result		Opponent
8/9	L	26-27	at Detroit
8/18	L	19-27	New Orleans
8/27	L	19-24	at Atlanta
8/31	W	14-6	Indianapolis

REGULAR SEASON (7-9)

Date	Result		Opponent	Att.
9/10	W	27-20	Baltimore	66,093
9/16	L	45-51	at Cleveland	72,801
9/23	L	21-24	at Seattle	68,110
10/1	L	13-34	New England	66,113
10/14	L	20-27	at Kansas City	76,846
10/21	W	38-31	New York Jets	65,868
10/28	L	13-24	Pittsburgh	66,188
11/4	L	21-33	at Buffalo	70,745
11/11	W	21-7	at Baltimore	71,130
11/18	L	27-35	Arizona	65,403
11/25	W	35-6	Tennessee	65,489
12/2	L	10-24	at Pittsburgh	58,842
12/9	W	19-10	St. Louis	65,143
12/15	L	13-20	at San Francisco	68,053
12/23	W	19-14	Cleveland	66,023
12/30	W	38-25	at Miami	70,461

SCORE BY PERIODS

Bengals	78	109	90	103	0	—	380
Opponents	64	146	68	107	0	—	385

2007 TEAM STATISTICS

	Bengals	Opp.
Total First Downs	320	313
Rushing	81	98
Passing	213	200
Penalty	26	15
3rd Down: Made/Att	96/208	86/201
3rd Down Pct.	46.2	42.8
4th Down: Made/Att	4/12	9/17
4th Down Pct.	33.3	52.9
Possession Avg.	29:26	30:34
Total Net Yards	5568	5580
Avg. Per Game	348.0	348.8
Total Plays	1008	1011
Avg. Per Play	5.5	5.5
Net Yards Rushing	1556	1893
Avg. Per Game	97.3	118.3
Total Rushes	416	449
Net Yards Passing	4012	3687
Avg. Per Game	250.8	230.4
Sacked/Yards Lost	17/119	22/128
Gross Yards	4131	3815
Att./Completions	575/373	540/353
Completion Pct.	64.9	65.4
Had Intercepted	20	19
Punts/Average	59/41.3	58/39.7
Net Punting Avg.	59/35.2	58/36.4
Penalties/Yards	90/670	88/712
Fumbles/Ball Lost	20/10	28/16
Touchdowns	41	44
Rushing	10	11
Passing	26	29
Returns	5	4

2007 INDIVIDUAL STATISTICS

PASSING

	Att.	Comp.	Yds.	Pct.	TD	Int.	Tkld.	Rate
Palmer	575	373	4131	64.9	26	20	17/119	86.7
Bengals	575	373	4131	64.9	26	20	17/119	86.7
Opponents	540	353	3815	65.4	29	19	22/128	89.2

SCORING

	TD R	TD P	TD Rt	PAT	FG	Saf	PTS
Graham	0	0	0	37/37	31/34	0	130
Houshmandzadeh	0	12	0	0/0	0/0	0	72
C. Johnson	0	8	0	0/0	0/0	0	48
Watson	7	0	0	0/0	0/0	0	42
R. Johnson	3	1	0	0/0	0/0	0	26
Henry	0	2	0	0/0	0/0	0	12
Holt	0	1	1	0/0	0/0	0	12
Chatman	0	1	0	0/0	0/0	0	6
Dorsey	0	0	1	0/0	0/0	0	6
J. Johnson	0	1	0	0/0	0/0	0	6
L. Johnson	0	0	1	0/0	0/0	0	6
Joseph	0	0	1	0/0	0/0	0	6
Ndukwe	0	0	1	0/0	0/0	0	6
Marshall	0	0	0	0/0	0/0	1	2
Larson	0	0	0	0/1	0/0	0	0
Bengals	10	26	5	37/38	31/34	1	380
Opponents	11	29	4	42/42	25/27	0	385

2-Pt. Conversions: R. Johnson, Bengals 1-3, Opponents 2-2

RUSHING

	No.	Yds	Avg	LG	TD
Watson	178	763	4.3	24	7
R. Johnson	170	497	2.9	22	3
Dorsey	21	183	8.7	46	0
C. Johnson	6	47	7.8	16	0
J. Johnson	7	25	3.6	12	0
Houshmandzadeh	5	14	2.8	8	0
Palmer	24	10	0.4	10	0
T. Perry	1	9	9.0	9	0
Chatman	1	5	5.0	5	0
Holt	2	2	1.0	1	0
Green	1	1	1.0	1	0
Bengals	416	1556	3.7	45	10
Opponents	449	1893	4.2	66t	11

RECEIVING

	No.	Yds	Avg	LG	TD
Houshmandzadeh	112	1143	10.2	42t	12
C. Johnson	93	1440	15.5	70t	8
Watson	52	374	7.2	43	0
Henry	21	343	16.3	52t	2
Kelly	20	211	10.6	26	0
Chatman	19	149	7.8	15	1
Holt	16	143	8.9	22	1
R. Johnson	13	110	8.5	33	1
Coats	12	122	10.2	25	0
J. Johnson	6	32	5.3	14	1
Dorsey	4	19	4.8	17	0
Green	3	33	11.0	18	0
T. Perry	1	7	7.0	7	0
M. Maxwell	1	5	5.0	5	0
Bengals	373	4131	11.1	70t	26
Opponents	353	3815	10.8	73	29

INTERCEPTIONS

	No.	Yds	Avg	LG	TD
Hall	5	16	3.2	12	0
Joseph	4	76	19.0	42t	1
Ndukwe	3	44	14.7	44	0
M. Williams	2	40	20.0	35	0
Jackson	2	7	3.5	7	0
Geathers	1	30	30.0	30	0
O'Neal	1	7	7.0	7	0
Myers	1	0	0.0	0	0
Bengals	19	220	11.6	44	1
Opponents	20	294	14.7	55t	3

PUNTING

	No.	Yds.	Avg.	In 20	LG
Larson	59	2437	41.3	21	55
Bengals	59	2437	41.3	21	55
Opponents	58	2302	39.7	20	58

PUNT RETURNS

	Ret	FC	Yds	Avg	LG	TD
Chatman	18	8	93	5.2	19	0
Green	9	10	38	4.2	9	0
Bengals	27	18	131	4.9	19	0
Opponents	33	10	299	9.1	63t	1

KICKOFF RETURNS

	No.	Yds	Avg	LG	TD
Holt	59	1432	24.3	100t	1
T. Perry	7	145	20.7	26	0
Kelly	3	38	12.7	15	0
Chatman	2	49	24.5	34	0
Dorsey	2	20	10.0	20	0
Bengals	73	1684	23.1	100t	1
Opponents	76	1732	22.8	85	0

FIELD GOALS

	1-19	20-29	30-39	40-49	50+
Graham	1/1	11/12	13/13	6/7	0/1
Bengals	1/1	11/12	13/13	6/7	0/1
Opponents	1/1	11/11	9/9	3/4	1/2

SACKS

	No.
Geathers	3.5
Ndukwe	2.0
Smith	2.0
M. Williams	2.0
Peko	1.5
Robinson	1.5
B. Adams	1.0
Brooks	1.0
Fanene	1.0
L. Johnson	1.0
Dh. Jones	1.0
Marshall	1.0
Myers	1.0
Thornton	1.0
(group)	1.0
Jackson	0.5
Bengals	22.0
Opponents	17.0

RECORD HOLDERS
INDIVIDUAL RECORDS—CAREER

Category	Name	Performance
Rushing (Yds.)	Corey Dillon, 1997-2003	8,061
Passing (Yds.)	Ken Anderson, 1971-1986	32,838
Passing (TDs)	Ken Anderson, 1971-1986	197
Receiving (No.)	Chad Johnson, 2001-07	559
Receiving (Yds.)	Chad Johnson, 2001-07	8,365
Interceptions	Ken Riley, 1969-1983	65
Punting (Avg.)	Dave Lewis, 1970-73	43.8
Punt Return (Avg.)	Mike Martin, 1983-89	9.9
Kickoff Return (Avg.)	Lemar Parrish, 1970-77	24.7
Field Goals	Jim Breech, 1980-1992	225
Touchdowns (Tot.)	Pete Johnson, 1977-1983	70
Points	Jim Breech, 1980-1992	1,151

INDIVIDUAL RECORDS—SINGLE SEASON

Category	Name	Performance
Rushing (Yds.)	Rudi Johnson, 2005	1,458
Passing (Yds.)	Carson Palmer, 2007	4,131
Passing (TDs)	Carson Palmer, 2005	32
Receiving (No.)	T.J. Houshmandzadeh, 2007	112
Receiving (Yds.)	Chad Johnson, 2007	1,440
Interceptions	Deltha O'Neal, 2005	10
Punting (Avg.)	Dave Lewis, 1970	46.2
Punt Return (Avg.)	Lemar Parrish, 1974	18.8
Kickoff Return (Avg.)	Tremain Mack, 1999	27.1
Field Goals	Shayne Graham, 2007	31
Touchdowns (Tot.)	Carl Pickens, 1995	17
Points	Shayne Graham, 2005	131

INDIVIDUAL RECORDS—SINGLE GAME

Category	Name	Performance
Rushing (Yds.)	Corey Dillon, 10-22-00	278
Passing (Yds.)	Boomer Esiason, 10-7-90	490
Passing (TDs)	Carson Palmer, 9-16-07	6
Receiving (No.)	Carl Pickens, 10-11-98	13
Receiving (Yds.)	Chad Johnson, 11-12-06	260
Interceptions	Many times	3
	Last time by Deltha O'Neal, 9-18-05	
Field Goals	Shayne Graham, 11-11-07	7
Touchdowns (Tot.)	Larry Kinnebrew, 10-28-84	4
	Corey Dillon, 12-4-97	4
Points	Larry Kinnebrew, 10-28-84	24
	Corey Dillon, 12-4-97	24

2008 VETERAN ROSTER

No.	Name	Pos.	Ht.	Wt.	Age	NFL Exp.	College	Hometown	How Acq.	'07 Games/ Starts
46	Adams, Blue	CB	5-10	187	28	5	Cincinnati	Miami, Fla.	FA-'07	13/0
71	Anderson, Willie	T	6-5	340	33	13	Auburn	Mobile, Ala.	D1-'96	7/5
79	Andrews, Stacy	G/T	6-7	342	27	5	Mississippi	Camden, Ark.	D4c-'04	16/14
58	Blackstock, Darryl	LB	6-3	244	25	4	Virginia	Newport News, Va.	FA-'08	16/0*
55	Brooks, Ahmad	LB	6-3	259	24	3	Virginia	Woodbridge, Va.	SD3-'06	2/2
36	Busing, John	S	6-2	221	25	3	Miami (Ohio)	Johns Creek, Ga.	FA-'06	12/0
83	Chatman, Antonio	WR	5-8	182	29	6	Cincinnati	Los Angeles, Calif.	FA-'06	13/1
86	Coats, Daniel	TE	6-3	255	24	2	Brigham Young	Layton, Utah	FA-'07	15/3
27	Dorsey, DeDe	HB	5-11	196	24	3	Lindenwood	Broken Arrow, Okla.	FA-'07	12/2
7 #	Elling, Aaron	K	6-2	201	30	5	Wyoming	Waconia, Minn.	W(Jax)-'07	0*
68	Fanene, Jonathan	DE	6-4	295	26	4	Utah	Pago Pago (American Samoa)	D7-'05	14/0
11	Fitzpatrick, Ryan	QB	6-2	225	25	4	Harvard	Gilbert, Ariz.	T(StL)-'07	1/0
12	Gabriel, Doug	WR	6-2	215	28	5	Central Florida	Miami, Fla.	FA-'08	0*
91	Geathers, Robert	DE	6-3	265	25	5	Georgia	Georgetown, S.C.	D4b-'04	16/16
53	Ghiaciuc, Eric	C	6-4	300	27	4	Central Michigan	Oxford, Mich.	D4-'05	12/12
17	Graham, Shayne	K	6-0	200	30	8	Virginia Tech	Dublin, Va.	W(Car)-'03	16/0
29	Hall, Leon	CB	5-11	199	23	2	Michigan	Vista, Calif.	D1-'07	16/10
50	Henderson, Eric	LB	6-2	263	25	2	Georgia Tech	New Orleans, La.	FA-'06	0*
16	Holt, Glenn	WR	6-1	193	24	3	Kentucky	Miami, Fla.	FA-'06	16/0
84	Houshmandzadeh, T.J.	WR	6-1	199	30	8	Oregon State	Barstow, Calif.	D7-'01	16/15
30	Irons, Kenny	HB	5-11	200	24	2	Auburn	Dacula, Ga.	D2-'07	0*
28	Jackson, Dexter	S	6-0	210	31	10	Florida State	Quincy, Fla.	UFA(TB)-'06	14/14
93	Jeanty, Rashad	LB	6-2	245	25	3	Central Florida	Miami, Fla.	FA-'06	10/7
59	Johnson, Brandon	LB	6-5	224	25	3	Louisville	Birmingham, Ala.	FA-'08	6/0*
85	Johnson, Chad	WR	6-1	192	30	8	Oregon State	Miami, Fla.	D2-'01	16/16
31	Johnson, Jeremi	FB	5-11	260	28	6	Western Kentucky	Louisville, Ky.	D4b-'03	16/9
32	Johnson, Rudi	HB	5-10	214	28	8	Auburn	Ettrick, Va.	D4-'01	11/9
20	Jones, David	CB	6-0	196	22	2	Wingate	Greenville, S.C.	W(NO)-'07	7/0
57	Jones, Dhani	LB	6-1	240	30	9	Michigan	Potomac, Md.	FA-'07	14/9
44	Jones, Herana-Daze	S	5-11	205	26	3	Indiana	Louisville, Ky.	FA-'05	9/0
76	Jones, Levi	T	6-5	307	29	7	Arizona State	Eloy, Ariz.	D1-'02	15/13
22	Joseph, Johnathan	CB	5-11	193	24	3	South Carolina	Rock Hill, S.C.	D1-'06	15/14
82	Kelly, Reggie	TE	6-4	250	31	10	Mississippi State	Aberdeen, Miss.	UFA(Atl)-'03	15/15
43	Kilmer, Ethan	S	6-0	204	25	3	Penn State	Wyalusing, Pa.	D7a-'06	0*
75	Kooistra, Scott	T/G	6-6	335	27	6	North Carolina State	Cary, N.C.	D7a-'03	16/0
19	Larson, Kyle	P	6-1	204	28	5	Nebraska	Funk, Neb.	FA-'04	16/0
80	Lawrie, Nate	TE	6-7	255	26	4	Yale	Indianapolis, Ind.	FA-'07	3/2
95	Manning, Roy	LB	6-2	245	26	4	Michigan	Saginaw, Mich.	W(Jax)-'07	5/0
52 #	Marshall, Lemar	LB	6-2	225	31	7	Michigan State	Cincinnati, Ohio	FA-'07	4/3
52	Maxwell, Jim	LB	6-4	240	27	5	Gardner-Webb	Johnsonville, S.C.	FA-'07	3/0
10	Maxwell, Marcus	WR	6-4	205	25	3	Oregon	Hercules, Calif.	FA-'07	5/0
51	Mays, Corey	LB	6-1	245	24	3	Notre Dame	Chicago, Ill.	W(NE)-'07	11/1
58 #	Miller, Caleb	LB	6-3	225	28	5	Arkansas	Sulphur Springs, Texas	D3a-'04	3/1
96	Myers, Michael	DT	6-2	300	32	11	Alabama	Vicksburg, Miss.	UFA(Den)-'07	15/2
41	Ndukwe, Chinedum	S	6-2	218	23	2	Notre Dame	Powell, Ohio	D7b-'07	14/2
24	O'Neal, Deltha	CB	5-11	194	31	9	California	Milpitas, Calif.	T(Den)-'04	16/8
98	Odom, Antwan	DE	6-5	274	26	5	Alabama	Bayou La Batre, Ala.	UFA(Tenn)-'08	16/16*
9	Palmer, Carson	QB	6-5	230	28	6	Southern California	Mission Viejo, Calif.	D1-'03	16/16
94	Peko, Domata	DT	6-3	319	23	3	Michigan State	Pago Pago (American Samoa)	D4-'06	16/16
23	Perry, Chris	HB	6-0	224	26	5	Michigan	Advance, N.C.	D1-'04	0*
99	Pollack, David	LB	6-2	255	26	4	Georgia	Snellville, Ga.	D1-'05	0*
3	Rowe, Jeff	QB	6-5	221	24	2	Nevada	Reno, Nev.	D5-'07	0*
92	Rucker, Frostee	DE	6-3	280	24	3	Southern California	Tustin, Calif.	D3-'06	5/0
48	St. Louis, Brad	LS/TE	6-3	243	32	9	Southwest Missouri State	Belton, Mo.	D7-'00	16/0
65	Santucci, Dan	C	6-4	304	24	2	Notre Dame	Harwood Heights, Ill.	PS(Ind)-'07	2/0
56	Schlegel, Anthony	LB	6-1	251	27	3	Ohio State	Dallas, Texas	W(NYJ)-'07	13/5
97	Thornton, John	DT	6-3	297	31	10	West Virginia	Philadelphia, Pa.	UFA(Tenn)-'03	14/14
45	Thurman, Odell	LB	6-0	240	25	2	Georgia	Monticello, Ga.	D2-'05	0*
81	Utecht, Ben	TE	6-6	251	27	4	Minnesota	Hastings, Minn.	RFA(Ind)-'08	14/13*
33	Watson, Kenny	HB	6-0	218	30	7	Penn State	Harrisburg, Pa.	FA-'03	16/5
26	White, Marvin	S	6-1	199	24	2	Texas Christian	Port Barre, La.	D4-'07	15/3
77	Whitworth, Andrew	T/G	6-7	339	26	3	Louisiana State	West Monroe, La.	D2-'06	16/16
63	Williams, Bobbie	G	6-4	345	31	9	Arkansas	Jefferson, Texas	UFA(Phil)-'04	16/16

* Blackstock played 16 games with Arizona in '07; Elling missed '07 season because of injury; Gabriel last active with Oakland in '06; Henderson missed '07 season because of injury; Irons missed '07 season because of injury; B. Johnson played 6 games with Arizona;

Kilmer inactive for 5 games; Odom played 16 games with Tennessee; C. Perry was on the Reserve/Physically Unable to Perform list; Pollack was on the Reserve/Physically Unable to Perform list; Rowe was inactive for 16 games; Thurman was on the Reserve/Suspended by Commissioner list for 16 games in '07; Utecht played in 14 games with Indianapolis in '07.

\#   Unrestricted free agent; subject to developments.

Players lost through free agency (5): LB Landon Johnson (Car; 16 games in '07), DE/DT Bryan Robinson (Ariz; 16), DE Justin Smith (SF; 16), C Alex Stepanovich (Atl; 12), S Madieu Williams (Minn; 13).

Also played with Bengals in '07—HB Clifton Dawson (2 games), LB Andre Frazier (2), WR Skyler Green (7), WR Chris Henry (8), WR Tab Perry (2), CB Keiwan Ratliff (3), HB Quincy Wilson (1).

2008 FIRST-YEAR ROSTER

Name	Pos.	Ht.	Wt.	Age	College	Hometown	How Acq.
Adams, Titus (1)	DT	6-4	305	25	Nebraska	Omaha, Neb.	FA-'07
Blair, James	G	6-3	323	23	Western Michigan	Detroit, Mich.	FA
Britt, Justin	G-C	6-4	302	22	Alabama	Cullman, Ala.	FA
Brown, Travis	WR	6-3	202	22	New Mexico	West Covina, Calif.	W(Sea)
Caldwell, Andre	WR	6-0	204	23	Florida	Tampa, Fla.	D3b
Castille, Simeon	CB	6-0	195	22	Alabama	Birmingham, Ala.	FA
Collins, Anthony	OT-G	6-5	317	22	Kansas	Beaumont, Texas	D4
Cook, Kyle (1)	C	6-3	295	25	Michigan State	Macomb, Mich.	FA-'07
Craig, Angelo	DE	6-5	242	22	Cincinnati	Cleveland, Ohio	D7a
Glatthaar, Bradley	HB	5-11	245	22	Cincinnati	Cincinnati, Ohio	FA
Hebert, Kyries (1)	S	6-3	220	27	Louisiana-Lafayette	Lafayette, La.	FA
Hoke, Anthony	LB	6-0	238	22	Cincinnati	Warren, Ohio	FA
Howell, Dan	LB	6-0	247	22	Washington	Newhall, Calif.	FA
Johnson, James	HB	5-11	202	23	Kansas State	Port Arthur, Texas	FA
Livings, Nate (1)	G	6-5	335	26	Louisiana State	Lake Charles, La.	FA-'06
Logan, Clyde	WR	6-3	202	26	Idaho State	Charlotte, N.C.	FA
Lynch, Corey	S	6-0	206	23	Appalachian State	Cape Coral, Fla.	D6a
Marquardt, Michael	DT	6-3	292	26	Arizona State	Vista, Calif.	FA
Palmer, Jordan (1)	QB	6-5	232	24	Texas-El Paso	Mission Viejo, Calif.	FA
Rivers, Keith	LB	6-2	241	22	Southern California	Lake Mary, Fla.	D1
Sherry, Matt	TE	6-4	255	23	Villanova	Rumford, R.I.	D6b
Shirley, Jason	DT	6-5	338	22	Fresno State	Fontana, Calif.	D5
Simpson, Jerome	WR	6-2	199	22	Coastal Carolina	Reidsville, N.C.	D2
Sims, Pat	DT	6-2	310	22	Auburn	Ft. Lauderdale, Fla.	D3a
Uperesa, Dane (1)	OT	6-5	315	24	Hawaii	Hauula (Oahu), Hawaii	FA-'07
Urrutia, Mario	WR	6-5	232	22	Louisville	Louisville, Ky.	D7b
Whaley, Tyler	FB	5-11	252	23	Ohio State	Ironton, Ohio	FA

The term NFL Rookie is defined as a player who is in his first season of professional football and has not been on the roster of another professional football team for any regular-season or postseason games. A Rookie is designated by an "R" on NFL rosters. Players who have been active in another professional football league or players who have NFL experience, including either preseason training camp or being on an Active List or Inactive List, or on Reserve/Injured or Reserve/Physically Unable to Perform for fewer than six regular-season games, are termed NFL First-Year Players. An NFL First-Year Player is designated by a "1" on NFL rosters. Thereafter, a player is credited with an additional year of experience for each season in which he accumulates six games on the Active List or Inactive List, or on Reserve/Injured or Reserve/Physically Unable to Perform.

Log on to www.bengals.com for an up-to-date roster; Age listed is as of September 4, 2008.

COACHING STAFF
Head Coach,
Marvin Lewis

Pro Career: After establishing himself as a record-setting NFL defensive coordinator, Lewis was named the ninth head coach in Bengals history on January 14, 2003. Marvin Lewis is in his sixth season as Bengals head coach. Only Paul Brown and Sam Wyche have had longer tenures (eight seasons each), or more career victories. Lewis' record over five previous campaigns is 42-38 in regular season, 0-1 in postseason and 42-39 overall. He is 13 wins behind Paul Brown (55-59-1) and 22 wins behind Wyche (64-68). He is one of three Bengals coaches with a winning career record, joining Forrest Gregg (34-27) and Bill "Tiger" Johnson (18-15). With the departure of Brian Billick as head coach at Baltimore, Lewis enters 2008 as the senior head coach in the AFC North Division. Overall in the NFL, only eight coaches have longer current tenures with their teams. Lewis entered 2007 as the only Bengals head coach never to experience a losing season, but the '07 club got off to an injury-plagued 2-6 start and could rally to only a 7-9 finish. The 2005 Bengals were 11-5 and won the AFC North title. Prior to his arrival, Lewis was the Washington Redskins' defensive coordinator (2002), serving as assistant head coach in addition to his coordinator's role. He spent six seasons (1996-2001) as defensive coordinator with the Baltimore Ravens, a tenure that included a Super Bowl victory. In the 2000 season, Lewis' Baltimore defense set the NFL record for fewest points allowed in a 16-game campaign (165) and has been widely considered as one of the best NFL defenses of all time. The 970 rushing yards allowed was the fewest in NFL history for a 16-game season. The Ravens' four shutouts were the most in the NFL since 1976. Prior to joining Baltimore, he spent four seasons (1992-95) with Pittsburgh as linebackers coach. Career record: 42-39.

Background: Earned All-Big Sky Conference honors as a linebacker at Idaho State (1978-1980), and saw action at quarterback and free safety. Received his bachelor's degree in physical education from Idaho State in 1981, and earned his Master's degree in athletic administration in 1982. Inducted into Idaho State's Hall of Fame in 2001. Began his coaching career at Idaho State (1981-84). The team finished 12-1 during his first season and won the NCAA Division I-AA championship. Was also the linebackers coach at Long Beach State (1985-86), New Mexico (1987-89), and Pittsburgh (1990-91).

Personal: Age 49, born in McDonald, Pa. Lewis and his wife, Peggy, have two children—Whitney and Marcus.

ASSISTANT COACHES

Paul Alexander, asst. head coach/offensive line; born Rochester, N.Y. Tackle Cortland State 1979-1981. No pro playing experience. College coach: Penn State 1982-84, Michigan 1985-86, Central Michigan 1987-1991. Pro coach: New York Jets 1992-93, joined Bengals in 1994.

Jim Anderson, running backs; born Harrisburg, Pa. Linebacker/defensive end California Western 1967-69. No pro playing experience. College coach: California Western 1970-71, Scottsdale (Ariz.) C.C. 1973, Nevada-Las Vegas 1974-75, Southern Methodist 1976-1980, Stanford 1981-83. Pro coach: Joined Bengals in 1984.

Bob Bratkowski, offensive coordinator; born San Angelo, Texas. Wide receiver Washington State 1975-77. No pro playing experience. College coach: Missouri 1978-1980, Weber State 1986, Wyoming 1986, Washington State 1987-88, Miami 1989-1991. Pro coach: Seattle Seahawks 1992-98, Pittsburgh Steelers 1999-2000, joined Bengals in 2001.

Louie Cioffi, asst. defensive backs; born Greenlawn, N.Y. Attended SUNY-Stony Brook. No college or pro playing experience. College coach: C.W. Post 1995-96. Pro coach: New York Jets 1993-94, joined Bengals in 1997.

Kevin Coyle, defensive backs; born Staten Island, N.Y. Defensive back Massachusetts 1975-77. No pro playing experience. College coach: Cincinnati 1978-79, Arkansas 1980, U.S. Merchant Marine Academy 1981, Holy Cross 1982-1990, Syracuse 1991-93, Maryland 1994-96, Fresno State 1997-2000. Pro coach: Joined Bengals in 2001.

Jeff FitzGerald, linebackers; born Burbank, Calif. Linebacker Oregon State 1980. No pro playing experience. College coach: Cincinnati 1985, Alabama 1986-89, San Diego State 1994-97. Pro coach: Tampa Bay Buccaneers 1990-93, Washington Redskins 1998-99, Arizona Cardinals 2000-03, Baltimore Ravens 2004-07, joined Bengals in 2008.

Paul Guenther, staff assistant; born Richboro, Pa. Linebacker Ursinus College 1990-93. No pro playing experience. College coach: Western Maryland 1994-95, Ursinus College 1996, 1997-2001 (head coach 1997-2001), Jacksonville 1997. Pro coach: Washington Redskins 2002-03, joined Bengals in 2005.

Jay Hayes, defensive line; born South Fayette, Pa. Defensive end Idaho 1978-1981. Pro defensive end/linebacker Michigan Panthers (USFL) 1984, Memphis Showboats (USFL) 1985. College coach: Notre Dame 1988-1991, California 1992-94, Wisconsin 1995-98. Pro coach: Pittsburgh Steelers 1999-2001, Minnesota Vikings 2002, joined Bengals in 2003.

Jonathan Hayes, tight ends; born South Fayette, Pa. Linebacker/tight end Iowa 1981-84. Pro tight end Kansas City Chiefs 1985-1993, Pittsburgh Steelers 1994-96.

College coach: Oklahoma 1999-2002. Pro coach: Joined Bengals in 2003.

Chip Morton, strength and conditioning; born Hamden, Conn. Attended North Carolina. No college or pro playing experience. College coach: Ohio State 1985-86, Penn State 1987-1991. Pro coach: San Diego Chargers 1992-94, Carolina Panthers 1995-98, Baltimore Ravens 1999-2001, Washington Redskins 2002, joined Bengals in 2003.

Ray Oliver, asst. strength and conditioning; born Cincinnati. Defensive back Ohio State 1980-81. College coach: Pittsburgh 1985-88, Kentucky 1989-1991, South Carolina 1993-95, Memphis 2001-03. Pro coach: Tampa Bay Buccaneers 1992, New Jersey Nets (NBA) 1996-97, joined Bengals in 2004.

Mike Sheppard, wide receivers; born Tulsa, Okla. Wide receiver Cal Lutheran 1969-1972. No pro playing experience. College coach: Cal Lutheran 1974-76, Brigham Young 1977-78, U.S. International 1979, Idaho State 1980-81, Long Beach State 1982, 1984-86, Kansas 1983, New Mexico 1987-1991, California 1992. Pro coach: Cleveland Browns 1993-95, Baltimore Ravens 1996, San Diego Chargers 1997-98, Seattle Seahawks 1999-2000, Buffalo Bills 2001, New Orleans Saints 2002-05, joined Bengals in 2007.

Darrin Simmons, special teams; born Elkhart, Kan. Punter Kansas 1993-95. No pro playing experience. College coach: Kansas 1996, Minnesota 1997. Pro coach: Baltimore Ravens 1998, Carolina Panthers 1999-2002, joined Bengals in 2003.

Bob Surace, offensive assistant; born Harrisburg, Pa. Center Princeton 1987-89. No pro playing experience. College coach: Springfield College 1990-91, Maine Maritime Academy 1992-93, Rensselaer Polytechnic Institute 1995, Western Connecticut State 1996-2001 (head coach 2000-01). Pro coach: Shreveport Pirates (CFL) 1994, joined Bengals in 2002.

Ken Zampese, quarterbacks; born Santa Maria, Calif. Wide receiver San Diego 1985-88. No pro playing experience. College coach: San Diego 1989, Southern California 1990-91, Northern Arizona 1992-95, Miami (Ohio) 1996-97. Pro coach: Philadelphia Eagles 1998, Green Bay Packers 1999, St. Louis Rams 2000-02, joined Bengals in 2003.

Mike Zimmer, defensive coordinator; born Peoria, Ill. Quarterback/linebacker Illinois State 1974-76. No pro playing experience. College coach: Missouri 1979-1980, Weber State 1981-88, Washington State 1989-1993. Pro coach: Dallas Cowboys 1994-2006, Atlanta Falcons 2007, joined Bengals in 2008.

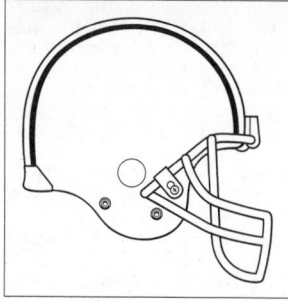

**American Football Conference
North Division
Team Colors:** Brown, Orange, and White
76 Lou Groza Blvd.
Berea, Ohio 44017
Telephone: (440) 891-5000

2008 SCHEDULE
PRESEASON
Aug. 7   **N.Y. Jets** 7:30
Aug. 18 at N.Y. Giants.....................8:00
Aug. 23 at Detroit 4:00
Aug. 28 **Chicago** 7:30

REGULAR SEASON
Sep. 7   **Dallas** 4:15
Sep. 14 **Pittsburgh** 8:15
Sep. 21 at Baltimore 4:15
Sep. 28 at Cincinnati 1:00
Oct. 5   BYE
Oct. 13 **N.Y. Giants** (Mon.) 8:30
Oct. 19 at Washington 4:15
Oct. 26 at Jacksonville 4:05
Nov. 2   **Baltimore** 1:00
Nov. 6   **Denver** (Thu.) 8:15
Nov. 17 at Buffalo (Mon.) 8:30
Nov. 23 **Houston** 1:00
Nov. 30 **Indianapolis** 1:00
Dec. 7   at Tennessee 12:00
Dec. 15 at Philadelphia (Mon.).........8:30
Dec. 21 **Cincinnati** 1:00
Dec. 28 at Pittsburgh 1:00

Stadium: Cleveland Browns Stadium
         (opened in 1999)
         • **Capacity:** 73,300
         100 Alfred Lerner Way
         Cleveland, Ohio 44114
Playing Surface: Grass
Headquarters/Training Camp:
         76 Lou Groza Boulevard
         Berea, Ohio 44017

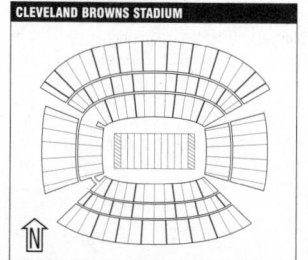

CLEVELAND BROWNS STADIUM

CLUB OFFICIALS
Owner: Randy Lerner
Vice Chairman: Bob Kain
Senior Vice President and General
   Manager: Phil Savage
Head Coach: Romeo Crennel
Senior Vice President: Lew Merletti
Senior Vice President, Business
   Operations: Mike Keenan
Executive Advisor: Jim Brown
Vice President, Communications:
   Bill Bonsiewicz
Vice President, Government Affairs:
   Diane Downing
Vice President, Finance & Administration:
   David Jenkins
Vice President, Team Operations &
   Security: Carl Meyer
Vice President, Sales & Marketing:
   Brett Reynolds
Director, Stadium Operations:
   Todd Argust
Director, New Media: Reagan Berube
Director, Player Development:
   Jerry Butler
Director, Information Technology:
   Gordon Foust
Director, Community Relations:
   Renee Harvey
Director, Alumni Relations: Dino Lucarelli
Director, Media Information: Ken Mather
Director, Football Administration:
   Trip MacCracken
Director, Scoreboard: Kathy McLain
Director, Marketing Services:
   George Muller
Director, Human Resources:
   Michael Nikolaus
Legal Counsel: Lorne Novick
Director, Communications: Amy Palcic
Director, Suite Operations: Joe Ricciuti
Controller: Laurie Rice
Director, Team Operations:
   Brendan Rowe
Director, Finance: Gregory Rush
Director, Direct Marketing and Customer
   Service: John Schulze
Director, Youth Development: Ed Suggs
Head Athletic Trainer: Marty Lauzon
Equipment Manager: Brad Melland
Video Director: Pat Dolan
Head Groundskeeper: Chris Powell

COACHING HISTORY
(435-380-10)
Records include postseason games
1950-1962 Paul Brown 115-49-5
1963-1970 Blanton Collier..............79-38-2
1971-74   Nick Skorich 30-26-2
1975-77   Forrest Gregg* 18-23-0
1977   Dick Modzelewski 0-1-0
1978-1984 Sam Rutigliano** 47-52-0
1984-88   Marty Schottenheimer ..46-31-0
1989-1990 Bud Carson*** 12-14-1
1990   Jim Shofner.....................1-6-0
1991-95   Bill Belichick 37-45-0
1999-2000 Chris Palmer 5-27-0
2001-04   Butch Davis****.........24-36-0
2004   Terry Robiskie 1-4-0
2005-07   Romeo Crennel 20-28-0
     *Resigned after 13 games in 1977
    **Released after eight games in 1984
   ***Released after nine games in 1990
  ****Resigned after 11 games in 2004

PAID ATTENDANCE
Home 570,751   Away 521,147
Total 1,091,898
Single-game home record,
   85,073 (9/21/70)
Single-season home record, 620,496
   (1980)

2008 DRAFT CHOICES

Round	Name	Pos.	College
4	Beau Bell	LB	Nevada-Las Vegas
	Martin Rucker	TE	Missouri
6	Ahtyba Rubin	NT	Iowa State
	Paul Hubbard	WR	Wisconsin
7	Alex Hall	LB	St. Augustine's (N.C.)

2007 TEAM RECORD
PRESEASON (3-1)

Date	Result	Opponent
8/11	W 16-12	Kansas City
8/18	L 20-23	Detroit
8/25	W 17-16	at Denver
8/30	W 19-9	at Chicago

REGULAR SEASON (10-6)

Date	Result	Opponent	Att.
9/9	L 7-34	Pittsburgh	73,089
9/16	W 51-45	Cincinnati	72,801
9/23	L 24-26	at Oakland	51,075
9/30	W 27-13	Baltimore	73,024
10/7	L 17-34	at New England	68,756
10/14	W 41-31	Miami	73,198
10/28	W 27-20	at St. Louis	62,777
11/4	W 33-30	Seattle (OT)	72,927
11/11	L 28-31	at Pittsburgh	64,781
11/18	W 33-30	at Baltimore (OT)	71,055
11/25	W 27-17	Houston	72,730
12/2	L 21-27	at Arizona	64,791
12/9	W 24-18	at New York Jets	76,822
12/16	W 8-0	Buffalo	73,196
12/23	L 14-19	at Cincinnati	66,023
12/30	W 20-7	San Francisco	73,041

(OT) Overtime

SCORE BY PERIODS

Browns	60	144	87	105	6 —	402
Opponents	85	112	82	103	0 —	382

2007 TEAM STATISTICS

	Browns	Opp.
Total First Downs	315	335
Rushing	110	100
Passing	192	211
Penalty	13	24
3rd Down: Made/Att	86/204	79/215
3rd Down Pct.	42.2	36.7
4th Down: Made/Att	6/15	11/25
4th Down Pct.	40.0	44.0
Possession Avg.	29:10	30:50
Total Net Yards	5621	5753
Avg. Per Game	351.3	359.6
Total Plays	1004	1066
Avg. Per Play	5.6	5.4
Net Yards Rushing	1895	2072
Avg. Per Game	118.4	129.5
Total Rushes	440	460
Net Yards Passing	3726	3681
Avg. Per Game	232.9	230.1
Sacked/Yards Lost	19/140	28/186
Gross Yards	3866	3867
Att./Completions	545/305	578/340
Completion Pct.	56.0	58.8
Had Intercepted	20	17
Punts/Average	69/42.0	69/40.2
Net Punting Avg.	69/35.8	69/32.9
Penalties/Yards	114/868	80/581
Fumbles/Ball Lost	22/9	19/10
Touchdowns	46	41
Rushing	13	8
Passing	29	29
Returns	4	4

2007 INDIVIDUAL STATISTICS

PASSING	Att.	Comp.	Yds.	Pct.	TD	Int.	Tkld.	Rate
Anderson	527	298	3787	56.5	29	19	14/109	82.5
Frye	10	4	34	40.0	0	1	5/31	10.0
Quinn	8	3	45	37.5	0	0	0/0	56.8
Browns	545	305	3866	56.0	29	20	19/140	80.7
Opponents	578	340	3867	58.8	29	17	28/186	83.4

SCORING	TD R	TD P	TD Rt	PAT	FG	Saf	PTS
Dawson	0	0	0	42/43	26/30	0	120
Edwards	0	16	0	0/0	0/0	0	96
Lewis	9	2	0	0/0	0/0	0	66
Winslow	0	5	0	0/0	0/0	0	32
Jurevicius	0	3	0	0/0	0/0	0	20
Anderson	3	0	0	0/0	0/0	0	18
Cribbs	0	0	3	0/0	0/0	0	18
Vickers	0	2	0	0/0	0/0	0	12
Carter	0	1	0	0/0	0/0	0	6
Pool	0	0	1	0/0	0/0	0	6
J. Wright	1	0	0	0/0	0/0	0	6
Browns	13	29	4	42/43	26/30	1	402
Opponents	8	29	4	38/38	32/35	0	382

2-Pt. Conversions: Jurevicius, Winslow, Browns 2-3, Opponents 1-3

RUSHING	No.	Yds	Avg	LG	TD
Lewis	298	1304	4.4	66t	9
J. Wright	60	277	4.6	18	1
Harrison	23	142	6.2	17	0
Anderson	32	70	2.2	11	3
Cribbs	9	61	6.8	18	0
Vickers	15	43	2.9	7	0
Frye	1	1	1.0	1	0
Zastudil	2	-3	-1.5	0	0
Browns	440	1895	4.3	66t	13
Opponents	460	2072	4.5	37	8

RECEIVING	No.	Yds	Avg	LG	TD
Winslow	82	1106	13.5	49	5
Edwards	80	1289	16.1	78t	16
Jurevicius	50	614	12.3	50	3
Lewis	30	248	8.3	34	2
J. Wright	24	233	9.7	23	0
Vickers	13	91	7.0	25	2
Heiden	12	104	8.7	27	0
Carter	8	117	14.6	22	1
Cribbs	3	37	12.3	18	0
Harrison	2	19	9.5	15	0
Dinkins	1	8	8.0	8	0
Browns	305	3866	12.7	78t	29
Opponents	340	3867	11.4	42	29

INTERCEPTIONS	No.	Yds	Avg	LG	TD
Bodden	6	75	12.5	26	0
Jones	5	37	7.4	26	0
Pool	2	103	51.5	100t	1
McDonald	2	0	0.0	0	0
Jackson	1	1	1.0	1	0
E. Wright	1	0	0.0	0	0
Browns	17	216	12.7	100t	1
Opponents	20	422	21.1	71t	2

PUNTING	No.	Yds.	Avg.	In 20	LG
Zastudil	49	2046	41.8	14	64
Player	13	593	45.6	6	57
Ernster	7	256	36.6	2	43
Browns	69	2895	42.0	22	64
Opponents	69	2774	40.2	19	69

PUNT RETURNS	Ret	FC	Yds	Avg	LG	TD
Cribbs	30	10	405	13.5	76t	1
Browns	30	10	405	13.5	76t	1
Opponents	34	8	308	9.1	94t	1

KICKOFF RETURNS	No.	Yds	Avg	LG	TD
Cribbs	59	1809	30.7	100t	2
Dinkins	7	62	8.9	19	0
J. Wright	3	49	16.3	20	0
Friedman	2	14	7.0	13	0
Jurevicius	1	9	9.0	9	0
Browns	72	1943	27.0	100t	2
Opponents	76	1590	20.9	65	0

FIELD GOALS	1-19	20-29	30-39	40-49	50+
Dawson	2/2	9/10	7/8	7/8	1/2
Browns	2/2	9/10	7/8	7/8	1/2
Opponents	1/1	12/12	11/11	8/11	0/0

SACKS	No.
Wimbley	5.0
Peek	4.0
R. Smith	4.0
Williams	4.0
McGinest	3.0
S. Smith	2.0
M. Adams	1.0
Jackson	1.0
Kelley	1.0
Thompson	1.0
E. Wright	1.0
Jones	0.5
Roye	0.5
Browns	28.0
Opponents	19.0

RECORD HOLDERS
INDIVIDUAL RECORDS—CAREER

Category	Name	Performance
Rushing (Yds.)	Jim Brown, 1957-1965	12,312
Passing (Yds.)	Brian Sipe, 1974-1983	23,713
Passing (TDs)	Brian Sipe, 1974-1983	154
Receiving (No.)	Ozzie Newsome, 1978-1990	662
Receiving (Yds.)	Ozzie Newsome, 1978-1990	7,980
Interceptions	Thom Darden, 1972-74, 1976-1981	45
Punting (Avg.)	Horace Gilliam, 1950-56	43.8
Punt Return (Avg.)	Greg Pruitt, 1973-1981	11.8
Kickoff Return (Avg.)	Joshua Cribbs, 2005-07	26.6
Field Goals	Lou Groza, 1950-59, 1961-67	234
Touchdowns (Tot.)	Jim Brown, 1957-1965	126
Points	Lou Groza, 1950-59, 1961-67	1,349

INDIVIDUAL RECORDS—SINGLE SEASON

Category	Name	Performance
Rushing (Yds.)	Jim Brown, 1963	1,863
Passing (Yds.)	Brian Sipe, 1980	4,132
Passing (TDs)	Brian Sipe, 1980	30
Receiving (No.)	Ozzie Newsome, 1983	89
	Ozzie Newsome, 1984	89
	Kellen Winslow, 2006	89
Receiving (Yds.)	Braylon Edwards, 2007	1,289
Interceptions	Thom Darden, 1978	10
	Anthony Henry, 2001	10
Punting (Avg.)	Gary Collins, 1965	46.7
Punt Return (Avg.)	Leroy Kelly, 1965	15.6
Kickoff Return (Avg.)	Billy Lefear, 1975	31.7
Field Goals	Matt Stover, 1995	29
Touchdowns (Tot.)	Jim Brown, 1965	21
Points	Jim Brown, 1965	126

INDIVIDUAL RECORDS—SINGLE GAME

Category	Name	Performance
Rushing (Yds.)	Jim Brown, 11-24-57	237
	Jim Brown, 11-19-61	237
Passing (Yds.)	Brian Sipe, 10-25-81	444
Passing (TDs)	Frank Ryan, 12-12-64	5
	Bill Nelsen, 11-2-69	5
	Brian Sipe, 10-7-79	5
	Kelly Holcomb, 11-28-04	5
	Derek Anderson, 9-16-07	5
Receiving (No.)	Ozzie Newsome, 10-14-84	14
Receiving (Yds.)	Ozzie Newsome, 10-14-84	191
Interceptions	Many times	3
	Last time by Anthony Henry, 11-18-01	
Field Goals	Phil Dawson, 11-5-06	6
Touchdowns (Tot.)	Dub Jones, 11-25-51	*6
Points	Dub Jones, 11-25-51	36

*NFL Record

2008 VETERAN ROSTER

No.	Name	Pos.	Ht.	Wt.	Age	NFL Exp.	College	Hometown	How Acq.	'07 Games/ Starts
20	Adams, Mike	DB	5-11	196	27	5	Delaware	Paterson, N.J.	UFA(SF)-'07	3/0
41	Ali, Charles	FB	6-2	265	23	2	Arkansas-Pine Bluff	St. Louis, Mo.	FA-'07	13/0
3	Anderson, Derek	QB	6-6	230	24	4	Oregon State	Portland, Ore.	W(Balt)-'05	16/15
23	Baxter, Gary	DB	6-2	210	29	8	Baylor	Tyler, Texas	UFA(Balt)-'05	0*
57	Bentley, LeCharles	OL	6-2	309	28	7	Ohio State	Cleveland, Ohio	UFA(NO)-'06	0*
38	Cargile, Steve	DB	6-2	210	25	2	Columbia	Cleveland, Ohio	W(Den)-'08	12/0*
85	Cieslak, Brad	TE	6-3	262	25	3	Northern Illinois	Long Grove, Ill.	FA-'07	2/0*
16	Cribbs, Joshua	WR	6-1	215	23	4	Kent State	Washington, D.C.	FA-'05	16/2
54	Davis, Andra	LB	6-1	250	29	7	Florida	Live Oak, Fla.	D5-'02	16/10
4	Dawson, Phil	K	5-11	205	33	10	Texas	Dallas, Texas	FA-'99	16/0
87	Dinkins, Darnell	TE	6-4	258	31	7	Pittsburgh	Pittsburgh, Pa.	UFA(Balt)-'06	15/0
11	Dorsey, Ken	QB	6-4	220	27	6	Miami	Orinda, Calif.	FA-'07	0*
17	Edwards, Braylon	WR	6-3	215	25	4	Michigan	Detroit, Mich.	D1-'05	16/16
66	Fraley, Hank	OL	6-2	315	30	9	Robert Morris	Gaithersburg, Md.	T(Phil)-'06	16/16
62	Friedman, Lennie	OL	6-3	295	31	10	Duke	Milford, N.J.	T(Chi)-'07	16/0
53	Griffin, Kris	LB	6-3	245	26	4	Indiana (Pa.)	Beaver, Pa.	W(KC)-'07	12/0
70	Hadnot, Rex	OL	6-2	325	26	5	Houston	Lufkin, Texas	UFA(Mia)-'08	16/16*
35	Harrison, Jerome	RB	5-9	210	25	3	Washington State	Kalamazoo, Mich.	D5a-'06	8/0
82	Heiden, Steve	TE	6-5	275	31	10	South Dakota St.	Rushford, Minn.	T(SD)-'02	16/6
39	Holly, Daven	DB	5-10	185	25	4	Cincinnati	Clairton, Pa.	FA-'06	15/6
52	Jackson, D'Qwell	LB	6-0	240	24	3	Maryland	Largo, Fla.	D2-'06	14/13
26	Jones, Sean	DB	6-1	225	26	5	Georgia	Atlanta, Ga.	D2-'04	16/16
84	Jurevicius, Joe	WR	6-5	232	33	11	Penn State	Mentor, Ohio	UFA(Sea)-'06	16/12
88	Kasper, Kevin	WR	6-1	202	30	5	Iowa	Hinsdale, Ill.	FA-'08	0*
93	Leonard, Louis	DL	6-4	330	23	2	Fresno State	Los Angeles, Calif.	W(StL)-'07	4/0
31	Lewis, Jamal	RB	5-11	245	28	9	Tennessee	Atlanta, Ga.	UFA(Balt)-'07	15/15
22	McDonald, Brandon	DB	5-10	184	22	2	Memphis	Collins, Miss.	D5-'07	16/2
55	McGinest, Willie	LB	6-5	270	36	15	Southern California	Long Beach, Calif.	UFA(NE)-'06	13/12
68	McKinney, Seth	OL	6-3	315	28	7	Texas A&M	Buffalo, Texas	UFA(Mia)-'07	8/8
90	McMillan, David	LB	6-3	250	26	4	Kansas	Killeen, Texas	D5-'05	15/0
51	Orr, Shantee	LB	6-1	246	26	5	Michigan	Detroit, Mich.	UFA(Jax)-'08	3/0*
56	Peek, Antwan	LB	6-3	255	28	6	Cincinnati	Cincinnati, Ohio	UFA(Hou)-'07	14/4
50	Philip, Marvin	OL	6-1	307	26	3	California	Redwood City, Calif.	W(Pitt)-'07	0*
64	Pontbriand, Ryan	LS	6-2	255	28	6	Rice	Houston, Texas	D5a-'03	16/0
21	Pool, Brodney	DB	6-2	205	23	4	Oklahoma	Houston, Texas	D2-'05	16/16
10	Quinn, Brady	QB	6-3	235	23	2	Notre Dame	Dublin, Ohio	D1b-'07	1/0
92	Rogers, Shaun	DL	6-4	340	29	8	Texas	LaPorte, Texas	T(Det)-'08	16/16*
28	Sandy, Justin	DB	6-0	210	26	2	Northern Iowa	Wayne, Neb.	FA-'07	0*
77	Shaffer, Kevin	OL	6-5	325	28	7	Tulsa	Salisbury, Md.	UFA(Atl)-'06	16/16
98	Smith, Robaire	DL	6-4	320	30	9	Michigan State	Flint, Mich.	UFA(Tenn)-'07	16/16
91	Smith, Shaun	DL	6-2	325	26	5	South Carolina	Brooklyn, N.Y.	RFA(Cin)-'07	15/11
27	Sorensen, Nick	DB	6-3	205	29	8	Virginia Tech	Winter Haven, Fla.	FA-'07	9/0
61	Sowells, Isaac	OL	6-3	325	26	3	Indiana	Louisville, Ky.	D4b-'06	0*
18	Stallworth, Donte'	WR	6-0	200	27	7	Tennessee	Sacramento, Calif.	UFA(NE)-'08	16/9*
65	Steinbach, Eric	OL	6-6	295	28	6	Iowa	Lockport, Ill.	UFA(Cin)-'07	16/16
73	Thomas, Joe	OL	6-6	315	23	2	Wisconsin	Brookfield, Wisc.	D1a-'07	16/16
72	Tucker, Ryan	OL	6-6	320	32	12	TCU	Midland, Texas	UFA(StL)-'02	12/8
47	Vickers, Lawrence	FB	6-0	252	25	3	Colorado	Houston, Texas	D6a-'06	16/14
99	Williams, Corey	DL	6-4	320	27	5	Arkansas State	Camden, Ark.	T(GB)-'08	16/9*
94	Williams, Leon	LB	6-2	250	24	3	Miami	Brooklyn, N.Y.	D4a-'06	16/10
81	Wilson, Travis	WR	6-1	215	24	3	Oklahoma	Carrollton, Texas	D3-'06	0*
95	Wimbley, Kamerion	LB	6-3	260	24	3	Florida State	Wichita, Kan.	D1-'06	16/16
80	Winslow, Kellen	TE	6-4	250	25	5	Miami	San Diego, Calif.	D1-'04	16/14
24	Wright, Eric	DB	5-10	193	22	2	Nevada-Las Vegas	San Francisco, Calif.	D2-'07	14/13
29	Wright, Jason	RB	5-10	214	25	4	Northwestern	Diamond Bar, Calif.	FA-'05	16/1
25	Wright, Kenny	DB	6-1	205	30	10	Northwestern St.	Ruston, La.	UFA(Wash)-'07	7/1
15	Zastudil, Dave	P	6-3	227	29	7	Ohio University	Bay Village, Ohio	UFA(Balt)-'06	12/0

* Baxter missed '07 season because of injury; Bentley missed '07 season because of injury; Cargile played 12 games with Denver; Cieslak played 2 games with Buffalo; K. Dorsey inactive for 15 games in '07; Hadnot played 16 games with Miami; Kasper last active with Detroit in '06; Orr played 3 games with Jacksonville; Philip inactive for 3 games; Rogers played 16 games with Detroit; Sandy last active with Tennessee in '05; Sowells did not play in 1 game; Stallworth played 16 games with New England; C. Williams played 16 games with Green Bay; Wilson inactive for 16 games.

Players lost through free agency (3): Ricardo Colclough (Car; 3 games in '07), LB Matt Stewart (Ari; 0), LB Chaun Thompson (Hou; 0).

Also played with Browns in '07—S Mike Adams (15 games), Colby Bockwoldt (1), DB Leigh Bodden (16), WR Tim Carter (16), K Paul Ernster (1), DL Simon Fraser (16), QB Charlie Frye (1), Kris Griffin (12), DE Bobby Hamilton (1), DL Ethan Kelley (13), P Scott Player (3), DL Orpheus Roye (13), NT Ted Washington (5).

2008 FIRST-YEAR ROSTER

Name	Pos.	Ht.	Wt.	Age	College	Hometown	How Acq.
Bell, Beau	LB	6-1	244	22	Nevada-Las Vegas	Tustin, Calif.	D4a
Bennett, Nathan	OL	6-4	300	24	Clemson	Dallas, Ga.	FA
Davis, AJ (1)	DB	5-10	193	25	North Carolina State	Durham, N.C.	FA-'07
Hall, Alex	LB	6-5	243	23	St. Augustine	Glenarden, Md.	D7
Hill, Efrem (1)	WR	6-0	188	25	Samford	Atlanta, Ga.	W(TB)-'07
Hubbard, Paul	WR	6-2	221	23	Wisconsin	Colorado Springs, Colo.	D6b
Hughes, Nate	WR	6-0	186	23	Alcorn State	Macon, Miss.	FA
James, Mil'Von	DB	5-10	196	22	Nevada-Las Vegas	Los Angeles, Calif.	FA
Jenkins, Damon	DB	5-10	190	23	Fresno State	Concord, Calif.	FA
Kapanui, Kolomona	TE	6-3	271	24	West Texas A&M	Palolo, Hawaii	FA
Lawson, Gerard	DB	5-10	195	23	Oregon State	Las Vegas, Nev.	FA
Lee, James	OL	6-4	300	23	South Carolina State	Belle Glade, Fla.	FA
Leggett, Lance	WR	6-3	189	23	Miami	Bartow, Fla.	FA
Louis, Cliff (1)	OL	6-8	300	24	Morgan State	Stanford, Conn.	FA-'07
Matthews, Asa	LB	6-2	239	24	Northern Colorado	Thornton, Colo.	FA
Mitchell, Xavier	LB	6-2	258	22	Tennessee	Long Beach, Miss.	FA
Ortiz, Chase	LB	6-2	249	23	Texas Christian	League City, Texas	FA
Pittman, Chase (1)	DE	6-5	275	25	Louisiana State	Minden, La.	D7a-'07
Purcell, Melila (1)	DE	6-5	285	24	Hawaii	Leone, American Samoa	D6-'07
Reda, Jason	K	6-1	200	23	Illinois	Rock Island, Ill.	FA
Rubin, Ahtyba	DL	6-2	215	22	Iowa State	Fort Belvoir, Virg.	D6a
Rucker, Martin	TE	6-4	251	23	Missouri	St. Joseph, Mo.	D4b
Sanders, Steve (1)	WR	6-3	201	25	Bowling Green	Cleveland, Ohio	FA-'06
Schaefering, Brian	DL	6-4	286	25	Lindenwood	St. Louis, Mo.	FA
Scott, Austin	RB	5-11	210	23	Penn State	Allentown, Pa.	FA
Steptoe, Syndric (1)	WR	5-9	195	23	Arizona	Bryan, Texas	D7b-'07
Terrell, Darnell	DB	6-1	203	24	Missouri	St. Louis, Mo.	FA
Thomas, Travis	RB	5-11	217	23	Notre Dame	Washington, Pa.	FA
West, Zach (1)	DL	6-5	305	24	Texas-El Paso	Ocala, Fla.	FA-'07
Young, Eric	OL	6-3	310	24	Tennessee	Union, S.C.	FA

The term NFL Rookie is defined as a player who is in his first season of professional football and has not been on the roster of another professional football team for any regular-season or postseason games. A Rookie is designated by an "R" on NFL rosters. Players who have been active in another professional football league or players who have NFL experience, including either preseason training camp or being on an Active List or Inactive List, or on Reserve/Injured or Reserve/Physically Unable to Perform for fewer than six regular-season games, are termed NFL First-Year Players. An NFL First-Year Player is designated by a "1" on NFL rosters. Thereafter, a player is credited with an additional year of experience for each season in which he accumulates six games on the Active List or Inactive List, or on Reserve/Injured or Reserve/Physically Unable to Perform.

Log on to www.clevelandbrowns.com for an up-to-date roster; Age listed is as of September 4, 2008.

COACHING STAFF

Head Coach,
Romeo Crennel
Pro Career: Romeo Crennel was named head coach of the Cleveland Browns on Feb. 8, 2005, the eleventh full-time head coach in team history. Crennel led the Browns to a 10-6 record in 2007, including a franchise-best seven consecutive home wins, and witnessed six Browns selected to the Pro Bowl. Crennel led the Browns to a 6-10 record in 2005 and posted a 4-12 mark in 2006. His résumé includes 38 years of coaching experience, including 27 years in the NFL, and has appeared in six Super Bowls, including five Super Bowl rings. Crennel crafted the defense for the New England Patriots and helped the Patriots win three Super Bowl's (2001, 2003-04). Crennel had previously coached in the NFL with Cleveland (2000), the Jets (1997-99), New England (1993-96), and the Giants (1981-1992), where he was the defensive line coach for the Giants' Super Bowl XXV title. Career record: 20-28.
Background: Crennel was a four-year starter (1966-69) as a defensive lineman at Western Kentucky. He earned team MVP honors as a senior. Earned his bachelor's degree in physical education, along with a master's degree, from Western Kentucky. Crennel coached collegiately at Western Kentucky (1970-74), Texas Tech (1975-77), Mississippi (1978-79), and Georgia Tech (1980).
Personal: Age 61, born in Lynchburg, Va. He and his wife, Rosemary, have three daughters, Lisa Tulley, Tiffany Crennel and Kristin Cullinane.

ASSISTANT COACHES

Dave Atkins, senior offensive assistant; born Victoria, Texas. Running back Texas El-Paso 1970-72. Pro running back San Francisco 49ers 1973, Honolulu Hawaiians (WFL) 1974, San Diego Chargers 1975. College coach: Texas El-Paso 1979-1980, San Diego State 1981-85. Pro coach: Philadelphia Eagles 1986-1992, New England Patriots 1993, Arizona Cardinals 1994-95, New Orleans Saints 1996, 2000-04, Minnesota Vikings 1997-99, joined Browns in 2005.

Chris Caminiti, head coach liaison and asst. special teams; born Enfield, Conn. No pro playing experience. College coach San Diego 1996, Occidental College 1997-99, Nevada-Las Vegas 2000. Pro coach: Joined Browns in 2007.

Wes Chandler, wide receivers; born New Smyrna Beach, Fla. Wide receiver Florida 1974-77. Pro wide receiver New Orleans Saints 1978-1981, San Diego Chargers 1981-87. College coach: Central Florida 1994-95. Pro coach: Orlando Thunder (WL) 1991-92, Rhein Fire (NFLE) 1995-97, Frankfurt Galaxy (NFLE) 1998, Berlin Thunder (NFLE) 1999, Dallas Cowboys 2000-02, Minnesota Vikings 2005, joined Browns in 2007.

Rob Chudzinski, offensive coordinator; born Toledo, Ohio. Tight end Miami 1986-1990. No pro playing experience. College coach: Miami 1994-2003. Pro coach: Cleveland Browns 2004, San Diego Chargers 2005-06, re-joined Browns in 2007.

Ted Daisher, special teams coordinator; born Taylor Mich. College experience: Wide receiver/defensive back Western Michigan 1975-77. No pro playing experience. College coach: Illinois 1980-84, Eastern Michigan 1985-88, Cincinnati 1989-1992, Army 1995-97, Indiana 1998-2000, East Carolina 2001-02. Pro coach: Philadelphia Eagles 2004-05, Oakland Raiders 2006, joined Browns in 2007.

Alan DeGennaro, asst. strength and conditioning coach; born Altoona, Pa. Attended Pittsburgh. No college or pro playing experience. Pro coach: Joined Browns in 2007.

Mike Haluchak, linebackers; born Concord, Calif. Linebacker Southern California 1967-1970. No pro playing experience. College coach: Southern California 1976-77, Cal State-Fullerton 1978, Pacific 1979-1980, California 1981, North Carolina State 1982. Pro coach: Oakland Invaders (USFL) 1983-85, San Diego Chargers 1986-1991, Cincinnati Bengals 1992-93, Washington Redskins 1994-96, New York Giants 1997-99, St. Louis Rams 2000-02, Jacksonville Jaguars 2003-04, joined Browns in 2005.

Umberto Leone, defensive quality control; born Garfield Heights, Ohio. Attended Ohio State. No college or pro playing experience. Pro coach: Joined Browns in 2005.

Anthony Lynn, running backs; born McKinney, Texas. Fullback Texas Tech 1987-1990. Pro fullback Denver Broncos 1993, 1997-99, San Francisco 49ers 1995-96. Pro coach: Denver Broncos 2000-02, Jacksonville Jaguars 2003-04, Dallas Cowboys 2005-06, joined Browns in 2007.

Steve Marshall, offensive line; born Hartford, Conn. Guard/tight end Louisville 1976-78. No pro playing experience. College coach: Plymouth State 1979, Tennessee 1980-81, Marshall 1982-83, Louisville 1984, Murray State 1985-86, Virginia Tech 1987-1992, Tennessee 1993-95, UCLA 1996, Texas A&M 1997, North Carolina 1998-99, Colorado 2000-01, Alabama 2007. Pro coach: Houston Texans 2002-05, joined Browns in 2007.

Richard McNutt, asst. defensive backs; born Park Forest, Ill. Defensive back Ohio State 2000-02. No pro playing experience. College coach Washington and Jefferson College 2004-05, Virginia Military Institute 2006, Toledo 2007. Pro coach: Joined Browns in 2008.

Randy Melvin, defensive line; born Aurora, Ill. Defensive line Eastern Illinois 1978-1981. No pro playing experience. College coach: Eastern Illinois 1988-1994, Wyoming 1995-96, Purdue 1997-99, Rutgers 2002-04, Illinois 2005. Pro coach: New England 2000-01,

joined Browns in 2005.

Tom Myslinski, strength and conditioning; born Rome, N.Y. Guard Tennessee 1989-1992. Pro guard Chicago Bears 1993-94, Pittsburgh Steelers 1996-97, 2000, Indianapolis Colts 1998. College coach: North Florida 1996, Pittsburgh 1998-2001, 2007, Robert Morris 2005-06. Pro coach: Cleveland Browns 2001-04, re-joined Browns in 2007.

Alfredo Roberts, tight ends; born Ft. Lauderdale, Fla. Tight end Miami 1983-87. Pro playing experience: Kansas City Chiefs 1988-1990, Dallas Cowboys 1991-93. College coach: Florida Atlantic 1999-2002. Pro coach: Jacksonville Jaguars 2003-06, joined Browns in 2007.

Rip Scherer, asst. head coach/quarterbacks; Quarterback William & Mary 1970-74. No pro playing experience. College coach: Penn State 1977-78, Virginia 1979, Georgia Tech 1980-86, Alabama 1987, Arizona 1988-1990, James Madison 1991-94, Memphis 1995-2000, Kansas 2001, Southern Mississippi 2003-04. Pro coach: Joined Browns in 2005.

Mike Sullivan, asst. offensive line; born Chicago. Offensive lineman Miami 1986-1990. Pro offensive lineman Dallas Cowboys 1991, Tampa Bay Buccaneers 1992-95. College coach: Miami 2000, Western Michigan 2005-06. Pro coach: Cleveland Browns 2001-04, re-joined Browns in 2007.

Bob Trott, defensive assistant; born Concord, N.C. College safety North Carolina 1973-75. No pro playing experience. College coach: North Carolina 1976-77, Air Force 1978-1983, Arkansas 1984-89, Clemson 1990, Duke 1996-2001, Baylor 2002, Louisiana-Monroe 2003-04. Pro coach: New York Giants 1991-92, New England Patriots 1993-95, joined Browns in 2005.

Mel Tucker, defensive coordinator; born Cleveland. College defensive back Wisconsin 1992-95. No pro playing experience. College coach: Michigan State 1997, Miami (Ohio) 1998-99, Louisiana State 2000, Ohio State 2001-04. Pro coach: Joined Browns in 2005.

Cory Undlin, defensive backs; born St. Cloud, Minn. Safety California Lutheran 1990-94. No pro playing experience. College coach: California Lutheran 1998-2002, Fresno State 2002-03. Pro coach: New England Patriots 2004, joined Browns in 2005.

Frank Verducci, offensive assistant; born Glen Ridge, N.J. Tight end/fullback U.S. Merchant Marine Academy-Kings Point 1975. No pro playing experience. College coach: Colorado State 1980, Maryland 1981-83, Northern Illinois 1984, Iowa 1985-86, 1989-1998, Northwestern 1987-88. Pro coach: Cincinnati Bengals 1999-2001, Dallas Cowboys 2002, Buffalo Bills 2004-05, joined Browns in 2007.

American Football Conference
West Division
Team Colors: Orange,
Broncos Navy Blue, and White
13655 Broncos Parkway
Englewood, Colorado 80112
Telephone: (303) 649-9000

2008 SCHEDULE
PRESEASON
Aug. 9   at Houston 7:00
Aug. 16   **Dallas**..............................7:00
Aug. 22   **Green Bay** 7:00
Aug. 29   at Arizona............................7:00

REGULAR SEASON
Sep. 8   at Oakland (Mon.) 7:15
Sep. 14   **San Diego** 2:15
Sep. 21   **New Orleans** 2:05
Sep. 28   at Kansas City 12:00
Oct. 5   **Tampa Bay** 2:05
Oct. 12   **Jacksonville** 2:05
Oct. 20   at New England (Mon.).....8:30
Oct. 26   BYE
Nov. 2   **Miami** 2:05
Nov. 6   at Cleveland (Thu.)...........8:15
Nov. 16   at Atlanta 1:00
Nov. 23   **Oakland** 2:05
Nov. 30   at N.Y. Jets.......................1:00
Dec. 7   **Kansas City** 2:05
Dec. 14   at Carolina 1:00
Dec. 21   **Buffalo** 2:05
Dec. 28   at San Diego 1:15

Stadium: INVESCO Field at Mile High
(opened in 2001)
• **Capacity:** 76,125
1701 Bryant Street
Denver, Colorado 80204
Playing Surface: DD Grassmaster
Training Camp: 13655 Broncos Parkway
Englewood, Colorado
80112

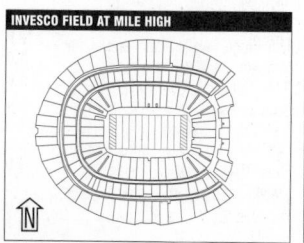

INVESCO FIELD AT MILE HIGH

CLUB OFFICIALS
President-Chief Executive Officer:
Pat Bowlen
Executive Vice President of Football
Operations/ Head Coach:
Mike Shanahan
Chief Operating Officer: Joe Ellis
FOOTBALL STAFF
Director of Player Personnel:
Jim Goodman
Assistant General Manager:
Jeff Goodman
Assistant General Manager:
Brian Xanders
Director of Football Administration:
Mike Bluem
Head Athletic Trainer: Steve Antonopulos
Director of Football Technology:
Kent Erickson
BUSINESS STAFF
General Counsel/Senior Vice President of
Administration: Rich Slivka
Vice President of Public Relations:
Jim Saccomano
Vice President of Marketing: Greg Carney
Vice President of Finance: Jim Barlow
Vice President of Community
Development: Cindy Galloway-Kellogg
STADIUM MANAGEMENT COMPANY
Vice President of Stadium Operations:
Mac Freeman

COACHING HISTORY
(395-351-10)
Records include postseason games
1960-61	Frank Filchock	7-20-1
1962-63	Jack Faulkner*	9-22-1
1964-66	Mac Speedie**	6-19-1
1966	Ray Malavasi	4-8-0
1967-1971	Lou Saban***	20-42-3
1971	Jerry Smith	2-3-0
1972-76	John Ralston	34-33-3
1977-1980	Robert (Red) Miller	42-25-0
1981-1992	Dan Reeves	117-79-1
1993-94	Wade Phillips	16-17-0
1995-2007	Mike Shanahan	138-83-0

  *Released after four games in 1964
  **Resigned after two games in 1966
  ***Resigned after nine games in 1971

PAID ATTENDANCE
Home 597,984   Away 523,012
Total 1,120,996
Single-game home record,
76,645 (10/29/07)
Single-season home record, 597,984
(2007)

2008 DRAFT CHOICES
Round	Name	Pos.	College
1	Ryan Clady	T	Boise State
2	Eddie Royal	WR	Virginia Tech
4	Kory Lichtensteiger	G	Bowling Green
	Jack Williams	DB	Kent State
5	Ryan Torain	RB	Arizona State
	Carlton Powell	DT	Virginia Tech
6	Spencer Larsen	LB	Arizona
7	Josh Barrett	DB	Arizona State
	Peyton Hillis	RB	Arkansas

DENVER BRONCOS

2007 TEAM RECORD
PRESEASON (2-2)
Date	Result	Opponent
8/13	W 17-13	at San Francisco
8/18	L 20-31	at Dallas
8/25	L 16-17	Cleveland
8/30	W 21-3	Arizona

REGULAR SEASON (7-9)
Date	Result	Opponent	Att.
9/9	W 15-14	at Buffalo	71,132
9/16	W 23-20	Oakland (OT)	76,784
9/23	L 14-23	Jacksonville	76,463
9/30	L 20-38	at Indianapolis	57,274
10/7	L 3-41	San Diego	76,879
10/21	W 31-28	Pittsburgh	77,038
10/29	L 13-19	Green Bay (OT)	77,160
11/4	L 7-44	at Detroit	60,783
11/11	W 27-11	at Kansas City	77,368
11/19	W 34-20	Tennessee	76,590
11/25	L 34-37	at Chicago (OT)	62,148
12/2	L 20-34	at Oakland	61,990
12/9	W 41-7	Kansas City	75,895
12/13	L 13-31	at Houston	70,747
12/24	L 3-23	at San Diego	65,477
12/30	W 22-19	Minnesota (OT)	76,084

(OT) Overtime

SCORE BY PERIODS
Broncos	75	89	94	56	6	—	320
Opponents	68	103	114	115	9	—	409

2007 TEAM STATISTICS
	Broncos	Opp.
Total First Downs	305	306
Rushing	96	119
Passing	187	168
Penalty	22	19
3rd Down: Made/Att	80/198	91/213
3rd Down Pct.	40.4	42.7
4th Down: Made/Att	7/22	10/13
4th Down Pct.	31.8	76.9
Possession Avg.	29:09	30:51
Total Net Yards	5541	5376
Avg. Per Game	346.3	336.0
Total Plays	976	992
Avg. Per Play	5.7	5.4
Net Yards Rushing	1957	2282
Avg. Per Game	122.3	142.6
Total Rushes	429	501
Net Yards Passing	3584	3094
Avg. Per Game	224.0	193.4
Sacked/Yards Lost	32/175	33/203
Gross Yards	3759	3297
Att./Completions	515/326	458/279
Completion Pct.	63.3	60.9
Had Intercepted	15	14
Punts/Average	60/43.8	60/43.9
Net Punting Avg.	60/36.3	60/38.7
Penalties/Yards	90/610	82/628
Fumbles/Ball Lost	30/14	34/16
Touchdowns	34	46
Rushing	10	14
Passing	21	25
Returns	3	7

2007 INDIVIDUAL STATISTICS
PASSING
	Att.	Comp.	Yds.	Pct.	TD	Int.	Tkld.	Rate
Cutler	467	297	3497	63.6	20	14	27/153	88.1
Ramsey	48	29	262	60.4	1	1	3/13	73.4
Marshall	0	0	0	—	0	0	2/9	—
Broncos	515	326	3759	63.3	21	15	32/175	86.7
Opponents	458	279	3297	60.9	25	14	33/203	88.3

SCORING
	TD R	TD P	TD Rt	PAT	FG	Saf	PTS
Elam	0	0	0	33/33	27/31	0	114
Marshall	0	7	0	0/0	0/0	0	42
Scheffler	0	5	0	0/0	0/0	0	30
Stokley	0	5	0	0/0	0/0	0	30
Henry	4	0	0	0/0	0/0	0	24
Sapp	2	1	0	0/0	0/0	0	18
Graham	0	2	0	0/0	0/0	0	12
Hall	2	0	0	0/0	0/0	0	12
Crowder	0	0	1	0/0	0/0	0	6
Cutler	1	0	0	0/0	0/0	0	6
Jackson	0	1	0	0/0	0/0	0	6
Jacobs	0	1	0	0/0	0/0	0	6
Martinez	0	0	1	0/0	0/0	0	6
Webster	0	0	1	0/0	0/0	0	6
Young	1	0	0	0/0	0/0	0	6
Prater	0	0	0	1/1	1/4	0	4
Broncos	10	21	3	33/33	27/31	1	320
Opponents	14	25	7	42/42	27/33	2	409

2-Pt. Conversions: Broncos 0-1, Opponents 3-3

RUSHING
	No.	Yds	Avg	LG	TD
Young	140	729	5.2	50	1
Henry	167	691	4.1	33	4
Hall	44	216	4.9	62t	2
Cutler	44	205	4.7	31	1
Sapp	18	59	3.3	12	2
Marshall	5	57	11.4	24	0
Ramsey	2	6	3.0	4	0
Bell	6	3	0.5	3	0
Walker	2	-3	-1.5	-1	0
Stokley	1	-6	-6.0	-6	0
Broncos	429	1957	4.6	62t	10
Opponents	501	2282	4.6	74t	14

RECEIVING
	No.	Yds	Avg	LG	TD
Marshall	102	1325	13.0	68t	7
Scheffler	49	549	11.2	41	5
Stokley	40	635	15.9	58	5
Young	35	231	6.6	24	0
Walker	26	287	11.0	24	0
Graham	24	246	10.3	28	2
Martinez	14	175	12.5	23	0
Sapp	14	51	3.6	16	1
Henry	7	65	9.3	21	0
Mustard	5	62	12.4	15	0
Clark	4	23	5.8	7	0
Jackson	3	34	11.3	24	1
Hall	2	69	34.5	65	0
Bell	1	7	7.0	7	0
Broncos	326	3759	11.5	68t	21
Opponents	279	3297	11.8	82t	25

INTERCEPTIONS
	No.	Yds	Avg	LG	TD
Bly	5	71	14.2	37	0
Bailey	3	3	1.0	3	0
Paymah	2	0	0.0	0	0
Dumervil	1	27	27.0	27	0
Gold	1	6	6.0	6	0
Williams	1	0	0.0	0	0
Thomas	1	-2	-2.0	-2	0
Broncos	14	105	7.5	37	0
Opponents	15	229	15.3	66t	2

PUNTING
	No.	Yds.	Avg.	In 20	LG
Sauerbrun	47	2200	46.8	14	65
Ernster	5	178	35.6	1	59
Paulescu	5	221	44.2	1	51
Elam	1	31	31	1	31
Broncos	60	2630	43.8	17	65
Opponents	60	2633	43.9	26	63

PUNT RETURNS
	Ret	FC	Yds	Avg	LG	TD
Martinez	14	12	157	11.2	80t	1
Hixon	7	5	32	4.6	14	0
Bly	2	0	20	10.0	10	0
Broncos	23	17	209	9.1	80t	1
Opponents	31	3	334	10.8	75t	2

KICKOFF RETURNS
	No.	Yds	Avg	LG	TD
Hall	19	475	25.0	34	0
Martinez	15	330	22.0	35	0
Hixon	12	274	22.8	35	0
Clark	3	70	23.3	26	0
Jacobs	3	35	11.7	15	0
Young	3	56	18.7	25	0
Sapp	2	30	15.0	22	0
Bly	1	23	23.0	23	0
Broncos	58	1293	22.3	35	0
Opponents	62	1424	23.0	88t	1

FIELD GOALS
	1-19	20-29	30-39	40-49	50+
Elam	0/0	11/11	6/6	9/12	1/2
Broncos	0/0	11/11	6/6	9/12	1/2
Opponents	3/3	8/8	8/9	6/7	2/6

SACKS
	No.
Dumervil	12.5
Crowder	4.0
Mallard	3.5
McKinley	2.5
Gold	2.0
(group)	2.0
Bly	1.0
Engelberger	1.0
Lynch	1.0
Moss	1.0
Peterson	1.0
Williams	1.0
Winborn	0.5
Broncos	33.0
Opponents	32.0

RECORD HOLDERS
INDIVIDUAL RECORDS—CAREER

Category	Name	Performance
Rushing (Yds.)	Terrell Davis, 1995-2002	7,607
Passing (Yds.)	John Elway, 1983-1998	51,475
Passing (TDs)	John Elway, 1983-1998	300
Receiving (No.)	Rod Smith, 1995-2007	849
Receiving (Yds.)	Rod Smith, 1995-2007	11,389
Interceptions	Steve Foley, 1976-1986	44
Punting (Avg.)	Jim Fraser, 1962-64	45.2
Punt Return (Avg.)	Darrien Gordon, 1997-98	12.5
Kickoff Return (Avg.)	Abner Haynes, 1965-66	26.3
Field Goals	Jason Elam, 1993-2007	395
Touchdowns (Tot.)	Rod Smith, 1995-2007	71
Points	Jason Elam, 1993-2007	1,786

INDIVIDUAL RECORDS—SINGLE SEASON

Category	Name	Performance
Rushing (Yds.)	Terrell Davis, 1998	2,008
Passing (Yds.)	Jake Plummer, 2004	4,089
Passing (TDs)	John Elway, 1997	27
	Jake Plummer, 2004	27
Receiving (No.)	Rod Smith, 2001	113
Receiving (Yds.)	Rod Smith, 2000	1,602
Interceptions	Goose Gonsoulin, 1960	11
Punting (Avg.)	Tom Rouen, 1998	46.9
Punt Return (Avg.)	Floyd Little, 1967	16.9
Kickoff Return (Avg.)	Bill Thompson, 1969	28.5
Field Goals	Jason Elam, 1995, 2001	31
Touchdowns (Tot.)	Terrell Davis, 1998	23
Points	Terrell Davis, 1998	138

INDIVIDUAL RECORDS—SINGLE GAME

Category	Name	Performance
Rushing (Yds.)	Mike Anderson, 12-3-00	251
Passing (Yds.)	Jake Plummer, 10-31-04	499
Passing (TDs)	Frank Tripucka, 10-28-62	5
	John Elway, 11-18-84	5
	Gus Frerotte, 11-19-00	5
Receiving (No.)	Rod Smith, 9-23-01	14
Receiving (Yds.)	Shannon Sharpe, 10-20-02	214
Interceptions	Goose Gonsoulin, 9-18-60	*4
	Willie Brown, 11-15-64	*4
	Delta O'Neal, 10-7-01	*4
Field Goals	Gene Mingo, 10-6-63	5
	Rich Karlis, 11-20-83	5
	Jason Elam, 9-3-95, 10-13-02	5
Touchdowns (Tot.)	Clinton Portis, 12-7-03	5
Points	Clinton Portis, 12-7-03	30

*NFL Record

2008 VETERAN ROSTER

No.	Name	Pos.	Ht.	Wt.	Age	NFL Exp.	College	Hometown	How Acq.	'07 Games/ Starts
21	Abdullah, Hamza	S	6-2	216	25	4	Washington State	Pomona, Calif.	W(TB)-'05	11/8
69	Alexander, P.J.	G	6-4	297	29	6	Syracuse	Tallahassee, Fla.	FA-'07	11/0
	Archer, Brandon	LB	6-0	239	24	2	Kansas State	St. Paul, Minn.	W(Ind)-'08	6/0*
	Bailey, Boss	LB	6-3	235	28	6	Georgia	Folkston, Ga.	UFA(Det)-'08	15/12*
24	Bailey, Champ	CB	6-0	192	30	10	Georgia	Folkston, Ga.	T(Wash)-'04	15/15
57	Beck, Jordan	LB	6-2	233	25	4	Cal Poly-San Luis Obispo	Mount Hermon, Calif.	FA-'07	11/0*
30	Bell, Mike	RB	6-0	225	25	3	Arizona	Tolleson, Ariz.	CFA-'06	5/0
77	Birdine, Larry	DE	6-4	265	24	2	Oklahoma	Lawton, Okla.	W(Tenn)-'07	0*
32	Bly, Dré	CB	5-10	188	31	10	North Carolina	Chesapeake, Va.	T(Det)-'07	16/16
90	Carrington, Paul	DE	6-7	250	25	3	Central Florida	Springfield, Ga.	FA-'07	0*
78	Clemons, Nic	DE	6-6	278	28	2	Georgia	Griffin, Ga.	FA-'08	0*
13	Colbert, Keary	WR	6-1	200	26	5	Southern California	Oxnard, Calif.	UFA(Car)-'08	12/8*
96	Crowder, Tim	DE	6-4	275	23	2	Texas	Tyler, Texas	D2-'07	13/1
6	Cutler, Jay	QB	6-3	233	25	3	Vanderbilt	Lincoln City, Ind.	D1-'06	16/16
92	Dumervil, Elvis	DE	5-11	260	24	3	Louisville	Miami, Fla.	D4b-'06	16/16
91	Ekuban, Ebenezer	DE	6-4	275	32	10	North Carolina	Bladensburg, Md.	T(Cle)-'05	0*
60	Engelberger, John	DE	6-4	260	31	9	Virginia Tech	Springfield, Va.	T(SF)-'05	16/15
8	Finnerty, Cullen	QB	6-2	223	26	2	Grand Valley State	Brighton, Mich.	FA-'08	0*
22	Foxworth, Domonique	CB	5-11	180	25	4	Maryland	Catonsville, Md.	D3b-'05	14/6
89	Graham, Daniel	TE	6-3	257	29	7	Colorado	Denver, Colo.	UFA(NE)-'07	15/15
53	Green, Louis	LB	6-3	237	28	5	Alcorn State	Fayette, Miss.	FA-'03	16/0
4	Hackney, Darrell	QB	6-0	248	25	2	Alabama-Birmingham	Atlanta, Ga.	FA-'07	0*
23	Hall, Andre	RB	5-10	212	26	2	South Florida	St. Petersburg, Fla.	FA-'06	10/1
50	Hamilton, Ben	G/C	6-4	290	31	8	Minnesota	Minneapolis, Minn.	D4a-'01	0*
74	Harris, Ryan	T	6-5	300	23	2	Notre Dame	St. Paul, Minn.	D3-'07	11/0
68	Harris, Steven	DT	6-5	305	24	2	Florida	Coral Gables, Fla.	FA-'07	4/0
20	Henry, Travis	RB	5-9	230	29	8	Tennessee	Frostproof, Fla.	FA-'07	12/7
70	Holland, Montrae	G	6-2	322	28	6	Florida State	Ore, Texas	UFA(NO)-'07	16/16
82	Jackson, Darrell	WR	5-11	206	29	9	Florida	Tampa, Fla.	FA-'08	15/15*
81	Jackson, Nate	TE	6-3	235	29	6	Menlo College	San Jose, Calif.	T(SF)-'03	5/1
19	Jacobs, Taylor	WR	6-1	210	27	6	Florida	Tallahassee, Fla.	FA-'07	10/0*
75	Jenkins, Julian	DE	6-3	277	24	2	Stanford	Atlanta, Ga.	FA-'08	0*
	Koutouvides, Niko	LB	6-2	238	27	5	Purdue	Plainville, Conn.	UFA(Sea)-'08	15/0*
73	Kuper, Chris	G	6-4	302	25	3	North Dakota	Anchorage, Alaska	D5-'06	16/11
83	Leach, Mike	TE/LS	6-2	240	31	9	William & Mary	Jefferson Township, N.J.	FA-'02	16/0
47	Lynch, John	S	6-2	220	36	16	Stanford	Del Mar, Calif.	FA-'04	13/12
98	Mallard, Josh	DT	6-2	259	29	4	Georgia	Savannah, Ga.	FA-'07	11/0*
33	Manuel, Marquand	S	6-0	209	29	7	Florida	Miami, Fla.	UFA(Car)-'08	16/2*
15	Marshall, Brandon	WR	6-4	230	24	3	Central Florida	Winter Park, Fla.	D4a-'06	16/16
17	Martinez, Glenn	WR	6-1	190	26	3	Saginaw Valley State	Auburndale, Fla.	FA-'07	12/1
28	McCree, Marlon	S	5-11	202	31	8	Kentucky	Port Orange, Fla.	FA-'08	16/16*
99	McKinley, Alvin	DT	6-3	294	30	9	Mississippi State	Weir, Miss.	UFA(Cle)-'07	15/10
25	Morton, Christian	CB	6-0	190	27	4	Illinois	St. Louis, Mo.	FA-'08	0*
94	Moss, Jarvis	DE	6-6	265	24	2	Florida	Denton, Texas	D1-'07	6/1
85	Mustard, Chad	TE	6-6	277	30	5	North Dakota	Columbus, Neb.	FA-'07	12/2
66	Nalen, Tom	C	6-3	286	37	15	Boston College	Foxboro, Mass.	D7c-'94	5/5
12	Parker, Samie	WR	5-11	190	27	5	Oregon	Long Beach, Calif.	UFA(KC)-'08	15/7*
2	Paulescu, Sam	P	6-0	189	24	2	Oregon State	La Habra, Calif.	FA-'07	1/0*
41	Paymah, Karl	CB	6-0	195	25	4	Washington State	Culver City, Calif.	D3a-'05	15/3
64	Pears, Erik	T	6-8	305	26	3	Colorado State	Denver, Colo.	FA-'05	16/16
97	Peterson, Kenny	DL	6-3	285	29	6	Ohio State	Canton, Ohio	FA-'07	7/0
84	Pierce, Brett	TE	6-5	263	27	3	Stanford	Vancouver, Wash.	FA-'08	0*
5	Prater, Matt	K	5-10	180	24	2	Central Florida	Estero, Fla.	W(Mia)-'07	4/0*
11	Ramsey, Patrick	QB	6-2	225	29	7	Tulane	Ruston, La.	FA-'07	2/0
40	Reid, Lamont	CB	5-11	195	26	2	North Carolina State	Concord, N.C.	FA-'07	0*
63 t-	Robertson, Dewayne	DT	6-1	310	26	6	Kentucky	Memphis, Tenn.	T(NYJ)-'08	16/15*
43	Rogers, Roderick	S	6-2	187	23	2	Wisconsin	Stone Mountain, Ga.	FA-'07	2/0
	Russell, Clifford	WR	5-11	195	29	6	Utah	Ewa Beach, Hawaii	FA-'08	0*
37	Sapp, Cecil	RB	5-11	229	26	6	Colorado State	Miami, Fla.	FA-'03	16/8
88	Scheffler, Tony	TE	6-5	250	25	3	Western Michigan	Morenci, Mich.	D2-'06	16/7
	Shepherd, Edell	WR	6-1	175	28	5	San Jose State	Los Angeles, Calif.	FA-'08	0*
72	Snell, Isaac	G	6-6	328	28	3	North Dakota State	Pipestone, Minn.	W(Tenn)-'07	0*
14	Stokley, Brandon	WR	5-11	192	32	10	Southwestern Louisiana	Lafayette, La.	FA-'07	13/9
79	Thomas, Marcus	DT	6-3	315	22	2	Florida	Jacksonville, Fla.	D4-'07	16/5
31	Underwood, Marviel	S	5-10	200	26	4	San Diego State	San Leandro, Calif.	FA-'07	0*
34	Vaughn, Vickiel	S	6-0	204	24	2	Arkansas	Plano, Texas	FA-'08	0/0*

No.	Name	Pos.	Ht.	Wt.	Age	NFL Exp.	College	Hometown	How Acq.	'07 Games/ Starts
58	Webster, Nate	LB	6-0	232	30	9	Miami	Miami, Fla.	UFA(Cin)-'06	16/13
62	Wiegmann, Casey	C	6-2	285	35	13	Iowa	Parkersburg, Iowa	UFA(KC)-'08	16/16*
55	Williams, D.J.	LB	6-1	242	26	5	Miami	Concord, Calif.	D1-'04	16/16
51	Winborn, Jamie	LB	5-11	242	29	8	Vanderbilt	Wetumpka, Ala.	FA-'07	14/2
35	Young, Selvin	RB	5-11	207	24	2	Texas	Jersey Village, Texas	FA-'07	15/8

Archer played 6 games with Indianapolis in '07; B. Bailey played 15 games with Detroit; Birdine was inactive for 8 games; Carrington was inactive for 8 games; Clemons was last active with Washington in '05; Colbert played 12 games with Carolina; Ekuban missed the '07 season because of injury; Finnerty was last active with Baltimore in '07; Hackney was inactive for 8 games; Hamilton was inactive for 3 games; D. Jackson played 15 games with San Francisco; Jacobs played 4 games with San Francisco and 6 games with Denver; Jenkins was last active with Tampa Bay in '06; Koutouvides played 15 games with Seattle; Mallard played 3 games with Atlanta and 11 with Denver; Manuel played 16 games with Carolina; McCree played 16 games with Carolina; Morton was last active with Carolina in '06; Parker played 15 games with Kansas City; Pierce was last active with Dallas in '05; Prater played 2 games with Atlanta and 2 with Denver; Reid last active with Arizona in '05; Robertson played 16 games with N.Y. Jets; Russell was last active with Miami in '06; Shepherd was last active with Houston in '06; Snell was inactive for 10 games; Underwood was inactive for 1 game; Vaughn missed '06 season with because of injury; Wiegmann played 16 games with Kansas City.

t- Broncos traded for Robertson (NYJ).

Traded—C/G Chris Myers (16 games in '07) to Houston.

Players lost through free agency (2): K Jason Elam (Atl; 16 games in '07), S Nick Ferguson (Hou; 12).

Also played with Broncos in '07—DT Sam Adams (11 games), DT Antwon Burton (6), S Steve Cargile (12), WR Brian Clark (4), S Curome Cox (7), P Paul Ernster (1), LB Ian Gold (14), DT Amon Gordon (4), WR Domenik Hixon (4), FB Kyle Johnson (1), T Matt Lepsis (16), LB D.D. Lewis (5), DE Simeon Rice (6), P Todd Sauerbrun (14), CB Jeff Shoate (7), RB Paul Smith (14), WR Javon Walker (8).

2008 FIRST-YEAR ROSTER

Name	Pos.	Ht.	Wt.	Age	College	Hometown	How Acq.
Alridge, Anthony	RB	5-9	170	24	Houston	Denton, Texas	FA
Barrett, Josh	S	6-3	231	23	Arizona State	Reno, Nev.	D7
Baugher, Danny (1)	P	5-10	194	24	Arizona	Phoenix, Ariz.	FA
Clady, Ryan	T	6-6	317	21	Boise State	Rialto, Calif.	D1
Erickson, Mitch	G	6-6	285	23	South Dakota State	Hutchinson, Minn.	FA
Hartley, Garrett	K	5-8	204	22	Oklahoma	Southlake, Texas	FA
Hillis, Peyton	FB	6-2	243	22	Arkansas	Conway, Ark.	D7b
Kern, Brett	P	6-3	195	22	Toledo	Grand Island, N.Y.	FA
Larsen, Spencer	LB	6-2	242	24	Arizona	Gilbert, Ariz.	D6
Lichtensteiger, Kory	C	6-3	300	23	Bowling Green	Van Wert, Ohio	D4a
McDaniel, Marquay (1)	WR	5-10	205	24	Hampton	Virginia Beach, Va.	FA-'07
Polumbus, Tyler	T	6-8	300	23	Colorado	Greenwood Village, Colo.	FA
Powell, Carlton	DT	6-2	301	23	Virginia Tech	Chesapeake, Va.	D5b
Royal, Eddie	WR	5-10	181	22	Virginia Tech	Chantilly, Va.	D2
Sam, Lorne	WR	6-3	215	23	Texas-El Paso	Buford, Ga.	FA
Torain, Ryan	RB	6-1	222	22	Arizona State	Shawnee Mission, Kan.	D5a
Williams, Jack	CB	5-9	181	23	Kent State	Norfolk, Va.	D4b
Woodyard, Wesley	LB	6-1	227	22	Kentucky	LaGrange, Ga.	FA

The term NFL Rookie is defined as a player who is in his first season of professional football and has not been on the roster of another professional football team for any regular-season or postseason games. A Rookie is designated by an "R" on NFL rosters. Players who have been active in another professional football league or players who have NFL experience, including either preseason training camp or being on an Active List or Inactive List, or on Reserve/Injured or Reserve/Physically Unable to Perform for fewer than six regular-season games, are termed NFL First-Year Players. An NFL First-Year Player is designated by a "1" on NFL rosters. Thereafter, a player is credited with an additional year of experience for each season in which he accumulates six games on the Active List or Inactive List, or on Reserve/Injured or Reserve/Physically Unable to Perform.

Log on to www.denverbroncos.com for an up-to-date roster; Age listed is as of September 4, 2008.

COACHING STAFF

Head Coach,
Mike Shanahan

Pro Career: Became the eleventh head coach in Broncos history on January 31, 1995. Mike Shanahan led the Broncos to back-to-back Super Bowl championships in 1997 and 1998, becoming just the fifth head coach to accomplish that feat, and is the only coach to win seven consecutive postseason games in a two-year period. No NFL head coach has won more game than Mike Shanahan's 146 victories since the start of the 1995 season. During his NFL career, Shanahan has been a part of teams that have played in nine conference championship games and six Super Bowls. In 29 seasons as a pro and college coach, Shanahan's teams have participated in postseason or bowl games 22 times. Under Shanahan's guidance, Denver set an NFL record by posting the most victories in both a two-year (33, 1997-98) and three-year (46, 1996-98) period. In the last sixteen years (thirteen with Denver and three as offensive coordinator with the San Francisco 49ers), Shanahan's offenses have finished number one in the NFL four times, second twice, and third twice. Shanahan was an assistant with Denver (1984-87, 1989-1991) and San Francisco (1992-94). Returned to Denver as quarterbacks coach on October 16, 1989, after posting 8-12 record as the Los Angeles Raiders' head coach. Career record: 146-95.

Background: Shanahan coached at Oklahoma (1975-76), Northern Arizona (1977), Eastern Illinois (1978), Minnesota (1979), and Florida (1980-83).

Personal: Age 56, born in Oak Park, Illinois. He was a wishbone quarterback-defensive back at Eastern Illinois. Mike and his wife, Peggy, have two children—Kyle and Krystal.

ASSISTANT COACHES

Joe Baker, offensive assistant; born Glen Ridge, N.J. Wide receiver Princeton 1987-1990. No pro playing experience. College coach: East Stroudsburg 1991, Samford 1993, Wisconsin 1999. Pro coach: Birmingham Fire (WLAF) 1992, Jacksonville Jaguars 1994-98, New Orleans Saints 2000-04, Green Bay Packers 2005, St. Louis Rams 2006, joined Broncos in 2007.

Jeremy Bates, quarterbacks; born Manhattan, Kan. Quarterback Tennessee 1995, Rick 1996-99. No pro playing experience. Pro coach: Tampa Bay Buccaneers 2002-04, New York Jets 2005, joined Broncos in 2006.

Ronnie Bradford, defensive backs; born Minot, N.D. Defensive back Colorado 1989-1992. Pro defensive back Denver Broncos 1993-95, Arizona Cardinals 1996, Atlanta Falcons 1997-2001, Minnesota Vikings 2002. Pro coach: Joined Broncos in 2003.

Jacob Burney, defensive line; born Chattanooga, Tenn. Defensive tackle Tennessee-Chattanooga 1977-1980. No pro playing experience. College coach: New Mexico 1983-86, Tulsa 1987, Mississippi State 1988, Wisconsin 1989, UCLA 1990-92, Tennessee 1993. Pro coach: Cleveland Browns/Baltimore Ravens 1994-98, Carolina Panthers 1999-2001, joined Broncos in 2002.

Keith Burns, special teams assistant; born Greeleyville, S.C. Linebacker Oklahoma State 1991-94. Pro linebacker Denver Broncos 1994-98, 2000-03, 2005-06, Chicago Bears 1999, Tampa Bay Buccaneers 2004. Pro coach: Joined Broncos in 2007.

Dwayne Chandler, asst. strength & conditioning; born Aberdeen, Miss. Fullback Oklahoma 1991-1995. No pro playing experience. College coach: Oklahoma 1999, Minnesota 2001-2006. Pro coach: Dallas Cowboys 2000, joined Broncos in 2007.

Rick Dennison, offensive coordinator/offensive line; born Kalispell, Mont. Tight end Colorado State 1976-79. Pro linebacker Denver Broncos 1982-1990. Pro coach: Joined Broncos in 1995.

Jedd Fisch, wide receivers; born Livingston, N.J. Attended Florida. No college or pro playing experience. College coach: Florida 1999-2000. Pro coach: Houston Texans 2001-2003, Baltimore Ravens 2004-07, joined Broncos in 2008.

Charlie Jackson, defensive assistant; born Vienna, Ga. Defensive back Air Force Academy 1997-99. No pro playing experience. College coach: UCLA 2002-03, Air Force Academy 2004. Pro coach: Green Bay Packers 2005, joined Broncos in 2007.

Bill Johnson, defensive line; born Monroe, La. Defensive lineman Northwestern (La.) State 1976-79. No pro playing experience. College coach: North western (La.) State 1980-81, McNeese State 1985-86, Miami 1987, Louisiana Tech 1988-89, Arkansas 1990-91, 2000, Texas A&M 1992-99. Pro coach: Atlanta Falcons 2001-06, joined Broncos in 2007.

Pat McPherson, tight ends; born Santa Clara, Calif. Linebacker Santa Clara 1991-92. No pro playing experience. Pro coach: Joined Broncos in 1998.

Scott O'Brien, special teams coordinator; born Superior, Wis. Linebacker Wisconsin-Superior 1975-78. No pro playing experience. College coach: Wisconsin-Superior 1980-82, Nevada-Las Vegas 1983-85, Rice 1986, Pittsburgh 1987-1990. Pro coach: Cleveland Browns 1991-95, Baltimore Ravens 1996-98, Carolina Panthers 1999-2004, Miami Dolphins 2005-06, joined Broncos in 2007.

Jim Ryan, linebackers; born Bellmawr, N.J. Linebacker William & Mary 1974-1978. Linebacker Denver Broncos 1979-

1988. Pro coach: Joined Broncos in 2005.

Greg Saporta, asst. strength and conditioning; born New York, N.Y. Wide receiver Buffalo State 1977-79. No pro playing experience. College coach: Florida 1981-88, 1993-94, North Carolina 1989-1992. Pro coach: Joined Broncos in 1995.

Bob Slowik, defensive coordinator; born Pittsburgh. Defensive back Delaware 1973-76. No pro playing experience. College coach: Delaware 1977-78, Florida 1979-1982, Drake 1983, Rutgers 1984-89, East Carolina 1990-91. Pro coach: Dallas Cowboys 1992, Chicago Bears 1993-98, Cleveland Browns 1999, Green Bay Packers 2000-04, joined Broncos in 2005.

Ryan Slowik, asst. defensive backs; born Chicago. Safety Wisconsin-Oshkosh 2002-03. No pro playing experience. College coach: Wisconsin-Oshkosh 2004. Pro coach: Joined Broncos in 2005.

Bobby Turner, running backs; born East Chicago, Ind. Defensive back Indiana State 1968-1971. No pro playing experience. College coach: Indiana State 1975-1982, Fresno State 1983-88, Ohio State 1989-1990, Purdue 1991-94. Pro coach: Joined Broncos in 1995.

Rich Tuten, strength and conditioning; born Columbia, S.C. Nose guard Clemson 1976-78. No pro playing experience. College coach: Florida 1979-1988, 1993-94, North Carolina 1989-1992. Pro coach: Joined Broncos in 1995.

Steve Watson, associate head coach; born Baltimore. Wide receiver Temple 1975-78. Pro wide receiver Denver 1979-1987. Pro coach: Joined Broncos in 2001.

**American Football Conference
South Division
Team Colors:** Deep Steel Blue, Battle
Red, and Liberty White
**Two Reliant Park
Houston, Texas 77054
Telephone:** (832) 667-2000

2008 SCHEDULE
PRESEASON
Aug. 9 **Denver** 7:00
Aug. 16 at New Orleans 7:00
Aug. 22 at Dallas 7:00
Aug. 28 **Tampa Bay** 7:00

REGULAR SEASON
Sep. 7 at Pittsburgh 1:00
Sep. 14 **Baltimore** 3:15
Sep. 21 at Tennessee 12:00
Sep. 28 at Jacksonville 1:00
Oct. 5 **Indianapolis** 12:00
Oct. 12 **Miami** 12:00
Oct. 19 **Detroit** 3:05
Oct. 26 BYE
Nov. 2 at Minnesota 12:00
Nov. 6 **Cincinnati** 12:00
Nov. 16 at Indianapolis 1:00
Nov. 23 at Cleveland 1:00
Dec. 1 **Jacksonville** (Mon.) 7:30
Dec. 7 at Green Bay 12:00
Dec. 14 **Tennessee** 12:00
Dec. 21 at Oakland 1:05
Dec. 28 **Chicago** 12:00

Stadium: Reliant Stadium
(opened in 2002)
•**Capacity:** 71,054
Houston, Texas 77054
Playing Surface: Grass
Training Camp: Methodist Training
Center

RELIANT STADIUM

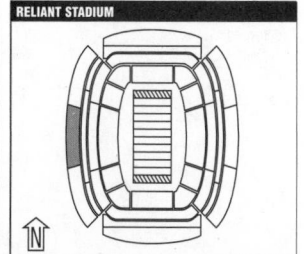

CLUB OFFICIALS
Chairman and CEO: Robert C. McNair
Vice Chairman: Philip J. Burguiéres
Vice Chairman: D. Cal McNair
General Manager: Rick Smith
President: Jamey Rootes
Senior Vice President, Treasurer and
CFO: Scott Schwinger
Senior Vice President, General Counsel
and CAO: Suzie Thomas
Vice President and Controller:
Marilan Logan
Vice President, Ticketing and Event
Management: John Schriever
Vice President, Sales and Marketing:
John Vidalin
Vice President, Finance: Greg Watson
Vice President, Communications:
Tony Wyllie
Director of Football Administration:
Chris Olsen
Director of Security: Ryan Reichert
Director of Football Operations:
Lloyd Richards
Director of Player Development:
Sean Washington
Director of College Scouting: Dale Strahm
Director of Pro Personnel: Brian Gardner
Associate Director of Pro Scouting:
Bobby Grier
Pro Scouts: Brandon Hunt, Kevin Murphy
Coordinator of College Scouting:
Mike Maccagnan
National College Scout: Ed Lambert
College Scouts: Bob Beers, Larry Bryan,
Jon Carr, Brian Hudspeth, Mike Martin,
Bob Merritt
Head Athletic Trainer: Kevin Bastin
Coordinator of Rehabilitation: Tom Colt
Assistant Athletic Trainer: Jon Ishop
Director of Equipment Services:
Jay Brunetti
Assistant Director of Equipment Services:
Matt Grupp
Equipment Services Assistant:
Christian Snell
Director of Video Operations: Joe Malota
Video Operations Assistant: Robert Wells
Director of Media Relations: Kevin Cooper
Director of Corporate Development:
Greg Grissom
Risk Manager: Jan Kelly
Corporate Counsel: Greg Kondritz
Director of Production and Entertainment:
Scott MacKerron
Director of Human Resources: Glenda
Morrison
Director of Ticket Services: Bryan Moynihan
Director of Event Services: Diane Ozzolek
Director of Advertising and Branding:
Melissa Rentz
Director of Media Products: Nick Schenck
Director of Information Technology:
Jeff Schmitz
Assistant Treasurer: Jon Southern
Director of Community Development:
Nicole Streeter
Director of Premium Seating:
Brian Varnadoe

COACHING HISTORY
(32-64-0)
2002-05 Dom Capers 18-46-0
2006-07 Gary Kubiak 14-18-0

PAID ATTENDANCE
Home 552,544   Away 506,095
Total 1,058,639
Single-game home record,
70,758 (12/21/03)
Single-season home record,
555,421 (2004)

2008 DRAFT CHOICES
Round	Name	Pos.	College
1	Duane Brown	T	Virginia Tech
3	Antwaun Molden	DB	Eastern Kentucky
	Steve Slaton	RB	West Virginia
4	Xavier Adibi	LB	Virginia Tech
5	Frank Okam	DT	Texas
6	Dominique Barber	DB	Minnesota
7	Alex Brink	QB	Washington State

HOUSTON TEXANS

2007 TEAM RECORD
PRESEASON (2-2)

Date	Result	Opponent
8/11	L 19-20	Chicago
8/18	W 33-20	at Arizona
8/25	W 28-16	Dallas
8/30	L 24-31	at Tampa Bay

REGULAR SEASON (8-8)

Date	Result	Opponent	Att.
9/9	W 20-3	Kansas City	70,080
9/16	W 34-21	at Carolina	73,665
9/23	L 24-30	Indianapolis	70,765
9/30	L 16-26	at Atlanta	69,312
10/7	W 22-19	Miami	70,156
10/14	L 17-37	at Jacksonville	63,715
10/21	L 36-38	Tennessee	70,734
10/28	L 10-35	at San Diego	60,439
11/4	W 24-17	at Oakland	49,603
11/18	W 23-10	New Orleans	70,780
11/25	L 17-27	at Cleveland	72,730
12/2	L 20-28	at Tennessee	69,143
12/9	W 28-14	Tampa Bay	70,237
12/13	W 31-13	Denver	70,747
12/23	L 15-38	at Indianapolis	57,262
12/30	W 42-28	Jacksonville	70,660

SCORE BY PERIODS

Texans	87	92	61	139	0 —	379
Opponents	81	132	90	81	0 —	384

2007 TEAM STATISTICS

	Texans	Opp.
Total First Downs	295	325
Rushing	96	107
Passing	190	197
Penalty	9	21
3rd Down: Made/Att	86/193	83/198
3rd Down Pct.	44.6	41.9
4th Down: Made/Att	11/15	8/16
4th Down Pct.	73.3	50.0
Possession Avg.	29:41	30:19
Total Net Yards	5337	5507
Avg. Per Game	333.6	344.2
Total Plays	968	994
Avg. Per Play	5.5	5.5
Net Yards Rushing	1586	1825
Avg. Per Game	99.1	114.1
Total Rushes	417	417
Net Yards Passing	3751	3682
Avg. Per Game	234.4	230.1
Sacked/Yards Lost	22/174	31/196
Gross Yards	3925	3878
Att./Completions	529/346	546/361
Completion Pct.	65.4	66.1
Had Intercepted	21	11
Punts/Average	55/41.7	59/43.0
Net Punting Avg.	55/37.9	59/37.1
Penalties/Yards	82/636	81/614
Fumbles/Ball Lost	26/17	24/14
Touchdowns	43	43
Rushing	12	15
Passing	24	25
Returns	7	3

2007 INDIVIDUAL STATISTICS

PASSING

	Att.	Comp.	Yds.	Pct.	TD	Int.	Tkld.	Rate
Schaub	289	192	2241	66.4	9	9	16/126	87.2
Rosenfels	240	154	1684	64.2	15	12	6/48	84.8
Texans	529	346	3925	65.4	24	21	22/174	86.1
Opponents	546	361	3878	66.1	25	11	31/196	93.6

SCORING

	TD R	TD P	TD Rt	PAT	FG	Saf	PTS
K. Brown	0	0	0	40/40	25/29	0	115
A. Johnson	0	8	0	0/0	0/0	0	48
Davis	0	3	3	0/0	0/0	0	38
Dayne	6	0	0	0/0	0/0	0	36
Walter	0	4	1	0/0	0/0	0	30
Daniels	0	3	0	0/0	0/0	0	18
Leach	1	2	0	0/0	0/0	0	18
Dreessen	2	0	0	0/0	0/0	0	12
Green	2	0	0	0/0	0/0	0	12
Gado	1	0	0	0/0	0/0	0	8
Walker	1	0	0	0/0	0/0	0	8
D. Anderson	0	1	0	0/0	0/0	0	6
Mathis	0	0	1	0/0	0/0	0	6
Putzier	0	1	0	0/0	0/0	0	6
Rosenfels	1	0	0	0/0	0/0	0	6
Ryans	0	0	1	0/0	0/0	0	6
M. Williams	0	0	1	0/0	0/0	0	6
Texans	12	24	7	40/40	25/29	0	379
Opponents	15	25	3	42/43	28/33	0	384

2-Pt. Conversions: Davis, Gado, Walker,
Texans 3-3, Opponents 0-0

RUSHING

	No.	Yds	Avg	LG	TD
Dayne	194	773	4.0	39	6
Walker	58	264	4.6	41	1
Green	70	260	3.7	18	2
Echemandu	20	85	4.3	20	0
Schaub	17	52	3.1	12	0
Rosenfels	21	51	2.4	19	1
Gado	18	46	2.6	7	1
Walter	5	30	6.0	13	0
Cook	8	24	3.0	9	0
Leach	2	2	1.0	1t	1
Turk	1	0	0.0	0	0
Jones	3	-1	-.3	4	0
Texans	417	1586	3.8	41	12
Opponents	417	1825	4.4	76	15

RECEIVING

	No.	Yds	Avg	LG	TD
Walter	65	800	12.3	46	4
Daniels	63	768	12.2	29	3
A. Johnson	60	851	14.2	77t	8
Davis	33	583	17.7	53t	3
Leach	25	108	4.3	15	2
Dayne	17	112	6.6	17	0
Jones	15	149	9.9	26	0
Green	14	123	8.8	53	0
Walker	13	81	6.2	9	0
D. Anderson	12	131	10.9	24	1
Gado	8	59	7.4	20	0
Cook	8	40	5.0	9	0
Putzier	6	39	6.5	11	1
Dreessen	4	55	13.8	28t	2
Echemandu	2	11	5.5	7	0
Mathis	1	15	15.0	15	0
Texans	346	3925	11.3	77t	24
Opponents	361	3878	10.7	74t	25

INTERCEPTIONS

	No.	Yds	Avg	LG	TD
Bennett	3	47	15.7	33	0
Du. Robinson	2	6	3.0	10	0
C. Brown	1	9	9.0	9	0
Hutchins	1	8	8.0	8	0
Greenwood	1	3	3.0	3	0
Clark	1	1	1.0	1	0
Ryans	1	1	1.0	1	0
T. Johnson	1	0	0	0	0
Texans	11	75	6.8	33	0
Opponents	21	267	12.7	70t	1

PUNTING

	No.	Yds.	Avg.	In 20	LG
Turk	55	2296	41.7	24	59
Texans	55	2296	41.7	24	59
Opponents	59	2535	43.0	24	64

PUNT RETURNS

	Ret	FC	Yds	Avg	LG	TD
Jones	30	7	286	9.5	74	0
Wynn	2	1	1	0.5	4	0
D. Anderson	1	0	0	0	0	0
Texans	33	8	287	8.7	74	0
Opponents	19	17	151	7.9	22	0

KICKOFF RETURNS

	No.	Yds	Avg	LG	TD
Davis	32	968	30.3	104t	3
Wynn	22	523	23.8	39	0
Mathis	11	320	29.1	84t	1
Jones	4	78	19.5	23	0
Cook	2	33	16.5	21	0
Leach	2	26	13.0	14	0
Walter	1	7	7.0	7	0
Boulware	0	6	—	6	0
Texans	74	1961	26.5	104t	4
Opponents	69	1593	23.1	52	0

FIELD GOALS

	1-19	20-29	30-39	40-49	50+
K. Brown	1/1	6/7	6/6	7/10	5/5
Texans	1/1	6/7	6/6	7/10	5/5
Opponents	0/0	14/14	6/7	6/8	2/4

SACKS

	No.
M. Williams	14.0
Okoye	5.5
Kalu	3.0
C. Anderson	2.0
Maddox	2.0
Ryans	2.0
Cochran	1.0
Greenwood	1.0
Hutchins	0.5
Texans	31.0
Opponents	22.0

RECORD HOLDERS
INDIVIDUAL RECORDS—CAREER

Category	Name	Performance
Rushing (Yds.)	Domanick Williams, 2003-06	3,195
Passing (Yds.)	David Carr, 2002-06	13,391
Passing (TDs)	David Carr, 2002-06	59
Receiving (No.)	Andre Johnson, 2003-07	371
Receiving (Yds.)	Andre Johnson, 2003-07	4,804
Interceptions	Marcus Coleman, 2002-06	11
	Aaron Glenn, 2002-04	11
	Dunta Robinson, 2004-07	11
Punting (Avg.)	Chad Stanley, 2002-06	41.0
Punt Return (Avg.)	Jacoby Jones, 2007	9.5
Kickoff Return (Avg.)	J.J. Moses, 2003-04	22.7
Field Goals	Kris Brown, 2002-07	122
Touchdowns (Tot.)	Domanick Williams, 2003-06	28
Points	Kris Brown, 2002-07	537

INDIVIDUAL RECORDS—SINGLE SEASON

Category	Name	Performance
Rushing (Yds.)	Domanick Williams, 2004	1,188
Passing (Yds.)	David Carr, 2004	3,531
Passing (TDs)	David Carr, 2004	16
Receiving (No.)	Andre Johnson, 2006	103
Receiving (Yds.)	Andre Johnson, 2006	1,147
Interceptions	Marcus Coleman, 2003	7
Punting (Avg.)	Matt Turk, 2007	41.7
Punt Return (Avg.)	Avion Black, 2002	13.4
Kickoff Return (Avg.)	André Davis, 2007	30.3
Field Goals	Kris Brown, 2005	26
Touchdowns (Tot.)	Domanick Williams, 2004	14
Points	Kris Brown, 2007	115

INDIVIDUAL RECORDS—SINGLE GAME

Category	Name	Performance
Rushing (Yds.)	Domanick Williams, 12-26-04	158
Passing (Yds.)	David Carr, 10-10-04	372
Passing (TDs)	Sage Rosenfels, 10-21-07	4
Receiving (No.)	Andre Johnson, 10-10-04, 11-27-05	12
	Kevin Walter, 10-14-07	12
Receiving (Yds.)	Andre Johnson, 10-10-04	170
Interceptions	Aaron Glenn, 12-8-02	2
	Marcus Coleman, 9-7-03	2
	Kenny Wright, 9-28-03	2
	Dunta Robinson, 10-3-04	2
Field Goals	Kris Brown, 9-7-03, 12-4-05, 10-7-07	5
Touchdowns (Tot.)	Many times	2
	Last time by André Davis and Ron Dayne, 12-30-07	
Points	Kris Brown, 10-7-07	16

2008 VETERAN ROSTER

No.	Name	Pos.	Ht.	Wt.	Age	NFL Exp.	College	Hometown	How Acq.	'07 Games/ Starts
47	Abbate, Jon	FB	5-11	245	23	2	Wake Forest	Powder Springs, Ga.	FA-'07	0*
20 #	Alexander, Roc	CB	5-10	190	26	5	Washington	Colorado Springs, Co.	W(Den)-'06	0*
89	Anderson, David	WR	5-10	197	25	3	Colorado State	Thousand Oaks, Calif.	D7-'06	7/0
32	Bennett, Fred	CB	6-1	194	24	2	South Carolina	Manning, S.C.	D4-'07	13/8
57	Bentley, Kevin	LB	6-0	238	28	7	Northwestern	North Hills, Calif.	UFA(Sea)-'08	14/2*
71	Black, Jordan	T	6-5	298	28	6	Notre Dame	Dallas, Texas	UFA(KC)-'07	8/0
24	Brown, C.C.	FS	6-0	208	25	4	Louisiana-Lafayette	Greenwood, Miss.	D6-'05	16/16
29	Brown, Chris	RB	6-3	220	27	6	Colorado	Naperville, Ill.	UFA(Tenn)-'08	12/1*
3	Brown, Kris	PK	5-11	209	31	10	Nebraska	Southlake, Texas	RFA(Pitt)-'02	16/0
87	Bruener, Mark	TE	6-4	252	35	14	Washington	Olympia, Wash.	UFA(Pitt)-'04	14/1
93	Bulman, Tim	DT	6-4	279	25	2	Boston College	Dorchester, Mass.	FA-'06	2/0
78	Butler, Rashad	T	6-4	270	25	3	Miami	West Palm Beach, Fla.	W(Car)-07	8/0
96	Cochran, Earl	DE	6-5	281	27	3	Alabama State	Bessemer, Ala.	FA-'06	15/1
43	Cook, Jameel	FB	5-10	238	29	8	Illinois	Miami, Fla.	UFA(TB)-'06	16/0
40	Cox, Curome	S	6-1	204	27	4	Maryland	Washington, D.C.	FA-'07	14/0
81	Daniels, Owen	TE	6-3	243	25	3	Wisconsin	Naperville, Ill.	D4-'06	16/16
11	Davis, André	WR	6-1	194	29	7	Virginia Tech	Niskayuna, N.Y.	UFA(Buff)-'07	14/8
36 #	Dayne, Ron	RB	5-10	244	30	9	Wisconsin	Berlin, N.J.	FA-'06	13/8
47	Demps, Will	FS	6-0	208	28	7	San Diego State	Charleston, S.C.	FA-'07	15/8
54	Diles, Zac	LB	6-2	240	23	2	Kansas State	Tulare, Calif.	D7-'07	11/0
85	Dreessen, Joel	TE	6-4	260	26	3	Colorado State	Ida Grove, Ia.	FA-'07	13/0
26	Earl, Glenn	SS	6-1	213	27	5	Notre Dame	Naperville, Ill.	D4-'04	0*
60	Eslinger, Greg	C	6-3	291	25	2	Minnesota	Bismarck, N.D.	FA-'07	0*
38	Faggins, DeMarcus	CB	5-10	178	29	7	Kansas State	Irving, Texas	D6a-'02	16/8
28	Ferguson, Nick	SS	5-11	201	33	9	Georgia Tech	Miami, Fla.	UFA(Den)-'08	12/7*
21	Fletcher, Jamar	CB	5-10	172	29	8	Wisconsin	St. Louis, Mo.	UFA(Den)-'07	10/2
75	Frye, Brandon	T	6-4	298	25	2	Virginia Tech	Myrtle Beach, S.C.	D5b-'07	0*
5	Gray, Quinn	QB	6-3	246	29	5	Florida A&M	Ft. Lauderdale, Fla.	UFA(Jax)-'08	8/4*
30	Green, Ahman	RB	6-0	220	31	11	Nebraska	Omaha, Neb.	UFA(GB)-'07	6/5
56	Greenwood, Morlon	LB	6-0	241	30	8	Syracuse	Freeport, N.Y.	UFA(Mia)-'05	16/15
31	Harrison, Brandon	FS	6-2	227	24	2	Stanford	Baton Rouge, La.	D5a-'07	0*
62	Jackson, Scott	T	6-4	302	29	4	Brigham Young	Rancho Palos Verdes, Calif.	FA-'07	0*
80	Johnson, Andre	WR	6-3	223	27	6	Miami	Miami, Fla.	D1-'03	9/9
29	Johnson, Derrick	CB	5-10	188	26	4	Washington	Riverside, Calif.	FA-'07	0*
99	Johnson, Travis	DT	6-3	303	26	4	Florida State	Sherman Oaks, Calif.	D1-'05	15/13
12	Jones, Jacoby	WR	6-2	207	24	2	Lane College	New Orleans, La.	D3-'07	14/3
94	Kalu, N.D.	DE	6-3	257	33	12	Rice	San Antonio, Texas	UFA(Phil)-'06	14/1
44	Leach, Vonta	FB	6-0	253	26	5	East Carolina	Rowland, N.C.	FA-'06	16/13
95	Maddox, Anthony	DT	6-1	290	29	4	Delta State	Albany, Ga.	FA-'06	16/3
17	McCoy, LeRon	WR	6-1	219	26	3	Indiana (Pa.)	Harrisburg, Pa.	FA-'08	0*
55 t-	Myers, Chris	C	6-4	300	26	4	Miami	Miami, Fla.	T(Den)-'08	16/16*
58	Okobi, Chukki	C	6-1	305	29	8	Purdue	Pawling, N.Y.	FA-'08	1/0*
91	Okoye, Amobi	DT	6-2	302	21	2	Louisville	Huntsville, Ala.	D1-'07	16/14
48	Pittman, Bryan	LS	6-3	264	31	6	Washington	Auburn, Wash.	FA-'03	16/0
69	Pitts, Chester	G	6-4	318	29	7	San Diego State	Inglewood, Calif.	D2-'02	16/16
35	Reeves, Jaques	CB	5-11	192	25	5	Purdue	Lancaster, Texas	UFA(Dall)-'08	16/13*
23	Robinson, Dunta	CB	5-10	176	26	5	South Carolina	Athens, Ga.	D1a-'04	9/9
18	Rosenfels, Sage	QB	6-4	222	30	8	Iowa State	Maquoketa, Ia.	UFA(Mia)-'06	9/5
59	Ryans, DeMeco	LB	6-1	239	24	3	Alabama	Bessemer, Ala.	D2-'06	16/16
74	Salaam, Ephraim	T	6-7	298	32	11	San Diego State	Sacramento, Calif.	UFA(Jax)-'06	16/16
8	Schaub, Matt	QB	6-5	231	27	5	Virginia	West Chester, Pa.	T(Atl)-'07	11/11
22 #	Simmons, Jason	SS	5-9	202	32	11	Arizona State	Lawndale, Calif.	UFA(Pitt)-'02	1/1
77	Spencer, Charles	T	6-4	338	26	3	Pittsburgh	Poughkeepsie, N.Y.	D3a-'06	0*
64	Studdard, Kasey	G	6-3	299	24	2	Texas	Lone Tree, Colo.	D6-'07	3/0
27	Taylor, Chris	RB	6-0	224	24	3	Indiana	Memphis, Tenn.	FA-'07	0*
51	Thompson, Chaun	LB	6-2	255	28	6	West Texas A&M	Mount Pleasant, Texas	UFA(Cle)-'08	16/0*
1	Turk, Matt	P	6-5	245	38	13	Wisconsin-Whitewater	Greenfield, Wisc.	FA-'07	16/0
37	Walker, Darius	RB	5-11	204	22	2	Notre Dame	Buford, Ga.	FA-'07	4/2
83	Walter, Kevin	WR	6-3	215	27	6	Eastern Michigan	Vernon Hills, Ill.	RFA(Cin)-'06	16/15
70 #	Weary, Fred	G	6-4	298	30	7	Tennessee	Montgomery, Ala.	D3a-'02	12/12
98	Weaver, Anthony	DE	6-3	276	28	7	Notre Dame	Saratoga, N.Y.	UFA(Balt)-'06	15/13
63	White, Chris	C	6-2	284	25	4	Southern Mississippi	Winona, Miss.	FA-'06	6/0
86	Williams, Harry	WR	6-2	196	26	2	Tuskegee	Birmingham, Ala.	FA-'06	2/0
90	Williams, Mario	DE	6-6	286	23	3	North Carolina State	Richlands, N.C.	D1-'06	16/16
73	Winston, Eric	T	6-5	310	24	3	Miami	Midland, Texas	D3b-'06	16/16
25 #	Wynn, Dexter	CB	5-9	171	27	5	Colorado State	Colorado Springs, Colo.	FA-'06	8/1
92	Zgonina, Jeff	DT	6-2	276	38	16	Purdue	Chicago, Ill.	UFA(Mia)-'07	16/1

* Abate missed '07 season because of injury; Alexander missed '07 season because of injury; Bentley played 14 games with Seattle in '07; Ch. Brown played 12 games with Tennessee in '07; Earl missed '07 season because of injury; Eslinger inactive for 4 games with Cleveland; Ferguson played in 12 games with Denver in '07; Gray played eight games with Jacksonville in '07; Harrison missed '07 season because of injury; Jackson missed '07 season because of injury; D. Johnson last active with Atlanta in '06; Myers played 16 games with Denver in '07; Okobi played one game with Arizona in '07; Spencer missed '07 season because of injury; Taylor missed '07 season because of injury; Thompson played 16 games with Cleveland in '07

\# Unrestricted free agent; subject to developments.

t- Texans traded for Myers (Den).

Players lost through free agency (4): LB Charlie Anderson (Mia; 7 games in '07), S Michael Boulware (Minn; 16), LB Danny Clark (NYG; 13), CB Von Hutchins (Atl; 16).

Also played with Texans in '07—LB Shawn Barber (6 games), G Mike Brisel (5), RB Adimchinobi Echemandu (9), C Mike Flanagan (14), RB Samkon Gado (4), C Drew Hodgdon (2), LB William Kershaw (2), DT Cedric Killings (2), WR Jerome Mathis (3), C Steve McKinney (3), LB Shantee Orr (5), TE Jeb Putzier (9).

2008 FIRST-YEAR ROSTER

Name	Pos.	Ht.	Wt.	Age	College	Hometown	How Acq.
Adibi, Xavier	LB	6-2	220	23	Virginia Tech	Hampton, Va.	D4
Barber, Dominique	S	6-0	210	22	Minnesota	Wayzata, Minn.	D6
Beach, Arliss (1)	RB	5-10	219	24	Kentucky	Ashland, Ky.	FA-'07
Bennett, Cole	TE	6-4	258	24	Auburn	Dalton, Ga.	FA
Boyd, Shane (1)	QB	6-1	222	25	Kentucky	Lexington, Ky.	FA-'07
Brink, Alex	QB	6-2	212	23	Washington State	Eugene, Ore.	D7
Brisiel, Mike (1)	G	6-5	296	25	Colorado State	Fayetteville, Ark.	FA-'06
Brown, Duane	T	6-4	315	23	Virginia Tech	Richmond, Va.	D1
Coley, Kevis (1)	LB	6-1	228	26	Southern Mississippi	Palatka, Fla.	FA-'07
Grice-Mullen, Ryan	WR	5-11	180	21	Hawaii	Rialto, Calif.	FA
Jenkins, Darnell	WR	5-10	188	25	Miami	Miami, Fla.	FA
Long, Gabe	DT	6-3	290	23	Utah	Anaheim, Calif.	FA
Mitchell, Brandon (1)	S	6-3	205	24	Ohio State	Atlanta, Ga.	FA-'07
Moffitt, Ben	LB	6-2	245	23	South Florida	Bushnell, Fla.	FA
Molden, Antwaun	CB	6-1	198	23	Eastern Kentucky	Cleveland, Ohio	D3a
Nading, Jesse	DE	6-5	258	23	Colorado State	Highlands Ranch, Colo.	FA
Okam, Frank	DT	6-5	320	22	Texas	Dallas, Texas	D5
Powell, Eric (1)	DE	6-3	284	28	Florida State	Orlando, Fla.	FA-'07
Richardson, Marcus	LB	6-0	235	23	Troy	Pensacola, Fla.	FA
Roberson, Derrick (1)	CB	5-10	175	23	Rutgers	Oakland Park, Fla.	FA-'07
Robinson, DelJuan (1)	DT	6-3	304	24	Mississippi State	Hernando, Miss.	FA-'07
Slaton, Steve	RB	5-9	197	22	West Virginia	Levittown, Pa.	D3b
Stevenson, Dan (1)	G	6-5	300	25	Notre Dame	Barrington, Ill.	FA-'07

The term NFL Rookie is defined as a player who is in his first season of professional football and has not been on the roster of another professional football team for any regular-season or postseason games. A Rookie is designated by an "R" on NFL rosters. Players who have been active in another professional football league or players who have NFL experience, including either preseason training camp or being on an Active List or Inactive List, or on Reserve/Injured or Reserve/Physically Unable to Perform for fewer than six regular-season games, are termed NFL First-Year Players. An NFL First-Year Player is designated by a "1" on NFL rosters. Thereafter, a player is credited with an additional year of experience for each season in which he accumulates six games on the Active List or Inactive List, or on Reserve/Injured or Reserve/Physically Unable to Perform.

Log on to www.houstontexans.com for an up-to-date roster; Age listed is as of September 4, 2008.

COACHING STAFF

Head Coach,
Gary Kubiak

Pro Career: Gary Kubiak was introduced as the second head coach in Houston Texans history on January 26, 2006. Kubiak returned to Houston after spending 20 of the previous 23 years in the Denver area. Kubiak's record as Texans head coach is 14-18, leaving him just five wins away from becoming the franchise's winningest head coach. In his first year as a head coach, Kubiak guided the Texans to a 6-10 record, tripling the team's win total of the year before. In 2007, the Texans broke even for the first time, finishing at 8-8. Houston went 7-3 outside of the AFC West and set a franchise record with a 6-2 mark at home. It was the first time the Texans posted a winning mark at Reliant Stadium. From 1995-2005, Kubiak served as Denver's offensive coordinator. Kubiak began his coaching career as the running backs coach at Texas A&M (1992-93). Kubiak started his NFL coaching career with the San Francisco 49ers as the quarterbacks coach, winning Super Bowl XXIX in hi s only seson (1994). Kubiak is a veteran of six Super Bowls—three as a player and three as a coach. Career record: 14-18.

Background: Kubiak starred at quarterback for Texas A&M from 1979-1982, earning all-Southwest Conference honors as a senior. He played for the Broncos from 1983-1991 as John Elway's backup. Kubiak played in 119 career games, tossed 14 touchdowns, and was a part of three teams that reached the Super Bowl.

Personal: Age 47, born in Houston. He and his wife, Rhonda, have three sons—Klint, Klay, and Klein.

ASSISTANT COACHES

John Benton, offensive line; born Los Angeles. Offensive lineman Colorado State 1986-1990. No pro playing experience. College coach: California University (Pa.) 1990-94, Colorado State 1996-2003. Pro coach: St. Louis Rams 2004-05, joined Texans in 2006.

Frank Bush, senior defensive assistant; born Athens, Ga. Linebacker North Carolina State 1981-84. Pro linebacker Houston Oilers 1985-86. Pro coach: Houston Oilers 1987-1991 (scout), 1992-94, Denver Broncos 1995-2003, Arizona Cardinals 2004-06, joined Texans in 2007.

Perry Carter, defensive assistant; born McComb, Miss. Defensive back Southern Mississippi 1989-1993. Pro defensive back Arizona Cardinals 1994, Kansas City Chiefs 1995, Oakland Raiders 1996-98, Edmonton Eskimos (CFL) 2000-01, Montreal Alouettes (CFL) 2002, British Columbia Lions (CFL) 2003-04. College coach: Texas A&M-Commerce 2004. Pro coach: Hamburg Sea Devils (NFLEL) 2006, joined Texans in 2006.

Jethro Franklin, defensive line; born St. Lazaire, France. Defensive lineman San Jose (Calif.) Community College 1984-85, Fresno State 1986-87. Pro defensive lineman Houston Oilers 1988-1990. College coach: Fresno State 1991-98, UCLA 1999, Southern California 2005. Pro coach: Green Bay Packers 2000-04, Tampa Bay Buccaneers 2006, joined Texans in 2007.

Alex Gibbs, asst. head coach/offense; born Morganton, N.C. Running back/defensive back Davidson College 1959-1963. No pro playing experience. College coach: Duke 1969-1970, Kentucky 1971-72, West Virginia 1973-74, Ohio State 1975-78, Auburn 1979-1981, Georgia 1982-83. Pro coach: Denver Broncos 1984-87, Oakland Raiders 1988-89, San Diego Chargers 1990-91, Indianapolis Colts 1992, Kansas City Chiefs 1993-94, Denver Broncos 1995-2003, Atlanta Falcons 2004-06, joined Texans in 2008.

Chick Harris, running backs; born Durham, N.C. Running back Northern Arizona 1966-69. No pro playing experience. College coach: Colorado State 1970-71, Long Beach State 1972-73, Washington 1975-1980. Pro coach: Detroit Wheels (WFL) 1974, Buffalo Bills 1981-82, Seattle Seahawks 1983-1991, Los Angeles Rams 1992-94, Carolina Panthers 1995-2001, joined Texans in 2002.

Richard Hightower, special teams assistant; born Houston. Wide receiver/defensive back Texas 1998-2002. No pro playing experience. Pro coach: Joined Texans in 2006.

Jon Hoke, defensive backs; born Kettering, Ohio. Defensive back Ball State 1976-79. Pro defensive back Chicago Bears 1980. College coach: Bowling Green 1983-86, San Diego State 1987-88, Kent State 1989-1993, Missouri 1994-98, Florida 1999-2001. Pro coach: Joined Texans in 2002.

Johnny Holland, linebackers; born Belleville, Texas. Linebacker Texas A&M 1983-86. Pro linebacker Green Bay Packers 1987-1993. Pro coach: Green Bay Packers 1995-99, Seattle Seahawks 2000-02, Detroit Lions 2003-05, joined Texans in 2006.

Larry Kirksey, wide receivers; born Harlan, Ky. Wide receiver Eastern Kentucky 1970-73. No pro playing experience. College coach: Miami (Ohio) 1974-76, Kentucky 1977-1981, Kansas 1982, Kentucky State 1983 (head coach), Florida 1984-88, Pittsburgh 1989, Alabama 1990-93, Texas A&M 2000, Middle Tennessee State 2006. Pro coach: San Francisco 49ers 1994-99, Detroit Lions 2001-02, Jacksonville Jaguars 2003, Denver Broncos 2004, joined Texans in 2007.

Matt LaFleur, offensive assistant; born Mt. Pleasant, Mich. QB/WR Western Michigan 1998-99, Saginaw Valley State 2000-02. Pro QB Omaha Beef (NIFL) 2002, Billings Outlaws (NIFL) 2002. College coach: Saginaw Valley State 2003, Central Michigan 2004-05, Northern Michigan 2006, Ashland 2007. Pro coach: Joined Texans in 2006.

Joe Marciano, special teams coordinator; born Dunmore, Pa. Quarterback Temple 1972-75. No pro playing experience. College coach: East Stroudsburg State 1977, Rhode Island 1978-79, Villanova 1980, Penn State 1981, Temple 1982. Pro coach: Philadelphia/Baltimore Stars (USFL) 1983-85, New Orleans Saints 1986-1995, Tampa Bay Buccaneers 1996-2001, joined Texans in 2002.

Mike McDaniel, offensive assistant; born Greeley, Colo. Wide receiver Yale 2001-04. No pro playing experience. Pro coach: Joined Texans in 2006.

Brian Pariani, tight ends; born San Francisco. No college or pro playing experience. College coach: UCLA 1989, Syracuse 2005. Pro coach: San Francisco 49ers 1991-94, Denver Broncos 1994-2004, joined Texans in 2006.

Frank Pollack, asst. offensive line; born Camp Springs, Md. Offensive lineman Northern Arizona 1985-89. Pro offensive lineman San Francisco 49ers 1990-97. College coach: Northern Arizona 2005-06. Pro coach: Joined Texans in 2008.

Ray Rhodes, asst. defensive backs; born Mexia, Texas. Running back Texas Christian 1969-1970, wide receiver/defensive back/kick returner Tulsa 1972-73. Pro wide receiver/defensive back New York Giants 1974-79, San Francisco 49ers 1980. Pro coach: San Francisco 49ers 1981-1991, 1994, Green Bay Packers 1992-93, 1999 (head coach 1999), Philadelphia Eagles 1995-98 (head coach), Washington Redskins 2000, Denver Broncos 2001-02, Seattle Seahawks 2003-07, joined Texans in 2008.

Robert Saleh, defensive assistant; born Dearborn, Mich. Tight end Northern Michigan 1997-2000. No pro playing experience. College coach: Michigan State 2002-03, Central Michigan 2004. Pro coach: Joined Texans in 2005.

Kyle Shanahan, offensive coordinator/quarterbacks; born Minneapolis. Wide receiver Duke 1998-99, Texas 2000-02. No pro playing experience. College coach: UCLA 2003. Pro coach: Tampa Bay Buccaneers 2004-05, joined Texans in 2006.

Richard Smith, defensive coordinator; born Los Angeles. Offensive lineman Rio Hondo (Calif.) J.C. 1975-76, Fresno State 1977-78. No pro playing experience. College coach: Rio Hondo (Calif.) J.C. 1979-1980, Cal State-Fullerton 1981-83, California 1984-86, Arizona 1987. Pro coach: Houston Oilers 1988-1992, Denver Broncos 1993-96, San Francisco 49ers 1997-2002, Detroit Lions 2003-04, Miami Dolphins 2005, joined Texans in 2006.

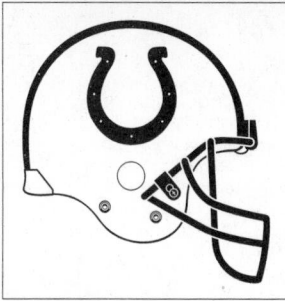

American Football Conference
South Division
Team Colors: Royal Blue and White
P.O. Box 535000
Indianapolis, Indiana 46253
Telephone: (317) 297-2658

2008 SCHEDULE
PRESEASON
Aug. 3	vs. Washington at Canton, OH.	8:00
Aug. 9	at Carolina	7:30
Aug. 16	at Atlanta	7:30
Aug. 24	**Buffalo**	8:00
Aug. 28	**Cincinnati**	7:00

REGULAR SEASON
Sep. 7	**Chicago**	8:15
Sep. 14	at Minnesota	12:00
Sep. 21	**Jacksonville**	4:15
Sep. 28	BYE	
Oct. 5	at Houston	12:00
Oct. 12	**Baltimore**	1:00
Oct. 19	at Green Bay	3:15
Oct. 27	at Tennessee (Mon.)	7:30
Nov. 2	**New England**	8:15
Nov. 9	at Pittsburgh	4:15
Nov. 16	**Houston**	1:00
Nov. 23	at San Diego *	5:15
Nov. 30	at Cleveland	1:00
Dec. 7	**Cincinnati**	1:00
Dec. 14	**Detroit**	1:00
Dec. 18	at Jacksonville (Thu.)	8:15
Dec. 28	**Tennessee**	1:00

Sunday night games in Weeks 11-17 subject to change

Stadium: Lucas Oil Stadium (opened in
2008) •**Capacity:** 63,000
500 South Capitol Avenue
Indianapolis, Indiana 46225
Playing Surface: FieldTurf
Training Camp: Rose-Hulman Institute
5500 Wabash Avenue
Terre Haute, IN 47803

LUCAS OIL STADIUM

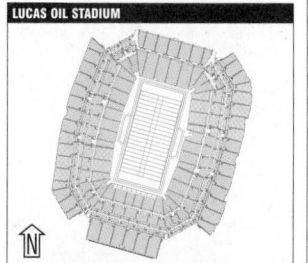

CLUB OFFICIALS
Owner and CEO: James Irsay
President: Bill Polian
Head Coach: Tony Dungy
Vice President: Casey Irsay
Senior Executive Vice President:
Pete Ward
Executive Vice President: Bob Terpening
Senior Vice President of Sales and
Marketing: Tom Zupancic
Vice President of Football Operations:
Chris Polian
Vice President-Finance: Kurt Humphrey
Vice President-Ticket Operations/Guest
Services: Larry Hall
Vice President-Public Relations:
Craig Kelley
Vice President of Sponsorship Sales:
Jay Souers
Vice President of Premium Seating and
Ticket Sales: Greg Hylton
Director of Football Administration:
Steve Champlin
Director of Pro Player Personnel:
Clyde Powers
Executive Director of Administration:
Bill Brooks
Executive Director of Community
Relations: Nicole Duncan
Equipment Manager: Jon Scott
Video Director: Marty Heckscher
Head Athletic Trainer: Hunter Smith
Assistant Director of Public Relations:
Vernon Cheek
Assistant Equipment Managers:
Mike Mays, Sean Sullivan,
Brian Seabrooks
Associate Head Athletic Trainer:
Dave Hammer
Assistant Trainers: Dave Walston,
Bryant Baugh
Assistant Video Director: John Starliper
Purchasing Administrator: Dave Filar

COACHING HISTORY
Baltimore 1953-1983
(432-401-7)
Records include postseason games
1953	Keith Molesworth	3-9-0
1954-1962	Weeb Ewbank	61-52-1
1963-69	Don Shula	73-26-4
1970-72	Don McCafferty*	26-11-1
1972	John Sandusky	4-5-0
1973-74	Howard Schnellenberger**	4-13-0
1974	Joe Thomas	2-9-0
1975-79	Ted Marchibroda	41-36-0
1980-81	Mike McCormack	9-23-0
1982-84	Frank Kush***	11-28-1
1984	Hal Hunter	0-1-0
1985-86	Rod Dowhower****	5-24-0
1986-1991	Ron Meyer#	36-36-0
1991	Rick Venturi	1-10-0
1992-95	Ted Marchibroda	32-35-0
1996-97	Lindy Infante	12-21-0
1998-2001	Jim Mora	32-34-0
2002-07	Tony Dungy	80-28-0

*Released after five games in 1972
**Released after three games in 1974
***Resigned after 15 games in 1984
****Released after 13 games in 1986
#Released after five games in 1991

PAID ATTENDANCE
Home 444,653   Away 538,318
Total 1,058,639
Single-game home record,
61,139 (10/20/97)
Single-season home record, 481,305
(1984)

2008 DRAFT CHOICES
Round	Name	Pos.	College
2	Mike Pollak	G	Arizona State
3	Philip Wheeler	LB	Georgia Tech
4	Jacob Tamme	TE	Kentucky
5	Marcus Howard	DE	Georgia
6	Tom Santi	TE	Virginia
	Steve Justice	C	Wake Forest
	Mike Hart	RB	Michigan
	Pierre Garcon	WR	Mount Union
7	Jamey Richard	G	Buffalo

2007 TEAM RECORD
PRESEASON (1-3)

Date	Result	Opponent
8/9	L 10-23	at Dallas
8/20	L 24-27	Chicago
8/25	W 37-10	Detroit
8/31	L 6-14	at Cincinnati

REGULAR SEASON (13-3)

Date	Result	Opponent	Att.
9/6	W 41-10	New Orleans	57,361
9/16	W 22-20	at Tennessee	69,143
9/23	W 30-24	at Houston	70,765
9/30	W 38-20	Denver	57,274
10/7	W 33-14	Tampa Bay	57,202
10/22	W 29-7	at Jacksonville	67,164
10/28	W 31-7	at Carolina	74,005
11/4	L 20-24	New England	57,540
11/11	L 21-23	at San Diego	67,726
11/18	W 13-10	Kansas City	57,294
11/22	W 31-13	at Atlanta	69,845
12/2	W 28-25	Jacksonville	57,302
12/9	W 44-20	at Baltimore	70,513
12/16	W 21-14	at Oakland	62,000
12/23	W 38-15	Houston	57,262
12/30	L 10-16	Tennessee	57,202

POSTSEASON (0-1)

1/13	L 24-28	San Diego	56,950

SCORE BY PERIODS

Colts	90	146	118	96	0	—	450
Opponents	67	67	41	87	0	—	262

2007 TEAM STATISTICS

	Colts	Opp.
Total First Downs	357	288
Rushing	119	111
Passing	212	162
Penalty	26	15
3rd Down: Made/Att	100/203	94/208
3rd Down Pct.	49.3	45.2
4th Down: Made/Att	6/10	14/25
4th Down Pct.	60.0	56.0
Possession Avg.	29:49	30:11
Total Net Yards	5739	4475
Avg. Per Game	358.7	279.7
Total Plays	1020	980
Avg. Per Play	5.6	4.6
Net Yards Rushing	1706	1711
Avg. Per Game	106.6	106.9
Total Rushes	446	454
Net Yards Passing	4033	2764
Avg. Per Game	252.1	172.8
Sacked/Yards Lost	23/139	28/162
Gross Yards	4172	2926
Att./Completions	551/355	498/325
Completion Pct.	64.4	65.3
Had Intercepted	14	22
Punts/Average	52/41.9	56/44.2
Net Punting Avg.	52/34.2	56/38.5
Penalties/Yards	67/515	85/722
Fumbles/Ball Lost	14/5	27/15
Touchdowns	54	31
Rushing	19	10
Passing	32	16
Returns	3	5

2007 INDIVIDUAL STATISTICS

PASSING

	Att.	Comp.	Yds.	Pct.	TD	Int.	Tkld.	Rate
Manning	515	337	4040	65.4	31	14	21/124	98.0
Sorgi	36	18	132	50.0	1	0	2/15	68.3
Colts	551	355	4172	64.4	32	14	23/139	96.1
Opponents	498	325	2926	65.3	16	22	28/162	73.3

SCORING

	TD R	TD P	TD Rt	PAT	FG	Saf	PTS
Vinatieri	0	0	0	49/51	23/29	0	118
Addai	12	3	0	0/0	0/0	0	92
Clark	0	11	0	0/0	0/0	0	66
Wayne	0	10	0	0/0	0/0	0	60
Keith	3	1	0	0/0	0/0	0	24
Gonzalez	0	3	0	0/0	0/0	0	18
Manning	3	0	0	0/0	0/0	0	18
Brackett	0	0	1	0/0	0/0	0	6
C. Dawson	1	0	0	0/0	0/0	0	6
Giordano	0	0	1	0/0	0/0	0	6
Harrison	0	1	0	0/0	0/0	0	6
Lawton	0	1	0	0/0	0/0	0	6
Rushing	0	0	1	0/0	0/0	0	6
Thorpe	0	1	0	0/0	0/0	0	6
Utecht	0	1	0	0/0	0/0	0	6
Fletcher	0	0	0	0/0	0/0	0	2
Freeney	0	0	0	0/0	0/0	1	2
Colts	19	32	3	49/51	23/29	2	450
Opponents	10	16	5	27/27	15/20	0	262

2-Pt. Conversions: Addai, Fletcher, Colts 2-3, Opponents 2-4

RUSHING

	No.	Yds	Avg	LG	TD
Addai	261	1072	4.1	23	12
Keith	121	533	4.4	22	3
C. Dawson	30	64	2.1	12	1
Clark	2	29	14.5	15	0
Lawton	5	13	2.6	4	0
Wayne	1	4	4.0	4	0
Sorgi	6	-4	-.7	1	0
Manning	20	-5	-.3	4	3
Colts	446	1706	3.8	23	19
Opponents	454	1711	3.8	32	10

RECEIVING

	No.	Yds	Avg	LG	TD
Wayne	104	1510	14.5	64	10
Clark	58	616	10.6	39	11
Addai	41	364	8.9	73t	3
Gonzalez	37	576	15.6	57t	3
Utecht	31	364	11.7	30	1
Harrison	20	247	12.4	42	1
Fletcher	18	143	7.9	21	0
Keith	13	77	5.9	14	1
Thorpe	12	70	5.8	12	1
Moorehead	8	65	8.1	16	0
Aromashodu	7	96	13.7	28	0
Lawton	4	29	7.3	11	1
C. Dawson	2	15	7.5	9	0
Colts	355	4172	11.8	73t	32
Opponents	325	2926	9.0	55	16

INTERCEPTIONS

	No.	Yds	Avg	LG	TD
Brackett	4	128	32.0	49	0
Bethea	4	47	11.8	30	0
Hayden	3	17	5.7	20	0
Giordano	2	89	44.5	83t	1
Sanders	2	32	16.0	29	0
Boiman	2	28	14.0	26	0
Session	2	3	1.5	3	0
Keiaho	1	11	11.0	11	0
Bullitt	1	0	0.0	0	0
Jackson	1	0	0.0	0	0
Colts	22	355	16.1	83t	1
Opponents	14	136	9.7	37	0

PUNTING

	No.	Yds	Avg.	In 20	LG
H. Smith	52	2181	41.9	18	63
Colts	52	2181	41.9	18	63
Opponents	56	2474	44.2	24	65

PUNT RETURNS

	Ret	FC	Yds	Avg	LG	TD
Rushing	19	14	249	13.1	90t	1
Thorpe	6	0	31	5.2	29	0
Colts	25	14	280	11.2	90t	1
Opponents	22	13	305	13.9	74	1

KICKOFF RETURNS

	No.	Yds	Avg	LG	TD
Rushing	31	714	23.0	47	0
Thorpe	15	318	21.2	40	0
Lawton	5	95	19.0	22	0
Keith	1	15	15.0	15	0
Reid	1	15	15.0	15	0
Colts	53	1157	21.8	47	0
Opponents	81	2029	25.0	94t	3

FIELD GOALS

	1-19	20-29	30-39	40-49	50+
Vinatieri	1/1	14/15	8/10	0/2	0/1
Colts	1/1	14/15	8/10	0/2	0/1
Opponents	0/0	1/1	10/10	3/7	1/2

SACKS

	No.
Mathis	7.0
Freeney	3.5
Sanders	3.5
Brock	2.5
Pitcock	1.5
Charleston	1.0
K. Dawson	1.0
Hagler	1.0
E. Johnson	1.0
Klecko	1.0
Rice	1.0
Thomas	1.0
(group)	1.0
Brackett	0.5
Jackson	0.5
Keiaho	0.5
Reid	0.5
Colts	28.0
Opponents	23.0

RECORD HOLDERS
INDIVIDUAL RECORDS—CAREER

Category	Name	Performance
Rushing (Yds.)	Edgerrin James, 1999-2005	9,226
Passing (Yds.)	Peyton Manning, 1998-2007	41,626
Passing (TDs)	Peyton Manning, 1998-2007	306
Receiving (No.)	Marvin Harrison, 1996-2007	1,042
Receiving (Yds.)	Marvin Harrison, 1996-2007	13,944
Interceptions	Bob Boyd, 1960-68	57
Punting (Avg.)	Chris Gardocki, 1995-98	44.8
Punt Return (Avg.)	Ron Gardin, 1970-71	13.5
Kickoff Return (Avg.)	Jim Duncan, 1969-1971	32.6
Field Goals	Mike Vanderjagt, 1998-2005	217
Touchdowns (Tot.)	Marvin Harrison, 1996-2007	123
Points	Mike Vanderjagt, 1998-2005	995

INDIVIDUAL RECORDS—SINGLE SEASON

Category	Name	Performance
Rushing (Yds.)	Edgerrin James, 2000	1,709
Passing (Yds.)	Peyton Manning, 2004	4,557
Passing (TDs)	Peyton Manning, 2004	49
Receiving (No.)	Marvin Harrison, 2002	*143
Receiving (Yds.)	Marvin Harrison, 2002	1,722
Interceptions	Tom Keane, 1953	11
Punting (Avg.)	Rohn Stark, 1985	45.9
Punt Return (Avg.)	T.J. Rushing, 2007	13.1
Kickoff Return (Avg.)	Jim Duncan, 1970	35.4
Field Goals	Mike Vanderjagt, 2003	37
Touchdowns (Tot.)	Lenny Moore, 1964	20
Points	Mike Vanderjagt, 2003	157

INDIVIDUAL RECORDS—SINGLE GAME

Category	Name	Performance
Rushing (Yds.)	Edgerrin James, 10-15-00	219
Passing (Yds.)	Peyton Manning, 10-31-04	472
Passing (TDs)	Peyton Manning, 9-28-03, 11-25-04	6
Receiving (No.)	Marvin Harrison, 12-26-99, 11-17-02	14
Receiving (Yds.)	Raymond Berry, 11-10-57	224
Interceptions	Many times	3
	Last time by Mike Prior, 12-20-92	
Field Goals	Many times	5
	Last time by Mike Vanderjagt, 12-7-03	
Touchdowns (Tot.)	Many times	4
	Last time by Joseph Addai, 11-26-06	
Points	Many times	24
	Last time by Joseph Addai, 11-26-06	

*NFL Record

2008 VETERAN ROSTER

No.	Name	Pos.	Ht.	Wt.	Age	NFL Exp.	College	Hometown	How Acq.	'07 Games/ Starts
29	Addai, Joseph	RB	5-11	214	25	3	Louisiana State	Houston, Texas	D1-'06	15/15
80	Aromashodu, Devin	WR	6-2	200	24	2	Auburn	Miami, Fla.	FA-'07	6/1
41	Bethea, Antoine	DB	5-11	203	24	3	Howard	Newport News, Va.	D6b-'06	13/13
58	Brackett, Gary	LB	5-11	235	28	6	Rutgers	Glassboro, N.J.	FA-'03	16/16
79	Brock, Raheem	DE	6-4	274	30	7	Temple	Philadelphia, Pa.	FA-'02	11/11
33	Bullitt, Melvin	DB	6-1	201	23	2	Texas A&M	Bryan, Texas	FA-'07	15/0
60	Charleston, Jeff	DE	6-4	265	25	2	Idaho State	Oregon City, Ore.	FA-'07	13/3
44	Clark, Dallas	TE/FB	6-3	252	29	6	Iowa	Livermore, Iowa	D1-'03	15/15
25	Coe, Michael	DB	6-0	190	24	2	Alabama State	Memphis, Tenn.	D5b-'07	6/0
42	Condren, Brannon	DB	6-1	205	25	2	Troy	Ft. Walton Beach, Fla.	D4b-'07	8/0
30	Dawson, Clifton	RB	5-10	212	24	2	Harvard	Scarborough, Ont.	FA-'07	13/0*
96	Dawson, Keyunta	DE	6-3	254	22	2	Texas Tech	Shreveport, La,	D7-'07	16/4
71	Diem, Ryan	T	6-6	331	29	8	Northern Illinois	Carol Stream, Ill.	D4-'01	10/10
76	Federkeil, Dan	T	6-6	290	24	3	Calgary	Medicine Hat, Alberta	FA-'06	8/0
81	Fletcher, Bryan	TE	6-5	230	29	4	UCLA	St. Louis, Mo.	FA-'05	15/3
93	Freeney, Dwight	DE	6-1	268	28	7	Syracuse	Hartford, Conn.	D1-'02	9/9
57	Gandy, Dylan	G	6-3	302	26	4	Texas Tech	Harlingen, Texas	D4a-'05	10/1
43	Giordano, Matt	DB	5-11	192	25	4	California	Fresno, Calif.	D4b-'05	12/4
11	Gonzalez, Anthony	WR	6-0	193	23	2	Ohio State	Cleveland, Ohio	D1-'07	13/9
52	Guzman, Ramon	LB	6-2	232	25	2	Buffalo	Bronx, N.Y.	FA-'07	16/0
56	Hagler, Tyjuan	LB	6-0	236	26	3	Cincinnati	Kankakee, Ill.	D5c-'05	9/0
83	Hall, Roy	WR	6-3	240	24	2	Ohio State	Lyndhurst, Ohio	D5a-'07	3/0
88	Harrison, Marvin	WR	6-0	175	36	13	Syracuse	Philadelphia, Pa.	D1-'96	5/5
26	Hayden, Kelvin	DB	6-0	195	25	4	Illinois	Chicago, Ill.	D2-'05	16/16
72	Hilliard, Corey	T	6-6	305	23	2	Oklahoma State	New Orleans, La.	FA-'07	3/0
20	Hughes, Dante	DB	5-10	190	22	2	California	Los Angeles, Calif.	D3a-'07	10/0
28	Jackson, Marlin	DB	6-0	196	25	4	Michigan	Sharon, Pa.	D1-'05	16/16
27	Jennings, Tim	DB	5-8	185	24	3	Georgia	Orangeburg, S.C.	D2-'06	11/4
74	Johnson, Charlie	T	6-4	305	24	3	Oklahoma State	Sherman, Texas	D6a-'06	14/10
99	Johnson, Ed	DT	6-2	296	24	2	Penn State	Detroit, Mich.	FA-'07	16/16
54	Keiaho, Freddy	LB	5-11	226	25	3	San Diego State	Ventura, Calif.	D3-'06	11/11
36	Keith, Kenton	RB	5-11	198	28	2	New Mexico State	Lincoln, Neb.	FA-'07	16/1
45	Lawton, Luke	RB	6-0	245	28	3	McNeese State	New Iberia, La.	FA-'07	11/0
65	Lilja, Ryan	G	6-2	285	26	5	Kansas State	Shawnee, Kan.	W(KC)-04	16/16
18	Manning, Peyton	QB	6-5	230	32	11	Tennessee	New Orleans, La.	D1-98	16/16
98	Mathis, Robert	DE	6-2	235	27	6	Alabama A&M	Atlanta, Ga.	D5a-'03	13/12
85	#Moorehead, Aaron	WR	6-3	200	27	6	Illinois	Deerfield, Ill.	FA-'03	8/2
97	Pitcock, Quinn	DT	6-2	299	24	2	Ohio State	Piqua, Ohio	D3b-'07	9/1
35	Ratliff, Keiwan	DB	5-11	188	27	5	Florida	Youngstown, Ohio	W(TB)-'07	4/0*
95	Reid, Darrell	DT	6-2	288	26	4	Minnesota	Freehold, N.J.	FA-'05	16/1
34	Rushing, T.J.	DB	5-9	186	25	3	Stanford	Pauls Valley, Okla.	D7-'06	14/0
21	Sanders, Bob	DB	5-8	206	27	5	Iowa	Erie, Pa.	D2b-'04	15/15
63	Saturday, Jeff	C	6-2	295	33	10	North Carolina	Tucker, Ga.	FA-'99	16/16
42	#Seidman, Mike	TE	6-4	261	27	6	UCLA	Westlake Village, Calif.	UFA(Car)-'07	0*
55	Session, Clint	LB	6-0	235	23	2	Pittsburgh	Pompano Beach, Fla.	D4c-'07	13/1
37	Smith, Antonio	DB	5-9	192	24	2	Ohio State	Columbus, Ohio	FA-'07	0*
17	Smith, Hunter	P	6-2	209	31	10	Notre Dame	Sherman, Texas	D7a-'99	16/0
48	Snow, Justin	TE	6-3	240	31	9	Baylor	Abilene, Texas	FA-'00	16/0
12	Sorgi, Jim	QB	6-5	196	27	5	Wisconsin	Fraser, Mich.	D6b-'04	4/0
91	Thomas, Josh	DE	6-5	271	27	5	Syracuse	Orchard Park, N.Y.	FA-'04	15/7
75	Toudouze, Michael	T	6-6	303	25	2	TCU	San Antonio, Texas	D5-'06	4/0
67	Ugoh, Tony	T	6-5	301	24	2	Arkansas	Houston, Texas	D2a-'07	11/11
4	Vinatieri, Adam	K	6-0	202	35	13	South Dakota State	Rapid City, S.D.	UFA(NE)-'06	16/0
87	Wayne, Reggie	WR	6-0	198	29	8	Miami	New Orleans, La.	D1b-'01	16/16
51	Worsley, Victor	LB	6-1	234	24	2	North Carolina	Battleboro, N.C.	FA-'07	3/0

C. Dawson played 2 games with Cincinnati and 11 with Indianapolis in '07; Ratliff played in 3 games with Cincinnati and 1 with Indianapolis; Rice played 6 games with Denver; Seidman missed '07 season because of injury; A. Smith missed '07 season because of injury.

\#   Unrestricted free agent; subject to developments.

Players lost through free agency (4): LB Rocky Boiman (Phil; 16 games in '07), DT Dan Klecko (Phil; 8), G Jake Scott (Tenn; 16).

Also played with Colts in '07—LB Brandon Archer (6 games), LB Rob Morris (2), DE Simeon Rice (2), WR Craphonso Thorpe (5), TE Ben Utecht (14).

2008 FIRST-YEAR ROSTER

Name	Pos.	Ht.	Wt.	Age	College	Hometown	How Acq.
Andrus, Shane (1)	K	5-10	190	27	Murray State	Murray, Kent.	W(NYG)
Betts, Josh (1)	QB	6-2	217	26	Miami (Ohio)	Vandalia, Ohio	FA
Bradley, Joe (1)	DT	6-3	305	25	Louisianan-Lafayette	Los Angeles, Calif.	FA
Burgess, Rudy	WR	5-10	186	23	Arizona State	Brooklyn, N.Y.	FA
Davis, Dan	DT	6-1	275	22	Connecticut	Newark, N.J.	FA
Dillon, Charles	WR	6-0	193	22	Washington State	Oxnard, Calif.	FA
Elgin, Mike (1)	G	6-4	295	24	Iowa	Bankston, Iowa	FA
Esera, Tala (1)	OL	6-3	315	24	Hawaii	Honolulu, Hawaii	FA
Ferrell, Colin	DT	6-0	301	23	Kent State	Hamilton, N.J.	FA
Foster, Brandon	DB	5-8	185	23	Texas	Arlington, Texas	FA
Foster, Eric	DT	6-2	265	23	Rutgers	Homestead, Fla.	FA
Garcon, Pierre	WR	6-0	210	22	Mount Union	West Palm Beach, Fla.	D6d
Giguere, Sam	WR	5-11	211	23	Sherbrooke	Sherbrooke, Quebec	FA
Hairston, Justise (1)	RB	6-1	220	25	Central Connecticut State	New Britain, Conn.	FA
Hart, Mike	RB	5-9	206	22	Michigan	Syracuse, N.Y.	D6c
Herold, Zac (1)	TE	6-5	251	24	Nebraska-Omaha	Cedar Rapids, Iowa	FA
Howard, Marcus	DE	6-0	237	22	Georgia	Huger, S.C.	D5
Ishola, Ben (1)	DE	6-3	255	28	Indiana	Berlin, Germany	FA
Johnson, Curtis	DE	6-3	237	23	Clark College	Lauderhill, Fla.	FA
Jones, Onrea (1)	WR	6-0	202	24	Hampton	Williamsburg, Va.	FA
Justice, Steve	C	6-3	293	24	Wake Forest	Lancaster, Pa.	D6b
Marquez, Darren	T	6-3	308	23	Southern Illinois	New Orleans, La.	FA
Milan, J.J. (1)	DE	6-5	265	24	Nevada	Reno, Nev.	FA
Pollak, Mike	G	6-3	301	23	Arizona State	Scottsdale, Ariz.	D2
Richard, Jamey	G	6-5	295	23	Buffalo	Weston, Conn.	D7
Robinson, Gijon (1)	TE	6-1	255	23	Missouri West State	Waynesville, Mo.	FA
Roby, Courtney	WR	6-0	189	25	Indiana	Indianapolis, Ind.	FA
Ross, Patrick (1)	C	6-4	300	25	Boston College	Reading, Ohio	FA
Santi, Tom	TE	6-3	250	22	Virginia	Nashville, Tenn.	D6a
Senn, Jordan	LB	5-11	224	24	Portland State	Beaverton, Ore.	FA
Shotwell, Kyle (1)	LB	6-1	235	24	Cal Poly-San Luis Obispo	Santa Barbara, Calif.	FA
Silva, Jamie	DB	5-11	204	23	Boston College	East Providence, R.I.	FA
Simpson, Chad	RB	5-9	216	23	Morgan State	Miami, Fla.	FA
Tafralis, Adam	QB	6-1	221	25	San Jose State	Daly City, Calif.	FA
Tamme, Jacob	TE	6-3	236	23	Kentucky	Danville, Kent.	D4
Wheeler, Philip	LB	6-2	240	23	Georgia Tech	Columbus, Ga.	D3

The term NFL Rookie is defined as a player who is in his first season of professional football and has not been on the roster of another professional football team for any regular-season or postseason games. A Rookie is designated by an "R" on NFL rosters. Players who have been active in another professional football league or players who have NFL experience, including either preseason training camp or being on an Active List or Inactive List, or on Reserve/Injured or Reserve/Physically Unable to Perform for fewer than six regular-season games, are termed NFL First-Year Players. An NFL First-Year Player is designated by a "1" on NFL rosters. Thereafter, a player is credited with an additional year of experience for each season in which he accumulates six games on the Active List or Inactive List, or on Reserve/Injured or Reserve/Physically Unable to Perform.

Log on to www.colts.com for an up-to-date roster; Age listed is as of September 4, 2008.

COACHING STAFF

Head Coach,
Tony Dungy

Pro Career: Tony Dungy was named head coach of the club on January 22, 2002. The 2008 season marks Dungy's seventh with the Colts and 13th as an NFL head coach. Dungy is 73-23 at the Colts' helm. With an overall mark of 80-28 with the Colts, Dungy became the winningest coach in franchise history at Carolina October 28, 2007. Dungy directed the Colts to a 29-17 win over Chicago in Super Bowl XLI on February 4, 2007, the fourth championship in club history. Dungy joined Tom Flores and Mike Ditka as the only people to earn Super Bowl titles as a player and a head coach. In 2005, Dungy became only the sixth head coach to win 100-plus regular-season games in the first 10 years. He is the NFL's winningest head coach from 1999-2007, and his .661 winning percentage ranks first among active head coaches with 50-plus victories. In 2007, the Colts became the first NFL team with five consecutive 12-plus-win seasons. Dungy held a 54-42 record as head coach with Tampa Bay (1996-2001), with four playoff appearances. At 25, Dungy was the NFL's youngest assistant coach with Pittsburgh in 1981. In 1982, he was promoted from defensive assistant to defensive backs coach, before becoming the league's youngest defensive coordinator in 1984 at age 28. He served as defensive backs coach at Kansas City (1989-1991) and as defensive coordinator at Minnesota (1992-95). Dungy signed with Pittsburgh as a free agent in 1977 and played safety for two seasons. He had 9 interceptions in 30 games for Pittsburgh and played in the club's Super Bowl XIII victory. He was traded to San Francisco in 1979. Career record: 136-74.

Background: Starred as a quarterback at University of Minnesota from 1973-76. Finished career as school's all-time leader in attempts, completions, passing yards and touchdown passes. Two-time team most valuable player, played in Hula Bowl, East-West Shrine Game and Japan Bowl.

Personal: Age 52, born in Jackson, Mich. Tony and his wife, Lauren, are the parents of six children, daughters Tiara and Jade, and sons, Eric, Jordan, and Justin, and the late James Dungy.

ASSISTANT COACHES

Jim Caldwell, associate head coach; born Beloit, Wis. Defensive back Iowa 1973-76. No pro playing experience. College coach: Iowa 1977, Southern Illinois 1978-1980, Northwestern 1981, Colorado 1982-84, Louisville 1985, Penn State 1986-1992, Wake Forest 1993-2000 (head coach). Pro coach: Tampa Bay Buccaneers 2001, joined Colts in 2002.

Clyde Christensen, wide receivers; born Covina, Calif. Quarterback Fresno City College 1975, North Carolina 1976-78. No pro playing experience. College coach: Mississippi 1979, East Tennessee State 1980-82, Temple 1983-85, East Carolina 1986-88, Holy Cross 1989-1990, South Carolina 1991, Maryland 1992-93, Clemson 1994-95. Pro coach: Tampa Bay Buccaneers 1996-2001, joined Colts in 2002.

Richard Howell, asst. strength and conditioning; born Bladenboro, N.C. Quarterback Davidson 1990-93. No pro playing experience. College coach: Davidson 1994-98, North Carolina 1998-99. Pro coach: Barcelona Dragons (NFLE) 1999, joined Colts in 2000.

Gene Huey, running backs; born Uniontown, Pa. Defensive back-wide receiver Wyoming 1965-68. Pro running back San Diego Chargers 1969. College coach: Wyoming 1970-73, New Mexico 1974-76, Nebraska 1977-1986, Arizona State 1987, Ohio State 1988-1991. Pro coach: Joined Colts in 1992.

Ron Meeks, defensive coordinator; born Jacksonville. Defensive back Arkansas State 1972-76. Pro defensive back Hamilton Tiger-Cats (CFL) 1977-79, Ottawa Rough Riders (CFL) 1979, Toronto Argonauts (CFL) 1980-81. College coach: Arkansas State 1984-85, Miami 1986-87, New Mexico State 1988, Fresno State 1989-1990. Pro coach: Dallas Cowboys 1991, Cincinnati Bengals 1992-96, Atlanta Falcons 1997-99, Washington Redskins 2000, St. Louis Rams 2001, joined Colts in 2002.

Pete Metzelaars, offensive quality control/asst. offensive line; born Three Rivers, Mich. Tight end Wabash College 1978-1981. Pro tight end Seattle Seahawks 1982-84, Buffalo Bills 1985-1994, Carolina Panthers 1995, Detroit Lions 1996-97. College coach: Wingate 2003. Pro coach: Barcelona Dragons (NFLE) 2003, joined Colts in 2004.

Tom Moore, offensive coordinator; born Owatanna, Minn. Quarterback Iowa 1957-1960. No pro playing experience. College coach: Iowa 1961-62, Dayton 1965-68, Wake Forest 1969, Georgia Tech 1970-71, Minnesota 1972-73, 1975-76. Pro coach: New York Stars (WFL) 1974, Pittsburgh Steelers 1977-1989, Minnesota Vikings 1990-93, Detroit Lions 1994-96, New Orleans Saints 1997, joined Colts in 1998.

Howard Mudd, offensive line; born Midland, Mich. Guard Hillsdale (Mich.) College 1960-63. Pro offensive lineman San Francisco 49ers 1964-69, Chicago Bears 1969-1971. College coach: California 1972-73. Pro coach: San Diego Chargers 1974-76, San Francisco 49ers 1977, Seattle Seahawks 1978-1982, 1993-97, Cleveland Browns 1983-88, Kansas City Chiefs 1989-1992, joined Colts in 1998.

Mike Murphy, linebackers; born New York, N.Y. Guard/linebacker Huron (S.D.) 1963-66. No pro playing experience. College coach: Vermont 1970-73, Idaho State 1974-76, Western Illinois 1977-78. Pro coach: Saskatchewan Roughriders (CFL) 1979-1983, Chicago Blitz (USFL) 1984, Detroit Lions 1985-89, Arizona Cardinals 1990-93, Seattle Seahawks 1995-97, joined Colts in 1998.

Rod Perry, special assistant to the defense; born Fresno, Calif. Defensive back Colorado 1972-74. Pro cornerback Los Angeles Rams 1975-1982, Cleveland Browns 1983-84. College coach: Columbia 1985, Fresno City College 1986, Fresno State 1987-88. Pro coach: Seattle Seahawks 1989-1991, Los Angeles Rams 1992-94, Houston Oilers 1995-96, San Diego Chargers 1997-2001, Carolina Panthers 2002-06, joined Colts in 2007.

Russ Purnell, special teams; born Chicago. Center Orange Coast (Calif.) J.C. 1966-67, Whittier College 1968-69. No pro playing experience. College coach: Whittier College 1970-71, Southern California 1982-85. Pro coach: Seattle Seahawks 1986-1994, Tennessee Oilers/Titans 1995-98, Baltimore Ravens 1999-2001, joined Colts in 2002.

Bill Teerlinck, defensive assistant; born Champaign, Ill. Defensive end Chadron State 2000-02. No pro playing experience. College coach: Indiana 2003-04, Illinois State 2005-06. Pro coach: Joined Colts in 2007.

John Teerlinck, defensive line; born Rochester, N.Y. Defensive lineman Western Illinois 1970-73. Pro defensive tackle San Diego Chargers 1974-77. College coach: Iowa Lakes J.C. 1977, Eastern Illinois 1978-79, Illinois 1980-82. Pro coach: Chicago Blitz (USFL) 1983-84, Arizona Wranglers/Outlaws (USFL) 1985-86, Cleveland Browns 1989-1990, Los Angeles Rams 1991, Minnesota Vikings 1992-94, Detroit Lions 1995-96, Denver Broncos 1997-2001, joined Colts in 2002.

Ricky Thomas, tight ends; born London, England. Safety Alabama 1983-86. No pro playing experience. College coach: Kentucky 1996, Gardner-Webb 1997. Pro coach: Tampa Bay Buccaneers 1997-2001, joined Colts in 2002.

Jon Torine, strength and conditioning; born Livingston, N.J. Linebacker Springfield (Mass.) College 1991. No pro playing experience. Pro coach: Buffalo Bills 1995-97, joined Colts in 1998.

Alan Williams, defensive backs; born Norfolk, Va. Running back William & Mary 1988-1991. No pro playing experience. College coach: William & Mary 1996-2000. Pro coach: Tampa Bay Buccaneers 2001, joined Colts in 2002.

Carlos Woods, defensive quality control; born Virginia Beach, Va. Linebacker/defensive end Delaware State 1998-2002. No pro playing experience. College coach: Penn State 2004-05. Pro coach: Joined Colts in 2007.

American Football Conference
South Division
Team Colors: Teal, Black, and Gold
Jacksonville Municipal Stadium
One Stadium Place
Jacksonville, Florida 32202
Telephone: (904) 633-6000

2008 SCHEDULE
PRESEASON
Aug. 9   **Atlanta**...............................7:30
Aug. 16 **Miami**...............................7:30
Aug. 23 at Tampa Bay....................7:30
Aug. 28 at **Washington**...................7:00

REGULAR SEASON
Sep. 7   at Tennessee 12:00
Sep. 14 **Buffalo** 1:00
Sep. 21 at Indianapolis 4:15
Sep. 28 **Houston** 1:00
Oct. 5   **Pittsburgh** 8:15
Oct. 12 at Denver 2:05
Oct. 19 BYE
Oct. 26 **Cleveland** 4:05
Nov. 2   at Cincinnati 1:00
Nov. 9   at Detroit 1:00
Nov. 16 **Tennessee** 1:00
Nov. 23 **Minnesota** 1:00
Dec. 1   at Houston (Mon.)..............7:30
Dec. 7   at Chicago 12:00
Dec. 14 **Green Bay** 1:00
Dec. 18 **Indianapolis** (Thu.) 8:15
Dec. 28 at Baltimore 1:00

Stadium: Jacksonville Municipal Stadium
   (opened in 1995)
   •**Capacity:** 67,164
   One Stadium Place
   Jacksonville, Florida 32202
Playing Surface: Grass
Training Camp: Jacksonville Municipal Stadium
   One Stadium Place
   Jacksonville, Florida 32202

JACKSONVILLE MUNICIPAL STADIUM

CLUB OFFICIALS
Chairman and Chief Executive Officer:
   Wayne Weaver
Senior Vice President/Football
   Operations: Paul Vance
Senior Vice President/Chief Financial
   Officer: Bill Prescott
Senior Vice President/Business
   Development: Tim Connolly
Vice President/Player Personnel:
   James Harris
Vice President/Communications and
   Media: Dan Edwards
Executive Director of Corporate
   Sponsorship: Macky Weaver
Executive Director of Football Operations:
   Skip Richardson
Executive Director of Information
   Technology: Bruce Swindell
Executive Director, College and Pro
   Personnel: Gene Smith
Director of Ticket Operations: Tim Bishko
Associate General Counsel: Sashi Brown
Head Athletic Trainer: Michael Ryan
Video Director: Mike Perkins
Equipment Manager: Drew Hampton
Assistant Director of Pro Personnel:
   Louis Clark
Executive Scouts: Terry McDonough,
   Tim Mingey
Regional Scouts: Andy Dengler,
   Chris Driggers, Art Perkins
BLESTO Representative:
   Jason DesJarlais
Scouts: Marty Miller, Larry Wright
Scouting Assistant: Chris Prescott
Coordinator, Communications:
   Hunter Robinson
Manger, Communications:
   Ryan Robinson
Executive Assistant to VP,
   Communications and Media:
   Alisa Abbott
Chair & Chief Executive Officer, Jaguars
   Foundation: Delores Barr Weaver
Executive Director: Peter Racine

COACHING HISTORY
(118-101-0)
Records include postseason games
1995-2002 Tom Coughlin 72-64-0
2003-07   Jack Del Rio 46-37-0

PAID ATTENDANCE
Home 486,791   Away 536,997
Total 1,023,788
Single-game home record,
   74,143 (12/28/98)
Single-season home record,
   561,472 (1998)

2008 DRAFT CHOICES
Round	Name	Pos.	College
1	Derrick Harvey	DE	Florida
2	Quentin Groves	DE	Auburn
5	Thomas Williams	LB	Southern California
	Trae Williams	DB	South Florida
7	Chauncey Washington	RB	Southern California

2007 TEAM RECORD

PRESEASON (3-1)

Date	Result	Opponent
8/11	L 17-18	at Miami
8/18	W 31-19	Tampa Bay
8/23	W 21-13	at Green Bay
8/30	W 31-14	Washington

REGULAR SEASON (11-5)

Date	Result	Opponent	Att.
9/9	L 10-13	Tennessee	65,437
9/16	W 13-7	Atlanta	61,821
9/23	W 23-14	at Denver	76,463
10/7	W 17-7	at Kansas City	76,917
10/14	W 37-17	Houston	63,715
10/22	L 7-29	Indianapolis	67,164
10/28	W 24-23	at Tampa Bay	65,133
11/4	L 24-41	at New Orleans	70,009
11/11	W 28-13	at Tennessee	69,143
11/18	W 24-17	San Diego	66,732
11/25	W 36-14	Buffalo	64,546
12/2	L 25-28	at Indianapolis	57,302
12/9	W 37-6	Carolina	66,090
12/16	W 29-22	at Pittsburgh	58,793
12/23	W 49-11	Oakland	66,905
12/30	L 28-42	at Houston	70,660

POSTSEASON (1-1)

Date	Result	Opponent	Att.
1/5	W 31-29	at Pittsburgh	63,629
1/12	L 20-31	at New England	68,756

SCORE BY PERIODS

Jaguars	92	108	76	135	0	—	411
Opponents	47	104	67	86	0	—	304

2007 TEAM STATISTICS

	Jaguars	Opp.
Total First Downs	328	286
Rushing	127	92
Passing	180	181
Penalty	21	13
3rd Down: Made/Att	100/219	80/201
3rd Down Pct.	45.7	39.8
4th Down: Made/Att	19/33	11/23
4th Down Pct.	57.6	47.8
Possession Avg.	32:08	27:52
Total Net Yards	5719	5021
Avg. Per Game	357.4	313.8
Total Plays	1022	970
Avg. Per Play	5.6	5.2
Net Yards Rushing	2391	1605
Avg. Per Game	149.4	100.3
Total Rushes	522	390
Net Yards Passing	3328	3416
Avg. Per Game	208.0	213.5
Sacked/Yards Lost	31/167	37/244
Gross Yards	3495	3660
Att./Completions	469/288	543/319
Completion Pct.	61.4	58.7
Had Intercepted	8	20
Punts/Average	54/41.6	66/43.5
Net Punting Avg.	54/36.9	66/37.3
Penalties/Yards	76/594	82/636
Fumbles/Ball Lost	18/13	20/10
Touchdowns	50	35
Rushing	18	12
Passing	28	20
Returns	4	3

2007 INDIVIDUAL STATISTICS

PASSING

	Att.	Comp.	Yds.	Pct.	TD	Int.	Tkld.	Rate
Garrard	325	208	2509	64.0	18	3	21/99	102.2
Gray	144	80	986	55.6	10	5	10/68	85.6
Jaguars	469	288	3495	61.4	28	8	31/167	97.1
Opponents	543	319	3660	58.7	20	20	37/244	76.1

SCORING

	TD R	TD P	TD Rt	PAT	FG	Saf	PTS
Scobee	0	0	0	26/27	12/13	0	62
Jones-Drew	9	0	1	0/0	0/0	0	60
R. Williams	0	10	0	0/0	0/0	0	60
Carney	0	0	0	20/21	9/11	0	47
Taylor	5	0	0	0/0	0/0	0	30
G. Jones	2	2	0	0/0	0/0	0	24
M. Jones	0	4	0	0/0	0/0	0	24
Northcutt	0	4	0	0/0	0/0	0	24
Wilford	0	3	0	0/0	0/0	0	18
Lewis	0	2	0	0/0	0/0	0	12
Garrard	1	0	0	0/0	0/0	0	8
Angulo	0	1	0	0/0	0/0	0	6
Broussard	0	1	0	0/0	0/0	0	6
Glenn	0	0	1	0/0	0/0	0	6
Ingram	0	0	1	0/0	0/0	0	6
D. Smith	0	0	1	0/0	0/0	0	6
Toefield	1	0	0	0/0	0/0	0	6
Wrighster	0	1	0	0/0	0/0	0	6
Jaguars	18	28	4	46/48	21/24	0	411
Opponents	12	20	3	32/32	18/23	1	304

2-Pt. Conversions: Garrard, Jaguars 1-2,
Opponents 3-3

RUSHING

	No.	Yds	Avg	LG	TD
Taylor	223	1202	5.4	80t	5
Jones-Drew	167	768	4.6	57t	9
Garrard	49	185	3.8	19	1
G. Jones	42	119	2.8	11	2
Gray	19	57	3.0	15	0
Northcutt	6	27	4.5	8	0
Toefield	13	27	2.1	7	1
R. Williams	1	8	8.0	8	0
Podlesh	2	-2	-1.0	0	0
Jaguars	522	2391	4.6	80t	18
Opponents	390	1605	4.1	42	12

RECEIVING

	No.	Yds	Avg	LG	TD
Wilford	45	518	11.5	35	3
Northcutt	44	601	13.7	55t	4
Jones-Drew	40	407	10.2	43	0
R. Williams	38	629	16.6	80t	10
Lewis	37	391	10.6	25	2
M. Jones	24	317	13.2	48	4
Wrighster	17	123	7.2	36	1
G. Jones	11	99	9.0	27	2
Estandia	9	136	15.1	30	0
Taylor	9	58	6.4	18	0
Angulo	8	81	10.1	22	1
Broussard	4	126	31.5	56	1
Smolko	1	5	5.0	5	0
Toefield	1	4	4.0	4	0
Jaguars	288	3495	12.1	80t	28
Opponents	319	3660	11.5	58t	20

INTERCEPTIONS

	No.	Yds	Avg	LG	TD
Nelson	5	76	15.2	37	0
Knight	4	31	7.8	15	0
B. Williams	3	10	3.3	6	0
Ingram	1	39	39.0	39t	1
Glenn	1	28	28.0	28t	1
Mathis	1	23	23.0	23	0
Peterson	1	12	12.0	12	0
Cousin	1	9	9.0	9	0
Starks	1	7	7.0	7	0
Durant	1	2	2.0	2	0
Fudge	1	0	0.0	0	0
Jaguars	20	237	11.9	39t	2
Opponents	8	215	26.9	75t	1

PUNTING

	No.	Yds	Avg	In 20	LG
Podlesh	54	2249	41.6	14	76
Jaguars	54	2249	41.6	14	76
Opponents	66	2868	43.5	24	70

PUNT RETURNS

	Ret	FC	Yds	Avg	LG	TD
Northcutt	26	13	240	9.2	37	0
Jones-Drew	3	0	28	9.3	17	0
Hawkins	1	0	0	0.0	0	0
Nkang	1	0	0	0.0	0	0
C. Owens	1	1	0	0.0	0	0
Starks	0	0	56	—	56	0
Jaguars	32	14	324	10.1	56	0
Opponents	28	4	218	7.8	24	0

KICKOFF RETURNS

	No.	Yds	Avg	LG	TD
Jones-Drew	31	811	26.2	100t	1
C. Owens	5	94	18.8	31	0
Starks	5	81	16.2	22	0
Toefield	3	57	19.0	26	0
Wrighster	2	35	17.5	29	0
Broussard	1	20	20.0	20	0
Landri	1	0	0.0	0	0
Smolko	1	12	12.0	12	0
Jaguars	49	1110	22.7	100t	1
Opponents	67	1323	19.7	104t	2

FIELD GOALS

	1-19	20-29	30-39	40-49	50+
Scobee	0/0	6/6	3/3	3/4	0/0
Carney	2/2	3/3	3/3	1/3	0/0
Jaguars	2/2	9/9	6/6	4/7	0/0
Opponents	0/0	5/6	7/8	6/8	0/1

SACKS

	No.
Spicer	7.5
Meier	4.0
Hawkins	3.5
Hayward	3.5
McCray	3.0
Stroud	3.0
Henderson	2.0
Peterson	2.0
D. Smith	1.5
Cousin	1.0
Durant	1.0
Ingram	1.0
Mincey	1.0
Nelson	1.0
Pettway	1.0
(group)	1.0
Jaguars	37.0
Opponents	31.0

RECORD HOLDERS
INDIVIDUAL RECORDS—CAREER

Category	Name	Performance
Rushing (Yds.)	Fred Taylor, 1998-2007	10,715
Passing (Yds.)	Mark Brunell, 1995-2003	25,698
Passing (TDs)	Mark Brunell, 1995-2003	144
Receiving (No.)	Jimmy Smith, 1995-2005	862
Receiving (Yds.)	Jimmy Smith, 1995-2005	12,287
Interceptions	Rashean Mathis, 2003-07	21
Punting (Avg.)	Bryan Barker, 1995-2000	43.5
Punt Return (Avg.)	Chris Hudson, 1995-98	10.9
Kickoff Return (Avg.)	Maurice Jones-Drew, 2006-07	27.0
Field Goals	Mike Hollis, 1995-2001	175
Touchdowns (Tot.)	Jimmy Smith, 1995-2005	69
	Fred Taylor, 1998-2007	69
Points	Mike Hollis, 1995-2001	764

INDIVIDUAL RECORDS—SINGLE SEASON

Category	Name	Performance
Rushing (Yds.)	Fred Taylor, 2003	1,572
Passing (Yds.)	Mark Brunell, 1996	4,367
Passing (TDs)	Mark Brunell, 1998	20
Receiving (No.)	Jimmy Smith, 1999	116
Receiving (Yds.)	Jimmy Smith, 1999	1,636
Interceptions	Rashean Mathis, 2006	8
Punting (Avg.)	Bryan Barker, 1998	45.0
Punt Return (Avg.)	Reggie Barlow, 1998	12.9
Kickoff Return (Avg.)	Maurice Jones-Drew, 2006	27.7
Field Goals	Mike Hollis, 1997, 1999	31
Touchdowns (Tot.)	Fred Taylor, 1998	17
Points	Mike Hollis, 1997	134

INDIVIDUAL RECORDS—SINGLE GAME

Category	Name	Performance
Rushing (Yds.)	Fred Taylor, 11-19-00	234
Passing (Yds.)	Mark Brunell, 9-22-96	432
Passing (TDs)	Mark Brunell, 11-29-98	4
	Quinn Gray, 12-30-07	4
Receiving (No.)	Keenan McCardell, 10-20-96	16
Receiving (Yds.)	Jimmy Smith, 9-10-00	291
Interceptions	Many times	2
	Last time by Rashean Mathis, 11-5-06	
Field Goals	Mike Hollis, 12-1-96, 11-30-97, 9-10-00	5
	Josh Scobee, 11-25-07	5
Touchdowns (Tot.)	James Stewart, 10-12-97	5
Points	James Stewart, 10-12-97	30

2008 VETERAN ROSTER

No.	Name	Pos.	Ht.	Wt.	Age	NFL Exp.	College	Hometown	How Acq.	'07 Games/ Starts
85	Angulo, Richard	TE	6-8	266	27	5	Western New Mexico	Albuquerque, N.M.	FA-'07	5/0
69	Barnes, Khalif	T	6-5	325	26	4	Washington	Spring Valley, Calif.	D2 '05	16/14
4	Bouman, Todd	QB	6-2	226	36	10	St. Cloud State	Ruthton, Minn.	FA-'07	0
15	Broussard, John	WR	6-1	176	24	2	San Jose State	Kingwood, Texas	D7a-'07	8/0
76	Collier, Richard	T	6-7	350	26	3	Valdosta State	Shreveport, La.	FA-'06	4/1
56	Durant, Justin	LB	6-1	232	22	2	Hampton	Florence, S.C.	D2-'07	13/8
83	Estandia, Greg	TE	6-8	265	25	2	Nevada-Las Vegas	Moorpark, Calif.	FA-'06	10/0
21	Florence, Drayton	CB	6-0	195	27	6	Tuskegee	Ocala, Fla.	UFA(SD)-'08	16/10
23	Fudge, Jamaal	S	5-9	194	25	3	Clemson	Jacksonville, Fla.	FA-'06	14/0
9	Garrard, David	QB	6-1	245	30	7	East Carolina	Durham, N.C.	D4-'02	12/12
50	Gilbert, Tony	LB	6-0	255	28	6	Georgia	Macon, Ga.	ps(Ariz)-'03	0*
57	Hawkins, Brent	LB	6-2	250	25	3	Illinois State	Godfrey, Ill.	D5-'06	14/0
97	Hayward, Reggie	DE	6-5	275	29	8	Iowa State	Dolton, Ill.	UFA(Den)-'05	12/10
98	Henderson, John	DT	6-7	335	29	7	Tennessee	Nashville, Tenn.	D1-'02	15/15
51	Ingram, Clint	LB	6-2	238	25	3	Oklahoma	Hallsville, Texas	D3-'06	13/11
59	Iwuh, Brian	LB	6-0	235	24	3	Colorado	Houston, Texas	FA-'06	16/1
33	Jones, Greg	FB/RB	6-1	254	27	5	Florida State	Beaufort, S.C.	D2b-'04	16/11
18	Jones, Matt	WR	6-6	232	25	4	Arkansas	Fort Smith, Ark.	D1-'05	12/0
32	Jones-Drew, Maurice	RB/KR	5-7	208	23	3	UCLA	Antioch, Calif.	D2-'06	15/0
73	Kennedy, Jimmy	DT	6-4	320	29	6	Penn State	Yonkers, N.Y.	UFA(Chi)-'08	3/0
66	Landri, Derek	DT	6-2	282	24	2	Notre Dame	Huntington Beach, Calif.	D5c-'07	13/0
17	Lemon, Cleo	QB	6-2	215	29	5	Arkansas State	Greenwood, Miss.	UFA(Mia)-'08	9/7
89	Lewis, Marcedes	TE	6-6	270	24	3	UCLA	Lakewood, Calif.	D1 '06	16/16
67	Manuwai, Vince	G	6-2	336	28	6	Hawaii	Honolulu, Hawaii	D3-'03	15/15
27	Mathis, Rashean	CB	6-1	190	28	6	Bethune-Cookman	Jacksonville, Fla.	D2-'03	14/14
96	McDaniel, Tony	DT	6-7	310	23	3	Tennessee	Columbia, S.C.	FA-'06	4/0
63	Meester, Brad	C	6-3	295	31	9	Northern Iowa	Parkersburg, Iowa	D2-'00	11/11
92	Meier, Rob	DE/DT	6-5	308	31	9	Washington State	W. Vancouver, B.C.	D7b-'00	16/9
94	Mincey, Jeremy	DE	6-3	265	24	2	Florida	Statesboro, Ga.	FA-'06	6/0
25	Nelson, Reggie	S	5-11	198	24	2	Florida	Melbourne, Fla.	D1-'07	16/15
42	Nkang, Chad	DB	5-11	215	23	2	Elon	Hyattsville, Mary.	D7b-'07	16/0
62	Norman, Dennis	C/G	6-5	322	28	8	Princeton	Marlton, N.J.	FA-'04	15/5
86	Northcutt, Dennis	WR/KR	5-11	172	30	9	Arizona	Los Angeles, Calif.	UFA(Cle)-'07	15/11
77	Nwaneri, Uche	G	6-3	320	24	2	Purdue	Garland, Texas	D5a-'07	9/1
24	Owens, Montell	FB	5-10	225	24	3	Maine	Wilmington, Del.	FA-'06	16/0
79	Pashos, Tony	T	6-6	325	28	6	Illinois	Lock Port, Ill.	UFA(Balt)-'07	15/15
54	Peterson, Mike	LB	6-1	238	32	10	Florida	Gainesville, Fla.	UFA(Ind)-'03	10/10
55	Pettway, Kenny	DE	6-4	248	25	3	Grambling State	Gilmer, Texas	FA-'06	10/0
3	Podlesh, Adam	P	5-11	198	25	2	Maryland	Pittsford, N.Y.	D4a-'07	16/0
80	Porter, Jerry	WR	6-2	220	30	9	West Virginia	Washington, D.C.	UFA(Oak)-'08	16/16
	Prioleau, Preston	S	5-11	185	31	10	Virginia Tech	Alvin, S.C.	UFA(Wash)	15/4*
78	Reyes, Tutan	OL	6-3	310	30	9	Mississippi	Queens, N.Y.	FA-'07	1/0
10	Scobee, Josh	K	6-1	192	26	5	Louisiana Tech	Longview, Texas	D5a-'04	8/0
43	Sensabaugh, Gerald	S	6-0	204	25	4	North Carolina	Kingsport, Tenn.	D5-'05	2/2
52	Smith, Daryl	LB	6-2	245	26	5	Georgia Tech	Albany, Ga.	D2a-'04	15/15
47	Smolko, Isaac	TE	6-5	260	25	2	Penn State	Youngstown, Ohio	FA-'07	6/0
95	Spicer, Paul	DE	6-4	295	33	9	Saginaw Valley St.	Indianapolis, Ind.	FA-'00	15/12
31	Starks, Scott	CB	5-9	176	25	4	Wisconsin	St. Louis, Mo.	D3-'05	16/0
28	Taylor, Fred	RB	6-1	228	32	11	Florida	Belle Glade, Fla.	D1a-'98	15/15
81	Walker, Mike	WR	6-2	208	23	2	Central Florida	Orlando, Fla.	D3-'07	0*
29	Williams, Brian	CB	5-11	202	29	7	North Carolina St.	High Point, N.C.	UFA(Minn)-'06	14/14
74	Williams, Maurice	T/G	6-5	302	29	8	Michigan	Detroit, Mich.	D2-'01	15/10
11	Williams, Reggie	WR	6-4	212	25	5	Washington	Tacoma, Wash.	D1-'04	15/6
84	Williamson, Troy	WR	6-1	203	25	4	South Carolina	Jackson, S.C.	T(Minn)-'08	11/8
87	Wrighster, George	TE	6-3	265	27	6	Oregon	Van Nuys, Calif.	D4a-'03	11/6
90	Wyche, James	DE	6-5	275	26	3	Syracuse	Roosevelt, N.Y.	D7a-'06	0*
88	Zelenka, Joe	LS/TE	6-3	256	32	10	Wake Forest	Cleveland, Ohio	FA-'01	16/0

* Bouman did not play in 3 games in '07; Gilbert missed '07 season because of injury; Florence played 16 games with San Diego; Kennedy played 3 games with Chicago; Lemon played 9 games with Miami; Porter played 16 games with Oakland; Prioleau played 15 games with Washington; B. Smith missed '07 season because of injury; Walker missed '07 season because of injury; Williamson played 11 games with Minnesota; Wyche missed '07 season because of injury.

Players lost through free agency (7): CB Aaron Glenn (NO; 5 games in '07), QB Quinn Gray (Hou; 8), S Sammy Knight (NYG; 16), DE Bobby McCray (NO; 14), LB Shantee Orr (Clev; 3), RB LaBrandon Toefield (Car; 2), WR Ernest Wilford (Mia; 16).

Traded—DT Marcus Stroud (9 games in '07) to Buffalo.

Also played with the Jaguars in '07—K John Carney (8 games), LB Marquis Cooper (1), LB Jorge Cordova (2), CB Terry Cousin (16), DT Grady Jackson (9), G Chris Naeole (8), WR Chad Owens (1), LB Pat Thomas (4), S Lamont Thompson (3).

2008 FIRST-YEAR ROSTER

Name	Pos.	Ht.	Wt.	Age	College	Hometown	How Acq.
Bishop, Adam	TE	6-5	248	23	Nevada	Santa Rosa, Calif.	FA
Boston, Alex	DE	6-3	261	23	Florida State	Bartow, Fla.	FA
Brown, Chris	TE	6-0	239	22	Tennessee	Destrehan, La.	FA
Carnahan, Andrew (1)	T	6-7	305	24	Arizona State	Hereford, Texas	D7c-'07
Cotrone, Anthony	FB	6-2	260	22	Maine	Valley Stream, N.Y.	FA
Davis, Charles (1)	TE	6-6	260	25	Purdue	Fraser, Michigan	FA-'07
Edwards, Clyde	WR	5-10	181	22	Grambling	Houston, Texas	FA
Gardner, Isaiah	CB	5-11	197	23	Maryland	Virginia Beach, Va.	FA
Gibbons, Ryan (1)	T	6-6	318	25	Northeastern	Marshfield, Mass.	FA-'06
Goode, Brett (1)	LS	6-1	246	23	Arkansas	Fort Smith, Ark.	FA-'07
Grant, Michael	CB	5-10	193	22	Arkansas	Stone Mountain, Ga.	FA
Groves, Quentin	DE	6-3	259	24	Auburn	Greenville, Miss.	D2-
Harvey, Derrick	DE	6-5	271	21	Florida	Greenbelt, Mary.	D1
Harvey, Jeron	WR	6-5	224	24	Houston	Jacksonville, Fla.	FA
Horrocks, Theo	DT	6-3	282	22	Vanderbilt	Fayetteville, Tenn.	FA
McMahon, Pete (1)	G	6-8	330	26	Iowa	Iowa City, Iowa	FA-'06
Miller, Drew	C/G	6-5	303	23	Florida	Sarasota, Fla.	FA
Moulton, Rashod (1)	CB	5-11	184	27	Fort Valley State	St. Petersburg, Fla.	FA-'07
Myles, Lamar	LB	5-11	230	22	Louisville	Winterhaven, Fla.	FA
Smith, Paul	QB	6-1	208	24	Tulsa	Owasso, Okla.	FA
Terry, D.D. (1)	RB	6-1	202	24	Sam Houston	Willis, Texas	FA-'07
Washington, Chauncey	RB	5-11	224	22	Southern California	Torrance, Calif.	D7
Williams, Thomas	LB	6-1	225	23	Southern California	Vacaville, Calif.	D5a
Williams, Trae	DB	5-10	195	23	South Florida	Plant City, Fla.	D5b
Witherspoon, Brian	CB	5-10	175	23	Stillman	Butler, Ala.	FA
Woods, D'Juan (1)	WR	6-1	210	24	Oklahoma State	Oklahoma City, Okla.	FA-'07

The term NFL Rookie is defined as a player who is in his first season of professional football and has not been on the roster of another professional football team for any regular-season or postseason games. A Rookie is designated by an "R" on NFL rosters. Players who have been active in another professional football league or players who have NFL experience, including either preseason training camp or being on an Active List or Inactive List, or on Reserve/Injured or Reserve/Physically Unable to Perform for fewer than six regular-season games, are termed NFL First-Year Players. An NFL First-Year Player is designated by a "1" on NFL rosters. Thereafter, a player is credited with an additional year of experience for each season in which he accumulates six games on the Active List or Inactive List, or on Reserve/Injured or Reserve/Physically Unable to Perform.

Log on to www.jaguars.com for an up-to-date roster; Age listed is as of September 4, 2008.

COACHING STAFF
Head Coach,
Jack Del Rio

Pro Career: Jack Del Rio was named head coach of the Jaguars on January 17, 2003, becoming the second head coach in franchise history. In 2007, the Jaguars posted an 11-5 record and won the franchise's first playoff game since 1999. In 2006, the Jaguars finished second in the NFL in total defense and third in rushing offense but fell just shy of the playoffs with an 8-8 record. Jacksonville finished with a 12-4 record in 2005 and Del Rio guided the franchise to its first postseason appearance since 1999. In 2004, the Jaguars registered a 9-7 record for the franchise's first winning season since 1999. In 2003, six of the Jaguars' eleven losses were by seven points or less. Del Rio was the defensive coordinator for the Carolina Panthers in 2002, and the team's defense ranked second in the league after finishing thirty-first in 2001. From 1999-2001, he was the linebackers coach for the Baltimore Ravens, helping the team win Super Bowl XXXV. Del Rio previously coached in New Orleans (1997-98). He previously spent 11 years as an NFL linebacker. In 1985, he was a third-round choice of the New Orleans Saints and was named to the NFL's All-Rookie team. Del Rio also played for the Kansas City Chiefs (1987-88), Dallas Cowboys (1989-1991), and Minnesota Vikings (1992-95). He played in the Pro Bowl following the 1994 season. Career record: 46-37.

Background: Four-year starter at linebacker from 1981-84 at Southern California, where he earned consensus All-America honors as a senior and was runner-up for the Lombardi Award. He was co-MVP of the 1985 Rose Bowl. Drafted by baseball's Toronto Blue Jays in 1981, Del Rio batted .340 while playing catcher on USC's baseball team. He has a political science degree from Kansas.

Personal: Age 45, born in Castro Valley, Calif. Jack and his wife, Linda, live in Jacksonville, and have three daughters, Lauren, Hope, and Aubrey, and a son, Luke.

ASSISTANT COACHES

Mark Asanovich, strength and conditioning; born Duluth, Minn. Attended St. Cloud State. No college or pro playing experience. College coach: Ohio State 1984-85, The Citadel 1986. Pro coach: Minnesota Vikings 1995, Tampa Bay Buccaneers 1996-2001, Baltimore Ravens 2002, joined Jaguars in 2003.

Joe DeCamillis, special teams coordinator; born Arvada, Colo. Attended Wyoming. No college or pro playing experience. College coach: Wyoming 1988. Pro coach: Denver Broncos 1989, Miami Dolphins 1990, New York Giants 1993-96, Atlanta Falcons 1997-2006, joined Jaguars in 2007.

Mark Duffner, linebackers; born Annandale, Va. Defensive lineman William & Mary 1972-74. No pro playing experience. College coach: Ohio State 1975-76, Cincinnati 1977-1980, Holy Cross 1981-1991 (head coach 1986-1991), Maryland 1992-1996 (head coach). Pro coach: Cincinnati Bengals 1997-2002, Green Bay Packers 2003-2005, joined Jaguars in 2006.

Les Ebert, asst. strength and conditioning; born Brainerd, Minn. Attended Minnesota-Duluth. No college or pro playing experience. Pro coach: Tampa Bay Buccaneers 1999-2002, joined Jaguars in 2003.

Andy Heck, offensive line; born Fargo, N.D. Tackle Notre Dame 1985-88. Pro tackle Seattle 1989-1993, Chicago 1994-98, Washington 1999-2000. College coach: Virginia 2001-03. Pro coach: Joined Jaguars in 2003.

Donnie Henderson, defensive backs; born Baltimore. Defensive back Utah State 1978-79. No pro playing experience. College coach: Utah State 1983-88, Idaho 1989-1990, California 1992-97, Houston 1998. Pro coach: Baltimore Ravens 1999-2003, N.Y. Jets 2004-05, Detroit Lions 2006-07, joined Jaguars in 2008.

Nate Kaczur, special teams assistant; born Scott City, Kan. Center Utah State 1986-89. No pro playing experience. College coach: Utah State 1991-99, Nebraska-Kerney 2000-03, Idaho 2004-05, Louisiana-Monroe 2006-07. Pro coach: Joined Jaguars in 2008.

Thom Kaumeyer, asst. defensive backs; born LaJolla, Calif. Safety Palomar (JC) College 1985-86, Oregon 1987-88. Pro safety Seattle Seahawks 1989-1990, New York Giants 1991-92. College coach: Palomar College 1991-94, 1998-2000 (head coach 1994), Onward Kashiyama Ltd. (head coach, Tokyo, Japan) 1995-96, San Diego State 2002-06, Tulane 2007, Kentucky 2008. Pro coach: Atlanta Falcons 2001-02, joined Jaguars in 2008.

Dirk Koetter, offensive coordinator; born Pocatello, Idaho. Quarterback Idaho State 1978-1981. No pro playing experience. College coach: San Francisco State 1985, Texas El-Paso 1986-88, Missouri 1989-1993, Boston College 1994-95, Oregon 1996-97, Boise State 1998-2000 (head coach), Arizona State 2001-06 (head coach). Pro coach: Joined Jaguars in 2007.

Ted Monachino, defensive line; born Council Bluffs, Iowa. Defensive lineman Missouri 1988-1990. No pro playing experience. College coach: Texas Christian 1998, Southwest Missouri State 1999, Boise State 2000, Arizona State 2001-2005. Pro coach: Joined Jaguars in 2006.

Todd Monken, wide receivers; born Wheaton, Ill. Quarterback Knox College 1987-1989. No pro playing experience. College coach: Grand Valley State 1989-1990, Notre Dame 1991-92, Eastern Michigan 1993-99, Louisiana Tech 2000-01, Oklahoma State 2002-04, Louisiana State 2005-06. Pro coach: Joined Jaguars in 2007.

Kennedy Pola, running backs; born Pago, Pago, American Samoa. Fullback Southern California 1982-85. No pro playing experience. College coach: UCLA 1992-93, San Diego State 1994-96, Colorado 1997-98, San Diego State 1999, Southern California 2000-2003. Pro coach: Cleveland Browns 2004, joined Jaguars in 2005.

Robert Prince, asst. wide receivers; born Okinawa, Japan. Wide receiver Humboldt State 1985-86. No pro playing experience. College coach: Humboldt State 1989-1990, Montana State 1991, Sacramento State 1992-93, Fort Lewis College 1994-95, Recruit Seagulls (Japan) 1996-97, Portland State 1998-2000, Boise State 2001-03. Pro coach: Atlanta Falcons, 2004-06, joined Jaguars in 2007.

Mike Shula, quarterbacks; born Baltimore. Quarterback Alabama 1984-86. No pro playing experience. College coach: Alabama 2003-06 (head coach). Pro coach: Miami Dolphins 1991-92, Chicago Bears 1993-95, Tampa Bay Buccaneers 1996-99, Miami Dolphins 2000-02, joined Jaguars in 2007.

Mike Tice, asst. head coach/offense; born Bayshore, N.Y. Quarterback Maryland 1977-1980. Pro tight end Seattle Seahawks 1981-1988, 1990-91, Washington Redskins 1989, Minnesota Vikings 1992-1993, 1995. Pro coach: Minnesota Vikings 1996-2005 (head coach 2001-2005), joined Jaguars in 2006.

Gregg Williams, defensive coordinator/ asst. head coach/defense; born Excelsior Springs, Mo. Quarterback Northeast Missouri State 1976-1979. No pro playing experience. College Coach: Houston 1988-89. Pro coach: Houston Oilers/Tennessee Titans 1990-2000, Buffalo Bills (head coach) 2001-03, Washington Redskins 2004-07, joined Jaguars in 2008.

Tom Williams, defensive assistant; born Fort Worth, Texas. Linebacker Stanford 1989-1992. No pro playing experience. College coach: Hawaii 1996-98, Washington 1999-2001, Stanford 2002-04, San Jose State 2005-06. Pro coach: Joined Jaguars in 2007.

American Football Conference
West Division
Team Colors: Red, Gold, and White
One Arrowhead Drive
Kansas City, Missouri 64129
Telephone: (816) 920-9300

2008 SCHEDULE
PRESEASON
Aug. 7   at Chicago..........................7:00
Aug. 16   **Arizona**.............................7:00
Aug. 23   at Miami...........................7:30
Aug. 28   **St. Louis**...........................7:00

REGULAR SEASON
Sep. 7   at New England 1:00
Sep. 14   **Oakland** 12:00
Sep. 21   at Atlanta 1:00
Sep. 28   **Denver** 12:00
Oct. 5   at Carolina 1:00
Oct. 12   BYE
Oct. 19   **Tennessee** 12:00
Oct. 26   at N.Y. Jets.......................1:00
Nov. 2   **Tampa Bay** 12:00
Nov. 9   at San Diego 1:15
Nov. 16   **New Orleans** 12:00
Nov. 23   **Buffalo** 12:00
Nov. 30   at Oakland 1:15
Dec. 7   at Denver 2:05
Dec. 14   **San Diego** 12:00
Dec. 21   **Miami** 12:00
Dec. 28   at Cincinnati 1:00

Stadium: Arrowhead Stadium
            (opened in 1972)
            •**Capacity:** 79,451
            One Arrowhead Drive
            Kansas City, Missouri 64129
Playing Surface: Grass
Training Camp: University of
                Wisconsin-River Falls
                River Falls, WI 54022

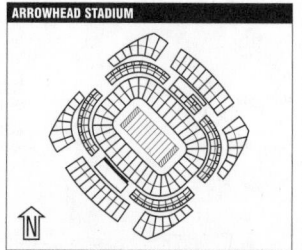

ARROWHEAD STADIUM

CLUB OFFICIALS
Chairman of the Board: Clark Hunt
President: Carl Peterson
Executive Vice President/Chief Operating
    Officer: Denny Thum
Vice President of Player Personnel:
    Bill Kuharich
Assistant to the President - Football
    Operations: Lynn Stiles
Senior Vice President of Administration:
    Bill Newman
Secretary: Jim Seigfreid
Director of Finance/Treasurer: Dale Young
Vice President of Sales and Marketing:
    Tammy Fruits
Director of College Scouting: Chuck Cook
Director of Public Relations: Bob Moore
Associate Director of Public Relations:
    Pete Moris
Director of Stadium Operations:
    Steve Schneider
Director of Development: Ken Blume
Director of Customer Relations:
    Anita Bailey
Director of Ticket and Event Marketing:
    Gary Spani
Executive Director of Player
    Development: Lamonte Winston
Director of Community Relations:
    Brenda Sniezek
Director of Ticket Operations:
    Doug Hopkins
Director of Salary Cap/General Counsel:
    Woodie Dixon
Director of Sales and Marketing:
    David Steffano
Equipment Manager: Mike Davidson
Asst. Equipment Managers: Allen Wright,
    Chris Shropshire, Kyle Crumbaugh
Head Athletic Trainer: David Price
Assistant Athletic Trainers: David Glover,
    Jimmy Ntelekos, Owen Stanley
Director of Video Operations: Pat Brazil
Assistant Director Video Operations:
    Ken Radino
Video Assistant: Josh Schmitt

COACHING HISTORY
Dallas Texans 1960-62
(387-346-12)
Records include postseason games
1960-1974 Hank Stram 129-79-10
1975-77   Paul Wiggin* 11-24-0
1977   Tom Bettis 1-6-0
1978-1982 Marv Levy 31-42-0
1983-86   John Mackovic 30-35-0
1987-88   Frank Gansz...................8-22-1
1989-1998 Marty Schottenheimer...104-65-1
1999-2000 Gunther Cunningham 16-16-0
2001-05   Dick Vermeil..................44-37-0
2006-07   Herm Edwards.............13-20-0
*Released after seven games in 1977

PAID ATTENDANCE
Home 622,541   Away 523,397
Total 1,145,938
Single-game home record,
    *82,893 (10/2/00)
Single-season home record,
    629,569 (1999)
*Arrowhead Stadium attendance: 78,502
Kauffman Stadium attendance: 4,391

2008 DRAFT CHOICES
Round	Name	Pos.	College
1	Glenn Dorsey	DT	Louisiana State
	Branden Albert	T	Virginia
2	Brandon Flowers	DB	Virginia Tech
3	Jamaal Charles	RB	Texas
	Brad Cottam	TE	Tennessee
	DaJuan Morgan	DB	North Carolina St.
4	William Franklin	WR	Missouri
5	Brandon Carr	DB	Grand Valley St.
6	Barry Richardson	T	Clemson
	Kevin Robinson	WR	Utah State
7	Brian Johnston	DE	Gardner-Webb
	Mike Merritt	TE	Central Florida

2007 TEAM RECORD
PRESEASON (0-4)

Date	Result	Opponent
8/11	L 12-16	at Cleveland
8/16	L 10-11	Miami
8/23	L 7-30	New Orleans
8/30	L 3-10	at St. Louis

REGULAR SEASON (4-12)

Date	Result	Opponent	Att.
9/9	L 3-20	at Houston	70,080
9/16	L 10-20	at Chicago	62,095
9/23	W 13-10	Minnesota	78,038
9/30	W 30-16	at San Diego	65,175
10/7	L 7-17	Jacksonville	76,917
10/14	W 27-20	Cincinnati	76,846
10/21	W 12-10	at Oakland	62,240
11/4	L 22-33	Green Bay	78,988
11/11	L 11-27	Denver	77,368
11/18	L 10-13	at Indianapolis	57,294
11/25	L 17-20	at Oakland	76,210
12/2	L 10-24	San Diego	74,874
12/9	L 7-41	at Denver	75,895
12/16	L 17-26	Tennessee	74,976
12/23	L 20-25	at Detroit	59,938
12/30	L 10-13	at N.Y. Jets (OT)	76,737

(OT) Overtime

SCORE BY PERIODS

Chiefs	26	92	39	69	0	—	226
Opponents	66	98	89	79	3	—	335

2007 TEAM STATISTICS

	Chiefs	Opp.
Total First Downs	255	278
Rushing	66	104
Passing	171	156
Penalty	18	18
3rd Down: Made/Att	79/232	65/208
3rd Down Pct.	34.1	31.3
4th Down: Made/Att	13/18	2/11
4th Down Pct.	72.2	18.2
Possession Avg.	29:52	30:08
Total Net Yards	4429	5111
Avg. Per Game	276.8	319.4
Total Plays	1001	980
Avg. Per Play	4.4	5.2
Net Yards Rushing	1248	2089
Avg. Per Game	78.0	130.6
Total Rushes	383	481
Net Yards Passing	3181	3022
Avg. Per Game	198.8	188.9
Sacked/Yards Lost	55/344	37/252
Gross Yards	3525	3274
Att./Completions	563/335	462/276
Completion Pct.	59.5	59.7
Had Intercepted	20	14
Punts/Average	96/45.0	84/44.8
Net Punting Avg.	96/39.1	84/39.5
Penalties/Yards	101/697	95/695
Fumbles/Ball Lost	22/13	21/8
Touchdowns	24	33
Rushing	6	11
Passing	17	17
Returns	1	5

2007 INDIVIDUAL STATISTICS

PASSING	Att.	Comp.	Yds.	Pct.	TD	Int.	Tkld.	Rate
Huard	332	206	2257	62.0	11	13	36/234	76.8
Croyle	224	127	1227	56.7	6	6	17/101	69.9
Thigpen	6	2	41	33.3	0	1	1/9	18.8
L. Johnson	1	0	0	0.0	0	0	0/0	39.6
Kennison	0	0	0	—	0	0	1/0	—
Chiefs	563	335	3525	59.5	17	20	55/344	73
Opponents	462	276	3274	59.7	17	14	37/252	81

SCORING	TD R	TD P	TD Rt	PAT	FG	Saf	PTS
Rayner	0	0	0	14/14	15/22	0	59
Bowe	0	5	0	0/0	0/0	0	30
Gonzalez	0	5	0	0/0	0/0	0	30
L. Johnson	3	1	0	0/0	0/0	0	24
Carney	0	0	0	7/7	3/3	0	16
Allen	0	2	0	0/0	0/0	0	12
Parker	0	2	0	0/0	0/0	0	12
Ko. Smith	2	0	0	0/0	0/0	0	12
Battle	1	0	0	0/0	0/0	0	6
Brackenridge	0	0	1	0/0	0/0	0	6
Webb	0	1	0	0/0	0/0	0	6
Wilson	0	1	0	0/0	0/0	0	6
Medlock	0	0	0	0/0	1/2	0	3
Holmes	0	0	0	0/0	0/0	0	2
Pollard	0	0	0	0/0	0/0	1	2
Chiefs	6	17	1	21/21	19/27	1	226
Opponents	11	17	5	33/33	34/39	1	335

2-Pt. Conversions: Holmes, Chiefs 1-3, Opponents 0-0

RUSHING	No.	Yds	Avg	LG	TD
L. Johnson	158	559	3.5	54	3
Ko. Smith	112	407	3.6	19	2
Holmes	46	137	3.0	11	0
Bennett	20	52	2.6	12	0
Battle	14	47	3.4	6	1
Croyle	7	18	2.6	6	0
G. Harris	9	9	1.0	4	0
Wilson	3	7	2.3	5	0
Kennison	1	5	5.0	5	0
Webb	1	5	5.0	5	0
McGraw	1	4	4.0	4	0
Parker	1	2	2.0	2	0
Huard	9	-1	-0.1	2	0
Drummond	1	-3	-3.0	-3	0
Chiefs	383	1248	3.3	54	6
Opponents	481	2089	4.3	53	11

RECEIVING	No.	Yds	Avg	LG	TD
Gonzalez	99	1172	11.8	31	5
Bowe	70	995	14.2	58	5
L. Johnson	30	186	6.2	30t	1
Webb	28	313	11.2	32	1
Parker	24	298	12.4	24	2
Wilson	24	180	7.5	31	1
Ko. Smith	22	148	6.7	17	0
Kennison	13	101	7.8	18	0
Bennett	10	47	4.7	9	0
Holmes	5	17	3.4	8	0
G. Harris	3	38	12.7	19	0
Grigsby	2	14	7.0	9	0
Dunn	2	9	4.5	8	0
Allen	2	3	1.5	2t	2
Battle	1	4	4.0	4	0
Chiefs	335	3525	10.5	58	17
Opponents	276	3274	11.9	77t	17

INTERCEPTIONS	No.	Yds	Avg	LG	TD
Page	3	37	12.3	37	0
Surtain	2	25	12.5	23	0
Pollard	2	23	11.5	21	0
D. Johnson	2	18	9.0	12	0
Law	2	2	1.0	2	0
D. Edwards	1	18	18.0	18	0
Sapp	1	15	15.0	15	0
Nap. Harris	1	4	4.0	4	0
Chiefs	14	142	10.1	37	0
Opponents	20	231	11.6	61t	0

PUNTING	No.	Yds.	Avg.	In 20	LG
Colquitt	95	4322	45.5	27	81
Chiefs	96	4322	45.0	27	81
Opponents	84	3762	44.8	32	70

PUNT RETURNS	Ret	FC	Yds	Avg	LG	TD
Drummond	32	11	222	6.9	22	0
Kennison	8	3	80	10.0	21	0
Chiefs	40	14	302	7.6	22	0
Opponents	50	19	387	7.7	73t	1

KICKOFF RETURNS	No.	Yds	Avg	LG	TD
Drummond	37	785	21.2	39	0
Sapp	15	251	16.7	32	0
Webb	10	204	20.4	28	0
McBride	4	40	10.0	14	0
Sippio	1	6	6.0	6	0
Chiefs	67	1286	19.2	39	0
Opponents	51	1105	21.7	42	0

FIELD GOALS	1-19	20-29	30-39	40-49	50+
Rayner	0/0	3/3	7/10	5/8	0/1
Carney	0/0	0/0	2/2	1/1	0/0
Medlock	0/0	1/1	0/1	0/0	0/0
Chiefs	0/0	4/4	9/13	6/9	0/1
Opponents	0/0	12/12	11/12	8/11	3/4

SACKS	No.
Allen	15.5
Hali	7.5
D. Johnson	4.0
R. Edwards	3.0
D. Edwards	2.0
Nap. Harris	1.5
Boone	1.0
McBride	1.0
Pollard	1.0
Wilkerson	0.5
Chiefs	37.0
Opponents	55.0

RECORD HOLDERS
INDIVIDUAL RECORDS—CAREER

Category	Name	Performance
Rushing (Yds.)	Priest Holmes, 2001-07	6,070
Passing (Yds.)	Len Dawson, 1962-1975	28,507
Passing (TDs)	Len Dawson, 1962-1975	237
Receiving (No.)	Tony Gonzalez, 1997-2007	820
Receiving (Yds.)	Tony Gonzalez, 1997-2007	9,882
Interceptions	Emmitt Thomas, 1966-1978	58
Punting (Avg.)	Jerrel Wilson, 1963-1977	43.4
Punt Return (Avg.)	Noland Smith, 1967-69	11.1
Kickoff Return (Avg.)	Noland Smith, 1967-69	26.8
Field Goals	Nick Lowery, 1980-1993	329
Touchdowns (Tot.)	Priest Holmes, 2001-07	83
Points	Nick Lowery, 1980-1993	1,466

INDIVIDUAL RECORDS—SINGLE SEASON

Category	Name	Performance
Rushing (Yds.)	Larry Johnson, 2006	1,789
Passing (Yds.)	Trent Green, 2004	4,591
Passing (TDs)	Len Dawson, 1964	30
Receiving (No.)	Tony Gonzalez, 2004	102
Receiving (Yds.)	Derrick Alexander, 2000	1,391
Interceptions	Emmitt Thomas, 1974	12
Punting (Avg.)	Dustin Colquitt, 2007	45.5
Punt Return (Avg.)	Dante Hall, 2003	16.3
Kickoff Return (Avg.)	Dave Grayson, 1962	29.7
Field Goals	Nick Lowery, 1990	34
Touchdowns (Tot.)	Priest Holmes, 2003	27
Points	Priest Holmes, 2003	162

INDIVIDUAL RECORDS—SINGLE GAME

Category	Name	Performance
Rushing (Yds.)	Larry Johnson, 11-20-05	211
Passing (Yds.)	Elvis Grbac, 11-5-00	504
Passing (TDs)	Len Dawson, 11-1-64	6
Receiving (No.)	Tony Gonzalez, 1-2-05	14
Receiving (Yds.)	Stephone Paige, 12-22-85	309
Interceptions	Bobby Ply, 12-16-62	*4
	Bobby Hunt, 10-4-64	*4
	Deron Cherry, 9-29-85	*4
Field Goals	Many times	5
	Last time by Nick Lowery, 9-20-93	
Touchdowns (Tot.)	Abner Haynes, 11-26-61	5
Points	Abner Haynes, 11-26-61	30

*NFL Record

2008 VETERAN ROSTER

No.	Name	Pos.	Ht.	Wt.	Age	NFL Exp.	College	Hometown	How Acq.	'07 Games/ Starts
79	Alabi, Anthony	T	6-5	315	27	4	TCU	San Antonio, Texas	W(Mia)-'08	9/0*
57	Baldwin, Johnny	LB	6-1	230	24	2	Alabama A&M	Bessemer, Ala.	W(Det)-'07	3/0
35	Barksdale, Rashad	CB	6-0	208	24	2	Albany	Hudson, N.Y.	W(Phil)-'07	6/0
70	Boone, Alfonso	DE	6-3	305	32	8	Mt. San Antonio J.C.	Saginaw, Mich.	UFA(Chi)-'07	15/15
82	Bowe, Dwayne	WR	6-2	221	23	2	Louisiana State	Miami, Fla.	D1-'07	16/15
34	Brackenridge, Tyron	CB	5-11	189	24	2	Washington State	Ontario, Calif.	CFA-'07	13/1
2	Colquitt, Dustin	P	6-3	210	26	4	Tennessee	Knoxville, Tenn.	D3-'05	16/0
12	Croyle, Brodie	QB	6-2	206	25	3	Alabama	Rainbow City, Ala.	D3-'06	9/6
1	Cundiff, Billy	K	6-1	201	28	5	Drake	Harlan, Iowa	FA-'08	0*
51	Darche, Jean-Philippe	LS	6-0	242	33	9	McGill	Montreal, Quebec	UFA(Sea)-'07	16/0
89	Darling, Devard	WR	6-1	213	26	5	Washington State	Houston, Texas	UFA(Balt)-'08	16/1*
59	Edwards, Donnie	LB	6-2	224	35	13	UCLA	Chula Vista, Calif.	UFA(SD)-'07	16/16
95	Edwards, Ron	DT	6-3	315	29	8	Texas A&M	Houston, Texas	UFA(Buff)-'06	16/15
84	Foschi, John Paul	TE	6-3	266	26	2	Georgia Tech	Queens, N.Y.	FA-'08	0*
88	Gonzalez, Tony	TE	6-5	251	32	12	California	Huntington Beach, Calif.	D1-'97	16/16
8	Greene, David	QB	6-3	226	26	3	Georgia	Snellville, Ga.	FA-'07	0*
91	Hali, Tamba	DE	6-3	275	24	3	Penn State	Teaneck, N.J.	D1-'06	16/16
50	Harris, Napoleon	LB	6-3	253	29	7	Northwestern	Harvey, Ill.	UFA(Minn)-'07	16/13
98	Harris, Nate	LB	6-0	230	25	2	Louisville	Miami, Fla.	CFA-'07	15/0
46	Hoyte, Oliver	FB	6-3	252	23	3	North Carolina State	Tampa, Fla.	W(Dall)-'08	10/9*
11	Huard, Damon	QB	6-3	218	35	12	Washington	Puyallup, Wash.	FA-'04	11/10
99	Jackson, T.J.	DT	6-0	304	24	2	Auburn	Opelika, Ala.	FA-'08	0*
56	Johnson, Derrick	LB	6-3	242	25	4	Texas	Waco, Texas	D1-'05	16/16
27	Johnson, Larry	RB	6-1	230	28	6	Penn State	State College, Pa.	D1-'03	8/8
73	Jones, Adrian	T	6-4	296	27	5	Kansas	Dallas, Texas	W(NYJ)-'07	7/0*
90	McBride, Turk	DE	6-4	278	23	2	Tennessee	Camden, N.J.	D2-'07	16/1
47	McGraw, Jon	S	6-3	208	29	7	Kansas State	Manhattan, Kan.	UFA(Det)-'07	13/0
77	McIntosh, Damion	T	6-4	320	31	9	Kansas State	Hollywood, Fla.	UFA(Mia)-'07	15/15
64	Niswanger, Rudy	C	6-5	301	25	3	Louisiana State	Monroe, La.	CFA-'06	12/0
9	Novak, Nick	K	5-11	191	27	3	Maryland	Charlottesville, Va.	FA-'08	0*
44	Page, Jarrad	S	6-0	225	23	3	UCLA	San Leandro, Calif.	D7-'06	16/16
22	Patterson, Dimitri	CB	5-10	190	25	3	Tuskegee	Orlando, Fla.	FA-'07	13/0
49	Pollard, Bernard	S	6-1	224	23	3	Purdue	Ft. Wayne, Ind.	D2-'06	16/15
17	Price, Maurice	WR	6-1	197	22	2	Charleston Southern	Orlando, Fla.	CFA-'07	0*
30	Sams, B.J.	KR	5-10	185	27	5	McNeese State	Mandeville, La.	UFA(Balt)-'08	1/0*
83	Sippio, Bobby	WR	6-3	214	27	3	Western Kentucky	Kissimmee, Fla.	FA-'07	9/0
21	Smith, Kolby	RB	5-11	219	23	2	Louisville	Tallahassee, Fla.	D5a-'07	16/6
74	Smith, Wade	C	6-4	296	27	6	Memphis	Dallas, Texas	UFA(NYJ)-'08	14/0*
61	Stallings, Tre	G	6-3	315	25	2	Mississippi	Magnolia, Miss.	D6a-'06	1/0
23	Surtain, Patrick	CB	5-11	195	32	11	Southern Mississippi	New Orleans, La.	T(Mia)-'05	16/16
71	Svitek, Will	T	6-6	300	26	4	Stanford	Newbury, Calif.	D6a-'05	13/4
65	Taylor, Herb	G	6-3	295	23	2	TCU	Houston, Texas	D6-'07	2/0
4	Thigpen, Tyler	QB	6-1	224	24	2	Coastal Carolina	Winnsboro, S.C.	W(Minn)-'07	1/0
55	Thomas, Pat	LB	6-1	237	25	4	North Carolina State	Miami, Fla.	FA-'07	8/1*
93	Tyler, Tank	DT	6-2	306	23	2	North Carolina State	Fayetteville, N.C.	D3-'07	15/1
54	Waters, Brian	G	6-3	320	31	9	North Texas	Waxahachie, Texas	FA-'00	16/16
80	Webb, Jeff	WR	6-2	211	26	3	San Diego State	La Quinta, Calif.	D6b-'06	16/2
25	Wesley, Greg	S	6-2	206	30	9	Arkansas - Pine Bluff	England, Ark.	D3-'00	15/1
53	Williams, Demorrio	LB	6-1	232	28	5	Nebraska	Beckville, Texas	UFA(Atl)-'08	16/16*

* Alabi played 9 games with Miami in '07; Cundiff last active with New Orleans in '06; Darling played 16 games with Baltimore; Foschi last active with Oakland in '06; Greene inactive for 1 game; Hoyte played 10 games with Dallas; Jackson last active with Atlanta in '06; Jones played 7 games with the N.Y. Jets; Novak last active with Washington in '06; Price missed '07 season because of injury; Sams played 1 game with Baltimore; W. Smith played 14 games with N.Y. Jets; Thomas played 4 games with Jacksonville and 4 games with Kansas City; Williams played 16 games with Atlanta.

Traded—DE Jared Allen (16 games in '07) to Minnesota.

Players lost through free agency (7): LB Keyaron Fox (Pitt; 10 games in '07), FB Boomer Grigsby (Mia; 13), WR Samie Parker (Den; 15), CB Benny Sapp (Minn; 14), C Casey Wiegmann (Den; 16), DE Jimmy Wilkerson (TB; 16), TE Kris Wilson (Phil; 16).

Also played with Chiefs in '07—LB Kendrell Bell (11 games), K John Carney (5), WR Eddie Drummond (12), TE Jason Dunn (16), FB Greg Hanoian (0), RB Gilbert Harris (4), RB Priest Holmes (4), WR Eddie Kennison (8), LB William Kershaw (1), CB Ty Law (16), K Justin Medlock (1), K Dave Rayner (10), DT James Reed (4), DE Khreem Smith (2), T Chris Terry (11 games), T Kyle Turley (7), G John Welbourn (16).

2008 FIRST-YEAR ROSTER

Name	Pos.	Ht.	Wt.	Age	College	Hometown	How Acq.
Albert, Branden	T/G	6-5	316	23	Virginia	Glen Burnia, Md.	D1b
Allan, Michael (1)	TE	6-6	254	24	Whitworth	Bellevue, Wash.	D7-'07
Arthur, Jabari	WR	6-4	219	26	Akron	Montreal, Quebec	FA
Barth, Connor	K	5-11	193	22	North Carolina	Wilmington, N.C.	FA
Battle, Jackie (1)	RB	6-2	238	24	Houston	Humble, Texas	FA-'07
Carr, Brandon	CB	6-0	207	22	Grand Valley State	Flint, Mich.	D5
Charles, Jamaal	RB	5-11	199	21	Texas	Port Arthur, Texas	D3a
Cottam, Brad	TE	6-7	269	23	Tennessee	Germantown, Tenn.	D3b
Cox, Mike	FB	6-0	252	23	Georgia Tech	Lewisberry, Pa.	FA
Dingle, Johnny	DE	6-1	265	23	West Virginia	Miami, Fla.	FA
Dorsey, Glenn	DT	6-1	297	23	Louisiana State	Gonzalez, La.	D1a
Flowers, Brandon	CB	5-9	187	22	Virginia Tech	Delray Beach, Fla.	D2
Franklin, Will	WR	6-0	209	22	Missouri	St. Louis, Mo.	D4
Girault, Ron	S	5-10	204	22	Rutgers	Montvale, N.J.	FA
Harris, Erick (1)	S	5-11	208	25	Liberty	Crestview, Fla.	FA
Jackson, Steven (1)	FB	6-2	246	24	Clemson	Columbia, S.C.	FA
Johnston, Brian	DE	6-4	269	22	Gardner-Webb	San Diego, Calif.	D7a
Kuale, E.J. (1)	LB	6-1	229	25	Louisiana State	Daytona Beach, Fla.	FA
Leffew, Travis (1)	T	6-4	292	25	Louisville	Lexington, Ky.	FA-'07
Leggett, Maurice	CB	5-11	188	21	Valdosta	Pittsburgh, Pa.	FA
Lokey, Derek	DT	6-1	287	22	Texas	Denton, Texas	FA
Manderino, Chris (1)	FB	6-0	231	25	California	Newport Beach, Calif.	FA
McDuffie, Chris	G	6-4	330	24	Clemson	Danville, Va.	FA
McMahan, Kevin (1)	WR	6-2	192	25	Maine	Rochester, N.Y.	FA
McRae, Kalvin	RB	5-9	203	23	Ohio	Avondale Estates, Ga.	FA
Merritt, Michael	TE	6-4	263	24	Central Florida	West Palm Beach, Fla.	D7b
Morgan, DaJuan	S	6-0	203	22	North Carolina State	Riviera Beach, Fla.	D3c
Murray, Maurice	DT	6-3	334	23	New Mexico State	Long Beach, Calif.	FA
Octavien, Steve	LB	6-0	238	23	Nebraska	Naples, Fla.	FA
Parker, Jason	DE	6-3	258	23	Arizona	San Diego, Calif.	FA
Richardson, Barry	T	6-6	319	22	Clemson	Mount Pleasant, S.C.	D6a
Robinson, Kevin	WR	5-11	196	23	Utah State	Fresno, Calif.	D6b
Saint-Dic, Jonal	DE	6-0	253	23	Michigan State	Elizabeth, N.J.	FA
Shackleford, Ken (1)	T	6-5	365	23	Georgia	Villa Rica, Ga.	FA
Smith, Rob (1)	G	6-3	311	24	Tennessee	Ft. Thomas, Ky.	FA
Swan, Luke	WR	5-11	191	23	Wisconsin	Fennimore, Wisc.	FA

The term NFL Rookie is defined as a player who is in his first season of professional football and has not been on the roster of another professional football team for any regular-season or postseason games. A Rookie is designated by an "R" on NFL rosters. Players who have been active in another professional football league or players who have NFL experience, including either preseason training camp or being on an Active List or Inactive List, or on Reserve/Injured or Reserve/Physically Unable to Perform for fewer than six regular-season games, are termed NFL First-Year Players. An NFL First-Year Player is designated by a "1" on NFL rosters. Thereafter, a player is credited with an additional year of experience for each season in which he accumulates six games on the Active List or Inactive List, or on Reserve/Injured or Reserve/Physically Unable to Perform.

Log on to www.kcchiefs.com for an up-to-date roster; Age listed is as of September 4, 2008.

COACHING STAFF

Head Coach,
Herm Edwards

Pro Career: Herm Edwards was named the tenth head coach in Chiefs franchise history on January 9, 2006. He enters his eighth season as an NFL head coach and his 29th season in the league as either a player, a scout or coach. He rejoined the Chiefs in 2006 after spending six seasons with Kansas City as a scout (1990-91), defensive backs coach (1992-94) and pro personnel scout (1995). Since the start of the 2001 campaign, only Tony Dungy (seven) and Bill Belichick (six) have guided their clubs to more playoff appearances than Edwards (four). In 2006, he became the first head coach in franchise history to guide the Chiefs to the playoffs in his initial season with the club. His 9-7 record tied for the most victories by a first-year coach in franchise annals as the Chiefs became the fifth team since 2000 to bounce back from an 0-2 start and still earn a spot in the postseason. After leading the Chiefs to the playoffs in 2006, Edwards became one of just five coaches in NFL history to guide two different squads to a playoff berth in their debut campaign with those teams. Edwards also led the N.Y. Jets to the postseason in 2001. Edwards began his pro coaching career as a participant of the NFL's Minority Coaching Fellowship program with Kansas City in 1989 and is the first graduate of the program to go on to become the head coach of the franchise for which he served his fellowship. He joined Tony Dungy's staff in Tampa Bay as assistant head coach/defensive backs coach, spending five seasons (1996-2000) in that capacity and was part of a Tampa Bay squad that reached the NFC Championship Game for the first time in 20 years in 1999. Edwards then enjoyed a five-year stint (2001-05) as the head coach of the N.Y. Jets. He led the Jets to 39 regular season wins and coached the club in a franchise-record five postseason contests. Career record: 54-64.

Background: Edwards played cornerback collegiately for California (1972, 1974), Monterey Peninsula (Calif.) J.C. (1973), and San Diego State (1976). Edwards entered the NFL as a rookie free agent with Philadelphia in 1977 and went on to start 135 consecutive regular season contests at cornerback for the Eagles, producing a franchise-record 38 combined INTs in regular and postseason action. He also started seven postseason contests for Philadelphia, including Super Bowl XV. He concluded his NFL playing career with the L.A. Rams and Atlanta in 1986. Collegiately, he was the defensive backs coach at San Jose State (1987-89).

Personal: Age 54, born in Fort Monmouth, N.J. He and his wife Lia have a son, Marcus and two daughters, Gabrielle and Vivian.

ASSISTANT COACHES

Bob Bicknell, offensive line; born Holliston, Mass. Tight end Boston College 1988-1991. No pro playing experience. College coach: Boston 1993-97, Temple 2006. Pro coach: Frankfurt Galaxy (NFLEL) 1998-99, Berlin Thunder (NFLEL) 2000-03, Cologne Centurions (NFLEL) 2004-05, joined Chiefs in 2007.

Gunther Cunningham, defensive coordinator/linebackers; born Munich, Germany. Linebacker/placekicker Oregon 1966-68. No pro playing experience. College coach: Oregon 1969-1971, Arkansas 1972, Stanford 1973-76, California 1977-1980. Pro coach: Hamilton Tiger-Cats (CFL) 1981, Baltimore/Indianapolis Colts 1982-84, San Diego Chargers 1985-1990, L.A. Raiders 1991-94, Kansas City Chiefs 1995-2000 (head coach 1999-2000), Tennessee Titans 2001-03, rejoined Chiefs in 2004.

Dick Curl, asst. head coach/quarterbacks; born Chester, Pa. Quarterback Richmond 1958-1962. No pro playing experience. College coach: Trenton State 1973-74 (head coach 1974), Rutgers 1975-1980, 1983-89, Virginia 1981-82, Boston College 1990. Pro coach: Barcelona Dragons (NFLEL) 1991-97, Frankfurt Galaxy (NFLEL) 1998-2000 (head coach), New York Jets 2003-05, joined Chiefs in 2006.

Joe D'Alessandris, asst. offensive line, born Aliquippa, Pa. Guard Western Carolina 1972-76. No pro playing experience. College coach: Western Carolina 1977-78, Livingston 1979-1983, Memphis 1984-85, UT-Chattanooga 1986-89, Samford 1993, Texas A&M 1994, Pittsburgh 1996, Duke 1997-2001, Georgia Tech 2002-07. Pro coach: Ottawa Rough Riders (CFL) 1990, Birmingham Fire (WLAF) 1991-92, Memphis 1995, joined Chiefs in 2008.

Jon Embree, tight ends; born Los Angeles. Tight end Colorado 1983-86. Pro tight end Los Angeles Rams 1987-88. College coach: Colorado 1991, 1993-2002, UCLA 2003-05. Pro coach: Joined Chiefs in 2006.

Chan Gailey, offensive coordinator; born Gainesville, Ga. Quarterback Florida 1971-73. No pro playing experience. College coach: Florida 1974-75, Troy State 1976-78, 1983-84 (head coach 1983-84), Air Force 1979-1982, Samford 1993 (head coach), Georgia Tech 2002-07 (head coach). Pro coach: Denver Broncos 1985-1990, Birmingham Fire (WLAF) 1991-92 (head coach), Pittsburgh Steelers 1994-97, Dallas Cowboys 1998-99 (head coach), Miami Dolphins 2000-01, joined Chiefs in 2008.

David Gibbs, defensive backs; born Mount Airy, N.C. Defensive back Colorado 1987-1990. No pro playing experience. College coach: Oklahoma 1991-92, Colorado 1993-94, Kansas 1995-96, Minnesota 1997-2000, Auburn 2005. Pro coach: Denver Broncos 2001-04, joined Chiefs in 2006.

Mike Ketchum, defensive quality control/asst. linebackers; born Ft. Benning, Ga. Offensive/defensive lineman University of the South 1995-98. College coach: Cumberland 1999-2000, Vanderbilt 2001-02, Iowa 2003-05. Pro coach: Joined Chiefs in 2006.

Tim Krumrie, defensive line; born Menomonie, Wis. Defensive tackle Wisconsin 1979-1982, Pro defensive tackle Cincinnati Bengals 1983-1994, Pro coach: Cincinnati Bengals 1995-2002, Buffalo Bills 2003-05, joined Chiefs in 2006.

Curtis Modkins, running backs; born Marlin, Texas. Running back TCU 1989-1992. No pro playing experience. College coach: TCU 1995-97, New Mexico 1998-2001, Georgia Tech 2002-07. Pro coach: Joined Chiefs in 2008.

Kevin Patullo, offensive assistant/quality control; born Hillsborough, N.J. Quarterback/wide receiver South Florida 1999-2001. College coach: South Florida 2002-03, Arizona 2004-06. Pro coach: Joined Chiefs in 2007.

Eric Price, wide receivers, born Pullman, Wash. Wide receiver Dixie (Utah) J.C. 1986-87, Weber State 1988-89. No pro playing experience. College coach: Weber State 1990, Hawaii 1991, Miami 1992-93, Cal Poly-San Luis Obispo 1994-95, Northern Arizona 1996-97, Washington State 1998-2000, Texas-El Paso 2004-07. Pro coach: N.Y. Jets 2001-02, joined Chiefs in 2008.

Mike Priefer, special teams; born Cleveland. Attended U.S. Naval Academy. No college or pro playing experience. College coach: Navy 1994-96, Youngstown State 1997-98, Virginia Military Institute 1999, Northern Illinois 2000-01. Pro coach: Jacksonville Jaguars 2002, New York Giants 2003-05, joined Chiefs in 2006.

Brent Salazar, asst. strength and conditioning; born Denver. Attended New Mexico. No college or pro playing experience. College coach: New Mexico 2002-03, Nevada-Las Vegas 2004, Pacific 2006. Pro coach: Joined Chiefs in 2007.

Cedric Smith, strength and conditioning; born Enterprise, Alabama. Fullback Florida 1986-89. Pro fullback Minnesota Vikings 1990, New Orleans Saints 1991, Washington Redskins 1994-95, Arizona Cardinals 1996-98. Pro coach: Denver Broncos 2001-06, joined Chiefs in 2007.

Nate Wainwright, manager of football administration; born Wilton, Iowa. Attended Iowa. No college or pro playing experience. Pro coach: N.Y. Jets 2001-05, joined Chiefs in 2006.

**American Football Conference
East Division**
Team Colors: Aqua, Coral, Blue, and
White
**7500 S.W. 30th Street
Davie, Florida 33314
Telephone:** (954) 452-7000

2008 SCHEDULE
PRESEASON

Aug. 9	**Tampa Bay**	7:30
Aug. 16	at Jacksonville	7:30
Aug. 23	**Kansas City**	7:30
Aug. 28	at New Orleans	7:00

REGULAR SEASON

Sep. 7	**N.Y. Jets**	1:00
Sep. 14	at Arizona	1:15
Sep. 21	at New England	1:00
Sep. 28	BYE	
Oct. 5	**San Diego**	1:00
Oct. 12	at Houston	12:00
Oct. 19	**Baltimore**	1:00
Oct. 26	**Buffalo**	1:00
Nov. 2	at Denver	2:05
Nov. 9	**Seattle**	1:00
Nov. 16	**Oakland**	1:00
Nov. 23	**New England**	1:00
Nov. 30	at St. Louis	12:00
Dec. 7	at Buffalo (Toronto)	4:05
Dec. 14	**San Francisco**	1:00
Dec. 21	at Kansas City	12:00
Dec. 28	at N.Y. Jets	1:00

Stadium: Dolphin Stadium
(opened in 1987)
• **Capacity:** 75,192
2269 Dan Marino Blvd.
Miami Gardens, Florida 33056
Playing Surface: Grass (PAT)
Training Camp: Nova Southeastern Univ.
7500 S.W. 30th Street
Davie, Florida 33314

DOLPHIN STADIUM

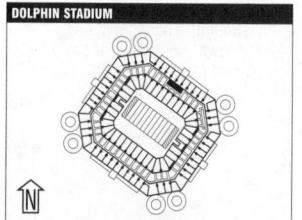

CLUB OFFICIALS
Owner/Chairman of the Board:
H. Wayne Huizenga
Owner: Stephen M. Ross
Chief Executive Officer, Dolphins
Enterprises: Joe Bailey
President & Chief Operating Officer:
Bryan Wiedmeier
Executive Vice President-Football
Operations: Bill Parcells
General Manager: Jeff Ireland
Head Coach: Tony Sparano
Senior Vice President-Finance &
Administration: Jill R. Strafaci
Senior Vice President-Operations:
Bill Galante
Senior Vice President-Media Relations:
Harvey Greene
Vice President-Information Technology:
Tery Howard
General Counsel/Football Administration:
Matt Thomas
Assistant Director of Player Personnel:
Brian Gaine
Director of College Scouting:
Chris Grier
Director of Player Development:
John Gamble
Senior Director of Internet & Publications:
Scott Stone
Alumni, Youth & Special Projects:
Nat Moore
Director of Youth Programs: Twan Russell
Director of Media Relations: Neal Gulkis
Director of Event Entertainment:
Dorie Grogan
Director of Programming & Production:
Jeff Griffith
Director of Cheerleaders: Emily Snow
Director of Records & Archives:
Kristin Hingston
Director of Community Relations:
Ilona Wolpin
Head Athletic Trainer: Kevin O'Neill
Equipment Manager: Joe Cimino
Video Director: Dave Hack
Team Security Investigator:
Stuart Weinstein

COACHING HISTORY
(389-286-4)
Records include postseason games

1966-69	George Wilson	15-39-2
1970-1995	Don Shula	274-147-2
1996-99	Jimmy Johnson	38-31-0
2000-04	Dave Wannstedt*	43-33-0
2004	Jim Bates	3-4-0
2005-06	Nick Saban	15-17-0
2007	Cam Cameron	1-15-0

*Resigned after nine games in 2004

PAID ATTENDANCE
Home 576,959   Away 579,803
Total 1,116,079
Single-game home record,
75,283 (10/27/96)
Single-season home record, 592,161
(1999)

2008 DRAFT CHOICES

Round	Name	Pos.	College
1	Jake Long	T	Michigan
2	Phillip Merling	DE	Clemson
	Chad Henne	QB	Michigan
3	Kendall Langford	DE	Hampton
4	Shawn Murphy	G	Utah State
6	Jalen Parmele	RB	Toledo
	Donald Thomas	G	Connecticut
	Lex Hilliard	RB	Montana
7	Lionel Dotson	DE	Arizona

2007 TEAM RECORD
PRESEASON (2-2)

Date	Result		Opponent
8/11	W	18-17	Jacksonville
8/16	W	11-10	at Kansas City
8/25	L	28-31	Tampa Bay
8/30	L	0-7	at New Orleans

REGULAR SEASON (1-15)

Date	Result		Opponent	Att.
9/9	L	13-16	at Washington (OT)	90,163
9/16	L	20-37	Dallas	71,615
9/23	L	28-31	at New York Jets	77,197
9/30	L	17-35	Oakland	70,621
10/7	L	19-22	at Houston	70,156
10/14	L	31-41	at Cleveland	73,198
10/21	L	28-49	New England	71,951
10/28	L	10-13	New York Giants	81,176
11/11	L	10-13	Buffalo	70,615
11/18	L	7-17	at Philadelphia	68,934
11/26	L	0-3	at Pittsburgh	57,704
12/2	L	13-40	New York Jets	71,109
12/9	L	17-38	at Buffalo	71,018
12/16	W	22-16	Baltimore (OT)	70,287
12/23	L	7-28	at New England	68,756
12/30	L	25-38	Cincinnati	70,461

(OT) Overtime

SCORE BY PERIODS

Dolphins	32	77	68	84	6 —	267
Opponents	110	146	52	126	3 —	437

2007 TEAM STATISTICS

	Dolphins	Opp.
Total First Downs	283	318
Rushing	107	129
Passing	162	165
Penalty	14	24
3rd Down: Made/Att	81/218	98/208
3rd Down Pct.	37.2	47.1
4th Down: Made/Att	13/22	6/10
4th Down Pct.	59.1	60.0
Possession Avg.	29:05	30:55
Total Net Yards	4600	5475
Avg. Per Game	287.5	342.2
Total Plays	989	983
Avg. Per Play	4.7	5.6
Net Yards Rushing	1569	2456
Avg. Per Game	98.1	153.5
Total Rushes	389	544
Net Yards Passing	3031	3019
Avg. Per Game	189.4	188.7
Sacked/Yards Lost	42/288	30/167
Gross Yards	3319	3186
Att./Completions	558/318	409/242
Completion Pct.	57.0	59.2
Had Intercepted	16	14
Punts/Average	77/43.2	62/43.3
Net Punting Avg.	77/36.6	62/37.3
Penalties/Yards	91/732	73/604
Fumbles/Ball Lost	25/13	20/8
Touchdowns	29	50
Rushing	14	18
Passing	12	28
Returns	3	4

2007 INDIVIDUAL STATISTICS

PASSING

PASSING	Att.	Comp.	Yds.	Pct.	TD	Int.	Tkld.	Rate
Lemon	309	173	1773	56.0	6	6	25/166	71.0
Green	141	85	987	60.3	5	7	7/53	72.6
Beck	107	60	559	56.1	1	3	10/69	62.0
M. Booker	1	0	0	0.0	0	0	0/0	39.6
Dolphins	558	318	3319	57.0	12	16	42/288	69.6
Opponents	409	242	3186	59.2	28	14	30/167	92.4

SCORING

SCORING	TD R	TD P	TD Rt	PAT	FG	Saf	PTS
Feely	0	0	0	26/26	21/23	0	89
Brown	4	1	0	0/0	0/0	0	32
Lemon	4	0	0	0/0	0/0	0	24
Ginn	0	2	1	0/0	0/0	0	18
Hagan	0	2	0	0/0	0/0	0	14
Gado	3	0	0	0/0	0/0	0	18
Camarillo	0	2	0	0/0	0/0	0	12
Martin	0	2	0	0/0	0/0	0	12
Peelle	0	2	0	0/0	0/0	0	12
Beck	1	0	0	0/0	0/0	0	6
M. Booker	0	1	0	0/0	0/0	0	6
Chatman	1	0	0	0/0	0/0	0	6
Cobbs	1	0	0	0/0	0/0	0	6
Lehan	0	0	1	0/0	0/0	0	6
Taylor	0	0	1	0/0	0/0	0	6
Dolphins	14	12	3	26/26	21/23	0	267
Opponents	18	28	4	49/49	28/33	1	437

2-Pt. Conversions: Brown, Hagan,
Dolphins 2-2, Opponents 1-1

RUSHING

RUSHING	No.	Yds	Avg	LG	TD
Brown	119	602	5.1	60	4
Chatman	128	515	4.0	30	1
L. Booker	28	125	4.5	22	0
Gado	35	104	3.0	20t	3
Lemon	31	102	3.3	11	4
Cobbs	15	47	3.1	12	1
Green	7	32	4.6	23	0
R. Williams	6	15	2.5	6	0
Beck	9	12	1.3	8	1
M. Booker	2	12	6.0	12	0
Mauia	4	5	1.3	3	0
Ginn	4	3	0.8	7	0
Chambers	1	-5	-5.0	-5	0
Dolphins	389	1569	4.0	60	14
Opponents	544	2456	4.5	59t	18

RECEIVING

RECEIVING	No.	Yds	Avg	LG	TD
M. Booker	50	556	11.1	26	1
Brown	39	389	10.0	43	1
Ginn	34	420	12.4	54	2
Martin	34	303	8.9	28	2
Chambers	31	415	13.4	28	0
Hagan	29	373	12.9	22t	2
Peelle	29	228	7.9	35	2
L. Booker	28	237	8.5	22	0
Chatman	27	161	6.0	22	0
Gado	12	106	8.8	35	0
Camarillo	8	160	20.0	64t	2
Cobbs	2	20	10.0	11	0
Mauia	2	5	2.5	5	0
Halterman	1	7	7.0	7	0
Hadnot	0	-2	—	-2	0
Dolphins	318	3319	10.4	64t	12
Opponents	242	3186	13.2	70t	28

INTERCEPTIONS

INTERCEPTIONS	No.	Yds	Avg	LG	TD
J. Allen	3	15	5.0	13	0
Goodman	2	23	11.5	18	0
Porter	2	19	9.5	14	0
Pope	2	0	0.0	0	0
Taylor	1	36	36.0	36t	1
Daniels	1	29	29.0	29	0
Hill	1	24	24.0	24	0
W. Allen	1	14	14.0	14	0
Lehan	1	0	0.0	0	0
Dolphins	14	160	11.4	36t	1
Opponents	16	232	14.5	36	0

PUNTING

PUNTING	No.	Yds.	Avg.	In 20	LG
Fields	77	3327	43.2	10	61
Dolphins	77	3327	43.2	10	61
Opponents	62	2682	43.3	25	64

PUNT RETURNS

PUNT RETURNS	Ret	FC	Yds	Avg	LG	TD
Ginn	24	15	230	9.6	87t	1
Dolphins	24	15	230	9.6	87t	1
Opponents	39	7	387	9.9	49	0

KICKOFF RETURNS

KICKOFF RETURNS	No.	Yds	Avg	LG	TD
Ginn	63	1433	22.7	52	0
Cobbs	5	44	8.8	11	0
M. Booker	2	3	1.5	3	0
Chatman	2	31	15.5	21	0
Hagan	2	25	12.5	14	0
Fifita	1	0	0.0	0	0
Mauia	1	4	4.0	4	0
Mruczkowski	1	9	9.0	9	0
Peelle	1	0	0.0	0	0
Camarillo	0	3	—	3	0
Dolphins	78	1552	19.9	52	0
Opponents	50	1292	25.8	98t	2

FIELD GOALS

FIELD GOALS	1-19	20-29	30-39	40-49	50+
Feely	0/0	7/7	6/6	7/9	1/1
Dolphins	0/0	7/7	6/6	7/9	1/1
Opponents	1/1	10/11	7/7	6/9	4/5

SACKS

SACKS	No.
Taylor	11.0
Porter	5.5
Roth	3.0
W. Allen	2.0
Holliday	2.0
Moses	1.5
R. Wright	1.5
Lehan	1.0
Thomas	1.0
Traylor	1.0
Crowder	0.5
Dolphins	30.0
Opponents	42.0

RECORD HOLDERS
INDIVIDUAL RECORDS—CAREER

Category	Name	Performance
Rushing (Yds.)	Larry Csonka, 1968-1974, 1979	6,737
Passing (Yds.)	Dan Marino, 1983-1999	61,361
Passing (TDs)	Dan Marino, 1983-1999	420
Receiving (No.)	Mark Clayton, 1983-1992	550
Receiving (Yds.)	Mark Duper, 1982-1992	8,869
Interceptions	Jake Scott, 1970-75	35
Punting (Avg.)	John Kidd, 1994-97	44.2
Punt Return (Avg.)	Jeff Ogden, 2000-01	13.7
Kickoff Return (Avg.)	Mercury Morris, 1969-1975	26.5
Field Goals	Olindo Mare, 1997-2006	245
Touchdowns (Tot.)	Mark Clayton, 1983-1992	82
Points	Olindo Mare, 1997-2006	1,048

INDIVIDUAL RECORDS—SINGLE SEASON

Category	Name	Performance
Rushing (Yds.)	Ricky Williams, 2002	1,853
Passing (Yds.)	Dan Marino, 1984	*5,084
Passing (TDs)	Dan Marino, 1984	48
Receiving (No.)	O.J. McDuffie, 1998	90
Receiving (Yds.)	Mark Clayton, 1984	1,389
Interceptions	Dick Westmoreland, 1967	10
Punting (Avg.)	John Kidd, 1996	46.3
Punt Return (Avg.)	Jeff Ogden, 2000	17.0
Kickoff Return (Avg.)	Duriel Harris, 1976	32.9
Field Goals	Olindo Mare, 1999	39
Touchdowns (Tot.)	Mark Clayton, 1984	18
Points	Olindo Mare, 1999	144

INDIVIDUAL RECORDS—SINGLE GAME

Category	Name	Performance
Rushing (Yds.)	Ricky Williams, 12-1-02	228
Passing (Yds.)	Dan Marino, 10-23-88	521
Passing (TDs)	Bob Griese, 11-24-77	6
	Dan Marino, 9-21-86	6
Receiving (No.)	Chris Chambers, 12-4-05	15
Receiving (Yds.)	Chris Chambers, 12-4-05	238
Interceptions	Dick Anderson, 12-3-73	*4
Field Goals	Olindo Mare, 10-17-99	6
Touchdowns (Tot.)	Paul Warfield, 12-15-73	4
	Mark Ingram, 11-27-94	4
Points	Paul Warfield, 12-15-73	24
	Mark Ingram, 11-27-94	24

*NFL Record

MIAMI DOLPHINS

2008 VETERAN ROSTER

No.	Name	Pos.	Ht.	Wt.	Age	NFL Exp.	College	Hometown	How Acq.	'07 Games/Starts
32	Allen, Jason	S	6-1	213	25	3	Tennessee	Muscle Shoals, Ala.	D1-'06	16/9
25	Allen, Will	CB	5-10	196	30	8	Syracuse	Syracuse, N.Y.	UFA(NYG)-'06	16/16
56	Anderson, Charlie	LB	6-4	245	26	5	Mississippi	Jackson, Miss.	UF(Hou)-'08	16/5*
51 t-	Ayodele, Akin	LB	6-2	250	29	7	Purdue	Irving, Texas	T(Dall)-'08	16/14*
9	Beck, John	QB	6-2	216	27	2	Brigham Young	Mesa, Ariz.	D2a-'07	5/4
37	Bell, Yeremiah	S	6-0	200	30	5	Eastern Kentucky	Winchester, Ky.	D6-03	1/1
23	Brown, Ronnie	RB	6-0	232	26	4	Auburn	Cartersville, Ga.	D1-'05	7/7
47	Bryan, Courtney	S	6-0	202	23	2	New Mexico State	San Jose, Calif.	FA-'07	12/0
83	Camarillo, Greg	WR	6-1	190	26	3	Stanford	Menlo Park, Calif.	W(SD)-'07	15/0
72	Carey, Vernon	T	6-5	335	27	5	Miami	Miami, FL	D1-'04	16/16
38	Cobbs, Patrick	RB	5-8	210	25	3	North Texas	Tecumseh, Okla.	FA-'06	14/0
26	Crocker, Chris	S	5-11	192	28	6	Marshall	Chesapeake, Va.	UFA(Atl)-'08	14/14*
52	Crowder, Channing	LB	6-2	245	24	4	Florida	Atlanta, Ga.	D3-'05	11/10
29	Daniels, Travis	CB	6-1	192	25	4	Louisiana State	Hollywood, Fla.	D4-'05	16/5
69	Darilek, Trey	G-C	6-5	310	27	3	Texas-El Paso	San Antonio, Texas	FA-'08	0*
28	Davis, Keith	S	5-11	207	29	6	Sam Houston State	Italy, Texas	UFA(Dall)-'08	14/1*
92	Denney, John	LS	6-5	270	29	4	Brigham Young	Thornton, Colo.	FA-'05	16/0
81 t-	Fasano, Anthony	TE	6-4	265	24	3	Notre Dame	Verona, N.J.	T(Dall)-'08	16/6*
3	Feely, Jay	K	5-10	210	32	8	Michigan	Tampa, Fla.	UFA(NYG)-'07	16/0
95 t-	Ferguson, Jason	DT	6-3	312	33	12	Georgia	Nettleton, Miss.	T(Dall)-'08	1/1*
2	Fields, Brandon	P	6-5	236	24	2	Michigan State	Toledo, Ohio	D7b-'07	16/0
19	Ginn, Ted Jr.	WR	5-11	178	23	2	Ohio State	Cleveland, Ohio	D1-'07	16/9
43	Glymph, Junior	LB	6-5	270	28	4	Carson-Newman	Newberry, S.C.	FA-'08	0*
21	Goodman, André	CB	5-10	185	30	7	South Carolina	Greenville, S.C.	UFA(Det)-'06	13/4
46	Grigsby, Boomer	FB	5-11	249	26	4	Illinois State	Canton, Ill.	FA-'08	13/1*
82	Hagan, Derek	WR	6-2	203	23	3	Arizona State	Palmdale, Calif.	D3-'06	16/1
80	Halterman, Aaron	TE	6-5	255	26	2	Indiana	Greenwood, Ind.	FA-'07	9/0
24	Hill, Renaldo	S	5-11	190	29	8	Michigan State	Detroit, Mich.	UFA(Oak)-'06	7/7
91	Holliday, Vonnie	DE	6-5	288	32	11	North Carolina	Camden, S.C.	FA-'05	12/12
33	Jones, Nathan	CB	5-10	183	26	5	Rutgers	Scotch Plains, N.J.	UFA(Dall)-'08	15/0*
85	Kircus, David	WR	6-0	190	28	4	Grand Valley State	Imlay City, Mich.	FA-'08	0*
30	Lehan, Michael	CB	6-0	190	28	6	Minnesota	Hopkins, Minn.	FA-'06	15/14
#	Liewinski, Chris	G	6-5	325	33	10	Indiana	Sterling Heights, Mich.	UFA(Ariz)-'07	16/14
88	Martin, David	TE	6-4	265	29	8	Tennessee	Norfolk, Va.	UFA(GB)-'07	15/15
45	Mauia, Reagan	FB	6-0	270	24	2	Hawaii	Lodi, Calif.	D6a-'07	16/9
4	McCown, Josh	QB	6-4	215	29	7	Sam Houston State	Jacksonville, Texas	UFA(Oak)-'08	9/9*
50	Miles, Edmond	LB	6-0	230	24	2	Iowa	Tallahassee, Fla.	FA-'07	16/0
74	Moses, Quentin	DE	6-5	260	24	2	Georgia	Athens, Ga.	FA-'07	7/1
#	Murczkowski, Gene	G	6-2	305	28	5	Purdue	Cleveland, Ohio	WAI(NE)-'07	15/0
68	Ndukwe, Ikechuku	G/C	6-4	338	26	2	Northwestern	Dublin, Ohio	FA-'07	0*
93	Ninkovich, Rob	DE	6-2	252	24	3	Purdue	New Lenox, Ill.	WAI(NO)-'07	4/0
87	Peelle, Justin	TE	6-4	255	29	7	Oregon	Dublin, Calif.	UFA(SD)-'06	16/10
17	Perry, Tab	WR	6-3	208	26	4	UCLA	Milpitas, Calif.	FA-'08	2/1*
55	Porter, Joey	LB	6-3	250	31	10	Colorado State	Bakersfield, Calif.	FA-'07	16/15
16	Rayner, Dave	K	6-2	210	25	4	Michigan State	Oxford, Mich.	FA-'08	11/0*
#	Rosenthal, Mike	T	6-7	320	31	10	Notre Dame	Mishawaka, Ind.	FA-'07	0*
98	Roth, Matt	DE	6-4	272	25	4	Iowa	Villa Park, Ill.	D2-'05	13/9
89	Ryan, Sean	TE	6-5	265	28	5	Boston College	Buffalo, N.Y.	UFA(NYJ)-'08	10/1*
64	Satele, Samson	C	6-3	300	23	2	Hawaii	Kailua, Hawaii	D2b-'07	16/16
#	Schulters, Lance	S	6-2	202	33	11	Hofstra	Brooklyn, N.Y.	FA-'07	7/4
65	Smiley, Justin	G	6-3	311	26	5	Alabama	Ellabell, Ga.	UFA(SF)-'08	8/8*
96	Soliai, Paul	DE	6-4	344	24	2	Utah	Pago Pago, American Samoa	D4-'07	8/0
#	Spragan, Donnie	LB	6-3	242	32	8	Stanford	Union City, Calif.	UFA(Den)-'05	16/5
94	Starks, Randy	DE	6-3	312	24	5	Maryland	Waldorf, Md.	UFA(Tenn)-'08	14/4*
99	Taylor, Jason	DE	6-6	255	34	12	Akron	Woodland Hills, Pa.	D3a-'97	16/16
41	Thomas, Joey	CB	6-1	190	28	3	Montana State	Burien, Wash.	FA-'08	0*
#	Tillman, Travares	S	6-1	205	30	8	Georgia Tech	Lyons, Ga.	UFA(Car)-'05	3/1
59	Torbor, Reggie	LB	6-2	250	27	5	Auburn	Baton Rouge, La.	UFA(NYG)-'08	16/6*
18	Wilford, Ernest	WR	6-4	218	29	5	Virginia Tech	Richmond, Va.	UFA(Jax)-'08	16/14*
34	Williams, Ricky	RB	5-10	225	31	8	Texas	San Diego, Calif.	T(NO)-'02	1/0
90	Wright, Rodrique	DE	6-5	300	24	2	Texas	Houston, Texas	D7b-'06	13/9

* Anderson played 16 games with Houston in '07; Ayodele played 16 games with Dallas; Crocker played 14 games with Atlanta; Darilek inactive 4 games in '06 with Miami; Glymph last active with Dallas in '06; Jones played 15 games with Dallas; Kircus last active with Denver in '06; McCown played 9 games with Oakland; Ndukwe inactive for 1 game; Perry played 2 games with Cincinnati; Rayner played 10 games with Kansas City and 1 game with San Diego; Rosenthal last active with Minnesota in '06; Ryan played 10 games with N.Y. Jets; Smiley played 8 games with San Francisco; Starks played 14 games with Tennessee; Thomas last active with New Orleans in '05; Torbor played 16 games with N.Y. Giants; Wilford played 16 games with Jacksonville.

t- Dolphins traded for Ayodele (Dall), Fasano (Dall), Ferguson (Dall).

Traded—RB Lorenzo Booker (7 games in '07) to Philadelphia.

Players lost through free agency (4): RB Jesse Chatman (NYJ; 14 games in '07), G Rex Hadnot (Cle; 16), QB Cleo Lemon (Jax; 9), LB Derrick Pope (Minn; 16).

Also played with Dolphins in '07—T Anthony Alabi (10 games), WR Marty Booker (16), Anthony Bryant (1), WR Chris Chambers (6), S Donovin Darius (3), NT Steve Fifita (13), RB Samkon Gado (5), DE Akbar Gbaja-Biamila (1), QB Trent Green (5), CB Tuff Harris (1), G Cory Lekkerkerker (11), DT Chas Page (6), Jerem Perry (4), WR Kerry Reed (1), DE Derreck Robinson (6), T L.J. Shelton (16), LB Kelvin Smith (4), LB Zach Thomas (5), Lamont Thompson (3), DT Keith Traylor (15), Mark Washington (3), S Cameron Worrell (12).

2008 FIRST-YEAR ROSTER

Name	Pos.	Ht.	Wt.	Age	College	Hometown	How Acq.
Babers, Scorpio	CB	5-11	195	24	Sam Houston State	Italy, Texas	FA
Bess, Davone	WR	5-10	190	22	Hawaii	Oakland, Calif.	FA
Billingsley, Will	CB	5-10	195	24	North Carolina A&T	Fort Wayne, Ind.	FA
Brown, Titus	LB	6-3	247	22	Mississippi State	Tuscaloosa, Ala.	FA
Byrne, Mike	CB	6-5	303	21	Delaware	Lititz, Pa.	FA
Carpenter, Dan	K	6-2	216	22	Montana	Helena, Mont.	FA
Dotson, Lionel	DE	6-4	295	23	Arizona	Houston, Texas	D7
Foster, Jayson	WR	5-7	170	23	Georgia Southern	Canton, Ga.	FA
Gore, Dan	T	6-5	290	23	Boise State	Prosser, Wash.	FA
Heerspink, Daren	T	6-6	314	24	Portland State	Lynden, Wash.	FA
Henne, Chad	QB	6-3	228	23	Michigan	Wyomissing, Pa.	D2b
Hilliard, Lex	RB	5-11	234	24	Montana	Kalispell, Mont.	D6c
Langford, Kendall	DE	6-6	287	22	Hampton	Petersburg, Va.	D3
Long, Jake	T	6-7	315	23	Michigan	Lapeer, Mich.	D1
Lymon, Selwyn	WR	6-3	216	21	Purdue	Fort Wayne, Ind.	FA
Merling, Phillip	DE	6-4	275	23	Clemson	St. Matthews, S.C.	D2a
Mormino, Drew (1)	C/G	6-3	299	24	Central Michigan	Buffalo Grove, Ill.	D6b-'07
Mulligan, Matthew	TE	6-4	258	23	Maine	Enfield, Me.	FA
Murphy, Shawn	G	6-4	314	25	Utah State	Alpine, Utah	D4
Parmele, Jalen	RB	5-11	225	22	Toledo	Midland, Mich.	D6a
Poppinga, Kelly	LB	6-1	240	26	Brigham Young	Evanston, Wyo.	FA
Robertson, Kory	DT	6-2	345	23	Virginia Tech	Martinsville, Va.	FA
Saunders, Keith	LB	6-3	240	23	Alabama	Willingboro, N.J.	FA
Smith, Kelvin (1)	LB	6-2	233	24	Syracuse	Spring Valley, N.Y.	D7a-'07
Thomas, Donald	G	6-4	305	22	Connecticut	New Haven, Conn.	D6b
Toribio, Anthony	DT	6-1	305	23	Carson-Newman	Miami, Fla.	FA
Wilson, Julius (1)	T	6-4	327	24	Alabama-Birmingham	Bradenton, Fla.	FA-'07
Wynn, Justin	WR	6-2	190	23	Grand Rapids (Mich.) C.C.	Fort Wayne, Ind.	FA

The term NFL Rookie is defined as a player who is in his first season of professional football and has not been on the roster of another professional football team for any regular-season or postseason games. A Rookie is designated by an "R" on NFL rosters. Players who have been active in another professional football league or players who have NFL experience, including either preseason training camp or being on an Active List or Inactive List, or on Reserve/Injured or Reserve/Physically Unable to Perform for fewer than six regular-season games, are termed NFL First-Year Players. An NFL First-Year Player is designated by a "1" on NFL rosters. Thereafter, a player is credited with an additional year of experience for each season in which he accumulates six games on the Active List or Inactive List, or on Reserve/Injured or Reserve/Physically Unable to Perform.

Log on to www.miamidolphins.com for an up-to-date roster; Age listed is as of September 4, 2008.

MIAMI DOLPHINS

COACHING STAFF
Head Coach,
Tony Sparano
Pro Career: Became the eighth head coach in Dolphins history on January 16, 2008. Had spent the previous five seasons (2003-07) on the staff of the Dallas Cowboys, during which time the team made three playoff appearances. He tutored the Cowboys' offensive line the last three years while also holding the title of assistant head coach the past two seasons. He coached the team's tight ends his first two seasons in Dallas. Prior to joining the Cowboys, Sparano had NFL stops in Cleveland (1999-2000), Washington (2001) and Jacksonville (2002). Career record: 0-0.
Background: Sparano was a four-year letterman as a center at the University of New Haven, where he earned his degree in criminal law. He began his coaching career at his alma mater in 1984 before moving on to Boston University as offensive coordinator in 1989. He returned to New Haven as the school's head coach in 1994, and manned that spot for the next five years.
Personal: Age 46, born in West Haven, Conn. He and his wife, Jeanette, have two sons, Tony and Andrew, and one daughter, Ryan Leigh.

ASSISTANT COACHES
John Bonamego, special teams coordinator; born Waynesboro, Pa. Wide receiver/quarterback Central Michigan 1985-86. No pro playing experience. College coach: Maine 1988-91, Lehigh 1992, Army 1993-98. Pro coach: Jacksonville Jaguars 1999-2002, Green Bay Packers 2003-05, New Orleans Saints 2006-07, joined Dolphins in 2008.
Todd Bowles, asst. head coach/secondary; born Elizabeth, N.J. Defensive back Temple 1982-85. Pro defensive back Washington Redskins 1986-1990, 1992-93, San Francisco 49ers 1991. College coach: Morehouse College 1997, Grambling State 1998-99. Pro coach: New York Jets 2000, Cleveland Browns 2001-04, Dallas Cowboys 2005-07, joined Dolphins in 2008.
Steve Bush, offensive quality control; born Denville, N.J. Defensive back Southern Connecticut State 1978-1981. No pro playing experience. College coach: Southern Connecticut State 1982-83, Springfield College 1984-85, New Haven 1986-87, Boston University 1988-89, Syracuse 2000-04. Pro coach: Joined Dolphins in 2008.
David Corrao, defensive quality control; Running back University of San Diego 1992. No pro playing experience. College coach: Syracuse 2000-03, Northeastern 2004, Mississippi 2005-07. Pro coach: Joined Dolphins in 2008.
George DeLeone, tight ends; born New Haven, Conn. Offensive lineman Connecticut 1966-67. No pro playing experience. College coach: Southern Connecticut State 1970-79, Rutgers 1980-83, Holy Cross 1984, Syracuse 1985-1996, 1998-2004, Mississippi 2005, Temple 2006-07. Pro coach: San Diego Chargers 1997, joined Dolphins in 2008.
Karl Dorrell, wide receivers; born Alameda, Calif. Wide receiver UCLA 1982-86. No pro playing experience. College coach: UCLA 1988, 2003-07 (head coach 2003-07), Central Florida 1989, Northern Arizona 1990-91, Colorado 1992-93, 1995-98, Arizona State 1994, Washington 1999. Pro coach: Denver Broncos 2000-02, joined Dolphins in 2008.
George Edwards, inside linebackers; born Siler City, N.C. Linebacker Duke 1985-89. No pro playing experience. College coach: Florida 1990-91, Appalachian State 1992-95, Duke 1996, Georgia 1997. Pro coach: Dallas Cowboys 1998-2001, Washington Redskins 2002-03, Cleveland Browns 2004, joined Dolphins in 2005.
Dan Henning, offensive coordinator; born Bronx, N.Y. Quarterback William & Mary 1962-64. Pro quarterback San Diego Chargers 1964, 1966-67. College coach: Florida State 1968-1970, 1974, Virginia Tech 1971, 1973, Boston College 1994-96 (head coach). Pro coach: Houston Oilers 1972, New York Jets 1976-78, 1998-2000, Miami Dolphins 1979-1980, Washington Redskins 1981-82, 1987-88, Atlanta Falcons 1983-86 (head coach), San Diego Chargers 1989-1991 (head coach), Detroit Lions 1992-93, Buffalo Bills 1997, Carolina Panthers 2002-06, re-joined Dolphins in 2008.
Steve Hoffman, kicking; born Camden, N.J. Quarterback/running back/wide receiver Dickinson College 1977-1980. Pro punter Washington Federals (USFL) 1983. College coach: Miami 1985-87. Pro coach: Dallas Cowboys 1989-2004, Atlanta Falcons 2006, joined Dolphins in 2007.
David Lee, quarterbacks; born Cape Girardeau, Mo. Quarterback Vanderbilt 1971-74. No pro playing experience. College coach: Tennessee-Martin 1975-76, Vanderbilt 1977, Mississippi 1978-1982, New Mexico 1983, Arkansas 1984-88, 2001-02, 2007, Texas-El Paso 1989-1993 (head coach), Rice 1994-2000. Pro coach: Dallas Cowboys 2003-06, joined Dolphins in 2008.
Evan Marcus, head strength and conditioning; born Cranford, N.J. Tackle Ithaca College 1986-1990. No pro playing experience. College coach: Arizona State 1991-92, Rutgers 1993, Maryland 1994, Texas 1995-97, Louisville 1998-99, Virginia 2003-06. Pro coach: New Orleans Saints 2000-02, Atlanta Falcons 2007, joined Dolphins in 2008.
Mike Maser, offensive line; born Clayton,

N.Y. Guard Buffalo 1967-1970. No pro playing experience. College coach: Marshall 1973, Bluefield State College 1974-78, Maine 1979-1980, Boston College 1981-93. Pro coach: Jacksonville Jaguars 1994-2002, Carolina Panthers 2003-06, joined Dolphins in 2008.
Paul Pasqualoni, defensive coordinator; born New Haven, Conn. Linebacker Penn State 1968-1971. No pro playing experience. College coach: Southern Connecticut State 1976-81, Western Connecticut 1982-86 (head coach), Syracuse 1987-2004 (head coach 1991-2004). Pro coach: Dallas Cowboys 2005-07, joined Dolphins in 2008.
Dave Puloka, asst. strength and conditioning; born Arlington, Mass. Linebacker Holy Cross 1997-2000. No pro playing experience College coach: Stevens Institute of Technology 2005, Virginia 2006. Pro coach: Atlanta Falcons 2007, joined Dolphins in 2008.
Jim Reid, outside linebackers; Defensive back Maine 1970-72. No pro playing experience. College coach: Massachusetts 1973-1991, Richmond 1992-93, 1995-2003 (head coach 1995-2003), Boston College 1994, Syracuse 2004, Bucknell 2005, VMI 2006-07 (head coach). Pro coach: Joined Dolphins in 2008.
Kacy Rodgers, defensive line; born Humboldt, Tennessee. Linebacker/defensive end Tennessee 1988-1991. Pro linebacker Shreveport Pirates (CFL) 1994. College coach: Tennessee-Martin 1994-97, Louisiana-Monroe 1998, Middle Tennessee State 1999-2001, Arkansas 2002. Pro coach: Dallas Cowboys 2003-07, joined Dolphins in 2008.
James Saxon, running backs; born Beaufort, S.C. Running back American River (Calif.) J.C. 1984-85, San Jose State 1986-87. Pro running back Kansas City Chiefs 1988-1991, Miami Dolphins 1992-94, Philadelphia Eagles 1995. College coach: Rutgers 1997-98, Menlo College 1999. Pro coach: Buffalo Bills 2000, Kansas City Chiefs 2001-07, joined Dolphins in 2008.

American Football Conference
East Division
Team Colors: Blue, Red, Silver, and White
Gillette Stadium
One Patriot Place
Foxborough, Massachusetts 02035
Telephone: (508) 543-8200

2008 SCHEDULE
PRESEASON
Aug. 7	**Baltimore**	7:30
Aug. 17	at Tampa Bay	8:00
Aug. 22	**Philadelphia**	7:30
Aug. 28	at N.Y. Giants	7:00

REGULAR SEASON
Sep. 7	**Kansas City**	1:00
Sep. 14	at N.Y. Jets	4:15
Sep. 21	**Miami**	1:00
Sep. 28	BYE	
Oct. 5	at San Francisco	1:15
Oct. 12	at San Diego	5:15
Oct. 20	**Denver** (Mon.)	8:30
Oct. 26	**St. Louis**	1:00
Nov. 2	at Indianapolis	8:15
Nov. 9	**Buffalo**	1:00
Nov. 13	**N.Y. Jets** (Thu.)	8:15
Nov. 23	at Miami	1:00
Nov. 30	**Pittsburgh**	4:15
Dec. 7	at Seattle *	5:15
Dec. 14	at Oakland	1:15
Dec. 21	**Arizona**	1:00
Dec. 28	at Buffalo	1:00

* Sunday night games in Weeks 11-17 subject to change

Stadium: Gillette Stadium
   (opened in 2002)
   • **Capacity:** 68,756
   One Patriot Place
   Foxborough, Massachusetts 02035
Playing Surface: FieldTurf
Training Camp: Gillette Stadium
            Foxborough, MA 02035

GILLETTE STADIUM

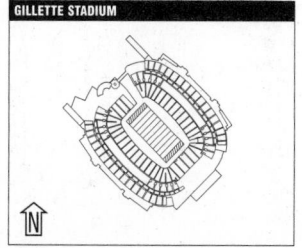

CLUB OFFICIALS
Chairman & CEO: Robert K. Kraft
President: Jonathan A. Kraft
Vice President of Player Personnel:
   Scott Pioli
Chief Administrative Officer:
   Jim Hausmann
Director of Strategic Initiatives and Retail
   Operations: Brian Bilello
Vice President of Human Resources:
   Robin Boudreau
Chief Operating Officer of TeamOps
   Security: Mark Briggs
Equipment Manager: Don Brocher
Vice President of Information
   Technology: Pat Curley
Video Director: Jimmy Dee
Vice President of Marketing Operations:
   Jennifer Ferron
Director of New Business Development &
   Operational Initiatives: Jessica Gelman
Director of Ticket Operations:
   Maryruth Hughey
Vice President of Media Relations:
   Stacey James
General Counsel: Richard Karelitz
Publisher / Editor-in-Chief and Director of
   Interactive Media: Fred Kirsch
Vice President of Sales: Murray Kohl
President of New England Patriots
   Charitable Foundation: Josh Kraft
Chief Financial Officer: John Mitchell
Vice President of Stadium Business
   Development and External Affairs:
   Dan Murphy
Director of Football/Head Coach
   Administration: Berj Najarian
Vice President of Stadium Operations:
   Jim Nolan
Executive Director of Corporate
   Development: David Pearlstein
Executive Producer of Broadcast
   Production: Matt Smith
Director of Cheerleaders: Tracy Sormanti
Executive Director of Community Affairs:
   Andre Tippett
Head Athletic Trainer: Jim Whalen

COACHING HISTORY
Boston 1960-1970
(387-362-9)
Records include postseason games
1960-61	Lou Saban*	7-12-0
1961-68	Mike Holovak	53-47-9
1969-1970	Clive Rush**	5-16-0
1970-72	John Mazur***	9-21-0
1972	Phil Bengtson	1-4-0
1973-78	Chuck Fairbanks****	46-41-0
1978	Hank Bullough-Ron Erhardt#	0-1-0
1979-1981	Ron Erhardt	21-27-0
1982-84	Ron Meyer##	18-16-0
1984-89	Raymond Berry	51-41-0
1990	Rod Rust	1-15-0
1991-92	Dick MacPherson	8-24-0
1993-96	Bill Parcells	34-34-0
1997-99	Pete Carroll	28-23-0
2000-07	Bill Belichick	105-40-0

Records include postseason games
   *Released after five games in 1961
   **Released after seven games in 1970
   ***Resigned after nine games in 1972
****Suspended for final regular-season game in 1978
   #Co-coaches
   ##Released after eight games in 1984

PAID ATTENDANCE
Home 579,182   Away 551,845
Total 1,131,207
Single-game home record,
   70,262 (12/12/04)
Single-season home record,
   579,182 (2007)

2008 DRAFT CHOICES
Round	Name	Pos.	College
1	Jerod Mayo	LB	Tennessee
2	Terrence Wheatley	DB	Colorado
3	Shawn Crable	LB	Michigan
	Kevin O'Connell	QB	San Diego St.
4	Jonathan Wilhite	DB	Auburn
5	Matt Slater	WR	UCLA
6	Bo Ruud	LB	Nebraska

2007 TEAM RECORD
PRESEASON (2-2)

Date	Result	Opponent
8/10	L 10-13	at Tampa Bay
8/17	L 24-27	Tennessee
8/24	W 24-7	at Carolina
8/30	W 27-20	N.Y. Giants

REGULAR SEASON (16-0)

Date	Result	Opponent	Att.
9/9	W 38-14	at N.Y. Jets	77,900
9/16	W 38-14	San Diego	68,756
9/23	W 38-7	Buffalo	68,756
10/1	W 34-13	at Cincinnati	66,113
10/7	W 34-17	Cleveland	68,756
10/14	W 48-27	at Dallas	63,984
10/21	W 49-28	at Miami	71,951
10/28	W 52-7	Washington	68,756
11/4	W 24-20	at Indianapolis	57,540
11/18	W 56-10	at Buffalo	71,338
11/25	W 31-28	Philadelphia	68,756
12/3	W 27-24	at Baltimore	71,382
12/9	W 34-13	Pittsburgh	68,756
12/16	W 20-10	N.Y. Jets	68,756
12/23	W 28-7	Miami	68,756
12/29	W 38-35	at N.Y. Giants	79,110

POSTSEASON (2-1)

1/12	W 31-20	Jacksonville	68,756
1/20	W 21-12	San Diego	68,756
2/3	L 14-17	vs. N.Y. Giants,	71,101
		at Glendale, Arizona	

SCORE BY PERIODS

Patriots	134	199	104	152	0	—	589
Opponents	41	96	58	79	0	—	274

2007 TEAM STATISTICS

	Patriots	Opp.
Total First Downs	393	278
Rushing	124	91
Passing	243	172
Penalty	26	15
3rd Down: Made/Att	92/191	63/187
3rd Down Pct.	48.2	33.7
4th Down: Made/Att	15/21	11/20
4th Down Pct.	71.4	55.0
Possession Avg.	32:33	27:27
Total Net Yards	6580	4613
Avg. Per Game	411.3	288.3
Total Plays	1058	933
Avg. Per Play	6.2	4.9
Net Yards Rushing	1849	1572
Avg. Per Game	115.6	98.3
Total Rushes	451	360
Net Yards Passing	4731	3041
Avg. Per Game	295.7	190.1
Sacked/Yards Lost	21/128	47/340
Gross Yards	4859	3381
Att./Completions	586/403	526/314
Completion Pct.	68.8	59.7
Had Intercepted	9	19
Punts/Average	45/40.5	76/43.4
Net Punting Avg.	45/36.1	76/36.9
Penalties/Yards	78/690	96/764
Fumbles/Ball Lost	14/6	25/12
Touchdowns	75	34
Rushing	17	7
Passing	50	23
Returns	8	4

2007 INDIVIDUAL STATISTICS
PASSING

PASSING	Att.	Comp.	Yds.	Pct.	TD	Int.	Tkld.	Rate
T. Brady	578	398	4806	68.9	50	8	21/128	117.2
Cassel	7	4	38	57.1	0	1	0/0	32.7
Gutierrez	1	1	15	100.0	0	0	0/0	118.8
Patriots	586	403	4859	68.8	50	9	21/128	116.0
Opponents	526	314	3381	59.7	23	19	47/340	78.1

SCORING

SCORING	TD R	TD P	TD Rt	PAT	FG	Saf	PTS
Moss	0	23	0	0/0	0/0	0	138
Gostkowski	0	0	0	74/74	21/24	0	137
Welker	0	8	0	0/0	0/0	0	48
Maroney	6	0	0	0/0	0/0	0	38
Watson	0	6	0	0/0	0/0	0	36
Gaffney	0	5	0	0/0	0/0	0	30
Evans	3	0	0	0/0	0/0	0	18
Morris	3	0	0	0/0	0/0	0	18
Stallworth	0	3	0	0/0	0/0	0	18
K. Brady	0	2	0	0/0	0/0	0	12
T. Brady	2	0	0	0/0	0/0	0	12
Eckel	2	0	0	0/0	0/0	0	12
Hobbs	0	0	2	0/0	0/0	0	12
Vrabel	0	2	0	0/0	0/0	0	12
Andrews	0	0	1	0/0	0/0	0	6
Cassel	1	0	0	0/0	0/0	0	6
Colvin	0	0	1	0/0	0/0	0	6
Faulk	0	1	0	0/0	0/0	0	6
Gay	0	0	1	0/0	0/0	0	6
Samuel	0	0	1	0/0	0/0	0	6
A. Thomas	0	0	1	0/0	0/0	0	6
Wilson	0	0	1	0/0	0/0	0	6
Patriots	17	50	8	74/74	21/24	0	589
Opponents	7	23	4	34/34	12/14	0	274

2-Pt. Conversions: Maroney, Patriots 1-1, Opponents 0-0

RUSHING

RUSHING	No.	Yds	Avg	LG	TD
Maroney	185	835	4.5	59t	6
Morris	85	384	4.5	49	3
Faulk	62	265	4.3	14	0
Evans	34	121	3.6	11	3
T. Brady	37	98	2.6	19	2
Eckel	33	90	2.7	14	2
Welker	4	34	8.5	27	0
Cassel	4	12	3.0	15t	1
Stallworth	1	12	12.0	12	0
Watson	1	11	11.0	11	0
Gutierrez	5	-13	-2.6	-1	0
Patriots	451	1849	4.1	59t	17
Opponents	360	1572	4.4	49	7

RECEIVING

RECEIVING	No.	Yds	Avg	LG	TD
Welker	112	1175	10.5	42	8
Moss	98	1493	15.2	65t	23
Faulk	47	383	8.1	23	1
Stallworth	46	697	15.2	69t	3
Gaffney	36	449	12.5	56t	5
Watson	36	389	10.8	35	6
K. Brady	9	70	7.8	20	2
Morris	6	35	5.8	18	0
Maroney	4	116	29.0	43	0
Evans	4	43	10.8	29	0
Vrabel	2	3	1.5	2t	2
D. Thomas	1	9	9.0	9	0
Eckel	1	6	6.0	6	0
Mankins	1	-9	-9.0	-9	0
Patriots	403	4859	12.1	69t	50
Opponents	314	3381	10.8	73t	23

INTERCEPTIONS

INTERCEPTIONS	No.	Yds	Avg	LG	TD
Samuel	6	89	14.8	42	1
Gay	3	52	17.3	31	0
Seau	3	28	9.3	23	0
Sanders	2	43	21.5	42	0
A. Thomas	1	65	65.0	65t	1
Wilson	1	5	5.0	5t	1
Colvin	1	4	4.0	4	0
Harrison	1	2	2.0	2	0
Hobbs	1	0	0.0	0	0
Patriots	19	288	15.2	65t	3
Opponents	9	131	14.6	36t	1

PUNTING

PUNTING	No.	Yds.	Avg.	In 20	LG
Hanson	44	1821	41.4	13	64
Patriots	45	1821	40.5	13	64
Opponents	76	3297	43.4	16	75

PUNT RETURNS

PUNT RETURNS	Ret	FC	Yds	Avg	LG	TD
Welker	25	7	249	10.0	35	0
T. Brown	6	2	55	9.2	28	0
C. Jackson	2	0	7	3.5	6	0
Faulk	0	9	0	—	—	0
Patriots	33	18	311	9.4	35	0
Opponents	14	8	75	5.4	33	0

KICKOFF RETURNS

KICKOFF RETURNS	No.	Yds	Avg	LG	TD
Hobbs	35	911	26.0	108t	1
Welker	7	176	25.1	33	0
C. Jackson	5	85	17.0	39	0
Andrews	4	149	37.3	77t	1
Faulk	2	47	23.5	27	0
Evans	1	13	13.0	13	0
Vrabel	1	3	3.0	3	0
Patriots	55	1384	25.2	108t	2
Opponents	92	2030	22.1	74t	1

FIELD GOALS

FIELD GOALS	1-19	20-29	30-39	40-49	50+
Gostkowski	0/0	10/10	8/9	3/5	0/0
Patriots	0/0	10/10	8/9	3/5	0/0
Opponents	0/0	5/5	2/3	4/4	1/2

SACKS

SACKS	No.
Vrabel	12.5
Green	6.5
A. Thomas	6.5
Colvin	4.0
Warren	4.0
Seau	3.5
Bruschi	2.0
Harrison	2.0
Wilfork	2.0
Seymour	1.5
Hobbs	1.0
(group)	1.0
Wright	0.5
Patriots	47.0
Opponents	21.0

RECORD HOLDERS
INDIVIDUAL RECORDS—CAREER

Category	Name	Performance
Rushing (Yds.)	Sam Cunningham, 1973-79, 1981-82	5,453
Passing (Yds.)	Drew Bledsoe, 1993-2001	29,657
Passing (TDs)	Tom Brady, 2000-07	197
Receiving (No.)	Troy Brown, 1993-2007	557
Receiving (Yds.)	Stanley Morgan, 1977-1989	10,352
Interceptions	Raymond Clayborn, 1977-1989	36
	Ty Law, 1995-2004	36
Punting (Avg.)	Tom Tupa, 1996-98	44.7
Punt Return (Avg.)	Mack Herron, 1973-75	12.0
Kickoff Return (Avg.)	Allen Carter, 1975-76	27.2
Field Goals	Adam Vinatieri, 1996-2005	263
Touchdowns (Tot.)	Stanley Morgan, 1977-1989	68
Points	Adam Vinatieri, 1996-2005	1,158

INDIVIDUAL RECORDS—SINGLE SEASON

Category	Name	Performance
Rushing (Yds.)	Corey Dillon, 2004	1,635
Passing (Yds.)	Tom Brady, 2007	4,806
Passing (TDs)	Tom Brady, 2007	*50
Receiving (No.)	Wes Welker, 2007	112
Receiving (Yds.)	Randy Moss, 2007	1,493
Interceptions	Ron Hall, 1964	11
Punting (Avg.)	Tom Tupa, 1997	45.8
Punt Return (Avg.)	Mack Herron, 1974	14.8
Kickoff Return (Avg.)	Raymond Clayborn, 1977	31.0
Field Goals	Tony Franklin, 1986	32
Touchdowns (Tot.)	Randy Moss, 2007	23
Points	Gino Cappelletti, 1964	155

INDIVIDUAL RECORDS—SINGLE GAME

Category	Name	Performance
Rushing (Yds.)	Tony Collins, 9-18-83	212
Passing (Yds.)	Drew Bledsoe, 11-13-94	426
Passing (TDs)	Tom Brady, 10-21-07	6
Receiving (No.)	Troy Brown, 9-22-02	16
Receiving (Yds.)	Terry Glenn, 10-3-99	214
Interceptions	Many times	3
	Last time by Asante Samuel, 11-26-06	
Field Goals	Gino Cappelletti, 10-4-64	6
Touchdowns (Tot.)	Randy Moss, 11-18-07	4
Points	Gino Cappelletti, 12-18-65	28

*NFL Record

NEW ENGLAND PATRIOTS

2008 VETERAN ROSTER

No.	Name	Pos.	Ht.	Wt.	Age	NFL Exp.	College	Hometown	How Acq.	'07 Games/ Starts
88	Aiken, Sam	WR	6-2	215	27	6	North Carolina	Kenansville, N.C.	UFA(Buff)-'08	12/0*
52	Alexander, Eric	LB	6-2	240	26	4	Louisiana State	Port Arthur, Texas	FA-'04	12/0
23	Andrews, Willie	DB	5-10	190	24	3	Baylor	Longview, Texas	D7-'06	15/0
12	Brady, Tom	QB	6-4	225	31	9	Michigan	San Mateo, Calif.	D6b-'00	16/16
65	Britt, Wesley	T	6-8	320	26	3	Alabama	Cullman, Ala.	FA-'06	4/1
54	Bruschi, Tedy	LB	6-1	247	35	13	Arizona	Roseville, Calif.	D3-96	16/16
25	Bryant, Fernando	CB	5-10	175	31	10	Alabama	Murfeesboro, Tenn.	FA-'08	16/16*
16	Cassel, Matt	QB	6-4	230	26	4	Southern California	Northridge, Calif.	D7a-'05	6/0
63	Connolly, Dan	G	6-4	313	26	3	Southeast Missouri St.	St. Louis, Mo.	FA-'08	0*
38	Eckel, Kyle	FB	5-11	237	26	2	Navy	Haverford, Pa.	FA-'07	12/0
44	Evans, Heath	RB	6-0	250	29	8	Auburn	West Palm Beach, Fla.	FA-'05	16/1
33	Faulk, Kevin	RB	5-8	202	32	10	Louisiana State	Carencro, La.	D2-99	16/8
10	Gaffney, Jabar	WR	6-1	200	27	7	Florida	Jacksonville, Fla.	FA-'06	16/7
3	Gostkowski, Stephen	K	6-1	210	24	3	Memphis	Madison, Miss.	D4b-'06	16/0
97	Green, Jarvis	DL	6-3	285	29	7	Louisiana State	Donaldsonville, La.	D4b-'02	16/10
7	Gutierrez, Matt	QB	6-4	230	24	2	Idaho State	Concord, Calif.	FA-'07	5/0
6	Hanson, Chris	P	6-2	202	31	10	Marshall	Sharpsburg, Ga.	FA-'07	16/0
37	Harrison, Rodney	S	6-1	220	35	15	Western Illinois	Chicago, Ill.	FA(SD)-'03	12/11
27	Hobbs, Ellis	CB	5-9	195	25	4	Iowa State	DeSoto, Texas	D3a-'05	16/16
59	Hobson, Victor	LB	6-0	252	28	6	Michigan	Mt. Laurel, N.J.	UFA(NYJ)-'08	16/14*
71	Hochstein, Russ	G/C	6-4	305	30	8	Nebraska	Hartington, Neb.	FA-'02	16/8
53	Izzo, Larry	LB	5-10	228	33	13	Rice	Houston, Texas	UFA(Mia)-'01	16/0
17	Jackson, Chad	WR	6-1	215	23	3	Florida	Hoover, Ala.	D2-'06	2/0
19	Jones, C.J.	WR	5-11	195	27	2	Iowa	Boynton Beach, Fla.	FA-'08	0*
77	Kaczur, Nick	T	6-4	315	29	4	Toledo	Brantford, Ontario	D3b-'05	15/15
67	Koppen, Dan	C	6-2	296	28	6	Boston College	Whitehall, Pa.	D5-'03	15/15
72	Light, Matt	T	6-4	305	30	8	Purdue	Greenville, Ohio	D2-'01	16/16
70	Mankins, Logan	G	6-4	310	26	4	Fresno State	Catheys Valley, Calif.	D1-'05	16/16
39	Maroney, Laurence	RB	5-11	220	23	3	Minnesota	St. Louis, Mo.	D1-'06	13/6
31	Meriweather, Brandon	DB	5-11	200	24	2	Miami	Apopka, Fla.	D1-'07	16/0
34	Morris, Sammy	RB	6-0	220	31	9	Texas Tech	San Antonio, Texas	UFA(Mia)-'07	6/2
81	Moss, Randy	WR	6-4	210	31	11	Marshall	Rand, W. Va.	T(Oak)-'07	16/16
61	Neal, Stephen	G	6-4	305	31	7	Cal State-Bakersfield	San Diego, Calif.	FA-'01	8/8
68	O'Callaghan, Ryan	T	6-7	330	25	3	California	Redding, Calif.	D5-'06	14/1
66	Paxton, Lonie	LS	6-2	260	30	9	Sacramento State	Corona, Calif.	FA-'00	16/0
2	Player, Scott	P	6-1	211	38	11	Florida State	St. Augustine, Fla.	FA-'08	3/0*
87	Pollard, Marcus	TE	6-3	265	36	14	Bradley	Valley, Ala.	UFA(Sea)-'08	14/10*
35	Richardson, Mike	CB	5-11	190	24	2	Notre Dame	Warner Robins, Ga.	D6-'07	0*
36	Sanders, James	S	5-10	210	24	4	Fresno State	Porterville, Calif.	D4-'05	15/15
29	Sanders, Lewis	CB	6-1	210	30	9	Maryland	Staten Island, N.Y.	FA-'08	14/6*
93	Seymour, Richard	DL	6-6	310	28	8	Georgia	Gadsden, S.C.	D1-'01	9/8
95	Smith, Kenny	DL	6-4	303	30	6	Alabama	Meridian, Miss.	FA-'08	0*
90	Smith, Le Kevin	DL	6-3	308	26	3	Nebraska	Macon, Ga.	D6c-'06	13/0
82	Spach, Stephen	TE	6-4	250	26	3	Fresno State	Clovis, Calif.	FA-'07	3/0
28	Spann, Antwain	CB	6-0	195	25	3	Louisiana-Lafayette	Oceanside, Calif.	FA-'07	1/0
96	Thomas, Adalius	LB	6-2	270	31	9	Southern Mississippi	Equality, Ala.	UFA(Balt)-'07	16/15
86	Thomas, David	TE	6-3	248	25	3	Texas	Wolfforth, Texas	D3-'06	2/0
92	Thomas, Santonio	DL	6-4	305	27	2	Miami	Belle Glade, Fla.	FA-'05	4/0
41	Ventrone, Ray	DB	5-10	200	25	3	Villanova	Pittsburgh, Pa.	FA-'07	2/0
50	Vrabel, Mike	LB	6-4	261	33	12	Ohio State	Akron, Ohio	UFA(Pitt)-'01	16/15
94	Warren, Ty	DL	6-5	300	27	6	Texas A&M	Bryan, Texas	D1-'03	16/16
15	Washington, Kelley	WR	6-3	215	29	6	Tennessee	Stephens City, Va.	UFA(Cin)-'07	14/0
84	Watson, Benjamin	TE	6-3	255	27	5	Georgia	Rock Hill, S.C.	D1b-'04	12/8
21	Webster, Jason	CB	5-9	187	30	9	Texas A&M	Houston, Texas	UFA(Buff)-'08	1/1*
83	Welker, Wes	WR	5-9	185	27	5	Texas Tech	Oklahoma City, Okla.	T(Mia)-'07	16/13
75	Wilfork, Vince	DL	6-2	325	26	5	Miami	Boynton Beach, Fla.	D1a-'04	16/16
26	Williams, Tank	S	6-2	223	28	7	Stanford	Bay St. Louis, Miss.	UFA(Minn)-'08	13/2*
58	Woods, Pierre	LB	6-5	250	26	3	Michigan	Cleveland, Ohio	FA-'06	16/0
99	Wright, Mike	DL	6-4	295	26	4	Cincinnati	Cincinnati, Ohio	FA-'05	8/1
74	Yates, Billy	G	6-2	305	28	5	Texas A&M	Fort Worth, Texas	FA-'05	7/1

* Aiken played 12 games with Buffalo; Bryant played 16 games with Detroit; Connolly last active with Jacksonville in '05; Hobson played 16 games with N.Y. Jets; Jones last active with Cleveland in '03; Player played 3 games with Cleveland; Pollard played 14 games with Seattle; Richardson missed '07 season because of injury; L. Sanders played 14 games with Atlanta; K. Smith last active with New Orleans in '03; Webster played 1 game with Buffalo; Williams played 13 games with Minnesota.

Players lost through free agency (4): DB Randall Gay (NO; 16 games in '07); CB Asante Samuel (Phil; 16); WR Donte Stallworth (Cle; 16); S Eugene Wilson (TB; 11).

Also played with Patriots in '07—S Rashad Baker (8 games), TE Kyle Brady (14), LB Chad Brown (2), WR Troy Brown (1), LB Rosevelt Colvin (11); CB Eddie Jackson (3), LB Corey Mays (1), S Mel Mitchell (10), DL Rashad Moore (1), TE Marcellus Rivers (3), LB Junior Seau (16).

2008 FIRST-YEAR ROSTER

Name	Pos.	Ht.	Wt.	Age	College	Hometown	How Acq.
Crable, Shawn	LB	6-5	243	23	Michigan	Massillon, Ohio	D3a
DeVree, Tyson	TE	6-6	245	23	Colorado	Hudsonville, Mich.	FA
Dillard, Mark	S	5-11	210	21	Louisiana Tech	Baton Rouge, La.	FA
Dragosavich, Mike	P	6-5	190	23	North Dakota State	Oak Lawn, Ill.	FA
Green-Ellis, BenJarvus	RB	5-11	215	23	Mississippi	New Orleans, La.	FA
Guyton, Gary	LB	6-3	242	22	Georgia Tech	Hinesville, Ga.	FA
Martin, Jimmy (1)	OL	6-5	306	25	Virginia Tech	Chantilly, Va.	FA
Mayo, Jerod	LB	6-1	242	22	Tennessee	Hampton, Va.	D1
Norwell, Chris	DE	6-6	303	23	Illinois	Cincinnati, Ohio	FA
O'Connell, Kevin	QB	6-5	225	23	San Diego State	Carlsbad, Calif.	D3b
Redd, Vince	LB	6-6	260	23	Liberty	Elizabethton, Tenn.	FA
Ruud, Bo	LB	6-3	235	24	Nebraska	Lincoln, Neb.	D6
Slater, Matthew	WR	6-0	198	22	UCLA	Anaheim, Calif.	D5
Smith, Henry	NT	6-3	315	25	Texas A&M	Aliceville, Ala.	FA
Stupar, Jonathan	TE	6-3	254	24	Virginia	State College, Pa.	FA
Tyler, Casey	DE	6-6	310	23	Portland State	Edmonds, Wash.	FA
Wendell, Ryan	C	6-2	275	22	Fresno State	Diamond Bar, Calif.	FA
Wheatley, Terrence	CB	5-9	183	23	Colorado	Plano, Texas	D2
Wilhite, Jonathan	CB	5-11	185	24	Auburn	Monroe, La.	D4

The term NFL Rookie is defined as a player who is in his first season of professional football and has not been on the roster of another professional football team for any regular-season or postseason games. A Rookie is designated by an "R" on NFL rosters. Players who have been active in another professional football league or players who have NFL experience, including either preseason training camp or being on an Active List or Inactive List, or on Reserve/Injured or Reserve/Physically Unable to Perform for fewer than six regular-season games, are termed NFL First-Year Players. An NFL First-Year Player is designated by a "1" on NFL rosters. Thereafter, a player is credited with an additional year of experience for each season in which he accumulates six games on the Active List or Inactive List, or on Reserve/Injured or Reserve/Physically Unable to Perform.

Log on to www.patriots.com for an up-to-date roster; Age listed is as of September 4, 2008.

COACHING STAFF
Head Coach,
Bill Belichick

Pro Career: Bill Belichick is in his 34th season as an NFL coach and is the only head coach in NFL history to win three Super Bowl titles in a four-year span. Hired by Chairman and CEO Robert Kraft on January 27, 2000, Belichick is in his ninth season as New England's head coach. In the 2007 season, Belichick led the Patriots to the NFL's first 16-0 regular season and just the fourth undefeated and untied regular season in the league's 88-year history. He has led the Patriots to the Super Bowl four times in the last seven seasons and has produced five straight AFC East titles and six division championships in the last seven seasons. Belichick directed the Patriots to victories in Super Bowls XXXVI (2001), XXXVIII (2003) and XXXIX (2004). Only one coach (Pittsburgh's Chuck Noll, 4) has won more Super Bowls than Belichick, and his three Super Bowl titles tie Washington's Joe Gibbs and San Francisco's Bill Walsh for second place on the NFL's all-time list. Belichick's Patriots teams own the all-time NFL records for consecutive total victories (21 from 2003-04), consecutive regular-season victories (19 from 2006-07) and consecutive playoff victories (10 from 2001-05). Belichick owns the second best postseason record in NFL history (15-4) and is the winningest NFL head coach since 2001 (100-29). From 2003-04, he directed the Patriots to back-to-back Super Bowl titles while posting consecutive 17-win campaigns. Belichick has spent more seasons in the league than any other current NFL head coach, and in that time has been a part of five Super Bowl championship teams. His overall record of 105-40 with the Patriots gives him the most victories and the best winning percentage of any head coach in franchise history. Coach Belichick's overall career winning percentage of .626 (142-85-0) ranks fifth among the 18 NFL coaches with 140 or more wins. He trails only George Halas (324-151-31, .682), Don Shula (347-173-6, .666), Curly Lambeau (229-134-22, .631), and Joe Gibbs (171-101-0, .629). Belichick's recent accomplishments are the latest triumphs in a career during which he has helped produce five Super Bowl titles, seven conference championships and 13 division titles since entering the NFL in 1975. He won his first two Super Bowls as the defensive coordinator for the New York Giants in 1986 and 1990 before claiming three Super Bowl championships with the Patriots. George Seifert is the only other man to have won multiple Super Bowls both as a head coach and as an assistant coach. Belichick launched his career in 1975 as a special assistant with the Baltimore Colts, then became an assistant special teams coach with Detroit

(1976-77) and Denver (1978). In 1979, he joined the New York Giants to begin a 12-season stint in which he contributed to two Super Bowl championships as New York's defensive coordinator. Belichick was named head coach of the Cleveland Browns in 1991, becoming the youngest head coach in the NFL at age 38. By 1994, Belichick brought the Browns back to the playoffs, finishing 11-5 and advancing to the second round of the playoffs, while allowing a league-low 204 total points. In 1996, Belichick joined New England and was a key contributor to the team's rebound from a 6-10 season in 1995 to an 11-5 season and the team's first division title in 10 years en route to the Patriots' appearance in Super Bowl XXXI. Belichick then spent three seasons with the New York Jets from 1997 to 1999, helping New York improve from a 1-15 season in 1996 to an appearance in the AFC Championship Game in 1998. Career record: 142-85.

Background: Belichick was a center/tight end at Wesleyan 1971-74.

Personal: Age 56, born in Nashville.

ASSISTANT COACHES

Dom Capers, special assistant/secondary; born Cambridge, Ohio. Defensive back Mount Union College 1968-1971. No pro playing experience. College coach: Kent State 1972-74, Hawaii 1975-76, San Jose State 1977, California 1978-79, Tennessee 1980-81, Ohio State 1982-83. Pro coach: Philadelphia/Baltimore Stars (USFL) 1984-85, New Orleans Saints 1986-1991, Pittsburgh Steelers 1992-94, Carolina Panthers 1995-98 (head coach), Jacksonville Jaguars 1999-2000, Houston Texans 2001-05 (head coach), Miami Dolphins 2006-07, joined Patriots in 2008.

Don Davis, asst. strength and conditioning; born Olathe, Kansas. Linebacker Kansas 1991-94. Pro linebacker New Orleans Saints 1996-98, Tampa Bay Buccaneers 1998-2000, St. Louis Rams 2001-02, New England Patriots 2003-06. Pro coach: Joined Patriots in 2007.

Ivan Fears, running backs; born Portsmouth, Va. Running back William & Mary 1973-75. No pro playing experience. College coach: William & Mary 1977-79, Syracuse 1980-1990. Pro coach: New England Patriots 1991-92, Chicago Bears 1993-98, re-joined Patriots in 1999.

Pepper Johnson, defensive line; born Detroit. Linebacker Ohio State 1982-85. Pro linebacker New York Giants 1986-1992, Cleveland Browns 1993-95, Detroit Lions 1996, New York Jets 1997-98. Pro coach: Joined Patriots in 2001.

Pete Mangurian, tight ends; born Los Angeles. Defensive lineman Louisiana State. No pro playing experience. College coach: Southern Methodist 1979-1980, New Mexico State 1981, Stanford 1982-83, Louisiana State 1984-87, Cornell 1998-2000 (head coach). Pro coach: Denver

Broncos 1988-1992, New York Giants 1993-96, Atlanta Falcons 1997, Atlanta Falcons 2001-03, joined Patriots in 2005.

Josh McDaniels, offensive coordinator/quarterbacks; born Barberton, Ohio. Quarterback/wide receiver John Carroll 1995-98. No pro playing experience. College coach: Michigan State 1999. Pro coach: Joined Patriots in 2001.

Harold Nash, asst. strength and conditioning; born New Orleans. Defensive back Louisiana-Lafayette 1988-1993. Pro defensive back Shreveport Pirates (CFL) 1994-95, Montreal Alouettes (CFL) 1996-99, Winnipeg Blue Bombers (CFL) 1999-2003, Edmonton Eskimos (CFL) 2004. Pro coach: Joined Patriots in 2005.

Bill O'Brien, wide receivers; born Andover, Mass. Linebacker/defensive end Brown 1990-92. No pro playing experience. College coach: Brown 1993-94, Georgia Tech 1995-2002, Maryland 2003-04, Duke 2005-06. Pro Coach: Joined Patriots in 2007.

Matt Patricia, linebackers; Center-guard Rensselaer 1992-96. No pro playing experience. College coach: Rensselaer 1996, Amherst 1999-2000, Syracuse 2001-03. Pro coach: Joined Patriots in 2004.

Dean Pees, defensive coordinator; born Dunkirk, Ohio. Attended Bowling Green. No college or pro playing experience. College coach: Findlay 1979-1982, Miami (Ohio) 1983-86, Navy 1987-89, Toledo 1990-93, Notre Dame 1994, Michigan State 1995-97, Kent State 1998-2003. Pro coach: Joined Patriots in 2004.

Dante Scarnecchia, asst. head coach/offensive line; born Los Angeles. Center-guard California Western 1968-1970. No pro playing experience. College coach: California Western 1970-72, Iowa State 1973-74, Southern Methodist 1975-76, Pacific 1977-78, Northern Arizona 1979, Southern Methodist 1980-81. Pro coach: New England Patriots 1982-88, Indianapolis Colts 1989-1990, re-joined Patriots in 1991.

Brad Seely, special teams; born Vinton, Iowa. Tackle-guard South Dakota State 1974-77. No pro playing experience. College coach: Colorado State 1979-1980, Southern Methodist 1981, North Carolina State 1982, Pacific 1983, Oklahoma State 1984-88. Pro coach: Indianapolis Colts 1989-1993, New York Jets 1994, Carolina Panthers 1995-98, joined Patriots in 1999.

Mike Woicik, strength and conditioning; born Baltimore. Attended Boston College. No college or pro playing experience. College coach: Springfield College 1978-1980, Syracuse 1980-89. Pro coach: Dallas Cowboys 1990-96, New Orleans Saints 1997-99, joined Patriots in 2000.

American Football Conference
East Division
Team Colors: Green and White
1000 Fulton Avenue
Hempstead, New York 11550
Telephone: (516) 560-8100

2008 SCHEDULE
PRESEASON
Aug. 7	at Cleveland	7:30
Aug. 16	**Washington**	7:00
Aug. 23	**N.Y. Giants**	7:00
Aug. 28	at Philadelphia	6:30

REGULAR SEASON
Sep. 7	at Miami	1:00
Sep. 14	**New England**	4:15
Sep. 22	at San Diego (Mon.)	5:30
Sep. 28	**Arizona**	1:00
Oct. 5	BYE	
Oct. 12	**Cincinnati**	1:00
Oct. 19	at Oakland	1:15
Oct. 26	**Kansas City**	1:00
Nov. 2	at Buffalo	1:00
Nov. 9	**St. Louis**	1:00
Nov. 13	at New England (Thu.)	8:15
Nov. 23	at Tennessee	12:00
Nov. 30	**Denver**	1:00
Dec. 7	at San Francisco	1:05
Dec. 14	**Buffalo**	1:00
Dec. 21	at Seattle	1:05
Dec. 28	**Miami**	1:00

Stadium: Meadowlands
(opened in 1976)
•**Capacity:** 80,062
East Rutherford, New Jersey
07073
Playing Surface: FieldTurf
Training Camp: 1000 Fulton Avenue
Hempstead, NY 11550

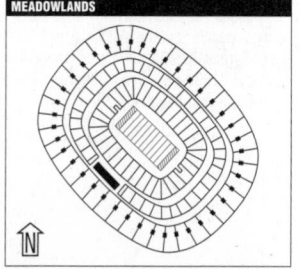

MEADOWLANDS

CLUB OFFICIALS
Owner and CEO:
Robert Wood Johnson IV
President: L. Jay Cross
General Manager: Mike Tannenbaum
Senior V.P., Business Operations:
Matt Higgins
Senior V.P., New Meadowlands Stadium
Project: Bill Senn
Senior V.P., Finance: Thad Sheely
V.P. Broadcasting and Production:
Bob Parente
V.P. Corporate Sales: Mark Ricco
Senior Director, Media Relations:
Bruce Speight
Director, Player Personnel: Terry Bradway
Asst. Director, Player Personnel:
JoJo Wooden
Director, Pro Personnel: Brendan Prophett
Pro Scout: Brock Sunderland
Pro Personnel Assistant: Cole Hufnagel
Director, College Scouting:
Joey Clinkscales
Coordinator, College Scouting:
Jay Mandolesi
National Scout: Jim Cochran,
Michael Davis
Personnel Scouts: Jeff Bauer,
Matt Bazirgan, Joe Bommarito,
Jesse Kaye, Gary Smith,
Kirwin Watson
Scouting Consultant: Dick Haley
Assistant, Player Personnel:
Kathryn Smith
Director, Football Administration:
Ari Nissim
Manager, Football Administration:
Jacqueline Davidson
Senior Director, Athletic Training:
John Mellody
Assistant Athletic Trainers: Josh Koch,
Dave Zuffelato
Director, Equipment: Gus Granneman
Manager, Equipment: Vito Contento
Assistant, Equipment: Cortez Robinson
Senior Director, Information &
Technology: Tom Murphy
Senior Director, Operations:
Clay Hampton
Senior Director, Security: Steve Yarnell
Director, Video: Steve Scarnecchia
Director, Player Development:
Dave Szott
Director, Ticket Sales: Jeff Hecker
Director, Community Relations:
Jesse Linder

COACHING HISTORY
New York Titans 1960-62
(330-405-8)
Records include postseason games
1960-61	Sammy Baugh	14-14-0
1962	Clyde (Bulldog) Turner	5-9-0
1963-1973	Weeb Ewbank	73-78-6
1974-75	Charley Winner*	9-14-0
1975	Ken Shipp	1-4-0
1976	Lou Holtz**	3-10-0
1976	Mike Holovak	0-1-0
1977-1982	Walt Michaels	41-49-1
1983-89	Joe Walton	54-59-1
1990-93	Bruce Coslet	26-39-0
1994	Pete Carroll	6-10-0
1995-96	Rich Kotite	4-28-0
1997-99	Bill Parcells	30-20-0
2000	Al Groh	9-7-0
2001-05	Herman Edwards	41-44-0
2006-07	Eric Mangini	14-19-0

*Released after nine games in 1975
**Resigned after 13 games in 1976

PAID ATTENDANCE
Home 616,756   Away 554,808
Total 1,171,564
Single-game home record,
79,572 (11/19/06)
Single-season home record,
628,773 (2002)

2008 DRAFT CHOICES
Round	Name	Pos.	College
1	Vernon Gholston	LB	Ohio State
	Dustin Keller	TE	Purdue
4	Dwight Lowery	DB	San Jose St.
5	Erik Ainge	QB	Tennessee
6	Marcus Henry	WR	Kansas
7	Nate Garner	T	Arkansas

2007 TEAM RECORD
PRESEASON (3-1)

Date	Result	Opponent
8/10	W 31-16	Atlanta
8/17	L 20-37	Minnesota
8/25	W 20-12	at N.Y. Giants
8/30	W 13-11	at Philadelphia

REGULAR SEASON (4-12)

Date	Result	Opponent	Att.
9/9	L 14-38	New England	77,900
9/16	L 13-20	at Baltimore	71,246
9/23	W 31-28	Miami	77,197
9/30	L 14-17	at Buffalo	70,600
10/7	L 24-35	at N.Y. Giants	78,809
10/14	L 9-16	Philadelphia	77,189
10/21	L 31-38	at Cincinnati	65,868
10/28	L 3-13	Buffalo	76,688
11/4	L 20-23	Washington (OT)	76,663
11/18	W 19-16	Pittsburgh (OT)	77,659
11/22	L 3-34	at Dallas	63,315
12/2	W 40-13	at Miami	71,109
12/9	L 18-24	Cleveland	76,822
12/16	L 10-20	at New England	68,756
12/23	L 6-10	at Tennessee	69,143
12/30	W 13-10	Kansas City (OT)	76,737

SCORE BY PERIODS

Jets	51	105	33	73	6	—	268
Opponents	47	111	70	124	3	—	355

2007 TEAM STATISTICS

	Jets	Opp.
Total First Downs	286	315
Rushing	92	128
Passing	173	174
Penalty	21	13
3rd Down: Made/Att	85/226	89/211
3rd Down Pct.	37.6	42.2
4th Down: Made/Att	10/21	8/10
4th Down Pct.	47.6	80.0
Possession Avg.	28:35	31:25
Total Net Yards	4715	5310
Avg. Per Game	294.7	331.9
Total Plays	1011	1016
Avg. Per Play	4.7	5.2
Net Yards Rushing	1701	2156
Avg. Per Game	106.3	134.8
Total Rushes	446	517
Net Yards Passing	3014	3154
Avg. Per Game	188.4	197.1
Sacked/Yards Lost	53/316	29/208
Gross Yards	3330	3362
Att./Completions	512/310	470/289
Completion Pct.	60.5	61.5
Had Intercepted	19	15
Punts/Average	72/42.5	68/42.7
Net Punting Avg.	72/36.6	68/35.9
Penalties/Yards	63/486	93/761
Fumbles/Ball Lost	20/6	15/6
Touchdowns	26	38
Rushing	6	14
Passing	15	18
Returns	5	6

2007 INDIVIDUAL STATISTICS

PASSING

PASSING	Att.	Comp.	Yds.	Pct.	TD	Int.	Tkld.	Rate
Pennington	260	179	1765	68.8	10	9	26/178	86.1
Clemens	250	130	1529	52.0	5	10	27/138	60.9
B. Smith	1	0	0	0.0	0	0	0/0	39.6
L. Washington	1	1	36	100	0	0	0/0	118.8
Jets	512	310	3330	60.5	15	19	53/316	73.9
Opponents	470	289	3362	61.5	18	15	29/208	82.6

SCORING

SCORING	TD R	TD P	TD Rt	PAT	FG	Saf	PTS
Nugent	0	0	0	23/24	29/36	0	110
L. Washington	3	0	3	0/0	0/0	0	38
Coles	0	6	0	0/0	0/0	0	36
Baker	0	3	0	0/0	0/0	0	18
Cotchery	0	2	0	0/0	0/0	0	12
T. Jones	1	1	0	0/0	0/0	0	12
B. Smith	0	2	0	0/0	0/0	0	12
Bowens	0	0	1	0/0	0/0	0	6
Clemens	1	0	0	0/0	0/0	0	6
Kowalewski	0	1	0	0/0	0/0	0	6
Pennington	1	0	0	0/0	0/0	0	6
Rhodes	0	0	1	0/0	0/0	0	6
Jets	6	15	5	23/24	29/36	0	268
Opponents	14	18	6	36/36	29/32	0	355

2-Pt. Conversions: L. Washington, Jets 1-2, Opponents 2-2

RUSHING

RUSHING	No.	Yds	Avg	LG	TD
T. Jones	310	1119	3.6	36	1
L. Washington	71	353	5.0	49	3
Clemens	27	111	4.1	18	1
B. Smith	12	45	3.8	11	0
Cotchery	5	38	7.6	16	0
Pennington	20	32	1.6	5	1
Davis	1	3	3.0	3	0
Jets	446	1701	3.8	49	6
Opponents	517	2156	4.2	32	14

RECEIVING

RECEIVING	No.	Yds	Avg	LG	TD
Cotchery	82	1130	13.8	50	2
Coles	55	646	11.7	57t	6
Baker	41	409	10.0	22	3
L. Washington	36	213	5.9	18	0
B. Smith	32	325	10.2	29	2
T. Jones	28	217	7.8	25	1
McCareins	19	232	12.2	51	0
Wright	6	87	14.5	36	0
Kowalewski	5	18	3.6	6	1
Ryan	3	46	15.3	22	0
Pociask	1	7	7.0	7	0
Davis	1	3	3.0	3	0
Mangold	1	-3	-3.0	-3	0
Jets	310	3330	10.7	57t	15
Opponents	289	3362	11.6	85t	18

INTERCEPTIONS

INTERCEPTIONS	No.	Yds	Avg	LG	TD
Rhodes	5	76	15.2	36	0
Revis	3	20	6.7	19	0
Poteat	2	11	5.5	11	0
Barton	1	1	1.0	1	0
D. Coleman	1	1	1.0	1	0
Vilma	1	1	1.0	1	0
Barrett	1	0	0.0	0	0
Dyson	1	0	0.0	0	0
Jets	15	110	7.3	36	0
Opponents	19	196	10.3	50t	4

PUNTING

PUNTING	No.	Yds.	Avg.	In 20	LG
Graham	66	2855	43.3	23	62
Kapinos	5	208	41.6	2	48
Jets	72	3063	42.5	25	62
Opponents	68	2901	42.7	23	64

PUNT RETURNS

PUNT RETURNS	Ret	FC	Yds	Avg	LG	TD
L. Washington	20	14	183	9.2	33	0
Jets	20	14	183	9.2	33	0
Opponents	32	13	268	8.4	32	0

KICKOFF RETURNS

KICKOFF RETURNS	No.	Yds	Avg	LG	TD
L. Washington	47	1291	27.5	98t	3
B. Smith	9	183	20.3	27	0
Cotchery	4	56	14.0	32	0
Baker	3	18	6.0	10	0
Bowens	3	30	10.0	17	0
McCareins	2	15	7.5	12	0
Miller	2	48	24.0	26	0
Wright	2	31	15.5	28	0
Chatham	1	5	5.0	5	0
Ryan	1	18	18.0	18	0
Jets	74	1695	22.9	98t	3
Opponents	51	1270	24.9	108t	1

FIELD GOALS

FIELD GOALS	1-19	20-29	30-39	40-49	50+
Nugent	1/1	11/11	10/12	6/8	1/4
Jets	1/1	11/11	10/12	6/8	1/4
Opponents	0/0	8/8	7/7	13/16	1/1

SACKS

SACKS	No.
Ellis	5.0
Harris	5.0
Robertson	4.0
Bowens	2.5
Mosley	2.5
B. Thomas	2.5
Barton	2.0
Hobson	2.0
Rhodes	2.0
K. Coleman	1.5
Jets	29.0
Opponents	53.0

RECORD HOLDERS
INDIVIDUAL RECORDS—CAREER

Category	Name	Performance
Rushing (Yds.)	Curtis Martin, 1998-2005	10,302
Passing (Yds.)	Joe Namath, 1965-1976	27,057
Passing (TDs)	Joe Namath, 1965-1976	170
Receiving (No.)	Don Maynard, 1960-1972	627
Receiving (Yds.)	Don Maynard, 1960-1972	11,732
Interceptions	Bill Baird, 1963-69	34
Punting (Avg.)	Ben Graham, 2005-07	43.7
Punt Return (Avg.)	Dick Christy, 1961-63	16.2
Kickoff Return (Avg.)	Justin Miller, 2005-07	27.1
Field Goals	Pat Leahy, 1974-1991	304
Touchdowns (Tot.)	Don Maynard, 1960-1972	88
Points	Pat Leahy, 1974-1991	1,470

INDIVIDUAL RECORDS—SINGLE SEASON

Category	Name	Performance
Rushing (Yds.)	Curtis Martin, 2004	1,697
Passing (Yds.)	Joe Namath, 1967	4,007
Passing (TDs)	Vinny Testaverde, 1998	29
Receiving (No.)	Al Toon, 1988	93
Receiving (Yds.)	Don Maynard, 1967	1,434
Interceptions	Dainard Paulson, 1964	12
Punting (Avg.)	Curley Johnson, 1965	45.3
Punt Return (Avg.)	Dick Christy, 1961	21.3
Kickoff Return (Avg.)	Bobby Humphery, 1984	30.7
Field Goals	Jim Turner, 1968	34
Touchdowns (Tot.)	Art Powell, 1960	14
	Don Maynard, 1965	14
	Emerson Boozer, 1972	14
	Curtis Martin, 2004	14
Points	Jim Turner, 1968	145

INDIVIDUAL RECORDS—SINGLE GAME

Category	Name	Performance
Rushing (Yds.)	Curtis Martin, 12-3-00	203
Passing (Yds.)	Joe Namath, 9-24-72	496
Passing (TDs)	Joe Namath, 9-24-72	6
Receiving (No.)	Clark Gaines, 9-21-80	17
Receiving (Yds.)	Don Maynard, 11-17-68	228
Interceptions	Many times	3
	Last time by Ty Law, 1-1-06	
Field Goals	Jim Turner, 11-3-68	6
	Bobby Howfield, 12-3-72	6
Touchdowns (Tot.)	Wesley Walker, 9-21-86	4
Points	Wesley Walker, 9-21-86	24

2008 VETERAN ROSTER

No.	Name	Pos.	Ht.	Wt.	Age	NFL Exp.	College	Hometown	How Acq.	'07 Games/ Starts
86	Baker, Chris	TE	6-3	258	28	7	Michigan State	Queens, N.Y.	D5-'02	15/15
36	Barrett, David	CB	5-10	195	30	9	Arkansas	Osceola, Ark.	UFA(Ariz)-04	16/9
50	Barton, Eric	LB	6-2	245	30	10	Maryland	Alexandria, Va.	UFA(Oak)-'04	16/15
72	Bender, Jacob	OL	6-6	315	23	2	Nicholls State	Mayo, Md.	D6-'07	2/0
23	Bing, Darnell	S	6-2	230	23	2	Southern California	Long Beach, Calif.	FA-'08	0*
96	Bowens, David	LB	6-3	265	31	10	Western Illinois	Detroit, Mich.	UFA(Mia)-'07	16/2
98	Brown, Kareem	DL	6-4	295	24	2	Miami	Miami, Fla.	W(NE)-'07	1/0
58	Chatham, Matt	LB	6-4	250	31	9	South Dakota	Sioux City, Iowa	UFA(NE)-'06	9/0
22	Chatman, Jesse	RB	5-8	225	28	5	Eastern Washington	Seattle, Wash.	UFA(Mia)-'08	14/6*
11	Clemens, Kellen	QB	6-2	223	25	3	Oregon	Burns, Ore.	D2-'06	10/8
30	Coleman, Drew	CB	5-9	175	25	3	TCU	Henderson, Texas	D6-'06	11/0
93	Coleman, Kenyon	DE	6-5	295	29	7	UCLA	Alta Loma, Calif.	UFA(Dall)-'07	16/14
87	Coles, Laveranues	WR	5-11	193	30	9	Florida State	Jacksonville, Fla.	T(Wash)-'05	12/10
89	Cotchery, Jerricho	WR	6-0	207	26	5	North Carolina State	Birmingham, Ala.	D4a-'04	15/15
19	Davis, Chris	WR	5-10	180	24	2	Wake Forest	St. Petersburg, Fla.	FA-'07	2/0
85	Dearth, James	TE/LS	6-4	270	32	8	Tarleton State	Scurry, Texas	FA-'01	16/0
70	DeVito, Mike	DE	6-3	298	24	2	Maine	Wellfleet, Mass.	FA-'07	7/0
27	Elam, Abram	S	6-0	207	26	3	Kent State	West Palm Beach, Fla.	FA-'07	13/8
92	Ellis, Shaun	DE	6-5	285	31	9	Tennessee	Anderson, S.C.	D1a-'00	16/16
66	Faneca, Alan	G	6-5	307	31	11	Louisiana State	New Orleans, La.	UFA(Pitt)-'08	16/16*
60	Ferguson, D'Brickashaw	T	6-6	312	24	3	Virginia	Freeport, N.Y.	D1a-'06	16/16
88	Franks, Bubba	TE	6-6	265	30	9	Miami	Riverside, Calif.	FA-'08	8/1*
7	Graham, Ben	P	6-5	235	34	4	Deakin (Australia)	Geelong/Victoria Australia	FA-'05	15/0
52	Harris, David	LB	6-2	243	24	2	Michigan	Grand Rapids, Mich.	D2-'07	16/9
26	Hawkins, Artrell	SS	5-10	195	31	11	Cincinnati	Johnstown, Pa.	FA-'08	0*
78	Hunter, Wayne	OT	6-5	303	27	5	Hawaii	Honolulu, Hawaii	FA-'07	0*
44	Ihedigbo, James	DB	6-1	202	24	2	Massachusetts	Northampton, Mass.	FA-'07	0*
77 t-	Jenkins, Kris	DT	6-4	349	29	8	Maryland	Ypsilanti, Mich.	T(Car)-'08	16/15*
95	Johnson, Thomas	DT	6-2	298	27	3	Middle Tennessee State	Memphis, Tenn.	FA-'08	0*
20	Jones, Thomas	RB	5-10	215	30	9	Virginia	Big Stone Gap, Va.	T(Chi)-'07	16/14
55	Kassell, Brad	LB	6-3	242	28	7	North Texas	Llano, Texas	UFA(Tenn)-'06	16/1
74	Mangold, Nick	C	6-4	300	24	3	Ohio State	Centerville, Ohio	D1b-'06	16/16
62	McChesney, Matt	OL	6-4	307	26	2	Colorado	Santa Cruz, Calif.	FA-'05	0*
21	Miller, Justin	CB/KR	5-10	196	24	4	Clemson	Owensboro, Ky.	FA-'06	2/0
68	Montgomery, Will	OL	6-3	312	25	3	Virginia Tech	Clifton, Va.	FA-'07	7/1
65	Moore, Brandon	G	6-3	295	28	6	Illinois	Gary, Ind.	FA-'03	16/16
69	Mosley, C.J.	DT	6-2	314	25	4	Missouri	Fort Knox, Ky.	T(Minn)-'06	14/2
94	Murrell, Marques	LB	6-2	246	23	2	Appalachian State	Fayetteville, N.C.	FA-'07	4/0
1	Nugent, Mike	K	5-9	188	26	4	Ohio State	Centerville, Ohio	D2a-'05	16/0
97	Pace, Calvin	LB	6-4	270	27	6	Wake Forest	Douglasville, Ga.	UFA(Ariz)-'08	16/16*
10	Pennington, Chad	QB	6-3	225	32	9	Marshall	Knoxville, Tenn.	D1c-'00	9/8
82	Pociask, Jason	TE	6-2	259	25	3	Wisconsin	Plainfield, Ind.	D5-'06	4/0
	Poteat, Hank	CB	5-10	195	31	8	Pittsburgh	Harrisburg, Pa.	FA-'06	16/9
91	Pouha, Sione	DT	6-3	325	29	4	Utah	Salt Lake City, Utah	D3-'05	16/1
24	Revis, Darrelle	DB/PR	5-11	204	23	2	Pittsburgh	Aliquippa, Pa.	D1-'07	16/16
25	Rhodes, Kerry	S	6-3	210	26	4	Louisville	Bessemer, Ala.	D4-'05	16/16
49	Richardson, Tony	FB	6-1	238	36	13	Auburn	Daleville, Ala.	UFA(Minn)-'08	14/3*
16	Smith, Brad	QB	6-2	210	24	3	Missouri	Liberty, Ohio	D4a-'06	16/9
33	Smith, Eric	S	6-1	209	25	3	Michigan State	Groveport, Ohio	D3b-'06	15/4
53	Spencer, Cody	LB	6-2	245	27	5	North Texas	Grapevine, Texas	FA-'06	1/0
83	Stuckey, Chansi	WR	6-0	196	24	2	Clemson	Warner Robins, Ga.	D7-'07	0*
99	Thomas, Bryan	LB	6-4	266	29	7	Alabama-Birmingham	Birmingham, Ala.	D1-'02	16/14
57	Trusnik, Jason	LB	6-4	250	24	2	Ohio Northern	Macedonia, Ohio	FA-'07	6/0
29	Washington, Leon	RB/KR	5-8	202	26	3	Florida State	Jacksonville, Fla.	D4b-'06	16/4
67	Woody, Damien	OL	6-3	335	30	10	Boston College	Beaveram, Va.	UFA(Det)-'08	13/8*
38	Woolfolk, Andre	CB	6-2	197	28	5	Oklahoma	Denver, Colo.	FA-'08	0*
15	Wright, Wallace	WR	6-1	191	24	2	North Carolina	Fayetteville, N.C.	FA-'06	16/0

*   Bing did not play in 1 game for Oakland; Chatman played 14 games with Miami; Faneca played 16 games with Pittsburgh; Franks played 8 games with Green Bay; Hawkins last active with New England in '06; Hunter last active with Jacksonville in '06; Ihedigbo did not play in 1 game; Jenkins played 16 games with Carolina; Johnson last active with Houston in '06; McChesney last active with N.Y. Jets in '05; Pace played 16 games with Arizona; Richardson played 14 games with Minnesota; Stuckey did not play in 1 game; Woody played 13 games with Detroit; Woolfolk was last active with Tennessee in '06.

t-   Jets traded for Jenkins (Car).

Traded—DT Dewayne Robertson (16 games in '07) to Denver; LB Jonathan Vilma (7) to New Orleans.

Players lost through free agency (4): S Erik Coleman (Atl; 15 games in '07), LB Victor Hobson (NE; 16), OL Wade Smith (KC; 14), TE Sean Ryan (Mia; 10).

Also played with Jets in '07—FB Darian Barnes (5 games), G Adrian Clarke (14), CB Andre Dyson (10), DE Eric Hicks (11), T Adrien Jones (7), TE Joe Kowalewski (13), WR Justin McCareins (16), FB Stacy Tutt (9), S Rashad Washington (9).

2008 FIRST-YEAR ROSTER

Name	Pos.	Ht.	Wt.	Age	College	Hometown	How Acq.
Ainge, Erik	QB	6-5	221	22	Tennessee	Hillsboro, Ore.	D5
Ball, David (1)	WR	6-0	197	24	New Hampshire	Berlin, Vt.	FA-'07
Boulay, Etienne	DB	5-9	187	25	New Hampshire	Montreal, Canada	FA
Caulcrick, Jehuu	RB	6-0	254	25	Michigan State	Findley Lake, N.Y.	FA
Clowney, David (1)	WR	6-0	188	23	Virginia Tech	Delray Beach, Fla.	FA-'07
Cummings, Kenwin	DE	6-3	270	22	Wingate	Maxton, N.C.	FA
Daniels, Stanley (1)	OL	6-4	320	23	Washington	San Diego, Calif.	FA
Garner, Nate	OL	6-7	318	23	Arkansas	Roland, Ark.	D7
Gholston, Vernon	LB	6-3	264	23	Ohio State	Detroit, Mich.	D1a
Henry, Marcus	WR	6-4	207	22	Kansas	Lawton, Okla.	D6
Kapinos, Jeremy (1)	P	6-1	235	24	Penn State	Springfield, Va.	FA-'07
Keller, Dustin	TE	6-2	248	23	Purdue	Lafayette, Ind.	D1b
Lowery, Dwight	CB	5-11	201	22	San Jose State	Santa Cruz, Calif.	D4
Lyles, Nate	DB	6-0	203	22	Virginia	Chicago, Ill.	FA
Mattison, Bryan	DE	6-3	272	24	Iowa	Mishawaka, Ind.	FA
McMackin, Shawn	OL	6-3	287	23	Hofstra	River Vale, N.J.	FA
Myers, Mark	K	6-2	195	26	Florida Atlantic	Rockledge, Fla.	FA
Oldenburg, Clint (1)	OL	6-5	300	24	Colorado State	Gillette, Wyo.	FA-'07
Pitoitua, Ropati	DE	6-8	290	23	Washington State	Spanaway, Wash.	FA
Ratliff, Brett (1)	QB	6-4	224	23	Utah	Chico, Calif.	FA-'07
Raymond, Paul	WR	5-10	170	22	Brown	Miami, Fla.	FA
Turner, Robert (1)	OL	6-4	308	24	New Mexico	Austin, Texas	FA-'07
Valentine, Justin	FB	6-1	230	23	Minnesota	Columbus, Ohio	FA
Woodhead, Danny	RB	5-9	200	23	Chadron State	North Platte, Neb.	FA

The term NFL Rookie is defined as a player who is in his first season of professional football and has not been on the roster of another professional football team for any regular-season or postseason games. A Rookie is designated by an "R" on NFL rosters. Players who have been active in another professional football league or players who have NFL experience, including either preseason training camp or being on an Active List or Inactive List, or on Reserve/Injured or Reserve/Physically Unable to Perform for fewer than six regular-season games, are termed NFL First-Year Players. An NFL First-Year Player is designated by a "1" on NFL rosters. Thereafter, a player is credited with an additional year of experience for each season in which he accumulates six games on the Active List or Inactive List, or on Reserve/Injured or Reserve/Physically Unable to Perform.

Log on to www.newyorkjets.com for an up-to-date roster; Age listed is as of September 4, 2008.

COACHING STAFF

Head Coach,
Eric Mangini

Pro Career: Eric Mangini was named the fourteenth full-time head coach of the New York Jets on January 17, 2006. Mangini guided the Jets to a 10-6 record and the Jets 12th postseason berth in franchise history in 2006. The 10-6 record tied him with the Saints' Sean Payton for the best record among first-year head coaches in 2006. He joined the Jets following six seasons with the New England Patriots (2000-05), the first five of which he served as the defensive backs coach before earning a promotion to defensive coordinator. Mangini is entering his fourteenth season in the NFL and his third as a head coach. He has been a part of five division titles and three Super Bowl championships in his career. Prior to joining the Patriots, Mangini served as an assistant on Bill Parcells' coaching staff with the Jets (1997-1999), where he worked primarily as the defensive assistant/quality control coach. In 1996, he served as a quality control/offensive assistant on Ted Marchibroda's coaching staff with the Baltimore Ravens. Mangini's first NFL coaching opportunity came in 1995 as an assistant on Belichick's Cleveland Browns staff. While completing his Wesleyan degree in Melbourne, Australia, Mangini served as the head coach and defensive coordinator for the Kew Colts, a semi-professional football team, and led them to back-to-back titles. Career record: 14-19.

Background: Mangini set a school record with 36.5 sacks as a nose tackle in college for Wesleyan (Conn.) from 1989-1990, 1992-93. He was voted a first-team all-star by NESCAC and ECAC New England Division III.

Personal: Age 37, born in Hartford, Conn. Mangini and his wife, Julie, have two sons, Jake and Luke.

ASSISTANT COACHES

Sal Alosi, head strength and conditioning; born Massapequa, N.Y. Linebacker Hofstra 1996-2000. No pro playing experience. College coach: Hofstra 2001. Pro coach: New York Jets 2002-05, Atlanta Falcons 2006, re-joined Jets in 2007.

Mike Bloomgren, quality control/offense; born Tallahassee, Fl.a Attended Florida State. No college or pro playing experience. College coach: Florida State 1997-98 Alabama 1999-2001, Catawba College 2002-04, Delta State 2005-06. Pro coach: Joined Jets in 2007.

Bill Callahan, asst. head coach/offense; born Chicago. Quarterback Benedictine 1975-77. No pro playing experience. College coach: Illinois 1980-86, Northern Arizona 1987-88, Southern Illinois 1989, Wisconsin 1990-94, Nebraska 2004-2007 (head coach). Pro coach: Philadelphia Eagles 1995-97, Oakland Raiders 1998-

2003 (head coach 2002-03), joined Jets in 2008.

Bryan Cox, asst. defensive line; born East St. Louis, Ill. Linebacker Western Illinois 1987-1990. Pro linebacker Miami Dolphins 1991-95, Chicago Bears 1996-97, New York Jets 1998-2000, New England Patriots 2001, New Orleans Saints 2002. Pro coach: Joined Jets in 2006.

Brian Daboll, quarterbacks; born Welland, Ontario, Canada. Safety Rochester 1994-96. No pro playing experience. College coach: William & Mary 1997, Michigan State 1998-99. Pro coach: New England Patriots 2000-2006, joined Jets in 2007.

Mike Devlin, tight ends/asst. offensive line; born Blacksburg, Va. Offensive line Iowa 1989-1992. Pro offensive lineman Buffalo Bills 1993-95, Arizona Cardinals 1996-99. College coach: Toledo 2004-05. Pro coach: Arizona Cardinals 2000-03, joined Jets in 2006.

Andy Dickerson, quality control/defense; born Wilmington, Del. Offensive lineman Tufts 1999-2002. No pro playing experience. College coach: Tufts 2003. Pro coach: Joined Jets in 2006.

Jerome Henderson; defensive backs; born Portsmouth, Va. Defensive back Clemson 1987-1990. Pro cornerback New England Patriots 1991-93, 1996, Buffalo Bills 1993-94, Philadelphia Eagles 1995, New York Jets 1997-98. Pro coach: Joined Jets in 2006.

Jim Herrmann, linebackers; born Hollywood, Calif. Linebacker Michigan 1979-1982. No pro playing experience. College coach: Michigan 1983, 1986-2005. Pro coach: Joined Jets in 2006.

Mike Jones, asst. strength and conditioning; born Thomasville, Ga. Safety Georgia 1989-1992. No pro experience. College coach: Arizona State 2006. Pro coach: Joined Jets in 2007.

Ben Kotwica, quality control/special teams and defense; born Tinley Park, Ill. Linebacker Army 1995-97. No pro playing experience. Pro coach: Joined Jets in 2007.

Rick Lyle, asst. strength and conditioning; born Monroe, La. Defensive lineman Missouri 1989-1993. Pro defensive lineman Cleveland Browns 1994-95, Baltimore Ravens 1996, New York Jets 1997-2001, New England Patriots 2002-03. Pro coach: Joined Jets in 2006.

Noel Mazzone, wide receivers; born Mt. Vernon, Wash. Quarterback New Mexico 1975-79. No pro playing experience. College coach: New Mexico 1980-81, Colorado State 1982-86, Texas Christian 1987-1991, Minnesota 1992-94, Mississippi 1994-98, Auburn 1999-2001, Oregon State 2002, North Carolina State 2003-05. Pro coach: Joined Jets in 2006.

Kevin O'Dea, special teams coordinator; born Williamsport, Pa. Wide receiver/defensive back Lock Haven 1984-85. No

pro playing experience. College coach: Lock Haven 1986, Cornell 1987, Virginia 1988-1990, Penn State 1991-93. Pro coach: San Diego Chargers 1994-95, Tampa Bay Buccaneers 1996-2001, Detroit Lions 2002-03, Arizona Cardinals 2004-05, Chicago Bears 2006-07, joined Jets in 2008.

Dan Quinn, defensive line; born Orange, N.J. Defensive lineman Salisbury State 1990-93. No pro playing experience. College coach: William & Mary 1994, Virginia Military Institute 1995, Hofstra 1997-2000. Pro coach: San Francisco 49ers 2001-04, Miami Dolphins 2005-06, joined Jets in 2007.

Jimmy Raye, running backs; born Fayetteville, N.C. Quarterback Michigan State 1964-68. Pro defensive back Philadelphia Eagles 1969. College coach: Michigan State 1971-75, Wyoming 1976. Pro coach: San Francisco 49ers 1977, Detroit Lions 1978-79, Atlanta Falcons 1980-82, 1987-89, Los Angeles Rams 1983-84, 1991, Tampa Bay Buccaneers 1985-86, New England Patriots 1990, Kansas City Chiefs 1992-2000, Washington Redskins 2001, New York Jets 2002-03, Oakland Raiders 2004-2005, re-joined Jets in 2006.

Brian Schottenheimer, offensive coordinator; born Denver. Quarterback Kansas 1992, Florida 1993-96. No pro playing experience. College coach: Syracuse 1999, Southern California 2000. Pro coach: St. Louis Rams 1997, Kansas City Chiefs 1998, Washington Redskins 2001, San Diego Chargers 2002-05, joined Jets in 2006.

Bob Sutton, defensive coordinator; born Ypsilanti, Mich. Attended Eastern Michigan. No college or pro playing experience. College coach: Michigan 1972-73, Syracuse 1974, Western Michigan 1975-76, 1980-81, Illinois 1977-79, North Carolina State 1982, Army 1983-1999 (head coach 1991-99). Pro coach: Joined Jets in 2000.

Brian Smith, quality control/offense; born Wilmington, Del. Defensive back Massachusetts 1997-2000. No pro playing experience. College coach: Massachusetts 2004-06. Pro coach: Joined Jets in 2007.

American Football Conference
West Division
Team Colors: Silver and Black
1220 Harbor Bay Parkway
Alameda, California 94502
Telephone: (510) 864-5000

2008 SCHEDULE
PRESEASON
Aug. 8   **San Francisco** 7:00
Aug. 15 at Tennessee. 7:00
Aug. 23 **Arizona**. 6:00
Aug. 29 at Seattle. 7:00

REGULAR SEASON
Sep. 8   **Denver** (Mon.) 7:15
Sep. 14 at Kansas City 12:00
Sep. 21 at Buffalo 1:00
Sep. 28 **San Diego** 1:05
Oct. 5   BYE
Oct. 12 at New Orleans 12:00
Oct. 19 **N.Y. Jets**. 1:15
Oct. 26 at Baltimore 1:00
Nov. 2   **Atlanta** 1:15
Nov. 9   **Carolina** 1:05
Nov. 16 at Miami 1:00
Nov. 23 at Denver 2:05
Nov. 30 **Kansas City** 1:15
Dec. 4   at San Diego (Thu.). 5:15
Dec. 14 **New England** 1:15
Dec. 21 **Houston** 1:05
Dec. 28 at Tampa Bay 1:00

Stadium: McAfee Coliseum
    (opened in 1966)
    • **Capacity:** 63,132
    7000 Coliseum Way
    Oakland, CA 94621-1917
Playing Surface: Grass
Training Camp: Napa Valley Marriott
    Napa, California 94558

McAFEE COLISEUM

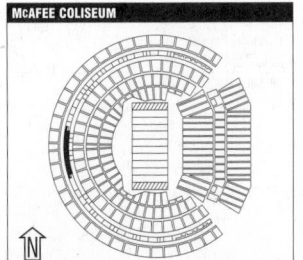

CLUB OFFICIALS
Owner: Al Davis
Chief Executive: Amy Trask
Legal: Jeff Birren, Dan Ventrelle
Finance: Marc Badain, Tom Blanda,
  Ed Villanueva, Derek Person
Special Projects: Jim Otto
Senior Administrator: Morris Bradshaw
Senior Executive: John Herrera
Public Relations: Mike Taylor
Tickets, Suites & Premium Seats:
  Rob Sullivan
Multi-Cultural Initiatives: Patty Herrera,
  Elena Valenzuela
Internet: Jerry Knaak
Marketing: Robert Kinnard
Community Relations: Scott Fink
Youth Initiatives: Rosie Bone
Raiderettes: Karen Kovac
Trainers: H. Rod Martin, Scott Touchet
Equipment: Bob Romanski,
  Richard Romanski, Danny Molina
Video Operations: Dave Nash, Jim Otten,
  John Otten
Broadcasting: Chris Gargano,
  Vittorio DeBartolo
Computer Operations: Matt Pasco

COACHING HISTORY
Oakland 1960-1981
Los Angeles 1982-1994
(425-331-11)
Records include postseason games
1960-61   Eddie Erdelatz* 6-10-0
1961-62   Marty Feldman** 2-15-0
1962   Red Conkright 1-8-0
1963-65   Al Davis 23-16-3
1966-68   John Rauch 35-10-1
1969-1978 John Madden 112-39-7
1979-1987 Tom Flores 91-56-0
1988-89   Mike Shanahan*** 8-12-0
1989-1994 Art Shell 56-41-0
1995-96   Mike White 15-17-0
1997   Joe Bugel 4-12-0
1998-2001 Jon Gruden 40-28-0
2002-03   Bill Callahan 17-18-0
2004-05   Norv Turner 9-23-0
2006   Art Shell 2-14-0
2007   Lane Kiffin 4-12-0
  *Released after two games in 1961
  **Released after five games in 1962
***Released after four games in 1989

PAID ATTENDANCE
Home 451,967   Away 554,193
Total 1,006,160
Single-game home record,
  62,660 (11/3/02)
Single-season home record,
  471,151 (2002)

2008 DRAFT CHOICES
Round	Name	Pos.	College
1	Darren McFadden	RB	Arkansas
4	Tyvon Branch	DB	Connecticut
	Arman Shields	WR	Richmond
6	Trevor Scott	DE	Buffalo
7	Chaz Schilens	WR	San Diego St.

OAKLAND RAIDERS

2007 TEAM RECORD
PRESEASON (2-2)

Date	Result	Opponent
8/11	W 27-23	Arizona
8/18	L 21-26	at San Francisco
8/24	W 20-10	St. Louis
8/30	L 14-19	at Seattle

REGULAR SEASON (4-12)

Date	Result	Opponent	Att.
9/9	L 21-36	Detroit	61,547
9/16	L 20-23	at Denver (OT)	76,784
9/23	W 26-24	Cleveland	51,075
9/30	W 35-17	at Miami	70,621
10/14	L 14-28	at San Diego	67,523
10/21	L 10-12	Kansas City	62,240
10/28	L 9-13	at Tennessee	69,143
11/4	L 17-24	Houston	49,603
11/11	L 6-17	Chicago	62,715
11/18	L 22-29	at Minnesota	62,960
11/25	W 20-17	at Kansas City	76,210
12/2	W 34-20	Denver	61,990
12/9	L 7-38	at Green Bay	70,828
12/16	L 14-21	Indianapolis	62,000
12/23	L 11-49	at Jacksonville	66,905
12/30	L 17-30	San Diego	61,706

(OT) Overtime

SCORE BY PERIODS

Raiders	43	75	69	96	0	—	283
Opponents	88	101	91	115	3	—	398

2007 TEAM STATISTICS

	Raiders	Opp.
Total First Downs	267	292
Rushing	111	121
Passing	133	156
Penalty	23	15
3rd Down: Made/Att	82/229	82/210
3rd Down Pct.	35.8	39.0
4th Down: Made/Att	10/24	6/11
4th Down Pct.	41.7	54.5
Possession Avg.	31:09	28:51
Total Net Yards	4717	5466
Avg. Per Game	294.8	341.6
Total Plays	1000	952
Avg. Per Play	4.7	5.7
Net Yards Rushing	2086	2334
Avg. Per Game	130.4	145.9
Total Rushes	508	486
Net Yards Passing	2631	3132
Avg. Per Game	164.4	195.8
Sacked/Yards Lost	41/262	27/186
Gross Yards	2893	3318
Att./Completions	451/260	439/261
Completion Pct.	57.6	59.5
Had Intercepted	20	18
Punts/Average	73/49.1	71/42.9
Net Punting Avg.	73/41.1	71/39.4
Penalties/Yards	120/864	99/734
Fumbles/Ball Lost	42/17	19/8
Touchdowns	30	46
Rushing	11	24
Passing	17	17
Returns	2	5

2007 INDIVIDUAL STATISTICS

PASSING

PASSING	Att.	Comp.	Yds.	Pct.	TD	Int.	Tkld.	Rate
McCown	190	111	1151	58.4	10	11	14/92	69.4
Culpepper	186	108	1331	58.1	5	5	21/130	78.0
Russell	66	36	373	54.5	2	4	6/40	55.9
Walter	8	5	38	62.5	0	0	0/0	74.0
Curry	1	0	0	0.0	0	0	0/0	39.6
Raiders	451	260	2893	57.6	17	20	41/262	70.9
Opponents	439	261	3318	59.5	17	18	27/186	78.9

SCORING

SCORING	TD R	TD P	TD Rt	PAT	FG	Saf	PTS
Janikowski	0	0	0	28/28	23/32	0	97
Porter	0	6	0	0/0	0/0	0	36
Curry	0	4	0	0/0	0/0	0	28
Fargas	4	0	0	0/0	0/0	0	24
Culpepper	3	0	0	0/0	0/0	0	18
Jordan	3	0	0	0/0	0/0	0	18
Miller	0	3	0	0/0	0/0	0	18
Dwight	0	2	0	0/0	0/0	0	12
Howard	0	0	2	0/0	0/0	0	12
Griffith	0	1	0	0/0	0/0	0	6
Madsen	0	1	0	0/0	0/0	0	6
Rhodes	1	0	0	0/0	0/0	0	6
Warren	0	0	0	0/0	0/0	1	2
Raiders	11	17	2	28/28	23/32	1	283
Opponents	24	17	5	43/43	25/34	1	398

2-Pt. Conversions: Curry 2, Raiders 2-2, Opponents 1-3

RUSHING

RUSHING	No.	Yds	Avg	LG	TD
Fargas	222	1009	4.5	48	4
Jordan	144	549	3.8	33	3
Rhodes	75	302	4.0	25	1
McCown	29	143	4.9	24	0
Culpepper	20	40	2.0	9	3
Griffith	7	27	3.9	6	0
Dwight	2	12	6.0	10	0
Russell	5	4	0.8	7	0
Higgins	2	3	1.5	8	0
Curry	1	1	1.0	1	0
Lechler	1	-4	-4.0	-4	0
Raiders	508	2086	4.1	48	11
Opponents	486	2334	4.8	62t	24

RECEIVING

RECEIVING	No.	Yds	Avg	LG	TD
Curry	55	717	13.0	49	4
Porter	44	705	16.0	59	6
Miller	44	444	10.1	28	3
Jordan	28	247	8.8	27	0
Griffith	26	165	6.3	29	1
Fargas	23	188	8.2	17	0
Rhodes	11	70	6.4	17	0
Madsen	8	102	12.8	39	1
M. Williams	7	90	12.9	24	0
Dwight	6	98	16.3	28t	2
Higgins	6	47	7.8	16	0
McFoy	1	19	19.0	19	0
O'Neal	1	1	1.0	1	0
Raiders	260	2893	11.1	59	17
Opponents	261	3318	12.7	80t	17

INTERCEPTIONS

INTERCEPTIONS	No.	Yds	Avg	LG	TD
Howard	6	172	28.7	66t	2
Morrison	4	94	23.5	45	0
Routt	3	31	10.3	31	0
Schweigert	2	10	5.0	10	0
Asomugha	1	10	10.0	10	0
Huff	1	4	4.0	4	0
Washington	1	0	0.0	0	0
Raiders	18	321	17.8	66t	2
Opponents	20	143	7.2	37	0

PUNTING

PUNTING	No.	Yds.	Avg.	In 20	LG
Lechler	73	3585	49.1	25	70
Raiders	73	3585	49.1	25	70
Opponents	71	3044	42.9	28	62

PUNT RETURNS

PUNT RETURNS	Ret	FC	Yds	Avg	LG	TD
Higgins	20	6	103	5.2	54	0
Dwight	9	3	54	6.0	16	0
Carr	8	7	52	6.5	24	0
Asomugha	1	0	0	0.0	0	0
Raiders	38	16	209	5.5	54	0
Opponents	40	12	445	11.1	90t	2

KICKOFF RETURNS

KICKOFF RETURNS	No.	Yds	Avg	LG	TD
Carr	59	1327	22.5	43	0
Rhodes	16	312	19.5	31	0
Brayton	1	6	6.0	6	0
Dwight	1	30	30.0	30	0
Griffith	1	11	11.0	11	0
Raiders	78	1686	21.6	43	0
Opponents	43	963	22.4	99t	11

FIELD GOALS

FIELD GOALS	1-19	20-29	30-39	40-49	50+
Janikowski	0/0	4/4	6/7	7/10	6/11
Raiders	0/0	4/4	6/7	7/10	6/11
Opponents	1/1	10/10	8/10	6/10	0/3

SACKS

SACKS	No.
Burgess	8.0
Clemons	8.0
Warren	4.0
Sapp	2.0
Howard	1.0
Huff	1.0
Kelly	1.0
Morrison	1.0
Richardson	1.0
Raiders	27.0
Opponents	41.0

RECORD HOLDERS
INDIVIDUAL RECORDS—CAREER

Category	Name	Performance
Rushing (Yds.)	Marcus Allen, 1982-1992	8,545
Passing (Yds.)	Ken Stabler, 1970-79	19,078
Passing (TDs)	Ken Stabler, 1970-79	150
Receiving (No.)	Tim Brown, 1988-2003	1,070
Receiving (Yds.)	Tim Brown, 1988-2003	14,734
Interceptions	Willie Brown, 1967-1978	39
	Lester Hayes, 1977-1986	39
Punting (Avg.)	Shane Lechler, 2000-07	*46.5
Punt Return (Avg.)	Claude Gibson, 1963-65	12.6
Kickoff Return (Avg.)	Jack Larscheid, 1960-61	28.4
Field Goals	Chris Bahr, 1980-88	162
Touchdowns (Tot.)	Tim Brown, 1988-2003	104
Points	George Blanda, 1967-1975	863

INDIVIDUAL RECORDS—SINGLE SEASON

Category	Name	Performance
Rushing (Yds.)	Marcus Allen, 1985	1,759
Passing (Yds.)	Rich Gannon, 2002	4,689
Passing (TDs)	Daryle Lamonica, 1969	34
Receiving (No.)	Tim Brown 1997	104
Receiving (Yds.)	Tim Brown, 1997	1,408
Interceptions	Lester Hayes, 1980	13
Punting (Avg.)	Shane Lechler, 2007	49.1
Punt Return (Avg.)	Claude Gibson, 1964	14.4
Kickoff Return (Avg.)	Harold Hart, 1975	30.5
Field Goals	Jeff Jaeger, 1993	35
Touchdowns (Tot.)	Marcus Allen, 1984	18
Points	Jeff Jaeger, 1993	132

INDIVIDUAL RECORDS—SINGLE GAME

Category	Name	Performance
Rushing (Yds.)	Napoleon Kaufman, 10-19-97	227
Passing (Yds.)	Cotton Davidson, 10-25-64	427
Passing (TDs)	Tom Flores, 12-22-63	6
	Daryle Lamonica, 10-19-69	6
Receiving (No.)	Tim Brown, 12-21-97	14
Receiving (Yds.)	Art Powell, 12-22-63	247
Interceptions	Many times	3
	Last time by Rod Woodson, 9-29-02	
Field Goals	Jeff Jaeger, 12-11-94	5
	Sebastian Janikowski, 10-29-00	5
Touchdowns (Tot.)	Art Powell, 12-22-63	4
	Marcus Allen, 9-24-84	4
	Harvey Williams, 11-16-97	4
Points	Art Powell, 12-22-63	24
	Marcus Allen, 9-24-84	24
	Harvey Williams, 11-16-97	24

*NFL Record

2008 VETERAN ROSTER

No.	Name	Pos.	Ht.	Wt.	Age	NFL Exp.	College	Hometown	How Acq.	'07 Games/ Starts
47	Alston, Jon	LB	6-0	225	25	3	Stanford	Los Angeles, Calif.	FA-'07	13/0
21	Asomugha, Nnamdi	CB	6-2	210	27	6	California	Los Angeles, Calif.	D1-'03	15/15
28	Baker, Rashad	S	5-10	200	26	5	Tennessee	Camden, N.J.	W(NE)-'07	8/0*
35	Bowie, John	CB	5-11	190	24	2	Cincinnati	Columbus, Ohio	D4-'07	3/0
57	Brown, Ricky	LB	6-2	235	24	3	Boston College	Cincinnati, Ohio	FA-'06	16/1
56	Burgess, Derrick	DE	6-2	260	30	8	Mississippi	Greenbelt, Md.	UFA(Phil)-'05	14/14
66	Carlisle, Cooper	G	6-5	295	31	9	Florida	McComb, Miss.	UFA(Den)-'07	16/16
18	Carter, Drew	WR	6-4	205	26	5	Ohio State	Solon, Ohio	UFA(Car)-'08	16/7*
59	Condo, Jon	LS/LB	6-3	250	27	2	Maryland	Philipsburg, Pa.	FA-'06	16/0
40	Cooper, Jarrod	S	6-1	215	30	7	Kansas State	Pearland, Texas	FA-'04	6/0
8 #	Culpepper, Daunte	QB	6-4	260	31	9	Central Florida	Ocala, Fla.	FA-'07	7/5
89	Curry, Ronald	WR	6-2	210	29	7	North Carolina	Hampton, Va.	D7-'02	16/13
17 #	Dwight, Tim	WR	5-8	185	33	10	Iowa	Iowa City, Iowa	FA-'06	8/1
38	Echemandu, Adimchinobi	RB	5-10	225	27	5	California	Hawthorne, Calif.	FA-'08	9/0*
58	Edwards, Kalimba	DE	6-6	265	28	7	South Carolina	East Point, Ga.	UFA-'08	8/6*
50	Ekejiuba, Isaiah	LB	6-4	240	26	4	Virginia	Somerset, N.J.	FA-'05	10/0
31	Eugene, Hiram	S	6-2	200	27	3	Louisiana Tech	Jeanerette, La.	FA-'06	16/5
25	Fargas, Justin	RB	6-1	220	28	6	Southern California	Sherman Oaks, Calif.	D3-'03	14/7
76	Gallery, Robert	G	6-7	325	28	5	Iowa	Masonville, Iowa	D1-'04	16/16
94	Gbaja-Biamila, Akbar	LB	6-5	260	29	3	San Diego State	Los Angeles, Calif.	FA-'08	1/0*
74	Green, Cornell	T	6-6	315	32	10	Central Florida	St. Petersburg, Fla.	UFA(TB)-'07	10/10
36	Griffith, Justin	RB	6-0	230	28	6	Mississippi State	Magee, Miss.	UFA(Atl)-'07	16/13
64	Grove, Jake	C	6-4	300	28	5	Virginia Tech	Forest, Va.	D2-'04	7/2
23 t-	Hall, DeAngelo	CB	5-10	195	24	5	Virginia Tech	Chesapeake, Va.	T(Atl)-'08	16/15*
77	Harris, Kwame	T	6-7	320	26	5	Stanford	Newark, Del.	UFA(SF)-'08	12/0*
44	Hartwell, Edgerton	LB	6-2	250	30	8	Western Illinois	Las Vegas, Nev.	FA-'08	0*
75	Henderson, Mario	T	6-7	300	23	2	Florida State	Lehigh Acres, Fla.	D3-'07	1/0
15	Higgins, Johnnie Lee	WR	5-11	185	24	2	Texas-El Paso	Sweeny, Texas	D3-'07	16/1
53	Howard, Thomas	LB	6-3	240	25	3	Texas-El Paso	Lubbock, Texas	D2-'06	16/16
24	Huff, Michael	S	6-1	205	25	3	Texas	Irving, Texas	D1-'06	16/16
11	Janikowski, Sebastian	K	6-2	250	30	9	Florida State	Daytona Beach, Fla.	D1-'00	16/0
37	Johnson, Chris	CB	6-1	200	28	6	Louisville	Longview, Texas	UFA(KC)-'07	13/0
34	Jordan, LaMont	RB	5-10	230	29	8	Maryland	Suitland, Md.	UFA(NYJ)-'05	13/7
96	Joseph, William	DT	6-5	310	29	5	Miami	Miami, Fla.	UFA(Oak)-'08	0*
93	Kelly, Tommy	DT	6-6	300	27	5	Mississippi State	Jackson, Miss.	FA-'04	7/6
9	Lechler, Shane	P	6-2	225	32	9	Texas A&M	Sealy, Texas	D5-'00	16/0
42 #	Lee, ReShard	RB	5-10	220	27	4	Middle Tennessee St.	Brunswick, Ga.	FA-'06	0*
85	Madsen, John	TE	6-5	240	25	3	Utah	West Valley City, Utah	FA-'06	16/3
14	McFoy, Chris	WR	6-1	200	25	2	Southern California	Chino, Calif.	FA-'07	3/0
79	McQuistan, Paul	G	6-6	315	25	3	Weber State	Lebanon, Ore.	D3-'06	16/6
80	Miller, Zach	TE	6-5	255	22	2	Arizona State	Phoenix, Ariz.	D2-'07	16/16
51	Morris , Chris	C	6-4	305	25	3	Michigan State	Temperance, Mich.	D7-'06	10/0
52	Morrison, Kirk	LB	6-2	240	26	4	San Diego State	Oakland, Calif.	D3-'05	16/16
62 #	Newberry, Jeremy	C	6-5	315	32	10	California	Antioch, Calif.	UFA(SF)-'07	13/13
46	O'Neal, Oren	RB	5-11	245	24	2	Arkansas State	Stuttgart, Ark.	D6-'07	13/1
98	Richardson, Jay	DE	6-6	280	24	2	Ohio State	Washington D.C.	D5-'07	15/10
26	Routt, Stanford	CB	6-1	195	25	4	Houston	Austin, Texas	D2-'05	15/12
2	Russell, JaMarcus	QB	6-6	255	23	2	Louisiana State	Mobile, Ala.	D1-'07	3/0
90	Sands, Terdell	DT	6-7	335	28	6	Tenn. Chattanooga	Chattanooga, Tenn.	FA-'03	15/10
30	Schweigert, Stuart	S	6-2	210	27	5	Purdue	Saginaw, Mich.	D3-'04	14/10
95	Shaw, Josh	DT	6-4	320	28	5	Michigan State	Ft. Lauderdale, Fla.	FA-'07	1/0
94	Spires, Greg	DE	6-1	265	34	11	Florida State	Cape Coral, Fla.	FA-'07	10/8*
86	Stewart, Tony	TE	6-5	260	29	8	Penn State	Allentown, Pa.	UFA(Cin)-'07	15/0
55	Thomas, Robert	LB	6-0	235	28	7	UCLA	El Centro, Calif.	FA-'06	13/11
32	Waddell, Michael	CB	5-10	180	27	4	North Carolina	Elerbe, N.C.	FA-'08	0*
71	Wade, John	C	6-5	300	33	11	Marshall	Harrisonburg, Va.	UFA(TB)-'08	0*
87	Wakefield, Fred	TE	6-7	295	29	8	Illinois	Tuscola, Ill.	UFA(Ariz)-'07	0*
17	Walker, Javon	WR	6-3	215	29	7	Florida State	Lafayette, La.	FA-'08	0*
16	Walter, Andrew	QB	6-6	230	26	4	Arizona State	Grand Junction, Colo.	D3-'05	1/0
72	Wand , Seth	T	6-7	330	29	6	NW Missouri State	Springfield, Mo.	FA-'07	0*
61	Warren, Gerard	DT	6-4	325	30	8	Florida	Lake City, Fla.	T(Den)-'07	11/3
54	Williams, Sam	LB	6-5	260	28	6	Fresno State	Clayton, Calif.	D3-'03	10/4
28	Wilson, Gibril	S	6-0	210	26	5	Tennessee	San Jose, Calif.	UFA(NYG)-'08	0*
	Wilson, Mark	T	6-7	320	27	3	California	McArthur, Calif.	FA-'06	0*

*   Baker played 8 games with New England in '07; Carter played 16 games with Carolina; Echemandu played 9 games with Houston; Edwards played 8 games with Detroit; Gbaja-Biamila played 1 game with Miami; Hall played 16 games with Atlanta; Harris played 12 games with San Francisco; Hartwell last active with Atlanta in '06; Joseph missed '07 season because of injury with N.Y. Giants; Lee missed '07 season; Starks inactive for 3 games; Waddell last active with Tennessee in '05; Wade played 16 games with Tampa Bay; Wakefield missed '07 season because of injury with N.Y. Giants; Walker played 8 games with Denver; Wand did not play in 4 games; G. Wilson played 13 games with N.Y. Giants; M. Wilson inactive for 1 game.

t- Raiders traded for Hall (Atl).

\#   Unrestricted Free Agent; subject to developments.

Retired—Warren Sapp, 13-year defensive tackle, 16 games in '07.

Players lost through free agency (3): DE Tyler Brayton (Car; 16 games in '07), DE Chris Clemons (Phil; 16), QB Josh McCown (Mia; 9).

Also played with Raiders in '07—CB Chris Carr (16 games), WR Jerry Porter (16), RB Dominic Rhodes (10), T Barry Sims (16), WR Travis Taylor (1), S B.J. Ward (4), CB Fabian Washington (15), WR Mike Williams (6).

2008 FIRST-YEAR ROSTER

Name	Pos.	Ht.	Wt.	Age	College	Hometown	How Acq.
Boone, Jesse	C	6-5	300	26	Utah	Fillmore, Utah	FA-'07
Branch, Tyvon	S	6-0	205	21	Connecticut	Cicero, N.Y.	D4
Brown, Darrick	DB	6-3	200	24	McNeese State	Tangipahoa, La.	FA
Buchanon, Will (1)	WR	6-3	190	25	Southern California	Oceanside, Calif.	FA-'06
Bush, Michael (1)	RB	6-1	245	24	Louisville	Louisville, Ky.	D4-'07
Gray, Derrick	DE	6-4	265	22	Texas Southern	Silver Spring, Md.	FA
Gunheim, Greyson	DE	6-5	260	22	Washington	Sebastopol, Calif.	FA
Holland, Johnathan (1)	WR	6-1	195	23	Louisiana Tech	Archibald, La.	D7-'07
Jackson, Malik	LB	6-2	230	23	Louisville	Dunwoody, Ga.	FA
James, Drisan (1)	WR	5-11	185	23	Boise State	Phoenix, Ariz.	FA
McFadden, Darren	RB	6-2	210	21	Arkansas	North Little Rock, Ark.	D1
Meyer, Erik (1)	QB	6-1	215	25	Eastern Washington	La Mirada, Calif.	FA
Otis, Jeff (1)	QB	6-2	210	25	Columbia	St. Louis, Mo.	FA
Palmer, Jonathan (1)	T	6-5	335	24	Auburn	Decatur, Ga.	FA
Rankin, Louis	RB	6-1	205	23	Washington	Stockton, Calif.	FA
Reece, Marcel	WR	6-3	240	23	Washington	Hesperia, Calif.	FA
Rodd, Brandon	G	6-4	305	22	Arizona State	Aiea, Hawaii	FA
Schilens, Chaz	WR	6-4	225	22	San Diego State	Mesa, Ariz.	D7
Scott, Trevor	DE	6-5	255	24	Buffalo	Potsdam, N.Y.	D6
Shields, Arman	WR	6-1	195	23	Richmond	Washington, D.C.	D4
Simmons, Shane	LB	6-1	230	23	Western Washington	Kent, Wash.	FA
Strong, Darrell	TE	6-5	265	22	Pittsburgh	Fort Lauderdale, Fla.	FA
Wagner, Chris	TE	6-6	255	23	South Dakota State	Brookings, S.D.	FA
Watkins, Todd (1)	WR	6-3	195	25	Brigham Young	La Mesa, Calif.	FA
White, Brian	QB	6-5	225	23	Portland State	Mission Viejo, Calif.	FA

The term NFL Rookie is defined as a player who is in his first season of professional football and has not been on the roster of another professional football team for any regular-season or postseason games. A Rookie is designated by an "R" on NFL rosters. Players who have been active in another professional football league or players who have NFL experience, including either preseason training camp or being on an Active List or Inactive List, or on Reserve/Injured or Reserve/Physically Unable to Perform for fewer than six regular-season games, are termed NFL First-Year Players. An NFL First-Year Player is designated by a "1" on NFL rosters. Thereafter, a player is credited with an additional year of experience for each season in which he accumulates six games on the Active List or Inactive List, or on Reserve/Injured or Reserve/Physically Unable to Perform.

Log on to www.raiders.com for an up-to-date roster; Age listed is as of September 4, 2008.

COACHING STAFF
Head Coach,
Lane Kiffin

Pro Career: In 2007, named the sixteenth head coach in Raiders history. Upon being hired, he was the youngest head coach (31) in the modern NFL era. He was an assistant for Jacksonville in 2000. No pro playing experience. Career redord: 4-12.

Background: Lettered three seasons at quarterback for Fresno State (1994-96). Coached at Fresno State (1997-98), Colorado State (1999), and the University of Southern California (2001-06). He was offensive coordinator and recruiting coordinator in addition to coaching wide receivers at Southern California from 2005-06; was receivers coach/passing game coordinator in 2004; wide receivers coach from 2002-03 and was the Trojans' tight ends coach in 2001. Kiffin's play-calling, structure, and offensive design helped the Trojans produce two Heisman Trophy winners—Matt Leinart in 2004 and Reggie Bush in 2005—and two national championships (2003 and 2004).

Personal: Age 33, born in Bloomington, Minn. Lane and his wife Layla have two daughters, Landry and Pressley. Father, Monte, is currently Tampa Bay's defensive coordinator.

ASSISTANT COACHES
Willie Brown, squad development, defensive backs; born Yazoo City, Miss. Defensive back Grambling State 1959-1962. Pro defensive back Denver Broncos 1963-66, Oakland Raiders 1967-1978. Inducted into Pro Football Hall of Fame in 1984. College coach: Long Beach State 1990-91 (head coach 1991). Pro coach: Oakland/Los Angeles Raiders 1979-1988, rejoined Raiders in 1995.

Tom Cable, offensive line; born Merced, Calif. Offensive lineman Idaho 1982-86. Pro offensive lineman Indianapolis Colts 1987. College coach: Idaho 1987-88, San Diego State 1989, Cal State-Fullerton 1990, Nevada-Las Vegas 1991, California 1992-97, Colorado 1998-99, Idaho 2000-03, UCLA 2004-05. Pro coach: Atlanta Falcons 2006, joined Raiders in 2007.

James Cregg, asst. offensive line; born Syracuse, N.Y. Offensive lineman Colorado State 1992-95. No pro playing experience. College coach: Colorado State 1997-99, Colgate 2000-03, Idaho 2004-06. Pro coach: Joined Raiders in 2007.

John DeFilippo, quarterbacks; born Youngstown, Ohio. Quarterback James Madison 1996-99. No pro playing experience. College coach: Fordham 2000, Notre Dame 2001-02, Columbia 2003-04. Pro coach: New York Giants 2005-06, joined Raiders in 2007.

John Fassel, quality control, special teams; born Anaheim, Calif. Wide receiver/quarterback Pacific 1994-95, Weber State 1996-98. No pro playing experience. College coach: Bucknell 1999, 2001, Idaho State 2000, New Mexico Highlands 2002-03. Pro coach: Amsterdam Admirals (NFLE) 2000, Baltimore Ravens 2005-07; joined Raiders in 2008.

Jeff Fish, strength & conditioning; born Ithaca, N.Y. Wide receiver Western Carolina 1986-88. No pro playing experience. College coach: Clemson 1991-92, Kent State 1993-94, Tulsa 1995-96, Missouri 2001-02. Pro coach: Tampa Bay Buccaneers 1997, Kansas City Chiefs 1998-2000, joined Raiders in 2004.

Randy Hanson, asst. defensive backs; born Burlington, Wash. Quarterback Delta (Calif.) J.C. 1987, Walla Walla (Wash.) 1988-89, Pacific University (Ore.) 1990-91. No pro playing experience. College coach: Eastern Washington 1993-95, Washington 1996-97, Eastern Washington 1998-99, Portland State 2000-02. Pro coach: Minnesota Vikings 2003-05, St. Louis Rams 2006, joined Raiders in 2007.

Adam Henry, quality control, offense; born Beaumont, Texas. Wide receiver McNeese State 1992-93. Pro receiver New Orleans Saints 1995. College coach: McNeese State 1996-2006. Pro coach: joined Raiders in 2007.

Mark Jackson, director of football development; born Boston, Mass. Defensive back Colby (Maine) 1991-1994. No pro playing experience. College coach: Trinity 1995-96, Southern California 2001-2005. Pro coach: New England Patriots 1998-2000, joined Raiders in 2007.

Don Johnson, asst. defensive line; born Newark, N.J. Linebacker Jersey City State 1973-76. College coach: Jersey City State 1984-85. Riverside (Calif.) C.C. 1987-1990, Cal State-Fullerton 1991-92, Nevada 1995-98, UCLA 1999-2004, Pro coach: Chicago Bears 2005-06, joined Raiders in 2007.

Greg Knapp, offensive coordinator; born Long Beach, Calif. Quarterback Sacramento State 1982-85. No pro playing experience. College coach: Sacramento State 1986-1994. Pro coach: San Francisco 49ers 1995-2003, Atlanta Falcons 2004-06, joined Raiders in 2007.

Sanjay Lal, quality control, offense; born London, England. Wide receiver UCLA 1989, Washington, 1990-92. Pro wide receiver St. Louis Rams 1998, Scottish Claymores (World League) 1999. College coach: Los Medanos (Calif.) College 2003, Saint Mary's College 2004, California 2005-06, joined Raiders in 2007.

James Lofton, wide receivers; born Fort Ord, Calif. Wide receiver Stanford 1975-77. Pro wide receiver Green Bay Packers 1978-1986, Los Angeles Raiders 1987-88, Buffalo Bills 1989-1992, Los Angeles Rams 1993, Philadelphia Eagles 1993. Pro coach: San Diego Chargers 2002-2007, joined Raiders in 2008.

Don Martindale, linebackers; born Dayton, Ohio. Linebacker Defiance College 1984-86. No pro playing experience. College coach: Defiance College 1987, Notre Dame 1994-95, Cincinnati 1996-98, Western Illinois 1999, Western Kentucky 2000-02. Pro coach: Joined Raiders in 2004.

George Martinez, quality control, defense; born Fort Bragg, N.C. Quarterback Northwestern Oklahoma State 1969-1972. No pro playing experience. College coach: East Central (Okla.) 1981-87, Panhandle State 1988. New Mexico Highlands 1989-1991 (head coach). Pro coach: Arizona Cardinals 1993-94, joined Raiders in 2006.

Keith Millard, defensive line; born Pleasanton, Calif. Defensive lineman Washington State 1980-84. Pro defensive lineman Minnesota Vikings 1985-1991, Seattle Seahawks 1992, Green Bay Packers 1992, Philadelphia Eagles 1993. College coach: Fort Lewis 1996, Menlo College 1997-2000. Pro coach: San Francisco Demons (XFL) 2001, Denver Broncos 2002-04, joined Raiders in 2005.

Darren Perry, defensive backs; born Norfolk, Va. Safety Penn State 1989-1991. Pro safety Pittsburgh Steelers 1992-98, San Diego Chargers 1999, New Orleans Saints 2000. Pro coach: Cincinnati Bengals 2002, Pittsburgh Steelers 2003-06, joined Raiders in 2007.

Tom Rathman, running backs; born Grand Island, Neb. Running back Nebraska 1983-85. Pro running back San Francisco 49ers 1986-1993, Los Angeles Raiders 1994. College coach: Menlo College (Calif.) 1996. Pro coach: San Francisco 1997-2002, Detroit Lions 2003-05, joined Raiders in 2007.

Brad Roll, strength & conditioning; July 4, 1958, Houston. Center Blinn (Tex.) J.C. 1976-77, Stephen F. Austin 1978-79. No pro playing experience. College coach: Stephen F. Austin 1980, Southwestern Louisiana 1981-86, Kansas 1987-88, Miami 1989-1992. Pro coach: Tampa Bay Buccaneers 1993-95, Miami Dolphins 1996-2003, Buffalo Bills 2004-05, St. Louis Rams 2006-07, joined Raiders in 2008.

Rob Ryan, defensive coordinator; born Ardmore, Okla. Linebacker Oklahoma State 1984, Southwestern Oklahoma State 1985-86. No pro playing experience. College coach: Western Kentucky 1987, Ohio State 1988, Tennessee State 1989-1993, Hutchinson (Kan.) C.C. 1996, Oklahoma State 1997- 99. Pro coach: Arizona Cardinals 1994-95, New England Patriots 2000-03, joined Raiders in 2004.

Brian Schneider, special teams; born San Diego. Linebacker Colorado State 1989-1993. No pro playing experience. College coach: Colorado State 1994-2002, UCLA 2003-05, Iowa State 2006, Air Force 2007. Pro coach: Joined Raiders in 2007.

Kelly Skipper, tight ends; born Brawley, Calif. Running back Fresno State 1985-88. No pro playing experience. College coach: Fresno State 1989-1997, UCLA 1998-2002, Washington State 2003-06. Pro coach: Joined Raiders in 2007.

**American Football Conference
North Division**
Team Colors: Black and Gold
3400 South Water Street
Pittsburgh, Pennsylvania 15203
Telephone: (412) 432-7800

2008 SCHEDULE
PRESEASON
Aug. 8	**Philadelphia**	7:30
Aug. 14	at Buffalo (Toronto)	7:30
Aug. 23	at Minnesota	7:00
Aug. 28	**Carolina**	7:30

REGULAR SEASON
Sep. 7	**Houston**	1:00
Sep. 14	at Cleveland	8:15
Sep. 21	at Philadelphia	4:15
Sep. 29	**Baltimore** (Mon.)	8:30
Oct. 5	at Jacksonville	8:15
Oct. 12	BYE	
Oct. 19	at Cincinnati	1:00
Oct. 26	**N.Y. Giants**	4:15
Nov. 3	at Washington (Mon.)	8:30
Nov. 9	**Indianapolis**	4:15
Nov. 16	**San Diego**	4:15
Nov. 20	**Cincinnati** (Thu.)	8:15
Nov. 30	at New England	4:15
Dec. 7	**Dallas**	4:15
Dec. 14	at Baltimore	1:00
Dec. 21	at Tennessee	12:00
Dec. 28	**Cleveland**	1:00

Stadium: Heinz Field (opened in 2001)
 • **Capacity:** 65,050
 100 Art Rooney Avenue
 Pittsburgh, Pennsylvania 15212
Playing Surface: DD GrassMaster
Training Camp: St. Vincent College
 Latrobe, PA 15650

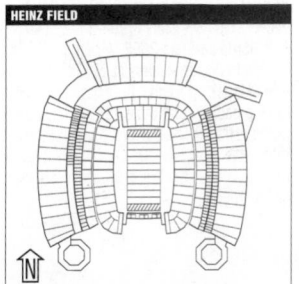

HEINZ FIELD

CLUB OFFICIALS
Chairman: Daniel M. Rooney
President: Arthur J. Rooney II
Vice President: John R. McGinley
Vice President: Arthur J. Rooney Jr.
Administration Advisor: Charles H. Noll
Director of Business: Mark Hart
Business Operations: Omar Khan
Director of Football Operations:
 Kevin Colbert
College Scouting Coordinator:
 Ron Hughes
Pro Scouting Coordinator: Doug Whaley
Head Athletic Trainer: John Norwig
Director of Marketing: Tony Quatrini
Communications Coordinator:
 Dave Lockett
Public Relations/Media Manager:
 Burt Lauten
Director of Stadium Management:
 Jim Sacco
Video Coordinator: Bob McCartney
Human Relations/Office Coordinator:
 Geraldine Glenn
Ticket Manager: Ben Lentz

COACHING HISTORY
**Pittsburgh Pirates 1933-39
(541-517-21)**
Records include postseason games
1933	Forrest (Jap) Douds	3-6-2
1934	Luby DiMelio	2-10-0
1935-36	Joe Bach	10-14-0
1937-39	Johnny (Blood) McNally*	6-19-0
1939-1940	Walt Kiesling	3-13-3
1941	Bert Bell**	0-2-0
	Aldo (Buff) Donelli***	0-5-0
1941-44	Walt Kiesling****	13-20-2
1945	Jim Leonard	2-8-0
1946-47	Jock Sutherland	13-10-1
1948-1951	Johnny Michelosen	20-26-2
1952-53	Joe Bach	11-13-0
1954-56	Walt Kiesling	14-22-0
1957-1964	Raymond (Buddy) Parker	51-47-6
1965	Mike Nixon	2-12-0
1966-68	Bill Austin	11-28-3
1969-1991	Chuck Noll	209-156-1
1992-2006	Bill Cowher	161-99-1
2007	Mike Tomlin	10-7-0

 *Released after three games in 1939
 **Resigned after two games in 1941
 ***Released after five games in 1941
 ****Co-coach with Earle (Greasy) Neale in
 Philadelphia-Pittsburgh merger in 1943 and
 with Phil Handler in Chicago Cardinals-
 Pittsburgh merger in 1944

PAID ATTENDANCE
Home 513,982   Away 559,125
Total 1,073,107
Single-game home record,
 64,420 (11/11/07)
Single-season home record,
 514,151 (2006)

2008 DRAFT CHOICES
Round	Name	Pos.	College
1	Rashard Mendenhall	RB	Illinois
2	Limas Sweed	WR	Texas
3	Bruce Davis	LB	UCLA
4	Tony Hills	T	Texas
5	Dennis Dixon	QB	Oregon
6	Mike Humpal	LB	Iowa
	Ryan Mundy	DB	West Virginia

PITTSBURGH STEELERS

2007 TEAM RECORD

PRESEASON (4-1)

Date	Result	Opponent
8/5	W 20-7	vs. New Orleans at Canton, OH
8/11	L 9-13	Green Bay
8/18	W 12-10	at Washington
8/26	W 27-13	Philadelphia
8/30	W 19-3	at Carolina

REGULAR SEASON (10-6)

Date	Result	Opponent	Att.
9/9	W 34-7	at Cleveland	73,089
9/16	W 26-3	Buffalo	64,307
9/23	W 37-16	San Francisco	64,313
9/30	L 14-21	at Arizona	64,844
10/7	W 21-0	Seattle	64,478
10/21	L 28-31	at Denver	77,038
10/28	W 24-13	at Cincinnati	66,188
11/5	W 38-7	Baltimore	63,457
11/11	W 31-28	Cleveland	64,781
11/18	L 16-19	at N.Y. Jets (OT)	77,659
11/26	W 3-0	Miami	57,704
12/2	W 24-10	Cincinnati	58,842
12/9	L 13-34	at New England	68,756
12/16	L 22-29	Jacksonville	58,793
12/20	W 41-24	at St. Louis	65,705
12/30	L 21-27	at Baltimore	71,353

(OT) Overtime

POSTSEASON (0-1)

Date	Result	Opponent	Att.
1/5	L 29-31	Jacksonville	63,629

SCORE BY PERIODS

Steelers	75	129	68	121	0	—	393
Opponents	67	78	70	51	3	—	269

2007 TEAM STATISTICS

	Steelers	Opp.
Total First Downs	298	249
Rushing	108	74
Passing	179	158
Penalty	11	17
3rd Down: Made/Att	103/220	87/215
3rd Down Pct.	46.8	40.5
4th Down: Made/Att	7/13	6/19
4th Down Pct.	53.8	31.6
Possession Avg.	33:18	26:42
Total Net Yards	5239	4262
Avg. Per Game	327.4	266.4
Total Plays	1000	933
Avg. Per Play	5.2	4.6
Net Yards Rushing	2168	1438
Avg. Per Game	135.5	89.9
Total Rushes	511	361
Net Yards Passing	3071	2824
Avg. Per Game	191.9	176.5
Sacked/Yards Lost	47/347	36/243
Gross Yards	3418	3067
Att./Completions	442/282	536/292
Completion Pct.	63.8	54.5
Had Intercepted	14	11
Punts/Average	68/42.4	82/43.0
Net Punting Avg.	68/37.9	82/38.6
Penalties/Yards	80/651	73/556
Fumbles/Ball Lost	21/8	30/14
Touchdowns	46	31
Rushing	9	6
Passing	34	22
Returns	3	3

2007 INDIVIDUAL STATISTICS

PASSING

	Att.	Comp.	Yds.	Pct.	TD	Int.	Tkld.	Rate
Roethlisberger	404	264	3154	65.3	32	11	47/347	104.1
Batch	36	17	232	47.2	2	3	0/0	52.1
Parker	1	0	0	0.0	0	0	0/0	39.6
Sepulveda	1	1	32	100.0	0	0	0/0	118.8
Steelers	442	282	3418	63.8	34	14	47/347	99.9
Opponents	536	292	3067	54.5	22	11	36/243	76.5

SCORING

	TD R	TD P	TD Rt	PAT	FG	Saf	PTS
Reed	0	0	0	44/44	23/25	0	113
Holmes	0	8	0	0/0	0/0	0	50
Ward	0	7	0	0/0	0/0	0	44
Davenport	5	2	0	0/0	0/0	0	42
Miller	0	7	0	0/0	0/0	0	42
Washington	0	5	0	0/0	0/0	0	30
Spaeth	0	3	0	0/0	0/0	0	18
Parker	2	0	0	0/0	0/0	0	12
Roethlisberger	2	0	0	0/0	0/0	0	12
McFadden	0	0	1	0/0	0/0	0	6
Rossum	0	0	1	0/0	0/0	0	6
Taylor	0	0	1	0/0	0/0	0	6
Tuman	0	1	0	0/0	0/0	0	6
Wilson	0	1	0	0/0	0/0	0	6
Steelers	9	34	3	44/44	23/25	0	393
Opponents	6	22	3	29/30	18/22	0	269

2-Pt. Conversions: Holmes, Ward,
Steelers 2-2, Opponents 0-1

RUSHING

	No.	Yds	Avg	LG	TD
Parker	321	1316	4.1	32	2
Davenport	107	499	4.7	45	5
Roethlisberger	35	204	5.8	30t	2
Davis	17	68	4.0	12	0
Wilson	2	37	18.5	37	0
Russell	7	21	3.0	8	0
Holmes	5	17	3.4	11	0
Ward	3	11	3.7	7	0
Kreider	1	2	2.0	2	0
Washington	1	0	0.0	0	0
Batch	12	-7	-0.6	0	0
Steelers	511	2168	4.2	45	9
Opponents	361	1438	4.0	38	6

RECEIVING

	No.	Yds	Avg	LG	TD
Ward	71	732	10.3	25	7
Holmes	52	942	18.1	83	8
Miller	47	566	12.0	29	7
Washington	29	450	15.5	40	5
Parker	23	164	7.1	22	0
Wilson	18	207	11.5	18	1
Davenport	18	184	10.2	32t	2
Davis	12	49	4.1	10	0
Spaeth	5	34	6.8	13t	3
Reid	4	54	13.5	25	0
Kreider	1	15	15.0	15	0
Haynes	1	12	12.0	12	0
Tuman	1	9	9.0	9t	1
Steelers	282	3418	12.1	83	34
Opponents	292	3067	10.5	63t	22

INTERCEPTIONS

	No.	Yds	Avg	LG	TD
Taylor	3	56	18.7	51t	1
An. Smith	2	50	25.0	50	0
Townsend	2	44	22.0	23	0
McFadden	1	50	50.0	50t	1
J. Harrison	1	20	20.0	20	0
Foote	1	14	14.0	14	0
Farrior	1	0	0.0	0	0
Steelers	11	234	21.3	51t	2
Opponents	14	110	7.9	29	0

PUNTING

	No.	Yds.	Avg.	In 20	LG
Sepulveda	68	2880	42.4	28	59
Steelers	68	2880	42.4	28	59
Opponents	82	3525	43.0	25	66

PUNT RETURNS

	Ret	FC	Yds	Avg	LG	TD
Rossum	36	8	232	6.4	49	0
Wilson	2	1	6	3.0	6	0
Gay	1	0	0	0.0	0	0
Steelers	39	9	238	6.1	49	0
Opponents	31	14	266	8.6	73t	1

KICKOFF RETURNS

	No.	Yds	Avg	LG	TD
Rossum	38	885	23.3	98t	1
Davenport	7	123	17.6	29	0
Reid	6	127	21.2	30	0
Eason	1	10	10.0	10	0
Steelers	52	1145	22.0	98t	1
Opponents	73	1647	22.6	100t	1

FIELD GOALS

	1-19	20-29	30-39	40-49	50+
Reed	0/0	9/9	10/10	4/5	0/1
Steelers	0/0	9/9	10/10	4/5	0/1
Opponents	1/1	8/8	5/5	2/4	2/4

SACKS

	No.
J. Harrison	8.5
Farrior	6.5
Haggans	4.0
Woodley	4.0
Foote	3.0
Aa. Smith	2.5
Keisel	2.0
Kirschke	2.0
Clark	1.0
Taylor	1.0
Carter	0.5
Hampton	0.5
Hoke	0.5
Steelers	36.0
Opponents	47.0

RECORD HOLDERS
INDIVIDUAL RECORDS—CAREER

Category	Name	Performance
Rushing (Yds.)	Franco Harris, 1972-1983	11,950
Passing (Yds.)	Terry Bradshaw, 1970-1983	27,989
Passing (TDs)	Terry Bradshaw, 1970-1983	212
Receiving (No.)	Hines Ward, 1998-2007	719
Receiving (Yds.)	Hines Ward, 1998-2007	8,737
Interceptions	Mel Blount, 1970-1983	57
Punting (Avg.)	Bobby Joe Green, 1960-61	45.7
Punt Return (Avg.)	Bobby Gage, 1949-1950	14.9
Kickoff Return (Avg.)	Lynn Chandnois, 1950-56	29.6
Field Goals	Gary Anderson, 1982-1994	309
Touchdowns (Tot.)	Franco Harris, 1972-1983	100
Points	Gary Anderson, 1982-1994	1,343

INDIVIDUAL RECORDS—SINGLE SEASON

Category	Name	Performance
Rushing (Yds.)	Barry Foster, 1992	1,690
Passing (Yds.)	Terry Bradshaw, 1979	3,724
Passing (TDs)	Ben Roethlisberger, 2007	32
Receiving (No.)	Hines Ward, 2002	112
Receiving (Yds.)	Yancey Thigpen, 1997	1,398
Interceptions	Mel Blount, 1975	11
Punting (Avg.)	Bobby Joe Green, 1961	47.0
Punt Return (Avg.)	Bobby Gage, 1949	16.0
Kickoff Return (Avg.)	Lynn Chandnois, 1952	35.2
Field Goals	Norm Johnson, 1995	34
Touchdowns (Tot.)	Willie Parker, 2006	16
Points	Norm Johnson, 1995	141

INDIVIDUAL RECORDS—SINGLE GAME

Category	Name	Performance
Rushing (Yds.)	Willie Parker, 12-7-06	223
Passing (Yds.)	Tommy Maddox, 11-10-02	473
Passing (TDs)	Terry Bradshaw, 11-15-81	5
	Mark Malone, 9-8-85	5
	Ben Roethlisberger, 11-5-07	5
Receiving (No.)	Courtney Hawkins, 11-1-98	14
Receiving (Yds.)	Plaxico Burress, 11-10-02	253
Interceptions	Jack Butler, 12-13-53	*4
Field Goals	Gary Anderson, 10-23-88	6
	Jeff Reed, 12-1-02	6
Touchdowns (Tot.)	Ray Mathews, 10-17-54	4
	Roy Jefferson, 11-3-68	4
Points	Ray Mathews, 10-17-54	24
	Roy Jefferson, 11-3-68	24

*NFL Record

2008 VETERAN ROSTER

No.	Name	Pos.	Ht.	Wt.	Age	NFL Exp.	College	Hometown	How Acq.	'07 Games/ Starts
16	Batch, Charlie	QB	6-2	216	33	11	Eastern Michigan	Homestead, Pa.	FA-'02	7/1
11	Bloom, Jeremy	WR	5-9	180	26	2	Colorado	Loveland, Colo.	FA-'07	0*
48	Boyd, Cody	TE	6-8	264	24	2	Washington State	Bellingham, Wash.	FA-'08	0*
69	Capizzi, Jason	T	6-9	315	25	2	Indiana (Pa.)	Gibsonia, Pa.	FA-'07	0*
23	Carter, Tyrone	S	5-9	195	32	9	Minnesota	Pompano Beach, Fla.	FA-'04	16/5
25	Clark, Ryan	S	5-11	205	28	7	Louisiana State	Merraro, La.	UFA(Wash)-'06	6/6
74	Colon, Willie	T	6-3	315	25	3	Hofstra	Bronx, N.Y.	D4a-'06	16/16
44	Davenport, Najeh	RB	6-1	247	29	7	Miami	Raleigh, N.C.	FA-'06	15/1
38	Davis, Carey	RB	5-10	225	27	2	Illinois	St. Louis, Mo.	FA-'06	16/7
88	Dekker, Jon	TE	6-5	250	25	2	Princeton	Greenfield, Wisc.	FA-'06	3/0
93	Eason, Nick	DE	6-3	305	28	6	Clemson	Lyons, Ga.	FA-'07	16/1
79	Essex, Trai	T	6-4	324	25	4	Northwestern	Fort Wayne, Ind.	D3-'05	3/0
51	Farrior, James	LB	6-2	243	33	12	Virginia	Ettrick, Va.	UFA(NYJ)-'02	16/16
50	Foote, Larry	LB	6-1	239	28	7	Michigan	Detroit, Mich.	D4-'02	16/16
57	Fox, Keyaron	LB	6-3	235	26	5	Georgia Tech	Atlanta, Ga.	FA-'08	10/0*
54	Frazier, Andre	LB	6-5	255	26	4	Cincinnati	Cincinnati, Ohio	FA-'07	10/0
22	Gay, William	CB	5-10	190	23	2	Louisville	Tallahassee, Fla.	D5b-'07	16/0
98	Hampton, Casey	DT	6-1	325	31	8	Texas	Galveston, Texas	D1-'01	15/15
97	Harrison, Arnold	LB	6-3	241	25	3	Georgia	Augusta, Ga.	FA-'05	13/0
92	Harrison, James	LB	6-0	242	30	5	Kent State	Akron, Ohio	FA-'04	16/16
62	Hartwig, Justin	C	6-4	312	29	7	Kansas	Mankato, Minn.	UFA(Car)-'08	15/15*
76	Hoke, Chris	DT	6-2	305	32	8	Brigham Young	Long Beach, Calif.	FA-'02	16/1
10	Holmes, Santonio	WR	5-11	189	24	3	Ohio State	Belle Glade, Fla.	D1-'06	13/13
99	Keisel, Brett	DE	6-5	285	29	7	Brigham Young	Greybull, Wyo.	D7b-'02	16/16
68	Kemoeatu, Chris	G	6-3	344	25	4	Utah	Kahuka, Hawaii	D6-'05	15/0
90	Kirschke, Travis	DE	6-3	298	33	12	UCLA	Highland Ranch, Colo.	UFA(SF)-'04	16/4
37	Madison, Anthony	CB	5-9	180	26	3	Alabama	Thomasville, Ala.	FA-'07	9/0
61	Mahan, Sean	C	6-3	301	28	6	Notre Dame	Jenks, Okla.	FA-'07	16/16
41	Mason, Grant	CB	6-0	192	25	2	Michigan	Pontiac, Mich.	FA-'07	5/0
95	McBean, Ryan	DE	6-5	290	24	2	Oklahoma State	Trinity, Texas	D4b-'07	1/0
20	McFadden, Bryant	CB	6-0	190	26	4	Florida State	Hollywood, Fla.	D2-'05	13/0
83	Miller, Heath	TE	6-5	256	25	4	Virginia	Swords Creek, Va.	D1-'05	16/16
21	Moore, Mewelde	RB	5-11	209	26	5	Tulane	Hammond, La.	UFA(Minn)-'08	12/0*
39	Parker, Willie	RB	5-10	209	27	5	North Carolina	Clinton, N.C.	FA-'04	15/15
65	Parquet, Jeremy	OL	6-6	321	26	3	Southern Mississippi	Norco, La.	FA-'07	0*
43	Polamalu, Troy	S	5-10	207	27	6	Southern California	Tenmile, Ore.	D1-'03	11/11
3	Reed, Jeff	K	5-11	225	29	7	North Carolina	Charlotte, N.C.	FA-'02	16/0
15	Reid, Willie	WR	5-10	186	25	3	Florida State	Kathleen, Ga.	D3b-'06	6/0
7	Roethlisberger, Ben	QB	6-5	241	26	5	Miami (Ohio)	Findlay, Ohio	D1-'04	15/15
33	Russell, Gary	RB	5-11	215	21	2	Minnesota	Columbus, Ohio	FA-'07	3/0
9	Sepulveda, Daniel	P	6-3	230	24	2	Baylor	Dallas, Texas	D4a-'07	16/0
27	Smith, Anthony	S	5-11	192	24	3	Syracuse	Hubbard, Ohio	D3a-'06	16/10
73	Simmons, Kendall	G	6-3	315	29	7	Auburn	Ripley, Miss.	D1-'02	16/16
91	Smith, Aaron	DE	6-5	298	32	10	Northern Colorado	Colorado Springs, Colo.	D4-'99	11/11
77	Smith, Marvel	T	6-5	321	30	9	Arizona State	Oakland, Calif.	D2-'00	12/12
89	Spaeth, Matt	TE	6-7	270	23	2	Minnesota	St. Michael, Minn.	D3-'07	14/6
72	Stapleton, Darnell	G/C	6-3	285	22	2	Rutgers	Union, N.J.	FA-'07	0*
78	Starks, Max	T	6-8	337	26	5	Florida	Orlando, Fla.	D3-'04	16/4
24	Taylor, Ike	CB	6-1	191	28	6	Louisiana-Lafayette	Gretna, La.	D4-'03	16/16
94	Timmons, Lawrence	LB	6-1	234	22	2	Florida State	Florence, S.C.	D1-'07	16/0
26	Townsend, Deshea	CB	5-10	190	32	11	Alabama	Batesville, Miss.	D4a-'98	16/16
86	Ward, Hines	WR	6-0	205	32	11	Georgia	Forest Park, Ga.	D3b-'98	13/13
60	Warren, Greg	LS	6-3	252	26	4	North Carolina	Goldsboro, N.C.	FA-'05	16/0
85	Washington, Nate	WR	6-1	185	25	4	Tiffin	Toledo, Ohio	FA-'05	16/4
56	Woodley, LaMarr	LB	6-2	265	23	2	Michigan	Saginaw, Mich.	D2-'07	13/0

* Bloom missed '06 season because of injury with Philadelphia; Boyd inactive 3 games for Washington in '07; Capizzi inactive for AFC Wild Card Game; Fox played 10 games with Kansas City; Hartwig played 15 games with Carolina; Moore played 12 games with Minnesota; Parquet inactive for 2 games with St. Louis and AFC Wild Card Game.

Players lost through free agency (3): G Alan Faneca (NYJ; 16 games in '07), LB Clark Haggans (Ariz; 16), QB Brian St. Pierre (Ariz; 0).

Also played with Steelers in '07—CB Ricardo Colclough (3 games), LB Marquis Cooper (3), RB Verron Haynes (1), FB Dan Kreider (10), LB Clint Kriewaldt (14), CB Allen Rossum (15), TE Jerame Tuman (6), WR Cedrick Wilson (16).

2008 FIRST-YEAR ROSTER

Name	Pos.	Ht.	Wt.	Age	College	Hometown	How Acq.
Bailey, Patrick	LB	6-4	235	22	Duke	Elmendorf, Texas	FA
Baker, Dallas (1)	WR	6-3	206	25	Florida	New Smyrna Beach, Fla.	D7-'07
Clement, Kyle	DL	6-3	315	23	Northwood	Hudsonville, Mich.	FA
Davis, Bruce	LB	6-3	252	23	UCLA	Houston, Texas	D3
Dixon, Dennis	QB	6-3	195	23	Oregon	San Leandro, Calif.	D5
Hills, Tony	T	6-5	304	23	Texas	Houston, Texas	D4
Humpal, Mike	LB	6-3	240	23	Iowa	New Hampton, Iowa	D6a
Latsko, Billy (1)	FB	5-10	233	24	Florida	Gainesville, Fla.	FA
Legursky, Doug	C	6-1	323	22	Marshall	Frankfurt, Germany	FA
Lentz, Matt (1)	OG	6-6	320	25	Michigan	Ortonville, Mich.	FA-'07
Lewis, Roy	CB	5-10	190	23	Washington	Los Angeles, Calif.	FA
Lorello, Mike (1)	DB	5-11	208	23	West Virginia	Powell, Ohio	FA-'07
Marion, Kevin	WR	5-10	168	24	Wake Forest	St. Petersburg, Fla.	FA
Mendenhall, Rashard	RB	5-10	225	21	Illinois	Skokie, Ill.	D1
Mundy, Ryan	S	6-1	215	23	West Virginia	Pittsburgh, Pa.	D6b
Paxson, Scott (1)	DT	6-4	292	25	Penn State	Philadelphia, Pa.	FA-'06
Potts, Mike	QB	6-4	220	23	William and Mary	Pittsburgh, Pa.	FA
Prince, Martavius	DL	6-2	282	23	Southern Miss	Ft. Pierce, Fla.	FA
Rauch, Julian	K	5-11	207	23	Appalachian State	Gastonia, N.C.	FA
Reffett, Jordan	DL	6-4	292	23	Washington	Moses Lake, Wash.	FA
Retkofsky, Jared (1)	LS	6-5	260	25	TCU	Justin, Texas	FA
Rucker, Micah	WR	6-6	221	23	Eastern Illinois	Bonita Springs, Fla.	FA
Sherrod, Dezmond	TE	6-2	250	23	Mississippi State	Newport, R.I.	FA
Sweed, Limas	WR	6-4	220	23	Texas	Brenham, Texas	D2
Trannon, Matt (1)	WR	6-6	235	25	Michigan State	Flint, Mich.	FA
Trucks, Anthony (1)	LB	6-1	230	24	Oregon	Martinez, Calif.	FA-'07
Vincent, Justin (1)	RB	5-10	219	25	Louisiana State	Lake Charles, La.	FA-'07
Walker, Gerran (1)	WR	5-10	185	24	Lehigh	Atlanta, Ga.	FA-'07
Williams, Travis	CB	5-9	180	23	East Carolina	Daytona Beach, Fla.	FA
Woods, Donovan	LB	6-2	230	23	Oklahoma State	Oklahoma City, Okla.	FA
Zabransky, Jared (1)	QB	6-2	219	24	Boise State	Hermiston, Ore.	FA

The term NFL Rookie is defined as a player who is in his first season of professional football and has not been on the roster of another professional football team for any regular-season or postseason games. A Rookie is designated by an "R" on NFL rosters. Players who have been active in another professional football league or players who have NFL experience, including either preseason training camp or being on an Active List or Inactive List, or on Reserve/Injured or Reserve/Physically Unable to Perform for fewer than six regular-season games, are termed NFL First-Year Players. An NFL First-Year Player is designated by a "1" on NFL rosters. Thereafter, a player is credited with an additional year of experience for each season in which he accumulates six games on the Active List or Inactive List, or on Reserve/Injured or Reserve/Physically Unable to Perform.

Log on to www.steelers.com for an up-to-date roster; Age listed is as of September 4, 2008.

COACHING STAFF
Head Coach,
Mike Tomlin

Pro Career: Became the sixteenth head coach in Steelers history when he replaced Bill Cowher on January 22, 2007. In his first season, Tomlin guided the Steelers to a 10-6 record and their first AFC North title since 2004. Tomlin was the Minnesota Vikings defensive coordinator in 2006 after spending the previous five seasons (2001-05) as defensive backs coach for the Tampa Bay Buccaneers. Tomlin coached one of the top defensive backfields in the NFL for the Buccaneers, culminating with its performance in Super Bowl XXXVII. The secondary recorded four interceptions, returning two for touchdowns to help Tampa Bay capture the franchise's first Super Bowl title. Tomlin served two seasons as the defensive backs coach at the University of Cincinnati (1999-2000) before going to Tampa Bay. Prior to joining the Cincinnati staff, Tomlin had a short stint on the coaching staff at Tennessee-Martin and then spent two seasons at Arkansas State. He spent the 1996 season as a graduate assistant at Memphis. Tomlin began his coaching career in 1995 as wide receivers coach at Virginia Military Institute. Career record: 10-7.

Background: Was a three-year starter at wide receiver at William & Mary (1990-94) and finished his career with 101 receptions for 2,046 yards and a school-record 20 touchdown receptions. A first-team All-Yankee Conference selection in 1994, he established a school record with a 20.2 yards per catch average. Tomlin was a teammate of current Viking Pro Bowl safety Darren Sharper at William and Mary. Graduated in 1994 with a degree in sociology.

Personal: Age 36, born in Hampton, Va. He and his wife, Kiya, have two sons, Dino and Mason, and a daughter Harlyn Quinn.

ASSISTANT COACHES

Ken Anderson, quarterbacks; born Batavia, Ill. Quarterback Augustana (Ill.) 1967-1970. Pro quarterback Cincinnati Bengals 1971-1986. Pro coach: Cincinnati Bengals 1992-2002, Jacksonville Jaguars 2003-2006, joined Steelers in 2007.

Bruce Arians, offensive coordinator; born Paterson, N.J. Quarterback Virginia Tech 1970-74. No pro playing experience. College coach: Virginia Tech 1975-77, Mississippi State 1978-1980, Alabama 1981-82, Temple 1983-88 (head coach), Mississippi State 1993-95, Alabama 1997. Pro coach: Kansas City Chiefs 1989-1992, New Orleans Saints 1996, Indianapolis Colts 1998-2000, Cleveland Browns 2001-03, joined Steelers in 2004.

Keith Butler, linebackers; born Anniston, Ala. Linebacker Memphis 1974-77. Pro linebacker Seattle Seahawks 1978-1987. College coach: Memphis 1990-97, Arkansas State 1998. Pro coach: Cleveland Browns 1999-2002, joined Steelers in 2003.

James Daniel, tight ends; born Wetumpka, Ala. Guard Alabama State 1970-73. No pro playing experience. College coach: Auburn 1981-1992. Pro coach: New York Giants 1993-96, Atlanta Falcons 1997-2003, joined Steelers in 2004.

Randy Fichtner, wide receivers; born Cleveland. Defensive back Purdue 1982-85. No pro playing experience. College coach: Michigan 1986-87, Southern California 1988, Nevada-Las Vegas 1989, Memphis 1990-93, Purdue 1994-96, Arkansas State 1997-2000, Memphis 2001-06. Pro coach: Joined Steelers in 2007.

Ray Horton, defensive backs; born Tacoma, Wash. Defensive back Washington 1979-1982. Pro defensive back Cincinnati Bengals 1983-88, Dallas Cowboys 1989-1992. Pro coach: Washington Redskins 1994-96, Cincinnati Bengals 1997-2001, Detroit Lions 2002-03, joined Steelers in 2004.

Amos Jones, asst. special teams; born Tallahassee, Fla.. Safety/running back Alabama 1978-1980. No pro playing experience. College coach: Alabama 1981-82, Temple 1983-88, Alabama 1990-91, Pittsburgh 1992, Tulane 1995-96, Cincinnati 1999-2002, James Madison 2003, Mississippi State 2004-06. Pro coach: British Columbia (CFL) 1997, joined Steelers in 2007.

Dick LeBeau, defensive coordinator; born London, Ohio. Defensive back Ohio State 1955-58. Pro cornerback Detroit Lions 1959-1972. Pro coach: Philadelphia Eagles 1973-75, Green Bay Packers 1976-79, Cincinnati Bengals 1980-1991, 1997-2002 (head coach 2000-02), Pittsburgh Steelers 1992-96, Buffalo Bills 2003, re-joined Steelers in 2004.

Bob Ligashesky, special teams; born Pittsburgh. Linebacker Indiana (Pa.) 1983-84. No pro playing experience. College coach: Wake Forest 1985, Arizona State 1986-89, Kent State 1990, Bowling Green 1991-99, Pittsburgh 2000-03. Pro coach: Jacksonville Jaguars 2004, St. Louis Rams 2005-06, joined Steelers in 2007.

John Mitchell, defensive line; born Mobile, Ala. Defensive end Eastern Arizona J.C. 1969-1970, Alabama 1971-72. No pro playing experience. College coach: Alabama 1973-76, Arkansas 1977-1982, Temple 1986, Louisiana State 1987-1990. Pro coach: Birmingham Stallions (USFL) 1983-85, Cleveland Browns 1991-93, joined Steelers in 1994.

Kirby Wilson, running backs; born Los Angeles. Running back/wide receiver Pasadena (Calif.) C.C. 1979-1980, Illinois 1981-82. Pro cornerback Winnipeg Blue Bombers (CFL) 1983, Toronto Argonauts (CFL) 1984. College coach: Pasadena (Calif.) C.C. 1989-1990, Southern Illinois 1991-92, Wyoming 1993-94, Iowa State 1995-96, Southern California 2001. Pro coach: New England Patriots 1997-99, Washington Redskins 2000, Tampa Bay Buccaneers 2002-03, Arizona Cardinals 2004-06, joined Steelers in 2007.

Larry Zierlein, offensive line; born Norton, Kan. Linebacker/tight end Pratt (Kan.) J.C. 1967-68, linebacker Fort Hays State (Kan.) 1969-1970. No pro playing experience. College coach: Fort Hays State (Kan.) 1970-71, Houston 1978-1986, Tulane 1988-1990, 1995-96, Louisiana State 1993-94, Cincinnati 1997-2000. Pro coach: Washington (AFL) 1987, New York/New JerseyKnights (WLAF) 1991-92, Cleveland Browns 2001-04, Buffalo Bills 2006, joined Steelers in 2007.

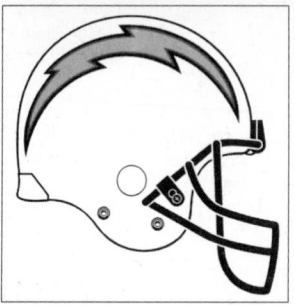

American Football Conference
West Division
Team Colors: Navy Blue, Powder Blue, White, and Gold
P.O. Box 609609
San Diego, California 92160-9609
Telephone: (858) 874-4500

2008 SCHEDULE
PRESEASON
Aug. 9	**Dallas**	7:00
Aug. 16	at St. Louis	7:00
Aug. 25	**Seattle**	5:00
Aug. 29	at San Francisco	7:00

REGULAR SEASON
Sep. 7	**Carolina**	1:15
Sep. 14	at Denver	2:15
Sep. 22	**N.Y. Jets** (Mon.)	5:30
Sep. 28	at Oakland	1:05
Oct. 5	at Miami	1:00
Oct. 12	**New England**	5:15
Oct. 19	at Buffalo	1:00
Oct. 26	at New Orleans (London)	5:00
Nov. 2	BYE	
Nov. 9	**Kansas City**	1:15
Nov. 16	at Pittsburgh	4:15
Nov. 23	**Indianapolis** *	5:15
Nov. 30	**Atlanta**	1:05
Dec. 4	**Oakland** (Thu.)	5:15
Dec. 14	at Kansas City	12:00
Dec. 21	at Tampa Bay *	8:15
Dec. 28	**Denver**	1:15

* Sunday night games in Weeks 11-17 subject to change

Stadium: Qualcomm Stadium
(opened in 1967)
• **Capacity:** 70,000 (app.)
9449 Friars Road
San Diego, California 92108
Playing Surface: Grass
Training Camp: Chargers Park
4020 Murphy Canyon Rd.
San Diego, CA 92123

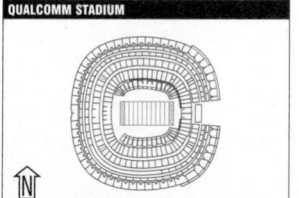

QUALCOMM STADIUM

CLUB OFFICIALS
Owner: Alex G. Spanos
President/CEO: Dean A. Spanos
Executive Vice President:
Michael A. Spanos
Executive Vice President-General
Manager: A.J. Smith
Executive Vice President-Chief Operating
Officer: Jim Steeg
Executive Vice President:
Jeremiah T. Murphy
Executive Vice President of Football
Operations-Assistant General
Manager: Ed McGuire
Executive Vice President-Chief Financial
Officer: Jeanne M. Bonk
Vice President-Chief Marketing Officer:
Ken Derrett
Director of Player Personnel:
Jimmy Raye
Director of College Scouting:
John Spanos
Director of Pro Scouting:
Dennis Abraham
Senior Executive: Randy Mueller
Head Athletic Trainer: James Collins
Director of Video Operations:
Brian Duddy
Equipment Manager: Bob Wick
Director of Player Development:
Arthur Hightower
Senior Director of Marketing
Partnerships: Dennis O'Leary
Senior Director of Ticket Sales and
Service: Todd Poulsen
Director of Marketing Programs and
Business Development: A.G. Spanos
Director of Business Operations:
John Hinek
Director of Public Relations: Bill Johnston
Director of Public Affairs &
Corporate/Community Relations:
Kimberley Layton
Director of Security: Dick Lewis
Director of Stadium/Game Operations &
Events: Sean O'Connor
Controller: Marsha Wells
Director of Ticket Operations:
Michael L. Dougherty

COACHING HISTORY
Los Angeles 1960
(363-373-11)
Records include postseason games
1960-69	Sid Gillman*	83-51-6
1969-1970	Charlie Waller	9-7-3
1971	Sid Gillman**	4-6-0
1971-73	Harland Svare***	7-17-2
1973	Ron Waller	1-5-0
1974-78	Tommy Prothro****	21-39-0
1978-1986	Don Coryell#	72-60-0
1986-88	Al Saunders	17-22-0
1989-1991	Dan Henning	16-32-0
1992-96	Bobby Ross	50-36-0
1997-98	Kevin Gilbride	6-16-0
1998	June Jones	3-7-0
1999-2001	Mike Riley	14-34-0
2002-06	Marty Schottenheimer	47-35-0
2007	Norv Turner	13-6-0

*Retired after nine games in 1969
**Resigned after 10 games in 1971
***Resigned after eight games in 1973
****Resigned after four games in 1978
#Resigned after eight games in 1986
##Released after six games in 1998

PAID ATTENDANCE
Home 546,866   Away 540,673
Total 1,087,539
Single-game home record,
69,288 (11/7/99)
Single-season home record,
547,937 (2005)

2008 DRAFT CHOICES
Round	Name	Pos.	College
1	Antoine Cason	DB	Arizona
3	Jacob Hester	RB	Louisiana St.
5	Marcus Thomas	RB	Texas-El Paso
6	DeJuan Tribble	DB	Boston College
7	Corey Clark	T	Texas A&M

2007 TEAM RECORD
PRESEASON (3-1)

Date	Result	Opponent
8/12	L 16-24	Seattle
8/18	W 30-13	at St. Louis
8/25	W 33-13	at Arizona
8/30	W 16-13	San Francisco

REGULAR SEASON (11-5)

Date	Result	Opponent	Att.
9/9	W 14-3	Chicago	67,837
9/16	L 14-38	at New England	68,756
9/23	L 24-31	at Green Bay	70,733
9/30	L 16-30	Kansas City	65,175
10/7	W 41-3	at Denver	76,879
10/14	W 28-14	Oakland	67,523
10/28	W 35-10	Houston	60,439
11/4	L 17-35	at Minnesota	63,043
11/11	W 23-21	Indianapolis	67,726
11/18	L 17-24	at Jacksonville	66,732
11/25	W 32-14	Baltimore	63,337
12/2	W 24-10	at Kansas City	74,874
12/9	W 23-17	at Tennessee (OT)	69,143
12/16	W 51-14	Detroit	66,505
12/24	W 23-3	Denver	65,477
12/30	W 30-17	at Oakland	61,706

(OT) Overtime

POSTSEASON (2-1)

Date	Result	Opponent	Att.
1/6	W 17-6	Tennessee	65,640
1/13	W 28-24	at Indianapolis	56,950
1/20	L 12-21	at New England	68,756

SCORE BY PERIODS

Chargers	119	116	93	78	6 —	412
Opponents	47	84	69	84	0 —	284

2007 TEAM STATISTICS

	Chargers	Opp.
Total First Downs	278	297
Rushing	104	89
Passing	158	185
Penalty	16	23
3rd Down: Made/Att	84/214	83/211
3rd Down Pct.	39.3	39.3
4th Down: Made/Att	6/10	9/26
4th Down Pct.	60.0	34.6
Possession Avg.	29:50	30:10
Total Net Yards	5044	5124
Avg. Per Game	315.3	320.3
Total Plays	980	1013
Avg. Per Play	5.1	5.1
Net Yards Rushing	2039	1712
Avg. Per Game	127.4	107.0
Total Rushes	485	416
Net Yards Passing	3005	3412
Avg. Per Game	187.8	213.3
Sacked/Yards Lost	24/170	42/272
Gross Yards	3175	3684
Att./Completions	471/281	555/338
Completion Pct.	59.7	60.9
Had Intercepted	16	30
Punts/Average	82/45.5	69/42.9
Net Punting Avg.	82/39.6	69/37.4
Penalties/Yards	94/761	86/665
Fumbles/Ball Lost	17/8	27/18
Touchdowns	49	35
Rushing	19	11
Passing	22	20
Returns	8	4

2007 INDIVIDUAL STATISTICS

PASSING

PASSING	Att.	Comp.	Yds.	Pct.	TD	Int.	Tkld.	Rate
Rivers	460	277	3152	60.2	21	15	22/163	82.4
Volek	10	3	6	30.0	0	1	2/7	0.0
Tomlinson	1	1	17	100.0	1	0	0/0	158.3
Chargers	471	281	3175	59.7	22	16	24/170	81.3
Opponents	555	338	3684	60.9	20	30	42/272	70.0

SCORING

SCORING	TD R	TD P	TD Rt	PAT	FG	Saf	PTS
Kaeding	0	0	0	46/46	24/27	0	118
Tomlinson	15	3	0	0/0	0/0	0	108
Gates	0	9	0	0/0	0/0	0	54
Chambers	0	4	0	0/0	0/0	0	24
Sproles	2	0	2	0/0	0/0	0	24
Cromartie	0	0	3	0/0	0/0	0	18
V. Jackson	0	3	0	0/0	0/0	0	18
Davis	0	1	0	0/0	0/0	0	6
Manumaleuna	0	1	0	0/0	0/0	0	6
Neal	0	1	0	0/0	0/0	0	6
Phillips	0	0	1	0/0	0/0	0	6
Rivers	1	0	0	0/0	0/0	0	6
Siler	0	0	1	0/0	0/0	0	6
Tucker	0	0	1	0/0	0/0	0	6
Turner	1	0	0	0/0	0/0	0	6
Chargers	19	22	8	46/46	24/27	0	412
Opponents	11	20	4	33/33	13/19	0	284

2-Pt. Conversions: Chargers 0-2, Opponents 1-2

RUSHING

RUSHING	No.	Yds	Avg	LG	TD
Tomlinson	315	1474	4.7	49	15
Turner	71	316	4.5	74t	1
Sproles	37	164	4.4	34	2
Rivers	29	33	1.1	10	1
Neal	13	32	2.5	10	0
Chambers	2	17	8.5	9	0
Davis	3	9	3.0	6	0
Pinnock	4	1	0.3	5	0
Volek	11	-7	-0.6	0	0
Chargers	485	2039	4.2	74t	19
Opponents	416	1712	4.1	64t	11

RECEIVING

RECEIVING	No.	Yds	Avg	LG	TD
Gates	75	984	13.1	49t	9
Tomlinson	60	475	7.9	36	3
V. Jackson	41	623	15.2	45	3
Chambers	35	555	15.9	44	4
Davis	20	188	9.4	18	1
Manumaleuna	10	86	8.6	40	1
Sproles	10	31	3.1	14	0
Naanee	8	69	8.6	22	0
Neal	8	23	2.9	9	1
Floyd	7	97	13.9	25	0
Turner	4	16	4.0	12	0
Osgood	2	23	11.5	15	0
Pinnock	1	5	5.0	5	0
Chargers	281	3175	11.3	49t	22
Opponents	338	3684	10.9	57t	20

INTERCEPTIONS

INTERCEPTIONS	No.	Yds	Avg	LG	TD
Cromartie	10	144	14.4	70t	1
Hart	5	73	14.6	22	0
McCree	3	20	6.7	19	0
Wilhelm	3	11	3.7	7	0
Phillips	2	36	18.0	18t	1
Cooper	2	23	11.5	18	0
Florence	2	4	2.0	4	0
Jammer	1	0	0.0	0	0
Olshansky	1	0	0.0	0	0
Weddle	1	0	0.0	0	0
Chargers	30	311	10.4	70t	2
Opponents	16	283	17.7	66t	2

PUNTING

PUNTING	No.	Yds.	Avg.	In 20	LG
Scifres	81	3735	46.1	36	70
Chargers	82	3735	45.5	36	70
Opponents	69	2961	42.9	16	81

PUNT RETURNS

PUNT RETURNS	Ret	FC	Yds	Avg	LG	TD
Sproles	24	2	229	9.5	45t	1
Davis	6	6	52	8.7	24	0
Osgood	2	0	0	0.0	0	0
Chargers	32	8	281	8.8	45t	1
Opponents	29	19	311	10.7	54	0

KICKOFF RETURNS

KICKOFF RETURNS	No.	Yds	Avg	LG	TD
Sproles	37	1008	27.2	89t	1
Turner	6	139	23.2	28	0
Cromartie	3	67	22.3	26	0
Manumaleuna	1	6	6.0	6	0
Neal	1	4	4.0	4	0
Chargers	48	1224	25.5	89t	1
Opponents	75	1566	20.9	62	0

FIELD GOALS

FIELD GOALS	1-19	20-29	30-39	40-49	50+
Kaeding	0/0	11/11	5/6	7/8	1/2
Chargers	0/0	11/11	5/6	7/8	1/2
Opponents	0/0	6/8	2/2	4/7	1/2

SACKS

SACKS	No.
Merriman	12.5
Phillips	8.5
Olshansky	3.5
Tucker	3.5
Castillo	2.5
Cesaire	2.5
Cooper	2.0
Bingham	1.5
Harris	1.5
Hart	1.0
Polk	1.0
Weddle	1.0
Wilhelm	1.0
Chargers	42.0
Opponents	24.0

RECORD HOLDERS
INDIVIDUAL RECORDS—CAREER

Category	Name	Performance
Rushing (Yds.)	LaDainian Tomlinson, 2001-07	10,650
Passing (Yds.)	Dan Fouts, 1973-1987	43,040
Passing (TDs)	Dan Fouts, 1973-1987	254
Receiving (No.)	Charlie Joiner, 1976-1986	586
Receiving (Yds.)	Lance Alworth, 1962-1970	9,585
Interceptions	Gill Byrd, 1983-1992	42
Punting (Avg.)	Darren Bennett, 1995-2003	43.8
	Mike Scifres, 2003-07	43.8
Punt Return (Avg.)	Darrien Gordon, 1993-96	13.6
Kickoff Return (Avg.)	Darren Sproles, 2005-07	25.4
Field Goals	John Carney, 1990-2000	261
Touchdowns (Tot.)	LaDainian Tomlinson, 2001-07	129
Points	John Carney, 1990-2000	1,076

INDIVIDUAL RECORDS—SINGLE SEASON

Category	Name	Performance
Rushing (Yds.)	LaDainian Tomlinson, 2006	1,815
Passing (Yds.)	Dan Fouts, 1981	4,802
Passing (TDs)	Dan Fouts, 1981	33
Receiving (No.)	LaDainian Tomlinson, 2003	100
Receiving (Yds.)	Lance Alworth, 1965	1,602
Interceptions	Antonio Cromartie, 2007	10
Punting (Avg.)	Darren Bennett, 2000	46.2
Punt Return (Avg.)	Leslie (Speedy) Duncan, 1965	15.5
Kickoff Return (Avg.)	Keith Lincoln, 1962	28.4
Field Goals	John Carney, 1994	34
Touchdowns (Tot.)	LaDainian Tomlinson, 2006	*31
Points	LaDainian Tomlinson, 2006	*186

INDIVIDUAL RECORDS—SINGLE GAME

Category	Name	Performance
Rushing (Yds.)	LaDainian Tomlinson, 12-28-03	243
Passing (Yds.)	Dan Fouts, 10-19-80, 12-11-82	444
Passing (TDs)	Dan Fouts, 11-22-81	6
Receiving (No.)	Kellen Winslow, 10-7-84	15
Receiving (Yds.)	Wes Chandler, 12-20-82	260
Interceptions	Many times	3
	Last time by Antonio Cromartie, 11-11-07	
Field Goals	John Carney, 9-5-93, 9-18-93	6
	Greg Davis, 10-5-97	6
Touchdowns (Tot.)	Kellen Winslow, 11-22-81	5
Points	Kellen Winslow, 11-22-81	30

*NFL Record

2008 VETERAN ROSTER

No.	Name	Pos.	Ht.	Wt.	Age	NFL Exp.	College	Hometown	How Acq.	'07 Games/ Starts
97	Bingham, Ryon	DT	6-3	303	27	4	Nebraska	Sandy, Utah	D7A-'04	16/2
50	Binn, David	LS	6-3	223	36	15	California	San Mateo, Calif.	FA-'94	16/0
93	Castillo, Luis	DE	6-3	290	25	4	Northwestern	Garfield, N.J.	D1B-'05	10/9
74	Cesaire, Jacques	DE	6-2	295	28	6	So. Connecticut St.	Gardner, Mass.	FA-'03	16/6
89	Chambers, Chris	WR	5-11	210	30	8	Wisconsin	Bedford, Ohio	T(Mia)-'07	16/12*
87	Chandler, Scott	TE	6-7	265	23	2	Iowa	Southlake, Texas	D4-'07	1/0
66	Clary, Jeromey	T	6-6	306	24	2	Kansas State	Mansfield, Texas	D6A-'06	16/6
54	Cooper, Stephen	LB	6-1	235	29	6	Maine	Wareham, Mass.	FA-'03	16/16
31	Cromartie, Antonio	CB	6-2	203	24	3	Florida State	Tallahassee, Fla.	D1-'06	16/8
84	Davis, Buster	WR	6-1	202	22	2	Louisiana State	New Orleans, La.	D1-'07	14/1
68	Dielman, Kris	G	6-4	310	27	6	Indiana	Troy, Ohio	FA-'03	16/16
51	Dobbins, Tim	LB	6-1	246	25	3	Iowa State	Nashville, Tenn.	D5-'06	16/0
80	Floyd, Malcom	WR	6-5	225	26	3	Wyoming	Sacramento, Calif.	FA-'04	6/1
85	Gates, Antonio	TE	6-4	260	28	6	Kent State	Detroit, Mich.	FA-'03	16/16
79	Goff, Mike	G	6-5	311	32	11	Iowa	Peru, Ill.	UFA(Cin)-'04	16/16
24	Gordon, Cletis	CB	6-1	197	25	3	Jackson State	Amite City, La.	FA-'06	14/0
28	Gregory, Steve	CB/S	5-11	185	25	3	Syracuse	Staten Island, N.Y.	FA-'06	16/0
61	Hardwick, Nick	C	6-4	295	27	5	Purdue	Indianapolis, Ind.	D3B-'04	12/12
92	Harris, Marques	LB	6-1	231	26	4	Southern Utah	Grand Junction, Colo.	FA-'05	15/2
42	Hart, Clinton	S	6-0	205	31	6	Central Florida C.C.	Bushnell, Fla.	W(Phi)-'04	16/16
83	Jackson, Vincent	WR	6-5	241	25	4	Northern Colorado	Colorado Springs, Colo.	D2-'05	16/16
23	Jammer, Quentin	CB	6-0	204	29	7	Texas	Angleton, Texas	D1-'02	15/14
10	Kaeding, Nate	K	6-0	187	26	5	Iowa	Coralville, Iowa	D3A-'04	16/0
86	Manumaleuna, Brandon	TE	6-2	288	28	8	Arizona	Torrance, Calif.	T(StL)-'06	16/12
91	McKinney, Brandon	DT	6-2	324	25	3	Michigan State	Dayton, Ohio	FA-'06	14/2
73	McNeill, Marcus	T	6-7	336	24	3	Auburn	Ellenwood, Ga.	D2-'06	16/16
56	Merriman, Shawne	LB	6-4	272	24	4	Maryland	Upper Marlboro, Md.	D1A-'05	15/15
63	Mruczkowski, Scott	C/G	6-5	318	26	4	Bowling Green	Garfield Heights, Ohio	D7-'05	15/0
11	Naanee, Legedu	TE/WR	6-2	226	24	2	Boise State	Portland, Ore.	D5-'07	13/0
27	Oliver, Paul	CB	5-10	195	24	2	Georgia	Kennesaw, Ga.	D4(Supp)-'07	0*
99	Olshansky, Igor	DE	6-6	309	26	5	Oregon	San Francisco, Calif.	D2-'04	16/16
81	Osgood, Kassim	WR	6-5	220	28	6	San Diego State	Salinas, Calif.	FA-'03	16/0
88	Parker, Eric	WR	6-0	180	29	7	Tennessee	Shorewood, Ill.	FA-'02	0*
95	Phillips, Shaun	LB	6-3	262	27	5	Purdue	Willingboro, N.J.	D4-'04	15/15
34	Pinnock, Andrew	FB	5-10	250	28	6	South Carolina	Bloomfield, Conn.	D7-'03	10/3
52	Polk, Carlos	LB	6-2	262	31	8	Nebraska	Rockford, Ill.	D4-'01	10/2
16	Race, Germaine	RB	5-10	218	23	2	Pittsburg State (Kan.)	Warrensburg, Mo.	FA-'07	0*
17	Rivers, Philip	QB	6-5	228	26	5	North Carolina State	Athens, Ala.	T(NYG)-'04	16/16
5	Scifres, Mike	P	6-2	236	27	6	Western Illinois	Destrehan, La.	D5-'03	16/0
	Shelton, L.J.	T	6-6	345	32	10	Eastern Michigan	Monrovia, Calif.	FA-'08	16/16*
59	Siler, Brandon	LB	6-2	239	22	2	Florida	Orlando, Fla.	D7-'07	15/0
58	Smith, Derek	LB	6-2	240	33	12	Arizona State	American Fork, Utah	FA-'08	15/14*
43	Sproles, Darren	RB/KR	5-6	181	25	4	Kansas State	Olathe, Kan.	D4-'05	15/0
21	Tomlinson, LaDainian	RB	5-10	221	29	8	Texas Christian	Waco, Texas	D1-'01	16/16
94	Tucker, Jyles	LB	6-3	258	24	2	Wake Forest	Dover, N.J.	FA-'07	6/0
7	Volek, Billy	QB	6-2	214	32	9	Fresno State	Fresno, Calif.	T(Tenn)-'06	5/0
53	Waters, Anthony	LB	6-3	238	24	2	Clemson	Lake View, S.C.	D3-'07	0*
32	Weddle, Eric	S	5-11	200	23	2	Utah	Alta Loma, Calif.	D2-'07	15/0
6	Whitehurst, Charlie	QB	6-4	227	26	3	Clemson	Alpharetta, Ga.	D3-'06	0*
57	Wilhelm, Matt	LB	6-4	245	27	6	Ohio State	Lorain, Ohio	D4-'03	14/14
76	Williams, Jamal	DT	6-3	348	32	11	Oklahoma State	Washington, D.C.	D2(Supp)-'98	13/13
65	Withrow, Cory	C/G	6-2	287	33	9	Washington State	Spokane, Wash.	FA-'06	13/4

* Chambers played 6 games with Miami and 10 games with San Diego in '07; Oliver inactive for 16 games; Parker inactive for 6 games; Race missed '07 season because of injury; Shelton played 16 games with Miami; Smith played 15 games with San Francisco; Waters inactive for 16 games; Whitehurst inactive for 16 games.

Players lost through free agency (2): CB Drayton Florence (Jax; 16 games in '07), RB Michael Turner (Atl; 16).

Also played with Chargers in '07—WR Malcom Floyd (6 games), S Marlon McCree (16), FB Lorenzo Neal (13), T Roman Oben (4), T Shane Olivea (13), K Dave Rayner (1).

2008 FIRST-YEAR ROSTER

Name	Pos.	Ht.	Wt.	Age	College	Hometown	How Acq.
Applewhite, Antwan (1)	LB	6-3	246	22	San Diego State	Los Angeles, Calif.	FA-'07
Bakhtiari, Eric	LB	6-3	258	23	San Diego	Burlingame, Calif.	FA
Banks, Gary	WR	6-0	193	26	Troy	Melvin, Ala.	FA
Battle, Tra (1)	S	5-11	173	23	Georgia	Forsyth, Ga.	FA-'07
Bell, Josh	CB	5-11	177	23	Baylor	Dallas, Texas	FA
Betschart, Wade	HB	6-2	248	23	Wyoming	Torrington, Wyo.	FA
Bonner, Brian	S	5-11	200	24	Texas Christian	Beeville, Texas	FA
Bramlet, Casey	QB	6-4	225	27	Wyoming	Casper, Wyo.	FA
Buckley, Eldra (1)	RB	5-9	207	23	Tennessee-Chattanooga	Charleston, Miss.	FA-'07
Cason, Antoine	CB	6-0	190	22	Arizona	Long Beach, Calif	D1
Clark, Corey	T	6-5	305	24	Texas A&M	Spring Branch, Texas	D7
Coleman, Andre (1)	DE	6-3	287	24	Albany	Buffalo, N.Y.	FA-'07
Divens, Lamar	DT	6-3	333	22	Tennessee State	Fayetteville, Tenn.	FA
Dombrowski, Brandyn	G	6-5	323	23	San Diego State	Henderson, Nev.	FA
Franks, Stanley	CB	5-9	177	22	Idaho	Long Beach, Calif.	FA
Grennan, Keith (1)	DE	6-4	298	24	Eastern Washington	Edmonds, Wash.	FA-'07
Hester, Jacob	RB	2-11	225	23	Louisiana State	Shreveport, La.	D3
Jackson, Brandon	WR	6-0	206	22	North Texas	Ft. Bend, Texas	FA
Jackson, Keith (1)	DT	6-0	315	23	Arkansas	Little Rock, Ark.	FA-'07
Luellen, Tyler	T	6-6	302	24	Missouri	Bethany, Mo.	FA
Manu, Charles	G	6-3	310	23	Nevada	Reno, Nev.	FA
Nande, Terna (1)	LB	6-0	230	25	Miami (Ohio)	Grand Rapids, Mich.	FA-'07
Pape, Tony (1)	G/T	6-6	302	26	Michigan	Darien, Ill.	FA-'07
Pittman, Billy	WR	6-0	195	23	Texas	Cameron, Texas	FA
Robertson, Erik (1)	G	6-2	310	23	California	Apple Valley, Calif.	FA
Shologan, Keith	DT	6-2	297	22	Central Florida	Edmonton, Alberta	FA
Tereshinski, John	TE	6-3	245	23	Wake Forest	Athens, Ga.	FA
Thomas, Marco (1)	WR	5-11	190	24	Western Illinois	Chicago, Ill.	FA
Thomas, Marcus	RB	6-0	215	24	Texas-El Paso	Phoenix, Ariz.	D5
Tolbert, Mike	FB	5-9	243	22	Coastal Carolina	Douglasville, Ga.	FA
Tribble, DeJuan	CB	5-9	190	23	Boston College	Cincinnati, Ohio	D6
Vinnedge, Billy	P/K	6-1	202	23	Wyoming	Arroyo Grande, Calif.	FA

The term NFL Rookie is defined as a player who is in his first season of professional football and has not been on the roster of another professional football team for any regular-season or postseason games. A Rookie is designated by an "R" on NFL rosters. Players who have been active in another professional football league or players who have NFL experience, including either preseason training camp or being on an Active List or Inactive List, or on Reserve/Injured or Reserve/Physically Unable to Perform for fewer than six regular-season games, are termed NFL First-Year Players. An NFL First-Year Player is designated by a "1" on NFL rosters. Thereafter, a player is credited with an additional year of experience for each season in which he accumulates six games on the Active List or Inactive List, or on Reserve/Injured or Reserve/Physically Unable to Perform.

Log on to www.sandiegochargers.com for an up-to-date roster; Age listed is as of September 4, 2008.

COACHING STAFF

Head Coach,
Norv Turner

Pro Career: A veteran coach of 23 NFL seasons, Turner became the 14th head coach in team history on February 19, 2007. In his first season, Turner led the Chargers (11-5) to the AFC West title, the team's third in the last four years. In the postseason, he led the Chargers to the AFC Championship Game. The Chargers' playoff wins over Tennessee and Indianapolis were the team's first since the 1994 season. A two-time Super Bowl champion as an offensive coordinator with the Dallas Cowboys, Turner was the offensive coordinator for the San Francisco 49ers in 2006. A Bay Area native from Martinez, California, this is Turner's second stint with the Chargers. He spent the 2001 season as the Bolts' offensive coordinator. Turner's previous 23 years of coaching experience include 10 as a head coach—seven for the Washington Redskins (1994-2000), two with the Oakland Raiders (2004-05), and one with the Chargers (2007). In 1999, he led the Redskins to a division title. He spent 13 seasons as an NFL assistant coach, including seven as an offensive coordinator with the Cowboys (1991-93), Chargers (2001), Dolphins (2002-03), and 49ers (2006). Turner began his NFL coaching career as an assistant with the Rams in 1985. He coached wide receivers from 1985-86 before adding the responsibility of the team's tight ends from 1987-1990. Turner made his coaching mark during his three seasons in Dallas as the Cowboys won back-to-back Super Bowls (XXVII and XXVIII) following the 1992 and 1993 seasons. Career record: 72-89-1.

Background: Turner played quarterback at Oregon, spending two seasons behind former Charger and NFL Hall of Fame quarterback Dan Fouts. Turner coached at Oregon (1975) and Southern California (1976-1984). During his nine-year tenure at USC, the Trojans played in four Rose Bowls, winning all four. One of those was a win over Michigan after the 1978 season that capped a 12-1 season and gave USC the National Championship.

Personal: Age 56, born in LeJeune, N.C. Turner and his wife, Nancy, have three children—Scott, Stephanie, and Drew.

ASSISTANT COACHES

Clancy Barone, tight ends; born San Andreas, Calif. Offensive lineman Cal State-Sacramento 1981-82, Nevada 1985-86. No pro playing experience. College coach: American River (Calif.) J.C. 1987-89, Cal State-Sacramento 1990-92, Texas A&M 1993, Eastern Illinois 1994-96, Wyoming 1997-99, Houston 2000-02, Texas State 2003. Pro coach: Atlanta Falcons 2004-06, joined Chargers in 2007.

Bill Bradley, secondary; born Palestine, Texas. Quarterback/ defensive back Texas

1966-68. Pro safety/punter/kick returner Philadelphia Eagles 1969-1977, St. Louis Cardinals 1978. College coach: Texas 1987, Baylor 2004-06. Pro coach: San Antonio Gunslingers (USFL) 1983-84, Memphis Showboats (USFL) 1985, Calgary Stampeders (CFL) 1988-1990, San Antonio Riders (WLAF) 1991-92, Sacramento Gold Miners (CFL) 1994, San Antonio Texans (CFL) 1995, Toronto Argonauts (CFL) 1996-97, Buffalo Bills 1998-2000, New York Jets 2001-03, joined Chargers in 2007.

Ted Cottrell, defensive coordinator; born Chester, Pa. Linebacker Delaware Valley College 1966-68. Pro linebacker Atlanta Falcons 1969-1970, Winnipeg Blue Bombers (CFL) 1971. College coach: Rutgers 1973-1980, 1983. Pro coach: Kansas City Chiefs 1981-82, New Jersey Generals (USFL) 1983-84, Buffalo Bills 1986-89, 1995-2000, Arizona Cardinals 1990-94, New York Jets 2001-03, Minnesota Vikings 2004-05, joined Chargers in 2007.

Steve Crosby, special teams; born Great Bend, Kan. Running back Fort Hays State 1970-73. Pro running back New York Giants 1974-76. College coach: Vanderbilt 1998-2001. Pro coach: Miami Dolphins 1979-1982, Atlanta Falcons 1983-84, 1986-89, Cleveland Browns 1985, 1991-95, New England Patriots 1990, joined Chargers in 2002.

John (Jack) Henry, offensive line; born Houston, Pa. Linebacker Penn State 1964-65, guard Indiana (Pa.) 1967-68. No pro playing experience. College coach: West Virginia 1970, 1978-79, Edinboro 1973, Louisville 1974, Millersville 1975-76, Southern Illinois 1977, Appalachian State 1980, Wake Forest 1981-85, Indiana (Pa.) 1986-89, Pittsburgh 1993-95. Pro coach: Pittsburgh Steelers 1990-91, San Diego Chargers 1996, Detroit Lions 1997-99, New Orleans Saints 2000-05, re-joined Chargers in 2006.

Hal Hunter, offensive line; born Canonsburg, Pa. Linebacker Northwestern 1978. College coach: William & Mary 1982, Pittsburgh 1983-84, Columbia 1985, Indiana (Pa.) 1986, Akron 1987-1990, Vanderbilt 1991-94, Louisiana State 1995-99, Indiana 2000-01, North Carolina 2002-05. Pro coach: Joined Chargers in 2006.

Jeff Hurd, strength and conditioning; born Pomona, Calif. No college or pro playing experience. College coach: Fort Hays State 1984, Delta State 1985-86, Clemson 1986-87, Western Michigan 1987-1992, Tulsa 1994. Pro coach: Jacksonville Jaguars 1995-97, Kansas City Chiefs 1998-2006, joined Chargers in 2007.

Charlie Joiner, receivers; born Many, La. Wide receiver Grambling State 1965-68. Pro defensive back/wide receiver Houston Oilers 1969-1972, Cincinnati Bengals 1972-75, San Diego Chargers 1976-1986. Inducted into Pro Football Hall of Fame

1996. Pro coach: San Diego Chargers 1987-1991, Buffalo Bills 1992-2000, Kansas City Chiefs 2001-07, re-joined Chargers in 2008.

Wayne Nunnely, defensive line; born Los Angeles. Fullback Nevada-Las Vegas 1972-75. No pro playing experience. College coach: Nevada-Las Vegas 1976, 1982-89 (head coach 1986-89), Cal Poly-Pomona 1977-78, Cal State-Fullerton 1979, Pacific 1980-81, Southern California 1991-92, UCLA 1993-94. Pro coach: New Orleans Saints 1995-96, joined Chargers in 1997.

John Pagano, outside linebackers; born Boulder, Colo. Linebacker Mesa State College 1985-88. No pro playing experience. College coach: Mesa State College 1989, Nevada-Las Vegas 1990-91, Louisiana Tech 1994, Mississippi 1995. Pro coach: New Orleans Saints 1996-97, Indianapolis Colts 1998-2001, joined Chargers in 2002.

John Ramsdell, quarterbacks; born Lafayette, Ind. Running back Springfield (Mass.) College 1972-75. No pro playing experience. College coach: San Francisco State 1976-77, Long Beach State 1978, Pacific 1979-1982, Oregon 1983-1994. Pro coach: St. Louis Rams 1995-2005, joined Chargers in 2006.

Ron Rivera, inside linebackers; born Fort Ord, Calif. Linebacker California 1980-83. Pro linebacker Chicago Bears 1984-1992. Pro coach: Chicago Bears 1997-98, 2004-06, Philadelphia Eagles 1999-2003, joined Chargers in 2007.

Kevin Ross, asst. secondary/quality control; born Camden, N.J. Defensive back Temple 1980-83. Pro defensive back Kansas City Chiefs 1984-1993, 1997, Atlanta Falcons 1994-95, San Diego Chargers 1996. Pro coach: Minnesota Vikings 2003-05, joined Chargers in 2007.

Clarence Shelmon, offensive coordinator; born Bossier City, La. Running back Houston 1971-75. No pro playing experience. College coach: Army 1978-1980, Indiana 1981-83, Arizona 1984-86, Southern California 1987-1990. Pro coach: Los Angeles Rams 1991, Seattle Seahawks 1992-97, Dallas Cowboys 1998-2001, joined Chargers in 2002.

Vernon Stephens, asst. strength and conditioning; born Jacksonville. No college or pro playing experience. College coach: North Florida 1999-2002, Colorado 2003-06. Pro coach: Jacksonville Jaguars 2002-03, joined Chargers in 2007.

Ollie Wilson, running backs; born Worcester, Mass. Wide receiver Springfield 1971-73. No pro playing experience. College coach: Springfield 1975, Northeastern 1976-1982, California 1983-1990. Pro coach: Atlanta Falcons 1991-96, 2002-07, San Diego Chargers 1997-2001, re-joined Chargers in 2008.

American Football Conference
South Division
Team Colors: Navy, Titans Blue, Red, Silver
460 Great Circle Road
Nashville, Tennessee 37228
Telephone: (615) 565-4000

2008 SCHEDULE
PRESEASON
Aug. 9   **St. Louis** 7:00
Aug. 15   **Oakland** 7:00
Aug. 22   at Atlanta.............................7:30
Aug. 28   at Green Bay 7:00

REGULAR SEASON
Sep. 7   **Jacksonville** 12:00
Sep. 14   at Cincinnati 1:00
Sep. 21   **Houston** 12:00
Sep. 28   **Minnesota** 12:00
Oct. 5   at Baltimore 1:00
Oct. 12   BYE
Oct. 19   at Kansas City 12:00
Oct. 27   **Indianapolis** (Mon.) 7:30
Nov. 2   **Green Bay** 12:00
Nov. 9   at Chicago 12:00
Nov. 16   at Jacksonville 1:00
Nov. 23   **N.Y. Jets** 12:00
Nov. 27   at Detroit (Thu.)...............12:30
Dec. 7   **Cleveland** 12:00
Dec. 14   at Houston 12:00
Dec. 21   **Pittsburgh** 12:00
Dec. 28   at Indianapolis 1:00

Stadium: LP Field
          (opened in 1999)
          • **Capacity:** 69,143
          One Titans Way
          Nashville, Tennessee 37213
Playing Surface: Natural Grass
Training Camp: Baptist Sports Park
          460 Great Circle Road
          Nashville, Tennessee
          37228

LP FIELD

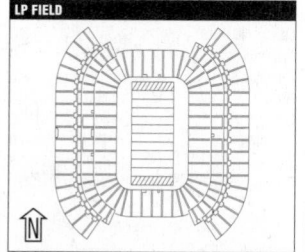

CLUB OFFICIALS
Owner/Chairman of the Board/CEO/
  President: K.S. (Bud) Adams, Jr.
Senior Executive V.P./General Counsel:
  Steve Underwood
Executive V.P./General Manager:
  Mike Reinfeldt
Executive V.P. of Administration/Facilities:
  Don MacLachlan
Vice President/Asst. General Counsel:
  Elza Bullock
Vice President/Finance and CFO:
  Robert McBurnett
Vice President/Community Affairs:
  Bob Hyde
Senior Director of Football
  Administration: Vincent Marino
National Supervisor of College Scouting:
  C.O. Brocato
Eastern Director of College Scouting:
  Mike Ackerley
Senior Director of Sales and Operations:
  Stuart Spears
Operations Manager: Brent Akers
Director of Broadcasting: Mike Keith
Vice President/Marketing:
  Ralph Ockenfels
Controller: Jenneen Kaufman
Director of Information Systems:
  Russ Hudson
Director of Internet
  Operations/Publications: Gary Glenn
Director of Media Relations:
  Robbie Bohren
Asst. Director of Media Relations:
  Dwight Spradlin
Director of Security: Steve Berk
Senior Director of Ticketing:
  Marty Collins
Director of Pro Personnel: Lake Dawson
Director of Player Development:
  Tina Tuggle
Director of Cheerleading: Stacie Kinder
Director of Suite and Club Services:
  Bill Wainwright
Marketing Manager: Brad McClanahan
Head Athletic Trainer: Brad Brown
Assistant Athletic Trainers:
  Don Moseley, Geoff Kaplan
Equipment Manager: Paul Noska
Video Director: Anthony Pastrana
General Manager of LP Field:
  Walter Overton

COACHING HISTORY
Houston 1960-1996
(364-386-6)
Records include postseason games
1960-61   Lou Rymkus* 12-7-1
1961   Wally Lemm 10-0-0
1962-63   Frank (Pop) Ivy 17-12-0
1964   Sammy Baugh...............4-10-0
1965   Hugh Taylor 4-10-0
1966-1970 Wally Lemm 28-40-4
1971   Ed Hughes.......................4-9-1
1972-73   Bill Peterson** 1-18-0
1973-74   Sid Gillman 8-15-0
1975-1980 O.A. (Bum) Phillips 59-38-0
1981-83   Ed Biles*** 8-23-0
1983   Chuck Studley 2-8-0
1984-85   Hugh Campbell**** 8-22-0
1985-89   Jerry Glanville.............35-35-0
1990-94   Jack Pardee#.............44-35-0
1994-2007 Jeff Fisher..................120-104-0
   * Released after five games in 1961
  ** Released after five games in 1973
 *** Resigned after six games in 1983
**** Released after 14 games in 1985
   \# Released after 10 games in 1994

PAID ATTENDANCE
Home 536,745   Away 530,131
Total 1,066,876
Single-game home record,
  69,149, many times (last: 12/18/05)
Single-season home record,
  553,192 (2005)

2008 DRAFT CHOICES

Round	Name	Pos.	College
1	Chris Johnson	RB	East Carolina
2	Jason Jones	DL	Eastern Michigan
3	Craig Stevens	TE	California
4	William Hayes	DE	Winston-Salem St.
	Lavelle Hawkins	WR	California
	Stanford Keglar	LB	Purdue
7	Cary Williams	DB	Washburn

TENNESSEE TITANS

2007 TEAM RECORD

PRESEASON (3-1)

Date	Result	Opponent
8/11	L 6-14	Washington
8/17	W 27-24	at New England
8/24	W 28-17	at Buffalo
8/30	W 30-14	Green Bay

REGULAR SEASON (10-6)

Date	Result	Opponent	Att.
9/9	W 13-10	at Jacksonville	65,437
9/16	L 20-22	Indianapolis	69,143
9/24	W 31-14	at New Orleans	70,002
10/7	W 20-13	Atlanta	69,143
10/14	L 10-13	at Tampa Bay	65,347
10/21	W 38-36	at Houston	70,734
10/28	W 13-9	Oakland	69,143
11/4	W 20-7	Carolina	69,143
11/11	L 13-28	at Jacksonville	69,143
11/19	L 20-34	at Denver	76,590
11/25	L 6-35	at Cincinnati	65,489
12/2	W 28-20	Houston	69,143
12/9	L 17-23	San Diego (OT)	69,143
12/16	W 26-17	at Kansas City	74,976
12/23	W 10-6	New York Jets	69,143
12/30	W 16-10	at Indianapolis	57,202

POSTSEASON (0-1)

1/6	L 6-17	at San Diego	65,640

SCORE BY PERIODS

Titans	59	64	98	80	0	—	301
Opponents	65	78	64	84	6	—	297

2007 TEAM STATISTICS

	Titans	Opp.
Total First Downs	306	268
Rushing	118	80
Passing	171	165
Penalty	17	23
3rd Down: Made/Att	89/217	97/230
3rd Down Pct.	41.0	42.2
4th Down: Made/Att	2/11	8/16
4th Down Pct.	18.2	50.0
Possession Avg.	31:38	28:22
Total Net Yards	4987	4665
Avg. Per Game	311.7	291.6
Total Plays	1037	978
Avg. Per Play	4.8	4.8
Net Yards Rushing	2109	1478
Avg. Per Game	131.8	92.4
Total Rushes	543	369
Net Yards Passing	2878	3187
Avg. Per Game	179.9	199.2
Sacked/Yards Lost	30/199	40/241
Gross Yards	3077	3428
Att./Completions	464/288	569/349
Completion Pct.	62.1	61.3
Had Intercepted	17	22
Punts/Average	73/41.9	81/44.6
Net Punting Avg.	73/36.5	81/37.6
Penalties/Yards	101/773	90/745
Fumbles/Ball Lost	32/17	26/12
Touchdowns	28	35
Rushing	17	11
Passing	9	21
Returns	2	3

2007 INDIVIDUAL STATISTICS

PASSING	Att.	Comp.	Yds.	Pct.	TD	Int.	Tkld.	Rate
Young	382	238	2546	62.3	9	17	25/157	71.1
Collins	82	50	531	61.0	0	0	5/42	79.9
Titans	464	288	3077	62.1	9	17	30/199	72.6
Opponents	569	349	3428	61.3	21	22	40/241	74.5

SCORING	TD R	TD P	TD Rt	PAT	FG	Saf	PTS
Bironas	0	0	0	28/28	35/39	0	133
White	7	0	0	0/0	0/0	0	42
C. Brown	5	0	0	0/0	0/0	0	30
R. Williams	0	4	0	0/0	0/0	0	24
Young	3	0	0	0/0	0/0	0	18
Fuller	0	0	2	0/0	0/0	0	12
Gage	0	2	0	0/0	0/0	0	12
Henry	2	0	0	0/0	0/0	0	12
B. Jones	0	2	0	0/0	0/0	0	12
Scaife	0	1	0	0/0	0/0	0	6
Titans	17	9	2	28/28	35/39	0	301
Opponents	11	21	3	31/33	18/25	0	297

2-Pt. Conversions: Titans 0-0, Opponents 1-1

RUSHING	No.	Yds	Avg	LG	TD
White	303	1110	3.7	28	7
C. Brown	102	462	4.5	42	5
Young	93	395	4.2	21	3
Henry	31	119	3.8	24t	2
B. Jones	2	37	18.5	19	0
Davis	2	19	9.5	14	0
Hall	1	8	8.0	8	0
Barclay	1	3	3.0	3	0
Troupe	1	-1	-1.0	-1	0
Collins	3	-3	-1.0	-1	0
Hentrich	1	-8	-8.0	-8	0
Bell	1	-15	-15.0	-15	0
R. Williams	2	-17	-8.5	-6	0
Titans	543	2109	3.9	42	17
Opponents	369	1478	4.0	62t	11

RECEIVING	No.	Yds	Avg	LG	TD
Gage	55	750	13.6	73	2
R. Williams	55	719	13.1	48	4
Scaife	46	421	9.2	26	1
Moulds	32	342	10.7	46	0
B. Jones	21	248	11.8	35t	2
White	20	114	5.7	15	0
C. Brown	19	128	6.7	16	0
Hartsock	12	138	11.5	27	0
Hall	9	60	6.7	11	0
Henry	6	53	8.8	18	0
Troupe	5	47	9.4	13	0
Davis	5	38	7.6	13	0
Barclay	2	13	6.5	7	0
Ealy	1	6	6.0	6	0
Titans	288	3077	10.7	73	9
Opponents	349	3428	9.8	69t	21

INTERCEPTIONS	No.	Yds	Avg	LG	TD
Bulluck	5	63	12.6	35	0
Harper	3	62	20.7	32	0
Griffin	3	3	1.0	3	0
Fuller	2	137	68.5	76t	2
Hope	2	45	22.5	45	0
Lowry	2	18	9.0	17	0
Thornton	2	16	8.0	11	0
Finnegan	1	14	14.0	14	0
Hill	1	0	0.0	0	0
LaBoy	1	0	0.0	0	0
Titans	22	358	16.3	76t	2
Opponents	17	116	6.8	23	0

PUNTING	No.	Yds.	Avg.	In 20	LG
Hentrich	70	2939	42.0	24	66
Miller	3	121	40.3	1	52
Titans	73	3060	41.9	25	66
Opponents	81	3615	44.6	23	70

PUNT RETURNS	Ret	FC	Yds	Avg	LG	TD
Davis	31	12	293	9.5	39	0
B. Jones	6	0	29	4.8	13	0
Barclay	3	1	34	11.3	19	0
Finnegan	2	3	11	5.5	9	0
Titans	42	16	367	8.7	39	0
Opponents	31	16	274	8.8	80t	1

KICKOFF RETURNS	No.	Yds	Avg	LG	TD
Griffin	18	422	23.4	48	0
Barclay	14	304	21.7	37	0
Henry	13	272	20.9	46	0
Davis	2	37	18.5	19	0
Troupe	2	21	10.5	12	0
Cramer	1	13	13.0	13	0
Hartsock	1	14	14.0	14	0
Lowry	1	15	15.0	15	0
Titans	52	1098	21.1	48	0
Opponents	58	1404	24.2	76	0

FIELD GOALS	1-19	20-29	30-39	40-49	50+
Bironas	0/0	10/12	12/12	9/10	4/5
Titans	0/0	10/12	12/12	9/10	4/5
Opponents	0/0	7/8	5/6	3/5	3/6

SACKS	No.
Vanden Bosch	12.0
Odom	8.0
Haynesworth	6.0
LaBoy	6.0
T. Brown	4.0
Finnegan	1.0
Fuller	1.0
Nickey	1.0
Thornton	1.0
Titans	40.0
Opponents	30.0

RECORD HOLDERS
INDIVIDUAL RECORDS—CAREER

Category	Name	Performance
Rushing (Yds.)	Eddie George, 1996-2003	10,009
Passing (Yds.)	Warren Moon, 1984-1993	33,685
Passing (TDs)	Warren Moon, 1984-1993	196
Receiving (No.)	Ernest Givins, 1986-1994	542
Receiving (Yds.)	Ernest Givins, 1986-1994	7,935
Interceptions	Jim Norton, 1960-68	45
Punting (Avg.)	Greg Montgomery, 1988-1993	43.6
Punt Return (Avg.)	Billy Johnson, 1974-1980	13.2
Kickoff Return (Avg.)	Bobby Jancik, 1962-67	26.5
Field Goals	Al Del Greco, 1991-2000	246
Touchdowns (Tot.)	Eddie George, 1996-2003	74
Points	Al Del Greco, 1991-2000	1,060

INDIVIDUAL RECORDS—SINGLE SEASON

Category	Name	Performance
Rushing (Yds.)	Earl Campbell, 1980	1,934
Passing (Yds.)	Warren Moon, 1991	4,690
Passing (TDs)	George Blanda, 1961	36
Receiving (No.)	Charley Hennigan, 1964	101
Receiving (Yds.)	Charley Hennigan, 1961	1,746
Interceptions	Fred Glick, 1963	12
	Mike Reinfeldt, 1979	12
Punting (Avg.)	Craig Hentrich, 1998	47.2
Punt Return (Avg.)	Billy Johnson, 1977	15.4
Kickoff Return (Avg.)	Ken Hall, 1960	31.3
Field Goals	Al Del Greco, 1998	36
Touchdowns (Tot.)	Earl Campbell, 1979	19
Points	Al Del Greco, 1998	136

INDIVIDUAL RECORDS—SINGLE GAME

Category	Name	Performance
Rushing (Yds.)	Billy Cannon, 12-10-61	216
	Eddie George, 8-31-97	216
Passing (Yds.)	Warren Moon, 12-16-90	527
Passing (TDs)	George Blanda, 11-19-61	*7
Receiving (No.)	Charley Hennigan, 10-13-61	13
	Haywood Jeffires, 10-13-91	13
	Drew Bennett, 12-19-04	13
Receiving (Yds.)	Charley Hennigan, 10-13-61	272
Interceptions	Many times	3
	Last time by Keith Bulluck, 9-24-07	
Field Goals	Rob Bironas, 10-21-07	*8
Touchdowns (Tot.)	Billy Cannon, 12-10-61	5
Points	Billy Cannon, 12-10-61	30

*NFL Record

2008 VETERAN ROSTER

No.	Name	Pos.	Ht.	Wt.	Age	NFL Exp.	College	Hometown	How Acq.	'07 Games/ Starts
54	Amano, Eugene	C/G	6-3	310	26	5	SE Missouri St.	San Diego, Calif.	D7-'04	16/5
58	Amato, Ken	LB/LS	6-2	245	31	6	Montana State	Miami, Fla.	FA-'03	7/0
98	Ball, Dave	DE	6-5	277	27	4	UCLA	Fairfield, Calif.	FA-'08	0*
2	Bironas, Rob	K	6-0	205	30	4	Georgia Southern	Louisville, Kent.	FA-'05	16/0
84	Blakley, Dwayne	TE	6-4	257	29	5	Missouri	St. Joseph, Mo.	UFA(Atl)-'08	12/3*
97	Brown, Tony	DT	6-3	285	27	4	Memphis	Chattanooga, Tenn.	FA-'06	16/16
53	Bulluck, Keith	LB	6-3	235	31	9	Syracuse	New City, N.Y.	D1-'00	16/16
28	Carr, Chris	DB	5-10	180	25	4	Boise State	Reno, Nev.	RFA(Oak)-'08	16/2*
40	Cain, Jeremy	FB/LS	6-1	240	28	3	Massachusetts	Fort Lauderdale, Fla.	FA-'07	9/0
49	Campbell, Kurt	LB	6-1	227	26	3	Albany	Kingston, Jamaica	FA-'07	0*
5	Collins, Kerry	QB	6-5	245	35	14	Penn. State	Lebanon, Pa.	UFA(Oak)-'06	6/1
77	Conover, Sean	DE	6-5	262	24	3	Bucknell	Whitman, Mass.	FA-'06	4/0
51	Cordova, Jorge	LB	6-1	244	26	4	Nevada	San Diego, Calif.	FA-'07	2/0
48	Cramer, Casey	FB	6-2	250	26	4	Dartmouth	Middleton, Wisc.	W(Car)-'06	5/1
83	Crumpler, Alge	TE	6-2	262	30	8	North Carolina	Wilmington, N.C.	FA-'08	14/10*
17	Davis, Chris	WR	5-10	181	24	2	Florida State	St. Petersburg, Fla.	D4b-'07	12/0
82	Ealy, Biren	WR	6-3	207	24	2	Houston	Houston, Texas	FA-'07	4/0
31	Finnegan, Cortland	CB	5-10	188	24	3	Samford	Milton, Fla.	D7a-'06	16/16
94	Fisher, Bryce	DE	6-3	265	31	8	Air Force	Renton, Wash.	T(Sea)-'07	9/0
78	Ford, Jacob	DE	6-4	251	25	2	Central Arkansas	Memphis, Tenn.	D6b-'07	0*
52	Fowler, Ryan	LB	6-3	250	26	5	Duke	Redington Shores, Fla.	RFA(Dall)-'07	14/14
22	Fuller, Vincent	S	6-1	190	26	4	Virginia Tech	Baltimore, Md.	D4a-'05	16/0
12	Gage, Justin	WR	6-4	212	27	6	Missouri	Jefferson City, Mo.	UFA(Chi)-'07	16/8
33	Griffin, Michael	DB	6-0	202	23	2	Texas	Austin, Texas	D1-'07	16/10
45	Hall, Ahmard	FB	5-11	242	28	3	Texas	Angleton, Texas	FA-'06	11/4
20	Harper, Nick	CB	5-10	182	33	8	Fort Valley St.	Baldwin, Ga.	UFA(Ind)-'07	14/14
64	Harris, Leroy	G/C	6-3	302	24	2	N.C. State	Raleigh, N.C.	D4a-'07	5/0
92	Haynesworth, Albert	DT	6-6	320	27	7	Tennessee	Hartsville, S.C.	D1-'02	13/12
42	Henry, Chris	RB	5-11	230	23	2	Arizona	Oakland, Calif.	D2-'07	7/0
15	Hentrich, Craig	P/K	6-3	213	37	15	Notre Dame	Alton, Ill.	UFA(GB)-'98	15/0
21	Hill, Reynaldo	CB	5-11	185	26	4	Florida	Ft. Lauderdale, Fla.	D7-'05	13/2
24	Hope, Chris	S	6-0	208	27	7	Florida State	Rock Hill, S.C.	UFA(Pitt)-'06	11/11
99	Johnson, Antonio	DT	6-3	310	23	2	Mississippi State	Leland, Miss.	D5-'07	0*
81	Jones, Brandon	WR	6-1	212	25	4	Oklahoma	Texarkana, Texas	D3b-'05	9/2
90	Kearse, Jevon	DE	6-4	265	32	10	Florida	Ft. Myers, Fla.	FA-'08	14/8*
30	King, Eric	CB	5-10	185	26	4	Wake Forest	Woodstock, Md.	W(Buff)-'06	15/1
70	Loper, Daniel	T	6-6	320	26	4	Texas Tech	Houston, Texas	D5b-'05	16/0
37	Lowry, Calvin	S	5-11	200	25	3	Penn. State	Fayetteville, N.C.	D4a-'06	16/11
3	Martin, Ingle	QB	6-2	220	26	2	Furman	Nashville, Tenn.	FA-'07	0*
68	Mawae, Kevin	C	6-4	289	37	15	Louisiana State	Leesville, La.	UFA(NYJ)-'06	14/14
19	McCareins, Justin	WR	6-2	215	29	8	Northern Illinois	Naperville, Tenn.	FA-'08	16/6*
4	Miller, Josh	P	6-4	225	38	12	Arizona	Rockaway, N.Y.	FA-'07	1/0
23	Nickey, Donnie	S	6-3	210	28	6	Ohio State	Plain City, Ohio	D5-'03	16/0
71	Roos, Michael	T	6-7	315	25	4	Eastern Washington	Vancouver, Wash.	D2-'05	16/16
80	Scaife, Bo	TE	6-3	249	27	4	Texas	Denver, Colo.	D6-'05	16/15
73	Scott, Jake	G	6-5	295	27	5	Idaho	Lewiston, Idaho	UFA(Ind)-'08	16/16*
57	Stamer, Josh	LB	6-2	242	30	6	South Dakota	Sutherland, Iowa	UFA(Buff)-'08	16/0*
44	Stephens, Leonard	TE	6-3	252	30	3	Howard	Brooklyn, N.Y.	FA-'07	0*
76	Stewart, David	T	6-7	318	26	4	Mississippi State	Moulton, Ala.	D4b-'05	16/16
50	Thornton, David	LB	6-2	225	29	7	North Carolina	Goldsboro, N.C.	UFA(Ind)-'06	16/16
55	Tulloch, Stephen	LB	5-11	235	23	3	N.C. State	Miami, Fla.	D4b-'06	16/1
93	Vanden Bosch, Kyle	DE	6-4	278	29	8	Nebraska	Larchwood, Iowa	UFA(Ariz)-'05	16/16
96	Vickerson, Kevin	DT	6-5	305	25	3	Michigan State	Detroit, Mich.	FA-'07	4/0
25	White, LenDale	RB	6-1	235	23	3	Southern California	Denver, Colo.	D2-'06	16/16
18	Williams, Mike	WR	6-5	242	24	4	Southern California	Tampa, Fla.	FA-'07	2/0
11	Williams, Paul	WR	6-1	205	24	2	Fresno State	Avenal, Calif.	D3-'07	0*
86	Williams, Roydell	WR	6-0	187	27	4	Tulane	LaPlace, La.	D4c-'05	16/14
10	Young, Vince	QB	6-5	233	25	3	Texas	Houston, Texas	D1-'06	15/15

* Ball last active with N.Y. Jets in '06; Blakley played 12 games with Atlanta; Carr played 16 games with Oakland; Campbell last active with Green Bay in '06; Crumpler played 14 games with Atlanta; Ford missed '07 season because of injury; Johnson missed '07 season because of injury; Kearse played 14 games with Philadelphia; Martin last active with Green Bay in '06; McCareins played 16 games with N.Y. Jets; Scott played 16 games with Indianapolis; Stamer played 16 games with Buffalo; Stephens last active with Washington in '02; P. Williams inactive for 16 games.

Players lost through free agency (8): G Jacob Bell (StL; 16 games in '07); RB Chris Brown (Hou; 12); LB Gilbert Gardner (Det; 13); TE Ben Hartsock (Atl; 16); DE Travis LaBoy (Ariz; 13); DE Antwan Odom (Cin; 16); DT Randy Starks (Mia; 14); TE Ben Troupe (TB; 16).

Also played with the Titans in '07—RB Chris Barclay (4 games), RB Quinton Ganther (2), CB Kelly Herndon (3), CB Chidi Iwuoma (1), G Benji Olson (13), LB Rich Scanlon (9), DT Corey Simon (4), DT Demetrin Veal (3), LB Levar Woods (8).

2008 FIRST-YEAR ROSTER

Name	Pos.	Ht.	Wt.	Age	College	Hometown	How Acq.
Allred, Colin (1)	LB	6-1	238	25	Baylor	Dallas, Texas	FA-'07
Booker, Barry	DT	6-4	285	22	Virginia Tech	Amherst, Va.	FA
Cole, Marquice (1)	CB	5-10	190	24	Northwestern	Hazel Crest, Ill.	FA-'07
Cuff, Omar	RB	5-10	195	23	Delaware	Landover, Md.	FA
Freeman, Jerrell	LB	6-0	220	22	Mary-Hardin Baylor	Waco, Texas	FA
Ganther, Quinton (1)	RB	5-9	214	24	Utah	Richmond, Calif.	D7c-'06
Hawkins, Lavelle	WR	5-11	190	22	California	Stockton, Calif.	D4b
Hayes, William	DE	6-3	272	23	Winston-Salem State	High Point, N.C.	D4a
Johnson, Chris	RB	5-11	200	22	East Carolina	Orlando, Fla.	D1
Joiner, Tony	S	6-0	210	22	Florida	Haines City, Fla.	FA
Jones, Jason	DL	6-5	275	22	Eastern Michigan	Detroit, Mich.	D2
Keglar, Stanford	LB	6-2	240	23	Purdue	Indianapolis, Ind.	D4c
Little, Rafael	RB	5-9	195	21	Kentucky	Anderson, S.C.	FA
Lucas, Enoka (1)	C/G	6-3	299	24	Oregon	Honolulu, Hawaii	FA
Mitchell, Shirdonya (1)	CB	5-11	183	26	Missouri	Dallas, Texas	FA
Muncy, Matt (1)	LB	6-1	238	25	Ohio	Miamisburg, Ohio	FA
Murphy, Jason (1)	C	6-2	304	26	Virginia Tech	Baltimore, Md.	FA-'07
Otto, Mike (1)	T	6-5	308	25	Purdue	Kokomo, Ind.	D7-'07
Pasteur, Brock	T	6-5	300	24	Stephen F. Austin	Orlando, Fla.	FA
Petrowski, Jamie (1)	TE	6-4	250	26	Indiana State	Terre Haute, Ind.	FA-'07
Rivers, Jason	WR	6-1	200	24	Hawaii	Honolulu, Hawaii	FA
Scott, Eric	C	6-3	300	24	Kentucky	Woodstock, Ga.	FA
Stevens, Craig	TE	6-3	255	24	California	San Pedro, Calif.	D3
Taylor, Eric (1)	DT	6-2	309	26	Memphis	Winchester, Tenn.	FA
Thompson, Paul (1)	QB	6-4	216	24	Oklahoma	Leander, Texas	FA
Velasco, Fernando	C/G	6-4	304	23	Georgia	Wrens, Ga.	FA
Williams, Cary	CB	6-1	185	23	Washburn	Hollywood, Fla.	D7
Williams, Edward	WR	6-4	215	25	Lane College	Montgomery, Ala.	FA
Winkler, Ulrich (1)	DE	6-5	265	24	None	Munich, Germany	FA-'07

The term NFL Rookie is defined as a player who is in his first season of professional football and has not been on the roster of another professional football team for any regular-season or postseason games. A Rookie is designated by an "R" on NFL rosters. Players who have been active in another professional football league or players who have NFL experience, including either preseason training camp or being on an Active List or Inactive List, or on Reserve/Injured or Reserve/Physically Unable to Perform for fewer than six regular-season games, are termed NFL First-Year Players. An NFL First-Year Player is designated by a "1" on NFL rosters. Thereafter, a player is credited with an additional year of experience for each season in which he accumulates six games on the Active List or Inactive List, or on Reserve/Injured or Reserve/Physically Unable to Perform.

Log on to www.titansonline.com for an up-to-date roster; Age listed is as of September 4, 2008.

COACHING STAFF
Head Coach,
Jeff Fisher
Pro Career: Officially became the franchise's fifteenth head coach on January 5, 1995, after closing his first campaign with the Oilers as head coach/defensive coordinator. He replaced Jack Pardee on November 14, 1994, coaching the remaining six games as head coach. Fisher holds the franchise mark for wins with 120 over his 13-year coaching career. In 2007, Fisher led the Titans to their fifth playoff appearance in the past nine years. In 2006, he became the first coach in franchise history and the 28th head coach in NFL history to reach 200 games. Only 11 other coaches in history have coached 200 games with one team. In 2005, he became the 34th coach in NFL history to reach the 100-win plateau. In 2004, he became the fourth youngest coach (46) since 1960 to reach 90 regular-season victories (John Madden, Don Shula, and Bill Cowher). Over the last nine seasons, Fisher has led the Titans to five playoff appearances, two AFC Championship Games, two division titles and a berth in Super Bowl XXXIV. In 2000, Fisher became only the fifth coach in NFL history to lead his team to consecutive 13-win seasons, joining Mike Holmgren, George Seifert, Marv Levy, and Mike Ditka. Fisher originally joined the Oilers in 1994 as the defensive coordinator, after serving as defensive backs coach for the San Francisco 49ers (1992-93). Prior to heading up the 49ers secondary, Fisher served as the defensive coordinator for the Los Angeles Rams (1991). He began his coaching career with the Philadelphia Eagles in 1986, where he handled defensive backs until becoming the NFL's youngest defensive coordinator in 1988. Drafted by Chicago in seventh round in 1981, he spent five seasons as a cornerback and kick returner for the Bears (1981-85). Assisted defensive coordinator Buddy Ryan in Bears' 1985 Super Bowl championship season after being placed on injured reserve with ankle injury. Career record: 120-104.
Background: Played at Southern California (1977-1980) for John Robinson in a star-studded defensive backfield that included Ronnie Lott, Dennis Smith, and Joey Browner. Member of the USC team that won the national championship in 1978. Also served as the Trojans' backup placekicker and was a Pac-10 All-Academic selection in 1980.
Personal: Age 50, born in Culver City, Calif. Fisher has three children, sons Brandon and Trenton, and daughter Tara.

ASSISTANT COACHES
Matt Burke, defensive assistant/quality control, born Hudson, Mass. Safety Dartmouth 1994-97. No pro playing experience. College coach: Boston College 2000-02, Harvard 2003. Pro coach: Joined Titans in 2006.
Earnest Byner, running backs; born Milledgeville, Ga. Running back East Carolina 1980-83. Pro running back Cleveland Browns 1984-88, 1994-95, Washington Redskins 1989-1993, Baltimore Ravens 1996-97. Pro coach: Washington Redskins 2004-07, joined Titans in 2008.
Chuck Cecil, defensive backs; born Red Bluff, Calif. Defensive back Arizona 1983-87. Pro safety Green Bay Packers 1988-1992, Phoenix Cardinals 1993, Houston Oilers 1995. Pro coach: Joined Titans in 2001.
Marty Galbraith, asst. special teams; born Joplin, Mo. Defensive back Missouri Southern 1971-73. No pro playing experience. College coach: Purdue 1977, Wake Forest 1978-1982, Louisiana State 1987-88, Wake Forest 1989-1990, Pittsburgh 1991, Georgia Tech 1992-93, Marshall 1998-99, North Carolina State 2000-02, Duke 2004. Pro coach: Tampa Bay Bandits (USFL) 1983-84, Kansas City Chiefs 1985, Arizona Outlaws (USFL) 1986, Arizona Cardinals 2003, joined Titans in 2005.
Fred Graves, wide receivers; born Los Angeles, Calif. Halfback/ split end Utah 1968-1971. Pro halfback California Suns 1973 (World Football League). College coach: Northeast Missouri State 1975-76, Western Illinois 1977-78, New Mexico State 1979-1981, Utah 1982-2000. Pro coach: Buffalo Bills 2001-03, Cleveland Browns 2004, Detroit Lions 2005, joined Titans in 2007.
Mike Heimerdinger, offensive coordinator; born DeKalb, Ill. Wide receiver Eastern Illinois 1970-74. No pro playing experience. College coach: Florida 1980, Air Force 1981, North Texas State 1982, Florida 1983-87, Cal State-Fullerton 1988, Rice 1989-1993, Duke 1994. Pro coach: Denver Broncos 1995-99, Tennessee Titans 2000-04, N.Y. Jets 2005, Denver Broncos 2006-07, re-joined Titans in 2008.
Craig Johnson, quarterbacks; born Rome, N.Y. Quarterback Wyoming 1978-1982. No pro playing experience. College coach: Wyoming 1983, Arkansas 1984, Army 1985, Rutgers 1986-88, Virginia Military Institute 1989-1991, Northwestern 1992-96, Maryland 1997-99. Pro coach: Joined Titans in 2000.
Alan Lowry, special teams; born Miami, Okla. Defensive back/quarterback Texas 1970-72. No pro playing experience. College coach: Virginia Tech 1974, Wyoming 1975, Texas 1977-1981. Pro coach: Dallas Cowboys 1982-1990, Tampa Bay Buccaneers 1991, San Francisco 49ers 1992-95, joined Titans/Oilers in 1996.
Dave McGinnis, linebackers; born Independence, Kan. Defensive back Texas Christian 1970-72. No pro playing experi-

ence. College coach: Texas Christian 1973-74, 1982, Missouri 1975-77, Indiana State 1978, 1980-81, Kansas State 1983-85. Pro coach: Chicago Bears 1986-1995, Arizona Cardinals 1996-2003 (head coach 2000-2003), joined Titans in 2004.
Mike Munchak, offensive line; born Scranton, Pa. Guard-tackle Penn State 1979-1981. Pro guard Houston Oilers 1982-1993. Inducted into Pro Football Hall of Fame 2001. Pro coach: Joined Titans/Oilers in 1994.
Marcus Robertson, asst. secondary; born Pasadena, Calif. Defensive back Iowa State 1987-1990. Pro safety Houston Oilers/Tennessee Titans 1991-2000, Seattle Seahawks 2001-02. Pro coach: Joined Titans in 2007.
Jim Schwartz, defensive coordinator; born Baltimore. Linebacker Georgetown 1984-88. No pro playing experience. College coach: Maryland 1989, Minnesota 1990, North Carolina Central 1991, Colgate 1992. Pro coach: Cleveland Browns/Baltimore Ravens 1995-98, joined Titans in 1999.
Jim Washburn, defensive line; born Shelby, N.C. Offensive lineman Gardner-Webb 1969-1973. No pro playing experience. College coach: Southern Methodist 1976, Lees McRae (N.C.) J.C. 1977-78, Livingston 1979, New Mexico 1980-82, South Carolina 1983-88, Purdue 1989, Arkansas 1994-97, Houston 1998. Pro coach: London Monarchs (WLAF) 1991, Charlotte Rage (AFL) 1993, joined Titans in 1999.
Steve Watterson, strength and rehabilitation; born Newport, R.I. Attended Rhode Island. No college or pro playing experience. Pro coach: Philadelphia Eagles 1984-85, joined Titans/Oilers in 1986.
John Zernhelt, tight ends, born Pottsville, Pa. Offensive lineman Maryland 1974-77. No pro playing experience. College coach: Ferrum 1977-1980, Marshall 1981, East Carolina 1982-86, Maryland 1987-1991, Rice 1992-93, Duke 1994-95, South Carolina 1996-98, James Madison 1999-2002, The Citadel 2003-04. Pro coach: New York Jets 2005, joined Titans in 2006.

The NFC

National Football Conference
West Division
Team Colors: Cardinal Red, Black, and
White
P.O. Box 888
Phoenix, Arizona 85001-0888
Telephone: (602) 379-0101

2008 SCHEDULE
PRESEASON
Aug. 7	**New Orleans**	5:00
Aug. 16	at Kansas City	7:00
Aug. 23	at Oakland	6:00
Aug. 29	**Denver**	7:00

REGULAR SEASON
Sep. 7	at San Francisco	1:15
Sep. 14	**Miami**	1:15
Sep. 21	at Washington	1:00
Sep. 28	at N.Y. Jets	1:00
Oct. 5	**Buffalo**	1:15
Oct. 12	**Dallas**	1:15
Oct. 19	BYE	
Oct. 26	at Carolina	1:00
Nov. 2	at St. Louis	12:00
Nov. 10	**San Francisco** (Mon.)	6:30
Nov. 16	at Seattle	1:05
Nov. 23	**N.Y. Giants**	2:15
Nov. 27	at Philadelphia (Thu.)	8:15
Dec. 7	**St. Louis**	2:15
Dec. 14	**Minnesota**	2:05
Dec. 21	at New England	1:00
Dec. 28	**Seattle**	2:15

Stadium: University of Phoenix Stadium
(opened in 2006)
• **Capacity:** 65,000
1 Cardinals Drive
Glendale, Arizona 85305
Playing Surface: Grass
Training Camp: Northern Arizona University
Flagstaff, Arizona 86011

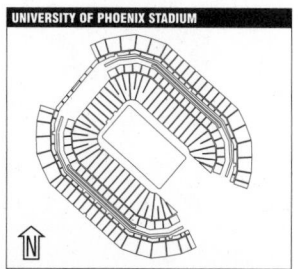

UNIVERSITY OF PHOENIX STADIUM

CLUB OFFICIALS
Owner: William V. Bidwill
President: Michael Bidwill
Vice President: William V. Bidwill, Jr.
General Manager: Rod Graves
Executive Vice President/Chief Business
Officer: Ron Minegar
Chief Financial Officer: Adrian Bracy
Vice President of Media Relations:
Mark Dalton
Vice President of Marketing:
Lisa Manning
Vice President of Business Development:
Steve Ryan
Vice President of Information
Technology: Mark Feller
Vice President of Security: Rick Knight
Senior Director of Players Programs:
Anthony Edwards
Senior Director of Community Relations:
Luis Zendejas
Senior Director of Ticketing: Steve Bomar
Senior Director of Ticket Sales:
Jamie Brandt
Senior Director of Stadium Operations:
John Drum
Director of Player Personnel: Steve Keim
Director of Football Administration:
Reggie Terry
Director of Cardinals Charities:
Pat Tankersley
Director of Broadcasting/Executive
Producer: Tom Hanny
Director of Cheerleading: Heather Karberg
Website Manager: Darren Urban
Video Director: Rob Brakel
Head Athletic Trainer: John Omohundro
Assistant Athletic Trainers:
Jim Shearer, Jeff Herndon,
Freddie Carbajal
Equipment Manager: Mark Ahlemeier
Assistant Equipment Manager:
Steve Christensen
Equipment Coordinator: Chris Janczewski

COACHING HISTORY
Chicago 1920-1959, St. Louis 1960-1987
(466-672-39)
Records include postseason games
1920-22	John (Paddy) Driscoll	17-8-4
1923-24	Arnold Horween	13-8-1
1925-26	Norman Barry	16-8-2
1927	Guy Chamberlin	3-7-1
1928	Fred Gillies	1-5-0
1929	Dewey Scanlon	6-6-1
1930	Ernie Nevers	5-6-2
1931	LeRoy Andrews*	0-1-0
1931	Ernie Nevers	5-3-0
1932	Jack Chevigny	2-6-2
1933-34	Paul Schissler	6-15-1
1935-38	Milan Creighton	16-26-4
1939	Ernie Nevers	1-10-0
1940-42	Jimmy Conzelman	8-22-3
1943-45	Phil Handler**	1-29-0
1946-48	Jimmy Conzelman	27-10-0
1949	Phil Handler-Buddy Parker***	2-4-0
1949	Raymond (Buddy) Parker	4-1-1
1950-51	Earl (Curly) Lambeau****	7-15-0
1951	Phil Handler-Cecil Isbell#	1-1-0
1952	Joe Kuharich	4-8-0
1953-54	Joe Stydahar	3-20-1
1955-57	Ray Richards	14-21-1
1958-1961	Frank (Pop) Ivy##	15-31-2
1961	Chuck Drulis-Ray Prochaska-	
	Ray Willsey###	2-0-0
1962-65	Wally Lemm	27-26-3
1966-1970	Charley Winner	35-30-5
1971-72	Bob Hollway	8-18-2
1973-77	Don Coryell	42-29-1
1978-79	Bud Wilkinson####	9-20-0
1979	Larry Wilson	2-1-0
1980-85	Jim Hanifan	39-50-1
1986-89	Gene Stallings@	23-34-1
1989	Hank Kuhlmann	0-5-0
1990-93	Joe Bugel	20-44-0
1994-95	Buddy Ryan	12-20-0
1996-2000	Vince Tobin@@	29-44-0
2000-03	Dave McGinnis	17-40-0
2004-06	Dennis Green	16-32-0
2007	Ken Whisenhunt	8-8-0

      * Resigned after one game in 1931
   ** Co-coach with Walt Kiesling in Chicago
      Cardinals-Pittsburgh merger in 1944
 *** Co-coaches for first six games in 1949
**** Resigned after 10 games in 1951
    # Co-coaches
  ## Resigned after 12 games in 1961
 ### Co-coaches
Released after 13 games in 1979
   @ Released after 11 games in 1989
 @@ Released after seven games in 2000

PAID ATTENDANCE
Home 504,272   Away 542,278
Total 1,046,550
Single-game home record, 73,025*
(9/19/93)
Single-season home record, 516,646
(2007)
*Team holds NFL attendance record of 103,467 for
home game at Azteca Stadium, Mexico City, Mexico

2008 DRAFT CHOICES
Round	Name	Pos.	College
1	D. Rodgers-Cromartie	DB	Tennessee St.
2	Calais Campbell	DE	Miami
3	Early Doucet	WR	Louisiana St.
4	Kenny Iwebema	DE	Iowa
5	Tim Hightower	RB	Richmond
6	Chris Harrington	DE	Texas A&M
7	Brandon Keith	T	Northern Iowa

2007 TEAM RECORD
PRESEASON (0-4)

Date	Result	Opponent
8/11	L 23-27	at Oakland
8/18	L 20-33	Houston
8/25	L 31-33	San Diego
8/30	L 3-21	at Denver

REGULAR SEASON (8-8)

Date	Result	Opponent	Att.
9/10	L 17-20	at San Francisco	68,111
9/16	W 23-20	Seattle	64,542
9/23	L 23-26	at Baltimore	71,372
9/30	W 21-14	Pittsburgh	64,844
10/7	W 34-31	at St. Louis	61,788
10/14	L 10-25	Carolina	64,403
10/21	L 19-21	at Washington	85,640
11/4	L 10-17	at Tampa Bay	65,267
11/11	W 31-21	Detroit	64,753
11/18	W 35-27	at Cincinnati	65,403
11/25	L 31-37	San Francisco (OT)	64,483
12/2	W 27-21	Cleveland	64,791
12/9	L 21-42	at Seattle	68,193
12/16	L 24-31	at New Orleans	70,007
12/23	W 30-27	Atlanta (OT)	64,159
12/30	W 48-19	St. Louis	64,671

(OT) Overtime

SCORE BY PERIODS

Cardinals	57	148	65	131	3 —	404
Opponents	88	114	99	92	6 —	399

2007 TEAM STATISTICS

	Cardinals	Opp.
Total First Downs	308	298
Rushing	70	90
Passing	210	185
Penalty	28	23
3rd Down: Made/Att	75/203	87/218
3rd Down Pct.	36.9	39.9
4th Down: Made/Att	12/14	7/15
4th Down Pct.	85.7	46.7
Possession Avg.	30:10	29:50
Total Net Yards	5505	5283
Avg. Per Game	344.1	330.2
Total Plays	1016	1013
Avg. Per Play	5.4	5.2
Net Yards Rushing	1440	1567
Avg. Per Game	90.0	97.9
Total Rushes	402	407
Net Yards Passing	4065	3716
Avg. Per Game	254.1	232.3
Sacked/Yards Lost	24/163	36/242
Gross Yards	4228	3958
Att./Completions	590/356	570/361
Completion Pct.	60.3	63.3
Had Intercepted	24	18
Punts/Average	80/40.0	73/43.6
Net Punting Avg.	80/32.0	73/37.1
Penalties/Yards	137/1128	118/881
Fumbles/Ball Lost	27/12	23/11
Touchdowns	49	45
Rushing	9	13
Passing	32	26
Returns	8	6

2007 INDIVIDUAL STATISTICS

PASSING

PASSING	Att.	Comp.	Yds.	Pct.	TD	Int.	Tkld.	Rate
Warner	451	281	3417	62.3	27	17	20/140	89.8
Leinart	112	60	647	53.6	2	4	4/23	61.9
Rattay	27	15	164	55.6	3	3	0/0	71.1
Cardinals	590	356	4228	60.3	32	24	24/163	83.4
Opponents	570	361	3958	63.3	26	18	36/242	85.8

SCORING

SCORING	TD R	TD P	TD Rt	PAT	FG	Saf	PTS
Rackers	0	0	0	47/48	21/30	0	110
Fitzgerald	0	10	0	0/0	0/0	0	60
Boldin	0	9	0	0/0	0/0	0	54
James	7	0	0	0/0	0/0	0	42
Pope	0	5	0	0/0	0/0	0	30
Rolle	0	0	3	0/0	0/0	0	18
Hood	0	0	2	0/0	0/0	0	12
Bry. Johnson	0	2	0	0/0	0/0	0	12
Patrick	0	2	0	0/0	0/0	0	12
Urban	0	2	0	0/0	0/0	0	12
Arrington	0	1	0	0/0	0/0	0	6
Bienemann	0	1	0	0/0	0/0	0	6
Breaston	0	0	1	0/0	0/0	0	6
Hayes	0	0	1	0/0	0/0	0	6
Shipp	1	0	0	0/0	0/0	0	6
Warner	1	0	0	0/0	0/0	0	6
Wells	0	0	1	0/0	0/0	0	6
Cardinals	9	32	8	47/48	21/30	0	404
Opponents	13	26	6	39/39	28/33	1	399

2-Pt. Conversions: Cardinals 0-1, Opponents 2-5

RUSHING

RUSHING	No.	Yds	Avg	LG	TD
James	324	1222	3.8	27	7
Arrington	26	78	3.0	12	0
Leinart	11	42	3.8	20	0
Shipp	15	41	2.7	14	1
Warner	17	15	0.9	9	1
Boldin	1	14	14.0	14	0
Morey	1	13	13.0	13	0
Breaston	2	8	4.0	10	0
Rattay	2	5	2.5	5	0
T. Smith	1	3	3.0	3	0
Berger	1	0	0.0	0	0
Hasselbeck	1	-1	-1.0	-1	0
Cardinals	402	1440	3.6	27	9
Opponents	407	1567	3.9	75	13

RECEIVING

RECEIVING	No.	Yds	Avg	LG	TD
Fitzgerald	100	1409	14.1	48t	10
Boldin	71	853	12.0	44t	9
Bry. Johnson	46	528	11.5	30	2
Arrington	29	241	8.3	32	1
James	24	204	8.5	26	0
Pope	23	238	10.3	31	5
Urban	22	329	15.0	42	2
Morey	8	131	16.4	62	0
Breaston	8	92	11.5	22	0
Patrick	7	73	10.4	21	2
T. Smith	7	59	8.4	16	0
Bienemann	7	46	6.6	13	1
Shipp	4	25	6.3	9	0
Cardinals	356	4228	11.9	62	32
Opponents	361	3958	11.0	74t	26

INTERCEPTIONS

INTERCEPTIONS	No.	Yds	Avg	LG	TD
Rolle	5	231	46.2	57	3
Hood	5	196	39.2	71t	2
Dansby	3	55	18.3	28	0
Wilson	2	20	10.0	20	0
Hayes	1	30	30.0	30t	1
Pace	1	14	14.0	14	0
R. Brown	1	5	5.0	5	0
Cardinals	18	551	30.6	71t	6
Opponents	24	380	15.8	84t	3

PUNTING

PUNTING	No.	Yds.	Avg.	In 20	LG
Barr	59	2385	40.4	15	61
Berger	20	813	40.7	6	56
Cardinals	80	3198	40.0	21	61
Opponents	73	3181	43.6	20	60

PUNT RETURNS

PUNT RETURNS	Ret	FC	Yds	Avg	LG	TD
Breaston	42	6	395	9.4	73t	1
Cardinals	42	6	395	9.4	73t	1
Opponents	38	15	496	13.1	75t	1

KICKOFF RETURNS

KICKOFF RETURNS	No.	Yds	Avg	LG	TD
Breaston	62	1391	22.4	59	0
Arrington	11	251	22.8	56	0
Morey	1	40	40.0	40	0
Cardinals	74	1682	22.7	59	0
Opponents	60	1389	23.2	80	0

FIELD GOALS

FIELD GOALS	1-19	20-29	30-39	40-49	50+
Rackers	2/2	5/5	6/8	5/6	3/9
Cardinals	2/2	5/5	6/8	5/6	3/9
Opponents	1/1	9/10	10/10	8/10	0/2

SACKS

SACKS	No.
Dockett	9.0
Pace	6.5
A. Smith	5.5
Hayes	4.0
Dansby	3.5
Blackstock	3.0
Berry	2.5
Tafoya	2.0
Cardinals	36.0
Opponents	24.0

RECORD HOLDERS
INDIVIDUAL RECORDS—CAREER

Category	Name	Performance
Rushing (Yds.)	Ottis Anderson, 1979-1986	7,999
Passing (Yds.)	Jim Hart, 1966-1983	34,639
Passing (TDs)	Jim Hart, 1966-1983	209
Receiving (No.)	Larry Centers, 1990-98	535
Receiving (Yds.)	Roy Green, 1979-1990	8,497
Interceptions	Larry Wilson, 1960-1972	52
Punting (Avg.)	Jerry Norton, 1959-1961	44.9
Punt Return (Avg.)	Charley Trippi, 1947-1955	13.7
Kickoff Return (Avg.)	Ollie Matson, 1952, 1954-58	28.5
Field Goals	Jim Bakken, 1962-1978	282
Touchdowns (Tot.)	Roy Green, 1979-1990	70
Points	Jim Bakken, 1962-1978	1,380

INDIVIDUAL RECORDS—SINGLE SEASON

Category	Name	Performance
Rushing (Yds.)	Ottis Anderson, 1979	1,605
Passing (Yds.)	Neil Lomax, 1984	4,614
Passing (TDs)	Charley Johnson, 1963	28
	Neil Lomax, 1984	28
Receiving (No.)	Larry Fitzgerald, 2005	103
Receiving (Yds.)	David Boston, 2001	1,598
Interceptions	Bob Nussbaumer, 1949	12
Punting (Avg.)	Jerry Norton, 1960	45.6
Punt Return (Avg.)	John (Red) Cochran, 1949	20.9
Kickoff Return (Avg.)	Ollie Matson, 1958	35.5
Field Goals	Neil Rackers, 2005	*40
Touchdowns (Tot.)	John David Crow, 1962	17
Points	Neil Rackers, 2005	140

INDIVIDUAL RECORDS—SINGLE GAME

Category	Name	Performance
Rushing (Yds.)	LeShon Johnson, 9-22-96	214
Passing (Yds.)	Boomer Esiason, 11-10-96 (OT)	522
Passing (TDs)	Jim Hardy, 10-2-50	6
	Charley Johnson, 9-26-65, 11-2-69	6
Receiving (No.)	Sonny Randle, 11-4-62	16
Receiving (Yds.)	Sonny Randle, 11-4-62	256
Interceptions	Bob Nussbaumer, 11-13-49	*4
	Jerry Norton, 11-20-60	*4
	Kwamie Lassiter, 12-27-98	*4
Field Goals	Jim Bakken, 9-24-67	7
Touchdowns (Tot.)	Ernie Nevers, 11-28-29	*6
Points	Ernie Nevers, 11-28-29	*40

*NFL Record

2008 VETERAN ROSTER

No.	Name	Pos.	Ht.	Wt.	Age	NFL Exp.	College	Hometown	How Acq.	'07 Games/ Starts
27	Adams, Michael	CB	5-8	181	23	2	Louisiana-Lafayette	Dallas, Texas	FA-'07	7/0
28	Arrington, J.J.	RB	5-9	212	25	4	California	Nashville, N.C.	D2-'05	16/0
52	Beisel, Monty	LB	6-3	244	30	8	Kansas State	Douglass, Kan.	FA-'06	16/2
92	Berry, Bertrand	DE	6-3	264	33	11	Notre Dame	Houston, Texas	UFA(Den)-'04	9/9
83	Bienemann, Troy	TE	6-5	253	25	2	Washington State	Mountain View, Calif.	FA-'07	16/4
81	Boldin, Anquan	WR	6-1	217	27	6	Florida State	Pahokee, Fla.	D2-'03	12/11
78	Branch, Alan	DT	6-5	332	23	2	Michigan	Rio Rancho, N.M.	D2-'07	11/0
15	Breaston, Steve	WR	6-0	189	25	2	Michigan	North Braddock, Pa	D5-'07	16/0
61	Brown, Elton	G/T	6-5	332	26	4	Virginia	Hampton, Va.	D4-'05	9/5
75	Brown, Levi	T	6-5	322	24	2	Penn State	Norfolk, Va.	D1-'07	13/11
20	Brown, Ralph	CB	5-10	185	29	9	Nebraska	LaPuenta, Calif.	UFA(Cle)-'07	16/0
46	Castille, Tim	FB	5-11	234	24	2	Alabama	Birmingham, Ala.	FA-'07	0*
35	Celestin, Oliver	S	6-0	207	27	5	Texas Southern	New Orleans, La	FA-'07	15/4
58	Dansby, Karlos	LB	6-4	250	26	5	Auburn	Birmingham, Ala.	D2-'04	14/14
90	Dockett, Darnell	DT	6-4	285	27	5	Florida State	Burtonsville, Md.	D3-'04	16/16
11	Fitzgerald, Larry	WR	6-3	226	25	5	Pittsburgh	Minneapolis, Minn.	D1-'04	15/15
47	Francisco, Aaron	S	6-2	207	25	4	Brigham Young	Laie, Hawaii	FA-'05	10/3
69	Gandy, Mike	T	6-4	308	29	8	Notre Dame	Dallas, Texas	UFA(Buff)-'07	16/16
25	Green, Eric	CB	5-11	195	26	4	Virginia Tech	Clewiston, Fla.	D3a-'05	11/11
53	Haggans, Clark	LB	6-4	243	31	9	Colorado State	Torrance, Calif.	UFA(Pitt)-'08	16/16*
54	Hayes, Gerald	LB	6-1	249	27	6	Pittsburgh	Paterson, N.J.	D3-'03	16/16
48	Hodel, Nathan	LS	6-2	238	30	7	Illinois	Fairview Heights, Ill.	FA-'01	16/0
26	Hood, Roderick	CB	5-11	198	26	6	Auburn	Columbus, Ga.	UFA(Phil)-'07	16/16
32	James, Edgerrin	RB	6-0	220	30	10	Miami	Immokalee, Fla.	UFA(Ind)-'06	16/16
50	Johnson, Al	C	6-5	305	29	6	Wisconsin	Brussels, Wisc.	UFA(Dall)-'07	14/14
9	Johnson, Dirk	P	6-0	205	33	6	Northern Colorado	Montrose, Col.	FA-'08	1/0*
55	LaBoy, Travis	DE/LB	6-3	260	27	5	Hawaii	San Rafeal, Calif.	UFA(Tenn)-'08	13/0*
7	Leinart, Matt	QB	6-5	232	25	3	Southern California	Santa Ana, Calif.	D1-'06	5/5
76	Lutui, Deuce	G	6-4	328	25	3	Southern California	Mesa, Ariz.	D2-'06	15/15
86	Merritt, Ahmad	WR	5-10	197	31	5	Wisconsin	Chicago, Ill.	FA-'07	0*
23	Minter, DeMario	CB	5-11	195	24	2	Georgia	Stone Mountain, Ga.	FA-'07	0*
87	Morey, Sean	WR	5-11	193	32	7	Brown	Marshfield, Mass.	UFA(Pitt)-'07	15/0
56	Okeafor, Chike	OLB	6-5	247	32	10	Purdue	Grand Rapids, Mich.	UFA(Sea)-'05	0*
89	Patrick, Ben	TE	6-3	252	24	2	Delaware	Savannah, Ga.	D7-'07	8/3
64	Peters, Scott	C/G	6-3	312	29	3	Arizona State	Pleasanton, Calif.	FA-'07	0*
82	Pope, Leonard	TE	6-8	258	24	3	Georgia	Americus, Ga.	D3-'06	13/11
1	Rackers, Neil	K	6-1	202	32	9	Illinois	St. Louis, Mo.	FA-'03	16/0
10	Rector, Jamaica	WR	5-10	183	27	3	NW Missouri State	Celeste, Texas	FA-'07	2/0
97	Robinson, Bryan	DE	6-4	304	34	12	Fresno State	Toledo, Ohio	UFA(Cin)-'08	16/4*
21	Rolle, Antrel	CB	6-0	208	25	4	Miami	Homestead, Fla.	D1-'05	16/8
95	Schobel, Bo	DE	6-5	264	27	5	TCU	Columbus, Texas	FA-'07	2/0
63	Sendlein, Lyle	G	6-2	300	24	2	Texas	Scottsdale, Ariz.	FA-'07	14/2
31	Shipp, Marcel	RB	5-11	224	30	8	Massachusetts	Paterson, N.J.	FA-'01	16/0
94	Smith, Antonio	DE	6-4	282	26	5	Oklahoma State	Oklahoma City, Okla.	D5-'04	16/13
45	Smith, Terrelle	FB	6-0	250	30	9	Arizona State	West Covina, Calif.	UFA(Cle)-'07	16/10
2	St. Pierre, Brian	QB	6-3	230	28	6	Boston College	Salem, Mass.	UFA(Pitt)-'08	0*
51	Stewart, Matt	LB	6-3	239	29	8	Vanderbilt	Columbus, Ohio	UFA(Cle)-'08	0*
96	Tafoya, Joe	DE	6-4	258	29	7	Arizona	Pittsburg, Calif.	UFA(Sea)-'07	13/7
84	Tuman, Jerame	TE	6-4	253	32	10	Michigan	Liberal, Kansas	FA-'08	6/0*
85	Urban, Jerheme	WR	6-3	212	27	5	Trinity	Victoria, Texas	W(Dall)-'07	10/2
22	Ware, Matt	S	6-2	214	25	5	UCLA	Los Angeles, Calif.	W(Phil)-'06	15/0
13	Warner, Kurt	QB	6-2	222	37	11	Northern Iowa	Burlington, Iowa	UFA(NYG)-'05	14/11
98	Watson, Gabe	DT	6-3	332	24	3	Michigan	Southfield, Mich.	D4-'06	16/16
74	Wells, Reggie	G	6-4	305	27	6	Clarion (Pa.)	Library, Pa.	D6a-'03	16/16
24	Wilson, Adrian	S	6-3	230	28	8	North Carolina State	High Point, N.C.	D3-'01	9/9

* Castille inactive for 16 games in '07; Haggans played 16 games with Pittsburgh; D. Johnson played 1 game with Chicago; LaBoy played 13 games with Tennessee; Merritt missed '07 season because of injury; Minter missed '06 season because of injury with Cleveland; Okeafor missed '07 season because of injury; Peters missed '06 season because of injury with Carolina; Robinson played 16 games with Cincinnati; St. Pierre did not play in 1 game with Pittsburgh; Stewart missed '07 season because of injury with Cleveland; Tuman played 6 games with Pittsburgh.

Players lost through free agency (2): LB Calvin Pace (NYJ; 16 games in '07), G Keydrick Vincent (Car; 8).

Also played with Cardinals in '07—T Brad Badger (1 game), DE Rodney Bailey (6), Mike Barr (10), P Mitch Berger (5), LB Darryl Blackstock (16), TE Tim Euhus (10), QB Tim Hasselbeck (1), S Terrence Holt (16), LB Brandon Johnson (6), WR Bryant Johnson (16), S Bhawoh Jue (1), DT Ross Kolodzieg (3), Chucky Okobi (1), QB Tim Rattay (4).

2008 FIRST-YEAR ROSTER

Name	Pos.	Ht.	Wt.	Age	College	Hometown	How Acq.
Bain, Travrous (1)	CB	6-0	175	24	Hampton	Miami, Fla.	FA-'07
Banks, Jason	DE	6-5	300	23	Grambling State	Baton Rouge, La.	FA
Baylark, Steve (1)	RB	6-0	225	25	Massachusetts	Apopka, Fla.	FA-'07
Brown, Marcus	CB	6-2	200	22	McNeese State	Tangipahoa, La.	FA
Campbell, Calais	DE	6-8	282	22	Miami	Aurora, Colo.	D2
Clifford, Peter	T	6-7	312	24	Michigan State	Salem, N.H.	FA
Coleman, Thaddeus	T	6-8	308	23	Mississippi Valley State	North Chicago, Ill.	FA
Cornelius, Jemalle	WR	5-11	185	24	Florida	Fort Meade, Fla.	FA
Doucet, Early	WR	6-0	211	22	Louisiana State	St. Martinville, La.	D3
Dykes, Keilen	DT	6-3	294	23	West Virginia	Youngstown, Ohio	FA
Harrington, Chris	LB	6-5	264	23	Texas A&M	Houston	D6
Highsmith, Ali	LB	6-1	223	23	Louisiana State	Miami, Fla.	FA
Hightower, Tim	RB	6-0	224	22	Richmond	Alexandria, Va.	D5
Holloway, David (1)	LB	6-2	230	24	Maryland	Stephentown, N.Y.	FA-'07
Iwebema, Kenny	DE	6-4	274	23	Iowa	Arlington, Texas	D4
Johnson, Dionte	FB	6-0	238	22	Ohio State	Columbus, Ohio	FA
Keith, Brandon	T	6-5	343	23	Northern Iowa	McAlester, Okla.	D7
Keyes, Dennis	S	6-2	199	23	UCLA	Canoga Park, Calif.	FA
Long, Lance	WR	5-11	186	23	Mississippi State	Macomb, Mich.	FA
Medder, Carlton	G	6-5	319	23	Florida	Clermont, Fla.	FA
Morelli, Anthony	QB	6-4	231	23	Penn State	Pittsburgh, Pa.	FA
Robinson, Bryan	DE	6-3	297	22	Wesley	Dover, Del.	FA
Rodgers-Cromartie, Dominique	CB	6-2	182	22	Tennessee State	Bradenton, Fla.	D1
Satele, Hercules	G	6-2	308	23	Hawaii	Honolulu, Hawaii	FA
Shor, Alex (1)	TE	6-7	250	25	Syracuse	Panama City, Fla.	FA-'06
Vallejo, Elliott (1)	T	6-7	315	24	Cal-Davis	Salinas, Calif.	FA-'07
Vincent, Chris (1)	RB	6-1	224	27	Oregon	Philadelphia, Pa.	FA

The term NFL Rookie is defined as a player who is in his first season of professional football and has not been on the roster of another professional football team for any regular-season or postseason games. A Rookie is designated by an "R" on NFL rosters. Players who have been active in another professional football league or players who have NFL experience, including either preseason training camp or being on an Active List or Inactive List, or on Reserve/Injured or Reserve/Physically Unable to Perform for fewer than six regular-season games, are termed NFL First-Year Players. An NFL First-Year Player is designated by a "1" on NFL rosters. Thereafter, a player is credited with an additional year of experience for each season in which he accumulates six games on the Active List or Inactive List, or on Reserve/Injured or Reserve/Physically Unable to Perform.

Log on to www.azcardinals.com for an up-to-date roster; Age listed is as of September 4, 2008.

COACHING STAFF

Head Coach,
Ken Whisenhunt

Pro Career: Became an NFL head coach for the first time when hired by Arizona on January 14, 2007. Led the team to an 8-8 record in his first season in Arizona, the first coach to do that since 1994. Improved the Cardinals record by three wins, the largest improvement of any of the NFL's five rookie head coaches in 2007. Came to the Cardinals with 10 years of experience as an NFL assistant coach and also played nine seasons in the league as a tight end. Whisenhunt spent the previous six seasons as an assistant on Bill Cowher's staff with the Pittsburgh Steelers, the first three as tight ends coach and the last three as offensive coordinator. Whisenhunt took over as Pittsburgh's offensive coordinator in 2004, the same year the team drafted quarterback Ben Roethlisberger, who went on to set an NFL record with wins in his first 13 career starts en route to Offensive Rookie of the Year honors. The next season he became the youngest quarterback in NFL history to win a Super Bowl and finished third in the league in passer rating (98.6). In Whisenhunt's first year as coordinator, the Steelers rushing attack improved from thirty-first to second and the overall offense ranked sixteenth. His second year ended with an NFL title after the Steelers offense averaged 26.8 points per game in the playoffs. He joined the Steelers in January of 2001 as tight ends coach. Whisenhunt previously coached at the pro level with the New York Jets (tight ends, 2000), Cleveland Browns (special teams, 1999) and Baltimore Ravens (tight ends, 1997-98). He began his coaching career in the collegiate ranks with Vanderbilt for two seasons (1995-96). Whisenhunt was selected in the 12th round of the 1985 NFL Draft by the Atlanta Falcons out of Georgia Tech. He went on to play nine NFL seasons with the Falcons (1985-88), Washington Redskins (1989-90), and New York Jets (1991-93). In 74 career games (37 starts), he caught 62 passes for 601 yards and 6 touchdowns. Career record: 8-8.

Background: After going to Georgia Tech as a walk-on, he played four seasons as a tight end/H-back. He finished his college playing career ranked second on the Yellow Jackets' receiving yardage list (1,264 yards) and fourth in career receptions (82). Whisenhunt was a consensus All-ACC and honorable mention All-America selection as a senior in 1984 when he averaged 19.1 yards-per-catch.

Personal: Age 46, born in Atlanta. Whisenhunt earned a degree in civil engineering from Georgia Tech. Ken and his wife, Alice, have two children—son, Kenneth, Jr. and daughter, Mary Ashley.

ASSISTANT COACHES

Ron Aiken, defensive line; born Moncks Corner, S.C. Guard/center North Carolina A&T 1973-76. No pro playing experience. College coach: Bethany College 1980-81, Tarkio College 1982-84, Rensselaer Polytechnic Institute 1985, Langston 1986-1990, New Mexico 1991-94, Vanderbilt 1995-96, Texas 1997, San Diego State 1998, Iowa 1999-2006. Pro coach: Joined Cardinals in 2007.

Teryl Austin, defensive backs; born Sharon, Pa. Defensive back Pittsburgh 1984-87. Pro defensive back Montreal Machine (WLAF) 1991. College coach: Penn State 1991-92, Wake Forest 1993-95, Syracuse 1996-98, Michigan 1999-2002. Pro coach: Seattle Seahawks 2003-06, joined Cardinals in 2007.

Maurice Carthon, running backs; born Chicago. Running back Arkansas State 1979-1982. Pro running back New Jersey Generals (USFL) 1983-85, New York Giants 1985-1991, Indianapolis Colts 1992. Pro coach: New England Patriots 1994-96, New York Jets 1997-2000, Detroit Lions 2001-02, Dallas Cowboys 2003-04, Cleveland Browns 2005-06, joined Cardinals in 2007.

Rick Courtright, asst. defensive backs; born Miami. Linebacker Wheaton College 1980-83. No pro playing experience. College coach: Washington 1991-92, Minnesota-Morris 1993, Ohio 1994, Idaho State 1995, Idaho 1996-99, Murray State 2000, Western Illinois 2001-03. Pro coach: Joined Cardinals in 2004.

Bill Davis, linebackers; born Youngstown, Ohio. Quarterback Cincinnati 1985-88. College coach: Michigan State 1990-91. Pro coach: Pittsburgh Steelers 1992-94, Carolina Panthers 1995-98, Cleveland Browns 1999, Green Bay Packers 2000, Atlanta Falcons 2001-03, New York Giants 2004, San Francisco 49ers 2005-06, joined Cardinals in 2007.

Russ Grimm, asst. head coach/offensive line; born Scottdale, Pa. Center Pittsburgh 1977-1980. Pro guard Washington Redskins 1981-1991. Pro coach: Washington Redskins 1992-2000, Pittsburgh Steelers 2001-06, joined Cardinals in 2007.

Todd Haley, offensive coordinator; born Atlanta. Attended Florida and Miami. No college or pro playing experience. Pro coach: New York Jets 1997-2000, Chicago Bears 2001-03, Dallas Cowboys 2004-06, joined Cardinals in 2007.

Freddie Kitchens, tight ends; born Gadsden, Ala. Quarterback Alabama 1994-97. No pro playing experience. College coach: Glenville State College 1999, Louisiana State 2000, North Texas 2001-03, Mississippi State 2004-05. Pro coach: Dallas Cowboys 2006, joined Cardinals in 2007.

John Lott, strength and conditioning; born Denton, Texas. Offensive lineman North Texas 1983-86. Pro offensive lineman

Pittsburgh Steelers 1987. College coach: Texas 1988, North Texas 1989-1990, Houston 1991-96. Pro coach: New York Jets 1997-2004, Cleveland Browns 2005-06, joined Cardinals in 2007.

Mike Miller, wide receivers; born Plum Borough, Pa. Attended Clarion. No college or pro playing experience. College coach: Robert Morris 1997-98, 2006. Pro coach: Pittsburgh Steelers 1999-2003, Buffalo Bills 2004-05, Berlin Thunder (NFLE) 2006, joined Cardinals in 2007.

Clancy Pendergast, defensive coordinator; born Phoenix. Attended Arizona. No college or pro playing experience. College coach: Mississippi State 1991, Southern California 1992, Oklahoma 1993-94, Alabama-Birmingham 1995. Pro coach: Houston Oilers 1995, Dallas Cowboys 1996-2002, Cleveland Browns 2003, joined Cardinals in 2004.

Matt Raich, defensive assistant; born Monaca, Pa. Middle linebacker Westminster College 1989-1992. No pro playing experience. College coach: Westminster 1993-94, Robert Morris 1996-98, 2000-02, Glenville State 1999. Pro coach: Pittsburgh Steelers 2004-06, joined Cardinals in 2007.

Jeff Rutledge, quarterbacks; born Birmingham, Ala. Quarterback Alabama 1975-78. Pro quarterback Los Angeles Rams 1979-1981, New York Giants 1982-89, Washington Redskins 1990-92. College coach: Vanderbilt 1995-2001. Pro coach: Joined Cardinals in 2007.

Kevin Spencer, special teams; born Queens, N.Y. Outside linebacker Springfield College 1971. No pro playing experience. College coach: SUNY-Cortland 1975-76, Cornell 1979-1980, Ithaca 1981-86, Wesleyan 1987-1991. Pro coach: Cleveland Browns 1991-94, Oakland Raiders 1995-97, Indianapolis Colts 1998-2001, Pittsburgh Steelers 2002-06, joined Cardinals in 2007.

Dedric Ward, offensive quality control; born Cedar Rapids, Iowa. Wide receiver Northern Iowa 1993-96. Pro wide receiver New York Jets 1997-2000, Miami Dolphins 2001-02, New England Patriots 2003, Dallas Cowboys 2004. College coach: Missouri State 2006. Pro coach: Joined Cardinals in 2007.

**National Football Conference
South Division**
Team Colors: Black, Red, Silver, and White
4400 Falcon Parkway
Flowery Branch, Georgia 30542
Telephone: (770) 965-3115

2008 SCHEDULE
PRESEASON
Aug. 9   at Jacksonville.....................7:30
Aug. 16   **Indianapolis**.......................7:30
Aug. 22   **Tennessee** 7:30
Aug. 28   at Baltimore.......................7:00

REGULAR SEASON
Sep. 7   **Detroit** 1:00
Sep. 14   at Tampa Bay 4:05
Sep. 21   **Kansas City** 1:00
Sep. 28   at Carolina 1:00
Oct. 5   at Green Bay 12:00
Oct. 12   **Chicago** 1:00
Oct. 19   BYE
Oct. 26   at Philadelphia 1:00
Nov. 2   at Oakland 1:15
Nov. 9   **New Orleans** 1:00
Nov. 16   **Denver** 1:00
Nov. 23   **Carolina** 1:00
Nov. 30   at San Diego 1:05
Dec. 7   at New Orleans 12:00
Dec. 14   **Tampa Bay** 1:00
Dec. 21   at Minnesota 12:00
Dec. 28   **St. Louis** 1:00

Stadium: Georgia Dome
        (opened in 1992)
        • **Capacity:** 71,228
        One Georgia Dome Drive
        Atlanta, Georgia 30313
Playing Surface: FieldTurf
Training Camp: Atlanta Falcons
            4400 Falcon Parkway
            Flowery Branch, GA 30542

GEORGIA DOME

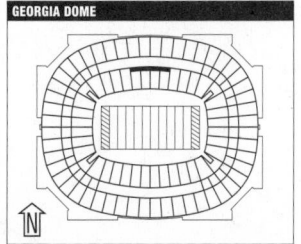

CLUB OFFICIALS
Owner & CEO: Arthur M. Blank
President: Rich McKay
General Manager: Thomas Dimitroff
Head Coach: Mike Smith
Executive Vice President-Marketing:
  Dick Sullivan
Director of Human Resources:
  Karen Walters
Vice President & CFO: Greg Beadles
Controller: Rob Geoffroy
Vice President of Football
  Communications: Reggie Roberts
Vice President of Information
  Technology: Danny Branch
Vice President of Marketing: Jim Smith
Vice President of Sales: Dave Cohen
Senior Director of Media Relations:
  Frank Kleha
Senior Director of Player Development:
  Kevin Winston
Director of Logistics and Facilities:
  Spencer Treadwell
Director of Ticket Operations:
  Jack Ragsdale
Director of Event Marketing: Roddy White
Director of Football Operations: Nick Polk
Director of Pro Personnel: Les Snead
Director of College Scouting:
  David Caldwell
Director of Community Relations:
  Kendyl Baugh Moss
Assistant Director of Player Personnel:
  Lionel Vital
Eastern Regional Scout: Phil Emery
Area Scouts: Matt Berry, Boyd Dowler,
  Bob Harrison, Taylor Morton,
  Mark Olson, Alex Page,
  Bruce Plummer, Chris Vaszily
Pro Scouts: Shepley Heard, DeJuan Polk
Head Athletic Trainer: Ron Medlin
Assistant Athletic Trainers:
  Roland Ramirez, Tom Reed
Video Director: Mike Crews
Video Assistants: Phil Tieman,
  Daniel Crews
Equipment Manager: Brian Boigner
Director of Sponsorship Sales:
  Tim Zulawski
Director of Retail: Chris DiPierri
Director of New Media: Dan Levak
Football Communications Manager:
  Ted Crews
Football Communications Coordinator:
  Matt Conti
Football Communications Coordinator:
  Brian Cearns

COACHING HISTORY
(262-386-6)
Records include postseason games
1966-68   Norb Hecker* 4-26-1
1968-1974   Norm Van Brocklin**..37-49-3
1974-76   Marion Campbell***.....6-19-0
1976   Pat Peppler 3-6-0
1977-1982   Leeman Bennett..........47-44-0
1983-86   Dan Henning..............22-41-1
1987-89   Marion Campbell****.11-32-0
1989   Jim Hanifan 0-4-0
1990-93   Jerry Glanville...........28-38-0
1994-96   June Jones 19-30-0
1997-2003   Dan Reeves# 52-61-1
2003   Wade Phillips.................2-1-0
2004-06   Jim Mora 27-23-0
2007   Bobby Petrino##......3-10-0
2007   Emmitt Thomas 1-2-0
    *Released after three games in 1968
  **Released after eight games in 1974
 ***Released after five games in 1976
****Retired after 12 games in 1989
    #Released after 13 games in 2003
  ##Resigned after 13 games in 2007

PAID ATTENDANCE
Home 534,588   Away 508,906
Total 1,043,494
Single-game home record,
  71,151 (10/22/06)
Single-season home record,
  553,979 (1992)

2008 DRAFT CHOICES

Round	Name	Pos.	College
1	Matt Ryan	QB	Boston College
	Sam Baker	T	Southern California
2	Curtis Lofton	LB	Oklahoma
3	Chevis Jackson	DB	Louisiana St.
	Harry Douglas	WR	Louisville
	Thomas DeCoud	DB	California
5	Robert James	LB	Arizona State
	Kroy Biermann	DE	Montana
6	Thomas Brown	RB	Georgia
7	Wilrey Fontenot	DB	Arizona
	Keith Zinger	TE	Louisiana St.

2007 TEAM RECORD
PRESEASON (3-1)

Date	Result	Opponent
8/10	L 16-31	at New York Jets
8/17	W 13-10	at Buffalo
8/27	W 24-19	Cincinnati
8/31	W 13-10	Baltimore

REGULAR SEASON (4-12)

Date	Result	Opponent	Att.
9/9	L 3-24	at Minnesota	62,815
9/16	L 7-13	at Jacksonville	61,821
9/23	L 20-27	Carolina	68,175
9/30	W 26-16	Houston	69,312
10/7	L 13-20	at Tennessee	69,143
10/15	L 10-31	New York Giants	69,828
10/21	L 16-22	at New Orleans	69,994
11/4	W 20-16	San Francisco	66,049
11/11	W 20-13	at Carolina	73,340
11/18	L 7-31	Tampa Bay	69,480
11/22	L 13-31	Indianapolis	69,845
12/2	L 16-28	at St. Louis	62,051
12/10	L 14-34	New Orleans	69,553
12/16	L 3-37	at Tampa Bay	65,133
12/23	L 27-30	at Arizona (OT)	64,159
12/30	W 44-41	Seattle	64,925

(OT) Overtime

SCORE BY PERIODS

Falcons	71	74	22	92	0 —	259
Opponents	105	121	90	95	3 —	414

2007 TEAM STATISTICS

	Falcons	Opp.
Total First Downs	248	320
Rushing	73	105
Passing	161	190
Penalty	14	25
3rd Down: Made/Att	86/237	78/210
3rd Down Pct.	36.3	37.1
4th Down: Made/Att	7/19	11/21
4th Down Pct.	36.8	52.4
Possession Avg.	28:34	31:26
Total Net Yards	4816	5688
Avg. Per Game	301.0	355.5
Total Plays	987	1042
Avg. Per Play	4.9	5.5
Net Yards Rushing	1520	2033
Avg. Per Game	95.0	127.1
Total Rushes	385	481
Net Yards Passing	3296	3655
Avg. Per Game	206.0	228.4
Sacked/Yards Lost	47/277	25/146
Gross Yards	3573	3801
Att./Completions	555/336	536/336
Completion Pct.	60.5	62.7
Had Intercepted	15	16
Punts/Average	88/43.5	74/41.4
Net Punting Avg.	88/38.8	74/37.5
Penalties/Yards	105/891	91/808
Fumbles/Ball Lost	18/9	21/12
Touchdowns	26	47
Rushing	7	12
Passing	18	27
Returns	1	8

2007 INDIVIDUAL STATISTICS

PASSING	Att.	Comp.	Yds.	Pct.	TD	Int.	Tkld.	Rate
Harrington	348	215	2215	61.8	7	8	32/192	77.2
Redman	149	89	1079	59.7	10	5	9/51	90.4
Leftwich	58	32	279	55.2	1	2	6/34	59.5
Falcons	555	336	3573	60.5	18	15	47/277	78.9
Opponents	536	336	3801	62.7	27	16	25/146	88.2

SCORING	TD R	TD P	TD Rt	PAT	FG	Saf	PTS
Andersen	0	0	0	24/24	25/28	0	99
White	0	6	0	0/0	0/0	0	36
Crumpler	0	5	0	0/0	0/0	0	30
Dunn	4	0	0	0/0	0/0	0	24
Jenkins	0	4	0	0/0	0/0	0	24
Hall	0	0	1	0/0	0/0	0	6
Horn	0	1	0	0/0	0/0	0	6
Jennings	0	1	0	0/0	0/0	0	6
Mughelli	1	0	0	0/0	0/0	0	6
Norwood	1	0	0	0/0	0/0	0	6
Robinson	0	1	0	0/0	0/0	0	6
Snelling	1	0	0	0/0	0/0	0	6
Prater	0	0	0	1/1	1/4	0	4
Koenen	0	0	0	0/0	0/2	0	0
Falcons	7	18	1	25/25	26/34	0	259
Opponents	12	27	8	46/46	28/30	0	414

2-Pt. Conversions: Falcons 0-1,
Opponents 1-1

RUSHING	No.	Yds	Avg	LG	TD
Dunn	227	720	3.2	38	4
Norwood	103	613	6.0	67t	1
Pinner	5	46	9.2	49	0
Snelling	13	43	3.3	17	1
T. Williams	1	37	37.0	37	0
Harrington	14	33	2.4	13	0
Redman	8	16	2.0	7	0
Leftwich	6	7	1.2	7	0
Mughelli	6	7	1.2	3	1
Koenen	1	0	0.0	0	0
White	1	-2	-2.0	-2	0
Falcons	385	1520	3.9	67t	7
Opponents	481	2033	4.2	50t	12

RECEIVING	No.	Yds	Avg	LG	TD
White	83	1202	14.5	69t	6
Jenkins	53	532	10.0	29	4
Crumpler	42	444	10.6	55t	5
Robinson	37	437	11.8	74t	1
Dunn	37	238	6.4	35	0
Norwood	28	277	9.9	46	0
Horn	27	243	9.0	26	1
Milner	9	50	5.6	15	0
Blakley	7	48	6.9	11	0
Jennings	6	62	10.3	28	1
Mughelli	6	36	6.0	12	0
Harrington	1	4	4.0	4	0
Falcons	336	3573	10.6	74t	18
Opponents	336	3801	11.3	60t	27

INTERCEPTIONS	No.	Yds	Avg	LG	TD
Hall	5	80	16.0	33	0
Crocker	3	40	13.3	18	0
Milloy	2	24	12.0	19	0
Boley	2	12	6.0	12	0
D. Williams	2	3	1.5	8	0
J. Williams	1	11	11.0	11	0
Lewis	1	4	4.0	4	0
Falcons	16	174	10.9	33	0
Opponents	15	292	19.5	76t	5

PUNTING	No.	Yds.	Avg.	In 20	LG
Koenen	88	3824	43.5	30	63
Falcons	88	3824	43.5	30	63
Opponents	74	3060	41.4	28	61

PUNT RETURNS	Ret	FC	Yds	Avg	LG	TD
Jennings	30	17	186	6.2	23	0
Hall	5	1	41	8.2	16	0
Harris	1	0	1	1.0	1	0
Falcons	36	18	228	6.3	23	0
Opponents	41	31	307	7.5	48	0

KICKOFF RETURNS	No.	Yds	Avg	LG	TD
Norwood	52	1317	25.3	76	0
Jennings	17	428	25.2	61	0
Mughelli	2	28	14.0	18	0
Babineaux	1	8	8.0	8	0
Falcons	72	1781	24.7	76	0
Opponents	50	1148	23.0	90t	1

FIELD GOALS	1-19	20-29	30-39	40-49	50+
Andersen	0/0	9/9	12/12	4/7	0/0
Prater	0/0	0/1	0/0	1/3	0/0
Koenen	0/0	0/0	0/0	0/0	0/2
Falcons	0/0	9/10	12/12	5/10	0/2
Opponents	1/1	8/9	11/11	6/7	2/2

SACKS	No.
Abraham	10.0
Babineaux	3.0
Boley	3.0
Brooking	2.0
Coleman	2.0
Davis	2.0
Crocker	1.0
Jackson	1.0
Nicholas	1.0
Falcons	25.0
Opponents	47.0

RECORD HOLDERS
INDIVIDUAL RECORDS—CAREER

Category	Name	Performance
Rushing (Yds.)	Gerald Riggs, 1982-88	6,631
Passing (Yds.)	Steve Bartkowski, 1975-1985	23,468
Passing (TDs)	Steve Bartkowski, 1975-1985	154
Receiving (No.)	Terance Mathis, 1994-2001	573
Receiving (Yds.)	Terance Mathis, 1994-2001	7,349
Interceptions	Rolland Lawrence, 1973-1980	39
Punting (Avg.)	Rick Donnelly, 1985-89	42.6
Punt Return (Avg.)	Darrien Gordon, 2001	14.1
Kickoff Return (Avg.)	Darrick Vaughn, 2000-01	25.7
Field Goals	Morten Andersen, 1995-2000, 2006-07	184
Touchdowns (Tot.)	Terance Mathis, 1994-2001	57
Points	Morten Andersen, 1995-2000, 2006-07	806

INDIVIDUAL RECORDS—SINGLE SEASON

Category	Name	Performance
Rushing (Yds.)	Jamal Anderson, 1998	1,846
Passing (Yds.)	Jeff George, 1995	4,143
Passing (TDs)	Steve Bartkowski, 1980	31
Receiving (No.)	Terance Mathis, 1994	111
Receiving (Yds.)	Alfred Jenkins, 1981	1,358
Interceptions	Scott Case, 1988	10
Punting (Avg.)	Billy Lothridge, 1968	44.3
Punt Return (Avg.)	Darrien Gordon, 2001	14.1
Kickoff Return (Avg.)	Darrick Vaughn, 2000	27.7
Field Goals	Jay Feely, 2002	32
Touchdowns (Tot.)	Jamal Anderson, 1998	16
Points	Jay Feely, 2002	138

INDIVIDUAL RECORDS—SINGLE GAME

Category	Name	Performance
Rushing (Yds.)	Gerald Riggs, 9-2-84	202
Passing (Yds.)	Steve Bartkowski, 11-15-81	416
Passing (TDs)	Wade Wilson, 12-13-92	5
Receiving (No.)	William Andrews, 11-15-81	15
Receiving (Yds.)	Terance Mathis, 12-13-98	198
Interceptions	Many times	2
	Last time by DeAngelo Hall, 9-17-06	
Field Goals	Norm Johnson, 11-13-94	6
Touchdowns (Tot.)	T.J. Duckett, 12-12-04	4
Points	T.J. Duckett, 12-12-04	24

2008 VETERAN ROSTER

No.	Name	Pos.	Ht.	Wt.	Age	NFL Exp.	College	Hometown	How Acq.	'07 Games/ Starts
55	Abraham, John	DE	6-4	266	30	9	South Carolina	Timmonsville, S.C.	T(NYJ)-'06	16/16
98	Anderson, Jamaal	DE	6-6	283	22	2	Arkansas	Little Rock, Ark.	D1-'07	16/16
93	Anderson, Tim	DT	6-3	304	27	5	Ohio State	Clyde, Ohio	FA-'07	5/0
95	Babineaux, Jonathan	DT	6-2	288	26	4	Iowa	Port Arthur, Texas	D2-'05	14/9
70	Batiste, D'Anthony	OL	6-4	318	26	2	Louisiana-Lafayette	Marksville, La.	FA-'07	4/4
63	Blalock, Justin	G	6-4	329	24	2	Texas	Dallas, Texas	D2a-'07	14/14
59	Boley, Michael	LB	6-3	242	26	4	Southern Miss	Gadsen, Ala.	D5a-'05	16/16
56	Brooking, Keith	LB	6-2	243	32	11	Georgia Tech	Senoia, Ga.	D1-'98	16/16
77	Clabo, Tyson	G	6-6	319	26	3	Wake Forest	Knoxville, Tenn.	FA-'06	11/11
26	Coleman, Erik	S	5-10	200	26	5	Washington State	Sacramento, Calif.	UFA(NYJ)-'08	15/4*
73	Dahl, Harvey	OL	6-5	313	27	2	Nevada	Fallon, Nev.	FA-'07	1/0
92	Davis, Chauncey	DE	6-2	271	25	4	Florida State	Bartow, Fla.	D4-'05	16/0
1	Elam, Jason	K	5-11	200	38	16	Hawaii	Ft. Walton Beach, Fla.	UFA(Den)-'08	16/0*
86	Finneran, Brian	WR	6-5	217	32	9	Villanova	Mission Viejo, Calif.	FA-'00	0*
65	Forney, Kynan	G	6-3	311	29	8	Hawaii	Nacogdoches, Texas	D7b-'01	14/14
79	Foster, Renardo	OL	6-7	326	24	2	Louisville	Ripley, Tenn.	FA-'07	7/2
75	Fraser, Simon	DE	6-6	300	25	4	Ohio State	Upper Arlington, Ohio	FA-'08	16/1*
13	Harrington, Joey	QB	6-4	222	29	7	Oregon	Portland, Ore.	FA-'07	12/10
41	Harris, Antoine	CB	5-10	200	26	2	Louisville	Columbus, Ohio	FA-'07	13/0
89	Hartsock, Ben	TE	6-4	265	28	5	Ohio State	Chillicothe, Ohio	UFA(Tenn)-'08	16/9*
87	Horn, Joe	WR	6-1	208	36	13	Itawamba (Miss.) J.C.	New Haven, Conn.	FA-'07	12/12
23	Houston, Chris	CB	5-11	183	23	2	Arkansas	Austin, Texas	D2b-'07	16/11
25	Hutchins, Von	CB	5-10	180	27	5	Mississippi	Natchez, Miss.	UFA(Hou)-'08	16/15*
30	Irons, David	CB	5-11	190	25	2	Auburn	Dacula, Ga.	D6b-'07	15/0
12	Jenkins, Michael	WR	6-4	208	26	5	Ohio State	Tampa, Fla.	D1b-'04	15/6
81	Jennings, Adam	WR	5-9	176	25	3	Fresno State	Granite Bay, Calif.	D6-'06	16/2
9	Koenen, Michael	P	5-11	194	26	4	Western Washington	Ferndale, Wash.	FA-'05	16/0
97	Lewis, Trey	DT	6-3	317	23	2	Washburn	Topeka, Kan.	D6a-'07	9/5
62	McClure, Todd	C	6-1	295	31	10	Louisiana State	Baton Rouge, La.	D7a-'99	16/16
64	McCoy, Pat	OL	6-5	328	27	2	West Texas A&M	Fairfield, Calif.	FA-'07	0*
38	McIntyre, Corey	FB	6-0	244	29	4	West Virginia	Indiantown, Fla.	FA-'06	14/0
36	Milloy, Lawyer	S	6-0	213	34	13	Washington	St. Louis, Mo.	FA-'06	16/16
88	Milner, Martrez	TE	6-4	260	24	2	Georgia	Gainesville, Ga.	D4b-'07	8/2
90	Moore, Rashad	DT	6-3	325	29	5	Tennessee	Huntsville, Ala.	FA-'08	1/0*
94	Moorehead, Kindal	DT	6-2	285	29	6	Alabama	Memphis, Tenn.	UFA(Car)-'07	16/1*
34	Mughelli, Ovie	FB	6-1	254	28	6	Wake Forest	Boston, Mass.	UFA(Balt)-'07	16/7
54	Nicholas, Stephen	LB	6-3	232	25	2	South Florida	Jacksonville, Fla.	D4a-'07	13/0
32	Norwood, Jerious	RB	5-11	202	25	3	Mississippi State	Jackson, Miss.	D3-'06	15/2
76	Ojinnaka, Quinn	T	6-5	312	24	3	Syracuse	Seabrook, Md.	D5-'06	11/7
66	Pennington, Terrance	T	6-7	325	24	2	New Mexico	Compton, Calif.	FA-'07	5/0
85	Rader, Jason	TE	6-4	260	27	3	Marshall	St. Albans, W. Va.	FA-'08	0*
8	Redman, Chris	QB	6-3	223	31	6	Louisville	Louisville, Kent.	FA-'07	7/4
19	Robinson, Laurent	WR	6-2	201	23	2	Illinois State	Fort Lewis, Wash.	D3-'07	15/6
46	Schneck, Mike	LS	6-1	237	31	10	Wisconsin	Whitefish Bay, Wis.	FA-'07	12/0
3	Shockley, D.J.	QB	6-0	220	25	2	Georgia	College Park, Ga.	D7-'06	0*
44	Snelling, Jason	RB	5-11	231	24	2	Virginia	Chester, Va.	D7-'07	7/0
96	Stanley, Montavious	DT	6-2	308	26	3	Louisville	Albany, Ga.	W(Dall)-'07	14/6
69	Stepanovich, Alex	C	6-4	300	26	5	Ohio State	Berea, Ohio	UFA(Cin)-'08	12/4*
39	Stone, Daren	S	6-3	218	23	2	Maine	Lockport, N.Y.	D6d-'07	12/0
53	Taylor, Tony	LB	6-0	241	24	2	Georgia	Watkinsville, Ga.	FA-'07	16/0
27	Turnbull, Nick	S	6-2	222	27	2	Florida International	Pembroke Pines, Fla.	FA-'08	0*
33	Turner, Michael	RB	5-10	237	26	5	Northern Illinois	Waukegan, Ill.	UFA(SD)-'08	16/0*
74	Weiner, Todd	T	6-4	314	32	11	Kansas State	Coral Springs, Fla.	UFA(Sea)-'02	8/7
84	White, Roddy	WR	6-0	206	26	4	Alabama-Birmingham	James Island, S.C.	D1-'05	16/14
67	Wilkerson, Ben	C	6-4	305	25	3	Louisiana State	Port Arthur, Texas	FA-'07	16/0
24	Williams, Jimmy	S	6-3	212	24	3	Virginia Tech	Hampton, Va.	D2-'06	14/2
52	Williams, Travis	LB	6-1	224	26	2	Auburn	Columbia, S.C.	FA-'07	6/0

* E. Coleman played 15 games with N.Y. Jets in '07; Elam played 16 games with Denver; Finneran missed '07 season because of injury; Fraser played 16 games with Cleveland; Hartsock played 16 games with Tennessee; Hutchins played 16 games with Houston; McCoy inactive for 3 games; Moore played 1 game with New England; Moorehead played 16 games with Carolina; Rader spent the '07 season on New England's practice squad; Shockley missed the '07 season because of injury; Stepanovich played 12 games with Cincinnati; Turnbull last active with Cincinnati; Turner played 16 games with San Diego.

Traded—CB DeAngelo Hall (16 games in '07) to Oakland.

Players lost through free agency (5): TE Courtney Anderson (Buff; 2 games in '07), TE Dwayne Blakley (Tenn; 12), S Chris Crocker (Mia; 14), CB Omare Lowe (Sea; 0), LB Demorrio Williams (KC; 16).

Also played with Falcons in '07—K Morten Anderson (14 games), DT Rod Coleman (5), TE Alge Crumpler (14), RB Warrick Dunn (16), OL Wayne Gandy (5), DE Kevin Huntley (5), DT Grady Jackson (7), QB Byron Leftwich (3), DL Jesse Mahelona (1), DE Josh Mallard (3), RB Artose Pinner (7), K Matt Prater (2), CB Lewis Sanders (14), LS Boone Stutz (4), LB Marcus Wilkins (15).

2008 FIRST-YEAR ROSTER

Name	Pos.	Ht.	Wt.	Age	College	Hometown	How Acq.
Baker, Sam	T	6-5	314	23	Southern California	Tustin, Calif.	D1b
Biermann, Kroy	DE	6-3	241	22	Montana	Hardin, Mont.	D5b
Brittingham, Jamar	RB	6-0	203	24	Bloomsburg	Langhorne, Pa.	FA
Brown, Isaac	LB	5-11	203	23	Central Michigan	Saginaw, Mich.	FA
Brown, Thomas	RB	5-8	204	22	Georgia	Tucker, Ga.	D6
Butterworth, Michael	T	6-7	330	23	Slippery Rock	Northern Cambria, Pa.	FA
Cooper, George (1)	TE	6-5	263	24	Georgia Tech	Westerville, Ohio	FA-'07
Datish, Doug (1)	C	6-5	306	25	Ohio State	Warren, Ohio	D6c-'07
DeCoud, Thomas	S	6-0	196	23	California	Vallejo, Calif.	D3c
Douglas, Harry	WR	5-11	169	22	Louisville	Jonesboro, Ga.	D3b
Evans, Willie (1)	DE	6-1	269	24	Mississippi State	Waynesboro, Miss.	FA
Everett, Earl (1)	LB	6-3	231	23	Florida	Webster, Fla.	FA-'07
Fontenot, Wilrey	CB	5-9	174	23	Arizona	Humble, Texas	D7a
Grimes, Brent (1)	CB	5-10	180	25	Shippensburg	Philadelphia, Pa.	FA-'07
Jackson, Chevis	CB	5-11	188	22	Louisiana State	Mobile, Ala.	D3a
James, Robert	LB	5-10	226	24	Arizona State	Glendale, Ariz.	D5a
Jones, Derrick (1)	DE	6-4	282	22	Grand Valley State	Barstow, Calif.	FA-'07
Kaylor, Jimmie	P	6-3	198	24	Colorado State	Northglenn, Colo.	FA
Lofton, Curtis	LB	6-0	238	22	Oklahoma	Kingfisher, Okla.	D2
Lovell, Kevin (1)	K	5-9	155	24	Cincinnati	Hawthorne, Calif.	
Miller, Brandon	DE	6-4	254	22	Georgia	Colquitt, Ga.	FA
Patterson, David (1)	DL	6-5	285	23	Ohio State	Warrensville Heights, Ohio	FA-'07
Quarterman, Kurt (1)	OL	6-5	342	22	Louisville	Albany, Ga.	FA-'07
Ryan, Matt	QB	6-4	221	23	Boston College	Exton, Pa.	D1a
Sharpe, Glenn	CB	6-0	185	24	Miami	Miami, Fla.	FA
Turnbull, Nick (1)	S	6-2	222	27	Florida International	Pembroke Pines, Fla.	FA
Vaughn, Cameron (1)	LB	6-4	241	24	Louisiana State	Marrero, La.	FA-'07
Weems, Eric (1)	WR	5-9	190	23	Bethune-Cookman	Ormond Beach, Fla.	FA-'07
Williams, Chandler (1)	WR	5-11	184	23	Florida International	Miami, Fla.	FA
Wolfe, D.J.	S	5-11	201	22	Oklahoma	Lawton, Okla.	FA
Zinger, Keith	TE	6-4	250	23	Louisiana State	Leesville, La.	D7b

The term NFL Rookie is defined as a player who is in his first season of professional football and has not been on the roster of another professional football team for any regular-season or postseason games. A Rookie is designated by an "R" on NFL rosters. Players who have been active in another professional football league or players who have NFL experience, including either preseason training camp or being on an Active List or Inactive List, or on Reserve/Injured or Reserve/Physically Unable to Perform for fewer than six regular-season games, are termed NFL First-Year Players. An NFL First-Year Player is designated by a "1" on NFL rosters. Thereafter, a player is credited with an additional year of experience for each season in which he accumulates six games on the Active List or Inactive List, or on Reserve/Injured or Reserve/Physically Unable to Perform.

Log on to www.atlantafalcons.com for an up-to-date roster; Age listed is as of September 4, 2008.

COACHING STAFF
Head Coach,
Mike Smith
Pro Career: Mike Smith was named the 14th head coach in Atlanta Falcons franchise history on January 23, 2008. From 2003-07, Smith served as the defensive coordinator for the Jaguars and led a defensive unit which ranked fourth in overall defense (296.6), third in offensive points allowed (16.1) and fifth in rushing defense (99.3) from 2003-06. Last year, the Jaguars' defense ranked twelfth. Prior to joining the Jaguars, Smith spent four seasons with the Baltimore Ravens and was the defensive assistant/defensive line coach from 1999-2001, which included the team's 2000 Super Bowl season. The Ravens defense set an NFL 16-game record by allowing only 165 points en route to the team's first championship. In 2002, Smith served as the Ravens' linebackers coach. Before joining the NFL ranks, Smith coached at San Diego State (1982-85), Morehead State (1986), and Tennessee Tech (1987-1998). Career record: 0-0.
Background: Smith played linebacker for the Winnipeg Blue Bombers of the CFL in 1982. He played at East Tennessee (1977-1981) and was named defensive MVP twice at his position. Smith led the team with 186 tackles as a senior.
Personal: Age 48, born in Chicago, and a native of Daytona Beach, Florida. He and his wife Julie have one daughter, Logan, who is seven years old.

ASSISTANT COACHES
Keith Armstrong, special teams coordinator; born Levittown, Pa. Running back Temple 1983-86. No pro playing experience. College coach: Temple 1987, Miami 1988, Akron 1989, Oklahoma State 1990-92, Notre Dame 1993. Pro coach: Atlanta Falcons 1994-96, Chicago Bears 1997-2000, Miami Dolphins 2001-2007, re-joined Falcons 2008.
Paul Boudreau, offensive line; born Arlington, Mass. Guard Boston College 1970-73. No pro playing experience. Pro coach: New Orleans Saints 1987-1993, Detroit Lions 1994-96, New England Patriots 1997-98, Miami Dolphins 1999-2000, Carolina Panthers 2001-02, Jacksonville Jaguars 2003-05, St. Louis Rams 2006-07, joined Falcons in 2008.
Gerald Brown, running backs; born Sweetwater, Tenn. Attended Memphis State. No college or pro playing experience. College coach: Tennessee Tech 1991-2000, Indiana 2002-07. Pro coach: Joined Falcons in 2008.
Joe Danna, defensive assistant; born Midland, Mich. Wide receiver Central Michigan 1995-98. No pro playing experience. College coach: Central Michigan 1999-2000, 2002-05, Georgia 2001, Georgia Southern 2006, James Madison 2007. Pro coach: Joined Falcons in 2008.
Paul Dunn, asst. offensive line; born

Philadelphia. Offensive lineman Pittsburgh 1978-1982. No pro playing experience. College coach: Pittsburgh 1983, 2005-07, Penn State 1984-85, Edinboro 1986-88, Rutgers 1989, Maine 1990-93, Cincinnati 1994-95, Vanderbilt 1996-97, Kansas State 1998-2002, Kentucky 2003-04. Pro coach: Joined Falcons in 2008.
Jeff Fish, strength and conditioning; born Ithaca, N.Y. Wide receiver Western Carolina 1985-88. No pro playing experience. College coach: Western Michigan 1989, Clemson 1991-92, Kent State 1993-94, Tulsa 1995-97, Missouri 2001-03. Pro coach: Tampa Bay Buccaneers 1997, Kansas City Chiefs 1998-2000, Oakland Raiders 2004-07, joined Falcons in 2008.
Ray Hamilton, defensive line; born Omaha, Neb. Nose tackle Oklahoma 1969-1972. Pro defensive lineman New England Patriots 1973-1981. College coach: Tennessee 1992. Pro coach: New England Patriots 1985-89, Tampa Bay Buccaneers 1991, Los Angeles Raiders 1993-94, New York Jets 1994-96, 2000, New England Patriots 1997-99, Cleveland Browns 2001-02, Jacksonville Jaguars 2003-07, joined Falcons in 2008.
Bill Hughan, asst. strength and conditioning; born Oxford, Conn. Attended Springfield College. No college or pro playing experience. College coach: Yale 1997-98, Columbia 1999-2000, Missouri 2001-03. Pro coach: Oakland Raiders 2004-07, joined Falcons in 2008.
Tom McMahon, asst. special teams; born Helena, Mont. Quarterback Carroll College 1988-1991. No pro playing experience. College coach: Carroll College 1992, 1994, Utah State 1995-2005, Louisville 2006. Pro coach: Joined Falcons in 2007.
Mike Mularkey, offensive coordinator; born Ft. Lauderdale, Fla. Tight end Florida 1979-1982. Pro tight end Minnesota Vikings 1983-88, Pittsburgh Steelers 1989-1991. College coach: Concordia 1993. Pro coach: Tampa Bay Buccaneers 1994-1995, Pittsburgh Steelers 1996-2003, Buffalo Bills 2004-05 (head coach), Miami Dolphins 2006-07, joined Falcons in 2008.
Bill Musgrave, quarterbacks; born Grand Junction, Colo. Quarterback Oregon 1987-1990. Pro quarterback San Francisco 49ers 1991-94, Denver Broncos 1995-96. College coach: Virginia 2001-02. Pro coach: Oakland Raiders 1997, Philadelphia Eagles 1998, Carolina Panthers 1999-2000, Jacksonville Jaguars 2003-04, Washington Redskins 2005, joined Falcons in 2006.
Glenn Pires, linebackers; born New Bedford, Mass. Offensive lineman Springfield College 1976-79. No pro playing experience. College coach: Dartmouth 1985-88, Syracuse 1989-1994, Michigan State 1995. Pro coach: Arizona Cardinals 1996-2000, Detroit Lions 2001-02, Miami Dolphins 2003-07, joined Falcons in 2008.

Alvin Reynolds, defensive backs; born Pineville, La. Safety Indiana State 1978-1981. No pro playing experience. College coach: Indiana State 1982-1992. Pro coach: Denver Broncos 1993-95, Baltimore Ravens 1996-98, Carolina Panthers 1999-2002, Jacksonville Jaguars 2003-07, joined Falcons in 2008.
Terry Robiskie, wide receivers; born New Orleans. Running back Louisiana State 1973-76. Pro running back Oakland Raiders 1977-79, Miami Dolphins 1980-81. Pro coach: Los Angeles Raiders 1982-1993, Washington Redskins 1994-2000 (interim head coach 2000), Cleveland Browns 2001-06 (interim head coach 2004), Miami Dolphins 2007, joined Falcons in 2008.
Chris Scelfo, tight ends; born New Iberia, La. Center Northeast Louisiana 1981-84. No pro playing experience. College coach: Northeast Louisiana 1986-87, Oklahoma 1988-89, Marshall 1990-95, Georgia 1996-98, Tulane 1998-2006. Pro coach: Joined Falcons in 2008.
Emmitt Thomas, asst. head coach/secondary; born Angleton, Texas. Quarterback/receiver Bishop (Texas) College 1963-65. Pro defensive back Kansas City Chiefs 1966-1978. College coach: Central Missouri State 1979-1980. Pro coach: St. Louis Cardinals 1981-85, Washington Redskins 1986-1994, Philadelphia Eagles 1995-1998, Green Bay Packers 1999, Minnesota Vikings 2000-01, joined Falcons in 2002 (interim head coach 2007).
Glenn Thomas, offensive assistant; born Eastland, Texas. Attended Texas Tech. No college or pro playing experience. College coach: Texas Tech 1998-2001, Midwestern State 2001-07. Pro coach: Joined Falcons in 2008.
Brian VanGorder, defensive coordinator; born Jackson, Mich. Linebacker Wayne State 1979-1980. No pro playing experience. College coach: Grand Valley State 1989-1991, Wayne State 1992-94 (head coach), Central Florida 1995-97, Central Michigan 1998-99, Western Illinois 2000, Georgia 2001-04, Georgia Southern 2006 (head coach). Pro coach: Jacksonville Jaguars 2005, joined Falcons in 2007.

National Football Conference
South Division
Team Colors: Black, Panther Blue, and
Silver
800 South Mint Street
Charlotte, North Carolina 28202-1502
Telephone: (704) 358-7000

2008 SCHEDULE
PRESEASON
Aug. 9	**Indianapolis**	7:30
Aug. 14	at Philadelphia	8:00
Aug. 23	**Washington**	7:30
Aug. 28	at Pittsburgh	7:30

REGULAR SEASON
Sep. 7	at San Diego	1:15
Sep. 14	**Chicago**	1:00
Sep. 21	at Minnesota	12:00
Sep. 28	**Atlanta**	1:00
Oct. 5	**Kansas City**	1:00
Oct. 12	at Tampa Bay	1:00
Oct. 19	**New Orleans**	1:00
Oct. 26	**Arizona**	1:00
Nov. 2	BYE	
Nov. 9	at Oakland	1:05
Nov. 16	**Detroit**	1:00
Nov. 23	at Atlanta	1:00
Nov. 30	at Green Bay	12:00
Dec. 8	**Tampa Bay** (Mon.)	8:30
Dec. 14	**Denver**	1:00
Dec. 21	at N.Y. Giants	1:00
Dec. 28	at New Orleans	12:00

Stadium: Bank of America Stadium
(opened in 1996)
• **Capacity:** 73,504
Charlotte, North Carolina
28202-1502
Playing Surface: Grass
Training Camp: Wofford College
Spartanburg,
South Carolina 29303

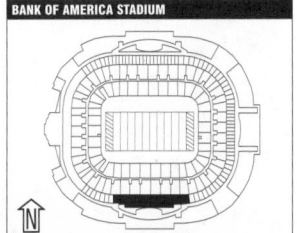

BANK OF AMERICA STADIUM

CLUB OFFICIALS
Owner/Founder: Jerry Richardson
President, Panthers Football LLC:
Mark Richardson
President Panthers Stadium LLC:
Jon Richardson
General Manager: Marty Hurney
General Counsel: Richard Thigpen
Chief Financial Officer: Dave Olsen
Controller: Mike Dudan
Director of Pro Scouting: Mark Koncz
Pro Scouts: Trent Kirchner, Tag Ribary
Director of College Scouting:
Don Gregory
College Scouts: Brian Adams,
Ryan Cowden, Khary Darlington,
Jeff Morrow, Joe Schoen,
Mike Szabo, Gerald Williams
Director of Communications:
Charlie Dayton
Media Relations Manager:
Steven Drummond
Public Relations Assistant: Deedee Mills
Communications Assistant:
Colin Murray
Director of Ticket Operations:
Phil Youtsey
Director of Player Development:
Donnie Shell
Director of Community Relations and
Cheerleader/Mascot Programs:
Riley Fields
Director of Sponsor Sales and Services:
Kyle Caddell
Director of Broadcast Administration:
Henry Thomas
Executive Producer-Television:
Greg Brannon
Executive Producer-Radio: David Langton
Director of Team Administration:
Rob Rogers
Director of Team Operations:
Brandon Beane
Video Director: Mark Hobbs
Assistant Video Director: Jeff Mueller
Head Trainer: Ryan Vermillion
Assistant Trainers: Mark Shermansky,
Reggie Scott
Equipment Manager: Jackie Miles
Assistant Equipment Manager: Don Toner
Director of Security: Gene Brown
Stadium Operations Manager: Scott Paul
Director of Entertainment and
Panthervision: Kyle Ritchie
Facility Manager: Matthew Getz
Head Groundskeeper: Tom Vaughan
Director of Human Resources:
Jackie Jeffries

COACHING HISTORY
(103-114-0)
Records include postseason games
1995-98	Dom Capers	31-35-0
1999-2001	George Seifert	16-32-0
2002-07	John Fox	56-47-0

PAID ATTENDANCE
Home 579,051   Away 521,096
Total 1,100,147
Single-game home record,
76,136 (12/10/95)
Single-season home record, 579,192
(2006)

2008 DRAFT CHOICES
Round	Name	Pos.	College
1	Jonathan Stewart	RB	Oregon
	Jeff Otah	T	Pittsburgh
3	Charles Godfrey	DB	Iowa
	Dan Connor	LB	Penn State
5	Gary Barnidge	TE	Louisville
6	Nick Hayden	DT	Wisconsin
7	Hilee Taylor	DE	North Carolina
	Geoff Schwartz	T	Oregon
	Mackenzy Bernadeau	G	Bentley

CAROLINA PANTHERS

2007 TEAM RECORD

PRESEASON (1-3)

Date	Result	Opponent
8/11	W 24-21	at N.Y. Giants
8/17	L 10-27	at Philadelphia
8/24	L 7-24	New England
8/30	L 3-19	Pittsburgh

REGULAR SEASON (7-9)

Date	Result	Opponent	Att.
9/9	W 27-13	at St. Louis	65,307
9/16	L 21-34	Houston	73,665
9/23	W 27-20	at Atlanta	68,175
9/30	L 7-20	Tampa Bay	73,707
10/7	W 16-13	at New Orleans	70,001
10/14	W 25-10	at Arizona	64,403
10/28	L 7-31	Indianapolis	74,005
11/4	L 7-20	at Tennessee	69,143
11/11	L 13-20	Atlanta	73,340
11/18	L 17-31	at Green Bay	70,805
11/25	L 6-31	New Orleans	72,032
12/2	W 31-14	San Francisco	73,191
12/9	L 6-37	at Jacksonville	66,090
12/16	W 13-10	Seattle	73,421
12/22	L 13-20	Dallas	73,860
12/30	W 31-23	at Tampa Bay	65,609

SCORE BY PERIODS

Panthers	50	66	48	103	0	— 267
Opponents	79	89	110	69	0	— 347

2007 TEAM STATISTICS

	Panthers	Opp.
Total First Downs	255	302
Rushing	85	100
Passing	142	174
Penalty	28	28
3rd Down: Made/Att	85/235	96/226
3rd Down Pct.	36.2	42.5
4th Down: Made/Att	6/14	7/14
4th Down Pct.	42.9	50.0
Possession Avg.	28:44	31:16
Total Net Yards	4559	5197
Avg. Per Game	284.9	324.8
Total Plays	989	1032
Avg. Per Play	4.6	5.0
Net Yards Rushing	1824	1771
Avg. Per Game	114.0	110.7
Total Rushes	451	472
Net Yards Passing	2735	3426
Avg. Per Game	170.9	214.1
Sacked/Yards Lost	33/206	23/177
Gross Yards	2941	3603
Att./Completions	505/285	537/337
Completion Pct.	56.4	62.8
Had Intercepted	17	14
Punts/Average	92/43.9	76/42.7
Net Punting Avg.	92/36.5	76/36.8
Penalties/Yards	95/801	100/904
Fumbles/Ball Lost	25/12	30/16
Touchdowns	28	38
Rushing	7	13
Passing	19	22
Returns	2	3

2007 INDIVIDUAL STATISTICS

PASSING	Att.	Comp.	Yds.	Pct.	TD	Int.	Tkld.	Rate
Testaverde	172	94	952	54.7	5	6	9/46	65.8
Carr	136	73	635	53.7	3	5	13/74	58.3
Moore	111	63	730	56.8	3	5	6/40	67.0
Delhomme	86	55	624	64.0	8	1	5/46	111.8
Panthers	505	285	2941	56.4	19	17	33/206	71.9
Opponents	537	337	3603	62.8	22	14	23/177	85.1

SCORING	TD R	TD P	TD Rt	PAT	FG	Saf	PTS
Kasay	0	0	0	27/27	24/28	0	99
Smith	0	7	0	0/0	0/0	0	42
Williams	4	1	0	0/0	0/0	0	30
D. Carter	0	4	0	0/0	0/0	0	24
Foster	3	1	0	0/0	0/0	0	24
Fauria	0	2	0	0/0	0/0	0	12
King	0	2	0	0/0	0/0	0	12
Rosario	0	2	0	0/0	0/0	0	12
Lucas	0	0	1	0/0	0/0	0	6
Marshall	0	0	1	0/0	0/0	0	6
Panthers	7	19	2	27/27	24/28	0	267
Opponents	13	22	3	38/38	27/32	0	347

2-Pt. Conversions: Panthers 0-1, Opponents 0-0

RUSHING	No.	Yds	Avg	LG	TD
Foster	247	876	3.5	20	3
Williams	144	717	5.0	75	4
Smith	9	66	7.3	22	0
Carr	17	59	3.5	15	0
Hoover	12	39	3.3	10	0
Delhomme	6	26	4.3	13	0
Testaverde	9	22	2.4	16	0
Jarrett	1	11	11.0	11	0
Moore	3	5	1.7	5	0
Haynes	3	3	1.0	3	0
Panthers	451	1824	4.0	75	7
Opponents	472	1771	3.8	80t	13

RECEIVING	No.	Yds	Avg	LG	TD
Smith	87	1002	11.5	74t	7
King	46	406	8.8	29	2
D. Carter	38	517	13.6	49	4
Colbert	32	332	10.4	43	0
Foster	25	182	7.3	23	1
Williams	23	175	7.6	30	1
Hoover	10	58	5.8	14	0
Rosario	6	108	18.0	54	2
Jarrett	6	73	12.2	22	0
Fauria	5	39	7.8	16	2
Robinson	4	35	8.8	12	0
Haynes	3	14	4.7	6	0
Panthers	285	2941	10.3	74t	19
Opponents	337	3603	10.7	69t	22

INTERCEPTIONS	No.	Yds	Avg	LG	TD
Marshall	3	107	35.7	73t	1
Cooper	3	19	6.3	19	0
Lucas	2	1	0.5	1	0
Harris	1	30	30.0	30	0
Manuel	1	4	4.0	4	0
Gamble	1	2	2.0	2	0
Beason	1	0	0.0	0	0
Th. Davis	1	0	0.0	0	0
Peppers	1	0	0.0	0	0
Panthers	14	163	11.6	73t	1
Opponents	17	150	8.8	45	1

PUNTING	No.	Yds.	Avg.	In 20	LG
Baker	90	3978	44.2	22	64
Kasay	2	60	30.0	1	32
Panthers	92	4038	43.9	23	64
Opponents	76	3243	42.7	31	66

PUNT RETURNS	Ret	FC	Yds	Avg	LG	TD
Robinson	30	19	262	8.7	34	0
Smith	2	0	7	3.5	6	0
Panthers	32	19	269	8.4	34	0
Opponents	55	16	579	10.5	94t	1

KICKOFF RETURNS	No.	Yds	Avg	LG	TD
Robinson	26	598	23.0	60	0
Williams	13	231	17.8	29	0
Goings	9	174	19.3	29	0
Moorehead	4	46	11.5	17	0
Hangartner	3	42	14.0	16	0
Rosario	2	39	19.5	25	0
King	1	16	16.0	16	0
Marshall	1	0	0.0	0	0
McClover	1	0	0.0	0	0
Panthers	60	1146	19.1	60	0
Opponents	56	1333	23.8	84	0

FIELD GOALS	1-19	20-29	30-39	40-49	50+
Kasay	2/2	6/6	8/9	6/9	2/2
Panthers	2/2	6/6	8/9	6/9	2/2
Opponents	0/0	13/14	5/5	7/9	2/4

SACKS	No.
Diggs	3.5
Lewis	3.5
Th. Davis	3.0
Rucker	3.0
Jenkins	2.5
Peppers	2.5
Moorehead	2.0
Manuel	1.0
Marshall	1.0
McClover	1.0
Panthers	23.0
Opponents	33.0

RECORD HOLDERS
INDIVIDUAL RECORDS—CAREER

Category	Name	Performance
Rushing (Yds.)	DeShaun Foster, 2002-07	3,336
Passing (Yds.)	Jake Delhomme, 2003-07	13,955
Passing (TDs)	Jake Delhomme, 2003-07	97
Receiving (No.)	Muhsin Muhammad, 1996-2004	578
Receiving (Yds.)	Muhsin Muhammad, 1996-2004	7,751
Interceptions	Eric Davis, 1996-2000	25
Punting (Avg.)	Todd Sauerbrun, 2001-04	45.5
Punt Return (Avg.)	Winslow Oliver, 1996-98	10.7
Kickoff Return (Avg.)	Michael Bates, 1996-2000	25.7
Field Goals	John Kasay, 1995-2007	276
Touchdowns (Tot.)	Steve Smith, 2001-07	45
Points	John Kasay, 1995-2007	1,163

INDIVIDUAL RECORDS—SINGLE SEASON

Category	Name	Performance
Rushing (Yds.)	Stephen Davis, 2003	1,444
Passing (Yds.)	Steve Beuerlein, 1999	4,436
Passing (TDs)	Steve Beuerlein, 1999	36
Receiving (No.)	Steve Smith, 2005	103
Receiving (Yds.)	Steve Smith, 2005	1,563
Interceptions	Doug Evans, 2001	8
Punting (Avg.)	Todd Sauerbrun, 2001	47.5
Punt Return (Avg.)	Winslow Oliver, 1996	11.5
Kickoff Return (Avg.)	Michael Bates, 1996	30.2
Field Goals	John Kasay, 1996	37
Touchdowns (Tot.)	Muhsin Muhammad, 2004	16
Points	John Kasay, 1996	145

INDIVIDUAL RECORDS—SINGLE GAME

Category	Name	Performance
Rushing (Yds.)	Stephen Davis, 10-26-03	178
Passing (Yds.)	Chris Weinke, 12-10-06	423
Passing (TDs)	Steve Beuerlein, 1-2-00	5
Receiving (No.)	Steve Smith, 11-20-05	14
Receiving (Yds.)	Steve Smith, 10-30-05	201
Interceptions	Deon Grant, 9-22-02	3
Field Goals	John Kasay, 12-5-04	6
Touchdowns (Tot.)	Many times	3
	Last time by Steve Smith, 9-16-07	
Points	Fred Lane, 11-2-97	18
	Tshimanga Biakabutuka, 10-3-99	18
	Muhsin Muhammad, 12-18-99, 11-14-04	18
	Steve Smith, 12-8-02, 9-25-05, 9-16-07	18
	Nick Goings, 11-21-04	18
	Stephen Davis, 9-18-05	18

2008 VETERANS ROSTER

No.	Name	Pos.	Ht.	Wt.	Age	NFL Exp.	College	Hometown	How Acq.	'07 Games/ Starts
50	Anderson, James	LB	6-2	235	24	3	Virginia Tech	Chesapeake, Va.	D3a-'06	10/1
7	Baker, Jason	P	6-2	205	30	8	Iowa	Fort Wayne, Ind.	T(Den)-'05	16/0
14	Basanez, Brett	QB	6-2	210	25	2	Northwestern	Arlington Heights, Ill.	FA-'06	0*
52	Beason, Jon	LB	6-0	237	23	2	Miami	Miramar, Fla.	D1-'07	16/16
96	Brayton, Tyler	DE	6-6	280	28	6	Colorado	Pasco, Wash.	UFA(Oak)-'08	16/0*
73	Bridges, Jeremy	G	6-4	326	28	6	Southern Mississippi	McComb, Miss.	FA-'06	13/10
61	Brown, Milford	G	6-5	330	28	7	Florida State	Montgomery, Ala.	UFA(StL)-'08	16/15*
22	Colclough, Ricardo	CB	5-11	195	26	5	Tusculum	Sumter, S.C.	UFA(Cle)-'08	3/0*
35 #	Cooper, Deke	S	6-2	210	30	6	Notre Dame	Evansville, Ind.	UFA(SF)-'07	16/15
55	Curry, Donte	LB	6-1	240	30	6	Morris Brown	Savannah, Ga.	FA-'07	7/0
58	Davis, Thomas	LB	6-0	240	25	4	Georgia	Shellman, Ga.	D1-'05	16/16
17	Delhomme, Jake	QB	6-2	215	33	10	Louisiana-Lafayette	Lafayette, La.	UFA(NO)-'03	3/3
41 #	Deloatch, Curtis	CB	6-2	214	26	5	North Carolina A&T	Ahoskie, N.C.	FA-'07	6/0
53	Diggs, Na'il	LB	6-4	240	30	9	Ohio State	Los Angeles, Calif.	FA-'06	16/10
86 #	Fauria, Christian	TE	6-4	250	36	14	Colorado	Encino, Calif.	FA-'07	15/3
32	Fleming, Troy	FB	6-0	245	27	3	Nebraska	Franklin, Tenn.	FA-'08	0*
77	Fonoti, Toniu	G	6-4	350	26	6	Nebraska	Hauula, Hawaii	FA-'08	0*
20	Gamble, Chris	CB	6-1	200	25	5	Ohio State	Sunrise, Fla.	D1-'04	15/12
91	Gibson, Gary	DT	6-3	285	26	3	Rutgers	Jamesville, N.Y.	FA-'07	1/0
37	Goings, Nick	RB	6-0	225	30	8	Pittsburgh	Dublin, Ohio	FA-'01	4/0
69	Gross, Jordan	T	6-4	300	28	6	Utah	Fruitland, Idaho	D1-'03	16/16
18	Hackett, D.J.	WR	6-2	208	27	5	Colorado	San Dimas, Calif.	UFA(Sea)-'08	6/6*
63	Hangartner, Geoff	C	6-5	301	26	4	Texas A&M	New Braunfels, Texas	D5b-'05	16/4
43	Harris, Chris	S	6-0	205	26	4	Louisiana-Monroe	Little Rock, Ark.	T(Chi)-'07	15/15
24	Haynes, Alex	RB	5-10	225	26	2	Central Florida	Orlando, Fla.	FA-'05	9/0
42	Holt, Terrence	S	6-2	208	28	6	North Carolina State	Gibsonville, N.C.	FA-'08	16/16*
45	Hoover, Brad	FB	6-0	245	31	9	Western Carolina	Thomasville, N.C.	FA-'00	16/12
57	Jamison, Brandon	LB	6-1	232	27	3	West Georgia	Hopkins, S.C.	W(Atl)-'06	15/0
80	Jarrett, Dwayne	WR	6-4	219	21	2	Southern California	New Brunswick, N.J.	D2a-'07	7/0
95	Johnson, Charles	DE	6-2	270	22	2	Georgia	Hawkinsville, Ga.	D3-'07	3/2
94	Johnson, Landon	LB	6-2	232	27	5	Purdue	Lubbock, Texas	UFA(Cin)-'08	16/16*
67	Kalil, Ryan	C	6-2	295	23	2	Southern California	Corona, Calif.	D2b-'07	5/3
4	Kasay, John	K	5-10	210	38	18	Georgia	Athens, Ga.	UFA(Sea)-'95	16/0
99	Kemoeatu, Maake	DT	6-5	345	29	7	Utah	Kahuku, Hawaii	FA-'06	16/13
47	King, Jeff	TE	6-3	260	25	3	Virginia Tech	Pulaski, Va.	D5-'06	16/16
56	Kyle, Jason	LB	6-3	242	36	14	Arizona State	Tempe, Ariz.	UFA(SF)-'01	16/0
92	Lewis, Damione	DT	6-2	301	30	8	Miami	Sulphur Springs, Texas	UFA(StL)-'06	15/2
5	Lloyd, Rhys	K	5-11	231	26	2	Minnesota	Dover, England	W(Balt)-'07	3/0
21	Lucas, Ken	CB	6-0	205	29	8	Mississippi	Cleveland, Miss.	UFA(Sea)-'05	16/16
31	Marshall, Richard	CB	5-11	189	23	3	Fresno State	Los Angeles, Calif.	D2-'06	16/5
71	Mathis, Evan	G	6-5	304	26	4	Alabama	Homewood, Ala.	D3a-'05	1/0
75	McClover, Stanley	DE	6-2	263	23	3	Auburn	Fort Lauderdale, Fla.	D7b-'06	11/0
54 #	Melton, Terrence	LB	6-1	235	31	5	Rice	Houston, Texas	FA-'08	0*
3	Moore, Matt	QB	6-3	202	24	2	Oregon State	Valencia, Calif.	W(Dall)-'07	9/3
87	Muhammad, Muhsin	WR	6-2	215	35	13	Michigan State	Lansing, Mich.	FA-'08	16/16*
76	Omiyale, Frank	T	6-4	310	25	4	Tennessee Tech	Whites Creek, Tenn.	W(Atl)-'07	0*
90	Peppers, Julius	DE	6-7	283	28	7	North Carolina	Bailey, N.C.	D1-'02	14/14
10	Robinson, Ryne	WR	5-9	179	23	2	Miami (Ohio)	Toledo, Ohio	D4-'07	16/0
88	Rosario, Dante	TE	6-4	250	23	2	Oregon	Dayton, Ore.	D5a-'07	16/2
25	Salley, Nate	S	6-1	216	24	3	Ohio State	Ft. Lauderdale, Fla.	D4-'06	0*
	Scott, Ian	DT	6-3	302	26	5	Florida	Gainesville, Fla.	UFA(Phil)-'08	0*
59 +	Seward, Adam	LB	6-2	248	26	4	Nevada-Las Vegas	Las Vegas, Nev.	D5a-'05	11/0
97	Shaw, Tim	LB	6-1	236	24	2	Penn State	Livonia, Mich.	D5b-'07	14/0
89	Smith, Steve	WR	5-9	185	29	8	Utah	Lynwood, Calif.	D3-'01	15/15
19	Taylor, Travis	WR	6-1	210	29	9	Florida	Jacksonville, Fla.	FA-'07	2/0
28	Teal, Quinton	S	6-1	187	24	2	Coastal Carolina	Bennettsville, S.C.	FA-'07	15/1
33	Toefield, LaBrandon	RB	5-11	235	27	6	Louisiana State	Independence, La.	UFA(Jax)-'08	2/1*
68	Vincent, Keydrick	G	6-5	325	30	8	Mississippi	Lakeland, Fla.	UFA(Ariz)-'08	7/1*
23	Wesley, Dante	CB	6-1	210	29	7	Arkansas Pine-Bluff	Pine Bluff, Ark.	FA-'07	2/0
70	Wharton, Travelle	T	6-4	312	27	5	South Carolina	Simpsonville, S.C.	D3-'04	16/16
34	Williams, DeAngelo	RB	5-9	217	25	3	Memphis	Wynne, Ark.	D1-'06	16/0
98	Williams, Stephen	DT	6-2	306	26	2	NW Missouri State	Bolingbrook, Ill.	FA-'07	0*
27	Wilson, C.J.	S	6-1	195	23	2	Baylor	Terrell, Texas	FA-'07	4/0

*   Basanez last active with Carolina in '06; Brayton played 16 games with Oakland in '07; Brown played 16 games with St. Louis; Colclough played 3 games with Pittsburgh; Fleming last active with Tennessee in '05; Fonoti last active with Miami in '06; Hackett played 6 games with Seattle; Holt played 16 games with Arizona; L. Johnson played 16 games with Cincinnati; Muhammad played 16 games with Chicago; Omiyale inactive for 16 games; Salley inactive for 2 games; Scott missed '07 season because of injury with Philadelphia; Toefield played 2 games with Jacksonville; Vincent played in 7 games with Arizona; S. Williams last active with Kansas City in '06.

\#   Unrestricted free agent, subject to developments.

+   Restricted free agent, subject to developments.

Players lost through free agency (4): WR Drew Carter (Oak; 16 games in '07), WR Keary Colbert (Den; 12), S Marquand Manuel (Den; 15), DT Kindal Moorehead (Atl; 16).

Also played with Panthers in '07—QB David Carr (6 games), CB Patrick Dendy (7), RB DeShaun Foster (16), DE Otis Grigsby (4), C Justin Hartwig (15), DT Kris Jenkins (16), LB Dan Morgan (3), DE Mike Rucker (16), QB Vinny Testaverde (7), G Mike Wahle (16).

2008 FIRST-YEAR ROSTER

Name	Pos.	Ht.	Wt.	Age	College	Hometown	How Acq.
Barnidge, Gary	TE	6-5	247	22	Louisville	Middleburg, Fla.	D5
Bernadeau, Mackenzy	G	6-4	308	22	Bentley	Waltham, Mass.	D7c
Birmingham, Decori (1)	RB	5-10	210	25	Arkansas	Atlanta, Texas	FA-'07
Brinkley, Casper	DE	6-2	259	23	South Carolina	Thomson, Ga.	FA
Conklin, Chris	TE	6-3	249	21	Wingate	Graham, N.C.	FA
Connor, Dan	LB	6-2	231	22	Penn State	Wallingford, Pa.	D3b
Davis, Josh (1)	WR	6-1	188	27	Marshall	York, S.C.	FA-'07
Evans, Breyone	FB	5-11	238	22	Massachusetts	Bristol, Conn.	FA
Fields, Joe	S	6-0	201	22	Syracuse	Houston, Texas	FA
Godfrey, Charles	S	5-11	205	22	Iowa	Baytown, Texas	D3a
Grixby, Cortney	CB	5-8	165	22	Nebraska	Omaha, Neb.	FA
Hannon, Chris (1)	WR	6-3	205	24	Tennessee	Sarasota, Fla.	FA-'07
Harris, Anthony (1)	DT	6-3	287	26	Western New Mexico	Mayersville, Miss.	FA
Hayden, Nick	DT	6-4	292	22	Wisconsin	Hartland, Wisc.	D6
Morton, Damon	WR	5-10	176	22	Colorado State	Riverside, Calif.	FA
Otah, Jeff	T	6-6	324	22	Pittsburgh	New Castle, Del.	D1b
Riley, Rueben (1)	G	6-4	305	23	Michigan	Grand Rapids, Mich.	FA-'07
Schwartz, Geoff	T	6-6	331	22	Oregon	Los Angeles, Calif.	D7b
Stewart, Jonathan	RB	5-10	235	21	Oregon	Fort Lewis, Wash.	D1a
Taylor, Hilee	DE	6-2	244	22	North Carolina	Laurinburg, N.C.	D7a
Tharp, Taylor	QB	6-1	203	23	Boise State	Boulder, Colo.	FA
Thompson, Dominique (1)	WR	5-11	205	25	William & Mary	Durham, N.C.	FA
Toney, Darren	CB	5-11	185	24	Arkansas State	Lake Village, Ark.	FA
Tunney, Eric	G	6-3	296	23	Central Michigan	Whittemore, Mich.	FA
Upshaw, Chad (1)	TE	6-4	246	24	Buffalo	Southport, Conn.	FA
Zeidman, Dan	P	6-0	201	22	Idaho State	Spring Valley, Calif.	FA

The term NFL Rookie is defined as a player who is in his first season of professional football and has not been on the roster of another professional football team for any regular-season or postseason games. A Rookie is designated by an "R" on NFL rosters. Players who have been active in another professional football league or players who have NFL experience, including either preseason training camp or being on an Active List or Inactive List, or on Reserve/Injured or Reserve/Physically Unable to Perform for fewer than six regular-season games, are termed NFL First-Year Players. An NFL First-Year Player is designated by a "1" on NFL rosters. Thereafter, a player is credited with an additional year of experience for each season in which he accumulates six games on the Active List or Inactive List, or on Reserve/Injured or Reserve/Physically Unable to Perform.

Log on to www.panthers.com for an up-to-date roster; Age listed is as of September 4, 2008.

COACHING STAFF

Head Coach,
John Fox

Pro Career: Became third coach in Carolina Panthers history on January 25, 2002. During tenure from 2002-07, 56 overall victories stand as the third-highest total in the NFC. Since arrival in 2002, Panthers are one of five teams that have ranked among the NFL's top 10 in total defense in at least four of the last six seasons. In 2005, directed team to second NFC championship appearance in three seasons. Became the fifth head coach in NFL history to record four career postseason road wins. Equaled an NFL record with four consecutive postseason road wins. In 2004, directed Carolina team that overcame a 1-7 record to end the regular season with mark of 7-9. Of the 28 NFL teams that began season with 1-7 record since 1990, Panthers became only third team to finish season with seven victories. In 2003, guided Panthers to Super Bowl XXXVIII two years after inheriting team that won one game in 2001. Joined Vince Lombardi and Bill Parcells as the only coaches in NFL history to inherit a one-win team and guide it to the playoffs in their second season. In 2002, engineered a six-game turn-around that ranks second for rookie head coaches since 1978. In 2002, the Panthers became the only team since 1970 to improve from thirty-first to second in total defense in one season. Prior to joining Carolina he served as the defensive coordinator for the N.Y. Giants (1997-2001). In 2000, Fox helped the Giants reach Super Bowl XXXV, including posting the first shutout in a conference title game since 1986. Before joining the Giants, Fox was a consultant for the Rams (1996), defensive coordinator for the Raiders (1994-95), defensive backs coach for the Chargers (1992-93) and Steelers (1989-1991), and secondary coach for the USFL's Los Angeles Express (1985). Career record: 56-47.

Background: Defensive back at San Diego State (1976-77). Coached at San Diego State (1978), U.S. International (1979), Boise State (1980), Long Beach State (1981), Utah (1982), Kansas (1983), Iowa State (1984), and Pittsburgh (1986-88). Received bachelor's degree in physical education and earned a teaching credential from San Diego State.

Personal: Age 53, born in Virginia Beach, Va. He and his wife, Robin, have four children—Mathew, Mark, Cody, and Halle.

ASSISTANT COACHES

Geep Chryst, tight ends/quality control-offense; born Madison, Wis. Linebacker Princeton 1981-84. Pro linebacker Orlando Thunder (WFL) 1992. College coach: Wisconsin-Platteville 1987, Wisconsin 1988, Wyoming 1989-1990. Pro coach: Orlando Thunder (WL) 1991, Chicago Bears 1991-95, Arizona Cardinals 1996-98, 2001-03, San Diego Chargers 1999-

2000, joined Panthers in 2006.

Danny Crossman, special teams; born El Paso, Texas. Defensive back Kansas 1985, Pittsburgh 1987-89. Pro defensive back Washington Redskins 1990, Detroit Lions 1991-92. College coach: U.S. Coast Guard Academy 1993, Western Kentucky 1994-96, Central Florida 1997-98, Georgia Tech 1999-2001, Michigan State 2002. Pro coach: Joined Panthers in 2003.

Jeff Davidson, offensive coordinator; born Akron, Ohio. Offensive lineman Ohio State 1986-89. Pro offensive lineman Denver Broncos 1990-92, New Orleans Saints 1994. Pro coach: New Orleans Saints 1995-96, New England Patriots 1997-2004, Cleveland Browns 2005-06, joined Panthers in 2007.

Ken Flajole, linebackers; born Seattle. Linebacker Wenatchee Valley (Wash.) C.C. 1973-74, Pacific Lutheran 1975-76. No pro playing experience. College coach: Pacific Lutheran 1977-78, Washington 1979, Montana 1980-85, Texas-El Paso 1986-88, Missouri 1989-1993, Richmond 1994, Hawaii 1995, Nevada 1996-97. Pro coach: Green Bay Packers 1998, Seattle Seahawks 1999-2002, joined Panthers in 2003.

Mike Gillhamer, secondary/safeties; born Oakland. Defensive back Carroll College 1972, Wenatchee (Wash.) J.C. 1973, Humboldt State 1974-75. No pro playing experience. College coach: College of the Sequoias 1979-1983, Weber State 1984, Utah 1985-89, San Jose State 1990-93, Nevada 1994-95, Oregon 2001-02, Louisville 2003. Pro coach: New York Giants 1997-2000, joined Panthers in 2004.

Matt House, special teams assistant/asst. strength and conditioning; born Harrison, Mich. No college or pro playing experience. College coach: Michigan State 2000-03, North Carolina 2003-04, Gardner-Webb 2005, Buffalo 2006-07. Pro coach: Joined Panthers in 2008.

Tim Lewis, secondary; born Quakertown, Pa. Defensive back Pittsburgh 1979-1982. Pro cornerback Green Bay Packers 1983-86. College coach: Texas A&M 1987-88, Southern Methodist 1989-1992, Pittsburgh 1993-94. Pro coach: Pittsburgh Steelers 1995-2003, New York Giants 2004-06, joined Panthers in 2007.

David Magazu, offensive line; born Taunton Mass. Defensive tackle Springfield College 1976-79. No pro playing experience. College coach: Ithaca 1980, Western Michigan 1981, Eastern Michigan 1982, Michigan 1983, Northern Illinois 1984, Ball State 1985-86, Navy 1987-89, Indiana State 1990-91, Colorado State 1992-94, Kentucky 1995-96, Memphis 1997-98, Boston College 1999-2002. Pro coach: Joined Panthers in 2003.

Mike McCoy, passing game coordinator/quarterbacks; born San Francisco. Quarterback Long Beach State 1990-91,

Utah 1992-94. Pro quarterback Amsterdam Admirals (NFLE) 1997, Calgary Stampeders (CFL) 1999. Pro coach: Joined Panthers in 1999.

Sam Mills III, quality control/defense; born Long Branch, N.J. Cornerback Montclair State 1997-98. No pro playing experience. Pro coach: Joined Panthers in 2006.

Jerry Simmons, strength and conditioning; born Elkhart, Kan. Linebacker Fort Hays State 1976-77. No pro playing experience. College coach: Fort Hays State 1978, Clemson 1980, Rice 1981-82, Southern California 1983-87. Pro coach: New England Patriots 1988-1990, Cleveland Browns/Baltimore Ravens 1991-98, joined Panthers in 1999.

Jim Skipper, asst. head coach/running backs; born Breaux Bridge, La. Defensive back Whittier College 1971-72. No pro playing experience. College coach: Cal Poly-Pomona 1974-76, San Jose State 1977-78, Pacific 1979, Oregon 1980-82. Pro coach: Philadelphia/Baltimore Stars (USFL) 1983-85, New Orleans Saints 1986-1995, Arizona Cardinals 1996, New York Giants 1997-2000, San Francisco Demons (XFL) 2001 (head coach), joined Panthers in 2002.

Sal Sunseri, defensive line; born Pittsburgh. Linebacker Pittsburgh 1979-1981. College coach: Pittsburgh 1985-1992, Iowa Wesleyan 1993, Louisville 1995-97, Alabama A&M 1998-99, Louisiana State 2000, Michigan State 2001. Pro coach: Joined Panthers in 2002.

Mike Trgovac, defensive coordinator; born Youngstown, Ohio. Defensive lineman Michigan 1977-1980. No pro playing experience. College coach: Michigan 1984-85, Ball State 1986-88, Navy 1989, Colorado State 1990-91, Notre Dame 1992-94. Pro coach: Philadelphia Eagles 1995-98, Green Bay Packers 1999, Washington Redskins 2000-01, joined Panthers in 2002.

Richard Williamson, wide receivers; born Ft. Deposit, Ala. Receiver Alabama 1961-62. No pro playing experience. College coach: Alabama 1963-67, 1970-71, Arkansas 1968-69, 1972-74, Memphis State 1975-1980 (head coach). Pro coach: Kansas City Chiefs 1983-86, Tampa Bay Buccaneers 1987-1991 (interim head coach 1990, head coach 1991), Cincinnati Bengals 1992-94, joined Panthers in 1995.

**National Football Conference
North Division**
Team Colors: Navy Blue, Orange, and
White
Halas Hall at Conway Park
1000 Football Drive
Lake Forest, Illinois 60045
Telephone: (847) 295-6600

2008 SCHEDULE
PRESEASON
Aug. 7　**Kansas City** 7:00
Aug. 16　at Seattle............................6:00
Aug. 21　**San Francisco** 7:00
Aug. 28　at Cleveland 7:30

REGULAR SEASON
Sep. 7　at Indianapolis 8:15
Sep. 14　at Carolina 1:00
Sep. 21　**Tampa Bay** 12:00
Sep. 28　**Philadelphia** 7:15
Oct. 5　at Detroit 1:00
Oct. 12　at Atlanta 1:00
Oct. 19　**Minnesota** 12:00
Oct. 26　BYE
Nov. 2　**Detroit** 12:00
Nov. 9　**Tennessee** 12:00
Nov. 16　at Green Bay 12:00
Nov. 23　at St. Louis 12:00
Nov. 30　at Minnesota * 7:15
Dec. 7　**Jacksonville** 12:00
Dec. 11　**New Orleans** (Thu.) 7:15
Dec. 22　**Green Bay** (Mon.) 7:30
Dec. 28　at Houston 12:00
Sunday night games in Weeks 11-17 subject to change

Stadium: Soldier Field
(opened in 1924)
　•**Capacity:** 61,500
1410 S. Museum Campus Dr.
Chicago, Illinois 60605
Playing Surface: Natural Grass
Training Camp: Olivet-Nazarene Univ.
Bourbonnais, Illinois
60901

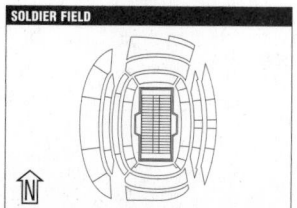

SOLDIER FIELD

CLUB OFFICIALS
Chairman of the Board:
　Michael B. McCaskey
Secretary: Virginia H. McCaskey
President and CEO: Ted Phillips
General Manager: Jerry Angelo
Vice President: Tim McCaskey
Senior Director of Special Projects:
　Pat McCaskey
Senior Director of Ticket Operations:
　George McCaskey
Senior Director of Business Development
　& Alumni Relations: Brian McCaskey
Senior Director of Administration:
　John Bostrom
Senior Director of Finance & Treasurer:
　Karen Murphy
Senior Director of Corporate Sales &
　Marketing: Chris Hibbs
Senior Director of Corporate
　Communications: Scott Hagel
Director of Pro Personnel: Bobby DePaul
Director of College Scouting:
　Greg Gabriel
Senior Director of Football Administration
　and General Counsel: Cliff Stein
Assistant Director of Pro Personnel:
　Morocco Brown
Director of Player Development:
　Isaiah Harris
Director of Community Relations:
　Caroline Guip
Director of Broadcasting & Scoreboard
　Operations: Greg Miller
Media Services Manager: Jim Christman
Media Relations Assistant: Mike Corbo
Media Relations Assistant: Cary Dohman
Director of Video Services: Dean Pope
Assistant Video Directors:
　Dave Hendrickson, Dan Tuohy
Head Athletic Trainer: Tim Bream
Assistant Trainers: Scott DeGraff,
　Chris Hanks
Director of Rehabilitation: Bobby Slater
Head Equipment Manager: Tony Medlin
Assistant Equipment Managers:
　Carl Piekarski, John Perkins
Scouts: Chris Ballard, Marty Barrett,
　Rex Hogan, Ted Monago,
　Mark Sadowski, Jeff Shiver
Director of Human Resources: Ann Quint
Director of Finance: Jake Jones
Director of Security & Safety Services:
　Tom Dillon
Director of Stadium Operations:
　Bryan Pett
Director of Football Systems Technology:
　Brian Wright
Director of Corporate Sales: Ryan Huzjak
Director of Client Services:
　Rebecca Coffey
Director of Stadium Sales & Services:
　Adam Kellner
Director of Creative Services:
　John Conroy
Director of Events & Advertising:
　Julie White
Director of Bears Care: Marge Hamm

COACHING HISTORY
Decatur Staleys 1920,
Chicago Staleys 1921
(693-508-42)
Records include postseason games
1920-29　George Halas 84-31-19
1930-32　Ralph Jones 24-10-7
1933-1942 George Halas* 88-24-4
1942-45　Hunk Anderson-
　　　　　Luke Johnsos**......24-12-2
1946-1955 George Halas 76-43-2
1956-57　John (Paddy) Driscoll......14-10-1
1958-1967 George Halas 76-53-6
1968-1971 Jim Dooley...................20-36-0
1972-74　Abe Gibron..................11-30-1
1975-77　Jack Pardee 20-23-0
1978-1981 Neill Armstrong 30-35-0
1982-1992 Mike Ditka.................112-68-0
1993-98　Dave Wannstedt..........41-57-0
1999-2003 Dick Jauron.................35-46-0
2004-07　Lovie Smith.................38-30-0
　*Retired after five games to enter U.S. Navy
**Co-coaches

PAID ATTENDANCE
Home 485,303　　　　　Away 547,170
Total 1,032,473
Single-game home record,
　66,900 (9/5/93)
Single-season home record, 527,769
　(1999)

2008 DRAFT CHOICES

Round	Name	Pos.	College
1	Chris Williams	T	Vanderbilt
2	Matt Forté	RB	Tulane
3	Earl Bennett	WR	Vanderbilt
	Marcus Harrison	DT	Arkansas
4	Craig Steltz	DB	Louisiana St.
5	Zackary Bowman	DB	Nebraska
	Kellen Davis	TE	Michigan State
7	Ervin Baldwin	DE	Michigan State
	Chester Adams	G	Georgia
	Joey LaRocque	LB	Oregon State
	Kirk Barton	T	Ohio State
	Marcus Monk	WR	Arkansas

2007 TEAM RECORD
PRESEASON (3-1)
Date	Result	Opponent
8/11	W 20-19	at Houston
8/20	W 27-24	at Indianapolis
8/25	W 31-28	San Francisco
8/30	L 9-19	Cleveland

REGULAR SEASON (7-9)
Date	Result	Opponent	Att.
9/9	L 3-14	at San Diego	67,837
9/16	W 20-10	Kansas City	62,095
9/23	L 10-34	Dallas	62,099
9/30	L 27-37	at Detroit	60,811
10/7	W 27-20	at Green Bay	70,904
10/14	L 31-34	Minnesota	62,174
10/21	W 19-16	at Philadelphia	67,806
10/28	L 7-16	Detroit	62,171
11/11	W 17-6	at Oakland	62,715
11/18	L 23-30	at Seattle	68,249
11/25	W 37-34	Denver (OT)	62,148
12/2	L 16-21	New York Giants	62,244
12/6	L 16-24	at Washington	82,213
12/17	L 13-20	at Minnesota	63,800
12/23	W 35-7	Green Bay	62,272
12/30	W 33-25	New Orleans	62,064

(OT) Overtime

SCORE BY PERIODS
Bears	46	97	85	103	3 —	334
Opponents	33	110	68	137	0 —	348

2007 TEAM STATISTICS
	Bears	Opp.
Total First Downs	266	305
Rushing	74	100
Passing	168	185
Penalty	24	20
3rd Down: Made/Att	81/238	73/223
3rd Down Pct.	34.0	32.7
4th Down: Made/Att	7/16	8/13
4th Down Pct.	43.8	61.5
Possession Avg.	28:22	31:38
Total Net Yards	4692	5675
Avg. Per Game	293.3	354.7
Total Plays	1035	1036
Avg. Per Play	4.5	5.5
Net Yards Rushing	1330	1967
Avg. Per Game	83.1	122.9
Total Rushes	423	454
Net Yards Passing	3362	3708
Avg. Per Game	210.1	231.8
Sacked/Yards Lost	43/339	41/245
Gross Yards	3701	3953
Att./Completions	569/327	541/343
Completion Pct.	57.5	63.4
Had Intercepted	21	16
Punts/Average	94/41.9	94/40.5
Net Punting Avg.	94/37.2	94/32.3
Penalties/Yards	111/839	92/670
Fumbles/Ball Lost	34/13	34/17
Touchdowns	34	39
Rushing	8	17
Passing	18	19
Returns	8	3

2007 INDIVIDUAL STATISTICS
PASSING
	Att.	Comp.	Yds.	Pct.	TD	Int.	Tkld.	Rate
Griese	262	161	1803	61.5	10	12	15/114	75.6
Grossman	225	122	1411	54.2	4	7	25/198	66.4
Orton	80	43	478	53.8	3	2	2/12	73.9
Gould	1	0	0	0.0	0	0	0/0	39.6
Peterson	1	1	9	100.0	1	0	0/0	143.8
Hester	0	0	0	—	0	0	1/15	—
Bears	569	327	3701	57.5	18	21	43/339	72.2
Opponents	541	343	3953	63.4	19	16	41/245	84.7

SCORING
	TD R	TD P	TD Rt	PAT	FG	Saf	PTS
Gould	0	0	0	33/33	31/36	0	126
Hester	0	2	6	0/0	0/0	0	48
Berrian	0	5	0	0/0	0/0	0	30
Benson	4	0	0	0/0	0/0	0	24
Clark	0	4	0	0/0	0/0	0	24
Muhammad	0	3	0	0/0	0/0	0	18
Peterson	3	0	0	0/0	0/0	0	18
Olsen	0	2	0	0/0	0/0	0	14
Bradley	0	1	0	0/0	0/0	0	6
Graham	0	0	1	0/0	0/0	0	6
McKie	1	0	0	0/0	0/0	0	6
St. Clair	0	1	0	0/0	0/0	0	6
Urlacher	0	0	1	0/0	0/0	0	6
Bears	8	18	8	33/33	31/36	1	334
Opponents	17	19	3	35/37	25/33	0	348

2-Pt. Conversions: Olsen, Bears 1-1, Opponents 2-2

RUSHING
	No.	Yds	Avg	LG	TD
Benson	196	674	3.4	43t	4
Peterson	151	510	3.4	21	3
Wolfe	31	85	2.7	25	0
Griese	13	28	2.2	9	0
Grossman	14	27	1.9	12	0
McKie	6	17	2.8	6	1
Orton	5	-1	-.2	1	0
Hester	7	-10	-1.4	5	0
Bears	423	1330	3.1	43t	8
Opponents	454	1967	4.3	73t	17

RECEIVING
	No.	Yds	Avg	LG	TD
Berrian	71	951	13.4	59t	5
Peterson	51	420	8.2	30	0
Clark	44	545	12.4	52	4
Muhammad	40	570	14.3	44	3
Olsen	39	391	10.0	31	2
Hester	20	299	15.0	81t	2
Davis	17	165	9.7	36	0
Benson	17	123	7.2	19	0
Wolfe	9	117	13.0	33	0
McKie	9	33	3.7	10	0
Bradley	6	71	11.8	19t	1
Gilmore	3	14	4.7	7	0
St. Clair	1	2	2.0	2t	1
Bears	327	3701	11.3	81t	18
Opponents	343	3953	11.5	71	19

INTERCEPTIONS
	No.	Yds	Avg	LG	TD
Urlacher	5	101	20.2	85t	1
Tillman	3	24	8.0	20	0
D. Manning	2	33	16.5	33	0
McGowan	2	5	2.5	5	0
Vasher	1	34	34.0	34	0
M. Brown	1	27	27.0	27	0
A. Brown	1	7	7.0	7	0
Archuleta	1	4	4.0	4	0
Bears	16	235	14.7	85t	1
Opponents	21	285	13.6	64t	2

PUNTING
	No.	Yds	Avg	In 20	LG
Maynard	88	3682	41.8	27	56
Johnson	4	199	49.8	1	60
Gould	2	53	26.5	1	28
Bears	94	3934	41.9	29	60
Opponents	94	3808	40.5	23	64

PUNT RETURNS
	Ret	FC	Yds	Avg	LG	TD
Hester	42	6	651	15.5	89t	4
Idonije	1	0	0	0.0	0	0
McGowan	1	0	0	0.0	0	0
Bears	44	6	651	14.8	89t	4
Opponents	40	19	236	5.9	25	0

KICKOFF RETURNS
	No.	Yds	Avg	LG	TD
Hester	43	934	21.7	97t	2
Davis	12	168	14.0	34	0
Gilmore	3	25	8.3	15	0
D. Manning	3	61	20.3	21	0
Peterson	3	17	5.7	14	0
Idonije	2	2	1.0	2	0
Wolfe	1	27	27.0	27	0
Bears	67	1234	18.4	97t	2
Opponents	71	1370	19.3	65	1

FIELD GOALS
	1-19	20-29	30-39	40-49	50+
Gould	0/0	7/7	12/13	12/14	0/2
Bears	0/0	7/7	12/13	12/14	0/2
Opponents	0/0	7/9	6/9	9/12	3/3

SACKS
	No.
Ogunleye	9.0
Harris	8.0
Anderson	5.0
Urlacher	5.0
A. Brown	4.5
Archuleta	2.0
Briggs	2.0
R. Manning	1.0
Vasher	1.0
Walker	1.0
Williams	1.0
(group)	1.0
Adams	0.5
Bears	41.0
Opponents	43.0

RECORD HOLDERS
INDIVIDUAL RECORDS—CAREER

Category	Name	Performance
Rushing (Yds.)	Walter Payton, 1975-1987	16,726
Passing (Yds.)	Sid Luckman, 1939-1950	14,686
Passing (TDs)	Sid Luckman, 1939-1950	137
Receiving (No.)	Walter Payton, 1975-1987	492
Receiving (Yds.)	Johnny Morris, 1958-1967	5,059
Interceptions	Gary Fencik, 1976-1987	38
Punting (Avg.)	George Gulyanics, 1947-1952	44.5
Punt Return (Avg.)	Devin Hester, 2006-07	*14.1
Kickoff Return (Avg.)	Gale Sayers, 1965-1971	*30.6
Field Goals	Kevin Butler, 1985-1995	243
Touchdowns (Tot.)	Walter Payton, 1975-1987	125
Points	Kevin Butler, 1985-1995	1,116

INDIVIDUAL RECORDS—SINGLE SEASON

Category	Name	Performance
Rushing (Yds.)	Walter Payton, 1977	1,852
Passing (Yds.)	Erik Kramer, 1995	3,838
Passing (TDs)	Erik Kramer, 1995	29
Receiving (No.)	Marty Booker, 2001	100
Receiving (Yds.)	Marcus Robinson, 1999	1,400
Interceptions	Mark Carrier, 1990	10
Punting (Avg.)	Bobby Joe Green, 1963	46.5
Punt Return (Avg.)	Harry Clark, 1943	15.8
Kickoff Return (Avg.)	Gale Sayers, 1967	37.7
Field Goals	Robbie Gould, 2006	32
Touchdowns (Tot.)	Gale Sayers, 1965	22
Points	Kevin Butler, 1985	144

INDIVIDUAL RECORDS—SINGLE GAME

Category	Name	Performance
Rushing (Yds.)	Walter Payton, 11-20-77	275
Passing (Yds.)	Johnny Lujack, 12-11-49	468
Passing (TDs)	Sid Luckman, 11-14-43	*7
Receiving (No.)	Jim Keane, 10-23-49	14
Receiving (Yds.)	Harlon Hill, 10-31-54	214
Interceptions	Many times	3
	Last time by Mark Carrier, 12-9-90	
Field Goals	Roger LeClerc, 12-3-61	5
	Mac Percival, 10-20-68	5
Touchdowns (Tot.)	Gale Sayers, 12-12-65	*6
Points	Gale Sayers, 12-12-65	36

*NFL Record

2008 VETERAN ROSTER

No.	Name	Pos.	Ht.	Wt.	Age	NFL Exp.	College	Hometown	How Acq.	'07 Games/ Starts
95	Adams, Anthony	DT	6-0	300	28	6	Penn State	Detroit, Mich.	UFA(SF)-'07	11/8
97	Anderson, Mark	DE	6-4	255	25	3	Alabama	Tulsa, Okla.	D5-'06	14/14
73	Bazuin, Dan	DE	6-3	260	25	2	Central Michigan	McBain, Mich.	D2-'07	0*
67	Beekman, Josh	G/C	6-2	310	25	2	Boston College	Amsterdam, N.Y.	D4-'07	1/0
32	Benson, Cedric	RB	5-11	220	25	4	Texas	Midland, Texas	D1-'05	11/11
86	Booker, Marty	WR	6-0	210	32	10	Louisiana-Monroe	Jonesboro, La.	FA-'08	15/15*
16	Bradley, Mark	WR	6-2	198	26	4	Oklahoma	Pine Bluff, Ark.	D2-'05	15/0
55	Briggs, Lance	LB	6-1	240	27	6	Arizona	Sacramento, Calif.	D3-'03	14/14
96	Brown, Alex	DE	6-3	260	29	7	Florida	White Springs, Fla.	D4-'02	16/2
30	Brown, Mike	S	5-10	207	30	9	Nebraska	Scottsdale, Ariz.	D2-'00	1/1
88	Clark, Desmond	TE	6-3	249	31	10	Wake Forest	Lakeland, Fla.	UFA(Mia)-'03	16/16
81	Davis, Rashied	WR	5-9	187	29	4	San Jose State	Granada Hills, Calif.	UFA(AFL)-'05	16/1
98	Dvoracek, Dusty	DT	6-3	303	25	3	Oklahoma	Lake Dallas, Texas	D3-'06	1/1
63	Garza, Roberto	G/C	6-2	310	29	8	Texas A&M-Kingsville	Rio Hondo, Texas	UFA(Atl)-'05	16/16
43	Gattis, Josh	S	6-1	207	24	2	Wake Forest	Durham, N.C.	FA-'07	4/0
9	Gould, Robbie	K	6-0	183	26	4	Penn State	Lock Haven, Pa.	FA-'05	16/0
21	Graham, Corey	CB	6-0	195	23	2	New Hampshire	Buffalo, N.Y.	D5b-'07	13/0
8	Grossman, Rex	QB	6-1	217	28	6	Florida	Bloomington, Ind.	D1b-'03	8/7
91	Harris, Tommie	DT	6-3	295	25	5	Oklahoma	Killeen, Texas	D1-'04	16/13
83	Hass, Mike	WR	6-1	206	25	2	Oregon State	Portland, Ore.	FA-'06	1/0
23	Hester, Devin	KR/PR	5-11	186	25	3	Miami	Riviera Beach, Fla.	D2b-'06	16/0
92	Hillenmeyer, Hunter	LB	6-4	238	27	6	Vanderbilt	Nashville, Tenn.	FA-'03	16/14
71	Idonije, Israel	DL	6-6	275	27	5	Manitoba	Lagos, Nigeria	FA-'03	16/3
57	Kreutz, Olin	C	6-2	292	31	11	Washington	Honolulu, Hawaii	D3-'98	16/16
80	Lloyd, Brandon	WR	6-0	200	27	6	Illinois	Blue Springs, Mo.	FA-'08	8/1*
65	Mannelly, Patrick	LS	6-5	265	33	11	Duke	Atlanta, Ga.	D6b-'98	16/0
38	Manning, Danieal	S	5-11	198	26	3	Abilene Christian	Corsicana, Texas	D2a-'06	16/15
24	Manning, Jr., Ricky	CB	5-9	193	27	6	UCLA	Fresno, Calif.	RFA(Car)-'06	16/5
4	Maynard, Brad	P	6-1	188	34	12	Ball State	Sheridan, Ind.	UFA(NYG)-'01	15/0
26	McBride, Trumaine	CB	5-9	185	22	2	Mississippi	Clarksdale, Miss.	D7a-'07	16/9
58	McClover, Darrell	LB	6-1	226	27	5	Miami	Coconut Creek, Fla.	FA-'06	5/0
36	McGowan, Brandon	S	5-11	207	24	4	Maine	Jersey City, N.J.	FA-'05	14/9
37	McKie, Jason	FB	5-11	245	28	7	Temple	Gulf Breeze, Fla.	W(Dall)-'03	16/11
60	Metcalf, Terrence	G	6-4	318	30	7	Mississippi	Clarksdale, Miss.	D3-'02	16/5
68	Oakley, Anthony	C/G	6-4	298	27	3	Western Kentucky	Houston, Texas	FA-'05	3/0
93	Ogunleye, Adewale	DE	6-4	260	31	8	Indiana	Staten Island, N.Y.	T(Mia)-'04	16/16
62	Okwo, Michael	LB	5-11	232	23	2	Stanford	Redondo Beach, Calif.	D3b-'07	0*
82	Olsen, Greg	TE	6-5	254	23	2	Miami	Wayne, N.J.	D1-'07	14/4
18	Orton, Kyle	QB	6-4	217	25	4	Purdue	Runnels, Iowa	D4-'05	3/3
44	Payne, Kevin	S	6-0	212	24	2	Louisiana-Monroe	Junction City, Ark.	D5a-'07	3/1
29	Peterson, Adrian	RB	5-10	210	29	7	Georgia Southern	Alachua, Fla.	D6a-'02	16/5
39	Polite, Lousaka	FB	6-0	242	26	4	Pittsburgh	Woodland Hills, Pa.	FA-'07	5/0
47	Pope, P.J.	RB	5-9	212	24	2	Bowling Green	Fairfield, Ohio	FA-'07	0*
84	Rideau, Brandon	WR	6-3	200	25	2	Kansas	Beaumont, Texas	FA-'06	0*
53	Roach, Nick	LB	6-0	234	23	2	Northwestern	Milwaukee, Wis.	FA-'07	3/0
48	Runnels, J.D.	FB	5-11	240	26	3	Oklahoma	Midwest City, Okla.	D6a-'06	0*
78	St. Clair, John	T	6-5	315	31	9	Virginia	Roanoke, Va.	FA-'05	16/5
76	Tait, John	T	6-6	312	33	10	Brigham Young	Tempe, Ariz.	RFA(KC)-'04	15/15
33	Tillman, Charles	CB	6-1	196	27	6	Louisiana-Lafayette	Copperas Cove, Texas	D2-'03	15/15
54	Urlacher, Brian	LB	6-4	258	30	9	New Mexico	Lovington, N.M.	D1-'00	16/16
31	Vasher, Nathan	CB	5-10	183	26	5	Texas	Texarkana, Texas	D4a-'04	4/2
52	Williams, Jamar	LB	6-0	237	24	3	Arizona State	Houston, Texas	D4-'06	16/1
59	Wilson, Rod	LB	6-2	230	26	3	South Carolina	Cross, S.C.	D7-'05	15/0
25	Wolfe, Garrett	RB	5-7	186	24	2	Northern Illinois	Chicago, Ill.	D3a-'07	13/0

* Bazuin missed '07 season because of injury; Booker played 15 games with Miami in '07; Lloyd played 8 games with Washington; Okwo missed '07 season because of injury; Pope last active with Green Bay in '06; Rideau inactive 1 game; Runnels missed '07 season because of injury.

Players lost through free agency (3): LB Brendon Ayanbadejo (Balt; 16 games in '07), WR Bernard Berrian (Minn; 16), TE John Gilmore (TB; 15), .

Also played with Bears in '07—S Adam Archuleta (15 games), G Ruben Brown (8), DT Antonio Garay (6), QB Brian Griese (7), CB Ade Jimoh (6), P Dirk Johnson (1), DT Jimmy Kennedy (3), T Fred Miller (15), WR Muhsin Muhammad (16), DT Babatunde Oshinowo (1), DT Matt Toeaina (3), DT Darwin Walker (13).

2008 FIRST-YEAR ROSTER

Name	Pos.	Ht.	Wt.	Age	College	Hometown	How Acq.
Adams, Chester	G	6-4	335	23	Georgia	Luverne, Ala.	D7b
Atterberry, Zacrey	P	6-2	186	24	Lindenwood	Lewisville, Texas	FA
Baldwin, Ervin	DE	6-2	270	22	Michigan State	Oglethorpe, Ga.	D7a
Balogh, Cody	T	6-7	328	22	Montana	Steilacoom, Wash.	FA
Barton, Kirk	T	6-5	310	23	Ohio State	Massillon, Ohio	D7d
Bennett, Earl	WR	6-0	209	21	Vanderbilt	Birmingham, Ala.	D3a
Bowman, Zackary	CB	6-1	197	23	Nebraska	Anchorage, Alaska	D5a
Brown, Trey	DB	5-9	189	23	UCLA	Overland Park, Kan.	FA
Clermond, Joe	DE	6-3	250	23	Pittsburgh	Tampa, Fla.	FA
Davis, Kellen	TE	6-7	262	22	Michigan State	Adrian, Mich.	D5b
Forté, Matt	RB	6-2	222	22	Tulane	Slidell, La.	D2
Hamilton, Curtis	WR	6-0	195	22	Western Kentucky	West Paducah, Kent.	FA
Hanie, Caleb	QB	6-2	236	22	Colorado State	Forney, Texas	FA
Harrison, Marcus	DT	6-3	310	24	Arkansas	Little Rock, Ark.	D3b
Hill, Nick	QB	6-3	210	23	Southern Illinois	DuQuoin, Ill.	FA
LaRocque, Joey	LB	6-2	226	22	Oregon State	Agoura, Calif.	D7c
Lawrence, Matthew	RB	6-1	210	23	Massachusetts	Bloomfield, Conn.	FA
Lee, Gerard	DE	6-1	280	22	Oregon State	New Orleans, La.	FA
Longest, Shane	K	5-11	180	22	St. Xavier	Wilmington, Ill.	FA
Majors, Leslie	CB	5-10	175	22	Indiana	South Holland, Ill.	FA
Mines, Fontel (1)	TE	6-4	244	23	Virginia	Richmond, Va.	FA-'07
Monk, Marcus	WR	6-4	222	22	Arkansas	Lepanto, Ark.	D7e
Osborn, Nick	DE	6-4	260	23	San Diego State	Kensington, Calif.	FA
Pakulak, Glenn (1)	P	6-3	220	28	Kentucky	Lapper, Mich.	FA
Peters, Leonard (1)	S	6-1	199	26	Hawai'i	Kahuku, Hawai'i	FA-'07
Poles, Ryan	G	6-4	290	22	Boston College	Canandaigua, N.Y.	FA
Reed, Tyler (1)	G	6-4	307	25	Penn State	Jefferson Borough, Pa.	D6b-'06
Steltz, Craig	S	6-1	210	22	Louisiana State	Metairie, La.	D4
Stone, Marcus	TE	6-2	239	23	NC State	Steelton, Pa.	FA
Toeaina, Matt (1)	DT	6-2	311	23	Oregon	Utulei, American Samoa	FA-'07
Williams, Chris	T	6-6	315	23	Vanderbilt	Glynn, La.	D1

The term NFL Rookie is defined as a player who is in his first season of professional football and has not been on the roster of another professional football team for any regular-season or postseason games. A Rookie is designated by an "R" on NFL rosters. Players who have been active in another professional football league or players who have NFL experience, including either preseason training camp or being on an Active List or Inactive List, or on Reserve/Injured or Reserve/Physically Unable to Perform for fewer than six regular-season games, are termed NFL First-Year Players. An NFL First-Year Player is designated by a "1" on NFL rosters. Thereafter, a player is credited with an additional year of experience for each season in which he accumulates six games on the Active List or Inactive List, or on Reserve/Injured or Reserve/Physically Unable to Perform.

Log on to www.chicagobears.com for an up-to-date roster; Age listed is as of September 4, 2008.

COACHING STAFF

**Head Coach,
Lovie Smith**

Pro Career: Named the thirteenth head coach in Chicago Bears history on January 15, 2004. Smith enters his fifth season as the head coach of the Chicago Bears with a regular season coaching record of 36-28 (.563). Those 36 wins are tied with Hall of Famer Mike Ditka for second-most wins in a coach's first four seasons with the franchise, one behind Hall of Famer George Halas. Smith also has a 2-2 postseason record, including an NFC Championship and the Bears first Super Bowl appearance in 21 years (2006), to give him the third-most playoff victories in team history behind the six of Halas and Ditka. Registering a career-high 13 wins in 2006 to tie predecessor Dick Jauron for the most victories by a Bears head coach in his third season, Smith led Chicago to home-field advantage in the NFC Playoffs and the team's first NFC Championship since its Super Bowl season of 1985. A year earlier, Smith earned the 2005 AP NFL Coach of the Year Award after turning a 1-3 start to the season into 11 victories, the most by a second-year coach in club annals, and the second seed in the NFC Playoffs. Fueled by an eight-game win streak, Smith led a worst-to-first revival in the NFC North division as the Bears six-win improvement from the previous season was tied for the biggest in the NFL in 2005. In Smith's first season, Chicago posted a 5-11 record. The Bears rank second in the NFL from 2004-07 with 140 takeaways and 14 touchdowns scored via defensive return. Smith came to Chicago from St. Louis (2001-03), where he served as defensive coordinator. In 2001 he helped the Rams return to the Super Bowl after missing the playoffs the previous season. Smith previously coached the linebackers for the Tampa Bay Buccaneers (1996-2000). Career record: 38-30.

Background: Played at Tulsa (1976-79), where he was a linebacker before moving to strong safety and earning two-time All-America and three-time All-Missouri Conference defensive back honors. Began his coaching career at his hometown high school (Big Sandy, Texas) in 1980 before moving to Cascia Hall Prep in Tulsa the following year. Two years later Smith began coaching collegiately at Tulsa (1983-86), Wisconsin (1987), Arizona State (1988-1991), Kentucky (1992), Tennessee (1993-94), and Ohio State (1995).

Personal: Age 50, born in Gladewater, Texas. Lovie and his wife MaryAnne have three sons—Mikal, Matthew and Miles and twin grandsons—Malachi and Noah.

ASSISTANT COACHES

Jim Arthur, strength and conditioning assistant; Attended Springfield (Mass.) College. No college or pro playing experience. College coach: Springfield (Mass.)

College 2000, Louisiana Tech 2001, Boston College 2002. Pro coach: Joined Bears in 2005.

Bob Babich, defensive coordinator; born Aliquippa, Pa. Linebacker Mesa (Colo.) C.C. 1979-1980, Tulsa 1981-82. No pro playing experience. College coach: Tulsa 1984-87, 1990, Wisconsin 1988-89, Bowling Green 1991, East Carolina 1992-93, Pittsburgh 1994-96, North Dakota State 1997-2002 (head coach). Pro coach: St. Louis Rams 2003, joined Bears in 2004.

Rob Boras, tight ends; born Glen Ellyn, Ill. Center DePauw 1988-1991. No pro playing experience. College coach: DePauw 1992-93, Texas 1994-97, Benedictine 1998 (head coach), Nevada-Las Vegas 1999-2003. Pro coach: Joined Bears in 2004.

Luke Butkus, offensive assistant/asst. offensive line; born Steger, Ill. Center Illinois 1998-2001. Pro center San Diego Chargers 2002-03. College coach: Oregon 2005-06. Pro coach: Joined Bears in 2007.

Gill Byrd, asst. defensive backs/safeties; born San Francisco. Cornerback San Jose State 1979-1982. Pro cornerback San Diego Chargers 1983-1992. Pro coach: St. Louis Rams 2003-05, joined Bears in 2006.

Darryl Drake, wide receivers; born Louisville, Ky. Wide receiver Western Kentucky 1975-78. Pro wide receiver Washington Redskins 1979, Ottawa Rough Riders (CFL) 1981, Cincinnati Bengals 1983. College coach: Western Kentucky 1983-1991, Georgia 1992-96, Baylor 1997, Texas 1998-2003. Pro coach: Joined Bears in 2004.

Brick Haley, defensive line; born Gadsen, Ala. Linebacker Alabama A&M 1984-88. No pro playing experience. College coach: Arkansas 1990, Austin Peay 1991-93, Troy State 1994-96, Houston 1997, Clemson 1998, Baylor 1999-2001, Georgia Tech 2002-03, Mississippi State 2004-06. Pro coach: Joined Bears in 2007.

Pep Hamilton, quarterbacks; born Charlotte, N.C. Quarterback Howard 1993-96. No pro playing experience. College coach: Howard 1997-2002. Pro coach: New York Jets 2003-05, San Francisco 49ers 2006, joined Bears in 2007.

Harry Hiestand, offensive line; born Malvern, Pa. Offensive lineman Springfield College 1978-79, East Stroudsburg 1980. No pro playing experience. College coach: East Stroudsburg 1981-85, Pennsylvania 1986, Southern California 1987, Toledo 1988, Cincinnati 1989-1993, Missouri 1994-96, Illinois 1997-2004. Pro coach: Joined Bears in 2005.

Rusty Jones, strength and conditioning coordinator; Attended Springfield (Mass.) College. No college or pro playing experience. College coach: Springfield (Mass.) College 1979-1982. Pro coach: Buffalo

Bills 1985-2004, joined Bears in 2005.

Lloyd Lee, linebackers; born Minneapolis. Safety Dartmouth 1994-97. Pro safety San Diego Chargers 1998-99. Pro coach: Tampa Bay Buccaneers (scout) 2001-03, joined Bears in 2004.

Charles London, offensive assistant/asst. wide receivers; born Dunwoody, Ga. Running back Duke 1994-96. No pro playing experience. College coach: Duke 2004-06. Pro coach: Joined Bears in 2007.

Tim Spencer, running backs; born Martin Ferry, Ohio. Running back Ohio State 1979-1982. Pro running back Chicago Blitz (USFL) 1983, Arizona Wranglers (USFL) 1984, Memphis Showboats (USFL) 1985, San Diego Chargers 1985-1990. College coach: Ohio State 1994-2003. Pro coach: Joined Bears in 2004.

Chris Tabor, asst. special teams; born St. Joseph, Mo. Quarterback Benedictine College 1989-1992. No pro playing experience. College coach: Hutchinson (Kan.) C.C. 1994, Central Methodist College 1995-96, Missouri 1997-2000, Culver-Stockton College 2001 (head coach), Utah State 2002-04, Western Michigan 2005-07. Pro coach: Joined Bears in 2008.

Dave Toub, special teams coordinator; born Ossining, N.Y. Offensive lineman Springfield College 1980-81, Texas-El Paso 1983-84. No pro playing experience. College coach: Texas El-Paso 1987-89, Missouri 1989-2000. Pro coach: Philadelphia Eagles 2001-03, joined Bears in 2004.

Ron Turner, offensive coordinator; born Martinez, Calif. Wide receiver Diablo Valley (Calif.) C.C. 1973-74, Pacific 1975-76. No pro playing experience. College coach: Pacific 1977, Arizona 1978-1980, Northwestern 1981-82, Pittsburgh 1983-84, Southern California 1985-87, Texas A&M 1988, Stanford 1989-1991, San Jose State 1992 (head coach), Illinois 1997-2004 (head coach). Pro coach: Chicago Bears 1993-96, re-joined Bears in 2005.

Eric Washington, defensive assistant/asst. defensive line; born Shreveport, La. Grambling State 1989-1991. No pro playing experience. College coach: Texas A&M 1997-98, Ohio 2001-03, Northwestern 2004-07. Pro coach: Joined Bears in 2008.

Steven Wilks, defensive backs; born Charlotte. Defensive back Appalachian State 1987-1991. Pro defensive back/wide receiver Charlotte Rage (AFL) 1993. College coach: Johnson C. Smith 1995-96, Savannah State 1997-99, Illinois State 2000, Appalachian State 2001, East Tennessee State 2002, Bowling Green State 2003, Notre Dame 2004, Washington 2005. Pro coach: Joined Bears in 2006.

**National Football Conference
East Division
Team Colors:** Royal Blue, Metallic Silver
Blue, and White
**Cowboys Center
One Cowboys Parkway
Irving, Texas 75063
Telephone:** (972) 556-9900

**2008 SCHEDULE
PRESEASON**
Aug. 9   at San Diego 7:00
Aug. 16 at Denver............................7:00
Aug. 22 **Houston** 7:00
Aug. 28 **Minnesota** 7:00

REGULAR SEASON
Sep. 7   at Cleveland 4:15
Sep. 15 **Philadelphia** (Mon.) 7:30
Sep. 21 at Green Bay 7:15
Sep. 28 **Washington** 3:15
Oct. 5   **Cincinnati** 3:15
Oct. 12 at Arizona 1:15
Oct. 19 at St. Louis 12:00
Oct. 26 **Tampa Bay** 12:00
Nov. 2   at N.Y. Giants....................4:15
Nov. 9   BYE
Nov. 16 at Washington * 8:15
Nov. 23 **San Francisco** 12:00
Nov. 27 **Seattle** (Thu.).....................3:15
Dec. 7   at Pittsburgh 4:15
Dec. 14 **N.Y. Giants** * 7:15
Dec. 20 **Baltimore** (Sat.) 7:15
Dec. 28 at Philadelphia 1:00
Sunday night games in Weeks 11-17 subject to change
Stadium: Texas Stadium (opened in 1971)
•**Capacity:** 65,529
2401 E. Airport Freeway
Irving, Texas 75062
Playing Surface: Sportfield Realgrass
Training Camp: Marriott Residence Inn
Oxnard, California 93030

TEXAS STADIUM

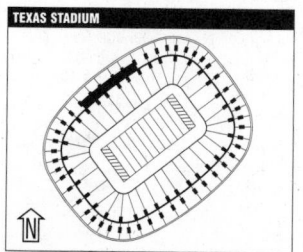

CLUB OFFICIALS
Owner/President/General Manager:
Jerry Jones
Chief Operating Officer/Executive Vice
President/Director of Player Personnel:
Stephen Jones
Vice President/Director of Charities and
Special Events: Charlotte Anderson
Chief Sales and Marketing Officer/Vice
President: Jerry Jones Jr.
CFO: George Mitchell
Vice President, Sales and Marketing:
Greg McElroy
General Counsel: Alec Scheiner
Director of Public Relations:
Rich Dalrymple
Director of Corporate Communications:
Brett Daniels
Director of Community Relations:
Emily Robbins
Assistant Director of College Scouting:
Tom Ciskowski
Director of Operations: Bruce Mays
Director of Player Development:
Bryan Wansley
Chief Diversity Officer:
Vincent Thompson
Director of Information Technology:
Peter Walsh
Director of Broadcasting: Scott Purcel
Internet Director: Derek Eagleton
Director of Ticket Operations:
Carol Padgett
Head Athletic Trainer: Jim Maurer
Equipment Manager: Mike McCord
Video Director: Robert Blackwell
Cheerleader Director: Kelli Finglass

COACHING HISTORY
(446-326-6)
Records include postseason games
1960-1988 Tom Landry 270-178-6
1989-1993 Jimmy Johnson 51-37-0
1994-97   Barry Switzer 45-26-0
1998-99   Chan Gailey 18-16-0
2000-02   Dave Campo 15-33-0
2003-06   Bill Parcells 34-32-0
2007   Wade Phillips 13-4-0

PAID ATTENDANCE
Home 500,479   Away 574,220
Total 1,074,699
Single-game home record,
65,180 (11/12/95)
Single-season home record,
518,167 (1995)

2008 DRAFT CHOICES

Round	Name	Pos.	College
1	Felix Jones	RB	Arkansas
	Mike Jenkins	DB	South Florida
2	Martellus Bennett	TE	Texas A&M
4	Tashard Choice	RB	Georgia Tech
5	Orlando Scandrick	DB	Boise State
6	Erik Walden	LB	Middle Tenn. St.

DALLAS COWBOYS

2007 TEAM RECORD
PRESEASON (2-2)

Date	Result	Opponent
8/9	W 23-10	Indianapolis
8/18	W 31-20	Denver
8/25	L 16-28	at Houston
8/30	L 14-23	at Minnesota

REGULAR SEASON (13-3)

Date	Result	Opponent	Att.
9/9	W 45-35	N.Y. Giants	63,031
9/16	W 37-20	at Miami	71,615
9/23	W 34-10	at Chicago	62,099
9/30	W 35-7	St. Louis	62,866
10/8	W 25-24	at Buffalo	71,575
10/14	L 27-48	New England	63,984
10/21	W 24-14	Minnesota	63,432
11/4	W 38-17	at Philadelphia	67,688
11/11	W 31-20	at N.Y. Giants	78,964
11/18	W 28-23	Washington	63,706
11/22	W 34-3	New York Jets	63,315
11/29	W 37-27	Green Bay	64,167
12/9	W 28-27	at Detroit	62,759
12/16	L 6-10	Philadelphia	63,777
12/22	W 20-13	at Carolina	73,860
12/30	L 6-27	at Washington	90,910

POSTSEASON (0-1)

Date	Result	Opponent	Att.
1/13	L 17-21	N.Y. Giants	63,660

SCORE BY PERIODS

Cowboys	61	147	117	130	0	—	455
Opponents	88	97	64	76	0	—	325

2007 TEAM STATISTICS

	Cowboys	Opp.
Total First Downs	322	304
Rushing	83	86
Passing	217	195
Penalty	22	23
3rd Down: Made/Att	84/199	85/216
3rd Down Pct.	42.2	39.4
4th Down: Made/Att	10/14	10/18
4th Down Pct.	71.4	55.6
Possession Avg.	30:34	29:27
Total Net Yards	5851	4922
Avg. Per Game	365.7	307.6
Total Plays	975	1008
Avg. Per Play	6.0	4.9
Net Yards Rushing	1746	1513
Avg. Per Game	109.1	94.6
Total Rushes	419	381
Net Yards Passing	4105	3409
Avg. Per Game	256.6	213.1
Sacked/Yards Lost	25/185	46/319
Gross Yards	4290	3728
Att./Completions	531/342	581/342
Completion Pct.	64.4	58.9
Had Intercepted	19	19
Punts/Average	63/47.1	73/45.0
Net Punting Avg.	63/38.5	73/39.1
Penalties/Yards	104/815	85/785
Fumbles/Ball Lost	21/5	26/10
Touchdowns	54	36
Rushing	14	12
Passing	36	19
Returns	4	5

2007 INDIVIDUAL STATISTICS

PASSING

PASSING	Att.	Comp.	Yds.	Pct.	TD	Int.	Tkld.	Rate
Romo	520	335	4211	64.4	36	19	24/176	97.4
B. Johnson	11	7	79	63.6	0	0	1/9	85.0
Cowboys	531	342	4290	64.4	36	19	25/185	97.1
Opponents	581	342	3728	58.9	19	19	46/319	75.1

SCORING

SCORING	TD R	TD P	TD Rt	PAT	FG	Saf	PTS
Folk	0	0	0	53/53	26/31	0	131
Owens	0	15	0	0/0	0/0	0	90
Barber	10	2	0	0/0	0/0	0	72
Crayton	0	7	0	0/0	0/0	0	42
Witten	0	7	0	0/0	0/0	0	42
Curtis	0	3	0	0/0	0/0	0	18
J. Jones	2	0	0	0/0	0/0	0	12
Romo	2	0	0	0/0	0/0	0	12
Fasano	0	1	0	0/0	0/0	0	6
Hatcher	0	0	1	0/0	0/0	0	6
Henry	0	0	1	0/0	0/0	0	6
Hurd	0	1	0	0/0	0/0	0	6
Newman	0	0	1	0/0	0/0	0	6
Watkins	0	0	1	0/0	0/0	0	6
Cowboys	14	36	4	53/53	26/31	0	455
Opponents	12	19	5	34/34	25/31	0	325

2-Pt. Conversions: Cowboys 0-1,
Opponents 0-2

RUSHING

RUSHING	No.	Yds	Avg	LG	TD
Barber	204	975	4.8	54	10
J. Jones	164	588	3.6	25	2
Romo	31	129	4.2	17	2
Thompson	14	54	3.9	23	0
Owens	1	5	5.0	5	0
B. Johnson	5	-5	-1.0	0	0
Cowboys	419	1746	4.2	54	14
Opponents	381	1513	4.0	62t	12

RECEIVING

RECEIVING	No.	Yds	Avg	LG	TD
Witten	96	1145	11.9	53	7
Owens	81	1355	16.7	52t	15
Crayton	50	697	13.9	59t	7
Barber	44	282	6.4	29	2
J. Jones	23	203	8.8	24	0
Hurd	19	314	16.5	51t	1
Fasano	14	143	10.2	26t	1
Anderson	6	55	9.2	17	0
Austin	5	76	15.2	35	0
Curtis	3	18	6.0	15t	3
Hoyte	1	2	2.0	2	0
Cowboys	342	4290	12.5	59t	36
Opponents	342	3728	10.9	69t	19

INTERCEPTIONS

INTERCEPTIONS	No.	Yds	Avg	LG	TD
Henry	6	81	13.5	28t	1
Hamlin	5	93	18.6	35	0
Newman	4	129	32.3	70	1
Williams	2	10	5.0	10	0
Reeves	1	18	18.0	18	0
Watkins	1	0	0.0	0	0
Cowboys	19	331	17.4	70	2
Opponents	19	191	10.1	38	2

PUNTING

PUNTING	No.	Yds.	Avg.	In 20	LG
McBriar	63	2970	47.1	17	64
Cowboys	63	2970	47.1	17	64
Opponents	73	3284	45.0	27	66

PUNT RETURNS

PUNT RETURNS	Ret	FC	Yds	Avg	LG	TD
Crayton	22	20	201	9.1	49	0
Newman	4	1	26	6.5	13	0
Cowboys	26	21	227	8.7	49	0
Opponents	35	9	406	11.6	85t	1

KICKOFF RETURNS

KICKOFF RETURNS	No.	Yds	Avg	LG	TD
Austin	24	612	25.5	60	0
Thompson	20	471	23.6	72	0
N. Jones	6	122	20.3	27	0
Stanback	3	78	26.0	35	0
Curtis	3	27	9.0	16	0
Crayton	3	26	8.7	13	0
McQuistan	1	12	12.0	12	0
Anderson	1	10	10.0	10	0
Cowboys	61	1358	22.3	72	0
Opponents	86	1979	23.0	103t	1

FIELD GOALS

FIELD GOALS	1-19	20-29	30-39	40-49	50+
Folk	0/0	10/12	7/7	7/7	2/5
Cowboys	0/0	10/12	7/7	7/7	2/5
Opponents	1/1	8/9	5/6	10/12	1/3

SACKS

SACKS	No.
Ware	14.0
Ellis	12.5
Canty	3.5
James	3.0
Ratliff	3.0
Spencer	3.0
Hatcher	2.0
T. Johnson	2.0
Spears	2.0
N. Jones	1.0
Cowboys	46.0
Opponents	25.0

RECORD HOLDERS
INDIVIDUAL RECORDS—CAREER

Category	Name	Performance
Rushing (Yds.)	Emmitt Smith, 1990-2002	*17,162
Passing (Yds.)	Troy Aikman, 1989-2000	32,942
Passing (TDs)	Troy Aikman, 1989-2000	165
Receiving (No.)	Michael Irvin, 1988-1999	750
Receiving (Yds.)	Michael Irvin, 1988-1999	11,904
Interceptions	Mel Renfro, 1964-1977	52
Punting (Avg.)	Mat McBriar, 2004-07	44.7
Punt Return (Avg.)	Deion Sanders, 1995-99	13.3
Kickoff Return (Avg.)	Mel Renfro, 1964-1977	26.4
Field Goals	Rafael Septien, 1978-1986	162
Touchdowns (Tot.)	Emmitt Smith, 1990-2002	164
Points	Emmitt Smith, 1990-2002	986

INDIVIDUAL RECORDS—SINGLE SEASON

Category	Name	Performance
Rushing (Yds.)	Emmitt Smith, 1995	1,773
Passing (Yds.)	Tony Romo, 2007	4,211
Passing (TDs)	Tony Romo, 2007	36
Receiving (No.)	Michael Irvin, 1995	111
Receiving (Yds.)	Michael Irvin, 1995	1,603
Interceptions	Everson Walls, 1981	11
Punting (Avg.)	Mat McBriar, 2006	48.2
Punt Return (Avg.)	Bob Hayes, 1968	20.8
Kickoff Return (Avg.)	Mel Renfro, 1965	30.0
Field Goals	Richie Cunningham, 1997	34
Touchdowns (Tot.)	Emmitt Smith, 1995	25
Points	Emmitt Smith, 1995	150

INDIVIDUAL RECORDS—SINGLE GAME

Category	Name	Performance
Rushing (Yds.)	Emmitt Smith, 10-31-93	237
Passing (Yds.)	Don Meredith, 11-10-63	460
Passing (TDs)	Many times	5
	Last time by Tony Romo, 11-23-06	
Receiving (No.)	Jason Witten, 12-9-07	15
Receiving (Yds.)	Bob Hayes, 11-13-66	246
Interceptions	Many times	3
	Last time by Terance Newman, 12-14-03	
Field Goals	Chris Boniol, 11-18-96	7
	Billy Cundiff, 9-15-03	7
Touchdowns (Tot.)	Many times	4
	Last time by Terrell Owens, 11-18-07	
Points	Many times	24
	Last time by Terrell Owens, 11-18-07	

*NFL Record

2008 VETERAN ROSTER

No.	Name	Pos.	Ht.	Wt.	Age	NFL Exp.	College	Hometown	How Acq.	'07 Games/ Starts
76	Adams, Flozell	T	6-7	340	33	11	Michigan State	Bellwood, Ill.	D2-'98	16/16
34	Anderson, Deon	FB	5-10	236	25	2	Connecticut	Providence, R.I	D6b-'07	8/4
19	Austin, Miles	WR	6-3	216	24	3	Monmouth University	Garfield, N.J.	FA-'06	16/0
92	Ayodele, Remi	NT	6-2	300	25	2	Oklahoma	Grand Prairie, Texas	FA-'06	7/0
24	#Barber, Marion	RB	6-0	221	25	4	Minnesota	Wayzata, Minn.	D4a-'05	16/0
67	Berger, Joe	G	6-5	304	26	4	Michigan Tech	Newaygo, Mich.	W(Mia)-'06	1/0
72	Bowen, Stephen	DE	6-5	303	24	3	Hofstra	Wheatley Heights, N.Y.	FA-'06	16/0
27	Brown, Courtney	S	6-1	203	24	2	Cal Poly	Berkeley, Calif.	D7a-'07	8/0
57	Burnett, Kevin	LB	6-3	227	25	4	Tennessee	Carson, Calif.	D2-'05	16/2
99	#Canty, Chris	DE	6-7	299	25	4	Virginia	Charlotte, N.C.	D4b-'05	16/16
54	Carpenter, Bobby	LB	6-2	248	25	3	Ohio State	Lancaster, Ohio	D1-'06	16/0
75	Colombo, Marc	T	6-8	315	29	7	Boston College	Bridgewater, Mass.	FA-'05	16/16
84	Crayton, Patrick	WR	6-0	205	29	5	Northwestern Okla. St.	DeSoto, Texas	D7b-'04	15/13
45	Cruz, Ronnie	FB	6-0	237	27	3	Northern State	Lakeport, Calif.	FA-'08	0*
89	Curtis, Tony	TE	6-5	265	25	3	Portland State	Seaside, Calif.	FA-'05	16/0
70	Davis, Leonard	G	6-6	354	29	8	Texas	Wortham, Texas	UFA(Ari)-'07	16/16
98	Ellis, Greg	LB	6-6	265	33	11	North Carolina	Wendell, N.C.	D1-'98	13/10
6	Folk, Nick	K	6-1	225	23	2	Arizona	Sherman Oaks, Calif.	D6a-'07	16/0
68	Free, Doug	T	6-6	324	24	2	Northern Illinois	Manitowoc, Wisc.	D4b-'07	1/0
83	Glenn, Terry	WR	5-11	196	34	13	Ohio State	Columbus, Ohio	T(GB)-'03	1/0
65	Gurode, Andre	C	6-4	316	30	7	Colorado	Houston, Texas	D2a-'02	14/14
26	Hamlin, Ken	S	6-2	206	27	6	Arkansas	Memphis, Tenn.	UFA(Sea)-'07	16/16
97	Hatcher, Jason	DE	6-6	298	26	3	Grambling State	Alexandria, La.	D3-'06	16/0
42	Henry, Anthony	CB	6-1	205	31	8	South Florida	Fort Myers, Fla.	UFA(Cle)-'05	13/10
17	Hurd, Sam	WR	6-2	196	23	3	Northern Illinois	San Antonio, Texas	FA-'06	16/2
56	James, Bradie	LB	6-2	239	27	6	Louisiana State	Monroe, La.	D4-'03	16/16
14	Johnson, Brad	QB	6-5	238	39	17	Florida State	Marietta, Ga.	FA-'07	16/0
66	Johnson, Tank	DT	6-3	300	26	5	Washington	Tempe, Ariz.	FA-'07	8/1
21	t-Jones, Pacman	CB	5-10	185	24	3	West Virginia	Atlanta, Ga.	T(Tenn)-'08	0*
63	Kosier, Kyle	G	6-5	294	29	7	Arizona State	Peoria, Ariz.	UFA(Det)-'06	16/16
91	Ladouceur, Louis-Philippe	LS	6-4	251	27	4	California	Pointe-Claire, Quebec	FA-'05	16/0
78	Marten, James	T	6-7	303	24	2	Boston College	Indianapolis, Ind.	D3-'07	0*
1	McBriar, Mat	P	6-1	224	29	5	Hawaii	East Brighton, Australia	FA-'04	16/0
77	McQuistan, Pat	T	6-6	311	25	3	Weber State	Lebanon, Ore.	D7-'06	16/0
41	Newman, Terence	CB	5-11	181	30	6	Kansas State	Salina, Kan.	D1-'03	13/11
23	Oglesby, Evan	CB	5-10	185	26	3	North Alabama	Toccoa, Ga.	FA-'07	8/0
81	Owens, Terrell	WR	6-3	218	34	13	Tennessee-Chattanooga	Alexander City, Ala.	FA-'06	15/15
71	Procter, Cory	C	6-4	297	25	4	Montana	Gig Harbor, Wash.	FA-'05	16/2
90	Ratliff, Jay	NT	6-4	298	27	4	Auburn	Valdosta. Ga.	FA-'05	15/14
50	Rogers, Justin	LB	6-4	250	25	2	Southern Methodist	Commerce, Texas	FA-'07	16/0
9	Romo, Tony	QB	6-2	224	28	6	Eastern Illinois	Burlington, Wisc.	FA-'03	16/8
64	Siavii, Junior	DT	6-5	330	29	3	Oregon	Pago Pago, African Samoa	FA-'07	0*
96	Spears, Marcus	DE	6-4	305	25	4	Louisiana State	Baton Rouge, La.	D1b-'05	16/16
93	Spencer, Anthony	LB	6-3	265	24	2	Purdue	Fort Wayne, Ind.	D1-'07	16/6
86	Stanback, Isaiah	WR	6-2	216	24	2	Washington	Seattle, Wash.	D4a-'07	2/0
55	Thomas, Zach	LB	5-11	228	35	13	Texas Tech	Pampa, Texas	FA-'08	5/5*
94	Ware, DeMarcus	LB	6-4	252	26	4	Troy	Auburn, Ala.	D1a-'05	16/16
25	Watkins, Patrick	S	6-5	208	25	3	Florida State	Tallahassee, Fla.	D5-'06	14/0
38	Williams, Roy	S	6-0	225	28	7	Oklahoma	Union City, Calif.	D1-'02	15/13
43	Wishom, Jerron	CB	6-0	197	26	2	Louisiana Tech	Lutcher, La.	FA-'08	0*
82	Witten, Jason	TE	6-5	266	26	6	Tennessee	Elizabethton, Tenn.	D3-'03	16/16

* Cruz last active with Kansas City in '06; Jones last active with Tennessee in '06; Marten inactive for 16 games; Siavii last active with Kansas City in '05; Thomas played 5 games with Miami in '07; Wishom last active with Green Bay in '05.

\# Unrestricted free agent, subject to development.

t- Cowboys traded for Jones (Tenn).

Traded—LB Akin Ayodele (16 games in '07) to Miami; TE Anthony Fasano (16) to Miami; DT Jason Ferguson (1) to Miami.

Players lost through free agency (4): S Keith Davis (Mia; 14 games in '07), RB Julius Jones (Sea; 16), CB Nathan Jones (Mia; 15), CB Jacques Reeves (Hou; 16).

Also played with Cowboys in '07—FB Oliver Hoyte (10 games), RB Tyson Thompson (8).

2008 FIRST-YEAR ROSTER

Name	Pos.	Ht.	Wt.	Age	College	Hometown	How Acq.
Amendola, Danny	WR	5-11	183	22	Texas Tech	The Woodlands, Texas	FA
Atchison, Drew	TE	6-6	247	23	William & Mary	Charlottesville, Va.	FA
Ball, Alan (1)	CB	6-1	176	23	Illinois	Detroit, Mich.	D7b-'07
Bartel, Richard (1)	QB	6-3	246	25	Tarleton State	Grapevine, Texas	FA-'07
Bennett, Martellus	TE	6-6	260	21	Texas A&M	Alief, Texas	D2
Bradford, Mark	WR	6-2	215	23	Stanford	Fremont, Calif.	FA
Butler, Quincy (1)	CB	6-1	190	24	Texas Christian	San Antonio, Texas	FA-'06
Choice, Tashard	RB	5-10	215	23	Georgia Tech	Riverdale, Ga.	D4
Coleman, Alonzo (1)	RB	5-9	207	24	Hampton	South Boston, Va.	FA-'07
Crosslin, Julius	FB	5-11	245	24	Oklahoma State	Amarillo, Texas	FA
Davis, Dowayne	S	6-0	202	22	Syracuse	Bronx, N.Y.	FA
Dixon, Marcus	DE	6-4	294	23	Hampton	Rome, Ga.	FA
Everett, Tyler (1)	CB	5-11	202	24	Ohio State	Canton, Ohio	FA-'07
George, Tearrius (1)	LB	6-4	270	25	Kansas State	Fayetteville, N.C.	FA-'07
Hale, Brandon	G	6-3	311	22	Sam Houston State	Grand Prairie, Texas	FA
Hannah, Rodney (1)	TE	6-6	256	24	Houston	Roseville, Calif.	FA-'07
Jefferson, Mike (1)	WR	6-1	215	25	Montana State	El Paso, Texas	FA-'07
Jenkins, Mike	CB	5-10	197	23	South Florida	Bradenton, Fla.	D1b
Jones, Felix	RB	5-10	207	21	Arkansas	Tulsa, Okla.	D1a
Karatepeyan, Alain	LB	6-0	245	23	Tulsa	Chatsworth, Calif.	FA
Lattimore, Keon	RB	5-11	222	24	Maryland	Owings Mills, Md.	FA
Long, Khari (1)	LB	6-4	257	26	Baylor	Wichita Falls, Texas	FA-'07
Ottovegio, Jay	P	5-11	197	23	Stanford	Coral Springs, Fla.	FA
Phinisee, Justin (1)	CB	5-11	199	25	Oregon	Long Beach, Calif.	FA
Polk, Daniel	WR	6-1	202	23	Midwestern State	Dallas, Tex.	FA
Robertson, Darrell	DE	6-4	255	22	Georgia Tech	Jonesboro, Ga.	FA
Scandrick, Orlando	CB	5-10	192	21	Boise St.	Los Alamitos, Calif.	D5
Smith, Marcus (1)	DE	6-4	281	24	Arizona	San Diego, Calif.	FA-'07
Smith, Tyson (1)	LB	6-2	240	26	Iowa State	Des Moines, Iowa	FA-'07
Walden, Erik	LB	6-2	242	24	Middle Tennessee State	Dublin, Ga.	D6
West, Joe	WR	6-1	215	24	Texas-El Paso	Garland, Texas	FA

The term NFL Rookie is defined as a player who is in his first season of professional football and has not been on the roster of another professional football team for any regular-season or postseason games. A Rookie is designated by an "R" on NFL rosters. Players who have been active in another professional football league or players who have NFL experience, including either preseason training camp or being on an Active List or Inactive List, or on Reserve/Injured or Reserve/Physically Unable to Perform for fewer than six regular-season games, are termed NFL First-Year Players. An NFL First-Year Player is designated by a "1" on NFL rosters. Thereafter, a player is credited with an additional year of experience for each season in which he accumulates six games on the Active List or Inactive List, or on Reserve/Injured or Reserve/Physically Unable to Perform.

Log on to www.dallascowboys.com for an up-to-date roster; Age listed is as of September 4, 2008.

DALLAS COWBOYS

COACHING STAFF

Head Coach,
Wade Phillips

Pro Career: Was named the seventh coach in club history on February 8, 2007. He led the Cowboys to a 13-3 record in 2007 becoming the third head coach since the NFL merger to reach 13 wins in his first season with a club. In guiding the Cowboys to the playoffs, he has now reached the playoffs in the first season in each of the last seven times he has taken over as a head coach or defensive coordinator. Phillips brought 30 years of NFL coaching experience, including five as a head coach and 20 as a defensive coordinator, to the Cowboys. In his six full seasons as a head coach, Phillips has produced a 58-38 record and guided his teams to four playoff appearances. He has had only one non-winning season as a head coach. His .604 career winning percentage in the regular season is already in the top 10 (currently sixth) among active NFL head coaches with four years of head coaching experience. Over the last 19 years as a head coach or coordinator, he has been a part of only four teams that have had non-winning records. During that time he has worked with a defense that ranked in the NFL's top 10 eight times. Phillips served as the defensive coordinator for the San Diego Chargers (2004-06) and Atlanta Falcons (2002-03), finishing the 2003 season as interim head coach. Phillips also served as interim head coach in New Orleans for four games in 1985 (1-3 record) and Atlanta for three games in 2003 (2-1). During the 1998-2000 seasons as head coach in Buffalo, the Bills compiled a record of 29-19. Phillips took the reins after a 6-10 finish in 1997 and reversed the team's fortunes by leading it to a 10-6 record and the playoffs in 1998. His 1999 team led the NFL in total defense, went 11-5 and earned another trip to the postseason. Before becoming the Bills head coach in 1998, he was the team's defensive coordinator (1995-97). Phillips had a two-year stint at Denver's head coach (1993-94), after serving as defensive coordinator the previous four seasons. He led the Broncos to a playoff berth in his first season (1993). He was the Philadelphia Eagles defensive coordinator and linebackers coach (1986-88). His first coordinator's position came with the New Orleans Saints (1981-85). He began his NFL coaching career with the Houston Oilers (1976-1980) under his father, longtime NFL coach Bum Phillips. Career record: 61-46.

Background: Played linebacker at Houston (1966-68). Served as a college coach at Houston (1969), Oklahoma State (1973-74), and Kansas (1975).

Personal: Age 61, born in Orange, Texas. He and his wife Laurie, have one son, Wesley, and one daughter, Tracy.

ASSISTANT COACHES

Dave Campo, secondary; born Groton, Conn. Defensive back Central Connecticut State 1967-1970. No pro playing experience. College coach: Central Connecticut State 1971-72; Albany 1973, Bridgeport 1974, Pittsburgh 1975, Washington State 1976, Boise State 1977-79, Oregon State 1980, Weber State 1981-82, Iowa State 1983, Syracuse 1984-86, Miami 1987-88. Pro coach: Dallas Cowboys 1989-2002 (head coach 2000-02), Cleveland Browns 2003-04, Jacksonville Jaguars 2005-07, re-joined Cowboys in 2008.

Jason Garrett, asst. head coach/offensive coordinator; born Abington, Pa. Quarterback Princeton 1987-88. Pro quarterback San Antonio Riders (World League) 1991, Ottawa RoughRiders (CFL) 1991, Dallas Cowboys 1993-99, New York Giants 2000-03, Tampa Bay Buccaneers 2004, Miami Dolphins 2004. College coach: Princeton 1990. Pro coach: Miami Dolphins 2005-06, joined Cowboys in 2007.

John Garrett, tight ends; born Danville, Pa. Wide receiver Columbia 1983-85, Princeton 1986-87. Pro wide receiver Cincinnati Bengals 1989, Buffalo Bills 1991, San Antonio Riders (World League) 1991. College coach: Virginia 2004-06. Pro coach: Cincinnati Bengals 1995-98, 2001-02, Arizona Cardinals 1999-2000, joined Cowboys in 2007.

Todd Grantham, defensive line; born Pulaski, Va. Offensive lineman Virginia Tech 1984-88. No pro playing experience. College coach: Virginia Tech 1990-95, Michigan State 1996-98. Pro coach: Indianapolis Colts 1999-2001, Houston Texans 2002-04, Cleveland Browns 2005-07, joined Cowboys in 2008.

Reggie Herring, linebackers; born Myrtle Beach, S.C. Linebacker Florida State 1978-1980. No pro playing experience. College coach: Oklahoma State 1981-85, Auburn 1986-1991, Texas Christian 1992-93, Clemson 1994-2001, North Carolina State 2004, Arkansas 2005-07 (interim head coach 2007). Pro coach: Houston Texans 2002-03, joined Cowboys in 2008.

Hudson Houck, offensive line; born Los Angeles. Center Southern California 1962-64. No pro playing experience. College coach: Southern California 1970-72, 1976-1982, Stanford 1973-75. Pro coach: Los Angeles Rams 1983-1991, Seattle Seahawks 1992, Dallas Cowboys 1993-2001, San Diego Chargers 2002-04, Miami Dolphins 2005-07, re-joined Cowboys in 2008.

Joe Juraszek, strength and conditioning; born Chicago. Linebacker/defensive end New Mexico 1976-1980. No pro playing experience. College coach: Oklahoma 1981-86, 1993-96, Texas Tech 1987-1992. Pro coach: Joined Cowboys in 1997.

Brett Maxie, asst. secondary; born Dallas. Safety Texas Southern 1982-84. Pro safety New Orleans Saints 1985-1993, Atlanta Falcons 1994, Carolina Panthers 1995-96, San Francisco 49ers 1997. Pro coach: Carolina Panthers 1998, San Francisco 49ers 1999-2003, Miami Dolphins 2007, joined Cowboys in 2008.

Dat Nguyen, asst. linebackers/defensive quality control; born Rockport, Texas. Linebacker Texas A&M 1994-1998. Pro linebacker Dallas Cowboys 1999-2005. Pro coach: Joined Cowboys in 2007.

Skip Peete, running backs; born Mesa, Ariz. Wide receiver Arizona 1981-82, Kansas 1984-85. Pro wide receiver New York Jets 1987. College coach: Pittsburgh 1988-1992, Michigan State 1993-94, Rutgers 1995, UCLA 1996-97. Pro coach: Oakland Raiders 1998-2006, joined Cowboys in 2007.

Wes Phillips, offensive assistant/offensive quality control; born Houston. Quarterback Texas-El Paso 1997-2001. Pro quarterback San Diego Riptide (AFL2) 2002-03. College coach: Texas-El Paso 2003, West Texas A&M 2004-05, Baylor 2006. Pro coach: Joined Cowboys in 2007.

Bruce Read, special teams; born Santa Rosa, Calif. No pro playing experience. College coach: Montana 1985-1996, Oregon State 1997-98, 2004-06. Pro coach: San Diego Chargers 1999-2001, New York Giants 2002-03, joined Cowboys in 2007.

Ray Sherman, wide receivers; born Berkeley, Calif. Wide receiver/defensive back Fresno State 1971-72. No pro playing experience. College coach: San Jose State 1974, California 1975, 1981, Michigan State 1976-77, Wake Forest 1978-1980, Purdue 1982-85, Georgia 1986-87. Pro coach: Houston Oilers 1988-89, Atlanta Falcons 1990, San Francisco 49ers 1991-93, New York Jets 1994, Minnesota Vikings 1995-97, 1999, Pittsburgh Steelers 1998, Green Bay Packers 2000-04, Tennessee Titans 2005-06, joined Cowboys in 2007.

Brian Stewart, defensive coordinator; born San Diego. Cornerback/free safety Northern Arizona 1983, 1986-87, Santa Monica City College 1984-85. No pro playing experience. College coach: Cal Poly-San Luis Obispo 1993-94, Northern Arizona 1995, Missouri 1996, 1999-2000, San Jose State 1997-98, Syracuse 2001. Pro coach: Houston Texans 2002-03, San Diego Chargers 2004-06, joined Cowboys in 2007.

Wade Wilson, quarterbacks; born Commerce, Texas. Quarterback East Texas State 1977-1980. Pro quarterback Minnesota Vikings 1981-1991, Atlanta Falcons 1992, New Orleans Saints 1993-94, Dallas Cowboys 1995-97, Oakland Raiders 1998-99. Pro coach: Dallas Cowboys 2000-02, Chicago Bears 2004-06, re-joined Cowboys in 2007.

National Football Conference
North Division
Team Colors: Honolulu Blue and Silver
Detroit Lions Practice &
Training Facility
222 Republic Drive
Allen Park, Michigan 48101
Telephone: (313) 216-4000

2008 SCHEDULE
PRESEASON
Aug. 7	**N.Y. Giants**	7:00
Aug. 17	at Cincinnati	7:35
Aug. 23	**Cleveland**	4:00
Aug. 28	at Buffalo	6:30

REGULAR SEASON
Sep. 7	at Atlanta	1:00
Sep. 14	**Green Bay**	1:00
Sep. 21	at San Francisco	1:05
Sep. 28	BYE	
Oct. 5	**Chicago**	1:00
Oct. 12	at Minnesota	12:00
Oct. 19	at Houston	3:05
Oct. 26	**Washington**	1:00
Nov. 2	at Chicago	12:00
Nov. 9	**Jacksonville**	1:00
Nov. 16	at Carolina	1:00
Nov. 23	**Tampa Bay**	1:00
Nov. 27	**Tennessee** (Thu.)	12:30
Dec. 7	**Minnesota**	1:00
Dec. 14	at Indianapolis	1:00
Dec. 20	**New Orleans**	1:00
Dec. 28	at Green Bay	12:00

Stadium: Ford Field (opened in 2002)
  • **Capacity:** 64,500
  2000 Brush Street
  Detroit, Michigan 48226
Playing Surface: FieldTurf
Training Camp: 222 Republic Drive
  Allen Park, Michigan
  48101

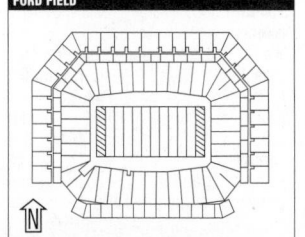

FORD FIELD

CLUB OFFICIALS
Chairman and Owner: William Clay Ford
Vice Chairman: William Clay Ford, Jr.
President and CEO: Matt Millen
Executive Vice President/COO:
  Tom Lewand
Senior Vice President & Assistant GM:
  Martin Mayhew
Senior Vice President: Bill Keenist
Senior Vice President/CFO: Tom Lesnau
Corporate Secretary: David Hempstead
Director of Pro Personnel: Sheldon White
Director of College Scouting:
  Scott McEwen
Scouts: Dave Boller, Mike Butler,
  Dennis Gentry, Chad Henry,
  Rob Lohman, Silas McKinnie,
  Lance Newmark, Charlie Sanders,
  Dave Sears, Dave Uyrus
Senior Director of Community Affairs:
  Tim Pendell
Director of Media Relations:
  Matt Barnhart
Director of Broadcasting and Production:
  Bryan Bender
Director of Ticket Operations:
  Mark Graham
Coordinator of Athletic Medicine/
  Athletic Trainer: Dean Kleinschmidt
Head Athletic Trainer: Al Bellamy
Equipment Manager: Tim O'Neill
Video Director: Robert Yanagi

COACHING HISTORY
Portsmouth Spartans 1930-33
(495-563-32)
Records include postseason games
1930	Hal (Tubby) Griffen	5-6-3
1931-36	George (Potsy) Clark	49-20-6
1937-38	Earl (Dutch) Clark	14-8-0
1939	Elmer (Gus) Henderson	6-5-0
1940	George (Potsy) Clark	5-5-1
1941-42	Bill Edwards*	4-9-1
1942	John Karcis	0-8-0
1943-47	Charles (Gus) Dorais	20-31-2
1948-1950	Alvin (Bo) McMillin	12-24-0
1951-56	Raymond (Buddy) Parker	50-24-2
1957-1964	George Wilson	55-45-6
1965-66	Harry Gilmer	10-16-2
1967-1972	Joe Schmidt	43-35-7
1973	Don McCafferty	6-7-1
1974-76	Rick Forzano**	15-17-0
1976-77	Tommy Hudspeth	11-13-0
1978-1984	Monte Clark	43-63-1
1985-88	Darryl Rogers***	18-40-0
1988-1996	Wayne Fontes	67-71-0
1997-2000	Bobby Ross****	27-32-0
2000	Gary Moeller	4-3-0
2001-02	Marty Mornhinweg	5-27-0
2003-05	Steve Mariucci#	15-28-0
2005	Dick Jauron	1-4-0
2006-07	Rod Marinelli	10-22-0

* Released after three games in 1942
** Resigned after four games in 1976
*** Released after 11 games in 1988
**** Resigned after nine games in 2000
# Released after 11 games in 2005

PAID ATTENDANCE
Home 484,304   Away 541,118
Total 1,025,422
Single-game home record,
  80,444 (12/20/81)
Single-season home record, 644,904
  (1980)

2008 DRAFT CHOICES
Round	Name	Pos.	College
1	Gosder Cherilus	T	Boston College
2	Jordon Dizon	LB	Colorado
3	Kevin Smith	RB	Central Florida
	Andre Fluellen	DT	Florida State
	Cliff Avril	DE	Purdue
5	Kenneth Moore	WR	Wake Forest
	Jerome Felton	RB	Furman
7	Landon Cohen	DT	Ohio
	Caleb Campbell	DB	Army

2007 TEAM RECORD
PRESEASON (2-2)

Date	Result	Opponent
8/9	W 27-26	Cincinnati
8/18	W 23-20	at Cleveland
8/25	L 10-37	at Indianapolis
8/30	L 13-16	Buffalo

REGULAR SEASON (7-9)

Date	Result	Opponent	Att.
9/9	W 36-21	at Oakland	61,547
9/16	W 20-17	Minnesota (OT)	61,771
9/23	L 21-56	at Philadelphia	67,570
9/30	W 37-27	Chicago	60,811
10/7	L 3-34	at Washington	88,944
10/21	W 23-16	Tampa Bay	60,442
10/28	W 16-7	at Chicago	62,171
11/4	W 44-7	Denver	60,783
11/11	L 21-31	at Arizona	64,753
11/18	L 10-16	New York Giants	60,675
11/22	L 26-37	Green Bay	63,257
12/2	L 10-42	at Minnesota	62,996
12/9	L 27-28	Dallas	62,759
12/16	L 14-51	at San Diego	66,505
12/23	W 25-20	Kansas City	59,938
12/30	L 13-34	at Green Bay	70,869

(OT) Overtime

SCORE BY PERIODS

Lions	61	107	67	108	3	—	346
Opponents	65	174	97	108	0	—	444

2007 TEAM STATISTICS

	Lions	Opp.
Total First Downs	303	363
Rushing	73	116
Passing	203	221
Penalty	27	26
3rd Down: Made/Att	62/190	97/213
3rd Down Pct.	32.6	45.5
4th Down: Made/Att	4/10	9/12
4th Down Pct.	40.0	75.0
Possession Avg.	27:33	32:27
Total Net Yards	5166	6042
Avg. Per Game	322.9	377.6
Total Plays	965	1087
Avg. Per Play	5.4	5.6
Net Yards Rushing	1288	1911
Avg. Per Game	80.5	119.4
Total Rushes	324	448
Net Yards Passing	3878	4131
Avg. Per Game	242.4	258.2
Sacked/Yards Lost	54/338	37/256
Gross Yards	4216	4387
Att./Completions	587/368	602/422
Completion Pct.	62.7	70.1
Had Intercepted	22	17
Punts/Average	68/44.3	61/44.9
Net Punting Avg.	68/36.4	61/39.6
Penalties/Yards	100/676	113/897
Fumbles/Ball Lost	35/14	40/18
Touchdowns	37	56
Rushing	13	19
Passing	19	32
Returns	5	5

2007 INDIVIDUAL STATISTICS

PASSING

	Att.	Comp.	Yds.	Pct.	TD	Int.	Tkld.	Rate
Kitna	561	355	4068	63.3	18	20	51/320	80.9
O'Sullivan	26	13	148	50.0	1	2	3/18	48.2
Lions	587	368	4216	62.7	19	22	54/338	79.4
Opponents	602	422	4387	70.1	32	17	37/256	96.8

SCORING

	TD R	TD P	TD Rt	PAT	FG	Saf	PTS
Hanson	0	0	0	35/36	29/35	0	122
Jones	8	0	0	0/0	0/0	0	48
McDonald	0	6	0	0/0	0/0	0	36
Johnson	1	4	0	0/0	0/0	0	30
Williams	0	5	0	0/0	0/0	0	30
Duckett	3	0	0	0/0	0/0	0	18
Fitzsimmons	0	1	1	0/0	0/0	1	14
Bell	1	0	0	0/0	0/0	0	6
Furrey	0	1	0	0/0	0/0	0	6
Lenon	0	0	1	0/0	0/0	0	6
Middleton	0	1	0	0/0	0/0	0	6
Rogers	0	0	1	0/0	0/0	0	6
K. Smith	0	0	1	0/0	0/0	0	6
Walters	0	1	0	0/0	0/0	0	6
White	0	0	1	0/0	0/0	0	6
Lions	13	19	5	35/36	29/35	1	346
Opponents	19	32	5	53/53	17/27	1	444

2-Pt. Conversions: Lions 0-1, Opponents 1-3

RUSHING

	No.	Yds	Avg	LG	TD
Jones	153	581	3.8	34	8
Duckett	65	335	5.2	53	3
Bell	44	182	4.1	24	1
Kitna	25	63	2.5	11	0
Johnson	4	52	13.0	32t	1
Cason	11	38	3.5	12	0
Calhoun	7	35	5.0	17	0
Bradley	5	9	1.8	3	0
McDonald	4	2	0.5	9	0
Williams	2	1	0.5	9	0
O'Sullivan	4	-10	-2.5	2	0
Lions	324	1288	4.0	53	13
Opponents	448	1911	4.3	49	19

RECEIVING

	No.	Yds	Avg	LG	TD
McDonald	79	943	11.9	49t	6
Williams	64	838	13.1	91t	5
Furrey	61	664	10.9	49	1
Johnson	48	756	15.8	49	4
Jones	32	197	6.2	16	0
McHugh	17	252	14.8	46	0
Cason	14	129	9.2	20	0
Bell	14	63	4.5	15	0
Walters	9	101	11.2	21	1
Fitzsimmons	8	85	10.6	22	1
Middleton	8	70	8.8	17	1
Calhoun	5	35	7.0	11	0
Duckett	4	54	13.5	22	0
Owens	1	9	9.0	9	0
Bradley	2	10	5.0	8	0
Kitna	1	9	9.0	9	0
Campbell	1	1	1.0	1	0
Lions	368	4216	11.5	91t	19
Opponents	422	4387	10.4	68t	32

INTERCEPTIONS

	No.	Yds	Avg	LG	TD
K. Smith	3	64	21.3	64t	1
Alexander	2	70	35.0	36	0
Kennedy	2	45	22.5	38	0
Fisher	2	25	12.5	13	0
Bryant	2	0	0.0	0	0
Rogers	1	66	66.0	66t	1
Lenon	1	61	61.0	61t	1
White	1	28	28.0	28	0
Sims	1	5	5.0	5	0
Bashir	1	0	0.0	0	0
Cody	1	-2	-2.0	-2	0
Lions	17	362	21.3	66t	3
Opponents	22	279	12.7	61t	2

PUNTING

	No.	Yds.	Avg.	In 20	LG
N. Harris	68	3010	44.3	26	58
Lions	68	3010	44.3	26	58
Opponents	61	2741	44.9	20	72

PUNT RETURNS

	Ret	FC	Yds	Avg	LG	TD
Walters	15	16	118	7.9	18	0
Furrey	3	4	30	10.0	13	0
Lions	18	20	148	8.2	18	0
Opponents	36	9	434	12.1	62	0

KICKOFF RETURNS

	No.	Yds	Avg	LG	TD
Cason	42	1041	24.8	74	0
Calhoun	10	221	22.1	33	0
Walters	8	172	21.5	39	0
Middleton	4	83	20.8	30	0
Fitzsimmons	3	62	20.7	41t	1
Furrey	2	25	12.5	15	0
Saipaia	2	23	11.5	12	0
B. Davis	1	1	1.0	1	0
Lions	72	1628	22.6	74	1
Opponents	65	1750	26.9	104t	2

FIELD GOALS

	1-19	20-29	30-39	40-49	50+
Hanson	1/1	4/5	10/12	11/13	3/4
Lions	1/1	4/5	10/12	11/13	3/4
Opponents	0/0	9/9	3/3	5/10	0/5

SACKS

	No.
Rogers	7.0
DeVries	6.5
White	6.5
Bailey	3.5
K. Edwards	3.0
C. Smith	2.5
Alexander	2.0
Lenon	2.0
Moore	2.0
Redding	1.0
Sims	1.0
Lions	37.0
Opponents	54.0

RECORD HOLDERS
INDIVIDUAL RECORDS—CAREER

Category	Name	Performance
Rushing (Yds.)	Barry Sanders, 1989-1998	15,269
Passing (Yds.)	Bobby Layne, 1950-58	15,710
Passing (TDs)	Bobby Layne, 1950-58	118
Receiving (No.)	Herman Moore, 1991-2001	670
Receiving (Yds.)	Herman Moore, 1991-2001	9,174
Interceptions	Dick LeBeau, 1959-1972	62
Punting (Avg.)	Yale Lary, 1952-53, 1956-1964	44.3
Punt Return (Avg.)	Jack Christiansen, 1951-58	12.8
Kickoff Return (Avg.)	Pat Studstill, 1961-67	25.7
Field Goals	Jason Hanson, 1992-2007	385
Touchdowns (Tot.)	Barry Sanders, 1989-1998	109
Points	Jason Hanson, 1992-2007	1,659

INDIVIDUAL RECORDS—SINGLE SEASON

Category	Name	Performance
Rushing (Yds.)	Barry Sanders, 1997	2,053
Passing (Yds.)	Scott Mitchell, 1995	4,338
Passing (TDs)	Scott Mitchell, 1995	32
Receiving (No.)	Herman Moore, 1995	123
Receiving (Yds.)	Herman Moore, 1995	1,686
Interceptions	Don Doll, 1950	12
	Jack Christiansen, 1953	12
Punting (Avg.)	Yale Lary, 1963	48.9
Punt Return (Avg.)	Pat Studstill, 1962	15.8
Kickoff Return (Avg.)	Mel Gray, 1994	28.4
Field Goals	Jason Hanson, 1993	34
Touchdowns (Tot.)	Barry Sanders, 1991	17
Points	Jason Hanson, 1995	132

INDIVIDUAL RECORDS—SINGLE GAME

Category	Name	Performance
Rushing (Yds.)	Barry Sanders, 11-13-94	237
Passing (Yds.)	Charlie Batch, 11-18-01	436
Passing (TDs)	Gary Danielson, 12-9-78	5
Receiving (No.)	Herman Moore, 12-4-95	14
Receiving (Yds.)	Cloyce Box, 12-3-50	302
Interceptions	Don Doll, 10-23-49	*4
Field Goals	Garo Yepremian, 11-13-66	6
	Jason Hanson, 10-17-99	6
Touchdowns (Tot.)	Dutch Clark, 10-22-34	4
	Cloyce Box, 12-3-50	4
	Barry Sanders, 11-24-91	4
Points	Dutch Clark, 10-22-34	24
	Cloyce Box, 12-3-50	24
	Barry Sanders, 11-24-91	24

*NFL Record

2008 VETERAN ROSTER

No.	Name	Pos.	Ht.	Wt.	Age	NFL Exp.	College	Hometown	How Acq.	'07 Games/ Starts
91	Alama-Francis, Ikaika	DE	6-5	280	23	2	Hawaii	Oahu, Hawaii	D2b-'07	6/0
42	Alexander, Gerald	S	6-2	204	24	2	Boise State	Rancho Cucamonga, Calif.	D2c-'07	16/16
76	Backus, Jeff	T	6-5	305	30	8	Michigan	Norcross, Ga.	D1-'01	16/16
28	Bell, Tatum	RB	5-11	213	27	5	Oklahoma State	DeSoto, Texas	T(Den)-'07	5/5
24	Blue, Greg	S	6-2	216	26	3	Georgia	College Park, Ga.	FA-'07	4/0
30	Bodden, Leigh	CB	6-1	193	26	6	Duquesne	Hyattsville, Md.	FA-'08	16/16*
40	Bradley, Jon	FB	6-0	301	27	5	Arkansas State	Barton, Ark.	FA-'07	15/6
27	Bullocks, Daniel	S	6-0	212	25	3	Nebraska	Chattanooga, Tenn.	D2-'06	0*
29	Calhoun, Brian	RB	5-10	208	24	3	Wisconsin	Oak Creek, Wisc.	D3-'06	4/0
89	Campbell, Dan	TE	6-5	265	32	10	Texas A&M	Glen Rose, Texas	UFA(Dall)-'06	2/1
52	Cannon, Anthony	LB	6-0	228	23	3	Tulane	Stone Mountain, Ga.	D7b-'06	11/0
36	Cason, Aveion	RB	5-10	204	29	8	Illinois State	St. Petersburg, Fla.	FA-'07	12/0
75	Cody, Shaun	DT	6-4	310	25	4	Southern California	Hacienda Heights, Calif.	D2-'05	15/0
94	Darby, Chuck	DT	6-0	297	32	8	South Carolina State	North, S.C.	UFA(Sea)-'08	6/6*
61	Davis, Frank	G	6-3	325	27	3	South Florida	Panama City, Panama	FA-'06	0*
95	DeVries, Jared	DE	6-4	275	32	10	Iowa	Aplington, Iowa	D3-'99	14/10
74	Dunn, Jon	T	6-7	324	26	2	Virginia Tech	Virginia Beach, Va.	FA-'07	0*
39	Edwards, Dovonte	CB	6-0	182	25	4	North Carolina State	Chapel Hill, N.C.	FA-'07	5/0
80	Ellis, Devale	WR	5-10	174	24	2	Hofstra	Brooklyn, N.Y.	FA-'06	0*
3	Ernster, Paul	K/P	6-0	212	26	2	Northern Arizona	Glendale, Ariz.	FA-'08	2/0*
58	Fincher, Alfred	LB	6-1	238	25	4	Connecticut	Norwood, Mass.	FA-'08	7/0*
21	Fisher, Travis	CB	5-10	189	28	7	Central Florida	Tallahassee, Fla.	UFA(StL)-'07	16/13
82	FitzSimmons, Casey	TE	6-4	258	27	6	Carroll College(Mont.)	Helena, Mont.	FA-'03	16/5
72	Foster, George	T	6-5	338	28	6	Georgia	Macon, Ga.	T(Den)-'07	15/9
87	Furrey, Mike	WR	6-0	195	31	5	Northern Iowa	Grove City, Ohio	UFA(StL)-'06	16/10
86	Gaines, Michael	TE	6-4	277	28	5	Central Florida	Tallahassee, Fla.	UFA(Buff)-'08	15/14*
54	Gardner, Gilbert	LB	6-1	228	26	5	Purdue	Angleton, Texas	UFA(Tenn)-'08	13/0*
4	Hanson, Jason	K	6-0	190	38	17	Washington State	Spokane, Wash.	D2b-'92	16/0
2	Harris, Nick	P	6-2	218	30	8	California	Avondale, Ariz.	W(Cin)-'03	16/0
35	Hicks, LaMarcus	S	6-0	189	25	2	Iowa State	Clarksdale, Miss.	FA-'07	5/0
43	Horne, Pacino	CB	5-11	191	24	2	Central Michigan	Ypsilanti, Mich.	FA-'08	0*
71	Hulsey, Corey	G	6-4	325	31	6	Clemson	Lula, Ga.	FA-'08	0*
81	Johnson, Calvin	WR	6-5	239	22	2	Georgia Tech	Tyrone, Ga.	D1-'07	15/10
25	Kelly, Brian	CB	5-11	193	32	11	Southern California	Las Vegas, Nev.	UFA(TB)-'08	11/4*
8	Kitna, Jon	QB	6-2	220	35	12	Central Washington	Tacoma, Wash.	UFA(Cin)-'06	16/16
53	Lenon, Paris	LB	6-2	235	30	7	Richmond	Lynchburg, Va.	UFA(GB)-'06	16/16
59	Lewis, Alex	LB	6-0	230	27	5	Wisconsin	Delran, N.J.	D5-'04	14/1
84	McDonald, Shaun	WR	5-10	183	27	6	Arizona State	Phoenix, Ariz.	UFA(StL)-'07	16/7
49	McHugh, Sean	TE/FB	6-5	265	26	3	Penn State	Springfield, Mass.	FA-'05	15/12
10	Middleton, Brandon	WR	5-10	190	27	2	Houston	Houston, Texas	FA-'07	5/0
79	Moore, Langston	DT	6-1	305	27	4	South Carolina	Charleston, S.C.	FA-'06	16/0
48	Muhlbach, Don	LS	6-4	265	27	5	Texas A&M	Lufkin, Texas	FA-'04	16/0
64	Mulitalo, Edwin	G	6-3	345	34	10	Arizona	Daly City, Calif.	FA-'07	15/15
6	Orlovsky, Dan	QB	6-3	230	25	4	Connecticut	Shelton, Conn.	D5-'05	0*
83	Owens, John	TE	6-3	255	28	4	Notre Dame	Bowie, Md.	FA-'07	7/0
32	Pearson, Kalvin	S	5-10	200	29	4	Grambling	Town Creek, Ala.	FA-'08	16/1*
66	Peterman, Stephen	G	6-4	323	26	4	Louisiana State	Gulfport, Miss.	FA-'06	13/13
51	Raiola, Dominic	C	6-1	295	29	8	Nebraska	Honolulu, Hawaii	D2a-'01	16/16
63	Ramirez, Manny	G	6-3	326	25	2	Texas Tech	Houston, Texas	D4b-'07	1/0
78	Redding, Cory	DT	6-4	295	27	6	Texas	Houston, Texas	D3-'03	16/16
38	Robinson, Ramzee	CB	5-10	186	24	2	Alabama	Huntsville, Ala.	FA-'07	6/0
73	Scott, Jonathan	T	6-6	318	25	3	Texas	Dallas, Texas	D5-'06	7/2
50	Sims, Ernie	LB	6-0	225	23	3	Florida State	Tallahassee, Fla.	D1-'06	16/16
93	Smith, Corey	DE	6-2	250	28	6	North Carolina State	Richmond, Va.	FA-'06	16/2
26	Smith, Dwight	S	5-10	201	30	9	Akron	Detroit, Mich.	D3-'01	14/13*
23	Smith, Keith	CB	5-11	191	28	5	McNeese State	Leesville, La.	D3-'04	15/1
99	White, Dewayne	DE	6-2	273	28	6	Louisville	Marbury, Ala.	UFA(TB)-'07	14/14
11	Williams, Roy	WR	6-3	211	26	5	Texas	Odessa, Texas	D1a-'04	12/12
31	Wilson, Stanley	CB	5-11	189	25	4	Stanford	Carson, Calif.	D3-'05	10/5

* Bodden played 16 games with Cleveland in '07; Bullocks missed '07 season because of injury ; Darby played 6 games with Seattle; F. Davis missed '07 season because of injury; Dunn last active with Cleveland in '05; Ernster played 1 game with Denver and 1 game with Cleveland; Fincher played 7 games with New Orleans; Gaines played 15 games with Buffalo; Gardner played 13 games with Tennessee; Kelly played 11 games with Tampa Bay; Orlovsky inactive for 16 games; Pearson played 16 games with Tampa Bay; D. Smith played 14 games with Minnesota.

Traded—DT Shaun Rogers (Cle; 16 games in '07).

Players lost through free agency (5): LB Boss Bailey (Den; 15 games in '07), RB T.J. Duckett (Sea; 12), LB Teddy Lehman (TB; 16), QB J.T. O'Sullivan (SF; 4), G Damien Woody (NYJ; 13).

Also played with Lions in '07—TE Courtney Anderson (2 games), S Idrees Bashir (9), CB Tony Beckham (6), CB Fernando Bryant (16), LB Donté Curry (2), DE Kalimba Edwards (8), S Eric Frampton (5), RB Kevin Jones (13), S Kenoy Kennedy (16), G Blaine Saipaia (14), TE Rudy Sylvan (3), WR Troy Walters (13).

2008 FIRST-YEAR ROSTER

Name	Pos.	Ht.	Wt.	Age	College	Hometown	How Acq.
Avril, Cliff	DE	6-3	253	22	Purdue	Green Cove Springs, Fla.	D3c
Ball, Reggie (1)	WR	5-11	195	23	Georgia Tech	Stone Mountain, Ga.	FA-'07
Bellamy, Ron (1)	WR	6-0	205	26	Michigan	Marrero, La.	FA-'07
Blackman, Darrell	WR	5-11	210	23	North Carolina State	Williamsport, Pa.	FA
Campbell, Caleb	LB	6-2	229	22	Army	Perryton, Texas	D7b
Cherilus, Gosder	T	6-7	319	24	Boston College	Somerville, Mass.	D1
Cohen, Landon	DT	6-3	296	22	Ohio	Spartanburg, S.C.	D7
Davis, Buster (1)	LB	5-9	239	24	Florida State	Daytona Beach, Fla.	FA-'07
DeGrate, Victor (1)	DE	6-3	294	23	Oklahoma State	DeSota, Texas	FA
Dizon, Jordon	LB	6-0	229	22	Colorado	Kauai, Hawaii	D2
Ervin, Allen	RB	5-10	224	23	Lambuth	Memphis, Tenn.	FA
Felton, Jerome	FB	6-0	246	22	Furman	Madisonville, Tenn.	D5b
Fluellen, Andre	DT	6-2	296	23	Florida State	Cartersville, Ga.	D3b
Hardie, Rudolph	DE	6-2	269	22	Howard	Hartford, Conn.	FA
Harriott, Claude (1)	DE	6-3	271	27	Pittsburgh	Belle Glade, Fla.	FA-'07
Harris, Clark (1)	TE	6-5	256	24	Rutgers	Manahawkin, N.J.	FA-'07
Madison, Carroll	G	6-2	308	23	Syracuse	Houston, Texas	FA
Moore, Kenneth	WR	5-11	195	23	Wake Forest	Charlotte, N.C.	D5
Patrick, Chris (1)	T	6-4	280	24	Nebraska	Ithaca, Mich.	FA
Pruitt, Tyrone	LB	5-11	220	22	Boston College	Brockton, Mass.	FA
Route, Israel (1)	CB	5-8	185	23	Tulane	Stone Mountain, Ga.	FA-'07
Smith, Kevin	RB	6-1	217	21	Central Florida	Miami, Fla.	D3
Standeford, John (1)	WR	6-4	206	26	Purdue	Monrovia, Ind.	FA
Stanton, Drew (1)	QB	6-3	226	24	Michigan State	Farmington Hills, Mich.	D2a-'07
Williams, Bobbie	CB	6-0	214	23	Bethune Cookman	Miami, Fla.	FA

The term NFL Rookie is defined as a player who is in his first season of professional football and has not been on the roster of another professional football team for any regular-season or postseason games. A Rookie is designated by an "R" on NFL rosters. Players who have been active in another professional football league or players who have NFL experience, including either preseason training camp or being on an Active List or Inactive List, or on Reserve/Injured or Reserve/Physically Unable to Perform for fewer than six regular-season games, are termed NFL First-Year Players. An NFL First-Year Player is designated by a "1" on NFL rosters. Thereafter, a player is credited with an additional year of experience for each season in which he accumulates six games on the Active List or Inactive List, or on Reserve/Injured or Reserve/Physically Unable to Perform.

Log on to www.detroitlions.com for an up-to-date roster; Age listed is as of September 4, 2008.

COACHING STAFF

Head Coach,
Rod Marinelli

Pro Career: Named Lions' twenty-fourth head coach January 19, 2006 and has re-shaped Detroit's roster with an emphasis on "football character." He led the Lions to a four-game improvement in his second season as head coach while continually emphasizing the importance in winning the turnover battle and minimizing penalties. Served as Tampa Bay's defensive line coach from 1996-2005 and assumed the additional role as assistant head coach in 2002. Throughout his 10-year tenure, the Buccaneers recorded 416 sacks, with 328.5 coming courtesy of his defensive line. The 328.5 sacks registered by Marinelli's line ranked first in the NFL among all defensive lines during that span. Additionally, the Buccaneers' defensive front four garnered top 5 rankings in sacks during six of the 10 seasons under Marinelli. Career record: 10-22.

Background: Marinelli's college playing career was split due to a one-year tour of duty in Vietnam. In 1968, he played offensive and defensive tackle at Utah. After his service in the military, he attended California Lutheran from 1970-72, earning NAIA All-America honors as an offensive tackle his senior season. He began his coaching career at his high school alma mater, Rosemead (San Gabriel Valley, Calif.) from 1973-75. Collegiately, Marinelli coached defensive line at Utah State (1976), California (1983-91), Arizona State (1992-94), and Southern California (1995).

Personal: Age 59, born in Rosemead, Calif., He and his wife, Barbara, have two daughters, Chris and Gina. Chris is married to Joe Barry, the Lions' defensive coordinator. Marinelli also has two granddaughters and two grandsons.

ASSISTANT COACHES

Jason Arapoff, director of physical development; born Weymouth, Mass. Defensive back Springfield College 1985-88. No college or pro playing experience. Pro coach: Washington Redskins 1992-2000, joined Lions in 2001.

Bradford Banta, asst. special teams; born Baton Rouge, La. Tight end Southern California 1990-93, Pro tight end/long snapper Indianapolis Colts 1993-99, New York Jets 2000, Detroit Lions 2001-03, Buffalo Bills 2004. College coach: Tennessee-Chattanooga 2007. Pro coach: Joined Lions in 2008.

Joe Barry, defensive coordinator; born Boulder, Colo. Linebacker Southern California 1991-93. No pro playing experience. College coach: Southern California 1994-95, Northern Arizona 1996-98, Nevada-Las Vegas 1999. Pro coach: San Francisco 49ers 2000, Tampa Bay Buccaneers 2001-2006, joined Lions in 2007.

Mike Barry, asst. offensive line; born Brooklyn, N.Y. Center Nebraska 1964-65, Southern Illinois 1966-68. No pro playing experience. College coach: Southern Illinois 1977-79, Arizona 1980-83, Iowa State 1986, Colorado 1987-1992, Southern California 1993-97, Tennessee 1998-2002, North Carolina State 2003-05. Pro coach: San Antonio Gunslingers (USFL) 1984, New Orleans/Portland Breakers (USFL) 1984-85, joined Lions in 2006.

Malcolm Blacken, strength and conditioning; born Richmond, Va. Running back Virginia Tech 1984-88. No pro playing experience. College coach: South Carolina 1990-91, George Mason 1992-94, Virginia 1995. Pro coach: Washington Redskins 1996-2000, joined Lions in 2001.

Kippy Brown, asst. head coach/passing game coordinator; born Sweetwater, Tenn. Quarterback Memphis State 1974-77. No pro playing experience. College coach: Memphis State 1978-1980, Louisville 1982, Tennessee 1983-89, 1993-94. Pro coach: New York Jets 1990-92, Tampa Bay Buccaneers 1995, Miami Dolphins 1996-99, Green Bay Packers 2000, Memphis Maniax (XFL head coach) 2001, Houston Texans 2002-05, joined Lions in 2006.

Pat Carter, tight ends; born Sarasota, Fla. Tight end Florida State 1984-87. Pro tight end Detroit Lions 1988, Los Angeles Rams 1989-1994, Houston Oilers 1995-96, Arizona Cardinals 1997. Pro coach: St. Louis Rams 2005, joined Lions in 2006.

Don Clemons, defensive quality control; born Newark, N.J. Defensive end Muhlenberg (Pa.) 1973-76. No pro playing experience. College coach: Kutztown State 1977-78, New Mexico 1979, Arizona State 1980-84. Pro coach: Joined Lions in 1985.

Jim Colletto, offensive coordinator; born San Francisco. Fullback/linebacker UCLA 1964-66. No pro playing experience. College coach: UCLA 1967-68, 1980-81, 2006, Brown 1969, Xavier 1970-71, Pacific 1972-74, Cal State Fullerton 1975-79 (head coach), Purdue 1982-84, Arizona State 1985-87, Ohio State 1988-90, Purdue 1991-96 (head coach), Notre Dame 1997-98. Pro coach: Baltimore Ravens 1999-2004, Oakland Raiders 2005, joined Lions in 2007.

Joe Cullen, defensive line; born Quincy, Mass. Nose Guard Massachusetts 1986-89. No pro playing experience. College coach: Massachusetts 1990-91, Richmond 1992-98, 2000, Louisiana State 1999, Memphis 2001, Indiana 2002-04, Illinois 2005. Pro coach: Joined Lions in 2006.

Sam Gash, running backs; born Henderson, N.C. Fullback Penn State 1987-1991. Pro fullback New England Patriots 1992-97, Buffalo Bills 1998-99,

2003, Baltimore Ravens 2000-02. Pro coach: New York Jets 2005-06, joined Lions in 2007.

Shawn Jefferson, wide receivers; born Jacksonville. Wide receiver Central Florida 1988-1990. Pro wide receiver San Diego Chargers 1991-95, New England Patriots 1996-99, Atlanta Falcons 2000-02, Detroit Lions 2003. Pro coach: Joined Lions in 2005.

Stan Kwan, special teams; born Phoenix. Attended South Mountain (Ariz.) C.C., San Diego State. No college or pro playing experience. Pro coach: San Diego Chargers 1991-96, Detroit Lions 1997-2000, Arizona Cardinals 2001-2003, re-joined Lions in 2004.

Jimmy Lake, secondary; born San Francisco. Safety Eastern Washington 1995-98. No pro playing experience. College coach: Eastern Washington 1999-2003, Washington 2004, Montana State 2005. Pro coach: Tampa Bay Buccaneers 2006-07, joined Lions in 2008.

Scot Loeffler, quarterbacks; born Barberton, Ohio. Quarterback Michigan 1993-95. No pro playing experience. College coach: Michigan 1996-99, Central Michigan 2000-01, Michigan 2002-07. Pro coach: Joined Lions in 2008.

Clayton Lopez, defensive backs; born Los Angeles. Safety Nevada 1991-94. No pro playing experience. College coach: Nevada 1995-98. Pro coach: Seattle Seahawks 1999-2003, Oakland Raiders 2004-2005, joined Lions in 2006.

Phil Snow, linebackers; born Woodland, Calif. Quarterback Sacramento City College 1974-75, Cal State Hayward 1977-78. No pro playing experience. College coach: Laney (Calif.) College 1979-1981, Boise State 1982-86, California 1987-1991, Arizona State 1992-2000, UCLA 2001-02, Washington 2003-04. Pro coach: Joined Lions in 2005.

Eric Sutulovich, quality control offense; born Kansas City, Kan. Tight end Louisiana Tech 1993-95. No pro playing experience. College coach: Louisiana Tech 1997-99, Pittsburgh 2000, Kansas 2006. Pro coach: Houston Texans 2002-05, joined Lions in 2008.

Kevin Tolbert, asst. strength and conditioning; No pro or college playing experience. College coach: Miami 1998-2000, Michigan 2001-07. Pro coach: Philadelphia Eagles 1996-97, joined Lions in 2008.

**National Football Conference
North Division**
Team Colors: Dark Green, Gold, and White
Lambeau Field Atrium
1265 Lombardi Avenue
Green Bay, Wisconsin 54304
Telephone: (920) 569-7500

2008 SCHEDULE
PRESEASON
Aug. 11 **Cincinnati** 7:00
Aug. 16 at San Francisco.................6:00
Aug. 22 at Denver...........................7:00
Aug. 28 **Tennessee** 7:00

REGULAR SEASON
Sep. 8 **Minnesota** (Mon.) 6:00
Sep. 14 at Detroit 1:00
Sep. 21 **Dallas** 7:15
Sep. 28 at Tampa Bay 1:00
Oct. 5 **Atlanta** 12:00
Oct. 12 at Seattle 1:15
Oct. 19 **Indianapolis** 3:15
Oct. 26 BYE
Nov. 2 at Tennessee 12:00
Nov. 9 at Minnesota 12:00
Nov. 16 **Chicago** 12:00
Nov. 24 at New Orleans (Mon.) 7:30
Nov. 30 **Carolina** 12:00
Dec. 7 **Houston** 12:00
Dec. 14 at Jacksonville 1:00
Dec. 22 at Chicago (Mon.) 7:30
Dec. 28 **Detroit** 12:00

Stadium: Lambeau Field (opened in 1957)
   • **Capacity:** 72,928
      1265 Lombardi Avenue
      Green Bay, Wisconsin 54304
Playing Surface: DD GrassMaster
Training Camp: St. Norbert College
      De Pere, Wisconsin 54115

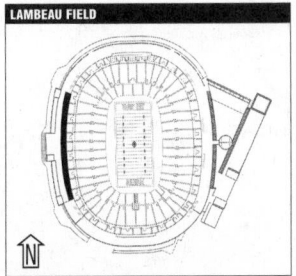
LAMBEAU FIELD

CLUB OFFICIALS
President and Chief Executive Officer:
   Mark Murphy
Executive Vice President/General
   Manager/Director of Football
   Operations: Ted Thompson
Vice President of Football Administration/
   Player Finance: Russ Ball
Vice President of Finance:
   Vicki Vannieuwenhoven
Vice President of Administration/
   Corporate Counsel: Jason Wied
Dir. of College Scouting: John Dorsey
Director-Football Operations:
   Reggie McKenzie
Director-Football Operations:
   John Schneider
Director of Player Development:
   Rob Davis
Director of Public Relations: Jeff Blumb
Assistant Directors of Public Relations:
   Sarah Quick, Adam Woullard
Public Relations Coordinator:
   Rob Crane
Manager of Corporate Communications:
   Aaron Popkey
Ticket Director: Mark Wagner
Director of Marketing and Corporate
   Sales: Craig Benzel
Director of Premium Sales and Guest
   Services: Jennifer Ark
Director of Retail Operations:
   Kate Hogan
Director of Administrative Affairs:
   Mark Schiefelbein
Director of Information Technology:
   Wayne Wichlacz
Director of Facility Operations:
   Ted Eisenreich
Director of Corporate Security:
   Doug Collins
Manager of Community Outreach:
   Cathy Dworak
Assistant Director of College Scouting:
   Shaun Herock
College Scouts: Lee Gissendaner,
   Brian Gutekunst, Alonzo Highsmith,
   Lenny McGill, Sam Seale,
   Jon-Eric Sullivan, Richie Williams
Scouting Coordinator: Danny Mock
Assistant Director of Pro Personnel:
   Tim Terry
Assistant Director of Pro Personnel:
   Eliot Wolf
Director of Research and Development:
   Mike Eayrs
Assistant Strength and Conditioning:
   Mark Lovat
Strength and Conditioning Assistant:
   Mondray Gee
Football Administration Coordinator:
   Matt Klein
Video Director: Bob Eckberg
Head Athletic Trainer: Pepper Burruss
Equipment Manager: Gordon (Red) Batty

COACHING HISTORY
(662-518-36)
Records include postseason games
1921-1949 Earl (Curly) Lambeau .212-106-21
1950-53   Gene Ronzani* 14-31-1
1953   Hugh Devore-
          Ray (Scooter) McLean**..0-2-0
1954-57   Lisle Blackbourn...........17-31-0
1958   Ray (Scooter) McLean....1-10-1
1959-1967 Vince Lombardi 98-30-4
1968-1970 Phil Bengtson 20-21-1
1971-74   Dan Devine...................25-28-4
1975-1983 Bart Starr 53-77-3
1984-87   Forrest Gregg 25-37-1
1988-1991 Lindy Infante................24-40-0
1992-98   Mike Holmgren..........84-42-0
1999   Ray Rhodes.....................8-8-0
2000-05   Mike Sherman 59-43-0
2006-07   Mike McCarthy............22-12-0
 *Resigned after 10 games in 1953
**Co-coaches

PAID ATTENDANCE
Home 566,418   Away 546,335
Total 1,112,753
Single-game home record,
   70,945 (11/11/07)
Single-season home record,
   566,418 (2007)

2008 DRAFT CHOICES

Round	Name	Pos.	College
2	Jordy Nelson	WR	Kansas State
	Brian Brohm	QB	Louisville
	Patrick Lee	DB	Auburn
3	Jermichael Finley	TE	Texas
4	Jeremy Thompson	DE	Wake Forest
	Josh Sitton	G	Central Florida
5	Breno Giacomini	T	Louisville
7	Matt Flynn	QB	Louisiana St.
	Brett Swain	WR	San Diego St.

GREEN BAY PACKERS

2007 TEAM RECORD
PRESEASON (2-2)
Date	Result	Opponent
8/11	W 13-9	at Pittsburgh
8/18	W 48-13	Seattle
8/23	L 13-21	Jacksonville
8/30	L 14-30	at Tennessee

REGULAR SEASON (13-3)
Date	Result	Opponent	Att.
9/9	W 16-13	Philadelphia	70,598
9/16	W 35-13	at N.Y. Giants	78,701
9/23	W 31-24	San Diego	70,733
9/30	W 23-16	at Minnesota	63,779
10/7	L 20-27	Chicago	70,904
10/14	W 17-14	Washington	70,761
10/29	W 19-13	at Denver (OT)	77,160
11/4	W 33-22	at Kansas City	78,988
11/11	W 34-0	Minnesota	70,945
11/18	W 31-17	Carolina	70,805
11/22	W 37-26	at Detroit	63,257
11/29	L 27-37	at Dallas	64,167
12/9	W 38-7	Oakland	70,828
12/16	W 33-14	at St. Louis	66,008
12/23	L 7-35	at Chicago	62,272
12/30	W 34-13	Detroit	70,869
(OT) Overtime			

POSTSEASON (1-1)
Date	Result	Opponent	Att.
1/12	W 42-20	Seattle	72,168
1/20	L 20-23	N.Y. Giants (OT)	72,740

SCORE BY PERIODS
Packers	86	128	112	103	6	—	435
Opponents	56	102	57	76	0	—	291

2007 TEAM STATISTICS
	Packers	Opp.
Total First Downs	307	297
Rushing	69	77
Passing	210	176
Penalty	28	44
3rd Down: Made/Att	86/202	69/209
3rd Down Pct.	42.6	33.0
4th Down: Made/Att	5/11	9/24
4th Down Pct.	45.5	37.5
Possession Avg.	30:19	29:41
Total Net Yards	5931	5013
Avg. Per Game	370.7	313.3
Total Plays	985	994
Avg. Per Play	6.0	5.0
Net Yards Rushing	1597	1647
Avg. Per Game	99.8	102.9
Total Rushes	388	424
Net Yards Passing	4334	3366
Avg. Per Game	270.9	210.4
Sacked/Yards Lost	19/127	36/218
Gross Yards	4461	3584
Att./Completions	578/383	534/295
Completion Pct.	66.3	55.2
Had Intercepted	15	19
Punts/Average	62/43.0	80/42.5
Net Punting Avg.	62/37.6	80/33.8
Penalties/Yards	113/1006	118/908
Fumbles/Ball Lost	25/9	17/9
Touchdowns	49	31
Rushing	13	6
Passing	30	23
Returns	6	2

2007 INDIVIDUAL STATISTICS
PASSING
PASSING	Att.	Comp.	Yds.	Pct.	TD	Int.	Tkld.	Rate
Favre	535	356	4155	66.5	28	15	15/93	95.7
Rodgers	28	20	218	71.4	1	0	3/24	106.0
Nall	15	7	88	46.7	1	0	1/10	87.6
Packers	578	383	4461	66.3	30	15	19/127	95.9
Opponents	534	295	3584	55.2	23	19	36/218	75.6

SCORING
SCORING	TD R	TD P	TD Rt	PAT	FG	Saf	PTS
Crosby	0	0	0	48/48	31/39	0	141
Jennings	0	12	0	0/0	0/0	0	72
Grant	8	0	0	0/0	0/0	0	48
Lee	0	6	0	0/0	0/0	0	36
Martin	0	4	0	0/0	0/0	0	24
Wynn	4	0	0	0/0	0/0	0	24
Franks	0	3	0	0/0	0/0	0	18
Blackmon	0	0	2	0/0	0/0	0	12
Driver	0	2	0	0/0	0/0	0	12
J. Jones	0	2	0	0/0	0/0	0	12
Woodson	0	0	2	0/0	0/0	0	12
Jackson	1	0	0	0/0	0/0	0	6
Robinson	0	1	0	0/0	0/0	0	6
T. White	0	0	1	0/0	0/0	0	6
T. Williams	0	0	1	0/0	0/0	0	6
Packers	13	30	6	48/48	31/39	0	435
Opponents	6	23	2	29/29	24/27	0	291

2-Pt. Conversions: Packers 0-0, Opponents 2-2

RUSHING
RUSHING	No.	Yds	Avg	LG	TD
Grant	188	956	5.1	66t	8
Jackson	75	267	3.6	46	1
Wynn	50	203	4.1	44	4
Morency	29	108	3.7	15	0
Rodgers	7	29	4.1	13	0
Favre	29	12	0.4	21	0
Ryan	2	7	3.5	7	0
Nall	5	6	1.2	8	0
Robinson	1	5	5.0	5	0
Driver	2	4	2.0	5	0
Packers	388	1597	4.1	66t	13
Opponents	424	1647	3.9	55	6

RECEIVING
RECEIVING	No.	Yds	Avg	LG	TD
Driver	82	1048	12.8	47	2
Jennings	53	920	17.4	82t	12
Lee	48	575	12.0	60	6
J. Jones	47	676	14.4	79t	2
Morency	30	199	6.6	18	0
Grant	30	145	4.8	21	0
Robinson	21	241	11.5	43	1
Franks	18	132	7.3	24	3
Martin	16	242	15.1	36	4
Jackson	16	130	8.1	16	0
Wynn	9	73	8.1	18	0
Hall	8	49	6.1	10	0
Krause	2	11	5.5	6	0
Kuhn	2	7	3.5	5	0
Bodiford	1	13	13.0	13	0
Packers	383	4461	11.6	82t	30
Opponents	295	3584	12.1	50	23

INTERCEPTIONS
INTERCEPTIONS	No.	Yds	Avg	LG	TD
Bigby	5	50	10.0	22	0
Woodson	4	48	12.0	46t	1
Barnett	2	40	20.0	38	0
Rouse	2	37	18.5	34	0
A. Harris	2	17	8.5	17	0
T. Williams	1	22	22.0	22	0
Hawk	1	10	10.0	10	0
C. Williams	1	9	9.0	9	0
Poppinga	1	0	0.0	0	0
Packers	19	233	12.3	46t	1
Opponents	15	166	11.1	85t	1

PUNTING
PUNTING	No.	Yds.	Avg.	In 20	LG
Ryan	60	2664	44.4	18	72
Packers	62	2664	43.0	18	72
Opponents	80	3397	42.5	22	61

PUNT RETURNS
PUNT RETURNS	Ret	FC	Yds	Avg	LG	TD
Woodson	33	5	268	8.1	34	0
Blackmon	8	0	106	13.3	57t	1
T. Williams	6	0	118	19.7	94t	1
Bush	1	0	0	0.0	0	0
Packers	48	5	492	10.3	94t	2
Opponents	19	14	113	5.9	26	0

KICKOFF RETURNS
KICKOFF RETURNS	No.	Yds	Avg	LG	TD
T. Williams	30	684	22.8	65	0
Robinson	25	596	23.8	67	0
Bodiford	2	41	20.5	22	0
Blackmon	1	3	3.0	3	0
Driver	1	4	4.0	4	0
Martin	1	6	6.0	6	0
Montgomery	1	0	0.0	0	0
Wynn	1	15	15.0	15	0
Packers	62	1349	21.8	67	0
Opponents	77	1610	20.9	74	0

FIELD GOALS
FIELD GOALS	1-19	20-29	30-39	40-49	50+
Crosby	1/1	8/8	10/11	9/14	3/5
Packers	1/1	8/8	10/11	9/14	3/5
Opponents	0/0	4/4	8/9	10/12	2/2

SACKS
SACKS	No.
Kampman	12.0
Gbaja-Biamila	9.5
C. Williams	7.0
Barnett	3.5
Hawk	1.0
Jenkins	1.0
Jolly	1.0
Pickett	1.0
Packers	36.0
Opponents	19.0

RECORD HOLDERS
INDIVIDUAL RECORDS—CAREER

Category	Name	Performance
Rushing (Yds.)	Jim Taylor, 1958-1966	8,207
Passing (Yds.)	Brett Favre, 1992-2007	*61,655
Passing (TDs)	Brett Favre, 1992-2007	*442
Receiving (No.)	Sterling Sharpe, 1988-1994	595
Receiving (Yds.)	James Lofton, 1978-1986	9,656
Interceptions	Bobby Dillon, 1952-59	52
Punting (Avg.)	Craig Hentrich, 1994-97	42.8
Punt Return (Avg.)	Desmond Howard, 1996, 1999	13.8
Kickoff Return (Avg.)	Travis Williams, 1967-1970	26.7
Field Goals	Ryan Longwell, 1997-2005	226
Touchdowns (Tot.)	Don Hutson, 1935-1945	105
Points	Ryan Longwell, 1997-2005	1,054

INDIVIDUAL RECORDS—SINGLE SEASON

Category	Name	Performance
Rushing (Yds.)	Ahman Green, 2003	1,883
Passing (Yds.)	Lynn Dickey, 1983	4,458
Passing (TDs)	Brett Favre, 1996	39
Receiving (No.)	Sterling Sharpe, 1993	112
Receiving (Yds.)	Robert Brooks, 1995	1,497
Interceptions	Irv Comp, 1943	10
Punting (Avg.)	Craig Hentrich, 1997	45.0
Punt Return (Avg.)	Billy Grimes, 1950	19.1
Kickoff Return (Avg.)	Travis Williams, 1967	*41.1
Field Goals	Chester Marcol, 1972	33
	Ryan Longwell, 2000	33
Touchdowns (Tot.)	Ahman Green, 2003	20
Points	Paul Hornung, 1960	176

INDIVIDUAL RECORDS—SINGLE GAME

Category	Name	Performance
Rushing (Yds.)	Ahman Green, 12-28-03	218
Passing (Yds.)	Lynn Dickey, 10-12-80	418
Passing (TDs)	Many times	5
	Last time by Brett Favre, 9-27-98	
Receiving (No.)	Don Hutson, 11-22-42	14
Receiving (Yds.)	Billy Howton, 10-21-56	257
Interceptions	Bobby Dillon, 11-26-53	*4
	Willie Buchanon, 9-24-78	*4
Field Goals	Chris Jacke, 11-11-90, 10-14-96	5
	Ryan Longwell, 9-24-00	5
Touchdowns (Tot.)	Paul Hornung, 12-12-65	5
Points	Paul Hornung, 10-8-61	33

*NFL Record

2008 VETERAN ROSTER

No.	Name	Pos.	Ht.	Wt.	Age	NFL Exp.	College	Hometown	How Acq.	'07 Games/ Starts
78	Barbre, Allen	G	6-4	300	24	2	Missouri Southern State	Granby, Mo.	D4-'07	7/0
56	Barnett, Nick	LB	6-2	232	27	6	Oregon State	Fontana, Calif.	D1-'03	16/16
20	Bigby, Atari	S	5-11	211	26	3	Central Florida	Miami, Fla.	FA-'06	16/16
55	Bishop, Desmond	LB	6-2	235	24	2	California	Fairfield, Calif.	D6b-'07	10/0
27	Blackmon, Will	CB	6-0	202	23	3	Boston College	Warwick, R.I.	D4b-'06	9/1
19	Bodiford, Shaun	WR	5-11	194	26	3	Portland State	Federal Way, Wash.	W(Det)-'06	6/0
24	Bush, Jarrett	CB	6-0	197	24	3	Utah State	Vacaville, Calif.	W(Car)-'06	14/1
54	Chillar, Brandon	LB	6-3	242	25	5	UCLA	Carlsbad, Calif.	UFA(StL)-'08	15/14*
76	Clifton, Chad	T	6-5	320	32	9	Tennessee	Martin, Tenn.	D2-'00	16/16
90	Cole, Colin	DT	6-1	320	28	4	Iowa	Ft. Lauderdale, Fla.	FA-'04	7/0
73	Colledge, Daryn	G	6-4	305	26	3	Boise State	North Pole, Alaska	D2a-'06	16/13
36	Collins, Nick	S	5-11	200	25	4	Bethune-Cookman	Cross City, Fla.	D2a-'05	13/13
62	Coston, Junius	G	6-3	313	24	4	North Carolina A&T	Raleigh, N.C.	D5a-'05	13/7
2	Crosby, Mason	K	6-1	212	24	2	Colorado	Georgetown, Texas	D6c-'07	16/0
29	Culver, Tyrone	S	6-1	200	25	3	Fresno State	Palmdale, Calif.	D6b-'06	0*
80	Driver, Donald	WR	6-0	190	33	10	Alcorn State	Houston, Texas	D7b-99	15/14
83	Francies, Chris	WR	6-1	193	26	2	Texas-El Paso	Houston, Texas	FA-'08	1/0
94	Gbaja-Biamila, Kabeer	DE	6-4	247	30	9	San Diego State	Los Angeles, Calif.	FA-'00 (D5a-'00)	15/2
25	Grant, Ryan	RB	6-1	224	25	2	Notre Dame	Ramsey, N.J.	T(NYG)-'07	15/7
35	Hall, Korey	FB	6-0	236	25	2	Boise State	Glenns Ferry, Idaho	D6a-'07	14/10
91	Harrell, Justin	DT	6-4	318	24	2	Tennessee	Martin, Tenn.	D1-'07	7/2
31	Harris, Al	CB	6-1	188	33	11	Texas A&M-Kingsville	Pompano Beach, Fla.	T(Phil)-'03	16/16
50	Hawk, A.J.	LB	6-1	247	24	3	Ohio State	Centerville, Ohio	D1-'06	16/16
23	Herron, Noah	RB	5-11	218	26	4	Northwestern	Mattawan, Mich.	FA-'05	0*
52	Hodge, Abdul	LB	6-0	229	25	3	Iowa	Lauderdale Lakes, Fla.	D3a-'06	0*
84	Humphrey, Tory	TE	6-2	250	25	3	Central Michigan	Saginaw, Mich.	FA-'05	0*
57	Hunter, Jason	DE	6-4	260	25	3	Appalachian State	Fayetteville, N.C.	FA-'06	16/0
32	Jackson, Brandon	RB	5-10	212	22	2	Nebraska	Horn Lake, Miss.	D2-'07	11/3
77	Jenkins, Cullen	DE	6-2	303	27	5	Central Michigan	Belleville, Mich.	FA-'04	16/15
85	Jennings, Greg	WR	5-11	197	24	3	Western Michigan	Kalamazoo, Mich.	D2b-'06	13/13
97	Jolly, Johnny	DT	6-3	318	25	3	Texas A&M	Houston, Texas	D6a-'06	10/7
89	Jones, James	WR	6-1	212	24	2	San Jose State	San Jose, Calif.	D3a-'07	16/9
74	Kampman, Aaron	DE	6-4	265	28	7	Iowa	Parkersburg, Iowa	D5a-'02	15/15
30	Kuhn, John	FB	6-0	250	25	3	Shippensburg	York, Pa.	W(Pitt)-'07	16/1
86	Lee, Donald	TE	6-4	248	28	6	Mississippi State	Maben, Miss.	FA-'05	15/12
82	Martin, Ruvell	WR	6-4	215	26	3	Saginaw Valley State	Muskegon, Mich.	FA-'06	15/5
75	Moll, Tony	T	6-5	304	25	3	Nevada	Sonoma, Calif.	D5b-'06	8/3
96	Montgomery, Michael	DE	6-5	270	25	4	Texas A&M	Center, Texas	D6a-'05	9/0
34	Morency, Vernand	RB	5-10	217	24	4	Oklahoma State	Miami, Fla.	T(Hou)-'06	13/0
95	Muir, Daniel	DT	6-2	312	24	2	Kent State	Riverdale, Md.	FA-'07	3/0
26	Peprah, Charlie	S	5-11	202	25	3	Alabama	Plano, Texas	W(NYG)-'06	16/0
79	Pickett, Ryan	DT	6-2	330	28	8	Ohio State	Zephyrhills, Fla.	UFA(StL)-'06	14/14
51	Poppinga, Brady	LB	6-3	245	28	4	Brigham Young	Evanston, Wyo.	D4b-'05	16/15
39	Powdrell, Ryan	FB	5-11	254	24	2	Southern California	Mission Viejo, Calif.	FA-'07	0*
12	Rodgers, Aaron	QB	6-2	223	24	4	California	Chico, Calif.	D1-'05	2/0
37	Rouse, Aaron	S	6-4	223	24	2	Virginia Tech	Virginia Beach, Va.	D3b-'07	11/3
9	Ryan, Jon	P	6-0	202	26	3	Regina (Canada)	Regina, Saskatchewan	FA-'06	16/0
72	Spitz, Jason	G/C	6-3	300	25	3	Louisville	Jacksonville, Fla.	D3b-'06	15/12
65	Tauscher, Mark	T	6-3	315	31	9	Wisconsin	Auburndale, Wis.	D7a-'00	16/16
70	Toledo, Joe	T	6-5	325	25	2	Washington	Carlsbad, Calif.	FA-'08	0*
63	Wells, Scott	C	6-2	295	27	5	Tennessee	Brentwood, Tenn.	FA-'04 (D7-'04)	14/13
59	White, Tracy	LB	6-0	234	27	6	Howard	St. Stephens, S.C.	FA-'06	13/0
38	Williams, Tramon	CB	5-11	185	25	2	Louisiana Tech	Napoleonville, La.	FA-'07	16/1
21	Woodson, Charles	CB	6-1	200	31	11	Michigan	Fremont, Ohio	UFA(Oak)-'06	14/14
42	Wynn, DeShawn	RB	5-10	232	24	2	Florida	Cincinnati, Ohio	D7a-'07	7/4

* Chillar played in 15 games with the St. Louis Rams in '07; Culver missed '07 season because of injury; Herron missed '07 season because of injury; Hodge missed '07 season because of injury; Humphrey missed '07 season because of injury; Powdrell missed '07 season because of injury; Toledo missed '07 season with Miami because of injury.

Retired (2)—Rob Davis, 12-year long snapper, 16 games with Green Bay in '07; Brett Favre, 17-year quarterback, 16 games.

Traded—DT Corey Williams (16 games in '07) to Cleveland.

Players lost through free agency (2): TE Bubba Franks (NYJ; 8 games in '07), CB Frank Walker (Balt; 12).

Also played with Packers in '07—WR Carlyle Holiday (1 game), TE Ryan Krause (9), QB Craig Nall (1), G Tony Palmer (2), WR Koren Robinson (9).

2008 FIRST-YEAR ROSTER

Name	Pos.	Ht.	Wt.	Age	College	Hometown	How Acq.
Allen, Condrew	CB	6-1	199	23	Portland State	Granite Bay, Calif.	FA
Bolston, Conrad (1)	DT	6-3	300	23	Maryland	Washington, D.C.	W(Minn)-'07
Brohm, Brian	QB	6-3	232	22	Louisville	Louisville, Ky.	D2b
Considine, Ryan	T	6-4	302	24	Louisiana Tech	Arlington, Texas	FA
Finley, Jermichael	TE	6-5	245	21	Texas	Diboll, Texas	D3
Flynn, Matt	QB	6-2	231	23	Louisiana State	Tyler, Texas	D7a
Gafford, Thomas (1)	LS	6-2	252	25	Houston	Houston, Texas	FA
Giacomini, Breno	T	6-7	303	22	Louisville	Malden, Mass.	D5
Havner, Spencer (1)	LB	6-3	244	25	UCLA	Grass Valley, Calif.	FA
Keenan, Ryan (1)	G	6-4	299	25	Northwestern	Lakewood, Ohio	FA
Lee, Pat	CB	6-0	200	24	Auburn	Miami, Fla.	D2c
Malone, Alfred (1)	DT	6-4	305	26	Troy	Frisco City, Ala.	FA
Nelson, Jordy	WR	6-3	217	23	Kansas State	Riley, Kan.	D2a
Porter, Joe (1)	CB	5-10	197	22	Rutgers	Franklin, N.J.	FA
Quinn, Johnny (1)	WR	6-0	197	24	North Texas	McKinney, Texas	FA
Sitton, Josh	G	6-3	319	22	Central Florida	Pensacola, Fla.	D4b
Stephenson, Cameron (1)	G	6-3	320	25	Rutgers	Hawthorne, Calif.	FA
Swain, Brett	WR	6-0	194	23	San Diego State	Carlsbad, Calif.	D7b
Thompson, Jeremy	DE	6-4	264	22	Wake Forest	Charlotte, N.C.	D4a
Thompson, Orrin (1)	T	6-6	322	25	Duke	Charlotte, N.C.	FA-'07
Ward, Kyle	CB	6-1	199	23	Louisiana-Lafayette	Dallas, Texas	FA
White, Corey (1)	FB	6-1	239	22	Alabama-Birmingham	Bessemer, Ala.	FA

The term NFL Rookie is defined as a player who is in his first season of professional football and has not been on the roster of another professional football team for any regular-season or postseason games. A Rookie is designated by an "R" on NFL rosters. Players who have been active in another professional football league or players who have NFL experience, including either preseason training camp or being on an Active List or Inactive List, or on Reserve/Injured or Reserve/Physically Unable to Perform for fewer than six regular-season games, are termed NFL First-Year Players. An NFL First-Year Player is designated by a "1" on NFL rosters. Thereafter, a player is credited with an additional year of experience for each season in which he accumulates six games on the Active List or Inactive List, or on Reserve/Injured or Reserve/Physically Unable to Perform.

Log on to www.packers.com for an up-to-date roster; Age listed is as of September 4, 2008.

COACHING STAFF
Head Coach,
Mike McCarthy
Pro Career: Named the fourteenth head coach in team history January 12, 2006. Named Motorola Coach of the Year, matched a franchise record with 13 wins, and won NFC North Division title in 2007. Became the first coach since Vince Lombardi to lead team to a championship game in his second season. Had returned to Green Bay after serving as the team's quarterbacks coach in 1999. Subsequently was a highly successful offensive coordinator for the New Orleans Saints (2000-04). With McCarthy calling plays, the Saints racked up 10 offensive team records and 26 individual marks. He was named NFC Assistant Coach of the Year by *USA Today* in 2000, and New Orleans led the league with 432 points and 49 touchdowns in 2002. The list of quarterbacks he has coached includes Joe Montana, Elvis Grbac, Rich Gannon, Brett Favre, Matt Hasselbeck, Aaron Brooks, Jake Delhomme and Marc Bulger—a collection that combines for 28 career Pro Bowl selections and eight Super Bowl starts. Career record: 22-12.
Background: Graduated with a degree in business administration from Baker University following a two-year playing career (1985-86). Was an all-conference tight end, helping the school to a NAIA Division II runner-up finish as a senior captain. Coached collegiately at Fort Hays State (1987-88) and Pittsburgh (1989-1992), before moving to the NFL with the Kansas City Chiefs (1993-98), Green Bay Packers (1999), New Orleans Saints (2000-04) and San Francisco 49ers (2005).
Personal: Age 45, born in Pittsburgh. Family includes daughter Alexandra, wife Jessica and two boys, George and Jack.

ASSISTANT COACHES
Edgar Bennett, running backs; born February 15, 1969, Jacksonville. Running back Florida State 1987, 1989-1991. Pro running back Green Bay Packers 1992-96, Chicago Bears 1998-99. Pro coach: Joined Packers in 2001.
James Campen, offensive line; born Sacramento, Calif. Center Sacramento City (Calif.) J.C. 1982-83, Tulane 1984-85. Pro center New Orleans Saints 1987-88, Green Bay Packers 1989-1993. Pro coach: Joined Packers in 2004.
Tom Clements, quarterbacks; born McKees Rocks, Pa. Quarterback Notre Dame 1972-74. Pro quarterback Ottawa Rough Riders (CFL) 1975-78, Hamilton Tiger-Cats (CFL) 1979, 1981-82, Kansas City Chiefs 1980, Winnipeg Blue Bombers (CFL) 1983-87. College coach: Notre Dame 1992-95. Pro coach: New Orleans Saints 1997-99, Kansas City Chiefs 2000, Pittsburgh Steelers 2001-03, Buffalo Bills 2004-05, joined Packers in 2006.

Jerry Fontenot, asst. offensive line; born Lafayette, La. Guard Texas A&M 1985-88. Pro center Chicago Bears 1989-1996, New Orleans Saints 1997-2003, Cincinnati Bengals 2004. Pro coach: Joined Packers in 2006.
Rock Gullickson, strength & conditioning; born Moorhead, Minn. Guard Moorhead (Minn.) State 1973-76. No pro playing experience. College coach: Moorhead State 1978, Mayville (N.D.) State 1979-1980, South Dakota State 1981, Montana State 1982-89, Rutgers 1990-92, Texas 1993-97, Louisville 1988-1999. Pro coach: New Orleans Saints 2000-05, joined Packers in 2006.
Carl Hairston, defensive ends; born Martinsville, Va. Defensive end Maryland-Eastern Shore 1972-75. Pro defensive end Philadelphia Eagles 1976-1983, Cleveland Browns 1984-89, Phoenix Cardinals 1990. Pro coach: Kansas City Chiefs 1995-96, 2001-05, St. Louis Rams 1997-2000, joined Packers in 2006.
Ty Knott, offensive quality control; born Los Angeles. Defensive back Oregon Tech 1988-89. No pro playing experience. College coach: Whittier College 1994-95, Indiana University (Pa.) 1997-99, Mt. San Antonio (Calif.) J.C. 2000, Greenville 2001. Pro coach: Jacksonville Jaguars 2002, New Orleans Saints 2003-05, joined Packers in 2006.
Ben McAdoo, tight ends; born Homer City, Pa. Attended Indiana University (Pa.). No college or pro playing experience. College coach: Michigan State 2001, Fairfield 2002, Pittsburgh 2003, Akron 2004, Stanford 2005. Pro coach: New Orleans Saints 2004, San Francisco 49ers 2005, joined Packers in 2006.
Winston Moss, asst. head coach/linebackers; born Miami. Linebacker Miami 1983-86. Pro linebacker Tampa Bay Buccaneers 1987-1990, Los Angeles Raiders 1991-94, Seattle Seahawks 1995-97. Pro coach: Seattle Seahawks 1998, New Orleans Saints 2000-05, joined Packers in 2006.
Robert Nunn, defensive tackles; born Apache, Okla. Linebacker Oklahoma State 1983-84, 1986-87. No pro playing experience. College coach: Northeastern Oklahoma 1988, Tennessee 1989-1990, Georgia Military College 1991-99 (head coach 1992-99). Pro coach: Miami Dolphins 2000-02, 2004, Washington Redskins 2003, joined Packers in 2005.
Joe Philbin, offensive coordinator; born Springfield, Mass. Tight end Washington & Jefferson 1980. No pro playing experience. College coach: Tulane 1984-85, Worcester Tech 1986-87, U.S. Merchant Marine Academy 1988-89, Allegheny 1990-93, Ohio University 1994, Northeastern 1995-96, Harvard 1997-98, Iowa 1999-2002. Pro coach: Joined Packers in 2003.
Jimmy Robinson, wide receivers; born

Atlanta. Wide receiver Georgia Tech 1972-74. Pro wide receiver New York Giants 1976-79, San Francisco 49ers 1980, Denver Broncos 1981. College coach: Georgia Tech 1987-89. Pro coach: Memphis Showboats (USFL) 1984-85, Atlanta Falcons 1990-93, Indianapolis Colts 1994-97, New York Giants 1998-2003, New Orleans Saints 2004-05, joined Packers in 2006.
Bob Sanders, defensive coordinator; born Jacksonville, N.C. Linebacker Davidson College 1973-75. No pro playing experience. College coach: Georgia Tech 1978, East Carolina 1980-82, Richmond 1983-84, Duke 1985-89, Florida 1990-2000. Pro coach: Miami Dolphins 2001-04, joined Packers in 2005.
Kurt Schottenheimer, secondary; born McDonald, Pa. Quarterback Coffeyville (Kan.) J.C. 1967-68, defensive back Miami (Fla.) 1969-70. No pro playing experience. College coach: William Paterson 1974, Michigan State 1978-1982, Tulane 1983, Louisiana State 1984-85, Notre Dame 1986. Pro coach: Cleveland Browns 1987-88, Kansas City Chiefs 1989-2000, Washington Redskins 2001, Detroit Lions 2002-03, Green Bay Packers 2004, St. Louis Rams 2005, rejoined Packers in 2006.
Shawn Slocum, asst. special teams; born Bryan, Texas. Linebacker Texas A&M 1983-84. No pro playing experience. College coach: Texas A&M 1989, 1991-97, 2000-02, Pittsburgh 1990, Southern California 1998-99, Mississippi 2005. Pro coach: Joined Packers in 2006.
Mike Stock, special teams coordinator; born Barberton, Ohio. Fullback Northwestern 1957-1960. Pro running back Saskatchewan Roughriders (CFL) 1961. College coach: Northwestern 1961, Buffalo 1966-67, Navy 1968, Notre Dame 1969-1974, 1983-86, Wisconsin 1975-77, Eastern Michigan 1978-1982 (head coach), Ohio State 1992-94. Pro coach: New Jersey Generals (USFL) 1983, Cincinnati Bengals 1987-1991, Kansas City Chiefs 1995-2000, Washington Redskins 2001-03, St. Louis Rams 2004, joined Packers in 2006.
Lionel Washington, defensive nickel package/cornerbacks; born New Orleans. Defensive back Tulane 1979-1982. Pro defensive back St. Louis Cardinals 1983-86, Los Angeles/Oakland Raiders 1987-1994, 1997, Denver Broncos 1995-96. Pro coach: Joined Packers in 1999.
Joe Whitt, Jr., defensive quality control; born Auburn, Ala. Wide receiver Auburn 1997-99. No pro playing experience. College coach: Auburn 2000-01, The Citadel 2002, Louisville 2003-06. Pro coach: Atlanta Falcons 2007, joined Packers in 2008.

**National Football Conference
North Division**
Team Colors: Purple, Gold, and White
9520 Viking Drive
Eden Prairie, Minnesota 55344
Telephone: (952) 828-6500

2008 SCHEDULE
PRESEASON
Aug. 8   **Seattle**...............................7:00
Aug. 16 at Baltimore.......................7:30
Aug. 23 **Pittsburgh**.........................7:00
Aug. 28 at Dallas............................7:00

REGULAR SEASON
Sep. 8   at Green Bay (Mon.)...........6:00
Sep. 14 **Indianapolis** 12:00
Sep. 21 **Carolina** 12:00
Sep. 28 at Tennessee 12:00
Oct. 6   at New Orleans (Mon.) 7:30
Oct. 12 **Detroit** 12:00
Oct. 19 at Chicago 12:00
Oct. 26 BYE
Nov. 2   **Houston** 12:00
Nov. 9   **Green Bay** 12:00
Nov. 16 at Tampa Bay 1:00
Nov. 23 at Jacksonville 1:00
Nov. 30 **Chicago** * 7:15
Dec. 7   at Detroit 1:00
Dec. 14 at Arizona 2:05
Dec. 21 **Atlanta** 12:00
Dec. 28 **N.Y. Giants**......................12:00
* Sunday night games in Weeks 11-17 subject to change
Stadium: Hubert H. Humphrey Metrodome
            (opened in 1982)
            •**Capacity:** 64,121
            500 11th Avenue South
            Minneapolis, Minnesota 55415
Playing Surface: FieldTurf
Training Camp: Minnesota State-Mankato
            Mankato, Minnesota
            56001

HUBERT H. HUMPHREY METRODOME

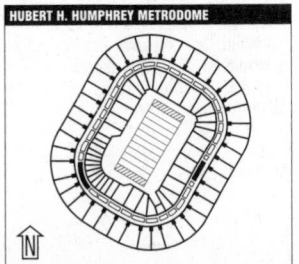

CLUB OFFICIALS
Owner/Chairman: Zygi Wilf
Owner/President: Mark Wilf
Owner/Vice Chairman: Leonard Wilf
Ownership Partners: Reggie Fowler,
    Alan Landis, David Mandelbaum
Vice President of Public Affairs/Stadium
    Development: Lester Bagley
Vice President of Football Operations:
    Rob Brzezinski
Vice President of Sales and Marketing:
    Steve LaCroix
Vice President of Finance: Steve Poppen
Vice President of Player Personnel:
    Rick Spielman
Vice President of Operations and Legal
    Counsel: Kevin Warren
Director of College Scouting:
    Scott Studwell
Director of Football Administration:
    Dave Blando
Director of Public Relations: Bob Hagan
Director of Community Relations:
    Brad Madson
Director of Operations/Team Travel:
    Luther Hippe
Director of Operations/Stadium and
    Logistics: Chad Lundeen
Director of Ticketing and Hospitality:
    Phil Huebner
Director of Video: Bob Marcus
Executive Director of Player
    Development/Legal: Les Pico
Director of Security: Kim Klawiter
Head Athletic Trainer: Eric Sugarman
Equipment Manager: Dennis Ryan
Director of Marketing & Business
    Development: Dannon Hulskotter
Director of Corporate Sales: Mike Slates
Director of Civic and Business Affairs:
    Kimberly Fields
Facilities Director: Nick Tigue

COACHING HISTORY
(403-340-9)
Records include postseason games
1961-66	Norm Van Brocklin	29-51-4
1967-1983	Bud Grant	161-99-5
1984	Les Steckel	3-13-0
1985	Bud Grant	7-9-0
1986-1991	Jerry Burns	55-46-0
1992-2001	Dennis Green*	101-70-0
2001-05	Mike Tice	33-34-0
2006-07	Brad Childress	14-18-0
*Resigned after 15 games in 2001

PAID ATTENDANCE
Home 496,046   Away 546,722
Total 1,042,768
Single-game home record,
    64,482 (11/2/03)
Single-season home record,
    510,741 (1998)

2008 DRAFT CHOICES
Round	Name	Pos.	College
2	Tyrell Johnson	DB	Arkansas State
5	John David Booty	QB	Southern California
	Letroy Guion	DT	Florida State
6	John Sullivan	C	Notre Dame
	Jaymar Johnson	WR	Jackson State

2007 TEAM RECORD
PRESEASON (2-2)

Date	Result	Opponent
8/10	L 10-13	St. Louis
8/17	W 37-20	at New York Jets
8/25	L 13-30	at Seattle
8/30	W 23-14	Dallas

REGULAR SEASON (8-8)

Date	Result	Opponent	Att.
9/9	W 24-3	Atlanta	62,815
9/16	L 17-20	at Detroit (OT)	61,771
9/23	L 10-13	at Kansas City	78,038
9/30	L 16-23	Green Bay	63,779
10/14	W 34-31	at Chicago	62,174
10/21	L 14-24	at Dallas	63,432
10/28	L 16-23	Philadelphia	63,019
11/4	W 35-17	San Diego	63,043
11/11	L 0-34	at Green Bay	70,945
11/18	W 29-22	Oakland	62,960
11/25	W 41-17	at N.Y. Giants	78,591
12/2	W 42-10	Detroit	62,996
12/9	W 27-7	at San Francisco	68,050
12/17	W 20-13	Chicago	63,800
12/23	L 21-32	Washington	63,634
12/30	L 19-22	at Denver (OT)	76,084

(OT) Overtime

SCORE BY PERIODS

Vikings	82	107	66	110	0 —	365
Opponents	63	110	60	72	6 —	311

2007 TEAM STATISTICS

	Vikings	Opp.
Total First Downs	294	305
Rushing	131	67
Passing	139	222
Penalty	24	16
3rd Down: Made/Att	69/200	94/234
3rd Down Pct.	34.5	40.2
4th Down: Made/Att	7/13	7/18
4th Down Pct.	53.8	38.9
Possession Avg.	29:22	30:38
Total Net Yards	5379	5410
Avg. Per Game	336.2	338.1
Total Plays	964	1063
Avg. Per Play	5.6	5.1
Net Yards Rushing	2634	1185
Avg. Per Game	164.6	74.1
Total Rushes	494	379
Net Yards Passing	2745	4225
Avg. Per Game	171.6	264.1
Sacked/Yards Lost	38/193	38/275
Gross Yards	2938	4500
Att./Completions	432/249	646/415
Completion Pct.	57.6	64.2
Had Intercepted	14	15
Punts/Average	81/44.7	82/46.1
Net Punting Avg.	81/37.0	82/40.5
Penalties/Yards	86/662	110/763
Fumbles/Ball Lost	27/16	37/16
Touchdowns	43	32
Rushing	22	7
Passing	12	22
Returns	9	3

2007 INDIVIDUAL STATISTICS

PASSING

PASSING	Att.	Comp.	Yds.	Pct.	TD	Int.	Tkld.	Rate
Jackson	294	171	1911	58.2	9	12	19/70	70.8
Holcomb	83	42	515	50.6	2	1	12/87	73.1
Bollinger	50	33	391	66.0	1	1	7/36	88.0
Rice	2	2	94	100.0	0	0	0/0	118.8
Kluwe	1	1	27	100.0	0	0	0/0	118.8
Moore	1	0	0	0.0	0	0	0/0	39.6
Taylor	1	0	0	0.0	0	0	0/0	39.6
Vikings	432	249	2938	57.6	12	14	38/193	74.2
Opponents	646	415	4500	64.2	22	15	38/275	86.3

SCORING

SCORING	TD R	TD P	TD Rt	PAT	FG	Saf	PTS
Longwell	0	0	0	39/40	20/24	0	99
Peterson	12	1	0	0/0	0/0	0	78
Taylor	7	0	0	0/0	0/0	0	42
Rice	0	4	0	0/0	0/0	0	24
Jackson	3	0	0	0/0	0/0	0	22
Wade	0	3	0	0/0	0/0	0	18
K. Williams	0	0	2	0/0	0/0	0	12
Allison	0	0	1	0/0	0/0	0	6
Edwards	0	0	1	0/0	0/0	0	6
Ferguson	0	1	0	0/0	0/0	0	6
Greenway	0	0	1	0/0	0/0	0	6
Griffin	0	0	1	0/0	0/0	0	6
Kleinsasser	0	1	0	0/0	0/0	0	6
Sharper	0	0	1	0/0	0/0	0	6
Shiancoe	0	1	0	0/0	0/0	0	6
Smith	0	0	1	0/0	0/0	0	6
Williamson	0	1	0	0/0	0/0	0	6
Winfield	0	0	1	0/0	0/0	0	6
Bollinger	0	0	0	0/0	0/0	0	2
Vikings	22	12	9	39/40	20/24	1	365
Opponents	7	22	3	31/31	28/32	2	311

2-Pt. Conversions: Jackson 2, Bollinger,
Vikings 3-3, Opponents 0-1

RUSHING

RUSHING	No.	Yds	Avg	LG	TD
Peterson	238	1341	5.6	73t	12
Taylor	157	844	5.4	84t	7
Jackson	54	260	4.8	32	3
Moore	20	113	5.7	17	0
Williamson	2	29	14.5	26	0
Bollinger	5	18	3.6	10	0
Tahi	6	15	2.5	6	0
Richardson	7	13	1.9	4	0
Dugan	2	7	3.5	4	0
Allison	2	3	1.5	3	0
Wade	1	-9	-9.0	-9	0
Vikings	494	2634	5.3	84t	22
Opponents	379	1185	3.1	30t	7

RECEIVING

RECEIVING	No.	Yds	Avg	LG	TD
Wade	54	647	12.0	40	3
Ferguson	32	391	12.2	71	1
Rice	31	396	12.8	60t	4
Taylor	29	281	9.7	50	0
Shiancoe	27	323	12.0	79	1
Peterson	19	268	14.1	60t	1
Williamson	18	240	13.3	60t	1
Richardson	11	89	8.1	12	0
Allison	8	122	15.3	35	0
Dugan	7	57	8.1	27	0
Moore	6	48	8.0	20	0
Kleinsasser	4	43	10.8	26	1
Mills	2	26	13.0	18	0
Tahi	1	7	7.0	7	0
Vikings	249	2938	11.8	79	12
Opponents	415	4500	10.8	81t	22

INTERCEPTIONS

INTERCEPTIONS	No.	Yds	Avg	LG	TD
Smith	4	112	28.0	93t	1
Sharper	4	61	15.3	41	1
K. Williams	2	72	36.0	54t	2
Greenway	2	39	19.5	37t	1
Winfield	1	14	14.0	14t	1
Gordon	1	0	0.0	0	0
Leber	1	0	0.0	0	0
Vikings	15	298	19.9	93t	6
Opponents	14	177	12.6	47	0

PUNTING

PUNTING	No.	Yds.	Avg.	In 20	LG
Kluwe	81	3621	44.7	34	70
Vikings	81	3621	44.7	34	70
Opponents	82	3780	46.1	33	69

PUNT RETURNS

PUNT RETURNS	Ret	FC	Yds	Avg	LG	TD
Wade	16	11	112	7.0	17	0
Moore	13	8	130	10.0	42	0
Vikings	29	19	242	8.3	42	0
Opponents	43	6	440	10.2	89t	0

KICKOFF RETURNS

KICKOFF RETURNS	No.	Yds	Avg	LG	TD
Allison	20	574	28.7	104t	1
Williamson	17	387	22.8	56	0
Peterson	16	412	25.8	53	0
Gordon	2	48	24.0	27	0
Dugan	1	18	18.0	18	0
Grigsby	1	2	2.0	2	0
Moore	1	20	20.0	20	0
Shiancoe	1	0	0.0	0	0
Vikings	59	1461	24.8	104t	1
Opponents	65	1441	22.2	55	0

FIELD GOALS

FIELD GOALS	1-19	20-29	30-39	40-49	50+
Longwell	0/0	3/3	6/6	10/11	1/4
Vikings	0/0	3/3	6/6	10/11	1/4
Opponents	0/0	7/7	10/10	10/12	1/3

SACKS

SACKS	No.
Edwards	5.0
Leber	5.0
Udeze	5.0
Henderson	4.5
Robison	4.5
S. Johnson	3.0
K. Williams	3.0
P. Williams	2.0
(group)	2.0
Evans	1.0
Grigsby	1.0
James	1.0
Mitchell	1.0
Vikings	38.0
Opponents	38.0

RECORD HOLDERS
INDIVIDUAL RECORDS—CAREER

Category	Name	Performance
Rushing (Yds.)	Robert Smith, 1993-2000	6,818
Passing (Yds.)	Fran Tarkenton, 1961-66, 1972-78	33,098
Passing (TDs)	Fran Tarkenton, 1961-66, 1972-78	239
Receiving (No.)	Cris Carter, 1990-2001	1,004
Receiving (Yds.)	Cris Carter, 1990-2001	12,383
Interceptions	Paul Krause, 1968-1979	53
Punting (Avg.)	Harry Newsome, 1990-93	43.8
Punt Return (Avg.)	David Palmer, 1994-2000	9.4
Kickoff Return (Avg.)	Charlie West, 1968-1973	25.5
Field Goals	Fred Cox, 1963-1977	282
Touchdowns (Tot.)	Cris Carter, 1990-2001	110
Points	Fred Cox, 1963-1977	1,365

INDIVIDUAL RECORDS—SINGLE SEASON

Category	Name	Performance
Rushing (Yds.)	Robert Smith, 2000	1,521
Passing (Yds.)	Daunte Culpepper, 2004	4,717
Passing (TDs)	Daunte Culpepper, 2004	39
Receiving (No.)	Cris Carter, 1994, 1995	122
Receiving (Yds.)	Randy Moss, 2003	1,632
Interceptions	Paul Krause, 1975	10
Punting (Avg.)	Bobby Walden, 1964	46.4
Punt Return (Avg.)	David Palmer, 1995	13.2
Kickoff Return (Avg.)	John Gilliam, 1972	26.3
Field Goals	Gary Anderson, 1998	35
Touchdowns (Tot.)	Chuck Foreman, 1975	22
Points	Gary Anderson, 1998	164

INDIVIDUAL RECORDS—SINGLE GAME

Category	Name	Performance
Rushing (Yds.)	Adrian Peterson, 11-4-07	*296
Passing (Yds.)	Tommy Kramer, 11-2-86	490
Passing (TDs)	Joe Kapp, 9-28-69	*7
Receiving (No.)	Rickey Young, 12-16-79	15
Receiving (Yds.)	Sammy White, 11-7-76	210
Interceptions	Many Times	3
	Last time by Darren Sharper, 11-13-05	
Field Goals	Rich Karlis, 11-5-89	7
Touchdowns (Tot.)	Chuck Foreman, 12-20-75	4
	Ahmad Rashad, 9-2-79	4
Points	Chuck Foreman, 12-20-75	24
	Ahmad Rashad, 9-2-79	24

*NFL Record

2008 VETERAN ROSTER

No.	Name	Pos.	Ht.	Wt.	Age	NFL Exp.	College	Hometown	How Acq.	'07 Games/ Starts
57	Alexander, Rufus	LB	6-1	232	25	2	Oklahoma	Baton Rouge, La.	D6-'07	0*
69 t-	Allen, Jared	DE	6-6	270	26	5	Idaho State	Los Gatos, Calif.	T(KC)-'08	14/14*
71	Allen, Kenderick	DT	6-5	328	29	5	Louisiana State	Bogalusa, La.	FA-'08	0*
84	Allison, Aundrae	WR	6-0	198	24	2	East Carolina	Kannapolis, N.C.	D5-'07	11/0
87	Berrian, Bernard	WR	6-1	185	27	5	Fresno State	Winton, Calif.	UFA(Chi)-'08	16/15*
78	Birk, Matt	C	6-4	309	32	11	Harvard	St. Paul, Minn.	D6-'98	16/16
9	Bollinger, Brooks	QB	6-1	205	28	6	Wisconsin	Grand Forks, N.D.	T(NYJ)-'06	5/1
27	Boulware, Michael	S	6-3	220	26	5	Florida State	Columbia, S.C.	UFA(Hou)-'08	16/0*
54	Ciurciu, Vinny	LB	6-0	235	28	6	Boston College	Paramus, N.J.	UFA(Car)-'07	13/0
62	Cook, Ryan	T	6-6	328	25	3	New Mexico	Albuquerque, N.M.	D2b-'06	16/16
83	Dugan, Jeff	FB	6-4	258	27	5	Maryland	Pittsburgh, Pa.	D7-'04	16/3
91	Edwards, Ray	DE	6-5	268	23	3	Purdue	Cincinnati OH	D4-'06	12/11
90	Evans, Fred	DT	6-4	305	24	3	Texas St.-San Marcos	Morgan Park, Ill.	FA-'07	11/0
59	Farwell, Heath	LB	6-0	235	26	4	San Diego State	Corona, Calif.	FA-'05	16/0
89	Ferguson, Robert	WR	6-1	219	28	8	Texas A&M	Houston, Texas	FA-'07	15/8
37	Frampton, Eric	S	5-11	205	24	2	Washington State	San Jose, Calif.	W(Det)-'07	14/0*
12	Frerotte, Gus	QB	6-3	233	37	15	Tulsa	Ford City, Pa.	FA-'08	8/3*
41	Gordon, Charles	CB	5-11	180	24	3	Kansas	Santa Monica, Calif.	FA-'06	16/3
52	Greenway, Chad	LB	6-2	242	25	3	Iowa	Mt. Vernon, S.D.	D1-'06	16/16
23	Griffin, Cedric	CB	6-0	203	25	3	Texas	San Antonio, Texas	D2a-'06	16/16
73	Grigsby, Otis	DE	6-3	260	27	2	Kentucky	Converse, Texas	W(Car)-'07	4/0
56	Henderson, E.J.	LB	6-1	245	28	6	Maryland	Aberdeen, Md.	D2-'03	16/16
64	Herrera, Anthony	G	6-2	315	28	5	Tennessee	Naples, Fla.	FA-'04	16/12
79	Hicks, Artis	G	6-4	335	29	7	Memphis	Jackson, Tenn.	T(Phil)-'06	14/4
43	Hicks, Maurice	RB	5-11	205	30	5	North Carolina A&T	Emporia, Va.	UFA(SF)-'08	16/0*
76	Hutchinson, Steve	G	6-5	313	30	8	Michigan	Ft. Lauderdale, Fla.	FA(Sea)-'06	16/16
7	Jackson, Tarvaris	QB	6-2	232	25	3	Alabama State	Montgomery, Ala.	D2c-'06	12/12
99	James, Erasmus	DE	6-4	266	25	4	Wisconsin	Hollywood, Fla.	D1b-'05	6/1
75	Johnson, Chase	T	6-8	330	24	2	Wyoming	Loveland, Colo.	FA-'07	0*
72	Johnson, Marcus	T	6-6	321	26	4	Mississippi	Coffeeville, Miss.	D2-'05	16/0
47	Jones, Braden	TE	6-3	260	25	2	Southern Illinois	Harrisburg, Ill.	FA-'07	0*
40	Kleinsasser, Jim	TE	6-3	272	31	10	North Dakota	Carrington, N.D.	D2-'99	16/10
5	Kluwe, Chris	P	6-4	215	26	4	UCLA	Los Alamitos, Calif.	W(Sea)-'05	16/0
51	Leber, Ben	LB	6-3	244	29	7	Kansas State	Vermillion, S.D.	UFA(SD)-'06	16/10
46	Loeffler, Cullen	LS	6-5	241	27	5	Texas	Ingram, Texas	FA-'04	16/0
8	Longwell, Ryan	K	6-0	200	34	12	California	Bend, Ore.	UFA(GB)-'06	16/0
21	McCauley, Marcus	CB	6-1	203	25	2	Fresno State	Sacramento, Calif.	D3-'07	16/9
74	McKinnie, Bryant	T	6-8	335	28	7	Miami	Woodbury, N.J.	D1-'02	16/16
45	Mills, Garrett	TE	6-1	235	24	3	Tulsa	Jenks, Okla.	W(NE)-'07	1/0
92	Mitchell, Jayme	DE	6-6	285	24	3	Mississippi	Jackson, Miss.	FA-'06	10/0
67	Mozes, Dan	G	6-3	293	24	2	West Virginia	Washington, Pa.	FA-'07	0*
28	Peterson, Adrian	RB	6-1	217	23	2	Oklahoma	Palestine, Texas	D1-'07	14/9
55	Pope, Derrick	LB	6-0	232	26	5	Alabama	Galveston, Texas	UFA(Mia)-'08	16/9*
18	Rice, Sidney	WR	6-4	202	22	2	South Carolina	Gaffney, S.C.	D2-'07	13/4
96	Robison, Brian	DE	6-3	259	25	2	Texas	Splendora, Texas	D4-'07	16/5
22	Sapp, Benny	CB	5-9	190	27	5	Northern Iowa	Ft. Lauderdale, Fla.	UFA(KC)-'08	14/2*
42	Sharper, Darren	S	6-2	210	32	12	William & Mary	Richmond, Va.	FA-'05	16/16
81	Shiancoe, Visanthe	TE	6-4	250	28	6	Morgan State	Laurel, Md.	UFA(NYG)'-07	16/15
38	Tahi, Naufahu	FB	6-0	254	26	3	Brigham Young	West Valley City, Utah	W(Cin)-'06	10/0
44	Tapeh, Thomas	FB	6-1	243	28	5	Minnesota	St. Paul, Minn.	UFA(Phil)-'08	16/8*
29	Taylor, Chester	RB	5-11	213	28	7	Toledo	River Rouge, Mich.	UFA(Balt)-'06	14/8
95	Udeze, Kenechi	DE	6-3	281	25	5	Southern California	Los Angeles, Calif.	D1-'04	16/15
19	Wade, Bobby	WR	5-10	186	27	6	Arizona	Phoenix, Ariz.	UFA(Tenn)-'07	16/12
93	Williams, Kevin	DT	6-5	311	28	6	Oklahoma State	Fordyce, Ark.	D1-'03	16/16
20	Williams, Madieu	S	6-1	203	26	5	Maryland	Lanham, Md.	UFA(Cin)-'08	13/13*
94	Williams, Pat	DT	6-3	317	35	12	Texas A&M	Monroe, La.	UFA(Buf)-'05	16/16
26	Winfield, Antoine	CB	5-9	180	31	10	Ohio State	Akron, Ohio	UFA(Buf)-'04	10/10
97	Wyms, Ellis	DT	6-3	290	29	8	Mississippi State	Indianola, Miss.	UFA(Sea)-'08	13/0*

* Alexander missed '07 season because of injury; J. Allen played 14 games with Kansas City; K. Allen last active with Green Bay in '06; Berrian played 16 games with Chicago; Boulware played 16 games with Houston; Frampton played 5 games with Detroit and 9 games with Minnesota; Frerotte played 8 games with St. Louis; Hicks played 16 games with San Francisco; C. Johnson inactive for 15 games; Jones missed '07 season because of injury; Mozes missed '07 season because of injury; Pope played 16 games with Miami; Sapp played 14 games with Kansas City; Tapeh played 16 games with Philadelphia; Williams played 13 games with Cincinnati; Wyms played 13 games with Seattle.

t-   Vikings traded for J. Allen (KC).

Traded—WR Troy Williamson (11 games in '07) to Jacksonville.

Players lost through free agency (5): DT Spencer Johnson (Buff; 16 games in '07), RB Mewelde Moore (Pitt; 12), FB Tony Richardson (NYJ; 14), LB Dontarrious Thomas (SF; 13), S Tank Williams (NE; 13).

Also played with Vikings in '07—DT Conrad Bolston (1 game), S Mike Doss (8), QB Kelly Holcomb (3), DE Darrion Scott (4), S Dwight Smith (14), CB Ronyell Whitaker (11).

2008 FIRST-YEAR ROSTER

Name	Pos.	Ht.	Wt.	Age	College	Hometown	How Acq.
Abdullah, Husain	S	6-0	204	23	Washington State	Pomona, Calif.	FA
Booty, John David	QB	6-3	213	23	Southern California	Shreveport, La.	D5
Burnett, Martail	DE	6-3	262	23	Utah	Los Angeles, Calif.	FA
Daniels, Brian (1)	G	6-4	303	23	Colorado	Denver, Colo.	FA
Douzable, Leger	DT	6-4	305	22	Central Florida	Tampa, Fla.	FA
Griffin, Marcus	S	5-10	201	23	Texas	Austin, Texas	FA
Guion, Letroy	DT	6-4	303	21	Florida State	Starke, Fla.	D5
Hauschka, Steven	K	6-2	185	23	North Carolina State	Needham, Ma.	FA
Henderson, Erin	LB	6-3	244	22	Maryland	Aberdeen, Md.	FA
Herron, David (1)	LB	6-1	239	24	Michigan State	Warren, Ohio	FA
Johnson, Jaymar	WR	6-0	176	24	Jackson State	Gary, Ind.	D6
Johnson, Tyrell	S	6-0	207	23	Arkansas State	Rison, Ark.	D2
Jones, Nate	WR	6-1	195	22	Texas	Texarkana, Texas	FA
Key, Travis	CB	5-10	185	22	Michigan State	Three Rivers, Mich.	FA
Leman, J	LB	6-2	240	23	Illinois	Champaign, Ill.	FA
Little, Brent (1)	WR	5-11	183	25	Southern Illinois	Poplar Bluff, Mo.	FA
Mattran, Tim	C	6-4	308	23	Stanford	Chaska, Minn.	FA
McCann, Dee	CB	5-10	200	25	West Virginia	Leakesville, Miss.	FA
Nance, Martin (1)	WR	6-3	212	25	Miami (Ohio)	Maryland Heights, Mo.	FA
Radovich, Drew	T	6-5	305	23	Southern California	Mission Viejo, Calif.	FA
Reynaud, Darius	WR	5-9	201	22	West Virginia	Boutte, La.	FA
Sullivan, John	C	6-4	301	23	Notre Dame	Old Greenwich, Conn.	D6
Sumrall, Brandon	CB	5-10	193	22	Southern Miss	Beaumont, Miss.	FA
Surrency, Justin (1)	WR	6-0	182	23	Northern Iowa	St. Paul, Minn.	FA
Walker, Marcus	CB	5-11	191	22	Oklahoma	Waco, Texas	FA
Whitlock, Arkee (1)	RB	5-9	203	24	Southern Illinois	Rock Hill, S.C.	FA
Wright, Kyle	QB	6-4	220	23	Miami	Danville, Calif.	FA
Young, Albert	RB	5-10	209	23	Iowa	Moorestown, N.J.	FA

The term NFL Rookie is defined as a player who is in his first season of professional football and has not been on the roster of another professional football team for any regular-season or postseason games. A Rookie is designated by an "R" on NFL rosters. Players who have been active in another professional football league or players who have NFL experience, including either preseason training camp or being on an Active List or Inactive List, or on Reserve/Injured or Reserve/Physically Unable to Perform for fewer than six regular-season games, are termed NFL First-Year Players. An NFL First-Year Player is designated by a "1" on NFL rosters. Thereafter, a player is credited with an additional year of experience for each season in which he accumulates six games on the Active List or Inactive List, or on Reserve/Injured or Reserve/Physically Unable to Perform.

Log on to www.vikings.com for an up-to-date roster; Age listed is as of September 4, 2008.

MINNESOTA VIKINGS

COACHING STAFF

Head Coach,
Brad Childress

Pro Career: Named the seventh head coach in Vikings' history on January 6, 2006. This marks Childress' 31st season coaching, including his eleventh on an NFL sideline, and his third with the Vikings. The 2007 Vikings became the first team in franchise history to rank No. 1 in the NFL in rushing offense and rushing defense. The offense in 2007 set franchise records by rushing for 2,634 yards (164.6 per game). The Vikings had seven players named to the Pro Bowl in '07, the most since 2000. Childress became the first head coach in team history to win his first two games when he accomplished the feat in 2006. Was an assistant coach with the Philadelphia Eagles (the last four as offensive coordinator), when the Eagles reached Super Bowl XXXIX and played in four straight NFC Championship Games. He began his NFL coaching career as the Colts' quarterbacks coach (1985). Career record: 14-18.

Background: Coached at Illinois (1978-1984), Northern Arizona (1986-89), Utah (1990), and Wisconsin (1991-98). Childress briefly played quarterback and wide receiver at Illinois before transferring to Eastern Illinois, where he graduated with a bachelor's degree in psychology.

Personal: Age 52, born in Aurora, Ill. He and his wife Dru-Ann have four children: Cara, Kyle, Andrew, and Christopher.

ASSISTANT COACHES

Juney Barnett, asst. strength and conditioning; born Philadelphia. Defensive back Bloomsburg 1997-2000. College coach: Bloomsburg 2001, Army 2005. Pro coach: Rhein Fire (NFLE) 2004-05, joined Vikings in 2006.

Darrell Bevell, offensive coordinator; born Yuma, Ariz. Quarterback Northern Arizona 1989, Wisconsin 1992-95. No pro playing experience. College coach: Westmar 1996, Iowa State 1997, Connecticut 1998-99. Pro coach: Green Bay Packers 2000-05, joined Vikings in 2006.

Eric Bieniemy, running backs; born New Orleans. Running back Colorado 1987-1990. Pro running back San Diego Chargers 1991-94, Cincinnati Bengals 1995-98, Philadelphia Eagles 1999. College coach: Colorado 2001-02, UCLA 2003-05. Pro coach: Joined Vikings in 2006.

Brendan Daly, defensive assistant/defensive line; born Chicago. Tight end Drake 1993-96. No pro playing experience. College coach: Drake 1998, Villanova 1999, 2005, Maryland 2000, Oklahoma State 2001-03, Illinois State 2004. Pro coach: Joined Vikings in 2006.

Karl Dunbar, defensive line; born Plaisance, La. Defensive lineman Louisiana State 1986-89. Pro defensive lineman Pittsburgh Steelers 1990, New Orleans Saints 1992-93, Arizona Cardinals 1994-95. College coach: Nicholls State 1998-99, Louisiana State 2000-01, 2005, Oklahoma State

2002-03. Pro coach: Chicago Bears 2004, joined Vikings in 2006.

Paul Ferraro, special teams coordinator; born Ridgewood, N.J. Defensive back Springfield College 1980-82. No pro playing experience. College coach: Massachusetts 1982, Syracuse 1983, Villanova 1984-86, Dartmouth 1987, Catholic 1988, Maine 1989, Ohio 1990, Bowling Green 1991-98, Georgia Tech 1999-2000, Rutgers 2001-04. Pro coach: Carolina Panthers 2005, joined Vikings in 2006.

Ryan Ficken, quality control-offense/running backs; born Aurora, Colo. Wide receiver Arizona State 1998-99. No pro playing experience. College coach: UCLA 2004-06. Pro coach: Joined Vikings in 2007.

Leslie Frazier, defensive coordinator/asst. head coach; born Columbus, Miss. Defensive back Alcorn State 1977-1980. Pro defensive back Chicago Bears 1981-86. College coach: Trinity (Ill.) College 1988-1996 (head coach), Illinois 1997-98. Pro coach Philadelphia Eagles 1999-2002, Cincinnati Bengals 2003-04, Indianapolis Colts 2005-06, joined Vikings in 2007.

Jim Hueber, asst. offensive line; born Philadelphia. Center South Dakota 1966-67. No pro playing experience. College coach: Cincinnati 1974, Dodge City (Kan.) C.C. 1975-78, Wichita State 1979-1980, Temple 1981-82, Memphis State 1983, Minnesota 1984-1991, Wisconsin 1992-2005. Pro coach: Joined Vikings in 2006.

Jeff Imamura, quality control-defense/linebackers; born Lubbock, Texas. Attended Texas Christian. No college or pro playing experience. College coach: Texas Christian 1997-99, Northern Arizona 2000-02, Saginaw Valley State 2003. Pro coach: Joined Vikings in 2006.

Jimmie Johnson, tight ends; born Augusta, Ga. Tight end Howard 1985-88. Pro tight end Washington Redskins 1989-1991, Detroit Lions 1992-93, Kansas City Chiefs 1994, Philadelphia Eagles 1995-98. College coach: South Carolina State 2001, Shaw 2002-03, Texas Southern 2004-05. Pro coach: Joined Vikings in 2006.

Tom Kanavy, strength and conditioning; born Archibald, Pa. Attended Penn State. No college or pro playing experience. College coach: Miami 1993, Penn State 1993-95. Pro coach: Philadelphia Eagles 1995-2005, joined Vikings in 2006.

Derek Mason, asst. defensive backs; born Phoenix. Defensive back Northern Arizona 1987-1991. No pro playing experience. College coach: Mesa C.C. 1994, Weber State 1995-96, Idaho State 1997-98, Bucknell 1999-2001, Utah 2002, St. Mary's (Calif.) 2003, New Mexico State 2004, Ohio 2005-06. Pro coach: Joined Vikings in 2007.

Pat Morris, offensive line; born Cleveland. Offensive lineman Southern California 1972-75. College coach: Southern California 1976-77, 1983-86, Northern Arizona 1978, Minnesota 1979-1982, Michigan State 1987-

1994, Stanford 1995-96. Pro coach: San Francisco 49ers 1997-2003, Detroit Lions 2004-05, joined Vikings in 2006.

Brian Murphy, asst. special teams; born Elmwood Park, Ill. Defensive lineman Lehigh 1988-1991. No pro playing experience. College coach: Benedictine 1992, Wisconsin 1994-96, 2002-05, Baylor 1997, San Diego 1998, Lehigh 1999. Pro coach: Joined Vikings in 2006.

Chad O'Shea, offensive assistant/wide receivers; born Houston. Quarterback Marshall 1991-93, Houston 1994-95. No pro playing experience. College coach: Houston 1996-99, Southern Mississippi 2000-02. Pro coach: Kansas City Chiefs 2004-05, joined Vikings in 2006.

Fred Pagac, linebackers; born Richeyville, Pa. Tight end Ohio State 1971-73. Pro tight end Chicago Bears 1974, Tampa Bay Buccaneers 1976. College coach: Ohio State 1978-2000. Pro coach: Oakland Raiders 2001-03, Kansas City Chiefs 2004-05, joined Vikings in 2006.

Kevin Rogers, quarterbacks; born Brooklyn, N.Y. Linebacker Massanutten Academy 1969-1970, William & Mary 1971-73. College coach: Ohio State 1977-78, William & Mary 1980-82, Navy 1983-1990, Syracuse 1991-98, Notre Dame 1999-2001, Virginia Tech 2002-05. Pro coach: Joined Vikings in 2006.

Ryan Silverfield, asst. offensive line; born Jacksonville, Fla. Attended Hampden-Sydney. No college or pro playing experience. College coach: Hampden-Sydney 2000-03, Jacksonville 2005, Central Florida 2006-07. Pro coach: Joined Vikings in 2008.

Kevin Stefanski, asst. to the head coach; born Philadelphia. Safety Pennsylvania 2000-04. College coach: Pennsylvania 2005. Pro coach: Joined Vikings in 2006.

George Stewart, wide receivers; born Little Rock, Ark. Guard Arkansas 1977-1980. No pro playing experience. College coach: Minnesota 1984-85, Notre Dame 1986-88. Pro coach: Pittsburgh Steelers 1989-1991, Tampa Bay Buccaneers 1992-95, San Francisco 49ers 1996-2002, Atlanta Falcons 2003-06, joined Vikings in 2007.

Martin Streight, asst. strength and conditioning; born Trenton, N.J. Attended Indiana (Penn.). No college or pro playing experience. College coach: Penn State 1994, Princeton 1995-96. Pro coach: Philadelphia Eagles 1995-96, Arizona Cardinals 1997-2003, Scottish Claymores (NFLE) 2003, Berlin Thunder (NFLE) 2004-05, joined Vikings in 2006.

Joe Woods, defensive backs; born Natrona Heights, Pa. Safety Illinois State 1988-1991. College coach: Muskingum 1992, Eastern Michigan 1993, Northwestern (La.) State 1994, Grand Valley State 1994-96, Kent State 1997, Hofstra 1998-2000, Western Michigan 2001-03. Pro coach: Tampa Bay Buccaneers 2004-05, joined Vikings in 2006.

National Football Conference
South Division
Team Colors: Old Gold, Black, and White
5800 Airline Drive
Metairie, Louisiana 70003
Telephone: (504) 733-0255

2008 SCHEDULE
PRESEASON
Aug. 10	at Arizona	5:00
Aug. 18	**Houston**	7:00
Aug. 23	at Cincinnati	7:35
Aug. 28	**Miami**	7:00

REGULAR SEASON
Sep. 7	**Tampa Bay**	12:00
Sep. 14	at Washington	1:00
Sep. 21	at Denver	2:05
Sep. 28	**San Francisco**	12:00
Oct. 6	**Minnesota** (Mon.)	7:30
Oct. 12	**Oakland**	12:00
Oct. 19	at Carolina	1:00
Oct. 26	**San Diego** (London)	5:00
Nov. 2	BYE	
Nov. 9	at Atlanta	1:00
Nov. 16	at Kansas City	12:00
Nov. 24	**Green Bay** (Mon.)	7:30
Nov. 30	at Tampa Bay	1:00
Dec. 7	**Atlanta**	12:00
Dec. 11	at Chicago (Thu.)	7:15
Dec. 21	at Detroit	1:00
Dec. 28	**Carolina**	12:00

Stadium: Louisiana Superdome
(opened in 1975)
• **Capacity:** 68,000
1500 Poydras Street
New Orleans, Louisiana 70112
Playing Surface: Sportexe Momentum
Training Camp: Millsaps College
Jackson, Mississippi 39210

LOUISIANA SUPERDOME

CLUB OFFICIALS
Owner/President: Tom Benson
Owner/Executive Vice President:
Rita Benson LeBlanc
Executive Vice President/General
Manager: Mickey Loomis
Senior Vice President/Chief Financial
Officer: Dennis Lauscha
Vice President of Player Personnel:
Rick Mueller
Vice President of Communications:
Greg Bensel
Vice President of Marketing and
Business Development: Ben Hales
Vice President/General Counsel:
Vicky Neumeyer
Vice President of Ticket and Suite Sales:
Mike Stanfield
Director of Football Administration:
Khai Harley
Director of Operations: James Nagaoka
Pro Scouting Director: Ryan Pace
Pro Scouts: Terry Fontenot, Ryan Powell
Director of College Scouting:
Rick Reiprish
College Scouting Coordinator:
Jason Mitchell
Area Scouts: David Hinson, Dwaune
Jones, Josh Lucas, Jim Monos,
Barrett Wiley, Terry Wooden
Combine Scout: Mike Siani
Scouting Administrative Assistant:
Joseph Laine
Scouting Assistant: Mike Henshaw
Equipment Manager: Dan Simmons
Assistant Equipment Manager:
Glennon (Silky) Powell
Equipment Assistant:
John Baumgartner
Head Athletic Trainer: Scottie B. Patton
Assistant Athletic Trainers:
Duane Brooks, Kevin Mangum
Video Director: Dave Desposito
Director of Player Development:
Fred McAfee
Coaching Assistants: Joe Alley,
Mike Cerullo, Carter Sheridan,
Adam Zimmer
Senior Director of New Media:
Doug Miller
Director of Communications: Ricky Zeller
Communications Manager:
Justin Macione
Communications Assistant:
Dave Lawrence
Director of Security: Geoff Santini
Director of Photography:
Michael C. Hebert
Director of Community Affairs: Nick Karl
Information Technology/Network
Manager: Jeff Huffman
Facilities Manager: Terry Ashburn

COACHING HISTORY
(256-373-5)
Records include postseason games
1967-70	Tom Fears*	13-34-2
1970-72	J.D. Roberts	7-25-3
1973-75	John North**	11-23-0
1975	Ernie Hefferle	1-7-0
1976-77	Hank Stram	7-21-0
1978-80	Dick Nolan***	15-29-0
1980	Dick Stanfel	1-3-0
1981-85	O.A. (Bum) Phillips****	27-42-0
1985	Wade Phillips	1-3-0
1986-96	Jim Mora#	93-78-0
1996	Rick Venturi	1-7-0
1997-99	Mike Ditka	15-33-0
2000-05	Jim Haslett	46-52-0
2006-07	Sean Payton	18-16-0

*Released after seven games in 1970
**Released after six games in 1975
***Released after 12 games in 1980
****Resigned after 12 games in 1985
#Resigned after eight games in 1996

PAID ATTENDANCE
Home 530,270   Away 521,368
Total 1,051,638
Single-game home record,
70,940 (9/2/79)
Single-season home record,
548,728 (1992)

2008 DRAFT CHOICES
Round	Name	Pos.	College
1	Sedrick Ellis	DT	Southern California
2	Tracy Porter	DB	Indiana
5	DeMario Pressley	DT	North Carolina St.
	Carl Nicks	T	Nebraska
6	Taylor Mehlhaff	K	Wisconsin
7	Adrian Arrington	WR	Michigan

2007 TEAM RECORD
PRESEASON (3-2)

Date	Result	Opponent
8/5	L 7-20	vs. Pittsburgh in Canton, OH
8/10	L 10-13	Buffalo
8/18	W 27-19	at Cincinnati
8/23	W 30-7	at Kansas City
8/30	W 7-0	Miami

REGULAR SEASON (7-9)

Date	Result	Opponent	Att.
9/6	L 10-41	at Indianapolis	57,361
9/16	L 14-31	at Tampa Bay	65,178
9/24	L 14-31	Tennessee	70,002
10/7	L 13-16	Carolina	70,001
10/14	W 28-17	at Seattle	68,296
10/21	W 22-16	Atlanta	69,994
10/28	W 31-10	at San Francisco	68,244
11/4	W 41-24	Jacksonville	70,009
11/11	L 29-37	St. Louis	70,003
11/18	L 10-23	at Houston	70,780
11/25	W 31-6	at Carolina	72,032
12/2	L 23-27	Tampa Bay	70,009
12/10	W 34-14	at Atlanta	69,553
12/16	W 31-24	Arizona	70,007
12/23	L 23-38	Philadelphia	70,011
12/30	L 25-33	at Chicago	62,064

SCORE BY PERIODS

Saints	89	130	94	66	0	—	379
Opponents	105	104	69	110	0	—	388

2007 TEAM STATISTICS

	Saints	Opp.
Total First Downs	346	288
Rushing	94	80
Passing	232	196
Penalty	20	12
3rd Down: Made/Att	99/214	86/206
3rd Down Pct.	46.3	41.7
4th Down: Made/Att	11/25	7/19
4th Down Pct.	44.0	36.8
Possession Avg.	31:09	28:51
Total Net Yards	5780	5570
Avg. Per Game	361.3	348.1
Total Plays	1060	964
Avg. Per Play	5.5	5.8
Net Yards Rushing	1466	1646
Avg. Per Game	91.6	102.9
Total Rushes	392	408
Net Yards Passing	4314	3924
Avg. Per Game	269.6	245.3
Sacked/Yards Lost	16/109	32/198
Gross Yards	4423	4122
Att./Completions	652/440	524/327
Completion Pct.	67.5	62.4
Had Intercepted	18	13
Punts/Average	63/43.8	67/43.6
Net Punting Avg.	63/37.2	67/39.8
Penalties/Yards	68/581	89/685
Fumbles/Ball Lost	25/12	27/10
Touchdowns	47	44
Rushing	14	7
Passing	28	32
Returns	5	5

2007 INDIVIDUAL STATISTICS

PASSING

PASSING	Att.	Comp.	Yds.	Pct.	TD	Int.	Tkld.	Rate
Brees	652	440	4423	67.5	28	18	16/109	89.4
Saints	652	440	4423	67.5	28	18	16/109	89.4
Opponents	524	327	4122	62.4	32	13	32/198	96.9

SCORING

SCORING	TD R	TD P	TD Rt	PAT	FG	Saf	PTS
Colston	0	11	0	0/0	0/0	0	66
Mare	0	0	0	34/34	10/17	0	64
Bush	4	2	0	0/0	0/0	0	42
Stecker	5	0	0	0/0	0/0	0	30
Gramatica	0	0	0	8/8	5/5	0	23
P. Thomas	1	1	1	0/0	0/0	0	20
Henderson	0	3	0	0/0	0/0	0	18
Moore	1	2	0	0/0	0/0	0	18
Patten	0	3	0	0/0	0/0	0	18
Copper	0	2	0	0/0	0/0	0	12
Johnson	0	2	0	0/0	0/0	0	12
Karney	2	0	0	0/0	0/0	0	12
McKenzie	0	0	2	0/0	0/0	0	12
Miller	0	2	0	0/0	0/0	0	12
Brees	1	0	0	0/0	0/0	0	6
David	0	0	1	0/0	0/0	0	6
Harper	0	0	1	0/0	0/0	0	6
W. Smith	0	0	0	0/0	0/0	1	2
Saints	14	28	5	42/42	15/22	1	379
Opponents	7	32	5	44/44	26/30	1	388

2-Pt. Conversions: Bush 3, P. Thomas, Saints 4-5, Opponents 0-0

RUSHING

RUSHING	No.	Yds	Avg	LG	TD
Bush	157	581	3.7	22	4
Stecker	115	448	3.9	26	5
P. Thomas	52	252	4.8	24t	1
McAllister	24	92	3.8	15	0
Brees	23	52	2.3	9	1
Henderson	2	20	10.0	15	0
Karney	11	17	1.5	10	2
Moore	2	7	3.5	7t	1
Weatherford	1	5	5.0	5	0
Martin	3	-3	-1.0	-1	0
Patten	2	-5	-2.5	1	0
Saints	392	1466	3.7	26	14
Opponents	408	1646	4.0	43	7

RECEIVING

RECEIVING	No.	Yds	Avg	LG	TD
Colston	98	1202	12.3	45	11
Bush	73	417	5.7	25	2
Patten	54	792	14.7	58	3
Johnson	48	378	7.9	22	2
Stecker	36	211	5.9	26	0
Moore	32	302	9.4	22	2
Miller	27	328	12.1	57	2
Henderson	20	409	20.5	54	3
P. Thomas	17	151	8.9	17	1
Copper	15	126	8.4	21	2
Karney	13	78	6.0	11	0
McAllister	4	15	3.8	7	0
Brees	2	10	5.0	8	0
Owens	1	4	4.0	4	0
Saints	440	4423	10.1	58	28
Opponents	327	4122	12.6	80t	32

INTERCEPTIONS

INTERCEPTIONS	No.	Yds	Avg	LG	TD
McKenzie	3	161	53.7	75t	2
Harper	3	58	19.3	31t	1
David	3	21	7.0	19	0
Craft	2	21	10.5	21	0
Bullocks	2	6	3.0	6	0
Saints	13	267	20.5	75t	3
Opponents	18	336	18.7	83t	2

PUNTING

PUNTING	No.	Yds.	Avg.	In 20	LG
Weatherford	63	2757	43.8	20	61
Saints	63	2757	43.8	20	61
Opponents	67	2924	43.6	28	60

PUNT RETURNS

PUNT RETURNS	Ret	FC	Yds	Avg	LG	TD
Moore	20	15	185	9.3	48	0
Bush	3	0	12	4.0	10	0
Craft	1	0	0	0.0	0	0
David	0	1	0	—	—	0
Saints	24	16	197	8.2	48	0
Opponents	35	11	335	9.6	64t	1

KICKOFF RETURNS

KICKOFF RETURNS	No.	Yds	Avg	LG	TD
P. Thomas	36	865	24.0	64	0
Barclay	5	98	19.6	28	0
Moore	17	318	18.7	32	0
Stecker	6	137	22.8	41	0
Copper	2	49	24.5	25	0
Patten	2	20	10.0	10	0
Cooper	1	8	8.0	8	0
Lake	1	10	10.0	10	0
Miller	1	8	8.0	8	0
Saints	71	1513	21.3	64	0
Opponents	56	1256	22.4	100t	1

FIELD GOALS

FIELD GOALS	1-19	20-29	30-39	40-49	50+
Mare	0/0	4/5	3/4	2/3	1/5
Gramatica	0/0	0/0	2/2	2/2	1/1
Saints	0/0	4/5	5/6	4/5	2/6
Opponents	0/0	10/11	10/10	3/4	3/5

SACKS

SACKS	No.
W. Smith	7.0
Harper	4.0
Wynn	3.5
Fujita	3.0
H. Thomas	3.0
B. Young	3.0
Grant	2.5
Simoneau	2.0
Bullocks	1.0
Lake	1.0
Simmons	1.0
Clancy	0.5
Cooper	0.5
Saints	32.0
Opponents	16.0

RECORD HOLDERS
INDIVIDUAL RECORDS—CAREER

Category	Name	Performance
Rushing (Yds.)	Deuce McAllister, 2001-07	5,678
Passing (Yds.)	Archie Manning, 1971-1982	21,734
Passing (TDs)	Aaron Brooks, 2000-05	120
Receiving (No.)	Eric Martin, 1985-1993	532
Receiving (Yds.)	Eric Martin, 1985-1993	7,854
Interceptions	Dave Waymer, 1980-89	37
Punting (Avg.)	Mark Royals, 1997-98	45.7
Punt Return (Avg.)	Mel Gray, 1986-88	13.4
Kickoff Return (Avg.)	Walter Roberts, 1967	26.3
Field Goals	Morten Andersen, 1982-1994	302
Touchdowns (Tot.)	Dalton Hilliard, 1986-1993	53
Points	Morten Andersen, 1982-1994	1,318

INDIVIDUAL RECORDS—SINGLE SEASON

Category	Name	Performance
Rushing (Yds.)	George Rogers, 1981	1,674
Passing (Yds.)	Drew Brees, 2007	4,423
Passing (TDs)	Aaron Brooks, 2002	27
Receiving (No.)	Marques Colston, 2007	98
Receiving (Yds.)	Joe Horn, 2004	1,399
Interceptions	Dave Whitsell, 1967	10
Punting (Avg.)	Mark Royals, 1997	45.9
Punt Return (Avg.)	Mel Gray, 1987	14.7
Kickoff Return (Avg.)	Don Shy, 1969	27.9
	Mel Gray, 1986	27.9
Field Goals	Morten Andersen, 1985	31
	John Carney, 2002	31
Touchdowns (Tot.)	Dalton Hilliard, 1989	18
Points	John Carney, 2002	130

INDIVIDUAL RECORDS—SINGLE GAME

Category	Name	Performance
Rushing (Yds.)	George Rogers, 9-4-83	206
Passing (Yds.)	Drew Brees, 11-19-06	510
Passing (TDs)	Billy Kilmer, 11-2-69	6
Receiving (No.)	Tony Galbreath, 9-10-78	14
Receiving (Yds.)	Wes Chandler, 9-2-79	205
Interceptions	Tommy Myers, 9-3-78	3
	Dave Waymer, 10-6-85	3
	Reggie Sutton, 10-18-87	3
	Gene Atkins, 12-22-91	3
	Sammy Knight, 9-9-01	3
Field Goals	Many times	5
	Last time by John Carney, 9-26-04	
Touchdowns (Tot.)	Joe Horn, 12-14-03	4
	Reggie Bush, 12-3-06	4
Points	Joe Horn, 12-14-03	24
	Reggie Bush, 12-3-06	24

2008 VETERAN ROSTER

No.	Name	Pos.	Ht.	Wt.	Age	NFL Exp.	College	Hometown	How Acq.	'07 Games/ Starts
65	Alleman, Andy	G	6-4	310	24	2	Akron	Greentown, Ohio	D3b-'07	0*
24	Barclay, Chris	RB	5-10	180	24	2	Wake Forest	Louisville, Ky.	W(Tenn)-'07	5/0*
9	Brees, Drew	QB	6-0	209	29	8	Purdue	Austin, Texas	UFA(SD)-'06	16/16
70	Brown, Jammal	T	6-6	313	27	4	Oklahoma	Lawton, Okla.	D1-'05	15/15
11	Brunell, Mark	QB	6-1	217	37	16	Washington	Santa Maria, Calif.	UFA(Wash)-'08	0*
29	Bullocks, Josh	S	6-1	207	25	4	Nebraska	Chattanooga, Tenn.	D2-'05	14/14
25	Bush, Reggie	RB	6-0	203	23	3	Southern California	Spring Valley, Calif.	D1-'06	12/10
74	Bushrod, Jermon	T	6-5	315	24	2	Towson	King George, Va.	D4-'07	1/0
80	Campbell, Mark	TE	6-6	260	32	10	Michigan	Clawson, Mich.	FA-'06	0*
71	Clancy, Kendrick	DT	6-1	305	30	9	Mississippi	Tuscaloosa, Ala.	FA-'07	14/2
12	Colston, Marques	WR	6-4	225	25	3	Hofstra	Harrisburg, Pa.	D7b-'06	16/14
18	Copper, Terrance	WR	6-0	207	26	5	East Carolina	Washington, N.C.	W(Dall)-'06	15/1
21	Craft, Jason	CB	5-10	187	32	10	Colorado State	Denver, Colo.	T(Jax)-'04	16/4
42	David, Jason	CB	5-8	180	26	5	Washington State	Covina, Calif.	RFA(Ind)-'07	13/12
73	Evans, Jahri	G	6-4	318	25	3	Bloomsburg	Philadelphia, Pa.	D4-'06	16/16
54	Evans, Troy	LB	6-3	238	30	7	Cincinnati	Cincinnati, Ohio	UFA(Hou)-'07	16/0
55	Fujita, Scott	LB	6-5	250	29	7	California	Oxnard, Calif.	UFA(Dall)-'06	15/15
20	Gay, Randall	CB	5-11	190	26	5	Louisiana State	Brusly, La.	UFA(NE)-'08	16/3*
85	Ghent, Ronnie	TE	6-2	253	28	2	Louisville	Lakeland, Fla.	FA-'07	8/0
31	Glenn, Aaron	CB	5-9	183	36	15	Texas A&M	Humble, Texas	UFA(Jax)-'08	5/4*
76	Goodwin, Jonathan	C/G	6-3	318	29	7	Michigan	Richland, S.C.	UFA(NYJ)-'06	13/2
1	Gramatica, Martin	K	5-8	170	32	9	Kansas State	LaBelle, Fla.	FA-'07	3/0
94	Grant, Charles	DE	6-3	285	30	7	Georgia	Colquitt, Ga.	D1b-'02	14/14
10	Green, Skyler	WR	5-9	190	23	3	Louisiana State	Avondale, La.	FA-'08	7/0*
41	Harper, Roman	S	6-1	200	25	3	Alabama	Prattville, Ala.	D2-'06	16/16
19	Henderson, Devery	WR	5-11	200	26	5	Louisiana State	Opelousas, La.	D2a-'04	16/9
47	Houser, Kevin	LS	6-2	252	31	9	Ohio State	Westlake, Ohio	D7-'00	16/0
82	Johnson, Eric	TE	6-3	252	28	8	Yale	Needham, Mass.	UFA(SF)-'07	14/12
43	Kaesviharn, Kevin	S	6-1	200	32	8	Augustana (S.D.)	Lakeville, Minn.	UFA(Cin)-'07	16/3
44	Karney, Mike	FB	5-11	255	27	5	Arizona State	Kent, Wash.	D5b-'04	16/9
96	Lake, Antwan	DT	6-4	308	29	6	West Virginia	Cambridge, Md.	W(Atl)-'06	15/7
68	Lehr, Matt	C/G	6-2	290	29	8	Virginia Tech	Woodbridge, Va.	UFA(TB)-'08	16/0*
26	McAllister, Deuce	RB	6-1	232	29	8	Mississippi	Lena, Miss	D1-'01	3/3
93	McCray, Bobby	DE	6-6	260	27	5	Florida	Homestead, Fla.	UFA(Jax)-'08	14/9*
34	McKenzie, Mike	CB	6-0	194	32	10	Memphis	Miami, Fla.	T(GB)-'04	16/16
17	Meachem, Robert	WR	6-2	210	23	2	Tennessee	Tulsa, Okla.	D1-'07	0*
83	Miller, Billy	TE	6-3	252	31	9	Southern California	Westlake Village, Calif.	FA-'06	16/6
50	Mitchell, Marvin	LB	6-3	249	23	2	Tennessee	Norfolk, Va.	FA-'07	10/0
16	Moore, Lance	WR	5-9	190	25	3	Toledo	Westerville, Ohio	FA-'07	16/4
52	Morgan, Dan	LB	6-2	245	29	8	Miami	Coral Springs, Fla.	FA-'08	3/3*
67	Nesbit, Jamar	G	6-4	328	31	10	South Carolina	Summerville, S.C.	UFA(Jax)-'04	16/16
81	Patten, David	WR	5-10	190	34	12	Western Carolina	Columbia, S.C.	FA-'07	16/5
39	Reis, Chris	S	6-1	215	24	2	Georgia Tech	Roswell, Ga.	FA-'07	14/0
95	Savage, Josh	DE	6-4	276	27	3	Utah	Midvale, Utah	FA-'07	1/0
58	Shanle, Scott	LB	6-2	245	28	6	Nebraska	St. Edward, Neb.	T(Dall)-'06	14/14
53	Simoneau, Mark	LB	6-0	245	31	9	Kansas State	Smith Center, Kan.	T(Phil)-'06	16/16
91	Smith, Will	DE	6-3	282	27	5	Ohio State	Utica, N.Y.	D1-'04	16/16
27	Stecker, Aaron	RB	5-10	213	32	9	Western Illinois	Green Bay, Wis.	UFA(TB)-'04	16/6
78	Stinchcomb, Jon	T	6-5	315	29	6	Georgia	Lilburn, Ga.	D2-'03	16/16
64	Strief, Zach	T	6-7	320	24	3	Northwestern	Milford, Ohio	D7a-'06	16/1
99	Thomas, Hollis	DT	6-0	335	34	13	Northern Illinois	St. Louis, Mo.	T(Phil)-'06	16/14
23	Thomas, Pierre	RB	5-11	215	23	2	Illinois	Lynwood, Ill.	FA-'07	12/1
51	t-Vilma, Jonathan	LB	6-1	230	26	5	Miami	Coral Gables, Fla.	T(NYJ)-'08	7/7*
7	Weatherford, Steve	P	6-3	215	25	3	Illinois	Terre Haute, Ind.	FA-'06	16/0
66	Young, Brian	DT	6-2	298	31	9	Texas-El Paso	El Paso, Texas	UFA(StL)-'04	16/16
28	Young, Usama	CB	6-0	200	23	2	Kent State	Largo, Md.	D3a-'07	14/0

* Alleman inactive for 16 games; Barclay played in 4 games with Tennessee and 1 game for New Orleans in '07; Brunell did not play in 3 games with Washington; Campbell inactive for 1 game; Gay played 16 games with New England; Glenn played 5 games with Jacksonville; Green played 7 games with Cincinnati; Lehr played 16 games with Tampa Bay; McCray played 14 games with Jacksonville; Meachem inactive for 16 games; Morgan played 3 games with Carolina; Vilma played 7 games with N.Y. Jets.

t- Saints traded for Vilma (NYJ).

Players lost to free agency (1): C Jeff Faine (TB; 14 games in '07).

Also played with Saints in '07—S Jay Bellamy (3 games), DT McKinley Boykin (3), RB Jamaal Branch (5), DE Josh Cooper (13), LB Alfred Fincher (7), K Olindo Mare (13), QB Jamie Martin (3), LB Matt McCoy (4), TE John Owens (8), LB Brian Simmons (16), CB Fred Thomas (7), DL Renaldo Wynn (12).

2008 FIRST-YEAR ROSTER

Name	Pos.	Ht.	Wt.	Age	College	Hometown	How Acq.
Arrington, Adrian	WR	6-3	192	22	Michigan	Cedar Rapids, Iowa	D7
Blythe, Todd	WR	6-5	214	23	Iowa State	Indianola, Iowa	FA
Boone, Jason	T	6-4	300	24	Utah	Fillmore, Utah	FA
Duckworth, Tim (1)	G	6-4	318	25	Auburn	Taylorsville, Miss.	FA
Dudley, Kevin (1)	FB	6-0	238	26	Michigan	Oxford, Ohio	FA
Dunbar, JoLonn	LB	6-0	226	23	Boston College	Syracuse, N.Y.	FA
Ellis, Sedrick	DT	6-1	307	23	Southern California	Chino, Calif.	D1
Fassitt, Greg (1)	CB	5-11	186	23	Grambling State	New Orleans, La.	FA
Geathers, Jeremy	DE	6-2	245	22	Nevada-Las Vegas	Andrews, S.C.	FA
Hamilton, Lynell	RB	6-0	235	23	San Diego State	Stockton, Calif.	FA
Harris, Orien (1)	DT	6-3	300	25	Miami	Newark, Del.	FA
Lulay, Travis (1)	QB	6-2	216	24	Montana State	Aumsville, Ore.	FA
Mehlhaff, Taylor	K	5-10	184	23	Wisconsin	Aberdeen, S.D.	D6
Nicks, Carl	T/G	6-5	343	25	Nebraska	Salinas, Calif.	D5b
Ortega, Buck (1)	TE	6-4	250	26	Miami	Miami, Fla.	FA
Palko, Tyler (1)	QB	6-1	215	25	Pittsburgh	Imperial, Pa.	FA
Phillips, Anwar (1)	CB	6-0	187	25	Penn State	St. Petersburg, Fla.	FA
Pittman, Marcus	DT	6-5	290	22	Troy	Broadway, N.C.	FA
Porter, Tracy	CB	5-11	186	22	Indiana	Port Allen, La.	D2
Prather, Waylon	P	6-3	225	23	San Jose State	Ben Lomond, Calif.	FA
Pressley, DeMario	DT	6-3	301	22	North Carolina State	Greensboro, N.C.	D5a
Roach, David	S	6-2	215	23	Texas Christian	Abliene, Texas	FA
Robinson, Carlos	WR	6-0	180	23	Grand Rapids (Mich.) C.C.	Grand Rapids, Mich.	FA
Ryan, Titus (1)	WR	6-0	193	24	Concordia (Ala.)	Tuscaloosa, Ala.	FA
Sanders, Luke	LB	6-5	242	23	Louisiana State	Monroe, La.	FA
Schwartz, Rocky	S	5-10	200	24	Houston	Bradenton, Fla.	FA
Senser, Ryan	LS	6-3	227	24	Ohio	Westerville, Ohio	FA
Sobomehin, Olaniyi	FB	6-1	230	23	Portland State	Portland, Ore.	FA
Tuminello, Kevin	C	6-4	285	24	Georgia Tech	Youngstown, Ohio	FA

The term NFL Rookie is defined as a player who is in his first season of professional football and has not been on the roster of another professional football team for any regular-season or postseason games. A Rookie is designated by an "R" on NFL rosters. Players who have been active in another professional football league or players who have NFL experience, including either preseason training camp or being on an Active List or Inactive List, or on Reserve/Injured or Reserve/Physically Unable to Perform for fewer than six regular-season games, are termed NFL First-Year Players. An NFL First-Year Player is designated by a "1" on NFL rosters. Thereafter, a player is credited with an additional year of experience for each season in which he accumulates six games on the Active List or Inactive List, or on Reserve/Injured or Reserve/Physically Unable to Perform.

Log on to www.neworleanssaints.com for an up-to-date roster; Age listed is as of September 4, 2008.

COACHING STAFF

Head Coach,
Sean Payton

Pro Career: Named the fourteenth head coach in Saints history on Jan. 18, 2006 and in his opening season led the Saints to the NFC Championship Game for the first time in club history. A unanimous choice for NFL coach of the year honors after also guiding the team to a 10-6 record and the NFC South title following a dramatic roster overhaul. Considered one of the NFL's brightest offensive minds, Payton has led a resurgence in his unit's productivity at each career stop, including in New Orleans, where the Saints featured the league's top-ranked offense in 2006 and ranked No. 4 in 2006. Came to New Orleans following a three-year stint with Dallas Cowboys, serving as the assistant head coach/passing game coordinator in 2005 after spending his first two seasons as assistant head coach/quarterbacks. Considered one of the NFL's brightest offensive minds, he has led a resurgence in his unit's productivity at each career stop, including in New Orleans, where the Saints featured the league's top-ranked offense in 2006. Additional experience includes four years with the New York Giants (1999-2002), the last three seasons as offensive coordinator. Also previously worked for the Philadelphia Eagles (1997-98) as quarterbacks coach. Career record: 18-16.

Background: Earned a degree in communications at Eastern Illinois, where he departed with a school-record 10,665 passing yards, then the third-highest total in NCAA Division I-AA history. A three-time All-American, Payton had brief playing stops with Chicago of the Arena Football League, the Ottawa Rough Riders of the Canadian Football League and the Chicago Bears in 1987. Inducted into the Eastern Illinois Hall of Fame in 2000, Payton entered the NFL after two coaching stints at San Diego State (1988-89, 1992-93) around a stop at Indiana State (1990-91). He also was quarterbacks coach/co-offensive coordinator at Miami (Ohio) from 1994-95.

Personal: Age 44, born in San Mateo, Calif. and raised in Naperville, Ill, Payton and his wife, Beth, have a daughter, Meghan, and a son, Connor.

ASSISTANT COACHES

Dennis Allen, secondary; born Atlanta. Safety Texas A&M 1992-95. No pro playing experience. College coach: Texas A&M 1996-99, Tulsa 2000-01. Pro coach: Atlanta Falcons 2002-05, joined Saints in 2006.

Adam Bailey, asst. strength and conditioning; born Tyler, Texas. Attended Louisville. No college or pro playing experience. College coach: Texas 1996-1997, Louisville 1998-1999, Auburn 2000-2001, Missouri 2002-2003. Pro coach:

New Orleans VooDoo (AFL) 2004-2005, joined Saints in 2005.

Pete Carmichael Jr., quarterbacks/passing game; born Farmingham, Mass. Attended Boston College. No college or pro playing experience. College coach: New Hampshire 1994, Louisiana Tech 1995-99. Pro coach: Cleveland Browns 2000, Washington Redskins 2001, San Diego Chargers 2002-05, joined Saints in 2006.

Dan Dalrymple, head strength and conditioning; born Cleveland. Offensive lineman Miami (Ohio) 1983-86. No pro playing experience. College coach: Miami (Ohio) 1987-2005. Pro coach: Joined Saints in 2006.

Gary Gibbs, defensive coordinator; born Beaumont, Texas. Linebacker Oklahoma 1972-75. No pro playing experience. College coach: Oklahoma 1975-1994 (head coach 1989-1994), Georgia 2000, Louisiana State 2001. Pro coach: Dallas Cowboys 2002-04, joined Saints in 2006.

Curtis Johnson, wide receivers; born New Orleans. Wide receiver Idaho 1979-1983. No pro playing experience. College coach: Idaho 1987-88, San Diego State 1989-1993, Southern Methodist 1994, California 1995, Miami 1996-2005. Pro coach: Joined Saints in 2006.

Travis Jones, asst. defensive line; born Milledgville, Ga. Linebacker Georgia 1991-94. Pro linebacker Baltimore Stallions (CFL) 1995. College coach: Georgia: 1997, Appalachian State 1998-2000, Kansas 2001-02, Louisiana State 2003-04. Pro coach: Miami Dolphins 2005-07, joined Saints in 2008.

Aaron Kromer, running backs; born Sandusky, Ohio. Offensive tackle Miami (Ohio) 1986-89. No pro playing experience. College coach: Miami (Ohio) 1990-98, Northwestern 1999-2000. Pro coach: Oakland Raiders 2001-04, Tampa Bay Buccaneers 2005-06, joined Saints in 2007.

Joe Lombardi, offensive assistant; born Seattle. Tight end Air Force 1992-94. No pro playing experience. College coach: Dayton 1996-98, Virginia Military Institute 1999, Bucknell 2000, Mercyhurst 2002-05. Pro coach: Atlanta Falcons 2006, joined Saints in 2007.

Mike Mallory, asst. special teams; born Bowling Green, Ohio. Linebacker Michigan 1982-85. No pro playing experience. College coach: Indiana 1986-87, Kent State 1989-1990, Eastern Illinois 1991-92, Rhode Island 1993-95, Northern Illinois 1996-99, Maryland 2000, Illinois 2001-05, Kansas 2006, Louisville 2007. Pro coach: Joined Saints in 2006.

Terry Malone, tight ends; born Buffalo. Tight end Holy Cross 1978-1982. No pro playing experience. College coach: Arizona 1983-84, Holy Cross 1985, Bowling Green 1986-1995, Boston College 1996, Michigan 1997-2005. Pro

coach: Joined Saints in 2006.

Doug Marrone, offensive coordinator/offensive line, born Bronx, N.Y. Offensive lineman Syracuse 1983-85. Pro offensive lineman Miami 1987, New Orleans Saints 1989, London Monarchs (NFLE) 1992. College coach: Cortland College 1992, U.S. Coast Guard Academy 1993, Northeastern 1994, Georgia Tech 1995-99, Georgia 2000, Tennessee 2001. Pro coach: New York Jets 2002-05, joined Saints in 2006.

Greg McMahon, special teams coordinator; born Rantoul, Ill. Defensive back Eastern Illinois 1978-1981. College coach: Eastern Illinois 1982, Minnesota 1983-84, North Alabama 1985-87, Southern Illinois 1988, Valdosta State 1989, Nevada Las-Vegas 1990-91, Illinois 1992-2004, East Carolina 2005. Pro coach: Joined Saints in 2006.

Tony Oden, asst. secondary; born Cleveland. Linebacker Baldwin-Wallace College 1991-95. No pro playing experience. College coach: Millersville (Penn.) 1996, Boston College 1997, Army 1998-99, East Carolina 2000-02, Eastern Michigan 2003. Pro coach: Houston Texans 2004-05, joined Saints in 2006.

Ed Orgeron, defensive line; born Larose, La. Defensive line Northwestern State (La.) University. No pro playing experience. College coach: Northwestern (La.) State 1984, McNeese State 1985, Arkansas 1986-87, Miami 1988-1992, Nicholls State 1994, Syracuse 1995-97, Southern California 1998-2004, Mississippi (head coach) 2005-07. Pro coach: Joined Saints in 2008.

Joe Vitt, asst. head coach/linebackers, born Syracuse, N.Y. Linebacker Towson State 1974-78. No pro playing experience. Pro coach: Baltimore Colts 1979-1981, Seattle Seahawks 1982-1991, Los Angeles Rams 1992-94, Philadelphia Eagles 1995-98, Green Bay Packers 1999, Kansas City Chiefs 2000-03, St. Louis Rams 2004-05 (head coach, final 11 games of 2005), joined Saints in 2006.

**National Football Conference
East Division**
Team Colors: Blue, Red, and White
Giants Stadium
East Rutherford, New Jersey 07073
Telephone: (201) 935-8111

2008 SCHEDULE
PRESEASON
Aug. 7   at Detroit 7:00
Aug. 18 **Cleveland** 8:00
Aug. 23 at N.Y. Jets 7:00
Aug. 28 **New England** 7:00

REGULAR SEASON
Sep. 4   **Washington** (Thu.) 7:00
Sep. 14 at St. Louis 12:00
Sep. 21 **Cincinnati** 1:00
Sep. 28 BYE
Oct. 5   **Seattle** 1:00
Oct. 13 at Cleveland (Mon.) 8:30
Oct. 19 **San Francisco** 1:00
Oct. 26 at Pittsburgh 4:15
Nov. 2   **Dallas** 4:15
Nov. 9   at Philadelphia 8:15
Nov. 16 **Baltimore** 1:00
Nov. 23 at Arizona 2:15
Nov. 30 at Washington 1:00
Dec. 7   **Philadelphia** 1:00
Dec. 14 at Dallas * 7:15
Dec. 21 **Carolina** 1:00
Dec. 28 at Minnesota 12:00
Sunday night games in Weeks 11-17 subject to change

Stadium: Giants Stadium (opened in 1976)
•**Capacity:** 80,242
East Rutherford, New Jersey
07073
Playing Surface: FieldTurf
Training Camp: University at Albany
1400 Washington Avenue
Albany, New York 12222

GIANTS STADIUM

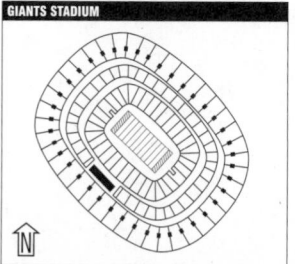

CLUB OFFICIALS
President/CEO: John K. Mara
Chairman/EVP: Steve Tisch
Treasurer: Jonathan Tisch
Senior Vice President-General Manager:
Jerry Reese
Senior Vice President and Chief
Marketing Officer: Michael Stevens
Vice President-Player Evaluations:
Chris Mara
Vice President and Chief Financial
Officer: Christine Procops
Vice President-Marketing: Rusty Hawley
VP/Medical Services: Ronnie Barnes
Vice-President-Communications:
Pat Hanlon
Vice President, Media and Partnerships:
Dan Lynch
Vice President and Executive Producer,
Giants Entertainment: Don Sperling
Assistant General Manager:
Kevin Abrams
Director of Player Personnel: TBD
Director of Pro Player Personnel:
David Gettleman
Assistant Director of Pro Player
Personnel: Ken Sternfeld
Director of College Scouting: Marc Ross
Director of Research and Development:
Raymond J. Walsh, Jr.
Director of Player Development:
Charles Way
Director of Marketing Partnerships:
Glenn Todd
Pro Personnel Assistants: Jeremy Breit,
Matthew Shauger
Director of Promotions: Frank Mara
Ticket Manager: John Gorman
Director of Administration: Jim Phelan
Controller: Steven Hamrahi
Director of Community Relations:
Allison Stangeby
Director of Creative Services:
Doug Murphy
Director of Public/Media Relations:
Peter John-Baptiste
Assistant Director of Communications:
Avis Roper
Head Athletic Trainer: Ronnie Barnes
Assistant Athletic Trainers:
Steve Kennelly, Byron Hansen,
Leigh Weiss
Equipment/Locker Room Manager:
Ed Wagner, Jr.
Equipment Director: Joseph Skiba
Assistant Equipment Managers:
Ed Skiba, Tim Slaman
Video Director: Dave Maltese
Assistant Video Directors:
Carmen Pizzano, Ed Triggs
Assistant Director of Community
Relations: Ethan Medley
Broadcast Production Manager:
Stephen Venditti
Directors of Information Technology:
Julie Glisky, Justin Warren
Director of Marketing Services & Youth
Programs: Beth Roche

COACHING HISTORY
(626-529-33)
Records include postseason games

Year	Coach	Record
1925	Bob Folwell	8-4-0
1926	Joe Alexander	8-4-1
1927-28	Earl Potteiger	15-8-3
1929-1930	LeRoy Andrews*	24-5-1
1930	Benny Friedman-Steve Owen	2-0-0
1931-1953	Steve Owen	153-108-17
1954-1960	Jim Lee Howell	55-29-4
1961-68	Allie Sherman	57-54-4
1969-1973	Alex Webster	29-40-1
1974-76	Bill Arnsparger**	7-28-0
1976-78	John McVay	14-23-0
1979-1982	Ray Perkins	24-35-0
1983-1990	Bill Parcells	85-52-1
1991-92	Ray Handley	14-18-0
1993-96	Dan Reeves	32-34-0
1997-2003	Jim Fassel	60-56-1
2004-07	Tom Coughlin	39-31-0

*Released after 15 games in 1930
**Released after seven games in 1976

PAID ATTENDANCE
Home 629,391   Away 558,524
Total 1,187,915
Single-game home record,
79,378 (1/8/06)
Single-season home record,
629,874 (2004)

2008 DRAFT CHOICES

Round	Name	Pos.	College
1	Kenny Phillips	DB	Miami
2	Terrell Thomas	DB	Southern California
3	Mario Manningham	WR	Michigan
4	Bryan Kehl	LB	Brigham Young
5	Jonathan Goff	LB	Vanderbilt
6	André Woodson	QB	Kentucky
	Robert Henderson	DE	So. Mississippi

2007 TEAM RECORD

PRESEASON (1-3)

Date	Result	Opponent
8/11	L 21-24	Carolina
8/19	W 13-12	at Baltimore
8/25	L 12-20	New York Jets
8/30	L 20-27	at New England

REGULAR SEASON (10-6)

Date	Result	Opponent	Att.
9/9	L 35-45	at Dallas	63,031
9/16	L 13-35	Green Bay	78,701
9/23	W 24-17	at Washington	90,803
9/30	W 16-3	Philadelphia	78,862
10/7	W 35-24	New York Jets	78,809
10/15	W 31-10	at Atlanta	69,828
10/21	W 33-15	San Francisco	78,912
10/28	W 13-10	at Miami	81,176
11/11	L 20-31	Dallas	78,964
11/18	W 16-10	at Detroit	60,675
11/25	L 17-41	Minnesota	78,591
12/2	W 21-16	at Chicago	62,244
12/9	W 16-13	at Philadelphia	68,594
12/16	L 10-22	Washington	77,899
12/23	W 38-21	at Buffalo	71,302
12/29	L 35-38	New England	79,110

POSTSEASON (4-0)

Date	Result	Opponent	Att.
1/6	W 24-14	at Tampa Bay	65,621
1/13	W 21-17	at Dallas	63,660
1/20	W 23-20	at Green Bay (OT)	72,740
2/3	W 17-14	vs. New England,	71,101
		at Glendale, Arizona	

(OT) Overtime

SCORE BY PERIODS

Giants	56	128	73	116	0	—	373
Opponents	82	100	72	97	0	—	351

2007 TEAM STATISTICS

	Giants	Opp.
Total First Downs	321	288
Rushing	119	83
Passing	167	185
Penalty	35	20
3rd Down: Made/Att	91/219	73/211
3rd Down Pct.	41.6	34.6
4th Down: Made/Att	6/17	10/16
4th Down Pct.	35.3	62.5
Possession Avg.	31:22	28:38
Total Net Yards	5302	4880
Avg. Per Game	331.4	305.0
Total Plays	1041	984
Avg. Per Play	5.1	5.0
Net Yards Rushing	2148	1563
Avg. Per Game	134.3	97.7
Total Rushes	469	408
Net Yards Passing	3154	3317
Avg. Per Game	197.1	207.3
Sacked/Yards Lost	28/222	53/349
Gross Yards	3376	3666
Att./Completions	544/302	523/306
Completion Pct.	55.5	58.5
Had Intercepted	20	15
Punts/Average	72/39.8	87/41.7
Net Punting Avg.	72/36.0	87/37.1
Penalties/Yards	77/652	118/874
Fumbles/Ball Lost	26/14	24/10
Touchdowns	44	41
Rushing	15	12
Passing	23	24
Returns	6	5

2007 INDIVIDUAL STATISTICS

PASSING	Att.	Comp.	Yds.	Pct.	TD	Int.	Tkld.	Rate
Manning	529	297	3336	56.1	23	20	27/217	73.9
Lorenzen	8	4	28	50.0	0	0	1/5	58.3
A. Wright	7	1	12	14.3	0	0	0/0	39.6
Giants	544	302	3376	55.5	23	20	28/222	73.0
Opponents	523	306	3666	58.5	24	15	53/349	83.4

SCORING	TD R	TD P	TD Rt	PAT	FG	Saf	PTS
Tynes	0	0	0	40/42	23/27	0	109
Burress	0	12	0	0/0	0/0	0	72
Droughns	6	0	0	0/0	0/0	0	36
Jacobs	4	2	0	0/0	0/0	0	36
Ward	3	1	0	0/0	0/0	0	24
Shockey	0	3	0	0/0	0/0	0	18
Toomer	0	3	0	0/0	0/0	0	18
Boss	0	2	0	0/0	0/0	0	12
Mitchell	0	0	2	0/0	0/0	0	12
Bradshaw	1	0	0	0/0	0/0	0	6
Hixon	0	0	1	0/0	0/0	0	6
Manning	1	0	0	0/0	0/0	0	6
Ross	0	0	1	0/0	0/0	0	6
Umenyiora	0	0	1	0/0	0/0	0	6
Webster	0	0	1	0/0	0/0	0	6
Giants	15	23	6	40/42	23/27	0	373
Opponents	12	24	5	38/38	21/29	1	351

2-Pt. Conversions: Giants 0-2, Opponents 1-3

RUSHING	No.	Yds	Avg	LG	TD
Jacobs	202	1009	5.0	43t	4
Ward	125	602	4.8	44	3
Droughns	85	275	3.2	45	6
Bradshaw	23	190	8.3	88t	1
Manning	29	69	2.4	18	1
Shockey	1	6	6.0	6	0
Moss	1	4	4.0	4	0
Lorenzen	1	2	2.0	2	0
A. Wright	1	-1	-1.0	-1	0
Hixon	1	-8	-8.0	-8	0
Giants	469	2148	4.6	88t	15
Opponents	408	1563	3.8	67t	12

RECEIVING	No.	Yds	Avg	LG	TD
Burress	70	1025	14.6	60t	12
Toomer	59	760	12.9	40	3
Shockey	57	619	10.9	29	3
Ward	26	179	6.9	17	1
Jacobs	23	174	7.6	34	2
Moss	21	225	10.7	20	0
Boss	9	118	13.1	23	2
S. Smith	8	63	7.9	12	0
Droughns	7	49	7.0	11	0
Hedgecock	6	45	7.5	9	0
Matthews	6	28	4.7	6	0
Tyree	4	35	8.8	24	0
Mix	3	39	13.0	21	0
Bradshaw	2	12	6.0	11	0
Hixon	1	5	5.0	5	0
Giants	302	3376	11.2	60t	23
Opponents	306	3666	12.0	65t	24

INTERCEPTIONS	No.	Yds	Avg	LG	TD
Madison	4	59	14.8	27	0
Wilson	4	12	3.0	10	0
Ross	3	51	17.0	43t	1
Webster	1	34	34.0	34t	1
Pierce	1	28	28.0	28	0
Mitchell	1	20	20.0	20t	1
Butler	1	0	0.0	0	0
Giants	15	204	13.6	43t	3
Opponents	20	336	16.8	93t	3

PUNTING	No.	Yds.	Avg.	In 20	LG
Feagles	71	2865	40.4	25	60
Giants	72	2865	39.8	25	60
Opponents	87	3631	41.7	27	64

PUNT RETURNS	Ret	FC	Yds	Avg	LG	TD
McQuarters	42	18	318	7.6	27	0
Bradshaw	1	0	1	1.0	1	0
Giants	43	18	319	7.4	27	0
Opponents	28	17	173	6.2	27	0

KICKOFF RETURNS	No.	Yds	Avg	LG	TD
Bradshaw	38	921	24.2	68	0
Droughns	20	437	21.9	34	0
Hixon	8	221	27.6	74t	1
Giants	66	1579	23.9	74t	1
Opponents	69	1596	23.1	98t	1

FIELD GOALS	1-19	20-29	30-39	40-49	50+
Tynes	1/1	9/10	5/8	8/8	0/0
Giants	1/1	9/10	5/8	8/8	0/0
Opponents	0/0	4/4	6/7	9/14	2/4

SACKS	No.
Umenyiora	13.0
Tuck	10.0
Strahan	9.0
Robbins	5.5
Kiwanuka	4.5
Mitchell	3.5
Ross	1.5
Alford	1.0
Cofield	1.0
Madison	1.0
Pierce	1.0
Torbor	1.0
(group)	1.0
Giants	53.0
Opponents	28.0

RECORD HOLDERS
INDIVIDUAL RECORDS—CAREER

Category	Name	Performance
Rushing (Yds.)	Tiki Barber, 1997-2006	10,449
Passing (Yds.)	Phil Simms, 1979-1993	33,462
Passing (TDs)	Phil Simms, 1979-1993	199
Receiving (No.)	Amani Toomer, 1996-2007	620
Receiving (Yds.)	Amani Toomer, 1996-2007	8,917
Interceptions	Emlen Tunnell, 1948-1958	74
Punting (Avg.)	Don Chandler, 1956-1964	43.8
Punt Return (Avg.)	Ward Cuff, 1941-45	12.1
Kickoff Return (Avg.)	Rocky Thompson, 1971-73	27.2
Field Goals	Pete Gogolak, 1966-1974	126
Touchdowns (Tot.)	Frank Gifford, 1952-1964	78
Points	Pete Gogolak, 1966-1974	646

INDIVIDUAL RECORDS—SINGLE SEASON

Category	Name	Performance
Rushing (Yds.)	Tiki Barber, 2005	1,860
Passing (Yds.)	Kerry Collins, 2002	4,073
Passing (TDs)	Y.A. Tittle, 1963	36
Receiving (No.)	Amani Toomer, 2002	82
Receiving (Yds.)	Amani Toomer, 2002	1,343
Interceptions	Otto Schnellbacher, 1951	11
	Jim Patton, 1958	11
Punting (Avg.)	Don Chandler, 1959	46.6
Punt Return (Avg.)	Merle Hapes, 1942	15.5
Kickoff Return (Avg.)	John Salscheider, 1949	31.6
Field Goals	Ali Haji-Sheikh, 1983	35
	Jay Feely, 2005	35
Touchdowns (Tot.)	Joe Morris, 1985	21
Points	Jay Feely, 2005	148

INDIVIDUAL RECORDS—SINGLE GAME

Category	Name	Performance
Rushing (Yds.)	Tiki Barber, 12-30-06	234
Passing (Yds.)	Phil Simms, 10-13-85	513
Passing (TDs)	Y.A. Tittle, 10-28-62	*7
Receiving (No.)	Tiki Barber, 1-2-00	13
Receiving (Yds.)	Del Shofner, 10-28-62	269
Interceptions	Many times	3
	Last time by Terry Kinard, 9-20-87	
Field Goals	Joe Danelo, 10-18-81	6
Touchdowns (Tot.)	Ron Johnson, 10-2-72	4
	Earnest Gray, 9-7-80	4
	Rodney Hampton, 9-24-95	4
Points	Ron Johnson, 10-2-72	24
	Earnest Gray, 9-7-80	24
	Rodney Hampton, 9-24-95	24

*NFL Record

2008 VETERAN ROSTER

No.	Name	Pos.	Ht.	Wt.	Age	NFL Exp.	College	Hometown	How Acq.	'07 Games/ Starts
93	Alford, Jay	DT	6-3	304	25	2	Penn State	Orange, N.J.	D3-'07	16/0
57	Blackburn, Chase	LB	6-3	247	25	4	Akron	Marysville, Ohio	FA-'05	16/0
77	Boothe, Kevin	G	6-5	315	25	3	Cornell	Fort Lauderdale, Fla.	W(Oak)-'07	1/0
89	Boss, Kevin	TE	6-6	253	24	2	Western Oregon	Philomath, Ore.	D5-'07	13/2
44	Bradshaw, Ahmad	RB	5-9	198	22	2	Marshall	Bluefield, Va.	D7b-'07	13/0
17	Burress, Plaxico	WR	6-5	232	31	9	Michigan State	Virginia Beach, Va.	UFA(Pitt)-'05	16/16
37	Butler, James	S	6-3	215	25	4	Georgia Tech	Climax, Ga.	FA-'05	13/12
8	Carr, David	QB	6-3	216	29	7	Fresno State	Bakersfield, Calif.	UFA-'08	0*
55	Clark, Daniel	LB	6-2	245	31	9	Illinois	Country Club Hills, Ill.	UFA(Hou)-'08	13/8*
96	Cofield, Barry	DT	6-4	306	24	3	Northwestern	Cleveland Heights, Ohio	D4a-'06	16/15
86	Collins, Jerome	TE	6-4	267	26	3	Notre Dame	Warrenville, Ill.	FA'-07	0*
52	Daniels, Tank	LB	6-3	248	26	3	Harding	Clarendon, Ark.	FA-'07	4/0
51	DeOssie, Zak	LB	6-4	249	24	2	Brown	No. Andover, Mass.	D4-'07	16/0
66	Diehl, David	T	6-5	319	27	6	Illinois	Oak Lawn, Ill.	D5-'03	16/16
35	Dockery, Kevin	CB	5-8	188	24	3	Mississippi State	Hernando, Miss.	FA-'06	13/4
24	Douglas, Robert	RB	6-1	230	26	2	Memphis	St. Louis, Mo.	FA-'07	1/0
22	Droughns, Reuben	RB	5-11	220	30	9	Oregon	Anaheim, Calif.	T(Cle)-'07	16/2
18	Feagles, Jeff	P	6-1	215	42	21	Miami	Phoenix, Ariz.	UFA(Sea)-'03	16/0
39	Hedgecock, Madison	FB	6-3	266	27	4	North Carolina	Wallburg, N.C.	W(StL)-'07	16/9*
87	Hixon, Domenik	WR	6-2	182	23	3	Akron	Columbus, Ohio	W(Den)-'07	12/1
27	Jacobs, Brandon	RB	6-4	264	26	4	Southern Illinois	Napoleanville, La.	D4-'05	11/9
20	Johnson, Michael	S	6-2	207	24	2	Arizona	Round Rock, Texas	D7a-'07	16/5
97	Kiwanuka, Mathias	LB	6-5	265	25	3	Boston College	Indianapolis, Ind.	D1-'06	10/10
26	Knight, Sammy	S	6-1	215	32	12	Southern California	Riverside, Calif.	UFA(Jax)-'08	16/15*
74	Leisle, Rodney	DT	6-3	315	27	3	UCLA	Bakersfield, Calif.	FA-'08	0*
13	Lorenzen, Jared	QB	6-4	285	27	4	Kentucky	Ft. Thomas, Ky.	FA-'04	2/0
29	Madison, Sam	CB	5-11	180	34	12	Louisville	Tallahassee, Fla.	FA-'06	16/15
10	Manning, Eli	QB	6-4	225	27	5	Mississippi	New Orleans, La.	T(SD)-'04	16/16
88	Matthews, Michael	TE	6-4	270	24	2	Georgia Tech	Cincinatti, Ohio	FA-'07	16/5
67	McKenzie, Kareem	T	6-6	327	29	8	Penn State	Willingboro, N.J.	UFA(NYJ)-'05	16/16
25	McQuarters, R.W.	CB	5-10	194	31	11	Oklahoma State	Tulsa, Okla.	UFA(Det)-'06	16/2
83	Moss, Sinorice	WR	5-8	185	24	3	Miami	Miami, Fla.	D2-'06	13/2
60	O'Hara, Shaun	C	6-3	303	31	9	Rutgers	Hillsborough, N.J.	UFA(Cle)-'04	16/16
54	O'Neil, Keith	LB	6-0	240	28	3	Northern Arizona	Angerst, N.Y.	FA-'08	0*
58	Pierce, Antonio	LB	6-1	238	29	8	Arizona	Ontario, Calif.	UFA(Wash)-'05	16/16
98	Robbins, Fred	DT	6-4	317	31	9	Wake Forest	Pensacola, Fla.	UFA(Minn)-'04	16/15
31	Ross, Aaron	CB	6-0	197	25	2	Texas	Tyler, Texas	D1-'07	16/9
65	Ruegamer, Grey	G	6-4	299	32	10	Arizona State	Las Vegas, Nev.	FA-'06	16/0
69	Seubert, Rich	G	6-3	310	29	8	Western Illinois	Marshfield, Wis.	FA-'01	16/16
80	Shockey, Jeremy	TE	6-5	251	28	6	Miami	Ada, Okla.	D1-'02	14/14
12	Smith, Steve	WR	5-11	195	23	2	Southern California	Woodland Hills, Calif.	D2-'07	5/0
76	Snee, Chris	G	6-3	317	26	5	Boston College	Montrose, Pa.	D2-'04	16/16
92	Strahan, Michael	DE	6-5	255	36	16	Texas Southern	Westbury, Texas	D2-'93	16/15
71	Tollefson, Dave	DE	6-4	255	26	2	N.W. Missouri State	Concord, Calif.	FA-'07	6/0
81	Toomer, Amani	WR	6-3	203	33	13	Michigan	Berkeley, Calif.	D2-'96	16/15
91	Tuck, Justin	DE	6-5	274	25	4	Notre Dame	Kellyton, Ala.	D3-'05	16/2
9	Tynes, Lawrence	PK	6-1	202	30	5	Troy State	Milton, Fla.	T(KC)-'07	16/0
85	Tyree, David	WR	6-0	206	28	6	Syracuse	Montclair, N.J.	D6c-'03	12/0
72	Umenyiora, Osi	DE	6-3	261	26	6	Troy State	Auburn, Ala.	D2-'03	16/16
28	Ware, Danny	RB	6-0	234	23	2	Georgia	Rockmart, Ga.	FA-'07	1/0
23	Webster, Corey	CB	6-0	202	26	4	Louisiana State	Vacherie, La.	D2-'05	14/3
79	Whimper, Guy	T	6-5	302	25	3	East Carolina	Havelock, N.C.	D4b-'06	16/0
59	Wilkinson, Gerris	LB	6-3	231	25	3	Georgia Tech	Oakland, Calif.	D3-'06	13/0
2	Wright, Anthony	QB	6-1	211	32	10	South Carolina	Vanceboro, N.C.	FA-'07	3/0
75	Wright, Manny	DT	6-5	345	24	4	Southern California	Long Beach, Calif.	FA-'07	6/0

* Carr played 6 games with Carolina in '07; Clark played 13 games with Houston; Collins inactive for 2 games; Hedgecock played 1 game with St. Louis and 15 games with N.Y. Giants; Knight played 16 games with Jacksonville; Leisle last active with New Orleans in '06; O'Neil last active with Indianapolis in '06.

Players lost through free agency (4): NT William Joseph (Oak; 0 games in '07), LB Kawika Mitchell (Buff; 16), LB Reggie Torbor (Mia; 16), S Gibril Wilson (Oak; 13).

Also played with Giants in '07—DE Adrian Awasom (2 games), S Craig Dahl(9), DT Russell Davis (11), Anthony Mix (4), RB Patrick Pass (1), RB Derrick Ward (8).

2008 FIRST-YEAR ROSTER

Name	Pos.	Ht.	Wt.	Age	College	Hometown	How Acq.
Bain, Andrew	G	6-3	344	22	Miami	Pampano Beach, Fla.	FA
Barnett, Darren (1)	CB	6-0	181	24	Missouri State	Cincinnati, Ohio	FA-'07
Bujnoch, Digger	C	6-5	285	23	Cincinnati	Cincinnati, Ohio	FA
Gilberry, Wallace	DE	6-3	267	23	Alabama	Bay Minette, Ala.	FA
Goff, Jonathan	LB	6-2	236	22	Vanderbilt	Lynn, Mass.	D5
Hall, DJ	WR	6-2	195	22	Alabama	Fort Walton Beach, Fla.	FA
Henderson, Robert	DE	6-3	278	24	Southern Miss	Ponchatoula, La.	D6
Hobbs, Jacob	OL	6-3	303	25	Albany	Schenectady, N.Y.	FA
Kehl, Bryan	LB	6-2	237	24	Brigham Young	Salt Lake City, Utah	D4
Leeson, Nick	LS	6-1	249	25	Virginia Tech	Abingdon, Va.	FA
London, Brandon (1)	WR	6-4	210	23	Massachusetts	Charlottesville, Va.	FA-'07
Lowber, Todd	WR	6-3	205	26	Ramapo	Delran, N.J.	FA
Manningham, Mario	WR	5-11	183	22	Michigan	Warren, Ohio	D3
Morrow, Alex	DE	6-6	270	23	Southern California	Rohnert Park, Calif.	FA
Nwagbuo, Ogemdi	DT	6-4	290	22	Michigan State	San Deigo, Calif.	FA
Phillips, Kenny	S	6-2	210	21	Miami	Miami, Fla.	D1
Pope, Geoffrey (1)	DB	6-0	186	24	Howard	Detroit, Mich.	FA-'07
Reynolds, Antonio	DE	6-3	270	24	Tennessee	Akron, Ohio	FA
Robinson, Nate	DT	6-5	315	23	Akron	Irvington, N.J.	FA
Scott, Miguel	DB	6-0	203	23	North Carolina State	Miami, Fla.	FA
Soi, Brian	DT	6-3	315	23	Utah	Provo, Utah	FA
Stringer, Terrance	DB	6-3	213	22	Tuskegee	Smith, Ala.	FA
Thiry, Dylan	T	6-8	315	23	Northwestern	Louisville, Ky.	FA
Thomas, Terrell	CB	6-0	199	23	Southern California	Alto Loma, Calif.	D2
Torrey, Brandon (1)	OL	6-4	295	25	Howard	Durham, N.C.	FA-'07
Warrick, Nehemiah	S	6-1	208	23	Michigan State	Bradenton, Fla.	FA
Woodson, André	QB	6-4	227	24	Kentucky	Radcliff, Ky.	D6

The term NFL Rookie is defined as a player who is in his first season of professional football and has not been on the roster of another professional football team for any regular-season or postseason games. A Rookie is designated by an "R" on NFL rosters. Players who have been active in another professional football league or players who have NFL experience, including either preseason training camp or being on an Active List or Inactive List, or on Reserve/Injured or Reserve/Physically Unable to Perform for fewer than six regular-season games, are termed NFL First-Year Players. An NFL First-Year Player is designated by a "1" on NFL rosters. Thereafter, a player is credited with an additional year of experience for each season in which he accumulates six games on the Active List or Inactive List, or on Reserve/Injured or Reserve/Physically Unable to Perform.

Log on to www.giants.com for an up-to-date roster; Age listed is as of September 4, 2008.

COACHING STAFF

Head Coach,
Tom Coughlin
Pro Career: Was named the sixteenth head coach in Giants history on January 6, 2004. This season marks Coughlin's fifth with the Giants and thirteenth as an NFL head coach. Coughlin directed the Giants 17-14 win over the New England Patriots in Super Bowl XLII on February 3, 2008, the third championship in the teams history. The Giants finished the 2007 regular season with a 10-6 record. Coached the Giants to an 11-5 record and the NFC East title in 2005, and guided the club to the playoffs in 2006, his second and third seasons with the team. Coughlin previously spent eight years (1995-2002) with the Jacksonville Jaguars. Under Coughlin, the Jaguars had the most victories of any NFL expansion team in its first seven seasons. They were also the only expansion team in NFL history to advance to the playoffs four times in their first five seasons. Coughlin's team went 9-7 in 1996 and an NFL-best 14-2 in 1999, both times reaching the AFC Championship Game. Coughlin previously coached the Philadelphia Eagles (1984-85), Green Bay Packers (1986-87), and Giants (1988-1990). He was a member of the Giants' Super Bowl XXV champion coaching staff. Career record: 111-95.

Background: Served as head coach at Boston College (1991-93), and coached at Syracuse (1969, 1974-1980), Rochester Institute of Technology 1970-73 (head coach), and Boston College (1981-83). Played wingback for Syracuse (1965-67).

Personal: Age 62, born in Waterloo, N.Y. Tom and his wife Judy have two daughters, Keli and Katie; two son-in-laws named Chris; two sons, Brian and Tim; two daughters-in-law, Andrea (Tim's wife) and Susie (Brian's wife); and five grandchildren, Emma Rose, Dylan, Shea, Cooper, and Caroline.

ASSISTANT COACHES

Andre Curtis, defensive assistant; born Richmond, Va. Linebacker Virginia Military Institute 1996-1999. No pro playing experience. College coach: Virginia Military Institute 2002-03, Georgia Southern 2004-05. Pro coach: Joined Giants in 2006.

Dave DeGuglielmo, asst. offensive line; born Cambridge, Mass. Attended Boston University. No college or pro playing experience. College coach: Boston College 1991-92, Boston University 1993-96, Connecticut 1997-98, South Carolina 1999-2003. Pro coach: Joined Giants in 2004.

Pat Flaherty, offensive line; born Hanover, Pa. Center East Stroudsburg 1974-77. No pro playing experience. College coach: East Stroudsburg 1980-81, Penn State 1982-83, Rutgers 1984-1991, East Carolina 1992, Wake Forest 1993-98, Iowa 1999. Pro coach: Washington Redskins 2000, Chicago Bears 2001-03, joined Giants in 2004.

Kevin Gilbride, offensive coordinator; born New Haven, Conn. Quarterback/tight end Southern Connecticut State 1971-73. No pro playing experience. College coach: Idaho State 1974-75, Tufts 1976-77, American International 1978-79. Southern Connecticut State 1980-84, East Carolina 1987-88. Pro coach: Ottawa Rough Riders (CFL) 1985-86, Houston Oilers 1989-1994, Jacksonville Jaguars 1995-96, San Diego Chargers 1997-98 (head coach), Pittsburgh Steelers 1999-2000, Buffalo Bills 2002-2003, joined Giants in 2004.

Peter Giunta, secondary/corners; born Salem, Mass. Running back/defensive back Northeastern 1974-77. No pro playing experience. College coach: Penn State 1981-83, Brown 1984-87, Lehigh 1988-1990. Pro coach: Philadelphia Eagles 1991-94, N.Y. Jets 1995-96, St. Louis Rams 1997-2000, Kansas City Chiefs 2001-2005, joined Giants in 2006.

Jerald Ingram, running backs; born Dayton, Ohio. Fullback Michigan 1979-1983. College coach: Michigan 1984, Ball State 1985-1990, Boston College 1991-93. Pro coach: Jacksonville Jaguars 1994-2002, joined Giants in 2004.

Thomas McGaughey, asst. special teams coordinator; born Chicago. Safety Houston 1991-95. Pro safety Philadelphia Eagles 1996, Barcelona Dragons (NFLE) 1997. College coach Houston 1997, 2003-04. Pro coach: Scottish Claymores (NFLE) 2002, Kansas City Chiefs 2002, Denver Broncos 2005-06, joined Giants in 2007.

David Merritt Sr., secondary/safeties; born Raleigh, N.C. Linebacker North Carolina State 1989-1992. Pro linebacker Miami Dolphins 1993, Arizona Cardinals 1993-96, Rhein Fire (NFLE) 1997. College coach: Chattanooga 1997, Virginia Military Institute 1998-2000. Pro coach: New York Jets 2001-2003, joined Giants in 2004.

Chris Palmer, quarterbacks; born Brewster, N.Y. Quarterback Southern Connecticut State 1968-1971. No pro playing experience. College coach: Connecticut 1972-74, Lehigh 1975, Colgate 1976-1982, New Haven 1985-87 (head coach), Boston 1988-89 (head coach). Pro coach: Montreal Concordes (CFL) 1983, New Jersey Generals (USFL) 1984-85, Houston Oilers 1990-92, New England Patriots 1993-96, Jacksonville Jaguars 1997-98, Cleveland Browns 1999-2000 (head coach), Houston Texans 2001-05, Dallas Cowboys 2006, joined Giants in 2007.

Jerry Palmieri, strength and conditioning; born Englewood, N.J. Attended Montclair State. No college or pro playing experience. College coach: North Carolina 1982-83, Oklahoma State 1984-86, Kansas State 1987-1992, Boston College 1993-94. Pro coach: Jacksonville Jaguars 1995-2002, New Orleans Saints 2003, joined Giants in 2004.

Marcus Paul, asst. strength and conditioning; born Orlando, Fla. Safety Syracuse 1984-88. Pro safety Chicago Bears 1989-1993, Tampa Buccaneers 1993. Pro coach: New Orleans Saints 1998-99, New England Patriots 2000-04, New York Jets 2005-2006, joined Giants in 2007.

Michael Pope, tight ends; born Monroe, N.C. Quarterback Lenoir-Rhyne 1962-64. No pro playing experience. College coach: Florida State 1970-74, Texas Tech 1975-77, Mississippi 1978-1982. Pro coach: New York Giants 1983-1991, Cincinnati Bengals 1992-93, New England Patriots 1994-96, Washington Redskins 1997-99, re-joined Giants in 2000.

Tom Quinn, special teams coordinator; born Pasadena, Calif. Linebacker Arizona 1986-1990. No pro playing experience. College coach; Davidson College 1991, James Madison 1992-94, Boston 1995, Holy Cross 1996-98, San Jose State 1999-2001, Stanford 2002-05. Pro coach: Joined Giants in 2006.

Sean Ryan, offensive quality control; born Glenn Falls, N.Y. Defensive back Hamilton College 1994. No pro playing experience. College coach: Albany 1998-99, Colgate 2000, Boston College 2001-02, Columbia 2003-04, Harvard 2006. Pro coach: Joined Giants in 2007.

Bill Sheridan, linebackers; born Detroit. Linebacker Grand Valley State 1979-1982. No pro playing experience. College coach: Michigan 1985-86, Maine 1987-88, Cincinnati 1989-1991, Army 1992-97, Michigan State 1998-2000, Notre Dame 2001, Michigan 2002-04. Pro coach. Joined Giants in 2005.

Steve Spagnuolo, defensive coordinator; born Witinville, Mass. Wide receiver Springfield College 1979-1981. No pro playing experience. College coach: Massachusetts 1982-83, Lafayette 1984-86, Connecticut 1987-1991, Maine 1993, Rutgers 1994-95, Bowling Green 1996-97. Pro coach: Barcelona Dragons (World League) 1992, Frankfurt Galaxy (NFLE) 1988, Philadelphia Eagles 1999-2006, joined Giants in 2007.

Mike Sullivan, wide receivers; born Santa Maria, Calif. Defensive back Army 1987-88. No pro playing experience. College coach: Mt. San Jacinto (Calif.) J.C. 1993, Humboldt State 1994, Army 1995-96, 1999-2000, Youngstown State 1997-98, Ohio 2001. Pro coach: Jacksonville Jaguars 2002-03, joined Giants in 2004.

Mike Waufle, defensive line; born Hornell, N.Y. U.S. Marines 1972-75. Defensive lineman Bakersfield (Calif.) J.C. 1975-76, Utah State 1977-78. No pro playing experience. College coach: Alfred 1979, Utah State 1980-84, Fresno State 1985-88, UCLA 1989, Oregon State 1990-91, California 1992-97. Pro coach: Oakland Raiders 1998-2003, joined Giants in 2004.

**National Football Conference
East Division**
Team Colors: Midnight Green, Silver, Black,
and White
**NovaCare Complex
One NovaCare Way
Philadelphia, Pennsylvania 19145
Telephone:** (215) 463-2500

2008 SCHEDULE
PRESEASON
Aug. 8   at Pittsburgh.........................7:30
Aug. 14 **Carolina**............................8:00
Aug. 22 at New England 7:30
Aug. 28 **N.Y. Jets** 6:30

REGULAR SEASON
Sep. 7   **St. Louis** 1:00
Sep. 15 at Dallas (Mon.) 7:30
Sep. 21 **Pittsburgh** 4:15
Sep. 28 at Chicago 7:15
Oct. 5   **Washington** 1:00
Oct. 12 at San Francisco 1:15
Oct. 19 BYE
Oct. 26 **Atlanta** 1:00
Nov. 2   at Seattle 1:15
Nov. 9   **N.Y. Giants**......................8:15
Nov. 16 at Cincinnati 1:00
Nov. 23 at Baltimore 1:00
Nov. 27 **Arizona** (Thu.)...................8:15
Dec. 7   at N.Y. Giants....................1:00
Dec. 15 **Cleveland** (Mon.) 8:30
Dec. 21 at Washington 1:00
Dec. 28 **Dallas** 1:00

Stadium: Lincoln Financial Field
(opened in 2003)
•**Capacity:** 67,594
One Lincoln Financial Field Way
Philadelphia, Pennsylvania 19148
Playing Surface: Natural Grass
Training Camp: Lehigh University
Bethlehem, PA 18015

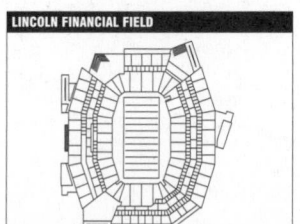

CLUB OFFICIALS
Chairman/Chief Executive Officer:
Jeffrey Lurie
President: Joe Banner
Head Coach/Executive Vice President of
Football Operations: Andy Reid
General Manager: Tom Heckert
Vice President of Player Personnel:
Jason Licht
Senior Vice President of Business
Operations: Mark Donovan
Senior Vice President/Chief Financial
Officer: Don Smolenski
Vice President of Football Administration:
Howie Roseman
Vice President of Sales and Service:
Bill Manning
Executive Director of Eagles Youth
Partnership: Sarah Martinez-Helfman
Director of Pro Personnel: Scott Cohen
Director of Football Media Relations:
Derek Boyko
Assistant Director of Football Media
Services: Bob Lange
Director of Marketing: Mike Malo
Director of Human Resources:
Kristie Pappal
Manager of Community Relations:
Julie Hirshey
Director of Stadium Operations:
Dave Duernberger
Director, Broadcasting: Rob Alberino
Director of Events: Leonard Bonacci
Director of Ticket Operations:
Laini Delawter
Director of Ticket Client Relations:
Leo Carlin
Director of Merchandise:
Brendan McQuillen
Travel Manager: Tracey Leinen
Director of Team Security:
Anthony (Butch) Buchanico
Head Athletic Trainer: Rick Burkholder
Asst. Athletic Trainers: Steve Condon,
Chris Peduzzi
Video Director: Mike Dougherty
Head Equipment Manager: John Hatfield

COACHING HISTORY
(496-541-25)
Records include postseason games
1933-35   Lud Wray 9-21-1
1936-1940 Bert Bell 10-44-2
1941-1950 Earle (Greasy) Neale*...66-44-5
1951   Alvin (Bo) McMillin**........2-0-0
1951   Wayne Millner..................2-8-0
1952-55   Jim Trimble..................25-20-3
1956-57   Hugh Devore 7-16-1
1958-1960 Lawrence (Buck) Shaw..20-16-1
1961-63   Nick Skorich 15-24-3
1964-68   Joe Kuharich 28-41-1
1969-1971 Jerry Williams*** 7-22-2
1971-72   Ed Khayat.....................8-15-2
1973-75   Mike McCormack 16-25-1
1976-1982 Dick Vermeil 57-51-0
1983-85   Marion Campbell**** ..17-29-1
1985   Fred Bruney.....................1-0-0
1986-1990 Buddy Ryan.................43-38-1
1991-94   Rich Kotite..................37-29-0
1995-98   Ray Rhodes..................30-36-1
1999-2007 Andy Reid...................96-62-0
      *Co-coach with Walt Kiesling in Philadelphia-
      Pittsburgh merger in 1943
    **Retired after two games in 1951
  ***Released after three games in 1971
 ****Released after 15 games in 1985

PAID ATTENDANCE
Home 541,280   Away 578,810
Total 1,120,090
Single-game home record,
72,111 (11/1/81)
Single-season home record,
557,325 (1980)

2008 DRAFT CHOICES
Round	Name	Pos.	College
2	Trevor Laws	DT	Notre Dame
	DeSean Jackson	WR	California
3	Bryan Smith	DE	McNeese State
4	Mike McGlynn	G	Pittsburgh
	Quintin Demps	DB	Texas-El Paso
	Jack Ikegwuonu	DB	Wisconsin
6	Mike Gibson	G	California
	Joe Mays	LB	North Dakota St.
	Andy Studebaker	DE	Wheaton
7	King Dunlap	T	Auburn

2007 TEAM RECORD

PRESEASON (1-3)

Date	Result	Opponent
8/13	L 3-29	at Baltimore
8/17	W 27-10	Carolina
8/26	L 13-27	at Pittsburgh
8/30	L 11-13	N.Y. Jets

REGULAR SEASON (8-8)

Date	Result	Opponent	Att.
9/9	L 13-16	at Green Bay	70,598
9/17	L 12-20	Washington	67,726
9/23	W 56-21	Detroit	67,570
9/30	L 3-16	at N.Y. Giants	78,862
10/14	W 16-9	at N.Y. Jets	77,189
10/21	L 16-19	Chicago	67,806
10/28	W 23-16	at Minnesota	63,019
11/4	L 17-38	Dallas	67,688
11/11	W 33-25	at Washington	90,218
11/18	W 17-7	Miami	68,934
11/25	L 28-31	at New England	68,756
12/2	L 24-28	Seattle	68,445
12/9	L 13-16	N.Y. Giants	68,594
12/16	W 10-6	at Dallas	63,777
12/23	W 38-23	at New Orleans	70,011
12/30	W 17-9	Buffalo	68,594

SCORE BY PERIODS

Eagles	100	97	69	70	0	—	336
Opponents	86	95	64	55	0	—	300

2007 TEAM STATISTICS

	Eagles	Opp.
Total First Downs	323	279
Rushing	118	80
Passing	186	177
Penalty	19	22
3rd Down: Made/Att	97/229	81/218
3rd Down Pct.	42.4	37.2
4th Down: Made/Att	9/15	3/13
4th Down Pct.	60.0	23.1
Possession Avg.	30:56	29:04
Total Net Yards	5729	4982
Avg. Per Game	358.1	311.4
Total Plays	1047	979
Avg. Per Play	5.5	5.1
Net Yards Rushing	1974	1533
Avg. Per Game	123.4	95.8
Total Rushes	421	403
Net Yards Passing	3755	3449
Avg. Per Game	234.7	215.6
Sacked/Yards Lost	49/250	37/244
Gross Yards	4005	3693
Att./Completions	577/350	539/312
Completion Pct.	60.7	57.9
Had Intercepted	15	11
Punts/Average	73/42.0	76/41.6
Net Punting Avg.	73/34.5	76/35.8
Penalties/Yards	83/649	81/616
Fumbles/Ball Lost	24/12	16/8
Touchdowns	38	30
Rushing	12	10
Passing	24	16
Returns	2	4

2007 INDIVIDUAL STATISTICS

PASSING	Att.	Comp.	Yds.	Pct.	TD	Int.	Tkld.	Rate
McNabb	473	291	3324	61.5	19	7	44/227	89.9
Feeley	103	59	681	57.3	5	8	3/10	61.2
Lewis	1	0	0	0.0	0	0	0/0	39.6
Kolb	0	0	0	—	0	0	2/13	—
Eagles	577	350	4005	60.7	24	15	49/250	84.6
Opponents	539	312	3693	57.9	16	11	37/244	80.3

SCORING	TD R	TD P	TD Rt	PAT	FG	Saf	PTS
Akers	0	0	0	36/36	24/32	0	108
Westbrook	7	5	0	0/0	0/0	0	72
Curtis	0	6	2	0/0	0/0	0	48
R. Brown	0	4	0	0/0	0/0	0	24
Buckhalter	4	0	0	0/0	0/0	0	24
Lewis	0	3	0	0/0	0/0	0	18
Avant	0	2	0	0/0	0/0	0	12
Baskett	0	1	0	0/0	0/0	0	6
Celek	0	1	0	0/0	0/0	0	6
Hunt	1	0	0	0/0	0/0	0	6
Schobel	0	1	0	0/0	0/0	0	6
Smith	0	1	0	0/0	0/0	0	6
Eagles	12	24	2	36/36	24/32	0	336
Opponents	10	16	4	27/29	31/38	0	300

2-Pt. Conversions: Eagles 0-2, Opponents 0-1

RUSHING	No.	Yds	Avg	LG	TD
Westbrook	278	1333	4.8	36	7
Buckhalter	62	313	5.0	30t	4
McNabb	50	236	4.7	40	0
R. Brown	5	36	7.2	12	0
Feeley	7	23	3.3	7	0
Tapeh	5	18	3.6	11	0
Hunt	10	16	1.6	4	1
Avant	1	1	1.0	1	0
Kolb	3	-2	-0.7	0	0
Eagles	421	1974	4.7	40	12
Opponents	403	1533	3.8	56	10

RECEIVING	No.	Yds	Avg	LG	TD
Westbrook	90	771	8.6	57t	5
Curtis	77	1110	14.4	75t	6
R. Brown	61	780	12.8	45t	4
Avant	23	267	11.6	31	2
Smith	22	236	10.7	26	1
Celek	16	178	11.1	29	1
Baskett	16	142	8.9	25	1
Lewis	13	265	20.4	50	3
Buckhalter	12	87	7.3	14	0
Schobel	11	108	9.8	18	1
Tapeh	8	50	6.3	9	0
Mahe	1	11	11.0	11	0
Eagles	350	4005	11.4	75t	24
Opponents	312	3693	11.8	91t	16

INTERCEPTIONS	No.	Yds	Avg	LG	TD
S. Brown	3	3	1.0	3	0
Sheppard	2	25	12.5	16	0
Gaither	1	49	49.0	49	0
Mikell	1	20	20.0	20	0
Bradley	1	13	13.0	13	0
Dawkins	1	1	1.0	1	0
Considine	1	0	0.0	0	0
James	1	0	0.0	0	0
Eagles	11	111	10.1	49	0
Opponents	15	198	13.2	49	1

PUNTING	No.	Yds	Avg	In 20	LG
Rocca	73	3066	42.0	24	65
Eagles	73	3066	42.0	24	65
Opponents	76	3162	41.6	21	61

PUNT RETURNS	Ret	FC	Yds	Avg	LG	TD
Mahe	31	11	249	8.0	32	0
Lewis	4	1	4	1.0	5	0
Westbrook	4	0	79	19.8	64	0
Reed	2	0	8	4.0	8	0
Graham	1	0	0	0.0	0	0
Eagles	42	12	340	8.1	64	0
Opponents	36	14	409	11.4	87t	1

KICKOFF RETURNS	No.	Yds	Avg	LG	TD
Buckhalter	37	798	21.6	35	0
Reed	31	701	22.6	34	0
Lewis	1	3	3.0	3	0
Mahe	1	19	19.0	19	0
Reagor	1	14	14.0	14	0
Baskett	0	4	—	4	0
Eagles	71	1539	21.7	35	0
Opponents	69	1536	22.3	51	0

FIELD GOALS	1-19	20-29	30-39	40-49	50+
Akers	0/0	12/12	10/10	1/6	1/4
Eagles	0/0	12/12	10/10	1/6	1/4
Opponents	1/1	13/13	10/13	5/9	2/2

SACKS	No.
T. Cole	12.5
J. Thomas	5.0
Patterson	4.0
Kearse	3.5
Bunkley	3.0
(group)	2.0
Bradley	1.0
Gocong	1.0
Hanson	1.0
Howard	1.0
Mikell	1.0
Reagor	1.0
Spikes	1.0
Eagles	37.0
Opponents	49.0

RECORD HOLDERS
INDIVIDUAL RECORDS—CAREER

Category	Name	Performance
Rushing (Yds.)	Wilbert Montgomery, 1977-1984	6,538
Passing (Yds.)	Ron Jaworski, 1977-1986	26,963
Passing (TDs)	Ron Jaworski, 1977-1986	175
Receiving (No.)	Harold Carmichael, 1971-1983	589
Receiving (Yds.)	Harold Carmichael, 1971-1983	8,978
Interceptions	Bill Bradley, 1969-1976	34
	Eric Allen, 1988-1994	34
Punting (Avg.)	Joe Muha, 1946-1950	42.9
Punt Return (Avg.)	Ernie Steele, 1942-48	16.8
Kickoff Return (Avg.)	Steve Van Buren, 1944-1951	26.7
Field Goals	David Akers, 1999-2007	197
Touchdowns (Tot.)	Harold Carmichael, 1971-1983	79
Points	David Akers, 1999-2007	897

INDIVIDUAL RECORDS—SINGLE SEASON

Category	Name	Performance
Rushing (Yds.)	Wilbert Montgomery, 1979	1,512
Passing (Yds.)	Donovan McNabb, 2004	3,875
Passing (TDs)	Sonny Jurgensen, 1961	32
Receiving (No.)	Brian Westbrook, 2007	90
Receiving (Yds.)	Mike Quick, 1983	1,409
Interceptions	Bill Bradley, 1971	11
Punting (Avg.)	Joe Muha, 1948	47.2
Punt Return (Avg.)	Steve Van Buren, 1944	15.3
Kickoff Return (Avg.)	Al Nelson, 1972	29.1
Field Goals	Paul McFadden, 1984	30
	David Akers, 2002	30
Touchdowns (Tot.)	Steve Van Buren, 1945	18
Points	David Akers, 2002	133

INDIVIDUAL RECORDS—SINGLE GAME

Category	Name	Performance
Rushing (Yds.)	Steve Van Buren, 11-27-49	205
Passing (Yds.)	Donovan McNabb, 12-5-04	464
Passing (TDs)	Adrian Burk, 10-17-54	*7
Receiving (No.)	Don Looney, 12-1-40	14
	Brian Westbrook, 11-4-07	14
Receiving (Yds.)	Tommy McDonald, 12-10-60	237
Interceptions	Russ Craft, 9-24-50	*4
Field Goals	Tom Dempsey, 11-12-72	6
Touchdowns (Tot.)	Many times	4
	Last time by Irving Fryar, 10-20-96	
Points	Bobby Walston, 10-17-54	25

*NFL Record

2008 VETERAN ROSTER

No.	Name	Pos.	Ht.	Wt.	Age	NFL Exp.	College	Hometown	How Acq.	'07 Games/ Starts
78	Abiamiri, Victor	DE	6-4	267	22	2	Notre Dame	Baltimore, Md.	D2b-'07	6/1
2	Akers, David	K	5-10	200	33	10	Louisville	Lexington, Kent.	FA-'99	16/0
73	Andrews, Shawn	G/T	6-4	335	25	5	Arkansas	Camden, Ark.	D1-'04	15/15
81	Avant, Jason	WR	6-0	212	25	3	Michigan	Chicago, Ill.	D4b-'06	15/5
84	Baskett, Hank	WR	6-4	220	26	3	New Mexico	Clovis, N.M.	T(Minn)-'06	16/0
50	Boiman, Rocky	LB	6-3	236	28	7	Notre Dame	Cincinnati, Ohio	UFA(Ind)-'08	16/7*
25 t-	Booker, Lorenzo	RB	5-10	191	24	2	Florida State	Ventura, Calif.	T(Mia)-'08	7/1*
55	Bradley, Stewart	LB	6-4	255	24	2	Nebraska	Salt Lake City, Utah	D3a-'07	16/1
86	Brown, Reggie	WR	6-1	197	27	4	Georgia	Carrollton, Ga.	D2a-'05	16/14
24	Brown, Sheldon	CB	5-10	200	29	7	South Carolina	Ft. Lawn, S.C.	D2b-'02	16/16
28	Buckhalter, Correll	RB	6-0	217	29	8	Nebraska	Collins, Miss.	D4-'01	14/2
97	Bunkley, Brodrick	DT	6-2	306	24	3	Florida State	Tampa, Fla.	D1-'06	15/15
87	Celek, Brent	TE	6-4	255	23	2	Cincinnati	Cincinnati, Ohio	D5b-'07	16/4
11	Childress, Bam	WR	5-10	185	26	2	Ohio State	Warrensville Heights, Ohio	FA-'08	0*
91	Clemons, Chris	DE	6-2	240	26	5	Georgia	Griffin, Ga.	UFA(Oak)-'08	16/2*
59	Cole, Nick	C	6-0	350	24	3	New Mexico State	Lawton, Okla.	FA-'06	16/1
58	Cole, Trent	LB/DE	6-3	270	25	4	Cincinnati	Xenia, Ohio	D5a-'05	16/16
37	Considine, Sean	S	6-0	212	26	4	Iowa	Byron, Ill.	D4a-'05	8/8
80	Curtis, Kevin	WR	6-0	186	30	6	Utah State	South Jordan, Utah	UFA(StL)-'07	16/16
34	Davis, Jason	FB	5-10	245	24	2	Illinois	St. Louis, Mo.	FA-'07	0*
20	Dawkins, Brian	S	6-0	210	34	13	Clemson	Jacksonville, Fla.	D2b-'96	10/10
46	Dorenbos, Jon	LS	6-0	250	28	6	Texas-El Paso	Garden Grove, Calif.	FA-'06	16/0
14	Feeley, A.J.	QB	6-3	220	31	8	Oregon	Ontario, Ore.	FA-'06	3/2
96	Gaither, Omar	LB	6-2	245	24	3	Tennessee	Charlotte, N.C.	D5b-'06	16/16
57	Gocong, Chris	LB	6-2	263	24	3	Cal Poly San Luis Obispo	Carpinteria, Calif.	D3-'06	16/12
35	Graham, Nick	CB	5-10	191	24	2	Tulsa	Oklahoma City, Okla.	FA-'07	15/0
21	Hanson, Joselio	CB	5-9	185	27	4	Texas Tech	Playa Del Rey, Calif.	FA-'06	16/4
79	Herremans, Todd	G/T	6-6	321	25	4	Saginaw Valley State	Ravenna, Mich.	D4b-'05	16/15
90	Howard, Darren	DE	6-3	275	31	9	Kansas State	St. Petersburg, Fla.	UFA(NO)-'06	16/0
29	Hunt, Tony	RB	6-1	227	22	2	Penn State	Alexandria, Va.	D3b-'07	8/0
67	Jackson, Jamaal	C	6-4	330	28	5	Delaware State	Miami, Fla.	FA-'03	16/16
62	Jean-Gilles, Max	G	6-3	358	24	3	Georgia	Miami, Fla.	D4a-'06	4/1
85	Jones, Jamal	WR	5-11	205	27	2	North Carolina A&T	Hyattsville, Md.	FA-'08	0*
56	Jordan, Akeem	LB	6-1	226	23	2	James Madison	Harrisonburg, Va.	FA-'07	9/1
74	Justice, Winston	T	6-6	320	23	3	Southern California	Long Beach, Calif.	D2-'06	7/1
49	Klecko, Dan	FB	5-11	275	27	6	Temple	Marlboro, N.J.	UFA(Ind)-'08	8/0*
4	Kolb, Kevin	QB	6-3	218	24	2	Houston	Stephenville, Texas	D2a-'07	1/0
83	Lewis, Greg	WR	6-0	180	28	6	Illinois	Richton Park, Ill.	FA-'03	15/1
25 #	Mahe, Reno	RB	5-10	212	28	6	Brigham Young	Salt Lake City, Utah	FA-'03	15/0
95	McDougle, Jerome	DE	6-2	264	29	6	Miami	Pompano Beach, Fla.	D1-'03	0*
5	McNabb, Donovan	QB	6-2	240	31	10	Syracuse	Chicago, Ill.	D1-'99	14/14
27	Mikell, Quintin	S	5-10	206	27	6	Boise State	Eugene, Ore.	FA-'03	14/11
23	Moats, Ryan	RB	5-8	210	25	4	Louisiana Tech	Dallas, Texas	D3-'05	0*
75	Parker, Juqua	DE	6-2	250	30	8	Oklahoma State	Houston, Texas	FA-'05	16/7
32	Paschal, Marcus	S	6-0	201	24	2	Iowa	Largo, Fla.	FA-'07	3/0
98	Patterson, Mike	DT	6-0	292	25	4	Southern California	Los Alamitos, Calif.	D1-'05	16/15
77	Ramsey, LaJuan	DT	6-3	300	24	3	Southern California	Compton, Calif.	D6-'06	9/0
94	Reagor, Montae	DT	6-3	285	31	10	Texas Tech	Waxahachie, Texas	FA-'07	7/0
30	Reed, J.R.	S	5-11	202	26	5	South Florida	Tampa, Fla.	FA-'07	15/3
6	Rocca, Sav	P	6-5	265	34	2	None	Lakeside, Australia	FA-'07	16/0
64	Rodgers, Stefan	G	6-5	310	26	3	Lambuth	North Little Rock, Ark.	FA-'06	0*
69	Runyan, Jon	T	6-7	330	34	13	Michigan	Flint, Mich.	UFA(Ten)-'00	16/16
22	Samuel, Asante	CB	5-10	185	27	6	Central Florida	Lauderdale Lakes, Fla.	UFA(NE)-'08	16/16*
61	Schable, A.J.	DE	6-4	273	24	2	South Dakota	Ida Grove, Iowa	FA-'08	0*
89	Schobel, Matt	TE	6-5	255	29	7	TCU	Columbus, Texas	UFA(Cin)-'06	15/6
26	Sheppard, Lito	CB	5-10	194	27	7	Florida	Jacksonville, Fla.	D1-'02	11/11
82	Smith, L.J.	TE	6-3	258	28	6	Rutgers	Highland Park, N.J.	D2-'03	10/9
72	Thomas, Tra	T	6-7	335	33	11	Florida State	Deland, Fla.	D1-'98	15/15
52	Togafau, Pago	LB	5-10	250	24	2	Idaho State	Long Beach, Calif.	W(Arz)-'07	7/0
66 #	von Oelhoffen, Kimo	DT	6-4	299	37	15	Boise State	Kaunakakai, Hawaii	FA-'07	8/1
36	Westbrook, Brian	RB	5-10	203	29	7	Villanova	Ft. Washington, Md.	D3-'02	15/15
88	Wilson, Kris	TE	6-2	251	27	5	Pittsburgh	Lancaster, Pa.	UFA(KC)-'08	16/12*
71	Young, Scott	G	6-4	312	27	4	Brigham Young	Salt Lake City, Utah	D5b-'05	1/0

* Boiman played 16 games with Indianapolis in '07; Booker played 7 games with Miami; Childress last active with New England in '06; Clemons played 16 games with Oakland; Davis missed '06 season due to injury; Jones last active with New Orleans in '06; Klecko played 8 games with Indianapolis; McDougle missed '07 season due to injury; Moats missed '07 season due to injury; Rodgers missed '07 season due to injury; Samuel played 16 game with New England; Schable last active with Arizona in '06; Wilson played 16 games with Kansas City.

t- Eagles traded for Booker (Mia).

\# Unrestricted free agent; subject to developments.

Players lost through free agency (2): CB William James (Buff; 14 games in '06), DT Ian Scott (Car; 0), FB Thomas Tapeh (Minn; 16).

Also played with Eagles in '07—DE Jevon Kearse (15 games), LB Matt McCoy (7), LB Takeo Spikes (14).

2008 FIRST-YEAR ROSTER

Name	Pos.	Ht.	Wt.	Age	College	Hometown	How Acq.
Arrington, Kyle	CB	5-10	196	22	Hofstra	Brandywine, Md.	FA
Clark, Jeremy (1)	DT	6-3	309	24	Alabama	Daphne, Al.	FA-'07
Collins, Jed	FB	6-1	249	22	Washington State	Mission Viejo, Ca.	FA
Davis, Tanard (1)	CB	5-9	184	25	Miami	Miami, Fl.	FA-'07
Demps, Quintin	S	5-11	206	23	Texas-El Paso	San Antonio, Tx.	D4b
Dunbar, Franklin	T	6-4	327	23	Middle Tennessee State	Waycross, Ga.	FA
Dunlap, King	T	6-8	310	22	Auburn	Brentwood, Tn.	D7
Fontenot, Therrian (1)	CB	5-11	185	26	Fresno State	Lawndale, Ca.	FA-'07
Gasperson, Michael (1)	WR	6-4	220	26	San Diego	Monterey, Ca.	FA-'05
Gibson, Mike	G	6-3	305	22	California	Napa, Ca.	D6a
Golden, Terrell	WR	6-2	216	23	Penn State	Norfolk, Va.	FA
Hardy, Frantz	WR	6-0	180	23	Nebraska	Miami, Fl.	FA
Ikegwuonu, Jack	CB	5-10	194	22	Wisconsin	Madison, Wi.	D4c
Jackson, DeSean	WR	5-10	169	21	California	Long Beach, Ca.	D2b
Jackson, Xzavie (1)	DE	6-3	287	23	Missouri	Vacaville, Ca.	FA-'07
Laws, Trevor	DT	6-1	304	23	Notre Dame	Apple Valley, Minn.	D2a
Mays, Joe	LB	5-11	246	23	North Dakota State	Chicago, Il.	D6b
McBride, Shaheer	WR	6-1	205	23	Delaware State	Chester, Pa.	FA
McGee, Richmond	P/K	6-4	203	25	Texas	Garland, Tx.	FA
McGlynn, Mike	G	6-4	311	23	Pittsburgh	Austintown, Oh.	D4a
Roland, Justin	LB	5-11	242	22	Kansas State	Ponca City, Ok.	FA
Sampy, Bill (1)	WR	5-11	192	25	Louisiana Lafayette	Carencro, La	FA-'06
Smith, Bryan	DE	6-2	231	24	McNeese State	Newton, Tx.	D3
Studebaker, Andy	LB	6-3	251	22	Wheaton	Eureka, Il.	D6c

The term NFL Rookie is defined as a player who is in his first season of professional football and has not been on the roster of another professional football team for any regular-season or postseason games. A Rookie is designated by an "R" on NFL rosters. Players who have been active in another professional football league or players who have NFL experience, including either preseason training camp or being on an Active List or Inactive List, or on Reserve/Injured or Reserve/Physically Unable to Perform for fewer than six regular-season games, are termed NFL First-Year Players. An NFL First-Year Player is designated by a "1" on NFL rosters. Thereafter, a player is credited with an additional year of experience for each season in which he accumulates six games on the Active List or Inactive List, or on Reserve/Injured or Reserve/Physically Unable to Perform.

Log on to www.philadelphiaeagles.com for an up-to-date roster; Age listed is as of September 4, 2008.

COACHING STAFF

Head Coach/Executive Vice President of Football Operations, Andy Reid

Pro Career: Reid has earned NFL coach of the year honors twice, compiled the best win total (96), winning percentage (.608) and playoff victory total (8) in team history. He has captured five division titles and four trips to the NFC Championship game. Since he was hired in 1999, no other franchise has earned more divisional playoff round appearances (6) than Philadelphia. Among coaches with 100 games under their belt entering 2008, Reid's .608 overall winning percentage is 16th in NFL history and third among active coaches behind Indianapolis' Tony Dungy (.648) and New England's Bill Belichick (.626). In his 16-year NFL coaching career, Reid's teams have made the playoffs 12 times (17-11 record). He has coached in the Super Bowl three times, the NFC Championship game seven times, and in the Pro Bowl four times. Reid became the 20th head coach in franchise history on January 11, 1999, and was promoted to head coach/executive vice president of football operations in 2001. He was named NFL coach of the year in 2000 and 2002. He joined the Eagles after a seven-year stint as an assistant coach with Green Bay (1992-98) under Mike Holmgren. With Green Bay, Reid helped the Packers earn a Super Bowl XXXI victory over New England. Career record: 96-62.

Background: Coached at Brigham Young (1982), San Francisco State (1983-85), Northern Arizona (1986), Texas-El Paso (1987-88), and Missouri (1989-1991). Reid first met Holmgren, who was a member of BYU's coaching staff, when Reid was an offensive tackle and guard on three Cougar Holiday Bowl teams. Reid graduated with a bachelor's degree in physical education. He also received a master's degree in professional leadership in physical education and athletics.

Personal: Age 50, born in Los Angeles, Reid and his wife Tammy have five children—Garrett, Britt, Crosby, Drew Ann, and Spencer.

ASSISTANT COACHES

Mike Caldwell, defensive quality control; Linebacker Middle Tennessee State 1989-1992. Pro linebacker Cleveland Browns 1993-95, Baltimore Ravens 1996, Arizona Cardinals 1997, Philadelphia Eagles 1998-2001, Chicago Bears 2002, Carolina Panthers 2003. Pro coach: Joined Eagles in 2008.

Juan Castillo, offensive line; born Port Isabel, Texas. Linebacker Texas A&I (now Texas A&M-Kingsville) 1978-1980. Pro linebacker San Antonio Gunslingers (USFL) 1984-85. College coach: Texas A&I/Texas A&M-Kingsville 1982-85, 1990-94. Pro coach: Joined Eagles in

1995.

David Culley, wide receivers; born Sparta, Tenn. Quarterback Vanderbilt 1973-77. No pro playing experience. College coach: Austin Peay 1978, Vanderbilt 1979-1981, Middle Tennessee State 1982, Tennessee-Chattanooga 1983, Western Kentucky 1984, Southwestern Louisiana 1985-88, Texas-El Paso 1989-1990, Texas A&M 1991-93. Pro coach: Tampa Bay Buccaneers 1994-95, Pittsburgh Steelers 1996-1998, joined Eagles in 1999.

Pete Jenkins, defensive line; born Macon, Ga. Linebacker/nose tackle Western Carolina 1963-64. No pro playing experience. College coach: Troy State 1968-1970, South Carolina 1971-74, Southern Mississippi 1975-77, Oklahoma State 1978, Florida 1979, Louisiana State 1980-1990, 2000-02, Mississippi State 1991-94, Auburn 1995-1999. Pro coach: Joined Eagles in 2006.

Jim Johnson, defensive coordinator; born Maywood, Ill. Quarterback Missouri 1959-1962. Pro tight end Buffalo Bills 1963-64. College coach: Missouri Southern 1967-68 (head coach), Drake 1969-1972, Indiana 1973-76, Notre Dame 1977-1980. Pro coach: Oklahoma Outlaws (USFL) 1984, Jacksonville Bulls (USFL) 1985, Phoenix Cardinals 1986-1993, Indianapolis Colts 1994-97, Seattle Seahawks 1998, joined Eagles in 1999.

Sean McDermott, secondary; born Omaha, Neb. Safety William & Mary 1994-97. No pro playing experience. College coach: William & Mary 1998. Pro coach: Joined Eagles in 1998.

Tom Melvin, tight ends; born Redwood City, Calif. Offensive lineman San Francisco State 1982-83. No pro playing experience. College coach: San Francisco State 1984-85, Northern Arizona 1986-87, California-Santa Barbara 1988-1990, Occidental College 1991-98. Pro coach: Joined Eagles in 1999.

Marty Mornhinweg, asst. head coach/offensive coordinator; born Edmond, Okla. Quarterback Montana 1981-84. Pro quarterback Denver Dynamite (AFL) 1987. College coach: Montana 1985, Texas-El Paso 1986-87, Northern Arizona 1988, 1994, Southeast Missouri State 1989-1990, Missouri 1991-93. Pro coach: Green Bay Packers 1995-96, San Francisco 49ers 1997-2000, Detroit Lions 2001-02 (head coach), joined Eagles in 2003.

Jeff Nixon, special teams quality control; born Rochester, Pa. Running back West Virginia 1993-94, Penn State 1996. No pro playing experience. College coach: Penn State 1997, Princeton 1998, Shippensburg 1999-2002, Tennessee-Chattanooga 2003-05, Temple 2006. Pro coach: Joined Eagles in 2007.

Rory Segrest, special teams coordinator; born Waycross, Ga. Tackle Alabama 1991-93. No pro playing experience.

College coach: Alabama 1994-97, Auburn 1997-98, Southeast Missouri State 1999-2001, Samford 2002-05. Pro coach: Joined Eagles in 2006.

Bill Shuey, linebackers; born Bethlehem, Pa. Attended Slippery Rock. No college or pro playing experience. Pro coach: Joined Eagles in 2003.

Pat Shurmur, quarterbacks; born Dearborn Heights, Mich. Center Michigan State 1983-87. No pro playing experience. College coach: Michigan State 1988-1997, Stanford 1998. Pro coach: Joined Eagles in 1999.

Otis Smith, assistant secondary; Cornerback Missouri 1988-89. Pro cornerback Philadelphia Eagles 1991-94, New York Jets 1995, 1997-99, New England Patriots 1996, 2000-02, Detroit Lions 2003. Pro coach: Joined Eagles in 2008.

James Urban, offensive assistant/quality control; born Mechanicsburg, Pa. Wide receiver Washington and Lee 1993-96. No pro playing experience. College coach: Clarion 1997-98, Pennsylvania 1999-2004. Pro coach: Joined Eagles in 2007.

Mark Whipple, offensive assistant; Quarterback Brown 1976-78. No pro playing experience. College coach: St. Lawrence 1980, Union 1981-82, Brown 1983, New Hampshire 1986-87, New Haven 1988-93, Brown 1994-97, Massachusetts 1998-03. Pro coach: Arizona Wranglers (USFL) 1984, Pittsburgh Steelers 2004-06, Joined Eagles in 2008.

Ted Williams, running backs; born Lyons, Texas. Attended Cal Poly-Pomona. No college or pro playing experience. College coach: UCLA 1980-89, Washington State 1991-93, Arizona 1994. Pro coach: Joined Eagles in 1995.

Mike Wolf, strength and conditioning; born Allentown, Pa. Center Penn State 1983-87. No pro playing experience. College coach: Vanderbilt 1988-89, Lehigh 1990, Penn State 1991. Pro coach: Minnesota Vikings 1992-94, joined Eagles in 1995.

**National Football Conference
West Division**
Team Colors: New Century Gold,
Millennium Blue, and White
One Rams Way
St. Louis, Missouri 63045
Telephone: (314) 982-7267

2008 SCHEDULE
PRESEASON
Aug. 9   at Tennessee 7:00
Aug. 16 **San Diego**...........................7:00
Aug. 23 **Baltimore**............................7:00
Aug. 28 at Kansas City 7:00

REGULAR SEASON
Sep. 7   at Philadelphia 1:00
Sep. 14 **N.Y. Giants**.......................12:00
Sep. 21 at Seattle 1:05
Sep. 28 **Buffalo** 3:05
Oct. 5   BYE
Oct. 12 at Washington 1:00
Oct. 19 **Dallas** 12:00
Oct. 26 at New England 1:00
Nov. 2   **Arizona** 12:00
Nov. 9   at N.Y. Jets 1:00
Nov. 16 at San Francisco 1:05
Nov. 23 **Chicago** 12:00
Nov. 30 **Miami** 12:00
Dec. 7   at Arizona 2:15
Dec. 14 **Seattle** 12:00
Dec. 21 **San Francisco** 12:00
Dec. 28 at Atlanta 1:00

Stadium: Edward Jones Dome
(opened in 1995)
 • **Capacity:** 66,000
701 Convention Plaza
St. Louis, Missouri 63101
Playing Surface: FieldTurf
Training Camp: Russell Training Center
1 Rams Way
St. Louis, Missouri 63045

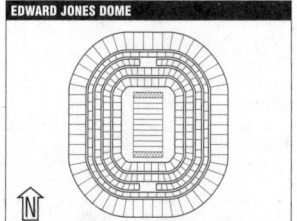

EDWARD JONES DOME

CLUB OFFICIALS
Owner/Chairman:
Dale "Chip" Rosenbloom
Owner/Partner: Lucia Rodriguez
Owner/Vice Chairman: Stan Kroenke
President: John Shaw
President, Football Operations/General
Manager: Jay Zygmunt
Executive Vice President of Player
Personnel: Billy Devaney
Vice President of Player Personnel:
Tony Softli
Executive Vice President and General
Counsel: Bob Wallace
Treasurer: Jeff Brewer
Chief Marketing Officer: Bob Reif
Vice President of Business Affairs:
Jim McCallum
Vice President of Finance & Ticketing:
Michael T. Naughton
Vice President of Operations:
John Oswald
Vice President of Public Relations:
Rick Smith
Vice President of Sales: Mike O'Keefe
Director of Football Operations:
Samir Suleiman
Director of Player Personnel:
Lawrence McCutcheon
Head Trainer: Jim Anderson
Assistant Trainers: Dake Walden,
James Lomax
Equipment Manager: Todd Hewitt
Assistant Equipment Manager: Jim Lake.
Scouts: Ray Agnew, Cary Conklin,
Dick Daniels, Luke Driscoll, Mel Foels,
Brad Holmes, Steve Kazor,
John Mancini

COACHING HISTORY
Cleveland 1937-1945,
Los Angeles 1946-1994
(520-478-20)
Records include postseason games
1937-38   Hugo Bezdek*............1-13-0
1938   Art Lewis 4-4-0
1939-1942   Earl (Dutch) Clark......16-26-2
1944   Aldo (Buff) Donelli.........4-6-0
1945-46   Adam Walsh 16-5-1
1947   Bob Snyder.................6-6-0
1948-49   Clark Shaughnessy 14-8-3
1950-52   Joe Stydahar**...........19-9-0
1952-54   Hamp Pool.................23-11-2
1955-59   Sid Gillman 28-32-1
1960-62   Bob Waterfield*** 9-24-1
1962-65   Harland Svare 14-31-3
1966-1970   George Allen 49-19-4
1971-72   Tommy Prothro 14-12-2
1973-77   Chuck Knox 57-20-1
1978-1982   Ray Malavasi 43-36-0
1983-1991   John Robinson.........79-74-0
1992-94   Chuck Knox 15-33-0
1995-96   Rich Brooks..............13-19-0
1997-99   Dick Vermeil...............25-26-0
2000-05   Mike Martz****........56-36-0
2005   Joe Vitt 4-7-0
2006-07   Scott Linehan............11-21-0
 * Released after three games in 1938
 ** Resigned after one game in 1952
 *** Resigned after eight games in 1962
 **** Took medical leave after five games in 2005

PAID ATTENDANCE
Home 500,699   Away 517,442
Total 1,018,141
Single-game home record,
66,273 (12/10/00)
Single-season home record,
520,926 (1999)

2008 DRAFT CHOICES

Round	Name	Pos.	College
1	Chris Long	DE	Virginia
2	Donnie Avery	WR	Houston
3	John Greco	T	Toledo
4	Justin King	DB	Penn State
	Keenan Burton	WR	Kentucky
5	Roy Schuening	G	Oregon State
7	Chris Chamberlain	LB	Tulsa
	David Vobora	LB	Idaho

2007 TEAM RECORD
PRESEASON (2-2)

Date	Result	Opponent
8/10	W 13-10	at Minnesota
8/18	L 13-30	San Diego
8/24	L 10-20	at Oakland
8/30	W 10-3	Kansas City

REGULAR SEASON (3-13)

Date	Result	Opponent	Att.
9/9	L 13-27	Carolina	65,307
9/16	L 16-17	San Francisco	65,295
9/23	L 3-24	at Tampa Bay	65,267
9/30	L 7-35	at Dallas	62,866
10/7	L 31-34	Arizona	61,788
10/14	L 3-22	at Baltimore	71,175
10/21	L 6-33	at Seattle	68,164
10/28	L 20-27	Cleveland	62,777
11/11	W 37-29	at New Orleans	70,003
11/18	W 13-9	at San Francisco	68,039
11/25	L 19-24	Seattle	65,423
12/2	W 28-16	Atlanta	62,051
12/9	L 10-19	at Cincinnati	65,143
12/16	L 14-33	Green Bay	66,008
12/20	L 24-41	Pittsburgh	65,705
12/30	L 19-48	at Arizona	64,671

SCORE BY PERIODS

Rams	95	72	56	40	0	—	263
Opponents	64	116	111	147	0	—	438

2007 TEAM STATISTICS

	Rams	Opp.
Total First Downs	281	316
Rushing	65	105
Passing	193	190
Penalty	23	21
3rd Down: Made/Att	81/223	78/201
3rd Down Pct.	36.3	38.8
4th Down: Made/Att	7/20	6/10
4th Down Pct.	35.0	60.0
Possession Avg.	30:08	29:52
Total Net Yards	4760	5457
Avg. Per Game	297.5	341.1
Total Plays	1026	999
Avg. Per Play	4.6	5.5
Net Yards Rushing	1527	1844
Avg. Per Game	95.4	115.3
Total Rushes	404	445
Net Yards Passing	3233	3613
Avg. Per Game	202.1	225.8
Sacked/Yards Lost	48/328	31/234
Gross Yards	3561	3847
Att./Completions	574/333	523/318
Completion Pct.	58.0	60.8
Had Intercepted	28	18
Punts/Average	78/47.2	66/47.7
Net Punting Avg.	78/39.3	66/39.8
Penalties/Yards	94/794	95/732
Fumbles/Ball Lost	25/9	23/9
Touchdowns	27	48
Rushing	5	16
Passing	19	25
Returns	3	7

2007 INDIVIDUAL STATISTICS

PASSING

	Att.	Comp.	Yds.	Pct.	TD	Int.	Tkld.	Rate
Bulger	378	221	2392	58.5	11	15	37/269	70.3
Frerotte	167	94	1014	56.3	7	12	11/59	58.3
Berlin	28	17	153	60.7	0	1	0/0	60.6
S. Jackson	1	1	2	100.0	1	0	0/0	118.8
Rams	574	333	3561	58.0	19	28	48/328	67.0
Opponents	523	318	3847	60.8	25	18	31/234	85.0

SCORING

	TD R	TD P	TD Rt	PAT	FG	Saf	PTS
Wilkins	0	0	0	25/25	24/32	0	97
Holt	0	7	0	0/0	0/0	0	44
S. Jackson	5	1	0	0/0	0/0	0	36
Bruce	0	4	0	0/0	0/0	0	24
Bennett	0	3	0	0/0	0/0	0	18
McMichael	0	3	0	0/0	0/0	0	18
Atogwe	0	0	1	0/0	0/0	0	6
F. Brown	0	0	1	0/0	0/0	0	6
D. Hall	0	0	1	0/0	0/0	0	6
Klopfenstein	0	1	0	0/0	0/0	0	6
Carriker	0	0	0	0/0	0/0	1	2
Rams	5	19	3	25/25	24/32	1	263
Opponents	16	25	7	44/44	34/39	0	438

2-Pt. Conversions: Holt, Rams 1-2, Opponents 2-4

RUSHING

	No.	Yds	Avg	LG	TD
S. Jackson	237	1002	4.2	54	5
B. Leonard	86	303	3.5	31	0
Pittman	38	139	3.7	43	0
Minor	17	68	4.0	13	0
D. Hall	3	18	6.0	9	0
Bulger	9	13	1.4	14	0
Stanley	1	5	5.0	5	0
Frerotte	6	3	0.5	2	0
Bruce	2	-4	-2.0	-1	0
Hagans	2	-4	-2.0	-2	0
Berlin	3	-16	-5.3	0	0
Rams	404	1527	3.8	54	5
Opponents	445	1844	4.1	46	16

RECEIVING

	No.	Yds	Avg	LG	TD
Holt	93	1189	12.8	40	7
Bruce	55	733	13.3	37	4
McMichael	39	429	11.0	29t	3
S. Jackson	38	271	7.1	37	1
Bennett	33	375	11.4	24	3
B. Leonard	30	183	6.1	16	0
Minor	12	86	7.2	20	0
Hagans	8	101	12.6	23	0
Looker	6	38	6.3	10	0
D. Hall	5	27	5.4	12	0
Byrd	4	44	11.0	14	0
Pittman	3	15	5.0	11	0
Klopfenstein	2	37	18.5	36t	1
Walker	2	13	6.5	8	0
Owens	1	9	9.0	9	0
Hedgecock	1	7	7.0	7	0
Taylor	1	4	4.0	4	0
Rams	333	3561	10.7	40	19
Opponents	318	3847	12.1	83	25

INTERCEPTIONS

	No.	Yds	Avg	LG	TD
Atogwe	8	125	15.6	52t	1
F. Brown	4	48	12.0	36t	1
Tinoisamoa	2	15	7.5	15	0
Bartell	2	10	5.0	9	0
Wade	1	2	2.0	2	0
Hill	1	0	0.0	0	0
Rams	18	200	11.1	52t	2
Opponents	28	427	15.3	68t	4

PUNTING

	No.	Yds.	Avg.	In 20	LG
Jones	78	3684	47.2	18	80
Rams	78	3684	47.2	18	80
Opponents	66	3147	47.7	19	71

PUNT RETURNS

	Ret	FC	Yds	Avg	LG	TD
D. Hall	19	6	286	15.1	85t	1
Williams	8	7	66	8.3	15	0
Looker	2	0	5	2.5	5	0
Hagans	1	1	0	0.0	0	0
Rams	30	14	357	11.9	85t	1
Opponents	48	8	437	9.1	37	0

KICKOFF RETURNS

	No.	Yds	Avg	LG	TD
D. Hall	29	729	25.1	84	0
Williams	22	508	23.1	37	0
Stanley	20	509	25.5	49	0
Hagans	7	130	18.6	22	0
Minor	2	24	12.0	21	0
Looker	1	19	19.0	19	0
Wade	1	19	19.0	19	0
Rams	82	1938	23.6	84	0
Opponents	58	1578	27.2	91t	2

FIELD GOALS

	1-19	20-29	30-39	40-49	50+
Wilkins	0/0	7/8	6/7	8/13	3/4
Rams	0/0	7/8	6/7	8/13	3/4
Opponents	0/0	8/8	12/13	12/14	2/4

SACKS

	No.
Witherspoon	7.0
Glover	6.0
Chavous	3.5
Chillar	2.5
J. Hall	2.5
Carriker	2.0
Ryan	2.0
Bartell	1.0
Draft	1.0
Tr. Johnson	1.0
Little	1.0
Moore	1.0
Wroten	0.5
Rams	31.0
Opponents	48.0

RECORD HOLDERS
INDIVIDUAL RECORDS—CAREER

Category	Name	Performance
Rushing (Yds.)	Eric Dickerson, 1983-87	7,245
Passing (Yds.)	Jim Everett, 1986-1993	23,758
Passing (TDs)	Roman Gabriel, 1962-1972	154
Receiving (No.)	Isaac Bruce, 1994-2007	942
Receiving (Yds.)	Isaac Bruce, 1994-2007	14,109
Interceptions	Ed Meador, 1959-1970	46
Punting (Avg.)	Danny Villanueva, 1960-64	44.3
Punt Return (Avg.)	Az-Zahir Hakim, 1998-2001	11.4
Kickoff Return (Avg.)	Ron Brown, 1984-89, 1991	26.3
Field Goals	Jeff Wilkins, 1997-2007	265
Touchdowns (Tot.)	Marshall Faulk, 1999-2005	85
Points	Jeff Wilkins, 1997-2007	1,223

INDIVIDUAL RECORDS—SINGLE SEASON

Category	Name	Performance
Rushing (Yds.)	Eric Dickerson, 1984	*2,105
Passing (Yds.)	Kurt Warner, 2001	4,830
Passing (TDs)	Kurt Warner, 1999	41
Receiving (No.)	Isaac Bruce, 1995	119
Receiving (Yds.)	Isaac Bruce, 1995	1,781
Interceptions	Dick (Night Train) Lane, 1952	*14
Punting (Avg.)	Donnie Jones, 2007	47.2
Punt Return (Avg.)	Woodley Lewis, 1952	18.5
Kickoff Return (Avg.)	Verda (Vitamin T) Smith, 1950	33.7
Field Goals	Jeff Wilkins, 2003	39
Touchdowns (Tot.)	Marshall Faulk, 2000	26
Points	Jeff Wilkins, 2003	163

INDIVIDUAL RECORDS—SINGLE GAME

Category	Name	Performance
Rushing (Yds.)	Willie Ellison, 12-5-71	247
Passing (Yds.)	Norm Van Brocklin, 9-28-51	*554
Passing (TDs)	Many times	5
	Last time by Kurt Warner, 10-10-99	
Receiving (No.)	Tom Fears, 12-3-50	18
Receiving (Yds.)	Willie Anderson, 11-26-89	*336
Interceptions	Many times	3
	Last time by Keith Lyle, 12-15-96	
Field Goals	Bob Waterfield, 12-9-51	5
	Jeff Wilkins, 10-1-00	5
Touchdowns (Tot.)	Many times	4
	Last time by Marshall Faulk, 10-20-02	
Points	Many times	24
	Last time by Marshall Faulk, 10-20-02	

*NFL Record

2008 VETERAN ROSTER

No.	Name	Pos.	Ht.	Wt.	Age	NFL Exp.	College	Hometown	How Acq.	'07 Games/ Starts
94	Adeyanju, Victor	DE	6-4	280	25	3	Indiana	Chicago, Ill.	D4-'06	15/7
21	Atogwe, Oshiomogho	S	5-11	210	27	4	Stanford	Windsor, Ontario	D3A-'05	16/16
24	Bartell, Ron	CB	6-1	205	26	4	Howard	Detroit, Mich.	D2-'05	16/12
70	Barron, Alex	T	6-7	315	25	4	Florida State	Orangeburg, S.C.	D1-'05	16/16
41	Bassey, Eric	S	6-1	200	25	2	Oklahoma	Garland, Texas	FA-'07	8/0
87	Becht, Anthony	TE	6-5	280	31	9	West Virginia	Drexel Hill, Pa.	UFA(TB)-'08	16/2*
63	Bell, Jacob	G	6-4	295	27	5	Miami (Ohio)	Cleveland, Ohio	UFA(Tenn)-'08	16/16*
83	Bennett, Drew	WR	6-5	206	30	8	UCLA	Orinda, Calif.	UFA(Tenn)-'07	14/1
34	Brown, Fakhir	CB	5-11	195	30	9	Grambling	Mansfield, La.	UFA(NO)-'06	12/12
3	Brown, Josh	K	6-0	212	29	6	Nebraska	Foyil, Okla.	UFA(Sea)-'08	16/0*
10	Bulger, Marc	QB	6-3	212	31	8	West Virginia	Pittsburgh, Pa.	FA-'01	12/12
17	Caldwell, Reche	WR	6-0	210	29	7	Florida	Tampa, Fla.	UFA(Wash)-'08	8/1*
90	Carriker, Adam	DL	6-6.	308	24	2	Nebraska	Kennewick, Wash.	D1-'07	16/16
42	Carter, Jerome	S	5-11	219	25	4	Florida State	Lake City, Fla.	D4A-'05	5/1
25	Chavous, Corey	S	6-1	208	32	11	Vanderbilt	Aiken, S.C.	UFA(Minn)-'06	14/14
53	Culberson, Quinton	LB	6-1	236	22	2	Mississippi State	Jackson, Miss.	FA-'07	14/1
52	Draft, Chris	LB	5-11	236	32	10	Stanford	Placentia, Calif.	UFA(Car)-'07	16/7
62	Fry, Dustin	C	6-3	314	24	2	Clemson	Summerville, S.C.	D5A-'07	4/0
97	Glover, La'Roi	DT	6-2	290	34	13	San Diego State	San Diego, Calif.	FA-'06	16/16
73	Goldberg, Adam	G	6-7	318	28	6	Wyoming	Edina, Minn.	T(Minn)-'06	4/2
77	Gorin, Brandon	T	6-6	308	30	7	Purdue	Muncie, Ind.	FA-'07	11/8
12	Green, Trent	QB	6-3	217	38	15	Indiana	Kirkwood, Mo.	FA-'08	5/5*
15	Hagans, Marques	WR	5-10	205	25	2	Virginia	Hampton, Va.	D5-'06	4/1
82	Hall, Dante	WR	5-8	187	29	9	Texas A&M	Houston, Texas	T(KC)-'07	7/1
96	Hall, James	DE	6-2	280	31	9	Michigan	New Orleans, La.	T(Det)-'07	15/15
26	Hill, Tye	CB	5-10	185	26	3	Clemson	St. George, S.C.	D1-'06	8/7
81	Holt, Torry	WR	6-0	190	32	10	North Carolina State	Greensboro, N.C.	D1-'99	16/16
68	Incognito, Richie	G	6-3	330	25	4	Nebraska	Glendale, Ariz.	D3B-'05	4/4
39	Jackson, Steven	RB	6-2	231	25	5	Oregon State	Las Vegas, Nev.	D1-'04	12/12
35	Johnson, Todd	S	6-1	202	29	6	Florida	Sarasota, Fla.	UFA(Chi)-'07	16/1
5	Jones, Donnie	P	6-3	222	28	5	Louisiana State	Baton Rouge, La.	RFA(Mia)-'07	16/0
88	Klopfenstein, Joe	TE	6-5	262	24	3	Colorado	Aurora, Colo.	D2-'06	16/11
60	Leckey, Nick	C	6-3	291	26	5	Kansas State	Grapevine, Texas	FA-'07	3/2
23	Leonard, Brian	RB	6-1	226	24	2	Rutgers	Gouverneur, N.Y.	D2-'07	16/7
75	LeVoir, Mark	T	6-7	306	26	2	Notre Dame	Eden Prairie, Minn.	FA-'07	0/0
91	Little, Leonard	DE	6-3	263	33	11	Tennessee	Asheville, N.C.	D3-'98	7/7
89	Looker, Dane	WR	6-0	194	32	8	Washington	Puyallup, Wash.	FA-'02	13/0
27	Macklin, David	CB	5-10	197	30	9	Penn State	Newport News, Va.	UFA(Wash)-'08	6/0*
45	Massey, Chris	LS	6-0	245	29	7	Marshall	Chesapeake, W. Va.	D7-'02	16/0
59	McGarigle, Tim	LB	6-0	240	24	2	Northwestern	Chicago, Ill.	D7A-'06	12/0
84	McMichael, Randy	TE	6-3	255	29	7	Georgia	Fort Valley, Ga.	FA-'07	16/15
22	Minor, Travis	RB	5-10	203	29	8	Florida State	Baton Rouge, La.	UFA(Mia)-'07	14/0
92	Moore, Eric	DE	6-4	270	27	4	Florida State	Pahokee, Fla.	FA-'06	7/1
49	Owens, Richard	FB	6-4	273	27	5	Louisville	Middleburg, Fla.	FA-'07	14/1
76	Pace, Orlando	T	6-7	325	32	12	Ohio State	Sandusky, Ohio	D1-'97	1/1
71	Petitti, Rob	T	6-6	327	26	4	Pittsburgh	Rumson, N.J.	FA-'07	5/1
30	Pittman, Antonio	RB	5-11	207	22	2	Ohio State	Akron, Ohio	W(NO)-'07	11/0
65	Romberg, Brett	C	6-2	298	28	5	Miami	Windsor, Ontario	FA-'06	9/9
95	Ryan, Clifton	DT	6-3	310	24	2	Michigan State	Saginaw, Mich.	D5B-'07	16/0
66	Setterstrom, Mark	G	6-4	314	24	3	Minnesota	Northfield, Minn.	D7B-'06	3/3
50	Tinoisamoa, Pisa	LB	6-1	240	27	6	Hawaii	Vista, Calif.	D2-'03	9/9
31	Vinnett, Darius	CB	5-8	170	23	2	Arkansas	Destrehan, La.	FA-'07	8/0
20	Wade, Jonathan	CB	5-10	195	24	2	Tennessee	Shreveport, La.	D3-'07	16/1
16	Williams, Brandon	WR	5-11	183	24	3	Wisconsin	St. Louis, Mo.	FA-'07	7/0
51	Witherspoon, Will	LB	6-1	240	28	7	Georgia	Panama City, Fla.	UFA(Car)-'06	16/16
99	Wroten, Claude	DT	6-2	295	24	3	Louisiana State	Bastrop, La.	D3A-'06	11/0

* Becht played 16 games with Tampa Bay in '07; J. Bell played 16 games with Tennessee; J. Brown palyed 16 games with Seattle; Caldwell played 8 games with Washington; Green played 5 games with Miami; Macklin played 6 games with Washington.

Retired—Jeff Wilkins, 14-year kicker, 16 games in '07.

Players lost through free agency (2): G Milford Brown (Car; 16 games in '07), LB Brandon Chillar (GB; 15).

Also played with Rams in '07—RB Rich Alexis (1 game), WR Isaac Bruce (14),TE Dominique Byrd (9), QB Gus Frerotte (8), FB Madison Hedgecock (1), DE Trevor Johnson (9), S Bhawoh Jue (1), C Andy McCollum (15), S Hanik Milligan (7), LB Raonall Smith (4), T Todd Steussie (6), WR Travis Taylor (1), TE Aaron Walker (7), CB Lenny Walls (5).

2008 FIRST-YEAR ROSTER

Name	Pos.	Ht.	Wt.	Age	College	Hometown	How Acq.
Ah You, C.J. (1)	DE	6-4	275	26	Oklahoma	Highland, Utah	FA-'07
Avery, Donnie	WR	5-11	190	24	Houston	Houston, Texas	D2
Berlin, Brock (1)	QB	6-1	215	27	Miami	Shreveport, La.	FA-'07
Bryant, Vernon	DT	6-2	285	24	Hampton	Courtland, Va.	FA
Burton, Keenan	WR	6-0	202	23	Kentucky	Louisville, Ky.	D4b
Caddell, Matt	WR	6-0	187	23	Alabama	McCalla, Ala.	FA
Chamberlain, Chris	LB	6-1	226	22	Tulsa	Bethany, Okla.	D7A
Douglas, Sean (1)	P	6-1	216	24	Washington	Bellevue, Neb.	FA
Fowler, Eric (1)	WR	6-2	208	23	Grand Valley State	New Haven, Mich.	FA-'07
Greco, John	T	6-4	326	23	Toledo	Youngstown, Ohio	D3
Hall, Vince	LB	5-11	238	23	Virginia Tech	Chesapeake, Va.	FA
Hardeway, Rodney	DE	6-3	230	22	Louisiana-Lafayette	Tyler, Texas	FA
Harrington, Dedrick	TE	6-3	248	24	Missouri	Mexico, Mo.	FA
Hyman, Josh	WR	5-11	191	25	Virginia Tech	Chesapeake, Va.	FA
Jones, Doug	TE	6-4	275	23	Cincinnati	Erlanger, Ky.	FA
King, Justin	CB	5-11	192	21	Penn State	Pittsburgh, Pa.	D4a
Long, Chris	DE	6-3	279	23	Virginia	Ivy, Va.	D1
Magro, Marc	LB	6-3	240	24	West Virginia	Morgantown, W. Va.	FA
McAnderson, Brandon	FB	5-11	238	23	Kansas	Lawrence, Kan.	FA
McKinney, Justin	CB	5-10	188	24	Kansas State	Sanford, Fla.	FA
Medlock, Justin (1)	K	5-11	201	24	UCLA	Fremont, Calif.	FA
Raiola, Donovan (1)	C	6-2	293	24	Wisconsin	Honolulu, Hawaii	FA-'07
Schuening, Roy	G	6-3	320	24	Oregon State	Pendleton, Ore.	D5
Sene, Stephen	T	6-5	326	24	Liberty	Irmo, S.C.	FA
Stanley, Derek (1)	WR	5-11	179	23	Wisconsin-Whitewater	Verona, Wisc.	D7b-'07
Thompson, Josh	DT	6-0	301	23	Auburn	Statesboro, Ga.	FA
Vobora, David	LB	6-1	236	22	Idaho	Eugene, Ore.	D7b
Weil, Russ	FB	6-0	241	23	Illinois	Minooka, Ill.	FA

The term NFL Rookie is defined as a player who is in his first season of professional football and has not been on the roster of another professional football team for any regular-season or postseason games. A Rookie is designated by an "R" on NFL rosters. Players who have been active in another professional football league or players who have NFL experience, including either preseason training camp or being on an Active List or Inactive List, or on Reserve/Injured or Reserve/Physically Unable to Perform for fewer than six regular-season games, are termed NFL First-Year Players. An NFL First-Year Player is designated by a "1" on NFL rosters. Thereafter, a player is credited with an additional year of experience for each season in which he accumulates six games on the Active List or Inactive List, or on Reserve/Injured or Reserve/Physically Unable to Perform.

Log on to www.stlouisrams.com for an up-to-date roster; Age listed is as of September 4, 2008.

COACHING STAFF
Head Coach,
Scott Linehan
Pro Career: Named twenty-second head coach in franchise history by Georgia Frontiere on January 19, 2006. In 2007, the team struggled through an injury epidemic. Only 18 of 80 possible starts were made by the projected opening day offensive line starters. Starting players missed 95 games, and 26 players missed a total of 155 games. Wide receiver Torry Holt earned his seventh Pro Bowl selection, accepting passes from three different quarterbacks. Pro Bowl quarterback Marc Bulger finished season on reserve/injured. In 2006, Bulger enjoyed the best season of his career, with 4,301 yards passing and 24 touchdowns. Balancing the offensive attack, running back Steven Jackson led the league with 2,234 combined yards, and set a Rams record for a running back with 90 catches in 2006. The Rams became only the fourth team in league history to have a 4,000-yard passer, 1,500-yard rusher, and two 1,000-yard receivers in one season, 2006. Prior to joining the Rams Linehan was offensive coordinator of the Miami Dolphins; the Dolphins improved from 29th in 2004 to 14th in total offense in 2005. Linehan spent three seasons (2002-04) as offensive coordinator for the Minnesota Vikings. In 2004, Daunte Culpepper posted the fourth-highest single season passer rating in NFL history (110.9). A college quarterback, Linehan was a free agent signee with the Dallas Cowboys before a shoulder injury ended his active career. Career record: 11-21.
Background: Linehan was an assistant coach on the collegiate level at Idaho (1989-1990, 1992-93), Nevada-Las Vegas (1991), Washington (1994-1998) and Louisville (1999-2001). Played quarterback at Idaho under Dennis Erickson (1982-86). The Vandals won the Big Sky Championship (1985) and made three consecutive playoff appearances (1984-86).
Personal: Age 44 born in Sunnyside, Wash. He and his wife, Kristen, have three sons: Matthew, Michael, and Marcus.

ASSISTANT COACHES
Brian Baker, defensive line; born Baltimore. Linebacker Maryland 1980-83. No pro playing experience. College coach: Maryland 1984-85, Army 1986, Georgia Tech 1987-1995. Pro coach: San Diego Chargers 1996, Detroit Lions 1997-2000, Minnesota Vikings 2001-05, joined Rams in 2006.
Jim Chaney, tight ends; born Warrensburg, Mo. Guard Central Missouri State 1981-85. No pro playing experience. College coach: Cal State-Fullerton 1985-1992, Wyoming 1993-1996, Purdue 1997-2005. Pro coach: Joined Rams in 2006.
Mike Cox, asst. secondary; born Coeur d' Alene, Idaho. Linebacker Idaho 1983-86.

No pro playing experience. College coach: Idaho 1987-1994, Utah State 1995-97, Louisville 1998-2002, Michigan State 2002-06. Pro coach: Joined Rams in 2007.
Todd Downing, defensive quality control; born Eden Prairie, Minn. Attended Minnesota. No college or pro playing experience. Pro coach: Minnesota Vikings 2003-05, joined Rams in 2006.
Henry Ellard, wide receivers; born Fresno, Calif. Wide receiver Fresno State 1979-1982. Pro wide receiver/punt returner Los Angeles Rams 1983-1993, Washington Redskins 1994-97, New England Patriots 1998, Washington Redskins 1998. College coach: Fresno State 2000. Pro coach: Joined Rams in 2001.
Chuck Faucette, asst. strength and conditioning; born Willingboro, N.J. Linebacker Maryland 1983-86. Pro linebacker San Diego Chargers 1987-89. College coach: Texas 1999-2001, SMU 2002-07. Pro coach: Hamilton TigerCats (CFL) 1990-92, joined Rams in 2008.
Jim Haslett, defensive coordinator; born Pittsburgh. Defensive end Indiana (Pa.) 1975-1978. Pro linebacker Buffalo Bills 1979-1986, N.Y. Jets 1987. College coach: Buffalo 1988-1990, Pittsburgh 1997-99. Pro coach: Sacramento Surge (NFLE) 1991-92, Los Angeles Raiders 1993-94, New Orleans Saints 1995-96, 2000-05 (head coach 2000-05), joined Rams in 2006.
Jeff Horton, special assistant/offense; born Tulsa, Okla. Attended Nevada. No college or pro playing experience. College coach: Minnesota 1984, Nevada 1985-89, 1992-93, Nevada-Las Vegas 1990-91, 1994-98 (head coach 1994-98), Wisconsin 1999-2005, Iowa State 2006. Pro coach: Joined Rams in 2006.
Dana LeDuc, strength and conditioning; born Tacoma, Wash. Attended Texas. No college or pro playing experience. College coach: Texas 1977-1992, Miami 1993-94. Pro coach: Seattle Seahawks 1995-98, joined Rams in 1999.
Steve Loney, offensive line; born Marshalltown, Iowa. Tackle Iowa State 1971-72. No pro playing experience. College coach: Iowa State 1974, 1995-97, Missouri Western 1975-76, Morehead State 1979-83, Citadel 1984-86, Colorado State 1989-92, Connecticut 1994, Minnesota 1998-99, Iowa State 2000-01, Drake 2007. Pro coach: Arizona Cardinals 1993, Minnesota Vikings 2002-05, Arizona Cardinals 2006, joined Rams in 2008.
Ron Milus, secondary; born Tacoma, Wash. Cornerback-punt returner Washington 1982-1985. No pro playing experience. College coach: Washington 1991-98, Texas A&M 1999. Pro coach: Denver Broncos 2000-02, Arizona Cardinals 2003, New York Giants 2004-05, joined Rams in 2006.
Keith Murphy, quality control/asst. special teams; born Seattle. Wide receiver

Washington 1992-95. No pro playing experience. College coach: Washington 1997-98, Eastern Washington 1999-2006. Pro coach: Joined Rams in 2007.
Al Roberts, special teams coordinator; born Fresno, Calif. Running back Washington 1964-65, Puget Sound. No pro playing experience. College coach: Washington 1977-1982, 1996, Wyoming 1986, Purdue 1987. Pro coach: L.A. Express (USFL) 1983-84, Houston Oilers 1984-85, Philadelphia Eagles 1988-1990, New York Jets 1991-93, Arizona Cardinals 1994-95, Cincinnati Bengals 1997-2002, joined Rams in 2007.
Al Saunders, offensive coordinator; born London, England. Defensive back San Jose State 1966-68. No pro playing experience. College coach: Southern California 1970-71, Missouri 1972, Utah State 1973-75, California 1976-1981, Tennessee 1982. Pro coach: San Diego Chargers 1983-88, Kansas City Chiefs 1989-1998, St. Louis Rams 1999-2000, Kansas City Chiefs 2001-05, Washington Redskins 2006-07, joined Rams in 2008.
Bob Saunders, offensive assistant/assistant wide receivers; born Walnut Creek, Calif. Attended Missouri-Kansas City. No college or pro experience. Pro coach: Kansas City Chiefs 2002-05, Washington Redskins 2006-07, joined Rams in 2008.
Terry Shea, quarterbacks; born San Mateo, Calif. Quarterback Oregon 1964-67. No experience. College coach: Oregon 1968-69, Mt. Hood Community College 1970-75, Utah State 1976-1983, San Jose State 1990-91, Stanford 1992-94, Rutgers 1996-2000. Pro coach: British Columbia Lions (CFL) 1995, Kansas City Chiefs 2001-03, 2005-06, Chicago Bears 2004, Miami Dolphins 2007, joined Rams in 2008.
Art Valero, asst. head coach/running backs; born LaMirada, Calif. Guard Boise State 1979-1980. No pro playing experience. College coach: Boise State 1981-82, Iowa State 1983, Long Beach State 1984-86, New Mexico 1987-89, Idaho 1990-94, Utah State 1995-97, Louisville 1998-2001. Pro coach: Tampa Bay Buccaneers 2002-2007, joined Rams in 2008.
Rick Venturi, asst. head coach/linebackers; born Taylorville, Ill. Quarterback/defensive back Northwestern 1965-67. No pro playing experience. College coach: Northwestern 1968-1972, 1978-1980 (head coach 1978-1980), Purdue 1973-76, Illinois 1977. Pro coach: Hamilton Tiger-Cats (CFL) 1981, Indianapolis Colts 1982-1993 (interim head coach for final 11 games of 1991), Cleveland Browns 1994-95, Saints 1996-2005 (interim head coach for final eight games of 1996), joined Rams in 2006.

National Football Conference
West Division
Team Colors: Metallic Gold,
      Cardinal Red, and Beige
4949 Centennial Boulevard
Santa Clara, California 95054
Telephone: (408) 562-4949

2008 SCHEDULE
PRESEASON
Aug. 8   at Oakland..........................7:00
Aug. 16 **Green Bay** 6:00
Aug. 21 at Chicago..........................7:00
Aug. 29 **San Diego**..........................7:00

REGULAR SEASON
Sep. 7   **Arizona** 1:15
Sep. 14 at Seattle 1:05
Sep. 21 **Detroit** 1:05
Sep. 28 at New Orleans 12:00
Oct. 5   **New England** 1:15
Oct. 12 **Philadelphia** 1:15
Oct. 19 at N.Y. Giants.....................1:00
Oct. 26 **Seattle** 1:15
Nov. 2   BYE
Nov. 10 at Arizona (Mon.) 6:30
Nov. 16 **St. Louis** 1:05
Nov. 23 at Dallas 12:00
Nov. 30 at Buffalo 1:00
Dec. 7   **N.Y. Jets** 1:05
Dec. 14 at Miami 1:00
Dec. 21 at St. Louis 12:00
Dec. 28 **Washington** 1:15

Stadium: Candlestick Park
   (opened in 1960)
   •**Capacity:** 69,732
   San Francisco, California 94124
Playing Surface: Natural Grass
Training Camp: Marie P. DeBartolo
            Sports Center
            4949 Centennial Boulevard
            Santa Clara, CA 95054

CANDLESTICK PARK

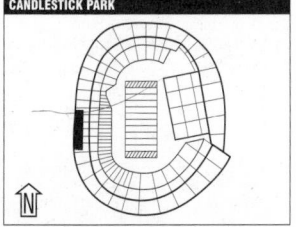

CLUB OFFICIALS
OWNERSHIP
Owner: Denise DeBartolo York
Owner: John York
Vice President of Strategic
   Planning/Owner: Jed York
Limited Partner: Franklin Mieuli
Limited Partner: Rick and Carla Morabito
MANAGEMENT
General Manager: Scot McCloughan
Chief Operating Officer: Andy Dolich
Executive Vice President of Football
   Operations: Lal Heneghan
Director of Player Personnel: Trent Baalke
Director of Pro Personnel: Tom Gamble
Director of College Scouting:
   David McCloughan
Vice President/Operations: Murlan Fowell
Vice President Communications:
   Lisa Lang
Vice President/CFO: Larry MacNeil
Director of Football Operations:
   Paraag Marathe
Director of Football Administration:
   Terry Tumey
Senior Manager of Ticket Office:
   Lynn Carrozzi
Director of Security: Fred Formosa
Director of Information Technology:
   Alexander Ignacio
Director of Stadium Operations:
   Jim Mercurio
Director of Public Relations: Aaron Salkin
Director of Public Relations Operations:
   Jason Jenkins
Director of Marketing: Michael P. Williams
Director of Player Development:
   Guy McIntrye
Director of Business Partnerships:
   Patrick Streko
Director of Human Resources:
   Annette Snyder
Director of Video Operations:
   Keith Yanagi
Controller: Debye Whelchel
Head Athletic Trainer: Jeff Ferguson
Equipment Manager: Steve Urbaniak

COACHING HISTORY
(475-396-13)
Records include postseason games
1950-54   Lawrence (Buck) Shaw..33-25-2
1955   Norman (Red) Strader 4-8-0
1956-58   Frankie Albert..............19-17-1
1959-1963 Howard (Red) Hickey* .27-27-1
1963-67   Jack Christiansen 26-38-3
1968-1975 Dick Nolan...................56-56-5
1976   Monte Clark.....................8-6-0
1977   Ken Meyer.......................5-9-0
1978   Pete McCulley** 1-8-0
1978   Fred O'Connor 1-6-0
1979-1988 Bill Walsh 102-63-1
1989-1996 George Seifert 108-35-0
1997-2002 Steve Mariucci............60-43-0
2003-04   Dennis Erickson 9-23-0
2005-07   Mike Nolan 16-32-0
   *Resigned after three games in 1963
   **Released after nine games in 1978

PAID ATTENDANCE
Home 530,225   Away 544,405
Total 1,074,630
Single-game home record,
   69,014 (11/13/94)
Single-season home record,
   544,228 (1999)

2008 DRAFT CHOICES

Round	Name	Pos.	College
1	Kentwan Balmer	DT	North Carolina
2	Chilo Rachal	G	Southern California
3	Reggie Smith	DB	Oklahoma
4	Cody Wallace	C	Texas A&M
6	Josh Morgan	WR	Virginia Tech
7	Larry Grant	LB	Ohio State

2007 TEAM RECORD
PRESEASON (1-3)

Date	Result	Opponent
8/13	L 13-17	Denver
8/18	W 26-21	Oakland
8/25	L 28-31	at Chicago
8/30	L 13-16	at San Diego

REGULAR SEASON (5-11)

Date	Result	Opponent	Att.
9/10	W 20-17	Arizona	68,111
9/16	W 17-16	at St. Louis	65,295
9/23	L 16-37	at Pittsburgh	64,313
9/30	L 3-23	Seattle	67,651
10/7	L 7-9	Baltimore	67,885
10/21	L 15-33	at N.Y. Giants	78,912
10/28	L 10-31	New Orleans	68,244
11/4	L 16-20	at Atlanta	66,049
11/12	L 0-24	at Seattle	68,331
11/18	L 9-13	St. Louis	68,039
11/25	W 37-31	at Arizona (OT)	64,483
12/2	L 14-31	at Carolina	73,191
12/9	L 7-27	Minnesota	68,050
12/15	W 20-13	Cincinnati	68,053
12/23	W 21-19	Tampa Bay	68,193
12/30	L 7-20	at Cleveland	73,041

(OT) Overtime

SCORE BY PERIODS

49ers	30	55	75	53	6	—	219
Opponents	87	158	27	92	0	—	364

2007 TEAM STATISTICS

	49ers	Opp.
Total First Downs	218	308
Rushing	65	94
Passing	140	187
Penalty	13	27
3rd Down: Made/Att	69/220	97/241
3rd Down Pct.	31.4	40.2
4th Down: Made/Att	5/17	7/13
4th Down Pct.	29.4	53.8
Possession Avg.	26:51	33:09
Total Net Yards	3797	5539
Avg. Per Game	237.3	346.2
Total Plays	925	1078
Avg. Per Play	4.1	5.1
Net Yards Rushing	1477	1896
Avg. Per Game	92.3	118.5
Total Rushes	357	504
Net Yards Passing	2320	3643
Avg. Per Game	145.0	227.7
Sacked/Yards Lost	55/365	31/183
Gross Yards	2685	3826
Att./Completions	513/274	543/345
Completion Pct.	53.4	63.5
Had Intercepted	17	12
Punts/Average	105/47.3	89/40.9
Net Punting Avg.	105/41.0	89/33.9
Penalties/Yards	97/702	89/661
Fumbles/Ball Lost	36/17	17/10
Touchdowns	24	39
Rushing	8	9
Passing	15	24
Returns	1	6

2007 INDIVIDUAL STATISTICS

PASSING	Att.	Comp.	Yds.	Pct.	TD	Int.	Tkld.	Rate
Dilfer	219	113	1166	51.6	7	12	27/182	55.1
A. Smith	193	94	914	48.7	2	4	17/121	57.2
S. Hill	79	54	501	68.4	5	1	6/31	101.3
Weinke	22	13	104	59.1	1	0	5/31	86.2
49ers	513	274	2685	53.4	15	17	55/365	64.3
Opponents	543	345	3826	63.5	24	12	31/183	89.9

SCORING	TD R	TD P	TD Rt	PAT	FG	Saf	PTS
Nedney	0	0	0	22/22	17/19	0	73
Battle	1	5	0	0/0	0/0	0	36
Gore	5	1	0	0/0	0/0	0	36
Davis	0	4	0	0/0	0/0	0	24
Jackson	0	3	0	0/0	0/0	0	18
Banta-Cain	0	0	1	0/0	0/0	0	6
Hicks	1	0	0	0/0	0/0	0	6
S. Hill	1	0	0	0/0	0/0	0	6
Jacobs	0	1	0	0/0	0/0	0	6
Walker	0	1	0	0/0	0/0	0	6
Norris	0	0	0	0/0	0/0	1	2
49ers	8	15	1	22/22	17/19	1	219
Opponents	9	24	6	37/38	31/35	0	364

2-Pt. Conversions: 49ers 0-1, Opponents 0-1

RUSHING	No.	Yds	Avg	LG	TD
Gore	260	1102	4.2	43t	5
Robinson	26	121	4.7	28	0
Hicks	21	117	5.6	18	1
A. Smith	13	89	6.8	25	0
Dilfer	10	25	2.5	11	0
Norris	7	17	2.4	6	0
S. Hill	12	14	1.2	12	1
Battle	4	4	1.0	8	1
Keasey	2	4	2.0	3	0
Gilmore	1	-8	-8.0	-8	0
Jacobs	1	-8	-8.0	-8	0
49ers	357	1477	4.1	43t	8
Opponents	504	1896	3.8	84t	9

RECEIVING	No.	Yds	Avg	LG	TD
Gore	53	436	8.2	23t	1
Davis	52	509	9.8	31	4
Battle	50	600	12.0	57t	5
Jackson	46	497	10.8	34	3
Walker	21	174	8.3	26	1
Hicks	14	86	6.1	11	0
Robinson	11	73	6.6	20	0
Lelie	10	115	11.5	47	0
Gilmore	7	111	15.9	42	0
Norris	6	38	6.3	13	0
Jacobs	3	40	13.3	21t	1
J. Hill	1	6	6.0	6	0
49ers	274	2685	9.8	57t	15
Opponents	345	3826	11.1	65	24

INTERCEPTIONS	No.	Yds	Avg	LG	TD
Clements	4	74	18.5	62	0
W. Harris	4	42	10.5	23	0
Michael M. Lewis	2	18	9.0	18	0
D. Smith	1	4	4.0	4	0
Spencer	1	0	0.0	0	0
49ers	12	138	11.5	62	0
Opponents	17	298	17.5	73t	3

PUNTING	No.	Yds	Avg	In 20	LG
Lee	105	4968	47.3	42	74
49ers	105	4968	47.3	42	74
Opponents	89	3644	40.9	26	63

PUNT RETURNS	Ret	FC	Yds	Avg	LG	TD
Michael L. Lewis	44	4	336	7.6	51	0
Clements	7	0	115	16.4	41	0
Williams	5	5	32	6.4	12	0
49ers	56	9	483	8.6	51	0
Opponents	53	16	402	7.6	76t	1

KICKOFF RETURNS	No.	Yds	Avg	LG	TD
Hicks	63	1502	23.8	55	0
Michael L. Lewis	5	86	17.2	24	0
Walker	3	63	21.0	30	0
Robinson	2	51	25.5	30	0
49ers	73	1702	23.3	55	0
Opponents	45	982	21.8	98t	0

FIELD GOALS	1-19	20-29	30-39	40-49	50+
Nedney	1/1	5/5	6/6	4/4	1/3
49ers	1/1	5/5	6/6	4/4	1/3
Opponents	2/2	12/13	10/11	6/6	1/3

SACKS	No.
Young	6.5
Willis	4.0
Banta-Cain	3.5
Douglas	3.0
Haralson	2.5
B. Moore	2.5
Green	2.0
Michael M. Lewis	1.5
Sopoaga	1.5
Clements	1.0
Fields	1.0
McDonald	1.0
Navies	1.0
49ers	31.0
Opponents	55.0

RECORD HOLDERS
INDIVIDUAL RECORDS—CAREER

Category	Name	Performance
Rushing (Yds.)	Joe Perry, 1950-1960, 1963	7,344
Passing (Yds.)	Joe Montana, 1979-1992	35,124
Passing (TDs)	Joe Montana, 1979-1992	244
Receiving (No.)	Jerry Rice, 1985-2000	1,281
Receiving (Yds.)	Jerry Rice, 1985-2000	19,247
Interceptions	Ronnie Lott, 1981-1990	51
Punting (Avg.)	Tommy Davis, 1959-1969	44.7
Punt Return (Avg.)	Dana McLemore, 1982-87	10.8
Kickoff Return (Avg.)	Abe Woodson, 1958-1964	29.4
Field Goals	Ray Wersching, 1977-1987	190
Touchdowns (Tot.)	Jerry Rice, 1985-2000	187
Points	Jerry Rice, 1985-2000	1,130

INDIVIDUAL RECORDS—SINGLE SEASON

Category	Name	Performance
Rushing (Yds.)	Frank Gore, 2006	1,695
Passing (Yds.)	Jeff Garcia, 2000	4,278
Passing (TDs)	Steve Young, 1998	36
Receiving (No.)	Jerry Rice, 1995	122
Receiving (Yds.)	Jerry Rice, 1995	*1,848
Interceptions	Dave Baker, 1960	10
	Ronnie Lott, 1986	10
Punting (Avg.)	Andy Lee, 2007	47.3
Punt Return (Avg.)	Dana McLemore, 1982	22.3
Kickoff Return (Avg.)	Joe Arenas, 1953	34.4
Field Goals	Jeff Wilkins, 1996	30
Touchdowns (Tot.)	Jerry Rice, 1987	23
Points	Jerry Rice, 1987	138

INDIVIDUAL RECORDS—SINGLE GAME

Category	Name	Performance
Rushing (Yds.)	Frank Gore, 11-19-06	212
Passing (Yds.)	Joe Montana, 10-14-90	476
Passing (TDs)	Joe Montana, 10-14-90	6
Receiving (No.)	Terrell Owens, 12-17-00	*20
Receiving (Yds.)	Jerry Rice, 12-18-95	289
Interceptions	Dave Baker, 12-4-60	*4
Field Goals	Ray Wersching, 10-16-83	6
	Jeff Wilkins, 9-29-96	6
Touchdowns (Tot.)	Jerry Rice, 10-14-90	5
Points	Jerry Rice, 10-14-90	30

*NFL Record

2008 VETERAN ROSTER

No.	Name	Pos.	Ht.	Wt.	Age	NFL Exp.	College	Hometown	How Acq.	'07 Games/ Starts
71 #	Allen, Larry	G	6-3	325	36	15	Sonoma State	Los Angeles, Calif.	FA-'06	16/16
64	Baas, David	G	6-4	331	26	4	Michigan	Sarasota, Fla.	D2-'05	15/8
47	Bajema, Billy	TE	6-4	258	25	4	Oklahoma State	Oklahoma City, Okla.	D7d-'05	14/2
95	Banta-Cain, Tully	LB	6-2	280	28	6	California	Sunnyvale, Calif.	UFA(NE)-'07	16/10
83	Battle, Arnaz	WR	6-1	213	28	6	Notre Dame	Shreveport, La.	D6-'03	16/15
25	Brown, Tarell	CB	5-10	194	23	2	Texas	Mesquite, Texas	D5-'07	9/0
88	Bruce, Isaac	WR	6-0	188	35	15	Memphis	Fort Lauderdale, Fla.	FA-'08	16/13*
22	Clements, Nate	CB	6-0	215	28	8	Ohio State	Shaker Heights, Ohio	UFA(Buff)-'07	16/16
76	Cohen, Joe	DT	6-2	315	24	2	Florida	Melbourne, Fla.	D4c-'07	0*
85	Davis, Vernon	TE	6-3	253	24	3	Maryland	Washington, D.C.	D1a-'06	14/14
63	Duckett, Damane	T	6-6	318	27	4	East Carolina	Lexington, N.C.	FA-'07	0*
78	Ellison, Atiyyah	DE/DT	6-3	318	26	3	Missouri	St. Louis, Mo.	FA-'07	0*
93	Fields, Ronald	DT	6-2	321	26	4	Mississippi State	Bogalusa, La.	D5a-'05	16/0
29	Foster, DeShaun	RB	6-0	222	28	7	UCLA	Charlotte, N.C.	FA-'08	16/16*
92	Franklin, Aubrayo	DT	6-1	334	28	6	Tennessee	Johnson City, Tenn.	UFA(Balt)-'07	14/13
38	Goldson, Dashon	S	6-2	208	23	2	Washington	Carson, Calif.	D4b-'07	Oct-00
21	Gore, Frank	RB	5-9	223	25	4	Miami	Coral Gables, Fla.	D3a-'05	15/15
54	Green, Roderick	LB	6-2	270	26	5	Central Missouri	Brenham, Texas	FA-'07	7/0
55	Haley, Dennis	LB	6-1	247	26	3	Virginia	Salem, Va.	FA-'08	2/0*
98	Haralson, Parys	LB	6-0	260	24	3	Tennessee	Flora, Miss.	D5a-'06	16/11
27	Harris, Walt	CB	5-11	199	34	13	Mississippi State	LaGrange, Ga.	FA-'07	15/15
66	Heitmann, Eric	C	6-3	318	28	7	Stanford	Katy, Texas	D7a-'02	16/16
89	Hill, Jason	WR	6-0	204	23	2	Washington State	San Francisco, Calif.	D3a-'07	5/0
13	Hill, Shaun	QB	6-3	235	28	7	Maryland	Parsons, Kan.	FA-'06	3/2
23	Hudson, Marcus	CB	6-2	198	25	3	North Carolina State	Miami, Fla.	D6b-'06	11/0
86	Jennings, Brian	TE-LS	6-5	228	31	9	Arizona State	Mesa, Ariz.	D7b-'00	16/0
75	Jennings, Jonas	T	6-3	325	30	8	Georgia	College Park, Ga.	UFA(Buff)-'05	5/5
82	Johnson, Bryant	WR	6-3	216	27	6	Penn State	Baltimore, Md.	UFA(Ariz)-'08	16/8*
45	Keasey, Zak	FB	6-0	245	26	2	Princeton	Lake Orion, Mich.	FA-'07	13/0
99	Lawson, Manny	LB	6-5	247	24	3	North Carolina State	Goldsboro, N.C.	D1b-'06	2/2
4	Lee, Andy	P	6-0	185	26	5	Pittsburgh	Westminster, S.C.	D6a-'04	16/0
18	Lelie, Ashley	WR	6-3	193	28	7	Hawaii	Bellflower, Calif.	UFA(Atl)-'07	15/3
28	Lewis, Keith	S	6-0	228	26	5	Oregon	Sacramento, Calif.	D6b-'04	12/0
32	Lewis, Michael	S	6-1	226	28	7	Colorado	Houston, Texas	UFA(Phil)-'07	16/16
91	McDonald, Ray	DE	6-3	282	24	2	Florida	Belle Glade, Fla.	D3b-'07	9/0
61	Mitchell, Qasim	T	6-5	347	28	5	North Carolina A&T	Jacksonville, N.C.	FA-'08	0*
56	Moore, Brandon	LB	6-1	255	29	7	Oklahoma	Baldwin, N.Y.	FA-'02	16/1
58	Moore, Jay	LB	6-4	270	25	2	Nebraska	Elkhorn, Neb.	D4a-'07	0*
6	Nedney, Joe	K	6-5	233	35	13	San Jose State	San Jose, Calif.	FA-'05	16/0
44	Norris, Moran	FB	6-1	252	30	8	Kansas	Houston, Texas	FA-'06	16/5
96	Oliver, Melvin	DE	6-3	279	25	3	Louisiana State	Opelika, Ala.	D6c-'06	0*
14	O'Sullivan, J.T.	QB	6-2	227	29	6	UC Davis	Burbank, Calif.	UFA(Det)-'08	4/0*
24	Robinson, Michael	RB	6-1	228	25	3	Penn State	Richmond, Va.	D4-'06	15/1
26	Roman, Mark	S	5-11	203	31	9	Louisiana State	Lafayette, La.	FA-'06	16/16
20	Rossum, Allen	CB	5-8	178	32	11	Notre Dame	Dallas, Texas	FA-'08	15/0*
11	Smith, Alex	QB	6-4	212	24	4	Utah	San Diego, Calif.	D1-'05	7/7
94	Smith, Justin	DE	6-4	275	28	8	Missouri	Jefferson City, Mo.	UFA(Cin)-'08	16/16*
68	Snyder, Adam	T/G	6-6	326	26	4	Oregon	Fullerton, Calif.	D3b-'05	16/11
90	Sopoaga, Isaac	DT	6-2	325	27	5	Hawaii	Pago Pago, American Samoa	D4a-'04	16/5
36	Spencer, Shawntae	CB	6-1	181	26	5	Pittsburgh	Rankin, Pa.	D2b-'04	11/1
74	Staley, Joe	T	6-5	306	24	2	Central Michigan	Rockford, Mich.	D1b-'07	16/16
30	Strickland, Donald	S	5-10	187	24	6	Colorado	San Francisco, Calif.	FA-'06	13/4
77	Terry, Jeb	G	6-5	311	27	4	North Carolina	Dallas, Texas	FA-'08	0*
51	Thomas, Dontarrious	LB	6-2	241	28	5	Auburn	Perry, Ga.	UFA(Minn)-'08	13/0*
53	Ulbrich, Jeff	LB	6-0	246	31	9	Hawaii	San Jose, Calif.	D3b-'00	16/2
46	Walker, Delanie	TE	6-0	244	24	3	Central Missouri	Pomona, Calif.	D6a-'06	16/10
52	Willis, Patrick	LB	6-1	242	23	2	Mississippi	Bruceton, Tenn.	D1a-'07	16/16
69	Wragge, Tony	G	6-4	320	29	4	New Mexico State	Creighton, Neb.	FA-'05	5/0

* Bruce played 16 games with St. Louis in '07; Cohen missed '07 because of injury; Duckett inactive 2 games; Ellison inactive for 16 games; Foster played 16 games with Carolina; Haley played 2 games with Baltimore; Johnson played 16 games with Arizona; Mitchell last active with Chicago in '05; J. Moore missed 07 because of injury; Oliver missed '07 because of injury; O'Sullivan played 4 games with Detroit; Rossum played 15 games with Pittsburgh; J. Smith played 16 games with Cincinnati; Terry last active with Tampa Bay in '06; Thomas played 13 games with Minnesota.

\# - Unrestricted Free Agent; subject to developments.

Players lost through free agency (4): DE Marques Douglas (TB; 16 games in '07), T Kwame Harris (Oak; 12), RB Maurice Hicks (Minn; 16), G Justin Smiley (Mia; 8).

Also played with 49ers in '07—QB Trent Dilfer (7 games), T Patrick Estes (1), WR Bryan Gilmore (10), WR Darrell Jackson (15), WR Taylor Jacobs (4), WR Michael Lewis (13), LB Hannibal Navies (5), LB Derek Smith (15), QB Chris Weinke (2), WR Brandon Williams (3), DT Bryant Young (16).

2008 FIRST-YEAR ROSTER

Name	Pos.	Ht.	Wt.	Age	College	Hometown	How Acq.
Baker, Lewis	S	6-3	203	23	Oklahoma	Bremerhaven, Germany	FA
Balmer, Kentwan	DT	6-5	292	21	North Carolina	Weldon, N.C.	D1
Booker, John	G	6-4	313	21	San Jose State	Hayward, Calif.	FA
Butler, Ezra	LB	6-2	245	23	Nevada	South Africa	FA
Clayton, Thomas (1)	RB	5-11	225	24	Kansas State	Alexandria, Va.	D6-'07
Curry, Markus (1)	CB	5-11	181	27	Michigan	Detroit, Mich.	FA-'07
Curry, Walter (1)	DT	6-4	241	27	Albany State (Ga.)	Crescent City, Fla.	FA
De La Puente, Brian	G	6-3	308	23	California	Los Angeles, Calif.	FA
Finley, J.J.	TE	6-6	254	23	Oklahoma	Arlington, Texas	FA
Grant, Larry	LB	6-1	235	23	Ohio State	Santa Rosa, Calif.	D7
Holmes, Louis	DE	6-4	263	23	Arizona	Fort Lauderdale, Fla.	FA
Jordan, Robert	WR	5-11	172	22	California	Hayward, Calif.	FA
Morgan, Josh	WR	6-0	219	23	Virginia Tech	Washington, D.C.	D6
Olson, Drew (1)	QB	6-2	222	25	UCLA	Piedmont, Calif.	FA-'07
Parker, D.J.	S	5-11	192	23	Virginia Tech	Hampton, Va.	FA
Rabb, Jerard (1)	WR	6-2	199	24	Boise State	El Modena, Calif.	FA-'07
Rachal, Chilo	G	6-4	319	22	Southern California	Compton, Calif.	D2
Richardson, Shaun	LB	6-1	248	23	Tennessee State	St. Louis, Mo.	FA
Schmitt, Ricky (1)	P	6-3	200	23	Shepherd College	Virginia Beach, Va.	FA
Smith, Reggie	CB	6-1	197	21	Oklahoma	Edmond, Okla.	D3
Wallace, Cody	C	6-4	290	23	Texas A&M	Cuero, Texas	D4
Wallace, Cooper (1)	TE	6-3	258	26	Auburn	Nashville, Tenn.	FA
Zeigler, Dominique (1)	WR	6-3	185	23	Baylor	Kalamazoo, Mich.	FA-'07

The term NFL Rookie is defined as a player who is in his first season of professional football and has not been on the roster of another professional football team for any regular-season or postseason games. A Rookie is designated by an "R" on NFL rosters. Players who have been active in another professional football league or players who have NFL experience, including either preseason training camp or being on an Active List or Inactive List, or on Reserve/Injured or Reserve/Physically Unable to Perform for fewer than six regular-season games, are termed NFL First-Year Players. An NFL First-Year Player is designated by a "1" on NFL rosters. Thereafter, a player is credited with an additional year of experience for each season in which he accumulates six games on the Active List or Inactive List, or on Reserve/Injured or Reserve/Physically Unable to Perform.

Log on to www.sf49ers.com for an up-to-date roster; Age listed is as of September 4, 2008.

COACHING STAFF

Head Coach,
Mike Nolan

Pro Career: Named the fifteenth head coach in 49ers history on January 19, 2005, Mike Nolan enters his fourth season as head coach of the San Francisco 49ers. Nolan is in his twenty-first year in the league and twenty-seventh year in coaching. Nolan joins San Francisco after an impressive stint as defensive coordinator of the Baltimore Ravens, a position he has held with three other teams: New York Jets (2000), Washington Redskins (1997-99), and New York Giants (1993-96). In Baltimore, Nolan's defense was among the NFL's best, finishing third overall. Baltimore ranked first in the AFC with 17 fumble recoveries and led the NFL in sacks (47) and tied for first in the AFC and second in the NFL with 41 takeaways. Nolan joined the Ravens after a one-year stay as the Jets defensive coordinator in 2000. From 1997-99 Nolan was the defensive coordinator of the Redskins. He also spent four seasons as defensive coordinator under then-head coach Dan Reeves for the New York Giants (1993-96). In his first season, the Giants' defense allowed the fewest points in the NFL (205). Nolan also worked on Reeves' staff from 1987-1992 with the Broncos as linebackers coach and as special teams coach/defensive assistant. Career record: 16-32.

Background: Nolan participated in the Broncos' 1981 training camp as a defensive back under Dan Reeves. He joined the Broncos after earning three letters at free safety for the Oregon Ducks (1978-1980). Nolan graduated from Woodside (Calif.) high school. He is the son of former NFL head coach Dick Nolan (San Francisco and New Orleans).

Personal: Age 49, born in Baltimore. He and wife Kathy, have four children: sons, Michael and Christopher, and daughters, Laura and Jennifer.

ASSISTANT COACHES

Duane Carlisle, strength and conditioning; born Haverhill, Mass. Attended Maryland. No college or pro playing experience. Pro coach: Speed development consultant for Philadelphia Eagles 2000-04, joined 49ers in 2005.

Shane Day, quality control; born Manhattan, Kan. Attended Kansas State. Wide receiver Rhodes College 1995-96. No pro playing experience. College coach: Michigan 2005-06. Pro coach: Joined 49ers in 2007.

Al Everest, special teams coordinator; born Santa Barbara, Calif. Safety Southern Methodist 1970-71. No pro playing experience. College coach: Southern Methodist 1972, North Texas 1973-74, Cameron University 1974-75. Pro coach: Arizona Cardinals 1996-99, New Orleans Saints 2000-05, joined 49ers in 2007.

Dave Fipp, asst. special teams; born Albuquerque, N.M. Safety Arizona 1994-

97. No pro playing experience. College coach: Holy Cross 1998-99, Arizona 2000, Cal Poly 2001-03, Nevada 2004, San Jose State 2005-07. Pro coach: Joined 49ers in 2008.

Chris Foerster, offensive line; born Milwaukee, Wis. Center Colorado State 1979-1982. No pro playing experience. College coach: Colorado State 1983-87, Stanford 1988-1991, Minnesota 1992. Pro coach: Minnesota Vikings 1993-95, Tampa Bay Buccaneers 1996-2001, Indianapolis Colts 2002-03, Miami Dolphins 2004, Baltimore Ravens 2005-07, joined 49ers in 2008.

Adam Gase, offensive assistant; born Ypsilanti, Mich. Attended Michigan State. No college or pro playing experience. College coach: Louisiana State 2000-02. Pro coach: Detroit Lions 2003-07, joined 49ers in 2008.

Pete Hoener, tight ends; born Peoria, Ill. Tight end/defensive end Bradley 1969-1970. College coach: Missouri 1975-76, Illinois State 1977, Indiana State 1978-1984, Illinois 1986-88, Purdue 1989-1990, Texas Christian 1991-97, Iowa State 1998-99, Texas A&M 2000. Pro coach: St. Louis Cardinals 1985-86, Arizona Cardinals 2003, Chicago Bears 2004, joined 49ers in 2005.

Vance Joseph, secondary assistant; born Marrero, La. Defensive back Colorado 1990-94. Pro defensive back New York Jets 1995, Indianapolis Colts 1996. College coach: Colorado 1999-2001, 2002-03, Wyoming 2002, Bowling Green State 2004. Pro coach: Joined 49ers in 2005.

Johnnie Lynn, secondary; born Los Angeles. Defensive back UCLA 1975-78. Pro defensive back New York Jets 1979-1986. College coach: Arizona 1988-1993. Pro coach: Tampa Bay Buccaneers 1994-95, San Francisco 49ers 1996, New York Giants 1997-2003, Baltimore Ravens 2004-05, joined 49ers in 2006.

Greg Manusky, defensive coordinator; born Wilkes-Barre, Pa. Linebacker Colgate 1983-87. Pro linebacker Washington Redskins 1988-1990, Minnesota Vikings 1991-93, Kansas City Chiefs 1994-99. Pro coach: Washington Redskins 2001, San Diego Chargers 2002-06, joined 49ers in 2007.

Mike Martz, offensive coordinator; born Sioux Falls, S.D. Tight end Fresno State 1972. No pro playing experience. College coach: San Diego Mesa C.C. 1974, 1976-77, San Jose State 1975, Santa Ana College 1978, Fresno State 1979, Pacific 1980-81, Minnesota 1982, Arizona State 1983-1991. Pro coach: L.A./St. Louis Rams 1992-96, 1999-2005 (head coach 2000-05), Washington Redskins 1997-98, Detroit Lions 2006-07, joined 49ers in 2008.

Tony Nathan, running backs; born Birmingham, Ala. Running back Alabama 1975-78. Pro running back Miami Dolphins 1979-1987. College coach: Florida

International 2003-05. Pro coach: Miami Dolphins 1988-1995, Tampa Bay Buccaneers 1996-2001, Baltimore Ravens 2006-07, joined 49ers in 2008.

Mike Singletary, asst. head coach/defense; born Houston. Linebacker Baylor 1977-1980. Pro linebacker Chicago Bears 1981-1992. Inducted into Pro Football Hall of Fame 1998. Pro coach: Baltimore Ravens 2003-04, joined 49ers in 2005.

Jerry Sullivan, wide receivers/senior assistant; born Miami, Fla. Quarterback Florida State 1963-64. No pro playing experience. College coach: Kansas State 1971-72, Texas Tech 1973-75, South Carolina 1976-1982, Indiana 1983, Louisiana State 1984-1990, Ohio State 1991. Pro coach: San Diego Chargers 1992-96, Detroit Lions 1997-2000, Arizona Cardinals 2001-03, Miami Dolphins 2004, joined 49ers in 2005.

Jason Tarver, outside linebackers/defensive assistant; born Stanford, Calif. Defensive back West Valley College 1994-95. No pro playing experience. College coach: West Valley College 1996-97, UCLA 1998-2000. Pro coach: Joined 49ers in 2001.

Ted Tollner, quarterbacks/assistant to head coach; born San Francisco, Calif. Quarterback Cal Poly-San Luis Obispo 1959-61. No pro playing experience. College coach: College of San Mateo 1971-72 (head coach), San Diego State (1973-80), 1994-2001 (head coach 1994-2001), Brigham Young 1981, Southern California 1982-86 (head coach 1983-86). Pro coach: Buffalo Bills 1987-88, San Diego Chargers 1989-91, San Francisco 2002-04, Detroit Lions 2005, re-joined 49ers in 2007.

Jim Tomsula, defensive line; born Homestead, Pa. Middle Tennessee State 1985-86, Catawba College 1987-1990. No pro playing experience College coach: Charleston Southern 1997. Pro coach: England Monarchs (NFL Europe) 1998, Scottish Claymores (NFL Europe) 1999-2003, Berlin Thunder (NFL Europe) 2004-05, Rhein Fire (NFL Europa head coach) 2006, joined 49ers in 2007.

Mark Uyeyama, asst. strength and conditioning; born Vancouver, B.C. Nose Guard Butte C.C. 1994-95, Northern State 1996-97. No pro playing experience. College coach: Arizona State 2001-03, Utah State 2004-07. Pro coach: joined 49ers in 2008.

George Warhop, offensive line; born Riverside, Ca. Guard/center Mt. San Jacinto (Calif.) J.C. 1979-1980, Cincinnati 1981-82. College coach: Cincinnati 1983, Kansas 1984-86, Vanderbilt 1987-89, New Mexico 1990, Southern Methodist 1993, Boston College 1994-95. Pro coach: London Monarchs (WL) 1991-92, St. Louis Rams 1996-97, Arizona Cardinals 1998-2002, Dallas Cowboys 2003-04, joined 49ers in 2005.

**National Football Conference
West Division**
Team Colors: Seahawks Blue, Seahawks
Navy, Seahawks Bright Green
Virginia Mason Athletic Center
12 Seahawks Way
Renton, Washington 98056
Telephone: (425) 827-9777

2008 SCHEDULE
PRESEASON
Aug. 8   at Minnesota 7:00
Aug. 16   **Chicago** 6:00
Aug. 25   at San Diego 5:00
Aug. 29   **Oakland** 7:00

REGULAR SEASON
Sep. 7   at Buffalo 1:00
Sep. 14   **San Francisco** 1:05
Sep. 21   **St. Louis** 1:05
Sep. 28   BYE
Oct. 5   at N.Y. Giants......................1:00
Oct. 12   **Green Bay**........................1:15
Oct. 19   at Tampa Bay 8:15
Oct. 26   at San Francisco 1:15
Nov. 2   **Philadelphia** 1:15
Nov. 9   at Miami 1:00
Nov. 16   **Arizona** 1:05
Nov. 23   **Washington** 1:15
Nov. 27   at Dallas (Thu.)...................3:15
Dec. 7   **New England** * 5:15
Dec. 14   at St. Louis 12:00
Dec. 21   **N.Y. Jets** 1:05
Dec. 28   at Arizona 2:15
Sunday night games in Weeks 11-17 subject to change
Stadium: Qwest Field
(opened in 2002)
•**Capacity:** 67,000
Playing Surface: FieldTurf
Training Camp: Seahawks Headquarters
Kirkland, WA 98033

QWEST FIELD

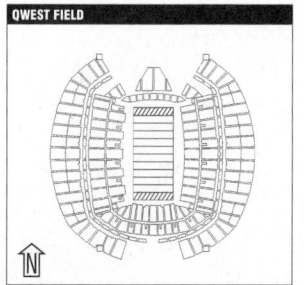

CLUB OFFICIALS
Chairman: Paul Allen
CEO: Tod Leiweke
President of Football Operations:
Tim Ruskell
Executive VP of Football Operations/
Head Coach: Mike Holmgren
Senior VP/CMO: John Rizzardini
Senior VP/CFO: Martha Fuller
VP/Football Administration: John Izdik
VP/Player Personnel: Ruston Webster
VP/Community Outreach: Mike Flood
VP/Corporate Partnership/Legal Affairs:
Lance Lopes
VP/Corporate Sales: Scott Patrick
Director of Marketing: Bill Chapin
Director of Corp. Hospitality, Suite Sales
& Service: Amy Sprangers
Director of Pro Personnel: Will Lewis
Director of Communications and
Broadcasting: Dave Pearson
Asst. Director of Communications:
Lane Gammel
Director of Community Outreach:
Sandy Gregory
Director of Ticket Sales/Operations:
Chuck Arnold
Gameday Presentation: Rick Crawford
Video Director Football: Thom Fermstad
Head Athletic Trainer: Sam Ramsden
Equipment Manager: Erik Kennedy
Team Travel: Jeremy Young

COACHING HISTORY
(253-264-0)
Records include postseason games
1976-1982 Jack Patera* 35-59-0
1982   Mike McCormack 4-3-0
1983-1991 Chuck Knox 83-67-0
1992-94   Tom Flores...................14-34-0
1995-98   Dennis Erickson..........31-33-0
1999-2007 Mike Holmgren 86-68-0
Released after two games in 1982

PAID ATTENDANCE
Home 533,657   Away 531,382
Total 1,065,039
Single-game home record,
68,681 (12/16/00)
Single-season home record,
533,657 (2007)

2008 DRAFT CHOICES
Round	Name	Pos.	College
1	Lawrence Jackson	DE	Southern California
2	John Carlson	TE	Notre Dame
4	Red Bryant	DT	Texas A&M
5	Owen Schmitt	RB	West Virginia
6	Tyler Schmitt	LS	San Diego St.
7	Justin Forsett	RB	California
	Brandon Coutu	K	Georgia

2007 TEAM RECORD
PRESEASON (3-1)

Date	Result	Opponent
8/12	W 24-16	at San Diego
8/18	L 13-48	at Green Bay
8/25	W 30-13	Minnesota
8/30	W 19-14	Oakland

REGULAR SEASON (10-6)

Date	Result	Opponent	Att.
9/9	W 20-6	Tampa Bay	68,044
9/16	L 20-23	at Arizona	64,542
9/23	W 24-21	Cincinnati	68,110
9/30	W 23-3	at San Francisco	67,651
10/7	L 0-21	at Pittsburgh	64,478
10/14	L 17-28	New Orleans	68,296
10/21	W 33-6	St. Louis	68,164
11/4	L 30-33	at Cleveland (OT)	72,927
11/12	W 24-0	San Francisco	68,331
11/18	W 30-23	Chicago	68,249
11/25	W 24-19	at St. Louis	65,423
12/2	W 28-24	at Philadelphia	68,445
12/9	W 42-21	Arizona	68,193
12/16	L 10-13	at Carolina	73,421
12/23	W 27-6	Baltimore	68,164
12/30	L 41-44	at Atlanta	64,925

(OT) Overtime

POSTSEASON (1-1)

1/5	W 35-14	Washington	68,297
1/12	L 20-42	at Green Bay	72,168

SCORE BY PERIODS

Seahawks	76	136	73	108	0	—	393
Opponents	62	95	39	92	3	—	291

2007 TEAM STATISTICS

	Seahawks	Opp.
Total First Downs	323	278
Rushing	93	78
Passing	211	183
Penalty	19	17
3rd Down: Made/Att	75/215	88/232
3rd Down Pct.	34.9	37.9
4th Down: Made/Att	6/14	5/17
4th Down Pct.	42.9	29.4
Possession Avg.	29:49	30:11
Total Net Yards	5583	5149
Avg. Per Game	348.9	321.8
Total Plays	1056	1035
Avg. Per Play	5.3	5.0
Net Yards Rushing	1619	1644
Avg. Per Game	101.2	102.8
Total Rushes	430	422
Net Yards Passing	3964	3505
Avg. Per Game	247.8	219.1
Sacked/Yards Lost	36/217	45/303
Gross Yards	4181	3808
Att./Completions	590/371	568/333
Completion Pct.	62.9	58.6
Had Intercepted	13	20
Punts/Average	86/40.0	93/46.5
Net Punting Avg.	86/34.3	93/37.0
Penalties/Yards	59/428	99/756
Fumbles/Ball Lost	21/11	31/14
Touchdowns	44	32
Rushing	9	16
Passing	30	15
Returns	5	1

2007 INDIVIDUAL STATISTICS

PASSING

	Att.	Comp.	Yds.	Pct.	TD	Int.	Tkld.	Rate
Hasselbeck	562	352	3966	62.6	28	12	33/204	91.4
S. Wallace	28	19	215	67.9	2	1	3/13	99.6
Seahawks	590	371	4181	62.9	30	13	36/217	91.8
Opponents	568	333	3808	58.6	15	20	45/303	73.0

SCORING

	TD R	TD P	TD Rt	PAT	FG	Saf	PTS
Brown	0	0	0	43/43	28/34	0	127
Burleson	0	9	2	0/0	0/0	0	66
Engram	0	6	0	0/0	0/0	0	36
Alexander	4	1	0	0/0	0/0	0	30
Morris	4	1	0	0/0	0/0	0	30
Branch	0	4	0	0/0	0/0	0	24
Hackett	0	3	0	0/0	0/0	0	18
Heller	0	3	0	0/0	0/0	0	18
Pollard	0	2	0	0/0	0/0	0	12
Hill	0	0	1	0/0	0/0	0	6
Obomanu	0	1	0	0/0	0/0	0	6
Trufant	0	0	1	0/0	0/0	0	6
Weaver	1	0	0	0/0	0/0	0	6
Wilson	0	0	1	0/0	0/0	0	6
Scobey	0	0	0	0/0	0/0	1	2
Seahawks	9	30	5	43/43	28/34	1	393
Opponents	16	15	1	27/28	22/27	2	291

2-Pt. Conversions: Seahawks 0-1,
Opponents 1-4

RUSHING

	No.	Yds	Avg	LG	TD
Alexander	207	716	3.5	25	4
Morris	140	628	4.5	46	4
Weaver	33	146	4.4	37	1
Hasselbeck	39	89	2.3	12	0
Strong	4	19	4.8	9	0
S. Wallace	4	17	4.3	11	0
Burleson	2	4	2.0	3	0
Plackemeier	1	0	0.0	0	0
Seahawks	430	1619	3.8	46	9
Opponents	422	1644	3.9	53t	16

RECEIVING

	No.	Yds	Avg	LG	TD
Engram	94	1147	12.2	49	6
Burleson	50	694	13.9	45t	9
Branch	49	661	13.5	65	4
Weaver	39	313	8.0	46	0
Hackett	32	384	12.0	59	3
Pollard	28	273	9.8	22	2
Morris	23	213	9.3	34t	1
Alexander	14	76	5.4	18	1
Heller	13	82	6.3	25	3
Obomanu	12	180	15.0	30	1
Strong	9	72	8.0	15	0
Taylor	5	38	7.6	12	0
S. Wallace	2	47	23.5	29	0
Pearman	1	1	1.0	1	0
Seahawks	371	4181	11.3	65	30
Opponents	333	3808	11.4	79t	15

INTERCEPTIONS

	No.	Yds	Avg	LG	TD
Trufant	7	150	21.4	84t	1
Tatupu	4	116	29.0	49	0
Grant	3	34	11.3	34	0
Peterson	2	3	1.5	3	0
Babineaux	1	0	0.0	0	0
Kerney	1	0	0.0	0	0
Russell	1	0	0.0	0	0
Tapp	1	-4	-4.0	-4	0
Seahawks	20	299	15.0	84t	1
Opponents	13	144	11.1	35	0

PUNTING

	No.	Yds.	Avg.	In 20	LG
Plackemeier	86	3436	40.0	30	62
Seahawks	86	3436	40.0	30	62
Opponents	93	4322	46.5	24	80

PUNT RETURNS

	Ret	FC	Yds	Avg	LG	TD
Burleson	58	8	658	11.3	94t	1
Seahawks	58	8	658	11.3	94t	1
Opponents	37	15	362	9.8	64	0

KICKOFF RETURNS

	No.	Yds	Avg	LG	TD
Burleson	27	590	21.9	91t	1
Wilson	14	385	27.5	89t	1
Obomanu	4	88	22.0	25	0
Pearman	3	71	23.7	33	0
Engram	1	12	12.0	12	0
Taylor	1	27	27.0	27	0
Terrill	1	0	0.0	0	0
C. Wallace	1	0	0.0	0	0
Willis	1	0	0.0	0	0
Seahawks	53	1173	22.1	91t	2
Opponents	72	1790	24.9	61	0

FIELD GOALS

	1-19	20-29	30-39	40-49	50+
Brown	0/0	12/12	5/5	8/12	3/5
Seahawks	0/0	12/12	5/5	8/12	3/5
Opponents	1/1	5/5	9/10	5/7	2/4

SACKS

	No.
Kerney	14.5
Peterson	9.5
Tapp	7.0
Bernard	3.5
Hill	3.0
Mebane	2.0
Wyms	2.0
Babineaux	1.0
Russell	1.0
Tatupu	1.0
Darby	0.5
Seahawks	45.0
Opponents	36.0

RECORD HOLDERS
INDIVIDUAL RECORDS—CAREER

Category	Name	Performance
Rushing (Yds.)	Shaun Alexander, 2000-07	9,429
Passing (Yds.)	Dave Krieg, 1980-1991	26,132
Passing (TDs)	Dave Krieg, 1980-1991	195
Receiving (No.)	Steve Largent, 1976-1989	819
Receiving (Yds.)	Steve Largent, 1976-1989	13,089
Interceptions	Dave Brown, 1976-1986	50
Punting (Avg.)	Rick Tuten, 1991-97	43.8
Punt Return (Avg.)	Charlie Rogers, 1999-2001	12.7
Kickoff Return (Avg.)	Steve Broussard, 1995-98	23.2
Field Goals	Norm Johnson, 1982-1990	159
Touchdowns (Tot.)	Shaun Alexander, 2000-07	112
Points	Norm Johnson, 1982-1990	810

INDIVIDUAL RECORDS—SINGLE SEASON

Category	Name	Performance
Rushing (Yds.)	Shaun Alexander, 2005	1,880
Passing (Yds.)	Matt Hasselbeck, 2007	3,966
Passing (TDs)	Dave Krieg, 1984	32
Receiving (No.)	Bobby Engram, 2007	94
Receiving (Yds.)	Steve Largent, 1985	1,287
Interceptions	John Harris, 1981	10
	Kenny Easley, 1984	10
Punting (Avg.)	Ryan Plackemeier, 2006	45.0
Punt Return (Avg.)	Charlie Rogers, 1999	14.5
Kickoff Return (Avg.)	Charlie Rogers, 2000	24.9
Field Goals	Todd Peterson, 1999	34
Touchdowns (Tot.)	Shaun Alexander, 2005	28
Points	Shaun Alexander, 2005	168

INDIVIDUAL RECORDS—SINGLE GAME

Category	Name	Performance
Rushing (Yds.)	Shaun Alexander, 11-11-01	266
Passing (Yds.)	Matt Hasselbeck, 12-29-02	449
Passing (TDs)	Dave Krieg, 12-2-84, 9-15-85, 11-28-88	5
	Warren Moon, 10-26-97	5
	Matt Hasselbeck, 11-23-03, 9-24-06	5
Receiving (No.)	Steve Largent, 10-18-87	15
Receiving (Yds.)	Steve Largent, 10-18-87	261
Interceptions	Kenny Easley, 9-3-84	3
	Eugene Robinson, 12-6-92	3
	Darryl Williams, 9-21-97	3
	Lofa Tatupu, 12-2-07	3
	Marcus Trufant, 12-9-07	3
Field Goals	Norm Johnson, 9-20-87, 12-18-88	5
Touchdowns (Tot.)	Shaun Alexander, 9-29-02	5
Points	Shaun Alexander, 9-29-02	30

2008 VETERAN ROSTER

No.	Name	Pos.	Ht.	Wt.	Age	NFL Exp.	College	Hometown	How Acq.	'07 Games/ Starts
47	Alcorn, Zac	TE	6-4	255	28	3	Black Hills State	Chadron, Neb.	FA-'08	0*
98	Atkins, Baraka	DE	6-4	268	23	2	Miami	Sarasota, Fla.	D4a-'07	12/0
52 t-	Babin, Jason	DE	6-3	267	28	5	Western Michigan	Paw Paw, Mich.	T(Hou)-'07	2/0
27	Babineaux, Jordan	CB	6-0	206	26	5	Southern Arkansas	Port Arthur, Texas	FA-'04	16/0
99	Bernard, Rocky	DT	6-3	308	29	7	Texas A&M	Baytown, Texas	D5a-'02	14/14
83	Branch, Deion	WR	5-9	192	29	7	Louisville	Albany, Ga.	T(NE)-'06	11/11
81	Burleson, Nate	WR	6-0	198	27	6	Nevada	Seattle, Wash.	RFA(Minn)-'06	16/12
91	Cooper, Chris	DE	6-5	285	30	8	Nebraska-Omaha	Lincoln, Neb.	FA-'08	12/0*
45	Duckett, T.J.	RB	6-0	254	27	7	Michigan State	Kalamazoo, Mich.	UFA(Det)-'08	12/1*
84	Engram, Bobby	WR	5-10	192	35	13	Penn State	Camden, S.C.	UFA(Chi)-'01	16/15
5 t-	Frye, Charlie	QB	6-4	217	27	4	Akron	Willard, Ohio	T(Cle)-'07	1/1*
24	Grant, Deon	S	6-2	215	29	9	Tennessee	Augusta, Ga.	UFA(Jax)-'07	16/16
62	Gray, Chris	G	6-4	305	38	16	Auburn	Birmingham, Ala.	UFA(Chi)-'98	16/16
94	Green, Howard	DT	6-2	320	29	4	Louisiana State	Donaldsonville, La.	FA-'07	5/0
42	Green, Mike	S	6-0	200	31	9	Northwestern St. (La.)	Ruston, La.	T(Chi)-'06	15/1
8	Hasselbeck, Matt	QB	6-4	225	32	10	Boston College	Westwood, Mass.	T(GB)-'01	16/16
85	Heller, Will	TE	6-6	270	27	6	Georgia Tech	Dunwoody, Ga.	UFA(TB)-'06	16/6
54	Herring, Will	LB	6-3	235	25	2	Auburn	Opelika, Ala.	D5-'07	12/0
56	Hill, Leroy	LB	6-1	238	25	4	Clemson	Haddock, Ga.	D3b-'05	14/14
32	Hobbs, Kevin	CB	6-0	188	25	2	Auburn	Tampa, Fla.	FA-'07	6/0
3	Hodges, Reggie	P	6-0	226	26	4	Ball State	Champaign, Ill.	FA-'08	0*
21	Jennings, Kelly	CB	5-11	180	25	3	Miami	Live Oak, Fla.	D1-'06	16/15
22	Jones, Julius	RB	5-10	208	27	5	Notre Dame	Big Stone Gap, Va.	UFA(Dall)-'08	16/16*
71	Jones, Walter	T	6-5	325	34	12	Florida State	Aliceville, Ala.	D1b-'97	15/15
97	Kerney, Patrick	DE	6-5	272	31	10	Virginia	Newtown, Pa.	UFA(Atl)-'07	16/16
34	Kirtman, David	FB	6-0	238	25	3	Southern California	Mercer Island, Wash.	D5-'06	6/0
50	Laury, Lance	LB	6-2	237	26	3	South Carolina	Hopkins, S.C.	FA-'06	16/0
58	Lewis, D.D.	LB	6-1	241	29	7	Texas	Houston, Texas	FA-'08	5/0*
75	Locklear, Sean	T	6-4	308	27	5	North Carolina State	Lumberton, N.C.	D3-'04	16/16
31	Lowe, Omare	CB	6-1	195	30	7	Washington	Maple Valley, Wash.	UFA(Atl)-'08	0*
53	Mallard, Wesly	LB	6-1	230	29	6	Oregon	Hinesville, Ga.	FA-'08	0*
10	Mare, Olindo	K	5-11	190	35	13	Syracuse	Cooper City, Fla.	FA-'08	13/0*
92	Mebane, Brandon	DT	6-1	314	23	2	California	Los Angeles, Calif.	D3-'07	16/10
20	Morris, Maurice	RB	5-11	216	28	7	Oregon	Chester, S.C.	D2a-'02	14/5
87	Obomanu, Ben	WR	6-0	206	24	3	Auburn	Selma, Ala.	D7b-'06	13/0
59	Peterson, Julian	LB	6-3	240	30	9	Michigan State	Washington, D.C.	UFA(SF)-'06	16/16
1	Plackemeier, Ryan	P	6-3	247	24	3	Wake Forest	Bonsall, Calif.	D7a-'06	16/0
88	Putzier, Jeb	TE	6-4	251	29	7	Boise State	Eagle, Idaho	UFA(Hou)-'08	8/1*
25	Russell, Brian	S	6-2	210	30	7	San Diego State	West Covina, Calif.	UFA(Cle)-'07	16/16
67	Sims, Rob	G	6-3	312	24	3	Ohio State	Macedonia, Ohio	D4-'06	16/16
65	Spencer, Chris	C	6-3	312	26	4	Mississippi	Madison, Miss.	D1-'05	16/16
55	Tapp, Darryl	DE	6-1	270	23	3	Virginia Tech	Chesapeake, Va.	D2-'06	16/16
51	Tatupu, Lofa	LB	6-0	242	25	4	Southern California	Wrentham, Mass.	D2-'05	16/16
86	Taylor, Courtney	WR	6-1	205	24	2	Auburn	Carrollton, Ala.	D6a-'07	8/0
93	Terrill, Craig	DT	6-2	295	28	5	Purdue	Lebanon, Ind.	D6-'04	16/2
96	Tripplett, Larry	DT	6-2	296	29	7	Washington	Los Angeles, Calif.	FA-'08	16/16*
23	Trufant, Marcus	CB	5-11	197	27	6	Washington State	Tacoma, Wash.	D1-'03	16/16
90	Tubbs, Marcus	DT	6-3	318	27	5	Texas	DeSoto, Texas	D1-'04	0*
68	Wahle, Mike	G	6-6	304	31	11	Navy	Lake Arrowhead, Calif.	FA-'08	16/16*
39	Wallace, C.J.	S	6-0	218	23	2	Washington	Sacramento, Calif.	FA-'07	9/0
15	Wallace, Seneca	QB	5-11	205	28	6	Iowa State	Sacramento, Calif.	D4a-'03	10/0
43	Weaver, Leonard	FB	6-0	242	25	4	Carson-Newman	Melbourne, Fla.	FA-'05	16/4
74	Willis, Ray	T	6-6	315	26	4	Florida State	Angleton, Texas	D4-'05	5/0
26	Wilson, Josh	CB	5-9	192	23	2	Maryland	Upper Marlboro, Md.	D2-'07	12/0
77	Womack, Floyd	T	6-4	328	29	8	Mississippi State	Cleveland, Miss.	D4c-'01	14/1
66	Wrotto, Mansfield	G	6-3	320	23	2	Georgia Tech	Snellville, Ga.	D4b-'07	0*

* Alcorn last active with Green Bay in '06; Cooper played 12 games with Arizona in '07; Duckett played 12 games with Detroit; Frye played 1 game with Cleveland; Hodges last active with Philadelphia in '05; J. Jones played 16 games with Dallas; Lewis played 5 games with Denver; Lowe missed '07 season because of injury; Mallard last active with Tampa Bay in '06; Mare played 13 games with New Orleans; Putzier played 8 games with Houston; Tripplett played 16 games with Buffalo; Tubbs missed '07 season because of injury; Wahle played 16 games with Carolina; Wrotto did not play in 1 game.

Players lost through free agency (6): K Josh Brown (StL; 16 games in '07), DT Chartric Darby (Det; 6), WR D.J. Hackett (Car; 6), LB Niko Koutouvides (Den; 15), TE Marcus Pollard (NE; 14), DT Ellis Wyms (Minn; 13).

Retired—Mack Strong, 14-year fullback, 5 games in '07.

Also played with Seahawks in '07—RB Shaun Alexander (13 games), T Tom Ashworth (13), LB Kevin Bentley (14), DE Bryce Fisher (1), TE Bennie Joppru (13), FB Fred McCrary (6), TE Derek Rackley (5), LS Jeff Robinson (3), RB Josh Scobey (4), LS Boone Stutz (8).

2008 FIRST-YEAR ROSTER

Name	Pos.	Ht.	Wt.	Age	College	Hometown	How Acq.
Adams, Jamar	S	6-2	212	22	Michigan	Charlotte, N.C.	FA
Alexander, Donovan	CB	5-11	185	23	North Dakota	Winnipeg, Manitoba	FA
Bell, Dalton (1)	QB	6-3	210	25	West Texas A&M	Canyon, Texas	W(Car)
Brown, Kevin	DT	6-2	303	23	UCLA	Los Angeles, Calif.	FA
Bryant, Red	DT	6-4	318	24	Texas A&M	Jasper, Texas	D4
Bumpus, Michael	WR	5-11	194	22	Washington State	Culver City, Calif.	FA
Carlson, John	TE	6-5	251	24	Notre Dame	Litchfield, Minn.	D2
Castelo, Matt	LB	5-10	225	22	San Jose State	San Jose, Calif.	FA
Coutu, Brandon	K	5-11	188	23	Georgia	Lawrenceville, Ga.	D7b
Curran, Dan	FB	6-0	240	31	New Hampshire	Chelmsford, Mass.	FA
Dickinson, Dustin	G	6-3	298	23	Houston	Springtown, Texas	FA
Dizer, DeMichael	CB	5-11	183	23	Grambling State	Sterlington, La.	FA
Filani, Joel	WR	6-2	216	24	Texas Tech	Tempe, Ariz.	FA
Forsett, Justin	RB	5-8	194	22	California	Arlington, Texas	D7a
Hawthorne, David	LB	6-0	240	23	Texas Christian	Corsicana, Texas	FA
Jackson, Lawrence	DE	6-4	271	23	Southern California	Inglewood, Calif.	D1
Johnson, Kelin	S	6-0	197	23	Georgia	Daytona Beach, Fla.	FA
Jones, Nick	C	6-3	305	23	Georgia	Bowdon, Ga.	FA
Kent, Jordan (1)	WR	6-4	219	24	Oregon	Eugen, Ore.	D6b-'07
Murray, Pat	G	6-3	310	23	Truman State	Pocahontas, Iowa	FA
Newton, Joe (1)	TE	6-7	258	24	Oregon Stte	Roseburg, Ore.	FA-'07
Payne, Logan (1)	WR	6-2	205	23	Minnesoa	Lutz, Fla.	FA-'07
Robinson, William	T	6-5	297	23	San Diego State	Pomona, Calif.	FA
Russo, Anthony	WR	5-10	191	23	Washington	Lakewood, Wash.	FA
Schmitt, Owen	FB	6-2	247	23	West Virginia	Fairfax, Va.	D5
Schmitt, Tyler	LS	6-2	231	22	San Diego State	Peoria, Ariz.	D6
Tafisi, Nu'u	DE	6-2	268	27	California	Salt Lake City, Utah	FA-'07
Vallos, Steve	G	6-3	312	24	Wake Forest	Boardman, Ohio	D7-'07
White, Chris	C	6-3	321	24	South Carolina	Chester, S.C.	FA
Wicks, Eric	S	6-0	217	23	West Virginia	Pittsburgh, Pa.	FA
Williams, Kyle (1)	T	6-6	295	24	Southern California	Dallas, Texas	FA-'07

The term NFL Rookie is defined as a player who is in his first season of professional football and has not been on the roster of another professional football team for any regular-season or postseason games. A Rookie is designated by an "R" on NFL rosters. Players who have been active in another professional football league or players who have NFL experience, including either preseason training camp or being on an Active List or Inactive List, or on Reserve/Injured or Reserve/Physically Unable to Perform for fewer than six regular-season games, are termed NFL First-Year Players. An NFL First-Year Player is designated by a "1" on NFL rosters. Thereafter, a player is credited with an additional year of experience for each season in which he accumulates six games on the Active List or Inactive List, or on Reserve/Injured or Reserve/Physically Unable to Perform.

Log on to www.seahawks.com for an up-to-date roster; Age listed is as of September 4, 2008.

COACHING STAFF

Executive Vice President of Football Operations/Head Coach,

Mike Holmgren

Pro Career: Named as the Seahawks' sixth head coach on January 8, 1999. In 2007, the Seahawks won their fourth consecutive NFC West crown and sixth-ever division title. In 2005, led them to a franchise-best record 13-3 finish, and their first-ever Super Bowl berth. In 2003, the Seahawks posted their first double-digit victory total since 1986. Holmgren joined Seattle after serving as the head coach of the Packers (1992-98). By winning at least one game in five consecutive postseasons (1993-97) Holmgren joined John Madden (1973-77) as the only coaches in league history to accomplish that feat. In 22 NFL seasons (1999-2007 head coach Seattle, 1992-98 head coach Green Bay, 1986-1991 assistant coach San Francisco) Holmgren's teams have a 228-122-1 (.650) record, posted double-digit win totals 13 times, made the postseason 17 times, won three Super Bowls (XXIII, XXIV, and XXXI), and reached two others (XXXII and XL). Career record: 170-110.

Background: Quarterback at Southern California (1966-69) and was drafted by the St. Louis Cardinals in the eighth round of the 1970 NFL Draft. He served as an assistant coach at San Francisco State (1981) and Brigham Young (1982-85). Earned his bachelor degree in business finance at Southern California.

Personal: Age 60, born in San Francisco. He and his wife, Kathy, have four daughters—Calla, Jenny, Emily, and Gretchen.

ASSISTANT COACHES

Chris Beake, offensive quality control; born Kansas City, Mo. Quarterback Air Force 1991-92. No pro playing experience. College coach: Air Force 1993-94. Pro coach: San Francisco 49ers 1999-2003, Atlanta Falcons 2004-2007, joined Seahawks in 2008.

Dwaine Board, defensive line; born Rocky Mount, Va. Defensive lineman North Carolina A&T 1974-77. Pro defensive lineman San Francisco 49ers 1979-1987, New Orleans Saints 1988. Pro coach: San Francisco 49ers 1990-2002, joined Seahawks in 2003.

Mike Clark, strength and conditioning; born Wichita, Kan. Linebacker Ottawa College 1973-76. No pro playing experience. College coach: Kansas 1977-78, 1982, Wyoming 1981, Oregon 1983-87, Southern California 1988-89, Texas A&M 2000-2003. Pro coach: Joined Seahawks in 2004.

Mike DeBord, offensive assistant/offensive line; born Muncie, Ind. No college or pro playing experience. College coach: Franklin 1982-83, Fort Hays State 1984-86, Eastern Illinois 1987-88, Ball State 1989, Colorado State 1990-91, Northwestern 1992, Michigan 1992-99,

Central Michigan 2000-03 (head coach), Michigan 2004-2007. Pro coach: Joined Seahawks in 2008.

Bruce DeHaven, special teams; born Trousdale, Kan. Attended Southwestern (Kan.) College. No college or pro playing experience. College coach: Kansas 1979-1981, New Mexico State 1982. Pro coach: New Jersey Generals (USFL) 1983, Pittsburgh Maulers (USFL) 1984, Orlando Renegades (USFL) 1985, Buffalo Bills 1987-1999, San Francisco 49ers 2000-02, Dallas Cowboys 2003-2006, joined Seahawks in 2007.

Kasey Dunn, running backs; born San Diego. Wide receiver Idaho 1987-1991. Pro wide receiver Houston Oilers 1992, British Columbia Lions (CFL) 1992, Edmonton Eskimos (CFL) 1993. College coach: Idaho 1993, 1995, San Diego 1994, New Mexico 1996-97, Washington State 1998-2002, Texas Christian 2003, Arizona 2004-2006, Baylor 2007, Maryland 2008. Pro coach: Joined Seahawks in 2008.

Keith Gilbertson, wide receivers; born Snohomish, Wash. Defensive line Central Washington 1967, Columbia Basin (Wash.) J.C. 1968, Hawaii 1969-1970. No pro playing experience. College coach: Idaho State 1971-74, Western Washington 1975, Washington 1976, Utah State 1977-1981, Idaho 1982, 1986-88, Washington 1989-1991, 1999-2004 (head coach 2003-04), California 1992-95 (head coach). Pro coach: L.A. Express (USFL) 1983-85, Seattle Seahawks 1996-98, re-joined Seahawks in 2005.

Gil Haskell, asst. head coach/offensive coordinator; born San Francisco. Defensive back San Francisco State 1961, 1963-65. No pro playing experience. College coach: Southern California 1978-1982. Pro coach: Los Angeles Rams 1983-1991, Green Bay Packers 1992-97, Carolina Panthers 1998-99, joined Seahawks in 2000.

Tom Headlee, quality control/defense; born Bothell, Wash. Attended Washington State. No college or pro playing experience. Pro coach: Joined Seahawks in 2006.

John Jamison, special teams assistant; born San Francisco. Wide receiver California 1968. No pro playing experience. Pro coach: Joined Seahawks in 2005.

Darren Krein, asst. strength & conditioning; born Aurora, Colo. Linebacker/defensive end Miami 1989-1993. Pro linebacker San Diego Chargers 1994, Barcelona Dragons (NFLE) 1996. Pro coach: Seattle Seahawks 1997-98, re-joined Seahawks in 2002.

Bill Lazor, quarterbacks; born Scranton, Pa. Quarterback Cornell 1991-93. No pro playing experience. College coach: Cornell 1994-2000, Buffalo 2001-02. Pro coach: Atlanta Falcons 2003, Washington

Redskins 2004-2007, joined Seahawks in 2008.

Jim Lind, tight ends; born Isle, Minn. Linebacker Bethel College 1965-66, defensive back Bemidji State 1971-72. No pro playing experience. College coach: St. Cloud State 1977-78, St. John's (Minn.) 1979-1980, Brigham Young 1981-82, Minnesota-Morris 1983-86 (head coach), Wisconsin-Eau Claire 1987-1991 (head coach). Pro coach: Green Bay Packers 1992-98, joined Seahawks in 1999.

Larry Marmie, defensive assistant/secondary; born Berea, Kent. Quarterback Eastern Kentucky 1962-65. No pro playing experience. College coach: Morehead State 1968-1971, Eastern Kentucky 1972-76, Tulsa 1977-78, North Carolina 1979-1982, Tennessee 1983-84, Arizona State 1985-1991 (head coach 1988-1991), Tennessee 1992-94, UCLA 1995. Pro coach: Arizona Cardinals 1996-2003, St. Louis Rams 2004-05, joined Seahawks in 2006.

John Marshall, defensive coordinator; born Arroyo Grande, Calif. Linebacker Washington State 1964. No pro playing experience. College coach: Oregon 1970-76, Southern California 1977-79. Pro coach: Green Bay Packers 1980-82, Indianapolis Colts 1986-88, San Francisco 49ers 1989-1998, Carolina Panthers 1999-2001, Detroit Lions 2002, joined Seahawks in 2003.

Jim Mora, asst. head coach/defensive backs; born Los Angeles. Linebacker Washington 1980-83. No pro playing experience. College coach: Washington 1984. Pro coach: San Diego Chargers 1986-1991, New Orleans Saints 1992-1996, San Francisco 49ers 1997-2003, Atlanta Falcons 2004-2006 (head coach), joined Seahawks in 2007.

Zerick Rollins, linebackers; born Houston. Defensive end Texas A&M 1995-97. No pro playing experience. Graduate assistant Texas A&M 1997-2000. Pro coach: Joined Seahawks in 2001.

Mike Solari, offensive line; born Daly City, Calif. Offensive lineman San Diego State 1972-75. No pro playing experience. College coach: Mira Costa (Calif.) J.C. 1978, U.S. International 1979, Boise State 1980, Cincinnati 1981-82, Kansas 1983-85, Pittsburgh 1986, Alabama 1990-91. Pro coach: Dallas Cowboys 1987-88, Phoenix Cardinals 1989, San Francisco 49ers 1992-1996, Kansas City Chiefs 1997-2007, joined Seahawks in 2008.

National Football Conference
South Division
Team Colors: Buccaneer Red, Pewter,
Black, and Orange
One Buccaneer Place
Tampa, Florida 33607
Telephone: (813) 870-2700

2008 SCHEDULE
PRESEASON

Aug. 9   at Miami.............................7:30
Aug. 17 **New England** 8:00
Aug. 23 **Jacksonville** 7:30
Aug. 28 at Houston 7:00

REGULAR SEASON

Sep. 7   at New Orleans 12:00
Sep. 14 **Atlanta** 4:05
Sep. 21 at Chicago 12:00
Sep. 28 **Green Bay** 1:00
Oct. 5   at Denver 2:05
Oct. 12 **Carolina** 1:00
Oct. 19 **Seattle** 8:15
Oct. 26 at Dallas 12:00
Nov. 2   at Kansas City 12:00
Nov. 9   BYE
Nov. 16 **Minnesota** 1:00
Nov. 23 at Detroit 1:00
Nov. 30 **New Orleans** 1:00
Dec. 8   at Carolina (Mon.) 8:30
Dec. 14 at Atlanta 1:00
Dec. 21 **San Diego** * 8:15
Dec. 28 **Oakland** 1:00
Sunday night games in Weeks 11-17 subject to change

Stadium: Raymond James Stadium
(opened in 1998)
• **Capacity:** 65,908
Tampa, Florida 33607
Playing Surface: Grass
Training Camp: Disney's Wide World of
Sports
Lake Buena Vista, Florida
92830

RAYMOND JAMES STADIUM

CLUB OFFICIALS
Owner/President: Malcolm Glazer
Executive Vice President: Bryan Glazer
Executive Vice President: Joel Glazer
Executive Vice President: Edward Glazer
General Manager: Bruce Allen
Director of Business Administration:
Brian Ford
Director of Football Operations:
Mark Arteaga
Director of College Scouting:
Dennis Hickey
Director of Pro Personnel: Mark Dominik
Personnel Executive: Doug Williams
General Counsel: Roxanne Kosarzycki
Director of Player Development:
Eric Vance
National College Scout: Jim Abrams
College Scouts: Reggie Cobb,
Frank Dorazio, Dominic Green,
Thomas Throckmorton, Seth Turner
National Combine Scout: Byron Kiefer
Pro Scout: Shelton Quarles
Director of Accounting: Anne Ansley
Director of Community Relations:
Miray Holmes
Director of Marketing and Business
Development: Jeff Ajluni
Director of Public Relations: Jeff Kamis
Director of Security and Facilities:
Andre Trescastro
Director of Special Events and Team
Operations: Killeen Mullen
Director of Ticketing and Sales:
Jason Layton
Broadcasting Operations Manager:
Jeff Ryan
Director of Creative Services:
Darren Morgan
Website Manager: Scott Smith
Public Relations Manager: Jason Wahlers
Trainer: Todd Toriscelli
Director of Rehabilitation:
Shannon Merrick
Equipment Manager: James Sorenson
Assistant Equipment Manager:
Larry Hoyt
Video Director: Dave Levy
Assistant Video Director: Chris Bryan

COACHING HISTORY
(202-312-1)
Records include postseason games

1976-1984	John McKay	45-91-1
1985-86	Leeman Bennett	4-28-0
1987-1990	Ray Perkins*	19-41-0
1990-91	Richard Williamson	4-15-0
1992-95	Sam Wyche	23-41-0
1996-2001	Tony Dungy	56-46-0
2002-07	Jon Gruden	51-50-0

*Released after 13 games in 1990

PAID ATTENDANCE
Home 491,951   Away 524,264
Total 1,016,215
Single-game home record,
73,523 (12/7/97)
Single-season home record,
545,980 (1979)

2008 DRAFT CHOICES

Round	Name	Pos.	College
1	Aqib Talib	DB	Kansas
2	Dexter Jackson	WR	Appalachian St.
3	Jeremy Zuttah	G	Rutgers
4	Dre Moore	DT	Maryland
5	Josh Johnson	QB	San Diego
6	Geno Hayes	LB	Florida State
7	Cory Boyd	RB	South Carolina

2007 TEAM RECORD

PRESEASON (3-1)

Date	Result	Opponent
8/10	W 13-10	New England
8/18	L 19-31	at Jacksonville
8/25	W 31-28	at Miami
8/30	W 31-24	Houston

REGULAR SEASON (9-7)

Date	Result	Opponent	Att.
9/9	L 6-20	at Seattle	68,044
9/16	W 31-14	New Orleans	65,178
9/23	W 24-3	St. Louis	65,267
9/30	W 20-7	at Carolina	73,707
10/7	L 14-33	at Indianapolis	57,202
10/14	W 13-10	Tennessee	65,347
10/21	L 16-23	at Detroit	60,442
10/28	L 23-24	Jacksonville	65,133
11/4	W 17-10	Arizona	65,267
11/18	W 31-7	at Atlanta	69,480
11/25	W 19-13	Washington	65,596
12/2	W 27-23	at New Orleans	70,009
12/9	L 14-28	at Houston	70,237
12/16	W 37-3	Atlanta	65,133
12/23	L 19-21	at San Francisco	68,193
12/30	L 23-31	Carolina	65,609

POSTSEASON (0-1)

1/6	L 14-24	N.Y. Giants	65,621

SCORE BY PERIODS

Buccaneers	84	109	72	69	0	—	334
Opponents	51	66	55	98	0	—	270

2007 TEAM STATISTICS

	Buccaneers	Opp.
Total First Downs	281	258
Rushing	98	93
Passing	162	158
Penalty	21	7
3rd Down: Made/Att	82/213	92/224
3rd Down Pct.	38.5	41.1
4th Down: Made/Att	5/13	9/16
4th Down Pct.	38.5	56.3
Possession Avg.	30:27	29:33
Total Net Yards	5229	4454
Avg. Per Game	326.8	278.4
Total Plays	975	977
Avg. Per Play	5.4	4.6
Net Yards Rushing	1872	1726
Avg. Per Game	117.0	107.9
Total Rushes	449	454
Net Yards Passing	3357	2728
Avg. Per Game	209.8	170.5
Sacked/Yards Lost	36/222	33/207
Gross Yards	3579	2935
Att./Completions	490/316	490/297
Completion Pct.	64.5	60.6
Had Intercepted	8	16
Punts/Average	78/43.4	83/43.5
Net Punting Avg.	78/37.2	83/38.3
Penalties/Yards	81/614	86/706
Fumbles/Ball Lost	18/12	31/19
Touchdowns	36	32
Rushing	15	11
Passing	18	18
Returns	3	3

2007 INDIVIDUAL STATISTICS

PASSING

	Att.	Comp.	Yds.	Pct.	TD	Int.	Tkld.	Rate
Garcia	327	209	2440	63.9	13	4	19/104	94.6
McCown	139	94	1009	67.6	5	3	15/104	91.7
Gradkowski	24	13	130	54.2	0	1	2/14	52.4
Buccaneers	490	316	3579	64.5	18	8	36/222	91.7
Opponents	490	297	2935	60.6	18	16	33/207	76.2

SCORING

	TD R	TD P	TD Rt	PAT	FG	Saf	PTS
Bryant	0	0	0	34/34	28/33	0	118
Graham	10	0	0	0/0	0/0	0	60
Galloway	0	6	0	0/0	0/0	0	36
Stevens	0	4	0	0/0	0/0	0	24
A. Smith	0	3	0	0/0	0/0	0	18
Williams	3	0	0	0/0	0/0	0	18
Barber	0	0	2	0/0	0/0	0	12
Becht	0	2	0	0/0	0/0	0	12
M. Bennett	1	1	0	0/0	0/0	0	12
Garcia	1	0	0	0/0	0/0	0	6
Hilliard	0	1	0	0/0	0/0	0	6
Spurlock	0	0	1	0/0	0/0	0	6
Stovall	0	1	0	0/0	0/0	0	6
Buccaneers	15	18	3	34/34	28/33	0	334
Opponents	11	18	3	31/32	15/18	1	270

2-Pt. Conversions: Buccaneers 0-2
Opponents 0-0

RUSHING

	No.	Yds	Avg	LG	TD
Graham	222	898	4.0	28t	10
Pittman	68	286	4.2	29	0
Williams	54	208	3.9	20	3
M. Bennett	41	189	4.6	28	1
McCown	12	117	9.8	31	0
Garcia	35	116	3.3	21	1
Clayton	5	22	4.4	20	0
Gradkowski	7	20	2.9	13	0
Darby	2	9	4.5	7	0
Hilliard	1	6	6.0	6	0
Galloway	1	1	1.0	1	0
Crockett	1	0	0.0	0	0
Buccaneers	449	1872	4.2	31	15
Opponents	454	1726	3.8	32t	11

RECEIVING

	No.	Yds	Avg	LG	TD
Hilliard	62	722	11.6	56	1
Galloway	57	1014	17.8	69t	6
Graham	49	324	6.6	21	0
A. Smith	32	385	12.0	33	3
Pittman	26	191	7.3	16	0
Clayton	22	301	13.7	39	0
Stevens	18	189	10.5	24t	4
Askew	18	175	9.7	22	0
Stovall	10	86	8.6	13	1
C. Lucas	5	82	16.4	52	0
M. Bennett	5	54	10.8	23t	1
Becht	5	20	4.0	9	2
Williams	3	17	5.7	8	0
Darby	2	16	8.0	9	0
Storer	2	3	1.5	2	0
Buccaneers	316	3579	11.3	69t	18
Opponents	297	2935	9.9	58	18

INTERCEPTIONS

	No.	Yds	Avg	LG	TD
Phillips	4	2	0.5	2	0
Buchanon	3	22	7.3	19	0
Barber	2	32	16.0	29t	1
Jackson	2	26	13.0	26	0
Ruud	2	7	3.5	5	0
Kelly	2	0	0.0	0	0
June	1	0	0.0	0	0
Buccaneers	16	89	5.6	29t	1
Opponents	8	167	20.9	62	2

PUNTING

	No.	Yds.	Avg.	In 20	LG
Bidwell	77	3382	43.9	30	61
Buccaneers	78	3382	43.4	30	61
Opponents	83	3613	43.5	26	76

PUNT RETURNS

	Ret	FC	Yds	Avg	LG	TD
Buchanon	16	0	55	3.4	24	0
Hilliard	15	4	92	6.1	20	0
Jones	12	6	143	11.9	35	0
Spurlock	4	3	30	7.5	15	0
Galloway	3	0	14	4.7	10	0
Buccaneers	50	13	334	6.7	35	0
Opponents	38	11	280	7.4	56	0

KICKOFF RETURNS

	No.	Yds	Avg	LG	TD
Spurlock	16	444	27.8	90t	1
Jones	10	286	28.6	36	0
Clayton	8	172	21.5	26	0
Graham	4	90	22.5	31	0
Buchanon	2	15	7.5	16	0
Cox	2	41	20.5	27	0
Darby	2	11	5.5	14	0
C. Lucas	2	35	17.5	18	0
Hilliard	1	3	3.0	3	0
Stovall	1	22	22.0	22	0
Buccaneers	48	1119	23.3	90t	1
Opponents	68	1328	19.5	97t	1

FIELD GOALS

	1-19	20-29	30-39	40-49	50+
Bryant	0/0	11/12	11/11	6/7	0/3
Buccaneers	0/0	11/12	11/11	6/7	0/3
Opponents	1/1	3/3	5/6	6/8	0/0

SACKS

	No.
White	8.0
Adams	6.0
Haye	6.0
Carter	3.0
Spires	2.0
Hovan	1.5
Peterson	1.5
Barber	1.0
Chukwurah	1.0
Phillips	1.0
Sims	1.0
(group)	1.0
Buccaneers	33.0
Opponents	36.0

RECORD HOLDERS
INDIVIDUAL RECORDS—CAREER

Category	Name	Performance
Rushing (Yds.)	James Wilder, 1981-89	5,957
Passing (Yds.)	Vinny Testaverde, 1987-1992	14,820
Passing (TDs)	Vinny Testaverde, 1987-1992	77
Receiving (No.)	James Wilder, 1981-89	430
Receiving (Yds.)	Mark Carrier, 1987-1992	5,018
Interceptions	Ronde Barber, 1997-2007	33
Punting (Avg.)	Josh Bidwell, 2004-07	43.8
Punt Return (Avg.)	Jacquez Green, 1998-2001	12.0
Kickoff Return (Avg.)	Aaron Stecker, 2000-03	23.8
Field Goals	Martín Gramatica, 1999-2004	137
Touchdowns (Tot.)	Mike Alstott, 1996-2006	71
Points	Martín Gramatica, 1999-2004	592

INDIVIDUAL RECORDS—SINGLE SEASON

Category	Name	Performance
Rushing (Yds.)	James Wilder, 1984	1,544
Passing (Yds.)	Brad Johnson, 2003	3,811
Passing (TDs)	Brad Johnson, 2003	26
Receiving (No.)	Keyshawn Johnson, 2001	106
Receiving (Yds.)	Mark Carrier, 1989	1,422
Interceptions	Ronde Barber, 2001	10
Punting (Avg.)	Josh Bidwell, 2005	45.6
Punt Return (Avg.)	Karl Williams, 1996	21.1
Kickoff Return (Avg.)	Mark Jones, 2007	28.6
Field Goals	Martín Gramatica, 2002	32
Touchdowns (Tot.)	James Wilder, 1984	13
Points	Martín Gramatica, 2002	128

INDIVIDUAL RECORDS—SINGLE GAME

Category	Name	Performance
Rushing (Yds.)	James Wilder, 11-6-83	219
Passing (Yds.)	Doug Williams, 11-16-80	486
Passing (TDs)	Steve DeBerg, 9-13-87	5
	Brad Johnson, 11-3-02	5
Receiving (No.)	James Wilder, 9-15-85	13
	Earnest Graham, 10-21-07	13
Receiving (Yds.)	Mark Carrier, 12-6-87	212
Interceptions	Ronde Barber, 12-23-01, 12-4-05	3
Field Goals	Martín Gramatica, 12-29-02	5
Touchdowns (Tot.)	Jimmie Giles, 10-20-85	4
Points	Jimmie Giles, 10-20-85	24

2008 VETERAN ROSTER

No.	Name	Pos.	Ht.	Wt.	Age	NFL Exp.	College	Hometown	How Acq.	'07 Games/ Starts
90	Adams, Gaines	DE	6-5	258	25	2	Clemson	Greenwood, S.C.	D1-'07	16/8
26	Allen, Will	S	6-1	200	26	5	Ohio State	Dayton, Ohio	D4-'04	15/0
35	Askew, B.J.	FB	6-3	233	28	6	Michigan	Cincinnati, Ohio	UFA(NYJ)-'07	13/9
20	Barber, Ronde	CB	5-10	184	33	12	Virginia	Roanoke, Va.	D3b-'97	16/16
92	Bennett, Charles	DE	6-3	254	25	3	Clemson	Camden, S.C.	D7a-'06	0*
29	Bennett, Michael	RB	5-9	207	30	8	Wisconsin	Milwaukee, Wisc.	T(KC)-'07	14/1*
10	Biddle, Taye	WR	6-1	185	25	2	Mississippi	Decatur, Ala.	W(Car)-'07	0*
9	Bidwell, Josh	P	6-3	220	32	9	Oregon	Winston, Ore.	UFA(GB)-'04	16/0
58	Black, Quincy	LB	6-2	240	24	2	New Mexico	Chicago, Ill.	D3-'07	15/0
55	Brooks, Derrick	LB	6-0	235	35	14	Florida State	Pensacola, Fla.	D1b-'95	16/16
89	Bryant, Antonio	WR	6-1	191	27	6	Pittsburgh	Miami, Fla.	FA-'08	0*
3	Bryant, Matt	K	5-9	200	33	7	Baylor	Orange, Texas	FA-'05	16/0
31	Buchanon, Phillip	CB	5-11	186	27	7	Miami	Ft. Myers, Fla.	FA-'06	16/13
72	Buenning, Dan	G	6-4	320	26	4	Wisconsin	Green Bay, Wisc.	D4-'05	0
93	Carter, Kevin	DE/DT	6-6	305	34	14	Florida	Tallahassee, Fla.	FA-'07	16/14
50	Cash, Antoine	LB	6-1	223	26	3	Southern Mississippi	Anguilla, Miss.	FA-'05	0*
54	Chukwurah, Patrick	DE/LB	6-1	250	29	7	Wyoming	Irving, Texas	UFA(Den)-'07	9/0
18	Clark, Brian	WR	6-2	204	24	2	North Carolina State	Tampa, Fla.	FA-'07	5/0*
80	Clayton, Michael	WR	6-4	215	25	5	Louisiana State	Baton Rouge, La.	D1-'04	14/4
27	Cox, Torrie	CB	5-10	192	27	6	Pittsburgh	Miami, Fla.	D6-'03	4/0
69	Davis, Anthony	G/T	6-4	322	28	5	Virginia Tech	Victoria, Va.	FA-'03	9/0
22	Davis, Sammy	CB	6-1	195	28	6	Texas A&M	Humble, Texas	FA-'07	14/1
74	Denman, Chris	T	6-7	315	24	2	Fresno State	Tehachapi, Calif.	D7a-'07	0*
94	Douglas, Marques	DE	6-2	292	31	8	Howard	Greensboro, N.C.	UFA(SF)-'08	16/16*
28	Dunn, Warrick	RB	5-9	187	33	12	Florida State	Baton Rouge, La.	FA-'08	16/15*
48	Economos, Andrew	LS	6-1	250	26	3	Georgia Tech	Atlanta, Ga.	FA-'06	16/0
52	Faine, Jeff	C	6-3	291	27	6	Notre Dame	Sanford, Fla.	UFA(NO)-'08	14/14*
46	Fells, Daniel	TE	6-4	252	24	2	Cal-Davis	Fullerton, Calif.	FA-'08	0*
84	Galloway, Joey	WR	5-11	197	36	14	Ohio State	Bellaire, Ohio	T(DAL)-'04	15/15
7	Garcia, Jeff	QB	6-1	205	38	10	San Jose State	Gilroy, Calif.	UFA(Phil)-'07	13/13
88	Gilmore, John	TE	6-5	257	28	7	Penn State	West Lawn, Pa.	UFA(Chi)-'07	15/1*
5	Gradkowski, Bruce	QB	6-1	220	25	3	Toledo	Pittsburgh, Pa.	D6a-'06	4/0
34	Graham, Earnest	RB	5-9	225	28	5	Florida	Ft. Myers, Fla.	FA-'03	15/10
8	t-Griese, Brian	QB	6-3	214	33	11	Michigan	Miami, Fla.	T(Chi)-'08	7/6*
14	Hankton, Cortez	WR	6-0	200	27	5	Texas Southern	New Orleans, La.	FA-'08	0*
71	Haye, Jovan	DT	6-2	285	26	4	Vanderbilt	Ft. Lauderdale, Fla.	FA-'06	16/16
57	Hayward, Adam	LB	6-0	235	24	2	Portland State	Westminster, Calif.	D6-'07	12/0
87	Heinrich, Keith	TE	6-6	255	29	6	Sam Houston State	Tomball, Texas	FA-'06	4/0
19	Hilliard, Ike	WR	5-11	210	32	12	Florida	Patterson, La.	FA-'05	15/1
95	Hovan, Chris	DT	6-2	296	30	9	Boston College	Rocky River, Ohio	FA-'05	16/16
36	Jackson, Tanard	S	6-0	200	23	2	Syracuse	Potomac, Md.	D4-'07	16/16
49	Joe, Leon	LB	6-1	235	26	5	Maryland	Xenia, Ohio	UFA(Buff)-'08	8/0*
75	Joseph, Davin	G	6-3	313	24	3	Oklahoma	Hallandale, Fla.	D1-'06	16/16
59	June, Cato	LB	6-0	227	28	6	Michigan	Washington, D.C.	UFA(Ind)-'07	16/14
53	Lehman, Teddy	LB	6-2	238	26	5	Oklahoma	Fort Gibson, Okla.	UFA(Det)-'08	16/0*
12	McCown, Luke	QB	6-3	212	27	5	Louisiana Tech	Jacksonville, Texas	T(Cle)-'05	5/3
41	McCoy, Matt	LB	5-11	230	25	4	San Diego State	Tustin, Calif.	UFA(NO)-'08	4/0*
56	Nece, Ryan	LB	6-3	224	29	7	UCLA	San Bernardino, Calif.	FA-'02	15/0
30	Nicholson, Donte	S	6-1	216	26	2	Oklahoma	Diamond Bar, Calif.	D5a-'05	1/0
70	Penn, Donald	T	6-5	305	25	3	Utah State	Playa Del Rey, Calif.	FA-'06	16/12
96	Peterson, Greg	DT	6-5	286	24	2	North Carolina Central	East Duplin, N.C.	D5-'07	10/0
77	Petitgout, Luke	T	6-6	310	32	10	Notre Dame	Georgetown, Del.	FA-'07	4/4
23	Phillips, Jermaine	S	6-2	220	29	7	Georgia	Roswell, Ga.	D5-'02	15/15
21	Piscitelli, Sabby	S	6-3	224	25	2	Oregon State	Boca Raton, Fla.	D2b-'07	3/0
51	Ruud, Barrett	LB	6-2	241	25	4	Nebraska	Lincoln, Neb.	D2-'05	15/15
78	Sears, Arron	G	6-3	319	23	2	Tennessee	Russellville, Ala.	D2a-'07	16/16
2	Simms, Chris	QB	6-4	220	28	6	Texas	Ramapo, N.J.	D3-'03	0*
98	Sims, Ryan	DT	6-4	315	28	7	North Carolina	Spartanburg, S.C.	T(KC)-'07	9/0
81	Smith, Alex	TE	6-4	258	26	4	Stanford	Denver, Colo.	D3a-'05	14/14
17	Spurlock, Micheal	WR	5-10	214	25	2	Mississippi	Indianola, Miss.	FA-'07	7/0
44	Storer, Byron	FB	6-1	219	24	2	California	Modesto, Calif.	FA-'07	9/3
85	Stovall, Maurice	WR	6-5	220	23	3	Notre Dame	Philadelphia, Pa.	D3-'06	15/1
83	Troupe, Ben	TE	6-4	270	26	5	Florida	Augusta, Ga.	UFA(Tenn)-'08	16/2*
65	Trueblood, Jeremy	T	6-8	320	25	3	Boston College	Indianapolis, Ind.	D2-'06	16/16
82	Warren, Paris	WR	6-0	213	25	4	Utah	Sacramento, Calif.	D7b-'05	0*

No.	Name	Pos.	Ht.	Wt.	Age	NFL Exp.	College	Hometown	How Acq.	'07 Games/ Starts
91	White, Greg	DE	6-3	270	29	2	Minnesota	Newark, N.J.	FA-'07	16/2
97	Wilkerson, Jimmy	DL	6-2	290	27	6	Oklahoma	Naples, Texas	UFA(KC)-'08	16/2*
24	Williams, Carnell	RB	5-11	217	26	4	Auburn	Attalla, Ala.	D1-'05	4/4
38	Wilson, Eugene	DB	5-10	195	28	6	Illinois	Merrillville, Ind.	UFA(NE)-'08	11/6*

* C. Bennett missed '07 season because of injury; M. Bennett played 6 games with Kansas City and eight games with Tampa Bay in '07; Biddle last active with Carolina in '06; A. Bryant last active with San Francisco in '06; Cash missed '07 season because of injury; Clark played 4 games with Denver and 1 game with Tampa Bay; Denman missed '07 season because of injury; Douglas played 16 games with San Francisco; Dunn played 16 games with Atlanta; Faine played 14 games with New Orleans; Fells inactive for 16 games with Atlanta in '06; Gilmore played 15 games with Chicago; Griese played 7 games with Chicago; Hankton last active with Jacksonville in '06; Joe played 8 games with Buffalo; Lehman played 16 games with Detroit; McCoy played 4 games with New Orleans; Simms inactive for 5 games in '07; Troupe played 16 games with Tennessee; Warren missed '07 season because of injury; Wilkerson played 16 games with Kansas City; Wilson played 11 games with New England.

t- Buccaneers traded for Griese (Chi).

Retired-Mike Alstott, 12-year fullback, missed '07 season because of injury.

Players lost through free agency (4): TE Anthony Becht (StL; 16 games in '07), CB Brian Kelly (Det; 11), C/G Matt Lehr (NO; 16), C John Wade (Oak; 16).

Also played with Buccaneers '07—FB Zack Crockett (1 game), RB Lionel Gates (1), WR Chas Gessner (1), WR Mark Jones (6), S Kalvin Pearson (16), RB Michael Pittman (10), DE Greg Spires (10), TE Jerramy Stevens (15), LB Jeremiah Trotter (3).

2008 FIRST-YEAR ROSTER

Name	Pos.	Ht.	Wt.	Age	College	Hometown	How Acq.
Boyd, Cory	RB	6-1	218	23	South Carolina	Orange, N.J.	D7
Bradwell, Chris	DT	6-4	280	24	Troy	Johns Creek, Ga.	FA
Clark, Chris	T	6-5	290	22	Southern Mississippi	New Orleans, La.	FA
Darby, Kenneth (1)	RB	5-10	211	25	Alabama	Huntsville, Ala.	D7c-'07
Gunn, Marquies (1)	DE	6-4	264	24	Auburn	Alexander City, Ala.	FA-'07
Hamilton, Marcus (1)	CB	5-11	188	24	Virginia	Centreville, Va.	D7b-'07
Hayes, Geno	LB	6-1	226	21	Florida State	Greenville, Fla.	D6
Hefney, Jonathan	CB	5-9	185	23	Tennessee	Rock Hill, S.C.	FA
Hunter, Darrell (1)	CB	5-11	211	24	Miami (Ohio)	Middletown, Ohio	FA-'07
Jackson, Amarri	WR	6-5	202	23	South Florida	Sarasota, Fla.	FA
Jackson, Dexter	WR	5-9	182	22	Appalachian State	Dunwoody, Ga.	D2
Johnson, Brian (1)	G	6-4	307	24	Louisiana State	Godby, Fla.	FA-'07
Johnson, Josh	QB	6-2	201	22	San Diego	Oakland, Calif.	D5
Lucas, Chad (1)	WR	6-1	201	26	Alabama State	Tuskegee, Ala.	FA-'06
Mack, Elbert	CB	5-10	175	22	Troy	Wichita, Kan.	FA
Moore, Dre	DT	6-4	305	23	Maryland	Charlotte, N.C.	D4
Rochford, John	C	6-2	273	24	Miami	Linwood, N.J.	FA
Roland, Dennis (1)	T	6-9	325	25	Georgia	Bolivar, Mo.	FA-'06
Smith, Clifton	RB	5-8	180	23	Fresno State	Huntington Beach, Calif.	FA
Spiller, Charles (1)	WR	6-0	183	23	Alcorn State	Woodville, Miss.	FA
Stewart, Carl	FB	6-3	254	23	Auburn	Maryville, Tenn.	FA
Talib, Aqib	CB	6-1	205	22	Kansas	Richardson, Texas	D1
Thompson, Tyrice	TE	6-5	220	23	Arizona State	Phoenix, Ariz.	FA
Zuttah, Jeremy	OL	6-4	303	22	Rutgers	Edison, N.J.	D3

The term NFL Rookie is defined as a player who is in his first season of professional football and has not been on the roster of another professional football team for any regular-season or postseason games. A Rookie is designated by an "R" on NFL rosters. Players who have been active in another professional football league or players who have NFL experience, including either preseason training camp or being on an Active List or Inactive List, or on Reserve/Injured or Reserve/Physically Unable to Perform for fewer than six regular-season games, are termed NFL First-Year Players. An NFL First-Year Player is designated by a "1" on NFL rosters. Thereafter, a player is credited with an additional year of experience for each season in which he accumulates six games on the Active List or Inactive List, or on Reserve/Injured or Reserve/Physically Unable to Perform.

Log on to www.buccaneers.com for an up-to-date roster; Age listed is as of September 4, 2008.

COACHING STAFF

Head Coach,
Jon Gruden

Pro Career: Gruden was named the seventh head coach in Buccaneers history on February 18, 2002, when he signed a five-year contract. Gruden led Tampa Bay to its first Super Bowl title in his first season as head coach in 2002. Gruden set two NFL records—he became the youngest head coach (39) to win a Super Bowl, and was the first veteran head coach to lead his team to the Super Bowl in his first season with a new team. In 2007, the Buccaneers won the NFC South for the third time in five seasons. Prior to joining the Buccaneers, Gruden guided the Oakland Raiders to division titles in each of his final two seasons. He steered the Raiders to a 40-28 mark in four seasons (1998-2001), with postseason appearances in 2000 and 2001. Under Gruden, the Raiders advanced to the AFC title game in 2000 and in 2001 lost a divisional playoff game to eventual Super Bowl champion New England. Prior to his four seasons in Oakland, Gruden spent 1995-97 as offensive coordinator for the Philadelphia Eagles and three years (1992-94) as wide receivers coach for Green Bay Packers. He worked as offensive assistant for the San Francisco 49ers in 1990. Career record: 91-78.

Background: Quarterback at Dayton (1982-84), graduating with a degree in communications. The Flyers had a 24-7 record in Gruden's three varsity seasons. Coach collegiately at Tennessee (1986-87), Southeast Missouri State (1988), Pacific (1989), and Pittsburgh (1991).

Personal: Age 45, born in Sandusky, Ohio. Jon and his wife Cindy, have three sons, Jon II, Michael, and Jayson.

ASSISTANT COACHES

Tim Berbenich, asst. running backs; born Huntington, N.Y. Wide receiver Hamilton College 1998-2001. No pro playing experience. Pro coach: New York Jets 2003-05, joined Buccaneers in 2006.

Richard Bisaccia, associate head coach/special teams/running backs; born Yonkers, N.Y. Defensive back Yankton College 1979-1982, Philadelphia Stars (USFL) 1983. College coach: Wayne State College 1983-87, South Carolina 1988-1993, Clemson 1994-98, Mississippi 1999-2001. Pro coach: Joined Buccaneers in 2002.

Casey Bradley, linebackers; born Zumbrota, Minn. Safety/punter North Dakota State 1984-1988. No pro playing experience. College coach: North Dakota State 1990-1991, 1996-2005, Fort Lewis College 1992-1996. Pro coach: Joined Buccaneers in 2006.

Bob Casullo, tight ends; born Little Falls, N.Y. Running back Brockport (N.Y.) State College 1970-73. No pro playing experience. College coach: Syracuse 1985-

1994, Georgia Tech 1995-98, Michigan State 1999. Pro coach: Oakland Raiders 2000-03, New York Jets 2004, Seattle Seahawks 2005-06, joined Buccaneers in 2007.

Larry Coyer, asst. head coach; born Huntington, W. Va. Linebacker Marshall 1962-64. No pro playing experience. College coach: Marshall 1965-67, Iowa 1974-77, Oklahoma State 1978, Iowa State 1979-1983, 1995-96, UCLA 1987-89, Houston 1990, Ohio State 1991-92, East Carolina 1993, Pittsburgh 1997-99. Pro coach: Michigan Panthers (USFL) 1984-85, New York Jets 1994, Denver Broncos 2000-06, joined Buccaneers in 2007.

Ejiro Evero, defensive quality control; born Colchester, England. Safety California-Davis 2000-2003. No pro playing experience. College coach: California-Davis 2005-2006. Pro coach: Joined Buccaneers in 2007.

Jay Gruden, offensive assistant; Quarterback Louisville 1985-88. Pro quarterback Tampa Bay Storm (AFL) 1991-96, Orlando Predators (AFL) 2002-03. Pro coach: Nashville Kats (AFL) 1997, Orlando Predators (AFL) 1998-2001, 2004-06, joined Buccaneers in 2002.

Monte Kiffin, defensive coordinator; born Lexington, Neb. Offensive/defensive tackle Nebraska 1959-1963. Pro defensive end Winnipeg Blue Bombers (CFL) 1965. College coach: Nebraska 1966-1976, Arkansas 1977-79, North Carolina State 1980-82 (head coach). Pro coach: Green Bay Packers 1983, Buffalo Bills 1984-85, Minnesota Vikings 1986-89, 1991-94, New York Jets 1990, New Orleans Saints 1995, joined Buccaneers in 1996.

Richard Mann, wide receivers; born Aliquippa, Pa. Wide receiver Arizona State 1966-68. No pro playing experience. College coach: Arizona State 1974-79, Louisville 1980-81. Pro coach: Baltimore/Indianapolis Colts 1982-84, Cleveland Browns 1985-1993, New York Jets 1994-96, Baltimore Ravens 1997-98, Kansas City Chiefs 1999-2000, Washington Redskins 2001, joined Buccaneers in 2002.

Mike Morris, head strength and conditioning; born Ayer, Mass. Wide receiver Syracuse 1981-85. No pro playing experience. Pro coach: New England Patriots 1997-99, joined Buccaneers in 2002.

Raheem Morris, defensive backs; born Irvington, N.J. Safety Hofstra 1994-97. No pro playing experience. College coach: Hofstra 1998, 2000-2001, Cornell 1999, Kansas State 2006. Pro coach: New York Jets 2001, Tampa Bay Buccaneers 2002-05, re-joined Buccaneers in 2007.

Bill Muir, offensive coordinator/offensive line; born Pittsburgh. Tackle Susquehanna 1962-64. No pro playing experience. College coach: Susquehanna 1965, Delaware Valley 1966-67, Rhode Island 1970-71, Idaho State 1972-73, Southern

Methodist 1976-77. Pro coach: Orlando (Continental Football League) 1968-69, Houston Shreveport Steamer (WFL) 1975, New England Patriots 1982-88, Indianapolis Colts 1989-1991, Philadelphia Eagles 1992-94, New York Jets 1995-2001, joined Buccaneers in 2002.

Greg Olson, quarterbacks; born Richland, Wash. Quarterback, Spokane Falls (Wash.) J.C. 1981-82. No pro playing experience. College coach: Washington State 1987-1989, Central Washington 1990-1993, Idaho 1994-1996, Purdue 1997-2000, 2002. Pro coach: San Francisco 49ers 2001, Chicago Bears 2003, Detroit Lions 2004-2005, St. Louis Rams 2006-2007, joined Buccaneers in 2008.

Kurt Shultz, asst. strength and conditioning; born Baltimore. Attended Maryland. No college or pro playing experience. College coach: Loyola (Md.) 1995-98, Maryland and Johns Hopkins 1999-2002. Pro coach: Cincinnati Bengals 2003, Minnesota Vikings 2004-05, joined Buccaneers in 2006.

Dwayne Stukes, special teams quality; born Portsmith, Va. Cornerback/safety Virginia 1996-1999. Pro safety Berlin Thunder (NFL Europe) 2001-2002, Colorado Crush (AFL) 2004. Pro coach: Joined Buccaneers in 2006.

Todd Wash, defensive line; born Miles City, Mont. Linebacker North Dakota State 1988-1991. No pro playing experience. College coach: Fort Lewis College 1996-99, Nebraska-Kearney 2000-01, North Dakota State 2002-03, 2005-06, Missouri Southern State 2004. Pro coach: Joined Buccaneers in 2006.

George Yarno, asst. offensive line, born Spokane, Wash. Offensive line Washington State 1975-1978. Pro offensive line Tampa Bay Buccaneers 1979-1983, 1985-1987, Denver Gold (USFL) 1984-1985, Atlanta Falcons 1988, Houston Oilers 1989, Green Bay 1990. College coach: Louisiana State 2001-2002, Washington State 2003-2007. Pro coach: Joined Buccaneers in 2008.

**National Football Conference
East Division
Team Colors:** Burgundy and Gold
**Redskins Park
21300 Redskins Park Drive
Ashburn, Virginia 20147
Telephone: (703) 726-7000**

2008 SCHEDULE
PRESEASON
Aug. 3   vs. Indianapolis at Canton, OH .8:00
Aug. 9   **Buffalo**...............................7:00
Aug. 16 at N.Y. Jets 7:00
Aug. 23 at Carolina...........................7:30
Aug. 28 **Jacksonville**......................7:00

REGULAR SEASON
Sep. 4   at N.Y. Giants (Thu.) 7:00
Sep. 14 **New Orleans** 1:00
Sep. 21 **Arizona** 1:00
Sep. 28 at Dallas 3:15
Oct. 5   at Philadelphia 1:00
Oct. 12 **St. Louis** 1:00
Oct. 19 **Cleveland** 4:15
Oct. 26 at Detroit 1:00
Nov. 3   **Pittsburgh** (Mon.) 8:30
Nov. 9   BYE
Nov. 16 **Dallas** * 8:15
Nov. 23 at Seattle 1:15
Nov. 30 **N.Y. Giants**.......................1:00
Dec. 7   at Baltimore 1:00
Dec. 14 at Cincinnati 1:00
Dec. 21 **Philadelphia** 1:00
Dec. 28 at San Francisco 1:15
Sunday night games in Weeks 11-17 subject to change

Stadium: FedExField (opened in 1997)
     • **Capacity:** 91,704
     1600 FedEx Way
     Landover, Maryland 20785
Playing Surface: Natural Grass
Training Camp: Redskins Park
           Ashburn, Virginia 20147

FEDEXFIELD

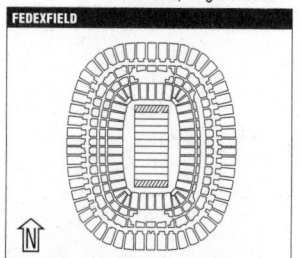

CLUB OFFICIALS
Owner: Daniel M. Snyder
Chief Operating Officer: Mitch Gershman
Chief Financial Officer: Jay Sloan
Executive Vice President, Football
     Operations: Vinny Cerrato
General Counsel: Dave Donovan
Senior Vice President: Karl Swanson
Senior Vice President, Marketing:
     Janice Schmidt
Senior Vice President, Stadium
     Operations: Michael Dillow
Director of Ticket Operations: Matt King
Director of Player Personnel:
     Scott Campbell
Director of Pro Personnel: Louis Riddick
Pro Scout: Donnie Warren
College Scouts: Chip Flanagan,
     Tim Gribble, Shemy Schembechler,
     Jim Zeches
National Scouts: Russ Bolinger,
     Joel Patten
Vice President, Football Administration:
     Eric Schaffer
Director of Player Development:
     John "JJ" Jefferson
Executive Director of Communications:
     Zack Bolno
Leadership Council/Community Affairs:
     BJ Corriveau
Director of Team Administration:
     Derrick Crawford
Video Director: Mike Bracken
Video Department: Todd Davis,
     George Claiborne
Director of Sports Medicine: Bubba Tyer
Head Athletic Trainer: John Burrell
Assistant Athletic Trainers: Eric Steward,
     Larry Hess, Elliott Jermyn
Equipment Manager: Brad Berlin
Assistant Equipment Manager:
     Anders Beutel, Chris Collins

COACHING HISTORY
**Boston 1932-36
(552-503-27)**
Records include postseason games

1932	Lud Wray	4-4-2
1933-34	William (Lone Star) Dietz	11-11-2
1935	Eddie Casey	2-8-1
1936-1942	Ray Flaherty	56-23-3
1943	Arthur (Dutch) Bergman	7-4-1
1944-45	Dudley DeGroot	14-6-1
1946-48	Glen (Turk) Edwards	16-18-1
1949	John Whelchel*	3-3-1
1949-1951	Herman Ball**	4-16-0
1951	Dick Todd	5-4-0
1952-53	Earl (Curly) Lambeau	10-13-1
1954-58	Joe Kuharich	26-32-2
1959-1960	Mike Nixon	4-18-2
1961-65	Bill McPeak	21-46-3
1966-68	Otto Graham	17-22-3
1969	Vince Lombardi	7-5-2
1970	Bill Austin	6-8-0
1971-77	George Allen	69-35-1
1978-1980	Jack Pardee	24-24-0
1981-1992	Joe Gibbs	140-65-0
1993	Richie Petitbon	4-12-0
1994-2000	Norv Turner***	50-60-1
2000	Terry Robiskie	1-2-0
2001	Marty Schottenheimer	8-8-0
2002-03	Steve Spurrier	12-20-0
2004-07	Joe Gibbs	31-36-0

     *Released after seven games in 1949
     **Released after three games in 1951
     ***Released after 13 games in 2000

PAID ATTENDANCE
Home 711,471   Away 553,419
Total 1,264,890
Single-game home record,
     90,910 (12/30/07)
Single-season home record,
     * 711,471 (2007)
NFL Record

2008 DRAFT CHOICES
Round	Name	Pos.	College
2	Devin Thomas	WR	Michigan State
	Fred Davis	TE	Southern California
	Malcolm Kelly	WR	Oklahoma
3	Chad Rinehart	T	Northern Iowa
4	Justin Tryon	DB	Arizona State
6	Durant Brooks	P	Georgia Tech
	Kareem Moore	DB	Nicholls State
	Colt Brennan	QB	Hawaii
7	Rob Jackson	DE	Kansas State
	Chris Horton	DB	UCLA

2007 TEAM RECORD

PRESEASON (2-2)

Date	Result	Opponent
8/11	W 14-6	at Tennessee
8/18	L 10-12	Pittsburgh
8/25	W 13-7	Baltimore
8/30	L 14-31	at Jacksonville

REGULAR SEASON (9-7)

Date	Result	Opponent	Att.
9/9	W 16-13	Miami (OT)	90,163
9/17	W 20-12	at Philadelphia	67,726
9/23	L 17-24	New York Giants	90,803
10/7	W 34-3	Detroit	88,944
10/14	L 14-17	at Green Bay	70,761
10/21	W 21-19	Arizona	85,640
10/28	L 7-52	at New England	68,756
11/4	W 23-20	at N.Y. Jets (OT)	76,663
11/11	L 25-33	Philadelphia	90,218
11/18	L 23-28	at Dallas	63,706
11/25	L 13-19	at Tampa Bay	65,596
12/2	L 16-17	Buffalo	85,831
12/6	W 24-16	Chicago	82,213
12/16	W 22-10	at N.Y. Giants	77,899
12/23	W 32-21	at Minnesota	63,634
12/30	W 27-6	Dallas	90,910

(OT) Overtime

POSTSEASON (0-1)

1/5	L 14-35	at Seattle	68,297

SCORE BY PERIODS

Redskins	76	94	55	76	6	—	307
Opponents	69	126	95	80	6	—	376

2007 TEAM STATISTICS

	Redskins	Opp.
Total First Downs	307	291
Rushing	103	89
Passing	192	174
Penalty	12	28
3rd Down: Made/Att	92/226	78/218
3rd Down Pct.	40.7	35.8
4th Down: Made/Att	6/15	10/17
4th Down Pct.	40.0	58.8
Possession Avg.	30:46	29:14
Total Net Yards	5334	4884
Avg. Per Game	333.4	305.3
Total Plays	1052	1026
Avg. Per Play	5.1	4.8
Net Yards Rushing	1871	1460
Avg. Per Game	116.9	91.3
Total Rushes	498	391
Net Yards Passing	3463	3424
Avg. Per Game	216.4	214.0
Sacked/Yards Lost	29/159	33/198
Gross Yards	3622	3622
Att./Completions	525/319	602/351
Completion Pct.	60.8	58.3
Had Intercepted	11	14
Punts/Average	75/41.0	81/43.0
Net Punting Avg.	75/36.4	81/36.9
Penalties/Yards	90/751	88/684
Fumbles/Ball Lost	35/18	27/10
Touchdowns	35	33
Rushing	15	10
Passing	18	20
Returns	2	3

2007 INDIVIDUAL STATISTICS

PASSING	Att.	Comp.	Yds.	Pct.	TD	Int.	Tkld.	Rate
J. Campbell	417	250	2700	60.0	12	11	21/110	77.6
Collins	105	67	888	63.8	5	0	7/47	106.4
Randle El	2	1	19	50.0	0	0	0/0	83.3
Portis	1	1	15	100.0	1	0	1/2	158.3
Redskins	525	319	3622	60.8	18	11	29/159	84.2
Opponents	602	351	3622	58.3	20	14	33/198	77.1

SCORING	TD R	TD P	TD Rt	PAT	FG	Saf	PTS
Suisham	0	0	0	29/30	29/35	0	116
Portis	11	0	0	0/0	0/0	0	66
Cooley	0	8	0	0/0	0/0	0	50
Moss	0	3	0	0/0	0/0	0	18
Sellers	2	1	0	0/0	0/0	0	18
Betts	1	1	0	0/0	0/0	0	12
Thrash	0	2	0	0/0	0/0	0	12
Randle El	0	1	0	0/0	0/0	0	8
J. Campbell	1	0	0	0/0	0/0	0	6
Fletcher	0	0	1	0/0	0/0	0	6
McCardell	0	1	0	0/0	0/0	0	6
Rogers	0	0	1	0/0	0/0	0	6
Yoder	0	1	0	0/0	0/0	0	6
Carter	0	0	0	0/0	0/0	1	2
Golston	0	0	0	0/0	0/0	1	2
Redskins	15	18	2	29/30	29/35	2	334
Opponents	10	20	3	29/30	27/37	1	310

2-Pt. Conversions: Cooley, Randle El, Redskins 2-5, Opponents 0-3

RUSHING	No.	Yds	Avg	LG	TD
Betts	245	1154	4.7	26	4
Portis	127	523	4.1	38t	7
Duckett	38	132	3.5	19	2
Randle El	19	118	6.2	20	0
J. Campbell	24	107	4.5	15	0
Moss	7	82	11.7	35	0
Sellers	12	51	4.3	13	0
Brunell	13	34	2.6	12	0
Cartwright	5	15	3.0	9	0
Redskins	490	2,216	4.5	38t	13
Opponents	492	2,197	4.5	69t	9

RECEIVING	No.	Yds	Avg	LG	TD
Cooley	57	734	12.9	66t	6
Moss	55	790	14.4	68t	6
Betts	53	445	8.4	34	1
Randle El	32	351	11.0	34t	3
Lloyd	23	365	15.9	52	0
Sellers	18	105	5.8	15	1
Portis	17	170	10.0	74	0
Thrash	12	151	12.6	27	1
Fauria	2	17	8.5	11	0
Duckett	2	16	8.0	19	0
Patten	1	25	25.0	25	0
Yoder	1	4	4.0	4t	1
Kozlowski	1	1	1.0	1	0
Redskins	274	3,174	11.6	74	19
Opponents	289	3,586	12.4	84t	30

INTERCEPTIONS	No.	Yds	Avg	LG	TD
Taylor	1	25	25.0	25	0
Springs	1	4	4.0	4	0
Daniels	1	0	0.0	0	0
Rogers	1	0	0.0	0	0
Wright	1	0	0.0	0	0
Fox	1	-4	-4.0	-4	0
Redskins	6	25	4.2	25	0
Opponents	10	272	27.2	84t	2

PUNTING	No.	Yds.	Avg.	In 20	LG
Frost	81	3,471	42.9	27	60
Redskins	82	3,471	42.3	27	60
Opponents	79	3,316	42.0	19	70

PUNT RETURNS	Ret	FC	Yds	Avg	LG	TD
Randle El	39	11	342	8.8	87t	1
Redskins	39	11	342	8.8	87t	1
Opponents	45	12	319	7.1	33	0

KICKOFF RETURNS	No.	Yds	Avg	LG	TD
Cartwright	64	1,541	24.1	100t	1
Sellers	4	53	13.3	22	0
Betts	2	27	13.5	27	0
Evans	1	0	0.0	0	0
Golston	1	0	0.0	0	0
Thrash	1	10	10.0	10	0
Redskins	73	1,631	22.3	100t	1
Opponents	67	1,396	20.8	44	0

FIELD GOALS	1-19	20-29	30-39	40-49	50+
Hall	0/0	3/3	4/4	2/4	0/0
Suisham	0/0	1/1	5/5	1/1	1/2
Novak	0/0	1/1	1/3	3/6	0/0
Redskins	0/0	5/5	1,0/12	6/11	1/2
Opponents	1/1	6/6	1,3/14	8/10	2/3

SACKS	No.
A. Carter	6.0
Daniels	3.0
Washington	2.5
Evans	2.0
Marshall	1.5
Archuleta	1.0
Griffin	1.0
Holdman	1.0
Golston	0.5
Montgomery	0.5
Redskins	19.0
Opponents	19.0

RECORD HOLDERS
INDIVIDUAL RECORDS—CAREER

Category	Name	Performance
Rushing (Yds.)	John Riggins, 1976-79, 1981-85	7,472
Passing (Yds.)	Joe Theismann, 1974-1985	25,206
Passing (TDs)	Sammy Baugh, 1937-1952	187
Receiving (No.)	Art Monk, 1980-1993	888
Receiving (Yds.)	Art Monk, 1980-1993	12,028
Interceptions	Darrell Green, 1983-2001	54
Punting (Avg.)	Sammy Baugh, 1937-1952	45.1
Punt Return (Avg.)	Johnny Williams, 1952-53	12.8
Kickoff Return (Avg.)	Bobby Mitchell, 1962-68	28.5
Field Goals	Mark Moseley, 1974-1986	263
Touchdowns (Tot.)	Charley Taylor, 1964-1977	90
Points	Mark Moseley, 1974-1986	1,206

INDIVIDUAL RECORDS—SINGLE SEASON

Category	Name	Performance
Rushing (Yds.)	Clinton Portis, 2005	1,516
Passing (Yds.)	Jay Schroeder, 1986	4,109
Passing (TDs)	Sonny Jurgensen, 1967	31
Receiving (No.)	Art Monk, 1984	106
Receiving (Yds.)	Santana Moss, 2005	1,483
Interceptions	Dan Sandifer, 1948	13
Punting (Avg.)	Sammy Baugh, 1940	*51.4
Punt Return (Avg.)	Johnny Williams, 1952	15.3
Kickoff Return (Avg.)	Mike Nelms, 1981	29.7
Field Goals	Mark Moseley, 1983	33
Touchdowns (Tot.)	John Riggins, 1983	24
Points	Mark Moseley, 1983	161

INDIVIDUAL RECORDS—SINGLE GAME

Category	Name	Performance
Rushing (Yds.)	Gerald Riggs, 9-17-89	221
Passing (Yds.)	Sammy Baugh, 10-31-43	446
Passing (TDs)	Sammy Baugh, 10-31-43, 11-23-47	6
	Mark Rypien, 11-10-91	6
Receiving (No.)	Art Monk, 12-15-85, 11-4-90	13
	Kelvin Bryant, 12-7-86	13
Receiving (Yds.)	Anthony Allen, 10-4-87	255
Interceptions	Sammy Baugh, 11-14-43	*4
	Dan Sandifer, 10-31-48	*4
Field Goals	Many times	5
	Last time by Shaun Suisham, 11-4-07	
Touchdowns (Tot.)	Dick James, 12-17-61	4
	Larry Brown, 12-16-73	4
Points	Dick James, 12-17-61	24
	Larry Brown, 12-16-73	24

*NFL Record

2008 VETERAN ROSTER

No.	Name	Pos.	Ht.	Wt.	Age	NFL Exp.	College	Hometown	How Acq.	'07 Games/ Starts
67	Albright, Ethan	LS	6-5	257	37	14	North Carolina	Greensboro, N.C.	UFA(Buff)-'01	16/0
79	Alexander, Lorenzo	DL	6-1	300	25	2	California	Berkeley, Calif.	FA-'07	13/1
91	Askew, Matthias	DT	6-5	302	26	2	Michigan State	Fort Lauderdale, Fla.	FA-'07	0*
46	Betts, Ladell	RB	5-11	225	29	7	Iowa	Blue Springs, Mo.	D2-'02	16/0
54	Blades , H.B.	LB	5-10	250	23	2	Pittsburgh	Plantation, Fla.	D6-'07	16/0
73	Boschetti, Ryan	DT	6-4	311	26	5	UCLA	Belmont, Calif.	FA-'04	1/0
36	Broughton, Nehemiah	FB	5-11	255	26	2	The Citadel	North Charleston, S.C.	D7-'05	0*
17	Campbell, Jason	QB	6-5	233	26	4	Auburn	Taylorsville, Miss.	D1-'05	13/13
50	Campbell, Khary	LB	6-2	232	29	7	Bowling Green	Toledo, Ohio	FA-'03	16/0
99	Carter, Andre	DE	6-4	252	29	8	California	Denver, Colo.	UFA(SF)-'06	16/16
31	Cartwright, Rock	RB	5-8	218	28	7	Kansas State	Conroe, Texas	D7-'02	15/0
15	Collins, Todd	QB	6-4	225	36	14	Michigan	Walpole, Mass.	UFA(KC)-'06	4/3
47	Cooley, Chris	TE	6-3	249	26	5	Utah State	Powell, Utah	D3-'04	16/16
93	Daniels, Phillip	DE	6-4	276	35	13	Georgia	Donalson, Ga.	UFA(Chi)-'04	15/15
37	Doughty, Reed	S	6-1	209	25	3	Northern Colorado	Johnstown, Colo.	D6-'06	16/6
25	Eubanks, John	CB	5-10	173	25	2	Southern Mississippi	Mound Bayou, Miss.	FA-'07	6/0
92	Evans, Demetric	DL	6-4	275	29	7	Georgia	Haynesville, La.	FA-'04	16/1
69	Fabini, Jason	OL	6-7	309	34	11	Cincinnati	Fort Wayne, Ind.	FA-'08	16/13
59	Fletcher, London	LB	5-10	245	33	11	John Carroll	Cleveland, Ohio	UFA(Buff)-'07	16/16
39	Fox, Vernon	S	5-10	203	28	7	Fresno State	Las Vegas, Nev.	FA-'06	14/0
4	Frost, Derrick	P	6-2	201	27	5	Northern Iowa	St. Louis, Mo.	FA-'08	16/0
68	Geisinger, Justin	OL	6-2	315	26	2	Vanderbilt	Pittsburgh, Pa.	FA-'07	0*
64	Golston, Kedric	DT	6-4	320	25	3	Georgia	Tyrone, Ga.	D6-'06	15/0
96	Griffin, Cornelius	DT	6-3	311	31	9	Alabama	Brundidge, Ala.	UFA(NYG)-'04	16/16
74	Heyer, Stephon	OL	6-6	325	24	2	Maryland	Lawrenceville, Ga.	FA-'07	12/5
97	Huntley, Kevin	DE	6-7	270	26	3	Kansas State	Washington D.C.	FA-'08	5/0*
32	Jackson, Eddie	CB	6-'0	200	27	5	Arkansas	Americus, Ga.	FA-'08	3/0*
76	Jansen, Jon	OT	6-6	297	32	10	Michigan	Clawson, Mich.	D2-'99	1/1
66	Kendall, Pete	OL	6-5	292	35	13	Boston College	Weymouth, Mass.	T(NYJ)-'07	16/16
30	Landry, LaRon	S	6-0	213	23	2	Louisiana State	Ama, La.	D1-'07	16/16
13	Mathis, Jerome	WR	5-11	184	25	3	Hampton	Petersburg, Va.	UFA(Hou)-'08	3/0*
52	McIntosh, Rocky	LB	6-2	232	25	3	Miami	Gaffney, S.C.	D2-'06	14/13
16	McMullen, Billy	WR	6-4	215	28	5	Virginia	Richmond, Va.	FA-'08	0*
19	Mix, Anthony	WR	6-5	235	25	2	Auburn	Bay Minette, Ala.	W(NYG)-'07	9/0
94	Montgomery, Anthony	DT	6-6	315	24	3	Minnesota	Cleveland, Ohio	D5-'06	16/15
89	Moss, Santana	WR	5-10	200	29	8	Miami	Miami, Fla.	T(NYJ)-'05	14/14
26	Portis, Clinton	RB	5-11	223	27	7	Miami	Gainesville, Fla.	T(Den)-'04	16/16
61	Rabach, Casey	OL	6-4	296	30	8	Wisconsin	Sturgeon Bay, Wisc.	UFA(Balt)-'05	15/15
82	Randle El, Antwaan	WR	5-10	190	29	7	Indiana	Riverdale, Ill.	UFA(Pitt)-'06	15/13
22	Rogers, Carlos	CB	6-'0	194	27	4	Auburn	Augusta, Ga.	D1-'05	7/7
60	Samuels, Chris	OT	6-5	317	31	9	Alabama	Mobile, Ala.	D1-'00	16/16
45	Sellers, Mike	FB	6-3	284	33	9	Walla Walla (Wash.) CC	North Thurston, Wash.	FA-'04	14/12
35	Shelton, Eric	RB	6-1	246	25	2	Louisville	Lexington, Kent.	FA-'08	0*
58	Sinclair, Matt	LB	6-2	245	26	2	Illinois	St. Louis, Mo.	FA-'07	4/0
27	Smoot, Fred	CB	5-11	190	29	8	Mississippi State	Jackson, Miss.	FA-'07	13/11
24	Springs, Shawn	CB	6-0	204	33	12	Ohio State	Silver Spring, Md.	UFA(Sea)-'04	16/14
6	Suisham, Shaun	K	6-0	197	26	3	Bowling Green	Wallaceburg, Ontario	FA-'06	16/0
77	Thomas, Randy	OG	6-5	317	32	10	Mississippi State	East Point, Ga.	UFA(NYJ)-'03	3/3
83	Thrash, James	WR	6-0	204	33	12	Missouri Southern	Wewoka, Okla.	T(Phil)-'04	13/5
29	Torrence, Leigh	CB	5-11	179	26	3	Stanford	Atlanta, Ga.	FA-'06	16/1
71	Wade, Todd	OL	6-8	314	31	9	Mississippi	Jackson, Miss.	FA-'06	11/10
55	Wallace, Rian	LB	6-3	243	26	3	Temple	Pottstown, Pa.	FA-'08	0*
53	Washington, Marcus	LB	6-3	248	30	9	Auburn	Auburn, Ala.	UFA(Ind)-'04	12/11
95	Wilson, Chris	DE	6-4	246	26	2	Northwood	Flint, Mich.	FA-'07	16/0
87	Yoder, Todd	TE	6-4	253	30	9	Vanderbilt	New Palestine, Ind.	UFA(Jax)-'06	15/1

* Askew last active in Cincinnati in '05; Broughton missed '07 season because of injury; Geisinger last active with Tennessee '06; Huntley played 5 games with Atlanta; Jackson played 3 games with New England in '07; Mathis played 3 games with Houston; McMullen last active with Minnesota in '06; Shelton last active with Carolina in '06; Wallace last active with Pittsburgh in '06.

Players lost through free agency (4): QB Mark Brunell (NO; 0 games in '07), WR Reche Caldwell (StL; 9), CB David Macklin (StL; 6), S Pierson Prioleau (Jax; 15).

Also played with Redskins in '07—G Rick DeMulling (5 games), WR Jimmy Farris (2), LB Randall Godfrey (11), TE Brian Kozlowski (2), WR Brandon Lloyd (8), WR Keenan McCardell (10), OL Mike Pucillo (11), S Omar Stoutmire (3), S Sean Taylor (9).

2008 FIRST-YEAR ROSTER

Name	Pos.	Ht.	Wt.	Age	College	Hometown	How Acq.
Brennan, Colt	QB	6-3	201	25	Hawaii	Irvine, Calif.	D6
Brooks, Durant	P	6-2	204	23	Georgia Tech	Macon, Ga.	D6
Brown, Kerry	OL	6-6	310	23	Appalachian State	Marietta, Ga.	FA
Buzbee, Alex (1)	DE	6-3	265	22	Georgetown	Chester, N.J.	FA-'07
Clark, Devin	OL	6-4	312	22	New Mexico	Mesa, Ariz.	FA
Davis, Tommy (1)	DE	6-2	257	25	North Carolina	Goldsboro, N.C.	FA-'07
Davis, Fred	TE	6-4	247	22	Southern California	Toledo, Ohio	D2
DeVan, Kyle	OL	6-2	306	23	Oregon State	Vacaville, Calif.	FA
Devine, Derek (1)	QB	6-3	222	24	Marshall	Wilsonville, Ore.	FA
Ecker, Tyler (1)	TE	6-6	248	26	Michigan	El Dorado Hills, Calif.	D7-'07
Gant, Horace	WR	6-3	218	23	St. Olaf	Pensacola, Fla.	FA
Gatewood, Curtis	LB	6-3	245	23	Vanderbilt	Memphis, Tenn.	FA
Ghee, Patrick (1)	S	6-1	210	24	Wake Forest	Kingsport, Tenn.	FA
Hollenbach, Sam (1)	QB	6-4	218	24	Maryland	Perkasie, Pa.	FA-'07
Holt, Cedrick (1)	CB	5-11	171	24	North Carolina	Waynesboro, N.C.	FA
Horton, Chris	S	6-1	216	23	UCLA	New Orleans, La.	D7
Jackson, Rob	DE	6-4	259	22	Kansas State	West Haven, Conn.	D7
Kelly, Malcolm	WR	6-4	219	21	Oklahoma	Longview, Texas	D2
Mann, Maurice (1)	WR	6-1	190	25	Nevada	Seaside, Calif.	FA
Mason, Marcus (1)	RB	5-9	218	24	Youngstown State	Potomac, Md.	FA-'07
Moore, Kareem	S	5-11	213	24	Nicholls State	Okolona, Miss.	D6
Richardson, Matteral	CB	6-'0	197	23	Arkansas	Marlin, Texas	FA
Rinehart, Chad	OL	6-5	311	23	Iowa	Boone, Iowa	D3
Schmitt, Pete (1)	TE	6-3	252	23	Wisconsin-Whitewater	Mount Horeb, Wisc.	FA
Smith, Dorian	DE	6-3	260	23	Oregon State	Van Nuys, Calif.	FA
Thomas, Devin	WR	6-2	218	21	Michigan State	Ann Arbor, Mich.	D2
Toler, Burl (1)	WR	6-2	190	25	California	Berkeley, Calif.	FA-'07
Tryon, Justin	CB	5-9	190	24	Arizona State	Palmdale, Calif.	D4
Verdun-Wheeler, Danny (1)	LB	6-2	244	23	Georgia	Thomson, Ga.	FA-'07
Washington, Tavares (1)	OL	6-3	320	25	Florida	Greenville, Miss.	FA
Westbrook, Byron (1)	CB	5-10	202	23	Salisbury	Washington D.C.	FA-'07
Wilson, Bryan	LB	6-3	250	23	Morgan State	Temple Hills, Md.	FA

The term NFL Rookie is defined as a player who is in his first season of professional football and has not been on the roster of another professional football team for any regular-season or postseason games. A Rookie is designated by an "R" on NFL rosters. Players who have been active in another professional football league or players who have NFL experience, including either preseason training camp or being on an Active List or Inactive List, or on Reserve/Injured or Reserve/Physically Unable to Perform for fewer than six regular-season games, are termed NFL First-Year Players. An NFL First-Year Player is designated by a "1" on NFL rosters. Thereafter, a player is credited with an additional year of experience for each season in which he accumulates six games on the Active List or Inactive List, or on Reserve/Injured or Reserve/Physically Unable to Perform.

Log on to www.washingtonredskins.com for an up-to-date roster; Age listed is as of September 4, 2008.

COACHING STAFF

Head Coach,
Jim Zorn

Pro Career: On February 9, 2008, Jim Zorn was announced as the Washington Redskins head coach. Zorn began his NFL coaching career as an offensive assistant with the Seattle Seahawks (1997), and then moved to the Detroit Lions as quarterbacks coach (1998-2000), where he was instrumental in the development of rookie quarterback Charlie Batch. Zorn returned to the Seattle Seahawks in 2001, as quarterbacks coach, where he remained until 2007 while helping to develop quarterbacks Matt Hasselbeck, Trent Dilfer, and Brock Huard. Career record: 0-0.

Background: Played quarterback at Cal Poly-Pomona. Broke into the NFL in 1976 as the first quarterback for the expansion Seahawks. Played nine years for Seattle, then one year each with the Green Bay Packers (1985), the Winnipeg Blue Bombers of the CFL (1986), and the Tampa Bay Buccaneers (1987). Coached at Boise State (1989-1991), Utah State (1992-1994), and Minnesota (1995-1996).

Personal: Age 55, born in Whittier, Calif. Jim and his wife, Joy, have four children, daughters, Rachel, Sarah, Danielle, and son, Isaac. Rachel is married to Neal Mitchell, and they have a daughter: Hollis Joy.

ASSISTANT COACHES

Harrison Bernstein, strength and conditioning; born Brooklyn, N.Y. Defensive back Johns Hopkins 1996-99. No pro playing experience. Pro coach: Joined Redskins in 2007.

Greg Blache, defensive coordinator/defensive line; born New Orleans. Attended Notre Dame. No college or pro playing experience. College coach: Notre Dame 1972-75, 1981-83, Tulane 1976-1980, Southern 1986, Kansas 1987. Pro coach: Jacksonville Bulls (USFL) 1984-85, Green Bay Packers 1988-1993, Indianapolis Colts 1994-98, Chicago Bears 1999-2003, joined Redskins in 2004.

Joe Bugel, asst. head coach-offense; born Pittsburgh. Guard/linebacker Western Kentucky 1960-63. No pro playing experience. College coach: Western Kentucky 1964-68, Navy 1969-1972, Iowa State 1973, Ohio State 1974. Pro coach: Detroit Lions 1975-76, Houston Oilers 1977-1980, Washington Redskins 1981-89, Phoenix Cardinals 1990-1993 (head coach), Oakland Raiders 1995-97 (head coach 1997), San Diego Chargers 1998-2001, re-joined Redskins in 2004.

Bobby Crumpler, strength and conditioning; born Newton Grove, N.C. Running back North Carolina State 1983-87. No pro playing experience. College coach: North Carolina State 1989, 1992-96,

2000-01, Kansas 2002. Pro coach: Joined Redskins in 2003.

Jerry Gray, secondary-cornerbacks; born Lubbock, Texas. Safety Texas 1981-84. Pro defensive back Los Angeles Rams 1985-1991, Houston Oilers 1992, Tampa Bay Buccaneers 1993. College coach: Southern Methodist 1995-96. Pro coach: Tennessee Titans 1997-2000, Buffalo Bills 2001-05, joined Redskins in 2006.

John Hastings, strength and conditioning; born Newport News, Va. Attended Ohio University. No college or pro playing experience. Pro coach: San Diego Chargers 1990-2001, joined Redskins in 2002.

Stan Hixon, wide receivers; born Lakeland, Fla. Wide receiver Iowa State 1975-78. No pro playing experience. College coach: Morehead State 1980-82, Appalachian State 1983-88, South Carolina 1989-1992, Wake Forest 1993-94, Georgia Tech 1995-99, Louisiana State 2000-03. Pro coach: Joined Redskins in 2004.

Steve Jackson, passing game-safeties; born Houston. Defensive back Purdue 1987-1990. Pro defensive back Houston Oilers/Tennessee Titans 1991-99. Pro coach: Buffalo Bills 2001-03, joined Redskins in 2004.

Bill Khayat, offensive quality control; born York, Pa. Tight end Duke 1992-95. Pro tight end Kansas City Chiefs 1996, Carolina Panthers 1997, Barcelona Dragons (NFLE) 1998. College coach: Tennessee State 2000-03. Pro coach: Arizona Cardinals 2004-06, joined Redskins in 2007.

Chris Meidt, offensive assistant; born Fergus Falls, Minn. Attended Bethel College. No college or pro playing experience. College coach: Bethel University 1995-2001, St. Olaf College 2002-07. Pro coach: Joined Redskins in 2008.

Stump Mitchell, asst. head coach/running backs; born St. Mary's, Ga. Tailback The Citadel 1977-1980. Pro running back St. Louis/Phoenix Cardinals 1981-89. College coach: Morgan State 1995-98 (head coach 1996-98). Pro coach: San Antonio Rough Riders (WLAF) 1991, Seattle Seahawks 1999-2007, joined Redskins in 2008.

Kirk Olivadotti, linebackers; born Wilmington, Del. Wide receiver Purdue 1992-1996. No pro playing experience. College coach: Maine Maritime Academy 1997, Indiana State 1998-99. Pro coach: Joined Redskins in 2000.

John Palermo, defensive line; born Newburgh, N.Y. Defensive tackle Florida State 1972-73. No pro playing experience. College coach: Memphis State 1980-82, Appalachian State 1983-84, Minnesota 1984-87, Notre Dame 1988-89, Austin Peay 1990, Wisconsin 1991-2005, Miami 2006, Tennessee Tech 2007. Pro coach: Joined Redskins in 2008.

Warren (Rennie) Simmons, tight end; born Poughkeepsie, N.Y. Center San Diego State 1961-65. No pro playing experi-

ence. College coach: Cal State-Fullerton 1974-78, Cerritos (Calif.) J.C. 1978-1980, Vanderbilt 1995. Pro coach: Washington Redskins 1981-1993, Los Angeles Rams 1994, Houston Oilers 1996, Atlanta Falcons 1997-2003, re-joined Redskins in 2004.

Arthur Smith, defensive quality control; born Memphis, Tenn. Offensive lineman North Carolina 2001-05. No pro playing experience. Pro coach: Joined Redskins in 2007.

Danny Smith, special teams; born Pittsburgh. Defensive back Edinboro State 1972-75. No pro playing experience. College coach: Edinboro State 1976, Clemson 1979, William & Mary 1980-83, The Citadel 1984-86, Georgia Tech 1987-1994. Pro coach: Philadelphia Eagles 1995-98, Detroit Lions 1999-2000, Buffalo Bills 2001-03, joined Redskins in 2004.

Sherman Smith, offensive coordinator; born Youngstown, Ohio. Quarterback Miami (Ohio) 1972-75. Pro running back Seattle Seahawks 1976-1982, San Diego Chargers 1983-84. College coach: Miami (Ohio) 1990-91, Illinois 1992-94. Pro coach: Houston Oilers/Tennessee Titans 1995-2007, joined Redskins in 2008.

2007 Season in Review

2007 TRADES

Running back **Tatum Bell**, tackle **George Foster**, and Broncos' fifth-round selection in 2007 (LB **Johnny Baldwin**) from Denver to Detroit for cornerback **Dre' Bly** and the Lions' sixth-round selection in 2007 (#176). (3/2)

Defensive end **James Hall** from Detroit to St. Louis for the Rams' fifth-round selection in 2007 (#154). (3/2)

Quarterback **Jake Plummer** from Denver to Tampa Bay for an unannounced selection. (3/3)

Defensive tackle **Dan Wilkinson** from Miami to Denver for the Broncos' sixth-round selection in 2007 (#198). (3/3)

Wide receiver **Wes Welker** from Miami to New England for the Patriots' second-round selection in 2007 (G **Samson Satele**) and seventh-round selection (DE **Abraham Wright**). (3/5)

Running back **Thomas Jones** and the Bears' second-round selection in 2007 (#63) from Chicago to New York Jets for the Redskins' second-round selection in 2007 (#37). (3/7)

Running back **Willie McGahee** from Buffalo to Baltimore for the Ravens' third-round selection (QB **Trent Edwards**) and seventh-round selection in 2007 (DE **C.J. Ah You**). (3/8)

Wide receiver **Tim Carter** from New York Giants to Cleveland for running back **Reuben Droughns**. (3/9)

Quarterback **Matt Schaub** and the Falcons' first-round selection in 2007 (DT **Amobi Okoye**) from Atlanta to Houston for the Texans' first-round selection (DE **Jamaal Anderson**), second-round selection (G **Justin Blalock**) in 2007, and an unannounced selection choice. (3/22)

Defensive back **Adam Archuleta** from Washington to Chicago for the Bears' sixth-round selection in 2007 (QB **Jordan Palmer**). (3/22)

Linebacker **Takeo Spikes** and quarterback **Kelly Holcomb** from Buffalo to Philadelphia for defensive tackle **Darwin Walker** and an unannounced selection choice. (3/28)

Kicker **Olindo Mare** from Miami to New Orleans for the Saints' sixth-round selection in 2007 (DE **Drew Mormino**). (4/3)

Wide receiver **Dante Hall** and Kansas City's third-round selection in 2007 (DB **Jonathan Wade**) from the Chiefs to St. Louis for the Rams' third-round selection in 2007 (DT **DeMarcus Tyler**) and Buffalo's fifth-round selection in 2007 (RB **Kolby Smith**). (4/25)

Carolina's first-round selection (DB **Darrelle Revis**) and sixth-round selection (#191) in 2007 from Carolina to New York Jets for the Jets' first-round selection in 2007 (LB **Jon Beason**), second-round selection in 2007 (C **Ryan Kalil**), and fifth-round selection in 2007 (LB **Tim Shaw**). (4/28)

Jacksonville's first-round selection in 2007 (DE **Jarvis Moss**) from Jacksonville to Denver for the Broncos' first-round selection in 2007 (DB **Reggie Nelson**), third-round selection in 2007 (#86), and sixth-round selection in 2007 (#198). (4/28)

Dallas' first-round selection in 2007 (QB **Brady Quinn**) from Dallas to Cleveland for the Browns' second-round selection in 2007 (#36), and first-round selection in 2008 (RB **Felix Jones**). (4/28)

Philadelphia's first-round selection in 2007 (LB **Anthony Spencer**) from Philadelphia to Dallas for the Browns' second-round selection in 2007 (QB **Kevin Kolb**), and the Cowboys' third-round selection in 2007 (LB **Stewart Bradley**) and fifth-round selection in 2007 (DB **C.J. Gaddis**). (4/28)

New England's first-round selection in 2007 (T **Joe Staley**) from New England to San Francisco for the 49ers' fourth-round selection in 2007 (#110) and first-round selection in 2008 (#7). (4/28)

Oakland's second-round selection in 2007 (DT **Alvin Branch**) from Oakland to Arizona for the Cardinals' second-round selection in 2007 (TE **Zach Miller**) and fourth-round selection in 2007 (#105). (4/28)

Detroit's second-round selection in 2007 (LB **Paul Posluszny**) from Detroit to Buffalo for the Bills' second-round selection in 2007 (QB **Drew Stanton**) and third-round selection in 2007 (#74). (4/28)

Washington's second-round selection in 2007 (DB **Eric Weddle**) from Chicago to San Diego for the Chargers' second-round selection in 2007 (DE **Dan Bazuin**), third-round selection in 2007 (RB **Garrett Wolfe**), fifth-round selection in 2007 (DB **Kevin Payne**), and third-round selection in 2008 (DT **Marcus Harrison**). (4/28)

Minnesota's second-round selection in 2007 (DB **Chris Houston**) from Minnesota to Atlanta for the Falcons' second-round selection in 2007 (WR **Sidney Rice**) and the Broncos' fourth-round selection in 2007 (#121). (4/28)

San Francisco's second-round selection in 2007 (T **Tony Ugoh**) from San Francisco to Indianapolis for the Saints' fourth-round selection in 2007 (DB **Dashon Goldson**) and the Colts' first-round selection in 2008 (DT **Kentwan Balmer**). (4/28)

Green Bay's second-round selection in 2007 (LB **David Harris**) and the Jets' seventh-round selection in 2007 (WR **Chansi Stuckey**) from Green Bay to New York Jets for the Bears' second-round selection in 2007 (RB **Brandon Jackson**), third-round selection in 2007 (DB **Aaron Rouse**), and the Panthers' sixth-round selection in 2007 (LB **Korey Hall**). (4/28)

Quarterback **Josh McCown** and wide receiver Mike Williams from Detroit to Oakland for the Cardinals' fourth-round selection in 2007 (DB **A.J. Davis**). (4/28)

Dallas' second-round selection in 2007 (DB **Eric Wright**) and sixth-round selection in 2007 (#195) from the Dallas to Cleveland for the Browns' third-round selection in 2007 (T **James Marten**), fourth-round selection in 2007 (QB **Isaiah Stanback**), and sixth-round selection in 2007 (K **Nick Folk**). (4/28)

New Orleans' second-round selection in 2007 (DE **Ikaika Alama-Francis**) from New Orleans to Detroit for the Lions' third-round selection in 2007 (DB **Usama Young**), and the Dolphins' fifth-round selection in 2007 (DB **David Jones**). (4/28)

Baltimore's second-round selection in 2007 (DB **Gerald Alexander**) from Baltimore to Detroit for the Bills' fifth-round selection in 2007 (WR **Yamon Figurs**) and the Lions' fourth-round selection in 2007 (#101). (4/29)

Denver's third-round selection in 2007 (T **Marshal Yanda**) from Jacksonville to Baltimore for the Lions' fourth-round selection in 2007 (P **Adam Podlesh**), and the Ravens' fifth-round selection in 2007 (DT **Derek Landri**) and sixth-round selection in 2007 (#203). (4/28)

New England's third-round selection in 2007 (T **Mario Henderson**) from New England to Oakland for the Raiders' seventh-round selection in 2007 (LB **Oscar Lua**) and third-round selection in 2008 (#69). (4/28)

Wide receiver **Darrell Jackson** from Seattle to San Francisco for the Jets' fourth-round selection in 2007 (G **Mansfield Wrotto**). (4/29)

Tampa Bay's fourth-round selection in 2007 (DE **Brian Robison**) from Tampa Bay to Minnesota for the Vikings' fourth-round selection in 2007 (DB **Tanard Jackson**) and sixth-round selection in 2007 (LB **Adam Hayward**). (4/29)

Wide receiver **Randy Moss** from Oakland to New England for the 49ers' fourth-round selection in 2007 (DB **John Bowie**). (4/29)

Houston's fourth-round selection in 2007 (RB **Antonio Pittman**) from Houston to New Orleans for the Chiefs' fourth-round selection

in 2007 (DB **Fred Bennett**) and fifth-round selection in 2007 (T **Brandon Frye**). (4/29)

Green Bay's fourth-round selection in 2007 (P **Daniel Sepulveda**) from Green Bay to Pittsburgh for the Steelers' fourth-round selection in 2007 (T **Allen Barbre**) and sixth-round selection in 2007 (LB **Desmond Bishop**). (4/29)

St. Louis' fourth-round selection in 2007 (G **Manuel Ramirez**) from St. Louis to Detroit for the Lions' fifth-round selection in 2007 (C **Dustin Fry**) and the Rams' fifth-round selection in 2007 (DT **Clifton Ryan**). (4/29)

Denver's fourth-round selection in 2007 (DT **Marcus Thomas**) from Minnesota to Denver for the Lions' sixth-round selection in 2007 (LB **Rufus Alexander**), and the Broncos' seventh-round selection in 2007 (WR **Chandler Williams**) and third-round selection in 2008 (#73). (4/29)

Atlanta's fifth-round selection in 2007 (G **Uche Nwaneri**) from Atlanta to Jacksonville for the Jaguars' sixth-round selection in 2007 (DB **David Irons**), the Broncos' sixth-round selection in 2007 (C **Doug Datish**), and the Ravens' sixth-round selection in 2007 (DB **Daren Stone**). (4/29)

Dallas' sixth-round selection in 2007 (RB **Deon Anderson**) from Cleveland to Dallas for the Jets' sixth-round selection in 2007 (DE **Melila Purcell**) and the Cowboys' seventh-round selection in 2007 (WR **Syndric Steptoe**). (4/29)

Defensive tackle **Ryan Sims** from Kansas City to Tampa Bay for an unannounced selection choice. (5/2)

Kicker **Lawrence Tynes** from Kansas City to the New York Giants for an unannounced selection choice. (5/22)

Quarterback **Trent Green** from Kansas City to Miami for an unannounced selection choice. (6/6)

Defensive tackle **Jimmy Kennedy** from St. Louis to Denver for an unannounced selection choice. (6/8)

Defensive tackle **Darwin Walker** from Buffalo to Chicago for an unannounced selection choice. (7/30)

Defensive back **Chris Harris** from Chicago to Carolina for an unannounced selection choice. (8/2)

Defensive back **Dante Wesley** from Chicago to New England for an unannounced selection choice. (8/7)

Defensive tackle **Gerard Warren** from Denver to Oakland for an unannounced selection choice. (8/20)

Linebacker **Jerry Mackey** from the New York Jets to Tampa Bay for an unannounced selection choice. (8/21)

Guard **Pete Kendall** from the New York Jets to Washington for an unannounced selection choice. (8/23)

Quarterback **Kelly Holcomb** from Philadelphia to Minnesota for an unannounced selection choice. (8/27)

Defensive back **Allen Rossum** from Atlanta to Pittsburgh for an unannounced selection choice. (9/1)

Defensive end **Jason Babin** from Houston to Seattle for defensive back **Michael Boulware**. (9/1)

Running back **Alvin Pearman** and an unannounced selection choice from the Jaguars to Seattle for an unannounced selection choice. (9/1)

Running back **Ryan Grant** from the New York Giants to Green Bay for an unannounced selection choice. (9/1)

Quarterback **Ryan Fitzpatrick** from St. Louis to Cincinnati for an unannounced selection choice. (9/1)

Quarterback **Charlie Frye** from Cleveland to Seattle for an unannounced selection choice. (9/11)

Defensive end **Bryce Fisher** from Seattle to Tennessee for an unannounced selection choice. (9/11)

Running back **Michael Bennett** and an unannounced selection choice from Kansas City to Tampa Bay for an unannounced selection choice. (10/16)

Wide receiver **Chris Chambers** from Miami to San Diego for an unannounced selection choice. (10/16)

* Draft choice number is listed if club later traded the pick.

2008 TRADES

Defensive tackle **Kris Jenkins** from Carolina to N.Y. Jets for the Jets' third-round selection in 2008 (DB **Charles Godfrey**) and the Jets' fifth-round selection in 2008 (TE **Gary Barnidge**). (2/29)

Defensive tackle **Jason Ferguson** and the Cowboys' sixth-round selection in 2008 (G **Donald Thomas**) from Dallas to Miami for the Dolphins' sixth-round selection in 2008 (LB **Erik Walden**). (2/29)

Wide receiver **Troy Williamson** from Minnesota to Jacksonville for the Jaguars' sixth-round selection in 2008 (WR **Jaymar Johnson**). (2/29)

Linebacker **Jonathan Vilma** from N.Y. Jets to New Orleans for the Saints' sixth-round selection in 2008 (DB **Dwight Lowery**). (2/29)

Defensive tackle **Jason Ferguson** and the Cowboys' sixth-round selection in 2008 (G **Donald Thomas**) from Dallas to Miami for the Dolphins' sixth-round selection in 2008 (LB **Erik Walden**). (2/29)

Defensive back **Leigh Bodden** and the Browns' third-round selection in 2008 (DT **Andre Fluellen**) from Cleveland to Detroit for defensive tackle **Shaun Rogers**. (3/1)

Defensive tackle **Corey Williams** from Green Bay to Cleveland for the Browns' sixth-round selection in 2008 (QB **Brian Brohm**). (3/1)

Defensive tackle **Marcus Stroud** from Jacksonville to Buffalo for the Ravens' third-round selection in 2008 (#71) and the Bears' fifth-round selection in 2008 (#143). (3/1)

Quarterback **Brian Griese** from Chicago to Tampa Bay for two unannounced selections. (3/3)

Center **Chris Myers** from Denver to Houston for the Texans' sixth-round selection in 2008 (LB **Spencer Larsen**). (3/17)

Defensive back **DeAngelo Hall** from Atlanta to Oakland for the Raiders' second-round selection in 2008 (#34) and an unannounced selection. (3/21)

Defensive end **Jared Allen** and the Buccaneers' sixth-round selection in 2008 (C **John Sullivan**) from Kansas City to Minnesota for the Vikings' first-round selection in 2008 (#17), the Broncos' third-round selection in 2008 (RB **Jamaal Charles**), the Vikings' third-round selection in 2008 (DB **DaJuan Morgan**), and the Vikings' sixth-round selection in 2008 (WR **Kevin Robinson**). (4/23)

Defensive tackle **Dewayne Robertson** from N.Y. Jets to Denver for an unannounced selection. (4/26)

Linebacker **Akin Ayodele** and tight end **Anthony Fasano** from Dallas to Miami for the Dolphins' fourth-round selection in 2008 (#100). (4/26)

New Orleans' first-round selection in 2008 (LB **Jerod Mayo**) and second-round selection in 2008 (LB **Shawn Crable**) from New Orleans to New England for the 49ers' first-round selection in 2008 (DT **Sedrick Ellis**) and the Patriots' fifth-round selection in 2008 (T **Carl Nicks**). (4/26)

Baltimore's first-round selection in 2008 (DE **Derrick Harvey**) from Baltimore to Jacksonville for the Jaguars' first-round selection in 2008 (#26), the Ravens' third-round selection in 2008 (LB **Tavares Gooden**), third-round selection in 2008 (#89), and the Jaguars' fourth-round selection in 2008 (#125). (4/26)

Detroit's first-round selection in 2008 (T **Branden Albert**) and the Lions' third-round

selection in 2008 (TE **Brad Cottam**) from Detroit to Kansas City for the Vikings' first-round selection in 2008 (T **Gosder Cherilus**), the Chiefs' third-round selection in 2008 (#66), and the Dolphins' fifth-round selection in 2008 (WR **Kenneth Moore**). (4/26)

Houston's first-round selection in 2008 (QB **Joe Flacco**) from Houston to Baltimore for the Jaguars' first-round selection in 2008 (#26), the Jaguars' third-round selection in 2008 (RB **Steve Slaton**), and the Ravens' sixth-round selection in 2008 (DB **Dominique Barber**). (4/26)

Philadelphia's first-round selection in 2008 (T **Jeff Otah**) from Philadelphia to Carolina for the Panthers' second-round selection in 2008 (G **Mike McGlynn**), and the Panthers' first-round selection in 2009. (4/26)

Washington's first-round selection in 2008 (T **Sam Baker**), the Redskins' third-round selection in 2008 (WR **Harry Douglas**), and the Redskins' fifth-round selection in 2008 (DE **Kroy Biermann**) from Washington to Atlanta for the Raiders' second-round selection in 2008 (WR **Devin Thomas**), the Texans' second-round selection (TE **Fred Davis**), and the Falcons' fourth-round selection (#103). (4/26)

Seattle's first-round selection in 2008 (DB **Mike Jenkins**) from Seattle to Dallas for the Cowboys' first-round selection in 2008 (DE **Lawrence Jackson**), fifth-round selection in 2008 (RB **Owen Schmitt**), and seventh-round selection in 2008 (K **Brandon Coutu**). (4/26)

Green Bay's first-round selection in 2008 (DT **Dustin Keller**) from Green Bay to N.Y. Jets for the Jets' second-round selection in 2008 (WR **Jordy Nelson**) and the Saints' fourth-round selection in 2008 (#113). (4/26)

Baltimore's second-round selection in 2008 (TE **John Carlson**) from Baltimore to Seattle for the Seahawks' second-round selection in 2008 (RB **Ray Rice**), and third-round selection in 2008 (DB **Tom Zbikowski**). (4/26)

Running back **Lorenzo Booker** from Miami to Philadelphia for the Eagles' fourth-round selection in 2008 (#115). (4/26)

Minnesota's second-round selection in 2008 (DT **Trevor Laws**) and fourth-round selection in 2008 (DB **Quintin Demps**) from Minnesota to Philadelphia for the Panthers' second-round selection in 2008 (DB **Tyrell Johnson**) and the Eagles' fifth-round selection in 2008 (DT **Letroy Guion**). (4/26)

Tampa Bay's second-round selection in 2008 (DE **Quentin Groves**) from Tampa Bay to Jacksonville for the Jaguars' second-round selection in 2008 (WR **Dexter Jackson**), the Seahawks' fifth-round selection in 2008 (#158), and the Jaguars' seventh-round selection in 2009. (4/26)

Miami's third-round selection in 2008 (RB **Kevin Smith**) from Miami to Detroit for the Chiefs' third-round selection in 2008 (DE **Kendall Langford**) and the Lions' sixth-round selection in 2008 (RB **Jalen Parmele**). (4/27)

New England's third-round selection in 2008 (RB **Jacob Hester**) from New England to San Diego for the Chargers' fifth-round selection in 2008 (#160) and second-round selection in 2009. (4/27)

Dallas' third-round selection in 2008 (DE **Cliff Avril**) from Dallas to Detroit for the Lions' fourth-round selection in 2008 (#111) and second-round selection in 2009. (4/27)

Defensive back **Adam Jones** from Tennessee to Dallas for the Cowboys' fourth-round selection in 2008 (WR **Lavelle Hawkins**). (4/27)

Tennessee's fourth-round selection in 2008 (DB **Justin Tryon**) and fifth-round selection in 2008 (#157) from Tennessee to Washington for the Falcons' fourth-round selection in 2008 (DE **William Hayes**). (4/27)

Oakland's fourth-round selection in 2008 (#104) and seventh-round selection in 2008 (#213) from Oakland to Dallas for the Dol-

phins' fourth-round selection in 2008 (DB **Tyvon Branch**). (4/27)

New York Jets' fourth-round selection in 2008 (DE **Jeremy Thompson**) from N.Y. Jets to Green Bay for the Saints' fourth-round selection in 2008 (DB **Dwight Lowery**) and the Packers' fifth-round selection in 2008 (QB **Erik Ainge**). (4/27)

Cleveland's fourth-round selection in 2008 (RB **Tashard Choice**) and fifth-round selection in 2008 (#155) from Cleveland to Dallas for the Raiders' fourth-round selection in 2008 (LB **Beau Bell**). (4/27)

Defensive back **Fabian Washington** from Oakland to Baltimore for the Jaguars' fourth-round selection in 2008 (WR **Arman Shields**). (4/27)

Chicago's fourth-round selection in 2008 (G **Shawn Murphy**) from Chicago to Miami for the Eagles' fourth-round selection in 2008 (#115), and the Dolphins' seventh-round selection in 2008 (DE **Ervin Baldwin**). (4/27)

Cleveland's third-round selection in 2009 from Cleveland to Dallas for the Lions' fourth-round selection in 2008 (TE **Martin Rucker**). (4/27)

Tampa Bay's fourth-round selection in 2008 (DB **Craig Steltz**) and the Seahawks' fifth-round selection in 2008 (TE **Kellen Davis**) from Tampa Bay to Chicago for the Eagles' fourth-round selection in 2008 (DT **Dre Moore**) and the Bears' sixth-round selection in 2008 (LB **Geno Hayes**). (4/27)

Pittsburgh's fourth-round selection in 2008 (LB **Bryan Kehl**) from Pittsburgh to N.Y. Giants for the Giants' fourth-round selection in 2008 (T **Tony Hills**) and the Packers' sixth-round selection in 2008 (#194). (4/27)

Green Bay's fourth-round selection in 2008 (WR **Keenan Burton**) from Green Bay to St. Louis for the Rams' fifth-round selection in 2008 (#137) and the Bengals' seventh-round selection in 2008 (WR **Brett Swain**). (4/27)

Minnesota's fifth-round selection in 2008 (T **Breno Giacomini**) and the Rams' seventh-round selection in 2008 (QB Matt Flynn) from Minnesota to Green Bay for the Rams' fifth-round selection in 2008 (QB **John David Booty**). (4/27)

Bears' fifth-round selection in 2008 (DB **Orlando Scandrick**) from Jacksonville to Dallas for the Browns' fifth-round selection in 2008 (LB **Thomas Williams**) and the Raiders' seventh-round selection in 2008 (RB **Chauncey Washington**). (4/27)

Detroit's fifth-round selection in 2008 (DT **DeMario Pressley**) from Detroit to New Orleans for the Saints' fifth-round selection in 2008 (RB **Jerome Felton**) and seventh-round selection in 2008 (DB **Caleb Campbell**). (4/27)

Tampa Bay's fifth-round selection in 2008 (WR **Matt Slater**) from Tampa Bay to New England for the Chargers' fifth-round selection in 2008 (QB **Josh Johnson**) and the Patriots' seventh-round selection in 2008 (RB **Cory Byrd**). (4/27)

St. Louis' sixth-round selection in 2008 (P **Durant Brooks**) and the Broncos' sixth-round selection in 2008 (DB **Kareem Moore**) from St. Louis to Washington for the Titans' fifth-round selection in 2008 (G **Roy Schuening**) and the Redskins' seventh-round selection in 2008 (LB **Chris Chamberlain**). (4/27)

Cleveland's fifth-round selection in 2009 from Cleveland to Philadelphia for the Browns' sixth-round selection in 2008 (WR **Paul Hubbard**). (4/27)

Green Bay's seventh-round selection in 2008 (WR **Adrian Arrington**) from Green Bay to New Orleans for the Saints' sixth-round selection in 2009. (4/27)

* Draft choice number is listed if club later traded the pick.

PRESEASON STANDINGS
AMERICAN FOOTBALL CONFERENCE

East Division

	W	L	T	Pct.	Pts.	OP
NY Jets	3	1	0	.750	84	76
Miami	2	2	0	.500	57	65
New England	2	2	0	.500	85	67
Buffalo	2	2	0	.500	56	64

North Division

	W	L	T	Pct.	Pts.	OP
Pittsburgh	4	1	0	.800	87	46
Cleveland	3	1	0	.750	72	60
Cincinnati	1	3	0	.250	78	84
Baltimore	1	3	0	.250	58	42

South Division

	W	L	T	Pct.	Pts.	OP
Tennessee	3	1	0	.750	91	69
Jacksonville	3	1	0	.750	100	64
Houston	2	2	0	.500	104	87
Indianapolis	1	3	0	.250	77	74

West Division

	W	L	T	Pct.	Pts.	OP
San Diego	3	1	0	.750	95	81
Oakland	2	2	0	.500	82	78
Denver	2	2	0	.500	74	64
Kansas City	0	4	0	.000	32	67

AFC PRESEASON RECORDS—TEAM BY TEAM

East Division

BUFFALO (2-2)

13	at New Orleans	10
10	Atlanta	13
17	Tennessee	28
16	at Detroit	13
56		**64**

MIAMI (2-2)

18	Jacksonville	17
11	at Kansas City	10
28	Tampa Bay	31
0	at New Orleans	7
57		**65**

NEW ENGLAND (2-2)

10	at Tampa Bay	13
24	Tennessee	27
24	at Carolina	7
27	New York Giants	20
85		**67**

N.Y. JETS (3-1)

31	Atlanta	16
20	Minnesota	37
20	at New York Giants	12
13	at Philadelphia	11
84		**76**

North Division

BALTIMORE (1-3)

29	Philadelphia	3
12	New York Giants	13
7	at Washington	13
10	at Atlanta	13
58		**42**

CINCINNATI (1-3)

26	at Detroit	27
19	New Orleans	27
19	at Atlanta	24
14	Indianapolis	6
78		**84**

CLEVELAND (3-1)

16	Kansas City	12
20	Detroit	23
17	at Denver	16
19	at Chicago	9
72		**60**

PITTSBURGH (4-1)

20	New Orleans (a)	7
9	Green Bay	13
12	at Washington	10
27	Philadelphia	13
19	at Carolina	3
87		**46**

South Division

HOUSTON (2-2)

19	Chicago	20
33	at Arizona	20
28	Dallas	16
24	at Tampa Bay	31
104		**87**

INDIANAPOLIS (1-3)

10	at Dallas	23
24	Chicago	27
37	Detroit	10
6	at Cincinnati	14
77		**74**

JACKSONVILLE (3-1)

17	at Miami	18
31	Tampa Bay	19
21	at Green Bay	13
31	Washington	14
100		**64**

TENNESSEE (3-1)

6	Washington	14
27	at New England	24
28	at Buffalo	17
30	Green Bay	14
91		**69**

West Division

DENVER (2-2)

17	at San Francisco	13
20	at Dallas	31
16	Cleveland	17
21	Arizona	3
74		**64**

KANSAS CITY (0-4)

12	at Cleveland	16
10	Miami	11
7	New Orleans	30
3	at St. Louis	10
32		**67**

OAKLAND (2-2)

27	Arizona	23
21	at San Francisco	26
20	St. Louis	10
14	at Seattle	19
82		**78**

SAN DIEGO (3-1)

16	Seattle	24
30	at St. Louis	13
33	at Arizona	31
16	San Francisco	13
95		**81**

(a) Pro Football Hall of Fame Game at Canton, Ohio

NFC PRESEASON RECORDS—TEAM BY TEAM

East Division

DALLAS (2-2)

23	Indianapolis	10
31	Denver	20
16	at Houston	28
14	at Minnesota	23
84		81

N.Y. GIANTS (1-3)

21	Carolina	24
13	at Baltimore	12
12	New York Jets	20
20	at New England	27
66		83

PHILADELPHIA (1-3)

3	at Baltimore	29
27	Carolina	10
13	at Pittsburgh	27
11	New York Jets	13
54		79

WASHINGTON (2-2)

14	at Tennessee	6
10	Pittsburgh	12
13	Baltimore	7
14	at Jacksonville	31
51		56

North Division

CHICAGO BEARS (3-1)

20	at Houston	19
27	at Indianapolis	24
31	San Francisco	28
9	Cleveland	19
87		90

DETROIT (2-2)

27	Cincinnati	26
23	at Cleveland	20
10	at Indianapolis	37
13	Buffalo	16
73		99

GREEN BAY (2-2)

13	at Pittsburgh	9
48	Seattle	13
13	Jacksonville	21
14	at Tennessee	30
88		73

MINNESOTA VIKINGS (2-2)

10	St. Louis	13
37	at New York Jets	20
13	at Seattle	30
23	Dallas	14
83		77

South Division

ATLANTA (3-1)

16	at New York Jets	31
13	at Buffalo	10
24	Cincinnati	19
13	Baltimore	10
66		70

CAROLINA (1-3)

24	at New York Giants	21
10	at Philadelphia	27
7	New England	24
3	Pittsburgh	19
44		91

NEW ORLEANS (3-2)

7	at Pittsburgh (a)	20
10	Buffalo	13
27	at Cincinnati	19
30	at Kansas City	7
7	Miami	0
81		59

TAMPA BAY (3-1)

13	New England	10
19	at Jacksonville	31
31	at Miami	28
31	Houston	24
94		93

West Division

ARIZONA (0-4)

23	at Oakland	27
20	Houston	33
31	San Diego	33
3	at Denver	21
77		114

ST. LOUIS (2-2)

13	at Minnesota	10
13	San Diego	30
10	at Oakland	20
10	Kansas City	3
46		63

SAN FRANCISCO (1-3)

13	Denver	17
26	Oakland	21
28	at Chicago	31
13	at San Diego	16
80		85

SEATTLE (3-1)

24	at San Diego	16
13	at Green Bay	48
30	Minnesota	13
19	Oakland	14
86		91

PRESEASON STANDINGS
NATIONAL FOOTBALL CONFERENCE

East Division

	W	L	T	Pct.	Pts.	OP
Dallas	2	2	0	.500	84	81
Washington	2	2	0	.500	51	56
Philadelphia	1	3	0	.250	54	79
NY Giants	1	3	0	.250	66	83

North Division

	W	L	T	Pct.	Pts.	OP
Chicago	3	1	0	.750	87	90
Green Bay	2	2	0	.500	88	73
Minnesota	2	2	0	.500	83	77
Detroit	2	2	0	.500	73	99

South Division

	W	L	T	Pct.	Pts.	OP
Tampa Bay	3	1	0	.750	94	93
Atlanta	3	1	0	.750	66	70
New Orleans	3	2	0	.600	81	59
Carolina	1	3	0	.250	44	91

West Division

	W	L	T	Pct.	Pts.	OP
Seattle	3	1	0	.750	86	91
St. Louis	2	2	0	.500	46	63
San Francisco	1	3	0	.250	80	85
Arizona	0	4	0	.000	77	114

(a) Pro Football Hall of Fame Game at Canton, Ohio

AMERICAN FOOTBALL CONFERENCE

BALTIMORE (5-11)
20	at Cincinnati	27
20	New York Jets	13
26	Arizona	23
13	at Cleveland	27
9	at San Francisco	7
22	St. Louis	3
14	at Buffalo	19
7	at Pittsburgh	38
7	Cincinnati	21
30	Cleveland (OT)	33
14	at San Diego	32
24	New England	27
20	Indianapolis	44
16	at Miami (OT)	22
6	at Seattle	27
27	Pittsburgh	21
275		384

BUFFALO (7-9)
14	Denver	15
3	at Pittsburgh	26
7	at New England	38
17	New York Jets	14
24	Dallas	25
19	Baltimore	14
13	at N.Y. Jets	3
33	Cincinnati	21
13	at Miami	10
10	New England	56
14	at Jacksonville	36
17	at Washington	16
38	Miami	17
0	at Cleveland	8
21	New York Giants	38
9	at Philadelphia	17
252		354

CINCINNATI (7-9)
27	Baltimore	20
45	at Cleveland	51
21	at Seattle	24
13	New England	34
20	at Kansas City	27
38	New York Jets	31
13	Pittsburgh	24
21	at Buffalo	33
21	at Baltimore	7
27	Arizona	35
35	Tennessee	6
10	at Pittsburgh	24
13	St. Louis	10
13	at San Francisco	20
19	Cleveland	14
38	at Miami	25
380		385

CLEVELAND (10-6)
7	Pittsburgh	34
51	Cincinnati	45
24	at Oakland	26
27	Baltimore	13
17	at New England	34
41	Miami	31
27	at St. Louis	20
33	Seattle (OT)	30
28	at Pittsburgh	31
33	at Baltimore (OT)	30
27	Houston	17
21	at Arizona	27
24	at N.Y. Jets	18
8	Buffalo	0
14	at Cincinnati	19
20	San Francisco	7
402		382

DENVER (7-9)
15	at Buffalo	14
23	Oakland (OT)	20
14	Jacksonville	23
20	at Indianapolis	38
3	San Diego	41
31	Pittsburgh	28
13	Green Bay (OT)	19
7	at Detroit	44
27	at Kansas City	11
34	Tennessee	20
34	at Chicago (OT)	37
20	at Oakland	34
41	Kansas City	7
13	at Houston	31
3	at San Diego	23
22	Minnesota (OT)	19
320		409

HOUSTON (8-8)
20	Kansas City	3
34	at Carolina	21
24	Indianapolis	30
16	at Atlanta	26
22	Miami	19
17	at Jacksonville	37
36	Tennessee	38
10	at San Diego	35
24	at Oakland	17
23	New Orleans	10
17	at Cleveland	27
20	at Tennessee	28
28	Tampa Bay	14
31	Denver	13
15	at Indianapolis	38
42	Jacksonville	28
379		384

INDIANAPOLIS (13-3)
41	New Orleans	10
22	at Tennessee	20
30	at Houston	24
38	Denver	20
33	Tampa Bay	14
29	at Jacksonville	7
31	at Carolina	7
20	New England	24
21	at San Diego	23
13	Kansas City	10
31	at Atlanta	13
28	Jacksonville	25
44	at Baltimore	20
21	at Oakland	14
38	Houston	15
10	Tennessee	16
450		262

KANSAS CITY (4-12)
3	at Houston	20
10	at Chicago	20
13	Minnesota	10
30	at San Diego	16
7	Jacksonville	17
27	Cincinnati	20
12	at Oakland	10
22	Green Bay	33
11	Denver	27
10	at Indianapolis	13
17	Oakland	20
10	San Diego	24
7	at Denver	41
17	Tennessee	26
20	at Detroit	25
10	at N.Y. Jets (OT)	13
226		335

MIAMI (1-15)
13	at Washington (OT)	16
20	Dallas	37
28	at N.Y. Jets	31
17	Oakland	35
19	at Houston	22
31	at Cleveland	41
28	New England	49
10	New York Giants	13
10	Buffalo	13
7	at Philadelphia	17
0	at Pittsburgh	3
13	New York Jets	40
17	at Buffalo	38
22	Baltimore (OT)	16
7	at New England	28
25	Cincinnati	38
267		437

NEW ENGLAND (16-0)
38	at N.Y. Jets	14
38	San Diego	14
38	Buffalo	7
34	at Cincinnati	13
34	Cleveland	17
48	at Dallas	27
49	at Miami	28
52	Washington	7
24	at Indianapolis	20
56	at Buffalo	10
31	Philadelphia	28
27	at Baltimore	24
34	Pittsburgh	13
20	New York Jets	10
28	Miami	7
38	at N.Y. Giants	35
589		274

JACKSONVILLE (11-5)
10	Tennessee	13
13	Atlanta	7
23	at Denver	14
17	at Kansas City	7
37	Houston	17
7	Indianapolis	29
24	at Tampa Bay	23
24	at New Orleans	41
28	at Tennessee	13
24	San Diego	17
36	Buffalo	14
25	at Indianapolis	28
37	Carolina	6
29	at Pittsburgh	22
49	Oakland	11
28	at Houston	42
411		304

NEW YORK JETS (4-12)
14	New England	38
13	at Baltimore	20
31	Miami	28
14	at Buffalo	17
24	at N.Y. Giants	35
9	Philadelphia	16
31	at Cincinnati	38
3	Buffalo	13
20	Washington (OT)	23
19	Pittsburgh (OT)	16
3	at Dallas	34
40	at Miami	13
18	Cleveland	24
10	at New England	20
6	at Tennessee	10
13	Kansas City (OT)	10
268		355

OAKLAND (4-12)
21	Detroit	36
20	at Denver (OT)	23
26	Cleveland	24
35	at Miami	17
14	at San Diego	28
10	Kansas City	12
9	at Tennessee	13
17	Houston	24
6	Chicago	17
22	at Minnesota	29
20	at Kansas City	17
34	Denver	20
7	at Green Bay	38
14	Indianapolis	21
11	at Jacksonville	49
17	San Diego	30
283		398

PITTSBURGH (10-6)
34	at Cleveland	7
26	Buffalo	3
37	San Francisco	16
14	at Arizona	21
21	Seattle	0
28	at Denver	31
24	at Cincinnati	13
38	Baltimore	7
31	Cleveland	28
16	at N.Y. Jets (OT)	19
3	Miami	0
24	Cincinnati	10
13	at New England	34
22	Jacksonville	29
41	at St. Louis	24
21	at Baltimore	27
393		269

SAN DIEGO (11-5)
14	Chicago	3
14	at New England	38
24	at Green Bay	31
16	Kansas City	30
41	at Denver	3
28	Oakland	14
35	Houston	10
17	at Minnesota	35
23	Indianapolis	21
17	at Jacksonville	24
32	Baltimore	14
24	at Kansas City	10
23	at Tennessee (OT)	17
51	Detroit	14
23	Denver	3
30	at Oakland	17
412		284

TENNESSEE (10-6)
13	at Jacksonville	10
20	Indianapolis	22
31	at New Orleans	14
20	Atlanta	13
10	at Tampa Bay	13
38	at Houston	36
13	Oakland	9
20	Carolina	7
13	Jacksonville	28
20	at Denver	34
6	at Cincinnati	35
28	Houston	20
17	San Diego (OT)	23
26	at Kansas City	17
10	New York Jets	6
16	at Indianapolis	10
301		297

NATIONAL FOOTBALL CONFERENCE

ARIZONA (8-8)
17	at San Francisco	20
23	Seattle	20
23	at Baltimore	26
21	Pittsburgh	14
34	at St. Louis	31
10	Carolina	25
19	at Washington	21
10	at Tampa Bay	17
31	Detroit	21
35	at Cincinnati	27
31	San Francisco (OT)	37
27	Cleveland	21
21	at Seattle	42
24	at New Orleans	31
30	Atlanta (OT)	27
48	St. Louis	19
404		**399**

DALLAS (13-3)
45	New York Giants	35
37	at Miami	20
34	at Chicago	10
35	St. Louis	7
25	at Buffalo	24
27	New England	48
24	Minnesota	14
38	at Philadelphia	17
31	at N.Y. Giants	20
28	Washington	23
34	New York Jets	3
37	Green Bay	27
28	at Detroit	27
6	Philadelphia	10
20	at Carolina	13
6	at Washington	27
455		**325**

NEW ORLEANS (7-9)
10	at Indianapolis	41
14	at Tampa Bay	31
14	Tennessee	31
13	Carolina	16
28	at Seattle	17
22	Atlanta	16
31	at San Francisco	10
41	Jacksonville	24
29	St. Louis	37
10	at Houston	23
31	at Carolina	6
23	Tampa Bay	27
34	at Atlanta	14
31	Arizona	24
23	Philadelphia	38
25	at Chicago	33
379		**388**

SAN FRANCISCO (5-11)
20	Arizona	17
17	at St. Louis	16
16	at Pittsburgh	37
3	Seattle	23
7	Baltimore	9
15	at N.Y. Giants	33
10	New Orleans	31
16	at Atlanta	20
0	at Seattle	24
9	St. Louis	13
37	at Arizona (OT)	31
14	at Carolina	31
7	Minnesota	27
20	Cincinnati	13
21	Tampa Bay	19
7	at Cleveland	20
219		**364**

ATLANTA (4-12)
3	at Minnesota	24
7	at Jacksonville	13
20	Carolina	27
26	Houston	16
13	at Tennessee	20
10	New York Giants	31
16	at New Orleans	22
20	San Francisco	16
20	at Carolina	13
7	Tampa Bay	31
13	Indianapolis	31
16	at St. Louis	28
14	New Orleans	34
3	at Tampa Bay	37
27	at Arizona (OT)	30
44	Seattle	41
259		**414**

DETROIT (7-9)
36	at Oakland	21
20	Minnesota (OT)	17
21	at Philadelphia	56
37	Chicago	27
3	at Washington	34
23	Tampa Bay	16
16	at Chicago	7
44	Denver	7
21	at Arizona	31
10	New York Giants	16
26	Green Bay	37
10	at Minnesota	42
27	Dallas	28
14	at San Diego	51
25	Kansas City	20
13	at Green Bay	34
346		**444**

NEW YORK GIANTS (10-6)
35	at Dallas	45
13	Green Bay	35
24	at Washington	17
16	Philadelphia	3
35	New York Jets	24
31	at Atlanta	10
33	San Francisco	15
13	at Miami	10
20	Dallas	31
16	at Detroit	10
17	Minnesota	41
21	at Chicago	16
16	at Philadelphia	13
10	Washington	22
38	at Buffalo	21
35	New England	38
373		**351**

SEATTLE (10-6)
20	Tampa Bay	6
20	at Arizona	23
24	Cincinnati	21
23	at San Francisco	3
0	at Pittsburgh	21
17	New Orleans	28
33	St. Louis	6
30	at Cleveland (OT)	33
24	San Francisco	0
30	Chicago	23
24	at St. Louis	19
28	at Philadelphia	24
42	Arizona	21
10	at Carolina	13
27	Baltimore	6
41	at Atlanta	44
393		**291**

CAROLINA (7-9)
27	at St. Louis	13
21	Houston	34
27	at Atlanta	20
7	Tampa Bay	20
16	at New Orleans	13
25	at Arizona	10
7	Indianapolis	31
7	at Tennessee	20
13	Atlanta	20
17	at Green Bay	31
6	New Orleans	31
31	San Francisco	14
6	at Jacksonville	37
13	Seattle	10
13	Dallas	20
31	at Tampa Bay	23
267		**347**

GREEN BAY (13-3)
16	Philadelphia	13
35	at N.Y. Giants	13
31	San Diego	24
23	at Minnesota	16
20	Chicago	27
17	Washington	14
19	at Denver (OT)	13
33	at Kansas City	22
34	Minnesota	0
31	Carolina	17
37	at Detroit	26
27	at Dallas	37
38	Oakland	7
33	at St. Louis	14
7	at Chicago	35
34	Detroit	13
435		**291**

PHILADELPHIA (8-8)
13	at Green Bay	16
12	Washington	20
56	Detroit	21
3	at N.Y. Giants	16
16	at N.Y. Jets	9
16	Chicago	19
23	at Minnesota	16
17	Dallas	38
33	at Washington	25
17	Miami	7
28	at New England	31
24	Seattle	28
13	New York Giants	16
10	at Dallas	6
38	at New Orleans	23
17	Buffalo	9
336		**300**

TAMPA BAY (9-7)
6	at Seattle	20
31	New Orleans	14
24	St. Louis	3
20	at Carolina	7
14	at Indianapolis	33
13	Tennessee	10
16	at Detroit	23
23	Jacksonville	24
17	Arizona	10
31	at Atlanta	7
19	Washington	13
27	at New Orleans	23
14	at Houston	28
37	Atlanta	3
19	at San Francisco	21
23	Carolina	31
334		**270**

CHICAGO (7-9)
3	at San Diego	14
20	Kansas City	10
10	Dallas	34
27	at Detroit	37
27	at Green Bay	20
31	Minnesota	34
19	at Philadelphia	16
7	Detroit	16
17	at Oakland	6
23	at Seattle	30
37	Denver (OT)	34
16	New York Giants	21
16	at Washington	24
13	at Minnesota	20
35	Green Bay	7
33	New Orleans	25
334		**348**

MINNESOTA (8-8)
24	Atlanta	3
17	at Detroit (OT)	20
10	at Kansas City	13
16	Green Bay	23
34	at Chicago	31
14	at Dallas	24
16	Philadelphia	23
35	San Diego	17
0	at Green Bay	34
29	Oakland	22
41	at N.Y. Giants	17
42	Detroit	10
27	at San Francisco	7
20	Chicago	13
21	Washington	32
19	at Denver (OT)	22
365		**311**

ST. LOUIS (3-13)
13	Carolina	27
16	San Francisco	17
3	at Tampa Bay	24
7	at Dallas	35
31	Arizona	34
3	at Baltimore	22
6	at Seattle	33
20	Cleveland	27
37	at New Orleans	29
13	at San Francisco	9
19	Seattle	24
28	Atlanta	16
10	at Cincinnati	19
14	Green Bay	33
24	Pittsburgh	41
19	at Arizona	48
263		**438**

WASHINGTON (9-7)
16	Miami (OT)	13
20	at Philadelphia	12
17	New York Giants	24
34	Detroit	3
14	at Green Bay	17
21	Arizona	19
7	at New England	52
23	at N.Y. Jets (OT)	20
25	Philadelphia	33
23	at Dallas	28
13	at Tampa Bay	19
16	Buffalo	17
24	Chicago	16
22	at N.Y. Giants	10
32	at Minnesota	21
27	Dallas	6
334		**310**

FINAL STANDINGS

AMERICAN FOOTBALL CONFERENCE

East Division	W	L	T	Pct.	Pts.	OP
* New England	16	0	0	1.000	589	274
Buffalo	7	9	0	.438	252	354
New York Jets	4	12	0	.250	268	355
Miami	1	15	0	.063	267	437
North Division	**W**	**L**	**T**	**Pct.**	**Pts.**	**OP**
* Pittsburgh	10	6	0	.625	393	269
Cleveland	10	6	0	.625	402	382
Cincinnati	7	9	0	.438	380	385
Baltimore	5	11	0	.313	275	384
South Division	**W**	**L**	**T**	**Pct.**	**Pts.**	**OP**
* Indianapolis	13	3	0	.813	450	262
# Jacksonville	11	5	0	.688	411	304
# Tennessee	10	6	0	.625	301	297
Houston	8	8	0	.500	379	384
West Division	**W**	**L**	**T**	**Pct.**	**Pts.**	**OP**
* San Diego	11	5	0	.688	412	284
Denver	7	9	0	.438	320	409
Kansas City	4	12	0	.250	226	335
Oakland	4	12	0	.250	283	398

NATIONAL FOOTBALL CONFERENCE

East Division	W	L	T	Pct.	Pts.	OP
* Dallas	13	3	0	.813	455	325
# New York Giants	10	6	0	.625	373	351
# Washington	9	7	0	.563	334	310
Philadelphia	8	8	0	.500	336	300
North Division	**W**	**L**	**T**	**Pct.**	**Pts.**	**OP**
* Green Bay	13	3	0	.813	435	291
Minnesota	8	8	0	.500	365	311
Detroit	7	9	0	.438	346	444
Chicago	7	9	0	.438	334	348
South Division	**W**	**L**	**T**	**Pct.**	**Pts.**	**OP**
* Tampa Bay	9	7	0	.563	334	270
Carolina	7	9	0	.438	267	347
New Orleans	7	9	0	.438	379	388
Atlanta	4	12	0	.250	259	414
West Division	**W**	**L**	**T**	**Pct.**	**Pts.**	**OP**
* Seattle	10	6	0	.625	393	291
Arizona	8	8	0	.500	404	399
San Francisco	5	11	0	.313	219	364
St. Louis	3	13	0	.188	263	438

* *Division champion*
\# *Wild Card team*

Pittsburgh finished ahead of Cleveland based on head-to-head sweep (2-0). Tennessee finished ahead of Cleveland based on better record vs. common opponents (4-1 to Browns' 3-2). Kansas City finished ahead of Oakland based on better record vs. common opponents (2-10 to Raiders' 1-11). Dallas finished ahead of Green Bay based on head-to-head victory. Detroit finished ahead of Chicago based on head-to-head sweep (2-0). Carolina finished ahead of New Orleans based on better conference record (7-5 to Saints' 6-6).

WILD-CARD PLAYOFFS

AFC
Jacksonville 31, PITTSBURGH 29
SAN DIEGO 17, Tennessee 6

NFC
SEATTLE 35, Washington 14
N.Y. Giants 24, TAMPA BAY 14

DIVISIONAL PLAYOFFS

AFC
NEW ENGLAND 31, Jacksonville 20
San Diego 28, INDIANAPOLIS 24

NFC
GREEN BAY 42, Seattle 20
N.Y. Giants 21, DALLAS 17

CHAMPIONSHIP GAMES

AFC
NEW ENGLAND 21, San Diego 12

NFC
N.Y. Giants 23, GREEN BAY 20 (OT)

SUPER BOWL XLII

N.Y. Giants (NFC) 17, New England (AFC) 14
at University of Phoenix Stadium, Glendale, Arizona

AFC-NFC PRO BOWL

NFC 42, AFC 30
at Aloha Stadium, Honolulu, Hawaii

Home teams in playoff games are indicated in CAPS.

FIRST WEEK SUMMARIES

American Football Conference

East Division	**W**	**L**	**T**	**Pct.**	**Pts.**	**OP**
New England	1	0	0	1.000	38	14
Buffalo	0	1	0	.000	14	15
Miami	0	1	0	.000	13	16
N.Y. Jets	0	1	0	.000	14	38
North Division	**W**	**L**	**T**	**Pct.**	**Pts.**	**OP**
Cincinnati	1	0	0	1.000	27	20
Pittsburgh	1	0	0	1.000	34	7
Baltimore	0	1	0	.000	20	27
Cleveland	0	1	0	.000	7	34
South Division	**W**	**L**	**T**	**Pct.**	**Pts.**	**OP**
Indianapolis	1	0	0	1.000	41	10
Houston	1	0	0	1.000	20	3
Tennessee	1	0	0	1.000	13	10
Jacksonville	0	1	0	.000	10	13
West Division	**W**	**L**	**T**	**Pct.**	**Pts.**	**OP**
Denver	1	0	0	1.000	15	14
San Diego	1	0	0	1.000	14	3
Kansas City	0	1	0	.000	3	20
Oakland	0	1	0	.000	21	36

National Football Conference

East Division	**W**	**L**	**T**	**Pct.**	**Pts.**	**OP**
Dallas	1	0	0	1.000	45	35
Washington	1	0	0	1.000	16	13
N.Y. Giants	0	1	0	.000	35	45
Philadelphia	0	1	0	.000	13	16
North Division	**W**	**L**	**T**	**Pct.**	**Pts.**	**OP**
Detroit	1	0	0	1.000	36	21
Green Bay	1	0	0	1.000	16	13
Minnesota	1	0	0	1.000	24	3
Chicago	0	1	0	.000	3	14
South Division	**W**	**L**	**T**	**Pct.**	**Pts.**	**OP**
Carolina	1	0	0	1.000	27	13
Atlanta	0	1	0	.000	3	24
New Orleans	0	1	0	.000	10	41
Tampa Bay	0	1	0	.000	6	20
West Division	**W**	**L**	**T**	**Pct.**	**Pts.**	**OP**
San Francisco	1	0	0	1.000	20	17
Seattle	1	0	0	1.000	20	6
Arizona	0	1	0	.000	17	20
St. Louis	0	1	0	.000	13	27

THURSDAY NIGHT, SEPTEMBER 6

INDIANAPOLIS 41, NEW ORLEANS 10—at RCA Dome, attendance 57,361. Peyton Manning passed for 288 yards and 3 touchdowns as the defending Super Bowl-champion Colts held the Saints without an offensive touchdown. The Colts had 452 yards of offense, including 263 in the second half, as they scored the games final 34 points. A 42-yard pass to Marvin Harrison set up Joseph Addai's 2-yard touchdown run to being the second half and give the Colts a 17-10 lead. The Colts scored on their next three possessions as well, the second set up by Freddie Keiaho's interception, and Matt Giordano capped the scoring with an 83-yard interception return for a touchdown with 55 seconds to play. Manning was 18 of 30 for 288 yards and 3 touchdowns. Reggie Wayne had 7 catches for 115 yards and Addai rushed 23 times for 118 yards. Drew Brees was 28 of 41 for 192 yards, with 2 interceptions.

New Orleans	0	10	0	0	—	10
Indianapolis	7	3	14	17	—	41

Ind — Harrison 27 pass from P. Manning (Vinatieri kick)
NO — David 55 fumble return (Mare kick)
NO — FG Mare 34
Ind — FG Vinatieri 33
Ind — Addai 2 run (Viantieri kick)
Ind — Wayne 28 pass from P. Manning (Vinatieri kick)
Ind — FG Vinatieri 33
Ind — Wayne 45 pass from P. Manning (Vinatieri kick)
Ind — Giordano 83 interception return (Vinatieri kick)

SUNDAY, SEPTEMBER 9

DENVER 15, BUFFALO 14—at Ralph Wilson Stadium, attendance 71,132. Jason Elam kicked a 42-yard field goal as time expired to lift the Broncos past the Bills. The Broncos outgained the Bills 470-184 in total yards, and drove into Buffalo territory on eight of their 10 possessions. Jim Leonhard intercepted a pass at the Bills' 8 with 27 seconds left in the half to help the Bills maintain a 7-6 lead. Elam missed a 50-yard field-goal attempt in the third quarter, and Marshawn Lynch scored on a 23-yard run nine plays later to give Buffalo a 14-6 lead. The Broncos responded with Jay Cutler's 5-yard touchdown pass to Brandon Marshall, but his 2-point attempt pass to Javon Walker was incomplete. The score remained 14-12 as the Broncos began their final drive on their own 34 with 2:13 to play. The Broncos twice completed fourth-and-2 situations on the final drive, once when Cutler ran for 7 yards and the second time on an 8-yard pass to Walker. On third-and-10 from the Bills' 35 with 18 seconds left Cutler completed an 11-yard pass to Walker. The Broncos rushed their special-teams unit on the field, and just before the clock struck zero Mike Leach snapped the ball and Elam nailed the 42-yard field goal. Cutler was 23 of 39 for 304 yards and 1 touchdown, with 1 interception. Walker had 9 receptions for 119 yards. J.P. Losman was 14 of 21 for 97 yards, with 1 interception.

Denver	3	3	6	3	—	15
Buffalo	7	0	7	0	—	14

Buff — Parrish 74 punt return (Lindell kick)
Den — FG Elam 21
Den — FG Elam 48
Buff — Lynch 23 run (Lindell kick)
Den — Marshall 5 pass from Cutler (pass failed)
Den — FG Elam 42

PITTSBURGH 34, CLEVELAND 7—at Cleveland Browns Stadium, attendance 73,089. The Steelers' defense registered 6 sacks and forced 5 turnovers as Mike Tomlin won his NFL head-coaching debut. On offense, the Steelers rushed 42 times for 206 yard and maintained possession for 36 minutes, 16 seconds. Of their 14 drives, the Browns only had one possession inside the Steelers' 35, and that is when Lawrence Vickers caught a 1-yard touchdown pass to cut the deficit to 24-7. The Steelers scored on their next two possessions to complete the scoring. Ben Roethlisberger was 12 of 23 for 161 yards and 4 touchdowns. Willie Parker rushed 27 times for 109 yards. Charlie Frye started and was 4 of 10 for 34 yards, with 1 interception. Derek Anderson entered in the second quarter and was 13 of 28 for 184 yards and 1 touchdown, with 1 interception.

Pittsburgh	17	0	14	3	—	34
Cleveland	0	0	7	0	—	7

Pitt — Ward 5 pass from Roethlisberger (Reed kick)
Pitt — FG Reed 26
Pitt — Holmes 40 pass from Roethlisberger (Reed kick)
Pitt — Spaeth 5 pass from Roethlisberger (Reed kick)
Cle — Vickers 1 pass from Anderson (Dawson kick)
Pitt — Miller 22 pass from Roethlisberger (Reed kick)
Pitt — FG Reed 31

GREEN BAY 16, PHILADELPHIA 13—at Lambeau Field, attendance 70,598. Rookie Mason Crosby kicked a 42-yard field goal with two seconds remaining as the Packers outlasted the Eagles. The Packers took advantage of two misplayed punts by the Eagles. Less than two minutes into the game Greg Lewis muffed a Jon Ryan punt at the Eagles' 21-yard line. A wild scramble ensued on the wet field and Tracy White recovered the football in the end zone for a Packers' touchdown and 7-0 lead. An interception by Nick Barnett at the Eagles' 34 moments later set up Crosby's first field goal for a 10-0 lead. With the score 13-13 with 1:09 to play, Ryan punted to J.R. Reed, who attempted to run up and catch the 29-yard punt. Instead, Reed muffed the ball and Jarrett Bush recovered at the Eagles' 31 with 59 seconds left. After two running plays and a kneeldown netted 6 yards, Crosby drilled the game-winning 42-yard field goal. Brett Favre was 23 of 42 for 206 yards, with 1 interception. Donovan McNabb was 15 of 33 for 184 yards and 1 touchdown, with 1 interception.

Philadelphia	0	10	3	0	—	13
Green Bay	10	0	3	3	—	16

GB — White fumble recovery in end zone (Crosby kick)
GB — FG Crosby 53
Phil — FG Akers 33
Phil — Avant 9 pass from McNabb (Akers kick)
Phil — FG Akers 47
GB — FG Crosby 37
GB — FG Crosby 42

HOUSTON 20, KANSAS CITY 3—at Reliant Stadium, attendance 70,080. Matt Schaub passed for 225 yards and 1 touchdown in his first game with the Texans. The Texans' forced 4 turnovers, and the Chiefs drove into Houston territory just two times. Schaub connected with Andre Johnson on a 77-yard touchdown pass in the second quarter. Three plays into the second half, Jamar Fletcher forced Kris Wilson to fumble. Mario Williams picked up the fumble and raced 38 yards for a touchdown. The Chiefs kicked a field goal late in the third quarter, but the Texans responded with a 15-play, 65-yard drive that consumed exactly 10 minutes and was capped by Kris Brown's 28-yard field goal with 5:05 to play for a 20-3 lead. Schaub was 16 of 22 for 225 yards and 1 touchdown, with 1 interception. Damon Huard was 22 of 33 for 168 yards, with 2 interceptions.

Kansas City	0	0	3	0	—	3
Houston	0	10	7	3	—	20

Hou — FG K. Brown 26
Hou — A. Johnson 77 pass from Schaub (K. Brown kick)
Hou — M. Williams 38 fumble return (K. Brown kick)
KC — FG Medlock 27
Hou — FG K. Brown 28

TENNESSEE 13, JACKSONVILLE 10—at Jacksonville Municipal Stadium, attendance 65,437. The Titans rushed for a club-record 282 yards as Tennessee maintained possession for 36 minutes, 55 seconds to beat the Jaguars. In his first game as the newly-anointed starter, David Garrard completed a perfectly placed 47-yard deep pass down the middle to rookie John Broussard for a touchdown and a 7-3 lead. Early in the second quarter, Gerald Sensabaugh recovered LenDale White's fumble at the Jaguars' 1 to quell a scoring threat. Josh Scobee kicked a 22-yard field goal in the second quarter, but Scobee had injured his quadricep in pregame warmups. Thus, in the third quarter with Jacksonville leading 10-7, Scobee was unable to attempt a 37-yard field goal. The Jaguars had to go for it on fourth-and-10 from the Titans' 19, and Garrard's pass to Maurice Jones-Drew lost two yards. The Titans responded with a 12-play, 79-yard drive capped by Vince Young's 2-yard touchdown run for a 13-10 Titans' lead. The Jaguars drove deep into Titans' territory, but Jones-Drew ran into teammate Marcedes Lewis, fumbled and Chris Hope recovered. The Jaguars never threatened again. Young was 11 of 18 for 78 yards, with 1 interception. Chris Brown had 19 carries for 175 yards. Garrard was 17 of 30 for 204 yards and 1 touchdown.

Tennessee	3	3	7	0	—	13
Jacksonville	7	3	0	0	—	10

Tenn — FG Bironas 20
Jax — Broussard 47 pass from Garrard (Scobee kick)
Jax — FG Scobee 22
Tenn — FG Bironas 31
Tenn — Young 2 run (Bironas kick)

MINNESOTA 24, ATLANTA 3—at Metrodome, attendance 62,815. Rookie Adrian Peterson rushed for 103 yards and turned a screen pass into a 60-yard touchdown as the Vikings defeated the Falcons. Kevin Williams ended Joey Harrington's first drive as the Falcons' quarterback with an interception and 54-yard return for a touchdown and 7-0 lead. Rookie Matt Prater missed a 44-yard field-goal attempt in the second quarter, but made a 45-yard field goal in the fourth quarter to pull the Falcons within 10-3. However, four plays later, on third-and-5, Peterson temporarily bobbled the screen pass, then burst through the secondary and raced 60 yards for a touchdown and 17-3 lead. Antoine Winfield's interception return for a touchdown with 2:37 to play finished the scoring. All five of Chris Kluwe's punts pinned the Falcons' inside the 20-yard line. Tarvaris Jackson was 13 of 23 for 163 yards and 1 touchdown, with 1 interception. Peterson rushed 19 times for 103 yards. Harrington was 23 of 32 for 199 yards, with 2 interceptions.

Atlanta	0	0	0	3	—	3
Minnesota	7	0	3	14	—	24

Minn — K. Williams 54 interception return (Longwell kick)
Minn — FG Longwell 49
Atl — FG Prater 45

Minn	—	Peterson 60 pass from Jackson (Longwell kick)
Minn	—	Winfield 14 interception return (Longwell kick)

NEW ENGLAND 38, N.Y. JETS 14—at The Meadowlands, attendance 77,900. Tom Brady passed for 3 touchdowns as the Patriots downed the Jets. New England outgained the Jets 431-227 in total yards. Chad Pennington's 7-yard touchdown pass to Laveranues Coles tied the game 7-7 with 4:15 remaining in the second quarter. The Patriots responded by scoring on five consecutive possessions, highlighted by Ellis Hobbs' NFL-record-setting 108-yard kickoff return to begin the second half. The Patriots' other five scoring drives were 91, 73, 85, 75, and 53 yards. Brady was 22 of 28 for 297 yards and 3 touchdowns. Randy Moss, in his first game with the Patriots, had 9 receptions for 183 yards and a long 51-yard touchdown catch in the third quarter. Pennington was 16 of 21 for 167 yards and 2 touchdowns. Kellen Clemens replaced an injured Pennington and was 5 of 10 for 35 yards.

New England	7	7	14	10	—	38
N.Y. Jets	0	7	0	7	—	14

NE	—	Welker 11 pass from Brady (Gostkowski kick)
NYJ	—	Coles 7 pass from Pennington (Nugent kick)
NE	—	Watson 5 pass from Brady (Gostkowski kick)
NE	—	Hobbs 108 kickoff return (Gostkowski kick)
NE	—	R. Moss 51 pass from Brady (Gostkowski kick)
NYJ	—	Coles 1 pass from Pennington (Nugent kick)
NE	—	FG Gostkowski 22
NE	—	Evans 1 run (Gostkowski kick)

DETROIT 36, OAKLAND 21—at McAfee Coliseum, attendance 61,547. Jon Kitna passed for 3 touchdowns as the Lions matched their road-win total from the past season. Travis Fisher intercepted a pass on the Raiders' first drive of the second half, setting up rookie Calvin Johnson's 16-yard touchdown catch to give the Lions a 17-0 lead. Late in the third quarter, trailing 17-7, Stanford Routt intercepted a pass from Kitna and returned it 31 yards to set up LaMont Jordan's 12-yard touchdown run to pull the Raiders within 17-14. The Lions responded with a field goal, but Josh McCown responded by completing all 5 of his pass attempts on the ensuing possession, capped by Justin Griffith's 7-yard touchdown catch, to give Oakland a 21-20 lead with 7:43 to play. The Lions answered with an 80-yard drive, highlighted by Kitna's 13-yard pass to Shaun McDonald on third-and-9, and capped by the duo's 32-yard touchdown, for a 26-21 lead with 4:15 remaining. Dewayne White intercepted a pass to set up Jason Hanson's third field goal with 1:56 to play, and then forced McCown to fumble with 1:37 remaining. Kalimba Edwards recovered the fumble, and Tatum Bell scored with 1:16 left to finish the scoring. Kitna was 27 of 36 for 289 yards and 3 touchdowns, with 2 interceptions. McCown was 30 of 40 for 313 yards and 2 touchdowns, with 2 interceptions. Ronald Curry had 10 catches for 133 yards.

Detroit	0	10	7	19	—	36
Oakland	0	0	14	7	—	21

Det	—	R. Williams 13 pass from Kitna (Hanson kick)
Det	—	FG Hanson 46
Det	—	C. Johnson 16 pass from Kitna (Hanson kick)
Oak	—	Curry 4 pass from McCown (Janikowski kick)
Oak	—	Jordan 12 run (Janikowski kick)
Det	—	FG Hanson 46
Oak	—	Griffith 7 pass from McCown (Janikowski kick)
Det	—	McDonald 32 pass from Kitna (pass failed)
Det	—	FG Hanson 23
Det	—	T. Bell 14 run (Hanson kick)

CAROLINA 27, ST. LOUIS 13—at Edward Jones Dome, attendance 65,307. Jake Delhomme passed for 3 touchdowns as the Panthers knocked off the Rams. Trailing 13-7 in the third quarter, the Panthers scored on four of their final five possessions. The Panthers took the lead 14-13 on Delhomme's 68-yard touchdown pass

to Steve Smith. Delhomme's 9-yard touchdown pass to Drew Carter with 7:15 remaining gave the Panthers a 24-13 lead, and Marc Bulger's fourth-and-2 pass intended for Isaac Bruce fell incomplete with 5:07 to play. Delhomme was 18 of 27 for 199 yards and 3 touchdowns. Smith had 7 catches for 118 yards. Bulger was 22 of 42 for 167 yards and 1 touchdown.

Carolina	7	0	7	13	—	27
St. Louis	7	3	3	0	—	13

Car	—	Carter 10 pass from Delhomme (Kasay kick)
StL	—	Holt 3 pass from Bulger (Wilkins kick)
StL	—	FG Wilkins 42
StL	—	FG Wilkins 28
Car	—	Smith 68 pass from Delhomme (Kasay kick)
Car	—	FG Kasay 34
Car	—	Carter 9 pass from Delhomme (Kasay kick)
Car	—	FG Kasay 32

SAN DIEGO 14, CHICAGO 3—at Qualcomm Stadium, attendance 67,837. The Chargers' defense limited the Bears to 11 first downs and forced 4 turnovers as San Diego rallied to defeat Chicago. The Chargers maintained possession for 37:03, including 21:21 of the second half. The Bears ran just 21 plays in the second half, and fumbled three times, leading to both San Diego touchdowns. Brandon McGowan fumbled a punt late in the third quarter. Matt Wilhelm recovered and LaDainian Tomlinson tossed a halfback-option pass to Antonio Gates for a 17-yard touchdown and 7-3 lead. Six plays later, Adrian Peterson fumbled and Clinton Hart recovered at the Chargers' 44. Tomlinson scored eight plays later for a 14-3 lead with 9:09 left. Cedric Benson was stopped for no gain on fourth-and-1 at the Chargers' 35 with 6:02 left, ending their final scoring opportunity. Philip Rivers was 22 of 31 for 190 yards, with 1 interception. Gates had 9 receptions for 107 yards. Grossman was 12 of 23 for 145 yards, with 1 interception.

Chicago	0	3	0	0	—	3
San Diego	0	0	7	7	—	14

Chi	—	FG Gould 27
SD	—	Gates 17 pass from Tomlinson (Kaeding kick)
SD	—	Tomlinson 7 run (Kaeding kick)

SEATTLE 20, TAMPA BAY 6—at Qwest Field, attendance 68,044. Shaun Alexander rushed for 105 yards and 1 touchdown as the Seahawks defeated the Buccaneers. Matt Bryant kicked 2 first-quarter field goals for the Buccaneers, but the Seahawks' defense stymied Tampa Bay the remainder of the game. The Buccaneers drove inside the Seahawks' 44 just once in their final nine possessions. By that point, the Seahawks already led 20-6, and the drive ended when Lofa Tatupu forced Earnest Graham to fumble. Kelly Jennings recovered at the Seahawks' 8-yard line with 3:38 to play to secure the victory. Matt Hasselbeck was 17 of 24 for 222 yards and 1 touchdown. Alexander had 27 carries for 105 yards. Jeff Garcia was 19 of 27 for 201 yards.

Tampa Bay	6	0	0	0	—	6
Seattle	0	10	0	10	—	20

TB	—	FG Bryant 38
TB	—	FG Bryant 32
Sea	—	FG J. Brown 28
Sea	—	Alexander 1 run (J. Brown kick)
Sea	—	FG J. Brown 28
Sea	—	Morris 34 pass from Hasselbeck (J. Brown kick)

WASHINGTON 16, MIAMI 13 (OT)—at FedExField, attendance 90,163. Shaun Suisham kicked a 39-yard field goal in overtime as the Redskins fought off the Dolphins. Trent Green completed a 1-yard touchdown pass to Justin Peelle on the final play of the first half to give the Dolphins a 7-3 halftime lead. Suisham gave the Redskins a 44-yard field goal with 5:30 remaining, but Green completed 4 of 5 pass-attempts to set up Jay Feely's game-tying field goal with 1:55 to play. On the final play of regulation, from the Redskins' 43, Jason Campbell unloaded a long pass for the end zone. Jason Taylor knocked down the pass, but Antwaan Randle El, trailing the play, caught the ball at the Dolphins' 7. Randle El managed to get into the end zone, but Taylor pushed him out of bounds at the 3-yard line as time expired. In overtime, the Redskins won the toss and Clinton Portis carried four times for 34 yards to set up Suisham's game-winning kick. Campbell was 12 of 21 for 222

yards, with 2 interceptions. Randle El had 5 receptions for 162 yards. Green was 24 of 38 for 219 yards and 1 touchdown.

Miami	0	7	3	0	—	13
Washington	0	3	7	3	—	16

Wash	—	FG Suisham 31
Mia	—	Peelle 1 pass from Green (Feely kick)
Wash	—	Portis 19 run (Suisham kick)
Mia	—	FG Feely 20
Wash	—	FG Suisham 44
Mia	—	FG Feely 36
Wash	—	FG Suisham 39

SUNDAY NIGHT, SEPTEMBER 9

DALLAS 45, N.Y. GIANTS 35—at Texas Stadium, attendance 63,031. Tony Romo passed for 345 yards and 4 touchdowns, and ran for another score, as the Cowboys outscored the Giants. During a stretch from the second through fourth quarter, the Giants scored six times on seven possessions, yet trailed 38-35. An interception by Jacques Reeves set up Romo's 12-yard touchdown pass to Jason Witten for a 17-6 lead in the second quarter. The Giants answered with a 75-yard touchdown drive, capped by Plaxico Burress' 4-yard scoring catch with 14 seconds left in the half. Kevin Dockery recovered Tyson Thompson's fumble on the ensuing kickoff to set up Lawrence Tynes' 44-yard field goal to give the Giants 10 points in the final 14 seconds of the first half and pull within 17-16. Tynes' third field goal cut the deficit to 31-22 early in the fourth quarter, but the Cowboys only needed three plays to counter, with Romo's 47-yard touchdown pass to Terrell Owens giving Dallas a 38-22 lead with 11:43 to play. The Giants countered with an 80-yard touchdown drive, but Eli Manning was sacked on the 2-point conversion attempt. On the next play, Gibril Wilson intercepted Romo's pass. Five plays later, Manning connected with Burress on the pair's third-touchdown connection of the game to pull within 38-35 with 4:09 remaining. Thompson returned the ensuing kickoff 46 yards, and three plays later, on third-and-seven, Romo hit a slanting Sam Hurd for a 51-yard touchdown pass and 45-35 lead with 3:03 to play. Jared Lorenzen suffered an injured Manning, and was sacked on fourth down by Roy Williams with 2:08 to play to end the final threat. Romo was 15 of 24 for 345 yards and 4 touchdowns, with 1 interception. Witten had 6 receptions for 116 yards. Manning was 28 of 41 for 312 yards and 4 touchdowns, with 1 interception. Burress had 8 receptions for 144 yards.

N.Y. Giants	6	10	3	16	—	35
Dallas	3	14	14	14	—	45

NYG	—	Burress 60 pass from E. Manning (mishandled snap)
Dall	—	FG Folk 31
Dall	—	Barber 18 run (Folk kick)
Dall	—	Witten 12 pass from Romo (Folk kick)
NYG	—	Burress 4 pass from E. Manning (Tynes kick)
NYG	—	FG Tynes 44
Dall	—	Owens 22 pass from Romo (Folk kick)
NYG	—	FG Tynes 48
Dall	—	Romo 9 run (Folk kick)
NYG	—	FG Tynes 24
Dall	—	Owens 47 pass from Romo (Folk kick)
NYG	—	Ward 9 pass from E. Manning (pass failed)
NYG	—	Burress 10 pass from E. Manning (Tynes kick)
Dall	—	Hurd 51 pass from Romo (Folk kick)

MONDAY NIGHT, SEPTEMBER 10

CINCINNATI 27, BALTIMORE 20—at Paul Brown Stadium, attendance 66,093. Michael Myers intercepted a pass in the end zone with 1:13 remaining as the Bengals won an AFC North battle. The Bengals' defense forced 6 turnovers, including 2 fourth-quarter interceptions, to hold off the Ravens. Landon Johnson had 11 tackles and recovered 2 fumbles, the latter of which was generated by Robert Geathers' sack that forced Steve McNair to fumble and was returned by Johnson 34 yards for a touchdown and 19-10 third-quarter lead. Matt Stover's second field goal, from 23 yards early in the fourth quarter, cut the deficit to 19-13. The Ravens' defense then forced a three-and-out, and Ed Reed returned the ensuing punt 63 yards for a touchdown and 20-19 Ravens' lead with 12:07 to play. The Ravens' defense forced another punt, but Geathers intercepted a McNair pass three plays later and returned it 30 yard to the Ravens' 22 to set up T.J. Houshmandzadeh's 7-yard touchdown catch from Carson Palmer with 8:53 to play. With 1:19 to play, on third-and-goal from the Bengals' 2, Kyle Boller, who was in for an injured McNair, fired a short pass for Todd Heap. The ball deflected off Heap and Johnson before Myers dove and intercepted the pass for a touchback. Palmer was 20 of 32 for 194 yards and 2 touchdowns. McNair was 20 of 34 for 203 yards, with 1 interception.

| Baltimore | 0 | 10 | 0 | 10 | — | 20 |
| Cincinnati | 9 | 3 | 7 | 8 | — | 27 |

Cin	—	C. Johnson 39 pass from Palmer (kick blocked)
Cin	—	FG Graham 23
Balt	—	M. Smith 6 run (Stover kick)
Cin	—	FG Graham 40
Balt	—	FG Stover 36
Cin	—	L. Johnson 34 fumble return (Graham kick)
Balt	—	FG Stover 23
Balt	—	Reed 63 punt return (Stover kick)
Cin	—	Houshmandzadeh 7 pass from Palmer (R. Johnson run)

MONDAY NIGHT, SEPTEMBER 10
SAN FRANCISCO 20, ARIZONA 17—at Monster Park, attendance 68,111. Arnaz Battle scored on a 1-yard run with 22 seconds remaining as the 49ers rallied to defeat the Cardinals. Walt Harris' 23-yard interception return to he Cardinals' 6-yard line set up Frank Gore's 6-yard scoring run for a 7-0 San Francisco lead. Arizona took a 10-7 lead on Edgerrin James' 7-yard run, which had been set up by Antonio Smith's recovery of an Alex Smith fumble. A 20-yard scramble by Matt Leinart on third down set up Leinart's 5-yard touchdown pass to Anquan Boldin to give the Cardinals a 17-13 lead with 6:40 remaining. The 49ers' offense had accumulated just 108 yards of total offense the entire night when they began their final drive at their own 14-yard line with 2:58 to play. Smith completed 4 consecutive passes to get into Cardinals' territory. Then, on fourth-and-13, Smith completed a pass deep over the middle to Battle. Just before Battle crossed the goal line, Terrence Holt forced Battle to fumble. Darrell Jackson recovered the ball in the end zone. Since an offensive teammate cannot advance a fumble in the final two minutes, the ball was placed on the 1-yard line with 26 seconds left. On the next play, with Battle coming in motion, he received the handoff and went around left end for the winning score. Shawntae Spencer intercepted Leinart's deep pass on the next play to secure the victory. Smith was 15 of 31 for 126 yards. Leinart was 14 of 28 for 102 yards and 1 touchdown, with 2 interceptions.

| Arizona | 0 | 10 | 0 | 7 | — | 17 |
| San Francisco | 7 | 3 | 3 | 7 | — | 20 |

SF	—	Gore 6 run (Nedney kick)
Ari	—	FG Rackers 35
Ari	—	James 7 run (Rackers kick)
SF	—	FG Nedney 33
SF	—	FG Nedney 30
Ari	—	Boldin 5 pass from Leinart (Rackers kick)
SF	—	Battle 1 run (Nedney kick)

SECOND WEEK SUMMARIES
American Football Conference

East Division	W	L	T	Pct.	Pts.	OP
New England	2	0	0	1.000	76	28
Buffalo	0	2	0	.000	17	41
N.Y. Jets	0	2	0	.000	27	58
Miami	0	2	0	.000	33	53
North Division	**W**	**L**	**T**	**Pct.**	**Pts.**	**OP**
Pittsburgh	2	0	0	1.000	60	10
Baltimore	1	1	0	.500	40	48
Cincinnati	1	1	0	.500	72	71
Cleveland	1	1	0	.500	58	79
South Division	**W**	**L**	**T**	**Pct.**	**Pts.**	**OP**
Indianapolis	2	0	0	1.000	63	30
Houston	2	0	0	1.000	54	24
Jacksonville	1	1	0	.500	23	24
Tennessee	1	1	0	.500	33	32
West Division	**W**	**L**	**T**	**Pct.**	**Pts.**	**OP**
Denver	2	0	0	1.000	38	34
San Diego	1	1	0	.500	28	41
Kansas City	0	2	0	.000	13	40

| Oakland | 0 | 2 | 0 | .000 | 41 | 59 |

National Football Conference

East Division	W	L	T	Pct.	Pts.	OP
Dallas	2	0	0	1.000	82	55
Washington	2	0	0	1.000	36	25
N.Y. Giants	0	2	0	.000	48	80
Philadelphia	.0	2	0	.000	25	36
North Division	**W**	**L**	**T**	**Pct.**	**Pts.**	**OP**
Detroit	2	0	0	1.000	56	38
Green Bay	2	0	0	1.000	51	26
Chicago	1	1	0	.500	23	24
Minnesota	1	1	0	.500	41	23
South Division	**W**	**L**	**T**	**Pct.**	**Pts.**	**OP**
Carolina	1	1	0	.500	48	47
Tampa Bay	1	1	0	.500	37	34
Atlanta	0	2	0	.000	10	37
New Orleans	0	2	0	.000	24	72
West Division	**W**	**L**	**T**	**Pct.**	**Pts.**	**OP**
San Francisco	2	0	0	1.000	37	33
Arizona	1	1	0	.500	40	40
Seattle	1	1	0	.500	40	29
St. Louis	0	2	0	.000	29	44

SUNDAY, SEPTEMBER 16
ARIZONA 23, SEATTLE 20—at University of Phoenix Stadium, attendance 64,542. Neil Rackers kicked a 42-yard field goal with one second remaining as the Cardinals gave Ken Whisenhunt his first NFL victory. Edgerrin James scored on a 17-yard run with 5:43 left in the first half to give the Cardinals a 17-0 lead. The Seahawks scored on their next four possessions, on drives of 80, 52, 51, and 78 yards to take a 20-17 lead with 9:52 remaining. Rackers kicked a 52-yard field goal to tie the game. With 1:48 remaining, Matt Hasselbeck and Shaun Alexander bumped into each other during a handoff attempt. Darnell Dockett recovered the ball at the Seahawks' 46, and four carries by Edgerrin James, totaling 22 yards, set up Rackers' 42-yard field goal one second later. Matt Leinart was 23 of 37 for 299 yards and 1 touchdown, with 1 interception. James carried 24 times for 128 yards. Hasselbeck was 22 of 36 for 281 yards and 1 touchdown. Deion Branch had 7 receptions for 122 yards.

| Seattle | 0 | 7 | 10 | 3 | — | 20 |
| Arizona | 3 | 14 | 0 | 6 | — | 23 |

Ari	—	FG Rackers 28
Ari	—	Pope 30 pass from Leinart (Rackers kick)
Ari	—	James 17 run (Rackers kick)
Sea	—	Burleson 24 pass from Hasselbeck (J. Brown kick)
Sea	—	Alexander 16 run (J. Brown kick)
Sea	—	FG J. Brown 28
Sea	—	FG J. Brown 28
Ari	—	FG Rackers 52
Ari	—	FG Rackers 42

BALTIMORE 20, N.Y. JETS 13—at M & T Bank Stadium, attendance 71,246. Ray Lewis intercepted a pass in the end zone for a touchback with 1:03 remaining as the Ravens held off the Jets. On third-and-goal from the Jets' 4-yard line, Kyle Boller completed a touchdown pass to Todd Heap with six seconds remaining in the first half to give Baltimore a 17-3 halftime lead. The Ravens led 20-3 early in the fourth quarter when Kellen Clemens, who was making his first NFL start for an injured Chad Pennington, went to a No Huddle offense and went 68 and 81 yards on their next two drives, capped by Clemens' 3-yard touchdown pass to Chris Baker. The Jets got the ball back and drove to the Ravens' 7 with 1:03 left. After an incompletion, Lewis stepped in front of a pass intended for Jerricho Cotchery. Kyle Boller was 23 of 35 for 185 yards and 2 touchdowns. Clemens was 19 of 37 for 260 yards and 1 touchdown, with 2 interceptions. Cotchery had 7 catches for 165 yards.

| N.Y. Jets | 0 | 3 | 0 | 10 | — | 13 |
| Baltimore | 7 | 10 | 0 | 3 | — | 20 |

Balt	—	McGahee 2 run (Stover kick)
NYJ	—	FG Nugent 50
Balt	—	FG Stover 28
Balt	—	Heap 4 pass from Boller (Stover kick)
Balt	—	FG Stover 43
NYJ	—	FG Nugent 21
NYJ	—	Baker 3 pass from Clemens (Nugent kick)

HOUSTON 34, CAROLINA 21—at Bank of America Stadium, attendance 73,665. The Texans scored 34 consecutive points to stun the Panthers and post the franchise's first-ever 2-0 start. Steve Smith caught touchdown passes to conclude each of the Panthers' first two possessions. However, the Texans put together consecutive touchdown drives of their own, capped by scoring catches by Andre Johnson, an took a 17-14 lead into the locker room. In the second half, the Texans scored on their on first possession to take a 24-14 lead. On the ensuing kickoff, Demarcus Faggins forced Nick Goings to fumble. Kevin Walter recovered the ball in the end zone for a touchdown, giving the Texans 14 points in a 12-second span, and a 31-14 lead. Matt Schaub was 20 of 28 for 227 yards and 2 touchdowns. Johnson had 7 receptions for 120 yards. Jake Delhomme was 27 of 41 for 316 yards and 3 touchdowns, with 1 interception. Smith had 8 catches for 153 yards.

| Houston | 7 | 10 | 14 | 3 | — | 34 |
| Carolina | 14 | 0 | 0 | 7 | — | 21 |

Car	—	Smith 7 pass from Delhomme (Kasay kick)
Car	—	Smith 12 pass from Delhomme (Kasay kick)
Hou	—	A. Johnson 31 pass from Schaub (K. Brown kick)
Hou	—	A. Johnson 9 pass from Schaub (K. Brown kick)
Hou	—	FG K. Brown 25
Hou	—	Green 13 run (K. Brown kick)
Hou	—	Walter fumble recovery in end zone (K. Brown kick)
Hou	—	FG K. Brown 33
Car	—	Smith 74 pass from Delhomme (Kasay kick)

CHICAGO 20, KANSAS CITY 10—at Soldier Field, attendance 62,095. Devin Hester returned a punt for a touchdown as the Bears won their home opener. The Chiefs gained just 2 first downs on their first five possessions to fall behind 17-0. The Bears scored on Hester's return, which had been preceded by lineman John St. Clair's first-ever touchdown catch on a tackle eligible play. A third-quarter interception by Napoleon Harris set up David Rayner's field goal to cut the deficit to 20-10. Rayner had a chance to pull the Chiefs within seven points, but his 48-yard field-goal attempt was blocked by Israel Idonije with 10:01 remaining. Donnie Edwards intercepted Rex Grossman's pass moments later to give the Chiefs another chance, but Danieal Manning intercepted Damon Huard's pass in the end zone with 7:47 to play. Lance Briggs recovered a fumble by Michael Bennett, that was forced by Charles Tillman, at the Bears' 16 with 2:21 remaining to seal the victory. Grossman was 20 of 34 for 160 yards and 1 touchdown, with 2 interceptions. Huard was 19 of 28 for 175 yards and 1 touchdown, with 1 interception.

| Kansas City | 0 | 7 | 3 | 0 | — | 10 |
| Chicago | 0 | 17 | 3 | 0 | — | 20 |

Chi	—	St. Clair 2 pass from Grossman (Gould kick)
Chi	—	Hester 73 punt return (Gould kick)
Chi	—	FG Gould 47
KC	—	Bowe 16 pass from Huard (Rayner kick)
Chi	—	FG Gould 38
KC	—	FG Rayner 45

CLEVELAND 51, CINCINNATI 45—at Cleveland Browns Stadium, attendance 72,801. Derek Anderson passed for 5 touchdowns to outduel Carson Palmer and defeat the Bengals. Palmer passed for 401 yards and 6 touchdowns in the defeat. The teams amassed 1,085 total yards, 554 of them by the Browns, while the Bengals had 33 of the 56 first downs in the game. During the second and third quarters, both teams had a stretch of scoring on five of six possessions. Cleveland capped its scoring spree when Jamal Lewis broke free for a 66-yard touchdown run to give the Browns a 41-31 lead with 5:54 left in the third quarter. The Browns immediately scored to pull within 41-38, but the Browns answered in the fourth quarter when Anderson connected on his fifth touchdown with a wide open Braylon Edwards for a 37-yard touchdown with 9:59 to play for a 48-38 lead. The Browns forced a punt and added a field goal for a 51-38 lead. Undaunted, Palmer guided the Bengals on a 64-yard drive, capped by his sixth touchdown, a 7-yard pass to Glenn Holt with 3:39 remaining, to pull within 51-45. The Bengals forced a punt and reached midfield with 33 seconds to play.

Leigh Bodden intercepted Palmer's pass down the right sideline at the 27-yard line to clinch the victory. Anderson was 20 of 33 for 328 yards and 5 touchdowns, with 1 interception. Lewis carried 27 times for 216 yards. Edwards had 8 receptions for 146 yards, and Kellen Winslow added 6 catches for 100 yards. Palmer was 33 of 50 for 401 yards and 6 touchdowns, with 2 interceptions. Chad Johnson had 11 receptions for 209 yards.

Cincinnati	7	14	17	7	—	45
Cleveland	6	21	14	10	—	51

Cin	—	R. Johnson 13 pass from Palmer (Graham kick)
Cle	—	FG Dawson 39
Cle	—	FG Dawson 39
Cle	—	Jurevicius 17 pass from Anderson (Dawson kick)
Cin	—	Houshmandzadeh 23 pass from Palmer (Graham kick)
Cle	—	Jurevicius 9 pass from Anderson (Dawson kick)
Cin	—	C. Johnson 22 pass from Palmer (Graham kick)
Cle	—	Winslow 25 pass from Anderson (Dawson kick)
Cin	—	FG Graham 20
Cle	—	Edwards 34 pass from Anderson (Dawson kick)
Cin	—	C. Johnson 14 pass from Palmer (Graham kick)
Cle	—	J. Lewis 66 run (Dawson kick)
Cin	—	Houshmandzadeh 5 pass from Palmer (Graham kick)
Cle	—	Edwards 37 pass from Anderson (Dawson kick)
Cle	—	FG Dawson 18
Cin	—	Holt 7 pass from Palmer (Graham kick)

DENVER 23, OAKLAND 20 (OT)—at INVESCO Field at Mile High, attendance 76,784. Jason Elam kicked a 23-yard field goal in overtime, after Sebastian Janikowski missed a game-winning field-goal attempt moments earlier, as the Broncos avoided a division loss to the rival Raiders. The Broncos outgained the Raiders 441-253 total yards, including a 208-85 advantage in the first half as Denver took a 17-3 halftime lead. Elam missed a 45-yard field-goal attempt to begin the second half, and the Raiders answered with Josh McCown's 46-yard touchdown pass to Jerry Porter. Early in the fourth quarter, Gerard Warren sacked Jay Cutler for a safety, and on the Broncos' next possession Thomas Howard intercepted Cutler's pass and returned it 44 yards for a touchdown and 20-17 lead with 8:55 to play. Elam tied the game with a 20-yard field goal with 2:18 remaining. In overtime, the Broncos won the toss, but were forced to punt. LaMont Jordan raced 33 yards on the Raiders' first play of overtime to set up Janikowski's potential game-winning kick. Janikowski made the initial attempt from 52 yards, but Mike Shanahan had called time out just before the snap. Janikowski's official attempt then hit high off the left upright. A 22-yard pass from Cutler to Brandon Marshall set up Elam's game-winning kick with 5:48 left in overtime. Cutler was 23 of 33 for 269 yard and 1 touchdown, with 2 interceptions. Travis Henry had 26 carries for 128 yards. Javon Walker had 8 receptions for 101 yards. McCown was 8 of 16 for 73 yards and 1 touchdown, with 3 interceptions. Jordan rushed 25 times for 159 yards.

Oakland	0	3	7	10	0	— 20
Denver	7	10	0	3	3	— 23

Den	—	Stokley 9 pass from Cutler (Elam kick)
Oak	—	FG Janikowski 38
Den	—	Sapp 4 run (Elam kick)
Den	—	FG Elam 23
Oak	—	Porter 46 pass from McCown (Janikowski kick)
Den	—	Safety, Warren sacked Cutler in end zone
Oak	—	Howard 44 interception return (Curry pass from McCown)
Den	—	FG Elam 20
Den	—	FG Elam 23

DETROIT 20, MINNESOTA 17 (OT)—at Ford Field, attendance 61,771. Jason Hanson made a 37-yard field goal in overtime as the Lions defeated the Vikings in Detroit for the first time since 2001.

The Lions' defense converted 5 turnovers into 17 points. Jon Kitna's second-quarter touchdown pass followed Keith Smith's interception and gave the Lions a 7-0 lead. Kitna left the game after the pass, having suffered a concussion. J.T. O'Sullivan replaced him, and completed a touchdown pass to Calvin Johnson, which had been set up by Gerald Alexander's interception, to take a 17-7 third-quarter lead. Later in the quarter, the Vikings scored 10 points in 49 seconds, the latter score occurring when Kevin Williams sacked O'Sullivan, forced him to fumble, and Ray Edwards recovered and returned the ball 9 yards for a touchdown to tie the game 17-17. Kitna returned in the fourth quarter, and guided the Lions downfield to set up a potential game-winning field-goal attempt, but Jason Hanson's boot from 48 yards was wide left with 45 seconds left. The Vikings drove to the Lions' 34, but Ryan Longwell's 52-yard attempt hit the left upright, forcing overtime. On the first play of overtime, Tarvaris Jackson was knocked out of the game. Brooks Bollinger entered the game, and seven plays later he fumbled the snap. Shaun Rogers recovered at midfield. Brian Calhoun broke off a 17-yard run to set up Hanson's winning kick. Kitna was 22 of 32 for 245 yards and 1 touchdown, with 1 interception. O'Sullivan was 13 of 24 for 148 yards and 1 touchdown, with 2 interceptions. Roy Williams had 7 receptions for 111 yards. Jackson was 17 of 33 for 166 yards, with 4 interceptions.

Minnesota	0	7	10	0	0	— 17
Detroit	0	10	7	0	3	— 20

Det	—	Williams 9 pass from Kitna (Hanson kick)
Minn	—	Jackson 1 run (Longwell kick)
Det	—	FG Hanson 30
Det	—	C. Johnson 7 pass from O'Sullivan (Hanson kick)
Minn	—	FG Longwell 32
Minn	—	Edwards 9 fumble return (Longwell kick)
Det	—	FG Hanson 37

JACKSONVILLE 13, ATLANTA 7—at Jacksonville Municipal Stadium, attendance 61,821. David Garrard passed for 272 yards and 1 touchdown as the Jaguars rallied to defeat the Falcons. Despite Matt Prater's missed 43-yard field goal attempt, the Falcons had a 7-3 halftime lead on the strength of a 12-play, 77-yard touchdown drive. The Falcons had a chance to add to the lead, but Prater missed a 26-yard attempt in the third quarter. On the ensuing possession, Garrard connected with Reggie Williams on third-and-goal from the 14-yard line with 14:10 remaining to take a 10-7 lead. The Jaguars' defense forced a punt, and the offense responded with a 13-play, 50-yard drive that consumed 8:03 off the clock, highlighted by Maurice Jones-Drew's 6-yard run on fourth-and-1 and capped by John Carney's 27-yard field goal with 3:39 to play. With 1:54 remaining, facing fourth-and-16 from their own 22-yard line, the Falcons punted. Fred Taylor gained the game-clinching first down that allowed the Jaguars to run out the clock. Garrard was 17 of 25 for 272 yards and 1 touchdown. Joey Harrington was 12 of 20 for 200 yards.

Atlanta	0	7	0	0	—	7
Jacksonville	0	3	10	0	—	13

Jax	—	FG Carney 35
Atl	—	Dunn 4 run (Prater kick)
Jax	—	R. Williams 14 pass from Garrard (Carney kick)
Jax	—	FG Carney 27

DALLAS 37, MIAMI 20—at Dolphin Stadium, attendance 71,615. Tony Romo passed for 2 touchdowns as the Cowboys scored 20 unanswered points in the second half to defeat the Dolphins. Trent Green's 18-yard touchdown pass to Marty Booker capped a 73-yard drive to begin the second half and gave the Dolphins a 13-10 lead. A 49-yard punt return later in the quarter by Patrick Crayton ignited the Cowboys. Romo completed a 2-yard touchdown pass to Tony Curtis for a 17-13 lead. The Dolphins then turned it over on consecutive possessions, the first was an interception by Ken Hamlin and the second a fumble recovery by Jay Ratliff, to set up a pair of Nick Folk field goals for a 23-13 lead with 11:00 left. An Anthony Henry interception later in the quarter led to Romo's 34-yard touchdown pass to Terrell Owens. Green answered with a 21-yard touchdown pass to Derek Hagan with 3:26 left. Henry then recovered the ensuing onside kick and, on the next play, Marion Barber scored on a 40-yard run to clinch the victory. Romo was 14 of 29 for 186 yards and 2 touchdowns. Green was 23 of 40 for 287 yards and 2 touchdowns, with 4 interceptions. Chris Chambers had 9 receptions for 109 yards.

Dallas	3	7	10	17	—	37
Miami	3	3	7	7	—	20

Mia	—	FG Feely 37
Dall	—	FG Folk 26
Dall	—	Barber 1 run (Folk kick)
Mia	—	FG Feely 45
Mia	—	Booker 18 pass from Green (Feely kick)
Dall	—	Curtis 2 pass from Romo (Folk kick)
Dall	—	FG Folk 28
Dall	—	FG Folk 47
Dall	—	Owens 34 pass from Romo (Folk kick)
Mia	—	Hagan 21 pass from Green (Feely kick)
Dall	—	Barber 40 run (Folk kick)

GREEN BAY 35, N.Y. GIANTS 13—at Giants Stadium, attendance 78,701. Brett Favre passed for 3 touchdowns as the Packers rallied to improve to 2-0 for the first time since 2001. Tramon Williams returned the second half's opening kickoff 42 yards to set up Favre's 2-yard touchdown pass to Bubba Franks for a 14-10 lead. The Giants responded with a field goal to pull within 14-13. Favre answered with a 10-play, 80-yard drive, capped by his 3-yard touchdown pass to Donald Lee. Charlie Peprah forced Ahmad Bradshaw to fumble the ensuing kickoff. Tracy White recovered, and five plays later Favre tossed a 10-yard touchdown pass to Donald Driver for a 28-13 lead with 11:41 remaining. Corey Williams intercepted Eli Manning's pass at the Packers' 38 with 6:35 to play. Five plays later, Dexter Wynn scored on a 38-yard run to ice the game. Favre was 29 of 38 for 286 yards and 3 touchdowns, with 1 interception. Manning was 16 of 29 for 211 yards and 1 touchdown, with 1 interception.

Green Bay	0	7	21	7	—	35
N.Y. Giants	0	10	3	0	—	13

GB	—	Wynn 6 run (Crosby kick)
NYG	—	Burress 26 pass from E. Manning (Tynes kick)
NYG	—	FG Tynes 48
GB	—	Franks 2 pass from Favre (Crosby kick)
NYG	—	FG Tynes 32
GB	—	Lee 3 pass from Favre (Crosby kick)
GB	—	Driver 10 pass from Favre (Crosby kick)
GB	—	Wynn 38 run (Crosby kick)

PITTSBURGH 26, BUFFALO 3—at Heinz Field, attendance 64,307. The Steelers' defense registered 4 sacks and allowed just 223 yards en route to victory. Jeff Reed kicked 4 field goals in the first half as Pittsburgh's offense maintained possession for 21:35 of the 30 minutes. Terrence McGee's 63-yard kickoff return to begin the second half set up Rian Lindell's 24-yard field goal, but the Steelers answered with a 62-yard drive, capped by Ben Roethlisberger's 1-yard touchdown pass to Matt Spaeth. Roethlisberger's 29-yard pass to Heath Miller set up Willie Parker's 11-yard touchdown run with 7:13 to play to finish the scoring. Roethlisberger was 21 of 34 for 242 yards and 1 touchdown, with 1 interception. Parker rushed 23 times for 126 yards. J.P. Losman was 15 of 25 for 154 yards.

Buffalo	0	0	3	0	—	3
Pittsburgh	3	9	7	7	—	26

Pitt	—	FG Reed 34
Pitt	—	FG Reed 28
Pitt	—	FG Reed 39
Pitt	—	FG Reed 31
Buff	—	FG Lindell 24
Pitt	—	Spaeth 1 pass from Roethlisberger (Reed kick)
Pitt	—	Parker 11 run (Reed kick)

SAN FRANCISCO 17, ST. LOUIS 16—at Edward Jones Dome, attendance 65,295. Frank Gore, playing four days after the death of his mother, rushed for 2 touchdowns as the 49ers improved to 2-0 for the first time since 1998. The Rams dominated the game statistically, outgaining the 49ers 392-186 in total yards and 20-8 in first downs. Gore's 43-yard touchdown run on fourth-and-1 in the third quarter gave the 49ers a 14-13 lead. Rookie Clifton Ryan pulled the trifecta in the fourth quarter. He sacked Alex Smith, forced him to fumble, and recovered the ball at the 49ers' 41. Four plays later, Jeff Wilkins made a 53-yard field goal to give the Rams a 16-14 lead with 10:04 remaining. The Rams then forced a punt, but Dante Hall muffed it and Marcus Hudson recovered at the Rams' 25. Joe Nedney kicked a 40-yard field goal with 3:23 to allow the 49ers to retake the lead, 17-16. Wilkins attempted a 56-yard field goal with 1:04 to play, but it fell short. Smith was 11 of 17 for 126 yards. Marc Bulger was 24 of 41 for 368 yards and 1 touchdown.

San Francisco	0	7	7	3	—	17
St. Louis	7	6	0	3	—	16

StL	—	Holt 12 pass from Bulger (Wilkins kick)
SF	—	Gore 1 run (Nedney kick)
StL	—	FG Wilkins 27
StL	—	FG Wilkins 29
SF	—	Gore 43 run (Nedney kick)
StL	—	FG Wilkins 53
SF	—	FG Nedney 40

TAMPA BAY 31, NEW ORLEANS 14—at Raymond James Stadium, attendance 65,178. Jeff Garcia connected with Joey Galloway on 2 receptions as the Buccaneers scored the game's first 28 points to defeat the Saints. The Buccaneers took a 14-0 lead on Garcia's 69-yard touchdown pass to Galloway. Just before halftime, Garcia completed a 41-yard pass to Ike Hilliard, followed by a 24-yard scoring as to Galloway for a 21-0 lead. Cato June intercepted a pass to stop the Saints' initial third-quarter drive, and Galloway caught a 41-yard pass to set up Carnell Williams' 1-yard touchdown run for a 28-0 lead with 4:26 left in the third quarter. Garcia was 10 of 16 for 243 yards and 2 touchdowns. Galloway had 4 receptions for 135 yards. Drew Brees was 26 of 44 for 260 yards and 1 touchdown, with 1 interception.

New Orleans	0	0	7	7	—	14
Tampa Bay	7	14	7	3	—	31

TB	—	Williams 1 run (Bryant kick)
TB	—	Galloway 69 pass from Garcia (Bryant kick)
TB	—	Galloway 24 pass from Garcia (Bryant kick)
TB	—	Williams 1 run (Bryant kick)
NO	—	Karney 1 run (Mare kick)
TB	—	FG Bryant 27
NO	—	Colston 4 pass from Brees (Mare kick)

INDIANAPOLIS 22, TENNESSEE 20—at LP Field, attendance 69,143. The Colts improved to 2-0 by holding off a late Titans' rally. The Colts scored on four of their first six possessions to take a 19-6 lead with 9:41 left in the third quarter. The Colts' defense then forced a punt, but Cortland Finnegan intercepted a pass from Peyton Manning and returned it 14 yards to the Colts' 15. Three plays later, LenDale White scored on a 3-yard touchdown run to pull within 19-13. The Colts answered with a 12-play, 70-yard drive that resulted in Adam Vinatieri's third field goal for a 22-13 lead. The Colts then recovered a fumble, but Vinatieri missed a 36-yard field-goal attempt, and the Titans responded with a 11-play, 74-yard drive capped by Vince Young's 1-yard touchdown pass to Roydell Williams to cut the deficit to 22-20 with 6:02 to play. The Colts drove to the Titans' 31, but on third down Kyle Vanden Bosch sacked Manning and returned a four-yard loss forcing the Colts to punt with 1:37 to play. Tennessee drove to the Colts' 47, but on fourth-and-4 Young attempted to lateral as he was being sacked. Darrell Reid recovered the ball to seal the victory. Manning was 28 of 42 for 312 yards and 1 touchdown, with 1 interception. Young was 17 of 27 for 184 yards and 1 touchdown.

Indianapolis	6	10	6	0	—	22
Tennessee	3	3	7	7	—	20

Ind	—	Addai 8 run (kick blocked)
Tenn	—	FG Bironas 30
Ind	—	Clark 22 pass from P. Manning (Vinatieri kick)
Tenn	—	FG Bironas 36
Ind	—	FG Vinatieri 22
Ind	—	FG Vinatieri 39
Tenn	—	White 3 run (Bironas kick)
Ind	—	FG Vinatieri 20
Tenn	—	Williams 1 pass from Young (Bironas kick)

NEW ENGLAND 38, SAN DIEGO 14—at Gillette Stadium, attendance 68,756. Tom Brady passed for 279 yards and 3 touchdowns as the Patriots rolled past the Chargers in a rematch of a 2006 AFC Divisional Playoff Game. The Patriots outgained the Chargers 407-201 in total yards and maintained possession for 35:46. New England posted scoring drives of 69, 75, and 50 yards on three of its first four possessions for a 17-0 lead, and Adalius Thomas, in just his second game with the Patriots, capped the half with a 65-yard interception return for a touchdown. The Chargers drove 72 yards in 16 plays to begin the second half with a touchdown, but the Patriots needed just seven plays to respond with a 75-yard touchdown drive, capped by Randy Moss' 24-yard touchdown catch for a 31-7 lead with 2:56 left in the third quarter. Brady was 25 of 31 for 279 yards and 3 touchdowns, with 1 interception. Moss had 8 receptions for 105 yards. Philip Rivers was 19 of 30 for 179 yards and 2 touchdowns, with 2 interceptions.

San Diego	0	0	7	7	—	14
New England	14	10	7	7	—	38

NE	—	Watson 7 pass from Brady (Gostkowski kick)
NE	—	Moss 23 pass from Brady (Gostkowski kick)
NE	—	FG Gostkowski 24
NE	—	Thomas 65 interception return (Gostkowski kick)
SD	—	Neal 1 pass from Rivers (Kaeding kick)
NE	—	Moss 24 pass from Brady (Gostkowski kick)
SD	—	Gates 12 pass from Rivers (Kaeding kick)
NE	—	Morris 3 run (Gostkowski kick)

WASHINGTON 20, PHILADELPHIA 12—at Lincoln Financial Field, attendance 67,726. The Redskins converted on 8 of 15 third-down situations to improve their record to 2-0. Jason Campbell engineered a 10-play, 73-yard touchdown drive in the final 1:42 of the first half, capped by his 16-yard touchdown pass to Chris Cooley, for a 10-6 halftime lead. Campbell's 28-yard pass to Ladell Betts and 18-yard connection with Todd Yoder set up Clinton Portis' 6-yard touchdown run with 12:02 to play for a 20-9 lead. David Akers' fourth field goal, from 22 yards, cut the deficit to 20-12 with 6:30 remaining. The Eagles' defense then forced a punt, and Donovan McNabb completed 5 of 6 passes to reach the Redskins' 13. But McNabb misfired on two of his next three attempts, and his fourth-and-6 pass for Kevin Curtis was knocked loose and incomplete due to a jarring hit from LaRon Landry. Campbell was 16 of 29 for 209 yards and 1 touchdown, with 1 interception. McNabb was 28 of 46 for 240 yards.

Washington	3	7	3	7	—	20
Philadelphia	0	6	3	3	—	12

Wash	—	FG Suisham 35
Phil	—	FG Akers 24
Phil	—	FG Akers 39
Wash	—	Cooley 16 pass from Campbell (Suisham kick)
Wash	—	FG Suisham 37
Phil	—	FG Akers 26
Wash	—	Portis 6 run (Suisham kick)
Phil	—	FG Akers 25

THIRD WEEK SUMMARIES
American Football Conference

East Division	W	L	T	Pct.	Pts.	OP
New England	3	0	0	1.000	114	35
N.Y. Jets	1	2	0	.333	58	86
Buffalo	0	3	0	.000	24	79
Miami	0	3	0	.000	61	84
North Division	W	L	T	Pct.	Pts.	OP
Pittsburgh	3	0	0	1.000	97	26
Baltimore	2	1	0	.667	66	63
Cincinnati	1	2	0	.333	93	95
Cleveland	1	2	0	.333	82	105
South Division	W	L	T	Pct.	Pts.	OP
Indianapolis	3	0	0	1.000	93	54
Houston	2	1	0	.667	78	54
Jacksonville	2	1	0	.667	46	34
Tennessee	2	1	0	.667	64	46

West Division	W	L	T	Pct.	Pts.	OP
Denver	2	1	0	.667	52	57
Kansas City	1	2	0	.333	26	50
Oakland	1	2	0	.333	67	83
San Diego	1	2	0	.333	52	72

National Football Conference

East Division	W	L	T	Pct.	Pts.	OP
Dallas	3	0	0	1.000	116	65
Washington	2	1	0	.667	53	49
N.Y. Giants	1	2	0	.333	72	97
Philadelphia	1	2	0	.333	81	57
North Division	W	L	T	Pct.	Pts.	OP
Green Bay	3	0	0	1.000	82	50
Detroit	2	1	0	.667	77	94
Chicago	1	2	0	.333	33	58
Minnesota	1	2	0	.333	51	36
South Division	W	L	T	Pct.	Pts.	OP
Carolina	2	1	0	.667	75	67
Tampa Bay	2	1	0	.667	61	37
Atlanta	0	3	0	.000	30	64
New Orleans	0	3	0	.000	38	103
West Division	W	L	T	Pct.	Pts.	OP
San Francisco	2	1	0	.667	53	70
Seattle	2	1	0	.667	64	50
Arizona	1	2	0	.333	63	66
St. Louis	0	3	0	.000	32	68

CAROLINA 27, ATLANTA 20—at Georgia Dome, attendance 68,175. Deshaun Foster rushed for 122 yards and scored 2 touchdowns as the Panthers held off the Falcons. Atlanta outgained the Panthers 442-313 in total yards, including a 278-127 total yardage edge in the first half, but the game was tied 10-10 at halftime. In the third quarter, Joey Harrington completed a 13-yard touchdown pass to Alge Crumpler on third down to give the Falcons a 17-10 lead. The Panthers answered with a 6-play, 80-yard drive, enhanced by three penalties, totalling 67 yards, on DeAngelo Hall, to tie the game, capped by John Kasay's 49-yard field goal to take a 27-17 lead. Morten Andersen's 25-yard field goal pulled the Falcons to within 27-20 with 3:03 left, but Foster rushed for three first downs in the final moments to clinch the victory. Jake Delhomme was 10 of 18 for 109 yards and 2 touchdowns. Delhomme suffered a torn elbow ligament late in the third quarter and was replaced by David Carr, who was 3 of 4 for 56 yards. Foster carried 20 times for 122 yards. Harrington was 31 of 44 for 361 yards and 2 touchdowns. Roddy White had 7 receptions for 127 yards.

Carolina	0	10	14	3	—	27
Atlanta	0	10	7	3	—	20

Car	—	FG Kasay 45
Atl	—	R. White 69 pass from Harrington (Andersen kick)
Car	—	Foster 13 pass from Delhomme (Kasay kick)
Atl	—	FG Andersen 24
Atl	—	Crumpler 13 pass from Harrington (Andersen kick)
Car	—	King 5 pass from Delhomme (Kasay kick)
Car	—	Foster 10 run (Kasay kick)
Car	—	FG Kasay 49
Atl	—	FG Andersen 25

BALTIMORE 26, ARIZONA 23—at M & T Bank Stadium, attendance 71,372. Matt Stover kicked a 46-yard field goal as time expired as the Ravens held off a late comeback. Baltimore scored on three of its first four possessions, and has a 78-yard punt returned for a touchdown by Yamon Figurs, to take a 20-3 halftime lead. The Ravens led 23-6 entering the fourth quarter. Kurt Warner, who had played in one first half drive that resulted in a field goal, engineered a 71-yard touchdown drive, capped by his 5-yard scoring pass to Anquan Boldin. After a three-and-out, Warner completed a 32-yard touchdown pass to Boldin two plays later to pull within 23-20 with 10:19 to play. After another punt, Neil Rackers tied the game with a 41-yard field goal with 1:50 remaining. Kyle Boller, who replaced an injured Steve McNair, completed two key passes to Derrick Mason to set up Stover's winning kick. McNair was 20 of 27 for 198 yards and 1 touchdown. Boller was 8 of 10 for 83 yards. Matt Leinart started and was 9 of 20 for 53 yards. Warner was 15 of 24 for 258 yards and 2 touchdowns. Boldin had 14 receptions for 181 yards.

Arizona	0	3	3	17	—	23
Baltimore	3	17	3	3	—	26

Balt — FG Stover 21
Balt — FG Stover 28
Ari — FG Rackers 48
Balt — Mason 13 pass from McNair (Stover kick)
Balt — Figurs 75 punt return (Stover kick)
Ari — FG Rackers 40
Balt — FG Stover 43
Ari — Boldin 5 pass from Warner (Rackers kick)
Ariz — Boldin 32 pass from Warner (Rackers kick)
Ari — FG Rackers 41
Balt — FG Stover 46

JACKSONVILLE 23, DENVER 14—at INVESCO Field at Mile High, attendance 76,463. The Jaguars' offense maintained possession for 38:42 by outgaining the Broncos 186-47 on the ground en route to victory. The Jaguars' defense limited the Broncos to just 11 first downs. Jacksonville had an 18-play, 80-yard drive that consumed 11 minutes, 44 seconds that resulted in their first touchdown, and had four other drives that were at least seven plays. The Broncos pulled within 20-14 with 12:41 to play. The Jaguars drove to the Broncos' 1, but Maurice Jones-Drew fumbled and Curome Cox recovered. However, four plays later, faced with fourth-and-5 from their own 9-yard line with 4:19 to play, the Broncos went for the first down and Jay Cutler's pass for Daniel Graham was incomplete. John Carney tacked on a field goal with 2:10 left to secure the victory. David Garrard was 14 of 20 for 154 yards and 1 touchdown. Cutler was 16 of 23 for 222 yards and 1 touchdown, with 1 interception. Brandon Marshall had 7 receptions for 133 yards.

Jacksonville	0	17	3	3	—	23
Denver	0	7	0	7	—	14

Jax — R. Williams 3 pass from Garrard (Carney kick)
Den — Jackson 1 pass from Cutler (Elam kick)
Jax — Jones 4 run (Carney kick)
Jax — FG Carney 19
Jax — FG Carney 27
Den — Henry 6 run (Elam kick)
Jax — FG Carney 18

GREEN BAY 31, SAN DIEGO 24—at Lambeau Field, attendance 70,733. The Packers scored 14 points in the final 2:03, highlighted by Brett Favre's record-tying 420th career touchdown pass, to rally and defeat the Chargers. Favre completed a pair of 5-yard touchdown passes in the first half, but the Chargers drove 80 yards in the final three minutes of the first half, and 80 yards in 12 plays to begin the second half, both resulting in touchdowns to give the Chargers a 21-17 lead. In the fourth quarter, the Packers drove to the Chargers' 1, but Favre's fourth-down pass for Bubba Franks fell incomplete with 5:48 to play. The Packers forced a punt, and on second-and-10 from the Packers' 43 with 2:13 remaining, Favre completed a quick slant pass to Greg Jennings, who caught the ball near the Chargers' 45 and ran untouched diagonally across the field for a 57-yard touchdown with 2:03 to play to give the Packers a 24-21 lead. The scoring pass allowed Favre to tie Dan Marino for first on the NFL's all-time passing touchdown list. Nick Barnett intercepted a pass moments later and returned it 38 yards to the Chargers' 2. Brandon Jackson scored two plays later for a 31-21 lead with 59 seconds left. Nate Kaeding kicked a 44-yard field goal with 20 seconds left, but Donald Driver recovered the onside kick to secure the victory. Favre was 28 of 45 for 369 yards and 3 touchdowns. Driver had 6 receptions for 126 yards. Rivers was 27 of 36 for 306 yards and 3 touchdowns, with 1 interception. Antonio Gates had 11 catches for 113 yards.

San Diego	7	7	7	3	—	24
Green Bay	3	14	0	14	—	31

SD — V. Jackson 27 pass from Rivers (Kaeding kick)
GB — FG Crosby 28
GB — Driver 5 pass from Favre (Crosby kick)
GB — Franks 5 pass from Favre (Crosby kick)
SD — Davis 9 pass from Rivers (Kaeding kick)
SD — Tomlinson 21 pass from Rivers (Kaeding kick)
GB — Jennings 57 pass from Favre (Crosby kick)
GB — B. Jackson 1 run (Crosby kick)
SD — FG Kaeding 44

INDIANAPOLIS 30, HOUSTON 24—at Reliant Stadium, attendance 70,765. Joseph Addai rushed for 2 touchdowns as the Colts remained undefeated by holding off the Texans. The Colts, not counting a one-play possession at the end of the first half, had nine possessions, drove into the red zone six times, and scored on all six of those possessions. Houston's Jerome Mathis returned the opening kickoff 84 yards for a touchdown, but the Colts led 14-10 at halftime, and scored twice in the first 6:22 of the second half, with Rocky Boiman's interception leading to Addai's 8-yard touchdown run for a 24-10 lead. Jacoby Jones' 74-yard punt return gave the Texans a scoring chance later in the third quarter, but Gary Brackett intercepted a pass to set up Adam Vinatieri's second field goal. The Texans scored twice in the fourth quarter, including a 14-play, 75-yard drive capped by Matt Schaub's 1-yard touchdown pass to Vonta Leach with 2:49 to play to pull within 30-24. The Texans didn't get the ball back until 19 seconds remained, and Schaub was sacked deep in Texans' territory as the clock expired. Manning was 20 of 29 for 273 yards and 1 touchdown. Schaub was 27 of 33 for 236 yards and 1 touchdown, with 2 interceptions.

Indianapolis	7	7	13	3	—	30
Houston	7	3	0	14	—	24

Hou — Mathis 84 kickoff return (K. Brown kick)
Ind — Clark 2 pass from Manning (Vinatieri kick)
Hou — FG K. Brown 33
Ind — Addai 4 run (Vinatieri kick)
Ind — FG Vinatieri 36
Ind — Addai 8 run (Vinatieri kick)
Ind — FG Vinatieri 28
Hou — Gado 1 run (K. Brown kick)
Ind — FG Vinatieri 35
Hou — Leach 1 pass from Schaub (K. Brown kick)

KANSAS CITY 13, MINNESOTA 10—at Arrowhead Stadium, attendance 78,038. The Chiefs' defense had 5 sacks and rookie Dwayne Bowe caught his second touchdown in as many weeks for the victorious Chiefs. The Vikings opened the game with a 50-yard touchdown drive, which wound up being their longest drive of the day. A fumble recovery by Chad Greenway at the Chiefs' 33 in the second quarter set up Ryan Longwell's field goal for a 10-0 lead. The Chiefs took the lead when Damon Huard engineered a 12-play, 84-yard drive, highlighted by 2 third-down completions, and capped by Bowe's 16-yard touchdown catch, in which he outleaped Cedric Griffin in the end zone, for a 13-10 lead with 9:23 remaining. In the final three possessions, the Vikings did not run a play in Chiefs' territory. Huard was 20 of 29 for 206 yards and 1 touchdown. Kelly Holcomb, who started for the injured Tarvaris Jackson, was 14 of 28 for 169 yards. Adrian Peterson rushed 25 times for 102 yards.

Minnesota	7	3	0	0	—	10
Kansas City	0	3	3	7	—	13

Minn — Peterson 11 run (Longwell kick)
Minn — FG Longwell 22
KC — FG Rayner 39
KC — FG Rayner 49
KC — Bowe 16 pass from Huard (Rayner kick)

NEW ENGLAND 38, BUFFALO 7—at Gillette Stadium, attendance 68,756. Tom Brady passed for 4 touchdowns as the Patriots posted 38 points for the third consecutive game. J.P. Losman was injured on the first play from scrimmage, and left a few plays later when Ellis Hobbs sacked him and Jarvis Green recovered the ball. The turnover led to Stephen Gostkowski's 24-yard field goal. The Bills answered as reserve rookie Trent Edwards engineered a 12-play, 80-yard drive capped by rookie Marshawn Lynch's 8-yard touchdown run for a 7-3 lead. The Patriots' defense allowed Buffalo just 15 yards on their next 17 plays, and by the time the Bills' offense regrouped the Patriots led 31-7. The Patriots had touchdown drives of 89 and 98 yards in the second half, capped by Randy Moss' 45-yard touchdown catch in stride deep down the right sideline. Brady was 23 of 29 for 311 yards and 4 touchdowns. Moss had 5 receptions for 115 yards and became the first player in NFL history to have at least 100 receiving yards in each of his first three games with a new club. Laurence Maroney rushed 19 times for 103 yards. Edwards was 10 of 20 for 97 yards, with 1 interception.

Buffalo	7	0	0	0	—	7
New England	3	14	14	7	—	38

NE — FG Gostkowski 24
Buff — Lynch 8 run (Lindell kick)
NE — Watson 8 pass from Brady (Gostkowski kick)
NE — Moss 3 pass from Brady (Gostkowski kick)
NE — Gaffney 4 pass from Brady (Gostkowski kick)
NE — Morris 4 run (Gostkowski kick)
NE — Moss 45 pass from Brady (Gostkowski kick)

N.Y. JETS 31, MIAMI 28—at The Meadowlands, attendance 77,197. Chad Pennington passed for 2 touchdowns and ran for another as the Jets notched their first victory. The Dolphins amassed 424 yards of offense, and allowed just 256 yards, but Leon Washington returned a kickoff 98 yards for a touchdown to give the Jets a 14-7 lead. The Dolphins cut the deficit to 14-13 just before halftime, but afraid to kick deep to Washington, Jay Feely's squib kick allowed the Jets to start at their own 43-yard line. Pennington completed 7 of 8 passes, capped by his 4-yard scoring pass to Chris Baker with two seconds left in the half for a 21-13 lead. The Jets' first two drives of the second half were 13 plays, 67 yards and 15 plays, 74 yards, capped by Pennington's 2-yard run on third-and-goal for a 31-13 lead with 12:51 to play. Ronnie Brown scored twice, and added a 2-point conversion, to pull the Dolphins within 31-28 with 1:15 remaining, but Feely's onside kick attempt went out of bounds and the Jets' ran out the clock. Pennington was 15 of 22 for 124 yards and 2 touchdowns. Thomas Jones had 25 carries for 110 yards. Trent Green was 23 of 36 for 318 yards and 1 touchdown, with 1 interception. Brown rushed 23 times for 112 yards. Chris Chambers had 6 receptions for 101 yards.

Miami	0	13	0	15	—	28
N.Y. Jets	7	14	3	7	—	31

NYJ — Coles 3 pass from Pennington (Nugent kick)
Mia — R. Brown 1 run (Feely kick)
NYJ — Washington 98 kickoff return (Nugent kick)
Mia — FG Feely 31
Mia — FG Feely 39
NYJ — Baker 4 pass from Pennington (Nugent kick)
NYJ — FG Nugent 21
NYJ — Pennington 2 run (Nugent kick)
Mia — R. Brown 2 run (R. Brown run)
Mia — R. Brown 22 pass from Green (Feely kick)

OAKLAND 26, CLEVELAND 24—at McAfee Coliseum, attendance 51,075. Tommy Kelly blocked Phil Dawson's 40-yard game-winning field-goal attempt as time expired as the Raiders held off the Browns. Interception returns of 26 yards by Thomas Howard and 45 yards by Kirk Morrison set up a pair of field goals by Sebastian Janikowski to stake the Raiders to a 16-0 lead. Joshua Cribbs returned the ensuing kickoff 99 yards to spark the Browns. In the third quarter, Daven Holly recovered Mike Williams' fumble to set up Derek Anderson's 21-yard touchdown pass to Braylon Edwards for a 17-16 Cleveland lead. The Raiders responded with a 15-play, 80-yard drive that culminated with Jordan's 1-yard run for a 23-17 lead. After a three-and-out, the Raiders consumed another 6:49 off the clock with an 11-play drive capped by Janikowski's fourth field goal for a 26-17 lead with 8:11 to play. The Browns answered with Anderson's 1-yard touchdown run, and then forced a punt. Starting from his own 9-yard line with 1:04 to play, Anderson connected on passes of 33 and 23 yards to Kellen Winslow. A 13-yard pass to Joe Jurevicius to the Raiders' 22 with three seconds left set up Dawson's field-goal attempt. Raiders coach Lane Kiffin called timeout just before Dawson made a 40-yard field goal. After the timeout, Tommy Kelly blocked Dawson's kick as time expired. Josh McCown was 6 of 12 for 108 yards and 1 touchdown. Daunte Culpepper was 8 of 14 for 118 yards. LaMont Jordan rushed 29 times for 121 yards. Anderson was 18 of 37 for 248 yards and 1 touchdown, with 2 interceptions.

Cleveland		0	10	7	7	—	24
Oakland		3	13	7	3	—	26

Oak — FG Janikowski 32
Oak — FG Janikowski 22
Oak — Curry 41 pass from McCown (Janikowski kick)
Oak — FG Janikowski 23
Cle — Cribbs 99 kickoff return (Dawson kick)
Cle — FG Dawson 23
Cle — Edwards 21 pass from Anderson (Dawson kick)
Oak — Jordan 1 run (Janikowski kick)
Oak — FG Janikowski 48
Cle — Anderson 1 run (Dawson kick)

PHILADELPHIA 56, DETROIT 21—at Lincoln Financial Field, attendance 67,570. Donovan McNabb passed for 381 yards and 4 touchdowns as the Eagles scored a franchise-best 42 first-half points en route to victory. The Eagles had 536 of the combined 968 yards, while Jon Kitna passed for a franchise-best 446 yards in defeat. The Eagles scored touchdowns on each of their first five possessions, including 1-play drives of 68 and 43 yards that resulted in scoring passes to a wide open Kevin Curtis, for a 35-7 lead with 11:32 left in the second quarter. Two quick touchdown passes by Kitna, including a 91-yard touchdown to Roy Williams, cut the deficit to 35-21 with 5:01 remaining in the half. Brian Westbrook took a short pass and turned it into a 43-yard touchdown for a 42-21 lead. An interception for a touchback by Sean Considine ended the Lions' drive just before halftime, and the Lions drove inside the Eagles' 30 four times in the second half, but Detroit missed a field goal, fumbled, and was twice stopped on downs. McNabb was 21 of 26 for 381 yards and 4 touchdowns. Curtis had 11 receptions for 221 yards. Westbrook had 14 carries for 110 yards and 5 receptions for 111 yards. Kitna was 29 of 46 for 446 yards and 2 touchdowns, with 1 interception. Williams had 9 catches for 204 yards.

Detroit		7	14	0	0	—	21
Philadelphia		21	21	7	7	—	56

Phil — Westbrook 25 run (Akers kick)
Det — K. Jones 2 run (Hanson kick)
Phil — Westbrook 5 run (Akers kick)
Phil — Curtis 68 pass from McNabb (Akers kick)
Phil — Curtis 12 pass from McNabb (Akers kick)
Phil — Curtis 43 pass from McNabb (Akers kick)
Det — McDonald 11 pass from Kitna (Hanson kick)
Det — R. Williams 91 pass from Kitna (Hanson kick)
Phil — Westbrook 43 pass from McNabb (Akers kick)
Phil — Buckhalter 1 run (Akers kick)
Phil — Hunt 1 run (Akers kick)

PITTSBURGH 37, SAN FRANCISCO 16—at Heinz Field, attendance 64,313. The Steelers scored on a kickoff return and interception return to register their first 3-0 start since 1992. Allen Rossum's 98-yard kickoff return was the first kickoff return for a touchdown by a Steelers' player in Heinz Field history. Pittsburgh drove 80 yards in 12 plays, capped by Ben Roethlisberger's 9-yard touchdown pass to Jerame Tuman with 37 seconds left in the half to give the Steelers a 14-6 lead. The Steelers scored on their first four possessions of the second half, along with a 50-yard cross-field interception return by Ryan McFadden that gave the Steelers a 30-9 lead with 4:01 to play. Roethlisberger was 13 of 20 for 160 yards and 1 touchdown. Willie Parker rushed 24 times for 133 yards. Alex Smith was 17 of 35 for 209 yards and 1 touchdown, with 1 interception.

San Francisco		6	0	3	7	—	16
Pittsburgh		7	7	3	20	—	37

SF — FG Nedney 32
Pitt — Rossum 98 kickoff return (Reed kick)
SF — FG Nedney 22
Pitt — Tuman 9 pass from Roethlisberger (Reed kick)
Pitt — FG Reed 36
SF — FG Nedney 50
Pitt — FG Reed 49
Pitt — FG Reed 35
Pitt — McFadden 50 interception return (Reed kick)
SF — Jacobs 21 pass from Smith (Nedney kick)
Pitt — Davenport 39 run (Reed kick)

SEATTLE 24, CINCINNATI 21—at Qwest Field, attendance 68,110. Matt Hasselbeck passed for 3 touchdowns for the Seahawks. In the third quarter, Kyle Larson's 38-yard punt was downed by Marvin White at the Seahawks' 2. Two plays later, Lemar Marshall sacked Hasselbeck for a safety to cut the deficit to 14-12. In the fourth quarter, Madieu Williams' interception and 35-yard return led to Shayne Graham's 24-yard field goal to give the Bengals a 15-14 lead with 9:57 to play. Josh Brown kicked a 23-yard field goal, but the Bengals answered with a 68-yard drive capped by Kenny Watson's 8-yard run with 2:42 to play. The Bengals went for two points, but Watson was stopped. On the ensuing drive, Shaun Alexander rushed for 14 yards on third-and-1, and Hasselbeck fired a 22-yard touchdown pass to Nate Burleson on the next play for a 24-21 lead with 1:00 left. Glenn Holt fumbled the ensuing kickoff, Deon Grant recovered, and Alexander added a 20-yard run to ice the game. Hasselbeck was 24 of 37 for 248 yards and 3 touchdowns, with 2 interceptions. Alexander rushed 21 times for 100 yards. Carson Palmer was 27 of 43 for 342 yards and 1 touchdown, with 2 interceptions. T.J. Houshmandzadeh had 12 receptions for 141 yards, and Chad Johnson added 9 catches for 138 yards.

Cincinnati		7	3	2	9	—	21
Seattle		7	7	0	10	—	24

Sea — Engram 18 pass from Hasselbeck (J. Brown kick)
Cin — Houshmandzadeh 35 pass from Palmer (Graham kick)
Cin — FG Graham 43
Sea — Branch 42 pass from Hasselbeck (J. Brown kick)
Cin — Safety, Marshall sacked Hasselbeck in end zone
Cin — FG Graham 24
Sea — FG J. Brown 23
Cin — Watson 8 run (run failed)
Sea — Burleson 22 pass from Hasselbeck (J. Brown kick)

TAMPA BAY 24, ST. LOUIS 3—at Raymond James Stadium, attendance 65,267. The Buccaneers' defense allowed just 245 yards and intercepted 3 passes to defeat the Rams. Jeff Wilkins missed a 42-yard field-goal attempt in the second quarter, and the Buccaneers answered with a 12-play drive to set up Matt Bryant's 27-yard field goal just before halftime for a 3-0 lead. The Rams cut the deficit to 10-3 with 11:31 to play. The Buccaneers responded with touchdown drives of 80 and 40 yards., The latter was set up by Mark Jones' 35-yard punt return and both drives ended with scoring runs by Earnest Graham for a 24-3 lead with 5:00 left. Jeff Garcia was 14 of 22 for 151 yards. Marc Bulger was 17 of 26 for 116 yards, with 3 interceptions. Steven Jackson had 30 carries for 115 yards.

St. Louis		0	0	0	3	—	3
Tampa Bay		0	3	7	14	—	24

TB — FG Bryant 27
TB — Williams 7 run (Bryant kick)
StL — FG Wilkins 25
TB — Graham 8 run (Bryant kick)
TB — Graham 28 run (Bryant kick)

N.Y. GIANTS 24, WASHINGTON 17—at FedExField, attendance 90,803. The Giants scored 21 unanswered points in the second half and used a goal-line stand in the final minute to register their first victory. In the first quarter, London Fletcher recovered a fumble to set up a touchdown, and just before halftime he intercepted a pass that led to Shaun Suisham's 47-yard field goal as the half expired to give the Redskins a 17-3 lead. Reuben Droughns began the second half with a 34-yard kickoff return and ended the drive with a 1-yard touchdown run to cap a 61-yard drive, that included three key third-down passes by Eli Manning, to trim the deficit to 17-10. Early in the fourth quarter, the Redskins recovered a fumble at their own 5-yard line, but the call was reversed and Droughns scored two plays later to tie the game with 12:33 to play. Midway through the quarter, Antonio Pierce recovered a fumble at the Red-

skins' 44, and Manning completed a short pass to Plaxico Burress, who broke free and scored on a 33-yard play to take a 24-17 lead with 5:32 remaining. The Redskins drove to the Giants' 1, and Campbell spiked the ball with 51 seconds left. On second down, Campbell's pass for Mike Sellers was incomplete. Ladell Betts was stopped for no gain on third down, and Betts lost 2 yards on fourth down as the Giants held on. Manning was 21 of 36 for 232 yards and 1 touchdown, with 2 interceptions. Campbell was 16 of 34 for 190 yards and 1 touchdown.

N.Y. Giants		3	0	7	14	—	24
Washington		7	10	0	0	—	17

NYG — FG Tynes 34
Wash — Portis 1 run (Suisham kick)
Wash — Cooley 8 pass from Campbell (Suisham kick)
Wash — FG Suisham 47
NYG — Droughns 1 run (Tynes kick)
NYG — Droughns 1 run (Tynes kick)
NYG — Burress 33 pass from E. Manning (Tynes kick)

SUNDAY NIGHT, SEPTEMBER 23
DALLAS 34, CHICAGO 10—at Soldier Field, attendance 62,099. Anthony Henry intercepted 2 passes as the Cowboys remained undefeated. Dallas' 116 points after three games are the second-most by a club since 1970, trailing only the 2000 St. Louis Rams' 119 points. The Cowboys had 431 yards of offense and allowed just 239 yards, and the defense forced 4 turnovers. With the score 3-3 late in the first half, Israel Idonije blocked Nick Folk's 23-yard field-goal attempt. Six plays later, the Bears lined up for a 52-yard field-goal attempt, but instead holder Brad Maynard tossed the ball to kicker Robbie Gould, who attempted a deep pass for Desmond Clark that fell incomplete. The Cowboys answered by scoring on their first three second-half possessions to take a 20-10 lead. On the Bears' next play from scrimmage, Henry intercepted a pass and returned it 28 yards for a touchdown and 27-10 lead with 11:49 to play. The Bears did not run another play in Cowboys' territory. Tony Romo was 22 of 35 for 329 yards and 2 touchdowns, with 1 interception. Marion Barber rushed 15 times for 102 yards. Terrell Owens had 8 receptions for 145 yards. Rex Grossman was 15 of 32 for 195 yards, with 3 interceptions.

Dallas		0	3	14	17	—	34
Chicago		3	0	7	0	—	10

Chi — FG Gould 20
Dall — FG Folk 30
Dall — Witten 3 pass from Romo (Folk kick)
Chi — Benson 1 run (Gould kick)
Dall — Barber 10 pass from Romo (Folk kick)
Dall — FG Folk 44
Dall — Henry 28 interception return (Folk kick)
Dall — Barber 1 run (Folk kick)

MONDAY NIGHT, SEPTEMBER 24
TENNESSEE 31, NEW ORLEANS 14—at Louisiana Superdome, attendance 70,002. Keith Bulluck intercepted 3 passes to lead a Titans' defense that forced 5 turnovers, including 4 in the fourth quarter, en route to victory. Reggie Bush's second 1-yard touchdown run, which capped a 62-yard drive, gave the Saints their first lead at 14-10 with 7:55 left in the third quarter. The Titans answered with a 57-yard drive, which was helped by a third-down offside penalty by the Saints that resulted in a first down, and was capped by LenDale White's 1-yard run for a 17-14 lead. On the Saints' next possession, Travis Laboy stripped Drew Brees of the football and Randy Starks recovered. Vince Young culminated the ensuing 10-play drive with a 3-yard touchdown pass to Bo Scaife. Bulluck's second interception halted the following drive, and Vincent Fuller's 61-yard interception return with 2:39 to play finished the scoring. Young was 14 of 22 for 164 yards and 2 touchdowns, with 1 interception. Brees was 29 of 45 for 225 yards, with 4 interceptions.

Tennessee		3	7	14	7	—	31
New Orleans		0	7	7	0	—	14

Tenn — FG Bironas 33
Tenn — B. Jones 35 pass from Young (Bironas kick)
NO — Bush 1 run (Mare kick)
NO — Bush 1 run (Mare kick)
Tenn — White 1 run (Bironas kick)

Tenn	—	Scaife 3 pass from Young (Bironas kick)
Tenn	—	Fuller 61 interception return (Bironas kick)

FOURTH WEEK SUMMARIES
American Football Conference

East Division

	W	L	T	Pct.	Pts.	OP
New England	4	0	0	1.000	148	48
Buffalo	1	3	0	.250	41	93
N.Y. Jets	1	3	0	.250	72	103
Miami	0	4	0	.000	78	119
North Division	W	L	T	Pct.	Pts.	OP
Pittsburgh	3	1	0	.750	111	47
Baltimore	2	2	0	.500	79	90
Cleveland	2	2	0	.500	109	118
Cincinnati	1	3	0	.250	106	129
South Division	W	L	T	Pct.	Pts.	OP
Indianapolis	4	0	0	1.000	131	74
Jacksonville	2	1	0	.667	46	34
Tennessee	2	1	0	.667	64	46
Houston	2	2	0	.500	94	80
West Division	W	L	T	Pct.	Pts.	OP
Denver	2	2	0	.500	72	95
Kansas City	2	2	0	.500	56	66
Oakland	2	2	0	.500	102	100
San Diego	1	3	0	.250	68	102

National Football Conference

East Division	W	L	T	Pct.	Pts.	OP
Dallas	4	0	0	1.000	151	72
Washington	2	1	0	.667	53	49
N.Y. Giants	2	2	0	.500	88	100
Philadelphia	1	3	0	.250	84	73
North Division	W	L	T	Pct.	Pts.	OP
Green Bay	4	0	0	1.000	105	66
Detroit	3	1	0	.750	114	121
Chicago	1	3	0	.250	60	95
Minnesota	1	3	0	.250	67	59
South Division	W	L	T	Pct.	Pts.	OP
Tampa Bay	3	1	0	.750	81	44
Carolina	2	2	0	.500	82	87
Atlanta	1	3	0	.250	56	80
New Orleans	0	3	0	.000	38	103
West Division	W	L	T	Pct.	Pts.	OP
Seattle	3	1	0	.750	87	53
Arizona	2	2	0	.500	84	80
San Francisco	2	2	0	.500	56	93
St. Louis	0	4	0	.000	39	103

SUNDAY, SEPTEMBER 30

ARIZONA 21, PITTSBURGH 14—at University of Phoenix Stadium, attendance 64,844. Former Steelers' assistant, and current Cardinals head coach, Ken Whisenhunt rallied to hand Mike Tomlin his first loss. The Cardinals improved to their record to 2-2 for the first time since 2002. Trailing 7-0 at halftime, the Cardinals drove 70 yards with their first possession of the second half to tie the game. Early in the fourth quarter, rookie Steve Breaston returned a punt 73 yards for a touchdown. The Cardinals forced a punt, and Matt Leinart engineered a 13-play, 82-yard drive, which included a 1-yard sneak by Leinart on fourth down and was capped by Edgerrin James' 2-yard run with 4:14 to play. The Steelers drove near midfield to clinch the victory. Leinart started and was 7 of 14 for 93 yards. Kurt Warner engineered the first touchdown drive, and was 14 of 21 for 132 yards and 1 touchdown. Roethlisberger was 17 of 32 for 244 yards and 2 touchdowns, with 2 interceptions. Holmes had 6 receptions for 128 yards.

Pittsburgh	7	0	0	7	—	14
Arizona	0	0	7	14	—	21
Pitt	—	Holmes 43 pass from Roethlisberger (Reed kick)				
Ariz	—	Urban 6 pass from Warner (Rackers kick)				
Ariz	—	Breaston 73 punt return (Rackers kick)				
Ariz	—	James 1 run (Rackers kick)				
Pitt	—	Holmes 7 pass from Roethlisberger (Reed kick)				

ATLANTA 26, HOUSTON 16—at Georgia Dome, attendance 69,312. Joey Harrington passed for 2 touchdowns as the Falcons won their first game and defeated Matt Schaub, the quarterback they had traded during the offseason. Stephen Nicholas recovered a fumble in the second quarter to set up a 34-yard drive that culminated with Michael Jenkins' 7-yard touchdown catch for a 17-7 lead. The Falcons led 20-10 at halftime, and both teams had consecutive drives of at least nine plays to begin the second half, capped by Morten Andersen's 46-yard field goal for a 26-16 lead with 8:16 to play. The Texans drove to the Falcons' 1 with 2:16 to play, but Schaub fumbled a third-down snap to lose six yards, and Kris Brown's 25-yard field-goal attempt went wide left to finish the final scoring threat. Harrington was 23 of 29 for 223 yards and 2 touchdowns. Schaub was 28 of 40 for 317 yards and 1 touchdown.

Houston	7	3	3	3	—	16
Atlanta	10	10	3	3	—	26
Atl	—	FG Andersen 28				
Hou	—	Davis 35 pass from Schaub (K. Brown kick)				
Atl	—	Jenkins 5 pass from Harrington (Andersen kick)				
Atl	—	Jenkins 7 pass from Harrington (Andersen kick)				
Atl	—	FG Andersen 22				
Hou	—	FG K. Brown 42				
Hou	—	FG K. Brown 37				
Atl	—	FG Andersen 36				
Hou	—	FG K. Brown 19				
Atl	—	FG Andersen 46				

BUFFALO 17, N.Y. JETS 14—at Ralph Wilson Stadium, attendance 70,600. Rookie Trent Edwards passed for a touchdown in his first NFL start as the Bills held off the Jets. In a scoreless first half, the Jets had the best scoring chance, but Mike Nugent's 37-yard field-goal attempt hit the right upright as the half expired. The Bills began the second half with scoring drives of 56 and 65 yards to take a 10-7 lead. Then Jabari Greer intercepted Chad Pennington's pass at the Jets' 25 and six plays later Edwards lofted a 1-yard touchdown pass to Michael Gaines on fourth-and-goal with 6:56 to play. The Jets went to a No Huddle offense and Leon Washington scored on an 8-yard run with 3:02 to play. The Jets then forced a punt and got the ball on their own 26 with 1:43 left. The Jets drove to the Bills' 39, but Terrence McGee intercepted Pennington's pass with six seconds left to clinch the victory. Edwards was 22 of 28 for 234 yards and 1 touchdown, with 1 interception. Pennington was 32 of 39 for 291 yards and 1 touchdown, with 2 interceptions. Jerricho Cotchery had 8 catches for 107 yards.

N.Y. Jets	0	0	7	7	—	14
Buffalo	0	0	7	10	—	17
Buff	—	Lynch 10 run (Lindell kick)				
NYJ	—	Coles 5 pass from Pennington (Nugent kick)				
Buff	—	FG Lindell 46				
Buff	—	Gaines 1 pass from Edwards (Lindell kick)				
NYJ	—	Washington 8 run (Nugent kick)				

TAMPA BAY 20, CAROLINA 7—at Bank of America Stadium, attendance 73,707. The Buccaneers rushed for 189 yards to defeat the Panthers. In the first half the Buccaneers outgained the Panthers 248-77 in total yards and had scoring drives of 71, 48, and 61 yards for a 17-0 lead. The Panthers ran just two plays in Buccaneers' territory prior to the two-minute warning. Jeff Garcia was 15 of 25 for 176 yards. Ike Hilliard had 7 receptions for 114 yards. David Carr, making his first start in place of injured Jake Delhomme, was 19 of 41 for 155 yards and 1 touchdown, with 1 interception.

Tampa Bay	14	3	0	3	—	20
Carolina	0	0	0	7	—	7
TB	—	Garcia 1 run (Bryant kick)				
TB	—	Graham 1 run (Bryant kick)				
TB	—	FG Bryant 25				
TB	—	FG Bryant 38				
Car	—	Williams 24 pass from Carr (Kasay kick)				

CLEVELAND 27, BALTIMORE 13—at Cleveland Browns Stadium, attendance 73,024. Derek Anderson passed for 2 touchdowns as the Browns downed the Ravens. Leigh Bodden intercepted a pass from Steve McNair in the first quarter. On the next play, Anderson connected with Braylon Edwards on a 78-yard touchdown for a 14-

0 lead. In the second quarter, Phil Dawson made a 41-yard field goal. On the ensuing kickoff, Yamon Figurs fumbled and David McMillan recovered at the Ravens' 31. Jamal Lewis scored eight plays later for an insurmountable 24-3 lead, with 4:52 left in the second quarter. The Browns' defense forced 2 turnovers, 2 missed field goals, and twice stopped the Ravens on downs in Browns' territory. Anderson was 10 of 18 for 204 yards and 2 touchdowns, with 1 interception. Steve McNair was 34 of 53 for 307 yards and 1 touchdown, with 1 interception. Derrick Mason had 10 receptions for 78 yards.

Baltimore	0	6	0	7	—	13
Cleveland	14	10	3	0	—	27
Cle	—	Jurevicius 2 pass from Anderson (Dawson kick)				
Cle	—	Edwards 78 pass from Anderson (Dawson kick)				
Balt	—	FG Stover 21				
Cle	—	FG Dawson 41				
Cle	—	Lewis 1 run (Dawson kick)				
Balt	—	FG Stover 29				
Cle	—	FG Dawson 20				
Balt	—	Sypniewski 4 pass from McNair (Stover kick)				

DALLAS 35, ST. LOUIS 7—at Texas Stadium, attendance 62,866. Tony Romo passed for 3 touchdowns and ran for another as the Cowboys remained undefeated. The Cowboys' defense did not allow an offensive touchdown, and outgained the Rams 502-187 in total yards. The Rams drove into the red zone twice. The first drive resulted in Jeff Wilkins' missed 28-yard field goal with the game scoreless early in the second quarter. The Cowboys responded with touchdown drives of 80, 83, 59, and 52 yards on four of their next five possessions. The Rams, trailing 28-7, drove inside the red zone late in the third quarter, but Ken Hamlin intercepted Marc Bulger's pass for a touchdown. Romo completed a 17-yard touchdown pass to Jason Witten five plays later as the Cowboys capped a 35-point outburst that lasted 19 minutes, 53 seconds. Romo was 21 of 33 for 339 yards and 3 touchdowns, with 1 interception. Patrick Crayton had 7 receptions for 184 yards. Bulger was 11 of 24 for 114 yards, with 1 interception. Gus Frerotte finished the game, completing 3 of 6 for 29 yards.

St. Louis	0	7	0	0	—	7
Dallas	0	14	21	0	—	35
Dall	—	J. Jones 2 run (Folk kick)				
StL	—	Hall 85 punt return (Wilkins kick)				
Dall	—	Romo 15 run (Folk kick)				
Dall	—	Crayton 59 pass from Romo (Folk kick)				
Dall	—	Crayton 37 pass from Romo (Folk kick)				
Dall	—	Witten 17 pass from Romo (Folk kick)				

DETROIT 37, CHICAGO 27—at Ford Field, attendance 60,811. The Lions scored an NFL-record 34-fourth-quarter points to improve their record to 3-1, matching their victory total from the previous season. The Bears, with Brian Griese making his first start in place of Rex Grossman, led 7-3 at halftime thanks to Griese's 15-yard touchdown pass to Muhsin Muhammad, and extended the lead to 13-3 with 49 seconds left in the third quarter. On the first play of the fourth quarter, Jon Kitna completed a 4-yard touchdown pass to Shaun McDonald. Four plays later, Keith Smith intercepted a pass and returned it 64 yards for a touchdown and 17-13 lead with 13:14 to play. Devin Hester returned the ensuing kickoff for a touchdown, but the Lions answered with Kitna's 49-yard pass to Mike Furrey setting up his 15-yard scoring toss to Troy Walters for a 24-20 lead with 10:06 remaining. The Lions' defense forced a three-and-out, and the offense drove 62 yards in eight plays, capped by Kevin Jones' 5-yard scoring run for a 30-20 lead with 3:34 left. Griese engineered a 12-play, 73-yard drive, capped by his 1-yard touchdown pass to Desmond Clark with 52 seconds left to pull within 30-27. But Casey FitzSimmons recovered the onside kick and returned it 41 yards for the game-clinching touchdown with 45 seconds remaining. Kitna was 20 of 24 for 247 yards and 2 touchdowns. Griese was 34 of 52 for 286 yards and 2 touchdowns, with 3 interceptions.

Chicago	0	7	6	14	—	27
Detroit	3	0	0	34	—	37
Det	—	FG Hanson 49				

Chi	—	Muhammad 15 pass from Griese (Gould kick)
Chi	—	FG Gould 49
Chi	—	FG Gould 41
Det	—	McDonald 4 pass from Kitna (Hanson kick)
Det	—	K. Smith 64 interception return (Hanson kick)
Chi	—	Hester 97 kickoff return (Gould kick)
Det	—	Walters 15 pass from Kitna (Hanson kick)
Det	—	K. Jones 5 run (kick blocked)
Chi	—	Clark 1 pass from Griese (Gould kick)
Det	—	FitzSimmons 41 kickoff return (Hanson kick)

INDIANAPOLIS 38, DENVER 20—at RCA Dome, attendance 57,274. Peyton Manning passed for 3 touchdowns and ran for another as the Colts improved to 4-0 for the third consecutive season. The Broncos scored on their first three possessions, but by halftime the Colts led 14-13. The Colts opened the second half with a seven-play, 73-yard drive, capped by Manning's 1-yard sneak. Two plays later, Marlin Jackson intercepted Jay Cutler's pass at the Broncos' 24 to set up a four-play drive that resulted in Dallas Clark's 3-yard touchdown catch for a 28-13 lead with 8:55 left in the third quarter. The Broncos answered with a 14-play, 79-yard drive to pull within 28-20, but the Colts scored on their next two possessions, capped by Adam Vinatieri's 22-yard field goal at 2:34 to play. Manning was 20 of 27 for 193 yards and 3 touchdowns. Joseph Addai had 19 carries for 136 yards. Cutler was 13 of 21 for 131 yards and 1 touchdown, with 1 interception.

Denver	10	3	7	0	— 20
Indianapolis	0	14	14	10	— 38

Den	—	FG Elam 35
Den	—	Marshall 7 pass from Cutler (Elam kick)
Ind	—	Addai 14 run (Vinatieri kick)
Den	—	FG Elam 22
Ind	—	Clark 9 pass from Manning (Vinatieri kick)
Ind	—	Manning 1 run (Vinatieri kick)
Ind	—	Clark 3 pass from Manning (Vinatieri kick)
Den	—	Cutler 2 run (Elam kick)
Ind	—	Wayne 5 pass from Manning (Vinatieri kick)
Ind	—	FG Vinatieri 22

OAKLAND 35, MIAMI 17—at Dolphin Stadium, attendance 70,621. Daunte Culpepper passed for 2 touchdowns and ran for 2 more scores against his former team as the Raiders pulled away from the Dolphins. The Raiders rushed for 299 yards and maintained possession for more than 35 minutes. Thomas Howard's first-quarter interception set up the Raiders' first touchdown, and Stanford Routt's interception near the goal line in the second quarter helped Oakland maintain a 14-7 lead. The Dolphins cut the lead to 14-10, but the Raiders answered with touchdowns on their final three drives. Justin Fargas' 48-yard run set up Culpepper's 5-yard scramble on third-and-goal for a 21-10 lead. Culpepper's 27-yard touchdown pass to Jerry Porter on third-and-7 early in the fourth quarter gave Oakland a 28-17 lead, and Fargas had runs of 32 and 27 yards on the final drive that was capped by Culpepper's 3-yard run on fourth-and-goal with 23 seconds to play. Culpepper was 5 of 12 for 75 yards and 2 touchdowns. Fargas carried 22 times for 179 yards. Trent Green was 14 of 25 for 158 yards and 1 touchdown, with 2 interceptions. Ronnie Brown carried 15 times for 134 yards.

Oakland	14	0	7	14	— 35
Miami	0	7	10	0	— 17

Oak	—	Porter 7 pass from Culpepper (Janikowski kick)
Oak	—	Culpepper 2 run (Janikowski kick)
Mia	—	Brown 9 run (Feely kick)
Mia	—	FG Feely 29
Oak	—	Culpepper 5 run (Janikowski kick)
Mia	—	Peelle 3 pass from Green (Feely kick)
Oak	—	Porter 27 pass from Culpepper (Janikowski kick)

Oak	—	Culpepper 3 run (Janikowski kick)

GREEN BAY 23, MINNESOTA 16—at Metrodome, attendance 63,779. Brett Favre set the NFL record for career touchdown passes as the Packers remained undefeated, matching the club's best start since 1998. Favre completed his record-setting 421st career touchdown pass by hitting Greg Jennings over the middle for a 16-yard touchdown on third-and-7 with 4:56 left in the first quarter. Mason Crosby kicked a 28-yard field goal just before halftime for a 10-6 lead, and then added a 44-yard field goal to cap the 8-minute, 56-second drive that began the second half to extend Green Bay's lead to 13-6. The Packers led 16-9 in the fourth quarter when Favre completed 6 of 8 passes on an 82-yard drive, capped by his 33-yard touchdown pass deep down the right side to James Jones on third-and-9 for a 23-9 lead with 5:46 to play. The Vikings responded with a 72-yard touchdown drive, and Chad Greenway recovered Favre's fumble moments later to give the Vikings the ball on their own 46-yard line with 1:40 to play. But Atari Bigby intercepted Kelly Holcomb's pass at the Packers' 23 with 1:06 remaining to clinch the victory. Favre was 32 of 45 for 344 yards and 2 touchdowns. Holcomb was 21 of 39 for 258 yards and 1 touchdown, with 1 interception. Adrian Peterson had 12 carries for 112 yards.

Green Bay	7	3	3	10	— 23
Minnesota	0	6	3	7	— 16

GB	—	Jennings 16 pass from Favre (Crosby kick)
Minn	—	FG Longwell 44
Minn	—	FG Longwell 35
GB	—	FG Crosby 28
GB	—	FG Crosby 44
Minn	—	FG Longwell 48
GB	—	FG Crosby 33
GB	—	J. Jones 33 pass from Favre (Crosby kick)
Minn	—	Rice 15 pass from Holcomb (Longwell kick)

KANSAS CITY 30, SAN DIEGO 16—at Qualcomm Stadium, attendance 65,175. The Chiefs scored the game's final 24 points to rally and surprise the Chargers. The Chiefs' defense forced 4 turnovers which led to 20 points. Despite 2 first-half turnovers, the Chargers took a 16-6 lead into the locker room thanks to Nate Kaeding's 38-yard field goal as the half expired. In the third quarter, trailing 16-9, Derrick Johnson intercepted a Philip Rivers pass. Three plays later, Damon Huard completed a 22-yard touchdown pass to Tony Gonzalez deep in the right corner of the end zone to tie the game. The Chiefs' defense forced a three-and-out, and the offense responded. On third-and-19, Dwayne Bowe took a short pass and split the secondary for a 51-yard and 23-16 lead. Later in the fourth quarter, Johnson sacked Rivers and forced him to fumble. Tyron Brackenridge recovered and raced 50 yards for a touchdown for 7:24 to play. The Chargers reached the Chiefs' 5-yard line with 4:03 to play, but Rivers threw four consecutive incomplete passes. Huard was 17 of 29 for 284 yards and 2 touchdowns, with 2 interceptions. Johnson had 25 carries for 123 yards, and Bowe had 8 catches for 164 yards. Rivers was 21 of 42 for 211 yards, with 3 interceptions. LaDainian Tomlinson had 20 carries for 132 yards.

Kansas City	0	6	10	14	— 30
San Diego	10	6	0	0	— 16

SD	—	FG Kaeding 24
SD	—	Tomlinson 5 run (Kaeding kick)
KC	—	FG Rayner 21
SD	—	FG Kaeding 51
KC	—	FG Rayner 25
SD	—	FG Kaeding 38
KC	—	FG Rayner 41
KC	—	Gonzalez 22 pass from Huard (Rayner kick)
KC	—	Bowe 51 pass from Huard (Rayner kick)
KC	—	Brackenridge 50 fumble return (Rayner kick)

SEATTLE 23, SAN FRANCISCO 3—at Monster Park, attendance 67,651. The Seahawks' defense allowed just 9 first downs, 184 yards, and registered 6 sacks to defeat the 49ers. Marcus Trufant had 2 interceptions, and Julian Peterson added 3 sacks. The 49ers had eight first half possessions, and the Seahawks' defense did not allow them across the Seattle 45-yard line en route to a 13-0 lead. The 49ers' onside kicked to begin the second half and recovered, but Trufant intercepted a pass on the next play. Matt Hasselbeck's

14-yard touchdown pass to Marcus Pollard six plays later increased the lead to 20-0. Nate Clements' interception set up Joe Nedney's 43-yard field goal late in the third quarter, but the 49ers failed to cross midfield on their final four possessions. Hasselbeck was 23 of 31 for 281 yards and 2 touchdowns, with 1 interception. Deion Branch had 7 receptions for 130 yards. Trent Dilfer was 12 of 33 for 128 yards, with 2 interceptions.

Seattle	0	13	7	3	— 23
San Francisco	0	0	3	0	— 3

Sea	—	FG J. Brown 23
Sea	—	Engram 17 pass from Hasselbeck (J. Brown kick)
Sea	—	FG J. Brown 31
Sea	—	Pollard 14 pass from Hasselbeck (J. Brown kick)
SF	—	FG Nedney 43
Sea	—	FG J. Brown 25

SUNDAY NIGHT, SEPTEMBER 30
N.Y. GIANTS 16, PHILADELPHIA 3—at Giants Stadium, attendance 78,862. Osi Umenyiora had 6 of the Giants' 12 sacks as New York frustrated the Eagles. The teams combined for just 402 total yards, 212 by the Giants. Leading 7-0, Lawrence Tynes capped a 55-yard drive, which was highlighted by a 32-yard pass interference penalty, with a 29-yard field goal late in the third quarter. On the next play, Donovan McNabb fumbled the snap. Kawika Mitchell recovered the ball, got up and ran 17 yards for a touchdown as 16-0 lead. The Eagles cut the deficit to 16-3 and late in the fourth quarter McNabb had a 19-yard touchdown passed nullified because he was beyond the line of scrimmage. On the next play, on fourth-and-18, Umenyiora capped his night by sacking McNabb with 2:19 to play, marking just the fourth time in NFL history a player had at least 6 sacks in a game. Mathias Kiwanuka added 3 sacks, and Justin Tuck chipped in with 2 sacks. Eli Manning was 14 of 26 for 135 yards and 1 touchdown, with 1 interception. McNabb was 15 of 31 for 138 yards, with 1 interception. Correll Buckhalter had 17 carries for 103 yards.

Philadelphia	0	0	0	3	— 3
N.Y. Giants	0	7	9	0	— 16

NYG	—	Burress 9 pass from E. Manning (Tynes kick)
NYG	—	FG Tynes 29
NYG	—	Mitchell 17 fumble return (kick failed)
Phil	—	FG Akers 53

MONDAY NIGHT, OCTOBER 1
NEW ENGLAND 34, CINCINNATI 13—at Paul Brown Stadium, attendance 66,113. Tom Brady passed for 3 touchdowns as the Patriots improved their record to 4-0. Asante Samuel intercepted Carson Palmer's pass at the Patriots' 2 just before halftime to turn away a scoring threat and allow the Patriots to take a 17-7 lead into the locker room. The Patriots opened the second half by forcing a punt and the offense answered with an 8-play, 81-yard drive, keyed by Wes Welker's 27-yard end around on third-and-3, and capped by Sammy Morris' 7-yard run for a 24-7 lead. The Bengals pulled within 27-13 with 9:04 remaining, but Brady responded by completing all 6 of his pass attempts on the ensuing 85-yard drive, capped by his 14-yard touchdown pass to Randy Moss on third-and-5 with 3:18 to play. Brady was 25 of 32 for 231 yards and 3 touchdowns, with 1 interception. Moss had 9 receptions for 102 yards. Palmer was 21 of 35 for 234 yards and 1 touchdown, with 2 interceptions. T.J. Houshmandzadeh had 10 catches for 100 yards.

New England	10	7	7	10	— 34
Cincinnati	0	7	3	3	— 13

NE	—	FG Gostkowski 31
NE	—	Vrabel 1 pass from Brady (Gostkowski kick)
Cin	—	Houshmandzadeh 1 pass from Palmer (Graham kick)
NE	—	Moss 7 pass from Brady (Gostkowski kick)
NE	—	Morris 7 run (Gostkowski kick)
Cin	—	FG Graham 40
NE	—	FG Gostkowski 36
Cin	—	FG Graham 48
NE	—	Moss 14 pass from Brady (Gostkowski kick)

2008 NFL Record & Fact Book

FIFTH WEEK SUMMARIES
American Football Conference

East Division	**W**	**L**	**T**	**Pct.**	**Pts.**	**OP**
New England	5	0	0	1.000	182	65
Buffalo	1	4	0	.200	65	118
N.Y. Jets	1	4	0	.200	96	138
Miami	0	5	0	.000	97	141
North Division	**W**	**L**	**T**	**Pct.**	**Pts.**	**OP**
Pittsburgh	4	1	0	.800	132	47
Baltimore	3	2	0	.600	88	97
Cleveland	2	3	0	.400	126	152
Cincinnati	1	3	0	.250	106	129
South Division	**W**	**L**	**T**	**Pct.**	**Pts.**	**OP**
Indianapolis	5	0	0	1.000	164	88
Jacksonville	3	1	0	.750	63	41
Tennessee	3	1	0	.750	84	59
Houston	3	2	0	.600	116	99
West Division	**W**	**L**	**T**	**Pct.**	**Pts.**	**OP**
Oakland	2	2	0	.500	102	100
Denver	2	3	0	.400	75	136
Kansas City	2	3	0	.400	63	83
San Diego	2	3	0	.400	109	105

National Football Conference

East Division	**W**	**L**	**T**	**Pct.**	**Pts.**	**OP**
Dallas	5	0	0	1.000	176	90
Washington	3	1	0	.750	87	52
N.Y. Giants	3	2	0	.600	123	124
Philadelphia	1	3	0	.250	84	73
North Division	**W**	**L**	**T**	**Pct.**	**Pts.**	**OP**
Green Bay	4	1	0	.800	125	93
Detroit	3	2	0	.600	117	155
Chicago	2	3	0	.400	87	115
Minnesota	1	3	0	.250	67	59
South Division	**W**	**L**	**T**	**Pct.**	**Pts.**	**OP**
Carolina	3	2	0	.600	98	100
Tampa Bay	3	2	0	.600	95	77
Atlanta	1	4	0	.200	69	100
New Orleans	0	4	0	.000	51	119
West Division	**W**	**L**	**T**	**Pct.**	**Pts.**	**OP**
Arizona	3	2	0	.600	118	111
Seattle	3	2	0	.600	87	74
San Francisco	2	3	0	.400	63	102
St. Louis	0	5	0	.000	70	137

SUNDAY, OCTOBER 7

SAN DIEGO 41, DENVER 3—at INVESCO Field at Mile High, attendance 76,879. Philip Rivers passed for 2 touchdowns and ran for another score as the Chargers snapped their three-game losing streak. The Chargers had a 484-296 advantage in total yards, and forced 3 turnovers that resulted in 17 points. The Chargers scored on five of their first six possessions, along with a 23-yard fumble return for a touchdown by Brandon Siler, to take a 34-3 lead before the third quarter had ended. Rivers was 13 of 18 for 270 yards and 2 touchdowns. Michael Turner carried 10 times for 147 yards. Antonio Gates had 7 receptions for 113 yards. Jay Cutler was 23 of 36 for 232 yards, with 1 interception.

San Diego	14	6	14	7	—	41
Denver	0	3	0	0	—	3

SD — Rivers 2 run (Kaeding kick)
SD — Siler 23 fumble return (Kaeding kick)
SD — FG Kaeding 26
Den — FG Elam 30
SD — FG Kaeding 45
SD — Gates 9 pass from Rivers (Kaeding kick)
SD — Jackson 15 pass from Rivers (Kaeding kick)
SD — Turner 74 run (Kaeding kick)

HOUSTON 22, MIAMI 19—at Reliant Stadium, attendance 70,156. Kris Brown made a 57-yard field goal with one second remaining as the Texans improved to 3-2 for the first time in franchise history. Brown became the first kicker in NFL history to make three field goals of at least 54 yards in the same game. Early in the game, Trent Green was suffered a season-ending concussion while trying to make a low block on Travis Johnson. Cleo Lemon replaced Green, and the Dolphins scored on each of their first four possessions to take a 16-7 lead. Brown ended the first half with a field goal, and C.C. Brown intercepted a pass two plays into the second half to set up Brown's 43-yard field goal to trim the deficit to 16-13. Brown tied the game 19-19 with a 20-yard field goal with 5:25 to play. The Dolphins punted and the Texan began on their own 3-yard line with 1:33 remaining. Matt Schaub connected on four of six passes, including two catches by Owen Daniels, a 19-yard grab by David Anderson and a 6-yard catch to Kevin Walter at the Dolphins' 38 with six seconds left. Brown then made the game-winning kick from a career-long 57 yards. Schaub was 20 of 34 for 294 yards, with 1 interception. Green was 1 of 2 for 5 yards, and Lemon was 15 of 27 for 151 yards, with 1 interception. Ronnie Brown carried 23 times for 114 yards, his third consecutive 100-yard rushing game.

Miami	10	6	0	3	—	19
Houston	7	3	6	6	—	22

Hou — Dayne 1 run (K. Brown kick)
Mia — FG Feely 23
Mia — R. Brown 3 run (Feely kick)
Mia — FG Feely 40
Mia — FG Feely 33
Hou — FG K. Brown 54
Hou — FG K. Brown 43
Hou — FG K. Brown 54
Mia — FG Feely 48
Hou — FG K. Brown 20
Hou — FG K. Brown 57

INDIANAPOLIS 33, TAMPA BAY 14—at RCA Dome, attendance 57,202. Making his first NFL start, rookie Kenton Keith rushed for a career-high 121 yards and 2 touchdowns as the Colts won their franchise-best twelfth consecutive home game. The Colts outgained the Buccaneers 400-177 in total yards, and maintained possession for 38 minutes, 15 seconds despite playing without injured Marvin Harrison and Joseph Addai. The Buccaneers cut the lead to 13-7 in the second quarter, and forced a punt. However, the Colts' defense forced a three-and-out, and the next time Tampa Bay had the ball it trailed 23-7, due to Adam Vinatieri's field goal as the half expired and Keith's 7-yard scoring run to cap the 13-play drive to begin the second half. The Colts' defense forced another punt, and the offense strung together and 11-play drive that culminated with Peyton Manning's 9-yard touchdown pass to Reggie Wayne on third-and-goal to open the fourth quarter for a 30-7 lead. Manning was 29 of 37 for 253 yards and 2 touchdowns, with 1 interception. Keith had 28 carries for 121 yards. Jeff Garcia was 18 of 23 for 143 yards and 2 touchdowns.

Tampa Bay	0	7	0	7	—	14
Indianapolis	7	9	7	10	—	33

Ind — Clark 10 pass from P. Manning (Vinatieri kick)
Ind — Keith 1 run (kick blocked)
TB — A. Smith 3 pass from Garcia (Bryant kick)
Ind — FG Vinatieri 27
Ind — Keith 7 run (Vinatieri kick)
Ind — Wayne 9 pass from P. Manning (Vinatieri kick)
TB — A. Smith 3 pass from Garcia (Bryant kick)
Ind — FG Vinatieri 35

JACKSONVILLE 17, KANSAS CITY 7—at Arrowhead Stadium, attendance 76,917. The Jaguars won their third consecutive game and nearly handed the Chiefs their first shutout at home since 1994. The Jaguars had a 18-play, 77-yard scoring drive to being the game, followed by an 80-yard drive for a touchdown for a 10-0 lead. In the fourth quarter, David Garrard engineered an 81-yard drive, highlighted by his 40-yard pass to Dennis Northcutt and capped by the duo's 3-yard touchdown with 8:26 to play for a 17-0 lead. The Chiefs avoided the shutout with a touchdown on the game's final play. Garrard was 20 of 27 for 218 yards and 1 touchdown. Damon Huard was 19 of 30 for 196 yards, with 1 interception, and Brodie Croyle was 6 of 13 for 83 yards and 1 touchdown.

Jacksonville	3	7	0	7	—	17
Kansas City	0	0	0	7	—	7

Jax — FG Carney 20
Jax — Jones-Drew 52 run (Carney kick)
Jax — Northcutt 3 pass from Garrard (Carney kick)
KC — Parker 13 pass from Croyle (Rayner kick)

NEW ENGLAND 34, CLEVELAND 17—at Gillette Stadium, attendance 68,756. Tom Brady passed for 3 touchdowns and the Patriots' defense forced 4 turnovers which resulted in 21 points as New England remained undefeated. Junior Seau intercepted his first 2 passes since 2002. The first interception came in the end zone and thwarted the Browns' opening drive. After a punt, Derek Anderson's next pass was intercepted as well, this time by Asante Samuel. On the following play, Brady fired a short pass to Donte' Stallworth, who broke free for a 34-yard touchdown. The Patriots scored on three of their next four possession to take a 20-0 halftime lead. Anderson completed a 21-yard touchdown pass to Tim Carter two plays into the fourth quarter to cut the deficit to 20-10, but the Patriots answered with a 71-yard drive, which included a 4-yard run by Sammy Morris on fourth-and-1 from the Browns' 29, and was capped by Brady's 25-yard touchdown pass to Ben Watson with 9:40 to play. Brady was 22 of 38 for 265 yards and 3 touchdowns. Morris had 21 carries for 102 yards. Watson had 6 receptions for 107 yards. Anderson was 22 of 43 for 287 yards and 2 touchdowns, with 3 interceptions. Braylon Edwards added 6 catches for 110 yards.

Cleveland	0	0	3	14	—	17
New England	10	10	0	14	—	34

NE — FG Gostkowski 20
NE — Stallworth 34 pass from Brady (Gostkowski kick)
NE — FG Gostkowski 25
NE — Watson 7 pass from Brady (Gostkowski kick)
Cle — FG Dawson 42
Cle — Carter 21 pass from Anderson (Dawson kick)
NE — Watson 25 pass from Brady (Gostkowski kick)
Cle — Winslow 14 pass from Anderson (Dawson kick)
NE — Gay 15 fumble return (Gostkowski kick)

CAROLINA 16, NEW ORLEANS 13—at Louisiana Superdome, attendance 70,001. John Kasay kicked a 52-yard field goal as time expired to rally the Panthers past the Saints. The Saints had the ball for more than 35 minutes and outgained the Panthers 341-243 in total yards, but Carolina capitalized on a few big plays. Kasay's first field goal came after an interception by Richard Marshall. David Carr was injured in the first quarter and briefly left the game, but Matt Moore completed a 43-yard pass to Keary Colbert to set up Kasay's second field goal. The Saints scored a touchdown to conclude their opening drive of the second half to take a 13-6 lead, and then had a 24-play, 93-yard drive that took more than 10 minutes off the clock. However, that drive stalled at the Panthers' 2, and Julius Peppers blocked Olindo Mare's 20-yard field-goal attempt. The Panthers responded with a 12-play, 85-yard drive, capped by Carr's 17-yard touchdown pass to Steve Smith on third-and-3 with 3:53 remaining to tie the game. The Saints had a chance to take the lead, but Mare missed a 54-yard field-goal attempt wide left with 2:14 left. Carr completed two key third-down passes on the ensuing drive, one to Colbert and the other to Smith with 21 seconds left to set up Kasay's winning kick. Carr was 10 of 17 for 119 yards and 1 touchdown, with 1 interception. Moore was 1 for 2 for 43 yards. Drew Brees was 29 of 47 for 252 yards, with 2 interceptions.

Carolina	3	3	0	10	—	16
New Orleans	3	3	7	0	—	13

Car — FG Kasay 23
NO — FG Mare 25
Car — FG Kasay 35
NO — FG Mare 28
NO — Karney 2 run (Mare kick)
Car — S. Smith 17 pass from Carr (Kasay kick)
Car — FG Kasay 52

N.Y. GIANTS 35, N.Y. JETS 24—at Giants Stadium, attendance 78,809. Rookie Aaron Ross intercepted 2 fourth-quarter passes as the Giants rallied to defeat the Jets. The Giants outgained the Jets in the second half 277-87 in total yards en route to outscoring them 28-7, including the game's final 21 points. The Jets dominated the first half, but a missed field goal and interception in Giants' territory limited their halftime lead to 17-7. A 33-yard pass to Plaxico Burress set up Brandon Jacobs' 19-yard touchdown run to cap the opening drive of the second half. However, Leon Washington returned the ensuing kickoff 98 yards for a touchdown and the Jets led 24-14 with 11:03 left in the third quarter. Leading 24-21 early in the fourth quarter, the Jets drove to the Giants' 23, but Ross intercepted Chad Pennington's pass at the 2-yard line to stop the drive. Eight plays later, Manning completed a 98-yard drive with a 53-yard touchdown pass to Burress, who took a short pass, went down the left sideline and stiff-armed a defender en route to the end zone with 7:52 remaining. After an exchange of punts, Ross intercepted Pennington's short pass on the right side intended for Jerricho Cotchery and returned it 43 yards for a 35-24 lead with 3:15 to play. Manning was 13 of 25 for 186 yards and 2 touchdowns, with 1 interception. Jacobs carried 20 times for 100 yards and Burress had 5 receptions for 124 yards. Pennington was 21 of 36 for 229 yards and 1 touchdown, with 3 interceptions.

N.Y. Jets	7	10	7	0	—	24
N.Y. Giants	0	7	14	14	—	35

NYJ — Rhodes 11 fumble return (Nugent kick)
NYG — Ward 8 run (Tynes kick)
NYJ — B. Smith 16 pass from Pennington (Nugent kick)
NYJ — FG Nugent 47
NYG — Jacobs 19 run (Tynes kick)
NYJ — Washington 98 kickoff return (Nugent kick)
NYG — Shockey 13 pass from E. Manning (Tynes kick)
NYG — Burress 53 pass from E. Manning (Tynes kick)
NYG — Ross 43 interception return (Tynes kick)

PITTSBURGH 21, SEATTLE 0—at Heinz Field, attendance 64,478. The Steelers' defense allowed just 144 yards and 8 first downs to hand the Seahawks their first shutout loss since 2000. The Steelers maintained possession for 40 minutes, 45 seconds, including 24 minutes and 53 seconds of the second half, to completely throttle the Seahawks. The Steelers led 7-0 late in the first half when the Seahawks drove to the Steelers' 14-yard line with seven seconds left. The Seahawks attempted one pass into the end zone, but Ike Taylor intercepted the pass to end the half. Pittsburgh opened the second half with a 17-play, 80-yard drive, which included 3 third-down pass conversions by Roethlisberger, including 2 to Cedric Wilson, to set up Najeh Davenport's 1-yard run for a 14-0 lead. The Seahawks had just four possessions in the second half, ran only 13 plays, and failed to cross their own 34-yard line. Roethlisberger was 18 of 22 for 206 yards and 1 touchdown. Willie Parker rushed 28 times for 102 yards. Matt Hasselbeck was 13 of 27 for 116 yards, with 1 interception.

Seattle	0	0	0	0	—	0
Pittsburgh	0	7	7	7	—	21

Pitt — Miller 13 pass from Roethlisberger (Reed kick)
Pitt — Davenport 1 run (Reed kick)
Pitt — Davenport 5 run (Reed kick)

ARIZONA 34, ST. LOUIS 31—at Edward Jones Dome, attendance 61,778. Roderick Hood had 2 interceptions, including 1 he returned for a touchdown, as the Cardinals outscored the Rams. In a game that featured three ties and three lead changes, the Cardinals took advantage of a break just before halftime. Trailing 13-10, the Cardinals had the ball on the Rams' 1-yard line with 14 seconds remaining and no timeouts. Edgerrin James was stopped for no gain. As the teams quickly lined up and the clock neared zero, Ron Bartell was flagged for a delay of game penalty when he kicked the ball. Given one play with zero time on the clock, the Cardinals went for the touchdown, and Kurt Warner scored on a 1-yard sneak for a 17-13 halftime lead. With the score tied 20-20 early in the fourth quarter, the Rams drove to the Cardinals' 37, but Gus Frerotte's short pass was intercepted by Hood and returned 68 yards for a touchdown. The Rams trailed 27-23 and were driving later in the quarter when Adrian Wilson intercepted Frerotte's pass and Warner capitalized with a 7-yard touchdown pass to Larry Fitzgerald with 3:11 to play. The Rams added a touchdown and 2-point conversion with 13 seconds left, but Fitzgerald recovered the onside kick to clinch the victory. Matt Leinart started and was 7 of 13 for 100 yards, with 1 interception. Warner replaced an injured Leinart in the second quarter, and was 14 of 28 for 190 yards and 1 touchdown, with 1 interception. Fitzgerald had 9 receptions for 136 yards. Frerotte was 24 of 43 for 262 yards and 3 touchdowns, with 3 interceptions. Brian Leonard, playing in place of injured Steven Jackson, had 18 carries for 102 yards.

Arizona	3	14	3	14	—	34
St. Louis	3	10	7	11	—	31

StL — FG Wilkins 46
Ari — FG Rackers 50
StL — Bennett 16 pass from Frerotte (Wilkins kick)
Ari — Wells fumble recovery in end zone (Rackers kick)
StL — FG Wilkins 35
Ari — Warner 1 run (Rackers kick)
StL — Holt 11 pass from Frerotte (Wilkins kick)
Ari — FG Rackers 32
Ari — Hood 68 interception return (Rackers kick)
StL — FG Wilkins 31
Ari — Fitzgerald 7 pass from Warner (Rackers kick)
StL — McMichael 29 pass from Frerotte (Holt pass from Frerotte)

BALTIMORE 9, SAN FRANCISCO 7—at Monster Park, attendance 67,885. The Ravens' defense allowed just 163 yards and 6 first downs as the offense held onto the ball for 38 minutes to hand the 49ers their third consecutive defeat. The Ravens had scoring drives of 68 and 54 plays in the second quarter, both capped by Matt Stover field goals, for a 6-0 halftime lead. Ed Reed intercepted a pass to stop the 49ers' opening possession of the second half to set up Stover's 49-yard field goal for a 9-0 lead, at which point the 49ers had not run a play inside the Ravens' 46-yard line. Trent Dilfer responded with a 42-yard pass to Bryan Gilmore followed by a 23-yard touchdown pass to Arnaz Battle to cut the deficit to 9-7. In the fourth quarter, a 19-yard screen pass to Frank Gore gave the 49ers a chance, but Joe Nedney's 52-yard field-goal attempt was wide right with 2:37 to play. Steve McNair completed an 18-yard pass to Derrick Mason for a first down with just over two minutes remaining, and added a 1-yard sneak on third-and-1 for the game-clinching first down with 1:00 left. McNair was 29 of 43 for 214 yards. Dilfer was 12 of 19 for 126 yards and 1 touchdown, with 1 interception.

Baltimore	0	6	3	0	—	9
San Francisco	0	0	7	0	—	7

Balt — FG Stover 26
Balt — FG Stover 32
Balt — FG Stover 49
SF — Battle 23 pass from Dilfer (Nedney kick)

TENNESSEE 20, ATLANTA 13—at LP Field, attendance 69,143. The Titans' defense allowed just 198 yards and 9 first downs, and Vincent Fuller returned an interception 76 yards for a touchdown. Rob Bironas' 30-yard field goal as the half expired tied the game 10-10. Trey Lewis intercepted a pass three plays into the second half to set up Morten Andersen's 28-yard field goal for a 13-10 Atlanta lead. With the scored tied 13-13 late in the third quarter, Corey McIntyre recovered a fumble at the Titans' 42. However, five plays later Fuller stepped in front of a pass intended for Michael Jenkins and returned in 76 yards for a touchdown and 20-13 lead. After an exchange of missed field goals, Byron Leftwich replaced Joey Harrington. David Thornton ended one scoring threat with an interception at the Titans' 14 with 3:20 left. The Titans were forced to punt, and a bad snap gave them the ball at the Titans' 19. Warrick Dunn ran for 18 yards on the next play. However, Leftwich fumbled on the next play, losing eight yards. Three plays later, on fourth and goal, Kyle Vanden Bosch sacked Leftwich with 1:00 remaining to clinch the victory. Young was 20 of 33 for 157 yards, with 3 interceptions. Harrington was 16 of 31 for 87 yards, with 1 interception. Leftwich was 2 of 8 for 28 yards, with 1 interception.

Atlanta	7	3	3	0	—	13
Tennessee	7	3	10	0	—	20

Atl — Hall 56 fumble return (Andersen kick)
Tenn — C.Brown 3 run (Bironas kick)
Atl — FG Andersen 32
Tenn — FG Bironas 30
Atl — FG Andersen 28
Tenn — FG Bironas 40
Tenn — Fuller 76 interception return (Bironas kick)

WASHINGTON 34, DETROIT 3—at FedExField, attendance 88,944. The Redskins' defense allowed just 144 yards, registered 6 sacks, a safety, and returned an interception for a touchdown as the Redskins defeated the Lions for the twenty-first consecutive time in Washington. The Lions did not cross midfield with their first six possessions. Once they did, Jason Hanson kicked a 39-yard field goal, and the Lions trailed just 14-3 with 2:27 left in the third quarter. The Lions' defense then forced a punt, but Derrick Frost's 52-yard punt was fair caught at the Lions' 8. Two plays later, Andre Carter sacked Jon Kitna for a safety. Early in the fourth quarter, James Thrash returned a punt 62 yards, fumbled at the 25-yard line and Rock Cartwright fell on the bouncing ball at the Lions' 3. Two plays later, Mike Sellers scored his second touchdown for a 24-3 lead with 10:47 remaining. Jason Campbell was 23 of 29 for 248 yards and 2 touchdowns. Antwaan Randle El had 7 catches for 100 yards. Kitna was 16 of 29 for 106 yards, with 2 interceptions.

Detroit	0	0	3	0	—	3
Washington	0	14	2	18	—	34

Wash — Cooley 7 pass from Campbell (Suisham kick)
Wash — Sellers 1 run (Suisham kick)
Det — FG Hanson 39
Wash — Safety, Carter sacked Kitna in end zone
Wash — Sellers 8 pass from Campbell (Cooley pass from Campbell)
Wash — FG Suisham 28
Wash — Rogers 61 interception return (Suisham kick)

SUNDAY NIGHT, OCTOBER 7

CHICAGO 27, GREEN BAY 20—at Lambeau Field, attendance 70,904. Brian Griese connected on a 34-yard touchdown pass to Desmond Clark with 2:05 remaining as the Bears scored the final 17 points to win on the road. The Packers scored on their last two possession of the first half to take a 17-7 halftime lead. The Bears began the second half with a field goal, but Tramon Williams returned the ensuing kickoff 65 yards to set up Mason Crosby's second field goal and a 20-10 lead. The Packers then forced a punt, but Brian Urlacher intercepted Brett Favre's short pass at the Packers' 19 and Greg Olsen caught a touchdown pass on the next play to pull the Bears within 20-17. The Packers' went three-and-out on their next four possessions. With the score 20-20 the Bears began the winning drive from their own 21-yard line with 5:27 to play. A 27-yard catch by Olsen set up Griese's winning 34-pass to Clark on third-and-2 with 2:05 remaining. The Packers drove to the Bears' 32, but Brandon McGowan intercepted Favre's Hail Mary pass in the end zone with one second to play. Griese was 15 of 25 for 214 yards and 2 touchdowns, with 1 interception. Favre was 29 of 40 for 322 yards and 1 touchdown, with 2 interceptions.

Chicago	0	7	10	10	—	27
Green Bay	7	10	3	0	—	20

GB — Wynn 2 run (Crosby kick)
Chi — Benson 10 run (Gould kick)
GB — Jennings 41 pass from Favre (Crosby kick)
GB — FG Crosby 37
Chi — FG Gould 44
GB — FG Crosby 37
Chi — Olsen 19 pass from Griese (Gould kick)
Chi — FG Gould 36
Chi — Clark 34 pass from Griese (Gould kick)

MONDAY NIGHT, OCTOBER 8

DALLAS 25, BUFFALO 24—at Ralph Wilson Stadium, attendance 71,575. Nick Folk kicked a 53-yard field goal as time expired as the Cowboys rallied to remain undefeated. The Cowboys outgained the Bills 385-229 in total yards, but the Bills' defense had 5 interceptions. George Wilson returned an interception 25 yards for a touchdown to stop the Cowboys first drive. The Bills had three more first-half interceptions, but Folk's 47-yard field goal as the half expired cut the deficit to 17-10. The Cowboys added a field goal to begin the second half, but Terrence McGee returned the ensuing kickoff 103 yards for a touchdown and 24-13 lead. The Bills led 24-16 in the middle of the fourth quarter when Terance Newman returned an interception 70 yards to stop the Bills' drive. However, John DiGiorgio intercepted Romo's pass two plays later to maintain the eight-point lead. The Cowboys' defense forced a punt, and Romo completed a 4-yard touchdown pass to Patrick Crayton with 20 seconds left. However, Jabari Greer batted away Romo's 2-point conversion pass intended for Terrell Owens to keep the score 24-22. Tony Curtis recovered the onside kick for Dallas. Romo completed two short passes, the second an 8-yard pass to Crayton with two seconds left to set up Folk's winning 53-yard attempt. The Bills called time out just before Folk made his first attempt, but Folk was undaunted and drilled the second try to win the game. Romo was 29 of 50 for 309 yards, with 5 interceptions. Jason Witten had 9 catches for 103 yards. Trent Edwards was 23 of 31 for 176 yards, with 1 interception.

Dallas	0	10	3	12	—	25
Buffalo	7	10	7	0	—	24

Buff	—	Wilson 25 interception return (Lindell kick)
Dall	—	Witten 22 pass from Romo (Folk kick)
Buff	—	FG Lindell 24
Buff	—	Kelsay interception in end zone (Lindell kick)
Dall	—	FG Folk 47
Dall	—	FG Folk 29
Buff	—	McGee 103 kickoff return (Lindell kick)
Dall	—	FG Folk 37
Dall	—	Crayton 4 pass from Romo (pass failed)
Dall	—	FG Folk 53

SIXTH WEEK SUMMARIES
American Football Conference

East Division	W	L	T	Pct.	Pts.	OP
New England	6	0	0	1.000	230	92
Buffalo	1	4	0	.200	65	118
N.Y. Jets	1	5	0	.167	105	154
Miami	0	6	0	.000	128	182
North Division	W	L	T	Pct.	Pts.	OP
Pittsburgh	4	1	0	.800	132	47
Baltimore	4	2	0	.667	110	100
Cleveland	3	3	0	.500	167	183
Cincinnati	1	4	0	.200	126	156
South Division	W	L	T	Pct.	Pts.	OP
Indianapolis	5	0	0	1.000	164	88
Jacksonville	4	1	0	.800	100	58
Tennessee	3	2	0	.600	94	72
Houston	3	3	0	.500	133	136
West Division	W	L	T	Pct.	Pts.	OP
Kansas City	3	3	0	.500	90	103
San Diego	3	3	0	.500	137	119
Denver	2	3	0	.400	75	136
Oakland	2	3	0	.400	116	128

National Football Conference

East Division	W	L	T	Pct.	Pts.	OP
Dallas	5	1	0	.833	203	144
N.Y. Giants	3	2	0	.600	123	143
Washington	3	2	0	.600	101	69
Philadelphia	2	3	0	.400	100	82
North Division	W	L	T	Pct.	Pts.	OP
Green Bay	5	1	0	.833	142	107
Detroit	3	2	0	.600	117	155
Minnesota	2	3	0	.400	101	90
Chicago	2	4	0	.333	118	149
South Division	W	L	T	Pct.	Pts.	OP
Carolina	4	2	0	.667	123	110
Tampa Bay	4	2	0	.667	108	87
Atlanta	1	4	0	.200	69	100
New Orleans	1	4	0	.200	79	136
West Division	W	L	T	Pct.	Pts.	OP
Arizona	3	3	0	.500	128	136
Seattle	3	3	0	.500	104	102
San Francisco	2	3	0	.400	63	102
St. Louis	0	6	0	.000	73	159

SUNDAY, OCTOBER 14

CAROLINA 25, ARIZONA 10—at University of Phoenix Stadium, attendance 64,403. Forty-three year-old Vinny Testaverde passed for 206 yards and a touchdown to become the oldest starting quarterback to win a game in NFL history. Testaverde, who had just signed with the Panthers four days earlier, earned the start after David Carr's back locked up on the flight from Charlotte. Arizona lost quarterback Kurt Warner in the first quarter when he injured his left shoulder scrambling for a loose ball. The defenses allowed just a combined 24 first downs, but Carolina's defense forced 5 turnovers, which the offense turned into 13 points. The Cardinals led 10-9 when the Panthers took over at their own 10-yard-line with

---

5:52 to play. A 25-yard pass interference penalty on the first play was followed by Testaverde's 65-yard pass deep down the right sideline to Steve Smith for a touchdown and 15-10 lead. The touchdown, which came with 5:40 to play, marked the 21st consecutive season that Testaverde had thrown a touchdown pass, extending his own NFL record. On the next play from scrimmage, Tim Rattay's pass was intercepted by Ken Lucas and set up John Kasay's 45-yard field goal with 4:26 remaining. Deke Cooper intercepted Rattay's pass with 3:19 to play, and DeAngelo Williams responded with a 75-yard run to set up his 13-yard scoring run with 2:07 left. Testaverde was 20 of 33 for 206 yards and 1 touchdown. Williams rushed 10 times for 121 yards, and Smith had 10 catches for 136 yards. Warner was 2 of 2 for 21 yards, and Rattay was 12 of 24 for 159 yards, with 3 interceptions.

Carolina	3	3	3	16	—	25
Arizona	0	7	3	0	—	10

Car	—	FG Kasay 33
Car	—	FG Kasay 43
Ariz	—	James 23 run (Rackers kick)
Car	—	FG Kasay 24
Ariz	—	FG Rackers 50
Car	—	S. Smith 65 pass from Testaverde (pass failed)
Car	—	FG Kasay 45
Car	—	D. Williams 13 run (Kasay kick)

BALTIMORE 22, ST. LOUIS 3—at M & T Bank Stadium, attendance 71,175. The Ravens' defense forced 6 turnovers and registered 4 sacks to stifle the Rams. The Rams trailed 6-0 in the second quarter when Jeff Wilkins missed a 35-yard-field-goal attempt. Eight plays later, Willis McGahee scored on a 6-yard run, one play after a 27-yard pass-interference penalty, to give the Ravens a 13-0 lead. Two plays into the second half, Corey Ivy intercepted Gus Frerotte's pass to set up Matt Stover's third field goal. Kyle Boller was 18 of 30 for 184 yards, with 1 interception. Frerotte, making his second start in place of injured Marc Bulger, was 19 of 36 for 208 yards, with 5 interceptions.

St. Louis	0	0	3	0	—	3
Baltimore	3	10	3	6	—	22

Balt	—	FG Stover 43
Balt	—	FG Stover 42
Balt	—	McGahee 6 run (Stover kick)
Balt	—	FG Stover 23
StL	—	FG Wilkins 32
Balt	—	FG Stover 31
Balt	—	FG Stover 36

MINNESOTA 34, CHICAGO 31—at Soldier Field, attendance 62,174. Rookie Adrian Peterson rushed for a Vikings' record 224 yards and Ryan Longwell kicked a 55-yard field goal as time expired to lift Minnesota past the Bears. Peterson's 67-yard run with 2:19 left in the first half tied the game 14-14. With 2:31 remaining in the third quarter, Peterson raced 73 yards for a touchdown and 21-14 lead. After an exchange of field goals, Peterson scampered 35 yards around left end for a touchdown and 31-17 lead with 4:10 remaining. With 2:36 to play, Brian Griese connected on a 35-yard touchdown pass to Muhsin Muhammad. The Bears' defense forced a three-and-out, and two plays later Griese lofted a deep pass down the right side to Devin Hester, who raced the remaining 35 yards for an 81-yard touchdown to tie the game with 1:38 left. Peterson returned the ensuing kickoff 53 yards to set up Longwell's winning kick. Griese was 26 of 45 for 381 yards and 3 touchdowns, with 2 interceptions. Peterson rushed 20 times for 224 yards and 1 touchdown.

Minnesota	7	7	7	13	—	34
Chicago	7	7	0	17	—	31

Chi	—	Hester 89 punt return (Gould kick)
Minn	—	Williamson 60 pass from T. Jackson (Longwell kick)
Chi	—	Berrian 39 pass from Griese (Gould kick)
Minn	—	Peterson 67 run (Longwell kick)
Minn	—	Peterson 73 run (Longwell kick)
Minn	—	FG Longwell 48
Chi	—	FG Gould 32
Minn	—	Peterson 35 run (Longwell kick)
Chi	—	Muhammad 33 pass from Griese (Gould kick)
Chi	—	Hester 81 pass from Griese (Gould kick)

Minn	—	FG Longwell 55

CLEVELAND 41, MIAMI 31—at Cleveland Browns Stadium, attendance 73,198. Braylon Edwards handed the Dolphins their club-record ninth consecutive defeat. The Browns scored on five of their six first-half possessions to take a 27-10 halftime lead. The Dolphins began the second half with a 14-play, 75-yard touchdown drive, forced a three-and-out, and then drove 62 yards in nine plays, which included a fourth-and-1 sneak for a first down by Cleo Lemon, and was capped by Lemon's 1-yard run to pull within 27-24 with 2:44 left in the third quarter. The Browns responded with a 12-play, 66-yard touchdown drive, capped by Edwards' second scoring catch. The Browns' defense then forced a three-and-out, and Edwards capped the ensuing 67-yard drive with a 16-yard scoring grab for a 41-24 lead with 4:34 to play. Both of Edwards' fourth-quarter touchdowns came on third down. Derek Anderson was 18 of 25 for 245 yards and 3 touchdowns. Lemon was 24 of 43 for 256 yards and 2 touchdowns, with 2 interceptions. Ronnie Brown had 19 carries for 101 yards.

Miami	3	7	14	7	—	31
Cleveland	14	13	0	14	—	41

Cle	—	Wright 1 run (Dawson kick)
Mia	—	FG Feely 43
Cle	—	Anderson 1 run (Dawson kick)
Cle	—	FG Dawson 40
Cle	—	Edwards 24 pass from Anderson (Dawson kick)
Mia	—	Martin 14 pass from Lemon (Feely kick)
Cle	—	FG Dawson 20
Mia	—	Lemon 5 run (Feely kick)
Mia	—	Lemon 1 run (Feely kick)
Cle	—	Edwards 5 pass from Anderson (Dawson kick)
Cle	—	Edwards 16 pass from Anderson (Dawson kick)
Mia	—	Martin 4 pass from Lemon (Feely kick)

NEW ENGLAND 48, DALLAS 27—at Texas Stadium, attendance 63,984. Tom Brady passed for 388 yards and 5 touchdowns as the Patriots handed the Cowboys their first loss. The game marked just the fifth time in NFL history that teams with records of at least 5-0 played each other. Brady became the first quarterback in NFL history to pass for at least 3 touchdowns in each of the seasons' first six games. The Patriots outgained the Cowboys 448-285 in total yards, and maintained possession for 38 minutes, 15 seconds. New England jumped to a 14-0 lead, but a fumble return for a touchdown by Jason Hatcher and Tony Romo's 12-yard touchdown pass to Terrell Owens to cap an 84-yard drive with just 46 seconds left in the half cut the Patriots lead to 21-17. The Patriots took the second half opening kickoff, went three-and-out, and the Cowboys answered with a 74-yard touchdown drive, capped by Patrick Crayton's 8-yard scoring catch to give the Cowboys a 24-21 lead with 10:20 remaining in the third quarter. The Patriots, trailing in the second half for the first time all season, responded by scoring on their final five possessions. The key play in the second half may have been Brady's 3-yard scramble on third-and-2 at the Patriots' 28 with New England leading 31-24 early in the fourth quarter. On the next play after the first down, Brady completed a 69-yard touchdown pass to Donte' Stallworth for a 38-24 lead. Leading 41-27, Junior Seau intercepted a pass with 3:45 to play to set up Kyle Eckel's first NFL touchdown with 19 seconds to play. Brady was 31 of 46 for 388 yards and 5 touchdowns. Wes Welker had 11 receptions for 124 yards. Romo was 18 of 29 for 199 yards and 2 touchdowns, with 1 interception.

New England	14	7	10	17	—	48
Dallas	0	17	3	7	—	27

NE	—	Moss 6 pass from T. Brady (Gostkowski kick)
NE	—	Welker 35 pass from T. Brady (Gostkowski kick)
Dall	—	FG Folk 38
Dall	—	Hatcher 29 fumble return (Folk kick)
NE	—	Welker 2 pass from T. Brady (Gostkowski kick)
Dall	—	Owens 12 pass from Romo (Folk kick)
Dall	—	Crayton 8 pass from Romo (Folk kick)

NE — K. Brady 1 pass from T. Brady (Gostkowski kick)
NE — FG Gostkowski 45
NE — Stallworth 69 pass from T. Brady (Gostkowski kick)
Dall — FG Folk 23
NE — FG Gostkowski 22
NE — Eckel 1 run (Gostkowski kick)

GREEN BAY 17, WASHINGTON 14—at Lambeau Field, attendance 70,761. Charles Woodson returned a fumble 57 yards for a touchdown as the Packers rallied to improve their record to 5-1. The Redskins took a 14-7 lead with 1:11 left in the second quarter when Jason Campbell completed a 14-yard touchdown pass to Chris Cooley on third-and-9. The Packers converted two third-down situations in the third quarter to set up Mason Crosby's 37-yard field goal. Two plays later, playing in the rain, Santana Moss fumbled the ball and Charles Woodson recovered. Woodson got up and raced 57 yards for a touchdown and 17-14 lead. Crosby had a 38-yard field-goal attempt hit off the left upright in the fourth quarter, and the Redskins responded by driving to the Packers' 33, but Campbell's fourth-and-2 pass for Ladell Betts fell incomplete. The Packers' defense allowed just 96 yards on nine Redskins' second-half possessions. Brett Favre was 19 of 37 for 188 yards, with 2 interception. Campbell was 21 of 37 for 217 yards and 1 touchdown, with 1 interception. Cooley had 9 receptions for 105 yards.

Washington	7	7	0	0	—	14
Green Bay	7	0	10	0	—	17

GB — Wynn 3 run (Crosby kick)
Wash — Campbell 6 run (Suisham kick)
Wash — Cooley 14 pass from Campbell (Suisham kick)
GB — FG Crosby 37
GB — Woodson 57 fumble return (Crosby kick)

JACKSONVILLE 37, HOUSTON 17—at Jacksonville Municipal Stadium, attendance 63,715. The Jaguars rushed for 244 yards, highlighted by Maurice Jones-Drew's 125 yards and 2 touchdowns, to overpower the Texans. Houston took a 6-0 lead in the second quarter, but the Jaguars responded by scoring on five consecutive possessions, on touchdown drives of 76, 81, 78, and 77 yards. In the fourth quarter, the Texans trailed 23-9 but drove to the Jaguars' 21. Paul Spicer sacked Matt Schaub and forced him to fumble. Daryl Smith recovered and returned the ball 77 yards for a touchdown and 30-9 lead with 8:55 to play. David Garrard was 22 of 34 for 221 yards and 2 touchdowns. Jones-Drew had 12 carries for 125 yards. Schaub was 19 of 31 for 259 yards, with 1 interception. Sage Rosenfels was 11 of 12 for 82 yards and 1 touchdown. Kevin Walter has 12 receptions for 160 yards.

Houston	3	3	3	8	—	17
Jacksonville	0	10	6	21	—	37

Hou — FG K. Brown 20
Hou — FG K. Brown 35
Jax — Wrighster 1 pass from Garrard (Carney kick)
Jax — FG Carney 37
Jax — R. Williams 9 pass from Garrard (kick blocked)
Hou — FG K. Brown 33
Jax — Jones-Drew 7 run (Carney kick)
Jax — D. Smith 77 fumble return (Carney kick)
Jax — Jones-Drew 57 run (Carney kick)
Hou — Leach 1 pass from Rosenfels (Gado run)

KANSAS CITY 27, CINCINNATI 20—at Arrowhead Stadium, attendance 76,846. Tony Gonzalez set the record for most career touchdown catches by a tight end as the Chiefs handed the Bengals their fourth consecutive defeat. Gonzalez' record 63rd career touchdown catch came on a 3-yard catch with 53 seconds left in the first quarter and allowed him to surpass Shannon Sharpe's record. Patrick Surtain intercepted a pass at the Bengals' 44 in the second quarter to set up Larry Johnson's 8-yard run for a 17-7 lead. In the fourth quarter, Damon Huard completed a 26-yard touchdown pass to Tony Gonzalez for a 27-10 lead with 8:03 to play. The Bengals cut the deficit to 27-17 and got the ball back, but Bernard Pollard intercepted Carson Palmer's pass with 3:18 to play. Shayne Graham kicked a 36-yard field goal with 18 seconds left, but Jarrad Page recovered the onside kick to seal the victory. Huard was 25 of 35 for 264 yards and 2 touchdowns. Gonzalez had 9 receptions for 102 yards. Johnson carried 31 times for 119 yards. Palmer was 26 of 43 for 320 yards and 2 touchdowns, with 2 interceptions. T.J. Houshmandzadeh had 8 receptions for 145 yards.

Cincinnati	7	0	0	13	—	20
Kansas City	10	10	0	7	—	27

KC — FG Rayner 32
Cin — Houshmandzadeh 42 pass from Palmer (Graham kick)
KC — Gonzalez 3 pass from Huard (Rayner kick)
KC — L. Johnson 8 run (Rayner kick)
KC — FG Rayner 20
Cin — FG Graham 33
KC — Gonzalez 26 pass from Huard (Rayner kick)
Cin — Houshmandzadeh 30 pass from Palmer (Graham kick)
Cin — FG Graham 36

PHILADELPHIA 16, N.Y. JETS 9—at The Meadowlands, attendance 77,189. Kevin Curtis caught a 75-yard touchdown to help the Eagles defeat the Jets. The Eagles had 413 total yards, but had to settle for five field goal attempts, with David Akers converting on three field goals to take a 16-6 lead with 1:40 remaining in the third quarter. The Jets had a chance to get back into the game when Hank Poteat intercepted a pass and returned it 11 yards to the Eagles' 7 with 11:24 to play. But the Jets were unable to get a first down, and Mike Nugent's 30-yard field goal cut the deficit to 16-9 with 9:28 to play. The Jets' defense forced a three-and-out, and the offense drove to the Eagles' 4. Thomas Jones was stopped for no gain on second down, and Chad Pennington's sneak did not gain any yards on third-and-1. On fourth-and-1, Pennington's pass for Lavernaues Coles fell incomplete with 3:27 to play. Brian Westbrook's 21-yard run on third-and-2 with 55 seconds left iced the game. Donovan McNabb was 22 of 35 for 278 yards and 1 touchdown, with 1 interception. Westbrook had 20 carries for 120 yards. Curtis had 5 receptions for 121 yards. Pennington was 11 of 21 for 128 yards, with 1 interception. Jones had 24 carries for 130 yards.

Philadelphia	7	3	6	0	—	16
N.Y. Jets	3	3	0	3	—	9

NYJ — FG Nugent 30
Phil — Curtis 75 pass from McNabb (Akers kick)
Phil — FG Akers 22
NYJ — FG Nugent 21
Phil — FG Akers 31
Phil — FG Akers 25
NYJ — FG Nugent 30

SAN DIEGO 28, OAKLAND 14—at Qualcomm Stadium, attendance 67,523. LaDainian Tomlinson rushed for 198 yards and 4 touchdowns as the Chargers won their second consecutive game. The Chargers' defense registered 5 sacks, forced 3 turnovers, and allowed just 245 total yards. San Diego opened the game with an 11-play, 80-yard touchdown drive. Thee plays later, Drayton Florence intercepted Daunte Culpepper's pass to set up Tomlinson's second touchdown for a 14-0 lead just 8:09 into the game. Thomas Howard intercepted a short pass and returned it 66 yards for a touchdown to cut the deficit to 14-7. Leading 21-7, Nate Kaeding missed a 50-yard field-goal attempt early in the fourth quarter. The Raiders answered with an 17-play, 60-yard touchdown drive, capped by Culpepper's 1-yard pass to Zach Miller on fourth-and-goal with 5:18 to play. On third-and-3 with 2:48 to play, Tomlinson broke free over right tackle and scored on a 41-yard run with 2:43 to play. Philip Rivers was 14 of 21 for 156 yards, with 1 interception. Culpepper was 24 of 37 for 229 yards and 1 touchdown, with 2 interceptions.

Oakland	0	7	0	7	—	14
San Diego	14	0	7	7	—	28

SD — Tomlinson 3 run (Kaeding kick)
SD — Tomlinson 27 run (Kaeding kick)
Oak — Howard 66 interception return (Janikowski kick)
SD — Tomlinson 13 run (Kaeding kick)
Oak — Miller 1 pass from Culpepper (Janikowski kick)
SD — Tomlinson 41 run (Kaeding kick)

TAMPA BAY 13, TENNESSEE 10—at Raymond James Stadium, attendance 65,347. Matt Bryant kicked a 43-yard field goal with 11 seconds remaining to lift the Buccaneers past the Titans. Tennessee held the ball for 37 minutes, 37 seconds, but committed 3 turnovers. With the score 3-3 in the third quarter, Vince Young injured his quad on a 2-yard run. Kerry Collins entered, the Buccaneers' forced a punt, and three plays later Jeff Garcia connected on a long pass with Joey Galloway for a 69-yard touchdown. The Titans had a chance early in the fourth quarter, but on third down from the Buccaneers' 24, Kevin Carter sacked Collins for a 13-yard loss, forcing the Titans to punt. Later in the fourth quarter, the Titans converted three third downs on a 13-play, 86-yard drive, including a 17-yard pass from Collins to Bo Scaife, to set up LenDale White's game-tying 2-yard touchdown run with 1:17 to play. Three plays later, on third-and-10 from his own 20, Garcia completed a 28-yard pass to Ike Hilliard. A 10-yard pass to Hilliard three plays later set up Bryant's winning kick. Garcia was 20 of 31 for 274 yards and 1 touchdown. Young was 11 of 14 for 120 yards, with 1 interception. Collins was 10 of 20 for 125 yards.

Tennessee	0	0	3	7	—	10
Tampa Bay	0	3	7	3	—	13

TB — FG Bryant 23
Tenn — FG Bironas 48
TB — Galloway 69 pass from Garcia (Bryant kick)
Tenn — L. White 2 run (Bironas kick)
TB — FG Bryant 43

SUNDAY NIGHT, OCTOBER 14

NEW ORLEANS 28, SEATTLE 17—at Qwest Field, attendance 68,296. The Saints scored 28 first-half points to snap their four-game losing streak. The Seahawks were stopped on their first possesison, and Boone Stutz' snap was fumbled, picked up by Pierre Thomas and returned 5 yards for a touchdown. An 86-yard touchdown drive gave New Orleans a 14-0 lead. Josh Bullocks then blocked Josh Brown's 44-yard field-goal attempt to set up Lance Moore's 7-yard end around for a touchdown a 21-0 lead. The Saints led 28-10 and drove to the Seahawks' 15 late in the third quarter, but Reggie Bush fumbled and Baraka Atkins recovered. The Seahawks went for a first down on fourth-and-3 from their own 34 with 9:03 to play, but Leonard Weaver was stopped for 2 yards. The Seahawks got the ball back and Matt Hasselbeck completed three consecutive passes of at least 20 yards, capped by Nate Burleson's 22-yard scoring catch with 6:39 to play. The Seahawks' defense forced another punt, but Bullocks intercepted Hasselbeck's long pass with 3:49 to play. On Seattle's final possession, on fourth-and-9 from the Saints' 14 with 1:21 to play, Hasselbeck's pass for Ben Obomanu fell incomplete. Drew Brees was 25 of 36 for 246 yards and 2 touchdowns. David Patten had 8 receptions for 113 yards. Hasselbeck was 26 of 43 for 362 yards and 2 touchdowns, with 1 interception. Bobby Engram had 9 catches for 120 yards.

New Orleans	7	21	0	0	—	28
Seattle	0	10	0	7	—	17

NO — P. Thomas 5 fumble return (Mare kick)
NO — E. Johnson 3 pass from Brees (Mare kick)
NO — Moore 7 run (Mare kick)
Sea — Obomanu 17 pass from Hasselbeck (J. Brown kick)
NO — Colston 2 pass from Brees (Mare kick)
Sea — FG J. Brown 52
Sea — Burleson 22 pass from Hasselbeck (J. Brown kick)

MONDAY NIGHT, OCTOBER 15

N.Y. GIANTS 31, ATLANTA 10—at Georgia Dome, attendance 69,828. Eli Manning passed for 303 yards and 2 touchdowns as the Giants won their fourth consecutive game. The Giants outgained the Falcons 491-284 in total yards, and maintained possession for 39 minutes, 38 seconds. Atlanta scored on its first two possessions to take a 10-7 lead with 5:14 left in the first quarter. In the second quarter, John Abraham forced Manning to fumble and Chris Crocker recovered at the Giants' 28. However, Morten Andersen's 48-yard field-goal attempt was short, and three plays later Manning completed a 43-yard touchdown pass to Plaxico Burress for a 21-10 lead. The Falcons failed to run a play inside the Giants' 30 on their final nine possessions. Manning was 27 of 39 for 303 yards and 2 touchdowns, with 2 interceptions. Joey Harrington was 18 of 39 for 209 yards, with 1 interception.

N.Y. Giants	14	7	0	10	—	31
Atlanta	10	0	0	0	—	10

Atl — FG Andersen 47
NYG — Toomer 5 pass from E. Manning (Tynes kick)
Atl — Norwood 67 run (Andersen kick)
NYG — Droughns 1 run (Tynes kick)
NYG — Burress 43 pass from E. Manning (Tynes kick)
NYG — FG Tynes 32
NYG — Ward 9 run (Tynes kick)

SEVENTH WEEK SUMMARIES

American Football Conference

East Division	**W**	**L**	**T**	**Pct.**	**Pts.**	**OP**
New England	7	0	0	1.000	279	120
Buffalo	2	4	0	.333	84	132
N.Y. Jets	1	6	0	.143	136	192
Miami	0	7	0	.000	156	231
North Division	**W**	**L**	**T**	**Pct.**	**Pts.**	**OP**
Pittsburgh	4	2	0	.667	160	78
Baltimore	4	3	0	.571	124	119
Cleveland	3	3	0	.500	167	183
Cincinnati	2	4	0	.333	164	187
South Division	**W**	**L**	**T**	**Pct.**	**Pts.**	**OP**
Indianapolis	6	0	0	1.000	193	95
Jacksonville	4	2	0	.667	107	87
Tennessee	4	2	0	.667	132	108
Houston	3	4	0	.429	169	174
West Division	**W**	**L**	**T**	**Pct.**	**Pts.**	**OP**
Kansas City	4	3	0	.571	102	113
Denver	3	3	0	.500	106	164
San Diego	3	3	0	.500	137	119
Oakland	2	4	0	.333	126	140

National Football Conference

East Division	**W**	**L**	**T**	**Pct.**	**Pts.**	**OP**
Dallas	6	1	0	.857	227	158
N.Y. Giants	5	2	0	.714	187	149
Washington	4	2	0	.667	122	88
Philadelphia	2	4	0	.333	116	101
North Division	**W**	**L**	**T**	**Pct.**	**Pts.**	**OP**
Green Bay	5	1	0	.833	142	107
Detroit	4	2	0	.667	140	171
Chicago	3	4	0	.429	137	165
Minnesota	2	4	0	.333	115	114
South Division	**W**	**L**	**T**	**Pct.**	**Pts.**	**OP**
Carolina	4	2	0	.667	123	110
Tampa Bay	4	3	0	.571	124	110
New Orleans	2	4	0	.333	101	152
Atlanta	1	6	0	.143	95	153
West Division	**W**	**L**	**T**	**Pct.**	**Pts.**	**OP**
Seattle	4	3	0	.571	137	108
Arizona	3	4	0	.429	147	157
San Francisco	2	4	0	.333	78	135
St. Louis	0	7	0	.000	79	192

SUNDAY, OCTOBER 21

BUFFALO 19, BALTIMORE 14—at Ralph Wilson Stadium, attendance 70,727. Rian Lindell kicked 4 field goals and Marshawn Lynch ran for a touchdown for the Bills. Lindell kicked 3 field goals in a span of less than nine minutes, with the third set up by John DiGiorgio's fumble recovery at the Ravens' 23, to take a 9-0 lead. Willis McGahee, playing his first game in Buffalo as a visiting player, scored on a 46-yard run to begin the second half, but the Bills scored on their next two possessions, with Trent Edwards' 54-yard pass on the latter drive setting up Lynch's touchdown run, to give Buffalo a 19-7 lead with 2:14 left in the third quarter. The Ravens responded by driving to the Bills' 8, but Boller's fourth-down pass was incomplete. Samari Rolle intercepted Edwards' pass three plays later, and Boller completed a 15-yard touchdown pass to Derrick Mason on fourth-and-11 with 6:34 remaining to pull the Ravens within 19-14. With 2:00 to play, the Ravens were faced with second-and-1 at the Bills' 49. Boller, however, threw three consecutive incomplete passes to end their final threat. Edwards was 11 of 21 of 153 yards, with 1 interception. Boller was 21 of 36 for 191 yards and 1 touchdown. McGahee had 19 carries for 114 yards.

Baltimore	0	0	7	7	—	14
Buffalo	3	6	10	0	—	19

Buff — FG Lindell 29
Buff — FG Lindell 26
Buff — FG Lindell 35
Balt — McGahee 46 run (Stover kick)
Buff — FG Lindell 41
Buff — Lynch 1 run (Lindell kick)
Balt — Mason 15 pass from Boller (Stover kick)

CINCINNATI 38, N.Y. JETS 31—at Paul Brown Stadium, attendance 65,868. Kenny Watson rushed for 3 touchdowns and the Bengals scored 28 unanswered points in the second half to defeat the Jets. With three drives of at least 60 yards, the Jets scored on their first five possessions en route to a 23-10 lead with 11:15 left in the third quarter. The Bengals then answered with scoring drives of 76, 57, and 50 yards, the last of which was set up by Domata Peko's fumble recovery at midfield, to take a 31-23 lead with 6:09 to play. With 37 seconds left, Johnathan Joseph intercepted Chad Pennington's short pass and returned it 42 yards for a touchdown and 38-23 lead. Jerricho Cotchery caught a deflected pass that had bounced off teammate Brad Smith for a touchdown as time expired. Carson Palmer was 14 of 21 for 226 yards and 1 touchdown, with 1 interception. Chad Johnson had 3 receptions for 102 yards. Watson rushed 31 times for 130 yards. Pennington was 20 of 31 for 272 yards and 3 touchdowns, with 1 interception. Laveranues Coles had 8 receptions for 133 yards.

N.Y. Jets	7	13	3	8	—	31
Cincinnati	3	7	7	21	—	38

NYJ — Coles 57 pass from Pennington (Nugent kick)
Cin — FG Graham 20
NYJ — FG Nugent 24
NYJ — FG Nugent 35
Cin — Watson 3 run (Graham kick)
NYJ — Coles 36 pass from Pennington (Nugent kick)
NYJ — FG Nugent 43
Cin — Houshmandzadeh 3 pass from Palmer (Graham kick)
Cin — Watson 1 run (Graham kick)
Cin — Watson 2 run (Graham kick)
Cin — Joseph 42 interception return (Graham kick)
NYJ — Cotchery 32 pass from Pennington (Washington pass from Pennington)

DALLAS 24, MINNESOTA 14—at Texas Stadium, attendance 63,432. Patrick Watkins returned Chris Canty's blocked field goal 68 yards for a touchdown to break a third-quarter tie and propel the Cowboys to victory. The Cowboys outgained the Vikings 381-196 in total yards, but trailed 14-7 at intermission thanks to two fumbles, one at the Vikings' 9 and the other returned 28 yards for a touchdown by Cedric Griffin on a play in which Griffin also fumbled, but recovered, on his way to the end zone. With the score 14-14 late in the third quarter, Canty blocked Ryan Longwell's 48-yard field goal attempt. Watkins recovered the ball and returned it 68 yards for a touchdown, marking the Cowboys' first blocked field goal return for a touchdown in 24 years. In the fourth quarter, Bradie James recovered Adrian Peterson's fumble at the Vikings' 22 to set up Nick Folk's 45-yard field goal with 10:34 remaining for a 24-14 lead. Tony Romo was 31 of 39 for 277 yards and 1 touchdown. Terrell Owens had 7 receptions for 103 yards. Jason Witten had 10 catches for 86 yards. Tarvaris Jackson was 6 of 19 for 72 yards.

Minnesota	7	7	0	0	—	14
Dallas	7	0	14	3	—	24

Dall — Owens 5 pass from Romo (Folk kick)
Minn — Peterson 20 run (Longwell kick)
Minn — Griffin 28 fumble return (Longwell kick)
Dall — Barber 1 run (Folk kick)
Dall — Watkins 68 return of blocked field goal (Folk kick)
Dall — FG Folk 45

DETROIT 23, TAMPA BAY 16—at Ford Field, attendance 60,442. The Buccaneers outgained the Lions 422-278 in total yards, but the Lions recovered 2 fumbles and blocked a punt. The Lions' 13 first-half points were set up by a blocked punt, fumble, and missed field goal en route to a 13-7 halftime lead. Trailing 16-7 early in the fourth quarter, the Buccaneers drove to the Lions' 1, but a mishandled snap was recovered by Jared DeVries. The fumble recovery sparked a 9-play, 93-yard drive, capped by Calvin Johnson's 32-yard touchdown run on an end around for 23-7 lead with 6:28 remaining. The Buccaneers scored a touchdown with 2:03 to play, recovered the onside kick, and Matt Bryant kicked a 48-yard field goal with 1:04 remaining to pull within 23-16. However, Casey FitzSimmons recovered the ensuing onside kick to clinch the victory. Jon Kitna was 16 of 20 for 147 yards. Jeff Garcia was 37 of 45 for 316 yards and 2 touchdowns. Earnest Graham had 13 receptions for 99 yards.

Tampa Bay	0	7	0	9	—	16
Detroit	10	3	3	7	—	23

Det — FG Hanson 34
Det — K. Jones 1 run (Hanson kick)
TB — Hilliard 5 pass from Garcia (Bryant kick)
Det — FG Hanson 42
Det — FG Hanson 32
Det — C. Johnson 32 run (Hanson kick)
TB — Stovall 4 pass from Garcia (pass failed)
TB — FG Bryant 48

TENNESSEE 38, HOUSTON 36—at Reliant Stadium, attendance 70,734. Rob Bironas kicked an NFL-record 8 field goals, including the game-winner from 29 yards as time expired, to offset a wild fourth-quarter comeback by the Texans. The Titans' defense forced 6 turnovers, all inside the Texans' 40, which led to 12 points. The Titans scored on seven consecutive possessions to take a 32-7 lead with 3:01 left in the third quarter. At that point, the Texans had failed to cross the Titans' 40 on any of their first nine possessions, with their lone score coming on DeMeco Ryans' 26-yard fumble return for a touchdown. Sage Rosenfels, who had replaced an injured Matt Schaub in the first quarter, capped a 70-yard drive with a touchdown pass to David Anderson with 13:43 to play. The Texans' defense forced a three-and-out, and Rosenfels completed all seven pass attempts on the ensuing 98-yard drive, which culminated with Kevin Walter's 6-yard touchdown catch to pull within 32-22 with 8:15 to play. The Texans got the ball back with 4:30 to play, but Nick Harper intercepted a pass to set up Bironas' record-tying seventh field goal, from 29 yards, for a 35-22 lead with 3:47 remaining. The Texans answered with a 12-play, 75-yard drive capped by Jeb Putzier's 7-yard catch to pull within 35-29 with 1:37 left. Zac Diles then recovered the ensuing onside kick, and Rosenfels completed a 53-yard touchdown pass to Andre Davis for a 36-35 lead with 57 seconds left. It was Houston's fourth touchdown in a span of 12:46. Kerry Collins, playing for an injured Vince Young, completed passes of 17 and 46 yards to Roydell Williams to set up Bironas' game-winning, and record-setting, 29-yard field goal as time expired. Collins was 25 of 42 for 280 yards. Williams had 5 receptions for 124 yards. LenDale White rushed 27 times for 104 yards. Schaub was 5 of 9 for 23 yards. Rosenfels was 22 of 35 for 290 yards and 4 touchdowns, with 3 interceptions.

Tennessee	6	16	10	6	—	38
Houston	7	0	0	29	—	36

Tenn — FG Bironas 52
Hou — Ryans 26 fumble return (K. Brown kick)
Tenn — FG Bironas 25
Tenn — FG Bironas 21
Hou — L. White 1 run (Bironas kick)
Tenn — FG Bironas 30
Tenn — FG Bironas 28
Tenn — FG Bironas 43
Tenn — C. Henry 4 run (Bironas kick)
Hou — Anderson 7 pass from Rosenfels (A. Davis pass from Rosenfels)
Hou — Walter 6 pass from Rosenfels (K. Brown kick)
Tenn — FG Bironas 29
Hou — Putzier 7 pass from Rosenfels (K. Brown kick)
Hou — A. Davis 53 pass from Rosenfels (K. Brown kick)
Tenn — FG Bironas 29

NEW ENGLAND 49, MIAMI 28—at Dolphin Stadium, attendance 71,951. Tom Brady passed for 6 touchdowns as the Patriots remained undefeated. New England scored on its first five possessions en route to a 42-7 halftime lead. Four of the six scoring drives were longer than 71 yards, but only one drive took more than three minutes. Brady was the first player with at least 5 touchdown passes in consecutive games since Daunte Culpepper in 2004. The

Dolphins drove 80 yards for a touchdown to pull within 42-14 with 11:35 to play. Matt Cassel came in at quarterback for New England, and three plays later Jason Taylor intercepted his pass and returned it 36 yards for a touchdown to pull within 42-21. The Patriots immediately reinserted Brady, who engineered a four-play, 59-yard drive, capped by his 16-yard touchdown pass to Wes Welker for a 49-21 lead with 8:11 to play. Brady was 21 of 25 for 354 yards and 6 touchdowns. Welker, in his first game against his former team, had 9 catches for 138 yards, and Randy Moss had 4 receptions for 122 yards. Cleo Lemon was 24 of 37 for 236 yards, with 1 interception.

| New England | 14 | 28 | 0 | 7 | — | 49 |
| Miami | 0 | 7 | 0 | 21 | — | 28 |

NE	—	Stallworth 30 pass from Brady (Gostkowski kick)
NE	—	K. Brady 2 pass from T. Brady (Gostkowski kick)
Mia	—	Lemon 4 run (Feely kick)
NE	—	Andrews 77 kickoff return (Gostkowski kick)
NE	—	Moss 35 pass from T. Brady (Gostkowski kick)
NE	—	Moss 50 pass from T. Brady (Gostkowski kick)
NE	—	Welker 14 pass from T. Brady (Gostkowski kick)
Mia	—	Cobbs 1 run (Feely kick)
Mia	—	Taylor 36 interception return (Feely kick)
NE	—	Welker 16 pass from T. Brady (Gostkowski kick)
Mia	—	Chatman 7 run (Feely kick)

N.Y. GIANTS 33, SAN FRANCISCO 15—at Giants Stadium, attendance 78,912. Osi Umenyiora returned a fumble 75 yards for a touchdown as the Giants won their fourth consecutive game. The Giants' defense registered 6 sacks and forced 4 turnovers which led to 24 points. Lawrence Tynes kicked 2 field goals in the final three minutes of the first half to take a 19-7 lead. The 49ers opened the second half by driving to the Giants' 15. But Umenyiora sacked Trent Dilfer from the blindside, forced him to fumble, scooped up the ball, and raced 75 yards for a touchdown and 26-7 lead. Antonio Pierce's fourth-quarter interception at the 49ers' 33 set up Jeremy Shockey's 2-yard touchdown catch for a 33-9 lead with 10:50 to play. Eli Manning was 18 of 31 for 146 yards and 2 touchdowns, with 1 interception. Brandon Jacobs had 18 carries for 107 yards. Dilfer was 23 of 38 for 209 yards and 2 touchdowns, with 2 interceptions.

| San Francisco | 0 | 7 | 2 | 6 | — | 15 |
| N.Y. Giants | 6 | 13 | 7 | 7 | — | 33 |

NYG	—	Toomer 4 pass from E. Manning (kick failed)
SF	—	Battle 17 pass from Dilfer (Nedney kick)
NYG	—	Jacobs 5 run (Tynes kick)
NYG	—	FG Tynes 29
NYG	—	FG Tynes 39
NYG	—	Umenyiora 75 fumble return (Tynes kick)
SF	—	Safety, Norris blocked punt out of end zone
NYG	—	Shockey 2 pass from E. Manning (Tynes kick)
SF	—	D. Jackson 1 pass from Dilfer (pass failed)

NEW ORLEANS 22, ATLANTA 16—at Louisiana Superdome, attendance 69,994. Drew Brees passed for 2 touchdowns as the Saints rallied to win their second consecutive game. The Falcons led 13-7 at halftime, but the Saints drove 80 yards to begin the second half, capped by Pierre Thomas' first-ever NFL rushing touchdown, a 24-yard run up the middle, for a 14-13 lead. Two plays later Joey Harrington replaced him, and in the fourth quarter engineered a 10-play drive capped by Morten Andersen's 21-yard field goal, his third of the game, for a 16-14 lead with 10:19 remaining. On the ensuing 11-play, 69-yard drive, Brees completed 3 third-down passes, capped by Reggie Bush's 4-yard touchdown grab on third-and-goal, followed by Bush's 2-point conversion run, for a 22-16 lead with 5:04 to play. Faced with fourth-and-13 from near midfield with 1:58 to play, and with all three timeouts, the Falcons punted. But Bush gained a first down to run out the clock. Brees was 22

of 34 for 219 yards and 2 touchdowns, with 1 interception. Leftwich was 15 of 23 for 145 yards and 1 touchdown. Harrington was 12 of 18 for 128 yards. Roddy White had 8 catches for 110 yards.

| Atlanta | 3 | 10 | 0 | 3 | — | 16 |
| New Orleans | 7 | 0 | 7 | 8 | — | 22 |

NO	—	Henderson 37 pass from Brees (Mare kick)
Atl	—	FG Andersen 38
Atl	—	FG Andersen 33
Atl	—	R. White 9 pass from Leftwich (Andersen kick)
NO	—	Thomas 24 run (Mare kick)
Atl	—	FG Andersen 21
NO	—	Bush 4 pass from Brees (Bush run)

KANSAS CITY 12, OAKLAND 10—at McAfee Coliseum, attendance 62,240. The Chiefs led 6-0 at halftime, with LaMont Jordan being stopped on fourth-and-1 from the Chiefs' 17 to thwart their lone scoring threat. Dave Rayner missed a 30-yard field goal in the third quarter, and Daunte Culpepper responded with a 59-yard pass to Jerry Porter and 21-yard touchdown pass to Ronald Curry to complete the two-play, 80-yard drive and take a 7-6 lead with 2:37 left the quarter. Damon Huard answered with a 58-yard pass to Dwayne Bowe, followed a few plays later by Larry Johnson's 1-yardtouchdown run with 11:30 to play. Sebastian Janikowski kicked a 37-yard field goal on the next drive to pull the Raiders within 12-10 with 5:49 remaining. The Raiders got the ball back with 1:46 to play and drove to the Raiders' 44 before Page intercepted Culpepper's pass to clinch the victory. Huard was 16 of 31 for 177 yards, with 1 interception. Johnson carried 24 times for 112 yards. Culpepper was 18 of 30 for 228 yards and 1 touchdown, with 1 interception.

| Kansas City | 3 | 3 | 0 | 6 | — | 12 |
| Oakland | 0 | 0 | 7 | 3 | — | 10 |

KC	—	FG Rayner 20
KC	—	FG Rayner 31
Oak	—	Curry 21 pass from Culpepper (Janikowski kick)
KC	—	L. Johnson 1 run (pass failed)
Oak	—	FG Janikowski 37

CHICAGO 19, PHILADELPHIA 16—at Lincoln Financial Field, attendance 67,806. Muhsin Muhammad caught a 15-yard touchdown pass with nine seconds remaining to cap a 97-yard drive for the Bears. The Eagles led 9-3 at halftime, but the Bears scored on each of their first three possessions of the second half, averaging nearly 10 plays a drive, but settling for field goals each time en route to a 12-9 lead with 9:21 remaining. The Eagles responded with a 74-yard drive, keyed by Donovan McNabb's 23-yard pass to Kevin Curtis on third-down, and capped by Matt Schobel's 13-yard touchdown catch with 4:57 to play for a 16-12 lead. After an exchange of punts, the Bears, beginning from their own 3, converted a pair of third-downs, including a 25-yard pass from Brian Griese to Bernard Berrian, to reach the Eagles' 36 with 31 seconds left. Griese then completed a 21-yard pass to Devin Hester to set up Muhammad's touchdown catch over the middle with nine seconds to play. Griese was 27 of 41 for 322 yards and 1 touchdown. McNabb was 21 of 34 for 226 yards and 1 touchdown.

| Chicago | 0 | 3 | 3 | 13 | — | 19 |
| Philadelphia | 3 | 6 | 0 | 7 | — | 16 |

Phil	—	FG Akers 24
Phil	—	FG Akers 33
Chi	—	FG Gould 31
Phil	—	FG Akers 37
Chi	—	FG Gould 22
Chi	—	FG Gould 41
Chi	—	FG Gould 45
Phil	—	Schobel 13 pass from McNabb (Akers kick)
Chi	—	Muhammad 15 pass from Griese (Gould kick)

SEATTLE 33, ST. LOUIS 6—at Qwest Field, attendance 68,164. Darryl Tapp registered 4 sacks and forced a fumble as the Seahawks' defense forced 5 turnovers and registered 7 sacks to keep the Rams winless. Leading 10-3 at halftime, Nate Burleson returned the second half's opening kickoff 91 yards for a touchdown and 17-3 lead. The Rams responded with a field goal, but the Seahawks scored on four of their next five possessions, with three turnovers leading to 13 Seahawks' points, for a 33-6 lead with 6:08 to play.

Matt Hasselbeck was 18 of 35 for 195 yards and 2 touchdowns, with 1 interception. Marc Bulger was 21 of 40 for 225 yards, with 3 interceptions.

| St. Louis | 3 | 0 | 3 | 0 | — | 6 |
| Seattle | 7 | 3 | 13 | 10 | — | 33 |

Sea	—	Heller 1 pass from Hasselbeck (J. Brown kick)
StL	—	FG Wilkins 31
Sea	—	FG J. Brown 38
Sea	—	Burleson 91 kickoff return (J. Brown kick)
StL	—	FG Wilkins 29
Sea	—	FG J. Brown 48
Sea	—	FG J. Brown 45
Sea	—	FG J. Brown 43
Sea	—	Heller 11 pass from Hasselbeck (J. Brown kick)

WASHINGTON 21, ARIZONA 19—at FedExField, attendance 85,640. Neil Rackers missed a 55-yard field-goal attempt with two seconds remaining as the Redskins held off the Cardinals. The Cardinals outgained the Redskins 364-160 in total yards, but London Fletcher's 27-yard interception return for a touchdown helped stake Washington a 14-0 lead. The Cardinals scored on the final play of the half, but Kedric Golston blocked Rackers' extra-point attempt. The Cardinals trailed 21-13 in the fourth quarter and drove to the Redskins' 10. On third-and-9, Andre Carter sacked Kurt Warner, forced him to fumble, and Phillip Daniels recovered with 7:14 to play. The Cardinals got the ball back and Warner completed 11- and 29-yard passes to J.J. Arrington to reach the Redskins' 2-yard-line with 1:21 to play. Marcel Shipp and Arrington combined to gain a yard. On third-and-goal, Tim Rattay came in and attempted his lone pass of the day, which was caught by Leonard Pope for a touchdown with 21 seconds left. On the 2-point conversion attempt, wide receiver Anquan Boldin took a direct snap, rolled right, but his pass fell incomplete. However, Jerheme Urban recovered the onside kick, and Warner completed 15- and 7-yard passes to Bryant Johnson to set up Rackers' 55-yard field-goal attempt, which sailed wide left. Jason Campbell was 12 of 18 for 95 yards, with 1 interception. Warner was 27 of 41 for 282 yards and 2 touchdowns, with 2 interceptions.

| Arizona | 0 | 6 | 0 | 13 | — | 19 |
| Washington | 7 | 7 | 7 | 0 | — | 21 |

Wash	—	Portis 2 run (Suisham kick)
Wash	—	Fletcher 27 interception return (Suisham kick)
Ari	—	Boldin 2 pass from Warner (kick blocked)
Wash	—	Portis 1 run (Suisham kick)
Ari	—	Boldin 10 pass from Warner (Rackers kick)
Ari	—	Pope 1 pass from Rattay (pass failed)

SUNDAY NIGHT, OCTOBER 21
DENVER 31, PITTSBURGH 28—at INVESCO Field at Mile High, attendance 77,038. Jason Elam kicked a 49-yard field goal as time expired to give the Broncos a victory. The Steelers opened the game with a 60-yard touchdown drive, but then the Broncos' defense clamped down, capped by Tim Crowder's 50-yard fumble return for a touchdown. The fumble was forced by Elvis Dumervil's sack of Ben Roethlisberger and staked the Broncos to a 21-7 lead. The Steelers scored touchdowns on all three of their second half possessions, on drives of 41, 94, and 78 yards. On the last drive, Roethlisberger completed all eight pass attempts, including two on third down, and capped by Heath Miller's 12-yard catch with 1:10 to play that tied the game. The Broncos began to drive, and a replay challenge overturned an incomplete pass and gave Daniel Graham a 9-yard catch at the Steelers' 30 with 20 seconds to play, setting up Elam's winning kick. Jay Cutler was 22 of 29 for 248 yards and 3 touchdowns, with 2 interceptions. Roethlisberger was 24 of 35 for 290 yards and 4 touchdowns, with 2 interceptions.

| Pittsburgh | 7 | 0 | 7 | 14 | — | 28 |
| Denver | 7 | 14 | 3 | 7 | — | 31 |

Pitt	—	Miller 1 pass from Roethlisberger (Reed kick)
Den	—	Stokley 15 pass from Cutler (Elam kick)
Den	—	C. Sapp 1 pass from Cutler (Elam kick)

Den — Crowder 50 fumble return (Elam kick)
Pitt — Holmes 13 pass from Roethlisberger (Reed kick)
Den — Scheffler 1 pass from Cutler (Elam kick)
Pitt — Spaeth 13 pass from Roethlisberger (Reed kick)
Pitt — Miller 12 pass from Roethlisberger (Reed kick)
Den — FG Elam 49

MONDAY NIGHT, OCTOBER 22
INDIANAPOLIS 29, JACKSONVILLE 7—at Jacksonville Municipal Stadium, attendance 67,164. Peyton Manning passed for 1 touchdown and ran for another as the Colts remained undefeated and took a two-game lead over the Jaguars. With the Colts leading 7-0 early in the second quarter, Ed Johnson sacked David Garrard, who injured his ankle on the play. Quinn Gray replaced him, and two plays later Bob Sanders intercepted his pass. The Colts drove 76 yards for a touchdown, and then on the next drive Sanders and Darrell Reid combined to stop Maurice Jones-Drew for a loss of 1 yard on fourth-and-1, setting up Adam Vinatieri for a field goal just before halftime for a 17-0 lead. The Jaguars opened the second half with a touchdown, and the defense forced a punt. However, Hunter Smith's punt was downed at the 4-yard line, and two plays later Dwight Freeney sacked Gray for a safety. The offense received the free kick and drove 55 yards for a field goal and 22-7 lead with 13:34 to play. Manning was 23 of 37 for 259 yards and 1 touchdown, with 1 interception. Reggie Wayne had 9 catches for 131 yards. Garrard was 8 of 12 for 72 yards. Gray was 9 of 24 for 56 yards, with 2 interceptions.

Indianapolis	7	10	2	10	—	29
Jacksonville	0	0	7	0	—	7

Ind — Keith 3 run (Vinatieri kick)
Ind — Manning 1 run (Vinatieri kick)
Ind — FG Vinatieri 36
Jax — Jones-Drew 1 run (Carney kick)
Ind — Safety, Freeney sacked Gray in end zone
Ind — FG Vinatieri 20
Ind — Clark 35 pass from Manning (Vinatieri kick)

EIGHTH WEEK SUMMARIES
American Football Conference

East Division	**W**	**L**	**T**	**Pct.**	**Pts.**	**OP**
New England	8	0	0	1.000	331	127
Buffalo	3	4	0	.429	97	135
N.Y. Jets	1	7	0	.125	139	205
Miami	0	8	0	.000	166	244
North Division	**W**	**L**	**T**	**Pct.**	**Pts.**	**OP**
Pittsburgh	5	2	0	.714	184	91
Baltimore	4	3	0	.571	124	119
Cleveland	4	3	0	.571	194	203
Cincinnati	2	5	0	.286	177	211
South Division	**W**	**L**	**T**	**Pct.**	**Pts.**	**OP**
Indianapolis	7	0	0	1.000	224	102
Jacksonville	5	2	0	.714	131	110
Tennessee	5	2	0	.714	145	117
Houston	3	5	0	.375	179	209
West Division	**W**	**L**	**T**	**Pct.**	**Pts.**	**OP**
Kansas City	4	3	0	.571	102	113
San Diego	4	3	0	.571	172	129
Denver	3	4	0	.429	119	183
Oakland	2	5	0	.286	135	153

National Football Conference

East Division	**W**	**L**	**T**	**Pct.**	**Pts.**	**OP**
Dallas	6	1	0	.857	227	158
N.Y. Giants	6	2	0	.750	200	159
Washington	4	3	0	.571	129	140
Philadelphia	3	4	0	.429	139	117
North Division	**W**	**L**	**T**	**Pct.**	**Pts.**	**OP**
Green Bay	6	1	0	.857	161	120
Detroit	5	2	0	.714	156	178
Chicago	3	5	0	.375	144	181
Minnesota	2	5	0	.286	131	137
South Division	**W**	**L**	**T**	**Pct.**	**Pts.**	**OP**
Carolina	4	3	0	.571	130	141
Tampa Bay	4	4	0	.500	147	134
New Orleans	3	4	0	.429	132	162
Atlanta	1	6	0	.143	95	153
West Division	**W**	**L**	**T**	**Pct.**	**Pts.**	**OP**
Seattle	4	3	0	.571	137	108
Arizona	3	4	0	.429	147	157
San Francisco	2	5	0	.286	88	166
St. Louis	0	8	0	.000	99	219

SUNDAY, OCTOBER 28
INDIANAPOLIS 31, CAROLINA 7—at Bank of America Stadium, attendance 74,005. Joseph Addai scored 3 touchdowns as the Colts became the second team in NFL history, and first since the Packers from 1929-1931, to begin three consecutive seasons with a 7-0 record. The Panthers began the game with an 18-play, 80-yard drive that lasted 11 minutes, and one second to take a 7-0 lead. In the second quarter the Panthers led 7-3 and had the ball at the Colts' 9, but Vinny Testaverde's third-and-4 pass was intercepted in the end zone by Antoine Bethea. Late in the quarter, Peyton Manning connected with Reggie Wayne on passes of 23 and 32 yards to set up Addai's 2-yard run just before halftime for a 10-7 lead. The Colts scored on a 60-yard drive to begin the second half, and Manning completed a long 59-yard touchdown pass to Wayne, hitting him in stride near the 15-yard line, for a 24-7 lead. Manning was 14 of 30 for 255 yards and 2 touchdowns. Wayne had 7 receptions for 168 yards. Addai carried 23 times for 100 yards. Testaverde started and was 12 of 20 for 82 yards, with 1 interception. David Carr replaced an injured Testaverde in the third quarter and was 16 of 25 for 103 yards. Jeff King had 10 receptions for 82 yards.

Indianapolis	3	7	14	7	—	31
Carolina	7	0	0	0	—	7

Car — Foster 3 run (Kasay kick)
Ind — FG Vinatieri 20
Ind — Addai 2 run (Vinatieri kick)
Ind — Addai 4 pass from Manning (Vinatieri kick)
Ind — Wayne 59 pass from Manning (Vinatieri kick)
Ind — Addai 12 run (Vinatieri kick)

DETROIT 16, CHICAGO 7—at Soldier Field, attendance 62,171. Kevin Jones rushed for 105 yards and 1 touchdown, and the Lions' defense intercepted 3 passes in the end zone, as Detroit swept the Bears for just the second time in the past ten seasons. Robbie Gould missed a 40-yard field goal in the first quarter. In the second quarter, Kenoy Kennedy intercepted Brian Griese's pass in the end zone, and the Lions answered with a 93-yard touchdown drive, highlighted by 2 catches for 44 yards and an 11-yard reverse by Calvin Johnson, and capped by Jones' touchdown run with 1:53 left in the half. The Lions' defense forced a three-and-out, and Jon Kitna's 24-yard pass to Roy Williams set up Jason Hanson's 52-yard field goal with five seconds left in the half for a 13-0 lead. Devin Hester's 39-yard punt return in the third quarter set up Griese's 20-yard touchdown pass to Greg Olsen, but the Lions responded with a 12-play, 67-yard drive for a field goal and 16-7 lead with 14:42 remaining. Gerald Alexander intercepted a pass in the end zone the 6:42 to play, and Fernando Bryant intercepted a pass in the end zone for a touchback with 45 seconds remaining. Kitna was 24 of 35 for 268 yards. Jones carried 23 times for 105 yards. Griese was 22 of 40 for 208 yards and 1 touchdown, with 4 interceptions.

Detroit	0	13	0	3	—	16
Chicago	0	0	7	0	—	7

Det — FG Hanson 26
Det — K. Jones 4 run (Hanson kick)
Det — FG Hanson 52
Chi — Olsen 20 pass from Griese (Gould kick)
Det — FG Hanson 20

PITTSBURGH 24, CINCINNATI 13—at Paul Brown Stadium, attendance 66,188. Hines Ward caught 2 touchdowns and Willie Parker rushed for 126 yards and a touchdown as the Steelers won their seventh consecutive game in Cincinnati. The Steelers scored touchdowns on three consecutive first-half drives, covering 80, 80, and 67 yards, capped by Parker's 1-yard run with four seconds left in the half, for a 21-6 lead. Ward had the touchdown catches to conclude the first two drives, and was tackled on the 1-yard line to set up Parker's run for the third touchdown. On the drive prior to Parker's score, the Bengals settled for a field goal on fourth-and-1 from the Steelers' 2 with 2:16 left in the half. The Bengals pulled within 21-13 when Carson Palmer completed a 9-yard touchdown pass to T.J. Houshmandzadeh. The 17-play, 88-yard drive was highlighted by Palmer's 14-yard pass to Chad Johnson on fourth-and-8. The Steelers answered with a six-minute, 53-second drive, capped by Jeff Reed's 40-yard field goal with 6:09 to play. James Harrison forced Kenny Watson to fumble, and Harrison recovered the ball as he was falling to the ground at the Steelers' 12-yard line with 3:16 remaining to clinch the victory. Ben Roethlisberger was 19 of 26 for 230 yards and 2 touchdowns, with 1 interception. Parker had 22 carries for 126 yards. Palmer was 23 of 31 for 205 yards and 1 touchdown.

Pittsburgh	7	14	0	3	—	24
Cincinnati	3	3	0	7	—	13

Cin — FG Graham 31
Pitt — Ward 21 pass from Roethlisberger (Reed kick)
Pitt — Ward 6 pass from Roethlisberger (Reed kick)
Cin — FG Graham 20
Pitt — Parker 1 run (Reed kick)
Cin — Houshmandzadeh 9 pass from Palmer (Graham kick)
Pitt — FG Reed 40

N.Y. GIANTS 13, MIAMI 10—at Wembley Stadium, London, England, attendance 81,176. In the first NFL regular-season game ever played outside of North America, Brandon Jacobs rushed for a career-high 131 yards as the Giants won their sixth consecutive game. In a game played in the rain, the teams combined for 483 yards (245 by the Dolphins). The Dolphins moved the ball on their first possession, but Jay Feely's 48-yard field-goal attempt sailed wide right. The Giants responded with a field goal, as the NFL's first-ever Scottish-born player, Lawrence Tynes, connected on a 20-yard kick with 3:33 left in the first quarter to cap an 11-play, 59-yard drive. The Giants used a 14-play, 69-yard drive, highlighted by Reuben Droughns' 2-yard run on fourth-and-1 near midfield, and capped by Eli Manning's 10-yard scramble to the left pylon for a 10-0 lead with 59 seconds left in the half. Three plays later, Michael Strahan sacked Cleo Lemon, forced him to fumble, and recovered the ball at the Dolphins' 34 with 26 seconds left to set up Tynes' 41-yard field goal with two seconds remaining in the half for a 13-0 lead. In the third quarter, Matt Roth's sack of Manning forced him to fumble, and Jason Taylor recovered near midfield to set up Feely's 29-yard field goal. Tynes missed a 29-yard field goal early in the fourth quarter, and the Dolphins pulled to within three points when Lemon fired a 21-yard pass to a slanting Ted Ginn Jr. in the end zone with 1:54 to play. But on the wet field, Feely's onside kick attempt slid out of bounds and the Giants ran out the clock. Manning was 8 of 22 for 59 yards. Jacobs carried 23 times for 131 yards. Lemon was 17 of 30 for 149 yards and 1 touchdown.

N.Y. Giants	3	10	0	0	—	13
Miami	0	0	3	7	—	10

NYG — FG Tynes 20
NYG — E. Manning 10 run (Tynes kick)
NYG — FG Tynes 41
Mia — FG Feely 29
Mia — Ginn 21 pass from Lemon (Feely kick)

PHILADELPHIA 23, MINNESOTA 16—at Metrodome, attendance 63,019. Donovan McNabb passed for 333 yards and 1 touchdown as Philadelphia defeated former Eagles' offensive coordinator, and current Vikings' head coach, Brad Childress. The Eagles had three consecutive scoring drives in the first half, highlighted by a 12-play, 93-yard touchdown drive, en route to a 17-10 halftime lead. McNabb's 25-yard pass to Brian Westbrook set up David Akers' 27-yard field goal in the third quarter for a 20-10 lead. Juqua Thomas sacked Kelly Holcomb late in the third quarter, knocking him out of the game. Brooks Bollinger replaced Holcomb and immediately engineered 11- and nine-play scoring drives that both led to field goals to cut the deficit to 20-16 with 8:53 to play. The Eagles responded, as McNabb's 31-yard pass to Kevin Curtis led to Akers' 25-yard field goal with 5:09 left. Faced with fourth-and-16 from their own 42-yard line with 3:29 to play, the Vikings punted. The Eagles maintained possession until Sav Rocca's 65-yard punt with 15 seconds to play pinned the Vikings inside their own 10-yard line. McNabb was 23 of 36 for 333 yards and 1 touchdown. Reggie Brown had 8 receptions for 105 yards. Holcomb was 7 of 16 for 88 yards and 1 touchdown. Bollinger was 7 of 10 for 94 yards.

Philadelphia	3	14	3	3	—	23
Minnesota	7	3	3	3	—	16

Minn — Shiancoe 9 pass from Holcomb (Longwell kick)
Phil — FG Akers 20
Phil — Westbrook 6 pass from McNabb (Akers kick)
Phil — Westbrook 1 run (Akers kick)
Minn — FG Longwell 39
Phil — FG Akers 27
Minn — FG Longwell 32
Minn — FG Longwell 48
Phil — FG Akers 25

NEW ENGLAND 52, WASHINGTON 7—at Gillette Stadium, attendance 68,756. Mike Vrabel had 3 sacks, forced 3 fumbles, and caught his 10th career touchdown as the Patriots jumped to a 52-0 lead and remained undefeated. The Patriots outgained the Redskins 486-224 in total yards, and the defense forced 4 turnovers that resulted in 17 points. The Patriots lead 17-0 when the Redskins put together their best drive of the half, but Vrabel sacked Jason Campbell and forced him to fumble. Ty Warren recovered at the Patriots' 27, and Tom Brady's 6-yard touchdown pass to Randy Moss eight plays later gave the Patriots a 24-0 lead with 17 seconds left in the half. The scoring pass was Brady's 29th of the season, giving him a new career high. The Patriots scored twice in a one-minute, 27-second span of the third quarter. First, Brady scored on a 2-yard scramble, marking his first career 2-rushing touchdown game. Three plays later, Vrabel sacked Campbell and forced him to fumble again. Rosevelt Colvin recovered and returned the ball 11 yards for a touchdown and 38-0 lead with 5:47 left in the third quarter. The Patriots scored on their next two possessions as well, with Matt Cassel engineering the second drive and capping it with a 15-yard scramble with 5:53 to play. Chris Cooley's 15-yard touchdown catch came with 3:00 remaining. Brady was 29 of 38 for 306 yards and 3 touchdowns. Campbell was 21 of 36 for 197 yards and 1 touchdown, with 1 interceptions.

Washington	0	0	0	7	—	7
New England	7	17	14	14	—	52

NE — Brady 3 run (Gostkowski kick)
NE — Vrabel 2 pass from Brady (Gostkowski kick)
NE — FG Gostkowski 36
NE — Moss 6 pass from Brady (Gostkowski kick)
NE — Brady 2 run (Gostkowski kick)
NE — Colvin 11 fumble return (Gostkowski kick)
NE — Welker 2 pass from Brady (Gostkowski kick)
NE — Cassel 15 run (Gostkowski kick)
Wash — Cooley 15 pass from Campbell (Suisham kick)

BUFFALO 13, N.Y. JETS 3—at The Meadowlands, attendance 76,688. J.P. Losman came off the bench to engineer two fourth-quarter scoring drives that resulted in the Jets' fifth consecutive defeat. The Bills began the game with a 16-play drive that resulted in a field goal. The Jets answered with a 15-play drive that also resulted in a field goal, tying the game 3-3 on Mike Nugent's kick with 10:28 left in the half. The Jets had a chance to take the lead just before halftime, but Aaron Schobel forced Leon Washington to fumble and Chris Kelsay recovered at the Bills' 17. Late in the third quarter, J.P. Losman replaced an injured Trent Edwards. On his second possession, Losman completed a 19-yard pass to Lee Evans to set up Rian Lindell's 40-yard field goal for a 6-3 lead with 10:06 remaining. After another Jets' punt, Losman fired a long pass deep down the right sideline that Evans caught amidst two defenders for an 85-yard touchdown for a 13-3 lead with 3:38 to play. Kellen Clemens entered the game, but was intercepted to end both of his drives. Edwards was 14 of 21 for 130 yards, with 1 interception. Losman was 3 of 5 for 113 yards and 1 touchdown. Evans had 5 receptions for 138 yards. Chad Pennington was 13 of 20 for 106 yards. Clemens was 5 of 12 for 67 yards, with 2 interceptions.

Buffalo	3	0	0	10	—	13
N.Y. Jets	0	3	0	0	—	3

Buff — FG Lindell 30
NYJ — FG Nugent 27
Buff — FG Lindell 40
Buff — Evans 85 pass from Losman (Lindell kick)

CLEVELAND 27, ST. LOUIS 20—at Edward Jones Dome, attendance 62,777. Derek Anderson passed for 3 touchdowns as the Browns posted consecutive victories for the first time in 64 games. The Rams scored touchdowns on their first two drives, but Steven Jackson left the game with an injury, and the Rams failed to pierce the end zone the remainder of the game despite driving into Browns' territory on eight of their nine possessions. Trailing 14-0, the Browns scored on five consecutive possessions, capped by Phil Dawson's 45-yard field goal with 10:35 remaining, for a 27-20 lead. After an exchange of punts, the Rams drove to the Browns' 16, but Brian Leonard was stopped for no gain on both third-and-1 and fourth-and-1 at the Browns' 16 with 1:52 to play. The Rams' defense forced a punt, and St. Louis drove to the Browns' 46, but Marc Bulger's pass was intercepted by Leigh Bodden at the Browns' 28 with 38 seconds to play. Anderson was 18 of 25 for 248 yards and 3 touchdowns. Braylon Edwards had 8 receptions for 117 yards. Bulger was 24 of 36 for 310 yards and 1 touchdown, with 1 interception. Torry Holt had 6 receptions for 110 yards.

Cleveland	3	14	7	3	—	27
St. Louis	14	3	3	0	—	20

StL — Jackson 2 run (Wilkins kick)
StL — Holt 1 pass from Bulger (Wilkins kick)
Cle — FG Dawson 35
Cle — Edwards 12 pass from Anderson (Dawson kick)
Cle — Winslow 21 pass from Anderson (Dawson kick)
StL — FG Wilkins 40
Cle — Edwards 5 pass from Anderson (Dawson kick)
StL — FG Wilkins 46
Cle — FG Dawson 45

SAN DIEGO 35, HOUSTON 10—at Qualcomm Stadium, attendance 60,439. In a week in which the Chargers practiced in Arizona because of the wildfires that struck San Diego, the Chargers scored 35 points in a span of 18 minutes, 18 seconds to win their third consecutive game. Antonio Cromartie had 2 interceptions and scored 2 touchdowns. A wide-open Antonio Gates caught a 49-yard touchdown pass with 5:49 left in the first quarter to open the scoring. Moments later, the punt snap sailed over Matt Turk's head. Turk chased after the ball but missed it, with Cromartie diving on the non-moving ball in the end zone for a 14-0 lead. After a Texans' field goal, Gates capped the next drive with a 31-yard touchdown catch. Cromartie intercepted Matt Schaub's pass on the next possession and weaved his way 70 yards for a touchdown and 28-3 lead. Cromartie's second interception came on the next drive, and led to Chris Chambers' 14-yard touchdown catch on third-and-12 for a 35-3 lead with 2:31 left in the half. It was Chambers' first game with the Chargers since being traded from Miami. Rivers was 7 of 11 for 130 yards and 3 touchdowns. Schaub was 11 of 18 for 77 yards, with 2 interceptions. Sage Rosenfels was 17 of 27 for 176 yards and 1 touchdown, with 2 interceptions.

Houston	0	3	0	7	—	10
San Diego	14	21	0	0	—	35

SD — Gates 49 pass from Rivers (Kaeding kick)
SD — Cromartie recovered fumble in end zone (Kaeding kick)
Hou — FG K. Brown 40
SD — Gates 31 pass from Rivers (Kaeding kick)
SD — Cromartie 70 interception return (Kaeding kick)
SD — Chambers 14 pass from Rivers (Kaeding kick)
Hou — Dreessen 28 pass from Rosenfels (K. Brown kick)

NEW ORLEANS 31, SAN FRANCISCO 10—at Monster Park, attendance 68,244. Drew Brees passed for 4 touchdowns, 3 to Marques Colston, as the Saints won their third consecutive game. The Saints outgained the 49ers 438-260 in total yards, including a 266-115 advantage in total yards in the first half as the 49ers lost their fifth consecutive game. The Saints scored on four of their six first-half possessions, capped by touchdown drives of 91 and 80 yards, to take a 24-0 lead even before the 49ers had crossed midfield. Brees was 31 of 39 for 336 yards and 4 touchdowns. Alex Smith was 22 of 43 for 190 yards and 1 touchdown.

New Orleans	10	14	0	7	—	31
San Francisco	0	0	3	7	—	10

NO — Colston 17 pass from Brees (Mare kick)
NO — FG Mare 26
NO — Copper 2 pass from Brees (Mare kick)
NO — Colston 3 pass from Brees (Mare kick)
SF — FG Nedney 29
NO — Colston 15 pass from Brees (Mare kick)
SF — Davis 7 pass from Smith (Nedney kick)

JACKSONVILLE 24, TAMPA BAY 23—at Raymond James Stadium, attendance 65,133. Replacing the injured David Garrard, Quinn Gray completed an 8-yard touchdown pass to Matt Jones to cap a comeback in his first NFL start. The Jaguars had 14 possessions, gained just 219 yards, but 103 of those came on their two touchdown-scoring drives. Their third-best drive, of 34 yards, led to John Carney's field goal and a 10-3 lead. Aaron Glenn jumped in front of Jeff Garcia's pass 16 seconds later and returned it 28 yards for a touchdown and 17-3 lead. The Buccaneers needed just three plays to respond with Garcia's long 58-yard touchdown pass to a streaking Joey Galloway. The Buccaneers scored twice in the third quarter to take a 23-17 lead, but Tampa Bay wound up scoring on just two of their seven second-half possessions, despite driving into Jaguars' territory six times. The missed opportunities caught up with the Buccaneers as the Jaguars drove 53 yards in eight plays, keyed by Ernest Wilford's 13-yard catch on third-and-6 to set up Jones' leaping 8-yard touchdown catch with 11:37 to play for a 24-23 lead. Faced with fourth-and-1 from the Jaguars' 45 with 30 seconds left, Reggie Nelson's interception clinched the victory. Gray was 7 of 16 for 100 yards and 1 touchdown. Garcia was 19 of 41 for 267 yards and 1 touchdown, with 3 interceptions. Galloway had 6 catches for 115 yards.

Jacksonville	7	10	0	7	—	24
Tampa Bay	3	10	10	0	—	23

TB — FG Bryant 44
Jax — Toefield 1 run (Carney kick)
Jax — FG Carney 41
Jax — A. Glenn 28 interception return (Carney kick)
TB — Galloway 58 pass from Garcia (Bryant kick)
TB — FG Bryant 22
TB — M. Bennett 19 run (Bryant kick)
TB — FG Bryant 42
Jax — M. Jones 8 pass from Gray (Carney kick)

TENNESSEE 13, OAKLAND 9—at LP Field, attendance 69,143. The Titans' defense registered 5 sacks and forced 2 turnovers to hand the Raiders their third consecutive defeat. The Raiders' defense allowed just 70 first-half yards en route to a 9-3 halftime lead. Late in the third quarter, LenDale White had runs of 27 and 14 yards on consecutive plays to set up Chris Henry, who on the ensuing play went around the left side 24 yards and dove into the end zone. Early in the fourth quarter, Travis LaBoy sacked Daunte Culpepper, forced him to fumble, and recovered the ball at the Raiders' 9 to set up Rob Bironas' 23-yard field goal to give the Titans a 13-9 lead with 11:22 to play. Chris Hope intercepted Culpepper's long pass at the Titans' 9 with 2:33 to play, and, following a punt, Culpepper's fourth-and-14 pass to Mike Williams fell incomplete with 1:17 remaining. Vince Young was 6 of 14 for 42 yards. White had 25 carries for 133 yards. Culpepper was 15 of 32 for 167 yards, with 1 interception.

Oakland	3	6	0	0	—	9
Tennessee	3	0	7	3	—	13

Oak — FG Janikowski 50
Tenn — FG Bironas 35
Oak — FG Janikowski 43
Oak — FG Janikowski 54
Tenn — C. Henry 24 run (Bironas kick)
Tenn — FG Bironas 23

MONDAY NIGHT, OCTOBER 29

GREEN BAY 19, DENVER 13 (OT)—at INVESCO Field at Mile High, attendance 77,160. After nearly losing at the end of regulation, Brett Favre completed an 82-yard touchdown pass to Greg Jennings on the first play from scrimmage in overtime as the Packers improved to 6-1 for the first time since 2002. With the score 7-

7, the Broncos drove to the Packers' 1, but a mishandled snap was recovered by Nick Barnett and the Packers drove 98 yards to kick a field goal. Green Bay led 13-7 at halftime, but never drove inside the Broncos' 44 on their three second-half possessions. Trailing 13-10, the Broncos began on their own 7-yard line with 2:27 to play. Jay Cutler completed a 7-yard pass to Brandon Stokley on fourth-and-2, and then connected on consecutive 35- and 13-yard passes to Brandon Marshall to reach the Packers' 13. Selvin Young gained 9 yards and the Broncos used their final timeout with 25 seconds left. Cutler's second-and-1 pass fell incomplete, and on third-and-1 with 22 seconds left Cutler tried to sneak for the first down but was stopped. The Broncos' field-goal unit raced onto the field, and Jason Elam kicked a 21-yard field goal as time expired. On the first play of overtime, Favre hit Jennings in stride at the Broncos' 40-yard line and Jennings outran Dre' Bly for the 82-yard touchdown. Favre was 21 of 27 for 331 yards and 2 touchdowns. Ryan Grant had 22 carries for 104 yards. Jennings had 6 catches for 141 yards. James Jones had 3 receptions for 107 yards. Cutler was 21 of 34 for 264 yards and 1 touchdown.

Green Bay	7	6	0	0	6	—	19
Denver	7	0	3	3	0	—	13

Den — Scheffler 5 pass from Cutler (Elam kick)
GB — J. Jones 79 pass from Favre (Crosby kick)
GB — FG Crosby 19
GB — FG Crosby 26
Den — FG Elam 45
Den — FG Elam 21
GB — Jennings 82 pass from Favre

NINTH WEEK SUMMARIES
American Football Conference

East Division	**W**	**L**	**T**	**Pct.**	**Pts.**	**OP**
New England	9	0	0	1.000	355	147
Buffalo	4	4	0	.500	130	156
N.Y. Jets	1	8	0	.111	159	228
Miami	0	8	0	.000	166	244
North Division	**W**	**L**	**T**	**Pct.**	**Pts.**	**OP**
Pittsburgh	6	2	0	.750	222	98
Cleveland	5	3	0	.625	227	233
Baltimore	4	4	0	.500	131	157
Cincinnati	2	6	0	.250	198	244
South Division	**W**	**L**	**T**	**Pct.**	**Pts.**	**OP**
Indianapolis	7	1	0	.875	244	126
Tennessee	6	2	0	.750	165	124
Jacksonville	5	3	0	.625	155	151
Houston	4	5	0	.444	203	226
West Division	**W**	**L**	**T**	**Pct.**	**Pts.**	**OP**
Kansas City	4	4	0	.500	124	146
San Diego	4	4	0	.500	189	164
Denver	3	5	0	.375	126	227
Oakland	2	6	0	.250	152	177

National Football Conference

East Division	**W**	**L**	**T**	**Pct.**	**Pts.**	**OP**
Dallas	7	1	0	.875	265	175
N.Y. Giants	6	2	0	.750	200	159
Washington	5	3	0	.625	152	160
Philadelphia	3	5	0	.375	156	155
North Division	**W**	**L**	**T**	**Pct.**	**Pts.**	**OP**
Green Bay	7	1	0	.875	194	142
Detroit	6	2	0	.750	200	185
Chicago	3	5	0	.375	144	181
Minnesota	3	5	0	.375	166	154
South Division	**W**	**L**	**T**	**Pct.**	**Pts.**	**OP**
Tampa Bay	5	4	0	.556	164	144
Carolina	4	4	0	.500	137	161
New Orleans	4	4	0	.500	173	186
Atlanta	2	6	0	.250	115	169
West Division	**W**	**L**	**T**	**Pct.**	**Pts.**	**OP**
Seattle	4	4	0	.500	167	141
Arizona	3	5	0	.375	157	174
San Francisco	2	6	0	.250	104	186
St. Louis	0	8	0	.000	99	219

SUNDAY, NOVEMBER 4

ATLANTA 20, SAN FRANCISCO 16—at Georgia Dome, attendance 66,049. The Falcons' defense allowed just 251 yards and forced 4 turnovers to hand the 49ers their sixth consecutive defeat. The 49ers opened the game with a 59-yard touchdown drive, but failed to pierce the end zone the remainder of the day. With the score 7-7 in the second quarter, Joey Harrington completed a 6-yard pass to Joe Horn on fourth-and-4 to keep alive a drive that resulted in Ovie Mughelli's 1-yard touchdown run with 3:48 left in the half. The 49ers opened the second half with two field goals, and had the ball near midfield when John Abraham sacked Alex Smith and forced him to fumble. Montavious Stanley recovered the ball to set up Morten Andersen's 33-yard field goal three plays into the fourth quarter for a 17-13 lead. The 49ers cut the deficit to 17-16 and had the ball deep in their own territory with 2:29 remaining when DeAngelo Hall intercepted Smith's pass to set up Andersen's second field goal with 1:10 to play. Jimmy Williams clinched the victory with an interception at the Falcons' 30 with nine second left. Harrington was 14 of 25 for 138 yards, with 1 interception. Warrick Dunn had 27 carries for 100 yards. Smith was 17 of 38 for 149 yards, with 3 interceptions.

San Francisco	7	0	6	3	—	16
Atlanta	7	7	0	6	—	20

SF — Hicks 9 run (Nedney kick)
Atl — Dunn 9 run (Andersen kick)
Atl — Mughelli 1 run (Andersen kick)
SF — FG Nedney 49
SF — FG Nedney 32
Atl — FG Andersen 33
SF — FG Nedney 22
Atl — FG Andersen 27

BUFFALO 33, CINCINNATI 21—at Ralph Wilson Stadium, attendance 70,745. Marshawn Lynch rushed for 153 yards and the game-clinching 56-yard touchdown with 2:22 remaining as the Bills outlasted the Bengals. The Bills outgained the Bengals 479-299 in total yards and had possession for 35 minutes, 42 seconds. Cincinnati remained in the game thanks to plays such as Glenn Holt's 100-yard kickoff return in the second quarter that helped the Bengals take a 14-13 halftime lead. The Bills opened the second half with Rian Lindell's third field goal, but Cincinnati answered with a 10-play, 70-yard drive capped by Carson Palmer's 1-yard pass to Jeremi Johnson for a 21-16 lead. Trailing 21-19, Lynch carried six consecutive times to reach the Bengals' 8-yard line. On the seventh play, on second-and-goal, Lynch ran right, stopped, and lofted a touchdown pass to Robert Royal for a 26-21 lead with 5:51 to play. The Bills' defense forced a punt, J.P. Losman completed a key third-and-7 pass to Lee Evans, and on the next play, Lynch broke a tackle behind the line of scrimmage, and raced 56 yards down the right side for the game-clinching score. Losman was 24 of 34 for 295 yards and 1 touchdown, with 1 interception. Evans had 9 receptions for 165 yards. Palmer was 26 of 39 for 271 yards and 2 touchdowns, with 1 interception.

Cincinnati	7	7	7	0	—	21
Buffalo	7	6	3	17	—	33

Buff — Evans 8 pass from Losman (Lindell kick)
Cin — Houshmandzadeh 15 pass from Palmer (Graham kick)
Buff — FG Lindell 23
Cin — Holt 100 kickoff return (Graham kick)
Buff — FG Lindell 21
Buff — FG Lindell 29
Cin — J. Johnson 1 pass from Palmer (Graham kick)
Buff — FG Lindell 38
Buff — Royal 8 pass from Lynch (Lindell kick)
Buff — Lynch 56 run (Lindell kick)

CLEVELAND 33, SEATTLE 30 (OT)—at Cleveland Browns Stadium, attendance 72,927. Phil Dawson's 25-yard field goal in overtime gave the Browns their first three-game winning streak since 2001. Nate Burleson's 94-yard punt return gave the Seahawks a 21-6 lead with 3:49 left in the first half. The Browns responded with a late field goal, and then drove 69 yards in 11 plays to being the second half, capped by Lewis' 1-yard run, to pull within 21-16. Trailing 24-16, Derek Anderson completed a 14-yard pass to Kellen Winslow on third-and-8, and then a 2-yard pass to Winslow on fourth-and-1, to set up Lewis' third touchdown, a 2-yard run with 12:42 remaining. The 2-point conversion attempt failed, and the Seahawks led 24-22. The Seahawks answered with Josh Brown's 26-yard field goal with 7:55 left, and the Browns came right back with a 14-play, 89-yard drive, that included three third-down conversions, including a 14-yard grab by Winslow to the Seahawks' 1, that led to Lewis' fourth touchdown with 2:17 remaining. Anderson completed a 2-point conversion pass to Joe Jurevicius for a 30-27 lead. Brown kicked a 22-yard field goal as regulation expired to force overtime, and the Seahawks started with the ball. On fourth-and-1 from the Browns' 33, Maurice Morris was stopped for no gain. Two plays later, Anderson's screen pass to Lewis resulted in a 34-yard gain to set up Dawson's winning kick with 9:19 left in overtime. Anderson was 29 of 48 for 364 yards, with 1 interception. Winslow had 11 receptions for 125 yards. Matt Hasselbeck was 30 of 47 for 318 yards and 2 touchdowns, with 1 interception. Bobby Engram had 14 catches for 139 yards.

Seattle	7	14	3	6	0	—	30
Cleveland	0	9	7	14	3	—	33

Sea — Engram 5 pass from Hasselbeck (J. Brown kick)
Cle — J. Lewis 2 run (kick failed)
Sea — Hackett 6 pass from Hasselbeck (J. Brown kick)
Sea — Burleson 94 punt return (J. Brown kick)
Cle — FG Dawson 19
Cle — J. Lewis 1 run (Dawson kick)
Sea — FG J. Brown 39
Cle — J. Lewis 2 run (pass failed)
Sea — FG J. Brown 26
Cle — J. Lewis 1 run (Jurevicius pass from Anderson)
Sea — FG J. Brown 22
Cle — FG Dawson 25

DETROIT 44, DENVER 7—at Ford Field, attendance 60,783. The Lions' defense registered 5 sacks and forced 4 turnovers to improve their record to 6-2 for the first time since 1999. The Lions scored on all four of their first half possessions, each lasting at least 10 plays and consuming 18 minutes, 44 seconds of the first 30 minutes, for a 16-0 halftime lead. In the second quarter, Shaun Rogers sacked Jay Cutler and knocked him out of the game. Patrick Ramsey replaced Cutler, and in the third quarter Corey Smith sacked Ramsey and forced him to fumble. Dewayne White recovered the ball and ran 3 yards for a touchdown and 23-0 lead. The Broncos then drove to the Lions' 4, but Ramsey threw three consecutive incomplete passes. Jon Kitna responded with a 46-yard pass to Sean McHugh and on the next play completed a 49-yard touchdown pass to Shaun McDonald for a 30-0 advantage. Rogers intercepted a screen pass in the fourth quarter and rumbled 66 yards for a touchdown. Kitna was 16 of 31 for 252 yards and 2 touchdowns. Cutler was 3 of 4 for 20 yards, and Ramsey was 29 of 46 for 262 yards and 1 touchdown, with 1 interception.

Denver	0	0	0	7	—	7
Detroit	3	13	14	14	—	44

Det — FG Hanson 43
Det — FG Hanson 53
Det — Furrey 15 pass from Kitna (Hanson kick)
Det — FG Hanson 38
Det — White 3 fumble return (Hanson kick)
Det — McDonald 49 pass from Kitna (Hanson kick)
Det — Rogers 66 interception return (Hanson kick)
Det — Duckett 3 run (Hanson kick)
Den — Stokley 2 pass from Ramsey (Elam kick)

NEW ENGLAND 24, INDIANAPOLIS 20—at RCA Dome, attendance 57,540. Tom Brady passed for 3 touchdowns as the Patriots rallied to defeat the Colts in a game in the first-ever game that featured two teams with at least 7-0 records. The Colts moved the ball at will in the first half, doubling the Patriots 229-114 in total yards, but settled for 1 touchdown, 2 field goals, and a missed 50-yard field-goal attempt for a 13-7 halftime lead. Trailing 13-10, the Patriots moved into Colts' territory early in the fourth quarter, but Gary Brackett made a juggling interception and returned the ball 28 yards to set up Peyton Manning's 1-yard sneak for a 20-10 lead with 9:42 to play. Four plays later, Brady completed a long 55-yard pass to Randy Moss down to the Colts' 3 to set up Brady's third-and-goal 3-yard touchdown pass to Wes Welker at the front left pylon to pull within 20-17 with 7:59 left. The Patriots' defense forced a punt, and Welker returned it 23 yards to the Patriots' 49 with 3:58 remaining. Brady completed a 5-yard pass to Moss, 33-yard pass to Donte' Stallworth, and then dumped a short pass to Kevin Faulk which resulted in a 13-yard touchdown for a 24-20 lead with 3:15 to play. The Colts drove to midfield, but on third-and-9 Jarvis Green sacked Manning from behind. Manning fumbled the ball into the air and Rosevelt Colvin recovered with 2:25 left. On third-and-6, Brady completed a 10-yard pass to Welker to clinch the victory. Brady was 21 of 32 for 255 yards and 3 touchdowns, with 2 interceptions. Moss had 9 catches for 145 yards. Manning was 16 of 27 for 225 yards and 1 touchdown, with 1 interception. Addai carried 26 times for 112 yards, and had 5 receptions for 114 yards to become the first player in franchise history with at least 100 yards rushing and receiving in the same game.

New England	0	7	3	14	—	24
Indianapolis	3	10	0	7	—	20

Ind — FG Vinatieri 21
NE — Moss 4 pass from Brady (Gostkowski kick)
Ind — FG Vinatieri 25
Ind — Addai 73 pass from Manning (Vinatieri kick)
NE — FG Gostkowski 34
Ind — Manning 1 run (Vinatieri kick)
NE — Welker 3 pass from Brady (Gostkowski kick)
NE — Faulk 13 pass from Brady (Gostkowski kick)

GREEN BAY 33, KANSAS CITY 22—at Arrowhead Stadium, attendance 78,988. The Packers scored 17 points in the final 3:05, capped by Charles Woodson's 46-yard interception return, to improve to 7-1 for the first time since 2002. The Packers outgained the Chiefs 432-234 in total yards, but needed to rally for the victory. Benny Sapp intercepted a pass with 25 seconds left in the half and returned it to the Packers' 30. A 29-yard pass interference penalty on the next play set up Larry Johnson's 1-yard touchdown run for a 7-6 Kansas City halftime lead. A.J. Hawk's interception at the Chiefs' 30 late in the third quarter led to Brett Favre's 13-yard touchdown pass to Greg Jennings on third-and-8 for a 13-7 lead. Johnson scored on a 30-yard screen pass, but the Packers retook the lead on Mason Crosby's 32-yard field goal with 8:52 left. The Chiefs answered with an 82-yard touchdown drive, capped by Tony Gonzalez's 17-yard touchdown catch and Priest Holmes' 2-point conversion run for a 22-16 lead with 5:18 to play. Favre connected on a long 60-yard scoring pass to Jennings with 3:05 left for a 23-22 lead, which was the fifth lead change in the span of 12 minutes, six seconds. The Packers then forced a three-and-out, Woodson returned the punt 27 yards to set up Crosby's 45-yard field goal with 1:40 to play for a 26-22 lead, and three plays later Woodson intercepted Huard's pass and returned it 46 yards with 59 seconds remaining for the clinching points. Favre was 24 of 34 for 360 yards and 2 touchdowns, with 2 interceptions. Huard was 19 of 32 for 213 yards and 2 touchdowns, with 2 interceptions. Gonzalez had 10 receptions for 109 yards.

Green Bay	0	6	7	20	—	33
Kansas City	0	7	0	15	—	22

GB — FG Crosby 48
GB — FG Crosby 36
KC — L. Johnson 1 run (Rayner kick)
GB — Jennings 13 pass from Favre (Crosby kick)
KC — L. Johnson 30 pass from Huard (Rayner kick)
GB — FG Crosby 32
KC — Gonzalez 17 pass from Huard (Holmes run)
GB — Jennings 60 pass from Favre (Crosby kick)
GB — FG Crosby 45
GB — Woodson 46 interception return (Crosby kick)

MINNESOTA 35, SAN DIEGO 17—at Metrodome, attendance 63,043. Adrian Peterson rushed for an NFL record 296 yards as the Vikings rallied to snap the Chargers' three-game winning streak. A second NFL records was established on the last play of the first half. With the score 7-7, Ryan Longwell attempted a 57-yard field goal. The kick was short and Antonio Cromartie leapt in the air and caught the ball just shy of the end line. Cromartie then ran up the middle of the field for about 30 yards, cut to this right, and raced untouched up the sideline for a 109-yard missed field goal return, marking the longest play in NFL history. Peterson, who had carried 13 times for 43 yards in the first half, capped the opening drive of the second half with a 64-yard touchdown run. In the middle of the quarter, Peterson gained 34 yards on four carries to set up Brooks Bollinger's 40-yard touchdown pass to a sprinting Sidney Rice to give the Vikings a 21-14 lead. Leading 21-17 with 14:09 left, the Vikings began on their own 20 and Peterson gained 55 yards on five carries, but fumbled and Drayton Florence recovered with 10:07 to play. The Vikings' defense forced a punt, and Mewelde Moore's 42-yard punt return was followed one play later by Peterson's 46-yard touchdown run down the right sideline for a 28-17 lead with 7:44 to play. Charles Gordon intercepted a pass on the next possession and Chester Taylor carried on four consecutive plays, capped by a 2-yard touchdown run, for a 35-17 lead with 4:28 remaining. The Vikings got the ball back with 1:58 to play, and Peterson gained 35 yards down the left sideline. On second-and-4 with 1:04 to play, Peterson gained 3 yards up the middle to the Chargers' 31 to break Jamal Lewis' record by one yard. Peterson had 146 rushing yards in the fourth quarter, and a total of 253 yards in the second half. Tarvaris Jackson was 6 of 12 for 63 yards for being injured just before halftime. Bollinger replaced him and was 7 of 10 for 95 yards and 1 touchdown. Philip Rivers was 19 of 42 for 197 yards, with 1 interception.

San Diego	7	7	0	3	—	17
Minnesota	7	0	14	14	—	35

SD — Tomlinson 1 run (Kaeding kick)
Minn — Peterson 1 run (Longwell kick)
SD — Cromartie 109 missed FG return (Kaeding kick)
Minn — Peterson 64 run (Longwell kick)
Minn — Rice 40 pass from Bollinger (Longwell kick)
SD — FG Kaeding 36
Minn — Peterson 46 run (Longwell kick)
Minn — Taylor 2 run (Longwell kick)

NEW ORLEANS 41, JACKSONVILLE 24—at Louisiana Superdome, attendance 70,009. Drew Brees passed for 445 yards and 3 touchdowns as the Saints won their fourth consecutive game. The Saints outgained the Jaguars 538-432 in total yards. The Saints began the game with a 40-yard drive for a field goal, then Terrance Copper recovered an onside kick and the Saints drove 57 yards for a touchdown and 10-0 lead before the Jaguars had the ball. The Jaguars scored on their next two possessions, the Saints answered with a 57-yard pass from Brees to Billy Miller that set up Reggie Bush's touchdown run, and then Maurice Jones-Drew returned the ensuing kickoff 100 yards for a touchdown as the first quarter expired with the score 17-17. Trailing 24-17, the Jaguars opened the second half with a 10-play drive to the Saints' 34. Facing fourth-and-4, Quinn Gray attempted a pass for Ernest Wilford that was intercepted by Mike McKenzie and returned 75 yards for a touchdown and 31-17 lead. The Saints' defense then forced a three-and-out, and the offense answered with a 67-yard drive, capped by Brees' 4-yard touchdown pass to David Patten for a 38-17 lead with 2:02 left in the third quarter. Brees was 35 of 49 for 445 yards and 3 touchdowns. Marques Colston had 10 receptions for 159 yards. Gray was 20 of 33 for 354 yards and 2 touchdowns, with 3 interceptions. Reggie Williams had 6 catches for 128 yards.

Jacksonville	17	0	0	7	—	24
New Orleans	17	7	14	3	—	41

NO — FG Mare 46
NO — Bush 1 run (Mare kick)
Jax — R. Williams 80 pass from Gray (Carney kick)
Jax — FG Carney 30
NO — Bush 2 pass from Brees (Mare kick)
Jax — Jones-Drew 100 kickoff return (Carney kick)
NO — Moore 8 pass from Brees (Mare kick)
NO — McKenzie 75 interception return (Mare kick)
NO — Patten 4 pass from Brees (Mare kick)
Jax — Northcutt 15 pass from Gray (Carney kick)
NO — FG Mare 34

WASHINGTON 23, N.Y. JETS 20 (OT)—at The Meadowlands, attendance 76,663. Clinton Portis rushed for 196 yards and Shaun Suisham kicked 5 field goal, including the game-winner in overtime, as the Redskins rallied to defeat the Jets. Leon Washington's 86-yard kickoff return to open the game was his franchise-best third of the season. With Kellen Clemens anointed as the new starting quarterback, replacing Chad Pennington, the Jets scored on their next two drives, capped by Clemens' 1-yard touchdown pass to Joe Kowalewski for a 17-3 lead. The Redskins moved the ball well, driving into Jets' territory on each of its first seven possessions. Four of the first five ended in field goals, and the sixth drive ended when Eric Barton intercepted a pass at the Jets' 18 to allow New York to maintain a 17-12 lead. Clemens then guided the Jets to the Redskins' 25, but Jerricho Cotchery fumbled on third down and LaRon Landry recovered. A 32-yard run by Portis set up Portis' 1-yard run, along with a 2-point conversion, for a 20-17 lead with 11:06 to play. With 5:13 to play, starting from their own 25-yard line, Clemens was 3-for-3 on third-down passes, and then scrambled for 6 yards on third-and-5 from the Redskins' 26 with 52 seconds left, to set up Mike Nugent's game-tying 30-yard field goal with 10 seconds to play. In overtime, Clemens completed a 39-yard pass to Cotchery on the first play to the Redskins' 42, but the drive stalled and the Jets punted. Starting from their own 10-yard line, Jason Campbell completed a key 17-yard pass to Chris Cooley on third-and-4, and Portis carried for 37 yards on the drive, capped by Suisham's 46-yard field goal 7:17 into overtime. Campbell was 12 of 23 for 142 yards, with 1 interception. Portis carried 36 times for 196 yards. Clemens was 23 of 42 for 226 yards and 1 touchdown.

Washington	3	6	3	8	3	—	23
N.Y. Jets	10	7	0	3	0	—	20

NYJ — Washington 86 kickoff return (Nugent kick)
Wash — FG Suisham 46
NYJ — FG Nugent 29
NYJ — Kowalewski 1 pass from Clemens (Nugent kick)
Wash — FG Suisham 40
Wash—FG Suisham 22
Wash — FG Suisham 40
Wash — Portis 1 run (Randle El pass from Campbell)
NYJ — FG Nugent 30
Wash — FG Suisham 46

HOUSTON 24, OAKLAND 17—at McAfee Stadium, attendance 49,603. Ron Dayne rushed for 122 yards as the Texans jumped to a 17-0 lead before having to hold on against the Raiders. Fred Bennett intercepted a pass and returned it 14 yards to set up Dayne's 14-yard touchdown run for a 14-0 lead. With 1:10 left in the half, Sebastian Janikowski attempted what would have been a record 64-yard field goal, only to have the ball hit halfway up the right upright and bounce away. The Texans responded with a 24-yard drive, capped by Kris Brown's 40-yard field goal for a 17-0 lead. The Texans opened the second half with another strong drive, but Jay Richardson blocked Brown's 43-yard field-goal attempt, which sparked 10 straight points for the Raiders. Clinging to a 17-10 lead in the middle of the fourth quarter and facing third-and-2, Sage Rosenfels completed a pass deep down the left sideline to Andre Davis for a 42-yard touchdown and 24-10 lead. DeMeco Ryans intercepted a pass at the Texans' 6 to thwart the next drive, but Tim Dwight scored on the following possession to pull within 24-17. Kevin Walter recovered the onside kick with 1:30 to play, and the Texans ran out the clock. Rosenfels, starting in place of injured Matt Schaub, was 11 of 19 for 181 yards and 1 touchdown, with 1 interception. Dayne has 21 carries for 122 yards. Josh McCown was 13 of 27 for 158 yards and 1 touchdown, with 3 interceptions. Justin Fargas had 23 carries for 104 yards.

Houston	7	10	0	7	—	24
Oakland	0	0	3	14	—	17

Hou — Green 8 run (K. Brown kick)
Hou — Dayne 14 run (K. Brown kick)
Hou — FG K. Brown 40
Oak — FG Janikowski 22
Oak — Fargas 1 run (Janikowski kick)
Hou — Davis 42 pass from Rosenfels (K. Brown kick)
Oak — Dwight 28 pass from McCown (Janikowski kick)

TAMPA BAY 17, ARIZONA 10—at Raymond James Stadium, attendance 65,267. Earnest Graham rushed for 124 yards and 1 touchdown as the Buccaneers limited the Cardinals to 195 yards. Tampa Bay held onto the ball for 43 minutes, seven seconds, and after allowing the Cardinals to open the game with a field goal, Tampa Bay's defense did not allow the Cardinals to cross midfield again until the third quarter when Arizona trailed 17-3. The Buccaneers had begun the first half and second half with 10-play touchdown drives, and had a chance to add to their lead, but Matt Bryant missed a 26-yard field goal early in the fourth quarter. The Cardinals responded with an 80-yard drive, capped by Edgerrin James' 3-yard run to pull within 17-10 within 7:30 to play. The Cardinals got the ball back twice, punting once and Jermaine Phillips intercepted Kurt Warner's long pass near midfield with 2:31 to play to thwart the other drive. Graham gained 15 yards for a first down to enable the Buccaneers run out the clock. Jeff Garcia was 18 of 28 for 196 yards and 1 touchdown. Graham had 34 carries for 124 yards. Warner was 10 of 30 for 172 yards, with 2 interceptions.

Arizona	3	0	0	7	—	10
Tampa Bay	7	3	7	0	—	17

Ari — FG Rackers 47
TB — Galloway 37 pass from Garcia (Bryant kick)
TB — FG Bryant 32
TB — Graham 2 run (Bryant kick)
Ari — James 3 run (Rackers kick)

TENNESSEE 20, CAROLINA 7—at LP Field, attendance 69,143. LenDale White rushed for 100 yards and 1 touchdown as the Titans moved to within one game of the Colts. The Titans' defense allowed just 191 yards and registered 7 sacks, including 3 by Albert Haynesworth. A 46-yard kickoff return by Chris Henry to begin the game set up a 52-yard touchdown drive for the Titans, and Rob Bironas' 53-yard field goal as the half expired gave the Titans a 13-0 lead. White scored early in the fourth to cap a 13-play, 86-yard drive before the Panthers finally scored. Carolina drove to the Titans' 34 later in fourth quarter, but Chris Hope intercepted Matt Moore's pass with 2:13 to play to clinch the victory. Vince Young was 14 of 23 for 110 yards, with 2 interceptions. White had 31 carries for 100 yards. David Carr was 15 of 27 for 107 yards and 1 touchdown, with 1 interception, and Moore replaced an injured Carr on the final drive and was 2 of 5 for 36 yards, with 1 interception.

Carolina	0	0	0	7	—	7
Tennessee	10	3	0	7	—	20

Tenn — Young 3 run (Bironas kick)
Tenn — FG Bironas 47
Tenn — FG Bironas 53
Tenn — White 1 run (Bironas kick)
Car — Carter 18 pass from Carr (Kasay kick)

SUNDAY NIGHT, NOVEMBER 4

DALLAS 38, PHILADELPHIA 17—at Lincoln Financial Field, attendance 67,688. Tony Romo passed for 324 yards and 3 touchdowns as the Cowboys improved to 7-1 for the first time since 1995. The Cowboys' offense gained 434 yards, while the defense registered 3 sacks and forced 3 turnovers. Donovan McNabb was sacked by Marcus Spears and DeMarcus Ware to being the game and fumbled. Bradie James recovered, and Julius Jones scored six plays later for a 7-0 lead. The Cowboys led 14-7 late in the first half when Ken Hamlin intercepted McNabb's third-down pass and returned the ball 14 yards to the Eagles' 14. Marion Barber scored three plays later for a 21-7 halftime lead. The Cowboys scored touchdowns on their first two drives of the second half, capped by Romo's 20-yard scoring pass to Jason Witten, for a 35-10 lead with 4:28 left in the third quarter. Romo was 20 of 25 for 324 yards and 3 touchdowns, with 1 interception. Terrell Owens had 10 catches for 174 yards. McNabb was 27 of 46 for 264 yards and 1 touchdown, with 2 interceptions. Brian Westbrook had 14 receptions for 90 yards.

Dallas	14	7	14	3	—	38
Philadelphia	7	0	3	7	—	17

Dall — J. Jones 2 run (Folk kick)
Phil — Westbrook 3 run (Akers kick)
Dall — Curtis 1 pass from Romo (Folk kick)
Dall — Barber 5 run (Folk kick)
Dall — Owens 45 pass from Romo (Folk kick)
Phil — FG Akers 36
Dall — Witten 20 pass from Romo (Folk kick)
Dall — FG Folk 22
Phil — Baskett 10 pass from McNabb (Akers kick)

MONDAY NIGHT, NOVEMBER 5

PITTSBURGH 38, BALTIMORE 7—at Heinz Field, attendance 63,457. Ben Roethlisberger passed for 209 yards and equalled a franchise record with 5 touchdown passes, all in the first half, as the Steelers took a two-game lead over the Ravens. The Steelers' defense allowed just 5 first downs, 104 total yards, had 6 sacks, and forced 4 turnovers. The longest drive of Pittsburgh's 5 first-half touchdowns was 50 yards. The first three touchdowns were set up by fumbles, and James Harrison's interception and 20-yard return led to Roethlisberger's 7-yard touchdown pass to Nate Washington with 1:51 left in the half for a 35-0 lead. The Steelers' defense did not allow the Ravens to pass their own 40-yard line on seven second-half possessions, all which ended in punts. Roethlisberger was 13 of 16 for 209 yards and 5 touchdowns for a perfect 158.3 passer rating. Santonio Holmes had 4 catches for 110 yards. Steve McNair was 13 of 22 for 63 yards, with 1 interception, and Kyle Boller was 3 of 9 for 21 yards.

Baltimore	0	7	0	0	—	7
Pittsburgh	14	21	3	0	—	38

Pitt — Miller 17 pass from Roethlisberger (Reed kick)
Pitt — Holmes 15 pass from Roethlisberger (Reed kick)
Pitt — Washington 30 pass from Roethlisberger (Reed kick)
Pitt — Holmes 35 pass from Roethlisberger (Reed kick)
Pitt — Washington 7 pass from Roethlisberger (Reed kick)
Balt — McGahee 33 run (Stover kick)
Pitt — FG Reed 22

TENTH WEEK SUMMARIES

American Football Conference

East Division	**W**	**L**	**T**	**Pct.**	**Pts.**	**OP**
New England	9	0	0	1.000	355	147
Buffalo	5	4	0	.556	143	166
N.Y. Jets	1	8	0	.111	159	228
Miami	0	9	0	.000	176	257
North Division	**W**	**L**	**T**	**Pct.**	**Pts.**	**OP**
Pittsburgh	7	2	0	.778	253	126
Cleveland	5	4	0	.556	225	264
Baltimore	4	5	0	.444	138	178
Cincinnati	3	6	0	.333	219	251
South Division	**W**	**L**	**T**	**Pct.**	**Pts.**	**OP**
Indianapolis	7	2	0	.778	265	149
Jacksonville	6	3	0	.667	183	164
Tennessee	6	3	0	.667	178	152
Houston	4	5	0	.444	203	226
West Division	**W**	**L**	**T**	**Pct.**	**Pts.**	**OP**
San Diego	5	4	0	.556	212	185
Denver	4	5	0	.444	153	238
Kansas City	4	5	0	.444	135	173
Oakland	2	7	0	.222	158	194

National Football Conference

East Division	**W**	**L**	**T**	**Pct.**	**Pts.**	**OP**
Dallas	8	1	0	.889	296	195
N.Y. Giants	6	3	0	.667	220	190
Washington	5	4	0	.556	177	193
Philadelphia	4	5	0	.444	189	180
North Division	**W**	**L**	**T**	**Pct.**	**Pts.**	**OP**
Green Bay	8	1	0	.889	228	142
Detroit	6	3	0	.667	221	216
Chicago	4	5	0	.444	161	187
Minnesota	3	6	0	.333	166	188
South Division	**W**	**L**	**T**	**Pct.**	**Pts.**	**OP**
Tampa Bay	5	4	0	.556	164	144
Carolina	4	5	0	.444	150	181
New Orleans	4	5	0	.444	202	223
Atlanta	3	6	0	.333	135	182
West Division	**W**	**L**	**T**	**Pct.**	**Pts.**	**OP**
Seattle	5	4	0	.556	191	141
Arizona	4	5	0	.444	188	195
San Francisco	2	7	0	.222	104	210
St. Louis	1	8	0	.111	136	248

SUNDAY, NOVEMBER 11

ARIZONA 31, DETROIT 21—at University of Phoenix Stadium, attendance 64,753. The Cardinals' defense limited the Lions to an NFL-record low minus-18 rushing yards as Arizona snapped its three-game losing streak. In addition to limiting the Lions to minus-18 rushing yards on 8 carries, the Cardinals forced 5 of the game's 9 turnovers, and sacked Jon Kitna 4 times. The Lions started the game with a touchdown, but then allowed 24 straight points. The Lions trailed 17-3 at halftime, but had driven to the Cardinals' 26. But Karlos Dansby forced Shaun McDonald to fumble on an end around that lost 15 yards. Antonio Smith recovered the ball, and five plays later Kurt Warner completed a 16-yard touchdown pass to Leonard Pope for a 24-7 lead. The Lions responded with a touchdown, and then recovered a fumble to get the ball back. However, Kitna fumbled the snap two plays later, and Darnell Dockett recovered to set up Warner's third touchdown pass, to Larry Fitzgerald from 20 yards, for a 31-14 lead with 13:23 remaining. Warner was 26 of 36 for 259 yards and 3 touchdowns, with 1 interception. Tim Rattay came in for one snap and completed a 2-yard touchdown pass to Pope just before halftime. Kitna was 32 of 45 for 296 yards and 2 touchdowns, with 2 interceptions.

Detroit	7	0	7	7	—	21
Arizona	3	14	7	7	—	31

Det — K. Jones 4 run (Hanson kick)
Ari — FG Rackers 23
Ari — Fitzgerald 1 pass from Warner (Rackers kick)
Ari — Pope 2 pass from Rattay (Rackers kick)
Ari — Pope 16 pass from Warner (Rackers kick)
Det — R. Williams 7 pass from Kitna (Hanson kick)
Ari — Fitzgerald 20 pass from Warner (Rackers kick)
Det — R. Williams 7 pass from Kitna (Hanson kick)

CINCINNATI 21, BALTIMORE 7—at M&T Bank Stadium, attendance 71,130. Shayne Graham kicked a club-record 7 field goals and the Bengals' defense forced 6 turnovers to hand the Ravens their third consecutive defeat. The Bengals led 6-0, but the Ravens drove to the Bengals' 2 just before halftime. On third down, Leon Hall intercepted Steve McNair's pass in the end zone for a touchback to preserve the 6-0 halftime lead. Graham kicked 5 field goals on the Bengals' first five possessions of the second half. The five kicks were in a span of exactly 14 minutes. Four of the field goals came after a Ravens' turnover, with three of the Bengals' drives covering less than 15 yards. Incredibly, the Ravens ran only two plays from scrimmage in between Graham's final three field goals, with Baltimore twice fumbling on the first play and muffing the kickoff on the other possession. Kyle Boller entered with the Ravens trailing 21-0 and guided them to their lone touchdown. Carson Palmer was 23 of 34 for 271 yards. McNair was 17 of 26 for 128 yards, with 1 interception. Boller was 6 of 8 for 89 yards, with 1 interception. Mark Clayton had 8 catches for 107 yards.

Cincinnati	0	6	3	12	—	21
Baltimore	0	0	0	7	—	7

Cin — FG Graham 34
Cin — FG Graham 19
Cin — FG Graham 22
Cin — FG Graham 35
Cin — FG Graham 35
Cin — FG Graham 21
Cin — FG Graham 33
Balt — McGahee 1 run (Stover kick)

ATLANTA 20, CAROLINA 13—at Bank of America Stadium, attendance 73,340. Joey Harrington completed a 30-yard touchdown pass to Alge Crumpler with 20 seconds to play to lift the Falcons to their second consecutive victory. The defenses allowed just 22 combined first downs and forced 17 punts. The Panthers used a fumble return for a touchdown by Ken Lucas and a 33-yard punt return by Ryne Robinson to set up John Kasay's field goal as the half expired for a 10-7 lead. The Falcons strung together consecutive scoring drives to take a 13-10 lead, but Vinny Testaverde responded with a 66-yard drive, keyed by Drew Carter's 14-yard catch on third down, to set up Kasay's tying field goal with 3:35 to play. A 23-yard punt return by Adam Jennings with 53 seconds left gave Atlanta the ball at the Panthers' 45. On second-and-5 from the Panthers' 30 with 26 seconds to play, Joey Harrington beat the blitz, with a short pass to Crumpler, who cut between the safeties and raced into the end zone for a 20-13 lead. Matt Moore came in for the final play, and his desperation pass was intercepted by Chris Crocker at the Falcons' 10. Harrington was 19 of 26 for 192 yards and 1 touchdown. Testaverde was 13 of 28 for 153 yards.

Atlanta	7	0	3	10	—	20
Carolina	0	10	0	3	—	13

Atl — Dunn 30 run (Andersen kick)
Car — Lucas 27 fumble return (Kasay kick)
Car — FG Kasay 29
Atl — FG Andersen 36
Atl — FG Andersen 47
Car — FG Kasay 31
Atl — Crumpler 30 pass from Harrington (Andersen kick)

GREEN BAY 34, MINNESOTA 0—at Lambeau Field, attendance 70,945. Brett Favre passed for 351 yards and 3 touchdowns as the Packers posted their first shutout since 2002. The Packers outgained the Vikings 488-247 in total yards and held the ball for 40 minutes, 40 seconds. The Vikings punted to conclude their first five possessions, and did not run a play inside the Packers' 42. By the time the Vikings received the kickoff for their sixth possession, they trailed 27-0. An interception by Charles Woodson at the Packers' 4 with 11:32 remaining helped preserve the shutout and sparked a 9-play, 96-yard fourth-quarter drive, capped by Favre's 17-yard touchdown pass to Ruvell Martin with 5:38 to play. Adrian Peterson, who set the NFL single-game rushing mark the previous week, was limited to 11 carries for 45 yards and injured his knee while being tackled in the third quarter. Favre was 33 of 46 for 351 yards and 3 touchdowns. Ryan Grant had 25 carries for 119 yards. Brooks Bollinger was 16 of 26 for 176 yards, with 1 interception.

Minnesota	0	0	0	0	—	0
Green Bay	7	6	14	7	—	34

GB — Grant 30 run (Crosby kick)
GB — FG Crosby 39
GB — FG Crosby 24
GB — Lee 1 pass from Favre (Crosby kick)
GB — Martin 8 pass from Favre (Crosby kick)
GB — Martin 17 pass from Favre (Crosby kick)

DENVER 27, KANSAS CITY 11—at Arrowhead Stadium, attendance 77,368. Undrafted rookie Selvin Young, making just his second start, rushed for 109 yards and 1 touchdown as the Broncos caught the Chiefs for second place in the AFC West. Bernard Pollard's blocked punt out of the end zone for a safety early in the second quarter was the difference as the Chiefs led 8-6 at halftime. Three plays into the second half, Damon Huard's pass was tipped by Hamza Abdullah and intercepted by Dre' Bly. Young scored three plays late for a 13-8 lead. On the next play, Elvis Dumervil sacked Huard, forced him to fumble, and Nate Webster recovered the ball and returned it 17 yards for a touchdown. The Broncos had scored 14 points in nine seconds and took a 20-8 lead. Brodie Croyle replaced Huard, and the Chiefs kicked a field goal on their next possession, and drove into Broncos' territory on their following drive, but Dave Rayner's 53-yard field-goal attempt sailed wide left. The Broncos responded with a 6-play drive, which was kept alive by a third-down pass interference penalty, and was capped by Jay Cutler's 18-yard touchdown pass to Daniel Graham for a 27-11 lead with 10:44 to play. Cutler was 17 of 29 for 192 yards and 1 touchdown, with 1 interception. Young carried 20 times for 109 yards. Huard was 6 of 15 for 83 yards, with 2 interceptions. Croyle was 17 of 30 for 162 yards, with 1 interception. Dwayne Bowe had 9 catches for 105 yards.

Denver	3	3	14	7	—	27
Kansas City	3	5	3	0	—	11

Den — FG Elam 44
KC — FG Rayner 38
KC — Safety, Pollard blocked punt out of end zone
Den — FG Elam 50
KC — FG Rayner 36
Den — S. Young 20 run (Elam kick)
Den — Webster 17 fumble return (Elam kick)
KC — FG Rayner 39
Den — Graham 18 pass from Cutler (Elam kick)

BUFFALO 13, MIAMI 10—at Dolphin Stadium, attendance 70,615. Rian Lindell kicked a 34-yard field goal with 46 seconds left as the Bills rallied to defeat the Dolphins. The Dolphins rushed for 143 yards and maintained possession for 36 minutes, 59 seconds. Will Allen intercepted a pass in the end zone late in the first half to help the Dolphins maintain a 3-0 lead. Early in the third quarter, John Wendling downed Brian Moorman's 36-yard punt at the Dolphins' 2. Three plays later, Chris Kelsay sacked Cleo Lemon for a safety. The Dolphins, however, forced a punt and then went on an 18-play, 80-yard drive that consumed 9 minutes, 45 seconds and was capped by Lemon's 5-yard scramble on third down to take a 10-2 lead into the fourth quarter. On the ensuing drive, the Bills went 66 yards in 10 plays, keyed by J.P. Losman's 1-yard sneak on fourth-and-1, and capped by Marshawn Lynch's 3-yard run. On the 2-point conversion attempt, Lynch took numerous hits before crossing the goal-line to tie the game 10-10 with 9:46 to play. The Bills' defense forced a punt, and Roscoe Parrish returned it 40 yards to midfield. The Bills used 10 plays to moved 34 yards, capped by Lindell's field goal with 46 seconds to play. Faced with second-and-6 from their own 49-yard line with 35 seconds to play, Lemon threw three consecutive incomplete passes. Losman was 12 of 23 for 157 yards, with 1 interception. Lemon was 16 of 29 for 131 yards. Jesse Chatman had 27 carries for 124 yards.

Buffalo	0	0	2	11	—	13
Miami	3	0	7	0	—	10

Mia — FG Feely 38
Buff — Safety, Lemon sacked by Kelsay in end zone
Mia — Lemon 5 run (Feely kick)
Buff — Lynch 3 run (Lynch run)
Buff — FG Lindell 34

ST. LOUIS 37, NEW ORLEANS 29—at Louisiana Superdome, attendance 70,003. The Rams rattled off 34 unanswered points to post their first victory of the season. The Rams had 409 yards of offense and maintained possession for 39 minutes, 42 seconds. Trailing 7-0 early, Oshiomogho Atogwe intercepted Drew Brees' pass at the Rams' 38 to spark St. Louis. Other than the Rams' four-play possession at the end of the half, the Rams responded to Atogwe's interception by scoring on six consecutive possessions, capped by Marc Bulger's 3-yard touchdown pass to Drew Bennett, for a 34-7 lead with 14:18 to play. The Saints scored on their next two possessions to pull within 34-21. Olindo Mare's onside kick attempt went out of bounds with 4:42 remaining, and Jeff Wilkins kicked a 44-yard field goal with 1:55 left for a 37-21 lead. Bulger was 27 of 33 for 302 yards and 2 touchdowns. Torry Holt had 8 catches for 124 yards. Brees was 25 of 36 for 272 yards and 2 touchdowns, with 2 interceptions. Marques Colston had 8 catches for 129 yards.

St. Louis	7	10	10	10	—	37
New Orleans	7	0	0	22	—	29

NO — Bush 7 run (Mare kick)
StL — Jackson 1 run (Wilkins kick)
StL — McMichael 2 pass from Jackson (Wilkins kick)
StL — FG Wilkins 49
StL — FG Wilkins 21
StL — Bruce 9 pass from Bulger (Wilkins kick)
StL — Bennett 3 pass from Bulger (Wilkins kick)
NO — Miller 1 pass from Brees (Bush run)
NO — Stecker 2 run (pass failed)
StL — FG Wilkins 44
NO — Johnson 7 pass from Brees (Bush run)

DALLAS 31, N.Y. GIANTS 20—at Giants Stadium, attendance 78,964. Tony Romo passed for 4 touchdowns as the Cowboys snapped the Giants' six-game winning streak. Both teams scored on their first possession. In the second quarter, Gibril Wilson intercepted a pass from Romo to set up a 60-yard drive capped by Rebuen Droughns' 1-yard touchdown run for a 14-10 lead. The Cowboys scored with 27 seconds left in the half to take the lead, and the Giants were content to run out the clock, but a 15-yard taunting penalty on the Cowboys and 29-yard pass from Eli Manning to Jeremy Shockey set up Lawrence Tynes' 40-yard field goal to tie the game 17-17. To begin the second half the Cowboys forced a three-and-out and the offense drove 86 yards, with 2 key third-down passes from Romo to Patrick Crayton keeping alive the drive, and capped by Terrell Owens' 25-yard touchdown for a 24-17 lead. The Giants answered with a 16-play, 75-yard drive, but had to settle for a field goal. The Cowboys quickly answered with Romo's 50-yard touchdown pass to a wide open Owens deep down the middle for a 31-20 lead with 10:43 remaining. Manning's fourth-and-4 pass from the Cowboys' 31 fell incomplete with 2:58 to play to end their final threat. Romo was 20 of 28 for 247 yards and 4 touchdowns, with 1 interception. Owens had 6 receptions for 125 yards. Manning was 23 of 34 for 236 yards and 1 touchdown, with 2 interceptions. Shockey had 12 catches for 129 yards.

Dallas	7	10	7	7	—	31
N.Y. Giants	7	10	0	3	—	20

Dall — Curtis 15 pass from Romo (Folk kick)
NYG — Shockey 8 pass from E. Manning (Tynes kick)
Dall — FG Folk 44
NYG — Droughns 1 run (Tynes kick)
Dall — Crayton 20 pass from Romo (Folk kick)
NYG — FG Tynes 40
Dall — Owens 25 pass from Romo (Folk kick)
NYG — FG Tynes 26
Dall — Owens 50 pass from Romo (Folk kick)

CHICAGO 17, OAKLAND 6—at McAfee Coliseum, attendance 62,715. Rex Grossman came off the bench to rally the Bears with 2 fourth-quarter touchdowns. Brian Griese started for the Bears, but with the score 3-3 he was knocked from the game when Kirk Morrison sacked him just before halftime. A 12-yard punt return by Tim Dwight, signed just 13 days earlier, and Josh McCown's 9-yard pass on third-and-7 to Zach Miller, set up Sebastian Janikowski's 52-yard field goal for a 6-3 lead with 4:04 to play. Three plays later, Grossman heaved a long pass deep down the left sideline that hit Bernard Berrian in stride for a 59-yard touchdown and 10-6 lead with 3:11 remaining. With 1:48 to play, Adewale Ogunleye sacked McCown, forced him to fumble, and Israel Idonije recovered at the Bears' 3. Cedric Benson scored on the next play to finalize the comeback. The Bears' defense allowed just 193 yards and forced 3 turnovers. Griese was 10 of 14 for 97 yards and Grossman was 7 of 14 for 142 yards and 1 touchdown. McCown was 14 of 27 for 108 yards, with 1 interception.

Chicago	0	3	0	14	—	17
Oakland	3	0	0	3	—	6

Oak — FG Janikowski 37
Chi — FG Gould 32
Oak — FG Janikowski 52
Chi — Berrian 59 pass from Grossman (Gould kick)
Chi — Benson 3 run (Gould kick)

PITTSBURGH 31, CLEVELAND 28—at Heinz Field, attendance 64,781. Ben Roethlisberger passed for 2 touchdowns and ran 30 yards for a fourth-quarter touchdown as the Steelers rallied to victory. The Steelers outgained the Browns 401-163 in total yards, and 71 of Cleveland's yards came on its game-opening touchdown drive. But Joshua Cribbs kept Cleveland in the game. Leading 7-3, Cribbs returned a kickoff 90 yards to set up Derek Anderson's 2-yard touchdown pass to Lawrence Vickers for a 14-3 lead. In the middle of the second quarter, Brodney Pool intercepted a pass at the Steelers' 18, and three plays later Braylon Edwards made a tip-toe-dragging 16-yard touchdown catch on the left side of the end zone for a 21-6 lead. In the third quarter, James Harrison forced Jamal Lewis to fumble, and Ike Taylor recovered to set up Hines Ward's 12-yard touchdown catch to cut the deficit to 21-16. In the fourth quarter, faced with third-and-10, Roethlisberger scrambled up the middle 30 yards for a touchdown and 24-21 lead. Cribbs responded by avoiding four of five Steelers near the 10-yard line and returning the ensuing kickoff 100 yards down the right sideline to give Cleveland 28-24 lead with 11:14 to play. The Steelers drove 78 yards on the next drive, with Roethlisberger completing 2 key third-down passes, including a 20-yard pass to Heath Miller on third-and-18, and scramble for 10 yards on third-and-9, to set up Miller's 2-yard touchdown catch with 3:13 remaining. The Browns drove to the Steelers 35, but Phil Dawson's 52-yard field-goal attempt was straight but short with six seconds to play. Roethlisberger was 23 of 34 for 278 yards and 2 touchdowns, with 1 interception. Willie Parker had 25 carries for 105 yards. Anderson was 16 of 35 for 123 yards and 3 touchdowns.

Cleveland	7	14	0	7	—	28
Pittsburgh	3	6	7	15	—	31

Cle — Winslow 4 pass from Anderson (Dawson kick)
Pitt — FG Reed 28
Cle — Vickers 2 pass from Anderson (Dawson kick)
Pitt — FG Reed 35
Cle — Edwards 16 pass from Anderson (Dawson kick)
Pitt — FG Reed 30
Pitt — Ward 12 pass from Roethlisberger (Reed kick)
Pitt — Roethlisberger 30 run (Ward pass from Roethlisberger)
Cle — Cribbs 100 kickoff return (Dawson kick)
Pitt — Miller 2 pass from Roethlisberger (Reed kick)

JACKSONVILLE 28, TENNESSEE 13—at LP Field, attendance 69,143. Maurice Jones-Drew rushed for 101 yards and 1 touchdown the Jaguars caught the Titans in the AFC South standings. The Jaguars had two 13-play drives out of their first three possessions to jump to a 14-0 lead. In the third quarter, Mike Peterson intercepted Vince Young's pass and Fred Taylor scored three plays later to stake the Jaguars to a 21-3 lead. The Titans scored on their next two possessions, with Justin Gage's 20-yard touchdown catch capping a 10-play drive to pull the Titans to within 21-13 six seconds into the fourth quarter. After an exchange of punts, the Jaguars were faced with fourth-and-2 from the Titans' 39 with 9:02 to play. Jacksonville went for the first down, and Quinn Gray completed a 4-yard pass to Dennis Northcutt. Later in the drive, Gray scrambled for 15 yards on third-and-12 to set up Greg Jones' second touchdown for a 28-13 lead with 4:47 remaining. Brian WIlliams intercepted Young's pass near the goal line with 1:14 to play to secure the victory. Gray was 13 of 23 for 101 yards and 1 touchdown. Jones-Drew had 19 carries for 101 yards and 1 touchdown. Young was 24 of 41 for 257 yards and 1 touchdown, with 2 interceptions.

Jacksonville	7	7	7	7	—	28
Tennessee	0	3	3	7	—	13

Jax — G. Jones 2 pass from Gray (Carney kick)
Jax — Jones-Drew 8 run (Carney kick)
Tenn — FG Bironas 37
Jax — Taylor 4 run (Carney kick)
Tenn — FG Bironas 49
Tenn — Gage 20 pass from Young (Bironas kick)
Jax — G. Jones 3 run (Carney kick)

PHILADELPHIA 33, WASHINGTON 25—at FedExField, attendance 90,218. Donovan McNabb passed for 4 touchdowns and Brian Westbrook scored 3 times as the Eagles remained in the playoff hunt. The Redskins led 12-7 at halftime and both teams scored on each of their first two second-half possessions as the Eagles cut the deficit to 22-20 with 10:35 remaining. After an exchange of turnovers, Shaun Suisham kicked a 21-yard field goal with 4:15 to play to give the Redskins a 25-20 lead. Three plays later, McNabb dumped a short screen pass to Westbrook, who cut down the right sideline, before slicing back to the middle of the field to complete a 57-yard touchdown. The Eagles went for two points, but McNabb's pass fell incomplete and Philadelphia led 26-24 with 3:16 remaining. Four plays later, on fourth-and-13, Mike Patterson sacked Jason Campbell and forced him to fumble. Brodrick Bunkley recovered and on the next play Westbrook scored on a 10-yard run. Moments later, Campbell's fourth-and-15 pass from his own 40 fell incomplete. McNabb was 20 of 28 for 251 yards and 4 touchdowns. Westbrook carried 20 times for 100 yards. Campbell was 23 of 34 for 215 yards and 3 touchdowns.

Philadelphia	7	0	6	20	—	33
Washington	0	12	3	10	—	25

Phil — Westbrook 4 pass from McNabb (Akers kick)
Wash — Thrash 4 pass from Campbell (kick failed)
Wash — Thrash 12 pass from Campbell (pass failed)
Wash — FG Suisham 23
Phil — Smith 8 pass from McNabb (pass failed)
Wash — McCardell 6 pass from Campbell (Suisham kick)
Phil — R. Brown 45 pass from McNabb (Akers kick)
Wash — FG Suisham 21
Phil — Westbrook 57 pass from McNabb (pass failed)
Phil — Westbrook 10 run (Akers kick)

SUNDAY NIGHT, NOVEMBER 11

SAN DIEGO 23, INDIANAPOLIS 21—at Qualcomm Stadium, attendance 67,726. Adam Vinatieri missed a 29-yard field-goal attempt with 1:31 to play as the Chargers nearly blew a 23-0 lead but held on for the victory. The Chargers' defense intercepted 6 passes and Darren Sproles became just the eleventh player in NFL history to return both a punt and kickoff for a touchdown in the same game. Sproles turned the trick in the first quarter, and the Chargers' defense intercepted Peyton Manning on four of their first five possessions en route to a 23-0 lead with 8:47 left in the first half. Trailing 23-7 at halftime, the Colts' defense allowed just 65 yards in the second half, and forced two turnovers. The first turnover came three plays after the Colts had pulled within 23-15. Philip Rivers, on a rainy night, had the ball slip out of his hand as he began to throw. Gray Brackett fell on the ball in the end zone for a touchdown to cut the deficit to 23-21 with 14:28 to play. Joseph Addai attempted the 2-point conversion run, but he was stopped shy of the goal line. The second turnover came with 5:50 remaining, when Clint Session intercepted Rivers' pass at the Chargers' 42. The Colts drove to the Chargers' 9, and on third-and-3, Addai was initially credited with a first down before a replay review marked the ball a foot shy. With 1:34 to play, the Colts lined up to go for the first down, but a false start penalty moved the ball back, forcing the Colts to attempt a field goal, which Vinatieri pushed wide right. The Colts got the ball back on their own 33 with 22 seconds left, but after two incomplete passes Clinton Hart picked off Manning to end the game. Rivers was 13 of 24 for 104 yards, with 2 interceptions. Antonio Cromartie had 3 interceptions. Manning was 34 of 56 for 328 yards and 2 touchdowns, with 6 interceptions. Reggie Wayne had 10 catches for 140 yards.

Indianapolis	0	7	0	14	—	21
San Diego	16	7	0	0	—	23

SD — Sproles 89 kickoff return (Kaeding kick)
SD — FG Kaeding 33
SD — Sproles 45 punt return (pass failed)
SD — Tomlinson 4 run (Kaeding kick)
Ind — Wayne 8 pass from Manning (Vinatieri kick)
Ind — Keith 7 pass from Manning (Fletcher pass from Manning)
Ind — Brackett fumble recovery in end zone (run failed)

MONDAY NIGHT, NOVEMBER 12

SEATTLE 24, SAN FRANCISCO 0—at Qwest Field, attendance 68,331. The Seahawks' defense allowed just 6 first downs while handing the 49ers their seventh consecutive defeat. Seattle outgained the 49ers 380-173 in total yards while maintaining possession for 39 minutes, 54 seconds. The Seahawks scored on three of their first four possessions to jump to a 17-0 lead. The Seahawks had the game's initial 17 first downs, at which point they had outgained the 49ers 247-31 in total yards. An interception by Nate Clements early in the third quarter gave the 49ers the ball at the Seahawks' 23. San Francisco drove to the Seahawks' 2, but on fourth-and-1 Frank Gore was stopped for no gain. Later in the third quarter, the 49ers reached the Seahawks' 23, but Alex Smith's fourth-and-3 pass fell incomplete. The Seahawks responded with a 12-play, 77-yard touchdown drive, capped by D.J. Hackett's 10-yard touchdown catch on the first play of the fourth quarter. Matt Hasselbeck was 27 of 40 for 278 yards and 2 touchdowns, with 1 interception. Hackett had 8 catches for 101 yards. Alex Smith was 12 of 28 for 114 yards.

San Francisco	0	0	0	0	—	0
Seattle	10	7	0	7	—	24

Sea — Heller 1 pass from Hasselbeck (J. Brown kick)
Sea — FG J. Brown 20
Sea — Morris 6 run (J. Brown kick)
Sea — Hackett 10 pass from Hasselbeck (J. Brown kick)

ELEVENTH WEEK SUMMARIES

American Football Conference

East Division	**W**	**L**	**T**	**Pct.**	**Pts.**	**OP**
New England	10	0	0	1.000	411	157
Buffalo	5	5	0	.500	153	222
N.Y. Jets	2	8	0	.200	178	244
Miami	0	10	0	.000	183	274
North Division	**W**	**L**	**T**	**Pct.**	**Pts.**	**OP**
Pittsburgh	7	3	0	.700	269	145
Cleveland	6	4	0	.600	288	294
Baltimore	4	6	0	.400	168	211
Cincinnati	3	7	0	.300	246	286
South Division	**W**	**L**	**T**	**Pct.**	**Pts.**	**OP**
Indianapolis	8	2	0	.800	278	159
Jacksonville	7	3	0	.700	207	181
Tennessee	6	4	0	.600	198	186
Houston	5	5	0	.500	226	236
West Division	**W**	**L**	**T**	**Pct.**	**Pts.**	**OP**
Denver	5	5	0	.500	187	258
San Diego	5	5	0	.500	229	209
Kansas City	4	6	0	.400	145	186
Oakland	2	8	0	.200	180	223

National Football Conference

East Division	**W**	**L**	**T**	**Pct.**	**Pts.**	**OP**
Dallas	9	1	0	.900	324	218
N.Y. Giants	7	3	0	.700	236	200
Philadelphia	5	5	0	.500	206	187
Washington	5	5	0	.500	200	221
North Division	**W**	**L**	**T**	**Pct.**	**Pts.**	**OP**
Green Bay	9	1	0	.900	259	159
Detroit	6	4	0	.600	231	232
Chicago	4	6	0	.400	184	217
Minnesota	4	6	0	.400	195	210
South Division	**W**	**L**	**T**	**Pct.**	**Pts.**	**OP**
Tampa Bay	6	4	0	.600	195	151
Carolina	4	6	0	.400	167	212
New Orleans	4	6	0	.400	212	246
Atlanta	3	7	0	.300	142	213
West Division	**W**	**L**	**T**	**Pct.**	**Pts.**	**OP**
Seattle	6	4	0	.600	221	164
Arizona	5	5	0	.500	223	222
St. Louis	2	8	0	.200	149	257
San Francisco	2	8	0	.200	113	223

SUNDAY, NOVEMBER 18

TAMPA BAY 31, ATLANTA 7—at Georgia Dome, attendance 69,480. Jeff Garcia passed for 2 touchdowns, Earnest Graham rushed for 102 yards, and the Buccaneers' defense forced 4 turnovers and registered 5 sacks to post a divisional road victory. Barrett Ruud's first-quarter interception of a Byron Leftwich pass led to one touchdown, and Greg White's sack in the second quarter forced Leftwich to fumble. Ronde Barber recovered the ball and returned it 41 yards for a touchdown and 14-0 lead. In the third quarter, Barber tackled Warrick Dunn for no gain on fourth-and-1 near midfield to set up a field goal, and Gaines Adams forced Leftwich to fumble on the ensuing possession. Chris Hovan recovered, and three plays later Garcia completed a 21-yard touchdown pass to Alex Smith for a 24-0 lead with 4:51 left in the third quarter. The Buccaneers forced a punt and scored on their next possession, and the Falcons did not break the shutout until reserve Joey Harrington completed a 7-yard touchdown pass to Adam Jennings on third-and-goal with 1:10 to play. Garcia was 10 of 20 for 159 yards and 2 touchdowns. Graham rushed 17 times for 102 yards. Leftwich was 15 of 27 for 106 yards, with 1 interception. Harrington was 16 of 20 for 139 yards and 1 touchdown.

Tampa Bay	7	7	10	7	—	31
Atlanta	0	0	0	7	—	7

TB — Galloway 44 pass from Garcia (Bryant kick)
TB — R. Barber 41 fumble return (Bryant kick)
TB — FG Bryant 23
TB — A. Smith 21 pass from Garcia (Bryant kick)
TB — Graham 26 run (Bryant kick)
Atl — Jennings 7 pass from Harrington (Andersen kick)

CLEVELAND 33, BALTIMORE 30 (OT)—at M & T Bank Stadium, attendance 71,055. In one of the most bizarre plays seen on a football field, Phil Dawson's goalpost-pinball-bouncing 51-yard field goal tied the game as regulation expired, and then Dawson added a 33-yard field goal in overtime for the victory. The Ravens' offense struggled in the first half, but Baltimore trailed just 13-7 thanks to Ray Lewis' 35-yard interception return for a touchdown. The Ravens then opened the second half with a 75-yard touchdown drive to take a 14-13 lead. The Browns answered with a touchdown. The Ravens had a chance to take the lead late in the third quarter, but Brodney Pool intercepted Kyle Boller's pass and returned the ball 100 yards for a touchdown and 27-14 lead. Undaunted, the Ravens responded with four consecutive scoring drives, capped by Matt Stover's 47-yard field goal with 26 seconds to play for a 30-27 lead. Joshua Cribbs returned the ensuing kickoff 39 yards to the Browns' 43, and Derek Anderson completed a key 18-yard pass to Braylon Edwards with three seconds left to set up Dawson's 51-yard attempt. The kick hit the left upright, hit the extension bar, about a foot inside the goal post, and then the ball bounced forward and back into the end zone. The referees originally ruled the kick no good, but then overturned their decision, thus forcing overtime. In overtime, the Browns won the toss, Cribbs returned the kickoff 41 yards, and Anderson completed a key 18-yard pass to Kellen Winslow on third-and-10 to help set up Dawson's game-winning 33-yard field goal. Anderson was 24 of 38 for 274 yards, with 1 interception. Boller was 22 of 41 for 279 yards and 1 touchdown, with 2 interceptions. Willis McGahee had 21 carries for 102 yards. Devard Darling had 4 receptions for 107 yards.

Cleveland	3	10	14	3	3	—	33
Baltimore	0	7	7	16	0	—	30

Cle — FG Dawson 28
Cle — J. Lewis 1 run (Dawson kick)
Balt — R. Lewis 35 interception return (Stover kick)
Cle — FG Dawson 39
Balt — McGahee 2 run (Stover kick)
Cle — Anderson 1 run (Dawson kick)
Cle — Pool 100 interception return (Dawson kick)
Balt — FG Stover 34
Balt — FG Stover 41
Balt — Darling 27 pass from Boller (Stover kick)
Balt — FG Stover 47
Cle — FG Dawson 51
Cle — FG Dawson 33

ARIZONA 35, CINCINNATI 27—at Paul Brown Stadium, attendance 65,403. Antrel Rolle tied an NFL record with 2 interception returns for touchdowns, and had a third called back by a penalty, as the Cardinals outlasted the Bengals. The Bengals outgained the Cardinals 396-247 in total yards, but the Bengals committed 5 turnovers, including 3 interceptions by Rolle. In the first quarter, Rolle intercepted a short pass and returned it 55 yards for a touchdown to tie the game 7-7. Kurt Warner's 5-yard touchdown pass to Larry Fitzgerald with 13 seconds left in the half staked the Cardinals to a 21-13 halftime lead. Karlos Dansby intercepted Carson Palmer's pass on the first play of the second half to set up Edgerrin James' 3-yard touchdown run for a 28-13 lead. The Bengals then drove to the Cardinals' 17. Chad Johnson caught a short pass, dropped the ball while running, and Terrence Holt recovered at the Cardinals' 9. The Bengals defense forced a punt, and Chris Henry caught a 37-yard touchdown pass a few plays later. Less than two minutes after Henry's touchdown, the Bengals' defense forced a punt, and DeDe Dorsey blocked Mike Barr's punt and returned the ball 19 yards for a touchdown to pull within 28-27. The Bengals forced another punt, but Rolle intercepted a short pass intended for Johnson and returned it 54 yards for a touchdown and 35-27 lead. In the fourth quarter, the Bengals twice drove in side the Cardinals' 40, but Palmer fourth-and-6 and fourth-and-5 passes fell incomplete. On their final possession, Rolle intercepted a pass deep down the middle at the Cardinals' 29 with 33 seconds left and returned it 71 yards, but a personal foul penalty nullified the touchdown but did preserve the victory. Warner was 16 of 28 for 211 yards and 2 touchdowns. Palmer was 37 of 52 for 329 yards and 2 touchdowns, with 4 interceptions.

Arizona	7	14	14	0	—	35
Cincinnati	7	6	14	0	—	27

Cin — Houshmandzadeh 19 pass from Palmer (Graham kick)
Ari — Rolle 55 interception return (Rackers kick)
Cin — FG Graham 41
Ari — Boldin 44 pass from Warner (Rackers kick)
Cin — FG Graham 38
Ari — Fitzgerald 5 pass from Warner (Rackers kick)
Ari — James 3 run (Rackers kick)
Cin — Henry 37 pass from Palmer (Graham kick)
Cin — Dorsey 19 return of blocked punt (Graham kick)
Ari — Rolle 54 interception return (Rackers kick)

DALLAS 28, WASHINGTON 23—at Texas Stadium, attendance 63,706. Terrell Owens had 4 touchdown catches and on defense knocked down a Hail Mary pass in the end zone as time expired as the Cowboys improved to 9-1 for the first time since 1983. The Redskins led 10-7 late in the third quarter when a 51-yard interference penalty on a pass intended for Patrick Crayton gave the Cowboys' the ball at the Redskins' 22. On third-and-19 moments later, Tony Romo found Owens open deep down the middle for a 31-yard touchdown and 14-10 lead. After a Redskins' field goal, Owens completed the ensuing 87-yard drive with a 46-yard touchdown catch on a post pattern for a 21-13 lead. After another field goal, it took just four plays for Romo to find a wide-open Owens deep down the right sideline for a 52-yard touchdown a 28-16 lead with 7:50 to play. The Redskins responded with a 74-yard drive, highlighted by Jason Campbell's 10-yard pass to Chris Cooley on fourth-and-4, and capped by Santana Moss' 5-yard touchdown catch with 3:45 remaining to pull within 28-23. The Redskins then forced a three-and-out and marched down to the Cowboys' 19, but Terence Newman intercepted Campbell's pass with 1:39 left. The Redskins' defense forced another punt, and from midfield as time expired Campbell lofted a pass into the end zone that Owens knocked down. Romo was 22 of 32 for 293 yards and 4 touchdowns, with 1 interception. Owens had 8 receptions for 173 yards. Campbell was 33 of 54 for 348 yards and 2 touchdowns, with 1 interception. Moss had 9 catches for 121 yards.

Washington	7	3	3	10	—	23
Dallas	0	7	7	14	—	28

Wash — Cooley 19 pass from Campbell (Suisham kick)
Dall — Owens 4 pass from Romo (Folk kick)
Wash — FG Suisham 45
Dall — Owens 31 pass from Romo (Folk kick)
Wash — FG Suisham 39
Dall — Owens 46 pass from Romo (Folk kick)
Wash — FG Suisham 44
Dall — Owens 52 pass from Romo (Folk kick)
Wash — S. Moss 5 pass from Campbell (Suisham kick)

N.Y. GIANTS 16, DETROIT 10—at Ford Field, 60,675. Eli Manning passed or 283 yards as the Giants held off the Lions. The Giants led 10-0 at halftime, but Jason Hanson kicked a 42-yard field goal to begin the second half and was lining up for a 52-yard field goal later in the quarter when Fred Robbins blocked the kick. Six plays later, Lawrence Tynes kicked a 46-yard field goal to give the Giants a 13-3 lead. Gibril Wilson intercepted a pass on the next drive to set up Tynes' 20-yard field goal for a 16-3 lead with 11:15 to play. Jon Kitna completed all 4 pass attempts on a four-play, 82-yard drive, capped by Calvin Johnson's 35-yard touchdown catch with 4:34 remaining, to pull within 16-10. The Lions' defense then forced a three-and-out, but James Butler intercepted Kitna's long pass with 1:54 remaining to thwart one drive. The Lions forced another punt and drove to the Giants' 43 with 56 seconds left, but Sam Madison intercepted Kitna's pass to clinch the victory. Manning was 28 of 39 for 283 yards and 1 touchdown. Kitna was 28 of 43 for 377 yards and 1 touchdown, with 3 interceptions. Shaun McDonald had 7 receptions for 113 yards. Roy Williams had 6 catches for 106 yards.

N.Y. Giants	3	7	3	3	—	16
Detroit	0	0	3	7	—	10

NYG — FG Tynes 28
NYG — Jacobs 10 pass from E. Manning (Tynes kick)
Det — FG Hanson 42
NYG — FG Tynes 46
NYG — FG Tynes 20
Det — C. Johnson 35 pass from Kitna (Hanson kick)

GREEN BAY 31, CAROLINA 17—at Lambeau Field, attendance 70,805. Brett Favre passed for 3 touchdowns as the Packers improved to 9-1 for its best start in 45 years. Tramon Williams had a 94-yard punt return for a touchdown in the first quarter, and the Packers had 71- and 73-yard touchdown drives in the second quarter, needing just six and seven plays, respectively, and capped by Favre touchdown passes, for a 21-3 halftime lead. Koren Robinson returned the opening kickoff of the second half 67 yards to set up Favre's 12-yard touchdown pass to Donald Lee for a 28-3 lead with 12:46 left in the third quarter. Vinny Testaverde's second touchdown pass cut the deficit to 28-17 with 4:22 remaining, but Donald Driver recovered the ensuing onside kick and Mason Crosby made a 47-yard field goal with 2:41 left. Favre was 22 of 30 for 218 yards and 3 touchdowns. Testaverde was 19 of 37 for 258 yards and 2 touchdowns, with 2 interceptions.

Carolina	3	0	7	7	—	17
Green Bay	7	14	7	3	—	31

GB — T. Williams 94 punt return (Crosby kick)
Car — FG Kasay 26
GB — Jennings 4 pass from Favre (Crosby kick)
GB — Lee 26 pass from Favre (Crosby kick)
GB — Lee 12 pass from Favre (Crosby kick)
Car — Fauria 2 pass from Testaverde (Kasay kick)
Car — D. Carter 5 pass from Testaverde (Kasay kick)
GB — FG Crosby 47

HOUSTON 23, NEW ORLEANS 10—at Reliant Stadium, attendance 70,780. Matt Schaub passed for 2 touchdowns as the Texans improved to 5-5, marking the latest in the season they have had a .500 record. Trailing 10-7, Schaub completed all 3 passes for 55 yards on a 70-yard drive, capped by his 10-yard touchdown pass to Joel Dreessen for a 14-10 lead with 2:10 left in the second quarter. The Texans' defense forced a three-and-out, and Jacoby Jones' 17-yard punt return led to Kris Brown's 36-yard field goal as the half expired for a 17-10 lead. Morlon Greenwood's interception early in the fourth quarter set up Brown's 53-yard field goal. The Saints drove to the Texans' 43 with 7:21 left, and on fourth-and-2, Drew Brees' pass for David Patten was incomplete. The Texans then executed a 10-play, 52-yard drive, which featured 6 carries by Ron Dayne, to set up Brown's 23-yard field goal with 1:57 remaining. Schaub was 21 of 33 for 293 yards and 2 touchdowns. Andre Johnson had 6 receptions for 120 yards. Brees was 33 of 49 for 290 yards and 1 touchdown, with 2 interceptions. Reggie Bush had 12 catches for 70 yards and Marques Colston added 9 receptions for 118 yards.

New Orleans	3	7	0	0	—	10
Houston	7	10	0	6	—	23

NO — FG Mare 52
Hou — A. Johnson 73 pass from Schaub (K. Brown kick)
NO — Henderson 6 pass from Brees (Mare kick)
Hou — Dreessen 10 pass from Schaub (K. Brown kick)
Hou — FG K. Brown 36
Hou — FG K. Brown 53
Hou — FG K. Brown 23

INDIANAPOLIS 13, KANSAS CITY 10—at RCA Dome, attendance 57,294. Adam Vinatieri kicked a 24-yard field goal with three seconds left as the Colts escaped with a hard-earned home victory. The defenses allowed a total of 450 yards, 234 by the Chiefs. Both kickers made just 1 of 3 field-goal attempts in the first half to make the score 3-3 at halftime. Joseph Addai carried 5 times for 35 yards on a 64-yard drive, capped by Addai's 3-yard touchdown run for a 10-3 lead. The Chiefs answered with a 11-play, 77-yard touchdown drive, which included 3 key third-down completions by Brodie Croyle, the last of which was a 19-yard touchdown pass to Dwayne Bowe in the corner of the end zone to tie the game. With 6:59 remaining, the Colts forced a punt and began on their own 33-yard line. Peyton Manning completed all 4 pass attempts on the drive as the Colts reached the Chiefs' 3. On fourth-and-1 with 2:00 left, Manning gained 1 yards on a quarterback sneak. The Colts then ran the clock down and Vinatieri kicked a 24-yard field goal with three seconds remaining. Manning was 16 of 32 for 163 yards, with 1 interception. Croyle was 19 of 27 for 169 yards and 1 touchdown.

Kansas City	0	3	7	0	— 10
Indianapolis	0	3	7	3	— 13

KC — FG Rayner 47
Ind — FG Vinatieri 27
Ind — Addai 3 run (Vinatieri kick)
KC — Bowe 19 pass from Croyle (Rayner kick)
Ind — FG Vinatieri 24

JACKSONVILLE 24, SAN DIEGO 17—at Jacksonville Municipal Stadium, attendance 66,732. David Garrard returned from a high ankle sprain that had cost him three game and passed for 2 touchdowns to lift the Jaguars to victory. Jacksonville scored on its first three possessions to take a 17-3 lead. The Chargers drove 60 yards in five plays for a touchdown to begin the second half, but the Jaguars answered with an 87-yard drive later in the quarter, keyed by three consecutive passes by Garrard covering 22, 36, and 36 yards, to set up his 1-yard scoring toss to Marcedes Lewis for a 24-10 lead with 5:02 left in the third quarter. Early in the fourth quarter, the Jaguars' defense made two big plays. LaDainian Tomlinson was dropped for a 1-yard loss on fourth-and-2 with 14:14 left, and Reggie Nelson intercepted a pass with 9:28 remaining. Antonio Gates did catch a 24-yard touchdown pass with 5:06 left to cut the deficit to 24-17, and the Chargers' defense forced a punt, but Sammy Knight intercepted Philip Rivers' pass at the Chargers' 48 with 1:26 left to clinch the victory. Garrard was 15 of 24 for 189 yards and 2 touchdowns. Rivers was 22 of 40 for 309 yards and 1 touchdown, with 2 interceptions.

San Diego	0	3	7	7	— 17
Jacksonville	10	7	7	0	— 24

Jax — FG Scobee 48
Jax — Jones-Drew 1 run (Scobee kick)
SD — FG Kaeding 23
Jax — Williams 36 pass from Garrard (Scobee kick)
SD — Tomlinson 6 run (Kaeding kick)
Jax — Lewis 1 pass from Garrard (Scobee kick)
SD — Gates 24 pass from Rivers (Kaeding kick)

MINNESOTA 29, OAKLAND 22—at Metrodome, attendance 62,960. Chester Taylor, starting in place of injured NFL-rushing leader Adrian Peterson, ran for 164 yards and 3 touchdowns for the Vikings. Minnesota compiled 478 yards of offense, but committed 5 turnovers to keep the game close. The Raiders scored on five of their last six first-half possessions, including three tallies set up by fumble recoveries, but settled for 4 field goals. The last field goal was a 49-yard boot by Sebastian Janikowski as the half expired to tie the game 19-19. With Minnesota leading 22-19 late in the third quarter, Brian Robison sacked Daunte Culpepper and forced him to fumble. Chad Greenway recovered at the Vikings' 26, and Minnesota drove 74 yards in six plays, capped by Taylor's 6-yard run to begin the fourth quarter, for a 29-19 lead. Janikowski made a 52-yard field goal with 3:23 left to pull within 29-22, and the Raiders' defense forced a punt. Greenway intercepted Culpepper's pass at the Raiders' 18, but fumbled and Paul McQuistan recovered. The Raiders drove to the Vikings' 41, but Culpepper's last-play desperation pass fell incomplete. Tarvaris Jackson was 17 of 22 for 171 yards, with 1 interception. Taylor carried 22 times for 164 yards. Culpepper was 23 of 39 for 344 yards and 1 touchdown, with 1 interception.

Oakland	3	16	0	3	— 22
Minnesota	9	10	3	7	— 29

Minn — Taylor 10 run (Longwell kick)
Minn — Safety, Culpepper flagged for intentional grounding in end zone
Oak — FG Janikowski 42
Minn — FG Longwell 30
Oak — Madsen 10 pass from Culpepper (Janikowski kick)
Oak — FG Janikowski 30
Minn — Taylor 38 run (Longwell kick)
Oak — FG Janikowski 42
Oak — FG Janikowski 49
Minn — FG Longwell 38
Minn — Taylor 6 run (Longwell kick)
Oak — FG Janikowski 52

N.Y. JETS 19, PITTSBURGH 16 (OT)—at The Meadowlands, attendance 77,659. Mike Nugent kicked a field goal with 23 seconds left in regulation and the game-winner in overtime as the Jets snapped a six-game losing streak. The Steelers finished their first three second-half possessions with Jeff Reed field goals to take a 16-13 lead with 8:41 to play. DeShea Townsend intercepted Kellen Clemens' pass to stop one drive, and Clemens' fourth-and-5 pass for Justin McCareins fell incomplete with 4:15 remaining. The Jets' defense forced a punt, and starting on their own 14-yard line, Clemens completed 5 passes and had a 15-yard scramble that enabled Nugent to kick a 28-yard field goal with 23 seconds left. The Jets won the overtime coin toss, but had to punt. The Jets' defense then also forced a punt, and Leon Washington returned the ball 33 yards to the Steelers' 26 to set up Nugent's game-winning 38-yard field goal. Clemens was 14 of 31 for 162 yards and 1 touchdown, with 1 interception. Thomas Jones had 30 carries for 117 yards. Ben Roethlisberger was 15 of 25 for 195 yards and 1 touchdown, with 1 interception.

Pittsburgh	0	7	6	3	0	— 16
N.Y. Jets	10	3	0	3	3	— 19

NYJ — Baker 1 pass from Clemens (Nugent kick)
NYJ — FG Nugent 25
Pitt — Holmes 7 pass from Roethlisberger (Reed kick)
NYJ — FG Nugent 19
Pitt — FG Reed 37
Pitt — FG Reed 33
Pitt — FG Reed 48
NYJ — FG Nugent 28
NYJ — FG Nugent 38

PHILADELPHIA 17, MIAMI 7—at Lincoln Financial Field, attendance 68,934. The Eagles' defense allowed just 186 total yards and 9 first downs to as Philadelphia improved to .500 for the first time. Rookie Ted Ginn returned a punt 87 yards for a touchdown for the Dolphins, and Donovan McNabb suffered an injured ankle in the second quarter. A.J. Feeley came off the bench to rally the Eagles. Philadelphia drove 62 yards to begin the second half, keyed by Feeley's 17-yard pass to Kevin Curtis on third-and-7, to set up Correll Buckhalter's 8-yard touchdown run for a 10-7 lead. Jason Avant's 4-yard touchdown catch early in the fourth quarter capped a 77-yard drive and extended the Eagles' lead to 17-7. The Dolphins drove to the Eagles' 1, but Jesse Chatman was dropped for a 1-yard loss, John Beck threw an incomplete pass, Chatman gained 1 yard, and on fourth down Chatman was dropped for a 13-yard loss with 6:40 remaining. McNabb was 3 of 11 for 34 yards, with 2 interceptions. Feeley was 13 of 19 for 116 yards and 1 touchdown, with 1 interception. Brian Westbrook had 32 carries for 148 yards. Beck, making his first NFL start, was 9 of 22 for 109 yards.

Miami	0	7	0	0	— 7
Philadelphia	0	3	7	7	— 17

Mia — Ginn 87 punt return (Feely kick)
Phil — FG Akers 34
Phil — Buckhalter 8 run (Akers kick)
Phil — Avant 4 pass from Feeley (Akers kick)

ST. LOUIS 13, SAN FRANCISCO 9—at Monster Park, attendance 68,039. Oshiomongho Atogwe intercepted a pass in the end zone as time expired to give the Rams their second consecutive victory. The 49ers' defense limited the Rams to 207 yards and sacked Bulger 6 times, but the offense gained just 244 yards and committed 2 turnovers. The Rams took the opening kickoff and marched downfield with a 79-yard drive, capped by Bulger's 3-yard touchdown pass to Torry Holt. The Rams led 10-3 at halftime, and Dante Hall's 29-yard punt return early in the fourth quarter set up Jeff Wilkins' second field goal for a 13-3 lead with 10:22 to play. The 49ers responded with consecutive field-goal drives. The latter field goal by Joe Nedney came on fourth-and-10 from the Rams' 28 with 1:55 remaining. The 49ers' defense then forced a three-and-out, using all their timeouts, and got the ball back on their own 11-yard line with 1:28 remaining. Trent Dilfer completed passes to four different receivers to reach the Rams' 21. As time expired, Dilfer's pass into the end zone was intercepted by Atogwe. Bulger was 21 of 32 for 155 yards and 1 touchdown. Dilfer was 20 of 42 for 231 yards, with 2 interceptions.

St. Louis	7	3	0	3	— 13
San Francisco	3	0	0	6	— 9

StL — Holt 3 pass from Bulger (Wilkins kick)
SF — FG Nedney 28
StL — FG Wilkins 49
StL — FG Wilkins 35
SF — FG Nedney 38
SF — FG Nedney 46

SEATTLE 30, CHICAGO 23—at Qwest Field, attendance 68,249. Matt Hasselbeck passed for 2 touchdowns as the Seahawks maintained their one-game lead in the NFC West. The Seahawks scored on their last two possessions of the first half to tie the game 17-17. Nate Burleson returned the second half's opening kickoff 44 yards, on fourth-and-1 from the Bears' 40 Hasselbeck completed a short pass to Marcus Pollard that produced 20 yards, and Burleson caught a 4-yard touchdown pass moments later for a 24-17 lead. The Bears trailed 27-20 and had the ball when Patrick Kerney sacked Rex Grossman and forced him to fumble. Darryl Tapp recovered at the Bears' 47 and Josh Brown booted a 46-yard field goal with 3:31 to play for a 30-20 lead. Robbie Gould kicked a 48-yard field goal with 13 seconds left, but his onside kick went out of bounds. Hasselbeck was 30 of 44 for 337 yards and 2 touchdowns. D.J. Hackett had 9 receptions for 136 yards. Grossman, making his first start in seven games, was 24 of 37 for 266 yards. Bernard Berrian had 9 catches for 102 yards.

Chicago	10	7	0	6	— 23
Seattle	7	10	7	6	— 30

Chi — Benson 43 run (Gould kick)
Chi — FG Gould 31
Sea — Hackett 19 pass from Hasselbeck (J. Brown kick)
Sea — Morris 19 run (J. Brown kick)
Chi — Peterson 5 run (Gould kick)
Sea — FG J. Brown 40
Sea — Burleson 4 pass from Hasselbeck (J. Brown kick)
Chi — FG Gould 47
Sea — FG J. Brown 23
Sea — FG J. Brown 46
Chi — FG Gould 48

SUNDAY NIGHT, NOVEMBER 18

NEW ENGLAND 56, BUFFALO 10—at Ralph Wilson Stadium, attendance 71,338. Randy Moss had a career-high 4 touchdown catches as the Patriots won their tenth consecutive game. New England's 56 points were the most points scored by a road team in the NFL since 1973. The Patriots outgained the Bills 510-229 in total yards, completed 8 of 11 third-down situations, and were 2-of-2 on fourth-down conversions. Thus, the Patriots were only stopped once, scoring touchdowns on each of their first seven possessions and punting with 3:49 left in the game. Randall Gay's interception 2:09 into the game set up the first touchdown, while the Patriots' other six scoring drives covered 63, 72, 84, 72, 73, and 75 yards. Kyle Eckel capped the latter drive with a 1-yard touchdown run on the first play of the fourth quarter for a 49-10 lead. Two plays later, Ellis Hobbs returned Dwayne Wright's fumble 35 yards for a touchdown and 56-10 lead with 13:59 remaining. Brady was 31 of 39 for 373 yards and 5 touchdowns. Moss had 10 catches for 128 yards. J.P. Losman was 15 of 26 for 173 yards and 1 touchdown, with 1 interception.

New England	14	21	7	14	— 56
Buffalo	7	0	3	0	— 10

NE — Maroney 6 run (Gostkowski kick)
NE — Moss 43 pass from Brady (Gostkowski kick)
Buff — Parrish 47 pass from Losman (Lindell kick)
NE — Moss 16 pass from Brady (Gostkowski kick)
NE — Moss 6 pass from Brady (Gostkowski kick)
NE — Moss 17 pass from Brady (Gostkowski kick)
Buff — FG Lindell 52
NE — Eckel 1 run (Gostkowski kick)
NE — Hobbs 35 fumble return (Gostkowski kick)

MONDAY NIGHT, NOVEMBER 19
DENVER 34, TENNESSEE 20—at INVESCO Field at Mile High, attendance 76,590. The Broncos used 4 long plays to move into a tie for first place in the AFC West. Tennessee outgained the Broncos 423-359 in total yards, had a 28-15 advantage in first downs, and controlled the ball for 35 minutes, 33 seconds, but Denver made four big plays. Jay Cutler's 48-yard touchdown pass to Brandon Stokley came on third-and-7 for a 7-0 lead. One minute, 40 seconds later, Glenn Martinez returned a punt 80 yards for a touchdown. On the opening drive of the second half, faced with third-and-6, Cutler completed a long 41-yard touchdown pass to Brandon Marshall deep down the right sideline for a 27-10 lead. Early in the fourth quarter, the Titans pulled within 27-20, but three plays later Andre Hall raced up the middle 62 yards for a touchdown and 34-20 lead with 12:48 remaining. Cutler was 16 of 21 for 200 yards and 2 touchdowns. Vince Young was 26 of 41 for 305 yards and 1 touchdown, with 2 interceptions.

Tennessee	0	10	7	3	—	20
Denver	14	6	7	7	—	34

Den	—	Stokley 48 pass from Cutler (Elam kick)
Den	—	Martinez 80 punt return (Elam kick)
Tenn	—	B. Jones 21 pass from Young (Bironas kick)
Den	—	FG Elam 21
Den	—	FG Elam 39
Tenn	—	FG Bironas 56
Den	—	Marshall 41 pass from Cutler (Elam kick)
Tenn	—	Young 4 run (Bironas kick)
Tenn	—	FG Bironas 37
Den	—	Hall 62 run (Elam kick)

TWELFTH WEEK SUMMARIES
American Football Conference

East Division	W	L	T	Pct.	Pts.	OP
New England*	11	0	0	1.000	442	185
Buffalo	5	6	0	.455	167	258
N.Y. Jets	2	9	0	.182	181	278
Miami	0	11	0	.000	183	277
North Division	**W**	**L**	**T**	**Pct.**	**Pts.**	**OP**
Pittsburgh	8	3	0	.727	272	145
Cleveland	7	4	0	.636	315	311
Baltimore	4	7	0	.364	182	243
Cincinnati	4	7	0	.364	281	292
South Division	**W**	**L**	**T**	**Pct.**	**Pts.**	**OP**
Indianapolis	9	2	0	.818	309	172
Jacksonville	8	3	0	.727	243	195
Tennessee	6	5	0	.545	204	221
Houston	5	6	0	.455	243	263
West Division	**W**	**L**	**T**	**Pct.**	**Pts.**	**OP**
San Diego	6	5	0	.545	261	223
Denver	5	6	0	.455	221	295
Kansas City	4	7	0	.364	162	206
Oakland	3	8	0	.273	200	240

National Football Conference

East Division	W	L	T	Pct.	Pts.	OP
Dallas	10	1	0	.909	358	221
N.Y. Giants	7	4	0	.636	253	241
Philadelphia	5	6	0	.455	234	218
Washington	5	6	0	.455	213	240
North Division	**W**	**L**	**T**	**Pct.**	**Pts.**	**OP**
Green Bay	10	1	0	.909	296	185
Detroit	6	5	0	.545	257	269
Chicago	5	6	0	.455	221	251
Minnesota	5	6	0	.455	236	227
South Division	**W**	**L**	**T**	**Pct.**	**Pts.**	**OP**
Tampa Bay	7	4	0	.636	214	164
New Orleans	5	6	0	.455	243	252
Carolina	4	7	0	.364	173	243
Atlanta	3	8	0	.273	155	244
West Division	**W**	**L**	**T**	**Pct.**	**Pts.**	**OP**
Seattle	7	4	0	.636	245	183
Arizona	5	6	0	.455	254	259
San Francisco	3	8	0	.273	150	254
St. Louis	2	9	0	.182	168	281

*Clinched division title

THURSDAY, NOVEMBER 22
GREEN BAY 37, DETROIT 26—at Ford Field, attendance 63,257.

Brett Favre passed for 3 touchdowns and set a club record with 20 consecutive completions, as the Packers improved to 10-1 for the first time in 45 years. The Lions drove inside the Packers' 40 on each of their first three possessions, but came away with just 2 field goals. Aaron Rouse's 34-yard interception return on the first play of the second quarter led immediately to Favre's 11-yard touchdown pass to Greg Jennings. Mason Crosby's 20-yard field goal as the half expired gave the Packers a 17-9 lead, and Green Bay drove 80 yards on their first two possessions of the second half, capped by Ruvell Martin's 3-yard touchdown catch, for a 31-12 lead with 1:48 left in the third quarter. The Lions had consecutive touchdown drives of 75 and 67 yards in the fourth quarter to pull within 34-26 with 6:34 to play. The Packers responded with a 10-play, 72-yard drive, highlighted by Ryan Grant's 27-yard run, to set up Crosby's 26-yard field goal to put the game out of reach with 1:44 to play. Favre was 31 of 41 for 381 yards and 3 touchdowns. Ryan Grant rushed 15 times for 101 yards. Donald Driver had 10 receptions for 147 yards. Kitna was 19 of 40 for 224 yards and 1 touchdown, with 1 interception.

Green Bay	0	17	14	6	—	37
Detroit	6	3	3	14	—	26

Det	—	FG Hanson 47
Det	—	FG Hanson 41
GB	—	Jennings 11 pass from Favre (Crosby kick)
GB	—	Grant 5 run (Crosby kick)
GB	—	FG Hanson 45
GB	—	FG Crosby 20
GB	—	Jennings 4 pass from Favre (Crosby kick)
Det	—	FG Hanson 52
GB	—	Martin 3 pass from Favre (Crosby kick)
GB	—	FG Crosby 20
Det	—	Johnson 6 pass from Kitna (Hanson kick)
Det	—	Jones 1 run (Hanson kick)
GB	—	FG Crosby 26

DALLAS 34, N.Y. JETS 3—at Texas Stadium, attendance 63,315. The Cowboys' defense limited the Jets to 180 yards, and Terence Newman returned an interception for a touchdown, as the Dallas improved to 10-1 for the first time in franchise history. The Cowboys maintained possession for 37 minutes, 52 seconds while gaining 344 yards. The Jets did not cross midfield until their sixth possession, by which point they trailed 21-0. The Cowboys had successive 71-yard scoring drives in the second half, capped by Tony Romo's 29th touchdown pass of the season, equaling Danny White's club record. Romo was 21 of 28 for 195 yards and 2 touchdowns, with 1 interception. Marion Barber carried 18 times for 103 yards. Kellen Clemens was 12 of 27 for 142 yards, with 1 interception.

N.Y. Jets	0	3	0	0	—	3
Dallas	7	14	3	10	—	34

Dall	—	Barber 7 run (Folk kick)
Dall	—	Witten 25 pass from Romo (Folk kick)
Dall	—	Newman 50 interception return (Folk kick)
NYJ	—	FG Nugent 40
Dall	—	FG Folk 46
Dall	—	FG Folk 27
Dall	—	Owens 22 pass from Romo (Folk kick)

THURSDAY NIGHT, NOVEMBER 22
INDIANAPOLIS 31, ATLANTA 13—at Georgia Dome, attendance 69,845. Peyton Manning passed for 3 touchdowns as the Colts improved to 9-2. The Falcons scored on their first two possessions, highlighted by Joey Harrington's 48-yard touchdown pass to Roddy White, for a 10-0 lead. The Falcons led 13-7 after Morten Andresen's second field goal, early in the second quarter, but Atlanta failed to cross the Colts' 40 on any of its remaining seven possessions. The Colts took the lead 14-13 late in the first half when Kelvin Hayden intercepted a pass. Four plays later, Manning connected with Ben Utecht on a 5-yard touchdown pass for a 21-13 lead. Rocky Boiman's interception in the second half set up Adam Vinatieri's field goal for a 31-13 lead with 32 seconds left in the third quarter. Manning was 22 of 32 for 272 yards and 3 touchdowns, with 1 interception. Anthony Gonzalez had 6 receptions for 105 yards. Harrington was 14 of 30 for 155 yards and 1 touchdown,

with 2 interceptions. Roddy White had 6 catches for 104 yards. Warrick Dunn became the 22nd player in NFL history with 10,000 rushing yards, eclipsing the mark on a 2-yard run in the second quarter.

Indianapolis	0	21	10	0	—	31
Atlanta	10	3	0	0	—	13

Atl	—	FG Andersen 34
Atl	—	White 48 pass from Harrington (Andersen kick)
Ind	—	Wayne 23 pass from P. Manning (Vinatieri kick)
Ind	—	FG Andersen 30
Atl	—	FG Andersen 34
Ind	—	Clark 8 pass from P. Manning (Vinatieri kick)
Ind	—	Utecht 5 pass from P. Manning (Vinatieri kick)
Ind	—	Addai 4 run (Vinatieri kick)
Ind	—	FG Vinatieri 24

SUNDAY, NOVEMBER 25
SAN FRANCISCO 37, ARIZONA 31 (OT)—at University of Phoenix Stadium, attendance 64,483. In overtime, Ronald Fields sacked Kurt Warner in the end zone which forced him to fumble, and Tully Banta-Cain recovered the ball for a touchdown as the 49ers snapped an eight-game losing streak. The Cardinals gained 552 yards, including 484 passing yards by Warner, but committed 4 turnovers while not forcing any. Walt Harris' interception set up the 49ers first touchdown, and Mark Roman's fumble recovery led to the second as the 49ers jumped to a 17-7 lead. However, Warner's 48-yard Hail Mary pass as the first half ended was caught in the end zone by Larry Fitzgerald to give Arizona a 21-17 lead. Trailing 24-21 and faced with fourth-and-1 on the 49ers' 2 with 10:00 to play, Tim Rattay came in to play quarterback and tossed a 2-yard touchdown pass to Ben Patrick for a 28-24 Arizona lead. Frank Gore gave the 490ers a 31-28 lead with a 35-yard touchdown run with 1:15 remaining. Beginning on their own 15-yard line, Warner completed five consecutive passes, capped by a 30-yard pass to Bryant Johnson who came down with the ball and was knocked out of bounds inches from the goal line with six seconds to play. With the clock stopped, Arizona used its final timeout, then Warner attempted a pass to Johnson that was incomplete. With two seconds left, Arizona opted for Neil Rackers' 19-yard field goal to force overtime. Sean Morey's 62-yard catch set up Rackers for a game-winning 27-yard field-goal attempt. Rackers made the kick, but the Cardinals were flagged for delay of game. Rackers then missed a 32-yard attempt wide left. Moments later, Andy Lee's 59-yard punt and an illegal block penalty on the return put the Cardinals on their own 3-yard line. Warner dropped back to pass and Fields wrapped up his arms, forcing Warner to fumble, and Banta-Cain fell on the ball for the victory. Trent Dilfer, staring in place of injured Alex Smith, was 25 of 39 for 256 yards and 2 touchdowns. Gore carried 21 times for 116 yards, and caught 11 passes for 98 yards. Warner, playing with a torn ligament in his non-throwing elbow, was 34 of 48 for a career-high 484 yards and 2 touchdowns, with 2 interceptions. Fitzgerald had 9 catches for 156 yards.

San Francisco	7	10	7	7	6	—	37
Arizona	7	14	0	10	0	—	31

Ari	—	Fitzgerald 28 pass from Warner (Rackers kick)
SF	—	Davis 2 pass from Dilfer (Nedney kick)
SF	—	FG Nedney 19
SF	—	Gore 11 run (Nedney kick)
Ari	—	Shipp 1 run (Rackers kick)
Ari	—	Fitzgerald 48 pass from Warner (Rackers kick)
SF	—	Battle 57 pass from Dilfer (Nedney kick)
Ari	—	Patrick 2 pass from Rattay (Rackers kick)
SF	—	Gore 35 run (Nedney kick)
Ari	—	FG Rackers 19
SF	—	Banta-Cain fumble recovery in end zone

NEW ORLEANS 31, CAROLINA 6—at Bank of America Stadium, attendance 72,032. Drew Brees passed for 3 touchdowns, and ran for another, as the Saints handed the Panthers their fifth consecutive home loss. The Saints' defense allowed just 195 yards and forced 4 turnovers, while the offense held onto the ball for 39 minutes, 23 seconds. The Saints led 10-6 at halftime, and opened the second half with touchdown drives of 73, 58, and 42 yards, the latter set up by Roman Harper's fumble recovery of DeShaun Foster's fumble, to take a 31-6 lead on Marques Colston's 4-yard touchdown catch with 47 seconds left in the third quarter. The three touchdown drives included five third-down conversions. Brees was 24 of 36 for 260 yards and 3 touchdowns, with 1 interception. David Carr started and was 10 of 22 for 95 yards, with 2 interceptions. Matt Moore replaced him and was 8 of 14 for 66 yards, with 1 interception.

New Orleans	0	10	21	0	—	31
Carolina	3	3	0	0	—	6

Car — FG Kasay 45
NO — L. Moore 1 pass from Brees (Mare kick)
NO — FG Mare 46
Car — FG Kasay 29
NO — Miller 1 pass from Brees (Mare kick)
NO — Brees 8 run (Mare kick)
NO — Colston 4 pass from Brees (Mare kick)

CHICAGO 37, DENVER 34 (OT)—at Soldier Field, attendance 62,148. Devin Hester had 2 scoring returns, the Bears scored twice in the final 5:17 of regulation to force overtime, and Robbie Gould made a game-winning 39-yard field goal to lift Chicago to an improbable victory. The Broncos outgained the Bears 430-293 in total yards, and forced 4 turnovers while only committing two, but Hester proved to be the equalizer. The Broncos led 13-6 at halftime, but Hester returned a punt 75 yards for a touchdown 2:11 into the third quarter to tie the game. After the Broncos drove 84 yards for a touchdown later in the third quarter, Hester returned the ensuing kickoff 88 yards for a touchdown, becoming just the ninth player in NFL history to return a punt and kickoff for a touchdown in the same game. Undaunted, on the next play from scrimmage Jay Cutler completed a 68-yard touchdown pass to Brandon Marshall for a 27-20 lead. The Broncos led 34-20 with 7:14 left when Charles Tillman blocked Todd Sauerbrun's punt. Adrian Peterson scored four plays later to cap the 18-yard drive and pull within 34-27. The Bears' defense forced another punt, and the offense drove to the Broncos' 3. On fourth-and-goal with 32 seconds left, Rex Grossman fired a pass to Bernard Berrian, who made a lunging catch and kept his foot and knee inbounds, for a touchdown to tie the game. In overtime, the Bears won the toss, and on the first play Grossman completed a 39-yard pass to Desmond Clark. Peterson then carried four times for 14 yards to set up Gould's 39-yard field goal. Grossman was 17 of 33 for 193 yards and 1 touchdown, with 1 interception. Cutler was 17 of 31 for 302 yards and 2 touchdowns, with 1 interception.

Denver	3	10	14	7	0	—	34
Chicago	3	3	14	14	3	—	37

Chi — FG Gould 24
Den — FG Elam 23
Den — Hall 16 run (Elam kick)
Chi — FG Gould 44
Den — FG Elam 22
Chi — Hester 75 punt return (Gould kick)
Den — Sapp 5 run (Elam kick)
Chi — Hester 88 kick return (Gould kick)
Den — Marshall 68 pass from Cutler (Elam kick)
Den — Scheffler 14 pass from Cutler (Elam kick)
Chi — Peterson 4 run (Gould kick)
Chi — Berrian 3 pass from Grossman (Gould kick)
Chi — FG Gould 39

CINCINNATI 35, TENNESSEE 6—at Paul Brown Stadium, attendance 65,489. Carson Palmer completed 3 touchdown passes, all to Chad Johnson, to hand the Titans their third consecutive defeat. The Bengals had 30 first downs, compared to 10 by the Titans, while compiling 426 total yards and controlling the ball for 38 minutes, 30 seconds. Rob Bironas' 23-yard field goal just before halftime cut the Titans' deficit to 14-6, but the Bengals drove 76, 52, and 82 yards with their first three drives of the second half, all resulting in touchdowns, for a 35-6 lead with 12:58 to play. Palmer was 32 of 38 for 283 yards and 3 touchdowns, with 1 interception. Johnson had 12 receptions for 103 yards, and his 531st career catch, which came in the second quarter, allowed Johnson to pass Carl Pickens for first on the club's all-time reception list. Young was 19 of 31 for 246 yards, with 1 interception.

Tennessee	0	6	0	0	—	6
Cincinnati	7	7	14	7	—	35

Cin — R. Johnson 5 run (Graham kick)
Tenn — FG Bironas 28
Cin — C. Johnson 10 pass from Palmer (Graham kick)
Tenn — FG Bironas 23
Cin — Watson 6 run (Graham kick)
Cin — C. Johnson 2 pass from Palmer (Graham kick)
Cin — C. Johnson 3 pass from Palmer (Graham kick)

CLEVELAND 27, HOUSTON 17—at Cleveland Browns Stadium, attendance 72,730. Derek Anderson passed for 2 touchdowns as the Browns won their fifth consecutive home game. The Texans led 10-7 in the second quarter when Kris Brown missed a 46-yard field-goal attempt. The Browns answered with an 11-play, 64-yard drive, keyed by Anderson's 9-yard pass to Braylon Edwards on fourth-and-3, and capped by Kellen Winslow's 7-yard touchdown catch for a 14-10 lead with 16 seconds left in the half. Winslow's 21-yard catch in the fourth quarter led to Phil Dawson's 27-yard field goal for a 20-10 lead with 8:32 remaining. Brandon McDonald intercepted a pass moments later, and Winslow caught a 20-yard pass to set up Jamal Lewis' 1-yard run for a 27-10 lead with 5:48 to play. Anderson was 24 of 35 for 253 yards and 2 touchdowns, with 1 interception. Lewis had 29 carries for 134 yards. Winslow had 10 catches for 107 yards. Matt Schaub was 22 of 36 for 256 yards and 2 touchdowns, with 2 interceptions.

Houston	7	3	0	7	—	17
Cleveland	0	14	3	10	—	27

Hou — Walter 17 pass from Schaub (K. Brown kick)
Cle — Edwards 19 pass from Anderson (Dawson kick)
Hou — FG K. Brown 41
Cle — Winslow 7 pass from Anderson (Dawson kick)
Cle — FG Dawson 25
Cle — FG Dawson 27
Cle — J. Lewis 1 run (Dawson kick)
Hou — Daniels 6 pass from Schaub (K. Brown kick)

JACKSONVILLE 36, BUFFALO 14—at Jacksonville Municipal Stadium, attendance 64,546. The Jaguars' defense forced 3 turnovers, David Garrard passed for 296 yards, and Josh Scobee kicked 5 field goals as the Jaguars won their third successive game. Jacksonville scored on four of its first five drives, taking a 16-7 halftime lead. The Jaguars added Scobee's fourth and fifth field goals on their first two possessions of the second half to take a 22-14 lead with 14:10 to play. The Bills then drove to the Jaguars' 33, but Justin Durant intercepted J.P. Losman's pass with 7:50 remaining. After an exchange of punts, the Jaguars faced third-and-7 from their own 41-yard line. Garrard fired a short pass over the middle to Reggie Williams, who raced upfield for a 59-yard touchdown and 29-14 lead with 2:39 left. The Jaguars' defense forced a four-and-out, and on the next play Maurice Jones-Drew ran up the middle for 17 yards and a touchdown with 1:43 remaining. Garrard was 23 of 37 for 296 yards and 1 touchdown. Fred Taylor rushed 14 times for 104 yards. Losman was 27 of 40 for 211 yards and 1 touchdown, with 2 interceptions.

Buffalo	0	7	7	0	—	14
Jacksonville	10	6	3	17	—	36

Jax — Taylor 50 run (Scobee kick)
Jax — FG Scobee 46
Jax — FG Scobee 33
Buff — Thomas 10 pass from Losman (Lindell kick)
Jax — FG Scobee 22
Jax — FG Scobee 23
Buff — Parrish 24 run (Lindell kick)
Jax — FG Scobee 20
Jax — Williams 59 pass from Garrard (Scobee kick)
Jax — Jones-Drew 17 run (Scobee kick)

OAKLAND 20, KANSAS CITY 17—at Arrowhead Stadium, attendance 76,210. Justin Fargas rushed for 139 yards as the Raiders snapped a six-game losing streak and 17-game losing skid to AFC West teams. Rookie Kolby Smith, making his first NFL start in place of injured Larry Johnson and the retired Priest Holmes, rushed for 94 yards and a touchdown in the first half as Kansas City led 10-6. Smith's second touchdown capped a 63-yard drive late in the third quarter and gave the Chiefs a 17-13 lead. The Chiefs then forced a punt, but Dave Rayner missed a 33-yard field goal wide left with 10:51 remaining. Culpepper then completed a 28-yard pass to Zach Miller, a 35-yard pass to Jerry Porter, and Fargas ran 14 yards for a touchdown to cap the 3-play, 77-yard drive for a 20-17 lead with 9:34 left. The Chiefs drove to the Raiders' 23, but Smith was dropped for a 1-yard loss on fourth-and-1 with 4:22 to play. Fargas' 21-yard run on third-and-11 with 1:54 remaining iced the game. Culpepper was 15 of 22 for 170 yards. Fargas had 22 carries for 139 yards. Brodie Croyle was 12 of 23 for 145 yards, with 1 interception. Smith had 31 carries for 150 yards.

Oakland	3	3	7	7	—	20
Kansas City	7	3	7	0	—	17

Oak — FG Janikowski 25
KC — Smith 10 run (Rayner kick)
Oak — FG Janikowski 54
KC — FG Rayner 30
Oak — Jordan 5 run (Janikowski kick)
KC — Smith 5 run (Rayner kick)
Oak — Fargas 14 run (Janikowski kick)

MINNESOTA 41, N.Y. GIANTS 17—at Giants Stadium, attendance 78,591. The Vikings returned 3 interceptions for a touchdown, equaling the second-most in NFL history, to defeat the Giants. On the game's second play, Tarvaris Jackson completed a 60-yard touchdown pass to Sidney Rice. Later in the quarter, Darren Sharper intercepted Eli Manning's pass an returned it 20 yards for a touchdown. Dwight Smith's interception in the second quarter was followed on the next play by Chester Taylor's 8-yard touchdown run for a 21-7 lead. Trailing 27-10, the Giants drove to the Vikings' 11 early in the fourth quarter, but Smith intercepted another pass and raced 93 yards for a touchdown. Two plays later, Chad Greenway intercepted Manning's short pass and returned it 37 yards for a touchdown and 41-10 lead with 12:59 to play. Jackson was 10 of 12 for 129 yards and 1 touchdown. Manning was 21 of 49 for 273 yards and 1 touchdown, with 4 interceptions.

Minnesota	14	10	3	14	—	41
N.Y. Giants	7	0	3	7	—	17

Minn — Rice 60 pass from Jackson (Longwell kick)
NYG — Droughns 1 run (Tynes kick)
Minn — Sharper 20 interception return (Longwell kick)
Minn — Taylor 8 run (Longwell kick)
Minn — FG Longwell 46
NYG — FG Tynes 48
Minn — FG Longwell 26
Minn — Smith 93 interception return (Longwell kick)
Minn — Greenway 37 interception return (Longwell kick)
NYG — Burress 6 pass from E. Manning (Tynes kick)

SEATTLE 24, ST. LOUIS 19—at Edward Jones Dome, attendance 65,423. Gus Frerotte fumbled a snap on fourth-and-goal from the Seahawks' 1 with 27 seconds left to allow Seattle to post its third consecutive victory. The Rams led 19-10 in the third quarter, with the Seahawks only touchdown coming on Josh Wilson's 89-yard kickoff return, when Marcus Trufant intercepted Frerotte at the Seahawks' 33. Maurice Morris' 46-yard run moments later set up Deion Branch's 9-yard touchdown catch to pull within 19-17. In the fourth quarter, Matt Hasselbeck completed all five of his pass attempts, for 61 yards on a 10-play, 80-yard drive, capped by Leonard Weaver's 56-yard touchdown run with 5:57 to play for a 24-19 Seattle lead. The Seahawks forced a punt, but Josh Brown's 52-yard field-goal attempt was wide right with 2:44 remaining. St. Louis drove to the Seahawks' 1 with 30 seconds left. Each team took a time out before Frerotte mishandled the snap. Frerotte did recover the loose ball, but he was tackled by Darryl Tapp for a 4-yard loss. Hasselbeck was 21 of 38 for 249 yards and 1 touchdown, with 1 interception. Frerotte was 20 of 32 for 161 yards and 1 touchdown, with 1 interception.

Seattle	7	0	10	7	—	24
St. Louis	16	3	0	0	—	19

StL — Safety, Carriker tackled Morris in end zone
StL — Jackson 53 run (Wilkins kick)
Sea — Wilson 89 kickoff return (J. Brown kick)
StL — Bruce 17 pass from Frerotte (Wilkins kick)
StL — FG Wilkins 23
Sea — FG J. Brown 33
Sea — Branch 9 pass from Hasselbeck (J. Brown kick)
Sea — Weaver 5 run (J. Brown kick)

SAN DIEGO 32, BALTIMORE 14—at Qualcomm Stadium, attendance 63,337. Philip Rivers passed for 3 touchdowns and the Chargers' defense allowed just 210 yards and registered 4 sacks to hand the Ravens their fifth consecutive loss. The Chargers scored on six consecutive possessions spanning 16 minutes, 41 seconds. Two of the scores were set up by fumbles, while the other four were quick-strike drives of 47, 60, 49, and 72 yards. LaDainian Tomlinson passed the 10,000-rushing yards mark on his 36-yard run in the third quarter, becoming the 23rd player in NFL history to reach the five-digit milestone. Three plays after Tomlinson's run, Rivers completed a 25-yard touchdown pass to Antonio Gates for a 29-7 lead with 11:30 left in the third quarter. Rivers was 25 of 35 for 249 yards and 3 touchdowns. Gates had 6 receptions for 105 yards and 2 touchdowns. Kyle Boller was 21 of 33 for 191 yards and 1 touchdown.

| Baltimore | 0 | 7 | 7 | 0 | — | 14 |
| San Diego | 0 | 22 | 7 | 3 | — | 32 |

SD — FG Kaeding 27
Balt — McGahee 1 run (Stover kick)
SD — Gates 35 pass from Rivers (kick failed)
SD — FG Kaeding 46
SD — Chambers 5 pass from Rivers (Kaeding kick)
SD — FG Kaeding 41
SD — Gates 25 pass from Rivers (Kaeding kick)
Balt — McClain 24 pass from Boller (Stover kick)
SD — FG Kaeding 41

TAMPA BAY 19, WASHINGTON 13—at Raymond James Stadium, attendance 65,596. Despite Jeff Garcia's first-quarter injury and the Redskins outgaining the Buccaneers 412-192 in total yards, Tampa Bay forced 6 turnovers and Brian Kelly intercepted a pass in the end zone with 17 seconds left to hold off the Redskins. Washington fumbled on four of its first five possessions. All four were recovered inside the Redskins' 32, and Tampa Bay converted them into a touchdown and three field goals to take a 16-0 lead. Matt Bryant's fourth field goal of the half came as time expired to give Tampa Bay a 19-3 lead. Washington drove 73 yards to begin the second half, capped by Jason Campbell's 39-yard touchdown pass to Chris Cooley on third-and-9 to pull within 19-10. The Redskins drove to the Buccaneers' 4 late in the third quarter, but on fourth-and-1 Derrick Brooks stopped Clinton Portis for no gain. The Redskins kicked a field goal, and then drove to the Buccaneers' 32, but Ronde Barber intercepted Campbell's pass with 3:40 to play. The Redskins' defense forced a punt and the offense drove to the Tampa Bay 16-yard line when Kelly intercepted Campbell's pass in the end zone with 17 seconds remaining to clinch the game. Garcia was 2 of 4 for 9 yards. He injured his back on the first play, and did return in the fourth quarter. Bruce Gradkowski replaced him and was 9 of 19 for 106 yards. Campbell was 30 of 49 for 301 yards and 1 touchdown, with 2 interceptions.

| Washington | 0 | 3 | 7 | 3 | — | 13 |
| Tampa Bay | 10 | 9 | 0 | 0 | — | 19 |

TB — Graham 1 run (Bryant kick)
TB — FG Bryant 35
TB — FG Bryant 27
TB — FG Bryant 48
Wash — FG Suisham 43
TB — FG Bryant 49
Wash — Cooley 39 pass from Campbell (Suisham kick)
Wash — FG Suisham 38

SUNDAY NIGHT, NOVEMBER 25
NEW ENGLAND 31, PHILADELPHIA 28—at Gillette Stadium,

attendance 68,756. Asante Samuel intercepted 2 passes as the Patriots overcame a scare to improve their record to 11-0. Three plays into the game, Samuel intercepted A.J. Feeley's pass and returned it 40 yards for a touchdown. The Patriots scored on all three of their first-half possessions, on drives of 78, 75, and 54 yards, but the Eagles had touchdown drives of 77, 76, and 68 yards and trailed just 24-21. Stephen Gostkowski missed a 32-yard field-goal attempt in the third quarter. On the ensuing drive Feeley, starting in place of injured Donovan McNabb, completed 3 key passes, and capped the possession with an 8-yard touchdown pass to Reggie Brown on third down for a 28-24 lead with 1:34 left in the third quarter. Laurence Maroney scored on a 4-yard run to cap a 10-play, 69-yard drive to take a 31-28 lead with 7:20 to play. The Eagles methodically drove to the Patriots' 29, but Feeley overthrew Kevin Curtis and Samuel intercepted a pass in the end zone for a touchback with 3:52 to play. The Eagles did not get the ball back until their were 18 seconds left, on their own 22, and James Sanders intercepted Feeley's final pass. Brady was 34 of 54 for 380 yards and 1 touchdown. Wes Welker had 13 catches for 149 yards. Feeley was 27 of 42 for 345 yards and 3 touchdowns, with 3 interceptions.

| Philadelphia | 7 | 14 | 7 | 0 | — | 28 |
| New England | 14 | 10 | 0 | 7 | — | 31 |

NE — Samuel 40 interception (Gostkowski kick)
Phil — Westbrook 1 run (Akers kick)
NE — Evans 1 run (Gostkowski kick)
Phil — G. Lewis 28 pass from Feeley (Akers kick)
NE — FG Gostkowski 23
Phil — G. Lewis 18 pass from Feeley (Akers kick)
NE — Gaffney 19 pass from Brady (Gostkowski kick)
Phil — R. Brown 8 pass from Feeley (Akers kick)
NE — Maroney 4 run (Gostkowski kick)

MONDAY NIGHT, NOVEMBER 26
PITTSBURGH 3, MIAMI 0—at Heinz Field, attendance 57,704. Jeff Reed kicked a 24-yard field goal with 17 seconds left as the Steelers won a game played in a downpour. The game was scoreless for 59 minutes, 43 seconds, the deepest a game had no points since a scoreless tie 64 years earlier, in 1943. The Steelers outgained the Dolphins 216-159 in total yards, while forcing two of the games three turnovers. Joey Porter intercepted Ben Roethlisberger's pass at the Dolphins' 21 to stop the game's opening drive, but neither team drove inside the opponents' 35 the remainder of the half. In the third quarter, on fourth-and-15 from the Steelers' 31, James Farrior and Larry Foote combined to sack John Beck. Later in the third quarter, the Steelers attempted a 44-yard field-goal attempt, but Jeff Reed's kick sailed wide left. The Dolphins drove to the Steelers' 25 early in the fourth quarter, but James Harrison sacked Beck on fourth-and-11. Roethlisberger's 21-yard pass to Hines Ward, and his 6-yard pass to Willie Reid on third-and-3 to the Dolphins' 6 with 1:19 left set up Reed's game-winning kick. Roethlisberger was 18 of 21 for 165 yards, with 1 interception. Beck was 14 of 23 for 132 yards.

| Miami | 0 | 0 | 0 | 0 | — | 0 |
| Pittsburgh | 0 | 0 | 0 | 3 | — | 3 |

Pitt — FG Reed 24

THIRTEENTH WEEK SUMMARIES
American Football Conference

East Division	W	L	T	Pct.	Pts.	OP
New England*	12	0	0	1.000	469	209
Buffalo	6	6	0	.500	184	274
N.Y. Jets	3	9	0	.250	221	291
Miami	0	12	0	.000	196	317
North Division	**W**	**L**	**T**	**Pct.**	**Pts.**	**OP**
Pittsburgh	9	3	0	.750	296	155
Cleveland	7	5	0	.583	336	338
Baltimore	4	8	0	.333	206	270
Cincinnati	4	8	0	.333	291	316
South Division	**W**	**L**	**T**	**Pct.**	**Pts.**	**OP**
Indianapolis	10	2	0	.833	337	197
Jacksonville	8	4	0	.667	268	223
Tennessee	7	5	0	.583	232	241
Houston	5	7	0	.417	263	291
West Division	**W**	**L**	**T**	**Pct.**	**Pts.**	**OP**
San Diego	7	5	0	.583	285	233

Denver	5	7	0	.417	241	329
Kansas City	4	8	0	.333	172	230
Oakland	4	8	0	.333	234	260

National Football Conference

East Division	W	L	T	Pct.	Pts.	OP
Dallas#	11	1	0	.917	395	248
N.Y. Giants	8	4	0	.667	274	257
Philadelphia	5	7	0	.417	258	246
Washington	5	7	0	.417	229	257
North Division	**W**	**L**	**T**	**Pct.**	**Pts.**	**OP**
Green Bay	10	2	0	.833	323	222
Detroit	6	6	0	.500	267	311
Minnesota	6	6	0	.500	278	237
Chicago	5	7	0	.417	237	272
South Division	**W**	**L**	**T**	**Pct.**	**Pts.**	**OP**
Tampa Bay	8	4	0	.667	241	187
Carolina	5	7	0	.417	204	257
New Orleans	5	7	0	.417	266	279
Atlanta	3	9	0	.250	171	272
West Division	**W**	**L**	**T**	**Pct.**	**Pts.**	**OP**
Seattle	8	4	0	.667	273	207
Arizona	6	6	0	.500	281	280
St. Louis	3	9	0	.250	196	297
San Francisco	3	9	0	.250	164	265

*Clinched division title
#Clinched playoff berth

THURSDAY NIGHT, NOVEMBER 29
DALLAS 37, GREEN BAY 27—at Georgia Dome, attendance 64,167. In the first matchup of 10-1 teams since 1990, Tony Romo passed for 4 touchdowns as the Cowboys clinched their first five possessions to clinch a playoff berth. Ken Hamlin's interception late in the first quarter set up Romo's first touchdown pass, a 3-yard strike to Patrick Crayton for a 13-3 lead. Terence Newman intercepted a Brett Favre pass in the second quarter. Favre was hit by blitzing cornerback Nate Jones while throwing the pass and injured his throwing elbow and separated his left shoulder. Two plays later Romo set the Cowboys' single-season record with his 32nd touchdown pass, finding Terrell Owens from 10 yards, for a 27-10 lead with still 9:53 left in the first half. Third-year backup Aaron Rodgers entered the game and completed his first NFL touchdown pass, an 11-yard pass to Greg Jennings just before halftime, to cut the deficit to 27-17. The Packers' defense opened the second half by stopping Julius Jones for 1 yard on fourth-and-2, and the offense drove 69 yards, capped by Ryan Grant's second touchdown to pull within 27-24 with 5:15 left in the third quarter. Al Harris then intercepted a pass for a touchback, but the Cowboys broke through on the ensuing possession with a 7-play, 75-yard drive, capped by Romo's 4-yard scoring pass to Crayton on third-and-goal for a 34-24 lead with 7:51 to play. Rodgers engineered another drive to set up Mason Crosby's 52-yard field goal with 5:03 remaining, but Marion Barber carried seven times on the ensuing nine-play drive, capped by Nick Folk's 25-yard field goal with 1:03 left. Romo was 19 of 30 for 309 yards and 4 touchdowns, with 1 interception. Owens had 7 receptions for 156 yards. Favre was 5 of 14 for 56 yards, with 2 interceptions. Rodgers was 18 of 26 for 201 yards and 1 touchdown.

| Green Bay | 10 | 7 | 7 | 3 | — | 27 |
| Dallas | 13 | 14 | 0 | 10 | — | 37 |

GB — FG Crosby 47
Dall — FG Folk 26
Dall — FG Folk 51
Dall — Crayton 3 pass from Romo (Folk kick)
GB — Grant 62 run (Crosby kick)
Dall — Fasano 26 pass from Romo (Folk kick)
Dall — Owens 10 pass from Romo (Folk kick)
GB — Jennings 11 pass from Rodgers (Crosby kick)
GB — Grant 1 run (Crosby kick)
Dall — Crayton 4 pass from Romo (Folk kick)
GB — FG Crosby 52
Dall — FG Folk 25

SUNDAY, DECEMBER 2
ARIZONA 27, CLEVELAND 21—at University of Phoenix Stadium, attendance 64,791. Kellen Winslow nearly landed inbounds with a 37-yard touchdown catch as time expired, but the pass was incom-

plete as the Cardinals held off the Browns. The Cardinals' defense forced 4 turnovers that were converted into 21 points, including a 71-yard interception return by Roderick Hood less than five minutes into the game. Three plays after Hood's return, Derek Anderson fumbled and Antonio Smith recovered to set up Kurt Warner's 5-yard touchdown pass to Leonard Pope for a 14-0 lead. Late in the third quarter, Joshua Cribbs muffed a punt. Ralph Brown recovered at the Browns' 22, and eight plays later Bryant Johnson caught a 1-yard touchdown pass for a 21-10 lead. Arizona was leading 24-21 with two minutes left and the ball on the Browns' 1, and facing second-and-goal, but Edgerrin James was twice stopped for no gain, so the Cardinals had to settle for Neil Rackers' 19-yard field goal for a 27-21 advantage with 1:48 to play. The Browns drove to the Cardinals' 37, and on the game's final play, Anderson lofted a pass to the left side of the end zone, where Winslow faced double coverage. Winslow leapt in the air and caught the ball, over the defenders, but came down just out of bounds. Warner was 18 of 30 for 169 yards and 2 touchdowns, with 1 interception. James had 24 carries for 114 yards. Anderson was 21 of 41 for 304 yards and 2 touchdowns,with 2 interceptions. Braylon Edwards had 7 catches for 149 yards.

Cleveland	3	7	8	3	—	21
Arizona	14	0	7	6	—	27

Ari — Hood 71 interception return (Rackers kick)
Ari — Pope 5 pass from Warner (Rackers kick)
Cle — FG Dawson 37
Cle — J. Lewis 6 pass from Anderson (Dawson kick)
Ari — Bry. Johnson 1 pass from Warner (Rackers kick)
Cle — Edwards 67 pass from Anderson (Winslow pass from Cribbs)
Ari — FG Rackers 33
Cle — FG Dawson 22
Ari — FG Rackers 19

CAROLINA 31, SAN FRANCISCO 14—at Bank of America Stadium, attendance 73,191. The Panthers' defense forced 6 turnovers, registered 6 sacks, and limited the 49ers to 195 total yards en route to their first home victory of the season. The Panthers had 51- and 80-yard scoring drives before Richard Marshall intercepted a pass and returned it 73 yards for a touchdown and 17-0 lead with 6:43 remaining in the first half. The 49ers scored touchdowns on their first two possessions of the second half, thanks to an interception by Michael Lewis and a 41-yard punt return by Nate Clements, to pull within 17-14. But Lewis muffed a punt later in the quarter at the 49ers' 11, and DeShaun Foster scored four plays later for a 24-14 lead. The Panthers then put the game away with a 14-play, 83-yard drive, which included four third-down conversions, capped by Vinny Testaverde's 1-yard scoring pass to Jeff King with 10:26 to play. Testaverde was 17 of 26 for 169 yards and 2 touchdowns, with 2 interceptions. At 44 years, 19 days, the victory proved the last of Testaverde's career, bettering his own record as the oldest winning starting quarterback in an NFL game. Trent Dilfer was 14 of 29 for 171 yards and 2 touchdowns, with 4 interceptions.

San Francisco	0	0	14	0	—	14
Carolina	3	14	7	7	—	31

Car — FG Kasay 19
Car — Rosario 5 pass from Testaverde (Kasay kick)
Car — Marshall 73 interception return (Kasay kick)
SF — Battle 20 pass from Dilfer (Nedney kick)
SF — Walker 21 pass from Dilfer (Nedney kick)
Car — Foster 1 run (Kasay kick)
Car — King 1 pass from Testaverde (Kasay kick)

N.Y. GIANTS 21, CHICAGO 16—at Soldier Field, attendance 62,244. The Giants scored twice in the final seven minutes, culminated by Reuben Droughns' 2-yard touchdown run with 1:33 to play, to overcome four turnovers and defeat the Bears. In the third quarter, Adewale Ogunleye recovered Derrick Ward's fumble at the Giants' 24 to set up Robbie Gould's 41-yard field goal for a 16-7 Bears lead. Late in the quarter, the Giants drove to the Bears' 1, but Charles Tillman intercepted Eli Manning's pass to thwart the drive. Manning rebounded by engineering an 11-play, 75-yard drive, capped by Amani Toomer's 6-yard touchdown catch to cut the deficit to 16-14 with 6:54 to play. The Giants' defense then forced a three-and-out and Manning completed a 24-yard pass to David Tyree and 15-yard pass to Plaxico Burress to reach the Bears' 2. Droughns scored on the next play to cap the 9-play, 77-yard drive for a 21-16 lead with 1:33 remaining. The Bears drove to the Giants' 28, but Rex Grossman's final three passes fell incomplete, the last one broken up by James Butler. Manning was 16 of 27 for 195 yards and 1 touchdown, with 2 interceptions. Ward had 24 carries for 154 yards. Grossman was 25 of 46 for 296 yards and 1 touchdowns.

N.Y. Giants	0	7	0	14	—	21
Chicago	7	6	3	0	—	16

Chi — Clark 1 pass from Grossman (Gould kick)
NYG — Ward 2 run (Tynes kick)
Chi — FG Gould 35
Chi — FG Gould 46
Chi — FG Gould 41
NYG — Toomer 6 pass from E. Manning (Tynes kick)
NYG — Droughns 2 run (Tynes kick)

INDIANAPOLIS 28, JACKSONVILLE 25—at RCA Dome, attendance 57,302. Peyton Manning passed for 4 touchdowns as the Colts extended their lead over the Jaguars in the AFC South to two games. The Colts scored on their final three first-half possessions, capped by Dallas Clark's touchdown catch with six seconds left in the half, for a 21-7 lead. The Jaguars opened the second half with scoring drives of 12 and 13 plays, the latter set up by Reggie Nelson's interception, to pull within 21-17 with 11:36 to play. The Colts answered with a 7-play, 63-yard drive, culminated with Manning's 1-yard shovel touchdown pass to Luke Lawton, who had just re-signed with the Colts that week, with 8:26 remaining. Antoine Bethea intercepted a pass at the Colts' 2 to stop the next drive, but following a punt, David Garrard completed a 17-yard touchdown pass to Dennis Northcutt. Garrard's 2-point conversion run cut the deficit to 28-25 with 2:47 left. Joseph Addai's 2-yard run on third-and-1 with 1:58 to play clinched the victory. Manning was 20 of 29 for 288 yards and 4 touchdowns, with 1 interception. Reggie Wayne had 8 catches for 158 yards. Garrard was 24 of 29 for 257 yards and 2 touchdowns, with 1 interception. Fred Taylor had 14 carries for 104 yards.

Jacksonville	0	7	7	11	—	25
Indianapolis	14	7	0	7	—	28

Ind — Clark 5 pass from P. Manning (Vinatieri kick)
Ind — Wayne 48 pass from P. Manning (Vinatieri kick)
Jax — Jones-Drew 12 run (Scobee kick)
Ind — Clark 15 pass from P. Manning (Vinatieri kick)
Jax — M. Lewis 2 pass from Garrard (Scobee kick)
Jax — FG Scobee 47
Ind — Lawton 1 pass from P. Manning (Vinatieri kick)
Jax — Northcutt 17 pass from Garrard (Garrard run)

SAN DIEGO 24, KANSAS CITY 10—at Arrowhead Stadium, attendance 74,874. LaDainian Tomlinson rushed for 177 yards and 2 touchdowns, and the Chargers' defense registered 9 sacks and forced 4 turnovers, to hand the Chiefs their fifth consecutive defeat. Defensive end Jared Allen, lined up as a tight end, caught a 2-yard touchdown pas in the second quarter to give the Chiefs a 10-3 lead. The Chargers answered with a Philip Rivers' 38-yard touchdown pass to Vincent Jackson to tie the game, and Tomlinson scored on a 31-yard run to open the second half to take a 17-10 lead. The Chiefs drove the the Chargers' 28, but Damon Huard's fourth-and-3 pass fell incomplete. In the fourth quarter, Tomlinson had a 34-yard run, and three plays later broke for for a 28-yard run over left tackle for a 24-10 lead. The touchdown was his 111th rushing touchdown, moving him past Walter Payton for third on the all-time list. Drayton Florence intercepted Huard's pass at the Chargers' 21 with 5:19 to play. Huard was injured on the play, and, after a punt, Tyler Thigpen made his first NFL appearance. He drove the Chiefs to the Chargers' 11, but Antonio Cromartie's interception in the end zone with 2:47 left clinched the victory. Rivers was 10 of 21 for 157 yards and 1 touchdown, with 1 interception. Tomlinson had 23 carries for 177 yards. Huard was 19 of 34 for 186 yards and 1 touchdown, with 2 interceptions. Thigpen was 2 of 6 for 41 yards, with 1 interception. Tony Gonzalez had 10 catches for 140 yards.

San Diego	3	7	7	7	—	24
Kansas City	3	7	0	0	—	10

KC — FG Carney 38
SD — FG Kaeding 25
KC — Allen 2 pass from Huard (Carney kick)
SD — Jackson 38 pass from Rivers (Kaeding kick)
SD — Tomlinson 31 run (Kaeding kick)
SD — Tomlinson 28 run (Kaeding kick)

N.Y. JETS 40, MIAMI 13—at Dolphin Stadium, attendance 71,109. Leon Washington scored twice and the Jets' defense allowed just 187 yards and forced 5 turnovers to defeat the Dolphins. In the second quarter, Will Allen sacked Kellen Clemens and forced him to fumble. Michael Lehan recovered the ball and returned it 43 yards for a touchdown and 13-10 Dolphins lead. However, the Jets scored twice in the final 2:39 of the half, the latter set up by Kerry Rhodes' interception and 36-yard return, to take a 20-13 lead. In the third quarter, Bryan Thomas sacked John Beck and forced him to fumble. Victor Hobson recovered to set up Mike Nugent's third field goal for a 23-13 lead. Moments later, rookie David Harris pulled a hat trick as he sacked Beck, forced him to fumble and recovered the ball. Thomas Jones scored eight plays later for a commanding 30-13 lead. Clemens was 15 of 24 for 236 yards and 1 touchdown, with 1 interception. Beck was 23 of 39 for 177 yards, with 3 interceptions.

N.Y. Jets	7	13	3	17	—	40
Miami	3	10	0	0	—	13

NYJ — L. Washington 18 run (Nugent kick)
Mia — FG Feely 53
Mia — FG Feely 44
NYJ — FG Nugent 29
Mia — Lehan 43 fumble return (Feely kick)
NYJ — B. Smith 19 pass from Clemens (Nugent kick)
NYJ — FG Nugent 40
NYJ — FG Nugent 35
NYJ — T. Jones 1 run (Nugent kick)
NYJ — FG Nugent 26
NYJ — L. Washington 12 run (Nugent kick)

MINNESOTA 42, DETROIT 10—at Metrodome, attendance 62,996. After missing two games with an injured knee, Adrian Peterson rushed for 116 yards and 2 touchdowns as the Vikings scored touchdowns on their first six possessions to post their third successive victory. The Vikings outgained the Lions 443-253 in total yards. Leading 14-10, Aundrae Allison returned a kickoff 104 yards for a touchdown with 9:23 left in the half. The Vikings' defense then forced a three-and-out, and Tarvaris Jackson engineered a 51-yard drive, capped by Bobby Wade's 6-yard touchdown catch with 2:17 left in the second quarter. Ray Edwards sacked Jon Kitna five plays later. Kenechi Udeze recovered and returned the ball 37 yards to set up Sidney Rice's 2-yard touchdown catch with five seconds left for a 35-10 halftime lead. Peterson capped the 66-yard opening drive of the second half with a dazzling 13-yard touchdown run. Jackson was 18 of 24 for 204 yards and 2 touchdowns, with 1 interception. Peterson carried 15 times for 116 yards. Kitna was 27 of 35 for 260 yards and 1 touchdown.

Detroit	3	7	0	0	—	10
Minnesota	7	28	7	0	—	42

Minn — Taylor 2 run (Longwell kick)
Det — FG Hanson 37
Minn — Peterson 16 run (Longwell kick)
Det — FitzSimmons 1 pass from Kitna (Hanson kick)
Minn — Allison 104 kickoff return (Longwell kick)
Minn — Wade 6 pass from Jackson (Longwell kick)
Minn — Rice 2 pass from Jackson (Longwell kick)
Minn — Peterson 13 run (Longwell kick)

TAMPA BAY 27, NEW ORLEANS 23—at Louisiana Superdome,

attendance 70,009. Jerramy Stevens caught a 1-yard touchdown pass with 14 seconds left as the Buccaneers took advantage of a late Saints turnover to take a commanding three-game lead in the NFC South. With Luke McCown starting in place of injured Jeff Garcia, McCown completed his first 15 passes as the Buccaneers rolled up 466 yards of offense and scored on three of their first four possessions. However, the Saints had scoring drives of 57 and 67 yards for a 14-13 halftime lead. Earnest Graham scored on a 25-yard run in the third quarter for a 20-14 lead, and the Buccaneers' defense then forced a punt. But Mike McKenzie stepped in front of McCown's short pass and returned it 53 yards for a touchdown and 21-20 Saints lead. Steve Weatherford's 53-yard punt bounced out of bounds at the Buccaneers' 2 with 3:56 left, and two plays later Will Smith sacked McCown for a safety. But two plays after the free kick, from the Saints' 49, New Orleans attempted a reverse. Reggie Bush tossed the ball to Devery Henderson, but the toss was low and Jovan Haye recovered. McCown's 21-yard pass to Graham got the Buccaneers to the Saints' 5, and on third-and-goal McCown found Stevens in the end zone for a touchdown with 14 seconds to play. McCown was 29 of 37 for 313 yards and 2 touchdowns, with 1 interception. Graham rushed 22 times for 106 yards, and Joey Galloway had 7 catches for 159 yards. Drew Brees was 17 of 23 for 179 yards and 2 touchdowns.

Tampa Bay	3	10	7	7	—	27
New Orleans	7	7	7	2	—	23

TB — FG Bryant 27
NO — Copper 4 pass from Brees (Mare kick)
TB — Becht 1 pass from L. McCown (Bryant kick)
TB — FG Bryant 31
NO — Henderson 45 pass from Brees (Mare kick)
TB — Graham 25 run (Bryant kick)
NO — McKenzie 53 interception return (Mare kick)
NO — Safety, W. Smith sacked L. McCown in end zone
TB — Stevens 4 pass from L. McCown (Bryant kick)

OAKLAND 34, DENVER 20—at McAfee Coliseum, attendance 61,990. Josh McCown passed for 3 touchdowns as the Raiders built a 17-point lead before withstanding a late rally to post back-to-back victories. The Raiders defense forced 4 turnovers, which resulted in 24 points. Robert Thomas' fumble recovery in the second quarter at the Broncos' 35 led to Zach Miller's 13-yard touchdown catch for a 14-7 lead. The Raiders scored twice within 1:45 of the third quarter, with Jerry Porter's 13-yard touchdown catch, which was set up by Chris Clemons' fumble recovery, giving the Raiders a 24-7 lead. The Broncos scored on their next three possessions to pull within 24-20 with 11:21 remaining. But the Raiders responded as McCown completed 26- and 19-yards passes to Miller to set up Sebastian Janikowski's 44-yard field goal. On the next play, Fabian Washington intercepted Jay Cutler's pass to spark a 10-play, 43-yard drive, which featured seven carries by Justin Fargas and culminated with his 5-yard touchdown run with 3:04 to play. McCown was 14 of 21 for 141 yards and 3 touchdowns. First overall draft pick JaMarcus Russell made his NFL debut in the second quarter, and was 4 of 7 for 56 yards. Fargas rushed 33 times for 146 yards. Cutler was 16 of 32 for 214 yards, with 2 interceptions. Brandon Stokley had 3 catches for 102 yards.

Denver	7	0	6	7	—	20
Oakland	7	7	10	10	—	34

Oak — Dwight 15 pass from J. McCown (Janikowski kick)
Den — T. Henry 4 run (Elam kick)
Oak — Miller 13 pass from J. McCown (Janikowski kick)
Oak — FG Janikowski 38
Oak — Porter 13 pass from J. McCown (Janikowski kick)
Den — FG Elam 29
Den — FG Elam 44
Den — T. Henry 3 run (Elam kick)
Oak — FG Janikowski 44
Oak — Fargas 5 run (Janikowski kick)

SEATTLE 28, PHILADELPHIA 24—at Lincoln Financial Field, attendance 68,445. Lofa Tatupu intercepted 3 passes as the Seahawks won in the rain. With A.J. Feeley playing in place of injured Donovan McNabb for a second consecutive week, Tatupu intercepted him on the first play of he game to set up Shaun Alexander's touchdown run. Tatupu's second interception, later in the first quarter, was returned 49 yards to set up Bobby Engram's 21-yard touchdown catch. Late in the first half, the Eagles drove to the Seahawks' 1. Trailing 21-17, Brian Westbrook was stopped for no gain, Feeley threw an incomplete pass, and Westbrook again was stopped for no gain. On fourth-and-goal, Westbrook was submarined by Rocky Bernard for no gain as the Seahawks went into the locker room with the lead. Maurice Morris' 45-yard touchdown run in the third quarter gave the Seahawks a 28-24 lead. The Eagles forced a punt with 1:16 to play, and Westbrook returned it 64 yards to the Seahawks' 14. But on third-and-7, Tatupu intercepted Feeley's pass with 14 seconds left to clinch the victory. Hasselbeck was 19 of 34 for 187 yards and 2 touchdowns, with 1 interception. Feeley was 19 of 42 for 220 yards and 1 touchdown, with 4 interceptions.

Seattle	14	7	7	0	—	28
Philadelphia	10	7	7	0	—	24

Sea — Alexander 2 run (J. Brown kick)
Phil — Buckhalter 30 run (Akers kick)
Sea — Engram 12 pass from Hasselbeck (J. Brown kick)
Phil — FG Akers 31
Sea — Burleson 43 pass from Hasselbeck (J. Brown kick)
Phil — Curtis 24 pass from Feeley (Akers kick)
Phil — Westbrook 29 run (Akers kick)
Sea — Morris 45 run (J. Brown kick)

ST. LOUIS 28, ATLANTA 16—at Edward Jones Dome, attendance 62,051. Gus Frerotte passed for 3 touchdowns as the Rams posted their first home victory. The Rams had touchdown drives of 75, 95, and 80 yards in the first half for a 21-0 lead. The Falcons gained 283 of their 435 yards after halftime as Chris Redman sparked a fierce rally. Trailing 21-3, Redman engineered scoring drives of 80 and 72 yards to pull within 21-16 with 7:17 to play. Two plays later, Chris Crocker intercepted Frerotte's pass to give the Falcons the ball on the Rams' 33. Atlanta drove to the Rams' 9, but on fourth-and-7 Redman's pass fell incomplete. The Falcons' defense forced a three-and-out to give Atlanta the ball near midfield, but on the next play Oshiomogho Atogwe intercepted Redman's pass. Steven Jackson scored on a 50-yard run two plays later to ice the game. Frerotte was 23 of 35 for 311 yards and 3 touchdowns, with 2 interceptions. Torry Holt had 6 catches for 135 yards. Joey Harrington was 17 of 34 for 184 yards, with 1 interception. Redman replaced him in the third quarter and was 16 of 24 for 172 yards and 2 touchdowns, with 1 interception. Roddy White had 10 receptions for 146 yards.

Atlanta	0	0	3	13	—	16
St. Louis	14	7	0	7	—	28

StL — McMichael 1 pass from Frerotte (Wilkins kick)
StL — Holt 31 pass from Frerotte (Wilkins kick)
StL — Bruce 8 pass from Frerotte (Wilkins kick)
Atl — FG Andersen 41
Atl — R. White 15 pass from Redman (pass failed)
Atl — Jenkins 5 pass from Redman (Andersen kick)
StL — Jackson 50 run (Wilkins kick)

TENNESSEE 28, HOUSTON 20—at LP Field, attendance 69,143. Vince Young passed for 248 yards and 2 touchdowns at the Titans snapped a three-game losing skid. With the score 7-7 in the first quarter, Matt Schaub was injured on a sack by Antwan Odom and left the game, but the Texans led 10-7 at halftime. Young's 43-yard touchdown pass to Roydell Williams on a deep fly pattern early in the third quarter gave the Titans their first lead in four games. Tennessee forced a punt, and Young engineered a 12-play, 87-yard drive, capped by Justin Gage's 11-yard touchdown for a 21-10 lead. The Texans cut the deficit to 21-17, and then forced a punt but Jacoby Jones muffed it and Donnie Nickey recovered. Two plays later, Chris Brown scored on a 7-yard run for a 28-17 lead with 9:49 to play. The Texans cut the deficit to 28-20 and got the ball back with 2:50 left, but Michael Griffin intercepted Sage Rosenfels' pass to secure the victory. Young was 21 of 31 for 248 yards and 2 touchdowns, with 1 interception. Schaub was 3 of 5 for 34 yards, while Rosenfels was 17 of 30 for 185 yards and 1 touchdown, with 1 interception. Andre Johnson had 9 catches for 116 yards.

Houston	7	3	0	10	—	20
Tennessee	7	0	14	7	—	28

Hou — Dayne 1 run (K. Brown kick)
Tenn — L. White 1 run (Bironas kick)
Hou — FG K. Brown 45
Tenn — R. Williams 43 pass from Young (Bironas kick)
Tenn — Gage 11 pass from Young (Bironas kick)
Hou — A. Johnson 28 pass from Rosenfels (K. Brown kick)
Tenn — C. Brown 7 run (Bironas kick)
Hou — FG K. Brown 50

BUFFALO 17, WASHINGTON 16—at FedExField, attendance 85,831. A 15-yard penalty by the Redskins set up Rian Lindell to make a 36-yard field goal with four seconds left as the Bills shocked the Redskins. The defeat came five days after the death of Sean Taylor. Clinton Portis capped a 57-yard drive in the third quarter with a touchdown for a 16-5 lead. Angelo Crowell, who had sacked Jason Campbell for a safety in the first half, recovered a fumble late in the third quarter to set up Lindell's second field goal, and Larry Tripplett's interception led to Lindell's third field goal. Trent Edwards' 54-yard pass to Fred Jackson on the Bills' next possession set up Lindell's 33-yard field goal to pull within 16-14 with 6:33 to play. Starting from their own 22-yard line with 56 seconds left and no timeouts, Edwards completed three straight passes, the third a 30-yard strike to Josh Reed to reach the Redskins' 33 with eight seconds left. The Redskins then called consecutive time outs to ice Lindell, which is an unsportsmanlike conduct penalty. Lindell made the ensuing 36-yard field goal. Edwards was 22 of 36 for 257 yards. Campbell was 21 of 37 for 236 yards, with 1 interception.

Buffalo	0	2	6	9	—	17
Washington	3	6	7	0	—	16

Wash — FG Suisham 27
Wash — FG Suisham 28
Buff — Safety, Crowell sacked Campbell in end zone
Wash — FG Suisham 33
Buff — FG Lindell 38
Wash — Portis 3 run (Suisham kick)
Buff — FG Lindell 43
Buff — FG Lindell 24
Buff — FG Lindell 33
Buff — FG Lindell 36

SUNDAY NIGHT, DECEMBER 2

PITTSBURGH 24, CINCINNATI 10—at Heinz Field, attendance 58,842. Hines Ward caught 2 touchdown passes, the second of which was his 64th and allowed him to pass John Stallworth for first on the franchise's all-time touchdown reception list, as the Steelers improved to 7-0 at home. The Bengals drove 75 yards to open the game, and had a chance for a 10-point lead, but Shayne Graham's 43-yard field-goal attempt in the rain sailed wide right. The Steelers responded by scoring on all three of their second-quarter possessions, the second being set up by Carey Davis' recovery of Glenn Holt's kickoff return, to take a 17-7 lead. Deltha O'Neal's fumble recovery in the third quarter led to Graham's 24-yard field goal, but Ben Roethlisberger completed 3 third-down conversion passes on the ensuing 10-play, 61-yard drive, capped by Ward's record-setting 8-yard touchdown catch with 1:22 left in the third quarter for a 24-10 lead. Carson Palmer's fourth-and-goal pass from the 3-yard line fell incomplete with 6:18 remaining to end their final threat. Roethlisberger was 21 of 32 for 184 yards and 2 touchdowns, with 2 interceptions. Ward had 11 catches for 90 yards. Palmer was 17 of 44 for 183 yards.

Cincinnati	7	0	3	0	—	10
Pittsburgh	0	17	7	0	—	24

Cin — R. Johnson 1 run (Graham kick)
Pitt — Roethlisberger 6 run (Reed kick)
Pitt — FG Reed 21
Pitt — Ward 2 pass from Roethlisberger (Reed kick)
Cin — FG Graham 24
Pitt — Ward 8 pass from Roethlisberger (Reed kick)

MONDAY NIGHT, DECEMBER 3

NEW ENGLAND 27, BALTIMORE 24—at M&T Bank Stadium,

attendance 71,382. In the closest scare yet of losing their perfect season, Jabar Gaffney caught an 8-yard touchdown pass from Tom Brady with 44 seconds left to complete a bizarre drive and keep the Patriots undefeated. Willis McGahee's 17-yard touchdown run capped an 8-play, 73-yard drive to begin the second half and gave the Ravens a 17-10 lead. The Patriots responded with an 11-play, 72-yard drive to tie the game, but the Ravens answered with another scoring drive to take a 24-17 lead on Daniel Wilcox's 1-yard touchdown catch two plays into the fourth quarter. The Ravens' defense then forced a punt, and Yamon Figurs returned the ball to the Patriots' 31. But on third down, James Sanders intercepted Kyle Boller's pass to set up Stephen Gostkowski's 38-yard field goal with 8:41 remaining. With 3:30 left, beginning on their own 27, New England began its winning drive. Faced with fourth-and-1 on the Ravens' 30 with 1:48 to play, Brady was stopped on a sneak-attempt, but the Ravens' sideline had called time out just before the snap. After a false start penalty, Brady scrambled for 12 yards. Moments later, on fourth-and-5, a defensive holding negated Brady's incomplete pass. On the next play, Brady found Gaffney for an 8-yard touchdown catch, in which Gaffney dragged his toes to stay in bounds, with 44 seconds left. Boller's Hail Mary pass from the Ravens' 45 was caught by Mark Clayton at the Patriots' 3, but Eric Alexander quickly tackled him before he could get into the end zone. Brady was 18 of 38 for 257 yards and 2 touchdowns, with 1 interception. Boller was 15 of 23 for 210 yards and 2 touchdowns, with 1 interception. McGahee had 30 carries for 138 yards.

New England	3	7	7	10	—	27
Baltimore	7	3	7	7	—	24

NE — FG Gostkowski 21
Balt — Mason 4 pass from Boller (Stover kick)
Balt — FG Stover 29
NE — Evans 1 run (Gostkowski kick)
Balt — McGahee 17 run (Stover kick)
NE — R. Moss 3 pass from Brady (Gostkowski kick)
Balt — Wilcox 1 pass from Boller (Stover kick)
NE — FG Gostkowski 38
NE — Gaffney 8 pass from Brady (Gostkowski kick)

FOURTEENTH WEEK SUMMARIES
American Football Conference

East Division	**W**	**L**	**T**	**Pct.**	**Pts.**	**OP**
New England*	13	0	0	1.000	503	222
Buffalo	7	6	0	.538	222	291
N.Y. Jets	3	10	0	.231	239	315
Miami	0	13	0	.000	213	355
North Division	**W**	**L**	**T**	**Pct.**	**Pts.**	**OP**
Pittsburgh	9	4	0	.692	309	189
Cleveland	8	5	0	.615	360	356
Cincinnati	5	8	0	.385	310	326
Baltimore	4	9	0	.308	226	314
South Division	**W**	**L**	**T**	**Pct.**	**Pts.**	**OP**
Indianapolis#	11	2	0	.846	381	217
Jacksonville	9	4	0	.692	305	229
Tennessee	7	6	0	.538	249	264
Houston	6	7	0	.462	291	305
West Division	**W**	**L**	**T**	**Pct.**	**Pts.**	**OP**
San Diego	8	5	0	.615	308	250
Denver	6	7	0	.462	282	336
Kansas City	4	9	0	.308	179	271
Oakland	4	9	0	.308	241	298

National Football Conference

East Division	**W**	**L**	**T**	**Pct.**	**Pts.**	**OP**
Dallas*	12	1	0	.923	423	275
N.Y. Giants	9	4	0	.692	290	270
Washington	6	7	0	.462	253	273
Philadelphia	5	8	0	.385	271	262
North Division	**W**	**L**	**T**	**Pct.**	**Pts.**	**OP**
Green Bay*	11	2	0	.846	361	229
Minnesota	7	6	0	.538	305	244
Detroit	6	7	0	.462	294	339
Chicago	5	8	0	.385	253	296
South Division	**W**	**L**	**T**	**Pct.**	**Pts.**	**OP**
Tampa Bay	8	5	0	.615	255	215
New Orleans	6	7	0	.462	300	293
Carolina	5	8	0	.385	210	294
Atlanta	3	10	0	.231	185	306
West Division	**W**	**L**	**T**	**Pct.**	**Pts.**	**OP**
Seattle*	9	4	0	.692	315	228
Arizona	6	7	0	.462	302	322
St. Louis	3	10	0	.231	206	316
San Francisco	3	10	0	.231	171	312

**Clinched division title*
#Clinched playoff berth

THURSDAY NIGHT, DECEMBER 6
WASHINGTON 24, CHICAGO 16—at FedExField, attendance 82,213. Todd Collins came off the bench to pass for 2 touchdowns as the Redskins posted an emotional victory three days after Sean Taylor's funeral. Both teams lost their starting quarterbacks to season-ending knee injuries in the first half. Brian Griese replaced Rex Grossman, but was intercepted by Shawn Springs, who returned the ball 53 yards to the Redskins' 21 with 24 seconds left in the half. Jason Campbell's replacement, Todd Collins, then connected on a 21-yard touchdown pass Todd Yoder. It was Collins' first scoring pass in five years. Collins opened the second half with a 54-yard pass to Clinton Portis to set up Mike Sellers' touchdown run for a 14-0 lead. With Griese leading the way, the Bears scored on all four of their second-half possessions, but Collins engineered scoring drives of 64 and 70 yards in the fourth quarter, capped by Ladell Betts' 16-yard touchdown catch on third-and-6 with 2:41 to play. Robbie Gould's third field goal cut the deficit to 24-16 with 30 seconds left, but his onside-kick attempt went out of bounds. Campbell was 10 of 16 for 100 yards, while Collins was 15 of 20 for 224 yards and 2 touchdowns. Grossman was 2 of 6 for 14 yards, and Griese was 27 of 45 for 295 yards and 1 touchdown, with 2 interceptions.

Chicago	0	0	10	6	—	16
Washington	0	7	7	10	—	24

Wash — Yoder 21 pass from T. Collins (Suisham kick)
Wash — Sellers 1 run (Suisham kick)
Chi — FG Gould 30
Chi — Berrian 17 pass from Griese (Gould kick)
Wash — FG Suisham 23
Chi — FG Gould 22
Wash — Betts 16 pass from T. Collins (Suisham kick)
Chi — FG Gould 21

SUNDAY, DECEMBER 9
BUFFALO 38, MIAMI 17—at Ralph Wilson Stadium, attendance 71,018. With a 24-degree wind chill along with some sleet, the Bills scored 31 points in the first 21 minutes to stay in the wild-card race. John Wendling recovered Ted Ginn Jr.'s muffed punt 95 seconds into the game to set up the first of Trent Edwards' 4 touchdown passes. Trailing 14-0, John Beck had the ball squirt out of hands as he reared back to throw. A blitzing George Wilson snared the fumble out of the air and ran 20 yards for a touchdown and 21-0 with 4:35 left in the first quarter. Donte Whitner's interception in the second quarter led to Lee Evans' 9-yard touchdown catch to give the Bills a 31-7 lead with 9:33 left in the half. Edwards was 11 of 23 for 165 yards and 4 touchdowns. Fred Jackson had 15 carries for 115 yards, and Marshawn Lynch rushed 23 times for 107 yards. It marked the first time in 11 years that the Bills had teammates run for 100 yards in the same game, since Thurman Thomas and Darick Holmes turned the feat. Beck was 1 of 2 for 6 yards, and was sacked 3 times. Cleo Lemon replaced him and was 22 of 42 for 241 yards, with 2 interceptions.

Miami	7	0	10	0	—	17
Buffalo	24	7	0	7	—	38

Buff — Royal 13 pass from Edwards (Lindell kick)
Buff — Royal 28 pass from Edwards (Lindell kick)
Buff — Wilson 20 fumble return (Lindell kick)
Mia — Gado 12 run (Feely kick)
Buff — FG Lindell 51
Buff — Evans 9 pass from Edwards (Lindell kick)
Mia — Gado 20 run (Feely kick)
Mia — FG Feely 41
Buff — Evans 70 pass from Edwards (Lindell kick)

CINCINNATI 19, ST. LOUIS 10—at Paul Brown Stadium, attendance 65,143. Shayne Graham made 4 field goals as the Bengals won a game played in a steady rain. With Brock Berlin making his first NFL start, the Bengals' defense permitted just 10 first downs, 241 yards, and the Rams were 3-of-13 on third-down conversions. Despite their offensive struggles, Fakhir Brown's 36-yard interception return for a touchdown 54 seconds into the second half pulled the Rams to within just three points, at 10-7. But the Bengals responded with field goals on their next two possessions, including a 15-play drive, for a 16-7 lead. Jeff Wilkins made a 50-yard field goal with 5:08 remaining to cut the deficit to 16-10, but Rudi Johnson carried six consecutive times, for 48 yards, to set up Graham's fourth field goal, from 46 yards, with 2:22 left. Dexter Jackson clinched the game with his interception with 1:38 to play. Carson Palmer was 21 of 29 for 189 yards, with 2 interceptions. Berlin, playing for injured Marc Bulger and Gus Frerotte, was 17 of 28 for 153 yards, with 1 interception.

St. Louis	0	0	7	3	—	10
Cincinnati	7	3	6	3	—	19

Cin — R. Johnson 1 run (Graham kick)
Cin — FG Graham 27
StL — F. Brown 36 interception return (Wilkins kick)
Cin — FG Graham 38
Cin — FG Graham 32
StL — FG Wilkins 50
Cin — FG Graham 46

DENVER 41, KANSAS CITY 7—at INVESCO Field at Mile High, attendance 75,895. Jay Cutler passed for 4 touchdowns and Selvin Young ran for 156 yards as the Broncos handed the Chiefs their sixth consecutive defeat. With the termperature near 20 degrees and snow surrounding the field, the Broncos had more first downs (23-7), total yards (453-129), and time of possession (34:27-25:33). The Chiefs had the ball for 12 possessions. The Broncos' defense limited 10 of the first 11 possessions to three plays or fewer. The Broncos' offense began the game with touchdown drives of 77 and 84 yards. After the Chiefs pulled to within 14-7, the Broncos scored on their next five drives, two of which were set up by turnovers, to take a 41-7 lead with 40 seconds left in the third quarter. Cutler was 20 of 27 for 244 yards and 4 touchdowns. Young rushed 17 times for 156 yards, and Brandon Marshall had 10 receptions for 115 yards. Brodie Croyle was 15 of 29 for 132 yards and 1 touchdown, with 1 interception.

Kansas City	0	7	0	0	—	7
Denver	14	10	17	0	—	41

Den — Stokley 21 pass from Cutler (Elam kick)
Den — Henry 1 run (Elam kick)
KC — Gonzalez 15 pass from Croyle (Carney kick)
Den — Marshall 8 pass from Cutler (Elam kick)
Den — FG Elam 37
Den — FG Elam 37
Den — Graham 2 pass from Cutler (Elam kick)
Den — Marshall 13 pass from Cutler (Elam kick)

DALLAS 28, DETROIT 27—at Ford Field, attendance 62,759. Tony Romo completed a 16-yard touchdown pass to Jason Witten with 18 seconds remaining as the Cowboys won their first NFC East title in nine years. The Lions scored on their first four possessions, all on drives of at least 55 yards, and capped by Kevin Jones' 2-yard touchdown run with 1:41 left in the half for a 20-7 lead. The Cowboys needed just 72 seconds to march 65 yards, with Romo completing all 6 pass attempts and scrambling for 15 yards on the other play. Marion Barber's 8-yard touchdown catch capped the drive, pulling Dallas to within 20-14. The teams exchanged touchdowns, and leading 27-21, the Lions drove to the Cowboys' 13 with 11:25 to play. However, the Lions' drive stalled, and Jason Hanson's 35-yard field-goal attempt sailed wide right. The Cowboys promptly drove downfield, but Witten fumbled at the 1-yard line after catching a pass. Greg Blue recovered with 5:47 to play. The Lions gained 2 first downs, but were forced to punt. Beginning from their own 17 with 3:15 to play, the Cowboys drove to their own 40. On fourth-and-6, Romo completed a 13-yard pass to Barber. After spiking the ball, Romo completed his final four passes, the last finding Witten in the end zone with 18 seconds to play. Romo was 35 of 44 for 302 yards and 2 touchdowns. Witten had 15 receptions for 138 yards and Barber added 10 catches for 61 yards. Kitna was 22 of

36 for 248 yards.

| Dallas | 0 | 14 | 0 | 14 | — | 28 |
| Detroit | 10 | 10 | 7 | 0 | — | 27 |

Det	—	Duckett 32 run (Hanson kick)
Det	—	FG Hanson 19
Dall	—	Barber 20 run (Folk kick)
Det	—	FG Hanson 36
Det	—	K. Jones 2 run (Hanson kick)
Dall	—	Barber 8 pass from Romo (Folk kick)
Det	—	K. Jones 3 run (Hanson kick)
Dall	—	Barber 1 run (Folk kick)
Dall	—	Witten 16 pass from Romo (Folk kick)

GREEN BAY 38, OAKLAND 7—at Lambeau Field, attendance 70,828. Ryan Grant rushed for 156 yards and Will Blackmon scored 2 special-teams touchdowns to clinch the NFC North. The Packers had a decided advantage in first downs (21-10) and total yards (445-233). With the temperature at 18 degrees, Blackmon's 57-yard punt return in the second quarter gave Green Bay a 14-0 lead, and moments later Al Harris intercepted a pass. But Mason Crosby's 43-yard field-goal attempt was wide left, and Jerry Porter's 25-yard touchdown catch with 16 seconds left in the half cut the deficit to 14-7. The Packers began the second half with a 56-yard drive, capped by Crosby's 44-yard field goal. The defense then forced a three-and-out, and on the first play Brett Favre launched a long pass that Greg Jennings caught for an 80-yard touchdown and 24-7 lead with 9:11 remaining in the third quarter. Later in the quarter, Jason Hunter forced Tim Dwight to fumble during a punt return. Blackmon recovered the ball in the end zone for a touchdown and 31-7 lead. Favre was 15 of 23 for 266 yards and 2 touchdowns, with 1 interception. Jennings had 2 receptions for 100 yards. Josh McCown was 7 of 15 for 110 yards and 1 touchdown with 2 interceptions. Andrew Walter entered in the fourth quarter and was 5 of 8 for 38 yards.

| Oakland | 0 | 7 | 0 | 0 | — | 7 |
| Green Bay | 0 | 14 | 17 | 7 | — | 38 |

GB	—	Grant 6 run (Crosby kick)
GB	—	Blackmon 57 punt return (Crosby kick)
Oak	—	Porter 25 pass from J. McCown (Janikowski kick)
GB	—	FG Crosby 44
GB	—	Jennings 80 pass from Favre (Crosby kick)
GB	—	Blackmon fumble recovery in end zone (Crosby kick)
GB	—	Lee 46 pass from Favre (Crosby kick)

HOUSTON 28, TAMPA BAY 14—at Reliant Stadium, attendance 70,237. Sage Rosenfels passed for 3 touchdowns as the Texans snapped the Buccaneers' four-game winning streak. With the score 7-7 in the second quarter, Will Demps recovered Ike Hilliard's fumble at the Buccaneers' 23. Three plays later, Rosenfels connected on an 8-yard touchdown pass to Kevin Walter. Andre Davis opened the second half with a 97-yard kickoff return for a touchdown. The Buccaneers needed just four plays to pull back within seven points, at 21-14. Houston scored on the first play of the fourth quarter, and the Buccaneers did not run another play inside the Texans' 38 until the final two minutes. Mario Williams' 13-yard sack of Luke McCown with 1:04 to play put the Buccaneers in a fourth-and-15 position from the Texans' 20, and McCown's long pass for Joey Galloway fell incomplete with 30 seconds remaining. Rosenfels was 27 of 36 for 209 yards and 3 touchdowns. McCown, playing in place of injured Jeff Garcia, was 25 of 38 for 266 yards.

| Tampa Bay | 0 | 7 | 0 | 7 | — | 14 |
| Houston | 7 | 7 | 7 | 7 | — | 28 |

Hou	—	A. Johnson 4 pass from Rosenfels (K. Brown kick)
TB	—	Graham 4 run (Bryant kick)
Hou	—	Walter 8 pass from Rosenfels (K. Brown kick)
Hou	—	Davis 97 kickoff return (K. Brown kick)
TB	—	Graham 11 run (Bryant kick)
Hou	—	Daniels 4 pass from Rosenfels (K. Brown kick)

JACKSONVILLE 37, CAROLINA 6—at Jacksonville Municipal Sta-

dium, attendance 66,090. The Jaguars' defense allowed just 149 total yards as Jacksonville handed the Panthers their sixth loss in seven games. John Kasay's 39-yard field goal with 1:03 left in the half cut the Jaguars' lead to 10-6. The Panthers had the ball to begin the second half, but on the first play from scrimmage John Henderson forced DeShaun Foster to fumble. Daryl Smith recovered the ball, and moments later Matt Jones caught a 6-yard touchdown pass from David Garrard, on third-and-5, for a 17-6 lead. The Jaguars forced a punt, drove 72 yards in 14 plays for a field goal, and on the first play of the fourth quarter Clint Ingram intercepted Vinny Testaverde's pass and returned it 39 yards for a touchdown and 27-6 lead. With 10:01 to play, Fred Taylor set a franchise-record with an 80-yard touchdown run up the middle for a 34-6 advantage. Garrard was 20 of 36 for 230 yards and 2 touchdowns. Taylor had 14 carries for 132 yards. Testaverde was 13 of 28 for 84 yards, with 1 interception. Matt Moore was 3 of 10 for 21 yards.

| Carolina | 0 | 6 | 0 | 0 | — | 6 |
| Jacksonville | 7 | 3 | 10 | 17 | — | 37 |

Jax	—	R. Williams 22 pass from Garrard (Scobee kick)
Car	—	FG Kasay 49
Jax	—	FG Scobee 21
Car	—	FG Kasay 39
Jax	—	M. Jones 6 pass from Garrard (Scobee kick)
Jax	—	FG Scobee 20
Jax	—	Ingram 39 interception return (Scobee kick)
Jax	—	Taylor 80 run (Scobee kick)
Jax	—	FG Scobee 33

NEW ENGLAND 34, PITTSBURGH 13—at Gillette Stadium, attendance 68,756. Tom Brady passed for 399 yards and 4 touchdowns as the Patriots improved to 13-0. The Steelers scored on three of their first four possessions, yet still trailed 14-13 when Jeff Reed's 44-yard field goal went through the uprights with 2:29 left in the half. On the ensuing possession, Brady completed a key 32-yard pass to Jabar Gaffney to set up Stephen Gostkowski's 42-yard field goal just before halftime for a 17-13 lead. The Steelers had the ball to begin the second half, but the Patriots' defense forced a punt. Four plays later, Brady threw a lateral to Randy Moss, who lateraled the ball back across the field to Brady, who then completed a long 56-yard touchdown pass to Gaffney for a 24-13 lead. With the score 31-13, the Steelers drove to the Patriots 1 early in the fourth quarter, but on fourth-and-goal, Hines Ward took a handoff, while in motion, and was unable to turn upfield. He was stopped for no gain with 13:27 to play. Brady was 32 of 46 for 399 yards and 4 touchdowns. Moss had 7 receptions for 135 yards, and Gaffney added 7 catches for 122 yards. Roethlisberger was 19 of 32 for 187 yards and 2 touchdowns. Willie Parker had 21 carries for 124 yards.

| Pittsburgh | 3 | 10 | 0 | 0 | — | 13 |
| New England | 7 | 10 | 14 | 3 | — | 34 |

Pitt	—	FG Reed 23
NE	—	R. Moss 4 pass from Brady (Gostkowski kick)
NE	—	R. Moss 63 pass from Brady (Gostkowski kick)
Pitt	—	Davenport 32 pass from Roethlisberger (Reed kick)
Pitt	—	FG Reed 44
NE	—	FG Gostkowski 42
NE	—	Gaffney 56 pass from Brady (Gostkowski kick)
NE	—	Welker 2 pass from Brady (Gostkowski kick)
NE	—	FG Gostkowski 28

CLEVELAND 24, N.Y. JETS 18—at The Meadowlands, attendance 76,822. Jamal Lewis scored 2 touchdowns, including a 31-yard run with 1:22 to play, as the Browns stayed in the playoff hunt. The Browns drove 80 yards for a touchdown just before halftime. Mike Nugent kicked a 35-yard field goal as time expired for the Jets, but the Browns took the second-half's opening kickoff and marched 61 yards for a touchdown and 14-3 lead. Trailing 17-6, the Jets drove 69 yards in nine plays, capped by Kellen Clemens' 1-yard run with 2:59 remaining, to pull within five points. The Jets went for the 2-point conversion, but Clemens' pass for Chris Baker fell incomplete. The Jets' Brad Kassell recovered the onside kick, and the Jets drove to the Browns' 20. But faced with fourth-and-20 with 1:43 to play, Nugent kicked a 38-yard field goal to cut the deficit to 17-15. Joe

Jurevicius recovered the next onside kick, and three plays later, on third-and-4, Lewis broke five tackles en route to his 31-yard touchdown run with 1:22 to play. Jerricho Cotchery's 37-yard catch set up Nugent's 35-yard field goal with 32 seconds left, which was the Jets' third score in the span of 2 minutes, 27 seconds. And for the second time in the final two minutes, Jurevicius recovered the onside kick, this time to secure the victory. Derek Anderson was 16 of 29 for 185 yards and 2 touchdowns, with 1 interception. Clemens was 24 of 41 for 286 yards, with 2 interceptions. Cotchery had 6 catches for 119 yards.

| Cleveland | 0 | 7 | 7 | 10 | — | 24 |
| N.Y. Jets | 0 | 3 | 3 | 12 | — | 18 |

Cle	—	J. Lewis 7 pass from Anderson (Dawson kick)
NYJ	—	FG Nugent 35
Cle	—	Edwards 4 pass from Anderson (Dawson kick)
NYJ	—	FG Nugent 41
Cle	—	FG Dawson 49
NYJ	—	Clemens 1 run (pass failed)
NYJ	—	FG Nugent 38
Cle	—	J. Lewis 31 run (Dawson kick)
NYJ	—	FG Nugent 35

N.Y. GIANTS 16, PHILADELPHIA 13—at Lincoln Financial Field, attendance 68,594. David Akers' 57-yard field-goal attempt hit the right upright with one second left as the Giants won their sixth successive road game. The Eagles opened each half with a score, the latter set up by Mike Patterson's fumble recovery at the Giants' 8, to take a 10-6 lead early in the third quarter. Later in the quarter Sam Madison recovered Brian Westbrook's fumble at the Eagles' 37. Eli Manning completed a 19-yard pass to Amani Toomer to set up his 20-yard touchdown pass to Plaxico Burress for a 13-10 lead. The Giants' defense then forced a three-and-out, and Burress caught the next pass for a 41-yard gain that led to Lawrence Tynes' 23-yard field goal in the final minute of the third quarter for a 16-10 lead. The Eagles responded with a field goal with 8:26 left. The Giants drove the Eagles' 31, but Brandon Jacobs fumbled on a long run and Juqua Thomas recovered at the Eagles' 5 with 5:51 remaining. With 2:00 left, Donovan McNabb's fumble and 6-yard pass from the Giants' 44 fell incomplete. The Eagles' defense forced a punt, and McNabb completed three passes to reach the Giants' 39 with five seconds left. Akers attempted a 57-yard field goal, but hit the right upright. Manning was 17 of 31 for 219 yards and 1 touchdown. Burress had 7 catches for 136 yards. McNabb was 20 of 30 for 179 yards and 1 touchdown.

| N.Y. Giants | 0 | 6 | 10 | 0 | — | 16 |
| Philadelphia | 7 | 0 | 3 | 3 | — | 13 |

Phil	—	Westbrook 18 pass from McNabb (Akers kick)
NYG	—	FG Tynes 19
NYG	—	FG Tynes 23
Phil	—	FG Akers 29
NYG	—	Burress 20 pass from E. Manning (Tynes kick)
NYG	—	FG Tynes 23
Phil	—	FG Akers 39

MINNESOTA 27, SAN FRANCISCO 7—at Monster Park, attendance 68,050. The Vikings scored 27 points in the game's first 24 minutes, eight seconds to win their fourth consecutive game. The 49ers actually outgained the Vikings by two yards, but committed 5 turnovers while forcing just one. One the first play from scrimmage, Kevin Williams intercepted Trent Dilfer's pass and returned it 18 yards for a touchdown just 14 seconds into the game. The Vikings scored on four of their first five possessions, capped by Chester Taylor's 84-yard touchdown run, for a 27-0 lead with 5:52 left in the second quarter. Sixth-year reserve Shaun Hill played the second half, and not only attempted his first career NFL passes, but drove the 49ers 61 yards for a touchdown on his first drive, capped by a 5-yard touchdown pass to Arnaz Battle. Tarvaris Jackson was 16 of 25 for 163 yards and 1 touchdown. Taylor had 6 carries for 101 yards. Dilfer was 7 of 19 for 45 yards, with 1 interception. Hill was 22 of 27 for 181 yards and 1 touchdown.

| Minnesota | 10 | 17 | 0 | 0 | — | 27 |
| San Francisco | 0 | 0 | 7 | 0 | — | 7 |

Minn	—	K. Williams 18 interception return (Longwell kick)
Minn	—	FG Longwell 48
Minn	—	Ferguson 19 pass from Jackson (Longwell kick)

Minn — FG Longwell 46
Minn — Taylor 84 run (Longwell kick)
SF — Battle 5 pass from S. Hill
(Nedney kick)

SEATTLE 42, ARIZONA 21—at Qwest Field, attendance 68,193. Matt Hasselbeck passed for 4 touchdowns and Marcus Trufant had 3 of the Seahawks' 5 interceptions as Seattle clinched its fourth consecutive NFC West title. The Seahawks scored on their first four possessions for a 24-0 lead with 7:44 left in the second quarter. The Cardinals used a 13-play, 83-yard drive in the third quarter to pull within 27-14, and Neil Rackers then recovered his own onside kick. But on the next play Trufant intercepted Kurt Warner's pass and Seattle drove 62 yards to Marcus Pollard's 3-yard touchdown catch to take a 34-14 lead. Hasselbeck was 22 of 33 for 272 yards and 4 touchdowns. Warner was 28 of 46 for 337 yards and 3 touchdowns, with 5 interceptions. Jerheme Urban had 6 catches for 123 yards.

Arizona	0	7	7	7	—	21
Seattle	10	17	0	15	—	42

Sea	—	FG J. Brown 23
Sea	—	Burleson 7 pass from Hasselbeck (J. Brown kick)
Sea	—	Engram 15 pass from Hasselbeck (J. Brown kick)
Sea	—	Branch 17 pass from Hasselbeck (J. Brown kick)
Ari	—	B. Johnson 5 pass from Warner (Rackers kick)
Sea	—	FG J. Brown 41
Ari	—	Urban 2 pass from Warner (Rackers kick)
Sea	—	Pollard 3 pass from Hasselbeck (J. Brown kick)
Sea	—	Safety, Scobey forced Berger out of bounds in end zone
Sea	—	Trufant 84 interception return (bad snap)
Ari	—	Fitzgerald 11 pass from Warner (Rackers kick)

SAN DIEGO 23, TENNESSEE 17 (OT)—at LP Field, attendance 69,143. Antonio Gates caught the tying touchdown pass with nine seconds left, and LaDainian Tomlinson ran for the game-winning touchdown in overtime as the Chargers won their third successive game. The Chargers ran just two plays in Titans' territory in the first half, trailing just 3-0. Three plays into the second half, Matt Wilhelm intercepted a pass to set up Nate Kaeding's 20-yard field goal. Nick Harper's interception later in the quarter, and 32-yard return, led to Chris Brown's 7-yard touchdown run. The Titans' defense then forced a punt. Chris Barclay returned it 19 yards, and Justin Gage caught a 12-yard pass on third-and-72 to set up LenDale White's 7-yard touchdown run for a 17-3 lead with 14:21 to play. The Chargers were forced to punt, but Kassim Osgood downed Mike Scifres' punt at the 1-yard line. The Titans did not get a first down, and San Diego needed to drive just 48 yards, capped by Tomlinson's 7-yard touchdown catch with 7:29 remaining, to pull within 17-10. Starting from their own 20 with 2:24 to play, Philip Rivers engineered a 14-play drive, highlighted by his 19-yard pass to Chris Chambers on fourth-and-5, and capped by Gates' 2-yard touchdown catch on a fade pattern with nine seconds to play to tie the game. The Chargers won the overtime toss but were forced to punt. Scifres' 51-yard punt was downed by Osgood and Antonio Cromartie at the 2-yard line. The Chargers' defense did not allow a first down and Tennessee punted. Faced with third-and-4, Gates caught a 12-yard pass, and three plays later Tomlinson scored on a 16-yard run around left end to win the game with 7:29 left in overtime. Rivers was 21 of 40 for 228 yards and 2 touchdowns, with 2 interceptions. Tomlinson had 26 carries for 146 yards. Vince Young was 13 of 21 for 121 yards, with 2 interceptions.

San Diego	0	0	3	14	6	—	23
Tennessee	3	0	7	7	0	—	17

Tenn	—	FG Bironas 44
SD	—	FG Kaeding 20
Tenn	—	C. Brown 7 run (Bironas kick)
Tenn	—	L. White 7 run (Bironas kick)
SD	—	Tomlinson 7 pass from Rivers (Kaeding kick)
SD	—	Gates 2 pass from Rivers (Kaeding kick)
SD	—	Tomlinson 16 run

SUNDAY NIGHT, DECEMBER 9
INDIANAPOLIS 44, BALTIMORE 20—at M&T Bank Stadium, attendance 70,513. Peyton Manning passed for 4 touchdowns as the Colts scored 37 first-half points to clinch their sixth consecutive postseason berth. The Colts scored touchdowns on their first four possessions, two of which were drives of 12 and 19 yards set up by turnovers, and Michael Coe added a blocked punt for a safety, to take a 30-0 lead. Anthony Gonzalez's 57-yard touchdown catch with 6:30 left in the half gave the Colts a 37-7 lead. At halftime the Colts had outgained the Ravens 255-57 in yardage. Manning was 13 of 17 for 249 yards and 4 touchdowns. Gonzalez had 6 catches for 134 yards. Kyle Boller was 19 of 25 for 132 yards and 1 touchdown, with 3 interceptions. Rookie Troy Smith made his NFL debut on the final drive, and scored on a 6-yard run with 59 seconds left.

Indianapolis	23	14	7	0	—	44
Baltimore	0	7	0	13	—	20

Ind	—	Wayne 34 pass from P. Manning (Vinatieri kick)
Ind	—	Addai 1 run (Vinatieri kick)
Ind	—	Addai 19 pass from P. Manning (Vinatieri kick)
Ind	—	Safety, punt blocked by Coe out of bounds in end zone
Ind	—	Addai 11 run (Vinatieri kick)
Balt	—	Figurs 94 kickoff return (Stover kick)
Ind	—	Gonzalez 57 pass from P. Manning (Vinatieri kick)
Ind	—	Gonzalez 40 pass from P. Manning (Vinatieri kick)
Balt	—	Darling 4 pass from Boller (pass failed)
Balt	—	T. Smith 6 run (Stover kick)

MONDAY NIGHT, DECEMBER 10
NEW ORLEANS 34, ATLANTA 14—at Georgia Dome, attendance 69,553. Drew Brees passed for 3 touchdowns as the Saints handed the Falcons their fourth consecutive loss. Less than 24 hours later, Bobby Petrino resigned as the Falcons' coach to take the head-coaching position at Arkansas. After scoring on the last three possession of the first half, on drives of 99, 75, and 94 yards, to take a 17-7 lead. The Saints then opened the second half with an 11-play, 80-yard drive for a 24-7 advantage, and two plays later Roman Harper stepped in front of Chris Redman's short pass and returned it 24 yards for a touchdown and 31-7 lead with 8:30 left in the third quarter. Brees was 28 of 41 for 328 yards and 3 touchdowns. Aaron Stecker had 20 carries for 100 yards. David Patten had 9 catches for 122 yards. Redman, making his first start in five seasons, was 23 of 40 for 298 yards and 2 touchdowns, with 1 interception.

New Orleans	7	10	14	3	—	34
Atlanta	7	0	0	7	—	14

NO	—	Patten 25 pass from Brees (Mare kick)
Atl	—	R. White 33 pass from Redman (Andersen kick)
NO	—	FG Mare 33
NO	—	Colston 15 pass from Brees (Mare kick)
NO	—	Colston 2 pass from Brees (Mare kick)
NO	—	Harper 31 interception return (Mare kick)
Atl	—	Jenkins 13 pass from Redman (Andersen kick)
NO	—	FG Mare 36

FIFTEENTH WEEK SUMMARIES
American Football Conference

East Division	W	L	T	Pct.	Pts.	OP
New England*	14	0	0	1.000	523	232
Buffalo	7	7	0	.500	222	299
N.Y. Jets	3	11	0	.214	249	335
Miami	1	13	0	.071	235	371
North Division	**W**	**L**	**T**	**Pct.**	**Pts.**	**OP**
Pittsburgh	9	5	0	.643	331	218
Cleveland	9	5	0	.643	368	356
Cincinnati	5	9	0	.357	323	346
Baltimore	4	10	0	.286	242	336

South Division	W	L	T	Pct.	Pts.	OP
Indianapolis*	12	2	0	.857	402	231
Jacksonville	10	4	0	.714	334	251
Tennessee	8	6	0	.571	275	281
Houston	7	7	0	.500	322	318
West Division	**W**	**L**	**T**	**Pct.**	**Pts.**	**OP**
San Diego*	9	5	0	.643	359	264
Denver	6	8	0	.429	295	367
Kansas City	4	10	0	.286	196	297
Oakland	4	10	0	.286	255	319

National Football Conference

East Division	W	L	T	Pct.	Pts.	OP
Dallas*	12	2	0	.857	429	285
N.Y. Giants	9	5	0	.643	300	292
Washington	7	7	0	.500	275	263
Philadelphia	6	8	0	.429	281	268
North Division	**W**	**L**	**T**	**Pct.**	**Pts.**	**OP**
Green Bay*	12	2	0	.857	394	243
Minnesota	8	6	0	.538	325	257
Detroit	6	8	0	.429	308	390
Chicago	5	9	0	.357	266	316
South Division	**W**	**L**	**T**	**Pct.**	**Pts.**	**OP**
Tampa Bay*	9	5	0	.643	292	218
New Orleans	7	7	0	.500	331	317
Carolina	6	8	0	.429	223	304
Atlanta	3	11	0	.214	188	343
West Division	**W**	**L**	**T**	**Pct.**	**Pts.**	**OP**
Seattle*	9	5	0	.643	325	241
Arizona	6	8	0	.429	326	353
San Francisco	4	10	0	.286	191	325
St. Louis	3	11	0	.214	220	349

*Clinched division title
#Clinched playoff berth

THURSDAY NIGHT, DECEMBER 13
HOUSTON 31, DENVER 13—at Reliant Stadium, attendance 70,747. Mario Williams had 3.5 of the Texans' 5 sacks as Houston matched the franchise record for victories (7) in a season. Trailing 10-6 at halftime, the Broncos drove to the Texans' 38. On fourth-and-7, Denver went for the first down, but Jay Cutler's pass to Selvin Young gained just 4 yards. The Texans took over, and Ron Dayne's 6-yard touchdown run capped the nine-play drive to take a 17-6 lead. Dre' Bly's interception later in the quarter set up a 27-yard drive, that culminated with Tony Scheffler's 12-yard touchdown catch to pull within 17-13. The Texans responded with a 74-yard touchdown drive, that included 2 key third-down passes by Sage Rosenfels, the latter a 4-yard touchdown pass to Andre Johnson on third-and-goal to take a 24-13 lead with 10:06 to play. The Texans' defense forced a three-and-out, and Johnson caught a 28-yard pass to set up Vonta Leach's 1-yard run for a 31-13 lead with 3:20 left. Rosenfels was 16 of 27 for 200 yards and 1 touchdown, with 1 interception. Cutler was 27 of 39 for 254 yards and 1 touchdown. Brandon Marshall had 11 catches for 107 yards, and Scheffler had 7 receptions for 100 yards.

Denver	0	6	7	0	—	13
Houston	7	3	14	7	—	31

Hou	—	Rosenfels 5 run (K. Brown kick)
Den	—	FG Elam 41
Hou	—	FG K. Brown 41
Den	—	FG Elam 47
Hou	—	Dayne 6 run (K. Brown kick)
Den	—	Scheffler 1 pass from Cutler (Elam kick)
Hou	—	A. Johnson 4 pass from Rosenfels (K. Brown kick)
Hou	—	Leach 1 run (K. Brown kick)

SATURDAY NIGHT, DECEMBER 15
SAN FRANCISCO 20, CINCINNATI 13—at Monster Park, attendance 68,053. Making his first career start, sixth-year quarterback Shaun Hill passed for 197 yards and a touchdown, and ran for another as the 49ers won for just the second time in 12 games. The 49ers converted 9 of 15 third-down situations for the game, including 7-of-7 on their four scoring drives. The 49ers had two 76-yard drives in the first half, one of 13 plays and another of 10 plays, that both resulted in touchdowns. In the third quarter, the 49ers controlled the ball for all but 2:06 of the clock, driving 12 plays for 61 yards and 11 plays for 48 yards for a pair of field goal and 20-10 lead. The Bengals responded with a field goal, and the ball back with 6:15 to play. Carson Palmer drove the Bengals to the 49ers' 24, but on fourth-and-3 Chad Johnson could not hold onto

Palmer's pass in the end zone. Frank Gore ran for 10 yards on third-and-9 with 1:59 to play to clinch the victory. Hill was 21 of 28 for 197 yards and 1 touchdown. Gore had 29 carries for 138 yards. Palmer was 19 of 31 for 252 yards and 1 touchdown.

Cincinnati	0	10	0	3	—	13
San Francisco	0	14	6	0	—	20

SF — Hill 3 run (Nedney kick)
Cin — FG Graham 24
Cin — Henry 52 pass from Palmer (Graham kick)
SF — Davis 17 pass from Hill (Nedney kick)
SF — FG Nedney 29
SF — FG Nedney 38
Cin — FG Graham 35

SUNDAY, DECEMBER 16

CAROLINA 13, SEATTLE 10—at Bank of America Stadium, attendance 73,421. DeAngelo Williams scored on a 35-yard run with 1:17 left as the Panthers snapped the Seahawks' five-game winning streak. In a game played with gusty winds, John Kasay missed a 37-yard field goal in the first half, otherwise neither team had a scoring opportunity in the first three quarters. The clubs then exchanged field goals, and Kasay added a 37-yard boot with 2:59 to play for a 6-3 lead. The Panthers' defense then forced the lone turnover of the game, as Thomas Davis sacked Matt Hasselbeck, forced him to fumble, and Richard Marshall recovered at the Seahawks' 40 with 1:38 left. Three plays later, on third-and-5, Williams broke free for a 35-yard touchdown run. Deion Branch caught a 15-yard touchdown pass with one second left to complete the scoring. Rookie Matt Moore made his first career start and was 19 of 27 for 208 yards. Hasselbeck was 27 of 41 for 274 yards and 1 touchdown.

Seattle	0	0	0	10	—	10
Carolina	0	0	0	13	—	13

Car — FG Kasay 53
Sea — FG J. Brown 23
Car — FG Kasay 37
Car — D. Williams 35 run (Kasay kick)
Sea — Branch 15 pass from Hasselbeck (J. Brown kick)

CLEVELAND 8, BUFFALO 0—at Cleveland Browns Stadium, attendance 73,196. Jamal Lewis rushed for 163 yards and Phil Dawson made 2 field goals as the Browns won in the snow and wind. It was the first 8-0 game in the NFL in 78 years. With a 16-degree wind chill, snow, and 32-mile-per-hour winds, neither team committed a turnover while the Browns outgained the Bills 304-232 yards. In the first quarter, Derek Anderson's pass deflected off Braylon Edwards into Joe Jurevicius' hands for a 25-yard catch to set up Dawson's 35-yard field goal. Early in the second quarter Ryan Neill's punt snap from the Bills' 24 sailed over Brian Moorman's head. Moorman kicked the loose ball through the end zone for a safety. Just before halftime, Dawson's 49-yard field goal weaved its way through the wind and skimmed the support bar just beyond the crossbar to give the Browns an 8-0 lead. The Bills did not cross midfield in the second half until their final drive. They reached the Browns' 10, but on fourth-and-5 Trent Edwards' short pass to Fred Jackson was held to no gain. Anderson was 9 of 24 for 137 yards. Lewis carried 33 times for 163 yards. Edwards was 13 of 33 for 124 yards.

Buffalo	0	0	0	0	—	0
Cleveland	3	5	0	0	—	8

Cle — FG Dawson 35
Cle — Safety, Neill fumbled out of end zone
Cle — FG Dawson 49

PHILADELPHIA 10, DALLAS 6—at Texas Stadium, attendance 63,777. The Eagles' defense registered 4 sacks and intercepted 3 passes as Philadelphia snapped the Cowboys' seven-game winning streak and kept its faint playoff hopes alive. The Cowboys led 3-0 and had the ball late in the first half when Lito Sheppard intercepted Tony Romo's pass. Donovan McNabb's 28-yard scramble a few plays later led to his 1-yard touchdown pass to Reggie Brown with 16 seconds left in the half for a 7-3 lead. Late in the fourth quarter trailing 10-6, the Cowboys were beginning to drive when Brian Dawkins intercepted a pass near midfield with 2:50 to play. McNabb then completed a key 29-yard pass to Brent Celek for a first down. With 2:19 to play from the Cowboys' 25, Brian Westbrook broke through the line and had an easy touchdown. Instead, per tackle Jon Runyan's advice in the huddle, Westbrook stopped and took a knee at the 1-yard line. The strategy worked. Since the Cowboys were out of timeouts, they could not get the ball back and the Eagles kneeled on the ball three times to end the game. McNabb was 23 of 41 for 208 yards and 1 touchdown. Romo was 13 of 36 for 214 yards, with 3 interceptions. Jason Witten had 8 catches for 113 yards.

Philadelphia	0	7	0	3	—	10
Dallas	0	3	3	0	—	6

Dall — FG Folk 33
Phil — R. Brown 1 pass from McNabb (Akers kick)
Dall — FG Folk 23
Phil — FG Akers 21

TENNESSEE 26, KANSAS CITY 17—at Arrowhead Stadium, attendance 74,976. Rob Bironas kicked 4 field goals and Vince Young completed 2 touchdown passes to Roydell Williams as the Titans stayed within a game of the Browns for the final wild-card berth. The Chiefs had 12- and 14-play drives in the first half to take a 14-10 lead. Williams' 35-yard catch in the third quarter set up Bironas' second field goal, but the Chiefs answered with a 14-play drive that resulted in John Carney's 36-yard field goal for a 17-13 lead. However, Carney's ensuing kickoff went out of bounds and three plays later, Young threw a deep pass down the left sideline that hit Williams in stride for a 41-yard touchdown to give the Titans a 20-17 lead. On the next play, Michael Griffin intercepted a pass that resulted in Bironas' 40-yard field goal. The Titans forced a punt and Bironas kicked a 25-yard field goal with 5:42 remaining for a 26-17 lead. David Thornton intercepted Brodie Croyle's pass moments later and the Titans ran the final 4:10 off the clock. Young was 16 of 26 for 191 yards and 2 touchdowns. Croyle was 25 of 43 for 217 yards and 2 touchdowns, with 2 interceptions.

Tennessee	7	3	10	6	—	26
Kansas City	0	14	3	0	—	17

Tenn — R. Williams 16 pass from Young (Bironas kick)
KC — Parker 10 pass from Croyle (Carney kick)
Tenn — FG Bironas 37
KC — Wilson 9 pass from Croyle (Carney kick)
Tenn — FG Bironas 37
KC — FG Carney 36
Tenn — R. Williams 41 pass from Young (Bironas kick)
Tenn — FG Bironas 40
Tenn — FG Bironas 25

MIAMI 22, BALTIMORE 16 (OT)—at Dolphin Stadium, attendance 70,287. Greg Camarillo scored on a 64-yard pass from Cleo Lemon in overtime as the Dolphins won their first game of the season. With members of the Dolphins' 1972 perfect season in attendance for their 35-year reunion, they saw Miami snap a 16-game losing streak, and celebrated the first touchdown of Camarillo's career. The Ravens scored on three of their first four possessions to take a 13-3 lead. In the third quarter, Lemon completed a key 21-yard pass to Derek Hagan on third-and-10, and moments later Lorenzo Booker gained 3 yards on fourth-and-1. On the next play, Samkon Gado scored on a 7-yard run to pull the Dolphins within 13-10. Michael Lehan stopped the next drive with an interception of Kyle Boller's pass, and the Dolphins drove 82 yards to tie the game with Jay Feely's 22-yard field goal with 12:06 to play. Feely added a 29-yard field goal with 1:56 left to give Miami a 16-13 lead. With Troy Smith in the game for his second drive, the Ravens drove to the Dolphins' 10. On third-and-goal, Smith completed a 9-yard pass to Devard Darling, who was knocked out of bounds inches shy of the pylon. Faced with fourth-and-goal with 12 seconds left, the Ravens decided to kick, and Matt Stover made an 18-yard field goal to force overtime. The Ravens won the toss, and drove to the Dolphins' 26. On fourth-and-11, Stover's 44-yard field-goal attempt sailed wide left. Three plays later, on third-and-8, a slanting Camarillo caught Lemon's pass near midfield and kept running for the 64-yard touchdown. Lemon was 23 of 39 for 315 yards and 1 touchdown. Camarillo had 3 catches for 109 yards. Boller was 10 of 19 for 159 yards and 1 touchdown, with 1 interception. Smith was 5 of 11 for 49 yards. McGahee carried 29 times for 104 yards.

Baltimore	3	10	0	3	0	—	16
Miami	0	3	7	6	6	—	22

Balt — FG Stover 27
Balt — FG Stover 39
Mia — FG Feely 23
Balt — Mason 17 pass from Boller (Stover kick)
Mia — Gado 7 run (Feely kick)
Mia — FG Feely 22
Mia — FG Feely 29
Balt — FG Stover 18
Mia — Camarillo 64 pass from Lemon

NEW ENGLAND 20, N.Y. JETS 10—at Gillette Stadium, attendance 68,756. In 25-degree wind chill with gusty winds, the Patriots became just the second team to post a 14-0 record. With the Jets backed up on their 3-yard line on the first play from scrimmage, Richard Seymour hit Kellen Clemens as he threw a pass. Eugene Wilson intercepted it and walked 5 yards into the end zone for a touchdown. Clemens suffered an injured rib and left the game. In the second quarter, David Bowens blocked Chris Hanson's punt and returned it 26 yards for a touchdown to pull the Jets within 10-7. Just before halftime, Kelley Washington blocked Ben Graham's punt. The Patriots took over on the three-yard line, and Laurence Maroney scored two plays later for a 17-7 halftime lead. The Jets used a 17-play, 70-yard drive in the fourth quarter to pull within 17-10 on Mike Nugent's 33-yard field goal with 6:13 to play. Tom Brady completed a key 16-yard pass to Wes Welker on the ensuing drive to set up Stephen Gostkowski's 34-yard field goal with 3:21 left. Leon Washington gave the Jets a chance by returning the kickoff 49 yards, but Nugent's 35-yard field-goal attempt sailed wide left with 2:12 remaining. Brady was 14 of 27 for 140 yards, with 1 interception. Maroney rushed 26 times for 104 yards. Chad Pennington came off the bench and was 25 of 38 for 184 yards.

N.Y. Jets	0	7	0	3	—	10
New England	7	10	0	3	—	20

NE — Wilson 5 interception return (Gostkowski kick)
NE — FG Gostkowski 26
NYJ — Bowens 26 blocked punt return (Nugent kick)
NE — Maroney 1 run (Gostkowski kick)
NYJ — FG Nugent 33
NE — FG Gostkowski 34

NEW ORLEANS 31, ARIZONA 24—at Louisiana Superdome, attendance 70,007. In a game in which a loss would severely hamper the loser's postseason chances, Aaron Stecker rushed for 2 touchdowns and Drew Brees passed for a pair of scores for the Saints. With the score 14-14, Roman Harper intercepted a tipped pass and returned it 31 yards. Three plays later, Brees completed a 19-yard pass to Marques Colston on third-and-6, and on the next play found David Patten in the end zone for a 32-yard touchdown and 21-14 lead with 1:56 left in the first half. Arizona had the ball to begin the second half, but Scott Fujita sacked Kurt Warner and forced him to fumble. Scott Shanle recovered the ball and returned it 26 yards. Two plays later, Stecker scored on a 6-yard run for a 28-14 advantage. The Cardinals scored on their next two drives, and got the ball back with 7:06 remaining trailing 31-24. The Saints' defense forced a three-and-out, and the offense ran the final 5:54 off the clock, highlighted by 11- and 22-yard passes to Billy Miller and capped by Pierre Thomas' 11-yard run for a first down with 2:16 left. Brees was 26 of 30 for 315 yards and 2 touchdowns. Colston had 8 receptions for 114 yards. Warner was 19 of 30 for 233 yards and 3 touchdowns, with 1 interception.

Arizona	7	7	7	3	—	24
New Orleans	7	14	10	0	—	31

Ari — Bienemann 1 pass from Warner (Rackers kick)
NO — Colston 19 pass from Brees (Gramatica kick)
NO — Stecker 1 run (Gramatica kick)
Ari — Fitzgerald 18 pass from Warner (Rackers kick)
NO — Patten 32 pass from Brees (Gramatica kick)
NO — Stecker 6 run (Gramatica kick)
Ari — Patrick 3 pass from Warner (Rackers kick)
NO — FG Gramatica 31
Ari — FG Rackers 26

INDIANAPOLIS 21, OAKLAND 14—at McAfee Coliseum, attendance 62,000. Peyton Manning passed for a touchdown as the Colts clinched their fifth consecutive AFC South title, secured a first-round bye, and became the first team to ever post five consecutive 12-win seasons. T.J. Rushing's 90-yard punt return for a touchdown in the first quarter gave the Colts a 10-0 lead. The Colts had a chance to extend the lead, but Manning's fourth-and-goal pass from the Raiders' 1 fell incomplete. The Raiders responded with a 20-play, 99-yard drive that consumed 11 minutes, 49 seconds, capped by Josh McCown's 3-yard touchdown pass to Ronald Curry with 3:06 left in the half that cut the deficit to 10-7. Trailing 13-7, the Raiders drove 60 yards in 13 plays, including three key third-down conversions, capped by Justin Fargas' 2-yard run for a 14-13 lead with 10:29 left. Manning responded by completing all seven of his pass attempts on the ensuing 11-play, 91-yard drive, that culminated with his 20-yard scoring pass to Anthony Gonzalez. Joseph Addai ran up the middle for the 2-point conversion for a 21-14 lead with 4:49 remaining. The Raiders drove to the Colts' 16, but McCown's last two passes fell incomplete. Manning was 22 of 39 for 276 yards and 1 touchdown, with 1 interception. McCown was 13 of 24 for 94 yards and 1 touchdown, while JaMarcus Russell played in three series and was 2 of 5 for 10 yards.

Indianapolis	10	0	3	8	—	21
Oakland	0	7	0	7	—	14

Ind — FG Vinatieri 22
Ind — Rushing 90 punt return (Vinatieri kick)
Oak — Curry 3 pass from J. McCown (Janikowski kick)
Ind — FG Vinatieri 19
Oak — Fargas 2 run (Janikowski kick)
Ind — Gonzalez 20 pass from P. Manning (Addai run)

JACKSONVILLE 29, PITTSBURGH 22—at Heinz Field, attendance 58,793. Fred Taylor rushed for 147 yards and the tie-breaking touchdown with 1:57 to play as the Jaguars solidified their playoff position and handed the Steelers their first home loss of the season. The Jaguars dominated statistically, outgaining the Steelers 421-217 in yards, 25-13 in first downs, and time of possession (37:39-22:21) while converting all 3 fourth-down situations in which they went for the first down. With snow beginning to fall just before halftime, Jacksonville drove 68 yards for a touchdown to take a 10-7 lead. The Jaguars opened the second half with a 20-play, 74-yard touchdown drive, forced a three-and-out, and Garrard completed a 55-yard touchdown pass to Dennis Northcutt on the next play. However, a mishandled snap and missed extra-point attempt on the two touchdowns gave the Jaguars just a 22-7 lead. Anthony Smith's interception and 50-yard return two plays into the fourth quarter gave the Steelers a chance, and Ben Roethlisberger completed an 11-yard touchdown pass to Hines Ward three plays later to pull within 22-14. The Steelers' defense forced a punt, and the offense drove 84 yards, highlighted by Santonio Holmes' 18-yard catch on third-and-18, and capped by Nate Washington's 30-yard touchdown catch in the end zone. On the 2-point conversion attempt, wide receiver Cedrick Wilson took the handoff and completed a pass to Santonio Holmes to tie the game with 5:46 left. The Jaguars answered with a 73-yard drive, that culminated with Taylor's 12-yard run for a 29-22 lead with 1:57 left. On fourth-and-7, Heath Miller caught a pass for six yards with 41 seconds left as Jacksonville held on. Garrard was 17 of 33 for 197 yards and 3 touchdowns, with 1 interception. Taylor rushed 25 times for 147 yards. Roethlisberger was 15 of 32 for 142 yards and 3 touchdowns. Willie Parker carried 14 times for 100 yards.

Jacksonville	3	7	12	7	—	29
Pittsburgh	0	7	0	15	—	22

Jax — FG Scobee 36
Pitt — Miller 18 pass from Roethlisberger (Reed kick)
Jax — Wilford 12 pass from Garrard (Scobee kick)
Jax — R. Williams 3 pass from Garrard (bad snap)
Jax — Northcutt 55 pass from Garrard (kick failed)
Pitt — Ward 11 pass from Roethlisberger (Reed kick)
Pitt — Washington 30 pass from Roethlisberger (Holmes pass from Wilson)
Jax — Taylor 12 run (Scobee kick)

GREEN BAY 33, ST. LOUIS 14—at Edward Jones Dome, attendance 66,008. Brett Favre passed for 2 touchdowns and became the NFL's all-time leader in passing yards as the Packers secured a first-round bye for the first time in 10 seasons. The Rams had touchdowns drives of 67 and 84 yards on successive possessions to tie the game 14-14 with 10:09 left in the half. The Rams didn't run a play inside the Packers' 30 on any of their final nine possessions. The Packers led 17-14 at halftime, and scored on their first three second-half drives, taking a 30-14 lead on Mason Crosby's field goal with 11:22 remaining. Favre set the record moments earlier, when he completed a 7-yard pass to Donald Driver on first-and-10 from the Packers' 38 with 14:45 to play. He passed Dan Marino's record of 61,361 passing yards. Favre was 19 of 30 for 225 yards and 2 touchdowns, with 2 interceptions. Marc Bulger was 20 of 39 for 219 yards and 1 touchdown, with 2 interceptions. Steven Jackson had 24 carries for 143 yards.

Green Bay	7	10	10	6	—	33
St. Louis	7	7	0	0	—	14

GB — Grant 1 run (Crosby kick)
StL — Holt 4 pass from Bulger (Wilkins kick)
GB — Lee 4 pass from Favre (Crosby kick)
StL — Jackson 46 run (Wilkins kick)
GB — FG Crosby 44
GB — FG Crosby 50
GB — Jennings 44 pass from Favre (Crosby kick)
GB — FG Crosby 25
GB — FG Crosby 46

SAN DIEGO 51, DETROIT 14—at Qualcomm Stadium, attendance 66,505. The Chargers' defense forced 6 turnovers that resulted in 27 points as San Diego won its third AFC West title in four years. The Chargers rushed for 274 yards and held the ball for 41 minutes, 32 seconds. LaDainian Tomlinson and Darren Sproles each rushed for 100 yards, becoming the first pair of Chargers to do so in the same game. The Chargers scored on their first eight possessions, including Shaun Phillips' 18-yard interception return, to take a 44-7 lead with 5:52 left in the third quarter. Of the seven offensive drives, three were 77 yards or longer. Philip Rivers was 14 of 21 for 142 yards and 1 touchdown. Sproles had 25 carries for 122 yards. Tomlinson played just the first half and had 15 carries for 116 yards. Jon Kitna was 26 of 45 for 302 yards and 2 touchdowns, with 5 interceptions. Calvin Johnson had 5 catches for 102 yards.

Detroit	0	7	7	0	—	14
San Diego	17	17	10	7	—	51

SD — Tomlinson 6 run (Kaeding kick)
SD — FG Kaeding 22
SD — Tomlinson 2 run (Kaeding kick)
SD — FG Kaeding 22
SD — Phillips 18 interception return (Kaeding kick)
Det — Middleton 9 pass from Kitna (Hanson kick)
SD — Manumaleuna 1 pass from Rivers (Kaeding kick)
SD — Sproles 1 run (Kaeding kick)
SD — FG Kaeding 45
Det — McDonald 17 pass from Kitna (Hanson kick)
SD — Sproles 11 run (Kaeding kick)

TAMPA BAY 37, ATLANTA 3—at Raymond James Stadium, attendance 65,133. Micheal Spurlock had the first kickoff return for a touchdown in Buccaneers' history to highlight Tampa Bay's NFC South-clinching victory. The Falcons were playing their first game for interim coach Emmitt Thomas, who had replaced Bobby Petrino after Petrino resigned on Tuesday to take the Arkansas head-coaching position. Three plays into the game, Ronde Barber returned an interception 29 yards for a touchdown. Morten Andersen's first-quarter filed goal capped the Falcons' best drive, 59 yards, to pull within 7-3. Spurlock took the ensuing kickoff and returned it 90 yards for a touchdown. It was the first kickoff return for a touchdown in the franchise's 32 seasons. A pair of second-quarter fumbles led to 10 points, the second forced and recovered by Greg White with 55 seconds left in the half. Matt Bryant ended that possession with a 28-yard field goal as the half expired for a 27-3 lead. Tampa Bay's defense did not allow the Falcons to cross their own 40 in the second half, and for the game allowed just 133 yards and 5 first downs. Jeff Garcia was 15 of 25 for 109 yards and 1 touchdown, with 1 interception. Chris Redman was 4 of 15 for 34 yards, with 2 interceptions.

Atlanta	3	0	0	0	—	3
Tampa Bay	14	13	3	7	—	37

TB — Barber 29 interception return (Bryant kick)
Atl — FG Andersen 33
TB — Spurlock 90 kickoff return (Bryant kick)
TB — FG Bryant 33
TB — Graham 1 run (Bryant kick)
TB — FG Bryant 28
TB — FG Bryant 34
TB — Becht 1 pass from Garcia (Bryant kick)

SUNDAY NIGHT, DECEMBER 16

WASHINGTON 22, N.Y. GIANTS 10—at Giants Stadium, attendance 77,899. Making his first start in 10 years, Todd Collins engineered five scoring drives as the Redskins stayed in the playoff chase. Lawrence Tynes kicked a 35-yard field goal with 1:16 left in the half to pull within 13-3, but Clinton Portis had a 31-yard run to help set up Shaun Suisham's third field goal of the half, as time expired, for a 16-3 lead. Washington then opened the second half with a 46-yard touchdown drive, highlighted by 15- and 19-yard passes by Collins, and capped by Portis' 5-yard touchdown run for a 22-3 lead. The Giants pulled within 20-10, and had a chance to get closer, but Tynes' 38-yard field-goal attempt early in the fourth quarter sailed wide left, and Eli Manning's fourth-and-5 pass from the Redskins' 20 fell incomplete with 5:22 to play. Collins was 8 of 25 for 166 yards. Portis had 25 carries for 126 yards. Manning was 18 of 53, with at least eight passes being dropped, for 184 yards and 1 touchdown. Brandon Jacobs carried 25 times for 130 yards.

Washington	3	13	6	0	—	22
N.Y. Giants	0	3	7	0	—	10

Wash — FG Suisham 49
Wash — FG Suisham 31
Wash — Betts 14 run (Suisham kick)
NYG — FG Tynes 35
Wash — FG Suisham 28
Wash — Portis 5 run (pass failed)
NYG — Boss 19 pass from E. Manning (Tynes kick)

MONDAY NIGHT, DECEMBER 17

MINNESOTA 20, CHICAGO 13—at Metrodome, attendance 63,800. Adrian Peterson scored 2 second-half touchdowns as the Vikings won their fifth consecutive game to remain in the wild-card chase. The Vikings outgained the Bears 372-209 in total yards, but committed 4 turnovers. Trailing 6-3 with 54 seconds left in the half, Tarvaris Jackson's deep pass was intercepted by Nathan Vasher and returned 34 yards to the Vikings' 12. Two plays later Jason McKie scored on a 1-yard run for a 13-3 lead with 30 seconds left in the half. However, Jackson completed two passes, and along with an unsportsmanlike conduct penalty, set up Ryan Longwell's 48-yard field goal to pull within 13-6. Jackson's 71-yard pass to Robert Ferguson set up Peterson's 1-yard touchdown run, but Longwell's extra-point attempt went wide left, allowing Chicago to maintain a 13-12 lead. Early in the fourth quarter, the Vikings drove to the Bears' 8. On second-and-goal, Jackson injured himself rolling to his right. Brooks Bollinger came into the game, and on the next play, Peterson ran up the middle for an 8-yard touchdown. Bollinger then ran up the middle for the 2-point conversion for a 20-13 lead with 10:56 to play. Darren Sharper intercepted Kyle Orton's long pass in the end zone with 1:38 to play to clinch the victory. Jackson was 18 of 29 for 249 yards, with 3 interceptions. Orton was 22 of 38 for 184 yards, with 1 interception.

Chicago	3	10	0	0	—	13
Minnesota	0	6	6	8	—	20

Chi — FG Gould 29
Minn — FG Longwell 42
Chi — FG Gould 47
Chi — McKie 1 run (Gould kick)
Minn — FG Longwell 48
Minn — Peterson 1 run (kick failed)
Minn — Peterson 8 run (Bollinger run)

SIXTEENTH WEEK SUMMARIES

American Football Conference

East Division	**W**	**L**	**T**	**Pct.**	**Pts.**	**OP**
New England*	15	0	0	1.000	551	239
Buffalo	7	8	0	.467	243	337

	W	L	T	Pct.	Pts.	OP
N.Y. Jets	3	12	0	.200	255	345
Miami	1	14	0	.067	242	399
North Division	**W**	**L**	**T**	**Pct.**	**Pts.**	**OP**
Pittsburgh*	10	5	0	.667	372	242
Cleveland	9	6	0	.600	382	375
Cincinnati	6	9	0	.400	342	360
Baltimore	4	11	0	.267	248	363
South Division	**W**	**L**	**T**	**Pct.**	**Pts.**	**OP**
Indianapolis*	13	2	0	.867	440	246
Jacksonville#	11	4	0	.733	383	262
Tennessee	9	6	0	.600	285	287
Houston	7	8	0	.467	337	356
West Division	**W**	**L**	**T**	**Pct.**	**Pts.**	**OP**
San Diego*	10	5	0	.667	382	267
Denver	6	9	0	.400	298	390
Kansas City	4	11	0	.267	216	322
Oakland	4	11	0	.267	266	368
National Football Conference						
East Division	**W**	**L**	**T**	**Pct.**	**Pts.**	**OP**
Dallas*	13	2	0	.867	449	298
N.Y. Giants#	10	5	0	.667	338	313
Washington	8	7	0	.533	307	304
Philadelphia	7	8	0	.467	319	291
North Division	**W**	**L**	**T**	**Pct.**	**Pts.**	**OP**
Green Bay*	12	3	0	.800	401	278
Minnesota	8	7	0	.533	346	289
Detroit	7	8	0	.467	333	410
Chicago	6	9	0	.400	301	323
South Division	**W**	**L**	**T**	**Pct.**	**Pts.**	**OP**
Tampa Bay*	9	6	0	.600	311	239
New Orleans	7	8	0	.467	354	355
Carolina	6	9	0	.400	236	324
Atlanta	3	12	0	.200	215	373
West Division	**W**	**L**	**T**	**Pct.**	**Pts.**	**OP**
Seattle*	10	5	0	.667	352	247
Arizona	7	8	0	.467	356	380
San Francisco	5	10	0	.333	212	344
St. Louis	3	12	0	.200	244	390

**Clinched division title*
#Clinched playoff berth

THURSDAY NIGHT, DECEMBER 20

PITTSBURGH 41, ST. LOUIS 24—at Edward Jones Dome, attendance 65,705. Making his first start for the injured Willie Parker, Najeh Davenport rushed for 123 yards and scored 2 touchdowns for the Steelers. Three days later, the Steelers clinched a playoff berth when Cleveland lost to Cincinnati. The Steelers amassed 425 yards for the game, and scored on their first four possessions, all on drives in excess of 65 yards. The Rams scored three times themselves, capped by Jeff Wilkins' 52-yard field goal with 1:01 left in the first half to cut the deficit to 24-17. The Steelers opened the second half with a 10-play, 69-yard drive, capped by Davenport's 1-yard run for a 31-17 lead. The Rams answered with a touchdown, but Jeff Reed kicked a 29-yard field goal to cap a 13-play drive with 4:38 remaining to take a 34-24 lead. Faced with fourth-and-10 from their own 34, Marc Bulger's pass was intercepted by Ike Taylor, who returned it 51 yards for a touchdown and 41-24 lead with 3:46 remaining. Ben Roethlisberger was 16 of 20 for 261 yards and 3 touchdowns. Davenport rushed 24 times for 123 yards. Santonio Holmes had 4 receptions for 133 yards. Bulger was 18 of 35 for 208 yards and 3 touchdowns, with 2 interceptions.

Pittsburgh	7	17	7	10	—	41
St. Louis	7	10	7	0	—	24

Pitt — N. Washington 17 pass from Roethlisberger (Reed kick)
StL — Jackson 12 pass from Bulger (Wilkins kick)
Pitt — FG Reed 21
StL — Bruce 12 pass from Bulger (Wilkins kick)
Pitt — N. Washington 33 pass from Roethlisberger (Reed kick)
Pitt — Davenport 12 pass from Roethlisberger (Reed kick)
StL — FG Wilkins 52
Pitt — Davenport 1 run (Reed kick)
StL — Bennett 23 pass from Bulger (Wilkins kick)
Pitt — FG Reed 29
Pitt — Taylor 51 interception return (Reed kick)

SATURDAY NIGHT, DECEMBER 22

DALLAS 20, CAROLINA 13—at Bank of America Stadium, attendance 73,860. Marion Barber rushed for 110 yards and 1 touchdown for the Cowboys, who the next day were assured home-field advantage throughout the playoffs when Green Bay lost to the Bears. Dallas outgained Carolina 405-216 in total yards and maintained possession for exactly 39 minutes. The Cowboys led 14-0 early in the second quarter, but Terrell Owens suffered a high ankle sprain on the play previous to the second touchdown, and the Cowboys seemed to struggle thereafter. The Panthers cut the deficit to 17-7 and reached the Cowboys' 1 in the third quarter. But a false start penalty, and consecutive sacks by the Cowboys, forced the Panthers to settle for John Kasay's 37-yard field goal. Thomas Davis' interception at the Panthers' 3 early in the fourth quarter kept the score 17-10, but the Cowboys forced a three-and-out and Patrick Crayton's 16-yard catch set up Nick Folk's 23-yard field goal for a 20-10 lead with 8:17 to play. Steve Smith caught a 57-yard pass to set up Kasay's 25-yard field goal with 3:01 remaining, but Barber rushed for 2 first downs in the final minutes to ensure the victory. Tony Romo was 28 of 42 for 257 yards and 1 touchdown, with 1 interception. Barber rushed 22 times for 110 yards. Matt Moore, making his second start, was 15 of 28 for 182 yards and 1 touchdown, with 1 interception. Smith had 9 receptions for 137 yards. No other Panthers' receiver had more than one catch.

Dallas	7	10	0	3	—	20
Carolina	0	7	3	3	—	13

Dall — Owens 10 pass from Romo (Folk kick)
Dall — Barber 5 run (Folk kick)
Car — S. Smith 11 pass from Moore (Kasay kick)
Dall — FG Folk 42
Car — FG Kasay 37
Dall — FG Folk 23
Car — FG Kasay 25

SUNDAY, DECEMBER 23

ARIZONA 30, ATLANTA 27 (OT)—at University of Phoenix Stadium, attendance 64,159. Neil Rackers made a field goal to end regulation and the game-winning kick in overtime as the Cardinals rallied to defeat the Falcons. The clubs combined for 842 yards, including 437 by the Cardinals. Arizona scored on its last three possessions of the first half, capped by J.J. Arrington's 4-yard touchdown reception just 16 seconds before halftime, to take a 24-14 lead. The Falcons pulled to within 24-17 on the strength of a 16-play, 83-yard drive. The Faclons' defense then forced a three-and-out, and DeAngelo Hall returned the punt 16 yards. Chris Redman then completed 6 of 8 passes on the ensuing 48-yard drive, capped by Alge Crumpler's 7-yard catch with 4:45 remaining, to tie the game. The Falcons' defense forced another three-and-out, and Redman completed four consecutive passes to set up Morten Andersen's 21-yard field goal for a 27-24 lead with 1:38 left. Kurt Warner completed two key third-down passes that led to Rackers' game-tying 29-yard field goal as regulation expired. In overtime, the Cardinals won the toss and Warner completed 25- and 9-yard passes to Anquan Boldin, and a 19-yard pass to Larry Fitzgerald, to set up Rackers' game-winning 31-yard field goal. Warner was 35 of 52 for 369 yards and 3 touchdowns. Boldin had 13 receptions for 162 yards. Redman was 28 of 42 for 315 yards and 2 touchdowns, with 1 interception. Roddy White had 12 catches for 141 yards, and Laurent Robinson added 7 receptions for 114 yards.

Atlanta	7	7	0	13	0	—	27
Arizona	7	17	0	3	3	—	30

Ari — Boldin 4 pass from Warner (Rackers kick)
Atl — Snelling 1 run (Andersen kick)
Ari — Boldin 13 pass from Warner (Rackers kick)
Atl — Robinson 74 pass from Redman (Andersen kick)
Ari — FG Rackers 32
Ari — Arrington 4 pass from Warner (Rackers kick)
Atl — FG Andersen 23
Atl — Crumpler 7 pass from Redman (Andersen kick)
Atl — FG Andersen 21
Ari — FG Rackers 29
Ari — FG Rackers 31

N.Y. GIANTS 38, BUFFALO 21—at Ralph Wilson Stadium, attendance 71,302. Ahmad Bradshaw and Brandon Jacobs combined to rush for 294 yards and 3 touchdowns as the Giants secured a playoff berth with their franchise-best seventh consecutive road victory. With wind gusts of 50 miles per hour and snow falling, the teams only scored in the two quarters that they were going to the west end zone. In the poor conditions, each team committed 4 turnovers. The Giants led 17-14 at halftime, but Keith Ellison intercepted Eli Manning's pass on the first play of the second half. Marshawn Lynch scored two plays later for a 21-17 lead. Despite driving east, the Giants drove to the Bills' 1, but Reuben Droughns was stopped twice, Bradshaw stopped once, and on fourth-and-goal from the 1-yard line Droughns was dropped by John McCargo for a 4-yard loss. The Giants drove to the Bills' 11 to begin the fourth quarter, but Manning fumbled and Larry Tripplett recovered. Two plays later, Kawika Mitchell intercepted a tipped pass and returned it 20 yards for a touchdown and 24-21 Giants lead. With 6:27 left, pinned on their own 12-yard line, Bradshaw broke a few tackles and raced 88 yards through the snow for a touchdown and 31-21 lead. Two plays later, Corey Webster intercepted Trent Edwards' pass and returned it 34 yards for a touchdown. Manning was 7 of 15 for 111 yards, with 2 interceptions. Bradshaw carried 17 times for 151 yards, and Jacobs rushed 25 times for 143 yards. Edwards was 9 of 26 for 161 yards and 2 touchdowns, with 3 interceptions.

N.Y. Giants	0	17	0	21	—	38
Buffalo	14	0	7	0	—	21

Buff — Gaines 3 pass from Edwards (Lindell kick)
Buff — Evans 4 pass from Edwards (Lindell kick)
NYG — Jacobs 6 run (Tynes kick)
NYG — Jacobs 43 run (Tynes kick)
NYG — FG Tynes 42
Buff — Lynch 3 run (Lindell kick)
NYG — Mitchell 20 interception return (Tynes kick)
NYG — Bradshaw 88 run (Tynes kick)
NYG — Webster 34 interception return (Tynes kick)

CHICAGO 35, GREEN BAY 7—at Soldier Field, attendance 62,272. The Bears blocked 2 punts and intercepted a pair of passes as Chicago battled through a minus-18 wind chill to defeat the Packers. Ryan Grant's 66-yard touchdown run in the second quarter gave the Packers a 7-6 lead, but the Bears responded late in the half with Garrett Wolfe's 33-yard screen pass to set up Adrian Peterson's 8-yard touchdown run for a 13-7 lead. Alex Brown intercepted Brett Favre's short pass three plays into the second half. Jason McKie gained 2 yards on fourth-and-1 moments later to set up Kyle Orton's 3-yard touchdown pass to Desmond Clark. Orton's 2-point conversion pass to Greg Olsen extended the lead to 21-7. The Bears' defense forced a three-and-out, and Charles Tillman blocked Jon Ryan's punt. Corey Graham recovered and ran 7 yards for his fist NFL touchdown and 28-7 lead. In the fourth quarter, eighth-year linebacker Brian Urlacher had his first career interception return for a touchdown when he took Favre's slant pass 85 yards the other way. Orton was 9 of 15 for 104 yards and 1 touchdown. Peterson carried 30 times for 102 yards. Favre was 17 of 32 for 153 yards, with 2 interceptions. Grant carried 14 times for 100 yards.

Green Bay	0	7	0	0	—	7
Chicago	3	10	15	7	—	35

Chi — FG Gould 31
Chi — FG Gould 35
GB — Grant 66 run (Crosby kick)
Chi — Peterson 8 run (Gould kick)
Chi — Clark 3 pass from Orton (Olsen pass from Orton)
Chi — Graham 7 blocked punt return (Gould kick)
Chi — Urlacher 85 interception return (Gould kick)

CINCINNATI 19, CLEVELAND 14—at Paul Brown Stadium, attendance 66,023. Kenny Watson ran for 130 yards and the Bengals' defense intercepted 4 passes to keep the Browns from clinching a playoff berth. The Bengals led 6-0 with 1:27 left in the half when Chinedum Ndukwe intercepted Derek Anderson's pass and returned it 44 yards. Carson Palmer completed a 5-yard touchdown pass to T.J. Houshmandzadeh on the next play for a 13-0 lead. On the next play from scrimmage, Leon Hall intercepted Anderson's pass and returned it 12 yards. Three plays later, Watson scored on a 1-yard run with 26 seconds left in the half, giving the Bengals 13 points in 39 seconds for a 19-0 lead. The Browns drove the length of the field to being the second half, but Ndukwe intercepted Anderson's pass, which was tipped by Marvin White, for a touchback. Leigh Bodden's interception in the middle of the fourth quarter set up Braylon Edwards' second touchdown catch to pull the Browns within 19-14 with 5:57 to play. The Bengals were attempting to run out the clock when Andra Davis forced Watson to fumble. D'Qwell Jackson recovered at the Browns' 17 with 1:48 remaining. Anderson completed 6 of 8 passes, and then scrambled for a first down, getting out of bounds with one second remaining. Passing from the Bengals' 29 and with a victory putting the Browns in the playoffs, Anderson's pass into the end zone was batted down by Johnathan Joseph. Palmer was 11 of 21 for 115 yards and 1 touchdown, with 2 interceptions. Watson had 30 carries for 130 yards. Anderson was 29 of 48 for 251 yards and 2 touchdowns, with 4 interceptions.

Cleveland	0	0	7	7	—	14
Cincinnati	0	19	0	0	—	19

Cin — FG Graham 29
Cin — FG Graham 38
Cin — Houshmandzadeh 5 pass from Palmer (Graham kick)
Cin — Watson 1 run (pass failed)
Cle — Edwards 12 pass from Anderson (Dawson kick)
Cle — Edwards 5 pass from Anderson (Dawson kick)

DETROIT 25, KANSAS CITY 20—at Ford Field, attendance 59,938. Paris Lenon's 19-yard interception return for a touchdown highlighted a 19-0 start as the Lions snapped a six-game losing streak and handed the Chiefs their eighth consecutive defeat. Less than two minutes after T.J. Duckett gave the Lions a 7-0 lead, Casey FitzSimmons blocked Dustin Colquitt's punt for a safety and 9-0 lead. The Lions drove 47 yards after the free kick, capped by Jason Hanson's 46-yard field goal. Three plays later, Lenon intercepted Brodie Croyle's pass and returned it 61 yards for a touchdown. The Lions scored 19 points in eight minutes, three seconds and led 19-0. Croyle was injured on Lenon's return, and Damon Huard replaced him. Huard promptly engineered two touchdown drives, and later on his 10-play, 70-yard drive, capped by Dwayne Bowe's 34-yard touchdown catch, pulled the Chiefs to within 22-20 with 13:28 to play. The Chiefs went for the tying 2-point conversion, but Jared DeVries knocked down Huard's pass. With 1:54 to play, Huard's fourth-down pass from the Chiefs' 29 fell incomplete. Hanson's third field goal, from 47 yards with 43 seconds left, extended the lead to 25-20. Samie Parker was tackled at the Lions' 30 during a last-play lateral attempt by the Chiefs. Jon Kitna was 9 of 16 for 115 yards, with 1 interception. Duckett had 15 carries for 102 yards. Croyle was 9 of 12 for 69 yards, with 1 interception. Huard was 24 of 36 for 305 yards and 2 touchdowns. Tony Gonzalez had 10 catches for 137 yards.

Kansas City	0	14	0	6	—	20
Detroit	9	10	3	3	—	25

Det — Duckett 11 run (Hanson kick)
Det — Safety, FitzSimmons blocked punt out of bounds in end zone
Det — FG Hanson 46
Det — Lenon 61 interception return (Hanson kick)
KC — Battle 3 run (Carney kick)
KC — Allen 1 pass from Huard (Carney kick)
Det — FG Hanson 20
KC — Bowe 34 pass from Huard (pass failed)
Det — FG Hanson 47

INDIANAPOLIS 38, HOUSTON 15—at RCA Dome, attendance 57,262. Peyton Manning passed for 3 touchdowns as the Colts scored 38 unanswered points to defeat the Texans. The Colts rolled up 458 total yards, allowing just 299 yards. The Texans opened the game with a touchdown drive of 76 yards, but the Colts responded by scoring on their first four possessions, which included consecutive 92-yard touchdown drives. Bob Sanders' interception led to Dallas Clark's 11-yard touchdown catch for a 24-7 lead with 3:39 left in the half. The Colts scored on their first two drives of the second half, capped by Reggie Wayne's 7-yard touchdown catch with 3:08 left in the third quarter, for a 38-7 lead. Manning was 28 of 35 for 311 yards and 3 touchdowns. Wayne had 10 receptions for 143 yards. Sage Rosenfels was 22 of 36 for 233 yards and 2 touchdowns, with 3 interceptions.

Houston	7	0	0	8	—	15
Indianapolis	3	21	14	0	—	38

Hou — Walter 17 pass from Rosenfels (K. Brown kick)
Ind — FG Vinatieri 29
Ind — Addai 2 run (Vinatieri kick)
Ind — Clark 6 pass from Manning (Vinatieri kick)
Ind — Clark 11 pass from Manning (Vinatieri kick)
Ind — Dawson 4 run (Vinatieri kick)
Ind — Wayne 7 pass from Manning (Vinatieri kick)
Hou — A. Johnson 6 pass from Rosenfels (D. Walker run)

JACKSONVILLE 49, OAKLAND 11—at Jacksonville Municipal Stadium, attendance 66,905. The Jaguars' defense registered 4 sacks and forced 4 turnovers as Jacksonville secured a postseason berth and won for the sixth time in seven games. The Jaguars doubled the Raiders in first downs (26-13) and total yards (437-215) while scoring touchdowns on four of their first five possessions for a 28-3 lead. David Garrard completed a long 37-yard touchdown pass to a leaping Matt Jones in the third quarter, and Jamaal Fudge's interception led to Reggie Williams' 9-yard touchdown catch with 13:00 remaining for a 42-3 lead. Garrard was 11 of 18 for 199 yards and 2 touchdowns, with 1 interception. Quinn Gray replaced him in the second half and was 5 of 8 for 54 yards and 2 touchdowns. Fred Taylor rushed for 111 yards on just seven carries, posting his fifth consecutive 100-yard game. Josh McCown started and was 6 of 8 for 46 yards. JaMarcus Russell was 7 of 23 for 83 yards and his first NFL touchdown, a 2-yard pass to Zach Miller with six seconds remaining, along with 3 interceptions.

Oakland	0	3	0	8	—	11
Jacksonville	14	14	7	14	—	49

Jax — Taylor 62 run (Scobee kick)
Jax — Jones-Drew 14 run (Scobee kick)
Oak — FG Janikowski 41
Jax — G. Jones 2 pass from Garrard (Scobee kick)
Jax — Garrard 2 run (Scobee kick)
Jax — M. Jones 37 pass from Garrard (Scobee kick)
Jax — R. Williams 9 pass from Gray (Scobee kick)
Jax — Angulo 7 pass from Gray (Scobee kick)
Oak — Miller 2 pass from Russell (Curry pass from Russell)

NEW ENGLAND 28, MIAMI 7—at Gillette Stadium, attendance 68,756. Tom Brady passed for 3 touchdowns and Laurence Maroney rushed for 156 yards and a score as the Patriots became the first team with a 15-0 regular-season record and tied their own NFL record by posting their 18th consecutive victory. The Patriots accumulated 304 of their 400 total yards in the first half, as they scored on touchdown drives of 70, 79, 68, and 80 yards and converted 6 of 7 third-down situations. Jabar Gaffney's 48-yard touchdown catch with 3:33 left in the second quarter was the Patriots' NFL-record seventy-first of the season and gave New England a 28-0 lead. Brady was 18 of 33 for 215 yards and 3 touchdowns, with 2 interceptions. Maroney rushed 14 times for 156 yards. Cleo Lemon was 18 of 41 for 171 yards and 1 touchdown.

Miami	0	0	7	0	—	7
New England	7	21	0	0	—	28

NE — Moss 11 pass from Brady (Gostkowski kick)
NE — Moss 1 pass from Brady (Gostkowski kick)
NE — Maroney 59 run (Gostkowski kick)
NE — Gaffney 48 pass from Brady (Gostkowski kick)
Mia — Camarillo 21 pass from Lemon (Feely kick)

PHILADELPHIA 38, NEW ORLEANS 23—at Louisiana Superdome, attendance 70,011. Five touchdowns were scored in the first quarter. Donovan McNabb passed for 263 yards and 3 touchdowns as the Eagles delivered a severe blow to the Saints' playoff hopes. The Eagles needed just three, six, and four plays to drive 73, 63, and 85 yards to take a 21-14 lead. The Saints cut the deficit to 24-17 with a field goal as the half expired, and New Orleans opened the second half by driving to the Eagles' 1. But Mike Karney was stopped for no gain on second down, and Aaron Stecker failed to score on third and fourth down. The Eagles responded with a 15-play, 98-yard drive, which included 3 third-down conversions, and was capped by Greg Lewis' 9-yard touchdown catch to take a 31-17 lead with 2:55 left in the third quarter. The Saints answered with a pair of field goals to pull within 31-23 with 7:19 to play, but the Eagles drove 56 yards in nine plays, capped by McNabb's 7-yard touchdown pass to Kevin Curtis on third-and-goal for a 38-23 lead with 2:28 left. McNabb was 24 of 35 for 263 yards and 3 touchdowns. Brian Westbrook had 17 carries for 100 yards. Drew Brees was 27 of 42 for 284 yards, with 1 interception.

Philadelphia	21	3	7	7	—	38
New Orleans	14	3	0	6	—	23

Phil — Curtis fumble recovery in end zone (Akers kick)
NO — Stecker 3 run (Gramatica kick)
NO — Stecker 1 run (Gramatica kick)
Phil — Buckhalter 20 run (Akers kick)
Phil — R. Brown 31 pass from McNabb (Akers kick)
Phil — FG Akers 24
NO — FG Gramatica 55
Phil — Lewis 9 pass from McNabb (Akers kick)
NO — FG Gramatica 35
NO — FG Gramatica 46
Phil — Curtis 7 pass from McNabb (Akers kick)

SAN FRANCISCO 21, TAMPA BAY 19—at Monster Park, attendance 68,193. Shaun Hill passed for 3 touchdowns to improve to 2-0 as a starter. The 49ers won despite being outgained 434-213 in total yards. The Buccaneers led 13-7 at halftime, but in the third quarter the 49ers' Patrick Willis sacked Luke McCown deep in Buccaneers' territory and forced him to fumble. Mark Roman recovered, and four plays later Hill completed a 5-yard touchdown pass to Vernon Davis for a 14-13 lead. Early in the fourth quarter, Nate Clements intercepted a pass and returned it 62 yards. On the next play, Hill tossed a short pass to Frank Gore which resulted in a 23-yard touchdown and 21-13 lead. The Buccaneers drove to the 49ers' 25, but McCown's fourth-and-6 pass fell incomplete with 5:20 left. The Buccaneers' defense forced a punt, and beginning from their own 39-yard line with 2:45 remaining, McCown completed 5 of 7 passes, including an 18-yard pass to Michael Clayton on fourth down, and capped by Jerramy Stevens' 24-yard touchdown catch with 1:20 left. The Buccaneers' went for the 2-point conversion, and Clayton caught the pass, but landed on the back end line. The onside kick bounded out of bounds, ensuring the 49ers' victory. Hill was 11 of 24 for 123 yards and 3 touchdowns, with 1 interception. Jeff Garcia was 12 of 20 for 196 yards and 1 touchdown. Luke McCown, with the Buccaneers' fourth-seed in the NFC playoffs already secured, played the second half and was 18 of 32 for 185 yards and 1 touchdown, with 1 interception.

Tampa Bay	6	7	0	6	—	19
San Francisco	0	7	7	7	—	21

TB — FG Bryant 34
TB — FG Bryant 22
SF — D. Jackson 21 pass from Hill (Nedney kick)
TB — Stevens 24 pass from Garcia (Bryant kick)
SF — Davis 5 pass from Hill (Nedney kick)
SF — Gore 23 pass from Hill (Nedney kick)
TB — Stevens 24 pass from L. McCown (pass failed)

SEATTLE 27, BALTIMORE 6—at Qwest Field, attendance 68,164. Matt Hasselbeck passed for 2 touchdowns as the Seahawks secured the third seed in the NFC while handing the Ravens their ninth consecutive defeat. Seattle scored three touchdowns in the second quarter, with Leroy Hill's 20-yard fumble return for a score sandwiched between 89- and 70-yard drives, to take a 21-0 lead.

The Ravens failed to run a play inside the Seahawks' 35-yard line, with their lone touchdown coming on rookie Troy Smith's 79-yard pass to Derrick Mason with 4:41 remaining. Hasselbeck was 18 of 27 for 199 yards and 2 touchdowns, with 2 interceptions. Smith, making his first NFL start, was 16 of 33 for 199 yards and 1 touchdown.

Baltimore	0	0	0	6	—	6
Seattle	0	21	6	0	—	27

Sea	—	Burleson 21 pass from Hasselbeck (J. Brown kick)
Sea	—	Hill 20 fumble return (J. Brown kick)
Sea	—	Alexander 14 pass from Hasselbeck (J. Brown kick)
Sea	—	FG J. Brown 42
Sea	—	FG J. Brown 39
Balt	—	Mason 79 pass from T. Smith (pass failed)

TENNESSEE 10, N.Y. JETS 6—at LP Field, attendance 69,143. Antwan Odom blocked an extra-point attempt in the first half, allowing the Titans to maintain their lead and hold on for the victory. By winning, the Titans guaranteed their own destiny for the playoffs, as a victory in their final game would ensure them the sixth seed in the postseason. Reynaldo Hill's interception at the Jets' 40 late in the first quarter set up Chris Brown's 4-yard touchdown run for a 7-0 lead. The Jets responded with a 77-yard touchdown drive, but Odom blocked Mike Nugent's extra-point attempt. The Jets had two chances to score before halftime, but Keith Bulluck intercepted a pass in the end zone for a touchback to thwart one drive, and Nugent's 51-yard field-goal attempt sailed wide left to end the other possession. The Titans opened the second half with a defensive stop and then the offense drove 58 yards to Rob Bironas' 46-yard field goal for a 10-6 lead. The Jets' drove to the Titans' 45 with 1:50 to play, but on fourth-and-4, Tony Brown sacked Chad Pennington. It was the Titans' sixth sack of the day. LenDale White gained seven yards on third-and-6 with 1:40 remaining to secure the victory. Young was 12 of 22 for 166 yards, with 1 interception. White had 23 carries for 103 yards. Pennington was 26 of 32 for 264 yards and 1 touchdown, with 2 interceptions. Jerricho Cotchery had 8 receptions for 152 yards.

N.Y. Jets	0	6	0	0	—	6
Tennessee	0	7	3	0	—	10

Tenn	—	C. Brown 4 run (Bironas kick)
NYJ	—	Cotchery 9 pass from Pennington (kick blocked)
Tenn	—	FG Bironas 46

SUNDAY NIGHT, DECEMBER 23

WASHINGTON 32, MINNESOTA 21—at Metrodome, attendance 63,634. Todd Collins passed for 254 yards and 2 touchdowns, and Clinton Portis passed and ran for a touchdown, as the Redskins put themselves in the driver's seat for the NFC's final playoff berth. The Vikings would have secured the NFC's sixth seed with a victory, but the Redskins jumped to a 25-0 lead. Kedric Golston started the scoring spree by stuffing Tony Richardson in the end zone for a safety less than five minutes into the game. Leading 9-0 in the second quarter, Shawn Springs intercepted a pass. Two plays later, Collins hit Santana Moss in stride in the end zone for a 32-yard touchdown and 16-0 lead. The Redskins' defense forced a punt, and Collins engineered a 10-play, 80-yard drive. The possession ended when Portis rolled right and completed a 15-yard halfback option pass to a wide open Antwaan Randle El for a touchdown and 22-0 lead with 44 seconds left in the half. The Redskins led 25-7 entering the fourth quarter, but Mewelde Moore ignited the Vikings with a 17-yard punt return and Tarvaris Jackson scored on a 6-yard scramble with 10:18 to play. Two plays later, Moss caught a 23-yard pass pass along the sideline for a first down. Unsure if Moss had been in bounds, the Redskins ran up to the line and quickly snapped the ball, but Collins mishandled the snap and Kevin Williams recovered. However, the Redskins challenged, and the referee agreed, that Minnesota had 12 players on the field. Seven plays later, Portis scored on a 13-yard run for a 32-14 lead with 5:06 remaining. Collins was 22 of 29 for 254 yards and 2 touchdowns. Jackson was 25 of 41 for 220 yards and 1 touchdown, with 2 interceptions.

Washington	9	13	3	7	—	32
Minnesota	0	0	7	14	—	21

Wash	—	Safety, Golston tackled Richardson in end zone
Wash	—	Cooley 33 pass from Collins (Suisham kick)
Wash	—	S. Moss 32 pass from Collins (Suisham kick)
Wash	—	Randle El 15 pass from Portis (pass failed)
Wash	—	FG Suisham 26
Minn	—	Kleinsasser 2 pass from Jackson (Longwell kick)
Minn	—	Jackson 6 run (Longwell kick)
Wash	—	Portis 13 run (Suisham kick)
Minn	—	Jackson 1 run (Longwell kick)

MONDAY NIGHT, DECEMBER 24

SAN DIEGO 23, DENVER 3—at Qualcomm Stadium, attendance 65,477. The Chargers' defense registered 4 sacks and forced 3 turnovers as San Diego throttled the Broncos. Denver opened the game by driving to the Chargers' 18, but on third down Igor Olshansky sacked Jay Cutler and forced him to fumble. Shawne Merriman recovered the ball, and the Broncos did not threaten the rest of the half. The Chargers' offense, meanwhile, scored on five of its first six possessions, capped by Philip Rivers' 14-yard touchdown pass to Chris Chambers that concluded an 11-play, 84-yard drive to open the second half, to take a 23-0 lead with 7:56 left in the third quarter. The Broncos cut the deficit to 23-3 and drove to the Chargers' 2 early in the fourth quarter, but Matt Wilhelm stuffed Cecil Sapp for a 1-yard loss on fourth-and-1 with 11:44 to play. Rivers was 17 of 25 for 189 yards and 1 touchdown. LaDainian Tomlinson rushed 19 times for 107 yards. Cutler was 14 of 32 for 155 yards, with 2 interceptions.

Denver	0	0	3	0	—	3
San Diego	10	6	7	0	—	23

SD	—	FG Kaeding 40
SD	—	Tomlinson 17 run (Kaeding kick)
SD	—	FG Kaeding 23
SD	—	FG Kaeding 29
SD	—	Chambers 14 pass from Rivers (Kaeding kick)
Den	—	FG Elam 23

SEVENTEENTH WEEK SUMMARIES

American Football Conference

East Division	**W**	**L**	**T**	**Pct.**	**Pts.**	**OP**
New England*	16	0	0	1.000	589	274
Buffalo	7	9	0	.438	252	354
N.Y. Jets	4	12	0	.250	268	355
Miami	1	15	0	.063	267	437
North Division	**W**	**L**	**T**	**Pct.**	**Pts.**	**OP**
Pittsburgh*	10	6	0	.625	393	269
Cleveland	10	6	0	.625	402	382
Cincinnati	7	9	0	.438	380	385
Baltimore	5	11	0	.313	275	384
South Division	**W**	**L**	**T**	**Pct.**	**Pts.**	**OP**
Indianapolis*	13	3	0	.813	450	262
Jacksonville#	11	5	0	.688	411	304
Tennessee#	10	6	0	.625	301	297
Houston	8	8	0	.500	379	384
West Division	**W**	**L**	**T**	**Pct.**	**Pts.**	**OP**
San Diego*	11	5	0	.688	412	284
Denver	7	9	0	.438	320	409
Kansas City	4	12	0	.250	226	335
Oakland	4	12	0	.250	283	398

National Football Conference

East Division	**W**	**L**	**T**	**Pct.**	**Pts.**	**OP**
Dallas*	13	3	0	.813	455	325
N.Y. Giants#	10	6	0	.625	373	351
Washington#	9	7	0	.563	334	310
Philadelphia	8	8	0	.500	336	300
North Division	**W**	**L**	**T**	**Pct.**	**Pts.**	**OP**
Green Bay*	13	3	0	.813	435	291
Minnesota	8	8	0	.500	365	311
Detroit	7	9	0	.438	346	444
Chicago	7	9	0	.438	334	348
South Division	**W**	**L**	**T**	**Pct.**	**Pts.**	**OP**
Tampa Bay*	9	7	0	.563	334	270
Carolina	7	9	0	.438	267	347
New Orleans	7	9	0	.438	379	388
Atlanta	4	12	0	.250	259	414
West Division	**W**	**L**	**T**	**Pct.**	**Pts.**	**OP**
Seattle*	10	6	0	.625	393	291
Arizona	8	8	0	.500	404	399
San Francisco	5	11	0	.313	219	364
St. Louis	3	13	0	.188	263	438

**Clinched division title*
#Clinched playoff berth

SATURDAY NIGHT, DECEMBER 29

NEW ENGLAND 38, N.Y. GIANTS 35—at Giants Stadium, attendance 79,110. The Patriots overcame a 12-point second-half deficit to become the first team to produce a 16-0 regular-season record. Both teams had already secured their postseason berths, the Patriots with their first seed in the AFC and the Giants with the fifth seed in the NFC, and would meet five weeks later in Super Bowl XLII. The Patriots scored on their first four first-half possessions, but the Giants had touchdown drives of 74 and 85 yards, along with Domenik Hixon's 74-yard kickoff return, to take a 21-16 halftime lead. The Giants' defense forced a three-and-out to begin the second half, and Brandon Jacobs had runs of 16 and 15 yards to set up Eli Manning's 19-yard touchdown pass to Plaxico Burress, on third-and-9, to take a 28-16 lead with 9:12 remaining in the third quarter. Tom Brady responded by completing five consecutive passes to set up Laurence Maroney's 6-yard touchdown run to pull within 28-23. In the fourth quarter, on second-and-10 from their own 35-yard line, Brady attempted a long pass to a wide open Randy Moss that was dropped near the 20-yard line. Undaunted, on the next play Brady attempted the same pass and Moss caught it for a 65-yard touchdown with 11:06 to play. Not only did the Patriots take a 31-28 lead with the touchdown, it was also Moss' record 23rd touchdown catch (breaking Jerry Rice's record of 22 in 1987) and Brady's 50th touchdown pass (surpassing Peyton Manning's mark of 49 set in 2004). Two plays later, Ellis Hobbs intercepted Eli Manning's pass to set up Maroney's 5-yard touchdown run for a 38-28 lead with 4:36 to play. Brady had continued the drive with a 13-yard pass to Kevin Faulk on third-and-11 and a 12-yard pass to Wes Welker on third-and-9. Manning's 3-yard touchdown pass to Burress cut the deficit to 38-35 with 1:04 remaining, but Mike Vrabel recovered the ensuing onside kick to secure the victory. The Patriots finished the season with an NFL-record 589 points and the victory was their nineteenth in a row, also setting a league record. Brady was 32 of 42 for 356 yards and 2 touchdowns. Welker had 11 receptions for 122 yards. Manning was 22 of 32 for 251 yards and 4 touchdowns, with 1 interception.

New England	3	13	7	15	—	38
N.Y. Giants	7	14	7	7	—	35

NYG	—	Jacobs 7 pass from Manning (Tynes kick)
NE	—	FG Gostkowski 37
NE	—	Moss 4 pass from Brady (Gostkowski kick)
NYG	—	Hixon 74 kickoff return (Tynes kick)
NE	—	FG Gostkowski 45
NE	—	FG Gostkowski 37
NYG	—	Boss 3 pass from Manning (Tynes kick)
NYG	—	Burress 19 pass from Manning (Tynes kick)
NE	—	Maroney 6 run (Gostkowski kick)
NE	—	Moss 65 pass from Brady (Maroney run)
NE	—	Maroney 5 run (Gostkowski kick)
NYG	—	Burress 3 pass from Manning (Tynes kick)

SUNDAY, DECEMBER 30

ARIZONA 48, ST. LOUIS 19—at University of Phoenix Stadium, attendance 64,671. Kurt Warner passed for 3 touchdowns as the Cardinals scored their most points in a game in 30 years and finished 8-8, their best record since 1998. The Cardinals outgained the Rams 422-234 in total yards and forced 3 turnovers. Edgerrin James' 2-yard touchdown run gave Arizona a 10-3 second-quarter lead. Just 1:05 later, Antrel Rolle intercepted Marc Bulger's pass and returned it 47 yards for a touchdown. The Cardinals' defense then forced a punt and Warner completed a 21-yard touchdown pass to Larry Fitzgerald for a 24-3 lead. Arizona lead 31-13 late in the third quarter when Oshiomogho Atogwe intercepted Warner's pass and returned it 52 yards for a touchdown to pull within 31-19. But Warner answered by completing all four pass attempts on the ensuing 6-play, 71-yard drive, capped by Anquan Boldin's 20-yard touchdown catch with 13:37 remaining for a 38-19 lead. Warner was 23 of 39 for 300 yards and 3 touchdowns, with 2 interceptions. Fitzgerald had 11 catches for 171 yards. James rushed 24 times for 102 yards. Bulger was 13 of 25 for 176 yards and 1 touchdown, with 2 interceptions.

St. Louis	3	3	13	0	—	19
Arizona	3	21	7	17	—	48

StL	—	FG Wilkins 37
Ari	—	FG Rackers 23
Ari	—	James 2 run (Rackers kick)
Ari	—	Rolle 47 interception return (Rackers kick)
Ari	—	Fitzgerald 21 pass from Warner (Rackers kick)
StL	—	FG Wilkins 42
StL	—	Klopfenstein 36 pass from Bulger (Wilkins kick)
Ari	—	Fitzgerald 6 pass from Warner (Rackers kick)
StL	—	Atogwe 52 interception return (pass failed)
Ari	—	Boldin 20 pass from Warner (Rackers kick)
Ari	—	FG Rackers 33
Ari	—	Hayes 30 interception return (Rackers kick)

ATLANTA 44, SEATTLE 41—at Georgia Dome, attendance 64,925. Chris Redman passed for 4 touchdowns as Emmitt Thomas won his first game as the Falcons' interim coach. The Falcons snapped a six-game losing streak despite the Seahawks accumulating 501 total yards (opposed to Atlanta's 364 yards). Seattle led 10-0, but the Falcons scored on eight of their nine possessions. With the third seed in the NFC playoffs already secured, Matt Hasselbeck was removed in the third quarter. Seattle still led 27-20 when Redman completed a 55-yard touchdown pass to Alge Crumpler to tie the game on the first play of the fourth quarter. Seneca Wallace was sacked by Jonathan Babineaux on the next play, fumbled, and Montavious Stanley recovered. Three plays later Crumpler caught a 7-yard touchdown pass for a 34-27 lead. Chris Crocker intercepted Wallace's pass on the next play, and Roddy White caught a 10-yard touchdown pass on the following play for a 41-27 lead with 13:15 to play. Redman had completed three touchdown passes in a span of 1:37. The Seahawks drove 80 and 81 yards for touchdowns on their next two possessions, with Morten Andersen's 32-yard field goal mixed in, to pull within 44-41 with 54 seconds remaining. Atlanta recovered the onside kick to secure the victory. Redman was 17 of 27 for 251 yards and 4 touchdowns. Hasselbeck was 15 of 25 for 147 yards and 1 touchdown. Wallace was 17 of 22 for 206 yards and 2 touchdowns, with 1 interception. Nate Burleson had 7 catches for 119 yards.

Seattle	7	10	10	14	—	41
Atlanta	0	17	3	24	—	44

Sea	—	Alexander 2 run (J. Brown kick)
Sea	—	FG J. Brown 54
Atl	—	Horn 4 pass from Redman (Andersen kick)
Atl	—	Dunn 5 run (Andersen kick)
Sea	—	Engram 30 pass from Hasselbeck (J. Brown kick)
Atl	—	FG Andersen 30
Sea	—	FG J. Brown 51
Atl	—	FG Andersen 37
Sea	—	Morris 29 run (J. Brown kick)
Atl	—	Crumpler 55 pass from Redman (Andersen kick)
Atl	—	Crumpler 7 pass from Redman (Andersen kick)
Atl	—	White 10 pass from Redman (Andersen kick)
Sea	—	Burleson 45 pass from Wallace (J. Brown kick)
Atl	—	FG Andersen 32
Sea	—	Burleson 13 pass from Wallace (J. Brown kick)

BALTIMORE 27, PITTSBURGH 21—at M&T Bank Stadium, attendance 71,353. Troy Smith passed for a touchdown as the Ravens snapped their franchise-record nine-game losing streak. The Steelers could have finished with the third seed in the AFC with a win and Chargers' loss, but decided to rest Ben Roethlisberger and Hines Ward. In turn, the offense only managed one substantial drive in the first three quarters. The Ravens' offense scored on its first three possessions to take a 17-0 lead with 13:27 left in the half. In the

third quarter, Smith's 15-yard touchdown pass to Devard Darling capped a 74-yard drive and increased the lead to 27-7. Smith was 16 of 27 for 171 yards and 1 touchdown. Charlie Batch was 16 of 31 for 218 yards and 2 touchdowns, with 2 interceptions.

Pittsburgh	0	7	0	14	—	21
Baltimore	10	10	7	0	—	27

Balt	—	M. Smith 2 run (Stover kick)
Balt	—	FG Stover 28
Balt	—	Ross 32 run (Stover kick)
Pitt	—	Davenport 1 run (Reed kick)
Balt	—	FG Stover 31
Balt	—	Darling 15 pass from T. Smith (Stover kick)
Pitt	—	Holmes 59 pass from Batch (Reed kick)
Pitt	—	Wilson 7 pass from Batch (Reed kick)

CHICAGO 33, NEW ORLEANS 25—at Soldier Field, attendance 62,064. Devin Hester scored twice as the Bears ended the Saints' playoff hopes. New Orleans needed a victory and a loss by both the Vikings and the Redskins later in the day to reach the playoffs. The Saints outgained the Bears 413-275 in total yards, but a safety and Hester's punt return, his 11th career NFL punt return for a touchdown in two seasons, were the difference. The Bears led 10-0 before 31 points were scored in the final 8:35 of the first half. Drew Brees passed for a pair of touchdowns, while Adrian Peterson threw a halfback-option pass to Bernard Berrian and Hester caught a 55-yard long pass to give Chicago a 24-17 halftime lead. The Bears' defense forced a three-and-out to begin the second half, and Hester returned the ensuing punt 64 yards for a touchdown an 31-17 lead. Jahri Evans was flagged for holding in the end zone with 5:14 to play to increase the lead to 33-17. Pierre Thomas caught a touchdown pass and scored on a 2-point conversion with seven seconds left, but Rashied Davis recovered the ensuing onside kick. Kyle Orton was 12 of 27 for 190 yards and 2 touchdowns, with 1 interception. Brees was 35 of 60 for 320 yards and 3 touchdowns, with 2 interceptions. Thomas rushed 20 times for 105 yards and had 12 catches for 121 yards.

New Orleans	0	17	0	8	—	25
Chicago	10	14	7	2	—	33

Chi	—	FG Gould 39
Chi	—	Bradley 19 pass from Orton (Gould kick)
NO	—	Colston 3 pass from Brees (Gramatica kick)
Chi	—	Berrian 9 pass from Peterson (Gould kick)
NO	—	Colston 21 pass from Brees (Gramatica kick)
Chi	—	Hester 55 pass from Orton (Gould kick)
NO	—	FG Gramatica 48
Chi	—	Hester 64 punt return (Gould kick)
Chi	—	Safety, Evans flagged for offensive holding in end zone
NO	—	Thomas 11 pass from Brees (Thomas run)

CLEVELAND 20, SAN FRANCISCO 7—at Cleveland Browns Stadium, attendance 73,041. Jamal Lewis rushed for 128 yards and the Browns' defense registered 5 sacks to post the franchise's first-ever 7-1 home record. Win or lose, the Browns needed the Titans to lose Sunday night in order to reach the playoffs. Joshua Cribbs returned a punt 76 yards for a first-quarter touchdown, and Braylon Edwards caught a 45-yard touchdown pass in the second quarter for a 14-0 lead. Brady Quinn made his NFL debut with 3:20 remaining in the second quarter and the Browns up 14-7. Quinn replaced an injured Derek Anderson and led the Browns to a field goal while completing 3 of 8 passes for 45 yards. Anderson, who returned for the second half, was 11 of 20 for 152 yards and 1 touchdown, with 1 interception. Chris Weinke, the 49ers' fourth starting quarterback of the season, playing in place of injured Shaun Hill, was 13 of 22 for 104 yards and 1 touchdown.

San Francisco	0	7	0	0	—	7
Cleveland	7	10	0	3	—	20

Cle	—	Cribbs 76 punt return (Dawson kick)
Cle	—	Edwards 45 pass from Anderson (Dawson kick)

SF	—	Jackson 7 pass from Weinke (Nedney kick)
Cle	—	FG Dawson 23
Cle	—	FG Dawson 49

DENVER 22, MINNESOTA 19 (OT)—at INVESCO Field at Mile High, attendance 76,084. Jason Elam kicked his fourth game-winning field goal of the season for the Broncos. The Vikings needed a victory and a Redskins' loss to reach the playoffs. The Redskins, however, were playing at the same time and led 13-3 at halftime and 27-3 early in the fourth quarter of their game. The Broncos led 14-3 at halftime, and drove 52 yards in 13 plays to begin the second half with a field goal to take a 17-3 lead. An offensive facemask penalty in the end zone by Ryan Cook increased Denver's lead to 19-3 early in the fourth quarter. However, Tarvaris Jackson engineered successive scoring drives of 69 and 65 yards, both ending with touchdown passes to Bobby Wade and Jackson 2-point conversion runs, to tie the game with 2:21 remaining. The Vikings won the overtime coin toss, but two plays into the extra session, Alvin McKinley and Jamie Winborn sacked Jackson and forced him to fumble. Elvis Dumervil recovered at the Vikings' 13, and Elam kicked the game-winning 30-yard field goal on the next play. Cutler was 26 of 37 for 246 yards and 2 touchdowns. Brandon Marshall had 10 catches for 114 yards. Jackson was 16 of 31 for 175 yards and 2 touchdowns.

Minnesota	0	3	0	16	0	—	19
Denver	0	14	3	2	3	—	22

Minn	—	FG Longwell 22
Den	—	Marshall 15 pass from Cutler (Elam kick)
Den	—	Scheffler 2 pass from Cutler (Elam kick)
Den	—	FG Elam 43
Den	—	Safety, Cook facemask penalty in end zone
Minn	—	Wade 5 pass from T. Jackson (T. Jackson run)
Minn	—	Wade 22 pass from T. Jackson (T. Jackson run)
Den	—	FG Elam 30

GREEN BAY 34, DETROIT 13—at Lambeau Field, attendance 70,869. Brett Favre passed for 2 touchdowns as the second-seeded Packers tied the franchise record with their 13th victory. The Packers drove 62, 97, and 41 yards on their first three possessions, all resulting in touchdowns. The latter drive was set up by Atari Bigby's interception and capped by Favre's 4-yard touchdown pass to Bubba Franks two plays into the second quarter for a 21-3 lead. Craig Nall replaced Favre after that scoring drive, and competed a 32-yard touchdown pass to Ruvell Martin on fourth-and-2 with 2:48 left in the third quarter for a 31-13 lead. Favre was 9 of 11 for 99 yards and 2 touchdowns. Nall was 7 of 15 for 88 yards and 1 touchdown. Brandon Jackson rushed 20 times for 113 yards. Jon Kitna was 22 of 48 for 246 yards and 1 touchdown, with 2 interceptions.

Detroit	3	7	3	0	—	13
Green Bay	14	7	10	3	—	34

Det	—	FG Hanson 35
GB	—	Grant 27 run (Crosby kick)
GB	—	Robinson 5 pass from Favre (Crosby kick)
GB	—	Franks 4 pass from Favre (Crosby kick)
Det	—	McDonald 30 pass from Kitna (Hanson kick)
GB	—	FG Crosby 33
Det	—	FG Hanson 38
GB	—	Martin 32 pass from Nall (Crosby kick)
GB	—	FG Crosby 35

HOUSTON 42, JACKSONVILLE 28—at Reliant Stadium, attendance 70,660. Andre' Davis returned two kickoffs for touchdowns just 28 seconds apart as the Texans scored a team-record 42 points and finished with the best record (8-8) in franchise history. The Jaguars had already secured the fifth seed in the AFC playoffs, so reserve Quinn Gray started. Gray did well, passing for 4 touchdowns, however, the Texans, after punting to end their first two drives, scored touchdowns on their next six possessions. With 29 seconds left in the first half, Gray completed a 6-yard touchdown pass to Ernest Wilford. Davis returned the ensuing kickoff 97 yards down the left side for a touchdown with 15 seconds left in half. The Jaguars kicked off to begin the second half, and Davis this time returned the kick up the middle 104 yards for a touchdown and 28-14 lead with 14:47 left in the third quarter. He became the seventh player to return two kickoffs for touchdowns in the same game. Darius Walker's 1-yard scoring run capped a 71-yard drive early in the fourth quarter and gave Houston a 42-21 lead. Sage Rosenfels was 11 of 18 for 128 yards and 1 touchdown, with 1 interception. Gray was 25 of 39 for 302 yards and 4 touchdowns. Matt Jones had 8 catches for 138 yards.

| Jacksonville | 7 | 7 | 7 | 7 | — | 28 |
| Houston | 0 | 21 | 14 | 7 | — | 42 |

Jax	—	R. Williams 22 pass from Gray (Scobee kick)
Hou	—	Dayne 2 run (K. Brown kick)
Hou	—	Daniels 2 pass from Rosenfels (K. Brown kick)
Jax	—	Wilford 6 pass from Gray (Scobee kick)
Hou	—	A. Davis 97 kickoff return (K. Brown kick)
Hou	—	A. Davis 104 kickoff return (K. Brown kick)
Hou	—	Dayne 12 run (K. Brown kick)
Jax	—	M. Jones 5 pass from Gray (Scobee kick)
Hou	—	Walker 1 run (K. Brown kick)
Jax	—	Wilford 17 pass from Gray (Scobee kick)

CINCINNATI 38, MIAMI 25—at Dolphin Stadium, attendance 70,461. Carson Palmer passed for 3 touchdowns for the Bengals. Cincinnati led 14-10 late in the first half when Palmer completed 4 of 5 passes in a 63-yard drive, capped by Antonio Chatman's 4-yard scoring grab with four seconds remaining, for a 21-10 halftime lead. Cleo Lemon was injured on the Dolphins' second play of the second half. John Beck came in and fumbled his first snap. Chinedum Ndukwe recovered and returned the ball 54 yards for a touchdown and 28-10 lead. Beck's 2-yard scoring run cut the deficit to 28-17, but Palmer completed a 43-yard pass to Chad Johnson on the next play that led to Kenny Watson's 2-yard touchdown run and a 35-17 lead with 10:03 left. Palmer was 23 of 32 for 316 yards and 3 touchdowns, with 1 interception. Johnson had 4 catches for 131 yards. Lemon was 14 of 21 for 123 yards and 1 touchdown. Beck played the second half and was 13 of 21 for 135 yards and 1 touchdown.

| Cincinnati | 7 | 14 | 7 | 10 | — | 38 |
| Miami | 3 | 7 | 0 | 15 | — | 25 |

Mia	—	FG Feely 49
Cin	—	C. Johnson 2 pass from Palmer (Graham kick)
Mia	—	Ginn Jr. 5 pass from Lemon (Feely kick)
Cin	—	C. Johnson 70 pass from Palmer (Graham kick)
Cin	—	Chatman 4 pass from Palmer (Graham kick)
Cin	—	Ndukwe 54 fumble return (Graham kick)
Mia	—	Beck 2 run (Feely kick)
Cin	—	Watson 2 run (Graham kick)
Cin	—	FG Graham 30
Mia	—	Hagan 22 pass from Beck (Hagan pass from Beck)

N.Y. JETS 13, KANSAS CITY 10 (OT)—at The Meadowlands, attendance 76,737. Mike Nugent kicked a 43-yard field goal in the freezing rain in overtime as the Chiefs dropped their ninth consecutive game. The Chiefs trailed 10-3 when they took over at their own 17-yard line with 6:57 to play. Brodie Croyle completed 6 of 8 passes on the ensuing 9-play, 83-yard drive, capped by Jeff Webb's 26-yard scoring catch to tie the game with 2:59 to play. The Jets won the overtime coin toss. Kellen Clemens ran for a pair of first downs, and Thomas Jones had runs of 9, 8, 10, and 8 yards to set up Nugent's game-winning 33-yard kick. Nugent made the kick, but a holding penalty forced him to attempt a 43-yard kick, which he also made with 9:47 left in overtime. Clemens was 13 of 25 for 115 yards and 1 touchdown. Croyle was 20 of 43 for 195 yards and 1 touchdown.

| Kansas City | 0 | 3 | 0 | 7 | 0 | — | 10 |
| N.Y. Jets | 0 | 10 | 0 | 0 | 3 | — | 13 |

NYJ	—	T. Jones 15 pass from Clemens (Nugent kick)
KC	—	FG Carney 40
NYJ	—	FG Nugent 27
KC	—	Webb 26 pass from Croyle (Carney kick)
NYJ	—	FG Nugent 43

SAN DIEGO 30, OAKLAND 17—at McAfee Coliseum, attendance 61,706. The Chargers' defense registered 4 sacks and forced 4 fumbles, which led to 17 points, and gave the Chargers their sixth consecutive win and secured the third seed in the AFC playoffs. Making his first-ever NFL start, JaMarcus Russell's first starting quarterback pass was intercepted by Igor Olshansky. Nine player later, Philip Rivers completed a 7-yard touchdown pass to LaDainian Tomlinson. In the third quarter Jyles Tucker sacked Russell in the end zone, forced him to fumble and recovered the ball for a touchdown and 24-10 lead. Russell's 32-yard touchdown pass to Jerry Porter cut the deficit to 24-17, but Darren Sproles returned the ensuing kickoff 54 yards to set up Nate Kaeding's 31-yard field goal for a 27-17 lead with 13:36 remaining. Rivers was 13 of 23 for 135 yards and 2 touchdowns. JaMarcus Russell was 23 of 31 for 224 yards and 1 touchdown with 1 interception. Dominic Rhodes carried 29 times for 122 yards.

| San Diego | 7 | 7 | 10 | 6 | — | 30 |
| Oakland | 7 | 3 | 0 | 7 | — | 17 |

SD	—	Tomlinson 7 pass from Rivers (Kaeding kick)
Oak	—	Rhodes 1 run (Janikowski kick)
SD	—	Chambers 19 pass from Rivers (Kaeding kick)
Oak	—	FG Janikowski 53
SD	—	FG Kaeding 36
SD	—	Tucker fumble recovery in end zone (Kaeding kick)
Oak	—	Porter 32 pass from Russell (Janikowski kick)
SD	—	FG Kaeding 31
SD	—	FG Kaeding 24

PHILADELPHIA 17, BUFFALO 9—at Lincoln Financial Field, attendance 68,594. Donovan McNabb passed for 345 yards as the Eagles finished the season with three successive victories. The Eagles led 10-6 late in the third quarter when McNabb completed a 32-yard pass to Reggie Brown, who fumbled at the Bills' 1-yard line. For the second consecutive week, Kevin Curtis recovered a fumble in the end zone for a touchdown and 17-6 lead. The Bills added a third field goal, and drove to the Eagles' 19 early in the fourth quarter trailing 17-9, but Marshawn Lynch was stopped by Akeem Jordan for no gain on fourth-and-1 from the Eagles' 19. The Eagles forced a punt with 3:35 left and the offense ran all but the final 10 seconds off the clock. McNabb was 29 of 41 for 345 yards and 1 touchdown, with 1 interception. Trent Edwards was 16 of 30 for 133 yards. Lynch had 22 carries for 105 yards.

| Buffalo | 0 | 3 | 6 | 0 | — | 9 |
| Philadelphia | 3 | 7 | 0 | 7 | — | 17 |

Phil	—	Celek 2 pass from McNabb (Akers kick)
Buff	—	FG Lindell 29
Phil	—	FG Akers 38
Buff	—	FG Lindell 23
Phil	—	Curtis fumble recovery in end zone (Akers kick)
Buff	—	FG Lindell 22

CAROLINA 31, TAMPA BAY 23—at Raymond James Stadium, attendance 65,609. DeAngelo Williams rushed for 121 yards and 2 touchdowns and Matt Moore passed for 2 touchdowns for the Panthers. Moore won two of his three starts for Carolina, while Tampa Bay had the fourth seed secured for the NFC playoffs and rested Jeff Garcia among others. Luke McCown engineered a 98-yard drive in the third quarter, highlighted by his 31-yard scramble and capped by his 23-yard screen pass to Michael Bennett for a touchdown and 20-17 lead. Moore responded with a 46-yard pass to Drew Carter that was followed by Williams' 1-yard run for a 24-20 lead. Nursing a 24-23 lead in the fourth quarter, Moore completed a 13-yard pass to Carter on third-and-7, and on the next play Williams scored on a 32-yard run for a 31-23 lead with 6:24 to play. Richard Marshall intercepted a pass at the Panthers' 7 moments later to end the Buccaneers' final threat. Moore was 15 of 24 for 174 yards and 2 touchdowns, with 1 interception. Williams rushed

20 times for 121 yards. McCown was 21 of 28 for 236 yards and 2 touchdowns, with 1 interception.

| Carolina | 7 | 10 | 7 | 7 | — | 31 |
| Tampa Bay | 7 | 6 | 7 | 3 | — | 23 |

TB	—	Stevens 3 pass from McCown (Bryant kick)
Car	—	Fauria 2 pass from Moore (Kasay kick)
TB	—	FG Bryant 23
Car	—	Rosario 20 pass from Moore (Kasay kick)
TB	—	FG Bryant 23
Car	—	FG Kasay 19
TB	—	M. Bennett 23 pass from McCown (Bryant kick)
Car	—	D. Williams 1 run (Kasay kick)
TB	—	FG Bryant 49
Car	—	D. Williams 32 run (Kasay kick)

WASHINGTON 27, DALLAS 6—at FedExField, attendance 90,910. The Redskins' defense permitted just 1 rushing yard and only 147 total yards as Washington won its fourth consecutive game and clinched the NFC's final playoff berth. The Redskins led just 10-3 with 49 seconds left in the hal when Todd Collins completed a 15-yard pass to Santana Moss and 19-yard pass to Reche Caldwell to set up Shaun Suisham's 21-yard field goal for a 13-3 halftime lead. The Redskins' defense forced a punt to begin the second half, and the offense marched 63 yards in 12 plays, with 3 third-down conversions, capped by Clinton Portis' 1-yard run for a 20-3 lead with 6:48 left in the third quarter. Collins' 42-yard touchdown pass to Moss came two plays after Mat McBriar's sixth punt and staked the Redskins to a 27-3 lead with 11:58 remaining. Collins was 22 of 31 for 244 yards and 1 touchdown. Portis rushed 25 times for 104 yards and Moss had 8 catches for 115 yards. Romo was 7 of 16 for 86 yards, with 1 interceptions. Brad Johnson replaced him in the third quarter and was 7 of 11 for 79 yards.

| Dallas | 0 | 3 | 0 | 3 | — | 6 |
| Washington | 7 | 6 | 7 | 7 | — | 27 |

Wash	—	Portis 23 run (Suisham kick)
Wash	—	FG Suisham 46
Dall	—	FG Folk 37
Wash	—	FG Suisham 21
Wash	—	Portis 1 run (Suisham kick)
Wash	—	Moss 42 pass from Collins (Suisham kick)
Dall	—	FG Folk 30

SUNDAY NIGHT, DECEMBER 30
TENNESSEE 16, INDIANAPOLIS 10—at RCA Dome, attendance 57,202. Rob Bironas kicked 3 field goals, including 2 in the fourth quarter, as the Titans earned the sixth and final AFC playoff spot. The victory knocked Cleveland from the playoffs and gave Tennessee its first postseason berth since 2003. The Colts had secured the second seed in the AFC and removed Peyton Manning in the second quarter trailing 7-3. In the third quarter, Rocky Boiman recovered a fumble and four plays later Jim Sorgi completed a 3-yard touchdown pass to Craphonso Thorpe for a 10-7 lead. Vince Young injured his quadricep during the ensuing drive and Kerry Collins replaced him. Playing on his 35th birthday, Collins' first two passes went for first downs to keep alive the drive and set up Bironas' game-tying 40-yard field goal. The Titans' defense forced punts on the Colts' next two possessions, and Collins responded by engineering scoring drives of 58 and 32 yards, both capped by Bironas' field goals, for a 16-10 lead with 2:56 remaining. The Colts failed to gain a first down on their final possession. Young was 14 of 18 for 157 yards. Collins was 10 of 13 for 106 yards. Justin Gage had 7 receptions for 104 yards. Manning was 14 of 16 for 95 yards. Sorgi was 11 of 24 for 68 yards and 1 touchdown. Reggie Wayne had 12 catches for 87 yards.

| Tennessee | 7 | 0 | 3 | 6 | — | 16 |
| Indianapolis | 0 | 3 | 7 | 0 | — | 10 |

Tenn	—	C. Brown 8 run (Bironas kick)
Ind	—	FG Vinatieri 37
Ind	—	Thorpe 3 pass from Sorgi (Vinatieri kick)
Tenn	—	FG Bironas 40
Tenn	—	FG Bironas 54
Tenn	—	FG Bironas 33

For postseason summaries, please refer to pages 522 and 537-548.

2007 PRO FOOTBALL AWARDS

ASSOCIATED PRESS
Most Valuable Player	Tom Brady
Offensive Player of the Year	Tom Brady
Defensive Player of the Year	Bob Sanders
Offensive Rookie of the Year	Adrian Peterson
Defensive Rookie of the Year	Patrick Willis
Coach of the Year	Bill Belichick
Comeback Player of the Year	Greg Ellis

THE SPORTING NEWS
Player of the Year	Tom Brady
Rookie of the Year	Adrian Peterson
Coach of the Year	Bill Belichick

PRO FOOTBALL WEEKLY/PFWA
Executive of the Year	Scott Pioli
Most Valuable Player	Tom Brady
Defensive Most Valuable Player	Bob Sanders
Offensive Rookie of the Year	Adrian Peterson
Defensive Rookie of the Year	Patrick Willis
Coach of the Year	Bill Belichick
Assistant Coach of the Year	Jason Garrett
Golden Toe	Rob Bironas
Comeback Player of the Year	Randy Moss
Most Improved Player of the Year	Derek Anderson

SPORTS ILLUSTRATED
Most Valuable Player	Tom Brady
Rookie of the Year	Adrian Peterson
Coach of the Year	Bill Belichick

MAXWELL CLUB PLAYER OF THE YEAR
(Bert Bell Trophy)	Tom Brady

MAXWELL CLUB COACH OF THE YEAR
(Earle "Greasy" Neale Trophy)	Bill Belichick

DIET PEPSI ROOKIE OF THE YEAR
Rookie of the Year	Adrian Peterson

FEDEX AIR & GROUND NFL PLAYERS OF THE YEAR
FedEx Express NFL Player of the Year	Brett Favre
FedEx Ground NFL Player of the Year	Fred Taylor

GMC SIERRA DEFENSIVE PLAYER OF THE YEAR
Defensive Player of the Year	Bob Sanders

MOTOROLA NFL COACH OF THE YEAR
Motorola Coach of the Year	Mike McCarthy

WALTER PAYTON/ NFL MAN OF THE YEAR
Man of the Year	Jason Taylor
Man of the Year Finalist	Hines Ward
Man of the Year Finalist	Brian Waters
Man of the Year Finalist	Jason Witten

SUPER BOWL XLII MOST VALUABLE PLAYER
Pete Rozelle Trophy	Eli Manning

AFC-NFC 2008 PRO BOWL MOST VALUABLE PLAYER
Dan McGuire Award	Adrian Peterson

2007 ALL-PRO TEAMS

2007 PFW/PFWA ALL-PRO TEAM
Selected by *Pro Football Weekly* and the Professional Football Writers of America

Offense:
Tom Brady, New England	Quarterback
LaDainian Tomlinson, San Diego	Running Back
Brian Westbrook, Philadelphia	Running Back
Jason Witten, Dallas	Tight End
Randy Moss, New England	Wide Receiver
Terrell Owens, Dallas	Wide Receiver
Matt Light, New England	Tackle
Walter Jones, Seattle	Tackle
Steve Hutchinson, Minnesota	Guard
Logan Mankins, New England	Guard
Jeff Saturday, Indianapolis	Center

Defense:
Jared Allen, Kansas City	End
Patrick Kerney, Seattle	End
Albert Haynesworth, Tennessee	Tackle
Kevin Williams, Minnesota	Tackle
DeMarcus Ware, Dallas	Outside Linebacker
Mike Vrabel, New England	Outside Linebacker
Patrick Willis, San Francisco	Middle Linebacker
Asante Samuel, New England	Cornerback
Antonio Cromartie, San Diego	Cornerback
Ed Reed, Baltimore	Safety
Bob Sanders, Indianapolis	Safety

Special Teams:
Rob Bironas, Tennessee	Kicker
Andy Lee, San Francisco	Punter
Josh Cribbs, Cleveland	Kick Returner
Devin Hester, Chicago	Punt Returner
Kassim Osgood, San Diego	Special Teams Player

2007 ASSOCIATED PRESS ALL-PRO TEAM
Selected by the Associated Press

Offense:
Tom Brady, New England	Quarterback
LaDainian Tomlinson, San Diego	Running Back
Brian Westbrook, Philadelphia	Running Back
Lorenzo Neal, San Diego	Fullback
Jason Witten, Dallas	Tight End
Randy Moss, New England	Wide Receiver
Terrell Owens, Dallas	Wide Receiver
Matt Light, New England	Tackle
Walter Jones, Seattle	Tackle
Steve Hutchinson, Minnesota	Guard
Alan Faneca, Pittsburgh	Guard
Jeff Saturday, Indianapolis	Center

Defense:
Jared Allen, Kansas City	End
Patrick Kerney, Seattle	End
Albert Haynesworth, Tennessee	Tackle
Kevin Williams, Minnesota	Tackle
DeMarcus Ware, Dallas	Outside Linebacker
Mike Vrabel, New England	Outside Linebacker
Patrick Willis, San Francisco	Inside Linebacker
Lofa Tatupu, Seattle	Inside Linebacker
Asante Samuel, New England	Cornerback
Antonio Cromartie, San Diego	Cornerback
Ed Reed, Baltimore	Safety
Bob Sanders, Indianapolis	Safety

Special Teams:
Rob Bironas, Tennessee	Kicker
Andy Lee, San Francisco	Punter

2007 ALL-NFL TEAM

Selected by the *Associated Press, Pro Football Weekly,* and the Professional Football Writers of America

Offense:

Tom Brady, New England (PFW, AP)	Quarterback
LaDainian Tomlinson, San Diego (PFW, AP)	Running Back
Brian Westbrook, Philadelphia (PFW, AP)	Running Back
Lorenzo Neal, San Diego (AP)	Fullback
Jason Witten, Dallas (PFW, AP)	Tight End
Randy Moss, New England (PFW, AP)	Wide Receiver
Terrell Owens, Dallas (PFW, AP)	Wide Receiver
Matt Light, New England (PFW, AP)	Tackle
Walter Jones, Seattle (PFW, AP)	Tackle
Steve Hutchinson, Minnesota (PFW, AP)	Guard
Logan Mankins, New England (PFW)	Guard
Alan Faneca, Pittsburgh (AP)	Guard
Jeff Saturday, Indianapolis (PFW, AP)	Center

Defense:

Jared Allen, Kansas City (PFW, AP)	End
Patrick Kerney, Seattle (PFW, AP)	End
Albert Haynesworth, Tennessee (PFW, AP)	Tackle
Kevin Williams, Minnesota (PFW, AP)	Tackle
DeMarcus Ware, Dallas (PFW, AP)	Outside Linebacker
Mike Vrabel, New England (PFW, AP)	Outside Linebacker
Patrick Willis, San Francisco (PFW, AP)	Inside Linebacker
Lofa Tatupu, Seattle (AP)	Inside Linebacker
Asante Samuel, New England (PFW, AP)	Cornerback
Antonio Cromartie, San Diego (PFW, AP)	Cornerback
Ed Reed, Baltimore (PFW, AP)	Safety
Bob Sanders, Indianapolis (PFW, AP)	Safety

Special Teams:

Rob Bironas, Tennessee (PFW, AP)	Kicker
Andy Lee, San Francisco (PFW, AP)	Punter
Josh Cribbs, Cleveland (PFW)	Kick Returner
Devin Hester, Chicago (PFW)	Punt Returner
Kassim Osgood, San Diego (PFW)	Special Teams Player

2007 PFW/PFWA ALL-ROOKIE TEAM

Selected by *Pro Football Weekly* and the Professional Football Writers of America

Offense:

Trent Edwards, Buffalo	Quarterback
Adrian Peterson, Minnesota	Running Back
Marshawn Lynch, Buffalo	Running Back
Greg Olsen, Chicago	Tight End
Dwayne Bowe, Kansas City	Wide Receiver
Calvin Johnson, Detroit	Wide Receiver
Joe Thomas, Cleveland	Tackle
Tony Ugoh, Indianapolis	Tackle
Arron Sears, Tampa Bay	Guard
Ben Grubbs, Baltimore	Guard
Samson Satele, Miami	Center

Defense:

Gaines Adams, Tampa Bay	End
Brian Robison, Minnesota	End
Amobi Okoye, Houston	Defensive Tackle
Ed Johnson, Indianapolis	Nose Tackle
Jon Beason, Carolina	Outside Linebacker
David Harris, N.Y. Jets	Outside Linebacker
Patrick Willis, San Francisco	Middle Linebacker
Darrelle Revis, N.Y. Jets	Cornerback
Leon Hall, Cincinnati	Cornerback
LaRon Landry, Washington	Safety
Reggie Nelson, Jacksonville	Safety

Special Teams:

Nick Folk, Dallas	Kicker
Daniel Sepulveda, Pittsburgh	Punter
Ted Ginn Jr., Miami	Punt Returner
Yamon Figurs, Baltimore	Kickoff Returner
Brandon Siler, San Diego	Special Teams Player

2007 AFC PLAYERS OF THE WEEK

	Offense		Defense		Special Teams	
Week 1	RB	Chris Brown, Tennessee	DE	Mario Williams, Houston	KR/CB	Ellis Hobbs, New England
Week 2	QB	Derek Anderson, Cleveland	S	Bob Sanders, Indianapolis	K	Jason Elam, Denver
Week 3	QB	Tom Brady, New England	LB	Keith Bulluck, Tennessee	WR/KR	Yamon Figurs, Baltimore
Week 4	QB	Daunte Culpepper, Oakland	CB	Jabari Greer, Buffalo	K	Dave Rayner, Kansas City
Week 5	QB	Philip Rivers, San Diego	CB	Ike Taylor, Pittsburgh	K	Kris Brown, Houston
Week 6	QB	Tom Brady, New England	DE	Paul Spicer, Jacksonville	K	Matt Stover, Baltimore
Week 7	QB	Tom Brady, New England	DE	Dwight Freeney, Indianapolis	K	Rob Bironas, Tennessee
Week 8	RB	Joseph Addai, Indianapolis	LB	Mike Vrabel, New England	P	Mike Scifres, San Diego
Week 9	WR	Randy Moss, New England	LB	James Harrison, Pittsburgh	CB	Antonio Cromartie, San Diego
Week 10	QB	Ben Roethlisberger, Pittsburgh	CB	Antonio Cromartie, San Diego	KR/PR	Darren Sproles, San Diego
Week 11	WR	Randy Moss, New England	DE	Shaun Ellis, N.Y. Jets	WR/PR	Glenn Martinez, Denver
Week 12	WR	Chad Johnson, Cincinnati	CB	Asante Samuel, New England	K	Josh Scobee, Jacksonville
Week 13	QB	Peyton Manning, Indianapolis	LB	Shawne Merriman, San Diego	K	Rian Lindell, Buffalo
Week 14	QB	Tom Brady, New England	DE	Elvis Dumervil, Denver	WR/KR	Andre Davis, Houston
Week 15	QB	Cleo Lemon, Miami	DE	Mario Williams, Houston	KR/DB	T.J. Rushing, Indianapolis
Week 16	QB	Ben Roethlisberger, Pittsburgh	DE	Kyle Vanden Bosch, Tennessee	DT	Darrell Reid, Indianapolis
Week 17	QB	Tom Brady, New England	LB	Jyles Tucker, San Diego	K	Rob Bironas, Tennessee

2007 AFC PLAYERS OF THE MONTH

	Offense		Defense		Special Teams	
September	QB	Tom Brady, New England	LB	Kirk Morrison, Oakland	KR/PR	Joshua Cribbs, Cleveland
October	QB	Tom Brady, New England	DE	Jared Allen, Kansas City	K	Rob Bironas, Tennessee
November	WR	Randy Moss, New England	LB	James Harrison, Pittsburgh	KR/PR	Joshua Cribbs, Cleveland
December	RB	Fred Taylor, Jacksonville	CB	Antonio Cromartie, San Diego	WR/KR	Andre Davis, Houston

2007 NFC PLAYERS OF THE WEEK

	Offense		Defense		Special Teams	
Week 1	QB	Tony Romo, Dallas	DE	Dewayne White, Tampa Bay	K	Mason Crosby, Green Bay
Week 2	QB	Brett Favre, Green Bay	LB	Barrett Ruud, Tampa Bay	PR/KR	Devin Hester, Chicago
Week 3	RB	Brian Westbrook, Philadelphia	CB	Anthony Henry, Dallas	LB	Lance Laury, Seattle
Week 4	QB	Brett Favre, Green Bay	DE	Osi Umenyiora, N.Y. Giants	PR/KR	Steve Breaston, Arizona
Week 5	QB	Jason Campbell, Washington	CB	Rod Hood, Arizona	K	Nick Folk, Dallas
Week 6	RB	Adrian Peterson, Minnesota	CB	Charles Woodson, Green Bay	WR/KR/PR	Devin Hester, Chicago
Week 7	QB	Brian Griese, Chicago	DE	Osi Umenyiora, N.Y. Giants	WR/KR/PR	Nate Burleson, Seattle
Week 8	QB	Drew Brees, New Orleans	DE	Trent Cole, Philadelphia	K	Jason Hanson, Detroit
Week 9	RB	Adrian Peterson, Minnesota	DT	Shaun Rogers, Detroit	K	Shaun Suisham, Washington
Week 10	QB	Marc Bulger, St. Louis	LB	Karlos Dansby, Arizona	K	Morten Andersen, Atlanta
Week 11	WR	Terrell Owens, Dallas	CB	Antrel Rolle, Arizona	PR	Tramon Williams, Green Bay
Week 12	RB	Frank Gore, San Francisco	S	Dwight Smith, Minnesota	WR/KR/PR	Aundrae Allison, Minnesota
Week 13	QB	Tony Romo, Dallas	LB	Lofa Tatupu, Seattle	KR/WR	Aundrae Allison, Minnesota
Week 14	QB	Todd Collins, Washington	CB	Marcus Trufant, Seattle	CB/PR	Will Blackmon, Green Bay
Week 15	QB	Drew Brees, New Orleans	CB	Lito Sheppard, Philadelphia	KR/WR	Micheal Spurlock, Tampa Bay
Week 16	RB	Clinton Portis, Washington	LB	Kawika Mitchell, N.Y. Giants	P	Brad Maynard, Chicago
Week 17	QB	Chris Redman, Atlanta	CB	Antrel Rolle, Arizona	WR/KR/PR	Devin Hester, Chicago

2007 NFC PLAYERS OF THE MONTH

	Offense		Defense		Special Teams	
September	QB	Tony Romo, Dallas	LB	Barrett Ruud, Tampa Bay	KR/PR	Devin Hester, Chicago
October	RB	Brandon Jacobs, N.Y. Giants	DE	Aaron Kampman, Green Bay	K	David Akers, Philadelphia
November	WR	Terrell Owens, Dallas	DE	Patrick Kerney, Seattle	K	Mason Crosby, Green Bay
December	QB	Todd Collins, Washington	S	Atari Bigby, Green Bay	K	Matt Bryant, Tampa Bay

2007 NFL ROOKIES OF THE MONTH

	Offense (College)		Defense (College)	
September	RB	Adrian Peterson, Minnesota (Oklahoma)	DT	Amobi Okoye, Houston (Louisville)
October	RB	Adrian Peterson, Minnesota (Oklahoma)	LB	Patrick Willis, San Francisco (Mississippi)
November	T	Joe Thomas, Cleveland (Wisconsin)	LB	David Harris, N.Y. Jets (Michigan)
December	QB	Matt Moore, Carolina (Oregon State)	LB	Patrick Willis, San Francisco (Mississippi)

TEN BEST RUSHING PERFORMANCES, 2007

	Att.	Yards	TD
1. Adrian Peterson Minnesota vs. San Diego, Nov. 4	30	*296	3
2. Adrian Peterson Minnesota vs. Chicago, Oct. 14	20	224	3
3. Jamal Lewis Cleveland vs. Cincinnati, Sept. 16	27	216	1
4. LaDainian Tomlinson San Diego vs. Oakland, Oct. 14	24	198	4
5. Clinton Portis Washington vs. New York Jets, Nov. 4	36	196	1
6. Justin Fargas Oakland vs. Miami, Sept. 30	22	179	0
7. LaDainian Tomlinson San Diego vs. Kansas City, Dec. 2	23	177	2
8. Chris Brown Tennessee vs. Jacksonville, Sept. 9	19	175	0
9. Chester Taylor Minnesota vs. Oakland, Nov. 18	22	164	3
10. Jamal Lewis Cleveland vs. Buffalo, Dec. 16	33	163	0

* NFL Record

100-YARD RUSHING PERFORMANCES, 2007

First Week

Chris Brown, Tennessee	175 yards vs. Jacksonville
Travis Henry, Denver	139 yards vs. Buffalo
Joseph Addai, Indianapolis	118 yards vs. New Orleans
Willie Parker, Pittsburgh	109 yards vs. Cleveland
Shaun Alexander, Seattle	105 yards vs. Tampa Bay
Adrian Peterson, Minnesota	103 yards vs. Atlanta

Second Week

Jamal Lewis, Cleveland	216 yards vs. Cincinnati
LaMont Jordan, Oakland	159 yards vs. Denver
Travis Henry, Denver	128 yards vs. Oakland
Edgerrin James, Arizona	138 yards vs. Seattle
Willie Parker, Pittsburgh	126 yards vs. Buffalo
Rudi Johnson, Cincinnati	116 yards vs. Cleveland
Cedric Benson, Chicago	101 yards vs. Kansas City

Third Week

Willie Parker, Pittsburgh	133 yards vs. San Francisco
DeShaun Foster, Carolina	122 yards vs. Atlanta
LaMont Jordan, Oakland	121 yards vs. Cleveland
Steven Jackson, St. Louis	115 yards vs. Tampa Bay
Ronnie Brown, Miami	112 yards vs. New York Jets
Thomas Jones, New York Jets	110 yards vs. Miami
Brian Westbrook, Philadelphia	110 yards vs. Detroit
Laurence Maroney, New England	103 yards vs. Buffalo
Marion Barber, Dallas	102 yards vs. Dallas
Adrian Peterson, Minnesota	102 yards vs. Minnesota
Shaun Alexander, Seattle	100 yards vs. Cincinnati

Fourth Week

Justin Fargas, Oakland	179 yards vs. Miami
Joseph Addai, Indianapolis	136 yards vs. Denver
Ronnie Brown, Miami	134 yards vs. Oakland
LaDainian Tomlinson, San Diego	132 yards vs. Kansas City
Travis Henry, Denver	131 yards vs. Indianapolis
Larry Johnson, Kansas City	123 yards vs. San Diego
Sammy Morris, New England	117 yards vs. Cincinnati
Adrian Peterson, Minnesota	112 yards vs. Green Bay
Willis McGahee, Baltimore	112 yards vs. Cleveland
Correll Buckhalter, Philadelphia	103 yards vs. New York Giants

Fifth Week

Michael Turner, San Diego	147 yards vs. Denver
Kenton Keith, Indianapolis	121 yards vs. Tampa Bay
Ronnie Brown, Miami	114 yards vs. Houston
Brian Leonard, St. Louis	102 yards vs. Arizona
Sammy Morris, New England	102 yards vs. Cleveland
Willie Parker, Pittsburgh	102 yards vs. Seattle
Brandon Jacobs, New York Giants	100 yards vs. New York Jets

Sixth Week

Adrian Peterson, Minnesota	224 yards vs. Chicago
LaDainian Tomlinson, San Diego	198 yards vs. Oakland
Thomas Jones, New York Jets	130 yards vs. Philadelphia
Maurice Jones-Drew, Jacksonville	125 yards vs. Houston
DeAngelo Williams, Carolina	121 yards vs. Arizona
Brian Westbrook, Philadelphia	120 yards vs. New York Jets
Larry Johnson, Kansas City	119 yards vs. Cincinnati
Ronnie Brown, Miami	101 yards vs. Cleveland

Seventh Week

Kenny Watson, Cincinnati	130 yards vs. New York Jets
Willis McGahee, Baltimore	114 yards vs. Buffalo
Larry Johnson, Kansas City	112 yards vs. Oakland
Brandon Jacobs, New York Giants	107 yards vs. San Francisco
LenDale White, Tennessee	104 yards vs. Houston

Eighth Week

LenDale White, Tennessee	133 yards vs. Oakland
Brandon Jacobs, New York Giants	131 yards vs. Miami
Willie Parker, Pittsburgh	126 yards vs. Cincinnati
Kevin Jones, Detroit	105 yards vs. Chicago
Ryan Grant, Green Bay	104 yards vs. Denver
Joseph Addai, Indianapolis	100 yards vs. Indianapolis

Ninth Week

Adrian Peterson, Minnesota	*296 yards vs. San Diego
Clinton Portis, Washington	196 yards vs. New York Jets
Marshawn Lynch, Buffalo	153 yards vs. Cincinnati
Earnest Graham, Tampa Bay	124 yards vs. Arizona
Ron Dayne, Houston	122 yards vs. Oakland
Joseph Addai, Indianapolis	112 yards vs. New England
Justin Fargas, Oakland	104 yards vs. Houston
Warrick Dunn, Atlanta	100 yards vs. San Francisco
LenDale White, Tennessee	100 yards vs. Carolina

Tenth Week

Clinton Portis, Washington	137 yards vs. Philadelphia
Jesse Chatman, Miami	124 yards vs. Buffalo
Ryan Grant, Green Bay	119 yards vs. Minnesota
Selvin Young, Denver	109 yards vs. Kansas City
Willie Parker, Pittsburgh	105 yards vs. Cleveland
Maurice Jones-Drew, Jacksonville	101 yards vs. Tennessee
Brian Westbrook, Philadelphia	100 yards vs. Washington

Eleventh Week

Chester Taylor, Minnesota	164 yards vs. Oakland
Brian Westbrook, Philadelphia	148 yards vs. Miami
Thomas Jones, New York Jets	117 yards vs. Pittsburgh
Earnest Graham, Tampa Bay	102 yards vs. Atlanta
Willis McGahee, Baltimore	102 yards vs. Cleveland

Twelfth Week

Kolby Smith, Kansas City	150 yards vs. Oakland
Justin Fargas, Oakland	139 yards vs. Kansas City
Jamal Lewis, Cleveland	134 yards vs. Houston
Frank Gore, San Francisco	116 yards vs. Arizona
Fred Taylor, Jacksonville	104 yards vs. Buffalo
Marion Barber, Dallas	103 yards vs. New York Jets
Ryan Grant, Green Bay	101 yards vs. Detroit

Thirteenth Week

LaDainian Tomlinson, San Diego	177 yards vs. Kansas City
Derrick Ward, New York Giants	154 yards vs. Chicago
Justin Fargas, Oakland	146 yards vs. Denver
Willis McGahee, Baltimore	138 yards vs. New England
Adrian Peterson, Minnesota	116 yards vs. Minnesota
Edgerrin James, Arizona	114 yards vs. Cleveland
Earnest Graham, Tampa Bay	106 yards vs. New Orleans
Fred Taylor, Jacksonville	104 yards vs. Indianapolis

Fourteenth Week

Ryan Grant, Green Bay	156 yards vs. Oakland
Selvin Young, Denver	156 yards vs. Kansas City
LaDainian Tomlinson, San Diego	146 yards vs. Tennessee
Fred Taylor, Jacksonville	132 yards vs. Carolina
Willie Parker, Pittsburgh	124 yards vs. New England
Jamal Lewis, Cleveland	118 yards vs. New York Jets
Brian Westbrook, Philadelphia	116 yards vs. New York Giants

Fred Jackson, Buffalo — 115 yards vs. Miami
LenDale White, Tennessee — 113 yards vs. San Diego
Marshawn Lynch, Buffalo — 107 yards vs. Miami
Thomas Jones, New York Jets — 106 yards vs. Cleveland
Chester Taylor, Minnesota — 101 yards vs. San Francisco
Aaron Stecker, New Orleans — 100 yards vs. Atlanta

Fifteenth Week
Jamal Lewis, Cleveland — 163 yards vs. Buffalo
Fred Taylor, Jacksonville — 147 yards vs. Pittsburgh
Steven Jackson, St. Louis — 143 yards vs. Green Bay
Frank Gore, San Francisco — 138 yards vs. Cincinnati
Brandon Jacobs, New York Giants — 130 yards vs. Washington
Clinton Portis, Washington — 126 yards vs. New York Giants
Darren Sproles, San Diego — 122 yards vs. Detroit
LaDainian Tomlinson, San Diego — 116 yards vs. Detroit
Laurence Maroney, New England — 104 yards vs. New York Jets
Willis McGahee, Baltimore — 104 yards vs. Miami
Willie Parker, Pittsburgh — 100 yards vs. Jacksonville

Sixteenth Week
Laurence Maroney, New England — 156 yards vs. Miami
Ahmad Bradshaw, New York Giants — 151 yards vs. Buffalo
Brandon Jacobs, New York Giants — 143 yards vs. Buffalo
Kenny Watson, Cincinnati — 130 yards vs. Cleveland
Najeh Davenport, Pittsburgh — 123 yards vs. St. Louis
Dominic Rhodes, Oakland — 115 yards vs. Jacksonville
Fred Taylor, Jacksonville — 111 yards vs. Oakland
Marion Barber, Dallas — 110 yards vs. Carolina
LaDainian Tomlinson, San Diego — 107 yards vs. Denver
LenDale White, Tennessee — 103 yards vs. New York Jets
T.J. Duckett, Detroit — 102 yards vs. Kansas City
Adrian Peterson, Chicago — 102 yards vs. Green Bay
Ryan Grant, Green Bay — 100 yards vs. Chicago
Brian Westbrook, Philadelphia — 100 yards vs. Philadelphia

Seventeenth Week
Jamal Lewis, Cleveland — 128 yards vs. San Francisco
Dominic Rhodes, Oakland — 122 yards vs. San Diego
DeAngelo Williams, Carolina — 121 yards vs. Tampa Bay
Brandon Jackson, Green Bay — 113 yards vs. Detroit
Marshawn Lynch, Buffalo — 105 yards vs. Philadelphia
Pierre Thomas, New Orleans — 105 yards vs. Chicago
Clinton Portis, Washington — 104 yards vs. Dallas
Edgerrin James, Arizona — 102 yards vs. Arizona
* NFL Record

Times 100 or More (159)
Parker, 8; Peterson (Min.), Tomlinson, Westbrook, 6;
Grant, Jacobs, Lewis, McGahee, F. Taylor, White, 5;
Addai, R. Brown, T. Jones, Fargas, Portis, 4; Barber,
Graham, Henry, James, L. Johnson, Lynch, Maroney, 3;
Alexander, Gore, S. Jackson, Jones-Drew, Jordan, Morris,
Rhodes, C. Taylor, Watson, D. Williams, Young, 2

TEN BEST PASSING PERFORMANCES, 2007

	Att.	Comp.	Yards	TD
1. Kurt Warner	34	48	484	2
Arizona vs. San Francisco, Nov. 25				
2. Jon Kitna	29	46	446	2
Detroit vs. Philadelphia, Sept. 23				
3. Drew Brees	35	49	445	3
New Orleans vs. Jacksonville, Nov. 4				
4. Carson Palmer	33	50	401	6
Cincinnati vs. Cleveland, Sept. 16				
5. Tom Brady	32	46	399	4
New England vs. Pittsburgh, Dec. 9				
6. Tom Brady	31	46	388	5
New England vs. Dallas, Oct. 14				
7. Brian Griese	26	45	381	3
Chicago vs. Minnesota, Oct. 14				
Brett Favre	31	41	381	3
Green Bay vs. Detroit, Nov. 22				
Donovan McNabb	21	26	381	4
Philadelphia vs. Detroit, Sept. 23				
10. Tom Brady	34	54	380	1
New England vs. Philadelphia, Nov. 25				

300-YARD PASSING PERFORMANCES, 2007

First Week
Tony Romo, Dallas — 345 yards vs. New York Giants
Josh McCown, Oakland — 313 yards vs. Detroit
Eli Manning, New York Giants — 312 yards vs. Dallas
Jay Cutler, Denver — 304 yards vs. Buffalo

Second Week
Carson Palmer, Cincinnati — 401 yards vs. Cleveland
Marc Bulger, St. Louis — 368 yards vs. San Francisco
Derek Anderson, Cleveland — 328 yards vs. Cincinnati
Jake Delhomme, Carolina — 316 yards vs. Houston
Peyton Manning, Indianapolis — 312 yards vs. Tennessee

Third Week
Jon Kitna, Detroit — 446 yards vs. Philadelphia
Donovan McNabb, Philadelphia — 381 yards vs. Detroit
Brett Favre, Green Bay — 369 yards vs. San Diego
Joey Harrington, Atlanta — 361 yards vs. Carolina
Carson Palmer, Cincinnati — 342 yards vs. Seattle
Tony Romo, Dallas — 329 yards vs. Chicago
Trent Green, Miami — 318 yards vs. New York Jets
Tom Brady, New England — 311 yards vs. Buffalo
Philip Rivers, San Diego — 306 yards vs. San Diego

Fourth Week
Brett Favre, Green Bay — 344 yards vs. Minnesota
Tony Romo, Dallas — 339 yards vs. Dallas
Matt Schaub, Houston — 317 yards vs. Atlanta
Steve McNair, Baltimore — 307 yards vs. Cleveland

Fifth Week
Brett Favre, Green Bay — 322 yards vs. Chicago
Tony Romo, Dallas — 309 yards vs. Buffalo

Sixth Week
Tom Brady, New England — 388 yards vs. Dallas
Brian Griese, Chicago — 381 yards vs. Minnesota
Matt Hasselbeck, Seattle — 362 yards vs. New Orleans
Carson Palmer, Cincinnati — 320 yards vs. Kansas City
Eli Manning, New York Giants — 303 yards vs. Atlanta

Seventh Week
Tom Brady, New England — 354 yards vs. Miami
Brian Griese, Chicago — 322 yards vs. Philadelphia
Jeff Garcia, Tampa Bay — 316 yards vs. Detroit

Eighth Week
Drew Brees, New Orleans — 336 yards vs. San Francisco
Donovan McNabb, Philadelphia — 333 yards vs. Minnesota
Brett Favre, Green Bay — 331 yards vs. Denver
Marc Bulger, St. Louis — 310 yards vs. Cleveland
Tom Brady, New England — 306 yards vs. Washington

Ninth Week

Drew Brees, New Orleans	445 yards vs. Jacksonville
Derek Anderson, Cleveland	364 yards vs. Seattle
Brett Favre, Green Bay	360 yards vs. Kansas City
Quinn Gray, Jacksonville	354 yards vs. New Orleans
Tony Romo, Dallas	324 yards vs. Philadelphia
Matt Hasselbeck, Seattle	318 yards vs. Cleveland

Tenth Week

Brett Favre, Green Bay	351 yards vs. Minnesota
Peyton Manning, Indianapolis	328 yards vs. San Diego
Marc Bulger, St. Louis	302 yards vs. New Orleans

Eleventh Week

Jon Kitna, Detroit	377 yards vs. New York Giants
Tom Brady, New England	373 yards vs. Buffalo
Jason Campbell, Washington	348 yards vs. Dallas
Daunte Culpepper, Oakland	344 yards vs. Minnesota
Matt Hasselbeck, Seattle	337 yards vs. Chicago
Carson Palmer, Cincinnati	329 yards vs. Arizona
Philip Rivers, San Diego	309 yards vs. Jacksonville
Vince Young, Tennessee	305 yards vs. Denver

Twelfth Week

Kurt Warner, Arizona	484 yards vs. San Francisco
Brett Favre, Green Bay	381 yards vs. Detroit
Tom Brady, New England	380 yards vs. Philadelphia
A.J. Feeley, Philadelphia	345 yards vs. New England
Jay Cutler, Denver	302 yards vs. Chicago
Jason Campbell, Washington	301 yards vs. Tampa Bay

Thirteenth Week

Luke McCown, Tampa Bay	313 yards vs. New Orleans
Gus Frerotte, St. Louis	311 yards vs. Atlanta
Tony Romo, Dallas	309 yards vs. Green Bay
Derek Anderson, Cleveland	304 yards vs. Cleveland

Fourteenth Week

Tom Brady, New England	399 yards vs. Pittsburgh
Kurt Warner, Arizona	337 yards vs. Seattle
Drew Brees, New Orleans	328 yards vs. Atlanta
Tony Romo, Dallas	302 yards vs. Detroit

Fifteenth Week

Drew Brees, New Orleans	315 yards vs. Arizona
Cleo Lemon, Miami	315 yards vs. Baltimore
Jon Kitna, Detroit	302 yards vs. San Diego

Sixteenth Week

Kurt Warner, Arizona	369 yards vs. Atlanta
Chris Redman, Atlanta	315 yards vs. Arizona
Peyton Manning, Indianapolis	311 yards vs. Houston
Damon Huard, Kansas City	305 yards vs. Detroit

Seventeenth Week

Tom Brady, New England	356 yards vs. New York Giants
Donovan McNabb, Philadelphia	345 yards vs. Buffalo
Drew Brees, New Orleans	320 yards vs. Chicago
Carson Palmer, Cincinnati	316 yards vs. Miami
Quinn Gray, Jacksonville	302 yards vs. Houston
Kurt Warner, Arizona	300 yards vs. St. Louis

Times 300 or More (71)

Brady, 8; Favre, Romo, 7; Brees, Palmer, 5; Warner, 4; Anderson, Bulger, Hasselbeck, Kitna, P. Manning, McNabb, 3; Campbell, Cutler, Gray, Griese, E. Manning, Rivers, 2

TEN BEST RECEIVING PERFORMANCES, 2007

	No.	Yards	TD
1. Kevin Curtis	11	221	3
Philadelphia vs. Detroit, Sept. 23			
2. Chad Johnson	11	209	2
Cincinnati vs. Cleveland, Sept. 16			
3. Roy Williams	9	204	1
Detroit vs. Philadelphia, Sept. 23			
4. Patrick Crayton	7	184	2
Dallas vs. St. Louis, Sept. 30			
5. Randy Moss	9	183	1
New England vs. New York Jets, Sept. 9			
6. Anquan Boldin	14	181	2
Arizona vs. Baltimore, Sept. 23			
7. Terrell Owens	10	174	1
Dallas vs. Philadelphia, Nov. 4			
8. Terrell Owens	8	173	4
Dallas vs. Washington, Nov. 18			
9. Larry Fitzgerald	11	171	2
Arizona vs. St. Louis, Dec. 30			
10. Reggie Wayne, Oct. 28	7	168	1
Indianapolis vs. Carolina, Oct. 28			

100-YARD RECEIVING PERFORMANCES, 2007

First Week

Randy Moss, New England	183 yards vs. New York Jets
Antwaan Randle El, Washington	162 yards vs. Miami
Plaxico Burress, New York Giants	144 yards vs. Dallas
Andre Johnson, Houston	142 yards vs. Kansas City
Ronald Curry, Oakland	133 yards vs. Detroit
Javon Walker, Denver	119 yards vs. Buffalo
Steve Smith, Carolina	118 yards vs. St. Louis
Jason Witten, Dallas	116 yards vs. New York Giants
Reggie Wayne, Indianapolis	115 yards vs. New Orleans
Antonio Gates, San Diego	107 yards vs. Chicago

Second Week

Chad Johnson, Cincinnati	209 yards vs. Cleveland
Jerricho Cotchery, New York Jets	165 yards vs. Baltimore
Steve Smith, Carolina	153 yards vs. Houston
Braylon Edwards, Cleveland	146 yards vs. Cincinnati
Isaac Bruce, St. Louis	145 yards vs. San Francisco
Joey Galloway, Tampa Bay	135 yards vs. New Orleans
Deion Branch, Seattle	122 yards vs. Arizona
Andre Johnson, Houston	120 yards vs. Carolina
Roy Williams, Detroit	111 yards vs. Minnesota
Chris Chambers, Miami	109 yards vs. Dallas
Randy Moss, New England	105 yards vs. San Diego
Javon Walker, Denver	101 yards vs. Oakland
Kellen Winslow, Cleveland	100 yards vs. Cincinnati

Third Week

Kevin Curtis, Philadelphia	221 yards vs. Detroit
Roy Williams, Detroit	204 yards vs. Philadelphia
Anquan Boldin, Arizona	181 yards vs. Baltimore
Terrell Owens, Dallas	145 yards vs. Chicago
T.J. Houshmandzadeh, Cincinnati	141 yards vs. Seattle
Chad Johnson, Cincinnati	138 yards vs. Seattle
Brandon Marshall, Denver	133 yards vs. Jacksonville
Roddy White, Atlanta	127 yards vs. Carolina
Donald Driver, Green Bay	126 yards vs. San Diego
Randy Moss, New England	115 yards vs. Buffalo
Antonio Gates, San Diego	113 yards vs. Green Bay
Brian Westbrook, Philadelphia	111 yards vs. Detroit
Chris Chambers, Miami	101 yards vs. New York Jets

Fourth Week

Patrick Crayton, Dallas	184 yards vs. St. Louis
Dwayne Bowe, Kansas City	164 yards vs. San Diego
Deion Branch, Seattle	130 yards vs. San Francisco
Santonio Holmes, Pittsburgh	128 yards vs. Arizona
Larry Fitzgerald, Arizona	120 yards vs. Pittsburgh
André Davis, Houston	117 yards vs. Atlanta
Ike Hilliard, Tampa Bay	114 yards vs. Carolina
Jerricho Cotchery, New York Jets	107 yards vs. Buffalo
Randy Moss, New England	102 yards vs. Cincinnati
T.J. Houshmandzadeh, Cincinnati	100 yards vs. New England

Fifth Week

Larry Fitzgerald, Arizona	136 yards vs. St. Louis
Plaxico Burress, New York Giants	124 yards vs. New York Jets
Antonio Gates, San Diego	113 yards vs. Denver

Braylon Edwards, Cleveland	110 yards vs. New England
Benjamin Watson, New England	107 yards vs. Cleveland
Jason Witten, Dallas	103 yards vs. Buffalo
Devery Henderson, New Orleans	101 yards vs. Carolina
Tony Gonzalez, Kansas City	100 yards vs. Jacksonville
Antwaan Randle El, Washington	100 yards vs. Detroit

Sixth Week

Kevin Walter, Houston	160 yards vs. Jacksonville
T.J. Houshmandzadeh, Cincinnati	145 yards vs. Kansas City
Steve Smith, Carolina	136 yards vs. Arizona
Donte' Stallworth, New England	136 yards vs. Dallas
Wes Welker, New England	124 yards vs. Dallas
Kevin Curtis, Philadelphia	121 yards vs. New York Jets
Bobby Engram, Seattle	120 yards vs. New Orleans
David Patten, New Orleans	113 yards vs. Seattle
Chris Cooley, Washington	105 yards vs. Green Bay
Tony Gonzalez, Kansas City	102 yards vs. Cincinnati

Seventh Week

Wes Welker, New England	138 yards vs. Miami
Laveranues Coles, New York Jets	133 yards vs. Cincinnati
Reggie Wayne, Indianapolis	131 yards vs. Jacksonville
Roydell Williams, Tennessee	124 yards vs. Houston
Randy Moss, New England	122 yards vs. Miami
Roddy White, Atlanta	110 yards vs. New Orleans
Terrell Owens, Dallas	103 yards vs. Minnesota
Chad Johnson, Cincinnati	102 yards vs. New York Jets

Eighth Week

Reggie Wayne, Indianapolis	168 yards vs. Carolina
Greg Jennings, Green Bay	141 yards vs. Denver
Lee Evans, Buffalo	138 yards vs. New York Jets
Braylon Edwards, Cleveland	117 yards vs. St. Louis
Joey Galloway, Tampa Bay	115 yards vs. Jacksonville
Torry Holt, St. Louis	110 yards vs. Cleveland
David Patten, New Orleans	109 yards vs. San Francisco
James Jones, Green Bay	107 yards vs. Denver
Reggie Brown, Philadelphia	105 yards vs. Minnesota

Ninth Week

Terrell Owens, Dallas	174 yards vs. Philadelphia
Lee Evans, Buffalo	165 yards vs. Cincinnati
Marques Colston, New Orleans	159 yards vs. Jacksonville
Randy Moss, New England	145 yards vs. Indianapolis
Bobby Engram, Seattle	139 yards vs. Cleveland
Reggie Williams, Jacksonville	128 yards vs. New Orleans
Kellen Winslow, Cleveland	125 yards vs. Seattle
Joseph Addai, Indianapolis	114 yards vs. New England
Santonio Holmes, Pittsburgh	110 yards vs. Pittsburgh
Tony Gonzalez, Kansas City	109 yards vs. Green Bay

Tenth Week

Reggie Wayne, Indianapolis	140 yards vs. San Diego
Marques Colston, New Orleans	129 yards vs. St. Louis
Jeremy Shockey, New York Giants	129 yards vs. Dallas
Terrell Owens, Dallas	125 yards vs. New York Giants
Torry Holt, St. Louis	124 yards vs. New Orleans
Mark Clayton, Baltimore	107 yards vs. Cincinnati
Dwayne Bowe, Kansas City	105 yards vs. Denver
D.J. Hackett, Seattle	101 yards vs. San Francisco

Eleventh Week

Terrell Owens, Dallas	173 yards vs. Washington
D.J. Hackett, Seattle	136 yards vs. Chicago
Drew Carter, Carolina	132 yards vs. Green Bay
Randy Moss, New England	128 yards vs. Buffalo
Santana Moss, Washington	121 yards vs. Dallas
Ronald Curry, Oakland	120 yards vs. Minnesota
Andre Johnson, Houston	120 yards vs. New Orleans
Marques Colston, New Orleans	118 yards vs. Houston
Shaun McDonald, Detroit	113 yards vs. New York Giants
Devard Darling, Baltimore	107 yards vs. Cleveland
Roy Williams, Detroit	106 yards vs. New York Giants
Bernard Berrian, Chicago	102 yards vs. Seattle

Twelfth Week

Larry Fitzgerald, Arizona	156 yards vs. San Francisco
Wes Welker, New England	149 yards vs. Philadelphia
Donald Driver, Green Bay	147 yards vs. Detroit
Kellen Winslow, Cleveland	107 yards vs. Houston
Antonio Gates, San Diego	105 yards vs. Baltimore
Anthony Gonzalez, Indianapolis	105 yards vs. Atlanta
Roddy White, Atlanta	104 yards vs. Indianapolis
Chad Johnson, Cincinnati	103 yards vs. Tennessee

Thirteenth Week

Joey Galloway, Tampa Bay	159 yards vs. New Orleans
Reggie Wayne, Indianapolis	158 yards vs. Jacksonville
Terrell Owens, Dallas	156 yards vs. Green Bay
Braylon Edwards, Cleveland	149 yards vs. Arizona
Roddy White, Atlanta	146 yards vs. St. Louis
Tony Gonzalez, Kansas City	140 yards vs. San Diego
Torry Holt, St. Louis	135 yards vs. Atlanta
Andre Johnson, Houston	116 yards vs. Tennessee
Kevin Curtis, Philadelphia	111 yards vs. Seattle
Brandon Stokley, Denver	102 yards vs. Oakland

Fourteenth Week

Jason Witten, Dallas	138 yards vs. Detroit
Plaxico Burress, New York Giants	136 yards vs. Philadelphia
Randy Moss, New England	135 yards vs. Pittsburgh
Anthony Gonzalez, Indianapolis	134 yards vs. Baltimore
Jerheme Urban, Arizona	123 yards vs. Seattle
Jabar Gaffney, New England	122 yards vs. Pittsburgh
David Patten, New Orleans	122 yards vs. Atlanta
Jerricho Cotchery, New York Jets	119 yards vs. Cleveland
Brandon Marshall, Denver	115 yards vs. Kansas City
Greg Jennings, Green Bay	100 yards vs. Oakland

Fifteenth Week

Marques Colston, New Orleans	114 yards vs. Arizona
Jason Witten, Dallas	113 yards vs. Philadelphia
Greg Camarillo, Miami	109 yards vs. Baltimore
Brandon Marshall, Denver	107 yards vs. Houston
Calvin Johnson, Detroit	102 yards vs. San Diego
Tony Scheffler, Denver	100 yards vs. Houston

Sixteenth Week

Anquan Boldin, Arizona	162 yards vs. Atlanta
Jerricho Cotchery, New York Jets	152 yards vs. Tennessee
Reggie Wayne, Indianapolis	143 yards vs. Houston
Roddy White, Atlanta	141 yards vs. Arizona
Tony Gonzalez, Kansas City	137 yards vs. Detroit
Steve Smith, Carolina	137 yards vs. Dallas
Santonio Holmes, Pittsburgh	133 yards vs. St. Louis
Laurent Robinson, Atlanta	114 yards vs. Arizona

Seventeenth Week

Larry Fitzgerald, Arizona	171 yards vs. St. Louis
Matt Jones, Jacksonville	138 yards vs. Houston
Chad Johnson, Cincinnati	131 yards vs. Miami
Wes Welker, New England	122 yards vs. New York Giants
Pierre Thomas, New Orleans	121 yards vs. Chicago
Nate Burleson, Seattle	119 yards vs. Atlanta
Santana Moss, Washington	115 yards vs. Dallas
Brandon Marshall, Denver	114 yards vs. Minnesota
Justin Gage, Tennessee	104 yards vs. Indianapolis
Randy Moss, New England	100 yards vs. New York Giants

Times 100 or more (164)

R. Moss, 9; Wayne, Owens, 6; T. Gonzalez, C. Johnson, White, 5; Colston, Cotchery, Edwards, Fitzgerald, Gates, A. Johnson, Marshall, S. Smith, Welker, Witten, 4; Burress, Curtis, Galloway, Holt, Holmes, Houshmandzadeh, Patten, Roy Williams, Winslow, 3; Boldin, Bowe, Branch, Chambers, Curry, Driver, Engram, Evans, A. Gonzalez, Hackett, Jennings, S. Moss, Randle El, Walker, 2

TOP QUARTERBACK SACK PERFORMANCES, 2007
(3.0 or More Sacks Per Game Needed to Qualify)

First Week
None

Second Week
Bryant Young, San Francisco   3.0 vs. St. Louis

Third Week
Trent Cole, Philadelphia   3.5 vs. Detroit

Fourth Week
Osi Umenyiora, New York Giants   6.0 vs. Philadelphia
Jared DeVries, Detroit   3.0 vs. Chicago
Kabeer Gbaja-Biamila, Green Bay   3.0 vs. Minnesota
Mathias Kiwanuka, New York Giants   3.0 vs. Philadelphia
Julian Peterson, Seattle   3.0 vs. San Francisco

Fifth Week
None

Sixth Week
None

Seventh Week
Darryl Tapp, Seattle   4.0 vs. St. Louis
Dewayne White, Detroit   3.0 vs. Tampa Bay

Eighth Week
Aaron Kampman, Green Bay   3.0 vs. Denver
Mike Vrabel, New England   3.0 vs. Washington

Ninth Week
James Harrison, Pittsburgh   3.5 vs. Baltimore
Albert Haynesworth, Tennessee   3.0 vs. Carolina

Tenth Week
Adewale Ogunleye, Chicago   3.0 vs. Oakland

Eleventh Week
Patrick Kerney, Seattle   3.0 vs. Chicago
Michael Strahan, New York Giants   3.0 vs. Detroit

Twelfth Week
Michael Boley, Atlanta   3.0 vs. Indianapolis
Patrick Kerney, Seattle   3.0 vs. St. Louis

Thirteenth Week
Shawne Merriman, San Diego   3.0 vs. Kansas City

Fourteenth Week
Elvis Dumervil, Denver   3.0 vs. Kansas City
Patrick Kerney, Seattle   3.0 vs. Arizona
Kyle Vanden Bosch, Tennessee   3.0 vs. San Diego

Fifteenth Week
Mario Williams, Houston   3.5 vs. Denver

Sixteenth Week
Kyle Vanden Bosch, Tennessee   3.0 vs. New York Jets
Mike Vrabel, New England   3.0 vs. Miami

Seventeenth Week
Jyles Tucker, San Diego   3.0 vs. Oakland

Times 3.0 or more (26)
Kerney, 3; Vanden Bosch, Vrabel, 2

2008 PLAYER RANKINGS AND PROJECTIONS

The *NFL.com 2008 Fantasy Football Preview*, available at newsstands now, contains 160 pages of fantasy football facts, tips, and projections for the upcoming season. The following eight pages display the projections for the running backs, wide receivers, quarterbacks, tight ends, and kickers for the 2008 season, as devised by the magazine's experts. Page 293 provides the statistical average for each team's defense over the past three seasons, allowing you a comprehensive look at which team defense can consistently help lead your fantasy team to the title. Pick up a copy of the *NFL.com 2008 Fantasy Football Preview* today.

RUNNING BACKS	Rushing Yards	Rushing Touchdowns	Receiving	Receiving Yards	Receiving Touchdowns	Total Touchdowns
1. LaDainian Tomlinson, San Diego	1525	16	57	440	2	18
2. Adrian Peterson, Minnesota	1575	15	24	320	2	17
3. Brian Westbrook, Philadelphia	1225	8	83	700	4	12
4. Steven Jackson, St. Louis	1350	11	51	470	2	13
5. Joseph Addai, Indianapolis	1175	13	43	365	2	15
6. Lary Johnson, Kansas City	1300	9	54	400	2	11
7. Frank Gore, San Francisco	1275	8	67	525	1	9
8. Marshawn Lynch, Buffalo	1350	9	48	385	0	9
9. Clinton Portis, Washington	1225	9	42	340	1	10
10. Ryan Grant, Green Bay	1225	9	44	310	0	9
11. Marion Barber, Dallas	1080	9	37	265	1	10
12. Willis McGahee, Baltimore	1275	8	38	215	0	8
13. Jamal Lewis, Cleveland	1200	7	23	155	1	8
14. Maurice Jones-Drew, Jacksonville	825	8	43	415	1	9
15. Brandon Jacobs, N.Y. Giants	1125	7	29	195	1	8
16. Michael Turner, Atlanta	1095	6	33	345	0	6
17. Ronnie Brown, Miami	1020	6	41	305	1	7
18. Willie Parker, Pittsburgh	1350	7	28	185	0	7
19. Reggie Bush, New Orleans	675	5	82	625	2	7
20. Earnest Graham, Tampa Bay	940	7	33	295	0	7
21. Laurence Maroney, New England	975	7	18	170	0	7
22. Julius Jones, Seattle	955	4	19	220	0	4
23. LenDale White, Tennessee	1075	6	23	120	0	6
24. Rudi Johnson, Cincinnati	1000	6	16	120	0	6
25. Edgerrin James, Arizona	960	5	27	195	0	5
26. Thomas Jones, N.Y. Jets	980	4	25	165	0	4
27. Travis Henry, Denver	850	7	13	105	0	7
28. Fred Taylor, Jacksonville	1025	4	13	75	0	4
29. Shaun Alexander, Free Agent	875	5	11	70	0	5
30. Cedric Benson, Chicago	775	5	15	145	0	5
31. Deuce McAllister, New Orleans	905	4	15	90	0	4
32. Selvin Young, Denver	700	4	41	235	0	4
33. Tatum Bell, Detroit	720	5	18	110	0	5
34. Chester Taylor, Minnesota	695	4	23	195	0	4
35. Ahman Green, Houston	600	4	19	155	0	4
36. Justin Fargas, Oakland	975	4	11	205	0	4
37. DeAngelo Williams, Carolina	720	3	23	235	0	3
38. Carnell Williams, Tampa Bay	650	3	18	185	0	3
39. Jerious Norwood, Atlanta	600	2	24	175	0	2
40. Warrick Dunn, Tampa Bay	545	3	25	200	0	3
41. Chris Brown, Houston	605	3	15	120	0	3
42. DeShaun Foster, San Francisco	545	2	22	155	1	3
43. Ahmad Bradshaw, N.Y. Giants	445	4	11	140	0	4
44. Kenny Watson, Cincinnati	420	3	28	225	0	3
45. Sammy Morris, New England	480	2	7	130	0	2
46. Leon Washington, N.Y. Jets	375	2	31	190	1	3
47. Kenton Keith, Indianapolis	465	2	10	95	0	2
48. Ricky Williams, Miami	425	3	14	95	0	3
49. Maurice Morris, Seattle	415	2	19	155	0	2
50. Ladell Betts, Washington	375	1	15	195	1	2
51. T.J. Duckett, Seattle	325	4	3	35	0	4
52. Brian Calhoun, Detroit	295	2	8	75	0	2
53. Adrian Peterson, Chicago	405	3	40	335	0	3
54. Chris Taylor, Houston	235	3	5	65	0	3
55. Kevin Jones, Free Agent	605	4	34	210	0	4
56. Correll Buckhalter, Philadelphia	340	3	15	130	0	3
57. LaMont Jordan, Oakland	485	2	21	155	0	2
58. Kevin Faulk, New England	185	0	44	355	1	1

	Rushing Yards	Rushing Touchdowns	Receiving	Receiving Yards	Receiving Touchdowns	Total Touchdowns
59. Dominic Rhodes, Indianapolis	535	3	12	115	0	3
60. Derrick Ward, N.Y. Giants	350	2	18	125	0	2
61. Brian Leonard, St. Louis	305	1	21	155	0	1
62. Kolby Smith, Kansas City	390	1	6	75	0	1
63. Fred Jackson, Buffalo	375	1	5	50	0	1
64. Brandon Jackson, Green Bay	275	2	19	110	0	2
65. Najeh Davenport, Pittsburgh	340	3	12	115	0	3
66. Chris Henry, Tennessee	345	3	13	100	0	3
67. Pierre Thomas, New Orleans	250	1	20	250	1	2
68. Darren Sproles, San Diego	285	2	9	65	0	2
69. Jason Wright, Cleveland	265	1	5	40	0	1
70. Jesse Chatman, Miami	220	1	20	180	0	1
71. Ron Dayne, Free Agent	320	3	9	85	0	3
72. Michael Pittman, Free Agent	295	1	24	145	0	1
73. Reuben Droughns, N.Y. Giants	175	4	5	45	0	4
74. DeShawn Wynn, Green Bay	255	2	10	80	0	2
75. Michael Bennett, Tampa Bay	225	1	10	85	1	2
76. Lorenzo Booker, Philadelphia	75	0	25	275	1	1
77. Leonard Weaver, Seattle	125	1	20	205	0	1
78. Michael Robinson, San Francisco	150	1	15	170	0	1
79. Aaron Stecker, New Orleans	125	1	15	175	0	1
80. Michael Bush, Oakland	120	0	10	180	1	1
81. Vernand Morency, Green Bay	100	0	20	185	1	1
82. Justin Griffith, Oakland	75	1	15	125	0	1
83. Heath Evans, New England	140	1	5	45	0	1
84. Chris Perry, Cincinnati	75	0	15	175	0	0
85. Cecil Sapp, Denver	75	1	10	110	0	1
86. Mewelde Moore, Pittsburgh	125	1	5	45	0	1
87. Mike Bell, Denver	125	1	5	45	0	1
88. Andre Hall, Denver	145	1	1	10	0	1
89. Greg Jones, Jacksonville	125	1	5	30	0	1
90. Vonta Leach, Houston	15	1	15	145	2	3
91. J.J. Arrington, Arizona	125	0	8	80	0	0
92. Marcel Shipp, Arizona	75	1	8	65	0	1
93. Mike Sellers, Washington	55	1	10	75	0	1
94. Darius Walker, Houston	125	1	0	0	0	1
95. Jerome Harrison, Cleveland	100	0	5	35	0	0
96. Kyle Eckel, New England	55	1	0	0	0	1

ROOKIES

	Rushing Yards	Rushing Touchdowns	Receiving	Receiving Yards	Receiving Touchdowns	Total Touchdowns
A. *Darren McFadden, Oakland*	1055	8	25	265	1	9
B. *Jonathan Stewart, Carolina*	650	4	30	285	0	4
C. *Matt Forté, Chicago*	585	3	18	155	0	3
D. *Rashard Mendenhall, Pittsburgh*	530	5	35	315	1	6
E. *Felix Jones, Dallas*	655	4	30	295	1	5
F. *Kevin Smith, Detroit*	500	2	15	135	0	2
G. *Chris Johnson, Tennessee*	485	3	20	185	0	3
H. *Ray Rice, Baltimore*	350	3	35	380	1	4

Players in bold/italics are rookies who could have significantly higher value.

For more in-depth analysis, pick up a copy of the NFL.com 2008 Fantasy Football Preview, *available at newsstands today.*

WIDE RECEIVERS	Receiving	Yards	Touchdowns
1. Randy Moss, New England	89	1395	16
2. Terrell Owens, Dallas	79	1280	14
3. Reggie Wayne, Indianapolis	97	1435	9
4. Andre Johnson, Houston	107	1295	10
5. Braylon Edwards, Cleveland	83	1285	10
6. Chad Johnson, Cincinnati	89	1360	8
7. Larry Fitzgerald, Arizona	94	1295	9
8. T.J. Houshmandzadeh, Cincinnati	98	1195	9
9. Steve Smith, Carolina	103	1200	8
10. Marques Colston, New Orleans	91	1195	9
11. Plaxico Burress, N.Y. Giants	73	1120	10
12. Brandon Marshall, Denver	100	1215	8
13. Torry Holt, St. Louis	98	1210	8
14. Wes Welker, New England	81	1095	7
15. Roy Williams, Detroit	73	1095	7
16. Anquan Boldin, Arizona	81	1070	7
17. Greg Jennings, Green Bay	67	1020	8
18. Santonio Holmes, Pittsburgh	64	1025	8
19. Roddy White, Atlanta	77	1120	6
20. Marvin Harrison, Indianapolis	81	1020	7
21. Dwayne Bowe, Kansas City	78	1020	6
22. Hines Ward, Pittsburgh	77	945	7
23. Donald Driver, Green Bay	84	1020	5
24. Javon Walker, Oakland	73	1045	5
25. Calvin Johnson, Detroit	65	945	6
26. Laveranues Coles, N.Y. Jets	68	975	6
27. Bobby Engram, Seattle	79	1010	5
28. Lee Evans, Buffalo	64	955	6
29. Kevin Curtis, Philadelphia	68	1000	5
30. Chris Chambers, San Diego	58	870	6
31. Joey Galloway, Tampa Bay	54	950	5
32. Santana Moss, Washington	68	900	5
33. Jerricho Cotchery, N.Y. Jets	78	975	4
34. Derrick Mason, Baltimore	84	975	4
35. Bernard Berrian, Minnesota	66	850	5
36. Jerry Porter, Jacksonville	66	875	5
37. Donte' Stallworth, Cleveland	53	850	5
38. Patrick Crayton, Dallas	58	785	6
39. Nate Burleson, Seattle	61	840	5
40. Reggie Brown, Philadelphia	64	820	4
41. D.J. Hackett, Carolina	56	750	5
42. Jabar Gaffney, New England	58	715	4
43. Anthony Gonzalez, Indianapolis	45	740	4
44. Devin Hester, Chicago	51	720	4
45. Bryant Johnson, San Francisco	65	780	3
46. Ted Ginn Jr., Miami	53	710	3
47. Reggie Williams, Jacksonville	49	625	5
48. Ronald Curry, Oakland	57	705	4
49. Isaac Bruce, San Francisco	60	745	3
50. Deion Branch, Seattle	43	670	3
51. Sidney Rice, Minnesota	55	635	4
52. Vincent Jackson, San Diego	47	670	3
53. Mark Clayton, Baltimore	59	655	3
54. Justin Gage, Tennessee	51	725	2
55. Amani Toomer, N.Y. Giants	50	645	3
56. Ernest Wilford, Miami	57	665	3
57. Antwaan Randle El, Washington	46	635	2
58. Marty Booker, Chicago	61	650	3
59. Darrell Jackson, Denver	53	580	4
60. Drew Bennett, St. Louis	49	640	3
61. Brandon Stokley, Denver	52	625	3
62. Shaun McDonald, Detroit	44	635	3
63. David Patten, New Orleans	41	625	3
64. Kevin Walter, Houston	46	595	3
65. James Jones, Green Bay	52	615	3
66. Antonio Bryant, Tampa Bay	41	605	3
67. Steve Smith, N.Y. Giants	53	595	3
68. Roydell Williams, Tennessee	47	655	2
69. Muhsin Muhammad, Carolina	49	595	3

WIDE RECEIVERS	Receiving	Yards	Touchdowns
70. Laurent Robinson, Atlanta	44	615	2
71. Arnaz Battle, San Francisco	46	535	3
72. Brad Smith, N.Y. Jets	30	400	2
73. Drew Carter, Oakland	41	520	3
74. Joe Jurevicius, Cleveland	41	475	3
75. Keary Colbert, Denver	47	520	2
76. Michael Jenkins, Atlanta	40	545	2
77. Nate Washington, Pittsburgh	34	405	4
78. Jeff Webb, Kansas City	35	445	3
79. Mark Bradley, Chicago	41	480	2
80. Josh Reed, Buffalo	40	525	1
81. Mike Furrey, Detroit	49	505	1
82. Devery Henderson, New Orleans	30	425	2
83. David Givens, Tennessee	34	420	2
84. Andre' Davis, Houston	29	425	2
85. Dennis Northcutt, Jacksonville	32	435	2
86. Derek Hagan, Miami	38	425	2
87. Ruvell Martin, Green Bay	25	345	3
88. Bobby Wade, Minnesota	30	380	2
89. Roscoe Parrish, Buffalo	25	375	2
90. Dwayne Jarrett, Carolina	30	385	2
91. Joe Horn, Atlanta	35	420	1
92. Samie Parker, Denver	30	375	1
93. Jason Avant, Philadelphia	30	325	2
94. Sinorice Moss, N.Y. Giants	35	375	1
95. Matt Jones, Jacksonville	30	280	3
96. Ashley Lelie, San Francisco	25	385	1
97. Ike Hilliard, Tampa Bay	35	380	1
98. Hank Baskett, Philadelphia	20	285	2
99. Demetrius Williams, Baltimore	25	275	2
100. Justin McCareins, Tennessee	25	275	2

Rookies

A. *James Hardy, Buffalo*	*54*	*735*	*4*
B. *Devin Thomas, Washington*	*45*	*620*	*6*
C. *Limas Sweed, Pittsburgh*	*42*	*680*	*5*
D. *DeSean Jackson, Philadelphia*	*35*	*515*	*4*
E. *Jerome Simpson, Cincinnati*	*30*	*485*	*3*
F. *Jordy Nelson, Green Bay*	*38*	*505*	*2*

Players in bold/italics are rookies who could have significantly higher value.

For more in-depth analysis, pick up a copy of the NFL.com 2008 Fantasy Football Preview, available at newsstands today.

QUARTERBACKS	Passing Yards	Passing Touchdowns	Rushing Yards	Rushing Touchdowns
1. Tom Brady, New England	4325	36	95	1
2. Peyton Manning, Indianapolis	4125	24	55	0
3. Tony Romo, Dallas	4075	29	120	2
4. Drew Brees, New Orleans	4275	27	100	0
5. Carson Palmer, Cincinnati	4075	28	25	0
6. Ben Roethlisberger, Pittsburgh	3425	27	150	2
7. Matt Hasselbeck, Seattle	3725	25	95	0
8. Derek Anderson, Cleveland	3525	24	85	2
9. Donovan McNabb, Philadelphia	3425	20	235	2
10. David Garrard, Jacksonville	3275	21	210	2
11. Marc Bulger, St. Louis	3825	22	35	0
12. Eli Manning, N.Y. Giants	3400	24	55	0
13. Jay Cutler, Denver	3525	22	135	0
14. Philip Rivers, San Diego	3275	23	45	0
15. Vince Young, Tennessee	2325	14	470	4
16. Matt Schaub, Houston	3225	19	90	0
17. Jon Kitna, Detroit	3425	17	110	0
18. Jake Delhomme, Carolina	3075	19	35	0
19. Aaron Rodgers, Green Bay	2925	16	120	1
20. Matt Leinart, Arizona	2850	18	135	0
21. Jeff Garcia, Tampa Bay	2825	14	105	1
22. Jason Campbell, Washington	3025	15	190	0
23. Tarvaris Jackson, Minnesota	2375	12	325	4
24. JaMarcus Russell, Oakland	2725	17	95	1
25. Alex Smith, San Francisco	2750	15	135	1
26. Trent Edwards, Buffalo	2675	15	85	0
27. Rex Grossman, Chicago	2525	15	55	0
28. Kellen Clemens, N.Y. Jets	2400	12	195	1
29. Brodie Croyle, Kansas City	2450	14	85	0
30. Kyle Boller, Baltimore	2375	13	85	0
31. Chris Redman, Atlanta	2170	13	60	0
32. John Beck, Miami	2295	12	45	0
33. Kurt Warner, Arizona	1425	8	15	0
34. Chad Pennington, N.Y. Jets	1650	8	40	0
35. Shaun Hill, San Francisco	1525	8	25	0
36. Kyle Orton, Chicago	1575	7	20	0
37. Sage Rosenfels, Houston	1250	6	20	0
38. Damon Huard, Kansas City	1325	4	10	0
39. Brady Quinn, Cleveland	1175	4	15	0
40. J.P. Losman, Buffalo	1025	3	45	0
41. Troy Smith, Baltimore	875	4	75	1
42. Drew Stanton, Detroit	850	4	15	0
43. Cleo Lemon, Jacksonville	900	1	110	1
44. Josh McCown, Miami	800	3	75	0
45. Kerry Collins, Tennessee	725	3	5	0
46. Seneca Wallace, Seattle	380	2	125	0
47. Gus Frerotte, Minnesota	750	2	15	0
48. Joey Harrington, Atlanta	680	2	25	0
49. Charlie Batch, Pittsburgh	425	2	0	0
50. A.J. Feeley, Philadelphia	375	2	50	0
51. Matt Moore, Carolina	375	2	5	0
52. Brooks Bollinger, Minnesota	275	2	20	0
53. Trent Green, St. Louis	375	2	10	0
54. Charlie Frye, Seattle	200	2	10	0
55. Todd Collins, Washington	325	1	0	0
56. Matt Cassel, New England	175	2	15	0
57. Patrick Ramsey, Denver	375	1	0	0
58. Brad Johnson, Dallas	125	2	0	0
59. Luke McCown, Tampa Bay	225	1	15	0
60. Quinn Gray, Houston	200	1	20	0

Rookies

A. *Matt Ryan, Atlanta*	*1325*	*7*	*20*	*0*
B. *Joe Flacco, Baltimore*	*775*	*3*	*0*	*0*

Players in bold/italics are rookies who could have significantly higher value.

TIGHT ENDS	Receiving	Yards	Touchdowns
1. Antonio Gates, San Diego	83	975	8
2. Jason Witten, Dallas	88	1000	7
3. Kellen Winslow, Cleveland	84	1025	6
4. Tony Gonzalez, Kansas City	87	975	5
5. Chris Cooley, Washington	68	750	7
6. Todd Heap, Baltimore	71	775	6
7. Dallas Clark, Indianapolis	51	575	7
8. Jeremy Shockey, N.Y. Giants	63	650	5
9. Vernon Davis, San Francisco	66	650	5
10. Owen Daniels, Houston	57	675	4
11. Greg Olsen, Chicago	47	575	5
12. Heath Miller, Pittsburgh	43	525	5
13. Tony Scheffler, Denver	51	510	5
14. Alge Crumpler, Tennessee	53	550	4
15. Benjamin Watson, New England	43	450	5
16. Donald Lee, Green Bay	40	485	4
17. L.J. Smith, Philadelphia	48	470	3
18. Zach Miller, Oakland	47	450	3
19. Ben Utecht, Cincinnati	39	450	2
20. Randy McMichael, St. Louis	35	410	2
21. Desmond Clark, Chicago	39	430	2
22. Eric Johnson, New Orleans	53	405	2
23. Leonard Pope, Arizona	34	315	4
24. Marcedes Lewis, Jacksonville	41	400	2
25. Chris Baker, N.Y. Jets	38	350	3
26. Jeff King, Carolina	35	325	3
27. Bo Scaife, Tennessee	35	375	2
28. Billy Miller, New Orleans	30	345	2
29. Alex Smith, Tampa Bay	30	225	2
30. Visanthe Shiancoe, Minnesota	25	280	1
31. David Martin, Miami	25	275	1
32. Kevin Boss, N.Y. Giants	20	240	1
33. Michael Gaines, Detroit	15	225	1
34. Bryan Fletcher, Indianapolis	22	215	1
35. Robert Royal, Buffalo	20	200	1
36. George Wrighster, Jacksonville	25	205	1
37. Steve Heiden, Cleveland	15	180	1
38. Daniel Coats, Cincinnati	20	185	1
39. Ben Patrick, Arizona	15	180	1
40. Anthony Fasano, Miami	20	175	1
41. Marcus Pollard, New England	25	275	1
42. Delanie Walker, San Francisco	15	175	1
43. Brent Celek, Philadelphia	15	145	1
44. Reggie Kelly, Cincinnati	15	140	1
45. Bubba Franks, N.Y. Jets	15	125	3
46. Ben Troupe, Tampa Bay	10	85	1
47. Brandon Manumaleuna, San Diego	10	80	1
48. Justin Peelle, Miami	20	225	1
49. Matt Schobel, Philadelphia	10	85	1
50. Daniel Graham, Denver	10	100	0

Rookie

A. *Dustin Keller, N.Y. Jets*	*37*	*417*	*4*
B. *John Carlson, Seattle*	*35*	*380*	*2*
C. *Fred Davis, Washington*	*22*	*265*	*3*

Players in bold/italics are rookies who could have significantly higher value.

For more in-depth analysis, pick up a copy of the NFL.com 2008 Fantasy Football Preview, available at newsstands today.

KICKERS	PTS	XP/XPA	FG/FGA
1. Nick Folk, Dallas	139	49/49	30/35
2. Josh Brown, St. Louis	130	43/43	29/36
3. Stephen Gostkowski, New England	129	57/57	24/29
4. Mason Crosby, Green Bay	125	38/38	29/34
5. Nate Kaeding, San Diego	125	47/47	26/29
6. Robbie Gould, Chicago	124	34/34	30/35
7. Shayne Graham, Cincinnati	124	40/40	28/33
8. Adam Vinatieri, Indianapolis	121	49/49	24/31
9. Rob Bironas, Tennessee	120	33/33	29/35
10. Josh Scobee, Jacksonville	119	38/39	27/32
11. Phil Dawson, Cleveland	118	40/40	26/31
12. Kris Brown, Houston	117	39/39	26/33
13. Neil Rackers, Arizona	114	33/33	27/35
14. Jason Hanson, Detroit	113	29/29	28/34
15. Jason Elam, Atlanta	112	34/34	26/34
16. David Akers, Philadelphia	110	41/41	23/30
17. Shaun Suisham, Washington	109	31/31	26/33
18. Jeff Reed, Pittsburgh	108	42/42	22/28
19. Matt Stover, Baltimore	107	23/23	28/31
20. Martin Gramatica, New Orleans	106	36/36	23/28
21. Matt Bryant, Tampa Bay	103	31/31	24/29
22. Mike Nugent, N.Y. Jets	102	24/25	26/32
23. Olindo Mare, Seattle	102	36/36	22/29
24. Ryan Longwell, Minnesota	101	35/36	22/27
25. Lawrence Tynes, N.Y. Giants	99	33/35	22/29
26. John Kasay, Carolina	98	32/32	22/27
27. Rian Lindell, Buffalo	98	29/29	23/29
28. Sebastian Janikowski, Oakland	96	30/30	22/25
29. Joey Nedney, San Francisco	95	23/23	24/29
30. Jay Feely, Miami	95	29/29	22/28

DEFENSE/ SPECIAL TEAMS*	Yards Per Game	Points Per Game	Takeaways	Sacks	Safeties	Touchdowns DEF & RET
1. Chargers	314.3	18.6	39	46	0	7
2. Patriots	299.3	18.2	29	45	0	6
3. Vikings	329.5	20.7	33	36	0	8
4. Cowboys	309.4	19.9	31	44	0	5
5. Steelers	273.5	17.3	28	39	1	4
6. Giants	319.9	22.1	28	49	0	5
7. Seahawks	324.5	18.5	29	43	0	4
8. Buccaneers	297.2	18.9	33	36	0	4
9. Bears	317.2	18.4	34	39	1	7
10. Packers	307.1	19.4	29	39	0	5
11. Jaguars	302.1	18.5	29	38	1	3
12. Ravens	292.3	20.4	25	41	1	5
13. Eagles	311.5	21.0	23	38	0	4
14. Colts	303.6	17.6	35	32	0	3
15. Redskins	318.6	21.7	26	34	0	3
16. Titans	316.3	22.1	31	38	1	4
17. Cardinals	323.9	23.8	31	38	0	5
18. Bills	338.3	20.9	29	33	1	5
19. Browns	346.4	21.9	25	32	0	3
20. Texans	341.4	23.6	25	34	0	5
21. 49ers	332.5	21.2	26	38	1	3
22. Raiders	328.6	21.6	34	29	1	4
23. Broncos	324.3	22.5	29	36	0	3
24. Panthers	313.6	19.8	28	30	0	3
25. Chiefs	322.4	20.6	25	35	0	2
26. Dolphins	326.2	23.4	25	34	1	3
27. Jets	327.1	21.5	28	33	0	4
28. Saints	329.5	23.2	22	30	0	3
29. Bengals	345.9	23.2	34	27	0	4
30. Lions	363.5	25.2	32	33	1	4
31. Rams	339.8	26.5	25	34	0	3
32. Falcons	342.7	24.6	27	31	0	2

Defense/Special Team statistics reflect an average of the past three seasons (2005-07); clubs are ranked in projected order.

For more in-depth analysis, pick up a copy of the NFL.com 2008 Fantasy Football Preview, available at newsstands today.

AMERICAN FOOTBALL CONFERENCE OFFENSE

	Balt.	Buff.	Cin.	Cle.	Den.	Hou.	Ind.	Jax.	KC	Mia.	NE	NYJ	Oak.	Pitt.	SD	Tenn.
First Downs	291	248	320	315	305	295	357	328	255	283	393	286	267	298	278	306
Rushing	96	91	81	110	96	96	119	127	66	107	124	92	111	108	104	118
Passing	175	141	213	192	187	190	212	180	171	162	243	173	133	179	158	171
Penalty	20	16	26	13	22	9	26	21	18	14	26	21	23	11	16	17
Rushes	446	448	416	440	429	417	446	522	383	389	451	446	508	511	485	543
Net Yds. Gained	1797	1800	1556	1895	1957	1586	1706	2391	1248	1569	1849	1701	2086	2168	2039	2109
Avg. Gain	4.0	4.0	3.7	4.3	4.6	3.8	3.8	4.6	3.3	4.0	4.1	3.8	4.1	4.2	4.2	3.9
Avg. Yds. per Game	112.3	112.5	97.3	118.4	122.3	99.1	106.6	149.4	78.0	98.1	115.6	106.3	130.4	135.5	127.4	131.8
Passes Attempted	557	445	575	545	515	529	551	469	563	558	586	512	451	442	471	464
Completed	341	263	373	305	326	346	355	288	335	318	403	310	260	282	281	288
% Completed	61.2	59.1	64.9	56.0	63.3	65.4	64.4	61.4	59.5	57.0	68.8	60.5	57.6	63.8	59.7	62.1
Total Yds. Gained	3308	2842	4131	3866	3759	3925	4172	3495	3525	3319	4859	3330	2893	3418	3175	3077
Times Sacked	39	26	17	19	32	22	23	31	55	42	21	53	41	47	24	30
Yds. Lost	273	208	119	140	175	174	139	167	344	288	128	316	262	347	170	199
Net Yds. Gained	3035	2634	4012	3726	3584	3751	4033	3328	3181	3031	4731	3014	2631	3071	3005	2878
Avg. Yds. per Game	189.7	164.6	250.8	232.9	224.0	234.4	252.1	208.0	198.8	189.4	295.7	188.4	164.4	191.9	187.8	179.9
Net Yds. per Pass Play	5.09	5.59	6.78	6.61	6.55	6.81	7.03	6.66	5.15	5.05	7.79	5.33	5.35	6.28	6.07	5.83
Yds. Gained per Comp.	9.70	10.81	11.08	12.68	11.53	11.34	11.75	12.14	10.52	10.44	12.06	10.74	11.13	12.12	11.30	10.68
Combined Net																
Yds. Gained	4832	4434	5568	5621	5541	5337	5739	5719	4429	4600	6580	4715	4717	5239	5044	4987
% Total Yds. Rushing	37.2	40.6	27.9	33.7	35.3	29.7	29.7	41.8	28.2	34.1	28.1	36.1	44.2	41.4	40.4	42.3
% Total Yds. Passing	62.8	59.4	72.1	66.3	64.7	70.3	70.3	58.2	71.8	65.9	71.9	63.9	55.8	58.6	59.6	57.7
Avg. Yds. per Game	302.0	277.1	348.0	351.3	346.3	333.6	358.7	357.4	276.8	287.5	411.3	294.7	294.8	327.4	315.3	311.7
Ball Control Plays	1042	919	1008	1004	976	968	1020	1022	1001	989	1058	1011	1000	1000	980	1037
Avg. Yds. per Play	4.6	4.8	5.5	5.6	5.7	5.5	5.6	5.6	4.4	4.7	6.2	4.7	4.7	5.2	5.1	4.8
Avg. Time of Poss.	30:46	28:51	29:26	29:10	29:09	29:41	29:49	32:08	29:52	29:05	32:33	28:35	31:09	33:18	29:50	31:38
Third Down Efficiency	38.5	33.3	46.2	42.2	40.4	44.6	49.3	45.7	34.1	37.2	48.2	37.6	35.8	46.8	39.3	41.0
Had Intercepted	14	14	20	20	15	21	14	8	20	16	9	19	20	14	16	17
Yds. Opp Returned	293	291	294	422	229	267	136	215	231	232	131	196	143	110	283	116
Ret. by Opp. for TD	1	2	3	2	2	1	0	1	2	0	1	4	0	0	2	0
Punts	79	81	59	69	60	55	52	54	96	77	45	72	73	68	82	73
Yds. Punted	3397	3302	2437	2895	2630	2296	2181	2249	4322	3327	1821	3063	3585	2880	3735	3060
Avg. Yds. per Punt	43.0	40.8	41.3	42.0	43.8	41.7	41.9	41.6	45.0	43.2	40.5	42.5	49.1	42.4	45.5	41.9
Punt Returns	35	31	27	30	23	33	25	32	40	24	33	20	38	39	32	42
Yds. Returned	338	476	131	405	209	287	280	324	302	230	311	183	209	238	281	367
Avg. Yds. per Return	9.7	15.4	4.9	13.5	9.1	8.7	11.2	10.1	7.6	9.6	9.4	9.2	5.5	6.1	8.8	8.7
Returned for TD	2	1	0	1	1	0	1	0	0	1	0	0	0	0	1	0
Kickoff Returns	65	70	73	72	58	74	53	49	67	78	55	74	78	52	48	52
Yds. Returned	1525	1448	1684	1943	1293	1961	1157	1110	1286	1552	1384	1695	1686	1145	1224	1098
Avg. Yds. per Return	23.5	20.7	23.1	27.0	22.3	26.5	21.8	22.7	19.2	19.9	25.2	22.9	21.6	22.0	25.5	21.1
Returned for TD	1	1	1	2	0	4	0	1	0	0	2	3	0	1	1	0
Fumbles	35	20	20	22	30	26	14	18	22	25	14	20	42	21	17	32
Lost	26	7	10	9	14	17	5	13	13	13	6	6	17	8	8	17
Out of Bounds	0	2	1	5	1	3	0	1	3	3	2	0	2	2	2	1
Own Rec. for TD	0	0	0	0	0	0	0	0	0	0	0	0	0	0	0	0
Opp. Rec. by	6	12	15	10	15	14	15	9	8	8	12	6	8	14	18	12
Opp. Rec. for TD	0	1	2	0	2	3	1	1	1	1	3	1	0	0	3	0
Penalties	107	78	90	114	90	82	67	76	101	91	78	63	120	80	94	101
Yds. Penalized	873	633	670	868	610	636	515	594	697	732	690	486	864	651	761	773
Total Points Scored	275	252	380	402	320	379	450	411	226	267	589	268	283	393	412	301
Total TDs	28	25	41	46	34	43	54	50	24	29	75	26	30	46	49	28
TDs Rushing	11	8	10	13	10	12	19	18	6	14	17	6	11	9	19	17
TDs Passing	13	12	26	29	21	24	32	28	17	12	50	15	17	34	22	9
TDs on Ret. and Rec.	4	5	5	4	3	7	3	4	1	3	8	5	2	3	8	2
Extra Point Kicks	26	24	37	42	33	40	49	46	21	26	74	23	28	44	46	28
Extra Point Kicks Att.	26	24	38	43	33	40	51	48	21	26	74	24	28	44	46	28
2Pt Conversions	0	1	1	2	0	3	2	1	1	2	1	1	2	2	0	0
2Pt Conversions Att.	2	1	3	3	1	3	3	2	3	2	1	2	2	2	2	0
Safeties	0	2	1	1	1	0	2	0	1	0	0	1	0	0	0	1
Field Goals Made	27	24	31	26	27	25	23	21	19	21	21	29	23	23	24	35
Field Goals Attempted	32	27	34	30	31	29	29	24	27	23	24	36	32	25	27	39
% Successful	84.4	88.9	91.2	86.7	87.1	86.2	79.3	87.5	70.4	91.3	87.5	80.6	71.9	92.0	88.9	89.7

AMERICAN FOOTBALL CONFERENCE DEFENSE

	Balt.	Buff.	Cin.	Cle.	Den.	Hou.	Ind.	Jax.	KC	Mia.	NE	NYJ	Oak.	Pitt.	SD	Tenn.
First Downs	258	322	313	335	306	325	288	286	278	318	278	315	292	249	297	268
Rushing	69	104	98	100	119	107	111	92	104	129	91	128	121	74	89	80
Passing	162	203	200	211	168	197	162	181	156	165	172	174	156	158	185	165
Penalty	27	15	15	24	19	21	15	13	18	24	15	13	15	17	23	23
Rushes	446	454	449	460	501	417	454	390	481	544	360	517	486	361	416	369
Net Yds. Gained	1268	1993	1893	2072	2282	1825	1711	1605	2089	2456	1572	2156	2334	1438	1712	1478
Avg. Gain	2.8	4.4	4.2	4.5	4.6	4.4	3.8	4.1	4.3	4.5	4.4	4.2	4.8	4.0	4.1	4.0
Avg. Yds. per Game	79.3	124.6	118.3	129.5	142.6	114.1	106.9	100.3	130.6	153.5	98.3	134.8	145.9	89.9	107.0	92.4
Passes Attempted	490	567	540	578	458	546	498	543	462	409	526	470	439	536	555	569
Completed	293	354	353	340	279	361	325	319	276	242	314	289	261	292	338	349
% Completed	59.8	62.4	65.4	58.8	60.9	66.1	65.3	58.7	59.7	59.2	59.7	61.5	59.5	54.5	60.9	61.3
Total Yds. Gained	3740	3958	3815	3867	3297	3878	2926	3660	3274	3186	3381	3362	3318	3067	3684	3428
Times Sacked	32	26	22	28	33	31	28	37	37	30	47	29	27	36	42	40
Yds. Lost	183	144	128	186	203	196	162	244	252	167	340	208	186	243	272	241
Net Yds. Gained	3557	3814	3687	3681	3094	3682	2764	3416	3022	3019	3041	3154	3132	2824	3412	3187
Avg. Yds. per Game	222.3	238.4	230.4	230.1	193.4	230.1	172.8	213.5	188.9	188.7	190.1	197.1	195.8	176.5	213.3	199.2
Net Yds. per Pass Play	6.81	6.43	6.56	6.07	6.30	6.38	5.25	5.89	6.06	6.88	5.31	6.32	6.72	4.94	5.72	5.23
Yds. Gained per Comp.	12.76	11.18	10.81	11.37	11.82	10.74	9.00	11.47	11.86	13.17	10.77	11.63	12.71	10.50	10.90	9.82
Combined Net Yds. Gained	4825	5807	5580	5753	5376	5507	4475	5021	5111	5475	4613	5310	5466	4262	5124	4665
% Total Yds. Rushing	26.3	34.3	33.9	36.0	42.4	33.1	38.2	32.0	40.9	44.9	34.1	40.6	42.7	33.7	33.4	31.7
% Total Yds. Passing	73.7	65.7	66.1	64.0	57.6	66.9	61.8	68.0	59.1	55.1	65.9	59.4	57.3	66.3	66.6	68.3
Avg. Yds. per Game	301.6	362.9	348.8	359.6	336.0	344.2	279.7	313.8	319.4	342.2	288.3	331.9	341.6	266.4	320.3	291.6
Ball Control Plays	968	1047	1011	1066	992	994	980	970	980	983	933	1016	952	933	1013	978
Avg. Yds. per Play	5.0	5.5	5.5	5.4	5.4	5.5	4.6	5.2	5.2	5.6	4.9	5.2	5.7	4.6	5.1	4.8
Avg. Time of Poss.	29:14	31:09	30:34	30:50	30:51	30:19	30:11	27:52	30:08	30:55	27:27	31:25	28:51	26:42	30:10	28:22
Third Down Efficiency	36.6	45.1	42.8	36.7	42.7	41.9	45.2	39.8	31.3	47.1	33.7	42.2	39.0	40.5	39.3	42.2
Intercepted By	17	18	19	17	14	11	22	20	14	14	19	15	18	11	30	22
Yds. Returned By	212	193	220	216	105	75	355	237	142	160	288	110	321	234	311	358
Returned for TD	1	2	1	1	0	0	1	2	0	1	3	0	2	2	2	2
Punts	76	61	58	69	60	59	56	66	84	62	76	68	71	82	69	81
Yds. Punted	3277	2598	2302	2774	2633	2535	2474	2868	3762	2682	3297	2901	3044	3525	2961	3615
Avg. Yds. per Punt	43.1	42.6	39.7	40.2	43.9	43.0	44.2	43.5	44.8	43.3	43.4	42.7	42.9	43.0	42.9	44.6
Punt Returns	38	37	33	34	31	19	22	28	50	39	14	32	40	31	29	31
Yds. Returned	375	196	299	308	334	151	305	218	387	387	75	268	445	266	311	274
Avg. Yds. per Return	9.9	5.3	9.1	9.1	10.8	7.9	13.9	7.8	7.7	9.9	5.4	8.4	11.1	8.6	10.7	8.8
Returned for TD	0	0	1	1	2	0	1	0	1	0	0	0	2	1	0	1
Kickoff Returns	61	56	76	76	62	69	81	67	51	50	92	51	43	73	75	58
Yds. Returned	1444	1150	1732	1590	1424	1593	2029	1323	1105	1292	2030	1270	963	1647	1566	1404
Avg. Yds. per Return	23.7	20.5	22.8	20.9	23.0	23.1	25.0	19.7	21.7	25.8	22.1	24.9	22.4	22.6	20.9	24.2
Returned for TD	0	1	0	0	1	0	3	2	0	2	1	1	1	1	0	0
Fumbles	12	29	28	19	34	24	27	20	21	20	25	15	19	30	27	26
Lost	6	12	16	10	16	14	15	10	8	8	12	6	8	14	18	12
Out of Bounds	2	2	3	3	3	2	1	2	1	2	0	1	2	2	0	0
Own Rec. for TD	0	1	0	0	0	0	0	0	0	0	0	0	0	0	0	0
Opp. Rec. by	26	7	10	9	14	16	5	13	12	13	6	6	17	8	8	17
Opp. Rec. for TD	2	1	0	1	2	2	1	0	2	2	1	1	2	1	2	2
Penalties	84	73	88	80	82	81	85	82	95	73	96	93	99	73	86	90
Yds. Penalized	728	567	712	581	628	614	722	636	695	604	764	761	734	556	665	745
Total Points Scored	384	354	385	382	409	384	262	304	335	437	274	355	398	269	284	297
Total TDs	39	39	44	41	46	43	31	35	33	50	34	38	46	31	35	35
TDs Rushing	9	15	11	8	14	15	10	12	11	18	7	14	24	6	11	11
TDs Passing	27	19	29	29	25	25	16	20	17	28	23	18	17	22	20	21
TDs on Ret. and Rec.	3	5	4	4	7	3	5	3	5	4	4	6	5	3	4	3
Extra Point Kicks	35	37	42	38	42	42	27	32	33	49	34	36	43	29	33	31
Extra Point Kicks Att.	36	37	42	38	42	43	27	32	33	49	34	36	43	30	33	33
2Pt Conversions	1	0	2	1	3	0	2	3	0	1	0	2	1	0	1	1
2Pt Conversions Att.	2	2	2	3	3	0	4	3	0	1	0	2	3	1	2	1
Safeties	1	1	0	0	2	0	0	1	1	1	0	0	1	0	0	0
Field Goals Made	37	27	25	32	27	28	15	18	34	28	12	29	25	18	13	18
Field Goals Attempted	43	30	27	35	33	33	20	23	39	33	14	32	34	22	19	25
% Successful	86.0	90.0	92.6	91.4	81.8	84.8	75.0	78.3	87.2	84.8	85.7	90.6	73.5	81.8	68.4	72.0

NATIONAL FOOTBALL CONFERENCE OFFENSE

	Ariz.	Atl.	Car.	Chi.	Dall.	Det.	GB	Minn.	NO	NYG	Phil.	StL	SF	Sea.	TB	Wash.
First Downs	308	248	255	266	322	303	307	294	346	321	323	281	218	323	281	307
Rushing	70	73	85	74	83	73	69	131	94	119	118	65	65	93	98	103
Passing	210	161	142	168	217	203	210	139	232	167	186	193	140	211	162	192
Penalty	28	14	28	24	22	27	28	24	20	35	19	23	13	19	21	12
Rushes	402	385	451	423	419	324	388	494	392	469	421	404	357	430	449	498
Net Yds. Gained	1440	1520	1824	1330	1746	1288	1597	2634	1466	2148	1974	1527	1477	1619	1872	1871
Avg. Gain	3.6	3.9	4.0	3.1	4.2	4.0	4.1	5.3	3.7	4.6	4.7	3.8	4.1	3.8	4.2	3.8
Avg. Yds. per Game	90.0	95.0	114.0	83.1	109.1	80.5	99.8	164.6	91.6	134.3	123.4	95.4	92.3	101.2	117.0	116.9
Passes Attempted	590	555	505	569	531	587	578	432	652	544	577	574	513	590	490	525
Completed	356	336	285	327	342	368	383	249	440	302	350	333	274	371	316	319
% Completed	60.3	60.5	56.4	57.5	64.4	62.7	66.3	57.6	67.5	55.5	60.7	58.0	53.4	62.9	64.5	60.8
Total Yds. Gained	4228	3573	2941	3701	4290	4216	4461	2938	4423	3376	4005	3561	2685	4181	3579	3622
Times Sacked	24	47	33	43	25	54	19	38	16	28	49	48	55	36	36	29
Yds. Lost	163	277	206	339	185	338	127	193	109	222	250	328	365	217	222	159
Net Yds. Gained	4065	3296	2735	3362	4105	3878	4334	2745	4314	3154	3755	3233	2320	3964	3357	3463
Avg. Yds. per Game	254.1	206.0	170.9	210.1	256.6	242.4	270.9	171.6	269.6	197.1	234.7	202.1	145.0	247.8	209.8	216.4
Net Yds. per Pass Play	6.62	5.48	5.08	5.49	7.38	6.05	7.26	5.84	6.46	5.51	6.00	5.20	4.08	6.33	6.38	6.25
Yds. Gained per Comp.	11.88	10.63	10.32	11.32	12.54	11.46	11.65	11.80	10.05	11.18	11.44	10.69	9.80	11.27	11.33	11.35
Combined Net Yds. Gained	5505	4816	4559	4692	5851	5166	5931	5379	5780	5302	5729	4760	3797	5583	5229	5334
% Total Yds. Rushing	26.2	31.6	40.0	28.3	29.8	24.9	26.9	49.0	25.4	40.5	34.5	32.1	38.9	29.0	35.8	35.1
% Total Yds. Passing	73.8	68.4	60.0	71.7	70.2	75.1	73.1	51.0	74.6	59.5	65.5	67.9	61.1	71.0	64.2	64.9
Avg. Yds. per Game	344.1	301.0	284.9	293.3	365.7	322.9	370.7	336.2	361.3	331.4	358.1	297.5	237.3	348.9	326.8	333.4
Ball Control Plays	1016	987	989	1035	975	965	985	964	1060	1041	1047	1026	925	1056	975	1052
Avg. Yds. per Play	5.4	4.9	4.6	4.5	6.0	5.4	6.0	5.6	5.5	5.1	5.5	4.6	4.1	5.3	5.4	5.1
Avg. Time of Poss.	30:10	28:34	28:44	28:22	30:34	27:33	30:19	29:22	31:09	31:22	30:56	30:08	26:51	29:49	30:27	30:46
Third Down Efficiency	36.9	36.3	36.2	34.0	42.2	32.6	42.6	34.5	46.3	41.6	42.4	36.3	31.4	35.0	38.5	40.7
Had Intercepted	24	15	17	21	19	22	15	14	18	20	15	28	17	13	8	11
Yds. Opp Returned	380	292	150	285	191	279	166	177	336	336	198	427	298	144	167	78
Ret. by Opp. for TD	3	5	1	2	2	2	1	0	2	3	1	4	3	0	2	0
Punts	80	88	92	94	63	68	62	81	63	72	73	78	105	86	78	75
Yds. Punted	3198	3824	4038	3934	2970	3010	2664	3621	2757	2865	3066	3684	4968	3436	3382	3072
Avg. Yds. per Punt	40.0	43.5	43.9	41.9	47.1	44.3	43.0	44.7	43.8	39.8	42.0	47.2	47.3	40.0	43.4	41.0
Punt Returns	42	36	32	44	26	18	48	29	24	43	42	30	56	58	50	40
Yds. Returned	395	228	269	651	227	148	492	242	197	319	340	357	483	658	334	299
Avg. Yds. per Return	9.4	6.3	8.4	14.8	8.7	8.2	10.3	8.3	8.2	7.4	8.1	11.9	8.6	11.3	6.7	7.5
Returned for TD	1	0	0	4	0	0	2	0	0	0	0	1	0	1	0	0
Kickoff Returns	74	72	60	67	61	72	62	59	71	66	71	82	73	53	48	65
Yds. Returned	1682	1781	1146	1234	1358	1628	1349	1461	1513	1579	1539	1938	1702	1173	1119	1544
Avg. Yds. per Return	22.7	24.7	19.1	18.4	22.3	22.6	21.8	24.8	21.3	23.9	21.7	23.6	23.3	22.1	23.3	23.8
Returned for TD	0	0	0	2	0	1	0	1	0	1	0	0	0	2	1	0
Fumbles	27	18	25	34	21	35	25	27	25	26	24	25	36	21	18	35
Lost	12	9	12	13	5	14	9	16	12	14	12	9	17	11	12	18
Out of Bounds	1	2	2	5	0	6	3	1	1	0	1	3	1	1	0	3
Own Rec. for TD	1	0	0	0	0	0	0	0	0	2	0	0	0	0	0	0
Opp. Rec. by	11	11	16	17	10	18	9	16	10	10	8	9	9	14	19	10
Opp. Rec. for TD	0	1	1	0	1	1	3	2	2	2	0	0	1	1	1	0
Penalties	137	105	95	111	104	100	113	86	68	77	83	94	97	59	81	90
Yds. Penalized	1128	891	801	839	815	676	1006	662	581	652	649	794	702	428	614	751
Total Points Scored	404	259	267	334	455	346	435	365	379	373	336	263	219	393	334	334
Total TDs	49	26	28	34	54	37	49	43	47	44	38	27	24	44	36	35
TDs Rushing	9	7	7	8	14	13	13	22	14	15	12	5	8	9	15	15
TDs Passing	32	18	19	18	36	19	30	12	28	23	24	19	15	30	18	18
TDs on Ret. and Rec.	8	1	2	8	4	5	6	9	5	6	2	3	1	5	3	2
Extra Point Kicks	47	25	27	33	53	35	48	39	42	40	36	25	22	43	34	29
Extra Point Kicks Att.	48	25	27	33	53	36	48	40	42	42	36	25	22	43	34	30
2Pt Conversions	0	0	0	1	0	0	0	3	4	0	0	1	0	0	0	2
2Pt Conversions Att.	1	0	1	1	1	1	0	3	5	2	2	2	1	1	2	5
Safeties	0	0	0	1	0	0	0	1	1	0	0	1	1	1	0	0
Field Goals Made	21	26	24	31	26	29	31	20	15	23	24	24	17	28	28	29
Field Goals Attempted	30	34	28	36	31	35	39	24	22	27	32	32	19	34	33	35
% Successful	70.0	76.5	85.7	86.1	83.9	82.9	79.5	83.3	68.2	85.2	75.0	75.0	89.5	82.4	84.8	82.9

NATIONAL FOOTBALL CONFERENCE DEFENSE

	Ariz.	Atl.	Car.	Chi.	Dall.	Det.	GB	Minn.	NO	NYG	Phil.	StL	SF	Sea.	TB	Wash.
First Downs	298	320	302	305	304	363	297	305	288	288	279	316	308	278	258	291
Rushing	90	105	100	100	86	116	77	67	80	83	80	105	94	78	93	89
Passing	185	190	174	185	195	221	176	222	196	185	177	190	187	183	158	174
Penalty	23	25	28	20	23	26	44	16	12	20	22	21	27	17	7	28
Rushes	407	481	472	454	381	448	424	379	408	408	403	445	504	422	454	391
Net Yds. Gained	1567	2033	1771	1967	1513	1911	1647	1185	1646	1563	1533	1844	1896	1644	1726	1460
Avg. Gain	3.9	4.2	3.8	4.3	4.0	4.3	3.9	3.1	4.0	3.8	3.8	4.1	3.8	3.9	3.8	3.7
Avg. Yds. per Game	97.9	127.1	110.7	122.9	94.6	119.4	102.9	74.1	102.9	97.7	95.8	115.3	118.5	102.8	107.9	91.3
Passes Attempted	570	536	537	541	581	602	534	646	524	523	539	523	543	568	490	602
Completed	361	336	337	343	342	422	295	415	327	306	312	318	345	333	297	351
% Completed	63.3	62.7	62.8	63.4	58.9	70.1	55.2	64.2	62.4	58.5	57.9	60.8	63.5	58.6	60.6	58.3
Total Yds. Gained	3958	3801	3603	3953	3728	4387	3584	4500	4122	3666	3693	3847	3826	3808	2935	3622
Times Sacked	36	25	23	41	46	37	36	38	32	53	37	31	31	45	33	33
Yds. Lost	242	146	177	245	319	256	218	275	198	349	244	234	183	303	207	198
Net Yds. Gained	3716	3655	3426	3708	3409	4131	3366	4225	3924	3317	3449	3613	3643	3505	2728	3424
Avg. Yds. per Game	232.3	228.4	214.1	231.8	213.1	258.2	210.4	264.1	245.3	207.3	215.6	225.8	227.7	219.1	170.5	214.0
Net Yds. per Pass Play	6.13	6.52	6.12	6.37	5.44	6.46	5.91	6.18	7.06	5.76	5.99	6.52	6.35	5.72	5.22	5.39
Yds. Gained per Comp.	10.96	11.31	10.69	11.52	10.90	10.40	12.15	10.84	12.61	11.98	11.84	12.10	11.09	11.44	9.88	10.32
Combined Net Yds. Gained	5283	5688	5197	5675	4922	6042	5013	5410	5570	4880	4982	5457	5539	5149	4454	4884
% Total Yds. Rushing	29.7	35.7	34.1	34.7	30.7	31.6	32.9	21.9	29.6	32.0	30.8	33.8	34.2	31.9	38.8	29.9
% Total Yds. Passing	70.3	64.3	65.9	65.3	69.3	68.4	67.1	78.1	70.4	68.0	69.2	66.2	65.8	68.1	61.2	70.1
Avg. Yds. per Game	330.2	355.5	324.8	354.7	307.6	377.6	313.3	338.1	348.1	305.0	311.4	341.1	346.2	321.8	278.4	305.3
Ball Control Plays	1013	1042	1032	1036	1008	1087	994	1063	964	984	979	999	1078	1035	977	1026
Avg. Yds. per Play	5.2	5.5	5.0	5.5	4.9	5.6	5.0	5.1	5.8	5.0	5.1	5.5	5.1	5.0	4.6	4.8
Avg. Time of Poss.	29:50	31:26	31:16	31:38	29:27	32:27	29:41	30:38	28:51	28:38	29:04	29:52	33:09	30:11	29:33	29:14
Third Down Efficiency	40.1	37.1	42.5	32.7	39.4	45.5	33.0	40.2	41.7	34.6	37.2	38.8	40.2	37.9	41.1	35.8
Intercepted By	18	16	14	16	19	17	19	15	13	15	11	18	12	20	16	14
Yds. Returned By	551	174	163	235	331	362	233	298	267	204	111	200	138	299	89	301
Returned for TD	6	0	1	1	2	3	1	6	3	3	0	2	0	1	1	2
Punts	73	74	76	94	73	61	80	82	67	87	76	66	89	93	83	81
Yds. Punted	3181	3060	3243	3808	3284	2741	3397	3780	2924	3631	3162	3147	3644	4322	3613	3484
Avg. Yds. per Punt	43.6	41.4	42.7	40.5	45.0	44.9	42.5	46.1	43.6	41.7	41.6	47.7	40.9	46.5	43.5	43.0
Punt Returns	38	41	55	40	35	36	19	43	35	28	36	48	53	37	38	32
Yds. Returned	496	307	579	236	406	434	113	440	335	173	409	437	402	362	280	202
Avg. Yds. per Return	13.1	7.5	10.5	5.9	11.6	12.1	5.9	10.2	9.6	6.2	11.4	9.1	7.6	9.8	7.4	6.3
Returned for TD	1	0	1	0	1	0	0	1	1	0	1	0	1	0	0	0
Kickoff Returns	60	50	56	71	86	65	77	65	56	69	69	58	45	72	68	66
Yds. Returned	1389	1148	1333	1370	1979	1750	1610	1441	1256	1596	1536	1578	982	1790	1328	1289
Avg. Yds. per Return	23.2	23.0	23.8	19.3	23.0	26.9	20.9	22.2	22.4	23.1	22.3	27.2	21.8	24.9	19.5	19.5
Returned for TD	0	1	0	1	1	2	0	0	1	1	0	2	1	0	1	1
Fumbles	23	21	30	34	26	40	17	37	27	24	16	23	17	31	31	27
Lost	11	12	16	17	10	18	9	16	10	10	8	9	10	14	19	10
Out of Bounds	0	3	2	2	2	4	0	5	2	3	1	1	2	2	0	3
Own Rec. for TD	0	0	0	0	0	0	0	0	1	0	0	1	0	0	0	0
Opp. Rec. by	12	9	11	13	5	14	9	15	12	14	12	8	17	11	12	18
Opp. Rec. for TD	1	2	1	0	1	1	0	0	0	1	2	0	1	1	0	2
Penalties	118	91	100	92	85	113	118	110	89	118	81	95	89	99	86	88
Yds. Penalized	881	808	904	670	785	897	908	763	685	874	616	732	661	756	706	684
Total Points Scored	399	414	347	348	325	444	291	311	388	351	300	438	364	291	270	310
Total TDs	45	47	38	39	36	56	31	32	44	41	30	48	39	32	32	33
TDs Rushing	13	12	13	17	12	19	6	7	7	12	10	16	9	16	11	10
TDs Passing	26	27	22	19	19	32	23	22	32	24	16	25	24	15	18	20
TDs on Ret. and Rec.	6	8	3	3	5	5	2	3	5	5	4	7	6	1	3	3
Extra Point Kicks	39	46	38	35	34	53	29	31	44	38	27	44	37	27	31	29
Extra Point Kicks Att.	39	46	38	37	34	53	29	31	44	38	29	44	38	28	32	30
2Pt Conversions	2	1	0	2	0	1	2	0	0	1	0	2	0	1	0	0
2Pt Conversions Att.	5	1	0	2	2	3	2	1	0	3	1	4	1	4	0	3
Safeties	1	0	0	0	0	1	0	2	1	1	0	0	0	2	1	1
Field Goals Made	28	28	27	25	25	17	24	28	26	21	31	34	31	22	15	27
Field Goals Attempted	33	30	32	33	31	27	27	32	30	29	38	39	35	27	18	37
% Successful	84.8	93.3	84.4	75.8	80.6	63.0	88.9	87.5	86.7	72.4	81.6	87.2	88.6	81.5	83.3	73.0

AFC, NFC, AND NFL SUMMARY

	AFC Offense Total	AFC Offense Average	AFC Defense Total	AFC Defense Average	NFC Offense Total	NFC Offense Average	NFC Defense Total	NFC Defense Average	NFL Total	NFL Average
First Downs	4825	301.6	4728	295.5	4703	293.9	4800	300.0	9528	297.8
Rushing	1646	102.9	1616	101.0	1413	88.3	1443	90.2	3059	95.6
Passing	2880	180.0	2815	175.9	2933	183.3	2998	187.4	5813	181.7
Penalty	299	18.7	297	18.6	357	22.3	359	22.4	656	20.5
Rushes	7280	455.0	7105	444.1	6706	419.1	6881	430.1	13986	437.1
Net Yds. Gained	29457	1841.1	29884	1867.8	27333	1708.3	26906	1681.6	56790	1774.7
Avg. Gain	—	4.0	—	4.2	—	4.1	—	3.9	—	4.1
Avg. Yds. per Game	—	115.1	—	116.7	—	106.8	—	105.1	—	110.9
Passes Attempted	8233	514.6	8186	511.6	8812	550.8	8859	553.7	17045	532.7
Completed	5074	317.1	4985	311.6	5351	334.4	5440	340.0	10425	325.8
% Completed	—	61.6	—	60.9	—	60.7	—	61.4	—	61.2
Total Yds. Gained	57094	3568.4	55841	3490.1	59780	3736.3	61033	3814.6	116874	3652.3
Times Sacked	522	32.6	525	32.8	580	36.3	577	36.1	1102	34.4
Yds. Lost	3449	215.6	3355	209.7	3700	231.3	3794	237.1	7149	223.4
Net Yds. Gained	53645	3352.8	52486	3280.4	56080	3505.0	57239	3577.4	109725	3428.9
Avg. Yds. per Game	—	209.6	—	205.0	—	219.1	—	223.6	—	214.3
Net Yds. per Pass Play	—	6.13	—	6.03	—	5.97	—	6.07	—	6.05
Yds. Gained per Comp.	—	11.25	—	11.20	—	11.17	—	11.22	—	11.21
Combined Net Yds. Gained	83102	5193.9	82370	5148.1	83413	5213.3	84145	5259.1	166515	5203.6
% Total Yds. Rushing	—	35.4	—	36.3	—	32.8	—	32.0	—	34.1
% Total Yds. Passing	—	64.6	—	63.7	—	67.2	—	68.0	—	65.9
Avg. Yds. per Game	—	324.6	—	321.8	—	325.8	—	328.7	—	325.2
Ball Control Plays	16035	1002.2	15816	988.5	16098	1006.1	16317	1019.8	32133	1004.2
Avg. Yds. per Play	—	5.2	—	5.2	—	5.2	—	5.2	—	5.2
Third Down Efficiency	—	41.1	—	40.4	—	38.0	—	38.6	—	39.5
Interceptions	257	16.1	281	17.6	277	17.3	253	15.8	534	16.7
Yds. Returned	3589	224.3	3537	221.1	3904	244.0	3956	247.3	7493	234.2
Returned for TD	21	1.3	20	1.3	31	1.9	32	2.0	52	1.6
Punts	1095	68.4	1098	68.6	1258	78.6	1255	78.4	2353	73.5
Yds. Punted	47180	2948.8	47248	2953.0	54489	3405.6	54421	3401.3	101669	3177.2
Avg. Yds. per Punt	—	43.1	—	43.0	—	43.3	—	43.4	—	43.2
Punt Returns	504	31.5	508	31.8	618	38.6	614	38.4	1122	35.1
Yds. Returned	4571	285.7	4599	287.4	5639	352.4	5611	350.7	10210	319.1
Avg. Yds. per Return	—	9.1	—	9.1	—	9.1	—	9.1	—	9.1
Returned for TD	8	0.5	10	0.6	9	0.6	7	0.4	17	0.5
Kickoff Returns	1018	63.6	1041	65.1	1056	66.0	1033	64.6	2074	64.8
Yds. Returned	23191	1449.4	23562	1472.6	23746	1484.1	23375	1460.9	46937	1466.8
Avg. Yds. per Return	—	22.8	—	22.6	—	22.5	—	22.6	—	22.6
Returned for TD	17	1.1	13	0.8	8	0.5	12	0.8	25	0.8
Fumbles	378	23.6	376	23.5	422	26.4	424	26.5	800	25.0
Lost	189	11.8	185	11.6	195	12.2	199	12.4	384	12.0
Out of Bounds	28	1.8	26	1.6	30	1.9	32	2.0	58	1.8
Own Rec. for TD	0	0.0	1	0.1	3	0.2	2	0.1	3	0.1
Opp. Rec.	182	11.4	187	11.7	197	12.3	192	12.0	379	11.8
Opp. Rec. for TD	19	1.2	22	1.4	16	1.0	13	0.8	35	1.1
Penalties	1432	89.5	1360	85.0	1500	93.8	1572	98.3	2932	91.6
Yds. Penalized	11053	690.8	10712	669.5	11989	749.3	12330	770.6	23042	720.1
Total Points Scored	5608	350.5	5513	344.6	5496	343.5	5591	349.4	11104	347.0
Total TDs	628	39.3	620	38.8	615	38.4	623	38.9	1243	38.8
TDs Rushing	200	12.5	196	12.3	186	11.6	190	11.9	386	12.1
TDs Passing	361	22.6	356	22.3	359	22.4	364	22.8	720	22.5
TDs on Ret. and Rec.	67	4.2	68	4.3	70	4.4	69	4.3	137	4.3
Extra Point Kicks	587	36.7	583	36.4	578	36.1	582	36.4	1165	36.4
Extra Point Kicks Att.	594	37.1	588	36.8	584	36.5	590	36.9	1178	36.8
2Pt Conversions	19	1.2	18	1.1	11	0.7	12	0.8	30	0.9
2Pt Conversions Att.	32	2.0	29	1.8	29	1.8	32	2.0	61	1.9
Safeties	9	0.6	8	0.5	9	0.6	10	0.6	18	0.6
Field Goals Made	399	24.9	386	24.1	396	24.8	409	25.6	795	24.8
Field Goals Attempted	469	29.3	462	28.9	491	30.7	498	31.1	960	30.0
% Successful	—	85.1	—	83.5	—	80.7	—	82.1	—	82.8

CLUB LEADERS

	Offense	Defense
First Downs	New England 393	Pittsburgh 249
Rushing	Minnesota 131	Minnesota 67
Passing	New England 243	Kansas City &
		Oakland 156
Penalty	N.Y. Giants 35	Tampa Bay 7
Rushes	Tennessee 543	New England 360
Net Yds. Gained	Minnesota 2634	Minnesota 1185
Avg. Gain	Minnesota 5.3	Baltimore 2.8
Passes Attempted	New Orleans 652	Miami 409
Completed	New Orleans 440	Miami 242
% Completed	New England 68.8	Pittsburgh 54.5
Total Yds. Gained	New England 4859	Indianapolis 2926
Times Sacked	New Orleans 16	N.Y. Giants 53
Yds. Lost	New Orleans 109	N.Y. Giants 349
Net Yds. Gained	New England 4731	Tampa Bay 2728
Net Yds. per Pass Play	New England 7.8	Pittsburgh 4.9
Yds. Gained per Comp.	Cleveland 12.7	Indianapolis 9.0
Combined Net Yds. Gained	New England 6580	Pittsburgh 4262
% Total Yds. Rushing	Minnesota 49.0	Minnesota 21.9
% Total Yds. Passing	Detroit 75.1	Miami 55.1
Ball Control Plays	New Orleans 1060	New England &
		Pittsburgh 933
Avg. Yds. per Play	New England 6.2	Tampa Bay 4.6
Avg. Time of Poss.	Pittsburgh 33:18	—
Third Down Efficiency	Indianapolis 49.3	Kansas City 31.3
Interceptions	—	San Diego 30
Yds. Returned	—	Arizona 551
Returned for TD	—	Arizona &
		Minnesota 6
Punts	San Francisco 105	—
Yds. Punted	San Francisco 4968	—
Avg. Yds. per Punt	Oakland 49.1	—
Punt Returns	Seattle 58	New England 14
Yds. Returned	Seattle 658	New England 75
Avg. Yds. per Return	Buffalo 15.4	Buffalo 5.3
Returned for TD	Chicago 4	—
Kickoff Returns	St. Louis 82	Oakland 43
Yds. Returned	Houston 1961	Oakland 963
Avg. Yds. per Return	Cleveland 27.0	Chicago 19.3
Returned for TD	Houston 4	—
Total Points Scored	New England 589	Indianapolis 262
Total TDs	New England 75	Philadelphia 30
TDs Rushing	Minnesota 22	Green Bay &
		Pittsburgh 6
TDs Passing	New England 50	Seattle 15
TDs on Ret. and Rec.	Minnesota 9	Seattle 1
Extra Point Kicks	New England 74	Indianapolis &
		Philadelphia &
		Seattle 27
2-Point Conversions	New Orleans 4	—
Safeties	Buffalo & Indianapolis	—
	& Washington 2	
Field Goals Made	Tennessee 35	New England 12
Field Goals Attempted	Green Bay &	New England 14
	Tennessee 39	
% Successful	Pittsburgh 92.0	Detroit 63.0

NFL CLUB RANKINGS BY YARDS

	Offense			Defense		
	Total	Rush	Pass	Total	Rush	Pass
Arizona	12	29	5	17	9	28
Atlanta	23	26	18	29	26	23
Baltimore	22	16	23	6	2	20
Buffalo	30	15	30	31	25	29
Carolina	29	14	29	16	18	17
Chicago	27	30	15	28	24	27
Cincinnati	10	24	7	27	21	26
Cleveland	8	10	12	30	27	24
Dallas	3	17	4	9	6	13
Denver	11	9	13	19	30	7
Detroit	19	31	9	32	23	31
Green Bay	2	21	2	11	14	12
Houston	14	22	11	24	19	25
Indianapolis	5	18	6	3	15	2
Jacksonville	7	2	17	12	11	15
Kansas City	31	32	20	13	28	5
Miami	28	23	24	23	32	4
Minnesota	13	*1	28	20	*1	32
New England	*1	13	*1	4	10	6
New Orleans	4	28	3	26	13	30
New York Giants	16	4	21	7	8	11
New York Jets	26	19	25	18	29	9
Oakland	25	6	31	22	31	8
Philadelphia	6	8	10	10	7	18
Pittsburgh	17	3	22	*1	3	3
St. Louis	24	25	19	21	20	21
San Diego	20	7	26	14	16	14
San Francisco	32	27	32	25	22	22
Seattle	9	20	8	15	12	19
Tampa Bay	18	11	16	2	17	*1
Tennessee	21	5	27	5	5	10
Washington	15	12	14	8	4	16

T = Tied for position * = League Leader

AFC TAKEAWAYS/GIVEAWAYS

	Takeaways			Giveaways			Net
	Int	Fum	Total	Int	Fum	Total	Diff.
San Diego	30	18	48	16	8	24	+24
Indianapolis	22	15	37	14	5	19	+18
New England	19	12	31	9	6	15	+16
Buffalo	18	12	30	14	7	21	+9
Jacksonville	20	10	30	8	13	21	+9
Cincinnati	19	16	35	20	10	30	+5
Pittsburgh	11	14	25	14	8	22	+3
Denver	14	16	30	15	14	29	+1
Tennessee	22	12	34	17	17	34	0
Cleveland	17	10	27	20	9	29	-2
N.Y. Jets	15	6	21	19	6	25	-4
Miami	14	8	22	16	13	29	-7
Kansas City	14	8	22	20	13	33	-11
Oakland	18	8	26	20	17	37	-11
Houston	11	14	25	21	17	38	-13
Baltimore	17	6	23	14	26	40	-17
Totals	**281**	**185**	**466**	**257**	**189**	**446**	**+20**

NFC TAKEAWAYS/GIVEAWAYS

	Takeaways			Giveaways			Net
	Int	Fum	Total	Int	Fum	Total	Diff.
Tampa Bay	16	19	35	8	12	20	+15
Seattle	20	14	34	13	11	24	+10
Dallas	19	10	29	19	5	24	+5
Atlanta	16	12	28	15	9	24	+4
Green Bay	19	9	28	15	9	24	+4
Carolina	14	16	30	17	12	29	+1
Minnesota	15	16	31	14	16	30	+1
Chicago	16	17	33	21	13	34	-1
Detroit	17	18	35	22	14	36	-1
Washington	14	10	24	11	18	29	-5
Arizona	18	11	29	24	12	36	-7
New Orleans	13	10	23	18	12	30	-7
Philadelphia	11	8	19	15	12	27	-8
N.Y. Giants	15	10	25	20	14	34	-9
St. Louis	18	9	27	28	9	37	-10
San Francisco	12	10	22	17	17	34	-12
Totals	**253**	**199**	**452**	**277**	**195**	**472**	**-20**

SCORING

POINTS
- NFC: 141 * Mason Crosby, Green Bay
- AFC: 138 Randy Moss, New England

TOUCHDOWNS
- AFC: 23 Randy Moss, New England
- NFC: 15 Terrell Owens, Dallas

EXTRA POINT KICKS
- AFC: 74 Stephen Gostkowski, New England
- NFC: 53 * Nick Folk, Dallas

TWO-POINT EXTRA POINT PLAYS
- NFC: 3 Reggie Bush, New Orleans
- AFC: 2 Ronald Curry, Oakland

FIELD GOALS
- AFC: 35 Rob Bironas, Tennessee
- NFC: 31 * Mason Crosby, Green Bay
- 31 Robbie Gould, Chicago

FIELD GOAL ATTEMPTS
- AFC: 39 Rob Bironas, Tennessee
- NFC: 39 * Mason Crosby, Green Bay

LONGEST FIELD GOAL
- AFC: 57 Kris Brown, Houston vs. Miami, October 7
- NFC: 55 Ryan Longwell, Minnesota at Chicago, October 14
- 55 Martin Gramatica, New Orleans vs. Philadelphia, December 23

MOST POINTS, GAME
- AFC: 26 Rob Bironas, Tennessee at Houston, October 21 (8-8 FG, 2-2 PAT)
- NFC: 24 Terrell Owens, Dallas vs. Washington, November 18 (4 TD)

TEAM LEADERS, POINTS
- AFC: BALTIMORE, 107, Matt Stover; BUFFALO, 96, Rian Lindell; CINCINNATI, 130, Shayne Graham; CLEVELAND, 120, Phil Dawson; DENVER, 114, Jason Elam; HOUSTON, 115, Kris Brown; INDIANAPOLIS, 118, Adam Vinatieri; JACKSONVILLE, 62, Josh Scobee; KANSAS CITY, 59, Dave Rayner; MIAMI, 89, Jay Feely; NEW ENGLAND, 138, Randy Moss; N.Y. JETS, 110, Mike Nugent; OAKLAND, 97, Sebastian Janikowski; PITTSBURGH, 113, Jeff Reed; SAN DIEGO, 118, Nate Kaeding; TENNESSEE, 133, Rob Bironas

- NFC: ARIZONA, 110, Neil Rackers; ATLANTA, 99, Morten Andersen; CAROLINA, 99, John Kasay; CHICAGO, 126, Robbie Gould; DALLAS, 131, *Nick Folk; DETROIT, 122, Jason Hanson; GREEN BAY, 141, *Mason Crosby; MINNESOTA, 99, Ryan Longwell; NEW ORLEANS, 66, Marques Colston; N.Y. GIANTS, 109, Lawrence Tynes; PHILADELPHIA, 108, David Akers; ST. LOUIS, 97, Jeff Wilkins; SAN FRANCISCO, 73, Joe Nedney; SEATTLE, 127, Josh Brown; TAMPA BAY, 118, Matt Bryant; WASHINGTON, 116, Shaun Suisham

TEAM CHAMPION
- AFC: 589 New England
- NFC: 455 Dallas

NFL TOP TEN SCORERS—KICKERS

	XP	XPA	FG	FGA	PTS
* Crosby, Mason, G.B.	48	48	31	39	141
Gostkowski, Stephen, N.E.	74	74	21	24	137
Bironas, Rob, Ten.	28	28	35	39	133
* Folk, Nick, Dal.	53	53	26	31	131
Graham, Shayne, Cin.	37	37	31	34	130
Brown, Josh, Sea.	43	43	28	34	127
Gould, Robbie, Chi.	33	33	31	36	126
Hanson, Jason, Det.	35	36	29	35	122
Dawson, Phil, Cle.	42	43	26	30	120
Bryant, Matt, T.B.	34	34	28	33	118
Kaeding, Nate, S.D.	46	46	24	27	118
Vinatieri, Adam, Ind.	49	51	23	29	118

NFL TOP TEN SCORERS—NONKICKERS

	TD	TDR	TDP	TDM	2-PT.	PTS
Moss, Randy, N.E.	23	0	23	0	0	138
Tomlinson, LaDainian, S.D.	18	15	3	0	0	108
Edwards, Braylon, Cle.	16	0	16	0	0	96
Addai, Joseph, Ind.	15	12	3	0	1	92
Owens, Terrell, Dal.	15	0	15	0	0	90
* Peterson, Adrian, Min.	13	12	1	0	0	78
Barber, Marion, Dal.	12	10	2	0	0	72
Burress, Plaxico, NY-G	12	0	12	0	0	72
Houshmandzadeh, T.J., Cin.	12	0	12	0	0	72
Jennings, Greg, G.B.	12	0	12	0	0	72
Westbrook, Brian, Phi.	12	7	5	0	0	72

AFC—INDIVIDUAL SCORERS

KICKERS

	XP	XPA	FG	FGA	PTS
Gostkowski, Stephen, N.E.	74	74	21	24	137
Bironas, Rob, Ten.	28	28	35	39	133
Graham, Shayne, Cin.	37	37	31	34	130
Dawson, Phil, Cle.	42	43	26	30	120
Kaeding, Nate, S.D.	46	46	24	27	118
Vinatieri, Adam, Ind.	49	51	23	29	118
Brown, Kris, Hou.	40	40	25	29	115
Elam, Jason, Den.	33	33	27	31	114
Reed, Jeff, Pit.	44	44	23	25	113
Nugent, Mike, NYJ	23	24	29	36	110
Stover, Matt, Bal.	26	26	27	32	107
Janikowski, Sebastian, Oak.	28	28	23	32	97
Lindell, Rian, Buf.	24	24	24	27	96
Feely, Jay, Mia.	26	26	21	23	89
Carney, John, Jac.-K.C.	27	28	12	14	63
Scobee, Josh, Jac.	26	27	12	13	62
Rayner, Dave, K.C.	14	14	15	22	59
* Medlock, Justin, K.C.	0	0	1	2	3
Larson, Kyle, Cin.	0	1	0	0	0

NONKICKERS

	TD	TDR	TDP	TDM	2-PT.	PTS
Moss, Randy, N.E.	23	0	23	0	0	138
Tomlinson, LaDainian, S.D.	18	15	3	0	0	108
Edwards, Braylon, Cle.	16	0	16	0	0	96
Addai, Joseph, Ind.	15	12	3	0	1	92
Houshmandzadeh, T.J., Cin.	12	0	12	0	0	72
Clark, Dallas, Ind.	11	0	11	0	0	66
Lewis, Jamal, Cle.	11	9	2	0	0	66
Jones-Drew, Maurice, Jac.	10	9	0	1	0	60
Wayne, Reggie, Ind.	10	0	10	0	0	60
Williams, Reggie, Jac.	10	0	10	0	0	60
Gates, Antonio, S.D.	9	0	9	0	0	54
Holmes, Santonio, Pit.	8	0	8	0	1	50
Johnson, Andre, Hou.	8	0	8	0	0	48
Johnson, Chad, Cin.	8	0	8	0	0	48
McGahee, Willis, Bal.	8	7	1	0	0	48
Welker, Wes, N.E.	8	0	8	0	0	48

Name	TD	TDR	TDP	TDM	2-PT.	PTS
* Lynch, Marshawn, Buf.	7	7	0	0	1	44
Ward, Hines, Pit.	7	0	7	0	1	44
Davenport, Najeh, Pit.	7	5	2	0	0	42
Marshall, Brandon, Den.	7	0	7	0	0	42
Miller, Heath, Pit.	7	0	7	0	0	42
Watson, Kenny, Cin.	7	7	0	0	0	42
White, LenDale, Ten.	7	7	0	0	0	42
Davis, Andre, Hou.	6	0	3	3	1	38
Maroney, Laurence, N.E.	6	6	0	0	1	38
Washington, Leon, NYJ	6	3	0	3	1	38
Coles, Laveranues, NYJ	6	0	6	0	0	36
Dayne, Ron, Hou.	6	6	0	0	0	36
Porter, Jerry, Oak.	6	0	6	0	0	36
Watson, Benjamin, N.E.	6	0	6	0	0	36
Brown, Ronnie, Mia.	5	4	1	0	1	32
Winslow, Kellen, Cle.	5	0	5	0	1	32
* Bowe, Dwayne, K.C.	5	0	5	0	0	30
Brown, Chris, Ten.	5	5	0	0	0	30
Evans, Lee, Buf.	5	0	5	0	0	30
Gaffney, Jabar, N.E.	5	0	5	0	0	30
Gonzalez, Tony, K.C.	5	0	5	0	0	30
Mason, Derrick, Bal.	5	0	5	0	0	30
Scheffler, Tony, Den.	5	0	5	0	0	30
Stokley, Brandon, Den.	5	0	5	0	0	30
Taylor, Fred, Jac.	5	5	0	0	0	30
Walter, Kevin, Hou.	5	0	4	1	0	30
Washington, Nate, Pit.	5	0	5	0	0	30
Curry, Ronald, Oak.	4	0	4	0	2	28
Gado, Samkon, Hou.-Mia.	4	4	0	0	1	26
Johnson, Rudi, Cin.	4	3	1	0	1	26
Chambers, Chris, S.D.	4	0	4	0	0	24
Fargas, Justin, Oak.	4	4	0	0	0	24
Henry, Travis, Den.	4	4	0	0	0	24
Johnson, Larry, K.C.	4	3	1	0	0	24
Jones, Greg, Jac.	4	2	2	0	0	24
Jones, Matt, Jac.	4	0	4	0	0	24
Keith, Kenton, Ind.	4	3	1	0	0	24
Lemon, Cleo, Mia.	4	4	0	0	0	24
Northcutt, Dennis, Jac.	4	0	4	0	0	24
Sproles, Darren, S.D.	4	2	0	2	0	24
Williams, Roydell, Ten.	4	0	4	0	0	24
Jurevicius, Joe, Cle.	3	0	3	0	1	20
Anderson, Derek, Cle.	3	3	0	0	0	18
Baker, Chris, NYJ	3	0	3	0	0	18
Cribbs, Josh, Cle.	3	0	0	3	0	18
Cromartie, Antonio, S.D.	3	0	0	3	0	18
Culpepper, Daunte, Oak.	3	3	0	0	0	18
Daniels, Owen, Hou.	3	0	3	0	0	18
Darling, Devard, Bal.	3	0	3	0	0	18
Evans, Heath, N.E.	3	3	0	0	0	18
* Ginn, Ted Jr., Mia.	3	0	2	1	0	18
* Gonzalez, Anthony, Ind.	3	0	3	0	0	18
Jackson, Vincent, S.D.	3	0	3	0	0	18
Jordan, LaMont, Oak.	3	3	0	0	0	18
Leach, Vonta, Hou.	3	1	2	0	0	18
Manning, Peyton, Ind.	3	3	0	0	0	18
* Miller, Zach, Oak.	3	0	3	0	0	18
Morris, Sammy, N.E.	3	3	0	0	0	18
Parrish, Roscoe, Buf.	3	1	1	1	0	18
Royal, Robert, Buf.	3	0	3	0	0	18
Sapp, Cecil, Den.	3	2	1	0	0	18
* Spaeth, Matt, Pit.	3	0	3	0	0	18
Stallworth, Donte', N.E.	3	0	3	0	0	18
Wilford, Ernest, Jac.	3	0	3	0	0	18
Young, Vince, Ten.	3	3	0	0	0	18
Hagan, Derek, Mia.	2	0	2	0	1	14
Allen, Jared, K.C.	2	0	2	0	0	12
Brady, Kyle, N.E.	2	0	2	0	0	12

Name	TD	TDR	TDP	TDM	2-PT.	PTS
Brady, Tom, N.E.	2	2	0	0	0	12
Camarillo, Greg, Mia.	2	0	2	0	0	12
Cotchery, Jerricho, NYJ	2	0	2	0	0	12
Dreessen, Joel, Hou.	2	0	2	0	0	12
Dwight, Tim, Oak.	2	0	2	0	0	12
Eckel, Kyle, N.E.	2	2	0	0	0	12
* Figurs, Yamon, Bal.	2	0	0	2	0	12
Fuller, Vincent, Ten.	2	0	0	2	0	12
Gage, Justin, Ten.	2	0	2	0	0	12
Gaines, Michael, Buf.	2	0	2	0	0	12
Graham, Daniel, Den.	2	0	2	0	0	12
Green, Ahman, Hou.	2	2	0	0	0	12
Hall, Andre, Den.	2	2	0	0	0	12
Henry, Chris, Cin.	2	0	2	0	0	12
* Henry, Chris, Ten.	2	2	0	0	0	12
Hobbs, Ellis, N.E.	2	0	0	2	0	12
Holt, Glenn, Cin.	2	0	1	1	0	12
Howard, Thomas, Oak.	2	0	0	2	0	12
Jones, Brandon, Ten.	2	0	2	0	0	12
Jones, Thomas, NYJ	2	1	1	0	0	12
Lewis, Marcedes, Jac.	2	0	2	0	0	12
Martin, David, Mia.	2	0	2	0	0	12
Parker, Samie, K.C.	2	0	2	0	0	12
Parker, Willie, Pit.	2	2	0	0	0	12
Peelle, Justin, Mia.	2	0	2	0	0	12
Roethlisberger, Ben, Pit.	2	2	0	0	0	12
Smith, Brad, NYJ	2	0	2	0	0	12
* Smith, Kolby, K.C.	2	2	0	0	0	12
Smith, Musa, Bal.	2	2	0	0	0	12
Vickers, Lawrence, Cle.	2	0	2	0	0	12
Vrabel, Mike, N.E.	2	0	2	0	0	12
Wilson, George, Buf.	2	0	0	2	0	12
Garrard, David, Jac.	1	1	0	0	1	8
Kelsay, Chris, Buf.	1	0	0	1	0	^8
* Walker, Darius, Hou.	1	1	0	0	1	8
Anderson, David, Hou.	1	0	1	0	0	6
Andrews, Willie, N.E.	1	0	1	0	0	6
Angulo, Richard, Jac.	1	0	1	0	0	6
* Battle, Jackie, K.C.	1	1	0	0	0	6
* Beck, John, Mia.	1	1	0	0	0	6
Booker, Marty, Mia.	1	0	1	0	0	6
Bowens, David, NYJ	1	0	0	1	0	6
* Brackenridge, Tyron, K.C.	1	0	0	1	0	6
Brackett, Gary, Ind.	1	0	0	1	0	6
* Broussard, John, Jac.	1	0	1	0	0	6
Carter, Tim, Cle.	1	0	1	0	0	6
Cassel, Matt, N.E.	1	1	0	0	0	6
Chatman, Antonio, Cin.	1	0	1	0	0	6
Chatman, Jesse, Mia.	1	1	0	0	0	6
Clemens, Kellen, NYJ	1	1	0	0	0	6
Cobbs, Patrick, Mia.	1	1	0	0	0	6
Colvin, Rosevelt, N.E.	1	0	0	1	0	6
* Crowder, Tim, Den.	1	0	0	1	0	6
Cutler, Jay, Den.	1	1	0	0	0	6
* Davis, Craig, S.D.	1	0	1	0	0	6
* Dawson, Clifton, Ind.	1	1	0	0	0	6
Dorsey, DeDe, Cin.	1	0	0	1	0	6
Faulk, Kevin, N.E.	1	0	1	0	0	6
Gay, Randall, N.E.	1	0	0	1	0	6
Giordano, Matt, Ind.	1	0	0	1	0	6
Glenn, Aaron, Jac.	1	0	0	1	0	6
Griffith, Justin, Oak.	1	0	1	0	0	6
Harrison, Marvin, Ind.	1	0	1	0	0	6
Heap, Todd, Bal.	1	0	1	0	0	6
Ingram, Clint, Jac.	1	0	0	1	0	6
Jackson, Nate, Den.	1	0	1	0	0	6
Johnson, Jeremi, Cin.	1	0	1	0	0	6
Johnson, Landon, Cin.	1	0	0	1	0	6

	TD	TDR	TDP	TDM	2-PT	PTS
Joseph, Johnathan, Cin.	1	0	0	1	0	6
Kowalewski, Joe, NYJ	1	0	1	0	0	6
Lawton, Luke, Ind.	1	0	1	0	0	6
Lehan, Michael, Mia.	1	0	0	1	0	6
Lewis, Ray, Bal.	1	0	0	1	0	6
Madsen, John, Oak.	1	0	1	0	0	6
Manumaleuna, Brandon, S.D.	1	0	1	0	0	6
Martinez, Glenn, Den.	1	0	0	1	0	6
Mathis, Jerome, Hou.	1	0	0	1	0	6
* McClain, Le'Ron, Bal.	1	0	1	0	0	6
McFadden, Bryant, Pit.	1	0	0	1	0	6
McGee, Terrence, Buf.	1	0	0	1	0	6
* Ndukwe, Nedu, Cin.	1	0	0	1	0	6
Neal, Lorenzo, S.D.	1	0	1	0	0	6
Pennington, Chad, NYJ	1	1	0	0	0	6
Phillips, Shaun, S.D.	1	0	0	1	0	6
Pool, Brodney, Cle.	1	0	0	1	0	6
Putzier, Jeb, Hou.	1	0	1	0	0	6
Reed, Ed, Bal.	1	0	0	1	0	6
Rhodes, Dominic, Oak.	1	1	0	0	0	6
Rhodes, Kerry, NYJ	1	0	0	1	0	6
Rivers, Philip, S.D.	1	1	0	0	0	6
Rosenfels, Sage, Hou.	1	1	0	0	0	6
Ross, Cory, Bal.	1	1	0	0	0	6
Rossum, Allen, Pit.	1	0	0	1	0	6
Rushing, T.J., Ind.	1	0	0	1	0	6
Ryans, DeMeco, Hou.	1	0	0	1	0	6
Samuel, Asante, N.E.	1	0	0	1	0	6
Scaife, Bo, Ten.	1	0	1	0	0	6
* Siler, Brandon, S.D.	1	0	0	1	0	6
Smith, Daryl, Jac.	1	0	0	1	0	6
* Smith, Troy, Bal.	1	1	0	0	0	6
Sypniewski, Quinn, Bal.	1	0	1	0	0	6
Taylor, Ike, Pit.	1	0	0	1	0	6
Taylor, Jason, Mia.	1	0	0	1	0	6
Thomas, Adalius, N.E.	1	0	0	1	0	6
Thomas, Anthony, Buf.	1	0	1	0	0	6
Thorpe, Craphonso, Ind.	1	0	1	0	0	6
Toefield, LaBrandon, Jac.	1	1	0	0	0	6
* Tucker, Jyles, S.D.	1	0	0	1	0	6
Tuman, Jerame, Pit.	1	0	1	0	0	6
Turner, Michael, S.D.	1	1	0	0	0	6
Utecht, Ben, Ind.	1	0	1	0	0	6
Webb, Jeff, K.C.	1	0	1	0	0	6
Webster, Nate, Den.	1	0	0	1	0	6
Wilcox, Daniel, Bal.	1	0	1	0	0	6
Williams, Mario, Hou.	1	0	0	1	0	6
Wilson, Cedrick, Pit.	1	0	1	0	0	6
Wilson, Eugene, N.E.	1	0	0	1	0	6
Wilson, Kris, K.C.	1	0	1	0	0	6
Wrighster, George, Jac.	1	0	1	0	0	6
Wright, Jason, Cle.	1	1	0	0	0	6
* Young, Selvin, Den.	1	1	0	0	0	6
Crowell, Angelo, Buf.	0	0	0	0	0	^2
Fletcher, Bryan, Ind.	0	0	0	0	1	2
Freeney, Dwight, Ind.	0	0	0	0	0	^2
Holmes, Priest, K.C.	0	0	0	0	1	2
Marshall, Lemar, Cin.	0	0	0	0	0	^2
Pollard, Bernard, K.C.	0	0	0	0	0	^2
Warren, Gerard, Oak.	0	0	0	0	0	^2

^ Safety; *Player that was a rookie in 2007
Team safety credited to Cleveland, Denver, and Indianapolis

NFC—INDIVIDUAL SCORERS
KICKERS

	XP	XPA	FG	FGA	PTS
* Crosby, Mason, G.B.	48	48	31	39	141

	XP	XPA	FG	FGA	PTS
* Folk, Nick, Dal.	53	53	26	31	131
Brown, Josh, Sea.	43	43	28	34	127
Gould, Robbie, Chi.	33	33	31	36	126
Hanson, Jason, Det.	35	36	29	35	122
Bryant, Matt, T.B.	34	34	28	33	118
Suisham, Shaun, Was.	29	30	29	35	116
Rackers, Neil, Ariz	47	48	21	30	110
Tynes, Lawrence, NY-G	40	42	23	27	109
Akers, David, Phi.	36	36	24	32	108
Andersen, Morten, Atl.	24	24	25	28	99
Kasay, John, Car.	27	27	24	28	99
Longwell, Ryan, Min.	39	40	20	24	99
Wilkins, Jeff, St.L	25	25	24	32	97
Nedney, Joe, S.F.	22	22	17	19	73
Mare, Olindo, N.O.	34	34	10	17	64
Gramatica, Martin, N.O.	8	8	5	5	23
Prater, Matt, Atl.	1	1	1	4	4
Koenen, Michael, Atl.	0	0	0	2	0

NONKICKERS

	TD	TDR	TDP	TDM	X2G	PTS
Owens, Terrell, Dal.	15	0	15	0	0	90
* Peterson, Adrian, Min.	13	12	1	0	0	78
Barber, Marion, Dal.	12	10	2	0	0	72
Burress, Plaxico, NY-G	12	0	12	0	0	72
Jennings, Greg, G.B.	12	0	12	0	0	72
Westbrook, Brian, Phi.	12	7	5	0	0	72
Burleson, Nate, Sea.	11	0	9	2	0	66
Colston, Marques, N.O.	11	0	11	0	0	66
Portis, Clinton, Was.	11	11	0	0	0	66
Fitzgerald, Larry, Ariz	10	0	10	0	0	60
Graham, Earnest, T.B.	10	10	0	0	0	60
Boldin, Anquan, Ariz	9	0	9	0	0	54
Cooley, Chris, Was.	8	0	8	0	1	50
Curtis, Kevin, Phi.	8	0	6	2	0	48
Grant, Ryan, G.B.	8	8	0	0	0	48
Hester, Devin, Chi.	8	0	2	6	0	48
Jones, Kevin, Det.	8	8	0	0	0	48
Holt, Torry, St.L	7	0	7	0	1	44
Bush, Reggie, N.O.	6	4	2	0	3	42
Crayton, Patrick, Dal.	7	0	7	0	0	42
James, Edgerrin, Ariz	7	7	0	0	0	42
Smith, Steve, Car.	7	0	7	0	0	42
Taylor, Chester, Min.	7	7	0	0	0	42
Witten, Jason, Dal.	7	0	7	0	0	42
Battle, Arnaz, S.F.	6	1	5	0	0	36
Droughns, Reuben, NY-G	6	6	0	0	0	36
Engram, Bobby, Sea.	6	0	6	0	0	36
Galloway, Joey, T.B.	6	0	6	0	0	36
Gore, Frank, S.F.	6	5	1	0	0	36
Jackson, Steven, St.L	6	5	1	0	0	36
Jacobs, Brandon, NY-G	6	4	2	0	0	36
Lee, Donald, G.B.	6	0	6	0	0	36
McDonald, Shaun, Det.	6	0	6	0	0	36
White, Roddy, Atl.	6	0	6	0	0	36
Alexander, Shaun, Sea.	5	4	1	0	0	30
Berrian, Bernard, Chi.	5	0	5	0	0	30
Crumpler, Alge, Atl.	5	0	5	0	0	30
* Johnson, Calvin, Det.	5	1	4	0	0	30
Morris, Maurice, Sea.	5	4	1	0	0	30
Pope, Leonard, Ariz	5	0	5	0	0	30
Stecker, Aaron, N.O.	5	5	0	0	0	30
Williams, DeAngelo, Car.	5	4	1	0	0	30
Williams, Roy, Det.	5	0	5	0	0	30
Benson, Cedric, Chi.	4	4	0	0	0	24
Branch, Deion, Sea.	4	0	4	0	0	24
Brown, Reggie, Phi.	4	0	4	0	0	24
Bruce, Isaac, St.L	4	0	4	0	0	24

	TD	TDR	TDP	TDM	2-PT.	PTS		TD	TDR	TDP	TDM	2-PT.	PTS
Buckhalter, Correll, Phi.	4	4	0	0	0	24	Arrington, J.J., Ariz	1	0	1	0	0	6
Carter, Drew, Car.	4	0	4	0	0	24	Atogwe, O.J., St.L	1	0	0	1	0	6
Clark, Desmond, Chi.	4	0	4	0	0	24	Banta-Cain, Tully, S.F.	1	0	0	1	0	6
Davis, Vernon, S.F.	4	0	4	0	0	24	Baskett, Hank, Phi.	1	0	1	0	0	6
Dunn, Warrick, Atl.	4	4	0	0	0	24	Bell, Tatum, Det.	1	1	0	0	0	6
Foster, DeShaun, Car.	4	3	1	0	0	24	Bienemann, Troy, Ariz	1	0	1	0	0	6
Jenkins, Michael, Atl.	4	0	4	0	0	24	Bradley, Mark, Chi.	1	0	1	0	0	6
Martin, Ruvell, G.B.	4	0	4	0	0	24	* Bradshaw, Ahmad, NY-G	1	1	0	0	0	6
* Rice, Sidney, Min.	4	0	4	0	0	24	* Breaston, Steve, Ariz	1	0	0	1	0	6
Stevens, Jerramy, T.B.	4	0	4	0	0	24	Brees, Drew, N.O.	1	1	0	0	0	6
Ward, Derrick, NY-G	4	3	1	0	0	24	Brown, Fakhir, St.L	1	0	0	1	0	6
* Wynn, DeShawn, G.B.	4	4	0	0	0	24	Campbell, Jason, Was.	1	1	0	0	0	6
Jackson, Tarvaris, Min.	3	3	0	0	2	22	* Celek, Brent, Phi.	1	0	1	0	0	6
* Thomas, Pierre, N.O.	3	1	1	1	1	20	David, Jason, N.O.	1	0	0	1	0	6
Bennett, Drew, St.L	3	0	3	0	0	18	Edwards, Ray, Min.	1	0	0	1	0	6
Curtis, Tony, Dal.	3	0	3	0	0	18	Fasano, Anthony, Dal.	1	0	1	0	0	6
Duckett, T.J., Det.	3	3	0	0	0	18	Ferguson, Robert, Min.	1	0	1	0	0	6
Franks, Bubba, G.B.	3	0	3	0	0	18	Fletcher, London, Was.	1	0	0	1	0	6
Hackett, D.J., Sea.	3	0	3	0	0	18	Furrey, Mike, Det.	1	0	1	0	0	6
Heller, Will, Sea.	3	0	3	0	0	18	Garcia, Jeff, T.B.	1	1	0	0	0	6
Henderson, Devery, N.O.	3	0	3	0	0	18	* Graham, Corey, Chi.	1	0	0	1	0	6
Jackson, Darrell, S.F.	3	0	3	0	0	18	Greenway, Chad, Min.	1	0	0	1	0	6
Lewis, Greg, Phi.	3	0	3	0	0	18	Griffin, Cedric, Min.	1	0	0	1	0	6
McMichael, Randy, St.L	3	0	3	0	0	18	Hall, Dante, St.L	1	0	0	1	0	6
Moore, Lance, N.O.	3	1	2	0	0	18	Hall, DeAngelo, Atl.	1	0	0	1	0	6
Moss, Santana, Was.	3	0	3	0	0	18	Harper, Roman, N.O.	1	0	0	1	0	6
Muhammad, Muhsin, Chi.	3	0	3	0	0	18	Hatcher, Jason, Dal.	1	0	0	1	0	6
Patten, David, N.O.	3	0	3	0	0	18	Hayes, Gerald, Ariz	1	0	0	1	0	6
Peterson, Adrian, Chi.	3	3	0	0	0	18	Henry, Anthony, Dal.	1	0	0	1	0	6
Rolle, Antrel, Ariz	3	0	0	3	0	18	Hicks, Maurice, S.F.	1	1	0	0	0	6
Sellers, Mike, Was.	3	2	1	0	0	18	Hill, Leroy, Sea.	1	0	0	1	0	6
Shockey, Jeremy, NY-G	3	0	3	0	0	18	Hill, Shaun, S.F.	1	1	0	0	0	6
Smith, Alex, T.B.	3	0	3	0	0	18	Hilliard, Ike, T.B.	1	0	1	0	0	6
Toomer, Amani, NY-G	3	0	3	0	0	18	Hixon, Domenik, NY-G	1	0	0	1	0	6
Wade, Bobby, Min.	3	0	3	0	0	18	Horn, Joe, Atl.	1	0	1	0	0	6
Williams, Cadillac, T.B.	3	3	0	0	0	18	* Hunt, Tony, Phi.	1	1	0	0	0	6
Fitzsimmons, Casey, Det.	2	0	1	1	0	^14	Hurd, Sam, Dal.	1	0	1	0	0	6
* Olsen, Greg, Chi.	2	0	2	0	1	14	* Jackson, Brandon, G.B.	1	1	0	0	0	6
Avant, Jason, Phi.	2	0	2	0	0	12	Jacobs, Taylor, S.F.	1	0	1	0	0	6
Barber, Ronde, T.B.	2	0	0	2	0	12	Jennings, Adam, Atl.	1	0	1	0	0	6
Becht, Anthony, T.B.	2	0	2	0	0	12	Kleinsasser, Jimmy, Min.	1	0	1	0	0	6
Bennett, Michael, T.B.	2	1	1	0	0	12	Klopfenstein, Joe, St.L	1	0	1	0	0	6
Betts, Ladell, Was.	2	1	1	0	0	12	Lenon, Paris, Det.	1	0	0	1	0	6
Blackmon, Will, G.B.	2	0	0	2	0	12	Lucas, Ken, Car.	1	0	0	1	0	6
* Boss, Kevin, NY-G	2	0	2	0	0	12	Manning, Eli, NY-G	1	1	0	0	0	6
Copper, Terrance, N.O.	2	0	2	0	0	12	Marshall, Richard, Car.	1	0	0	1	0	6
Driver, Donald, G.B.	2	0	2	0	0	12	McCardell, Keenan, Was.	1	0	1	0	0	6
Fauria, Christian, Car.	2	0	2	0	0	12	McKie, Jason, Chi.	1	1	0	0	0	6
Hood, Roderick, Ariz	2	0	0	2	0	12	Middleton, Brandon, Det.	1	0	1	0	0	6
Johnson, Bryant, Ariz	2	0	2	0	0	12	Mughelli, Ovie, Atl.	1	1	0	0	0	6
Johnson, Eric, N.O.	2	0	2	0	0	12	Newman, Terence, Dal.	1	0	0	1	0	6
* Jones, James, G.B.	2	0	2	0	0	12	Norwood, Jerious, Atl.	1	1	0	0	0	6
Jones, Julius, Dal.	2	2	0	0	0	12	Obomanu, Ben, Sea.	1	0	1	0	0	6
Karney, Mike, N.O.	2	2	0	0	0	12	Robinson, Koren, G.B.	1	0	1	0	0	6
King, Jeff, Car.	2	0	2	0	0	12	* Robinson, Laurent, Atl.	1	0	1	0	0	6
McKenzie, Mike, N.O.	2	0	0	2	0	12	Rogers, Carlos, Was.	1	0	0	1	0	6
Miller, Billy, N.O.	2	0	2	0	0	12	Rogers, Shaun, Det.	1	0	0	1	0	6
Mitchell, Kawika, NY-G	2	0	0	2	0	12	* Ross, Aaron, NY-G	1	0	0	1	0	6
* Patrick, Ben, Ariz	2	0	2	0	0	12	Schobel, Matt, Phi.	1	0	1	0	0	6
Pollard, Marcus, Sea.	2	0	2	0	0	12	Sharper, Darren, Min.	1	0	0	1	0	6
Romo, Tony, Dal.	2	2	0	0	0	12	Shiancoe, Visanthe, Min.	1	0	1	0	0	6
* Rosario, Dante, Car.	2	0	2	0	0	12	Shipp, Marcel, Ariz	1	1	0	0	0	6
Thrash, James, Was.	2	0	2	0	0	12	Smith, Dwight, Min.	1	0	0	1	0	6
Urban, Jerheme, Ariz	2	0	2	0	0	12	Smith, L.J., Phi.	1	0	1	0	0	6
Williams, Kevin, Min.	2	0	0	2	0	12	Smith, Keith, Det.	1	0	1	0	0	6
Woodson, Charles, G.B.	2	0	0	2	0	12	* Snelling, Jason, Atl.	1	1	0	0	0	6
Randle El, Antwaan, Was.	1	0	1	0	1	8	Spurlock, Micheal, T.B.	1	0	0	1	0	6
* Allison, Aundrae, Min.	1	0	0	1	0	6	St. Clair, John, Chi.	1	0	1	0	0	6

Stovall, Maurice, T.B.	1	0	1	0	0	6		Wilson, Josh, Sea.	1	0	0	1	0	6
Trufant, Marcus, Sea.	1	0	0	1	0	6		Winfield, Antoine, Min.	1	0	0	1	0	6
Umenyiora, Osi, NY-G	1	0	0	1	0	6		Yoder, Todd, Was.	1	0	1	0	0	6
Urlacher, Brian, Chi.	1	0	0	1	0	6		Bollinger, Brooks, Min.	0	0	0	0	1	2
Walker, Delanie, S.F.	1	0	1	0	0	6		Carriker, Adam, St.L	0	0	0	0	0	^2
Walters, Troy, Det.	1	0	1	0	0	6		Carter, Andre, Was.	0	0	0	0	0	^2
Warner, Kurt, Ariz	1	1	0	0	0	6		Golston, Kedric, Was.	0	0	0	0	0	^2
Watkins, Pat, Dal.	1	0	0	1	0	6		Norris, Moran, S.F.	0	0	0	0	0	^2
Weaver, Leonard, Sea.	1	1	0	0	0	6		Scobey, Josh, Sea.	0	0	0	0	0	^2
Webster, Corey, NY-G	1	0	0	1	0	6		Smith, Will, N.O.	0	0	0	0	0	^2
Wells, Reggie, Ariz	1	0	0	1	0	6								
White, Dewayne, Det.	1	0	0	1	0	6		^ Safety						
White, Tracy, G.B.	1	0	0	1	0	6		Team safety credited to Chicago and Minnesota						
Williams, Tramon, G.B.	1	0	0	1	0	6		* Player that was a rookie in 2007						
Williamson, Troy, Min.	1	0	1	0	0	6								

AMERICAN FOOTBALL CONFERENCE—SCORING

	TD	TDR	TDP	TDM	XKG	XKAtt	X2G	X2Att	FG	FGA	SAF	POINTS
New England	75	17	50	8	74	74	1	1	21	24	0	589
Indianapolis	54	19	32	3	49	51	2	3	23	29	2	450
San Diego	49	19	22	8	46	46	0	2	24	27	0	412
Jacksonville	50	18	28	4	46	48	1	2	21	24	0	411
Cleveland	46	13	29	4	42	43	2	3	26	30	1	402
Pittsburgh	46	9	34	3	44	44	2	2	23	25	0	393
Cincinnati	41	10	26	5	37	38	1	3	31	34	1	380
Houston	43	12	24	7	40	40	3	3	25	29	0	379
Denver	34	10	21	3	33	33	0	1	27	31	1	320
Tennessee	28	17	9	2	28	28	0	0	35	39	0	301
Oakland	30	11	17	2	28	28	2	2	23	32	1	283
Baltimore	28	11	13	4	26	26	0	2	27	32	0	275
N.Y. Jets	26	6	15	5	23	24	1	2	29	36	0	268
Miami	29	14	12	3	26	26	2	2	21	23	0	267
Buffalo	25	8	12	5	24	24	1	1	24	27	2	252
Kansas City	24	6	17	1	21	21	1	3	19	27	1	226
AFC Total	628	200	361	67	587	594	19	32	399	469	9	5608
AFC Average	39.3	12.5	22.6	4.2	36.7	37.1	1.2	2.0	24.9	29.3	0.6	350.5

NATIONAL FOOTBALL CONFERENCE—SCORING

	TD	TDR	TDP	TDM	XKG	XKAtt	X2G	X2Att	FG	FGA	SAF	POINTS
Dallas	54	14	36	4	53	53	0	1	26	31	0	455
Green Bay	49	13	30	6	48	48	0	0	31	39	0	435
Arizona	49	9	32	8	47	48	0	1	21	30	0	404
Seattle	44	9	30	5	43	43	0	1	28	34	1	393
New Orleans	47	14	28	5	42	42	4	5	15	22	1	379
N.Y. Giants	44	15	23	6	40	42	0	2	23	27	0	373
Minnesota	43	22	12	9	39	40	3	3	20	24	1	365
Detroit	37	13	19	5	35	36	0	1	29	35	1	346
Philadelphia	38	12	24	2	36	36	0	2	24	32	0	336
Chicago	34	8	18	8	33	33	1	1	31	36	1	334
Tampa Bay	36	15	18	3	34	34	0	2	28	33	0	334
Washington	35	15	18	2	29	30	2	5	29	35	2	334
Carolina	28	7	19	2	27	27	0	1	24	28	0	267
St. Louis	27	5	19	3	25	25	1	2	24	32	1	263
Atlanta	26	7	18	1	25	25	0	1	26	34	0	259
San Francisco	24	8	15	1	22	22	0	1	17	19	1	219
NFC Total	615	186	359	70	578	584	11	29	396	491	9	5496
NFC Average	38.4	11.6	22.4	4.4	36.1	36.5	0.7	1.8	24.8	30.7	0.6	343.5
NFL Total	1243	386	720	137	1165	1178	30	61	795	960	18	11104
NFL Average	38.8	12.1	22.5	4.3	36.4	36.8	0.9	1.9	24.8	30.0	0.6	347.0

FIELD GOALS

FIELD GOAL PERCENTAGE
AFC:	.920	Jeff Reed, Pittsburgh
NFC:	.895	Joe Nedney, San Francisco

FIELD GOALS
AFC:	35	Rob Bironas, Tennessee
NFC:	31	* Mason Crosby, Green Bay
	31	Robbie Gould, Chicago

FIELD GOAL ATTEMPTS
AFC:	39	Rob Bironas, Tennessee
NFC:	39	* Mason Crosby, Green Bay

FIELD GOALS, GAME
AFC:	8	Rob Bironas, Tennessee at Houston, October 21 (8 attempts)
NFC:	5	Shaun Suisham, Washington at N.Y. Jets, November 4 (5 attempts) - (OT)

LONGEST FIELD GOAL
AFC:	57	Kris Brown, Houston vs. Miami, October 7
NFC:	55	Ryan Longwell, Minnesota at Chicago, October 14
	55	Martin Gramatica, New Orleans vs. Philadelphia, December 23

AVERAGE YARDS MADE
AFC:	40.3	Sebastian Janikowski, Oakland
NFC:	39.9	Ryan Longwell, Minnesota

AMERICAN FOOTBALL CONFERENCE—FIELD GOALS

	FG	FGA	Pct	Long
Pittsburgh	23	25	.920	49
Miami	21	23	.913	53
Cincinnati	31	34	.912	48
Tennessee	35	39	.897	56
Buffalo	24	27	.889	52
San Diego	24	27	.889	51
Jacksonville	21	24	.875	48
New England	21	24	.875	45
Denver	27	31	.871	50
Cleveland	26	30	.867	51
Houston	25	29	.862	57
Baltimore	27	32	.844	49
N.Y. Jets	29	36	.806	50
Indianapolis	23	29	.793	39
Oakland	23	32	.719	54
Kansas City	19	27	.704	49
AFC Total	399	469	—	57
AFC Average	24.9	29.3	.851	—

NATIONAL FOOTBALL CONFERENCE—FIELD GOALS

	FG	FGA	Pct	Long
San Francisco	17	19	.895	50
Chicago	31	36	.861	49
Carolina	24	28	.857	53
N.Y. Giants	23	27	.852	48
Tampa Bay	28	33	.848	49
Dallas	26	31	.839	53
Minnesota	20	24	.833	55
Detroit	29	35	.829	53
Washington	29	35	.829	50
Seattle	28	34	.824	54
Green Bay	31	39	.795	53
Atlanta	26	34	.765	47
Philadelphia	24	32	.750	53
St. Louis	24	32	.750	53
Arizona	21	30	.700	52
New Orleans	15	22	.682	55
NFC Total	396	491	—	55
NFC Average	24.8	30.7	.807	—
League Total	795	960	—	57
League Average	24.8	30.0	.828	—

AFC—INDIVIDUAL FIELD GOALS

	1-19 Yards	20-29 Yards	30-39 Yards	40-49 Yards	50 or Longer	Totals	Avg Yds Att	Avg Yds Made	Avg Yds Miss	Long
Reed, Jeff, Pit.	0-0 —	9-9 1.000	10-10 1.000	4-5 .800	0-1 .000	23-25 .920	34.1	32.3	54.5	49
Feely, Jay, Mia.	0-0 —	7-7 1.000	6-6 1.000	7-9 .778	1-1 1.000	21-23 .913	36.8	35.8	47.5	53
Graham, Shayne, Cin.	1-1 1.000	11-12 .917	13-13 1.000	6-7 .857	0-1 .000	31-34 .912	32.4	31.6	40.7	48
Bironas, Rob, Ten.	0-0 —	10-12 .833	12-12 1.000	9-10 .900	4-5 .800	35-39 .897	36.5	36.2	39.0	56
Kaeding, Nate, S.D.	0-0 —	11-11 1.000	5-6 .833	7-8 .875	1-2 .500	24-27 .889	34.1	33.0	42.7	51
Lindell, Rian, Buf.	0-0 —	11-11 1.000	7-7 1.000	4-6 .667	2-3 .667	24-27 .889	34.7	33.0	48.3	52
Gostkowski, Stephen, N.E.	0-0 —	10-10 1.000	8-9 .889	3-5 .600	0-0 —	21-24 .875	32.1	31.0	40.3	45
Elam, Jason, Den.	0-0 —	11-11 1.000	6-6 1.000	9-12 .750	1-2 .500	27-31 .871	35.3	33.7	46.5	50
Dawson, Phil, Cle.	2-2 1.000	9-10 .900	7-8 .875	7-8 .875	1-2 .500	26-30 .867	34.2	33.6	38.0	51
Brown, Kris, Hou.	1-1 1.000	6-7 .857	6-6 1.000	7-10 .700	5-5 1.000	25-29 .862	37.6	37.1	40.8	57
Stover, Matt, Bal.	1-1 1.000	11-11 1.000	7-7 1.000	8-12 .667	0-1 .000	27-32 .844	35.0	33.1	45.4	49
Nugent, Mike, NYJ	1-1 1.000	11-11 1.000	10-12 .833	6-8 .750	1-4 .250	29-36 .806	34.9	32.4	45.0	50
Vinatieri, Adam, Ind.	1-1 1.000	14-15 .933	8-10 .800	0-2 .000	0-1 .000	23-29 .793	30.3	27.6	40.7	39
Janikowski, Sebastian, Oak.	0-0 —	4-4 1.000	6-7 .857	7-10 .700	6-11 .545	23-32 .719	43.2	40.3	50.6	54
Rayner, Dave, K.C.	0-0 —	3-3 1.000	7-10 .700	5-8 .625	0-1 .000	15-22 .682	37.1	35.6	40.4	49
(Nonqualifiers)										
Carney, John, Jac.-K.C.	2-2 1.000	3-3 1.000	5-5 1.000	2-4 .500	0-0 —	12-14 .857	32.7	30.7	45.0	41
Scobee, Josh, Jac.	0-0 —	6-6 1.000	3-3 1.000	3-4 .750	0-0 —	12-13 .923	32.1	30.9	46.0	48
* Medlock, Justin, K.C.	0-0 —	1-1 1.000	0-1 .000	0-0 —	0-0 —	1-2 .500	28.5	27.0	30.0	27
AFC Totals	9-9 1.000	148-154 .961	126-138 .913	94-128 .734	22-40 .550	399-469 .851	35.1	33.5	43.8	57
NFL Totals	17-17 1.000	270-284 .951	253-279 .907	208-280 .743	47-100 .470	795-960 .828	36.2	34.4	44.5	57

Leader based on overall percentage, minimum 16 field goals

NFC—INDIVIDUAL FIELD GOALS

	1-19 Yards	20-29 Yards	30-39 Yards	40-49 Yards	50 or Longer	Totals	Avg Yds Att	Avg Yds Made	Avg Yds Miss	Long
Nedney, Joe, S.F.	1-1 1.000	5-5 1.000	6-6 1.000	4-4 1.000	1-3 .333	17-19 .895	36.2	34.1	53.5	50
Andersen, Morten, Atl.	0-0 —	9-9 1.000	12-12 1.000	4-7 .571	0-0 —	25-28 .893	33.6	32.2	46.0	47
Gould, Robbie, Chi.	0-0 —	7-7 1.000	12-13 .923	12-14 .857	0-2 .000	31-36 .861	37.4	35.9	46.4	49
Kasay, John, Car.	2-2 1.000	6-6 1.000	8-9 .889	6-9 .667	2-2 1.000	24-28 .857	36.5	35.5	42.3	53
Tynes, Lawrence, NY-G	1-1 1.000	9-10 .900	5-8 .625	8-8 1.000	0-0 —	23-27 .852	33.5	33.5	33.8	48
Bryant, Matt, T.B.	0-0 —	11-12 .917	11-11 1.000	6-7 .857	0-3 .000	28-33 .848	35.0	33.0	46.2	49
* Folk, Nick, Dal.	0-0 —	10-12 .833	7-7 1.000	7-7 1.000	2-5 .400	26-31 .839	35.8	34.9	40.4	53
Longwell, Ryan, Min.	0-0 —	3-3 1.000	6-6 1.000	10-11 .909	1-4 .250	20-24 .833	42.0	39.9	52.5	55
Hanson, Jason, Det.	1-1 1.000	4-5 .800	10-12 .833	11-13 .846	3-4 .750	29-35 .829	39.0	38.4	41.5	53
Suisham, Shaun, Was.	0-0 —	10-10 1.000	8-10 .800	10-13 .769	1-2 .500	29-35 .829	36.7	35.2	43.7	50
Brown, Josh, Sea.	0-0 —	12-12 1.000	5-5 1.000	8-12 .667	3-5 .600	28-34 .824	37.1	35.0	46.7	54
* Crosby, Mason, G.B.	1-1 1.000	8-8 1.000	10-11 .909	9-14 .643	3-5 .600	31-39 .795	38.6	36.6	46.4	53
Akers, David, Phi.	0-0 —	12-12 1.000	10-10 1.000	1-6 .167	1-4 .250	24-32 .750	35.3	30.8	48.5	53
Wilkins, Jeff, St.L	0-0 —	7-8 .875	6-7 .857	8-13 .615	3-4 .750	24-32 .750	38.5	37.3	42.0	53
Rackers, Neil, Ariz	2-2 1.000	5-5 1.000	6-8 .750	5-6 .833	3-9 .333	21-30 .700	39.0	34.9	48.4	52
Mare, Olindo, N.O.	0-0 —	4-5 .800	3-4 .750	2-3 .667	1-5 .200	10-17 .588	39.2	35.0	45.1	52
(Nonqualifiers)										
Gramatica, Martin, N.O.	0-0 —	0-0 —	2-2 1.000	2-2 1.000	1-1 1.000	5-5 1.000	43.0	43.0	—	55
Prater, Matt, Atl.	0-0 —	0-1 .000	0-0 —	1-3 .333	0-0 —	1-4 .250	39.5	45.0	37.7	45
Koenen, Michael, Atl.	0-0 —	0-0 —	0-0 —	0-0 —	0-2 .000	0-2 .000	51.5	—	51.5	0
NFC Totals	8-8 1.000	122-130 .938	127-141 .901	114-152 .750	25-60 .417	396-491 .807	37.2	35.3	45.0	55
NFL Totals	17-17 1.000	270-284 .951	253-279 .907	208-280 .743	47-100 .470	795-960 .828	36.2	34.4	44.5	57

Leader based on overall percentage, minimum 16 field goals
* Player that was a rookie in 2007

RUSHING

YARDS
AFC: 1474 LaDainian Tomlinson, San Diego
NFC: 1341 * Adrian Peterson, Minnesota

YARDS, GAME
NFC: 296 * Adrian Peterson, Minnesota vs. San Diego, November 4 (30 attempts, 3 TD)
AFC: 216 Jamal Lewis, Cleveland vs. Cincinnati, September 16 (27 attempts, 1 TD)

LONGEST
NFC: 88 * Ahmad Bradshaw, N.Y. Giants at Buffalo, December 23 - TD
AFC: 80 Fred Taylor, Jacksonville vs. Carolina, December 9 - TD

ATTEMPTS
NFC: 325 Clinton Portis, Washington
AFC: 321 Willie Parker, Pittsburgh

ATTEMPTS, GAME
NFC: 36 Clinton Portis, Washington at N.Y. Jets, November 4 (196 yards, 1 TD) - (OT)
AFC: 33 Justin Fargas, Oakland vs. Denver, December 2 (146 yards, 1 TD)
33 Jamal Lewis, Cleveland vs. Buffalo, December 16 (163 yards, 0 TD)

YARDS PER ATTEMPT
NFC: 6.0 Jerious Norwood, Atlanta
AFC: 5.4 Fred Taylor, Jacksonville

TOUCHDOWNS
AFC: 15 LaDainian Tomlinson, San Diego
NFC: 12 * Adrian Peterson, Minnesota

TEAM LEADERS, YARDS
AFC BALTIMORE, 1207, Willis McGahee; BUFFALO, 1115, *Marshawn Lynch; CINCINNATI, 763, Kenny Watson; CLEVELAND, 1304, Jamal Lewis; DENVER, 729, *Selvin Young; HOUSTON, 773, Ron Dayne; INDIANAPOLIS, 1072, Joseph Addai; JACKSONVILLE, 1202, Fred Taylor; KANSAS CITY, 559, Larry Johnson; MIAMI, 602, Ronnie Brown; NEW ENGLAND, 835, Laurence Maroney; N.Y. JETS, 1119, Thomas Jones; OAKLAND, 1009, Justin Fargas; PITTSBURGH, 1316, Willie Parker; SAN DIEGO, 1474, LaDainian Tomlinson; TENNESSEE, 1110, LenDale White

NFC: ARIZONA, 1222, Edgerrin James; ATLANTA, 720, Warrick Dunn; CAROLINA, 876, DeShaun Foster; CHICAGO, 674, Cedric Benson; DALLAS, 975, Marion Barber; DETROIT, 581, Kevin Jones; GREEN BAY, 956, Ryan Grant; MINNESOTA, 1341, *Adrian Peterson; NEW ORLEANS, 581, Reggie Bush; N.Y. GIANTS, 1009, Brandon Jacobs; PHILADELPHIA, 1333, Brian Westbrook; ST. LOUIS, 1002, Steven Jackson; SAN FRANCISCO, 1102, Frank Gore; SEATTLE, 716, Shaun Alexander; TAMPA BAY, 898, Earnest Graham; WASHINGTON, 1262, Clinton Portis

TEAM CHAMPION
NFC: 2634 Minnesota
AFC: 2391 Jacksonville

Player that was a rookie in 2007

NFL TOP TEN RUSHERS

	Att	Yards	Avg	Long	TD
Tomlinson, LaDainian, S.D.	315	1474	4.7	49	15
* Peterson, Adrian, Min.	238	1341	5.6	73t	12
Westbrook, Brian, Phi.	278	1333	4.8	36	7
Parker, Willie, Pit.	321	1316	4.1	32	2
Lewis, Jamal, Cle.	298	1304	4.4	66t	9
Portis, Clinton, Was.	325	1262	3.9	32	11
James, Edgerrin, Ariz	324	1222	3.8	27	7
McGahee, Willis, Bal.	294	1207	4.1	46t	7
Taylor, Fred, Jac.	223	1202	5.4	80t	5
Jones, Thomas, NYJ	310	1119	3.6	36	1

AFC—INDIVIDUAL RUSHERS

	Att	Yards	Avg	Long	TD
Tomlinson, LaDainian, S.D.	315	1474	4.7	49	15
Parker, Willie, Pit.	321	1316	4.1	32	2
Lewis, Jamal, Cle.	298	1304	4.4	66t	9
McGahee, Willis, Bal.	294	1207	4.1	46t	7
Taylor, Fred, Jac.	223	1202	5.4	80t	5
Jones, Thomas, NYJ	310	1119	3.6	36	1
* Lynch, Marshawn, Buf.	280	1115	4.0	56t	7
White, LenDale, Ten.	303	1110	3.7	28	7
Addai, Joseph, Ind.	261	1072	4.1	23	12
Fargas, Justin, Oak.	222	1009	4.5	48	4
Maroney, Laurence, N.E.	185	835	4.5	59t	6
Dayne, Ron, Hou.	194	773	4.0	39	6
Jones-Drew, Maurice, Jac.	167	768	4.6	57t	9
Watson, Kenny, Cin.	178	763	4.3	24	7
* Young, Selvin, Den.	140	729	5.2	50	1
Henry, Travis, Den.	167	691	4.1	33	4
Brown, Ronnie, Mia.	119	602	5.1	60	4
Johnson, Larry, K.C.	158	559	3.5	54	3
Jordan, LaMont, Oak.	144	549	3.8	33	3
Keith, Kenton, Ind.	121	533	4.4	22	3
Chatman, Jesse, Mia.	128	515	4.0	30	1
Davenport, Najeh, Pit.	107	499	4.7	45	5
Johnson, Rudi, Cin.	170	497	2.9	22	3
Brown, Chris, Ten.	102	462	4.5	42	5
* Smith, Kolby, K.C.	112	407	3.6	19	2
Young, Vince, Ten.	93	395	4.2	21	3
Morris, Sammy, N.E.	85	384	4.5	49	3
Washington, Leon, NYJ	71	353	5.0	49	3
Turner, Michael, S.D.	71	316	4.5	74t	1
Rhodes, Dominic, Oak.	75	302	4.0	25	1
Jackson, Fred, Buf.	58	300	5.2	27	0
Wright, Jason, Cle.	60	277	4.6	18	1
Faulk, Kevin, N.E.	62	265	4.3	14	0
Smith, Musa, Bal.	75	264	3.5	24	2
* Walker, Darius, Hou.	58	264	4.6	41	1
Green, Ahman, Hou.	70	260	3.7	18	2
Hall, Andre, Den.	44	216	4.9	62t	2
Cutler, Jay, Den.	44	205	4.7	31	1
Roethlisberger, Ben, Pit.	35	204	5.8	30t	2
Garrard, David, Jac.	49	185	3.8	19	1
Dorsey, DeDe, Cin.	21	183	8.7	45	0
Sproles, Darren, S.D.	37	164	4.4	34	2
Gado, Samkon, Hou.-Mia.	53	150	2.8	20t	4
McCown, Josh, Oak.	29	143	4.9	24	0
Harrison, Jerome, Cle.	23	142	6.2	17	0
Holmes, Priest, K.C.	46	137	3.0	11	0
* Booker, Lorenzo, Mia.	28	125	4.5	22	0
Evans, Heath, N.E.	34	121	3.6	11	3
* Henry, Chris, Ten.	31	119	3.8	24t	2
Jones, Greg, Jac.	42	119	2.8	11	2
Clemens, Kellen, NYJ	27	111	4.1	18	1
Losman, J.P., Buf.	20	110	5.5	17	0
Lemon, Cleo, Mia.	31	102	3.3	11	4
Brady, Tom, N.E.	37	98	2.6	19	2
* Wright, Dwayne, Buf.	29	94	3.2	15	0

	Att	Yards	Avg	Long	TD
Eckel, Kyle, N.E.	33	90	2.7	14	2
Boller, Kyle, Bal.	19	89	4.7	15	0
Thomas, Anthony, Buf.	36	89	2.5	9	0
Echemandu, Adimchinobe, Hou.	20	85	4.3	20	0
Ross, Cory, Bal.	12	72	6.0	32t	1
Anderson, Derek, Cle.	32	70	2.2	11	3
Davis, Carey, Pit.	17	68	4.0	12	0
* Dawson, Clifton, Ind.	30	64	2.1	12	1
Anderson, Mike, Bal.	15	62	4.1	16	0
Cribbs, Josh, Cle.	9	61	6.8	18	0
Sapp, Cecil, Den.	18	59	3.3	12	2
Gray, Quinn, Jac.	19	57	3.0	15	0
Marshall, Brandon, Den.	5	57	11.4	24	0
* Smith, Troy, Bal.	12	54	4.5	14	1
Schaub, Matt, Hou.	17	52	3.1	12	0
Rosenfels, Sage, Hou.	21	51	2.4	19	1
* Edwards, Trent, Buf.	14	49	3.5	14	0
* Battle, Jackie, K.C.	14	47	3.4	6	1
Cobbs, Patrick, Mia.	15	47	3.1	12	1
Johnson, Chad, Cin.	6	47	7.8	16	0
Smith, Brad, NYJ	12	45	3.8	11	0
Vickers, Lawrence, Cle.	15	43	2.9	7	0
Culpepper, Daunte, Oak.	20	40	2.0	9	3
Cotchery, Jerricho, NYJ	5	38	7.6	16	0
Jones, Brandon, Ten.	2	37	18.5	16	0
Wilson, Cedrick, Pit.	2	37	18.5	37	0
Welker, Wes, N.E.	4	34	8.5	27	0
Rivers, Philip, S.D.	29	33	1.1	10	1
Green, Trent, Mia.	7	32	4.6	23	0
McNair, Steve, Bal.	10	32	3.2	13	0
Neal, Lorenzo, S.D.	13	32	2.5	10	0
Pennington, Chad, NYJ	20	32	1.6	5	1
Walter, Kevin, Hou.	5	30	6.0	13	0
Clark, Dallas, Ind.	2	29	14.5	15	0
Griffith, Justin, Oak.	7	27	3.9	6	0
Northcutt, Dennis, Jac.	6	27	4.5	8	0
Toefield, LaBrandon, Jac.	13	27	2.1	7	1
Johnson, Jeremi, Cin.	7	25	3.6	12	0
Cook, Jameel, Hou.	8	24	3.0	9	0
* Russell, Gary, Pit.	7	21	3.0	8	0
* Davis, Chris, Ten.	2	19	9.5	14	0
Parrish, Roscoe, Buf.	3	19	6.3	24t	1
Croyle, Brodie, K.C.	7	18	2.6	6	0
* McClain, Le'Ron, Bal.	8	18	2.3	4	0
Holmes, Santonio, Pit.	5	17	3.4	11	0
Williams, Ricky, Mia.	6	15	2.5	6	0
Houshmandzadeh, T.J., Cin.	5	14	2.8	8	0
Moorman, Brian, Buf.	4	14	3.5	10	0
Lawton, Luke, Ind.	5	13	2.6	4	0
* Beck, John, Mia.	9	12	1.3	8	1
Booker, Marty, Mia.	2	12	6.0	12	0
Cassel, Matt, N.E.	4	12	3.0	15t	1
Chambers, Chris, Mia.-S.D.	3	12	4.0	9	0
Dwight, Tim, Oak.	2	12	6.0	10	0
Stallworth, Donte', N.E.	1	12	12.0	12	0
Ward, Hines, Pit.	3	11	3.7	7	0
Watson, Benjamin, N.E.	1	11	11.0	11	0
Palmer, Carson, Cin.	24	10	0.4	10	0
Reed, Josh, Buf.	4	10	2.5	12	0
* Davis, Craig, S.D.	3	9	3.0	6	0
* Harris, Gilbert, K.C.	9	9	1.0	4	0
Perry, Tab, Cin.	1	9	9.0	9	0
Hall, Ahmard, Ten.	1	8	8.0	8	0
Williams, Reggie, Jac.	1	8	8.0	8	0
Wilson, Kris, K.C.	3	7	2.3	5	0
Ramsey, Patrick, Den.	2	6	3.0	4	0
Chatman, Antonio, Cin.	1	5	5.0	5	0
Kennison, Eddie, K.C.	1	5	5.0	5	0
* Mauia, Reagan, Mia.	4	5	1.3	3	0
Webb, Jeff, K.C.	1	5	5.0	5	0
McGraw, Jon, K.C.	1	4	4.0	4	0
* Russell, JaMarcus, Oak.	5	4	0.8	7	0
Wayne, Reggie, Ind.	1	4	4.0	4	0
Barclay, Chris, Ten.	1	3	3.0	3	0
Bell, Mike, Den.	6	3	0.5	3	0
* Davis, Chris, NYJ	1	3	3.0	3	0
* Ginn, Ted Jr., Mia.	4	3	0.8	7	0
* Higgins, Johnnie Lee, Oak.	2	3	1.5	8	0
Holt, Glenn, Cin.	2	2	1.0	1	0
Kreider, Dan, Pit.	1	2	2.0	2	0
Leach, Vonta, Hou.	2	2	1.0	1t	1
Parker, Samie, K.C.	1	2	2.0	2	0
Curry, Ronald, Oak.	1	1	1.0	1	0
Frye, Charlie, Cle.	1	1	1.0	1	0
Green, Skyler, Cin.	1	1	1.0	1	0
Pinnock, Andrew, S.D.	4	1	0.3	5	0
Turk, Matt, Hou.	1	0	0.0	0	0
Washington, Nate, Pit.	1	0	0.0	0	0
* Figurs, Yamon, Bal.	1	-1	-1.0	-1	0
Huard, Damon, K.C.	9	-1	-.1	2	0
* Jones, Jacoby, Hou.	3	-1	-.3	4	0
Troupe, Ben, Ten.	1	-1	-1.0	-1	0
* Podlesh, Adam, Jac.	2	-2	-1.0	-1	0
Collins, Kerry, Ten.	3	-3	-1.0	-1	0
Drummond, Eddie, K.C.	1	-3	-3.0	-3	0
Walker, Javon, Den.	2	-3	-1.5	-1	0
Zastudil, Dave, Cle.	2	-3	-1.5	0	0
Lechler, Shane, Oak.	1	-4	-4.0	-4	0
Sorgi, Jim, Ind.	6	-4	-.7	1	0
Manning, Peyton, Ind.	20	-5	-.3	4	3
Stokley, Brandon, Den.	1	-6	-6.0	-6	0
Batch, Charlie, Pit.	12	-7	-.6	0	0
Volek, Billy, S.D.	11	-7	-.6	0	0
Hentrich, Craig, Ten.	1	-8	-8.0	-8	0
* Gutierrez, Matt, N.E.	5	-13	-2.6	-1	0
Bell, Jacob, Ten.	1	-15	-15.0	-15	0
Williams, Roydell, Ten.	2	-17	-8.5	-6	0

t = Touchdown
Leader based on most yards gained
* Player that was a rookie in 2007

NFC—INDIVIDUAL RUSHERS

	Att	Yards	Avg	Long	TD
* Peterson, Adrian, Min.	238	1341	5.6	73t	12
Westbrook, Brian, Phi.	278	1333	4.8	36	7
Portis, Clinton, Was.	325	1262	3.9	32	11
James, Edgerrin, Ariz	324	1222	3.8	27	7
Gore, Frank, S.F.	260	1102	4.2	43t	5
Jacobs, Brandon, NY-G	202	1009	5.0	43t	4
Jackson, Steven, St.L	237	1002	4.2	54	5
Barber, Marion, Dal.	204	975	4.8	54	10
Grant, Ryan, G.B.	188	956	5.1	66t	8
Graham, Earnest, T.B.	222	898	4.0	28t	10
Foster, DeShaun, Car.	247	876	3.5	20	3
Taylor, Chester, Min.	157	844	5.4	84t	7
Dunn, Warrick, Atl.	227	720	3.2	38	4
Williams, DeAngelo, Car.	144	717	5.0	75	4
Alexander, Shaun, Sea.	207	716	3.5	25	4
Benson, Cedric, Chi.	196	674	3.4	43t	4
Morris, Maurice, Sea.	140	628	4.5	46	4
Norwood, Jerious, Atl.	103	613	6.0	67t	1
Ward, Derrick, NY-G	125	602	4.8	44	3
Jones, Julius, Dal.	164	588	3.6	25	2
Bush, Reggie, N.O.	157	581	3.7	22	4
Jones, Kevin, Det.	153	581	3.8	34	8

2007 INDIVIDUAL STATISTICS—RUSHING

	Att	Yards	Avg	Long	TD
Peterson, Adrian, Chi.	151	510	3.4	21	3
Stecker, Aaron, N.O.	115	448	3.9	26	5
Betts, Ladell, Was.	93	335	3.6	20	1
Duckett, T.J., Det.	65	335	5.2	53	3
Buckhalter, Correll, Phi.	62	313	5.0	30t	4
* Leonard, Brian, St.L	86	303	3.5	31	0
Pittman, Michael, T.B.	68	286	4.2	29	0
Droughns, Reuben, NY-G	85	275	3.2	45	6
* Jackson, Brandon, G.B.	75	267	3.6	46	1
Jackson, Tarvaris, Min.	54	260	4.8	32	3
* Thomas, Pierre, N.O.	52	252	4.8	24t	1
Bennett, Michael, K.C.-T.B.	61	241	4.0	28	1
McNabb, Donovan, Phi.	50	236	4.7	40	0
Williams, Cadillac, T.B.	54	208	3.9	20	3
* Wynn, DeShawn, G.B.	50	203	4.1	44	4
* Bradshaw, Ahmad, NY-G	23	190	8.3	88t	1
Campbell, Jason, Was.	36	185	5.1	29	1
Bell, Tatum, Det.	44	182	4.1	24	1
Weaver, Leonard, Sea.	33	146	4.4	37	1
* Pittman, Antonio, St.L	38	139	3.7	43	0
Romo, Tony, Dal.	31	129	4.2	17	2
Robinson, Michael, S.F.	26	121	4.7	28	0
Hicks, Maurice, S.F.	21	117	5.6	18	1
McCown, Luke, T.B.	12	117	9.8	31	0
Garcia, Jeff, T.B.	35	116	3.3	21	1
Moore, Mewelde, Min.	20	113	5.7	17	0
Morency, Vernand, G.B.	29	108	3.7	15	0
McAllister, Deuce, N.O.	24	92	3.8	15	0
Hasselbeck, Matt, Sea.	39	89	2.3	12	0
Smith, Alex, S.F.	13	89	6.8	25	0
* Wolfe, Garrett, Chi.	31	85	2.7	25	0
Arrington, J.J., Ariz	26	78	3.0	12	0
Sellers, Mike, Was.	26	78	3.0	15	2
Manning, Eli, NY-G	29	69	2.4	18	1
Minor, Travis, St.L	17	68	4.0	13	0
Smith, Steve, Car.	9	66	7.3	22	0
Kitna, Jon, Det.	25	63	2.5	11	0
Carr, David, Car.	17	59	3.5	15	0
Thompson, Tyson, Dal.	14	54	3.9	23	0
Brees, Drew, N.O.	23	52	2.3	9	1
* Johnson, Calvin, Det.	4	52	13.0	32t	1
Pinner, Artose, Atl.	5	46	9.2	49	0
* Snelling, Jason, Atl.	13	43	3.3	17	1
Leinart, Matt, Ariz	11	42	3.8	20	0
Shipp, Marcel, Ariz	15	41	2.7	14	1
Hoover, Brad, Car.	12	39	3.3	10	0
Cason, Aveion, Det.	11	38	3.5	12	0
Williams, Travis, Atl.	1	37	37.0	37	0
Brown, Reggie, Phi.	5	36	7.2	12	0
Calhoun, Brian, Det.	7	35	5.0	17	0
Harrington, Joey, Atl.	14	33	2.4	13	0
Rodgers, Aaron, G.B.	7	29	4.1	13	0
Williamson, Troy, Min.	2	29	14.5	26	0
Griese, Brian, Chi.	13	28	2.2	9	0
Grossman, Rex, Chi.	14	27	1.9	12	0
Delhomme, Jake, Car.	6	26	4.3	13	0
Dilfer, Trent, S.F.	10	25	2.5	11	0
Feeley, A.J., Phi.	7	23	3.3	7	0
Clayton, Michael, T.B.	5	22	4.4	20	0
Testaverde, Vinny, Car.	9	22	2.4	16	0
Gradkowski, Bruce, T.B.	7	20	2.9	13	0
Henderson, Devery, N.O.	2	20	10.0	15	0
Strong, Mack, Sea.	4	19	4.8	9	0
Bollinger, Brooks, Min.	5	18	3.6	10	0
Hall, Dante, St.L	3	18	6.0	9	0
Tapeh, Thomas, Phi.	5	18	3.6	11	0
Karney, Mike, N.O.	11	17	1.5	10	2
McKie, Jason, Chi.	6	17	2.8	6	1
Norris, Moran, S.F.	7	17	2.4	6	0
Wallace, Seneca, Sea.	4	17	4.3	11	0
* Hunt, Tony, Phi.	10	16	1.6	4	1
Redman, Chris, Atl.	8	16	2.0	7	0
Tahi, Naufahu, Min.	6	15	2.5	6	0
Warner, Kurt, Ariz	17	15	0.9	9	1
Boldin, Anquan, Ariz	1	14	14.0	14	0
Hill, Shaun, S.F.	12	14	1.2	12	1
Bulger, Marc, St.L	9	13	1.4	14	0
Morey, Sean, Ariz	1	13	13.0	13	0
Moss, Santana, Was.	3	13	4.3	11	0
Richardson, Tony, Min.	7	13	1.9	4	0
Favre, Brett, G.B.	29	12	0.4	21	0
* Jarrett, Dwayne, Car.	1	11	11.0	11	0
Bradley, Jon, Det.	5	9	1.8	3	0
* Darby, Kenneth, T.B.	2	9	4.5	7	0
* Breaston, Steve, Ariz	2	8	4.0	10	0
Dugan, Jeff, Min.	2	7	3.5	4	0
Leftwich, Byron, Atl.	6	7	1.2	7	0
Moore, Lance, N.O.	2	7	3.5	7t	1
Mughelli, Ovie, Atl.	6	7	1.2	3	1
Ryan, Jon, G.B.	2	7	3.5	7	0
Hilliard, Ike, T.B.	1	6	6.0	6	0
Nall, Craig, G.B.	5	6	1.2	8	0
Shockey, Jeremy, NY-G	1	6	6.0	6	0
* Moore, Matt, Car.	3	5	1.7	5	0
Owens, Terrell, Dal.	1	5	5.0	5	0
Rattay, Tim, Ariz	2	5	2.5	5	0
Robinson, Koren, G.B.	1	5	5.0	5	0
* Stanley, Derek, St.L	1	5	5.0	5	0
Weatherford, Steven, N.O.	1	5	5.0	5	0
Battle, Arnaz, S.F.	4	4	1.0	8	1
Burleson, Nate, Sea.	2	4	2.0	3	0
Driver, Donald, G.B.	2	4	2.0	5	0
Keasey, Zak, S.F.	2	4	2.0	3	0
Moss, Sinorice, NY-G	1	4	4.0	4	0
* Allison, Aundrae, Min.	2	3	1.5	3	0
Frerotte, Gus, St.L	6	3	0.5	2	0
Haynes, Alex, Car.	3	3	1.0	3	0
Smith, Terrelle, Ariz	1	3	3.0	3	0
Lorenzen, Jared, NY-G	1	2	2.0	2	0
McDonald, Shaun, Det.	4	2	0.5	9	0
Avant, Jason, Phi.	1	1	1.0	1	0
Collins, Todd, Was.	8	1	0.1	4	0
Galloway, Joey, T.B.	1	1	1.0	1	0
Williams, Roy, Det.	2	1	0.5	9	0
Berger, Mitch, Ariz	1	0	0.0	0	0
Cartwright, Rock, Was.	2	0	0.0	1	0
Crockett, Zack, T.B.	1	0	0.0	0	0
Frost, Derrick, Was.	1	0	0.0	0	0
Koenen, Michael, Atl.	1	0	0.0	0	0
Plackemeier, Ryan, Sea.	1	0	0.0	0	0
Hasselbeck, Tim, Ariz	1	-1	-1.0	-1	0
Orton, Kyle, Chi.	5	-1	-.2	1	0
Wright, Anthony, NY-G	1	-1	-1.0	-1	0
* Kolb, Kevin, Phi.	3	-2	-.7	0	0
White, Roddy, Atl.	1	-2	-2.0	-2	0
Martin, Jamie, N.O.	3	-3	-1.0	-1	0
Randle El, Antwaan, Was.	4	-3	-.8	1	0
Bruce, Isaac, St.L	2	-4	-2.0	-1	0
Hagans, Marques, St.L	2	-4	-2.0	-2	0
Johnson, Brad, Dal.	5	-5	-1.0	0	0
Patten, David, N.O.	2	-5	-2.5	1	0
Gilmore, Bryan, S.F.	1	-8	-8.0	-8	0
Hixon, Domenik, NY-G	1	-8	-8.0	-8	0
Jacobs, Taylor, S.F.	1	-8	-8.0	-8	0
Wade, Bobby, Min.	1	-9	-9.0	-9	0
Hester, Devin, Chi.	7	-10	-1.4	5	0

	Att	Yards	Avg	Long	TD
O'Sullivan, J.T., Det.	4	-10	-2.5	2	0
Berlin, Brock, St.L	3	-16	-5.3	0	0

t = Touchdown
Leader based on most yards gained
* Player that was a rookie in 2007

AMERICAN FOOTBALL CONFERENCE—RUSHING

	Att	Yards	Avg	Long	TD
Jacksonville	522	2391	4.6	80t	18
Pittsburgh	511	2168	4.2	45	9
Tennessee	543	2109	3.9	42	17
Oakland	508	2086	4.1	48	11
San Diego	485	2039	4.2	74t	19
Denver	429	1957	4.6	62t	10
Cleveland	440	1895	4.3	66t	13
New England	451	1849	4.1	59t	17
Buffalo	448	1800	4.0	56t	8
Baltimore	446	1797	4.0	46t	11
Indianapolis	446	1706	3.8	23	19
N.Y. Jets	446	1701	3.8	49	6
Houston	417	1586	3.8	41	12
Miami	389	1569	4.0	60	14
Cincinnati	416	1556	3.7	45	10
Kansas City	383	1248	3.3	54	6
AFC Total	7280	29457	4.0	80t	200
AFC Average	455.0	1841.1	4.0	—	12.5

NATIONAL FOOTBALL CONFERENCE—RUSHING

	Att	Yards	Avg	Long	TD
Minnesota	494	2634	5.3	84t	22
N.Y. Giants	469	2148	4.6	88t	15
Philadelphia	421	1974	4.7	40	12
Tampa Bay	449	1872	4.2	31	15
Washington	498	1871	3.8	32	15
Carolina	451	1824	4.0	75	7
Dallas	419	1746	4.2	54	14
Seattle	430	1619	3.8	46	9
Green Bay	388	1597	4.1	66t	13
St. Louis	404	1527	3.8	54	5
Atlanta	385	1520	3.9	67t	7
San Francisco	357	1477	4.1	43t	8
New Orleans	392	1466	3.7	26	14
Arizona	402	1440	3.6	27	9
Chicago	423	1330	3.1	43t	8
Detroit	324	1288	4.0	53	13
NFC Total	6706	27333	4.1	88t	186
NFC Average	419.1	1708.3	4.1	—	11.6
League Total	13986	56790	—	88t	386
League Average	437.1	1774.7	4.1	—	12.1

PASSING

HIGHEST RATING
AFC: 117.2   Tom Brady, New England
NFC: 97.4   Tony Romo, Dallas

COMPLETION PERCENTAGE
AFC: 68.9   Tom Brady, New England
NFC: 67.5   Drew Brees, New Orleans

ATTEMPTS
NFC: 652   Drew Brees, New Orleans
AFC: 578   Tom Brady, New England

COMPLETIONS
NFC: 440   Drew Brees, New Orleans
AFC: 398   Tom Brady, New England

YARDS
AFC: 4806   Tom Brady, New England
NFC: 4423   Drew Brees, New Orleans

YARDS, GAME
NFC: 484   Kurt Warner, Arizona vs. San Francisco, November 25 (34-48, 2 TD) - (OT)
AFC: 401   Carson Palmer, Cincinnati at Cleveland, September 16 (33-50, 6 TD)

LONGEST
NFC: 91   Jon Kitna (to Roy Williams), Detroit at Philadelphia, September 23 - TD
AFC: 85   J.P. Losman (to Lee Evans), Buffalo at N.Y. Jets, October 28 - TD

YARDS PER ATTEMPT
AFC: 8.31   Tom Brady, New England
NFC: 8.10   Tony Romo, Dallas

TOUCHDOWN PASSES
AFC: 50   Tom Brady, New England
NFC: 36   Tony Romo, Dallas

TOUCHDOWN PASSES, GAME
AFC: 6   Carson Palmer, Cincinnati at Cleveland, September 16 (33-50, 401 yards)
    6   Tom Brady, New England at Miami, October 21 (21-25, 354 yards)
NFC: 4   Eli Manning, N.Y. Giants at Dallas, September 9 (28-41, 312 yards)
    4   Tony Romo, Dallas vs. N.Y. Giants, September 9 (15-24, 345 yards)
    4   Donovan McNabb, Philadelphia vs. Detroit, September 23 (21-26, 381 yards)
    4   Drew Brees, New Orleans at San Francisco, October 28 (31-39, 336 yards)
    4   Donovan McNabb, Philadelphia at Washington, November 11 (20-28, 251 yards)
    4   Tony Romo, Dallas at N.Y. Giants, November 11 (20-28, 247 yards)
    4   Tony Romo, Dallas vs. Washington, November 18 (22-32, 293 yards)
    4   Tony Romo, Dallas vs. Green Bay, November 29 (19-30, 309 yards)
    4   Matt Hasselbeck, Seattle vs. Arizona, December 9 (22-33, 272 yards)
    4   Eli Manning, N.Y. Giants vs. New England, December 29 (22-32, 251 yards)
    4   Chris Redman, Atlanta vs. Seattle, December 30 (17-27, 251 yards)

LOWEST INTERCEPTION PERCENTAGE
NFC: 1.2   Jeff Garcia, Tampa Bay
AFC: 0.9   David Garrard, Jacksonville

TEAM CHAMPION (MOST NET YARDS)
AFC: 4731   New England
NFC: 4334   Green Bay

NFL TOP TEN PASSERS

	Att	Comp	Pct Comp	Yds	Avg Gain	TD	Pct TD	Long	Int	Pct Int	Sack	Yds Lost	Rating Points
Brady, Tom, N.E.	578	398	68.9	4806	8.31	50	8.7	69t	8	1.4	21	128	117.2
Roethlisberger, Ben, Pit.	404	264	65.3	3154	7.81	32	7.9	83	11	2.7	47	347	104.1
Garrard, David, Jac.	325	208	64.0	2509	7.72	18	5.5	59t	3	0.9	21	99	102.2
Manning, Peyton, Ind.	515	337	65.4	4040	7.84	31	6.0	73t	14	2.7	21	124	98.0
Romo, Tony, Dal.	520	335	64.4	4211	8.10	36	6.9	59t	19	3.7	24	176	97.4
Favre, Brett, G.B.	535	356	66.5	4155	7.77	28	5.2	82t	15	2.8	15	93	95.7
Garcia, Jeff, T.B.	327	209	63.9	2440	7.46	13	4.0	69t	4	1.2	19	104	94.6
Hasselbeck, Matt, Sea.	562	352	62.6	3966	7.06	28	5.0	65	12	2.1	33	204	91.4
McNabb, Donovan, Phi.	473	291	61.5	3324	7.03	19	4.0	75t	7	1.5	44	227	89.9
Warner, Kurt, Ariz.	451	281	62.3	3417	7.58	27	6.0	62	17	3.8	20	140	89.8

AMERICAN FOOTBALL CONFERENCE—PASSING

	Att	Comp	Pct Comp	Gross Yards	Sacked	Yds Lost	Net Yards	Yds/ Att	Yards/ Comp	TD	Pct TD	Long	Int	Pct Int
New England	586	403	68.8	4859	21	128	4731	8.29	12.06	50	8.53	69t	9	1.5
Indianapolis	551	355	64.4	4172	23	139	4033	7.57	11.75	32	5.81	73t	14	2.5
Cincinnati	575	373	64.9	4131	17	119	4012	7.18	11.08	26	4.52	70t	20	3.5
Houston	529	346	65.4	3925	22	174	3751	7.42	11.34	24	4.54	77t	21	4.0
Cleveland	545	305	56.0	3866	19	140	3726	7.09	12.68	29	5.32	78t	20	3.7
Denver	515	326	63.3	3759	32	175	3584	7.30	11.53	21	4.08	68t	15	2.9
Kansas City	563	335	59.5	3525	55	344	3181	6.26	10.52	17	3.02	58	20	3.6
Jacksonville	469	288	61.4	3495	31	167	3328	7.45	12.14	28	5.97	80t	8	1.7
Pittsburgh	442	282	63.8	3418	47	347	3071	7.73	12.12	34	7.69	83	14	3.2
N.Y. Jets	512	310	60.5	3330	53	316	3014	6.50	10.74	15	2.93	57t	19	3.7
Miami	558	318	57.0	3319	42	288	3031	5.95	10.44	12	2.15	64t	16	2.9
Baltimore	557	341	61.2	3308	39	273	3035	5.94	9.70	13	2.33	79t	14	2.5
San Diego	471	281	59.7	3175	24	170	3005	6.74	11.30	22	4.67	49t	16	3.4
Tennessee	464	288	62.1	3077	30	199	2878	6.63	10.68	9	1.94	73	17	3.7
Oakland	451	260	57.6	2893	41	262	2631	6.41	11.13	17	3.77	59	20	4.4
Buffalo	445	263	59.1	2842	26	208	2634	6.39	10.81	12	2.70	85t	14	3.1
AFC Total	8233	5074	—	57094	522	3449	53645	—	—	361	—	85t	257	—
AFC Average	514.6	317.1	61.6	3568.4	32.6	215.6	3352.8	6.93	11.25	22.6	4.4	—	16.1	3.1

NATIONAL FOOTBALL CONFERENCE—PASSING

	Att	Comp	Pct Comp	Gross Yards	Sacked	Yds Lost	Net Yards	Yds/ Att	Yards/ Comp	TD	Pct TD	Long	Int	Pct Int
Green Bay	578	383	66.3	4461	19	127	4334	7.72	11.65	30	5.19	82t	15	2.6
New Orleans	652	440	67.5	4423	16	109	4314	6.78	10.05	28	4.29	58	18	2.8
Dallas	531	342	64.4	4290	25	185	4105	8.08	12.54	36	6.78	59t	19	3.6
Arizona	590	356	60.3	4228	24	163	4065	7.17	11.88	32	5.42	62	24	4.1
Detroit	587	368	62.7	4216	54	338	3878	7.18	11.46	19	3.24	91t	22	3.7
Seattle	590	371	62.9	4181	36	217	3964	7.09	11.27	30	5.08	65	13	2.2
Philadelphia	577	350	60.7	4005	49	250	3755	6.94	11.44	24	4.16	75t	15	2.6
Chicago	569	327	57.5	3701	43	339	3362	6.50	11.32	18	3.16	81t	21	3.7
Washington	525	319	60.8	3622	29	159	3463	6.90	11.35	18	3.43	54	11	2.1
Tampa Bay	490	316	64.5	3579	36	222	3357	7.30	11.33	18	3.67	69t	8	1.6
Atlanta	555	336	60.5	3573	47	277	3296	6.44	10.63	18	3.24	74t	15	2.7
St. Louis	574	333	58.0	3561	48	328	3233	6.20	10.69	19	3.31	40	28	4.9
N.Y. Giants	544	302	55.5	3376	28	222	3154	6.21	11.18	23	4.23	60t	20	3.7
Carolina	505	285	56.4	2941	33	206	2735	5.82	10.32	19	3.76	74t	17	3.4
Minnesota	432	249	57.6	2938	38	193	2745	6.80	11.80	12	2.78	79	14	3.2
San Francisco	513	274	53.4	2685	55	365	2320	5.23	9.80	15	2.92	57t	17	3.3
NFC Total	8812	5351	—	59780	580	3700	56080	—	—	359	—	91t	277	—
NFC Average	550.8	334.4	60.7	3736.3	36.3	231.3	3505.0	6.78	11.17	22.4	4.1	—	17.3	3.1
League Total	17045	10425	—	116874	1102	7149	109725	—	—	720	—	91t	534	—
League Average	532.7	325.8	61.2	3652.3	34.4	223.4	3428.9	6.86	11.21	22.5	4.2	—	16.7	3.1

AFC—INDIVIDUAL PASSERS

	Att	Comp	Pct Comp	Yds	Avg Gain	TD	Pct TD	Long	Int	Pct Int	Sack	Yds Lost	Rating Points
Brady, Tom, N.E.	578	398	68.9	4806	8.31	50	8.7	69t	8	1.4	21	128	117.2
Roethlisberger, Ben, Pit.	404	264	65.3	3154	7.81	32	7.9	83	11	2.7	47	347	104.1
Garrard, David, Jac.	325	208	64.0	2509	7.72	18	5.5	59t	3	0.9	21	99	102.2
Manning, Peyton, Ind.	515	337	65.4	4040	7.84	31	6.0	73t	14	2.7	21	124	98.0
Cutler, Jay, Den.	467	297	63.6	3497	7.49	20	4.3	68t	14	3.0	27	153	88.1
Schaub, Matt, Hou.	289	192	66.4	2241	7.75	9	3.1	77t	9	3.1	16	126	87.2
Palmer, Carson, Cin.	575	373	64.9	4131	7.18	26	4.5	70t	20	3.5	17	119	86.7
Pennington, Chad, NYJ	260	179	68.8	1765	6.79	10	3.8	57t	9	3.5	26	178	86.1
Rosenfels, Sage, Hou.	240	154	64.2	1684	7.02	15	6.3	53t	12	5.0	6	48	84.8
Anderson, Derek, Cle.	527	298	56.5	3787	7.19	29	5.5	78t	19	3.6	14	109	82.5
Rivers, Philip, S.D.	460	277	60.2	3152	6.85	21	4.6	49t	15	3.3	22	163	82.4
Huard, Damon, K.C.	332	206	62.0	2257	6.80	11	3.3	58	13	3.9	36	234	76.8
Boller, Kyle, Bal.	275	168	61.1	1743	6.34	9	3.3	53	10	3.6	24	159	75.2
Young, Vince, Ten.	382	238	62.3	2546	6.66	9	2.4	73	17	4.5	25	157	71.1
Lemon, Cleo, Mia.	309	173	56.0	1773	5.74	6	1.9	64t	6	1.9	25	166	71.0
* Edwards, Trent, Buf.	269	151	56.1	1630	6.06	7	2.6	70t	8	3.0	12	105	70.4
Croyle, Brodie, K.C.	224	127	56.7	1227	5.48	6	2.7	35	6	2.7	17	101	69.9
Clemens, Kellen, NYJ	250	130	52.0	1529	6.12	5	2.0	56	10	4.0	27	138	60.9
(Nonqualifiers)													
Gray, Quinn, Jac.	144	80	55.6	986	6.85	10	6.9	80t	5	3.5	10	68	85.6
Collins, Kerry, Ten.	82	50	61.0	531	6.48	0	0.0	46	0	0.0	5	42	79.9
* Smith, Troy, Bal.	76	40	52.6	452	5.95	2	2.6	79t	0	0.0	4	29	79.5
Culpepper, Daunte, Oak.	186	108	58.1	1331	7.16	5	2.7	59	5	2.7	21	130	78.0
Losman, J.P., Buf.	175	111	63.4	1204	6.88	4	2.3	85t	6	3.4	14	103	76.9
McNair, Steve, Bal.	205	133	64.9	1113	5.43	2	1.0	30	4	2.0	11	85	73.9
Ramsey, Patrick, Den.	48	29	60.4	262	5.46	1	2.1	21	1	2.1	3	13	73.4
Green, Trent, Mia.	141	85	60.3	987	7.00	5	3.5	43	7	5.0	7	53	72.6
McCown, Josh, Oak.	190	111	58.4	1151	6.06	10	5.3	46t	11	5.8	14	92	69.4
Sorgi, Jim, Ind.	36	18	50.0	132	3.67	1	2.8	12	0	0.0	2	15	68.3
* Beck, John, Mia.	107	60	56.1	559	5.22	1	0.9	22t	3	2.8	10	69	62.0
* Russell, JaMarcus, Oak.	66	36	54.5	373	5.65	2	3.0	32t	4	6.1	6	40	55.9
Batch, Charlie, Pit.	36	17	47.2	232	6.44	2	5.6	59t	3	8.3	0	0	52.1
Frye, Charlie, Cle.	10	4	40.0	34	3.40	0	0.0	15	1	10.0	5	31	10.0
Volek, Billy, S.D.	10	3	30.0	6	0.60	0	0.0	4	1	10.0	2	7	0.0
(Fewer than 10 attempts)													
Booker, Marty, Mia.	1	0	0.0	0	0.00	0	0.0	0	0	0.0	0	0	39.6
Cassel, Matt, N.E.	7	4	57.1	38	5.43	0	0.0	21	1	14.3	0	0	32.7
Clayton, Mark, Bal.	1	0	0.0	0	0.00	0	0.0	0	0	0.0	0	0	39.6
Curry, Ronald, Oak.	1	0	0.0	0	0.00	0	0.0	0	0	0.0	0	0	39.6
* Gutierrez, Matt, N.E.	1	1	100.0	15	15.00	0	0.0	15	0	0.0	0	0	118.8
Johnson, Larry, K.C.	1	0	0.0	0	0.00	0	0.0	0	0	0.0	0	0	39.6
Kennison, Eddie, K.C.	0	0	—	0	—	0	—	—	0	—	1	0	—
* Lynch, Marshawn, Buf.	1	1	100.0	8	8.00	1	100.0	8t	0	0.0	0	0	139.6
Marshall, Brandon, Den.	0	0	—	0	—	0	—	—	0	—	2	9	-1.0
Parker, Willie, Pit.	1	0	0.0	0	0.00	0	0.0	0	0	0.0	0	0	39.6
* Quinn, Brady, Cle.	8	3	37.5	45	5.63	0	0.0	18	0	0.0	0	0	56.8
* Sepulveda, Daniel, Pit.	1	1	100.0	32	32.00	0	0.0	32	0	0.0	0	0	118.8
Smith, Brad, NYJ	1	0	0.0	0	0.00	0	0.0	—	0	0.0	0	0	39.6
* Thigpen, Tyler, K.C.	6	2	33.3	41	6.83	0	0.0	22	1	16.7	1	9	18.8
Tomlinson, LaDainian, S.D.	1	1	100.0	17	17.00	1	100.0	17t	0	0.0	0	0	158.3
Walter, Andrew, Oak.	8	5	62.5	38	4.75	0	0.0	19	0	0.0	0	0	74.0
Washington, Leon, NYJ	1	1	100.0	36	36.00	0	0.0	36	0	0.0	0	0	118.8

t = Touchdown
Leader based on rating points, minimum 224 attempts
* Player that was a rookie in 2007

NFC—INDIVIDUAL PASSERS

	Att	Comp	Pct Comp	Yds	Avg Gain	TD	Pct TD	Long	Int	Pct Int	Sack	Yds Lost	Rating Points
Romo, Tony, Dal.	520	335	64.4	4211	8.10	36	6.9	59t	19	3.7	24	176	97.4
Favre, Brett, G.B.	535	356	66.5	4155	7.77	28	5.2	82t	15	2.8	15	93	95.7
Garcia, Jeff, T.B.	327	209	63.9	2440	7.46	13	4.0	69t	4	1.2	19	104	94.6
Hasselbeck, Matt, Sea.	562	352	62.6	3966	7.06	28	5.0	65	12	2.1	33	204	91.4
McNabb, Donovan, Phi.	473	291	61.5	3324	7.03	19	4.0	75t	7	1.5	44	227	89.9
Warner, Kurt, Ariz	451	281	62.3	3417	7.58	27	6.0	62	17	3.8	20	140	89.8
Brees, Drew, N.O.	652	440	67.5	4423	6.78	28	4.3	58	18	2.8	16	109	89.4
Kitna, Jon, Det.	561	355	63.3	4068	7.25	18	3.2	91t	20	3.6	51	320	80.9
Campbell, Jason, Was.	417	250	60.0	2700	6.47	12	2.9	54	11	2.6	21	110	77.6
Harrington, Joey, Atl.	348	215	61.8	2215	6.36	7	2.0	69t	8	2.3	32	192	77.2
Griese, Brian, Chi.	262	161	61.5	1803	6.88	10	3.8	81t	12	4.6	15	114	75.6
Manning, Eli, NY-G	529	297	56.1	3336	6.31	23	4.3	60t	20	3.8	27	217	73.9
Jackson, Tarvaris, Min.	294	171	58.2	1911	6.50	9	3.1	71	12	4.1	19	70	70.8
Bulger, Marc, St.L	378	221	58.5	2392	6.33	11	2.9	40	15	4.0	37	269	70.3
Grossman, Rex, Chi.	225	122	54.2	1411	6.27	4	1.8	59t	7	3.1	25	198	66.4
(Nonqualifiers)													
Delhomme, Jake, Car.	86	55	64.0	624	7.26	8	9.3	74t	1	1.2	5	46	111.8
Collins, Todd, Was.	105	67	63.8	888	8.46	5	4.8	54	0	0.0	7	47	106.4
Rodgers, Aaron, G.B.	28	20	71.4	218	7.79	1	3.6	43	0	0.0	3	24	106.0
Hill, Shaun, S.F.	79	54	68.4	501	6.34	5	6.3	26	1	1.3	6	31	101.3
Wallace, Seneca, Sea.	28	19	67.9	215	7.68	2	7.1	45t	1	3.6	3	13	99.6
McCown, Luke, T.B.	139	94	67.6	1009	7.26	5	3.6	60	3	2.2	15	104	91.7
Redman, Chris, Atl.	149	89	59.7	1079	7.24	10	6.7	74t	5	3.4	9	51	90.4
Bollinger, Brooks, Min.	50	33	66.0	391	7.82	1	2.0	50	1	2.0	7	36	88.0
Nall, Craig, G.B.	15	7	46.7	88	5.87	1	6.7	32t	0	0.0	1	10	87.6
Weinke, Chris, S.F.	22	13	59.1	104	4.73	1	4.5	21	0	0.0	5	31	86.2
Johnson, Brad, Dal.	11	7	63.6	79	7.18	0	0.0	35	0	0.0	1	9	85.0
Orton, Kyle, Chi.	80	43	53.8	478	5.98	3	3.8	55t	2	2.5	2	12	73.9
Holcomb, Kelly, Min.	83	42	50.6	515	6.20	2	2.4	40	1	1.2	12	87	73.1
Rattay, Tim, Ariz	27	15	55.6	164	6.07	3	11.1	42	3	11.1	0	0	71.1
* Moore, Matt, Car.	111	63	56.8	730	6.58	3	2.7	57	5	4.5	6	40	67.0
Testaverde, Vinny, Car.	172	94	54.7	952	5.53	5	2.9	65t	6	3.5	9	46	65.8
Leinart, Matt, Ariz	112	60	53.6	647	5.78	2	1.8	40	4	3.6	4	23	61.9
Feeley, A.J., Phi.	103	59	57.3	681	6.61	5	4.9	47	8	7.8	3	10	61.2
Berlin, Brock, St.L	28	17	60.7	153	5.46	0	0.0	23	1	3.6	0	0	60.6
Leftwich, Byron, Atl.	58	32	55.2	279	4.81	1	1.7	23	2	3.4	6	34	59.5
Frerotte, Gus, St.L	167	94	56.3	1014	6.07	7	4.2	38	12	7.2	11	59	58.3
Carr, David, Car.	136	73	53.7	635	4.67	3	2.2	38	5	3.7	13	74	58.3
Smith, Alex, S.F.	193	94	48.7	914	4.74	2	1.0	45	4	2.1	17	121	57.2
Dilfer, Trent, S.F.	219	113	51.6	1166	5.32	7	3.2	57t	12	5.5	27	182	55.1
Gradkowski, Bruce, T.B.	24	13	54.2	130	5.42	0	0.0	20	1	4.2	2	14	52.4
O'Sullivan, J.T., Det.	26	13	50.0	148	5.69	1	3.8	42	2	7.7	3	18	48.2
(Fewer than 10 attempts)													
Gould, Robbie, Chi.	1	0	0.0	0	0.00	0	0.0	0	0	0.0	0	0	39.6
Hester, Devin, Chi.	0	0	—	0	—	0	—	—	0	—	1	15	—
Jackson, Steven, St.L	1	1	100.0	2	2.00	1	100.0	2t	0	0.0	0	0	118.8
Kluwe, Chris, Min.	1	1	100.0	27	27.00	0	0.0	27	0	0.0	0	0	118.8
* Kolb, Kevin, Phi.	0	0	—	0	—	0	—	—	0	—	2	13	—
Lewis, Greg, Phi.	1	0	0.0	0	0.00	0	0.0	0	0	0.0	0	0	39.6
Lorenzen, Jared, NY-G	8	4	50.0	28	3.50	0	0.0	9	0	0.0	1	5	58.3
Moore, Mewelde, Min.	1	0	0.0	0	0.00	0	0.0	0	0	0.0	0	0	39.6
Peterson, Adrian, Chi.	1	1	100.0	9	9.00	1	100.0	9t	0	0.0	0	0	143.8
Portis, Clinton, Was.	1	1	100.0	15	15.00	1	100.0	15t	0	0.0	1	2	158.3
Randle El, Antwaan, Was.	2	1	50.0	19	9.50	0	0.0	19	0	0.0	0	0	83.3
* Rice, Sidney, Min.	2	2	100.0	94	47.00	0	0.0	79	0	0.0	0	0	118.8
Taylor, Chester, Min.	1	0	0.0	0	0.00	0	0.0	0	0	0.0	0	0	39.6
Wright, Anthony, NY-G	7	1	14.3	12	1.71	0	0.0	12	0	0.0	0	0	39.6

t = Touchdown
Leader based on rating points, minimum 224 attempts
* Player that was a rookie in 2007

PASS RECEIVING

RECEPTIONS
AFC:	112	T.J. Houshmandzadeh, Cincinnati
	112	Wes Welker, New England
NFC:	100	Larry Fitzgerald, Arizona

RECEPTIONS, GAME
NFC:	15	Jason Witten, Dallas at Detroit, December 9 (138 yards, 1 TD)
AFC:	13	Wes Welker, New England vs. Philadelphia, November 25 (149 yards, 0 TD)

YARDS
AFC:	1510	Reggie Wayne, Indianapolis
NFC:	1409	Larry Fitzgerald, Arizona

YARDS, GAME
NFC:	221	Kevin Curtis, Philadelphia vs. Detroit, September 23 (11 receptions, 3 TD)
AFC:	209	Chad Johnson, Cincinnati at Cleveland, September 16 (11 receptions, 2 TD)

LONGEST
NFC:	91	Roy Williams (from Jon Kitna), Detroit at Philadelphia, September 23 - TD
AFC:	85	Lee Evans (from J.P. Losman), Buffalo at N.Y. Jets, October 28 - TD

YARDS PER RECEPTION
AFC:	18.1	Santonio Holmes, Pittsburgh
NFC:	17.8	Joey Galloway, Tampa Bay

TOUCHDOWNS
AFC:	23	Randy Moss, New England
NFC:	15	Terrell Owens, Dallas

TEAM LEADERS, RECEPTIONS
AFC: BALTIMORE, 103, Derrick Mason; BUFFALO, 55, Lee Evans; CINCINNATI, 112, T.J. Houshmandzadeh; CLEVELAND, 82, Kellen Winslow; DENVER, 102, Brandon Marshall; HOUSTON, 65, Kevin Walter; INDIANAPOLIS, 104, Reggie Wayne; JACKSONVILLE, 45, Ernest Wilford; KANSAS CITY, 99, Tony Gonzalez; MIAMI, 50, Marty Booker; NEW ENGLAND, 112, Wes Welker; N.Y. JETS, 82, Jerricho Cotchery; OAKLAND, 55, Ronald Curry; PITTSBURGH, 71, Hines Ward; SAN DIEGO, 75, Antonio Gates; TENNESSEE, 55, Justin Gage, Roydell Williams

NFC: ARIZONA, 100, Larry Fitzgerald; ATLANTA, 83, Roddy White; CAROLINA, 87, Steve Smith; CHICAGO, 71, Bernard Berrian; DALLAS, 96, Jason Witten; DETROIT, 79, Shaun McDonald; GREEN BAY, 82, Donald Driver; MINNESOTA, 54, Bobby Wade; NEW ORLEANS, 98, Marques Colston; N.Y. GIANTS, 70, Plaxico Burress; PHILADELPHIA, 90, Brian Westbrook; ST. LOUIS, 93, Torry Holt; SAN FRANCISCO, 53, Frank Gore; SEATTLE, 94, Bobby Engram; TAMPA BAY, 62, Ike Hilliard; WASHINGTON, 66, Chris Cooley

Player that was a rookie in 2007

NFL TOP TEN PASS RECEIVERS
	No	Yards	Avg	Long	TD
Houshmandzadeh, T.J., Cin.	112	1143	10.2	42t	12
Welker, Wes, N.E.	112	1175	10.5	42	8
Wayne, Reggie, Ind.	104	1510	14.5	64	10
Mason, Derrick, Bal.	103	1087	10.6	79t	5
Marshall, Brandon, Den.	102	1325	13	68t	7
Fitzgerald, Larry, Ariz	100	1409	14.1	48t	10
Gonzalez, Tony, K.C.	99	1172	11.8	31	5
Colston, Marques, N.O.	98	1202	12.3	45	11
Moss, Randy, N.E.	98	1493	15.2	65t	23
Witten, Jason, Dal.	96	1145	11.9	53	7

NFL TOP TEN RECEIVERS BY YARDS
	Yards	No	Avg	Long	TD
Wayne, Reggie, Ind.	1510	104	14.5	64	10
Moss, Randy, N.E.	1493	98	15.2	65t	23
Johnson, Chad, Cin.	1440	93	15.5	70t	8
Fitzgerald, Larry, Ariz	1409	100	14.1	48t	10
Owens, Terrell, Dal.	1355	81	16.7	52t	15
Marshall, Brandon, Den.	1325	102	13	68t	7
Edwards, Braylon, Cle.	1289	80	16.1	78t	16
Colston, Marques, N.O.	1202	98	12.3	45	11
White, Roddy, Atl.	1202	83	14.5	69t	6
Holt, Torry, St.L	1189	93	12.8	40	7

AFC—INDIVIDUAL RECEIVERS
	No	Yards	Avg	Long	TD
Welker, Wes, N.E.	112	1175	10.5	42	8
Houshmandzadeh, T.J., Cin.	112	1143	10.2	42t	12
Wayne, Reggie, Ind.	104	1510	14.5	64	10
Mason, Derrick, Bal.	103	1087	10.6	79t	5
Marshall, Brandon, Den.	102	1325	13.0	68t	7
Gonzalez, Tony, K.C.	99	1172	11.8	31	5
Moss, Randy, N.E.	98	1493	15.2	65t	23
Johnson, Chad, Cin.	93	1440	15.5	70t	8
Cotchery, Jerricho, NYJ	82	1130	13.8	50	2
Winslow, Kellen, Cle.	82	1106	13.5	49	5
Edwards, Braylon, Cle.	80	1289	16.1	78t	16
Gates, Antonio, S.D.	75	984	13.1	49t	9
Ward, Hines, Pit.	71	732	10.3	25	7
* Bowe, Dwayne, K.C.	70	995	14.2	58	5
Chambers, Chris, Mia.-S.D.	66	970	14.7	44	4
Walter, Kevin, Hou.	65	800	12.3	46	4
Daniels, Owen, Hou.	63	768	12.2	29	3
Johnson, Andre, Hou.	60	851	14.2	77t	8
Tomlinson, LaDainian, S.D.	60	475	7.9	36	3
Clark, Dallas, Ind.	58	616	10.6	39	11
Evans, Lee, Buf.	55	849	15.4	85t	5
Gage, Justin, Ten.	55	750	13.6	73	2
Williams, Roydell, Ten.	55	719	13.1	48	4
Curry, Ronald, Oak.	55	717	13.0	49	4
Coles, Laveranues, NYJ	55	646	11.7	57t	6
Holmes, Santonio, Pit.	52	942	18.1	83	8
Watson, Kenny, Cin.	52	374	7.2	43	0
Reed, Josh, Buf.	51	578	11.3	30	0
Jurevicius, Joe, Cle.	50	614	12.3	50	3
Booker, Marty, Mia.	50	556	11.1	26	1
Scheffler, Tony, Den.	49	549	11.2	41	5
Clayton, Mark, Bal.	48	531	11.1	52	0
Miller, Heath, Pit.	47	566	12.0	29	7
Faulk, Kevin, N.E.	47	383	8.1	23	1
Stallworth, Donte', N.E.	46	697	15.2	69t	3
Scaife, Bo, Ten.	46	421	9.2	26	1
Wilford, Ernest, Jac.	45	518	11.5	35	3
Porter, Jerry, Oak.	44	705	16.0	59	6
Northcutt, Dennis, Jac.	44	601	13.7	55t	4
* Miller, Zach, Oak.	44	444	10.1	28	3
McGahee, Willis, Bal.	43	231	5.4	30	1
Jackson, Vincent, S.D.	41	623	15.2	45	3

	No	Yards	Avg	Long	TD		No	Yards	Avg	Long	TD
Baker, Chris, NYJ	41	409	10.0	22	3	Sapp, Cecil, Den.	14	51	3.6	16	1
Addai, Joseph, Ind.	41	364	8.9	73t	3	Johnson, Rudi, Cin.	13	110	8.5	33	1
Stokley, Brandon, Den.	40	635	15.9	58	5	Kennison, Eddie, K.C.	13	101	7.8	18	0
Jones-Drew, Maurice, Jac.	40	407	10.2	43	0	Vickers, Lawrence, Cle.	13	91	7.0	25	2
Brown, Ronnie, Mia.	39	389	10.0	43	1	* Walker, Darius, Hou.	13	81	6.2	9	0
Williams, Reggie, Jac.	38	629	16.6	80t	10	Keith, Kenton, Ind.	13	77	5.9	14	1
* Gonzalez, Anthony, Ind.	37	576	15.6	57t	3	Hartsock, Ben, Ten.	12	138	11.5	27	1
Lewis, Marcedes, Jac.	37	391	10.6	25	2	Anderson, David, Hou.	12	131	10.9	24	1
Gaffney, Jabar, N.E.	36	449	12.5	56t	5	* Coats, Daniel, Cin.	12	122	10.2	25	0
Watson, Benjamin, N.E.	36	389	10.8	35	6	Gado, Samkon, Hou.-Mia.	12	106	8.8	35	0
Washington, Leon, NYJ	36	213	5.9	18	0	Heiden, Steve, Cle.	12	104	8.7	27	0
Parrish, Roscoe, Buf.	35	352	10.1	47t	1	Thorpe, Craphonso, Ind.	12	70	5.8	12	1
* Young, Selvin, Den.	35	231	6.6	24	0	Davis, Carey, Pit.	12	49	4.1	10	0
* Ginn, Ted Jr., Mia.	34	420	12.4	54	2	Jones, Greg, Jac.	11	99	9.0	27	2
Martin, David, Mia.	34	303	8.9	28	2	Rhodes, Dominic, Oak.	11	70	6.4	17	0
Sypniewski, Quinn, Bal.	34	246	7.2	13	1	Manumaleuna, Brandon, S.D.	10	86	8.6	40	1
Davis, Andre, Hou.	33	583	17.7	53t	3	Sproles, Darren, S.D.	10	31	3.1	14	0
Moulds, Eric, Ten.	32	342	10.7	46	0	Estandia, Greg, Jac.	9	136	15.1	30	0
Smith, Brad, NYJ	32	325	10.2	29	2	Brady, Kyle, N.E.	9	70	7.8	20	2
Utecht, Ben, Ind.	31	364	11.7	30	1	Hall, Ahmard, Ten.	9	60	6.7	11	0
Lewis, Jamal, Cle.	30	248	8.3	34	2	Taylor, Fred, Jac.	9	58	6.4	18	0
Johnson, Larry, K.C.	30	186	6.2	30t	1	* McClain, Le'Ron, Bal.	9	55	6.1	13t	1
Washington, Nate, Pit.	29	450	15.5	40	5	Camarillo, Greg, Mia.	8	160	20.0	64t	2
Hagan, Derek, Mia.	29	373	12.9	22t	2	Carter, Tim, Cle.	8	117	14.6	22	1
Peelle, Justin, Mia.	29	228	7.9	35	2	Madsen, John, Oak.	8	102	12.8	39	1
Webb, Jeff, K.C.	28	313	11.2	32	1	Angulo, Richard, Jac.	8	81	10.1	22	1
Jordan, LaMont, Oak.	28	247	8.8	27	0	* Naanee, Legedu, S.D.	8	69	8.6	22	0
* Booker, Lorenzo, Mia.	28	237	8.5	22	0	Moorehead, Aaron, Ind.	8	65	8.1	16	0
Jones, Thomas, NYJ	28	217	7.8	25	1	Cook, Jameel, Hou.	8	40	5.0	9	0
Smith, Musa, Bal.	27	192	7.1	29	0	Neal, Lorenzo, S.D.	8	23	2.9	9	1
Chatman, Jesse, Mia.	27	161	6.0	22	0	Floyd, Malcom, S.D.	7	97	13.9	25	0
Walker, Javon, Den.	26	287	11.0	24	0	Aromashodu, Devin, Ind.	7	96	13.7	28	0
Griffith, Justin, Oak.	26	165	6.3	29	1	Williams, Mike, Oak.	7	90	12.9	24	0
Royal, Robert, Buf.	25	248	9.9	28t	3	Price, Peerless, Buf.	7	68	9.7	22	0
Gaines, Michael, Buf.	25	215	8.6	20	2	Henry, Travis, Den.	7	65	9.3	21	0
Leach, Vonta, Hou.	25	108	4.3	15	2	Dwight, Tim, Oak.	6	98	16.3	28t	2
Jones, Matt, Jac.	24	317	13.2	48	4	Wright, Wallace, NYJ	6	87	14.5	36	0
Parker, Samie, K.C.	24	298	12.4	24	2	* Henry, Chris, Ten.	6	53	8.8	18	0
Graham, Daniel, Den.	24	246	10.3	28	2	* Higgins, Johnnie Lee, Oak.	6	47	7.8	16	0
Wright, Jason, Cle.	24	233	9.7	23	0	Putzier, Jeb, Hou.	6	39	6.5	11	1
Wilson, Kris, K.C.	24	180	7.5	31	1	Morris, Sammy, N.E.	6	35	5.8	18	0
Heap, Todd, Bal.	23	239	10.4	37	1	Johnson, Jeremi, Cin.	6	32	5.3	14	1
Fargas, Justin, Oak.	23	188	8.2	17	0	Wilcox, Daniel, Bal.	6	18	3.0	7	1
Parker, Willie, Pit.	23	164	7.1	22	0	Mustard, Chad, Den.	5	62	12.4	15	0
Jackson, Fred, Buf.	22	190	8.6	54	0	Troupe, Ben, Ten.	5	47	9.4	13	0
* Smith, Kolby, K.C.	22	148	6.7	17	0	* Davis, Chris, Ten.	5	38	7.6	13	0
Henry, Chris, Cin.	21	343	16.3	52t	2	* Spaeth, Matt, Pit.	5	34	6.8	13t	3
Jones, Brandon, Ten.	21	248	11.8	35t	2	Kowalewski, Joe, NYJ	5	18	3.6	6	1
Williams, Demetrius, Bal.	20	290	14.5	34	0	Holmes, Priest, K.C.	5	17	3.4	8	0
Harrison, Marvin, Ind.	20	247	12.4	42	1	* Broussard, John, Jac.	4	126	31.5	56	1
Kelly, Reggie, Cin.	20	211	10.6	26	0	Maroney, Laurence, N.E.	4	116	29.0	43	0
* Davis, Craig, S.D.	20	188	9.4	18	1	Dreessen, Joel, Hou.	4	55	13.8	28t	2
White, LenDale, Ten.	20	114	5.7	15	0	Reid, Willie, Pit.	4	54	13.5	25	0
McCareins, Justin, NYJ	19	232	12.2	51	0	Evans, Heath, N.E.	4	43	10.8	29	0
Chatman, Antonio, Cin.	19	149	7.8	15	1	Lawton, Luke, Ind.	4	29	7.3	11	1
Brown, Chris, Ten.	19	128	6.7	16	0	Anderson, Mike, Bal.	4	26	6.5	10	0
Darling, Devard, Bal.	18	326	18.1	53	3	Clark, Brian, Den.	4	23	5.8	7	0
Wilson, Cedrick, Pit.	18	207	11.5	18	1	Dorsey, DeDe, Cin.	4	19	4.8	17	0
Davenport, Najeh, Pit.	18	184	10.2	32t	2	Turner, Michael, S.D.	4	16	4.0	12	0
* Lynch, Marshawn, Buf.	18	184	10.2	30	0	Ryan, Sean, NYJ	3	46	15.3	22	0
Fletcher, Bryan, Ind.	18	143	7.9	21	0	* Harris, Gilbert, K.C.	3	38	12.7	19	0
Wrighster, George, Jac.	17	123	7.2	36	1	Cribbs, Josh, Cle.	3	37	12.3	18	0
Dayne, Ron, Hou.	17	112	6.6	17	0	Jackson, Nate, Den.	3	34	11.3	24	1
Holt, Glenn, Cin.	16	143	8.9	22	1	Green, Skyler, Cin.	3	33	11.0	18	0
* Jones, Jacoby, Hou.	15	149	9.9	26	0	* Schouman, Derek, Buf.	3	19	6.3	10	0
Thomas, Anthony, Buf.	15	95	6.3	11	1	* Wright, Dwayne, Buf.	3	17	5.7	8	0
Martinez, Glenn, Den.	14	175	12.5	23	0	Hall, Andre, Den.	2	69	34.5	65	0
Green, Ahman, Hou.	14	123	8.8	53	0	Osgood, Kassim, S.D.	2	23	11.5	15	0

	No	Yards	Avg	Long	TD
Cobbs, Patrick, Mia.	2	20	10.0	11	0
Harrison, Jerome, Cle.	2	19	9.5	15	0
Green, Justin, Bal.	2	16	8.0	10	0
* Dawson, Clifton, Ind.	2	15	7.5	9	0
Grigsby, Boomer, K.C.	2	14	7.0	9	0
Neufeld, Ryan, Buf.	2	14	7.0	8	0
Barclay, Chris, Ten.	2	13	6.5	7	0
Echemandu, Adimchinobe, Hou.	2	11	5.5	7	0
Dunn, Jason, K.C.	2	9	4.5	9	0
* Mauia, Reagan, Mia.	2	5	2.5	5	0
Vickers, Lee, Bal.	2	4	2.0	5	0
Allen, Jared, K.C.	2	3	1.5	2t	2
Vrabel, Mike, N.E.	2	3	1.5	2t	2
Figurs, Yamon, Bal.	1	36	36.0	36	0
* McFoy, Chris, Oak.	1	19	19.0	19	0
Kreider, Dan, Pit.	1	15	15.0	15	0
Mathis, Jerome, Hou.	1	15	15.0	15	0
Haynes, Verron, Pit.	1	12	12.0	12	0
* Willis, Matt, Bal.	1	11	11.0	11	0
Aiken, Sam, Buf.	1	10	10.0	10	0
Thomas, David, N.E.	1	9	9.0	9	0
Tuman, Jerame, Pit.	1	9	9.0	9t	1
Dinkins, Darnell, Cle.	1	8	8.0	8	0
Bell, Mike, Den.	1	7	7.0	7	0
Halterman, Aaron, Mia.	1	7	7.0	7	0
Perry, Tab, Cin.	1	7	7.0	7	0
Pociask, Jason, NYJ	1	7	7.0	7	0
* Ealy, Biren, Ten.	1	6	6.0	6	0
Eckel, Kyle, N.E.	1	6	6.0	6	0
Maxwell, Marcus, Cin.	1	5	5.0	5	0
Pinnock, Andrew, S.D.	1	5	5.0	5	0
Smolko, Isaac, Jac.	1	5	5.0	5	0
* Battle, Jackie, K.C.	1	4	4.0	4	0
Toefield, LaBrandon, Jac.	1	4	4.0	4	0
* Davis, Chris, NYJ	1	3	3.0	3	0
Everett, Kevin, Buf.	1	3	3.0	3	0
* O'Neal, Oren, Oak.	1	1	1.0	1	0
Mangold, Nick, NYJ	1	-3	-3.0	-3	0
Mankins, Logan, N.E.	1	-9	-9.0	-9	0
Hadnot, Rex, Mia.	0	-2	—	-2	0

*t = Touchdown; * Player that was a rookie in 2007*
Leader based on receptions

NFC—INDIVIDUAL RECEIVERS

	No	Yards	Avg	Long	TD
Fitzgerald, Larry, Ariz	100	1409	14.1	48t	10
Colston, Marques, N.O.	98	1202	12.3	45	11
Witten, Jason, Dal.	96	1145	11.9	53	7
Engram, Bobby, Sea.	94	1147	12.2	49	6
Holt, Torry, St.L	93	1189	12.8	40	7
Westbrook, Brian, Phi.	90	771	8.6	57t	5
Smith, Steve, Car.	87	1002	11.5	74t	7
White, Roddy, Atl.	83	1202	14.5	69t	6
Driver, Donald, G.B.	82	1048	12.8	47	2
Owens, Terrell, Dal.	81	1355	16.7	52t	15
McDonald, Shaun, Det.	79	943	11.9	49t	6
Curtis, Kevin, Phi.	77	1110	14.4	75t	6
Bush, Reggie, N.O.	73	417	5.7	25	2
Berrian, Bernard, Chi.	71	951	13.4	59t	5
Boldin, Anquan, Ariz	71	853	12.0	44t	9
Burress, Plaxico, NY-G	70	1025	14.6	60t	12
Cooley, Chris, Was.	66	786	11.9	39t	8
Williams, Roy, Det.	64	838	13.1	91t	5
Hilliard, Ike, T.B.	62	722	11.6	56	1
Moss, Santana, Was.	61	808	13.2	49	3
Brown, Reggie, Phi.	61	780	12.8	45t	4

	No	Yards	Avg	Long	TD
Furrey, Mike, Det.	61	664	10.9	49	1
Toomer, Amani, NY-G	59	760	12.9	40	3
Galloway, Joey, T.B.	57	1014	17.8	69t	6
Shockey, Jeremy, NY-G	57	619	10.9	29	3
Bruce, Isaac, St.L	55	733	13.3	37	4
Patten, David, N.O.	54	792	14.7	58	3
Wade, Bobby, Min.	54	647	12.0	40	3
Jennings, Greg, G.B.	53	920	17.4	82t	12
Jenkins, Michael, Atl.	53	532	10.0	29	4
Gore, Frank, S.F.	53	436	8.2	23t	1
Davis, Vernon, S.F.	52	509	9.8	31	4
Randle El, Antwaan, Was.	51	728	14.3	54	1
Peterson, Adrian, Chi.	51	420	8.2	30	0
Crayton, Patrick, Dal.	50	697	13.9	59t	7
Burleson, Nate, Sea.	50	694	13.9	45t	9
Battle, Arnaz, S.F.	50	600	12.0	57t	5
Branch, Deion, Sea.	49	661	13.5	65	4
Graham, Earnest, T.B.	49	324	6.6	21	0
* Johnson, Calvin, Det.	48	756	15.8	49	4
Lee, Donald, G.B.	48	575	12.0	60	6
Johnson, Eric, N.O.	48	378	7.9	22	2
* Jones, James, G.B.	47	676	14.4	79t	2
Portis, Clinton, Was.	47	389	8.3	54	0
Johnson, Bryant, Ariz	46	528	11.5	30	2
Jackson, Darrell, S.F.	46	497	10.8	34	3
King, Jeff, Car.	46	406	8.8	29	2
Clark, Desmond, Chi.	44	545	12.4	52	4
Barber, Marion, Dal.	44	282	6.4	29	2
Crumpler, Alge, Atl.	42	444	10.6	55t	5
Muhammad, Muhsin, Chi.	40	570	14.3	44	3
McMichael, Randy, St.L	39	429	11.0	29t	3
* Olsen, Greg, Chi.	39	391	10.0	31	2
Weaver, Leonard, Sea.	39	313	8.0	46	0
Carter, Drew, Car.	38	517	13.6	49	4
Jackson, Steven, St.L	38	271	7.1	37	1
* Robinson, Laurent, Atl.	37	437	11.8	74t	1
Dunn, Warrick, Atl.	37	238	6.4	35	0
Stecker, Aaron, N.O.	36	211	5.9	26	0
Bennett, Drew, St.L	33	375	11.4	24	3
Ferguson, Robert, Min.	32	391	12.2	71	1
Smith, Alex, T.B.	32	385	12.0	33	3
Hackett, D.J., Sea.	32	384	12.0	59	3
Colbert, Keary, Car.	32	332	10.4	43	0
Moore, Lance, N.O.	32	302	9.4	22	2
Jones, Kevin, Det.	32	197	6.2	16	0
* Rice, Sidney, Min.	31	396	12.8	60t	4
Morency, Vernand, G.B.	30	199	6.6	18	0
* Leonard, Brian, St.L	30	183	6.1	16	0
Grant, Ryan, G.B.	30	145	4.8	21	0
Taylor, Chester, Min.	29	281	9.7	50	0
Arrington, J.J., Ariz	29	241	8.3	32	1
Norwood, Jerious, Atl.	28	277	9.9	46	0
Pollard, Marcus, Sea.	28	273	9.8	22	2
Miller, Billy, N.O.	27	328	12.1	57	2
Shiancoe, Visanthe, Min.	27	323	12.0	79	1
Horn, Joe, Atl.	27	243	9.0	26	1
Pittman, Michael, T.B.	26	191	7.3	16	0
Ward, Derrick, NY-G	26	179	6.9	17	1
Foster, DeShaun, Car.	25	182	7.3	23	1
James, Edgerrin, Ariz	24	204	8.5	26	0
Avant, Jason, Phi.	23	267	11.6	31	2
Pope, Leonard, Ariz	23	238	10.3	31	5
Morris, Maurice, Sea.	23	213	9.3	34t	1
Jones, Julius, Dal.	23	203	8.8	24	0
Williams, DeAngelo, Car.	23	175	7.6	30	1
Jacobs, Brandon, NY-G	23	174	7.6	34	2
Urban, Jerheme, Ariz	22	329	15.0	42	2
Clayton, Michael, T.B.	22	301	13.7	39	0

	No	Yards	Avg	Long	TD		No	Yards	Avg	Long	TD
McCardell, Keenan, Was.	22	256	11.6	32	1	Bienemann, Troy, Ariz	7	46	6.6	13	1
Smith, L.J., Phi.	22	236	10.7	26	1	* Rosario, Dante, Car.	6	108	18.0	54	2
Robinson, Koren, G.B.	21	241	11.5	43	1	* Jarrett, Dwayne, Car.	6	73	12.2	22	0
Moss, Sinorice, NY-G	21	225	10.7	20	0	Bradley, Mark, Chi.	6	71	11.8	19t	1
Betts, Ladell, Was.	21	174	8.3	28	1	Jennings, Adam, Atl.	6	62	10.3	28	1
Walker, Delanie, S.F.	21	174	8.3	26	1	* Anderson, Deon, Dal.	6	55	9.2	17	0
Henderson, Devery, N.O.	20	409	20.5	54	3	Moore, Mewelde, Min.	6	48	8.0	20	0
Hester, Devin, Chi.	20	299	15.0	81t	2	Looker, Dane, St.L	6	38	6.3	10	0
Hurd, Sam, Dal.	19	314	16.5	51t	1	Norris, Moran, S.F.	6	38	6.3	13	0
* Peterson, Adrian, Min.	19	268	14.1	60t	1	Mughelli, Ovie, Atl.	6	36	6.0	12	0
Williamson, Troy, Min.	18	240	13.3	60t	1	* Matthews, Michael, NY-G	6	28	4.7	6	0
Stevens, Jerramy, T.B.	18	189	10.5	24t	4	Lucas, Chad, T.B.	5	82	16.4	52	0
Askew, B.J., T.B.	18	175	9.7	22	0	Austin, Miles, Dal.	5	76	15.2	35	0
Franks, Bubba, G.B.	18	132	7.3	24	3	Fauria, Christian, Car.	5	39	7.8	16	2
McHugh, Sean, Det.	17	252	14.8	46	0	* Taylor, Courtney, Sea.	5	38	7.6	12	0
Davis, Rashied, Chi.	17	165	9.7	36	0	Calhoun, Brian, Det.	5	35	7.0	11	0
* Thomas, Pierre, N.O.	17	151	8.9	17	1	Hall, Dante, St.L	5	27	5.4	12	0
Benson, Cedric, Chi.	17	123	7.2	19	0	Becht, Anthony, T.B.	5	20	4.0	9	2
Sellers, Mike, Was.	17	117	6.9	24	1	Duckett, T.J., Det.	4	54	13.5	22	0
Martin, Ruvell, G.B.	16	242	15.1	36	4	Byrd, Dominique, St.L	4	44	11.0	14	0
* Celek, Brent, Phi.	16	178	11.1	29	1	Kleinsasser, Jimmy, Min.	4	43	10.8	26	1
Baskett, Hank, Phi.	16	142	8.9	25	1	* Robinson, Ryne, Car.	4	35	8.8	12	0
* Jackson, Brandon, G.B.	16	130	8.1	16	0	Tyree, David, NY-G	4	35	8.8	24	0
Caldwell, Reche, Was.	15	141	9.4	19	0	Shipp, Marcel, Ariz	4	25	6.3	9	0
Copper, Terrance, N.O.	15	126	8.4	21	2	McAllister, Deuce, N.O.	4	15	3.8	7	0
Bennett, Michael, K.C.-T.B.	15	101	6.7	23t	1	Jacobs, Taylor, S.F.	3	40	13.3	21t	1
Fasano, Anthony, Dal.	14	143	10.2	26t	1	Mix, Anthony, NY-G	3	39	13.0	21	0
Cason, Aveion, Det.	14	129	9.2	20	0	Curtis, Tony, Dal.	3	18	6.0	15t	3
Hicks, Maurice, S.F.	14	86	6.1	11	0	Williams, Cadillac, T.B.	3	17	5.7	8	0
Alexander, Shaun, Sea.	14	76	5.4	18	1	* Pittman, Antonio, St.L	3	15	5.0	11	0
Bell, Tatum, Det.	14	63	4.5	15	0	Gilmore, John, Chi.	3	14	4.7	7	0
Lewis, Greg, Phi.	13	265	20.4	50	3	Haynes, Alex, Car.	3	14	4.7	6	0
Heller, Will, Sea.	13	82	6.3	25	3	Wallace, Seneca, Sea.	2	47	23.5	29	0
Karney, Mike, N.O.	13	78	6.0	11	0	Klopfenstein, Joe, St.L	2	37	18.5	36t	1
Obomanu, Ben, Sea.	12	180	15.0	30	1	Mills, Garrett, Min.	2	26	13.0	18	0
Buckhalter, Correll, Phi.	12	87	7.3	14	0	* Darby, Kenneth, T.B.	2	16	8.0	9	0
Minor, Travis, St.L	12	86	7.2	20	0	Lloyd, Brandon, Was.	2	14	7.0	9	0
Schobel, Matt, Phi.	11	108	9.8	18	1	Owens, John, N.O.-Det.	2	13	6.5	9	0
Richardson, Tony, Min.	11	89	8.1	12	0	Walker, Aaron, St.L	2	13	6.5	8	0
Robinson, Michael, S.F.	11	73	6.6	20	0	* Bradshaw, Ahmad, NY-G	2	12	6.0	11	0
Lelie, Ashley, S.F.	10	115	11.5	47	0	Krause, Ryan, G.B.	2	11	5.5	6	0
Stovall, Maurice, T.B.	10	86	8.6	13	1	Bradley, Jon, Det.	2	10	5.0	8	0
Hoover, Brad, Car.	10	58	5.8	14	0	Brees, Drew, N.O.	2	10	5.0	8	0
* Boss, Kevin, NY-G	9	118	13.1	23	2	Kuhn, John, G.B.	2	7	3.5	5	0
* Wolfe, Garrett, Chi.	9	117	13.0	33	0	* Storer, Byron, T.B.	2	3	1.5	2	0
Thrash, James, Was.	9	107	11.9	31	2	Bodiford, Shaun, G.B.	1	13	13.0	13	0
Walters, Troy, Det.	9	101	11.2	21	1	Mahe, Reno, Phi.	1	11	11.0	11	0
* Wynn, DeShawn, G.B.	9	73	8.1	18	0	Kitna, Jon, Det.	1	9	9.0	9	0
Strong, Mack, Sea.	9	72	8.0	15	0	Owens, Richard, St.L	1	9	9.0	9	0
* Milner, Martrez, Atl.	9	50	5.6	15	0	Tahi, Naufahu, Min.	1	7	7.0	7	0
McKie, Jason, Chi.	9	33	3.7	10	0	* Hill, Jason, S.F.	1	6	6.0	6	0
Morey, Sean, Ariz	8	131	16.4	62	0	Hixon, Domenik, NY-G	1	5	5.0	5	0
* Allison, Aundrae, Min.	8	122	15.3	35	0	Kozlowski, Brian, Was.	1	5	5.0	5	0
Hagans, Marques, St.L	8	101	12.6	23	0	Harrington, Joey, Atl.	1	4	4.0	4	0
* Breaston, Steve, Ariz	8	92	11.5	22	0	Taylor, Travis, St.L	1	4	4.0	4	0
Fitzsimmons, Casey, Det.	8	85	10.6	22	1	Hoyte, Oliver, Dal.	1	2	2.0	2	0
Middleton, Brandon, Det.	8	70	8.8	17	1	St. Clair, John, Chi.	1	2	2.0	2t	1
* Smith, Steve, NY-G	8	63	7.9	12	0	Campbell, Dan, Det.	1	1	1.0	1	0
Tapeh, Thomas, Phi.	8	50	6.3	9	0	Pearman, Alvin, Sea.	1	1	1.0	1	0
* Hall, Korey, G.B.	8	49	6.1	10	0						
Gilmore, Bryan, S.F.	7	111	15.9	42	0						
Yoder, Todd, Was.	7	97	13.9	30	1						
* Patrick, Ben, Ariz	7	73	10.4	21	2						
Smith, Terrelle, Ariz	7	59	8.4	16	0						
Dugan, Jeff, Min.	7	57	8.1	27	0						
Hedgecock, Madison, St.L-NY-G	7	52	7.4	9	0						
Droughns, Reuben, NY-G	7	49	7.0	11	0						
Blakley, Dwayne, Atl.	7	48	6.9	11	0						

t = Touchdown; * Player that was a rookie in 2007
Leader based on receptions

INTERCEPTIONS

IINTERCEPTIONS
AFC: 10 Antonio Cromartie, San Diego
NFC: 8 O.J. Atogwe, St. Louis

INTERCEPTIONS, GAME
AFC: 3 Keith Bulluck, Tennessee at New Orleans, September 24 (51 yards, 0 TD)
3 Antonio Cromartie, San Diego vs. Indianapolis, November 11 (27 yards, 0 TD)
NFC: 3 Antrel Rolle, Arizona at Cincinnati, November 18 (127 yards, 2 TD)
3 Lofa Tatupu, Seattle at Philadelphia, December 2 (100 yards, 0 TD)
3 Marcus Trufant, Seattle vs. Arizona, December 9 (96 yards, 1 TD)

YARDS
NFC: 231 Antrel Rolle, Arizona
AFC: 172 Thomas Howard, Oakland

LONGEST
AFC: 100 Brodney Pool, Cleveland at Baltimore, November 18 - TD - (OT)
NFC: 93 Dwight Smith, Minnesota at N.Y. Giants, November 25 - TD

TOUCHDOWNS
NFC: 3 Antrel Rolle, Arizona
AFC: 2 Vincent Fuller, Tennessee
2 Thomas Howard, Oakland

TEAM LEADERS, INTERCEPTIONS
AFC: BALTIMORE, 7, Ed Reed; BUFFALO, 4, Terrence McGee; CINCINNATI, 5, *Leon Hall; CLEVELAND, 6, Leigh Bodden; DENVER, 5, Dre' Bly; HOUSTON, 3, *Fred Bennett; INDIANAPOLIS, 4, Antoine Bethea, Gary Brackett; JACKSONVILLE, 5, *Reggie Nelson; KANSAS CITY, 3, Jarrad Page; MIAMI, 3, Jason Allen; NEW ENGLAND, 6, Asante Samuel; N.Y. JETS, 5, Kerry Rhodes; OAKLAND, 6, Thomas Howard; PITTSBURGH, 3, Ike Taylor; SAN DIEGO, 10, Antonio Cromartie; TENNESSEE, 5, Keith Bulluck

NFC: ARIZONA, 5, Roderick Hood, Antrel Rolle; ATLANTA, 5, DeAngelo Hall; CAROLINA, 3, Deke Cooper, Richard Marshall; CHICAGO, 5, Brian Urlacher; DALLAS, 6, Anthony Henry; DETROIT, 3, Keith Smith; GREEN BAY, 5, Atari Bigby; MINNESOTA, 4, Darren Sharper, Dwight Smith; NEW ORLEANS, 4, Jason David, Roman Harper, Mike McKenzie; N.Y. GIANTS, 4, Sam Madison, Gibril Wilson; PHILADELPHIA, 3, Sheldon Brown; ST. LOUIS, 8, O.J. Atogwe; SAN FRANCISCO, 4, Nate Clements, Walt Harris; SEATTLE, 7, Marcus Trufant; TAMPA BAY, 4, Jermaine Phillips; WASHINGTON, 5, Sean Taylor

TEAM CHAMPION
AFC: 30 San Diego
NFC: 20 Seattle

NFL TOP TEN INTERCEPTORS

	No	Yards	Avg	Long	TD
Cromartie, Antonio, S.D.	10	144	14.4	70t	1
Atogwe, O.J., St.L	8	125	15.6	52t	1
Reed, Ed, Bal.	7	130	18.6	32	0
Trufant, Marcus, Sea.	7	150	21.4	84t	1
Bodden, Leigh, Cle.	6	75	12.5	26	0
Henry, Anthony, Dal.	6	81	13.5	28t	1
Howard, Thomas, Oak.	6	172	28.7	66t	2
Samuel, Asante, N.E.	6	89	14.8	42	1
14 tied	5				

AFC—INDIVIDUAL INTERCEPTORS

	No	Yards	Avg	Long	TD
Cromartie, Antonio, S.D.	10	144	14.4	70t	1
Reed, Ed, Bal.	7	130	18.6	32	0
Howard, Thomas, Oak.	6	172	28.7	66t	2
Samuel, Asante, N.E.	6	89	14.8	42	1
Bodden, Leigh, Cle.	6	75	12.5	26	0
* Nelson, Reggie, Jac.	5	76	15.2	37	0
Rhodes, Kerry, NYJ	5	76	15.2	36	0
Hart, Clinton, S.D.	5	73	14.6	22	0
Bly, Dre', Den.	5	71	14.2	37	0
Bulluck, Keith, Ten.	5	63	12.6	35	0
Jones, Sean, Cle.	5	37	7.4	26	0
* Hall, Leon, Cin.	5	16	3.2	12	0
Brackett, Gary, Ind.	4	128	32.0	49	0
Morrison, Kirk, Oak.	4	94	23.5	45	0
Joseph, Johnathan, Cin.	4	76	19.0	42t	1
Bethea, Antoine, Ind.	4	47	11.8	30	0
Knight, Sammy, Jac.	4	31	7.8	15	0
McGee, Terrence, Buf.	4	4	1.0	2	0
Harper, Nick, Ten.	3	62	20.7	32	0
Taylor, Ike, Pit.	3	56	18.7	51t	1
Gay, Randall, N.E.	3	52	17.3	31	0
* Bennett, Fred, Hou.	3	47	15.7	33	0
* Ndukwe, Nedu, Cin.	3	44	14.7	44	0
Page, Jarrad, K.C.	3	37	12.3	37	0
Routt, Stanford, Oak.	3	31	10.3	31	0
Seau, Junior, N.E.	3	28	9.3	23	0
McCree, Marlon, S.D.	3	20	6.7	19	0
* Revis, Darrelle, NYJ	3	20	6.7	19	0
Hayden, Kelvin, Ind.	3	17	5.7	20	0
Allen, Jason, Mia.	3	15	5.0	13	0
Wilhelm, Matt, S.D.	3	11	3.7	7	0
Williams, Brian, Jac.	3	10	3.3	6	0
Bailey, Champ, Den.	3	3	1.0	3	0
* Griffin, Michael, Ten.	3	3	1.0	3	0
Fuller, Vincent, Ten.	2	137	68.5	76t	2
Pool, Brodney, Cle.	2	103	51.5	100t	1
Giordano, Matt, Ind.	2	89	44.5	83t	1
Leonhard, Jim, Buf.	2	60	30.0	36	0
Smith, Anthony, Pit.	2	50	25.0	50	0
Hope, Chris, Ten.	2	45	22.5	45	0
Townsend, Deshea, Pit.	2	44	22.0	23	0
Sanders, James, N.E.	2	43	21.5	42	0
Williams, Madieu, Cin.	2	40	20.0	35	0
Phillips, Shaun, S.D.	2	36	18.0	18t	1
Lewis, Ray, Bal.	2	35	17.5	35t	1
Sanders, Bob, Ind.	2	32	16.0	29	0
Boiman, Rocky, Ind.	2	28	14.0	26	0
Surtain, Patrick, K.C.	2	25	12.5	23	0
Wilson, George, Buf.	2	25	12.5	25t	1
Cooper, Stephen, S.D.	2	23	11.5	18	0
Goodman, Andre', Mia.	2	23	11.5	18	0
Pollard, Bernard, K.C.	2	23	11.5	21	0
Pittman, David, Bal.	2	21	10.5	29	0
Porter, Joey, Mia.	2	19	9.5	14	0
Johnson, Derrick, K.C.	2	18	9.0	12	0
Lowry, Calvin, Ten.	2	18	9.0	17	0

	No	Yards	Avg	Long	TD
Thornton, David, Ten.	2	16	8.0	11	0
Poteat, Hank, NYJ	2	11	5.5	11	0
Schweigert, Stuart, Oak.	2	10	5.0	10	0
Jackson, Dexter, Cin.	2	7	3.5	7	0
Robinson, Dunta, Hou.	2	6	3.0	10	0
Florence, Drayton, S.D.	2	4	2.0	4	0
Martin, Derrick, Bal.	2	3	1.5	3	0
* Session, Clint, Ind.	2	3	1.5	3	0
Law, Ty, K.C.	2	2	1.0	2	0
Greer, Jabari, Buf.	2	1	0.5	2	0
* McDonald, Brandon, Cle.	2	0	0.0	0	0
Paymah, Karl, Den.	2	0	0.0	0	0
Pope, Derrick, Mia.	2	0	0.0	0	0
Thomas, Adalius, N.E.	1	65	65.0	65t	1
McFadden, Bryant, Pit.	1	50	50.0	50t	1
Ingram, Clint, Jac.	1	39	39.0	39t	1
DiGiorgio, John, Buf.	1	38	38.0	38	0
Taylor, Jason, Mia.	1	36	36.0	36t	1
Geathers, Robert, Cin.	1	30	30.0	30	0
Daniels, Travis, Mia.	1	29	29.0	29	0
Whitner, Donte, Buf.	1	29	29.0	29	0
Glenn, Aaron, Jac.	1	28	28.0	28t	1
Dumervil, Elvis, Den.	1	27	27.0	27	0
Hill, Renaldo, Mia.	1	24	24.0	24	0
Mathis, Rashean, Jac.	1	23	23.0	23	0
Ivy, Corey, Bal.	1	22	22.0	22	0
Harrison, James, Pit.	1	20	20.0	20	0
Youboty, Ashton, Buf.	1	19	19.0	19	0
Edwards, Donnie, K.C.	1	18	18.0	18	0
Sapp, Benny, K.C.	1	15	15.0	15	0
Allen, Will, Mia.	1	14	14.0	14	0
Finnegan, Cortland, Ten.	1	14	14.0	14	0
Foote, Larry, Pit.	1	14	14.0	14	0
Peterson, Mike, Jac.	1	12	12.0	12	0
Keiaho, Freddie, Ind.	1	11	11.0	11	0
Asomugha, Nnamdi, Oak.	1	10	10.0	10	0
Brown, C.C., Hou.	1	9	9.0	9	0
Cousin, Terry, Jac.	1	9	9.0	9	0
Hutchins, Von, Hou.	1	8	8.0	8	0
Thomas, Kiwaukee, Buf.	1	8	8.0	8	0
O'Neal, Deltha, Cin.	1	7	7.0	7	0
Starks, Scott, Jac.	1	7	7.0	7	0
Gold, Ian, Den.	1	6	6.0	6	0
Crowell, Angelo, Buf.	1	5	5.0	5	0
Wilson, Eugene, N.E.	1	5	5.0	5t	1
Colvin, Rosevelt, N.E.	1	4	4.0	4	0
Ellison, Keith, Buf.	1	4	4.0	4	0
Harris, Napoleon, K.C.	1	4	4.0	4	0
Huff, Michael, Oak.	1	4	4.0	4	0
Greenwood, Morlon, Hou.	1	3	3.0	3	0
* Durant, Justin, Jac.	1	2	2.0	2	0
Harrison, Rodney, N.E.	1	2	2.0	2	0
Barton, Eric, NYJ	1	1	1.0	1	0
Clark, Danny, Hou.	1	1	1.0	1	0
Coleman, Drew, NYJ	1	1	1.0	1	0
Edwards, Dwan, Bal.	1	1	1.0	1	0
Jackson, D'Qwell, Cle.	1	1	1.0	1	0
Ryans, DeMeco, Hou.	1	1	1.0	1	0
Vilma, Jonathan, NYJ	1	1	1.0	1	0
Barrett, David, NYJ	1	0	0.0	0	0
* Bullitt, Melvin, Ind.	1	0	0.0	0	0
Dyson, Andre, NYJ	1	0	0.0	0	0
Farrior, James, Pit.	1	0	0.0	0	0
Fudge, Jamaal, Jac.	1	0	0.0	0	0
Hill, Reynaldo, Ten.	1	0	0.0	0	0
Hobbs, Ellis, N.E.	1	0	0.0	0	0
Jackson, Marlin, Ind.	1	0	0.0	0	0
Jammer, Quentin, S.D.	1	0	0.0	0	0
Johnson, Travis, Hou.	1	0	0.0	0	0
Kelsay, Chris, Buf.	1	0	0.0	0t	1
LaBoy, Travis, Ten.	1	0	0.0	0	0
Lehan, Michael, Mia.	1	0	0.0	0	0
McAlister, Chris, Bal.	1	0	0.0	0	0
Myers, Michael, Cin.	1	0	0.0	0	0
Olshansky, Igor, S.D.	1	0	0.0	0	0
Rolle, Samari, Bal.	1	0	0.0	0	0
Tripplett, Larry, Buf.	1	0	0.0	0	0
Washington, Fabian, Oak.	1	0	0.0	0	0
* Weddle, Eric, S.D.	1	0	0.0	0	0
Williams, D.J., Den.	1	0	0.0	0	0
* Wright, Eric, Cle.	1	0	0.0	0	0
* Thomas, Marcus, Den.	1	-2	-2.0	-2	0

*t = Touchdown; *Player that was a rookie in 2007*
Leader based on interceptions

NFC—INDIVIDUAL INTERCEPTORS

	No	Yards	Avg	Long	TD
Atogwe, O.J., St.L	8	125	15.6	52t	1
Trufant, Marcus, Sea.	7	150	21.4	84t	1
Henry, Anthony, Dal.	6	81	13.5	28t	1
Rolle, Antrel, Ariz	5	231	46.2	57	3
Hood, Roderick, Ariz	5	196	39.2	71t	2
Urlacher, Brian, Chi.	5	101	20.2	85t	1
Taylor, Sean, Was.	5	98	19.6	48	0
Hamlin, Ken, Dal.	5	93	18.6	35	0
Hall, DeAngelo, Atl.	5	80	16.0	33	0
Bigby, Atari, G.B.	5	50	10.0	22	0
Newman, Terence, Dal.	4	129	32.3	70	1
Tatupu, Lofa, Sea.	4	116	29.0	49	0
Smith, Dwight, Min.	4	112	28.0	93t	1
Clements, Nate, S.F.	4	74	18.5	62	0
Springs, Shawn, Was.	4	63	15.8	53	0
Sharper, Darren, Min.	4	61	15.3	41	1
Madison, Sam, NY-G	4	59	14.8	27	0
Brown, Fakhir, St.L	4	48	12.0	36t	1
Woodson, Charles, G.B.	4	48	12.0	46t	1
Harris, Walt, S.F.	4	42	10.5	23	0
Wilson, Gibril, NY-G	4	12	3.0	10	0
Phillips, Jermaine, T.B.	4	2	0.5	2	0
McKenzie, Mike, N.O.	3	161	53.7	75t	2
Marshall, Richard, Car.	3	107	35.7	73t	1
Smith, Keith, Det.	3	64	21.3	64t	1
Harper, Roman, N.O.	3	58	19.3	31t	1
Dansby, Karlos, Ariz	3	55	18.3	28	0
* Ross, Aaron, NY-G	3	51	17.0	43t	1
Crocker, Chris, Atl.	3	40	13.3	18	0
Fletcher, London, Was.	3	36	12.0	27t	1
Grant, Deon, Sea.	3	34	11.3	34	0
Tillman, Charles, Chi.	3	24	8.0	20	0
Buchanon, Phillip, T.B.	3	22	7.3	19	0
David, Jason, N.O.	3	21	7.0	19	0
Cooper, Deke, Car.	3	19	6.3	19	0
Brown, Sheldon, Phi.	3	3	1.0	3	0
Williams, Kevin, Min.	2	72	36.0	54t	2
* Alexander, Gerald, Det.	2	70	35.0	36	0
Kennedy, Kenoy, Det.	2	45	22.5	38	0
Barnett, Nick, G.B.	2	40	20.0	38	0
Greenway, Chad, Min.	2	39	19.5	37t	1
* Rouse, Aaron, G.B.	2	37	18.5	34	0
Manning, Danieal, Chi.	2	33	16.5	33	0
Barber, Ronde, T.B.	2	32	16.0	29t	1
* Jackson, Tanard, T.B.	2	26	13.0	26	0
Fisher, Travis, Det.	2	25	12.5	13	0
Sheppard, Lito, Phi.	2	25	12.5	16	0
Milloy, Lawyer, Atl.	2	24	12.0	19	0
Craft, Jason, N.O.	2	21	10.5	21	0
Wilson, Adrian, Ariz	2	20	10.0	20	0

	No	Yards	Avg	Long	TD
Lewis, Michael M., S.F.	2	18	9.0	18	0
Harris, Al, G.B.	2	17	8.5	17	0
Tinoisamoa, Pisa, St.L	2	15	7.5	15	0
Boley, Michael, Atl.	2	12	6.0	12	0
Bartell, Ronald, St.L	2	10	5.0	9	0
Williams, Roy, Dal.	2	10	5.0	10	0
Ruud, Barrett, T.B.	2	7	3.5	5	0
Bullocks, Josh, N.O.	2	6	3.0	6	0
McGowan, Brandon, Chi.	2	5	2.5	5	0
Peterson, Julian, Sea.	2	3	1.5	3	0
Williams, Demorrio, Atl.	2	3	1.5	8	0
Lucas, Ken, Car.	2	1	0.5	1	0
Bryant, Fernando, Det.	2	0	0.0	0	0
Kelly, Brian, T.B.	2	0	0.0	0	0
Rogers, Shaun, Det.	1	66	66.0	66t	1
Lenon, Paris, Det.	1	61	61.0	61t	1
Rogers, Carlos, Was.	1	61	61.0	61t	1
Gaither, Omar, Phi.	1	49	49.0	49	0
Smoot, Fred, Was.	1	47	47.0	47	0
Vasher, Nathan, Chi.	1	34	34.0	34	0
Webster, Corey, NY-G	1	34	34.0	34t	1
Harris, Chris, Car.	1	30	30.0	30	0
Hayes, Gerald, Ariz	1	30	30.0	30t	1
Pierce, Antonio, NY-G	1	28	28.0	28	0
White, Dewayne, Det.	1	28	28.0	28	0
Brown, Mike, Chi.	1	27	27.0	27	0
Williams, Tramon, G.B.	1	22	22.0	22	0
Mikell, Quintin, Phi.	1	20	20.0	20	0
Mitchell, Kawika, NY-G	1	20	20.0	20t	1
Reeves, Jacques, Dal.	1	18	18.0	18	0
Pace, Calvin, Ariz	1	14	14.0	14	0
Winfield, Antoine, Min.	1	14	14.0	14t	1
* Bradley, Stewart, Phi.	1	13	13.0	13	0
Williams, Jimmy, Atl.	1	11	11.0	11	0
Hawk, A.J., G.B.	1	10	10.0	10	0
Williams, Corey, G.B.	1	9	9.0	9	0
Brown, Alex, Chi.	1	7	7.0	7	0
Brown, Ralph, Ariz	1	5	5.0	5	0
Sims, Ernie, Det.	1	5	5.0	5	0
Archuleta, Adam, Chi.	1	4	4.0	4	0
* Lewis, Trey, Atl.	1	4	4.0	4	0
Manuel, Marquand, Car.	1	4	4.0	4	0
Smith, Derek M., S.F.	1	4	4.0	4	0
Gamble, Chris, Car.	1	2	2.0	2	0
* Wade, Jonathan, St.L	1	2	2.0	2	0
Dawkins, Brian, Phi.	1	1	1.0	1	0
Babineaux, Jordan, Sea.	1	0	0.0	0	0
Bashir, Idrees, Det.	1	0	0.0	0	0
* Beason, Jon, Car.	1	0	0.0	0	0
Butler, James, NY-G	1	0	0.0	0	0
Considine, Sean, Phi.	1	0	0.0	0	0
Davis, Thomas, Car.	1	0	0.0	0	0
Gordon, Charles, Min.	1	0	0.0	0	0
Hill, Tye, St.L	1	0	0.0	0	0
James, William, Phi.	1	0	0.0	0	0
June, Cato, T.B.	1	0	0.0	0	0
Kerney, Patrick, Sea.	1	0	0.0	0	0
Leber, Ben, Min.	1	0	0.0	0	0
Peppers, Julius, Car.	1	0	0.0	0	0
Poppinga, Brady, G.B.	1	0	0.0	0	0
Russell, Brian, Sea.	1	0	0.0	0	0
Spencer, Shawntae, S.F.	1	0	0.0	0	0
Watkins, Pat, Dal.	1	0	0.0	0	0
Cody, Shaun, Det.	1	-2	-2.0	-2	0
Tapp, Darryl, Sea.	1	-4	-4.0	-4	0
McIntosh, Rocky, Was.	0	-4	—	-4	0

t = Touchdown; Leader based on interceptions
* Player that was a rookie in 2007

AMERICAN FOOTBALL CONFERENCE—INTERCEPTIONS

	No	Yards	Avg	Long	TD
San Diego	30	311	10.4	70t	2
Indianapolis	22	355	16.1	83t	1
Tennessee	22	358	16.3	76t	2
Jacksonville	20	237	11.9	39t	2
Cincinnati	19	220	11.6	44	1
New England	19	288	15.2	65t	3
Buffalo	18	193	10.7	38	2
Oakland	18	321	17.8	66t	2
Baltimore	17	212	12.5	35t	1
Cleveland	17	216	12.7	100t	1
N.Y. Jets	15	110	7.3	36	0
Denver	14	105	7.5	37	0
Kansas City	14	142	10.1	37	0
Miami	14	160	11.4	36t	1
Houston	11	75	6.8	33	0
Pittsburgh	11	234	21.3	51t	2
AFC Total	281	3537	12.6	100t	20
AFC Average	17.6	221.1	12.6	—	1.3

NATIONAL FOOTBALL CONFERENCE—INTERCEPTIONS

	No	Yards	Avg	Long	TD
San	20	299	15.0	84t	1
Dallas	19	331	17.4	70	2
Green Bay	19	233	12.3	46t	1
Arizona	18	551	30.6	71t	6
St. Louis	18	200	11.1	52t	2
Detroit	17	362	21.3	66t	3
Atlanta	16	174	10.9	33	0
Chicago	16	235	14.7	85t	1
Tampa Bay	16	89	5.6	29t	1
Minnesota	15	298	19.9	93t	6
N.Y. Giants	15	204	13.6	43t	3
Carolina	14	163	11.6	73t	1
Washington	14	301	21.5	61t	2
New Orleans	13	267	20.5	75t	3
San Francisco	12	138	11.5	62	0
Philadelphia	11	111	10.1	49	0
NFC Total	253	3956	15.6	93t	32
NFC Average	15.8	247.3	15.6	—	2.0
League Total	534	7493	—	100t	52
League Average	16.7	234.2	14.0	—	1.6

KICKOFF RETURNS

YARDS PER RETURN
AFC: 30.7 Josh Cribbs, Cleveland
NFC: 28.7* Aundrae Allison, Minnesota

YARDS
AFC: 1809 Josh Cribbs, Cleveland
NFC: 1502 Maurice Hicks, San Francisco

YARDS, GAME
AFC: 245 Josh Cribbs, Cleveland at Baltimore,
November 18 (7 returns, 0 TD)- (OT)
NFC: 233 * Pierre Thomas, New Orleans vs. St. Louis,
November 11 (8 returns, 0 TD)

LONGEST
AFC: 108 Ellis Hobbs, New England at N.Y. Jets,
September 9 - TD
NFC: 104 * Aundrae Allison, Minnesota vs. Detroit,
December 2 - TD

RETURNS
AFC: 63 * Ted Ginn Jr., Miami
NFC: 63 Maurice Hicks, San Francisco

RETURNS, GAME
NFC: 9 Aveion Cason, Detroit at San Diego,
December 16 (150 yards, 0 TD)
AFC: 8 Terrence McGee, Buffalo vs. New England,
November 18 (147 yards, 0 TD)
8 * Ted Ginn Jr., Miami vs. N.Y. Jets, December 2
(198 yards, 0 TD)

TOUCHDOWNS
AFC: 3 Andre Davis, Houston
3 Leon Washington, N.Y. Jets
NFC: 2 Devin Hester, Chicago

TEAM CHAMPION
AFC: 27.0 Cleveland
NFC: 24.8 Minnesota

NFL TOP TEN KICKOFF RETURNERS

	No	Yards	Avg	Long	TD
Cribbs, Josh, Cle.	59	1809	30.7	100t	2
Davis, Andre, Hou.	32	968	30.3	104t	3
* Allison, Aundrae, Min.	20	574	28.7	104t	1
Washington, Leon, NYJ	47	1291	27.5	98t	3
Sproles, Darren, S.D.	37	1008	27.2	89t	1
Jones-Drew, Maurice, Jac.	31	811	26.2	100t	1
Hobbs, Ellis, N.E.	35	911	26.0	108t	1
Cartwright, Rock, Was.	52	1339	25.8	80	0
Austin, Miles, Dal.	24	612	25.5	60	0
* Stanley, Derek, St.L	20	509	25.5	49	0

AFC—INDIVIDUAL KICKOFF RETURNERS

	No	Yards	Avg	Long	TD
Cribbs, Josh, Cle.	59	1809	30.7	100t	2
Davis, Andre, Hou.	32	968	30.3	104t	3
Washington, Leon, NYJ	47	1291	27.5	98t	3
Sproles, Darren, S.D.	37	1008	27.2	89t	1
Jones-Drew, Maurice, Jac.	31	811	26.2	100t	1
Hobbs, Ellis, N.E.	35	911	26.0	108t	1
* Figurs, Yamon, Bal.	46	1138	24.7	94t	1
Holt, Glenn, Cin.	59f	1432	24.3	100t	1
McGee, Terrence, Buf.	45	1082	24.0	103t	1
Wynn, Dexter, Hou.	22	523	23.8	39	0
Rossum, Allen, Pit.	38	885	23.3	98t	1
Rushing, T.J., Ind.	31	714	23.0	47	0
* Ginn, Ted Jr., Mia.	63	1433	22.7	52	0

	No	Yards	Avg	Long	TD
Carr, Chris, Oak.	59	1327	22.5	43	0
Drummond, Eddie, K.C.	37	785	21.2	39	0
(Nonqualifiers)					
Hall, Andre, Den.	19	475	25.0	34	0
* Griffin, Michael, Ten.	18	422	23.4	48	0
Rhodes, Dominic, Oak.	16	312	19.5	31	0
Martinez, Glenn, Den.	15	330	22.0	35	0
Thorpe, Craphonso, Ind.	15	318	21.2	40	0
Sapp, Benny, K.C.	15	251	16.7	32	0
* Henry, Chris, Ten.	13	272	20.9	46	0
Mathis, Jerome, Hou.	11	320	29.1	84t	1
Webb, Jeff, K.C.	10	204	20.4	28	0
Smith, Brad, NYJ	9	183	20.3	27	0
Ross, Cory, Bal.	9	148	16.4	25	0
Welker, Wes, N.E.	7	176	25.1	33	0
Perry, Tab, Cin.	7	145	20.7	26	0
Davenport, Najeh, Pit.	7	123	17.6	29	0
Dinkins, Darnell, Cle.	7	62	8.9	19	0
Turner, Michael, S.D.	6	139	23.2	28	0
Reid, Willie, Pit.	6	127	21.2	30	0
Parrish, Roscoe, Buf.	6	126	21.0	24	0
Sams, B.J., Bal.	5	140	28.0	47	0
Lawton, Luke, Ind.	5	95	19.0	22	0
Owens, Chad, Jac.	5	94	18.8	31	0
Jackson, Chad, N.E.	5	85	17.0	39	0
Starks, Scott, Jac.	5	81	16.2	22	0
Cobbs, Patrick, Mia.	5	44	8.8	11	0
Andrews, Willie, N.E.	4	149	37.3	77t	1
* Jones, Jacoby, Hou.	4	78	19.5	23	0
Cotchery, Jerricho, NYJ	4	56	14.0	32	0
* McBride, Turk, K.C.	4	40	10.0	14	0
Smith, Musa, Bal.	3	89	29.7	52	0
Clark, Brian, Den.	3	70	23.3	26	0
Cromartie, Antonio, S.D.	3	67	22.3	26	0
Toefield, LaBrandon, Jac.	3	57	19.0	26	0
* Young, Selvin, Den.	3	56	18.7	25	0
Wright, Jason, Cle.	3	49	16.3	20	0
Jackson, Fred, Buf.	3	46	15.3	19	0
Kelly, Reggie, Cin.	3f	38	12.7	15	0
Jacobs, Taylor, Den.	3	35	11.7	15	0
Bowens, David, NYJ	3	30	10.0	17	0
Baker, Chris, NYJ	3	18	6.0	10	0
Neufeld, Ryan, Buf.	3	6	2.0	7	0
Chatman, Antonio, Cin.	2	49	24.5	34	0
Miller, Justin, NYJ	2	48	24.0	26	0
Faulk, Kevin, N.E.	2	47	23.5	27	0
* Davis, Chris, Ten.	2	37	18.5	19	0
Wrighster, George, Jac.	2	35	17.5	29	0
Cook, Jameel, Hou.	2	33	16.5	21	0
Leonhard, Jim, Buf.	2	32	16.0	17	0
Chatman, Jesse, Mia.	2	31	15.5	21	0
Wright, Wallace, NYJ	2	31	15.5	28	0
Sapp, Cecil, Den.	2	30	15.0	22	0
Leach, Vonta, Hou.	2	26	13.0	14	0
Thomas, Anthony, Buf.	2	26	13.0	15	0
Hagan, Derek, Mia.	2	25	12.5	14	0
Troupe, Ben, Ten.	2	21	10.5	12	0
Dorsey, DeDe, Cin.	2	20	10.0	20	0
McCareins, Justin, NYJ	2	15	7.5	12	0
Friedman, Lennie, Cle.	2	14	7.0	13	0
Anderson, Mike, Bal.	2	10	5.0	10	0
Booker, Marty, Mia.	2	3	1.5	3	0
Dwight, Tim, Oak.	1	30	30.0	30	0
Bly, Dre', Den.	1	23	23.0	23	0
* Broussard, John, Jac.	1	20	20.0	20	0
Ryan, Sean, NYJ	1	18	18.0	18	0
Keith, Kenton, Ind.	1	15	15.0	15	0
Lowry, Calvin, Ten.	1	15	15.0	15	0

	No	Yards	Avg	Long	TD		No	Yards	Avg	Long	TD
Reid, Darrell, Ind.	1	15	15.0	15	0	Williams, DeAngelo, Car.	13	231	17.8	29	0
Hartsock, Ben, Ten.	1	14	14.0	14	0	Davis, Rashied, Chi.	12	168	14.0	34	0
Cramer, Casey, Ten.	1	13	13.0	13	0	Arrington, J.J., Ariz	11	251	22.8	56	0
Evans, Heath, N.E.	1	13	13.0	13	0	Jones, Mark, T.B.	10	286	28.6	36	0
Preston, Duke, Buf.	1	12	12.0	12	0	Calhoun, Brian, Det.	10	221	22.1	33	0
Smolko, Isaac, Jac.	1	12	12.0	12	0	Goings, Nick, Car.	9	174	19.3	29	0
Griffith, Justin, Oak.	1	11	11.0	11	0	Clayton, Michael, T.B.	8	172	21.5	26	0
Eason, Nick, Pit.	1	10	10.0	10	0	Walters, Troy, Det.	8	172	21.5	39	0
Jurevicius, Joe, Cle.	1	9	9.0	9	0	Hagans, Marques, St.L	7	130	18.6	22	0
Mruczkowski, Gene, Mia.	1	9	9.0	9	0	Stecker, Aaron, N.O.	6	137	22.8	41	0
Walter, Kevin, Hou.	1	7	7.0	7	0	Jones, Nate, Dal.	6	122	20.3	27	0
Brayton, Tyler, Oak.	1	6	6.0	6	0	Scobey, Josh, Buf.	5	112	22.4	29	0
Chambers, Kirk, Buf.	1	6	6.0	6	0	Betts, Ladell, Was.	5	108	21.6	36	0
Manumaleuna, Brandon, S.D.	1	6	6.0	6	0	Lewis, Michael L., S.F.	5	86	17.2	24	0
Sippio, Bobby, K.C.	1	6	6.0	6	0	Graham, Earnest, T.B.	4	90	22.5	31	0
Chatham, Matt, NYJ	1	5	5.0	5	0	Obomanu, Ben, Sea.	4	88	22.0	25	0
* Mauia, Reagan, Mia.	1f	4	4.0	4	0	Middleton, Brandon, Det.	4	83	20.8	30	0
Neal, Lorenzo, S.D.	1	4	4.0	4	0	Moorehead, Kindal, Car.	4	46	11.5	17	0
Vrabel, Mike, N.E.	1	3	3.0	3	0	* Stanback, Isaiah, Dal.	3	78	26.0	35	0
Fifita, Steve, Mia.	1	0	0.0	0	0	Pearman, Alvin, Sea.	3	71	23.7	33	0
* Landri, Derek, Jac.	1	0	0.0	0	0	Walker, Delanie, S.F.	3	63	21.0	30	0
Peelle, Justin, Mia.	1	0	0.0	0	0	Fitzsimmons, Casey, Det.	3	62	20.7	41t	1
Wilson, George, Buf.	1	0	0.0	0	0	Manning, Danieal, Chi.	3	61	20.3	21	0
* Wright, Dwayne, Buf.	1	0	0.0	0	0	Hangartner, Geoff, Car.	3	42	14.0	16	0
Boulware, Michael, Hou.	0	6	—	6	0	Curtis, Tony, Dal.	3	27	9.0	16	0
Camarillo, Greg, Mia.	0	3	—	3	0	Crayton, Patrick, Dal.	3	26	8.7	13	0
Cesaire, Jacques, S.D.	0f	0	—	0	0	Gilmore, John, Chi.	3	25	8.3	15	0
Ninkovich, Rob, Mia.	0f	0	—	0	0	Peterson, Adrian, Chi.	3	17	5.7	14	0
Spaeth, Matt, Pit.	0f	0	—	0	0	Robinson, Michael, S.F.	2	51	25.5	30	0
Sypniewski, Quinn, Bal.	0f	0	—	0	0	Copper, Terrance, N.O.	2	49	24.5	25	0
Thomas, David, N.E.	0f	0	—	0	0	Gordon, Charles, Min.	2	48	24.0	27	0
Woods, Pierre, N.E.	0f	0	—	0	0	Bodiford, Shaun, G.B.	2	41	20.5	22	0
						Cox, Torrie, T.B.	2	41	20.5	27	0
						* Rosario, Dante, Car.	2	39	19.5	25	0
						Thrash, James, Was.	2	36	18.0	20	0
						Lucas, Chad, T.B.	2	35	17.5	18	0
						Mughelli, Ovie, Atl.	2	28	14.0	18	0
						Furrey, Mike, Det.	2	25	12.5	15	0

t = Touchdown; f = Fair Catch
Leader based on average return, minimum 20 returns
* Player that was a rookie in 2007

NFC—INDIVIDUAL KICKOFF RETURNERS

	No	Yards	Avg	Long	TD
* Allison, Aundrae, Min.	20	574	28.7	104t	1
Cartwright, Rock, Was.	52	1339	25.8	80	0
Austin, Miles, Dal.	24	612	25.5	60	0
* Stanley, Derek, St.L	20	509	25.5	49	0
Norwood, Jerious, Atl.	52	1317	25.3	76	0
Hall, Dante, St.L	29	729	25.1	84	0
Cason, Aveion, Det.	42	1041	24.8	74	0
Hixon, Domenik, Den.-NY-G	20	495	24.8	74t	1
* Bradshaw, Ahmad, NY-G	38	921	24.2	68	0
* Thomas, Pierre, N.O.	36	865	24.0	64	0
Hicks, Maurice, S.F.	63	1502	23.8	55	0
Robinson, Koren, G.B.	25	596	23.8	67	0
Thompson, Tyson, Dal.	20	471	23.6	72	0
Williams, Brandon, St.L	22	508	23.1	37	0
* Robinson, Ryne, Car.	26	598	23.0	60	0
Williams, Tramon, G.B.	30	684	22.8	65	0
Reed, J.R., Phi.	31	701	22.6	34	0
* Breaston, Steve, Ariz	62	1391	22.4	59	0
Burleson, Nate, Sea.	27	590	21.9	91t	1
Droughns, Reuben, NY-G	20	437	21.9	34	0
Hester, Devin, Chi.	43	934	21.7	97t	2
Buckhalter, Correll, Phi.	37	798	21.6	35	0
(Nonqualifiers)					
Barclay, Chris, Ten.-N.O.	19	402	21.2	37	0
Jennings, Adam, Atl.	17	428	25.2	61	0
Williamson, Troy, Min.	17	387	22.8	56	0
Moore, Lance, N.O.	17	318	18.7	32	0
Spurlock, Micheal, T.B.	16	444	27.8	90t	1
* Peterson, Adrian, Min.	16	412	25.8	53	0
* Wilson, Josh, Sea.	14	385	27.5	89t	1

	No	Yards	Avg	Long	TD
Minor, Travis, St.L	2	24	12.0	21	0
Saipaia, Blaine, Det.	2	23	11.5	12	0
Patten, David, N.O.	2	20	10.0	10	0
Buchanon, Phillip, T.B.	2	15	7.5	16	0
Eubanks, John, Was.	2	14	7.0	14	0
* Darby, Kenneth, T.B.	2	11	5.5	14	0
Idonije, Israel, Chi.	2	2	1.0	2	0
Morey, Sean, Ariz	1	40	40.0	40	0
* Taylor, Courtney, Sea.	1	27	27.0	27	0
* Wolfe, Garrett, Chi.	1	27	27.0	27	0
Stovall, Maurice, T.B.	1	22	22.0	22	0
Moore, Mewelde, Min.	1	20	20.0	20	0
Looker, Dane, St.L	1	19	19.0	19	0
Mahe, Reno, Phi.	1	19	19.0	19	0
* Wade, Jonathan, St.L	1	19	19.0	19	0
Dugan, Jeff, Min.	1	18	18.0	18	0
Randle El, Antwaan, Was.	1	17	17.0	17	0
King, Jeff, Car.	1f	16	16.0	16	0
* Wynn, DeShawn, G.B.	1	15	15.0	15	0
Reagor, Montae, Phi.	1	14	14.0	14	0
Engram, Bobby, Sea.	1	12	12.0	12	0
McQuistan, Pat, Dal.	1	12	12.0	12	0
Moss, Santana, Was.	1	12	12.0	12	0
Alexander, Lorenzo, Was.	1	10	10.0	10	0
* Anderson, Deon, Dal.	1	10	10.0	10	0
Lake, Antwan, Was.	1	10	10.0	10	0
Babineaux, Jonathan, Atl.	1	8	8.0	8	0
Cooper, Josh, N.O.	1	8	8.0	8	0
Miller, Billy, N.O.	1	8	8.0	8	0
Yoder, Todd, Was.	1	8	8.0	8	0
Martin, Ruvell, G.B.	1	6	6.0	6	0

	No	Yards	Avg	Long	TD
Driver, Donald, G.B.	1	4	4.0	4	0
Blackmon, Will, G.B.	1	3	3.0	3	0
Hilliard, Ike, T.B.	1	3	3.0	3	0
Lewis, Greg, Phi.	1	3	3.0	3	0
Grigsby, Otis, Min.	1	2	2.0	2	0
* Davis, Buster, Det.	1	1	1.0	1	0
Marshall, Richard, Car.	1	0	0.0	0	0
McClover, Stanley, Car.	1	0	0.0	0	0
Montgomery, Mike, G.B.	1	0	0.0	0	0
Shiancoe, Visanthe, Min.	1	0	0.0	0	0
Terrill, Craig, Sea.	1	0	0.0	0	0
* Wallace, C.J., Sea.	1	0	0.0	0	0
Willis, Ray, Sea.	1	0	0.0	0	0
Baskett, Hank, Phi.	0	4	—	4	0
Ashworth, Tom, Sea.	0f	0	—	0	0
Bentley, Kevin, Sea.	0f	0	—	0	0

t = Touchdown; f = Fair Catch
Leader based on average return, minimum 20 returns
* Player that was a rookie in 2007

AMERICAN FOOTBALL CONFERENCE—KICKOFF RETURNS

	No	Yards	Avg	Long	TD
Cleveland	72	1943	27.0	100t	2
Houston	74	1961	26.5	104t	4
San Diego	48	1224	25.5	89t	1
New England	55	1384	25.2	108t	2
Baltimore	65	1525	23.5	94t	1
Cincinnati	73	1684	23.1	100t	1
N.Y. Jets	74	1695	22.9	98t	3
Jacksonville	49	1110	22.7	100t	1
Denver	58	1293	22.3	35	0
Pittsburgh	52	1145	22.0	98t	1
Indianapolis	53	1157	21.8	47	0
Oakland	78	1686	21.6	43	0
Tennessee	52	1098	21.1	48	0
Buffalo	70	1448	20.7	103t	1
Miami	78	1552	19.9	52	0
Kansas City	67	1286	19.2	39	0
AFC Total	1018	23191	22.8	108t	17
AFC Average	63.6	1449.4	22.8	—	1.1

NATIONAL FOOTBALL CONFERENCE—KICKOFF RETURNS

	No	Yards	Avg	Long	TD
Minnesota	59	1461	24.8	104t	1
Atlanta	72	1781	24.7	76	0
N.Y. Giants	66	1579	23.9	74t	1
Washington	65	1544	23.8	80	0
St. Louis	82	1938	23.6	84	0
San Francisco	73	1702	23.3	55	0
Tampa Bay	48	1119	23.3	90t	1
Arizona	74	1682	22.7	59	0
Detroit	72	1628	22.6	74	1
Dallas	61	1358	22.3	72	0
Seattle	53	1173	22.1	91t	2
Green Bay	62	1349	21.8	67	0
Philadelphia	71	1539	21.7	35	0
New Orleans	71	1513	21.3	64	0
Carolina	60	1146	19.1	60	0
Chicago	67	1234	18.4	97t	2
NFC Total	1056	23746	22.5	104t	8
NFC Average	66.0	1484.1	22.5	—	0.5
League Total	2074	46937	—	108t	25
League Average	64.8	1466.8	22.6	—	0.8

PUNTING

AVERAGE YARDS PER PUNT
AFC: 49.1 Shane Lechler, Oakland
NFC: 47.3 Andy Lee, San Francisco

NET AVERAGE YARDS PER PUNT
AFC: 41.1 Shane Lechler, Oakland
NFC: 41.0 Andy Lee, San Francisco

LONGEST
AFC: 81 Dustin Colquitt, Kansas City vs. San Diego, December 2
NFC: 80 Donnie Jones, St. Louis at Seattle, October 21

PUNTS
NFC: 105 Andy Lee, San Francisco
AFC: 95 Dustin Colquitt, Kansas City

PUNTS, GAME
AFC: 10 Sam Koch, Baltimore at Pittsburgh, November 5 (436 yards)
10 * Brandon Fields, Miami at New England, December 23 (446 yards)
10 Dustin Colquitt, Kansas City at N.Y. Jets, December 30 (442 yards) - (OT)
NFC: 10 Andy Lee, San Francisco vs. Seattle, September 30 (543 yards)

TEAM CHAMPION
AFC: 49.1 Oakland
NFC: 47.3 San Francisco

AMERICAN FOOTBALL CONFERENCE—PUNTING

	Total Punts	Yards	Long	Avg	TB	Blk	Opp Ret	Return Yards	In 20	Net Avg
Oakland	73	3585	70	49.1	7	0	40	445	25	41.1
San Diego	82	3735	70	45.5	9	1	29	311	36	39.6
Kansas City	96	4322	81	45.0	9	1	50	387	27	39.1
Denver	60	2630	65	43.8	6	2	31	334	17	36.3
Miami	77	3327	61	43.2	6	0	39	387	10	36.6
Baltimore	79	3397	64	43.0	9	1	38	375	20	36.0
N.Y. Jets	72	3063	62	42.5	8	1	32	268	25	36.6
Pittsburgh	68	2880	59	42.4	2	0	31	266	28	37.9
Cleveland	69	2895	64	42.0	6	0	34	308	22	35.8
Indianapolis	52	2181	63	41.9	5	0	22	305	18	34.2
Tennessee	73	3060	66	41.9	6	0	31	274	25	36.5
Houston	55	2296	59	41.7	3	0	19	151	24	37.9
Jacksonville	54	2249	76	41.6	2	0	28	218	14	36.9
Cincinnati	59	2437	55	41.3	3	0	33	299	21	35.2
Buffalo	81	3302	75	40.8	3	0	37	196	30	37.6
New England	45	1821	64	40.5	6	1	14	75	13	36.1
AFC Total	1095	47180	81	—	90	7	508	4599	355	—
AFC Average	68.4	2948.8	—	43.1	5.6	0.4	31.8	287.4	22.2	37.2

NATIONAL FOOTBALL CONFERENCE—PUNTING

	Total Punts	Yards	Long	Avg	TB	Blk	Opp Ret	Return Yards	In 20	Net Avg
San Francisco	105	4968	74	47.3	13	0	53	402	42	41.0
St. Louis	78	3684	80	47.2	9	0	48	437	18	39.3
Dallas	63	2970	64	47.1	7	0	35	406	17	38.5
Minnesota	81	3621	70	44.7	9	0	43	440	34	37.0
Detroit	68	3010	58	44.3	5	0	36	434	26	36.4
Carolina	92	4038	64	43.9	5	0	55	579	23	36.5
New Orleans	63	2757	61	43.8	4	0	35	335	20	37.2
Atlanta	88	3824	63	43.5	5	0	41	307	30	38.8
Tampa Bay	78	3382	61	43.4	10	1	38	280	30	37.2
Green Bay	62	2664	72	43.0	11	2	19	113	18	37.6
Philadelphia	73	3066	65	42.0	7	0	36	409	24	34.5
Chicago	94	3934	60	41.9	10	0	40	236	29	37.2
Washington	75	3072	64	41.0	7	0	32	202	23	36.4
Arizona	80	3198	61	40.0	7	1	38	496	21	32.0
Seattle	86	3436	62	40.0	6	0	37	362	30	34.3
N.Y. Giants	72	2865	60	39.8	5	1	28	173	25	36.0
NFC Total	1258	54489	80	—	120	5	614	5611	410	—
NFC Average	78.6	3405.6	—	43.3	7.5	0.3	38.4	350.7	25.6	36.9
NFL Total	2353	101669	81	—	210	12	1122	10210	765	—
NFL Average	73.5	3177.2	—	43.2	6.6	0.4	35.1	319.1	23.9	37.1

NFL TOP TEN PUNTERS

	No	Yards	Long	Avg	Total Punts	TB	Blk	Opp Ret	Return Yards	In 20	Net Avg
Lechler, Shane, Oak.	73	3585	70	49.1	73	7	0	40	445	25	41.1
Lee, Andy, S.F.	105	4968	74	47.3	105	13	0	53	402	42	41.0
Jones, Donnie, St.L	78	3684	80	47.2	78	9	0	48	437	18	39.3
McBriar, Mat, Dal.	63	2970	64	47.1	63	7	0	35	406	17	38.5
Sauerbrun, Todd, Den.	47	2200	65	46.8	49	6	2	28	313	14	36.1
Scifres, Mike, S.D.	81	3735	70	46.1	82	9	1	29	311	36	39.6
Colquitt, Dustin, K.C.	95	4322	81	45.5	96	9	1	50	387	27	39.1
Kluwe, Chris, Min.	81	3621	70	44.7	81	9	0	43	440	34	37.0
Ryan, Jon, G.B.	60	2664	72	44.4	62	11	2	19	113	18	37.6
Harris, Nick, Det.	68	3010	58	44.3	68	5	0	36	434	26	36.4

AFC—INDIVIDUAL PUNTERS

	No	Yards	Long	Avg	Total Punts	TB	Blk	Opp Ret	Return Yards	In 20	Net Avg
Lechler, Shane, Oak.	73	3585	70	49.1	73	7	0	40	445	25	41.1
Sauerbrun, Todd, Den.	47	2200	65	46.8	49	6	2	28	313	14	36.1
Scifres, Mike, S.D.	81	3735	70	46.1	82	9	1	29	311	36	39.6
Colquitt, Dustin, K.C.	95	4322	81	45.5	96	9	1	50	387	27	39.1
Koch, Sam, Bal.	78	3397	64	43.6	79	9	1	38	375	20	36.0
Graham, Ben, NYJ	66	2855	62	43.3	67	7	1	31	262	23	36.6
* Fields, Brandon, Mia.	77	3327	61	43.2	77	6	0	39	387	10	36.6
* Sepulveda, Daniel, Pit.	68	2880	59	42.4	68	2	0	31	266	28	37.9
Hentrich, Craig, Ten.	70	2939	66	42.0	70	6	0	30	264	24	36.5
Smith, Hunter, Ind.	52	2181	63	41.9	52	5	0	22	305	18	34.2
Zastudil, Dave, Cle.	49	2046	64	41.8	49	4	0	26	272	14	34.6
Turk, Matt, Hou.	55	2296	59	41.7	55	3	0	19	151	24	37.9
* Podlesh, Adam, Jac.	54	2249	76	41.6	54	2	0	28	218	14	36.9
Hanson, Chris, N.E.	44	1821	64	41.4	45	6	1	14	75	13	36.1
Larson, Kyle, Cin.	59	2437	55	41.3	59	3	0	33	299	21	35.2
Moorman, Brian, Buf.	81	3302	75	40.8	81	3	0	37	196	30	37.6
(Nonqualifiers)											
Player, Scott, Cle.	13	593	57	45.6	13	2	0	6	29	6	40.3
Ernster, Paul, Cle.-Den.	12	434	59	36.2	12	0	0	2	7	3	35.6
* Paulescu, Sam, hen.	5	221	51	44.2	5	0	0	3	21	1	40.0
* Kapinos, Jeremy, NYJ	5	208	48	41.6	5	1	0	1	6	2	36.4
Miller, Josh, Ten.	3	121	52	40.3	3	0	0	1	10	1	37.0
Elam, Jason, Den.	1	31	31	31.0	1	0	0	0	0	1	31.0

Leader based on average, minimum 40 punts

NFC—INDIVIDUAL PUNTERS

	No	Yards	Long	Avg	Total Punts	TB	Blk	Opp Ret	Return Yards	In 20	Net Avg
Lee, Andy, S.F.	105	4968	74	47.3	105	13	0	53	402	42	41.0
Jones, Donnie, St.L	78	3684	80	47.2	78	9	0	48	437	18	39.3
McBriar, Mat, Dal.	63	2970	64	47.1	63	7	0	35	406	17	38.5
Kluwe, Chris, Min.	81	3621	70	44.7	81	9	0	43	440	34	37.0
Ryan, Jon, G.B.	60	2664	72	44.4	62	11	2	19	113	18	37.6
Harris, Nick, Det.	68	3010	58	44.3	68	5	0	36	434	26	36.4
Baker, Jason, Car.	90	3978	64	44.2	90	5	0	54	485	22	37.7
Bidwell, Josh, T.B.	77	3382	61	43.9	78	10	1	38	280	30	37.2
Weatherford, Steven, N.O.	63	2757	61	43.8	63	4	0	35	335	20	37.2
Koenen, Michael, Atl.	88	3824	63	43.5	88	5	0	41	307	30	38.8
* Rocca, Save, Phi.	73	3066	65	42.0	73	7	0	36	409	24	34.5
Maynard, Brad, Chi.	88	3682	56	41.8	88	9	0	38	214	27	37.4
Frost, Derrick, Was.	75	3072	64	41.0	75	7	0	32	202	23	36.4
Barr, Mike, Ariz	59	2385	61	40.4	60	5	1	28	384	15	31.7
Feagles, Jeff, NY-G	71	2865	60	40.4	72	5	1	28	173	25	36.0
Plackemeier, Ryan, Sea.	86	3436	62	40.0	86	6	0	37	362	30	34.3
(Nonqualifiers)											
Berger, Mitch, Ariz	20	813	56	40.7	20	2	0	10	112	6	33.1
Johnson, Dirk, Chi.	4	199	60	49.8	4	1	0	2	22	1	39.3
Kasay, John, Car.	2	60	32	30.0	2	0	0	1	94	1	-17.0
Gould, Robbie, Chi.	2	53	28	26.5	2	0	0	0	0	1	26.5

Leader based on average, minimum 40 punts
* Player that was a rookie in 2007

PUNT RETURNS

YARDS PER RETURN
AFC: 16.3 Roscoe Parrish, Buffalo
NFC: 15.5 Devin Hester, Chicago

YARDS
NFC: 658 Nate Burleson, Seattle
AFC: 440 Roscoe Parrish, Buffalo

YARDS, GAME
NFC: 143 Devin Hester, Chicago vs. Kansas City,
September 16 (5 returns, 1 TD)
AFC: 135 Josh Cribbs, Cleveland vs. San Francisco,
December 30 (4 returns, 1 TD)

LONGEST
NFC: 94 Nate Burleson, Seattle at Cleveland,
November 4 - TD - (OT)
94 Tramon Williams, Green Bay vs. Carolina,
November 18 - TD
AFC: 90 T.J. Rushing, Indianapolis at Oakland,
December 16 - TD

RETURNS
NFC: 58 Nate Burleson, Seattle
AFC: 36 Allen Rossum, Pittsburgh

RETURNS, GAME
AFC: 7 Eddie Drummond, Kansas City at Oakland,
October 21 (52 yards, 0 TD)
NFC: 7 Michael L. Lewis, San Francisco vs.
St. Louis, November 18
(18 yards, 0 TD)

FAIR CATCHES
NFC: 20 Patrick Crayton, Dallas
AFC: 15 * Ted Ginn Jr., Miami

TOUCHDOWNS
NFC: 4 Devin Hester, Chicago
AFC: 1 Josh Cribbs, Cleveland
1 * Yamon Figurs, Baltimore
1 * Ted Ginn Jr., Miami
1 Glenn Martinez, Denver
1 Roscoe Parrish, Buffalo
1 Ed Reed, Baltimore
1 T.J. Rushing, Indianapolis
1 Darren Sproles, San Diego

TEAM CHAMPION
AFC: 15.4 Buffalo
NFC: 14.8 Chicago

NFL TOP TEN PUNT RETURNERS

	No	FC	Yards	Avg	Long	TD
Parrish, Roscoe, Buf.	27	2	440	16.3	74t	1
Hester, Devin, Chi.	42	6	651	15.5	89t	4
Cribbs, Josh, Cle.	30	10	405	13.5	76t	1
Burleson, Nate, Sea.	58	8	658	11.3	94t	1
Welker, Wes, N.E.	25	7	249	10.0	35	0
* Ginn, Ted Jr., Mia.	24	15	230	9.6	87t	1
Sproles, Darren, S.D.	24	2	229	9.5	45t	1
* Jones, Jacoby, Hou.	30	7	286	9.5	74	0
* Davis, Chris, Ten.	31	12	293	9.5	39	0
* Breaston, Steve, Ariz	42	6	395	9.4	73t	1

AFC—INDIVIDUAL PUNT RETURNERS

	No	FC	Yards	Avg	Long	TD
Parrish, Roscoe, Buf.	27	2	440	16.3	74t	1
Cribbs, Josh, Cle.	30	10	405	13.5	76t	1
Welker, Wes, N.E.	25	7	249	10.0	35	0
* Ginn, Ted Jr., Mia.	24	15	230	9.6	87t	1
Sproles, Darren, S.D.	24	2	229	9.5	45t	1
* Jones, Jacoby, Hou.	30	7	286	9.5	74	0
* Davis, Chris, Ten.	31	12	293	9.5	39	0
Northcutt, Dennis, Jac.	26	13	240	9.2	37	0
Washington, Leon, NYJ	20	14	183	9.2	33	0
Drummond, Eddie, K.C.	32	11	222	6.9	22	0
Rossum, Allen, Pit.	36	8	232	6.4	49	0
* Higgins, Johnnie Lee, Oak.	20	6	103	5.2	54	0
(Nonqualifiers)						
Rushing, T.J., Ind.	19	14	249	13.1	90t	1
Chatman, Antonio, Cin.	18	8	93	5.2	19	0
* Figurs, Yamon, Bal.	16	9	171	10.7	75t	1
Martinez, Glenn, Den.	14	12	157	11.2	80t	1
Reed, Ed, Bal.	10	3	94	9.4	63t	1
Dwight, Tim, Oak.	9	3	54	6.0	16	0
Green, Skyler, Cin.	9	10	38	4.2	9	0
Kennison, Eddie, K.C.	8	3	80	10.0	21	0
Carr, Chris, Oak.	8	7	52	6.5	24	0
Hixon, Domenik, Den.	7	5	32	4.6	14	0
Brown, Troy, N.E.	6	2	55	9.2	28	0
* Davis, Craig, S.D.	6	6	52	8.7	24	0
Thorpe, Craphonso, Ind.	6	0	31	5.2	29	0
Jones, Brandon, Ten.	6	0	29	4.8	13	0
Ross, Cory, Bal.	5	0	36	7.2	15	0
Sams, B.J., Bal.	4	0	37	9.3	16	0
Leonhard, Jim, Buf.	4	2	36	9.0	13	0
Barclay, Chris, Ten.	3	1	34	11.3	19	0
Jones-Drew, Maurice, Jac.	3	0	28	9.3	17	0
Bly, Dre', Den.	2	0	20	10.0	10	0
Finnegan, Cortland, Ten.	2	3	11	5.5	9	0
Jackson, Chad, N.E.	2	0	7	3.5	6	0
Wilson, Cedrick, Pit.	2	1	6	3.0	6	0
Wynn, Dexter, Hou.	2	1	1	0.5	4	0
Osgood, Kassim, S.D.	2	0	0	0.0	0	0
Anderson, David, Hou.	1	0	0	0.0	0	0
Asomugha, Nnamdi, Oak.	1	0	0	0.0	0	0
* Gay, William, Pit.	1	0	0	0.0	0	0
Hawkins, Brent, Jac.	1	0	0	0.0	0	0
* Nkang, Chad, Jac.	1	0	0	0.0	0	0
Owens, Chad, Jac.	1	1	0	0.0	0	0
Starks, Scott, Jac.	0	0	56	—	56	0
Faulk, Kevin, N.E.	0	9	0	—	—	0

t = Touchdown
Leader based on average return, minimum 20 returns
* Player that was a rookie in 2007

2007 INDIVIDUAL STATISTICS—PUNT RETURNS

NFC—INDIVIDUAL PUNT RETURNERS

	No	FC	Yards	Avg	Long	TD
Hester, Devin, Chi.	42	6	651	15.5	89t	4
Burleson, Nate, Sea.	58	8	658	11.3	94t	1
* Breaston, Steve, Ariz	42	6	395	9.4	73t	1
Moore, Lance, N.O.	20	15	185	9.3	48	0
Crayton, Patrick, Dal.	22	20	201	9.1	49	0
* Robinson, Ryne, Car.	30	19	262	8.7	34	0
Woodson, Charles, G.B.	33	5	268	8.1	34	0
Mahe, Reno, Phi.	31	11	249	8.0	32	0
Lewis, Michael L., S.F.	44	4	336	7.6	51	0
McQuarters, R.W., NY-G	42	18	318	7.6	27	0
Jennings, Adam, Atl.	30	17	186	6.2	23	0
Randle El, Antwaan, Was.	34	7	209	6.1	27	0

(Nonqualifiers)

	No	FC	Yards	Avg	Long	TD
Hall, Dante, St.L	19	6	286	15.1	85t	1
Wade, Bobby, Min.	16	11	112	7.0	17	0
Buchanon, Phillip, T.B.	16	0	55	3.4	24	0
Walters, Troy, Det.	15	16	118	7.9	18	0
Hilliard, Ike, T.B.	15	4	92	6.1	20	0
Moore, Mewelde, Min.	13	8	130	10.0	42	0
Williams, Brandon, S.F.-St.L	13	12	98	7.5	15	0
Jones, Mark, T.B.	12	6	143	11.9	35	0
Blackmon, Will, G.B.	8	0	106	13.3	57t	1
Clements, Nate, S.F.	7	0	115	16.4	41	0
Williams, Tramon, G.B.	6	0	118	19.7	94t	1
Hall, DeAngelo, Atl.	5	1	41	8.2	16	0
Westbrook, Brian, Phi.	4	0	79	19.8	64	0
Spurlock, Micheal, T.B.	4	3	30	7.5	15	0
Newman, Terence, Dal.	4	1	26	6.5	13	0
McCardell, Keenan, Was.	4	2	19	4.8	9	0
Lewis, Greg, Phi.	4	1	4	1.0	5	0
Furrey, Mike, Det.	3	4	30	10.0	13	0
Galloway, Joey, T.B.	3	0	14	4.7	10	0
Bush, Reggie, N.O.	3	0	12	4.0	10	0
Thrash, James, Was.	2	1	71	35.5	62	0
Reed, J.R., Phi.	2	0	8	4.0	8	0
Smith, Steve, Car.	2	0	7	3.5	6	0
Looker, Dane, St.L	2	0	5	2.5	5	0
* Bradshaw, Ahmad, NY-G	1	0	1	1.0	1	0
Harris, Antoine, Atl.	1	0	1	1.0	1	0
Bush, Jarrett, G.B.	1	0	0	0.0	0	0
Craft, Jason, N.O.	1	0	0	0.0	0	0
* Graham, Nick, Phi.	1	0	0	0.0	0	0
Hagans, Marques, St.L	1	1	0	0.0	0	0
Idonije, Israel, Chi.	1	0	0	0.0	0	0
McGowan, Brandon, Chi.	1	0	0	0.0	0	0
David, Jason, N.O.	0	1	0	—	—	0

t = Touchdown
Leader based on average return, minimum 20 returns
* Player that was a rookie in 2007

AMERICAN FOOTBALL CONFERENCE—PUNT RETURNS

	No	FC	Yards	Avg	Long	TD
Buffalo	31	4	476	15.4	74t	1
Cleveland	30	10	405	13.5	76t	1
Indianapolis	25	14	280	11.2	90t	1
Jacksonville	32	14	324	10.1	56	0
Baltimore	35	12	338	9.7	75t	2
Miami	24	15	230	9.6	87t	1
New England	33	18	311	9.4	35	0
N.Y. Jets	20	14	183	9.2	33	0
Denver	23	17	209	9.1	80t	1
San Diego	32	8	281	8.8	45t	1
Tennessee	42	16	367	8.7	39	0
Houston	33	8	287	8.7	74	0
Kansas City	40	14	302	7.6	22	0
Pittsburgh	39	9	238	6.1	49	0
Oakland	38	16	209	5.5	54	0
Cincinnati	27	18	131	4.9	19	0
AFC Total	504	207	4571	9.1	90t	8
AFC Average	31.5	12.9	285.7	9.1	—	0.5

NATIONAL FOOTBALL CONFERENCE—PUNT RETURNS

	No	FC	Yards	Avg	Long	TD
Chicago	44	6	651	14.8	89t	4
St. Louis	30	14	357	11.9	85t	1
Seattle	58	8	658	11.3	94t	1
Green Bay	48	5	492	10.3	94t	2
Arizona	42	6	395	9.4	73t	1
Dallas	26	21	227	8.7	49	0
San Francisco	56	9	483	8.6	51	0
Carolina	32	19	269	8.4	34	0
Minnesota	29	19	242	8.3	42	0
Detroit	18	20	148	8.2	18	0
New Orleans	24	16	197	8.2	48	0
Philadelphia	42	12	340	8.1	64	0
Washington	40	10	299	7.5	62	0
N.Y. Giants	43	18	319	7.4	27	0
Tampa Bay	50	13	334	6.7	35	0
Atlanta	36	18	228	6.3	23	0
NFC Total	618	214	5639	9.1	94t	9
NFC Average	38.6	13.4	352.4	9.1	—	0.6
League Total	1122	421	10210	—	94t	17
League Average	35.1	13.2	319.1	9.1	—	0.5

FUMBLES

MOST FUMBLES
NFC:	17	Jon Kitna, Detroit
AFC:	11	Jay Cutler, Denver
	11	Josh McCown, Oakland
	11	Philip Rivers, San Diego

MOST FUMBLES, GAME
NFC:	5	Eli Manning, N.Y. Giants at Buffalo, December 23
AFC:	4	Daunte Culpepper, Oakland at Tennessee, October 28
	4	Cleo Lemon, Miami at Buffalo, December 9

OWN FUMBLES RECOVERED
| AFC: | 7 | Vince Young, Tennessee |
| NFC: | 7 | Jon Kitna, Detroit |

OWN FUMBLES RECOVERED, GAME
| AFC: | 3 | Cleo Lemon, Miami at Buffalo, December 9 (0 yards, 0 TD) |
| NFC: | 3 | Eli Manning, N.Y. Giants at Buffalo, December 23 (0 yards, 0 TD) |

OPPONENTS' FUMBLES RECOVERED
NFC:	4	Chad Greenway, Minnesota
	4	Jovan Haye, Tampa Bay
AFC:	3	Leigh Bodden, Cleveland
	3	C.C. Brown, Houston
	3	Elvis Dumervil, Denver
	3	James Harrison, Pittsburgh
	3	DeMeco Ryans, Houston
	3	Jason Taylor, Miami
	3	Ty Warren, New England

OPPONENTS' FUMBLES RECOVERED, GAME
AFC:	2	Landon Johnson, Cincinnati vs. Baltimore, September 10 (34 yards, 1 TD)
	2	DeMeco Ryans, Houston vs. Tennessee, October 21 (26 yards, 1 TD)
	2	Ty Warren, New England vs. Washington, October 28 (0 yards, 0 TD)
	2	Elvis Dumervil, Denver vs. Minnesota, December 30 (0 yards, 0 TD) - (OT)
NFC:	2	Osi Umenyiora, N.Y. Giants vs. San Francisco, October 21 (75 yards, 1 TD)
	2 *	Tanard Jackson, Tampa Bay vs. Washington, November 25 (16 yards, 0 TD)
	2	Jovan Haye, Tampa Bay at Houston, December 9 (9 yards, 0 TD)
	2	E.J. Henderson, Minnesota at San Francisco, December 9 (16 yards, 0 TD)

YARDS
| AFC: | 77 | Daryl Smith, Jacksonville |
| NFC: | 75 | Osi Umenyiora, N.Y. Giants |

LONGEST
| AFC: | 77 | Daryl Smith, Jacksonville vs. Houston, October 14 - TD |
| NFC: | 75 | Osi Umenyiora, N.Y. Giants vs. San Francisco, October 21 - TD |

AFC—TOUCHDOWNS ON FUMBLE RECOVERIES
Brackenridge, Tyron, K.C.	1
Brackett, Gary, Ind.	1
Colvin, Rosevelt, N.E.	1
Cromartie, Antonio, S.D.	1
Crowder, Tim, Den.	1
Gay, Randall, N.E.	1
Hobbs, Ellis, N.E.	1
Johnson, Landon, Cin.	1
Lehan, Michael, Mia.	1
Ndukwe, Nedu, Cin.	1
Rhodes, Kerry, NYJ	1
Ryans, DeMeco, Hou.	1
Siler, Brandon, S.D.	1
Smith, Daryl, Jac.	1
Tucker, Jyles, S.D.	1
Walter, Kevin, Hou.	1
Webster, Nate, Den.	1
Williams, Mario, Hou.	1
Wilson, George, Buf.	1

NFC—TOUCHDOWNS ON FUMBLE RECOVERIES
Curtis, Kevin, Phi.	2
Banta-Cain, Tully, S.F.	1
Barber, Ronde, T.B.	1
Blackmon, Will, G.B.	1
David, Jason, N.O.	1
Edwards, Ray, Min.	1
Griffin, Cedric, Min.	1
Hall, DeAngelo, Atl.	1
Hatcher, Jason, Dal.	1
Hill, Leroy, Sea.	1
Lucas, Ken, Car.	1
Mitchell, Kawika, NY-G	1
Thomas, Pierre, N.O.	1
Umenyiora, Osi, NY-G	1
Wells, Reggie, Ariz	1
White, Dewayne, Det.	1
White, Tracy, G.B.	1
Woodson, Charles, G.B.	1

AFC FUMBLES—INDIVIDUAL
	Fum	Own Rec	Opp Rec	Yards	Tot Rec
Abdullah, Hamza, Den.	0	0	1	0	1
Adams, Mike, Cle.	0	0	1	0	1
Amano, Eugene, Ten.	0	1	0	0	1
Anderson, Charlie, Hou.	0	0	1	0	1
Anderson, David, Hou.	1	0	0	0	0
Anderson, Derek, Cle.	5	1	0	-3	1
Anderson, Mike, Bal.	2	0	0	0	0
Asomugha, Nnamdi, Oak.	1	0	0	0	0
Baker, Chris, NYJ	1	1	0	0	1
* Beck, John, Mia.	7	0	0	-17	0
Bell, Jacob, Ten.	1	0	0	0	0
Bell, Mike, Den.	1	0	0	0	0
Bennett, Michael, K.C.	2	0	0	0	0
Bodden, Leigh, Cle.	1	0	3	0	3
Boiman, Rocky, Ind.	0	0	1	5	1
Boller, Kyle, Bal.	5	0	0	0	0
Booker, Marty, Mia.	1	0	0	0	0
Boone, Alfonso, K.C.	0	0	1	0	1
* Brackenridge, Tyron, K.C.	0	0	1	50	1
Brackett, Gary, Ind.	0	0	1	0	1
Brady, Tom, N.E.	6	1	0	0	1
Brayton, Tyler, Oak.	0	0	1	0	1
Brock, Raheem, Ind.	0	0	2	0	2
Brown, C.C., Hou.	0	0	3	19	3
Brown, Chris, Ten.	1	0	0	0	0
Brown, Jason, Bal.	0	1	0	0	1

	Fum	Own Rec	Opp Rec	Yards	Tot Rec
Brown, Troy, N.E.	1	0	0	0	0
* Bryan, Courtney, Mia.	0	0	1	0	1
Bulluck, Keith, Ten.	1	0	1	2	1
Burgess, Derrick, Oak.	0	0	1	0	1
Camarillo, Greg, Mia.	0	1	0	0	1
Carlisle, Cooper, Oak.	0	2	0	0	2
Cassel, Matt, N.E.	1	1	0	-9	1
Chambers, Chris, S.D.	1	0	0	0	0
Chatman, Jesse, Mia.	1	0	0	0	0
Clark, Brian, Den.	2	0	0	0	0
Clark, Dallas, Ind.	0	1	0	0	1
Clarke, Adrien, NYJ	0	1	0	0	1
Clemens, Kellen, NYJ	4	1	0	-1	1
Clement, Anthony, NYJ	0	1	0	0	1
Clemons, Chris, Oak.	0	0	1	0	1
Cochran, Earl, Hou.	0	0	1	0	1
* Coe, Michael, Ind.	0	0	1	0	1
Collins, Kerry, Ten.	1	0	0	0	0
Colvin, Rosevelt, N.E.	0	0	2	16	2
Cooper, Jarrod, Oak.	0	0	1	0	1
Cooper, Stephen, S.D.	0	0	2	-1	2
Cotchery, Jerricho, NYJ	1	1	0	0	1
Cox, Curome, Den.	0	0	1	0	1
Cribbs, Josh, Cle.	5	2	0	0	2
Cromartie, Antonio, S.D.	0	0	2	2	2
* Crowder, Tim, Den.	0	0	2	50	2
Crowell, Angelo, Buf.	0	0	1	0	1
Croyle, Brodie, K.C.	4	1	0	0	1
Culpepper, Daunte, Oak.	9	4	0	-7	4
Cutler, Jay, Den.	11	3	0	-31	3
Daniels, Owen, Hou.	4	1	0	0	1
Darling, Devard, Bal.	0	0	1	0	1
Davenport, Najeh, Pit.	1	1	0	0	1
Davis, Andre, Hou.	1	0	1	1	1
Davis, Carey, Pit.	0	0	1	0	1
* Davis, Chris, Ten.	6	2	0	0	2
* Davis, Craig, S.D.	1	0	0	0	0
* Dawson, Keyunta, Ind.	0	0	2	10	2
Dayne, Ron, Hou.	1	1	0	0	1
Demps, Will, Hou.	0	0	2	3	2
Denney, Ryan, Buf.	0	0	1	0	1
Dielman, Kris, S.D.	0	1	0	0	1
DiGiorgio, John, Buf.	0	0	2	0	2
Dobbins, Tim, S.D.	0	1	1	0	2
Dockery, Derrick, Buf.	0	1	0	0	1
Drummond, Eddie, K.C.	2	0	0	0	0
Dumervil, Elvis, Den.	0	0	3	0	3
Dwight, Tim, Oak.	2	1	0	0	1
Echemandu, Adimchinobe, Hou.	1	0	0	0	0
Edwards, Braylon, Cle.	3	0	0	0	0
Edwards, Donnie, K.C.	0	0	1	0	1
Edwards, Ron, K.C.	0	0	1	0	1
* Edwards, Trent, Buf.	4	1	0	-6	1
Ellis, Shaun, NYJ	0	0	1	6	1
Faggins, Demarcus, Hou.	0	0	1	0	1
Faneca, Alan, Pit.	0	1	0	0	1
Fanene, Jonathan, Cin.	0	0	1	0	1
Fargas, Justin, Oak.	3	0	0	0	0
Faulk, Kevin, N.E.	1	0	0	0	0
Ferguson, D'Brickashaw, NYJ	0	1	0	0	1
Ferguson, Nick, Den.	0	1	1	0	2
Fifita, Steve, Mia.	1	0	0	0	0
* Figurs, Yamon, Bal.	4	2	0	0	2
Florence, Drayton, S.D.	0	0	1	7	1
Flynn, Mike, Bal.	0	1	0	0	1
Fowler, Melvin, Buf.	0	1	0	0	1
Fraley, Hank, Cle.	0	1	0	0	1
Fraser, Simon, Cle.	0	0	1	0	1
Frazier, Andre, Pit.	0	1	0	0	1
Fudge, Jamaal, Jac.	0	0	1	0	1
Fuller, Vincent, Ten.	0	0	1	0	1
Gado, Samkon, Hou.	1	0	0	0	0
Gage, Justin, Ten.	1	1	1	0	2
Garrard, David, Jac.	3	0	0	0	0
Gay, Randall, N.E.	0	0	1	15	1
* Gay, William, Pit.	1	0	1	0	1
Geathers, Robert, Cin.	0	0	1	0	1
* Ginn, Ted Jr., Mia.	3	2	0	-9	2
Goff, Mike, S.D.	0	1	0	0	1
Gold, Ian, Den.	0	0	2	0	2
Gray, Quinn, Jac.	2	1	0	0	1
Green, Jarvis, N.E.	0	0	1	0	1
Green, Trent, Mia.	2	1	0	-15	1
Gregg, Kelly, Bal.	0	0	1	4	1
Greisen, Nick, Bal.	0	1	0	0	1
* Griffin, Michael, Ten.	1	0	0	0	0
Grove, Jake, Oak.	0	1	0	0	1
* Guzman, Ramon, Ind.	0	1	1	13	2
Hagan, Derek, Mia.	0	1	0	0	1
Haggans, Clark, Pit.	0	0	1	0	1
Hagler, Tyjuan, Ind.	0	0	1	0	1
Hall, Andre, Den.	1	2	0	0	2
Harper, Nick, Ten.	0	1	1	0	2
* Harris, David, NYJ	0	0	1	0	1
* Harris, Gilbert, K.C.	1	0	0	0	0
Harris, Marques, S.D.	0	0	1	1	1
* Harris, Steven, Den.	0	0	1	0	1
Harrison, James, Pit.	0	0	3	0	3
Hart, Clinton, S.D.	0	0	1	0	1
Hartsock, Ben, Ten.	0	1	0	0	1
Hawkins, Brent, Jac.	1	0	1	0	1
Hayden, Kelvin, Ind.	1	0	1	0	1
Henry, Travis, Den.	3	1	0	0	1
* Higgins, Johnnie Lee, Oak.	4	0	0	0	0
Hill, Reynaldo, Ten.	0	0	1	0	1
Hixon, Domenik, Den.	1	0	0	0	0
Hobbs, Ellis, N.E.	1	0	1	35	1
Hobson, Victor, NYJ	0	0	2	0	2
Holly, Daven, Cle.	0	0	1	3	1
Holmes, Santonio, Pit.	2	0	0	0	0
Holt, Glenn, Cin.	3	1	0	0	1
Hope, Chris, Ten.	0	0	1	0	1
Houshmandzadeh, T.J., Cin.	2	0	0	0	0
Howard, Thomas, Oak.	0	1	0	0	1
Huard, Damon, K.C.	5	1	0	0	1
Huff, Michael, Oak.	0	1	0	0	1
Ivy, Corey, Bal.	0	0	1	0	1
Iwuh, Brian, Jac.	0	0	1	0	1
Jackson, Dexter, Cin.	0	0	2	19	2
Jackson, D'Qwell, Cle.	0	0	1	0	1
Jackson, Fred, Buf.	0	2	0	0	2
Jackson, Marlin, Ind.	0	0	2	21	2
Jammer, Quentin, S.D.	0	0	2	0	2
Jeanty, Rashad, Cin.	0	0	2	0	2
Jenkins, Justin, Buf.	0	0	1	0	1
Johnson, Andre, Hou.	1	0	0	0	0
Johnson, Chad, Cin.	2	0	0	0	0
Johnson, Charlie, Ind.	0	2	0	0	2
Johnson, Landon, Cin.	0	0	2	34	2
Johnson, Larry, K.C.	1	0	0	0	0
Johnson, Rudi, Cin.	3	0	0	0	0
Jones, Brandon, Ten.	1	0	0	0	0
* Jones, Jacoby, Hou.	2	1	0	5	1
Jones, Thomas, NYJ	2	2	0	0	2
Jones-Drew, Maurice, Jac.	2	0	0	0	0
Jordan, LaMont, Oak.	0	1	0	4	1

	Fum	Own Rec	Opp Rec	Yards	Tot Rec		Fum	Own Rec	Opp Rec	Yards	Tot Rec
Keith, Kenton, Ind.	1	0	0	0	0	Pittman, David, Bal.	1	0	0	0	0
Kelsay, Chris, Buf.	0	0	1	0	1	Pitts, Chester, Hou.	0	1	0	0	1
Kennison, Eddie, K.C.	1	1	0	0	1	* Podlesh, Adam, Jac.	1	0	0	-12	0
LaBoy, Travis, Ten.	0	0	1	0	1	Polamalu, Troy, Pit.	0	0	1	13	1
Leach, Vonta, Hou.	2	0	0	0	0	Pope, Derrick, Mia.	0	0	1	0	1
Lehan, Michael, Mia.	0	0	1	43	1	Ramsey, Patrick, Den.	2	1	0	0	1
Lemon, Cleo, Mia.	7	3	0	-1	3	Reed, Ed, Bal.	2	0	1	6	1
Leonhard, Jim, Buf.	1	0	0	0	0	Reid, Darrell, Ind.	0	0	2	0	2
Lepsis, Matt, Den.	0	2	0	0	2	Reid, Willie, Pit.	1	0	0	0	0
Lewis, Jamal, Cle.	4	1	0	0	1	* Revis, Darrelle, NYJ	0	1	0	0	1
Lewis, Ray, Bal.	0	0	1	0	1	Rhodes, Dominic, Oak.	2	1	0	0	1
Losman, J.P., Buf.	5	1	0	-2	1	Rhodes, Kerry, NYJ	0	0	1	11	1
* Lynch, Marshawn, Buf.	2	0	0	0	0	Rivers, Philip, S.D.	11	3	0	-4	3
Madison, Anthony, Pit.	0	1	0	0	1	Robertson, Dewayne, NYJ	0	0	1	0	1
Mangold, Nick, NYJ	1	0	0	-1	0	Roethlisberger, Ben, Pit.	9	4	0	-16	4
Manning, Peyton, Ind.	6	3	0	0	3	Rosenfels, Sage, Hou.	4	0	0	-2	0
Marshall, Brandon, Den.	3	3	0	0	3	Ross, Cory, Bal.	2	1	0	0	1
Martin, Derrick, Bal.	0	0	1	0	1	Rossum, Allen, Pit.	3	0	0	0	0
Martinez, Glenn, Den.	3	1	0	0	1	Royal, Robert, Buf.	2	0	0	0	0
Mason, Derrick, Bal.	1	0	0	0	0	Rucker, Frostee, Cin.	0	0	1	0	1
Mathis, Robert, Ind.	0	0	1	0	1	Rushing, T.J., Ind.	1	0	0	0	0
* Mauia, Reagan, Mia.	1	0	0	0	0	* Russell, JaMarcus, Oak.	4	1	0	-8	1
Mawae, Kevin, Ten.	2	0	0	-4	0	Ryans, DeMeco, Hou.	0	0	3	26	3
McCargo, John, Buf.	0	0	1	0	1	Sanders, Bob, Ind.	0	1	0	25	1
* McClain, Le'Ron, Bal.	1	1	0	0	1	Sanders, James, N.E.	0	0	1	0	1
McCown, Josh, Oak.	11	3	0	0	3	Sapp, Benny, K.C.	0	0	1	0	1
McCree, Marlon, S.D.	0	0	1	2	1	Sapp, Warren, Oak.	0	0	1	0	1
McFadden, Bryant, Pit.	0	0	1	0	1	* Satele, Samson, Mia.	1	0	0	-2	0
McGahee, Willis, Bal.	4	1	0	-10	1	Scaife, Bo, Ten.	2	0	0	0	0
McGinest, Willie, Cle.	0	0	1	0	1	Scanlon, Rich, Ten.	0	0	2	0	2
McGraw, Jon, K.C.	0	0	1	0	1	Schaub, Matt, Hou.	7	2	0	-6	2
McIntosh, Damion, K.C.	0	1	0	0	1	Scheffler, Tony, Den.	1	0	0	0	0
McMillan, David, Cle.	0	0	1	0	1	Schobel, Aaron, Buf.	0	0	1	0	1
McNair, Steve, Bal.	8	0	0	-3	0	Sensabaugh, Gerald, Jac.	0	0	1	0	1
McQuistan, Paul, Oak.	0	0	1	0	1	Shelton, L.J., Mia.	0	0	1	0	1
Merriman, Shawne, S.D.	0	0	2	0	2	* Siler, Brandon, S.D.	0	1	1	23	2
Miller, Heath, Pit.	0	1	0	0	1	Simmons, Kendall, Pit.	0	1	0	0	1
Miller, Justin, NYJ	1	0	0	0	0	Sims, Barry, Oak.	0	4	0	0	4
* Miller, Zach, Oak.	2	2	1	0	3	Smith, Aaron, Pit.	0	0	2	0	2
Moore, Brandon, NYJ	0	1	0	0	1	Smith, Anthony, Pit.	0	0	1	0	1
Moorman, Brian, Buf.	1	1	0	0	1	Smith, Brad, NYJ	1	0	0	-9	0
Morrison, Kirk, Oak.	1	0	1	0	1	Smith, Daryl, Jac.	0	0	2	77	2
Moss, Randy, N.E.	0	2	0	0	2	Smith, Eric, NYJ	0	1	0	0	1
Naeole, Chris, Jac.	0	1	0	2	1	Smith, Musa, Bal.	1	0	0	0	0
* Ndukwe, Nedu, Cin.	0	0	1	54	1	* Smith, Troy, Bal.	3	1	0	-3	1
Neal, Lorenzo, S.D.	1	0	0	0	0	Spicer, Paul, Jac.	0	0	1	0	1
Neill, Ryan, Buf.	2	0	0	-38	0	Spragan, Donnie, Mia.	0	0	1	0	1
* Nelson, Reggie, Jac.	1	0	0	0	0	Sproles, Darren, S.D.	1	0	0	0	0
Newberry, Jeremy, Oak.	2	1	0	-6	1	Starks, Randy, Ten.	0	0	1	0	1
Nickey, Donnie, Ten.	0	0	1	0	1	Stepanovich, Alex, Cin.	1	0	0	-2	0
* Nkang, Chad, Jac.	1	0	0	0	0	Stewart, David, Ten.	0	1	0	0	1
Norman, Dennis, Jac.	0	1	0	0	1	Stroud, Marcus, Jac.	0	0	1	0	1
Northcutt, Dennis, Jac.	1	1	0	0	1	Surtain, Patrick, K.C.	0	0	1	0	1
O'Neal, Deltha, Cin.	0	0	1	0	1	Sypniewski, Quinn, Bal.	1	0	0	0	0
Osgood, Kassim, S.D.	0	0	1	0	1	Taylor, Fred, Jac.	2	0	0	0	0
Owens, Chad, Jac.	1	0	0	0	0	Taylor, Ike, Pit.	0	0	1	0	1
Page, Jarrad, K.C.	0	0	1	0	1	Taylor, Jason, Mia.	0	0	3	0	3
Palmer, Carson, Cin.	5	2	0	-1	2	Thomas, Anthony, Buf.	0	2	0	0	2
Parker, Samie, K.C.	1	1	0	0	1	* Thomas, Joe, Cle.	0	1	0	0	1
Parker, Willie, Pit.	4	1	0	0	1	* Thomas, Marcus, Den.	0	0	1	0	1
Parrish, Roscoe, Buf.	1	1	0	0	1	Thornton, David, Ten.	0	0	1	0	1
Peek, Antwan, Cle.	0	0	1	0	1	Thornton, John, Cin.	0	0	1	0	1
Peko, Domata, Cin.	0	0	1	0	1	* Timmons, Lawrence, Pit.	0	0	2	5	2
Pennington, Chad, NYJ	5	2	0	-3	2	Tripplett, Larry, Buf.	0	0	1	0	1
Perry, Tab, Cin.	1	0	0	0	0	* Tucker, Jyles, S.D.	0	0	1	0	1
Peters, Jason, Buf.	0	1	0	0	1	Tucker, Ryan, Cle.	0	1	0	0	1
Peterson, Mike, Jac.	0	0	1	0	1	Turley, Kyle, K.C.	0	1	0	0	1
Pittman, Bryan, Hou.	1	0	0	-33	0	Turner, Michael, S.D.	1	0	0	0	0

	Fum	Own Rec	Opp Rec	Yards	Tot Rec
Utecht, Ben, Ind.	2	0	0	0	0
Volek, Billy, S.D.	1	0	0	-2	0
Walter, Kevin, Hou.	0	1	1	0	2
Warren, Ty, N.E.	0	0	3	0	3
Washington, Leon, NYJ	4	1	0	0	1
Watson, Benjamin, N.E.	1	0	1	0	1
Watson, Kenny, Cin.	3	3	0	0	3
Wayne, Reggie, Ind.	3	1	0	0	1
Webb, Jeff, K.C.	2	1	0	0	1
Webster, Nate, Den.	0	0	1	17	1
Welker, Wes, N.E.	3	2	0	0	2
* Wendling, John, Buf.	0	0	1	0	1
White, LenDale, Ten.	5	0	0	0	0
* White, Marvin, Cin.	0	0	1	0	1
Whitworth, Andrew, Cin.	0	1	0	0	1
Wiegmann, Casey, K.C.	1	0	0	-9	0
Wilfork, Vince, N.E.	0	0	1	0	1
Wilhelm, Matt, S.D.	0	0	1	0	1
Williams, Bobbie, Cin.	0	2	0	0	2
Williams, Ricky, Mia.	1	0	0	0	0
Williams, D.J., Den.	0	0	2	1	2
Williams, Jamal, S.D.	0	0	1	0	1
Williams, Kyle, Buf.	0	0	1	0	1
Williams, Madieu, Cin.	0	0	1	2	1
Williams, Mario, Hou.	0	0	1	38	1
Williams, Mike, Oak.	1	0	0	0	0
Williams, Reggie, Jac.	3	0	0	0	0
Wilson, Eugene, N.E.	0	0	1	4	1
Wilson, George, Buf.	1	0	1	20	1
Wilson, Kris, K.C.	2	0	0	0	0
Winslow, Kellen, Cle.	2	0	0	0	0
* Wright, Dwayne, Buf.	1	0	0	0	0
Wright, Jason, Cle.	1	0	0	0	0
Wright, Rodrique, Mia.	0	0	1	0	1
* Young, Selvin, Den.	2	1	0	0	1
Young, Vince, Ten.	10	7	0	-17	7
Zastudil, Dave, Cle.	1	1	0	-11	1

Yards includes aborted plays, own recoveries and opponents' recoveries.

* Player that was a rookie in 2007

NFC FUMBLES—INDIVIDUAL

	Fum	Own Rec	Opp Rec	Yards	Tot Rec
Adams, Anthony, Chi.	0	0	1	0	1
Adams, Flozell, Dal.	0	2	0	0	2
Adeyanju, Victor, St.L	0	0	1	24	1
* Alexander, Gerald, Det.	0	0	2	0	2
Alexander, Shaun, Sea.	2	1	0	0	1
Allen, Will, T.B.	0	1	1	0	2
* Allison, Aundrae, Min.	2	0	0	0	0
Andrews, Shawn, Phi.	0	1	0	0	1
Archuleta, Adam, Chi.	0	0	1	0	1
* Atkins, Baraka, Sea.	0	0	1	0	1
Atogwe, O.J., St.L	0	0	1	0	1
Ayanbadejo, Brendon, Chi.	0	1	0	-3	1
Babineaux, Jonathan, Atl.	1	0	1	11	1
Babineaux, Jordan, Sea.	0	0	1	0	1
Backus, Jeff, Det.	0	1	0	0	1
Banta-Cain, Tully, S.F.	0	0	1	0	1
Barber, Ronde, T.B.	1	0	2	33	2
Barber, Marion, Dal.	3	1	1	0	2
Barnett, Nick, G.B.	0	0	1	0	1
Bartell, Ronald, St.L	0	0	1	7	1
Bashir, Idrees, Det.	0	0	2	0	2

	Fum	Own Rec	Opp Rec	Yards	Tot Rec
Bassey, Eric, St.L	0	0	1	0	1
Batiste, D'Anthony, Atl.	0	1	0	0	1
Battle, Arnaz, S.F.	3	0	0	0	0
* Beason, Jon, Car.	0	0	1	2	1
Bell, Tatum, Det.	1	0	0	0	0
Bennett, Drew, St.L	1	1	0	0	1
Benson, Cedric, Chi.	3	2	0	0	2
Berger, Mitch, Ariz	1	1	0	-15	1
Berlin, Brock, St.L	2	0	0	-3	0
Bernard, Rocky, Sea.	0	0	2	0	2
Berrian, Bernard, Chi.	1	1	0	0	1
Berry, Bertrand, Ariz	0	0	1	0	1
Betts, Ladell, Was.	1	0	0	0	0
Birk, Matt, Min.	1	0	0	-16	0
Blackburn, Chase, NY-G	0	0	1	0	1
Blackmon, Will, G.B.	0	0	1	0	1
Blackstock, Darryl, Ariz	0	0	1	34	1
* Blalock, Justin, Atl.	0	1	0	0	1
Blue, Greg, Det.	0	0	1	0	1
Boldin, Anquan, Ariz	2	0	0	0	0
Bollinger, Brooks, Min.	1	0	0	0	0
Bradley, Jon, Det.	1	0	0	0	0
* Bradshaw, Ahmad, NY-G	2	1	0	0	1
Brees, Drew, N.O.	9	0	0	-6	0
Briggs, Lance, Chi.	0	0	1	0	1
Brooking, Keith, Atl.	0	0	1	2	1
Brown, Alex, Chi.	0	0	2	0	2
* Brown, Courtney, Dal.	0	0	1	0	1
Brown, Elton, Ariz	0	1	0	0	1
Brown, Mike, Chi.	0	0	1	0	1
Brown, Ralph, Ariz	0	0	1	0	1
Brown, Reggie, Phi.	1	0	0	0	0
Buchanon, Phillip, T.B.	1	0	0	0	0
Buckhalter, Correll, Phi.	1	0	0	0	0
Bulger, Marc, St.L	6	1	0	-3	1
Bunkley, Brodrick, Phi.	0	0	1	0	1
Burleson, Nate, Sea.	3	0	0	0	0
Bush, Jarrett, G.B.	1	0	1	0	1
Bush, Reggie, N.O.	8	3	0	-16	3
Butler, James, NY-G	0	0	1	4	1
Campbell, Jason, Was.	13	4	0	-9	4
Canty, Chris, Dal.	0	0	1	0	1
Carr, David, Car.	1	2	0	-6	2
* Carriker, Adam, St.L	0	0	1	0	1
Carter, Andre, Was.	0	0	1	0	1
Carter, Kevin, T.B.	0	0	1	0	1
Cartwright, Rock, Was.	0	1	0	0	1
Cason, Aveion, Det.	2	0	0	0	0
* Celek, Brent, Phi.	1	0	0	0	0
Chillar, Brandon, St.L	0	0	1	0	1
Chukwurah, Patrick, T.B.	0	0	1	0	1
Clark, Desmond, Chi.	1	0	0	0	0
Clayton, Michael, T.B.	1	0	0	0	0
Colbert, Keary, Car.	1	0	0	0	0
Cole, Trent, Phi.	0	0	1	0	1
Collins, Todd, Was.	4	1	0	-2	1
Colombo, Marc, Dal.	0	1	0	0	1
Colston, Marques, N.O.	1	0	0	0	0
Cooley, Chris, Was.	1	2	0	0	2
Crayton, Patrick, Dal.	2	1	0	0	1
Crocker, Chris, Atl.	0	0	1	0	1
Curtis, Kevin, Phi.	0	2	0	0	2
Daniels, Phillip, Was.	0	0	2	0	2
David, Jason, N.O.	0	0	1	55	1
Davis, Chauncey, Atl.	0	0	1	0	1
Davis, Thomas, Car.	0	0	1	0	1
Davis, Vernon, S.F.	1	1	0	0	1

	Fum	Own Rec	Opp Rec	Yards	Tot Rec		Fum	Own Rec	Opp Rec	Yards	Tot Rec
Delhomme, Jake, Car.	1	1	0	0	1	Hudson, Marcus, S.F.	0	1	1	-1	2
DeVries, Jared, Det.	0	0	3	0	3	* Hunt, Tony, Phi.	0	1	0	0	1
Diggs, Na'il, Car.	0	1	0	0	1	Hutchinson, Steve, Min.	0	2	0	1	2
Dilfer, Trent, S.F.	8	6	0	-13	6	Idonije, Israel, Chi.	0	0	1	0	1
Dockery, Kevin, NY-G	0	0	1	0	1	* Irons, David, Atl.	0	0	1	4	1
Dockett, Darnell, Ariz	0	0	2	0	2	Jackson, Darrell, S.F.	1	2	0	0	2
Driver, Donald, G.B.	1	0	0	0	0	Jackson, Jamaal, Phi.	1	0	0	-7	0
Droughns, Reuben, NY-G	1	1	0	0	1	Jackson, Steven, St.L	5	2	0	0	2
Duckett, T.J., Det.	1	1	0	0	1	* Jackson, Tanard, T.B.	0	1	2	16	3
Dugan, Jeff, Min.	1	0	0	0	0	Jackson, Tarvaris, Min.	5	0	0	-12	0
Dunn, Warrick, Atl.	2	2	0	0	2	Jacobs, Brandon, NY-G	5	0	0	0	0
Edwards, Kalimba, Det.	0	0	1	0	1	James, Bradie, Dal.	0	0	3	1	3
Edwards, Ray, Min.	0	0	1	9	1	James, Edgerrin, Ariz	5	1	0	0	1
Engram, Bobby, Sea.	1	1	0	0	1	Jennings, Adam, Atl.	1	0	0	0	0
Evans, Jahri, N.O.	0	1	0	0	1	Jennings, Greg, G.B.	1	1	0	0	1
Farwell, Heath, Min.	0	1	0	0	1	Jennings, Jonas, S.F.	0	1	0	0	1
Favre, Brett, G.B.	9	4	0	-18	4	Jennings, Kelly, Sea.	0	0	2	13	2
Feeley, A.J., Phi.	1	1	0	0	1	Johnson, Al, Ariz	1	1	0	-27	1
Fitzgerald, Larry, Ariz	3	0	0	0	0	Johnson, Bryant, Ariz	0	1	0	0	1
Fletcher, London, Was.	0	0	1	6	1	* Johnson, Calvin, Det.	1	0	0	0	0
Forney, Kynan, Atl.	0	1	0	0	1	Johnson, Eric, N.O.	1	3	0	16	3
Foster, DeShaun, Car.	7	1	0	0	1	Johnson, Spencer, Min.	0	0	2	0	2
Foster, George, Det.	0	1	0	0	1	Johnson, Tank, Dal.	0	0	1	0	1
Frerotte, Gus, St.L	3	2	0	-4	2	Jolly, Johnny, G.B.	0	0	1	19	1
Frost, Derrick, Was.	1	1	0	-8	1	* Jones, James, G.B.	3	0	0	0	0
Fujita, Scott, N.O.	0	0	2	0	2	Jones, Julius, Dal.	0	1	0	0	1
Gamble, Chris, Car.	0	0	1	0	1	Jones, Kevin, Det.	2	1	0	0	1
Gandy, Mike, Ariz	0	1	0	0	1	June, Cato, T.B.	1	0	0	4	0
Garcia, Jeff, T.B.	4	2	0	-11	2	Justice, Winston, Phi.	0	1	0	0	1
Garza, Roberto, Chi.	0	1	0	0	1	Kaesviharn, Kevin, N.O.	0	1	0	2	1
Goings, Nick, Car.	1	0	0	0	0	* Kalil, Ryan, Car.	1	0	0	-24	0
Golston, Kedric, Was.	0	0	1	0	1	Kampman, Aaron, G.B.	0	0	1	0	1
Gore, Frank, S.F.	4	1	0	0	1	Kearse, Jevon, Phi.	0	0	1	0	1
Graham, Earnest, T.B.	1	0	0	0	0	Kelly, Brian, T.B.	0	0	1	-2	1
* Graham, Nick, Phi.	1	1	0	0	1	Kennedy, Kenoy, Det.	0	0	1	0	1
Grant, Deon, Sea.	0	0	1	0	1	King, Jeff, Car.	2	1	0	0	1
Grant, Ryan, G.B.	1	1	0	0	1	Kitna, Jon, Det.	17	7	0	-3	7
Greenway, Chad, Min.	1	0	4	0	4	Koenen, Michael, Atl.	1	0	0	-1	0
Griese, Brian, Chi.	6	2	0	-4	2	* Kolb, Kevin, Phi.	1	0	0	0	0
Griffin, Cedric, Min.	1	1	1	50	2	Kosier, Kyle, Dal.	0	2	0	0	2
Gross, Jordan, Car.	0	1	0	0	1	Kreutz, Olin, Chi.	1	1	0	-3	1
Grossman, Rex, Chi.	6	1	0	-1	1	Lake, Antwan, N.O.	0	0	1	0	1
Gurode, Andre, Dal.	3	1	0	0	1	* Landry, LaRon, Was.	0	1	1	15	2
Hagans, Marques, St.L	2	0	0	0	0	Leber, Ben, Min.	0	0	1	10	1
Hall, Dante, St.L	2	1	0	0	1	Lee, Donald, G.B.	1	0	0	0	0
Hall, DeAngelo, Atl.	0	0	1	56	1	Leftwich, Byron, Atl.	6	0	0	-11	0
* Hall, Korey, G.B.	0	1	0	0	1	Lelie, Ashley, S.F.	1	1	0	0	1
Hanson, Joselio, Phi.	0	0	1	0	1	Lewis, Alex, Det.	0	0	1	0	1
Harris, Chris, Car.	1	0	3	2	3	Lewis, Damione, Car.	0	0	1	0	1
Hartwig, Justin, Car.	1	1	0	-13	1	Lewis, Greg, Phi.	2	0	0	0	0
Hasselbeck, Matt, Sea.	9	3	0	-8	3	Lewis, Michael L., S.F.	2	0	0	0	0
Hatcher, Jason, Dal.	0	0	1	29	1	Lewis, Michael M., S.F.	0	0	1	0	1
Hawk, A.J., G.B.	0	0	1	0	1	Locklear, Sean, Sea.	0	2	0	0	2
Haye, Jovan, T.B.	0	0	4	9	4	Looker, Dane, St.L	0	2	0	0	2
Heitmann, Eric, S.F.	2	0	0	-5	0	Lucas, Ken, Car.	0	0	2	43	2
Henderson, E.J., Min.	0	0	2	16	2	Madison, Sam, NY-G	0	0	1	6	1
Hester, Devin, Chi.	7	2	0	0	2	Mahe, Reno, Phi.	2	1	0	0	1
* Heyer, Stephon, Was.	0	1	0	0	1	Manning, Eli, NY-G	13	4	0	-5	4
Hicks, Maurice, S.F.	3	0	0	0	0	Manning, Ricky, Chi.	0	0	1	11	1
Hill, Leroy, Sea.	0	0	1	20	1	Marshall, Richard, Car.	0	0	2	0	2
Hill, Shaun, S.F.	3	2	0	0	2	Martin, Ruvell, G.B.	1	0	0	0	0
Hillenmeyer, Hunter, Chi.	0	0	1	0	1	Massey, Chris, St.L	0	0	1	0	1
Hilliard, Ike, T.B.	3	0	0	0	0	* Matthews, Michael, NY-G	0	1	0	0	1
Holcomb, Kelly, Min.	1	0	0	0	0	Maynard, Brad, Chi.	0	0	1	0	1
Holt, Terrence, Ariz	0	0	1	0	1	McAllister, Deuce, N.O.	1	0	0	0	0
Holt, Torry, St.L	2	2	0	0	2	* McBride, Trumaine, Chi.	0	0	1	0	1
* Houston, Chris, Atl.	0	1	0	0	1	McClure, Todd, Atl.	1	0	1	-16	1
Hovan, Chris, T.B.	0	0	1	3	1	McCown, Luke, T.B.	3	1	0	-2	1

	Fum	Own Rec	Opp Rec	Yards	Tot Rec		Fum	Own Rec	Opp Rec	Yards	Tot Rec
McDonald, Shaun, Det.	3	0	0	0	0	Shanle, Scott, N.O.	0	0	1	26	1
McGowan, Brandon, Chi.	1	0	1	0	1	Shiancoe, Visanthe, Min.	1	2	0	0	2
McIntosh, Rocky, Was.	0	0	1	0	1	Smith, Alex, S.F.	6	0	0	0	0
McIntyre, Corey, Atl.	0	0	1	0	1	Smith, Antonio, Ariz	0	0	3	10	3
McKenzie, Kareem, NY-G	0	1	0	0	1	Smith, Derek M., S.F.	0	0	1	-1	1
McKie, Jason, Chi.	1	1	0	0	1	Smith, Alex, T.B.	0	1	0	-1	1
McNabb, Donovan, Phi.	9	0	0	-5	0	Smith, L.J., Phi.	1	0	0	0	0
McQuarters, R.W., NY-G	1	1	0	0	1	Smith, Steve, Car.	1	0	0	0	0
* Mebane, Brandon, Sea.	0	1	1	0	2	Smith, Will, N.O.	0	0	3	0	3
Mikell, Quintin, Phi.	1	0	1	0	1	Snee, Chris, NY-G	0	1	0	0	1
Milligan, Hanik, St.L	0	1	0	0	1	Spencer, Chris, Sea.	1	0	0	0	0
Mitchell, Kawika, NY-G	0	0	1	17	1	Springs, Shawn, Was.	0	0	1	0	1
Moll, Tony, G.B.	0	2	0	0	2	* Staley, Joe, S.F.	0	1	0	0	1
Montgomery, Anthony, Was.	0	0	2	0	2	* Stanley, Derek, St.L	1	0	0	0	0
Moore, Lance, N.O.	2	1	1	0	2	Stanley, Montavious, Atl.	0	0	2	0	2
* Moore, Matt, Car.	2	3	0	-4	3	Stecker, Aaron, N.O.	1	1	0	0	1
Moore, Mewelde, Min.	1	0	0	0	0	Stinchcomb, Jonathan, N.O.	0	1	0	0	1
Morency, Vernand, G.B.	1	0	0	0	0	Strahan, Michael, NY-G	0	0	1	4	1
Morris, Maurice, Sea.	1	0	0	0	0	Stutz, Boone, Sea.	1	0	0	-26	0
Moss, Santana, Was.	2	0	0	0	0	Tapp, Darryl, Sea.	0	0	2	9	2
Moss, Sinorice, NY-G	1	0	0	0	0	Tauscher, Mark, G.B.	0	1	0	-5	1
Mughelli, Ovie, Atl.	0	1	0	0	1	Taylor, Chester, Min.	5	0	0	0	0
Mulitalo, Edwin, Det.	0	1	0	0	1	Taylor, Sean, Was.	1	0	0	0	0
Nall, Craig, G.B.	2	1	0	-3	1	Testaverde, Vinny, Car.	3	1	0	0	1
Navies, Hannibal, S.F.	0	0	1	0	1	* Thomas, Pierre, N.O.	0	0	1	5	1
Nesbit, Jamar, N.O.	0	1	0	0	1	Thomas, Juqua, Phi.	0	0	2	0	2
Newman, Terence, Dal.	1	0	0	0	0	Thompson, Tyson, Dal.	1	0	0	0	0
* Nicholas, Stephen, Atl.	0	0	1	0	1	Thrash, James, Was.	1	0	0	0	0
Norris, Moran, S.F.	0	1	0	0	1	Tillman, Charles, Chi.	1	0	0	0	0
Ogunleye, Adewale, Chi.	0	0	3	14	3	Udeze, Kenechi, Min.	0	0	1	37	1
Orton, Kyle, Chi.	2	2	0	-5	2	Ulbrich, Jeff, S.F.	0	1	0	0	1
O'Sullivan, J.T., Det.	3	1	0	-4	1	Umenyiora, Osi, NY-G	0	0	2	75	2
Owens, Richard, St.L	0	1	0	0	1	Urlacher, Brian, Chi.	0	0	2	0	2
Pace, Calvin, Ariz	0	0	2	4	2	Wade, Bobby, Min.	3	1	0	0	1
Patten, David, N.O.	2	0	0	0	0	Wallace, Seneca, Sea.	1	0	0	0	0
Patterson, Mike, Phi.	0	0	1	12	1	Walters, Troy, Det.	1	1	0	0	1
Peppers, Julius, Car.	0	0	2	0	2	Ward, Derrick, NY-G	2	0	0	0	0
* Peterson, Adrian, Min.	4	3	0	0	3	Warner, Kurt, Ariz	12	5	0	-28	5
Peterson, Adrian, Chi.	3	2	0	-2	2	Wells, Reggie, Ariz	0	1	0	0	1
* Peterson, Greg, T.B.	0	0	1	0	1	Wells, Scott, G.B.	2	0	0	-14	0
Peterson, Julian, Sea.	0	0	2	8	2	Westbrook, Brian, Phi.	2	0	0	0	0
Petitti, Rob, St.L	0	1	0	0	1	Whitaker, Ronyell, Min.	0	1	0	0	1
Pierce, Antonio, NY-G	0	1	1	0	2	White, Greg, T.B.	0	0	2	0	2
Pittman, Michael, T.B.	1	0	0	0	0	White, Dewayne, Det.	0	0	2	3	2
Pope, Leonard, Ariz	1	0	0	0	0	White, Roddy, Atl.	3	0	0	0	0
Portis, Clinton, Was.	6	1	0	-11	1	White, Tracy, G.B.	0	0	2	0	2
Rabach, Casey, Was.	1	0	0	-7	0	Williams, Brandon, S.F.-St.L	2	0	0	0	0
Randle El, Antwaan, Was.	3	2	0	0	2	Williams, Cadillac, T.B.	2	0	0	0	0
Ratliff, Jay, Dal.	0	1	1	0	2	Williams, DeAngelo, Car.	1	0	0	0	0
Rattay, Tim, Ariz	2	2	0	-1	2	Williams, Kevin, Min.	0	0	1	15	1
Redding, Cory, Det.	0	0	2	27	2	Williams, Pat, Min.	0	0	2	1	2
Redman, Chris, Atl.	2	0	0	0	0	Williams, Roy, Det.	2	0	0	0	0
Reed, J.R., Phi.	1	0	0	0	0	Williams, Roy, Dal.	0	0	1	0	1
Robinson, Michael, S.F.	1	0	0	0	0	Willis, Ray, Sea.	1	0	0	0	0
* Robinson, Laurent, Atl.	1	0	0	0	0	* Willis, Patrick, S.F.	0	0	1	0	1
* Robinson, Ryne, Car.	2	0	0	0	0	Wilson, Gibril, NY-G	1	0	1	0	1
Rogers, Shaun, Det.	1	1	3	10	4	* Wilson, Josh, Sea.	1	1	0	0	1
Roman, Mark, S.F.	0	0	3	44	3	Winfield, Antoine, Min.	0	0	1	0	1
Romo, Tony, Dal.	10	5	0	-4	5	Witherspoon, Will, St.L	0	0	1	0	1
* Rosario, Dante, Car.	0	0	1	0	1	Witten, Jason, Dal.	1	1	0	0	1
Rucker, Mike, Car.	0	0	2	3	2	* Wolfe, Garrett, Chi.	1	0	0	0	0
Runyan, Jon, Phi.	0	1	0	0	1	Woodson, Charles, G.B.	1	1	1	57	2
Russell, Brian, Sea.	0	0	1	0	1						
Ruud, Barrett, T.B.	0	0	3	3	3						
* Ryan, Clifton, St.L	0	0	1	0	1						
Ryan, Jon, G.B.	1	1	0	-10	1						
Sellers, Mike, Was.	1	0	0	0	0						
Seubert, Rich, NY-G	0	1	0	0	1						

Yards includes aborted plays, own recoveries and opponents' recoveries

* Player that was a rookie in 2007

AMERICAN FOOTBALL CONFERENCE—FUMBLES

	Fum	Own Rec	Fum OB	TD	Opp Rec	TD	Fum Yards	Tot Rec
Indianapolis	14	9	0	0	15	1	74	24
New England	14	6	2	0	12	3	61	18
San Diego	17	7	2	0	18	3	28	25
Jacksonville	18	4	1	0	9	1	67	13
Buffalo	20	11	2	0	12	1	-26	23
Cincinnati	20	9	1	0	15	2	106	24
N.Y. Jets	20	14	0	0	6	1	3	20
Pittsburgh	21	11	2	0	14	0	2	25
Cleveland	22	8	5	0	10	0	-11	18
Kansas City	22	7	3	0	8	1	41	15
Miami	25	9	3	0	8	1	-1	17
Houston	26	7	3	0	14	3	51	21
Denver	30	15	1	0	15	2	37	30
Tennessee	32	14	1	0	12	0	-19	26
Baltimore	35	9	0	0	6	0	-6	15
Oakland	42	23	2	0	8	0	-17	31
AFC Total	378	163	28	0	182	19	390	345
AFC Average	23.6	10.2	1.8	0.0	11.4	1.2	24.4	21.6

NATIONAL FOOTBALL CONFERENCE—FUMBLES

	Fum	Own Rec	Fum OB	TD	Opp Rec	TD	Fum Yards	Tot Rec
Atlanta	18	7	2	0	11	1	45	18
Tampa Bay	18	6	0	0	19	1	52	25
Dallas	21	16	0	0	10	1	26	26
Seattle	21	9	1	0	14	1	16	23
Philadelphia	24	11	1	2	8	0	0	19
Carolina	25	12	2	0	16	1	3	28
Green Bay	25	13	3	0	9	3	26	22
New Orleans	25	12	1	0	10	2	82	22
St. Louis	25	14	3	0	9	0	21	23
N.Y. Giants	26	12	0	0	10	2	101	22
Arizona	27	14	1	1	11	0	-23	25
Minnesota	27	11	1	0	16	2	111	27
Chicago	34	16	5	0	17	0	7	33
Detroit	35	15	6	0	18	1	33	33
Washington	35	14	3	0	10	0	-16	24
San Francisco	36	18	1	0	9	1	24	27
NFC Total	422	200	30	3	197	16	508	397
NFC Average	26.4	12.5	1.9	0.2	12.3	1.0	31.8	24.8
NFL Total	800	363	58	3	379	35	898	742
NFL Average	25.0	11.3	1.8	0.1	11.8	1.1	28.1	23.2

SACKS
MOST SACKS
AFC: 15.5 Jared Allen, Kansas City

NFC: 14.5 Patrick Kerney, Seattle

MOST SACKS, GAME
NFC: 6.0 Osi Umenyiora, N.Y. Giants vs. Philadelphia, September 30

AFC: 3.5 James Harrison, Pittsburgh vs. Baltimore, November 5

3.5 Mario Williams, Houston vs. Denver, December 13

TEAM LEADERS, SACKS
AFC: BALTIMORE, 5.0, Terrell Suggs; BUFFALO, 6.5, Aaron Schobel; CINCINNATI, 3.5, Robert Geathers; CLEVELAND, 5.0, Kamerion Wimbley; DENVER, 12.5, Elvis Dumervil; HOUSTON, 14.0, Mario Williams; INDIANAPOLIS, 7.0, Robert Mathis; JACKSONVILLE, 7.5, Paul Spicer; KANSAS CITY, 15.5, Jared Allen; MIAMI, 11.0, Jason Taylor; NEW ENGLAND, 12.5, Mike Vrabel; N.Y. JETS, 5.0, Shaun Ellis,*David Harris; OAKLAND, 8.0, Derrick Burgess, Chris Clemons; PITTSBURGH, 8.5, James Harrison; SAN DIEGO, 12.5, Shawne Merriman; TENNESSEE, 12.0, Kyle Vanden Bosch

NFC: ARIZONA, 9.0, Darnell Dockett; ATLANTA, 10.0, John Abraham; CAROLINA, 3.5, Na'il Diggs, Damione Lewis; CHICAGO, 9.0, Adewale Ogunleye; DALLAS, 14.0, DeMarcus Ware; DETROIT, 7.0, Shaun Rogers; GREEN BAY, 12.0, Aaron Kampman; MINNESOTA, 5.0, Ray Edwards, Ben Leber, Kenechi Udeze; NEW ORLEANS, 7.0, Will Smith; N.Y. GIANTS, 13.0, Osi Umenyiora; PHILADELPHIA, 12.5, Trent Cole; ST. LOUIS, 7.0, Will Witherspoon; SAN FRANCISCO, 6.5, Bryant Young; SEATTLE, 14.5, Patrick Kerney; TAMPA BAY, 8.0, Greg White; WASHINGTON, 10.5, Andre Carter

TEAM CHAMPION
NFC: 53 N.Y. Giants
AFC: 47 New England

NFL TOP TEN LEADERS—SACKS

	Sacks
Allen, Jared, K.C.	15.5
Kerney, Patrick, Sea.	14.5
Ware, DeMarcus, Dal.	14.0
Williams, Mario, Hou.	14.0
Umenyiora, Osi, NY-G	13.0
Cole, Trent, Phi.	12.5
Dumervil, Elvis, Den.	12.5
Ellis, Greg, Dal.	12.5
Merriman, Shawne, S.D.	12.5
Vrabel, Mike, N.E.	12.5

AMERICAN FOOTBALL CONFERENCE—SACKS

	Sacks	Yards
New England	47	340
San Diego	42	272
Tennessee	40	241
Jacksonville	37	244
Kansas City	37	252
Pittsburgh	36	243
Denver	33	203
Baltimore	32	183
Houston	31	196
Miami	30	167
N.Y. Jets	29	208
Cleveland	28	186
Indianapolis	28	162
Oakland	27	186
Buffalo	26	144
Cincinnati	22	128
AFC Total	525	3355
AFC Average	32.8	209.7

NATIONAL FOOTBALL CONFERENCE—SACKS

	Sacks	Yards
N.Y. Giants	53	349
Dallas	46	319
Seattle	45	303
Chicago	41	245
Minnesota	38	275
Detroit	37	256
Philadelphia	37	244
Arizona	36	242
Green Bay	36	218
Tampa Bay	33	207
Washington	33	198
New Orleans	32	198
St. Louis	31	234
San Francisco	31	183
Atlanta	25	146
Carolina	23	177
NFC Total	577	3794
NFC Average	36.1	237.1
League Total	1102	7149
League Average	34.4	223.4

AFC—INDIVIDUAL SACKS

	Sacks
Allen, Jared, K.C.	15.5
Williams, Mario, Hou.	14.0
Dumervil, Elvis, Den.	12.5
Merriman, Shawne, S.D.	12.5
Vrabel, Mike, N.E.	12.5
Vanden Bosch, Kyle, Ten.	12.0
Taylor, Jason, Mia.	11.0
Harrison, James, Pit.	8.5
Phillips, Shaun, S.D.	8.5
Burgess, Derrick, Oak.	8.0
Clemons, Chris, Oak.	8.0
Odom, Antwan, Ten.	8.0
Hali, Tamba, K.C.	7.5
Spicer, Paul, Jac.	7.5
Mathis, Robert, Ind.	7.0
Farrior, James, Pit.	6.5
Green, Jarvis, N.E.	6.5
Schobel, Aaron, Buf.	6.5
Thomas, Adalius, N.E.	6.5
Haynesworth, Albert, Ten.	6.0
LaBoy, Travis, Ten.	6.0
* Okoye, Amobi, Hou.	5.5
Porter, Joey, Mia.	5.5
Ellis, Shaun, NYJ	5.0
* Harris, David, NYJ	5.0
Suggs, Terrell, Bal.	5.0
Wimbley, Kamerion, Cle.	5.0
Brown, Tony, Ten.	4.0
Colvin, Rosevelt, N.E.	4.0
* Crowder, Tim, Den.	4.0
Haggans, Clark, Pit.	4.0
Johnson, Derrick, K.C.	4.0
Meier, Rob, Jac.	4.0
Peek, Antwan, Cle.	4.0
Robertson, Dewayne, NYJ	4.0
Smith, Robaire, Cle.	4.0
Warren, Gerard, Oak.	4.0
Warren, Ty, N.E.	4.0
Williams, Leon, Cle.	4.0
* Woodley, LaMarr, Pit.	4.0
Freeney, Dwight, Ind.	3.5
Geathers, Robert, Cin.	3.5
Hawkins, Brent, Jac.	3.5
Hayward, Reggie, Jac.	3.5
Mallard, Josh, Den.	3.5
Olshansky, Igor, S.D.	3.5
Sanders, Bob, Ind.	3.5
Seau, Junior, N.E.	3.5
* Tucker, Jyles, S.D.	3.5
Edwards, Ron, K.C.	3.0
Foote, Larry, Pit.	3.0
Gregg, Kelly, Bal.	3.0
Ivy, Corey, Bal.	3.0
Kalu, N. D., Hou.	3.0
McCray, Bobby, Jac.	3.0
McGinest, Willie, Cle.	3.0
Ngata, Haloti, Bal.	3.0
Roth, Matt, Mia.	3.0
Stroud, Marcus, Jac.	3.0
Bowens, David, NYJ	2.5
Brock, Raheem, Ind.	2.5
Castillo, Luis, S.D.	2.5
Cesaire, Jacques, S.D.	2.5
Kelsay, Chris, Buf.	2.5
McCargo, John, Buf.	2.5
McKinley, Alvin, Den.	2.5
Mosley, C.J., NYJ	2.5
Smith, Aaron, Pit.	2.5

	Sacks		Sacks	NFC—INDIVIDUAL SACKS	
Thomas, Bryan, NYJ	2.5	Huff, Michael, Oak.	1.0		Sacks
Allen, Will, Mia.	2.0	Ingram, Clint, Jac.	1.0	Kerney, Patrick, Sea.	14.5
Anderson, Charlie, Hou.	2.0	Jackson, D'Qwell, Cle.	1.0	Ware, DeMarcus, Dal.	14.0
Bannan, Justin, Bal.	2.0	* Johnson, Ed, Ind.	1.0	Umenyiora, Osi, NY-G	13.0
* Barnes, Antwan, Bal.	2.0	Johnson, Landon, Cin.	1.0	Cole, Trent, Phi.	12.5
Barton, Eric, NYJ	2.0	Jones, Dhani, Cin.	1.0	Ellis, Greg, Dal.	12.5
Bruschi, Tedy, N.E.	2.0	* Jones, Edgar, Bal.	1.0	Kampman, Aaron, G.B.	12.0
Cooper, Stephen, S.D.	2.0	Kelley, Ethan, Cle.	1.0	Carter, Andre, Was.	10.5
Crowell, Angelo, Buf.	2.0	Kelly, Tommy, Oak.	1.0	Abraham, John, Atl.	10.0
DiGiorgio, John, Buf.	2.0	Klecko, Dan, Ind.	1.0	Tuck, Justin, NY-G	10.0
Edwards, Donnie, K.C.	2.0	Landry, Dawan, Bal.	1.0	Gbaja-Biamila, Kabeer, G.B.	9.5
Gold, Ian, Den.	2.0	Lehan, Michael, Mia.	1.0	Peterson, Julian, Sea.	9.5
Harrison, Rodney, N.E.	2.0	Lynch, John, Den.	1.0	Dockett, Darnell, Ariz	9.0
Henderson, John, Jac.	2.0	Marshall, Lemar, Cin.	1.0	Ogunleye, Adewale, Chi.	9.0
Hobson, Victor, NYJ	2.0	* McBride, Turk, K.C.	1.0	Strahan, Michael, NY-G	9.0
Holliday, Vonnie, Mia.	2.0	Mincey, Jeremy, Jac.	1.0	Harris, Tommie, Chi.	8.0
Johnson, Jarret, Bal.	2.0	Morrison, Kirk, Oak.	1.0	White, Greg, T.B.	8.0
Keisel, Brett, Pit.	2.0	* Moss, Jarvis, Den.	1.0	Rogers, Shaun, Det.	7.0
Kirschke, Travis, Pit.	2.0	Myers, Michael, Cin.	1.0	Smith, Will, N.O.	7.0
Lewis, Ray, Bal.	2.0	* Nelson, Reggie, Jac.	1.0	Tapp, Darryl, Sea.	7.0
Maddox, Anthony, Hou.	2.0	Nickey, Donnie, Ten.	1.0	Williams, Corey, G.B.	7.0
* Ndukwe, Nedu, Cin.	2.0	Peterson, Kenny, Den.	1.0	Witherspoon, Will, St.L	7.0
Peterson, Mike, Jac.	2.0	Pettway, Kenneth, Jac.	1.0	DeVries, Jared, Det.	6.5
Pryce, Trevor, Bal.	2.0	Polk, Carlos, S.D.	1.0	Pace, Calvin, Ariz	6.5
Rhodes, Kerry, NYJ	2.0	Pollard, Bernard, K.C.	1.0	White, Dewayne, Det.	6.5
Ryans, DeMeco, Hou.	2.0	Rice, Simeon, Ind.	1.0	Young, Bryant, S.F.	6.5
Sapp, Gerome, Bal.	2.0	* Richardson, Jay, Oak.	1.0	* Adams, Gaines, T.B.	6.0
Sapp, Warren, Oak.	2.0	Scott, Bart, Bal.	1.0	Glover, La'Roi, St.L	6.0
Smith, Justin, Cin.	2.0	Stills, Gary, Bal.	1.0	Haye, Jovan, T.B.	6.0
Smith, Shaun, Cle.	2.0	Taylor, Ike, Pit.	1.0	Robbins, Fred, NY-G	5.5
Wilfork, Vince, N.E.	2.0	Thomas, Josh, Ind.	1.0	Smith, Antonio, Ariz	5.5
Williams, Kyle, Buf.	2.0	Thomas, Zach, Mia.	1.0	Anderson, Mark, Chi.	5.0
Williams, Madieu, Cin.	2.0	Thompson, Chaun, Cle.	1.0	Edwards, Ray, Min.	5.0
Bingham, Ryon, S.D.	1.5	Thornton, David, Ten.	1.0	Leber, Ben, Min.	5.0
Coleman, Kenyon, NYJ	1.5	Thornton, John, Cin.	1.0	Thomas, Juqua, Phi.	5.0
Hargrove, Anthony, Buf.	1.5	Traylor, Keith, Mia.	1.0	Udeze, Kenechi, Min.	5.0
Harris, Marques, S.D.	1.5	Tripplett, Larry, Buf.	1.0	Urlacher, Brian, Chi.	5.0
Harris, Napoleon, K.C.	1.5	* Weddle, Eric, S.D.	1.0	Washington, Marcus, Was.	5.0
* Moses, Quentin, Mia.	1.5	Wilhelm, Matt, S.D.	1.0	Brown, Alex, Chi.	4.5
Peko, Domata, Cin.	1.5	Williams, D.J., Den.	1.0	Henderson, E.J., Min.	4.5
* Pitcock, Quinn, Ind.	1.5	* Wright, Eric, Cle.	1.0	Kiwanuka, Mathias, NY-G	4.5
Robinson, Bryan, Cin.	1.5	Youboty, Ashton, Buf.	1.0	* Robison, Brian, Min.	4.5
Seymour, Richard, N.E.	1.5	Brackett, Gary, Ind.	0.5	Harper, Roman, N.O.	4.0
Smith, Daryl, Jac.	1.5	Carter, Tyrone, Pit.	0.5	Hayes, Gerald, Ariz	4.0
Wright, Rodrique, Mia.	1.5	Crowder, Channing, Mia.	0.5	Patterson, Mike, Phi.	4.0
Adams, Blue, Cin.	1.0	Hampton, Casey, Pit.	0.5	* Willis, Patrick, S.F.	4.0
Adams, Mike, Cle.	1.0	Hoke, Chris, Pit.	0.5	Wilson, Chris, Was.	4.0
Bly, Dre', Den.	1.0	Hutchins, Von, Hou.	0.5	Bailey, Boss, Det.	3.5
Boone, Alfonso, K.C.	1.0	Jackson, Dexter, Cin.	0.5	Banta-Cain, Tully, S.F.	3.5
Brooks, Ahmad, Cin.	1.0	Jackson, Marlin, Ind.	0.5	Barnett, Nick, G.B.	3.5
Charleston, Jeff, Ind.	1.0	Jones, Sean, Cle.	0.5	Bernard, Rocky, Sea.	3.5
Clark, Ryan, Pit.	1.0	Keiaho, Freddie, Ind.	0.5	Canty, Chris, Dal.	3.5
Cochran, Earl, Hou.	1.0	Reid, Darrell, Ind.	0.5	Chavous, Corey, St.L	3.5
Cousin, Terry, Jac.	1.0	Roye, Orpheus, Cle.	0.5	Dansby, Karlos, Ariz	3.5
* Dawson, Keyunta, Ind.	1.0	Wilkerson, Jimmy, K.C.	0.5	Diggs, Na'il, Car.	3.5
Denney, Ryan, Buf.	1.0	Winborn, Jamie, Den.	0.5	Kearse, Jevon, Phi.	3.5
* Durant, Justin, Jac.	1.0	Wright, Mike, N.E.	0.5	Lewis, Damione, Car.	3.5
Edwards, Dwan, Bal.	1.0			Mitchell, Kawika, NY-G	3.5
Ellison, Keith, Buf.	1.0	*Player that was a rookie in 2007*		Wynn, Renaldo, N.O.	3.5
Engelberger, John, Den.	1.0			Babineaux, Jonathan, Atl.	3.0
Fanene, Jonathan, Cin.	1.0			Blackstock, Darryl, Ariz	3.0
Finnegan, Cortland, Ten.	1.0			Boley, Michael, Atl.	3.0
Fuller, Vincent, Ten.	1.0			Bunkley, Brodrick, Phi.	3.0
Greenwood, Morlon, Hou.	1.0			Carter, Kevin, T.B.	3.0
Haggan, Mario, Buf.	1.0			Davis, Thomas, Car.	3.0
Hagler, Tyjuan, Ind.	1.0			Douglas, Marques, S.F.	3.0
Hart, Clinton, S.D.	1.0			Edwards, Kalimba, Det.	3.0
Hobbs, Ellis, N.E.	1.0			Fujita, Scott, N.O.	3.0
Howard, Thomas, Oak.	1.0			Hill, Leroy, Sea.	3.0

	Sacks		Sacks
James, Bradie, Dal.	3.0	Jenkins, Cullen, G.B.	1.0
Johnson, Spencer, Min.	3.0	Johnson, Trevor, St.L	1.0
McIntosh, Rocky, Was.	3.0	Jolly, Johnny, G.B.	1.0
Ratliff, Jay, Dal.	3.0	Jones, Nate, Dal.	1.0
Rucker, Mike, Car.	3.0	Lake, Antwan, N.O.	1.0
* Spencer, Anthony, Dal.	3.0	Little, Leonard, St.L	1.0
Thomas, Hollis, N.O.	3.0	Madison, Sam, NY-G	1.0
Williams, Kevin, Min.	3.0	Manning, Ricky, Chi.	1.0
Young, Brian, N.O.	3.0	Manuel, Marquand, Car.	1.0
Berry, Bertrand, Ariz	2.5	Marshall, Richard, Car.	1.0
Chillar, Brandon, St.L	2.5	McClover, Stanley, Car.	1.0
Daniels, Phillip, Was.	2.5	* McDonald, Ray, S.F.	1.0
Grant, Charles, N.O.	2.5	Mikell, Quintin, Phi.	1.0
Griffin, Cornelius, Was.	2.5	Mitchell, Jayme, Min.	1.0
Hall, James, St.L	2.5	Moore, Eric, St.L	1.0
Haralson, Parys, S.F.	2.5	Navies, Hannibal, S.F.	1.0
Jenkins, Kris, Car.	2.5	* Nicholas, Stephen, Atl.	1.0
Moore, Brandon, S.F.	2.5	Phillips, Jermaine, T.B.	1.0
Peppers, Julius, Car.	2.5	Pickett, Ryan, G.B.	1.0
Smith, Corey, Det.	2.5	Pierce, Antonio, NY-G	1.0
* Alexander, Gerald, Det.	2.0	Reagor, Montae, Phi.	1.0
Archuleta, Adam, Chi.	2.0	Redding, Cory, Det.	1.0
Briggs, Lance, Chi.	2.0	Russell, Brian, Sea.	1.0
Brooking, Keith, Atl.	2.0	Simmons, Brian, N.O.	1.0
* Carriker, Adam, St.L	2.0	Sims, Ernie, Det.	1.0
Coleman, Rod, Atl.	2.0	Sims, Ryan, T.B.	1.0
Davis, Chauncey, Atl.	2.0	Spikes, Takeo, Phi.	1.0
Green, Roderick, S.F.	2.0	Tatupu, Lofa, Sea.	1.0
Hatcher, Jason, Dal.	2.0	Torbor, Reggie, NY-G	1.0
Johnson, Tank, Dal.	2.0	Torrence, Leigh, Was.	1.0
Lenon, Paris, Det.	2.0	Vasher, Nathan, Chi.	1.0
* Mebane, Brandon, Sea.	2.0	Walker, Darwin, Chi.	1.0
Moore, Langston, Det.	2.0	Williams, Jamar, Chi.	1.0
Moorehead, Kindal, Car.	2.0	Adams, Anthony, Chi.	0.5
* Ryan, Clifton, St.L	2.0	Clancy, Kendrick, N.O.	0.5
Simoneau, Mark, N.O.	2.0	Cooper, Josh, N.O.	0.5
Spears, Marcus, Dal.	2.0	Darby, Chartric, Sea.	0.5
Spires, Greg, T.B.	2.0	Doughty, Reed, Was.	0.5
Tafoya, Joe, Ariz	2.0	Montgomery, Anthony, Was.	0.5
Williams, Pat, Min.	2.0	Wroten, Claude, St.L	0.5
Wyms, Ellis, Sea.	2.0		
Hovan, Chris, T.B.	1.5	*Player that was a rookie in 2007*	
* Landry, LaRon, Was.	1.5		
Lewis, Michael M., S.F.	1.5		
* Peterson, Greg, T.B.	1.5		
* Ross, Aaron, NY-G	1.5		
Sopoaga, Isaac, S.F.	1.5		
* Alford, Jay, NY-G	1.0		
Babineaux, Jordan, Sea.	1.0		
Barber, Ronde, T.B.	1.0		
Bartell, Ronald, St.L	1.0		
* Bradley, Stewart, Phi.	1.0		
Bullocks, Josh, N.O.	1.0		
Chukwurah, Patrick, T.B.	1.0		
Clements, Nate, S.F.	1.0		
Cofield, Barry, NY-G	1.0		
Crocker, Chris, Atl.	1.0		
Draft, Chris, St.L	1.0		
Evans, Demetric, Was.	1.0		
Evans, Fred, Min.	1.0		
Fields, Ronald, S.F.	1.0		
Gocong, Chris, Phi.	1.0		
Golston, Kedric, Was.	1.0		
Grigsby, Otis, Min.	1.0		
Hanson, Joselio, Phi.	1.0		
Hawk, A.J., G.B.	1.0		
Howard, Darren, Phi.	1.0		
Jackson, Grady, Atl.	1.0		
James, Erasmus, Min.	1.0		

2007 NFL PAID ATTENDANCE BREAKDOWN

	Games	Attendance	Average
NFL Preseason Total	65	4,119,278	63,374
NFL Regular-Season Total	256	17,345,205	67,755
NFL Postseason Total	12	792,019	66,002
NFL All Games	333	22,256,502	66,836

1.1-MILLION CLUB

During the 2007 season, 11 teams drew more than 1.1 million paid attendance home and away during the regular season. For the eighth consecutive year, the Washington Redskins led the league in regular-season paid attendance (1,264,890). The Redskins also set an NFL record for single-season home paid attendance (711,471).

Team	Total Paid Home Attendance	Total Paid Visiting Attendance	Total Paid Attendance
Washington	711,471	553,419	1,264,890
New York Giants	629,391	558,524	1,187,915
New York Jets	616,756	554,808	1,171,564
Miami	576,959	579,803	1,156,762
Kansas City	622,541	523,397	1,145,938
New England	579,182	551,845	1,131,027
Buffalo	557,058	571,994	1,129,052
Denver	597,984	523,012	1,120,996
Philadelphia	541,280	578,810	1,120,090
Green Bay	566,418	546,335	1,112,753
Carolina	579,051	521,096	1,100,147

For complete year-by-year attendance records, see pages 616-617.

Inside the Numbers

GREATEST COMEBACKS
IN NFL HISTORY
(Most Points Overcome To Win Game)

REGULAR SEASON GAMES

FROM 28 POINTS BEHIND TO WIN:
December 7, 1980, at San Francisco

New Orleans	14	21	0	0	0 —	35
San Francisco	0	7	14	14	3 —	38

NO — Harris 33 pass from Manning (Ricardo kick)
NO — Childs 21 pass from Manning (Ricardo kick)
NO — Holmes 1 run (Ricardo kick)
SF — Solomon 57 punt return (Wersching kick)
NO — Holmes 1 run (Ricardo kick)
NO — Harris 41 pass from Manning (Ricardo kick)
SF — Montana 1 run (Wersching kick)
SF — Clark 71 pass from Montana (Wersching kick)
SF — Solomon 14 pass from Montana (Wersching kick)
SF — Elliott 7 run (Wersching kick)
SF — FG Wersching 36

FROM 26 POINTS BEHIND TO WIN:
September 21, 1997, at Buffalo

Indianapolis	14	12	0	9 —	35
Buffalo	0	10	6	21 —	37

Ind — Bailey 10 pass from Harbaugh (Blanchard kick)
Ind — Faulk 10 run (Blanchard kick)
Ind — FG Blanchard 39
Ind — FG Blanchard 36
Ind — FG Blanchard 49
Ind — FG Blanchard 22
Buff — Johnson 16 pass from Collins (Christie kick)
Buff — FG Christie 27
Buff — A. Smith 15 run (2-pt attempt failed)
Ind — FG Blanchard 25
Buff — Early 4 pass from Collins (Christie kick)
Buff — A. Smith 1 run (Christie kick)
Buff — A. Smith 54 run (Christie kick)
Ind — Harrison 2 pass from Justin (2-pt attempt failed)

FROM 25 POINTS BEHIND TO WIN:
November 8, 1987, at St. Louis

Tampa Bay	7	7	14	0 —	28
St. Louis	0	3	0	28 —	31

TB — Carrier 5 pass from DeBerg (Igwebuike kick)
TB — Carter 3 pass from DeBerg (Igwebuike kick)
StL — FG Gallery 31
TB — Smith 34 pass from DeBerg (Igwebuike kick)
TB — Smith 3 run (Igwebuike kick)
StL — Awalt 4 pass from Lomax (Gallery kick)
StL — Noga 23 fumble recovery (Gallery kick)

StL — J. Smith 11 pass from Lomax (Gallery kick)
StL — J. Smith 17 pass from Lomax (Gallery kick)

FROM 24 POINTS BEHIND TO WIN:
October 27, 1946, at Washington

Philadelphia	0	0	14	14 —	28
Washington	10	14	0	0 —	24

Wash — Rosato 2 run (Poillon kick)
Wash — FG Poillon 28
Wash — Rosato 4 run (Poillon kick)
Wash — Lapka recovered fumble in end zone (Poillon kick)
Phil — Steele 1 run (Lio kick)
Phil — Pritchard 45 pass from Thompson (Lio kick)
Phil — Steinke 7 pass from Thompson (Lio kick)
Phil — Ferrante 30 pass from Thompson (Lio kick)

FROM 24 POINTS BEHIND TO WIN:
October 20, 1957, at Detroit

Baltimore	7	14	6	0 —	27
Detroit	0	3	7	21 —	31

Balt — Mutscheller 15 pass from Unitas (Rechichar kick)
Det — FG Martin 47
Balt — Moore 72 pass from Unitas (Rechichar kick)
Balt — Mutscheller 52 pass from Unitas (Rechichar kick)
Balt — Moore 4 pass from Unitas (kick failed)
Det — Junker 14 pass from Rote (Layne kick)
Det — Cassady 26 pass from Layne (Layne kick)
Det — Johnson 1 run (Layne kick)
Det — Cassady 29 pass from Layne (Layne kick)

FROM 24 POINTS BEHIND TO WIN:
October 25, 1959, at Minneapolis

Philadelphia	0	0	21	7 —	28
Chicago Cardinals	7	10	7	0 —	24

Cardinals — Crow 10 pass from Roach (Conrad kick)
Cardinals — J. Hill 77 blocked field goal return (Conrad kick)
Cardinals — FG Conrad 15
Cardinals — Lane 37 interception return (Conrad kick)
Phil — Barnes 1 run (Walston kick)
Phil — McDonald 29 pass from Van Brocklin (Walston kick)
Phil — Barnes 2 run (Walston kick)
Phil — McDonald 22 pass from Van Brocklin (Walston kick)

FROM 24 POINTS BEHIND TO WIN:
October 23, 1960, at Denver

Boston	10	7	7	0 —	24
Denver	0	0	14	17 —	31

Bos — FG Cappelletti 12
Bos — Colclough 10 pass from Songin (Cappelletti kick)
Bos — Wells 6 pass from Songin (Cappelletti kick)
Bos — Miller 47 pass from Songin (Cappelletti kick)
Den — Carmichael 21 pass from Tripucka (Mingo kick)

Den — Jessup 19 pass from Tripucka (Mingo kick)
Den — Carmichael 35 lateral from Taylor, pass from Tripucka (Mingo kick)
Den — Taylor 8 pass from Tripucka (Mingo kick)
Den — FG Mingo 9

FROM 24 POINTS BEHIND TO WIN:
December 15, 1974, at Miami

New England	21	3	0	3 —	27
Miami	0	17	7	10 —	34

NE — Hannah recovered fumble in end zone (J. Smith kick)
NE — Sanders 23 interception return (J. Smith kick)
NE — Herron 4 pass from Plunkett (J. Smith kick)
NE — FG J. Smith 46
Mia — Nottingham 1 run (Yepremian kick)
Mia — Baker 37 pass from Morrall (Yepremian kick)
Mia — FG Yepremian 28
Mia — Baker 46 pass from Morrall (Yepremian kick)
NE — FG J. Smith 34
Mia — Nottingham 2 run (Yepremian kick)
Mia — FG Yepremian 40

FROM 24 POINTS BEHIND TO WIN:
December 4, 1977, at Minnesota

San Francisco	0	10	14	3 —	27
Minnesota	0	0	7	21 —	28

SF — Delvin Williams 2 run (Wersching kick)
SF — FG Wersching 31
SF — Dave Williams 80 kickoff return (Wersching kick)
SF — Delvin Williams 5 run (Wersching kick)
Minn — McClanahan 15 pass from Lee (Cox kick)
Minn — Rashad 8 pass from Kramer (Cox kick)
Minn — Tucker 9 pass from Kramer (Cox kick)
SF — FG Wersching 31
Minn — S. White 69 pass from Kramer (Cox kick)

FROM 24 POINTS BEHIND TO WIN:
September 23, 1979, at Denver

Seattle	10	10	14	0 —	34
Denver	0	10	21	6 —	37

Sea — FG Herrera 28
Sea — Doornink 5 run (Herrera kick)
Den — FG Turner 27
Sea — Doornink 5 run (Herrera kick)
Den — Armstrong 2 run (Turner kick)
Sea — FG Herrera 22
Sea — McCullum 13 pass from Zorn (Herrera kick)
Den — Smith 1 run (Herrera kick)
Den — Studdard 2 pass from Morton (Turner kick)
Den — Moses 11 pass from Morton (Turner kick)
Den — Upchurch 35 pass from Morton (Turner kick)

Den — Lytle 1 run (kick failed)

FROM 24 POINTS BEHIND TO WIN:
September 23, 1979, at Cincinnati

Houston	0	10	17	0	3	—	30
Cincinnati	14	10	0	3	0	—	27

Cin — Johnson 1 run (Bahr kick)
Cin — Alexander 2 run (Bahr kick)
Cin — Johnson 1 run (Bahr kick)
Cin — FG Bahr 52
Hou — Burrough 35 pass from Pastorini (Fritsch kick)
Hou — FG Fritsch 33
Hou — Campbell 8 run (Fritsch kick)
Hou — Caster 22 pass from Pastorini (Fritsch kick)
Hou — FG Fritsch 47
Cin — FG Bahr 55
Hou — FG Fritsch 29

FROM 24 POINTS BEHIND TO WIN:
November 22, 1982, at Los Angeles

San Diego	10	14	0	0	—	24
L.A. Raiders	0	7	14	7	—	28

SD — FG Benirschke 19
SD — Scales 29 pass from Fouts (Benirschke kick)
SD — Muncie 2 run (Benirschke kick)
SD — Muncie 1 run (Benirschke kick)
Raiders — Christensen 1 pass from Plunkett (Bahr kick)
Raiders — Allen 3 run (Bahr kick)
Raiders — Allen 6 run (Bahr kick)
Raiders — Hawkins 1 run (Bahr kick)

FROM 24 POINTS BEHIND TO WIN:
September 26, 1988, at Denver

L.A. Raiders	0	0	14	13	3	—	30
Denver	7	17	0	3	0	—	27

Den — Dorsett 1 run (Karlis kick)
Den — Dorsett 1 run (Karlis kick)
Den — Sewell 7 pass from Elway (Karlis kick)
Den — FG Karlis 39
Raiders — Smith 40 pass from Schroeder (Bahr kick)
Raiders — Smith 42 pass from Schroeder (Bahr kick)
Raiders — FG Bahr 28
Raiders — Allen 4 run (Bahr kick)
Den — FG Karlis 25
Raiders — FG Bahr 44
Raiders — FG Bahr 35

FROM 24 POINTS BEHIND TO WIN:
December 6, 1992, at Tampa

L.A. Rams	0	3	21	7	—	31
Tampa Bay	6	21	0	0	—	27

TB — FG Murray 34
TB — FG Murray 47
TB — Armstrong 81 pass from Testaverde (Murray kick)
TB — Jones 26 fumble recovery (Murray kick)
Rams — FG Zendejas 18
TB — Carrier 10 pass from Testaverde (Murray kick)
Rams — Anderson 40 pass from Everett (Zendejas kick)
Rams — Chadwick 27 pass from Everett (Zendejas kick)
Rams — Lang 1 run (Zendejas kick)

Rams — Carter 8 pass from Everett (Zendejas kick)

POSTSEASON GAMES

FROM 32 POINTS BEHIND TO WIN:
AFC First-Round Playoff Game
January 3, 1993, at Buffalo

Houston	7	21	7	3	—	38
Buffalo	3	0	28	7	3	—	41

Hou — Jeffires 3 pass from Moon (Del Greco kick)
Buff — FG Christie 36
Hou — Slaughter 7 pass from Moon (Del Greco kick)
Hou — Duncan 26 pass from Moon (Del Greco kick)
Hou — Jeffires 27 pass from Moon (Del Greco kick)
Hou — McDowell 58 interception return (Del Greco kick)
Buff — Davis 1 run (Christie kick)
Buff — Beebe 38 pass from Reich (Christie kick)
Buff — Reed 26 pass from Reich (Christie kick)
Buff — Reed 18 pass from Reich (Christie kick)
Buff — Reed 17 pass from Reich (Christie kick)
Hou — FG Del Greco 26
Buff — FG Christie 32

FROM 24 POINTS BEHIND TO WIN:
NFC First-Round Playoff Game
January 5, 2003, at San Francisco

N.Y. Giants	7	21	10	0	—	38
San Francisco	7	7	8	17	—	39

SF — Owens 76 pass from Garcia (Chandler kick)
NYG — Toomer 12 pass from Collins (Bryant kick)
NYG — Shockey 2 pass from Collins (Bryant kick)
SF — Barlow 1 run (Chandler kick)
NYG — Toomer 8 pass from Collins (Bryant kick)
NYG — Toomer 24 pass from Collins (Bryant kick)
NYG — Barber 6 run (Bryant kick)
NYG — FG Bryant 21
SF — Owens 26 pass from Garcia (Owens from Garcia)
SF — Garcia 14 run (Owens from Garcia)
SF — Garcia 14 run (Owens from Garcia)
SF — FG Chandler 25
SF — Streets 13 pass from Garcia (2-pt attempt failed)

FROM 20 POINTS BEHIND TO WIN:
Western Conference Playoff Game
December 22, 1957, at San Francisco

Detroit	0	7	14	10	—	31
San Francisco	14	10	3	0	—	27

SF — Owens 34 pass from Tittle (Soltau kick)
SF — McElhenny 47 pass from Tittle (Soltau kick)
Det — Junker 4 pass from Rote (Martin kick)
SF — Wilson 12 pass from Tittle (Soltau kick)
SF — FG Soltau 25

SF — FG Soltau 10
Det — Tracy 2 run (Martin kick)
Det — Tracy 58 run (Martin kick)
Det — Gedman 3 run (Martin kick)
Det — FG Martin 14

FROM 18 POINTS BEHIND TO WIN:
NFC Divisional Playoff Game
December 23, 1972, at San Francisco

Dallas	3	10	0	17	—	30
San Francisco	7	7	14	0	—	28

SF — Washington 97 kickoff return (Gossett kick)
Dall — FG Fritsch 37
SF — Schreiber 1 run (Gossett kick)
SF — Schreiber 1 run (Gossett kick)
Dall — FG Fritsch 45
Dall — Alworth 28 pass from Morton (Fritsch kick)
SF — Schreiber 1 run (Gossett kick)
Dall — FG Fritsch 27
Dall — Parks 20 pass from Staubach (Fritsch kick)
Dall — Sellers 10 pass from Staubach (Fritsch kick)

FROM 18 POINTS BEHIND TO WIN:
AFC Divisional Playoff Game
January 4, 1986, at Miami

Cleveland	7	7	7	0	—	21
Miami	3	0	14	7	—	24

Mia — FG Reveiz 51
Cle — Newsome 16 pass from Kosar (Bahr kick)
Cle — Byner 21 run (Bahr kick)
Cle — Byner 66 run (Bahr kick)
Mia — Moore 6 pass from Marino (Reveiz kick)
Mia — Davenport 31 run (Reveiz kick)
Mia — Davenport 1 run (Reveiz kick)

FROM 18 POINTS BEHIND TO WIN:
AFC Divisional Playoff Game
January 21, 2007, at Indianapolis

New England	7	14	7	6	—	34
Indianapolis	3	3	15	17	—	38

NE — Mankins 0 fumble recovery (Gostkowski kick)
Ind — FG Vinatieri 42
NE — Dillon 7 run (Gostkowski kick)
NE — Samuel 39 interception return (Gostkowski kick)
Ind — FG Vinatieri 26
Ind — Manning 1 run (Vinatieri kick)
Ind — Klecko 1 pass from Manning (Harrison from Manning)
NE — Gaffney 6 pass from Brady (Gostkowski kick)
Ind — Saturday 0 fumble recovery (Vinatieri kick)
NE — FG Gostkowski 28
Ind — FG Vinatieri 36
NE — FG Gostkowski 43
Ind — Addai 3 run (Vinatieri kick)

RECORDS FOR NFL TEAMS FOR MOST POINTS IN A GAME (REGULAR SEASON ONLY)

Note: When the record has been achieved more than once, only the most recent game is shown; summaries are listed in alphabetical order by conference. Bold face indicates team holding record.

BALTIMORE RAVENS
December 19, 2005, at Baltimore

Green Bay	3	0	0	0	—	3
Baltimore	14	10	10	14	—	48

TD: Balt—Todd Heap 2, Mark Clayton, Randy Hymes, Jamal Lewis, Adalius Thomas. TD Passes: Balt—Kyle Boller 3. FG: Balt—Matt Stover 2; GB—Ryan Longwell.

BUFFALO BILLS
September 18, 1966, at Buffalo

Miami	3	7	0	14	—	24
Buffalo	21	27	3	7	—	58

TD: Buff—Bobby Burnett 2, Butch Byrd 2, Jack Spikes 2, Bobby Crockett, Jack Kemp; Mia—Dave Kocourek, Bo Roberson, John Roderick. TD Passes: Buff—Jack Kemp, Daryle Lamonica; Mia—George Wilson 3. FG: Buff—Booth Lusteg; Mia—Gene Mingo.

CINCINNATI BENGALS
December 17, 1989, at Cincinnati

Houston	0	0	0	7	—	7
Cincinnati	21	10	21	9	—	61

TD: Cin—Eddie Brown 2, Eric Ball, James Brooks, Ira Hillary, Rodney Holman, Tim McGee, Craig Taylor; Hou—Lorenzo White. TD Passes: Cin—Boomer Esiason 4, Erik Wilhelm. FG: Cin—Jim Breech 2.

CLEVELAND BROWNS
November 7, 1954, at Cleveland

Washington	0	3	0	0	—	3
Cleveland	13	14	21	14	—	62

TD: Cle—Darrell Brewster 2, Mo Bassett, Ken Gorgal, Otto Graham, Dub Jones, Dante Lavelli, Curley Morrison. TD Passes: Cle—George Ratterman 3, Otto Graham. FG: Cle—Lou Groza 2; Wash—Vic Janowicz.

DENVER BRONCOS
October 6, 1963, at Denver

San Diego	13	7	0	14	—	34
Denver	3	14	9	24	—	50

TD: Den—Lionel Taylor 2, Goose Gonsoulin, Gene Prebola, Donnie Stone; SD—Keith Lincoln 2, Lance Alworth, Paul Lowe, Jacque MacKinnon. TD Passes: Den—John McCormick 3; SD—Tobin Rote 3, John Hadl 2. FG: Den—Gene Mingo 5.

HOUSTON TEXANS
December 30, 2007 at Houston

Jacksonville	7	7	7	7	—	28
Houston	0	21	14	7	—	42

TD: Jax—Earnest Wilford 2, Matt Jones, Reggie Williams; Hou—Andre Davis 2, Ron Dayne 2, Owen Daniels, Darius Walker. TD Passes: Jax—Quinn Gray 4; Hou—Sage Rosenfels.

INDIANAPOLIS COLTS
December 12, 1976, at Baltimore

Buffalo	3	3	7	7	—	20
Baltimore Colts	7	13	28	10	—	58

TD: Balt—Roger Carr, Raymond Chester, Glenn Doughty, Roosevelt Leaks, Derrel Luce, Lydell Mitchell, Howard Stevens; Buff—Bob Chandler, O.J. Simpson. TD Passes: Balt—Bert Jones 3; Buff—Gary Marangi. FG: Balt—Toni Linhart 3; Buff—George Jakowenko 2.

JACKSONVILLE JAGUARS
December 23, 2007, at Jacksonville

Oakland	0	3	0	8	—	11
Jacksonville	14	14	7	14	—	49

TD: Oak—Zach Miller; Jac—Richard Angulo, David Garrard, Greg Jones, Matt Jones, Maurice Jones-Drew, Fred Taylor, Reggie Williams. TD Passes: Oak—JaMarcus Russell; Jac—David Garrard 2, Quinn Gray 2. FG: Oak—Sebastian Janikowski.

KANSAS CITY CHIEFS
September 7, 1963, at Denver

Kansas City	14	14	21	10	—	59
Denver	0	7	0	0	—	7

TD: KC—Chris Burford 2, Frank Jackson 2, Dave Grayson, Abner Haynes, Sherrill Headrick, Curtis McClinton; Den—Lionel Taylor. TD Passes: KC—Len Dawson 4, Curtis McClinton; Den—Mickey Slaughter. FG: KC—Tommy Brooker.

MIAMI DOLPHINS
November 24, 1977, at St. Louis

Miami	14	14	20	7	—	55
St. Louis Cardinals	7	0	0	7	—	14

TD: Mia—Nat Moore 3, Gary Davis, Duriel Harris, Leroy Harris, Benny Malone, Andre Tillman; StL—Ike Harris, Terry Metcalf. TD Passes: Mia—Bob Griese 6; StL—Jim Hart.

NEW ENGLAND PATRIOTS
November 18, 2007, at Buffalo

New England	14	21	7	14	—	56
Buffalo	7	0	3	0	—	10

TD: NE—Randy Moss 4, Kyle Eckel, Ellis Hobbs, Laurence Maroney, Benjamin Watson; Buff—Roscoe Parrish. TD Passes: NE—Tom Brady 5; Buff—J.P. Losman. FG: Buff—Rian Lindell.

NEW YORK JETS
November 17, 1985, at New York

Tampa Bay	14	7	7	0	—	28
New York Jets	17	24	14	7	—	62

TD: NYJ—Mickey Shuler 3, Johnny Hector 2, Tony Paige, Al Toon, Wesley Walker; TB—James Wilder 2, Kevin House, Calvin Magee. TD Passes: NYJ—Ken O'Brien 5; TB—Steve DeBerg 2. FG: NYJ—Pat Leahy 2.

OAKLAND RAIDERS
September 29, 2002 at Oakland

Tennessee	7	0	12	6	—	25
Oakland	21	10	7	14	—	52

TD: Oak—Tim Brown, Phillip Buchanon, Charlie Garner, Terry Kirby, Jerry Porter, Jim Rice, Rod Woodson; Tenn—Drew Bennett, Eddie George, Justin McCareins, John Simon. TD Passes: Oak—Rich Gannon 4; Tenn—Steve McNair 2. FG: Oak—Sebastian Janikowski.

PITTSBURGH STEELERS
November 30, 1952, at Pittsburgh

New York Giants	0	0	7	0	—	7
Pittsburgh	14	14	7	28	—	63

TD: Pitt—Lynn Chandnois 2, Dick Hensley 2, Jack Butler, George Hays, Ray Mathews, Ed Modzelewski, Elbie Nickel; NYG—Bill Stribling. TD Passes: Pitt—Jim Finks 4, Gary Kerkorian; NYG—Tom Landry.

SAN DIEGO CHARGERS
December 22, 1963, at San Diego

Denver	7	10	3	0	—	20
San Diego	10	16	10	22	—	58

TD: SD—Paul Lowe 2, Chuck Allen, Bobby Jackson, Dave Kocourek, Keith Lincoln, Jacque MacKinnon; Den—Billy Joe, Donnie Stone. TD Passes: SD—John Hadl, Tobin Rote; Den—Don Breaux. FG: SD—George Blair 3; Den—Gene Mingo 2.

TENNESSEE TITANS
December 9, 1990, at Houston

Cleveland	0	7	7	0	—	14
Houston Oilers	14	31	7	6	—	58

TD: Hou—Lorenzo White 4, Ernest Givins, Leonard Harris, Tony Jones, Terry Kinard; Cle—Eric Metcalf 2. TD Passes: Hou—Warren Moon 2, Cody Carlson; Cle—Bernie Kosar. FG: Hou—Teddy Garcia.

ARIZONA CARDINALS
November 13, 1949, at New York

Chicago Cardinals	7	31	14	13	— 65
New York Bulldogs	7	0	6	7	— 20

TD: Chi—Red Cochran 2, Pat Harder 2, Bill Dewell, Mel Kutner, Bob Ravensburg, Vic Schwall, Charlie Trippi; NY—Joe Golding, Frank Muehlheuser, Johnny Rauch. TD Passes: Chi—Paul Christman 3, Jim Hardy 3; NY—Bobby Layne. FG: Chi—Pat Harder.

ATLANTA FALCONS
September 16, 1973, at New Orleans

Atlanta	0	24	21	17	— 62
New Orleans	0	0	7	0	— 7

TD: Atl—Ken Burrow 2, Eddie Ray 2, Wes Chesson, Tom Hayes, Art Malone, Joe Profit; NO—Bill Butler. TD Passes: Atl—Dick Shiner 3, Bob Lee; NO—Archie Manning. FG: Atl—Nick Mike-Mayer 2.

Carolina Panthers
December 8, 2002, at Carolina

Cincinnati	7	10	14	0	— 31
Carolina	9	7	21	15	— 52

TD: Car—Steve Smith 3, Dee Brown, Muhsin Muhammad, Al Wallace, Wesley Walls; Cin—Peter Warrick 2, Jon Kitna, Takeo Spikes. TD Passes: Car—Rodney Peete 3; Cin—Jon Kitna 2. FG: Cin—Neil Rackers.

CHICAGO BEARS
December 7, 1980, at Chicago

Green Bay	0	7	0	0	— 7
Chicago	0	28	13	20	— 61

TD: Chi—Walter Payton 3, Brian Baschnagel, Robin Earl, Roland Harper, Willie McClendon, Len Walterscheid, Rickey Watts; GB—James Lofton. TD Passes: Chi—Vince Evans 3; GB—Lynn Dickey.

DALLAS COWBOYS
October 12, 1980, at Dallas

San Francisco	0	7	0	7	— 14
Dallas	14	24	14	7	— 59

TD: Dall—Drew Pearson 3, Ron Springs 2, Tony Dorsett, Billy Joe DuPree, Robert Newhouse; SF—Dwight Clark 2. TD Passes: Dall—Danny White 4; SF—Steve DeBerg 2. FG: Dall—Rafael Septien.

DETROIT LIONS
November 27, 1997, at Detroit

Chicago	14	6	0	0	— 20
Detroit	3	14	17	21	— 55

TD: Det—Herman Moore, Johnnie Morton, Ron Rivers, Barry Sanders 2, Tracy Scroggins; Chi—Raymont Harris, Ricky Proehl. TD Passes: Det—Scott Mitchell 2; Chi—Erik Kramer. FG: Det—Jason Hanson 2; Chi—Jeff Jaeger 2.

GREEN BAY PACKERS
October 7, 1945, at Milwaukee

Detroit	0	7	7	7	— 21
Green Bay	0	41	9	7	— 57

TD: GB—Don Hutson 4, Charley Brock, Irv Comp, Ted Fritsch, Clyde Goodnight; Det—Chuck Fenenbock, John Greene, Bob Westfall. TD Passes: GB—Tex McKay 4, Lou Brock, Irv Comp; Det—Dave Ryan.

MINNESOTA VIKINGS
October 18, 1970, at Minnesota

Dallas	3	3	0	7	— 13
Minnesota	14	20	17	3	— 54

TD: Minn—Clint Jones 2, Ed Sharockman 2, John Beasley, Dave Osborn; Dall—Calvin Hill. TD Pass: Minn—Gary Cuozzo. FG: Minn—Fred Cox 4; Dall—Mike Clark 2.

NEW ORLEANS SAINTS
November 21, 1976, at Seattle

New Orleans	3	17	28	3	— 51
Seattle	6	0	14	7	— 27

TD: NO—Bobby Douglass 2, Tony Galbreath, Chuck Muncie, Tom Myers, Elex Price; Sea—Sherman Smith 2, Steve Largent, Jim Zorn. TD Pass: Sea—Bill Munson. FG: NO—Rich Szaro 3.

NEW YORK GIANTS
November 26, 1972, at New York

Philadelphia	3	7	0	0	— 10
New York Giants	14	24	10	14	— 62

TD: NYG—Don Herrmann 2, Ron Johnson 2, Bob Tucker 2, Randy Johnson; Phil—Harold Jackson. TD Passes: NYG—Norm Snead 3, Randy Johnson 2; Phil—John Reaves. FG: NYG—Pete Gogolak 2; Phil—Tom Dempsey.

PHILADELPHIA EAGLES
November 6, 1934, at Philadelphia

Cincinnati Reds	0	0	0	0	— 0
Philadelphia	26	6	12	20	— 64

TD: Phil—Joe Carter 3, Swede Hanson 3, Marvin Ellstrom, Roger Kirkman, Ed Matesic, Ed Storm. TD Passes: Phil—Ed Matesic 2, Albert Weiner 2, Marvin Elstrom.

ST. LOUIS RAMS
October 22, 1950, at Los Angeles

Baltimore	13	0	7	7	— 27
Los Angeles Rams	21	14	14	21	— 70

TD: LA—Bob Boyd 2, Vitamin T. Smith 2, Tom Fears, Elroy (Crazylegs) Hirsch, Dick Hoerner, Ralph Pasquariello, Dan Towler, Bob Waterfield; Balt—Chet Mutryn 2, Adrian Burk, Billy Stone. TD Passes: LA—Norm Van Brocklin 2, Bob Waterfield 2, Glenn Davis; Balt—Adrian Burk 3.

SAN FRANCISCO 49ERS
October 18, 1992, at San Francisco

Atlanta	7	3	0	7	— 17
San Francisco	21	21	14	0	— 56

TD: SF—Jerry Rice 3, Ricky Watters 3, Brent Jones, Tom Rathman; Atl—Michael Haynes, Jason Phillips. TD Passes: SF—Steve Young 3; Atl—Chris Miller, Wade Wilson. FG: Atl—Norm Johnson.

SEATTLE SEAHAWKS
October 30, 1977, at Seattle

Buffalo	3	0	7	7	— 17
Seattle	14	28	7	7	— 56

TD: Sea—Steve Largent 2, Duke Fergerson, Al Hunter, David Sims, Sherman Smith, Don Testerman, Jim Zorn; Buff—Joe Ferguson, John Kimbrough. TD Passes: Sea—Jim Zorn 4; Buff—Joe Ferguson. FG: Buff—Carson Long.

TAMPA BAY BUCCANEERS
December 23, 2001, at Tampa Bay

New Orleans	0	0	7	14	— 21
Tampa Bay	17	13	3	15	— 48

TD: TB—Mike Alstott, Ronde Barber, Warrick Dunn, Dave Moore, Karl Williams; NO—Joe Horn 2, Eddie Williams. TD Passes: TB—Brad Johnson 3; NO—Aaron Brooks 3. FG: TB—Martin Gramatica 4.

WASHINGTON REDSKINS
November 27, 1966, at Washington

New York Giants	0	14	14	13	— 41
Washington	13	21	14	24	— 72

TD: Wash—A.D. Whitfield 3, Brig Owens 2, Charley Taylor 2, Rickie Harris, Joe Don Looney, Bobby Mitchell; NYG—Allen Jacobs, Homer Jones, Dan Lewis, Joe Morrison, Aaron Thomas, Gary Wood. TD Passes: Wash—Sonny Jurgensen 3; NYG—Gary Wood 2, Tom Kennedy. FG: Wash—Charlie Gogolak.

RECORDS OF NFL TEAMS SINCE 1970 AFL-NFL MERGER

AFC	W	L	T	Pct.	Division Titles	Playoff Berths	Postseason Record	Super Bowl Record
Miami	354	228	2	.608	12	21	20-19	2-3
Pittsburgh	351	231	2	.603	18	23	28-18	5-1
Denver	339	239	6	.586	10	17	17-15	2-4
Oakland	323	255	6	.559	12	18	22-15	3-1
Jacksonville**	113	95	0	.543	2	6	5-6	0-0
New England	303	281	0	.519	10	15	20-12	3-3
Kansas City	292	285	7	.506	5	11	3-11	0-0
Baltimore***	96	95	1	.503	2	4	5-3	1-0
Indianapolis	282	300	2	.485	11	16	13-14	2-0
Tennessee	280	302	2	.481	4	15	12-15	0-1
Buffalo	276	306	2	.474	7	13	12-13	0-4
San Diego	268	311	5	.463	8	10	8-10	0-1
Cleveland+	244	289	3	.458	6	11	4-11	0-0
Cincinnati	261	323	0	.447	6	8	5-8	0-2
N.Y. Jets	253	329	2	.435	2	10	6-10	0-0
Houston****	32	64	0	.333	0	0	0-0	0-0

NFC	W	L	T	Pct.	Division Titles	Playoff Berths	Postseason Record	Super Bowl Record
Dallas	347	237	0	.594	16	25	31-20	5-3
Minnesota	333	249	2	.572	14	22	16-22	0-3
San Francisco	330	251	3	.568	17	21	25-16	5-0
Washington	325	257	2	.558	6	16	20-13	3-2
St. Louis	310	270	4	.534	11	19	16-18	1-2
Philadelphia	295	282	7	.511	7	16	13-16	0-2
Green Bay	293	283	8	.509	8	13	13-12	1-1
Chicago	290	293	1	.497	9	13	9-12	1-1
Seattle*	246	254	0	.492	6	10	7-10	0-1
N.Y. Giants	282	299	3	.485	6	13	16-10	3-1
Carolina**	97	111	0	.466	2	3	6-3	0-1
Detroit	246	334	4	.425	3	9	1-9	0-0
Atlanta	244	335	5	.422	3	8	6-8	0-1
New Orleans	242	338	4	.417	3	6	2-6	0-0
Arizona	232	346	6	.402	2	4	1-4	0-0
Tampa Bay*	196	303	1	.393	6	10	6-9	1-0

*Entered NFL in 1976.
**Entered NFL in 1995.
***Entered NFL in 1996.
****Entered NFL in 2002.
+Did not play, 1996-98.
Oakland totals include L.A. Raiders, 1982-1994.
Tennessee totals include Houston, 1970-1996.
Indianapolis totals include Baltimore, 1970-1983.
St. Louis totals include L.A. Rams, 1970-1994.
Arizona totals include St. Louis, 1970-1987, and Phoenix, 1988-1993.
Tie games before 1972 are not calculated in won-lost percentage.

HOME RECORDS OF NFL TEAMS SINCE 1970 AFL-NFL MERGER

AFC	W	L	T	Pct.
Pittsburgh	210	81	1	.721
Denver	207	82	4	.715
Miami	204	86	1	.703
Jacksonville**	67	37	0	.644
Baltimore***	61	34	1	.641
Oakland	180	110	2	.620
Kansas City	178	110	3	.618
New England	173	119	0	.592
Buffalo	163	129	1	.558
Tennessee	160	131	1	.550
Cincinnati	160	132	0	.548
San Diego	154	135	2	.533
Indianapolis	150	140	2	.517
Cleveland+	136	129	2	.513
N.Y. Jets	136	154	1	.469
Houston****	20	28	0	.417

NFC	W	L	T	Pct.
Dallas	198	94	0	.678
Minnesota	196	96	1	.671
Washington	185	104	2	.640
San Francisco	178	112	2	.613
Green Bay	175	112	5	.608
St. Louis	171	119	2	.590
Chicago	171	120	1	.587
Seattle*	147	104	0	.586
Philadelphia	164	126	3	.565
Detroit	160	131	1	.550
N.Y. Giants	154	138	1	.527
Atlanta	146	146	1	.500
Carolina**	51	53	0	.490
Tampa Bay*	122	127	1	.490
Arizona	139	149	3	.483
New Orleans	128	163	1	.440

*Entered NFL in 1976.
**Entered NFL in 1995.
***Entered NFL in 1996.
****Entered NFL in 2002.
+Did not play, 1996-98.
Oakland totals include L.A. Raiders, 1982-1994.
Tennessee totals include Houston, 1970-1996.
Indianapolis totals include Baltimore, 1970-1983.
St. Louis totals include L.A. Rams, 1970-1994.
Arizona totals include St. Louis, 1970-1987, and Phoenix, 1988-1993.
Tie games before 1972 are not calculated in won-lost percentage.

ROAD RECORDS OF NFL TEAMS SINCE 1970 AFL-NFL MERGER

AFC	W	L	T	Pct.
Miami	150	142	1	.514
Oakland	143	145	4	.497
Pittsburgh	141	150	1	.485
Denver	132	157	2	.457
Indianapolis	132	160	0	.452
New England	130	162	0	.445
Jacksonville**	46	58	0	.442
Tennessee	120	171	1	.412
Cleveland+	108	160	1	.403
N.Y. Jets	117	175	1	.401
Kansas City	114	175	4	.396
San Diego	114	176	3	.394
Buffalo	113	177	1	.390
Baltimore***	35	61	0	.365
Cincinnati	101	191	0	.346
Houston****	12	36	0	.250

NFC	W	L	T	Pct.
San Francisco	152	139	1	.522
Dallas	149	143	0	.510
St. Louis	139	151	2	.479
Washington	140	153	0	.478
Minnesota	137	153	1	.473
Philadelphia	131	156	4	.457
N.Y. Giants	128	161	2	.443
Carolina**	46	58	0	.442
Green Bay	118	171	3	.409
Chicago	119	173	0	.408
Seattle*	99	150	0	.398
New Orleans	114	175	3	.395
Atlanta	98	189	4	.342
Arizona	93	197	3	.322
Detroit	86	203	3	.299
Tampa Bay**	74	176	0	.296

*Entered NFL in 1976.
**Entered NFL in 1995.
***Entered NFL in 1996.
****Entered NFL in 2002.
+Did not play, 1996-98.
Oakland totals include L.A. Raiders, 1982-1994.
Tennessee totals include Houston, 1970-1996.
Indianapolis totals include Baltimore, 1970-1983.
St. Louis totals include L.A. Rams, 1970-1994.
Arizona totals include St. Louis, 1970-1987, and Phoenix, 1988-1993.
Tie games before 1972 are not calculated in won-lost percentage.

RECORDS OF TEAMS ON KICKOFF WEEKEND

AFC	W	L	T	Pct.	Longest W Strk.	Longest L Strk.	Current Streak
Jacksonville	9	4	0	.692	6	2	L-1
Denver	30	17	1	.638	4	4	W-1
San Diego	28	20	0	.583	6	6	W-2
Miami	23	18	1	.561	11	5	L-2
Kansas City	26	22	0	.542	7	4	L-2
Pittsburgh	37	32	4	.536	5	3	W-5
Indianapolis	33	30	1	.524	8	8	W-3
Tennessee	25	23	0	.521	4	3	W-1
Houston	3	3	0	.500	2	3	W-1
New England	24	24	0	.500	6	3	W-4
Oakland	24	24	0	.500	5	5	L-5
Cleveland	27	28	0	.491	5	6	L-3
Cincinnati	19	21	0	.475	4	4	W-3
N.Y. Jets	20	28	0	.417	3	5	L-1
Buffalo	19	29	0	.396	6	5	L-2
Baltimore	4	8	0	.333	2	4	L-1

NFC	W	L	T	Pct.	Longest W Strk.	Longest L Strk.	Current Streak
Dallas	32	15	1	.681	17	5	W-1
Chicago	49	34	5	.590	9	6	L-1
N.Y. Giants	46	32	5	.590	4	3	L-2
Minnesota	27	19	1	.587	5	3	W-2
Green Bay	48	36	3	.571	5	6	W-1
Detroit	42	34	2	.553	10	4	W-1
St. Louis	38	32	0	.543	5	6	L-1
San Francisco	30	27	1	.526	5	3	W-1
Atlanta	22	20	0	.524	5	3	L-1
Washington	37	35	4	.514	6	5	W-1
Tampa Bay	13	19	0	.406	3	5	L-2
Arizona	34	51	2	.400	6	7	L-1
Philadelphia	29	44	1	.397	5	9	L-1
Carolina	5	8	0	.385	3	4	W-1
Seattle	11	21	0	.344	3	8	W-2
New Orleans	13	28	0	.317	2	6	L-1

Kansas City totals include Dallas Texans, 1960-62.
Oakland totals include L.A. Raiders, 1982-1994.
San Diego totals include L.A. Chargers, 1960.
Indianapolis totals include Baltimore, 1953-1983.
Tennessee totals include Houston, 1960-1996.
New England totals include Boston, 1960-1970.
St. Louis totals include Cleveland, 1937-1942 and 1944-45, and L.A. Rams, 1946-1994.
Detroit totals include Portsmouth, 1930-33.
Arizona totals include Chi. Cardinals, 1920-1959, St. Louis, 1960-1987, and Phoenix, 1988-1993.
Chicago totals include Decatur, 1920.
Washington totals include Boston Braves, 1932 and Boston Redskins, 1933-36.
NOTE: All tied games occurred prior to 1972, when calculation of ties in percentage as half-win

RECORDS OF NFL TEAMS, 1998-2007

AFC	W	L	T	Pct.	Division Titles	Playoff Berths	Postseason Record	Super Bowl Record
New England	108	52	0	.675	6	7	14-4	3-1
Indianapolis	105	55	0	.656	6	8	7-7	1-0
Denver	97	63	0	.606	2	5	4-4	1-0
Pittsburgh	95	64	1	.597	4	5	7-4	1-0
Tennessee	91	69	0	.569	2	5	5-5	0-1
Jacksonville	89	71	0	.556	2	4	3-4	0-0
Baltimore	86	74	0	.538	2	4	5-3	1-0
N.Y. Jets	82	78	0	.513	2	5	3-5	0-0
Kansas City	80	80	0	.500	1	2	0-2	0-0
Miami	80	80	0	.500	1	4	3-4	0-0
San Diego	77	83	0	.481	3	3	2-3	0-0
Buffalo	74	86	0	.463	0	2	0-2	0-0
Oakland	68	92	0	.425	3	3	4-3	0-1
Cincinnati	61	99	0	.381	1	1	0-1	0-0
Cleveland	50	94	0	.347	0	1	0-1	0-0
Houston	32	64	0	.333	0	0	0-0	0-0

Cleveland did not play in 1998.
Houston entered NFL in 2002.

NFC	W	L	T	Pct.	Division Titles	Playoff Berths	Postseason Record	Super Bowl Record
Green Bay	97	63	0	.606	4	6	3-6	0-0
Philadelphia	91	69	0	.569	5	6	8-6	0-1
Seattle	90	70	0	.563	5	6	4-6	0-1
Minnesota	87	73	0	.544	2	4	4-4	0-0
Tampa Bay	86	74	0	.538	4	6	4-5	1-0
St. Louis	85	75	0	.531	3	5	6-4	1-1
N.Y. Giants	83	77	0	.519	3	5	6-4	1-1
Dallas	80	80	0	.500	1	5	0-5	0-0
Chicago	75	85	0	.469	3	3	2-3	0-1
Atlanta	74	85	1	.466	2	3	4-3	0-1
Washington	74	86	0	.463	1	3	2-3	0-0
Carolina	71	89	0	.444	1	2	5-2	0-1
New Orleans	71	89	0	.444	2	2	2-2	0-0
San Francisco	69	91	0	.431	1	3	2-3	0-0
Arizona	58	102	0	.363	0	1	1-1	0-0
Detroit	53	107	0	.331	0	1	0-1	0-0

Seattle was in the AFC from 1998-2001.

HOME RECORDS, 1998-2007

AFC	W - L - T	Pct.
New England	59-21-0	.738
Denver	57-23-0	.713
Indianapolis	57-23-0	.713
Baltimore	54-26-0	.675
Pittsburgh	52-27-1	.656
Kansas City	52-28-0	.650
Jacksonville	51-29-0	.638
Miami	48-32-0	.600
Tennessee	48-32-0	.600
San Diego	46-34-0	.575
N.Y. Jets	45-35-0	.563
Buffalo	44-36-0	.550
Oakland	40-40-0	.500
Cincinnati	35-45-0	.438
Houston	20-28-0	.417
Cleveland	27-45-0	.375

NFC	W - L - T	Pct.
Seattle	56-24-0	.700
Green Bay	55-25-0	.688
Minnesota	55-25-0	.688
Tampa Bay	52-28-0	.650
Dallas	49-31-0	.613
St. Louis	49-31-0	.613
Philadelphia	47-33-0	.588
Chicago	44-36-0	.550
San Francisco	44-36-0	.550
Washington	43-37-0	.538
Atlanta	42-38-0	.525
N.Y. Giants	41-39-0	.513
Arizona	39-41-0	.488
Detroit	37-43-0	.463
Carolina	36-44-0	.450
New Orleans	33-47-0	.413

Cleveland did not play in 1998.
Houston entered the NFL in 2002.
Seattle was in the AFC from 1998-2001.

ROAD RECORDS, 1998-2007

AFC	W-L-T	Pct.
New England	49-31-0	.613
Indianapolis	48-32-0	.600
Pittsburgh	43-37-0	.538
Tennessee	43-37-0	.538
Denver	40-40-0	.500
Jacksonville	38-42-0	.475
N.Y. Jets	37-43-0	.463
Baltimore	32-48-0	.400
Miami	32-48-0	.400
San Diego	31-49-0	.388
Buffalo	30-50-0	.375
Kansas City	28-52-0	.350
Oakland	28-52-0	.350
Cincinnati	26-54-0	.325
Cleveland	23-49-0	.319
Houston	12-36-0	.250

NFC	W-L-T	Pct.
Philadelphia	44-36-0	.550
Green Bay	42-38-0	.525
N.Y. Giants	42-38-0	.525
New Orleans	38-42-0	.475
St. Louis	36-44-0	.450
Carolina	35-45-0	.438
Seattle	34-46-0	.425
Tampa Bay	34-46-0	.425
Atlanta	32-47-1	.406
Minnesota	32-48-0	.400
Chicago	31-49-0	.388
Dallas	31-49-0	.388
Washington	31-49-0	.388
San Francisco	25-55-0	.313
Arizona	19-61-0	.238
Detroit	16-64-0	.200

Cleveland did not play in 1998.
Houston entered the NFL in 2002.
Seattle was in the AFC from 1998-2001.

RECORDS BY MONTHS, 1998-2007

AFC	Sept. W-L-T	Oct. W-L-T	Nov. W-L-T	Dec. W-L-T	Total W-L-T	Pct.
New England	20-12-0	28-14-0	26-14-0	34-12-0	108- 52-0	.675
Indianapolis	24-9-0	26-11-0	26-16-0	29-19-0	105- 55-0	.656
Denver	23-12-0	24-17-0	25-12-0	25-22-0	97- 63-0	.606
Pittsburgh	17-15-0	26-12-0	22-19-1	30-18-0	95- 64-1	.597
Tennessee	14-18-0	25-16-0	21-17-0	31-18-0	91- 69-0	.569
Jacksonville	21-12-0	17-22-0	25-15-0	26-22-0	89- 71-0	.556
Baltimore	18-15-0	17-22-0	25-18-0	26-19-0	86- 74-0	.538
N.Y. Jets	13-19-0	18-22-0	24-15-0	27-22-0	82- 78-0	.513
Kansas City	18-16-0	24-15-0	14-26-0	24-23-0	80- 80-0	.500
Miami	18-14-0	18-21-0	22-19-0	22-26-0	80- 80-0	.500
San Diego	15-18-0	22-19-0	17-22-0	23-24-0	77- 83-0	.481
Buffalo	11-21-0	22-20-0	19-20-0	22-25-0	74- 86-0	.463
Oakland	18-15-0	18-21-0	17-23-0	15-33-0	68- 92-0	.425
Cincinnati	12-21-0	14-26-0	16-25-0	19-27-0	61- 99-0	.381
Cleveland	11-20-0	14-22-0	13-22-0	12-30-0	50- 94-0	.347
Houston	6-14-0	8-15-0	8-16-0	10-19-0	32- 64-0	.333

Cleveland did not play in 1998.
Houston entered the NFL in 2002.
September totals include August; December totals include January.

NFC	Sept. W-L-T	Oct. W-L-T	Nov. W-L-T	Dec. W-L-T	Total W-L-T	Pct.
Green Bay	22-13-0	17-18-0	24-19-0	34-13-0	97- 63-0	.606
Philadelphia	16-18-0	22-17-0	25-17-0	28-17-0	91- 69-0	.569
Seattle	23-11-0	14-22-0	27-15-0	26-22-0	90- 70-0	.563
Minnesota	19-15-0	23-15-0	24-17-0	21-26-0	87- 73-0	.544
Tampa Bay	18-15-0	18-21-0	23-17-0	27-21-0	86- 74-0	.538
St. Louis	17-17-0	23-16-0	19-20-0	26-22-0	85- 75-0	.531
N.Y. Giants	19-15-0	25-14-0	13-27-0	26-21-0	83- 77-0	.519
Dallas	18-14-0	21-19-0	23-19-0	18-28-0	80- 80-0	.500
Chicago	10-23-0	22-18-0	21-19-0	22-25-0	75- 85-0	.469
Atlanta	16-17-0	19-21-0	19-20-1	20-27-0	74- 85-1	.466
Washington	14-18-0	17-23-0	17-24-0	26-21-0	74- 86-0	.463
Carolina	14-17-0	15-27-0	17-23-0	25-22-0	71- 89-0	.444
New Orleans	16-15-0	20-22-0	16-23-0	19-29-0	71- 89-0	.444
San Francisco	14-18-0	16-24-0	17-23-0	22-26-0	69- 91-0	.431
Arizona	10-23-0	13-25-0	16-25-0	19-29-0	58-102-0	.363
Detroit	14-19-0	14-23-0	15-29-0	10-36-0	53-107-0	.331

Seattle was in the AFC from 1998-2001.
September totals include August; December totals include January.

TAKEAWAYS/GIVEAWAYS, 1998-2007

	Takeaways			Giveaways			
AFC	Int.	Fum.	Total	Int.	Fum.	Total	Net.Diff.
New England	190	120	310	145	106	251	59
Jacksonville	160	118	278	117	106	223	55
Kansas City	167	138	305	156	101	257	48
N.Y. Jets	183	106	289	157	89	246	43
Denver	164	131	295	161	94	255	40
Pittsburgh	161	136	297	163	103	266	31
Tennessee	163	125	288	149	113	262	26
Indianapolis	146	130	276	156	98	254	22
Baltimore	203	123	326	167	148	315	11
Cincinnati	159	127	286	176	113	289	-3
Miami	186	118	304	184	132	316	-12
Buffalo	149	111	260	153	120	273	-13
San Diego	179	104	283	190	115	305	-22
Houston	75	61	136	94	74	168	-32
Oakland	164	107	271	163	140	303	-32
Cleveland	150	93	243	178	119	297	-54

Cleveland did not play in 1998.
Houston entered NFL in 2002.

	Takeaways			Giveaways			
NFC	Int.	Fum.	Total	Int.	Fum.	Total	Net.Diff.
Tampa Bay	197	123	320	149	126	275	45
Seattle	191	123	314	162	123	285	29
Philadelphia	162	132	294	142	129	271	23
Atlanta	166	136	302	163	119	282	20
Carolina	185	142	327	177	141	318	9
Detroit	156	133	289	194	106	300	-11
N.Y. Giants	155	119	274	166	119	285	-11
Washington	162	109	271	147	136	283	-12
San Francisco	164	104	268	156	127	283	-15
Green Bay	185	120	305	196	125	321	-16
Chicago	164	142	306	179	144	323	-17
Minnesota	162	120	282	176	129	305	-23
New Orleans	156	134	290	180	133	313	-23
Dallas	160	112	272	179	117	296	-24
St. Louis	175	116	291	210	148	358	-67
Arizona	158	118	276	212	138	350	-74

Seattle was in the AFC from 1998-2001.

BEST TAKEAWAY/GIVEAWAY DIFFERENTIAL, SEASON
+43   Washington, 1983
+26   Kansas City, 1990
+25   N.Y. Giants, 1997

HIGH AND LOW SINGLE-GAME YARDAGE TOTALS, 1998-2007
Most Total Yards, Game
645   Pittsburgh vs. Atlanta, Nov. 10, 2002 (OT)
614   St. Louis vs. San Diego, Oct. 1, 2000
605   Minnesota at New Orleans, Oct. 17, 2004
595   New Orleans vs. Cincinnati, Nov. 19, 2006
591   Seattle at San Diego, Dec. 29, 2002 (OT)
Fewest Total Yards, Game
26   Cleveland at Buffalo, Dec. 12, 2004
40   Cleveland vs. Pittsburgh, Sept. 12, 1999
47   Houston at Pittsburgh, Dec. 8, 2002
53   Cleveland at Jacksonville, Dec. 3, 2000
94   Cincinnati at Baltimore, Sept. 24, 2000
Most Yards Rushing, Game
407   Cincinnati vs. Denver, Oct. 22, 2000
378   Minnesota vs. San Diego, Nov. 4, 2007
375   Jacksonville vs. Indianapolis, Dec. 10, 2006
343   Baltimore vs. Cleveland, Sept. 14, 2003
337   St. Louis vs. Carolina, Nov. 11, 2001
Fewest Yards Rushing, Game
-18   Detroit at Arizona, Nov. 11, 2007
-3   Detroit vs. Minnesota, Dec. 10, 2006
1   Dallas at Washington, Dec. 30, 2007

4   Cincinnati at Baltimore, Sept. 24, 2000
5   New England at Pittsburgh, Oct. 31, 2004
Most Yards Passing, Game
504   New Orleans vs. Cincinnati, Nov. 19, 2006
499   Denver vs. Atlanta, Oct. 31, 2004
474   Kansas City at Oakland, Nov. 5, 2000
473   N.Y. Jets at Baltimore, Dec. 24, 2000
472   Indianapolis at Kansas City, Oct. 31, 2004
Fewest Yards Passing, Game
-19   San Diego at Kansas City, Sept. 20, 1998
-9   Cleveland at Jacksonville, Dec. 3, 2000
-5   Houston at Oakland, Dec. 3, 2006
-3   Cleveland at Buffalo, Dec. 12, 2004
0   Oakland at San Diego, Dec. 28, 2003

NFL INDIVIDUAL LEADERS, 1998-2007

Points		Passing Yards	
Jason Elam	1,183	Peyton Manning	41,626
Adam Vinatieri	1,154	Brett Favre	39,064
Matt Stover	1,141	Trent Green	27,950
Ryan Longwell	1,123	Kerry Collins	27,422
Jeff Wilkins	1,116	Jake Plummer	27,050

Touchdowns		TD Passes	
LaDainian Tomlinson	129	Peyton Manning	306
Randy Moss	125	Brett Favre	260
Terrell Owens	119	Tom Brady	197
Shaun Alexander	112	Donovan McNabb	171
Marvin Harrison	109	Trent Green	162

Field Goals		Receptions	
Matt Stover	282	Marvin Harrison	905
Jason Elam	261	Torry Holt	805
Adam Vinatieri	259	Tony Gonzalez	787
Jason Hanson	246	Terrell Owens	787
Ryan Longwell	243	Randy Moss	774

Rushes		Reception Yards	
Edgerrin James	2,849	Marvin Harrison	12,242
Curtis Martin	2,560	Randy Moss	12,193
Corey Dillon	2,385	Torry Holt	11,864
LaDainian Tomlinson	2,365	Terrell Owens	11,614
Fred Taylor	2,285	Isaac Bruce	9,903

Rushing Yards		Receiving TDs	
Edgerrin James	11,607	Randy Moss	124
Fred Taylor	10,715	Terrell Owens	117
LaDainian Tomlinson	10,650	Marvin Harrison	109
Curtis Martin	10,302	Torry Holt	71
Corey Dillon	10,112	Hines Ward	65

Rushing TDs		Interceptions	
LaDainian Tomlinson	115	Darren Sharper	51
Shaun Alexander	100	Ty Law	43
Priest Holmes	86	Champ Bailey	42
Edgerrin James	77	Dre' Bly	38
Corey Dillon	72	Two tied	37

Pass Attempts		Sacks	
Brett Favre	5,553	Jason Taylor	112.0
Peyton Manning	5,405	Michael Strahan	109.5
Kerry Collins	4,076	Simeon Rice	104.5
Jake Plummer	4,054	Kevin Carter	77.5
Jon Kitna	3,949	Trevor Pryce	77.0

Completions	
Peyton Manning	3,468
Brett Favre	3,406
Steve McNair	2,388
Jon Kitna	2,363
Jake Plummer	2,327

NFL GAMES IN WHICH A TEAM HAS SCORED 60 OR MORE POINTS

(Home team in capitals)

Regular Season

WASHINGTON 72, New York Giants 41	November 27, 1966
LOS ANGELES RAMS 70, Baltimore 27	October 22, 1950
Chicago Cardinals 65, NEW YORK BULLDOGS 20	November 13, 1949
LOS ANGELES RAMS 65, Detroit 24	October 29, 1950
PHILADELPHIA 64, Cincinnati 0	November 6, 1934
CHICAGO CARDINALS 63, New York Giants 35	October 17, 1948
AKRON 62, Oorang 0	October 29, 1922
PITTSBURGH 62, New York Giants 7	November 30, 1952
CLEVELAND 62, New York Giants 14	December 6, 1953
CLEVELAND 62, Washington 3	November 7, 1954
NEW YORK GIANTS 62, Philadelphia 10	November 26, 1972
Atlanta 62, NEW ORLEANS 7	September 16, 1973
NEW YORK JETS 62, Tampa Bay 28	November 17, 1985
CHICAGO 61, San Francisco 20	December 12, 1965
Cincinnati 61, HOUSTON 17	December 17, 1972
CHICAGO 61, Green Bay 7	December 7, 1980
CINCINNATI 61, Houston 7	December 17, 1989
ROCK ISLAND 60, Evansville 0	October 15, 1922
CHICAGO CARDINALS 60, Rochester 0	October 7, 1923

Postseason

Chicago Bears 73, WASHINGTON 0	December 8, 1940
JACKSONVILLE 62, Miami 7	January 15, 2000

YOUNGEST AND OLDEST PLAYERS IN NFL IN 2007

10 Youngest Players	Age as of Sept. 6, 2007	Games	Starts	Position
Amobi Okoye, Houston	20	16	14	DT
Dwayne Jarrett, Carolina	20	7	0	WR
Gary Russell, Pittsburgh	20	3	0	RB
Sidney Rice, Minnesota	21	13	4	WR
Charles Johnson, Carolina	21	3	2	DE
Lawrence Timmons, Pittsburgh	21	16	0	LB
Marshawn Lynch, Buffalo	21	13	13	RB
Ahmad Bradshaw, N.Y. Giants	21	12	0	RB
Jared Gaither, Baltimore	21	6	2	T
Jamaal Anderson, Atlanta	21	16	16	DE

10 Oldest Players	Age as of Sept. 6, 2007	Games	Starts	Position
Morten Andersen, Atlanta	47	14	0	K
Vinny Testaverde, Carolina	43	7	6	QB
John Carney, Jac.-K.C.	43	13	0	K
Jeff Feagles, N.Y. Giants	41	16	0	P
Matt Stover, Baltimore	39	16	0	K
Ted Washington, Cleveland	39	5	1	NT
Matt Turk, Houston	39	16	0	P
Brad Johnson, Dallas	38	16	0	QB
Rob Davis, Green Bay	38	16	0	LS
Junior Seau, New England	38	16	4	LB

YOUNGEST AND OLDEST REGULAR STARTERS BY POSITION IN 2007

Minimum: 8 Games Started

	Youngest*			Oldest*	
QB	23	Trent Edwards, Buf.	37	Brett Favre, G.B.	
RB	21	Marshawn Lynch, Buf.	36	Lorenzo Neal, S.D.	
WR	21	Calvin Johnson, Det.	35	Joey Galloway, T.B.	
TE	21	Zach Miller, Oak.	35	Kyle Brady, N.E.	
T	22	Joe Thomas, Cle.	34	Fred Miller, Chi.	
G	22	Arron Sears, T.B.	37	Chris Gray, Sea.	
C	22	Samson Satele, Mia.	37	Andy McCollum, StL	
DE	21	Jamaal Anderson, Atl.	35	Michael Strahan, NYG	
DT	20	Amobi Okoye, Hou.	38	Keith Traylor, Mia.	
LB	21	Justin Durant, Jac.	35	Willie McGinest, Cle.	
CB	21	Trumaine McBride, Chi.	33	Ty Law, K.C.	
S	22	Donte Whitner, Buf.	35	John Lynch, Den.	

*Age as of Sept. 6, 2007

OLDEST INDIVIDUAL SINGLE-SEASON OR SINGLE-GAME RECORDS IN NFL RECORD & FACT BOOK

Most Points, Game—40, Ernie Nevers, Chi. Cardinals vs. Chi. Bears, Nov. 28, 1929 (6-td, 4-pat)

Most Touchdowns Rushing, Game—6, Ernie Nevers, Chi. Cardinals vs. Chi. Bears, Nov. 28, 1929

Highest Rushing Average Gain, Season (Qualifiers)—8.44, Beattie Feathers, Chi. Bears, 1934 (119-1,004)

Highest Punting Average, Season (Qualifiers)—51.40, Sammy Baugh, Washington, 1940 (35-1,799)

Highest Punting Average, Rookie, Season (Qualifiers)—45.92, Frank Sinkwich, Detroit, 1943 (12-551)

Highest Punting Average, Game (minimum: 4 punts)—61.75, Bob Cifers, Detroit vs. Chi. Bears, Nov. 24, 1946 (4-247)

Highest Average Gain, Pass Receptions, Season (minimum: 24 receptions)—32.58, Don Currivan, Boston, 1947 (24-782)

Highest Average Gain, Passing, Game (minimum: 20 passes)—18.58, Sammy Baugh, Washington vs. Boston, Oct. 31, 1948 (24-446)

Most Touchdowns, Fumble Recoveries, Game—2, Fred (Dippy) Evans, Chi. Bears vs. Washington, Nov. 28, 1948

Most Yards Gained, Intercepted Passes, Rookie, Season—301, Don Doll, Detroit, 1949

Most Passes Had Intercepted, Game—8, Jim Hardy, Chi. Cardinals vs. Philadelphia, Sept. 24, 1950

Highest Kickoff Return Average, Game (minimum: 3 returns)—73.50, Wally Triplett, Detroit vs. Los Angeles, Oct. 29, 1950 (4-294)

Highest Punt Return Average, Season (Qualifiers)—23.00, Herb Rich, Baltimore, 1950 (12-276)

Highest Punt Return Average, Rookie, Season (Qualifiers)—23.00, Herb Rich, Baltimore, 1950 (12-276)

Most Yards Passing, Game—554, Norm Van Brocklin, Los Angeles vs. N.Y. Yanks, Sept. 28, 1951

Most Touchdowns, Punt Returns, Rookie, Season—4, Jack Christiansen, Detroit, 1951

Most Interceptions By, Season—14, Dick (Night Train) Lane, Los Angeles, 1952

Most Interceptions By, Rookie, Season—14, Dick (Night Train) Lane, Los Angeles, 1952

Highest Average Gain, Passing, Season (Qualifiers)—11.17, Tommy O'Connell, Cleveland, 1957 (110-1,229)

Most Yards Gained, Pass Receptions, Rookie, Season—1,473, Bill Groman, Houston, 1960

NFL INDIVIDUAL LEADERS OVER RECENT SEASONS

Last 2 Seasons	Last 3 Seasons	Last 4 Seasons

Points

Last 2 Seasons		Last 3 Seasons		Last 4 Seasons	
294	LaDainian Tomlinson	414	LaDainian Tomlinson	522	LaDainian Tomlinson
269	Robbie Gould	376	Shayne Graham	498	Shayne Graham
254	Nate Kaeding	366	Nate Kaeding	480	Nate Kaeding
245	Shayne Graham	366	Neil Rackers	473	Jason Elam
240	Stephen Gostkowski	351	Robbie Gould	472	Adam Vinatieri

Touchdowns

49	LaDainian Tomlinson	69	LaDainian Tomlinson	87	LaDainian Tomlinson
28	Marion Barber	44	Larry Johnson	60	Shaun Alexander
28	Terrell Owens	40	Shaun Alexander	55	Larry Johnson
26	Maurice Jones-Drew	34	Randy Moss	48	Terrell Owens
26	Randy Moss	34	Terrell Owens	47	Randy Moss

Field Goals

63	Robbie Gould	89	Neil Rackers	114	Matt Stover
58	Jason Hanson	85	Matt Stover	111	Shayne Graham
57	Rob Bironas	84	Robbie Gould	111	Neil Rackers
56	Shayne Graham	84	Shayne Graham	107	Jason Elam
56	Jeff Wilkins	83	Jeff Wilkins	102	Jeff Wilkins

Rushes

663	LaDainian Tomlinson	1,021	Edgerrin James	1,355	Edgerrin James
661	Edgerrin James	1,002	LaDainian Tomlinson	1,341	LaDainian Tomlinson
658	Willie Parker	920	Thomas Jones	1,209	Rudi Johnson
612	Jamal Lewis	913	Willie Parker	1,182	Shaun Alexander
606	Thomas Jones	910	Larry Johnson	1,162	Willis McGahee

Rushing Yards

3,289	LaDainian Tomlinson	4,751	LaDainian Tomlinson	6,086	LaDainian Tomlinson
2,810	Willie Parker	4,098	Larry Johnson	5,435	Edgerrin James
2,797	Frank Gore	4,012	Willie Parker	5,188	Shaun Alexander
2,550	Brian Westbrook	3,887	Edgerrin James	5,040	Tiki Barber
2,530	Steven Jackson	3,664	Thomas Jones	4,718	Rudi Johnson

Rushing Touchdowns

43	LaDainian Tomlinson	61	LaDainian Tomlinson	78	LaDainian Tomlinson
24	Marion Barber	40	Larry Johnson	54	Shaun Alexander
22	Maurice Jones-Drew	38	Shaun Alexander	49	Larry Johnson
20	Larry Johnson	29	Marion Barber	39	Rudi Johnson
19	Joseph Addai	29	Clinton Portis	37	Corey Dillon

Passes

1,206	Drew Brees	1,755	Brett Favre	2,295	Brett Favre
1,157	Jon Kitna	1,706	Drew Brees	2,106	Drew Brees
1,148	Brett Favre	1,624	Tom Brady	2,098	Tom Brady
1,095	Carson Palmer	1,608	Eli Manning	2,036	Carson Palmer
1,094	Tom Brady	1,604	Carson Palmer	2,022	Peyton Manning

Completions

796	Drew Brees	1,119	Drew Brees	1,417	Brett Favre
727	Jon Kitna	1,071	Brett Favre	1,381	Drew Brees
717	Tom Brady	1,051	Tom Brady	1,340	Peyton Manning
699	Brett Favre	1,042	Carson Palmer	1,339	Tom Brady
699	Peyton Manning	1,004	Peyton Manning	1,305	Carson Palmer

Passing Yards

8,841	Drew Brees	12,445	Tom Brady	16,741	Peyton Manning
8,437	Peyton Manning	12,417	Drew Brees	16,137	Tom Brady
8,335	Tom Brady	12,184	Peyton Manning	16,009	Brett Favre
8,276	Jon Kitna	12,002	Carson Palmer	15,576	Drew Brees
8,166	Carson Palmer	11,921	Brett Favre	14,899	Carson Palmer

Last 2 Seasons		Last 3 Seasons		Last 4 Seasons	

Touchdown Passes

	Last 2 Seasons		Last 3 Seasons		Last 4 Seasons
74	Tom Brady	100	Tom Brady	139	Peyton Manning
62	Peyton Manning	90	Peyton Manning	128	Tom Brady
55	Tony Romo	86	Carson Palmer	105	Drew Brees
54	Drew Brees	78	Drew Brees	104	Carson Palmer
54	Carson Palmer	71	Eli Manning	96	Brett Favre

Receptions

202	T.J. Houshmandzadeh	288	Torry Holt	382	Torry Holt
190	Reggie Wayne	280	T.J. Houshmandzadeh	372	Chad Johnson
186	Torry Holt	277	Chad Johnson	353	T.J. Houshmandzadeh
180	Chad Johnson	273	Steve Smith	353	Derrick Mason
179	Wes Welker	273	Reggie Wayne	352	Tony Gonzalez

Receiving Yards

2,820	Reggie Wayne	4,241	Chad Johnson	5,515	Chad Johnson
2,809	Chad Johnson	3,875	Reggie Wayne	5,085	Reggie Wayne
2,535	Terrell Owens	3,764	Larry Fitzgerald	5,080	Torry Holt
2,377	Torry Holt	3,731	Steve Smith	4,772	Donald Driver
2,355	Larry Fitzgerald	3,708	Torry Holt	4,544	Larry Fitzgerald

Receiving Touchdowns

28	Terrell Owens	34	Randy Moss	48	Terrell Owens
26	Randy Moss	34	Terrell Owens	47	Randy Moss
22	Plaxico Burress	29	Plaxico Burress	41	Antonio Gates
22	Braylon Edwards	28	Antonio Gates	40	Marvin Harrison
21	T.J. Houshmandzadeh	28	T.J. Houshmandzadeh	36	Two tied

Interceptions

16	Asante Samuel	21	Champ Bailey	24	Champ Bailey
13	Champ Bailey	19	Asante Samuel	22	Ed Reed
12	Walt Harris	17	Darren Sharper	21	Darren Sharper
12	Ed Reed	16	Ty Law	20	Asante Samuel
12	Charles Woodson	15	DeAngelo Hall	19	Rashean Mathis

Sacks

29.5	Shawne Merriman	39.5	Shawne Merriman	46.0	Jason Taylor
27.5	Aaron Kampman	36.5	Jason Taylor	43.0	Jared Allen
25.5	DeMarcus Ware	35.0	Derrick Burgess	40.5	Aaron Schobel
24.5	Jason Taylor	34.0	Jared Allen	40.5	Osi Umenyiora
23.0	Jared Allen	34.0	Aaron Kampman	39.5	Shawne Merriman

NFL TEAM LEADERS OVER RECENT SEASONS

Highest Won-Lost Percentage

.875	New England	.813	Indianapolis	.813	New England
.781	Indianapolis	.792	New England	.797	Indianapolis
.781	San Diego	.708	San Diego	.719	San Diego
.688	Dallas	.667	Seattle	.688	Pittsburgh
.656	Green Bay	.646	Two tied	.641	Seattle

Most Points

974	New England	1,353	New England	1,838	Indianapolis
904	San Diego	1,322	San Diego	1,790	New England
880	Dallas	1,316	Indianapolis	1,768	San Diego
877	Indianapolis	1,205	Dallas	1,551	Seattle
792	New Orleans	1,180	Seattle	1,548	Cincinnati

Most Total Yards

12,044	New Orleans	17,608	Indianapolis	24,083	Indianapolis
11,949	New England	17,581	New England	23,303	New England
11,832	Philadelphia	17,075	New Orleans	22,864	Green Bay
11,809	Indianapolis	16,941	Philadelphia	22,590	Denver
11,623	Dallas	16,825	Dallas	22,559	Philadelphia

Last 2 Seasons	Last 3 Seasons	Last 4 Seasons

Most Rushing Yards

Last 2 Seasons		Last 3 Seasons		Last 4 Seasons	
4,932	Jacksonville	7,005	Atlanta	9,677	Atlanta
4,617	San Diego	6,891	Jacksonville	8,981	Denver
4,459	Atlanta	6,689	San Diego	8,874	San Diego
4,454	Minnesota	6,648	Denver	8,847	Pittsburgh
4,323	Tennessee	6,513	NY Giants	8,741	Jacksonville

Most Passing Yards

8,817	New Orleans	12,437	Indianapolis	17,060	Indianapolis
8,341	Indianapolis	12,251	New England	16,344	Green Bay
8,131	New England	12,164	Arizona	15,839	New England
8,129	Green Bay	12,160	New Orleans	15,747	New Orleans
7,941	Dallas	11,895	Green Bay	15,530	Philadelphia

Fewest Turnovers

38	Indianapolis	51	Indianapolis	74	Indianapolis
39	San Diego	61	Jacksonville	83	Jacksonville
42	New England	66	New England	85	San Diego
44	Atlanta	67	San Diego	93	New England
44	Jacksonville	73	Two tied	100	Two tied

Fewest Points Allowed

511	New England	805	Chicago	1,093	Pittsburgh
578	Jacksonville	842	Pittsburgh	1,109	New England
584	Pittsburgh	847	Jacksonville	1,127	Jacksonville
585	Baltimore	849	New England	1,136	Chicago
587	San Diego	869	Indianapolis	1,152	Baltimore

Fewest Total Yards Allowed

9,050	Baltimore	13,599	Baltimore	17,745	Pittsburgh
9,067	Pittsburgh	13,611	Pittsburgh	18,402	Baltimore
9,323	New England	14,169	Tampa Bay	18,721	Tampa Bay
9,559	Jacksonville	14,214	Jacksonville	19,348	Jacksonville
9,725	Tampa Bay	14,456	Carolina	19,578	New England

Fewest Rushing Yards Allowed

2,170	Minnesota	4,011	Minnesota	5,525	Pittsburgh
2,482	Baltimore	4,073	Baltimore	5,754	Baltimore
2,850	Pittsburgh	4,226	Pittsburgh	5,981	San Diego
3,065	Jacksonville	4,659	New England	6,017	Minnesota
3,079	New England	4,674	San Diego	6,231	New England

Fewest Passing Yards Allowed

5,312	Indianapolis	8,463	Indianapolis	11,590	Tampa Bay
5,545	Oakland	8,788	Oakland	11,925	Miami
6,026	Miami	9,011	Tampa Bay	12,220	Pittsburgh
6,082	Tampa Bay	9,131	NY Jets	12,355	Indianapolis
6,217	Pittsburgh	9,333	Miami	12,443	NY Jets

Most Opponents' Turnovers

77	Chicago	111	Chicago	146	Cincinnati
76	San Diego	110	Cincinnati	140	Chicago
67	Minnesota	102	Minnesota	132	Carolina
66	Cincinnati	96	Three tied	130	Indianapolis
66	New England			129	San Diego

SHAUN ALEXANDER'S CAREER RUSHING VS. EACH OPPONENT

Opponent	Games	Rushes	Yards	Yards Per Rush	Yards Per Game	TD
Arizona	12	226	1,070	4.7	89.2	16
Atlanta	5	86	387	4.5	77.4	5
Baltimore	2	35	145	4.1	72.5	0
Buffalo	3	43	174	4.0	58.0	1
Carolina	3	40	212	5.3	70.7	1
Chicago	1	21	101	4.8	101.0	2
Cincinnati	2	41	186	4.5	93.0	0
Cleveland	3	45	162	3.6	54.0	1
Dallas	4	72	229	3.2	57.3	5
Denver	6	86	295	3.4	49.2	3
Detroit	2	39	161	4.1	80.5	1
Green Bay	3	80	376	4.7	125.3	2
Houston	1	22	141	6.4	141.0	4
Indianapolis	2	26	159	6.1	79.5	2
Jacksonville	3	48	262	5.5	87.3	2
Kansas City	5	71	442	6.2	88.4	4
Miami	3	54	188	3.5	62.7	1
Minnesota	3	65	307	4.7	102.3	5
New England	1	16	77	4.8	77.0	1
New Orleans	4	71	297	4.2	74.3	3
N.Y. Giants	4	93	290	3.1	72.5	3
N.Y. Jets	1	19	77	4.1	77.0	0
Oakland	5	69	353	5.1	70.6	5
Philadelphia	4	59	243	4.1	60.8	3
Pittsburgh	2	31	73	2.4	36.5	1
St. Louis	10	202	968	4.8	96.8	9
San Diego	6	105	367	3.5	61.2	4
San Francisco	11	239	954	4.0	86.7	10
Tampa Bay	3	72	242	3.4	80.7	2
Tennessee	1	26	172	6.6	172.0	1
Washington	4	74	319	4.3	79.8	3
Totals	119	2,176	9,429	4.3	79.2	100

LADAINIAN TOMLINSON'S CAREER RUSHING VS. EACH OPPONENT

Opponent	Games	Rushes	Yards	Yards Per Rush	Yards Per Game	TD
Arizona	3	63	232	3.7	77.3	2
Atlanta	1	23	64	2.8	64.0	1
Baltimore	3	73	280	3.8	93.3	1
Buffalo	4	91	431	4.7	107.8	4
Carolina	1	17	47	2.8	47.0	1
Chicago	2	33	86	2.6	43.0	2
Cincinnati	4	80	420	5.3	105.0	9
Cleveland	4	89	585	6.6	146.3	7
Dallas	2	46	162	3.5	81.0	1
Denver	14	292	1,222	4.2	87.3	15
Detroit	2	40	204	5.1	102.0	2
Green Bay	2	42	113	2.7	56.5	0
Houston	3	70	295	4.2	98.3	1
Indianapolis	3	66	233	3.5	77.7	2
Jacksonville	3	45	156	3.5	52.0	2
Kansas City	13	251	1,261	5.0	97.0	10
Miami	3	59	182	3.1	60.7	1
Minnesota	2	32	202	6.3	101.0	3
New England	4	94	468	5.0	117.0	5
New Orleans	1	17	36	2.1	36.0	1
N.Y. Giants	1	21	192	9.1	192.0	3
N.Y. Jets	3	56	254	4.5	84.7	5
Oakland	14	357	1,709	4.8	122.1	16
Philadelphia	2	36	58	1.6	29.0	0
Pittsburgh	3	53	189	3.6	63.0	3
St. Louis	2	49	303	6.2	151.5	3
San Francisco	2	45	159	3.5	79.5	4
Seattle	4	77	315	4.1	78.8	1
Tampa Bay	1	25	131	5.2	131.0	1
Tennessee	3	62	364	5.9	121.3	4
Washington	2	61	297	4.9	148.5	5
Totals	111	2,365	10,650	4.5	95.9	115

EDGERRIN JAMES' CAREER RUSHING VS. EACH OPPONENT

Opponent	Games	Rushes	Yards	Yards Per Rush	Yards Per Game	TD
Atlanta	3	66	235	3.6	78.3	0
Baltimore	4	72	257	3.6	64.3	1
Buffalo	6	141	552	3.9	92.0	7
Carolina	1	21	78	3.7	78.0	1
Chicago	3	76	327	4.3	109.0	2
Cincinnati	4	94	253	2.7	63.3	6
Cleveland	5	104	434	4.2	86.8	4
Dallas	3	66	291	4.4	97.0	1
Denver	4	51	187	3.7	46.8	3
Detroit	4	94	400	4.3	100.0	1
Green Bay	3	62	217	3.5	72.3	2
Houston	8	190	879	4.6	109.9	4
Jacksonville	9	199	785	3.9	87.2	2
Kansas City	5	109	440	4.0	88.0	1
Miami	6	159	668	4.2	111.3	3
Minnesota	3	56	266	4.8	88.7	0
New England	9	232	950	4.1	105.6	3
New Orleans	1	16	84	5.3	84.0	0
N.Y. Giants	2	26	121	4.7	60.5	0
N.Y. Jets	6	156	627	4.0	104.5	6
Oakland	4	89	377	4.2	94.3	2
Philadelphia	1	22	152	6.9	152.0	2
Pittsburgh	3	70	263	3.8	87.7	1
St. Louis	5	123	542	4.4	108.4	5
San Diego	4	68	223	3.3	55.8	2
San Francisco	5	119	453	3.8	90.6	3
Seattle	6	132	613	4.6	102.2	5
Tampa Bay	1	9	15	1.7	15.0	1
Tennessee	7	164	713	4.3	101.9	8
Washington	3	63	205	3.3	68.3	1
Totals	128	2,849	11,607	4.1	90.7	77

FRED TAYLOR'S CAREER RUSHING VS. EACH OPPONENT

Opponent	Games	Rushes	Yards	Yards Per Rush	Yards Per Game	TD
Arizona	1	23	137	6.0	137.0	2
Atlanta	3	65	301	4.6	100.3	0
Baltimore	6	116	510	4.4	85.0	4
Buffalo	4	67	337	5.0	84.3	1
Carolina	3	45	230	5.1	76.7	1
Chicago	2	22	81	3.7	40.5	0
Cincinnati	7	144	660	4.6	94.3	5
Cleveland	3	79	462	5.8	154.0	5
Dallas	3	72	281	3.9	93.7	1
Denver	5	56	253	4.5	50.6	1
Detroit	2	55	327	5.9	163.5	2
Green Bay	1	22	165	7.5	165.0	1
Houston	10	152	765	5.0	76.5	3
Indianapolis	13	220	1,130	5.1	86.9	5
Kansas City	5	68	301	4.4	60.2	1
Miami	3	47	200	4.3	66.7	2
Minnesota	2	45	252	5.6	126.0	0
New England	1	16	57	3.6	57.0	0
New Orleans	2	47	248	5.3	124.0	1
N.Y. Giants	3	43	140	3.3	46.7	2
N.Y. Jets	4	111	470	4.2	117.5	3
Oakland	1	7	111	15.9	111.0	1
Philadelphia	2	36	151	4.2	75.5	1
Pittsburgh	10	205	915	4.5	91.5	7
St. Louis	1	22	165	7.5	165.0	1
San Diego	3	58	236	4.1	78.7	1
San Francisco	2	41	135	3.3	67.5	0
Seattle	2	41	179	4.4	89.5	1
Tampa Bay	3	73	314	4.3	104.7	3
Tennessee	17	237	980	4.1	57.6	5

Opponent	Games	Rushes	Yards	Yards Per Rush	Yards Per Game	TD
Washington	3	50	222	4.4	74.0	1
Totals	127	2,285	10,715	4.7	84.4	61

MARVIN HARRISON'S CAREER RECEIVING VS. EACH OPPONENT

Opponent	Games	Rec.	Yards	Yards/ Rec.	Yards/ Game	TD
Arizona	2	8	104	13.0	52.0	1
Atlanta	2	12	183	15.3	91.5	2
Baltimore	6	31	436	14.1	72.7	3
Buffalo	14	61	831	13.6	59.4	9
Carolina	1	8	119	14.9	119.0	0
Chicago	2	10	91	9.1	45.5	1
Cincinnati	6	44	597	13.6	99.5	6
Cleveland	4	38	407	10.7	101.8	2
Dallas	4	29	333	11.5	83.3	3
Denver	6	37	399	10.8	66.5	3
Detroit	3	24	266	11.1	88.7	5
Green Bay	3	15	191	12.7	63.7	2
Houston	11	67	858	12.8	78.0	5
Jacksonville	12	50	725	14.5	60.4	8
Kansas City	5	35	528	15.1	105.6	6
Miami	15	84	1,133	13.5	75.5	9
Minnesota	3	25	255	10.2	85.0	4
New England	16	102	1,458	14.3	91.1	14
New Orleans	4	23	391	17.0	97.8	4
N.Y. Giants	3	25	350	14.0	116.7	3
N.Y. Jets	13	73	826	11.3	63.5	5
Oakland	3	21	245	11.7	81.7	3
Philadelphia	4	18	311	17.3	77.8	4
Pittsburgh	3	15	256	17.1	85.3	2
St. Louis	2	9	135	15.0	67.5	1
San Diego	6	37	563	15.2	93.8	2
San Francisco	3	16	243	15.2	81.0	4
Seattle	2	11	172	15.6	86.0	0
Tampa Bay	2	14	233	16.6	116.5	2
Tennessee	11	76	1,020	13.4	92.7	8
Washington	4	24	285	11.9	71.3	2
Totals	175	1,042	13,944	13.4	79.7	123

ISAAC BRUCE'S CAREER RECEIVING VS. EACH OPPONENT

Opponent	Games	Rec.	Yards	Yards/ Rec.	Yards/ Game	TD
Arizona	13	52	823	15.8	63.3	6
Atlanta	17	75	1,314	17.5	77.3	11
Baltimore	3	21	334	15.9	111.3	2
Buffalo	2	12	194	16.2	97.0	1
Carolina	15	65	816	12.6	54.4	4
Chicago	7	38	518	13.6	74.0	1
Cincinnati	3	10	192	19.2	64.0	0
Cleveland	3	13	145	11.2	48.3	2
Dallas	3	5	84	16.8	28.0	1
Denver	5	16	204	12.8	40.8	0
Detroit	4	15	200	13.3	50.0	1
Green Bay	8	39	557	14.3	69.6	3
Houston	1	4	94	23.5	94.0	1
Indianapolis	2	13	256	19.7	128.0	2
Jacksonville	1	2	30	15.0	30.0	1
Kansas City	5	22	343	15.6	68.6	4
Miami	4	29	416	14.3	104.0	1
Minnesota	5	30	447	14.9	89.4	2
New England	2	11	189	17.2	94.5	1
New Orleans	15	83	1,459	17.6	97.3	12
N.Y. Giants	6	27	381	14.1	63.5	2
N.Y. Jets	4	18	254	14.1	63.5	3
Oakland	3	12	176	14.7	58.7	1
Philadelphia	6	28	382	13.6	63.7	2
Pittsburgh	3	17	268	15.8	89.3	1
San Diego	4	25	448	17.9	112.0	5

Opponent	Games	Rec.	Yards	Yards/ Rec.	Yards/ Game	TD
San Francisco	26	128	1,925	15.0	74.0	10
Seattle	13	61	813	13.3	62.5	3
Tampa Bay	5	14	177	12.6	35.4	0
Tennessee	2	7	64	9.1	32.0	1
Washington	7	50	606	12.1	86.6	1
Totals	197	942	14,109	15.0	71.6	84

KEENAN McCARDELL'S CAREER RECEIVING VS. EACH OPPONENT

Opponent	Games	Rec.	Yards	Yards/ Rec.	Yards/ Game	TD
Arizona	3	6	104	17.3	34.7	1
Atlanta	6	33	404	12.2	67.3	4
Baltimore	14	82	941	11.5	67.2	1
Buffalo	7	31	352	11.4	50.3	1
Carolina	6	28	381	13.6	63.5	3
Chicago	4	19	180	9.5	45.0	1
Cincinnati	18	73	997	13.7	55.4	10
Cleveland	8	43	482	11.2	60.3	2
Dallas	6	30	406	13.5	67.7	3
Denver	7	26	287	11.0	41.0	0
Detroit	4	9	162	18.0	40.5	1
Green Bay	5	21	286	13.6	57.2	1
Houston	1	5	59	11.8	59.0	0
Indianapolis	4	12	260	21.7	65.0	3
Jacksonville	3	16	161	10.1	53.7	0
Kansas City	10	34	484	14.2	48.4	1
Miami	2	10	144	14.4	72.0	3
Minnesota	3	7	58	8.3	19.3	1
New England	7	23	335	14.6	47.9	5
New Orleans	7	44	519	11.8	74.1	3
N.Y. Giants	5	28	365	13.0	73.0	2
N.Y. Jets	5	11	136	12.4	27.2	0
Oakland	7	29	432	14.9	61.7	2
Philadelphia	6	21	248	11.8	41.3	2
Pittsburgh	20	72	885	12.3	44.3	3
St. Louis	4	25	354	14.2	88.5	2
San Diego	1	9	97	10.8	97.0	0
San Francisco	4	17	262	15.4	65.5	1
Seattle	5	19	316	16.6	63.2	1
Tampa Bay	4	17	203	11.9	50.8	2
Tennessee	19	66	863	13.1	45.4	4
Washington	4	17	210	12.4	52.5	0
Totals	209	883	11,373	12.9	54.4	63

St. Louis totals include one game vs. L.A. Rams
Tennessee totals include seven games vs. Houston

TERRELL OWENS' CAREER RECEIVING VS. EACH OPPONENT

Opponent	Games	Rec.	Yards	Yards/ Rec.	Yards/ Game	TD
Arizona	5	30	432	14.4	86.4	5
Atlanta	13	60	930	15.5	71.5	11
Baltimore	3	15	192	12.8	64.0	1
Buffalo	3	12	166	13.8	55.3	1
Carolina	14	72	1,083	15.0	77.4	10
Chicago	5	49	710	14.5	142.0	2
Cincinnati	3	21	366	17.4	122.0	2
Cleveland	2	12	199	16.6	99.5	2
Dallas	8	39	537	13.8	67.1	7
Denver	4	14	266	19.0	66.5	2
Detroit	7	33	469	14.2	67.0	6
Green Bay	8	43	575	13.4	71.9	6
Houston	1	5	45	9.0	45.0	3
Indianapolis	3	17	252	14.8	84.0	2
Jacksonville	2	11	156	14.2	78.0	1
Kansas City	4	25	296	11.8	74.0	1
Miami	2	9	140	15.6	70.0	1
Minnesota	4	22	311	14.1	77.8	3
New England	2	9	127	14.1	63.5	2

Opponent	Games	Rec.	Yards	Yards/Rec.	Yards/Game	TD
New Orleans	14	61	994	16.3	71.0	12
N.Y. Giants	8	44	704	16.0	88.0	9
N.Y. Jets	3	13	163	12.5	54.3	2
Oakland	3	33	447	13.5	149.0	3
Philadelphia	8	38	579	15.2	72.4	5
Pittsburgh	4	20	268	13.4	67.0	2
St. Louis	16	68	1,004	14.8	62.8	9
San Diego	4	22	401	18.2	100.3	4
San Francisco	1	5	143	28.6	143.0	2
Seattle	4	17	202	11.9	50.5	2
Tampa Bay	3	15	271	18.1	90.3	2
Tennessee	3	12	163	13.6	54.3	2
Washington	9	36	479	13.3	53.2	7
Totals	173	882	13,070	14.8	75.5	129

Tennessee totals include one game vs. Houston

MORTEN ANDERSEN'S CAREER KICKING VS. EACH OPPONENT

Opponent	Games	FG	FGA	FG%	Long FG	XP	XPA	Pts.
Arizona	17	30	32	93.8	52	48	49	138
Atlanta	25	40	51	78.4	49	56	58	176
Baltimore	3	4	5	80.0	46	4	4	16
Buffalo	6	9	14	64.3	50	14	14	41
Carolina	15	27	33	81.8	51	27	27	108
Chicago	9	8	13	61.5	60	23	23	47
Cincinnati	7	10	14	71.4	49	20	20	50
Cleveland	7	13	14	92.9	53	17	17	56
Dallas	15	22	30	73.3	54	31	31	97
Denver	10	8	14	57.1	55	31	33	55
Detroit	14	12	19	63.2	50	33	33	69
Green Bay	10	15	17	88.2	52	29	29	74
Houston	3	4	5	80.0	46	12	12	24
Indianapolis	5	7	9	77.8	46	14	14	35
Jacksonville	4	6	7	85.7	46	7	7	25
Kansas City	6	11	12	91.7	50	10	10	43
Miami	6	7	9	77.8	50	21	21	42
Minnesota	12	18	23	78.3	51	20	20	74
New England	7	11	13	84.6	54	21	21	54
New Orleans	18	29	37	78.4	55	40	40	127
N.Y. Giants	12	18	23	78.3	47	19	19	73
N.Y. Jets	7	13	14	92.9	53	14	14	53
Oakland	10	13	16	81.3	51	21	21	60
Philadelphia	15	28	34	82.4	56	24	24	108
Pittsburgh	8	9	13	69.2	50	20	21	47
St. Louis	38	54	63	85.7	51	95	97	257
San Diego	7	7	11	63.6	46	20	20	41
San Francisco	39	64	76	84.2	59	62	64	254
Seattle	9	16	17	94.1	48	22	22	70
Tampa Bay	19	26	34	76.5	50	38	38	116
Tennessee	8	13	18	72.2	47	16	16	55
Washington	11	13	19	68.4	50	20	20	59
Totals	382	565	709	79.7	60	849	859	2,544

Arizona totals include five games vs. St. Louis and four games vs. Phoenix
Oakland totals include four games vs. L.A. Raiders
St. Louis totals include 23 games vs. L.A. Rams
Tennessee totals include five games vs. Houston

JOHN CARNEY'S CAREER KICKING VS. EACH OPPONENT

Opponent	Games	FG	FGA	FG%	Long FG	XP	XPA	Pts.
Arizona	4	5	5	100.0	50	9	9	24
Atlanta	16	25	33	75.8	51	37	37	112
Baltimore	4	4	4	100.0	47	8	8	20
Buffalo	5	10	12	83.3	54	9	9	39
Carolina	14	17	21	81.0	48	29	29	80
Chicago	6	7	13	53.8	50	12	12	33
Cincinnati	6	13	14	92.9	48	13	14	52
Cleveland	6	12	14	85.7	48	12	12	48
Dallas	4	4	4	100.0	44	11	11	23
Denver	23	40	46	87.0	50	34	35	154
Detroit	7	8	10	80.0	47	11	11	35
Green Bay	6	7	11	63.6	47	11	11	32
Houston	2	2	3	66.7	39	8	9	14
Indianapolis	10	17	20	85.0	50	24	24	75
Jacksonville	1	2	2	100.0	38	1	2	7
Kansas City	22	22	30	73.3	54	44	44	110
Miami	6	9	12	75.0	49	12	12	39
Minnesota	6	13	14	92.9	50	14	15	53
New England	6	3	8	37.5	46	9	9	18
New Orleans	5	11	11	100.0	49	14	14	47
N.Y. Giants	6	12	14	85.7	46	15	15	51
N.Y. Jets	7	6	7	85.7	53	17	17	35
Oakland	21	34	42	81.0	48	33	34	135
Philadelphia	5	6	7	85.7	39	9	9	27
Pittsburgh	10	15	18	83.3	48	18	18	63
St. Louis	7	16	19	84.2	53	16	16	64
San Diego	2	2	3	66.7	38	3	3	9
San Francisco	7	14	16	87.5	50	14	14	56
Seattle	23	49	57	86.0	54	35	36	182
Tampa Bay	16	20	24	83.3	48	38	39	98
Tennessee	6	10	11	90.9	48	8	8	38
Washington	5	10	14	71.4	41	9	9	39
Totals	274	425	519	81.9	54	537	545	1,812

Arizona totals include one game vs. Phoenix
Oakland totals include two games vs. L.A. Raiders
St. Louis totals include two games vs. L.A. Rams
Tennessee totals include two games vs. Houston

KURT WARNER'S CAREER PASSING VS. EACH OPPONENT

Opponent	Games	Att.	Cmp.	Pct.	Yards	Avg. Gain	TD	Int.	Sacked
Arizona	1	30	19	63.3	193	6.43	1	0	6/32
Atlanta	8	229	154	67.2	2,154	9.41	21	6	15/83
Baltimore	3	73	49	67.1	694	9.51	5	2	3/25
Carolina	6	141	93	66.0	1,206	8.55	8	12	8/56
Chicago	3	73	43	58.9	542	7.42	4	3	8/35
Cincinnati	2	49	33	67.3	521	10.63	5	0	5/25
Cleveland	3	86	60	69.8	658	7.65	5	1	3/12

Opponent	Games	Att.	Cmp.	Pct.	Yards	Avg. Gain	TD	Int.	Sacked
Dallas	2	35	19	54.3	234	6.69	1	1	3/6
Denver	2	76	57	75.0	756	9.95	3	4	5/28
Detroit	6	205	136	66.3	1,507	7.35	11	4	13/72
Green Bay	1	26	20	76.9	187	7.19	1	1	4/29
Houston	1	10	10	100.0	115	11.50	1	0	2/12
Indianapolis	1	30	23	76.7	359	11.97	3	1	2/0
Jacksonville	1	46	29	63.0	315	6.85	2	1	3/14
Kansas City	1	25	15	60.0	185	7.40	1	2	2/14
Miami	1	31	24	77.4	328	10.58	4	0	1/10
Minnesota	2	53	40	75.5	490	9.25	0	0	5/29
New England	1	42	30	71.4	401	9.55	3	2	1/5
New Orleans	6	184	119	64.7	1,648	8.96	13	7	13/99
N.Y. Giants	5	217	133	61.3	1,507	6.94	5	5	17/115
N.Y. Jets	1	27	18	66.7	215	7.96	1	0	2/4
Philadelphia	4	136	76	55.9	870	6.40	3	6	18/108
Pittsburgh	1	21	14	66.7	132	6.29	1	0	1/6
St. Louis	5	176	112	63.6	1,358	7.72	8	7	7/47
San Diego	2	62	46	74.2	746	12.03	5	0	3/24
San Francisco	10	328	214	65.2	2,816	8.59	19	10	20/141
Seattle	5	192	124	64.6	1,393	7.26	6	10	16/115
Tampa Bay	4	146	79	54.1	1,080	7.40	3	11	10/72
Tennessee	1	46	29	63.0	328	7.13	3	0	6/41
Washington	4	164	108	65.9	1,070	6.52	6	4	8/56
Totals	93	2,959	1,926	65.1	24,008	8.11	152	100	210/1,315

PEYTON MANNING'S CAREER PASSING VS. EACH OPPONENT

Opponent	Games	Att.	Cmp.	Pct.	Yards	Avg. Gain	TD	Int.	Sacked
Arizona	1	2	1	50.0	5	2.50	0	0	1/0
Atlanta	4	124	89	71.8	1,046	8.44	13	4	5/34
Baltimore	6	216	138	63.9	1,703	7.88	13	3	10/87
Buffalo	10	320	195	60.9	2,250	7.03	13	9	9/66
Carolina	3	98	54	55.1	773	7.89	4	3	5/18
Chicago	2	67	43	64.2	513	7.66	6	2	2/21
Cincinnati	5	169	108	63.9	1,365	8.08	14	3	3/12
Cleveland	4	143	93	65.0	992	6.94	2	4	2/10
Dallas	3	111	71	64.0	819	7.38	5	3	3/20
Denver	6	165	108	65.5	1,110	6.73	8	2	5/30
Detroit	2	61	45	73.8	524	8.59	9	2	1/7
Green Bay	2	84	53	63.1	687	8.18	8	1	4/27
Houston	12	375	270	72.0	3,292	8.78	29	4	14/79
Jacksonville	13	452	277	61.3	3,473	7.68	25	8	11/81
Kansas City	5	171	103	60.2	1,399	8.18	9	4	9/75
Miami	11	378	230	60.8	2,654	7.02	16	18	17/126
Minnesota	2	65	48	73.8	551	8.48	8	1	1/4
New England	13	461	282	61.2	3,414	7.41	26	18	20/128
New Orleans	4	115	75	65.2	1,173	10.20	11	4	5/26
N.Y. Giants	3	122	75	61.5	878	7.20	6	4	3/20
N.Y. Jets	10	373	233	62.5	2,503	6.71	13	11	13/85
Oakland	4	154	97	63.0	1,082	7.03	9	6	7/45
Philadelphia	3	69	48	69.6	737	10.68	7	1	1/8
Pittsburgh	2	73	47	64.4	549	7.52	3	4	4/15
St. Louis	2	60	37	61.7	386	6.43	2	1	4/21
San Diego	5	222	128	57.7	1,588	7.15	8	11	10/62
San Francisco	3	112	72	64.3	856	7.64	5	6	3/16
Seattle	3	81	52	64.2	732	9.04	2	1	3/6
Tampa Bay	2	84	63	75.0	639	7.61	4	2	1/5
Tennessee	12	374	264	70.6	3,079	8.23	20	10	11/72
Washington	3	104	69	66.3	854	8.21	8	3	4/26
Totals	160	5,405	3,468	64.2	41,626	7.70	306	153	191/1,232

TOM BRADY'S CAREER PASSING VS. EACH OPPONENT

Opponent	Games	Att.	Cmp.	Pct.	Yards	Avg. Gain	TD	Int.	Sacked
Arizona	1	26	15	57.7	219	8.42	2	2	2/12
Atlanta	2	58	43	74.1	600	10.34	6	1	4/22
Baltimore	2	68	33	48.5	429	6.31	2	1	4/23
Buffalo	14	411	268	65.2	3,220	7.83	30	10	31/190

Opponent	Games	Att.	Cmp.	Pct.	Yards	Avg. Gain	TD	Int.	Sacked
Carolina	2	73	40	54.8	468	6.41	2	3	3/23
Chicago	2	88	58	65.9	595	6.76	4	3	2/13
Cincinnati	3	84	58	69.0	679	8.08	7	2	1/3
Cleveland	4	119	72	60.5	899	7.55	4	3	6/29
Dallas	2	80	46	57.5	600	7.50	5	0	5/24
Denver	5	203	115	56.7	1,302	6.41	8	5	7/40
Detroit	3	71	46	64.8	521	7.34	0	2	2/21
Green Bay	2	75	44	58.7	427	5.69	5	3	3/21
Houston	2	70	45	64.3	477	6.81	4	2	5/28
Indianapolis	7	216	144	66.7	1,662	7.69	14	9	8/70
Jacksonville	2	73	50	68.5	477	6.53	3	0	3/23
Kansas City	3	120	78	65.0	973	8.11	6	5	8/33
Miami	14	387	221	57.1	2,447	6.32	25	13	29/161
Minnesota	2	77	50	64.9	611	7.94	7	1	5/47
New Orleans	2	55	34	61.8	480	8.73	7	0	7/45
N.Y. Giants	2	63	40	63.5	468	7.43	2	0	3/31
N.Y. Jets	14	407	260	63.9	2,840	6.98	15	6	25/169
Oakland	2	68	42	61.8	478	7.03	2	0	4/25
Philadelphia	2	98	64	65.3	635	6.48	4	0	5/26
Pittsburgh	4	173	117	67.6	1,336	7.72	9	3	9/68
St. Louis	2	58	37	63.8	419	7.22	3	2	4/15
San Diego	4	170	113	66.5	1,220	7.18	8	4	6/43
San Francisco	1	30	22	73.3	226	7.53	2	1	1/5
Seattle	1	30	19	63.3	231	7.70	1	1	1/7
Tampa Bay	1	31	20	64.5	258	8.32	3	0	1/5
Tennessee	3	84	46	54.8	578	6.88	2	1	7/48
Washington	2	76	54	71.1	595	7.83	5	3	2/8
Totals	112	3,642	2,294	63.0	26,370	7.24	197	86	203/1,278

DONOVAN McNABB'S CAREER PASSING VS. EACH OPPONENT

Opponent	Games	Att.	Cmp.	Pct.	Yards	Avg. Gain	TD	Int.	Sacked
Arizona	6	186	126	67.7	1,373	7.38	12	5	13/72
Atlanta	3	122	75	61.5	880	7.21	4	2	5/21
Baltimore	1	33	18	54.5	219	6.64	1	0	2/19
Buffalo	3	81	53	65.4	552	6.81	1	1	6/37
Carolina	3	72	40	55.6	459	6.38	1	3	6/39
Chicago	5	140	85	60.7	879	6.28	3	3	9/53
Cincinnati	1	40	23	57.5	198	4.95	1	1	2/15
Cleveland	2	79	51	64.6	766	9.70	8	1	7/49
Dallas	15	485	264	54.4	3,045	6.28	22	11	32/208
Denver	1	34	12	35.3	283	8.32	3	2	2/11
Detroit	2	68	50	73.5	737	10.84	6	0	3/18
Green Bay	5	168	93	55.4	1,252	7.45	9	2	15/91
Houston	2	77	48	62.3	573	7.44	4	2	4/30
Indianapolis	2	83	46	55.4	446	5.37	2	2	6/59
Jacksonville	2	82	46	56.1	391	4.77	2	0	9/42
Kansas City	2	74	51	68.9	638	8.62	5	2	3/19
Miami	2	38	18	47.4	270	7.11	0	3	1/0
Minnesota	3	93	61	65.6	801	8.61	6	0	5/37
New England	1	46	18	39.1	186	4.04	0	2	8/43
New Orleans	4	124	79	63.7	991	7.99	8	1	12/66
N.Y. Giants	14	390	222	56.9	2,561	6.57	16	4	43/255
N.Y. Jets	2	58	39	67.2	419	7.22	2	2	8/45
Oakland	2	79	42	53.2	498	6.30	2	1	5/16
Pittsburgh	2	79	41	51.9	322	4.08	2	1	7/30
St. Louis	3	83	50	60.2	527	6.35	6	3	8/58
San Diego	2	98	57	58.2	508	5.18	3	3	5/36
San Francisco	4	123	81	65.9	1,108	9.01	8	3	13/97
Seattle	1	37	24	64.9	283	7.65	2	0	5/41
Tampa Bay	5	107	57	53.3	603	5.64	4	5	12/87
Tennessee	3	80	42	52.5	529	6.61	3	3	11/64
Washington	15	473	277	58.6	3,107	6.57	25	11	32/171
Totals	118	3,732	2,18	58.7	25,404	6.81	171	79	299/1,829

The NFL rates its passers for statistical purposes against a fixed performance standard based on statistical achievements of all qualified pro passers since 1960. The current system replaced one that rated passers in relation to their position in a total group based on various criteria. The current system, which was adopted in 1973, removes inequities that existed in the former method and, at the same time, provides a means of comparing passing performances from one season to the next.

It is important to remember that the system is used to rate passers, not quarterbacks. Statistics do not reflect leadership, play-calling, and other intangible factors that go into making a successful professional quarterback. Four categories are used as a basis for compiling a rating:

—Percentage of completions per attempt
—Average yards gained per attempt
—Percentage of touchdown passes per attempt
—Percentage of interceptions per attempt

The average standard is 1.000. The bottom is .000. To earn a 2.000 rating, a passer must perform at exceptional levels, i.e., 70 percent in completions, 10 percent in touchdowns, 1.5 percent in interceptions, and 11 yards average gain per pass attempt. The maximum passer can receive in any category is 2.375.

For example, to gain a 2.375 in completion percentage, a passer would have to complete 77.5 percent of his passes. The NFL record is 70.55 by Ken Anderson (Cincinnati, 1982). To earn a 2.375 in percentage of touchdowns, a passer would have to achieve a percentage of 11.9. The record is 13.9 by Sid Luckman (Chicago, 1943). To gain 2.375 in percentage of interceptions, a passer would have to go the entire season without an interception. The 2.375 figure in average yards is 12.50, compared with the NFL record of 11.17 by Tommy O'Connell (Cleveland, 1957).

In order to make the rating more understandable, the point rating is then converted into a scale of 100, with 158.3 being the highest rating a passer can achieve. In cases where statistical performance has been superior, it is possible for a passer to sur-

pass a 100 rating. For example, take Peyton Manning's record-setting season in 2004 when he completed 336 of 497 passes for 4,557 yards, 49 touchdowns, and 10 interceptions. The four calculations would be:

—Percentage of Completions—336 of 497 is 67.60 percent. Subtract 30 from the completion percentage (37.60) and multiply the result by 0.05. The result is a point rating of 1.880.
Note: If the result is less than zero (Comp. Pct. less than 30.0), award zero points. If the results are greater than 2.375 (Comp. Pct. greater than 77.5), award 2.375.

—Average Yards Gained Per Attempt—4,557 yards divided by 497 attempts is 9.17. Subtract three yards from yards-per-attempt (6.17) and multiply the result by 0.25. The result is 1.543.
Note: If the result is less than zero (yards per attempt less than 3.0), award zero points. If the result is greater than 2.375 (yards per attempt greater than 12.5), award 2.375 points.

—Percentage of Touchdown Passes—49 touchdowns in 497 attempts is 9.86 percent. Multiply the touchdown percentage by 0.2. The result is 1.972.
Note: If the result is greater than 2.375 (touchdown percentage greater than 11.875), award 2.375.

—Percentage of Interceptions—10 interceptions in 497 attempts is 2.01 percent. Multiply the interception percentage by 0.25 (0.503) and subtract the number from 2.375. The result is 1.872.
Note: If the result is less than zero (interception percentage greater than 9.5), award zero points.

The sum of the four steps is (1.880 + 1.543 + 1.972 + 1.872) 7.267. The sum is then divided by six (1.211) and multiplied by 100. In this case, the result is 121.1. This same formula can be used to determine a passer rating for any player who attempts at least one pass.

Forty-two qualifying passers have had a single-season passer rating of 100 or higher. The following is a list of the Top 25 single-seasons passer ratings among qualifying players:

TOP 25 NFL SINGLE-SEASON PASSER RATINGS (QUALIFYING PLAYERS)

Player, Team	Season	Rating	Att.	Comp.	Pct.	Yds.	Yds. Avg.	TD	TD Pct.	Int.	Int. Pct.
Peyton Manning, Indianapolis	2004	*121.1	497	336	67.6	4,557	9.17	49	9.9	10	2.0
Tom Brady, New England	2007	117.2	578	398	68.9	4,806	8.31	*50	8.7	8	1.4
Steve Young, San Francisco	1994	112.8	461	324	70.2	3,969	8.61	35	7.6	10	2.2
Joe Montana, San Francisco	1989	112.4	386	271	70.2	3,521	9.12	26	6.7	8	2.1
Daunte Culpepper, Minnesota	2004	110.9	548	379	69.2	4,717	8.61	39	7.1	11	2.0
Milt Plum, Cleveland	1960	110.4	250	151	60.4	2,297	9.19	21	8.4	5	2.0
Sammy Baugh, Washington	1945	109.9	182	128	70.3	1,669	9.17	11	6.0	4	2.2
Kurt Warner, St. Louis	1999	109.2	499	325	65.1	4,353	8.72	41	8.2	13	2.6
Dan Marino, Miami	1984	108.9	564	362	64.2	*5,084	9.01	48	8.5	17	3.0
Sid Luckman, Chicago Bears	1943	107.5	202	110	54.5	2,194	10.86	28	13.9	12	5.9
Steve Young, San Francisco	1992	107.0	402	268	66.7	3,465	8.62	25	6.2	7	1.7
Randall Cunningham, Minnesota	1998	106.0	425	259	60.9	3,704	8.72	34	8.0	10	2.4
Bart Starr, Green Bay	1966	105.0	251	156	62.2	2,257	8.99	14	5.6	3	1.2
Drew Brees, San Diego	2004	104.8	400	262	65.5	3,159	7.90	27	6.8	7	1.8
Roger Staubach, Dallas	1971	104.8	211	126	59.7	1,882	8.92	15	7.1	4	1.9
Y.A. Tittle, N.Y. Giants	1963	104.8	367	221	60.2	3,145	8.57	36	9.8	14	3.8
Donovan McNabb, Philadelphia	2004	104.7	469	300	64.0	3,875	8.06	31	6.6	8	1.7
Steve Young, San Francisco	1997	104.7	356	241	67.7	3,029	8.51	19	5.3	6	1.7
Bart Starr, Green Bay	1968	104.3	171	109	63.7	1,617	9.46	15	8.8	8	4.7
Chad Pennington, N.Y. Jets	2002	104.2	399	275	68.9	3,120	7.82	22	5.5	6	1.5
Ben Roethlisberger, Pittsburgh	2007	104.1	404	264	65.3	3,154	7.81	32	7.9	11	2.7
Peyton Manning, Indianapolis	2005	104.1	453	305	67.3	3,747	8.27	28	6.2	10	2.2
Ken Stabler, Oakland	1976	103.4	291	194	66.7	2,737	9.41	27	9.3	17	5.8
Brian Griese, Denver	2000	102.9	336	216	64.3	2,688	8.00	19	5.7	4	1.2
Joe Montana, San Francisco	1984	102.9	432	279	64.6	3,630	8.40	28	6.5	10	2.3

*NFL Record

HIGHEST NFL POSTSEASON PASSER RATINGS (MINIMUM: 150 ATTEMPTS)

Player	Games	Att.	Cmp.	Pct.	Yards	Avg. Gain	TD	Int.	Rating
Bart Starr	10	213	130	61.0	1,753	8.23	15	3	104.8
Joe Montana	23	734	460	62.7	5,772	7.86	45	21	95.6
Jake Delhomme	7	192	113	58.9	1,642	8.55	11	5	95.0
Ken Anderson	6	166	110	66.3	1,321	7.96	9	6	93.5
Kurt Warner	7	268	169	63.1	2,221	8.29	15	10	92.3
Joe Theismann	10	211	128	60.7	1,782	8.45	11	7	91.4
Troy Aikman	16	502	320	63.7	3,849	7.67	23	17	88.3
Tom Brady	17	595	372	62.5	3,954	6.65	26	12	88.0
Steve Young	22	471	292	62.0	3,326	7.06	20	13	85.8
Brett Favre	22	721	438	60.6	5,311	7.37	39	28	85.2

HIGHEST NFL POSTSEASON PASSER RATINGS, ACTIVE PLAYERS (MINIMUM: 100 ATTEMPTS)

Player	Games	Att.	Cmp.	Pct.	Yards	Avg. Gain	TD	Int.	Rating
Jake Delhomme	7	192	113	58.9	1,642	8.55	11	5	95.0
Drew Brees	3	123	78	63.4	916	7.45	5	2	92.7
Kurt Warner	7	268	169	63.1	2,221	8.29	15	10	92.3
Tom Brady	17	595	372	62.5	3,954	6.65	26	12	88.0
Ben Roethlisberger	7	189	118	62.4	1,547	8.19	12	11	85.1
Peyton Manning	14	522	323	61.9	3,898	7.47	21	17	84.6
Eli Manning	6	164	98	59.8	1,128	6.88	8	5	84.1
Chad Pennington	5	178	107	60.1	1,166	6.55	7	4	83.2
Daunte Culpepper	4	134	73	54.5	980	7.31	8	5	82.3
Vinny Testaverde	7	189	114	60.3	1,320	6.98	6	5	81.0

ALL-TIME RANKINGS OF PLAYERS IN FOUR CATEGORIES THAT DETERMINE NFL PASSER RATING

Minimum: 1,500 Attempts

COMPLETION PERCENTAGE	Pct.	Att.	Comp.
Chad Pennington	65.61	1,919	1,259
Kurt Warner	65.09	2,959	1,926
Steve Young	64.28	4,149	2,667
Peyton Manning	64.16	5,405	3,468
Carson Palmer	64.10	2,036	1,305
Daunte Culpepper	63.79	2,927	1,867
Drew Brees	63.71	3,015	1,921
Marc Bulger	63.53	2,484	1,578
Joe Montana	63.24	5,391	3,409
Tom Brady	62.99	3,642	2,294

TOUCHDOWN PERCENTAGE	Pct.	Att.	TD
Sid Luckman	7.86	1,744	137
Frank Ryan	6.99	2,133	149
Len Dawson	6.39	3,741	239
Daryle Lamonica	6.31	2,601	164
Sammy Baugh	6.24	2,995	187
Charlie Conerly	6.11	2,833	173
Bob Waterfield	6.00	1,617	97
Earl Morrall	5.99	2,689	161
Sonny Jurgensen	5.98	4,262	255
Norm Van Brocklin	5.98	2,895	173

AVERAGE YARDS PER PASS	Avg.	Att.	Yards
Otto Graham	8.63	1,565	13,499
Sid Luckman	8.42	1,744	14,686
Norm Van Brocklin	8.16	2,895	23,611
Kurt Warner	8.11	2,959	24,008
Steve Young	7.98	4,149	33,124
Ed Brown	7.85	1,987	15,600
Bart Starr	7.85	3,149	24,718
Johnny Unitas	7.76	5,186	40,239
Earl Morrall	7.74	2,689	20,809
Peyton Manning	7.70	5,405	41,626

INTERCEPTION PERCENTAGE	Pct.	Att.	Int.
Neil O'Donnell	2.11	3,229	68
Donovan McNabb	2.12	3,732	79
Mark Brunell	2.31	4,594	106
Jeff Garcia	2.33	3,300	77
Tom Brady	2.36	3,642	86
Steve Bono	2.47	1,701	42
Rich Gannon	2.47	4,206	104
Joe Montana	2.58	5,391	139
Steve Young	2.58	4,149	107
Bernie Kosar	2.59	3,365	87

STARTING RECORDS OF ACTIVE NFL QUARTERBACKS

Minimum: 10 starts

	W - L - T	Pct.
Tom Brady	86-24-0	.782
Philip Rivers	25-7-0	.781
Tony Romo	19-7-0	.731
Ben Roethlisberger	39-16-0	.709
Kyle Orton	12-6-0	.667
Peyton Manning	105-55-0	.656
Donovan McNabb	73-39-0	.652
David Garrard	19-11-0	.633
Rex Grossman	19-11-0	.633
Vince Young	17-11-0	.607
Matt Hasselbeck	57-39-0	.594
Jake Delhomme	38-27-0	.585
Damon Huard	14-10-0	.583
Brad Johnson	71-51-0	.582
Tarvaris Jackson	8-6-0	.571
Kurt Warner	48-37-0	.565
Derek Anderson	10-8-0	.556
Eli Manning	30-25-0	.545
Brian Griese	42-36-0	.538
Marc Bulger	38-34-0	.528
Carson Palmer	32-29-0	.525
Chad Pennington	32-29-0	.525
Drew Brees	47-43-0	.522
Byron Leftwich	24-22-0	.522
Mark Brunell	78-72-0	.520
Trent Dilfer	58-55-0	.513
Todd Collins	10-10-0	.500
Trent Green	56-56-0	.500
Jeff Garcia	52-53-0	.495
Kyle Boller	20-22-0	.476
A.J. Feeley	7-8-0	.467
Chris Simms	7-8-0	.467
Gus Frerotte	37-44-1	.457
Daunte Culpepper	41-49-0	.456
Kerry Collins	67-82-0	.450
Charlie Batch	22-28-0	.440
Matt Leinart	7-9-0	.438
Jay Cutler	9-12-0	.429
Vinny Testaverde	90-123-1	.423
Anthony Wright	8-11-0	.421
Patrick Ramsey	10-14-0	.417
Jon Kitna	46-65-0	.414
Jason Campbell	8-12-0	.400
Chris Redman	4-6-0	.400
Josh McCown	12-19-0	.387
Alex Smith	11-19-0	.367
Joey Harrington	26-50-0	.342
Kelly Holcomb	8-16-0	.333
J.P. Losman	10-21-0	.323
Charlie Frye	6-13-0	.316
Matt Schaub	4-9-0	.308
Billy Volek	3-7-0	.300
David Carr	23-56-0	.291
Tim Rattay	5-13-0	.278
Bruce Gradkowski	3-8-0	.273
Brooks Bollinger	2-8-0	.200
Ken Dorsey	2-8-0	.200
Chris Weinke	2-18-0	.100

TEAMS THAT FINISHED IN FIRST PLACE IN THEIR DIVISION THE SEASON AFTER FINISHING IN LAST PLACE

Season	Team	Record	Prior Season
1967	Houston	9-4-1	*3-11-0
1968	Minnesota	8-6-0	3- 8-3
1970	Cincinnati	8-6-0	4- 9-1
1970	San Francisco	10-3-1	4- 8-2
1972	Green Bay	10-4-0	4- 8-2
1975	Baltimore	10-4-0	2-12-0

Season	Team	Record	Prior Season
1979	Tampa Bay	10-6-0	5-11-0
1981	Cincinnati	12-4-0	6-10-0
1987	Indianapolis	9-6-0	3-13-0
1988	Cincinnati	12-4-0	4-11-0
1990	Cincinnati	9-7-0	8- 8-0
1991	Denver	12-4-0	5-11-0
1992	San Diego	11-5-0	4-12-0
1993	Detroit	10-6-0	5-11-0
1997	N.Y. Giants	10-5-1	6-10-0
1999	Indianapolis	13-3-0	3-13-0
1999	St. Louis	13-3-0	4-12-0
2000	New Orleans	10-6-0	3-13-0
2001	Chicago	13-3-0	5-11-0
2001	New England	11-5-0	5-11-0
2003	Carolina	11-5-0	7- 9-0
2003	Kansas City	13-3-0	*8- 8-0
2004	Atlanta	11-5-0	5-11-0
2004	San Diego	12-4-0	*4-12-0
2005	Chicago	11-5-0	5-11-0
2005	Tampa Bay	11-5-0	5-11-0
2006	Baltimore	13-3-0	*6-10-0
2006	New Orleans	10-6-0	3-13-0
2006	Philadelphia	10-6-0	6-10-0
2007	Tampa Bay	9-7-0	4-12-0

*tied for last place

LONGEST WINNING STREAKS SINCE 1970

19	New England, 2006-07	(3 in 2006, 16 in 2007) (current)
18	New England, 2003-04	(12 in 2003, 6 in 2004)
16	Miami, 1971-73	(1 in 1971, 14 in 1972, 1 in 1973)
16	Miami, 1983-84	(5 in 1983, 11 in 1984)
16	Pittsburgh, 2004-05	(14 in 2004, 2 in 2005)
15	San Francisco, 1989-90	(5 in 1989, 10 in 1990)
14	Oakland, 1976-77	(10 in 1976, 4 in 1977)
14	Denver, 1997-98	(1 in 1997, 13 in 1998)
13	Minnesota, 1974-75	(3 in 1974, 10 in 1975)
13	Chicago, 1984-85	(1 in 1984, 12 in 1985)
13	N.Y. Giants, 1989-90	(3 in 1989, 10 in 1990)
13	Indianapolis, 2005	
12	Washington, 1990-91	(1 in 1990, 11 in 1991)
11	Pittsburgh, 1975	
11	Baltimore, 1975-76	(9 in 1975, 2 in 1976)
11	Chicago, 1986-87	(7 in 1986, 4 in 1987)
11	Houston, 1993	
11	San Francisco, 1997	
11	Jacksonville, 1999	
11	Indianapolis, 1999	
11	Seattle, 2005	
11	San Diego	(10 in 2006, 1 in 2007)
10	Miami, 1973	
10	Pittsburgh, 1976-77	(9 in 1976, 1 in 1977)
10	Denver, 1984	
10	San Francisco, 1994	
10	Minnesota, 1999-00	(3 in 1999, 7 in 2000)
10	Indianapolis, 2005-06	(1 in 2005, 9 in 2006)

NFL PLAYOFF APPEARANCES BY SEASONS

Team	Number of Seasons in Playoffs
Dallas	29
N.Y. Giants	29
St. Louis	27
Chicago	24
Cleveland	24
Green Bay	24
Minnesota	24
Pittsburgh	24
San Francisco	22
Washington	22
Indianapolis	21
Miami	21
Oakland	21
Philadelphia	20

Team	Number of Seasons in Playoffs
Tennessee	20
Buffalo	17
Denver	17
New England	16
Kansas City	15
San Diego	15
Detroit	14
N.Y. Jets	12
Seattle	10
Tampa Bay	10
Atlanta	8
Cincinnati	8
Arizona	6
Jacksonville	6
New Orleans	6
Baltimore	4
Carolina	3

TEAMS IN SUPER BOWL CONTENTION (1978-2007)

	With 3 Weeks to Play	With 2 Weeks to Play	With 1 Week to Play
2007	23	20	15
2006	25	24	*20
2005	18	17	14
2004	*27	*26	17
2003	22	17	14
2002	21	21	19
2001	23	16	13
2000	19	17	16
1999	23	20	16
1998	22	19	14
1997	22	18	14
1996	23	21	13
1995	*27	21	18
1994	25	22	15
1993	20	18	16
1992	20	16	14
1991	20	18	13
1990	23	20	15
1989	21	18	17
1988	21	18	15
1987	19	19	15
1986	19	17	14
1985	21	18	13
1984	18	14	13
1983	24	19	15
1982	20	17	16
1981	21	20	16
1980	20	14	12
1979	19	15	13
1978	20	17	12

RECORD OF TEAMS ON THE ROAD (1970-2007)

Year	W	L	T	Pct
1970	72	101	9	.420
1971	74	100	8	.429
1972	87	90	5	.492
1973	66	109	7	.382
1974	82	99	1	.453
1975	81	101	0	.445
1976	83	112	1	.426
1977	83	113	0	.423
1978	93	130	1	.417
1979	92	132	0	.411
1980	101	122	1	.453
1981	84	139	1	.377
1982	57	68	1	.456
1983	104	119	1	.467
1984	94	129	1	.422
1985	80	144	0	.357

Year	W	L	T	Pct
1986	104	118	2	.469
1987	95	114	1	.455
1988	92	131	1	.413
1989	95	128	1	.426
1990	93	131	0	.415
1991	92	132	0	.411
1992	88	136	0	.393
1993	101	123	0	.451
1994	96	128	0	.429
1995	96	144	0	.400
1996	91	149	0	.379
1997	93	145	2	.392
1998	89	151	0	.371
1999	100	148	0	.403
2000	110	138	0	.444
2001	112	136	0	.452
2002	107	148	1	.420
2003	99	157	0	.387
2004	111	145	0	.434
2005	105	151	0	.410
2006	120	136	0	.469
2007	109	147	0	.426

GAMES DECIDED BY 7 POINTS OR LESS AND 3 POINTS OR LESS (1970-2007)

	Games Decided by 7 Points or Less	Games Decided by 3 Points or Less
1970	59 of 182 (32.4%)	34 of 182 (18.7%)
1971	76 of 182 (41.8%)	35 of 182 (19.2%)
1972	71 of 182 (39.0%)	38 of 182 (20.9%)
1973	60 of 182 (32.9%)	28 of 182 (15.4%)
1974	91 of 182 (50.0%)	37 of 182 (20.3%)
1975	62 of 182 (34.1%)	35 of 182 (19.2%)
1976	73 of 196 (37.2%)	38 of 196 (19.4%)
1977	85 of 196 (43.4%)	36 of 196 (18.4%)
1978	108 of 224 (48.2%)	49 of 224 (21.9%)
1979	104 of 224 (46.4%)	51 of 224 (22.8%)
1980	108 of 224 (48.2%)	58 of 224 (25.9%)
1981	91 of 224 (40.6%)	60 of 224 (26.8%)
1982	61 of 126 (48.4%)	33 of 126 (26.2%)
1983	106 of 224 (47.3%)	54 of 224 (24.1%)
1984	95 of 224 (42.4%)	58 of 224 (25.9%)
1985	87 of 224 (38.8%)	38 of 224 (17.0%)
1986	106 of 224 (47.3%)	48 of 224 (21.4%)
1987	99 of 210 (47.1%)	40 of 210 (19.0%)
1988	113 of 224 (50.4%)	62 of 224 (27.7%)
1989	107 of 224 (47.8%)	55 of 224 (24.6%)
1990	97 of 224 (43.3%)	54 of 224 (24.1%)
1991	112 of 224 (50.0%)	57 of 224 (25.4%)
1992	88 of 224 (39.3%)	48 of 224 (21.4%)
1993	*105 of 224 (46.9%)	53 of 224 (23.7%)
1994	115 of 224 (51.3%)	60 of 224 (26.8%)
1995	115 of 240 (47.9%)	61 of 240 (25.4%)
1996	109 of 240 (45.4%)	47 of 240 (19.6%)
1997	111 of 240 (46.3%)	67 of 240 (27.9%)
1998	113 of 240 (47.1%)	50 of 240 (20.8%)
1999	115 of 248 (46.4%)	**64 of 248 (25.8%)
2000	109 of 248 (44.0%)	61 of 248 (24.6%)
2001	121 of 248 (48.8%)	62 of 248 (25.0%)
2002	126 of 256 (49.2%)	63 of 256 (24.6%)
2003	124 of 256 (48.4%)	60 of 256 (23.4%)
2004	116 of 256 (45.3%)	61 of 256 (23.8%)
2005	114 of 256 (44.5%)	60 of 256 (23.4%)
2006	117 of 256 (45.7%)	61 of 256 (23.8%)
2007	110 of 256 (43.0%)	55 of 256 (21.5%)

*Week record: Dec. 11-13, 1993 (Week 15), 12 of 14 games (86%) decided by 7 points or less.
**Week record: Oct. 10-11, 1999 (Week 5), 10 of 14 games (71%) decided by 3 points or less.

GAMES DECIDED BY 8 PTS. OR LESS (1994-2007)

1994	121 of 224 (54.0%)	2001	128 of 248 (51.6%)
1995	123 of 240 (51.3%)	2002	137 of 256 (53.5%)
1996	115 of 240 (47.9%)	2003	132 of 256 (51.6%)
1997	120 of 240 (50.0%)	2004	121 of 256 (47.3%)
1998	120 of 240 (50.0%)	2005	123 of 256 (48.0%)
1999	124 of 248 (50.0%)	2006	126 of 256 (49.2%)
2000	119 of 248 (48.0%)	2007	120 of 256 (46.9%)

TWO-POINT CONVERSION RESULTS (1994-2007)

1994	59 of 116 (50.9%)	2001	40 of 90 (44.4%)
1995	40 of 104 (38.5%)	2002	47 of 98 (48.0%)
1996	44 of 92 (47.8%)	2003	29 of 66 (43.9%)
1997	47 of 109 (43.1%)	2004	37 of 76 (48.7%)
1998	41 of 105 (39.1%)	2005	27 of 53 (50.9%)
1999	31 of 84 (36.9%)	2006	21 of 41 (51.2%)
2000	35 of 85 (41.2%)	2007	30 of 61 (49.2%)

RECORDS AFTER BYE WEEKS (1990-2007)

AFC		NFC	
Baltimore	7-5	Arizona	9-10
Buffalo	13-6	Atlanta	10-9
Cincinnati	4-15	Carolina	5-8
Cleveland	5-9	Chicago	12-7
Denver	15-4	Dallas	14-5
Houston	2-4	Detroit	9-10
Indianapolis	10-9	Green Bay	11-8
Jacksonville	7-6	Minnesota	15-4
Kansas City	12-7	New Orleans	8-11
Miami	11-8	N.Y. Giants	4-15
New England	10-9	Philadelphia	15-4
N.Y. Jets	10-9	San Francisco	8-11
Oakland	9-10	Seattle	5-14
Pittsburgh	10-9	St. Louis	10-9
San Diego	9-9	Tampa Bay	7-12
Tennessee	11-8	Washington	11-8

2007 RECORDS OF TEAMS IN CLOSE GAMES

AFC	Overall Record	Decided by 8 Pts. or Less	Decided By 3 Pts. or Less
Baltimore	5-11	4-5	2-2
Buffalo	7-9	4-4	3-2
Cincinnati	7-9	3-5	0-1
Cleveland	10-6	6-4	2-2
Denver	7-9	4-2	4-1
Houston	8-8	2-3	1-1
Indianapolis	13-3	5-3	3-1
Jacksonville	11-5	4-2	1-2
Kansas City	4-12	3-4	2-3
Miami	1-15	1-6	0-6
New England	16-0	4-0	3-0
N.Y. Jets	4-12	3-7	3-2
Oakland	4-12	2-6	2-2
Pittsburgh	10-6	2-5	2-2
San Diego	11-5	2-2	1-0
Tennessee	10-6	7-3	2-2

NFC	Overall Record	Decided by 8 Pts. or Less	Decided By 3 Pts. or Less
Arizona	8-8	6-6	3-3
Atlanta	4-12	3-5	1-1
Carolina	7-9	4-2	2-0
Chicago	7-9	4-5	2-1
Dallas	13-3	4-1	2-0
Detroit	7-9	3-2	1-1
Green Bay	13-3	5-1	2-0
Minnesota	8-8	3-5	1-3
New Orleans	7-9	2-4	0-1
N.Y. Giants	10-6	5-1	2-1
Philadelphia	8-8	5-6	0-4
San Francisco	5-11	5-3	3-1
Seattle	10-6	4-4	1-4
St. Louis	3-13	2-4	0-2
Tampa Bay	9-7	4-4	1-2
Washington	9-7	5-6	3-2

SUPER BOWL CHAMPIONS THAT DID NOT MAKE PLAYOFFS THE FOLLOWING YEAR

Pittsburgh—Super Bowl XL champions did not make playoffs in 2006 season.

Tampa Bay—Super Bowl XXXVII champions did not make playoffs in 2003 season.

New England—Super Bowl XXXVI champions did not make playoffs in the 2002 season.

Denver—Super Bowl XXXIII champions did not make playoffs in the 1999 season.

N.Y. Giants—Super Bowl XXV champions did not make playoffs in the 1991 season.

Washington—Super Bowl XXII champions did not make play-offs in the 1988 season.

N.Y. Giants—Super Bowl XXI champions did not make playoffs in the 1987 season.

San Francisco—Super Bowl XVI champions did not make playoffs in the 1982 season.

Oakland—Super Bowl XV champions did not make playoffs in the 1981 season.

Pittsburgh—Super Bowl XIV champions did not make playoffs in the 1980 season.

Kansas City—Super Bowl IV champions did not make playoffs in the 1970 season.

Green Bay—Super Bowl II champions did not make playoffs in the 1968 season.

NON-DIVISION WINNERS THAT PLAYED IN SUPER BOWL

2007	New York Giants	Super Bowl XLII
	(Defeated New England, 17-14)	
2005	Pittsburgh Steelers	Super Bowl XL
	(Defeated Seattle, 21-10)	
2000	Baltimore Ravens	Super Bowl XXXV
	(Defeated N.Y. Giants, 34-7)	
1999	Tennessee Titans	Super Bowl XXXIV
	(Lost to St. Louis, 23-16)	
1997	Denver Broncos	Super Bowl XXXII
	(Defeated Green Bay, 31-24)	
1992	Buffalo Bills	Super Bowl XXVII
	(Lost to Dallas, 52-17)	
1985	New England Patriots	Super Bowl XX
	(Lost to Chicago, 46-10)	
1980	Oakland Raiders	Super Bowl XV
	(Defeated Philadelphia, 27-10)	
1975	Dallas Cowboys	Super Bowl X
	(Lost to Pittsburgh, 21-17)	
1969	Kansas City Chiefs	Super Bowl IV
	(Defeated Minnesota, 23-7)	

TEAMS AT OR UNDER .500 IN POSTSEASON PLAY

2006	New York Giants	8-8
2004	Minnesota Vikings	8-8
2004	St. Louis Rams	8-8
1999	Dallas Cowboys	8-8
1999	Detroit Lions	8-8
1991	New York Jets	8-8
1990	New Orleans Saints	8-8
1985	Cleveland Browns	8-8
1982	Cleveland Browns	4-5
1982	Detroit Lions	4-5
1969	Houston Oilers	6-6-2

COLDEST NFL GAMES ON RECORD

-13 degrees (-48 degree wind chill)—December 31, 1967, Lambeau Field, Green Bay, Wisconsin, NFL Championship (Green Bay 21, Dallas 17)

-9 degrees (-59 degree wind chill)—January 10, 1982, Riverfront Stadium, Cincinnati, Ohio, AFC Championship (Cincinnati 27, San Diego 7)

0 degrees (-32 degree wind chill)—January 15, 1994, Rich Stadium, Orchard Park, New York, AFC Divisional Playoff (Buffalo 29, Los Angeles Raiders 23)

TEAM LEADERS

Offense	Most Scored		Fewest Scored	
1st Quarter	134	New England	26	Kansas City
2nd Quarter	199	New England	41	Buffalo
3rd Quarter	118	Indianapolis	22	Atlanta
4th Quarter	152	New England	40	St. Louis
Defense	**Most Scored**		**Fewest Scored**	
1st Quarter	110	Miami	33	Chicago
2nd Quarter	174	Detroit	66	Tampa Bay
3rd Quarter	114	Denver	27	San Francisco
4th Quarter	147	St. Louis	51	Pittsburgh

2007 NFL SCORE BY QUARTERS

AFC Offense	1	2	3	4	OT	PTS
New England	134	199	104	152	0	589
Indianapolis	90	146	118	96	0	450
San Diego	119	116	93	78	6	412
Jacksonville	92	108	76	135	0	411
Cleveland	60	144	87	105	6	402
Pittsburgh	75	129	68	121	0	393
Cincinnati	78	109	90	103	0	380
Houston	87	92	61	139	0	379
Denver	75	89	94	56	6	320
Tennessee	59	64	98	80	0	301
Oakland	43	75	69	96	0	283
Baltimore	33	110	44	88	0	275
N.Y. Jets	51	105	33	73	6	268
Miami	32	77	68	84	6	267
Buffalo	79	41	68	64	0	252
Kansas City	26	92	39	69	0	226

NFC Offense	1	2	3	4	OT	PTS
Dallas	61	147	117	130	0	455
Green Bay	86	128	112	103	6	435
Arizona	57	148	65	131	3	404
Seattle	76	136	73	108	0	393
New Orleans	89	130	94	66	0	379
N.Y. Giants	56	128	73	116	0	373
Minnesota	82	107	66	110	0	365
Detroit	61	107	67	108	3	346
Philadelphia	100	97	69	70	0	336
Chicago	46	97	85	103	3	334
Tampa Bay	84	109	72	69	0	334
Washington	56	117	65	90	6	334
Carolina	50	66	48	103	0	267
St. Louis	95	72	56	40	0	263
Atlanta	71	74	22	92	0	259
San Francisco	30	55	75	53	6	219

AFC Defense	1	2	3	4	OT	PTS
Indianapolis	67	67	41	87	0	262
Pittsburgh	67	78	70	51	3	269
New England	41	96	58	79	0	274
San Diego	47	84	69	84	0	284
Tennessee	65	78	64	84	6	297
Jacksonville	47	104	67	86	0	304
Kansas City	66	98	89	79	3	335
Buffalo	63	104	92	95	0	354
N.Y. Jets	47	111	70	124	3	355
Cleveland	85	112	82	103	0	382
Baltimore	69	136	87	83	9	384
Houston	81	132	90	81	0	384
Cincinnati	64	146	68	107	0	385
Oakland	88	101	91	115	3	398
Denver	68	103	114	115	9	409
Miami	110	146	52	126	3	437

NFC Defense	1	2	3	4	OT	PTS
Tampa Bay	51	66	55	98	0	270
Green Bay	56	102	57	76	0	291
Seattle	62	95	39	92	3	291
Philadelphia	86	95	64	55	0	300
Washington	44	67	83	116	0	310
Minnesota	63	110	60	72	6	311
Dallas	88	97	64	76	0	325
Carolina	79	89	110	69	0	347
Chicago	33	110	68	137	0	348
N.Y. Giants	82	100	72	97	0	351
San Francisco	87	158	27	92	0	364
New Orleans	105	104	69	110	0	388
Arizona	88	114	99	92	6	399
Atlanta	105	121	90	95	3	414
St. Louis	64	116	111	147	0	438
Detroit	65	174	97	108	0	444
NFL Totals	**2,233**	**3,414**	**2,369**	**3,031**	**57**	**11,104**

LARGEST TRADES IN NFL HISTORY
(Based on number of players or draft choices involved)

18—**October 13, 1989**—RB Herschel Walker from the Dallas Cowboys to Minnesota. Dallas also traded its third-round choice in 1990, its tenth-round choice in 1990, and its third-round choice in 1991 to Minnesota. Minnesota traded LB Jesse Solomon, LB David Howard, CB Issiac Holt, and DE Alex Stewart along with its first-round choice in 1990, its second-round choice in 1990, its sixth-round choice in 1990, its first-round choice in 1991, its second-round choice in 1991, its first-round choice in 1992, its second-round choice in 1992, and its third-round choice in 1992 to Dallas. Minnesota traded RB Darrin Nelson to Dallas, which traded Nelson to San Diego for the Chargers' fifth-round choice in 1990, which Dallas then sent to Minnesota.

15—**March 26, 1953**—T Mike McCormack, DT Don Colo, LB Tom Catlin, DB John Petitbon, and G Harry Agganis from Baltimore to Cleveland for DB Don Shula, DB Bert Rechichar, DB Carl Taseff, LB Ed Sharkey, E Gern Nagler, QB Harry Agganis, T Dick Batten, T Stu Sheets, G Art Spinney, and G Elmer Willhoite.

15—**January 28, 1971**—LB Marlin McKeever, first- and third-round choices in 1971, and third-, fourth-, fifth-, sixth-, and seventh-round choices in 1972 from Washington to the Los Angeles Rams for LB Maxie Baughan, LB Jack Pardee, LB Myron Pottios, RB Jeff Jordan, G John Wilbur, DT Diron Talbert, and a fifth-round choice in 1971.

12—**June 13, 1952**—Selection rights to Les Richter from the Dallas Texans to the Los Angeles Rams for RB Dick Hoerner, DB Tom Keane, DB George Sims, C Joe Reid, HB Billy Baggett, T Jack Halliday, FB Dick McKissack, LB Vic Vasicek, E Richard Wilkins, C Aubrey Phillips, and RB Dave Anderson.

10—**March 23, 1959**—HB Ollie Matson from the Chicago Cardinals to the Los Angeles Rams for T Frank Fuller, DE Glenn Holtzman, T Ken Panfil, DT Art Hauser, E John Tracey, FB Larry Hickman, HB Don Brown, the Rams second-round choice in 1960, and a player to be delivered during the 1959 training camp.

10—**October 31, 1987**—RB Eric Dickerson from the Los Angeles Rams to Indianapolis. The rights to LB Cornelius Bennett from Indianapolis to Buffalo. Indianapolis running back Owen Gill and the Colts' first- and second-round choices in 1988 and second-round choice in 1989, plus Bills running back Greg Bell and Buffalo's first-round choice in 1988 and first- and second-round choices in 1989 to the Rams.

2008 TOP 100 TELEVISION MARKETS
(NFL TEAM MARKETS IN BOLD)

RANK	MARKET	TV HOUSEHOLDS	% of U.S.
1	**New York**	**7,391,940**	**6.553**
2	Los Angeles	5,647,440	5.007
3	**Chicago**	**3,469,110**	**3.076**
4	**Philadelphia**	**2,939,950**	**2.606**
5	**Dallas-Ft. Worth**	**2,435,600**	**2.159**
6	**San Francisco-Oak-San Jose**	**2,419,440**	**2.145**
7	**Boston (Manchester)**	**2,393,960**	**2.122**
8	**Atlanta**	**2,310,490**	**2.048**
9	**Washington, DC (Hagrstwn)**	**2,308,290**	**2.046**
10	**Houston**	**2,050,550**	**1.818**
11	**Detroit**	**1,925,460**	**1.707**
12	**Phoenix (Prescott)**	**1,802,550**	**1.598**
13	**Tampa-St. Pete (Sarasota)**	**1,783,910**	**1.582**
14	**Seattle-Tacoma**	**1,782,040**	**1.580**
15	**Minneapolis-St. Paul**	**1,706,740**	**1.513**
16	**Miami-Ft. Lauderdale**	**1,536,020**	**1.362**
17	**Cleveland-Akron (Canton)**	**1,533,710**	**1.360**
18	**Denver**	**1,477,280**	**1.310**
19	Orlando-Daytona Bch-Melbrn	1,434,050	1.271
20	Sacramnto-Stkton-Modesto	1,391,790	1.234
21	**St. Louis**	**1,244,370**	**1.103**
22	**Pittsburgh**	**1,158,210**	**1.027**
23	Portland, OR	1,150,320	1.020
24	**Baltimore**	**1,095,490**	**0.971**
25	**Charlotte**	**1,085,640**	**0.962**
26	**Indianapolis**	**1,072,090**	**0.950**
27	**San Diego**	**1,051,210**	**0.932**
28	Raleigh-Durham (Fayetvlle)	1,039,890	0.922
29	Hartford & New Haven	1,007,490	0.893
30	**Nashville**	**966,170**	**0.857**
31	**Kansas City**	**927,060**	**0.822**
32	Columbus, OH	905,690	0.803
33	**Cincinnati**	**904,340**	**0.802**
34	Milwaukee	891,010	0.790
35	Salt Lake City	874,650	0.775
36	Greenvll-Spart-Ashevll-And	838,270	0.743
37	San Antonio	792,440	0.703
38	West Palm Beach-Ft. Pierce	775,340	0.687
39	Grand Rapids-Kalmzoo-B.Crk	739,640	0.656
40	Birmingham (Ann, Tusc)	730,430	0.648
41	Harrisburg-Lncstr-Leb-York	723,620	0.642
42	Norfolk-Portsmth-Newpt Nws	717,440	0.636
43	Las Vegas	707,470	0.627
44	Albuquerque-Santa Fe	677,740	0.601
45	Oklahoma City	676,850	0.600
46	Greensboro-H.Point-W.Salem	671,980	0.596
47	Memphis	667,890	0.592
48	Louisville	657,180	0.583
49	**Jacksonville**	**655,470**	**0.581**
50	**Buffalo**	**636,700**	**0.564**

2008 TOP 100 TELEVISION MARKETS
(NFL TEAM MARKETS IN BOLD)

RANK	MARKET	TV HOUSEHOLDS	% of U.S.
51	Austin	635,860	0.564
52	Providence-New Bedford	626,800	0.556
53	**New Orleans**	**600,150**	**0.532**
54	Wilkes Barre-Scranton	592,310	0.525
55	Fresno-Visalia	568,730	0.504
56	Albany-Schenectady-Troy	553,790	0.491
57	Little Rock-Pine Bluff	552,400	0.490
58	Knoxville	534,410	0.474
59	Richmond-Petersburg	526,760	0.467
60	Tulsa	519,820	0.461
61	Mobile-Pensacola (Ft Walt)	517,410	0.459
62	Dayton	511,220	0.453
63	Ft. Myers-Naples	491,760	0.436
64	Lexington	490,530	0.435
65	Charleston-Huntington	476,680	0.423
66	Flint-Saginaw-Bay City	469,980	0.417
67	Roanoke-Lynchburg	451,580	0.400
68	Tucson (Sierra Vista)	446,550	0.396
69	Wichita-Hutchinson Plus	446,520	0.396
70	**Green Bay-Appleton**	**439,940**	**0.390**
71	Des Moines-Ames	425,760	0.377
72	Toledo	424,670	0.376
73	Honolulu	424,010	0.376
74	Springfield, MO	410,930	0.364
75	Omaha	407,700	0.361
76	Portland-Auburn	407,560	0.361
77	Spokane	403,820	0.358
78	Rochester, NY	392,420	0.348
79	Paducah-Cape Girard-Harsbg	390,130	0.346
80	Syracuse	386,380	0.343
81	Columbia, SC	384,060	0.340
82	Shreveport	383,610	0.340
83	Huntsville-Decatur (Flor)	382,790	0.339
84	Champaign&Sprngfld-Decatur	378,870	0.336
85	Madison	372,990	0.331
86	Chattanooga	353,680	0.314
87	Cedar Rapids-Wtrlo-IWC&Dub	339,480	0.301
88	Harlingen-Wslco-Brnsvl-McA	338,550	0.300
89	South Bend-Elkhart	337,870	0.300
90	Jackson, MS	334,200	0.296
91	Tri-Cities, TN-VA	328,970	0.292
92	Burlington-Plattsburgh	328,050	0.291
93	Colorado Springs-Pueblo	326,380	0.289
94	Baton Rouge	317,550	0.282
95	Waco-Temple-Bryan	315,900	0.280
96	Davenport-R.Island-Moline	308,950	0.274
97	Savannah	306,680	0.272
98	El Paso (Las Cruces)	302,470	0.268
99	Johnstown-Altoona-St Colge	295,180	0.262
100	Charleston, SC	294,230	0.261
TOTAL NFL MARKETS		**53,103,880**	**47.079**
TOTAL TOP 100 MARKETS		**97,039,450**	**86.029**
TOTAL MARKETS		**112,798,170**	**100.000**

RETIRED UNIFORM NUMBERS IN NFL

AFC

Baltimore	None	
Buffalo	Jim Kelly	12
Cincinnati	Bob Johnson	54
Cleveland	Otto Graham	14
	Jim Brown	32
	Ernie Davis	45
	Don Fleming	46
	Lou Groza	76
Denver	John Elway	7
	Frank Tripucka	18
	Floyd Little	44
Houston	None	
Indianapolis	Johnny Unitas	19
	Buddy Young	22
	Lenny Moore	24
	Art Donovan	70
	Jim Parker	77
	Raymond Berry	82
	Gino Marchetti	89
Jacksonville	None	
Kansas City	Jan Stenerud	3
	Len Dawson	16
	Emmitt Thomas	18
	Abner Haynes	28
	Stone Johnson	33
	Mack Lee Hill	36
	Willie Lanier	63
	Bobby Bell	78
	Buck Buchanan	86
Miami	Bob Griese	12
	Dan Marino	13
	Larry Csonka	39
New England	Bruce Armstrong	78
	Gino Cappelletti	20
	Mike Haynes	40
	Steve Nelson	57
	John Hannah	73
	Jim Lee Hunt	79
	Bob Dee	89
New York Jets	Joe Namath	12
	Don Maynard	13
	Joe Klecko	73
Oakland	None	
Pittsburgh	Ernie Stautner	70
San Diego	Dan Fouts	14
	Lance Alworth	19
Tennessee	Warren Moon	1
	Earl Campbell	34
	Jim Norton	43
	Mike Munchak	63
	Elvin Bethea	65
	Bruce Matthews	74

NFC

Arizona	Larry Wilson	8
	Pat Tillman	40
	Stan Mauldin	77
	J.V. Cain	88
	Marshall Goldberg	99
Atlanta	Steve Bartkowski	10
	William Andrews	31
	Jeff Van Note	57
	Tommy Nobis	60
Carolina	Sam Mills	51
Chicago	Bronko Nagurski	3
	George McAfee	5
	George Halas	7
	Willie Galimore	28
	Walter Payton	34

	Gale Sayers	40
	Brian Piccolo	41
	Sid Luckman	42
	Dick Butkus	51
	Bill Hewitt	56
	Bill George	61
	Bulldog Turner	66
	Red Grange	77
Dallas	None	
Detroit	Dutch Clark	7
	Bobby Layne	22
	Doak Walker	37
	Joe Schmidt	56
	Chuck Hughes	85
Green Bay	Tony Canadeo	3
	Don Hutson	14
	Bart Starr	15
	Ray Nitschke	66
	Reggie White	92
Minnesota	Fran Tarkenton	10
	Mick Tingelhoff	53
	Jim Marshall	70
	Korey Stringer	77
	Cris Carter	80
	Alan Page	88
New Orleans	Jim Taylor	31
	Doug Atkins	81
New York Giants	Ray Flaherty	1
	Tuffy Leemans	4
	Mel Hein	7
	Phil Simms	11
	Y.A. Tittle	14
	Frank Gifford	16
	Al Blozis	32
	Joe Morrison	40
	Charlie Conerly	42
	Ken Strong	50
	Lawrence Taylor	56
Philadelphia	Steve Van Buren	15
	Tom Brookshier	40
	Pete Retzlaff	44
	Chuck Bednarik	60
	Al Wistert	70
	Reggie White	92
	Jerome Brown	99
St. Louis	Bob Waterfield	7
	Eric Dickerson	29
	Merlin Olsen	74
	Jackie Slater	78
	Jack Youngblood	85
San Francisco	John Brodie	12
	Joe Montana	16
	Joe Perry	34
	Jimmy Johnson	37
	Hugh McElhenny	39
	Ronnie Lott	42
	Charlie Krueger	70
	Leo Nomellini	73
	Bob St. Clair	79
	Dwight Clark	87
Seattle	"Fans/the twelfth man"	12
	Steve Largent	80
Tampa Bay	Lee Roy Selmon	63
Washington	Sammy Baugh	33

ALL-TIME REGULAR-SEASON RECORDS OF CURRENT NFL TEAMS

AFC

BALTIMORE RAVENS

Season	All Games			Home Games			Road Games		
	W	L	T	W	L	T	W	L	T
1996	4	12		4	4		0	8	
1997	6	9	1	3	4	1	3	5	
1998	6	10		4	4		2	6	
1999	8	8		4	4		4	4	
2000	12	4		6	2		6	2	
2001	10	6		6	2		4	4	
2002	7	9		4	4		3	5	
2003	10	6		7	1		3	5	
2004	9	7		6	2		3	5	
2005	6	10		6	2		0	8	
2006	13	3		7	1		6	2	
2007	5	11		4	4		1	7	
	96	95	1	61	34	1	35	61	

BUFFALO BILLS

Season	All Games			Home Games			Road Games		
	W	L	T	W	L	T	W	L	T
1960	5	8	1	3	4		2	4	1
1961	6	8		2	5		4	3	
1962	7	6	1	3	3	1	4	3	
1963	7	6	1	4	2	1	3	4	
1964	12	2		6	1		6	1	
1965	10	3	1	5	2		5	1	1
1966	9	4	1	4	2	1	5	2	
1967	4	10		2	5		2	5	
1968	1	12	1	1	6		0	6	1
1969	4	10		4	3		0	7	
1970	3	10	1	1	6		2	4	1
1971	1	13		1	6		0	7	
1972	4	9	1	2	4	1	2	5	
1973	9	5		5	2		4	3	
1974	9	5		5	2		4	3	
1975	8	6		3	4		5	2	
1976	2	12		1	6		1	6	
1977	3	11		1	6		2	5	
1978	5	11		4	4		1	7	
1979	7	9		3	5		4	4	
1980	11	5		6	2		5	3	
1981	10	6		7	1		3	5	
1982	4	5		4	1		0	4	
1983	8	8		3	5		5	3	
1984	2	14		2	6		0	8	
1985	2	14		2	6		0	8	
1986	4	12		3	5		1	7	
1987	7	8		4	4		3	4	
1988	12	4		8	0		4	4	
1989	9	7		6	2		3	5	
1990	13	3		8	0		5	3	
1991	13	3		7	1		6	2	
1992	11	5		6	2		5	3	
1993	12	4		6	2		6	2	
1994	7	9		4	4		3	5	
1995	10	6		6	2		4	4	
1996	10	6		7	1		3	5	
1997	6	10		4	4		2	6	
1998	10	6		6	2		4	4	
1999	11	5		6	2		5	3	
2000	8	8		5	3		3	5	
2001	3	13		1	7		2	6	
2002	8	8		5	3		3	5	
2003	6	10		4	4		2	6	
2004	9	7		5	3		4	4	
2005	5	11		4	4		1	7	
2006	7	9		4	4		3	5	
2007	7	9		4	4		3	5	
	341	375	8	197	162	4	144	213	4

CINCINNATI BENGALS

Season	All Games			Home Games			Road Games		
	W	L	T	W	L	T	W	L	T
1968	3	11		2	5		1	6	
1969	4	9	1	4	3		0	6	1
1970	8	6		5	2		3	4	
1971	4	10		3	4		1	6	
1972	8	6		4	3		4	3	
1973	10	4		7	0		3	4	
1974	7	7		4	3		3	4	
1975	11	3		6	1		5	2	
1976	10	4		6	1		4	3	
1977	8	6		5	2		3	4	
1978	4	12		3	5		1	7	
1979	4	12		4	4		0	8	
1980	6	10		3	5		3	5	
1981	12	4		6	2		6	2	
1982	7	2		4	0		3	2	
1983	7	9		4	4		3	5	
1984	8	8		5	3		3	5	
1985	7	9		5	3		2	6	
1986	10	6		6	2		4	4	
1987	4	11		1	7		3	4	
1988	12	4		8	0		4	4	
1989	8	8		5	3		3	5	
1990	9	7		5	3		4	4	
1991	3	13		3	5		0	8	
1992	5	11		3	5		2	6	
1993	3	13		3	5		0	8	
1994	3	13		2	6		1	7	
1995	7	9		3	5		4	4	
1996	8	8		6	2		2	6	
1997	7	9		6	2		1	7	
1998	3	13		1	7		2	6	
1999	4	12		2	6		2	6	
2000	4	12		3	5		1	7	
2001	6	10		4	4		2	6	
2002	2	14		1	7		1	7	
2003	8	8		5	3		3	5	
2004	8	8		5	3		3	5	
2005	11	5		5	3		6	2	
2006	8	8		4	4		4	4	
2007	7	9		5	3		2	6	
	268	343	1	166	140		102	203	1

CLEVELAND BROWNS*

Season	All Games			Home Games			Road Games		
	W	L	T	W	L	T	W	L	T
1950	10	2		5	1		5	1	
1951	11	1		6	0		5	1	
1952	8	4		4	2		4	2	
1953	11	1		6	0		5	1	
1954	9	3		5	1		4	2	
1955	9	2	1	5	1		4	1	1
1956	5	7		1	5		4	2	
1957	9	2	1	6	0		3	2	1
1958	9	3		4	2		5	1	
1959	7	5		3	3		4	2	
1960	8	3	1	4	2		4	1	1
1961	8	5	1	4	3		4	2	1
1962	7	6	1	4	2	1	3	4	
1963	10	4		5	2		5	2	
1964	10	3	1	5	1	1	5	2	
1965	11	3		5	2		6	1	
1966	9	5		5	2		4	3	

Season	All Games W	L	T	Home Games W	L	T	Road Games W	L	T
1967	9	5		6	1		3	4	
1968	10	4		5	2		5	2	
1969	10	3	1	5	1	1	5	2	
1970	7	7		4	3		3	4	
1971	9	5		4	3		5	2	
1972	10	4		4	3		6	1	
1973	7	5	2	5	1	1	2	4	1
1974	4	10		3	4		1	6	
1975	3	11		3	4		0	7	
1976	9	5		6	1		3	4	
1977	6	8		2	5		4	3	
1978	8	8		5	3		3	5	
1979	9	7		5	3		4	4	
1980	11	5		6	2		5	3	
1981	5	11		3	5		2	6	
1982	4	5		2	2		2	3	
1983	9	7		6	2		3	5	
1984	5	11		2	6		3	5	
1985	8	8		5	3		3	5	
1986	12	4		6	2		6	2	
1987	10	5		5	2		5	3	
1988	10	6		6	2		4	4	
1989	9	6	1	5	2	1	4	4	
1990	3	13		2	6		1	7	
1991	6	10		3	5		3	5	
1992	7	9		4	4		3	5	
1993	7	9		4	4		3	5	
1994	11	5		6	2		5	3	
1995	5	11		3	5		2	6	
1999	2	14		0	8		2	6	
2000	3	13		2	6		1	7	
2001	7	9		4	4		3	5	
2002	9	7		3	5		6	2	
2003	5	11		2	6		3	5	
2004	4	12		3	5		1	7	
2005	6	10		4	4		2	6	
2006	4	12		2	6		2	6	
2007	10	6		7	1		3	5	
	424	360	10	229	162	5	195	198	5

*Did not play from 1996-98.

DENVER BRONCOS

Season	All Games W	L	T	Home Games W	L	T	Road Games W	L	T
1960	4	9	1	2	4	1	2	5	
1961	3	11		2	5		1	6	
1962	7	7		3	4		4	3	
1963	2	11	1	2	5		0	6	1
1964	2	11	1	2	4	1	0	7	
1965	4	10		2	5		2	5	
1966	4	10		3	4		1	6	
1967	3	11		1	6		2	5	
1968	5	9		3	4		2	5	
1969	5	8	1	4	2	1	1	6	
1970	5	8	1	3	3	1	2	5	
1971	4	9	1	2	4	1	2	5	
1972	5	9		3	4		2	5	
1973	7	5	2	3	3	1	4	2	1
1974	7	6	1	3	3	1	4	3	
1975	6	8		5	2		1	6	
1976	9	5		6	1		3	4	
1977	12	2		6	1		6	1	
1978	10	6		6	2		4	4	
1979	10	6		6	2		4	4	
1980	8	8		4	4		4	4	
1981	10	6		8	0		2	6	
1982	2	7		1	4		1	3	
1983	9	7		6	2		3	5	

Season	All Games W	L	T	Home Games W	L	T	Road Games W	L	T
1984	13	3		7	1		6	2	
1985	11	5		6	2		5	3	
1986	11	5		7	1		4	4	
1987	10	4	1	7	1		3	3	1
1988	8	8		6	2		2	6	
1989	11	5		6	2		5	3	
1990	5	11		4	4		1	7	
1991	12	4		7	1		5	3	
1992	8	8		7	1		1	7	
1993	9	7		5	3		4	4	
1994	7	9		4	4		3	5	
1995	8	8		6	2		2	6	
1996	13	3		8	0		5	3	
1997	12	4		8	0		4	4	
1998	14	2		8	0		6	2	
1999	6	10		3	5		3	5	
2000	11	5		6	2		5	3	
2001	8	8		6	2		2	6	
2002	9	7		5	3		4	4	
2003	10	6		6	2		4	4	
2004	10	6		6	2		4	4	
2005	13	3		8	0		5	3	
2006	9	7		4	4		5	3	
2007	7	9		5	3		2	6	
	378	336	10	231	125	7	147	211	3

HOUSTON TEXANS

Season	All Games W	L	T	Home Games W	L	T	Road Games W	L	T
2002	4	12		2	6		2	6	
2003	5	11		3	5		2	6	
2004	7	9		3	5		4	4	
2005	2	14		2	6		0	8	
2006	6	10		4	4		2	6	
2007	8	8		6	2		2	6	
	32	64		20	28		12	36	

INDIANAPOLIS COLTS*

Season	All Games W	L	T	Home Games W	L	T	Road Games W	L	T
1953	3	9		2	4		1	5	
1954	3	9		2	4		1	5	
1955	5	6	1	4	1	1	1	5	
1956	5	7		4	2		1	5	
1957	7	5		4	2		3	3	
1958	9	3		6	0		3	3	
1959	9	3		4	2		5	1	
1960	6	6		4	2		2	4	
1961	8	6		5	2		3	4	
1962	7	7		3	4		4	3	
1963	8	6		4	3		4	3	
1964	12	2		7	1		5	1	
1965	10	3	1	5	2		5	1	1
1966	9	5		5	2		4	3	
1967	11	1	2	6	0	1	5	1	1
1968	13	1		6	1		7	0	
1969	8	5	1	4	2	1	4	3	
1970	11	2	1	5	1	1	6	1	
1971	10	4		5	2		5	2	
1972	5	9		2	5		3	4	
1973	4	10		3	4		1	6	
1974	2	12		0	7		2	5	
1975	10	4		5	2		5	2	
1976	11	3		6	1		5	2	
1977	10	4		6	1		4	3	
1978	5	11		2	6		3	5	
1979	5	11		3	5		2	6	
1980	7	9		2	6		5	3	

Season	All W	L	T	Home W	L	T	Road W	L	T
1981	2	14		1	7		1	7	
1982	0	8	1	0	3	1	0	5	
1983	7	9		3	5		4	4	
1984	4	12		2	6		2	6	
1985	5	11		4	4		1	7	
1986	3	13		1	7		2	6	
1987	9	6		4	4		5	2	
1988	9	7		6	2		3	5	
1989	8	8		6	2		2	6	
1990	7	9		3	5		4	4	
1991	1	15		0	8		1	7	
1992	9	7		4	4		5	3	
1993	4	12		2	6		2	6	
1994	8	8		5	3		3	5	
1995	9	7		5	3		4	4	
1996	9	7		6	2		3	5	
1997	3	13		2	6		1	7	
1998	3	13		3	5		0	8	
1999	13	3		7	1		6	2	
2000	10	6		6	2		4	4	
2001	6	10		3	5		3	5	
2002	10	6		5	3		5	3	
2003	12	4		5	3		7	1	
2004	12	4		7	1		5	3	
2005	14	2		7	1		7	1	
2006	12	4		8	0		4	4	
2007	13	3		6	2		7	1	
	415	384	7	225	174	5	190	210	2

*includes Baltimore Colts (1953-1983).

JACKSONVILLE JAGUARS

Season	All W	L	T	Home W	L	T	Road W	L	T
1995	4	12		2	6		2	6	
1996	9	7		7	1		2	6	
1997	11	5		7	1		4	4	
1998	11	5		7	1		4	4	
1999	14	2		7	1		7	1	
2000	7	9		4	4		3	5	
2001	6	10		3	5		3	5	
2002	6	10		3	5		3	5	
2003	5	11		5	3		0	8	
2004	9	7		4	4		5	3	
2005	12	4		6	2		6	2	
2006	8	8		6	2		2	6	
2007	11	5		6	2		5	3	
	113	95		67	37		46	58	

KANSAS CITY CHIEFS*

Season	All W	L	T	Home W	L	T	Road W	L	T
1960	8	6		5	2		3	4	
1961	6	8		4	3		2	5	
1962	11	3		6	1		5	2	
1963	5	7	2	4	3		1	4	2
1964	7	7		4	3		3	4	
1965	7	5	2	5	2		2	3	2
1966	11	2	1	4	2	1	7	0	
1967	9	5		4	3		5	2	
1968	12	2		6	1		6	1	
1969	11	3		6	1		5	2	
1970	7	5	2	4	1	2	3	4	
1971	10	3	1	7	0		3	3	1
1972	8	6		3	4		5	2	
1973	7	5	2	5	1	1	2	4	1
1974	5	9		1	6		4	3	
1975	5	9		3	4		2	5	
1976	5	9		1	6		4	3	

Season	All W	L	T	Home W	L	T	Road W	L	T
1977	2	12		1	6		1	6	
1978	4	12		3	5		1	7	
1979	7	9		3	5		4	4	
1980	8	8		3	5		5	3	
1981	9	7		5	3		4	4	
1982	3	6		2	2		1	4	
1983	6	10		5	3		1	7	
1984	8	8		5	3		3	5	
1985	6	10		5	3		1	7	
1986	10	6		6	2		4	4	
1987	4	11		3	4		1	7	
1988	4	11	1	4	4		0	7	1
1989	8	7	1	5	3		3	4	1
1990	11	5		6	2		5	3	
1991	10	6		6	2		4	4	
1992	10	6		7	1		3	5	
1993	11	5		7	1		4	4	
1994	9	7		5	3		4	4	
1995	13	3		8	0		5	3	
1996	9	7		5	3		4	4	
1997	13	3		8	0		5	3	
1998	7	9		5	3		2	6	
1999	9	7		6	2		3	5	
2000	7	9		5	3		2	6	
2001	6	10		3	5		3	5	
2002	8	8		6	2		2	6	
2003	13	3		8	0		5	3	
2004	7	9		4	4		3	5	
2005	10	6		7	1		3	5	
2006	9	7		6	2		3	5	
2007	4	12		2	6		2	6	
	379	333	12	226	131	4	153	202	8

*includes Dallas Texans (1960-62).

MIAMI DOLPHINS

Season	All W	L	T	Home W	L	T	Road W	L	T
1966	3	11		2	5		1	6	
1967	4	10		4	3		0	7	
1968	5	8	1	1	5	1	4	3	
1969	3	10	1	2	4	1	1	6	
1970	10	4		6	1		4	3	
1971	10	3	1	6	1		4	2	1
1972	14	0		7	0		7	0	
1973	12	2		7	0		5	2	
1974	11	3		7	0		4	3	
1975	10	4		5	2		5	2	
1976	6	8		3	4		3	4	
1977	10	4		6	1		4	3	
1978	11	5		7	1		4	4	
1979	10	6		6	2		4	4	
1980	8	8		5	3		3	5	
1981	11	4	1	6	1	1	5	3	
1982	7	2		4	0		3	2	
1983	12	4		7	1		5	3	
1984	14	2		7	1		7	1	
1985	12	4		8	0		4	4	
1986	8	8		4	4		4	4	
1987	8	7		4	3		4	4	
1988	6	10		4	4		2	6	
1989	8	8		4	4		4	4	
1990	12	4		7	1		5	3	
1991	8	8		5	3		3	5	
1992	11	5		6	2		5	3	
1993	9	7		4	4		5	3	
1994	10	6		6	2		4	4	
1995	9	7		5	3		4	4	
1996	8	8		4	4		4	4	

Season	All Games W	L	T	Home Games W	L	T	Road Games W	L	T
1997	9	7		6	2		3	5	
1998	10	6		7	1		3	5	
1999	9	7		5	3		4	4	
2000	11	5		5	3		6	2	
2001	11	5		7	1		4	4	
2002	9	7		7	1		2	6	
2003	10	6		4	4		6	2	
2004	4	12		3	5		1	7	
2005	9	7		5	3		4	4	
2006	6	10		4	4		2	6	
2007	1	15		1	7		0	8	
	369	267	4	213	103	3	156	164	1

NEW ENGLAND PATRIOTS*

Season	All Games W	L	T	Home Games W	L	T	Road Games W	L	T
1960	5	9		3	4		2	5	
1961	9	4	1	4	2	1	5	2	
1962	9	4	1	6	1		3	3	1
1963	7	6	1	5	1	1	2	5	
1964	10	3	1	4	2	1	6	1	
1965	4	8	2	1	4	2	3	4	
1966	8	4	2	4	2	1	4	2	1
1967	3	10	1	2	4		1	6	1
1968	4	10		2	5		2	5	
1969	4	10		2	5		2	5	
1970	2	12		1	6		1	6	
1971	6	8		5	2		1	6	
1972	3	11		2	5		1	6	
1973	5	9		3	4		2	5	
1974	7	7		3	4		4	3	
1975	3	11		2	5		1	6	
1976	11	3		6	1		5	2	
1977	9	5		6	1		3	4	
1978	11	5		5	3		6	2	
1979	9	7		6	2		3	5	
1980	10	6		6	2		4	4	
1981	2	14		2	6		0	8	
1982	5	4		3	1		2	3	
1983	8	8		5	3		3	5	
1984	9	7		5	3		4	4	
1985	11	5		7	1		4	4	
1986	11	5		4	4		7	1	
1987	8	7		5	3		3	4	
1988	9	7		7	1		2	6	
1989	5	11		3	5		2	6	
1990	1	15		0	8		1	7	
1991	6	10		4	4		2	6	
1992	2	14		1	7		1	7	
1993	5	11		3	5		2	6	
1994	10	6		5	3		5	3	
1995	6	10		3	5		3	5	
1996	11	5		6	2		5	3	
1997	10	6		6	2		4	4	
1998	9	7		6	2		3	5	
1999	8	8		5	3		3	5	
2000	5	11		3	5		2	6	
2001	11	5		6	2		5	3	
2002	9	7		5	3		4	4	
2003	14	2		8	0		6	2	
2004	14	2		8	0		6	2	
2005	10	6		5	3		5	3	
2006	12	4		5	3		7	1	
2007	16	0		8	0		8	0	
	366	349	9	206	149	6	160	200	3

*includes Boston Patriots (1960-1970).

NEW YORK JETS*

Season	All Games W	L	T	Home Games W	L	T	Road Games W	L	T
1960	7	7		3	4		4	3	
1961	7	7		5	2		2	5	
1962	5	9		2	5		3	4	
1963	5	8	1	4	2	1	1	6	
1964	5	8	1	5	1	1	0	7	
1965	5	8	1	3	3	1	2	5	
1966	6	6	2	4	3		2	3	2
1967	8	5	1	4	2	1	4	3	
1968	11	3		6	1		5	2	
1969	10	4		5	2		5	2	
1970	4	10		2	5		2	5	
1971	6	8		4	3		2	5	
1972	7	7		4	3		3	4	
1973	4	10		2	4		2	6	
1974	7	7		3	4		4	3	
1975	3	11		1	6		2	5	
1976	3	11		2	5		1	6	
1977	3	11		1	6		2	5	
1978	8	8		4	4		4	4	
1979	8	8		6	2		2	6	
1980	4	12		2	6		2	6	
1981	10	5	1	6	2		4	3	1
1982	6	3		3	1		3	2	
1983	7	9		2	6		5	3	
1984	7	9		3	5		4	4	
1985	11	5		7	1		4	4	
1986	10	6		5	3		5	3	
1987	6	9		4	4		2	5	
1988	8	7	1	5	2	1	3	5	
1989	4	12		1	7		3	5	
1990	6	10		3	5		3	5	
1991	8	8		4	4		4	4	
1992	4	12		3	5		1	7	
1993	8	8		3	5		5	3	
1994	6	10		4	4		2	6	
1995	3	13		2	6		1	7	
1996	1	15		0	8		1	7	
1997	9	7		5	3		4	4	
1998	12	4		7	1		5	3	
1999	8	8		4	4		4	4	
2000	9	7		5	3		4	4	
2001	10	6		3	5		7	1	
2002	9	7		5	3		4	4	
2003	6	10		4	4		2	6	
2004	10	6		6	2		4	4	
2005	4	12		4	4		0	8	
2006	10	6		4	4		6	2	
2007	4	12		3	5		1	7	
	322	394	8	177	179	5	145	215	3

*includes New York Titans (1960-62).

OAKLAND RAIDERS*

Season	All Games W	L	T	Home Games W	L	T	Road Games W	L	T
1960	6	8		3	4		3	4	
1961	2	12		1	6		1	6	
1962	1	13		1	6		0	7	
1963	10	4		6	1		4	3	
1964	5	7	2	5	2		0	5	2
1965	8	5	1	5	2		3	3	1
1966	8	5	1	3	3	1	5	2	
1967	13	1		7	0		6	1	
1968	12	2		6	1		6	1	
1969	12	1	1	7	0		5	1	1
1970	8	4	2	6	1		2	3	2
1971	8	4	2	5	1	1	3	3	1
1972	10	3	1	5	1	1	5	2	

Season	All Games W	L	T	Home Games W	L	T	Road Games W	L	T
1973	9	4	1	5	2		4	2	1
1974	12	2		6	1		6	1	
1975	11	3		6	1		5	2	
1976	13	1		7	0		6	1	
1977	11	3		6	1		5	2	
1978	9	7		4	4		5	3	
1979	9	7		6	2		3	5	
1980	11	5		6	2		5	3	
1981	7	9		4	4		3	5	
1982	8	1		4	0		4	1	
1983	12	4		6	2		6	2	
1984	11	5		6	2		5	3	
1985	12	4		7	1		5	3	
1986	8	8		3	5		5	3	
1987	5	10		3	5		2	5	
1988	7	9		3	5		4	4	
1989	8	8		7	1		1	7	
1990	12	4		6	2		6	2	
1991	9	7		5	3		4	4	
1992	7	9		5	3		2	6	
1993	10	6		5	3		5	3	
1994	9	7		4	4		5	3	
1995	8	8		4	4		4	4	
1996	7	9		4	4		3	5	
1997	4	12		2	6		2	6	
1998	8	8		4	4		4	4	
1999	8	8		5	3		3	5	
2000	12	4		7	1		5	3	
2001	10	6		5	3		5	3	
2002	11	5		6	2		5	3	
2003	4	12		4	4		0	8	
2004	5	11		3	5		2	6	
2005	4	12		2	6		2	6	
2006	2	14		2	6		0	8	
2007	4	12		2	6		2	6	
	400	313	11	224	135	3	176	178	8

*includes Los Angeles Raiders (1982-1994).

PITTSBURGH STEELERS*

Season	All Games W	L	T	Home Games W	L	T	Road Games W	L	T
1933	3	6	2	2	3		1	3	2
1934	2	10		1	5		1	5	
1935	4	8		2	5		2	3	
1936	6	6		4	1		2	5	
1937	4	7		2	4		2	3	
1938	2	9		0	5		2	4	
1939	1	9	1	1	4		0	5	1
1940	2	7	2	1	2	2	1	5	
1941	1	9	1	1	4		0	5	1
1942	7	4		3	2		4	2	
1945	2	8		1	4		1	4	
1946	5	5	1	4	1		1	4	1
1947	8	4		5	1		3	3	
1948	4	8		4	2		0	6	
1949	6	5	1	3	2	1	3	3	
1950	6	6		2	4		4	2	
1951	4	7	1	1	4	1	3	3	
1952	5	7		2	4		3	3	
1953	6	6		3	3		3	3	
1954	5	7		4	2		1	5	
1955	4	8		3	2		1	6	
1956	5	7		3	3		2	4	
1957	6	6		4	2		2	4	
1958	7	4	1	5	1		2	3	1
1959	6	5	1	3	2	1	3	3	
1960	5	6	1	4	2		1	4	1
1961	6	8		4	3		2	5	

Season	All Games W	L	T	Home Games W	L	T	Road Games W	L	T
1962	9	5		4	3		5	2	
1963	7	4	3	5	0	2	2	4	1
1964	5	9		2	5		3	4	
1965	2	12		1	6		1	6	
1966	5	8	1	3	3	1	2	5	
1967	4	9	1	1	6		3	3	1
1968	2	11	1	1	6		1	5	1
1969	1	13		1	6		0	7	
1970	5	9		4	3		1	6	
1971	6	8		5	2		1	6	
1972	11	3		7	0		4	3	
1973	10	4		7	1		3	3	
1974	10	3	1	5	2		5	1	1
1975	12	2		6	1		6	1	
1976	10	4		6	1		4	3	
1977	9	5		6	1		3	4	
1978	14	2		7	1		7	1	
1979	12	4		8	0		4	4	
1980	9	7		6	2		3	5	
1981	8	8		5	3		3	5	
1982	6	3		4	0		2	3	
1983	10	6		4	4		6	2	
1984	9	7		6	2		3	5	
1985	7	9		5	3		2	6	
1986	6	10		4	4		2	6	
1987	8	7		4	3		4	4	
1988	5	11		4	4		1	7	
1989	9	7		4	4		5	3	
1990	9	7		6	2		3	5	
1991	7	9		5	3		2	6	
1992	11	5		7	1		4	4	
1993	9	7		6	2		3	5	
1994	12	4		7	1		5	3	
1995	11	5		6	2		5	3	
1996	10	6		7	1		3	5	
1997	11	5		7	1		4	4	
1998	7	9		5	3		2	6	
1999	6	10		2	6		4	4	
2000	9	7		4	4		5	3	
2001	13	3		7	1		6	2	
2002	10	5	1	5	2	1	5	3	
2003	6	10		4	4		2	6	
2004	15	1		8	0		7	1	
2005	11	5		5	3		6	2	
2006	8	8		5	3		3	5	
2007	10	6		7	1		3	5	
	508	484	20	300	193	9	208	291	11

*includes Pittsburgh Pirates (1933-1940).

SAN DIEGO CHARGERS*

Season	All Games W	L	T	Home Games W	L	T	Road Games W	L	T
1960	10	4		5	2		5	2	
1961	12	2		6	1		6	1	
1962	4	10		3	4		1	6	
1963	11	3		6	1		5	2	
1964	8	5	1	4	3		4	2	1
1965	9	2	3	4	1	2	5	1	1
1966	7	6	1	5	2		2	4	1
1967	8	5	1	5	2	1	3	3	
1968	9	5		4	3		5	2	
1969	8	6		5	2		3	4	
1970	5	6	3	2	3	2	3	3	1
1971	6	8		6	1		0	7	
1972	4	9	1	2	5		2	4	1
1973	2	11	1	2	5		0	6	1
1974	5	9		3	4		2	5	
1975	2	12		1	6		1	6	

Season	All Games W	L	T	Home Games W	L	T	Road Games W	L	T
1976	6	8		3	4		3	4	
1977	7	7		3	4		4	3	
1978	9	7		5	3		4	4	
1979	12	4		7	1		5	3	
1980	11	5		6	2		5	3	
1981	10	6		5	3		5	3	
1982	6	3		3	1		3	2	
1983	6	10		4	4		2	6	
1984	7	9		4	4		3	5	
1985	8	8		6	2		2	6	
1986	4	12		2	6		2	6	
1987	8	7		4	3		4	4	
1988	6	10		3	5		3	5	
1989	6	10		4	4		2	6	
1990	6	10		3	5		3	5	
1991	4	12		3	5		1	7	
1992	11	5		6	2		5	3	
1993	8	8		4	4		4	4	
1994	11	5		5	3		6	2	
1995	9	7		5	3		4	4	
1996	8	8		5	3		3	5	
1997	4	12		2	6		2	6	
1998	5	11		4	4		1	7	
1999	8	8		4	4		4	4	
2000	1	15		1	7		0	8	
2001	5	11		4	4		1	7	
2002	8	8		5	3		3	5	
2003	4	12		2	6		2	6	
2004	12	4		7	1		5	3	
2005	9	7		4	4		5	3	
2006	14	2		8	0		6	2	
2007	11	5		7	1		4	4	
	354	359	11	201	156	5	153	203	6

*includes Los Angeles Chargers (1960).

TENNESSEE TITANS*

Season	All Games W	L	T	Home Games W	L	T	Road Games W	L	T
1960	10	4		6	1		4	3	
1961	10	3	1	6	1		4	2	1
1962	11	3		6	1		5	2	
1963	6	8		4	3		2	5	
1964	4	10		3	4		1	6	
1965	4	10		3	4		1	6	
1966	3	11		3	4		0	7	
1967	9	4	1	5	2		4	2	1
1968	7	7		3	4		4	3	
1969	6	6	2	4	2	1	2	4	1
1970	3	10	1	1	6		2	4	1
1971	4	9	1	3	3	1	1	6	
1972	1	13		1	6		0	7	
1973	1	13		0	7		1	6	
1974	7	7		3	4		4	3	
1975	10	4		5	2		5	2	
1976	5	9		3	4		2	5	
1977	8	6		5	2		3	4	
1978	10	6		5	3		5	3	
1979	11	5		6	2		5	3	
1980	11	5		6	2		5	3	
1981	7	9		5	3		2	6	
1982	1	8		1	4		0	4	
1983	2	14		2	6		0	8	
1984	3	13		2	6		1	7	
1985	5	11		4	4		1	7	
1986	5	11		4	4		1	7	
1987	9	6		5	2		4	4	
1988	10	6		7	1		3	5	
1989	9	7		6	2		3	5	
1990	9	7		6	2		3	5	
1991	11	5		7	1		4	4	
1992	10	6		5	3		5	3	
1993	12	4		7	1		5	3	
1994	2	14		2	6		0	8	
1995	7	9		3	5		4	4	
1996	8	8		2	6		6	2	
1997	8	8		6	2		2	6	
1998	8	8		3	5		5	3	
1999	13	3		8	0		5	3	
2000	13	3		7	1		6	2	
2001	7	9		3	5		4	4	
2002	11	5		6	2		5	3	
2003	12	4		7	1		5	3	
2004	5	11		2	6		3	5	
2005	4	12		3	5		1	7	
2006	8	8		4	4		4	4	
2007	10	6		5	3		5	3	
	350	368	6	203	157	2	147	211	4

*includes Houston (1960-1996) and Tennessee Oilers (1997-98).

NFC
ARIZONA CARDINALS*

Season	All Games W	L	T	Home Games W	L	T	Road Games W	L	T
1920	6	2	2	5	1	1	1	1	1
1921	3	3	2	3	3	1	0	0	1
1922	8	3		8	3		0	0	
1923	8	4		8	3		0	1	
1924	5	4	1	5	3	1	0	1	
1925	11	2	1	11	2		0	0	1
1926	5	6	1	3	3		2	3	1
1927	3	7	1	2	3	1	1	4	
1928	1	5		1	1		0	4	
1929	6	6	1	3	2		3	4	1
1930	5	6	2	3	2		2	4	2
1931	5	4		3	0		2	4	
1932	2	6	2	1	2	1	1	4	1
1933	1	9	1	0	4	1	1	5	
1934	5	6		2	2		3	4	
1935	6	4	2	2	2		4	2	2
1936	3	8	1	3	1	1	0	7	
1937	5	5	1	1	3		4	2	1
1938	2	9		1	4		1	5	
1939	1	10		0	4		1	6	
1940	2	7	2	2	1	1	0	6	1
1941	3	7	1	0	3	1	3	4	
1942	3	8		2	2		1	6	
1943	0	10		0	3		0	7	
1945	1	9		0	3		1	6	
1946	6	5		2	2		4	3	
1947	9	3		5	0		4	3	
1948	11	1		5	1		6	0	
1949	6	5	1	2	3	1	4	2	
1950	5	7		3	3		2	4	
1951	3	9		1	5		2	4	
1952	4	8		2	4		2	4	
1953	1	10	1	0	5	1	1	5	
1954	2	10		2	4		0	6	
1955	4	7	1	3	2	1	1	5	
1956	7	5		4	2		3	3	
1957	3	9		0	6		3	3	
1958	2	9	1	1	4	1	1	5	
1959	2	10		2	4		0	6	
1960	6	5	1	3	2	1	3	3	
1961	7	7		3	4		4	3	
1962	4	9	1	2	4	1	2	5	
1963	9	5		3	4		6	1	
1964	9	3	2	4	1	1	5	2	1

Season	All Games W	L	T	Home Games W	L	T	Road Games W	L	T
1965	5	9		2	5		3	4	
1966	8	5	1	5	1	1	3	4	
1967	6	7	1	3	3	1	3	4	
1968	9	4	1	4	2	1	5	2	
1969	4	9	1	3	4		1	5	1
1970	8	5	1	6	1		2	4	1
1971	4	9	1	1	5	1	3	4	
1972	4	9	1	2	5		2	4	1
1973	4	9	1	2	4	1	2	5	
1974	10	4		5	2		5	2	
1975	11	3		6	1		5	2	
1976	10	4		6	1		4	3	
1977	7	7		4	3		3	4	
1978	6	10		3	5		3	5	
1979	5	11		3	5		2	6	
1980	5	11		2	6		3	5	
1981	7	9		5	3		2	6	
1982	5	4		1	3		4	1	
1983	8	7	1	4	3	1	4	4	
1984	9	7		5	3		4	4	
1985	5	11		4	4		1	7	
1986	4	11	1	3	5		1	6	1
1987	7	8		4	3		3	5	
1988	7	9		4	4		3	5	
1989	5	11		2	6		3	5	
1990	5	11		3	5		2	6	
1991	4	12		2	6		2	6	
1992	4	12		3	5		1	7	
1993	7	9		4	4		3	5	
1994	8	8		5	3		3	5	
1995	4	12		3	5		1	7	
1996	7	9		5	3		2	6	
1997	4	12		3	5		1	7	
1998	9	7		5	3		4	4	
1999	6	10		4	4		2	6	
2000	3	13		3	5		0	8	
2001	7	9		3	5		4	4	
2002	5	11		3	5		2	6	
2003	4	12		4	4		0	8	
2004	6	10		5	3		1	7	
2005	5	11		3	5		2	6	
2006	5	11		3	5		2	6	
2007	8	8		6	2		2	6	
	464	657	39	272	284	22	192	373	17

*includes Chicago Cardinals (1920-1959), St. Louis Cardinals (1960-1987), and Phoenix Cardinals (1988-1993).

Season	All Games W	L	T	Home Games W	L	T	Road Games W	L	T
1984	4	12		2	6		2	6	
1985	4	12		3	5		1	7	
1986	7	8	1	2	5	1	5	3	
1987	3	12		2	6		1	6	
1988	5	11		2	6		3	5	
1989	3	13		3	5		0	8	
1990	5	11		5	3		0	8	
1991	10	6		6	2		4	4	
1992	6	10		5	3		1	7	
1993	6	10		4	4		2	6	
1994	7	9		5	3		2	6	
1995	9	7		7	1		2	6	
1996	3	13		2	6		1	7	
1997	7	9		3	5		4	4	
1998	14	2		8	0		6	2	
1999	5	11		4	4		1	7	
2000	4	12		3	5		1	7	
2001	7	9		3	5		4	4	
2002	9	6	1	5	3		4	3	1
2003	5	11		2	6		3	5	
2004	11	5		7	1		4	4	
2005	8	8		4	4		4	4	
2006	7	9		3	5		4	4	
2007	4	12		3	5		1	7	
	256	378	6	153	166	2	103	212	4

CAROLINA PANTHERS

Season	All Games W	L	T	Home Games W	L	T	Road Games W	L	T
1995	7	9		5	3		2	6	
1996	12	4		8	0		4	4	
1997	7	9		2	6		5	3	
1998	4	12		2	6		2	6	
1999	8	8		5	3		3	5	
2000	7	9		5	3		2	6	
2001	1	15		0	8		1	7	
2002	7	9		4	4		3	5	
2003	11	5		6	2		5	3	
2004	7	9		3	5		4	4	
2005	11	5		5	3		6	2	
2006	8	8		4	4		4	4	
2007	7	9		2	6		5	3	
	97	111		51	53		46	58	

CHICAGO BEARS*

Season	All Games W	L	T	Home Games W	L	T	Road Games W	L	T
1920	10	1	2	6	0	1	4	1	1
1921	9	1	1	9	1	1	0	0	
1922	9	3		7	1		2	2	
1923	9	2	1	7	1	1	2	1	
1924	6	1	4	5	0	3	1	1	1
1925	9	5	3	7	1	1	2	4	2
1926	12	1	3	10	0	2	2	1	1
1927	9	3	2	7	1	1	2	2	1
1928	7	5	1	6	3		1	2	1
1929	4	9	2	1	5	2	3	4	
1930	9	4	1	5	2	1	4	2	
1931	8	5		6	3		2	2	
1932	7	1	6	6	1	1	1	0	5
1933	10	2	1	6	0		4	2	1
1934	13	0		5	0		8	0	
1935	6	4	2	1	2	2	5	2	
1936	9	3		3	1		6	2	
1937	9	1	1	4	1		5	0	1
1938	6	5		2	3		4	2	
1939	8	3		4	1		4	2	
1940	8	3		5	0		3	3	

ATLANTA FALCONS

Season	All Games W	L	T	Home Games W	L	T	Road Games W	L	T
1966	3	11		1	6		2	5	
1967	1	12	1	1	5	1	0	7	
1968	2	12		1	6		1	6	
1969	6	8		4	3		2	5	
1970	4	8	2	3	4		1	4	2
1971	7	6	1	4	3		3	3	1
1972	7	7		4	3		3	4	
1973	9	5		4	3		5	2	
1974	3	11		2	5		1	6	
1975	4	10		3	4		1	6	
1976	4	10		3	4		1	6	
1977	7	7		4	3		3	4	
1978	9	7		7	1		2	6	
1979	6	10		3	5		3	5	
1980	12	4		6	2		6	2	
1981	7	9		4	4		3	5	
1982	5	4		2	3		3	1	
1983	7	9		4	4		3	5	

Season	All Games W	L	T	Home Games W	L	T	Road Games W	L	T
1941	10	1		5	1		5	0	
1942	11	0		6	0		5	0	
1943	8	1	1	5	0		3	1	1
1944	6	3	1	4	0	1	2	3	
1945	3	7		2	3		1	4	
1946	8	2	1	4	1	1	4	1	
1947	8	4		4	2		4	2	
1948	10	2		5	1		5	1	
1949	9	3		5	1		4	2	
1950	9	3		6	0		3	3	
1951	7	5		3	3		4	2	
1952	5	7		3	3		2	4	
1953	3	8	1	1	4	1	2	4	
1954	8	4		4	2		4	2	
1955	8	4		5	1		3	3	
1956	9	2	1	6	0		3	2	1
1957	5	7		2	4		3	3	
1958	8	4		5	1		3	3	
1959	8	4		4	2		4	2	
1960	5	6	1	4	2		1	4	1
1961	8	6		5	2		3	4	
1962	9	5		4	3		5	2	
1963	11	1	2	6	0	1	5	1	1
1964	5	9		2	5		3	4	
1965	9	5		5	2		4	3	
1966	5	7	2	4	1	2	1	6	
1967	7	6	1	3	3	1	4	3	
1968	7	7		2	5		5	2	
1969	1	13		1	6		0	7	
1970	6	8		3	4		3	4	
1971	6	8		4	3		2	5	
1972	4	9	1	1	5	1	3	4	
1973	3	11		1	6		2	5	
1974	4	10		4	3		0	7	
1975	4	10		3	4		1	6	
1976	7	7		4	3		3	4	
1977	9	5		5	2		4	3	
1978	7	9		4	4		3	5	
1979	10	6		6	2		4	4	
1980	7	9		5	3		2	6	
1981	6	10		4	4		2	6	
1982	3	6		2	2		1	4	
1983	8	8		5	3		3	5	
1984	10	6		6	2		4	4	
1985	15	1		8	0		7	1	
1986	14	2		7	1		7	1	
1987	11	4		6	2		5	2	
1988	12	4		7	1		5	3	
1989	6	10		4	4		2	6	
1990	11	5		7	1		4	4	
1991	11	5		6	2		5	3	
1992	5	11		4	4		1	7	
1993	7	9		3	5		4	4	
1994	9	7		5	3		4	4	
1995	9	7		5	3		4	4	
1996	7	9		6	2		1	7	
1997	4	12		2	6		2	6	
1998	4	12		3	5		1	7	
1999	6	10		3	5		3	5	
2000	5	11		3	5		2	6	
2001	13	3		7	1		6	2	
2002	4	12		3	5		1	7	
2003	7	9		6	2		1	7	
2004	5	11		2	6		3	5	
2005	11	5		7	1		4	4	
2006	13	3		6	2		7	1	
2007	7	9		4	4		3	5	
	677	491	42	398	205	24	279	286	18

*includes Decatur Staleys (1920) and Chicago Staleys (1921).

DALLAS COWBOYS

Season	All Games W	L	T	Home Games W	L	T	Road Games W	L	T
1960	0	11	1	0	6		0	5	1
1961	4	9	1	2	4	1	2	5	
1962	5	8	1	2	4	1	3	4	
1963	4	10		3	4		1	6	
1964	5	8	1	2	4	1	3	4	
1965	7	7		5	2		2	5	
1966	10	3	1	6	1		4	2	1
1967	9	5		5	2		4	3	
1968	12	2		5	2		7	0	
1969	11	2	1	6	0	1	5	2	
1970	10	4		6	1		4	3	
1971	11	3		6	1		5	2	
1972	10	4		5	2		5	2	
1973	10	4		6	1		4	3	
1974	8	6		5	2		3	4	
1975	10	4		5	2		5	2	
1976	11	3		6	1		5	2	
1977	12	2		6	1		6	1	
1978	12	4		7	1		5	3	
1979	11	5		6	2		5	3	
1980	12	4		8	0		4	4	
1981	12	4		8	0		4	4	
1982	6	3		3	2		3	1	
1983	12	4		6	2		6	2	
1984	9	7		5	3		4	4	
1985	10	6		7	1		3	5	
1986	7	9		3	5		4	4	
1987	7	8		3	4		4	4	
1988	3	13		1	7		2	6	
1989	1	15		0	8		1	7	
1990	7	9		5	3		2	6	
1991	11	5		6	2		5	3	
1992	13	3		7	1		6	2	
1993	12	4		6	2		6	2	
1994	12	4		6	2		6	2	
1995	12	4		6	2		6	2	
1996	10	6		6	2		4	4	
1997	6	10		5	3		1	7	
1998	10	6		6	2		4	4	
1999	8	8		7	1		1	7	
2000	5	11		3	5		2	6	
2001	5	11		4	4		1	7	
2002	5	11		4	4		1	7	
2003	10	6		6	2		4	4	
2004	6	10		4	4		2	6	
2005	9	7		5	3		4	4	
2006	9	7		4	4		5	3	
2007	13	3		6	2		7	1	
	414	302	6	234	123	4	180	179	2

DETROIT LIONS*

Season	All Games W	L	T	Home Games W	L	T	Road Games W	L	T
1930	5	6	3	5	1	2	0	5	1
1931	11	3		8	0		3	3	
1932	6	2	4	3	0	2	3	2	2
1933	6	5		4	1		2	4	
1934	10	3		6	2		4	1	
1935	7	3	2	5	0	1	2	3	1
1936	8	4		5	1		3	3	
1937	7	4		4	2		3	2	

Season	All Games W	L	T	Home Games W	L	T	Road Games W	L	T
1938	7	4		4	3		3	1	
1939	6	5		4	2		2	3	
1940	5	5	1	3	3		2	2	1
1941	4	6	1	3	2		1	4	1
1942	0	11		0	7		0	4	
1943	3	6	1	2	2	1	1	4	
1944	6	3	1	4	2		2	1	1
1945	7	3		4	1		3	2	
1946	1	10		1	5		0	5	
1947	3	9		2	4		1	5	
1948	2	10		2	4		0	6	
1949	4	8		2	4		2	4	
1950	6	6		4	2		2	4	
1951	7	4	1	3	3	1	4	1	
1952	9	3		6	1		3	2	
1953	10	2		5	1		5	1	
1954	9	2	1	5	0	1	4	2	
1955	3	9		3	4		0	5	
1956	9	3		5	1		4	2	
1957	8	4		5	1		3	3	
1958	4	7	1	2	4		2	3	1
1959	3	8	1	2	4		1	4	1
1960	7	5		5	1		2	4	
1961	8	5	1	2	5		6	0	1
1962	11	3		7	0		4	3	
1963	5	8	1	3	3	1	2	5	
1964	7	5	2	3	3	1	4	2	1
1965	6	7	1	2	4	1	4	3	
1966	4	9	1	3	4		1	5	1
1967	5	7	2	3	4		2	3	2
1968	4	8	2	1	4	2	3	4	
1969	9	4	1	5	2		4	2	1
1970	10	4		6	1		4	3	
1971	7	6	1	3	4		4	2	1
1972	8	5	1	5	2		3	3	1
1973	6	7	1	4	3		2	4	1
1974	7	7		5	2		2	5	
1975	7	7		4	3		3	4	
1976	6	8		5	2		1	6	
1977	6	8		5	2		1	6	
1978	7	9		5	3		2	6	
1979	2	14		2	6		0	8	
1980	9	7		6	2		3	5	
1981	8	8		7	1		1	7	
1982	4	5		2	3		2	2	
1983	9	7		6	2		3	5	
1984	4	11	1	2	5	1	2	6	
1985	7	9		6	2		1	7	
1986	5	11		1	7		4	4	
1987	4	11		1	6		3	5	
1988	4	12		2	6		2	6	
1989	7	9		4	4		3	5	
1990	6	10		3	5		3	5	
1991	12	4		8	0		4	4	
1992	5	11		3	5		2	6	
1993	10	6		5	3		5	3	
1994	9	7		6	2		3	5	
1995	10	6		7	1		3	5	
1996	5	11		4	4		1	7	
1997	9	7		6	2		3	5	
1998	5	11		4	4		1	7	
1999	8	8		6	2		2	6	
2000	9	7		4	4		5	3	
2001	2	14		2	6		0	8	
2002	3	13		3	5		0	8	
2003	5	11		5	3		0	8	
2004	6	10		3	5		3	5	
2005	5	11		3	5		2	6	

Season	All Games W	L	T	Home Games W	L	T	Road Games W	L	T
2006	3	13		2	6		1	7	
2007	7	9		5	3		2	6	
	488	553	32	305	228	14	183	325	18

includes Portsmouth Spartans (1930-33).

GREEN BAY PACKERS

Season	All Games W	L	T	Home Games W	L	T	Road Games W	L	T
1921	3	2	1	2	1		1	1	1
1922	4	3	3	4	1	1	0	2	2
1923	7	2	1	4	2	1	3	0	
1924	7	4		5	0		2	4	
1925	8	5		6	0		2	5	
1926	7	3	3	4	1	2	3	2	1
1927	7	2	1	6	1		1	1	1
1928	6	4	3	2	2	2	4	2	1
1929	12	0	1	5	0		7	0	1
1930	10	3	1	6	0		4	3	1
1931	12	2		8	0		4	2	
1932	10	3	1	5	0	1	5	3	
1933	5	7	1	3	2	1	2	5	
1934	7	6		4	2		3	4	
1935	8	4		5	2		3	2	
1936	10	1	1	5	1		5	0	1
1937	7	4		3	2		4	2	
1938	8	3		4	2		4	1	
1939	9	2		4	1		5	1	
1940	6	4	1	4	2		2	2	1
1941	10	1		4	1		6	0	
1942	8	2	1	4	1		4	1	1
1943	7	2	1	2	1	1	5	1	
1944	8	2		5	0		3	2	
1945	6	4		4	1		2	3	
1946	6	5		2	3		4	2	
1947	6	5	1	4	2		2	3	1
1948	3	9		2	4		1	5	
1949	2	10		1	5		1	5	
1950	3	9		3	3		0	6	
1951	3	9		2	4		1	5	
1952	6	6		3	3		3	3	
1953	2	9	1	1	5		1	4	1
1954	4	8		2	4		2	4	
1955	6	6		5	1		1	5	
1956	4	8		2	4		2	4	
1957	3	9		1	5		2	4	
1958	1	10	1	1	4	1	0	6	
1959	7	5		4	2		3	3	
1960	8	4		4	2		4	2	
1961	11	3		6	1		5	2	
1962	13	1		7	0		6	1	
1963	11	2	1	6	1		5	1	1
1964	8	5	1	4	3		4	2	1
1965	10	3	1	6	1		4	2	1
1966	12	2		6	1		6	1	
1967	9	4	1	4	2	1	5	2	
1968	6	7	1	2	5		4	2	1
1969	8	6		5	2		3	4	
1970	6	8		4	3		2	5	
1971	4	8	2	3	3	1	1	5	1
1972	10	4		4	3		6	1	
1973	5	7	2	3	2	2	2	5	
1974	6	8		4	3		2	5	
1975	4	10		3	4		1	6	
1976	5	9		4	3		1	6	
1977	4	10		2	5		2	5	
1978	8	7	1	5	2	1	3	5	
1979	5	11		4	4		1	7	
1980	5	10	1	4	4		1	6	1

Season	All Games W	L	T	Home Games W	L	T	Road Games W	L	T
1981	8	8		4	4		4	4	
1982	5	3	1	3	1		2	2	1
1983	8	8		5	3		3	5	
1984	8	8		5	3		3	5	
1985	8	8		5	3		3	5	
1986	4	12		1	7		3	5	
1987	5	9	1	2	5	1	3	4	
1988	4	12		2	6		2	6	
1989	10	6		6	2		4	4	
1990	6	10		3	5		3	5	
1991	4	12		2	6		2	6	
1992	9	7		6	2		3	5	
1993	9	7		6	2		3	5	
1994	9	7		7	1		2	6	
1995	11	5		7	1		4	4	
1996	13	3		8	0		5	3	
1997	13	3		8	0		5	3	
1998	11	5		7	1		4	4	
1999	8	8		5	3		3	5	
2000	9	7		6	2		3	5	
2001	12	4		7	1		5	3	
2002	12	4		8	0		4	4	
2003	10	6		5	3		5	3	
2004	10	6		4	4		6	2	
2005	4	12		3	5		1	7	
2006	8	8		3	5		5	3	
2007	13	3		7	1		6	2	
	637	503	36	366	205	16	271	298	20

MINNESOTA VIKINGS

Season	All Games W	L	T	Home Games W	L	T	Road Games W	L	T
1961	3	11		3	4		0	7	
1962	2	11	1	1	5	1	1	6	
1963	5	8	1	3	4		2	4	1
1964	8	5	1	4	3		4	2	1
1965	7	7		2	5		5	2	
1966	4	9	1	2	5		2	4	1
1967	3	8	3	1	4	2	2	4	1
1968	8	6		4	3		4	3	
1969	12	2		7	0		5	2	
1970	12	2		7	0		5	2	
1971	11	3		5	2		6	1	
1972	7	7		3	4		4	3	
1973	12	2		7	0		5	2	
1974	10	4		4	3		6	1	
1975	12	2		7	0		5	2	
1976	11	2	1	6	0	1	5	2	
1977	9	5		5	2		4	3	
1978	8	7	1	5	3		3	4	1
1979	7	9		5	3		2	6	
1980	9	7		5	3		4	4	
1981	7	9		5	3		2	6	
1982	5	4		4	1		1	3	
1983	8	8		3	5		5	3	
1984	3	13		2	6		1	7	
1985	7	9		4	4		3	5	
1986	9	7		5	3		4	4	
1987	8	7		5	3		3	4	
1988	11	5		7	1		4	4	
1989	10	6		8	0		2	6	
1990	6	10		4	4		2	6	
1991	8	8		4	4		4	4	
1992	11	5		5	3		6	2	
1993	9	7		4	4		5	3	
1994	10	6		6	2		4	4	
1995	8	8		6	2		2	6	
1996	9	7		5	3		4	4	

Season	All Games W	L	T	Home Games W	L	T	Road Games W	L	T
1997	9	7		5	3		4	4	
1998	15	1		8	0		7	1	
1999	10	6		6	2		4	4	
2000	11	5		7	1		4	4	
2001	5	11		5	3		0	8	
2002	6	10		4	4		2	6	
2003	9	7		6	2		3	5	
2004	8	8		5	3		3	5	
2005	9	7		6	2		3	5	
2006	6	10		3	5		3	5	
2007	8	8		5	3		3	5	
	385	316	9	223	129	4	162	187	5

NEW ORLEANS SAINTS

Season	All Games W	L	T	Home Games W	L	T	Road Games W	L	T
1967	3	11		2	5		1	6	
1968	4	9	1	3	4		1	5	1
1969	5	9		3	4		2	5	
1970	2	11	1	2	5		0	6	1
1971	4	8	2	2	4	1	2	4	1
1972	2	11	1	2	5		0	6	1
1973	5	9		5	2		0	7	
1974	5	9		4	3		1	6	
1975	2	12		2	5		0	7	
1976	4	10		2	5		2	5	
1977	3	11		2	5		1	6	
1978	7	9		3	5		4	4	
1979	8	8		3	5		5	3	
1980	1	15		0	8		1	7	
1981	4	12		2	6		2	6	
1982	4	5		2	3		2	2	
1983	8	8		5	3		3	5	
1984	7	9		3	5		4	4	
1985	5	11		3	5		2	6	
1986	7	9		4	4		3	5	
1987	12	3		6	1		6	2	
1988	10	6		5	3		5	3	
1989	9	7		5	3		4	4	
1990	8	8		5	3		3	5	
1991	11	5		6	2		5	3	
1992	12	4		6	2		6	2	
1993	8	8		4	4		4	4	
1994	7	9		3	5		4	4	
1995	7	9		4	4		3	5	
1996	3	13		2	6		1	7	
1997	6	10		3	5		3	5	
1998	6	10		4	4		2	6	
1999	3	13		3	5		0	8	
2000	10	6		3	5		7	1	
2001	7	9		3	5		4	4	
2002	9	7		4	4		5	3	
2003	8	8		5	3		3	5	
2004	8	8		3	5		5	3	
2005	3	13		1	7		2	6	
2006	10	6		4	4		6	2	
2007	7	9		3	5		4	4	
	254	367	5	136	176	1	118	191	4

NEW YORK GIANTS

Season	All Games W	L	T	Home Games W	L	T	Road Games W	L	T
1925	8	4		7	2		1	2	
1926	8	4	1	5	2	1	3	2	
1927	11	1	1	7	1		4	0	1
1928	4	7	2	1	2	2	3	5	
1929	13	1	1	7	1		6	0	1
1930	13	4		6	2		7	2	

Season	All Games W	L	T	Home Games W	L	T	Road Games W	L	T
1931	7	6	1	4	2	1	3	4	
1932	4	6	2	3	2	1	1	4	1
1933	11	3		7	0		4	3	
1934	8	5		5	1		3	4	
1935	9	3		4	2		5	1	
1936	5	6	1	3	3	1	2	3	
1937	6	3	2	4	2	1	2	1	1
1938	8	2	1	6	1		2	1	1
1939	9	1	1	6	0		3	1	1
1940	6	4	1	4	3		2	1	1
1941	8	3		5	2		3	1	
1942	5	5	1	3	2	1	2	3	
1943	6	3	1	4	2		2	1	1
1944	8	1	1	5	1		3	0	1
1945	3	6	1	2	4		1	2	1
1946	7	3	1	5	1	1	2	2	
1947	2	8	2	2	3	1	0	5	1
1948	4	8		2	4		2	4	
1949	6	6		2	4		4	2	
1950	10	2		5	1		5	1	
1951	9	2	1	5	1		4	1	1
1952	7	5		2	4		5	1	
1953	3	9		2	4		1	5	
1954	7	5		4	2		3	3	
1955	6	5	1	4	1	1	2	4	
1956	8	3	1	4	1	1	4	2	
1957	7	5		3	3		4	2	
1958	9	3		5	1		4	2	
1959	10	2		5	1		5	1	
1960	6	4	2	1	3	2	5	1	
1961	10	3	1	4	2	1	6	1	
1962	12	2		6	1		6	1	
1963	11	3		5	2		6	1	
1964	2	10	2	2	5		0	5	2
1965	7	7		3	4		4	3	
1966	1	12	1	1	6		0	6	1
1967	7	7		5	2		2	5	
1968	7	7		3	4		4	3	
1969	6	8		5	2		1	6	
1970	9	5		5	2		4	3	
1971	4	10		1	6		3	4	
1972	8	6		4	3		4	3	
1973	2	11	1	2	4	1	0	7	
1974	2	12		0	7		2	5	
1975	5	9		2	5		3	4	
1976	3	11		3	4		0	7	
1977	5	9		3	4		2	5	
1978	6	10		5	3		1	7	
1979	6	10		4	4		2	6	
1980	4	12		2	6		2	6	
1981	9	7		4	4		5	3	
1982	4	5		2	3		2	2	
1983	3	12	1	1	7		2	5	1
1984	9	7		6	2		3	5	
1985	10	6		6	2		4	4	
1986	14	2		8	0		6	2	
1987	6	9		5	3		1	6	
1988	10	6		5	3		5	3	
1989	12	4		7	1		5	3	
1990	13	3		7	1		6	2	
1991	8	8		5	3		3	5	
1992	6	10		4	4		2	6	
1993	11	5		6	2		5	3	
1994	9	7		4	4		5	3	
1995	5	11		3	5		2	6	
1996	6	10		3	5		3	5	
1997	10	5	1	6	2		4	3	1
1998	8	8		5	3		3	5	

Season	All Games W	L	T	Home Games W	L	T	Road Games W	L	T
1999	7	9		4	4		3	5	
2000	12	4		5	3		7	1	
2001	7	9		5	3		2	6	
2002	10	6		5	3		5	3	
2003	4	12		1	7		3	5	
2004	6	10		3	5		3	5	
2005	11	5		7	1		4	4	
2006	8	8		3	5		5	3	
2007	10	6		3	5		7	1	
	606	506	33	337	237	16	269	269	17

PHILADELPHIA EAGLES

Season	All Games W	L	T	Home Games W	L	T	Road Games W	L	T
1933	3	5	1	2	3	1	1	2	
1934	4	7		2	4		2	3	
1935	2	9		0	5		2	4	
1936	1	11		1	6		0	5	
1937	2	8	1	0	5	1	2	3	
1938	5	6		2	3		3	3	
1939	1	9	1	1	3	1	0	6	
1940	1	10		1	4		0	6	
1941	2	8	1	1	4	1	1	4	
1942	2	9		0	5		2	4	
1944	7	1	2	3	1	2	4	0	
1945	7	3		6	0		1	3	
1946	6	5		3	2		3	3	
1947	8	4		6	1		2	3	
1948	9	2	1	6	0		3	2	1
1949	11	1		6	0		5	1	
1950	6	6		2	4		4	2	
1951	4	8		1	5		3	3	
1952	7	5		4	2		3	3	
1953	7	4	1	5	0	1	2	4	
1954	7	4	1	5	1		2	3	1
1955	4	7	1	4	2		0	5	1
1956	3	8	1	2	3	1	1	5	
1957	4	8		3	3		1	5	
1958	2	9	1	2	4		0	5	1
1959	7	5		5	1		2	4	
1960	10	2		5	1		5	1	
1961	10	4		5	2		5	2	
1962	3	10	1	2	5		1	5	1
1963	2	10	2	1	5	1	1	5	1
1964	6	8		3	4		3	4	
1965	5	9		2	5		3	4	
1966	9	5		5	2		4	3	
1967	6	7	1	5	2		1	5	1
1968	2	12		1	6		1	6	
1969	4	9	1	2	5		2	4	1
1970	3	10	1	3	3	1	0	7	
1971	6	7	1	3	4		3	3	1
1972	2	11	1	0	6	1	2	5	
1973	5	8	1	4	3		1	5	1
1974	7	7		5	2		2	5	
1975	4	10		2	5		2	5	
1976	4	10		2	5		2	5	
1977	5	9		4	3		1	6	
1978	9	7		5	3		4	4	
1979	11	5		5	3		6	2	
1980	12	4		7	1		5	3	
1981	10	6		6	2		4	4	
1982	3	6		1	4		2	2	
1983	5	11		1	7		4	4	
1984	6	9	1	5	3		1	6	1
1985	7	9		4	4		3	5	
1986	5	10	1	2	5	1	3	5	
1987	7	8		4	4		3	4	

Season	All Games W	L	T	Home Games W	L	T	Road Games W	L	T
1988	10	6		5	3		5	3	
1989	11	5		6	2		5	3	
1990	10	6		6	2		4	4	
1991	10	6		4	4		6	2	
1992	11	5		8	0		3	5	
1993	8	8		3	5		5	3	
1994	7	9		5	3		2	6	
1995	10	6		6	2		4	4	
1996	10	6		5	3		5	3	
1997	6	9	1	6	2		0	7	1
1998	3	13		3	5		0	8	
1999	5	11		4	4		1	7	
2000	11	5		5	3		6	2	
2001	11	5		4	4		7	1	
2002	12	4		7	1		5	3	
2003	12	4		5	3		7	1	
2004	13	3		7	1		6	2	
2005	6	10		4	4		2	6	
2006	10	6		5	3		5	3	
2007	8	8		3	5		5	3	
	474	520	24	268	234	12	206	286	12

ST. LOUIS RAMS*

Season	All Games W	L	T	Home Games W	L	T	Road Games W	L	T
1937	1	10		0	5		1	5	
1938	4	7		2	2		2	5	
1939	5	5	1	3	2	1	2	3	
1940	4	6	1	3	1	1	1	5	
1941	2	9		1	4		1	5	
1942	5	6		3	2		2	4	
1944	4	6		1	2		3	4	
1945	9	1		4	0		5	1	
1946	6	4	1	3	2		3	2	1
1947	6	6		3	3		3	3	
1948	6	5	1	3	2	1	3	3	
1949	8	2	2	5	1		3	1	2
1950	9	3		5	1		4	2	
1951	8	4		5	2		3	2	
1952	9	3		5	1		4	2	
1953	8	3	1	5	1		3	2	1
1954	6	5	1	3	2	1	3	3	
1955	8	3	1	5	1		3	2	1
1956	4	8		4	2		0	6	
1957	6	6		5	1		1	5	
1958	8	4		4	2		4	2	
1959	2	10		0	6		2	4	
1960	4	7	1	2	3	1	2	4	
1961	4	10		4	3		0	7	
1962	1	12	1	0	7		1	5	1
1963	5	9		3	4		2	5	
1964	5	7	2	3	2	2	2	5	
1965	4	10		3	4		1	6	
1966	8	6		5	2		3	4	
1967	11	1	2	5	1	1	6	0	1
1968	10	3	1	5	2		5	1	1
1969	11	3		5	2		6	1	
1970	9	4	1	3	3	1	6	1	
1971	8	5	1	4	2	1	4	3	
1972	6	7	1	4	3		2	4	1
1973	12	2		7	0		5	2	
1974	10	4		6	1		4	3	
1975	12	2		6	1		6	1	
1976	10	3	1	5	2		5	1	1
1977	10	4		7	0		3	4	
1978	12	4		6	2		6	2	
1979	9	7		4	4		5	3	
1980	11	5		6	2		5	3	

(St. Louis Rams continued)

Season	All Games W	L	T	Home Games W	L	T	Road Games W	L	T
1981	6	10		4	4		2	6	
1982	2	7		1	4		1	3	
1983	9	7		5	3		4	4	
1984	10	6		5	3		5	3	
1985	11	5		6	2		5	3	
1986	10	6		6	2		4	4	
1987	6	9		3	4		3	5	
1988	10	6		4	4		6	2	
1989	11	5		6	2		5	3	
1990	5	11		2	6		3	5	
1991	3	13		2	6		1	7	
1992	6	10		4	4		2	6	
1993	5	11		3	5		2	6	
1994	4	12		3	5		1	7	
1995	7	9		4	4		3	5	
1996	6	10		4	4		2	6	
1997	5	11		2	6		3	5	
1998	4	12		2	6		2	6	
1999	13	3		8	0		5	3	
2000	10	6		5	3		5	3	
2001	14	2		6	2		8	0	
2002	7	9		6	2		1	7	
2003	12	4		8	0		4	4	
2004	8	8		6	2		2	6	
2005	6	10		3	5		3	5	
2006	8	8		4	4		4	4	
2007	3	13		1	7		2	6	
	501	454	20	278	194	10	223	260	10

*includes Cleveland Rams (1937-1942, 1944-45) and Los Angeles Rams (1946-1994).

SAN FRANCISCO 49ERS

Season	All Games W	L	T	Home Games W	L	T	Road Games W	L	T
1950	3	9		3	3		0	6	
1951	7	4	1	5	1		2	3	1
1952	7	5		3	3		4	2	
1953	9	3		5	1		4	2	
1954	7	4	1	4	2		3	2	1
1955	4	8		2	4		2	4	
1956	5	6	1	3	3		2	3	1
1957	8	4		5	1		3	3	
1958	6	6		4	2		2	4	
1959	7	5		4	2		3	3	
1960	7	5		3	3		4	2	
1961	7	6	1	5	1	1	2	5	
1962	6	8		1	6		5	2	
1963	2	12		2	5		0	7	
1964	4	10		3	4		1	6	
1965	7	6	1	4	2	1	3	4	
1966	6	6	2	4	2	1	2	4	1
1967	7	7		3	4		4	3	
1968	7	6	1	3	3	1	4	3	
1969	4	8	2	3	3	1	1	5	1
1970	10	3	1	5	1	1	5	2	
1971	9	5		4	3		5	2	
1972	8	5	1	4	2	1	4	3	
1973	5	9		3	4		2	5	
1974	6	8		3	4		3	4	
1975	5	9		2	5		3	4	
1976	8	6		4	3		4	3	
1977	5	9		3	4		2	5	
1978	2	14		2	6		0	8	
1979	2	14		2	6		0	8	
1980	6	10		4	4		2	6	
1981	13	3		7	1		6	2	
1982	3	6		0	5		3	1	
1983	10	6		4	4		6	2	

Season	All Games W	L	T	Home Games W	L	T	Road Games W	L	T
1984	15	1		7	1		8	0	
1985	10	6		5	3		5	3	
1986	10	5	1	6	2		4	3	1
1987	13	2		6	1		7	1	
1988	10	6		4	4		6	2	
1989	14	2		6	2		8	0	
1990	14	2		6	2		8	0	
1991	10	6		7	1		3	5	
1992	14	2		7	1		7	1	
1993	10	6		6	2		4	4	
1994	13	3		7	1		6	2	
1995	11	5		6	2		5	3	
1996	12	4		6	2		6	2	
1997	13	3		8	0		5	3	
1998	12	4		8	0		4	4	
1999	4	12		3	5		1	7	
2000	6	10		4	4		2	6	
2001	12	4		7	1		5	3	
2002	10	6		5	3		5	3	
2003	7	9		6	2		1	7	
2004	2	14		1	7		1	7	
2005	4	12		3	5		1	7	
2006	7	9		4	4		3	5	
2007	5	11		3	5		2	6	
	450	379	13	247	167	7	203	212	6

SEATTLE SEAHAWKS

Season	All Games W	L	T	Home Games W	L	T	Road Games W	L	T
1976	2	12		1	6		1	6	
1977	5	9		3	4		2	5	
1978	9	7		5	3		4	4	
1979	9	7		5	3		4	4	
1980	4	12		0	8		4	4	
1981	6	10		5	3		1	7	
1982	4	5		3	2		1	3	
1983	9	7		5	3		4	4	
1984	12	4		7	1		5	3	
1985	8	8		5	3		3	5	
1986	10	6		7	1		3	5	
1987	9	6		6	2		3	4	
1988	9	7		5	3		4	4	
1989	7	9		3	5		4	4	
1990	9	7		5	3		4	4	
1991	7	9		5	3		2	6	
1992	2	14		1	7		1	7	
1993	6	10		4	4		2	6	
1994	6	10		3	5		3	5	
1995	8	8		5	3		3	5	
1996	7	9		4	4		3	5	
1997	8	8		4	4		4	4	
1998	8	8		6	2		2	6	
1999	9	7		5	3		4	4	
2000	6	10		3	5		3	5	
2001	9	7		6	2		3	5	
2002	7	9		3	5		4	4	
2003	10	6		8	0		2	6	
2004	9	7		5	3		4	4	
2005	13	3		8	0		5	3	
2006	9	7		5	3		4	4	
2007	10	6		7	1		3	5	
	246	254		147	104		99	150	

TAMPA BAY BUCCANEERS

Season	All Games W	L	T	Home Games W	L	T	Road Games W	L	T
1976	0	14		0	7		0	7	
1977	2	12		1	6		1	6	

Season	All Games W	L	T	Home Games W	L	T	Road Games W	L	T
1978	5	11		3	5		2	6	
1979	10	6		5	3		5	3	
1980	5	10	1	2	5	1	3	5	
1981	9	7		6	2		3	5	
1982	5	4		4	1		1	3	
1983	2	14		1	7		1	7	
1984	6	10		6	2		0	8	
1985	2	14		2	6		0	8	
1986	2	14		1	7		1	7	
1987	4	11		2	5		2	6	
1988	5	11		3	5		2	6	
1989	5	11		2	6		3	5	
1990	6	10		4	4		2	6	
1991	3	13		3	5		0	8	
1992	5	11		3	5		2	6	
1993	5	11		3	5		2	6	
1994	6	10		4	4		2	6	
1995	7	9		5	3		2	6	
1996	6	10		5	3		1	7	
1997	10	6		5	3		5	3	
1998	8	8		6	2		2	6	
1999	11	5		7	1		4	4	
2000	10	6		6	2		4	4	
2001	9	7		5	3		4	4	
2002	12	4		6	2		6	2	
2003	7	9		3	5		4	4	
2004	5	11		4	4		1	7	
2005	11	5		6	2		5	3	
2006	4	12		3	5		1	7	
2007	9	7		6	2		3	5	
	196	303	1	122	127	1	74	176	

WASHINGTON REDSKINS*

Season	All Games W	L	T	Home Games W	L	T	Road Games W	L	T
1932	4	4	2	2	3	1	2	1	1
1933	5	5	2	4	2		1	3	2
1934	6	6		4	3		2	3	
1935	2	8	1	2	5		0	3	1
1936	7	5		4	3		3	2	
1937	8	3		4	2		4	1	
1938	6	3	2	3	1	1	3	2	1
1939	8	2	1	5	0	1	3	2	
1940	9	2		6	0		3	2	
1941	6	5		4	2		2	3	
1942	10	1		5	1		5	0	
1943	6	3	1	4	2		2	1	1
1944	6	3	1	4	2		2	1	1
1945	8	2		6	0		2	2	
1946	5	5	1	3	2	1	2	3	
1947	4	8		4	2		0	6	
1948	7	5		4	2		3	3	
1949	4	7	1	3	3		1	4	1
1950	3	9		1	5		2	4	
1951	5	7		2	4		3	3	
1952	4	8		1	5		3	3	
1953	6	5	1	3	3		3	2	1
1954	3	9		3	3		0	6	
1955	8	4		3	3		5	1	
1956	6	6		4	2		2	4	
1957	5	6	1	2	3	1	3	3	
1958	4	7	1	3	2	1	1	5	
1959	3	9		2	4		1	5	
1960	1	9	2	1	4	1	0	5	1
1961	1	12	1	1	6		0	6	1
1962	5	7	2	3	4		2	3	2
1963	3	11		1	6		2	5	
1964	6	8		4	3		2	5	

Season	All Games W	L	T	Home Games W	L	T	Road Games W	L	T
1965	6	8		3	4		3	4	
1966	7	7		4	3		3	4	
1967	5	6	3	2	4	1	3	2	2
1968	5	9		3	4		2	5	
1969	7	5	2	4	2	1	3	3	1
1970	6	8		4	3		2	5	
1971	9	4	1	4	2	1	5	2	
1972	11	3		6	1		5	2	
1973	10	4		7	0		3	4	
1974	10	4		6	1		4	3	
1975	8	6		5	2		3	4	
1976	10	4		5	2		5	2	
1977	9	5		5	2		4	3	
1978	8	8		5	3		3	5	
1979	10	6		6	2		4	4	
1980	6	10		4	4		2	6	
1981	8	8		5	3		3	5	
1982	8	1		3	1		5	0	
1983	14	2		7	1		7	1	
1984	11	5		7	1		4	4	
1985	10	6		5	3		5	3	
1986	12	4		7	1		5	3	
1987	11	4		6	1		5	3	
1988	7	9		4	4		3	5	
1989	10	6		4	4		6	2	
1990	10	6		7	1		3	5	
1991	14	2		7	1		7	1	
1992	9	7		6	2		3	5	
1993	4	12		3	5		1	7	
1994	3	13		0	8		3	5	
1995	6	10		4	4		2	6	
1996	9	7		5	3		4	4	
1997	8	7	1	5	2	1	3	5	
1998	6	10		4	4		2	6	
1999	10	6		6	2		4	4	
2000	8	8		4	4		4	4	
2001	8	8		4	4		4	4	
2002	7	9		5	3		2	6	
2003	5	11		3	5		2	6	
2004	6	10		3	5		3	5	
2005	10	6		6	2		4	4	
2006	5	11		3	5		2	6	
2007	9	7		5	3		4	4	
	529	486	27	306	213	11	223	273	16

*includes Boston Braves (1932) and Boston Redskins (1933-36).

ALL-TIME RECORDS OF NFL TEAMS

AFC	W	L	T	Pct.
Miami	369	267	4	.580
Oakland	400	313	11	.561
Jacksonville	113	95	0	.543
Cleveland	424	360	10	.541
Kansas City	379	333	12	.532
Denver	378	336	10	.529
Indianapolis	415	384	7	.519
Pittsburgh	508	484	20	.512
New England	366	349	9	.512
Baltimore	96	95	1	.503
San Diego	354	359	11	.497
Tennessee	350	368	6	.487
Buffalo	341	375	8	.476
N.Y. Jets	322	394	8	.450
Cincinnati	268	343	1	.439
Houston	32	64	0	.333

NFC	W	L	T	Pct.
Chicago	677	491	42	.580
Dallas	414	302	6	.578
Green Bay	637	503	36	.558
Minnesota	385	316	9	.549
N.Y. Giants	606	506	33	.545
San Francisco	450	379	13	.543
St. Louis	501	454	20	.525
Washington	529	486	27	.521
Seattle	246	254	0	.492
Philadelphia	474	520	24	.477
Detroit	488	553	32	.469
Carolina	97	111	0	.466
Arizona	464	657	39	.414
New Orleans	254	367	5	.409
Atlanta	256	378	6	.404
Tampa Bay	196	303	1	.393

From 1920-1971, tie games were not included in win percentage.

History

The Professional Football Hall of Fame is located in Canton, Ohio, site of the organizational meeting on September 17, 1920, from which the National Football League evolved. The NFL recognized Canton as the Hall of Fame site on April 27, 1961. Canton area individuals, foundations, and companies donated almost $400,000 in cash and services to provide funds for the construction of the original two-building complex, which was dedicated on September 7, 1963. Since that time, the Hall added three buildings with major expansion projects in 1971, 1978, and 1995. The Hall's largest-ever expansion, a $9.2 million project, was completed in early fall 1995. With the new fifth building, the Hall's size is now 82,307 square feet, more than four times its original size.

The expanded Hall represents the sport of pro football in many ways—through (1) GameDay Stadium, a dynamic two-part turntable theater featuring NFL action in Cinemascope for the first time, (2) a standard theater showing NFL films hourly, (3) six large exhibition areas where the history of pro football is detailed in memento, picture, and story form, (4) an extensive archive and information center, and (5) a large museum store.

Throughout the years, the Pro Football Hall of Fame has become an extremely popular tourist attraction. Since its opening, the Hall has had more than eight million visitors.

New members of the Pro Football Hall of Fame are elected annually by a 44-member National Board of Selectors, made up of media representatives from every league city, eleven at-large representatives, and a representative of the Pro Football Writers of America. Between four and seven new members are elected each year. An affirmative vote of approximately 80 percent is needed for election.

Any fan may nominate any eligible player or contributor simply by writing to the Pro Football Hall of Fame. Players and coaches must have last played or coached at least five years before he is eligible. Contributors (administrators, owners, *et al.*) may be elected

while they are still active.

The charter class of 17 enshrinees was elected in 1963 and the honor roll now stands at 247 (153 living as of May 15, 2008) with the election of a six-man class in 2008. That class consists of Fred Dean, Darrell Green, Art Monk, Emmitt Thomas, Andre Tippett, and Gary Zimmerman.

ROSTER OF MEMBERS

HERB ADDERLEY
Cornerback. 6-0, 205. Born in Philadelphia, Pennsylvania, June 8, 1939. Michigan State. Inducted in 1980. 1961-69 Green Bay Packers, 1970-72 Dallas Cowboys. **Highlights:** 48 interceptions, 7 touchdowns. Played in four Super Bowls, five Pro Bowls.

TROY AIKMAN
Quarterback. 6-4, 219. Born in West Covina, California, November 21, 1966. Oklahoma, UCLA. Inducted in 2006. 1989-2000 Dallas Cowboys. **Highlights:** His 90 wins in 1990s make him winningest quarterback of any decade. Led Cowboys to three Super Bowl wins. Passed for 32,942 yards, 165 touchdowns. Named to six Pro Bowls.

GEORGE ALLEN
Coach. Born in Detroit, Michigan, April 29, 1918. Died December 31, 1990. Alma College, Eastern Michigan, Marquette, Michigan. Inducted in 2002. 1966-1970 Los Angeles Rams, 1971-77 Washington Redskins. **Highlights:** 118-54-5 overall record. Never suffered a losing season, and ranked tenth in coaching victories at time of retirement.

MARCUS ALLEN
Running back. 6-2, 210. Born in San Diego, California, March 26, 1960. Southern California. Inducted in 2003. 1982-1992 Los Angeles Raiders, 1993-1997 Kansas City Chiefs. **Highlights:** First player in NFL history to tally 10,000 rushing yards and 5,000 receiving yards. MVP, Super Bowl XVIII.

LANCE ALWORTH
Wide receiver. 6-0, 184. Born in Houston, Texas, August 3, 1940. Arkansas. Inducted in 1978. 1962-1970 San Diego Chargers, 1971-72 Dallas Cowboys. **Highlights:** 542 receptions for 10,266 yards, 85 touchdowns. All-AFL seven times, seven All-Star games.

DOUG ATKINS
Defensive end. 6-8, 275. Born in Humboldt, Tennessee, May 8, 1930. Tennessee. Inducted in 1982. 1953-54 Cleveland Browns, 1955-1966 Chicago Bears, 1967-69 New Orleans Saints. **Highlights:** Eight Pro Bowls, All-NFL four times. Played for 17 years, 205 games.

MORRIS (RED) BADGRO
End. 6-0, 190. Born in Orillia, Washington, December 1, 1902. Died July 13, 1998. Southern California. Inducted in 1981. 1927-28 New York Yankees, 1930-35 New York Giants, 1936 Brooklyn Dodgers. **Highlights:** First- or second-team All-NFL four times. Scored first touchdown in NFL Championship Game series.

LEM BARNEY
Cornerback. 6-0, 190. Born in Gulfport, Mississippi, September 8, 1945. Jackson State. Inducted in 1992. 1967-1977 Detroit Lions. **Highlights:** 56 interceptions for 1,077 yards, 11 touchdowns (7 defensive, 4 special teams). Seven Pro Bowls, All-NFL/NFC four times.

CLIFF BATTLES
Halfback. 6-1, 195. Born in Akron, Ohio, May 1, 1910. Died April 28, 1981. West Virginia Wesleyan. Inducted in 1968. 1932 Boston Braves, 1933-36 Boston Redskins, 1937 Washington Redskins. **Highlights:** NFL rushing champion 1932, 1937. First to gain more than 200 yards in a game, 1933.

SAMMY BAUGH
Quarterback. 6-2, 180. Born in Temple, Texas, March 17, 1914. Texas Christian. Inducted in 1963. 1937-1952 Washington Redskins. **Highlights:** Charter enshrinee. Six-time NFL passing leader. NFL passing, punting, interception champ, 1943.

CHUCK BEDNARIK
Center-linebacker. 6-3, 230. Born in Bethlehem, Pennsylvania, May 1, 1925. Pennsylvania. Inducted in 1967. 1949-1962 Philadelphia Eagles. **Highlights:** Eight Pro Bowls. Missed three games in 14 years. Named NFL all-time center, 1969.

BERT BELL
Team owner. Commissioner. Born in Philadelphia, Pennsylvania, February 25, 1895. Died October 11, 1959. Pennsylvania. Inducted in 1963. 1933-1940 Philadelphia Eagles, 1941-42 Pittsburgh Steelers, 1943 Phil-Pitt, 1944 Card-Pitt, 1945-46 Pittsburgh Steelers. Commissioner, 1946-1959. **Highlights:** Charter enshrinee. Built NFL image as commissioner, 1946-1959. Set up long-term television policies.

BOBBY BELL
Linebacker. 6-4, 225. Born in Shelby, North Carolina, June 17, 1940. Minnesota. Inducted in 1983. 1963-1974 Kansas City Chiefs. **Highlights:** 26 interceptions. All-AFL/AFC eight times. Nine career touchdowns, 1 on onside kick return.

RAYMOND BERRY
End. 6-2, 187. Born in Corpus Christi, Texas, February 27, 1933. Southern Methodist. Inducted in 1973. 1955-1967 Baltimore Colts. **Highlights:** 631 receptions for 9,275 yards, 68 touchdowns. Set NFL title game mark with 12 catches for 178 yards, 1958.

ELVIN BETHEA
Defensive end. 6-2, 260. Born in Trenton, New Jersey, March 1, 1946. North Carolina A&T. Inducted in 2003. 1968-1983 Houston Oilers. **Highlights:** Led team in sacks six times. Elected to eight Pro Bowls. Played for 16 years, 210 games.

CHARLES W. BIDWILL SR.
Team owner. Born in Chicago, Illinois, September 16, 1895. Died April 19, 1947. Loyola of Chicago. Inducted in 1967. 1933-1943 Chicago Cardinals, 1944 Card-Pitt, 1945-47 Chicago Cardinals. **Highlights:** Guiding light for NFL during depression years. Built famous "Dream Backfield."

FRED BILETNIKOFF
Wide receiver. 6-1, 190. Born in Erie, Pennsylvania, February 23, 1943. Florida State. Inducted in 1988. 1965-1978 Oakland Raiders. **Highlights:** 589 receptions for 8,974 yards, 76 touchdowns. 40 catches 10 straight years. MVP, Super Bowl XI.

GEORGE BLANDA
Quarterback-kicker. 6-2, 215. Born in Youngwood, Pennsylvania, September 17, 1927. Kentucky. Inducted in 1981. 1949-1958 Chicago Bears, 1950 Baltimore Colts, 1960-66 Houston Oilers, 1967-1975 Oakland Raiders. **Highlights:** 2,002 career points. 26-season, 340-game career longest in NFL history.

MEL BLOUNT
Cornerback. 6-3, 205. Born in Vidalia, Georgia, April 10, 1948. Southern University. Inducted in 1989. 1970-1983 Pittsburgh Steelers. **Highlights:** 57 interceptions for 736 yards. NFL defensive MVP, 1975. Played in five Pro Bowls.

TERRY BRADSHAW
Quarterback. 6-3, 210. Born in Shreveport, Louisiana, September 2, 1948. Louisiana Tech. Inducted in 1989. 1970-1983 Pittsburgh Steelers. **Highlights:** 27,989 yards passing, 212 touchdowns. MVP in Super Bowls XIII, XIV.

BOB (BOOMER) BROWN
Tackle. 6-4, 280. Born in Cleveland, Ohio, December 8, 1941. Nebraska. Inducted in 2004. 1964-68 Philadelphia Eagles, 1969-1970 Los Angeles Rams, 1971-73 Oakland Raiders. **Highlights:** All-NFL seven of 10 seasons, six Pro Bowls. Named to 1960s All-Decade Team.

JIM BROWN
Fullback. 6-2, 228. Born in St. Simons, Georgia, February 17, 1936. Syracuse. Inducted in 1971. 1957-1965 Cleveland Browns. **Highlights:** 12,312 yards rushing, 756 points. Led NFL rushers eight years. Nine consecutive Pro Bowls.

PAUL BROWN
Coach. Born in Norwalk, Ohio, September 7, 1908. Died August 5, 1991. Miami (Ohio). Inducted in 1967. 1946-49 Cleveland Browns (AAFC), 1950-1962 Cleveland Browns. **Highlights:** Built Cleveland dynasty with 167-53-8 record, four AAFC titles, three NFL crowns. Returned to coaching with Cincinnati Bengals after induction, 1968-1975.

ROOSEVELT BROWN
Tackle. 6-3, 255. Born in Charlottesville, Virginia, October 20, 1932. Died June 9, 2004. Morgan State. Inducted in 1975. 1953-1965 New York Giants. **Highlights:** All-NFL eight consecutive years, nine Pro Bowls. NFL's lineman of year, 1956.

WILLIE BROWN
Cornerback. 6-1, 210. Born in Yazoo City, Mississippi, December 2, 1940. Grambling. Inducted in 1984. 1963-66 Denver Broncos, 1967-1978 Oakland Raiders. **Highlights:** 54 interceptions for 472 yards. Scored on 75-yard interception in Super Bowl XI.

BUCK BUCHANAN
Defensive tackle. 6-7, 274. Born in Gainesville, Alabama, September 10, 1940. Died July 16, 1992. Grambling. Inducted in 1990. 1963-1975 Kansas City Chiefs. **Highlights:** Led Chiefs defensive efforts in Super Bowl I, IV. Did not miss a game in 13 years.

NICK BUONICONTI
Linebacker. 5-11, 220. Born in Springfield, Massachusetts, December 15, 1940. Notre Dame. Inducted in 2001. 1962-68 Boston Patriots, 1969-1974, 1976 Miami Dolphins. **Highlights:** All-AFL/AFC eight times. Named to AFL's All-Time Team.

DICK BUTKUS
Linebacker. 6-3, 245. Born in Chicago, Illinois, December 9, 1942. Illinois. Inducted in 1979. 1965-1973 Chicago Bears. **Highlights:** All-NFL six years, eight consecutive Pro Bowls. 27 fumble recoveries.

EARL CAMPBELL
Running back. 5-11, 233. Born in Tyler, Texas, March 29, 1955. Texas. Inducted in 1991. 1978-1984 Houston Oilers, 1984-85 New Orleans Saints. **Highlights:** 9,407 yards rushing, 74 touchdowns. 1,934 yards rushing in 1980, including four games with at least 200 yards.

TONY CANADEO
Halfback. 5-11, 195. Born in Chicago, Illinois, May 5, 1919. Died November 29, 2003. Gonzaga. Inducted in 1974. 1941-44, 1946-1952 Green Bay Packers. **Highlights:** Two-way player. Third player to rush for 1,000 yards in single season, 1949.

JOE CARR
NFL president. Born in Columbus, Ohio, October 23, 1879. Died May 20, 1939. Did not attend college. Inducted in 1963. President, 1921-1939 National Football League. **Highlights:** Charter enshrinee. NFL co-organizer, 1920. Introduced standard player contract.

HARRY CARSON
Linebacker. 6-2, 237. Born in Florence, South Carolina, November 26, 1953. South Carolina State. Inducted in 2006. 1976-1988 New York Giants. **Highlights:** 11 career interceptions. Named to nine Pro Bowls. Named first- or second-team All-NFL six times.

DAVE CASPER
Tight end. 6-4, 240. Born in Bemidji, Minnesota, February 2, 1952. Notre Dame. Inducted in 2002. 1974-1980 Oakland Raiders, 1980-83 Houston Oilers, 1983 Minnesota Vikings, 1984 Los Angeles Raiders. **Highlights:** 378 receptions for 5,216 yards, 52 touchdowns. Five consecutive Pro Bowls.

GUY CHAMBERLIN
End. Coach. 6-2, 196. Born in Blue Springs, Nebraska, January 16, 1894. Died April 4, 1967. Nebraska. Inducted in 1965. 1919 Canton Bulldogs, 1920-21 Decatur Staleys/Chicago Staleys, player-coach 1922-23 Canton Bulldogs, 1924 Cleveland Bulldogs, 1925-26 Frankford Yellowjackets, 1927-28 Chicago Cardinals. **Highlights:** Player-coach of four NFL championship teams. Six-year coaching record of 58-16-7.

JACK CHRISTIANSEN
Safety. 6-1, 185. Born in Sublette, Kansas, December 20, 1928. Died June 29, 1986. Colorado State. Inducted in 1970. 1951-58 Detroit Lions. **Highlights:** 46 interceptions. NFL interception leader, 1953, 1957. Eight punt returns for touchdowns.

EARL (DUTCH) CLARK
Quarterback. 6-0, 185. Born in Fowler, Colorado, October 11, 1906. Died August 5, 1978. Colorado College. Inducted in 1963. 1931-32 Portsmouth Spartans, 1934-38 Detroit Lions. **Highlights:** Charter enshrinee. NFL scoring champion three years. Led Lions to 1935 NFL title.

GEORGE CONNOR
Tackle-linebacker. 6-3, 240. Born in Chicago, Illinois, January 21, 1925. Died March 31, 2003. Holy Cross, Notre Dame. Inducted in 1975. 1948-1955 Chicago Bears. **Highlights:** All-NFL at three positions—T, DT, LB. All-NFL five years. Played in first four Pro Bowls.

JIMMY CONZELMAN

Quarterback. Coach. Team owner. 6-0, 180. Born in St. Louis, Missouri, March 6, 1898. Died July 31, 1970. Washington of St. Louis. Inducted in 1964. 1920 Decatur Staleys, 1921-22 Rock Island Independents, 1922-24 Milwaukee Badgers; owner-coach 1925-26 Detroit Panthers; player-coach 1927-29, coach 1930 Providence Steam Roller; coach 1940-42, 1946-48 Chicago Cardinals. **Highlights:** Player-coach of four NFL teams in 1920's. Coached Cardinals to 1947 NFL crown.

LOU CREEKMUR

Tackle-guard. 6-4, 255. Born in Hopelawn, New Jersey. January 22, 1927. William & Mary. Inducted in 1996. 1950-59 Detroit Lions. **Highlights:** All-NFL six times, twice at guard and four times at tackle. Selected to eight Pro Bowls and played on three NFL championship teams.

LARRY CSONKA

Running back. 6-3, 235. Born in Stow, Ohio, December 25, 1946. Syracuse. Inducted in 1987. 1968-1974, 1979 Miami Dolphins, 1976-78 New York Giants. **Highlights:** 8,081 yards rushing, 68 touchdowns. MVP Super Bowl VIII. Only 21 fumbles in 1,891 carries and 106 receptions.

AL DAVIS

Team, League Administrator. Born in Brockton, Massachusetts, July 4, 1929. Wittenberg, Syracuse. Inducted in 1992. 1963-1981, 1995-present Oakland Raiders, 1982-1994 Los Angeles Raiders, 1966 American Football League. **Highlights:** Only person to serve in pros as personnel assistant, scout, assistant coach, head coach, general manager, commissioner, team owner/CEO.

WILLIE DAVIS

Defensive end. 6-3, 245. Born in Lisbon, Louisiana, July 24, 1934. Grambling. Inducted in 1981. 1958-59 Cleveland Browns, 1960-69 Green Bay Packers. **Highlights:** All-NFL five seasons, five Pro Bowls. Did not miss game in 12-year career.

LEN DAWSON

Quarterback. 6-0, 190. Born in Alliance, Ohio, June 20, 1935. Purdue. Inducted in 1987. 1957-59 Pittsburgh Steelers, 1960-61 Cleveland Browns, 1962 Dallas Texans, 1963-1975 Kansas City Chiefs. **Highlights:** 28,711 yards passing, 239 touchdowns. Four AFL passing crowns. MVP, Super Bowl IV.

FRED DEAN

Defensive end. 6-3, 230. Born in Arcadia, Louisiana, February 24, 1952. Louisiana Tech. Inducted in 2008. 1975-1981 San Diego Chargers, 1981-85 San Francisco 49ers. **Highlights:** Had career-high 17.5 sacks in 1983. Played on two Super Bowl championship teams with 49ers (Super Bowls XVI, XIX).

JOE DeLAMIELLEURE

Guard. 6-3, 254. Born in Detroit, Michigan, March 16, 1951. Michigan State. Inducted in 2003. 1973-1979, 1985 Buffalo Bills, 1980-1984 Cleveland Browns. **Highlights:** Selected All-Pro and All-AFC six consecutive times, 1975-1980. Named to six Pro Bowls. Played 13 years, 185 games.

ERIC DICKERSON

Running back. 6-3, 220. Born in Sealy, Texas, September 2, 1960. Southern Methodist. Inducted in 1999. 1983-87 Los Angeles Rams, 1987-1991 Indianapolis Colts, 1992 Los Angeles Raiders, 1993 Atlanta Falcons. **Highlights:** Rushed for 13,259 career yards, including an NFL record 2,105 yards in 1984. All-Pro five times, six Pro Bowls.

DAN DIERDORF

Tackle. 6-3, 290. Born in Canton, Ohio, June 29, 1949. Michigan. Inducted in 1996. 1971-1983 St. Louis Cardinals. **Highlights:** All-Pro five times, played in six Pro Bowls, named NFL's best blocker three times.

MIKE DITKA

Tight end. 6-3, 225. Born in Carnegie, Pennsylvania, October 18, 1939. Pittsburgh. Inducted in 1988. 1961-66 Chicago Bears, 1967-68 Philadelphia Eagles, 1969-1972 Dallas Cowboys. **Highlights:** 427 receptions for 5,812 yards, 43 touchdowns. First tight end selected to Hall of Fame. Five consecutive Pro Bowls.

ART DONOVAN

Defensive tackle. 6-3, 265. Born in Bronx, New York, June 5, 1925. Boston College. Inducted in 1968. 1950 Baltimore Colts, 1951 New York Yanks, 1952 Dallas Texans, 1953-1961 Baltimore Colts. **Highlights:** Five Pro Bowls. Vital part of Baltimore's climb to powerhouse status in 1950s.

TONY DORSETT

Running back. 5-11, 184. Born in Rochester, Pennsylvania, April 7, 1954. Pittsburgh. Inducted in 1994. 1977-1987 Dallas Cowboys, 1988 Denver Broncos. **Highlights:** 12,739 yards rushing, 398 receptions, 91 touchdowns. Ran record 99 yards for touchdown vs. Minnesota, January, 1983.

JOHN (PADDY) DRISCOLL

Quarterback. 5-11, 160. Born in Evanston, Illinois, January 11, 1896. Died June 29, 1968. Northwestern. Inducted in 1965. 1919 Hammond Pros, 1920 Decatur Staleys, 1920-25 Chicago Cardinals, 1926-29 Chicago Bears. **Highlights:** All-NFL seven times. Dropkicked record 4 field goals in one game, 1925.

BILL DUDLEY

Halfback. 5-10, 182. Born in Bluefield, Virginia, December 24, 1921. Virginia. Inducted in 1966. 1942, 1945-46 Pittsburgh Steelers, 1947-49 Detroit Lions, 1950-51, 1953 Washington Redskins. **Highlights:** Won NFL rushing, interception, punt return titles, 1946. All-NFL 1942, 1946, and 1947.

ALBERT GLEN (TURK) EDWARDS

Tackle. 6-2, 260. Born in Mold, Washington, September 28, 1907. Died January 12, 1973. Washington State. Inducted in 1969. 1932 Boston Braves, 1933-36 Boston Redskins, 1937-1940 Washington Redskins. **Highlights:** All-NFL 1932-34, 1936, 1937. Steamrolling blocker, smothering tackler.

CARL ELLER

Defensive end. 6-6, 247. Born in Winston-Salem, North Carolina, January 25, 1942. Minnesota. Inducted in 2004. 1964-1978 Minnesota Vikings, 1979 Seattle Seahawks. **Highlights:** Fixture on Vikings' "Purple People Eaters" defensive line, All-Pro five time, elected to six Pro Bowls.

JOHN ELWAY

Quarterback. 6-3, 215. Born in Port Angeles, Washington, June 28, 1960. Stanford. Inducted in 2004. 1983-1998 Denver Broncos. **Highlights:** Passed for 51,475 yards, 300 touchdowns. Named to nine Pro Bowls. NFL MVP, 1987; MVP, Super Bowl XXXIII.

WEEB EWBANK

Coach. Born in Richmond, Indiana, May 6, 1907. Died November 17, 1998. Miami (Ohio). Inducted in 1978. 1954-1962 Baltimore Colts, 1963-1973 New York Jets. **Highlights:** Only coach to win championships in both NFL, AFL. Led both Colts (1958 and 1959) and Jets (1968) to championships.

TOM FEARS

End. 6-2, 215. Born in Guadalajara, Mexico, December 3, 1922. Died January 4, 2000. Santa Clara, UCLA. Inducted in 1970. 1948-1956 Los Angeles Rams. **Highlights:** 400 receptions for 5,397 yards, 38 touchdowns. Led NFL receivers first three seasons. Had then-record 18 receptions in single game.

JIM FINKS
Administrator. Born in St. Louis, Missouri, August 31, 1927. Died May 8, 1994. Tulsa. Inducted 1995. 1964-1973 Minnesota Vikings, 1974-1982 Chicago Bears, 1986-1993 New Orleans Saints. **Highlights:** Developed Vikings, Bears, Saints—all teams with losing records—into winners.

RAY FLAHERTY
Coach. Born in Spokane, Washington, September 1, 1903. Died July 19, 1994. Gonzaga. Inducted in 1976. 1936-1942 Boston/Washington Redskins, 1946-48 New York Yankees (AAFC), 1949 Chicago Hornets (AAFC). **Highlights:** 82-41-5 coaching record. Introduced screen pass in 1937 title game and platoon system.

LEN FORD
Defensive end. 6-4, 260. Born in Washington, D.C., February 18, 1926. Died March 14, 1972. Morgan State, Michigan. Inducted in 1976. 1948-49 Los Angeles Dons (AAFC), 1950-57 Cleveland Browns, 1958 Green Bay Packers. **Highlights:** All-NFL five times, four Pro Bowls. Recovered 20 opponents' fumbles.

DAN FORTMANN
Guard. 6-0, 210. Born in Pearl River, New York, April 11, 1916. Died May 23, 1995. Colgate. Inducted in 1965. 1936-1943 Chicago Bears. **Highlights:** At 20, became youngest starter in NFL. First- or second-team All-NFL every season of career.

DAN FOUTS
Quarterback. 6-3, 210. Born in San Francisco, California, June 10, 1951. Oregon. Inducted in 1993. 1973-1987 San Diego Chargers. **Highlights:** 43,040 passing yards, 254 touchdowns. Six Pro Bowls, NFL MVP, 1982.

BENNY FRIEDMAN
Quarterback. 5-10, 183. Born in Cleveland, Ohio, March 18, 1905. Died November 23, 1982. Michigan. Inducted in 2005. 1927 Cleveland Bulldogs, 1928 Detroit Wolverines, 1929-1931 New York Giants, 1932-34 Brooklyn Dodgers. **Highlights:** NFL's first great passer. Set league mark for touchdowns with 20 in 1929. Led NFL in touchdown passes each of his first four seasons.

FRANK GATSKI
Center. 6-3, 240. Born in Farmington, West Virginia, March 18, 1919. Marshall, Auburn. Died November 22, 2005. Inducted in 1985. 1946-49 Cleveland Browns (AAFC), 1950-56 Cleveland Browns, 1957 Detroit Lions. **Highlights:** Never missed game in high school, college, or pro football. Played 11 championship games, winning eight.

BILL GEORGE
Linebacker. 6-2, 230. Born in Waynesburg, Pennsylvania, October 27, 1929. Died September 30, 1982. Wake Forest. Inducted in 1974. 1952-1965 Chicago Bears, 1966 Los Angeles Rams. **Highlights:** All-NFL eight years, eight consecutive Pro Bowls. 14 years of service, longest of any Bears player.

JOE GIBBS
Coach. Born in Mocksville, North Carolina, November 25, 1940. Cerritos (Calif.) J.C., San Diego State. Inducted in 1996. 1981-1992 Washington Redskins. **Highlights:** 124-60-0 record in regular season, 16-5 in postseason, including four Super Bowl appearances—winning three. Won 10 or more games eight times.

FRANK GIFFORD
Halfback. 6-1, 195. Born in Santa Monica, California, August 16, 1930. Southern California. Inducted in 1977. 1952-1960, 1962-64 New York Giants. **Highlights:** Starred on both offense and defense. Seven Pro Bowls, 1956 NFL player of the year.

SID GILLMAN
Coach. Born in Minneapolis, Minnesota, October 26, 1911. Died January 3, 2003. Ohio State. Inducted in 1983. 1955-59 Los Angeles Rams, 1960-69, 1971 Los Angeles/San Diego Chargers, 1973-74 Houston Oilers. **Highlights:** 123-104-7 coaching record. First to win division titles in both NFL, AFL.

OTTO GRAHAM
Quarterback. 6-1, 195. Born in Waukegan, Illinois, December 6, 1921. Died December 17, 2003. Northwestern. Inducted in 1965. 1946-49 Cleveland Browns (AAFC), 1950-55 Cleveland Browns. **Highlights:** 23,584 passing yards, 174 touchdowns. Guided Browns to 10 division or league crowns in 10 years.

HAROLD (RED) GRANGE
Halfback. 6-0, 185. Born in Forksville, Pennsylvania, June 13, 1903. Died January 28, 1991. Illinois. Inducted in 1963. 1925 Chicago Bears, 1926 New York Yankees (AFL), 1927 New York Yankees, 1929-1934 Chicago Bears. **Highlights:** Charter enshrinee. Nicknamed "Galloping Ghost." Name produced first huge pro football crowds.

BUD GRANT
Coach. Born in Superior, Wisconsin, May 20, 1927. Minnesota. Inducted in 1994. 1967-1983, 1985 Minnesota Vikings. **Highlights:** 168-108-5 coaching record. Led Vikings to 11 division championships, four Super Bowls.

DARRELL GREEN
Cornerback. 5-8, 176. Born in Houston, Texas, February 15, 1960. Texas A&I. Inducted in 2008. 1983-2002 Washington Redskins. **Highlights:** 54 interceptions, 621 yards, 6 TDs. Played 20 seasons. Recorded interception in NFL record 19 straight seasons. Selected to seven Pro Bowls.

JOE GREENE
Defensive tackle. 6-4, 260. Born in Temple, Texas, September 24, 1946. North Texas State. Inducted in 1987. 1969-1981 Pittsburgh Steelers. **Highlights:** NFL defensive player of the year, 1972, 1974. Four-time Super Bowl champion, 10 Pro Bowls.

FORREST GREGG
Tackle. 6-4, 250. Born in Birthright, Texas, October 18, 1933. Southern Methodist. Inducted in 1977. 1956, 1958-1970 Green Bay Packers, 1971 Dallas Cowboys. **Highlights:** Played 188 consecutive games. Nine Pro Bowls. Played on six NFL championship teams, three Super Bowl winners.

BOB GRIESE
Quarterback. 6-1, 190. Born in Evansville, Indiana, February 3, 1945. Purdue. Inducted in 1990. 1967-1980 Miami Dolphins. **Highlights:** 25,092 passing yards, 192 touchdowns. Led Miami to three AFC titles, Super Bowl VII, VIII wins.

LOU GROZA
Tackle-kicker. 6-3, 250. Born in Martins Ferry, Ohio, January 25, 1924. Died November 29, 2000. Ohio State. Inducted in 1974. 1946-49 Cleveland Browns (AAFC), 1950-59, 1961-67 Cleveland Browns. **Highlights:** 1,608 points in 21 years. Nine Pro Bowls, All-NFL six years. NFL player of the year, 1954.

JOE GUYON
Halfback. 6-1, 180. Born on White Earth Indian Reservation, Minnesota, November 26, 1892. Died November 27, 1971. Carlisle, Georgia Tech. Inducted in 1966. 1919-1920 Canton Bulldogs, 1921 Cleveland Indians, 1922-23 Oorang Indians, 1924 Rock Island Independents, 1924-25 Kansas City Cowboys, 1927 New York Giants. **Highlights:** Touchdown pass gave Giants victory over Bears to win 1927 championship.

GEORGE HALAS

End. Coach. Team owner. Born in Chicago, Illinois, February 2, 1895. Died October 31, 1983. Illinois. Inducted in 1963. Player-coach 1920 Decatur Staleys, 1921 Chicago Staleys, 1922-29 Chicago Bears; coach 1933-1942, 1946-1955, 1958-1967 Chicago Bears. **Highlights:** Charter enshrinee. 324 coaching wins. Only person associated with NFL throughout first 50 years. Coached Bears 40 seasons, won six NFL titles.

JACK HAM

Linebacker. 6-1, 225. Born in Johnstown, Pennsylvania, December 23, 1948. Penn State. Inducted in 1988. 1971-1982 Pittsburgh Steelers. **Highlights:** Won four Super Bowls, 21 opponents' fumbles recovered, 32 interceptions. Eight consecutive Pro Bowls.

DAN HAMPTON

Defensive tackle-defensive end. 6-5, 264. Born in Oklahoma City, Oklahoma, September 19, 1957. Arkansas. Inducted in 2002. 1979-1990 Chicago Bears. **Highlights:** A versatile player, he earned all-pro honors at both defensive tackle and defensive end. Named to four Pro Bowls.

JOHN HANNAH

Guard. 6-3, 265. Born in Canton, Georgia, April 4, 1951. Alabama. Inducted in 1991. 1973-1985 New England Patriots. **Highlights:** Renowned as premier guard of era. All-Pro 10 years, nine Pro Bowls.

FRANCO HARRIS

Running back. 6-2, 225. Born in Fort Dix, New Jersey, March 7, 1950. Penn State. Inducted in 1990. 1972-1983 Pittsburgh Steelers, 1984 Seattle Seahawks. **Highlights:** 12,120 rushing yards, 100 total touchdowns. 1,556 rushing yards in 19 postseason games. MVP in Super Bowl IX.

MIKE HAYNES

Cornerback. 6-2, 195. Born in Denison, Texas, July 1, 1953. Arizona State. Inducted in 1997. 1976-1982 New England Patriots, 1983-89 Los Angeles Raiders. **Highlights:** Defensive rookie of the year. Selected to nine Pro Bowls and intercepted 46 passes, plus one pick in Super Bowl XVIII.

ED HEALEY

Tackle. 6-3, 220. Born in Indian Orchard, Massachusetts, December 28, 1894. Died December 9, 1978. Dartmouth. Inducted in 1964. 1920-22 Rock Island Independents, 1922-27 Chicago Bears. **Highlights:** Two-way star. Perennial all-pro with Bears.

MEL HEIN

Center. 6-2, 225. Born in Redding, California, August 22, 1909. Died January 31, 1992. Washington State. Inducted in 1963. 1931-1945 New York Giants. **Highlights:** Charter enshrinee. 60-minute regular for 15 years. All-NFL eight consecutive years.

TED HENDRICKS

Linebacker. 6-7, 235. Born in Guatemala City, Guatemala, November 1, 1947. Miami. Inducted in 1990. 1969-1973 Baltimore Colts, 1974 Green Bay Packers, 1975-1981 Oakland Raiders, 1982-83 Los Angeles Raiders. **Highlights:** 25 blocked field goals, extra points, and punts, 26 interceptions. Played in 215 consecutive games.

WILBUR (PETE) HENRY

Tackle. 6-0, 250. Born in Mansfield, Ohio, October 31, 1897. Died February 7, 1952. Washington & Jefferson. Inducted in 1963. 1920-23, 1925-26 Canton Bulldogs, 1927 New York Giants, 1927-28 Pottsville Maroons. **Highlights:** Charter enshrinee. Largest player of his time at 250 pounds. Bulwark of Canton's championship lines.

ARNIE HERBER

Quarterback. 6-0, 200. Born in Green Bay, Wisconsin, April 2, 1910. Died October 14, 1969. Wisconsin, Regis College. Inducted in 1966. 1930-1940 Green Bay Packers, 1944-45 New York Giants. **Highlights:** NFL passing leader 1932, 1934, 1936. Came out of retirement to lead 1944 Giants to NFL Eastern crown.

BILL HEWITT

End. 5-11, 191. Born in Bay City, Michigan, October 8, 1909. Died January 14, 1947. Michigan. Inducted in 1971. 1932-36 Chicago Bears, 1937-39 Philadelphia Eagles, 1943 Phil-Pitt. **Highlights:** First to be named all-NFL with two teams—1933, 1934, 1936 Bears; 1937 Eagles.

GENE HICKERSON

Guard. 6-3, 248. Born in Trenton, Tennessee, February 15, 1935. Mississippi. Inducted in 2007. 1958-1973 Cleveland Browns. **Highlights:** Blocked for three Hall of Fame running backs. Voted to six straight Pro Bowls. Named to NFL's All-Decade Team of the 1960s.

CLARKE HINKLE

Fullback. 5-11, 201. Born in Toronto, Ohio, April 10, 1909. Died November 9, 1988. Bucknell. Inducted in 1964. 1932-1941 Green Bay Packers. **Highlights:** 3,860 yards rushing, 379 points. Fullback on offense, linebacker on defense.

ELROY (CRAZYLEGS) HIRSCH

Halfback-end. 6-2, 190. Born in Wausau, Wisconsin, June 17, 1923. Died January 28, 2004. Wisconsin, Michigan. Inducted in 1968. 1946-48 Chicago Rockets (AAFC), 1949-1957 Los Angeles Rams. **Highlights:** 387 receptions for 7,029 yards, 60 touchdowns. Key part of Rams' revolutionary "three end" offense, 1949.

PAUL HORNUNG

Halfback. 6-2, 220. Born in Louisville, Kentucky, December 23, 1935. Notre Dame. Inducted in 1986. 1957-1962, 1964-66 Green Bay Packers. **Highlights:** 760 points. Led NFL scorers three years, including record 176 points, 1960. Record 19 points scored in 1961 NFL title game.

KEN HOUSTON

Safety. 6-3, 198. Born in Lufkin, Texas, November 12, 1944. Prairie View A&M. Inducted in 1986. 1967-1972 Houston Oilers, 1973-1980 Washington Redskins. **Highlights:** 49 interceptions, 898 yards, 9 touchdowns. NFL's premier strong safety of 1970s. 12 Pro Bowls.

ROBERT (CAL) HUBBARD

Tackle. 6-5, 250. Born in Keytesville, Missouri, October 31, 1900. Died October 17, 1977. Centenary, Geneva. Inducted in 1963. 1927-28 New York Giants, 1929-1933, 1935 Green Bay Packers, 1936 New York Giants, 1936 Pittsburgh Pirates. **Highlights:** Charter enshrinee. Most feared lineman of his time. All-NFL six years, 1927-29, 1931-33.

SAM HUFF

Linebacker. 6-1, 230. Born in Morgantown, West Virginia, October 4, 1934. West Virginia. Inducted in 1982. 1956-1963 New York Giants, 1964-67, 1969 Washington Redskins. **Highlights:** 30 interceptions. Played in six NFL title games, five Pro Bowls. Redskins player-coach, 1969.

LAMAR HUNT

Team owner. Born in El Dorado, Arkansas, August 2, 1932. Died December 13, 2006. Southern Methodist. Inducted in 1972. 1959-present Dallas Texans/Kansas City Chiefs. **Highlights:** Driving force behind organization of AFL. Spearheaded merger negotiations with NFL, 1966.

DON HUTSON
End. 6-1, 180. Born in Pine Bluff, Arkansas, January 31, 1913. Died June 26, 1997. Alabama. Inducted in 1963. 1935-1945 Green Bay Packers. **Highlights:** Charter enshrinee. 488 receptions for 7,991 yards, 99 touchdowns. NFL receiving champion eight years. NFL MVP, 1941, 1942.

MICHAEL IRVIN
Wide Receiver. 6-2, 207. Born in Ft. Lauderdale, Florida, March 5, 1966. Inducted in 2007. 1988-1999 Dallas Cowboys. **Highlights:** 750 career receptions for 11,904 yards, 65 touchdowns. Had NFL record eleven 100-yard receiving games, 1995.

JIMMY JOHNSON
Cornerback. 6-2, 187. Born in Dallas, Texas, March 31, 1938. UCLA. Inducted in 1994. 1961-1976 San Francisco 49ers. **Highlights:** 47 interceptions for 615 yards. Five Pro Bowls. Opposing passers avoided throwing in his area.

JOHN HENRY JOHNSON
Fullback. 6-2, 225. Born in Waterproof, Louisiana, November 24, 1929. St. Mary's, Arizona State. Inducted in 1987. 1954-56 San Francisco 49ers, 1957-59 Detroit Lions, 1960-65 Pittsburgh Steelers, 1966 Houston Oilers. **Highlights:** 6,803 yards rushing, 55 total touchdowns. Member of San Francisco's "Million-Dollar" backfield.

CHARLIE JOINER
Wide receiver. 5-11, 180. Born in Many, Louisiana, October 14, 1947. Grambling. Inducted in 1996. 1969-1972 Houston Oilers, 1972-75 Cincinnati Bengals, 1976-1986 San Diego Chargers. **Highlights:** 750 receptions for 12,146 yards and 65 touchdowns. Played 18 seasons, 239 games, most ever for wide receiver at time of retirement.

DAVID (DEACON) JONES
Defensive end. 6-5, 260. Born in Eatonville, Florida, December 9, 1938. South Carolina State, Mississippi Vocational. Inducted in 1980. 1961-1971 Los Angeles Rams, 1972-73 San Diego Chargers, 1974 Washington Redskins. **Highlights:** Specialized in quarterback "sacks," a term he invented. Unanimous all-league five consecutive years.

STAN JONES
Guard-defensive tackle. 6-1, 250. Born in Altoona, Pennsylvania, November 24, 1931. Maryland. Inducted in 1991. 1954-1965 Chicago Bears, 1966 Washington Redskins. **Highlights:** Seven consecutive Pro Bowls. First to rely on weightlifting for football preparation.

HENRY JORDAN
Defensive tackle. 6-3, 240. Born in Emporia, Virginia, January 26, 1935. Died February 21, 1977. Virginia. Inducted in 1995. 1957-58 Cleveland Browns, 1959-1969 Green Bay Packers. **Highlights:** Fixture at DT during Packers' dynasty. Played in four Pro Bowls, seven NFL title games, Super Bowls I, II.

SONNY JURGENSEN
Quarterback. 6-0, 203. Born in Wilmington, North Carolina, August 23, 1934. Duke. Inducted in 1983. 1957-1963 Philadelphia Eagles, 1964-1974 Washington Redskins. **Highlights:** 32,224 yards passing, 255 touchdowns, 82.63 passer rating. Surpassed 3,000 yards passing in five seasons.

JIM KELLY
Quarterback. 6-3, 225. Born in Pittsburgh, Pennsylvania, February 14, 1960. Miami. Inducted in 2002. 1986-1996 Buffalo Bills. **Highlights:** Passed for more than 3,000 yards eight times. Mastered the no-huddle offense that propelled Bills to four consecutive Super Bowls.

LEROY KELLY
Running back. 6-0, 205. Born in Philadelphia, Pennsylvania, May 20, 1942. Morgan State. Inducted in 1994. 1964-1973 Cleveland Browns. **Highlights:** 7,274 yards rushing, 90 total touchdowns, 1,000-yard rusher first three years as starter. Punt return champion, 1965.

WALT KIESLING
Guard. Coach. 6-2, 245. Born in St. Paul, Minnesota, March 27, 1903. Died March 2, 1962. St. Thomas (Minnesota). Inducted in 1966. 1926-27 Duluth Eskimos, 1928 Pottsville Maroons, 1929-1933 Chicago Cardinals, 1934 Chicago Bears, 1935-36 Green Bay Packers, 1937-38 Pittsburgh Pirates; coach, 1939 Pittsburgh Pirates, 1940-42 Pittsburgh Steelers; co-coach, 1943 Phil-Pitt, 1944 Card-Pitt; coach, 1954-56 Pittsburgh Steelers. **Highlights:** 34-year career as pro player, assistant coach, head coach. Led Steelers to first winning season, 1942.

FRANK (BRUISER) KINARD
Tackle. 6-1, 210. Born in Pelahatchie, Mississippi, October 23, 1914. Died September 7, 1985. Mississippi. Inducted in 1971. 1938-1943 Brooklyn Dodgers, 1944 Brooklyn Tigers, 1946-47 New York Yankees (AAFC). **Highlights:** First man to earn both All-NFL, All-AAFC honors. Out because of injury only once.

PAUL KRAUSE
Safety. 6-3, 200. Born in Flint, Michigan, February 19, 1942. Iowa. Inducted in 1998. 1964-67 Washington Redskins, 1968-1979 Minnesota Vikings. **Highlights:** NFL all-time leader with 81 interceptions. Played in eight Pro Bowls. Starting safety in four Super Bowls.

EARL (CURLY) LAMBEAU
Coach. Born in Green Bay, Wisconsin, April 9, 1898. Died June 1, 1965. Notre Dame. Inducted in 1963. 1919-1949 Green Bay Packers, 1950-51 Chicago Cardinals, 1952-53 Washington Redskins. **Highlights:** Charter enshrinee. 229-134-22 coaching record with six NFL championships. Founded pre-NFL Packers, 1919.

JACK LAMBERT
Linebacker. 6-4, 220. Born in Mantua, Ohio, July 8, 1952. Kent State. Inducted in 1990. 1974-1984 Pittsburgh Steelers. **Highlights:** Leader of 'Steel Curtain.' NFL defensive player of year in 1976, nine Pro Bowls.

TOM LANDRY
Coach. Born in Mission, Texas, September 11, 1924. Died February 12, 2000. Texas. Inducted in 1990. 1960-1988 Dallas Cowboys. **Highlights:** 270-178-6 coaching record. 20 consecutive winning seasons. Innovator on offense and defense.

DICK (NIGHT TRAIN) LANE
Cornerback. 6-2, 210. Born in Austin, Texas, April 16, 1928. Died January 29, 2002. Scottsbluff Junior College. Inducted in 1974. 1952-53 Los Angeles Rams, 1954-59 Chicago Cardinals, 1960-65 Detroit Lions. **Highlights:** 68 interceptions for 1,207 yards, 5 touchdowns. Record 14 interceptions as rookie. Seven Pro Bowls.

JIM LANGER
Center. 6-2, 255. Born in Little Falls, Minnesota, May 16, 1948. South Dakota State. Inducted in 1987. 1970-79 Miami Dolphins, 1980-81 Minnesota Vikings. **Highlights:** Played every offensive down in Dolphins' perfect 1972 season. Six Pro Bowls.

WILLIE LANIER
Linebacker. 6-1, 245. Born in Clover, Virginia, August 21, 1945. Morgan State. Inducted in 1986. 1967-1977 Kansas City Chiefs. **Highlights:** 27 interceptions. Defensive star in Super Bowl IV upset. Nicknamed 'Contact' for ferocious tackling.

STEVE LARGENT
Wide receiver. 5-11, 191. Born in Tulsa, Oklahoma, September 28, 1954, Tulsa. Inducted in 1995. 1976-1989 Seattle Seahawks. **Highlights:** 819 receptions for 13,089 yards, 100 touchdowns. Receptions in 177 consecutive games.

YALE LARY
Defensive back-punter. 5-11, 189. Born in Fort Worth, Texas, November 24, 1930. Texas A&M. Inducted in 1979. 1952-53, 1956-1964 Detroit Lions. **Highlights:** 50 interceptions. Three NFL punting crowns, three touchdowns on punt returns. Nine Pro Bowls.

DANTE LAVELLI
End. 6-0, 199. Born in Hudson, Ohio, February 23, 1923. Ohio State. Inducted in 1975. 1946-49 Cleveland Browns (AAFC), 1950-56 Cleveland Browns. **Highlights:** 386 receptions for 6,488 yards, 62 touchdowns. 24 catches in six NFL title games.

BOBBY LAYNE
Quarterback. 6-2, 190. Born in Santa Anna, Texas, December 19, 1926. Died December 1, 1986. Texas. Inducted in 1967. 1948 Chicago Bears, 1949 New York Bulldogs, 1950-58 Detroit Lions, 1958-1962 Pittsburgh Steelers. **Highlights:** 26,768 yards passing, 196 touchdowns, 2,451 yards rushing. Late touchdown pass won 1953 NFL title game.

ALPHONSE (TUFFY) LEEMANS
Fullback. 6-0, 200. Born in Superior, Wisconsin, November 12, 1912. Died January 19, 1979. Oregon, George Washington. Inducted in 1978. 1936-1943 New York Giants. **Highlights:** 3,132 yards rushing, 2,318 yards passing, 422 yards receiving. Led NFL rushers as rookie, 1936.

MARV LEVY
Coach. Born in Chicago, Illinois, August 3, 1925. Wyoming, Coe College, Harvard. Inducted in 2001. 1978-1982 Kansas City Chiefs, 1986-1997 Buffalo Bills. **Highlights:** Led Bills to unprecedented four consecutive Super Bowls. Had 154-120 record. Coaching victories ranked 10th when retired.

BOB LILLY
Defensive tackle. 6-5, 260. Born in Olney, Texas, July 26, 1939. Texas Christian. Inducted in 1980. 1961-1974 Dallas Cowboys. **Highlights:** Eleven Pro Bowls. Played 196 consecutive games. Foundation of great Dallas defensive units.

LARRY LITTLE
Guard. 6-1, 265. Born in Groveland, Georgia, November 2, 1945. Bethune-Cookman. Inducted in 1993. 1967-68 San Diego Chargers, 1969-1980 Miami Dolphins. **Highlights:** Five Pro Bowls, started in three Super Bowls. Epitome of powerful Dolphins rushing game of 1970s.

JAMES LOFTON
Wide receiver. 6-3, 192. Born in Fort Ord, California, July 5, 1956. Stanford. Inducted in 2003. 1978-1986 Green Bay Packers, 1987-88 Los Angeles Raiders, 1989-1992 Buffalo Bills, 1993 Los Angeles Rams, 1993 Philadelphia Eagles. **Highlights:** Played 16 seasons, 233 games. Caught 764 passes for 75 touchdowns and a then-record 14,004 yards. All-Pro four times, eight Pro Bowls.

VINCE LOMBARDI
Coach. Born in Brooklyn, New York, June 11, 1913. Died September 3, 1970. Fordham. Inducted in 1971. 1959-1967 Green Bay Packers, 1969 Washington Redskins. **Highlights:** 105-35-6 coaching record in 10 years, including five NFL titles and victories in Super Bowls I and II.

HOWIE LONG
Defensive end. 6-5, 268. Born in Somerville, Massachusetts, January 6, 1960. Villanova. Inducted in 2000. 1981-1993 Oakland/Los Angeles Raiders. **Highlights:** All-Pro 1983, 1984, 1985. Named All-AFC four times, 1983-1986. Eight Pro Bowls.

RONNIE LOTT
Cornerback-safety. 6-0, 203. Born in Albuquerque, New Mexico, May 8, 1959. Southern California. Inducted in 2000. 1981-1990 San Francisco 49ers, 1991-92 Los Angeles Raiders, 1993-94 New York Jets. **Highlights:** Ten Pro Bowls, 63 career interceptions, and was named to the NFL's 75th Anniversary Team.

SID LUCKMAN
Quarterback. 6-0, 195. Born in Brooklyn, New York, November 21, 1916. Died July 5, 1998. Columbia. Inducted in 1965. 1939-1950 Chicago Bears. **Highlights:** 137 touchdown passes. All-NFL five times. League MVP in 1943.

WILLIAM ROY (LINK) LYMAN
Tackle. 6-2, 252. Born in Table Rock, Nebraska, November 30, 1898. Died December 28, 1972. Nebraska. Inducted in 1964. 1922-23, 1925 Canton Bulldogs, 1924 Cleveland Bulldogs, 1925 Frankford Yellowjackets, 1926-28, 1930-31, 1933-34 Chicago Bears. **Highlights:** Played for four NFL champions. In 16 seasons of college and pro football, played on one losing team.

TOM MACK
Guard. 6-3, 250. Born in Cleveland, Ohio, November 1, 1943. Michigan. Inducted in 1999. 1966-1978 Los Angeles Rams. **Highlights:** Never missed a game in entire 184-game career. Elected to 11 Pro Bowls.

JOHN MACKEY
Tight end. 6-2, 224. Born in New York, New York, September 24, 1941. Syracuse. Inducted in 1992. 1963-1971 Baltimore Colts, 1972 San Diego Chargers. **Highlights:** 331 receptions for 5,236 yards, 38 touchdowns. Second tight end to enter Hall of Fame.

JOHN MADDEN
Coach. Born in Austin, Minnesota, April 10, 1936. San Mateo Junior College, California Polytechnic College at San Luis Obispo. Inducted in 2006. 1969-1978 Oakland Raiders. **Highlights:** Became one of youngest coaches in history when hired at age 32. 112-39-7 overall record. Owns best regular season winning percentage among coaches with 100 wins.

TIM MARA
Team owner. Born in New York, New York, July 29, 1887. Died February 16, 1959. Did not attend college. Inducted in 1963. 1925-1959 New York Giants. **Highlights:** Charter enshrinee. Founder of New York Giants. Built team into powerhouse winning four NFL titles, 10 division titles.

WELLINGTON MARA
Team owner. Born in New York, New York, August 14, 1916. Died October 25, 2005. Fordham. Inducted in 1997. 1937-2005 New York Giants. **Highlights:** Lifetime contributor to NFL and New York Giants. Worked as Giants' ballboy, secretary, vice-president, president and co-CEO. NFC president 1984-present.

GINO MARCHETTI
Defensive end. 6-4, 245. Born in Smithers, West Virginia, January 2, 1927. San Francisco. Inducted in 1972. 1952 Dallas Texans, 1953-1964, 1966 Baltimore Colts. **Highlights:** Named top defensive end of NFL's first 50 years. 10 consecutive Pro Bowls. All-NFL seven times.

DAN MARINO
Quarterback. 6-4, 218. Born in Pittsburgh, Pennsylvania, September 15, 1961. Pittsburgh. Inducted in 2005. 1983-1999 Miami Dolphins. **Highlights:** Holds NFL records for career passing yardage (61,361), completions (4,967), attempts (8,358), and touchdowns (420). Voted to nine Pro Bowls.

GEORGE PRESTON MARSHALL
Team owner. Born in Grafton, West Virginia, October 11, 1896. Died August 9, 1969. Randolph-Macon. Inducted in 1963. 1932 Boston Braves, 1933-36 Boston Redskins, 1937-1969 Washington Redskins. **Highlights:** Charter enshrinee. Sponsored progressive rules changes. Organized first team band, pioneered halftime shows.

OLLIE MATSON
Halfback. 6-2, 220. Born in Trinity, Texas, May 1, 1930. San Francisco. Inducted in 1972. 1952, 1954-58 Chicago Cardinals, 1959-1962 Los Angeles Rams, 1963 Detroit Lions, 1964-66 Philadelphia Eagles. **Highlights:** Nine touchdowns on kickoff, punt returns. Traded for nine players in 1959.

BRUCE MATTHEWS
Guard-tackle-center. 6-5, 289. Born in Raleigh, North Carolina, August 8, 1961. Southern California. Inducted in 2007. 1983-2001 Houston Oilers/Tennessee Oilers/Tennessee Titans. **Highlights:** Played in 296 games, most ever by positional player at time of his retirement. Named to a record-tying 14 straight Pro Bowls. All-Pro nine times, All-AFC 12 times.

DON MAYNARD
Wide receiver. 6-1, 185. Born in Crosbyton, Texas, January 25, 1935. Texas Western. Inducted in 1987. 1958 New York Giants, 1960-62 New York Titans, 1963-1972 New York Jets, 1973 St. Louis Cardinals. **Highlights:** 633 receptions for 11,834 yards, 88 touchdowns. At least 50 catches and 1,000 yards in five different seasons.

GEORGE McAFEE
Halfback. 6-0, 177. Born in Corbin, Kentucky, March 13, 1918. Duke. Inducted in 1966. 1940-41, 1945-1950 Chicago Bears. **Highlights:** Two-way star. 25 interceptions, 234 points. Career punt-return average of 12.78 yards per return.

MIKE McCORMACK
Tackle. 6-4, 250. Born in Chicago, Illinois, June 21, 1930. Kansas. Inducted in 1984. 1951 New York Yanks, 1954-1962 Cleveland Browns. **Highlights:** Excelled as offensive right tackle for eight years. Six Pro Bowls.

TOMMY McDONALD
Wide receiver. 5-9, 175. Born in Roy, New Mexico, July 26, 1934. Oklahoma. Inducted in 1998. 1957-1963 Philadelphia Eagles, 1964 Dallas Cowboys, 1965-66 Los Angeles Rams, 1967 Atlanta Falcons, 1968 Cleveland Browns. **Highlights:** Recorded 495 receptions for 8,410 yards, 84 touchdowns.

HUGH McELHENNY
Halfback. 6-1, 198. Born in Los Angeles, California, December 31, 1928. Washington. Inducted in 1970. 1952-1960 San Francisco 49ers, 1961-62 Minnesota Vikings, 1963 New York Giants, 1964 Detroit Lions. **Highlights:** 5,281 rushing yards, 360 points. Totaled 11,369 yards rushing, receiving, and returning kicks.

JOHNNY (BLOOD) McNALLY
Halfback. 6-0, 185. Born in New Richmond, Wisconsin, November 27, 1903. Died November 28, 1985. Notre Dame, St. John's (Minnesota). Inducted in 1963. 1925-26 Milwaukee Badgers, 1926-27 Duluth Eskimos, 1928 Pottsville Maroons, 1929-1933, 1935-36 Green Bay Packers, 1934 Pittsburgh Pirates, 1934 Pittsburgh Pirates; player-coach, 1937-38 Pittsburgh Pirates. **Highlights:** Charter enshrinee. 49 touchdowns, 297 points in 14 seasons with five teams.

MIKE MICHALSKE
Guard. 6-0, 209. Born in Cleveland, Ohio, April 24, 1903. Died October 26, 1983. Penn State. Inducted in 1964. 1926 New York Yankees (AFL), 1927-28 New York Yankees, 1929-1935, 1937 Green Bay Packers. **Highlights:** Anchored Packers' championship lines, 1929-1931. First guard enshrined in Canton.

WAYNE MILLNER
End. 6-0, 191. Born in Roxbury, Massachusetts, January 31, 1913. Died November 19, 1976. Notre Dame. Inducted in 1968. 1936 Boston Redskins, 1937-1941, 1945 Washington Redskins. **Highlights:** Redskins' all-time leader with 124 catches when retired. 55- and 78-yard touchdown receptions in 1937 NFL Championship Game.

BOBBY MITCHELL
Running back-wide receiver. 6-0, 195. Born in Hot Springs, Arkansas, June 6, 1935. Illinois. Inducted in 1983. 1958-1961 Cleveland Browns, 1962-68 Washington Redskins. **Highlights:** 91 touchdowns, including 8 on kickoff and punt returns. 14,078 combined yards.

RON MIX
Tackle. 6-4, 255. Born in Los Angeles, California, March 10, 1938. Southern California. Inducted in 1979. 1960 Los Angeles Chargers, 1961-69 San Diego Chargers, 1971 Oakland Raiders. **Highlights:** All-AFL nine times. Only two holding penalties in 10 years with the Chargers.

ART MONK
Wide receiver. 6-3, 210. Born in White Plains, New York, December 5, 1957. Syracuse. Inducted in 2008. 1980-1993 Washington Redskins, 1994 New York Jets, 1995 Philadelphia Eagles. **Highlights:** 940 receptions, 12,721 yards, 68 TDs. Set then-single season record, 106 catches, 1984. Had 50 or more catches in a season nine times.

JOE MONTANA
Quarterback. 6-2, 200. Born in New Eagle, Pennsylvania, June, 11, 1956. Notre Dame. Inducted in 2000. 1979-1992 San Francisco 49ers, 1993-94 Kansas City Chiefs. **Highlights:** MVP in Super Bowl's XVI, XIX, and XXIV. Eight Pro Bowls and All-NFL three times.

WARREN MOON
Quarterback. 6-3, 212. Born in Los Angeles, California, November 18, 1956. West Los Angeles Junior College, Washington. Inducted in 2006. 1984-1993 Houston Oilers, 1994-1996 Minnesota Vikings, 1997-1998 Seattle Seahawks, 1999-2000 Kansas City Chiefs. **Highlights:** Passed for 49,325 yards and 291 touchdowns in 17 NFL seasons. Elected to nine Pro Bowls including eight straight. Threw for 3,000 yards in nine seasons.

LENNY MOORE
Flanker-running back. 6-1, 198. Born in Reading, Pennsylvania, November 25, 1933. Penn State. Inducted in 1975. 1956-1967 Baltimore Colts. **Highlights:** From 1963-65, scored touchdowns in record 18 consecutive games. 113 career touchdowns, 12,451 combined net yards.

MARION MOTLEY
Fullback. 6-1, 238. Born in Leesburg, Georgia, June 5, 1920. Died June 27, 1999. South Carolina State, Nevada. Inducted in 1968. 1946-49 Cleveland Browns (AAFC), 1950-53 Cleveland Browns, 1955 Pittsburgh Steelers. **Highlights:** AAFC's all-time rushing champion. Led league in rushing in first NFL season.

MIKE MUNCHAK
Guard. 6-3, 281. Born in Scranton, Pennsylvania, March 5, 1960. Penn State. Inducted in 2001. 1982-1993 Houston Oilers. **Highlights:** Devastating blocker, All-AFC seven times, elected to nine Pro Bowls.

ANTHONY MUÑOZ
Tackle. 6-6, 278. Born in Ontario, California, August 19, 1958. Southern California. Inducted in 1998. 1980-1992 Cincinnati Bengals. **Highlights:** All-Pro choice 11 consecutive years, 1981-1991. Selected to 11 straight Pro Bowls.

GEORGE MUSSO
Guard-tackle. 6-2, 270. Born in Collinsville, Illinois. April 8, 1910. Died September 5, 2000. Millikin. Inducted in 1982. 1933-1944 Chicago Bears. **Highlights:** First player to achieve All-NFL status at two positions—tackle in 1935 and guard in 1937.

BRONKO NAGURSKI
Fullback. 6-2, 225. Born in Rainy River, Ontario, Canada, November 3, 1908. Died January 7, 1990. Minnesota. Inducted in 1963. 1930-37, 1943 Chicago Bears. **Highlights:** Charter enshrinee. 2,778 rushing yards in nine seasons. All-NFL five times.

JOE NAMATH
Quarterback. 6-2, 200. Born in Beaver Falls, Pennsylvania, May 31, 1943. Alabama. Inducted in 1985. 1965-1976 New York Jets, 1977 Los Angeles Rams. **Highlights:** First quarterback to pass for more than 4,000 yards in season, 1967. Guaranteed, delivered victory over Colts in Super Bowl III.

EARLE (GREASY) NEALE
Coach. Born in Parkersburg, West Virginia, November 5, 1891. Died November 2, 1973. West Virginia Wesleyan. Inducted in 1969. 1941-42, 1944-1950 Philadelphia Eagles; co-coach, 1943 Phil-Pitt. **Highlights:** Turned Eagles into winners with three consecutive division crowns, NFL championships in 1948 and 1949.

ERNIE NEVERS
Fullback. 6-1, 205. Born in Willow River, Minnesota, June 11, 1903. Died May 3, 1976. Stanford. Inducted in 1963. 1926-27 Duluth Eskimos, 1929-1931 Chicago Cardinals. **Highlights:** Charter enshrinee. Holds NFL's longest-standing record, 40 points in one game in 1929.

OZZIE NEWSOME
Tight end. 6-2, 232. Born in Muscle Shoals, Alabama, March 16, 1956. Alabama. Inducted in 1999. 1978-1990 Cleveland Browns. **Highlights:** Finished career as all-time leader among tight ends with 662 receptions for 7,980 yards.

RAY NITSCHKE
Linebacker. 6-3, 235. Born in Elmwood Park, Illinois, December 29, 1936. Died March 8, 1998. Illinois. Inducted in 1978. 1958-1972 Green Bay Packers. **Highlights:** MVP of 1962 title game. Named NFL's all-time linebacker in 1969.

CHUCK NOLL
Coach. Born in Cleveland, Ohio, January 5, 1932. Dayton. Inducted in 1993. 1969-1991 Pittsburgh Steelers. **Highlights:** Coached for 23 years. Only coach to win four Super Bowl titles (IX, X, XIII, XIV).

LEO NOMELLINI
Defensive tackle. 6-3, 264. Born in Lucca, Italy, June 19, 1924. Died October 17, 2000. Minnesota. Inducted in 1969. 1950-1963 San Francisco 49ers. **Highlights:** Played every 49ers game for 14 seasons. 10 Pro Bowls.

MERLIN OLSEN
Defensive tackle. 6-5, 270. Born in Logan, Utah, September 15, 1940. Utah State. Inducted in 1982. 1962-1976 Los Angeles Rams. **Highlights:** Member of the Fearsome "Foursome. Named" to 14 consecutive Pro Bowls, Rams' all-time team.

JIM OTTO
Center. 6-2, 255. Born in Wausau, Wisconsin, January 5, 1938. Miami. Inducted in 1980. 1960-1974 Oakland Raiders. **Highlights:** Named AFL's all-time center. Played in 210 games, 12 AFL All-Star Games or Pro Bowls, six AFL/AFC title games.

STEVE OWEN
Tackle. Coach. 6-2, 235. Born in Cleo Springs, Oklahoma, April 21, 1898. Died May 17, 1964. Phillips. Inducted in 1966. 1924-25 Kansas City Cowboys, 1925 Cleveland Bulldogs, 1926-1931, 1933 New York Giants; coach, 1930-1953 New York Giants. **Highlights:** Both player and coach. Coached Giants to record of 155-108-17, eight divisional titles, two NFL championships.

ALAN PAGE
Defensive tackle. 6-4, 225. Born in Canton, Ohio, August 7, 1945. Notre Dame. Inducted in 1988. 1967-1978 Minnesota Vikings, 1978-1981 Chicago Bears. **Highlights:** Dominating defensive tackle played in 218 consecutive games, four Super Bowls. Won league MVP honors in 1971.

CLARENCE (ACE) PARKER
Quarterback. 5-11, 168. Born in Portsmouth, Virginia, May 17, 1912. Duke. Inducted in 1972. 1937-1941 Brooklyn Dodgers, 1945 Boston Yanks, 1946 New York Yankees (AAFC). **Highlights:** Two-way threat. Two-time All-NFL performer, league MVP in 1940.

JIM PARKER
Guard-tackle. 6-3, 273. Born in Macon, Georgia, April 3, 1934. Died July 18, 2005. Ohio State. Inducted in 1973. 1957-1967 Baltimore Colts. **Highlights:** First full-time offensive lineman elected to Hall of Fame. All-NFL eight consecutive years, eight Pro Bowls.

WALTER PAYTON
Running back. 5-10, 202. Born in Columbia, Mississippi, July 25, 1954. Died November 1, 1999. Jackson State. Inducted in 1993. 1975-1987 Chicago Bears. **Highlights:** NFL's all-time leading rusher with 16,726 yards and combined net yardage with 21,803 at time of retirement.

JOE PERRY
Fullback. 6-0, 200. Born in Stevens, Arkansas, January 22, 1927. Compton Junior College. Inducted in 1969. 1948-49 San Francisco 49ers (AAFC), 1950-1960, 1963 San Francisco 49ers, 1961-62 Baltimore Colts. **Highlights:** First player in NFL history to gain 1,000 yards two consecutive seasons. 12,532 combined yards.

PETE PIHOS
End. 6-1, 210. Born in Orlando, Florida, October 22, 1923. Indiana. Inducted in 1970. 1947-1955 Philadelphia Eagles. **Highlights:** Three-time NFL receiving champion. Caught winning touchdown in 1949 NFL Championship Game.

FRITZ POLLARD
Halfback-Coach. 5-9, 165. Born in Chicago, Illinois, January 27, 1894. Died May 11, 1986. Brown. Inducted in 2005. 1919-1921, 1925-26 Akron Pros/Indians, 1922 Milwaukee Badgers, 1923, 1925 Hammond Pros, 1925 Providence Steam Roller. **Highlights:** True pioneer as one of two African American players in the NFL in 1920 and helped lead Akron to league title that season. In 1921, became the league's first black head coach.

HUGH (SHORTY) RAY
Supervisor of officials 1938-1952. Born in Highland Park, Illinois, September 21, 1884. Died September 16, 1956. Illinois. Inducted in 1966. **Highlights:** Supervisor of Officials, 1938-1952. Streamlined rules to improve game tempo, player safety.

DAN REEVES
Team owner. Born in New York, New York, June 30, 1912. Died April 15, 1971. Georgetown. Inducted in 1967. 1941-45 Cleveland Rams, 1946-1971 Los Angeles Rams. **Highlights:** Moved Rams to Los Angeles in 1946 and opened up West Coast to pro football. First postwar owner to sign African-American player.

MEL RENFRO
Cornerback-safety. 6-0, 192. Born in Houston, Texas, December 30, 1941. Oregon. Inducted in 1996. 1964-1977 Dallas Cowboys. **Highlights:** 52 interceptions for 626 yards and 3 touchdowns. Also added 842 yards on punt returns, 2,246 yards on kickoff returns. Elected to Pro Bowl first 10 seasons.

JOHN RIGGINS
Running back. 6-2, 240. Born in Seneca, Kansas, August 4, 1949. Kansas. Inducted in 1992. 1971-75 New York Jets, 1976-79, 1981-85 Washington Redskins. **Highlights:** 11,352 rushing yards, 116 total touchdowns. MVP of Super Bowl XVII with 166 rushing yards including game-winning 43-yard touchdown.

JIM RINGO
Center. 6-2, 230. Born in Orange, New Jersey, November 21, 1931. Died November 19, 2007. Syracuse. Inducted in 1981. 1953-1963 Green Bay Packers, 1964-67 Philadelphia Eagles. **Highlights:** Ten-time Pro Bowl selection, seven-time All-NFL selection. Started in then-record 182 consecutive games.

ANDY ROBUSTELLI
Defensive end. 6-0, 230. Born in Stamford, Connecticut, December 6, 1925. Arnold College. Inducted in 1971. 1951-55 Los Angeles Rams, 1956-1964 New York Giants. **Highlights:** Anchored defense in eight championship games. Named NFL's top player in 1962.

ART ROONEY
Team owner. Born in Coulterville, Pennsylvania, January 27, 1901. Died August 25, 1988. Georgetown, Duquesne. Inducted in 1964. 1933-39 Pittsburgh Pirates, 1940-42, 1945-1988 Pittsburgh Steelers, 1943 Phil-Pitt, 1944 Card-Pitt. **Highlights:** Founded Pittsburgh Pirates in 1933 and renamed them Steelers in 1940. Team won four Super Bowls in 1970s.

DAN ROONEY
Team owner. Born in Pittsburgh, Pennsylvania, July, 20, 1932. Duquesne. Inducted in 2000. 1955-present Pittsburgh Steelers. **Highlights:** Has been on the board of directors for the NFL Trust Fund, NFL Films, and Scheduling Committee. Played a key role in the labor agreement reached in 1993 between the NFL owners and players.

PETE ROZELLE
Commissioner. Born in South Gate, California, March 1, 1926. Died December 6, 1996. Compton Junior College, San Francisco. Inducted in 1985. Commissioner, 1960-1989. **Highlights:** Negotiated first league-wide television contract in 1962. Generally recognized as premiere commissioner in all of sports. Credited with making NFL the nation's most popular sport.

BOB ST. CLAIR
Tackle. 6-9, 265. Born in San Francisco, California, February 18, 1931. San Francisco, Tulsa. Inducted in 1990. 1953-1963 San Francisco 49ers. **Highlights:** Exceptional offensive lineman. Also played goal-line defense and had 10 blocked field goals, 1956.

BARRY SANDERS
Running back. 5-8, 203. Born in Wichita, Kansas, July 16, 1968. Oklahoma State. Inducted in 2004. 1989-1998 Detroit Lions. **Highlights:** 15,269 rushing yards, 99 touchdowns. Rushed for 1,000 yards in each of 10 seasons. NFL co-MVP, 1997. Selected to 10 Pro Bowls.

CHARLIE SANDERS
Tight end. 6-4, 230. Born in Richlands, North Carolina, August 25, 1946. Minnesota. Inducted in 2007. 1968-1977 Detroit Lions. **Highlights:** 336 career receptions for 4,817 yards and 31 touchdowns. Selected to seven Pro Bowls. Named to the NFL's All-Decade Team of 1970s.

GALE SAYERS
Running back. 6-0, 200. Born in Wichita, Kansas, May 30, 1943. Kansas. Inducted in 1977. 1965-1971 Chicago Bears. **Highlights:** Broke into league by scoring rookie-record 22 touchdowns. Led league in rushing in 1966, 1969. MVP of three Pro Bowls.

JOE SCHMIDT
Linebacker. 6-0, 222. Born in Pittsburgh, Pennsylvania, January 18, 1932. Pittsburgh. Inducted in 1973. 1953-1965 Detroit Lions. **Highlights:** 24 interceptions. Lions' team captain for nine years. Mastered middle linebacker position that evolved in 1950s.

TEX SCHRAMM
Team president-general manager. Born in San Gabriel, California, June 2, 1920. Died July 15, 2003. Texas. Inducted in 1991. 1947-1956 Los Angeles Rams. 1960-1989 Dallas Cowboys. **Highlights:** Played prominent role in AFL-NFL merger. Chairman of Competition Committee from 1966-1988.

LEE ROY SELMON
Defensive end. 6-3, 250. Born in Eufaula, Oklahoma, October 20, 1954. Oklahoma. Inducted in 1995. 1976-1984 Tampa Bay Buccaneers. **Highlights:** 78½ sacks, 380 quarterback pressures, forced 28 fumbles. Six consecutive Pro Bowl selections.

BILLY SHAW
Guard. 6-2, 258. Born in Natchez, Mississippi, December 15, 1938. Georgia Tech. Inducted in 1999. 1961-69 Buffalo Bills. **Highlights:** First player who played entire career in AFL to be elected to Hall of Fame. Named to AFL's all-time team.

ART SHELL
Tackle. 6-5, 285. Born in Charleston, South Carolina, November 26, 1946. Maryland State-Eastern Shore. Inducted in 1989. 1968-82 Oakland/Los Angeles Raiders. **Highlights:** Cornerstone of Raiders' offensive line in 1970s. 207 regular-season games, 23 postseason games, eight Pro Bowls.

DON SHULA
Coach. Born in Grand River, Ohio, January 4, 1930. John Carroll. Inducted in 1997. 1963-69 Baltimore Colts, 1970-1995 Miami Dolphins. **Highlights:** Won more games (347) than any coach in NFL history. Won two Super Bowl titles, including Super Bowl VII when Dolphins recorded NFL's only perfect season (17-0).

O.J. SIMPSON
Running back. 6-1, 212. Born in San Francisco, California, July 9, 1947. City College (San Francisco), Southern California. Inducted in 1985. 1969-1977 Buffalo Bills, 1978-79 San Francisco 49ers. **Highlights:** In 1973, became first player to rush for 2,000 yards in season. Finished career with four rushing titles, 11,236 yards.

MIKE SINGLETARY
Linebacker. 6-0, 230. Born in Houston, Texas, October 9, 1958. Baylor. Inducted in 1998. 1981-1992 Chicago Bears. **Highlights:** All-Pro choice eight times and All-NFC nine consecutive seasons. Selected to 10 Pro Bowls.

JACKIE SLATER
Tackle. 6-4, 277. Born in Jackson, Mississippi, May 27, 1954. Jackson State. Inducted in 2001. 1976-1995 Los Angeles/St. Louis Rams. **Highlights:** Played 20 seasons, 259 games. Blocked for seven different 1,000-yard rushers. Seven Pro Bowls.

JACKIE SMITH
Tight end. 6-4, 232. Born in Columbia, Mississippi, February 23, 1940. Northwestern State (Louisiana). Inducted in 1994. 1963-1977 St. Louis Cardinals, 1978 Dallas Cowboys. **Highlights:** 480 receptions for 7,918 yards, 40 touchdowns. Third tight end to be elected to Hall of Fame.

JOHN STALLWORTH
Wide receiver. 6-2, 191. Born in Tuscaloosa, Alabama, July 15, 1952. Alabama A&M. Inducted in 2002. 1974-1987 Pittsburgh Steelers. **Highlights:** 537 receptions for 8,723 yards, 63 touchdowns. Scored go-ahead touchdown in Super Bowl XIV on 73-yard reception.

BART STARR
Quarterback. 6-1, 200. Born in Montgomery, Alabama, January 9, 1934. Alabama. Inducted in 1977. 1956-1971 Green Bay Packers. **Highlights:** Quarterbacked Packers to six division titles, five NFL titles, and first two Super Bowls in which he was MVP.

ROGER STAUBACH
Quarterback. 6-3, 202. Born in Cincinnati, Ohio, February 5, 1942. New Mexico Military Institute, Navy. Inducted in 1985. 1969-1979 Dallas Cowboys. **Highlights:** Led Cowboys to four NFC titles and victories in Super Bowls VI, XII. When retired, 83.4 career passer rating was best of all time.

ERNIE STAUTNER
Defensive tackle. 6-2, 235. Born in Prinzing-by-Cham, Bavaria, April 20, 1925. Died February 16, 2006. Boston College. Inducted in 1969. 1950-1963 Pittsburgh Steelers. **Highlights:** Played in nine Pro Bowls and won the best lineman award in 1957. Recorded 3 safeties.

JAN STENERUD
Kicker. 6-2, 190. Born in Fetsund, Norway, November 26, 1942. Montana State. Inducted in 1991. 1967-1979 Kansas City Chiefs, 1980-83 Green Bay Packers, 1984-85 Minnesota Vikings. **Highlights:** 1,699 points on 580 extra points, 373 field goals. First pure placekicker to enter Hall of Fame.

DWIGHT STEPHENSON
Center. 6-2, 255. Born in Murfreesboro, North Carolina, November 20, 1957. Alabama. Inducted in 1998. 1980-87 Miami Dolphins. **Highlights:** Recognized as premier center of his time. All-Pro, All-AFC five straight years. Selected to five Pro Bowls.

HANK STRAM
Coach. Born in Chicago, Illinois, January 3, 1923. Died July 4, 2005. Purdue. Inducted in 2003. 1960-1974 Dallas Texans/Kansas City Chiefs, 1976-1977 New Orleans Saints. **Highlights:** Overall record of 136-100-10. Recorded most wins in AFL history. Guided teams to titles in 1962, 1966, and 1969. Led Chiefs to AFL win in Super Bowl IV.

KEN STRONG
Halfback. 5-11, 210. Born in West Haven, Connecticut, April 21, 1906. Died October 5, 1979. New York University. Inducted in 1967. 1929-1932 Staten Island Stapletons, 1933-35, 1939, 1944-47 New York Giants, 1936-37 New York Yanks (AFL). **Highlights:** Scored 17 points to lead Giants to victory in 1934 'Sneakers' game, led NFL with 64 points, 1933.

JOE STYDAHAR
Tackle. 6-4, 230. Born in Kaylor, Pennsylvania, March 17, 1912. Died March 23, 1977. West Virginia. Inducted in 1967. 1936-1942, 1945-46 Chicago Bears. **Highlights:** One of stalwarts of Bears' 'Monsters of the Midway.' Played on five divisional, three NFL championship teams.

LYNN SWANN
Wide receiver. 5-11, 180. Born in Alcoa, Tennessee, March 7, 1952. Southern California. Inducted in 2001. 1974-1982 Pittsburgh Steelers. **Highlights:** All-AFC three times. Selected to three Pro Bowls. MVP, Super Bowl X.

FRAN TARKENTON
Quarterback. 6-0, 185. Born in Richmond, Virginia, February 3, 1940. Georgia. Inducted in 1986. 1961-66, 1972-78 Minnesota Vikings, 1967-1971 New York Giants. **Highlights:** At retirement, held NFL records for attempts (6,467), completions (3,686), yards (47,003), and touchdowns (342). Four touchdowns passes in first NFL game.

CHARLEY TAYLOR
Running back-wide receiver. 6-3, 210. Born in Grand Prairie, Texas, September 28, 1941. Arizona State. Inducted in 1984. 1964-1975, 1977 Washington Redskins. **Highlights:** Won rookie of year honors as running back. Switched to wide receiver and won receiving titles in 1966, 1967.

JIM TAYLOR
Fullback. 6-0, 216. Born in Baton Rouge, Louisiana, September 20, 1935. Louisiana State. Inducted in 1976. 1958-1966 Green Bay Packers, 1967 New Orleans Saints. **Highlights:** 8,597 rushing yards, 558 points. In 1962, led league in rushing and scoring with 19 touchdowns.

LAWRENCE TAYLOR
Linebacker. 6-3, 237. Born in Williamsburg, Virginia, February 4, 1959. North Carolina. Inducted in 1999. 1981-1993 New York Giants. **Highlights:** Redefined the position of outside linebacker. All-Pro nine times, 10 Pro Bowls. NFL MVP in 1986.

EMMITT THOMAS
Cornerback. 6-2, 192. Born in Angleton, Texas, June 3, 1943. Bishop. Inducted in 2008. 1966-1978 Kansas City Chiefs. **Highlights:** Undrafted free agent. 58 interceptions, 937 yards, 5 TDs. Ranked fifth all-time in interceptions at retirement. Interception leader – AFL, 1969 and NFL, 1974.

THURMAN THOMAS
Running back. 5-10, 198. Born in Houston, Texas, May 16, 1966. Oklahoma State. Inducted in 2007. 1988-1999 Buffalo Bills, 2000 Miami Dolphins. **Highlights:** Amassed 16,532 total yards including 12,074 yards rushing. Scored 88 touchdowns. Only player in history to lead league in yards from scrimmage four straight seasons.

JIM THORPE
Halfback. 6-1, 190. Born in Prague, Oklahoma, May 28, 1888. Died March 28, 1953. Carlisle. Inducted in 1963. 1915-17, 1919-1920, 1926 Canton Bulldogs, 1921 Cleveland Indians, 1922-23 Oorang Indians, 1924 Rock Island Independents, 1925 New York Giants, 1928 Chicago Cardinals. **Highlights:** Charter enshrinee. First president of American Professional Football Association, 1920. Played for 12 seasons.

ANDRE TIPPETT
Linebacker. 6-3, 240. Born in Birmingham, Alabama, December 27, 1959. Iowa; Ellsworth (IA) Jr. College. Inducted in 2008. 1982-1993 New England Patriots. **Highlights:** Recorded 100 career sacks including personal best 18.5 sacks, 1984. Named to five straight Pro Bowls, 1985-89.

Y.A. TITTLE
Quarterback. 6-0, 200. Born in Marshall, Texas, October 24, 1926. Louisiana State. Inducted in 1971. 1948-49 Baltimore Colts (AAFC), 1950 Baltimore Colts, 1951-1960 San Francisco 49ers, 1961-64 New York Giants. **Highlights:** 33,070 yards, 242 touchdowns. 33 touchdown passes in 1962 and 36 in 1963. Two-time league MVP.

GEORGE TRAFTON
Center. 6-2, 235. Born in Chicago, Illinois, December 6, 1896. Died September 5, 1971. Notre Dame. Inducted in 1964. 1920-1932 Decatur Staleys/Chicago Staleys/Chicago Bears. **Highlights:** First center to snap with one hand. Named top NFL center of 1920s.

CHARLEY TRIPPI
Halfback-quarterback. 6-0, 185. Born in Pittston, Pennsylvania, December 14, 1922. Georgia. Inducted in 1968. 1947-1955 Chicago Cardinals. **Highlights:** One of football's most versatile performers. Played halfback five years, quarterback for two, defense for two.

EMLEN TUNNELL
Safety. 6-1, 200. Born in Bryn Mawr, Pennsylvania, March 29, 1925. Died July 22, 1975. Toledo, Iowa. Inducted in 1967. 1948-1958 New York Giants, 1959-1961 Green Bay Packers. **Highlights:** 79 interceptions. Gained more yards on kickoff, punt, and interception returns (924) in 1952 than that season's NFL rushing leader.

CLYDE (BULLDOG) TURNER
Center. 6-2, 235. Born in Plains, Texas, March 10, 1919. Died October 30, 1998. Hardin-Simmons. Inducted in 1966. 1940-1952 Chicago Bears. **Highlights:** Anchored defense for four NFL championship teams, including 4 interceptions in five title games.

JOHNNY UNITAS
Quarterback. 6-1, 195. Born in Pittsburgh, Pennsylvania, May 7, 1933. Died September 11, 2002. Louisville. Inducted in 1979. 1956-1972 Baltimore Colts, 1973 San Diego Chargers. **Highlights:** 40,239 passing yards, 290 touchdowns. Led Colts to two NFL championships. Passed for at least one touchdown in 47 consecutive games.

GENE UPSHAW
Guard. 6-5, 255. Born in Robstown, Texas, August 15, 1945. Texas A & I. Inducted in 1987. 1967-1981 Oakland Raiders. **Highlights:** Premier guard of his era played in 10 AFL/AFC Championship Games, three Super Bowls, seven Pro Bowls.

NORM VAN BROCKLIN
Quarterback. 6-1, 190. Born in Eagle Butte, South Dakota, March 15, 1926. Died May 2, 1983. Oregon. Inducted in 1971. 1949-1957 Los Angeles Rams, 1958-1960 Philadelphia Eagles. **Highlights:** NFL-record 554 yards passing in 1951 season opener. Guided Eagles to NFL crown as league MVP in two.

STEVE VAN BUREN
Halfback. 6-1, 200. Born in La Ceiba, Honduras, December 28, 1920. Louisiana State. Inducted in 1965. 1944-1951 Philadelphia Eagles. **Highlights:** Four-time rushing champion. Won 1944 punt-return title and was 1945 kickoff-return champion.

DOAK WALKER
Halfback. 5-11, 173. Born in Dallas, Texas, January 1, 1927. Died September 27, 1998. Southern Methodist. Inducted in 1986. 1950-55 Detroit Lions. **Highlights:** 534 points. Won two NFL scoring titles. Had winning 67-yard scoring run in 1952 title game.

BILL WALSH
Coach. Born in Los Angeles, California, November 30, 1931. Died July 30, 2007. San Jose State. Inducted in 1993. 1979-1988 San Francisco 49ers. **Highlights:** 102-63-1 coaching record. Guided 49ers to three Super Bowl titles (XVI, XIX, XXIII) in 10 years.

PAUL WARFIELD
Wide receiver. 6-0, 188. Born in Warren, Ohio, November 28, 1942. Ohio State. Inducted in 1983. 1964-69, 1976-77 Cleveland Browns, 1970-74 Miami Dolphins. **Highlights:** 8,565 yards receiving, 85 touchdowns. Eight-time Pro Bowl player. Key to both Cleveland and Miami offenses.

BOB WATERFIELD
Quarterback. 6-2, 200. Born in Elmira, New York, July 26, 1920. Died March 25, 1983. UCLA. Inducted in 1965. 1945 Cleveland Rams, 1946-1952 Los Angeles Rams. **Highlights:** NFL MVP as rookie in 1945 and led Rams to NFL title. Grabbed 20 interceptions in limited defensive duties.

MIKE WEBSTER
Center. 6-2, 260. Born in Tomahawk, Wisconsin, March 18, 1952. Died September 24, 2002. Wisconsin. Inducted in 1997. 1974-1988 Pittsburgh Steelers, 1989-1990 Kansas City Chiefs. **Highlights:** Played in 245 games, nine Pro Bowls and won four Super Bowls during 17-year career.

ROGER WEHRLI
Cornerback. 6-0, 190. Born in New Point, Missouri, November 26, 1947. Missouri. Inducted in 2007. 1969-1982 St. Louis Cardinals. **Highlights:** 40 career interceptions. Named to the NFL's All-Decade Team of 1970s. All-Pro five times, selected to seven Pro Bowls.

ARNIE WEINMEISTER
Defensive tackle. 6-4, 235. Born in Rhein, Saskatchewan, Canada, March 23, 1923. Died June 29, 2000. Washington. Inducted in 1984. 1948-49 New York Yankees (AAFC), 1950-53 New York Giants. **Highlights:** Dominant defensive tackle of his time. Four-time All-NFL selection, four Pro Bowls.

RANDY WHITE
Defensive tackle. 6-4, 265. Born in Pittsburgh, Pennsylvania, January 15, 1953. Maryland. Inducted in 1994. 1975-1988 Dallas Cowboys. **Highlights:** Missed only one game in 14 seasons. Co-MVP of Super Bowl XII. Nine-time Pro Bowl selection.

REGGIE WHITE
Defensive tackle-defensive end. 6-5, 291. Born in Chattanooga, Tennessee, December 19, 1961. Died December 26, 2004. Tennessee. Inducted in 2006. 1985-1992 Philadelphia Eagles, 1993-1998 Green Bay Packers, 2000 Carolina Panthers. **Highlights:** Retired as all-time sack leader with 198. Named All-Pro 13 of 15 seasons including 10 as first-team selection. Named to 13 straight Pro Bowls.

DAVE WILCOX
Linebacker. 6-3, 241. Born in Ontario, Oregon, September, 29, 1942. Boise State, Oregon. Inducted in 2000. 1964-1974 San Francisco 49ers. **Highlights:** Seven Pro Bowls, All-NFL five times. Missed only one game because of injury.

BILL WILLIS
Guard. 6-2, 215. Born in Columbus, Ohio, October 5, 1921. Died November 27, 2007. Ohio State. Inducted in 1977. 1946-1953 Cleveland Browns (AAFC/NFL). **Highlights:** Two-way player who excelled on defense. Four-time All-NFL player, played in three Pro Bowls.

LARRY WILSON
Safety. 6-0, 190. Born in Rigby, Idaho, March 24, 1938. Utah. Inducted in 1978. 1960-1972 St. Louis Cardinals. **Highlights:** 52 interceptions. Had interception in seven consecutive games in 1966. Made "safety blitz" famous.

KELLEN WINSLOW
Tight end. 6-5, 250. Born in St. Louis, Missouri, November 5, 1957. Missouri. Inducted in 1995. 1979-1987 San Diego Chargers **Highlights:** 541 receptions for 6,741 yards, 45 touchdowns. 13 catches, blocked field goal in 1981 playoff win over Miami.

ALEX WOJCIECHOWICZ
Center. 6-0, 235. Born in South River, New Jersey, August 12, 1915. Died July 13, 1992. Fordham. Inducted in 1968. 1938-1946 Detroit Lions, 1946-1950 Philadelphia Eagles. **Highlights:** One of league's first iron men. Played both ways for eight years with Lions.

WILLIE WOOD
Safety. 5-10, 190. Born in Washington, D.C., December 23, 1936. Southern California. Inducted in 1989. 1960-1971 Green Bay Packers. **Highlights:** 48 interceptions. Competed in six NFL Championship Games and Super Bowls I and II.

RAYFIELD WRIGHT
Tackle. 6-6, 255. Born in Griffin, Georgia, August 23, 1945. Fort Valley State. Inducted in 2006. 1967-1979 Dallas Cowboys. **Highlights:** Named first- or second-team All-Pro and voted to Pro Bowl six straight seasons, 1971-76. Played in six NFC championship games and five Super Bowls. Named to NFL's All-Decade Team of 1970s.

RON YARY
Tackle. 6-5, 255. Born in Chicago, Illinois, July 16, 1946. Cerritos (Calif.) J.C., Southern California. Inducted in 2001. 1968-1981 Minnesota Vikings, 1982 Los Angeles Rams. **Highlights:** All-Pro six consecutive seasons, All-NFC eight consecutive years. Named to seven Pro Bowls. Started in four Super Bowls and five NFL/NFC Championship Games.

STEVE YOUNG
Quarterback. 6-2, 205. Born in Salt Lake City, Utah, October 11, 1961. Brigham Young. Inducted in 2005. 1985-86 Tampa Bay Buccaneers, 1987-1999 San Francisco 49ers. **Highlights:** Led the NFL in passing a record-tying six times. Passed for more than 33,000 yards and 232 touchdowns in career. MVP of Super Bowl XXIX. Elected to seven Pro Bowls.

JACK YOUNGBLOOD
Defensive end. 6-4, 247. Born in Jacksonville, Florida, January 26, 1950. Florida. Inducted in 2001. 1971-1984 Los Angeles Rams. **Highlights:** Played in club-record 201 consecutive games. Played in five NFC Championship Games, one Super Bowl. Named All-Pro five times, All-NFC seven times. Elected to seven consecutive Pro Bowls. Lions.

GARY ZIMMERMAN
Tackle. 6-6, 294. Born in Fullerton, California, December 13, 1961. Oregon. Inducted in 2008. 1986-1992 Minnesota Vikings, 1993-97 Denver Broncos. **Highlights:** Named to seven Pro Bowls. One of handful of players to be named to two NFL All-Decade Teams, 1980s and 1990s.

ENSHRINEES BY YEAR OF INDUCTION
*Deceased
(Date of enshrinement in parentheses)

1963 CHARTER CLASS
(September 7, 1963)
Sammy Baugh
Bert Bell*
Joe Carr*
Earl (Dutch) Clark*
Harold (Red) Grange*
George Halas*
Mel Hein*
Wilbur (Pete) Henry*
Robert (Cal) Hubbard*
Don Hutson*
Earl (Curly) Lambeau*
Tim Mara*
George Preston Marshall*
John (Blood) McNally*
Bronko Nagurski*
Ernie Nevers*
Jim Thorpe*

CLASS OF 1964
(September 6, 1964)
Jimmy Conzelman*
Ed Healey*
Clarke Hinkle*
William Roy (Link) Lyman*
Mike Michalske*
Art Rooney*
George Trafton*

CLASS OF 1965
(September 12, 1965)
Guy Chamberlin*
John (Paddy) Driscoll*
Dan Fortmann*
Otto Graham*
Sid Luckman*
Steve Van Buren*
Bob Waterfield*

CLASS OF 1966
(September 17, 1966)
Bill Dudley
Joe Guyon*
Arnie Herber*
Walt Kiesling*
George McAfee
Steve Owen*
Hugh (Shorty) Ray*
Clyde (Bulldog) Turner*

CLASS OF 1967
(August 5, 1967)
Chuck Bednarik
Charles W. Bidwill Sr.*
Paul Brown*
Bobby Layne*
Dan Reeves*
Ken Strong*
Joe Stydahar*
Emlen Tunnell*

CLASS OF 1968
(August 3, 1968)
Cliff Battles*
Art Donovan
Elroy (Crazylegs) Hirsch*
Wayne Millner*
Marion Motley*
Charley Trippi
Alex Wojciechowicz*

CLASS OF 1969
(September 13, 1969)
Albert Glen (Turk) Edwards*
Earle (Greasy) Neale*
Leo Nomellini*
Joe Perry
Ernie Stautner*

CLASS OF 1970
(August 8, 1970)
Jack Christiansen*
Tom Fears*
Hugh McElhenny
Pete Pihos

CLASS OF 1971
(July 31, 1971)
Jim Brown
Bill Hewitt*
Frank (Bruiser) Kinard*
Vince Lombardi*
Andy Robustelli
Y. A. Tittle
Norm Van Brocklin*

CLASS OF 1972
(July 29, 1972)
Lamar Hunt*
Gino Marchetti
Ollie Matson
Clarence (Ace) Parker

CLASS OF 1973
(July 28, 1973)
Raymond Berry
Jim Parker*
Joe Schmidt

CLASS OF 1974
(July 27, 1974)
Tony Canadeo*
Bill George*
Lou Groza*
Dick (Night Train) Lane*

CLASS OF 1975
(August 2, 1975)
Roosevelt Brown*
George Connor*
Dante Lavelli
Lenny Moore

CLASS OF 1976
(July 24, 1976)
Ray Flaherty*
Len Ford*
Jim Taylor

CLASS OF 1977
(July 30, 1977)
Frank Gifford
Forrest Gregg
Gale Sayers
Bart Starr
Bill Willis*

CLASS OF 1978
(July 29, 1978)
Lance Alworth
Weeb Ewbank*
Alphonse (Tuffy) Leemans*
Ray Nitschke*
Larry Wilson

CLASS OF 1979
(July 28, 1979)
Dick Butkus
Yale Lary
Ron Mix
Johnny Unitas*

CLASS OF 1980
(August 2, 1980)
Herb Adderley
David (Deacon) Jones
Bob Lilly
Jim Otto

CLASS OF 1981
(August 1, 1981)
Morris (Red) Badgro*
George Blanda
Willie Davis
Jim Ringo*

CLASS OF 1982
(August 7, 1982)
Doug Atkins
Sam Huff
George Musso*
Merlin Olsen

CLASS OF 1983
(July 30, 1983)
Bobby Bell
Sid Gillman*
Sonny Jurgensen
Bobby Mitchell
Paul Warfield

CLASS OF 1984
(July 28, 1984)
Willie Brown
Mike McCormack
Charley Taylor
Arnie Weinmeister*

CLASS OF 1985
(August 3, 1985)
Frank Gatski*
Joe Namath
Pete Rozelle*
O. J. Simpson
Roger Staubach

CLASS OF 1986
(August 2, 1986)
Paul Hornung
Ken Houston
Willie Lanier
Fran Tarkenton
Doak Walker*

CLASS OF 1987
(August 8, 1987)
Larry Csonka
Len Dawson
Joe Greene
John Henry Johnson
Jim Langer
Don Maynard
Gene Upshaw

CLASS OF 1988
(July 30, 1988)
Fred Biletnikoff
Mike Ditka
Jack Ham
Alan Page

CLASS OF 1989
(August 5, 1989)
Mel Blount
Terry Bradshaw
Art Shell
Willie Wood

CLASS OF 1990
(August 4, 1990)
Buck Buchanan*
Bob Griese
Franco Harris
Ted Hendricks
Jack Lambert
Tom Landry*
Bob St. Clair

CLASS OF 1991
(July 27, 1991)
Earl Campbell
John Hannah
Stan Jones
Tex Schramm*
Jan Stenerud

CLASS OF 1992
(August 1, 1992)
Lem Barney
Al Davis
John Mackey
John Riggins

CLASS OF 1993
(July 31, 1993)
Dan Fouts
Larry Little
Chuck Noll
Walter Payton*
Bill Walsh*

CLASS OF 1994
(July 30, 1994)
Tony Dorsett
Bud Grant
Jimmy Johnson
Leroy Kelly
Jackie Smith
Randy White

CLASS OF 1995
(July 29, 1995)
Jim Finks*
Henry Jordan*
Steve Largent
Lee Roy Selmon
Kellen Winslow

CLASS OF 1996
(July 27, 1996)
Lou Creekmur
Dan Dierdorf
Joe Gibbs
Charlie Joiner
Mel Renfro

CLASS OF 1997
(July 26, 1997)
Mike Haynes
Wellington Mara*
Don Shula
Mike Webster*

CLASS OF 1998
(August 1, 1998)
Paul Krause
Tommy McDonald
Anthony Muñoz
Mike Singletary
Dwight Stephenson

CLASS OF 1999
(August 7, 1999)
Eric Dickerson
Tom Mack
Ozzie Newsome
Billy Shaw
Lawrence Taylor

CLASS OF 2000
(July 29, 2000)
Howie Long
Ronnie Lott
Joe Montana
Dan Rooney
Dave Wilcox

CLASS OF 2001
(August 4, 2001)
Nick Buoniconti
Marv Levy
Mike Munchak
Jackie Slater
Lynn Swann
Ron Yary
Jack Youngblood

CLASS OF 2002
(August 3, 2002)
George Allen*
Dave Casper
Dan Hampton
Jim Kelly
John Stallworth

CLASS OF 2003
(August 3, 2003)
Marcus Allen
Elvin Bethea
Joe DeLamielleure
James Lofton
Hank Stram*

CLASS OF 2004
(August 8, 2004)
Bob (Boomer) Brown
Carl Eller
John Elway
Barry Sanders

CLASS OF 2005
(August 7, 2005)
Benny Friedman*
Dan Marino
Fritz Pollard*
Steve Young

CLASS OF 2006
(August 6, 2006)
Troy Aikman
Harry Carson
John Madden
Warren Moon
Reggie White*
Rayfield Wright

CLASS OF 2007
(August 4, 2007)
Gene Hickerson
Michael Irvin
Bruce Matthews
Charlie Sanders
Thurman Thomas
Roger Wehrli

CLASS OF 2008
(August 2, 2008)
Fred Dean
Darrell Green
Art Monk
Emmitt Thomas
Andre Tippett
Gary Zimmerman

1869
Rutgers and Princeton played a college soccer football game, the first ever, November 6. The game used modified London Football Association rules. During the next seven years, rugby gained favor with the major eastern schools over soccer, and modern football began to develop from rugby.

1876
At the Massasoit convention, the first rules for American football were written. Walter Camp, who would become known as the father of American football, first became involved with the game.

1892
In an era in which football was a major attraction of local athletic clubs, an intense competition between two Pittsburgh-area clubs, the Allegheny Athletic Association (AAA) and the Pittsburgh Athletic Club (PAC), led to the making of the first professional football player. Former Yale All-America guard William (Pudge) Heffelfinger was paid $500 by the AAA to play in a game against the PAC, becoming the first person to be paid to play football, November 12. The AAA won the game 4-0 when Heffelfinger picked up a PAC fumble and ran 35 yards for a touchdown.

1893
The Pittsburgh Athletic Club signed one of its players, probably halfback Grant Dibert, to the first known pro football contract, which covered all of the PAC's games for the year.

1895
John Brallier became the first football player to openly turn pro, accepting $10 and expenses to play for the Latrobe YMCA against the Jeannette Athletic Club.

1896
The Allegheny Athletic Association team fielded the first completely professional team for its abbreviated two-game season.

1897
The Latrobe Athletic Association football team went entire-ly professional, becoming the first team to play a full season with only professionals.

1898
A touchdown was changed from four points to five.

Chris O'Brien formed a neighborhood team, which played under the name the Morgan Athletic Club, on the south side of Chicago. The team later became known as the Normals, then the Racine (for a street in Chicago) Cardinals, the Chicago Cardinals, the St. Louis Cardinals, the Phoenix Cardinals, and, in 1994, the Arizona Cardinals. The team remains the oldest continuing operation in pro football.

1900
William C. Temple took over the team payments for the Duquesne Country and Athletic Club, becoming the first known individual club owner.

1902
Baseball's Philadelphia Athletics, managed by Connie Mack, and the Philadelphia Phillies formed professional football teams, joining the Pittsburgh Stars in the first attempt at a pro football league, named the National Football League. The Athletics won the first night football game ever played, 39-0 over Kanaweola AC at Elmira, New York, November 21.

All three teams claimed the pro championship for the year, but the league president, Dave Berry, named the Stars the champions. Pitcher Rube Waddell was with the Athletics, and pitcher Christy Mathewson a fullback for Pittsburgh.

The first World Series of pro football, actually a five-team tournament, was played among a team made up of players from both the Athletics and the Phillies, but simply named New York; the New York Knickerbockers; the Syracuse AC; the Warlow AC; and the Orange (New Jersey) AC at New York's original Madison Square Garden. New York and Syracuse played the first indoor football game before 3,000, December 28. Syracuse, with Glen (Pop) Warner at guard, won 6-0 and went on to win the tournament.

1903
The Franklin (Pa.) Athletic Club won the second and last World Series of pro football over the Oreos AC of Asbury Park, New Jersey; the Watertown Red and Blacks; and the Orange AC.

Pro football was popularized in Ohio when the Massillon Tigers, a strong amateur team, hired four Pittsburgh pros to play in the season-ending game against Akron. At the same time, pro football declined in the Pittsburgh area, and the emphasis on the pro game moved west from Pennsylvania to Ohio.

1904
A field goal was changed from five points to four.

Ohio had at least seven pro teams, with Massillon winning the Ohio Independent Championship, that is, the pro title. Talk surfaced about forming a state-wide league to end spiraling salaries brought about by constant bidding for players and to write universal rules for the game. The feeble attempt to start the league failed.

Halfback Charles Follis signed a contract with the Shelby (Ohio) AC, making him the first known black pro football player.

1905
The Canton AC, later to become known as the Bulldogs, became a professional team. Massillon again won the Ohio League championship.

1906
The forward pass was legalized. The first authenticated pass completion in a pro game came on October 27, when George (Peggy) Parratt of Massillon threw a completion to Dan (Bullet) Riley in a victory over a combined Benwood-Moundsville team.

Arch-rivals Canton and Massillon, the two best pro teams in America, played twice, with Canton winning the first game but Massillon winning the second and the Ohio League championship. A betting scandal and the financial disaster wrought upon the two clubs by paying huge salaries caused a temporary decline in interest in pro football in the two cities and, somewhat,

throughout Ohio.

1909
A field goal dropped from four points to three.

1912
A touchdown was increased from five points to six.

Jack Cusack revived a strong pro team in Canton.

1913
Jim Thorpe, a former football and track star at the Carlisle Indian School (Pa.) and a double gold medal winner at the 1912 Olympics in Stockholm, played for the Pine Village Pros in Indiana.

1915
Massillon again fielded a major team, reviving the old rivalry with Canton. Cusack signed Thorpe to play for Canton for $250 a game.

1916
With Thorpe and former Carlisle teammate Pete Calac starring, Canton went 9-0-1, won the Ohio League championship, and was acclaimed the pro football champion.

1917
Despite an upset by Massillon, Canton again won the Ohio League championship.

1919
Canton again won the Ohio League championship, despite the team having been turned over from Cusack to Ralph Hay. Thorpe and Calac were joined in the backfield by Joe Guyon.

Earl (Curly) Lambeau and George Calhoun organized the Green Bay Packers. Lambeau's employer at the Indian Packing Company provided $500 for equipment and allowed the team to use the company field for practices. The Packers went 10-1.

1920
Pro football was in a state of confusion due to three major problems: dramatically rising salaries; players continually jumping from one team to another following the highest offer; and the use of college players still enrolled in school. A league in which all the members would follow the same rules seemed the answer. An

organizational meeting, at which the Akron Pros, Canton Bulldogs, Cleveland Indians, and Dayton Triangles were represented, was held at the Jordan and Hupmobile auto showroom in Canton, Ohio, August 20. This meeting resulted in the formation of the American Professional Football Conference.

A second organizational meeting was held in Canton, September 17. The teams were from four states—Akron, Canton, Cleveland, and Dayton from Ohio; the Hammond Pros and Muncie Flyers from Indiana; the Rochester Jeffersons from New York; and the Rock Island Independents, Decatur Staleys, and Racine Cardinals from Illinois. The name of the league was changed to the American Professional Football Association. Hoping to capitalize on his fame, the members elected Thorpe president; Stanley Cofall of Cleveland was elected vice president. A membership fee of $100 per team was charged to give an appearance of respectability, but no team ever paid it. Scheduling was left up to the teams, and there were wide variations, both in the overall number of games played and in the number played against APFA member teams.

Four other teams—the Buffalo All-Americans, Chicago Tigers, Columbus Panhandles, and Detroit Heralds—joined the league sometime during the year. On September 26, the first game featuring an APFA team was played at Rock Island's Douglas Park. A crowd of 800 watched the Independents defeat the St. Paul Ideals 48-0. A week later, October 3, the first game matching two APFA teams was held. At Triangle Park, Dayton defeated Columbus 14-0, with Lou Partlow of Dayton scoring the first touchdown in a game between Association teams. The same day, Rock Island defeated Muncie 45-0.

By the beginning of December, most of the teams in the APFA had abandoned their hopes for a championship, and some of them, including the Chicago Tigers and the Detroit Heralds, had finished their seasons, disbanded, and

had their franchises canceled by the Association. Four teams—Akron, Buffalo, Canton, and Decatur—still had championship as-pirations, but a series of late-season games among them left Akron as the only undefeated team in the Association. At one of these games, Akron sold tackle Bob Nash to Buffalo for $300 and five percent of the gate receipts—the first APFA player deal.

1921
At the league meeting in Akron, April 30, the championship of the 1920 season was awarded to the Akron Pros. The APFA was reorganized, with Joe Carr of the Columbus Panhandles named president and Carl Storck of Dayton secretary-treasurer. Carr moved the Association's headquarters to Columbus, drafted a league constitution and by-laws, gave teams territorial rights, restricted player movements, developed membership criteria for the franchises, and issued standings for the first time, so that the APFA would have a clear champion.

The Association's membership increased to 22 teams, including the Green Bay Packers, who were awarded to John Clair of the Acme Packing Company.

Thorpe moved from Canton to the Cleveland Indians, but he was hurt early in the season and played very little.

A.E. Staley turned the Decatur Staleys over to player-coach George Halas, who moved the team to Cubs Park in Chicago. Staley paid Halas $5,000 to keep the name Staleys for one more year. Halas made halfback Ed (Dutch) Sternaman his partner.

Player-coach Fritz Pollard of the Akron Pros became the first black head coach.

The Staleys claimed the APFA championship with a 9-1-1 record, as did Buffalo at 9-1-2. Carr ruled in favor of the Staleys, giving Halas his first championship.

1922
After admitting the use of players who had college eligibility remaining during the 1921 season, Clair and the Green Bay management with-

drew from the APFA, January 28. Curly Lambeau promised to obey league rules and then used $50 of his own money to buy back the franchise. Bad weather and low attendance plagued the Packers, and Lambeau went broke, but local merchants arranged a $2,500 loan for the club. A public non-profit corporation was set up to operate the team, with Lambeau as head coach and manager.

The American Professional Football Association changed its name to the National Football League, June 24. The Chicago Staleys became the Chicago Bears.

The NFL fielded 18 teams, including the new Oorang Indians of Marion, Ohio, an all-Indian team featuring Thorpe, Joe Guyon, and Pete Calac, and sponsored by the Oorang dog kennels.

Canton, led by player-coach Guy Chamberlin and tackles Link Lyman and Wilbur (Pete) Henry, emerged as the league's first true powerhouse, going 10-0-2.

1923
For the first time, all of the franchises considered to be part of the NFL fielded teams. Thorpe played his second and final season for the Oorang Indians. Against the Bears, Thorpe fumbled, and Halas picked up the ball and returned it 98 yards for a touchdown, a record that would last until 1972.

Canton had its second consecutive undefeated season, going 11-0-1 for the NFL title.

1924
The league had 18 franchises, including new ones in Kansas City, Kenosha, and Frankford, a section of Philadelphia. League champion Canton, successful on the field but not at the box office, was purchased by the owner of the Cleveland franchise, who kept the Canton franchise inactive, while using the best players for his Cleveland team, which he renamed the Bulldogs. Cleveland won the title with a 7-1-1 record.

1925
Five new franchises were admitted to the NFL—the New York Giants, who were award-

ed to Tim Mara and Billy Gibson for $500; the Detroit Panthers, featuring Jimmy Conzelman as owner, coach, and tailback; the Providence Steam Roller; a new Canton Bulldogs team; and the Pottsville Maroons, who had been perhaps the most successful independent pro team. The NFL established its first player limit, at 16 players.

Late in the season, the NFL made its greatest coup in gaining national recognition. Shortly after the University of Illinois season ended in November, All-America halfback Harold (Red) Grange signed a contract to play with the Chicago Bears. On Thanksgiving Day, a crowd of 36,000—the largest in pro football history—watched Grange and the Bears play the Chicago Cardinals to a scoreless tie at Wrigley Field. At the beginning of December, the Bears left on a barnstorming tour that saw them play eight games in 12 days, in St. Louis, Philadelphia, New York City, Washington, Boston, Pittsburgh, Detroit, and Chicago. A crowd of 73,000 watched the game against the Giants at the Polo Grounds, helping assure the future of the troubled NFL franchise in New York. The Bears then played nine more games in the South and West, including a game in Los Angeles, in which 75,000 fans watched them defeat the Los Angeles Tigers in the Los Angeles Memorial Coliseum.

Pottsville and the Chicago Cardinals were the top contenders for the league title, with Pottsville winning a late-season meeting 21-7. Pottsville scheduled a game against a team of former Notre Dame players for Shibe Park in Philadelphia. Frankford lodged a protest not only because the game was in Frankford's protected territory, but because it was being played the same day as a Yellow Jackets home game. Carr gave three different notices forbidding Pottsville to play the game, but Pottsville played anyway, December 12. That day, Carr fined the club, suspended it from all rights and privileges (including the right to play for the NFL championship), and re-turned its franchise to the league. The Cardinals, who ended the season with the best record in the league, were named the 1925 champions.

1926

Grange's manager, C.C. Pyle, told the Bears that Grange wouldn't play for them unless he was paid a five-figure salary and given one-third ownership of the team. The Bears refused. Pyle leased Yankee Stadium in New York City, then petitioned for an NFL franchise. After he was refused, he started the first American Football League. It lasted one season and included Grange's New York Yankees and eight other teams. The AFL champion Philadelphia Quakers played a December game against the New York Giants, seventh in the NFL, and the Giants won 31-0. At the end of the season, the AFL folded.

Halas pushed through a rule that prohibited any team from signing a player whose college class had not graduated.

The NFL grew to 22 teams, including the Duluth Eskimos, who signed All-America fullback Ernie Nevers of Stanford, giving the league a gate attraction to rival Grange. The 15-member Eskimos, dubbed the Iron Men of the North, played 29 exhibition and league games, 28 on the road, and Nevers played in all but 29 minutes of them.

Frankford edged the Bears for the championship, despite Halas having obtained John (Paddy) Driscoll from the Cardinals. On December 4, the Yellow Jackets scored in the final two minutes to defeat the Bears 7-6 and move ahead of them in the standings.

1927

At a special meeting in Cleveland, April 23, Carr decided to secure the NFL's future by eliminating the financially weaker teams and consolidating the quality players onto a limited number of more successful teams. The new-look NFL dropped to 12 teams, and the center of gravity of the league left the Midwest, where the NFL had started, and began to emerge in the large cities of the East. One of the new teams was Grange's New

York Yankees, but Grange suffered a knee injury and the Yankees finished in the middle of the pack. The NFL championship was won by the crosstown rival New York Giants, who posted 10 shutouts in 13 games.

1928

Grange and Nevers both retired from pro football, and Duluth disbanded, as the NFL was reduced to only 10 teams. The Providence Steam Roller of Jimmy Conzelman and Pearce Johnson won the championship, playing in the Cyclodrome, a 10,000-seat oval that had been built for bicycle races.

1929

Chris O'Brien sold the Chicago Cardinals to David Jones, July 27.

The NFL added a fourth official, the field judge, July 28.

Grange and Nevers returned to the NFL. Nevers scored six rushing touchdowns and four extra points as the Cardinals beat Grange's Bears 40-6, November 28. The 40 points set a record that remains the NFL's oldest.

Providence became the first NFL team to host a game at night under floodlights, against the Cardinals, November 6.

The Packers added back Johnny Blood (McNally), tackle Cal Hubbard, and guard Mike Michalske, and won their first NFL championship, edging the Giants, who featured quarterback Benny Friedman.

1930

Dayton, the last of the NFL's original franchises, was purchased by William B. Dwyer and John C. Depler, moved to Brooklyn, and renamed the Dodgers. The Portsmouth, Ohio, Spartans entered the league.

The Packers edged the Giants for the title, but the most improved team was the Bears. Halas retired as a player and replaced himself as coach of the Bears with Ralph Jones, who refined the T-formation by introducing wide ends and a halfback in motion. Jones also introduced rookie All-America fullback-tackle Bronko Nagurski.

The Giants defeated a team of former Notre Dame players coached by Knute Rockne 22-0 before 55,000 at the Polo Grounds, December 14. The proceeds went to the New York Unemployment Fund to help those suffering because of the Great Depression, and the easy victory helped give the NFL credibility with the press and the public.

1931

The NFL decreased to 10 teams, and halfway through the season the Frankford franchise folded. Carr fined the Bears, Packers, and Portsmouth $1,000 each for using players whose college classes had not graduated.

The Packers won an unprecedented third consecutive title, beating out the Spartans, who were led by rookie backs Earl (Dutch) Clark and Glenn Presnell.

1932

George Preston Marshall, Vincent Bendix, Jay O'Brien, and M. Dorland Doyle were awarded a franchise for Boston, July 9. Despite the presence of two rookies—halfback Cliff Battles and tackle Glen (Turk) Edwards—the new team, named the Braves, lost money and Marshall was left as the sole owner at the end of the year.

NFL membership dropped to eight teams, the lowest in history. Official statistics were kept for the first time. The Bears and the Spartans finished the season in the first-ever tie for first place. After the season finale, the league office arranged for an additional regular-season game to determine the league champion. The game was moved indoors to Chicago Stadium because of bitter cold and heavy snow. The arena allowed only an 80-yard field that came right to the walls. The goal posts were moved from the end lines to the goal lines and, for safety, inbounds lines or hashmarks where the ball would be put in play were drawn 10 yards from the walls that butted against the sidelines. The Bears won 9-0, December 18, scoring the winning touchdown on a two-yard pass from Nagurski to Grange. The Spartans claimed Nagurski's pass was thrown

from less than five yards behind the line of scrimmage, violating the existing passing rule, but the play stood.

1933

The NFL, which long had followed the rules of college football, made a number of significant changes from the college game for the first time and began to develop rules serving its needs and the style of play it preferred. The innovations from the 1932 championship game—inbounds line or hashmarks and goal posts on the goal lines—were adopted. Also the forward pass was legalized from anywhere behind the line of scrimmage, February 25.

Marshall and Halas pushed through a proposal that divided the NFL into two divisions, with the winners to meet in an annual championship game, July 8.

Three new franchises joined the league—the Pittsburgh Pirates of Art Rooney, the Philadelphia Eagles of Bert Bell and Lud Wray, and the Cincinnati Reds. The Staten Island Stapletons suspended operations for a year, but never returned to the league.

Halas bought out Sternaman, became sole owner of the Bears, and reinstated himself as head coach. Marshall changed the name of the Boston Braves to the Redskins. David Jones sold the Chicago Cardinals to Charles W. Bidwill.

In the first NFL Championship Game scheduled before the season, the Western Division champion Bears defeated the Eastern Division champion Giants 23-21 at Wrigley Field, December 17.

1934

G.A. (Dick) Richards purchased the Portsmouth Spartans, moved them to Detroit, and renamed them the Lions.

Professional football gained new prestige when the Bears were matched against the best college football players in the first Chicago College All-Star Game, August 31. The game ended in a scoreless tie before 79,432 at Soldier Field.

The Cincinnati Reds lost their first eight games, then were suspended from the league for defaulting on payments. The St. Louis Gunners, an independent team, joined the NFL by buying the Cincinnati franchise and went 1-2 the last three weeks.

Rookie Beattie Feathers of the Bears became the NFL's first 1,000-yard rusher, gaining 1,004 on 101 carries. The Thanksgiving Day game between the Bears and the Lions became the first NFL game broadcast nationally, with Graham McNamee the announcer for NBC radio.

In the championship game, on an extremely cold and icy day at the Polo Grounds, the Giants trailed the Bears 13-3 in the third quarter before changing to basketball shoes for better footing. The Giants won 30-13 in what has come to be known as the Sneakers Game, December 9.

The player waiver rule was adopted, December 10.

1935
The NFL adopted Bert Bell's proposal to hold an annual draft of college players, to begin in 1936, with teams selecting in an inverse order of finish, May 19. The inbounds line or hashmarks were moved nearer the center of the field, 15 yards from the sidelines.

All-America end Don Hutson of Alabama joined Green Bay. The Lions defeated the Giants 26-7 in the NFL Championship Game, December 15.

1936
There were no franchise transactions for the first year since the formation of the NFL. It also was the first year in which all member teams played the same number of games.

The Eagles made University of Chicago halfback and Heisman Trophy winner Jay Berwanger the first player ever selected in the NFL draft, February 8. The Eagles traded his rights to the Bears, but Berwanger never played pro football. The first player selected to actually sign was the number-two pick, Riley Smith of Alabama, who was selected by Boston.

A rival league was formed, and it became the second to call itself the American Football League. The Boston Shamrocks were its champions.

Because of poor atten-

dance, Marshall, the owner of the host team, moved the Championship Game from Boston to the Polo Grounds in New York. Green Bay defeated the Redskins 21-6, December 13.

1937
Homer Marshman was granted a Cleveland franchise, named the Rams, February 12. Marshall moved the Redskins to Washington, D.C., February 13. The Redskins signed TCU All-America tailback Sammy Baugh, who led them to a 28-21 victory over the Bears in the NFL Championship Game, December 12.

The Los Angeles Bulldogs had an 8-0 record to win the AFL title, but then the 2-year-old league folded.

1938
At the suggestion of Halas, Hugh (Shorty) Ray became a technical advisor on rules and officiating to the NFL. A new rule called for a 15-yard penalty for roughing the passer.

Rookie Byron (Whizzer) White of the Pittsburgh Pirates led the NFL in rushing. The Giants defeated the Packers 23-17 for the NFL title, December 11.

Marshall, *Los Angeles Times* sports editor Bill Henry, and promoter Tom Gallery established the Pro Bowl game between the NFL champion and a team of pro all-stars.

1939
The New York Giants defeated the Pro All-Stars 13-10 in the first Pro Bowl, at Wrigley Field, Los Angeles, January 15.

Carr, NFL president since 1921, died in Columbus, May 20. Carl Storck was named acting president, May 25.

An NFL game was televised for the first time when NBC broadcast the Brooklyn Dodgers-Philadelphia Eagles game from Ebbets Field to the approximately 1,000 sets then in New York, October 22.

Green Bay defeated New York 27-0 in the NFL Championship Game, December 10 at Milwaukee. NFL attendance exceeded 1 million in a season for the first time, reaching 1,071,200.

1940
A six-team rival league, the third to call itself the American Football League, was formed, and the Columbus Bullies won its championship.

Halas' Bears, with additional coaching by Clark Shaughnessy of Stanford, defeated the Redskins 73-0 in the NFL Championship Game, December 8. The game, which was the most decisive victory in NFL history, popularized the Bears' T-formation with a man-in-motion. It was the first championship carried on network radio, broadcast by Red Barber to 120 stations of the Mutual Broadcasting System, which paid $2,500 for the rights.

Art Rooney sold the Pittsburgh franchise to Alexis Thompson, December 9, then bought part interest in the Philadelphia Eagles.

1941
Elmer Layden was named the first Commissioner of the NFL, March 1; Storck, the acting president, resigned, April 5. NFL headquarters were moved to Chicago.

Bell and Rooney traded the Eagles to Thompson for the Pirates, then re-named their new team the Steelers. Homer Marshman sold the Rams to Daniel F. Reeves and Fred Levy, Jr.

The league by-laws were revised to provide for playoffs in case there were ties in division races, and sudden-death overtimes in case a playoff game was tied after four quarters. An official *NFL Record Manual* was published for the first time.

Columbus again won the championship of the AFL, but the two-year-old league then folded.

The Bears and the Packers finished in a tie for the Western Division championship, setting up the first divisional playoff game in league history. The Bears won 33-14, then defeated the Giants 37-9 for the NFL championship, December 21.

1942
Players departing for service in World War II depleted the rosters of NFL teams. Halas left the Bears in midseason to join the Navy, and Luke John-

sos and Heartley (Hunk) Anderson served as co-coaches as the Bears went 11-0 in the regular season. The Redskins defeated the Bears 14-6 in the NFL Championship Game, December 13.

1943
The Cleveland Rams, with co-owners Reeves and Levy in the service, were granted permission to suspend operations for one season, April 6. Levy transferred his stock in the team to Reeves, April 16.

The NFL adopted free substitution, April 7. The league also made the wearing of helmets mandatory and approved a 10-game schedule for all teams.

Philadelphia and Pittsburgh were granted permission to merge for one season, June 19. The team, known as Phil-Pitt (and called the Steagles by fans), divided home games between the two cities, and Earle (Greasy) Neale of Philadelphia and Walt Kiesling of Pittsburgh served as co-coaches. The merger automatically dissolved the last day of the season, December 5.

Ted Collins was granted a franchise for Boston, to become active in 1944.

Sammy Baugh led the league in passing, punting, and interceptions. He led the Redskins to a tie with the Giants for the Eastern Division title, and then to a 28-0 victory in a divisional playoff game. The Bears beat the Redskins 41-21 in the NFL Championship Game, December 26.

1944
Collins, who had wanted a franchise in Yankee Stadium in New York, named his new team in Boston the Yanks. Cleveland resumed operations. The Brooklyn Dodgers changed their name to the Tigers.

Coaching from the bench was legalized, April 20.

The Cardinals and the Steelers were granted permission to merge for one year under the name Card-Pitt, April 21. Phil Handler of the Cardinals and Walt Kiesling of the Steelers served as co-coaches. The merger automatically dissolved the last day of the season, December 3.

In the NFL Championship Game, Green Bay defeated the New York Giants 14-7, December 17.

1945
The inbounds lines or hash-marks were moved from 15 yards away from the sidelines to nearer the center of the field—20 yards from the sidelines.

Brooklyn and Boston merged into a team that played home games in both cities and was known simply as The Yanks. The team was coached by former Boston head coach Herb Kopf. In December, the Brooklyn franchise withdrew from the NFL to join the new All-America Football Conference; all the players on its active and reserve lists were assigned to The Yanks, who once again became the Boston Yanks.

Halas rejoined the Bears late in the season after service with the U.S. Navy. Although Halas took over much of the coaching duties, Anderson and Johnsos remained the coaches of record throughout the season.

Steve Van Buren of Philadelphia led the NFL in rushing, kickoff returns, and scoring.

After the Japanese surrendered ending World War II, a count showed that the NFL service roster, limited to men who had played in league games, totaled 638, 21 of whom had died in action.

Rookie quarterback Bob Waterfield led Cleveland to a 15-14 victory over Washington in the NFL Championship Game, December 16.

1946
The contract of Commissioner Layden was not renewed, and Bert Bell, the co-owner of the Steelers, replaced him, January 11. Bell moved the league headquarters from Chicago to the Philadelphia suburb of Bala-Cynwyd.

Free substitution was withdrawn and substitutions were limited to no more than three men at a time. Forward passes were made automatically incomplete upon striking the goal posts, January 11.

The NFL took on a truly national appearance for the first time when Reeves was granted permission by the league to move his NFL champion Rams to Los Angeles.

Halfback Kenny Washington (March 21) and end Woody Strode (May 7) signed with the Los Angeles Rams to become the first African-Americans to play in the NFL in the modern era. Guard Bill Willis (August 6) and running back Marion Motley (August 9) joined the AAFC with the Cleveland Browns.

The rival All-America Football Conference began play with eight teams. The Cleveland Browns, coached by Paul Brown, won the AAFC's first championship, defeating the New York Yankees 14-9.

Bill Dudley of the Steelers led the NFL in rushing, interceptions, and punt returns, and won the league's most valuable player award.

Backs Frank Filchock and Merle Hapes of the Giants were questioned about an attempt by a New York man to fix the championship game with the Bears. Bell suspended Hapes but allowed Filchock to play; he played well, but Chicago won 24-14, December 15.

1947
The NFL added a fifth official, the back judge.

A bonus choice was made for the first time in the NFL draft. One team each year would select the special choice before the first round began. The Chicago Bears won a lottery and the rights to the first choice and drafted back Bob Fenimore of Oklahoma A&M.

The Cleveland Browns again won the AAFC title, defeating the New York Yankees 14-3.

Charles Bidwill, Sr., owner of the Cardinals, died April 19, but his wife and sons retained ownership of the team. On December 28, the Cardinals won the NFL Championship Game 28-21 over the Philadelphia Eagles, who had beaten Pittsburgh 21-0 in a playoff.

1948
Plastic helmets were prohibited. A flexible artificial tee was permitted at the kickoff. Officials other than the referee were equipped with whistles, not horns, January 14.

Fred Mandel sold the Detroit Lions to a syndicate headed by D. Lyle Fife, January 15.

Halfback Fred Gehrke of the Los Angeles Rams painted horns on the Rams' helmets, the first modern helmet emblems in pro football.

The Cleveland Browns won their third straight championship in the AAFC, going 14-0 and then defeating the Buffalo Bills 49-7.

In a blizzard, the Eagles defeated the Cardinals 7-0 in the NFL Championship Game, December 19.

1949
Alexis Thompson sold the champion Eagles to a syndicate headed by James P. Clark, January 15. The Boston Yanks became the New York Bulldogs, sharing the Polo Grounds with the Giants.

Free substitution was adopted for one year, January 20.

The NFL had two 1,000-yard rushers in the same season for the first time—Steve Van Buren of Philadelphia and Tony Canadeo of Green Bay.

The AAFC played its season with a one-division, seven-team format. On December 9, Bell announced a merger agreement in which three AAFC franchises—Cleveland, San Francisco, and Baltimore—would join the NFL in 1950. The Browns won their fourth consecutive AAFC title, defeating the 49ers 21-7, December 11.

In a heavy rain, the Eagles defeated the Rams 14-0 in the NFL Championship Game, December 18.

1950
Unlimited free substitution was restored, opening the way for the era of two platoons and specialization in pro football, January 20.

Curly Lambeau, founder of the franchise and Green Bay's head coach since 1921, resigned under fire, February 1.

The name National Football League was restored after about three months as the National-American Football League. The American and National conferences were created to replace the Eastern and Western divisions, March 3.

The New York Bulldogs became the Yanks and divided the players of the former AAFC Yankees with the Giants. A special allocation draft was held in which the 13 teams drafted the remaining AAFC players, with special consideration for Baltimore, which received 15 choices compared to 10 for other teams.

The Los Angeles Rams became the first NFL team to have all of its games—both home and away—televised. The Washington Redskins followed the Rams in arranging to televise their games; other teams made deals to put selected games on television.

In the first game of the season, former AAFC champion Cleveland defeated NFL champion Philadelphia 35-10. For the first time, deadlocks occurred in both conferences and playoffs were necessary. The Browns defeated the Giants in the American and the Rams defeated the Bears in the National. Cleveland defeated Los Angeles 30-28 in the NFL Championship Game, December 24.

1951
The Pro Bowl game, dormant since 1942, was revived under a new format matching the all-stars of each conference at the Los Angeles Memorial Coliseum. The American Conference defeated the National Conference 28-27, January 14.

Abraham Watner returned the Baltimore franchise and its player contracts back to the NFL for $50,000. Baltimore's former players were made available for drafting at the same time as college players, January 19.

A rule was passed that no tackle, guard, or center would be eligible to catch a forward pass, January 18.

The Rams reversed their television policy and televised only road games.

The NFL Championship Game was televised coast-to-coast for the first time, December 23. The DuMont Network paid $75,000 for the rights to the game, in which the Rams defeated the Browns 24-17.

1952
Ted Collins sold the New York Yanks' franchise back to the NFL, January 19. A new fran-

chise was awarded to a group in Dallas after it purchased the assets of the Yanks, January 24. The new Texans went 1-11, with the owners turning the franchise back to the league in midseason. For the last five games of the season, the commissioner's office operated the Texans as a road team, using Hershey, Pennsylvania, as a home base. At the end of the season the franchise was canceled, the last time an NFL team failed.

The Pittsburgh Steelers abandoned the Single-Wing for the T-formation, the last pro team to do so.

The Detroit Lions won their first NFL championship in 17 years, defeating the Browns 17-7 in the title game, December 28.

1953

A Baltimore group headed by Carroll Rosenbloom was granted a franchise and was awarded the holdings of the defunct Dallas organization, January 23. The team, named the Colts, put together the largest trade in league history, acquiring 10 players from Cleveland in exchange for five.

The names of the American and National conferences were changed to the Eastern and Western conferences, January 24.

Jim Thorpe died, March 28.

Mickey McBride, founder of the Cleveland Browns, sold the franchise to a syndicate headed by Dave R. Jones, June 10.

The NFL policy of blacking out home games was upheld by Judge Allan K. Grim of the U.S. District Court in Philadelphia, November 12.

The Lions again defeated the Browns in the NFL Championship Game, winning 17-16, December 27.

1954

The Canadian Football League began a series of raids on NFL teams, signing quarterback Eddie LeBaron and defensive end Gene Brito of Washington and defensive tackle Arnie Weinmeister of the Giants, among others.

Fullback Joe Perry of the 49ers became the first player in league history to gain 1,000 yards rushing in consecutive seasons.

Cleveland defeated Detroit 56-10 in the NFL Championship Game, December 26.

1955

The sudden-death overtime rule was used for the first time in a preseason game between the Rams and Giants at Portland, Oregon, August 28. The Rams won 23-17 three minutes into overtime.

A rule change declared the ball dead immediately if the ball carrier touched the ground with any part of his body except his hands or feet while in the grasp of an opponent.

The Baltimore Colts made an 80-cent phone call to Johnny Unitas and signed him as a free agent. Another quarterback, Otto Graham, played his last game as the Browns defeated the Rams 38-14 in the NFL Championship Game, December 26. Graham had quarterbacked the Browns to 10 championship-game appearances in 10 years.

NBC replaced DuMont as the network for the title game, paying a rights fee of $100,000.

1956

The NFL Players Association was founded.

Grabbing an opponent's facemask (other than the ball carrier) was made illegal. Using radio receivers to communicate with players on the field was prohibited. A natural leather ball with white end stripes replaced the white ball with black stripes for night games.

The Giants moved from the Polo Grounds to Yankee Stadium.

Halas retired as coach of the Bears, and was replaced by Paddy Driscoll.

CBS became the first network to broadcast some NFL regular-season games to selected television markets across the nation.

The Giants routed the Bears 47-7 in the NFL Championship Game, December 30.

1957

Pete Rozelle was named general manager of the Rams. Anthony J. Morabito, founder and co-owner of the 49ers, died of a heart attack during a game against the Bears at Kezar Stadium, October 28.

An NFL-record crowd of 102,368 saw the 49ers-Rams game at the Los Angeles Memorial Coliseum, November 10.

The Lions came from 20 points down to post a 31-27 playoff victory over the 49ers, December 22. Detroit defeated Cleveland 59-14 in the NFL Championship Game, December 29.

1958

The bonus selection in the draft was eliminated, January 29. The last selection was quarterback King Hill of Rice by the Chicago Cardinals.

Halas reinstated himself as coach of the Bears.

Jim Brown of Cleveland gained an NFL-record 1,527 yards rushing. In a divisional playoff game, the Giants held Brown to eight yards and defeated Cleveland 10-0.

Baltimore, coached by Weeb Ewbank, defeated the Giants 23-17 in the first sudden-death overtime in an NFL Championship Game, December 28. The game ended when Colts fullback Alan Ameche scored on a one-yard touchdown run after 8:15 of overtime.

1959

Vince Lombardi was named head coach of the Green Bay Packers, January 28. Tim Mara, the co-founder of the Giants, died, February 17.

Lamar Hunt of Dallas announced his intentions to form a second pro football league. The first meeting was held in Chicago, August 14, and consisted of Hunt representing Dallas; Bob Howsam, Denver; K.S. (Bud) Adams, Houston; Barron Hilton, Los Angeles; Max Winter and Bill Boyer, Minneapolis; and Harry Wismer, New York City. They made plans to begin play in 1960.

The new league was named the American Football League, August 22. Buffalo, owned by Ralph Wilson, became the seventh franchise, October 28. Boston, owned by William H. Sullivan, became the eighth team, November 22. The first AFL draft, lasting 33 rounds, was held, November 22. Joe Foss was named AFL Commissioner, November 30. An additional draft of 20 rounds

was held by the AFL, December 2.

NFL Commissioner Bert Bell died of a heart attack suffered at Franklin Field, Philadelphia, during the last two minutes of a game between the Eagles and the Steelers, October 11. Treasurer Austin Gunsel was named president in the office of the commissioner, October 14.

The Colts again defeated the Giants in the NFL Championship Game, 31-16, December 27.

1960

Pete Rozelle was elected NFL Commissioner as a compromise choice on the twenty-third ballot, January 26. Rozelle moved the league offices to New York City.

Hunt was elected AFL president for 1960, January 26. Minneapolis withdrew from the AFL, January 27, and the same ownership was given an NFL franchise for Minnesota (to start in 1961), January 28. Dallas received an NFL franchise for 1960, January 28. Oakland received an AFL franchise, January 30.

The AFL adopted the two-point option on points after touchdown, January 28. A no-tampering verbal pact, relative to players' contracts, was agreed to between the NFL and AFL, February 9.

The NFL owners voted to allow the transfer of the Chicago Cardinals to St. Louis, March 13.

The AFL signed a five-year television contract with ABC, June 9.

The Boston Patriots defeated the Buffalo Bills 28-7 before 16,000 at Buffalo in the first AFL preseason game, July 30. The Denver Broncos defeated the Patriots 13-10 before 21,597 at Boston in the first AFL regular-season game, September 9.

Philadelphia defeated Green Bay 17-13 in the NFL Championship Game, December 26.

1961

The Houston Oilers defeated the Los Angeles Chargers 24-16 before 32,183 in the first AFL Championship Game, January 1.

Detroit defeated Cleveland 17-16 in the first Playoff Bowl, or Bert Bell Benefit Bowl, between second-place teams in each conference in Miami, January 7.

End Willard Dewveall of the Bears played out his option and joined the Oilers, becoming the first player to play out his contract and jump from the NFL to the AFL, January 14.

Ed McGah, Wayne Valley, and Robert Osborne bought out their partners in the ownership of the Raiders, January 17. The Chargers were transferred to San Diego, February 10. Dave R. Jones sold the Browns to a group headed by Arthur B. Modell, March 22. The Howsam brothers sold the Broncos to a group headed by Calvin Kunz and Gerry Phipps, May 26.

NBC was awarded a two-year contract for radio and television rights to the NFL Championship Game for $615,000 annually, $300,000 of which was to go directly into the NFL Player Benefit Plan, April 5.

Canton, Ohio, where the league that became the NFL was formed in 1920, was chosen as the site of the Pro Football Hall of Fame, April 27. Dick McCann, a former Redskins executive, was named executive director.

A bill legalizing single-network television contracts by professional sports leagues was introduced in Congress by Representative Emanuel Celler. It passed the House and Senate and was signed into law by President John F. Kennedy, September 30.

Houston defeated San Diego 10-3 for the AFL championship, December 24. Green Bay won its first NFL championship since 1944, defeating the New York Giants 37-0, December 31.

1962

The Western Division defeated the Eastern Division 47-27 in the first AFL All-Star Game, played before 20,973 in San Diego, January 7.

Both leagues prohibited grabbing any player's facemask. The AFL voted to make the scoreboard clock the official timer of the game.

The NFL entered into a single-network agreement with CBS for telecasting all regular-season games for $4.65 million annually, January 10.

Judge Roszel Thompson of the U.S. District Court in Baltimore ruled against the AFL in its antitrust suit against the NFL, May 21. The AFL had charged the NFL with monopoly and conspiracy in areas of expansion, television, and player signings. The case lasted two and a half years, the trial two months.

McGah and Valley acquired controlling interest in the Raiders, May 24. The AFL assumed financial responsibility for the New York Titans, November 8. With Commissioner Rozelle as referee, Daniel F. Reeves regained the ownership of the Rams, outbidding his partners in sealed-envelope bidding for the team, November 27.

The Dallas Texans defeated the Oilers 20-17 for the AFL championship at Houston after 17 minutes, 54 seconds of overtime on a 25-yard field goal by Tommy Brooker, December 23. The game lasted a record 77 minutes, 54 seconds.

Judge Edward Weinfeld of the U.S. District Court in New York City upheld the legality of the NFL's television blackout within a 75-mile radius of home games and denied an injunction that would have forced the championship game between the Giants and the Packers to be televised in the New York City area, December 28. The Packers beat the Giants 16-7 for the NFL title, December 30.

1963

The Dallas Texans transferred to Kansas City, becoming the Chiefs, February 8. The New York Titans were sold to a five-man syndicate headed by David (Sonny) Werblin, March 28. Weeb Ewbank became the Titans' new head coach and the team's name was changed to the Jets, April 15. They began play in Shea Stadium.

NFL Properties, Inc., was founded to serve as the licensing arm of the NFL.

Rozelle indefinitely suspended Green Bay halfback Paul Hornung and Detroit defensive tackle Alex Karras for placing bets on their own teams and on other NFL games; he also fined five other Detroit players $2,000 each for betting on one game in

which they did not participate, and the Detroit Lions Football Company $2,000 on each of two counts for failure to report information promptly and for lack of sideline supervision.

Paul Brown, head coach of the Browns since their inception, was fired and replaced by Blanton Collier. Don Shula replaced Weeb Ewbank as head coach of the Colts.

The AFL allowed the Jets and Raiders to select players from other franchises in hopes of giving the league more competitive balance, May 11.

NBC was awarded exclusive network broadcasting rights for the 1963 AFL Championship Game for $926,000, May 23.

The Pro Football Hall of Fame was dedicated at Canton, Ohio, September 7.

The U.S. Fourth Circuit Court of Appeals reaffirmed the lower court's finding for the NFL in the $10-million suit brought by the AFL, ending three and a half years of litigation, November 21.

Jim Brown of Cleveland rushed for an NFL single-season record 1,863 yards.

Boston defeated Buffalo 26-8 in the first divisional playoff game in AFL history, December 28.

The Bears defeated the Giants 14-10 in the NFL Championship Game, a record sixth and last title for Halas in his thirty-sixth season as the Bears' coach, December 29.

1964

The Chargers defeated the Patriots 51-10 in the AFL Championship Game, January 5.

William Clay Ford, the Lions' president since 1961, purchased the team, January 10. A group representing the late James P. Clark sold the Eagles to a group headed by Jerry Wolman, January 21. Carroll Rosenbloom, the majority owner of the Colts since 1953, acquired complete ownership of the team, January 23.

The AFL signed a five-year, $36-million television contract with NBC to begin with the 1965 season, January 29.

Hornung and Karras were reinstated by Rozelle, March 16.

CBS submitted the winning bid of $14.1 million per year

for the NFL regular-season television rights for 1964 and 1965, January 24. CBS acquired the rights to championship games for 1964 and 1965 for $1.8 million per game, April 17.

Pete Gogolak of Cornell signed a contract with Buffalo, becoming the first soccer-style kicker in pro football.

Buffalo defeated San Diego 20-7 in the AFL Championship Game, December 26. Cleveland defeated Baltimore 27-0 in the NFL Championship Game, December 27.

1965

The NFL teams pledged not to sign college seniors until completion of all their games, including bowl games, and empowered the Commissioner to discipline the clubs up to as much as the loss of an entire draft list for a violation of the pledge, February 15.

The NFL added a sixth official, the line judge, February 19. The color of the officials' penalty flags was changed from white to bright gold, April 5.

Commissioner Rozelle negotiated an agreement on behalf of the NFL clubs to purchase Ed Sabol's Blair Motion Pictures, which was renamed NFL Films, April 5.

Atlanta was awarded an NFL franchise for 1966, with Rankin Smith, Sr., as owner, June 30. Miami was awarded an AFL franchise for 1966, with Joe Robbie and Danny Thomas as owners, August 16.

Field Judge Burl Toler became the first black official in NFL history, September 19.

According to a Harris survey, sports fans chose professional football (41 percent) as their favorite sport, overtaking baseball (38 percent) for the first time, October.

Green Bay defeated Baltimore 13-10 in sudden-death overtime in a Western Conference playoff game. Don Chandler kicked a 25-yard field goal for the Packers after 13 minutes, 39 seconds of overtime, December 26. The Packers then defeated the Browns 23-12 in the NFL Championship Game, January 2.

In the AFL Championship Game, the Bills again defeated the Chargers, 23-0, December 26.

CBS acquired the rights to

the NFL regular-season games in 1966 and 1967, with an option for 1968, for $18.8 million per year, December 29.

1966

The AFL-NFL war reached its peak, as the leagues spent a combined $7 million to sign their 1966 draft choices. The NFL signed 75 percent of its 232 draftees, the AFL 46 percent of its 181. Of the 111 common draft choices, 79 signed with the NFL, 28 with the AFL, and 4 went unsigned.

Buddy Young became the first African-American to work in the league office when Commissioner Rozelle named him director of player relations, February 1.

The rights to the 1966 and 1967 NFL Championship Games were sold to CBS for $2 million per game, February 14.

Foss resigned as AFL Commissioner, April 7. Al Davis, the head coach and general manager of the Raiders, was named to replace him, April 8.

Goal posts offset from the goal line, painted bright yellow, and with uprights 20 feet above the cross-bar were made standard in the NFL, May 16.

A series of secret meetings regarding a possible AFL-NFL merger were held in the spring between Hunt of Kansas City and Tex Schramm of Dallas. Rozelle announced the merger, June 8. Under the agreement, the two leagues would combine to form an expanded league with 24 teams, to be increased to 26 in 1968 and to 28 by 1970 or soon thereafter. All existing franchises would be retained, and no franchises would be transferred outside their metropolitan areas. While maintaining separate schedules through 1969, the leagues agreed to play an annual AFL-NFL World Championship Game beginning in January, 1967, and to hold a combined draft, also beginning in 1967. Preseason games would be held between teams of each league starting in 1967. Official regular-season play would start in 1970 when the two leagues would officially merge to form one league with two conferences. Rozelle was named Commissioner of the expanded league

setup.

Davis rejoined the Raiders, and Milt Woodard was named president of the AFL, July 25.

The St. Louis Cardinals moved into newly constructed Busch Memorial Stadium.

Barron Hilton sold the Chargers to a group headed by Eugene Klein and Sam Schulman, August 25.

Congress approved the AFL-NFL merger, passing legislation exempting the agreement itself from antitrust action, October 21.

New Orleans was awarded an NFL franchise to begin play in 1967, November 1. John Mecom, Jr., of Houston was designated majority stockholder and president of the franchise, December 15.

The NFL was realigned for the 1967-69 seasons into the Capitol and Century Divisions in the Eastern Conference and the Central and Coastal Divisions in the Western Conference, December 2. New Orleans and the New York Giants agreed to switch divisions in 1968 and return to the 1967 alignment in 1969.

The rights to the Super Bowl for four years were sold to CBS and NBC for $9.5 million, December 13.

1967

Green Bay earned the right to represent the NFL in the first AFL-NFL World Championship Game by defeating Dallas 34-27, January 1. The same day, Kansas City defeated Buffalo 31-7 to represent the AFL. The Packers defeated the Chiefs 35-10 before 61,946 fans at the Los Angeles Memorial Coliseum in the first game between AFL and NFL teams, January 15. The winning players' share for the Packers was $15,000 each, and the losing players' share for the Chiefs was $7,500 each. The game was televised by both CBS and NBC.

The "sling-shot" goal post and a six-foot-wide border around the field were made standard in the NFL, February 22.

Baltimore made Bubba Smith, a Michigan State defensive lineman, the first choice in the first combined AFL-NFL draft, March 14.

The AFL awarded a franchise to begin play in 1968 to

Cincinnati, May 23. A group with Paul Brown as part owner, general manager, and head coach, was awarded the Cincinnati franchise, September 27.

Arthur B. Modell, the president of the Cleveland Browns, was elected president of the NFL, May 28.

Defensive back Emlen Tunnell of the New York Giants became the first black player to enter the Pro Football Hall of Fame, August 5.

An AFL team defeated an NFL team for the first time, when Denver beat Detroit 13-7 in a preseason game, August 5.

Green Bay defeated Dallas 21-17 for the NFL championship on a last-minute 1-yard quarterback sneak by Bart Starr in 13-below-zero temperature at Green Bay, December 31. The same day, Oakland defeated Houston 40-7 for the AFL championship.

1968

Green Bay defeated Oakland 33-14 in Super Bowl II at Miami, January 14. The game had the first $3-million gate in pro football history.

Vince Lombardi resigned as head coach of the Packers, but remained as general manager, January 28.

Werblin sold his shares in the Jets to his partners Don Lillis, Leon Hess, Townsend Martin, and Phil Iselin, May 21. Lillis assumed the presidency of the club, but then died July 23. Iselin was appointed president, August 6.

Halas retired for the fourth and last time as head coach of the Bears, May 27.

The Oilers left Rice Stadium for the Astrodome and became the first NFL team to play its home games in a domed stadium.

The movie Heidi became a footnote in sports history when NBC didn't show the last 50 seconds of the Jets-Raiders game in order to permit the children's special to begin on time. The Raiders scored two touchdowns in the last 42 seconds to win 43-32, November 17.

Ewbank became the first coach to win titles in both the NFL and AFL when his Jets defeated the Raiders 27-23 for the AFL championship,

December 29. The same day, Baltimore defeated Cleveland 34-0.

1969

The AFL established a playoff format for the 1969 season, with the winner in one division playing the runner-up in the other, January 11.

An AFL team won the Super Bowl for the first time, as the Jets defeated the Colts 16-7 at Miami, January 12 in Super Bowl III. The title Super Bowl was recognized by the NFL for the first time.

Vince Lombardi became part owner, executive vice-president, and head coach of the Washington Redskins, February 7.

Wolman sold the Eagles to Leonard Tose, May 1.

Baltimore, Cleveland, and Pittsburgh agreed to join the 13-team American Football Conference of the NFL in 1970, May 17. The NFL also agreed on a playoff format that would include one "wild-card" team per conference—the second-place team with the best record.

The NFL announced a three-year agreement with ABC to televise Monday Night Football. The new series makes the NFL the first league with a regular series of national telecasts in prime time, May 26.

George Preston Marshall, president emeritus of the Redskins, died at 72, August 9.

The NFL marked its fiftieth year by the wearing of a special patch by each of the 16 teams.

1970

Kansas City defeated Minnesota 23-7 in Super Bowl IV at New Orleans, January 11. The gross receipts of approximately $3.8 million were the largest ever for a one-day sports event.

Four-year television contracts, under which CBS would televise all NFC games and NBC all AFC games (except Monday night games) and the two would divide televising the Super Bowl and AFC-NFC Pro Bowl games, were announced, January 26.

Art Modell resigned as president of the NFL, March 12. Milt Woodard resigned as president of the AFL, March

13. Lamar Hunt was elected president of the AFC and George Halas was elected president of the NFC, March 19.

The merged 26-team league adopted rules changes putting names on the backs of players' jerseys, making a point after touchdown worth only one point, and making the scoreboard clock the official timing device of the game, March 18.

The Players Negotiating Committee and the NFL Players Association announced a four-year agreement guaranteeing approximately $4,535,000 annually to player pension and insurance benefits, August 3. The owners also agreed to contribute $250,000 annually to improve or implement items such as disability payments, widows' benefits, maternity benefits, and dental benefits. The agreement also provided for increased preseason game and per diem payments, averaging approximately $2.6 million annually.

The Pittsburgh Steelers moved into Three Rivers Stadium. The Cincinnati Bengals moved to Riverfront Stadium.

Vince Lombardi died of cancer at 57, September 3.

The Super Bowl trophy was renamed the Vince Lombardi trophy, September 10.

Tom Dempsey of New Orleans kicked a game-winning NFL-record 63-yard field goal against Detroit, November 8.

1971
Baltimore defeated Dallas 16-13 on Jim O'Brien's 32-yard field goal with five seconds to go in Super Bowl V at Miami, January 17. The NBC telecast was viewed in an estimated 23,980,000 homes, the largest audience ever for a one-day sports event.

The NFC defeated the AFC 27-6 in the first AFC-NFC Pro Bowl at Los Angeles, January 24.

The Boston Patriots changed their name to the New England Patriots, March 25. Their new stadium, Schaefer Stadium, was dedicated in a 20-14 preseason victory over the Giants.

The Philadelphia Eagles left Franklin Field and played their games at the new Veterans Stadium.

The San Francisco 49ers left Kezar Stadium and moved their games to Candlestick Park.

Daniel F. Reeves, the president and general manager of the Rams, died at 58, April 15.

The Dallas Cowboys moved from the Cotton Bowl into their new home, Texas Stadium, October 24.

Miami defeated Kansas City 27-24 in sudden-death overtime in an AFC Divisional Playoff Game, December 25. Garo Yepremian kicked a 37-yard field goal for the Dolphins after 22 minutes, 40 seconds of overtime, as the game lasted 82 minutes, 40 seconds overall, making it the longest game in history.

1972
Dallas defeated Miami 24-3 in Super Bowl VI at New Orleans, January 16. The CBS telecast was viewed in an estimated 27,450,000 homes, the top-rated one-day telecast ever.

The inbounds lines or hashmarks were moved nearer the center of the field, 23 yards, 1 foot, 9 inches from the sidelines, March 23. The method of determining won-lost percentage in standings changed. Tie games, previously not counted in the standings, were made equal to a half-game won and a half-game lost, May 24.

Robert Irsay purchased the Los Angeles Rams and transferred ownership of the club to Carroll Rosenbloom in exchange for the Baltimore Colts, July 13.

William V. Bidwill purchased the stock of his brother Charles (Stormy) Bidwill to become the sole owner of the St. Louis Cardinals, September 2.

The National District Attorneys Association endorsed the position of professional leagues in opposing proposed legalization of gambling on professional team sports, September 28.

Franco Harris' "Immaculate Reception" gave the Steelers their first postseason win ever, 13-7 over the Raiders, December 23.

1973
Rozelle announced that all

Super Bowl VII tickets were sold and that the game would be telecast in Los Angeles, the site of the game, on an experimental basis, January 3.

Miami defeated Washington 14-7 in Super Bowl VII at Los Angeles, completing a 17-0 season, the first perfect-record regular-season and postseason mark in NFL history, January 14. The NBC telecast was viewed by approximately 75 million people.

The AFC defeated the NFC 33-28 in the Pro Bowl in Dallas, the first time since 1942 that the game was played outside Los Angeles, January 21.

A jersey numbering system was adopted, April 5: 1-19 for quarterbacks and specialists, 20-49 for running backs and defensive backs, 50-59 for centers and linebackers, 60-79 for defensive linemen and interior offensive linemen other than centers, and 80-89 for wide receivers and tight ends. Players who had been in the NFL in 1972 could continue to use old numbers.

NFL Charities, a nonprofit organization, was created to derive an income from monies generated from NFL Properties' licensing of NFL trademarks and team names, June 26. NFL Charities was set up to support education and charitable activities and to supply economic support to persons formerly associated with professional football who were no longer able to support themselves.

Congress adopted experimental legislation (for three years) requiring any NFL game that had been declared a sellout 72 hours prior to kickoff to be made available for local televising, September 14. The legislation provided for an annual review to be made by the Federal Communications Commission.

The Buffalo Bills moved their home games from War Memorial Stadium to Rich Stadium in nearby Orchard Park. The Giants tied the Eagles 23-23 in the final game in Yankee Stadium, September 23. The Giants played the rest of their home games at the Yale Bowl in New Haven, Connecticut.

A rival league, the World Football League, was formed and was reported in operation,

October 2. It had plans to start play in 1974.

O.J. Simpson of Buffalo became the first player to rush for more than 2,000 yards in a season, gaining 2,003.

1974
Miami defeated Minnesota 24-7 in Super Bowl VIII at Houston, the second consecutive Super Bowl championship for the Dolphins, January 13. The CBS telecast was viewed by approximately 75 million people.

Rozelle was given a 10-year contract effective January 1, 1973, February 27.

Tampa Bay was awarded the twenty-seventh franchise to begin operation in 1976, April 24.

Sweeping rules changes were adopted to add action and tempo to games: one sudden-death overtime period was added for preseason and regular-season games; the goal posts were moved from the goal line to the end lines; kickoffs were moved from the 40- to the 35-yard line; after missed field goals from beyond the 20, the ball was to be returned to the line of scrimmage; restrictions were placed on members of the punting team to open up return possibilities; roll-blocking and cutting of wide receivers was eliminated; the extent of downfield contact a defender could have with an eligible receiver was restricted; the penalties for offensive holding, illegal use of the hands, and tripping were reduced from 15 to 10 yards; wide receivers blocking back toward the ball within three yards of the line of scrimmage were prevented from blocking below the waist, April 25.

Seattle was awarded the twenty-eighth NFL franchise to begin play in 1976, June 4. Lloyd W. Nordstrom, president of the Seattle Seahawks, and Hugh Culverhouse, president of the Tampa Bay Buccaneers, signed franchise agreements, December 5.

The Birmingham Americans defeated the Florida Blazers 22-21 in the WFL World Bowl, winning the league championship, December 5.

1975
Pittsburgh defeated Minnesota

16-6 in Super Bowl IX at New Orleans, the Steelers' first championship since entering the NFL in 1933. The NBC telecast was viewed by approximately 78 million people.

The Memphis Southmen of the WFL signed Larry Csonka, Jim Kiick, and Paul Warfield of Miami, March 31.

The divisional winners with the highest won-loss percentage were made the home team for the divisional play-offs, and the surviving winners with the highest percentage made home teams for the championship games. Previously, the home sites were pre-determined by division on a rotating basis, June 26.

Referees were equipped with wireless microphones for all preseason, regular-season, and playoff games.

The Lions moved to the new Pontiac Silverdome. The Giants played their home games in Shea Stadium. The Saints moved into the Louisiana Superdome.

The World Football League folded, October 22.

1976

Pittsburgh defeated Dallas 21-17 in Super Bowl X in Miami. The Steelers joined Green Bay and Miami as the only teams to win two Super Bowls; the Cowboys became the first wild-card team to play in the Super Bowl. The CBS telecast was viewed by an estimated 80 million people, the largest television audience in history.

Lloyd Nordstrom, the president of the Seahawks, died at 66, January 20. His brother Elmer succeeded him as majority representative of the team.

The owners awarded Super Bowl XII, to be played on January 15, 1978, to New Orleans. They also adopted the use of two 30-second clocks for all games, visible to both players and fans to note the official time between the ready-for-play signal and snap of the ball, March 16.

A veteran player allocation was held to stock the Seattle and Tampa Bay franchises with 39 players each, March 30-31. In the college draft, Seattle and Tampa Bay each received eight extra choices,

April 8-9.

The Giants moved into new Giants Stadium in East Rutherford, New Jersey.

The Steelers defeated the College All-Stars in a storm-shortened Chicago College All-Star Game, the last of the series, July 23. St. Louis defeated San Diego 20-10 in a preseason game before 38,000 in Korakuen Stadium, Tokyo, in the first NFL game outside of North America, August 16.

1977

Oakland defeated Minnesota 32-14 in Super Bowl XI at Pasadena, January 9. The paid attendance was a pro record 103,438. The NBC telecast was viewed by 81.9 million people, the largest ever to view a sports event. The victory was the fifth consecutive for the AFC in the Super Bowl.

The NFL Players Association and the NFL Management Council ratified a collective bargaining agreement extending until 1982, covering five football seasons while continuing the pension plan—including years 1974, 1975, and 1976—with contributions totaling more than $55 million. The total cost of the agreement was estimated at $107 million. The agreement called for a college draft at least through 1986; contained a no-strike, no-suit clause; established a 43-man active player limit; reduced pension vesting to four years; provided for increases in minimum salaries and preseason and postseason pay; improved insurance, medical, and dental benefits; modified previous practices in player movement and control; and reaffirmed the NFL Commissioner's disciplinary authority. Additionally, the agreement called for the NFL member clubs to make payments totaling $16 million the next 10 years to settle various legal disputes, February 25.

The San Francisco 49ers were sold to Edward J. DeBartolo, Jr., March 28.

A 16-game regular season, 4-game preseason was adopted to begin in 1978, March 29. A second wild-card team was adopted for the playoffs beginning in 1978, with the wild-card teams to play each other and the win-

ners advancing to a round of eight postseason series.

The Seahawks were permanently aligned in the AFC Western Division and the Buccaneers in the NFC Central Division, March 31.

The owners awarded Super Bowl XIII, to be played on January 21, 1979, to Miami, to be played in the Orange Bowl; Super Bowl XIV, to be played January 20, 1980, was awarded to Pasadena, to be played in the Rose Bowl, June 14.

Rules changes were adopted to open up the passing game and to cut down on injuries. Defenders were permitted to make contact with eligible receivers only once; the head slap was outlawed; offensive linemen were prohibited from thrusting their hands to an opponent's neck, face, or head; and wide receivers were prohibited from clipping, even in the legal clipping zone.

Rozelle negotiated contracts with the three television networks to televise all NFL regular-season and postseason games, plus selected preseason games, for four years beginning with the 1978 season. ABC was awarded yearly rights to 16 Monday night games, four prime-time games, the AFC-NFC Pro Bowl, and the Hall of Fame games. CBS received the rights to all NFC regular-season and postseason games (except those in the ABC package) and to Super Bowls XIV and XVI. NBC received the rights to all AFC regular-season and postseason games (except those in the ABC package) and to Super Bowls XIII and XV. Industry sources considered it the largest single television package ever negotiated, October 12.

1978

Dallas defeated Denver 27-10 in Super Bowl XII, held indoors for the first time, at the Louisiana Superdome in New Orleans, January 15. The CBS telecast was viewed by more than 102 million people, meaning the game was watched by more viewers than any other show of any kind in the history of television. Dallas' victory was the first for the NFC in six years.

According to a Louis Harris Sports Survey, 70 percent of the nation's sports fans said they followed football, compared to 54 percent who followed baseball. Football increased its lead as the country's favorite, 26 percent to 16 percent for baseball, January 19.

A seventh official, the side judge, was added to the officiating crew, March 14.

The NFL continued a trend toward opening up the game. Rules changes permitted a defender to maintain contact with a receiver within five yards of the line of scrimmage, but restricted contact beyond that point. The pass-blocking rule was interpreted to permit the extending of arms and open hands, March 17.

A study on the use of instant replay as an officiating aid was made during seven nationally televised preseason games.

The NFL played for the first time in Mexico City, with the Saints defeating the Eagles 14-7 in a preseason game, August 5.

Bolstered by the expansion of the regular-season schedule from 14 to 16 weeks, NFL paid attendance exceeded 12 million (12,771,800) for the first time. The per-game average of 57,017 was the third-highest in league history and the most since 1973.

1979

Pittsburgh defeated Dallas 35-31 in Super Bowl XIII at Miami to become the first team ever to win three Super Bowls, January 21. The NBC telecast was viewed in 35,090,000 homes, by an estimated 96.6 million fans.

NFL rules changes emphasized additional player safety. The changes prohibited players on the receiving team from blocking below the waist during kickoffs, punts, and field-goal attempts; prohibited the wearing of torn or altered equipment and exposed pads that could be hazardous; extended the zone in which there could be no crackback blocks; and instructed officials to quickly whistle a play dead when a quarterback was clearly in the grasp of a tackler, March 16.

Carroll Rosenbloom, the president of the Rams, drowned at 72, April 2. His widow, Georgia, assumed control of the club.

1980

Pittsburgh defeated the Los Angeles Rams 31-19 in Super Bowl XIV at Pasadena to become the first team to win four Super Bowls, January 20. The game was viewed in a record 35,330,000 homes.

The AFC-NFC Pro Bowl, won 37-27 by the NFC, was played before 48,060 fans at Aloha Stadium in Honolulu, Hawaii. It was the first time in the 30-year history of the Pro Bowl that the game was played in a non-NFL city.

Rules changes placed greater restrictions on contact in the area of the head, neck, and face. Under the heading of "personal foul," players were prohibited from directly striking, swinging, or clubbing on the head, neck, or face. Starting in 1980, a penalty could be called for such contact whether or not the initial contact was made below the neck area.

CBS, with a record bid of $12 million, won the national radio rights to 26 NFL regular-season games, including Monday Night Football, and all 10 postseason games for the 1980-83 seasons.

The Los Angeles Rams moved their home games to Anaheim Stadium in nearby Orange County, California.

The Oakland Raiders joined the Los Angeles Coliseum Commission's antitrust suit against the NFL. The suit contended the league violated antitrust laws in declining to approve a proposed move by the Raiders from Oakland to Los Angeles.

The NFL Draft is televised for the first time by ESPN, April 29.

Television ratings in 1980 were the second-best in NFL history, trailing only the combined ratings of the 1976 season. All three networks posted gains, and NBC's 15.0 rating was its best ever. CBS and ABC had their best ratings since 1977, with 15.3 and 20.8 ratings, respectively. CBS Radio reported a record audience of 7 million for Monday night and special games.

1981

Oakland defeated Philadelphia 27-10 in Super Bowl XV at the Louisiana Superdome in New Orleans, to become the first wild-card team to win a Super Bowl, January 25.

Edgar F. Kaiser, Jr., purchased the Denver Broncos from Gerald and Allan Phipps, February 26.

The owners adopted a disaster plan for re-stocking a team should the club be involved in a fatal accident, March 20.

A CBS-New York Times poll showed that 48 percent of sports fans preferred football to 31 percent for baseball.

The NFL teams hosted 167 representatives from 44 predominantly black colleges during training camps for a total of 289 days. The program was adopted for renewal during each training camp period.

ABC and CBS set all-time rating highs. ABC finished with a 21.7 rating and CBS with a 17.5 rating. NBC was down slightly to 13.9.

1982

San Francisco defeated Cincinnati 26-21 in Super Bowl XVI at the Pontiac Silverdome, in the first Super Bowl held in the North, January 24. The CBS telecast achieved the highest rating of any televised sports event ever, 49.1 with a 73.0 share. The game was viewed by a record 110.2 million fans. CBS Radio reported a record 14 million listeners for the game.

The NFL signed a five-year contract with the three television networks (ABC, CBS, and NBC) to televise all NFL regular-season and postseason games starting with the 1982 season.

A jury ruled against the NFL in the antitrust trial brought by the Los Angeles Coliseum Commission and the Oakland Raiders, May 7. The verdict cleared the way for the Raiders to move to Los Angeles, where they defeated Green Bay 24-3 in their first preseason game, August 29.

The 1982 season was reduced from a 16-game schedule to nine as the result of a 57-day players' strike. The strike was called by the NFLPA at midnight on Monday, September 20, following the

Green Bay at New York Giants game. Play resumed November 21-22 following ratification of the Collective Bargaining Agreement by NFL owners, November 17 in New York.

Under the Collective Bargaining Agreement, which was to run through the 1986 season, the NFL draft was extended through 1992 and the veteran free-agent system was left basically unchanged. A minimum salary schedule for years of experience was established; training camp and postseason pay were increased; players' medical, insurance, and retirement benefits were increased; and a severance-pay system was introduced to aid in career transition, a first in professional sports.

Despite the players' strike, the average paid attendance in 1982 was 58,472, the fifth-highest in league history.

1983

Because of the shortened season, the NFL adopted a format of 16 teams competing in a Super Bowl Tournament for the 1982 playoffs. The NFC's number-one seed, Washington, defeated the AFC's number-two seed, Miami, 27-17 in Super Bowl XVII at the Rose Bowl in Pasadena, January 30.

Super Bowl XVII was the second-highest rated live television program of all time, giving the NFL a sweep of the top 10 live programs in television history. The game was viewed in more than 40 million homes, the largest ever for a live telecast.

George Halas, the owner of the Bears and the last surviving member of the NFL's second organizational meeting, died at 88, October 31.

1984

The Los Angeles Raiders defeated Washington 38-9 in Super Bowl XVIII at Tampa Stadium, January 22. The game achieved a 46.4 rating and 71.0 share.

An 11-man group headed by H.R. (Bum) Bright purchased the Dallas Cowboys from Clint Murchison, Jr., March 20. Club president Tex Schramm was designated as managing general partner.

Wellington Mara was named president of the NFC, March 20.

Patrick Bowlen purchased a majority interest in the Denver Broncos from Edgar Kaiser, Jr., March 21.

The Colts relocated to Indianapolis, March 28. Their new home became the Hoosier Dome.

The New York Jets moved their home games to Giants Stadium in East Rutherford, New Jersey.

Alex G. Spanos purchased a majority interest in the San Diego Chargers from Eugene V. Klein, August 28.

Houston defeated Pittsburgh 23-20 to mark the one-hundredth overtime game in regular-season play since overtime was adopted in 1974, December 2.

On the field, many all-time records were set: Dan Marino of Miami passed for 5,084 yards and 48 touchdowns; Eric Dickerson of the Los Angeles Rams rushed for 2,105 yards; Art Monk of Washington caught 106 passes; and Walter Payton of Chicago broke Jim Brown's career rushing mark, finishing the season with 13,309 yards.

According to a CBS Sports/New York Times survey, 53 percent of the nation's sports fans said they most enjoyed watching football, compared to 18 percent for baseball, December 2-4.

1985

San Francisco defeated Miami 38-16 in Super Bowl XIX at Stanford Stadium in Stanford, California, January 20. The game was viewed on television by more people than any other live event in history. President Ronald Reagan, who took his second oath of office before tossing the coin for the game, was one of 115,936,000 viewers. The game drew a 46.4 rating and a 63.0 share. In addition, 6 million people watched the Super Bowl in the United Kingdom and a similar number in Italy. Super Bowl XIX had a direct economic impact of $113.5 million on the San Francisco Bay area.

NBC Radio and the NFL entered into a two-year agreement granting NBC the radio rights to a 37-game package in each of the 1985-86 seasons, March 6. The package included 27 regular-season games and 10 postseason games.

Norman Braman, in partnership with Edward Leibowitz, bought the Philadelphia Eagles from Leonard Tose, April 29.

A group headed by Tom Benson, Jr., was approved to purchase the New Orleans Saints from John W. Mecom, Jr., June 3.

The NFL owners adopted a resolution calling for a series of overseas preseason games, beginning in 1986, with one game to be played in England/Europe and/or one game in Japan each year. The game would be a fifth preseason game for the clubs involved and all arrangements and selection of the clubs would be under the control of the Commissioner, May 23.

The league-wide conversion to videotape from movie film for coaching study was approved.

A Louis Harris poll in December revealed that pro football remained the sport most followed by Americans. Fifty-nine percent of those surveyed followed pro football, compared with 54 percent who followed baseball.

The Chicago-Miami Monday game had the highest rating, 29.6, and share, 46.0, of any prime-time game in NFL history, December 2. The game was viewed in more than 25 million homes.

The NFL showed a ratings increase on all three networks for the season, gaining 4 percent on NBC, 10 on CBS, and 16 on ABC.

1986
Chicago defeated New England 46-10 in Super Bowl XX at the Louisiana Superdome, January 26. The Patriots had earned the right to play the Bears by becoming the first wild-card team to win three consecutive games on the road. The NBC telecast replaced the final episode of M*A*S*H as the most-viewed television program in history, with an audience of 127 million viewers, according to A.C. Nielsen figures. In addition to drawing a 48.3 rating and a 70 percent share in the United

States, Super Bowl XX was televised to 59 foreign countries and beamed via satellite to the QE II. An estimated 300 million Chinese viewed a tape delay of the game in March. CBS Radio figures indicated an audience of 10 million for the game.

The owners adopted limited use of instant replay as an officiating aid, prohibited players from wearing or otherwise displaying equipment, apparel, or other items that carry commercial names, names of organizations, or personal messages of any type, March 11.

After an 11-week trial, a jury in U.S. District Court in New York awarded the United States Football League one dollar in its $1.7 billion antitrust suit against the NFL. The jury rejected all of the USFL's television-related claims, which were the self-proclaimed heart of the USFL's case. The jury deliberated five days, July 29.

Chicago defeated Dallas 17-6 at Wembley Stadium in London in the first American Bowl. The game drew a sellout crowd of 82,699 and the NBC national telecast in this country produced a 12.4 rating and 36 percent share, making it the highest daytime preseason television audience ever with 10.65-million viewers, August 3.

ABC's *NFL Monday Night Football*, in its seventeenth season, became the longest-running prime-time series in the history of the network.

1987
The New York Giants defeated Denver 39-20 in Super Bowl XXI and captured their first NFL title since 1956. The game, played in Pasadena's Rose Bowl, drew a sellout crowd of 101,063. According to A.C. Nielsen figures, the CBS broadcast of the game was viewed in the U.S. on television by 122.64-million people, making the telecast the second most-watched television audience of all-time behind Super Bowl XX. The game was watched live or on tape in 55 foreign countries and NBC Radio's broadcast of the game was heard by a record 10.1 million people.

New three-year TV con-

tracts with ABC, CBS, and NBC were announced for 1987-89 at the NFL annual meeting in Maui, Hawaii, March 15. Commissioner Rozelle and Broadcast Committee Chairman Art Modell also announced a three-year contract with ESPN to televise 13 prime-time games each season. The ESPN contract was the first with a cable network. However, NFL games on ESPN also were scheduled for regular television in the city of the visiting team and in the home city if the game was sold out 72 hours in advance.

A special payment program was adopted to benefit nearly 1,000 former NFL players who participated in the League before the current Bert Bell NFL Pension Plan was created and made retroactive to the 1959 season. Players covered by the new program spent at least five years in the League and played all or part of their career prior to 1959. Each vested player would receive $60 per month for each year of service in the League for life.

NFL and CBS Radio jointly announced agreement granting CBS the radio rights to a 40-game package in each of the next three NFL seasons, 1987-89, April 7.

Over 400 former NFL players from the pre-1959 era received first payments from NFL owners, July 1.

The NFL's debut on ESPN produced the two highest-rated and most-watched sports programs in basic cable history. The Chicago at Miami game on August 16 drew an 8.9 rating in 3.81 million homes. Those records fell two weeks later when the Los Angeles Raiders at Dallas game achieved a 10.2 cable rating in 4.36 million homes.

The 1987 season was reduced from a 16-game season to 15 as the result of a 24-day players' strike. The strike was called by the NFLPA on Tuesday, September 22, following the New England at New York Jets game. Games scheduled for the third weekend were canceled but the games of weeks four, five, and six were played with replacement teams. Striking players returned for the seventh week of the season, October 25.

In a three-team deal involving 10 players and/or draft choices, the Los Angeles Rams traded running back Eric Dickerson to the Indianapolis Colts for six draft choices and two players. Buffalo obtained the rights to linebacker Cornelius Bennett from Indianapolis, sending Greg Bell and three draft choices to the Rams. The Colts added Owen Gill and three draft choices of their own to complete the deal with the Rams, October 31.

The Chicago at Minnesota game became the highest-rated and most-watched sports program in basic cable history when it drew a 14.4 cable rating in 6.5 million homes, December 6.

1988
Washington defeated Denver 42-10 in Super Bowl XXII to earn its second victory this decade in the NFL Championship Game. The game, played for the first time in San Diego Jack Murphy Stadium, drew a sellout crowd of 73,302. According to A.C. Nielsen figures, the ABC broadcast of the game was viewed in the U.S. on television by 115,000,000 people. The game was seen live or on tape in 60 foreign countries, including the People's Republic of China, and CBS's radio broadcast of the game was heard by 13.7 million people.

In a unanimous 3-0 decision, the 2nd Circuit Court of Appeals in New York upheld the verdict of the jury that in July, 1986, had awarded the United States Football League one dollar in its $1.7 billion antitrust suit against the NFL. In a 91-page opinion, Judge Ralph K. Winter said the USFL sought through court decree the success it failed to gain among football fans, March 10.

By a 23-5 margin, owners voted to continue the instant replay system for the third consecutive season with the Instant Replay Official to be assigned to a regular seven-man, on-the-field crew. At the NFL annual meeting in Phoenix, Arizona, a 45-second clock was also approved to replace the 30-second clock. For a normal sequence of plays, the interval between plays was changed to 45 seconds from the time the ball is signaled dead until it is snapped on the succeeding play.

NFL owners approved the transfer of the Cardinals' franchise from St. Louis to Phoenix; approved two supplemental drafts each year—one prior to training camp and one prior to the regular season; and voted to initiate an annual series of games in Japan/Asia as early as the 1989 preseason, March 14-18.

The NFL Annual Selection Meeting returned to a separate two-day format and for the first time originated on a Sunday. ESPN drew a 3.6 rating during their seven-hour coverage of the draft, which was viewed in 1.6 million homes, April 24-25.

Art Rooney, founder and owner of the Steelers, died at 87, August 25.

Johnny Grier became the first African-American referee in NFL history, September 4.

Commissioner Rozelle announced that two teams would play a preseason game as part of the American Bowl series on August 6, 1989, in the Korakuen Tokyo Dome in Japan, December 16.

1989

San Francisco defeated Cincinnati 20-16 in Super Bowl XXIII. The game, played for the first time at Joe Robbie Stadium in Miami, was attended by a sellout crowd of 75,129. NBC's telecast of the game was watched by an estimated 110,780,000 viewers, according to A.C. Nielsen, making it the sixth most-watched program in television history. The game was seen live or on tape in 60 foreign countries, including an estimated 300 million in China. The CBS Radio broadcast of the game was heard by 11.2 million people.

Commissioner Rozelle announced his retirement, pending the naming of a successor, March 22 at the NFL annual meeting in Palm Desert, California.

Following the announcement, AFC president Lamar Hunt and NFC president Wellington Mara announced the formation of a six-man search committee composed

of Art Modell, Robert Parins, Dan Rooney, and Ralph Wilson. Hunt and Mara served as co-chairmen.

By a 24-4 margin, owners voted to continue the instant replay system for the fourth straight season. A strengthened policy regarding anabolic steroids and masking agents was announced by Commissioner Rozelle. NFL clubs called for strong disciplinary measures in cases of feigned injuries and adopted a joint proposal by the Long-Range Planning and Finance committees regarding player personnel rules, March 19-23.

Two hundred twenty-nine unconditional free agents signed with new teams under management's Plan B system, April 1.

Jerry Jones purchased a majority interest in the Dallas Cowboys from H.R. (Bum) Bright, April 18.

Tex Schramm was named president of the new World League of American Football to work with a six-man committee of Dan Rooney, chairman; Norman Braman, Lamar Hunt, Victor Kiam, Mike Lynn, and Bill Walsh, April 18.

NFL and CBS Radio jointly announced agreement extending CBS's radio rights to an annual 40-game package through the 1994 season, April 18.

As of opening day, September 10, of the 229 Plan B free agents, 111 were active and 23 others were on teams' reserve lists. Ninety-two others were waived and three retired.

Art Shell was named head coach of the Los Angeles Raiders making him the NFL's first black head coach since Fritz Pollard coached the Akron Pros in 1921, October 3.

The site of the New England Patriots at San Francisco 49ers game scheduled for Candlestick Park on October 22 was switched to Stanford Stadium in the aftermath of the Bay Area Earthquake of October 17. The change was announced on October 19.

Paul Tagliabue became the seventh chief executive of the NFL on October 26 when he was chosen to succeed Commissioner Pete Rozelle on the sixth ballot of a three-day

meeting in Cleveland, Ohio.

In all, 12 ballots were required to select Tagliabue. Two were conducted at a meeting in Chicago on July 6, and four at a meeting in Dallas on October 10-11. On the twelfth ballot, with Seattle absent, Tagliabue received more than the 19 affirmative votes required for election from among the 27 clubs present.

The transfer from Commissioner Rozelle to Commissioner Tagliabue took place at 12:01 A.M. on Sunday, November 5.

NFL Charities donated $1 million through United Way to benefit Bay Area earthquake victims, November 6.

1990

San Francisco defeated Denver 55-10 in Super Bowl XXIV at the Louisiana Superdome, January 28. San Francisco joined Pittsburgh as the NFL's only teams to win four Super Bowls.

The NFL announced revisions in its 1990 draft eligibility rules. College juniors became eligible but must renounce their collegiate football eligibility before applying for the NFL Draft, February 16.

Commissioner Tagliabue announced NFL teams will play their 16-game schedule over 17 weeks in 1990-92 and 16 games over 18 weeks in 1993, February 27.

The NFL revised its playoff format to include two additional wild-card teams (one per conference), which raised the total to six wild-card teams.

Commissioner Tagliabue and Broadcast Committee Chairman Art Modell announced a four-year contract with Turner Broadcasting to televise nine Sunday-night games.

New four-year TV agreements were ratified for 1990-93 for ABC, CBS, NBC, ESPN, and TNT at the NFL annual meeting in Orlando, Florida, March 12. The contracts totaled $3.6 billion, the largest in TV history.

The NFL announced plans to expand its American Bowl series of preseason games. In addition to games in London and Tokyo, American Bowl games were scheduled for Berlin, Germany, and Montre-

al, Canada, in 1990.

For the fifth straight year, NFL owners voted to continue a limited system of Instant Replay. Beginning in 1990, the replay official will have a two-minute time limit to make a decision. The vote was 21-7, March 12.

Commissioner Tagliabue announced the formation of a Committee on Expansion and Realignment, March 13. He also named a Player Advisory Council, comprised of 12 former NFL players, March 14.

One-hundred eighty-four Plan B unconditional free agents signed with new teams, April 2.

Commissioner Tagliabue appointed Dr. John Lombardo as the League's Drug Advisor for Anabolic Steroids, April 25 and named Dr. Lawrence Brown as the League's Advisor for Drugs of Abuse, May 17.

NFL International Week was celebrated with four preseason games in seven days in Tokyo, London, Berlin, and Montreal. More than 200,000 fans on three continents attended the four games, August 4-11.

Commissioner Tagliabue announced the NFL Teacher of the Month program in which the League furnishes grants and scholarships in recognition of teachers who provided a positive influence upon NFL players in elementary and secondary schools, September 20.

For the first time since 1957, every NFL club won at least one of its first four games, October 1.

The Super Bowl Most Valuable Player trophy was renamed the Pete Rozelle trophy, October 8.

1991

The New York Giants defeated Buffalo 20-19 in Super Bowl XXV to capture their second title in five years. The game was played before a sellout crowd of 73,813 at Tampa Stadium and became the first Super Bowl decided by one point, January 26. The ABC broadcast of the game was seen by more than 112-million people in the United States and was seen live or taped in 60 other countries.

NFL playoff games earned

the top television rating spot of the week for each week of the month-long playoffs, January 29.

New York businessman Robert Tisch purchased a 50 percent interest in the New York Giants from Mrs. Helen Mara Nugent and her children, Tim Mara and Maura Mara Concannon, February 2.

NFL clubs voted to continue a limited system of Instant Replay for the sixth consecutive year. The vote was 21-7, March 19.

The NFL launched the World League of American Football, the first sports league to operate on a weekly basis on two separate continents, March 23.

NFL Charities presented a $250,000 donation to the United Service Organization. The donation was the second largest single grant ever by NFL Charities, April 5.

Commissioner Tagliabue named Harold Henderson as Executive Vice President for Labor Relations and Chairman of the NFL Management Council Executive Committee, April 8.

NFL clubs approved a recommendation by the Expansion and Realignment Committee to add two teams for the 1994 season, resulting in six divisions of five teams each, May 22.

"NFL International Week" featured six 1990 playoff teams playing nationally televised games in London, Berlin, and Tokyo on July 28 and August 3-4. The games drew more than 150,000 fans.

Paul Brown, founder of the Cleveland Browns and Cincinnati Bengals, died at age 82, August 5.

NFL clubs approved a resolution establishing an international division. A three-year financial plan for the World League was approved by NFL clubs at a meeting in Dallas, October 23.

1992

The NFL agreed to provide a minimum of $2.5 million in financial support to the NFL Alumni Association and assistance to NFL Alumni-related programs. The agreement included contributions from NFL Charities to the Pre-59ers and Dire Need Programs for former players, January 25.

The Washington Redskins defeated the Buffalo Bills 37-24 in Super Bowl XXVI to capture their third world championship in 10 years, January 26. The game was played before a sellout crowd of 63,130 at the Hubert H. Humphrey Metrodome in Minneapolis and attracted the second largest television audience in Super Bowl history. The CBS broadcast was seen by more than 123 million people nationally, second only to the 127 million who viewed Super Bowl XX.

The use in officiating of a limited system of Instant Replay was not approved. The vote was 17-11 in favor of approval (21 votes were required). Instant Replay had been used for six consecutive years (1986-1991), March 18.

St. Louis businessman James Orthwein purchased controlling interest in the New England Patriots from Victor Kiam, May 11.

In a Harris Poll taken during the NFL offseason, professional football again was declared the nation's most popular sport. Professional football finished atop similar surveys conducted by Harris in 1985 and 1989, May 23.

NFL clubs accepted the report of the Expansion Committee at a league meeting in Pasadena. The report names five cities as finalists for the two expansion teams—Baltimore, Charlotte, Jacksonville, Memphis, and St. Louis, May 19.

At a league meeting in Dallas, NFL clubs approved a proposal by the World League Board of Directors to restructure the World League and place future emphasis on its international success, September 17.

NFL teams played their 16-game regular-season schedule over 18 weeks for the only time in league history.

1993

The NFL and lawyers for the players announced a settlement of various lawsuits and an agreement on the terms of a seven-year deal that included a new player system to be in place through the 1999 season, January 6.

Commissioner Tagliabue announced the establishment of the "NFL World Partnership Program" to develop amateur football internationally through a series of clinics conducted by former NFL players and coaches, January 14.

As part of Super Bowl XXVII, the NFL announced the creation of the first NFL Youth Education Town, a facility located in south central Los Angeles for inner city youth, January 25.

The Dallas Cowboys defeated the Buffalo Bills 52-17 in Super Bowl XXVII to capture their first NFL title since 1978. The game was played before a crowd of 98,374 at the Rose Bowl in Pasadena, California. The NBC broadcast of the game was the most watched program in television history and was seen by 133,400,000 people in the United States. The rating for the game was 45.1, the tenth highest for any televised sports event. The game also was seen live or taped in 101 other countries, January 31.

The NFL and the NFL Players Association officially signed a 7-year Collective Bargaining Agreement in Washington, D.C., which guarantees more than $1 billion in pension, health, and post-career benefits for current and retired players—the most extensive benefits plan in pro sports. It was the NFL's first CBA since the 1982 agreement expired in 1987, June 29.

NFL Enterprises, a newly formed division of the NFL responsible for NFL Films, home video, and special domestic and international television programming was announced, August 19.

NFL announced plans to allow fans, for the first time ever, to join players and coaches in selecting the annual AFC and NFC Pro Bowl teams, October 12.

NFL clubs unanimously awarded the league's twenty-ninth franchise to the Carolina Panthers and owner Jerry Richardson at a meeting in Chicago, October 26.

At the same meeting in Chicago, NFL clubs approved a plan to form a European league with joint venture partners, October 27.

Don Shula became the winningest coach in NFL history when Miami beat Philadelphia to give Shula his 325th victory, one more than George Halas, November 14.

NFL clubs awarded the league's thirtieth franchise to the Jacksonville Jaguars and owner Wayne Weaver at a meeting in Chicago, November 30.

The NFL announced new 4-year television agreements with NBC, ABC, ESPN, TNT, and NFL newcomer FOX, which took over the NFC package from CBS, December 18.

The NFL completed its new TV agreements by announcing that NBC would retain the rights to the AFC package, December 20.

1994

The Dallas Cowboys defeated the Buffalo Bills 30-13 in Super Bowl XXVIII to become the fifth team to win back-to-back Super Bowl titles. The game was viewed by the largest U.S. audience in television history—134.8 million people. The game's 45.5 rating was the highest for a Super Bowl since 1987 and the tenth highest-rated Super Bowl ever, January 30.

NFL clubs unanimously approved the transfer of the New England Patriots from James Orthwein to Robert Kraft at a meeting in Orlando, February 22.

In a move to increase offensive production, NFL clubs at the league's annual meeting in Orlando adopted a package of changes, including modifications in line play, chucking rules, and the roughing-the-passer rule, plus the adoption of the two-point conversion and moving the spot of the kickoff back to the 30-yard line, March 22.

NFL clubs approved the transfer of the majority interest in the Miami Dolphins from the Robbie family to H. Wayne Huizenga, March 23.

The NFL and FOX announced the formation of a joint venture to create a six-team World League to begin play in Europe in April, 1995, March 23.

The Carolina Panthers earned the right to select first in the 1995 NFL draft by winning a coin toss with the Jacksonville Jaguars. The Jaguars received the second selection in the 1995 draft, April 24.

NFL clubs approved the transfer of the Philadelphia Eagles from Norman Braman to Jeffrey Lurie, May 6.

The NFL launched "NFL Sunday Ticket," a new season subscription service for satellite television dish owners, June 1.

An all-time NFL record crowd of 112,376 attended the American Bowl game between Dallas and Houston in Mexico City. It concluded the biggest American Bowl series in NFL history with four games attracting a record 256,666 fans, August 15.

The NFL reached agreement on a new seven-year contract with its game officials, September 22.

The NFL Management Council and the NFL Players Association announced an agreement on the formulation and implementation of the most comprehensive drug and alcohol policy in sports, October 28.

At an NFL meeting in Chicago, Commissioner Tagliabue slotted the two new expansion teams into the AFC Central (Jacksonville Jaguars) and NFC West (Carolina Panthers) for the 1995 season only. He also appointed a special committee on realignment to make recommendations on the 1996 season and beyond, November 2.

1995

The San Francisco 49ers became the first team to win five Super Bowls when they defeated the San Diego Chargers 49-26 in Super Bowl XXIX at Joe Robbie Stadium in Miami, January 29.

Carolina and Jacksonville stocked their expansion rosters with a total of 66 players from other NFL teams in a veteran player allocation draft in New York, February 16.

CBS Radio and the NFL agreed to a new four-year contract for an annual 53-game package of games, continuing a relationship that spanned 15 of the past 17 years, February 22.

NFL clubs approved the transfer of the Tampa Bay Buccaneers from the estate of the late Hugh Culverhouse to South Florida businessman

Malcolm Glazer, March 13.

After a two-year hiatus, the World League of American Football returned to action with six teams in Europe, April 8.

The NFL became the first major sports league to establish a site on the Internet system of on-line computer communication, April 10.

The transfer of the Rams from Los Angeles to St. Louis was approved by a vote of the NFL clubs at a meeting in Dallas, April 12.

ABC's *NFL Monday Night Football* finished the 1994-95 television season as the fifth highest-rated show out of 146 with a 17.8 average rating, the highest finish in the 25-year history of the series, April 18.

The Frankfurt Galaxy defeated the Amsterdam Admirals 26-22 to win the 1995 World Bowl before a crowd of 23,847 in Amsterdam's Olympic Stadium, June 23.

The transfer of the Raiders from Los Angeles to Oakland was approved by a vote of the NFL clubs at a meeting in Chicago, July 22.

Jacksonville Municipal Stadium opened in Jacksonville, Florida before a sold-out crowd of more than 70,000 as the St. Louis Rams defeated the Jacksonville Jaguars 27-10 in their first preseason game, August 18.

NFL Charities and 50 NFL players donated $1 million to the United Negro College Fund in honor of the fiftieth anniversary of the UNCF and the integration of the modern NFL, September 15.

The Trans World Dome opened in St. Louis with a sold-out crowd of 65,598 as the Rams defeated the Carolina Panthers 28-17, November 12.

On the field, many significant records and milestones were achieved: Miami's Dan Marino surpassed Pro Football Hall of Famer Fran Tarkenton in four major passing categories—attempts, completions, yards, and touchdowns—to become the NFL's all-time career leader. San Francisco's Jerry Rice became the all-time reception and receiving-yardage leader.

1996

The Dallas Cowboys won their third Super Bowl title in four

years when they defeated the Pittsburgh Steelers 27-17 in Super Bowl XXX at Sun Devil Stadium in Tempe, Arizona. The game was viewed by the largest audience in U.S. television history—138.5 million people, January 28.

An agreement between the NFL and the city of Cleveland regarding the Cleveland Browns' relocation was approved by a vote of the NFL clubs, February 9. According to the agreement, the city of Cleveland retained the Browns' heritage and records, including the name, logo, colors, history, playing records, trophies, and memorabilia, and committed to building a new 72,000-seat stadium for a reactivated Browns' franchise to begin play there no later than 1999. Art Modell received approval to move his franchise to Baltimore and rename it.

The transfer of the Oilers from Houston to Nashville for the 1998 season was approved by a vote of the NFL clubs at a meeting in Atlanta, April 30.

The Scottish Claymores defeated the Frankfurt Galaxy 32-27 to win the 1996 World Bowl in front of 38,982 at Murrayfield Stadium in Edinburgh, Scotland, June 23.

The NFL returned to Baltimore when the new Baltimore Ravens defeated the Philadelphia Eagles 17-9 in a preseason game before a crowd of 63,804 at Memorial Stadium, August 3.

Ericsson Stadium opened in Charlotte, North Carolina with a crowd of 65,350 as the Carolina Panthers defeated the Chicago Bears 30-12 in a preseason game, August 3.

Former NFL Commissioner Pete Rozelle died at his home in Rancho Santa Fe, California. Rozelle, regarded as the premiere commissioner in sports history, led the NFL for 29 years, from 1960-1989, December 6.

1997

Indianapolis Colts owner Robert Irsay died from complications related to a stroke he suffered in 1995. Irsay acquired the club in 1972 when he traded his Los Angeles Rams to Carrol Rosenbloom for the Colts. He later moved

the Colts from Baltimore to Indianapolis in 1984, January 14.

The Green Bay Packers won their first NFL title in 29 years by defeating the New England Patriots 35-21 in Super Bowl XXXI at the Louisiana Superdome in New Orleans. The game was viewed by the fourth-largest audience in U.S. television history—128 million people, January 26.

The rules governing cross-ownership were modified, permitting NFL club owners to also own teams in other sports in their home market or markets without NFL teams. The vote was 24-5 (one abstention) in favor of approval, March 11.

Washington Redskins owner Jack Kent Cooke died at his home in Washington, D.C. Cooke became majority owner in 1974 and the Redskins won three Super Bowls under his leadership, April 6.

The Barcelona Dragons defeated the Rhein Fire 38-24 to win the 1997 World Bowl in front of 31,100 fans at Estadi Olimpic de Montjuic in Barcelona, Spain, June 22.

NFL clubs approved the transfer of the Seattle Seahawks from Ken Behring to Paul Allen, August 19.

Jack Kent Cooke Stadium opened in Raljon, Maryland with a crowd of 78,270 as the Washington Redskins defeated the Arizona Cardinals 19-13 in overtime, September 14.

The 10,000th regular-season game in NFL history was played when the Seattle Seahawks defeated the Tennessee Oilers 16-13 at the Kingdome in Seattle, October 5.

Atlanta Falcons owner Rankin Smith died of heart failure three days prior to his seventy-third birthday. Smith was the founder of the Falcons and was instrumental in bringing Super Bowls XXVIII and XXXIV to Atlanta, October 26.

1998

The NFL reached agreement on record eight-year television contracts with four networks. ABC (*NFL Monday Night Football*) and FOX (NFC) retained their previous rights, CBS took over the AFC package from NBC, and ESPN won the right to broadcast the entire Sunday night cable package, January 13.

The World League was renamed the NFL Europe League, January 22.

The Denver Broncos won their first Super Bowl by defeating the defending champion Green Bay Packers 31-24 in Super Bowl XXXII at Qualcomm Stadium in San Diego. The game tied Super Bowl XXVII for the third-largest audience in U.S. television history with 133.4 million viewers, January 25.

The NFL clubs approved an extension of the Collective Bargaining Agreement through 2003. The extended CBA also created a $100 million fund for youth football, March 22.

The NFL clubs unanimously approved an expansion team for Cleveland to fulfill the commitment to return the Browns to the field in 1999, March 23.

The Rhein Fire defeated the Frankfurt Galaxy 34-10 to win the 1998 World Bowl in front of 47,846 fans in Frankfurt's Waldstadion—the biggest crowd to witness a World Bowl since 1991, June 14.

NFL clubs approved the transfer of the Minnesota Vikings from a 10-man ownership group to Red McCombs, July 28.

The NFL Stadium at Camden Yards opened in Baltimore, Maryland before a crowd of 65,938 as the Baltimore Ravens defeated the Chicago Bears 19-14 in a preseason game, August 8.

Raymond James Stadium opened in Tampa, Florida before a crowd of 62,410 as the Tampa Bay Buccaneers defeated the Chicago Bears 27-15, September 20.

Tennessee Oilers owner Bud Adams announced the team will change its name to the Tennessee Titans following the 1998 season. The NFL announced that the name Oilers will be retired—a first in league history, November 14.

1999

The Denver Broncos won their second consecutive Super Bowl title by defeating the NFC champion Atlanta Falcons 34-19 in Super Bowl XXXIII at Pro Player Stadium in Miami. The game was viewed by 127.5 million viewers, the sixth most-watched program in U.S. television history, January 31.

Jim Pyne, a center allocated by the Detroit Lions, was the first selection of the Cleveland Browns in the 1999 NFL Expansion Draft. The Browns eventually selected 37 players, February 9.

CBS Radio/Westwood One agreed to a 3-year extension of their exclusive national radio rights to NFL games, March 11.

By a vote of 28-3, the owners adopted an instant replay system as an officiating aid for the 1999 season, March 17.

New York Jets owner Leon Hess died from complications of a blood disease. Hess had been involved in the ownership of the Jets since 1963 and was sole owner of the club since 1984, May 9.

A group led by Washington area businessman Daniel Snyder is approved by NFL clubs as the new owner of the Washington Redskins at a league meeting in Atlanta, May 25.

The Frankfurt Galaxy became the first team in NFL Europe League history to win a second World Bowl by defeating the Barcelona Dragons 38-24 at Rheinstadion, in Düsseldorf, Germany, June 27.

The Cleveland Browns returned to the field for the first time since 1995 and defeated the Dallas Cowboys 20-17 in overtime in the annual Hall of Fame Game at Canton, Ohio, August 9.

Cleveland Browns Stadium opened in Cleveland, Ohio before a crowd of 71,398 as the Minnesota Vikings defeated the Browns in a preseason game, 24-17, August 21.

Adelphia Coliseum opened in Nashville, Tennessee before a crowd of 65,729 with the Tennessee Titans defeating the Atlanta Falcons 17-3 in a preseason game, August 26.

Houston, Texas and owner Robert McNair were awarded the NFL's thirty-second franchise in a vote of the NFL clubs at a league meeting in Atlanta. The team will begin play in 2002. The NFL clubs also voted to realign into eight divisions of four teams each for the 2002 season, October 6.

Walter Payton, the NFL's all-time leading rusher, died of liver cancer at the age of 45.

Payton played for the Chicago Bears from 1975-1987 and rushed for an NFL-record 16,726 yards, November 1.

Former NFL Commissioner Pete Rozelle, who guided a still-developing league to its position today as America's most popular sport, was named by *The Sporting News* as the most powerful person in sports in the 20th Century, December 15.

2000

New York businessman Robert Wood Johnson IV was approved by NFL clubs as the new owner of the New York Jets at a league meeting, January 18.

The St. Louis Rams won their first Super Bowl by defeating the AFC champion Tennessee Titans 23-16 in Super Bowl XXXIV at the Georgia Dome in Atlanta. The game was viewed by 130.7 million viewers, the fifth most-watched program in U.S. television history, January 30.

For the first time in league history, paid attendance topped 16 million for the regular season and more than 65,000 per game, an increase of 1,300 per game over 1998. Paid attendance for all NFL games increased in 1999 for the third year in a row and was the highest ever in the 80-year history of the league. It marked the first time in league history that the 20-million paid attendance mark was reached for all games in a season, March 27.

The Rhein Fire won their second World Bowl in three years, defeating the Scottish Claymores 13-10 to win World Bowl 2000 in front of 35,680 at Frankfurt's Waldstadion, June 25.

More than 100 of the 136 living members of the Pro Football Hall of Fame gathered to celebrate Pro Football's Greatest Reunion in Canton, Ohio, July 28-31.

Paul Brown Stadium opened in Cincinnati, Ohio with a crowd of 56,180 as the Cincinnati Bengals defeated the Chicago Bears 24-20 in a preseason game, August 19.

Minnesota's Gary Anderson converted a 21-yard field goal against Buffalo to pass George Blanda as the NFL's all-time scoring leader with 2,004 points, October 22.

San Francisco's Terrell Owens set a single-game receiving record with 20 receptions (283 yards) against Chicago, surpassing the previous mark of 18 by Tom Fears of the Los Angeles Rams in 1950, December 17.

2001

NFL clubs approved additional league-wide revenue sharing at a special league meeting in Dallas. The teams agreed to pool the visiting team share of gate receipts for all preseason and regular-season games and divide the pool equally starting in 2002, January 17.

The Baltimore Ravens won their first Super Bowl by defeating the NFC champion New York Giants 34-7 in Super Bowl XXXV at Raymond James Stadium in Tampa. The game was witnessed by 131.2 million viewers, the fifth most-watched program in U.S. television history, January 28.

The *Sports Business Daily* named NFL Commissioner Paul Tagliabue the 2000 Sports Industrialist of the Year, February 28.

NFL owners unanimously approved a realignment plan for the league starting in 2002. With the addition of the Houston Texans, the league's 32 teams will be divided into eight four-team divisions. Seven clubs change divisions, and the Seattle Seahawks change conferences, moving from the AFC to the NFC. A new scheduling format ensures that every team meets every other team in the league at least once every four years, May 22.

The Berlin Thunder won their first World Bowl, defeating the Barcelona Dragons 24-17 to win World Bowl IX in front of 32,116 at Amsterdam ArenA, June 30.

Heinz Field opened in Pittsburgh, Pennsylvania before a crowd of 57,829 with the Pittsburgh Steelers defeating the Detroit Lions 20-7 in a preseason game; and INVESCO Field at Mile High opened in Denver, Colorado before a crowd of 74,063 with the Denver Broncos defeating the New Orleans Saints 31-24 in a preseason game, August 25.

President George W. Bush became the first United States

President to be involved in an NFL regular-season pregame coin toss as he helped kick off the 2001 season from the White House. Via satellite, President Bush tossed the coin for the 10 regular-season games that started at 1:00 P.M. ET, September 9.

In the wake of the September 11 terrorist attacks, Commissioner Paul Tagliabue postponed the games scheduled for September 16-17, September 13.

The league's 16-game regular season was retained when the postponed Week 2 games were rescheduled for the weekend of January 6-7, September 18.

The NFL and its game officials agreed to a new six-year Collective Bargaining Agreement, ending a two-week lockout of the regular officials, who returned to work on September 23, September 19.

The NFL announced that the league's prohibition of anabolic steroids and related substances had been strengthened to include supplements containing ephedrine and other high-risk supplements, September 27.

The NFL announced that the Super Bowl would be rescheduled from January 27 to February 3 in order to retain the full playoff format for the 2002 season. It will be the first Super Bowl played in February, October 3.

President Bush designated Super Bowl XXXVI as a "National Special Security Event," allowing all security for the game to be coordinated by the Secret Service, November 26.

2002

The NFL and the NFL Players Association agreed to a fourth extension of the 1993 Collective Bargaining Agreement through 2007, January 7.

In an AFC Wild Card matchup, the Oakland Raiders defeated the New York Jets 38-24 in the NFL's first-ever prime-time playoff game, January 12.

In a special meeting in New Orleans, NFL owners voted unanimously to approve the purchase of the Atlanta Falcons to Home Depot co-founder Arthur Blank, February 2.

The New England Patriots won their first Super Bowl by defeating the NFC champion St. Louis Rams 20-17 in Super Bowl XXXVI at the Louisiana Superdome in New Orleans. The game marked the first time in Super Bowl history that the winning points came on the final play, a 48-yard field goal by Patriots kicker Adam Vinatieri. Super Bowl XXXVI was viewed by 131.7 million viewers, the fifth-most watched program in U.S. television history, February 3.

Tony Boselli, a five-time Pro Bowl tackle allocated by the Jacksonville Jaguars, was the first selection of the Houston Texans in the 2002 NFL Expansion Draft. The Texans selected 19 players, February 18.

The NFL and Westwood One/CBS Radio Sports announced the renewal of a multiyear agreement for Westwood One/CBS Radio Sports to continue as the exclusive network radio home of the NFL, April 9.

NFL Europe kicked off its tenth season with a record 254 players allocated by NFL clubs, April 13-14.

The Berlin Thunder became the first team to win consecutive World Bowls, defeating the Rhein Fire 26-20 to win World Bowl X in front of 53,109 fans at Rheinstadion, June 22.

Seahawks Stadium opened in Seattle, Washington with an attendance of 52,902 fans as the Indianapolis Colts defeated the Seattle Seahawks 28-10 in a preseason game, August 10.

Gillette Stadium opened in Foxboro, Massachusetts with a crowd of 68,436 fans as the New England Patriots defeated the Philadelphia Eagles 16-15 in a preseason game, August 17.

Reliant Stadium opened in Houston, Texas with 69,432 fans in attendance, the largest non-Super Bowl crowd to ever watch an NFL game in Houston as the Miami Dolphins defeated the Houston Texans 24-3 in a preseason game, August 24.

For the first time, the NFL season kicked off on a Thursday night in prime time as the San Francisco 49ers defeated the New York Giants 16-13 at Giants Stadium. The game

was preceded by "NFL Kickoff Live From Times Square," presented by New York City and the NFL, a football and music festival honoring the resilient spirit of New York and America, September 5.

Week 1 of the 2002 season produced the highest-scoring and most competitive Kickoff Weekend in NFL history. The 16 games averaged 49.3 points per game. A total of 788 points and 89 touchdowns were scored, the most in league history for an opening weekend. Eleven of the 16 games were decided by one score (eight points or less), a Kickoff Weekend record, September 5-9.

Johnny Unitas, the legendary quarterback for the Baltimore Colts and a Pro Football Hall of Fame member, died of a heart attack at the age of 69, September 11.

Oakland Raiders wide receiver Jerry Rice became the all-time leader in yards from scrimmage, surpassing Pro Football Hall of Fame running back Walter Payton (21,281 yards), September 29.

Cleveland Browns owner Al Lerner, the NFL Finance Committee Chairman and Chairman and CEO of MBNA Corporation, died at the age of 69, October 23.

Dallas Cowboys running back Emmitt Smith became the NFL's all-time rushing leader, surpassing Pro Football Hall of Fame running back Walter Payton (16,726 yards), October 27.

The NFL and NFLPA announced the creation of USA Football, the first national advocacy organization representing all levels of amateur football, December 5.

The 2002 season concluded with 25 overtime games, the most in NFL history, December 30.

2003

The Tampa Bay Buccaneers won their first Super Bowl by defeating the AFC champion Oakland Raiders 48-21 in Super Bowl XXXVII at Qualcomm Stadium in San Diego. The game was witnessed by 138.9 million viewers, making Super Bowl XXXVII the most-watched program in U.S. television history, January 26.

Chicago Bears chairman emeritus Edward W. McCaskey died at the age of 83, April 8.

The Frankfurt Galaxy became the first team to win three World Bowls, defeating the Rhein Fire 35-16 to win World Bowl XI in front of 28,138 fans at Hampden Park, June 14.

Tex Schramm, the legendary team president and general manager of the Dallas Cowboys and a member of the Pro Football Hall of Fame, died at the age of 83, July 15.

Lincoln Financial Field opened in Philadelphia, Pennsylvania with an attendance of 66,279 fans as the New England Patriots defeated the Philadelphia Eagles 24-12 in a preseason game, August 22.

A renovated Lambeau Field opened in Green Bay, Wisconsin with a crowd of 69,831 fans as the Carolina Panthers defeated the Green Bay Packers 20-7 in a preseason game, August 23.

A renovated Soldier Field opened in Chicago, Illinois with an attendance of 61,500 fans as the Green Bay Packers defeated the Chicago Bears 38-23 in a regular season game on ABC's *NFL Monday Night Football*, September 29.

NFL Network, the first 24-hour, year-round television channel dedicated to the NFL and the sport of football, launched on DirecTV, November 4.

2004

The New England Patriots won their second Super Bowl in three years by defeating the NFC champion Carolina Panthers 32-29 in Super Bowl XXXVIII at Reliant Stadium in Houston. The game was witnessed by 144.4 million viewers, making Super Bowl XXXVIII the most-watched program in U.S. television history, February 1.

By a vote of 29-3, NFL owners extended the instant replay system for another five seasons through 2008, March 30.

Steve Bisciotti took over as the controlling owner of the Baltimore Ravens, succeeding Art Modell, who operated the franchise for 43 years, April 8.

Former Arizona Cardinals safety Pat Tillman was killed in

a firefight while on combat patrol with the U.S. Army Rangers in Afghanistan, April 22.

A federal appeals court formally ruled in favor of the NFL's draft eligibility rule in Maurice Clarett's lawsuit, citing federal labor policy in permitting the NFL and the Players Association to set rules for when players can enter the league, May 24.

The Berlin Thunder defeated the Frankfurt Galaxy 30-24 to win World Bowl XII in front of 35,413 fans at Arena Auf-Schalke, June 12.

The New England Patriots defeated the New York Jets 13-7 for their NFL-record 18th consecutive regular-season victory, October 24.

The NFL reached an agreement on six-year contract extensions with two of its network television partners—CBS and FOX—to run through the 2011 season, November 8.

The NFL and DirecTV announced a five-year extension on the NFL Sunday Ticket subscription television package to run through the 2010 season, November 8.

NFL Europe named the Hamburg Sea Devils as the league's newest team, November 24.

2005

Indianapolis Colts quarterback Peyton Manning set the NFL single-season record with 49 touchdown passes, January 2.

The New England Patriots became the second team in NFL history to win three Super Bowls in four seasons by defeating the Philadelphia Eagles 24-21 in Super Bowl XXXIX at ALLTEL Stadium in Jacksonville. The game was witnessed by 133.7 million viewers, making Super Bowl XXXIX the fifth-most watched program in U.S. television history, February 6.

The Pat Tillman USO Center opened in Afghanistan. The NFL donated $250,000 to the USO to honor the memory of the former Arizona Cardinals player who died in Afghanistan while serving in the U.S. Army, April 1.

The NFL reached long-term agreements for its Sunday and Monday primetime TV pack-

ages. NBC returned to the NFL by acquiring the Sunday night package for six years (2006-2011). ESPN agreed on an eight-year deal to televise *Monday Night Football* from 2006-2013, April 18.

The NFL strengthened its steroids program by adopting the Olympic testosterone testing standard, tripling the number of times a player can be randomly tested during the offseason from two to six, adding substances to the list of banned substances, and putting new language in the policy to allow for testing of designer drugs and other substances that may have evaded detection, April 27.

NFL owners voted unanimously to approve the sale of the Minnesota Vikings to real-estate developer Zygi Wilf, May 25.

NFL owners awarded Super Bowl XLIII, to be played on February 1, 2009 to Tampa, May 25.

The Amsterdam Admirals defeated the Berlin Thunder 27-21 to win World Bowl XIII in front of 35,134 fans at LTU Arena in Düsseldrof, Germany, June 11.

The NFL designated September 18-19 as "Hurricane Relief Weekend," which concluded with a telethon in conjunction with a Monday Night Football doubleheader on ABC and ESPN. The New York Giants-New Orleans Saints game, originally scheduled for the Louisiana Superdome, was moved to Giants Stadium following Hurricane Katrina. In total, the NFL, its owners, teams, players, and fans contributed $21 million to aid the Hurricane Katrina rebuilding effort, September 19.

An NFL record 103,467 fans attended the Arizona Cardinals' 31-14 victory over the San Francisco 49ers at Mexico City's Azteca Stadium, the first-ever regular-season NFL game played outside the United States, October 2.

Wellington Mara, the New York Giants' president and co-chief executive officer, died at the age of 89, October 25.

Preston Robert Tisch, the Giants' chairman and co-chief executive officer, died at the age of 79, November 15.

2006

The NFL announced that NFL Network would begin airing a "Road To The Playoffs" package of eight primetime regular season NFL games starting in 2006, January 28.

The Pittsburgh Steelers won their fifth Super Bowl, defeating the Seattle Seahawks 21-10 in Super Bowl XL at Ford Field in Detroit, Michigan. The game was witnessed by 141.1 million viewers, making it the second-most watched program in U.S. television history, February 5.

The NFL clubs approved an extension of the Collective Bargaining Agreement through 2012, March 8.

Commissioner Tagliabue announced his decision to retire by the end of July. The NFL enjoyed an era of unrivaled prosperity in the Tagliabue Era, including labor peace throughout his 17-year tenure, March 20.

NFL clubs unanimously decided to return the name of the official game ball to "The Duke" in honor of the late New York Giants owner Wellington Mara, March 27.

The Amsterdam Admirals defeated the Berlin Thunder 22-7 to win World Bowl XIV in front of 36,286 fans at LTU Arena in Düsseldorf, Germany, May 27.

Roger Goodell became the eighth chief executive of the NFL on August 8 when he was chosen to succeed Paul Tagliabue as commissioner by a unanimous vote of the clubs at a three-day meeting in Chicago, Illinois. The transfer from Commissioner Tagliabue to Commissioner Goodell took place at 6:00 A.M. on Friday, September 1.

Cardinals Stadium opened in Glendale, Arizona with a crowd of 63,400 fans on August 12 as the Arizona Cardinals defeated the Pittsburgh Steelers 21-13 in a preseason game. The facility was later renamed University of Phoenix Stadium on September 26.

President George W. Bush signed into law HR 4954, which included the Internet Gambling Prohibition and Enforcement Act. The bill prohibits online gamblers from using credit cards, checks and electronic fund transfers to place and settle bets,

strengthening enforcement of federal and state gambling laws that had been evaded by overseas gambling operations using the Internet, October 13.

NFL owners approved a resolution to stage a limited number of international regular-season games—up to two per season—beginning in 2007 and continuing through 2011, October 24.

The NFL Network broadcast its first-ever regular-season game as the Kansas City Chiefs defeated the Denver Broncos 19-10 at Arrowhead Stadium on Thanksgiving night, November 23.

San Diego Chargers running back LaDainian Tomlinson set the NFL single-season record for touchdowns with 29 on December 10. He finished the season with 31 touchdowns and also set a single-season record for points with 186.

Lamar Hunt, founder of the Kansas City Chiefs and the American Football League, died at the age of 74, December 13.

2007

The Indianapolis Colts won their second Super Bowl, defeating the Chicago Bears 29-17 in Super Bowl XLI at Dolphin Stadium in South Florida. The game was witnessed by 139.8 million viewers, making it the third-most watched program in U.S. television history, February 4.

NFL clubs approved additional league-wide revenue sharing at a league meeting in Phoenix, Arizona. The teams agreed to redistribute up to $430 million over a four-year span, retroactive to 2006, March 26.

The NFL announced changes to its long-standing personal conduct policy and programs for players, coaches, and other team and league employees. The modifications focus on expanded educational and support programs in addition to increased levels of discipline for violations of the policy, April 10.

The NFL, NFL Players Association, NFL Retired Players Association, NFL Alumni Association, NFL Charities and Pro Football Hall of Fame formed the first-ever Alliance to coordinate medical support services for former players, May 22.

The Hamburg Sea Devils defeated the Frankfurt Galaxy 37-28 to win World Bowl XV in front of 48,125 fans at Commerzbank-Arena in Frankfurt, Germany, June 23.

The NFL announced it will focus its international business strategy on reaching the widest possible global audience, including the staging of international regular-season games, and discontinued NFL Europa after 15 seasons of operation, June 29.

NFL owners unanimously approved $10 million in additional Alliance funding for retired players to help pay for joint replacement surgeries and other medical assistance, supplementing the initial $7 million committed in July by Alliance members, October 24.

The New York Giants defeated the Miami Dolphins 13-10 at London's in front of 81,176 fans at Wembley Stadium in the first regular-season game played outside of North America, October 28.

On the field in the 2007 season, many significant records and milestones were achieved: Green Bay quarterback Brett Favre surpassed Pro Football Hall of Famer Dan Marino in both passing categories—touchdowns and yards—to become the NFL's all-time career leader. Patriots quarterback Tom Brady set the single-season record with 50 touchdown passes, including 23 to wide receiver Randy Moss—also a record. New England, which became the first team ever to finish 16-0 in the regular season, scored a record 589 points.

2008
The NFL, United States Olympic Committee, United States Anti-Doping Agency and MLB announced a partnership to form a clean competition anti-doping research collaborative, January 10.

Georgia Frontiere, majority owner of the St. Louis Rams, died at the age of 80, January 18.

The NFL announced it will stage a regular-season game in the United Kingdom during each of the next three seasons, beginning with the New Orleans Saints hosting the San Diego Chargers on October 26, 2008 at London's Wembley Stadium, February 1.

The New York Giants scored with 35 seconds remaining to win their third Super Bowl, defeating the New England Patriots 17-14 in Super Bowl XLII at University of Phoenix Stadium in Glendale, Arizona. The game was witnessed by 148.3 million viewers, making it the most watched program in U.S. television history, February 3.

The NFL set an all-time paid attendance record in 2007 for the sixth consecutive season. Attendance for all 2007 games was 22,256,502, an increase of 56,790 over the previous mark. The Washington Redskins set an all-time NFL regular-season home paid attendance record of 711,471 for eight games, breaking their own record of 708,852 in 2006.

NFL owners voted unanimously to approve the sale of 50 percent of the Miami Dolphins, Dolphin Stadium, and the surrounding developable land to Stephen M. Ross. Wayne Huizenga holds the other 50 percent and remains operating owner, April 1.

NFL COMMISSIONERS AND PRESIDENTS*
1920 ....Jim Thorpe, President
1921-39....Joe Carr, President
1939-41 .Carl Storck, President
1941-46 ....Elmer Layden, Commissioner
1946-1959 ....Bert Bell, Commissioner
1960-1989.........Pete Rozelle, Commissioner
1989-2006 .....Paul Tagliabue, Commissioner
2006-present ..Roger Goodell, Commissioner
*NFL treasurer Austin Gunsel served as president in the office of the commissioner following the death of Bert Bell (Oct. 11, 1959) until the election of Pete Rozelle (Jan. 26, 1960).

2007

AMERICAN CONFERENCE

East Division

	W	L	T	Pct.	Pts.	OP
New England#	16	0	0	1.000	589	274
Buffalo	7	9	0	.438	252	354
New York Jets	4	12	0	.250	268	355
Miami	1	15	0	.063	267	437

North Division

	W	L	T	Pct.	Pts.	OP
Pittsburgh	10	6	0	.625	393	269
Cleveland	10	6	0	.625	402	382
Cincinnati	7	9	0	.438	380	385
Baltimore	5	11	0	.313	275	384

South Division

	W	L	T	Pct.	Pts.	OP
Indianapolis	13	3	0	.813	450	262
Jacksonville*	11	5	0	.688	411	304
Tennessee*	10	6	0	.625	301	297
Houston	8	8	0	.500	379	384

West Division

	W	L	T	Pct.	Pts.	OP
San Diego	11	5	0	.688	412	284
Denver	7	9	0	.438	320	409
Kansas City	4	12	0	.250	226	335
Oakland	4	12	0	.250	283	398

NATIONAL CONFERENCE

East Division

	W	L	T	Pct.	Pts.	OP
Dallas#	13	3	0	.813	455	325
New York Giants*	10	6	0	.625	373	351
Washington*	9	7	0	.563	334	310
Philadelphia	8	8	0	.500	336	300

North Division

	W	L	T	Pct.	Pts.	OP
Green Bay	13	3	0	.813	435	291
Minnesota	8	8	0	.500	365	311
Detroit	7	9	0	.438	346	444
Chicago	7	9	0	.438	334	348

South Division

	W	L	T	Pct.	Pts.	OP
Tampa Bay	9	7	0	.563	334	270
Carolina	7	9	0	.438	267	347
New Orleans	7	9	0	.438	379	388
Atlanta	4	12	0	.250	259	414

West Division

	W	L	T	Pct.	Pts.	OP
Seattle	10	6	0	.625	393	291
Arizona	8	8	0	.500	404	399
San Francisco	5	11	0	.313	219	364
St. Louis	3	13	0	.188	263	438

Wild Card qualifier for playoffs; #Top playoff seed in conference
Pittsburgh finished ahead of Cleveland based on head-to-head sweep (2-0). Tennessee finished ahead of Cleveland based on better record vs. common opponents (4-1 to Browns' 3-2). Kansas City finished ahead of Oakland based on better record vs. common opponents (2-10 to Raiders' 1-11). Dallas finished ahead of Green Bay based on head-to-head victory. Detroit finished ahead of Chicago based on head-to-head sweep (2-0). Carolina finished ahead of New Orleans based on better record (7-5 to Saints' 6-6).
Wild Card Playoff: Jacksonville 31, PITTSBURGH 29
  SAN DIEGO 17, Tennessee 6
Divisional Playoff: NEW ENGLAND 31, Jacksonville 20
  San Diego 28, INDIANAPOLIS 24
AFC Championship: NEW ENGLAND 21, San Diego 12
Wild Card Playoff: SEATTLE 35, Washington 14
  N.Y. Giants 24, TAMPA BAY 14
Divisional Playoff: GREEN BAY 42, Seattle 20
  N.Y. Giants 21, DALLAS 17
NFC Championship: N.Y. Giants 23, GREEN BAY 20 (OT)
Super Bowl XLII: N.Y. Giants (NFC) 17, New England (AFC) 14
  at University of Phoenix Stadium, Glendale, Arizona

In Past Standings section, home teams in playoff games are indicated by capital letters.

Playoff Seeds

AFC	NFC
1. New England	1. Dallas
2. Indianapolis	2. Green Bay
3. San Diego	3. Seattle
4. Pittsburgh	4. Tampa Bay
5. Jacksonville	**5. N.Y. Giants**
6. Tennessee	6. Washington

2006

AMERICAN CONFERENCE

East Division

	W	L	T	Pct.	Pts.	OP
New England	12	4	0	.750	385	237
New York Jets*	10	6	0	.625	316	295
Buffalo	7	9	0	.438	300	311
Miami	6	10	0	.375	260	283

North Division

	W	L	T	Pct.	Pts.	OP
Baltimore	13	3	0	.813	353	201
Cincinnati	8	8	0	.500	373	331
Pittsburgh	8	8	0	.500	353	315
Cleveland	4	12	0	.250	238	356

South Division

	W	L	T	Pct.	Pts.	OP
Indianapolis	12	4	0	.750	427	360
Tennessee	8	8	0	.500	324	400
Jacksonville	8	8	0	.500	371	274
Houston	6	10	0	.375	267	366

West Division

	W	L	T	Pct.	Pts.	OP
San Diego#	14	2	0	.875	492	303
Kansas City*	9	7	0	.563	331	315
Denver	9	7	0	.563	319	305
Oakland	2	14	0	.125	168	332

NATIONAL CONFERENCE

East Division

	W	L	T	Pct.	Pts.	OP
Philadelphia	10	6	0	.625	398	328
Dallas*	9	7	0	.563	425	350
New York Giants*	8	8	0	.500	355	362
Washington	5	11	0	.313	307	376

North Division

	W	L	T	Pct.	Pts.	OP
Chicago#	13	3	0	.813	427	255
Green Bay	8	8	0	.500	301	366
Minnesota	6	10	0	.375	282	327
Detroit	3	13	0	.188	305	398

South Division

	W	L	T	Pct.	Pts.	OP
New Orleans	10	6	0	.625	413	322
Carolina	8	8	0	.500	270	305
Atlanta	7	9	0	.438	292	328
Tampa Bay	4	12	0	.250	211	353

West Division

	W	L	T	Pct.	Pts.	OP
Seattle	9	7	0	.563	335	341
St. Louis	8	8	0	.500	367	381
San Francisco	7	9	0	.438	298	412
Arizona	5	11	0	.313	314	389

Wild Card qualifier for playoffs; #Top playoff seed in conference
Indianapolis finished ahead of New England based on head-to-head victory. Cincinnati finished ahead of Pittsburgh based on better division record (4-2 to Steelers' 3-3). Tennessee finished ahead of Jacksonville based on better division record (4-2 to Jaguars' 2-4). Kansas City finished ahead of Denver based on better division record (4-2 to Broncos' 3-3). New Orleans finished ahead of Philadelphia based on head-to-head victory. New York Giants finished ahead of Carolina and St. Louis based on better conference record (Giants' 7-5 to Panthers' 6-6 and Rams' 6-6) and ahead of Green Bay based on strength of victory (.422 to Packers' .383).
Wild Card Playoff: INDIANAPOLIS 23, Kansas City 8
  NEW ENGLAND 37, N.Y. Jets 16
Divisional Playoff: Indianapolis 15, BALTIMORE 6
  New England 24, SAN DIEGO 21
AFC Championship: INDIANAPOLIS 38, New England 34
Wild Card Playoff: SEATTLE 21, Dallas 20
  PHILADELPHIA 23, N.Y. Giants 20
Divisional Playoff: NEW ORLEANS 27, Philadelphia 24
  CHICAGO 27, Seattle 24 (OT)
NFC Championship: CHICAGO 39, New Orleans 14
Super Bowl XLI: Indianapolis (AFC) 29, Chicago (NFC) 17
  at Dolphin Stadium, Miami, Florida

Playoff Seeds

AFC	NFC
1. San Diego	**1. Chicago**
2. Baltimore	2. New Orleans
3. Indianapolis	3. Philadelphia
4. New England	4. Seattle
5. N.Y. Jets	5. Dallas
6. Kansas City	6. N.Y. Giants

2005

AMERICAN CONFERENCE

East Division

	W	L	T	Pct.	Pts.	OP
New England	10	6	0	.625	379	338
Miami	9	7	0	.563	318	317
Buffalo	5	11	0	.313	271	367
N.Y. Jets	4	12	0	.250	240	355

North Division

	W	L	T	Pct.	Pts.	OP
Cincinnati	11	5	0	.688	421	350
Pittsburgh*	11	5	0	.688	389	258
Baltimore	6	10	0	.375	265	299
Cleveland	6	10	0	.375	232	301

South Division

	W	L	T	Pct.	Pts.	OP
Indianapolis#	14	2	0	.875	439	247
Jacksonville*	12	4	0	.750	361	269
Tennessee	4	12	0	.250	299	421
Houston	2	14	0	.125	260	431

West Division

	W	L	T	Pct.	Pts.	OP
Denver	13	3	0	.813	395	258
Kansas City	10	6	0	.625	403	325
San Diego	9	7	0	.563	418	312
Oakland	4	12	0	.250	290	383

NATIONAL CONFERENCE

East Division

	W	L	T	Pct.	Pts.	OP
N.Y. Giants	11	5	0	.688	422	314
Washington*	10	6	0	.625	359	293
Dallas	9	7	0	.563	325	308
Philadelphia	6	10	0	.375	310	388

North Division

	W	L	T	Pct.	Pts.	OP
Chicago	11	5	0	.688	260	202
Minnesota	9	7	0	.563	306	344
Detroit	5	11	0	.313	254	345
Green Bay	4	12	0	.250	298	344

South Division

	W	L	T	Pct.	Pts.	OP
Tampa Bay	11	5	0	.688	300	274
Carolina*	11	5	0	.688	391	259
Atlanta	8	8	0	.500	351	341
New Orleans	3	13	0	.188	235	398

West Division

	W	L	T	Pct.	Pts.	OP
Seattle#	13	3	0	.813	452	271
St. Louis	6	10	0	.375	363	429
Arizona	5	11	0	.313	311	387
San Francisco	4	12	0	.250	239	428

*Wild Card qualifier for playoffs; #Top playoff seed in conference
Cincinnati finished ahead of Pittsburgh based on better division record (5-1 to Steelers' 4-2). Baltimore finished ahead of Cleveland based on better division record (2-4 to Browns' 1-5). Tampa Bay finished ahead of Carolina based on better division record (5-1 to Panthers' 4-2). Chicago finished ahead of Tampa Bay, and Tampa Bay finished ahead of the New York Giants, based on better conference record (Bears' 10-2 to Buccaneers' 9-3 to Giants' 8-4).

Wild Card playoff: NEW ENGLAND 28, Jacksonville 3
 Pittsburgh 31, CINCINNATI 17
Divisional playoff: DENVER 27, New England 13
 Pittsburgh 21, INDIANAPOLIS 18
AFC Championship: Pittsburgh 34, DENVER 17
Wild Card playoffs: Washington 17, TAMPA BAY 10
 Carolina 23, NEW YORK GIANTS 0
Divisional playoff: SEATTLE 20, Washington 10
 Carolina 29, CHICAGO 21
NFC Championship: SEATTLE 34, Carolina 14
Super Bowl XL: Pittsburgh (AFC) 21, Seattle (NFC) 10
 at Ford Field, Detroit, Michigan

Playoff Seeds

AFC	NFC
1. Indianapolis	1. Seattle
2. Denver	2. Chicago
3. Cincinnati	3. Tampa Bay
4. New England	4. New York Giants
5. Jacksonville	5. Carolina
6. Pittsburgh	6. Washington

2004

AMERICAN CONFERENCE

East Division

	W	L	T	Pct.	Pts.	OP
New England	14	2	0	.875	437	260
N.Y. Jets*	10	6	0	.625	333	261
Buffalo	9	7	0	.563	395	284
Miami	4	12	0	.250	275	354

North Division

	W	L	T	Pct.	Pts.	OP
Pittsburgh#	15	1	0	.938	372	251
Baltimore	9	7	0	.563	317	268
Cincinnati	8	8	0	.500	374	372
Cleveland	4	12	0	.250	276	390

South Division

	W	L	T	Pct.	Pts.	OP
Indianapolis	12	4	0	.750	522	351
Jacksonville	9	7	0	.563	261	280
Houston	7	9	0	.438	309	339
Tennessee	5	11	0	.313	344	439

West Division

	W	L	T	Pct.	Pts.	OP
San Diego	12	4	0	.750	446	313
Denver*	10	6	0	.625	381	304
Kansas City	7	9	0	.438	483	435
Oakland	5	11	0	.313	320	442

NATIONAL CONFERENCE

East Division

	W	L	T	Pct.	Pts.	OP
Philadelphia#	13	3	0	.813	386	260
N.Y. Giants	6	10	0	.375	303	347
Dallas	6	10	0	.375	293	405
Washington	6	10	0	.375	240	265

North Division

	W	L	T	Pct.	Pts.	OP
Green Bay	10	6	0	.625	424	380
Minnesota*	8	8	0	.500	405	395
Detroit	6	10	0	.375	296	350
Chicago	5	11	0	.313	231	331

South Division

	W	L	T	Pct.	Pts.	OP
Atlanta	11	5	0	.688	340	337
New Orleans	8	8	0	.500	348	405
Carolina	7	9	0	.438	355	339
Tampa Bay	5	11	0	.313	301	304

West Division

	W	L	T	Pct.	Pts.	OP
Seattle	9	7	0	.563	371	373
St. Louis*	8	8	0	.500	319	392
Arizona	6	10	0	.375	284	322
San Francisco	2	14	0	.125	259	452

*Wild Card qualifier for playoffs; #Top playoff seed in conference
Indianapolis finished ahead of San Diego based on head-to-head victory. N.Y. Jets finished ahead of Denver based on better record vs. common opponents (5-0 to Broncos' 3-2). St. Louis finished ahead of New Orleans and Minnesota based on best conference record (7-5 to Saints' 6-6 to Vikings' 5-7), and Minnesota finished ahead of New Orleans based on head-to-head victory. N.Y. Giants finished ahead of Dallas and Washington based on better head-to-head record (3-1 to Cowboys' 2-2 to Redskins' 1-3), and Dallas finished ahead of Washington based on head-to-head sweep (2-0).

Wild Card playoffs: N.Y. Jets 20, SAN DIEGO 17 (OT)
 INDIANAPOLIS 49, Denver 24
Divisional playoffs: PITTSBURGH 20, N.Y. Jets 17 (OT)
 NEW ENGLAND 20, Indianapolis 3
AFC Championship: New England 41, PITTSBURGH 27
Wild Card playoffs: St. Louis 27, SEATTLE 20
 Minnesota 31, GREEN BAY 17
Divisional playoffs: ATLANTA 47, St. Louis 17
 PHILADELPHIA 27, Minnesota 14
NFC Championship: PHILADELPHIA 27, Atlanta 10
Super Bowl XXXIX: New England (AFC) 24, Philadelphia (NFC) 21
 at Alltel Stadium, Jacksonville, Florida

Playoff Seeds

AFC	NFC
1. Pittsburgh	1. Philadelphia
2. New England	2. Atlanta
3. Indianapolis	3. Green Bay
4. San Diego	4. Seattle
5. N.Y. Jets	5. St. Louis
6. Denver	6. Minnesota

2003

AMERICAN CONFERENCE
East Division

	W	L	T	Pct.	Pts.	OP
New England#	14	2	0	.875	348	238
Miami	10	6	0	.625	311	261
Buffalo	6	10	0	.375	243	279
N.Y. Jets	6	10	0	.375	283	299

North Division

	W	L	T	Pct.	Pts.	OP
Baltimore	10	6	0	.625	391	281
Cincinnati	8	8	0	.500	346	384
Pittsburgh	6	10	0	.375	300	327
Cleveland	5	11	0	.313	254	322

South Division

	W	L	T	Pct.	Pts.	OP
Indianapolis	12	4	0	.750	447	336
Tennessee*	12	4	0	.750	435	324
Jacksonville	5	11	0	.313	276	331
Houston	5	11	0	.313	255	380

West Division

	W	L	T	Pct.	Pts.	OP
Kansas City	13	3	0	.813	484	332
Denver*	10	6	0	.625	381	301
Oakland	4	12	0	.250	270	379
San Diego	4	12	0	.250	313	441

NATIONAL CONFERENCE
East Division

	W	L	T	Pct.	Pts.	OP
Philadelphia#	12	4	0	.750	374	287
Dallas*	10	6	0	.625	289	260
Washington	5	11	0	.313	287	372
N.Y. Giants	4	12	0	.250	243	387

North Division

	W	L	T	Pct.	Pts.	OP
Green Bay	10	6	0	.625	442	307
Minnesota	9	7	0	.563	416	353
Chicago	7	9	0	.438	283	346
Detroit	5	11	0	.313	270	379

South Division

	W	L	T	Pct.	Pts.	OP
Carolina	11	5	0	.688	325	304
New Orleans	8	8	0	.500	340	326
Tampa Bay	7	9	0	.438	301	264
Atlanta	5	11	0	.313	299	422

West Division

	W	L	T	Pct.	Pts.	OP
St. Louis	12	4	0	.750	447	328
Seattle*	10	6	0	.625	404	327
San Francisco	7	9	0	.438	384	337
Arizona	4	12	0	.250	225	452

*Wild Card qualifier for playoffs; #Top playoff seed in conference

Buffalo finished ahead of N.Y. Jets based on better division record (2-4 to Jets' 1-5). Indianapolis finished ahead of Tennessee based on head-to-head sweep (2-0). Jacksonville finished ahead of Houston based on better division record (2-4 to Texans' 1-5). Denver finished ahead of Miami based on better conference record (9-3 to Dolphins' 7-5). Oakland finished ahead of San Diego based on better conference record (3-9 to Chargers' 2-10). Philadelphia finished ahead of St. Louis based on better conference record (9-3 to Rams' 8-4). Seattle finished ahead of Dallas based on better strength of victory (65-95 to Cowboys' 62-98).

Wild Card playoffs: Tennessee 20, BALTIMORE 17; INDIANAPOLIS 41, Denver 10

Divisional playoffs: NEW ENGLAND 17, Tennessee 14; Indianapolis 38, KANSAS CITY 31

AFC Championship: NEW ENGLAND 24, Indianapolis 14

Wild Card playoffs: CAROLINA 29, Dallas 10; GREEN BAY 33, Seattle 27 (OT)

Divisional playoffs: Carolina 29, ST. LOUIS 23 (2OT); PHILADELPHIA 20, Green Bay 17 (OT)

NFC Championship: Carolina 14, PHILADELPHIA 3

Super Bowl XXXVIII: New England (AFC) 32, Carolina (NFC) 29 at Reliant Stadium, Houston, Texas

Playoff Seeds

AFC	NFC
1. New England	1. Philadelphia
2. Kansas City	2. St. Louis
3. Indianapolis	**3. Carolina**
4. Baltimore	4. Green Bay
5. Tennessee	5. Seattle
6. Denver	6. Dallas

2002

AMERICAN CONFERENCE
East Division

	W	L	T	Pct.	Pts.	OP
N.Y. Jets	9	7	0	.563	359	336
New England	9	7	0	.563	381	346
Miami	9	7	0	.563	378	301
Buffalo	8	8	0	.500	379	397

North Division

	W	L	T	Pct.	Pts.	OP
Pittsburgh	10	5	1	.656	390	345
Cleveland*	9	7	0	.563	344	320
Baltimore	7	9	0	.438	316	354
Cincinnati	2	14	0	.125	279	456

South Division

	W	L	T	Pct.	Pts.	OP
Tennessee	11	5	0	.688	367	324
Indianapolis*	10	6	0	.625	349	313
Jacksonville	6	10	0	.375	328	315
Houston	4	12	0	.250	213	356

West Division

	W	L	T	Pct.	Pts.	OP
Oakland#	11	5	0	.688	450	304
Denver	9	7	0	.563	392	344
San Diego	8	8	0	.500	333	367
Kansas City	8	8	0	.500	467	399

NATIONAL CONFERENCE
East Division

	W	L	T	Pct.	Pts.	OP
Philadelphia#	12	4	0	.750	415	241
N.Y. Giants*	10	6	0	.625	320	279
Washington	7	9	0	.438	307	365
Dallas	5	11	0	.313	217	329

North Division

	W	L	T	Pct.	Pts.	OP
Green Bay	12	4	0	.750	398	328
Minnesota	6	10	0	.375	390	442
Chicago	4	12	0	.250	281	379
Detroit	3	13	0	.188	306	451

South Division

	W	L	T	Pct.	Pts.	OP
Tampa Bay	12	4	0	.750	346	196
Atlanta*	9	6	1	.594	402	314
New Orleans	9	7	0	.563	432	388
Carolina	7	9	0	.438	258	302

West Division

	W	L	T	Pct.	Pts.	OP
San Francisco	10	6	0	.625	367	351
St. Louis	7	9	0	.438	316	369
Seattle	7	9	0	.438	355	369
Arizona	5	11	0	.313	262	417

*Wild Card qualifier for playoffs; #Top playoff seed in conference

New York Jets finished ahead of New England based on better record in common games (8-4 to Patriots' 7-5) and Miami based on better division record (4-2 to Dolphins' 2-4). New England finished ahead of Miami based on better division record (4-2 to Dolphins' 2-4). Cleveland finished ahead of Denver and New England based on better conference record (7-5 to Broncos' 5-7 and Patriots' 6-6). Oakland finished ahead of Tennessee based on better head-to-head record (1-0). San Diego finished ahead of Kansas City based on better division record (3-3 to Chiefs' 2-4). Philadelphia finished ahead of Green Bay and Tampa Bay based on better conference record (11-1 to Packers' 9-3 and Buccaneers' 9-3). Tampa Bay finished ahead of Green Bay based on better head-to-head record (1-0). St. Louis finished ahead of Seattle based on better division record (4-2 to Seahawks' 2-4).

Wild Card playoffs: N.Y. JETS 41, Indianapolis 0; PITTSBURGH 36, Cleveland 33

Divisional playoffs: TENNESSEE 34, Pittsburgh 31 (OT); OAKLAND 30, N.Y. Jets 10

AFC Championship: OAKLAND 41, Tennessee 24

Wild Card playoffs: Atlanta 27, GREEN BAY 7; SAN FRANCISCO 39, N.Y. Giants 38

Divisional playoffs: PHILADELPHIA 20, Atlanta 6; TAMPA BAY 31, San Francisco 6

NFC Championship: Tampa Bay 27, PHILADELPHIA 10

Super Bowl XXXVII: Tampa Bay (NFC) 48, Oakland (AFC) 21 at Qualcomm Stadium, San Diego, California

Playoff Seeds

AFC	NFC
1. Oakland	1. Philadelphia
2. Tennessee	**2. Tampa Bay**
3. Pittsburgh	3. Green Bay
4. N.Y. Jets	4. San Francisco
5. Indianapolis	5. N.Y. Giants
6. Cleveland	6. Atlanta

2001

AMERICAN CONFERENCE

Eastern Division

	W	L	T	Pct.	Pts.	OP
New England	11	5	0	.688	371	272
Miami*	11	5	0	.688	344	290
N.Y. Jets*	10	6	0	.625	308	295
Indianapolis	6	10	0	.375	413	486
Buffalo	3	13	0	.188	265	420

Central Division

	W	L	T	Pct.	Pts.	OP
Pittsburgh#	13	3	0	.813	352	212
Baltimore*	10	6	0	.625	303	265
Cleveland	7	9	0	.438	285	319
Tennessee	7	9	0	.438	336	388
Jacksonville	6	10	0	.375	294	286
Cincinnati	6	10	0	.375	226	309

Western Division

	W	L	T	Pct.	Pts.	OP
Oakland	10	6	0	.625	399	327
Seattle	9	7	0	.563	301	324
Denver	8	8	0	.500	340	339
Kansas City	6	10	0	.375	320	344
San Diego	5	11	0	.313	332	321

NATIONAL CONFERENCE

Eastern Division

	W	L	T	Pct.	Pts.	OP
Philadelphia	11	5	0	.688	343	208
Washington	8	8	0	.500	256	303
N.Y. Giants	7	9	0	.438	294	321
Arizona	7	9	0	.438	295	343
Dallas	5	11	0	.313	246	338

Central Division

	W	L	T	Pct.	Pts.	OP
Chicago	13	3	0	.813	338	203
Green Bay*	12	4	0	.750	390	266
Tampa Bay*	9	7	0	.563	324	280
Minnesota	5	11	0	.313	290	390
Detroit	2	14	0	.125	270	424

Western Division

	W	L	T	Pct.	Pts.	OP
St. Louis#	14	2	0	.875	503	273
San Francisco*	12	4	0	.750	409	282
New Orleans	7	9	0	.438	333	409
Atlanta	7	9	0	.438	291	377
Carolina	1	15	0	.063	253	410

Wild Card qualifier for playoffs; #Top playoff seed in conference
New England finished ahead of Miami based on better division record (6-2 to Dolphins' 5-3). Baltimore was second Wild Card ahead of N.Y. Jets based on better record against common opponents (3-2 to Jets' 2-2). Cleveland finished ahead of Tennessee based on better division record (5-5 to Titans' 3-7). Jacksonville finished ahead of Cincinnati based on head-to-head record (2-0). N.Y. Giants finished ahead of Arizona based on head-to-head record (2-0). Green Bay was first Wild Card ahead of San Francisco based on better conference record (9-3 to 49ers' 8-4). New Orleans finished ahead of Atlanta based on better division record (4-4 to Falcons' 3-5).

Wild Card playoffs: OAKLAND 38, N.Y. Jets 24; Baltimore 20, MIAMI 3
Divisional playoffs: NEW ENGLAND 16, Oakland 13 (OT); PITTSBURGH 27, Baltimore 10
AFC Championship: New England 24, PITTSBURGH 17
Wild Card playoffs: PHILADELPHIA 31, Tampa Bay 9; GREEN BAY 25, San Francisco 15
Divisional playoffs: Philadelphia 33, CHICAGO 19; ST. LOUIS 45, Green Bay 17
NFC Championship: ST. LOUIS 29, Philadelphia 24
Super Bowl XXXVI: New England (AFC) 20, St. Louis (NFC) 17 at Louisiana Superdome, New Orleans, Louisiana

Playoff Seeds

AFC	NFC
1. Pittsburgh	**1. St. Louis**
2. New England	2. Chicago
3. Oakland	3. Philadelphia
4. Miami	4. Green Bay
5. Baltimore	5. San Francisco
6. N.Y. Jets	6. Tampa Bay

2000

AMERICAN CONFERENCE

Eastern Division

	W	L	T	Pct.	Pts.	OP
Miami	11	5	0	.688	323	226
Indianapolis*	10	6	0	.625	429	326
N.Y. Jets	9	7	0	.563	321	321
Buffalo	8	8	0	.500	315	350
New England	5	11	0	.313	276	338

Central Division

	W	L	T	Pct.	Pts.	OP
Tennessee#	13	3	0	.813	346	191
Baltimore*	12	4	0	.750	333	165
Pittsburgh	9	7	0	.563	321	255
Jacksonville	7	9	0	.438	367	327
Cincinnati	4	12	0	.250	185	359
Cleveland	3	13	0	.188	161	419

Western Division

	W	L	T	Pct.	Pts.	OP
Oakland	12	4	0	.750	479	299
Denver*	11	5	0	.688	485	369
Kansas City	7	9	0	.438	355	354
Seattle	6	10	0	.375	320	405
San Diego	1	15	0	.063	269	440

NATIONAL CONFERENCE

Eastern Division

	W	L	T	Pct.	Pts.	OP
N.Y. Giants#	12	4	0	.750	328	246
Philadelphia*	11	5	0	.688	351	245
Washington	8	8	0	.500	281	269
Dallas	5	11	0	.313	294	361
Arizona	3	13	0	.188	210	443

Central Division

	W	L	T	Pct.	Pts.	OP
Minnesota	11	5	0	.688	397	371
Tampa Bay*	10	6	0	.625	388	269
Green Bay	9	7	0	.563	353	323
Detroit	9	7	0	.563	307	307
Chicago	5	11	0	.313	216	355

Western Division

	W	L	T	Pct.	Pts.	OP
New Orleans	10	6	0	.625	354	305
St. Louis*	10	6	0	.625	540	471
Carolina	7	9	0	.438	310	310
San Francisco	6	10	0	.375	388	422
Atlanta	4	12	0	.250	252	413

Wild Card qualifier for playoffs; #Top playoff seed in conference
Green Bay finished ahead of Detroit based on better division record (5-3 to Lions' 3-5). New Orleans finished ahead of St. Louis based on better division record (7-1 to Rams' 5-3). Tampa Bay was second Wild Card based on head-to-head victory over St. Louis (1-0).

Wild Card playoffs: MIAMI 23, Indianapolis 17 (OT); BALTIMORE 21, Denver 3
Divisional playoffs: OAKLAND 27, Miami 0; Baltimore 24, TENNESSEE 10
AFC Championship: Baltimore 16, OAKLAND 3
Wild Card playoffs: NEW ORLEANS 31, St. Louis 28; PHILADELPHIA 21, Tampa Bay 3
Divisional playoffs: MINNESOTA 34, New Orleans 16; N.Y. GIANTS 20, Philadelphia 10
NFC Championship: N.Y. GIANTS 41, Minnesota 0
Super Bowl XXXV: Baltimore (AFC) 34, N.Y. Giants (NFC) 7 at Raymond James Stadium, Tampa, Florida

Playoff Seeds

AFC	NFC
1. Tennessee	**1. N.Y. Giants**
2. Oakland	2. Minnesota
3. Miami	3. New Orleans
4. Baltimore	4. Philadelphia
5. Denver	5. Tampa Bay
6. Indianapolis	6. St. Louis

1999

AMERICAN CONFERENCE

Eastern Division

	W	L	T	Pct.	Pts.	OP
Indianapolis	13	3	0	.813	423	333
Buffalo*	11	5	0	.688	320	229
Miami*	9	7	0	.563	326	336
N.Y. Jets	8	8	0	.500	308	309
New England	8	8	0	.500	299	284

Central Division

	W	L	T	Pct.	Pts.	OP
Jacksonville#	14	2	0	.875	396	217
Tennessee*	13	3	0	.813	392	324
Baltimore	8	8	0	.500	324	277
Pittsburgh	6	10	0	.375	317	320
Cincinnati	4	12	0	.250	283	460
Cleveland	2	14	0	.125	217	437

Western Division

	W	L	T	Pct.	Pts.	OP
Seattle	9	7	0	.563	338	298
Kansas City	9	7	0	.563	390	322
San Diego	8	8	0	.500	269	316
Oakland	8	8	0	.500	390	329
Denver	6	10	0	.375	314	318

NATIONAL CONFERENCE

Eastern Division

	W	L	T	Pct.	Pts.	OP
Washington	10	6	0	.625	443	377
Dallas*	8	8	0	.500	352	276
N.Y. Giants	7	9	0	.438	299	358
Arizona	6	10	0	.375	245	382
Philadelphia	5	11	0	.313	272	357

Central Division

	W	L	T	Pct.	Pts.	OP
Tampa Bay	11	5	0	.688	270	235
Minnesota*	10	6	0	.625	399	335
Detroit*	8	8	0	.500	322	323
Green Bay	8	8	0	.500	357	341
Chicago	6	10	0	.375	272	341

Western Division

	W	L	T	Pct.	Pts.	OP
St. Louis#	13	3	0	.813	526	242
Carolina	8	8	0	.500	421	381
Atlanta	5	11	0	.313	285	380
San Francisco	4	12	0	.250	295	453
New Orleans	3	13	0	.188	260	434

*Wild Card qualifier for playoffs; #Top playoff seed in conference
Miami was third Wild Card ahead of Kansas City based on better record against common opponents (6-1 to Chiefs' 5-3). N.Y. Jets finished ahead of New England based on better division record (4-4 to Patriots' 2-6). Seattle finished ahead of Kansas City based on head-to-head sweep (2-0). San Diego finished ahead of Oakland based on better division record (5-3 to Raiders' 3-5). Dallas was second Wild Card based on better record against common opponents (3-2 to Lions' 3-3) and better conference record than Carolina (7-5 to Panthers' 6-6). Detroit was third Wild Card based on better conference record than Green Bay (7-5 to Packers' 6-6) and better conference record than Carolina (7-5 to Panthers' 6-6).
Wild Card playoffs: TENNESSEE 22, Buffalo 16; Miami 20, SEATTLE 17
Divisional playoffs: JACKSONVILLE 62, Miami 7; Tennessee 19, INDIANAPOLIS 16
AFC Championship: Tennessee 33, JACKSONVILLE 14
Wild Card playoffs: WASHINGTON 27, Detroit 13; MINNESOTA 27, Dallas 10
Divisional playoffs: TAMPA BAY 14, Washington 13; ST. LOUIS 49, Minnesota 37
NFC Championship: ST. LOUIS 11, Tampa Bay 6
Super Bowl XXXIV: St. Louis (NFC) 23, Tennessee (AFC) 16 at Georgia Dome, Atlanta, Georgia

Playoff Seeds

AFC	NFC
1. Jacksonville	**1. St. Louis**
2. Indianapolis	2. Tampa Bay
3. Seattle	3. Washington
4. Tennessee	4. Minnesota
5. Buffalo	5. Dallas
6. Miami	6. Detroit

1998

AMERICAN CONFERENCE

Eastern Division

	W	L	T	Pct.	Pts.	OP
N.Y. Jets	12	4	0	.750	416	266
Miami*	10	6	0	.625	321	265
Buffalo*	10	6	0	.625	400	333
New England*	9	7	0	.563	337	329
Indianapolis	3	13	0	.188	310	444

Central Division

	W	L	T	Pct.	Pts.	OP
Jacksonville	11	5	0	.688	392	338
Tennessee	8	8	0	.500	330	320
Pittsburgh	7	9	0	.438	263	303
Baltimore	6	10	0	.375	269	335
Cincinnati	3	13	0	.188	268	452

Western Division

	W	L	T	Pct.	Pts.	OP
Denver#	14	2	0	.875	501	309
Oakland	8	8	0	.500	288	356
Seattle	8	8	0	.500	372	310
Kansas City	7	9	0	.438	327	363
San Diego	5	11	0	.313	241	342

NATIONAL CONFERENCE

Eastern Division

	W	L	T	Pct.	Pts.	OP
Dallas	10	6	0	.625	381	275
Arizona*	9	7	0	.563	325	378
N.Y. Giants	8	8	0	.500	287	309
Washington	6	10	0	.375	319	421
Philadelphia	3	13	0	.188	161	344

Central Division

	W	L	T	Pct.	Pts.	OP
Minnesota#	15	1	0	.938	556	296
Green Bay*	11	5	0	.688	408	319
Tampa Bay	8	8	0	.500	314	295
Detroit	5	11	0	.313	306	378
Chicago	4	12	0	.250	276	368

Western Division

	W	L	T	Pct.	Pts.	OP
Atlanta	14	2	0	.875	442	289
San Francisco*	12	4	0	.750	479	328
New Orleans	6	10	0	.375	305	359
Carolina	4	12	0	.250	336	413
St. Louis	4	12	0	.250	285	378

*Wild Card qualifier for playoffs; #Top playoff seed in conference
Miami finished ahead of Buffalo based on better net division points (6 to Bills' 0). Oakland finished ahead of Seattle based on head-to-head sweep (2-0). Carolina finished ahead of St. Louis based on head-to-head sweep (2-0).
Wild Card playoffs: MIAMI 24, Buffalo 17; JACKSONVILLE 25, New England 10
Divisional playoffs: DENVER 38, Miami 3; N.Y. JETS 34, Jacksonville 24
AFC Championship: DENVER 23, N.Y. Jets 10
Wild Card playoffs: Arizona 20, DALLAS 7; SAN FRANCISCO 30, Green Bay 27
Divisional playoffs: ATLANTA 20, San Francisco 18; MINNESOTA 41, Arizona 21
NFC Championship: Atlanta 30, MINNESOTA 27 (OT)
Super Bowl XXXIII: Denver (AFC) 34, Atlanta (NFC) 19, at Pro Player Stadium, Miami, Florida

Playoff Seeds

AFC	NFC
1. Denver	1. Minnesota
2. N.Y. Jets	**2. Atlanta**
3. Jacksonville	3. Dallas
4. Miami	4. San Francisco
5. Buffalo	5. Green Bay
6. New England	6. Arizona

1997

AMERICAN CONFERENCE
Eastern Division

	W	L	T	Pct.	Pts.	OP
New England	10	6	0	.625	369	289
Miami*	9	7	0	.563	339	327
N.Y. Jets	9	7	0	.563	348	287
Buffalo	6	10	0	.375	255	367
Indianapolis	3	13	0	.188	313	401

Central Division

	W	L	T	Pct.	Pts.	OP
Pittsburgh	11	5	0	.688	372	307
Jacksonville*	11	5	0	.688	394	318
Tennessee	8	8	0	.500	333	310
Cincinnati	7	9	0	.438	355	405
Baltimore	6	9	1	.406	326	345

Western Division

	W	L	T	Pct.	Pts.	OP
Kansas City	13	3	0	.813	375	232
Denver*	12	4	0	.750	472	287
Seattle	8	8	0	.500	365	362
Oakland	4	12	0	.250	324	419
San Diego	4	12	0	.250	266	425

NATIONAL CONFERENCE
Eastern Division

	W	L	T	Pct.	Pts.	OP
N.Y. Giants	10	5	1	.656	307	265
Washington	8	7	1	.531	327	289
Philadelphia	6	9	1	.406	317	372
Dallas	6	10	0	.375	304	314
Arizona	4	12	0	.250	283	379

Central Division

	W	L	T	Pct.	Pts.	OP
Green Bay	13	3	0	.813	422	282
Tampa Bay*	10	6	0	.625	299	263
Detroit*	9	7	0	.563	379	306
Minnesota*	9	7	0	.563	354	359
Chicago	4	12	0	.250	263	421

Western Division

	W	L	T	Pct.	Pts.	OP
San Francisco#	13	3	0	.813	375	265
Carolina	7	9	0	.438	265	314
Atlanta	7	9	0	.438	320	361
New Orleans	6	10	0	.375	237	327
St. Louis	5	11	0	.313	299	359

*Wild Card qualifier for playoffs; #Top playoff seed in conference
Miami finished ahead of N.Y. Jets based on head-to-head sweep (2-0). Pittsburgh finished ahead of Jacksonville based on better net division points (78 to Jaguars' 23). Oakland finished ahead of San Diego based on better division record (2-6 to Chargers' 1-7). San Francisco was top playoff seed based on better conference record than Green Bay (11-1 to Packers' 10-2). Detroit finished ahead of Minnesota based on head-to-head sweep (2-0). Carolina finished ahead of Atlanta based on head-to-head sweep (2-0).

Wild Card playoffs: DENVER 42, Jacksonville 17; NEW ENGLAND 17, Miami 3
Divisional playoffs: PITTSBURGH 7, New England 6; Denver 14, KANSAS CITY 10
AFC Championship: Denver 24, PITTSBURGH 21
Wild Card playoffs: Minnesota 23, N.Y. GIANTS 22; TAMPA BAY 20, Detroit 10
Divisional playoffs: SAN FRANCISCO 38, Minnesota 22; GREEN BAY 21, Tampa Bay 7
NFC Championship: Green Bay 23, SAN FRANCISCO 10
Super Bowl XXXII: Denver (AFC) 31, Green Bay (NFC) 24, at Qualcomm Stadium, San Diego, California

Playoff Seeds

AFC	NFC
1. Kansas City	1. San Francisco
2. Pittsburgh	**2. Green Bay**
3. New England	3. N.Y. Giants
4. Denver	4. Tampa Bay
5. Jacksonville	5. Detroit
6. Miami	6. Minnesota

1996

AMERICAN CONFERENCE
Eastern Division

	W	L	T	Pct.	Pts.	OP
New England	11	5	0	.688	418	313
Buffalo*	10	6	0	.625	319	266
Indianapolis*	9	7	0	.563	317	334
Miami	8	8	0	.500	339	325
N.Y. Jets	1	15	0	.063	279	454

Central Division

	W	L	T	Pct.	Pts.	OP
Pittsburgh	10	6	0	.625	344	257
Jacksonville*	9	7	0	.563	325	335
Cincinnati	8	8	0	.500	372	369
Houston	8	8	0	.500	345	319
Baltimore	4	12	0	.250	371	441

Western Division

	W	L	T	Pct.	Pts.	OP
Denver#	13	3	0	.813	391	275
Kansas City	9	7	0	.563	297	300
San Diego	8	8	0	.500	310	376
Oakland	7	9	0	.438	340	293
Seattle	7	9	0	.438	317	376

NATIONAL CONFERENCE
Eastern Division

	W	L	T	Pct.	Pts.	OP
Dallas	10	6	0	.625	286	250
Philadelphia*	10	6	0	.625	363	341
Washington	9	7	0	.563	364	312
Arizona	7	9	0	.438	300	397
N.Y. Giants	6	10	0	.375	242	297

Central Division

	W	L	T	Pct.	Pts.	OP
Green Bay#	13	3	0	.813	456	210
Minnesota*	9	7	0	.563	298	315
Chicago	7	9	0	.438	283	305
Tampa Bay	6	10	0	.375	221	293
Detroit	5	11	0	.313	302	368

Western Division

	W	L	T	Pct.	Pts.	OP
Carolina	12	4	0	.750	367	218
San Francisco*	12	4	0	.750	398	257
St. Louis	6	10	0	.375	303	409
Atlanta	3	13	0	.188	309	461
New Orleans	3	13	0	.188	229	339

*Wild Card qualifier for playoffs; #Top playoff seed in conference
Jacksonville was second Wild Card ahead of Indianapolis and Kansas City based on better conference record (7-5 to Colts' 6-6 and Chiefs' 5-7). Indianapolis was third Wild Card based on head-to-head victory over Kansas City (1-0). Cincinnati finished ahead of Houston based on better net division points (19 to Oilers' 11). Oakland finished ahead of Seattle based on better division record (3-5 to Seahawks' 2-6). Dallas finished ahead of Philadelphia based on better record against common opponents (8-5 to Eagles' 7-6). Minnesota was third Wild Card based on better conference record than Washington (8-4 to Redskins' 6-6). Carolina finished ahead of San Francisco based on head-to-head sweep (2-0). Atlanta finished ahead of New Orleans based on head-to-head sweep (2-0).

Wild Card playoffs: Jacksonville 30, BUFFALO 27; PITTSBURGH 42, Indianapolis 14
Divisional playoffs: Jacksonville 30, DENVER 27; NEW ENGLAND 28, Pittsburgh 3
AFC Championship: NEW ENGLAND 20, Jacksonville 6
Wild Card playoffs: DALLAS 40, Minnesota 15; SAN FRANCISCO 14, Philadelphia 0
Divisional playoffs: GREEN BAY 35, San Francisco 14; CAROLINA 26, Dallas 17
NFC Championship: GREEN BAY 30, Carolina 13
Super Bowl XXXI: Green Bay (NFC) 35, New England (AFC) 21, at Louisiana Superdome, New Orleans, Louisiana

Playoff Seeds

AFC	NFC
1. Denver	**1. Green Bay**
2. New England	2. Carolina
3. Pittsburgh	3. Dallas
4. Buffalo	4. San Francisco
5. Jacksonville	5. Philadelphia
6. Indianapolis	6. Minnesota

1995

AMERICAN CONFERENCE

Eastern Division

	W	L	T	Pct.	Pts.	OP
Buffalo	10	6	0	.625	350	335
Indianapolis*	9	7	0	.563	331	316
Miami*	9	7	0	.563	398	332
New England	6	10	0	.375	294	377
N.Y. Jets	3	13	0	.188	233	384

Central Division

	W	L	T	Pct.	Pts.	OP
Pittsburgh	11	5	0	.688	407	327
Cincinnati	7	9	0	.438	349	374
Houston	7	9	0	.438	348	324
Cleveland	5	11	0	.313	289	356
Jacksonville	4	12	0	.250	275	404

Western Division

	W	L	T	Pct.	Pts.	OP
Kansas City#	13	3	0	.813	358	241
San Diego*	9	7	0	.563	321	323
Seattle	8	8	0	.500	363	366
Denver	8	8	0	.500	388	345
Oakland	8	8	0	.500	348	332

NATIONAL CONFERENCE

Eastern Division

	W	L	T	Pct.	Pts.	OP
Dallas#	12	4	0	.750	435	291
Philadelphia*	10	6	0	.625	318	338
Washington	6	10	0	.375	326	359
N.Y. Giants	5	11	0	.313	290	340
Arizona	4	12	0	.250	275	422

Central Division

	W	L	T	Pct.	Pts.	OP
Green Bay	11	5	0	.688	404	314
Detroit*	10	6	0	.625	436	336
Chicago	9	7	0	.563	392	360
Minnesota	8	8	0	.500	412	385
Tampa Bay	7	9	0	.438	238	335

Western Division

	W	L	T	Pct.	Pts.	OP
San Francisco	11	5	0	.688	457	258
Atlanta*	9	7	0	.563	362	349
St. Louis	7	9	0	.438	309	418
Carolina	7	9	0	.438	289	325
New Orleans	7	9	0	.438	319	348

Wild Card qualifier for playoffs; #Top playoff seed in conference
Indianapolis finished ahead of Miami based on head-to-head sweep (2-0). San Diego was first Wild Card based on head-to-head victory over Indianapolis (1-0). Cincinnati finished ahead of Houston based on better division record (4-4 to Oilers' 3-5). Seattle finished ahead of Denver and Oakland based on best head-to-head record (3-1 to Broncos' 2-2 and Raiders' 1-3). Denver finished ahead of Oakland based on head-to-head sweep (2-0). Philadelphia was first Wild Card ahead of Detroit based on better conference record (9-3 to Lions' 7-5). San Francisco was second playoff seed ahead of Green Bay based on better conference record (8-4 to Packers' 7-5). Atlanta was third Wild Card ahead of Chicago based on better record against common opponents (4-2 to Bears' 3-3). St. Louis finished ahead of Carolina and New Orleans based on best head-to-head record (3-1 to Panthers' 1-3 and Saints' 2-2). Carolina finished ahead of New Orleans based on better conference record (4-8 to 3-9).

Wild Card playoffs: BUFFALO 37, Miami 22; Indianapolis 35, SAN DIEGO 20
Divisional playoffs: PITTSBURGH 40, Buffalo 21; Indianapolis 10, KANSAS CITY 7
AFC Championship: PITTSBURGH 20, Indianapolis 16
Wild Card playoffs: PHILADELPHIA 58, Detroit 37; GREEN BAY 37, Atlanta 20
Divisional playoffs: Green Bay 27, SAN FRANCISCO 17; DALLAS 30, Philadelphia 11
NFC Championship: DALLAS 38, Green Bay 27
Super Bowl XXX: Dallas (NFC) 27, Pittsburgh (AFC) 17, at Sun Devil Stadium, Tempe, Arizona

Playoff Seeds

AFC	NFC
1. Kansas City	1. Dallas
2. Pittsburgh	2. San Francisco
3. Buffalo	3. Green Bay
4. San Diego	4. Philadelphia
5. Indianapolis	5. Detroit
6. Miami	6. Atlanta

1994

AMERICAN CONFERENCE

Eastern Division

	W	L	T	Pct.	Pts.	OP
Miami	10	6	0	.625	389	327
New England*	10	6	0	.625	351	312
Indianapolis	8	8	0	.500	307	320
Buffalo	7	9	0	.438	340	356
N.Y. Jets	6	10	0	.375	264	320

Central Division

	W	L	T	Pct.	Pts.	OP
Pittsburgh#	12	4	0	.750	316	234
Cleveland*	11	5	0	.688	340	204
Cincinnati	3	13	0	.188	276	406
Houston	2	14	0	.125	226	352

Western Division

	W	L	T	Pct.	Pts.	OP
San Diego	11	5	0	.688	381	306
Kansas City*	9	7	0	.563	319	298
L.A. Raiders	9	7	0	.563	303	327
Denver	7	9	0	.438	347	396
Seattle	6	10	0	.375	287	323

NATIONAL CONFERENCE

Eastern Division

	W	L	T	Pct.	Pts.	OP
Dallas	12	4	0	.750	414	248
N.Y. Giants	9	7	0	.563	279	305
Arizona	8	8	0	.500	235	267
Philadelphia	7	9	0	.438	308	308
Washington	3	13	0	.188	320	412

Central Division

	W	L	T	Pct.	Pts.	OP
Minnesota	10	6	0	.625	356	314
Green Bay*	9	7	0	.563	382	287
Detroit*	9	7	0	.563	357	342
Chicago*	9	7	0	.563	271	307
Tampa Bay	6	10	0	.375	251	351

Western Division

	W	L	T	Pct.	Pts.	OP
San Francisco#	13	3	0	.813	505	296
New Orleans	7	9	0	.438	348	407
Atlanta	7	9	0	.438	317	385
L.A. Rams	4	12	0	.250	286	365

Wild Card qualifier for playoffs; #Top playoff seed in conference
Miami finished ahead of New England based on head-to-head sweep (2-0). Kansas City finished ahead of L.A. Raiders based on head-to-head sweep (2-0). Green Bay was first Wild Card based on best head-to-head record (3-1) vs. Detroit (2-2) and Chicago (1-3) and better conference record (8-4) than N.Y. Giants (6-6). Detroit was second Wild Card based on better division record (4-4) than Chicago (3-5) and head-to-head victory over N.Y. Giants (1-0). Chicago was third Wild Card based on better record against common opponents (4-4) than N.Y. Giants (3-5). New Orleans finished ahead of Atlanta based on head-to-head sweep (2-0).

Wild Card playoffs: MIAMI 27, Kansas City 17; CLEVELAND 20, New England 13
Divisional playoffs: PITTSBURGH 29, Cleveland 9; SAN DIEGO 22, Miami 21
AFC Championship: San Diego 17, PITTSBURGH 13
Wild Card playoffs: GREEN BAY 16, Detroit 12; Chicago 35, MINNESOTA 18
Divisional playoffs: SAN FRANCISCO 44, Chicago 15; DALLAS 35, Green Bay 9
NFC Championship: SAN FRANCISCO 38, Dallas 28
Super Bowl XXIX: San Francisco (NFC) 49, San Diego (AFC) 26, at Joe Robbie Stadium, Miami, Florida

Playoff Seeds

AFC	NFC
1. Pittsburgh	1. San Francisco
2. San Diego	2. Dallas
3. Miami	3. Minnesota
4. Cleveland	4. Green Bay
5. New England	5. Detroit
6. Kansas City	6. Chicago

1993

AMERICAN CONFERENCE

Eastern Division

	W	L	T	Pct.	Pts.	OP
Buffalo#	12	4	0	.750	329	242
Miami	9	7	0	.563	349	351
N.Y. Jets	8	8	0	.500	270	247
New England	5	11	0	.313	238	286
Indianapolis	4	12	0	.250	189	378

Central Division

	W	L	T	Pct.	Pts.	OP
Houston	12	4	0	.750	368	238
Pittsburgh*	9	7	0	.563	308	281
Cleveland	7	9	0	.438	304	307
Cincinnati	3	13	0	.188	187	319

Western Division

	W	L	T	Pct.	Pts.	OP
Kansas City	11	5	0	.688	328	291
L.A. Raiders*	10	6	0	.625	306	326
Denver*	9	7	0	.563	373	284
San Diego	8	8	0	.500	322	290
Seattle	6	10	0	.375	280	314

NATIONAL CONFERENCE

Eastern Division

	W	L	T	Pct.	Pts.	OP
Dallas#	12	4	0	.750	376	229
N.Y. Giants*	11	5	0	.688	288	205
Philadelphia	8	8	0	.500	293	315
Phoenix	7	9	0	.438	326	269
Washington	4	12	0	.250	230	345

Central Division

	W	L	T	Pct.	Pts.	OP
Detroit	10	6	0	.625	298	292
Minnesota*	9	7	0	.563	277	290
Green Bay*	9	7	0	.563	340	282
Chicago	7	9	0	.438	234	230
Tampa Bay	5	11	0	.313	237	376

Western Division

	W	L	T	Pct.	Pts.	OP
San Francisco	10	6	0	.625	473	295
New Orleans	8	8	0	.500	317	343
Atlanta	6	10	0	.375	316	385
L.A. Rams	5	11	0	.313	221	367

*Wild Card qualifier for playoffs; #Top playoff seed in conference
Buffalo was top playoff seed based on head-to-head victory over Houston (1-0). Denver was second Wild Card, and Pittsburgh was third Wild Card ahead of Miami, based on better conference record (8-4 to Steelers' 7-5 to Dolphins' 6-6). San Francisco was second playoff seed based on head-to-head victory over Detroit (1-0). Minnesota finished ahead of Green Bay based on head-to-head sweep (2-0).
Wild Card playoffs: KANSAS CITY 27, Pittsburgh 24 (OT); L.A. RAIDERS 42, Denver 24
Divisional playoffs: BUFFALO 29, L.A. Raiders 23; Kansas City 28, HOUSTON 20
AFC Championship: BUFFALO 30, Kansas City 13
Wild Card playoffs: Green Bay 28, DETROIT 24; N.Y. GIANTS 17, Minnesota 10
Divisional playoffs: SAN FRANCISCO 44, N.Y. Giants 3; DALLAS 27, Green Bay 17
NFC Championship: DALLAS 38, San Francisco 21
Super Bowl XXVIII: Dallas (NFC) 30, Buffalo (AFC) 13, at Georgia Dome, Atlanta, Georgia

Playoff Seeds

AFC	NFC
1. Buffalo	**1. Dallas**
2. Houston	2. San Francisco
3. Kansas City	3. Detroit
4. L.A. Raiders	4. N.Y. Giants
5. Denver	5. Minnesota
6. Pittsburgh	6. Green Bay

1992

AMERICAN CONFERENCE

Eastern Division

	W	L	T	Pct.	Pts.	OP
Miami	11	5	0	.688	340	281
Buffalo*	11	5	0	.688	381	283
Indianapolis	9	7	0	.563	216	302
N.Y. Jets	4	12	0	.250	220	315
New England	2	14	0	.125	205	363

Central Division

	W	L	T	Pct.	Pts.	OP
Pittsburgh#	11	5	0	.688	299	225
Houston*	10	6	0	.625	352	258
Cleveland	7	9	0	.438	272	275
Cincinnati	5	11	0	.313	274	364

Western Division

	W	L	T	Pct.	Pts.	OP
San Diego	11	5	0	.688	335	241
Kansas City*	10	6	0	.625	348	282
Denver	8	8	0	.500	262	329
L.A. Raiders	7	9	0	.438	249	281
Seattle	2	14	0	.125	140	312

NATIONAL CONFERENCE

Eastern Division

	W	L	T	Pct.	Pts.	OP
Dallas	13	3	0	.813	409	243
Philadelphia*	11	5	0	.688	354	245
Washington*	9	7	0	.563	300	255
N.Y. Giants	6	10	0	.375	306	367
Phoenix	4	12	0	.250	243	332

Central Division

	W	L	T	Pct.	Pts.	OP
Minnesota	11	5	0	.688	374	249
Green Bay	9	7	0	.563	276	296
Tampa Bay	5	11	0	.313	267	365
Chicago	5	11	0	.313	295	361
Detroit	5	11	0	.313	273	332

Western Division

	W	L	T	Pct.	Pts.	OP
San Francisco#	14	2	0	.875	431	236
New Orleans*	12	4	0	.750	330	202
Atlanta	6	10	0	.375	327	414
L.A. Rams	6	10	0	.375	313	383

*Wild Card qualifier for playoffs; #Top playoff seed in conference
Pittsburgh was top playoff seed, and Miami was second playoff seed based on San Diego, based on conference record (10-2 to Dolphins' 9-3 to Chargers' 9-5). Miami finished ahead of Buffalo based on better conference record (9-3 to Bills' 7-5). Houston was second Wild Card based on head-to-head victory over Kansas City (1-0). Washington was third Wild Card based on better conference record than Green Bay (7-5 to Packers' 6-6). Tampa Bay finished ahead of Chicago and Detroit based on better conference record (5-9 to Bears' 4-8 to Lions' 3-9). Atlanta finished ahead of L.A. Rams based on better record against common opponents (5-7 to Rams' 4-8).
Wild Card playoffs: SAN DIEGO 17, Kansas City 0; BUFFALO 41, Houston 38 (OT)
Divisional playoffs: Buffalo 24, PITTSBURGH 3; MIAMI 31, San Diego 0
AFC Championship: Buffalo 29, MIAMI 10
Wild Card playoffs: Washington 24, MINNESOTA 7; Philadelphia 36, NEW ORLEANS 20
Divisional playoffs: SAN FRANCISCO 20, Washington 13; DALLAS 34, Philadelphia 10
NFC Championship: Dallas 30, SAN FRANCISCO 20
Super Bowl XXVII: Dallas (NFC) 52, Buffalo (AFC) 17, at Rose Bowl, Pasadena, California

Playoff Seeds

AFC	NFC
1. Pittsburgh	1. San Francisco
2. Miami	**2. Dallas**
3. San Diego	3. Minnesota
4. Buffalo	4. New Orleans
5. Houston	5. Philadelphia
6. Kansas City	6. Washington

1991

AMERICAN CONFERENCE

Eastern Division

	W	L	T	Pct.	Pts.	OP
Buffalo#	13	3	0	.813	458	318
N.Y. Jets*	8	8	0	.500	314	293
Miami	8	8	0	.500	343	349
New England	6	10	0	.375	211	305
Indianapolis	1	15	0	.063	143	381

Central Division

	W	L	T	Pct.	Pts.	OP
Houston	11	5	0	.688	386	251
Pittsburgh	7	9	0	.438	292	344
Cleveland	6	10	0	.375	293	298
Cincinnati	3	13	0	.188	263	435

Western Division

	W	L	T	Pct.	Pts.	OP
Denver	12	4	0	.750	304	235
Kansas City*	10	6	0	.625	322	252
L.A. Raiders*	9	7	0	.563	298	297
Seattle	7	9	0	.438	276	261
San Diego	4	12	0	.250	274	342

NATIONAL CONFERENCE

Eastern Division

	W	L	T	Pct.	Pts.	OP
Washington#	14	2	0	.875	485	224
Dallas*	11	5	0	.688	342	310
Philadelphia	10	6	0	.625	285	244
N.Y. Giants	8	8	0	.500	281	297
Phoenix	4	12	0	.250	196	344

Central Division

	W	L	T	Pct.	Pts.	OP
Detroit	12	4	0	.750	339	295
Chicago*	11	5	0	.688	299	269
Minnesota	8	8	0	.500	301	306
Green Bay	4	12	0	.250	273	313
Tampa Bay	3	13	0	.188	199	365

Western Division

	W	L	T	Pct.	Pts.	OP
New Orleans	11	5	0	.688	341	211
Atlanta*	10	6	0	.625	361	338
San Francisco	10	6	0	.625	393	239
L.A. Rams	3	13	0	.188	234	390

*Wild Card qualifier for playoffs; #Top playoff seed in conference
N.Y. Jets finished ahead of Miami based on head-to-head sweep (2-0). Chicago was first Wild Card based on better conference record than Dallas (9-3 to Cowboys' 8-4). Atlanta finished ahead of San Francisco based on head-to-head sweep (2-0), and was third Wild Card ahead of Philadelphia based on better conference record (7-5 to Eagles' 6-6).
Wild Card playoffs: KANSAS CITY 10, L.A. Raiders 6; HOUSTON 17, N.Y. Jets 10
Divisional playoffs: DENVER 26, Houston 24; BUFFALO 37, Kansas City 14
AFC Championship: BUFFALO 10, Denver 7
Wild Card playoffs: Atlanta 27, NEW ORLEANS 20; Dallas 17, CHICAGO 13
Divisional playoffs: WASHINGTON 24, Atlanta 7; DETROIT 38, Dallas 6
NFC Championship: WASHINGTON 41, Detroit 10
Super Bowl XXVI: Washington (NFC) 37, Buffalo (AFC) 24, at Hubert H. Humphrey Metrodome, Minneapolis, Minnesota

Playoff Seeds

AFC	NFC
1. Buffalo	**1. Washington**
2. Denver	2. Detroit
3. Houston	3. New Orleans
4. Kansas City	4. Chicago
5. L.A. Raiders	5. Dallas
6. N.Y. Jets	6. Atlanta

1990

AMERICAN CONFERENCE

Eastern Division

	W	L	T	Pct.	Pts.	OP
Buffalo#	13	3	0	.813	428	263
Miami*	12	4	0	.750	336	242
Indianapolis	7	9	0	.438	281	353
N.Y. Jets	6	10	0	.375	295	345
New England	1	15	0	.063	181	446

Central Division

	W	L	T	Pct.	Pts.	OP
Cincinnati	9	7	0	.563	360	352
Houston*	9	7	0	.563	405	307
Pittsburgh	9	7	0	.563	292	240
Cleveland	3	13	0	.188	228	462

Western Division

	W	L	T	Pct.	Pts.	OP
L.A. Raiders	12	4	0	.750	337	268
Kansas City*	11	5	0	.688	369	257
Seattle	9	7	0	.563	306	286
San Diego	6	10	0	.375	315	281
Denver	5	11	0	.313	331	374

NATIONAL CONFERENCE

Eastern Division

	W	L	T	Pct.	Pts.	OP
N.Y. Giants	13	3	0	.813	335	211
Philadelphia*	10	6	0	.625	396	299
Washington*	10	6	0	.625	381	301
Dallas	7	9	0	.438	244	308
Phoenix	5	11	0	.313	268	396

Central Division

	W	L	T	Pct.	Pts.	OP
Chicago	11	5	0	.688	348	280
Tampa Bay	6	10	0	.375	264	367
Detroit	6	10	0	.375	373	413
Green Bay	6	10	0	.375	271	347
Minnesota	6	10	0	.375	351	326

Western Division

	W	L	T	Pct.	Pts.	OP
San Francisco#	14	2	0	.875	353	239
New Orleans*	8	8	0	.500	274	275
L.A. Rams	5	11	0	.313	345	412
Atlanta	5	11	0	.313	348	365

*Wild Card qualifier for playoffs; #Top playoff seed in conference
Cincinnati finished ahead of Houston and Pittsburgh based on best head-to-head record (3-1 to Oilers' 2-2 to Steelers' 1-3). Houston was Wild Card based on better conference record (8-4) than Seattle (7-5) and Pittsburgh (6-6). Philadelphia finished ahead of Washington based on better division record (5-3 to Redskins' 4-4). Tampa Bay was second in NFC Central based on best head-to-head record (5-1) against Detroit (2-4), Green Bay (3-3), and Minnesota (2-4). Detroit finished third based on best net division points (minus 8) against Green Bay (minus 40). Green Bay finished ahead of Minnesota based on better conference record (5-7 to Vikings' 4-8). The L.A. Rams finished ahead of Atlanta based on net points in division (plus 1 to Falcons' minus 31).
Wild Card playoffs: MIAMI 17, Kansas City 16; CINCINNATI 41, Houston 14
Divisional playoffs: BUFFALO 44, Miami 34; L.A. RAIDERS 20, Cincinnati 10
AFC Championship: BUFFALO 51, L.A. Raiders 3
Wild Card playoffs: Washington 20, PHILADELPHIA 6; CHICAGO 16, New Orleans 6
Divisional playoffs: SAN FRANCISCO 28, Washington 10; N.Y. GIANTS 31, Chicago 3
NFC Championship: N.Y. Giants 15, SAN FRANCISCO 13
Super Bowl XXV: N.Y. Giants (NFC) 20, Buffalo (AFC) 19, at Tampa Stadium, Tampa, Florida

Playoff Seeds

AFC	NFC
1. Buffalo	1. San Francisco
2. L.A. Raiders	**2. N.Y. Giants**
3. Cincinnati	3. Chicago
4. Miami	4. Philadelphia
5. Kansas City	5. Washington
6. Houston	6. New Orleans

1989

AMERICAN CONFERENCE
Eastern Division

	W	L	T	Pct.	Pts.	OP
Buffalo	9	7	0	.563	409	317
Indianapolis	8	8	0	.500	298	301
Miami	8	8	0	.500	331	379
New England	5	11	0	.313	297	391
N.Y. Jets	4	12	0	.250	253	411

Central Division

	W	L	T	Pct.	Pts.	OP
Cleveland	9	6	1	.594	334	254
Houston*	9	7	0	.563	365	412
Pittsburgh*	9	7	0	.563	265	326
Cincinnati	8	8	0	.500	404	285

Western Division

	W	L	T	Pct.	Pts.	OP
Denver#	11	5	0	.688	362	226
Kansas City	8	7	1	.531	318	286
L.A. Raiders	8	8	0	.500	315	297
Seattle	7	9	0	.438	241	327
San Diego	6	10	0	.375	266	290

NATIONAL CONFERENCE
Eastern Division

	W	L	T	Pct.	Pts.	OP
N.Y. Giants	12	4	0	.750	348	252
Philadelphia*	11	5	0	.688	342	274
Washington	10	6	0	.625	386	308
Phoenix	5	11	0	.313	258	377
Dallas	1	15	0	.063	204	393

Central Division

	W	L	T	Pct.	Pts.	OP
Minnesota	10	6	0	.625	351	275
Green Bay	10	6	0	.625	362	356
Detroit	7	9	0	.438	312	364
Chicago	6	10	0	.375	358	377
Tampa Bay	5	11	0	.313	320	419

Western Division

	W	L	T	Pct.	Pts.	OP
San Francisco#	14	2	0	.875	442	253
L.A. Rams*	11	5	0	.688	426	344
New Orleans	9	7	0	.563	386	301
Atlanta	3	13	0	.188	279	437

*Wild Card qualifier for playoffs; #Top playoff seed in conference
Indianapolis finished ahead of Miami based on better conference record (7-5 vs. Dolphins' 6-8). Houston finished ahead of Pittsburgh based on head-to-head sweep (2-0). The L.A. Rams did not play San Francisco in the divisional playoffs because, from 1970-1989, two teams from the same division could not meet prior to the conference championship game. Philadelphia was first Wild Card ahead of L.A. Rams based on better record against common opponents (6-3 to Rams' 5-4). Minnesota finished ahead of Green Bay based on better division record (6-2 vs. Packers' 5-3).
Wild Card playoff: Pittsburgh 26, HOUSTON 23 (OT)
Divisional playoffs: CLEVELAND 34, Buffalo 30;
  DENVER 24, Pittsburgh 23
AFC Championship: DENVER 37, Cleveland 21
Wild Card playoff: L.A. Rams 21, PHILADELPHIA 7
Divisional playoffs: L.A. Rams 19, N.Y. GIANTS 13 (OT);
  SAN FRANCISCO 41, Minnesota 13
NFC Championship: SAN FRANCISCO 30, L.A. Rams 3
Super Bowl XXIV: San Francisco (NFC) 55, Denver (AFC) 10,
  at Louisiana Superdome, New Orleans, Louisiana

1988

AMERICAN CONFERENCE
Eastern Division

	W	L	T	Pct.	Pts.	OP
Buffalo	12	4	0	.750	329	237
Indianapolis	9	7	0	.563	354	315
New England	9	7	0	.563	250	284
N.Y. Jets	8	7	1	.531	372	354
Miami	6	10	0	.375	319	380

Central Division

	W	L	T	Pct.	Pts.	OP
Cincinnati#	12	4	0	.750	448	329
Cleveland*	10	6	0	.625	304	288
Houston*	10	6	0	.625	424	365
Pittsburgh	5	11	0	.313	336	421

Western Division

	W	L	T	Pct.	Pts.	OP
Seattle	9	7	0	.563	339	329
Denver	8	8	0	.500	327	352
L.A. Raiders	7	9	0	.438	325	369
San Diego	6	10	0	.375	231	332
Kansas City	4	11	1	.281	254	320

NATIONAL CONFERENCE
Eastern Division

	W	L	T	Pct.	Pts.	OP
Philadelphia	10	6	0	.625	379	319
N.Y. Giants	10	6	0	.625	359	304
Washington	7	9	0	.438	345	387
Phoenix	7	9	0	.438	344	398
Dallas	3	13	0	.188	265	381

Central Division

	W	L	T	Pct.	Pts.	OP
Chicago#	12	4	0	.750	312	215
Minnesota*	11	5	0	.688	406	233
Tampa Bay	5	11	0	.313	261	350
Detroit	4	12	0	.250	220	313
Green Bay	4	12	0	.250	240	315

Western Division

	W	L	T	Pct.	Pts.	OP
San Francisco	10	6	0	.625	369	294
L.A. Rams*	10	6	0	.625	407	293
New Orleans	10	6	0	.625	312	283
Atlanta	5	11	0	.313	244	315

*Wild Card qualifier for playoffs; #Top playoff seed in conference
Cincinnati was top playoff seed ahead of Buffalo based on head-to-head victory (1-0). Indianapolis finished ahead of New England based on better record against common opponents (7-5 to Patriots' 6-6). Cleveland finished ahead of Houston based on better division record (4-2 to Oilers' 3-3). Houston did not play Cincinnati, and Minnesota did not play Chicago in the divisional playoffs because, from 1970-1989, two teams from the same division could not meet prior to the conference championship game. Philadelphia finished first in NFC East based on head-to-head sweep of N.Y. Giants (2-0). Washington finished third in NFC East based on better division record (4-4) than Phoenix (3-5). Detroit finished fourth in NFC Central based on head-to-head sweep of Green Bay (2-0). San Francisco finished first in NFC West based on better head-to-head record (3-1) against L.A. Rams (2-2) and New Orleans (1-3). L.A. Rams finished second in NFC West based on better division record (4-2) than New Orleans (3-3) and earned Wild-Card position based on better conference record (8-4) than N.Y. Giants (9-5) and New Orleans (6-6).
Wild Card playoff: Houston 24, CLEVELAND 23
Divisional playoffs: CINCINNATI 21, Seattle 13;
  BUFFALO 17, Houston 10
AFC Championship: CINCINNATI 21, Buffalo 10
Wild Card playoff: MINNESOTA 28, L.A. Rams 17
Divisional playoffs: CHICAGO 20, Philadelphia 12;
  SAN FRANCISCO 34, Minnesota 9
NFC Championship: San Francisco 28, CHICAGO 3
Super Bowl XXIII: San Francisco (NFC) 20, Cincinnati (AFC) 16,
  at Joe Robbie Stadium, Miami, Florida

1987

AMERICAN CONFERENCE

Eastern Division

	W	L	T	Pct.	Pts.	OP
Indianapolis	9	6	0	.600	300	238
New England	8	7	0	.533	320	293
Miami	8	7	0	.533	362	335
Buffalo	7	8	0	.467	270	305
N.Y. Jets	6	9	0	.400	334	360

Central Division

	W	L	T	Pct.	Pts.	OP
Cleveland	10	5	0	.667	390	239
Houston*	9	6	0	.600	345	349
Pittsburgh	8	7	0	.533	285	299
Cincinnati	4	11	0	.267	285	370

Western Division

	W	L	T	Pct.	Pts.	OP
Denver#	10	4	1	.700	379	288
Seattle*	9	6	0	.600	371	314
San Diego	8	7	0	.533	253	317
L.A. Raiders	5	10	0	.333	301	289
Kansas City	4	11	0	.267	273	388

NATIONAL CONFERENCE

Eastern Division

	W	L	T	Pct.	Pts.	OP
Washington	11	4	0	.733	379	285
Dallas	7	8	0	.467	340	348
St. Louis	7	8	0	.467	362	368
Philadelphia	7	8	0	.467	337	380
N.Y. Giants	6	9	0	.400	280	312

Central Division

	W	L	T	Pct.	Pts.	OP
Chicago	11	4	0	.733	356	282
Minnesota*	8	7	0	.533	336	335
Green Bay	5	9	1	.367	255	300
Tampa Bay	4	11	0	.267	286	360
Detroit	4	11	0	.267	269	384

Western Division

	W	L	T	Pct.	Pts.	OP
San Francisco#	13	2	0	.867	459	253
New Orleans*	12	3	0	.800	422	283
L.A. Rams	6	9	0	.400	317	361
Atlanta	3	12	0	.200	205	436

*Wild Card qualifier for playoffs; #Top playoff seed in conference
New England finished ahead of Miami based on head-to-head sweep (2-0). Houston was first Wild Card ahead of Seattle based on better conference record (7-4 to Seahawks' 5-6). Chicago was second playoff seed ahead of Washington based on better conference record (9-2 to Redskins' 9-3). Dallas finished ahead of St. Louis and Philadelphia based on better division record (4-4 to Cardinals' 3-5 and Eagles' 3-5). St. Louis finished ahead of Philadelphia based on better conference record (7-7 to Eagles' 4-7). Tampa Bay finished ahead of Detroit based on better division record (3-4 to Lions' 2-5).

Wild Card playoff: HOUSTON 23, Seattle 20 (OT)
Divisional playoffs: CLEVELAND 38, Indianapolis 21;
  DENVER 34, Houston 10
AFC Championship: DENVER 38, Cleveland 33
Wild Card playoff: Minnesota 44, NEW ORLEANS 10
Divisional playoffs: Minnesota 36, SAN FRANCISCO 24;
  Washington 21, CHICAGO 17
NFC Championship: WASHINGTON 17, Minnesota 10
Super Bowl XXII: Washington (NFC) 42, Denver (AFC) 10,
  at San Diego Jack Murphy Stadium, San Diego, California
Note: 1987 regular season was reduced from 16 to 15 games for each team due to players' strike.

1986

AMERICAN CONFERENCE

Eastern Division

	W	L	T	Pct.	Pts.	OP
New England	11	5	0	.688	412	307
N.Y. Jets*	10	6	0	.625	364	386
Miami	8	8	0	.500	430	405
Buffalo	4	12	0	.250	287	348
Indianapolis	3	13	0	.188	229	400

Central Division

	W	L	T	Pct.	Pts.	OP
Cleveland#	12	4	0	.750	391	310
Cincinnati	10	6	0	.625	409	394
Pittsburgh	6	10	0	.375	307	336
Houston	5	11	0	.313	274	329

Western Division

	W	L	T	Pct.	Pts.	OP
Denver	11	5	0	.688	378	327
Kansas City*	10	6	0	.625	358	326
Seattle	10	6	0	.625	366	293
L.A. Raiders	8	8	0	.500	323	346
San Diego	4	12	0	.250	335	396

NATIONAL CONFERENCE

Eastern Division

	W	L	T	Pct.	Pts.	OP
N.Y. Giants#	14	2	0	.875	371	236
Washington*	12	4	0	.750	368	296
Dallas	7	9	0	.438	346	337
Philadelphia	5	10	1	.344	256	312
St. Louis	4	11	1	.281	218	351

Central Division

	W	L	T	Pct.	Pts.	OP
Chicago	14	2	0	.875	352	187
Minnesota	9	7	0	.563	398	273
Detroit	5	11	0	.313	277	326
Green Bay	4	12	0	.250	254	418
Tampa Bay	2	14	0	.125	239	473

Western Division

	W	L	T	Pct.	Pts.	OP
San Francisco	10	5	1	.656	374	247
L.A. Rams*	10	6	0	.625	309	267
Atlanta	7	8	1	.469	280	280
New Orleans	7	9	0	.438	288	287

*Wild Card qualifier for playoffs; #Top playoff seed in conference
Denver was second playoff seed ahead of New England based on head-to-head victory (1-0). N.Y. Jets were first Wild Card based on better conference record (8-4) than Kansas City (9-5), Seattle (7-5), and Cincinnati (7-5). Kansas City was second Wild Card based on better conference record (9-5) than Seattle (7-5) and Cincinnati (7-5). N.Y. Giants were top playoff seed based on better conference record than Chicago (11-1 to Bears' 10-2). Washington did not play the N.Y. Giants in the divisional playoffs because, from 1970-1989, two teams from the same division could not meet prior to the conference championship game.

Wild Card playoff: N.Y. JETS 35, Kansas City 15
Divisional playoffs: CLEVELAND 23, N.Y. Jets 20 (OT);
  DENVER 22, New England 17
AFC Championship: Denver 23, CLEVELAND 20 (OT)
Wild Card playoff: WASHINGTON 19, L.A. Rams 7
Divisional playoffs: Washington 27, CHICAGO 13
  N.Y. GIANTS 49, San Francisco 3
NFC Championship: N.Y. GIANTS 17, Washington 0
Super Bowl XXI: N.Y. Giants (NFC) 39, Denver (AFC) 20,
  at Rose Bowl, Pasadena, California

1985

AMERICAN CONFERENCE

Eastern Division

	W	L	T	Pct.	Pts.	OP
Miami	12	4	0	.750	428	320
N.Y. Jets*	11	5	0	.688	393	264
New England*	11	5	0	.688	362	290
Indianapolis	5	11	0	.313	320	386
Buffalo	2	14	0	.125	200	381

Central Division

	W	L	T	Pct.	Pts.	OP
Cleveland	8	8	0	.500	287	294
Cincinnati	7	9	0	.438	441	437
Pittsburgh	7	9	0	.438	379	355
Houston	5	11	0	.313	284	412

Western Division

	W	L	T	Pct.	Pts.	OP
L.A. Raiders#	12	4	0	.750	354	308
Denver	11	5	0	.688	380	329
Seattle	8	8	0	.500	349	303
San Diego	8	8	0	.500	467	435
Kansas City	6	10	0	.375	317	360

NATIONAL CONFERENCE

Eastern Division

	W	L	T	Pct.	Pts.	OP
Dallas	10	6	0	.625	357	333
N.Y. Giants*	10	6	0	.625	399	283
Washington	10	6	0	.625	297	312
Philadelphia	7	9	0	.438	286	310
St. Louis	5	11	0	.313	278	414

Central Division

	W	L	T	Pct.	Pts.	OP
Chicago#	15	1	0	.938	456	198
Green Bay	8	8	0	.500	337	355
Minnesota	7	9	0	.438	346	359
Detroit	7	9	0	.438	307	366
Tampa Bay	2	14	0	.125	294	448

Western Division

	W	L	T	Pct.	Pts.	OP
L.A. Rams	11	5	0	.688	340	277
San Francisco*	10	6	0	.625	411	263
New Orleans	5	11	0	.313	294	401
Atlanta	4	12	0	.250	282	452

*Wild Card qualifier for playoffs; #Top playoff seed in conference

L.A. Raiders were top playoff seed ahead of Miami based on better record against common opponents (5-1 to 4-2). N.Y. Jets were first Wild Card based on better conference record (9-3) than New England (8-4) and Denver (8-4). New England was second Wild Card ahead of Denver based on better record against common opponents (4-2 to Broncos' 3-3). Cincinnati finished ahead of Pittsburgh based on head-to-head sweep (2-0). Seattle finished ahead of San Diego based on head-to-head sweep (2-0). Dallas finished ahead of N.Y. Giants and Washington based on better head-to-head record (4-0 to Giants' 1-3 and Redskins' 1-3). N.Y. Giants were first Wild Card based on better conference record (8-4) than San Francisco (7-5) and Washington (6-6). San Francisco was second Wild Card based on head-to-head victory over Washington (1-0). Minnesota finished ahead of Detroit based on better division record (3-5 to Lions' 2-6).

Wild Card playoff: New England 26, N.Y. JETS 14
Divisional playoffs: MIAMI 24, Cleveland 21;
   New England 27, L.A. RAIDERS 20
AFC Championship: New England 31, MIAMI 14
Wild Card playoff: N.Y. GIANTS 17, San Francisco 3
Divisional playoffs: L.A. RAMS 20, Dallas 0;
   CHICAGO 21, N.Y. Giants 0
NFC Championship: CHICAGO 24, L.A. Rams 0
Super Bowl XX: Chicago (NFC) 46, New England (AFC) 10,
   at Louisiana Superdome, New Orleans, Louisiana

1984

AMERICAN CONFERENCE

Eastern Division

	W	L	T	Pct.	Pts.	OP
Miami#	14	2	0	.875	513	298
New England	9	7	0	.563	362	352
N.Y. Jets	7	9	0	.438	332	364
Indianapolis	4	12	0	.250	239	414
Buffalo	2	14	0	.125	250	454

Central Division

	W	L	T	Pct.	Pts.	OP
Pittsburgh	9	7	0	.563	387	310
Cincinnati	8	8	0	.500	339	339
Cleveland	5	11	0	.313	250	297
Houston	3	13	0	.188	240	437

Western Division

	W	L	T	Pct.	Pts.	OP
Denver	13	3	0	.813	353	241
Seattle*	12	4	0	.750	418	282
L.A. Raiders*	11	5	0	.688	368	278
Kansas City	8	8	0	.500	314	324
San Diego	7	9	0	.438	394	413

NATIONAL CONFERENCE

Eastern Division

	W	L	T	Pct.	Pts.	OP
Washington	11	5	0	.688	426	310
N.Y. Giants*	9	7	0	.563	299	301
St. Louis	9	7	0	.563	423	345
Dallas	9	7	0	.563	308	308
Philadelphia	6	9	1	.406	278	320

Central Division

	W	L	T	Pct.	Pts.	OP
Chicago	10	6	0	.625	325	248
Green Bay	8	8	0	.500	390	309
Tampa Bay	6	10	0	.375	335	380
Detroit	4	11	1	.281	283	408
Minnesota	3	13	0	.188	276	484

Western Division

	W	L	T	Pct.	Pts.	OP
San Francisco#	15	1	0	.938	475	227
L.A. Rams*	10	6	0	.625	346	316
New Orleans	7	9	0	.438	298	361
Atlanta	4	12	0	.250	281	382

*Wild Card qualifier for playoffs; #Top playoff seed in conference

N.Y. Giants finished ahead of St. Louis and Dallas based on best head-to-head record (3-1 to Cardinals' 2-2 and Cowboys' 1-3). St. Louis finished ahead of Dallas based on better division record (5-3 to Cowboys' 3-5).

Wild Card playoff: SEATTLE 13, L.A. Raiders 7
Divisional playoffs: MIAMI 31, Seattle 10;
   Pittsburgh 24, DENVER 17
AFC Championship: MIAMI 45, Pittsburgh 28
Wild Card playoff: N.Y. Giants 16, L.A. RAMS 13
Divisional playoffs: SAN FRANCISCO 21, N.Y. Giants 10;
   Chicago 23, WASHINGTON 19
NFC Championship: SAN FRANCISCO 23, Chicago 0
Super Bowl XIX: San Francisco (NFC) 38, Miami (AFC) 16,
   at Stanford Stadium, Stanford, California

1983

AMERICAN CONFERENCE

Eastern Division

	W	L	T	Pct.	Pts.	OP
Miami	12	4	0	.750	389	250
New England	8	8	0	.500	274	289
Buffalo	8	8	0	.500	283	351
Baltimore	7	9	0	.438	264	354
N.Y. Jets	7	9	0	.438	313	331

Central Division

	W	L	T	Pct.	Pts.	OP
Pittsburgh	10	6	0	.625	355	303
Cleveland	9	7	0	.563	356	342
Cincinnati	7	9	0	.438	346	302
Houston	2	14	0	.125	288	460

Western Division

	W	L	T	Pct.	Pts.	OP
L.A. Raiders	12	4	0	.750	442	338
Seattle*	9	7	0	.563	403	397
Denver*	9	7	0	.563	302	327
San Diego	6	10	0	.375	358	462
Kansas City	6	10	0	.375	386	367

NATIONAL CONFERENCE

Eastern Division

	W	L	T	Pct.	Pts.	OP
Washington#	14	2	0	.875	541	332
Dallas*	12	4	0	.750	479	360
St. Louis	8	7	1	.531	374	428
Philadelphia	5	11	0	.313	233	322
N.Y. Giants	3	12	1	.219	267	347

Central Division

	W	L	T	Pct.	Pts.	OP
Detroit	9	7	0	.563	347	286
Green Bay	8	8	0	.500	429	439
Chicago	8	8	0	.500	311	301
Minnesota	8	8	0	.500	316	348
Tampa Bay	2	14	0	.125	241	380

Western Division

	W	L	T	Pct.	Pts.	OP
San Francisco	10	6	0	.625	432	293
L.A. Rams*	9	7	0	.563	361	344
New Orleans	8	8	0	.500	319	337
Atlanta	7	9	0	.438	370	389

*Wild Card qualifier for playoffs; #Top playoff seed in conference

L.A. Raiders were top playoff seed ahead of Miami based on head-to-head victory (1-0). Seattle was second Wild Card ahead of Denver based on better division record (5-3 to Broncos' 3-5) after Cleveland was eliminated from three-way tie based on head-to-head record (Seattle and Denver 2-1 to Browns' 0-2). Seattle did not play the L.A. Raiders in the divisional playoffs because, from 1970-1989, two teams from the same division could not meet prior to the conference championship game. New England finished ahead of Buffalo based on head-to-head sweep (2-0). Baltimore finished ahead of N.Y. Jets based on better conference record (5-9 to Jets' 4-8). San Diego finished ahead of Kansas City based on head-to-head sweep (2-0). Green Bay finished ahead of Chicago based on better record against common opponents (5-5 to Bears' 4-6) after Minnesota was eliminated from three-way tie based on conference record (Chicago 7-7 and Green Bay 6-6 to Vikings' 4-8).

Wild Card playoff: SEATTLE 31, Denver 7
Divisional playoffs: Seattle 27, MIAMI 20;
   L.A. RAIDERS 38, Pittsburgh 10
AFC Championship: L.A. RAIDERS 30, Seattle 14
Wild Card playoff: L.A. Rams 24, DALLAS 17
Divisional playoffs: SAN FRANCISCO 24, Detroit 23;
   WASHINGTON 51, L.A. Rams 7
NFC Championship: WASHINGTON 24, San Francisco 21
Super Bowl XVIII: L.A. Raiders (AFC) 38, Washington (NFC) 9,
   at Tampa Stadium, Tampa, Florida

1982

AMERICAN CONFERENCE

	W	L	T	Pct.	Pts.	OP
L.A. Raiders#	8	1	0	.889	260	200
Miami	7	2	0	.778	198	131
Cincinnati	7	2	0	.778	232	177
Pittsburgh	6	3	0	.667	204	146
San Diego	6	3	0	.667	288	221
N.Y. Jets	6	3	0	.667	245	166
New England	5	4	0	.556	143	157
Cleveland	4	5	0	.444	140	182
Buffalo	4	5	0	.444	150	154
Seattle	4	5	0	.444	127	147
Kansas City	3	6	0	.333	176	184
Denver	2	7	0	.222	148	226
Houston	1	8	0	.111	136	245
Baltimore	0	8	1	.056	113	236

NATIONAL CONFERENCE

	W	L	T	Pct.	Pts.	OP
Washington#	8	1	0	.889	190	128
Dallas	6	3	0	.667	226	145
Green Bay	5	3	1	.611	226	169
Minnesota	5	4	0	.556	187	198
Atlanta	5	4	0	.556	183	199
St. Louis	5	4	0	.556	135	170
Tampa Bay	5	4	0	.556	158	178
Detroit	4	5	0	.444	181	176
New Orleans	4	5	0	.444	129	160
N.Y. Giants	4	5	0	.444	164	160
San Francisco	3	6	0	.333	209	206
Chicago	3	6	0	.333	141	174
Philadelphia	3	6	0	.333	191	195
L.A. Rams	2	7	0	.222	200	250

As the result of a 57-day players' strike, the 1982 NFL regular season schedule was reduced from 16 weeks to 9. At the conclusion of the regular season, the NFL conducted a 16-team postseason Super Bowl Tournament. Eight teams from each conference were seeded 1-8 based on their records during the season.

#Top playoff seed in conference

Miami finished ahead of Cincinnati based on better conference record (6-1 to Bengals' 6-2). Pittsburgh finished ahead of San Diego based on better record against common opponents (3-1 to Chargers' 2-1) after N.Y. Jets were eliminated from three-way tie based on conference record (Pittsburgh and San Diego 5-3 to Jets' 2-3). Cleveland finished ahead of Buffalo and Seattle based on better conference record (4-3 to Bills' 3-3 to Seahawks' 3-5). Buffalo finished ahead of Seattle based on better conference record (3-3 to Seahawks' 3-5). Minnesota (4-1), Atlanta (4-3), St. Louis (5-4), Tampa Bay (3-3) seeds were determined by best won-lost record in conference games. Detroit finished ahead of New Orleans and the N.Y. Giants based on best conference record (4-4 to Saints' 3-5 to Giants' 3-5). San Francisco finished ahead of Chicago, and Chicago finished ahead of Philadelphia, based on conference record (49ers' 2-3 to Bears' 2-5 to Eagles' 1-5).

First round playoff: MIAMI 28, New England 13;
   L.A. RAIDERS 27, Cleveland 10;
   N.Y. Jets 44, CINCINNATI 17;
   San Diego 31, PITTSBURGH 28
Second round playoff: N.Y. Jets 17, L.A. RAIDERS 14;
   MIAMI 34, San Diego 13
AFC Championship: MIAMI 14, N.Y. Jets 0
First round playoff: WASHINGTON 31, Detroit 7;
   GREEN BAY 41, St. Louis 16;
   MINNESOTA 30, Atlanta 24;
   DALLAS 30, Tampa Bay 17
Second round playoff: WASHINGTON 21, Minnesota 7;
   DALLAS 37, Green Bay 26
NFC Championship: WASHINGTON 31, Dallas 17
Super Bowl XVII: Washington (NFC) 27, Miami (AFC) 17,
   at Rose Bowl, Pasadena, California

1981

AMERICAN CONFERENCE
Eastern Division

	W	L	T	Pct.	Pts.	OP
Miami	11	4	1	.719	345	275
N.Y. Jets*	10	5	1	.656	355	287
Buffalo*	10	6	0	.625	311	276
Baltimore	2	14	0	.125	259	533
New England	2	14	0	.125	322	370

Central Division

	W	L	T	Pct.	Pts.	OP
Cincinnati#	12	4	0	.750	421	304
Pittsburgh	8	8	0	.500	356	297
Houston	7	9	0	.438	281	355
Cleveland	5	11	0	.313	276	375

Western Division

	W	L	T	Pct.	Pts.	OP
San Diego	10	6	0	.625	478	390
Denver	10	6	0	.625	321	289
Kansas City	9	7	0	.563	343	290
Oakland	7	9	0	.438	273	343
Seattle	6	10	0	.375	322	388

NATIONAL CONFERENCE
Eastern Division

	W	L	T	Pct.	Pts.	OP
Dallas	12	4	0	.750	367	277
Philadelphia*	10	6	0	.625	368	221
N.Y. Giants*	9	7	0	.563	295	257
Washington	8	8	0	.500	347	349
St. Louis	7	9	0	.438	315	408

Central Division

	W	L	T	Pct.	Pts.	OP
Tampa Bay	9	7	0	.563	315	268
Detroit	8	8	0	.500	397	322
Green Bay	8	8	0	.500	324	361
Minnesota	7	9	0	.438	325	369
Chicago	6	10	0	.375	253	324

Western Division

	W	L	T	Pct.	Pts.	OP
San Francisco#	13	3	0	.813	357	250
Atlanta	7	9	0	.438	426	355
Los Angeles	6	10	0	.375	303	351
New Orleans	4	12	0	.250	207	378

*Wild Card qualifier for playoffs; #Top playoff seed in conference
Baltimore finished ahead of New England based on head-to-head sweep (2-0). San Diego finished ahead of Denver based on better division record (6-2 to Broncos' 5-3). Buffalo was second Wild Card based on head-to-head victory over Denver (1-0). Detroit finished ahead of Green Bay based on better record against common opponents (5-5 to Packers' 4-6).
Wild Card playoff: Buffalo 31, N.Y. JETS 27
Divisional playoffs: San Diego 41, MIAMI 38 (OT); CINCINNATI 28, Buffalo 21
AFC Championship: CINCINNATI 27, San Diego 7
Wild Card playoff: N.Y. Giants 27, PHILADELPHIA 21
Divisional playoffs: DALLAS 38, Tampa Bay 0; SAN FRANCISCO 38, N.Y. Giants 24
NFC Championship: SAN FRANCISCO 28, Dallas 27
Super Bowl XVI: San Francisco (NFC) 26, Cincinnati (AFC) 21, at Silverdome, Pontiac, Michigan

1980

AMERICAN CONFERENCE
Eastern Division

	W	L	T	Pct.	Pts.	OP
Buffalo	11	5	0	.688	320	260
New England	10	6	0	.625	441	325
Miami	8	8	0	.500	266	305
Baltimore	7	9	0	.438	355	387
N.Y. Jets	4	12	0	.250	302	395

Central Division

	W	L	T	Pct.	Pts.	OP
Cleveland	11	5	0	.688	357	310
Houston*	11	5	0	.688	295	251
Pittsburgh	9	7	0	.563	352	313
Cincinnati	6	10	0	.375	244	312

Western Division

	W	L	T	Pct.	Pts.	OP
San Diego#	11	5	0	.688	418	327
Oakland*	11	5	0	.688	364	306
Kansas City	8	8	0	.500	319	336
Denver	8	8	0	.500	310	323
Seattle	4	12	0	.250	291	408

NATIONAL CONFERENCE
Eastern Division

	W	L	T	Pct.	Pts.	OP
Philadelphia	12	4	0	.750	384	222
Dallas*	12	4	0	.750	454	311
Washington	6	10	0	.375	261	293
St. Louis	5	11	0	.313	299	350
N.Y. Giants	4	12	0	.250	249	425

Central Division

	W	L	T	Pct.	Pts.	OP
Minnesota	9	7	0	.563	317	308
Detroit	9	7	0	.563	334	272
Chicago	7	9	0	.438	304	264
Tampa Bay	5	10	1	.344	271	341
Green Bay	5	10	1	.344	231	371

Western Division

	W	L	T	Pct.	Pts.	OP
Atlanta#	12	4	0	.750	405	272
Los Angeles*	11	5	0	.688	424	289
San Francisco	6	10	0	.375	320	415
New Orleans	1	15	0	.063	291	487

*Wild Card qualifier for playoffs; #Top playoff seed in conference
San Diego was top playoff seed based on better conference record than Cleveland and Buffalo (9-3 to Browns' 8-4 and Bills' 8-4). Cleveland was second playoff seed based on better record against common opponents (5-2 to Bills' 5-3). Cleveland finished ahead of Houston based on better conference record (8-4 to Oilers' 7-5). Oakland was first Wild Card based on better conference record than Houston (9-3 to Oilers' 7-5). San Diego finished ahead of Oakland based on better net points in division games (plus 60 net points to Raiders' plus 37). Oakland did not play San Diego in the divisional playoffs because, from 1970-1989, two teams from the same division could not meet prior to the conference championship game. Kansas City finished ahead of Denver based on head-to-head sweep (2-0). Atlanta was top playoff seed based on head-to-head victory over Philadelphia (1-0). Philadelphia finished ahead of Dallas based on better net points in division games (plus 84 net points to Cowboys' plus 50). Minnesota finished ahead of Detroit based on better conference record (8-4 to Lions' 9-5). Tampa Bay finished ahead of Green Bay based on better head-to-head record (1-0-1 to Packers' 0-1-1).
Wild Card playoff: OAKLAND 27, Houston 7
Divisional playoffs: SAN DIEGO 20, Buffalo 14; Oakland 14, CLEVELAND 12
AFC Championship: Oakland 34, SAN DIEGO 27
Wild Card playoff: DALLAS 34, Los Angeles 13
Divisional playoffs: PHILADELPHIA 31, Minnesota 16; Dallas 30, ATLANTA 27
NFC Championship: PHILADELPHIA 20, Dallas 7
Super Bowl XV: Oakland (AFC) 27, Philadelphia (NFC) 10, at Louisiana Superdome, New Orleans, Louisiana

1979

AMERICAN CONFERENCE

Eastern Division

	W	L	T	Pct.	Pts.	OP
Miami	10	6	0	.625	341	257
New England	9	7	0	.563	411	326
N.Y. Jets	8	8	0	.500	337	383
Buffalo	7	9	0	.438	268	279
Baltimore	5	11	0	.313	271	351

Central Division

	W	L	T	Pct.	Pts.	OP
Pittsburgh	12	4	0	.750	416	262
Houston*	11	5	0	.688	362	331
Cleveland	9	7	0	.563	359	352
Cincinnati	4	12	0	.250	337	421

Western Division

	W	L	T	Pct.	Pts.	OP
San Diego	12	4	0	.750	411	246
Denver*	10	6	0	.625	289	262
Seattle	9	7	0	.563	378	372
Oakland	9	7	0	.563	365	337
Kansas City	7	9	0	.438	238	262

NATIONAL CONFERENCE

Eastern Division

	W	L	T	Pct.	Pts.	OP
Dallas#	11	5	0	.688	371	313
Philadelphia*	11	5	0	.688	339	282
Washington	10	6	0	.625	348	295
N.Y. Giants	6	10	0	.375	237	323
St. Louis	5	11	0	.313	307	358

Central Division

	W	L	T	Pct.	Pts.	OP
Tampa Bay	10	6	0	.625	273	237
Chicago*	10	6	0	.625	306	249
Minnesota	7	9	0	.438	259	337
Green Bay	5	11	0	.313	246	316
Detroit	2	14	0	.125	219	365

Western Division

	W	L	T	Pct.	Pts.	OP
Los Angeles	9	7	0	.563	323	309
New Orleans	8	8	0	.500	370	360
Atlanta	6	10	0	.375	300	388
San Francisco	2	14	0	.125	308	416

*Wild Card qualifier for playoffs; #Top playoff seed in conference
San Diego was top playoff seed based on head-to-head victory over
Pittsburgh (1-0). Seattle finished ahead of Oakland based on
head-to-head sweep (2-0). Dallas finished ahead of Philadelphia
based on better conference record (10-2 to Eagles' 9-3).
Philadelphia did not play Dallas in the divisional playoffs because,
from 1970-1989, two teams from the same division could not
meet prior to the conference championship game. Tampa Bay
finished ahead of Chicago based on a better division record
(6-2 to Bears' 5-3). Chicago was second Wild Card ahead of
Washington based on better net points in all games (57 to
Redskins' 53).
Wild Card playoff: HOUSTON 13, Denver 7
Divisional playoffs: Houston 17, SAN DIEGO 14;
   PITTSBURGH 34, Miami 14
AFC Championship: PITTSBURGH 27, Houston 13
Wild Card playoff: PHILADELPHIA 27, Chicago 17
Divisional playoffs: TAMPA BAY 24, Philadelphia 17;
   Los Angeles 21, DALLAS 19
NFC Championship: Los Angeles 9, TAMPA BAY 0
Super Bowl XIV: Pittsburgh (AFC) 31, Los Angeles (NFC) 19,
   at Rose Bowl, Pasadena, California

1978

AMERICAN CONFERENCE

Eastern Division

	W	L	T	Pct.	Pts.	OP
New England	11	5	0	.688	358	286
Miami*	11	5	0	.688	372	254
N.Y. Jets	8	8	0	.500	359	364
Buffalo	5	11	0	.313	302	354
Baltimore	5	11	0	.313	239	421

Central Division

	W	L	T	Pct.	Pts.	OP
Pittsburgh#	14	2	0	.875	356	195
Houston*	10	6	0	.625	283	298
Cleveland	8	8	0	.500	334	356
Cincinnati	4	12	0	.250	252	284

Western Division

	W	L	T	Pct.	Pts.	OP
Denver	10	6	0	.625	282	198
Oakland	9	7	0	.563	311	283
Seattle	9	7	0	.563	345	358
San Diego	9	7	0	.563	355	309
Kansas City	4	12	0	.250	243	327

NATIONAL CONFERENCE

Eastern Division

	W	L	T	Pct.	Pts.	OP
Dallas	12	4	0	.750	384	208
Philadelphia*	9	7	0	.563	270	250
Washington	8	8	0	.500	273	283
St. Louis	6	10	0	.375	248	296
N.Y. Giants	6	10	0	.375	264	298

Central Division

	W	L	T	Pct.	Pts.	OP
Minnesota	8	7	1	.531	294	306
Green Bay	8	7	1	.531	249	269
Detroit	7	9	0	.438	290	300
Chicago	7	9	0	.438	253	274
Tampa Bay	5	11	0	.313	241	259

Western Division

	W	L	T	Pct.	Pts.	OP
Los Angeles#	12	4	0	.750	316	245
Atlanta*	9	7	0	.563	240	290
New Orleans	7	9	0	.438	281	298
San Francisco	2	14	0	.125	219	350

*Wild Card qualifier for playoffs; #Top playoff seed in conference
New England finished ahead of Miami based on better division
record (6-2 to Dolphins' 5-3). Buffalo finished ahead of Baltimore
based on head-to-head sweep (2-0). Oakland finished ahead of
Seattle and San Diego based on better record against common
opponents (6-2 to Seahawks' 5-3 and Chargers' 4-4). Atlanta
was first Wild Card based on better conference record than
Philadelphia (8-4 to Eagles' 6-6). Houston did not play
Pittsburgh, and Atlanta did not play Los Angeles in the divisional
playoffs because, from 1970-1989, two teams from the same
division could not meet prior to the conference championship
game. St. Louis finished ahead of N.Y. Giants based on better
division record (3-5 to Giants' 2-6). Minnesota finished ahead of
Green Bay based on better head-to-head record (1-0-1). Detroit
finished ahead of Chicago based on better division record (4-4 to
Bears' 3-5).
Wild Card playoff: Houston 17, MIAMI 9
Divisional playoffs: Houston 31, NEW ENGLAND 14;
   PITTSBURGH 33, Denver 10
AFC Championship: PITTSBURGH 34, Houston 5
Wild Card playoff: ATLANTA 14, Philadelphia 13
Divisional playoffs: DALLAS 27, Atlanta 20;
   LOS ANGELES 34, Minnesota 10
NFC Championship: Dallas 28, LOS ANGELES 0
Super Bowl XIII: Pittsburgh (AFC) 35, Dallas (NFC) 31,
   at Orange Bowl, Miami, Florida

1977

AMERICAN CONFERENCE
Eastern Division

	W	L	T	Pct.	Pts.	OP
Baltimore	10	4	0	.714	295	221
Miami	10	4	0	.714	313	197
New England	9	5	0	.643	278	217
Buffalo	3	11	0	.214	160	313
N.Y. Jets	3	11	0	.214	191	300

Central Division

	W	L	T	Pct.	Pts.	OP
Pittsburgh	9	5	0	.643	283	243
Cincinnati	8	6	0	.571	238	235
Houston	8	6	0	.571	299	230
Cleveland	6	8	0	.429	269	267

Western Division

	W	L	T	Pct.	Pts.	OP
Denver#	12	2	0	.857	274	148
Oakland*	11	3	0	.786	351	230
San Diego	7	7	0	.500	222	205
Seattle	5	9	0	.357	282	373
Kansas City	2	12	0	.143	225	349

NATIONAL CONFERENCE
Eastern Division

	W	L	T	Pct.	Pts.	OP
Dallas#	12	2	0	.857	345	212
Washington	9	5	0	.643	196	189
St. Louis	7	7	0	.500	272	287
Philadelphia	5	9	0	.357	220	207
N.Y. Giants	5	9	0	.357	181	265

Central Division

	W	L	T	Pct.	Pts.	OP
Minnesota	9	5	0	.643	231	227
Chicago*	9	5	0	.643	255	253
Detroit	6	8	0	.429	183	252
Green Bay	4	10	0	.286	134	219
Tampa Bay	2	12	0	.143	103	223

Western Division

	W	L	T	Pct.	Pts.	OP
Los Angeles	10	4	0	.714	302	146
Atlanta	7	7	0	.500	179	129
San Francisco	5	9	0	.357	220	260
New Orleans	3	11	0	.214	232	336

*Wild Card qualifier for playoffs; #Top playoff seed in conference
Baltimore finished ahead of Miami based on better conference
record (9-3 to Dolphins' 8-4). Buffalo finished ahead of N.Y. Jets
based on better strength of schedule (.582 to Jets' .536).
Cincinnati finished ahead of Houston based on better division
record (6-3 to Oilers' 5-4). Oakland did not play Denver in the
divisional playoffs because, from 1970-1989, two teams from the
same division could not meet prior to the conference
championship game. Minnesota finished ahead of Chicago based
on fewer losses by common opponents (11 losses to 14 losses
by the Bears' opponents). Chicago won Wild Card ahead of
Washington based on better net points in conference games
(48 to Redskins' 4). Philadelphia finished ahead of N.Y. Giants
based on head-to-head sweep (2-0).
Divisional playoffs: DENVER 34, Pittsburgh 21;
Oakland 37, BALTIMORE 31 (OT)
AFC Championship: DENVER 20, Oakland 17
Divisional playoffs: DALLAS 37, Chicago 7;
Minnesota 14, LOS ANGELES 7
NFC Championship: DALLAS 23, Minnesota 6
Super Bowl XII: Dallas (NFC) 27, Denver (AFC) 10,
at Louisiana Superdome, New Orleans, Louisiana

1976

AMERICAN CONFERENCE
Eastern Division

	W	L	T	Pct.	Pts.	OP
Baltimore	11	3	0	.786	417	246
New England*	11	3	0	.786	376	236
Miami	6	8	0	.429	263	264
N.Y. Jets	3	11	0	.214	169	383
Buffalo	2	12	0	.143	245	363

Central Division

	W	L	T	Pct.	Pts.	OP
Pittsburgh	10	4	0	.714	342	138
Cincinnati	10	4	0	.714	335	210
Cleveland	9	5	0	.643	267	287
Houston	5	9	0	.357	222	273

Western Division

	W	L	T	Pct.	Pts.	OP
Oakland#	13	1	0	.929	350	237
Denver	9	5	0	.643	315	206
San Diego	6	8	0	.429	248	285
Kansas City	5	9	0	.357	290	376
Tampa Bay	0	14	0	.000	125	412

NATIONAL CONFERENCE
Eastern Division

	W	L	T	Pct.	Pts.	OP
Dallas	11	3	0	.786	296	194
Washington*	10	4	0	.714	291	217
St. Louis	10	4	0	.714	309	267
Philadelphia	4	10	0	.286	165	286
N.Y. Giants	3	11	0	.214	170	250

Central Division

	W	L	T	Pct.	Pts.	OP
Minnesota#	11	2	1	.821	305	176
Chicago	7	7	0	.500	253	216
Detroit	6	8	0	.429	262	220
Green Bay	5	9	0	.357	218	299

Western Division

	W	L	T	Pct.	Pts.	OP
Los Angeles	10	3	1	.750	351	190
San Francisco	8	6	0	.571	270	190
Atlanta	4	10	0	.286	172	312
New Orleans	4	10	0	.286	253	346
Seattle	2	12	0	.143	229	429

*Wild Card qualifier for playoffs; #Top playoff seed in conference
Baltimore finished ahead of New England based on better division
record (7-1 to Patriots' 6-2). Pittsburgh finished ahead of
Cincinnati based on head-to-head sweep (2-0). Washington
finished ahead of St. Louis based on head-to-head sweep (2-0).
Atlanta finished ahead of New Orleans based on better division
record (2-4 to Saints' 1-5).
Divisional playoffs: OAKLAND 24, New England 21;
Pittsburgh 40, BALTIMORE 14
AFC Championship: OAKLAND 24, Pittsburgh 7
Divisional playoffs: MINNESOTA 35, Washington 20;
Los Angeles 14, DALLAS 12
NFC Championship: MINNESOTA 24, Los Angeles 13
Super Bowl XI: Oakland (AFC) 32, Minnesota (NFC) 14,
at Rose Bowl, Pasadena, California

1975

AMERICAN CONFERENCE

Eastern Division

	W	L	T	Pct.	Pts.	OP
Baltimore	10	4	0	.714	395	269
Miami	10	4	0	.714	357	222
Buffalo	8	6	0	.571	420	355
N.Y. Jets	3	11	0	.214	258	433
New England	3	11	0	.214	258	358

Central Division

	W	L	T	Pct.	Pts.	OP
Pittsburgh#	12	2	0	.857	373	162
Cincinnati*	11	3	0	.786	340	246
Houston	10	4	0	.714	293	226
Cleveland	3	11	0	.214	218	372

Western Division

	W	L	T	Pct.	Pts.	OP
Oakland	11	3	0	.786	375	255
Denver	6	8	0	.429	254	307
Kansas City	5	9	0	.357	282	341
San Diego	2	12	0	.143	189	345

NATIONAL CONFERENCE

Eastern Division

	W	L	T	Pct.	Pts.	OP
St. Louis	11	3	0	.786	356	276
Dallas*	10	4	0	.714	350	268
Washington	8	6	0	.571	325	276
N.Y. Giants	5	9	0	.357	216	306
Philadelphia	4	10	0	.286	225	302

Central Division

	W	L	T	Pct.	Pts.	OP
Minnesota#	12	2	0	.857	377	180
Detroit	7	7	0	.500	245	262
Chicago	4	10	0	.286	191	379
Green Bay	4	10	0	.286	226	285

Western Division

	W	L	T	Pct.	Pts.	OP
Los Angeles	12	2	0	.857	312	135
San Francisco	5	9	0	.357	255	286
Atlanta	4	10	0	.286	240	289
New Orleans	2	12	0	.143	165	360

Wild Card qualifier for playoffs; #Top playoff seed in conference
Baltimore finished ahead of Miami based on head-to-head sweep (2-0). Cincinnati did not play Pittsburgh in the divisional playoffs because, from 1970-1989, two teams from the same division could not meet prior to the conference championship game. N.Y. Jets finished ahead of New England based on head-to-head sweep (2-0). Minnesota was top playoff seed based on better Point Rating system than Los Angeles (3 to 6). Chicago finished ahead of Green Bay based on better division record (2-4 to Bears' 1-5).

Divisional playoffs: PITTSBURGH 28, Baltimore 10; OAKLAND 31, Cincinnati 28
AFC Championship: PITTSBURGH 16, Oakland 10
Divisional playoffs: LOS ANGELES 35, St. Louis 23; Dallas 17, MINNESOTA 14
NFC Championship: Dallas 37, LOS ANGELES 7
Super Bowl X: Pittsburgh (AFC) 21, Dallas (NFC) 17, at Orange Bowl, Miami, Florida

1974

AMERICAN CONFERENCE

Eastern Division

	W	L	T	Pct.	Pts.	OP
Miami	11	3	0	.786	327	216
Buffalo*	9	5	0	.643	264	244
New England	7	7	0	.500	348	289
N.Y. Jets	7	7	0	.500	279	300
Baltimore	2	12	0	.143	190	329

Central Division

	W	L	T	Pct.	Pts.	OP
Pittsburgh	10	3	1	.750	305	189
Houston	7	7	0	.500	236	282
Cincinnati	7	7	0	.500	283	259
Cleveland	4	10	0	.286	251	344

Western Division

	W	L	T	Pct.	Pts.	OP
Oakland	12	2	0	.857	355	228
Denver	7	6	1	.536	302	294
Kansas City	5	9	0	.357	233	293
San Diego	5	9	0	.357	212	285

NATIONAL CONFERENCE

Eastern Division

	W	L	T	Pct.	Pts.	OP
St. Louis	10	4	0	.714	285	218
Washington*	10	4	0	.714	320	196
Dallas	8	6	0	.571	297	235
Philadelphia	7	7	0	.500	242	217
N.Y. Giants	2	12	0	.143	195	299

Central Division

	W	L	T	Pct.	Pts.	OP
Minnesota	10	4	0	.714	310	195
Detroit	7	7	0	.500	256	270
Green Bay	6	8	0	.429	210	206
Chicago	4	10	0	.286	152	279

Western Division

	W	L	T	Pct.	Pts.	OP
Los Angeles	10	4	0	.714	263	181
San Francisco	6	8	0	.429	226	236
New Orleans	5	9	0	.357	166	263
Atlanta	3	11	0	.214	111	271

Wild Card qualifier for playoffs
New England finished ahead of N.Y. Jets based on better record against common opponents (5-4 to Jets' 4-5). Houston finished ahead of Cincinnati based on head-to-head sweep (2-0). Kansas City finished ahead of San Diego based on better record against common opponents (4-6 to Chargers' 3-7). St. Louis finished ahead of Washington based on head-to-head sweep (2-0).

Divisional playoffs: OAKLAND 28, Miami 26; PITTSBURGH 32, Buffalo 14
AFC Championship: Pittsburgh 24, OAKLAND 13
Divisional playoffs: MINNESOTA 30, St. Louis 14; LOS ANGELES 19, Washington 10
NFC Championship: MINNESOTA 14, Los Angeles 10
Super Bowl IX: Pittsburgh (AFC) 16, Minnesota (NFC) 6, at Tulane Stadium, New Orleans, Louisiana

From 1933-1974, sites for league/conference championship games alternated by division.

1973

AMERICAN CONFERENCE

Eastern Division

	W	L	T	Pct.	Pts.	OP
Miami	12	2	0	.857	343	150
Buffalo	9	5	0	.643	259	230
New England	5	9	0	.357	258	300
N.Y. Jets	4	10	0	.286	240	306
Baltimore	4	10	0	.286	226	341

Central Division

	W	L	T	Pct.	Pts.	OP
Cincinnati	10	4	0	.714	286	231
Pittsburgh*	10	4	0	.714	347	210
Cleveland	7	5	2	.571	234	255
Houston	1	13	0	.071	199	447

Western Division

	W	L	T	Pct.	Pts.	OP
Oakland	9	4	1	.679	292	175
Kansas City	7	5	2	.571	231	192
Denver	7	5	2	.571	354	296
San Diego	2	11	1	.179	188	386

NATIONAL CONFERENCE

Eastern Division

	W	L	T	Pct.	Pts.	OP
Dallas	10	4	0	.714	382	203
Washington*	10	4	0	.714	325	198
Philadelphia	5	8	1	.393	310	393
St. Louis	4	9	1	.321	286	365
N.Y. Giants	2	11	1	.179	226	362

Central Division

	W	L	T	Pct.	Pts.	OP
Minnesota	12	2	0	.857	296	168
Detroit	6	7	1	.464	271	247
Green Bay	5	7	2	.429	202	259
Chicago	3	11	0	.214	195	334

Western Division

	W	L	T	Pct.	Pts.	OP
Los Angeles	12	2	0	.857	388	178
Atlanta	9	5	0	.643	318	224
San Francisco	5	9	0	.357	262	319
New Orleans	5	9	0	.357	163	312

Wild Card qualifier for playoffs

Cincinnati finished ahead of Pittsburgh based on better conference record (8-3 to Steelers' 7-4). N.Y. Jets finished ahead of Baltimore based on head-to-head sweep (2-0). Kansas City finished ahead of Denver based on better division record (4-2 to Broncos' 3-2-1). Dallas finished ahead of Washington based on better point differential in head-to-head games (13 points). San Francisco finished ahead of New Orleans based on better division record (2-4 to Saints' 1-5).

Divisional playoffs: OAKLAND 33, Pittsburgh 14;
  MIAMI 34, Cincinnati 16
AFC Championship: MIAMI 27, Oakland 10
Divisional playoffs: MINNESOTA 27, Washington 20;
  DALLAS 27, Los Angeles 16
NFC Championship: Minnesota 27, DALLAS 10
Super Bowl VIII: Miami (AFC) 24, Minnesota (NFC) 7,
  at Rice Stadium, Houston, Texas

1972

AMERICAN CONFERENCE

Eastern Division

	W	L	T	Pct.	Pts.	OP
Miami	14	0	0	1.000	385	171
N.Y. Jets	7	7	0	.500	367	324
Baltimore	5	9	0	.357	235	252
Buffalo	4	9	1	.321	257	377
New England	3	11	0	.214	192	446

Central Division

	W	L	T	Pct.	Pts.	OP
Pittsburgh	11	3	0	.786	343	175
Cleveland*	10	4	0	.714	268	249
Cincinnati	8	6	0	.571	299	229
Houston	1	13	0	.071	164	380

Western Division

	W	L	T	Pct.	Pts.	OP
Oakland	10	3	1	.750	365	248
Kansas City	8	6	0	.571	287	254
Denver	5	9	0	.357	325	350
San Diego	4	9	1	.321	264	344

NATIONAL CONFERENCE

Eastern Division

	W	L	T	Pct.	Pts.	OP
Washington	11	3	0	.786	336	218
Dallas*	10	4	0	.714	319	240
N.Y. Giants	8	6	0	.571	331	247
St. Louis	4	9	1	.321	193	303
Philadelphia	2	11	1	.179	145	352

Central Division

	W	L	T	Pct.	Pts.	OP
Green Bay	10	4	0	.714	304	226
Detroit	8	5	1	.607	339	290
Minnesota	7	7	0	.500	301	252
Chicago	4	9	1	.321	225	275

Western Division

	W	L	T	Pct.	Pts.	OP
San Francisco	8	5	1	.607	353	249
Atlanta	7	7	0	.500	269	274
Los Angeles	6	7	1	.464	291	286
New Orleans	2	11	1	.179	215	361

Wild Card qualifier for playoffs

Dallas did not play Washington in the divisional playoffs because, from 1970-1989, two teams from the same division could not meet prior to the conference championship game.

Divisional playoffs: PITTSBURGH 13, Oakland 7;
  MIAMI 20, Cleveland 14
AFC Championship: Miami 21, PITTSBURGH 17
Divisional playoffs: Dallas 30, SAN FRANCISCO 28;
  WASHINGTON 16, Green Bay 3
NFC Championship: WASHINGTON 26, Dallas 3
Super Bowl VII: Miami (AFC) 14, Washington (NFC) 7,
  at Memorial Coliseum, Los Angeles, California

1971

AMERICAN CONFERENCE

Eastern Division
	W	L	T	Pct.	Pts.	OP
Miami	10	3	1	.769	315	174
Baltimore*	10	4	0	.714	313	140
New England	6	8	0	.429	238	325
N.Y. Jets	6	8	0	.429	212	299
Buffalo	1	13	0	.071	184	394

Central Division
	W	L	T	Pct.	Pts.	OP
Cleveland	9	5	0	.643	285	273
Pittsburgh	6	8	0	.429	246	292
Houston	4	9	1	.308	251	330
Cincinnati	4	10	0	.286	284	265

Western Division
	W	L	T	Pct.	Pts.	OP
Kansas City	10	3	1	.769	302	208
Oakland	8	4	2	.667	344	278
San Diego	6	8	0	.429	311	341
Denver	4	9	1	.308	203	275

NATIONAL CONFERENCE

Eastern Division
	W	L	T	Pct.	Pts.	OP
Dallas	11	3	0	.786	406	222
Washington*	9	4	1	.692	276	190
Philadelphia	6	7	1	.462	221	302
St. Louis	4	9	1	.308	231	279
N.Y. Giants	4	10	0	.286	228	362

Central Division
	W	L	T	Pct.	Pts.	OP
Minnesota	11	3	0	.786	245	139
Detroit	7	6	1	.538	341	286
Chicago	6	8	0	.429	185	276
Green Bay	4	8	2	.333	274	298

Western Division
	W	L	T	Pct.	Pts.	OP
San Francisco	9	5	0	.643	300	216
Los Angeles	8	5	1	.615	313	260
Atlanta	7	6	1	.538	274	277
New Orleans	4	8	2	.333	266	347

Wild Card qualifier for playoffs
New England finished ahead of N.Y. Jets based on better strength of schedule (.537 to Jets' .510).
Divisional playoffs: Miami 27, KANSAS CITY 24 (OT); Baltimore 20, CLEVELAND 3
AFC Championship: MIAMI 21, Baltimore 0
Divisional playoffs: Dallas 20, MINNESOTA 12; SAN FRANCISCO 24, Washington 20
NFC Championship: DALLAS 14, San Francisco 3
Super Bowl VI: Dallas (NFC) 24, Miami (AFC) 3, at Tulane Stadium, New Orleans, Louisiana

From 1920-1971, tie games were not included in winning percentage.

1970

AMERICAN CONFERENCE

Eastern Division
	W	L	T	Pct.	Pts.	OP
Baltimore	11	2	1	.846	321	234
Miami*	10	4	0	.714	297	228
N.Y. Jets	4	10	0	.286	255	286
Buffalo	3	10	1	.231	204	337
Boston Patriots	2	12	0	.143	149	361

Central Division
	W	L	T	Pct.	Pts.	OP
Cincinnati	8	6	0	.571	312	255
Cleveland	7	7	0	.500	286	265
Pittsburgh	5	9	0	.357	210	272
Houston	3	10	1	.231	217	352

Western Division
	W	L	T	Pct.	Pts.	OP
Oakland	8	4	2	.667	300	293
Kansas City	7	5	2	.583	272	244
San Diego	5	6	3	.455	282	278
Denver	5	8	1	.385	253	264

NATIONAL CONFERENCE

Eastern Division
	W	L	T	Pct.	Pts.	OP
Dallas	10	4	0	.714	299	221
N.Y. Giants	9	5	0	.643	301	270
St. Louis	8	5	1	.615	325	228
Washington	6	8	0	.429	297	314
Philadelphia	3	10	1	.231	241	332

Central Division
	W	L	T	Pct.	Pts.	OP
Minnesota	12	2	0	.857	335	143
Detroit*	10	4	0	.714	347	202
Green Bay	6	8	0	.429	196	293
Chicago	6	8	0	.429	256	261

Western Division
	W	L	T	Pct.	Pts.	OP
San Francisco	10	3	1	.769	352	267
Los Angeles	9	4	1	.692	325	202
Atlanta	4	8	2	.333	206	261
New Orleans	2	11	1	.154	172	347

Wild Card qualifier for playoffs
Miami did not play Baltimore, and Detroit did not play Minnesota, in the divisional playoffs because, from 1970-1989, two teams from the same division could not meet prior to the conference championship game. Green Bay finished ahead of Chicago based on better division record (2-4 to Bears' 1-5).
Divisional playoffs: BALTIMORE 17, Cincinnati 0; OAKLAND 21, Miami 14
AFC Championship: BALTIMORE 27, Oakland 17
Divisional playoffs: DALLAS 5, Detroit 0; San Francisco 17, MINNESOTA 14
NFC Championship: Dallas 17, SAN FRANCISCO 10
Super Bowl V: Baltimore (AFC) 16, Dallas (NFC) 13, at Orange Bowl, Miami, Florida

1969 NFL

EASTERN CONFERENCE
Capitol Division

	W	L	T	Pct.	Pts.	OP
Dallas	11	2	1	.846	369	223
Washington	7	5	2	.583	307	319
New Orleans	5	9	0	.357	311	393
Philadelphia	4	9	1	.308	279	377

Century Division

	W	L	T	Pct.	Pts.	OP
Cleveland	10	3	1	.769	351	300
N.Y. Giants	6	8	0	.429	264	298
St. Louis	4	9	1	.308	314	389
Pittsburgh	1	13	0	.071	218	404

WESTERN CONFERENCE
Coastal Division

	W	L	T	Pct.	Pts.	OP
Los Angeles	11	3	0	.786	320	243
Baltimore	8	5	1	.615	279	268
Atlanta	6	8	0	.429	276	268
San Francisco	4	8	2	.333	277	319

Central Division

	W	L	T	Pct.	Pts.	OP
Minnesota	12	2	0	.857	379	133
Detroit	9	4	1	.692	259	188
Green Bay	8	6	0	.571	269	221
Chicago	1	13	0	.071	210	339

Conference championships: Cleveland 38, DALLAS 14;
  MINNESOTA 23, Los Angeles 20
NFL championship: MINNESOTA 27, Cleveland 7
Super Bowl IV: Kansas City (AFL) 23, Minnesota (NFL) 7,
  at Tulane Stadium, New Orleans, Louisiana

1969 AFL

EASTERN DIVISION

	W	L	T	Pct.	Pts.	OP
N.Y. Jets	10	4	0	.714	353	269
Houston	6	6	2	.500	278	279
Boston Patriots	4	10	0	.286	266	316
Buffalo	4	10	0	.286	230	359
Miami	3	10	1	.231	233	332

WESTERN DIVISION

	W	L	T	Pct.	Pts.	OP
Oakland	12	1	1	.923	377	242
Kansas City	11	3	0	.786	359	177
San Diego	8	6	0	.571	288	276
Denver	5	8	1	.385	297	344
Cincinnati	4	9	1	.308	280	367

Divisional playoffs: Kansas City 13, N.Y. JETS 6;
  OAKLAND 56, Houston 7
AFL championship: Kansas City 17, OAKLAND 7

1968 NFL

EASTERN CONFERENCE
Capitol Division

	W	L	T	Pct.	Pts.	OP
Dallas	12	2	0	.857	431	186
N.Y. Giants	7	7	0	.500	294	325
Washington	5	9	0	.357	249	358
Philadelphia	2	12	0	.143	202	351

Century Division

	W	L	T	Pct.	Pts.	OP
Cleveland	10	4	0	.714	394	273
St. Louis	9	4	1	.692	325	289
New Orleans	4	9	1	.308	246	327
Pittsburgh	2	11	1	.154	244	397

WESTERN CONFERENCE
Coastal Division

	W	L	T	Pct.	Pts.	OP
Baltimore	13	1	0	.929	402	144
Los Angeles	10	3	1	.769	312	200
San Francisco	7	6	1	.538	303	310
Atlanta	2	12	0	.143	170	389

Central Division

	W	L	T	Pct.	Pts.	OP
Minnesota	8	6	0	.571	282	242
Chicago	7	7	0	.500	250	333
Green Bay	6	7	1	.462	281	227
Detroit	4	8	2	.333	207	241

Conference championships: CLEVELAND 31, Dallas 20;
  BALTIMORE 24, Minnesota 14
NFL championship: Baltimore 34, CLEVELAND 0
Super Bowl III: N.Y. Jets (AFL) 16, Baltimore (NFL) 7,
  at Orange Bowl, Miami, Florida

1968 AFL

EASTERN DIVISION

	W	L	T	Pct.	Pts.	OP
N.Y. Jets	11	3	0	.786	419	280
Houston	7	7	0	.500	303	248
Miami	5	8	1	.385	276	355
Boston Patriots	4	10	0	.286	229	406
Buffalo	1	12	1	.077	199	367

WESTERN DIVISION

	W	L	T	Pct.	Pts.	OP
Oakland	12	2	0	.857	453	233
Kansas City	12	2	0	.857	371	170
San Diego	9	5	0	.643	382	310
Denver	5	9	0	.357	255	404
Cincinnati	3	11	0	.214	215	329

Western Division playoff: OAKLAND 41, Kansas City 6
AFL championship: N.Y. JETS 27, Oakland 23

1967 NFL

EASTERN CONFERENCE
Capitol Division

	W	L	T	Pct.	Pts.	OP
Dallas	9	5	0	.643	342	268
Philadelphia	6	7	1	.462	351	409
Washington	5	6	3	.455	347	353
New Orleans	3	11	0	.214	233	379

Century Division

	W	L	T	Pct.	Pts.	OP
Cleveland	9	5	0	.643	334	297
N.Y. Giants	7	7	0	.500	369	379
St. Louis	6	7	1	.462	333	356
Pittsburgh	4	9	1	.308	281	320

WESTERN CONFERENCE
Coastal Division

	W	L	T	Pct.	Pts.	OP
Los Angeles	11	1	2	.917	398	196
Baltimore	11	1	2	.917	394	198
San Francisco	7	7	0	.500	273	337
Atlanta	1	12	1	.077	175	422

Central Division

	W	L	T	Pct.	Pts.	OP
Green Bay	9	4	1	.692	332	209
Chicago	7	6	1	.538	239	218
Detroit	5	7	2	.417	260	259
Minnesota	3	8	3	.273	233	294

*Los Angeles finished ahead of Baltimore based on better point dif-
ferential in head-to-head games (net 24 points).*
Conference championships: DALLAS 52, Cleveland 14;
  GREEN BAY 28, Los Angeles 7
NFL championship: GREEN BAY 21, Dallas 17
Super Bowl II: Green Bay (NFL) 33, Oakland (AFL) 14,
  at Orange Bowl, Miami, Florida

1967 AFL

EASTERN DIVISION

	W	L	T	Pct.	Pts.	OP
Houston	9	4	1	.692	258	199
N.Y. Jets	8	5	1	.615	371	329
Buffalo	4	10	0	.286	237	285
Miami	4	10	0	.286	219	407
Boston Patriots	3	10	1	.231	280	389

WESTERN DIVISION

	W	L	T	Pct.	Pts.	OP
Oakland	13	1	0	.929	468	233
Kansas City	9	5	0	.643	408	254
San Diego	8	5	1	.615	360	352
Denver	3	11	0	.214	256	409

AFL championship: OAKLAND 40, Houston 7

1966 NFL

EASTERN CONFERENCE

	W	L	T	Pct.	Pts.	OP
Dallas	10	3	1	.769	445	239
Cleveland	9	5	0	.643	403	259
Philadelphia	9	5	0	.643	326	340
St. Louis	8	5	1	.615	264	265
Washington	7	7	0	.500	351	355
Pittsburgh	5	8	1	.385	316	347
Atlanta	3	11	0	.214	204	437
N.Y. Giants	1	12	1	.077	263	501

WESTERN CONFERENCE

	W	L	T	Pct.	Pts.	OP
Green Bay	12	2	0	.857	335	163
Baltimore	9	5	0	.643	314	226
Los Angeles	8	6	0	.571	289	212
San Francisco	6	6	2	.500	320	325
Chicago	5	7	2	.417	234	272
Detroit	4	9	1	.308	206	317
Minnesota	4	9	1	.308	292	304

NFL championship: Green Bay 34, DALLAS 27
Super Bowl I: Green Bay (NFL) 35, Kansas City (AFL) 10,
  at Memorial Coliseum, Los Angeles, California

1966 AFL

EASTERN DIVISION

	W	L	T	Pct.	Pts.	OP
Buffalo	9	4	1	.692	358	255
Boston Patriots	8	4	2	.677	315	283
N.Y. Jets	6	6	2	.500	322	312
Houston	3	11	0	.214	335	396
Miami	3	11	0	.214	213	362

WESTERN DIVISION

	W	L	T	Pct.	Pts.	OP
Kansas City	11	2	1	.846	448	276
Oakland	8	5	1	.615	315	288
San Diego	7	6	1	.538	335	284
Denver	4	10	0	.286	196	381

AFL championship: Kansas City 31, BUFFALO 7

1965 NFL

EASTERN CONFERENCE	W	L	T	Pct.	Pts.	OP	WESTERN CONFERENCE	W	L	T	Pct.	Pts.	OP
Cleveland	11	3	0	.786	363	325	Green Bay	10	3	1	.769	316	224
Dallas	7	7	0	.500	325	280	Baltimore	10	3	1	.769	389	284
N.Y. Giants	7	7	0	.500	270	338	Chicago	9	5	0	.643	409	275
Washington	6	8	0	.429	257	301	San Francisco	7	6	1	.538	421	402
Philadelphia	5	9	0	.357	363	359	Minnesota	7	7	0	.500	383	403
St. Louis	5	9	0	.357	296	309	Detroit	6	7	1	.462	257	295
Pittsburgh	2	12	0	.143	202	397	Los Angeles	4	10	0	.286	269	328

Western Conference playoff: GREEN BAY 13, Baltimore 10 (OT)
NFL championship: GREEN BAY 23, Cleveland 12

1965 AFL

EASTERN DIVISION	W	L	T	Pct.	Pts.	OP	WESTERN DIVISION	W	L	T	Pct.	Pts.	OP
Buffalo	10	3	1	.769	313	226	San Diego	9	2	3	.818	340	227
N.Y. Jets	5	8	1	.385	285	303	Oakland	8	5	1	.615	298	239
Boston Patriots	4	8	2	.333	244	302	Kansas City	7	5	2	.583	322	285
Houston	4	10	0	.286	298	429	Denver	4	10	0	.286	303	392

AFL championship: Buffalo 23, SAN DIEGO 0

1964 NFL

EASTERN CONFERENCE	W	L	T	Pct.	Pts.	OP	WESTERN CONFERENCE	W	L	T	Pct.	Pts.	OP
Cleveland	10	3	1	.769	415	293	Baltimore	12	2	0	.857	428	225
St. Louis	9	3	2	.750	357	331	Green Bay	8	5	1	.615	342	245
Philadelphia	6	8	0	.429	312	313	Minnesota	8	5	1	.615	355	296
Washington	6	8	0	.429	307	305	Detroit	7	5	2	.583	280	260
Dallas	5	8	1	.385	250	289	Los Angeles	5	7	2	.417	283	339
Pittsburgh	5	9	0	.357	253	315	Chicago	5	9	0	.357	260	379
N.Y. Giants	2	10	2	.167	241	399	San Francisco	4	10	0	.286	236	330

NFL championship: CLEVELAND 27, Baltimore 0

1964 AFL

EASTERN DIVISION	W	L	T	Pct.	Pts.	OP	WESTERN DIVISION	W	L	T	Pct.	Pts.	OP
Buffalo	12	2	0	.857	400	242	San Diego	8	5	1	.615	341	300
Boston Patriots	10	3	1	.769	365	297	Kansas City	7	7	0	.500	366	306
N.Y. Jets	5	8	1	.385	278	315	Oakland	5	7	2	.417	303	350
Houston	4	10	0	.286	310	355	Denver	2	11	1	.154	240	438

AFL championship: BUFFALO 20, San Diego 7

1963 NFL

EASTERN CONFERENCE	W	L	T	Pct.	Pts.	OP	WESTERN CONFERENCE	W	L	T	Pct.	Pts.	OP
N.Y. Giants	11	3	0	.786	448	280	Chicago	11	1	2	.917	301	144
Cleveland	10	4	0	.714	343	262	Green Bay	11	2	1	.846	369	206
St. Louis	9	5	0	.643	341	283	Baltimore	8	6	0	.571	316	285
Pittsburgh	7	4	3	.636	321	295	Detroit	5	8	1	.385	326	265
Dallas	4	10	0	.286	305	378	Minnesota	5	8	1	.385	309	390
Washington	3	11	0	.214	279	398	Los Angeles	5	9	0	.357	210	350
Philadelphia	2	10	2	.167	242	381	San Francisco	2	12	0	.143	198	391

NFL championship: CHICAGO 14, N.Y. Giants 10

1963 AFL

EASTERN DIVISION	W	L	T	Pct.	Pts.	OP	WESTERN DIVISION	W	L	T	Pct.	Pts.	OP
Boston Patriots	7	6	1	.538	327	257	San Diego	11	3	0	.786	399	255
Buffalo	7	6	1	.538	304	291	Oakland	10	4	0	.714	363	282
Houston	6	8	0	.429	302	372	Kansas City	5	7	2	.417	347	263
N.Y. Jets	5	8	1	.385	249	399	Denver	2	11	1	.154	301	473

Eastern Division playoff: Boston 26, BUFFALO 8
AFL championship: SAN DIEGO 51, Boston 10

1962 NFL

EASTERN CONFERENCE	W	L	T	Pct.	Pts.	OP	WESTERN CONFERENCE	W	L	T	Pct.	Pts.	OP
N.Y. Giants	12	2	0	.857	398	283	Green Bay	13	1	0	.929	415	148
Pittsburgh	9	5	0	.643	312	363	Detroit	11	3	0	.786	315	177
Cleveland	7	6	1	.538	291	257	Chicago	9	5	0	.643	321	287
Washington	5	7	2	.417	305	376	Baltimore	7	7	0	.500	293	288
Dallas Cowboys	5	8	1	.385	398	402	San Francisco	6	8	0	.429	282	331
St. Louis	4	9	1	.308	287	361	Minnesota	2	11	1	.154	254	410
Philadelphia	3	10	1	.231	282	356	Los Angeles	1	12	1	.077	220	334

NFL championship: Green Bay 16, N.Y. GIANTS 7

1962 AFL

EASTERN DIVISION	W	L	T	Pct.	Pts.	OP	WESTERN DIVISION	W	L	T	Pct.	Pts.	OP
Houston	11	3	0	.786	387	270	Dallas Texans	11	3	0	.786	389	233
Boston Patriots	9	4	1	.692	346	295	Denver	7	7	0	.500	353	334
Buffalo	7	6	1	.538	309	272	San Diego	4	10	0	.286	314	392
N.Y. Titans	5	9	0	.357	278	423	Oakland	1	13	0	.071	213	370

AFL championship: Dallas Texans 20, HOUSTON 17 (OT)

1961 NFL

EASTERN CONFERENCE	W	L	T	Pct.	Pts.	OP	WESTERN CONFERENCE	W	L	T	Pct.	Pts.	OP
N.Y. Giants	10	3	1	.769	368	220	Green Bay	11	3	0	.786	391	223
Philadelphia	10	4	0	.714	361	297	Detroit	8	5	1	.615	270	258
Cleveland	8	5	1	.615	319	270	Baltimore	8	6	0	.571	302	307
St. Louis	7	7	0	.500	279	267	Chicago	8	6	0	.571	326	302
Pittsburgh	6	8	0	.429	295	287	San Francisco	7	6	1	.538	346	272
Dallas Cowboys	4	9	1	.308	236	380	Los Angeles	4	10	0	.286	263	333
Washington	1	12	1	.077	174	392	Minnesota	3	11	0	.214	285	407

NFL championship: GREEN BAY 37, N.Y. Giants 0

1961 AFL

EASTERN DIVISION	W	L	T	Pct.	Pts.	OP	WESTERN DIVISION	W	L	T	Pct.	Pts.	OP
Houston	10	3	1	.769	513	242	San Diego	12	2	0	.857	396	219
Boston Patriots	9	4	1	.692	413	313	Dallas Texans	6	8	0	.429	334	343
N.Y. Titans	7	7	0	.500	301	390	Denver	3	11	0	.214	251	432
Buffalo	6	8	0	.429	294	342	Oakland	2	12	0	.143	237	458

AFL championship: Houston 10, SAN DIEGO 3

1960 NFL

EASTERN CONFERENCE	W	L	T	Pct.	Pts.	OP	WESTERN CONFERENCE	W	L	T	Pct.	Pts.	OP
Philadelphia	10	2	0	.833	321	246	Green Bay	8	4	0	.667	332	209
Cleveland	8	3	1	.727	362	217	Detroit	7	5	0	.583	239	212
N.Y. Giants	6	4	2	.600	271	261	San Francisco	7	5	0	.583	208	205
St. Louis	6	5	1	.545	288	230	Baltimore	6	6	0	.500	288	234
Pittsburgh	5	6	1	.455	240	275	Chicago	5	6	1	.455	194	299
Washington	1	9	2	.100	178	309	L.A. Rams	4	7	1	.364	265	297
							Dallas Cowboys	0	11	1	.000	177	369

NFL championship: PHILADELPHIA 17, Green Bay 13

1960 AFL

EASTERN CONFERENCE	W	L	T	Pct.	Pts.	OP	WESTERN CONFERENCE	W	L	T	Pct.	Pts.	OP
Houston	10	4	0	.714	379	285	L.A. Chargers	10	4	0	.714	373	336
N.Y. Titans	7	7	0	.500	382	399	Dallas Texans	8	6	0	.571	362	253
Buffalo	5	8	1	.385	296	303	Oakland	6	8	0	.429	319	388
Boston Patriots	5	9	0	.357	286	349	Denver	4	9	1	.308	309	393

AFL championship: HOUSTON 24, L.A. Chargers 16

1959

EASTERN CONFERENCE

	W	L	T	Pct.	Pts.	OP
N.Y. Giants	10	2	0	.833	284	170
Cleveland	7	5	0	.583	270	214
Philadelphia	7	5	0	.583	268	278
Pittsburgh	6	5	1	.545	257	216
Washington	3	9	0	.250	185	350
Chi. Cardinals	2	10	0	.167	234	324

WESTERN CONFERENCE

	W	L	T	Pct.	Pts.	OP
Baltimore	9	3	0	.750	374	251
Chi. Bears	8	4	0	.667	252	196
Green Bay	7	5	0	.583	248	246
San Francisco	7	5	0	.583	255	237
Detroit	3	8	1	.273	203	275
Los Angeles	2	10	0	.167	242	315

NFL championship: BALTIMORE 31, N.Y. Giants 16

1958

EASTERN CONFERENCE

	W	L	T	Pct.	Pts.	OP
N.Y. Giants	9	3	0	.750	246	183
Cleveland	9	3	0	.750	302	217
Pittsburgh	7	4	1	.636	261	230
Washington	4	7	1	.364	214	268
Chi. Cardinals	2	9	1	.182	261	356
Philadelphia	2	9	1	.182	235	306

WESTERN CONFERENCE

	W	L	T	Pct.	Pts.	OP
Baltimore	9	3	0	.750	381	203
Chi. Bears	8	4	0	.667	298	230
Los Angeles	8	4	0	.667	344	278
San Francisco	6	6	0	.500	257	324
Detroit	4	7	1	.364	261	276
Green Bay	1	10	1	.091	193	382

Eastern Conference playoff: N.Y. GIANTS 10, Cleveland 0
NFL championship: Baltimore 23, N.Y. GIANTS 17 (OT)

1957

EASTERN CONFERENCE

	W	L	T	Pct.	Pts.	OP
Cleveland	9	2	1	.818	269	172
N.Y. Giants	7	5	0	.583	254	211
Pittsburgh	6	6	0	.500	161	178
Washington	5	6	1	.455	251	230
Philadelphia	4	8	0	.333	173	230
Chi. Cardinals	3	9	0	.250	200	299

WESTERN CONFERENCE

	W	L	T	Pct.	Pts.	OP
Detroit	8	4	0	.667	251	231
San Francisco	8	4	0	.667	260	264
Baltimore	7	5	0	.583	303	235
Los Angeles	6	6	0	.500	307	278
Chi. Bears	5	7	0	.417	203	211
Green Bay	3	9	0	.250	218	311

Western Conference playoff: Detroit 31, SAN FRANCISCO 27
NFL championship: DETROIT 59, Cleveland 14

1956

EASTERN CONFERENCE

	W	L	T	Pct.	Pts.	OP
N.Y. Giants	8	3	1	.727	264	197
Chi. Cardinals	7	5	0	.583	240	182
Washington	6	6	0	.500	183	225
Cleveland	5	7	0	.417	167	177
Pittsburgh	5	7	0	.417	217	250
Philadelphia	3	8	1	.273	143	215

WESTERN CONFERENCE

	W	L	T	Pct.	Pts.	OP
Chi. Bears	9	2	1	.818	363	246
Detroit	9	3	0	.750	300	188
San Francisco	5	6	1	.455	233	284
Baltimore	5	7	0	.417	270	322
Green Bay	4	8	0	.333	264	342
Los Angeles	4	8	0	.333	291	307

NFL championship: N.Y. GIANTS 47, Chi. Bears 7

1955

EASTERN CONFERENCE

	W	L	T	Pct.	Pts.	OP
Cleveland	9	2	1	.818	349	218
Washington	8	4	0	.667	246	222
N.Y. Giants	6	5	1	.545	267	223
Chi. Cardinals	4	7	1	.364	224	252
Philadelphia	4	7	1	.364	248	231
Pittsburgh	4	8	0	.333	195	285

WESTERN CONFERENCE

	W	L	T	Pct.	Pts.	OP
Los Angeles	8	3	1	.727	260	231
Chi. Bears	8	4	0	.667	294	251
Green Bay	6	6	0	.500	258	276
Baltimore	5	6	1	.455	214	239
San Francisco	4	8	0	.333	216	298
Detroit	3	9	0	.250	230	275

NFL championship: Cleveland 38, LOS ANGELES 14

1954

EASTERN CONFERENCE

	W	L	T	Pct.	Pts.	OP
Cleveland	9	3	0	.750	336	162
Philadelphia	7	4	1	.636	284	230
N.Y. Giants	7	5	0	.583	293	184
Pittsburgh	5	7	0	.417	219	263
Washington	3	9	0	.250	207	432
Chi. Cardinals	2	10	0	.167	183	347

WESTERN CONFERENCE

	W	L	T	Pct.	Pts.	OP
Detroit	9	2	1	.818	337	189
Chi. Bears	8	4	0	.667	301	279
San Francisco	7	4	1	.636	313	251
Los Angeles	6	5	1	.545	314	285
Green Bay	4	8	0	.333	234	251
Baltimore	3	9	0	.250	131	279

NFL championship: CLEVELAND 56, Detroit 10

1953

EASTERN CONFERENCE

	W	L	T	Pct.	Pts.	OP
Cleveland	11	1	0	.917	348	162
Philadelphia	7	4	1	.636	352	215
Washington	6	5	1	.545	208	215
Pittsburgh	6	6	0	.500	211	263
N.Y. Giants	3	9	0	.250	179	277
Chi. Cardinals	1	10	1	.091	190	337

WESTERN CONFERENCE

	W	L	T	Pct.	Pts.	OP
Detroit	10	2	0	.833	271	205
San Francisco	9	3	0	.750	372	237
Los Angeles	8	3	1	.727	366	236
Chi. Bears	3	8	1	.273	218	262
Baltimore	3	9	0	.250	182	350
Green Bay	2	9	1	.182	200	338

NFL championship: DETROIT 17, Cleveland 16

1952

AMERICAN CONFERENCE

	W	L	T	Pct.	Pts.	OP
Cleveland	8	4	0	.667	310	213
N.Y. Giants	7	5	0	.583	234	231
Philadelphia	7	5	0	.583	252	271
Pittsburgh	5	7	0	.417	300	273
Chi. Cardinals	4	8	0	.333	172	221
Washington	4	8	0	.333	240	287

NATIONAL CONFERENCE

	W	L	T	Pct.	Pts.	OP
Detroit	9	3	0	.750	344	192
Los Angeles	9	3	0	.750	349	234
San Francisco	7	5	0	.583	285	221
Green Bay	6	6	0	.500	295	312
Chi. Bears	5	7	0	.417	245	326
Dallas Texans	1	11	0	.083	182	427

National Conference playoff: DETROIT 31, Los Angeles 21
NFL championship: Detroit 17, CLEVELAND 7

1951

AMERICAN CONFERENCE

	W	L	T	Pct.	Pts.	OP
Cleveland	11	1	0	.917	331	152
N.Y. Giants	9	2	1	.818	254	161
Washington	5	7	0	.417	183	296
Pittsburgh	4	7	1	.364	183	235
Philadelphia	4	8	0	.333	234	264
Chi. Cardinals	3	9	0	.250	210	287

NATIONAL CONFERENCE

	W	L	T	Pct.	Pts.	OP
Los Angeles	8	4	0	.667	392	261
Detroit	7	4	1	.636	336	259
San Francisco	7	4	1	.636	255	205
Chi. Bears	7	5	0	.583	286	282
Green Bay	3	9	0	.250	254	375
N.Y. Yanks	1	9	2	.100	241	382

NFL championship: LOS ANGELES 24, Cleveland 17

1950

AMERICAN CONFERENCE

	W	L	T	Pct.	Pts.	OP
Cleveland	10	2	0	.833	310	144
N.Y. Giants	10	2	0	.833	268	150
Philadelphia	6	6	0	.500	254	141
Pittsburgh	6	6	0	.500	180	195
Chi. Cardinals	5	7	0	.417	233	287
Washington	3	9	0	.250	232	326

NATIONAL CONFERENCE

	W	L	T	Pct.	Pts.	OP
Los Angeles	9	3	0	.750	466	309
Chi. Bears	9	3	0	.750	279	207
N.Y. Yanks	7	5	0	.583	366	367
Detroit	6	6	0	.500	321	285
Green Bay	3	9	0	.250	244	406
San Francisco	3	9	0	.250	213	300
Baltimore	1	11	0	.083	213	462

American Conference playoff: CLEVELAND 8, N.Y. Giants 3
National Conference playoff: LOS ANGELES 24, Chi. Bears 14
NFL championship: CLEVELAND 30, Los Angeles 28

1949

EASTERN DIVISION	W	L	T	Pct.	Pts.	OP	WESTERN DIVISION	W	L	T	Pct.	Pts.	OP
Philadelphia	11	1	0	.917	364	134	Los Angeles	8	2	2	.800	360	239
Pittsburgh	6	5	1	.545	224	214	Chi. Bears	9	3	0	.750	332	218
N.Y. Giants	6	6	0	.500	287	298	Chi. Cardinals	6	5	1	.545	360	301
Washington	4	7	1	.364	268	339	Detroit	4	8	0	.333	237	259
N.Y. Bulldogs	1	10	1	.091	153	368	Green Bay	2	10	0	.167	114	329

NFL championship: Philadelphia 14, LOS ANGELES 0

1948

EASTERN DIVISION	W	L	T	Pct.	Pts.	OP	WESTERN DIVISION	W	L	T	Pct.	Pts.	OP
Philadelphia	9	2	1	.818	376	156	Chi. Cardinals	11	1	0	.917	395	226
Washington	7	5	0	.583	291	287	Chi. Bears	10	2	0	.833	375	151
N.Y. Giants	4	8	0	.333	297	388	Los Angeles	6	5	1	.545	327	269
Pittsburgh	4	8	0	.333	200	243	Green Bay	3	9	0	.250	154	290
Boston	3	9	0	.250	174	372	Detroit	2	10	0	.167	200	407

NFL championship: PHILADELPHIA 7, Chi. Cardinals 0

1947

EASTERN DIVISION	W	L	T	Pct.	Pts.	OP	WESTERN DIVISION	W	L	T	Pct.	Pts.	OP
Philadelphia	8	4	0	.667	308	242	Chi. Cardinals	9	3	0	.750	306	231
Pittsburgh	8	4	0	.667	240	259	Chi. Bears	8	4	0	.667	363	241
Boston	4	7	1	.364	168	256	Green Bay	6	5	1	.545	274	210
Washington	4	8	0	.333	295	367	Los Angeles	6	6	0	.500	259	214
N.Y. Giants	2	8	2	.200	190	309	Detroit	3	9	0	.250	231	305

Eastern Division playoff: Philadelphia 21, PITTSBURGH 0
NFL championship: CHI. CARDINALS 28, Philadelphia 21

1946

EASTERN DIVISION	W	L	T	Pct.	Pts.	OP	WESTERN DIVISION	W	L	T	Pct.	Pts.	OP
N.Y. Giants	7	3	1	.700	236	162	Chi. Bears	8	2	1	.800	289	193
Philadelphia	6	5	0	.545	231	220	Los Angeles	6	4	1	.600	277	257
Washington	5	5	1	.500	171	191	Green Bay	6	5	0	.545	148	158
Pittsburgh	5	5	1	.500	136	117	Chi. Cardinals	6	5	0	.545	260	198
Boston	2	8	1	.200	189	273	Detroit	1	10	0	.091	142	310

NFL championship: Chi. Bears 24, N.Y. GIANTS 14

1945

EASTERN DIVISION	W	L	T	Pct.	Pts.	OP	WESTERN DIVISION	W	L	T	Pct.	Pts.	OP
Washington	8	2	0	.800	209	121	Cleveland	9	1	0	.900	244	136
Philadelphia	7	3	0	.700	272	133	Detroit	7	3	0	.700	195	194
N.Y. Giants	3	6	1	.333	179	198	Green Bay	6	4	0	.600	258	173
Boston	3	6	1	.333	123	211	Chi. Bears	3	7	0	.300	192	235
Pittsburgh	2	8	0	.200	79	220	Chi. Cardinals	1	9	0	.100	98	228

NFL championship: CLEVELAND 15, Washington 14

1944

EASTERN DIVISION	W	L	T	Pct.	Pts.	OP	WESTERN DIVISION	W	L	T	Pct.	Pts.	OP
N.Y. Giants	8	1	1	.889	206	75	Green Bay	8	2	0	.800	238	141
Philadelphia	7	1	2	.875	267	131	Chi. Bears	6	3	1	.667	258	172
Washington	6	3	1	.667	169	180	Detroit	6	3	1	.667	216	151
Boston	2	8	0	.200	82	233	Cleveland	4	6	0	.400	188	224
Brooklyn	0	10	0	.000	69	166	Card-Pitt	0	10	0	.000	108	328

NFL championship: Green Bay 14, N.Y. GIANTS 7

1943

EASTERN DIVISION	W	L	T	Pct.	Pts.	OP	WESTERN DIVISION	W	L	T	Pct.	Pts.	OP
Washington	6	3	1	.667	229	137	Chi. Bears	8	1	1	.889	303	157
N.Y. Giants	6	3	1	.667	197	170	Green Bay	7	2	1	.778	264	172
Phil-Pitt	5	4	1	.556	225	230	Detroit	3	6	1	.333	178	218
Brooklyn	2	8	0	.200	65	234	Chi. Cardinals	0	10	0	.000	95	238

Eastern Division playoff: Washington 28, N.Y. GIANTS 0
NFL championship: CHI. BEARS 41, Washington 21

1942

EASTERN DIVISION	W	L	T	Pct.	Pts.	OP	WESTERN DIVISION	W	L	T	Pct.	Pts.	OP
Washington	10	1	0	.909	227	102	Chi. Bears	11	0	0	1.000	376	84
Pittsburgh	7	4	0	.636	167	119	Green Bay	8	2	1	.800	300	215
N.Y. Giants	5	5	1	.500	155	139	Cleveland	5	6	0	.455	150	207
Brooklyn	3	8	0	.273	100	168	Chi. Cardinals	3	8	0	.273	98	209
Philadelphia	2	9	0	.182	134	239	Detroit	0	11	0	.000	38	263

NFL championship: WASHINGTON 14, Chi. Bears 6

1941

EASTERN DIVISION	W	L	T	Pct.	Pts.	OP	WESTERN DIVISION	W	L	T	Pct.	Pts.	OP
N.Y. Giants	8	3	0	.727	238	114	Chi. Bears	10	1	0	.909	396	147
Brooklyn	7	4	0	.636	158	127	Green Bay	10	1	0	.909	258	120
Washington	6	5	0	.545	176	174	Detroit	4	6	1	.400	121	195
Philadelphia	2	8	1	.200	119	218	Chi. Cardinals	3	7	1	.300	127	197
Pittsburgh	1	9	1	.100	103	276	Cleveland	2	9	0	.182	116	244

Western Division playoff: CHI. BEARS 33, Green Bay 14
NFL championship: CHI. BEARS 37, N.Y. Giants 9

1940

EASTERN DIVISION	W	L	T	Pct.	Pts.	OP	WESTERN DIVISION	W	L	T	Pct.	Pts.	OP
Washington	9	2	0	.818	245	142	Chi. Bears	8	3	0	.727	238	152
Brooklyn	8	3	0	.727	186	120	Green Bay	6	4	1	.600	238	155
N.Y. Giants	6	4	1	.600	131	133	Detroit	5	5	1	.500	138	153
Pittsburgh	2	7	2	.222	60	178	Cleveland	4	6	1	.400	171	191
Philadelphia	1	10	0	.091	111	211	Chi. Cardinals	2	7	2	.222	139	222

NFL championship: Chi. Bears 73, WASHINGTON 0

1939

EASTERN DIVISION	W	L	T	Pct.	Pts.	OP	WESTERN DIVISION	W	L	T	Pct.	Pts.	OP
N.Y. Giants	9	1	1	.900	168	85	Green Bay	9	2	0	.818	233	153
Washington	8	2	1	.800	242	94	Chi. Bears	8	3	0	.727	298	157
Brooklyn	4	6	1	.400	108	219	Detroit	6	5	0	.545	145	150
Philadelphia	1	9	1	.100	105	200	Cleveland	5	5	1	.500	195	164
Pittsburgh	1	9	1	.100	114	216	Chi. Cardinals	1	10	0	.091	84	254

NFL championship: GREEN BAY 27, N.Y. Giants 0

1938

EASTERN DIVISION	W	L	T	Pct.	Pts.	OP	WESTERN DIVISION	W	L	T	Pct.	Pts.	OP
N.Y. Giants	8	2	1	.800	194	79	Green Bay	8	3	0	.727	223	118
Washington	6	3	2	.667	148	154	Detroit	7	4	0	.636	119	108
Brooklyn	4	4	3	.500	131	161	Chi. Bears	6	5	0	.545	194	148
Philadelphia	5	6	0	.455	154	164	Cleveland	4	7	0	.364	131	215
Pittsburgh	2	9	0	.182	79	169	Chi. Cardinals	2	9	0	.182	111	168

NFL championship: N.Y. GIANTS 23, Green Bay 17

1937

EASTERN DIVISION	W	L	T	Pct.	Pts.	OP	WESTERN DIVISION	W	L	T	Pct.	Pts.	OP
Washington	8	3	0	.727	195	120	Chi. Bears	9	1	1	.900	201	100
N.Y. Giants	6	3	2	.667	128	109	Green Bay	7	4	0	.636	220	122
Pittsburgh	4	7	0	.364	122	145	Detroit	7	4	0	.636	180	105
Brooklyn	3	7	1	.300	82	174	Chi. Cardinals	5	5	1	.500	135	165
Philadelphia	2	8	1	.200	86	177	Cleveland	1	10	0	.091	75	207

NFL championship: Washington 28, CHI. BEARS 21

1936

EASTERN DIVISION	W	L	T	Pct.	Pts.	OP	WESTERN DIVISION	W	L	T	Pct.	Pts.	OP
Boston	7	5	0	.583	149	110	Green Bay	10	1	1	.909	248	118
Pittsburgh	6	6	0	.500	98	187	Chi. Bears	9	3	0	.750	222	94
N.Y. Giants	5	6	1	.455	115	163	Detroit	8	4	0	.667	235	102
Brooklyn	3	8	1	.273	92	161	Chi. Cardinals	3	8	1	.273	74	143
Philadelphia	1	11	0	.083	51	206							

NFL championship: Green Bay 21, Boston 6, at Polo Grounds, N.Y.

1935

EASTERN DIVISION	W	L	T	Pct.	Pts.	OP	WESTERN DIVISION	W	L	T	Pct.	Pts.	OP
N.Y. Giants	9	3	0	.750	180	96	Detroit	7	3	2	.700	191	111
Brooklyn	5	6	1	.455	90	141	Green Bay	8	4	0	.667	181	96
Pittsburgh	4	8	0	.333	100	209	Chi. Bears	6	4	2	.600	192	106
Boston	2	8	1	.200	65	123	Chi. Cardinals	6	4	2	.600	99	97
Philadelphia	2	9	0	.182	60	179							

NFL championship: DETROIT 26, N.Y. Giants 7
One game between Boston and Philadelphia was canceled.

1934

EASTERN DIVISION	W	L	T	Pct.	Pts.	OP	WESTERN DIVISION	W	L	T	Pct.	Pts.	OP
N.Y. Giants	8	5	0	.615	147	107	Chi. Bears	13	0	0	1.000	286	86
Boston	6	6	0	.500	107	94	Detroit	10	3	0	.769	238	59
Brooklyn	4	7	0	.364	61	153	Green Bay	7	6	0	.538	156	112
Philadelphia	4	7	0	.364	127	85	Chi. Cardinals	5	6	0	.455	80	84
Pittsburgh	2	10	0	.167	51	206	St. Louis	1	2	0	.333	27	61
							Cincinnati	0	8	0	.000	10	243

NFL championship: N.Y. GIANTS 30, Chi. Bears 13

1933

EASTERN DIVISION	W	L	T	Pct.	Pts.	OP	WESTERN DIVISION	W	L	T	Pct.	Pts.	OP
N.Y. Giants	11	3	0	.786	244	101	Chi. Bears	10	2	1	.833	133	82
Brooklyn	5	4	1	.556	93	54	Portsmouth	6	5	0	.545	128	87
Boston	5	5	2	.500	103	97	Green Bay	5	7	1	.417	170	107
Philadelphia	3	5	1	.375	77	158	Cincinnati	3	6	1	.333	38	110
Pittsburgh	3	6	2	.333	67	208	Chi. Cardinals	1	9	1	.100	52	101

NFL championship: CHI. BEARS 23, N.Y. Giants 21

1932

	W	L	T	Pct.
Chicago Bears	7	1	6	.875
Green Bay Packers	10	3	1	.769
Portsmouth Spartans	6	2	4	.750
Boston Braves	4	4	2	.500
New York Giants	4	6	2	.400
Brooklyn Dodgers	3	9	0	.250
Chicago Cardinals	2	6	2	.250
Staten Island Stapletons	2	7	3	.222

*Chicago Bears and Portsmouth finished
regularly scheduled games tied for first
place. Bears won playoff game, which
counted in standings, 9-0.*

1931

	W	L	T	Pct.
Green Bay Packers	12	2	0	.857
Portsmouth Spartans	11	3	0	.786
Chicago Bears	8	5	0	.615
Chicago Cardinals	5	4	0	.556
New York Giants	7	6	1	.538
Providence Steam Roller	4	4	3	.500
Staten Island Stapletons	4	6	1	.400
Cleveland Indians	2	8	0	.200
Brooklyn Dodgers	2	12	0	.143
Frankford Yellow Jackets	1	6	1	.143

1930

	W	L	T	Pct.
Green Bay Packers	10	3	1	.769
New York Giants	13	4	0	.765
Chicago Bears	9	4	1	.692
Brooklyn Dodgers	7	4	1	.636
Providence Steam Roller	6	4	1	.600
Staten Island Stapletons	5	5	2	.500
Chicago Cardinals	5	6	2	.455
Portsmouth Spartans	5	6	3	.455
Frankford Yellow Jackets	4	13	1	.222
Minneapolis Red Jackets	1	7	1	.125
Newark Tornadoes	1	10	1	.091

1929

	W	L	T	Pct.
Green Bay Packers	12	0	1	1.000
New York Giants	13	1	1	.929
Frankford Yellow Jackets	10	4	5	.714
Chicago Cardinals	6	6	1	.500
Boston Bulldogs	4	4	0	.500
Staten Island Stapletons	3	4	3	.429
Providence Steam Roller	4	6	2	.400
Orange Tornadoes	3	5	4	.375
Chicago Bears	4	9	2	.308
Buffalo Bisons	1	7	1	.125
Minneapolis Red Jackets	1	9	0	.100
Dayton Triangles	0	6	0	.000

1928

	W	L	T	Pct.
Providence Steam Roller	8	1	2	.889
Frankford Yellow Jackets	11	3	2	.786
Detroit Wolverines	7	2	1	.778
Green Bay Packers	6	4	3	.600
Chicago Bears	7	5	1	.583
New York Giants	4	7	2	.364
New York Yankees	4	8	1	.333
Pottsville Maroons	2	8	0	.200
Chicago Cardinals	1	5	0	.167
Dayton Triangles	0	7	0	.000

1927

	W	L	T	Pct.
New York Giants	11	1	1	.917
Green Bay Packers	7	2	1	.778
Chicago Bears	9	3	2	.750
Cleveland Bulldogs	8	4	1	.667
Providence Steam Roller	8	5	1	.615
New York Yankees	7	8	1	.467
Frankford Yellow Jackets	6	9	3	.400
Pottsville Maroons	5	8	0	.385
Chicago Cardinals	3	7	1	.300
Dayton Triangles	1	6	1	.143
Duluth Eskimos	1	8	0	.111
Buffalo Bisons	0	5	0	.000

1926

	W	L	T	Pct.
Frankford Yellow Jackets	14	1	2	.933
Chicago Bears	12	1	3	.923
Pottsville Maroons	10	2	2	.833
Kansas City Cowboys	8	3	0	.727
Green Bay Packers	7	3	3	.700
Los Angeles Buccaneers	6	3	1	.667
New York Giants	8	4	1	.667
Duluth Eskimos	6	5	3	.545
Buffalo Rangers	4	4	2	.500
Chicago Cardinals	5	6	1	.455
Providence Steam Roller	5	7	1	.417
Detroit Panthers	4	6	2	.400
Hartford Blues	3	7	0	.300
Brooklyn Lions	3	8	0	.273
Milwaukee Badgers	2	7	0	.222
Akron Indians	1	4	3	.200
Dayton Triangles	1	4	1	.200
Racine Tornadoes	1	4	0	.200
Columbus Tigers	1	6	0	.143
Canton Bulldogs	1	9	3	.100
Hammond Pros	0	4	0	.000
Louisville Colonels	0	4	0	.000

1925

	W	L	T	Pct.
Chicago Cardinals	11	2	1	.846
Pottsville Maroons	10	2	0	.833
Detroit Panthers	8	2	2	.800
New York Giants	8	4	0	.667
Akron Indians	4	2	2	.667
Frankford Yellow Jackets	13	7	0	.650
Chicago Bears	9	5	3	.643
Rock Island Independents	5	3	3	.625
Green Bay Packers	8	5	0	.615
Providence Steam Roller	6	5	1	.545
Canton Bulldogs	4	4	0	.500
Cleveland Bulldogs	5	8	1	.385
Kansas City Cowboys	2	5	1	.286
Hammond Pros	1	4	0	.200
Buffalo Bisons	1	6	2	.143
Duluth Kelleys	0	3	0	.000
Rochester Jeffersons	0	6	1	.000
Milwaukee Badgers	0	6	0	.000
Dayton Triangles	0	7	1	.000
Columbus Tigers	0	9	0	.000

1924

	W	L	T	Pct.
Cleveland Bulldogs	7	1	1	.875
Chicago Bears	6	1	4	.857
Frankford Yellow Jackets	11	2	1	.846
Duluth Kelleys	5	1	0	.833
Rock Island Independents	5	2	2	.714
Green Bay Packers	7	4	0	.636
Racine Legion	4	3	3	.571
Chicago Cardinals	5	4	1	.556
Buffalo Bisons	6	5	0	.545
Columbus Tigers	4	4	0	.500
Hammond Pros	2	2	1	.500
Milwaukee Badgers	5	8	0	.385
Akron Indians	2	6	0	.250
Dayton Triangles	2	6	0	.250
Kansas City Blues	2	7	0	.222
Kenosha Maroons	0	4	1	.000
Minneapolis Marines	0	6	0	.000
Rochester Jeffersons	0	7	0	.000

1923

	W	L	T	Pct.
Canton Bulldogs	11	0	1	1.000
Chicago Bears	9	2	1	.818
Green Bay Packers	7	2	1	.778
Milwaukee Badgers	7	2	3	.778
Cleveland Indians	3	1	3	.750
Chicago Cardinals	8	4	0	.667
Duluth Kelleys	4	3	0	.571
Buffalo All-Americans	5	4	3	.556
Columbus Tigers	5	4	1	.556
Racine Legion	4	4	2	.500
Toledo Maroons	3	3	2	.500
Rock Island Independents	2	3	3	.400
Minneapolis Marines	2	5	2	.286
St. Louis All-Stars	1	4	2	.200
Hammond Pros	1	5	1	.167
Dayton Triangles	1	6	1	.143
Akron Indians	1	6	0	.143
Oorang Indians	1	10	0	.091
Louisville Brecks	0	3	0	.000
Rochester Jeffersons	0	4	0	.000

1922

	W	L	T	Pct.
Canton Bulldogs	10	0	2	1.000
Chicago Bears	9	3	0	.750
Chicago Cardinals	8	3	0	.727
Toledo Maroons	5	2	2	.714
Rock Island Independents	4	2	1	.667
Racine Legion	6	4	1	.600
Dayton Triangles	4	3	1	.571
Green Bay Packers	4	3	3	.571
Buffalo All-Americans	5	4	1	.556
Akron Pros	3	5	2	.375
Milwaukee Badgers	2	4	3	.333
Oorang Indians	3	6	0	.333
Minneapolis Marines	1	3	0	.250
Louisville Brecks	1	3	0	.250
Evansville Crimson Giants	0	3	0	.000
Rochester Jeffersons	0	4	1	.000
Hammond Pros	0	5	1	.000
Columbus Panhandles	0	8	0	.000

1921

	W	L	T	Pct.
Chicago Staleys	9	1	1	.900
Buffalo All-Americans	9	1	2	.900
Akron Pros	8	3	1	.727
Canton Bulldogs	5	2	3	.714
Rock Island Independents	4	2	1	.667
Evansville Crimson Giants	3	2	0	.600
Green Bay Packers	3	2	1	.600
Dayton Triangles	4	4	1	.500
Chicago Cardinals	3	3	2	.500
Rochester Jeffersons	2	3	0	.400
Cleveland Indians	3	5	0	.375
Washington Senators	1	2	0	.333
Cincinnati Celts	1	3	0	.250
Hammond Pros	1	3	1	.250
Minneapolis Marines	1	3	0	.250
Detroit Tigers	1	5	1	.167
Columbus Panhandles	1	8	0	.111
Tonawanda Kardex	0	1	0	.000
Muncie Flyers	0	2	0	.000
Louisville Brecks	0	2	0	.000
New York Giants	0	2	0	.000

1920*

	W	L	T	Pct.
Akron Pros	8	0	3	1.000
Decatur Staleys	10	1	2	.909
Buffalo All-Americans	9	1	1	.900
Chicago Cardinals	6	2	2	.750
Rock Island Independents	6	2	2	.750
Dayton Triangles	5	2	2	.714
Rochester Jeffersons	6	3	2	.667
Canton Bulldogs	7	4	2	.636
Detroit Heralds	2	3	3	.400
Cleveland Tigers	2	4	2	.333
Chicago Tigers	2	5	1	.286
Hammond Pros	2	5	0	.286
Columbus Panhandles	2	6	2	.250
Muncie Flyers	0	1	0	.000

*No official standings were maintained for the 1920 season, and the championship was awarded to the Akron Pros in a League meeting on April 30, 1921. Clubs played schedules that included games against nonleague opponents.

PRO FOOTBALL HALL OF FAME GAME (45)

Date	Winner	Loser	Attendance
August 11, 1962	New York Giants 21 (tie)	St. Louis Cardinals 21 (tie)	14,000
September 8, 1963	Pittsburgh Steelers 16	Cleveland Browns 7	18,462
September 6, 1964	Baltimore Colts 48	Pittsburgh Steelers 17	11,479
September 12, 1965	Washington Redskins 20	Detroit Lions 3	14,416
1966	No game was played		
August 5, 1967	Philadelphia Eagles 28	Cleveland Browns 13	17,304
August 3, 1968	Chicago Bears 30	Dallas Cowboys 24	14,578
September 13, 1969	Green Bay Packers 38	Atlanta Falcons 24	17,411
August 8, 1970	New Orleans Saints 14	Minnesota Vikings 13	17,932
July 31, 1971	Los Angeles Rams (NFC) 17	Houston Oilers (AFC) 6	19,384
July 29, 1972	Kansas City Chiefs (AFC) 23	New York Giants (NFC) 17	19,304
July 28, 1973	San Francisco 49ers (NFC) 20	New England Patriots (AFC) 7	19,685
July 27, 1974	St. Louis Cardinals (NFC) 21	Buffalo Bills (AFC) 13	17,286
August 2, 1975	Washington Redskins (NFC) 17	Cincinnati Bengals (AFC) 9	19,360
July 24, 1976	Denver Broncos (AFC) 17	Detroit Lions (NFC) 7	17,639
July 30, 1977	Chicago Bears (NFC) 20	New York Jets (AFC) 6	19,057
July 29, 1978	Philadelphia Eagles (NFC) 17	Miami Dolphins (AFC) 3	19,255
July 28, 1979	Oakland Raiders (AFC) 20	Dallas Cowboys (NFC) 13	20,648
August 2, 1980*	San Diego Chargers (AFC) 0	Green Bay Packers (NFC) 0	19,972
August 1, 1981	Cleveland Browns (AFC) 24	Atlanta Falcons (NFC) 10	23,921
August 7, 1982	Minnesota Vikings (NFC) 30	Baltimore Colts (AFC) 14	23,379
July 30, 1983	Pittsburgh Steelers (AFC) 27	New Orleans Saints (NFC) 14	23,909
July 28, 1984	Seattle Seahawks (AFC) 38	Tampa Bay Buccaneers (NFC) 0	22,250
August 3, 1985	New York Giants (NFC) 21	Houston Oilers (AFC) 20	23,940
August 2, 1986	New England Patriots (AFC) 21	St. Louis Cardinals (NFC) 16	22,739
August 8, 1987	San Francisco 49ers (NFC) 20	Kansas City Chiefs (AFC) 7	23,826
July 30, 1988	Cincinnati Bengals (AFC) 14	Los Angeles Rams (NFC) 7	23,801
August 5, 1989	Washington Redskins (NFC) 31	Buffalo Bills (AFC) 6	23,948
August 4, 1990	Chicago Bears (NFC) 13	Cleveland Browns (AFC) 0	23,952
July 27, 1991	Detroit Lions (NFC) 14	Denver Broncos (AFC) 3	23,815
August 1, 1992	New York Jets (AFC) 41	Philadelphia Eagles (NFC) 14	23,853
July 31, 1993	Los Angeles Raiders (AFC) 19	Green Bay Packers (NFC) 3	23,863
July 30, 1994	Atlanta Falcons (NFC) 21	San Diego Chargers (AFC) 17	23,185
July 29, 1995	Carolina Panthers (NFC) 20	Jacksonville Jaguars (AFC) 14	24,625
July 27, 1996	Indianapolis Colts (AFC) 10	New Orleans Saints (NFC) 3	23,376
July 26, 1997	Minnesota Vikings (NFC) 28	Seattle Seahawks (AFC) 26	23,846
August 1, 1998	Tampa Bay Buccaneers (NFC) 30	Pittsburgh Steelers (AFC) 6	23,875
August 9, 1999	Cleveland Browns (AFC) 20	Dallas Cowboys (NFC) 17 (OT)	25,156
July 31, 2000	New England Patriots (AFC) 20	San Francisco 49ers (NFC) 0	22,840
August 6, 2001	St. Louis Rams (NFC) 17	Miami Dolphins (AFC) 10	22,736
August 5, 2002	New York Giants (NFC) 34	Houston Texans (AFC) 17	22,461
August 4, 2003**	Kansas City Chiefs (AFC) 9	Green Bay Packers (NFC) 0	22,385
August 9, 2004	Washington Redskins (NFC) 20	Denver Broncos (AFC) 17	22,177
August 8, 2005	Chicago Bears (NFC) 27	Miami Dolphins (AFC) 24	22,292
August 6, 2006	Oakland Raiders (AFC) 16	Philadelphia Eagles (NFC) 10	22,200
August 5, 2007	Pittsburgh Steelers (AFC) 20	New Orleans Saints (NFC) 7	22,302

*Game called with 5:29 remaining because of severe thunder and lightning.
**Game called with 5:49 remaining in the third quarter because of lightning and torrential rain.

RS=REGULAR SEASON
PS=POSTSEASON
*ARIZONA vs. ATLANTA
RS: Cardinals lead series, 14-10
1966—Falcons, 16-10 (A)
1968—Cardinals, 17-12 (StL)
1971—Cardinals, 26-9 (A)
1973—Cardinals, 32-10 (A)
1975—Cardinals, 23-20 (StL)
1978—Cardinals, 42-21 (StL)
1980—Falcons, 33-27 (StL) OT
1981—Falcons, 41-20 (A)
1982—Cardinals, 23-20 (A)
1986—Falcons, 33-13 (A)
1987—Cardinals, 34-21 (A)
1989—Cardinals, 34-20 (P)
1990—Cardinals, 24-13 (A)
1991—Cardinals, 16-10 (P)
1992—Falcons, 20-17 (A)
1993—Cardinals, 27-10 (A)
1994—Falcons, 10-6 (Atl)
1995—Cardinals, 40-37 (Ariz) OT
1997—Cardinals, 29-26 (Ariz)
1999—Falcons, 37-14 (Atl)
2001—Cardinals, 34-14 (Ariz)
2004—Falcons, 6-3 (Atl)
2006—Falcons, 32-10 (Atl)
2007—Cardinals, 30-27 (Ariz) OT
(RS Pts.—Cardinals 531, Falcons 518)
Franchise known as Phoenix prior to 1994 and in St. Louis prior to 1988
*ARIZONA vs. BALTIMORE
RS: Ravens lead series, 3-1
1997—Cardinals, 16-13 (B)
2000—Ravens, 13-7 (A)
2003—Ravens, 26-18 (A)
2007—Ravens, 26-23 (B)
(RS Pts.—Ravens 78, Cardinals 64)
*ARIZONA vs. BUFFALO
RS: Bills lead series, 5-3
1971—Cardinals, 28-23 (B)
1975—Bills, 32-14 (StL)
1981—Cardinals, 24-0 (StL)
1984—Cardinals, 37-7 (StL)
1986—Bills, 17-10 (B)
1990—Bills, 45-14 (B)
1999—Bills, 31-21 (A)
2004—Bills, 38-14 (B)
(RS Pts.—Bills 193, Cardinals 162)
Franchise known as Phoenix prior to 1994 and in St. Louis prior to 1988
ARIZONA vs. CAROLINA
RS: Panthers lead series, 5-2
1995—Panthers, 27-7 (C)
2001—Cardinals, 30-7 (C)
2002—Cardinals, 16-13 (C)
2003—Panthers, 20-17 (A)
2004—Panthers, 35-10 (C)
2005—Panthers, 24-20 (A)
2007—Panthers, 25-10 (A)
(RS Pts.—Panthers 151, Cardinals 110)
*ARIZONA vs. **CHICAGO
RS: Bears lead series, 55-26-6
(NP denotes Normal Park;
Wr denotes Wrigley Field;
Co denotes Comiskey Park;
So denotes Soldier Field;
all Chicago)
1920—Cardinals, 7-6 (NP)
    Staleys, 10-0 (Wr)

1921—Tie, 0-0 (Wr)
1922—Cardinals, 6-0 (Co)
    Cardinals, 9-0 (Co)
1923—Bears, 3-0 (Wr)
1924—Bears, 6-0 (Wr)
    Bears, 21-0 (Co)
1925—Cardinals, 9-0 (Co)
    Tie, 0-0 (Wr)
1926—Bears, 16-0 (Wr)
    Bears, 10-0 (So)
    Tie, 0-0 (Wr)
1927—Bears, 9-0 (NP)
    Cardinals, 3-0 (Wr)
1928—Bears, 15-0 (NP)
    Bears, 34-0 (Wr)
1929—Tie, 0-0 (Wr)
    Cardinals, 40-6 (Co)
1930—Bears, 32-6 (Co)
    Bears, 6-0 (Wr)
1931—Bears, 26-13 (Wr)
    Bears, 18-7 (Wr)
1932—Tie, 0-0 (Wr)
    Bears, 34-0 (Wr)
1933—Bears, 12-9 (Wr)
    Bears, 22-6 (Wr)
1934—Bears, 20-0 (Wr)
    Bears, 17-6 (Wr)
1935—Tie, 7-7 (Wr)
    Bears, 13-0 (Wr)
1936—Bears, 7-3 (Wr)
    Cardinals, 14-7 (Wr)
1937—Bears, 16-7 (Wr)
    Bears, 42-28 (Wr)
1938—Bears, 16-13 (So)
    Bears, 34-28 (Wr)
1939—Bears, 44-7 (Wr)
    Bears, 48-7 (Co)
1940—Cardinals, 21-7 (Co)
    Bears, 31-23 (Wr)
1941—Bears, 53-7 (Wr)
    Bears, 34-24 (Co)
1942—Bears, 41-14 (Wr)
    Bears, 21-7 (Co)
1943—Bears, 20-0 (Wr)
    Bears, 35-24 (Co)
1945—Cardinals, 16-7 (Wr)
    Bears, 28-20 (Co)
1946—Bears, 34-17 (Co)
    Cardinals, 35-28 (Wr)
1947—Cardinals, 31-7 (Co)
    Cardinals, 30-21 (Wr)
1948—Bears, 28-17 (Co)
    Cardinals, 24-21 (Wr)
1949—Bears, 17-7 (Co)
    Bears, 52-21 (Wr)
1950—Bears, 27-6 (Wr)
    Cardinals, 20-10 (Co)
1951—Cardinals, 28-14 (Co)
    Cardinals, 24-14 (Wr)
1952—Cardinals, 21-10 (Co)
    Bears, 10-7 (Wr)
1953—Cardinals, 24-17 (Wr)
1954—Bears, 29-7 (Co)
1955—Cardinals, 53-14 (Wr)
1956—Bears, 10-3 (Wr)
1957—Bears, 14-6 (Co)
1958—Bears, 30-14 (Wr)
1959—Bears, 31-7 (So)
1965—Bears, 34-13 (Wr)
1966—Cardinals, 24-17 (StL)

1967—Bears, 30-3 (Wr)
1969—Cardinals, 20-17 (StL)
1972—Bears, 27-10 (StL)
1975—Cardinals, 34-20 (So)
1977—Cardinals, 16-13 (StL)
1978—Bears, 17-10 (So)
1979—Bears, 42-6 (So)
1982—Cardinals, 10-7 (So)
1984—Cardinals, 38-21 (StL)
1990—Bears, 31-21 (P)
1994—Bears, 19-16 (A) OT
1998—Cardinals, 20-7 (A)
2001—Bears, 20-13 (C)
2003—Bears, 28-3 (C)
2006—Bears, 24-23 (A)
(RS Pts.—Bears 1,646, Cardinals 1,073)
Franchise known as Phoenix prior to 1994, in St. Louis prior to 1988, and in Chicago prior to 1960
**Franchise in Decatur prior to 1921 and known as Staleys prior to 1922*
*ARIZONA vs. CINCINNATI
RS: Bengals lead series, 5-4
1973—Bengals, 42-24 (C)
1979—Bengals, 34-28 (C)
1985—Cardinals, 41-27 (StL)
1988—Bengals, 21-14 (C)
1994—Cardinals, 28-7 (A)
1997—Bengals, 24-21 (C)
2000—Bengals, 24-13 (C)
2003—Cardinals, 17-14 (A)
2007—Cardinals, 35-27 (C)
(RS Pts.—Cardinals 221, Bengals 220)
Franchise known as Phoenix prior to 1994 and in St. Louis prior to 1988
*ARIZONA vs. CLEVELAND
RS: Browns lead series, 33-12-3
1950—Browns, 34-24 (Cle)
    Browns, 10-7 (Chi)
1951—Browns, 34-17 (Chi)
    Browns, 49-28 (Cle)
1952—Browns, 28-13 (Cle)
    Browns, 10-0 (Chi)
1953—Browns, 27-7 (Chi)
    Browns, 27-16 (Cle)
1954—Browns, 31-7 (Cle)
    Browns, 35-3 (Chi)
1955—Browns, 26-20 (Chi)
    Browns, 35-24 (Cle)
1956—Cardinals, 9-7 (Chi)
    Cardinals, 24-7 (Cle)
1957—Browns, 17-7 (Chi)
    Browns, 31-0 (Cle)
1958—Browns, 35-28 (Cle)
    Browns, 38-24 (Chi)
1959—Browns, 34-7 (Chi)
    Browns, 17-7 (Cle)
1960—Browns, 28-27 (Cle)
    Tie, 17-17 (StL)
1961—Browns, 20-17 (Cle)
    Browns, 21-10 (StL)
1962—Browns, 34-7 (StL)
    Browns, 38-14 (Cle)
1963—Cardinals, 20-14 (Cle)
    Browns, 24-10 (StL)
1964—Tie, 33-33 (Cle)
    Cardinals, 28-19 (StL)
1965—Cardinals, 49-13 (Cle)
    Browns, 27-24 (StL)
1966—Cardinals, 34-28 (Cle)

Browns, 38-10 (StL)
1967—Browns, 20-16 (Cle)
Browns, 20-16 (StL)
1968—Cardinals, 27-21 (Cle)
Cardinals, 27-16 (StL)
1969—Tie, 21-21 (Cle)
Browns, 27-21 (StL)
1974—Cardinals, 29-7 (StL)
1979—Browns, 38-20 (StL)
1985—Cardinals, 27-24 (Cle) OT
1988—Browns, 29-21 (P)
1994—Browns, 32-0 (Cle)
2000—Cardinals, 29-21 (A)
2003—Browns, 44-6 (Cle)
2007—Cardinals, 27-21 (A)
(RS Pts.—Browns 1,227, Cardinals 859)
*Franchise known as Phoenix prior to
1994, in St. Louis prior to 1988,
and in Chicago prior to 1960
ARIZONA vs. DALLAS
RS: Cowboys lead series, 55-27-1
PS: Cardinals lead series, 1-0
1960—Cardinals, 12-10 (StL)
1961—Cardinals, 31-17 (D)
Cardinals, 31-13 (StL)
1962—Cardinals, 28-24 (D)
Cardinals, 52-20 (StL)
1963—Cardinals, 34-7 (D)
Cowboys, 28-24 (StL)
1964—Cardinals, 16-6 (D)
Cowboys, 31-13 (StL)
1965—Cardinals, 20-13 (StL)
Cowboys, 27-13 (D)
1966—Tie, 10-10 (StL)
Cowboys, 31-17 (D)
1967—Cowboys, 46-21 (D)
1968—Cowboys, 27-10 (StL)
1969—Cowboys, 24-3 (D)
1970—Cardinals, 20-7 (StL)
Cardinals, 38-0 (D)
1971—Cowboys, 16-13 (StL)
Cowboys, 31-12 (D)
1972—Cowboys, 33-24 (D)
Cowboys, 27-6 (StL)
1973—Cowboys, 45-10 (D)
Cowboys, 30-3 (StL)
1974—Cardinals, 31-28 (StL)
Cowboys, 17-14 (D)
1975—Cowboys, 37-31 (D) OT
Cardinals, 31-17 (StL)
1976—Cardinals, 21-17 (StL)
Cowboys, 19-14 (D)
1977—Cowboys, 30-24 (StL)
Cardinals, 24-17 (D)
1978—Cowboys, 21-12 (D)
Cowboys, 24-21 (StL) OT
1979—Cowboys, 22-21 (StL)
Cowboys, 22-13 (D)
1980—Cowboys, 27-24 (StL)
Cowboys, 31-21 (D)
1981—Cowboys, 30-17 (D)
Cardinals, 20-17 (StL)
1982—Cowboys, 24-7 (StL)
1983—Cowboys, 34-17 (StL)
Cowboys, 35-17 (D)
1984—Cardinals, 31-20 (D)
Cowboys, 24-17 (StL)
1985—Cardinals, 21-10 (StL)
Cowboys, 35-17 (D)
1986—Cowboys, 31-7 (StL)

Cowboys, 37-6 (D)
1987—Cardinals, 24-13 (StL)
Cowboys, 21-16 (D)
1988—Cowboys, 17-14 (P)
Cardinals, 16-10 (D)
1989—Cardinals, 19-10 (D)
Cardinals, 24-20 (P)
1990—Cardinals, 20-3 (P)
Cowboys, 41-10 (D)
1991—Cowboys, 17-9 (P)
Cowboys, 27-7 (D)
1992—Cowboys, 31-20 (D)
Cowboys, 16-10 (P)
1993—Cowboys, 17-10 (P)
Cowboys, 20-15 (D)
1994—Cowboys, 38-3 (D)
Cowboys, 28-21 (A)
1995—Cowboys, 34-20 (D)
Cowboys, 37-13 (A)
1996—Cowboys, 17-3 (D)
Cowboys, 10-6 (A)
1997—Cardinals, 25-22 (A) OT
Cowboys, 24-6 (D)
1998—Cowboys, 38-10 (D)
Cowboys, 35-28 (A)
**Cardinals, 20-7 (D)
1999—Cowboys, 35-7 (D)
Cardinals, 13-9 (A)
2000—Cardinals, 32-31 (A)
Cowboys, 48-7 (D)
2001—Cowboys, 17-3 (D)
Cardinals, 17-10 (A)
2002—Cardinals, 9-6 (A) OT
2003—Cowboys, 24-7 (D)
2005—Cowboys, 34-13 (D)
2006—Cowboys, 27-10 (A)
(RS Pts.—Cowboys 1,936, Cardinals 1,407)
(PS Pts.—Cardinals 20, Cowboys 7)
*Franchise known as Phoenix prior to
1994 and in St. Louis prior to 1988
**NFC First-Round Playoff
ARIZONA vs. DENVER
RS: Broncos lead series, 7-0-1
1973—Tie, 17-17 (StL)
1977—Broncos, 7-0 (D)
1989—Broncos, 37-0 (P)
1991—Broncos, 24-19 (D)
1995—Broncos, 38-6 (D)
2001—Broncos, 38-17 (A)
2002—Broncos, 37-7 (D)
2006—Broncos, 37-20 (A)
(RS Pts.—Broncos 235, Cardinals 86)
*Franchise known as Phoenix prior to
1994 and in St. Louis prior to 1988
ARIZONA vs. **DETROIT
RS: Lions lead series, 31-23-5
1930—Tie, 0-0 (Port)
Cardinals, 23-0 (C)
1931—Spartans, 13-3 (Port)
Cardinals, 20-19 (C)
1932—Tie, 7-7 (Port)
1933—Spartans, 7-6 (Port)
1934—Lions, 6-0 (D)
Lions, 17-13 (C)
1935—Tie, 10-10 (D)
Lions, 7-6 (C)
1936—Lions, 39-0 (D)
Lions, 14-7 (C)
1937—Lions, 16-7 (C)
Lions, 16-7 (D)

1938—Lions, 10-0 (D)
Lions, 7-3 (C)
1939—Lions, 21-3 (D)
Lions, 17-3 (C)
1940—Tie, 0-0 (Buffalo)
Lions, 43-14 (C)
1941—Tie, 14-14 (C)
Lions, 21-3 (D)
1942—Cardinals, 13-0 (C)
Cardinals, 7-0 (D)
1943—Lions, 35-17 (D)
Lions, 7-0 (Buffalo)
1945—Lions, 10-0 (Milwaukee)
Lions, 26-0 (C)
1946—Cardinals, 34-14 (C)
Cardinals, 36-14 (D)
1947—Cardinals, 45-21 (C)
Cardinals, 17-7 (D)
1948—Cardinals, 56-20 (C)
Cardinals, 28-14 (D)
1949—Lions, 24-7 (C)
Cardinals, 42-19 (D)
1959—Lions, 45-21 (D)
1961—Lions, 45-14 (StL)
1967—Cardinals, 38-28 (StL)
1969—Lions, 20-0 (D)
1970—Lions, 16-3 (D)
1973—Lions, 20-16 (StL)
1975—Cardinals, 24-13 (D)
1978—Cardinals, 21-14 (StL)
1980—Lions, 20-7 (D)
Cardinals, 24-23 (StL)
1989—Cardinals, 16-13 (D)
1993—Cardinals, 26-20 (D)
Lions, 21-14 (Phx)
1995—Cardinals, 20-17 (D)
1998—Lions, 17-15 (D)
1999—Cardinals, 23-19 (A)
2001—Cardinals, 45-38 (A)
2002—Cardinals, 23-20 (A) OT
2003—Lions, 42-24 (D)
2004—Lions, 26-12 (D)
2005—Lions, 29-21 (D)
2006—Cardinals, 17-10 (A)
2007—Cardinals, 31-21 (A)
(RS Pts.—Lions 1,069, Cardinals 912)
*Franchise known as Phoenix prior to
1994, in St. Louis prior to 1988,
and in Chicago prior to 1960
**Franchise in Portsmouth prior to 1934
and known as the Spartans
ARIZONA vs. GREEN BAY
RS: Packers lead series, 42-22-4
PS: Packers lead series, 1-0
1921—Tie, 3-3 (C)
1922—Cardinals, 16-3 (C)
1924—Cardinals, 3-0 (C)
1925—Cardinals, 9-6 (C)
1926—Cardinals, 13-7 (GB)
Packers, 3-0 (C)
1927—Packers, 13-0 (GB)
Tie, 6-6 (C)
1928—Packers, 20-0 (GB)
1929—Packers, 9-2 (GB)
Packers, 7-6 (C)
Packers, 12-0 (C)
1930—Packers, 14-6 (GB)
Cardinals, 13-6 (C)
1931—Packers, 26-7 (GB)
Cardinals, 21-13 (C)

1932—Packers, 15-7 (GB)
    Packers, 19-9 (C)
1933—Packers, 14-6 (C)
1934—Packers, 15-0 (GB)
    Cardinals, 9-0 (Mil)
    Cardinals, 6-0 (C)
1935—Cardinals, 7-6 (GB)
    Cardinals, 3-0 (Mil)
    Cardinals, 9-7 (C)
1936—Packers, 10-7 (GB)
    Packers, 24-0 (Mil)
    Tie, 0-0 (C)
1937—Cardinals, 14-7 (GB)
    Packers, 34-13 (Mil)
1938—Packers, 28-7 (Mil)
    Packers, 24-22 (Buffalo)
1939—Packers, 14-10 (GB)
    Packers, 27-20 (Mil)
1940—Packers, 31-6 (Mil)
    Packers, 28-7 (C)
1941—Packers, 14-13 (Mil)
    Packers, 17-9 (GB)
1942—Packers, 17-13 (C)
    Packers, 55-24 (GB)
1943—Packers, 28-7 (C)
    Packers, 35-14 (Mil)
1945—Packers, 33-14 (GB)
1946—Packers, 19-7 (C)
    Cardinals, 24-6 (GB)
1947—Cardinals, 14-10 (GB)
    Cardinals, 21-20 (C)
1948—Cardinals, 17-7 (Mil)
    Cardinals, 42-7 (C)
1949—Cardinals, 39-17 (Mil)
    Cardinals, 41-21 (C)
1955—Packers, 31-14 (GB)
1956—Packers, 24-21 (C)
1962—Packers, 17-0 (Mil)
1963—Packers, 30-7 (StL)
1967—Packers, 31-23 (StL)
1969—Packers, 45-28 (GB)
1971—Tie, 16-16 (StL)
1973—Packers, 25-21 (GB)
1976—Cardinals, 29-0 (StL)
1982—**Packers, 41-16 (GB)
1984—Packers, 24-23 (GB)
1985—Cardinals, 43-28 (StL)
1988—Packers, 26-17 (P)
1990—Packers, 24-21 (P)
1999—Packers, 49-24 (GB)
2000—Packers, 29-3 (A)
2003—Cardinals, 20-13 (A)
2006—Packers, 31-14 (GB)
(RS Pts.—Packers 1,200, Cardinals 884)
(PS Pts.—Packers 41, Cardinals 16)
*Franchise known as Phoenix prior to 1994, in St. Louis prior to 1988, and in Chicago prior to 1960
**NFC First-Round Playoff
ARIZONA vs. HOUSTON
RS: Texans lead series, 1-0
2005—Texans, 30-19 (H)
(RS Pts.—Texans 30, Cardinals 19)
***ARIZONA vs. **INDIANAPOLIS**
RS: Colts lead series, 7-6
1961—Colts, 16-0 (B)
1964—Colts, 47-27 (B)
1968—Colts, 27-0 (B)
1972—Cardinals, 10-3 (B)
1976—Cardinals, 24-17 (StL)

1978—Colts, 30-17 (StL)
1980—Cardinals, 17-10 (B)
1981—Cardinals, 35-24 (B)
1984—Cardinals, 34-33 (I)
1990—Cardinals, 20-17 (P)
1992—Colts, 16-13 (I)
1996—Colts, 20-13 (I)
2005—Colts, 17-13 (I)
(RS Pts.—Colts 277, Cardinals 223)
*Franchise known as Phoenix prior to 1994 and in St. Louis prior to 1988
**Franchise in Baltimore prior to 1984
ARIZONA vs. JACKSONVILLE
RS: Jaguars lead series, 2-0
2000—Jaguars, 44-10 (J)
2005—Jaguars, 24-17 (A)
(RS Pts.—Jaguars 68, Cardinals 27)
***ARIZONA vs. KANSAS CITY**
RS: Chiefs lead series, 7-2-1
1970—Tie, 6-6 (KC)
1974—Chiefs, 17-13 (StL)
1980—Chiefs, 21-13 (StL)
1983—Chiefs, 38-14 (KC)
1986—Cardinals, 23-14 (StL)
1995—Chiefs, 24-3 (A)
1998—Chiefs, 34-24 (KC)
2001—Cardinals, 24-16 (A)
2002—Chiefs, 49-0 (KC)
2006—Chiefs, 23-20 (A)
(RS Pts.—Chiefs 242, Cardinals 140)
*Franchise known as Phoenix prior to 1994 and in St. Louis prior to 1988
***ARIZONA vs. MIAMI**
RS: Dolphins lead series, 8-1
1972—Dolphins, 31-10 (M)
1977—Dolphins, 55-14 (StL)
1978—Dolphins, 24-10 (M)
1981—Dolphins, 20-7 (StL)
1984—Dolphins, 36-28 (StL)
1990—Dolphins, 23-3 (M)
1996—Dolphins, 38-10 (A)
1999—Dolphins, 19-16 (M)
2004—Cardinals, 24-23 (M)
(RS Pts.—Dolphins 269, Cardinals 122)
*Franchise known as Phoenix prior to 1994 and in St. Louis prior to 1988
***ARIZONA vs. MINNESOTA**
RS: Series tied, 9-9
PS: Vikings lead series, 2-0
1963—Cardinals, 56-14 (M)
1967—Cardinals, 34-24 (M)
1969—Vikings, 27-10 (StL)
1972—Cardinals, 19-17 (M)
1974—Cardinals, 28-24 (StL)
    **Vikings, 30-14 (M)
1977—Cardinals, 27-7 (M)
1979—Cardinals, 37-7 (StL)
1981—Cardinals, 30-17 (StL)
1983—Cardinals, 41-31 (M)
1991—Vikings, 34-7 (M)
    Vikings, 28-0 (P)
1994—Cardinals, 17-7 (A)
1995—Vikings, 30-24 (A) OT
1996—Vikings, 41-17 (M)
1997—Vikings, 20-19 (A)
1998—**Vikings, 41-21 (M)
2000—Vikings, 31-14 (M)
2003—Cardinals, 18-17 (A)
2006—Vikings, 31-26 (M)
(RS Pts.—Cardinals 420, Vikings 411)

(PS Pts.—Vikings 71, Cardinals 35)
*Franchise known as Phoenix prior to 1994 and in St. Louis prior to 1988
**NFC Divisional Playoff
***ARIZONA vs. **NEW ENGLAND**
RS: Cardinals lead series, 6-5
1970—Cardinals, 31-0 (StL)
1975—Cardinals, 24-17 (StL)
1978—Patriots, 16-6 (StL)
1981—Cardinals, 27-20 (NE)
1984—Cardinals, 33-10 (NE)
1990—Cardinals, 34-14 (P)
1991—Cardinals, 24-10 (P)
1993—Patriots, 23-21 (P)
1996—Patriots, 31-0 (NE)
1999—Patriots, 27-3 (A)
2004—Patriots, 23-12 (A)
(RS Pts.—Cardinals 215, Patriots 191)
*Franchise known as Phoenix prior to 1994 and in St. Louis prior to 1988
**Franchise in Boston prior to 1971
***ARIZONA vs. NEW ORLEANS**
RS: Cardinals lead series, 13-12
1967—Cardinals, 31-20 (StL)
1968—Cardinals, 21-20 (NO)
    Cardinals, 31-17 (StL)
1969—Saints, 51-42 (StL)
1970—Cardinals, 24-17 (StL)
1974—Saints, 14-0 (NO)
1977—Cardinals, 49-31 (StL)
1980—Cardinals, 40-7 (NO)
1981—Cardinals, 30-3 (StL)
1982—Cardinals, 21-7 (NO)
1983—Saints, 28-17 (NO)
1984—Saints, 34-24 (NO)
1985—Cardinals, 28-16 (StL)
1986—Saints, 16-7 (StL)
1987—Cardinals, 24-19 (StL)
1990—Saints, 28-7 (NO)
1991—Saints, 27-3 (P)
1992—Saints, 30-21 (P)
1993—Saints, 20-17 (P)
1996—Cardinals, 28-14 (NO)
1997—Saints, 27-10 (NO)
1998—Cardinals, 19-17 (A)
2000—Saints, 21-10 (A)
2004—Cardinals, 34-10 (A)
2007—Saints, 31-24 (NO)
(RS Pts.—Cardinals 562, Saints 525)
*Franchise known as Phoenix prior to 1994 and in St. Louis prior to 1988
***ARIZONA vs. N.Y. GIANTS**
RS: Giants lead series, 78-41-2
1926—Giants, 20-0 (NY)
1927—Giants, 28-7 (NY)
1929—Giants, 24-21 (NY)
1930—Giants, 25-12 (NY)
    Giants, 13-7 (C)
1935—Cardinals, 14-13 (NY)
1936—Giants, 14-6 (NY)
1938—Giants, 6-0 (NY)
1939—Giants, 17-7 (NY)
1941—Cardinals, 10-7 (NY)
1942—Giants, 21-7 (NY)
1943—Giants, 24-13 (NY)
1946—Giants, 28-24 (NY)
1947—Giants, 35-31 (NY)
1948—Cardinals, 63-35 (NY)
1949—Giants, 41-38 (C)
1950—Cardinals, 17-3 (C)

Giants, 51-21 (NY)
1951—Giants, 28-17 (NY)
Giants, 10-0 (C)
1952—Cardinals, 24-23 (NY)
Giants, 28-6 (C)
1953—Giants, 21-7 (NY)
Giants, 23-20 (C)
1954—Giants, 41-10 (C)
Giants, 31-17 (NY)
1955—Cardinals, 28-17 (C)
Giants, 10-0 (NY)
1956—Cardinals, 35-27 (C)
Giants, 23-10 (NY)
1957—Giants, 27-14 (NY)
Giants, 28-21 (C)
1958—Giants, 37-7 (Buffalo)
Cardinals, 23-6 (NY)
1959—Giants, 9-3 (NY)
Giants, 30-20 (Minn)
1960—Giants, 35-14 (StL)
Cardinals, 20-13 (NY)
1961—Cardinals, 21-10 (NY)
Giants, 24-9 (StL)
1962—Giants, 31-14 (StL)
Giants, 31-28 (NY)
1963—Giants, 38-21 (StL)
Cardinals, 24-17 (NY)
1964—Giants, 34-17 (NY)
Tie, 10-10 (StL)
1965—Giants, 14-10 (NY)
Giants, 28-15 (StL)
1966—Cardinals, 24-19 (StL)
Cardinals, 20-17 (NY)
1967—Giants, 37-20 (StL)
Giants, 37-14 (NY)
1968—Cardinals, 28-21 (NY)
1969—Cardinals, 42-17 (StL)
Giants, 49-6 (NY)
1970—Giants, 35-17 (NY)
Giants, 34-17 (StL)
1971—Giants, 21-20 (StL)
Cardinals, 24-7 (NY)
1972—Giants, 27-21 (NY)
Giants, 13-7 (StL)
1973—Cardinals, 35-27 (StL)
Giants, 24-13 (New Haven)
1974—Cardinals, 23-21 (New Haven)
Cardinals, 26-14 (StL)
1975—Cardinals, 26-14 (StL)
Cardinals, 20-13 (NY)
1976—Cardinals, 27-21 (StL)
Cardinals, 17-14 (NY)
1977—Cardinals, 28-0 (StL)
Giants, 27-7 (NY)
1978—Cardinals, 20-10 (StL)
Giants, 17-0 (NY)
1979—Cardinals, 27-14 (NY)
Cardinals, 29-20 (StL)
1980—Giants, 41-35 (StL)
Cardinals, 23-7 (NY)
1981—Giants, 34-14 (NY)
Giants, 20-10 (StL)
1982—Cardinals, 24-21 (StL)
1983—Tie, 20-20 (StL) OT
Cardinals, 10-6 (NY)
1984—Giants, 16-10 (NY)
Cardinals, 31-21 (StL)
1985—Giants, 27-17 (NY)
Giants, 34-3 (StL)
1986—Giants, 13-6 (StL)

Giants, 27-7 (NY)
1987—Giants, 30-7 (NY)
Cardinals, 27-24 (StL)
1988—Cardinals, 24-17 (P)
Giants, 44-7 (NY)
1989—Giants, 35-7 (NY)
Giants, 20-13 (P)
1990—Giants, 20-19 (NY)
Giants, 24-21 (P)
1991—Giants, 20-9 (NY)
Giants, 21-14 (P)
1992—Giants, 31-21 (NY)
Cardinals, 19-0 (P)
1993—Giants, 19-17 (NY)
Cardinals, 17-6 (P)
1994—Giants, 20-17 (A)
Cardinals, 10-9 (NY)
1995—Giants, 27-21 (NY) OT
Giants, 10-6 (A)
1996—Giants, 16-8 (NY)
Cardinals, 31-23 (A)
1997—Giants, 27-13 (A)
Giants, 19-10 (NY)
1998—Giants, 34-7 (NY)
Giants, 23-19 (A)
1999—Cardinals, 14-3 (A)
Cardinals, 34-24 (NY)
2000—Giants, 21-16 (NY)
Giants, 31-7 (A)
2001—Giants, 17-10 (A)
Giants, 17-13 (NY)
2002—Cardinals, 21-7 (A)
2004—Cardinals, 17-14 (A)
2005—Giants, 42-19 (NY)
(RS Pts.—Giants 2,661, Cardinals 2,046)
Franchise known as Phoenix prior to 1994, in St. Louis prior to 1988, and in Chicago prior to 1960
*ARIZONA vs. N.Y. JETS
RS: Jets lead series, 4-2
1971—Cardinals, 17-10 (StL)
1975—Cardinals, 37-6 (NY)
1978—Jets, 23-10 (NY)
1996—Jets, 31-21 (A)
1999—Jets, 12-7 (NY)
2004—Jets, 13-3 (A)
(RS Pts.—Cardinals 95, Jets 95)
Franchise known as Phoenix prior to 1994 and in St. Louis prior to 1988
*ARIZONA vs. **OAKLAND
RS: Raiders lead series, 5-2
1973—Raiders, 17-10 (StL)
1983—Cardinals, 34-24 (LA)
1989—Raiders, 16-14 (LA)
1998—Raiders, 23-20 (A)
2001—Cardinals, 34-31 (O) OT
2002—Raiders, 41-20 (A)
2006—Raiders, 22-9 (O)
(RS Pts.— Raiders 174, Cardinals 141)
Franchise known as Phoenix prior to 1994 and in St. Louis prior to 1988
*Franchise in Los Angeles from 1982-1994
*ARIZONA vs. PHILADELPHIA
RS: Cardinals lead series, 53-52-5
PS: Series tied, 1-1
1935—Cardinals, 12-3 (C)
1936—Cardinals, 13-0 (C)
1937—Tie, 6-6 (P)
1938—Eagles, 7-0 (Erie, Pa.)

1941—Eagles, 21-14 (P)
1945—Eagles, 21-6 (P)
1947—Cardinals, 45-21 (P)
**Cardinals, 28-21 (C)
1948—Cardinals, 21-14 (C)
**Eagles, 7-0 (P)
1949—Eagles, 28-3 (P)
1950—Eagles, 45-7 (C)
Cardinals, 14-10 (P)
1951—Eagles, 17-14 (C)
1952—Eagles, 10-7 (P)
Cardinals, 28-22 (C)
1953—Eagles, 56-17 (C)
Eagles, 38-0 (P)
1954—Eagles, 35-16 (C)
Eagles, 30-14 (P)
1955—Tie, 24-24 (C)
Eagles, 27-3 (P)
1956—Cardinals, 20-6 (P)
Cardinals, 28-17 (C)
1957—Eagles, 38-21 (C)
Cardinals, 31-27 (P)
1958—Tie, 21-21 (C)
Eagles, 49-21 (P)
1959—Eagles, 28-24 (Minn)
Eagles, 27-17 (P)
1960—Eagles, 31-27 (P)
Eagles, 20-6 (StL)
1961—Cardinals, 30-27 (P)
Eagles, 20-7 (StL)
1962—Cardinals, 27-21 (P)
Cardinals, 45-35 (StL)
1963—Cardinals, 28-24 (P)
Cardinals, 38-14 (StL)
1964—Cardinals, 38-13 (P)
Cardinals, 36-34 (StL)
1965—Eagles, 34-27 (P)
Eagles, 28-24 (StL)
1966—Cardinals, 16-13 (StL)
Cardinals, 41-10 (P)
1967—Cardinals, 48-14 (StL)
Cardinals, 45-17 (P)
1968—Cardinals, 45-17 (P)
1969—Eagles, 34-30 (StL)
1970—Cardinals, 35-20 (P)
Cardinals, 23-14 (StL)
1971—Cardinals, 37-20 (StL)
Eagles, 19-7 (P)
1972—Tie, 6-6 (P)
Cardinals, 24-23 (StL)
1973—Cardinals, 34-23 (P)
Eagles, 27-24 (StL)
1974—Cardinals, 7-3 (StL)
Cardinals, 13-3 (P)
1975—Cardinals, 31-20 (StL)
Cardinals, 24-23 (P)
1976—Cardinals, 33-14 (StL)
Cardinals, 17-14 (P)
1977—Cardinals, 21-17 (P)
Cardinals, 21-16 (StL)
1978—Cardinals, 16-10 (P)
Eagles, 14-10 (StL)
1979—Eagles, 24-20 (StL)
Eagles, 16-13 (P)
1980—Cardinals, 24-14 (StL)
Eagles, 17-3 (P)
1981—Eagles, 52-10 (StL)
Eagles, 38-0 (P)
1982—Cardinals, 23-20 (P)
1983—Cardinals, 14-11 (P)
Cardinals, 31-7 (StL)

1984—Cardinals, 34-14 (P)
Cardinals, 17-16 (StL)
1985—Eagles, 30-7 (P)
Eagles, 24-14 (StL)
1986—Cardinals, 13-10 (StL)
Tie, 10-10 (P) OT
1987—Eagles, 28-23 (StL)
Cardinals, 31-19 (P)
1988—Eagles, 31-21 (P)
Eagles, 23-17 (Phx)
1989—Eagles, 17-5 (Phx)
Eagles, 31-14 (P)
1990—Cardinals, 23-21 (P)
Eagles, 23-21 (Phx)
1991—Cardinals, 26-10 (P)
Eagles, 34-14 (Phx)
1992—Eagles, 31-14 (Phx)
Eagles, 7-3 (P)
1993—Eagles, 23-17 (P)
Cardinals, 16-3 (Phx)
1994—Eagles, 17-7 (P)
Cardinals, 12-6 (A)
1995—Eagles, 31-19 (A)
Eagles, 21-20 (P)
1996—Cardinals, 36-30 (A)
Eagles, 29-19 (P)
1997—Eagles, 13-10 (P) OT
Cardinals, 31-21 (A)
1998—Cardinals, 17-3 (A)
Cardinals, 20-17 (P) OT
1999—Cardinals, 25-24 (P)
Cardinals, 21-17 (A)
2000—Eagles, 33-14 (A)
Eagles, 34-9 (P)
2001—Cardinals, 21-20 (P)
Eagles, 21-7 (A)
2002—Eagles, 38-14 (P)
2005—Cardinals, 27-21 (A)
(RS Pts.—Eagles 2,340, Cardinals 2,133)
(PS Pts.—Eagles 28, Cardinals 28)
*Franchise known as Phoenix prior to
1994, in St. Louis prior to 1988,
and in Chicago prior to 1960
**NFL Championship
ARIZONA vs. **PITTSBURGH
RS: Steelers lead series, 31-23-3
1933—Pirates, 14-13 (C)
1935—Pirates, 17-13 (P)
1936—Cardinals, 14-6 (C)
1937—Cardinals, 13-7 (P)
1939—Cardinals, 10-0 (P)
1940—Tie, 7-7 (P)
1942—Steelers, 19-3 (P)
1945—Steelers, 23-0 (P)
1946—Steelers, 14-7 (P)
1948—Cardinals, 24-7 (P)
1950—Steelers, 28-17 (C)
Steelers, 28-7 (P)
1951—Steelers, 28-14 (C)
1952—Steelers, 34-28 (C)
Steelers, 17-14 (P)
1953—Steelers, 31-28 (Chi)
Steelers, 21-17 (C)
1954—Cardinals, 17-14 (C)
Steelers, 20-17 (P)
1955—Steelers, 14-7 (P)
Cardinals, 27-13 (C)
1956—Steelers, 14-7 (P)
Cardinals, 38-27 (C)
1957—Steelers, 29-20 (P)

Steelers, 27-2 (C)
1958—Steelers, 27-20 (C)
Steelers, 38-21 (P)
1959—Cardinals, 45-24 (C)
Steelers, 35-20 (P)
1960—Steelers, 27-14 (P)
Cardinals, 38-7 (StL)
1961—Steelers, 30-27 (P)
Cardinals, 20-0 (StL)
1962—Steelers, 26-17 (StL)
Steelers, 19-7 (P)
1963—Steelers, 23-10 (P)
Cardinals, 24-23 (StL)
1964—Cardinals, 34-30 (StL)
Cardinals, 21-20 (P)
1965—Cardinals, 20-7 (P)
Cardinals, 21-17 (StL)
1966—Steelers, 30-9 (P)
Cardinals, 6-3 (StL)
1967—Cardinals, 28-14 (P)
Tie, 14-14 (StL)
1968—Tie, 28-28 (StL)
Cardinals, 20-10 (P)
1969—Cardinals, 27-14 (P)
Cardinals, 47-10 (StL)
1972—Steelers, 25-19 (StL)
1979—Steelers, 24-21 (StL)
1985—Steelers, 23-10 (P)
1988—Cardinals, 31-14 (Phx)
1994—Cardinals, 20-17 (A) OT
1997—Steelers, 26-20 (A) OT
2003—Steelers, 28-15 (P)
2007—Cardinals, 21-14 (A)
(RS Pts.—Steelers 1,106, Cardinals 1,059)
*Franchise known as Phoenix prior to
1994, in St. Louis prior to 1988,
and in Chicago prior to 1960
**Steelers known as Pirates prior to 1941
ARIZONA vs. **ST. LOUIS
RS: Rams lead series, 30-26-2
PS: Rams lead series, 1-0
1937—Cardinals, 6-0 (Clev)
Cardinals, 13-7 (Chi)
1938—Cardinals, 7-6 (Clev)
Cardinals, 31-17 (Chi)
1939—Rams, 24-0 (Chi)
Rams, 14-0 (Clev)
1940—Rams, 26-14 (Clev)
Cardinals, 17-7 (Chi)
1941—Rams, 10-6 (Chi)
Cardinals, 7-0 (Chi)
1942—Cardinals, 7-0 (Buffalo)
Rams, 7-3 (Clev)
1945—Rams, 21-0 (Clev)
Rams, 35-21 (Chi)
1946—Cardinals, 34-10 (Chi)
Rams, 17-14 (LA)
1947—Rams, 27-7 (LA)
Cardinals, 17-10 (Chi)
1948—Cardinals, 27-22 (LA)
Cardinals, 27-24 (Chi)
1949—Tie, 28-28 (Chi)
Cardinals, 31-27 (LA)
1951—Rams, 45-21 (LA)
1953—Tie, 24-24 (Chi)
1954—Rams, 28-17 (LA)
Rams, 20-14 (Chi)
1960—Cardinals, 43-21 (LA)
1965—Rams, 27-3 (StL)
1968—Rams, 24-13 (StL)

1970—Rams, 34-13 (LA)
1972—Cardinals, 24-14 (StL)
1975—***Rams, 35-23 (LA)
1976—Cardinals, 30-28 (LA)
1979—Rams, 21-0 (LA)
1980—Rams, 21-13 (StL)
1984—Rams, 16-13 (StL)
1985—Rams, 46-14 (LA)
1986—Rams, 16-10 (StL)
1987—Rams, 27-24 (StL)
1988—Cardinals, 41-27 (LA)
1989—Rams, 37-14 (LA)
1991—Cardinals, 24-14 (LA)
1992—Cardinals, 20-14 (LA)
1993—Cardinals, 38-10 (P)
1994—Rams, 14-12 (LA)
1996—Cardinals, 31-28 (A) OT
1998—Cardinals, 20-17 (StL)
2002—Rams, 27-14 (A)
Rams, 30-28 (StL)
2003—Rams, 37-13 (StL)
Rams, 30-27 (A) OT
2004—Rams, 17-10 (StL)
Cardinals, 31-7 (A)
2005—Rams, 17-12 (A)
Cardinals, 38-28 (StL)
2006—Rams, 16-14 (A)
Cardinals, 34-20 (StL)
2007—Cardinals, 34-31 (StL)
Cardinals, 48-19 (A)
(RS Pts.—Rams 1,191, Cardinals 1,096)
(PS Pts.—Rams 35, Cardinals 23)
*Franchise known as Phoenix prior to
1994, in St. Louis prior to 1988,
and in Chicago prior to 1960
**Franchise in Los Angeles prior to 1995
and in Cleveland prior to 1946
***NFC Divisional Playoff
ARIZONA vs. SAN DIEGO
RS: Chargers lead series, 8-3
1971—Chargers, 20-17 (SD)
1976—Chargers, 43-24 (SD)
1983—Cardinals, 44-14 (StL)
1987—Chargers, 28-24 (SD)
1989—Chargers, 24-13 (P)
1992—Chargers, 27-21 (P)
1995—Chargers, 28-25 (SD)
1998—Cardinals, 16-13 (A)
2001—Cardinals, 20-17 (SD)
2002—Chargers, 23-15 (A)
2006—Chargers, 27-20 (SD)
(RS Pts.—Chargers 264, Cardinals 239)
*Franchise known as Phoenix prior to
1994, in St. Louis prior to 1988,
ARIZONA vs. SAN FRANCISCO
RS: 49ers lead series, 19-14
1951—Cardinals, 27-21 (SF)
1957—Cardinals, 20-10 (SF)
1962—49ers, 24-17 (StL)
1964—Cardinals, 23-13 (SF)
1968—49ers, 35-17 (SF)
1971—49ers, 26-14 (SF)
1974—Cardinals, 34-9 (SF)
1976—Cardinals, 23-20 (StL) OT
1978—Cardinals, 16-10 (SF)
1979—Cardinals, 13-10 (StL)
1980—49ers, 24-21 (SF) OT
1982—49ers, 31-20 (SF)
1983—49ers, 42-27 (StL)
1986—49ers, 43-17 (SF)

1987—49ers, 34-28 (SF)
1988—Cardinals, 24-23 (P)
1991—49ers, 14-10 (SF)
1992—Cardinals, 24-14 (P)
1993—49ers, 28-14 (SF)
1999—49ers, 24-10 (A)
2000—49ers, 27-20 (SF)
2002—49ers, 38-28 (SF)
    49ers, 17-14 (A)
2003—Cardinals, 16-13 (A) OT
    49ers, 50-14 (SF)
2004—49ers, 31-28 (SF) OT
    49ers, 31-28 (A) OT
2005—Cardinals, 31-14 (Mex. City)
    Cardinals, 17-10 (SF)
2006—Cardinals, 34-27 (A)
    Cardinals, 26-20 (SF)
2007—49ers, 20-17 (SF)
    49ers, 37-31 (A) OT
(RS Pts.—49ers 790, Cardinals 703)
*Franchise known as Phoenix prior to
1994, in St. Louis prior to 1988,
and in Chicago prior to 1960
ARIZONA vs. SEATTLE
RS: Series tied, 9-9
1976—Cardinals, 30-24 (S)
1983—Cardinals, 33-28 (StL)
1989—Cardinals, 34-24 (S)
1993—Cardinals, 30-27 (S) OT
1995—Cardinals, 20-14 (A) OT
1998—Seahawks, 33-14 (S)
2002—Cardinals, 24-13 (S)
    Seahawks, 27-6 (A)
2003—Seahawks, 38-0 (A)
    Seahawks, 28-10 (S)
2004—Cardinals, 25-17 (A)
    Seahawks, 24-21 (S)
2005—Seahawks, 37-12 (S)
    Seahawks, 33-19 (A)
2006—Seahawks, 21-10 (S)
    Cardinals, 27-21 (A)
2007—Cardinals, 23-20 (A)
    Seahawks, 42-21 (S)
(RS Pts.—Seahawks 471, Cardinals 359)
*Franchise known as Phoenix prior to
1994 and in St. Louis prior to 1988
ARIZONA vs. TAMPA BAY
RS: Series tied, 8-8
1977—Buccaneers, 17-7 (TB)
1981—Buccaneers, 20-10 (TB)
1983—Cardinals, 34-27 (TB)
1985—Buccaneers, 16-0 (TB)
1986—Cardinals, 30-19 (TB)
    Cardinals, 21-17 (StL)
1987—Cardinals, 31-28 (StL)
    Cardinals, 31-14 (TB)
1988—Cardinals, 30-24 (TB)
1989—Buccaneers, 14-13 (P)
1992—Buccaneers, 23-7 (TB)
    Buccaneers, 7-3 (P)
1996—Cardinals, 13-9 (A)
1997—Buccaneers, 19-18 (TB)
2004—Cardinals, 12-7 (A)
2007—Buccaneers, 17-10 (TB)
(RS Pts.—Buccaneers 278, Cardinals 270)
*Franchise known as Phoenix prior to
1994 and in St. Louis prior to 1988
ARIZONA vs. **TENNESSEE
RS: Cardinals lead series, 5-3
1970—Cardinals, 44-0 (StL)

1974—Cardinals, 31-27 (H)
1979—Cardinals, 24-17 (H)
1985—Oilers, 20-10 (StL)
1988—Oilers, 38-20 (H)
1994—Cardinals, 30-12 (H)
1997—Oilers, 41-14 (A)
2005—Cardinals, 20-10 (A)
(RS Pts.—Cardinals 193, Titans 165)
*Franchise known as Phoenix prior to
1994 and in St. Louis prior to 1988
**Franchise in Houston prior to 1997;
known as Oilers prior to 1999
ARIZONA vs. **WASHINGTON
RS: Redskins lead series, 72-44-2
1932—Cardinals, 9-0 (B)
    Braves, 8-6 (C)
1933—Redskins, 10-0 (C)
    Tie, 0-0 (B)
1934—Redskins, 9-0 (B)
1935—Cardinals, 6-0 (B)
1936—Redskins, 13-10 (B)
1937—Cardinals, 21-14 (W)
1939—Redskins, 28-7 (W)
1940—Redskins, 28-21 (W)
1942—Redskins, 28-0 (W)
1943—Redskins, 13-7 (W)
1945—Redskins, 24-21 (W)
1947—Cardinals, 45-21 (W)
1949—Cardinals, 38-7 (C)
1950—Cardinals, 38-28 (W)
1951—Redskins, 7-3 (C)
    Redskins, 20-17 (W)
1952—Redskins, 23-7 (C)
    Cardinals, 17-6 (W)
1953—Cardinals, 24-13 (C)
    Redskins, 28-17 (W)
1954—Cardinals, 38-16 (C)
    Redskins, 37-20 (W)
1955—Cardinals, 24-10 (W)
    Redskins, 31-0 (C)
1956—Cardinals, 31-3 (W)
    Redskins, 17-14 (C)
1957—Redskins, 37-14 (C)
    Cardinals, 44-14 (W)
1958—Cardinals, 37-10 (C)
    Redskins, 45-31 (W)
1959—Cardinals, 49-21 (C)
    Redskins, 23-14 (W)
1960—Cardinals, 44-7 (StL)
    Cardinals, 26-14 (W)
1961—Cardinals, 24-0 (W)
    Cardinals, 38-24 (StL)
1962—Redskins, 24-14 (W)
    Tie, 17-17 (StL)
1963—Cardinals, 21-7 (W)
    Cardinals, 24-20 (StL)
1964—Cardinals, 23-17 (W)
    Cardinals, 38-24 (StL)
1965—Cardinals, 37-16 (W)
    Redskins, 24-20 (StL)
1966—Cardinals, 23-7 (StL)
    Redskins, 26-20 (W)
1967—Cardinals, 27-21 (W)
1968—Cardinals, 41-14 (StL)
1969—Redskins, 33-17 (W)
1970—Cardinals, 27-17 (StL)
    Redskins, 28-27 (W)
1971—Redskins, 24-17 (StL)
    Redskins, 20-0 (W)
1972—Redskins, 24-10 (W)

    Redskins, 33-3 (StL)
1973—Cardinals, 34-27 (StL)
    Redskins, 31-13 (W)
1974—Cardinals, 17-10 (W)
    Cardinals, 23-20 (StL)
1975—Redskins, 27-17 (W)
    Cardinals, 20-17 (StL) OT
1976—Redskins, 20-10 (W)
    Redskins, 16-10 (StL)
1977—Cardinals, 24-14 (W)
    Redskins, 26-20 (StL)
1978—Redskins, 28-10 (StL)
    Cardinals, 27-17 (W)
1979—Redskins, 17-7 (StL)
    Redskins, 30-28 (W)
1980—Redskins, 23-0 (W)
    Redskins, 31-7 (StL)
1981—Cardinals, 40-30 (StL)
    Redskins, 42-21 (W)
1982—Redskins, 12-7 (StL)
    Redskins, 28-0 (W)
1983—Redskins, 38-14 (StL)
    Redskins, 45-7 (W)
1984—Cardinals, 26-24 (StL)
    Redskins, 29-27 (W)
1985—Redskins, 27-10 (W)
    Redskins, 27-16 (StL)
1986—Redskins, 28-21 (W)
    Redskins, 20-17 (StL)
1987—Redskins, 28-21 (W)
    Redskins, 34-17 (StL)
1988—Cardinals, 30-21 (P)
    Redskins, 33-17 (W)
1989—Redskins, 30-28 (W)
    Redskins, 29-10 (P)
1990—Redskins, 31-0 (W)
    Redskins, 38-10 (P)
1991—Redskins, 34-0 (W)
    Redskins, 20-14 (P)
1992—Cardinals, 27-24 (P)
    Redskins, 41-3 (W)
1993—Cardinals, 17-10 (W)
    Cardinals, 36-6 (P)
1994—Cardinals, 19-16 (W) OT
    Cardinals, 17-15 (A)
1995—Redskins, 27-7 (W)
    Cardinals, 24-20 (A)
1996—Cardinals, 37-34 (W) OT
    Cardinals, 27-26 (A)
1997—Redskins, 19-13 (W) OT
    Redskins, 38-28 (A)
1998—Cardinals, 29-27 (A)
    Cardinals, 45-42 (W)
1999—Redskins, 24-10 (A)
    Redskins, 28-3 (W)
2000—Cardinals, 16-15 (A)
    Redskins, 20-3 (W)
2001—Redskins, 20-10 (A)
    Redskins, 20-17 (W)
2002—Redskins, 31-23 (W)
2005—Redskins, 17-13 (A)
2007—Redskins, 21-19 (W)
(RS Pts.—Redskins 2,621, Cardinals 2,186)
*Franchise known as Phoenix prior to
1994, in St. Louis prior to 1988,
and in Chicago prior to 1960
**Franchise in Boston prior to 1937 and
known as Braves prior to 1933

ATLANTA vs. ARIZONA

RS: Cardinals lead series, 14-10;
See Arizona vs. Atlanta

ATLANTA vs. BALTIMORE
RS: Ravens lead series, 2-1
1999—Ravens, 19-13 (A) OT
2002—Falcons, 20-17 (A)
2006—Ravens, 24-10 (B)
(RS Pts.—Ravens 60, Falcons 43)

ATLANTA vs. BUFFALO
RS: Falcons lead series, 5-4
1973—Bills, 17-6 (A)
1977—Bills, 3-0 (B)
1980—Falcons, 30-14 (B)
1983—Falcons, 31-14 (A)
1989—Falcons, 30-28 (A)
1992—Bills, 41-14 (B)
1995—Bills, 23-17 (B)
2001—Falcons, 33-30 (A)
2005—Falcons, 24-16 (B)
(RS Pts.—Bills 186, Falcons 185)

ATLANTA vs. CAROLINA
RS: Falcons lead series, 16-10
1995—Falcons, 23-20 (A) OT
          Panthers, 21-17 (C)
1996—Panthers, 29-6 (C)
          Falcons, 20-17 (A)
1997—Panthers, 9-6 (A)
          Panthers, 21-12 (C)
1998—Falcons, 19-14 (C)
          Falcons, 51-23 (A)
1999—Falcons, 27-20 (A)
          Panthers, 34-28 (C)
2000—Falcons, 15-10 (C)
          Falcons, 13-12 (A)
2001—Falcons, 24-16 (A)
          Falcons, 10-7 (C)
2002—Falcons, 30-0 (A)
          Falcons, 41-0 (C)
2003—Panthers, 23-3 (C)
          Falcons, 20-14 (A) OT
2004—Falcons, 27-10 (C)
          Falcons, 34-31 (A) OT
2005—Panthers, 24-6 (C)
          Panthers, 44-11 (A)
2006—Falcons, 20-6 (C)
          Panthers, 10-3 (A)
2007—Panthers, 27-20 (A)
          Falcons, 20-13 (C)
(RS Pts.—Falcons 506, Panthers 455)

ATLANTA vs. CHICAGO
RS: Bears lead series, 12-10
1966—Bears, 23-6 (C)
1967—Bears, 23-14 (A)
1968—Falcons, 16-13 (C)
1969—Falcons, 48-31 (A)
1970—Bears, 23-14 (A)
1972—Falcons, 37-21 (C)
1973—Falcons, 46-6 (A)
1974—Falcons, 13-10 (A)
1976—Falcons, 10-0 (C)
1977—Falcons, 16-10 (C)
1978—Bears, 13-7 (C)
1980—Falcons, 28-17 (A)
1983—Falcons, 20-17 (C)
1985—Bears, 36-0 (C)
1986—Bears, 13-10 (A)
1990—Bears, 30-24 (C)
1992—Bears, 41-31 (C)
1993—Bears, 6-0 (C)
1998—Falcons, 20-13 (A)

2001—Bears, 31-3 (A)
2002—Bears, 14-13 (A)
2005—Bears, 16-3 (C)
(RS Pts.—Bears 407, Falcons 379)

ATLANTA vs. CINCINNATI
RS: Bengals lead series, 7-4
1971—Falcons, 9-6 (C)
1975—Bengals, 21-14 (A)
1978—Bengals, 37-7 (C)
1981—Bengals, 30-28 (A)
1984—Bengals, 35-14 (C)
1987—Bengals, 16-10 (A)
1990—Falcons, 38-17 (A)
1993—Bengals, 21-17 (C)
1996—Bengals, 41-31 (C)
2002—Falcons, 30-3 (A)
2006—Falcons, 29-27 (C)
(RS Pts.—Bengals 254, Falcons 227)

ATLANTA vs. CLEVELAND
RS: Browns lead series, 10-2
1966—Browns, 49-17 (A)
1968—Browns, 30-7 (C)
1971—Falcons, 31-14 (C)
1976—Browns, 20-17 (A)
1978—Browns, 24-16 (A)
1981—Browns, 28-17 (C)
1984—Browns, 23-7 (A)
1987—Browns, 38-3 (C)
1990—Browns, 13-10 (A)
1993—Falcons, 17-14 (A)
2002—Browns, 24-16 (C)
2006—Browns, 17-13 (A)
(RS Pts.—Browns 294, Falcons 171)

ATLANTA vs. DALLAS
RS: Cowboys lead series, 13-8
PS: Cowboys lead series, 2-0
1966—Cowboys, 47-14 (A)
1967—Cowboys, 37-7 (D)
1969—Cowboys, 24-17 (A)
1970—Cowboys, 13-0 (D)
1974—Cowboys, 24-0 (A)
1976—Falcons, 17-10 (A)
1978—*Cowboys, 27-20 (D)
1980—*Cowboys, 30-27 (A)
1985—Cowboys, 24-10 (D)
1986—Falcons, 37-35 (A)
1987—Falcons, 21-10 (D)
1988—Cowboys, 26-20 (D)
1989—Falcons 27-21 (A)
1990—Falcons, 26-7 (A)
1991—Cowboys, 31-27 (D)
1992—Cowboys, 41-17 (A)
1993—Falcons, 27-14 (A)
1995—Cowboys, 28-13 (A)
1996—Cowboys, 32-28 (D)
1999—Cowboys, 24-7 (D)
2001—Falcons, 20-13 (A)
2003—Cowboys, 27-13 (D)
2006—Cowboys, 38-28 (A)
(RS Pts.—Cowboys 512, Falcons 390)
(PS Pts.—Cowboys 57, Falcons 47)
*NFC Divisional Playoff

ATLANTA vs. DENVER
RS: Broncos lead series, 7-4
PS: Broncos lead series, 1-0
1970—Broncos, 24-10 (D)
1972—Falcons, 23-20 (A)
1975—Falcons, 35-21 (A)
1979—Broncos, 20-17 (A) OT
1982—Falcons, 34-27 (D)

1985—Broncos, 44-28 (A)
1988—Broncos, 30-14 (D)
1994—Broncos, 32-28 (D)
1997—Broncos, 29-21 (A)
1998—*Broncos, 34-19 (South Florida)
2000—Broncos, 42-14 (D)
2004—Falcons, 41-28 (D)
(RS Pts.—Broncos 317, Falcons 265)
(PS Pts.—Broncos 34, Falcons 19)
*Super Bowl XXXIII

ATLANTA vs. DETROIT
RS: Lions lead series, 23-9
1966—Lions, 28-10 (D)
1967—Lions, 24-3 (D)
1968—Lions, 24-7 (A)
1969—Lions, 27-21 (D)
1971—Lions, 41-38 (D)
1972—Lions, 26-23 (A)
1973—Lions, 31-6 (D)
1975—Lions, 17-14 (A)
1976—Lions, 24-10 (D)
1977—Falcons, 17-6 (A)
1978—Falcons, 14-0 (A)
1979—Lions, 24-23 (D)
1980—Falcons, 43-28 (A)
1983—Falcons, 30-14 (D)
1984—Lions, 27-24 (A) OT
1985—Lions, 28-27 (A)
1986—Falcons, 20-6 (D)
1987—Lions, 30-13 (A)
1988—Lions, 31-17 (D)
1989—Lions, 31-24 (A)
1990—Lions, 21-14 (D)
1993—Lions, 30-13 (D)
1994—Lions, 31-28 (D) OT
1995—Falcons, 34-22 (A)
1996—Lions, 28-24 (D)
1997—Lions, 28-17 (D)
1998—Falcons, 24-17 (D)
2000—Lions, 13-10 (D)
2002—Falcons, 36-15 (A)
2004—Falcons, 17-10 (A)
2005—Falcons, 27-7 (D)
2006—Lions, 30-14 (D)
(RS Pts.—Lions 726, Falcons 635)

ATLANTA vs. GREEN BAY
RS: Packers lead series, 12-10
PS: Series tied, 1-1
1966—Packers, 56-3 (Mil)
1967—Packers, 23-0 (Mil)
1968—Packers, 38-7 (A)
1969—Packers, 28-10 (A)
1970—Packers, 27-24 (GB)
1971—Falcons, 28-21 (A)
1972—Falcons, 10-9 (Mil)
1974—Falcons, 10-3 (A)
1975—Packers, 22-13 (GB)
1976—Packers, 24-20 (A)
1979—Falcons, 25-7 (A)
1981—Falcons, 31-17 (GB)
1982—Packers, 38-7 (A)
1983—Falcons, 47-41 (A) OT
1988—Falcons, 20-0 (A)
1989—Packers, 23-21 (Mil)
1991—Falcons, 35-31 (A)
1992—Falcons, 24-10 (A)
1994—Packers, 21-17 (Mil)
1995—*Packers, 37-20 (GB)
2001—Falcons, 23-20 (GB)
2002—Packers, 37-34 (GB) OT

*Falcons, 27-7 (GB)
2005—Packers, 33-25 (A)
(RS Pts.—Packers 529, Falcons 434)
(PS Pts.—Falcons 47, Packers 44)
NFC First-Round Playoff
ATLANTA vs. HOUSTON
RS: Series tied, 1-1
2003—Texans, 17-13 (H)
2007—Falcons, 26-16 (A)
(RS Pts.—Falcons 39, Texans 33)
ATLANTA vs. *INDIANAPOLIS
RS: Colts lead series, 13-1
1966—Colts, 19-7 (A)
1967—Colts, 38-31 (B)
Colts, 49-7 (A)
1968—Colts, 28-20 (A)
Colts, 44-0 (B)
1969—Colts, 21-14 (A)
Colts, 13-6 (B)
1974—Colts, 17-7 (A)
1986—Colts, 28-23 (A)
1989—Colts, 13-9 (I)
1998—Falcons, 28-21 (A)
2001—Colts, 41-27 (I)
2003—Colts, 38-7 (I)
2007—Colts, 31-13 (A)
(RS Pts.—Colts 401, Falcons 199)
Franchise in Baltimore prior to 1984
ATLANTA vs. JACKSONVILLE
RS: Jaguars lead series, 3-1
1996—Jaguars, 19-17 (J)
1999—Jaguars, 30-7 (A)
2003—Falcons, 21-14 (A)
2007—Jaguars, 13-7 (J)
(RS Pts.—Jaguars 76, Falcons 52)
ATLANTA vs. KANSAS CITY
RS: Chiefs lead series, 5-1
1972—Chiefs, 17-14 (A)
1985—Chiefs, 38-10 (KC)
1991—Chiefs, 14-3 (KC)
1994—Chiefs, 30-10 (A)
2000—Falcons, 29-13 (A)
2004—Chiefs, 56-10 (KC)
(RS Pts.—Chiefs 168, Falcons 76)
ATLANTA vs. MIAMI
RS: Dolphins lead series, 7-3
1970—Dolphins, 20-7 (A)
1974—Dolphins, 42-7 (M)
1980—Dolphins, 20-17 (A)
1983—Dolphins, 31-24 (M)
1986—Falcons, 20-14 (M)
1992—Dolphins, 21-17 (M)
1995—Dolphins, 21-20 (M)
1998—Falcons, 38-16 (A)
2001—Dolphins, 21-14 (M)
2005—Falcons, 17-10 (M)
(RS Pts.—Dolphins 216, Falcons 181)
ATLANTA vs. MINNESOTA
RS: Vikings lead series, 15-8
PS: Series tied, 1-1
1966—Falcons, 20-13 (M)
1967—Falcons, 21-20 (A)
1968—Vikings, 47-7 (M)
1969—Falcons, 10-3 (A)
1970—Vikings, 37-7 (A)
1971—Vikings, 24-7 (A)
1973—Falcons, 20-14 (A)
1974—Vikings, 23-10 (M)
1975—Vikings, 38-0 (M)
1977—Vikings, 14-7 (A)

1980—Vikings, 24-23 (M)
1981—Falcons, 31-30 (A)
1982—*Vikings, 30-24 (M)
1984—Vikings, 27-20 (M)
1985—Falcons, 14-13 (A)
1987—Vikings, 24-13 (M)
1989—Vikings, 43-17 (M)
1991—Vikings, 20-19 (A)
1996—Vikings, 23-17 (A)
1998—**Falcons, 30-27 (M) OT
1999—Vikings, 17-14 (A)
2002—Falcons, 30-24 (M) OT
2003—Vikings, 39-26 (A)
2005—Falcons, 30-10 (A)
2007—Vikings, 24-3 (M)
(RS Pts.—Vikings 551, Falcons 366)
(PS Pts.—Vikings 57, Falcons 54)
NFC First-Round Playoff
*NFC Championship
ATLANTA vs. NEW ENGLAND
RS: Falcons lead series, 6-5
1972—Patriots, 21-20 (NE)
1977—Patriots, 16-10 (A)
1980—Falcons, 37-21 (NE)
1983—Falcons, 24-13 (A)
1986—Patriots, 25-17 (NE)
1989—Falcons, 16-15 (A)
1992—Falcons, 34-0 (A)
1995—Falcons, 30-17 (A)
1998—Falcons, 41-10 (NE)
2001—Patriots, 24-10 (A)
2005—Patriots, 31-28 (A)
(RS Pts.—Falcons 267, Patriots 193)
ATLANTA vs. NEW ORLEANS
RS: Falcons lead series, 43-34
PS: Falcons lead series, 1-0
1967—Saints, 27-24 (NO)
1969—Falcons, 45-17 (A)
1970—Falcons, 14-3 (NO)
Falcons, 32-14 (A)
1971—Falcons, 28-6 (A)
Falcons, 24-20 (NO)
1972—Falcons, 21-14 (NO)
Falcons, 36-20 (A)
1973—Falcons, 62-7 (NO)
Falcons, 14-10 (A)
1974—Saints, 14-13 (NO)
Saints, 13-3 (A)
1975—Falcons, 14-7 (A)
Saints, 23-7 (NO)
1976—Saints, 30-0 (NO)
Falcons, 23-20 (A)
1977—Saints, 21-20 (NO)
Falcons, 35-7 (A)
1978—Falcons, 20-17 (NO)
Falcons, 20-17 (A)
1979—Falcons, 40-34 (NO) OT
Saints, 37-6 (A)
1980—Falcons, 41-14 (NO)
Falcons, 31-13 (A)
1981—Falcons, 27-0 (A)
Falcons, 41-10 (NO)
1982—Falcons, 35-0 (A)
Saints, 35-6 (NO)
1983—Saints, 19-17 (A)
Saints, 27-10 (NO)
1984—Falcons, 36-28 (A)
Saints, 17-13 (A)
1985—Falcons, 31-24 (A)
Falcons, 16-10 (NO)

1986—Falcons, 31-10 (NO)
Saints, 14-9 (A)
1987—Saints, 38-0 (A)
1988—Saints, 29-21 (A)
Saints, 10-9 (NO)
1989—Saints, 20-13 (NO)
Saints, 26-17 (A)
1990—Falcons, 28-27 (A)
Saints, 10-7 (NO)
1991—Saints, 27-6 (A)
Falcons, 23-20 (NO) OT
*Falcons, 27-20 (NO)
1992—Saints, 10-7 (A)
Saints, 22-14 (NO)
1993—Saints, 34-31 (A)
Falcons, 26-15 (NO)
1994—Saints, 33-32 (NO)
Saints, 29-20 (A)
1995—Falcons, 27-24 (NO) OT
Falcons, 19-14 (A)
1996—Falcons, 17-15 (A)
Falcons, 31-15 (NO)
1997—Falcons, 23-17 (NO)
Falcons, 20-3 (A)
1998—Falcons, 31-23 (A)
Falcons, 27-17 (NO)
1999—Falcons, 20-17 (NO)
Falcons, 35-12 (A)
2000—Saints, 21-19 (A)
Saints, 23-7 (NO)
2001—Falcons, 20-13 (NO)
Saints, 28-10 (A)
2002—Falcons, 37-35 (NO)
Falcons, 24-17 (A)
2003—Saints, 45-17 (A)
Saints, 23-20 (NO) OT
2004—Falcons, 24-21 (A)
Saints, 26-13 (NO)
2005—Falcons, 34-31 (San Antonio)
Falcons, 36-17 (A)
2006—Saints, 23-3 (NO)
Saints, 31-13 (A)
2007—Saints, 22-16 (NO)
Saints, 34-14 (A)
(RS Pts.—Falcons 1,656, Saints 1,516)
(PS Pts.—Falcons 27, Saints 20)
NFC First-Round Playoff
ATLANTA vs. N.Y. GIANTS
RS: Falcons lead series, 10-9
1966—Falcons, 27-16 (NY)
1968—Falcons, 24-21 (A)
1971—Giants, 21-17 (A)
1974—Falcons, 14-7 (New Haven)
1977—Falcons, 17-3 (A)
1978—Falcons, 23-20 (A)
1979—Giants, 24-3 (NY)
1981—Giants, 27-24 (A) OT
1982—Falcons, 16-14 (NY)
1983—Giants, 16-13 (A) OT
1984—Giants, 19-7 (A)
1988—Giants, 23-16 (A)
1998—Falcons, 34-20 (NY)
2000—Giants, 13-6 (A)
2002—Falcons, 17-10 (NY)
2003—Falcons, 27-7 (NY)
2004—Falcons, 14-10 (NY)
2006—Giants, 27-14 (A)
2007—Giants, 31-10 (A)
(RS Pts.—Giants 329, Falcons 323)
ATLANTA vs. N.Y. JETS

RS: Falcons lead series, 5-4
1973—Falcons, 28-20 (NY)
1980—Jets, 14-7 (A)
1983—Falcons, 27-21 (NY)
1986—Jets, 28-14 (A)
1989—Jets, 27-7 (NY)
1992—Falcons, 20-17 (A)
1995—Falcons, 13-3 (A)
1998—Jets, 28-3 (NY)
2005—Falcons, 27-14 (A)
(RS Pts.—Jets 172, Falcons 146)

ATLANTA vs. *OAKLAND
RS: Raiders lead series, 7-4
1971—Falcons, 24-13 (A)
1975—Raiders, 37-34 (O) OT
1979—Raiders, 50-19 (O)
1982—Raiders, 38-14 (A)
1985—Raiders, 34-24 (A)
1988—Falcons, 12-6 (LA)
1991—Falcons, 21-17 (A)
1994—Raiders, 30-17 (LA)
1997—Raiders, 36-31 (A)
2000—Raiders, 41-14 (O)
2004—Falcons, 35-10 (A)
(RS Pts.—Raiders 312, Falcons 245)
Franchise in Los Angeles from 1982-1994

ATLANTA vs. PHILADELPHIA
RS: Eagles lead series, 12-10-1
PS: Eagles lead series, 2-1
1966—Eagles, 23-10 (P)
1967—Eagles, 38-7 (A)
1969—Falcons, 27-3 (P)
1970—Tie, 13-13 (P)
1973—Falcons, 44-27 (P)
1976—Eagles, 14-13 (A)
1978—*Falcons, 14-13 (A)
1979—Falcons, 14-10 (P)
1980—Falcons, 20-17 (P)
1981—Eagles, 16-13 (P)
1983—Eagles, 28-24 (A)
1984—Falcons, 26-10 (A)
1985—Eagles, 23-17 (P) OT
1986—Eagles, 16-0 (A)
1988—Falcons, 27-24 (P)
1990—Eagles, 24-23 (A)
1994—Eagles, 28-21 (A)
1996—Eagles, 33-18 (A)
1997—Falcons, 20-17 (A)
1998—Falcons, 17-12 (A)
2000—Eagles, 38-10 (A)
2002—**Eagles, 20-6 (P)
2003—Eagles, 23-16 (A)
2004—***Eagles, 27-10 (P)
2005—Falcons, 14-10 (A)
2006—Eagles, 24-17 (P)
(RS Pts.—Eagles 464, Falcons 418)
(PS Pts.—Eagles 60, Falcons 30)
NFC First-Round Playoff
**NFC Divisional Playoff*
***NFC Championship*

ATLANTA vs. PITTSBURGH
RS: Steelers lead series, 11-2-1
1966—Steelers, 57-33 (A)
1968—Steelers, 41-21 (A)
1970—Falcons, 27-16 (A)
1974—Steelers, 24-17 (P)
1978—Steelers, 31-7 (P)
1981—Steelers, 34-20 (A)
1984—Steelers, 35-10 (P)
1987—Steelers, 28-12 (A)

1990—Steelers, 21-9 (P)
1993—Steelers, 45-17 (A)
1996—Steelers, 20-17 (A)
1999—Steelers, 13-9 (P)
2002—Tie, 34-34 (P) OT
2006—Falcons, 41-38 (A) OT
(RS Pts.—Steelers 437, Falcons 274)

ATLANTA vs. *ST. LOUIS
RS: Rams lead series, 47-24-2
PS: Falcons lead series, 1-0
1966—Rams, 19-14 (A)
1967—Rams, 31-3 (A)
       Rams, 20-3 (LA)
1968—Rams, 27-14 (LA)
       Rams, 17-10 (A)
1969—Rams, 17-7 (LA)
       Rams, 38-6 (A)
1970—Tie, 10-10 (LA)
       Rams, 17-7 (A)
1971—Tie, 20-20 (LA)
       Rams, 24-16 (A)
1972—Falcons, 31-3 (A)
       Rams, 20-7 (LA)
1973—Rams, 31-0 (LA)
       Falcons, 15-13 (A)
1974—Rams, 21-0 (LA)
       Rams, 30-7 (A)
1975—Rams, 22-7 (LA)
       Rams, 16-7 (A)
1976—Rams, 30-14 (A)
       Rams, 59-0 (LA)
1977—Falcons, 17-6 (A)
       Rams, 23-7 (LA)
1978—Rams, 10-0 (LA)
       Falcons, 15-7 (A)
1979—Rams, 20-14 (LA)
       Rams, 34-13 (A)
1980—Rams, 13-10 (A)
       Rams, 20-17 (LA) OT
1981—Rams, 37-35 (A)
       Rams, 21-16 (LA)
1982—Falcons, 34-17 (A)
1983—Rams, 27-21 (A)
       Rams, 36-13 (A)
1984—Falcons, 30-28 (LA)
       Rams, 24-10 (A)
1985—Rams, 17-6 (LA)
       Falcons, 30-14 (A)
1986—Falcons, 26-14 (A)
       Rams, 14-7 (LA)
1987—Falcons, 24-20 (A)
       Rams, 33-0 (LA)
1988—Rams, 33-0 (A)
       Rams, 22-7 (LA)
1989—Rams, 31-21 (A)
       Rams, 26-14 (LA)
1990—Rams, 44-24 (LA)
       Falcons, 20-13 (A)
1991—Falcons, 31-14 (A)
       Falcons, 31-14 (LA)
1992—Falcons, 30-28 (A)
       Rams, 38-27 (LA)
1993—Falcons, 30-24 (A)
       Rams, 13-0 (LA)
1994—Falcons, 31-13 (A)
       Falcons, 8-5 (LA)
1995—Rams, 21-19 (StL)
       Falcons, 31-6 (A)
1996—Rams, 59-16 (StL)
       Rams, 34-27 (A)

1997—Falcons, 34-31 (A)
       Falcons, 27-21 (StL)
1998—Falcons, 37-15 (A)
       Falcons, 21-10 (StL)
1999—Rams, 35-7 (StL)
       Rams, 41-13 (A)
2000—Rams, 41-20 (A)
       Rams, 45-29 (StL)
2001—Rams, 35-6 (A)
       Rams, 31-13 (StL)
2003—Rams, 36-0 (StL)
2004—Rams, 34-17 (A)
       **Falcons, 47-17 (A)
2007—Rams, 28-16 (StL)
(RS Pts.—Rams 1,728, Falcons 1,183)
(PS Pts.—Falcons 47, Rams 17)
Franchise in Los Angeles prior to 1995
**NFC Divisional Playoff*

ATLANTA vs. SAN DIEGO
RS: Falcons lead series, 6-1
1973—Falcons, 41-0 (SD)
1979—Falcons, 28-26 (SD)
1988—Chargers, 10-7 (A)
1991—Falcons, 13-10 (SD)
1994—Falcons, 10-9 (A)
1997—Falcons, 14-3 (SD)
2004—Falcons, 21-20 (A)
(RS Pts.—Falcons 134, Chargers 78)

ATLANTA vs. SAN FRANCISCO
RS: 49ers lead series, 44-27-1
PS: Falcons lead series, 1-0
1966—49ers, 44-7 (A)
1967—49ers, 38-7 (A)
       49ers, 34-28 (A)
1968—49ers, 28-13 (SF)
       49ers, 14-12 (A)
1969—Falcons, 24-12 (A)
       Falcons, 21-7 (SF)
1970—Falcons, 21-20 (A)
       49ers, 24-20 (SF)
1971—Falcons, 20-17 (A)
       49ers, 24-3 (SF)
1972—49ers, 49-14 (A)
       49ers, 20-0 (SF)
1973—49ers, 13-9 (A)
       Falcons, 17-3 (SF)
1974—49ers, 16-10 (A)
       49ers, 27-0 (SF)
1975—Falcons, 17-3 (SF)
       Falcons, 31-9 (A)
1976—49ers, 15-0 (SF)
       Falcons, 21-16 (A)
1977—Falcons, 7-0 (SF)
       49ers, 10-3 (A)
1978—Falcons, 20-17 (SF)
       Falcons, 21-10 (A)
1979—49ers, 20-15 (SF)
       Falcons, 31-21 (A)
1980—Falcons, 20-17 (SF)
       Falcons, 35-10 (A)
1981—Falcons, 34-17 (A)
       49ers, 17-14 (SF)
1982—Falcons, 17-7 (SF)
1983—49ers, 24-20 (SF)
       Falcons, 28-24 (A)
1984—49ers, 14-5 (SF)
       49ers, 35-17 (A)
1985—49ers, 35-16 (SF)
       49ers, 38-17 (A)
1986—Tie, 10-10 (A) OT

49ers, 20-0 (SF)
1987—49ers, 25-17 (A)
49ers, 35-7 (SF)
1988—Falcons, 34-17 (SF)
49ers, 13-3 (A)
1989—49ers, 45-3 (SF)
49ers, 23-10 (A)
1990—49ers, 19-13 (SF)
49ers, 45-35 (A)
1991—Falcons, 39-34 (SF)
Falcons, 17-14 (A)
1992—49ers, 56-17 (SF)
49ers, 41-3 (A)
1993—49ers, 37-30 (SF)
Falcons, 27-24 (A)
1994—49ers, 42-3 (A)
49ers, 50-14 (SF)
1995—49ers, 41-10 (SF)
Falcons, 28-27 (A)
1996—49ers, 39-17 (SF)
49ers, 34-10 (A)
1997—49ers, 34-7 (SF)
49ers, 35-28 (A)
1998—49ers, 31-20 (SF)
Falcons, 31-19 (A)
*Falcons, 20-18 (A)
1999—49ers, 26-7 (SF)
Falcons, 34-29 (A)
2000—Falcons, 36-28 (A)
49ers, 16-6 (SF)
2001—49ers, 16-13 (SF) OT
49ers, 37-31 (A) OT
2004—Falcons, 21-19 (SF)
2007—Falcons, 20-16 (A)
(RS Pts.—49ers 1,746, Falcons 1,216)
(PS Pts.—Falcons 20, 49ers 18)
*NFC Divisional Playoff

ATLANTA vs. SEATTLE
RS: Seahawks lead series, 8-3
1976—Seahawks, 30-13 (S)
1979—Seahawks, 31-28 (A)
1985—Seahawks, 30-26 (S)
1988—Seahawks, 31-20 (A)
1991—Falcons, 26-13 (A)
1997—Falcons, 24-17 (S)
2000—Seahawks, 30-10 (A)
2002—Seahawks, 30-24 (A) OT
2004—Seahawks, 28-26 (S)
2005—Seahawks, 21-18 (S)
2007—Seahawks, 44-41 (A)
(RS Pts.—Seahawks 302, Falcons 259)

ATLANTA vs. TAMPA BAY
RS: Buccaneers lead series, 17-12
1977—Buccaneers, 17-0 (TB)
1978—Buccaneers, 14-9 (TB)
1979—Falcons, 17-14 (A)
1981—Buccaneers, 24-23 (TB)
1984—Buccaneers, 23-6 (TB)
1986—Falcons, 23-20 (TB) OT
1987—Buccaneers, 48-10 (TB)
1988—Falcons, 17-10 (A)
1990—Buccaneers, 23-17 (TB)
1991—Falcons, 43-7 (A)
1992—Falcons, 35-7 (TB)
1993—Buccaneers, 31-24 (A)
1994—Falcons, 34-13 (A)
1995—Buccaneers, 24-21 (TB)
1997—Buccaneers, 31-10 (A)
1999—Buccaneers, 19-10 (TB)
2000—Buccaneers, 27-14 (A)

2002—Buccaneers, 20-6 (A)
Buccaneers, 34-10 (TB)
2003—Buccaneers, 31-10 (A)
Falcons, 30-28 (TB)
2004—Falcons, 24-14 (A)
Buccaneers, 27-0 (TB)
2005—Buccaneers, 30-27 (A)
Buccaneers, 27-24 (TB) OT
2006—Falcons, 14-3 (A)
Falcons, 17-6 (TB)
2007—Buccaneers, 31-7 (A)
Buccaneers, 37-3 (TB)
(RS Pts.—Buccaneers 620, Falcons 505)

ATLANTA vs. *TENNESSEE
RS: Titans lead series, 7-5
1972—Falcons, 20-10 (A)
1976—Oilers, 20-14 (H)
1978—Falcons, 20-14 (A)
1981—Falcons, 31-27 (H)
1984—Falcons, 42-10 (A)
1987—Oilers, 37-33 (H)
1990—Falcons, 47-27 (A)
1993—Oilers, 33-17 (H)
1996—Oilers, 23-13 (A)
1999—Titans, 30-17 (T)
2003—Titans, 38-31 (A)
2007—Titans, 20-13 (T)
(RS Pts.—Falcons 298, Titans 289)
*Franchise in Houston prior to 1997; known as Oilers prior to 1999

ATLANTA vs. WASHINGTON
RS: Redskins lead series, 14-5-1
PS: Redskins lead series, 1-0
1966—Redskins, 33-20 (W)
1967—Tie, 20-20 (A)
1969—Redskins, 27-20 (W)
1972—Redskins, 24-13 (W)
1975—Redskins, 30-27 (A)
1977—Redskins, 10-6 (W)
1978—Falcons, 20-17 (A)
1979—Redskins, 16-7 (A)
1980—Falcons, 10-6 (A)
1983—Redskins, 37-21 (W)
1984—Redskins, 27-14 (W)
1985—Redskins, 44-10 (A)
1987—Falcons, 21-20 (A)
1989—Redskins, 31-30 (A)
1991—Redskins, 56-17 (W)
*Redskins, 24-7 (W)
1992—Redskins, 24-17 (W)
1993—Redskins, 30-17 (W)
1994—Falcons, 27-20 (W)
2003—Redskins, 33-31 (A)
2006—Falcons, 24-14 (W)
(RS Pts.—Redskins 519, Falcons 372)
(PS Pts.—Redskins 24, Falcons 7)
*NFC Divisional Playoff

BALTIMORE vs. ARIZONA
RS: Ravens lead series, 3-1;
See Arizona vs. Baltimore
BALTIMORE vs. ATLANTA
RS: Ravens lead series, 2-1;
See Atlanta vs. Baltimore
BALTIMORE vs. BUFFALO
RS: Series tied, 2-2
1999—Bills, 13-10 (Balt)
2004—Ravens, 20-6 (Balt)
2006—Ravens, 19-7 (Balt)
2007—Bills, 19-14 (Buf)

(RS Pts.—Ravens 63, Bills 45)
BALTIMORE vs. CAROLINA
RS: Panthers lead series, 3-0
1996—Panthers, 27-16 (C)
2002—Panthers, 10-7 (C)
2006—Panthers, 23-21 (B)
(RS Pts.—Panthers 60, Ravens 44)
BALTIMORE vs. CHICAGO
RS: Bears lead series, 2-1
1998—Bears, 24-3 (C)
2001—Ravens, 17-6 (B)
2005—Bears, 10-6 (C)
(RS Pts.—Bears 40, Ravens 26)
BALTIMORE vs. CINCINNATI
RS: Ravens lead series, 13-11
1996—Bengals, 24-21 (B)
Bengals, 21-14 (C)
1997—Ravens, 23-10 (B)
Bengals, 16-14 (C)
1998—Ravens, 31-24 (B)
Ravens, 20-13 (C)
1999—Ravens, 34-31 (C)
Ravens, 22-0 (B)
2000—Ravens, 37-0 (B)
Ravens, 27-7 (C)
2001—Bengals, 21-10 (C)
Ravens, 16-0 (B)
2002—Ravens, 38-27 (B)
Ravens, 27-23 (C)
2003—Bengals, 34-26 (C)
Ravens, 31-13 (B)
2004—Ravens, 23-9 (C)
Bengals, 27-26 (B)
2005—Bengals, 21-9 (B)
Bengals, 42-29 (C)
2006—Ravens, 26-20 (B)
Bengals, 13-7 (C)
2007—Ravens, 27-20 (C)
Bengals, 21-7 (B)
(RS Pts.—Ravens 538, Bengals 444)
BALTIMORE vs. CLEVELAND
RS: Ravens lead series, 11-7
1999—Ravens, 17-10 (B)
Ravens, 41-9 (C)
2000—Ravens, 12-0 (C)
Ravens, 44-7 (B)
2001—Ravens, 24-14 (C)
Browns, 27-17 (B)
2002—Ravens, 26-21 (C)
Browns, 14-13 (B)
2003—Ravens, 33-13 (B)
Ravens, 35-0 (C)
2004—Browns, 20-3 (C)
Ravens, 27-13 (B)
2005—Ravens, 16-3 (B)
Browns, 20-16 (C)
2006—Ravens, 15-14 (C)
Ravens, 27-17 (B)
2007—Browns, 27-13 (C)
Browns, 33-30 (B) OT
(RS Pts.—Ravens 399, Browns 272)
BALTIMORE vs. DALLAS
RS: Ravens lead series, 2-0
2000—Ravens, 27-0 (B)
2004—Ravens, 30-10 (B)
(RS Pts.—Ravens 57, Cowboys 10)
BALTIMORE vs. DENVER
RS: Series tied, 3-3
PS: Ravens lead series, 1-0
1996—Broncos, 45-34 (D)

2000—*Ravens, 21-3 (B)
2001—Ravens, 20-13 (D)
2002—Ravens, 34-23 (B)
2003—Ravens, 26-6 (B)
2005—Broncos, 12-10 (D)
2006—Broncos, 13-3 (D)
(RS Pts.—Ravens 127, Broncos 112)
(PS Pts.—Ravens 21, Broncos 3)
*AFC First-Round Playoff
BALTIMORE vs. DETROIT
RS: Series tied, 1-1
1998—Ravens, 19-10 (B)
2005—Lions, 35-17 (D)
(RS Pts.—Lions 45, Ravens 36)
BALTIMORE vs. GREEN BAY
RS: Packers lead series, 2-1
1998—Packers, 28-10 (GB)
2001—Packers, 31-23 (GB)
2005—Ravens, 48-3 (B)
(RS Pts.—Ravens 81, Packers 62)
BALTIMORE vs. HOUSTON
RS: Ravens lead series, 2-0
2002—Ravens, 23-19 (H)
2005—Ravens, 16-15 (B)
(RS Pts.—Ravens 39, Texans 34)
BALTIMORE vs. INDIANAPOLIS
RS: Colts lead series, 5-2
PS: Colts lead series, 1-0
1996—Colts, 26-21 (I)
1998—Ravens, 38-31 (B)
2001—Ravens, 39-27 (B)
2002—Colts, 22-20 (I)
2004—Colts, 20-10 (I)
2005—Colts, 24-7 (B)
2006—*Colts, 15-6 (B)
2007—Colts, 44-20 (B)
(RS Pts.—Colts 194, Ravens 155)
(PS Pts.—Colts 15, Ravens 6)
*AFC Divisional Playoff
BALTIMORE vs. JACKSONVILLE
RS: Jaguars lead series, 9-6
1996—Jaguars, 30-27 (J)
　　　Jaguars, 28-25 (B) OT
1997—Jaguars, 28-27 (B)
　　　Jaguars, 29-27 (J)
1998—Jaguars, 24-10 (J)
　　　Jaguars, 45-19 (B)
1999—Jaguars, 6-3 (J)
　　　Jaguars, 30-23 (B)
2000—Ravens, 39-36 (B)
　　　Ravens, 15-10 (J)
2001—Ravens, 18-17 (B)
　　　Ravens, 24-21 (J)
2002—Ravens, 17-10 (B)
2003—Ravens, 24-17 (B)
2005—Jaguars, 30-3 (J)
(RS Pts.—Jaguars 361, Ravens 301)
BALTIMORE vs. KANSAS CITY
RS: Chiefs lead series, 3-1
1999—Chiefs, 35-8 (B)
2003—Chiefs, 17-10 (B)
2004—Chiefs, 27-24 (B)
2006—Ravens, 20-10 (KC)
(RS Pts.—Chiefs 89, Ravens 62)
BALTIMORE vs. MIAMI
RS: Dolphins lead series, 5-1
PS: Ravens lead series, 1-0
1997—Dolphins, 24-13 (B)
2000—Dolphins, 19-6 (M)
2001—*Ravens, 20-3 (M)

2002—Dolphins, 26-7 (M)
2003—Dolphins, 9-6 (M) OT
2004—Ravens, 30-23 (B)
2007—Dolphins, 22-16 (M) OT
(RS Pts.—Dolphins 123, Ravens 78)
(PS Pts.—Ravens 20, Dolphins 3)
*AFC First-Round Playoff
BALTIMORE vs. MINNESOTA
RS: Ravens lead series, 2-1
1998—Vikings, 38-28 (B)
2001—Ravens, 19-3 (B)
2005—Ravens, 30-23 (B)
(RS Pts.—Ravens 77, Vikings 64)
BALTIMORE vs. NEW ENGLAND
RS: Patriots lead series, 4-0
1996—Patriots, 46-38 (B)
1999—Patriots, 20-3 (NE)
2004—Patriots, 24-3 (NE)
2007—Patriots, 27-24 (B)
(RS Pts.—Patriots 117, Ravens 68)
BALTIMORE vs. NEW ORLEANS
RS: Ravens lead series, 3-1
1996—Ravens, 17-10 (B)
1999—Ravens, 31-8 (B)
2002—Saints, 37-25 (B)
2006—Ravens, 35-22 (NO)
(RS Pts.—Ravens 108, Saints 77)
BALTIMORE vs. N.Y. GIANTS
RS: Ravens lead series, 2-0
PS: Ravens lead series, 1-0
1997—Ravens, 24-23 (NY)
2000—*Ravens, 34-7 (Tampa)
2004—Ravens, 37-14 (B)
(RS Pts.—Ravens 61, Giants 37)
(PS Pts.—Ravens 34, Giants 7)
*Super Bowl XXXV
BALTIMORE vs. N.Y. JETS
RS: Ravens lead series, 5-1
1997—Jets, 19-16 (NY) OT
1998—Ravens, 24-10 (NY)
2000—Ravens, 34-20 (B)
2004—Ravens, 20-17 (NY) OT
2005—Ravens, 13-3 (B)
2007—Ravens, 20-13 (B)
(RS Pts.—Ravens 127, Jets 82)
BALTIMORE vs. OAKLAND
RS: Ravens lead series, 3-1
PS: Ravens lead series, 1-0
1996—Ravens, 19-14 (B)
1998—Ravens, 13-10 (B)
2000—*Ravens, 16-3 (O)
2003—Raiders, 20-12 (O)
2006—Ravens, 28-6 (B)
(RS Pts.—Ravens 72, Raiders 50)
(PS Pts.—Ravens 16, Raiders 3)
*AFC Championship
BALTIMORE vs. PHILADELPHIA
RS: Eagles lead series, 1-0-1
1997—Tie, 10-10 (B) OT
2004—Eagles, 15-10 (P)
(RS Pts.—Eagles 25, Ravens 20)
BALTIMORE vs. PITTSBURGH
RS: Steelers lead series, 14-10
PS: Steelers lead series, 1-0
1996—Steelers, 31-17 (P)
　　　Ravens, 31-17 (B)
1997—Steelers, 42-34 (B)
　　　Steelers, 37-0 (P)
1998—Steelers, 20-13 (B)
　　　Steelers, 16-6 (P)

1999—Steelers, 23-20 (B)
　　　Ravens, 31-24 (P)
2000—Ravens, 16-0 (P)
　　　Steelers, 9-6 (B)
2001—Ravens, 13-10 (P)
　　　Steelers, 26-21 (B)
　　　*Steelers, 27-10 (P)
2002—Steelers, 31-18 (B)
　　　Steelers, 34-31 (P)
2003—Steelers, 34-15 (P)
　　　Ravens, 13-10 (B) OT
2004—Ravens, 30-13 (B)
　　　Steelers, 20-7 (P)
2005—Steelers, 20-19 (P)
　　　Ravens, 16-13 (B) OT
2006—Ravens, 27-0 (B)
　　　Ravens, 31-7 (P)
2007—Steelers, 38-7 (P)
　　　Ravens, 27-21 (B)
(RS Pts.—Steelers 496, Ravens 449)
(PS Pts.—Steelers 27, Ravens 10)
*AFC Divisional Playoff
BALTIMORE vs. ST. LOUIS
RS: Series tied, 2-2
1996—Ravens, 37-31 (B) OT
1999—Rams, 27-10 (StL)
2003—Rams, 33-22 (StL)
2007—Ravens, 22-3 (B)
(RS Pts.—Rams 94, Ravens 91)
BALTIMORE vs. SAN DIEGO
RS: Series tied, 3-3
1997—Chargers, 21-17 (SD)
1998—Chargers, 14-13 (SD)
2000—Ravens, 24-3 (B)
2003—Ravens, 24-10 (SD)
2006—Ravens, 16-13 (B)
2007—Chargers, 32-14 (SD)
(RS Pts.—Ravens 108, Chargers 93)
BALTIMORE vs. SAN FRANCISCO
RS: Ravens lead series, 2-1
1996—49ers, 38-20 (SF)
2003—Ravens, 44-6 (B)
2007—Ravens, 9-7 (SF)
(RS Pts.—Ravens 73, 49ers 51)
BALTIMORE vs. SEATTLE
RS: Ravens lead series, 2-1
1997—Ravens, 31-24 (B)
2003—Ravens, 44-41 (B) OT
2007—Seahawks, 27-6 (S)
(RS Pts.—Seahawks 92, Ravens 81)
BALTIMORE vs. TAMPA BAY
RS: Buccaneers lead series, 2-1
2001—Buccaneers, 22-10 (TB)
2002—Buccaneers, 25-0 (B)
2006—Ravens, 27-0 (B)
(RS Pts.—Buccaneers 47, Ravens 37)
BALTIMORE vs. *TENNESSEE
RS: Ravens lead series, 8-7
PS: Series tied, 1-1
1996—Oilers, 29-13 (H)
　　　Oilers, 24-21 (B)
1997—Ravens, 36-10 (T)
　　　Ravens, 21-19 (B)
1998—Oilers, 12-8 (B)
　　　Oilers, 16-14 (T)
1999—Titans, 14-11 (T)
　　　Ravens, 41-14 (B)
2000—Titans, 14-6 (B)
　　　Ravens, 24-23 (T)
　　　**Ravens, 24-10 (T)

2001—Ravens, 26-7 (B)
    Ravens, 16-10 (T)
2002—Ravens, 13-12 (B)
2003—***Titans, 20-17 (B)
2005—Titans, 25-10 (T)
2006—Ravens, 27-26 (T)
(RS Pts.—Ravens 287, Titans 255)
(PS Pts.—Ravens 41, Titans 30)
*Franchise in Houston prior to 1997;
known as Oilers prior to 1999
**AFC Divisional Playoff
***AFC First-Round Playoff

BALTIMORE vs. WASHINGTON
RS: Ravens lead series, 2-1
1997—Ravens, 20-17 (W)
2000—Redskins, 10-3 (W)
2004—Ravens, 17-10 (W)
(RS Pts.—Ravens 40, Redskins 37)

BUFFALO vs. ARIZONA
RS: Bills lead series, 5-3;
See Arizona vs. Buffalo
BUFFALO vs. ATLANTA
RS: Falcons lead series, 5-4;
See Atlanta vs. Buffalo
BUFFALO vs. BALTIMORE
RS: Series tied, 2-2;
See Baltimore vs. Buffalo
BUFFALO vs. CAROLINA
RS: Bills lead series, 3-1
1995—Bills, 31-9 (B)
1998—Bills, 30-14 (C)
2001—Bills, 25-24 (B)
2005—Panthers, 13-9 (B)
(RS Pts.—Bills 95, Panthers 60)
BUFFALO vs. CHICAGO
RS: Bears lead series, 6-4
1970—Bears, 31-13 (C)
1974—Bills, 16-6 (B)
1979—Bears, 7-0 (B)
1988—Bears, 24-3 (C)
1991—Bills, 35-20 (B)
1994—Bears, 20-13 (C)
1997—Bears, 20-3 (C)
2000—Bills, 20-3 (B)
2002—Bills, 33-27 (B) OT
2006—Bears, 40-7 (C)
(RS Pts.—Bears 198, Bills 143)
BUFFALO vs. CINCINNATI
RS: Bills lead series, 14-9
PS: Bengals lead series, 2-0
1968—Bengals, 34-23 (C)
1969—Bills, 16-13 (B)
1970—Bengals, 43-14 (B)
1973—Bengals, 16-13 (B)
1975—Bengals, 33-24 (C)
1978—Bills, 5-0 (B)
1979—Bills, 51-24 (B)
1980—Bills, 14-0 (C)
1981—Bengals, 27-24 (C) OT
    *Bengals, 28-21 (C)
1983—Bills, 10-6 (B)
1984—Bengals, 52-21 (C)
1985—Bengals, 23-17 (B)
1986—Bengals, 36-33 (C) OT
1988—Bengals, 35-21 (C)
    **Bengals, 21-10 (C)
1989—Bills, 24-7 (B)
1991—Bills, 35-16 (B)
1996—Bills, 31-17 (B)

1998—Bills, 33-20 (C)
2002—Bills, 27-9 (B)
2003—Bills, 22-16 (B) OT
2004—Bills, 33-17 (C)
2005—Bills, 37-27 (C)
2007—Bills, 33-21 (B)
(RS Pts.—Bills 561, Bengals 492)
(PS Pts.—Bengals 49, Bills 31)
*AFC Divisional Playoff
**AFC Championship
BUFFALO vs. CLEVELAND
RS: Browns lead series, 8-5
PS: Browns lead series, 1-0
1972—Browns, 27-10 (C)
1974—Bills, 15-10 (C)
1977—Browns, 27-16 (B)
1978—Browns, 41-20 (C)
1981—Bills, 22-13 (B)
1984—Browns, 13-10 (B)
1985—Browns, 17-7 (C)
1986—Browns, 21-17 (B)
1987—Browns, 27-21 (C)
1989—*Browns, 34-30 (C)
1990—Bills, 42-0 (C)
1995—Bills, 22-19 (C)
2004—Bills, 37-7 (B)
2007—Browns, 8-0 (C)
(RS Pts.—Bills 239, Browns 230)
(PS Pts.—Browns 34, Bills 30)
*AFC Divisional Playoff
BUFFALO vs. DALLAS
RS: Cowboys lead series, 5-3
PS: Cowboys lead series, 2-0
1971—Cowboys, 49-37 (B)
1976—Cowboys, 17-10 (D)
1981—Cowboys, 27-14 (D)
1984—Bills, 14-3 (B)
1992—*Cowboys, 52-17 (Pasadena)
1993—Bills, 13-10 (D)
    **Cowboys, 30-13 (Atlanta)
1996—Bills, 10-7 (B)
2003—Cowboys, 10-6 (B)
2007—Cowboys, 25-24 (B)
(RS Pts.—Cowboys 148, Bills 128)
(PS Pts.—Cowboys 82, Bills 30)
*Super Bowl XXVII
**Super Bowl XXVIII
BUFFALO vs. DENVER
RS: Bills lead series, 17-15-1
PS: Bills lead series, 1-0
1960—Broncos, 27-21 (B)
    Tie, 38-38 (D)
1961—Broncos, 22-10 (B)
    Bills, 23-10 (D)
1962—Broncos, 23-20 (B)
    Bills, 45-38 (D)
1963—Bills, 30-28 (D)
    Bills, 27-17 (B)
1964—Bills, 30-13 (B)
    Bills, 30-19 (D)
1965—Bills, 30-15 (D)
    Bills, 31-13 (B)
1966—Bills, 38-21 (B)
1967—Bills, 17-16 (D)
    Broncos, 21-20 (B)
1968—Broncos, 34-32 (D)
1969—Bills, 41-28 (B)
1970—Broncos, 25-10 (B)
1975—Bills, 38-14 (B)
1977—Broncos, 26-6 (D)

1979—Broncos, 19-16 (B)
1981—Bills, 9-7 (B)
1984—Broncos, 37-7 (B)
1987—Bills, 21-14 (B)
1989—Broncos, 28-14 (B)
1990—Bills, 29-28 (B)
1991—*Bills, 10-7 (B)
1992—Bills, 27-17 (B)
1994—Bills, 27-20 (B)
1995—Broncos, 22-7 (D)
1997—Broncos, 23-20 (B) OT
2002—Broncos, 28-23 (D)
2005—Broncos, 28-17 (B)
2007—Broncos, 15-14 (B)
(RS Pts.—Bills 768, Broncos 734)
(PS Pts.—Bills 10, Broncos 7)
*AFC Championship
BUFFALO vs. DETROIT
RS: Lions lead series, 4-3-1
1972—Tie, 21-21 (B)
1976—Lions, 27-14 (D)
1979—Bills, 20-17 (D)
1991—Lions, 17-14 (B) OT
1994—Lions, 35-21 (D)
1997—Bills, 22-13 (B)
2002—Bills, 24-17 (B)
2006—Lions, 20-17 (D)
(RS Pts.—Lions 167, Bills 153)
BUFFALO vs. GREEN BAY
RS: Bills lead series, 7-3
1974—Bills, 27-7 (GB)
1979—Bills, 19-12 (B)
1982—Packers, 33-21 (Mil)
1988—Bills, 28-0 (B)
1991—Bills, 34-24 (Mil)
1994—Bills 29-20 (B)
1997—Packers, 31-21 (GB)
2000—Bills 27-18 (B)
2002—Packers, 10-0 (GB)
2006—Bills, 24-10 (B)
(RS Pts.—Bills 230, Packers 165)
BUFFALO vs. HOUSTON
RS: Bills lead series, 3-1
2002—Bills, 31-24 (H)
2003—Texans, 12-10 (B)
2005—Bills, 22-7 (B)
2006—Bills, 24-21 (H)
(RS Pts.—Bills 87, Texans 64)
BUFFALO vs. *INDIANAPOLIS
RS: Bills lead series, 34-30-1
1970—Tie, 17-17 (Balt)
    Colts, 20-14 (Buff)
1971—Colts, 43-0 (Buff)
    Colts, 24-0 (Balt)
1972—Colts, 17-0 (Buff)
    Colts, 35-7 (Balt)
1973—Bills, 31-13 (Buff)
    Bills, 24-17 (Balt)
1974—Bills, 27-14 (Balt)
    Bills, 6-0 (Buff)
1975—Bills, 38-31 (Balt)
    Colts, 42-35 (Buff)
1976—Colts, 31-13 (Buff)
    Colts, 58-20 (Balt)
1977—Colts, 17-14 (Balt)
    Colts, 31-13 (Buff)
1978—Bills, 24-17 (Buff)
    Bills, 21-14 (Balt)
1979—Bills, 31-13 (Balt)
    Colts, 14-13 (Buff)

1980—Colts, 17-12 (Buff)
Colts, 28-24 (Balt)
1981—Bills, 35-3 (Balt)
Bills, 23-17 (Buff)
1982—Bills, 20-0 (Buff)
1983—Bills, 28-23 (Buff)
Bills, 30-7 (Balt)
1984—Colts, 31-17 (I)
Bills, 21-15 (Buff)
1985—Colts, 49-17 (I)
Bills, 21-9 (Buff)
1986—Bills, 24-13 (Buff)
Colts, 24-14 (I)
1987—Colts, 47-6 (Buff)
Bills, 27-3 (I)
1988—Bills, 34-23 (Buff)
Colts, 17-14 (I)
1989—Colts, 37-14 (I)
Bills, 30-7 (Buff)
1990—Bills, 26-10 (Buff)
Bills, 31-7 (I)
1991—Bills, 42-6 (Buff)
Bills, 35-7 (I)
1992—Bills, 38-0 (Buff)
Colts, 16-13 (I) OT
1993—Bills, 23-9 (Buff)
Bills, 30-10 (I)
1994—Colts, 27-17 (Buff)
Colts, 10-9 (I)
1995—Bills, 20-14 (Buff)
Bills, 16-10 (I)
1996—Bills, 16-13 (Buff) OT
Colts, 13-10 (I) OT
1997—Bills, 37-35 (B)
Bills, 9-6 (I)
1998—Bills, 31-24 (I)
Bills, 34-11 (B)
1999—Colts, 31-14 (I)
Bills, 31-6 (B)
2000—Colts, 18-16 (B)
Colts, 44-20 (I)
2001—Colts, 42-26 (I)
Colts, 30-14 (B)
2003—Colts, 17-14 (B)
2006—Colts, 17-16 (I)
(RS Pts.—Bills 1,347, Colts 1,271)
*Franchise in Baltimore prior to 1984
BUFFALO vs. JACKSONVILLE
RS: Bills lead series, 4-3
PS: Jaguars lead series, 1-0
1996—*Jaguars, 30-27 (B)
1997—Jaguars, 20-14 (B)
1998—Bills, 17-16 (B)
2001—Bills, 13-10 (J)
2003—Bills, 38-17 (J)
2004—Jaguars, 13-10 (B)
2006—Bills, 27-24 (B)
2007—Jaguars, 36-14 (J)
(RS Pts.—Jaguars 136, Bills 133)
(PS Pts.—Jaguars 30, Bills 27)
*AFC First-Round Playoff
BUFFALO vs. *KANSAS CITY
RS: Bills lead series, 19-16-1
PS: Bills lead series, 2-1
1960—Texans, 45-28 (B)
Texans, 24-7 (D)
1961—Bills, 27-24 (B)
Bills, 30-20 (D)
1962—Texans, 41-21 (D)
Bills, 23-14 (B)

1963—Tie, 27-27 (B)
Bills, 35-26 (KC)
1964—Bills, 34-17 (B)
Bills, 35-22 (KC)
1965—Bills, 23-7 (KC)
Bills, 34-25 (B)
1966—Chiefs, 42-20 (B)
Bills, 29-14 (KC)
**Chiefs, 31-7 (B)
1967—Chiefs, 23-13 (KC)
1968—Chiefs, 18-7 (B)
1969—Chiefs, 29-7 (B)
Chiefs, 22-19 (KC)
1971—Chiefs, 22-9 (KC)
1973—Bills, 23-14 (B)
1976—Bills, 50-17 (B)
1978—Bills, 28-13 (B)
Chiefs, 14-10 (KC)
1982—Bills, 14-9 (B)
1983—Bills, 14-9 (KC)
1986—Chiefs, 20-17 (B)
Bills, 17-14 (KC)
1991—Chiefs, 33-6 (KC)
***Bills, 37-14 (B)
1993—Chiefs, 23-7 (KC)
****Bills, 30-13 (B)
1994—Bills, 44-10 (B)
1996—Bills, 20-9 (B)
1997—Chiefs, 22-16 (KC)
2000—Bills, 21-17 (KC)
2002—Chiefs, 17-16 (KC)
2003—Chiefs, 38-5 (KC)
2005—Bills, 14-3 (B)
(RS Pts.—Bills 750, Chiefs 744)
(PS Pts.—Bills 74, Chiefs 58)
*Franchise in Dallas prior to 1963 and known as Texans
**AFL Championship
***AFC Divisional Playoff
****AFC Championship
BUFFALO vs. MIAMI
RS: Dolphins lead series, 49-34-1
PS: Bills lead series, 3-1
1966—Bills, 58-24 (B)
Bills, 29-0 (M)
1967—Bills, 35-13 (B)
Dolphins, 17-14 (M)
1968—Tie, 14-14 (M)
Dolphins, 21-17 (B)
1969—Dolphins, 24-6 (M)
Bills, 28-3 (B)
1970—Dolphins, 33-14 (B)
Dolphins, 45-7 (M)
1971—Dolphins, 29-14 (B)
Dolphins, 34-0 (M)
1972—Dolphins, 24-23 (M)
Dolphins, 30-16 (B)
1973—Dolphins, 27-6 (M)
Dolphins, 17-0 (B)
1974—Dolphins, 24-16 (B)
Dolphins, 35-28 (M)
1975—Dolphins, 35-30 (B)
Dolphins, 31-21 (M)
1976—Dolphins, 30-21 (B)
Dolphins, 45-27 (M)
1977—Dolphins, 13-0 (B)
Dolphins, 31-14 (M)
1978—Dolphins, 31-24 (M)
Dolphins, 25-24 (B)
1979—Dolphins, 9-7 (B)

Dolphins, 17-7 (M)
1980—Bills, 17-7 (B)
Dolphins, 17-14 (M)
1981—Bills, 31-21 (B)
Dolphins, 16-6 (M)
1982—Dolphins, 9-7 (B)
Dolphins, 27-10 (M)
1983—Dolphins, 12-0 (B)
Bills, 38-35 (B) OT
1984—Dolphins, 21-17 (B)
Dolphins, 38-7 (M)
1985—Dolphins, 23-14 (B)
Dolphins, 28-0 (M)
1986—Dolphins, 27-14 (M)
Dolphins, 34-24 (B)
1987—Bills, 34-31 (M) OT
Bills, 27-0 (B)
1988—Bills, 9-6 (B)
Bills, 31-6 (M)
1989—Bills, 27-24 (M)
Bills, 31-17 (B)
1990—Dolphins, 30-7 (M)
Bills, 24-14 (B)
*Bills, 44-34 (B)
1991—Bills, 35-31 (B)
Bills, 41-27 (M)
1992—Dolphins, 37-10 (B)
Bills, 26-20 (M)
**Bills, 29-10 (M)
1993—Dolphins, 22-13 (B)
Bills, 47-34 (M)
1994—Bills, 21-11 (M)
Bills, 42-31 (M)
1995—Dolphins, 23-6 (M)
Bills, 23-20 (B)
***Bills, 37-22 (B)
1996—Dolphins, 21-7 (B)
Dolphins, 16-14 (M)
1997—Bills, 9-6 (B)
Dolphins, 30-13 (M)
1998—Dolphins, 13-7 (M)
Bills, 30-24 (B)
***Dolphins, 24-17 (M)
1999—Bills, 23-18 (M)
Bills, 23-3 (B)
2000—Dolphins, 22-13 (M)
Dolphins, 33-6 (B)
2001—Dolphins, 34-27 (B)
Dolphins, 34-7 (M)
2002—Bills, 23-10 (M)
Bills, 38-21 (B)
2003—Dolphins, 17-7 (M)
Dolphins, 20-3 (B)
2004—Bills, 20-13 (B)
Bills, 42-32 (M)
2005—Bills, 20-14 (B)
Dolphins, 24-23 (M)
2006—Bills, 16-6 (M)
Bills, 21-0 (B)
2007—Bills, 13-10 (M)
Bills, 38-17 (B)
(RS Pts.—Dolphins 1,818, Bills 1,596)
(PS Pts.—Bills 127, Dolphins 90)
*AFC Divisional Playoff
**AFC Championship
***AFC First-Round Playoff
BUFFALO vs. MINNESOTA
RS: Vikings lead series, 7-4
1971—Vikings, 19-0 (M)
1975—Vikings, 35-13 (B)

1979—Vikings, 10-3 (M)
1982—Bills, 23-22 (B)
1985—Vikings, 27-20 (B)
1988—Bills, 13-10 (B)
1994—Vikings, 21-17 (B)
1997—Vikings, 34-13 (B)
2000—Vikings, 31-27 (M)
2002—Bills, 45-39 (M) OT
2006—Bills, 17-12 (B)
(RS Pts.—Vikings 260, Bills 191)
BUFFALO vs. *NEW ENGLAND
RS: Patriots lead series, 54-40-1
PS: Patriots lead series, 1-0
1960—Bills, 13-0 (Bos)
　　　Bills, 38-14 (Buff)
1961—Patriots, 23-21 (Buff)
　　　Patriots, 52-21 (Bos)
1962—Tie, 28-28 (Buff)
　　　Patriots, 21-10 (Bos)
1963—Bills, 28-21 (Buff)
　　　Patriots, 17-7 (Bos)
　　　**Patriots, 26-8 (Buff)
1964—Patriots, 36-28 (Buff)
　　　Bills, 24-14 (Bos)
1965—Bills, 24-7 (Buff)
　　　Bills, 23-7 (Bos)
1966—Patriots, 20-10 (Buff)
　　　Patriots, 14-3 (Bos)
1967—Patriots, 23-0 (Buff)
　　　Bills, 44-16 (Bos)
1968—Patriots, 16-7 (Buff)
　　　Patriots, 23-6 (Bos)
1969—Bills, 23-16 (Buff)
　　　Patriots, 35-21 (Buff)
1970—Bills, 45-10 (Bos)
　　　Patriots, 14-10 (Buff)
1971—Patriots, 38-33 (NE)
　　　Bills, 27-20 (Buff)
1972—Bills, 38-14 (Buff)
　　　Bills, 27-24 (NE)
1973—Bills, 31-13 (NE)
　　　Bills, 37-13 (Buff)
1974—Bills, 30-28 (Buff)
　　　Bills, 29-28 (NE)
1975—Bills, 45-31 (Buff)
　　　Bills, 34-14 (NE)
1976—Patriots, 26-22 (Buff)
　　　Patriots, 20-10 (NE)
1977—Bills, 24-14 (NE)
　　　Patriots, 20-7 (Buff)
1978—Patriots, 14-10 (Buff)
　　　Patriots, 26-24 (NE)
1979—Patriots, 26-6 (Buff)
　　　Bills, 16-13 (NE) OT
1980—Bills, 31-13 (Buff)
　　　Patriots, 24-2 (NE)
1981—Bills, 20-17 (Buff)
　　　Bills, 19-10 (NE)
1982—Patriots, 30-19 (NE)
1983—Patriots, 31-0 (Buff)
　　　Patriots, 21-7 (NE)
1984—Patriots, 21-17 (Buff)
　　　Patriots, 38-10 (NE)
1985—Patriots, 17-14 (Buff)
　　　Patriots, 14-3 (NE)
1986—Patriots, 23-3 (Buff)
　　　Patriots, 22-19 (NE)
1987—Patriots, 14-7 (NE)
　　　Patriots, 13-7 (Buff)
1988—Bills, 16-14 (NE)

Bills, 23-20 (Buff)
1989—Bills, 31-10 (Buff)
　　　Patriots, 33-24 (NE)
1990—Bills, 27-10 (NE)
　　　Bills, 14-0 (Buff)
1991—Bills, 22-17 (Buff)
　　　Patriots, 16-13 (NE)
1992—Bills, 41-7 (NE)
　　　Bills, 16-7 (Buff)
1993—Bills, 38-14 (Buff)
　　　Bills, 13-10 (NE) OT
1994—Bills, 38-35 (NE)
　　　Patriots, 41-17 (Buff)
1995—Patriots, 27-14 (NE)
　　　Patriots, 35-25 (Buff)
1996—Bills, 17-10 (Buff)
　　　Patriots, 28-25 (NE)
1997—Patriots, 33-6 (NE)
　　　Patriots, 31-10 (Buff)
1998—Bills, 13-10 (Buff)
　　　Patriots, 25-21 (NE)
1999—Bills, 17-7 (Buff)
　　　Bills, 13-10 (NE) OT
2000—Bills, 16-13 (NE) OT
　　　Patriots, 13-10 (Buff) OT
2001—Patriots, 21-11 (NE)
　　　Patriots, 12-9 (Buff) OT
2002—Patriots, 38-7 (Buff)
　　　Patriots, 27-17 (NE)
2003—Bills, 31-0 (Buff)
　　　Patriots, 31-0 (NE)
2004—Patriots, 31-17 (Buff)
　　　Patriots, 29-6 (NE)
2005—Patriots, 21-16 (NE)
　　　Patriots, 35-7 (Buff)
2006—Patriots, 19-17 (NE)
　　　Patriots, 28-6 (B)
2007—Patriots, 38-7 (NE)
　　　Patriots, 56-10 (Buff)
(RS Pts.—Patriots 1,979, Bills 1,743)
(PS Pts.—Patriots 26, Bills 8)
*Franchise in Boston prior to 1971
**Division Playoff
BUFFALO vs. NEW ORLEANS
RS: Series tied, 4-4
1973—Saints, 13-0 (NO)
1980—Bills, 35-26 (NO)
1983—Bills, 27-21 (B)
1989—Saints, 22-19 (B)
1992—Bills, 20-16 (NO)
1998—Bills, 45-33 (NO)
2001—Saints, 24-6 (B)
2005—Saints, 19-7 (San Antonio)
(RS Pts.—Saints 174, Bills 159)
BUFFALO vs. N.Y. GIANTS
RS: Bills lead series, 6-4
PS: Giants lead series, 1-0
1970—Giants, 20-6 (NY)
1975—Giants, 17-14 (B)
1978—Bills, 41-17 (B)
1987—Bills, 6-3 (B) OT
1990—Bills, 17-13 (NY)
　　　*Giants, 20-19 (Tampa)
1993—Bills, 17-14 (B)
1996—Bills, 23-20 (NY) OT
1999—Giants, 19-17 (B)
2003—Bills, 24-7 (NY)
2007—Giants, 38-21 (B)
(RS Pts.—Bills 186, Giants 168)
(PS Pts.—Giants 20, Bills 19)

*Super Bowl XXV
BUFFALO vs. *N.Y. JETS
RS: Bills lead series, 52-42
PS: Bills lead series, 1-0
1960—Titans, 27-3 (NY)
　　　Titans, 17-13 (B)
1961—Bills, 41-31 (B)
　　　Titans, 21-14 (NY)
1962—Titans, 17-6 (B)
　　　Bills, 20-3 (NY)
1963—Bills, 45-14 (B)
　　　Bills, 19-10 (NY)
1964—Bills, 34-24 (B)
　　　Bills, 20-7 (NY)
1965—Bills, 33-21 (B)
　　　Jets, 14-12 (NY)
1966—Bills, 33-23 (NY)
　　　Bills, 14-3 (B)
1967—Bills, 20-17 (B)
　　　Jets, 20-10 (NY)
1968—Bills, 37-35 (B)
　　　Jets, 25-21 (NY)
1969—Jets, 33-19 (B)
　　　Jets, 16-6 (NY)
1970—Bills, 34-31 (B)
　　　Bills, 10-6 (NY)
1971—Jets, 28-17 (NY)
　　　Jets, 20-7 (B)
1972—Bills, 41-24 (B)
　　　Jets, 41-3 (NY)
1973—Bills, 9-7 (B)
　　　Bills, 34-14 (NY)
1974—Bills, 16-12 (B)
　　　Jets, 20-10 (NY)
1975—Bills, 42-14 (B)
　　　Bills, 24-23 (NY)
1976—Jets, 17-14 (NY)
　　　Jets, 19-14 (B)
1977—Jets, 24-19 (B)
　　　Bills, 14-10 (NY)
1978—Jets, 21-20 (B)
　　　Jets, 45-14 (NY)
1979—Bills, 46-31 (B)
　　　Bills, 14-12 (NY)
1980—Bills, 20-10 (B)
　　　Bills, 31-24 (NY)
1981—Bills, 31-0 (B)
　　　Jets, 33-14 (NY)
　　　**Bills, 31-27 (NY)
1983—Jets, 34-10 (B)
　　　Bills, 24-17 (NY)
1984—Jets, 28-26 (B)
　　　Jets, 21-17 (NY)
1985—Jets, 42-3 (NY)
　　　Jets, 27-7 (B)
1986—Jets, 28-24 (B)
　　　Jets, 14-13 (NY)
1987—Jets, 31-28 (B)
　　　Bills, 17-14 (NY)
1988—Bills, 37-14 (NY)
　　　Bills, 9-6 (B) OT
1989—Bills, 34-3 (B)
　　　Bills, 37-0 (NY)
1990—Bills, 30-7 (B)
　　　Bills, 30-27 (B)
1991—Bills, 23-20 (NY)
　　　Bills, 24-13 (B)
1992—Bills, 24-20 (NY)
　　　Jets, 24-17 (B)
1993—Bills, 19-10 (NY)

Bills, 16-14 (B)
1994—Jets, 23-3 (B)
Jets, 22-17 (NY)
1995—Bills, 29-10 (B)
Bills, 28-26 (NY)
1996—Bills, 25-22 (NY)
Bills, 35-10 (B)
1997—Bills, 28-22 (NY)
Bills, 20-10 (B)
1998—Jets, 34-12 (NY)
Jets, 17-10 (B)
1999—Bills, 17-3 (B)
Jets, 17-7 (NY)
2000—Jets, 27-14 (NY)
Bills, 23-20 (B)
2001—Jets, 42-36 (B)
Bills, 14-9 (NY)
2002—Jets, 37-31 (B) OT
Jets, 31-13 (NY)
2003—Jets, 30-3 (NY)
Bills, 17-6 (B)
2004—Jets, 16-14 (NY)
Bills, 22-17 (B)
2005—Bills, 27-17 (B)
Jets, 30-26 (NY)
2006—Jets, 28-20 (B)
Bills, 31-13 (NY)
2007—Bills, 17-14 (B)
Bills, 13-3 (NY)
(RS Pts.—Bills 1,922, Jets 1,851)
(PS Pts.—Bills 31, Jets 27)
*Jets known as Titans prior to 1963
**AFC First-Round Playoff
BUFFALO vs. *OAKLAND
RS: Raiders lead series, 19-15
PS: Bills lead series, 2-0
1960—Bills, 38-9 (B)
Raiders, 20-7 (O)
1961—Raiders, 31-22 (B)
Bills, 26-21 (O)
1962—Bills, 14-6 (B)
Bills, 10-6 (O)
1963—Raiders, 35-17 (O)
Bills, 12-0 (B)
1964—Bills, 23-20 (B)
Raiders, 16-13 (O)
1965—Bills, 17-12 (B)
Bills, 17-14 (O)
1966—Bills, 31-10 (O)
1967—Raiders, 24-20 (B)
Raiders, 28-21 (O)
1968—Raiders, 48-6 (B)
Raiders, 13-10 (O)
1969—Raiders, 50-21 (O)
1972—Raiders, 28-16 (O)
1974—Bills, 21-20 (B)
1977—Raiders, 34-13 (O)
1980—Bills, 24-7 (B)
1983—Raiders, 27-24 (B)
1987—Raiders, 34-21 (LA)
1988—Bills, 37-21 (B)
1990—Bills, 38-24 (B)
**Bills, 51-3 (B)
1991—Bills, 30-27 (LA) OT
1992—Raiders, 20-3 (LA)
1993—Raiders, 25-24 (B)
***Bills, 29-23 (B)
1998—Bills, 44-21 (B)
1999—Raiders, 20-14 (B)
2002—Raiders, 49-31 (B)

2004—Raiders, 13-10 (O)
2005—Raiders, 38-17 (O)
(RS Pts.—Raiders 771, Bills 692)
(PS Pts.—Bills 80, Raiders 26)
*Franchise in Los Angeles from 1982-1994
**AFC Championship
***AFC Divisional Playoff
BUFFALO vs. PHILADELPHIA
RS: Eagles lead series, 6-5
1973—Bills, 27-26 (B)
1981—Eagles, 20-14 (B)
1984—Eagles, 27-17 (B)
1985—Eagles, 21-17 (P)
1987—Eagles, 17-7 (P)
1990—Bills, 30-23 (B)
1993—Bills, 10-7 (P)
1996—Bills, 24-17 (P)
1999—Bills, 26-0 (B)
2003—Eagles, 23-13 (B)
2007—Eagles, 17-9 (P)
(RS Pts.—Eagles 198, Bills 194)
BUFFALO vs. PITTSBURGH
RS: Steelers lead series, 11-8
PS: Steelers lead series, 2-1
1970—Steelers, 23-10 (P)
1972—Steelers, 38-21 (B)
1974—*Steelers, 32-14 (P)
1975—Bills, 30-21 (P)
1978—Steelers, 28-17 (B)
1979—Steelers, 28-0 (P)
1980—Bills, 28-13 (B)
1982—Bills, 13-0 (B)
1985—Steelers, 30-24 (P)
1986—Bills, 16-12 (B)
1988—Bills, 36-28 (B)
1991—Bills, 52-34 (B)
1992—Bills, 28-20 (B)
*Bills, 24-3 (P)
1993—Steelers, 23-0 (P)
1994—Steelers, 23-10 (P)
1995—*Steelers, 40-21 (P)
1996—Steelers, 24-6 (P)
1999—Bills, 24-21 (B)
2001—Steelers, 20-3 (B)
2004—Steelers, 29-24 (B)
2007—Steelers, 26-3 (P)
(RS Pts.—Steelers 441, Bills 345)
(PS Pts.—Steelers 75, Bills 59)
*AFC Divisional Playoff
BUFFALO vs. *ST. LOUIS
RS: Bills lead series, 5-4
1970—Rams, 19-0 (B)
1974—Rams, 19-14 (LA)
1980—Bills, 10-7 (B) OT
1983—Rams, 41-17 (LA)
1989—Bills, 23-20 (B)
1992—Bills, 40-7 (B)
1995—Bills, 45-27 (StL)
1998—Rams, 34-33 (B)
2004—Bills, 37-17 (B)
(RS Pts.—Bills 219, Rams 191)
*Franchise in Los Angeles prior to 1995
BUFFALO vs. *SAN DIEGO
RS: Chargers lead series, 20-9-2
PS: Bills lead series, 2-1
1960—Chargers, 24-10 (B)
Bills, 32-3 (LA)
1961—Chargers, 19-11 (B)
Chargers, 28-10 (SD)
1962—Bills, 35-10 (B)

Bills, 40-20 (SD)
1963—Chargers, 14-10 (SD)
Chargers, 23-13 (B)
1964—Bills, 30-3 (B)
Bills, 27-24 (SD)
**Bills, 20-7 (B)
1965—Chargers, 34-3 (B)
Tie, 20-20 (SD)
**Bills, 23-0 (SD)
1966—Chargers, 27-7 (SD)
Tie, 17-17 (B)
1967—Chargers, 37-17 (B)
1968—Chargers, 21-6 (B)
1969—Chargers, 45-6 (SD)
1971—Chargers, 20-3 (SD)
1973—Chargers, 34-7 (SD)
1976—Chargers, 34-13 (B)
1979—Chargers, 27-19 (SD)
1980—Bills, 26-24 (SD)
***Chargers, 20-14 (SD)
1981—Bills, 28-27 (B)
1985—Chargers, 14-9 (B)
Chargers, 40-7 (SD)
1998—Chargers, 16-14 (SD)
2000—Bills, 27-24 (B) OT
2001—Chargers, 27-24 (SD)
2002—Bills, 20-13 (B)
2005—Chargers, 48-10 (SD)
2006—Chargers, 24-21 (B)
(RS Pts.—Chargers 741, Bills 522)
(PS Pts.—Bills 57, Chargers 27)
*Franchise in Los Angeles prior to 1961
**AFL Championship
***AFC Divisional Playoff
BUFFALO vs. SAN FRANCISCO
RS: Bills lead series, 5-4
1972—Bills, 27-20 (B)
1980—Bills, 18-13 (SF)
1983—49ers, 23-10 (B)
1989—49ers, 21-10 (SF)
1992—Bills, 34-31 (SF)
1995—49ers, 27-17 (SF)
1998—Bills, 26-21 (B)
2001—49ers, 35-0 (SF)
2004—Bills, 41-7 (SF)
(RS Pts.—49ers 198, Bills 183)
BUFFALO vs. SEATTLE
RS: Seahawks lead series, 6-4
1977—Seahawks, 56-17 (S)
1984—Seahawks, 31-28 (S)
1988—Bills, 13-3 (S)
1989—Seahawks, 17-16 (S)
1995—Bills, 27-21 (B)
1996—Seahawks, 26-18 (S)
1999—Seahawks, 26-16 (S)
2000—Bills, 42-23 (S)
2001—Seahawks, 23-20 (B)
2004—Bills, 38-9 (S)
(RS Pts.—Bills 235, Seahawks 235)
BUFFALO vs. TAMPA BAY
RS: Buccaneers lead series, 6-2
1976—Bills, 14-9 (TB)
1978—Buccaneers, 31-10 (TB)
1982—Buccaneers, 24-23 (TB)
1986—Buccaneers, 34-28 (TB)
1988—Buccaneers, 10-5 (TB)
1991—Bills, 17-10 (TB)
2000—Buccaneers, 31-17 (TB)
2005—Buccaneers, 19-3 (TB)
(RS Pts.—Buccaneers 168, Bills 117)

BUFFALO vs. *TENNESSEE
RS: Titans lead series, 24-14
PS: Bills lead series, 2-1
1960—Bills, 25-24 (B)
Oilers, 31-23 (H)
1961—Bills, 22-12 (H)
Oilers, 28-16 (B)
1962—Oilers, 28-23 (B)
Oilers, 17-14 (H)
1963—Oilers, 31-20 (B)
Oilers, 28-14 (H)
1964—Bills, 48-17 (H)
Bills, 24-10 (B)
1965—Oilers, 19-17 (B)
Bills, 29-18 (H)
1966—Bills, 27-20 (B)
Bills, 42-20 (H)
1967—Oilers, 20-3 (B)
Oilers, 10-3 (H)
1968—Oilers, 30-7 (B)
Oilers, 35-6 (H)
1969—Oilers, 17-3 (B)
Oilers, 28-14 (H)
1971—Oilers, 20-14 (B)
1974—Oilers, 21-9 (B)
1976—Oilers, 13-3 (B)
1978—Oilers, 17-10 (H)
1983—Bills, 30-13 (B)
1985—Bills, 20-0 (B)
1986—Oilers, 16-7 (H)
1987—Bills, 34-30 (B)
1988—**Bills, 17-10 (B)
1989—Bills, 47-41 (H) OT
1990—Oilers, 27-24 (B)
1992—Oilers, 27-3 (H)
***Bills, 41-38 (B) OT
1993—Bills, 35-7 (B)
1994—Bills, 15-7 (H)
1995—Oilers, 28-17 (B)
1997—Oilers, 31-14 (T)
1999—***Titans, 22-16 (T)
2000—Bills, 16-13 (B)
2003—Titans, 28-26 (T)
2006—Titans, 30-29 (B)
(RS Pts.—Titans 812, Bills 733)
(PS Pts.—Bills 74, Titans 70)
*Franchise in Houston prior to 1997;
known as Oilers prior to 1999
**AFC Divisional Playoff
***AFC First-Round Playoff
BUFFALO vs. WASHINGTON
RS: Bills lead series, 7-4
PS: Redskins lead series, 1-0
1972—Bills, 24-17 (W)
1977—Redskins, 10-0 (B)
1981—Bills, 21-14 (B)
1984—Redskins, 41-14 (W)
1987—Redskins, 27-7 (B)
1990—Redskins, 29-14 (W)
1991—*Redskins, 37-24 (Minneapolis)
1993—Bills, 24-10 (B)
1996—Bills, 38-13 (B)
1999—Bills, 34-17 (W)
2003—Bills, 24-7 (B)
2007—Bills, 17-16 (W)
(RS Pts.—Bills 217, Redskins 201)
(PS Pts.—Redskins 37, Bills 24)
*Super Bowl XXVI

CAROLINA vs. ARIZONA

RS: Panthers lead series, 5-2;
See Arizona vs. Carolina
CAROLINA vs. ATLANTA
RS: Falcons lead series, 16-10;
See Atlanta vs. Carolina
CAROLINA vs. BALTIMORE
RS: Panthers lead series, 3-0;
See Baltimore vs. Carolina
CAROLINA vs. BUFFALO
RS: Bills lead series, 3-1;
See Buffalo vs. Carolina
CAROLINA vs. CHICAGO
RS: Bears lead series, 2-1
PS: Panthers lead series, 1-0
1995—Bears, 31-27 (Chi)
2002—Panthers, 24-14 (Car)
2005—Bears, 13-3 (Chi)
*Panthers, 29-21 (Chi)
(RS Pts.—Bears 58, Panthers 54)
(PS Pts.—Panthers 29, Bears 21)
*NFC Divisional Playoff
CAROLINA vs. CINCINNATI
RS: Panthers lead series, 2-1
1999—Panthers, 27-3 (Car)
2002—Panthers, 52-31 (Car)
2006—Bengals, 17-14 (Cin)
(RS Pts.—Panthers 93, Bengals 51)
CAROLINA vs. CLEVELAND
RS: Panthers lead series, 3-0
1999—Panthers, 31-17 (Cle)
2002—Panthers, 13-6 (Cle)
2006—Panthers, 20-12 (Car)
(RS Pts.—Panthers 64, Browns 35)
CAROLINA vs. DALLAS
RS: Cowboys lead series, 7-1
PS: Panthers lead series, 2-0
1996—*Panthers, 26-17 (C)
1997—Panthers, 23-13 (D)
1998—Cowboys, 27-20 (D)
2000—Cowboys, 16-13 (C) OT
2002—Cowboys, 14-13 (D)
2003—Cowboys, 24-20 (D)
**Panthers, 29-10 (C)
2005—Cowboys, 24-20 (C)
2006—Cowboys, 35-14 (C)
2007—Cowboys, 20-13 (C)
(RS Pts.—Cowboys 173, Panthers 136)
(PS Pts.—Panthers 55, Cowboys 27)
*NFC Divisional Playoff
*NFC First-Round Playoff
CAROLINA vs. DENVER
RS: Broncos lead series, 2-0
1997—Broncos, 34-0 (D)
2004—Broncos, 20-17 (D)
(RS Pts.—Broncos 54, Panthers 17)
CAROLINA vs. DETROIT
RS: Panthers lead series, 3-1
1999—Lions, 24-9 (C)
2002—Panthers, 31-7 (C)
2003—Panthers, 20-14 (C)
2005—Panthers, 21-20 (D)
(RS Pts.—Panthers 81, Lions 65)
CAROLINA vs. GREEN BAY
RS: Packers lead series, 6-3
PS: Packers lead series, 1-0
1996—*Packers, 30-13 (GB)
1997—Packers, 31-10 (C)
1998—Packers, 37-30 (C)
1999—Panthers, 33-31 (GB)
2000—Panthers, 31-14 (C)

2001—Packers, 28-7 (C)
2002—Packers, 17-14 (GB)
2004—Packers, 24-14 (C)
2005—Panthers, 32-29 (C)
2007—Packers, 31-17 (GB)
(RS Pts.—Packers 242, Panthers 188)
(PS Pts.—Packers 30, Panthers 13)
*NFC Championship
CAROLINA vs. HOUSTON
RS: Texans lead series, 2-0
2003—Texans, 14-10 (H)
2007—Texans, 34-21 (C)
(RS Pts.—Texans 48, Panthers 31)
CAROLINA vs. INDIANAPOLIS
RS: Panthers lead series, 3-1
1995—Panthers, 13-10 (C)
1998—Panthers, 27-19 (I)
2003—Panthers, 23-20 (I) OT
2007—Colts, 31-7 (C)
(RS Pts.—Colts 80, Panthers 70)
CAROLINA vs. JACKSONVILLE
RS: Jaguars lead series, 3-1
1996—Jaguars, 24-14 (J)
1999—Jaguars, 22-20 (C)
2003—Panthers, 24-23 (C)
2007—Jaguars, 37-6 (J)
(RS Pts.—Jaguars 106, Panthers 64)
CAROLINA vs. KANSAS CITY
RS: Chiefs lead series, 2-1
1997—Chiefs, 35-14 (C)
2000—Chiefs, 15-14 (KC)
2004—Panthers, 28-17 (KC)
(RS Pts.—Chiefs 67, Panthers 56)
CAROLINA vs. MIAMI
RS: Dolphins lead series, 3-0
1998—Dolphins, 13-9 (C)
2001—Dolphins, 23-6 (M)
2005—Dolphins, 27-24 (M)
(RS Pts.—Dolphins 63, Panthers 39)
CAROLINA vs. MINNESOTA
RS: Vikings lead series, 4-3
1996—Vikings, 14-12 (M)
1997—Vikings, 21-14 (M)
2000—Vikings, 31-17 (M)
2001—Panthers, 24-13 (M)
2002—Panthers, 21-14 (M)
2005—Panthers, 38-13 (C)
2006—Vikings, 16-13 (M) OT
(RS Pts.—Panthers 139, Vikings 122)
CAROLINA vs. NEW ENGLAND
RS: Panthers lead series, 2-1
PS: Patriots lead series, 1-0
1995—Panthers, 20-17 (NE) OT
2001—Patriots, 38-6 (C)
2003—*Patriots, 32-29 (Houston)
2005—Panthers, 27-17 (C)
(RS Pts.—Patriots 72, Panthers 53)
(PS Pts.—Patriots 32, Panthers 29)
*Super Bowl XXXVIII
CAROLINA vs. NEW ORLEANS
RS: Panthers lead series, 14-12
1995—Panthers, 20-3 (C)
Saints, 34-26 (NO)
1996—Panthers, 22-20 (NO)
Panthers, 19-7 (C)
1997—Panthers, 13-0 (NO)
Saints, 16-13 (C)
1998—Saints, 19-14 (NO)
Panthers, 31-17 (C)
1999—Saints, 19-10 (NO)

Panthers, 45-13 (C)
2000—Saints, 24-6 (NO)
Saints, 20-10 (C)
2001—Saints, 27-25 (C)
Saints, 27-23 (NO)
2002—Saints, 34-24 (C)
Panthers, 10-6 (NO)
2003—Panthers, 19-13 (C)
Panthers, 23-20 (NO) OT
2004—Panthers, 32-21 (NO)
Saints, 21-18 (C)
2005—Saints, 23-20 (C)
Panthers, 27-10 (Baton Rouge)
2006—Panthers, 21-18 (C)
Panthers, 31-21 (NO)
2007—Panthers, 16-13 (NO)
Saints, 31-6 (C)
(RS Pts.—Panthers 524, Saints 477)

CAROLINA vs. N.Y. GIANTS
RS: Panthers lead series, 2-1
PS: Panthers lead series, 1-0
1996—Panthers, 27-17 (C)
2003—Panthers, 37-24 (NY)
2005—*Panthers, 23-0 (NY)
2006—Giants, 27-13 (C)
(RS Pts.—Panthers 77, Giants 68)
(PS Pts.—Panthers 23, Giants 0)
*NFC First-Round Playoff

CAROLINA vs. N.Y. JETS
RS: Series tied, 2-2
1995—Panthers, 26-15 (C)
1998—Jets, 48-21 (NY)
2001—Jets, 13-12 (C)
2005—Panthers, 30-3 (C)
(RS Pts.—Panthers 89, Jets 79)

CAROLINA vs. OAKLAND
RS: Raiders lead series, 2-1
1997—Panthers, 38-14 (C)
2000—Raiders, 52-9 (O)
2004—Raiders, 27-24 (C)
(RS Pts.— Raiders 93, Panthers 71)

CAROLINA vs. PHILADELPHIA
RS: Eagles lead series, 4-1
PS: Panthers lead series, 1-0
1996—Eagles, 20-9 (C)
1999—Panthers, 33-7 (C)
2003—Eagles, 25-16 (C)
*Panthers, 14-3 (P)
2004—Eagles, 30-8 (P)
2006—Eagles, 27-24 (P)
(RS Pts.—Eagles 109, Panthers 90)
(PS Pts.—Panthers 14, Eagles 3)
*NFC Championship

CAROLINA vs. PITTSBURGH
RS: Steelers lead series, 3-1
1996—Panthers, 18-14 (C)
1999—Steelers, 30-20 (P)
2002—Steelers, 30-14 (P)
2006—Steelers, 37-3 (C)
(RS Pts.—Steelers 111, Panthers 55)

CAROLINA vs. ST. LOUIS
RS: Panthers lead series, 10-7
PS: Panthers lead series, 1-0
1995—Rams, 31-10 (C)
Rams, 28-17 (StL)
1996—Panthers, 45-13 (C)
Panthers, 20-10 (StL)
1997—Panthers, 16-10 (StL)
Rams, 30-18 (C)
1998—Panthers, 24-20 (StL)

Panthers, 20-13 (C)
1999—Rams, 35-10 (StL)
Rams, 34-21 (C)
2000—Panthers, 27-24 (StL)
Panthers, 16-3 (C)
2001—Rams, 48-14 (StL)
Rams, 38-32 (C)
2003—*Panthers, 29-23 (StL) 2OT
2004—Panthers, 20-7 (C)
2006—Panthers, 15-0 (C)
2007—Panthers, 27-13 (StL)
(RS Pts.—Rams 357, Panthers 352)
(PS Pts.—Panthers 29, Rams 23)
*NFC Divisional Playoff

CAROLINA vs. SAN DIEGO
RS: Panthers lead series, 2-1
1997—Panthers, 26-7 (SD)
2000—Panthers, 30-22 (C)
2004—Chargers, 17-6 (C)
(RS Pts.—Panthers 62, Chargers 46)

CAROLINA vs. SAN FRANCISCO
RS: Panthers lead series, 9-7
1995—Panthers, 13-7 (SF)
49ers, 31-10 (C)
1996—Panthers, 23-7 (C)
Panthers, 30-24 (SF)
1997—49ers, 34-21 (C)
49ers, 27-19 (SF)
1998—49ers, 25-23 (SF)
49ers, 31-28 (C) OT
1999—Panthers, 31-29 (SF)
Panthers, 41-24 (C)
2000—Panthers, 38-22 (SF)
Panthers, 34-16 (C)
2001—49ers, 24-14 (SF)
49ers, 25-22 (C) OT
2004—Panthers, 37-27 (SF)
2007—Panthers, 31-14 (C)
(RS Pts.—Panthers 415, 49ers 367)

CAROLINA vs. SEATTLE
RS: Panthers lead series, 2-1
PS: Seahawks lead series, 1-0
2000—Panthers, 26-3 (C)
2004—Seahawks, 23-17 (S)
2005—*Seahawks, 34-14 (S)
2007—Panthers, 13-10 (C)
(RS Pts.—Panthers 56, Seahawks 36)
(PS Pts.—Seahawks 34, Panthers 14)
*NFC Championship

CAROLINA vs. TAMPA BAY
RS: Panthers lead series, 9-6
1995—Buccaneers, 20-13 (C)
1996—Panthers, 24-0 (C)
1998—Buccaneers, 16-13 (TB)
2002—Buccaneers, 12-9 (C)
Buccaneers, 23-10 (TB)
2003—Panthers, 12-9 (TB) OT
Panthers, 27-24 (C)
2004—Panthers, 21-14 (C)
Panthers, 37-20 (TB)
2005—Panthers, 34-14 (TB)
Buccaneers, 20-10 (C)
2006—Panthers, 26-24 (TB)
Panthers, 24-10 (C)
2007—Buccaneers, 20-7 (C)
Panthers, 31-23 (TB)
(RS Pts.—Panthers 298, Buccaneers 249)

CAROLINA vs. *TENNESSEE
RS: Titans lead series, 2-1
1996—Panthers, 31-6 (H)

2003—Titans, 37-17 (C)
2006—Panthers, 26-24 (TB)
Panthers, 24-10 (C)
2007—Titans, 20-7 (T)
(RS Pts.—Titans 63, Panthers 55)
*Franchise in Houston prior to 1997;
known as Oilers prior to 1999

CAROLINA vs. WASHINGTON
RS: Redskins lead series, 7-1
1995—Redskins, 20-17 (W)
1997—Redskins, 24-10 (C)
1998—Redskins, 28-25 (C)
1999—Redskins, 38-36 (W)
2000—Redskins, 20-17 (W)
2001—Redskins, 17-14 (W) OT
2003—Panthers, 20-17 (C)
2006—Redskins, 17-13 (W)
(RS Pts.—Redskins 181, Panthers 152)

CHICAGO vs. ARIZONA
RS: Bears lead series, 55-26-6;
See Arizona vs. Chicago

CHICAGO vs. ATLANTA
RS: Bears lead series, 12-10;
See Atlanta vs. Chicago

CHICAGO vs. BALTIMORE
RS: Bears lead series, 2-1;
See Baltimore vs. Chicago

CHICAGO vs. BUFFALO
RS: Bears lead series, 6-4;
See Buffalo vs. Chicago

CHICAGO vs. CAROLINA
RS: Bears lead series, 2-1
PS: Panthers lead series, 1-0;
See Carolina vs. Chicago

CHICAGO vs. CINCINNATI
RS: Bengals lead series, 5-3
1972—Bengals, 13-3 (Chi)
1980—Bengals, 17-14 (Chi) OT
1986—Bears, 44-7 (Cin)
1989—Bears, 17-14 (Chi)
1992—Bengals, 31-28 (Chi) OT
1995—Bengals, 16-10 (Cin)
2001—Bears, 24-0 (Cin)
2005—Bengals, 24-7 (Chi)
(RS Pts.—Bears 147, Bengals 122)

CHICAGO vs. CLEVELAND
RS: Browns lead series, 9-4
1951—Browns, 42-21 (Chi)
1954—Browns, 39-10 (Chi)
1960—Browns, 42-0 (Cle)
1961—Bears, 17-14 (Chi)
1967—Browns, 24-0 (Chi)
1969—Browns, 28-24 (Chi)
1972—Bears, 17-0 (Cle)
1980—Browns, 27-21 (Cle)
1986—Bears, 41-31 (Cle)
1989—Browns, 27-7 (Cle)
1992—Browns, 27-14 (Cle)
2001—Bears, 27-21 (Chi) OT
2005—Browns, 20-10 (Cle)
(RS Pts.—Browns 342, Bears 209)

CHICAGO vs. DALLAS
RS: Cowboys lead series, 11-8
PS: Cowboys lead series, 2-0
1960—Bears, 17-7 (C)
1962—Bears, 34-33 (D)
1964—Cowboys, 24-10 (C)
1968—Cowboys, 34-3 (C)
1971—Bears, 23-19 (C)

1973—Cowboys, 20-17 (C)
1976—Cowboys, 31-21 (D)
1977—*Cowboys, 37-7 (D)
1979—Cowboys, 24-20 (D)
1981—Cowboys, 10-9 (D)
1984—Cowboys, 23-14 (C)
1985—Bears, 44-0 (D)
1986—Bears, 24-10 (D)
1988—Bears, 17-7 (C)
1991–**Cowboys, 17-13 (C)
1992—Cowboys, 27-14 (D)
1996—Bears, 22-6 (C)
1997—Cowboys, 27-3 (D)
1998—Bears, 13-12 (C)
2004—Cowboys, 21-7 (D)
2007—Cowboys, 34-10 (C)
(RS Pts.—Cowboys 369, Bears 322)
(PS Pts.—Cowboys 54, Bears 20)
*NFC Divisional Playoff
**NFC First-Round Playoff
CHICAGO vs. DENVER
RS: Bears lead series, 7-6
1971—Broncos, 6-3 (D)
1973—Bears, 33-14 (D)
1976—Broncos, 28-14 (C)
1978—Broncos, 16-7 (D)
1981—Bears, 35-24 (C)
1983—Bears, 31-14 (D)
1984—Bears, 27-0 (C)
1987—Broncos, 31-29 (D)
1990—Bears, 16-13 (D) OT
1993—Broncos, 13-3 (C)
1996—Broncos, 17-12 (D)
2003—Bears, 19-10 (D)
2007—Bears, 37-34 (C) OT
(RS Pts.—Bears 266, Broncos 220)
CHICAGO vs. *DETROIT
RS: Bears lead series, 87-64-5
1930—Spartans, 7-6 (P)
    Bears, 14-6 (C)
1931—Bears, 9-6 (C)
    Spartans, 3-0 (P)
1932—Tie, 13-13 (C)
    Tie, 7-7 (P)
    Bears, 9-0 (C)
1933—Bears, 17-14 (C)
    Bears, 17-7 (P)
1934—Bears, 19-16 (D)
    Bears, 10-7 (C)
1935—Tie, 20-20 (C)
    Lions, 14-2 (D)
1936—Bears, 12-10 (C)
    Lions, 13-7 (D)
1937—Bears, 28-20 (C)
    Bears, 13-0 (D)
1938—Lions, 13-7 (C)
    Lions, 14-7 (D)
1939—Lions, 10-0 (C)
    Bears, 23-13 (D)
1940—Bears, 7-0 (C)
    Lions, 17-14 (D)
1941—Bears, 49-0 (C)
    Bears, 24-7 (D)
1942—Bears, 16-0 (C)
    Bears, 42-0 (D)
1943—Bears, 27-21 (D)
    Bears, 35-14 (C)
1944—Tie, 21-21 (C)
    Lions, 41-21 (D)
1945—Lions, 16-10 (D)

Lions, 35-28 (C)
1946—Bears, 42-6 (C)
    Bears, 45-24 (D)
1947—Bears, 33-24 (C)
    Bears, 34-14 (D)
1948—Bears, 28-0 (C)
    Bears, 42-14 (D)
1949—Bears, 27-24 (C)
    Bears, 28-7 (D)
1950—Bears, 35-21 (D)
    Bears, 6-3 (C)
1951—Bears, 28-23 (D)
    Lions, 41-28 (C)
1952—Bears, 24-23 (C)
    Lions, 45-21 (D)
1953—Lions, 20-16 (C)
    Lions, 13-7 (D)
1954—Lions, 48-23 (D)
    Bears, 28-24 (C)
1955—Bears, 24-14 (D)
    Bears, 21-20 (C)
1956—Lions, 42-10 (D)
    Bears, 38-21 (C)
1957—Bears, 27-7 (D)
    Lions, 21-13 (C)
1958—Bears, 20-7 (D)
    Bears, 21-16 (C)
1959—Bears, 24-14 (D)
    Bears, 25-14 (C)
1960—Bears, 28-7 (C)
    Lions, 36-0 (D)
1961—Bears, 31-17 (D)
    Lions, 16-15 (C)
1962—Lions, 11-3 (D)
    Bears, 3-0 (C)
1963—Bears, 37-21 (D)
    Bears, 24-14 (C)
1964—Lions, 10-0 (C)
    Bears, 27-24 (D)
1965—Bears, 38-10 (C)
    Bears, 17-10 (D)
1966—Lions, 14-3 (D)
    Tie, 10-10 (C)
1967—Bears, 14-3 (C)
    Bears, 27-13 (D)
1968—Lions, 42-0 (D)
    Lions, 28-10 (C)
1969—Lions, 13-7 (D)
    Lions, 20-3 (C)
1970—Lions, 28-14 (D)
    Lions, 16-10 (C)
1971—Bears, 28-23 (D)
    Lions, 28-3 (C)
1972—Lions, 38-24 (C)
    Lions, 14-0 (D)
1973—Lions, 30-7 (C)
    Lions, 40-7 (D)
1974—Bears, 17-9 (C)
    Lions, 34-17 (D)
1975—Lions, 27-7 (D)
    Bears, 25-21 (C)
1976—Bears, 10-3 (C)
    Lions, 14-10 (D)
1977—Bears, 30-20 (C)
    Bears, 31-14 (D)
1978—Bears, 19-0 (D)
    Lions, 21-17 (C)
1979—Bears, 35-7 (C)
    Lions, 20-0 (D)
1980—Bears, 24-7 (C)

Bears, 23-17 (D) OT
1981—Lions, 48-17 (D)
    Lions, 23-7 (C)
1982—Lions, 17-10 (D)
    Bears, 20-17 (C)
1983—Lions, 31-17 (D)
    Lions, 38-17 (C)
1984—Bears, 16-14 (C)
    Bears, 30-13 (D)
1985—Bears, 24-3 (C)
    Bears, 37-17 (D)
1986—Bears, 13-7 (C)
    Bears, 16-13 (D)
1987—Bears, 30-10 (C)
1988—Bears, 24-7 (D)
    Bears, 13-12 (C)
1989—Bears, 47-27 (D)
    Lions, 27-17 (C)
1990—Bears, 23-17 (C) OT
    Lions, 38-21 (D)
1991—Bears, 20-10 (C)
    Lions, 16-6 (D)
1992—Bears, 27-24 (C)
    Lions, 16-3 (D)
1993—Bears, 10-6 (D)
    Lions, 20-14 (C)
1994—Lions, 21-16 (D)
    Bears, 20-10 (C)
1995—Lions, 24-17 (C)
    Lions, 27-7 (D)
1996—Lions, 35-16 (D)
    Bears, 31-14 (C)
1997—Lions, 32-7 (C)
    Lions, 55-20 (D)
1998—Bears, 31-27 (C)
    Lions, 26-3 (D)
1999—Lions, 21-17 (D)
    Bears, 28-10 (C)
2000—Lions, 21-14 (C)
    Bears, 23-20 (D)
2001—Bears, 13-10 (C)
    Bears, 24-0 (D)
2002—Lions, 23-20 (D) OT
    Bears, 20-17 (C) OT
2003—Bears, 24-16 (C)
    Lions, 12-10 (D)
2004—Lions, 20-16 (C)
    Lions, 19-13 (D)
2005—Bears, 38-6 (C)
    Bears, 19-13 (D) OT
2006—Bears, 34-7 (C)
    Bears, 26-21 (D)
2007—Bears, 37-27 (D)
    Lions, 16-7 (C)
(RS Pts.—Bears 2,927, Lions 2,716)
*Franchise in Portsmouth prior to 1934
and known as the Spartans
CHICAGO vs. GREEN BAY
RS: Bears lead series, 89-79-6
PS: Bears lead series, 1-0
1921—Staleys, 20-0 (C)
1923—Bears, 3-0 (GB)
1924—Bears, 3-0 (C)
1925—Packers, 14-10 (GB)
    Bears, 21-0 (C)
1926—Tie, 6-6 (GB)
    Bears, 19-13 (C)
    Tie, 3-3 (C)
1927—Bears, 7-6 (GB)
    Bears, 14-6 (C)

1928—Tie, 12-12 (GB)
 Packers, 16-6 (C)
 Packers, 6-0 (C)
1929—Packers, 23-0 (GB)
 Packers, 14-0 (C)
 Packers, 25-0 (C)
1930—Packers, 7-0 (GB)
 Packers, 13-12 (C)
 Bears, 21-0 (C)
1931—Packers, 7-0 (GB)
 Packers, 6-2 (C)
 Bears, 7-6 (C)
1932—Tie, 0-0 (GB)
 Packers, 2-0 (C)
 Bears, 9-0 (C)
1933—Bears, 14-7 (GB)
 Bears, 10-7 (C)
 Bears, 7-6 (C)
1934—Bears, 24-10 (GB)
 Bears, 27-14 (C)
1935—Packers, 7-0 (GB)
 Packers, 17-14 (C)
1936—Bears, 30-3 (GB)
 Packers, 21-10 (C)
1937—Bears, 14-2 (GB)
 Packers, 24-14 (C)
1938—Bears, 2-0 (GB)
 Packers, 24-17 (C)
1939—Packers, 21-16 (GB)
 Bears, 30-27 (C)
1940—Bears, 41-10 (GB)
 Bears, 14-7 (C)
1941—Bears, 25-17 (GB)
 Packers, 16-14 (C)
 **Bears, 33-14 (C)
1942—Packers, 44-28 (GB)
 Bears, 38-7 (C)
1943—Tie, 21-21 (GB)
 Bears, 21-7 (C)
1944—Packers, 42-28 (GB)
 Bears, 21-0 (C)
1945—Packers, 31-21 (GB)
 Bears, 28-24 (C)
1946—Bears, 30-7 (GB)
 Bears, 10-7 (C)
1947—Packers, 29-20 (GB)
 Bears, 20-17 (C)
1948—Bears, 45-7 (GB)
 Bears, 7-6 (C)
1949—Bears, 17-0 (GB)
 Bears, 24-3 (C)
1950—Packers, 31-21 (GB)
 Bears, 28-14 (C)
1951—Bears, 31-20 (GB)
 Bears, 24-13 (C)
1952—Bears, 24-14 (GB)
 Packers, 41-28 (C)
1953—Bears, 17-13 (GB)
 Tie, 21-21 (C)
1954—Bears, 10-3 (GB)
 Bears, 28-23 (C)
1955—Packers, 24-3 (GB)
 Bears, 52-31 (C)
1956—Bears, 37-21 (GB)
 Bears, 38-14 (C)
1957—Packers, 21-17 (GB)
 Bears, 21-14 (C)
1958—Bears, 34-20 (GB)
 Bears, 24-10 (C)
1959—Packers, 9-6 (GB)

Bears, 28-17 (C)
1960—Bears, 17-14 (GB)
 Packers, 41-13 (C)
1961—Packers, 24-0 (GB)
 Packers, 31-28 (C)
1962—Packers, 49-0 (GB)
 Packers, 38-7 (C)
1963—Bears, 10-3 (GB)
 Bears, 26-7 (C)
1964—Packers, 23-12 (GB)
 Packers, 17-3 (C)
1965—Packers, 23-14 (GB)
 Bears, 31-10 (C)
1966—Packers, 17-0 (C)
 Packers, 13-6 (GB)
1967—Bears, 13-10 (GB)
 Packers, 17-13 (C)
1968—Bears, 13-10 (GB)
 Packers, 28-27 (C)
1969—Packers, 17-0 (GB)
 Packers, 21-3 (C)
1970—Packers, 20-19 (GB)
 Bears, 35-17 (C)
1971—Packers, 17-14 (C)
 Packers, 31-10 (GB)
1972—Packers, 20-17 (GB)
 Packers, 23-17 (C)
1973—Bears, 31-17 (GB)
 Packers, 21-0 (C)
1974—Bears, 10-9 (C)
 Packers, 20-3 (Mil)
1975—Bears, 27-14 (C)
 Packers, 28-7 (GB)
1976—Bears, 24-13 (C)
 Bears, 16-10 (GB)
1977—Bears, 26-0 (GB)
 Bears, 21-10 (C)
1978—Packers, 24-14 (GB)
 Bears, 14-0 (C)
1979—Bears, 6-3 (C)
 Bears, 15-14 (GB)
1980—Packers, 12-6 (GB) OT
 Bears, 61-7 (C)
1981—Packers, 16-9 (C)
 Packers, 21-17 (GB)
1983—Packers, 31-28 (GB)
 Bears, 23-21 (C)
1984—Bears, 9-7 (GB)
 Packers, 20-14 (C)
1985—Bears, 23-7 (C)
 Bears, 16-10 (GB)
1986—Bears, 25-12 (GB)
 Bears, 12-10 (C)
1987—Bears, 26-24 (GB)
 Bears, 23-10 (C)
1988—Bears, 24-6 (GB)
 Bears, 16-0 (C)
1989—Packers, 14-13 (GB)
 Packers, 40-28 (C)
1990—Bears, 31-13 (GB)
 Bears, 27-13 (C)
1991—Bears, 10-0 (GB)
 Bears, 27-13 (C)
1992—Bears, 30-10 (GB)
 Packers, 17-3 (C)
1993—Packers, 17-3 (GB)
 Bears, 30-17 (C)
1994—Packers, 33-6 (C)
 Packers, 40-3 (GB)
1995—Packers, 27-24 (C)

Packers, 35-28 (GB)
1996—Packers, 37-6 (C)
 Packers, 28-17 (GB)
1997—Packers, 38-24 (GB)
 Packers, 24-23 (C)
1998—Packers, 26-20 (GB)
 Packers, 16-13 (C)
1999—Bears, 14-13 (GB)
 Packers, 35-19 (C)
2000—Bears, 27-24 (GB)
 Packers, 28-6 (C)
2001—Packers, 20-12 (C)
 Packers, 17-7 (GB)
2002—Packers, 34-21 (C)
 Packers, 30-20 (GB)
2003—Packers, 38-23 (C)
 Packers, 34-21 (GB)
2004—Bears, 21-10 (GB)
 Packers, 31-14 (C)
2005—Bears, 19-7 (C)
 Bears, 24-17 (GB)
2006—Bears, 26-0 (GB)
 Packers, 26-7 (C)
2007—Bears, 27-20 (GB)
 Bears, 35-7 (C)
(RS Pts.—Bears 2,985, Packers 2,825)
(PS Pts.—Bears 33, Packers 14)
*Bears known as Staleys prior to 1922
**Division Playoff
CHICAGO vs. HOUSTON
RS: Texans lead series, 1-0
2004—Texans, 24-5 (C)
(RS Pts.—Texans 24, Bears 5)
CHICAGO vs. *INDIANAPOLIS
RS: Colts lead series, 22-17
PS: Colts lead series, 1-0
1953—Colts, 13-9 (B)
 Colts, 16-14 (C)
1954—Bears, 28-9 (C)
 Bears, 28-13 (B)
1955—Colts, 23-17 (B)
 Bears, 38-10 (C)
1956—Colts, 28-21 (B)
 Bears, 58-27 (C)
1957—Colts, 21-10 (B)
 Colts, 29-14 (C)
1958—Colts, 51-38 (B)
 Colts, 17-0 (C)
1959—Bears, 26-21 (B)
 Colts, 21-7 (C)
1960—Colts, 42-7 (B)
 Colts, 24-20 (C)
1961—Colts, 24-10 (C)
 Bears, 21-20 (B)
1962—Bears, 35-15 (C)
 Bears, 57-0 (B)
1963—Bears, 10-3 (C)
 Bears, 17-7 (B)
1964—Colts, 52-0 (B)
 Colts, 40-24 (C)
1965—Colts, 26-21 (C)
 Bears, 13-0 (B)
1966—Bears, 27-17 (C)
 Colts, 21-16 (B)
1967—Colts, 24-3 (C)
1968—Colts, 28-7 (B)
1969—Colts, 24-21 (C)
1970—Colts, 21-20 (B)
1975—Colts, 35-7 (C)
1983—Colts, 22-19 (B) OT

1985—Bears, 17-10 (C)
1988—Bears, 17-13 (I)
1991—Bears, 31-17 (I)
2000—Bears, 27-24 (C)
2004—Colts, 41-10 (C)
2006—**Colts, 29-17 (South Florida)
(RS Pts.—Colts 835, Bears 779)
(PS: Pts.—Colts 29, Bears 17)
*Franchise in Baltimore prior to 1984
**Super Bowl XLI

CHICAGO vs. JACKSONVILLE
RS: Series tied, 2-2
1995—Bears, 30-27 (J)
1998—Jaguars, 24-23 (C)
2001—Bears, 33-13 (C)
2004—Jaguars, 22-3 (J)
(RS Pts.—Bears 89, Jaguars 86)

CHICAGO vs. KANSAS CITY
RS: Bears lead series, 6-4
1973—Chiefs, 19-7 (KC)
1977—Bears, 28-27 (C)
1981—Bears, 16-13 (KC) OT
1987—Bears, 31-28 (C)
1990—Chiefs, 21-10 (C)
1993—Bears, 19-17 (KC)
1996—Chiefs, 14-10 (KC)
1999—Bears, 20-17 (C)
2003—Chiefs, 31-3 (KC)
2007—Bears, 20-10 (C)
(RS Pts.—Chiefs 197, Bears 164)

CHICAGO vs. MIAMI
RS: Dolphins lead series, 7-3
1971—Dolphins, 34-3 (M)
1975—Dolphins, 46-13 (C)
1979—Dolphins, 31-16 (M)
1985—Dolphins, 38-24 (M)
1988—Bears, 34-7 (C)
1991—Dolphins, 16-13 (C) OT
1994—Bears, 17-14 (M)
1997—Dolphins, 36-33 (M) OT
2002—Dolphins, 27-9 (M)
2006—Dolphins, 31-13 (C)
(RS Pts.—Dolphins 277, Bears 178)

CHICAGO vs. MINNESOTA
RS: Vikings lead series, 50-41-2
PS: Bears lead series, 1-0
1961—Vikings, 37-13 (M)
        Bears, 52-35 (C)
1962—Bears, 13-0 (M)
        Bears, 31-30 (C)
1963—Bears, 28-7 (M)
        Tie, 17-17 (C)
1964—Bears, 34-28 (M)
        Vikings, 41-14 (C)
1965—Bears, 45-37 (M)
        Vikings, 24-17 (C)
1966—Vikings, 13-10 (M)
        Bears, 41-28 (C)
1967—Bears, 17-7 (M)
        Tie, 10-10 (C)
1968—Bears, 27-17 (M)
        Bears, 26-24 (C)
1969—Vikings, 31-0 (C)
        Vikings, 31-14 (M)
1970—Vikings, 24-0 (C)
        Vikings, 16-13 (M)
1971—Bears, 20-17 (M)
        Vikings, 27-10 (C)
1972—Bears, 13-10 (C)
        Vikings, 23-10 (M)

1973—Vikings, 22-13 (C)
        Vikings, 31-13 (M)
1974—Vikings, 11-7 (M)
        Vikings, 17-0 (C)
1975—Vikings, 28-3 (M)
        Vikings, 13-9 (C)
1976—Vikings, 20-19 (M)
        Bears, 14-13 (C)
1977—Vikings, 22-16 (M) OT
        Bears, 10-7 (C)
1978—Vikings, 24-20 (C)
        Vikings, 17-14 (M)
1979—Bears, 26-7 (C)
        Vikings, 30-27 (M)
1980—Vikings, 34-14 (C)
        Vikings, 13-7 (M)
1981—Vikings, 24-21 (M)
        Bears, 10-9 (C)
1982—Vikings, 35-7 (M)
1983—Vikings, 23-14 (C)
        Bears, 19-13 (M)
1984—Bears, 16-7 (C)
        Bears, 34-3 (M)
1985—Bears, 33-24 (M)
        Bears, 27-9 (C)
1986—Bears, 23-0 (C)
        Vikings, 23-7 (M)
1987—Bears, 27-7 (C)
        Bears, 30-24 (M)
1988—Vikings, 31-7 (C)
        Vikings, 28-27 (M)
1989—Bears, 38-7 (C)
        Vikings, 27-16 (M)
1990—Bears, 19-16 (C)
        Vikings, 41-13 (M)
1991—Bears, 10-6 (C)
        Bears, 34-17 (M)
1992—Vikings, 21-20 (M)
        Vikings, 38-10 (C)
1993—Vikings, 10-7 (M)
        Vikings, 19-12 (C)
1994—Vikings, 42-14 (C)
        Vikings, 33-27 (M) OT
        *Bears, 35-18 (M)
1995—Bears, 31-14 (C)
        Bears, 14-6 (M)
1996—Vikings, 20-14 (C)
        Bears, 15-13 (M)
1997—Vikings, 27-24 (C)
        Vikings, 29-22 (M)
1998—Vikings, 31-28 (C)
        Vikings, 48-22 (M)
1999—Bears, 24-22 (M)
        Vikings, 27-24 (C) OT
2000—Vikings, 30-27 (M)
        Vikings, 28-16 (C)
2001—Bears, 17-10 (C)
        Bears, 13-6 (M)
2002—Bears, 27-23 (C)
        Vikings, 25-7 (M)
2003—Vikings, 24-13 (M)
        Bears, 13-10 (C)
2004—Vikings, 27-22 (M)
        Bears, 24-14 (C)
2005—Bears, 28-3 (C)
        Vikings, 34-10 (M)
2006—Bears, 19-16 (M)
        Bears, 23-13 (C)
2007—Vikings, 34-31 (C)
        Vikings, 20-13 (M)

RS Pts.—Vikings 1,931, Bears 1,733)
(PS Pts.—Bears 35, Vikings 18)
*NFC First-Round Playoff

CHICAGO vs. NEW ENGLAND
RS: Patriots lead series, 7-3
PS: Bears lead series, 1-0
1973—Patriots, 13-10 (C)
1979—Patriots, 27-7 (C)
1982—Bears, 26-13 (C)
1985—Bears, 20-7 (C)
        *Bears, 46-10 (New Orleans)
1988—Patriots, 30-7 (NE)
1994—Patriots, 13-3 (C)
1997—Patriots, 31-3 (NE)
2000—Bears, 24-17 (C)
2002—Patriots, 33-30 (C)
2006—Patriots, 17-13 (NE)
(RS Pts.—Patriots 201, Bears 143)
(PS Pts.—Bears 46, Patriots 10)
*Super Bowl XX

CHICAGO vs. NEW ORLEANS
RS: Bears lead series, 12-11
PS: Bears lead series, 2-0
1968—Bears, 23-17 (NO)
1970—Bears, 24-3 (NO)
1971—Bears, 35-14 (C)
1973—Saints, 21-16 (NO)
1974—Bears, 24-10 (C)
1975—Bears, 42-17 (NO)
1977—Saints, 42-24 (C)
1980—Bears, 22-3 (C)
1982—Saints, 10-0 (C)
1983—Saints, 34-31 (NO) OT
1984—Bears, 20-7 (C)
1987—Saints, 19-17 (C)
1990—*Bears, 16-6 (C)
1991—Bears, 20-17 (NO)
1992—Saints, 28-6 (NO)
1994—Bears, 17-7 (C)
1996—Saints, 27-24 (NO)
1997—Saints, 20-17 (C)
1999—Bears, 14-10 (C)
2000—Saints, 31-10 (C)
2002—Saints, 29-23 (C)
2003—Saints, 23-13 (NO)
2005—Bears, 20-17 (Baton Rouge)
2006—**Bears, 39-14 (C)
2007—Bears, 33-25 (C)
(RS Pts.—Bears 475, Saints 428)
(PS Pts.—Bears 55, Saints 20)
*NFC First-Round Playoff
**NFC Championship

CHICAGO vs. N.Y. GIANTS
RS: Bears lead series, 27-18-2
PS: Bears lead series, 5-3
1925—Bears, 19-7 (NY)
        Giants, 9-0 (C)
1926—Bears, 7-0 (C)
1927—Giants, 13-7 (NY)
1928—Bears, 13-0 (C)
1929—Giants, 26-14 (C)
        Giants, 34-0 (NY)
        Giants, 14-9 (C)
1930—Giants, 12-0 (C)
        Bears, 12-0 (NY)
1931—Bears, 6-0 (C)
        Bears, 12-6 (NY)
        Giants, 25-6 (C)
1932—Bears, 28-8 (NY)
        Bears, 6-0 (C)

1933—Bears, 14-10 (C)
    Giants, 3-0 (NY)
    *Bears, 23-21 (C)
1934—Bears, 27-7 (C)
    Bears, 10-9 (NY)
    *Giants, 30-13 (NY)
1935—Bears, 20-3 (NY)
    Giants, 3-0 (C)
1936—Bears, 25-7 (NY)
1937—Tie, 3-3 (NY)
1939—Giants, 16-13 (NY)
1940—Bears, 37-21 (NY)
1941—*Bears, 37-9 (C)
1942—Bears, 26-7 (NY)
1943—Bears, 56-7 (NY)
1946—Giants, 14-0 (NY)
    *Bears, 24-14 (NY)
1948—Bears, 35-14 (C)
1949—Giants, 35-28 (NY)
1956—Tie, 17-17 (NY)
    *Giants, 47-7 (NY)
1962—Giants, 26-24 (C)
1963—*Bears, 14-10 (C)
1965—Bears, 35-14 (NY)
1967—Bears, 34-7 (C)
1969—Giants, 28-24 (NY)
1970—Bears, 24-16 (NY)
1974—Bears, 16-13 (C)
1977—Bears, 12-9 (NY) OT
1985—**Bears, 21-0 (C)
1987—Bears, 34-19 (C)
1990—**Giants, 31-3 (NY)
1991—Bears, 20-17 (C)
1992—Giants, 27-14 (C)
1993—Giants, 26-20 (C)
1995—Bears, 27-24 (NY)
2000—Giants, 14-7 (C)
2004—Bears, 28-21 (NY)
2006—Bears, 38-20 (NY)
2007—Giants, 21-16 (C)
(RS Pts.—Bears 823, Giants 632)
(PS Pts.—Giants 162, Bears 142)
*NFL Championship
**NFC Divisional Playoff
CHICAGO vs. N.Y. JETS
RS: Bears lead series, 6-3
1974—Jets, 23-21 (C)
1979—Bears, 23-13 (C)
1985—Bears, 19-6 (NY)
1991—Bears, 19-13 (C) OT
1994—Bears, 19-7 (NY)
1997—Jets, 23-15 (C)
2000—Jets, 17-10 (NY)
2002—Bears, 20-13 (C)
2006—Bears, 10-0 (NY)
(RS Pts.—Bears 156, Jets 115)
CHICAGO vs. *OAKLAND
RS: Series tied, 6-6
1972—Raiders, 28-21 (O)
1976—Raiders, 28-27 (C)
1978—Raiders, 25-19 (C) OT
1981—Bears, 23-6 (O)
1984—Bears, 17-6 (C)
1987—Bears, 6-3 (LA)
1990—Raiders, 24-10 (LA)
1993—Raiders, 16-14 (C)
1996—Bears, 19-17 (C)
1999—Raiders, 24-17 (O)
2003—Bears, 24-21 (C)
2007—Bears, 17-6 (O)

(RS Pts.—Bears 214, Raiders 204)
*Franchise in Los Angeles from 1982-1994
CHICAGO vs. PHILADELPHIA
RS: Bears lead series, 25-8-1
PS: Eagles lead series, 2-1
1933—Tie, 3-3 (P)
1935—Bears, 39-0 (P)
1936—Bears, 17-0 (P)
    Bears, 28-7 (P)
1938—Bears, 28-6 (P)
1939—Bears, 27-14 (C)
1941—Bears, 49-14 (P)
1942—Bears, 45-14 (C)
1944—Bears, 28-7 (P)
1946—Bears, 21-14 (C)
1947—Bears, 40-7 (C)
1948—Eagles, 12-7 (P)
1949—Bears, 38-21 (C)
1955—Bears, 17-10 (C)
1961—Eagles, 16-14 (P)
1963—Bears, 16-7 (C)
1968—Bears, 29-16 (P)
1970—Bears, 20-16 (C)
1972—Bears, 21-12 (P)
1975—Bears, 15-13 (C)
1979—*Eagles, 27-17 (P)
1980—Eagles, 17-14 (P)
1983—Bears, 7-6 (P)
    Bears, 17-14 (C)
1986—Bears, 13-10 (C) OT
1987—Bears, 35-3 (P)
1988—**Bears, 20-12 (C)
1989—Bears, 27-13 (C)
1993—Bears, 17-6 (P)
1994—Eagles, 30-22 (P)
1995—Bears, 20-14 (C)
1999—Eagles, 20-16 (C)
2000—Eagles, 13-9 (P)
2001—**Eagles, 33-19 (C)
2002—Eagles, 19-13 (C)
2004—Eagles, 19-9 (C)
2007—Bears, 19-16 (P)
(RS Pts.—Bears 740, Eagles 409)
(PS Pts.—Eagles 72, Bears 56)
*NFC First-Round Playoff
**NFC Divisional Playoff
CHICAGO vs. *PITTSBURGH
RS: Bears lead series, 16-7-1
1934—Bears, 28-0 (P)
1935—Bears, 23-7 (P)
1936—Bears, 27-9 (P)
    Bears, 26-6 (C)
1937—Bears, 7-0 (P)
1939—Bears, 32-0 (P)
1941—Bears, 34-7 (C)
1945—Bears, 28-7 (C)
1947—Bears, 49-7 (C)
1949—Bears, 30-21 (C)
1958—Steelers, 24-10 (P)
1959—Bears, 27-21 (C)
1963—Tie, 17-17 (P)
1967—Steelers, 41-13 (P)
1969—Bears, 38-7 (C)
1971—Bears, 17-15 (C)
1975—Steelers, 34-3 (P)
1980—Steelers, 38-3 (P)
1986—Bears, 13-10 (C) OT
1989—Bears, 20-0 (P)
1992—Bears, 30-6 (C)
1995—Steelers, 37-34 (C) OT

1998—Steelers, 17-12 (P)
2005—Steelers, 21-9 (P)
(RS Pts.—Bears 530, Steelers 352)
*Steelers known as Pirates prior to 1941
CHICAGO vs. *ST. LOUIS
RS: Bears lead series, 48-34-3
PS: Series tied, 1-1
1937—Bears, 20-2 (Clev)
    Bears, 15-7 (C)
1938—Rams, 14-7 (C)
    Rams, 23-21 (Clev)
1939—Bears, 30-21 (Clev)
    Bears, 35-21 (C)
1940—Bears, 21-14 (Clev)
    Bears, 47-25 (C)
1941—Bears, 48-21 (Clev)
    Bears, 31-13 (C)
1942—Bears, 21-7 (Clev)
    Bears, 47-0 (C)
1944—Rams, 19-7 (Clev)
    Bears, 28-21 (C)
1945—Rams, 17-0 (Clev)
    Rams, 41-21 (C)
1946—Tie, 28-28 (C)
    Bears, 27-21 (LA)
1947—Bears, 41-21 (LA)
    Rams, 17-14 (C)
1948—Bears, 42-21 (C)
    Bears, 21-6 (LA)
1949—Rams, 31-16 (C)
    Rams, 27-24 (LA)
1950—Bears, 24-20 (LA)
    Bears, 24-14 (C)
    **Rams, 24-14 (LA)
1951—Rams, 42-17 (C)
1952—Rams, 31-7 (LA)
    Rams, 40-24 (C)
1953—Rams, 38-24 (LA)
    Bears, 24-21 (C)
1954—Rams, 42-38 (LA)
    Bears, 24-13 (C)
1955—Bears, 31-20 (C)
    Bears, 24-3 (C)
1956—Bears, 35-24 (LA)
    Bears, 30-21 (C)
1957—Bears, 34-26 (C)
    Bears, 16-10 (LA)
1958—Bears, 31-10 (C)
    Rams, 41-35 (LA)
1959—Rams, 28-21 (C)
    Bears, 26-21 (LA)
1960—Bears, 34-27 (C)
    Tie, 24-24 (LA)
1961—Bears, 21-17 (LA)
    Bears, 28-24 (C)
1962—Bears, 27-23 (LA)
    Bears, 30-14 (C)
1963—Bears, 52-14 (LA)
    Bears, 6-0 (C)
1964—Bears, 38-17 (C)
    Bears, 34-24 (LA)
1965—Rams, 30-28 (LA)
    Bears, 31-6 (C)
1966—Rams, 31-17 (LA)
    Bears, 17-10 (C)
1967—Rams, 28-17 (C)
1968—Bears, 17-16 (LA)
1969—Rams, 9-7 (C)
1971—Rams, 17-3 (LA)
1972—Tie, 13-13 (C)

1973—Rams, 26-0 (C)
1975—Rams, 38-10 (LA)
1976—Rams, 20-12 (LA)
1977—Bears, 24-23 (C)
1979—Bears, 27-23 (C)
1981—Rams, 24-7 (C)
1982—Bears, 34-26 (LA)
1983—Rams, 21-14 (LA)
1984—Rams, 29-13 (LA)
1985—***Bears, 24-0 (C)
1986—Rams, 20-17 (C)
1988—Rams, 23-3 (LA)
1989—Bears, 20-10 (C)
1990—Bears, 38-9 (C)
1993—Rams, 20-6 (LA)
1994—Bears, 27-13 (C)
1995—Rams, 34-28 (StL)
1996—Bears, 35-9 (C)
1997—Bears, 13-10 (StL)
1998—Rams, 20-12 (C)
1999—Rams, 34-12 (StL)
2002—Rams, 21-16 (StL)
2003—Rams, 23-21 (C)
2006—Bears, 42-27 (StL)
(RS Pts.—Bears 1,976, Rams 1,750)
(PS Pts.—Bears 38, Rams 24)
*Franchise in Los Angeles prior to 1995
and in Cleveland prior to 1946
**Conference Playoff
***NFC Championship
CHICAGO vs. SAN DIEGO
RS: Series tied, 5-5
1970—Chargers, 20-7 (C)
1974—Chargers, 28-21 (SD)
1978—Chargers, 40-7 (SD)
1981—Bears, 20-17 (C) OT
1984—Chargers, 20-7 (SD)
1993—Bears, 16-13 (SD)
1996—Bears, 27-14 (C)
1999—Bears, 23-20 (SD) OT
2003—Bears, 20-7 (C)
2007—Chargers, 14-3 (SD)
(RS Pts.—Chargers 193, Bears 151)
CHICAGO vs. SAN FRANCISCO
RS: Bears lead series, 29-27-1
PS: 49ers lead series, 3-0
1950—Bears, 32-20 (SF)
        Bears, 17-0 (C)
1951—Bears, 13-7 (C)
1952—49ers, 40-16 (C)
        Bears, 20-17 (SF)
1953—49ers, 35-28 (C)
        49ers, 24-14 (SF)
1954—49ers, 31-24 (C)
        Bears, 31-27 (SF)
1955—49ers, 20-19 (C)
        Bears, 34-23 (SF)
1956—Bears, 31-7 (C)
        Bears, 38-21 (SF)
1957—49ers, 21-17 (C)
        49ers, 21-17 (SF)
1958—49ers, 28-6 (C)
        Bears, 27-14 (SF)
1959—49ers, 20-17 (SF)
        Bears, 14-3 (C)
1960—Bears, 27-10 (C)
        49ers, 25-7 (SF)
1961—Bears, 31-0 (C)
        49ers, 41-31 (SF)
1962—Bears, 30-14 (SF)

        49ers, 34-27 (C)
1963—49ers, 20-14 (SF)
        Bears, 27-7 (C)
1964—49ers, 31-21 (SF)
        Bears, 23-21 (C)
1965—49ers, 52-24 (SF)
        Bears, 61-20 (C)
1966—Tie, 30-30 (C)
        49ers, 41-14 (SF)
1967—Bears, 28-14 (SF)
1968—Bears, 27-19 (C)
1969—49ers, 42-21 (SF)
1970—49ers, 37-16 (C)
1971—49ers, 13-0 (SF)
1972—49ers, 34-21 (C)
1974—49ers, 34-0 (C)
1975—49ers, 31-3 (SF)
1976—Bears, 19-12 (SF)
1978—Bears, 16-13 (SF)
1979—Bears, 28-27 (SF)
1981—49ers, 28-17 (SF)
1983—Bears, 13-3 (C)
1984—*49ers, 23-0 (SF)
1985—Bears, 26-10 (C)
1987—49ers, 41-0 (SF)
1988—Bears, 10-9 (C)
        *49ers, 28-3 (C)
1989—49ers, 26-0 (SF)
1991—49ers, 52-14 (SF)
1994—**49ers, 44-15 (SF)
2000—49ers, 17-0 (SF)
2001—Bears, 37-31 (C) OT
2003—49ers, 49-7 (SF)
2004—Bears, 23-13 (C)
2005—Bears, 17-9 (C)
2006—Bears, 41-10 (C)
(RS Pts.—49ers 1,277, Bears 1,188)
(PS Pts.—49ers 95, Bears 18)
*NFC Championship
**NFC Divisional Playoff
CHICAGO vs. SEATTLE
RS: Seahawks lead series, 7-3
PS: Bears lead series, 1-0
1976—Bears, 34-7 (S)
1978—Seahawks, 31-29 (C)
1982—Seahawks, 20-14 (S)
1984—Seahawks, 38-9 (S)
1987—Seahawks, 34-21 (C)
1990—Bears, 17-0 (C)
1999—Seahawks, 14-13 (C)
2003—Seahawks, 24-17 (S)
2006—Bears, 37-6 (C)
        *Bears, 27-24 (C) OT
2007—Seahawks, 30-23 (S)
(RS Pts.—Bears 214, Seahawks 204)
(PS Pts.—Bears 27, Seahawks 24)
*NFC Divisional Playoff
CHICAGO vs. TAMPA BAY
RS: Bears lead series, 35-17
1977—Bears, 10-0 (TB)
1978—Buccaneers, 33-19 (TB)
        Bears, 14-3 (C)
1979—Buccaneers, 17-13 (C)
        Bears, 14-0 (TB)
1980—Bears, 23-0 (C)
        Bears, 14-13 (TB)
1981—Bears, 28-17 (C)
        Buccaneers, 20-10 (TB)
1982—Buccaneers, 26-23 (TB) OT
1983—Bears, 17-10 (C)

        Bears, 27-0 (TB)
1984—Bears, 34-14 (C)
        Bears, 44-9 (TB)
1985—Bears, 38-28 (C)
        Bears, 27-19 (TB)
1986—Bears, 23-3 (TB)
        Bears, 48-14 (C)
1987—Bears, 20-3 (C)
        Bears, 27-26 (TB)
1988—Bears, 28-10 (C)
        Bears, 27-15 (TB)
1989—Buccaneers, 42-35 (TB)
        Buccaneers, 32-31 (C)
1990—Bears, 26-6 (TB)
        Bears, 27-14 (C)
1991—Bears, 21-20 (TB)
        Bears, 27-0 (C)
1992—Bears, 31-14 (C)
        Buccaneers, 20-17 (TB)
1993—Bears, 47-17 (C)
        Buccaneers, 13-10 (TB)
1994—Bears, 21-9 (C)
        Bears, 20-6 (TB)
1995—Bears, 25-6 (TB)
        Bears, 31-10 (C)
1996—Bears, 13-10 (C)
        Buccaneers, 34-19 (TB)
1997—Bears, 13-7 (C)
        Buccaneers, 31-15 (TB)
1998—Buccaneers, 27-15 (TB)
        Buccaneers, 31-17 (C)
1999—Buccaneers, 6-3 (TB)
        Buccaneers, 20-6 (C)
2000—Buccaneers, 41-0 (TB)
        Bears, 13-10 (C)
2001—Bears, 27-24 (TB)
        Bears, 27-3 (C)
2002—Buccaneers, 15-0 (C)
2004—Buccaneers, 19-7 (TB)
2005—Bears, 13-10 (TB)
2006—Bears, 34-31 (C) OT
(RS Pts.—Bears 1,119, Buccaneers 808)
CHICAGO vs. *TENNESSEE
RS: Bears lead series, 5-4
1973—Bears, 15-14 (C)
1977—Oilers, 47-0 (H)
1980—Oilers, 10-6 (C)
1986—Bears, 20-7 (H)
1989—Oilers, 33-28 (C)
1992—Oilers, 24-7 (H)
1995—Bears, 35-32 (C)
1998—Bears, 23-20 (T)
2004—Bears, 19-17 (T) OT
(RS Pts.—Titans 204, Bears 173)
*Franchise in Houston prior to 1997;
known as Oilers prior to 1999
CHICAGO vs. *WASHINGTON
RS: Bears lead series, 20-18-1
PS: Redskins lead series, 4-3
1932—Tie, 7-7 (B)
1933—Bears, 7-0 (C)
        Redskins, 10-0 (B)
1934—Bears, 21-0 (B)
1935—Bears, 30-14 (B)
1936—Bears, 26-0 (B)
1937—**Redskins, 28-21 (C)
1938—Bears, 31-7 (C)
1940—Redskins, 7-3 (W)
        **Bears, 73-0 (W)
1941—Bears, 35-21 (C)

1942—**Redskins, 14-6 (W)
1943—Redskins, 21-7 (W)
    **Bears, 41-21 (C)
1945—Redskins, 28-21 (W)
1946—Bears, 24-20 (C)
1947—Bears, 56-20 (W)
1948—Bears, 48-13 (C)
1949—Bears, 31-21 (W)
1951—Bears, 27-0 (W)
1953—Bears, 27-24 (W)
1957—Redskins, 14-3 (C)
1964—Redskins, 27-20 (W)
1968—Redskins, 38-28 (C)
1971—Bears, 16-15 (C)
1974—Redskins, 42-0 (W)
1976—Bears, 33-7 (C)
1978—Bears, 14-10 (W)
1980—Bears, 35-21 (C)
1981—Redskins, 24-7 (C)
1984—***Bears, 23-19 (W)
1985—Bears, 45-10 (C)
1986—***Redskins, 27-13 (C)
1987—***Redskins, 21-17 (C)
1988—Bears, 34-14 (W)
1989—Redskins, 38-14 (W)
1990—Redskins, 10-9 (W)
1991—Redskins, 20-7 (C)
1996—Redskins, 10-3 (C)
1997—Redskins, 31-8 (C)
1999—Redskins, 48-22 (W)
2001—Bears, 20-15 (W)
2003—Bears, 27-24 (C)
2004—Redskins, 13-10 (C)
2005—Redskins, 9-7 (W)
2007—Redskins, 24-16 (W)
(RS Pts.—Bears 779, Redskins 677)
(PS Pts.—Bears 194, Redskins 130)
*Franchise in Boston prior to 1937 and
known as Braves prior to 1933
**NFL Championship
***NFC Divisional Playoff

CINCINNATI vs. ARIZONA
RS: Bengals lead series, 5-4;
See Arizona vs. Cincinnati
CINCINNATI vs. ATLANTA
RS: Bengals lead series, 7-4;
See Atlanta vs. Cincinnati
CINCINNATI vs. BALTIMORE
RS: Ravens lead series, 13-11;
See Baltimore vs. Cincinnati
CINCINNATI vs. BUFFALO
RS: Bills lead series, 14-9
PS: Bengals lead series, 2-0;
See Buffalo vs. Cincinnati
CINCINNATI vs. CAROLINA
RS: Panthers lead series, 2-1;
See Carolina vs. Cincinnati
CINCINNATI vs. CHICAGO
RS: Bengals lead series, 5-3;
See Chicago vs. Cincinnati
CINCINNATI vs. CLEVELAND
RS: Bengals lead series, 35-34
1970—Browns, 30-27 (Cle)
    Bengals, 14-10 (Cin)
1971—Browns, 27-24 (Cin)
    Browns, 31-27 (Cle)
1972—Browns, 27-6 (Cle)
    Browns, 27-24 (Cin)
1973—Browns, 17-10 (Cle)

    Bengals, 34-17 (Cin)
1974—Bengals, 33-7 (Cin)
    Bengals, 34-24 (Cle)
1975—Bengals, 24-17 (Cin)
    Browns, 35-23 (Cle)
1976—Bengals, 45-24 (Cle)
    Bengals, 21-6 (Cin)
1977—Browns, 13-3 (Cin)
    Bengals, 10-7 (Cle)
1978—Browns, 13-10 (Cle) OT
    Bengals, 48-16 (Cin)
1979—Bengals, 28-27 (Cle)
    Bengals, 16-12 (Cin)
1980—Browns, 31-7 (Cle)
    Browns, 27-24 (Cin)
1981—Browns, 20-17 (Cin)
    Bengals, 41-21 (Cle)
1982—Bengals, 23-10 (Cin)
1983—Browns, 17-7 (Cle)
    Bengals, 28-21 (Cin)
1984—Bengals, 12-9 (Cin)
    Bengals, 20-17 (Cle) OT
1985—Bengals, 27-10 (Cin)
    Browns, 24-6 (Cle)
1986—Bengals, 30-13 (Cle)
    Browns, 34-3 (Cin)
1987—Browns, 34-0 (Cin)
    Browns, 38-24 (Cle)
1988—Bengals, 24-17 (Cin)
    Browns, 23-16 (Cle)
1989—Bengals, 21-14 (Cin)
    Bengals, 21-0 (Cle)
1990—Bengals, 34-13 (Cle)
    Bengals, 21-14 (Cin)
1991—Browns, 14-13 (Cle)
    Bengals, 23-21 (Cin)
1992—Bengals, 30-10 (Cin)
    Browns, 37-21 (Cle)
1993—Browns, 27-14 (Cle)
    Browns, 28-17 (Cin)
1994—Browns, 28-20 (Cin)
    Browns, 37-13 (Cle)
1995—Browns, 29-26 (Cin) OT
    Browns, 26-10 (Cle)
1999—Bengals, 18-17 (Cin)
    Bengals, 44-28 (Cin)
2000—Browns, 24-7 (Cin)
    Bengals, 12-3 (Cle)
2001—Bengals, 24-14 (Cin)
    Browns, 18-0 (Cle)
2002—Browns, 20-7 (Cle)
    Browns, 27-20 (Cin)
2003—Bengals, 21-14 (Cle)
    Browns, 22-14 (Cin)
2004—Browns, 34-17 (Cle)
    Bengals, 58-48 (Cin)
2005—Bengals, 27-13 (Cle)
    Bengals, 23-20 (Cin)
2006—Bengals, 34-17 (Cin)
    Bengals, 30-0 (Cle)
2007—Browns, 51-45 (Cle)
    Bengals, 19-14 (Cin)
(RS Pts.—Bengals 1,473, Browns 1,436)
CINCINNATI vs. DALLAS
RS: Cowboys lead series, 5-4
1973—Cowboys, 38-10 (D)
1979—Cowboys, 38-13 (D)
1985—Bengals, 50-24 (C)
1988—Bengals, 38-24 (D)
1991—Cowboys, 35-23 (D)

1994—Cowboys, 23-20 (C)
1997—Bengals, 31-24 (C)
2000—Cowboys, 23-6 (D)
2004—Bengals, 26-3 (C)
(RS Pts.—Cowboys 232, Bengals 217)
CINCINNATI vs. DENVER
RS: Broncos lead series, 16-8
1968—Bengals, 24-10 (C)
    Broncos, 10-7 (D)
1969—Broncos, 30-23 (C)
    Broncos, 27-16 (D)
1971—Bengals, 24-10 (D)
1972—Bengals, 21-10 (C)
1973—Broncos, 28-10 (D)
1975—Bengals, 17-16 (D)
1976—Bengals, 17-7 (C)
1977—Broncos, 24-13 (C)
1979—Broncos, 10-0 (D)
1981—Bengals, 38-21 (C)
1983—Broncos, 24-17 (D)
1984—Broncos, 20-17 (D)
1986—Broncos, 34-28 (D)
1991—Broncos, 45-14 (D)
1994—Broncos, 15-13 (D)
1996—Broncos, 14-10 (D)
1997—Broncos, 38-20 (D)
1998—Broncos, 33-26 (C)
2000—Bengals, 31-21 (C)
2003—Broncos, 30-10 (C)
2004—Bengals, 23-10 (C)
2006—Broncos, 24-23 (D)
(RS Pts.—Broncos 511, Bengals 442)
CINCINNATI vs. DETROIT
RS: Bengals lead series, 6-3
1970—Lions, 38-3 (D)
1974—Lions, 23-19 (C)
1983—Bengals, 17-9 (C)
1986—Bengals, 24-17 (D)
1989—Bengals, 42-7 (C)
1992—Lions, 19-13 (C)
1998—Bengals, 34-28 (D) OT
2001—Bengals, 31-27 (D)
2005—Bengals, 41-17 (D)
(RS Pts.—Bengals 224, Lions 185)
CINCINNATI vs. GREEN BAY
RS: Series tied, 5-5
1971—Packers, 20-17 (GB)
1976—Bengals, 28-7 (C)
1977—Bengals, 17-7 (Mil)
1980—Packers, 14-9 (GB)
1983—Bengals, 34-14 (C)
1986—Bengals, 34-28 (Mil)
1992—Packers, 24-23 (GB)
1995—Packers, 24-10 (GB)
1998—Packers, 13-6 (C)
2005—Bengals, 21-14 (C)
(RS Pts.—Bengals 199, Packers 165)
CINCINNATI vs. HOUSTON
RS: Bengals lead series, 3-0
2002—Bengals, 38-3 (H)
2003—Bengals, 34-27 (C)
2005—Bengals, 16-10 (C)
(RS Pts.—Bengals 88, Texans 40)
CINCINNATI vs. *INDIANAPOLIS
RS: Colts lead series, 14-8
PS: Colts lead series, 1-0
1970—**Colts, 17-0 (B)
1972—Colts, 20-19 (C)
1974—Bengals, 24-14 (B)
1976—Colts, 28-27 (B)

1979—Colts, 38-28 (B)
1980—Bengals, 34-33 (C)
1981—Bengals, 41-19 (B)
1982—Bengals, 20-17 (B)
1983—Colts, 34-31 (C)
1987—Bengals, 23-21 (I)
1989—Colts, 23-12 (C)
1990—Colts, 34-20 (C)
1992—Colts, 21-17 (C)
1993—Colts, 9-6 (C)
1994—Colts, 17-13 (C)
1995—Bengals, 24-21 (I) OT
1996—Bengals, 31-24 (C)
1997—Bengals, 28-13 (I)
1998—Colts, 39-26 (I)
1999—Colts, 31-10 (I)
2002—Colts, 28-21 (I)
2005—Colts, 45-37 (C)
2006—Colts, 34-16 (I)
(RS Pts.—Colts 563, Bengals 508)
(PS Pts.—Colts 17, Bengals 0)
*Franchise in Baltimore prior to 1984
**AFC Divisional Playoff
CINCINNATI vs. JACKSONVILLE
RS: Jaguars lead series, 11-5
1995—Bengals, 24-17 (C)
          Bengals, 17-13 (J)
1996—Bengals, 28-21 (C)
          Jaguars, 30-27 (J)
1997—Jaguars, 21-13 (J)
          Bengals, 31-26 (C)
1998—Jaguars, 24-11 (J)
          Jaguars, 34-17 (C)
1999—Jaguars, 41-10 (C)
          Jaguars, 24-7 (J)
2000—Jaguars, 13-0 (C)
          Bengals, 17-14 (C)
2001—Jaguars, 30-13 (J)
          Jaguars, 14-10 (C)
2002—Jaguars, 29-15 (C)
2005—Jaguars, 23-20 (J)
(RS Pts.—Jaguars 374, Bengals 260)
CINCINNATI vs. KANSAS CITY
RS: Chiefs lead series, 13-11
1968—Chiefs, 13-3 (KC)
          Chiefs, 16-9 (C)
1969—Bengals, 24-19 (C)
          Chiefs, 42-22 (KC)
1970—Chiefs, 27-19 (C)
1972—Bengals, 23-16 (KC)
1973—Bengals, 14-6 (C)
1974—Bengals, 33-6 (C)
1976—Bengals, 27-24 (KC)
1977—Bengals, 27-7 (KC)
1978—Chiefs, 24-23 (C)
1979—Chiefs, 10-7 (C)
1980—Bengals, 20-6 (KC)
1983—Chiefs, 20-15 (KC)
1984—Chiefs, 27-22 (C)
1986—Chiefs, 24-14 (KC)
1987—Bengals, 30-27 (C) OT
1988—Chiefs, 31-28 (KC)
1989—Bengals, 21-17 (KC)
1993—Chiefs, 17-15 (KC)
2003—Bengals, 24-19 (C)
2005—Chiefs, 37-3 (KC)
2006—Bengals, 23-10 (KC)
2007—Chiefs, 27-20 (KC)
(RS Pts.—Chiefs 472, Bengals 466)
CINCINNATI vs. MIAMI

RS: Dolphins lead series, 12-5
PS: Dolphins lead series, 1-0
1968—Dolphins, 24-22 (C)
          Bengals, 38-21 (M)
1969—Bengals, 27-21 (C)
1971—Dolphins, 23-13 (C)
1973—*Dolphins, 34-16 (M)
1974—Dolphins, 24-3 (M)
1977—Bengals, 23-17 (C)
1978—Dolphins, 21-0 (M)
1980—Dolphins, 17-16 (M)
1983—Dolphins, 38-14 (M)
1987—Dolphins, 20-14 (C)
1989—Dolphins, 20-13 (C)
1991—Dolphins, 37-13 (M)
1994—Dolphins, 23-7 (C)
1995—Dolphins, 26-23 (C)
2000—Dolphins, 31-16 (C)
2004—Bengals, 16-13 (C)
2007—Bengals, 38-25 (M)
(RS Pts.—Dolphins 401, Bengals 296)
(PS Pts.—Dolphins 34, Bengals 16)
*AFC Divisional Playoff
CINCINNATI vs. MINNESOTA
RS: Series tied, 5-5
1973—Bengals, 27-0 (C)
1977—Vikings, 42-10 (M)
1980—Bengals, 14-0 (C)
1983—Vikings, 20-14 (M)
1986—Bengals, 24-20 (C)
1989—Vikings, 29-21 (M)
1992—Vikings, 42-7 (C)
1995—Bengals, 27-24 (C)
1998—Vikings, 24-3 (M)
2005—Bengals, 37-8 (C)
(RS Pts.—Vikings 209, Bengals 184)
CINCINNATI vs. *NEW ENGLAND
RS: Patriots lead series, 13-8
1968—Patriots, 33-14 (B)
1969—Patriots, 25-14 (C)
1970—Bengals, 45-7 (C)
1972—Bengals, 31-7 (NE)
1975—Bengals, 27-10 (C)
1978—Patriots, 10-3 (C)
1979—Patriots, 20-14 (C)
1984—Patriots, 20-14 (NE)
1985—Patriots, 34-23 (NE)
1986—Bengals, 31-7 (NE)
1988—Patriots, 27-21 (NE)
1990—Bengals, 41-7 (C)
1991—Bengals, 29-7 (C)
1992—Bengals, 20-10 (C)
1993—Patriots, 7-2 (NE)
1994—Patriots, 31-28 (C)
2000—Patriots, 16-13 (NE)
2001—Bengals, 23-17 (C)
2004—Patriots, 35-28 (NE)
2006—Patriots, 38-13 (C)
2007—Patriots, 34-13 (C)
(RS Pts.—Bengals 447, Patriots 402)
*Franchise in Boston prior to 1971
CINCINNATI vs. NEW ORLEANS
RS: Bengals lead series, 6-5
1970—Bengals, 26-6 (C)
1975—Bengals, 21-0 (NO)
1978—Saints, 20-18 (C)
1981—Saints, 17-7 (NO)
1984—Bengals, 24-21 (NO)
1987—Saints, 41-24 (C)
1990—Saints, 21-7 (C)

1993—Saints, 20-13 (NO)
1996—Bengals, 30-15 (C)
2002—Bengals, 20-13 (C)
2006—Bengals, 31-16 (NO)
(RS Pts.—Bengals 221, Saints 190)
CINCINNATI vs. N.Y. GIANTS
RS: Bengals lead series, 5-2
1972—Bengals, 13-10 (C)
1977—Bengals, 30-13 (C)
1985—Bengals, 35-30 (C)
1991—Bengals, 27-24 (C)
1994—Giants, 27-20 (NY)
1997—Giants, 29-27 (NY)
2004—Bengals, 23-22 (C)
(RS Pts.—Bengals 175, Giants 155)
CINCINNATI vs. N.Y. JETS
RS: Jets lead series, 12-7
PS: Jets lead series, 1-0
1968—Jets, 27-14 (NY)
1969—Jets, 21-7 (C)
          Jets, 40-7 (NY)
1971—Jets, 35-21 (NY)
1973—Bengals, 20-14 (C)
1976—Bengals, 42-3 (NY)
1981—Bengals, 31-30 (NY)
1982—*Jets, 44-17 (C)
1984—Jets, 43-23 (NY)
1985—Jets, 29-20 (C)
1986—Bengals, 52-21 (M)
1987—Jets, 27-20 (NY)
1988—Bengals, 36-19 (C)
1990—Bengals, 25-20 (C)
1992—Jets, 17-14 (NY)
1993—Jets, 17-12 (NY)
1997—Jets, 31-14 (C)
2001—Jets, 15-14 (NY)
2004—Jets, 31-24 (NY)
2007—Bengals, 38-31 (C)
(RS Pts.—Jets 471, Bengals 434)
(PS Pts.—Jets 44, Bengals 17)
*AFC First-Round Playoff
CINCINNATI vs. *OAKLAND
RS: Raiders lead series, 17-8
PS: Raiders lead series, 2-0
1968—Raiders, 31-10 (O)
          Raiders, 34-0 (C)
1969—Bengals, 31-17 (C)
          Raiders, 37-17 (O)
1970—Bengals, 31-21 (C)
1971—Raiders, 31-27 (O)
1972—Raiders, 20-14 (C)
1974—Raiders, 30-27 (O)
1975—Bengals, 14-10 (C)
          **Raiders, 31-28 (O)
1976—Raiders, 35-20 (O)
1978—Raiders, 34-21 (C)
1980—Raiders, 28-17 (O)
1982—Bengals, 31-17 (C)
1983—Raiders, 20-10 (C)
1985—Raiders, 13-6 (LA)
1988—Bengals, 45-21 (LA)
1989—Raiders, 28-7 (C)
1990—Raiders, 24-7 (LA)
          **Raiders, 20-10 (LA)
1991—Bengals, 38-14 (C)
1992—Raiders, 24-21 (C) OT
1993—Bengals, 16-10 (C)
1995—Raiders, 20-17 (C)
1998—Raiders, 27-10 (O)
2003—Raiders, 23-20 (O)

2006—Bengals, 27-10 (C)
(RS Pts.—Raiders 600, Bengals 463)
(PS Pts.—Raiders 51, Bengals 38)
Franchise in Los Angeles from 1982-1994
**AFC Divisional Playoff*

CINCINNATI vs. PHILADELPHIA
RS: Bengals lead series, 7-3
1971—Bengals, 37-14 (C)
1975—Bengals, 31-0 (P)
1979—Bengals, 37-13 (C)
1982—Bengals, 18-14 (P)
1988—Bengals, 28-24 (P)
1991—Eagles, 17-10 (P)
1994—Bengals, 33-30 (C)
1997—Eagles, 44-42 (P)
2000—Eagles, 16-7 (P)
2004—Bengals, 38-10 (P)
(RS Pts.—Bengals 281, Eagles 182)

CINCINNATI vs. PITTSBURGH
RS: Steelers lead series, 45-30
PS: Steelers lead series, 1-0
1970—Steelers, 21-10 (P)
    Bengals, 34-7 (C)
1971—Bengals, 21-10 (P)
    Steelers, 21-13 (C)
1972—Bengals, 15-10 (C)
    Steelers, 40-17 (P)
1973—Bengals, 19-7 (C)
    Steelers, 20-13 (P)
1974—Bengals, 17-10 (C)
    Steelers, 27-3 (P)
1975—Steelers, 30-24 (C)
    Steelers, 35-14 (P)
1976—Steelers, 23-6 (P)
    Steelers, 7-3 (C)
1977—Steelers, 20-14 (P)
    Bengals, 17-10 (C)
1978—Steelers, 28-3 (C)
    Steelers, 7-6 (P)
1979—Bengals, 34-10 (C)
    Steelers, 37-17 (P)
1980—Bengals, 30-28 (C)
    Bengals, 17-16 (P)
1981—Bengals, 34-7 (C)
    Bengals, 17-10 (P)
1982—Steelers, 26-20 (P) OT
1983—Steelers, 24-14 (C)
    Bengals, 23-10 (P)
1984—Steelers, 38-17 (P)
    Bengals, 22-20 (C)
1985—Bengals, 37-24 (P)
    Bengals, 26-21 (C)
1986—Bengals, 24-22 (C)
    Steelers, 30-9 (P)
1987—Steelers, 23-20 (P)
    Steelers, 30-16 (C)
1988—Bengals, 17-12 (P)
    Bengals, 42-7 (C)
1989—Bengals, 41-10 (C)
    Bengals, 26-16 (P)
1990—Bengals, 27-3 (C)
    Bengals, 16-12 (P)
1991—Steelers, 33-27 (C) OT
    Steelers, 17-10 (P)
1992—Steelers, 20-0 (P)
    Steelers, 21-9 (C)
1993—Steelers, 34-7 (P)
    Steelers, 24-16 (C)
1994—Steelers, 14-10 (P)
    Steelers, 38-15 (C)

1995—Bengals, 27-9 (P)
    Steelers, 49-31 (C)
1996—Steelers, 20-10 (P)
    Bengals, 34-24 (C)
1997—Steelers, 26-10 (C)
    Steelers, 20-3 (P)
1998—Bengals, 25-20 (C)
    Bengals, 25-24 (P)
1999—Steelers, 17-3 (C)
    Bengals, 27-20 (P)
2000—Steelers, 15-0 (C)
    Steelers, 48-28 (C)
2001—Steelers, 16-7 (P)
    Bengals, 26-23 (C) OT
2002—Steelers, 34-7 (C)
    Steelers, 29-21 (P)
2003—Steelers, 17-10 (C)
    Bengals, 24-20 (P)
2004—Steelers, 28-17 (P)
    Steelers, 19-14 (C)
2005—Steelers, 27-13 (C)
    Bengals, 38-31 (P)
    *Steelers, 31-17 (C)
2006—Bengals, 28-20 (P)
    Steelers, 23-17 (C) OT
2007—Steelers, 24-13 (C)
    Steelers, 24-10 (P)
(RS Pts.—Steelers 1,608, Bengals 1,346)
(PS Pts.—Steelers 31, Bengals 17)
AFC First-Round Playoff

CINCINNATI vs. *ST. LOUIS
RS: Bengals lead series, 6-5
1972—Rams, 15-12 (LA)
1976—Bengals, 20-12 (C)
1978—Bengals, 20-19 (LA)
1981—Bengals, 24-10 (C)
1984—Rams, 24-14 (C)
1990—Bengals, 34-31 (LA) OT
1993—Bengals, 15-3 (C)
1996—Rams, 26-16 (StL)
1999—Rams, 38-10 (C)
2003—Rams, 27-10 (StL)
2007—Bengals, 19-10 (C)
(RS Pts.—Rams 215, Bengals 194)
Franchise in Los Angeles prior to 1995

CINCINNATI vs. SAN DIEGO
RS: Chargers lead series, 18-10
PS: Bengals lead series, 1-0
1968—Bengals, 29-13 (SD)
    Chargers, 31-10 (C)
1969—Bengals, 34-20 (C)
    Chargers, 21-14 (SD)
1970—Bengals, 17-14 (SD)
1971—Bengals, 31-0 (C)
1973—Bengals, 20-13 (SD)
1974—Chargers, 20-17 (C)
1975—Bengals, 47-17 (C)
1977—Chargers, 24-3 (SD)
1978—Chargers, 22-13 (SD)
1979—Chargers, 26-24 (C)
1980—Chargers, 31-14 (C)
1981—Bengals, 40-17 (SD)
    *Bengals, 27-7 (C)
1982—Chargers, 50-34 (SD)
1985—Chargers, 44-41 (C)
1987—Chargers, 10-9 (C)
1988—Bengals, 27-10 (C)
1990—Bengals, 21-16 (SD)
1992—Chargers, 27-10 (SD)
1994—Chargers, 27-10 (SD)

1996—Chargers, 27-14 (SD)
1997—Bengals, 38-31 (C)
1999—Chargers, 34-7 (C)
2001—Chargers, 28-14 (SD)
2002—Chargers, 34-6 (C)
2003—Bengals, 34-27 (SD)
2006—Chargers, 49-41 (C)
(RS Pts.—Chargers 699, Bengals 603)
(PS Pts.—Bengals 27, Chargers 7)
AFC Championship

CINCINNATI vs. SAN FRANCISCO
RS: 49ers lead series, 8-3
PS: 49ers lead series, 2-0
1974—Bengals, 21-3 (SF)
1978—49ers, 28-12 (SF)
1981—49ers, 21-3 (C)
    *49ers, 26-21 (Detroit)
1984—49ers, 23-17 (SF)
1987—49ers, 27-26 (C)
1988—**49ers, 20-16 (South Florida)
1990—49ers, 20-17 (C) OT
1993—49ers, 21-8 (SF)
1996—49ers, 28-21 (SF)
1999—Bengals, 44-30 (C)
2003—Bengals, 41-38 (C)
2007—49ers, 20-13 (SF)
(RS Pts.—49ers 259, Bengals 223)
(PS Pts.—49ers 46, Bengals 37)
Super Bowl XVI
**Super Bowl XXIII*

CINCINNATI vs. SEATTLE
RS: Seahawks lead series, 9-8
PS: Bengals lead series, 1-0
1977—Bengals, 42-20 (C)
1981—Bengals, 27-21 (C)
1982—Bengals, 24-10 (C)
1984—Seahawks, 26-6 (C)
1985—Seahawks, 28-24 (C)
1986—Bengals, 34-7 (C)
1987—Bengals, 17-10 (S)
1988—*Bengals, 21-13 (C)
1989—Seahawks, 24-17 (C)
1990—Seahawks, 31-16 (S)
1991—Seahawks, 13-7 (C)
1992—Bengals, 21-3 (S)
1993—Seahawks, 19-10 (C)
1994—Bengals, 20-17 (S) OT
1995—Seahawks, 24-21 (S)
1999—Seahawks, 37-20 (S)
2003—Bengals, 27-24 (C)
2007—Seahawks, 24-21 (S)
(RS Pts.—Bengals 354, Seahawks 338)
(PS Pts.—Bengals 21, Seahawks 13)
AFC Divisional Playoff

CINCINNATI vs. TAMPA BAY
RS: Buccaneers lead series, 6-3
1976—Bengals, 21-0 (C)
1980—Buccaneers, 17-12 (C)
1983—Bengals, 23-17 (TB)
1989—Bengals, 56-23 (C)
1995—Buccaneers, 19-16 (TB)
1998—Buccaneers, 35-0 (C)
2001—Bengals, 16-13 (C) OT
2002—Buccaneers, 35-7 (C)
2006—Buccaneers, 14-13 (TB)
(RS Pts.— Buccaneers 176, Bengals 161)

CINCINNATI vs. *TENNESSEE
RS: Titans lead series, 38-31-1
PS: Bengals lead series, 1-0
1968—Oilers, 27-17 (C)

1969—Tie, 31-31 (H)
1970—Oilers, 20-13 (C)
Bengals, 30-20 (H)
1971—Oilers, 10-6 (H)
Bengals, 28-13 (C)
1972—Bengals, 30-7 (C)
Bengals, 61-17 (H)
1973—Bengals, 24-10 (C)
Bengals, 27-24 (H)
1974—Oilers, 34-21 (C)
Oilers, 20-3 (H)
1975—Bengals, 21-19 (H)
Bengals, 23-19 (C)
1976—Bengals, 27-7 (H)
Bengals, 31-27 (C)
1977—Bengals, 13-10 (C) OT
Oilers, 21-16 (H)
1978—Bengals, 28-13 (C)
Oilers, 17-10 (H)
1979—Oilers, 30-27 (C) OT
Oilers, 42-21 (H)
1980—Oilers, 13-10 (C)
Oilers, 23-3 (H)
1981—Oilers, 17-10 (H)
Bengals, 34-21 (C)
1982—Bengals, 27-6 (C)
Bengals, 35-27 (H)
1983—Bengals, 55-14 (H)
Bengals, 38-10 (C)
1984—Bengals, 13-3 (C)
Bengals, 31-13 (H)
1985—Oilers, 44-27 (H)
Bengals, 45-27 (C)
1986—Bengals, 31-28 (C)
Oilers, 32-28 (H)
1987—Oilers, 31-29 (C)
Oilers, 21-17 (H)
1988—Bengals, 44-21 (C)
Oilers, 41-6 (H)
1989—Oilers, 26-24 (H)
Bengals, 61-7 (C)
1990—Oilers, 48-17 (H)
Bengals, 40-20 (C)
**Bengals, 41-14 (C)
1991—Oilers, 30-7 (C)
Oilers, 35-3 (H)
1992—Oilers, 38-24 (C)
Oilers, 26-10 (H)
1993—Oilers, 28-12 (H)
Oilers, 38-3 (C)
1994—Oilers, 20-13 (H)
Bengals, 34-31 (C)
1995—Oilers, 38-28 (C)
Bengals, 32-25 (H)
1996—Oilers, 30-27 (C) OT
Bengals, 21-13 (H)
1997—Oilers, 30-7 (T)
Bengals, 41-14 (C)
1998—Oilers, 23-14 (C)
Oilers, 44-14 (T)
1999—Titans, 36-35 (T)
Titans, 24-14 (C)
2000—Titans, 23-14 (C)
Titans, 35-3 (T)
2001—Titans, 20-7 (C)
Bengals, 23-21 (T)
2002—Titans, 30-24 (C)
2004—Titans, 27-20 (T)
2005—Bengals, 31-23 (T)
2007—Bengals, 35-6 (C)

(RS Pts.—Titans 1,639, Bengals 1,629)
(PS Pts.—Bengals 41, Titans 14)
*Franchise in Houston prior to 1997;
known as Oilers prior to 1999
**AFC First-Round Playoff
CINCINNATI vs. WASHINGTON
RS: Redskins lead series, 4-3
1970—Redskins, 20-0 (W)
1974—Bengals, 28-17 (C)
1979—Redskins, 28-14 (W)
1985—Redskins, 27-24 (W)
1988—Bengals, 20-17 (C) OT
1991—Redskins, 34-27 (C)
2004—Bengals, 17-10 (W)
(RS Pts.—Redskins 153, Bengals 130)

CLEVELAND vs. ARIZONA
RS: Browns lead series, 33-12-3;
See Arizona vs. Cleveland
CLEVELAND vs. ATLANTA
RS: Browns lead series, 10-2;
See Atlanta vs. Cleveland
CLEVELAND vs. BALTIMORE
RS: Ravens lead series, 11-7;
See Baltimore vs. Cleveland
CLEVELAND vs. BUFFALO
RS: Browns lead series, 8-5
PS: Browns lead series, 1-0;
See Buffalo vs. Cleveland
CLEVELAND vs. CAROLINA
RS: Panthers lead series, 3-0;
See Carolina vs. Cleveland
CLEVELAND vs. CHICAGO
RS: Browns lead series, 9-4;
See Chicago vs. Cleveland
CLEVELAND vs. CINCINNATI
RS: Bengals lead series, 35-34;
See Cincinnati vs. Cleveland
CLEVELAND vs. DALLAS
RS: Browns lead series, 15-10
PS: Browns lead series, 2-1
1960—Browns, 48-7 (D)
1961—Browns, 25-7 (C)
Browns, 38-17 (D)
1962—Browns, 19-10 (C)
Cowboys, 45-21 (D)
1963—Browns, 41-24 (D)
Browns, 27-17 (C)
1964—Browns, 27-6 (C)
Browns, 20-16 (D)
1965—Browns, 23-17 (C)
Browns, 24-17 (D)
1966—Browns, 30-21 (C)
Cowboys, 26-14 (D)
1967—Cowboys, 21-14 (C)
*Cowboys, 52-14 (D)
1968—Cowboys, 28-7 (D)
*Browns, 31-20 (C)
1969—Browns, 42-10 (C)
*Browns, 38-14 (D)
1970—Cowboys, 6-2 (C)
1974—Cowboys, 41-17 (D)
1979—Browns, 26-7 (C)
1982—Cowboys, 31-14 (D)
1985—Cowboys, 20-7 (D)
1988—Browns, 24-21 (C)
1991—Cowboys, 26-14 (C)
1994—Browns, 19-14 (D)
2004—Cowboys, 19-12 (D)
(RS Pts.—Browns 555, Cowboys 474)

(PS Pts.—Cowboys 86, Browns 83)
*Conference Championship
CLEVELAND vs. DENVER
RS: Broncos lead series, 16-5
PS: Broncos lead series, 3-0
1970—Browns, 27-13 (D)
1971—Broncos, 27-0 (C)
1972—Browns, 27-20 (D)
1974—Browns, 23-21 (C)
1975—Broncos, 16-15 (D)
1976—Broncos, 44-13 (D)
1978—Broncos, 19-7 (C)
1980—Broncos, 19-16 (C)
1981—Broncos, 23-20 (D) OT
1983—Broncos, 27-6 (D)
1984—Broncos, 24-14 (C)
1986—*Broncos, 23-20 (C) OT
1987—*Broncos, 38-33 (D)
1988—Broncos, 30-7 (D)
1989—Browns, 16-13 (C)
*Broncos, 37-21 (D)
1990—Browns, 30-29 (D)
1991—Broncos, 17-7 (C)
1992—Broncos, 12-0 (C)
1993—Broncos, 29-14 (C)
1994—Broncos, 26-14 (D)
2000—Broncos, 44-10 (D)
2003—Broncos, 23-20 (D) OT
2006—Broncos, 17-7 (D)
(RS Pts.—Broncos 493, Browns 293)
(PS Pts.—Broncos 98, Browns 74)
*AFC Championship
CLEVELAND vs. DETROIT
RS: Lions lead series, 13-4
PS: Lions lead series, 3-1
1952—Lions, 17-6 (D)
*Lions, 17-7 (C)
1953—*Lions, 17-16 (D)
1954—Lions, 14-10 (C)
*Browns, 56-10 (C)
1957—Lions, 20-7 (D)
*Lions, 59-14 (D)
1958—Lions, 30-10 (C)
1963—Lions, 38-10 (D)
1964—Browns, 37-21 (C)
1967—Lions, 31-14 (D)
1969—Lions, 28-21 (C)
1970—Lions, 41-24 (D)
1975—Lions, 21-10 (D)
1983—Browns, 31-26 (D)
1986—Browns, 24-21 (C)
1989—Lions, 13-10 (D)
1992—Lions, 24-14 (D)
1995—Browns, 38-20 (C)
2001—Browns, 24-14 (C)
2005—Lions, 13-10 (C)
(RS Pts.—Lions 410, Browns 282)
(PS Pts.—Lions 103, Browns 93)
*NFL Championship
CLEVELAND vs. GREEN BAY
RS: Packers lead series, 9-7
PS: Packers lead series, 1-0
1953—Browns, 27-0 (Mil)
1955—Browns, 41-10 (C)
1956—Browns, 24-7 (Mil)
1961—Packers, 49-17 (C)
1964—Packers, 28-21 (Mil)
1965—*Packers, 23-12 (GB)
1966—Packers, 21-20 (C)
1967—Packers, 55-7 (Mil)

1969—Browns, 20-7 (C)
1972—Packers, 26-10 (C)
1980—Browns, 26-21 (C)
1983—Packers, 35-21 (Mil)
1986—Packers, 17-14 (C)
1992—Browns, 17-6 (C)
1995—Packers, 31-20 (C)
2001—Packers, 30-7 (GB)
2005—Browns, 26-24 (GB)
(RS Pts.—Packers 367, Browns 318)
(PS Pts.—Packers 23, Browns 12)
*NFL Championship
CLEVELAND vs. HOUSTON
RS: Browns lead series, 3-2
2002—Browns, 34-17 (C)
2004—Browns, 22-14 (H)
2005—Texans, 19-16 (H)
2006—Texans, 14-6 (H)
2007—Browns, 27-17 (C)
(RS Pts.—Browns 105, Texans 81)
CLEVELAND vs. *INDIANAPOLIS
RS: Browns lead series, 13-11
PS: Series tied, 2-2
1956—Colts, 21-7 (C)
1959—Browns, 38-31 (B)
1962—Colts, 36-14 (C)
1964—**Browns, 27-0 (C)
1968—Browns, 30-20 (B)
        **Colts, 34-0 (C)
1971—Browns, 14-13 (B)
        ***Colts, 20-3 (C)
1973—Browns, 24-14 (C)
1975—Colts, 21-7 (B)
1978—Browns, 45-24 (B)
1979—Browns, 13-10 (C)
1980—Browns, 28-27 (B)
1981—Browns, 42-28 (C)
1983—Browns, 41-23 (C)
1986—Browns, 24-9 (I)
1987—Colts, 9-7 (C)
        ***Browns, 38-21 (C)
1988—Browns, 23-17 (C)
1989—Colts, 23-17 (I) OT
1991—Browns, 31-0 (I)
1992—Colts, 14-3 (I)
1993—Colts, 23-10 (I)
1994—Browns, 21-14 (I)
1999—Colts, 29-28 (C)
2002—Colts, 28-23 (C)
2003—Colts, 9-6 (C)
2005—Colts, 13-6 (I)
(RS Pts.—Browns 502, Colts 456)
(PS Pts.—Colts 75, Browns 68)
*Franchise in Baltimore prior to 1984
**NFL Championship
***AFC Divisional Playoff
CLEVELAND vs. JACKSONVILLE
RS: Jaguars lead series, 8-2
1995—Jaguars, 23-15 (C)
        Jaguars, 24-21 (J)
1999—Jaguars, 24-7 (J)
        Jaguars, 24-14 (C)
2000—Jaguars, 27-7 (C)
        Jaguars, 48-0 (J)
2001—Browns, 23-14 (J)
        Jaguars, 15-10 (C)
2002—Browns, 21-20 (J)
2005—Jaguars, 20-14 (C)
(RS Pts.—Jaguars 239, Browns 132)
CLEVELAND vs. KANSAS CITY

RS: Series tied, 9-9-2
1971—Chiefs, 13-7 (KC)
1972—Chiefs, 31-7 (C)
1973—Tie, 20-20 (KC)
1975—Browns, 40-14 (C)
1976—Chiefs, 39-14 (KC)
1977—Browns, 44-7 (C)
1978—Chiefs, 17-3 (KC)
1979—Browns, 27-24 (KC)
1980—Browns, 20-13 (C)
1984—Chiefs, 10-6 (KC)
1986—Browns, 20-7 (C)
1988—Browns, 6-3 (KC)
1989—Tie, 10-10 (C) OT
1990—Chiefs, 34-0 (KC)
1991—Browns, 20-15 (C)
1994—Chiefs, 20-13 (KC)
1995—Browns, 35-17 (C)
2002—Chiefs, 40-39 (C)
2003—Chiefs, 41-20 (KC)
2006—Browns, 31-28 (C) OT
(RS Pts.—Chiefs 403, Browns 382)
CLEVELAND vs. MIAMI
RS: Dolphins lead series, 7-6
PS: Dolphins lead series, 2-0
1970—Browns, 28-0 (M)
1972—*Dolphins, 20-14 (M)
1973—Dolphins, 17-9 (C)
1976—Browns, 17-13 (C)
1979—Browns, 30-24 (C) OT
1985—*Dolphins, 24-21 (M)
1986—Browns, 26-16 (C)
1988—Dolphins, 38-31 (M)
1989—Dolphins, 13-10 (M) OT
1990—Dolphins, 30-13 (C)
1992—Dolphins, 27-23 (C)
1993—Dolphins, 24-14 (C)
2004—Dolphins, 10-7 (M)
2005—Browns, 22-0 (C)
2007—Browns, 41-31 (C)
(RS Pts.—Browns 271, Dolphins 243)
(PS Pts.—Dolphins 44, Browns 35)
*AFC Divisional Playoff
CLEVELAND vs. MINNESOTA
RS: Vikings lead series, 9-3
PS: Vikings lead series, 1-0
1965—Vikings, 27-17 (C)
1967—Browns, 14-10 (C)
1969—Vikings, 51-3 (M)
        *Vikings, 27-7 (M)
1973—Vikings, 26-3 (M)
1975—Vikings, 42-10 (C)
1980—Vikings, 28-23 (M)
1983—Vikings, 27-21 (C)
1986—Browns, 23-20 (M)
1989—Browns, 23-17 (C) OT
1992—Vikings, 17-13 (M)
1995—Vikings, 27-11 (M)
2005—Vikings, 24-12 (M)
(RS Pts.—Vikings 316, Browns 173)
(PS Pts.—Vikings 27, Browns 7)
*NFL Championship
CLEVELAND vs. NEW ENGLAND
RS: Browns lead series, 11-9
PS: Browns lead series, 1-0
1971—Browns, 27-7 (C)
1974—Browns, 21-14 (NE)
1977—Browns, 30-27 (C) OT
1980—Patriots, 34-17 (NE)
1982—Browns, 10-7 (C)

1983—Browns, 30-0 (NE)
1984—Patriots, 17-16 (C)
1985—Browns, 24-20 (C)
1987—Browns, 20-10 (NE)
1991—Browns, 20-0 (NE)
1992—Browns, 19-17 (NE)
1993—Patriots, 20-17 (C)
1994—Browns, 13-6 (C)
        *Browns, 20-13 (C)
1995—Patriots, 17-14 (NE)
1999—Browns, 19-7 (C)
2000—Browns, 19-11 (C)
2001—Patriots, 27-16 (NE)
2003—Patriots, 9-3 (NE)
2004—Patriots, 42-15 (C)
2007—Patriots, 34-17 (NE)
(RS Pts.—Browns 355, Patriots 338)
(PS Pts.—Browns 20, Patriots 13)
*AFC First-Round Playoff
CLEVELAND vs. NEW ORLEANS
RS: Browns lead series, 11-4
1967—Browns, 42-7 (NO)
1968—Browns, 24-10 (NO)
        Browns, 35-17 (C)
1969—Browns, 27-17 (NO)
1971—Browns, 21-17 (NO)
1975—Browns, 17-16 (C)
1978—Browns, 24-16 (NO)
1981—Browns, 20-17 (C)
1984—Saints, 16-14 (C)
1987—Saints, 28-21 (NO)
1990—Saints, 25-20 (NO)
1993—Browns, 17-13 (C)
1999—Browns, 21-16 (NO)
2002—Browns, 24-15 (NO)
2006—Saints, 19-14 (C)
(RS Pts.—Browns 341, Saints 249)
CLEVELAND vs. N.Y. GIANTS
RS: Browns lead series, 25-19-2
PS: Series tied, 1-1
1950—Giants, 6-0 (C)
        Giants, 17-13 (NY)
        *Browns, 8-3 (C)
1951—Browns, 14-13 (C)
        Browns, 10-0 (NY)
1952—Giants, 17-9 (C)
        Giants, 37-34 (NY)
1953—Browns, 7-0 (NY)
        Browns, 62-14 (C)
1954—Browns, 24-14 (C)
        Browns, 16-7 (NY)
1955—Browns, 24-14 (C)
        Tie, 35-35 (NY)
1956—Giants, 21-9 (C)
        Browns, 24-7 (NY)
1957—Browns, 6-3 (C)
        Browns, 34-28 (NY)
1958—Giants, 21-17 (C)
        Giants, 13-10 (NY)
        *Giants, 10-0 (NY)
1959—Giants, 10-6 (C)
        Giants, 48-7 (NY)
1960—Giants, 17-13 (C)
        Browns, 48-34 (NY)
1961—Giants, 37-21 (C)
        Tie, 7-7 (NY)
1962—Browns, 17-7 (C)
        Giants, 17-13 (NY)
1963—Browns, 35-24 (NY)
        Giants, 33-6 (C)

1964—Browns, 42-20 (C)
    Browns, 52-20 (NY)
1965—Browns, 38-14 (NY)
    Browns, 34-21 (C)
1966—Browns, 28-7 (NY)
    Browns, 49-40 (C)
1967—Giants, 38-34 (NY)
    Browns, 24-14 (C)
1968—Browns, 45-10 (C)
1969—Browns, 28-17 (C)
    Giants, 27-14 (NY)
1973—Browns, 12-10 (C)
1977—Browns, 21-7 (NY)
1985—Browns, 35-33 (NY)
1991—Giants, 13-10 (NY)
1994—Giants, 16-13 (C)
2000—Giants, 24-3 (C)
2004—Giants, 27-10 (NY)
(RS Pts.—Browns 1,013, Giants 859)
(PS Pts.—Giants 13, Browns 8)
*Conference Playoff
CLEVELAND vs. N.Y. JETS
RS: Browns lead series, 12-7
PS: Browns lead series, 1-0
1970—Browns, 31-21 (C)
1972—Browns, 26-10 (NY)
1976—Browns, 38-17 (C)
1978—Browns, 37-34 (C) OT
1979—Browns, 25-22 (NY) OT
1980—Browns, 17-14 (C)
1981—Jets, 14-13 (C)
1983—Browns, 10-7 (C)
1984—Jets, 24-20 (C)
1985—Jets, 37-10 (NY)
1986—*Browns, 23-20 (C) OT
1988—Jets, 23-3 (C)
1989—Browns, 38-24 (C)
1990—Jets, 24-21 (NY)
1991—Jets, 17-14 (C)
1994—Browns, 27-7 (C)
2002—Browns, 24-21 (NY)
2004—Jets, 10-7 (C)
2006—Browns, 20-13 (C)
2007—Browns, 24-18 (NY)
(RS Pts.—Browns 405, Jets 357)
(PS Pts.—Browns 23, Jets 20)
*AFC Divisional Playoff
CLEVELAND vs. *OAKLAND
RS: Raiders lead series, 10-7
PS: Raiders lead series, 2-0
1970—Raiders, 23-20 (O)
1971—Raiders, 34-20 (C)
1973—Browns, 7-3 (O)
1974—Raiders, 40-24 (C)
1975—Raiders, 38-17 (O)
1977—Raiders, 26-10 (C)
1979—Raiders, 19-14 (O)
1980—**Raiders, 14-12 (C)
1982—***Raiders, 27-10 (LA)
1985—Raiders, 21-20 (C)
1986—Raiders, 27-14 (LA)
1987—Browns, 24-17 (LA)
1992—Browns, 28-16 (LA)
1993—Browns, 19-16 (LA)
2000—Raiders, 36-10 (O)
2003—Browns, 13-7 (O)
2005—Browns, 9-7 (O)
2006—Browns, 24-21 (O)
2007—Raiders, 26-24 (O)
(RS Pts.—Raiders 377, Browns 297)

(PS Pts.—Raiders 41, Browns 22)
*Franchise in Los Angeles from 1982-1994
**AFC Divisional Playoff
***AFC First-Round Playoff
CLEVELAND vs. PHILADELPHIA
RS: Browns lead series, 31-14-1
1950—Browns, 35-10 (P)
    Browns, 13-7 (C)
1951—Browns, 20-17 (C)
    Browns, 24-9 (P)
1952—Browns, 49-7 (P)
    Eagles, 28-20 (C)
1953—Browns, 37-13 (C)
    Eagles, 42-27 (P)
1954—Eagles, 28-10 (P)
    Browns, 6-0 (C)
1955—Browns, 21-17 (C)
    Eagles, 33-17 (P)
1956—Browns, 16-0 (P)
    Browns, 17-14 (C)
1957—Browns, 24-7 (C)
    Eagles, 17-7 (P)
1958—Browns, 28-14 (C)
    Browns, 21-14 (P)
1959—Browns, 28-7 (C)
    Browns, 28-21 (P)
1960—Browns, 41-24 (P)
    Eagles, 31-29 (C)
1961—Eagles, 27-20 (P)
    Browns, 45-24 (C)
1962—Eagles, 35-7 (P)
    Tie, 14-14 (C)
1963—Browns, 37-7 (C)
    Browns, 23-17 (P)
1964—Browns, 28-20 (P)
    Browns, 38-24 (C)
1965—Browns, 35-17 (P)
    Browns, 38-34 (C)
1966—Browns, 27-7 (C)
    Eagles, 33-21 (P)
1967—Eagles, 28-24 (P)
1968—Browns, 47-13 (C)
1969—Browns, 27-20 (P)
1972—Browns, 27-17 (P)
1976—Browns, 24-3 (C)
1979—Browns, 24-19 (P)
1982—Eagles, 24-21 (C)
1988—Browns, 19-3 (C)
1991—Eagles, 32-30 (C)
1994—Browns, 26-7 (P)
2000—Eagles, 35-24 (C)
2004—Eagles, 34-31 (C) OT
(RS Pts.—Browns 1,175, Eagles 854)
CLEVELAND vs. PITTSBURGH
RS: Series tied, 55-55
PS: Steelers lead series, 2-0
1950—Browns, 30-17 (P)
    Browns, 45-7 (C)
1951—Browns, 17-0 (C)
    Browns, 28-0 (P)
1952—Browns, 21-20 (P)
    Browns, 29-28 (C)
1953—Browns, 34-16 (C)
    Browns, 20-16 (P)
1954—Steelers, 55-27 (P)
    Browns, 42-7 (C)
1955—Browns, 41-14 (C)
    Browns, 30-7 (P)
1956—Browns, 14-10 (P)
    Steelers, 24-16 (C)

1957—Browns, 23-12 (P)
    Browns, 24-0 (C)
1958—Browns, 45-12 (P)
    Browns, 27-10 (C)
1959—Steelers, 17-7 (P)
    Steelers, 21-20 (C)
1960—Browns, 28-20 (C)
    Steelers, 14-10 (P)
1961—Browns, 30-28 (C)
    Steelers, 17-13 (C)
1962—Browns, 41-14 (P)
    Browns, 35-14 (C)
1963—Browns, 35-23 (C)
    Steelers, 9-7 (P)
1964—Steelers, 23-7 (C)
    Browns, 30-17 (P)
1965—Browns, 24-19 (C)
    Browns, 42-21 (P)
1966—Browns, 41-10 (C)
    Steelers, 16-6 (P)
1967—Browns, 21-10 (C)
    Browns, 34-14 (P)
1968—Browns, 31-24 (C)
    Browns, 45-24 (P)
1969—Browns, 42-31 (C)
    Browns, 24-3 (P)
1970—Browns, 15-7 (C)
    Steelers, 28-9 (P)
1971—Browns, 27-17 (C)
    Steelers, 26-9 (P)
1972—Browns, 26-24 (C)
    Steelers, 30-0 (P)
1973—Browns, 33-6 (P)
    Browns, 21-16 (C)
1974—Steelers, 20-16 (P)
    Steelers, 26-16 (C)
1975—Steelers, 42-6 (C)
    Steelers, 31-17 (P)
1976—Steelers, 31-14 (P)
    Browns, 18-16 (C)
1977—Browns, 28-14 (C)
    Steelers, 35-31 (P)
1978—Steelers, 15-9 (P) OT
    Steelers, 34-14 (C)
1979—Steelers, 51-35 (C)
    Steelers, 33-30 (P) OT
1980—Browns, 27-26 (C)
    Steelers, 16-13 (P)
1981—Steelers, 13-7 (P)
    Steelers, 32-10 (C)
1982—Browns, 10-9 (C)
    Steelers, 37-21 (P)
1983—Steelers, 44-17 (P)
    Browns, 30-17 (C)
1984—Browns, 20-10 (C)
    Steelers, 23-20 (P)
1985—Browns, 17-7 (C)
    Steelers, 10-9 (P)
1986—Browns, 27-24 (P)
    Browns, 37-31 (C) OT
1987—Browns, 34-10 (C)
    Browns, 19-13 (P)
1988—Browns, 23-9 (P)
    Browns, 27-7 (C)
1989—Browns, 51-0 (P)
    Steelers, 17-7 (C)
1990—Browns, 13-3 (C)
    Steelers, 35-0 (P)
1991—Browns, 17-14 (C)
    Steelers, 17-10 (P)

1992—Browns, 17-9 (C)
    Steelers, 23-13 (P)
1993—Browns, 28-23 (C)
    Steelers, 16-9 (P)
1994—Steelers, 17-10 (C)
    Steelers, 17-7 (P)
    *Steelers, 29-9 (P)
1995—Steelers, 20-3 (P)
    Steelers, 20-17 (C)
1999—Steelers, 43-0 (C)
    Browns, 16-15 (P)
2000—Browns, 23-20 (C)
    Steelers, 22-0 (P)
2001—Steelers, 15-12 (C) OT
    Steelers, 28-7 (P)
2002—Steelers, 16-13 (P) OT
    Steelers, 23-20 (C)
    **Steelers, 36-33 (P)
2003—Browns, 33-13 (P)
    Steelers, 13-6 (C)
2004—Steelers, 34-23 (P)
    Steelers, 24-10 (C)
2005—Steelers, 34-21 (P)
    Steelers, 41-0 (C)
2006—Steelers, 24-20 (C)
    Steelers, 27-7 (P)
2007—Steelers, 34-7 (C)
    Steelers, 31-28 (P)
(RS Pts.—Browns 2,235, Steelers 2,213)
(PS Pts.—Steelers 65, Browns 42)
*AFC Divisional Playoff
**AFC First-Round Playoff
CLEVELAND vs. *ST. LOUIS
RS: Series tied, 9-9
PS: Browns lead series, 2-1
1950—**Browns, 30-28 (C)
1951—Browns, 38-23 (LA)
    **Rams, 24-17 (LA)
1952—Browns, 37-7 (C)
1955—**Browns, 38-14 (LA)
1957—Browns, 45-31 (C)
1958—Browns, 30-27 (LA)
1963—Browns, 20-6 (C)
1965—Rams, 42-7 (LA)
1968—Rams, 24-6 (C)
1973—Rams, 30-17 (LA)
1977—Rams, 9-0 (C)
1978—Browns, 30-19 (C)
1981—Rams, 27-16 (LA)
1984—Rams, 20-17 (LA)
1987—Browns, 30-17 (C)
1990—Rams, 38-23 (C)
1993—Browns, 42-14 (LA)
1999—Rams, 34-3 (StL)
2003—Rams, 26-20 (C)
2007—Browns, 27-20 (StL)
(RS Pts.—Rams 414, Browns 408)
(PS Pts.—Browns 85, Rams 66)
*Franchise in Los Angeles prior to 1995
**NFL Championship
CLEVELAND vs. SAN DIEGO
RS: Chargers lead series, 13-7-1
1970—Chargers, 27-10 (C)
1972—Browns, 21-17 (SD)
1973—Tie, 16-16 (C)
1974—Chargers, 36-35 (SD)
1976—Browns, 21-17 (C)
1977—Chargers, 37-14 (SD)
1981—Chargers, 44-14 (C)
1982—Chargers, 30-13 (C)

1983—Browns, 30-24 (SD) OT
1985—Browns, 21-7 (SD)
1986—Browns, 47-17 (C)
1987—Chargers, 27-24 (SD) OT
1990—Chargers, 24-14 (C)
1991—Browns, 30-24 (SD) OT
1992—Chargers, 14-13 (C)
1995—Chargers, 31-13 (SD)
1999—Chargers, 23-10 (SD)
2001—Browns, 20-16 (C)
2003—Chargers, 26-20 (C)
2004—Chargers, 21-0 (C)
2006—Chargers, 32-25 (SD)
(RS Pts.—Chargers 510, Browns 411)
CLEVELAND vs. SAN FRANCISCO
RS: Browns lead series, 11-6
1950—Browns, 34-14 (C)
1951—49ers, 24-10 (SF)
1953—Browns, 23-21 (C)
1955—Browns, 38-3 (SF)
1959—49ers, 21-20 (C)
1962—Browns, 13-10 (SF)
1968—Browns, 33-21 (SF)
1970—49ers, 34-31 (SF)
1974—Browns, 7-0 (C)
1978—Browns, 24-7 (C)
1981—Browns, 15-12 (SF)
1984—49ers, 41-7 (C)
1987—49ers, 38-24 (SF)
1990—49ers, 20-17 (SF)
1993—Browns, 23-13 (C)
2003—Browns, 13-12 (SF)
2007—Browns, 20-7 (C)
(RS Pts.—Browns 352, 49ers 298)
CLEVELAND vs. SEATTLE
RS: Seahawks lead series, 11-5
1977—Seahawks, 20-19 (S)
1978—Seahawks, 47-24 (S)
1979—Seahawks, 29-24 (C)
1980—Browns, 27-3 (S)
1981—Seahawks, 42-21 (S)
1982—Browns, 21-7 (S)
1983—Seahawks, 24-9 (C)
1984—Seahawks, 33-0 (S)
1985—Seahawks, 31-13 (S)
1988—Seahawks, 16-10 (C)
1989—Browns, 17-7 (S)
1993—Seahawks, 22-5 (S)
1994—Browns, 35-9 (C)
2001—Seahawks, 9-6 (C)
2003—Seahawks, 34-7 (S)
2007—Browns, 33-30 (C) OT
(RS Pts.—Seahawks 363, Browns 271)
CLEVELAND vs. TAMPA BAY
RS: Browns lead series, 5-2
1976—Browns, 24-7 (TB)
1980—Browns, 34-27 (TB)
1983—Browns, 20-0 (C)
1989—Browns, 42-31 (TB)
1995—Browns, 22-6 (C)
2002—Buccaneers 17-3 (TB)
2006—Buccaneers, 22-7 (C)
(RS Pts.—Browns 152, Buccaneers 110)
CLEVELAND vs. *TENNESSEE
RS: Browns lead series, 33-26
PS: Titans lead series, 1-0
1970—Browns, 28-14 (C)
    Browns, 21-10 (H)
1971—Browns, 31-0 (C)
    Browns, 37-24 (H)

1972—Browns, 23-17 (H)
    Browns, 20-0 (C)
1973—Browns, 42-13 (C)
    Browns, 23-13 (H)
1974—Browns, 20-7 (H)
    Oilers, 28-24 (H)
1975—Oilers, 40-10 (C)
    Oilers, 21-10 (H)
1976—Browns, 21-7 (H)
    Browns, 13-10 (C)
1977—Browns, 24-23 (H)
    Oilers, 19-15 (C)
1978—Oilers, 16-13 (C)
    Oilers, 14-10 (H)
1979—Oilers, 31-10 (H)
    Browns, 14-7 (C)
1980—Oilers, 16-7 (C)
    Browns, 17-14 (H)
1981—Oilers, 9-3 (C)
    Oilers, 17-13 (H)
1982—Browns, 20-14 (H)
1983—Browns, 25-19 (C) OT
    Oilers, 34-27 (H)
1984—Browns, 27-10 (C)
    Browns, 27-20 (H)
1985—Browns, 21-6 (H)
    Browns, 28-21 (C)
1986—Browns, 23-20 (H)
    Browns, 13-10 (C) OT
1987—Oilers, 15-10 (C)
    Browns, 40-7 (H)
1988—Oilers, 24-17 (H)
    Browns, 28-23 (C)
    **Oilers, 24-23 (C)
1989—Browns, 28-17 (C)
    Browns, 24-20 (H)
1990—Oilers, 35-23 (C)
    Oilers, 58-14 (H)
1991—Oilers, 28-24 (H)
    Oilers, 17-14 (C)
1992—Browns, 24-14 (H)
    Oilers, 17-14 (C)
1993—Oilers, 27-20 (C)
    Oilers, 19-17 (H)
1994—Browns, 11-8 (H)
    Browns, 34-10 (C)
1995—Browns, 14-7 (H)
    Oilers, 37-10 (C)
1999—Titans, 26-9 (T)
    Titans, 33-21 (C)
2000—Titans, 24-10 (T)
    Titans, 24-0 (C)
2001—Titans, 31-15 (C)
    Browns, 41-38 (T)
2002—Browns, 31-28 (T) OT
2005—Browns, 20-14 (C)
(RS Pts.—Browns 1,173, Titans 1,125)
(PS Pts.—Titans 24, Browns 23)
*Franchise in Houston prior to 1997;
known as Oilers prior to 1999
**AFC First-Round Playoff
CLEVELAND vs. WASHINGTON
RS: Browns lead series, 33-9-1
1950—Browns, 20-14 (C)
    Browns, 45-21 (W)
1951—Browns, 45-0 (C)
1952—Browns, 19-15 (C)
    Browns, 48-24 (W)
1953—Browns, 30-14 (W)
    Browns, 27-3 (C)

1954—Browns, 62-3 (C)
　　　Browns, 34-14 (W)
1955—Redskins, 27-17 (C)
　　　Browns, 24-14 (W)
1956—Redskins, 20-9 (W)
　　　Redskins, 20-17 (C)
1957—Browns, 21-17 (C)
　　　Tie, 30-30 (W)
1958—Browns, 20-10 (W)
　　　Browns, 21-14 (C)
1959—Browns, 34-7 (C)
　　　Browns, 31-17 (W)
1960—Browns, 31-10 (W)
　　　Browns, 27-16 (C)
1961—Browns, 31-7 (C)
　　　Browns, 17-6 (W)
1962—Redskins, 17-16 (C)
　　　Redskins, 17-9 (W)
1963—Browns, 37-14 (C)
　　　Browns, 27-20 (W)
1964—Browns, 27-13 (W)
　　　Browns, 34-24 (C)
1965—Browns, 17-7 (W)
　　　Browns, 24-16 (C)
1966—Browns, 38-14 (W)
　　　Browns, 14-3 (C)
1967—Browns, 42-37 (C)
1968—Browns, 24-21 (W)
1969—Browns, 27-23 (C)
1971—Browns, 20-13 (W)
1975—Redskins, 23-7 (C)
1979—Redskins, 13-9 (C)
1985—Redskins, 14-7 (C)
1988—Browns, 17-13 (W)
1991—Redskins, 42-17 (W)
2004—Browns, 17-13 (C)
(RS Pts.—Browns 1,090, Redskins 680)

DALLAS vs. ARIZONA
RS: Cowboys lead series, 55-27-1
PS: Cardinals lead series, 1-0;
See Arizona vs. Dallas
DALLAS vs. ATLANTA
RS: Cowboys lead series, 13-8
PS: Cowboys lead series, 2-0;
See Atlanta vs. Dallas
DALLAS vs. BALTIMORE
RS: Ravens lead series, 2-0;
See Baltimore vs. Dallas
DALLAS vs. BUFFALO
RS: Cowboys lead series, 5-3
PS: Cowboys lead series, 2-0;
See Buffalo vs. Dallas
DALLAS vs. CAROLINA
RS: Cowboys lead series, 7-1
PS: Panthers lead series, 2-0;
See Carolina vs. Dallas
DALLAS vs. CHICAGO
RS: Cowboys lead series, 11-8
PS: Cowboys lead series, 2-0;
See Chicago vs. Dallas
DALLAS vs. CINCINNATI
RS: Cowboys lead series, 5-4;
See Cincinnati vs. Dallas
DALLAS vs. CLEVELAND
RS: Browns lead series, 15-10
PS: Browns lead series, 2-1;
See Cleveland vs. Dallas
DALLAS vs. DENVER
RS: Broncos lead series, 5-4

PS: Cowboys lead series, 1-0
1973—Cowboys, 22-10 (Den)
1977—Cowboys, 14-6 (Dal)
　　　*Cowboys, 27-10 (New Orleans)
1980—Broncos, 41-20 (Den)
1986—Broncos, 29-14 (Den)
1992—Cowboys, 31-27 (Den)
1995—Cowboys, 31-21 (Dal)
1998—Broncos, 42-23 (Den)
2001—Broncos, 26-24 (Dal)
2005—Broncos, 24-21 (Dal) OT
(RS Pts.—Broncos 226, Cowboys 200)
(PS Pts.—Cowboys 27, Broncos 10)
*Super Bowl XII
DALLAS vs. DETROIT
RS: Cowboys lead series, 11-9
PS: Series tied, 1-1
1960—Lions, 23-14 (Det)
1963—Cowboys, 17-14 (Dal)
1968—Cowboys, 59-13 (Dal)
1970—*Cowboys, 5-0 (Dal)
1972—Cowboys, 28-24 (Dal)
1975—Cowboys, 36-10 (Det)
1977—Cowboys, 37-0 (Dal)
1981—Lions, 27-24 (Det)
1985—Lions, 26-21 (Dal)
1986—Cowboys, 31-7 (Det)
1987—Lions, 27-17 (Det)
1991—Lions, 34-10 (Det)
　　　*Lions, 38-6 (Det)
1992—Cowboys, 37-3 (Det)
1994—Lions, 20-17 (Dal) OT
2001—Lions, 15-10 (Det)
2002—Lions, 9-7 (Det)
2003—Cowboys, 38-7 (Det)
2004—Cowboys, 31-21 (Dal)
2005—Cowboys, 20-7 (Dal)
2006—Lions, 39-31 (Dal)
2007—Cowboys, 28-27 (Det)
(RS Pts.—Cowboys 513, Lions 353)
(PS Pts.—Lions 38, Cowboys 11)
*NFC Divisional Playoff
DALLAS vs. GREEN BAY
RS: Cowboys lead series, 11-10
PS: Cowboys lead series, 4-2
1960—Packers, 41-7 (GB)
1964—Packers, 45-21 (D)
1965—Packers, 13-3 (Mil)
1966—*Packers, 34-27 (D)
1967—*Packers, 21-17 (GB)
1968—Packers, 28-17 (D)
1970—Cowboys, 16-3 (D)
1972—Packers, 16-13 (Mil)
1975—Packers, 19-17 (D)
1978—Cowboys, 42-14 (Mil)
1980—Cowboys, 28-7 (Mil)
1982—**Cowboys, 37-26 (D)
1984—Cowboys, 20-6 (D)
1989—Packers, 31-13 (GB)
　　　Packers, 20-10 (D)
1991—Cowboys, 20-17 (Mil)
1993—Cowboys, 36-14 (D)
　　　***Cowboys, 27-17 (D)
1994—Cowboys, 42-31 (D)
　　　***Cowboys, 35-9 (D)
1995—Cowboys, 34-24 (D)
　　　****Cowboys, 38-27 (D)
1996—Cowboys, 21-6 (D)
1997—Packers, 45-17 (GB)
1999—Cowboys, 27-13 (D)

2004—Packers, 41-20 (GB)
2007—Cowboys, 37-27 (D)
(RS Pts.—Cowboys 461, Packers 461)
(PS Pts.—Cowboys 181, Packers 134)
*NFL Championship
**NFC Second-Round Playoff
***NFC Divisional Playoff
****NFC Championship
DALLAS vs. HOUSTON
RS: Series tied, 1-1
2002—Texans, 19-10 (H)
2006—Cowboys, 34-6 (D)
(RS Pts.—Cowboys 44, Texans 25)
DALLAS vs. *INDIANAPOLIS
RS: Cowboys lead series, 8-5
PS: Colts lead series, 1-0
1960—Colts, 45-7 (D)
1967—Colts, 23-17 (B)
1969—Cowboys, 27-10 (D)
1970—**Colts, 16-13 (Miami)
1972—Cowboys, 21-0 (B)
1976—Cowboys, 30-27 (D)
1978—Cowboys, 38-0 (D)
1981—Cowboys, 37-13 (B)
1984—Cowboys, 22-3 (D)
1993—Cowboys, 27-3 (I)
1996—Colts, 25-24 (D)
1999—Colts, 34-24 (I)
2002—Colts, 20-3 (I)
2006—Cowboys, 21-14 (D)
(RS Pts.—Cowboys 298, Colts 217)
(PS Pts.—Colts 16, Cowboys 13)
*Franchise in Baltimore prior to 1984
**Super Bowl V
DALLAS vs. JACKSONVILLE
RS: Series tied, 2-2
1997—Cowboys, 26-22 (D)
2000—Jaguars, 23-17 (D) OT
2002—Cowboys, 21-19 (D)
2006—Jaguars, 24-17 (J)
(RS Pts.—Jaguars 88, Cowboys 81)
DALLAS vs. KANSAS CITY
RS: Cowboys lead series, 5-3
1970—Cowboys, 27-16 (KC)
1975—Chiefs, 34-31 (D)
1983—Cowboys, 41-21 (D)
1989—Chiefs, 36-28 (KC)
1992—Cowboys, 17-10 (D)
1995—Cowboys, 24-12 (D)
1998—Chiefs, 20-17 (KC)
2005—Cowboys, 31-28 (D)
(RS Pts.—Cowboys 216, Chiefs 177)
DALLAS vs. MIAMI
RS: Dolphins lead series, 7-4
PS: Cowboys lead series, 1-0
1971—*Cowboys, 24-3 (New Orleans)
1973—Dolphins, 14-7 (D)
1978—Dolphins, 23-16 (M)
1981—Cowboys, 28-27 (D)
1984—Dolphins, 28-21 (M)
1987—Dolphins, 20-14 (D)
1989—Dolphins, 17-14 (D)
1993—Dolphins, 16-14 (D)
1996—Cowboys, 29-10 (M)
1999—Cowboys, 20-0 (D)
2003—Dolphins, 40-21 (D)
2007—Cowboys, 37-20 (M)
(RS Pts.—Cowboys 221, Dolphins 215)
(PS Pts.—Cowboys 24, Dolphins 3)
*Super Bowl VI

DALLAS vs. MINNESOTA
RS: Series tied, 10-10
PS: Cowboys lead series, 4-2
1961—Cowboys, 21-7 (D)
    Cowboys, 28-0 (M)
1966—Cowboys, 28-17 (D)
1968—Cowboys, 20-7 (M)
1970—Vikings, 54-13 (M)
1971—*Cowboys, 20-12 (M)
1973—**Vikings, 27-10 (D)
1974—Vikings, 23-21 (D)
1975—*Cowboys, 17-14 (M)
1977—Cowboys, 16-10 (D) OT
    **Cowboys, 23-6 (D)
1978—Vikings, 21-10 (D)
1979—Cowboys, 36-20 (M)
1982—Vikings, 31-27 (M)
1983—Cowboys, 37-24 (M)
1987—Vikings, 44-38 (D) OT
1988—Vikings, 43-3 (D)
1993—Cowboys, 37-20 (M)
1995—Cowboys, 23-17 (M) OT
1996—***Cowboys, 40-15 (D)
1998—Vikings, 46-36 (D)
1999—Vikings, 27-17 (M)
    ***Vikings, 27-10 (M)
2000—Vikings, 27-15 (D)
2004—Vikings, 35-17 (M)
2007—Cowboys, 24-14 (D)
(RS Pts.—Vikings 487, Cowboys 467)
(PS Pts.—Cowboys 120, Vikings 101)
*NFC Divisional Playoff
**NFC Championship
***NFC First-Round Playoff
DALLAS vs. NEW ENGLAND
RS: Cowboys lead series, 7-3
1971—Cowboys, 44-21 (D)
1975—Cowboys, 34-31 (NE)
1978—Cowboys, 17-10 (D)
1981—Cowboys, 35-21 (NE)
1984—Cowboys, 20-17 (D)
1987—Cowboys, 23-17 (NE) OT
1996—Cowboys, 12-6 (D)
1999—Patriots, 13-6 (NE)
2003—Patriots, 12-0 (NE)
2007—Patriots, 48-27 (D)
(RS Pts.—Cowboys 218, Patriots 196)
DALLAS vs. NEW ORLEANS
RS: Cowboys lead series, 14-8
1967—Cowboys, 14-10 (D)
    Cowboys, 27-10 (NO)
1968—Cowboys, 17-3 (NO)
1969—Cowboys, 21-17 (NO)
    Cowboys, 33-17 (D)
1971—Saints, 24-14 (NO)
1973—Cowboys, 40-3 (D)
1976—Cowboys, 24-6 (NO)
1978—Cowboys, 27-7 (D)
1982—Cowboys, 21-7 (D)
1983—Cowboys, 21-20 (D)
1984—Cowboys, 30-27 (D) OT
1988—Saints, 20-17 (NO)
1989—Saints, 28-0 (NO)
1990—Cowboys, 17-13 (D)
1991—Cowboys, 23-14 (D)
1994—Cowboys, 24-16 (NO)
1998—Saints, 22-3 (NO)
1999—Saints, 31-24 (NO)
2003—Saints, 13-7 (NO)
2004—Saints, 27-13 (D)

2006—Saints, 42-17 (D)
(RS Pts.—Cowboys 434, Saints 377)
DALLAS vs. N.Y. GIANTS
RS: Cowboys lead series, 54-35-2
PS: Giants lead series, 1-0
1960—Tie, 31-31 (NY)
1961—Giants, 31-10 (D)
    Cowboys, 17-16 (NY)
1962—Giants, 41-10 (D)
    Giants, 41-31 (NY)
1963—Giants, 37-21 (NY)
    Giants, 34-27 (D)
1964—Tie, 13-13 (NY)
    Cowboys, 31-21 (NY)
1965—Cowboys, 31-2 (D)
    Cowboys, 38-20 (NY)
1966—Cowboys, 52-7 (D)
    Cowboys, 17-7 (NY)
1967—Cowboys, 38-24 (D)
1968—Giants, 27-21 (D)
    Cowboys, 28-10 (NY)
1969—Cowboys, 25-3 (D)
1970—Cowboys, 28-10 (D)
    Giants, 23-20 (NY)
1971—Cowboys, 20-13 (D)
    Cowboys, 42-14 (NY)
1972—Cowboys, 23-14 (NY)
    Giants, 23-3 (D)
1973—Cowboys, 45-28 (D)
    Cowboys, 23-10 (New Haven)
1974—Giants, 14-6 (D)
    Cowboys, 21-7 (New Haven)
1975—Cowboys, 13-7 (NY)
    Cowboys, 14-3 (D)
1976—Cowboys, 24-14 (NY)
    Cowboys, 9-3 (D)
1977—Cowboys, 41-21 (D)
    Cowboys, 24-10 (NY)
1978—Cowboys, 34-24 (NY)
    Cowboys, 24-3 (D)
1979—Cowboys, 16-14 (NY)
    Cowboys, 28-7 (D)
1980—Cowboys, 24-3 (D)
    Giants, 38-35 (NY)
1981—Cowboys, 18-10 (D)
    Giants, 13-10 (NY) OT
1983—Cowboys, 28-13 (D)
    Cowboys, 38-20 (NY)
1984—Giants, 28-7 (NY)
    Giants, 19-7 (D)
1985—Cowboys, 30-29 (NY)
    Cowboys, 28-21 (D)
1986—Cowboys, 31-28 (D)
    Giants, 17-14 (NY)
1987—Cowboys, 16-14 (NY)
    Cowboys, 33-24 (D)
1988—Giants, 12-10 (D)
    Giants, 29-21 (NY)
1989—Giants, 30-13 (D)
    Giants, 15-0 (NY)
1990—Giants, 28-7 (D)
    Giants, 31-17 (NY)
1991—Cowboys, 21-16 (D)
    Giants, 22-9 (NY)
1992—Cowboys, 34-28 (NY)
    Cowboys, 30-3 (D)
1993—Cowboys, 31-9 (D)
    Cowboys, 16-13 (NY) OT
1994—Cowboys, 38-10 (D)
    Giants, 15-10 (NY)

1995—Cowboys, 35-0 (NY)
    Cowboys, 21-20 (D)
1996—Cowboys, 27-0 (D)
    Giants, 20-6 (NY)
1997—Giants, 20-17 (NY)
    Giants, 20-7 (D)
1998—Cowboys, 31-7 (NY)
    Cowboys, 16-6 (D)
1999—Giants, 13-10 (NY)
    Cowboys, 26-18 (D)
2000—Giants, 19-14 (NY)
    Giants, 17-13 (D)
2001—Giants, 27-24 (NY) OT
    Cowboys, 20-13 (D)
2002—Giants, 21-17 (D)
    Giants, 37-7 (NY)
2003—Cowboys, 35-32 (NY) OT
    Cowboys, 19-3 (D)
2004—Giants, 26-10 (D)
    Giants, 28-24 (NY)
2005—Cowboys, 16-13 (D) OT
    Giants, 17-10 (NY)
2006—Giants, 36-22 (D)
    Cowboys, 23-20 (NY)
2007—Cowboys, 45-35 (D)
    Cowboys, 31-20 (NY)
    *Giants, 21-17 (D)
(RS Pts.—Cowboys 2,001, Giants 1,653)
(PS Pts.—Giants 21, Cowboys 17)
*NFC Divisional Playoff
DALLAS vs. N.Y. JETS
RS: Cowboys lead series, 7-2
1971—Cowboys, 52-10 (D)
1975—Cowboys, 31-21 (NY)
1978—Cowboys, 30-7 (NY)
1987—Cowboys, 38-24 (NY)
1990—Jets, 24-9 (NY)
1993—Cowboys, 28-7 (NY)
1999—Jets, 22-21 (D)
2003—Cowboys, 17-6 (NY)
2007—Cowboys, 34-3 (D)
(RS Pts.—Cowboys 260, Jets 124)
DALLAS vs. *OAKLAND
RS: Raiders lead series, 6-3
1974—Raiders, 27-23 (O)
1980—Cowboys, 19-13 (O)
1983—Raiders, 40-38 (D)
1986—Raiders, 17-13 (D)
1992—Cowboys, 28-13 (LA)
1995—Cowboys, 34-21 (O)
1998—Raiders, 13-12 (O)
2001—Raiders, 28-21 (O)
2005—Raiders, 19-13 (O)
(RS Pts.—Cowboys 201, Raiders 191)
*Franchise in Los Angeles from 1982-1994
DALLAS vs. PHILADELPHIA
RS: Cowboys lead series, 52-42
PS: Cowboys lead series, 2-1
1960—Eagles, 27-25 (D)
1961—Eagles, 43-7 (D)
    Eagles, 35-13 (P)
1962—Cowboys, 41-19 (D)
    Eagles, 28-14 (P)
1963—Eagles, 24-21 (P)
    Cowboys, 27-20 (D)
1964—Eagles, 17-14 (D)
    Eagles, 24-14 (P)
1965—Eagles, 35-24 (D)
    Cowboys, 21-19 (P)
1966—Cowboys, 56-7 (D)

Eagles, 24-23 (P)
1967—Eagles, 21-14 (P)
Cowboys, 38-17 (D)
1968—Cowboys, 45-13 (P)
Cowboys, 34-14 (D)
1969—Cowboys, 38-7 (P)
Cowboys, 49-14 (D)
1970—Cowboys, 17-7 (P)
Cowboys, 21-17 (D)
1971—Cowboys, 42-7 (P)
Cowboys, 20-7 (D)
1972—Cowboys, 28-6 (D)
Cowboys, 28-7 (P)
1973—Eagles, 30-16 (P)
Cowboys, 31-10 (D)
1974—Eagles, 13-10 (P)
Cowboys, 31-24 (D)
1975—Cowboys, 20-17 (P)
Cowboys, 27-17 (D)
1976—Cowboys, 27-7 (D)
Cowboys, 26-7 (P)
1977—Cowboys, 16-10 (P)
Cowboys, 24-14 (D)
1978—Cowboys, 14-7 (D)
Cowboys, 31-13 (P)
1979—Eagles, 31-21 (D)
Cowboys, 24-17 (P)
1980—Eagles, 17-10 (P)
Cowboys, 35-27 (D)
*Eagles, 20-7 (P)
1981—Cowboys, 17-14 (P)
Cowboys, 21-10 (D)
1982—Eagles, 24-20 (P)
1983—Cowboys, 37-7 (D)
Cowboys, 27-20 (P)
1984—Cowboys, 23-17 (D)
Cowboys, 26-10 (P)
1985—Eagles, 16-14 (P)
Cowboys, 34-17 (D)
1986—Cowboys, 17-14 (P)
Eagles, 23-21 (D)
1987—Cowboys, 41-22 (D)
Eagles, 37-20 (P)
1988—Eagles, 24-23 (P)
Eagles, 23-7 (D)
1989—Eagles, 27-0 (D)
Eagles, 20-10 (P)
1990—Eagles, 21-20 (P)
Eagles, 17-3 (P)
1991—Eagles, 24-0 (D)
Cowboys, 25-13 (P)
1992—Eagles, 31-7 (P)
Cowboys, 20-10 (D)
**Cowboys, 34-10 (D)
1993—Cowboys, 23-10 (P)
Cowboys, 23-17 (D)
1994—Cowboys, 24-13 (D)
Cowboys, 31-19 (P)
1995—Cowboys, 34-12 (D)
Eagles, 20-17 (P)
**Cowboys, 30-11 (D)
1996—Cowboys, 23-19 (P)
Eagles, 31-21 (D)
1997—Cowboys, 21-20 (D)
Eagles, 13-12 (P)
1998—Cowboys, 34-0 (P)
Cowboys, 13-9 (D)
1999—Eagles, 13-10 (P)
Cowboys, 20-10 (D)
2000—Eagles, 41-14 (D)

Eagles, 16-13 (P) OT
2001—Eagles, 40-18 (P)
Eagles, 36-3 (D)
2002—Eagles, 44-13 (P)
Eagles, 27-3 (D)
2003—Cowboys, 23-21 (D)
Eagles, 36-10 (P)
2004—Eagles, 49-21 (D)
Eagles, 12-7 (P)
2005—Cowboys, 33-10 (D)
Cowboys, 21-20 (P)
2006—Eagles, 38-24 (P)
Eagles, 23-7 (D)
2007—Cowboys, 38-17 (P)
Eagles, 10-6 (D)
(RS Pts.—Cowboys 2,030, Eagles 1,807)
(PS Pts.—Cowboys 71, Eagles 41)
*NFC Championship
**NFC Divisional Playoff

DALLAS vs. PITTSBURGH
RS: Cowboys lead series, 14-12
PS: Steelers lead series, 2-1
1960—Steelers, 35-28 (D)
1961—Cowboys, 27-24 (D)
Steelers, 37-7 (P)
1962—Steelers, 30-28 (D)
Cowboys, 42-27 (P)
1963—Steelers, 27-21 (P)
Steelers, 24-19 (D)
1964—Steelers, 23-17 (P)
Cowboys, 17-14 (D)
1965—Steelers, 22-13 (P)
Cowboys, 24-17 (D)
1966—Cowboys, 52-21 (D)
Cowboys, 20-7 (P)
1967—Cowboys, 24-21 (P)
1968—Cowboys, 28-7 (D)
1969—Cowboys, 10-7 (P)
1972—Cowboys, 17-13 (D)
1975—*Steelers, 21-17 (Miami)
1977—Steelers, 28-13 (P)
1978—**Steelers, 35-31 (Miami)
1979—Steelers, 14-3 (P)
1982—Steelers, 36-28 (D)
1985—Cowboys, 27-13 (D)
1988—Steelers, 24-21 (P)
1991—Cowboys, 20-10 (D)
1994—Cowboys, 26-9 (P)
1995—***Cowboys, 27-17 (Tempe)
1997—Cowboys, 37-7 (P)
2004—Steelers, 24-20 (D)
(RS Pts.—Cowboys 589, Steelers 521)
(PS Pts.—Cowboys 75, Steelers 73)
*Super Bowl X
**Super Bowl XIII
***Super Bowl XXX

DALLAS vs. *ST. LOUIS
RS: Series tied, 10-10
PS: Series tied, 4-4
1960—Rams, 38-13 (D)
1962—Cowboys, 27-17 (LA)
1967—Rams, 35-13 (D)
1969—Rams, 24-23 (LA)
1971—Cowboys, 28-21 (D)
1973—Rams, 37-31 (LA)
**Cowboys, 27-16 (D)
1975—Cowboys, 18-7 (D)
***Cowboys, 37-7 (LA)
1976—**Rams, 14-12 (D)
1978—Rams, 27-14 (LA)

***Cowboys, 28-0 (LA)
1979—Cowboys, 30-6 (D)
**Rams, 21-19 (D)
1980—Rams, 38-14 (LA)
****Cowboys, 34-13 (D)
1981—Cowboys, 29-17 (D)
1983—****Rams, 24-17 (D)
1984—Cowboys, 20-13 (LA)
1985—**Rams, 20-0 (LA)
1986—Rams, 29-10 (LA)
1987—Cowboys, 29-21 (LA)
1989—Rams, 35-31 (D)
1990—Cowboys, 24-21 (LA)
1992—Rams, 27-23 (D)
2002—Cowboys, 13-10 (StL)
2005—Rams, 20-10 (D)
2007—Cowboys, 35-7 (D)
(RS Pts.—Rams 450, Cowboys 435)
(PS Pts.—Cowboys 174, Rams 115)
*Franchise in Los Angeles prior to 1995
**NFC Divisional Playoff
***NFC Championship
****NFC First-Round Playoff

DALLAS vs. SAN DIEGO
RS: Cowboys lead series, 6-2
1972—Cowboys, 34-28 (SD)
1980—Cowboys, 42-31 (D)
1983—Chargers, 24-23 (SD)
1986—Cowboys, 24-21 (SD)
1990—Cowboys, 17-14 (D)
1995—Cowboys, 23-9 (SD)
2001—Chargers, 32-21 (D)
2005—Cowboys, 28-24 (SD)
(RS Pts.—Cowboys 212, Chargers 183)

DALLAS vs. SAN FRANCISCO
RS: 49ers lead series, 14-9-1
PS: Cowboys lead series, 5-2
1960—Cowboys, 26-14 (D)
1963—49ers, 31-24 (SF)
1965—Cowboys, 39-31 (D)
1967—49ers, 24-16 (SF)
1969—Tie, 24-24 (D)
1970—*Cowboys, 17-10 (SF)
1971—*Cowboys, 14-3 (SF)
1972—49ers, 31-10 (D)
**Cowboys, 30-28 (SF)
1974—Cowboys, 20-14 (D)
1977—Cowboys, 42-35 (SF)
1979—Cowboys, 21-13 (SF)
1980—Cowboys, 59-14 (D)
1981—49ers, 45-14 (SF)
*49ers, 28-27 (SF)
1983—49ers, 42-17 (SF)
1985—49ers, 31-16 (SF)
1989—49ers, 31-14 (D)
1990—49ers, 24-6 (D)
1992—*Cowboys, 30-20 (SF)
1993—Cowboys, 26-17 (D)
*Cowboys, 38-21 (D)
1994—49ers, 21-14 (SF)
*49ers, 38-28 (SF)
1995—49ers, 38-20 (D)
1996—Cowboys, 20-17 (SF) OT
1997—49ers, 17-10 (SF)
2000—49ers, 41-24 (D)
2001—Cowboys, 27-21 (D)
2002—49ers, 31-27 (D)
2005—Cowboys, 34-31 (SF)
(RS Pts.—49ers 650, Cowboys 538)
(PS Pts.—Cowboys 184, 49ers 148)

*NFC Championship
**NFC Divisional Playoff
DALLAS vs. SEATTLE
RS: Cowboys lead series, 6-4
PS: Seahawks lead series, 1-0
1976—Cowboys, 28-13 (S)
1980—Cowboys, 51-7 (D)
1983—Cowboys, 35-10 (S)
1986—Seahawks, 31-14 (D)
1992—Cowboys, 27-0 (D)
1998—Cowboys, 30-22 (D)
2001—Seahawks, 29-3 (S)
2002—Cowboys, 17-14 (D)
2004—Cowboys, 43-39 (S)
2005—Seahawks, 13-10 (S)
2006—*Seahawks, 21-20 (S)
(RS Pts.—Cowboys 255, Seahawks 181)
(PS Pts.—Seahawks 21, Cowboys 20)
*NFC First-Round Playoff
DALLAS vs. TAMPA BAY
RS: Cowboys lead series, 7-3
PS: Cowboys lead series, 2-0
1977—Cowboys, 23-7 (D)
1980—Cowboys, 28-17 (D)
1981—*Cowboys, 38-0 (D)
1982—Cowboys, 14-9 (D)
      **Cowboys, 30-17 (D)
1983—Cowboys, 27-24 (D) OT
1990—Cowboys, 14-10 (D)
      Cowboys, 17-13 (TB)
2000—Buccaneers, 27-7 (TB)
2001—Buccaneers, 10-6 (D)
2003—Buccaneers, 16-0 (TB)
2006—Cowboys, 38-10 (D)
(RS Pts.—Cowboys 174, Buccaneers 143)
(PS Pts.—Cowboys 68, Buccaneers 17)
*NFC Divisional Playoff
**NFC First-Round Playoff
DALLAS vs. *TENNESSEE
RS: Cowboys lead series, 7-5
1970—Cowboys, 52-10 (D)
1974—Cowboys, 10-0 (H)
1979—Oilers, 30-24 (D)
1982—Cowboys, 37-7 (H)
1985—Cowboys, 17-10 (H)
1988—Oilers, 25-17 (D)
1991—Oilers, 26-23 (H) OT
1994—Cowboys, 20-17 (D)
1997—Oilers, 27-14 (D)
2000—Titans, 31-0 (T)
2002—Cowboys, 21-13 (D)
2006—Cowboys, 45-14 (T)
(RS Pts.—Cowboys 280, Titans 210)
*Franchise in Houston prior to 1997;
known as Oilers prior to 1999
DALLAS vs. WASHINGTON
RS: Cowboys lead series, 56-36-2
PS: Redskins lead series, 2-0
1960—Redskins, 26-14 (W)
1961—Tie, 28-28 (D)
      Redskins, 34-24 (W)
1962—Tie, 35-35 (D)
      Cowboys, 38-10 (W)
1963—Redskins, 21-17 (W)
      Cowboys, 35-20 (D)
1964—Cowboys, 24-18 (D)
      Redskins, 28-16 (W)
1965—Cowboys, 27-7 (D)
      Redskins, 34-31 (W)
1966—Cowboys, 31-30 (W)

Redskins, 34-31 (D)
1967—Cowboys, 17-14 (W)
      Redskins, 27-20 (D)
1968—Cowboys, 44-24 (W)
      Cowboys, 29-20 (D)
1969—Cowboys, 41-28 (W)
      Cowboys, 20-10 (D)
1970—Cowboys, 45-21 (W)
      Cowboys, 34-0 (D)
1971—Redskins, 20-16 (D)
      Cowboys, 13-0 (W)
1972—Redskins, 24-20 (W)
      Cowboys, 34-24 (D)
      *Redskins, 26-3 (W)
1973—Redskins, 14-7 (W)
      Cowboys, 27-7 (D)
1974—Redskins, 28-21 (W)
      Cowboys, 24-23 (D)
1975—Redskins, 30-24 (W) OT
      Cowboys, 31-10 (D)
1976—Cowboys, 20-7 (W)
      Redskins, 27-14 (D)
1977—Cowboys, 34-16 (D)
      Cowboys, 14-7 (W)
1978—Redskins, 9-5 (W)
      Cowboys, 37-10 (D)
1979—Redskins, 34-20 (W)
      Cowboys, 35-34 (D)
1980—Cowboys, 17-3 (W)
      Cowboys, 14-10 (D)
1981—Cowboys, 26-10 (W)
      Cowboys, 24-10 (D)
1982—Cowboys, 24-10 (W)
      *Redskins, 31-17 (W)
1983—Cowboys, 31-30 (W)
      Redskins, 31-10 (D)
1984—Redskins, 34-14 (W)
      Redskins, 30-28 (D)
1985—Cowboys, 44-14 (D)
      Cowboys, 13-7 (W)
1986—Cowboys, 30-6 (D)
      Redskins, 41-14 (W)
1987—Redskins, 13-7 (D)
      Redskins, 24-20 (W)
1988—Redskins, 35-17 (D)
      Cowboys, 24-17 (W)
1989—Redskins, 30-7 (D)
      Cowboys, 13-3 (W)
1990—Redskins, 19-15 (W)
      Cowboys, 27-17 (D)
1991—Redskins, 33-31 (D)
      Cowboys, 24-21 (W)
1992—Cowboys, 23-10 (D)
      Redskins, 20-17 (W)
1993—Redskins, 35-16 (D)
      Cowboys, 38-3 (D)
1994—Cowboys, 34-7 (W)
      Cowboys, 31-7 (D)
1995—Redskins, 27-23 (W)
      Redskins, 24-17 (D)
1996—Cowboys, 21-10 (D)
      Redskins, 37-10 (D)
1997—Redskins, 21-16 (W)
      Cowboys, 17-14 (D)
1998—Cowboys, 31-10 (W)
      Cowboys, 23-7 (D)
1999—Cowboys, 41-35 (W) OT
      Cowboys, 38-20 (D)
2000—Cowboys, 27-21 (W)
      Cowboys, 32-13 (D)

2001—Cowboys, 9-7 (D)
      Cowboys, 20-14 (W)
2002—Cowboys, 27-20 (D)
      Redskins, 20-14 (W)
2003—Cowboys, 21-14 (D)
      Cowboys, 27-0 (W)
2004—Cowboys, 21-18 (W)
      Cowboys, 13-10 (D)
2005—Redskins, 14-13 (D)
      Redskins, 35-7 (W)
2006—Cowboys, 27-10 (D)
      Redskins, 22-19 (W)
2007—Cowboys, 28-23 (D)
      Redskins, 27-6 (W)
(RS Pts.—Cowboys 2,178, Redskins 1,796)
(PS Pts.—Redskins 57, Cowboys 20)
*NFC Championship

DENVER vs. ARIZONA
RS: Broncos lead series, 7-0-1;
See Arizona vs. Denver
DENVER vs. ATLANTA
RS: Broncos lead series, 7-4
PS: Broncos lead series, 1-0;
See Atlanta vs. Denver
DENVER vs. BALTIMORE
RS: Series tied, 3-3
PS: Ravens lead series, 1-0;
See Baltimore vs. Denver
DENVER vs. BUFFALO
RS: Bills lead series, 17-15-1
PS: Bills lead series, 1-0;
See Buffalo vs. Denver
DENVER vs. CAROLINA
RS: Broncos lead series, 2-0;
See Carolina vs. Denver
DENVER vs. CHICAGO
RS: Bears lead series, 7-6;
See Chicago vs. Denver
DENVER vs. CINCINNATI
RS: Broncos lead series, 16-8;
See Cincinnati vs. Denver
DENVER vs. CLEVELAND
RS: Broncos lead series, 16-5
PS: Broncos lead series, 3-0;
See Cleveland vs. Denver
DENVER vs. DALLAS
RS: Broncos lead series, 6-4
PS: Cowboys lead series, 1-0;
See Dallas vs. Denver
DENVER vs. DETROIT
RS: Broncos lead series, 6-4
1971—Lions, 24-20 (Den)
1974—Broncos, 31-27 (Det)
1978—Lions, 17-14 (Det)
1981—Broncos, 27-21 (Den)
1984—Broncos, 28-7 (Det)
1987—Broncos, 34-0 (Den)
1990—Lions, 40-27 (Det)
1999—Broncos, 17-7 (Det)
2003—Broncos, 20-16 (Den)
2007—Lions, 44-7 (Det)
(RS Pts.—Broncos 225, Lions 203)
DENVER vs. GREEN BAY
RS: Series tied, 5-5-1
PS: Broncos lead series, 1-0
1971—Packers, 34-13 (Mil)
1975—Broncos, 23-13 (D)
1978—Broncos, 16-3 (D)
1984—Broncos, 17-14 (D)

1987—Tie, 17-17 (Mil) OT
1990—Broncos, 22-13 (D)
1993—Packers, 30-27 (GB)
1996—Packers, 41-6 (GB)
1997—*Broncos, 31-24 (San Diego)
1999—Broncos, 31-10 (D)
2003—Packers, 31-3 (GB)
2007—Packers, 19-13 (D) OT
(RS Pts.—Packers 225, Broncos 188)
(PS Pts.—Broncos 31, Packers 24)
*Super Bowl XXXII
DENVER vs. HOUSTON
RS: Series tied, 1-1
2004—Broncos, 31-13 (D)
2007—Texans, 31-13 (H)
(RS Pts.—Broncos 44, Texans 44)
DENVER vs. *INDIANAPOLIS
RS: Broncos lead series, 11-6
PS: Colts lead series, 2-0
1974—Broncos, 17-6 (B)
1977—Broncos, 27-13 (D)
1978—Colts, 7-6 (B)
1981—Broncos, 28-10 (D)
1983—Broncos, 17-10 (B)
        Broncos, 21-19 (D)
1985—Broncos, 15-10 (I)
1988—Colts, 55-23 (I)
1989—Broncos, 14-3 (D)
1990—Broncos, 27-17 (I)
1993—Broncos, 35-13 (D)
2001—Colts, 29-10 (I)
2002—Colts, 23-20 (D) OT
2003—Broncos, 31-17 (I)
        **Colts, 41-10 (I)
2004—Broncos, 33-14 (D)
        **Colts, 49-24 (I)
2006—Colts, 34-31 (D)
2007—Colts, 38-20 (I)
(RS Pts.—Broncos 375, Colts 318)
(PS Pts.—Colts 90, Broncos 34)
*Franchise in Baltimore prior to 1984
**AFC First-Round Playoff
DENVER vs. JACKSONVILLE
RS: Series tied, 3-3
PS: Series tied, 1-1
1995—Broncos, 31-23 (D)
1996—*Jaguars, 30-27 (D)
1997—**Broncos, 42-17 (D)
1998—Broncos, 37-24 (D)
1999—Jaguars, 27-24 (J)
2004—Jaguars, 7-6 (J)
2005—Broncos, 20-7 (J)
2007—Jaguars, 23-14 (D)
(RS Pts.—Broncos 132, Jaguars 111)
(PS Pts.—Broncos 69, Jaguars 47)
*AFC Divisional Playoff
**AFC First-Round Playoff
DENVER vs. *KANSAS CITY
RS: Chiefs lead series, 52-43
PS: Broncos lead series, 1-0
1960—Texans, 17-14 (D)
        Texans, 34-7 (Dal)
1961—Texans, 19-12 (D)
        Texans, 49-21 (Dal)
1962—Texans, 24-3 (D)
        Texans, 17-10 (Dal)
1963—Chiefs, 59-7 (D)
        Chiefs, 52-21 (KC)
1964—Broncos, 33-27 (D)
        Chiefs, 49-39 (KC)

1965—Chiefs, 31-23 (D)
        Chiefs, 45-35 (KC)
1966—Chiefs, 37-10 (KC)
        Chiefs, 56-10 (D)
1967—Chiefs, 52-9 (KC)
        Chiefs, 38-24 (D)
1968—Chiefs, 34-2 (KC)
        Chiefs, 30-7 (D)
1969—Chiefs, 26-13 (D)
        Chiefs, 31-17 (KC)
1970—Broncos, 26-13 (D)
        Chiefs, 16-0 (KC)
1971—Chiefs, 16-3 (D)
        Chiefs, 28-10 (KC)
1972—Chiefs, 45-24 (D)
        Chiefs, 24-21 (KC)
1973—Chiefs, 16-14 (KC)
        Broncos, 14-10 (D)
1974—Broncos, 17-14 (KC)
        Chiefs, 42-34 (D)
1975—Broncos, 37-33 (D)
        Chiefs, 26-13 (KC)
1976—Chiefs, 35-26 (KC)
        Broncos, 17-16 (D)
1977—Broncos, 23-7 (D)
        Broncos, 14-7 (KC)
1978—Broncos, 23-17 (KC) OT
        Broncos, 24-3 (D)
1979—Broncos, 24-10 (KC)
        Broncos, 20-3 (D)
1980—Chiefs, 23-17 (D)
        Chiefs, 31-14 (KC)
1981—Chiefs, 28-14 (KC)
        Broncos, 16-13 (D)
1982—Chiefs, 37-16 (D)
1983—Broncos, 27-24 (D)
        Chiefs, 48-17 (KC)
1984—Broncos, 21-0 (D)
        Chiefs, 16-13 (KC)
1985—Broncos, 30-10 (KC)
        Broncos, 14-13 (D)
1986—Broncos, 38-17 (D)
        Chiefs, 37-10 (KC)
1987—Broncos, 26-17 (KC)
        Broncos, 20-17 (D)
1988—Chiefs, 20-13 (KC)
        Broncos, 17-11 (D)
1989—Broncos, 34-20 (D)
        Broncos, 16-13 (KC)
1990—Broncos, 24-23 (D)
        Chiefs, 31-20 (KC)
1991—Broncos, 19-16 (D)
        Broncos, 24-20 (KC)
1992—Broncos, 20-19 (D)
        Chiefs, 42-20 (KC)
1993—Chiefs, 15-7 (KC)
        Broncos, 27-21 (D)
1994—Chiefs, 31-28 (D)
        Broncos, 20-17 (KC) OT
1995—Chiefs, 21-7 (D)
        Chiefs, 20-17 (KC)
1996—Chiefs, 17-14 (KC)
        Broncos, 34-7 (D)
1997—Broncos, 19-3 (D)
        Chiefs, 24-22 (KC)
        **Broncos, 14-10 (KC)
1998—Broncos, 30-7 (KC)
        Broncos, 35-31 (D)
1999—Chiefs, 26-10 (KC)
        Chiefs, 16-10 (D)

2000—Chiefs, 23-22 (D)
        Chiefs, 20-7 (KC)
2001—Broncos, 20-6 (D)
        Chiefs, 26-23 (KC) OT
2002—Chiefs, 37-34 (KC) OT
        Broncos, 31-24 (D)
2003—Chiefs, 24-23 (KC)
        Broncos, 45-27 (D)
2004—Broncos, 34-24 (D)
        Chiefs, 45-17 (KC)
2005—Broncos, 30-10 (D)
        Chiefs, 31-27 (KC)
2006—Broncos, 9-6 (D) OT
        Chiefs, 19-10 (KC)
2007—Broncos, 27-11 (KC)
        Broncos, 41-7 (D)
(RS Pts.—Chiefs 2,238, Broncos 1,893)
(PS Pts.—Broncos 14, Chiefs 10)
*Franchise in Dallas prior to 1963 and
known as Texans
**AFC Divisional Playoff
DENVER vs. MIAMI
RS: Dolphins lead series, 10-3-1
PS: Broncos lead series, 1-0
1966—Dolphins, 24-7 (M)
        Broncos, 17-7 (D)
1967—Dolphins, 35-21 (M)
1968—Broncos, 21-14 (D)
1969—Dolphins, 27-24 (M)
1971—Tie, 10-10 (D)
1975—Dolphins, 14-13 (M)
1985—Dolphins, 30-26 (D)
1998—Dolphins, 31-21 (M)
        *Broncos, 38-3 (D)
1999—Dolphins, 38-21 (D)
2001—Dolphins, 21-10 (M)
2002—Dolphins, 24-22 (D)
2004—Broncos, 20-17 (D)
2005—Dolphins, 34-10 (M)
(RS Pts.—Dolphins 326, Broncos 243)
(PS Pts.—Broncos 38, Dolphins 3)
*AFC Divisional Playoff
DENVER vs. MINNESOTA
RS: Vikings lead series, 7-5
1972—Vikings, 23-20 (D)
1978—Vikings, 12-9 (M) OT
1981—Broncos, 19-17 (D)
1984—Broncos, 42-21 (D)
1987—Vikings, 34-27 (M)
1990—Vikings, 27-22 (M)
1991—Broncos, 13-6 (D)
1993—Vikings, 26-23 (D)
1996—Broncos, 21-17 (M)
1999—Vikings, 23-20 (D)
2003—Vikings, 28-20 (M)
2007—Broncos, 22-19 (D) OT
(RS Pts.—Broncos 258, Vikings 253)
DENVER vs. *NEW ENGLAND
RS: Broncos lead series, 24-15
PS: Broncos lead series, 2-0
1960—Broncos, 13-10 (B)
        Broncos, 31-24 (D)
1961—Patriots, 45-17 (B)
        Patriots, 28-24 (D)
1962—Patriots, 41-16 (B)
        Patriots, 33-29 (D)
1963—Broncos, 14-10 (D)
        Patriots, 40-21 (B)
1964—Patriots, 39-10 (D)
        Patriots, 12-7 (B)

1965—Broncos, 27-10 (B)
Patriots, 28-20 (D)
1966—Patriots, 24-10 (D)
Broncos, 17-10 (B)
1967—Broncos, 26-21 (D)
1968—Patriots, 20-17 (D)
Broncos, 35-14 (B)
1969—Broncos, 35-7 (D)
1972—Broncos, 45-21 (D)
1976—Patriots, 38-14 (NE)
1979—Broncos, 45-10 (D)
1980—Patriots, 23-14 (NE)
1984—Broncos, 26-19 (D)
1986—Broncos, 27-20 (D)
**Broncos, 22-17 (D)
1987—Broncos, 31-20 (D)
1988—Broncos, 21-10 (D)
1991—Broncos, 9-6 (NE)
Broncos, 20-3 (D)
1995—Broncos, 37-3 (NE)
1996—Broncos, 34-8 (NE)
1997—Broncos, 34-13 (D)
1998—Broncos, 27-21 (D)
1999—Patriots, 24-23 (NE)
2000—Patriots, 28-19 (D)
2001—Broncos, 31-20 (D)
2002—Broncos, 24-16 (NE)
2003—Patriots, 30-26 (D)
2005—Broncos, 28-20 (D)
**Broncos, 27-13 (D)
2006—Broncos, 17-7 (NE)
(RS Pts.—Broncos 921, Patriots 776)
(PS Pts.—Broncos 49, Patriots 30)
*Franchise in Boston prior to 1971
**AFC Divisional Playoff
DENVER vs. NEW ORLEANS
RS: Broncos lead series, 6-2
1970—Broncos, 31-6 (NO)
1974—Broncos, 33-17 (D)
1979—Broncos, 10-3 (D)
1985—Broncos, 34-23 (D)
1988—Saints, 42-0 (NO)
1994—Saints, 30-28 (D)
2000—Broncos, 38-23 (NO)
2004—Broncos, 34-13 (NO)
(RS Pts.—Broncos 208, Saints 157)
DENVER vs. N.Y. GIANTS
RS: Giants lead series, 5-4
PS: Giants lead series, 1-0
1972—Giants, 29-17 (NY)
1976—Broncos, 14-13 (D)
1980—Broncos, 14-9 (NY)
1986—Giants, 19-16 (NY)
*Giants, 39-20 (Pasadena)
1989—Giants, 14-7 (D)
1992—Broncos, 27-13 (D)
1998—Giants, 20-16 (NY)
2001—Broncos, 31-20 (D)
2005—Giants, 24-23 (NY)
(RS Pts.—Broncos 165, Giants 161)
(PS Pts.—Giants 39, Broncos 20)
*Super Bowl XXI
DENVER vs. *N.Y. JETS
RS: Broncos lead series, 15-14-1
PS: Broncos lead series, 1-0
1960—Titans, 28-24 (NY)
Titans, 30-27 (D)
1961—Titans, 35-28 (NY)
Broncos, 27-10 (D)

1962—Broncos, 32-10 (NY)
Titans, 46-45 (D)
1963—Tie, 35-35 (NY)
Jets, 14-9 (D)
1964—Jets, 30-6 (NY)
Broncos, 20-16 (D)
1965—Broncos, 16-13 (D)
Jets, 45-10 (NY)
1966—Jets, 16-7 (D)
1967—Jets, 38-24 (D)
Broncos, 33-24 (NY)
1968—Broncos, 21-13 (NY)
1969—Broncos, 21-19 (D)
1973—Broncos, 40-28 (NY)
1976—Broncos, 46-3 (D)
1978—Jets, 31-28 (D)
1980—Broncos, 31-24 (D)
1986—Jets, 22-10 (NY)
1992—Broncos, 27-16 (D)
1993—Broncos, 26-20 (NY)
1994—Jets, 25-22 (NY) OT
1996—Broncos, 31-6 (D)
1998—**Broncos, 23-10 (D)
1999—Jets, 21-13 (D)
2000—Broncos, 30-23 (NY)
2002—Jets, 19-13 (NY)
2005—Broncos, 27-0 (D)
(RS Pts.—Broncos 729, Jets 660)
(PS Pts.—Broncos 23, Jets 10)
*Jets known as Titans prior to 1963
**AFC Championship
DENVER vs. *OAKLAND
RS: Raiders lead series, 54-39-2
PS: Series tied, 1-1
1960—Broncos, 31-14 (D)
Raiders, 48-10 (O)
1961—Raiders, 33-19 (O)
Broncos, 27-24 (D)
1962—Broncos, 44-7 (D)
Broncos, 23-6 (O)
1963—Raiders, 26-10 (D)
Raiders, 35-31 (O)
1964—Raiders, 40-7 (O)
Tie, 20-20 (D)
1965—Raiders, 28-20 (D)
Raiders, 24-13 (O)
1966—Raiders, 17-3 (D)
Raiders, 28-10 (O)
1967—Raiders, 51-0 (O)
Raiders, 21-17 (D)
1968—Raiders, 43-7 (D)
Raiders, 33-27 (O)
1969—Raiders, 24-14 (D)
Raiders, 41-10 (O)
1970—Raiders, 35-23 (O)
Raiders, 24-19 (D)
1971—Raiders, 27-16 (O)
Raiders, 21-13 (D)
1972—Broncos, 30-23 (O)
Raiders, 37-20 (D)
1973—Tie, 23-23 (D)
Raiders, 21-17 (O)
1974—Raiders, 28-17 (D)
Broncos, 20-17 (O)
1975—Raiders, 42-17 (D)
Raiders, 17-10 (O)
1976—Raiders, 17-10 (O)
Raiders, 19-6 (O)
1977—Broncos, 30-7 (O)
Raiders, 24-14 (D)

**Broncos, 20-17 (D)
1978—Broncos, 14-6 (D)
Broncos, 21-6 (O)
1979—Raiders, 27-3 (O)
Raiders, 14-10 (D)
1980—Raiders, 9-3 (O)
Raiders, 24-21 (D)
1981—Broncos, 9-7 (D)
Broncos, 17-0 (O)
1982—Raiders, 27-10 (LA)
1983—Raiders, 22-7 (D)
Raiders, 22-20 (LA)
1984—Raiders, 16-13 (D)
Broncos, 22-19 (LA) OT
1985—Raiders, 31-28 (LA) OT
Raiders, 17-14 (D) OT
1986—Broncos, 38-36 (D)
Broncos, 21-10 (LA)
1987—Broncos, 30-14 (D)
Broncos, 23-17 (LA)
1988—Raiders, 30-27 (D)
Raiders, 21-20 (LA)
1989—Broncos, 31-21 (D)
Raiders, 16-13 (LA) OT
1990—Raiders, 14-9 (LA)
Raiders, 23-20 (D)
1991—Raiders, 16-13 (LA)
Raiders, 17-16 (D)
1992—Broncos, 17-13 (D)
Raiders, 24-0 (LA)
1993—Raiders, 23-20 (D)
Raiders, 33-30 (LA) OT
***Raiders, 42-24 (LA)
1994—Raiders, 48-16 (D)
Raiders, 23-13 (LA)
1995—Broncos, 27-0 (D)
Broncos, 31-28 (O)
1996—Raiders, 22-21 (O)
Broncos, 24-19 (D)
1997—Raiders, 28-25 (O)
Broncos, 31-3 (D)
1998—Broncos, 34-17 (O)
Broncos, 40-14 (D)
1999—Broncos, 16-13 (O)
Broncos, 27-21 (D) OT
2000—Broncos, 33-24 (O)
Broncos, 27-24 (D)
2001—Raiders, 38-28 (O)
Broncos, 23-17 (D)
2002—Raiders, 34-10 (D)
Raiders, 28-16 (O)
2003—Raiders, 31-10 (D)
Broncos, 22-8 (O)
2004—Broncos, 31-3 (O)
Raiders, 25-24 (D)
2005—Broncos, 31-17 (O)
Broncos, 22-3 (D)
2006—Broncos, 13-3 (D)
Broncos, 17-13 (O)
2007—Broncos, 23-20 (D) OT
Raiders, 34-20 (O)
(RS Pts.—Raiders 2,053, Broncos 1,848)
(PS Pts.—Raiders 59, Broncos 44)
*Franchise in Los Angeles from 1982-1994
**AFC Championship
***AFC First-Round Playoff
DENVER vs. PHILADELPHIA
RS: Eagles lead series, 6-4
1971—Eagles, 17-16 (P)
1975—Broncos, 25-10 (D)

1980—Eagles, 27-6 (P)
1983—Eagles, 13-10 (D)
1986—Broncos, 33-7 (P)
1989—Eagles, 28-24 (D)
1992—Eagles, 30-0 (P)
1995—Eagles, 31-13 (P)
1998—Broncos, 41-16 (D)
2005—Broncos, 49-21 (D)
(RS Pts.—Broncos 217, Eagles 200)
DENVER vs. PITTSBURGH
RS: Broncos lead series, 13-6-1
PS: Series tied, 3-3
1970—Broncos, 16-13 (D)
1971—Broncos, 22-10 (D)
1973—Broncos, 23-13 (P)
1974—Tie, 35-35 (D) OT
1975—Steelers, 20-9 (P)
1977—Broncos, 21-7 (D)
　　　*Broncos, 34-21 (D)
1978—Steelers, 21-17 (D)
　　　*Steelers, 33-10 (P)
1979—Steelers, 42-7 (P)
1983—Broncos, 14-10 (P)
1984—*Steelers, 24-17 (D)
1985—Broncos, 31-23 (P)
1986—Broncos, 21-10 (D)
1988—Steelers, 39-21 (P)
1989—Broncos, 34-7 (D)
　　　*Broncos, 24-23 (D)
1990—Steelers, 34-17 (D)
1991—Broncos, 20-13 (D)
1993—Broncos, 37-13 (D)
1997—Steelers, 35-24 (P)
　　　**Broncos, 24-21 (P)
2003—Broncos, 17-14 (D)
2005—**Steelers, 34-17 (D)
2006—Broncos, 31-20 (P)
2007—Broncos, 31-28 (D)
(RS Pts.—Broncos 448, Steelers 407)
(PS Pts.—Steelers 156, Broncos 126)
*AFC Divisional Playoff
**AFC Championship
DENVER vs. *ST. LOUIS
RS: Rams lead series, 6-5
1972—Broncos, 16-10 (LA)
1974—Rams, 17-10 (D)
1979—Rams, 13-9 (D)
1982—Broncos, 27-24 (LA)
1985—Rams, 20-16 (LA)
1988—Broncos, 35-24 (D)
1994—Rams, 27-21 (LA)
1997—Broncos, 35-14 (D)
2000—Rams, 41-36 (StL)
2002—Broncos, 23-16 (D)
2006—Broncos, 18-10 (StL)
(RS Pts.—Broncos 238, Rams 224)
*Franchise in Los Angeles prior to 1995
DENVER vs. *SAN DIEGO
RS: Broncos lead series, 52-43-1
1960—Chargers, 23-19 (D)
　　　Chargers, 41-33 (LA)
1961—Chargers, 37-0 (SD)
　　　Chargers, 19-16 (D)
1962—Broncos, 30-21 (D)
　　　Broncos, 23-20 (SD)
1963—Broncos, 50-34 (D)
　　　Chargers, 58-20 (SD)
1964—Chargers, 42-14 (SD)
　　　Chargers, 31-20 (D)
1965—Chargers, 34-31 (SD)

Chargers, 33-21 (D)
1966—Chargers, 24-17 (SD)
　　　Broncos, 20-17 (D)
1967—Chargers, 38-21 (SD)
　　　Chargers, 24-20 (D)
1968—Chargers, 55-24 (SD)
　　　Chargers, 47-23 (D)
1969—Broncos, 13-0 (SD)
　　　Chargers, 45-24 (SD)
1970—Chargers, 24-21 (SD)
　　　Tie, 17-17 (D)
1971—Broncos, 20-16 (D)
　　　Chargers, 45-17 (SD)
1972—Chargers, 37-14 (SD)
　　　Broncos, 38-13 (D)
1973—Broncos, 30-19 (D)
　　　Broncos, 42-28 (SD)
1974—Broncos, 27-7 (D)
　　　Chargers, 17-0 (SD)
1975—Broncos, 27-17 (SD)
　　　Broncos, 13-10 (D) OT
1976—Broncos, 26-0 (D)
　　　Broncos, 17-0 (SD)
1977—Broncos, 17-14 (SD)
　　　Broncos, 17-9 (D)
1978—Broncos, 27-14 (D)
　　　Chargers, 23-0 (SD)
1979—Broncos, 7-0 (D)
　　　Chargers, 17-7 (SD)
1980—Chargers, 30-13 (D)
　　　Broncos, 20-13 (SD)
1981—Broncos, 42-24 (D)
　　　Chargers, 34-17 (SD)
1982—Chargers, 23-3 (D)
　　　Chargers, 30-20 (SD)
1983—Broncos, 14-6 (D)
　　　Chargers, 31-7 (SD)
1984—Broncos, 16-13 (SD)
　　　Broncos, 16-13 (D)
1985—Chargers, 30-10 (SD)
　　　Broncos, 30-24 (D) OT
1986—Broncos, 31-14 (SD)
　　　Chargers, 9-3 (D)
1987—Broncos, 31-17 (SD)
　　　Broncos, 24-0 (D)
1988—Broncos, 34-3 (D)
　　　Broncos, 12-0 (SD)
1989—Broncos, 16-10 (D)
　　　Chargers, 19-16 (SD)
1990—Chargers, 19-7 (SD)
　　　Broncos, 20-10 (D)
1991—Broncos, 27-19 (D)
　　　Broncos, 17-14 (SD)
1992—Broncos, 21-13 (D)
　　　Chargers, 24-21 (SD)
1993—Broncos, 34-17 (D)
　　　Chargers, 13-10 (SD)
1994—Chargers, 37-34 (D)
　　　Broncos, 20-15 (SD)
1995—Chargers, 17-6 (SD)
　　　Broncos, 30-27 (D)
1996—Broncos, 28-17 (D)
　　　Chargers, 16-10 (SD)
1997—Broncos, 38-28 (SD)
　　　Broncos, 38-3 (D)
1998—Broncos, 27-10 (D)
　　　Broncos, 31-16 (SD)
1999—Broncos, 33-17 (SD)
　　　Chargers, 12-6 (D)
2000—Broncos, 21-7 (SD)

Broncos, 38-37 (D)
2001—Chargers, 27-10 (SD)
　　　Broncos, 26-16 (D)
2002—Broncos, 26-9 (D)
　　　Chargers, 30-27 (SD) OT
2003—Broncos, 37-13 (SD)
　　　Broncos, 37-8 (D)
2004—Broncos, 23-13 (D)
　　　Chargers, 20-17 (SD)
2005—Broncos, 20-17 (D)
　　　Broncos, 23-7 (SD)
2006—Chargers, 35-27 (D)
　　　Chargers, 48-20 (SD)
2007—Chargers, 41-3 (D)
　　　Chargers, 23-3 (SD)
(RS Pts.—Broncos 2,014, Chargers 2,010)
*Franchise in Los Angeles prior to 1961
DENVER vs. SAN FRANCISCO
RS: Broncos lead series, 6-5
PS: 49ers lead series, 1-0
1970—49ers, 19-14 (SF)
1973—49ers, 36-34 (D)
1979—Broncos, 38-28 (SF)
1982—Broncos, 24-21 (D)
1985—Broncos, 17-16 (D)
1988—Broncos, 16-13 (SF) OT
1989—*49ers, 55-10 (New Orleans)
1994—49ers, 42-19 (SF)
1997—49ers, 34-17 (SF)
2000—Broncos, 38-9 (D)
2002—Broncos, 24-14 (SF)
2006—49ers, 26-23 (D) OT
(RS Pts.—Broncos 264, 49ers 258)
(PS Pts.—49ers 55, Broncos 10)
*Super Bowl XXIV
DENVER vs. SEATTLE
RS: Broncos lead series, 33-18
PS: Seahawks lead series, 1-0
1977—Broncos, 24-13 (S)
1978—Broncos, 28-7 (D)
　　　Broncos, 20-17 (S) OT
1979—Broncos, 37-34 (D)
　　　Seahawks, 28-23 (S)
1980—Broncos, 36-20 (D)
　　　Broncos, 25-17 (S)
1981—Seahawks, 13-10 (S)
　　　Broncos, 23-13 (D)
1982—Seahawks, 17-10 (D)
　　　Seahawks, 13-11 (S)
1983—Seahawks, 27-19 (S)
　　　Broncos, 38-27 (D)
　　　*Seahawks, 31-7 (S)
1984—Seahawks, 27-24 (D)
　　　Broncos, 31-14 (S)
1985—Broncos, 13-10 (D) OT
　　　Broncos, 27-24 (S)
1986—Broncos, 20-13 (D)
　　　Seahawks, 41-16 (S)
1987—Broncos, 40-17 (D)
　　　Seahawks, 28-21 (S)
1988—Seahawks, 21-14 (D)
　　　Seahawks, 42-14 (S)
1989—Broncos, 24-21 (S) OT
　　　Broncos, 41-14 (D)
1990—Broncos, 34-31 (D) OT
　　　Seahawks, 17-12 (S)
1991—Broncos, 16-10 (D)
　　　Seahawks, 13-10 (S)
1992—Seahawks, 16-13 (S) OT
　　　Broncos, 10-6 (D)

1993—Broncos, 28-17 (D)
 Broncos, 17-9 (S)
1994—Broncos, 16-9 (S)
 Broncos, 17-10 (D)
1995—Seahawks, 27-10 (S)
 Seahawks, 31-27 (D)
1996—Broncos, 30-20 (S)
 Broncos, 34-7 (D)
1997—Broncos, 35-14 (S)
 Broncos, 30-27 (D)
1998—Broncos, 21-16 (S)
 Broncos, 28-21 (D)
1999—Seahawks, 20-17 (S)
 Broncos, 36-30 (D) OT
2000—Broncos, 38-31 (S)
 Broncos, 31-24 (D)
2001—Seahawks, 34-21 (S)
 Broncos, 20-7 (D)
2002—Broncos, 31-9 (S)
2006—Seahawks, 23-20 (D)
(RS Pts.—Broncos 1,191, Seahawks 997)
(PS Pts.—Seahawks 31, Broncos 7)
*AFC First-Round Playoff
DENVER vs. TAMPA BAY
RS: Broncos lead series, 4-2
1976—Broncos, 48-13 (D)
1981—Broncos, 24-7 (TB)
1993—Buccaneers, 17-10 (D)
1996—Broncos, 27-23 (D)
1999—Buccaneers, 13-10 (TB)
2004—Broncos, 16-13 (TB)
(RS Pts.—Broncos 135, Buccaneers 86)
DENVER vs. *TENNESSEE
RS: Titans lead series, 20-13-1
PS: Broncos lead series, 2-1
1960—Oilers, 45-25 (D)
 Oilers, 20-10 (H)
1961—Oilers, 55-14 (D)
 Oilers, 45-14 (H)
1962—Broncos, 20-10 (D)
 Oilers, 34-17 (H)
1963—Oilers, 20-14 (H)
 Oilers, 33-24 (D)
1964—Oilers, 38-17 (D)
 Oilers, 34-15 (H)
1965—Oilers, 28-17 (D)
 Broncos, 31-21 (H)
1966—Oilers, 45-7 (H)
 Broncos, 40-38 (D)
1967—Oilers, 10-6 (H)
 Oilers, 20-18 (D)
1968—Oilers, 38-17 (H)
1969—Oilers, 24-21 (H)
 Tie, 20-20 (D)
1970—Oilers, 31-21 (H)
1972—Broncos, 30-17 (D)
1973—Broncos, 48-20 (H)
1974—Broncos, 37-14 (D)
1976—Oilers, 17-3 (H)
1977—Broncos, 24-14 (H)
1979—**Oilers, 13-7 (H)
1980—Oilers, 20-16 (D)
1983—Broncos, 26-14 (H)
1985—Broncos, 31-20 (H)
1987—Oilers, 40-10 (D)
 ***Broncos, 34-10 (D)
1991—Oilers, 42-14 (H)
 ***Broncos, 26-24 (D)
1992—Broncos, 27-21 (D)
1995—Oilers, 42-33 (H)

2004—Broncos, 37-16 (T)
2007—Broncos, 34-20 (D)
(RS Pts.—Titans 915, Broncos 749)
(PS Pts.—Broncos 67, Titans 47)
*Franchise in Houston prior to 1997;
known as the Oilers prior to 1999
**AFC First-Round Playoff
***AFC Divisional Playoff
DENVER vs. WASHINGTON
RS: Broncos lead series, 6-4
PS: Redskins lead series, 1-0
1970—Redskins, 19-3 (D)
1974—Redskins, 30-3 (W)
1980—Broncos, 20-17 (D)
1986—Broncos, 31-30 (D)
1987—*Redskins, 42-10 (San Diego)
1989—Broncos, 14-10 (W)
1992—Redskins, 34-3 (W)
1995—Broncos, 38-31 (D)
1998—Broncos, 38-16 (W)
2001—Redskins, 17-10 (D)
2005—Broncos, 21-19 (D)
(RS Pts.—Redskins 223, Broncos 181)
(PS Pts.—Redskins 42, Broncos 10)
*Super Bowl XXII

DETROIT vs. ARIZONA
RS: Lions lead series, 31-23-5;
See Arizona vs. Detroit
DETROIT vs. ATLANTA
RS: Lions lead series, 23-9;
See Atlanta vs. Detroit
DETROIT vs. BALTIMORE
RS: Series tied, 1-1;
See Baltimore vs. Detroit
DETROIT vs. BUFFALO
RS: Lions lead series, 4-3-1;
See Buffalo vs. Detroit
DETROIT vs. CAROLINA
RS: Panthers lead series, 3-1;
See Carolina vs. Detroit
DETROIT vs. CHICAGO
RS: Bears lead series, 87-64-5;
See Chicago vs. Detroit
DETROIT vs. CINCINNATI
RS: Bengals lead series, 6-3;
See Cincinnati vs. Detroit
DETROIT vs. CLEVELAND
RS: Lions lead series, 13-4
PS: Lions lead series, 3-1;
See Cleveland vs. Detroit
DETROIT vs. DALLAS
RS: Cowboys lead series, 11-9
PS: Series tied, 1-1;
See Dallas vs. Detroit
DETROIT vs. DENVER
RS: Broncos lead series, 6-4;
See Denver vs. Detroit
DETROIT vs. GREEN BAY
RS: Packers lead series, 84-64-7
PS: Packers lead series, 2-0
1930—Packers, 47-13 (GB)
 Tie, 6-6 (P)
1932—Packers, 15-10 (GB)
 Spartans, 19-0 (P)
1933—Packers, 17-0 (GB)
 Spartans, 7-0 (P)
1934—Lions, 3-0 (GB)
 Packers, 3-0 (D)
1935—Packers, 13-9 (Mil)

 Packers, 31-7 (GB)
 Lions, 20-10 (D)
1936—Packers, 20-18 (GB)
 Packers, 26-17 (D)
1937—Packers, 26-6 (GB)
 Packers, 14-13 (D)
1938—Lions, 17-7 (GB)
 Packers, 28-7 (D)
1939—Packers, 26-7 (GB)
 Packers, 12-7 (D)
1940—Lions, 23-14 (GB)
 Packers, 50-7 (D)
1941—Packers, 23-0 (GB)
 Packers, 24-7 (D)
1942—Packers, 38-7 (Mil)
 Packers, 28-7 (D)
1943—Packers, 35-14 (GB)
 Packers, 27-6 (D)
1944—Packers, 27-6 (Mil)
 Packers, 14-0 (D)
1945—Packers, 57-21 (Mil)
 Lions, 14-3 (D)
1946—Packers, 10-7 (Mil)
 Packers, 9-0 (D)
1947—Packers, 34-17 (GB)
 Packers, 35-14 (D)
1948—Packers, 33-21 (GB)
 Lions, 24-20 (D)
1949—Packers, 16-14 (Mil)
 Lions, 21-7 (D)
1950—Lions, 45-7 (GB)
 Lions, 24-21 (D)
1951—Lions, 24-17 (GB)
 Lions, 52-35 (D)
1952—Lions, 52-17 (GB)
 Lions, 48-24 (D)
1953—Lions, 14-7 (GB)
 Lions, 34-15 (D)
1954—Lions, 21-17 (GB)
 Lions, 28-24 (D)
1955—Packers, 20-17 (GB)
 Lions, 24-10 (D)
1956—Lions, 20-16 (GB)
 Packers, 24-20 (D)
1957—Lions, 24-14 (GB)
 Lions, 18-6 (D)
1958—Tie, 13-13 (GB)
 Lions, 24-14 (D)
1959—Packers, 28-10 (GB)
 Packers, 24-17 (D)
1960—Packers, 28-9 (GB)
 Lions, 23-10 (D)
1961—Lions, 17-13 (Mil)
 Packers, 17-9 (D)
1962—Packers, 9-7 (GB)
 Lions, 26-14 (D)
1963—Packers, 31-10 (Mil)
 Tie, 13-13 (D)
1964—Lions, 14-10 (D)
 Packers, 30-7 (GB)
1965—Packers, 31-21 (D)
 Lions, 12-7 (GB)
1966—Packers, 23-14 (GB)
 Packers, 31-7 (D)
1967—Tie, 17-17 (GB)
 Packers, 27-17 (D)
1968—Lions, 23-17 (GB)
 Tie, 14-14 (D)
1969—Packers, 28-17 (D)
 Lions, 16-10 (GB)

1970—Lions, 40-0 (GB)
    Lions, 20-0 (D)
1971—Lions, 31-28 (D)
    Tie, 14-14 (Mil)
1972—Packers, 24-23 (D)
    Packers, 33-7 (GB)
1973—Tie, 13-13 (GB)
    Lions, 34-0 (D)
1974—Packers, 21-19 (Mil)
    Lions, 19-17 (D)
1975—Lions, 30-16 (Mil)
    Lions, 13-10 (D)
1976—Packers, 24-14 (GB)
    Lions, 27-6 (D)
1977—Lions, 10-6 (D)
    Packers, 10-9 (GB)
1978—Packers, 13-7 (D)
    Packers, 35-14 (Mil)
1979—Packers, 24-16 (Mil)
    Packers, 18-13 (D)
1980—Lions, 29-7 (Mil)
    Lions, 24-3 (D)
1981—Lions, 31-27 (D)
    Packers, 31-17 (GB)
1982—Lions, 30-10 (GB)
    Lions, 27-24 (D)
1983—Lions, 38-14 (D)
    Lions, 23-20 (Mil) OT
1984—Packers, 41-9 (GB)
    Lions, 31-28 (D)
1985—Packers, 43-10 (GB)
    Packers, 26-23 (D)
1986—Lions, 21-14 (GB)
    Packers, 44-40 (D)
1987—Lions, 19-16 (GB) OT
    Packers, 34-33 (D)
1988—Lions, 19-9 (Mil)
    Lions, 30-14 (D)
1989—Packers, 23-20 (Mil) OT
    Lions, 31-22 (D)
1990—Packers, 24-21 (D)
    Lions, 24-17 (GB)
1991—Lions, 23-14 (D)
    Lions, 21-17 (GB)
1992—Packers, 27-13 (D)
    Packers, 38-10 (Mil)
1993—Packers, 26-17 (Mil)
    Lions, 30-20 (D)
    **Packers, 28-24 (D)
1994—Packers, 38-30 (Mil)
    Lions, 34-31 (D)
    **Packers, 16-12 (GB)
1995—Packers, 30-21 (GB)
    Lions, 24-16 (D)
1996—Packers, 28-18 (GB)
    Packers, 31-3 (D)
1997—Lions, 26-15 (D)
    Packers, 20-10 (GB)
1998—Packers, 38-19 (GB)
    Lions, 27-20 (D)
1999—Lions, 23-15 (D)
    Packers, 26-17 (GB)
2000—Lions, 31-24 (D)
    Packers, 26-13 (GB)
2001—Packers, 28-6 (GB)
    Packers, 29-27 (D)
2002—Packers, 37-31 (D)
    Packers, 40-14 (GB)
2003—Packers, 31-6 (GB)
    Lions, 22-14 (D)

2004—Packers, 38-10 (D)
    Packers, 16-13 (GB)
2005—Lions, 17-3 (D)
    Packers, 16-13 (GB) OT
2006—Packers, 31-24 (D)
    Packers, 17-9 (GB)
2007—Packers, 37-26 (D)
    Packers, 34-13 (GB)
(RS Pts.—Packers 3,216, Lions 2,798)
(PS Pts.—Packers 44, Lions 36)
*Franchise in Portsmouth prior to 1934
and known as the Spartans
**NFC First-Round Playoff
DETROIT vs. HOUSTON
RS: Lions lead series, 1-0
2004—Lions, 28-16 (D)
(RS Pts.—Lions 28, Texans 16)
DETROIT vs. *INDIANAPOLIS
RS: Colts lead series, 19-18-2
1953—Lions, 27-17 (B)
    Lions, 17-7 (D)
1954—Lions, 35-0 (D)
    Lions, 27-3 (B)
1955—Colts, 28-13 (B)
    Lions, 24-14 (D)
1956—Lions, 31-14 (B)
    Lions, 27-3 (D)
1957—Colts, 34-14 (B)
    Lions, 31-27 (D)
1958—Colts, 28-15 (B)
    Colts, 40-14 (D)
1959—Colts, 21-9 (B)
    Colts, 31-24 (D)
1960—Lions, 30-17 (D)
    Lions, 20-15 (B)
1961—Lions, 16-15 (B)
    Colts, 17-14 (D)
1962—Lions, 29-20 (B)
    Lions, 21-14 (D)
1963—Colts, 25-21 (D)
    Colts, 24-21 (B)
1964—Colts, 34-0 (D)
    Lions, 31-14 (B)
1965—Colts, 31-7 (B)
    Tie, 24-24 (D)
1966—Colts, 45-14 (B)
    Lions, 20-14 (D)
1967—Colts, 41-7 (B)
1968—Colts, 27-10 (D)
1969—Tie, 17-17 (B)
1973—Colts, 29-27 (D)
1977—Lions, 13-10 (B)
1980—Colts, 10-9 (D)
1985—Colts, 14-6 (I)
1991—Lions, 33-24 (I)
1997—Lions, 32-10 (I)
2000—Colts, 30-18 (I)
2004—Colts, 41-9 (D)
(RS Pts.—Colts 829, Lions 757)
*Franchise in Baltimore prior to 1984
DETROIT vs. JACKSONVILLE
RS: Jaguars lead series, 2-1
1995—Lions, 44-0 (D)
1998—Jaguars, 37-22 (J)
2004—Jaguars, 23-17 (J) OT
(RS Pts.—Lions 83, Jaguars 60)
DETROIT vs. KANSAS CITY
RS: Chiefs lead series, 7-4
1971—Lions, 32-21 (D)
1975—Chiefs, 24-21 (KC) OT

1980—Chiefs, 20-17 (KC)
1981—Lions, 27-10 (D)
1987—Chiefs, 27-20 (D)
1988—Lions, 7-6 (KC)
1990—Chiefs, 43-24 (KC)
1996—Chiefs, 28-24 (KC)
1999—Chiefs, 31-21 (KC)
2003—Chiefs, 45-17 (KC)
2007—Lions, 25-20 (D)
(RS Pts.—Chiefs 275, Lions 235)
DETROIT vs. MIAMI
RS: Dolphins lead series, 7-2
1973—Dolphins, 34-7 (M)
1979—Dolphins, 28-10 (D)
1985—Lions, 31-21 (D)
1991—Lions, 17-13 (D)
1994—Dolphins, 27-20 (M)
1997—Dolphins, 33-30 (M)
2000—Dolphins, 23-8 (D)
2002—Dolphins, 49-21 (M)
2006—Dolphins, 27-10 (D)
(RS Pts.—Dolphins 255, Lions 154)
DETROIT vs. MINNESOTA
RS: Vikings lead series, 61-30-2
1961—Lions, 37-10 (M)
    Lions, 13-7 (D)
1962—Lions, 17-6 (M)
    Lions, 37-23 (D)
1963—Lions, 28-10 (D)
    Vikings, 34-31 (M)
1964—Lions, 24-20 (M)
    Tie, 23-23 (D)
1965—Lions, 31-29 (M)
    Vikings, 29-7 (D)
1966—Lions, 32-31 (M)
    Vikings, 28-16 (D)
1967—Tie, 10-10 (M)
    Lions, 14-3 (D)
1968—Vikings, 24-10 (M)
    Vikings, 13-6 (D)
1969—Vikings, 24-10 (M)
    Vikings, 27-0 (D)
1970—Vikings, 30-17 (D)
    Vikings, 24-20 (M)
1971—Vikings, 16-13 (D)
    Vikings, 29-10 (M)
1972—Vikings, 34-10 (M)
    Vikings, 16-14 (M)
1973—Vikings, 23-9 (D)
    Vikings, 28-7 (M)
1974—Vikings, 7-6 (D)
    Lions, 20-16 (M)
1975—Vikings, 25-19 (M)
    Lions, 17-10 (D)
1976—Vikings, 10-9 (D)
    Vikings, 31-23 (M)
1977—Vikings, 14-7 (M)
    Vikings, 30-21 (D)
1978—Vikings, 17-7 (M)
    Lions, 45-14 (D)
1979—Vikings, 13-10 (D)
    Vikings, 14-7 (M)
1980—Lions, 27-7 (D)
    Vikings, 34-0 (M)
1981—Vikings, 26-24 (M)
    Lions, 45-7 (D)
1982—Vikings, 34-31 (D)
1983—Vikings, 20-17 (M)
    Lions, 13-2 (D)
1984—Vikings, 29-28 (D)

Lions, 16-14 (M)
1985—Vikings, 16-13 (M)
Lions, 41-21 (D)
1986—Lions, 13-10 (M)
Vikings, 24-10 (D)
1987—Vikings, 34-19 (M)
Vikings, 17-14 (D)
1988—Vikings, 44-17 (M)
Vikings, 23-0 (D)
1989—Vikings, 24-17 (M)
Vikings, 20-7 (D)
1990—Lions, 34-27 (M)
Vikings, 17-7 (D)
1991—Lions, 24-20 (D)
Lions, 34-14 (M)
1992—Lions, 31-17 (D)
Vikings, 31-14 (M)
1993—Lions, 30-27 (M)
Vikings, 13-0 (D)
1994—Vikings, 10-3 (M)
Lions, 41-19 (D)
1995—Vikings, 20-10 (M)
Lions, 44-38 (D)
1996—Vikings, 17-13 (M)
Vikings, 24-22 (D)
1997—Lions, 38-15 (D)
Lions, 14-13 (M)
1998—Vikings, 29-6 (M)
Vikings, 34-13 (D)
1999—Lions, 25-23 (D)
Vikings, 24-17 (M)
2000—Vikings, 31-24 (D)
Vikings, 24-17 (M)
2001—Vikings, 31-26 (M)
Lions, 27-24 (D)
2002—Vikings, 31-24 (M)
Vikings, 38-36 (D)
2003—Vikings, 23-13 (D)
Vikings, 24-14 (M)
2004—Vikings, 22-19 (M)
Vikings, 28-27 (D)
2005—Vikings, 27-14 (M)
Vikings, 21-16 (D)
2006—Vikings, 26-17 (M)
Vikings, 30-20 (D)
2007—Lions, 20-17 (D) OT
Vikings, 42-10 (M)
(RS Pts.—Vikings 2,029, Lions 1,733)
DETROIT vs. NEW ENGLAND
RS: Patriots lead series, 5-4
1971—Lions, 34-7 (NE)
1976—Lions, 30-10 (D)
1979—Patriots, 24-17 (NE)
1985—Patriots, 23-6 (NE)
1993—Lions, 19-16 (NE) OT
1994—Patriots, 23-17 (D)
2000—Lions, 34-9 (D)
2002—Patriots, 20-12 (D)
2006—Patriots, 28-21 (NE)
(RS Pts.—Lions 190, Patriots 160)
DETROIT vs. NEW ORLEANS
RS: Lions lead series, 9-8-1
1968—Tie, 20-20 (D)
1970—Saints, 19-17 (NO)
1972—Lions, 27-14 (D)
1973—Saints, 20-13 (NO)
1974—Lions, 19-14 (D)
1976—Saints, 17-16 (NO)
1977—Lions, 23-19 (D)
1979—Saints, 17-7 (NO)

1980—Lions, 24-13 (D)
1988—Saints, 22-14 (D)
1989—Lions, 21-14 (D)
1990—Lions, 27-10 (NO)
1992—Saints, 13-7 (D)
1993—Saints, 14-3 (NO)
1997—Saints, 35-17 (NO)
2000—Lions, 14-10 (NO)
2002—Lions, 26-21 (D)
2005—Lions, 13-12 (San Antonio)
(RS Pts.—Lions 308, Saints 304)
*DETROIT vs. N.Y. GIANTS
RS: Lions lead series, 20-18-1
PS: Lions lead series, 1-0
1930—Giants, 19-6 (P)
1931—Spartans, 14-6 (P)
Giants, 14-0 (NY)
1932—Spartans, 7-0 (P)
Spartans, 6-0 (NY)
1933—Spartans, 17-7 (P)
Giants, 13-10 (NY)
1934—Lions, 9-0 (D)
1935—**Lions, 26-7 (D)
1936—Giants, 14-7 (NY)
Lions, 38-0 (D)
1937—Lions, 17-0 (NY)
1939—Lions, 18-14 (D)
1941—Giants, 20-13 (NY)
1943—Tie, 0-0 (D)
1945—Giants, 35-14 (NY)
1947—Lions, 35-7 (D)
1949—Lions, 45-21 (NY)
1953—Lions, 27-16 (NY)
1955—Giants, 24-19 (D)
1958—Giants, 19-17 (D)
1962—Giants, 17-14 (NY)
1964—Lions, 26-3 (D)
1967—Lions, 30-7 (NY)
1969—Lions, 24-0 (D)
1972—Lions, 30-16 (D)
1974—Lions, 20-19 (D)
1976—Giants, 24-10 (NY)
1982—Giants, 13-6 (D)
1983—Lions, 15-9 (D)
1988—Giants, 30-10 (NY)
Giants, 13-10 (D) OT
1989—Giants, 24-14 (NY)
1990—Giants, 20-0 (NY)
1994—Lions, 28-25 (NY) OT
1996—Giants, 35-7 (D)
1997—Giants, 26-20 (D) OT
2000—Lions, 31-21 (NY)
2004—Lions, 28-13 (NY)
2007—Giants, 16-10 (D)
(RS Pts.—Lions 652, Giants 560)
(PS Pts.—Lions 26, Giants 7)
**Franchise in Portsmouth prior to 1934
and known as the Spartans*
**NFL Championship
DETROIT vs. N.Y. JETS
RS: Lions lead series, 6-5
1972—Lions, 37-20 (D)
1979—Jets, 31-10 (NY)
1982—Jets, 28-13 (D)
1985—Lions, 31-20 (D)
1988—Jets, 17-10 (D)
1991—Lions, 34-20 (D)
1994—Lions, 18-7 (NY)
1997—Lions, 13-10 (D)
2000—Lions, 10-7 (NY)

2002—Jets, 31-14 (D)
2006—Jets, 31-24 (NY)
(RS Pts.—Jets 222, Lions 214)
DETROIT vs. *OAKLAND
RS: Raiders lead series, 6-4
1970—Lions, 28-14 (D)
1974—Raiders, 35-13 (O)
1978—Raiders, 29-17 (O)
1981—Lions, 16-0 (D)
1984—Raiders, 24-3 (D)
1987—Raiders, 27-7 (LA)
1990—Raiders, 38-31 (D)
1996—Raiders, 37-21 (O)
2003—Lions, 23-13 (O)
2007—Lions, 36-21 (O)
(RS Pts.—Raiders 238, Lions 195)
*Franchise in Los Angeles from 1982-1994
*DETROIT vs. PHILADELPHIA
RS: Eagles lead series, 13-12-2
PS: Eagles lead series, 1-0
1933—Spartans, 25-0 (P)
1934—Lions, 10-0 (P)
1935—Lions, 35-0 (D)
1936—Lions, 23-0 (P)
1938—Eagles, 21-7 (D)
1940—Lions, 21-0 (P)
1941—Lions, 21-17 (D)
1945—Lions, 28-24 (D)
1948—Eagles, 45-21 (P)
1949—Eagles, 22-14 (D)
1951—Lions, 28-10 (P)
1954—Tie, 13-13 (D)
1957—Lions, 27-16 (P)
1960—Eagles, 28-10 (P)
1961—Eagles, 27-24 (D)
1965—Lions, 35-28 (P)
1968—Eagles, 12-0 (D)
1971—Eagles, 23-20 (D)
1974—Eagles, 28-17 (P)
1977—Lions, 17-13 (P)
1979—Eagles, 44-7 (P)
1984—Tie, 23-23 (D) OT
1986—Lions, 13-11 (P)
1995—**Eagles, 58-37 (P)
1996—Eagles, 24-17 (P)
1998—Eagles, 10-9 (P)
2004—Eagles, 30-13 (D)
2007—Eagles, 56-21 (P)
(RS Pts.—Eagles 525, Lions 499)
(PS Pts.—Eagles 58, Lions 37)
**Franchise in Portsmouth prior to 1934
and known as the Spartans*
**NFC First-Round Playoff
DETROIT vs. *PITTSBURGH
RS: Series tied, 14-14-1
1934—Lions, 40-7 (D)
1936—Lions, 28-3 (D)
1937—Lions, 7-3 (D)
1938—Lions, 16-7 (D)
1940—Pirates, 10-7 (D)
1942—Steelers, 35-7 (D)
1946—Lions, 17-7 (D)
1947—Steelers, 17-10 (P)
1948—Lions, 17-14 (D)
1949—Steelers, 14-7 (P)
1950—Lions, 10-7 (D)
1952—Lions, 31-6 (D)
1953—Lions, 38-21 (D)
1955—Lions, 31-28 (D)
1956—Lions, 45-7 (D)

1959—Tie, 10-10 (P)
1962—Lions, 45-7 (D)
1966—Steelers, 17-3 (P)
1967—Steelers, 24-14 (D)
1969—Steelers, 16-13 (P)
1973—Steelers, 24-10 (P)
1983—Lions, 45-3 (D)
1986—Steelers, 27-17 (P)
1989—Steelers, 23-3 (D)
1992—Steelers, 17-14 (P)
1995—Steelers, 23-20 (P)
1998—Lions, 19-16 (D) OT
2001—Steelers, 47-14 (P)
2005—Steelers, 35-21 (P)
(RS Pts.—Lions 559, Steelers 475)
Steelers known as Pirates prior to 1941
DETROIT vs. *ST. LOUIS
RS: Rams lead series, 41-37-1
PS: Lions lead series, 1-0
1937—Lions, 28-0 (C)
 Lions, 27-7 (D)
1938—Rams, 21-17 (C)
 Lions, 6-0 (D)
1939—Lions, 15-7 (D)
 Rams, 14-3 (C)
1940—Lions, 6-0 (D)
 Rams, 24-0 (C)
1941—Lions, 17-7 (D)
 Lions, 14-0 (C)
1942—Rams, 14-0 (D)
 Rams, 27-7 (C)
1944—Rams, 20-17 (D)
 Lions, 26-14 (C)
1945—Rams, 28-21 (D)
1946—Rams, 35-14 (LA)
 Rams, 41-20 (D)
1947—Rams, 27-13 (D)
 Rams, 28-17 (LA)
1948—Rams, 44-7 (LA)
 Rams, 34-27 (D)
1949—Rams, 27-24 (LA)
 Rams, 21-10 (D)
1950—Rams, 30-28 (D)
 Rams, 65-24 (LA)
1951—Rams, 27-21 (D)
 Lions, 24-22 (LA)
1952—Lions, 17-14 (LA)
 Lions, 24-16 (D)
 **Lions, 31-21 (D)
1953—Lions, 31-19 (D)
 Rams, 37-24 (LA)
1954—Lions, 21-3 (D)
 Lions, 27-24 (LA)
1955—Rams, 17-10 (D)
 Rams, 24-13 (LA)
1956—Lions, 24-21 (D)
 Lions, 16-7 (LA)
1957—Lions, 10-7 (D)
 Rams, 35-17 (LA)
1958—Rams, 42-28 (D)
 Lions, 41-24 (LA)
1959—Lions, 17-7 (LA)
 Lions, 23-17 (D)
1960—Rams, 48-35 (LA)
 Lions, 12-10 (D)
1961—Lions, 14-13 (D)
 Lions, 28-10 (LA)
1962—Lions, 13-10 (D)
 Lions, 12-3 (LA)
1963—Lions, 23-2 (LA)

Rams, 28-21 (D)
1964—Tie, 17-17 (LA)
 Lions, 37-17 (D)
1965—Lions, 20-0 (D)
 Lions, 31-7 (LA)
1966—Rams, 14-7 (D)
 Rams, 23-3 (LA)
1967—Rams, 31-7 (D)
1968—Rams, 10-7 (LA)
1969—Lions, 28-0 (D)
1970—Rams, 28-23 (LA)
1971—Rams, 21-13 (D)
1972—Lions, 34-17 (LA)
1974—Rams, 16-13 (LA)
1975—Rams, 20-0 (D)
1976—Rams, 20-17 (D)
1980—Lions, 41-20 (LA)
1981—Rams, 20-13 (LA)
1982—Lions, 19-14 (LA)
1983—Rams, 21-10 (LA)
1986—Rams, 14-10 (LA)
1987—Rams, 37-16 (D)
1988—Rams, 17-10 (LA)
1991—Rams, 21-10 (D)
1993—Lions, 16-13 (LA)
1999—Lions, 31-27 (D)
2001—Rams, 35-0 (D)
2003—Lions, 30-20 (D)
2006—Rams, 41-34 (StL)
(RS Pts.—Rams 1,559, Lions 1,435)
(PS Pts.—Lions 31, Rams 21)
Franchise in Los Angeles prior to 1995 and in Cleveland prior to 1946
**Conference Playoff*
DETROIT vs. SAN DIEGO
RS: Chargers lead series, 6-3
1972—Lions, 34-20 (D)
1977—Lions, 20-0 (D)
1978—Lions, 31-14 (D)
1981—Chargers, 28-23 (SD)
1984—Chargers, 27-24 (SD)
1996—Chargers, 27-21 (SD)
1999—Chargers, 20-10 (D)
2003—Chargers, 14-7 (D)
2007—Chargers, 51-14 (SD)
(RS Pts.—Chargers 201, Lions 184)
DETROIT vs. SAN FRANCISCO
RS: 49ers lead series, 32-26-1
PS: Series tied, 1-1
1950—Lions, 24-7 (D)
 49ers, 28-27 (SF)
1951—49ers, 20-10 (D)
 49ers, 21-17 (SF)
1952—49ers, 17-3 (SF)
 49ers, 28-0 (D)
1953—Lions, 24-21 (D)
 Lions, 14-10 (SF)
1954—49ers, 37-31 (SF)
 Lions, 48-7 (D)
1955—49ers, 27-24 (D)
 49ers, 38-21 (SF)
1956—Lions, 20-17 (D)
 Lions, 17-13 (SF)
1957—49ers, 35-31 (SF)
 Lions, 31-10 (D)
 *Lions, 31-27 (SF)
1958—49ers, 24-21 (SF)
 Lions, 35-21 (D)
1959—49ers, 34-13 (D)
 49ers, 33-7 (SF)

1960—49ers, 14-10 (D)
 Lions, 24-0 (SF)
1961—49ers, 49-0 (D)
 Tie, 20-20 (SF)
1962—Lions, 45-24 (D)
 Lions, 38-24 (SF)
1963—Lions, 26-3 (D)
 Lions, 45-7 (SF)
1964—Lions, 26-17 (SF)
 Lions, 24-7 (D)
1965—49ers, 27-21 (D)
 49ers, 17-14 (SF)
1966—49ers, 27-24 (SF)
 49ers, 41-14 (D)
1967—49ers, 45-3 (SF)
1968—49ers, 14-7 (D)
1969—Lions, 26-14 (SF)
1970—Lions, 28-7 (D)
1971—49ers, 31-27 (SF)
1973—Lions, 30-20 (D)
1974—Lions, 17-13 (D)
1975—Lions, 28-17 (SF)
1977—49ers, 28-7 (SF)
1978—Lions, 33-14 (D)
1980—Lions, 17-13 (D)
1981—Lions, 24-17 (D)
1983—**49ers, 24-23 (SF)
1984—49ers, 30-27 (D)
1985—Lions, 23-21 (D)
1988—49ers, 20-13 (SF)
1991—49ers, 35-3 (SF)
1992—49ers, 24-6 (SF)
1993—49ers, 55-17 (D)
1994—49ers, 27-21 (D)
1995—Lions, 27-24 (D)
1996—49ers, 24-14 (SF)
1998—49ers, 35-13 (D)
2001—49ers, 21-13 (SF)
2003—49ers, 24-17 (SF)
2006—49ers, 19-13 (D)
(RS Pts.—49ers 1,275, Lions 1,245)
(PS Pts.—Lions 54, 49ers 51)
Conference Playoff
**NFC Divisional Playoff*
DETROIT vs. SEATTLE
RS: Seahawks lead series, 6-4
1976—Lions, 41-14 (S)
1978—Seahawks, 28-16 (S)
1984—Seahawks, 38-17 (S)
1987—Seahawks, 37-14 (D)
1990—Seahawks, 30-10 (S)
1993—Lions, 30-10 (D)
1996—Lions, 17-16 (D)
1999—Lions, 28-20 (S)
2003—Seahawks, 35-14 (S)
2006—Seahawks, 9-6 (D)
(RS Pts.—Seahawks 237, Lions 193)
DETROIT vs. TAMPA BAY
RS: Lions lead series, 27-24
PS: Buccaneers lead series, 1-0
1977—Lions, 16-7 (D)
1978—Lions, 15-7 (TB)
 Lions, 34-23 (D)
1979—Buccaneers, 31-16 (TB)
 Buccaneers, 16-14 (D)
1980—Lions, 24-10 (TB)
 Lions, 27-14 (D)
1981—Buccaneers, 28-10 (TB)
 Buccaneers, 20-17 (D)
1982—Buccaneers, 23-21 (TB)

1983—Lions, 11-0 (TB)
    Lions, 23-20 (D)
1984—Buccaneers, 21-17 (TB)
    Lions, 13-7 (D) OT
1985—Lions, 30-9 (D)
    Buccaneers, 19-16 (TB) OT
1986—Buccaneers, 24-20 (D)
    Lions, 38-17 (TB)
1987—Buccaneers, 31-27 (D)
    Lions, 20-10 (TB)
1988—Buccaneers, 23-20 (D)
    Buccaneers, 21-10 (TB)
1989—Lions, 17-16 (TB)
    Lions, 33-7 (D)
1990—Buccaneers, 38-21 (D)
    Buccaneers, 23-20 (TB)
1991—Lions, 31-3 (D)
    Buccaneers, 30-21 (TB)
1992—Buccaneers, 27-23 (D)
    Lions, 38-7 (TB)
1993—Buccaneers, 27-10 (TB)
    Lions, 23-0 (D)
1994—Buccaneers, 24-14 (TB)
    Lions, 14-9 (D)
1995—Lions, 27-24 (D)
    Lions, 37-10 (TB)
1996—Lions, 21-6 (D)
    Lions, 27-0 (TB)
1997—Buccaneers, 24-17 (D)
    Lions, 27-9 (TB)
    *Buccaneers, 20-10 (TB)
1998—Lions, 27-6 (D)
    Lions, 28-25 (TB)
1999—Lions, 20-3 (D)
    Buccaneers, 23-16 (TB)
2000—Buccaneers, 31-10 (D)
    Lions, 28-14 (TB)
2001—Buccaneers, 20-17 (D)
    Buccaneers, 15-12 (TB)
2002—Buccaneers, 23-20 (D)
2005—Buccaneers, 17-13 (TB)
2007—Lions, 23-16 (D)
(RS Pts—Lions 1,074, Buccaneers 858)
(PS Pts.—Buccaneers 20, Lions 10)
*NFC First-Round Playoff
DETROIT vs. *TENNESSEE
RS: Titans lead series, 6-3
1971—Lions, 31-7 (H)
1975—Oilers, 24-8 (H)
1983—Oilers, 27-17 (H)
1986—Lions, 24-13 (D)
1989—Oilers, 35-31 (H)
1992—Oilers, 24-21 (D)
1995—Lions, 24-17 (H)
2001—Titans, 27-24 (D)
2004—Titans, 24-19 (T)
(RS Pts.—Lions 199, Titans 198)
*Franchise in Houston prior to 1997;
known as Oilers prior to 1999
DETROIT vs. **WASHINGTON
RS: Redskins lead series, 26-10
PS: Redskins lead series, 3-0
1932—Spartans, 10-0 (P)
1933—Spartans, 13-0 (B)
1934—Lions, 24-0 (D)
1935—Lions, 17-7 (B)
    Lions, 14-0 (D)
1938—Redskins, 7-5 (D)
1939—Redskins, 31-7 (W)
1940—Redskins, 20-14 (D)

1942—Redskins, 15-3 (D)
1943—Redskins, 42-20 (W)
1946—Redskins, 17-16 (W)
1947—Lions, 38-21 (D)
1948—Redskins, 46-21 (W)
1951—Lions, 35-17 (D)
1956—Redskins, 18-17 (W)
1965—Lions, 14-10 (D)
1968—Redskins, 14-3 (W)
1970—Redskins, 31-10 (W)
1973—Redskins, 20-0 (D)
1976—Redskins, 20-7 (W)
1978—Redskins, 21-19 (D)
1979—Redskins, 27-24 (D)
1981—Redskins, 33-31 (W)
1982—***Redskins, 31-7 (W)
1983—Redskins, 38-17 (W)
1984—Redskins, 28-14 (W)
1985—Redskins, 24-3 (W)
1987—Redskins, 20-13 (W)
1990—Redskins, 41-38 (D) OT
1991—Redskins, 45-0 (W)
    ****Redskins, 41-10 (W)
1992—Redskins, 13-10 (W)
1995—Redskins, 36-30 (W) OT
1997—Redskins, 30-7 (W)
1999—Lions, 33-17 (D)
    ***Redskins, 27-13 (W)
2000—Lions, 15-10 (D)
2004—Redskins, 17-10 (D)
2007—Redskins, 34-3 (W)
(RS Pts.—Redskins 770, Lions 555)
(PS Pts.—Redskins 99, Lions 30)
*Franchise in Portsmouth prior to 1934
and known as the Spartans.
**Franchise in Boston prior to 1937
***NFC First-Round Playoff
****NFC Championship

GREEN BAY vs. ARIZONA
RS: Packers lead series, 42-22-4
PS: Packers lead series, 1-0;
See Arizona vs. Green Bay
GREEN BAY vs. ATLANTA
RS: Packers lead series, 12-10
PS: Series tied, 1-1;
See Atlanta vs. Green Bay
GREEN BAY vs. BALTIMORE
RS: Packers lead series, 2-1;
See Baltimore vs. Green Bay
GREEN BAY vs. BUFFALO
RS: Bills lead series, 7-3;
See Buffalo vs. Green Bay
GREEN BAY vs. CAROLINA
RS: Packers lead series, 6-3
PS: Packers lead series, 1-0;
See Carolina vs. Green Bay
GREEN BAY vs. CHICAGO
RS: Bears lead series, 89-79-6
PS: Bears lead series, 1-0;
See Chicago vs. Green Bay
GREEN BAY vs. CINCINNATI
RS: Series tied, 5-5;
See Cincinnati vs. Green Bay
GREEN BAY vs. CLEVELAND
RS: Packers lead series, 9-7
PS: Packers lead series, 1-0;
See Cleveland vs. Green Bay
GREEN BAY vs. DALLAS
RS: Cowboys lead series, 11-10

PS: Cowboys lead series, 4-2;
See Dallas vs. Green Bay
GREEN BAY vs. DENVER
RS: Series tied, 5-5-1
PS: Broncos lead series, 1-0;
See Denver vs. Green Bay
GREEN BAY vs. DETROIT
RS: Packers lead series, 84-64-7
PS: Packers lead series, 2-0;
See Detroit vs. Green Bay
GREEN BAY vs. HOUSTON
RS: Packers lead series, 1-0
2004—Packers, 16-13 (H)
(RS Pts.—Packers 16, Texans 13)
GREEN BAY vs. *INDIANAPOLIS
RS: Colts lead series, 20-19-1
PS: Packers lead series, 1-0
1953—Packers, 37-14 (GB)
    Packers, 35-24 (B)
1954—Packers, 7-6 (B)
    Packers, 24-13 (Mil)
1955—Colts, 24-20 (Mil)
    Colts, 14-10 (B)
1956—Packers, 38-33 (Mil)
    Colts, 28-21 (B)
1957—Colts, 45-17 (Mil)
    Packers, 24-21 (B)
1958—Colts, 24-17 (Mil)
    Colts, 56-0 (B)
1959—Colts, 38-21 (B)
    Colts, 28-24 (Mil)
1960—Packers, 35-21 (GB)
    Colts, 38-24 (B)
1961—Packers, 45-7 (GB)
    Colts, 45-21 (B)
1962—Packers, 17-6 (B)
    Packers, 17-13 (GB)
1963—Packers, 31-20 (GB)
    Packers, 34-20 (B)
1964—Colts, 21-20 (GB)
    Colts, 24-21 (B)
1965—Packers, 20-17 (Mil)
    Packers, 42-27 (B)
    **Packers, 13-10 (GB) OT
1966—Packers, 24-3 (Mil)
    Packers, 14-10 (B)
1967—Colts, 13-10 (B)
1968—Colts, 16-3 (GB)
1969—Colts, 14-6 (B)
1970—Colts, 13-10 (Mil)
1974—Packers, 20-13 (B)
1982—Tie, 20-20 (B) OT
1985—Colts, 37-10 (I)
1988—Colts, 20-13 (GB)
1991—Packers, 14-10 (Mil)
1997—Colts, 41-38 (I)
2000—Packers, 26-24 (GB)
2004—Colts, 45-31 (I)
(RS Pts.—Colts 906, Packers 861)
(PS Pts.—Packers 13, Colts 10)
*Franchise in Baltimore prior to 1984
**Conference Playoff
GREEN BAY vs. JACKSONVILLE
RS: Packers lead series, 2-1
1995—Packers, 24-14 (J)
2001—Packers, 28-21 (J)
2004—Jaguars, 28-25 (GB)
(RS Pts.—Packers 77, Jaguars 63)
GREEN BAY vs. KANSAS CITY
RS: Chiefs lead series, 6-2-1

PS: Packers lead series, 1-0
1966—*Packers, 35-10 (Los Angeles)
1973—Tie, 10-10 (Mil)
1977—Chiefs, 20-10 (KC)
1987—Packers, 23-3 (KC)
1989—Chiefs, 21-3 (GB)
1990—Chiefs, 17-3 (GB)
1993—Chiefs, 23-16 (KC)
1996—Chiefs, 27-20 (KC)
2003—Chiefs, 40-34 (GB) OT
2007—Packers, 33-22 (KC)
(RS Pts.—Chiefs 183, Packers 152)
(PS Pts.—Packers 35, Chiefs 10)
*Super Bowl I
GREEN BAY vs. MIAMI
RS: Dolphins lead series, 9-3
1971—Dolphins, 27-6 (Mia)
1975—Dolphins, 31-7 (GB)
1979—Dolphins, 27-7 (Mia)
1985—Dolphins, 34-24 (GB)
1988—Dolphins, 24-17 (Mia)
1989—Dolphins, 23-20 (Mia)
1991—Dolphins, 16-13 (Mia)
1994—Dolphins, 24-14 (Mil)
1997—Packers, 23-18 (GB)
2000—Dolphins, 28-20 (Mia)
2002—Packers, 24-10 (GB)
2006—Packers, 34-24 (M)
(RS Pts.—Dolphins 286, Packers 209)
GREEN BAY vs. MINNESOTA
RS: Packers lead series, 48-44-1
PS: Vikings lead series, 1-0
1961—Packers, 33-7 (Minn)
　　　Packers, 28-10 (Mil)
1962—Packers, 34-7 (GB)
　　　Packers, 48-21 (Minn)
1963—Packers, 37-28 (Minn)
　　　Packers, 28-7 (GB)
1964—Vikings, 24-23 (GB)
　　　Packers, 42-13 (Minn)
1965—Packers, 38-13 (GB)
　　　Packers, 24-19 (GB)
1966—Vikings, 20-17 (GB)
　　　Packers, 28-16 (Minn)
1967—Vikings, 10-7 (Mil)
　　　Packers, 30-27 (Minn)
1968—Vikings, 26-13 (Mil)
　　　Vikings, 14-10 (Minn)
1969—Vikings, 19-7 (Minn)
　　　Vikings, 9-7 (Mil)
1970—Packers, 13-10 (Mil)
　　　Vikings, 10-3 (Minn)
1971—Vikings, 24-13 (GB)
　　　Vikings, 3-0 (Minn)
1972—Vikings, 27-13 (GB)
　　　Packers, 23-7 (Minn)
1973—Vikings, 11-3 (Minn)
　　　Vikings, 31-7 (GB)
1974—Vikings, 32-17 (GB)
　　　Packers, 19-7 (Minn)
1975—Vikings, 28-17 (GB)
　　　Vikings, 24-3 (Minn)
1976—Vikings, 17-10 (Mil)
　　　Vikings, 20-9 (Minn)
1977—Vikings, 19-7 (Minn)
　　　Vikings, 13-6 (GB)
1978—Vikings, 21-7 (Minn)
　　　Tie, 10-10 (GB) OT
1979—Vikings, 27-21 (Minn) OT
　　　Packers, 19-7 (Mil)

1980—Packers, 16-3 (GB)
　　　Packers, 25-13 (Minn)
1981—Vikings, 30-13 (Mil)
　　　Packers, 35-23 (Minn)
1982—Packers, 26-7 (Mil)
1983—Vikings, 20-17 (GB) OT
　　　Packers, 29-21 (Minn)
1984—Packers, 45-17 (Mil)
　　　Packers, 38-14 (Minn)
1985—Packers, 20-17 (Mil)
　　　Packers, 27-17 (Minn)
1986—Vikings, 42-7 (Minn)
　　　Vikings, 32-6 (GB)
1987—Packers, 23-16 (Minn)
　　　Packers, 16-10 (Mil)
1988—Packers, 34-14 (Minn)
　　　Packers, 18-6 (GB)
1989—Vikings, 26-14 (Minn)
　　　Packers, 20-19 (Mil)
1990—Packers, 24-10 (Mil)
　　　Vikings, 23-7 (Minn)
1991—Vikings, 35-21 (GB)
　　　Packers, 27-7 (Minn)
1992—Vikings, 23-20 (GB) OT
　　　Vikings, 27-7 (Minn)
1993—Vikings, 15-13 (Minn)
　　　Vikings, 21-17 (Mil)
1994—Packers, 16-10 (GB)
　　　Vikings, 13-10 (Minn) OT
1995—Packers, 38-21 (GB)
　　　Packers, 27-24 (Minn)
1996—Vikings, 30-21 (Minn)
　　　Packers, 38-10 (GB)
1997—Packers, 38-32 (GB)
　　　Packers, 27-11 (Minn)
1998—Vikings, 37-24 (GB)
　　　Vikings, 28-14 (Minn)
1999—Packers, 23-20 (GB)
　　　Vikings, 24-20 (Minn)
2000—Packers, 26-20 (GB) OT
　　　Packers, 33-28 (Minn)
2001—Vikings, 35-13 (Minn)
　　　Packers, 24-13 (GB)
2002—Vikings, 31-21 (Minn)
　　　Packers, 26-22 (GB)
2003—Vikings, 30-25 (GB)
　　　Packers, 30-27 (Minn)
2004—Packers, 34-31 (GB)
　　　Packers, 34-31 (Minn)
　　　*Vikings, 31-17 (GB)
2005—Vikings, 23-20 (Minn)
　　　Vikings, 20-17 (GB)
2006—Packers, 23-17 (Minn)
　　　Packers, 9-7 (GB)
2007—Packers, 23-16 (Minn)
　　　Packers, 34-0 (GB)
(RS Pts.—Packers 1,924, Vikings 1,760)
(PS Pts.—Vikings 31, Packers 17)
*NFC First-Round Playoff
GREEN BAY vs. NEW ENGLAND
RS: Series tied, 4-4
PS: Packers lead series, 1-0
1973—Patriots, 33-24 (NE)
1979—Packers, 27-14 (GB)
1985—Patriots, 26-20 (NE)
1988—Packers, 45-3 (Mil)
1994—Patriots, 17-16 (NE)
1996—*Packers, 35-21 (New Orleans)
1997—Packers, 28-10 (NE)
2002—Packers, 28-10 (NE)

2006—Patriots, 35-0 (GB)
(RS Pts.—Packers 188, Patriots 148)
(PS Pts.—Packers 35, Patriots 21)
*Super Bowl XXXI
GREEN BAY vs. NEW ORLEANS
RS: Packers lead series, 14-6
1968—Packers, 29-7 (Mil)
1971—Saints, 29-21 (Mil)
1972—Packers, 30-20 (NO)
1973—Packers, 30-10 (GB)
1975—Saints, 20-19 (NO)
1976—Packers, 32-27 (Mil)
1977—Packers, 24-20 (NO)
1978—Packers, 28-17 (Mil)
1979—Packers, 28-19 (Mil)
1981—Packers, 35-7 (NO)
1984—Packers, 23-13 (NO)
1985—Packers, 38-14 (Mil)
1986—Saints, 24-10 (NO)
1987—Saints, 33-24 (NO)
1989—Packers, 35-34 (GB)
1993—Packers, 19-17 (NO)
1995—Packers, 34-23 (NO)
2002—Saints, 35-20 (NO)
2005—Packers, 52-3 (GB)
2006—Saints, 34-27 (GB)
(RS Pts.—Packers 558, Saints 406)
GREEN BAY vs. N.Y. GIANTS
RS: Packers lead series, 25-21-2
PS: Packers lead series, 4-2
1928—Giants, 6-0 (GB)
　　　Packers, 7-0 (NY)
1929—Packers, 20-6 (NY)
1930—Packers, 14-7 (GB)
　　　Giants, 13-6 (NY)
1931—Packers, 27-7 (GB)
　　　Packers, 14-10 (NY)
1932—Packers, 13-0 (GB)
　　　Giants, 6-0 (NY)
1933—Giants, 10-7 (Mil)
　　　Giants, 17-6 (NY)
1934—Packers, 20-6 (Mil)
　　　Giants, 17-3 (NY)
1935—Packers, 16-7 (GB)
1936—Packers, 26-14 (NY)
1937—Giants, 10-0 (NY)
1938—Giants, 15-3 (NY)
　　　*Giants, 23-17 (NY)
1939—*Packers, 27-0 (Mil)
1940—Giants, 7-3 (NY)
1942—Tie, 21-21 (NY)
1943—Packers, 35-21 (NY)
1944—Giants, 24-0 (NY)
　　　*Packers, 14-7 (NY)
1945—Packers, 23-14 (NY)
1947—Tie, 24-24 (NY)
1948—Giants, 49-3 (Mil)
1949—Giants, 30-10 (GB)
1952—Packers, 17-3 (NY)
1957—Giants, 31-17 (GB)
1959—Giants, 20-3 (NY)
1961—Packers, 20-17 (Mil)
　　　*Packers, 37-0 (GB)
1962—*Packers, 16-7 (NY)
1967—Packers, 48-21 (NY)
1969—Packers, 20-10 (Mil)
1971—Packers, 42-40 (GB)
1973—Packers, 16-14 (New Haven)
1975—Packers, 40-14 (Mil)
1980—Giants, 27-21 (NY)

1981—Packers, 27-14 (NY)
          Packers, 26-24 (Mil)
1982—Packers, 27-19 (NY)
1983—Giants, 27-3 (NY)
1985—Packers, 23-20 (GB)
1986—Giants, 55-24 (NY)
1987—Giants, 20-10 (NY)
1992—Giants, 27-7 (NY)
1995—Packers, 14-6 (GB)
1998—Packers, 37-3 (NY)
2001—Packers, 34-25 (NY)
2004—Giants, 14-7 (GB)
2007—Packers, 35-13 (NY)
          **Giants, 23-20 (GB) OT
(RS Pts.—Packers 817, Giants 807)
(PS Pts.—Packers 131, Giants 60)
*NFL Championship
**NFC Championship Game
GREEN BAY vs. N.Y. JETS
RS: Jets lead series, 8-2
1973—Packers, 23-7 (Mil)
1979—Jets, 27-22 (GB)
1981—Jets, 28-3 (NY)
1982—Jets, 15-13 (NY)
1985—Jets, 24-3 (Mil)
1991—Jets, 19-16 (NY) OT
1994—Packers, 17-10 (GB)
2000—Jets, 20-16 (GB)
2002—Jets, 42-17 (NY)
2006—Jets, 38-10 (GB)
(RS Pts.—Jets 230, Packers 140)
GREEN BAY vs. *OAKLAND
RS: Series tied, 5-5
PS: Packers lead series, 1-0
1967—**Packers, 33-14 (Miami)
1972—Raiders, 20-14 (GB)
1976—Raiders, 18-14 (O)
1978—Raiders, 28-3 (GB)
1984—Raiders, 28-7 (LA)
1987—Raiders, 20-0 (GB)
1990—Packers, 29-16 (LA)
1993—Packers, 28-0 (GB)
1999—Packers, 28-24 (GB)
2003—Packers, 41-7 (O)
2007—Packers, 38-7 (GB)
(RS Pts.—Packers 202, Raiders 168)
(PS Pts.—Packers 33, Raiders 14)
*Franchise in Los Angeles from 1982-1994
**Super Bowl II
GREEN BAY vs. PHILADELPHIA
RS: Packers lead series, 23-13
PS: Eagles lead series, 2-0
1933—Packers, 35-9 (GB)
          Packers, 10-0 (P)
1934—Packers, 19-6 (GB)
1935—Packers, 13-6 (P)
1937—Packers, 37-7 (Mil)
1939—Packers, 23-16 (P)
1940—Packers, 27-20 (GB)
1942—Packers, 7-0 (P)
1946—Packers, 19-7 (P)
1947—Eagles, 28-14 (P)
1951—Packers, 37-24 (GB)
1952—Packers, 12-10 (Mil)
1954—Packers, 37-14 (P)
1958—Packers, 38-35 (GB)
1960—*Eagles, 17-13 (P)
1962—Packers, 49-0 (P)
1968—Packers, 30-13 (GB)
1970—Packers, 30-17 (Mil)

1974—Eagles, 36-14 (P)
1976—Packers, 28-13 (GB)
1978—Eagles, 10-3 (P)
1979—Eagles, 21-10 (GB)
1987—Packers, 16-10 (GB) OT
1990—Eagles, 31-0 (P)
1991—Eagles, 20-3 (GB)
1992—Packers, 27-24 (Mil)
1993—Eagles, 20-17 (GB)
1994—Eagles, 13-7 (P)
1996—Packers, 39-13 (GB)
1997—Eagles, 10-9 (P)
1998—Packers, 24-16 (GB)
2000—Packers, 6-3 (GB)
2003—Eagles, 17-14 (GB)
          **Eagles, 20-17 (P) OT
2004—Eagles, 47-17 (P)
2005—Eagles, 19-14 (P)
2006—Eagles, 31-9 (P)
2007—Packers, 16-13 (GB)
(RS Pts.—Packers 710, Eagles 579)
(PS Pts.—Eagles 37, Packers 30)
*NFL Championship
**NFC Divisional Playoff
GREEN BAY vs. *PITTSBURGH
RS: Packers lead series, 18-13
1933—Packers, 47-0 (GB)
1935—Packers, 27-0 (GB)
          Packers, 34-14 (P)
1936—Packers, 42-10 (Mil)
1938—Packers, 20-0 (GB)
1940—Packers, 24-3 (Mil)
1941—Packers, 54-7 (P)
1942—Packers, 24-21 (Mil)
1946—Packers, 17-7 (GB)
1947—Steelers, 18-17 (Mil)
1948—Steelers, 38-7 (P)
1949—Steelers, 30-7 (Mil)
1951—Packers, 35-33 (Mil)
          Steelers, 28-7 (P)
1953—Steelers, 31-14 (P)
1954—Steelers, 21-20 (GB)
1957—Packers, 27-10 (P)
1960—Packers, 19-13 (P)
1963—Packers, 33-14 (Mil)
1965—Packers, 41-9 (P)
1967—Steelers, 24-17 (GB)
1969—Packers, 38-34 (P)
1970—Packers, 20-12 (P)
1975—Steelers, 16-13 (Mil)
1980—Steelers, 22-20 (P)
1983—Steelers, 25-21 (GB)
1986—Steelers, 27-3 (P)
1992—Eagles, 17-3 (GB)
1995—Packers, 24-19 (GB)
1998—Steelers, 27-20 (P)
2005—Steelers, 20-10 (GB)
(RS Pts.—Packers 719, Steelers 536)
*Steelers known as Pirates prior to 1941
GREEN BAY vs. *ST. LOUIS
RS: Rams lead series, 45-41-2
PS: Series tied, 1-1
1937—Packers, 35-10 (C)
          Packers, 35-7 (GB)
1938—Packers, 26-17 (GB)
          Packers, 28-7 (C)
1939—Rams, 27-24 (GB)
          Packers, 7-6 (C)
1940—Packers, 31-14 (GB)
          Tie, 13-13 (C)

1941—Packers, 24-7 (Mil)
          Packers, 17-14 (C)
1942—Packers, 45-28 (GB)
          Packers, 30-12 (C)
1944—Packers, 30-21 (GB)
          Packers, 42-7 (C)
1945—Rams, 27-14 (GB)
          Rams, 20-7 (C)
1946—Rams, 21-17 (Mil)
          Rams, 38-17 (LA)
1947—Packers, 17-14 (Mil)
          Packers, 30-10 (LA)
1948—Packers, 16-0 (GB)
          Rams, 24-10 (LA)
1949—Rams, 48-7 (GB)
          Rams, 35-7 (LA)
1950—Rams, 45-14 (Mil)
          Rams, 51-14 (LA)
1951—Rams, 28-0 (Mil)
          Rams, 42-14 (LA)
1952—Rams, 30-28 (Mil)
          Rams, 45-27 (LA)
1953—Rams, 38-20 (Mil)
          Rams, 33-17 (LA)
1954—Packers, 35-17 (Mil)
          Rams, 35-27 (LA)
1955—Packers, 30-28 (Mil)
          Rams, 31-17 (LA)
1956—Packers, 42-17 (Mil)
          Rams, 49-21 (LA)
1957—Rams, 31-27 (Mil)
          Rams, 42-17 (LA)
1958—Rams, 20-7 (GB)
          Rams, 34-20 (LA)
1959—Rams, 45-6 (Mil)
          Packers, 38-20 (LA)
1960—Rams, 33-31 (Mil)
          Packers, 35-21 (LA)
1961—Packers, 35-17 (GB)
          Packers, 24-17 (LA)
1962—Packers, 41-10 (Mil)
          Packers, 20-17 (LA)
1963—Packers, 42-10 (GB)
          Packers, 31-14 (LA)
1964—Rams, 27-17 (Mil)
          Tie, 24-24 (LA)
1965—Packers, 6-3 (Mil)
          Rams, 21-10 (LA)
1966—Packers, 24-13 (GB)
          Packers, 27-23 (LA)
1967—Rams, 27-24 (LA)
          **Packers, 28-7 (Mil)
1968—Rams, 16-14 (Mil)
1969—Rams, 34-21 (LA)
1970—Rams, 31-21 (GB)
1971—Rams, 30-13 (LA)
1973—Rams, 24-7 (LA)
1974—Packers, 17-6 (Mil)
1975—Rams, 22-5 (LA)
1977—Rams, 24-6 (LA)
1978—Rams, 31-14 (LA)
1980—Rams, 51-21 (LA)
1981—Rams, 35-23 (LA)
1982—Packers, 35-23 (Mil)
1983—Packers, 27-24 (Mil)
1984—Packers, 31-6 (Mil)
1985—Packers, 34-17 (LA)
1988—Rams, 34-7 (GB)
1989—Rams, 41-38 (LA)
1990—Packers, 36-24 (GB)

1991—Rams, 23-21 (LA)
1992—Packers, 28-13 (GB)
1993—Packers, 36-6 (Mil)
1994—Packers, 24-17 (GB)
1995—Rams, 17-14 (GB)
1996—Packers, 24-9 (StL)
1997—Packers, 17-7 (GB)
2001—***Rams, 45-17 (StL)
2003—Rams, 34-24 (StL)
2004—Packers, 45-17 (GB)
2006—Rams, 23-20 (GB)
2007—Packers, 33-14 (StL)
(RS Pts.—Rams 2,055, Packers 1,980)
(PS Pts.—Rams 52, Packers 45)
*Franchise in Los Angeles prior to 1995
and in Cleveland prior to 1946
**Conference Championship
***NFC Divisional Playoff
GREEN BAY vs. SAN DIEGO
RS: Packers lead series, 8-1
1970—Packers, 22-20 (SD)
1974—Packers, 34-0 (GB)
1978—Packers, 24-3 (SD)
1984—Chargers, 34-28 (GB)
1993—Packers, 20-13 (SD)
1996—Packers, 42-10 (GB)
1999—Packers, 31-3 (SD)
2003—Packers, 38-21 (SD)
2007—Packers, 31-24 (GB)
(RS Pts.—Packers 270, Chargers 128)
GREEN BAY vs. SAN FRANCISCO
RS: Packers lead series, 28-25-1
PS: Packers lead series, 4-1
1950—Packers, 25-21 (GB)
        49ers, 30-14 (SF)
1951—49ers, 31-19 (SF)
1952—49ers, 24-14 (SF)
1953—49ers, 37-7 (Mil)
        49ers, 48-14 (SF)
1954—49ers, 23-17 (Mil)
        49ers, 35-0 (SF)
1955—Packers, 27-21 (Mil)
        Packers, 28-7 (SF)
1956—49ers, 17-16 (GB)
        49ers, 38-20 (SF)
1957—49ers, 24-14 (Mil)
        49ers, 27-20 (SF)
1958—49ers, 33-12 (Mil)
        49ers, 48-21 (SF)
1959—Packers, 21-20 (GB)
        Packers, 36-14 (SF)
1960—Packers, 41-14 (Mil)
        Packers, 13-0 (SF)
1961—Packers, 30-10 (GB)
        49ers, 22-21 (SF)
1962—Packers, 31-13 (Mil)
        Packers, 31-21 (SF)
1963—Packers, 28-10 (Mil)
        Packers, 21-17 (SF)
1964—Packers, 24-14 (Mil)
        49ers, 24-14 (SF)
1965—Packers, 27-10 (GB)
        Tie, 24-24 (SF)
1966—49ers, 21-20 (SF)
        Packers, 20-7 (Mil)
1967—Packers, 13-0 (GB)
1968—49ers, 27-20 (SF)
1969—Packers, 14-7 (Mil)
1970—49ers, 26-10 (SF)
1972—Packers, 34-24 (Mil)

1973—49ers, 20-6 (SF)
1974—49ers, 7-6 (SF)
1976—49ers, 26-14 (GB)
1977—Packers, 16-14 (Mil)
1980—Packers, 23-16 (Mil)
1981—49ers, 13-3 (Mil)
1986—49ers, 31-17 (Mil)
1987—49ers, 23-12 (GB)
1989—49ers, 21-17 (SF)
1990—49ers, 24-20 (GB)
1995—*Packers, 27-17 (SF)
1996—Packers, 23-20 (GB) OT
        *Packers, 35-14 (GB)
1997—**Packers, 23-10 (SF)
1998—Packers, 36-22 (GB)
        ***49ers, 30-27 (SF)
1999—Packers, 20-3 (SF)
2000—Packers, 31-28 (GB)
2001—***Packers, 25-15 (GB)
2002—Packers, 20-14 (SF)
2003—Packers, 20-10 (GB)
2006—Packers, 30-19 (SF)
(RS Pts.—49ers 1,096, Packers 1,079)
(PS Pts.—Packers 137, 49ers 86)
*NFC Divisional Playoff
**NFC Championship
***NFC First-Round Playoff
GREEN BAY vs. SEATTLE
RS: Packers lead series, 6-5
PS: Packers lead series, 2-0
1976—Packers, 27-20 (Mil)
1978—Packers, 45-28 (Mil)
1981—Packers, 34-24 (GB)
1984—Seahawks, 30-24 (Mil)
1987—Seahawks, 24-13 (S)
1990—Seahawks, 20-14 (Mil)
1996—Packers, 31-10 (S)
1999—Seahawks, 27-7 (GB)
2003—Packers, 35-13 (GB)
        *Packers, 33-27 (GB) OT
2005—Packers, 23-17 (GB)
2006—Seahawks, 34-24 (S)
2007—**Packers, 42-20 (GB)
(RS Pts.—Packers 277, Seahawks 247)
(PS Pts.—Packers 75, Seahawks 47)
*NFC First-Round Playoff
**NFC Divisional Playoff
GREEN BAY vs. TAMPA BAY
RS: Packers lead series, 29-19-1
PS: Packers lead series, 1-0
1977—Packers, 13-0 (TB)
1978—Packers, 9-7 (GB)
        Packers, 17-7 (TB)
1979—Buccaneers, 21-10 (GB)
        Buccaneers, 21-3 (TB)
1980—Tie, 14-14 (TB) OT
        Buccaneers, 20-17 (Mil)
1981—Buccaneers, 21-10 (GB)
        Buccaneers, 37-3 (TB)
1983—Packers, 55-14 (Mil)
        Packers, 12-9 (TB) OT
1984—Buccaneers, 30-27 (TB) OT
        Packers, 27-14 (GB)
1985—Packers, 21-0 (GB)
        Packers, 20-17 (TB)
1986—Packers, 31-7 (Mil)
        Packers, 21-7 (TB)
1987—Buccaneers, 23-17 (Mil)
1988—Packers, 13-10 (GB)
        Buccaneers, 27-24 (TB)

1989—Buccaneers, 23-21 (GB)
        Packers, 17-16 (TB)
1990—Buccaneers, 26-14 (TB)
        Packers, 20-10 (Mil)
1991—Packers, 15-13 (GB)
        Packers, 27-0 (TB)
1992—Buccaneers, 31-3 (TB)
        Packers, 19-14 (Mil)
1993—Packers, 37-14 (TB)
        Packers, 13-10 (GB)
1994—Packers, 30-3 (GB)
        Packers, 34-19 (TB)
1995—Packers, 35-13 (GB)
        Buccaneers, 13-10 (TB) OT
1996—Packers, 34-3 (TB)
        Packers, 13-7 (GB)
1997—Packers, 21-16 (GB)
        Packers, 17-6 (TB)
        *Packers, 21-7 (GB)
1998—Packers, 23-15 (GB)
        Buccaneers, 24-22 (TB)
1999—Packers, 26-23 (GB)
        Buccaneers, 29-10 (TB)
2000—Packers, 20-15 (TB)
        Packers, 17-14 (GB) OT
2001—Buccaneers, 14-10 (TB)
        Packers, 21-20 (GB)
2002—Buccaneers, 21-7 (TB)
2003—Packers, 20-13 (TB)
2005—Buccaneers, 17-16 (GB)
(RS Pts.—Packers 928, Buccaneers 756)
(PS Pts.—Packers 21, Buccaneers 7)
*NFC Divisional Playoff
GREEN BAY vs. TENNESSEE
RS: Titans lead series, 5-4
1972—Packers, 23-10 (H)
1977—Oilers, 16-10 (GB)
1980—Oilers, 22-3 (GB)
1983—Oilers, 41-38 (H) OT
1986—Oilers, 31-3 (GB)
1992—Packers, 16-14 (H)
1998—Packers, 30-22 (GB)
2001—Titans, 26-20 (T)
2004—Titans, 48-27 (GB)
(RS Pts.—Titans 227, Packers 173)
*Franchise in Houston prior to 1997;
known as Oilers prior to 1999
GREEN BAY vs. *WASHINGTON
RS: Packers lead series, 17-12-1
PS: Series tied, 1-1
1932—Packers, 21-0 (B)
1933—Tie, 7-7 (GB)
        Redskins, 20-7 (B)
1934—Packers, 10-0 (B)
1936—Packers, 31-2 (GB)
        Packers, 7-3 (B)
        **Packers, 21-6 (New York)
1937—Redskins, 14-6 (W)
1939—Packers, 24-14 (Mil)
1941—Packers, 22-17 (W)
1943—Redskins, 33-7 (Mil)
1946—Packers, 20-7 (W)
1947—Packers, 27-10 (Mil)
1948—Redskins, 23-7 (W)
1949—Redskins, 30-0 (W)
1950—Packers, 35-21 (Mil)
1952—Packers, 35-20 (Mil)
1958—Redskins, 37-21 (W)
1959—Packers, 21-0 (W)
1968—Packers, 27-7 (W)

1972—Redskins, 21-16 (W)
   ***Redskins, 16-3 (W)
1974—Redskins, 17-6 (GB)
1977—Redskins, 10-9 (W)
1979—Redskins, 38-21 (W)
1983—Packers, 48-47 (GB)
1986—Redskins, 16-7 (GB)
1988—Redskins, 20-17 (Mil)
2001—Packers, 37-0 (GB)
2002—Packers, 30-9 (GB)
2004—Packers, 28-14 (W)
2007—Packers, 17-14 (GB)
(RS Pts.—Packers 571, Redskins 471)
(PS Pts.—Packers 24, Redskins 22)
*Franchise in Boston prior to 1937 and
known as Braves prior to 1933
**NFL Championship
***NFC Divisional Playoff

HOUSTON vs. ARIZONA
RS: Texans lead series, 1-0;
See Arizona vs. Houston
HOUSTON vs. ATLANTA
RS: Series tied, 1-1;
See Atlanta vs. Houston
HOUSTON vs. BALTIMORE
RS: Ravens lead series, 2-0;
See Baltimore vs. Houston
HOUSTON vs. BUFFALO
RS: Bills lead series, 3-1;
See Buffalo vs. Houston
HOUSTON vs. CAROLINA
RS: Texans lead series, 2-0;
See Carolina vs. Houston
HOUSTON vs. CHICAGO
RS: Texans lead series, 1-0;
See Chicago vs. Houston
HOUSTON vs. CINCINNATI
RS: Bengals lead series, 3-0;
See Cincinnati vs. Houston
HOUSTON vs. CLEVELAND
RS: Browns lead series, 3-2;
See Cleveland vs. Houston
HOUSTON vs. DALLAS
RS: Series tied, 1-1;
See Dallas vs. Houston
HOUSTON vs. DENVER
RS: Series tied, 1-1;
See Denver vs. Houston
HOUSTON vs. DETROIT
RS: Lions lead series 1-0;
See Detroit vs. Houston
HOUSTON vs. GREEN BAY
RS: Packers lead series, 1-0;
See Green Bay vs. Houston
HOUSTON vs. INDIANAPOLIS
RS: Colts lead series, 11-1
2002—Colts, 23-3 (H)
   Colts, 19-3 (I)
2003—Colts, 30-21 (I)
   Colts, 20-17 (H)
2004—Colts, 49-14 (I)
   Colts, 23-14 (H)
2005—Colts, 38-20 (H)
   Colts, 31-17 (I)
2006—Colts, 43-24 (I)
   Texans, 27-24 (H)
2007—Colts, 30-24 (H)
   Colts, 38-15 (I)
(RS Pts.—Colts 368, Texans 199)

HOUSTON vs. JACKSONVILLE
RS: Texans lead series, 7-5
2002—Texans, 21-19 (J)
   Jaguars, 24-21 (H)
2003—Texans, 24-20 (H)
   Jaguars, 27-0 (J)
2004—Texans, 20-6 (H)
   Texans, 21-0 (J)
2005—Jaguars, 21-14 (J)
   Jaguars, 38-20 (H)
2006—Texans, 27-7 (H)
   Texans, 13-10 (J)
2007—Jaguars, 37-17 (J)
   Texans, 42-28 (H)
(RS Pts.—Texans 240, Jaguars 237)
HOUSTON vs. KANSAS CITY
RS: Series tied, 2-2
2003—Chiefs, 42-14 (H)
2004—Texans, 24-21 (KC)
2005—Chiefs, 45-17 (H)
2007—Texans, 20-3 (H)
(RS Pts.—Chiefs 111, Texans 75)
HOUSTON vs. MIAMI
RS: Texans lead series, 3-0
2003—Texans, 21-20 (M)
2006—Texans, 17-15 (H)
2007—Texans, 22-19 (H)
(RS Pts.—Texans 60, Dolphins 54)
HOUSTON vs. MINNESOTA
RS: Vikings lead series, 1-0
2004—Vikings, 34-28 (H) OT
(RS Pts.—Vikings 34, Texans 28)
HOUSTON vs. NEW ENGLAND
RS: Patriots lead series, 2-0
2003—Patriots, 23-20 (H) OT
2006—Patriots, 40-7 (NE)
(RS Pts.—Patriots 63, Texans 27)
HOUSTON vs. NEW ORLEANS
RS: Series tied, 1-1
2003—Saints, 31-10 (NO)
2007—Texans, 23-10 (H)
(RS Pts.—Saints 41, Texans 33)
HOUSTON vs. N.Y. GIANTS
RS: Series tied, 1-1
2002—Texans, 16-14 (H)
2006—Giants, 14-10 (NY)
(RS Pts.—Giants 28, Texans 26)
HOUSTON vs. N.Y. JETS
RS: Jets lead series, 3-0
2003—Jets, 19-14 (H)
2004—Jets, 29-7 (NY)
2006—Jets, 26-11 (NY)
(RS Pts.—Jets 74, Texans 32)
HOUSTON vs. OAKLAND
RS: Texans lead series, 3-0
2004—Texans, 30-17 (H)
2006—Texans, 23-14 (O)
2007—Texans, 24-17 (O)
(RS Pts.—Texans 77, Raiders 48)
HOUSTON vs. PHILADELPHIA
RS: Eagles lead series, 2-0
2002—Eagles, 35-17 (P)
2006—Eagles, 24-10 (H)
(RS Pts.—Eagles 59, Texans 27)
HOUSTON vs. PITTSBURGH
RS: Series tied, 1-1
2002—Texans, 24-6 (P)
2005—Steelers, 27-7 (H)
(RS Pts.—Steelers 33, Texans 31)
HOUSTON vs. ST. LOUIS

RS: Rams lead series, 1-0
2005—Rams, 33-27 (H) OT
(RS Pts.—Rams 33, Texans 27)
HOUSTON vs. SAN DIEGO
RS: Chargers lead series, 3-0
2002—Chargers, 24-3 (SD)
2004—Chargers, 27-20 (H)
2007—Chargers, 35-10 (SD)
(RS Pts.—Chargers 86, Texans 33)
HOUSTON vs. SAN FRANCISCO
RS: 49ers lead series, 1-0
2005—49ers, 20-17 (SF) OT
(RS Pts.—49ers 20, Texans 17)
HOUSTON vs. SEATTLE
RS: Seahawks lead series, 1-0
2005—Seahawks, 42-10
(RS Pts.—Seahawks 42, Texans 10)
HOUSTON vs. TAMPA BAY
RS: Series tied, 1-1
2003—Buccaneers, 16-3 (TB)
2007—Texans, 28-14 (H)
(RS Pts.—Texans 31, Buccaneers 30)
HOUSTON vs. TENNESSEE
RS: Titans lead series, 10-2
2002—Titans, 17-10 (T)
   Titans, 13-3 (H)
2003—Titans, 38-17 (T)
   Titans, 27-24 (H)
2004—Texans, 20-10 (T)
   Texans, 31-21 (H)
2005—Titans, 34-20 (H)
   Titans, 13-10 (T)
2006—Titans, 28-22 (T)
   Titans, 26-20 (H) OT
2007—Titans, 38-36 (H)
   Titans, 28-20 (T)
(RS Pts.—Titans 293, Texans 233)
HOUSTON vs. WASHINGTON
RS: Redskins lead series, 2-0
2002—Redskins, 26-10 (W)
2006—Redskins, 31-15 (H)
(RS Pts.—Redskins 57, Texans 25)

INDIANAPOLIS vs. ARIZONA
RS: Colts lead series, 7-6;
See Arizona vs. Indianapolis
INDIANAPOLIS vs. ATLANTA
RS: Colts lead series, 13-1;
See Atlanta vs. Indianapolis
INDIANAPOLIS vs. BALTIMORE
RS: Colts lead series, 5-2
PS: Colts lead series, 1-0;
See Baltimore vs. Indianapolis
INDIANAPOLIS vs. BUFFALO
RS: Bills lead series, 34-30-1;
See Buffalo vs. Indianapolis
INDIANAPOLIS vs. CAROLINA
RS: Panthers lead series, 3-1;
See Carolina vs. Indianapolis
INDIANAPOLIS vs. CHICAGO
RS: Colts lead series, 22-17
PS: Colts lead series, 1-0;
See Chicago vs. Indianapolis
INDIANAPOLIS vs. CINCINNATI
RS: Colts lead series, 14-8
PS: Colts lead series, 1-0;
See Cincinnati vs. Indianapolis
INDIANAPOLIS vs. CLEVELAND
RS: Browns lead series, 13-11
PS: Series tied, 2-2;

See Cleveland vs. Indianapolis
INDIANAPOLIS vs. DALLAS
RS: Cowboys lead series, 8-5
PS: Colts lead series, 1-0;
See Dallas vs. Indianapolis
INDIANAPOLIS vs. DENVER
RS: Broncos lead series, 11-6
PS: Colts lead series, 2-0;
See Denver vs. Indianapolis
INDIANAPOLIS vs. DETROIT
RS: Colts lead series, 19-18-2;
See Detroit vs. Indianapolis
INDIANAPOLIS vs. GREEN BAY
RS: Colts lead series, 20-19-1
PS: Packers lead series, 1-0;
See Green Bay vs. Indianapolis
INDIANAPOLIS vs. HOUSTON
RS: Colts lead series, 11-1;
See Houston vs. Indianapolis
INDIANAPOLIS vs. JACKSONVILLE
RS: Colts lead series, 11-3
1995—Colts, 41-31 (J)
2000—Colts, 43-14 (I)
2002—Colts, 28-25 (J)
    Colts, 20-13 (I)
2003—Colts, 23-13 (I)
    Jaguars, 28-23 (J)
2004—Colts, 24-17 (J)
    Jaguars, 27-24 (I)
2005—Colts, 10-3 (I)
    Colts, 26-18 (J)
2006—Colts, 21-14 (I)
    Jaguars, 44-17 (J)
2007—Colts, 29-7 (J)
    Colts, 28-25 (I)
(RS Pts.—Colts 357, Jaguars 279)
*INDIANAPOLIS vs. KANSAS CITY
RS: Colts lead series, 9-7
PS: Colts lead series, 3-0
1970—Chiefs, 44-24 (B)
1972—Chiefs, 24-10 (KC)
1975—Colts, 28-14 (B)
1977—Colts, 17-6 (KC)
1979—Chiefs, 14-0 (KC)
    Chiefs, 10-7 (B)
1980—Colts, 31-24 (KC)
    Chiefs, 38-28 (B)
1985—Chiefs, 20-7 (KC)
1990—Colts, 23-19 (I)
1995—**Colts, 10-7 (KC)
1996—Colts, 24-19 (KC)
1999—Colts, 25-17 (I)
2000—Colts, 27-14 (KC)
2001—Colts, 35-28 (KC)
2003—**Colts, 38-31 (KC)
2004—Chiefs, 45-35 (KC)
2006—***Colts, 23-8 (I)
2007—Colts, 13-10 (I)
(RS Pts.—Chiefs 346, Colts 334)
(PS Pts.—Colts 71, Chiefs 46)
*Franchise in Baltimore prior to 1984
**AFC Divisional Playoff
***AFC First-Round Playoff
*INDIANAPOLIS vs. MIAMI
RS: Dolphins lead series, 44-23
PS: Dolphins lead series, 2-0
1970—Colts, 35-0 (B)
    Dolphins, 34-17 (M)
1971—Dolphins, 17-14 (M)
    Colts, 14-3 (B)

    **Dolphins, 21-0 (M)
1972—Dolphins, 23-0 (B)
    Dolphins, 16-0 (M)
1973—Dolphins, 44-0 (M)
    Colts, 16-3 (B)
1974—Dolphins, 17-7 (M)
    Dolphins, 17-16 (B)
1975—Colts, 33-17 (M)
    Colts, 10-7 (B) OT
1976—Colts, 28-14 (B)
    Colts, 17-16 (M)
1977—Colts, 45-28 (B)
    Dolphins, 17-6 (M)
1978—Dolphins, 42-0 (B)
    Dolphins, 26-8 (M)
1979—Dolphins, 19-0 (M)
    Dolphins, 28-24 (B)
1980—Colts, 30-17 (M)
    Dolphins, 24-14 (B)
1981—Dolphins, 31-28 (B)
    Dolphins, 27-10 (M)
1982—Dolphins, 24-20 (M)
    Dolphins, 34-7 (B)
1983—Dolphins, 21-7 (B)
    Dolphins, 37-0 (M)
1984—Dolphins, 44-7 (M)
    Dolphins, 35-17 (I)
1985—Dolphins, 30-13 (M)
    Dolphins, 34-20 (I)
1986—Dolphins, 30-10 (M)
    Dolphins, 17-13 (I)
1987—Dolphins, 23-10 (I)
    Colts, 40-21 (M)
1988—Colts, 15-13 (I)
    Colts, 31-28 (M)
1989—Dolphins, 19-13 (M)
    Colts, 42-13 (I)
1990—Dolphins, 27-7 (I)
    Dolphins, 23-17 (M)
1991—Dolphins, 17-6 (M)
    Dolphins, 10-6 (I)
1992—Colts, 31-20 (M)
    Dolphins, 28-0 (I)
1993—Dolphins, 24-20 (I)
    Dolphins, 41-27 (M)
1994—Dolphins, 22-21 (M)
    Colts, 10-6 (I)
1995—Colts, 27-24 (M) OT
    Colts, 36-28 (I)
1996—Colts, 10-6 (I)
    Dolphins, 37-13 (M)
1997—Dolphins, 16-10 (M)
    Colts, 41-0 (I)
1998—Dolphins, 24-15 (I)
    Dolphins, 27-14 (M)
1999—Dolphins, 34-31 (I)
    Colts, 37-34 (M)
2000—Dolphins, 17-14 (I)
    Colts, 20-13 (M)
    ***Dolphins 23-17 (M) OT
2001—Dolphins, 27-24 (I)
    Dolphins, 41-6 (M)
2002—Dolphins, 21-13 (I)
2003—Colts, 23-17 (M)
2006—Colts, 27-22 (I)
(RS Pts.—Dolphins 1,516, Colts 1,143)
(PS Pts.—Dolphins 44, Colts 17)
*Franchise in Baltimore prior to 1984
**AFC Championship
***AFC First-Round Playoff

*INDIANAPOLIS vs. MINNESOTA
RS: Colts lead series, 13-7-1
PS: Colts lead series, 1-0
1961—Colts, 34-33 (B)
    Vikings, 28-20 (M)
1962—Colts, 34-7 (M)
    Colts, 42-17 (B)
1963—Colts, 37-34 (M)
    Colts, 41-10 (B)
1964—Vikings, 34-24 (M)
    Colts, 17-14 (B)
1965—Colts, 35-16 (M)
    Colts, 41-21 (M)
1966—Colts, 38-23 (M)
    Colts, 20-17 (B)
1967—Tie, 20-20 (M)
1968—Colts, 21-9 (B)
    **Colts, 24-14 (B)
1969—Vikings, 52-14 (M)
1971—Vikings, 10-3 (M)
1982—Vikings, 13-10 (M)
1988—Vikings, 12-3 (M)
1997—Vikings, 39-28 (M)
2000—Colts, 31-10 (I)
2004—Colts, 31-28 (I)
(RS Pts.—Colts 544, Vikings 447)
(PS Pts.—Colts 24, Vikings 14)
*Franchise in Baltimore prior to 1984
**Conference Championship
*INDIANAPOLIS vs. **NEW ENGLAND
RS: Patriots lead series, 42-26
PS: Patriots lead series, 2-1
1970—Colts, 14-6 (Bos)
    Colts, 27-3 (Balt)
1971—Colts, 23-3 (NE)
    Patriots, 21-17 (Balt)
1972—Colts, 24-17 (NE)
    Colts, 31-0 (Balt)
1973—Patriots, 24-16 (NE)
    Colts, 18-13 (Balt)
1974—Patriots, 42-3 (NE)
    Patriots, 27-17 (Balt)
1975—Patriots, 21-10 (NE)
    Colts, 34-21 (Balt)
1976—Colts, 27-13 (NE)
    Patriots, 21-14 (Balt)
1977—Patriots, 17-3 (NE)
    Colts, 30-24 (Balt)
1978—Colts, 34-27 (Balt)
    Patriots, 35-14 (NE)
1979—Colts, 31-26 (Balt)
    Patriots, 50-21 (NE)
1980—Patriots, 37-21 (Balt)
    Patriots, 47-21 (NE)
1981—Colts, 29-28 (NE)
    Colts, 23-21 (Balt)
1982—Patriots, 24-13 (Balt)
1983—Colts, 29-23 (NE) OT
    Colts, 12-7 (Balt)
1984—Patriots, 50-17 (I)
    Patriots, 16-10 (NE)
1985—Patriots, 34-15 (NE)
    Patriots, 38-31 (I)
1986—Patriots, 33-3 (NE)
    Patriots, 30-21 (I)
1987—Colts, 30-16 (I)
    Patriots, 24-0 (NE)
1988—Patriots, 21-17 (NE)
    Colts, 24-21 (I)
1989—Patriots, 23-20 (I) OT

Patriots, 22-16 (NE)
1990—Patriots, 16-14 (I)
Colts, 13-10 (NE)
1991—Patriots, 16-7 (I)
Patriots, 23-17 (NE) OT
1992—Patriots, 37-34 (I) OT
Colts, 6-0 (NE)
1993—Colts, 9-6 (I)
Patriots, 38-0 (NE)
1994—Patriots, 12-10 (I)
Patriots, 28-13 (NE)
1995—Colts, 24-10 (NE)
Colts, 10-7 (I)
1996—Patriots, 27-9 (I)
Patriots, 27-13 (NE)
1997—Patriots, 31-6 (I)
Patriots, 20-17 (NE)
1998—Patriots, 29-6 (NE)
Patriots, 21-16 (I)
1999—Patriots, 31-28 (NE)
Colts, 20-15 (I)
2000—Patriots, 24-16 (NE)
Colts, 30-23 (I)
2001—Patriots, 44-13 (NE)
Patriots, 38-17 (I)
2003—Patriots, 38-34 (I)
***Patriots, 24-14 (NE)
2004—Patriots, 27-24 (NE)
****Patriots, 20-3 (NE)
2005—Colts, 40-21 (NE)
2006—Colts, 27-20 (NE)
***Colts, 38-34 (I)
2007—Patriots, 24-20 (I)
(RS Pts.—Patriots 1,589, Colts 1,253)
(PS Pts.—Patriots 78, Colts 55)
*Franchise in Baltimore prior to 1984
**Franchise in Boston prior to 1971
***AFC Championship
****AFC Divisional Playoff
INDIANAPOLIS vs. NEW ORLEANS
RS: Series tied, 5-5
1967—Colts, 30-10 (B)
1969—Colts, 30-10 (NO)
1973—Colts, 14-10 (B)
1986—Saints, 17-14 (I)
1989—Saints, 41-6 (NO)
1995—Saints, 17-14 (NO)
1998—Saints, 19-13 (I) OT
2001—Saints, 34-20 (NO)
2003—Colts, 55-21 (NO)
2007—Colts, 41-10 (I)
(RS Pts.—Colts 237, Saints 189)
*Franchise in Baltimore prior to 1984
INDIANAPOLIS vs. N.Y. GIANTS
RS: Colts lead series, 7-6
PS: Colts lead series, 2-0
1954—Colts, 20-14 (B)
1955—Giants, 17-7 (NY)
1958—Giants, 24-21 (NY)
**Colts, 23-17 (NY) OT
1959—**Colts, 31-16 (B)
1963—Giants, 37-28 (B)
1968—Colts, 26-0 (NY)
1971—Colts, 31-7 (NY)
1975—Colts, 21-0 (NY)
1979—Colts, 31-7 (NY)
1990—Giants, 24-7 (I)
1993—Giants, 20-6 (NY)
1999—Colts, 27-19 (NY)
2002—Giants, 44-27 (I)

2006—Colts, 26-21 (NY)
(RS Pts.—Colts 278, Giants 234)
(PS Pts.—Colts 54, Giants 33)
*Franchise in Baltimore prior to 1984
**NFL Championship
INDIANAPOLIS vs. N.Y. JETS
RS: Colts lead series, 40-25
PS: Jets lead series, 2-0
1968—**Jets 16-7 (Miami)
1970—Colts, 29-22 (NY)
Colts, 35-20 (B)
1971—Colts, 22-0 (B)
Colts, 14-13 (NY)
1972—Jets, 44-34 (B)
Jets, 24-20 (NY)
1973—Jets, 34-10 (B)
Jets, 20-17 (NY)
1974—Colts, 35-20 (NY)
Jets, 45-38 (B)
1975—Colts, 45-28 (NY)
Colts, 52-19 (B)
1976—Colts, 20-0 (NY)
Colts, 33-16 (B)
1977—Colts, 20-12 (NY)
Colts, 33-12 (B)
1978—Jets, 33-10 (B)
Jets, 24-16 (NY)
1979—Colts, 10-8 (B)
Jets, 30-17 (NY)
1980—Colts, 17-14 (NY)
Colts, 35-21 (B)
1981—Jets, 41-14 (B)
Jets, 25-0 (NY)
1982—Jets, 37-0 (NY)
1983—Colts, 17-14 (NY)
Jets, 10-6 (B)
1984—Jets, 23-14 (I)
Colts, 9-5 (NY)
1985—Jets, 25-20 (NY)
Jets, 35-17 (I)
1986—Jets, 26-7 (I)
Jets, 31-16 (NY)
1987—Colts, 6-0 (I)
Jets, 19-14 (NY)
1988—Colts, 38-14 (I)
Jets, 34-16 (NY)
1989—Colts, 17-10 (NY)
Colts, 27-10 (I)
1990—Colts, 17-14 (I)
Colts, 29-21 (NY)
1991—Jets, 17-6 (I)
Colts, 28-27 (NY)
1992—Colts, 6-3 (I) OT
Colts, 10-6 (NY)
1993—Jets, 31-17 (I)
Colts, 9-6 (NY)
1994—Jets, 16-6 (NY)
Colts, 28-25 (I)
1995—Colts, 27-24 (NY) OT
Colts, 17-10 (I)
1996—Colts, 21-7 (NY)
Colts, 34-29 (I)
1997—Jets, 16-12 (I)
Colts, 22-14 (NY)
1998—Jets, 44-6 (NY)
Colts, 24-23 (I)
1999—Colts, 16-13 (NY)
Colts, 13-6 (I)
2000—Colts, 23-15 (I)
Jets, 27-17 (NY)

2001—Colts, 45-24 (NY)
Jets, 29-28 (I)
2002—***Jets, 41-0 (NY)
2003—Colts, 38-31 (I)
2006—Colts, 31-28 (NY)
(RS Pts.—Colts 1,335, Jets 1,319)
(PS Pts.—Jets 57, Colts 7)
*Franchise in Baltimore prior to 1984
**Super Bowl III
***AFC First-Round Playoff
INDIANAPOLIS vs. **OAKLAND
RS: Raiders lead series, 7-4
PS: Series tied, 1-1
1970—***Colts, 27-17 (B)
1971—Colts, 37-14 (O)
1973—Raiders, 34-21 (B)
1975—Raiders, 31-20 (B)
1977—****Raiders, 37-31 (B) OT
1984—Raiders, 21-7 (LA)
1986—Colts, 30-24 (LA)
1991—Raiders, 16-0 (LA)
1995—Raiders, 30-17 (O)
2000—Raiders, 38-31 (I)
2001—Raiders, 23-18 (I)
2004—Colts, 35-14 (I)
2007—Colts, 21-14 (O)
(RS Pts.—Raiders 259, Colts 237)
(PS Pts.—Colts 58, Raiders 54)
*Franchise in Baltimore prior to 1984
**Franchise in Los Angeles from 1982-1994
***AFC Championship
****AFC Divisional Playoff
INDIANAPOLIS vs. PHILADELPHIA
RS: Colts lead series, 10-6
1953—Eagles, 45-14 (P)
1965—Colts, 34-24 (B)
1967—Colts, 38-6 (P)
1969—Colts, 24-20 (B)
1970—Colts, 29-10 (B)
1974—Eagles, 30-10 (P)
1978—Eagles, 17-14 (B)
1981—Eagles, 38-13 (P)
1983—Colts, 22-21 (P)
1984—Eagles, 16-7 (P)
1990—Colts, 24-23 (P)
1993—Eagles, 20-10 (I)
1996—Colts, 37-10 (I)
1999—Colts, 44-17 (P)
2002—Colts, 35-13 (P)
2006—Colts, 45-21 (I)
(RS Pts.—Colts 400, Eagles 331)
*Franchise in Baltimore prior to 1984
INDIANAPOLIS vs. PITTSBURGH
RS: Steelers lead series, 13-5
PS: Steelers lead series, 5-0
1957—Steelers, 19-13 (B)
1968—Colts, 41-7 (P)
1971—Colts, 34-21 (B)
1974—Steelers, 30-0 (P)
1975—**Steelers, 28-10 (P)
1976—**Steelers, 40-14 (B)
1977—Colts, 31-21 (B)
1978—Steelers, 35-13 (P)
1979—Steelers, 17-13 (P)
1980—Steelers, 20-17 (B)
1983—Steelers, 24-13 (B)
1984—Colts, 17-16 (I)
1985—Steelers, 45-3 (P)
1987—Steelers, 21-7 (P)

1991—Steelers, 21-3 (I)
1992—Steelers, 30-14 (P)
1994—Steelers, 31-21 (P)
1995—***Steelers, 20-16 (P)
1996—****Steelers, 42-14 (P)
1997—Steelers, 24-22 (P)
2002—Steelers, 28-10 (P)
2005—Colts, 26-7 (I)
      **Steelers, 21-18 (I)
(RS Pts.—Steelers 417, Colts 298)
(PS Pts.—Steelers 151, Colts 72)
*Franchise in Baltimore prior to 1984
**AFC Divisional Playoff
***AFC Championship
****AFC First-Round Playoff
*INDIANAPOLIS vs. **ST. LOUIS
RS: Colts lead series, 22-17-2
1953—Rams, 21-13 (B)
      Rams, 45-2 (LA)
1954—Rams, 48-0 (B)
      Colts, 22-21 (LA)
1955—Tie, 17-17 (B)
      Rams, 20-14 (LA)
1956—Colts, 56-21 (B)
      Rams, 31-7 (LA)
1957—Colts, 31-14 (B)
      Rams, 37-21 (LA)
1958—Colts, 34-7 (B)
      Rams, 30-28 (LA)
1959—Colts, 35-21 (B)
      Colts, 45-26 (LA)
1960—Colts, 31-17 (B)
      Rams, 10-3 (LA)
1961—Colts, 27-24 (B)
      Rams, 34-17 (LA)
1962—Colts, 30-27 (B)
      Colts, 14-2 (LA)
1963—Rams, 17-16 (B)
      Colts, 19-16 (B)
1964—Colts, 35-20 (B)
      Colts, 24-7 (LA)
1965—Colts, 35-20 (B)
      Colts, 20-17 (LA)
1966—Colts, 17-3 (LA)
      Rams, 23-7 (B)
1967—Tie, 24-24 (B)
      Rams, 34-10 (LA)
1968—Colts, 27-10 (B)
      Colts, 28-24 (LA)
1969—Rams, 27-20 (B)
      Colts, 13-7 (LA)
1971—Colts, 24-17 (B)
1975—Rams, 24-13 (LA)
1986—Rams, 24-7 (I)
1989—Rams, 31-17 (LA)
1995—Colts, 21-18 (I)
2001—Rams, 42-17 (StL)
2005—Colts, 45-28 (I)
(RS Pts.—Rams 906, Colts 886)
*Franchise in Baltimore prior to 1984
**Franchise in Los Angeles prior to 1995
*INDIANAPOLIS vs. SAN DIEGO
RS: Chargers lead series, 14-8
PS: Series tied, 1-1
1970—Colts, 16-14 (SD)
1972—Chargers, 23-20 (B)
1976—Colts, 37-21 (SD)
1981—Chargers, 43-14 (B)
1982—Chargers, 44-26 (SD)
1984—Chargers, 38-10 (I)

1986—Chargers, 17-3 (I)
1987—Chargers, 16-13 (I)
      Colts, 20-7 (SD)
1988—Colts, 16-0 (SD)
1989—Colts, 10-6 (I)
1992—Chargers, 34-14 (I)
      Chargers, 26-0 (SD)
1993—Chargers, 31-0 (I)
1995—Chargers, 27-24 (I)
      **Colts, 35-20 (SD)
1996—Chargers, 26-19 (I)
1997—Chargers, 35-19 (SD)
1998—Colts, 17-12 (I)
1999—Colts, 27-19 (SD)
2004—Colts, 34-31 (I) OT
2005—Chargers, 26-17 (I)
2007—Chargers, 23-21 (SD)
      ***Chargers, 28-24 (I)
(RS Pts.—Chargers 519, Colts 377)
(PS Pts.—Colts 59, Chargers 48)
*Franchise in Baltimore prior to 1984
**AFC First-Round Playoff
***AFC Divisional Playoff
*INDIANAPOLIS vs. SAN FRANCISCO
RS: Colts lead series, 23-18
1953—49ers, 38-21 (B)
      49ers, 45-14 (SF)
1954—Colts, 17-13 (B)
      49ers, 10-7 (SF)
1955—Colts, 26-14 (B)
      49ers, 35-24 (SF)
1956—49ers, 20-17 (B)
      49ers, 30-17 (SF)
1957—Colts, 27-21 (B)
      49ers, 17-13 (SF)
1958—Colts, 35-27 (B)
      49ers, 21-12 (SF)
1959—Colts, 45-14 (B)
      Colts, 34-14 (SF)
1960—49ers, 30-22 (B)
      49ers, 34-10 (SF)
1961—Colts, 20-17 (B)
      Colts, 27-24 (SF)
1962—49ers, 21-13 (B)
      Colts, 22-3 (SF)
1963—Colts, 20-14 (SF)
      Colts, 20-3 (B)
1964—Colts, 37-7 (B)
      Colts, 14-3 (SF)
1965—Colts, 27-24 (B)
      Colts, 34-28 (SF)
1966—Colts, 36-14 (B)
      Colts, 30-14 (SF)
1967—Colts, 41-7 (B)
      Colts, 26-9 (SF)
1968—Colts, 27-10 (B)
      Colts, 42-14 (SF)
1969—49ers, 24-21 (B)
      49ers, 20-17 (SF)
1972—49ers, 24-21 (SF)
1986—49ers, 35-14 (SF)
1989—49ers, 30-24 (I)
1995—Colts, 18-17 (I)
1998—49ers, 34-31 (I)
2001—49ers, 40-21 (I)
2005—Colts, 28-3 (SF)
(RS Pts.—Colts 972, 49ers 822)
*Franchise in Baltimore prior to 1984
*INDIANAPOLIS vs. SEATTLE
RS: Colts lead series, 5-4

1977—Colts, 29-14 (S)
1978—Colts, 17-14 (S)
1991—Seahawks, 31-3 (S)
1994—Colts, 17-15 (I)
      Colts, 31-19 (S)
1997—Seahawks, 31-3 (I)
1998—Seahawks, 27-23 (S)
2000—Colts, 37-24 (S)
2005—Seahawks, 28-13 (S)
(RS Pts.—Seahawks 203, Colts 173)
*Franchise in Baltimore prior to 1984
*INDIANAPOLIS vs. TAMPA BAY
RS: Colts lead series, 7-4
1976—Colts, 42-17 (B)
1979—Buccaneers, 29-26 (B) OT
1985—Colts, 31-23 (TB)
1987—Colts, 24-6 (I)
1988—Colts, 35-31 (I)
1991—Buccaneers, 17-3 (TB)
1992—Colts, 24-14 (TB)
1994—Buccaneers, 24-10 (TB)
1997—Buccaneers, 31-28 (I)
2003—Colts, 38-35 (TB) OT
2007—Colts, 33-14 (I)
(RS Pts.—Colts 294, Buccaneers 241)
*Franchise in Baltimore prior to 1984
*INDIANAPOLIS vs. **TENNESSEE
RS: Colts lead series, 15-11
PS: Titans lead series, 1-0
1970—Colts, 24-20 (H)
1973—Oilers, 31-27 (H)
1976—Colts, 38-14 (B)
1979—Oilers, 28-16 (B)
1980—Oilers, 21-16 (H)
1983—Colts, 20-10 (B)
1984—Colts, 35-21 (H)
1985—Colts, 34-16 (I)
1986—Oilers, 31-17 (H)
1987—Colts, 51-27 (I)
1988—Oilers, 17-14 (I) OT
1990—Oilers, 24-10 (H)
1992—Oilers, 20-10 (I)
1994—Colts, 45-21 (I)
1999—***Titans, 19-16 (I)
2002—Titans, 23-15 (I)
      Titans, 27-17 (T)
2003—Colts, 33-7 (I)
      Colts, 29-27 (T)
2004—Colts, 31-17 (T)
      Colts, 51-24 (I)
2005—Colts, 31-10 (T)
      Colts, 35-3 (I)
2006—Colts, 14-13 (I)
      Titans, 20-17 (T)
2007—Colts, 22-20 (T)
      Titans, 16-10 (I)
(RS Pts.—Colts 662, Titans 508)
(PS Pts.—Titans 19, Colts 16)
*Franchise in Baltimore prior to 1984
**Franchise in Houston prior to 1997;
known as Oilers prior to 1999
***AFC Divisional Playoff
*INDIANAPOLIS vs. WASHINGTON
RS: Colts lead series, 18-10
1953—Colts, 27-17 (W)
1954—Redskins, 24-21 (W)
1955—Redskins, 14-13 (B)
1956—Colts, 19-17 (B)
1957—Colts, 21-17 (W)
1958—Colts, 35-10 (B)

1959—Redskins, 27-24 (W)
1960—Colts, 20-0 (B)
1961—Colts, 27-6 (W)
1962—Colts, 34-21 (B)
1963—Colts, 36-20 (W)
1964—Colts, 45-17 (B)
1965—Colts, 38-7 (W)
1966—Colts, 37-10 (B)
1967—Colts, 17-13 (W)
1969—Colts, 41-17 (B)
1973—Redskins, 22-14 (W)
1977—Colts, 10-3 (B)
1978—Colts, 21-17 (B)
1981—Redskins, 38-14 (W)
1984—Redskins, 35-7 (I)
1990—Colts, 35-28 (I)
1993—Redskins, 30-24 (W)
1994—Redskins, 41-27 (I)
1996—Redskins, 31-16 (W)
1999—Colts, 24-21 (I)
2002—Redskins, 26-21 (W)
2006—Colts, 36-22 (I)
(RS Pts.—Colts 704, Redskins 551)
*Franchise in Baltimore prior to 1984

JACKSONVILLE vs. ARIZONA
RS: Jaguars lead series, 2-0;
See Arizona vs. Jacksonville
JACKSONVILLE vs. ATLANTA
RS: Jaguars lead series, 3-1;
See Atlanta vs. Jacksonville
JACKSONVILLE vs. BALTIMORE
RS: Jaguars lead series, 9-6;
See Baltimore vs. Jacksonville
JACKSONVILLE vs. BUFFALO
RS: Bills lead series, 4-3
PS: Jaguars lead series, 1-0;
See Buffalo vs. Jacksonville
JACKSONVILLE vs. CAROLINA
RS: Jaguars lead series, 3-1;
See Carolina vs. Jacksonville
JACKSONVILLE vs. CHICAGO
RS: Series tied, 2-2;
See Chicago vs. Jacksonville
JACKSONVILLE vs. CINCINNATI
RS: Jaguars lead series, 11-5;
See Cincinnati vs. Jacksonville
JACKSONVILLE vs. CLEVELAND
RS: Jaguars lead series, 8-2;
See Cleveland vs. Jacksonville
JACKSONVILLE vs. DALLAS
RS: Series tied, 2-2;
See Dallas vs. Jacksonville
JACKSONVILLE vs. DENVER
RS: Series tied, 3-3
PS: Series tied, 1-1;
See Denver vs. Jacksonville
JACKSONVILLE vs. DETROIT
RS: Jaguars lead series, 2-1;
See Detroit vs. Jacksonville
JACKSONVILLE vs. GREEN BAY
RS: Packers lead series, 2-1;
See Green Bay vs. Jacksonville
JACKSONVILLE vs. HOUSTON
RS: Texans lead series, 7-5;
See Houston vs. Jacksonville
JACKSONVILLE vs. INDIANAPOLIS
RS: Colts lead series, 11-3;
See Indianapolis vs. Jacksonville
JACKSONVILLE vs. KANSAS CITY

RS: Jaguars lead series, 5-2
1997—Jaguars, 24-10 (J)
1998—Jaguars, 21-16 (J)
2001—Chiefs, 30-26 (J)
2002—Jaguars, 23-16 (KC)
2004—Jaguars, 22-16 (J)
2006—Chiefs, 35-30 (KC)
2007—Jaguars, 17-7 (KC)
(RS Pts.—Jaguars 163, Chiefs 130)
JACKSONVILLE vs. MIAMI
RS: Jaguars lead series, 2-1
PS: Jaguars lead series, 1-0
1998—Jaguars, 28-21 (J)
1999—*Jaguars, 62-7 (J)
2003—Dolphins, 24-10 (J)
2006—Jaguars, 24-10 (M)
(RS Pts.—Jaguars 62, Dolphins 55)
(PS Pts.—Jaguars 62, Dolphins 7)
*AFC Divisional Playoff
JACKSONVILLE vs. MINNESOTA
RS: Vikings lead series, 2-1
1998—Vikings, 50-10 (M)
2001—Jaguars, 33-3 (M)
2004—Vikings, 27-16 (M)
(RS Pts.—Vikings 80, Jaguars 59)
JACKSONVILLE vs. NEW ENGLAND
RS: Patriots lead series, 4-0
PS: Patriots lead series, 3-1
1996—Patriots, 28-25 (NE) OT
       *Patriots, 20-6 (NE)
1997—Patriots, 26-20 (J)
1998—**Jaguars, 25-10 (J)
2003—Patriots, 27-13 (NE)
2005—**Patriots, 28-3 (NE)
2006—Patriots, 24-21 (J)
2007—***Patriots, 31-20 (NE)
(RS Pts.—Patriots 105, Jaguars 79)
(PS Pts.—Patriots 89, Jaguars 54)
*AFC Championship
**AFC First-Round Playoff
***AFC Divisional Playoff
JACKSONVILLE vs. NEW ORLEANS
RS: Series tied, 2-2
1996—Saints, 17-13 (NO)
1999—Jaguars, 41-23 (J)
2003—Jaguars, 20-19 (J)
2007—Saints, 41-24 (NO)
(RS Pts.—Saints 100, Jaguars 98)
JACKSONVILLE vs. N.Y. GIANTS
RS: Series tied, 2-2
1997—Jaguars, 40-13 (J)
2000—Giants, 28-25 (NY)
2002—Giants, 24-17 (NY)
2006—Jaguars, 26-10 (J)
(RS Pts.—Jaguars 108, Giants 75)
JACKSONVILLE vs. N.Y. JETS
RS: Jaguars lead series, 5-2
PS: Jets lead series, 1-0
1995—Jets, 27-10 (NY)
1996—Jaguars, 21-17 (J)
1998—*Jets, 34-24 (NY)
1999—Jaguars, 16-6 (NY)
2002—Jaguars, 28-3 (J)
2003—Jets, 13-10 (NY)
2005—Jaguars, 26-20 (NY) OT
2006—Jaguars, 41-0 (J)
(RS Pts.—Jaguars 152, Jets 86)
(PS Pts.—Jets 34, Jaguars 24)
*AFC Divisional Playoff
JACKSONVILLE vs. OAKLAND

RS: Jaguars lead series, 3-1
1996—Raiders, 17-3 (O)
1997—Jaguars, 20-9 (O)
2004—Jaguars, 13-6 (O)
2007—Jaguars, 49-11 (J)
(RS Pts.—Jaguars 85, Raiders 43)
JACKSONVILLE vs. PHILADELPHIA
RS: Jaguars lead series, 3-0
1997—Jaguars, 38-21 (J)
2002—Jaguars, 28-25 (J)
2006—Jaguars, 13-6 (P)
(RS Pts.—Jaguars 79, Eagles 52)
JACKSONVILLE vs. PITTSBURGH
RS: Jaguars lead series, 11-8
PS: Jaguars lead series, 1-0
1995—Jaguars, 20-16 (J)
       Steelers, 24-7 (P)
1996—Jaguars, 24-9 (J)
       Steelers, 28-3 (P)
1997—Jaguars, 30-21 (J)
       Steelers, 23-17 (P) OT
1998—Steelers, 30-15 (P)
       Jaguars, 21-3 (J)
1999—Jaguars, 17-3 (P)
       Jaguars, 20-6 (J)
2000—Steelers, 24-13 (J)
       Jaguars, 34-24 (P)
2001—Jaguars, 21-3 (J)
       Steelers, 20-7 (P)
2002—Steelers, 25-23 (J)
2004—Steelers, 17-16 (J)
2005—Jaguars, 23-17 (P) OT
2006—Jaguars, 9-0 (J)
2007—Jaguars, 29-22 (P)
       *Jaguars, 31-29 (P)
(RS Pts.—Jaguars 349, Steelers 315)
(PS Pts.—Jaguars 31, Steelers 29)
*AFC First-Round Playoff
JACKSONVILLE vs. ST. LOUIS
RS: Rams lead series, 2-0
1996—Rams, 17-14 (StL)
2005—Rams, 24-21 (StL)
(RS Pts.—Rams 41, Jaguars 35)
JACKSONVILLE vs. SAN DIEGO
RS: Jaguars lead series, 2-1
2003—Jaguars, 27-21 (SD)
2004—Chargers, 34-21 (SD)
2007—Jaguars, 24-17 (J)
(RS Pts.—Chargers 72, Jaguars 72)
JACKSONVILLE vs. SAN FRANCISCO
RS: Jaguars lead series, 2-0
1999—Jaguars, 41-3 (J)
2005—Jaguars, 10-9 (J)
(RS Pts.—Jaguars 51, 49ers 12)
JACKSONVILLE vs. SEATTLE
RS: Seahawks lead series, 3-2
1995—Seahawks, 47-30 (J)
1996—Jaguars, 20-13 (J)
2000—Seahawks, 28-21 (J)
2001—Seahawks, 24-15 (S)
2005—Jaguars, 26-14 (J)
(RS Pts.—Seahawks 126, Jaguars 112)
JACKSONVILLE vs. TAMPA BAY
RS: Jaguars lead series, 3-1
1995—Buccaneers, 17-16 (TB)
1998—Jaguars, 29-24 (J)
2003—Jaguars, 17-10 (J)
2007—Jaguars, 24-23 (TB)
(RS Pts.—Jaguars 86, Buccaneers 74)
JACKSONVILLE vs. *TENNESSEE

RS: Titans lead series, 14-12
PS: Titans lead, 1-0
1995—Oilers, 10-3 (J)
    Jaguars, 17-16 (H)
1996—Oilers, 34-27 (J)
    Jaguars, 23-17 (H)
1997—Jaguars, 30-24 (T)
    Jaguars, 17-9 (J)
1998—Jaguars, 27-22 (T)
    Oilers, 16-13 (J)
1999—Titans, 20-19 (J)
    Titans, 41-14 (T)
    **Titans, 33-14 (J)
2000—Titans, 27-13 (T)
    Jaguars, 16-13 (J)
2001—Jaguars, 13-6 (J)
    Titans, 38-24 (T)
2002—Titans, 23-14 (T)
    Titans, 28-10 (J)
2003—Titans, 30-17 (J)
    Titans, 10-3 (T)
2004—Jaguars, 15-12 (T)
    Titans, 18-15 (J)
2005—Jaguars, 31-28 (T)
    Jaguars, 40-13 (J)
2006—Jaguars, 37-7 (J)
    Titans, 24-17 (T)
2007—Titans, 13-10 (J)
    Jaguars, 28-13 (T)
(RS Pts.—Titans 502, Jaguars 493)
(PS Pts.—Titans 33, Jaguars 14)
*Franchise in Houston prior to 1997;
known as Oilers prior to 1999
**AFC Championship
JACKSONVILLE vs. WASHINGTON
RS: Redskins lead series, 3-1
1997—Redskins, 24-12 (W)
2000—Redskins, 35-16 (J)
2002—Jaguars, 26-7 (J)
2006—Redskins, 36-30 (W) OT
(RS Pts.—Redskins 102, Jaguars 84)

KANSAS CITY vs. ARIZONA
RS: Chiefs lead series, 7-2-1;
See Arizona vs. Kansas City
KANSAS CITY vs. ATLANTA
RS: Chiefs lead series, 5-1;
See Atlanta vs. Kansas City
KANSAS CITY vs. BALTIMORE
RS: Chiefs lead series, 3-1;
See Baltimore vs. Kansas City
KANSAS CITY vs. BUFFALO
RS: Bills lead series, 19-16-1
PS: Bills lead series, 2-1;
See Buffalo vs. Kansas City
KANSAS CITY vs. CAROLINA
RS: Chiefs lead series, 2-1;
See Carolina vs. Kansas City
KANSAS CITY vs. CHICAGO
RS: Bears lead series, 6-4;
See Chicago vs. Kansas City
KANSAS CITY vs. CINCINNATI
RS: Chiefs lead series, 13-11;
See Cincinnati vs. Kansas City
KANSAS CITY vs. CLEVELAND
RS: Series tied, 9-9-2;
See Cleveland vs. Kansas City
KANSAS CITY vs. DALLAS
RS: Cowboys lead series, 5-3;
See Dallas vs. Kansas City

KANSAS CITY vs. DENVER
RS: Chiefs lead series, 52-43
PS: Broncos lead series, 1-0;
See Denver vs. Kansas City
KANSAS CITY vs. DETROIT
RS: Chiefs lead series, 7-4;
See Detroit vs. Kansas City
KANSAS CITY vs. GREEN BAY
RS: Chiefs lead series, 6-2-1
PS: Packers lead series, 1-0;
See Green Bay vs. Kansas City
KANSAS CITY vs. HOUSTON
RS: Series tied, 2-2;
See Houston vs. Kansas City
KANSAS CITY vs. INDIANAPOLIS
RS: Colts lead series, 9-7
PS: Colts lead series, 3-0;
See Indianapolis vs. Kansas City
KANSAS CITY vs. JACKSONVILLE
RS: Jaguars lead series, 5-2;
See Jacksonville vs. Kansas City
KANSAS CITY vs. MIAMI
RS: Chiefs lead series, 12-11
PS: Dolphins lead series, 3-0
1966—Chiefs, 34-16 (KC)
    Chiefs, 19-18 (M)
1967—Chiefs, 24-0 (M)
    Chiefs, 41-0 (KC)
1968—Chiefs, 48-3 (M)
1969—Chiefs, 17-10 (KC)
1971—*Dolphins, 27-24 (KC) OT
1972—Dolphins, 20-10 (KC)
1974—Dolphins, 9-3 (M)
1976—Chiefs, 20-17 (M) OT
1981—Dolphins, 17-7 (KC)
1983—Dolphins, 14-6 (M)
1985—Dolphins, 31-0 (M)
1987—Dolphins, 42-0 (M)
1989—Chiefs, 26-21 (KC)
    Chiefs, 27-24 (M)
1990—**Dolphins, 17-16 (M)
1991—Chiefs, 42-7 (KC)
1993—Dolphins, 30-10 (M)
1994—Dolphins, 45-28 (M)
    **Dolphins, 27-17 (M)
1995—Dolphins, 13-6 (M)
1997—Dolphins, 17-14 (M)
2002—Chiefs, 48-30 (KC)
2005—Chiefs, 30-20 (M)
2006—Dolphins, 13-10 (M)
(RS Pts.—Chiefs 470, Dolphins 417)
(PS Pts.—Dolphins 71, Chiefs 57)
*AFC Divisional Playoff
**AFC First-Round Playoff
KANSAS CITY vs. MINNESOTA
RS: Chiefs lead series, 5-4
PS: Chiefs lead series, 1-0
1969—*Chiefs, 23-7 (New Orleans)
1970—Vikings, 27-10 (M)
1974—Vikings, 35-15 (KC)
1981—Chiefs, 10-6 (M)
1990—Chiefs, 24-21 (KC)
1993—Vikings, 30-10 (M)
1996—Chiefs, 21-6 (M)
1999—Chiefs, 31-28 (KC)
2003—Vikings, 45-20 (M)
2007—Chiefs, 13-10 (KC)
(RS Pts.—Vikings 208, Chiefs 154)
(PS Pts.—Chiefs 23, Vikings 7)
*Super Bowl IV

*KANSAS CITY vs. **NEW ENGLAND
RS: Chiefs lead series, 16-11-3
1960—Patriots, 42-14 (B)
    Texans, 34-0 (D)
1961—Patriots, 18-17 (D)
    Patriots, 28-21 (B)
1962—Texans, 42-28 (D)
    Texans, 27-7 (B)
1963—Tie, 24-24 (B)
    Chiefs, 35-3 (KC)
1964—Patriots, 24-7 (B)
    Patriots, 31-24 (KC)
1965—Chiefs, 27-17 (KC)
    Tie, 10-10 (B)
1966—Chiefs, 43-24 (B)
    Tie, 27-27 (KC)
1967—Chiefs, 33-10 (B)
1968—Chiefs, 31-17 (KC)
1969—Chiefs, 31-0 (B)
1970—Chiefs, 23-10 (KC)
1973—Chiefs, 10-7 (NE)
1977—Patriots, 21-17 (NE)
1981—Patriots, 33-17 (NE)
1990—Chiefs, 37-7 (NE)
1992—Chiefs, 27-20 (NE)
1995—Chiefs, 31-26 (KC)
1998—Patriots, 40-10 (NE)
1999—Chiefs, 16-14 (KC)
2000—Patriots, 30-24 (NE)
2002—Patriots, 41-38 (NE) OT
2004—Patriots, 27-19 (KC)
2005—Chiefs, 26-16 (KC)
(RS Pts.—Chiefs 742, Patriots 602)
*Franchise located in Dallas prior to 1963
and known as Texans
**Franchise in Boston prior to 1971
KANSAS CITY vs. NEW ORLEANS
RS: Series tied, 4-4
1972—Chiefs, 20-17 (NO)
1976—Saints, 27-17 (KC)
1982—Saints, 27-17 (NO)
1985—Chiefs, 47-27 (NO)
1991—Saints, 17-10 (KC)
1994—Chiefs, 30-17 (NO)
1997—Chiefs, 25-13 (KC)
2004—Saints, 27-20 (NO)
(RS Pts.—Chiefs 186, Saints 172)
KANSAS CITY vs. N.Y. GIANTS
RS: Giants lead series, 9-2
1974—Giants, 33-27 (KC)
1978—Giants, 26-10 (NY)
1979—Giants, 21-17 (KC)
1983—Chiefs, 38-17 (KC)
1984—Giants, 28-27 (NY)
1988—Giants, 28-12 (NY)
1992—Giants, 35-21 (NY)
1995—Chiefs, 20-17 (KC) OT
1998—Giants, 28-7 (NY)
2001—Giants, 13-3 (KC)
2005—Giants, 27-17 (NY)
(RS Pts.—Giants 273, Chiefs 199)
*KANSAS CITY vs. **N.Y. JETS
RS: Chiefs lead series, 16-15-1
PS: Series tied, 1-1
1960—Titans, 37-35 (D)
    Titans, 41-35 (NY)
1961—Titans, 28-7 (NY)
    Texans, 35-24 (D)
1962—Texans, 20-17 (D)
    Texans, 52-31 (NY)

1963—Jets, 17-0 (NY)
　　Chiefs, 48-0 (KC)
1964—Jets, 27-14 (NY)
　　Chiefs, 24-7 (KC)
1965—Chiefs, 14-10 (NY)
　　Jets, 13-10 (KC)
1966—Chiefs, 32-24 (NY)
1967—Chiefs, 42-18 (KC)
　　Chiefs, 21-7 (NY)
1968—Jets, 20-19 (KC)
1969—Chiefs, 34-16 (NY)
　　***Chiefs, 13-6 (NY)
1971—Jets, 13-10 (NY)
1974—Chiefs, 24-16 (KC)
1975—Jets, 30-24 (NY)
1982—Chiefs, 37-13 (KC)
1984—Jets, 17-16 (NY)
　　Jets, 28-7 (NY)
1986—****Jets, 35-15 (NY)
1987—Jets, 16-9 (KC)
1988—Tie, 17-17 (NY)
　　Chiefs, 38-34 (KC)
1992—Chiefs, 23-7 (NY)
1998—Jets, 20-17 (KC)
2001—Jets, 27-7 (NY)
2002—Chiefs, 29-25 (NY)
2005—Chiefs, 27-7 (KC)
2007—Jets, 13-10 (NY) OT
(RS Pts.—Chiefs 737, Jets 620)
(PS Pts.—Jets 41, Chiefs 28)
*Franchise in Dallas prior to 1963 and
known as Texans
**Jets known as Titans prior to 1963
***Inter-Divisional Playoff
****AFC First-Round Playoff
KANSAS CITY vs. **OAKLAND
RS: Chiefs lead series, 50-43-2
PS: Chiefs lead series, 2-1
1960—Texans, 34-16 (O)
　　Raiders, 20-19 (D)
1961—Texans, 42-35 (O)
　　Texans, 43-11 (D)
1962—Texans, 26-16 (O)
　　Texans, 35-7 (D)
1963—Raiders, 10-7 (O)
　　Raiders, 22-7 (KC)
1964—Chiefs, 21-9 (O)
　　Chiefs, 42-7 (KC)
1965—Raiders, 37-10 (O)
　　Chiefs, 14-7 (KC)
1966—Chiefs, 32-10 (O)
　　Raiders, 34-13 (KC)
1967—Raiders, 23-21 (O)
　　Raiders, 44-22 (KC)
1968—Chiefs, 24-10 (KC)
　　Raiders, 38-21 (O)
　　***Raiders, 41-6 (O)
1969—Raiders, 27-24 (KC)
　　Raiders, 10-6 (O)
　　****Chiefs, 17-7 (O)
1970—Tie, 17-17 (KC)
　　Raiders, 20-6 (O)
1971—Tie, 20-20 (O)
　　Chiefs, 16-14 (KC)
1972—Chiefs, 27-14 (O)
　　Raiders, 26-3 (O)
1973—Chiefs, 16-3 (KC)
　　Raiders, 37-7 (O)
1974—Raiders, 27-7 (O)
　　Raiders, 7-6 (KC)

1975—Chiefs, 42-10 (KC)
　　Raiders, 28-20 (O)
1976—Raiders, 24-21 (KC)
　　Raiders, 21-10 (O)
1977—Raiders, 37-28 (KC)
　　Raiders, 21-20 (O)
1978—Raiders, 28-6 (O)
　　Raiders, 20-10 (KC)
1979—Chiefs, 35-7 (KC)
　　Chiefs, 24-21 (O)
1980—Raiders, 27-14 (KC)
　　Chiefs, 31-17 (O)
1981—Chiefs, 27-0 (KC)
　　Chiefs, 28-17 (O)
1982—Raiders, 21-16 (KC)
1983—Raiders, 21-20 (LA)
　　Raiders, 28-20 (KC)
1984—Raiders, 22-20 (KC)
　　Raiders, 17-7 (LA)
1985—Chiefs, 36-20 (KC)
　　Raiders, 19-10 (LA)
1986—Raiders, 24-17 (KC)
　　Chiefs, 20-17 (LA)
1987—Raiders, 35-17 (LA)
　　Chiefs, 16-10 (KC)
1988—Raiders, 27-17 (KC)
　　Raiders, 17-10 (LA)
1989—Chiefs, 24-19 (KC)
　　Raiders, 20-14 (LA)
1990—Chiefs, 9-7 (KC)
　　Chiefs, 27-24 (LA)
1991—Chiefs, 24-21 (KC)
　　Chiefs, 27-21 (LA)
　　*****Chiefs, 10-6 (KC)
1992—Chiefs, 27-7 (KC)
　　Raiders, 28-7 (LA)
1993—Chiefs, 24-9 (KC)
　　Chiefs, 31-20 (LA)
1994—Chiefs, 13-3 (KC)
　　Chiefs, 19-9 (LA)
1995—Chiefs, 23-17 (KC) OT
　　Chiefs, 29-23 (O)
1996—Chiefs, 19-3 (KC)
　　Raiders, 26-7 (O)
1997—Chiefs, 28-27 (O)
　　Chiefs, 30-0 (KC)
1998—Chiefs, 28-8 (KC)
　　Chiefs, 31-24 (O)
1999—Chiefs, 37-34 (O)
　　Raiders, 41-38 (KC) OT
2000—Raiders, 20-17 (KC)
　　Raiders, 49-31 (O)
2001—Raiders, 27-24 (KC)
　　Raiders, 28-26 (O)
2002—Chiefs, 20-10 (KC)
　　Raiders, 24-0 (O)
2003—Chiefs, 17-10 (O)
　　Chiefs, 27-24 (KC)
2004—Chiefs, 34-27 (O)
　　Chiefs, 31-30 (KC)
2005—Chiefs, 23-17 (O)
　　Chiefs, 27-23 (KC)
2006—Chiefs, 17-13 (KC)
　　Chiefs, 20-9 (O)
2007—Chiefs, 12-10 (O)
　　Raiders, 20-17 (KC)
(RS Pts.—Chiefs 1,989, Raiders 1,866)
(PS Pts.—Raiders 54, Chiefs 33)
*Franchise in Dallas prior to 1963 and
known as Texans

**Franchise in Los Angeles from
1982-1994
***Division Playoff
****AFL Championship
*****AFC First-Round Playoff
KANSAS CITY vs. PHILADELPHIA
RS: Eagles lead series, 3-2
1972—Eagles, 21-20 (KC)
1992—Chiefs, 24-17 (KC)
1998—Chiefs, 24-21 (P)
2001—Eagles, 23-10 (KC)
2005—Eagles, 37-31 (KC)
(RS Pts.—Eagles 119, Chiefs 109)
KANSAS CITY vs. PITTSBURGH
RS: Steelers lead series, 17-8
PS: Chiefs lead series, 1-0
1970—Chiefs, 31-14 (P)
1971—Chiefs, 38-16 (KC)
1972—Steelers, 16-7 (P)
1974—Steelers, 34-24 (KC)
1975—Steelers, 28-3 (P)
1976—Steelers, 45-0 (KC)
1978—Steelers, 27-24 (P)
1979—Steelers, 30-3 (KC)
1980—Steelers, 21-16 (P)
1981—Chiefs, 37-33 (P)
1982—Steelers, 35-14 (P)
1984—Chiefs, 37-27 (P)
1985—Chiefs, 36-28 (KC)
1986—Chiefs, 24-19 (P)
1987—Steelers, 17-16 (KC)
1988—Steelers, 16-10 (P)
1989—Steelers, 23-17 (P)
1992—Steelers, 27-3 (KC)
1993—*Chiefs, 27-24 (KC) OT
1996—Steelers, 17-7 (KC)
1997—Chiefs, 13-10 (KC)
1998—Chiefs, 20-13 (KC)
1999—Chiefs, 35-19 (KC)
2001—Steelers, 20-17 (KC)
2003—Chiefs, 41-20 (KC)
2006—Steelers, 45-7 (P)
(RS Pts.—Steelers 615, Chiefs 465)
(PS Pts.—Chiefs 27, Steelers 24)
*AFC First-Round Playoff
KANSAS CITY vs. *ST. LOUIS
RS: Chiefs lead series, 5-4
1973—Rams, 23-13 (KC)
1982—Rams, 20-14 (LA)
1985—Rams, 16-0 (KC)
1991—Chiefs, 27-20 (LA)
1994—Rams, 16-0 (KC)
1997—Chiefs, 28-20 (StL)
2000—Chiefs, 54-34 (KC)
2002—Chiefs, 49-10 (KC)
2006—Chiefs, 31-17 (StL)
(RS Pts.—Chiefs 216, Rams 176)
*Franchise in Los Angeles prior to 1995
KANSAS CITY vs. **SAN DIEGO
RS: Chiefs lead series, 50-44-1
PS: Chargers lead series, 1-0
1960—Chargers, 21-20 (LA)
　　Texans, 17-0 (D)
1961—Chargers, 26-10 (D)
　　Chargers, 24-14 (SD)
1962—Chargers, 32-28 (SD)
　　Texans, 26-17 (D)
1963—Chargers, 24-10 (SD)
　　Chargers, 38-17 (KC)
1964—Chargers, 28-14 (KC)

Chiefs, 49-6 (SD)
1965—Tie, 10-10 (SD)
Chiefs, 31-7 (KC)
1966—Chiefs, 24-14 (KC)
Chiefs, 27-17 (SD)
1967—Chargers, 45-31 (SD)
Chargers, 17-16 (KC)
1968—Chiefs, 27-20 (KC)
Chiefs, 40-3 (SD)
1969—Chiefs, 27-9 (SD)
Chiefs, 27-3 (SD)
1970—Chiefs, 26-14 (KC)
Chargers, 31-13 (SD)
1971—Chargers, 21-14 (SD)
Chiefs, 31-10 (KC)
1972—Chiefs, 26-14 (KC)
Chargers, 27-17 (KC)
1973—Chiefs, 19-0 (SD)
Chiefs, 33-6 (KC)
1974—Chiefs, 24-14 (SD)
Chargers, 14-7 (KC)
1975—Chiefs, 12-10 (SD)
Chargers, 28-20 (KC)
1976—Chargers, 30-16 (KC)
Chiefs, 23-20 (SD)
1977—Chargers, 23-7 (KC)
Chiefs, 21-16 (SD)
1978—Chargers, 29-23 (SD) OT
Chiefs, 23-0 (KC)
1979—Chargers, 20-14 (KC)
Chargers, 28-7 (SD)
1980—Chargers, 24-7 (KC)
Chargers, 20-7 (SD)
1981—Chargers, 42-31 (KC)
Chargers, 22-20 (SD)
1982—Chiefs, 19-12 (KC)
1983—Chargers, 17-14 (KC)
Chargers, 41-38 (SD)
1984—Chiefs, 31-13 (KC)
Chiefs, 42-21 (SD)
1985—Chargers, 31-20 (SD)
Chiefs, 38-34 (KC)
1986—Chiefs, 42-41 (KC)
Chiefs, 24-23 (SD)
1987—Chiefs, 20-13 (KC)
Chargers, 42-21 (SD)
1988—Chargers, 24-23 (KC)
Chargers, 24-13 (SD)
1989—Chargers, 21-6 (SD)
Chargers, 20-13 (KC)
1990—Chiefs, 27-10 (KC)
Chiefs, 24-21 (SD)
1991—Chiefs, 14-13 (SD)
Chiefs, 20-17 (KC) OT
1992—Chiefs, 24-10 (SD)
Chiefs, 16-14 (KC)
***Chargers, 17-0 (SD)
1993—Chiefs, 17-14 (SD)
Chiefs, 28-24 (KC)
1994—Chargers, 20-6 (SD)
Chargers, 14-13 (KC)
1995—Chiefs, 29-23 (KC) OT
Chiefs, 22-7 (SD)
1996—Chargers, 22-19 (SD)
Chargers, 28-14 (KC)
1997—Chiefs, 31-3 (SD)
Chiefs, 29-7 (SD)
1998—Chiefs, 23-7 (KC)
Chargers, 38-37 (SD)
1999—Chargers, 21-14 (SD)

Chiefs, 34-0 (KC)
2000—Chiefs, 42-10 (KC)
Chargers, 17-16 (SD)
2001—Chiefs, 25-20 (SD)
Chiefs, 20-17 (KC)
2002—Chargers, 35-34 (SD)
Chiefs, 24-22 (KC)
2003—Chiefs, 27-14 (KC)
Chiefs, 28-24 (SD)
2004—Chargers, 34-31 (KC)
Chargers, 24-17 (SD)
2005—Chargers, 28-20 (SD)
Chiefs, 20-7 (KC)
2006—Chiefs, 30-27 (KC)
Chargers, 20-9 (SD)
2007—Chiefs, 30-16 (SD)
Chargers, 24-10 (KC)
(RS Pts.—Chiefs 2,094, Chargers 1,853)
(PS Pts.—Chargers 17, Chiefs 0)
*Franchise in Dallas prior to 1963 and
known as Texans
**Franchise in Los Angeles prior to 1961
***AFC First-Round Playoff

KANSAS CITY vs. SAN FRANCISCO
RS: 49ers lead series, 6-4
1971—Chiefs, 26-17 (SF)
1975—49ers, 20-3 (KC)
1982—49ers, 26-13 (KC)
1985—49ers, 31-3 (SF)
1991—49ers, 28-14 (SF)
1994—Chiefs, 24-17 (KC)
1997—Chiefs, 44-9 (KC)
2000—49ers, 21-7 (SF)
2002—49ers, 17-13 (SF)
2006—Chiefs, 41-10 (KC)
(PS Pts.—Chiefs 188, 49ers 186)

KANSAS CITY vs. SEATTLE
RS: Chiefs lead series, 31-18
1977—Seahawks, 34-31 (KC)
1978—Seahawks, 13-10 (KC)
Seahawks, 23-19 (S)
1979—Chiefs, 24-6 (S)
Chiefs, 37-21 (KC)
1980—Seahawks, 17-16 (KC)
Chiefs, 31-30 (S)
1981—Chiefs, 20-14 (S)
Chiefs, 40-13 (KC)
1983—Chiefs, 17-13 (KC)
Seahawks, 51-48 (S) OT
1984—Seahawks, 45-0 (S)
Chiefs, 34-7 (KC)
1985—Chiefs, 28-7 (KC)
Seahawks, 24-6 (S)
1986—Seahawks, 23-17 (S)
Chiefs, 27-7 (KC)
1987—Seahawks, 43-14 (S)
Chiefs, 41-20 (KC)
1988—Seahawks, 31-10 (S)
Chiefs, 27-24 (KC)
1989—Chiefs, 20-16 (S)
Chiefs, 20-10 (KC)
1990—Seahawks, 19-7 (S)
Seahawks, 17-16 (KC)
1991—Chiefs, 20-13 (KC)
Chiefs, 19-6 (S)
1992—Chiefs, 26-7 (KC)
Chiefs, 24-14 (S)
1993—Chiefs, 31-16 (S)
Chiefs, 34-24 (KC)
1994—Chiefs, 38-23 (KC)

Seahawks, 10-9 (S)
1995—Chiefs, 34-10 (S)
Chiefs, 26-3 (KC)
1996—Chiefs, 35-17 (S)
Chiefs, 34-16 (KC)
1997—Chiefs, 20-17 (KC) OT
Chiefs, 19-14 (S)
1998—Chiefs, 17-6 (KC)
Seahawks, 24-12 (S)
1999—Seahawks, 31-19 (KC)
Seahawks, 23-14 (S)
2000—Chiefs, 24-17 (KC)
Chiefs, 24-19 (S)
2001—Chiefs, 19-7 (KC)
Seahawks, 21-18 (S)
2002—Seahawks, 39-32 (S)
2006—Chiefs, 35-28 (KC)
(RS Pts.—Chiefs 1,143, Seahawks 933)

KANSAS CITY vs. TAMPA BAY
RS: Chiefs lead series, 5-4
1976—Chiefs, 28-19 (TB)
1978—Buccaneers, 30-13 (KC)
1979—Buccaneers, 3-0 (TB)
1981—Chiefs, 19-10 (KC)
1984—Chiefs, 24-20 (KC)
1986—Chiefs, 27-20 (KC)
1993—Chiefs, 27-3 (TB)
1999—Buccaneers, 17-10 (TB)
2004—Buccaneers, 34-31 (TB)
(RS Pts.—Chiefs 179, Buccaneers 156)

*KANSAS CITY vs. **TENNESSEE
RS: Chiefs lead series, 25-19
PS: Chiefs lead series, 2-0
1960—Oilers, 20-10 (H)
Texans, 24-0 (D)
1961—Texans, 26-21 (D)
Oilers, 38-7 (H)
1962—Texans, 31-7 (H)
Oilers, 14-6 (D)
***Texans, 20-17 (H) OT
1963—Chiefs, 28-7 (KC)
Oilers, 28-7 (H)
1964—Chiefs, 28-7 (KC)
Chiefs, 28-19 (H)
1965—Chiefs, 52-21 (KC)
Oilers, 38-36 (H)
1966—Chiefs, 48-23 (KC)
1967—Chiefs, 25-20 (H)
Oilers, 24-19 (KC)
1968—Chiefs, 26-21 (H)
Chiefs, 24-10 (KC)
1969—Chiefs, 24-0 (KC)
1970—Chiefs, 24-9 (KC)
1971—Chiefs, 20-16 (H)
1973—Chiefs, 38-14 (KC)
1974—Chiefs, 17-7 (H)
1975—Oilers, 17-13 (KC)
1977—Oilers, 34-20 (H)
1978—Oilers, 20-17 (KC)
1979—Oilers, 20-6 (H)
1980—Chiefs, 21-20 (KC)
1981—Chiefs, 23-10 (KC)
1983—Chiefs, 13-10 (H) OT
1984—Oilers, 17-16 (KC)
1985—Oilers, 23-20 (H)
1986—Oilers, 27-13 (KC)
1988—Oilers, 7-6 (H)
1989—Chiefs, 34-0 (KC)
1990—Oilers, 27-10 (KC)
1991—Oilers, 17-7 (H)

1992—Oilers, 23-20 (H) OT
1993—Oilers, 30-0 (H)
    ****Chiefs, 28-20 (H)
1994—Chiefs, 31-9 (KC)
1995—Chiefs, 20-13 (KC)
1996—Chiefs, 20-19 (H)
2000—Titans, 17-14 (T) OT
2004—Chiefs, 49-38 (T)
2007—Titans, 26-17 (KC)
(RS Pts.—Chiefs 952, Titans 774)
(PS Pts.—Chiefs 48, Titans 37)
*Franchise in Dallas prior to 1963 and
known as Texans
**Franchise in Houston prior to 1997;
known as Oilers prior to 1999
***AFL Championship
****AFC Divisional Playoff
KANSAS CITY vs. WASHINGTON
RS: Chiefs lead series, 6-1
1971—Chiefs, 27-20 (KC)
1976—Chiefs, 33-30 (W)
1983—Redskins, 27-12 (W)
1992—Chiefs, 35-16 (KC)
1995—Chiefs, 24-3 (KC)
2001—Chiefs, 45-13 (W)
2005—Chiefs, 28-21, (KC)
(RS Pts.—Chiefs 204, Redskins 130)

MIAMI vs. ARIZONA
RS: Dolphins lead series, 8-1;
See Arizona vs. Miami
MIAMI vs. ATLANTA
RS: Dolphins lead series, 7-3;
See Atlanta vs. Miami
MIAMI vs. BALTIMORE
RS: Dolphins lead series, 5-1
PS: Ravens lead series, 1-0;
See Baltimore vs. Miami
MIAMI vs. BUFFALO
RS: Dolphins lead series, 49-34-1
PS: Bills lead series, 3-1;
See Buffalo vs. Miami
MIAMI vs. CAROLINA
RS: Dolphins lead series, 3-0;
See Carolina vs. Miami
MIAMI vs. CHICAGO
RS: Dolphins lead series, 7-3;
See Chicago vs. Miami
MIAMI vs. CINCINNATI
RS: Dolphins lead series, 12-5
PS: Dolphins lead series, 1-0;
See Cincinnati vs. Miami
MIAMI vs. CLEVELAND
RS: Dolphins lead series, 7-6
PS: Dolphins lead series, 2-0;
See Cleveland vs. Miami
MIAMI vs. DALLAS
RS: Dolphins lead series, 7-4
PS: Cowboys lead series, 1-0;
See Dallas vs. Miami
MIAMI vs. DENVER
RS: Dolphins lead series, 10-3-1
PS: Broncos lead series, 1-0;
See Denver vs. Miami
MIAMI vs. DETROIT
RS: Dolphins lead series, 7-2;
See Detroit vs. Miami
MIAMI vs. GREEN BAY
RS: Dolphins lead series, 9-3;
See Green Bay vs. Miami

MIAMI vs. HOUSTON
RS: Texans lead series, 3-0;
See Houston vs. Miami
MIAMI vs. INDIANAPOLIS
RS: Dolphins lead series, 44-23
PS: Dolphins lead series, 2-0;
See Indianapolis vs. Miami
MIAMI vs. JACKSONVILLE
RS: Jaguars lead series, 2-1
PS: Jaguars lead series, 1-0;
See Jacksonville vs. Miami
MIAMI vs. KANSAS CITY
RS: Chiefs lead series, 12-11
PS: Dolphins lead series, 3-0;
See Kansas City vs. Miami
MIAMI vs. MINNESOTA
RS: Dolphins lead series, 5-4
PS: Dolphins lead series, 1-0
1972—Dolphins, 16-14 (Minn)
1973—*Dolphins, 24-7 (Houston)
1976—Vikings, 29-7 (Mia)
1979—Dolphins, 27-12 (Minn)
1982—Dolphins, 22-14 (Mia)
1988—Dolphins, 24-7 (Mia)
1994—Vikings, 38-35 (Minn)
2000—Vikings, 13-7 (Minn)
2002—Vikings, 20-17 (Minn)
2006—Dolphins, 24-20 (Mia)
(RS Pts.—Dolphins 179, Vikings 167)
(PS Pts.—Dolphins 24, Vikings 7)
*Super Bowl VIII
MIAMI vs. *NEW ENGLAND
RS: Dolphins lead series, 47-35
PS: Patriots lead series, 2-1
1966—Patriots, 20-14 (M)
1967—Patriots, 41-10 (B)
    Dolphins, 41-32 (M)
1968—Dolphins, 34-10 (B)
    Dolphins, 38-7 (M)
1969—Dolphins, 17-16 (B)
    Patriots, 38-23 (Tampa)
1970—Patriots, 27-14 (B)
    Dolphins, 37-20 (M)
1971—Dolphins, 41-3 (M)
    Patriots, 34-13 (NE)
1972—Dolphins, 52-0 (M)
    Dolphins, 37-21 (NE)
1973—Dolphins, 44-23 (M)
    Dolphins, 30-14 (NE)
1974—Patriots, 34-24 (NE)
    Dolphins, 34-27 (M)
1975—Dolphins, 22-14 (NE)
    Dolphins, 20-7 (M)
1976—Patriots, 30-14 (NE)
    Dolphins, 10-3 (M)
1977—Dolphins, 17-5 (M)
    Patriots, 14-10 (NE)
1978—Patriots, 33-24 (M)
    Dolphins, 23-3 (M)
1979—Patriots, 28-13 (NE)
    Dolphins, 39-24 (M)
1980—Patriots, 34-0 (NE)
    Dolphins, 16-13 (M) OT
1981—Dolphins, 30-27 (NE) OT
    Dolphins, 24-14 (M)
1982—Patriots, 3-0 (NE)
    **Dolphins, 28-13 (M)
1983—Dolphins, 34-24 (M)
    Patriots, 17-6 (NE)
1984—Dolphins, 28-7 (M)

    Dolphins, 44-24 (NE)
1985—Patriots, 17-13 (NE)
    Dolphins, 30-27 (M)
    ***Patriots, 31-14 (M)
1986—Patriots, 34-7 (NE)
    Patriots, 34-27 (M)
1987—Patriots, 28-21 (NE)
    Patriots, 24-10 (M)
1988—Patriots, 21-10 (NE)
    Patriots, 6-3 (M)
1989—Dolphins, 24-10 (M)
    Dolphins, 31-10 (M)
1990—Dolphins, 27-24 (NE)
    Dolphins, 17-10 (M)
1991—Dolphins, 20-10 (NE)
    Dolphins, 30-20 (M)
1992—Dolphins, 38-17 (M)
    Dolphins, 16-13 (NE) OT
1993—Dolphins, 17-13 (M)
    Patriots, 33-27 (NE) OT
1994—Dolphins, 39-35 (M)
    Dolphins, 23-3 (NE)
1995—Dolphins, 20-3 (NE)
    Patriots, 34-17 (M)
1996—Dolphins, 24-10 (M)
    Patriots, 42-23 (NE)
1997—Patriots, 27-24 (NE)
    Patriots, 14-12 (M)
    **Patriots, 17-3 (NE)
1998—Dolphins, 12-9 (M) OT
    Patriots, 26-23 (NE)
1999—Dolphins, 31-30 (NE)
    Dolphins, 27-17 (M)
2000—Dolphins, 10-3 (M)
    Dolphins, 27-24 (NE)
2001—Dolphins, 30-10 (M)
    Dolphins, 20-13 (NE)
2002—Dolphins, 26-13 (M)
    Patriots, 27-24 (NE) OT
2003—Patriots, 19-13 (M) OT
    Patriots, 12-0 (NE)
2004—Dolphins, 29-28 (M)
    Patriots, 23-16 (M)
2005—Patriots, 23-16 (M)
    Dolphins, 28-26 (NE)
2006—Patriots, 20-10 (NE)
    Dolphins, 21-0 (M)
2007—Patriots, 49-28 (M)
    Patriots, 28-7 (NE)
(RS Pts.—Dolphins 1,812, Patriots 1,618)
(PS Pts.—Patriots 61, Dolphins 45)
*Franchise in Boston prior to 1971
**AFC First-Round Playoff
***AFC Championship
MIAMI vs. NEW ORLEANS
RS: Dolphins lead series, 6-3
1970—Dolphins, 21-10 (M)
1974—Dolphins, 21-0 (NO)
1980—Dolphins, 21-16 (M)
1983—Saints, 17-7 (NO)
1986—Dolphins, 31-27 (NO)
1992—Saints, 24-13 (NO)
1995—Saints, 33-30 (NO)
1998—Dolphins, 30-10 (M)
2005—Dolphins, 21-6 (Baton Rouge)
(RS Pts.—Dolphins 195, Saints 143)
MIAMI vs. N.Y. GIANTS
RS: Giants lead series, 4-2
1972—Dolphins, 23-13 (NY)
1990—Giants, 20-3 (NY)

1993—Giants, 19-14 (M)
1996—Giants, 17-7 (M)
2003—Dolphins, 23-10 (NY)
2007—Giants, 13-10 (London)
(RS Pts.—Giants 92, Dolphins 80)
MIAMI vs. N.Y. JETS
RS: Jets lead series, 45-38-1
PS: Dolphins lead series, 1-0
1966—Jets, 19-14 (M)
    Jets, 30-13 (NY)
1967—Jets, 29-7 (NY)
    Jets, 33-14 (M)
1968—Jets, 35-17 (NY)
    Jets, 31-7 (M)
1969—Jets, 34-31 (NY)
    Jets, 27-9 (M)
1970—Dolphins, 20-6 (NY)
    Dolphins, 16-10 (M)
1971—Jets, 14-10 (M)
    Dolphins, 30-14 (NY)
1972—Dolphins, 27-17 (NY)
    Dolphins, 28-24 (M)
1973—Dolphins, 31-3 (M)
    Dolphins, 24-14 (NY)
1974—Dolphins, 21-17 (M)
    Jets, 17-14 (NY)
1975—Dolphins, 43-0 (NY)
    Dolphins, 27-7 (M)
1976—Dolphins, 16-0 (M)
    Dolphins, 27-7 (NY)
1977—Dolphins, 21-17 (M)
    Dolphins, 14-10 (NY)
1978—Jets, 33-20 (NY)
    Jets, 24-13 (M)
1979—Jets, 33-27 (NY)
    Jets, 27-24 (M)
1980—Jets, 17-14 (NY)
    Jets, 24-17 (M)
1981—Tie, 28-28 (M) OT
    Jets, 16-15 (NY)
1982—Dolphins, 45-28 (NY)
    Dolphins, 20-19 (M)
    *Dolphins, 14-0 (M)
1983—Dolphins, 32-14 (NY)
    Dolphins, 34-14 (M)
1984—Dolphins, 31-17 (NY)
    Dolphins, 28-17 (M)
1985—Jets, 23-7 (NY)
    Dolphins, 21-17 (M)
1986—Jets, 51-45 (NY) OT
    Dolphins, 45-3 (M)
1987—Jets, 37-31 (NY) OT
    Dolphins, 37-28 (M)
1988—Jets, 44-30 (M)
    Jets, 38-34 (NY)
1989—Jets, 40-33 (M)
    Dolphins, 31-23 (NY)
1990—Dolphins, 20-16 (M)
    Dolphins, 17-3 (NY)
1991—Jets, 41-23 (NY)
    Jets, 23-20 (M) OT
1992—Jets, 26-14 (NY)
    Dolphins, 19-17 (M)
1993—Jets, 24-14 (M)
    Jets, 27-10 (NY)
1994—Dolphins, 28-14 (M)
    Dolphins, 28-24 (NY)
1995—Dolphins, 52-14 (M)
    Jets, 17-16 (NY)
1996—Dolphins, 36-27 (M)

Dolphins, 31-28 (NY)
1997—Dolphins, 31-20 (NY)
    Dolphins, 24-17 (M)
1998—Jets, 20-9 (NY)
    Jets, 21-16 (M)
1999—Jets, 28-20 (NY)
    Jets, 38-31 (M)
2000—Jets, 40-37 (NY) OT
    Jets, 20-3 (M)
2001—Jets, 21-17 (NY)
    Jets, 24-0 (M)
2002—Dolphins, 30-3 (M)
    Jets, 13-10 (NY)
2003—Dolphins, 21-10 (NY)
    Dolphins, 23-21 (M)
2004—Jets, 17-9 (M)
    Jets, 41-14 (NY)
2005—Jets, 17-7 (NY)
    Dolphins, 24-20 (M)
2006—Jets, 20-17 (NY)
    Jets, 13-10 (M)
2007—Jets, 31-28 (NY)
    Jets, 40-13 (M)
(RS Pts.—Dolphins 1,865, Jets 1,826)
(PS Pts.—Dolphins 14, Jets 0)
*AFC Championship
MIAMI vs. *OAKLAND
RS: Raiders lead series, 16-11-1
PS: Raiders lead series, 3-1
1966—Raiders, 23-14 (M)
    Raiders, 21-10 (O)
1967—Raiders, 31-17 (O)
1968—Raiders, 47-21 (M)
1969—Raiders, 20-17 (O)
    Tie, 20-20 (M)
1970—Dolphins, 20-13 (M)
    **Raiders, 21-14 (O)
1973—Raiders, 12-7 (O)
    ***Dolphins, 27-10 (M)
1974—**Raiders, 28-26 (O)
1975—Raiders, 31-21 (M)
1978—Dolphins, 23-6 (M)
1979—Raiders, 13-3 (O)
1980—Raiders, 16-10 (O)
1981—Raiders, 33-17 (M)
1983—Raiders, 27-14 (LA)
1984—Raiders, 45-34 (M)
1986—Raiders, 30-28 (M)
1988—Dolphins, 24-14 (LA)
1990—Raiders, 13-10 (M)
1992—Dolphins, 20-7 (M)
1994—Dolphins, 20-17 (M) OT
1996—Raiders, 17-7 (O)
1997—Dolphins, 34-16 (O)
1998—Dolphins, 27-17 (O)
1999—Dolphins, 16-9 (O)
2000—**Raiders, 27-0 (O)
2001—Dolphins, 18-15 (M)
2002—Dolphins, 23-17 (M)
2005—Dolphins, 33-21 (O)
2007—Raiders, 35-17 (M)
(RS Pts.—Raiders 586, Dolphins 525)
(PS Pts.—Raiders 86, Dolphins 67)
*Franchise in Los Angeles from 1982-1994
**AFC Divisional Playoff
***AFC Championship
MIAMI vs. PHILADELPHIA
RS: Dolphins lead series, 7-5
1970—Eagles, 24-17 (P)
1975—Dolphins, 24-16 (M)

1978—Eagles, 17-3 (P)
1981—Dolphins, 13-10 (M)
1984—Dolphins, 24-23 (M)
1987—Dolphins, 28-10 (P)
1990—Dolphins, 23-20 (M) OT
1993—Dolphins, 19-14 (P)
1996—Eagles, 35-28 (P)
1999—Dolphins, 16-13 (M)
2003—Eagles, 34-27 (M)
2007—Eagles, 17-7 (P)
(RS Pts.—Eagles 233, Dolphins 229)
MIAMI vs. PITTSBURGH
RS: Steelers lead series, 10-9
PS: Dolphins lead series, 2-1
1971—Dolphins, 24-21 (M)
1972—*Dolphins, 21-17 (P)
1973—Dolphins, 30-26 (M)
1976—Steelers, 14-3 (P)
1979—**Steelers, 34-14 (P)
1980—Steelers, 23-10 (P)
1981—Dolphins, 30-10 (M)
1984—Dolphins, 31-7 (P)
    *Dolphins, 45-28 (M)
1985—Dolphins, 24-20 (M)
1987—Dolphins, 35-24 (M)
1988—Steelers, 40-24 (P)
1989—Steelers, 34-14 (P)
1990—Dolphins, 28-6 (P)
1993—Steelers, 21-20 (M)
1994—Steelers, 16-13 (P) OT
1995—Dolphins, 23-10 (M)
1996—Steelers, 24-17 (M)
1998—Dolphins, 21-0 (M)
2004—Steelers, 13-3 (M)
2006—Steelers, 28-17 (P)
2007—Steelers, 3-0 (P)
(RS Pts.—Dolphins 367, Steelers 340)
(PS Pts.—Dolphins 80, Steelers 79)
*AFC Championship
**AFC Divisional Playoff
MIAMI vs. *ST. LOUIS
RS: Dolphins lead series, 8-2
1971—Dolphins, 20-14 (LA)
1976—Rams, 31-28 (M)
1980—Dolphins, 35-14 (LA)
1983—Dolphins, 30-14 (M)
1986—Dolphins, 37-31 (LA) OT
1992—Dolphins, 26-10 (M)
1995—Dolphins, 41-22 (StL)
1998—Dolphins, 14-0 (M)
2001—Rams, 42-10 (StL)
2004—Dolphins, 31-14 (M)
(RS Pts.—Dolphins 272, Rams 192)
*Franchise in Los Angeles prior to 1995
MIAMI vs. SAN DIEGO
RS: Dolphins lead series, 11-10
PS: Series tied, 2-2
1966—Chargers, 44-10 (SD)
1967—Chargers, 24-0 (SD)
    Dolphins, 41-24 (M)
1968—Chargers, 34-28 (SD)
1969—Chargers, 21-14 (M)
1972—Dolphins, 24-10 (M)
1974—Dolphins, 28-21 (SD)
1977—Chargers, 14-13 (M)
1978—Dolphins, 28-21 (SD)
1980—Chargers, 27-24 (M) OT
1981—*Chargers, 41-38 (M) OT
1982—**Dolphins, 34-13 (M)
1984—Chargers, 34-28 (SD) OT

1986—Chargers, 50-28 (SD)
1988—Dolphins, 31-28 (M)
1991—Chargers, 38-30 (SD)
1992—*Dolphins, 31-0 (M)
1993—Chargers, 45-20 (SD)
1994—*Chargers, 22-21 (SD)
1995—Dolphins, 24-14 (SD)
1999—Dolphins, 12-9 (M)
2000—Dolphins, 17-7 (SD)
2002—Dolphins, 30-3 (M)
2003—Dolphins, 26-10 (Ariz)
2005—Dolphins, 23-21 (SD)
(RS Pts.—Chargers 499, Dolphins 479)
(PS Pts.—Dolphins 124, Chargers 76)
*AFC Divisional Playoff
**AFC Second-Round Playoff
MIAMI vs. SAN FRANCISCO
RS: Dolphins lead series, 5-4
PS: 49ers lead series, 1-0
1973—Dolphins, 21-13 (M)
1977—Dolphins, 19-15 (SF)
1980—Dolphins, 17-13 (M)
1983—Dolphins, 20-17 (SF)
1984—*49ers, 38-16 (Stanford)
1986—49ers, 31-16 (M)
1992—49ers, 27-3 (SF)
1995—49ers, 44-20 (M)
2001—49ers, 21-0 (SF)
2004—Dolphins, 24-17 (SF)
(RS Pts.—49ers 198, Dolphins 140)
(PS Pts.—49ers 38, Dolphins 16)
*Super Bowl XIX
MIAMI vs. SEATTLE
RS: Dolphins lead series, 6-3
PS: Dolphins lead series, 2-1
1977—Dolphins, 31-13 (M)
1979—Dolphins, 19-10 (M)
1983—*Seahawks, 27-20 (M)
1984—*Dolphins, 31-10 (M)
1987—Seahawks, 24-20 (S)
1990—Dolphins, 24-17 (M)
1992—Dolphins, 19-17 (S)
1996—Seahawks, 22-15 (M)
1999—**Dolphins, 20-17 (S)
2000—Dolphins, 23-0 (M)
2001—Dolphins, 24-20 (S)
2004—Seahawks, 24-17 (S)
(RS Pts.—Dolphins 192, Seahawks 147)
(PS Pts.—Dolphins 71, Seahawks 54)
*AFC Divisional Playoff
**AFC First-Round Playoff
MIAMI vs. TAMPA BAY
RS: Series tied, 4-4
1976—Dolphins, 23-20 (TB)
1982—Buccaneers, 23-17 (TB)
1985—Dolphins, 41-38 (M)
1988—Dolphins, 17-14 (TB)
1991—Dolphins, 33-14 (M)
1997—Buccaneers, 31-21 (TB)
2000—Buccaneers, 16-13 (M)
2005—Buccaneers, 27-13 (TB)
(RS Pts.—Buccaneers 183, Dolphins 178)
MIAMI vs. *TENNESSEE
RS: Dolphins lead series, 17-13
PS: Titans lead series, 1-0
1966—Dolphins, 20-13 (H)
          Dolphins, 29-28 (M)
1967—Oilers, 17-14 (H)
          Oilers, 41-10 (M)
1968—Oilers, 24-10 (M)

          Dolphins, 24-7 (H)
1969—Oilers, 22-10 (H)
          Oilers, 32-7 (M)
1970—Dolphins, 20-10 (H)
1972—Dolphins, 34-13 (M)
1975—Oilers, 20-19 (H)
1977—Dolphins, 27-7 (M)
1978—Oilers, 35-30 (H)
          **Oilers, 17-9 (M)
1979—Oilers, 9-6 (M)
1981—Dolphins, 16-10 (H)
1983—Dolphins, 24-17 (H)
1984—Dolphins, 28-10 (H)
1985—Oilers, 26-23 (H)
1986—Dolphins, 28-7 (M)
1989—Oilers, 39-7 (H)
1991—Oilers, 17-13 (M)
1992—Dolphins, 19-16 (M)
1996—Dolphins, 23-20 (H)
1997—Dolphins, 16-13 (M) OT
1999—Dolphins, 17-0 (M)
2001—Dolphins, 31-23 (T)
2003—Titans, 31-7 (T)
2004—Titans, 17-7 (M)
2005—Dolphins, 24-10 (M)
2006—Dolphins, 13-10 (M)
(RS Pts.—Dolphins 556, Titans 544)
(PS Pts.—Titans 17, Dolphins 9)
*Franchise in Houston prior to 1997;
known as Oilers prior to 1999
**AFC First-Round Playoff
MIAMI vs. WASHINGTON
RS: Dolphins lead series, 6-4
PS: Series tied, 1-1
1972—*Dolphins, 14-7 (Los Angeles)
1974—Redskins, 20-17 (W)
1978—Dolphins, 16-0 (W)
1981—Dolphins, 13-10 (M)
1982—**Redskins, 27-17 (Pasadena)
1984—Dolphins, 35-17 (W)
1987—Dolphins, 23-21 (M)
1990—Redskins, 42-20 (W)
1993—Dolphins, 17-10 (M)
1999—Redskins, 21-10 (W)
2003—Dolphins, 24-23 (M)
2007—Redskins, 16-13 (W) OT
(RS Pts.—Dolphins 188, Redskins 180)
(PS Pts.—Redskins 34, Dolphins 31)
*Super Bowl VII
**Super Bowl XVII

MINNESOTA vs. ARIZONA
RS: Series tied, 9-9
PS: Vikings lead series, 2-0;
See Arizona vs. Minnesota
MINNESOTA vs. ATLANTA
RS: Vikings lead series, 15-8
PS: Series tied, 1-1;
See Atlanta vs. Minnesota
MINNESOTA vs. BALTIMORE
RS: Ravens lead series, 2-1;
See Baltimore vs. Minnesota
MINNESOTA vs. BUFFALO
RS: Vikings lead series, 7-4;
See Buffalo vs. Minnesota
MINNESOTA vs. CAROLINA
RS: Vikings lead series, 4-3;
See Carolina vs. Minnesota
MINNESOTA vs. CHICAGO
RS: Vikings lead series, 50-41-2

PS: Bears lead series, 1-0;
See Chicago vs. Minnesota
MINNESOTA vs. CINCINNATI
RS: Series tied, 5-5;
See Cincinnati vs. Minnesota
MINNESOTA vs. CLEVELAND
RS: Vikings lead series, 9-3
PS: Vikings lead series, 1-0;
See Cleveland vs. Minnesota
MINNESOTA vs. DALLAS
RS: Series tied, 10-10
PS: Cowboys lead series, 4-2;
See Dallas vs. Minnesota
MINNESOTA vs. DENVER
RS: Vikings lead series, 7-5;
See Denver vs. Minnesota
MINNESOTA vs. DETROIT
RS: Vikings lead series, 61-30-2;
See Detroit vs. Minnesota
MINNESOTA vs. GREEN BAY
RS: Packers lead series, 48-44-1
PS: Vikings lead series, 1-0;
See Green Bay vs. Minnesota
MINNESOTA vs. HOUSTON
RS: Vikings lead series, 1-0;
See Houston vs. Minnesota
MINNESOTA vs. INDIANAPOLIS
RS: Colts lead series, 13-7-1
PS: Colts lead series, 1-0;
See Indianapolis vs. Minnesota
MINNESOTA vs. JACKSONVILLE
RS: Vikings lead series, 2-1;
See Jacksonville vs. Minnesota
MINNESOTA vs. KANSAS CITY
RS: Chiefs lead series, 5-4
PS: Chiefs lead series, 1-0;
See Kansas City vs. Minnesota
MINNESOTA vs. MIAMI
RS: Dolphins lead series, 5-4
PS: Dolphins lead series, 1-0;
See Miami vs. Minnesota
MINNESOTA vs. *NEW ENGLAND
RS: Patriots lead series, 6-4
1970—Vikings, 35-14 (B)
1974—Patriots, 17-14 (M)
1979—Patriots, 27-23 (NE)
1988—Vikings, 36-6 (M)
1991—Patriots, 26-23 (NE) OT
1994—Patriots, 26-20 (NE) OT
1997—Vikings, 23-18 (M)
2000—Vikings, 21-13 (NE)
2002—Patriots, 24-17 (NE)
2006—Patriots, 31-7 (M)
(RS Pts.—Vikings 219, Patriots 202)
*Franchise in Boston prior to 1971
MINNESOTA vs. NEW ORLEANS
RS: Vikings lead series, 17-7
PS: Vikings lead series, 2-0
1968—Saints, 20-17 (NO)
1970—Vikings, 26-0 (M)
1971—Vikings, 23-10 (NO)
1972—Vikings, 37-6 (M)
1974—Vikings, 29-9 (M)
1975—Vikings, 20-7 (NO)
1976—Vikings, 40-9 (NO)
1978—Saints, 31-24 (NO)
1980—Vikings, 23-20 (NO)
1981—Vikings, 20-10 (NO)
1983—Saints, 17-16 (NO)
1985—Saints, 30-23 (M)

1986—Vikings, 33-17 (M)
1987—*Vikings, 44-10 (NO)
1988—Vikings, 45-3 (M)
1990—Vikings, 32-3 (M)
1991—Saints, 26-0 (NO)
1993—Saints, 17-14 (M)
1994—Vikings, 21-20 (M)
1995—Vikings, 43-24 (M)
1998—Vikings, 31-24 (M)
2000—**Vikings, 34-16 (M)
2001—Saints, 28-15 (NO)
2002—Vikings, 32-31 (NO)
2004—Vikings, 38-31 (NO)
2005—Vikings, 33-16 (M)
(RS Pts.—Vikings 635, Saints 409)
(PS Pts.—Vikings 78, Saints 26)
*NFC First-Round Playoff
**NFC Divisional Playoff

MINNESOTA vs. N.Y. GIANTS
RS: Vikings lead series, 11-8
PS: Giants lead series, 2-1
1964—Vikings, 30-21 (NY)
1965—Vikings, 40-14 (M)
1967—Vikings, 27-24 (M)
1969—Giants, 24-23 (NY)
1971—Vikings, 17-10 (NY)
1973—Vikings, 31-7 (New Haven)
1976—Vikings, 24-7 (M)
1986—Giants, 22-20 (M)
1989—Giants, 24-14 (NY)
1990—Giants, 23-15 (NY)
1993—*Giants, 17-10 (NY)
1994—Vikings, 27-10 (NY)
1996—Giants, 15-10 (NY)
1997—*Vikings, 23-22 (NY)
1999—Vikings, 34-17 (NY)
2000—**Giants, 41-0 (NY)
2001—Vikings, 28-16 (M)
2002—Giants, 27-20 (M)
2003—Giants, 29-17 (M)
2004—Giants, 34-13 (M)
2005—Vikings, 24-21 (M)
2007—Vikings, 41-17 (NY)
(RS Pts.—Vikings 455, Giants 362)
(PS Pts.—Giants 80, Vikings 33)
*NFC First-Round Playoff
**NFC Championship

MINNESOTA vs. N.Y. JETS
RS: Jets lead series, 7-1
1970—Jets, 20-10 (NY)
1975—Vikings, 29-21 (M)
1979—Jets, 14-7 (NY)
1982—Jets, 42-14 (M)
1994—Jets, 31-21 (M)
1997—Jets, 23-21 (NY)
2002—Jets, 20-7 (NY)
2006—Jets, 26-13 (M)
(RS Pts.—Jets 197, Vikings 122)

MINNESOTA vs. *OAKLAND
RS: Raiders lead series, 8-4
PS: Raiders lead series, 1-0
1973—Vikings, 24-16 (M)
1976—**Raiders, 32-14 (Pasadena)
1977—Raiders, 35-13 (O)
1978—Raiders, 27-20 (O)
1981—Raiders, 36-10 (M)
1984—Raiders, 23-20 (LA)
1987—Vikings, 31-20 (M)
1990—Raiders, 28-24 (M)
1993—Raiders, 24-7 (LA)

1996—Vikings, 16-13 (O) OT
1999—Raiders, 22-17 (M)
2003—Raiders, 28-18 (O)
2007—Vikings, 29-22 (M)
(RS Pts.—Raiders 294, Vikings 229)
(PS Pts.—Raiders 32, Vikings 14)
*Franchise in Los Angeles from 1982-1994
**Super Bowl XI

MINNESOTA vs. PHILADELPHIA
RS: Vikings lead series, 11-9
PS: Eagles lead series, 2-0
1962—Vikings, 31-21 (M)
1963—Vikings, 34-13 (P)
1968—Vikings, 24-17 (P)
1971—Vikings, 13-0 (P)
1973—Vikings, 28-21 (M)
1976—Vikings, 31-12 (P)
1978—Vikings, 28-27 (M)
1980—Eagles, 42-7 (M)
       *Eagles, 31-16 (P)
1981—Vikings, 35-23 (M)
1984—Eagles, 19-17 (P)
1985—Vikings, 28-23 (M)
       Eagles, 37-35 (M)
1988—Vikings, 23-21 (M)
1989—Eagles, 10-9 (P)
1990—Eagles, 32-24 (P)
1992—Eagles, 28-17 (P)
1997—Vikings, 28-19 (M)
2001—Eagles, 48-17 (P)
2004—Eagles, 27-16 (P)
       *Eagles, 27-14 (P)
2007—Eagles, 23-16 (M)
(RS Pts.—Eagles 463, Vikings 461)
(PS Pts.—Eagles 58, Vikings 30)
*NFC Divisional Playoff

MINNESOTA vs. PITTSBURGH
RS: Vikings lead series, 8-6
PS: Steelers lead series, 1-0
1962—Steelers, 39-31 (P)
1964—Vikings, 30-10 (M)
1967—Vikings, 41-27 (P)
1969—Vikings, 52-14 (M)
1972—Steelers, 23-10 (P)
1974—*Steelers, 16-6 (New Orleans)
1976—Vikings, 17-6 (M)
1980—Steelers, 23-17 (M)
1983—Vikings, 17-14 (P)
1986—Vikings, 31-7 (M)
1989—Steelers, 27-14 (P)
1992—Vikings, 6-3 (P)
1995—Vikings, 44-24 (M)
2001—Steelers, 21-16 (P)
2005—Steelers, 18-3 (M)
(RS Pts.—Vikings 329, Steelers 256)
(PS Pts.—Steelers 16, Vikings 6)
*Super Bowl IX

MINNESOTA vs. *ST. LOUIS
RS: Vikings lead series, 17-14-2
PS: Vikings lead series, 5-2
1961—Rams, 31-17 (LA)
       Vikings, 42-21 (M)
1962—Rams, 38-14 (LA)
       Tie, 24-24 (M)
1963—Rams, 27-24 (LA)
       Vikings, 21-13 (M)
1964—Rams, 22-13 (LA)
       Vikings, 34-13 (M)
1965—Vikings, 38-35 (LA)
       Vikings, 24-13 (M)

1966—Vikings, 35-7 (M)
       Rams, 21-6 (LA)
1967—Rams, 39-3 (LA)
1968—Rams, 31-3 (M)
1969—Vikings, 20-13 (LA)
       **Vikings, 23-20 (M)
1970—Vikings, 13-3 (M)
1972—Vikings, 45-41 (LA)
1973—Vikings, 10-9 (M)
1974—Rams, 20-17 (LA)
       ***Vikings, 14-10 (M)
1976—Tie, 10-10 (M) OT
       ***Vikings, 24-13 (M)
1977—Rams, 35-3 (LA)
       ****Vikings, 14-7 (LA)
1978—Rams, 34-17 (M)
       ****Rams, 34-10 (LA)
1979—Rams, 27-21 (LA) OT
1985—Rams, 13-10 (LA)
1987—Vikings, 21-16 (LA)
1988—*****Vikings, 28-17 (M)
1989—Vikings, 23-21 (M) OT
1991—Vikings, 20-14 (M)
1992—Vikings, 31-17 (LA)
1998—Vikings, 38-31 (StL)
1999—****Rams, 49-37 (StL)
2000—Rams, 40-29 (StL)
2003—Rams, 48-17 (StL)
2005—Vikings, 27-13 (M)
2006—Rams, 41-21 (M)
(RS Pts.—Rams 757, Vikings 715)
(PS Pts.—Rams 150, Vikings 150)
*Franchise in Los Angeles prior to 1995
**Conference Championship
***NFC Championship
****NFC Divisional Playoff
*****NFC First-Round Playoff

MINNESOTA vs. SAN DIEGO
RS: Series tied, 5-5
1971—Chargers, 30-14 (SD)
1975—Vikings, 28-13 (M)
1978—Chargers, 13-7 (M)
1981—Vikings, 33-31 (SD)
1984—Chargers, 42-13 (M)
1985—Vikings, 21-17 (M)
1993—Chargers, 30-17 (M)
1999—Vikings, 35-27 (M)
2003—Chargers, 42-28 (SD)
2007—Vikings, 35-17 (M)
(RS Pts.—Chargers 262, Vikings 231)

MINNESOTA vs. SAN FRANCISCO
RS: Vikings lead series, 19-18-1
PS: 49ers lead series, 4-1
1961—49ers, 38-24 (M)
       49ers, 38-28 (SF)
1962—49ers, 21-7 (SF)
       49ers, 35-12 (M)
1963—Vikings, 24-20 (SF)
       Vikings, 45-14 (M)
1964—Vikings, 27-22 (SF)
       Vikings, 24-7 (M)
1965—Vikings, 42-41 (SF)
       49ers, 45-24 (M)
1966—Tie, 20-20 (SF)
       Vikings, 28-3 (SF)
1967—49ers, 27-21 (M)
1968—Vikings, 30-20 (SF)
1969—Vikings, 10-7 (M)
1970—*49ers, 17-14 (M)
1971—49ers, 13-9 (M)

1972—49ers, 20-17 (SF)
1973—Vikings, 17-13 (SF)
1975—Vikings, 27-17 (M)
1976—49ers, 20-16 (SF)
1977—Vikings, 28-27 (M)
1979—Vikings, 28-22 (M)
1983—49ers, 48-17 (M)
1984—49ers, 51-7 (SF)
1985—Vikings, 28-21 (M)
1986—Vikings, 27-24 (SF) OT
1987—*Vikings, 36-24 (SF)
1988—49ers, 24-21 (SF)
　　　　*49ers, 34-9 (SF)
1989—*49ers, 41-13 (SF)
1990—49ers, 20-17 (M)
1991—Vikings, 17-14 (M)
1992—49ers, 20-17 (M)
1993—49ers, 38-19 (SF)
1994—Vikings, 21-14 (M)
1995—Vikings, 37-30 (M)
1997—49ers, 28-17 (SF)
　　　　*49ers, 38-22 (SF)
1999—Vikings, 40-16 (M)
2003—Vikings, 35-7 (M)
2006—49ers, 9-3 (SF)
2007—Vikings, 27-7 (SF)
(RS Pts.—49ers 868, Vikings 851)
(PS Pts.—49ers 154, Vikings 94)
*NFC Divisional Playoff
MINNESOTA vs. SEATTLE
RS: Seahawks lead series, 6-4
1976—Vikings, 27-21 (M)
1978—Seahawks, 29-28 (S)
1984—Seahawks, 20-12 (M)
1987—Seahawks, 28-17 (S)
1990—Vikings, 24-21 (S)
1996—Seahawks, 42-23 (S)
2002—Seahawks, 48-23 (S)
2003—Vikings, 34-7 (M)
2004—Seahawks, 27-23 (M)
2006—Vikings, 31-13 (S)
(RS Pts.—Seahawks 256, Vikings 242)
MINNESOTA vs. TAMPA BAY
RS: Vikings lead series, 31-19
1977—Vikings, 9-3 (TB)
1978—Buccaneers, 16-10 (M)
　　　　Vikings, 24-7 (TB)
1979—Buccaneers, 12-10 (M)
　　　　Vikings, 23-22 (TB)
1980—Vikings, 38-30 (M)
　　　　Vikings, 21-10 (TB)
1981—Buccaneers, 21-13 (TB)
　　　　Vikings, 25-10 (M)
1982—Vikings, 17-10 (M)
1983—Vikings, 19-16 (TB) OT
　　　　Buccaneers, 17-12 (M)
1984—Buccaneers, 35-31 (TB)
　　　　Vikings, 27-24 (M)
1985—Vikings, 31-16 (TB)
　　　　Vikings, 26-7 (M)
1986—Vikings, 23-10 (TB)
　　　　Vikings, 45-13 (M)
1987—Buccaneers, 20-10 (TB)
　　　　Vikings, 23-17 (M)
1988—Vikings, 14-13 (M)
　　　　Vikings, 49-20 (TB)
1989—Vikings, 17-3 (M)
　　　　Vikings, 24-10 (TB)
1990—Buccaneers, 23-20 (M) OT
　　　　Buccaneers, 26-13 (TB)

1991—Vikings, 28-13 (M)
　　　　Vikings, 26-24 (TB)
1992—Vikings, 26-20 (M)
　　　　Vikings, 35-7 (TB)
1993—Vikings, 15-0 (M)
　　　　Buccaneers, 23-10 (TB)
1994—Vikings, 36-13 (TB)
　　　　Buccaneers, 20-17 (M) OT
1995—Buccaneers, 20-17 (TB) OT
　　　　Vikings, 31-17 (M)
1996—Buccaneers, 24-13 (TB)
　　　　Vikings, 21-10 (M)
1997—Buccaneers, 28-14 (M)
　　　　Vikings, 10-6 (TB)
1998—Vikings, 31-7 (M)
　　　　Buccaneers, 27-24 (TB)
1999—Vikings, 21-14 (M)
　　　　Buccaneers, 24-17 (TB)
2000—Vikings, 30-23 (M)
　　　　Buccaneers, 41-13 (TB)
2001—Vikings, 20-16 (M)
　　　　Buccaneers, 41-14 (TB)
2002—Buccaneers, 38-24 (TB)
2005—Buccaneers, 24-13 (M)
(RS Pts.—Vikings 1,080, Buccaneers 891)
MINNESOTA vs. *TENNESSEE
RS: Vikings lead series, 7-3
1974—Vikings, 51-10 (M)
1980—Oilers, 20-16 (H)
1983—Vikings, 34-14 (M)
1986—Oilers, 23-10 (H)
1989—Vikings, 38-7 (M)
1992—Oilers, 17-13 (M)
1995—Vikings, 23-17 (M) OT
1998—Vikings, 26-16 (T)
2001—Vikings, 42-24 (M)
2004—Vikings, 20-3 (M)
(RS Pts.—Vikings 273, Titans 151)
*Franchise in Houston prior to 1997; known as Oilers prior to 1999
MINNESOTA vs. WASHINGTON
RS: Redskins lead series, 8-6
PS: Redskins lead series, 3-2
1968—Vikings, 27-14 (M)
1970—Vikings, 19-10 (M)
1972—Redskins, 24-21 (M)
1973—*Vikings, 27-20 (M)
1975—Redskins, 31-30 (W)
1976—*Vikings, 35-20 (M)
1980—Vikings, 39-14 (W)
1982—**Redskins, 21-7 (W)
1984—Redskins, 31-17 (M)
1986—Redskins, 44-38 (W) OT
1987—Redskins, 27-24 (M) OT
　　　　***Redskins, 17-10 (W)
1992—Redskins, 15-13 (M)
　　　　****Redskins, 24-7 (M)
1993—Vikings, 14-9 (W)
1998—Vikings, 41-7 (M)
2004—Redskins, 21-18 (W)
2006—Vikings, 19-16 (W)
2007—Redskins, 32-21 (M)
(RS Pts.—Vikings 341, Redskins 295)
(PS Pts.—Redskins 102, Vikings 86)
*NFC Divisional Playoff
**NFC Second-Round Playoff
***NFC Championship
****NFC First-Round Playoff

NEW ENGLAND vs. ARIZONA

RS: Cardinals lead series, 6-5;
See Arizona vs. New England
NEW ENGLAND vs. ATLANTA
RS: Falcons lead series, 6-5;
See Atlanta vs. New England
NEW ENGLAND vs. BALTIMORE
RS: Patriots lead series, 4-0;
See Baltimore vs. New England
NEW ENGLAND vs. BUFFALO
RS: Patriots lead series, 54-40-1
PS: Patriots lead series, 1-0;
See Buffalo vs. New England
NEW ENGLAND vs. CAROLINA
RS: Panthers lead series, 2-1
PS: Patriots lead series, 1-0;
See Carolina vs. New England
NEW ENGLAND vs. CHICAGO
RS: Patriots lead series, 7-3
PS: Bears lead series, 1-0;
See Chicago vs. New England
NEW ENGLAND vs. CINCINNATI
RS: Patriots lead series, 13-8;
See Cincinnati vs. New England
NEW ENGLAND vs. CLEVELAND
RS: Browns lead series, 11-9
PS: Browns lead series, 1-0;
See Cleveland vs. New England
NEW ENGLAND vs. DALLAS
RS: Cowboys lead series, 7-3;
See Dallas vs. New England
NEW ENGLAND vs. DENVER
RS: Broncos lead series, 24-15
PS: Broncos lead series, 2-0;
See Denver vs. New England
NEW ENGLAND vs. DETROIT
RS: Patriots lead series, 5-4;
See Detroit vs. New England
NEW ENGLAND vs. GREEN BAY
RS: Series tied, 4-4
PS: Packers lead series, 1-0;
See Green Bay vs. New England
NEW ENGLAND vs. HOUSTON
RS: Patriots lead series, 2-0;
See Houston vs. New England
NEW ENGLAND vs. INDIANAPOLIS
RS: Patriots lead series, 42-26
PS: Patriots lead series, 2-1;
See Indianapolis vs. New England
NEW ENGLAND vs. JACKSONVILLE
RS: Patriots lead series, 4-0
PS: Patriots lead series, 3-1;
See Jacksonville vs. New England
NEW ENGLAND vs. KANSAS CITY
RS: Chiefs lead series, 16-11-3;
See Kansas City vs. New England
NEW ENGLAND vs. MIAMI
RS: Dolphins lead series, 47-35
PS: Patriots lead series, 2-1;
See Miami vs. New England
NEW ENGLAND vs. MINNESOTA
RS: Patriots lead series, 6-4;
See Minnesota vs. New England
NEW ENGLAND vs. NEW ORLEANS
RS: Patriots lead series, 8-3
1972—Patriots, 17-10 (NO)
1976—Patriots, 27-6 (NE)
1980—Patriots, 38-27 (NE)
1983—Patriots, 7-0 (NE)
1986—Patriots, 21-20 (NO)
1989—Saints, 28-24 (NE)

1992—Saints, 31-14 (NE)
1995—Saints, 31-17 (NE)
1998—Patriots, 30-27 (NO)
2001—Patriots, 34-17 (NE)
2005—Patriots, 24-17 (NE)
(RS Pts.—Patriots 253, Saints 214)
*NEW ENGLAND vs. N.Y. GIANTS
RS: Patriots lead series, 5-3
PS: Giants lead series, 1-0;
1970—Giants, 16-0 (B)
1974—Patriots, 28-20 (New Haven)
1987—Giants, 17-10 (NY)
1990—Giants, 13-10 (NE)
1996—Patriots, 23-22 (NY)
1999—Patriots, 16-14 (NE)
2003—Patriots, 17-6 (NE)
2007—Patriots, 38-35 (NY)
      **Giants, 17-14 (Arizona)
(RS Pts.—Giants 143, Patriots 142)
(PS Pts.—Giants 17, Patriots 14)
*Franchise in Boston prior to 1971
**Super Bowl XLII
*NEW ENGLAND vs. **N.Y. JETS
RS: Jets lead series, 48-46-1
PS: Patriots lead series, 2-0
1960—Patriots, 28-24 (NY)
      Patriots, 38-21 (B)
1961—Titans, 21-20 (B)
      Titans, 37-30 (NY)
1962—Patriots, 43-14 (NY)
      Patriots, 24-17 (B)
1963—Patriots, 38-14 (B)
      Jets, 31-24 (NY)
1964—Patriots, 26-10 (B)
      Jets, 35-14 (NY)
1965—Jets, 30-20 (B)
      Patriots, 27-23 (NY)
1966—Tie, 24-24 (B)
      Jets, 38-28 (NY)
1967—Jets, 30-23 (NY)
      Jets, 29-24 (B)
1968—Jets, 47-31 (Birmingham)
      Jets, 48-14 (NY)
1969—Jets, 23-14 (B)
      Jets, 23-17 (NY)
1970—Jets, 31-21 (B)
      Jets, 17-3 (NY)
1971—Patriots, 20-0 (NE)
      Jets, 13-6 (NY)
1972—Jets, 41-13 (NE)
      Jets, 34-10 (NY)
1973—Jets, 9-7 (NE)
      Jets, 33-13 (NY)
1974—Patriots, 24-0 (NY)
      Jets, 21-16 (NE)
1975—Jets, 36-7 (NY)
      Jets, 30-28 (NE)
1976—Patriots, 41-7 (NE)
      Patriots, 38-24 (NY)
1977—Jets, 30-27 (NY)
      Patriots, 24-13 (NE)
1978—Patriots, 55-21 (NE)
      Patriots, 19-17 (NY)
1979—Patriots, 56-3 (NE)
      Jets, 27-26 (NY)
1980—Jets, 21-11 (NY)
      Patriots, 34-21 (NE)
1981—Jets, 28-24 (NY)
      Jets, 17-6 (NE)
1982—Jets, 31-7 (NE)

1983—Patriots, 23-13 (NE)
      Jets, 26-3 (NY)
1984—Patriots, 28-21 (NY)
      Patriots, 30-20 (NE)
1985—Patriots, 20-13 (NE)
      Jets, 16-13 (NY) OT
      ***Patriots, 26-14 (NY)
1986—Patriots, 20-6 (NY)
      Jets, 31-24 (NE)
1987—Jets, 43-24 (NY)
      Patriots, 42-20 (NE)
1988—Patriots, 28-3 (NE)
      Patriots, 14-13 (NY)
1989—Patriots, 27-24 (NY)
      Jets, 27-26 (NE)
1990—Jets, 37-13 (NE)
      Jets, 42-7 (NY)
1991—Jets, 28-21 (NE)
      Patriots, 6-3 (NY)
1992—Jets, 30-21 (NY)
      Patriots, 24-3 (NE)
1993—Jets, 45-7 (NY)
      Jets, 6-0 (NE)
1994—Jets, 24-17 (NY)
      Patriots, 24-13 (NE)
1995—Patriots, 20-7 (NY)
      Patriots, 31-28 (NE)
1996—Patriots, 31-27 (NY)
      Patriots, 34-10 (NE)
1997—Patriots, 27-24 (NE) OT
      Jets, 24-19 (NY)
1998—Jets, 24-14 (NE)
      Jets, 31-10 (NY)
1999—Patriots, 30-28 (NY)
      Jets, 24-17 (NE)
2000—Jets, 20-19 (NY)
      Jets, 34-17 (NE)
2001—Jets, 10-3 (NE)
      Patriots, 17-16 (NY)
2002—Patriots, 44-7 (NY)
      Jets, 30-17 (NE)
2003—Patriots, 23-16 (NE)
      Patriots, 21-16 (NY)
2004—Patriots, 13-7 (NE)
      Patriots, 23-7 (NY)
2005—Patriots, 16-3 (NE)
      Patriots, 31-21 (NY)
2006—Patriots, 24-17 (NY)
      Jets, 17-14 (NE)
      ***Patriots, 37-16 (NE)
2007—Patriots, 38-14 (NY)
      Patriots, 20-10 (NE)
(RS Pts.—Patriots 2,088, Jets 2,033)
(PS Pts.—Patriots 63, Jets 30)
*Franchise in Boston prior to 1971
**Jets known as Titans prior to 1963
***AFC First-Round Playoff
*NEW ENGLAND vs. **OAKLAND
RS: Raiders lead series, 14-13-1
PS: Patriots lead series, 2-1
1960—Raiders, 27-14 (O)
      Patriots, 34-28 (B)
1961—Patriots, 20-17 (B)
      Patriots, 35-21 (O)
1962—Patriots, 26-16 (B)
      Raiders, 20-0 (O)
1963—Patriots, 20-14 (O)
      Patriots, 20-14 (B)
1964—Patriots, 17-14 (O)
      Tie, 43-43 (B)

1965—Raiders, 24-10 (B)
      Raiders, 30-21 (O)
1966—Patriots, 24-21 (B)
1967—Raiders, 35-7 (O)
      Raiders, 48-14 (B)
1968—Raiders, 41-10 (O)
1969—Raiders, 38-23 (B)
1971—Patriots, 20-6 (NE)
1974—Raiders, 41-26 (O)
1976—Patriots, 48-17 (NE)
      ***Raiders, 24-21 (O)
1978—Patriots, 21-14 (O)
1981—Raiders, 27-17 (O)
1985—Raiders, 35-20 (NE)
      ***Patriots, 27-20 (LA)
1987—Patriots, 26-23 (NE)
1989—Raiders, 24-21 (LA)
1994—Raiders, 21-17 (NE)
2001—***Patriots, 16-13 (NE) OT
2002—Raiders, 27-20 (O)
2005—Patriots, 30-20 (NE)
(RS Pts.—Raiders 706, Patriots 604)
(PS Pts.—Patriots 64, Raiders 57)
*Franchise in Boston prior to 1971
**Franchise in Los Angeles from
1982-1994
***AFC Divisional Playoff
NEW ENGLAND vs. PHILADELPHIA
RS: Eagles lead series, 6-4
PS: Patriots lead series, 1-0
1973—Eagles, 24-23 (P)
1977—Patriots, 14-6 (NE)
1978—Patriots, 24-14 (NE)
1981—Eagles, 13-3 (P)
1984—Eagles, 27-17 (P)
1987—Eagles, 34-31 (NE) OT
1990—Eagles, 48-20 (P)
1999—Eagles, 24-9 (P)
2003—Patriots, 31-10 (P)
2004—*Patriots, 24-21 (Jacksonville)
2007—Patriots, 31-28 (NE)
(RS Pts.—Eagles 228, Patriots 203)
(PS Pts.—Patriots 24, Eagles 21)
*Super Bowl XXXIX
NEW ENGLAND vs. PITTSBURGH
RS: Steelers lead series, 12-7
PS: Patriots lead series, 3-1
1972—Steelers, 33-3 (P)
1974—Steelers, 21-17 (NE)
1976—Patriots, 30-27 (P)
1979—Steelers, 16-13 (NE) OT
1981—Steelers, 27-21 (P) OT
1982—Steelers, 37-14 (P)
1983—Patriots, 28-23 (P)
1986—Patriots, 34-0 (P)
1989—Steelers, 28-10 (P)
1990—Steelers, 24-3 (P)
1991—Steelers, 20-6 (P)
1993—Steelers, 17-14 (P)
1995—Steelers, 41-27 (P)
1996—*Patriots, 28-3 (NE)
1997—Steelers, 24-21 (NE) OT
      *Steelers, 7-6 (P)
1998—Patriots, 23-9 (P)
2001—**Patriots, 24-17 (P)
2002—Patriots, 30-14 (NE)
2004—Steelers, 34-20 (P)
      **Patriots, 41-27 (P)
2005—Patriots, 23-20 (P)
2007—Patriots, 34-13 (NE)

(RS Pts.—Steelers 428, Patriots 371)
(PS Pts.—Patriots 99, Steelers 54)
AFC Divisional Playoff
**AFC Championship*
NEW ENGLAND vs. *ST. LOUIS
RS: Rams lead series, 5-4
PS: Patriots lead series, 1-0
1974—Patriots, 20-14 (NE)
1980—Rams, 17-14 (NE)
1983—Patriots, 21-7 (LA)
1986—Patriots, 30-28 (LA)
1989—Rams, 24-20 (NE)
1992—Rams, 14-0 (LA)
1998—Rams, 32-18 (StL)
2001—Rams, 24-17 (NE)
**Patriots, 20-17 (New Orleans)
2004—Patriots, 40-22 (StL)
(RS Pts.—Rams 182, Patriots 180)
(PS Pts.—Patriots 20, Rams 17)
Franchise in Los Angeles prior to 1995
**Super Bowl XXXVI*
NEW ENGLAND vs. **SAN DIEGO
RS: Patriots lead series, 18-13-2
PS: Patriots lead series, 2-1
1960—Patriots, 35-0 (LA)
Chargers, 45-16 (B)
1961—Chargers, 38-27 (B)
Patriots, 41-0 (SD)
1962—Patriots, 24-20 (B)
Patriots, 20-14 (SD)
1963—Chargers, 17-13 (SD)
Chargers, 7-6 (B)
***Chargers, 51-10 (SD)
1964—Patriots, 33-28 (SD)
Chargers, 26-17 (B)
1965—Tie, 10-10 (B)
Patriots, 22-6 (SD)
1966—Chargers, 24-0 (SD)
Patriots, 35-17 (B)
1967—Chargers, 28-14 (SD)
Tie, 31-31 (SD)
1968—Chargers, 27-17 (B)
1969—Chargers, 13-10 (B)
Chargers, 28-18 (SD)
1970—Chargers, 16-14 (B)
1973—Patriots, 30-14 (NE)
1975—Patriots, 33-19 (SD)
1977—Patriots, 24-20 (SD)
1978—Patriots, 28-23 (NE)
1979—Patriots, 27-21 (NE)
1983—Patriots, 37-21 (NE)
1994—Patriots, 23-17 (NE)
1996—Patriots, 45-7 (SD)
1997—Patriots, 41-7 (NE)
2001—Patriots, 29-26 (NE) OT
2002—Chargers, 21-14 (SD)
2005—Chargers, 41-17 (NE)
2006—****Patriots, 24-21 (SD)
2007—Patriots, 38-14 (NE)
*****Patriots, 21-12 (NE)
(RS Pts.—Patriots 792, Chargers 649)
(PS Pts.—Chargers 84, Patriots 55)
Franchise in Boston prior to 1971
**Franchise in Los Angeles prior to 1961*
***AFL Championship*
****AFC Divisional Playoff*
*****AFC Championship*
NEW ENGLAND vs. SAN FRANCISCO
RS: 49ers lead series, 7-3
1971—49ers, 27-10 (SF)

1975—Patriots, 24-16 (NE)
1980—49ers, 21-17 (SF)
1983—Patriots, 33-13 (NE)
1986—49ers, 29-24 (NE)
1989—49ers, 37-20 (SF)
1992—49ers, 24-12 (NE)
1995—49ers, 28-3 (SF)
1998—Patriots, 24-21 (NE)
2004—Patriots, 21-7 (NE)
(RS Pts.—49ers 243, Patriots 168)
NEW ENGLAND vs. SEATTLE
RS: Series tied, 7-7
1977—Patriots, 31-0 (NE)
1980—Patriots, 37-31 (S)
1982—Patriots, 16-0 (S)
1983—Seahawks, 24-6 (S)
1984—Patriots, 38-23 (NE)
1985—Patriots, 20-13 (S)
1986—Seahawks, 38-31 (NE)
1988—Patriots, 13-7 (NE)
1989—Seahawks, 24-3 (NE)
1990—Seahawks, 33-20 (NE)
1992—Seahawks, 10-6 (NE)
1993—Patriots, 17-14 (NE)
Seahawks, 10-9 (S)
2004—Patriots, 30-20 (NE)
(RS Pts.—Patriots 274, Seahawks 250)
NEW ENGLAND vs. TAMPA BAY
RS: Patriots lead series, 4-2
1976—Patriots, 31-14 (TB)
1985—Patriots, 32-14 (TB)
1988—Patriots, 10-7 (NE) OT
1997—Buccaneers, 27-7 (TB)
2000—Buccaneers, 21-16 (NE)
2005—Patriots, 28-0 (NE)
(RS Pts.—Patriots 124, Buccaneers 83)
NEW ENGLAND vs. **TENNESSEE
RS: Patriots lead series, 20-15-1
PS: Series tied, 1-1
1960—Oilers, 24-10 (B)
Oilers, 37-21 (H)
1961—Tie, 31-31 (B)
Oilers, 27-15 (H)
1962—Patriots, 34-21 (B)
Oilers, 21-17 (H)
1963—Patriots, 45-3 (B)
Patriots, 46-28 (H)
1964—Patriots, 25-24 (B)
Patriots, 34-17 (H)
1965—Oilers, 31-10 (H)
Patriots, 42-14 (B)
1966—Patriots, 27-21 (B)
Patriots, 38-14 (H)
1967—Patriots, 18-7 (B)
Oilers, 27-6 (H)
1968—Oilers, 16-0 (B)
Oilers, 45-17 (H)
1969—Oilers, 24-0 (B)
Oilers, 27-23 (H)
1971—Patriots, 28-20 (NE)
1973—Patriots, 32-0 (H)
1975—Oilers, 7-0 (H)
1978—Patriots, 26-23 (NE)
***Oilers, 31-14 (NE)
1980—Oilers, 38-34 (H)
1981—Patriots, 38-10 (NE)
1982—Patriots, 29-21 (NE)
1987—Patriots, 21-7 (H)
1988—Oilers, 31-6 (H)
1989—Patriots, 23-13 (NE)

1991—Patriots, 24-20 (NE)
1993—Oilers, 28-14 (NE)
1998—Patriots, 27-16 (NE)
2002—Titans, 24-7 (T)
2003—Patriots, 38-30 (NE)
***Patriots, 17-14 (NE)
2006—Patriots, 40-23 (T)
(RS Pts.—Patriots 867, Titans 749)
(PS Pts.—Titans 45, Patriots 31)
Franchise in Boston prior to 1971
**Franchise in Houston prior to 1997;
known as Oilers prior to 1999*
***AFC Divisional Playoff*
NEW ENGLAND vs. WASHINGTON
RS: Redskins lead series, 6-2
1972—Patriots, 24-23 (NE)
1978—Redskins, 16-14 (NE)
1981—Redskins, 24-22 (W)
1984—Redskins, 26-10 (NE)
1990—Redskins, 25-10 (NE)
1996—Redskins, 27-22 (NE)
2003—Redskins, 20-17 (W)
2007—Patriots, 52-7 (NE)
(RS Pts.—Patriots 171, Redskins 168)

NEW ORLEANS vs. ARIZONA
RS: Cardinals lead series, 13-12;
See Arizona vs. New Orleans
NEW ORLEANS vs. ATLANTA
RS: Falcons lead series, 43-34
PS: Falcons lead series, 1-0;
See Atlanta vs. New Orleans
NEW ORLEANS vs. BALTIMORE
RS: Ravens lead series, 3-1;
See Baltimore vs. New Orleans
NEW ORLEANS vs. BUFFALO
RS: Series tied, 4-4;
See Buffalo vs. New Orleans
NEW ORLEANS vs. CAROLINA
RS: Panthers lead series, 14-12;
See Carolina vs. New Orleans
NEW ORLEANS vs. CHICAGO
RS: Bears lead series, 12-11
PS: Bears lead series, 2-0;
See Chicago vs. New Orleans
NEW ORLEANS vs. CINCINNATI
RS: Bengals lead series, 6-5;
See Cincinnati vs. New Orleans
NEW ORLEANS vs. CLEVELAND
RS: Browns lead series, 11-4;
See Cleveland vs. New Orleans
NEW ORLEANS vs. DALLAS
RS: Cowboys lead series, 14-8;
See Dallas vs. New Orleans
NEW ORLEANS vs. DENVER
RS: Broncos lead series, 6-2;
See Denver vs. New Orleans
NEW ORLEANS vs. DETROIT
RS: Lions lead series, 9-8-1;
See Detroit vs. New Orleans
NEW ORLEANS vs. GREEN BAY
RS: Packers lead series, 14-6;
See Green Bay vs. New Orleans
NEW ORLEANS vs. HOUSTON
RS: Series tied, 1-1;
See Houston vs. New Orleans
NEW ORLEANS vs. INDIANAPOLIS
RS: Series tied, 5-5;
See Indianapolis vs. New Orleans
NEW ORLEANS vs. JACKSONVILLE

RS: Series tied, 2-2;
See Jacksonville vs. New Orleans

NEW ORLEANS vs. KANSAS CITY
RS: Series tied, 4-4;
See Kansas City vs. New Orleans

NEW ORLEANS vs. MIAMI
RS: Dolphins lead series, 6-3;
See Miami vs. New Orleans

NEW ORLEANS vs. MINNESOTA
RS: Vikings lead series, 17-7
PS: Vikings lead series, 2-0;
See Minnesota vs. New Orleans

NEW ORLEANS vs. NEW ENGLAND
RS: Patriots lead series, 8-3;
See New England vs. New Orleans

NEW ORLEANS vs. N.Y. GIANTS
RS: Giants lead series, 14-10
1967—Giants, 27-21 (NY)
1968—Giants, 38-21 (NY)
1969—Saints, 25-24 (NY)
1970—Saints, 14-10 (NO)
1972—Giants, 45-21 (NY)
1975—Giants, 28-14 (NY)
1978—Saints, 28-17 (NO)
1979—Saints, 24-14 (NO)
1981—Giants, 20-7 (NY)
1984—Saints, 10-3 (NY)
1985—Giants, 21-13 (NO)
1986—Giants, 20-17 (NY)
1987—Saints, 23-14 (NO)
1988—Giants, 13-12 (NO)
1993—Giants, 24-14 (NO)
1994—Saints, 27-22 (NO)
1995—Giants, 45-29 (NY)
1996—Saints 17-3 (NY)
1997—Giants, 14-9 (NY)
1999—Giants, 31-3 (NY)
2001—Giants, 21-13 (NY)
2003—Saints, 45-7 (NO)
2005—Giants, 27-10 (NY*)
2006—Saints, 30-7 (NY)
(RS Pts.—Giants 495, Saints 447)
*Saints home game

NEW ORLEANS vs. N.Y. JETS
RS: Series tied, 5-5
1972—Jets, 18-17 (NY)
1977—Jets, 16-13 (NO)
1980—Saints, 21-20 (NY)
1983—Jets, 31-28 (NO)
1986—Jets, 28-23 (NY)
1989—Saints, 29-14 (NO)
1992—Saints, 20-0 (NY)
1995—Saints, 12-0 (NY)
2001—Jets, 16-9 (NO)
2005—Saints, 21-19 (NY)
(RS Pts.—Saints 193, Jets 162)

NEW ORLEANS vs. *OAKLAND
RS: Raiders lead series, 5-4-1
1971—Tie, 21-21 (NO)
1975—Raiders, 48-10 (O)
1979—Raiders, 42-35 (NO)
1985—Raiders, 23-13 (LA)
1988—Saints, 20-6 (NO)
1991—Saints, 27-0 (NO)
1994—Raiders, 24-19 (LA)
1997—Saints, 13-10 (O)
2000—Raiders, 31-22 (NO)
2004—Saints, 31-26 (O)
(RS Pts.—Raiders 231, Saints 211)
*Franchise in Los Angeles from 1982-1994

NEW ORLEANS vs. PHILADELPHIA
RS: Eagles lead series, 15-9
PS: Series tied, 1-1
1967—Saints, 31-24 (NO)
       Eagles, 48-21 (P)
1968—Eagles, 29-17 (P)
1969—Eagles, 13-10 (P)
       Saints, 26-17 (NO)
1972—Saints, 21-3 (NO)
1974—Saints, 14-10 (NO)
1977—Eagles, 28-7 (P)
1978—Eagles, 24-17 (NO)
1979—Eagles, 26-14 (NO)
1980—Eagles, 34-21 (NO)
1981—Eagles, 31-14 (NO)
1983—Saints, 20-17 (P) OT
1985—Saints, 23-21 (NO)
1987—Eagles, 27-17 (P)
1989—Saints, 30-20 (NO)
1991—Saints, 13-6 (P)
1992—Eagles, 15-13 (P)
       *Eagles, 36-20 (NO)
1993—Eagles, 37-26 (P)
1995—Eagles, 15-10 (NO)
2000—Eagles, 21-7 (NO)
2003—Eagles, 33-20 (P)
2006—Saints, 27-24 (NO)
       **Saints, 27-24 (NO)
2007—Eagles, 38-23 (NO)
(RS Pts.—Eagles 561, Saints 442)
(PS Pts.—Eagles 60, Saints 47)
*NFC First-Round Playoff
**NFC Divisional Playoff

NEW ORLEANS vs. PITTSBURGH
RS: Steelers lead series, 7-6
1967—Steelers, 14-10 (NO)
1968—Saints, 16-12 (P)
       Saints, 24-14 (NO)
1969—Saints, 27-24 (NO)
1974—Steelers, 28-7 (NO)
1978—Steelers, 20-14 (P)
1981—Steelers, 20-6 (NO)
1984—Saints, 27-24 (NO)
1987—Saints, 20-16 (P)
1990—Steelers, 9-6 (NO)
1993—Steelers, 37-14 (P)
2002—Saints, 32-29 (NO)
2006—Steelers, 38-31 (P)
(RS Pts.—Steelers 285, Saints 234)

NEW ORLEANS vs. *ST. LOUIS
RS: Rams lead series, 38-29
PS: Saints lead series, 1-0
1967—Rams, 27-13 (NO)
1969—Rams, 36-17 (LA)
1970—Rams, 30-17 (NO)
       Rams, 34-16 (LA)
1971—Saints, 24-20 (NO)
       Rams, 45-28 (LA)
1972—Rams, 34-14 (LA)
       Saints, 19-16 (NO)
1973—Rams, 29-7 (LA)
       Rams, 24-13 (NO)
1974—Rams, 24-0 (LA)
       Saints, 20-7 (NO)
1975—Rams, 38-14 (LA)
       Rams, 14-7 (NO)
1976—Rams, 16-10 (NO)
       Rams, 33-14 (LA)
1977—Rams, 14-7 (LA)
       Saints, 27-26 (NO)

1978—Rams, 26-20 (NO)
       Saints, 10-3 (LA)
1979—Rams, 35-17 (NO)
       Saints, 29-14 (LA)
1980—Rams, 45-31 (LA)
       Rams, 27-7 (NO)
1981—Saints, 23-17 (NO)
       Saints, 21-13 (LA)
1983—Rams, 30-27 (LA)
       Rams, 26-24 (NO)
1984—Rams, 28-10 (LA)
       Rams, 34-21 (LA)
1985—Rams, 28-10 (LA)
       Saints, 29-3 (NO)
1986—Saints, 6-0 (NO)
       Rams, 26-13 (LA)
1987—Rams, 37-10 (NO)
       Saints, 31-14 (LA)
1988—Rams, 12-10 (NO)
       Saints, 14-10 (LA)
1989—Rams, 40-21 (LA)
       Rams, 20-17 (NO) OT
1990—Saints, 24-20 (LA)
       Saints, 20-17 (NO)
1991—Saints, 24-7 (NO)
       Saints, 24-17 (LA)
1992—Saints, 13-10 (NO)
       Saints, 37-14 (LA)
1993—Saints, 37-6 (LA)
       Rams, 23-20 (NO)
1994—Saints, 37-34 (NO)
       Saints, 31-15 (LA)
1995—Rams, 17-13 (StL)
       Saints, 19-10 (NO)
1996—Rams, 26-10 (NO)
       Rams, 14-13 (StL)
1997—Rams, 38-24 (StL)
       Rams, 34-27 (NO)
1998—Rams, 24-17 (StL)
       Saints, 24-3 (NO)
1999—Rams, 43-12 (StL)
       Rams, 30-14 (NO)
2000—Saints, 31-24 (StL)
       Rams, 26-21 (NO)
       **Saints, 31-28 (NO)
2001—Saints, 34-31 (StL)
       Rams, 34-21 (NO)
2004—Saints, 28-25 (StL) OT
2005—Rams, 28-17 (StL)
2007—Rams, 37-29 (NO)
(RS Pts.—Rams 1,509, Saints 1,342)
(PS Pts.—Saints 31, Rams 28)
*Franchise in Los Angeles prior to 1995
**NFC First-Round Playoff

NEW ORLEANS vs. SAN DIEGO
RS: Chargers lead series, 7-2
1973—Chargers, 17-14 (SD)
1977—Chargers, 14-0 (NO)
1979—Chargers, 35-0 (NO)
1988—Saints, 23-17 (SD)
1991—Chargers, 24-21 (SD)
1994—Chargers, 36-22 (NO)
1997—Chargers, 20-6 (NO)
2000—Saints, 28-27 (SD)
2004—Chargers, 43-17 (SD)
(RS Pts.—Chargers 233, Saints 131)

NEW ORLEANS vs. SAN FRANCISCO
RS: 49ers lead series, 45-22-2
1967—49ers, 27-13 (SF)
1969—Saints, 43-38 (NO)

1970—Tie, 20-20 (SF)
    49ers, 38-27 (NO)
1971—49ers, 38-20 (NO)
    Saints, 26-20 (SF)
1972—49ers, 37-2 (NO)
    Tie, 20-20 (SF)
1973—49ers, 40-0 (SF)
    Saints, 16-10 (NO)
1974—49ers, 17-13 (NO)
    49ers, 35-21 (SF)
1975—49ers, 35-21 (SF)
    49ers, 16-6 (NO)
1976—49ers, 33-3 (SF)
    49ers, 27-7 (NO)
1977—49ers, 10-7 (NO) OT
    49ers, 20-17 (SF)
1978—Saints, 14-7 (SF)
    Saints, 24-13 (NO)
1979—Saints, 30-21 (SF)
    Saints, 31-20 (NO)
1980—49ers, 26-23 (NO)
    49ers, 38-35 (SF) OT
1981—49ers, 21-14 (SF)
    49ers, 21-17 (NO)
1982—Saints, 23-20 (SF)
1983—49ers, 32-13 (NO)
    49ers, 27-0 (SF)
1984—49ers, 30-20 (SF)
    49ers, 35-3 (NO)
1985—Saints, 20-17 (SF)
    49ers, 31-19 (NO)
1986—49ers, 26-17 (SF)
    Saints, 23-10 (NO)
1987—49ers, 24-22 (NO)
    Saints, 26-24 (NO)
1988—49ers, 34-33 (NO)
    49ers, 30-17 (SF)
1989—49ers, 24-20 (NO)
    49ers, 31-13 (SF)
1990—49ers, 13-12 (NO)
    Saints, 13-10 (SF)
1991—Saints, 10-3 (NO)
    49ers, 38-24 (SF)
1992—49ers, 16-10 (NO)
    49ers, 21-20 (SF)
1993—Saints, 16-13 (NO)
    49ers, 42-7 (SF)
1994—49ers, 24-13 (SF)
    49ers, 35-14 (NO)
1995—49ers, 44-22 (NO)
    Saints, 11-7 (SF)
1996—49ers, 27-11 (SF)
    49ers, 24-17 (NO)
1997—49ers, 33-7 (SF)
    49ers, 23-0 (NO)
1998—49ers, 31-0 (NO)
    49ers, 31-20 (SF)
1999—49ers, 28-21 (SF)
    Saints, 24-6 (NO)
2000—Saints, 31-15 (NO)
    Saints, 31-27 (SF)
2001—49ers, 28-27 (SF)
    49ers, 38-0 (NO)
2002—Saints, 35-27 (NO)
2004—Saints, 30-27 (NO)
2006—Saints, 34-10 (NO)
2007—Saints, 31-10 (SF)
(RS Pts.—49ers 1,674, Saints 1,230)
NEW ORLEANS vs. SEATTLE
RS: Series tied, 5-5

1976—Saints, 51-27 (S)
1979—Seahawks, 38-24 (S)
1985—Seahawks, 27-3 (NO)
1988—Saints, 20-19 (S)
1991—Saints, 27-24 (NO)
1997—Saints, 20-17 (NO) OT
2000—Seahawks, 20-10 (S)
2003—Seahawks, 27-10 (S)
2004—Seahawks, 21-7 (NO)
2007—Saints, 28-17 (S)
(RS Pts.—Seahawks 237, Saints 200)
NEW ORLEANS vs. TAMPA BAY
RS: Saints lead series, 19-13
1977—Buccaneers, 33-14 (NO)
1978—Saints, 17-10 (TB)
1979—Saints, 42-14 (TB)
1981—Buccaneers, 31-14 (NO)
1982—Buccaneers, 13-10 (NO)
1983—Saints, 24-21 (TB)
1984—Saints, 17-13 (NO)
1985—Saints, 20-13 (NO)
1986—Saints, 38-7 (NO)
1987—Saints, 44-34 (NO)
1988—Saints, 13-9 (NO)
1989—Buccaneers, 20-10 (TB)
1990—Saints, 35-7 (NO)
1991—Saints, 23-7 (NO)
1992—Saints, 23-21 (NO)
1994—Saints, 9-7 (TB)
1996—Buccaneers, 13-7 (TB)
1998—Saints, 9-3 (NO)
1999—Buccaneers, 31-16 (NO)
2001—Buccaneers, 48-21 (TB)
2002—Saints, 26-20 (TB) OT
    Saints, 23-20 (NO)
2003—Saints, 17-14 (TB)
    Buccaneers, 14-7 (NO)
2004—Buccaneers, 20-17 (NO)
    Saints, 21-17 (TB)
2005—Buccaneers, 10-3 (Baton Rouge)
    Buccaneers, 27-13 (TB)
2006—Saints, 24-21 (NO)
    Saints, 31-14 (TB)
2007—Buccaneers, 31-14 (TB)
    Buccaneers, 27-23 (NO)
(RS Pts.—Saints 625, Buccaneers 590)
NEW ORLEANS vs. *TENNESSEE
RS: Titans lead series, 7-4-1
1971—Tie, 13-13 (H)
1976—Oilers, 31-26 (NO)
1978—Oilers, 17-12 (NO)
1981—Saints, 27-24 (H)
1984—Saints, 27-10 (H)
1987—Saints, 24-10 (NO)
1990—Oilers, 23-10 (H)
1993—Saints, 33-21 (NO)
1996—Oilers, 31-14 (NO)
1999—Titans, 24-21 (NO)
2003—Titans, 27-12 (T)
2007—Titans, 31-14 (NO)
(RS Pts.—Titans 262, Saints 233)
*Franchise in Houston prior to 1997;
known as Oilers prior to 1999*
NEW ORLEANS vs. WASHINGTON
RS: Redskins lead series, 14-7
1967—Redskins, 30-10 (NO)
    Saints, 30-14 (W)
1968—Saints, 37-17 (NO)
1969—Redskins, 26-20 (NO)
    Redskins, 17-14 (W)

1971—Redskins, 24-14 (W)
1973—Saints, 19-3 (NO)
1975—Redskins, 41-3 (W)
1979—Saints, 14-10 (W)
1980—Redskins, 22-14 (W)
1982—Redskins, 27-10 (NO)
1986—Redskins, 14-6 (NO)
1988—Redskins, 27-24 (W)
1989—Redskins, 16-14 (NO)
1990—Redskins, 31-17 (W)
1992—Saints, 20-3 (NO)
1994—Redskins, 38-24 (NO)
2001—Redskins, 40-10 (NO)
2002—Saints, 43-27 (W)
2003—Saints, 24-20 (W)
2006—Redskins, 16-10 (NO)
(RS Pts.—Redskins 463, Saints 377)

N.Y. GIANTS vs. ARIZONA
RS: Giants lead series, 78-41-2;
See Arizona vs. N.Y. Giants
N.Y. GIANTS vs. ATLANTA
RS: Falcons lead series, 10-9;
See Atlanta vs. N.Y. Giants
N.Y. GIANTS vs. BALTIMORE
RS: Ravens lead series, 2-0
PS: Ravens lead series, 1-0;
See Baltimore vs. N.Y. Giants
N.Y. GIANTS vs. BUFFALO
RS: Bills lead series, 6-4
PS: Giants lead series, 1-0;
See Buffalo vs. N.Y. Giants
N.Y. GIANTS vs. CAROLINA
RS: Panthers lead series, 2-1
PS: Panthers lead series, 1-0;
See Carolina vs. N.Y. Giants
N.Y. GIANTS vs. CHICAGO
RS: Bears lead series, 27-18-2
PS: Bears lead series, 5-3;
See Chicago vs. N.Y. Giants
N.Y. GIANTS vs. CINCINNATI
RS: Bengals lead series, 5-2;
See Cincinnati vs. N.Y. Giants
N.Y. GIANTS vs. CLEVELAND
RS: Browns lead series, 25-19-2
PS: Series tied, 1-1;
See Cleveland vs. N.Y. Giants
N.Y. GIANTS vs. DALLAS
RS: Cowboys lead series, 54-35-2
PS: Giants lead series, 1-0;
See Dallas vs. N.Y. Giants
N.Y. GIANTS vs. DENVER
RS: Giants lead series, 5-4
PS: Giants lead series, 1-0;
See Denver vs. N.Y. Giants
N.Y. GIANTS vs. DETROIT
RS: Lions lead series, 20-18-1
PS: Lions lead series, 1-0;
See Detroit vs. N.Y. Giants
N.Y. GIANTS vs. GREEN BAY
RS: Packers lead series, 25-21-2
PS: Packers lead series, 4-2;
See Green Bay vs. N.Y. Giants
N.Y. GIANTS vs. HOUSTON
RS: Series tied, 1-1;
See Houston vs. N.Y. Giants
N.Y. GIANTS vs. INDIANAPOLIS
RS: Colts lead series, 7-6
PS: Colts lead series, 2-0;
See Indianapolis vs. N.Y. Giants

N.Y. GIANTS vs. JACKSONVILLE
RS: Series tied, 2-2;
See Jacksonville vs. N.Y. Giants
N.Y. GIANTS vs. KANSAS CITY
RS: Giants lead series, 9-2;
See Kansas City vs. N.Y. Giants
N.Y. GIANTS vs. MIAMI
RS: Giants lead series, 4-2;
See Miami vs. N.Y. Giants
N.Y. GIANTS vs. MINNESOTA
RS: Vikings lead series, 11-8
PS: Giants lead series, 2-1;
See Minnesota vs. N.Y. Giants
N.Y. GIANTS vs. NEW ENGLAND
RS: Patriots lead series, 5-3
PS: Giants lead series, 1-0;
See New England vs. N.Y. Giants
N.Y. GIANTS vs. NEW ORLEANS
RS: Giants lead series, 14-10;
See New Orleans vs. N.Y. Giants
N.Y. GIANTS vs. N.Y. JETS
RS: Giants lead series, 7-4
1970—Giants, 22-10 (NYJ)
1974—Jets, 26-20 (New Haven) OT
1981—Jets, 26-7 (NYG)
1984—Giants, 20-10 (NYJ)
1987—Giants, 20-7 (NYG)
1988—Jets, 27-21 (NYJ)
1993—Jets, 10-6 (NYG)
1996—Giants, 13-6 (NYJ)
1999—Giants, 41-28 (NYG)
2003—Giants, 31-28 (NYJ) OT
2007—Giants, 35-24 (NYG)
(RS Pts.—Giants 236, Jets 202)
N.Y. GIANTS vs. *OAKLAND
RS: Raiders lead series, 7-3
1973—Raiders, 42-0 (O)
1980—Raiders, 33-17 (NY)
1983—Raiders, 27-12 (LA)
1986—Giants, 14-9 (LA)
1989—Giants, 34-17 (NY)
1992—Raiders, 13-10 (LA)
1995—Raiders, 17-13 (NY)
1998—Raiders, 20-17 (O)
2001—Raiders, 28-10 (NY)
2005—Giants, 30-21 (O)
(RS Pts.—Raiders 227, Giants 157)
Franchise in Los Angeles from 1982-1994
N.Y. GIANTS vs. PHILADELPHIA
RS: Giants lead series, 78-66-2
PS: Giants lead series, 2-1
1933—Giants, 56-0 (NY)
    Giants, 20-14 (P)
1934—Giants, 17-0 (NY)
    Eagles, 6-0 (P)
1935—Giants, 10-0 (NY)
    Giants, 21-14 (P)
1936—Eagles, 10-7 (P)
    Giants, 21-17 (NY)
1937—Giants, 16-7 (P)
    Giants, 21-0 (NY)
1938—Eagles, 14-10 (P)
    Giants, 17-7 (NY)
1939—Giants, 13-3 (P)
    Giants, 27-10 (NY)
1940—Giants, 20-14 (P)
    Giants, 17-7 (NY)
1941—Giants, 24-0 (P)
    Giants, 16-0 (NY)
1942—Giants, 35-17 (NY)

    Giants, 14-0 (P)
1944—Eagles, 24-17 (NY)
    Tie, 21-21 (P)
1945—Eagles, 38-17 (P)
    Giants, 28-21 (NY)
1946—Eagles, 24-14 (P)
    Giants, 45-17 (NY)
1947—Eagles, 23-0 (P)
    Eagles, 41-24 (NY)
1948—Eagles, 45-0 (P)
    Eagles, 35-14 (NY)
1949—Eagles, 24-3 (NY)
    Eagles, 17-3 (P)
1950—Giants, 7-3 (NY)
    Giants, 9-7 (P)
1951—Giants, 26-24 (NY)
    Giants, 23-7 (P)
1952—Giants, 31-7 (P)
    Eagles, 14-10 (NY)
1953—Eagles, 30-7 (P)
    Eagles, 37-28 (NY)
1954—Giants, 27-14 (NY)
    Eagles, 29-14 (P)
1955—Eagles, 27-17 (P)
    Giants, 31-7 (NY)
1956—Giants, 20-3 (NY)
    Giants, 21-7 (P)
1957—Giants, 24-20 (P)
    Giants, 13-0 (NY)
1958—Eagles, 27-24 (P)
    Giants, 24-10 (NY)
1959—Eagles, 49-21 (P)
    Giants, 24-7 (NY)
1960—Eagles, 17-10 (NY)
    Eagles, 31-23 (P)
1961—Giants, 38-21 (NY)
    Giants, 28-24 (P)
1962—Giants, 29-13 (P)
    Giants, 19-14 (NY)
1963—Giants, 37-14 (NY)
    Giants, 42-14 (NY)
1964—Eagles, 38-7 (P)
    Eagles, 23-17 (NY)
1965—Giants, 16-14 (P)
    Giants, 35-27 (NY)
1966—Eagles, 35-17 (P)
    Eagles, 31-3 (NY)
1967—Giants, 44-7 (NY)
1968—Giants, 34-25 (P)
    Giants, 7-6 (NY)
1969—Eagles, 23-20 (NY)
1970—Giants, 30-23 (NY)
    Eagles, 23-20 (P)
1971—Eagles, 23-7 (P)
    Eagles, 41-28 (NY)
1972—Giants, 27-12 (P)
    Giants, 62-10 (NY)
1973—Tie, 23-23 (NY)
    Eagles, 20-16 (P)
1974—Eagles, 35-7 (P)
    Eagles, 20-7 (New Haven)
1975—Giants, 23-14 (P)
    Giants, 13-10 (NY)
1976—Eagles, 20-7 (P)
    Eagles, 10-0 (NY)
1977—Eagles, 28-10 (NY)
    Eagles, 17-14 (P)
1978—Eagles, 19-17 (NY)
    Eagles, 20-3 (P)
1979—Eagles, 23-17 (P)

    Eagles, 17-13 (NY)
1980—Eagles, 35-3 (P)
    Eagles, 31-16 (NY)
1981—Eagles, 24-10 (NY)
    Giants, 20-10 (P)
    *Giants, 27-21 (P)
1982—Giants, 23-7 (NY)
    Giants, 26-24 (P)
1983—Eagles, 17-13 (NY)
    Giants, 23-0 (P)
1984—Giants, 28-27 (NY)
    Eagles, 24-10 (P)
1985—Giants, 21-0 (NY)
    Giants, 16-10 (P) OT
1986—Giants, 35-3 (NY)
    Giants, 17-14 (P)
1987—Giants, 20-17 (P)
    Giants, 23-20 (NY) OT
1988—Eagles, 24-13 (P)
    Eagles, 23-17 (NY) OT
1989—Eagles, 21-19 (P)
    Eagles, 24-17 (NY)
1990—Giants, 27-20 (NY)
    Eagles, 31-13 (P)
1991—Giants, 30-7 (P)
    Eagles, 19-14 (NY)
1992—Eagles, 47-34 (NY)
    Eagles, 20-10 (P)
1993—Eagles, 21-10 (NY)
    Giants, 7-3 (P)
1994—Giants, 28-23 (NY)
    Giants, 16-13 (P)
1995—Eagles, 17-14 (NY)
    Eagles, 28-19 (P)
1996—Eagles, 19-10 (NY)
    Eagles, 24-0 (P)
1997—Giants, 31-17 (NY)
    Giants, 31-21 (P)
1998—Giants, 20-0 (NY)
    Giants, 20-10 (P)
1999—Giants, 16-15 (NY)
    Giants, 23-17 (P) OT
2000—Giants, 33-18 (P)
    Giants, 24-7 (NY)
    **Giants, 20-10 (NY)
2001—Eagles, 10-9 (NY)
    Eagles, 24-21 (P)
2002—Eagles, 17-3 (P)
    Giants, 10-7 (NY) OT
2003—Eagles, 14-10 (NY)
    Eagles, 28-10 (P)
2004—Eagles, 31-17 (P)
    Eagles, 27-6 (NY)
2005—Giants, 27-17 (NY)
    Giants, 26-23 (P) OT
2006—Giants, 30-24 (P) OT
    Eagles, 36-22 (NY)
    *Eagles, 23-20 (P)
2007—Giants, 16-3 (NY)
    Giants, 16-13 (P)
(RS Pts.—Giants 2,756, Eagles 2,616)
(PS Pts.—Giants 67, Eagles 54)
NFC First-Round Playoff
**NFC Divisional Playoff*
N.Y. GIANTS vs. *PITTSBURGH
RS: Giants lead series, 43-28-3
1933—Giants, 23-2 (P)
    Giants, 27-3 (NY)
1934—Giants, 14-12 (P)
    Giants, 17-7 (NY)

1935—Giants, 42-7 (P)
Giants, 13-0 (NY)
1936—Pirates, 10-7 (P)
1937—Giants, 10-7 (P)
Giants, 17-0 (NY)
1938—Giants, 27-14 (P)
Pirates, 13-10 (NY)
1939—Giants, 14-7 (P)
Giants, 23-7 (NY)
1940—Tie, 10-10 (P)
Giants, 12-0 (NY)
1941—Giants, 37-10 (P)
Giants, 28-7 (NY)
1942—Steelers, 13-10 (P)
Steelers, 17-9 (NY)
1945—Giants, 34-6 (P)
Steelers, 21-7 (NY)
1946—Steelers, 17-14 (P)
Giants, 7-0 (NY)
1947—Steelers, 38-21 (NY)
Steelers, 24-7 (P)
1948—Giants, 34-27 (NY)
Steelers, 38-28 (P)
1949—Steelers, 28-7 (P)
Steelers, 21-17 (NY)
1950—Giants, 18-7 (P)
Steelers, 17-6 (NY)
1951—Tie, 13-13 (P)
Giants, 14-0 (NY)
1952—Steelers, 63-7 (P)
1953—Steelers, 24-14 (P)
Steelers, 14-10 (NY)
1954—Giants, 30-6 (P)
Giants, 24-3 (NY)
1955—Steelers, 30-23 (P)
Steelers, 19-17 (NY)
1956—Giants, 38-10 (NY)
Giants, 17-14 (P)
1957—Giants, 35-0 (NY)
Steelers, 21-10 (P)
1958—Giants, 17-6 (NY)
Steelers, 31-10 (P)
1959—Giants, 21-16 (P)
Steelers, 14-9 (NY)
1960—Giants, 19-17 (P)
Giants, 27-24 (NY)
1961—Giants, 17-14 (P)
Giants, 42-21 (NY)
1962—Giants, 31-27 (P)
Steelers, 20-17 (NY)
1963—Steelers, 31-0 (P)
Giants, 33-17 (NY)
1964—Steelers, 27-24 (P)
Steelers, 44-17 (NY)
1965—Giants, 23-13 (P)
Giants, 35-10 (NY)
1966—Tie, 34-34 (P)
Steelers, 47-28 (NY)
1967—Giants, 27-24 (P)
Giants, 28-20 (NY)
1968—Giants, 34-20 (P)
1969—Giants, 10-7 (NY)
Giants, 21-17 (P)
1971—Steelers, 17-13 (NY)
1976—Steelers, 27-0 (NY)
1985—Giants, 28-10 (NY)
1991—Giants, 23-20 (P)
1994—Steelers, 10-6 (NY)
2000—Giants, 30-10 (NY)
2004—Steelers, 33-30 (NY)

(RS Pts.—Giants 1,459, Steelers 1,232)
Steelers known as Pirates prior to 1941
N.Y. GIANTS vs. *ST. LOUIS
RS: Rams lead series, 25-12
PS: Series tied, 1-1
1938—Giants, 28-0 (NY)
1940—Rams, 13-0 (NY)
1941—Giants, 49-14 (NY)
1945—Rams, 21-17 (NY)
1946—Rams, 31-21 (NY)
1947—Rams, 34-10 (LA)
1948—Rams, 52-37 (NY)
1953—Rams, 21-7 (LA)
1954—Rams, 17-16 (NY)
1959—Giants, 23-21 (LA)
1961—Giants, 24-14 (NY)
1966—Rams, 55-14 (LA)
1968—Rams, 24-21 (LA)
1970—Rams, 31-3 (NY)
1973—Rams, 40-6 (LA)
1976—Rams, 24-10 (LA)
1978—Rams, 20-17 (NY)
1979—Giants, 20-14 (LA)
1980—Rams, 28-7 (NY)
1981—Giants, 10-7 (NY)
1983—Rams, 16-6 (NY)
1984—Rams, 33-12 (LA)
**Giants, 16-13 (LA)
1985—Giants, 24-19 (NY)
1988—Rams, 45-31 (NY)
1989—Rams, 31-10 (LA)
***Rams, 19-13 (NY) OT
1990—Giants, 31-7 (LA)
1991—Rams, 19-13 (NY)
1992—Rams, 38-17 (LA)
1993—Giants, 20-10 (NY)
1994—Rams, 17-10 (LA)
1997—Rams, 13-3 (StL)
1999—Rams, 31-10 (StL)
2000—Rams, 38-24 (NY)
2001—Rams, 15-14 (StL)
2002—Giants, 26-21 (StL)
2003—Giants, 23-13 (NY)
2005—Giants, 44-24 (NY)
(RS Pts.—Rams 871, Giants 658)
(PS Pts.—Rams 32, Giants 29)
Franchise in Los Angeles prior to 1995 and in Cleveland prior to 1946
**NFC First-Round Playoff*
***NFC Divisional Playoff*
N.Y. GIANTS vs. SAN DIEGO
RS: Giants lead series, 5-4
1971—Giants, 35-17 (NY)
1975—Giants, 35-24 (NY)
1980—Chargers, 44-7 (SD)
1983—Chargers, 41-34 (NY)
1986—Giants, 20-7 (NY)
1989—Giants, 20-13 (SD)
1995—Chargers, 27-17 (NY)
1998—Giants, 34-16 (SD)
2005—Chargers, 45-23 (SD)
(RS Pts.—Chargers 234, Giants 225)
N.Y. GIANTS vs. SAN FRANCISCO
RS: Series tied, 13-13
PS: 49ers lead series, 4-3
1952—Giants, 23-14 (NY)
1956—Giants, 38-21 (SF)
1957—49ers, 27-17 (NY)
1960—Giants, 21-19 (SF)
1963—Giants, 48-14 (NY)

1968—49ers, 26-10 (NY)
1972—Giants, 23-17 (SF)
1975—Giants, 26-23 (SF)
1977—Giants, 20-17 (NY)
1978—Giants, 27-10 (NY)
1979—Giants, 32-16 (NY)
1980—49ers, 12-0 (SF)
1981—49ers, 17-10 (SF)
*49ers, 38-24 (SF)
1984—49ers, 31-10 (NY)
*49ers, 21-10 (SF)
1985—**Giants, 17-3 (NY)
1986—Giants, 21-17 (SF)
*Giants, 49-3 (NY)
1987—49ers, 41-21 (NY)
1988—49ers, 20-17 (NY)
1989—49ers, 34-24 (SF)
1990—49ers, 7-3 (SF)
***Giants, 15-13 (SF)
1991—Giants, 16-14 (NY)
1992—49ers, 31-14 (NY)
1993—*49ers, 44-3 (SF)
1995—49ers, 20-6 (SF)
1998—49ers, 31-7 (SF)
2002—Giants, 16-13 (NY)
**49ers, 39-38 (SF)
2005—Giants, 24-6 (SF)
2007—Giants, 33-15 (NY)
(RS Pts.—49ers 516, Giants 504)
(PS Pts.—49ers 161, Giants 156)
NFC Divisional Playoff
**NFC First-Round Playoff*
***NFC Championship*
N.Y. GIANTS vs. SEATTLE
RS: Giants lead series, 7-5
1976—Giants, 28-16 (NY)
1980—Giants, 27-21 (S)
1981—Giants, 32-0 (S)
1983—Seahawks, 17-12 (NY)
1986—Seahawks, 17-12 (S)
1989—Giants, 15-3 (NY)
1992—Giants, 23-10 (NY)
1995—Seahawks, 30-28 (S)
2001—Giants, 27-24 (NY)
2002—Giants, 9-6 (NY)
2005—Seahawks, 24-21 (S) OT
2006—Seahawks, 42-30 (S)
(RS Pts.—Giants 264, Seahawks 210)
N.Y. GIANTS vs. TAMPA BAY
RS: Giants lead series, 10-6
PS: Giants lead series, 1-0
1977—Giants, 10-0 (TB)
1978—Giants, 19-13 (TB)
Giants, 17-14 (NY)
1979—Giants, 17-14 (NY)
Buccaneers, 31-3 (TB)
1980—Buccaneers, 30-13 (TB)
1984—Giants, 17-14 (NY)
Buccaneers, 20-17 (TB)
1985—Giants, 22-20 (NY)
1991—Giants, 21-14 (TB)
1993—Giants, 23-7 (NY)
1997—Buccaneers, 20-8 (NY)
1998—Buccaneers, 20-3 (TB)
1999—Giants, 17-13 (TB)
2003—Buccaneers, 19-13 (TB)
2006—Giants, 17-3 (NY)
2007—*Giants, 24-14 (TB)
(RS Pts.—Buccaneers 252, Giants 237)
(PS Pts.—Giants 24, Buccaneers 14)

*NFC First-Round Playoff
N.Y. GIANTS vs. *TENNESSEE
RS: Giants lead series, 5-4
1973—Giants, 34-14 (NY)
1982—Giants, 17-14 (NY)
1985—Giants, 35-14 (H)
1991—Giants, 24-20 (NY)
1994—Giants, 13-10 (H)
1997—Oilers, 10-6 (T)
2000—Titans, 28-14 (T)
2002—Titans, 32-29 (NY) OT
2006—Titans, 24-21 (T)
(RS Pts.—Giants 193, Titans 166)
*Franchise in Houston prior to 1997;
known as Oilers prior to 1999
N.Y. GIANTS vs. *WASHINGTON
RS: Giants lead series, 85-61-4
PS: Series tied, 1-1
1932—Braves, 14-6 (B)
　　　Tie, 0-0 (NY)
1933—Redskins, 21-20 (B)
　　　Giants, 7-0 (NY)
1934—Giants, 16-13 (B)
　　　Giants, 3-0 (NY)
1935—Giants, 20-12 (B)
　　　Giants, 17-6 (NY)
1936—Giants, 7-0 (B)
　　　Redskins, 14-0 (NY)
1937—Redskins, 13-3 (W)
　　　Redskins, 49-14 (NY)
1938—Giants, 10-7 (W)
　　　Giants, 36-0 (NY)
1939—Tie, 0-0 (W)
　　　Giants, 9-7 (NY)
1940—Redskins, 21-7 (W)
　　　Giants, 21-7 (NY)
1941—Giants, 17-10 (W)
　　　Giants, 20-13 (NY)
1942—Giants, 14-7 (W)
　　　Redskins, 14-7 (NY)
1943—Giants, 14-10 (NY)
　　　Giants, 31-7 (W)
　　　**Redskins, 28-0 (NY)
1944—Giants, 16-13 (NY)
　　　Giants, 31-0 (W)
1945—Redskins, 24-14 (NY)
　　　Redskins, 17-0 (W)
1946—Redskins, 24-14 (NY)
　　　Giants, 31-0 (NY)
1947—Redskins, 28-20 (W)
　　　Giants, 35-10 (NY)
1948—Redskins, 41-10 (W)
　　　Redskins, 28-21 (NY)
1949—Giants, 45-35 (W)
　　　Giants, 23-7 (NY)
1950—Giants, 21-17 (W)
　　　Giants, 24-21 (NY)
1951—Giants, 35-14 (W)
　　　Giants, 28-14 (NY)
1952—Giants, 14-10 (W)
　　　Redskins, 27-17 (NY)
1953—Redskins, 13-9 (W)
　　　Redskins, 24-21 (NY)
1954—Giants, 51-21 (W)
　　　Giants, 24-7 (NY)
1955—Giants, 35-7 (NY)
　　　Giants, 27-20 (W)
1956—Redskins, 33-7 (W)
　　　Giants, 28-14 (NY)
1957—Giants, 24-20 (W)

Redskins, 31-14 (NY)
1958—Giants, 21-14 (W)
　　　Giants, 30-0 (NY)
1959—Giants, 45-14 (NY)
　　　Giants, 24-10 (W)
1960—Tie, 24-24 (NY)
　　　Giants, 17-3 (W)
1961—Giants, 24-21 (W)
　　　Giants, 53-0 (NY)
1962—Giants, 49-34 (NY)
　　　Giants, 42-24 (W)
1963—Giants, 24-14 (W)
　　　Giants, 44-14 (NY)
1964—Giants, 13-10 (NY)
　　　Redskins, 36-21 (W)
1965—Redskins, 23-7 (NY)
　　　Giants, 27-10 (W)
1966—Giants, 13-10 (NY)
　　　Redskins, 72-41 (W)
1967—Redskins, 38-34 (W)
1968—Giants, 48-21 (NY)
　　　Giants, 13-10 (W)
1969—Redskins, 20-14 (W)
1970—Giants, 35-33 (NY)
　　　Giants, 27-24 (W)
1971—Redskins, 30-3 (NY)
　　　Redskins, 23-7 (W)
1972—Redskins, 23-16 (NY)
　　　Redskins, 27-13 (W)
1973—Redskins, 21-3 (New Haven)
　　　Redskins, 27-24 (W)
1974—Redskins, 13-10 (New Haven)
　　　Redskins, 24-3 (W)
1975—Redskins, 49-13 (W)
　　　Redskins, 21-13 (NY)
1976—Redskins, 19-17 (W)
　　　Giants, 12-9 (NY)
1977—Giants, 20-17 (NY)
　　　Giants, 17-6 (W)
1978—Giants, 17-6 (NY)
　　　Redskins, 16-13 (W) OT
1979—Redskins, 27-0 (W)
　　　Giants, 14-6 (W)
1980—Redskins, 23-21 (NY)
　　　Redskins, 16-13 (W)
1981—Giants, 17-7 (W)
　　　Redskins, 30-27 (NY) OT
1982—Redskins, 27-17 (W)
　　　Redskins, 15-14 (W)
1983—Redskins, 33-17 (W)
　　　Redskins, 31-22 (W)
1984—Redskins, 30-14 (W)
　　　Giants, 37-13 (NY)
1985—Giants, 17-3 (NY)
　　　Redskins, 23-21 (W)
1986—Giants, 27-20 (NY)
　　　Giants, 24-14 (W)
　　　***Giants, 17-0 (NY)
1987—Redskins, 38-12 (NY)
　　　Redskins, 23-19 (W)
1988—Giants, 27-20 (NY)
　　　Giants, 24-23 (W)
1989—Giants, 27-24 (W)
　　　Giants, 20-17 (NY)
1990—Giants, 24-20 (W)
　　　Giants, 21-10 (NY)
1991—Redskins, 17-13 (NY)
　　　Redskins, 34-17 (W)
1992—Giants, 24-7 (W)
　　　Redskins, 28-10 (NY)

1993—Giants, 41-7 (W)
　　　Giants, 20-6 (NY)
1994—Giants, 31-23 (NY)
　　　Giants, 21-19 (W)
1995—Giants, 24-15 (W)
　　　Giants, 20-13 (W)
1996—Redskins, 31-10 (NY)
　　　Redskins, 31-21 (W)
1997—Tie, 7-7 (W) OT
　　　Giants, 30-10 (W)
1998—Giants, 31-24 (NY)
　　　Redskins, 21-14 (W)
1999—Redskins, 50-21 (NY)
　　　Redskins, 23-13 (W)
2000—Redskins, 16-6 (NY)
　　　Giants, 9-7 (W)
2001—Giants, 23-9 (W)
　　　Redskins, 35-21 (W)
2002—Giants, 19-17 (NY)
　　　Giants, 27-21 (W)
2003—Giants, 24-21 (W) OT
　　　Redskins, 20-7 (W)
2004—Giants, 20-14 (W)
　　　Redskins, 31-7 (W)
2005—Giants, 36-0 (W)
　　　Redskins, 35-20 (W)
2006—Giants, 19-3 (W)
　　　Giants, 34-28 (W)
2007—Giants, 24-17 (W)
　　　Redskins, 22-10 (NY)
(RS Pts.—Giants 2,979, Redskins 2,730)
(PS Pts.—Redskins 28, Giants 17)
*Franchise in Boston prior to 1937 and
known as Braves prior to 1933
**Division Playoff
***NFC Championship

N.Y. JETS vs. ARIZONA
RS: Jets lead series, 4-2;
See Arizona vs. N.Y. Jets
N.Y. JETS vs. ATLANTA
RS: Falcons lead series, 5-4;
See Atlanta vs. N.Y. Jets
N.Y. JETS vs. BALTIMORE
RS: Ravens lead series, 5-1;
See Baltimore vs. N.Y. Jets
N.Y. JETS vs. BUFFALO
RS: Bills lead series, 52-42
PS: Bills lead series, 1-0;
See Buffalo vs. N.Y. Jets
N.Y. JETS vs. CAROLINA
RS: Series tied, 2-2;
See Carolina vs. N.Y. Jets
N.Y. JETS vs. CHICAGO
RS: Bears lead series, 6-3;
See Chicago vs. N.Y. Jets
N.Y. JETS vs. CINCINNATI
RS: Jets lead series, 12-7
PS: Jets lead series, 1-0;
See Cincinnati vs. N.Y. Jets
N.Y. JETS vs. CLEVELAND
RS: Browns lead series, 12-7
PS: Browns lead series, 1-0;
See Cleveland vs. N.Y. Jets
N.Y. JETS vs. DALLAS
RS: Cowboys lead series, 7-2;
See Dallas vs. N.Y. Jets
N.Y. JETS vs. DENVER
RS: Broncos lead series, 15-14-1
PS: Broncos lead series, 1-0;

See Denver vs. N.Y. Jets
N.Y. JETS vs. DETROIT
RS: Lions lead series, 6-5;
See Detroit vs. N.Y. Jets
N.Y. JETS vs. GREEN BAY
RS: Jets lead series, 8-2;
See Green Bay vs. N.Y. Jets
N.Y. JETS vs. HOUSTON
RS: Jets lead series, 3-0;
See Houston vs. N.Y. Jets
N.Y. JETS vs. INDIANAPOLIS
RS: Colts lead series, 40-25
PS: Colts lead series, 2-0;
See Indianapolis vs. N.Y. Jets
N.Y. JETS vs. JACKSONVILLE
RS: Jaguars lead series, 5-2
PS: Jets lead series, 1-0;
See Jacksonville vs. N.Y. Jets
N.Y. JETS vs. KANSAS CITY
RS: Chiefs lead series, 16-15-1
PS: Series tied, 1-1;
See Kansas City vs. N.Y. Jets
N.Y. JETS vs. MIAMI
RS: Jets lead series, 45-38-1
PS: Dolphins lead series, 1-0;
See Miami vs. N.Y. Jets
N.Y. JETS vs. MINNESOTA
RS: Jets lead series, 7-1;
See Minnesota vs. N.Y. Jets
N.Y. JETS vs. NEW ENGLAND
RS: Jets lead series, 48-46-1
PS: Patriots lead series, 2-0;
See New England vs. N.Y. Jets
N.Y. JETS vs. NEW ORLEANS
RS: Series tied, 5-5;
See New Orleans vs. N.Y. Jets
N.Y. JETS vs. N.Y. GIANTS
RS: Giants lead series, 7-4;
See N.Y. Giants vs. N.Y. Jets
*N.Y. JETS vs. **OAKLAND
RS: Raiders lead series, 19-14-2
PS: Series tied, 2-2
1960—Raiders, 28-27 (NY)
　　　Titans, 31-28 (O)
1961—Titans, 14-6 (O)
　　　Titans, 23-12 (NY)
1962—Titans, 28-17 (O)
　　　Titans, 31-21 (NY)
1963—Jets, 10-7 (NY)
　　　Raiders, 49-26 (O)
1964—Jets, 35-13 (NY)
　　　Raiders, 35-26 (O)
1965—Tie, 24-24 (NY)
　　　Raiders, 24-14 (O)
1966—Raiders, 24-21 (NY)
　　　Tie, 28-28 (O)
1967—Jets, 27-14 (NY)
　　　Raiders, 38-29 (O)
1968—Raiders, 43-32 (O)
　　　***Jets, 27-23 (NY)
1969—Raiders, 27-14 (NY)
1970—Raiders, 14-13 (NY)
1972—Raiders, 24-16 (O)
1977—Raiders, 28-27 (NY)
1979—Jets, 28-19 (NY)
1982—****Jets, 17-14 (LA)
1985—Raiders, 31-0 (LA)
1989—Raiders, 14-7 (NY)
1993—Raiders, 24-20 (LA)
1995—Raiders, 47-10 (NY)

1996—Raiders, 34-13 (NY)
1997—Jets 23-22 (NY)
1999—Raiders, 24-23 (O)
2000—Raiders, 31-7 (O)
2001—Jets, 24-22 (O)
　　　*****Raiders, 38-24 (O)
2002—Raiders, 26-20 (O)
　　　****Raiders, 30-10 (O)
2003—Jets, 27-24 (O) OT
2005—Jets, 26-10 (NY)
2006—Jets, 23-3 (NY)
(RS Pts.—Raiders 835, Jets 747)
(PS Pts.—Raiders 105, Jets 78)
Jets known as Titans prior to 1963
***Franchise in Los Angeles from
1982-1994*
***AFL Championship
****AFC Second-Round Playoff
*****AFC First-Round Playoff
N.Y. JETS vs. PHILADELPHIA
RS: Eagles lead series, 8-0
1973—Eagles, 24-23 (P)
1977—Eagles, 27-0 (P)
1978—Eagles, 17-9 (P)
1987—Eagles, 38-27 (NY)
1993—Eagles, 35-30 (NY)
1996—Eagles, 21-20 (NY)
2003—Eagles, 24-17 (P)
2007—Eagles, 16-9 (NY)
(RS Pts.—Eagles 202, Jets 135)
N.Y. JETS vs. PITTSBURGH
RS: Steelers lead series, 15-3
PS: Steelers lead series, 1-0
1970—Steelers, 21-17 (P)
1973—Steelers, 26-14 (P)
1975—Steelers, 20-7 (NY)
1977—Steelers, 23-20 (NY)
1978—Steelers, 28-17 (NY)
1981—Steelers, 38-10 (P)
1983—Steelers, 34-7 (NY)
1984—Steelers, 23-17 (NY)
1986—Steelers, 45-24 (NY)
1988—Jets, 24-20 (NY)
1989—Steelers, 13-0 (NY)
1990—Steelers, 24-7 (NY)
1992—Steelers, 27-10 (P)
2000—Steelers, 20-3 (NY)
2001—Steelers, 18-7 (P)
2003—Jets, 6-0 (NY)
2004—Steelers, 17-6 (P)
　　　*Steelers, 20-17 (P) OT
2007—Jets, 19-16 (NY) OT
(RS Pts.—Steelers 413, Jets 215)
(PS Pts.—Steelers 20, Jets 17)
*AFC Divisional Playoff
N.Y. JETS vs. *ST. LOUIS
RS: Rams lead series, 9-2
1970—Jets, 31-20 (LA)
1974—Rams, 20-13 (NY)
1980—Rams, 38-13 (LA)
1983—Jets, 27-24 (NY) OT
1986—Rams, 17-3 (NY)
1989—Rams, 38-14 (LA)
1992—Rams, 18-10 (LA)
1995—Rams, 23-20 (NY)
1998—Rams, 30-10 (StL)
2001—Rams, 34-14 (NY)
2004—Rams, 32-29 (StL) OT
(RS Pts.—Rams 294, Jets 184)
*Franchise in Los Angeles prior to 1995

*N.Y. JETS vs. **SAN DIEGO
RS: Chargers lead series, 18-11-1
PS: Jets lead series, 1-0
1960—Chargers, 21-7 (NY)
　　　Chargers, 50-43 (LA)
1961—Chargers, 25-10 (NY)
　　　Chargers, 48-13 (SD)
1962—Chargers, 40-14 (SD)
　　　Titans, 23-3 (NY)
1963—Chargers, 24-20 (SD)
　　　Chargers, 53-7 (NY)
1964—Tie, 17-17 (NY)
　　　Chargers, 38-3 (SD)
1965—Chargers, 34-9 (NY)
　　　Chargers, 38-7 (SD)
1966—Jets, 17-16 (NY)
　　　Chargers, 42-27 (SD)
1967—Jets, 42-31 (SD)
1968—Jets, 23-20 (NY)
　　　Jets, 37-15 (SD)
1969—Chargers, 34-27 (SD)
1971—Chargers, 49-21 (SD)
1974—Jets, 27-14 (NY)
1975—Chargers, 24-16 (SD)
1983—Jets, 41-29 (SD)
1989—Jets, 20-17 (SD)
1990—Chargers, 39-3 (NY)
　　　Chargers, 38-17 (SD)
1991—Jets, 24-3 (NY)
1994—Chargers, 21-6 (NY)
2002—Jets, 44-13 (SD)
2004—Jets, 34-28 (SD)
　　　***Jets, 20-17 (SD) OT
2005—Chargers, 31-26 (NY)
(RS Pts.—Chargers 855, Jets 625)
(PS Pts.—Jets 20, Chargers 17)
Jets known as Titans prior to 1963
**Franchise in Los Angeles prior to 1961
***AFC First-Round Playoff
N.Y. JETS vs. SAN FRANCISCO
RS: 49ers lead series, 8-2
1971—49ers, 24-21 (NY)
1976—49ers, 17-6 (SF)
1980—49ers, 37-27 (NY)
1983—Jets, 27-13 (SF)
1986—49ers, 24-10 (SF)
1989—49ers, 23-10 (NY)
1992—49ers, 31-14 (NY)
1998—49ers, 36-30 (SF) OT
2001—49ers, 19-17 (NY)
2004—Jets, 22-14 (NY)
(RS Pts.—49ers 238, Jets 184)
N.Y. JETS vs. SEATTLE
RS: Series tied, 8-8
1977—Seahawks, 17-0 (NY)
1978—Seahawks, 24-17 (NY)
1979—Seahawks, 30-7 (S)
1980—Seahawks, 27-17 (NY)
1981—Seahawks, 19-3 (NY)
　　　Seahawks, 27-23 (S)
1983—Seahawks, 17-10 (NY)
1985—Jets, 17-14 (NY)
1986—Jets, 38-7 (S)
1987—Jets, 30-14 (NY)
1991—Seahawks, 20-13 (S)
1995—Jets, 16-10 (S)
1997—Jets, 41-3 (S)
1998—Jets, 32-31 (NY)
1999—Jets, 19-9 (NY)
2004—Jets, 37-14 (NY)

(RS Pts.—Jets 320, Seahawks 283)
N.Y. JETS vs. TAMPA BAY
RS: Jets lead series, 8-1
1976—Jets, 34-0 (NY)
1982—Jets, 32-17 (NY)
1984—Buccaneers, 41-21 (TB)
1985—Jets, 62-28 (NY)
1990—Jets, 16-14 (TB)
1991—Jets, 16-13 (NY)
1997—Jets, 31-0 (NY)
2000—Jets, 21-17 (TB)
2005—Jets, 14-12 (NY)
(RS Pts.—Jets 247, Buccaneers 142)
*N.Y. JETS vs. **TENNESSEE
RS: Titans lead series, 21-15-1
PS: Titans lead series, 1-0
1960—Oilers, 27-21 (H)
　　　Oilers, 42-28 (NY)
1961—Oilers, 49-13 (H)
　　　Oilers, 48-21 (NY)
1962—Oilers, 56-17 (H)
　　　Oilers, 44-10 (NY)
1963—Jets, 24-17 (NY)
　　　Oilers, 31-27 (H)
1964—Jets, 24-21 (NY)
　　　Oilers, 33-17 (H)
1965—Oilers, 27-21 (H)
　　　Jets, 41-14 (NY)
1966—Jets, 52-13 (NY)
　　　Oilers, 24-0 (H)
1967—Tie, 28-28 (NY)
1968—Jets, 20-14 (H)
　　　Jets, 26-7 (NY)
1969—Jets, 26-17 (NY)
　　　Jets, 34-26 (H)
1972—Oilers, 26-20 (H)
1974—Oilers, 27-22 (NY)
1977—Oilers, 20-0 (H)
1979—Oilers, 27-24 (H) OT
1980—Jets, 31-28 (NY) OT
1981—Jets, 33-17 (NY)
1984—Oilers, 31-20 (H)
1988—Jets, 45-3 (NY)
1990—Jets, 17-12 (H)
1991—Oilers, 23-20 (NY)
　　　***Oilers, 17-10 (H)
1993—Oilers, 24-0 (H)
1994—Oilers, 24-10 (H)
1995—Oilers, 23-6 (H)
1996—Oilers, 35-10 (NY)
1998—Jets, 24-3 (T)
2003—Jets, 24-17 (NY)
2006—Jets, 23-16 (T)
2007—Titans, 10-6 (T)
(RS Pts.—Titans 904, Jets 785)
(PS Pts.—Titans 17, Jets 10)
*Jets known as Titans prior to 1963
**Franchise in Houston prior to 1997;
known as Oilers prior to 1999
***AFC First-Round Playoff
N.Y. JETS vs. WASHINGTON
RS: Redskins lead series, 8-1
1972—Redskins, 35-17 (NY)
1976—Redskins, 37-16 (NY)
1978—Redskins, 23-3 (W)
1987—Redskins, 17-16 (W)
1993—Jets, 3-0 (W)
1996—Redskins, 31-16 (W)
1999—Redskins, 27-20 (NY)
2003—Redskins, 16-13 (W)

2007—Redskins 23-20 (NY) OT
(RS Pts.—Redskins 209, Jets 124)

OAKLAND vs. ARIZONA
RS: Raiders lead series, 5-2;
See Arizona vs. Oakland
OAKLAND vs. ATLANTA
RS: Raiders lead series, 7-4;
See Atlanta vs. Oakland
OAKLAND vs. BALTIMORE
RS: Ravens lead series, 3-1
PS: Ravens lead series, 1-0;
See Baltimore vs. Oakland
OAKLAND vs. BUFFALO
RS: Raiders lead series, 19-15
PS: Bills lead series, 2-0;
See Buffalo vs. Oakland
OAKLAND vs. CAROLINA
RS: Raiders lead series, 2-1;
See Carolina vs. Oakland
OAKLAND vs. CHICAGO
RS: Series tied, 6-6;
See Chicago vs. Oakland
OAKLAND vs. CINCINNATI
RS: Raiders lead series, 17-8
PS: Raiders lead series, 2-0;
See Cincinnati vs. Oakland
OAKLAND vs. CLEVELAND
RS: Raiders lead series, 10-7
PS: Raiders lead series, 2-0;
See Cleveland vs. Oakland
OAKLAND vs. DALLAS
RS: Raiders lead series, 6-3;
See Dallas vs. Oakland
OAKLAND vs. DENVER
RS: Raiders lead series, 54-39-2
PS: Series tied, 1-1;
See Denver vs. Oakland
OAKLAND vs. DETROIT
RS: Raiders lead series, 6-4;
See Detroit vs. Oakland
OAKLAND vs. GREEN BAY
RS: Series tied, 5-5
PS: Packers lead series, 1-0;
See Green Bay vs. Oakland
OAKLAND vs. HOUSTON
RS: Texans lead series, 3-0;
See Houston vs. Oakland
OAKLAND vs. INDIANAPOLIS
RS: Raiders lead series, 7-4
PS: Series tied, 1-1;
See Indianapolis vs. Oakland
OAKLAND vs. JACKSONVILLE
RS: Jaguars lead series, 3-1;
See Jacksonville vs. Oakland
OAKLAND vs. KANSAS CITY
RS: Chiefs lead series, 50-43-2
PS: Chiefs lead series, 2-1;
See Kansas City vs. Oakland
OAKLAND vs. MIAMI
RS: Raiders lead series, 16-11-1
PS: Raiders lead series, 3-1;
See Miami vs. Oakland
OAKLAND vs. MINNESOTA
RS: Raiders lead series, 8-4
PS: Raiders lead series, 1-0;
See Minnesota vs. Oakland
OAKLAND vs. NEW ENGLAND
RS: Raiders lead series, 14-13-1
PS: Patriots lead series, 2-1;

See New England vs. Oakland
OAKLAND vs. NEW ORLEANS
RS: Raiders lead series, 5-4-1;
See New Orleans vs. Oakland
OAKLAND vs. N.Y. GIANTS
RS: Raiders lead series, 7-3;
See N.Y. Giants vs. Oakland
OAKLAND vs. N.Y. JETS
RS: Raiders lead series, 19-14-2
PS: Series tied, 2-2;
See N.Y. Jets vs. Oakland
*OAKLAND vs. PHILADELPHIA
RS: Eagles lead series, 5-4
PS: Raiders lead series, 1-0
1971—Raiders, 34-10 (O)
1976—Raiders, 26-7 (P)
1980—Eagles, 10-7 (P)
　　　**Raiders, 27-10 (New Orleans)
1986—Eagles, 33-27 (LA) OT
1989—Eagles, 10-7 (P)
1992—Eagles, 31-10 (P)
1995—Raiders, 48-17 (O)
2001—Raiders, 20-10 (P)
2005—Eagles, 23-20 (P)
(RS Pts.—Raiders 199, Eagles 151)
(PS Pts.—Raiders 27, Eagles 10)
*Franchise in Los Angeles from 1982-1994
**Super Bowl XV
*OAKLAND vs. PITTSBURGH
RS: Raiders lead series, 9-8
PS: Series tied, 3-3
1970—Raiders, 31-14 (O)
1972—Steelers, 34-28 (P)
　　　**Steelers, 13-7 (P)
1973—Steelers, 17-9 (O)
　　　**Raiders, 33-14 (O)
1974—Raiders, 17-0 (P)
　　　***Steelers, 24-13 (O)
1975—***Steelers, 16-10 (P)
1976—Raiders, 31-28 (O)
　　　***Raiders, 24-7 (O)
1977—Raiders, 16-7 (P)
1980—Raiders, 45-34 (P)
1981—Raiders, 30-27 (O)
1983—**Raiders, 38-10 (LA)
1984—Steelers, 13-7 (LA)
1990—Raiders, 20-3 (LA)
1994—Steelers, 21-3 (LA)
1995—Steelers, 29-10 (O)
2000—Steelers, 21-20 (P)
2002—Raiders, 30-17 (P)
2003—Steelers, 27-7 (P)
2004—Steelers, 24-21 (P)
2006—Raiders, 20-13 (O)
(RS Pts.—Raiders 345, Steelers 329)
(PS Pts.—Steelers 125, Steelers 84)
*Franchise in Los Angeles from 1982-1994
**AFC Divisional Playoff
***AFC Championship
*OAKLAND vs. **ST. LOUIS
RS: Raiders lead series, 7-4
1972—Raiders, 45-17 (O)
1977—Rams, 20-14 (LA)
1979—Raiders, 24-17 (LA)
1982—Raiders, 37-31 (LA Raiders)
1985—Raiders, 16-6 (LA Rams)
1988—Rams, 22-17 (LA Raiders)
1991—Raiders, 20-17 (LA Raiders)
1994—Raiders, 20-17 (LA Rams)
1997—Raiders, 35-17 (O)

2002—Rams, 28-13 (StL)
2006—Rams, 20-0 (O)
(RS Pts.—Raiders 241, Rams 212)
Franchise in Los Angeles from 1982-1994
**Franchise in Los Angeles prior to 1995*
*OAKLAND vs. **SAN DIEGO
RS: Raiders lead series, 54-40-2
PS: Raiders lead series, 1-0
1960—Chargers, 52-28 (LA)
    Chargers, 41-17 (O)
1961—Chargers, 44-0 (SD)
    Chargers, 41-10 (O)
1962—Chargers, 42-33 (O)
    Chargers, 31-21 (SD)
1963—Raiders, 34-33 (SD)
    Raiders, 41-27 (O)
1964—Chargers, 31-17 (SD)
    Raiders, 21-20 (O)
1965—Chargers, 17-6 (O)
    Chargers, 24-14 (SD)
1966—Chargers, 29-20 (O)
    Raiders, 41-19 (SD)
1967—Raiders, 51-10 (O)
    Raiders, 41-21 (SD)
1968—Chargers, 23-14 (O)
    Raiders, 34-27 (SD)
1969—Raiders, 24-12 (SD)
    Raiders, 21-16 (O)
1970—Tie, 27-27 (SD)
    Raiders, 20-17 (O)
1971—Raiders, 34-0 (SD)
    Raiders, 34-33 (O)
1972—Tie, 17-17 (O)
    Raiders, 21-19 (SD)
1973—Raiders, 27-17 (SD)
    Raiders, 31-3 (O)
1974—Raiders, 14-10 (SD)
    Raiders, 17-10 (O)
1975—Raiders, 6-0 (SD)
    Raiders, 25-0 (O)
1976—Raiders, 27-17 (SD)
    Raiders, 24-0 (O)
1977—Raiders, 24-0 (O)
    Chargers, 12-7 (SD)
1978—Raiders, 21-20 (SD)
    Chargers, 27-23 (O)
1979—Chargers, 30-10 (SD)
    Raiders, 45-22 (O)
1980—Chargers, 30-24 (SD) OT
    Raiders, 38-24 (O)
    ***Raiders, 34-27 (SD)
1981—Chargers, 55-21 (O)
    Chargers, 23-10 (SD)
1982—Raiders, 28-24 (LA)
    Raiders, 41-34 (SD)
1983—Raiders, 42-10 (LA)
    Raiders, 30-14 (LA)
1984—Raiders, 33-30 (LA)
    Raiders, 44-37 (SD)
1985—Raiders, 34-21 (LA)
    Chargers, 40-34 (SD) OT
1986—Raiders, 17-13 (LA)
    Raiders, 37-31 (SD) OT
1987—Chargers, 23-17 (LA)
    Chargers, 16-14 (SD)
1988—Raiders, 24-13 (LA)
    Raiders, 13-3 (SD)
1989—Raiders, 40-14 (LA)
    Chargers, 14-12 (SD)
1990—Raiders, 24-9 (SD)

    Raiders, 17-12 (LA)
1991—Chargers, 21-13 (LA)
    Raiders, 9-7 (SD)
1992—Chargers, 27-3 (SD)
    Chargers, 36-14 (LA)
1993—Chargers, 30-23 (LA)
    Raiders, 12-7 (SD)
1994—Chargers, 26-24 (LA)
    Raiders, 24-17 (SD)
1995—Raiders, 17-7 (O)
    Chargers, 12-6 (SD)
1996—Chargers, 40-34 (O)
    Raiders, 23-14 (SD)
1997—Chargers, 25-10 (O)
    Raiders, 38-13 (SD)
1998—Raiders, 7-6 (O)
    Raiders, 17-10 (SD)
1999—Raiders, 28-9 (O)
    Chargers, 23-20 (SD)
2000—Raiders, 9-6 (O)
    Raiders, 15-13 (SD)
2001—Raiders, 34-24 (O)
    Raiders, 13-6 (SD)
2002—Chargers, 27-21 (O) OT
    Raiders, 27-7 (SD)
2003—Raiders, 34-31 (O) OT
    Chargers, 21-14 (SD)
2004—Chargers, 42-14 (SD)
    Chargers, 23-17 (O)
2005—Chargers, 27-14 (O)
    Chargers, 34-10 (SD)
2006—Chargers, 27-0 (O)
    Chargers, 21-14 (SD)
2007—Chargers, 28-14 ((SD)
    Chargers, 30-17 (O)
(RS Pts.—Raiders 2,125, Chargers 2,028)
(PS Pts.—Raiders 34, Chargers 27)
Franchise in Los Angeles from 1982-1994
**Franchise in Los Angeles prior to 1961*
***AFC Championship*
*OAKLAND vs. SAN FRANCISCO
RS: Raiders lead series, 6-5
1970—49ers, 38-7 (O)
1974—Raiders, 35-24 (SF)
1979—Raiders, 23-10 (O)
1982—Raiders, 23-17 (SF)
1985—49ers, 34-10 (LA)
1988—Raiders, 9-3 (SF)
1991—Raiders, 12-6 (LA)
1994—49ers, 44-14 (SF)
2000—Raiders, 34-28 (SF) OT
2002—49ers, 23-20 (O) OT
2006—49ers, 34-20 (SF)
(RS Pts.—49ers 261, Raiders 207)
Franchise in Los Angeles from 1982-1994
*OAKLAND vs. SEATTLE
RS: Raiders lead series, 27-23
PS: Series tied, 1-1
1977—Raiders, 44-7 (O)
1978—Seahawks, 27-7 (S)
    Seahawks, 17-16 (O)
1979—Seahawks, 27-10 (S)
    Seahawks, 29-24 (O)
1980—Raiders, 33-14 (O)
    Raiders, 19-17 (S)
1981—Raiders, 20-10 (O)
    Raiders, 32-31 (S)
1982—Raiders, 28-23 (LA)
1983—Seahawks, 38-36 (S)
    Seahawks, 34-21 (LA)

    **Raiders, 30-14 (LA)
1984—Raiders, 28-14 (LA)
    Seahawks, 17-14 (S)
    ***Seahawks, 13-7 (S)
1985—Seahawks, 33-3 (S)
    Raiders, 13-3 (LA)
1986—Raiders, 14-10 (LA)
    Seahawks, 37-0 (S)
1987—Seahawks, 35-13 (LA)
    Raiders, 37-14 (S)
1988—Seahawks, 35-27 (LA)
    Seahawks, 43-37 (LA)
1989—Seahawks, 24-20 (LA)
    Seahawks, 23-17 (S)
1990—Raiders, 17-13 (S)
    Raiders, 24-17 (LA)
1991—Raiders, 23-20 (S) OT
    Raiders, 31-7 (LA)
1992—Raiders, 19-0 (S)
    Raiders, 20-3 (LA)
1993—Raiders, 17-13 (S)
    Raiders, 27-23 (LA)
1994—Seahawks, 38-9 (LA)
    Raiders, 17-16 (S)
1995—Raiders, 34-14 (O)
    Seahawks, 44-10 (S)
1996—Raiders, 27-21 (S)
    Seahawks, 28-21 (O)
1997—Seahawks, 45-34 (S)
    Seahawks, 22-21 (O)
1998—Raiders, 31-18 (S)
    Raiders, 20-17 (O)
1999—Seahawks, 22-21 (S)
    Raiders, 30-21 (O)
2000—Raiders, 31-3 (O)
    Seahawks, 27-24 (S)
2001—Raiders, 38-14 (O)
    Seahawks, 34-27 (S)
2002—Raiders, 31-17 (O)
2006—Seahawks, 16-0 (S)
(RS Pts.—Raiders 1,117, Seahawks 1,075)
(PS Pts.—Raiders 37, Seahawks 27)
Franchise in Los Angeles from 1982-1994
**AFC Championship*
***AFC First-Round Playoff*
*OAKLAND vs. TAMPA BAY
RS: Raiders lead series, 5-1
PS: Buccaneers lead series, 1-0
1976—Raiders, 49-16 (O)
1981—Raiders, 18-16 (O)
1993—Raiders, 27-20 (LA)
1996—Buccaneers, 20-17 (TB) OT
1999—Raiders, 45-0 (O)
2002—**Buccaneers, 48-21 (San Diego)
2004—Raiders, 30-20 (O)
(RS Pts.—Raiders 186, Buccaneers 92)
(PS Pts.—Buccaneers 48, Raiders 21)
Franchise in Los Angeles from 1982-1994
**Super Bowl XXXVII*
*OAKLAND vs. **TENNESSEE
RS: Raiders lead series, 23-18
PS: Raiders lead series, 4-0
1960—Oilers, 37-22 (O)
    Raiders, 14-13 (H)
1961—Oilers, 55-0 (H)
    Oilers, 47-16 (O)
1962—Oilers, 28-20 (O)
    Oilers, 32-17 (H)
1963—Raiders, 24-13 (H)
    Raiders, 52-49 (O)

1964—Oilers, 42-28 (H)
  Raiders, 20-10 (O)
1965—Raiders, 21-17 (O)
  Raiders, 33-21 (H)
1966—Oilers, 31-0 (H)
  Raiders, 38-23 (O)
1967—Raiders, 19-7 (H)
  ***Raiders, 40-7 (O)
1968—Raiders, 24-15 (H)
1969—Raiders, 21-17 (O)
  ****Raiders, 56-7 (O)
1971—Raiders, 41-21 (O)
1972—Raiders, 34-0 (H)
1973—Raiders, 17-6 (H)
1975—Oilers, 27-26 (O)
1976—Raiders, 14-13 (H)
1977—Raiders, 34-29 (O)
1978—Raiders, 21-17 (O)
1979—Oilers, 31-17 (H)
1980—*****Raiders, 27-7 (O)
1981—Oilers, 17-16 (H)
1983—Raiders, 20-6 (LA)
1984—Raiders, 24-14 (H)
1986—Raiders, 28-17 (H)
1988—Oilers, 38-35 (H)
1989—Oilers, 23-7 (H)
1991—Raiders, 47-17 (H)
1994—Raiders, 17-14 (LA)
1997—Oilers, 24-21 (T) OT
1999—Titans, 21-14 (T)
2001—Titans, 13-10 (O)
2002—Raiders, 52-25 (O)
  ******Raiders, 41-24 (O)
2003—Titans, 25-20 (T)
2004—Raiders, 40-35 (O)
2005—Raiders, 34-25 (T)
2007—Titans, 13-9 (T)
(RS Pts.—Titans 958, Raiders 937)
(PS Pts.—Raiders 164, Titans 45)
*Franchise in Los Angeles from 1982-1994
**Franchise in Houston prior to 1997;
known as Oilers prior to 1999
***AFL Championship
****Inter-Divisional Playoff
*****AFC First-Round Playoff
******AFC Championship
OAKLAND vs. WASHINGTON
RS: Raiders lead series, 7-3
PS: Raiders lead series, 1-0
1970—Raiders, 34-20 (O)
1975—Raiders, 26-23 (W) OT
1980—Raiders, 24-21 (O)
1983—Redskins, 37-35 (W)
  **Raiders, 38-9 (Tampa)
1986—Redskins, 10-6 (W)
1989—Raiders, 37-24 (LA)
1992—Raiders, 21-20 (W)
1995—Raiders, 20-8 (W)
1998—Redskins, 29-19 (O)
2005—Raiders, 16-13 (W)
(RS Pts.—Raiders 238, Redskins 205)
(PS Pts.—Raiders 38, Redskins 9)
*Franchise in Los Angeles from
1982-1994
**Super Bowl XVIII

PHILADELPHIA vs. ARIZONA
RS: Cardinals lead series, 53-52-5
PS: Series tied, 1-1;
See Arizona vs. Philadelphia

PHILADELPHIA vs. ATLANTA
RS: Eagles lead series, 12-10-1
PS: Eagles lead series, 2-1;
See Atlanta vs. Philadelphia
PHILADELPHIA vs. BALTIMORE
RS: Eagles lead series, 1-0-1;
See Baltimore vs. Philadelphia
PHILADELPHIA vs. BUFFALO
RS: Eagles lead series, 6-5;
See Buffalo vs. Philadelphia
PHILADELPHIA vs. CAROLINA
RS: Eagles lead series, 4-1
PS: Panthers lead series, 1-0;
See Carolina vs. Philadelphia
PHILADELPHIA vs. CHICAGO
RS: Bears lead series, 25-8-1
PS: Eagles lead series, 2-1;
See Chicago vs. Philadelphia
PHILADELPHIA vs. CINCINNATI
RS: Bengals lead series, 7-3;
See Cincinnati vs. Philadelphia
PHILADELPHIA vs. CLEVELAND
RS: Browns lead series, 31-14-1;
See Cleveland vs. Philadelphia
PHILADELPHIA vs. DALLAS
RS: Cowboys lead series, 52-42
PS: Cowboys lead series, 2-1;
See Dallas vs. Philadelphia
PHILADELPHIA vs. DENVER
RS: Eagles lead series, 6-4;
See Denver vs. Philadelphia
PHILADELPHIA vs. DETROIT
RS: Eagles lead series, 13-12-2
PS: Eagles lead series, 1-0;
See Detroit vs. Philadelphia
PHILADELPHIA vs. GREEN BAY
RS: Packers lead series, 23-13
PS: Eagles lead series, 2-0;
See Green Bay vs. Philadelphia
PHILADELPHIA vs. HOUSTON
RS: Eagles lead series, 2-0;
See Houston vs. Philadelphia
PHILADELPHIA vs. INDIANAPOLIS
RS: Colts lead series, 10-6;
See Indianapolis vs. Philadelphia
PHILADELPHIA vs. JACKSONVILLE
RS: Jaguars lead series, 3-0;
See Jacksonville vs. Philadelphia
PHILADELPHIA vs. KANSAS CITY
RS: Eagles lead series, 3-2;
See Kansas City vs. Philadelphia
PHILADELPHIA vs. MIAMI
RS: Dolphins lead series, 7-5;
See Miami vs. Philadelphia
PHILADELPHIA vs. MINNESOTA
RS: Vikings lead series, 11-9
PS: Eagles lead series, 2-0;
See Minnesota vs. Philadelphia
PHILADELPHIA vs. NEW ENGLAND
RS: Eagles lead series, 6-4
PS: Patriots lead series, 1-0;
See New England vs. Philadelphia
PHILADELPHIA vs. NEW ORLEANS
RS: Eagles lead series, 15-9
PS; Series tied, 1-1;
See New Orleans vs. Philadelphia
PHILADELPHIA vs. N.Y. GIANTS
RS: Giants lead series, 78-66-2
PS: Giants lead series, 2-1;
See N.Y. Giants vs. Philadelphia

PHILADELPHIA vs. N.Y. JETS
RS: Eagles lead series, 8-0;
See N.Y. Jets vs. Philadelphia
PHILADELPHIA vs. OAKLAND
RS: Eagles lead series, 5-4
PS: Raiders lead series, 1-0;
See Oakland vs. Philadelphia
PHILADELPHIA vs. *PITTSBURGH
RS: Eagles lead series, 45-27-3
PS: Eagles lead series, 1-0
1933—Eagles, 25-6 (Phila)
1934—Eagles, 17-0 (Pitt)
  Pirates, 9-7 (Phila)
1935—Pirates, 17-7 (Phila)
  Eagles, 17-6 (Pitt)
1936—Pirates, 17-0 (Pitt)
  Pirates, 6-0 (Johnstown, Pa.)
1937—Pirates, 27-14 (Pitt)
  Pirates, 16-7 (Pitt)
1938—Eagles, 27-7 (Buffalo)
  Eagles, 14-7 (Charleston, W. Va.)
1939—Eagles, 17-14 (Phila)
  Pirates, 24-12 (Pitt)
1940—Pirates, 7-3 (Pitt)
  Eagles, 7-0 (Phila)
1941—Eagles, 10-7 (Pitt)
  Tie, 7-7 (Phila)
1942—Eagles, 24-14 (Pitt)
  Steelers, 14-0 (Phila)
1945—Eagles, 45-3 (Pitt)
  Eagles, 30-6 (Phila)
1946—Steelers, 10-7 (Pitt)
  Eagles, 10-7 (Phila)
1947—Steelers, 35-24 (Pitt)
  Eagles, 21-0 (Phila)
  **Eagles, 21-0 (Pitt)
1948—Eagles, 34-7 (Pitt)
  Eagles, 17-0 (Phila)
1949—Eagles, 38-7 (Pitt)
  Eagles, 34-17 (Phila)
1950—Eagles, 17-10 (Phila)
  Steelers, 9-7 (Phila)
1951—Eagles, 34-13 (Pitt)
  Steelers, 17-13 (Phila)
1952—Eagles, 31-25 (Pitt)
  Eagles, 26-21 (Phila)
1953—Eagles, 23-17 (Phila)
  Eagles, 35-7 (Pitt)
1954—Eagles, 24-22 (Phila)
  Steelers, 17-7 (Pitt)
1955—Steelers, 13-7 (Phila)
  Eagles, 24-0 (Phila)
1956—Eagles, 35-21 (Pitt)
  Eagles, 14-7 (Phila)
1957—Steelers, 6-0 (Pitt)
  Eagles, 7-6 (Phila)
1958—Steelers, 24-3 (Pitt)
  Steelers, 31-24 (Phila)
1959—Eagles, 28-24 (Phila)
  Steelers, 31-0 (Pitt)
1960—Eagles, 34-7 (Phila)
  Steelers, 27-21 (Pitt)
1961—Eagles, 21-16 (Phila)
  Eagles, 35-24 (Pitt)
1962—Steelers, 13-7 (Pitt)
  Steelers, 26-17 (Phila)
1963—Tie, 21-21 (Phila)
  Tie, 20-20 (Pitt)
1964—Eagles, 21-7 (Phila)
  Eagles, 34-10 (Pitt)

1965—Steelers, 20-14 (Phila)
    Eagles, 47-13 (Pitt)
1966—Eagles, 31-14 (Pitt)
    Eagles, 27-23 (Phila)
1967—Eagles, 34-24 (Phila)
1968—Steelers, 6-3 (Pitt)
1969—Eagles, 41-27 (Phila)
1970—Eagles, 30-20 (Phila)
1974—Steelers, 27-0 (Pitt)
1979—Eagles, 17-14 (Phila)
1988—Eagles, 27-26 (Phila)
1991—Eagles, 23-14 (Phila)
1994—Steelers, 14-3 (Pitt)
1997—Eagles, 23-20 (Phila)
2000—Eagles, 26-23 (Pitt) OT
2004—Steelers, 27-3 (Pitt)
(RS Pts.—Eagles 1,414, Steelers 1,091)
(PS Pts.—Eagles 21, Steelers 0)
*Steelers known as Pirates prior to 1941
**Division Playoff

PHILADELPHIA vs. *ST. LOUIS
RS: Rams lead series, 17-16-1
PS: Rams lead series, 2-1
1937—Rams, 21-3 (P)
1939—Rams, 35-13 (Colorado Springs)
1940—Rams, 21-13 (C)
1942—Rams, 24-14 (Akron)
1944—Eagles, 26-13 (P)
1945—Eagles, 28-14 (P)
1946—Eagles, 25-14 (LA)
1947—Eagles, 14-7 (P)
1948—Tie, 28-28 (LA)
1949—Eagles, 38-14 (P)
    **Eagles, 14-0 (LA)
1950—Eagles, 56-20 (P)
1955—Rams, 23-21 (P)
1956—Rams, 27-7 (LA)
1957—Rams, 17-13 (LA)
1959—Eagles, 23-20 (P)
1964—Rams, 20-10 (LA)
1967—Rams, 33-17 (LA)
1969—Rams, 23-17 (P)
1972—Rams, 34-3 (P)
1975—Rams, 42-3 (P)
1977—Rams, 20-0 (LA)
1978—Rams, 16-14 (P)
1983—Eagles, 13-9 (P)
1985—Rams, 17-6 (P)
1986—Eagles, 34-20 (P)
1988—Eagles, 30-24 (P)
1989—***Rams, 21-7 (P)
1990—Eagles, 27-21 (LA)
1995—Eagles, 20-9 (P)
1998—Eagles, 17-14 (P)
1999—Eagles, 38-31 (P)
2001—Rams, 20-17 (P) OT
    ****Rams, 29-24 (StL)
2002—Eagles, 10-3 (P)
2004—Rams, 20-7 (StL)
2005—Eagles, 17-16 (StL)
(RS Pts.—Rams 690, Eagles 622)
(PS Pts.—Rams 50, Eagles 45)
*Franchise in Los Angeles prior to 1995
and in Cleveland prior to 1946
**NFL Championship
***NFC First-Round Playoff
****NFC Championship

PHILADELPHIA vs. SAN DIEGO
RS: Chargers lead series, 5-4
1974—Eagles, 13-7 (SD)

1980—Chargers, 22-21 (SD)
1985—Chargers, 20-14 (SD)
1986—Eagles, 23-7 (P)
1989—Chargers, 20-17 (SD)
1995—Chargers, 27-21 (P)
1998—Chargers, 13-10 (SD)
2001—Eagles, 24-14 (P)
2005—Eagles, 20-17 (P)
(RS Pts.—Eagles 163, Chargers 147)

PHILADELPHIA vs. SAN FRANCISCO
RS: 49ers lead series, 16-9-1
PS: 49ers lead series, 1-0
1951—Eagles, 21-14 (P)
1953—49ers, 31-21 (SF)
1956—Tie, 10-10 (P)
1958—49ers, 30-24 (P)
1959—49ers, 24-14 (SF)
1964—49ers, 28-24 (P)
1966—Eagles, 35-34 (SF)
1967—49ers, 28-27 (P)
1969—49ers, 14-13 (SF)
1971—49ers, 31-3 (P)
1973—49ers, 38-28 (SF)
1975—Eagles, 27-17 (P)
1983—Eagles, 22-17 (SF)
1984—49ers, 21-9 (P)
1985—49ers, 24-13 (SF)
1989—49ers, 38-28 (P)
1991—49ers, 23-7 (P)
1992—Eagles, 20-14 (SF)
1993—Eagles, 37-34 (SF) OT
1994—Eagles, 40-8 (SF)
1996—*49ers, 14-0 (SF)
1997—49ers, 24-12 (P)
2001—49ers, 13-3 (SF)
2002—Eagles, 38-17 (SF)
2003—49ers, 31-28 (P) OT
2005—Eagles, 42-3 (P)
2006—Eagles, 38-24 (SF)
(RS Pts.—49ers 596, Eagles 578)
(PS Pts.—49ers 14, Eagles 0)
*NFC First-Round Playoff

PHILADELPHIA vs. SEATTLE
RS: Eagles lead series, 6-5
1976—Eagles, 27-10 (P)
1980—Eagles, 27-20 (S)
1986—Seahawks, 24-20 (S)
1989—Eagles, 31-7 (P)
1992—Eagles, 20-17 (S) OT
1995—Seahawks, 26-14 (S)
1998—Seahawks, 38-0 (P)
2001—Eagles, 27-3 (S)
2002—Eagles, 27-20 (S)
2005—Seahawks, 42-0 (P)
2007—Seahawks, 28-24 (P)
(RS Pts.—Seahawks 235, Eagles 217)

PHILADELPHIA vs. TAMPA BAY
RS: Series tied, 5-5
PS: Series tied, 2-2
1977—Eagles, 13-3 (P)
1979—*Buccaneers, 24-17 (TB)
1981—Eagles, 20-10 (P)
1988—Eagles, 41-14 (TB)
1991—Buccaneers, 14-13 (TB)
1995—Buccaneers, 21-6 (P)
1999—Buccaneers, 19-5 (P)
2000—**Eagles, 21-3 (P)
2001—Eagles, 17-13 (TB)
    **Eagles, 31-9 (P)
2002—Eagles, 20-10 (P)

    ***Buccaneers, 27-10 (P)
2003—Buccaneers, 17-0 (P)
2006—Buccaneers, 23-21 (TB)
(RS Pts.—Eagles 156, Buccaneers 144)
(PS Pts.—Eagles 79, Buccaneers 63)
*NFC Divisional Playoff
**NFC First-Round Playoff
***NFC Championship

PHILADELPHIA vs. *TENNESSEE
RS: Eagles lead series, 6-3
1972—Eagles, 18-17 (H)
1979—Eagles, 26-20 (H)
1982—Eagles, 35-14 (P)
1988—Eagles, 32-23 (P)
1991—Eagles, 13-6 (H)
1994—Eagles, 21-6 (P)
2000—Titans, 15-13 (P)
2002—Titans, 27-24 (T)
2006—Titans, 31-13 (P)
(RS Pts.—Eagles 195, Titans 159)
*Franchise in Houston prior to 1997;
known as Oilers prior to 1999

PHILADELPHIA vs. *WASHINGTON
RS: Redskins lead series, 75-65-5
PS: Redskins lead series, 1-0
1934—Redskins, 6-0 (B)
    Redskins, 14-7 (P)
1935—Eagles, 7-6 (B)
1936—Redskins, 26-3 (P)
    Redskins, 17-7 (B)
1937—Eagles, 14-0 (W)
    Redskins, 10-7 (P)
1938—Redskins, 26-23 (P)
    Redskins, 20-14 (W)
1939—Redskins, 7-0 (P)
    Redskins, 7-6 (W)
1940—Redskins, 34-17 (P)
    Redskins, 13-6 (W)
1941—Redskins, 21-17 (P)
    Redskins, 20-14 (W)
1942—Redskins, 14-10 (P)
    Redskins, 30-27 (W)
1944—Tie, 31-31 (P)
    Eagles, 37-7 (W)
1945—Redskins, 24-14 (W)
    Eagles, 16-0 (P)
1946—Eagles, 28-24 (W)
    Redskins, 27-10 (P)
1947—Eagles, 45-42 (P)
    Eagles, 38-14 (W)
1948—Eagles, 45-0 (W)
    Eagles, 42-21 (P)
1949—Eagles, 49-14 (P)
    Eagles, 44-21 (W)
1950—Eagles, 35-3 (P)
    Eagles, 33-0 (W)
1951—Redskins, 27-23 (P)
    Eagles, 35-21 (W)
1952—Eagles, 38-20 (P)
    Redskins, 27-21 (W)
1953—Tie, 21-21 (P)
    Redskins, 10-0 (W)
1954—Eagles, 49-21 (W)
    Eagles, 41-33 (P)
1955—Redskins, 31-30 (P)
    Redskins, 34-21 (W)
1956—Eagles, 13-9 (P)
    Redskins, 19-17 (W)
1957—Eagles, 21-12 (P)
    Redskins, 42-7 (W)

1958—Redskins, 24-14 (P)
Redskins, 20-0 (W)
1959—Eagles, 30-23 (P)
Eagles, 34-14 (W)
1960—Eagles, 19-13 (P)
Eagles, 38-28 (W)
1961—Eagles, 14-7 (P)
Eagles, 27-24 (W)
1962—Redskins, 27-21 (P)
Eagles, 37-14 (W)
1963—Eagles, 37-24 (W)
Redskins, 13-10 (P)
1964—Redskins, 35-20 (W)
Eagles, 21-10 (P)
1965—Redskins, 23-21 (W)
Eagles, 21-14 (P)
1966—Redskins, 27-13 (P)
Eagles, 37-28 (W)
1967—Eagles, 35-24 (P)
Tie, 35-35 (W)
1968—Redskins, 17-14 (W)
Redskins, 16-10 (P)
1969—Tie, 28-28 (W)
Redskins, 34-29 (P)
1970—Redskins, 33-21 (P)
Redskins, 24-6 (W)
1971—Tie, 7-7 (W)
Redskins, 20-13 (P)
1972—Redskins, 14-0 (W)
Redskins, 23-7 (P)
1973—Redskins, 28-7 (P)
Redskins, 38-20 (W)
1974—Redskins, 27-20 (P)
Redskins, 26-7 (W)
1975—Eagles, 26-10 (P)
Eagles, 26-3 (W)
1976—Redskins, 20-17 (P) OT
Redskins, 24-0 (W)
1977—Redskins, 23-17 (W)
Redskins, 17-14 (P)
1978—Redskins, 35-30 (W)
Eagles, 17-10 (P)
1979—Eagles, 28-17 (P)
Redskins, 17-7 (W)
1980—Eagles, 24-14 (P)
Eagles, 24-0 (W)
1981—Eagles, 36-13 (P)
Redskins, 15-13 (W)
1982—Redskins, 37-34 (P) OT
Redskins, 13-9 (W)
1983—Redskins, 23-13 (P)
Redskins, 28-24 (W)
1984—Redskins, 20-0 (W)
Eagles, 16-10 (P)
1985—Eagles, 19-6 (W)
Redskins, 17-12 (P)
1986—Redskins, 41-14 (W)
Redskins, 21-14 (P)
1987—Redskins, 34-24 (W)
Eagles, 31-27 (P)
1988—Redskins, 17-10 (W)
Redskins, 20-19 (P)
1989—Eagles, 42-37 (W)
Redskins, 10-3 (P)
1990—Redskins, 13-7 (W)
Eagles, 28-14 (P)
**Redskins, 20-6 (P)
1991—Eagles, 24-22 (P)
1992—Redskins, 16-12 (W)

Eagles, 17-13 (P)
1993—Eagles, 34-31 (P)
Eagles, 17-14 (W)
1994—Eagles, 21-17 (P)
Eagles, 31-29 (W)
1995—Eagles, 37-34 (P) OT
Eagles, 14-7 (W)
1996—Eagles, 17-14 (W)
Redskins, 26-21 (P)
1997—Eagles, 24-10 (P)
Redskins, 35-32 (W)
1998—Eagles, 17-12 (P)
Redskins, 28-3 (W)
1999—Eagles, 35-28 (P)
Redskins, 20-17 (W) OT
2000—Redskins, 17-14 (P)
Eagles, 23-20 (W)
2001—Redskins, 13-3 (P)
Eagles, 20-6 (W)
2002—Eagles, 37-7 (W)
Eagles, 34-21 (P)
2003—Eagles, 27-25 (P)
Eagles, 31-7 (W)
2004—Eagles, 28-6 (P)
Eagles, 17-14 (W)
2005—Redskins, 17-10 (W)
Redskins, 31-20 (P)
2006—Eagles, 27-3 (P)
Eagles, 21-19 (W)
2007—Redskins, 20-12 (P)
Eagles, 33-25 (W)
(RS Pts.—Eagles 2,973, Redskins 2,835)
(PS Pts.—Redskins 20, Eagles 6)
*Franchise in Boston prior to 1937
**NFC First-Round Playoff

PITTSBURGH vs. ARIZONA
RS: Steelers lead series, 31-23-3;
See Arizona vs. Pittsburgh
PITTSBURGH vs. ATLANTA
RS: Steelers lead series, 11-2-1;
See Atlanta vs. Pittsburgh
PITTSBURGH vs. BALTIMORE
RS: Steelers lead series, 14-10
PS: Steelers lead series, 1-0;
See Baltimore vs. Pittsburgh
PITTSBURGH vs. BUFFALO
RS: Steelers lead series, 11-8
PS: Steelers lead series, 2-1;
See Buffalo vs. Pittsburgh
PITTSBURGH vs. CAROLINA
RS: Steelers lead series, 3-1;
See Carolina vs. Pittsburgh
PITTSBURGH vs. CHICAGO
RS: Bears lead series, 16-7-1;
See Chicago vs. Pittsburgh
PITTSBURGH vs. CINCINNATI
RS: Steelers lead series, 45-30
PS: Steelers lead series, 1-0;
See Cincinnati vs. Pittsburgh
PITTSBURGH vs. CLEVELAND
RS: Series tied, 55-55
PS: Steelers lead series, 2-0;
See Cleveland vs. Pittsburgh
PITTSBURGH vs. DALLAS
RS: Cowboys lead series, 14-12
PS: Steelers lead series, 2-1;
See Dallas vs. Pittsburgh
PITTSBURGH vs. DENVER
RS: Broncos lead series, 13-6-1

PS: Series tied, 3-3;
See Denver vs. Pittsburgh
PITTSBURGH vs. DETROIT
RS: Series tied, 14-14-1;
See Detroit vs. Pittsburgh
PITTSBURGH vs. GREEN BAY
RS: Packers lead series, 18-13;
See Green Bay vs. Pittsburgh
PITTSBURGH vs. HOUSTON
RS: Series tied, 1-1;
See Houston vs. Pittsburgh
PITTSBURGH vs. INDIANAPOLIS
RS: Steelers lead series, 13-5
PS: Steelers lead series, 5-0;
See Indianapolis vs. Pittsburgh
PITTSBURGH vs. JACKSONVILLE
RS: Jaguars lead series, 11-8
PS: Jaguars lead series, 1-0;
See Jacksonville vs. Pittsburgh
PITTSBURGH vs. KANSAS CITY
RS: Steelers lead series, 17-8
PS: Chiefs lead series, 1-0;
See Kansas City vs. Pittsburgh
PITTSBURGH vs. MIAMI
RS: Steelers lead series, 10-9
PS: Dolphins lead series, 2-1;
See Miami vs. Pittsburgh
PITTSBURGH vs. MINNESOTA
RS: Vikings lead series, 8-6
PS: Steelers lead series, 1-0;
See Minnesota vs. Pittsburgh
PITTSBURGH vs. NEW ENGLAND
RS: Steelers lead series, 12-7
PS: Patriots lead series, 3-1;
See New England vs. Pittsburgh
PITTSBURGH vs. NEW ORLEANS
RS: Steelers lead series, 7-6;
See New Orleans vs. Pittsburgh
PITTSBURGH vs. N.Y. GIANTS
RS: Giants lead series, 43-28-3;
See N.Y. Giants vs. Pittsburgh
PITTSBURGH vs. N.Y. JETS
RS: Steelers lead series, 15-3
PS: Steelers lead series, 1-0;
See N.Y. Jets vs. Pittsburgh
PITTSBURGH vs. OAKLAND
RS: Raiders lead series, 9-8
PS: Series tied, 3-3;
See Oakland vs. Pittsburgh
PITTSBURGH vs. PHILADELPHIA
RS: Eagles lead series, 45-27-3
PS: Eagles lead series, 1-0;
See Philadelphia vs. Pittsburgh
*PITTSBURGH vs. **ST. LOUIS**
RS: Rams lead series, 15-6-2
PS: Steelers lead series, 1-0
1938—Rams, 13-7 (New Orleans)
1939—Tie, 14-14 (C)
1941—Rams, 17-14 (Akron)
1947—Rams, 48-7 (P)
1948—Rams, 31-14 (LA)
1949—Tie, 7-7 (P)
1952—Rams, 28-14 (LA)
1955—Rams, 27-26 (LA)
1956—Steelers, 30-13 (P)
1961—Rams, 24-14 (LA)
1964—Rams, 26-14 (P)
1968—Rams, 45-10 (LA)
1971—Rams, 23-14 (P)
1975—Rams, 10-3 (LA)

1978—Rams, 10-7 (LA)
1979—***Steelers, 31-19 (Pasadena)
1981—Steelers, 24-0 (P)
1984—Steelers, 24-14 (P)
1987—Rams, 31-21 (LA)
1990—Steelers, 41-10 (P)
1993—Rams, 27-0 (LA)
1996—Steelers, 42-6 (P)
2003—Rams, 33-21 (P)
2007—Steelers, 41-24 (StL)
(RS Pts.—Rams 481, Steelers 409)
(PS Pts.—Steelers 31, Rams 19)
*Steelers known as Pirates prior to 1941
**Franchise in Los Angeles prior to 1995
and in Cleveland prior to 1946
***Super Bowl XIV
PITTSBURGH vs. SAN DIEGO
RS: Steelers lead series, 19-6
PS: Chargers lead series, 2-0
1971—Steelers, 21-17 (P)
1972—Steelers, 24-2 (SD)
1973—Steelers, 38-21 (P)
1975—Steelers, 37-0 (SD)
1976—Steelers, 23-0 (P)
1977—Steelers, 10-9 (SD)
1979—Chargers, 35-7 (SD)
1980—Chargers, 26-17 (SD)
1982—*Chargers, 31-28 (P)
1983—Steelers, 26-3 (P)
1984—Steelers, 52-24 (P)
1985—Chargers, 54-44 (SD)
1987—Steelers, 20-16 (SD)
1988—Chargers, 20-14 (SD)
1989—Steelers, 20-17 (P)
1990—Steelers, 36-14 (P)
1991—Steelers, 26-20 (P)
1992—Steelers, 23-6 (SD)
1993—Steelers, 16-3 (P)
1994—Chargers, 37-34 (SD)
    **Chargers, 17-13 (P)
1995—Steelers, 31-16 (P)
1996—Steelers, 16-3 (P)
2000—Steelers, 34-21 (SD)
2003—Steelers, 40-24 (P)
2005—Steelers, 24-22 (SD)
2006—Chargers, 23-13 (SD)
(RS Pts.—Steelers 646, Chargers 433)
(PS Pts.—Chargers 48, Steelers 41)
*AFC First-Round Playoff
**AFC Championship
PITTSBURGH vs. SAN FRANCISCO
RS: 49ers lead series, 10-9
1951—49ers, 28-24 (P)
1952—Steelers, 24-7 (SF)
1954—49ers, 31-3 (SF)
1958—49ers, 23-20 (SF)
1961—Steelers, 20-10 (P)
1965—49ers, 27-17 (SF)
1968—49ers, 45-28 (P)
1973—Steelers, 37-14 (SF)
1977—Steelers, 27-0 (P)
1978—Steelers, 24-7 (SF)
1981—49ers, 17-14 (P)
1984—Steelers, 20-17 (SF)
1987—Steelers, 30-17 (P)
1990—49ers, 27-7 (SF)
1993—49ers, 24-13 (P)
1996—49ers, 25-15 (P)
1999—Steelers, 27-6 (SF)
2003—49ers, 30-14 (SF)

2007—Steelers, 37-16 (P)
(RS Pts.—Steelers 401, 49ers 371)
PITTSBURGH vs. SEATTLE
RS: Seahawks lead series, 8-7
PS: Steelers lead series, 1-0
1977—Steelers, 30-20 (P)
1978—Steelers, 21-10 (P)
1981—Seahawks, 24-21 (S)
1982—Seahawks, 16-0 (S)
1983—Steelers, 27-21 (S)
1986—Seahawks, 30-0 (S)
1987—Steelers, 13-9 (P)
1991—Seahawks, 27-7 (S)
1992—Steelers, 20-14 (P)
1993—Seahawks, 16-6 (S)
1994—Seahawks, 30-13 (S)
1998—Steelers, 13-10 (P)
1999—Seahawks, 29-10 (P)
2003—Seahawks, 23-16 (S)
2005—*Steelers, 21-10 (Detroit)
2007—Steelers, 21-0 (P)
(RS Pts.—Seahawks 279, Steelers 218)
(PS Pts.—Steelers 21, Seahawks 10)
*Super Bowl XL
PITTSBURGH vs. TAMPA BAY
RS: Steelers lead series, 7-1
1976—Steelers, 42-0 (P)
1980—Steelers, 24-21 (TB)
1983—Steelers, 17-12 (P)
1989—Steelers, 31-22 (TB)
1998—Buccaneers, 16-3 (TB)
2001—Steelers, 17-10 (TB)
2002—Steelers, 17-7 (TB)
2006—Steelers, 20-3 (P)
(RS Pts.—Steelers 171, Buccaneers 91)
PITTSBURGH vs. *TENNESSEE
RS: Steelers lead series, 38-28
PS: Steelers lead series, 3-1
1970—Oilers, 19-7 (P)
    Steelers, 7-3 (H)
1971—Steelers, 23-16 (P)
    Oilers, 29-3 (H)
1972—Steelers, 24-7 (P)
    Steelers, 9-3 (H)
1973—Steelers, 36-7 (H)
    Steelers, 33-7 (P)
1974—Steelers, 13-7 (H)
    Oilers, 13-10 (P)
1975—Steelers, 24-17 (P)
    Steelers, 32-9 (H)
1976—Steelers, 32-16 (P)
    Steelers, 21-0 (H)
1977—Oilers, 27-10 (H)
    Steelers, 27-10 (P)
1978—Oilers, 24-17 (P)
    Steelers, 13-3 (H)
    **Steelers, 34-5 (P)
1979—Steelers, 38-7 (P)
    Oilers, 20-17 (H)
    **Steelers, 27-13 (P)
1980—Steelers, 31-17 (P)
    Oilers, 6-0 (H)
1981—Steelers, 26-13 (P)
    Oilers, 21-20 (H)
1982—Steelers, 24-10 (H)
1983—Steelers, 40-28 (H)
    Steelers, 17-10 (P)
1984—Steelers, 35-7 (P)
    Oilers, 23-20 (H) OT
1985—Steelers, 20-0 (P)

Steelers, 30-7 (H)
1986—Steelers, 22-16 (H) OT
    Steelers, 21-10 (P)
1987—Oilers, 23-3 (P)
    Oilers, 24-16 (H)
1988—Oilers, 34-14 (P)
    Steelers, 37-34 (H)
1989—Oilers, 27-0 (H)
    Oilers, 23-16 (P)
    ***Steelers, 26-23 (H) OT
1990—Steelers, 20-9 (P)
    Oilers, 34-14 (H)
1991—Steelers, 26-14 (P)
    Oilers, 31-6 (H)
1992—Steelers, 29-24 (H)
    Steelers, 21-20 (P)
1993—Oilers, 23-3 (H)
    Oilers, 26-17 (P)
1994—Steelers, 30-14 (P)
    Steelers, 12-9 (H) OT
1995—Steelers, 34-17 (H)
    Steelers, 21-7 (P)
1996—Steelers, 30-16 (P)
    Oilers, 23-13 (H)
1997—Steelers, 37-24 (P)
    Oilers, 16-6 (T)
1998—Oilers, 41-31 (P)
    Oilers, 23-14 (T)
1999—Titans, 16-10 (T)
    Titans, 47-36 (P)
2000—Titans, 23-20 (P)
    Titans, 9-7 (T)
2001—Steelers, 34-7 (P)
    Steelers, 34-24 (T)
2002—Titans, 31-23 (T)
    ****Titans, 34-31 (T) OT
2003—Titans, 30-13 (P)
2005—Steelers, 34-7 (P)
(RS Pts.—Steelers 1,363, Titans 1,142)
(PS Pts.—Steelers 118, Titans 75)
*Franchise in Houston prior to 1997;
known as Oilers prior to 1999
**AFC Championship
***AFC First-Round Playoff
****AFC Divisional Playoff
PITTSBURGH vs. **WASHINGTON
RS: Redskins lead series, 42-30-3
1933—Redskins, 21-6 (P)
    Pirates, 16-14 (B)
1934—Redskins, 7-0 (P)
    Redskins, 39-0 (B)
1935—Pirates, 6-0 (P)
    Redskins, 13-3 (B)
1936—Pirates, 10-0 (P)
    Redskins, 30-0 (B)
1937—Redskins, 34-20 (P)
    Pirates, 21-13 (P)
1938—Redskins, 7-0 (P)
    Redskins, 15-0 (W)
1939—Redskins, 44-14 (W)
    Redskins, 21-14 (P)
1940—Redskins, 40-10 (P)
    Redskins, 37-10 (W)
1941—Redskins, 24-20 (P)
    Redskins, 23-3 (W)
1942—Redskins, 28-14 (W)
    Redskins, 14-0 (P)
1945—Redskins, 14-0 (P)
    Redskins, 24-0 (W)
1946—Tie, 14-14 (W)

Steelers, 14-7 (P)
1947—Redskins, 27-26 (W)
Steelers, 21-14 (P)
1948—Redskins, 17-14 (W)
Steelers, 10-7 (P)
1949—Redskins, 27-14 (P)
Redskins, 27-14 (W)
1950—Steelers, 26-7 (W)
Redskins, 24-7 (P)
1951—Redskins, 22-7 (P)
Steelers, 20-10 (W)
1952—Redskins, 28-24 (P)
Steelers, 24-23 (W)
1953—Redskins, 17-9 (P)
Steelers, 14-13 (W)
1954—Steelers, 37-7 (P)
Redskins, 17-14 (W)
1955—Redskins, 23-14 (P)
Redskins, 28-17 (W)
1956—Steelers, 30-13 (P)
Steelers, 23-0 (W)
1957—Steelers, 28-7 (P)
Redskins, 10-3 (W)
1958—Steelers, 24-16 (P)
Tie, 14-14 (W)
1959—Redskins, 23-17 (P)
Steelers, 27-6 (W)
1960—Tie, 27-27 (W)
Steelers, 22-10 (P)
1961—Steelers, 20-0 (P)
Steelers, 30-14 (W)
1962—Steelers, 23-21 (P)
Steelers, 27-24 (W)
1963—Steelers, 38-27 (P)
Steelers, 34-28 (W)
1964—Redskins, 30-0 (P)
Steelers, 14-7 (W)
1965—Steelers, 31-3 (P)
Redskins, 35-14 (W)
1966—Redskins, 33-27 (P)
Redskins, 24-10 (W)
1967—Redskins, 15-10 (P)
1968—Redskins, 16-13 (W)
1969—Redskins, 14-7 (P)
1973—Steelers, 21-16 (P)
1979—Steelers, 38-7 (P)
1985—Redskins, 30-23 (P)
1988—Redskins, 30-29 (W)
1991—Redskins, 41-14 (P)
1997—Steelers, 14-13 (P)
2000—Steelers, 24-3 (P)
2004—Steelers, 16-7 (P)
(RS Pts.—Redskins 1,413, Steelers 1,171)
*Steelers known as Pirates prior to 1941
**Franchise in Boston prior to 1937

ST. LOUIS vs. ARIZONA
RS: Rams lead series, 30-26-2
PS: Rams lead series, 1-0;
See Arizona vs. St. Louis
ST. LOUIS vs. ATLANTA
RS: Rams lead series, 47-24-2
PS: Falcons lead series, 1-0;
See Atlanta vs. St. Louis
ST. LOUIS vs. BALTIMORE
RS: Series tied, 2-2;
See Baltimore vs. St. Louis
ST. LOUIS vs. BUFFALO
RS: Bills lead series, 5-4;
See Buffalo vs. St. Louis

ST. LOUIS vs. CAROLINA
RS: Panthers lead series, 10-7
PS: Panthers lead series, 1-0;
See Carolina vs. St. Louis
ST. LOUIS vs. CHICAGO
RS: Bears lead series, 48-34-3
PS: Series tied, 1-1;
See Chicago vs. St. Louis
ST. LOUIS vs. CINCINNATI
RS: Bengals lead series, 6-5;
See Cincinnati vs. St. Louis
ST. LOUIS vs. CLEVELAND
RS: Series tied, 9-9
PS: Browns lead series, 2-1;
See Cleveland vs. St. Louis
ST. LOUIS vs. DALLAS
RS: Series tied, 10-10
PS: Series tied, 4-4;
See Dallas vs. St. Louis
ST. LOUIS vs. DENVER
RS: Rams lead series, 6-5;
See Denver vs. St. Louis
ST. LOUIS vs. DETROIT
RS: Rams lead series, 41-37-1
PS: Lions lead series, 1-0;
See Detroit vs. St. Louis
ST. LOUIS vs. GREEN BAY
RS: Rams lead series, 45-41-2
PS: Series tied, 1-1;
See Green Bay vs. St. Louis
ST. LOUIS vs. HOUSTON
RS: Rams lead series, 1-0;
See Houston vs. St. Louis
ST. LOUIS vs. INDIANAPOLIS
RS: Colts lead series, 22-17-2;
See Indianapolis vs. St. Louis
ST. LOUIS vs. JACKSONVILLE
RS: Rams lead series, 2-0;
See Jacksonville vs. St. Louis
ST. LOUIS vs. KANSAS CITY
RS: Chiefs lead series; 5-4;
See Kansas City vs. St. Louis
ST. LOUIS vs. MIAMI
RS: Dolphins lead series, 8-2;
See Miami vs. St. Louis
ST. LOUIS vs. MINNESOTA
RS: Vikings lead series, 17-14-2
PS: Vikings lead series, 5-2;
See Minnesota vs. St. Louis
ST. LOUIS vs. NEW ENGLAND
RS: Rams lead series, 5-4
PS: Patriots lead series, 1-0;
See New England vs. St. Louis
ST. LOUIS vs. NEW ORLEANS
RS: Rams lead series, 38-29
PS: Saints lead series, 1-0;
See New Orleans vs. St. Louis
ST. LOUIS vs. N.Y. GIANTS
RS: Rams lead series, 25-12
PS: Series tied, 1-1;
See N.Y. Giants vs. St. Louis
ST. LOUIS vs. N.Y. JETS
RS: Rams lead series, 9-2;
See N.Y. Jets vs. St. Louis
ST. LOUIS vs. OAKLAND
RS: Raiders lead series, 7-4;
See Oakland vs. St. Louis
ST. LOUIS vs. PHILADELPHIA
RS: Rams lead series, 17-16-1
PS: Rams lead series, 2-1;

See Philadelphia vs. St. Louis
ST. LOUIS vs. PITTSBURGH
RS: Rams lead series, 16-5-2
PS: Steelers lead series, 1-0;
See Pittsburgh vs. St. Louis
*ST. LOUIS vs. SAN DIEGO
RS: Rams lead series, 5-4
1970—Rams, 37-10 (LA)
1975—Rams, 13-10 (SD) OT
1979—Chargers, 40-16 (LA)
1988—Chargers, 38-24 (LA)
1991—Rams, 30-24 (LA)
1994—Chargers, 31-17 (SD)
2000—Rams, 57-31 (StL)
2002—Rams, 28-24 (StL)
2006—Chargers, 38-24 (SD)
(RS Pts.—Rams 246, Chargers 246)
*Franchise in Los Angeles prior to 1995
*ST. LOUIS vs. SAN FRANCISCO
RS: Rams lead series, 60-54-2
PS: 49ers lead series, 1-0
1950—Rams, 35-14 (SF)
Rams, 28-21 (LA)
1951—49ers, 44-17 (SF)
Rams, 23-16 (LA)
1952—Rams, 35-9 (LA)
Rams, 34-21 (SF)
1953—49ers, 31-30 (SF)
49ers, 31-27 (LA)
1954—Tie, 24-24 (LA)
Rams, 42-34 (SF)
1955—49ers, 23-14 (SF)
Rams, 27-14 (LA)
1956—49ers, 33-30 (SF)
Rams, 30-6 (LA)
1957—49ers, 23-20 (SF)
Rams, 37-24 (LA)
1958—Rams, 33-3 (SF)
Rams, 56-7 (LA)
1959—49ers, 34-0 (SF)
49ers, 24-16 (LA)
1960—49ers, 13-9 (SF)
Rams, 23-7 (LA)
1961—49ers, 35-0 (SF)
Rams, 17-7 (LA)
1962—Rams, 28-14 (SF)
49ers, 24-17 (LA)
1963—Rams, 28-21 (SF)
Rams, 21-17 (LA)
1964—Rams, 42-14 (LA)
49ers, 28-7 (SF)
1965—49ers, 45-21 (LA)
49ers, 30-27 (SF)
1966—Rams, 34-3 (LA)
49ers, 21-13 (SF)
1967—49ers, 27-24 (LA)
Rams, 17-7 (SF)
1968—Rams, 24-10 (LA)
Tie, 20-20 (SF)
1969—Rams, 27-21 (SF)
Rams, 41-30 (LA)
1970—49ers, 20-6 (LA)
Rams, 30-13 (SF)
1971—Rams, 20-13 (SF)
Rams, 17-6 (LA)
1972—Rams, 31-7 (LA)
Rams, 26-16 (SF)
1973—Rams, 40-20 (SF)
Rams, 31-13 (LA)
1974—Rams, 37-14 (LA)

Rams, 15-13 (SF)
1975—Rams, 23-14 (SF)
49ers, 24-23 (LA)
1976—49ers, 16-0 (LA)
Rams, 23-3 (SF)
1977—Rams, 34-14 (LA)
Rams, 23-10 (SF)
1978—Rams, 27-10 (LA)
Rams, 31-28 (SF)
1979—Rams, 27-24 (LA)
Rams, 26-20 (SF)
1980—Rams, 48-26 (LA)
Rams, 31-17 (SF)
1981—49ers, 20-17 (SF)
49ers, 33-31 (LA)
1982—49ers, 30-24 (LA)
Rams, 21-20 (SF)
1983—Rams, 10-7 (SF)
49ers, 45-35 (LA)
1984—49ers, 33-0 (LA)
49ers, 19-16 (SF)
1985—49ers, 28-14 (LA)
Rams, 27-20 (SF)
1986—Rams, 16-13 (LA)
49ers, 24-14 (SF)
1987—49ers, 31-10 (LA)
49ers, 48-0 (SF)
1988—49ers, 24-21 (LA)
Rams, 38-16 (SF)
1989—Rams, 13-12 (SF)
49ers, 30-27 (LA)
**49ers, 30-3 (SF)
1990—Rams, 28-17 (SF)
49ers, 26-10 (LA)
1991—49ers, 27-10 (SF)
49ers, 33-10 (LA)
1992—49ers, 27-24 (SF)
49ers, 27-10 (LA)
1993—49ers, 40-17 (SF)
49ers, 35-10 (LA)
1994—49ers, 34-19 (LA)
49ers, 31-27 (SF)
1995—49ers, 44-10 (StL)
49ers, 41-13 (SF)
1996—49ers, 34-0 (SF)
49ers, 28-11 (StL)
1997—49ers, 15-12 (StL)
49ers, 30-10 (SF)
1998—49ers, 28-10 (StL)
49ers, 38-19 (SF)
1999—Rams, 42-20 (StL)
Rams, 23-7 (SF)
2000—Rams, 41-24 (StL)
Rams, 34-24 (SF)
2001—Rams, 30-26 (StL)
Rams, 27-14 (StL)
2002—49ers, 37-13 (SF)
Rams, 31-20 (StL)
2003—Rams, 27-24 (StL) OT
49ers, 30-10 (SF)
2004—Rams, 24-14 (SF)
Rams, 16-6 (StL)
2005—49ers, 28-25 (SF)
49ers, 24-20 (StL)
2006—49ers, 20-13 (SF)
Rams, 20-17 (StL)
2007—49ers, 17-16 (StL)
Rams, 13-9 (SF)
(RS Pts.—Rams 2,569, 49ers 2,547)
(PS Pts.—49ers 30, Rams 3)

*Franchise in Los Angeles prior to 1995
**NFC Championship
**ST. LOUIS vs. SEATTLE*
RS: Seahawks lead series, 10-9
PS: Rams lead series, 1-0
1976—Rams, 45-6 (LA)
1979—Rams, 24-0 (S)
1985—Rams, 35-24 (S)
1988—Rams, 31-10 (LA)
1991—Seahawks, 23-9 (S)
1997—Seahawks, 17-9 (StL)
2000—Rams, 37-34 (Sea)
2002—Rams, 37-20 (StL)
Seahawks, 30-10 (Sea)
2003—Seahawks, 24-23 (Sea)
Rams, 27-22 (StL)
2004—Rams, 33-27 (Sea) OT
Rams, 23-12 (StL)
**Rams, 27-20 (Sea)
2005—Seahawks, 37-31 (StL)
Seahawks, 31-16 (Sea)
2006—Seahawks, 30-28 (StL)
Seahawks, 24-22 (Sea)
2007—Seahawks, 33-6 (Sea)
Seahawks, 24-19 (StL)
(RS Pts.—Rams 465, Seahawks 428)
(PS Pts.—Rams 27, Seahawks 20)
*Franchise in Los Angeles prior to 1995
**NFC First-Round Playoff
**ST. LOUIS vs. TAMPA BAY*
RS: Rams lead series, 9-7
PS: Rams lead series, 2-0
1977—Rams, 31-0 (LA)
1978—Rams, 26-23 (LA)
1979—Buccaneers, 21-6 (TB)
**Rams, 9-0 (TB)
1980—Buccaneers, 10-9 (TB)
1984—Rams, 34-33 (TB)
1985—Rams, 31-27 (TB)
1986—Rams, 26-20 (LA) OT
1987—Rams, 35-3 (LA)
1990—Rams, 35-14 (TB)
1992—Rams, 31-27 (TB)
1994—Buccaneers, 24-14 (TB)
1999—**Rams, 11-6 (StL)
2000—Buccaneers, 38-35 (TB)
2001—Buccaneers, 24-17 (StL)
2002—Buccaneers, 26-14 (StL)
2004—Rams, 28-21 (StL)
2007—Buccaneers, 24-3 (TB)
(RS Pts.—Rams 375, Buccaneers 335)
(PS Pts.—Rams 20, Buccaneers 6)
*Franchise in Los Angeles prior to 1995
**NFC Championship
**ST. LOUIS vs. **TENNESSEE*
RS: Rams lead series, 6-3
PS: Rams lead series, 1-0
1973—Rams, 31-26 (H)
1978—Rams, 10-6 (H)
1981—Oilers, 27-20 (LA)
1984—Rams, 27-16 (LA)
1987—Oilers, 20-16 (H)
1990—Rams, 17-13 (LA)
1993—Rams, 28-13 (H)
1999—Titans, 24-21 (T)
***Rams, 23-16 (Atlanta)
2005—Rams, 31-27 (StL)
(RS Pts.—Rams 201, Titans 172)
(PS Pts.—Rams 23, Titans 16)
*Franchise in Los Angeles prior to 1995

**Franchise in Houston prior to 1997;
known as Oilers prior to 1999
***Super Bowl XXXIV
**ST. LOUIS vs. WASHINGTON*
RS: Redskins lead series, 20-7-1
PS: Series tied, 2-2
1937—Redskins, 16-7 (C)
1938—Redskins, 37-13 (W)
1941—Redskins, 17-13 (W)
1942—Redskins, 33-14 (W)
1944—Redskins, 14-10 (W)
1945—**Rams, 15-14 (C)
1948—Rams, 41-13 (W)
1949—Rams, 53-27 (LA)
1951—Redskins, 31-21 (W)
1962—Redskins, 20-14 (W)
1963—Redskins, 37-14 (LA)
1967—Tie, 28-28 (LA)
1969—Rams, 24-13 (W)
1971—Redskins, 38-24 (LA)
1974—Redskins, 23-17 (LA)
***Rams, 19-10 (LA)
1977—Redskins, 17-14 (W)
1981—Redskins, 30-7 (LA)
1983—Redskins, 42-20 (LA)
***Redskins, 51-7 (W)
1986—****Redskins, 19-7 (W)
1987—Rams, 30-26 (W)
1991—Redskins, 27-6 (LA)
1993—Rams, 10-6 (LA)
1994—Redskins, 24-21 (LA)
1995—Rams, 35-23 (StL)
1996—Redskins, 17-10 (StL)
1997—Rams, 23-20 (W)
2000—Redskins, 33-20 (StL)
2002—Redskins, 20-17 (W)
2005—Redskins, 24-9 (StL)
2006—Rams, 37-31 (StL) OT
(RS Pts.—Redskins 699, Rams 540)
(PS Pts.—Redskins 94, Rams 48)
*Franchise in Los Angeles prior to 1995
and in Cleveland prior to 1946
**NFL Championship
***NFC Divisional Playoff
****NFC First-Round Playoff

SAN DIEGO vs. ARIZONA
RS: Chargers lead series, 8-3;
See Arizona vs. San Diego
SAN DIEGO vs. ATLANTA
RS: Falcons lead series, 6-1;
See Atlanta vs. San Diego
SAN DIEGO vs. BALTIMORE
RS: Series tied, 3-3;
See Baltimore vs. San Diego
SAN DIEGO vs. BUFFALO
RS: Chargers lead series, 20-9-2
PS: Bills lead series, 2-1;
See Buffalo vs. San Diego
SAN DIEGO vs. CAROLINA
RS: Panthers lead series, 2-1;
See Carolina vs. San Diego
SAN DIEGO vs. CHICAGO
RS: Series tied, 5-5;
See Chicago vs. San Diego
SAN DIEGO vs. CINCINNATI
RS: Chargers lead series, 18-10
PS: Bengals lead series, 1-0;
See Cincinnati vs. San Diego
SAN DIEGO vs. CLEVELAND

RS: Chargers lead series, 13-7-1;
See Cleveland vs. San Diego
SAN DIEGO vs. DALLAS
RS: Cowboys lead series, 6-2;
See Dallas vs. San Diego
SAN DIEGO vs. DENVER
RS: Broncos lead series, 52-43-1;
See Denver vs. San Diego
SAN DIEGO vs. DETROIT
RS: Chargers lead series, 6-3;
See Detroit vs. San Diego
SAN DIEGO vs. GREEN BAY
RS: Packers lead series, 8-1;
See Green Bay vs. San Diego
SAN DIEGO vs. HOUSTON
RS: Chargers lead series, 3-0;
See Houston vs. San Diego
SAN DIEGO vs. INDIANAPOLIS
RS: Chargers lead series, 14-8
PS: Series tied, 1-1;
See Indianapolis vs. San Diego
SAN DIEGO vs. JACKSONVILLE
RS: Jaguars lead series, 2-1;
See Jacksonville vs. San Diego
SAN DIEGO vs. KANSAS CITY
RS: Chiefs lead series, 50-44-1
PS: Chargers lead series, 1-0;
See Kansas City vs. San Diego
SAN DIEGO vs. MIAMI
RS: Dolphins lead series, 11-10
PS: Series tied, 2-2;
See Miami vs. San Diego
SAN DIEGO vs. MINNESOTA
RS: Series tied, 5-5;
See Minnesota vs. San Diego
SAN DIEGO vs. NEW ENGLAND
RS: Patriots lead series, 18-13-2
PS: Patriots lead series, 2-1;
See New England vs. San Diego
SAN DIEGO vs. NEW ORLEANS
RS: Chargers lead series, 7-2;
See New Orleans vs. San Diego
SAN DIEGO vs. N.Y. GIANTS
RS: Giants lead series, 5-4;
See N.Y. Giants vs. San Diego
SAN DIEGO vs. N.Y. JETS
RS: Chargers lead series, 18-11-1
PS: Jets lead series, 1-0;
See N.Y. Jets vs. San Diego
SAN DIEGO vs. OAKLAND
RS: Raiders lead series, 54-40-2
PS: Raiders lead series, 1-0;
See Oakland vs. San Diego
SAN DIEGO vs. PHILADELPHIA
RS: Chargers lead series, 5-4;
See Philadelphia vs. San Diego
SAN DIEGO vs. PITTSBURGH
RS: Steelers lead series, 19-6
PS: Chargers lead series, 2-0;
See Pittsburgh vs. San Diego
SAN DIEGO vs. ST. LOUIS
RS: Rams lead series, 5-4;
See St. Louis vs. San Diego
SAN DIEGO vs. SAN FRANCISCO
RS: 49ers lead series, 6-5
PS: 49ers lead series, 1-0
1972—49ers, 34-3 (SF)
1976—Chargers, 13-7 (SD) OT
1979—Chargers, 31-9 (SD)
1982—Chargers, 41-37 (SF)

1988—49ers, 48-10 (SD)
1991—49ers, 34-14 (SF)
1994—49ers, 38-15 (SD)
    *49ers, 49-26 (South Florida)
1997—49ers, 17-10 (SF)
2000—49ers, 45-17 (SD)
2002—Chargers, 20-17 (SD) OT
2006—Chargers, 48-19 (SF)
(RS Pts.—49ers 305, Chargers 222)
(PS Pts.—49ers 49, Chargers 26)
Super Bowl XXIX
SAN DIEGO vs. SEATTLE
RS: Seahawks lead series, 25-23
1977—Chargers, 30-28 (S)
1978—Chargers, 24-20 (S)
    Chargers, 37-10 (SD)
1979—Chargers, 33-16 (S)
    Chargers, 20-10 (SD)
1980—Chargers, 34-13 (S)
    Chargers, 21-14 (SD)
1981—Chargers, 24-10 (SD)
    Seahawks, 44-23 (S)
1983—Seahawks, 34-31 (S)
    Chargers, 28-21 (SD)
1984—Seahawks, 31-17 (S)
    Seahawks, 24-0 (SD)
1985—Seahawks, 49-35 (SD)
    Seahawks, 26-21 (S)
1986—Seahawks, 33-7 (S)
    Seahawks, 34-24 (SD)
1987—Seahawks, 34-3 (S)
1988—Chargers, 17-6 (SD)
    Seahawks, 17-14 (S)
1989—Seahawks, 17-16 (SD)
    Seahawks, 10-7 (S)
1990—Chargers, 31-14 (S)
    Seahawks, 13-10 (SD) OT
1991—Seahawks, 20-9 (S)
    Chargers, 17-14 (SD)
1992—Chargers, 17-6 (SD)
    Chargers, 31-14 (S)
1993—Chargers, 18-12 (SD)
    Seahawks, 31-14 (S)
1994—Chargers, 24-10 (S)
    Chargers, 35-15 (SD)
1995—Chargers, 14-10 (SD)
    Chargers, 35-25 (S)
1996—Chargers, 29-7 (SD)
    Seahawks, 32-13 (S)
1997—Seahawks, 26-22 (S)
    Seahawks, 37-31 (SD)
1998—Seahawks, 27-20 (SD)
    Seahawks, 38-17 (S)
1999—Chargers, 13-10 (SD)
    Chargers, 19-16 (S)
2000—Seahawks, 20-12 (SD)
    Seahawks, 17-15 (S)
2001—Seahawks, 13-10 (S) OT
    Seahawks, 25-22 (SD)
2002—Seahawks, 31-28 (SD) OT
2006—Chargers, 20-17 (Sea)
(RS Pts.—Seahawks 1,001, Chargers 992)
SAN DIEGO vs. TAMPA BAY
RS: Chargers lead series, 7-1
1976—Chargers, 23-0 (TB)
1981—Chargers, 24-23 (TB)
1987—Chargers, 17-13 (TB)
1990—Chargers, 41-10 (SD)
1992—Chargers, 29-14 (SD)
1993—Chargers, 32-17 (TB)

1996—Buccaneers, 25-17 (SD)
2004—Chargers, 31-24 (SD)
(RS Pts.—Chargers 214, Buccaneers 126)
***SAN DIEGO vs. **TENNESSEE*
RS: Chargers lead series, 22-13-1
PS: Titans lead series, 3-1
1960—Oilers, 38-28 (H)
    Chargers, 24-21 (LA)
    ***Oilers, 24-16 (H)
1961—Chargers, 34-24 (SD)
    Oilers, 33-13 (H)
    ***Oilers, 10-3 (SD)
1962—Oilers, 42-17 (SD)
    Oilers, 33-27 (H)
1963—Chargers, 27-0 (SD)
    Chargers 20-14 (H)
1964—Chargers, 27-21 (SD)
    Chargers, 20-17 (H)
1965—Chargers, 31-14 (SD)
    Chargers, 37-26 (H)
1966—Chargers, 28-22 (H)
1967—Chargers, 13-3 (SD)
    Oilers, 24-17 (H)
1968—Chargers, 30-14 (SD)
1969—Chargers, 21-17 (H)
1970—Tie, 31-31 (SD)
1971—Oilers, 49-33 (H)
1972—Chargers, 34-20 (SD)
1974—Oilers, 21-14 (H)
1975—Chargers, 33-17 (H)
1976—Chargers, 30-27 (SD)
1978—Chargers, 45-24 (H)
1979—****Oilers, 17-14 (SD)
1984—Chargers, 31-14 (SD)
1985—Oilers, 37-35 (H)
1986—Chargers, 27-0 (SD)
1987—Oilers, 33-18 (H)
1989—Oilers, 34-27 (SD)
1990—Oilers, 17-7 (SD)
1992—Oilers, 27-0 (H)
1993—Chargers, 18-17 (SD)
1998—Chargers, 13-7 (T)
2004—Chargers, 38-17 (SD)
2006—Chargers, 40-7 (SD)
2007—Chargers, 23-17 (T) OT
    *****Chargers, 17-6 (SD)
(RS Pts.—Chargers 895, Titans 795)
(PS Pts.—Titans 57, Chargers 50)
Franchise in Los Angeles prior to 1961
**Franchise in Houston prior to 1997;*
known as Oilers prior to 1999
***AFL Championship*
****AFC Divisional Playoff*
*****AFC First-Round Playoff*
SAN DIEGO vs. WASHINGTON
RS: Redskins lead series, 6-2
1973—Redskins, 38-0 (W)
1980—Redskins, 40-17 (W)
1983—Redskins, 27-24 (SD)
1986—Redskins, 30-27 (W)
1989—Redskins, 26-21 (W)
1998—Redskins, 24-20 (W)
2001—Chargers, 30-3 (SD)
2005—Chargers, 23-17 (W) OT
(RS Pts.—Redskins 205, Chargers 162)

SAN FRANCISCO vs. ARIZONA
RS: 49ers lead series, 19-14;
See Arizona vs. San Francisco
SAN FRANCISCO vs. ATLANTA

RS: 49ers lead series, 44-27-1
PS: Falcons lead series, 1-0;
See Atlanta vs. San Francisco
SAN FRANCISCO vs. BALTIMORE
RS: Ravens lead series, 2-1;
See Baltimore vs. San Francisco
SAN FRANCISCO vs. BUFFALO
RS: Bills lead series, 5-4;
See Buffalo vs. San Francisco
SAN FRANCISCO vs. CAROLINA
RS: Panthers lead series, 9-7;
See Carolina vs. San Francisco
SAN FRANCISCO vs. CHICAGO
RS: Bears lead series, 29-27-1
PS: 49ers lead series, 3-0;
See Chicago vs. San Francisco
SAN FRANCISCO vs. CINCINNATI
RS: 49ers lead series, 8-3
PS: 49ers lead series, 2-0;
See Cincinnati vs. San Francisco
SAN FRANCISCO vs. CLEVELAND
RS: Browns lead series, 11-6;
See Cleveland vs. San Francisco
SAN FRANCISCO vs. DALLAS
RS: 49ers lead series, 14-9-1
PS: Cowboys lead series, 5-2;
See Dallas vs. San Francisco
SAN FRANCISCO vs. DENVER
RS: Broncos lead series, 6-5
PS: 49ers lead series, 1-0;
See Denver vs. San Francisco
SAN FRANCISCO vs. DETROIT
RS: 49ers lead series, 32-26-1
PS: Series tied, 1-1;
See Detroit vs. San Francisco
SAN FRANCISCO vs. GREEN BAY
RS: Packers lead series, 28-25-1
PS: Packers lead series, 4-1;
See Green Bay vs. San Francisco
SAN FRANCISCO vs. HOUSTON
RS: 49ers lead series, 1-0;
See Houston vs. San Francisco
SAN FRANCISCO vs. INDIANAPOLIS
RS: Colts lead series, 23-18;
See Indianapolis vs. San Francisco
SAN FRANCISCO vs. JACKSONVILLE
RS: Jaguars lead series, 2-0;
See Jacksonville vs. San Francisco
SAN FRANCISCO vs. KANSAS CITY
RS: 49ers lead series, 6-4;
See Kansas City vs. San Francisco
SAN FRANCISCO vs. MIAMI
RS: Dolphins lead series, 5-4
PS: 49ers lead series, 1-0;
See Miami vs. San Francisco
SAN FRANCISCO vs. MINNESOTA
RS: Vikings lead series, 19-18-1
PS: 49ers lead series, 4-1;
See Minnesota vs. San Francisco
SAN FRANCISCO vs. NEW ENGLAND
RS: 49ers lead series, 7-3;
See New England vs. San Francisco
SAN FRANCISCO vs. NEW ORLEANS
RS: 49ers lead series, 45-22-2;
See New Orleans vs. San Francisco
SAN FRANCISCO vs. N.Y. GIANTS
RS: Series tied, 13-13
PS: 49ers lead series, 4-3;
See N.Y. Giants vs. San Francisco
SAN FRANCISCO vs. N.Y. JETS

RS: 49ers lead series, 8-2;
See N.Y. Jets vs. San Francisco
SAN FRANCISCO vs. OAKLAND
RS: Raiders lead series, 6-5;
See Oakland vs. San Francisco
SAN FRANCISCO vs. PHILADELPHIA
RS: 49ers lead series, 16-9-1
PS: 49ers lead series, 1-0;
See Philadelphia vs. San Francisco
SAN FRANCISCO vs. PITTSBURGH
RS: 49ers lead series, 10-9;
See Pittsburgh vs. San Francisco
SAN FRANCISCO vs. ST. LOUIS
RS: Rams lead series, 60-54-2
PS: 49ers lead series, 1-0;
See St. Louis vs. San Francisco
SAN FRANCISCO vs. SAN DIEGO
RS: 49ers lead series, 6-5
PS: 49ers lead series, 1-0;
See San Diego vs. San Francisco
SAN FRANCISCO vs. SEATTLE
RS: Seahawks lead series, 10-8
1976—49ers, 37-21 (Sea)
1979—Seahawks, 35-24 (SF)
1985—49ers, 19-6 (SF)
1988—49ers, 38-7 (Sea)
1991—49ers, 24-22 (Sea)
1997—Seahawks, 38-9 (Sea)
2002—49ers, 28-21 (Sea)
       49ers, 31-24 (SF)
2003—Seahawks, 20-19 (Sea)
       Seahawks, 24-17 (SF)
2004—Seahawks, 34-0 (Sea)
       Seahawks, 42-27 (SF)
2005—Seahawks, 27-25 (SF)
       Seahawks, 41-3 (Sea)
2006—49ers, 20-14 (SF)
       49ers, 24-14 (Sea)
2007—Seahawks, 23-3 (SF)
       Seahawks, 24-0 (Sea)
(RS Pts.—Seahawks 437, 49ers 348)
SAN FRANCISCO vs. TAMPA BAY
RS: 49ers lead series, 15-3
PS: Buccaneers lead series, 1-0
1977—49ers, 20-10 (SF)
1978—49ers, 6-3 (SF)
1979—49ers, 23-7 (SF)
1980—Buccaneers, 24-23 (SF)
1983—49ers, 35-21 (SF)
1984—49ers, 24-17 (SF)
1986—49ers, 31-7 (TB)
1987—49ers, 24-10 (TB)
1989—49ers, 20-16 (TB)
1990—49ers, 31-7 (SF)
1992—49ers, 21-14 (SF)
1993—49ers, 45-21 (TB)
1994—49ers, 41-16 (SF)
1997—Buccaneers, 13-6 (TB)
2002—*Buccaneers, 31-6 (TB)
2003—49ers, 24-7 (SF)
2004—Buccaneers, 35-3 (TB)
2005—49ers, 15-10 (SF)
2007—49ers, 21-19 (SF)
(RS Pts.—49ers 413, Buccaneers 257)
(PS Pts.—Buccaneers 31, 49ers 6)
*NFC Divisional Playoff
SAN FRANCISCO vs. *TENNESSEE
RS: 49ers lead series, 7-4
1970—49ers, 30-20 (H)
1975—Oilers, 27-13 (SF)

1978—Oilers, 20-19 (H)
1981—49ers, 28-6 (SF)
1984—49ers, 34-21 (H)
1987—49ers, 27-20 (SF)
1990—49ers, 24-21 (H)
1993—Oilers, 10-7 (SF)
1996—49ers, 10-9 (H)
1999—49ers, 24-22 (SF)
2005—Titans, 33-22 (T)
(RS Pts.—49ers 238, Titans 209)
*Franchise in Houston prior to 1997;
known as Oilers prior to 1999
SAN FRANCISCO vs. WASHINGTON
RS: 49ers lead series, 13-9-1
PS: 49ers lead series, 3-1
1952—49ers, 23-17 (W)
1954—49ers, 41-7 (SF)
1955—Redskins, 7-0 (W)
1961—49ers, 35-3 (SF)
1967—Redskins, 31-28 (W)
1969—Tie, 17-17 (SF)
1970—49ers, 26-17 (SF)
1971—*49ers, 24-20 (SF)
1973—Redskins, 33-9 (W)
1976—Redskins, 24-21 (SF)
1978—Redskins, 38-20 (W)
1981—49ers, 30-17 (W)
1983—**Redskins, 24-21 (W)
1984—49ers, 37-31 (SF)
1985—49ers, 35-8 (W)
1986—Redskins, 14-6 (W)
1988—49ers, 37-21 (SF)
1990—49ers, 26-13 (SF)
       *49ers, 28-10 (SF)
1992—*49ers, 20-13 (SF)
1994—49ers, 37-22 (W)
1996—49ers, 19-16 (W) OT
1998—49ers, 45-10 (W)
1999—Redskins, 26-20 (SF) OT
2002—49ers, 20-10 (SF)
2004—Redskins, 26-16 (SF)
2005—Redskins, 52-17 (W)
(RS Pts.—49ers 565, Redskins 460)
(PS Pts.—49ers 93, Redskins 67)
*NFC Divisional Playoff
**NFC Championship

SEATTLE vs. ARIZONA
RS: Series tied, 9-9;
See Arizona vs. Seattle
SEATTLE vs. ATLANTA
RS: Seahawks lead series, 8-3;
See Atlanta vs. Seattle
SEATTLE vs. BALTIMORE
RS: Ravens lead series, 2-1;
See Baltimore vs. Seattle
SEATTLE vs. BUFFALO
RS: Seahawks lead series, 6-4;
See Buffalo vs. Seattle
SEATTLE vs. CAROLINA
RS: Panthers lead series, 2-1
PS: Seahawks lead series, 1-0;
See Carolina vs. Seattle
SEATTLE vs. CHICAGO
RS: Seahawks lead series, 7-3
PS: Bears lead series, 1-0;
See Chicago vs. Seattle
SEATTLE vs. CINCINNATI
RS: Seahawks lead series, 9-8
PS: Bengals lead series, 1-0;

See Cincinnati vs. Seattle

SEATTLE vs. CLEVELAND
RS: Seahawks lead series, 11-5;
See Cleveland vs. Seattle

SEATTLE vs. DALLAS
RS: Cowboys lead series, 6-4;
PS: Seahawks lead series, 1-0;
See Dallas vs. Seattle

SEATTLE vs. DENVER
RS: Broncos lead series, 33-18;
PS: Seahawks lead series, 1-0;
See Denver vs. Seattle

SEATTLE vs. DETROIT
RS: Seahawks lead series, 6-4;
See Detroit vs. Seattle

SEATTLE vs. GREEN BAY
RS: Packers lead series, 6-5
PS: Packers lead series, 2-0;
See Green Bay vs. Seattle

SEATTLE vs. HOUSTON
RS: Seahawks lead series, 1-0;
See Houston vs. Seattle

SEATTLE vs. INDIANAPOLIS
RS: Colts lead series, 5-4;
See Indianapolis vs. Seattle

SEATTLE vs. JACKSONVILLE
RS: Seahawks lead series, 3-2;
See Jacksonville vs. Seattle

SEATTLE vs. KANSAS CITY
RS: Chiefs lead series, 31-18;
See Kansas City vs. Seattle

SEATTLE vs. MIAMI
RS: Dolphins lead series, 6-3
PS: Dolphins lead series, 2-1;
See Miami vs. Seattle

SEATTLE vs. MINNESOTA
RS: Seahawks lead series, 6-4;
See Minnesota vs. Seattle

SEATTLE vs. NEW ENGLAND
RS: Series tied, 7-7;
See New England vs. Seattle

SEATTLE vs. NEW ORLEANS
RS: Series tied, 5-5;
See New Orleans vs. Seattle

SEATTLE vs. N.Y. GIANTS
RS: Giants lead series, 7-5;
See N.Y. Giants vs. Seattle

SEATTLE vs. N.Y. JETS
RS: Series tied, 8-8;
See N.Y. Jets vs. Seattle

SEATTLE vs. OAKLAND
RS: Raiders lead series, 27-23
PS: Series tied, 1-1;
See Oakland vs. Seattle

SEATTLE vs. PHILADELPHIA
RS: Eagles lead series, 6-5;
See Philadelphia vs. Seattle

SEATTLE vs. PITTSBURGH
RS: Seahawks lead series, 8-7
PS: Steelers lead series, 1-0;
See Pittsburgh vs. Seattle

SEATTLE vs. ST. LOUIS
RS: Seahawks lead series, 10-9
PS: Rams lead series, 1-0;
See St. Louis vs. Seattle

SEATTLE vs. SAN DIEGO
RS: Seahawks lead series, 25-23;
See San Diego vs. Seattle

SEATTLE vs. SAN FRANCISCO
RS: Seahawks lead series, 10-8;

See San Francisco vs. Seattle

SEATTLE vs. TAMPA BAY
RS: Seahawks lead series, 7-1
1976—Seahawks, 13-10 (TB)
1977—Seahawks, 30-23 (S)
1994—Seahawks, 22-21 (S)
1996—Seahawks, 17-13 (TB)
1999—Buccaneers, 16-3 (S)
2004—Seahawks, 10-6 (TB)
2006—Seahawks, 23-7 (TB)
2007—Seahawks, 20-6 (S)
(RS Pts.—Seahawks 138, Buccaneers 102)

SEATTLE vs. *TENNESSEE
RS: Seahawks lead series, 9-4
PS: Titans lead series, 1-0
1977—Oilers, 22-10 (S)
1979—Seahawks, 34-14 (S)
1980—Seahawks, 26-7 (H)
1981—Oilers, 35-17 (H)
1982—Oilers, 23-21 (H)
1987—**Oilers, 23-20 (H) OT
1988—Seahawks, 27-24 (S)
1990—Seahawks, 13-10 (S) OT
1993—Oilers, 24-14 (H)
1994—Seahawks, 16-14 (H)
1996—Seahawks, 23-16 (S)
1997—Seahawks, 16-13 (S)
1998—Seahawks, 20-18 (S)
2005—Seahawks, 28-24 (T)
(RS Pts.—Seahawks 265, Titans 244)
(PS Pts.—Titans 23, Seahawks 20)
*Franchise in Houston prior to 1997;
known as Oilers prior to 1999
**AFC First-Round Playoff

SEATTLE vs. WASHINGTON
RS: Redskins lead series, 9-4
PS: Seahawks lead series, 2-0
1976—Redskins, 31-7 (W)
1980—Seahawks, 14-0 (W)
1983—Redskins, 27-17 (S)
1986—Redskins, 19-14 (W)
1989—Redskins, 29-0 (S)
1992—Redskins, 16-3 (S)
1994—Seahawks, 28-7 (W)
1995—Seahawks, 27-20 (W)
1998—Seahawks, 24-14 (S)
2001—Redskins, 27-14 (W)
2002—Redskins, 14-3 (S)
2003—Redskins, 27-20 (W)
2005—Redskins, 20-17 (W) OT
      *Seahawks, 20-10 (S)
2007—**Seahawks, 35-14 (S)
(RS Pts.—Redskins 251, Seahawks 188)
(PS Pts.—Seahawks 55, Redskins 24)
*NFC Divisional Playoff
**NFC First-Round Playoff

TAMPA BAY vs. ARIZONA
RS: Series tied, 8-8;
See Arizona vs. Tampa Bay

TAMPA BAY vs. ATLANTA
RS: Buccaneers lead series, 17-12;
See Atlanta vs. Tampa Bay

TAMPA BAY vs. BALTIMORE
RS: Buccaneers lead series, 2-1;
See Baltimore vs. Tampa Bay

TAMPA BAY vs. BUFFALO
RS: Buccaneers lead series, 6-2;
See Buffalo vs. Tampa Bay

TAMPA BAY vs. CAROLINA

RS: Panthers lead series, 9-6;
See Carolina vs. Tampa Bay

TAMPA BAY vs. CHICAGO
RS: Bears lead series, 35-17;
See Chicago vs. Tampa Bay

TAMPA BAY vs. CINCINNATI
RS: Buccaneers lead series, 6-3;
See Cincinnati vs. Tampa Bay

TAMPA BAY vs. CLEVELAND
RS: Browns lead series, 5-2;
See Cleveland vs. Tampa Bay

TAMPA BAY vs. DALLAS
RS: Cowboys lead series, 7-3
PS: Cowboys lead series, 2-0;
See Dallas vs. Tampa Bay

TAMPA BAY vs. DENVER
RS: Broncos lead series, 4-2;
See Denver vs. Tampa Bay

TAMPA BAY vs. DETROIT
RS: Lions lead series, 27-24
PS: Buccaneers lead series, 1-0;
See Detroit vs. Tampa Bay

TAMPA BAY vs. GREEN BAY
RS: Packers lead series, 29-19-1
PS: Packers lead series, 1-0;
See Green Bay vs. Tampa Bay

TAMPA BAY vs. HOUSTON
RS: Series tied, 1-1;
See Houston vs. Tampa Bay

TAMPA BAY vs. INDIANAPOLIS
RS: Colts lead series, 7-4;
See Indianapolis vs. Tampa Bay

TAMPA BAY vs. JACKSONVILLE
RS: Jaguars lead series, 3-1;
See Jacksonville vs. Tampa Bay

TAMPA BAY vs. KANSAS CITY
RS: Chiefs lead series, 5-4;
See Kansas City vs. Tampa Bay

TAMPA BAY vs. MIAMI
RS: Series tied, 4-4;
See Miami vs. Tampa Bay

TAMPA BAY vs. MINNESOTA
RS: Vikings lead series, 31-19;
See Minnesota vs. Tampa Bay

TAMPA BAY vs. NEW ENGLAND
RS: Patriots lead series, 4-2;
See New England vs. Tampa Bay

TAMPA BAY vs. NEW ORLEANS
RS: Saints lead series, 19-13;
See New Orleans vs. Tampa Bay

TAMPA BAY vs. N.Y. GIANTS
RS: Giants lead series, 10-6
PS: Giants lead series, 1-0;
See N.Y. Giants vs. Tampa Bay

TAMPA BAY vs. N.Y. JETS
RS: Jets lead series, 8-1;
See N.Y. Jets vs. Tampa Bay

TAMPA BAY vs. OAKLAND
RS: Raiders lead series, 5-1
PS: Buccaneers lead series, 1-0;
See Oakland vs. Tampa Bay

TAMPA BAY vs. PHILADELPHIA
RS: Series tied, 5-5
PS: Series tied, 2-2;
See Philadelphia vs. Tampa Bay

TAMPA BAY vs. PITTSBURGH
RS: Steelers lead series, 7-1;
See Pittsburgh vs. Tampa Bay

TAMPA BAY vs. ST. LOUIS
RS: Rams lead series, 9-7

PS: Rams lead series, 2-0;
See St. Louis vs. Tampa Bay
TAMPA BAY vs. SAN DIEGO
RS: Chargers lead series, 7-1;
See San Diego vs. Tampa Bay
TAMPA BAY vs. SAN FRANCISCO
RS: 49ers lead series, 15-3
PS: Buccaneers lead series, 1-0;
See San Francisco vs. Tampa Bay
TAMPA BAY vs. SEATTLE
RS: Seahawks lead series, 7-1;
See Seattle vs. Tampa Bay
TAMPA BAY vs. *TENNESSEE
RS: Titans lead series, 7-2
1976—Oilers, 20-0 (H)
1980—Oilers, 20-14 (H)
1983—Buccaneers, 33-24 (TB)
1989—Oilers, 20-17 (H)
1995—Oilers, 19-7 (H)
1998—Oilers, 31-22 (TB)
2001—Titans, 31-28 (Tenn) OT
2003—Titans, 33-13 (Tenn)
2007—Buccaneers, 13-10 (TB)
(RS Pts.—Titans 208, Buccaneers 147)
*Franchise in Houston prior to 1997;
known as Oilers prior to 1999*
TAMPA BAY vs. WASHINGTON
RS: Buccaneers lead series, 8-7
PS: Series tied, 1-1
1977—Redskins, 10-0 (TB)
1982—Redskins, 21-13 (TB)
1989—Redskins, 32-28 (W)
1993—Redskins, 23-17 (TB)
1994—Buccaneers, 26-21 (TB)
          Buccaneers, 17-14 (W)
1995—Buccaneers, 14-6 (TB)
1996—Buccaneers, 24-10 (TB)
1998—Redskins, 20-16 (W)
1999—*Buccaneers, 14-13 (TB)
2000—Redskins, 20-17 (W) OT
2003—Buccaneers, 35-13 (W)
2004—Redskins, 16-10 (W)
2005—Buccaneers, 36-35 (TB)
          **Redskins, 17-10 (TB)
2006—Buccaneers, 20-17 (TB)
2007—Buccaneers, 19-13 (TB)
(RS Pts.—Buccaneers 292, Redskins 271)
(PS Pts.—Redskins 30, Buccaneers 24)
*NFC Divisional Playoff
**NFC First-Round Playoff

TENNESSEE VS. ARIZONA
RS: Cardinals lead series, 5-3;
See Arizona vs. Tennessee
TENNESSEE vs. ATLANTA
RS: Titans lead series, 7-5;
See Atlanta vs. Tennessee
TENNESSEE vs. BALTIMORE
RS: Ravens lead series, 8-7
PS: Series tied, 1-1;
See Baltimore vs. Tennessee
TENNESSEE vs. BUFFALO
RS: Titans lead series, 24-14
PS: Bills lead series, 2-1;
See Buffalo vs. Tennessee
TENNESSEE vs. CAROLINA
RS: Titans lead series, 2-1;
See Carolina vs. Tennessee
TENNESSEE vs. CHICAGO
RS: Bears lead series, 5-4;

See Chicago vs. Tennessee
TENNESSEE vs. CINCINNATI
RS: Titans lead series, 38-31-1
PS: Bengals lead series, 1-0;
See Cincinnati vs. Tennessee
TENNESSEE vs. CLEVELAND
RS: Browns lead series, 33-26
PS: Titans lead series, 1-0;
See Cleveland vs. Tennessee
TENNESSEE vs. DALLAS
RS: Cowboys lead series, 7-5;
See Dallas vs. Tennessee
TENNESSEE vs. DENVER
RS: Titans lead series, 20-13-1
PS: Broncos lead series, 2-1;
See Denver vs. Tennessee
TENNESSEE vs. DETROIT
RS: Titans lead series, 6-3;
See Detroit vs. Tennessee
TENNESSEE vs. GREEN BAY
RS: Titans lead series, 5-4;
See Green Bay vs. Tennessee
TENNESSEE vs. HOUSTON
RS: Titans lead series, 10-2;
See Houston vs. Tennessee
TENNESSEE vs. INDIANAPOLIS
RS: Colts lead series, 15-11
PS: Titans lead series, 1-0;
See Indianapolis vs. Tennessee
TENNESSEE vs. JACKSONVILLE
RS: Titans lead series, 14-12
PS: Titans lead series, 1-0;
See Jacksonville vs. Tennessee
TENNESSEE vs. KANSAS CITY
RS: Chiefs lead series, 25-19
PS: Chiefs lead series, 2-0;
See Kansas City vs. Tennessee
TENNESSEE vs. MIAMI
RS: Dolphins lead series, 17-13
PS: Titans lead series, 1-0;
See Miami vs. Tennessee
TENNESSEE vs. MINNESOTA
RS: Vikings lead series, 7-3;
See Minnesota vs. Tennessee
TENNESSEE vs. NEW ENGLAND
RS: Patriots lead series, 20-15-1
PS: Series tied, 1-1;
See New England vs. Tennessee
TENNESSEE vs. NEW ORLEANS
RS: Titans lead series, 7-4-1;
See New Orleans vs. Tennessee
TENNESSEE vs. N.Y. GIANTS
RS: Giants lead series, 5-4;
See N.Y. Giants vs. Tennessee
TENNESSEE vs. N.Y. JETS
RS: Titans lead series, 21-15-1
PS: Titans lead series, 1-0;
See N.Y. Jets vs. Tennessee
TENNESSEE vs. OAKLAND
RS: Raiders lead series, 23-18
PS: Raiders lead series, 4-0;
See Oakland vs. Tennessee
TENNESSEE vs. PHILADELPHIA
RS: Eagles lead series, 6-3;
See Philadelphia vs. Tennessee
TENNESSEE vs. PITTSBURGH
RS: Steelers lead series, 38-28
PS: Steelers lead series, 3-1;
See Pittsburgh vs. Tennessee
TENNESSEE vs. ST. LOUIS

RS: Rams lead series, 6-3
PS: Rams lead series, 1-0;
See St. Louis vs. Tennessee
TENNESSEE vs. SAN DIEGO
RS: Chargers lead series, 22-13-1
PS: Titans lead series, 3-1;
See San Diego vs. Tennessee
TENNESSEE vs. SAN FRANCISCO
RS: 49ers lead series, 7-4;
See San Francisco vs. Tennessee
TENNESSEE vs. SEATTLE
RS: Seahawks lead series, 9-4
PS: Titans lead series, 1-0;
See Seattle vs. Tennessee
TENNESSEE vs. TAMPA BAY
RS: Titans lead series, 7-2;
See Tampa Bay vs. Tennessee
*TENNESSEE vs. WASHINGTON
RS: Titans lead series, 6-4
1971—Redskins, 22-13 (W)
1975—Oilers, 13-10 (H)
1979—Oilers, 29-27 (W)
1985—Redskins, 16-13 (W)
1988—Oilers, 41-17 (H)
1991—Redskins, 16-13 (W) OT
1997—Oilers, 28-14 (T)
2000—Titans, 27-21 (W)
2002—Redskins, 31-14 (T)
2006—Titans, 25-22 (W)
(RS—Titans 216, Redskins 196)
*Franchise in Houston prior to 1997;
known as Oilers prior to 1999*

WASHINGTON vs. ARIZONA
RS: Redskins lead series, 72-44-2;
See Arizona vs. Washington
WASHINGTON vs. ATLANTA
RS: Redskins lead series, 14-5-1
PS: Redskins lead series, 1-0;
See Atlanta vs. Washington
WASHINGTON vs. BALTIMORE
RS: Ravens lead series, 2-1;
See Baltimore vs. Washington
WASHINGTON vs. BUFFALO
RS: Bills lead series, 7-4
PS: Redskins lead series, 1-0;
See Buffalo vs. Washington
WASHINGTON vs. CAROLINA
RS: Redskins lead series, 7-1;
See Carolina vs. Washington
WASHINGTON vs. CHICAGO
RS: Bears lead series, 20-18-1
PS: Redskins lead series, 4-3;
See Chicago vs. Washington
WASHINGTON vs. CINCINNATI
RS: Redskins lead series, 4-3;
See Cincinnati vs. Washington
WASHINGTON vs. CLEVELAND
RS: Browns lead series, 33-9-1;
See Cleveland vs. Washington
WASHINGTON vs. DALLAS
RS: Cowboys lead series, 56-36-2
PS: Redskins lead series, 2-0;
See Dallas vs. Washington
WASHINGTON vs. DENVER
RS: Broncos lead series, 6-4
PS: Redskins lead series, 1-0;
See Denver vs. Washington
WASHINGTON vs. DETROIT
RS: Redskins lead series, 26-10

PS: Redskins lead series, 3-0;
See Detroit vs. Washington
WASHINGTON vs. GREEN BAY
RS: Packers lead series, 17-12-1
PS: Series tied, 1-1;
See Green Bay vs. Washington
WASHINGTON vs. HOUSTON
RS: Redskins lead series, 2-0;
See Houston vs. Washington
WASHINGTON vs. INDIANAPOLIS
RS: Colts lead series, 18-10;
See Indianapolis vs. Washington
WASHINGTON vs. JACKSONVILLE
RS: Redskins lead series, 3-1;
See Jacksonville vs. Washington
WASHINGTON vs. KANSAS CITY
RS: Chiefs lead series, 6-1;
See Kansas City vs. Washington
WASHINGTON vs. MIAMI
RS: Dolphins lead series, 6-4
PS: Series tied, 1-1;
See Miami vs. Washington
WASHINGTON vs. MINNESOTA
RS: Redskins lead series, 8-6
PS: Redskins lead series, 3-2;
See Minnesota vs. Washington
WASHINGTON vs. NEW ENGLAND
RS: Redskins lead series, 6-2;
See New England vs. Washington
WASHINGTON vs. NEW ORLEANS
RS: Redskins lead series, 14-7;
See New Orleans vs. Washington
WASHINGTON vs. N.Y. GIANTS
RS: Giants lead series, 85-61-4
PS: Series tied, 1-1;
See N.Y. Giants vs. Washington
WASHINGTON vs. N.Y. JETS
RS: Redskins lead series, 8-1;
See N.Y. Jets vs. Washington
WASHINGTON vs. OAKLAND
RS: Raiders lead series, 7-3
PS: Raiders lead series, 1-0;
See Oakland vs. Washington
WASHINGTON vs. PHILADELPHIA
RS: Redskins lead series, 75-65-5
PS: Redskins lead series, 1-0;
See Philadelphia vs. Washington
WASHINGTON vs. PITTSBURGH
RS: Redskins lead series, 42-30-3;
See Pittsburgh vs. Washington
WASHINGTON vs. ST. LOUIS
RS: Redskins lead series, 20-7-1
PS: Series tied, 2-2;
See St. Louis vs. Washington
WASHINGTON vs. SAN DIEGO
RS: Redskins lead series, 6-2;
See San Diego vs. Washington
WASHINGTON vs. SAN FRANCISCO
RS: 49ers lead series, 13-9-1
PS: 49ers lead series, 3-1;
See San Francisco vs. Washington
WASHINGTON vs. SEATTLE
RS: Redskins lead series, 9-4
PS: Seahawks lead series, 2-0;
See Seattle vs. Washington
WASHINGTON vs. TAMPA BAY
RS: Buccaneers lead series, 8-7
PS: Series tied, 1-1;
See Tampa Bay vs. Washington

WASHINGTON vs. TENNESSEE
RS: Titans lead series, 6-4;
See Tennessee vs. Washington

SUPER BOWL COMPOSITE STANDINGS

	W	L	Pct.	Pts.	OP
San Francisco 49ers	5	0	1.000	188	89
Baltimore Ravens	1	0	1.000	34	7
New York Jets	1	0	1.000	16	7
Tampa Bay Buccaneers	1	0	1.000	48	21
Pittsburgh Steelers	5	1	.833	141	110
Green Bay Packers	3	1	.750	127	76
New York Giants	3	1	.750	83	87
Indianapolis/Baltimore Colts	2	1	.667	52	46
Dallas Cowboys	5	3	.625	221	132
Oakland/L.A. Raiders	3	2	.600	132	114
Washington Redskins	3	2	.600	122	103
New England Patriots	3	3	.500	121	165
Chicago Bears	1	1	.500	63	39
Kansas City Chiefs	1	1	.500	33	42
Miami Dolphins	2	3	.400	74	103
Denver Broncos	2	4	.333	115	206
St. Louis/L.A. Rams	1	2	.333	59	67
Atlanta Falcons	0	1	.000	19	34
Carolina Panthers	0	1	.000	29	32
San Diego Chargers	0	1	.000	26	49
Seattle Seahawks	0	1	.000	10	21
Tennessee Titans	0	1	.000	16	23
Cincinnati Bengals	0	2	.000	37	46
Philadelphia Eagles	0	2	.000	31	51
Buffalo Bills	0	4	.000	73	139
Minnesota Vikings	0	4	.000	34	95

SUPER BOWL HOST CITIES

Miami/South Florida	9
New Orleans	9
Los Angeles	7 (LA Coliseum 2, Rose Bowl 5)
San Diego	3
Tampa	3
Arizona	2
Atlanta	2
Detroit	2
Houston	2
Jacksonville	1
Minneapolis	1
Stanford	1

FUTURE SUPER BOWL SITES

Super Bowl XLIII	Feb. 1, 2009	Raymond James Stadium, Tampa, Florida
Super Bowl XLIV	Feb. 7, 2010	Dolphin Stadium, South Florida
Super Bowl XLV	Feb. 6, 2011	Dallas Cowboys New Stadium, North Texas
Super Bowl XLVI	Feb. 5, 2012	Lucas Oil Stadium, Indianapolis, Indiana

PETE ROZELLE TROPHY/SUPER BOWL MVPs*

Super Bowl I	— QB Bart Starr, Green Bay
Super Bowl II	— QB Bart Starr, Green Bay
Super Bowl III	— QB Joe Namath, N.Y. Jets
Super Bowl IV	— QB Len Dawson, Kansas City
Super Bowl V	— LB Chuck Howley, Dallas
Super Bowl VI	— QB Roger Staubach, Dallas
Super Bowl VII	— S Jake Scott, Miami
Super Bowl VIII	— RB Larry Csonka, Miami
Super Bowl IX	— RB Franco Harris, Pittsburgh
Super Bowl X	— WR Lynn Swann, Pittsburgh
Super Bowl XI	— WR Fred Biletnikoff, Oakland
Super Bowl XII	— DT Randy White and DE Harvey Martin, Dallas
Super Bowl XIII	— QB Terry Bradshaw, Pittsburgh
Super Bowl XIV	— QB Terry Bradshaw, Pittsburgh
Super Bowl XV	— QB Jim Plunkett, Oakland
Super Bowl XVI	— QB Joe Montana, San Francisco
Super Bowl XVII	— RB John Riggins, Washington
Super Bowl XVIII	— RB Marcus Allen, L.A. Raiders
Super Bowl XIX	— QB Joe Montana, San Francisco
Super Bowl XX	— DE Richard Dent, Chicago
Super Bowl XXI	— QB Phil Simms, N.Y. Giants
Super Bowl XXII	— QB Doug Williams, Washington
Super Bowl XXIII	— WR Jerry Rice, San Francisco
Super Bowl XXIV	— QB Joe Montana, San Francisco
Super Bowl XXV	— RB Ottis Anderson, N.Y. Giants
Super Bowl XXVI	— QB Mark Rypien, Washington
Super Bowl XXVII	— QB Troy Aikman, Dallas
Super Bowl XXVIII	— RB Emmitt Smith, Dallas
Super Bowl XXIX	— QB Steve Young, San Francisco
Super Bowl XXX	— CB Larry Brown, Dallas
Super Bowl XXXI	— KR-PR Desmond Howard, Green Bay
Super Bowl XXXII	— RB Terrell Davis, Denver
Super Bowl XXXIII	— QB John Elway, Denver
Super Bowl XXXIV	— QB Kurt Warner, St. Louis
Super Bowl XXXV	— LB Ray Lewis, Baltimore
Super Bowl XXXVI	— QB Tom Brady, New England
Super Bowl XXXVII	— S Dexter Jackson, Tampa Bay
Super Bowl XXXVIII	— QB Tom Brady, New England
Super Bowl XXXIX	— WR Deion Branch, New England
Super Bowl XL	— WR Hines Ward, Pittsburgh
Super Bowl XLI	— QB Peyton Manning, Indianapolis
Super Bowl XLII	— QB Eli Manning, N.Y. Giants

Award named Pete Rozelle Trophy since Super Bowl XXV.

SUPER BOWL MVP BY POSITION

Quarterback	22
Running Back	7
Wide Receiver	5
Defensive End	2
Linebacker	2
Safety	2
Cornerback	1
Defensive Tackle	1
Kick Returner-Punt Returner	1

A defensive end and defensive tackle shared the Super Bowl XII MVP award.

RESULTS

NFC leads AFC, 22-20

Super Bowl	Date	Winner (Share)	Loser (Share)	Score	Site	Attendance
XLII	2-3-08	N.Y. Giants ($78,000)	New England ($40,000)	17-14	Glendale	71,101
XLI	2-4-07	Indianapolis ($73,000)	Chicago ($38,000)	29-17	South Florida	74,512
XL	2-5-06	Pittsburgh ($73,000)	Seattle ($38,000)	21-10	Detroit	68,206
XXXIX	2-6-05	New England ($68,000)	Philadelphia ($36,500)	24-21	Jacksonville	78,125
XXXVIII	2-1-04	New England ($68,000)	Carolina ($36,500)	32-29	Houston	71,525
* XXXVII	1-26-03	Tampa Bay ($63,000)	Oakland ($35,000)	48-21	San Diego	67,603
* XXXVI	2-3-02	New England ($63,000)	St. Louis ($34,500)	20-17	New Orleans	72,922
XXXV	1-28-01	Baltimore ($58,000)	N.Y. Giants ($34,500)	34-7	Tampa	71,921
* XXXIV	1-30-00	St. Louis ($58,000)	Tennessee ($33,000)	23-16	Atlanta	72,625
XXXIII	1-31-99	Denver ($53,000)	Atlanta ($32,500)	34-19	South Florida	74,803
XXXII	1-25-98	Denver ($48,000)	Green Bay ($29,000)	31-24	San Diego	68,912
XXXI	1-26-97	Green Bay ($48,000)	New England ($29,000)	35-21	New Orleans	72,301
XXX	1-28-96	Dallas ($42,000)	Pittsburgh ($27,000)	27-17	Tempe	76,347
XXIX	1-29-95	San Francisco ($42,000)	San Diego ($26,000)	49-26	South Florida	74,107
* XXVIII	1-30-94	Dallas ($38,000)	Buffalo ($23,500)	30-13	Atlanta	72,817
XXVII	1-31-93	Dallas ($36,000)	Buffalo ($18,000)	52-17	Pasadena	98,374
XXVI	1-26-92	Washington ($36,000)	Buffalo ($18,000)	37-24	Minneapolis	63,130
* XXV	1-27-91	N.Y. Giants ($36,000)	Buffalo ($18,000)	20-19	Tampa	73,813
XXIV	1-28-90	San Francisco ($36,000)	Denver ($18,000)	55-10	New Orleans	72,919
XXIII	1-22-89	San Francisco ($36,000)	Cincinnati ($18,000)	20-16	South Florida	75,129
XXII	1-31-88	Washington ($36,000)	Denver ($18,000)	42-10	San Diego	73,302
XXI	1-25-87	N.Y. Giants ($36,000)	Denver ($18,000)	39-20	Pasadena	101,063
XX	1-26-86	Chicago ($36,000)	New England ($18,000)	46-10	New Orleans	73,818
XIX	1-20-85	San Francisco ($36,000)	Miami ($18,000)	38-16	Stanford	84,059
XVIII	1-22-84	L.A. Raiders ($36,000)	Washington ($18,000)	38-9	Tampa	72,920
* XVII	1-30-83	Washington ($36,000)	Miami ($18,000)	27-17	Pasadena	103,667
XVI	1-24-82	San Francisco ($18,000)	Cincinnati ($9,000)	26-21	Pontiac	81,270
XV	1-25-81	Oakland ($18,000)	Philadelphia ($9,000)	27-10	New Orleans	76,135
XIV	1-20-80	Pittsburgh ($18,000)	Los Angeles ($9,000)	31-19	Pasadena	103,985
XIII	1-21-79	Pittsburgh ($18,000)	Dallas ($9,000)	35-31	Miami	79,484
XII	1-15-78	Dallas ($18,000)	Denver ($9,000)	27-10	New Orleans	75,583
XI	1-9-77	Oakland ($15,000)	Minnesota ($7,500)	32-14	Pasadena	103,438
X	1-18-76	Pittsburgh ($15,000)	Dallas ($7,500)	21-17	Miami	80,187
IX	1-12-75	Pittsburgh ($15,000)	Minnesota ($7,500)	16-6	New Orleans	80,997
VIII	1-13-74	Miami ($15,000)	Minnesota ($7,500)	24-7	Houston	71,882
VII	1-14-73	Miami ($15,000)	Washington ($7,500)	14-7	Los Angeles	90,182
VI	1-16-72	Dallas ($15,000)	Miami ($7,500)	24-3	New Orleans	81,023
V	1-17-71	Baltimore ($15,000)	Dallas ($7,500)	16-13	Miami	79,204
* IV	1-11-70	Kansas City ($15,000)	Minnesota ($7,500)	23-7	New Orleans	80,562
III	1-12-69	N.Y. Jets ($15,000)	Baltimore ($7,500)	16-7	Miami	75,389
II	1-14-68	Green Bay ($15,000)	Oakland ($7,500)	33-14	Miami	75,546
I	1-15-67	Green Bay ($15,000)	Kansas City ($7,500)	35-10	Los Angeles	61,946

* One week between conference championship games and Super Bowl; all others had two weeks between conference championship games and Super Bowl.

SUPER BOWL XLII

University of Phoenix Stadium, Glendale, Arizona
February 3, 2008, Attendance: 71,101

N.Y. GIANTS 17, NEW ENGLAND 14—Eli Manning completed a 13-yard touchdown pass to Plaxico Burress with 35 seconds remaining as the Giants outlasted the previously undefeated Patriots. The Giants won their first Super Bowl in 17 years, and their third overall, while the Patriots joined the 1934 and 1942 Chicago Bears as the only teams to go undefeated in the regular season but lose their championship game. The Giants opened the game with a 16-play, 63-yard drive that resulted in Lawrence Tynes' 32-yard field goal with 5:01 left in the first quarter. It was the longest game-opening drive in Super Bowl history. The Patriots responded as Laurence Maroney's 43-yard kickoff return

sparked a 56-yard drive, capped by Maroney's 1-yard touchdown run to begin the second quarter. The Giants drove to the Patriots' 14 on their next possession, but Ellis Hobbs intercepted Manning's deflected pass to stymie the drive. The Giants had the last scoring opportunity of the half, but Ahmad Bradshaw was flagged 10 yards for illegally batting forward a fumble, which took the Giants out of field-goal range. The Patriots drove to the Giants' 25 to begin the third quarter, but on third down Michael Strahan sacked Tom Brady for a 6-yard loss. On fourth-and-13 from the Giants' 31, Brady attempted a deep pass that sailed out of the end zone. With 14:52 to play beginning from their own 20-yard line, Manning connected on a 45-yard pass over the middle to Kevin Boss. Moments later

Steve Smith caught a 17-yard pass on third-and-4, and two plays later Manning found David Tyree open over the middle for a 5-yard touchdown for a 10-7 lead with 11:05 to play. After an exchange of punts, the Patriots took possession on their own 20-yard-line with 7:54 to play. Brady completed 8 of 11 passes on the 80-yard drive, none for more than 13 yards, capped by Randy Moss' 6-yard touchdown catch on third-and-goal with 2:42 to play. The Giants and Manning took possession on their own 17-yard-line with 2:39 left. Manning completed an 11-yard pass to Amani Toomer, and four plays later Brandon Jacobs gained 2 yards on fourth-and-1. Three plays later, faced with third-and-5 from their own 44 with 1:15 remaining, Manning dropped back to pass. He escaped the simultaneous grasps of Jarvis Green and Richard Seymour, spun away and then launched a pass deep down field. Tyree and Rodney Harrison both leapt for the ball, and Tyree caught the ball in the midair and cradled it against his helmet while falling to the ground with Harrison draped all over him. The 32-yard reception gave the Patriots' 24 gave the Giants a chance, and Smith's 12-yard catch on third-and-11 moments later put the ball at the Patriots' 13. On the next play, Burress caught a fade pass from Manning with 35 seconds left. The Patriots started from their own 26 with 29 seconds remaining, and on second down Jay Alford sacked Brady for a 10-yard loss. Brady's final two long pass attempts to Moss fell incomplete. Manning was 19 of 34 or 255 yards and 2 touchdowns, with 1 interception, and was named the game's most valuable player, one year after his brother, Peyton, won the award for the Colts. Brady was 29 of 48 for 266 yards and 1 touchdown. Wes Welker had 11 catches, which tied a Super Bowl record, for 103 yards.

N.Y. Giants (17)	Offense	New England (14)
Plaxico Burress	WR	Wes Welker
David Diehl	LT	Matt Light
Rich Seubert	LG	Logan Mankins
Shaun O'Hara	C	Dan Koppen
Chris Snee	RG	Stephen Neal
Kareem McKenzie	RT	Nick Kaczur
Kevin Boss	TE	Benjamin Watson
Amani Toomer	WR	Randy Moss
Eli Manning	QB	Tom Brady
Brandon Jacobs	RB	Laurence Maroney
Michael Matthews	TE	Kyle Brady
Defense		
Michael Strahan	LDE	Ty Warren
Barry Cofield	LDT	Vince Wilfork
Fred Robbins	RDT	Richard Seymour
Osi Umenyiora	RDE/OLB	Mike Vrabel
Reggie Torbor	SLB/MLB	Tedy Bruschi
Gary Brackett	MLB/OLB	Adalius Thomas
Kawika Mitchell	WLB/DB	Brandon Meriweather
Aaron Ross	LCB	Asante Samuel
Corey Webster	RCB	Ellis Hobbs
James Butler	SS	Rodney Harrison
Gibril Wilson	FS	James Sanders

SUBSTITUTIONS

N.Y. GIANTS—Specialists: K—Lawrence Tynes. P—Jeff Feagles. Offense: RB—Ahmad Bradshaw, Reuben Droughns. FB—Madison Hedgecock. WR—Domenik Hixon, Steve Smith, David Tyree. G—Kevin Boothe, Grey Ruegamer. T—Guy Whimper. Defense: DT—Jay Alford. DE—Dave Tollefson, Justin Tuck. LB—Chase Blackburn, Torrance Daniels, Zak DeOssie, Gerris Wilkinson. CB—Kevin Dockery, Sam Madison, R.W. McQuarters. S—Michael Johnson. DNP: QB—Anthony Wright. Not Active: QB—Jared Lorenzen. RB—Danny Ware. WR—Sinorice Moss. TE—Jerome Collins. T—Adam Koets. DT—Russell Davis, Manuel Wright. CB—Geoffrey Pope.

NEW ENGLAND—Specialists: K—Stephen Gostkowski. P—Chris Hanson. LS—Lonie Paxton. Offense: RB—Kyle Eckel, Heath Evans, Kevin Faulk. WR—Jabar Gaffney, Donte' Stallworth, Kelley Washington. G/C—Russ Hochstein T—Ryan O'Callaghan. Defense: DL—Jarvis Green, Rashad Moore, Le Kevin Smith. LB—Eric Alexander, Larry Izzo, Junior Seau, Pierre Woods. CB—Randall Gay. DB—Willie Andrews, Raymond Ventrone, Eugene Wilson. DNP: QB—Matt Cassel. Not Active: QB—Matt Gutierrez. WR—Troy Brown, Chad Jackson. TE—Stephen Spach. G—Billy Yates. T—Wesley Britt. DL—Santonio Thomas. CB—Antwain Spann.

OFFICIALS

Referee—Mike Carey. Umpire—Tony Michalek. Line Judge—Carl Johnson. Side Judge—Larry Rose. Head Linesman—Gary Slaughter. Back Judge—Scott Helverson. Field Judge—Boris Cheek. Replay Official—Ken Baker. Video Operator—Jim Grant.

SCORING

N.Y. Giants (NFC)	3	0	0	14	— 17
New England (AFC)	0	7	0	7	— 14

NYG— FG Tynes 32 (5:01)
NE — Maroney 1 run
  (Gostkowski kick) (14:57)
NYG— Tyree 5 pass from Manning
  (Gould kick) (11:05)
NE — Moss 6 pass from Brady
  (Gostkowski kick) (2:42)
NYG— Burress 13 pass from Manning
  (Tynes kick) (0:35)

TEAM STATISTICS	NYG	NE
Total First Downs	17	22
Rushing	4	3
Passing	13	17
Penalty	0	2
Total Net Yardage	338	274
Total Offensive Plays	63	69
Avg. Gain Per Offensive Play	5.4	4.0
Rushes	26	16
Yards Gained Rushing (Net)	91	45
Avg. Yards per Rush	3.5	2.8
Passes Attempted	34	48
Passes Completed	19	29
Had Intercepted	1	0
Tackled Attempting to Pass	3	5
Yards Lost Attempting to Pass	8	37
Yards Gained Passing (Net)	247	229
Punts	4	4
Avg. Distance	39.0	43.8
Punt Returns	3	1
Punt Return Yardage	25	15
Kickoff Returns	2	4
Kickoff Return Yardage	39	94
Interception Return Yardage	0	23
Total Return Yardage	25	38
Fumbles	2	1
Fumbles Lost	0	1
Own Fumbles Recovered	2	0
Opponent Fumbles Recovered	1	0
Penalties	4	5
Yards Penalized	36	35

Field Goals	1	0
Field Goals Attempted	1	0
Third-Down Efficiency	8/16	7/14
Fourth-Down Efficiency	1/1	0/2
Time of Possession	30:27	29:33

INDIVIDUAL STATISTICS

RUSHING: NYG: Bradshaw 9-45-0, Jacobs 14-42-0, Manning 3-4-0. NE: Maroney 14-36-1, Faulk 1-7-0, Evans 1-2-0.

PASSING: NYG: Manning 34-19-255-2-1. NE: Brady 48-29-266-1-0.

RECEIVING: NYG: Toomer 6-84-0, Smith 5-50-0, Tyree 3-43-1, Burress 2-27-1, Boss 1-45-0, Hedgecock 1-3-0, Bradshaw 1-3-0. NE: Welker 11-103-0, Faulk 7-52-0, Moss 5-62-1, Stallworth 3-34-0, Maroney 2-12-0, Brady 1-3-0.

KICKOFF RETURNS: NYG: Hixon 2-39-0. NE: Maroney 4-94-0.

PUNT RETURNS: NYG: McQuarters 3-25-0. NE: Welker 1-15-0, Faulk 0-0-0.

PUNTING: NYG: Feagles 4-156-39.0. NE: Hanson 4-175-43.8.

INTERCEPTIONS: NYG: none. NE: Hobbs 1-23-0.

SACKS: NYG: Tuck 2, Alford 1, Mitchell 1, Strahan 1. NE: Thomas 2, Green 1.

SUPER BOWL XLI

Dolphin Stadium, South Florida
February 4, 2007, Attendance: 74,512

INDIANAPOLIS 29, CHICAGO 17—Peyton Manning passed for 247 yards and 1 touchdown as the Colts won their first Super Bowl in 36 years. The Colts outgained the Bears 430-265 in total yards and maintained a 38:04-21:56 edge in time of possession. Devin Hester opened the game with a 92-yard kickoff return for a touchdown, the first time the Super Bowl began with a touchdown. Two possessions later, on third-and-10, Manning found Reggie Wayne wide open deep down the middle for a 53-yard touchdown to tie the score. A steady rain forced the teams to commit 4 first-quarter turnovers, and Hunter Smith mishandled the snap on the extra point, allowing the Bears to maintain a 7-6 lead. Later in the quarter, Thomas Jones' 52-yard run set up Rex Grossman's short touchdown pass to Muhsin Muhammad for a 14-6 lead. The Colts scored on back-to-back drives to begin the second quarter, capped by Dominic Rhodes' 1-yard run, for a 16-14 lead. To begin the second half, the Colts ran 7:34 off the clock with a 13-play, 56-yard drive that culminated with Adam Vinatieri's 24-yard field goal for a 19-14 lead. The teams then exchanged field goals, and the Bears forced a punt. On first-and-10 from the Bears' 38 with 11:59 to play, Grossman's pass intended for Muhammad was thrown high. Kelvin Hayden intercepted the pass, maneuvered up the far sideline while staying inbounds, and raced 56 yards for a touchdown. It was Hayden's first-ever professional interception. Four plays later, Bob Sanders intercepted Grossman's deep pass. The Bears got the ball back twice, but never ran a play across midfield. Manning, who won the Pete Rozelle MVP award, was 25 of 38 for 247 yards and 1 touchdown, with 1 interception. Rhodes carried 21 times for 113 yards. Joseph Addai had 10 receptions for 66 yards. Grossman was 20 of 28 for 165 yards and 1 touchdown, with 2 interceptions. Jones rushed 15 times for 112 yards.

Indianapolis (AFC)	6 10 6 7	— 29
Chicago (NFC)	14 0 3 0	— 17
Chi—	Hester 92 kickoff return (Gould kick) (14:46)	
Ind—	Wayne 53 pass from Manning (mishandled hold) (6:50)	
Chi—	Muhammad 4 pass from Grossman (Gould kick) (4:34)	
Ind—	FG Vinatieri 29 (11:17)	
Ind—	Rhodes 1 run (Vinatieri kick) (6:09)	
Ind—	FG Vinatieri 24 (7:26)	
Ind—	FG Vinatieri 20 (3:16)	
Chi—	FG Gould 44 (1:14)	
Ind—	Hayden 56 interception return (Vinatieri kick) (11:44)	

SUPER BOWL XL

Ford Field, Detroit, Michigan
February 5, 2006, Attendance: 68,206
PITTSBURGH 21, SEATTLE 10—at Ford Field, attendance 68,206. The Steelers made three big plays on offense and played a bend-but-don't-break defense to win their record-tying fifth Super Bowl title. The Seahawks lost despite winning the turnover battle (2-1), having more total yards (396-339), and consuming more of the clock (33:02-26:58). The Seahawks crossed midfield on 9 of their 12 possessions, but scored just twice. Late in the first quarter, Darrell Jackson's 16-yard touchdown catch was nullified by pass interference. The Seahawks settled for Josh Brown's 47-yard field goal. With 3:58 left in the second quarter, faced with third-and-28 from the Seahawks' 40, Ben Roethlisberger eluded the rush, rolled left and threw a deep pass across field. Hines Ward outleaped Michael Boulware at the 3-yard line for a 37-yard pass play. Two plays later, on a broken play, Roethlisberger dove over left tackle and reached the goal line for a touchdown. The Seahawks reached the Steelers' 40 with 54 seconds left, but Matt Hasselbeck's third-and-6 pass fell incomplete and Brown's 54-yard field-goal attempt sailed wide right. On the second play of the second half, Willie Parker set a Super Bowl record with his 75-yard touchdown run over right tackle. Brown's 50-yard field-goal attempt sailed wide left on the next possession, and the Steelers drove to the Seahawks' 7. On third-and-6, Roethlisberger's pass to the right flat was intercepted by Kelly Herndon, who returned the ball a Super Bowl-record 76 yards to the Steelers' 20.

Three plays later, Jerramy Stevens caught Hasselbeck's 16-yard touchdown pass to cut the deficit to 14-10 with 6:45 left in the third quarter. Early in the fourth quarter, the Seahawks drove to the Steelers' 19. On first down, Stevens caught an 18-yard pass, but a holding penalty nullified the catch and Ike Taylor intercepted Hasselbeck's pass a few plays later. Three plays later, Parker took a handoff and gave the ball to Antwaan Randle El on a reverse. Rolling to his right, Randle El fired a perfect 43-yard touchdown pass to Ward for a 21-10 lead with 8:56 to play. The Seahawks punted and then did not get the ball back until there was 1:51 remaining. Seattle reached the Steelers' 26 with 35 seconds left. From the Steelers' 23, Hasselbeck's fourth-and-7 pass to Stevens fell incomplete at the 2-yard line with three seconds remaining. Roethlisberger, who became the youngest quarterback to win the Super Bowl, was 9 of 21 for 123 yards, with 2 interceptions. Ward had 5 catches for 123 yards to earn the Pete Rozelle Trophy as the game's most valuable player. Hasselbeck was 26 of 49 for 273 yards and 1 touchdown, with 1 interception.

Seattle (NFC)	3 0 7 0	— 10
Pittsburgh (AFC)	0 7 7 7	— 21
Sea—	FG J. Brown 47 (0:22)	
Pitt—	Roethlisberger 1 run (Reed kick) (1:55)	
Pitt—	Parker 75 run (Reed kick) (14:38)	
Sea—	Stevens 16 pass from Hasselbeck (J. Brown kick) (6:45)	
Pitt—	Ward 43 pass from Randle El (Reed kick) (8:56)	

SUPER BOWL XXXIX

Alltel Stadium, Jacksonville, Florida
February 6, 2005, Attendance: 78,125
NEW ENGLAND 24, PHILADELPHIA 21—Deion Branch had 11 receptions for 133 yards and the Patriots' defense forced 4 turnovers en route to becoming the eighth team to post consecutive Super Bowl titles. The Patriots matched the Dallas Cowboys (XXVII, XXVIII, and XXX) as the only team with three Super Bowl victories in the span of four seasons. The Eagles threatened first, driving to the Patriots' 8 late in the first quarter. On first down, Mike Vrabel sacked Donovan McNabb for a 16-yard loss and, after a penalty overturned an interception, Rodney Harrison stepped in front of a pass for an interception at the Eagles' 4. Early in the second quarter the Eagles drove 81 yards, keyed by Todd Pinkston's 40-yard catch, and capped by McNabb's 6-yard touchdown pass to L.J. Smith on third-and-goal for a 7-0 lead. The Patriots responded by driving to the Eagles' 4, but Tom Brady fumbled on a fake handoff attempt and Darwin Walker recovered. Later in the quarter, a 29-yard punt by Dirk

Johnson allowed the Patriots to drive just 37 yards, keyed by Branch's 7-yard catch on third-and-3, and capped by Brady's pass to David Givens on the right side of the end zone to tie the game with 1:10 left in the half. New England began the second half with a 9-play, 69-yard drive, including 4 receptions, 2 on third down, by Branch, and capped by Vrabel's 2-yard catch. The Eagles put together a 10-play, 74-yard drive later in the third quarter, keyed by Brian Westbrook's 4-yard catch on third-and-3, and followed on the next play by his 10-yard touchdown catch to tie the game. On the ensuing drive, Kevin Faulk caught screen passes of 13 and 14 yards, and had a 12-yard run, and Corey Dillon capped the possession with a 2-yard run with 13:44 remaining for a 21-14 lead. The Patriots' defense forced a three-and-out, and Branch's 19-yard catch set up Adam Vinatieri's 22-yard field goal with 8:40 to play. Tedy Bruschi intercepted McNabb's pass at the Patriots' 24 with 7:20 remaining. The Eagles forced a punt and, beginning at their own 21 with 5:40 to play, needed 13 plays to drive 79 yards, capped by McNabb's 30-yard touchdown pass on a post-pattern to Greg Lewis with 1:48 to play. Christian Fauria recovered the onside kick, but the Eagles' defense forced a punt. Dexter Reid downed Josh Miller's 32-yard punt at the Eagles' 4 with 46 seconds left, and Harrison intercepted McNabb's pass three plays later to clinch the title. Brady was 23 of 33 for 236 yards and 2 touchdowns. Branch earned MVP honors with his Super Bowl-record-tying 11 catches. McNabb was 30 of 51 for 357 yards and 3 touchdowns, with 3 interceptions. Terrell Owens had 9 receptions for 122 yards.

New England (AFC)	0 7 7 10	— 24
Philadelphia (NFC)	0 7 7 7	— 21
Phil—	Smith 6 pass from McNabb (Akers kick) (9:55)	
NE—	Givens 4 pass from Brady (Vinatieri kick) (1:10)	
NE—	Vrabel 2 pass from Brady (Vinatieri kick) (11:04)	
Phil—	Westbrook 10 pass from McNabb (Akers kick) (3:35)	
NE—	Dillon 2 run (Vinatieri kick) (13:44)	
NE—	FG Vinatieri 22 (8:40)	
Phil—	G. Lewis 30 pass from McNabb (Akers kick) (1:48)	

SUPER BOWL XXXVIII

Reliant Stadium, Houston, Texas
February 1, 2004, Attendance: 71,525
NEW ENGLAND 32, CAROLINA 29—Adam Vinatieri kicked a 41-yard field goal with four seconds remaining as the Patriots won their second Super Bowl in three seasons. While it took a Super Bowl-record 26 minutes and 55 seconds for the first points to be scored, the teams combined for 868 yards (481 by New England) and the game also featured the high-

est scoring quarter (combined 37 points in the fourth). Vinatieri missed a 31-yard field goal on the Patriots' first possession, and had a 36-yard attempt blocked by Shane Burton with 6:00 left in the second quarter. But three plays later, Mike Vrabel sacked Jake Delhomme and forced him to fumble. Richard Seymour recovered at the Panthers' 20, and a 12-yard scramble by Tom Brady on third-and-7 set up his 5-yard touchdown pass to Deion Branch with 3:05 left in the first half. The Panthers responded with an 8-play, 95-yard drive capped by Delhomme's 39-yard perfectly placed touchdown pass to Steve Smith with 1:07 left in the half. Delhomme beat the blitz by lofting the pass deep down the left sideline. Brady's 52-yard pass to Branch with 37 seconds left in the half set up David Givens' 5-yard touchdown catch with 18 seconds left. New England squibbed the ensuing kickoff and Kris Mangum returned it 12 yards to the Panthers' 47. A 21-yard run by Stephen Davis set up John Kasay's 50-yard field goal as the half expired for a 14-10 New England lead. Neither team scored in the third quarter, but Antowain Smith's 2-yard touchdown run two plays into the final quarter capped a 71-yard drive and gave the Patriots a 21-10 lead. Undaunted, Carolina scored on its next two possessions. First, Delhomme completed passes of 18 and 22 yards to Smith to set up DeShaun Foster's 33-yard touchdown run to cut the deficit to 21-16 with 12:39 to play. Carolina went for the 2-point conversion, but Delhomme's pass was incomplete. New England marched to the Panthers' 9 with the ensuing kickoff, but Reggie Howard intercepted Brady's third-and-goal pass in the end zone. Two plays later, Delhomme rolled left and fired a Super Bowl-record 85-yard touchdown pass to Muhammad for a 22-21 lead with 6:53 left. Once again, the Panthers went for 2 points and Delhomme's pass was incomplete. New England drove 68 yards on its next possession, with Givens catching a 25-yard pass and 18-yard pass on third-and-9, to set up Brady's 1-yard touchdown pass to Vrabel, who was lined up as a tight end. A direct snap to Kevin Faulk resulted in a 2-point conversion for a 29-22 lead with 2:51 left. Delhomme completed passes of 19 yards to Muhammad and 31 yards to Ricky Proehl before finding Proehl from 12 yards with the tying touchdown with 1:08 remaining. Kasay's ensuing kickoff went out of bounds, giving New England the ball at their own 40. Five plays later, faced with third-and-3 from the Panthers' 40 with 14 seconds left, Brady fired a 17-yard pass to Branch to set up Vinatieri's Super Bowl-winning 41-yard field goal. Brady, who was named the Super Bowl most valuable player for the second time in his career, was 32 of 48 for 354 yards and 3 touchdowns, with 1 interception. Branch had 10 receptions for 143 yards.

Delhomme was 16 of 33 for 323 yards and 3 touchdowns, and Muhammad had 4 catches for 140 yards.

Carolina (NFC)	0 10 0 19 — 29
New England (AFC)	0 14 0 18 — 32

NE — Branch 5 pass from Brady (Vinatieri kick) (3:05)
Car — Smith 39 pass from Delhomme (Kasay kick) (1:07)
NE — Givens 5 pass from Brady (Vinatieri kick) (0:18)
Car — FG Kasay 50 (0:00)
NE — Smith 2 run (Vinatieri kick) (14:49)
Car — Foster 33 run (pass failed) (12:39)
Car — Muhammad 85 pass from Delhomme (pass failed) (6:53)
NE — Vrabel 1 pass from Brady (Faulk run) (2:51)
Car — Proehl 12 pass from Delhomme (Kasay kick) (1:08)
NE — FG Vinatieri 41 (0:04)

SUPER BOWL XXXVII

Qualcomm Stadium, San Diego, CA
January 26, 2003, Attendance: 67,603
TAMPA BAY 48, OAKLAND 21—The Buccaneers' defense intercepted 5 passes, 3 of which were returned for touchdowns, and recorded 5 sacks as Tampa Bay scored 34 unanswered points en route to its first Super Bowl victory. Charles Woodson intercepted Brad Johnson three plays into the game to give Oakland the ball at the Buccaneers' 36. But Simeon Rice sacked Rich Gannon on third down to force the Raiders to settle for Sebastian Janikowski's 40-yard field goal. On their next nine possessions, the Raiders registered just 2 first downs and did not run a play inside the Buccaneers' 40 as Tampa Bay scored the next 34 points. The Buccaneers answered Janikowski's field goal with Martín Gramatica's 31-yard boot to tie the game. An interception by Dexter Jackson set up Gramatica's go-ahead field goal early in the second quarter. Midway through the second quarter, a 25-yard punt return by Karl Williams and a 19-yard run by Michael Pittman led to Mike Alstott's 2-yard touchdown run. Late in the half, the Buccaneers drove 77 yards, aided by 3 defensive penalties and pass receptions of 16 and 12 yards by Alstott, to set up Brad Johnson's 5-yard touchdown pass to Keenan McCardell with 30 seconds left in the half, which gave Tampa Bay a 20-3 lead. With their first possession of the second half, the Buccaneers put together a 14-play, 89-yard drive that consumed 7:52 and was culminated by Johnson's 8-yard scoring toss to McCardell. Two plays later, Dwight Smith intercepted Gannon's pass and returned it 44 yards for a touchdown and a 34-3 lead with 4:47 left in the third quarter. Tampa Bay scored 4 touchdowns in a span of 16:37. Jerry Porter's 39-yard touchdown catch in the back of the end

zone made it 34-9. Less than three minutes later, Tim Johnson blocked Tom Tupa's punt. Eric Johnson caught the ball and dove into the end zone for a touchdown to cut the deficit to 34-15 with 14:16 remaining. The Buccaneers drove deep downfield again, but Tupa mishandled the snap for a field-goal attempt, allowing the Raiders to regain possession. Gannon hit Jerry Rice with a 48-yard touchdown pass with 6:06 left to trim the lead to 34-21. A 9-yard pass by Johnson to Alstott on third-and-7 allowed Tampa Bay to take another two minutes off the clock before Tupa punted with 2:44 remaining. On third-and-18 from the Raiders' 29, Derrick Brooks intercepted Gannon's pass and raced 44 yards down the left sideline for a touchdown with 1:18 remaining to give Tampa Bay a commanding 41-21 lead. Smith intercepted a tipped pass and returned it 50 yards for a touchdown with two seconds left to finish the scoring. Johnson was 18 of 34 for 215 yards and 2 touchdowns, with 1 interception. Pittman had 29 carries for 124 yards. Gannon was 24 of 44 for 272 yards and 2 touchdowns, with a Super Bowl record 5 interceptions. Jackson, who had the first 2 interceptions, 1 of which led to the go-ahead field goal, was named the game's most valuable player.

Oakland (AFC)	3 0 6 12 — 21
Tampa Bay (NFC)	3 17 14 14 — 48

Oak — FG Janikowski 40 (10:40)
TB — FG Gramatica 31 (7:51)
TB — FG Gramatica 43 (11:16)
TB — Alstott 2 run (Gramatica kick) (6:24)
TB — McCardell 5 pass from B. Johnson (Gramatica kick) (0:30)
TB — McCardell 8 pass from B. Johnson (Gramatica kick) (5:30)
TB — D. Smith 44 interception return (Gramatica kick) (4:47)
Oak — Porter 39 pass from Gannon (pass failed) (2:14)
Oak — E. Johnson 13 return of blocked punt (pass failed) (14:16)
Oak — Rice 48 pass from Gannon (pass failed) (6:06)
TB — Brooks 44 interception return (Gramatica kick) (1:18)
TB — D. Smith 50 interception return (Gramatica kick) (0:02)

SUPER BOWL XXXVI

Louisiana Superdome, New Orleans, LA
February 3, 2002, Attendance: 72,922
NEW ENGLAND 20, ST. LOUIS 17—Adam Vinatieri's 48-yard field goal as time expired gave the New England Patriots their first Super Bowl title. The Rams outgained the Patriots 427-267 in total yards, but the Patriots forced 3 turnovers, which resulted in 17 points, while committing no turnovers. Jeff Wilkins' 50-yard field goal

capped a 10-play, 48-yard drive midway through the first quarter to give the Rams a 3-0 lead. The first turnover came with 8:49 left in the second quarter, when Ty Law stepped in front of an out-pattern pass intended for Isaac Bruce and raced 47 yards untouched down the left sideline into the end zone. Late in the first half, Kurt Warner completed a 15-yard pass to Ricky Proehl to the Patriots' 40, but Antwan Harris forced Proehl to fumble and Terrell Buckley recovered. Five plays later, Tom Brady's 8-yard touchdown pass to David Patten with 31 seconds left in the quarter gave New England a 14-3 halftime lead. Late in the third quarter, Torry Holt slipped coming off the line of scrimmage, and Otis Smith intercepted Warner's pass and returned it 30 yards to the Rams' 33 to set up Vinatieri's 37-yard field goal and a 17-3 lead. The Rams responded by driving to the Patriots' 3. On fourth-and-goal, Warner scrambled, was tackled by Roman Phifer, and fumbled. Tebucky Jones picked up the ball and raced the length of the field for an apparent touchdown, but the play was negated by Willie McGinest's holding penalty. Warner scored two plays later to trim the deficit to 17-10 with 9:31 left. The Patriots went three and out on their next two possessions, giving the Rams the ball on their 45-yard-line with 1:51 left. Warner completed an 18-yard pass to Az-Zahir Hakim and an 11-yard pass to Yo Murphy before connecting on a 26-yard touchdown pass to Proehl with 1:30 left to tie the game. Operating without any time outs, Brady completed 3 short passes to J.R. Redmond to reach the Patriots' 41 with 33 seconds left. After an incompletion, Brady completed 23- and 16-yard passes to Troy Brown and Jermaine Wiggins, respectively, to reach the Rams' 30, and then spiked the ball with 7 seconds remaining. Vinatieri drilled the 48-yard field-goal attempt, marking the first time in Super Bowl history the game had been won on the final play. Brady, who earned most valuable player honors, was 16 of 27 for 145 yards and 1 touchdown. Warner was 28 of 44 for 365 yards and 1 touchdown, with 2 interceptions.

St. Louis (NFC)	3	0	0	14 — 17
New England (AFC)	0	14	3	3 — 20

StL — FG Wilkins 50 (3:10)
NE — Law 47 interception return (Vinatieri kick) (8:49)
NE — Patten 8 pass from Brady (Vinatieri kick) (0:31)
NE — FG Vinatieri 37 (1:18)
StL — Warner 2 run (Wilkins kick) (9:31)
StL — Proehl 26 pass from Warner (Wilkins kick) (1:30)
NE — FG Vinatieri 48 (0:00)

SUPER BOWL XXXV
Raymond James Stadium, Tampa, Florida
January 28, 2001, Attendance: 71,921
BALTIMORE 34, N.Y. GIANTS 7—The

Ravens' defense completed a dominating season by permitting just 152 yards, forcing 5 turnovers, recording 4 sacks, and not allowing an offensive touchdown en route to the franchise's first Super Bowl victory. Jermaine Lewis' punt return into Giants' territory midway through the first quarter was followed two plays later by Trent Dilfer's 38-yard touchdown pass to Brandon Stokley, which gave the Ravens a 7-0 lead. Early in the second quarter, Jessie Armstead intercepted a short pass by Dilfer and returned it 43 yards for a touchdown, but the play was nullified by a penalty. Dilfer's 36-yard pass to Qadry Ismail in the second quarter set up Matt Stover's 47-yard field goal with 1:48 left in the half. Tiki Barber's 27-yard run gave the Giants their deepest penetration of the game, to the Ravens' 29, but Chris McAlister intercepted Kerry Collins' pass on the next play to preserve a 10-0 lead. In the third quarter, Duane Starks stepped in front of Amani Toomer and intercepted Collins' pass. Starks returned it 49 yards untouched for a 17-0 lead. The Giants immediately cut the lead to 10 points when Ron Dixon returned the ensuing kickoff 97 yards for a touchdown. However, Jermaine Lewis then matched Dixon's kickoff return as he cut across the field and raced 84 yards for a 24-7 lead with 3:13 left in the third quarter. The 3 touchdowns in 36 seconds were a Super Bowl record. The Giants gained just 1 first down on their final four possessions. Jamal Lewis' 3-yard touchdown run midway through the fourth quarter gave Baltimore a 31-7 lead, and Robert Bailey recovered Dixon's fumble on the ensuing kickoff return to set up Stover's 34-yard field goal with 5:27 remaining to finish the scoring. Dilfer completed 12 of 25 passes for 153 yards and 1 touchdown. Jamal Lewis had 27 carries for 102 yards. Collins was 15 of 39 for 112 yards, with 4 interceptions. Ray Lewis was named Super Bowl most valuable player.

Baltimore (AFC)	7	3	14	10 — 34
N.Y. Giants (NFC)	0	0	7	0 — 7

Balt — Stokley 38 pass from Dilfer (Stover kick) (6:50)
Balt — FG Stover 47 (1:41)
Balt — Starks 49 interception return (Stover kick) (3:49)
NYG — Dixon 97 kickoff return (Daluiso kick) (3:31)
Balt — Je. Lewis 84 kickoff return (Stover kick) (3:13)
Balt — Ja. Lewis 3 run (Stover kick) (8:45)
Balt — FG Stover 34 (5:27)

SUPER BOWL XXXIV
Georgia Dome, Atlanta, Georgia
January 30, 2000, Attendance: 72,625
ST. LOUIS 23, TENNESSEE 16—Mike Jones tackled Kevin Dyson at the 1-yard line as time expired, preserving the Rams' first-ever Super Bowl title. The Rams

drove inside the Titans' 20 with each of their first six possessions, but compiled just 3 field goals and 1 touchdown to take a 16-0 lead. Holder Mike Horan's bobbled snap averted a 35-yard field-goal attempt to conclude the Rams' first drive. The Titans responded with a 42-yard drive, their longest of the half, but Al Del Greco missed a 47-yard attempt. Jeff Wilkins added 3 field goals and missed a 34-yard attempt while the Titans did not threaten the rest of the half, giving the Rams a 9-0 lead at intermission despite outgaining the Titans in total yards (294-89). Tennessee drove 43 yards with the second half's opening kickoff, but Todd Lyght blocked Del Greco's 47-yard attempt to keep the Titans off the board. Kurt Warner's 31-yard pass to Isaac Bruce keyed the ensuing drive that was capped by Warner's 9-yard touchdown pass to Torry Holt with 7:20 left in the third quarter to give the Rams a 16-0 lead. The Titans responded with touchdown drives in excess of seven minutes on each of their next two possessions. Steve McNair's 23-yard scramble set up Eddie George's 1-yard run in the final minute of the third quarter. McNair's 2-point conversion pass to Frank Wycheck was incomplete, but the Titans' defense forced a punt and the offense drove 79 yards in 13 plays, highlighted by 21-yard passes from McNair to Isaac Byrd and Jackie Harris, and capped by George's 2-yard run to cut the deficit to 16-13 with 7:21 remaining. The Rams once again failed to get a first down, and following a punt, the Titans needed just 28 yards to set up Del Greco's game-tying 43-yard kick with 2:12 left. On the next play from scrimmage, Warner fired a deep pass down the right sideline to Bruce, who caught the ball at the Titans' 38, cut toward the inside, and outran the defense to the end zone to give the Rams a 23-16 lead with 1:54 left. The Titans drove downfield, and McNair avoided a sack and completed a 16-yard pass to Kevin Dyson at the Rams' 10 with six seconds remaining. With no timeouts, McNair attempted a quick pass to a slanting Dyson, who caught the ball in stride at the Rams' 3. However, Jones reacted quickly and stepped up to tackle Dyson at the 1-yard line as time expired. Warner, who was named the game's most valuable player, was 24 of 45 for a Super Bowl-record 414 yards and 2 touchdowns. Bruce had 6 catches for 162 yards, and Holt had 7 for 109 yards. McNair was 22 of 36 for 214 yards. The Titans were the first team in Super Bowl history to come back from a 16-point deficit.

St. Louis (NFC)	3	6	7	7 — 23
Tennessee (AFC)	0	0	6	10 — 16

StL — FG Wilkins 27 (3:00)
StL — FG Wilkins 29 (4:16)
StL — FG Wilkins 28 (0:15)
StL — Holt 9 pass from Warner (Wilkins kick) (3:59)

Tenn — George 1 run (pass failed) (0:14)

Tenn — George 2 run (Del Greco kick) (7:21)

Tenn — FG Del Greco 43 (2:12)

StL — Bruce 73 pass from Warner (Wilkins kick) (1:54)

SUPER BOWL XXXIII

Pro Player Stadium, South Florida
January 31, 1999, Attendance: 74,803
DENVER 34, ATLANTA 19—John Elway, in his last game, passed for 336 yards and ran for a touchdown to earn most valuable player honors as the Broncos became the first AFC team to win consecutive Super Bowls since the Steelers won XIII and XIV. A 25-yard pass interference penalty on Ray Crockett assisted the Falcons' nine-play, 48-yard game-opening drive that was capped by Morten Andersen's 32-yard field goal. Elway's 41-yard pass to Rod Smith kept alive Denver's ensuing drive and led to Howard Griffith's 1-yard touchdown run. Ronnie Bradford's interception and return to the Broncos' 35 late in the first quarter gave Atlanta excellent field position. However, Jamal Anderson was stopped for no gain on third-and-1 and thrown for a 2-yard loss on fourth down. Denver capitalized on its defensive effort with Jason Elam's 26-yard field goal. The Falcons responded by driving to the Broncos' 8, but Andersen's 26-yard field-goal attempt sailed wide right and on the next play, Elway fired an 80-yard touchdown pass to Smith to turn a possible 10-6 game into a 17-3 Broncos lead. Andersen's 28-yard field goal and 2 misses by Elam on the Broncos' first two second-half possessions gave Atlanta an opportunity to climb back into the game. However, Darrien Gordon dashed the Falcons' hopes with interceptions on consecutive possessions inside the Broncos' 20 to stop drives and set up Broncos touchdowns. Gordon returned the first interception, on a tipped pass, 58 yards to the Falcons' 24 to set up Griffith's second touchdown five plays later, and picked the second pass off at the Broncos' 2 and returned it 50 yards. Terrell Davis turned a short pass into a 39-yard gain, and Elway scored two plays later to give Denver a 31-6 lead. Tim Dwight returned the ensuing kickoff for a touchdown, and, after a field goal by Elam, the Falcons' offense scored with 2:04 remaining on Chandler's 3-yard pass to Terance Mathis. Byron Chamberlain recovered the ensuing onside kick, but Tyrone Braxton recovered Anderson's fumble at the Falcons' 33 with 1:30 remaining to ice the game. The Falcons drove inside the Broncos' 30 seven times, but tallied just 1 touchdown and 2 field goals, throwing 2 interceptions, missing 1 field goal, and turning the ball over 1 time on downs during the other possessions. Elway was 18 of 29 for 336 yards and 1 touchdown, with 1 intercep-

tion. Davis had 25 carries for 102 yards. Smith had 5 receptions for 152 yards. Chandler was 19 of 35 for 219 yards and 1 touchdown, with 3 interceptions.

Denver (AFC)	7 10 0 17	— 34
Atlanta (NFC)	3 3 0 13	— 19

Atl — FG Andersen 32 (9:35)

Den — Griffith 1 run (Elam kick) (3:55)

Den — FG Elam 26 (9:17)

Den — R. Smith 80 pass from Elway (Elam kick) (4:54)

Atl — FG Andersen 28 (2:25)

Den — Griffith 1 run (Elam kick) (14:56)

Den — Elway 3 run (Elam kick) (11:20)

Atl — Dwight 94 kickoff return (Andersen kick) (11:01)

Den — FG Elam 37 (7:08)

Atl — Mathis 3 pass from Chandler (pass failed) (2:04)

SUPER BOWL XXXII

Qualcomm Stadium, San Diego, California
January 25, 1998, Attendance: 68,912
DENVER 31, GREEN BAY 24—Terrell Davis rushed for 157 yards and a Super Bowl-record 3 touchdowns to lead the Broncos to their first NFL championship and break the NFC's streak of Super Bowl victories at 13. The defending Super Bowl champion Packers took the opening kickoff and marched 76 yards in just over four minutes, scoring the first points on Brett Favre's 22-yard touchdown pass to Antonio Freeman. The Broncos responded with a 10-play, 58-yard drive capped by Davis' 1-yard run to tie the game. Tyrone Braxton intercepted Favre two plays later, and John Elway scored on a third-and-goal play to begin the second quarter. Steve Atwater forced Favre to fumble three plays later, and Neil Smith recovered at the Packers' 33. Jason Elam converted a 51-yard field goal, the second longest in Super Bowl history, to give the Broncos a 17-7 lead with 12:21 left in the half. After an exchange of punts, the Packers produced a 17-play, 95-yard drive that consumed 7:26 and finished with Favre's 6-yard touchdown pass to Mark Chmura on third-and-5 with 12 seconds left in the half. Tyrone Williams forced and recovered Davis' fumble at the Broncos' 26 on the first play from scrimmage in the second half. However, the Broncos' defense kept the Packers out of the end zone as Ryan Longwell's 27-yard field goal tied the game with 11:59 left in the third quarter. After another exchange of punts, Elway's 36-yard pass to Ed McCaffrey keyed a 13-play, 92-yard drive capped by Davis' 1-yard touchdown run with 34 seconds left in the third quarter. Tim McKyer recovered Freeman's fumble at the Packers' 22 on the ensuing kickoff return, giving the Broncos a golden opportunity, but Eugene Robinson intercepted Elway's pass in the end zone on the next play.

Sparked by Robinson's play, the Packers took just four plays, three on passes to Freeman, to score the tying touchdown with 13:32 remaining. Each defense stiffened, forcing two punts, but the Broncos got great field position following Craig Hentrich's 39-yard punt to the Packers' 49 with 3:27 left and the score tied 24-24. Davis rushed for 2 yards on the first play, but Darrius Holland's 15-yard facemask penalty moved the ball to the Packers' 32. Elway threw a 23-yard pass to Howard Griffith two plays later, and after a holding penalty, Davis rushed 17 yards to the Packers' 1 with 1:47 left. After a timeout, Davis waltzed into the end zone to give Denver a 31-24 lead with 1:45 remaining. Freeman returned the kickoff 22 yards to the Broncos' 30, and Favre completed 22- and 13-yard screen passes to Dorsey Levens to reach the Broncos' 35 with 1:04 left. But after a 4-yard pass to Levens and incompletions to Freeman and Brooks, John Mobley knocked away Favre's pass to Chmura with 32 seconds left to give the Broncos the Vince Lombardi Trophy. Elway was 12 of 22 for 123 yards, with 1 interception. Favre was 25 of 42 for 256 yards and 1 touchdown, with 1 interception. Freeman had 9 receptions for 126 yards. Davis was named the game's most valuable player.

Green Bay (NFC)	7 7 3 7	— 24
Denver (AFC)	7 10 7 7	— 31

GB — Freeman 22 pass from Favre (Longwell kick) (10:58)

Den — Davis 1 run (Elam kick) (5:39)

Den — Elway 1 run (Elam kick) (14:55)

Den — FG Elam 51 (12:21)

GB — Chmura 6 pass from Favre (Longwell kick) (0:12)

GB — FG Longwell 27 (11:59)

Den — Davis 1 run (Elam kick) (0:34)

GB — Freeman 13 pass from Favre (Longwell kick) (13:32)

Den — Davis 1 run (Elam kick) (1:45)

SUPER BOWL XXXI

Louisiana Superdome, New Orleans, LA
January 26, 1997, Attendance: 72,301
GREEN BAY 35, NEW ENGLAND 21—Desmond Howard returned a kickoff 99 yards for a touchdown and Brett Favre passed for 2 touchdowns and ran for a score as the Packers won their first Super Bowl in twenty-nine years. Howard, en route to garnering the MVP trophy, equaled a Super Bowl record with 244 total return yards. It was Favre's arm that struck first, as he hit Andre Rison on a 54-yard touchdown pass on the Packers' second play from scrimmage to take a 7-0 lead. Two plays later Doug Evans made a diving interception of Drew Bledsoe's pass at the 28-yard line, setting up Chris Jacke's field goal and giving the Packers a 10-0 lead just 6:18 into the Super Bowl. The Patriots answered with touchdowns on their next two posses-

sions. Craig Newsome's pass interference penalty set up the first touchdown and a 44-yard completion from Bledsoe to Terry Glenn preceding Ben Coates' touchdown gave New England its first and only lead. The 24 combined first quarter points were the most in Super Bowl history. Green Bay struck again 56 seconds into the second quarter as Favre hit Antonio Freeman with a Super Bowl-record 81-yard touchdown bomb. Jacke booted his second field goal on Green Bay's next possession. After a Mike Prior interception, Favre orchestrated a 74-yard, nearly 6-minute drive that concluded with a diving Favre touching the ball against the pylon to give Green Bay a 27-14 halftime lead. Curtis Martin brought the Patriots to within a score by running in from 18 yards out with 3:27 left in the third quarter. But Howard broke the Patriots' spirit by returning the ensuing kickoff a Super Bowl-record 99 yards. Favre found Mark Chmura for the 2-point conversion to finish the scoring. Bledsoe was intercepted twice in the fourth quarter as the Patriots never crossed midfield in 4 fourth-quarter possessions. Reggie White set a Super Bowl record with 3 sacks. Favre completed 14 of 27 passes for 246 yards, with no interceptions. Bledsoe completed 11 more passes than Favre, but for just 7 more yards, and threw 4 interceptions.

New England (AFC) 14 0 7 0 — 21
Green Bay (NFC)   10 17 8 0 — 35

GB — Rison 54 pass from Favre (Jacke kick) (11:28)
GB — FG Jacke 37 (8:42)
NE — Byars 1 pass from Bledsoe (Vinatieri kick) (6:35)
NE — Coates 4 pass from Bledsoe (Vinatieri kick) (2:33)
GB — Freeman 81 pass from Favre (Jacke kick) (14:04)
GB — FG Jacke 31 (8:15)
GB — Favre 2 run (Jacke kick) (1:11)
NE — Martin 18 run (Vinatieri kick) (3:27)
GB — Howard 99 kickoff return (Chmura pass from Favre) (3:10)

SUPER BOWL XXX
Sun Devil Stadium, Tempe, Arizona
January 28, 1996, Attendance: 76,347
DALLAS 27, PITTSBURGH 17—Cornerback Larry Brown's 2 interceptions led to 14 second-half points and helped lift the Cowboys to their third Super Bowl victory in the last four seasons and their record-tying fifth title overall. Brown's interceptions foiled the comeback efforts of the Steelers, and earned him the Pete Rozelle Trophy as the game's most valuable player. Dallas scored on each of its first three possessions, taking a 13-0 lead on Troy Aikman's 3-yard touchdown pass to Jay Novacek and a pair of field goals by Chris Boniol. Neil O'Donnell's 6-yard touch-

down pass to Yancey Thigpen 13 seconds before halftime pulled Pittsburgh within 6 points, and the Steelers had the ball near midfield midway through the third quarter. But O'Donnell's third-down pass was intercepted by Brown at the Cowboys' 38-yard line, and his 44-yard return carried to Pittsburgh's 18. After Aikman's 17-yard completion to Michael Irvin, Emmitt Smith ran 1 yard for the touchdown that put Dallas ahead again by 13 points. The Steelers rallied, though, behind Norm Johnson's 46-yard field goal, a successful surprise onside kick, and Byron (Bam) Morris' 1-yard touchdown run with 6:36 to play in the game. And when they forced a punt and took possession at their own 32-yard line trailing only 20-17 with 4:15 remaining, it appeared they might have a chance to break the NFC's recent domination in the Super Bowl. But on second down, Brown struck again, intercepting O'Donnell's pass at the 39 and returning it 33 yards to the 6. Two plays later, Smith barreled over from 4 yards out for the clinching touchdown with 3:43 to go. Pittsburgh limited the Cowboys' powerful running game to only 56 yards and enjoyed a whopping 201-61 advantage in total yards in the second half, but could not overcome the 3 interceptions (another came on the game's final play) thrown by O'Donnell, the NFL's career leader for fewest interceptions per pass attempt. In all, O'Donnell completed 28 of 49 passes for 239 yards. Morris rushed for a game-high 73 yards on 19 carries. For Dallas, Aikman completed 15 of 23 pass attempts for 209 yards. The Cowboys' victory was the twelfth in a row for NFC teams over AFC teams in the Super Bowl.

Dallas (NFC)   10 3 7 7 — 27
Pittsburgh (AFC) 0 7 0 10 — 17

Dall — FG Boniol 42 (12:05)
Dall — Novacek 3 pass from Aikman (Boniol kick) (5:23)
Dall — FG Boniol 35 (6:03)
Pitt — Thigpen 6 pass from O'Donnell (N. Johnson kick) (0:13)
Dall — E. Smith 1 run (Boniol kick) (6:42)
Pitt — FG N. Johnson 46 (11:20)
Pitt — Morris 1 run (N. Johnson kick) (6:36)
Dall — E. Smith 4 run (Boniol kick) (3:43)

SUPER BOWL XXIX
Joe Robbie Stadium, South Florida
January 29, 1995, Attendance: 74,107
SAN FRANCISCO 49, SAN DIEGO 26—Steve Young passed for a record 6 touchdowns, and the 49ers became the first team to win five Super Bowls when they routed the Chargers. Young, the game's most valuable player, directed an explosive offense that generated 7 touchdowns, 28 first downs, and 455 total yards. He completed 24 of 36 passes for

325 yards, and broke the record of 5 touchdown passes set by former 49ers quarterback Joe Montana in Super Bowl XXIV. San Francisco wasted little time scoring, taking the lead for good on Young's 44-yard touchdown pass to Jerry Rice only three plays and 1:24 into the game. The next time they had the ball, the 49ers marched 79 yards in four plays, taking a 14-0 lead when Young teamed with running back Ricky Watters on a 51-yard touchdown pass with 10:05 still to play in the opening period. San Diego then put together its most impressive possession of the game, a 13-play, 78-yard drive that consumed more than 7 minutes and was capped by Natrone Means' 1-yard touchdown run, to cut its deficit to 14-7 late in the quarter. But San Francisco countered with a 70-yard drive of its own, and Young's 5-yard touchdown pass to fullback William Floyd made it 21-7. Young's fourth touchdown pass of the half, 8 yards to Watters 4:44 before halftime, increased the advantage to 28-7, and the Chargers could get no closer than 18 points after that. Watters, who ran 9 yards for a touchdown in the third quarter, equaled the Super Bowl record with 3 touchdowns. Rice also scored 3 touchdowns (the second time in his career he'd done that in a Super Bowl) while catching 10 passes for 149 yards. He established career records for receptions, yards, and touchdowns in a Super Bowl. Young, who scrambled 21 yards and 15 yards to set up touchdowns in the first half, was the game's leading rusher with 49 yards on 5 carries. San Diego's Means, who rushed for 1,350 yards during the regular season, was limited to 33 yards on 13 attempts. Chargers quarterback Stan Humphries completed 24 of 49 passes for 275 yards. Rookie Andre Coleman became only the third player in Super Bowl history to return a kickoff for a touchdown, going 98 yards in the third quarter. The 75 points scored by the two teams established another record, breaking the previous mark of 69 set in Dallas' 52-17 victory over Buffalo in XXVII. The 49ers' victory was the eleventh straight for NFC teams over AFC teams in the Super Bowl.

San Diego (AFC)   7 3 8 8 — 26
San Francisco (NFC) 14 14 14 7 — 49

SF — Rice 44 pass from S. Young (Brien kick) (13:36)
SF — Watters 51 pass from S. Young (Brien kick) (10:05)
SD — Means 1 run (Carney kick) (2:44)
SF — Floyd 5 pass from S. Young (Brien kick) (13:02)
SF — Watters 8 pass from S. Young (Brien kick) (4:44)
SD — FG Carney 31 (1:44)
SF — Watters 9 run (Brien kick) (9:35)
SF — Rice 15 pass from S. Young (Brien kick) (3:18)

SD — Coleman 98 kickoff return (Seay pass from Humphries) (3:01)

SF — Rice 7 pass from S. Young (Brien kick) (13:49)

SD — Martin 30 pass from Humphries (Pupunu pass from Humphries) (2:25)

SUPER BOWL XXVIII

Georgia Dome, Atlanta, Georgia
January 30, 1994, Attendance: 72,817
DALLAS 30, BUFFALO 13—Emmitt Smith rushed for 132 yards and 2 second-half touchdowns to power the Cowboys to their second consecutive NFL title. By winning, Dallas joined San Francisco and Pittsburgh as the only franchises with four Super Bowl victories. The Bills, meanwhile, extended a dubious string by losing in the Super Bowl for the fourth consecutive year. To win, the Cowboys had to rally from a 13-6 halftime deficit. Buffalo had forged its lead on Thurman Thomas' 4-yard touchdown run and a pair of field goals by Steve Christie, including a 54-yard kick, the longest in Super Bowl history. But just 55 seconds into the second half, Thomas was stripped of the ball by Dallas defensive tackle Leon Lett. Safety James Washington recovered and weaved his way 46 yards for a touchdown to tie the game at 13-13. After forcing the Bills to punt, the Cowboys began their next possession on their 36-yard line and Smith, the game's most valuable player, took over. He carried 7 times for 61 yards on the ensuing 8-play, 64-yard drive, capping the march with a 15-yard touchdown run to give Dallas the lead for good with 8:42 remaining in the third quarter. Early in the fourth quarter, Washington intercepted Jim Kelly's pass and returned it 12 yards to Buffalo's 34. A penalty moved the ball back to the 39, but Smith carried twice for 10 yards and caught a screen pass for 9, and quarterback Troy Aikman completed a 16-yard pass to Alvin Harper to give the Cowboys a first-and-goal at the 6. Smith took it from there, cracking the end zone on fourth-and-goal from the 1 to put Dallas ahead 27-13 with 9:50 remaining. Eddie Murray's third field goal, from 20 yards with 2:50 left, ended any doubt about the game's outcome. Smith had 30 carries in all, with 19 of his attempts and 92 yards coming after intermission. Washington, normally a reserve who played most of the game because the Cowboys used five defensive backs to combat the Bills' No-Huddle offense, had 11 tackles and forced another fumble by Thomas in the first quarter. Aikman completed 19 of 27 passes for 207 yards. Buffalo's Kelly completed a Super Bowl-record 31 passes in 50 attempts for 260 yards. Dallas, the first team in NFL history to begin the regular season 0-2 and go on to win the Super Bowl, also became the fifth to win back-to-back titles, following

Green Bay, Miami, Pittsburgh (the Steelers did it twice), and San Francisco. Buffalo became the third team, along with Minnesota and Denver, to lose four Super Bowls. The Cowboys' victory was the tenth in succession for the NFC over the AFC.

Dallas (NFC)	6	0	14	10	— 30
Buffalo (AFC)	3	10	0	0	— 13

Dall — FG Murray 41 (12:41)
Buff — FG Christie 54 (10:19)
Dall — FG Murray 24 (3:55)
Buff — Thomas 4 run (Christie kick) (12:26)
Buff — FG Christie 28 (0:00)
Dall — Washington 46 fumble return (Murray kick) (14:05)
Dall — E. Smith 15 run (Murray kick) (8:42)
Dall — E. Smith 1 run (Murray kick) (9:50)
Dall — FG Murray 20 (2:50)

SUPER BOWL XXVII

Rose Bowl, Pasadena, California
January 31, 1993, Attendance: 98,374
DALLAS 52, BUFFALO 17—Troy Aikman passed for 4 touchdowns, Emmitt Smith rushed for 108 yards, and the Cowboys converted 9 turnovers into 35 points while coasting to the victory. Dallas' win was its third in its record sixth Super Bowl appearance; the Bills became the first team to drop three in succession. Buffalo led 7-0 until the first 2 of its record number of turnovers helped the Cowboys take the lead for good late in the opening quarter. First, Dallas safety James Washington intercepted Jim Kelly's pass and returned it 13 yards to the Bills' 47, setting up Aikman's 23-yard touchdown pass to tight end Jay Novacek with 1:36 remaining in the period. On the next play from scrimmage, Kelly was sacked by Charles Haley and fumbled at the Bills' 2-yard line where the Cowboys' Jimmie Jones picked up the loose ball and ran 2 yards for a touchdown. Dallas, which recovered 5 fumbles and intercepted 4 passes, struck just as quickly late in the first half, when Aikman tossed 19- and 18-yard touchdown passes to Michael Irvin 18 seconds apart to give the Cowboys a 28-10 lead at intermission. The second score was set up when Bills running back Thurman Thomas lost a fumble at his 19-yard line. Buffalo scored for the last time when backup quarterback Frank Reich, playing because Kelly was injured while attempting to pass midway through the second quarter, threw a 40-yard touchdown pass to Don Beebe on the final play of the third period to trim the deficit to 31-17. But Dallas put the game out of reach by scoring three times in a span of 2:33 of the fourth quarter. Aikman, the game's most valuable player, completed 22 of 30 passes for 273 yards. The victory was the ninth in succession for the NFC over the AFC.

Buffalo (AFC)	7	3	7	0	— 17
Dallas (NFC)	14	14	3	21	— 52

Buff — Thomas 2 run (Christie kick) (10:00)
Dall — Novacek 23 pass from Aikman (Elliott kick) (1:36)
Dall — J. Jones 2 fumble recovery return (Elliott kick) (1:21)
Buff — FG Christie 21 (3:24)
Dall — Irvin 19 pass from Aikman (Elliott kick) (1:54)
Dall — Irvin 18 pass from Aikman (Elliott kick) (1:36)
Dall — FG Elliott 20 (8:21)
Buff — Beebe 40 pass from Reich (Christie kick) (0:00)
Dall — Harper 45 pass from Aikman (Elliott kick) (10:04)
Dall — E. Smith 10 run (Elliott kick) (8:12)
Dall — Norton 9 fumble recovery return (Elliott kick) (7:31)

SUPER BOWL XXVI

Metrodome, Minneapolis, Minnesota
January 26, 1992, Attendance: 63,130
WASHINGTON 37, BUFFALO 24—Mark Rypien passed for 292 yards and 2 touchdowns as the Redskins overwhelmed the Bills to win their third Super Bowl in the past 10 years. Rypien, the game's most valuable player, completed 18 of 33 passes, including a 10-yard scoring strike to Earnest Byner and a 30-yard touchdown to Gary Clark. The latter came late in the third quarter after Buffalo had trimmed a 24-0 deficit to 24-10, and effectively put the game out of reach. Washington went on to lead by as much as 37-10 before the Bills made it close with a pair of touchdowns in the final six minutes. Though the Redskins struggled early, converting their first three drives inside the Bills' 20-yard line into only 3 points, they built a 17-0 halftime lead. And they made it 24-0 just 16 seconds into the second half, after Kurt Gouveia intercepted Buffalo quarterback Jim Kelly's pass on the first play of the third quarter and returned it 23 yards to the Bills' 2. One play later, Gerald Riggs scored his second touchdown of the game to make it 24-0. Kelly, forced to bring Buffalo from behind, completed 28 of a Super Bowl-record 58 passes for 275 yards and 2 touchdowns, but was intercepted 4 times. Bills running back Thurman Thomas, who had an AFC-high 1,407 yards rushing and an NFL-best 2,038 total yards from scrimmage during the regular season, ran for only 13 yards on 10 carries and was limited to 27 yards on 4 receptions. Clark had 7 catches for 114 yards and Art Monk added 7 for 113 for the Redskins, who amassed 417 yards of total offense while limiting the explosive Bills to 283. Washington's Joe Gibbs became only the third head coach to win three Super Bowls.

Washington (NFC)	0 17 14 6	— 37
Buffalo (AFC)	0 0 10 14	— 24

Wash — FG Lohmiller 34 (13:02)
Wash — Byner 10 pass from Rypien (Lohmiller kick) (9:54)
Wash — Riggs 1 run (Lohmiller kick) (7:17)
Wash — Riggs 2 run (Lohmiller kick) (14:44)
Buff — FG Norwood 21 (11:59)
Buff — Thomas 1 run (Norwood kick) (5:58)
Wash — Clark 30 pass from Rypien (Lohmiller kick) (1:24)
Wash — FG Lohmiller 25 (14:54)
Wash — FG Lohmiller 39 (11:36)
Buff — Metzelaars 2 pass from Kelly (Norwood kick) (5:59)
Buff — Beebe 4 pass from Kelly (Norwood kick) (3:55)

SUPER BOWL XXV
Tampa Stadium, Tampa, Florida
January 27, 1991, Attendance: 73,813
NEW YORK GIANTS 20, BUFFALO 19—
The NFC champion New York Giants won their second Super Bowl in five years with a 20-19 victory over AFC titlist Buffalo. New York, employing its ball-control offense, had possession for 40 minutes, 33 seconds, a Super Bowl record. The Bills, who scored 95 points in their previous two playoff games leading to Super Bowl XXV, had the ball for less than eight minutes in the second half and just 19:27 for the game. Fourteen of New York's 73 plays came on its initial drive of the third quarter, which covered 75 yards and consumed a Super Bowl-record 9:29 before running back Ottis Anderson ran 1 yard for a touchdown. Giants quarterback Jeff Hostetler kept the long drive going by converting three third-down plays—an 11-yard pass to running back David Meggett on third-and-eight, a 14-yard toss to wide receiver Mark Ingram on third-and-13, and a 9-yard pass to Howard Cross on third-and-four—to give New York a 17-12 lead in the third quarter. Buffalo jumped to a 12-3 lead midway through the second quarter before Hostetler completed a 14-yard scoring strike to wide receiver Stephen Baker to close the score to 12-10 at halftime. Buffalo's Thurman Thomas ran 31 yards for a touchdown on the opening play of the fourth quarter to help Buffalo recapture the lead 19-17. Matt Bahr's 21-yard field goal gave the Giants a 20-19 lead, but Buffalo's Scott Norwood had a chance to win the game with seconds remaining before his 47-yard field-goal attempt sailed wide right. Hostetler completed 20 of 32 passes for 222 yards and 1 touchdown. Anderson rushed 21 times for 102 yards and 1 touchdown to capture most-valuable-player honors. Thomas totaled 190 scrimmage yards, rushing 15 times for 135 yards and catching 5 passes for 55 yards.

Buffalo (AFC)	3 9 0 7	— 19
N.Y. Giants (NFC)	3 7 7 3	— 20

NYG — FG Bahr 28 (7:14)
Buff — FG Norwood 23 (5:51)
Buff — D. Smith 1 run (Norwood kick) (12:30)
Buff — Safety, B. Smith tackled Hostetler in end zone (8:27)
NYG — Baker 14 pass from Hostetler (Bahr kick) (0:25)
NYG — Anderson 1 run (Bahr kick) (5:31)
Buff — Thomas 31 run (Norwood kick) (14:52)
NYG — FG Bahr 21 (7:20)

SUPER BOWL XXIV
Louisiana Superdome, New Orleans, LA
January 28, 1990, Attendance: 72,919
SAN FRANCISCO 55, DENVER 10—NFC titlist San Francisco won its fourth Super Bowl championship with a 55-10 victory over AFC champion Denver. The 49ers, who also won Super Bowls XVI, XIX, and XXIII, tied the Pittsburgh Steelers for most Super Bowl victories. The Steelers captured Super Bowls IX, X, XIII, and XIV. San Francisco's 55 points broke the previous Super Bowl scoring mark of 46 points by Chicago in Super Bowl XX. San Francisco scored touchdowns on four of its six first-half possessions to hold a 27-3 lead at halftime. Interceptions by Michael Walter and Chet Brooks ended the Broncos' first two possessions of the second half. San Francisco quarterback Joe Montana was named the Super Bowl most valuable player for a record third time. Montana completed 22 of 29 passes for 297 yards and a Super Bowl-record 5 touchdowns. Jerry Rice, Super Bowl XXIII most valuable player, caught 7 passes for 148 yards and 3 touchdowns. The 49ers' domination included first downs (28 to 12), net yards (461 to 167), and time of possession (39:31 to 20:29).

San Francisco (NFC)	13 14 14 14	— 55
Denver (AFC)	3 0 7 0	— 10

SF — Rice 20 pass from Montana (Cofer kick) (10:06)
Den — FG Treadwell 42 (6:47)
SF — Jones 7 pass from Montana (kick failed) (0:03)
SF — Rathman 1 run (Cofer kick) (7:15)
SF — Rice 38 pass from Montana (Cofer kick) (0:34)
SF — Rice 28 pass from Montana (Cofer kick) (12:48)
SF — Taylor 35 pass from Montana (Cofer kick) (9:44)
Den — Elway 3 run (Treadwell kick) (6:53)
SF — Rathman 3 run (Cofer kick) (14:57)
SF — Craig 1 run (Cofer kick) (13:47)

SUPER BOWL XXIII
Joe Robbie Stadium, South Florida
January 22, 1989, Attendance: 75,129
SAN FRANCISCO 20, CINCINNATI 16—
NFC champion San Francisco captured its third Super Bowl of the 1980s by defeating AFC champion Cincinnati 20-16. The 49ers, who also won Super Bowls XVI and XIX, became the first NFC team to win three Super Bowls. Pittsburgh, with four Super Bowl titles (IX, X, XIII, and XIV), and the Oakland/Los Angeles Raiders, with three (XI, XV, and XVIII), lead AFC franchises. Even though San Francisco held an advantage in total net yards (453 to 229), the 49ers found themselves trailing the Bengals late in the game. With the score 13-13, Cincinnati took a 16-13 lead on Jim Breech's 40-yard field goal with 3:20 remaining. It was Breech's third field goal of the day, following earlier successes from 34 and 43 yards. The 49ers started their winning drive at their 8-yard line. Over the next 11 plays, San Francisco covered 92 yards with the decisive score coming on a 10-yard pass from quarterback Joe Montana to wide receiver John Taylor with 34 seconds remaining. At halftime, the score was 3-3, the first time in Super Bowl history the game was tied at intermission. After the teams traded third-period field goals, the Bengals jumped ahead 13-6 on Stanford Jennings' 93-yard kickoff return for a touchdown with 34 seconds remaining in the quarter. The 49ers didn't waste any time coming back as they covered 85 yards in four plays, concluding with Montana's 14-yard scoring pass to Jerry Rice 57 seconds into the final stanza. Rice was named the game's most valuable player after compiling 11 catches for a Super Bowl-record 215 yards. Montana completed 23 of 36 passes for a Super Bowl-record 357 yards and 2 touchdowns.

Cincinnati (AFC)	0 3 10 3	— 16
San Francisco (NFC)	3 0 3 14	— 20

SF — FG Cofer 41 (3:14)
Cin — FG Breech 34 (1:15)
Cin — FG Breech 43 (5:39)
SF — FG Cofer 32 (0:50)
Cin — Jennings 93 kickoff return (Breech kick) (0:34)
SF — Rice 14 pass from Montana (Cofer kick) (14:03)
Cin — FG Breech 40 (3:20)
SF — Taylor 10 pass from Montana (Cofer kick) (0:34)

SUPER BOWL XXII
San Diego Jack Murphy Stadium, San Diego, CA
January 31, 1988, Attendance: 73,302
WASHINGTON 42, DENVER 10—NFC champion Washington won Super Bowl XXII and its second NFL championship of the 1980s with a 42-10 decision over AFC champion Denver. The Redskins, who also won Super Bowl XVII, enjoyed a record-setting second quarter en route to the victory. The Broncos broke in front

10-0 when quarterback John Elway threw a 56-yard touchdown pass to wide receiver Ricky Nattiel on the Broncos' first play from scrimmage. Following a Washington punt, Denver's Rich Karlis kicked a 24-yard field goal to cap a seven-play, 61-yard scoring drive. The Redskins then erupted for 35 points on five straight possessions in the second period and coasted thereafter. The 35 points established an NFL postseason mark for most points in a period. Redskins quarterback Doug Williams led the second-period explosion by passing for a Super Bowl record-tying 4 touchdowns, including 80- and 50-yard passes to wide receiver Ricky Sanders, a 27-yard toss to wide receiver Gary Clark, and an 8-yard pass to tight end Clint Didier. Washington scored 5 touchdowns in 18 plays with total time of possession of only 5:47. Overall, Williams completed 18 of 29 passes for 340 yards and was named the game's most valuable player. His pass-yardage total eclipsed the Super Bowl record of 331 yards by Joe Montana of San Francisco in Super Bowl XIX. Sanders ended with 193 yards on 9 catches, breaking the previous Super Bowl yardage record of 161 yards by Lynn Swann of Pittsburgh in Game X. Rookie running back Timmy Smith was the game's leading rusher with 22 carries for a Super Bowl-record 204 yards, breaking the previous mark of 191 yards by Marcus Allen of the Raiders in Game XVIII. Smith also scored twice on runs of 58 and 4 yards. Washington's 6 touchdowns and 602 total yards gained also set Super Bowl records. Redskins cornerback Barry Wilburn had 2 of the team's 3 interceptions, and strong safety Alvin Walton had 2 of Washington's 5 sacks.

Washington (NFC)	0 35 0 7	—	42
Denver (AFC)	10 0 0 0	—	10

Den — Nattiel 56 pass from Elway (Karlis kick) (13:03)

Den — FG Karlis 24 (9:09)

Wash — Sanders 80 pass from Williams (Haji-Sheikh kick) (14:07)

Wash — Clark 27 pass from Williams (Haji-Sheikh kick) (10:15)

Wash — Smith 58 run (Haji-Sheikh kick) (6:27)

Wash — Sanders 50 pass from Williams (Haji-Sheikh kick) (3:42)

Wash — Didier 8 pass from Williams (Haji-Sheikh kick) (1:04)

Wash — Smith 4 run (Haji-Sheikh kick) (13:09)

SUPER BOWL XXI

Rose Bowl, Pasadena, California
January 25, 1987, Attendance: 101,063
NEW YORK GIANTS 39, DENVER 20—The NFC champion New York Giants captured their first NFL title since 1956 when they downed the AFC champion Denver Broncos 39-20 in Super Bowl XXI. The

victory marked the NFC's fifth NFL title in the past six seasons. The Broncos, behind the passing of quarterback John Elway, who was 13 of 20 for 187 yards in the first half, held a 10-9 lead at intermission, the narrowest halftime margin in Super Bowl history. Denver's Rich Karlis opened the scoring with a Super Bowl record-tying 48-yard field goal. New York drove 78 yards in nine plays on the next series to take a 7-3 lead on quarterback Phil Simms' 6-yard touchdown pass to tight end Zeke Mowatt. The Broncos came right back with a 58-yard scoring drive on six plays capped by Elway's 4-yard touchdown run. The only scoring in the second period was the sack of Elway in the end zone by defensive end George Martin for a New York safety. The Giants produced a key defensive stand early in the second quarter when the Broncos had a first down at the New York 1-yard line, but failed to score on three running plays and Karlis' 23-yard missed field-goal attempt. The Giants took command of the game in the third period en route to a 30-point second half, the most ever scored in one half of Super Bowl play. New York took the lead for good on tight end Mark Bavaro's 13-yard touchdown catch 4:52 into the third period. The nine-play, 63-yard scoring drive included the successful conversion of a fourth-and-1 play on the New York 46-yard line. Denver was limited to only 2 net yards on 10 offensive plays in the third period. Simms set Super Bowl records for most consecutive completions (10) and highest completion percentage (88 percent on 22 completions in 25 attempts). He also passed for 268 yards and 3 touchdowns and was named the game's most valuable player. New York running back Joe Morris was the game's leading rusher with 20 carries for 67 yards. Denver wide receiver Vance Johnson led all receivers with 5 catches for 121 yards.

Denver (AFC)	10 0 0 10	—	20
N.Y. Giants (NFC)	7 2 17 13	—	39

Den — FG Karlis 48 (10:51)

NYG — Mowatt 6 pass from Simms (Allegre kick) (5:27)

Den — Elway 4 run (Karlis kick) (2:06)

NYG — Safety, Martin tackled Elway in end zone (2:46)

NYG — Bavaro 13 pass from Simms (Allegre kick) (10:08)

NYG — FG Allegre 21 (3:54)

NYG — Morris 1 run (Allegre kick) (0:24)

NYG — McConkey 6 pass from Simms (Allegre kick) (10:56)

Den — FG Karlis 28 (6:01)

NYG — Anderson 2 run (kick failed) (4:18)

Den — V. Johnson 47 pass from Elway (Karlis kick) (2:06)

SUPER BOWL XX

Louisiana Superdome, New Orleans, LA
January 26, 1986, Attendance: 73,818
CHICAGO 46, NEW ENGLAND 10—The NFC champion Chicago Bears, seeking their first NFL title since 1963, scored a Super Bowl-record 46 points in downing AFC champion New England 46-10 in Super Bowl XX. The previous record for most points in a Super Bowl was 38, shared by San Francisco in XIX and the Los Angeles Raiders in XVIII. The Bears' league-leading defense tied the Super Bowl record for sacks (7) and limited the Patriots to a record-low 7 rushing yards. New England took the quickest lead in Super Bowl history when Tony Franklin kicked a 36-yard field goal with 1:19 elapsed in the first period. The score came about because of Larry McGrew's fumble recovery at the Chicago 19-yard line. However, the Bears rebounded for a 23-3 first-half lead, while building a yardage advantage of 236 total yards to New England's minus 19. Running back Matt Suhey rushed 8 times for 37 yards, including an 11-yard touchdown run, and caught 1 pass for 24 yards in the first half. After the Patriot's first drive of the second half ended with a punt to the Bears' 4-yard line, Chicago marched 96 yards in nine plays with quarterback Jim McMahon's 1-yard scoring run capping the drive. McMahon became the first quarterback in Super Bowl history to rush for a pair of touchdowns. The Bears completed their scoring via a 28-yard interception return by reserve cornerback Reggie Phillips, a 1-yard run by defensive tackle/fullback William Perry, and a safety when defensive end Henry Waechter tackled Patriots quarterback Steve Grogan in the end zone. Bears defensive end Richard Dent became the fourth defender to be named the game's most valuable player after contributing 1.5 sacks. The Bears' victory margin of 36 points was the largest in Super Bowl history, bettering the previous mark of 29 by the Los Angeles Raiders when they topped Washington 38-9 in Game XVIII. McMahon completed 12 of 20 passes for 256 yards before leaving the game in the fourth period with a wrist injury. The NFL's all-time leading rusher, Bears running back Walter Payton, carried 22 times for 61 yards. Wide receiver Willie Gault caught 4 passes for 129 yards, the fourth-most receiving yards in a Super Bowl. Chicago coach Mike Ditka became the second man (Tom Flores of Raiders was the other) to win a Super Bowl ring as a player and as a coach.

Chicago (NFC)	13 10 21 2	—	46
New England (AFC)	3 0 0 7	—	10

NE — FG Franklin 36 (13:41)

Chi — FG Butler 28 (9:20)

Chi — FG Butler 24 (1:26)

Chi — Suhey 11 run (Butler kick) (0:23)

Chi — McMahon 2 run (Butler kick)
(7:24)
Chi — FG Butler 24 (0:00)
Chi — McMahon 1 run (Butler kick)
(7:22)
Chi — Phillips 28 interception return
(Butler kick) (6:16)
Chi — Perry 1 run (Butler kick)
(3:22)
NE — Fryar 8 pass from Grogan
(Franklin kick) (13:14)
Chi — Safety, Waechter tackled
Grogan in end zone (5:36)

SUPER BOWL XIX
Stanford Stadium, Stanford, California
January 20, 1985, Attendance: 84,059
SAN FRANCISCO 38, MIAMI 16—The San Francisco 49ers captured their second Super Bowl title with a dominating offense and a defense that tamed Miami's explosive passing attack. The Dolphins held a 10-7 lead at the end of the first period, which represented the most points scored by two teams in an opening quarter of a Super Bowl. However, the 49ers used excellent field position in the second period to build a 28-16 halftime lead. Running back Roger Craig set a Super Bowl record by scoring 3 touchdowns on pass receptions of 8 and 16 yards and a run of 2 yards. San Francisco's Joe Montana was voted the game's most valuable player. He joined Green Bay's Bart Starr and Pittsburgh's Terry Bradshaw as the only two-time Super Bowl most valuable players. Montana completed 24 of 35 passes for a Super Bowl-record 331 yards and 3 touchdowns, and rushed 5 times for 59 yards, including a 6-yard touchdown. Craig had 58 yards on 15 carries and caught 7 passes for 77 yards. Wendell Tyler rushed 13 times for 65 yards and had 4 catches for 70 yards. Dwight Clark had 6 receptions for 77 yards, while Russ Francis had 5 for 60. San Francisco's 537 total net yards bettered the previous Super Bowl record of 429 yards by Oakland in Super Bowl XI. The 49ers also held a time of possession advantage over the Dolphins of 37:11 to 22:49.

Miami (AFC)   10 6 0 0 — 16
San Francisco (NFC)   7 21 10 0 — 38
Mia — FG von Schamann 37 (7:24)
SF — Monroe 33 pass from
Montana (Wersching kick)
(3:12)
Mia — D. Johnson 2 pass from
Marino (von Schamann kick)
(0:45)
SF — Craig 8 pass from Montana
(Wersching kick) (11:34)
SF — Montana 6 run
(Wersching kick) (6:58)
SF — Craig 2 run (Wersching kick)
(2:05)
Mia — FG von Schamann 31 (0:12)
Mia — FG von Schamann 30 (0:00)
SF — FG Wersching 27 (10:12)

SF — Craig 16 pass from Montana
(Wersching kick) (6:18)

SUPER BOWL XVIII
Tampa Stadium, Tampa, Florida
January 22, 1984, Attendance: 72,920
LOS ANGELES RAIDERS 38, WASHINGTON 9—The Los Angeles Raiders dominated the Washington Redskins from the beginning in Super Bowl XVIII and achieved the most lopsided victory in Super Bowl history, surpassing Green Bay's 35-10 win over Kansas City in Super Bowl I. The Raiders took a 7-0 lead 4:52 into the game when Derrick Jensen blocked Jeff Hayes' punt and recovered it in the end zone for a touchdown. With 9:14 remaining in the first half, Raiders quarterback Jim Plunkett fired a 12-yard touchdown pass to wide receiver Cliff Branch to complete a three-play, 65-yard drive. Washington cut the Raiders' lead to 14-3 on a 24-yard field goal by Mark Moseley. With seven seconds left in the first half, Raiders linebacker Jack Squirek intercepted Joe Theismann's pass at the Redskins' 5-yard line and ran it in for a touchdown to give Los Angeles a 21-3 halftime lead. In the third period, running back Marcus Allen, who rushed for a Super Bowl-record 191 yards on 20 carries, increased the Raiders' lead to 35-9 on touchdown runs of 5 and 74 yards, the latter erasing the Super Bowl record of 58 yards set by Baltimore's Tom Matte in Game III. Allen was named the game's most valuable player. The victory over Washington raised Raiders coach Tom Flores' playoff record to 8-1, including a 27-10 win against Philadelphia in Super Bowl XV. The 38 points scored by the Raiders were the highest total by a Super Bowl team. The previous high was 35 points by Green Bay in Game I.

Washington (NFC) 0 3 6 0 — 9
L.A. Raiders (AFC) 7 14 14 3 — 38
Raiders — Jensen recovered blocked
punt in end zone
(Bahr kick) (10:08)
Raiders — Branch 12 pass from
Plunkett (Bahr kick) (9:14)
Wash — FG Moseley 24 (3:05)
Raiders — Squirek 5 interception
return (Bahr kick) (0:07)
Wash — Riggins 1 run (kick
blocked) (10:52)
Raiders — Allen 5 run (Bahr kick)
(7:06)
Raiders — Allen 74 run (Bahr kick)
(0:00)
Raiders — FG Bahr 21 (2:24)

SUPER BOWL XVII
Rose Bowl, Pasadena, California
January 30, 1983, Attendance: 103,667
WASHINGTON 27, MIAMI 17—Fullback John Riggins ran for a Super Bowl-record 166 yards on 38 carries to spark Washington to a 27-17 victory over AFC champion Miami. It was Riggins' fourth straight

100-yard rushing game during the playoffs, also a record. The win marked Washington's first NFL title since 1942, and was only the second time in Super Bowl history NFL/NFC teams scored consecutive victories (Green Bay did it in Super Bowls I and II and San Francisco won Super Bowl XVI). The Redskins, under second-year head coach Joe Gibbs, used a balanced offense that accounted for 400 total yards (a Super Bowl-record 276 yards rushing and 124 passing), second in Super Bowl history to 429 yards by Oakland in Super Bowl XI. The Dolphins built a 17-10 halftime lead on a 76-yard touchdown pass from quarterback David Woodley to wide receiver Jimmy Cefalo 6:49 into the first period, a 20-yard field goal by Uwe von Schamann with 6:00 left in the half, and a Super Bowl-record 98-yard kickoff return by Fulton Walker with 1:38 remaining. Washington had tied the score at 10-10 with 1:51 left on a 4-yard touchdown pass from Joe Theismann to wide receiver Alvin Garrett. Mark Moseley started the Redskins' scoring with a 31-yard field goal late in the first period, and added a 20-yard field goal midway through the third period to cut the Dolphins' lead to 17-13. Riggins, who was voted the game's most valuable player, gave Washington its first lead of the game with 10:01 left when he ran 43 yards off left tackle for a touchdown in a fourth-and-1 situation. Wide receiver Charlie Brown caught a 6-yard scoring pass from Theismann with 1:55 left to complete the scoring. The Dolphins managed only 176 yards (142 in first half). Theismann completed 15 of 23 passes for 143 yards, with 2 touchdowns and 2 interceptions. For Miami, Woodley was 4 of 14 for 97 yards, with 1 touchdown, and 1 interception. Don Strock was 0 for 3 in relief.

Miami (AFC)   7 10 0 0 — 17
Washington (NFC) 0 10 3 14 — 27
Mia — Cefalo 76 pass from Woodley
(von Schamann kick) (8:11)
Wash — FG Moseley 31 (0:39)
Mia — FG von Schamann 20 (6:00)
Wash — Garrett 4 pass from Theismann (Moseley kick) (1:51)
Mia — Walker 98 kickoff return (von
Schamann kick) (1:38)
Wash — FG Moseley 20 (8:09)
Wash — Riggins 43 run (Moseley kick)
(10:01)
Wash — Brown 6 pass from
Theismann (Moseley kick)
(1:55)

SUPER BOWL XVI
Pontiac Silverdome, Pontiac, Michigan
January 24, 1982, Attendance: 81,270
SAN FRANCISCO 26, CINCINNATI 21—Ray Wersching's Super Bowl record-tying 4 field goals and Joe Montana's controlled passing helped lift the San Francisco 49ers to their first NFL championship with a 26-21 victory over Cincinnati. The 49ers

built a game-record 20-0 halftime lead via Montana's 1-yard touchdown run, which capped an 11-play, 68-yard drive; fullback Earl Cooper's 11-yard scoring pass from Montana, which climaxed a Super Bowl record 92-yard drive on 12 plays; and Wersching's 22- and 26-yard field goals. The Bengals rebounded in the second half, closing the gap to 20-14 on quarterback Ken Anderson's 5-yard run and Dan Ross' 4-yard reception from Anderson, who established Super Bowl passing records for completions (25) and completion percentage (73.5 percent on 25 of 34). Wersching added two fourth-period field goals of 40 and 23 yards to increase the 49ers' lead to 26-14. The Bengals managed to score on an Anderson-to-Ross 3-yard pass with only 16 seconds remaining. Ross set a Super Bowl record with 11 receptions for 104 yards. Montana, the game's most valuable player, completed 14 of 22 passes for 157 yards. Cincinnati compiled 356 yards to San Francisco's 275, which marked the first time in Super Bowl history that the team that gained the most yards from scrimmage lost the game.

San Francisco (NFC)	7 13 0 6	— 26
Cincinnati (AFC)	0 0 7 14	— 21

SF — Montana 1 run (Wersching kick) (5:52)
SF — Cooper 11 pass from Montana (Wersching kick) (6:53)
SF — FG Wersching 22 (0:15)
SF — FG Wersching 26 (0:02)
Cin — Anderson 5 run (Breech kick) (11:25)
Cin — Ross 4 pass from Anderson (Breech kick) (10:06)
SF — FG Wersching 40 (5:25)
SF — FG Wersching 23 (1:57)
Cin — Ross 3 pass from Anderson (Breech kick) (0:16)

SUPER BOWL XV
Louisiana Superdome, New Orleans, LA
January 25, 1981, Attendance: 76,135
OAKLAND 27, PHILADELPHIA 10—Jim Plunkett passed for 3 touchdowns, including an 80-yard strike to Kenny King, as the Raiders became the first wild-card team to win the Super Bowl. Plunkett's touchdown bomb to King—the longest play in Super Bowl history—gave Oakland a decisive 14-0 lead with nine seconds left in the first period. Linebacker Rod Martin had set up Oakland's first touchdown, a 2-yard reception by Cliff Branch, with a 17-yard interception return to the Eagles' 30-yard line. The Eagles never recovered from that early deficit, managing only Tony Franklin's field goal (30 yards) and an 8-yard touchdown pass from Ron Jaworski to Keith Krepfle. Plunkett, who became a starter in the sixth game of the season, completed 13 of 21 for 261 yards and was named the game's most valuable player. Oakland won 9 of 11 games with Plunkett starting, but that was good enough only for second place in the AFC West, although they tied division winner San Diego with an 11-5 record. The Raiders, who had previously won Super Bowl XI over Minnesota, had to win three playoff games to get to the championship game. Oakland defeated Houston 27-7 at home followed by road victories over Cleveland (14-12) and San Diego (34-27). Oakland's Mark van Eeghen was the game's leading rusher with 75 yards on 18 carries. Philadelphia's Wilbert Montgomery led all receivers with 6 receptions for 91 yards. Branch had 5 for 67 and Harold Carmichael of Philadelphia 5 for 83. Martin finished the game with 3 interceptions, a Super Bowl record.

Oakland (AFC)	14 0 10 3	— 27
Philadelphia (NFC)	0 3 0 7	— 10

Oak — Branch 2 pass from Plunkett (Bahr kick) (8:56)
Oak — King 80 pass from Plunkett (Bahr kick) (0:09)
Phil — FG Franklin 30 (10:28)
Oak — Branch 29 pass from Plunkett (Bahr kick) (12:24)
Oak — FG Bahr 46 (4:35)
Phil — Krepfle 8 pass from Jaworski (Franklin kick) (13:59)
Oak — FG Bahr 35 (8:29)

SUPER BOWL XIV
Rose Bowl, Pasadena, California
January 20, 1980, Attendance: 103,985
PITTSBURGH 31, LOS ANGELES 19—Terry Bradshaw completed 14 of 21 passes for 309 yards and set two passing records as the Steelers became the first team to win four Super Bowls. Despite 3 interceptions by the Rams, Bradshaw kept his poise and brought the Steelers from behind twice in the second half. Trailing 13-10 at halftime, Pittsburgh went ahead 17-13 when Bradshaw hit Lynn Swann with a 47-yard touchdown pass after 2:48 of the third quarter. On the Rams' next possession Vince Ferragamo, who was 15 of 25 for 212 yards, responded with a 50-yard pass to Billy Waddy that moved Los Angeles from its 26 to the Steelers' 24. On the following play, Lawrence McCutcheon connected with Ron Smith on a halfback option pass that gave the Rams a 19-17 lead. On Pittsburgh's initial possession of the final period, Bradshaw lofted a 73-yard scoring pass to John Stallworth to put the Steelers in front to stay 24-19. Franco Harris scored on a 1-yard run later in the quarter to seal the verdict. A 45-yard pass from Bradshaw to Stallworth was the key play in the drive to Harris' score. Bradshaw, the game's most valuable player for the second straight year, set career Super Bowl records for most touchdown passes (9) and most passing yards (932). Larry Anderson gave the Steelers excellent field position throughout the game with 5 kickoff returns for a record 162 yards.

Los Angeles (NFC)	7 6 6 0	— 19
Pittsburgh (AFC)	3 7 7 14	— 31

Pitt — FG Bahr 41 (7:31)
LA — Bryant 1 run (Corral kick) (2:44)
Pitt — Harris 1 run (Bahr kick) (12:52)
LA — FG Corral 31 (7:21)
LA — FG Corral 45 (0:14)
Pitt — Swann 47 pass from Bradshaw (Bahr kick) (12:12)
LA — Smith 24 pass from McCutcheon (kick failed) (10:15)
Pitt — Stallworth 73 pass from Bradshaw (Bahr kick) (12:04)
Pitt — Harris 1 run (Bahr kick) (1:49)

SUPER BOWL XIII
Orange Bowl, Miami, Florida
January 21, 1979, Attendance: 79,484
PITTSBURGH 35, DALLAS 31—Terry Bradshaw passed for a record 4 touchdowns to lead the Steelers to victory. The Steelers became the first team to win three Super Bowls, mostly because of Bradshaw's accurate arm. Bradshaw, voted the game's most valuable player, completed 17 of 30 passes for 318 yards, a personal high. Four of those passes went for touchdowns—2 to John Stallworth and the third, with 26 seconds remaining in the second period, to Rocky Bleier for a 21-14 halftime lead. The Cowboys scored twice before intermission on Roger Staubach's 39-yard pass to Tony Hill and a 37-yard fumble return by linebacker Mike Hegman, who stole the ball from Bradshaw. The Steelers broke open the contest with 2 touchdowns in a span of 19 seconds midway through the final period. Franco Harris rambled 22 yards up the middle to give the Steelers a 28-17 lead with 7:10 left. Pittsburgh got the ball right back when Randy White fumbled the kickoff and Dennis Winston recovered for the Steelers. On first down, Bradshaw fired his fourth touchdown pass, an 18-yard pass to Lynn Swann to boost the Steelers' lead to 35-17 with 6:51 to play. The Cowboys refused to let the Steelers run away with the contest. Staubach connected with Billy Joe DuPree on a 7-yard scoring pass with 2:23 left. Then the Cowboys recovered an onside kick and Staubach took them in for another score, passing 4 yards to Butch Johnson with 22 seconds remaining. Bleier recovered another onside kick with 17 seconds left to seal the victory for the Steelers.

Pittsburgh (AFC)	7 14 0 14	— 35
Dallas (NFC)	7 7 3 14	— 31

Pitt — Stallworth 28 pass from Bradshaw (Gerela kick) (9:47)
Dall — Hill 39 pass from Staubach (Septien kick) (0:00)
Dall — Hegman 37 fumble recovery return (Septien kick) (12:08)

Pitt — Stallworth 75 pass from Bradshaw (Gerela kick) (10:25)

Pitt — Bleier 7 pass from Bradshaw (Gerela kick) (0:26)

Dall — FG Septien 27 (2:36)

Pitt — Harris 22 run (Gerela kick) (7:10)

Pitt — Swann 18 pass from Bradshaw (Gerela kick) (6:51)

Dall — DuPree 7 pass from Staubach (Septien kick) (2:23)

Dall — B. Johnson 4 pass from Staubach (Septien kick) (0:22)

SUPER BOWL XII
Louisiana Superdome, New Orleans, LA
January 15, 1978, Attendance: 75,583
DALLAS 27, DENVER 10—The Cowboys evened their Super Bowl record at 2-2 by defeating Denver before a sellout crowd plus 102,010,000 television viewers, the largest audience ever to watch a sporting event. Dallas converted 2 interceptions into 10 points and Efren Herrera added a 35-yard field goal for a 13-0 halftime advantage. In the third period Craig Morton engineered a drive to the Cowboys' 30 and Jim Turner's 47-yard field goal made the score 13-3. After an exchange of punts, Butch Johnson made a spectacular diving catch in the end zone to complete a 45-yard pass from Roger Staubach and put the Cowboys ahead 20-3. Following Rick Upchurch's 67-yard kickoff return, Norris Weese guided the Broncos to a touchdown to cut the deficit to 20-10. Dallas clinched the victory when running back Robert Newhouse tossed a 29-yard touchdown pass to Golden Richards with 7:04 left in the game. It was the first pass thrown by Newhouse since 1975. Harvey Martin and Randy White, who were named co-most valuable players, led the Cowboys' defense, which recovered 4 fumbles and intercepted 4 passes.

Dallas (NFC)   10 3 7 7 — 27
Denver (AFC)   0 0 10 0 — 10

Dall — Dorsett 3 run (Herrera kick) (4:29)

Dall — FG Herrera 35 (1:31)

Dall — FG Herrera 43 (11:16)

Den — FG Turner 47 (12:32)

Dall — Johnson 45 pass from Staubach (Herrera kick) (6:59)

Den — Lytle 1 run (Turner kick) (5:39)

Dall — Richards 29 pass from Newhouse (Herrera kick) (7:04)

SUPER BOWL XI
Rose Bowl, Pasadena, California
January 9, 1977, Attendance: 103,438
OAKLAND 32, MINNESOTA 14—The Raiders won their first NFL championship before a record Super Bowl crowd plus 81 million television viewers, the largest audience ever to watch a sporting event. The Raiders gained a record-breaking 429

yards, including running back Clarence Davis' 137 rushing yards. Wide receiver Fred Biletnikoff made 4 key receptions, which earned him the game's most valuable player trophy. Oakland scored on three successive possessions in the second quarter to build a 16-0 halftime lead. Errol Mann's 24-yard field goal opened the scoring, then the AFC champions put together drives of 64 and 35 yards, scoring on a 1-yard pass from Ken Stabler to Dave Casper and a 1-yard run by Pete Banaszak. The Raiders increased their lead to 19-0 on a 40-yard field goal in the third quarter, but Minnesota responded with a 12-play, 58-yard drive late in the period, with Fran Tarkenton passing 8 yards to wide receiver Sammy White to cut the deficit to 19-7. Two fourth-quarter interceptions clinched the title for the Raiders. One set up Banaszak's second touchdown run, the other resulted in cornerback Willie Brown's Super Bowl-record 75-yard interception return.

Oakland (AFC)   0 16 3 13 — 32
Minnesota (NFC) 0 0 7 7 — 14

Oak — FG Mann 24 (14:12)

Oak — Casper 1 pass from Stabler (Mann kick) (7:10)

Oak — Banaszak 1 run (kick failed) (3:33)

Oak — FG Mann 40 (5:16)

Minn — S. White 8 pass from Tarkenton (Cox kick) (0:47)

Oak — Banaszak 2 run (Mann kick) (7:39)

Oak — Brown 75 interception return (kick failed) (5:43)

Minn — Voigt 13 pass from Lee (Cox kick) (0:25)

SUPER BOWL X
Orange Bowl, Miami, Florida
January 18, 1976, Attendance: 80,187
PITTSBURGH 21, DALLAS 17—The Steelers won the Super Bowl for the second year in a row on Terry Bradshaw's 64-yard touchdown pass to Lynn Swann and an aggressive defense that snuffed out a late rally by the Cowboys with an end-zone interception on the final play of the game. In the fourth quarter, Pittsburgh ran on fourth down and gave up the ball on the Cowboys' 39 with 1:22 to play. Roger Staubach ran and passed for 2 first downs but his last desperation pass was picked off by Glen Edwards. Dallas' scoring was the result of 2 touchdown passes by Staubach, one to Drew Pearson for 29 yards and the other to Percy Howard for 34 yards. Howard's reception was the only catch of his NFL career. Toni Fritsch had a 36-yard field goal. The Steelers scored on 2 touchdown passes by Bradshaw, 1 to Randy Grossman for 7 yards and the long bomb to Swann. Roy Gerela had 36- and 18-yard field goals. Reggie Harrison blocked a punt through the end zone for a safety. Swann set a Super Bowl record by gaining 161 yards on his 4

receptions.

Dallas (NFC)   7 3 0 7 — 17
Pittsburgh (AFC) 7 0 0 14 — 21

Dall — D. Pearson 29 pass from Staubach (Fritsch kick) (10:24)

Pitt — Grossman 7 pass from Bradshaw (Gerela kick) (5:57)

Dall — FG Fritsch 36 (14:45)

Pitt — Safety, Harrison blocked Hoopes' punt through end zone (11:28)

Pitt — FG Gerela 36 (8:41)

Pitt — FG Gerela 18 (6:37)

Pitt — Swann 64 pass from Bradshaw (kick failed) (3:02)

Dall — P. Howard 34 pass from Staubach (Fritsch kick) (1:48)

SUPER BOWL IX
Tulane Stadium, New Orleans, Louisiana
January 12, 1975, Attendance: 80,997
PITTSBURGH 16, MINNESOTA 6—AFC champion Pittsburgh, in its initial Super Bowl appearance, and NFC champion Minnesota, making a third bid for its first Super Bowl title, struggled through a first half in which the only score was produced by the Steelers' defense when Dwight White downed Vikings' quarterback Fran Tarkenton in the end zone for a safety 7:49 into the second period. The Steelers forced another break and took advantage on the second-half kickoff when Minnesota's Bill Brown fumbled and Marv Kellum recovered for Pittsburgh on the Vikings' 30. After Rocky Bleier failed to gain on first down, Franco Harris carried 3 consecutive times for 24 yards, a loss of 3, and a 9-yard touchdown and a 9-0 lead. Though its offense was completely stymied by Pittsburgh's defense, Minnesota managed to move into a threatening position after 4:27 of the final period when Matt Blair blocked Bobby Walden's punt and Terry Brown recovered the ball in the end zone for a touchdown. Fred Cox's kick failed and the Steelers led 9-6. Pittsburgh wasted no time putting the victory away. The Steelers took the ensuing kickoff and marched 66 yards in 11 plays, climaxed by Terry Bradshaw's 4-yard scoring pass to Larry Brown with 3:31 left. Pittsburgh's defense permitted Minnesota only 119 yards total offense, including a Super Bowl low of 17 rushing yards. The Steelers, meanwhile, gained 333 yards, including Harris' record 158 yards on 34 carries.

Pittsburgh (AFC) 0 2 7 7 — 16
Minnesota (NFC)   0 0 0 6 — 6

Pitt — Safety, White downed Tarkenton in end zone (7:11)

Pitt — Harris 9 run (Gerela kick) (13:25)

Minn — T. Brown recovered blocked punt in end zone (kick failed) (10:33)

Pitt — L. Brown 4 pass from Bradshaw (Gerela kick) (3:31)

SUPER BOWL VIII

Rice Stadium, Houston, Texas
January 13, 1974, Attendance: 71,882
MIAMI 24, MINNESOTA 7—The defending NFL champion Dolphins, representing the AFC for the third straight year, scored the first two times they had possession on marches of 62 and 56 yards while the Miami defense limited the Vikings to only seven plays in the first period. Larry Csonka climaxed the initial 10-play drive with a 5-yard touchdown bolt through right guard after 5:27 had elapsed. Four plays later, Miami began another 10-play scoring drive, which ended with Jim Kiick bursting 1 yard through the middle for another touchdown after 13:38 of the period. Garo Yepremian added a 28-yard field goal midway in the second period for a 17-0 Miami lead. Minnesota then drove from its 20 to a second-and-2 situation on the Miami 7 yard line with 1:18 left in the half. But on two plays, Miami limited Oscar Reed to 1 yard. On fourth-and-1 from the 6, Reed went over right tackle, but Dolphins middle linebacker Nick Buoniconti jarred the ball loose and Jake Scott recovered for Miami to halt the Minnesota threat. The Vikings were unable to muster enough offense in the second half to threaten the Dolphins. Csonka rushed 33 times for a Super Bowl-record 145 yards. Bob Griese of Miami completed 6 of 7 passes for 73 yards.

Minnesota (NFC)		0 0 0 7 — 7	
Miami (AFC)		14 3 7 0 — 24	
Mia	—	Csonka 5 run (Yepremian kick) (5:27)	
Mia	—	Kiick 1 run (Yepremian kick) (1:22)	
Mia	—	FG Yepremian 28 (6:02)	
Mia	—	Csonka 2 run (Yepremian kick) (8:44)	
Minn	—	Tarkenton 4 run (Cox kick) (13:25)	

SUPER BOWL VII

Memorial Coliseum, Los Angeles, CA
January 14, 1973, Attendance: 90,182
MIAMI 14, WASHINGTON 7—The Dolphins played virtually perfect football in the first half as their defense permitted the Redskins to cross midfield only once and their offense turned good field position into 2 touchdowns. On its third possession, Miami opened its first scoring drive from the Dolphins' 37 yard line. An 18-yard pass from Bob Griese to Paul Warfield preceded by three plays Griese's 28-yard touchdown pass to Howard Twilley. After Washington moved from its 17 to the Miami 48 with two minutes remaining in the first half, Dolphins linebacker Nick Buoniconti intercepted Billy Kilmer's pass at the Miami 41 and returned it to the Washington 27. Jim Kiick ran for 3 yards, Larry Csonka for 3, Griese passed to Jim Mandich for 19, and Kiick gained 1 to the 1-yard line. With 18 seconds left until intermission, Kiick scored from the 1.

Washington's only touchdown came with 2:07 left in the game and resulted from a misplayed field-goal attempt and fumble by Garo Yepremian, with the Redskins' Mike Bass picking the ball out of the air and running 49 yards for the score. Dolphins safety Jake Scott, who had 2 interceptions, including 1 in the end zone to kill a Redskins' drive, was voted the game's most valuable player.

Miami (AFC)		7 7 0 0 — 14	
Washington (NFC)		0 0 0 7 — 7	
Mia	—	Twilley 28 pass from Griese (Yepremian kick) (0:01)	
Mia	—	Kiick 1 run (Yepremian kick) (0:18)	
Wash	—	Bass 49 fumble recovery return (Knight kick) (2:07)	

SUPER BOWL VI

Tulane Stadium, New Orleans, Louisiana
January 16, 1972, Attendance: 81,023
DALLAS 24, MIAMI 3—The Cowboys rushed for a record 252 yards and their defense limited the Dolphins to a low of 185 yards while not permitting a touchdown for the first time in Super Bowl history. Dallas converted Chuck Howley's recovery of Larry Csonka's first fumble of the season into a 3-0 advantage and led at halftime 10-3. After Dallas received the second-half kickoff, Duane Thomas led a 71-yard march in eight plays for a 17-3 margin. Howley intercepted Bob Griese's pass at the 50 and returned it to the Miami 9 early in the fourth period, and three plays later Roger Staubach passed 7 yards to Mike Ditka for the final touchdown. Thomas rushed for 95 yards and Walt Garrison gained 74. Staubach, voted the game's most valuable player, completed 12 of 19 passes for 119 yards and 2 touchdowns.

Dallas (NFC)		3 7 7 7 — 24	
Miami (AFC)		0 3 0 0 — 3	
Dall	—	FG Clark 9 (1:23)	
Dall	—	Alworth 7 pass from Staubach (Clark kick) (1:15)	
Mia	—	FG Yepremian 31 (0:04)	
Dall	—	D. Thomas 3 run (Clark kick) (9:43)	
Dall	—	Ditka 7 pass from Staubach (Clark kick) (11:42)	

SUPER BOWL V

Orange Bowl, Miami, Florida
January 17, 1971, Attendance: 79,204
BALTIMORE 16, DALLAS 13—A 32-yard field goal by rookie kicker Jim O'Brien brought the Baltimore Colts a victory over the Dallas Cowboys in the final five seconds of Super Bowl V. The game between the champions of the AFC and NFC was played on artificial turf for the first time. Dallas led 13-6 at the half but interceptions by Rick Volk and Mike Curtis set up a Baltimore touchdown and O'Brien's decisive kick in the fourth period. Earl Morrall relieved an injured Johnny Unitas late in the first half, although Unitas com-

pleted the Colts' only scoring pass. It caromed off receiver Eddie Hinton's fingertips, off Dallas defensive back Mel Renfro, and finally settled into the grasp of John Mackey, who went 45 yards to score on a 75-yard play.

Baltimore (AFC)		0 6 0 10 — 16	
Dallas (NFC)		3 10 0 0 — 13	
Dall	—	FG Clark 14 (5:32)	
Dall	—	FG Clark 30 (14:52)	
Balt	—	Mackey 75 pass from Unitas (kick blocked) (14:55)	
Dall	—	Thomas 7 pass from Morton (Clark kick) (7:53)	
Balt	—	Nowatzke 2 run (O'Brien kick) (7:35)	
Balt	—	FG O'Brien 32 (0:05)	

SUPER BOWL IV

Tulane Stadium, New Orleans, Louisiana
January 11, 1970, Attendance: 80,562
KANSAS CITY 23, MINNESOTA 7—The AFL squared the Super Bowl at two games apiece with the NFL, building a 16-0 halftime lead behind Len Dawson's superb quarterbacking and a powerful defense. Dawson, the fourth consecutive quarterback to be chosen the Super Bowl's top player, called an almost flawless game, completing 12 of 17 passes and hitting Otis Taylor on a 46-yard play for the final Chiefs touchdown. The Kansas City defense limited Minnesota's strong rushing game to 67 yards and had 3 interceptions and 2 fumble recoveries. The crowd of 80,562 set a Super Bowl record, as did the gross receipts of $3,817,872.69.

Minnesota (NFL)		0 0 7 0 — 7	
Kansas City (AFL)		3 13 7 0 — 23	
KC	—	FG Stenerud 48 (6:52)	
KC	—	FG Stenerud 32 (13:20)	
KC	—	FG Stenerud 25 (7:52)	
KC	—	Garrett 5 run (Stenerud kick) (5:34)	
Minn	—	Osborn 4 run (Cox kick) (4:32)	
KC	—	Taylor 46 pass from Dawson (Stenerud kick) (1:22)	

SUPER BOWL III

Orange Bowl, Miami, Florida
January 12, 1969, Attendance: 75,389
NEW YORK JETS 16, BALTIMORE 7—Jets quarterback Joe Namath "guaranteed" victory on the Thursday before the game, then went out and led the AFL to its first Super Bowl victory over a Baltimore team that had lost only once in 16 games all season. Namath, chosen the outstanding player, completed 17 of 28 passes for 206 yards and directed a steady attack that dominated the NFL champions after the Jets' defense had intercepted Colts quarterback Earl Morrall 3 times in the first half. The Jets had 337 total yards, including 121 rushing yards by Matt Snell. Johnny Unitas, who had missed most of the season with a sore elbow, came off the bench and led Baltimore to its only

touchdown late in the fourth quarter after New York led 16-0.

New York Jets (AFL) 0 7 6 3 — 16
Baltimore (NFL)   0 0 0 7 — 7

NYJ — Snell 4 run (Turner kick) (9:03)
NYJ — FG Turner 32 (10:08)
NYJ — FG Turner 30 (3:58)
NYJ — FG Turner 9 (13:26)
Balt — Hill 1 run (Michaels kick) (3:19)

SUPER BOWL II

Orange Bowl, Miami, Florida
January 14, 1968, Attendance: 75,546
GREEN BAY 33, OAKLAND 14—Green Bay, after winning its third consecutive NFL championship, won the Super Bowl title for the second straight year, defeating the AFL champion Raiders in a game that drew the first $3-million gate in football history. Bart Starr again was chosen the game's most valuable player as he completed 13 of 24 passes for 202 yards and 1 touchdown and directed a Packers' attack that was in control all the way after building a 16-7 halftime lead. Don Chandler kicked 4 field goals and all-pro cornerback Herb Adderley capped the Green Bay scoring with a 60-yard interception return. The game marked the last for Vince Lombardi as Packers coach, ending nine years at Green Bay in which he won six Western Conference championships, five NFL championships, and two Super Bowls.

Green Bay (NFL) 3 13 10 7 — 33
Oakland (AFL)   0 7 0 7 — 14

GB — FG Chandler 39 (9:53)
GB — FG Chandler 20 (11:52)
GB — Dowler 62 pass from Starr (Chandler kick) (10:50)
Oak — Miller 23 pass from Lamonica (Blanda kick) (6:15)
GB — FG Chandler 43 (0:01)
GB — Anderson 2 run (Chandler kick) (5:54)
GB — FG Chandler 31 (0:02)
GB — Adderley 60 interception return (Chandler kick) (11:03)
Oak — Miller 23 pass from Lamonica (Blanda kick) (9:13)

SUPER BOWL I

Memorial Coliseum, Los Angeles, CA
January 15, 1967, Attendance: 61,946
GREEN BAY 35, KANSAS CITY 10—The Green Bay Packers opened the Super Bowl series by defeating the AFL champion Chiefs behind the passing of Bart Starr, the receiving of Max McGee, and a key interception by all-pro safety Willie Wood. Green Bay broke open the game with 3 second-half touchdowns, the first of which was set up by Wood's 50-yard return of an interception. McGee, filling in for ailing Boyd Dowler after having caught only 4 passes all season, caught 7 from Starr for 138 yards and 2 touchdowns. Elijah Pitts ran for 2 other scores. The Chiefs' 10 points came in the second quarter, the only touchdown on a 7-yard pass from Len Dawson to Curtis McClinton. Starr completed 16 of 23 passes for 250 yards and 2 touchdowns and was chosen the most valuable player. The Packers collected $15,000 per man and the Chiefs $7,500—the largest single-game shares in the history of team sports.

Kansas City (AFL) 0 10 0 0 — 10
Green Bay (NFL)   7 7 14 7 — 35

GB — McGee 37 pass from Starr (Chandler kick) (6:04)
KC — McClinton 7 pass from Dawson (Mercer kick) (10:40)
GB — Taylor 14 run (Chandler kick) (4:37)
KC — FG Mercer 31 (0:54)
GB — Pitts 5 run (Chandler kick) (12:33)
GB — McGee 13 pass from Starr (Chandler kick) (0:51)
GB — Pitts 1 run (Chandler kick) (6:35)

AFC CHAMPIONSHIP GAME RESULTS
Includes AFL Championship Games (1960-69)

Season	Date	Winner (Share)	Loser (Share)	Score	Site	Attendance
2007	Jan. 20	New England ($37,500)	San Diego ($37,500)	21-12	Foxborough	68,756
2006	Jan. 21	Indianapolis ($37,000)	New England ($37,000)	38-34	Indianapolis	57,433
2005	Jan. 22	Pittsburgh ($37,000)	Denver ($37,000)	34-17	Denver	76,775
2004	Jan. 23	New England ($36,500)	Pittsburgh ($36,500)	41-27	Pittsburgh	65,242
2003	Jan. 18	New England ($36,500)	Indianapolis ($36,500)	24-14	Foxborough	68,436
2002	Jan. 19	Oakland ($35,000)	Tennessee ($35,000)	41-24	Oakland	62,544
2001	Jan. 27	New England ($34,500)	Pittsburgh ($34,500)	24-17	Pittsburgh	64,704
2000	Jan. 14	Baltimore ($34,500)	Oakland ($34,500)	16-3	Oakland	62,784
1999	Jan. 23	Tennessee ($33,000)	Jacksonville ($33,000)	33-14	Jacksonville	75,206
1998	Jan. 17	Denver ($32,500)	N.Y. Jets ($32,500)	23-10	Denver	75,482
1997	Jan. 11	Denver ($30,000)	Pittsburgh ($30,000)	24-21	Pittsburgh	61,382
1996	Jan. 12	New England ($29,000)	Jacksonville ($29,000)	20-6	Foxborough	60,190
1995	Jan. 14	Pittsburgh ($27,000)	Indianapolis ($27,000)	20-16	Pittsburgh	61,062
1994	Jan. 15	San Diego ($26,000)	Pittsburgh ($26,000)	17-13	Pittsburgh	61,545
1993	Jan. 23	Buffalo ($23,500)	Kansas City ($23,500)	30-13	Buffalo	76,642
1992	Jan. 17	Buffalo ($18,000)	Miami ($18,000)	29-10	Miami	72,703
1991	Jan. 12	Buffalo ($18,000)	Denver ($18,000)	10-7	Buffalo	80,272
1990	Jan. 20	Buffalo ($18,000)	L.A. Raiders ($18,000)	51-3	Buffalo	80,325
1989	Jan. 14	Denver ($18,000)	Cleveland ($18,000)	37-21	Denver	76,046
1988	Jan. 8	Cincinnati ($18,000)	Buffalo ($18,000)	21-10	Cincinnati	59,747
1987	Jan. 17	Denver ($18,000)	Cleveland ($18,000)	38-33	Denver	76,197
1986	Jan. 11	Denver ($18,000)	Cleveland ($18,000)	23-20*	Cleveland	79,973
1985	Jan. 12	New England ($18,000)	Miami ($18,000)	31-14	Miami	75,662
1984	Jan. 6	Miami ($18,000)	Pittsburgh ($18,000)	45-28	Miami	76,029
1983	Jan. 8	L.A. Raiders ($18,000)	Seattle ($18,000)	30-14	Los Angeles	91,445
1982	Jan. 23	Miami ($18,000)	N.Y. Jets ($18,000)	14-0	Miami	67,396
1981	Jan. 10	Cincinnati ($9,000)	San Diego ($9,000)	27-7	Cincinnati	46,302
1980	Jan. 11	Oakland ($9,000)	San Diego ($9,000)	34-27	San Diego	52,675
1979	Jan. 6	Pittsburgh ($9,000)	Houston ($9,000)	27-13	Pittsburgh	50,475
1978	Jan. 7	Pittsburgh ($9,000)	Houston ($9,000)	34-5	Pittsburgh	50,725
1977	Jan. 1	Denver ($9,000)	Oakland ($9,000)	20-17	Denver	75,044
1976	Dec. 26	Oakland ($8,500)	Pittsburgh ($5,500)	24-7	Oakland	53,821
1975	Jan. 4	Pittsburgh ($8,500)	Oakland ($5,500)	16-10	Pittsburgh	50,609
1974	Dec. 29	Pittsburgh ($8,500)	Oakland ($5,500)	24-13	Oakland	53,800
1973	Dec. 30	Miami ($8,500)	Oakland ($5,500)	27-10	Miami	79,325
1972	Dec. 31	Miami ($8,500)	Pittsburgh ($5,500)	21-17	Pittsburgh	50,845
1971	Jan. 2	Miami ($8,500)	Baltimore ($5,500)	21-0	Miami	76,622
1970	Jan. 3	Baltimore ($8,500)	Oakland ($5,500)	27-17	Baltimore	54,799
1969	Jan. 4	Kansas City ($7,755)	Oakland ($6,252)	17-7	Oakland	53,564
1968	Dec. 29	N.Y. Jets ($7,007)	Oakland ($5,349)	27-23	New York	62,627
1967	Dec. 31	Oakland ($6,321)	Houston ($4,996)	40-7	Oakland	53,330
1966	Jan. 1	Kansas City ($5,309)	Buffalo ($3,799)	31-7	Buffalo	42,080
1965	Dec. 26	Buffalo ($5,189)	San Diego ($3,447)	23-0	San Diego	30,361
1964	Dec. 26	Buffalo ($2,668)	San Diego ($1,738)	20-7	Buffalo	40,242
1963	Jan. 5	San Diego ($2,498)	Boston ($1,596)	51-10	San Diego	30,127
1962	Dec. 23	Dallas ($2,206)	Houston ($1,471)	20-17*	Houston	37,981
1961	Dec. 24	Houston ($1,792)	San Diego ($1,111)	10-3	San Diego	29,556
1960	Jan. 1	Houston ($1,025)	L.A. Chargers ($718)	24-16	Houston	32,183

Sudden death overtime

AFC CHAMPIONSHIP GAME COMPOSITE STANDINGS

	W	L	Pct.	Pts.	OP
Cincinnati Bengals	2	0	1.000	48	17
Baltimore Ravens	1	0	1.000	16	3
Buffalo Bills	6	2	.750	180	92
Denver Broncos	6	2	.750	189	166
New England Patriots**	6	2	.750	205	179
Kansas City Chiefs*	3	1	.750	81	61
Miami Dolphins	5	2	.714	152	115
Pittsburgh Steelers	6	7	.462	285	270
Indianapolis Colts#	2	3	.400	95	116
Tennessee Titans##	3	5	.375	133	195
Oakland Raiders###	5	9	.357	272	304
New York Jets	1	2	.333	37	60
San Diego Chargers***	2	7	.222	140	182
Seattle Seahawks	0	1	.000	14	30
Jacksonville Jaguars	0	2	.000	20	53
Cleveland Browns	0	3	.000	74	98

* One game played when franchise was in Dallas (Texans) (Won 20-17)

** One game played when franchise was in Boston (Lost 51-10)

*** One game played when franchise was in Los Angeles (Lost 24-16)

\# Two games played when franchise was in Baltimore (Won 27-17, Lost 21-0)

\#\# Six games played when franchise was in Houston and known as Oilers (Won 2, lost 4)

\#\#\# Two games played when franchise was in Los Angeles (Won 30-14, lost 51-3)

2007 AFC CHAMPIONSHIP GAME
Gillette Stadium, Foxborough, Massachusetts
January 20, 2008, Attendance: 68,756
NEW ENGLAND 21, SAN DIEGO 12—Laurence Maroney rushed for 122 yards and the Patriots played a bend-but-don't-break defense to advance to their fourth Super Bowl in seven seasons.

New England became the first team to win its first 18 games of a season. LaDainian Tomlinson, who injured his knee the previous week, attempted to play, but after 2 carries and a reception on the first two drives, he sat out the rest of the game. Philip Rivers, who also injured his knee against the Colts, played the entire game and three times drove the Chargers inside the Patriots' 10-yard line. It was not until afterward that it was revealed Rivers played despite having knee surgery six days earlier. Quentin Jammer's interception late in the first quarter led to Nate Kaeding's 26-yard field goal. The Patriots responded with a 65-yard touchdown drive. Vincent Jackson had catches of 15, 16, and 21 yards to reach the Patriots' 9 on their next drive, but San Diego again settled for Kaeding's field goal to pull within 7-6. With 4:36 left in the half, Asante Samuel intercepted Rivers' pass and two plays later Tom Brady completed a 12-yard touchdown pass to Jabar Gaffney for a 14-6 lead. A 26-yard run by Darren Sproles just before halftime led to Kaeding's 40-yard field goal, pulling the Chargers to within 14-9. Drayton Florence's interception to begin the second half led to the Chargers driving to the Patriots' 4. But on third-and-1, Junior Seau submarined Michael Turner for a 2-yard loss. Kaeding's fourth field goal cut the deficit to 14-12. The Patriots seemed poised to take a big lead on the next drive, but Antonio Cromartie intercepted Brady's pass in the end zone. New England forced a punt, and Maroney had a 20-yard run to set up Brady's 6-yard touchdown pass to Wes Welker for a 21-12 lead with 12:15 remaining. The Chargers punted on fourth-and-10 from the Patriots' 36 with 9:13 remaining and never got the ball back. Brady completed a swing pass to Kevin Faulk for exactly 11 yards on third-and-11, and then connected with Faulk for 14 yards on third-and-3. Maroney had a 5-yard run on third-and-2 with 3:36 left, and clinched the game with his 5-yard run on third-and-4 just after the two-minute warning. Brady was 22 of 33 for 209 yards and 2 touchdowns, with 3 interceptions. Maroney had 25 carries for 122 yards. Rivers was 19 of 37 for 211 yards, with 2 interceptions.

San Diego (12)	Offense	New England (21)
Brandon Manumaleuna	TE-WR	Wes Welker
Marcus McNeill	LT	Matt Light
Kris Dielman	LG	Logan Mankins
Nick Hardwick	C	Dan Koppen
Mike Goff	RG	Stephen Neal
Jeromey Clary	RT	Nick Kaczur
Antonio Gates	TE	Benjamin Watson
Vincent Jackson	WR	Randy Moss
Philip Rivers	QB	Tom Brady
Lorenzo Neal	RB	Kevin Faulk
LaDainian Tomlinson	FB/TE	Kyle Brady
	Defense	
Igor Olshansky	LE	Ty Warren
Jamal Williams	DT-NT	Vince Wilfork
Luis Castillo	RE-RE	Richard Seymour
Shaun Phillips	OLB	Mike Vrabel
Stephen Cooper	ILB	Junior Seau
Matt Wihelm	ILB	Tedy Bruschi
Shawne Merriman	OLB	Adalius Thomas
Quentin Jammer	LCB	Asante Samuel
Antonio Cromartie	RCB	Ellis Hobbs
Clinton Hart	SS	Rodney Harrison
Marlon McCree	FS	James Sanders

SUBSTITUTIONS
SAN DIEGO—Specialists: K—Nate Kaeding. P—Mike Scifres. LS—David Binn. Offense: RB—Darren Sproles, Michael Turner. FB—Andrew Pinnock. WR—Chris Chambers, Craig Davis, Kassim Osgood. TE/WR—Legedu Naanee. T—Shane Olivea. C/G—Scott Mruczkowski. Defense: DT—Ryon Bingham. DE—Jacques Cesaire. LB—Tim Dobbins, Marques Harris, Brandon Siler, Jyles Tucker. CB—Drayton Florence. CB/S—Steve Gregory. S—Eric Weddle. DNP: QB—Billy Volek. C/G—Cory Withrow. Not Active: K—David Rayner. QB—Charlie Whitehurst. WR—Malcolm Floyd. TE—Scott Chandler. DT—Brandon McKinney. LB—Anthony

Waters. CB—Cletis Gordon, Paul Oliver.
NEW ENGLAND—Specialists: K—Stephen Gostkowski. P—Chris Hanson. LS—Lonie Paxton. Offense: RB—Kyle Eckel, Heath Evans, Laurence Maroney. WR—Jabar Gaffney, Donte' Stallworth, Kelley Washington. TE—Stephen Spach. G/C—Russ Hochstein T—Ryan O'Callaghan. Defense: DL—Jarvis Green, Rashad Moore. LB—Eric Alexander, Larry Izzo, Pierre Woods. CB—Randall Gay. DB—Willie Andrews, Brandon Meriweather, Raymond Ventrone, Eugene Wilson. DNP: QB—Matt Cassel. Not Active: QB—Matt Gutierrez. WR—Troy Brown, Chad Jackson. G—Billy Yates. T—Wesley Britt. DL—Le Kevin Smith. CB—Antwan Spann. S—Mel Mitchell.

OFFICIALS
Referee—Jeff Triplette. Umpire—Butch Hannah. Line Judge—Gary Arthur. Side Judge—Greg Meyer. Head Linesman—Steve Stelljes. Back Judge—Gregory Steed. Field Judge—Tom Sifferman. Replay Official—Howard Slavin. Video Operator—Terry Sullivan.

SCORING

San Diego	3	6	3	0	—	12
New England	0	14	0	7	—	21

SD — FG Kaeding 26
NE — Maroney 1 run (Gostkowski kick)
SD — FG Kaeding 23
NE — Gaffney 12 pass from Brady (Gostkowski kick)
SD — FG Kaeding 40
SD — FG Kaeding 24
NE — Welker 6 pass from Brady (Gostkowski kick)

TEAM STATISTICS	SD	NE
Total First Downs	17	25
Rushing	4	13
Passing	12	11
Penalty	1	1
Total Net Yardage	311	347
Total Offensive Plays	60	66
Average Gain Per Offensive Play	5.2	5.3
Rushes	22	31
Yards Gained Rushing (Net)	104	149
Average Yards per Rush	4.7	4.8
Passes Attempted	37	33
Passes Completed	19	22
Had Intercepted	2	3
Tackled Attempting to Pass	1	2
Yards Lost Attempting to Pass	4	11
Yards Gained Passing (Net)	207	198
Punts	5	4
Average Distance	38.0	40.0
Punt Returns	3	0
Punt Return Yardage	16	0
Kickoff Returns	4	5
Kickoff Return Yardage	84	92
Interception Return Yardage	14	7
Total Return Yardage	30	7
Fumbles	1	1
Fumbles Lost	0	0
Own Fumbles Recovered	1	1
Opponent Fumbles Recovered	0	0
Penalties	1	2
Yards Penalized	5	19
Field Goals	4	0
Field Goals Attempted	4	0
Third-Down Efficiency	3/12	7/13
Fourth-Down Efficiency	0/0	0/0
Time of Possession	26:40	33:20

INDIVIDUAL STATISTICS
RUSHING: SD: Turner 17-65-0, Sproles 3-34-0, Tomlinson 2-5-0. NE: Maroney 25-122-1, Moss 1-14-0, Faulk 1-8-0, Evans 2-7-0,. T. Brady 2-(-2)-0.
PASSING: SD: Rivers 37-19-211-0-2. NE: Brady 33-22-209-2-3.

RECEIVING: SD: Chambers 7-90-0, Jackson 6-93-0, Gates 2-17-0, Sproles 2-5-0, Turner 1-5-0, Tomlinson 1-1-0. NE: Faulk 8-82-0, Welker 7-56-1, Stallworth 2-11-0, Moss 1-18-0, Evans 1-13-0, Gaffney 1-12-1, Maroney 1-9-0, Watson 1-8-0.
KICKOFF RETURNS: SD: Sproles 4-84-0. NE: Maroney 2-43-0, Hobbs 2-39-0, Andrews 1-10-0.

PUNT RETURNS: SD: Sproles 3-16-0. NE: Welker 0-0-0, Faulk 0-0-0.
PUNTING: SD: Scifres 5-190-38.0. NE: Hanson 4-160-40.0.
INTERCEPTIONS: SD: Florence 1-7-0, Cromartie 1-7-0, Jammer 1-0-0. NE: Samuel 1-10-0, Hobbs 1-(-3)-0.
SACKS: SD: Castillo 1, Cooper 0.5, Olshansky 0.5. NE: Seau 1.

NFC CHAMPIONSHIP GAME RESULTS
Includes NFL Championship Games (1933-1969)

Season	Date	Winner (Share)	Loser (Share)	Score	Site	Attendance
2007	Jan. 20	N.Y. Giants ($37,500)	Green Bay ($37,500)	23-20*	Green Bay	72,740
2006	Jan. 21	Chicago ($37,000)	New Orleans ($37,000)	39-14	Chicago	61,817
2005	Jan. 22	Seattle ($37,000)	Carolina ($37,000)	34-14	Seattle	67,837
2004	Jan. 23	Philadelphia ($36,500)	Atlanta ($36,500)	27-10	Philadelphia	67,717
2003	Jan. 18	Carolina ($36,500)	Philadelphia ($36,500)	14-3	Philadelphia	67,862
2002	Jan. 19	Tampa Bay ($35,000)	Philadelphia ($35,000)	27-10	Philadelphia	66,713
2001	Jan. 27	St. Louis ($34,500)	Philadelphia ($34,500)	29-24	St. Louis	66,502
2000	Jan. 14	N.Y. Giants ($34,500)	Minnesota ($34,500)	41-0	East Rutherford	79,310
1999	Jan. 23	St. Louis ($33,000)	Tampa Bay ($33,000)	11-6	St. Louis	66,396
1998	Jan. 17	Atlanta ($32,500)	Minnesota ($32,500)	30-27*	Minnesota	64,060
1997	Jan. 11	Green Bay ($30,000)	San Francisco ($30,000)	23-10	San Francisco	68,987
1996	Jan. 12	Green Bay ($29,000)	Carolina ($29,000)	30-13	Green Bay	60,216
1995	Jan. 14	Dallas ($27,000)	Green Bay ($27,000)	38-27	Dallas	65,135
1994	Jan. 15	San Francisco ($26,000)	Dallas ($26,000)	38-28	San Francisco	69,125
1993	Jan. 23	Dallas ($23,500)	San Francisco ($23,500)	38-21	Dallas	64,902
1992	Jan. 17	Dallas ($18,000)	San Francisco ($18,000)	30-20	San Francisco	64,920
1991	Jan. 12	Washington ($18,000)	Detroit ($18,000)	41-10	Washington	55,585
1990	Jan. 20	N.Y. Giants ($18,000)	San Francisco ($18,000)	15-13	San Francisco	65,750
1989	Jan. 14	San Francisco ($18,000)	L.A. Rams ($18,000)	30-3	San Francisco	65,634
1988	Jan. 8	San Francisco ($18,000)	Chicago ($18,000)	28-3	Chicago	66,946
1987	Jan. 17	Washington ($18,000)	Minnesota ($18,000)	17-10	Washington	55,212
1986	Jan. 11	New York Giants ($18,000)	Washington ($18,000)	17-0	East Rutherford	76,891
1985	Jan. 12	Chicago ($18,000)	L.A. Rams ($18,000)	24-0	Chicago	66,030
1984	Jan. 6	San Francisco ($18,000)	Chicago ($18,000)	23-0	San Francisco	61,336
1983	Jan. 8	Washington ($18,000)	San Francisco ($18,000)	24-21	Washington	55,363
1982	Jan. 22	Washington ($18,000)	Dallas ($18,000)	31-17	Washington	55,045
1981	Jan. 10	San Francisco ($9,000)	Dallas ($9,000)	28-27	San Francisco	60,525
1980	Jan. 11	Philadelphia ($9,000)	Dallas ($9,000)	20-7	Philadelphia	71,522
1979	Jan. 6	Los Angeles ($9,000)	Tampa Bay ($9,000)	9-0	Tampa	72,033
1978	Jan. 7	Dallas ($9,000)	Los Angeles ($9,000)	28-0	Los Angeles	71,086
1977	Jan. 1	Dallas ($9,000)	Minnesota ($9,000)	23-6	Dallas	64,293
1976	Dec. 26	Minnesota ($8,500)	Los Angeles ($5,500)	24-13	Minneapolis	48,379
1975	Jan. 4	Dallas ($8,500)	Los Angeles ($5,500)	37-7	Los Angeles	88,919
1974	Dec. 29	Minnesota ($8,500)	Los Angeles ($5,500)	14-10	Minneapolis	48,444
1973	Dec. 30	Minnesota ($8,500)	Dallas ($5,500)	27-10	Dallas	64,422
1972	Dec. 31	Washington ($8,500)	Dallas ($5,500)	26-3	Washington	53,129
1971	Jan. 2	Dallas ($8,500)	San Francisco ($5,500)	14-3	Dallas	63,409
1970	Jan. 3	Dallas ($8,500)	San Francisco ($5,500)	17-10	San Francisco	59,364
1969	Jan. 4	Minnesota ($7,930)	Cleveland ($5,118)	27-7	Minneapolis	46,503
1968	Dec. 29	Baltimore ($9,306)	Cleveland ($5,963)	34-0	Cleveland	78,410
1967	Dec. 31	Green Bay ($7,950)	Dallas ($5,299)	21-17	Green Bay	50,861
1966	Jan. 1	Green Bay ($9,813)	Dallas ($6,527)	34-27	Dallas	74,152
1965	Jan. 2	Green Bay ($7,819)	Cleveland ($5,288)	23-12	Green Bay	50,777
1964	Dec. 27	Cleveland ($8,052)	Baltimore ($5,571)	27-0	Cleveland	79,544
1963	Dec. 29	Chicago ($5,899)	New York ($4,218)	14-10	Chicago	45,801
1962	Dec. 30	Green Bay ($5,888)	New York ($4,166)	16-7	New York	64,892
1961	Dec. 31	Green Bay ($5,195)	New York ($3,339)	37-0	Green Bay	39,029
1960	Dec. 26	Philadelphia ($5,116)	Green Bay ($3,105)	17-13	Philadelphia	67,325
1959	Dec. 27	Baltimore ($4,674)	New York ($3,083)	31-16	Baltimore	57,545
1958	Dec. 28	Baltimore ($4,718)	New York ($3,111)	23-17*	New York	64,185
1957	Dec. 29	Detroit ($4,295)	Cleveland ($2,750)	59-14	Detroit	55,263
1956	Dec. 30	New York ($3,779)	Chi. Bears ($2,485)	47-7	New York	56,836
1955	Dec. 26	Cleveland ($3,508)	Los Angeles ($2,316)	38-14	Los Angeles	85,693
1954	Dec. 26	Cleveland ($2,478)	Detroit ($1,585)	56-10	Cleveland	43,827
1953	Dec. 27	Detroit ($2,424)	Cleveland ($1,654)	17-16	Detroit	54,577
1952	Dec. 28	Detroit ($2,274)	Cleveland ($1,712)	17-7	Cleveland	50,934
1951	Dec. 23	Los Angeles ($2,108)	Cleveland ($1,483)	24-17	Los Angeles	57,522
1950	Dec. 24	Cleveland ($1,113)	Los Angeles ($686)	30-28	Cleveland	29,751
1949	Dec. 18	Philadelphia ($1,094)	Los Angeles ($739)	14-0	Los Angeles	27,980
1948	Dec. 19	Philadelphia ($1,540)	Chi. Cardinals ($874)	7-0	Philadelphia	36,309
1947	Dec. 28	Chi. Cardinals ($1,132)	Philadelphia ($754)	28-21	Chicago	30,759

Season	Date	Winner (Share)	Loser (Share)	Score	Site	Attendance
1946	Dec. 15	Chi. Bears ($1,975)	New York ($1,295)	24-14	New York	58,346
1945	Dec. 16	Cleveland ($1,469)	Washington ($902)	15-14	Cleveland	32,178
1944	Dec. 17	Green Bay ($1,449)	New York ($814)	14-7	New York	46,016
1943	Dec. 26	Chi. Bears ($1,146)	Washington ($765)	41-21	Chicago	34,320
1942	Dec. 13	Washington ($965)	Chi. Bears ($637)	14-6	Washington	36,006
1941	Dec. 21	Chi. Bears ($430)	New York ($288)	.37-9	Chicago	13,341
1940	Dec. 8	Chi. Bears ($873)	Washington ($606)	73-0	Washington	36,034
1939	Dec. 10	Green Bay ($703.97)	New York ($455.57)	27-0	Milwaukee	32,279
1938	Dec. 11	New York ($504.45)	Green Bay ($368.81)	23-17	New York	48,120
1937	Dec. 12	Washington ($225.90)	Chi. Bears ($127.78)	28-21	Chicago	15,870
1936	Dec. 13	Green Bay ($250)	Boston ($180)	21-6	New York	29,545
1935	Dec. 15	Detroit ($313.35)	New York ($200.20)	26-7	Detroit	15,000
1934	Dec. 9	New York ($621)	Chi. Bears ($414.02)	30-13	New York	35,059
1933	Dec. 17	Chi. Bears ($210.34)	New York ($140.22)	23-21	Chicago	26,000

*Sudden death overtime

NFC CHAMPIONSHIP GAME COMPOSITE STANDINGS

	W	L	Pct.	Pts.	OP
Seattle Seahawks	1	0	1.000	34	14
Baltimore Colts	3	1	.750	88	60
Green Bay Packers	10	4	.714	323	200
Detroit Lions	4	2	.667	139	141
Washington Redskins*	7	5	.583	222	255
Chicago Bears	8	6	.571	325	259
Philadelphia Eagles	5	4	.556	143	128
Dallas Cowboys	8	8	.500	361	319
Minnesota Vikings	4	4	.500	135	151
Arizona Cardinals**	1	1	.500	28	28
Atlanta Falcons	1	1	.500	40	54
San Francisco 49ers	5	7	.417	245	222
New York Giants	7	11	.389	304	342
Cleveland Browns	4	7	.364	224	253
St. Louis Rams***	5	9	.357	163	300
Carolina Panthers	1	2	.333	41	67
Tampa Bay Buccaneers	1	2	.333	33	30
New Orleans Saints	0	1	.000	14	39

*One game played when franchise was in Boston (Lost 21-6)
**Both games played when franchise was in Chicago (Won 28-21, lost 7-0)
***One game played when franchise was in Cleveland (Won 15-14), and 11 games when franchise was in Los Angeles (Won 2, lost 9, scored 108 points, allowed 256 points).

2007 NFC CHAMPIONSHIP GAME

Lambeau Field, Green Bay, Wisconsin
January 20, 2008, Attendance: 72,740

N.Y. GIANTS 23, GREEN BAY 20 (OT)—After missing 2 fourth-quarter field goals, Lawrence Tynes made a 47-yard field goal 2:35 into overtime as the Giants earned their second Super Bowl appearance in 17 years. Playing in sub-zero temperatures, the kickoff wind chill of minus-23 made this the third coldest game in NFL postseason history, trailing just the 1967 NFL Championship Game (The Ice Bowl) and the 1981 AFC Championship Game. The Giants outgained the Packers 377-264 in total yards, and maintained possession for 40:01 of the game's 62:35. Tynes' second field goal of the first half gave the Giants a 6-0 lead. On the next play, Brett Favre completed a 90-yard touchdown pass to Donald Driver for a 7-6 lead. The Packers added a field goal just before halftime, but the Giants opened the second half with a 12-play, 69-yard touchdown drive, capped by Brandon Jacobs' 1-yard scoring plunge for a 13-10 lead. Tramon Williams returned the ensuing kickoff 49 yards, and Favre completed a 12-yard touchdown pass to Donald Lee moments later for a 17-13 lead with 5:00 left in the third quarter. Domenik Hixon answered with a 33-yard kickoff return, and Eli Manning completed a 23-yard pass to Amani Toomer to set up Ahmad Bradshaw's 4-yard scoring run for a 20-17 advantage. The Packers drove to the Giants' 31, but

R.W. McQuarters intercepted a pass. However, Ryan Grant forced McQuarters to fumble the return, and Mark Tauscher recovered at the Giants' 19. Mason Crosby tied the game four plays later with a 37-yard field goal with 11:46 remaining. Tynes misses a 43-yard field-goal attempt wide left with 6:49 left, and his 36-yard field-goal attempt as time expired went wide left, also, forcing overtime. The Packers won the coin toss, but on the second play of overtime Corey Webster intercepted Favre's pass and returned the ball 9 yards to the Packers' 34. On fourth-and-5, Tynes kicked a 47-yard field goal for victory. Manning was 21 of 40 for 251 yards. Plaxico Burress had 11 receptions for 151 yards. Favre was 19 of 35 for 236 yards and 2 touchdowns, with 2 interceptions. Driver had 5 catches for 141 yards.

N.Y. Giants (23)	Offense	Green Bay (20)
Plaxico Burress	WR	Donald Driver
David Diehl	LT	Chad Clifton
Rich Seubert	LG	Daryn Colledge
Shaun O'Hara	C	Scott Wells
Chris Snee	RG	Jason Spitz
Kareem McKenzie	RT	Mark Tauscher
Kevin Boss	TE	Donald Lee
Amani Toomer	WR/FB	Korey Hall
Eli Manning	QB	Brett Favre
Brandon Jacobs	RB	Ryan Grant
Madison Hedgecock	FB	John Kuhn
	Defense	
Michael Strahan	LE	Aaron Kampman
Barry Cofield	NT/LT	Ryan Pickett
Fred Robbins	DT/RT	Corey Williams
Osi Umenyiora	RE	Cullen Jenkins
Reggie Torbor	SLB	Brady Poppinga
Antonio Pierce	MLB	Nick Barnett
Kawika Mitchell	WLB	A.J. Hawk
R.W. McQuarters	LCB	Charles Woodson
Corey Webster	RCB	Al Harris
James Butler	SS	Atari Bigby
Gibril Wilson	FS	Nick Collins

SUBSTITUTIONS

N.Y. GIANTS—Specialists: K—Lawrence Tynes. P—Jeff Feagles. Offense: RB—Ahmad Bradshaw, Reuben Droughns. WR—Domenik Hixon, Steve Smith, David Tyree. TE—Michael Matthews. G—Kevin Boothe. T—Guy Whimper. C—Grey Ruegamer. Defense: DT—Jay Alford. DE—Dave Tollefson, Justin Tuck. LB—Chase Blackburn, Torrance Daniels, Zak DeOssie, Gerris Wilkinson. CB—Sam Madison, Geoffrey Pope, Aaron Ross. S—Michael Johnson. DNP: QB—Anthony Wright. Not Active: QB—Jared Lorenzen. RB—Danny Ware. WR—Sinorice Moss. TE—Jerome Collins. T—Adam Koets. DT—Russell Davis, Manuel Wright. CB—Kevin Dockery.

GREEN BAY—Specialists: K—Mason Crosby. P—Jon Ryan. LS—Rob Davis. Offense: RB—Brandon Jackson, Vernand

Morency. WR—Greg Jennings, James Jones, Ruvell Martin, Koren Robinson. TE—Bubba Franks. G—Allen Barbre. T—Tony Moll. Defense: DT—Justin Harrell. DE—Kabeer Gbaja-Biamila, Jason Hunter, Michael Montgomery. LB—Desmond Bishop, Tracy White. CB—Jarrett Bush, Charlie Peprah, Tramon Williams. S—Aaron Rouse. DNP: QB—Aaron Rodgers. Not Active: QB—Craig Nall. WR—Shaun Bodiford. TE—Ryan Krause. T—Orrin Thompson. DT—Conrad Bolston, Daniel Muir. CB—Will Blackmon, Frank Walker.

OFFICIALS
Referee—Terry McAulay. Umpire—Roy Ellison. Line Judge—Jeff Bergman. Side Judge—Rick Patterson. Head Linesman—Jim Mello. Back Judge—Perry Paganelli. Field Judge—Scott Steenson. Replay Official—Bobby Boylston. Video Operator—David Coleman.

SCORING

N.Y. Giants	3	3	14	0	3	—	23
Green Bay	0	10	7	3	0	—	20

NYG — FG Tynes 37
GB — Driver 90 pass from Favre (Crosby kick)
GB — FG Crosby 36
NYG — Jacobs 1 run (Tynes kick)
GB — Lee 12 pass from Favre (Crosby kick)
NYG — Bradshaw 4 run (Tynes kick)
GB — FG Crosby 37
NYG — FG Tynes 47

TEAM STATISTICS	NYG	GB
Total First Downs	24	13
Rushing	8	2
Passing	12	9
Penalty	4	2
Total Net Yardage	377	264
Total Offensive Plays	81	49
Average Gain Per Offensive Play	4.7	5.4
Rushes	39	14
Yards Gained Rushing (Net)	134	28
Average Yards per Rush	3.4	2.0
Passes Attempted	40	35
Passes Completed	21	19
Had Intercepted	0	2
Tackled Attempting to Pass	2	0
Yards Lost Attempting to Pass	8	0
Yards Gained Passing (Net)	243	236
Punts	4	6
Average Distance	32.5	32.2
Punt Returns	4	2
Punt Return Yardage	24	1
Kickoff Returns	5	5
Kickoff Return Yardage	121	103
Interception Return Yardage	20	0
Total Return Yardage	44	1
Fumbles	5	1
Fumbles Lost	1	0
Own Fumbles Recovered	4	1
Opponent Fumbles Recovered	0	1
Penalties	6	7
Yards Penalized	50	37
Field Goals	3	2
Field Goals Attempted	5	2
Third-Down Efficiency	6/16	1/10
Fourth-Down Efficiency	0/1	0/0
Time of Possession	40:01	22:34

INDIVIDUAL STATISTCS
RUSHING: NYG: Jacobs 21-67-1, Bradshaw 16-63-1, Manning 2-4-0. GB: Grant 13-29-0, Favre 1-(-1)-0.
PASSING: NYG: Manning 40-21-251-0-0. GB: Favre 35-19-236-0-2.
RECEIVING: NYG: Burress 11-151-0, Toomer 4-42-0, Smith 2-25-0, Boss 1-12-0, Bradshaw 1-9-0, Jacobs 1-8-0, Tyree 1-4-0. GB: Driver 5-141-1, Robinson 4-16-0, Lee 3-35-1, Morency 2-9-0, Jennings 1-14-0, Hall 1-12-0, Franks 1-11-0, Jackson 1-1-0, Grant 1-(-3)-0.
KICKOFF RETURNS: NYG: Hixon 5-121-0. GB: Robinson 4-54-0, T. Williams 1-49-0.
PUNT RETURNS: NYG: McQuarters 4-24-0. GB: T. Williams 2-1-0.
PUNTING: NYG: Feagles 4-130-32.5. GB: Ryan 6-193-32.2.
INTERCEPTIONS: NYG: McQuarters 1-11-0, Webster 1-9-0. GB: None.
SACKS: NYG: None. GB: Gbaja-Biamila 1, Hawk 1.

AFC DIVISIONAL PLAYOFFS RESULTS
Includes Second-Round Playoff Games (1982), AFC Inter-Divisional Games (1969), and special playoff games to break ties for AFL Division Championships (1963, 1968)

Season	Date	Winner (Share)	Loser (Share)	Score	Site	Attendance
2007	Jan. 12	New England ($20,000)	Jacksonville ($20,000)	31-20	Foxborough	68,756
	Jan. 13	San Diego ($20,000)	Indianapolis ($20,000)	28-24	Indianapolis	56,950
2006	Jan. 14	New England ($19,000)	San Diego ($19,000)	24-21	San Diego	68,810
	Jan. 13	Indianapolis ($19,000)	Baltimore ($19,000)	15-6	Baltimore	71,162
2005	Jan. 15	Pittsburgh ($19,000)	Indianapolis ($19,000)	21-18	Indianapolis	57,449
	Jan. 14	Denver ($19,000)	New England ($19,000)	27-13	Denver	76,238
2004	Jan. 16	New England ($18,000)	Indianapolis ($18,000)	20-3	Foxborough	68,756
	Jan. 15	Pittsburgh ($18,000)	N.Y. Jets ($18,000)	20-17*	Pittsburgh	64,915
2003	Jan. 11	Indianapolis ($18,000)	Kansas City ($18,000)	38-31	Kansas City	79,159
	Jan. 10	New England ($18,000)	Tennessee ($18,000)	17-14	Foxborough	68,436
2002	Jan. 12	Oakland ($17,000)	N.Y. Jets ($17,000)	30-10	Oakland	62,207
	Jan. 11	Tennessee ($17,000)	Pittsburgh ($17,000)	34-31*	Nashville	68,809
2001	Jan. 20	Pittsburgh ($17,000)	Baltimore ($17,000)	27-10	Pittsburgh	63,976
	Jan. 19	New England ($17,000)	Oakland ($17,000)	16-13*	Foxborough	60,292
2000	Jan. 7	Baltimore ($16,000)	Tennessee ($16,000)	24-10	Nashville	68,527
	Jan. 6	Oakland ($16,000)	Miami ($16,000)	27-0	Oakland	61,998
1999	Jan. 16	Tennessee ($16,000)	Indianapolis ($16,000)	19-16	Indianapolis	57,097
	Jan. 15	Jacksonville ($16,000)	Miami ($16,000)	62-7	Jacksonville	75,173
1998	Jan. 10	N.Y. Jets ($15,000)	Jacksonville ($15,000)	34-24	East Rutherford	78,817
	Jan. 9	Denver ($15,000)	Miami ($15,000)	38-3	Denver	75,729
1997	Jan. 4	Denver ($15,000)	Kansas City ($15,000)	14-10	Kansas City	76,965
	Jan. 3	Pittsburgh ($15,000)	New England ($15,000)	7-6	Pittsburgh	61,228
Season	**Date**	**Winner (Share)**	**Loser (Share)**	**Score**	**Site**	**Attendance**
1996	Jan. 5	New England ($14,000)	Pittsburgh ($14,000)	28-3	Foxborough	60,188
	Jan. 4	Jacksonville ($14,000)	Denver ($14,000)	30-27	Denver	75,678

1995	Jan. 7	Indianapolis ($13,000)	Kansas City ($13,000)	10-7	Kansas City	77,594
	Jan. 6	Pittsburgh ($13,000)	Buffalo ($13,000)	40-21	Pittsburgh	59,072
1994	Jan. 8	San Diego ($12,000)	Miami ($12,000)	22-21	San Diego	63,381
	Jan. 7	Pittsburgh ($12,000)	Cleveland ($12,000)	29-9	Pittsburgh	58,185
1993	Jan. 16	Kansas City ($12,000)	Houston ($12,000)	28-20	Houston	64,011
	Jan. 15	Buffalo ($12,000)	L.A. Raiders ($12,000)	29-23	Buffalo	61,923
1992	Jan. 10	Miami ($10,000)	San Diego ($10,000)	31-0	Miami	71,224
	Jan. 9	Buffalo ($10,000)	Pittsburgh ($10,000)	24-3	Pittsburgh	60,407
1991	Jan. 5	Buffalo ($10,000)	Kansas City ($10,000)	37-14	Buffalo	80,182
	Jan. 4	Denver ($10,000)	Houston ($10,000)	26-24	Denver	75,301
1990	Jan. 13	L.A. Raiders ($10,000)	Cincinnati ($10,000)	20-10	Los Angeles	92,045
	Jan. 12	Buffalo ($10,000)	Miami ($10,000)	44-34	Buffalo	77,087
1989	Jan. 7	Denver ($10,000)	Pittsburgh ($10,000)	24-23	Denver	75,477
	Jan. 6	Cleveland ($10,000)	Buffalo ($10,000)	34-30	Cleveland	78,921
1988	Jan. 1	Buffalo ($10,000)	Houston ($10,000)	17-10	Buffalo	79,532
	Dec. 31	Cincinnati ($10,000)	Seattle ($10,000)	21-13	Cincinnati	58,560
1987	Jan. 10	Denver ($10,000)	Houston ($10,000)	34-10	Denver	75,440
	Jan. 9	Cleveland ($10,000)	Indianapolis ($10,000)	38-21	Cleveland	79,372
1986	Jan. 4	Denver ($10,000)	New England ($10,000)	22-17	Denver	75,262
	Jan. 3	Cleveland ($10,000)	N.Y. Jets ($10,000)	23-20*	Cleveland	79,720
1985	Jan. 5	New England ($10,000)	L.A. Raiders ($10,000)	27-20	Los Angeles	87,163
	Jan. 4	Miami ($10,000)	Cleveland ($10,000)	24-21	Miami	74,667
1984	Dec. 30	Pittsburgh ($10,000)	Denver ($10,000)	24-17	Denver	74,981
	Dec. 29	Miami ($10,000)	Seattle ($10,000)	31-10	Miami	73,469
1983	Jan. 1	L.A. Raiders ($10,000)	Pittsburgh ($10,000)	38-10	Los Angeles	90,380
	Dec. 31	Seattle ($10,000)	Miami ($10,000)	27-20	Miami	74,136
1982	Jan. 16	Miami ($10,000)	San Diego ($10,000)	34-13	Miami	71,383
	Jan. 15	N.Y. Jets ($10,000)	L.A. Raiders ($10,000)	17-14	Los Angeles	90,038
1981	Jan. 3	Cincinnati ($5,000)	Buffalo ($5,000)	28-21	Cincinnati	55,420
	Jan. 2	San Diego ($5,000)	Miami ($5,000)	41-38*	Miami	73,735
1980	Jan. 4	Oakland ($5,000)	Cleveland ($5,000)	14-12	Cleveland	78,245
	Jan. 3	San Diego ($5,000)	Buffalo ($5,000)	20-14	San Diego	52,253
1979	Dec. 30	Pittsburgh ($5,000)	Miami ($5,000)	34-14	Pittsburgh	50,214
	Dec. 29	Houston ($5,000)	San Diego ($5,000)	17-14	San Diego	51,192
1978	Dec. 31	Houston ($5,000)	New England ($5,000)	31-14	Foxborough	60,735
	Dec. 30	Pittsburgh ($5,000)	Denver ($5,000)	33-10	Pittsburgh	50,230
1977	Dec. 24	Oakland ($5,000)	Baltimore ($5,000)	37-31*	Baltimore	59,925
	Dec. 24	Denver ($5,000)	Pittsburgh ($5,000)	34-21	Denver	75,059
1976	Dec. 19	Pittsburgh [$]	Baltimore [$]	40-14	Baltimore	59,296
	Dec. 18	Oakland [$]	New England [$]	24-21	Oakland	53,050
1975	Dec. 28	Oakland [$]	Cincinnati [$]	31-28	Oakland	53,030
	Dec. 27	Pittsburgh [$]	Baltimore [$]	28-10	Pittsburgh	49,557
1974	Dec. 22	Pittsburgh [$]	Buffalo [$]	32-14	Pittsburgh	49,841
	Dec. 21	Oakland [$]	Miami [$]	28-26	Oakland	53,023
1973	Dec. 23	Miami [$]	Cincinnati [$]	34-16	Miami	78,928
	Dec. 22	Oakland [$]	Pittsburgh [$]	33-14	Oakland	52,646
1972	Dec. 24	Miami [$]	Cleveland [$]	20-14	Miami	78,916
	Dec. 23	Pittsburgh [$]	Oakland [$]	13-7	Pittsburgh	50,327
1971	Dec. 26	Baltimore [$]	Cleveland [$]	20-3	Cleveland	70,734
	Dec. 25	Miami [$]	Kansas City [$]	27-24*	Kansas City	50,374
1970	Dec. 27	Oakland [$]	Miami [$]	21-14	Oakland	52,594
	Dec. 26	Baltimore [$]	Cincinnati [$]	17-0	Baltimore	49,694
1969	Dec. 21	Oakland [$]	Houston [$]	56-7	Oakland	53,539
	Dec. 20	Kansas City [$]	N.Y. Jets [$]	13-6	New York	62,977
1968	Dec. 22	Oakland [$]	Kansas City [$]	41-6	Oakland	53,605
1963	Dec. 28	Boston [$]	Buffalo [$]	26-8	Buffalo	33,044

*Sudden death overtime
$ Players received 1/14 of annual salary for playoff appearances.

2007 AFC DIVISIONAL PLAYOFF GAME

RCA Dome, Indianapolis, Indiana
January 13, 2008, Attendance: 56,950

SAN DIEGO 28, INDIANAPOLIS 24—Billy Volek scored on a quarterback sneak with 4:50 remaining, and the Chargers' defense made 2 fourth-down stops in the final 2:01 to advance to the AFC Championship Game for the first time in 13 years. The Colts outgained the Chargers 446-411 in total yards, but committed 3 turnovers compared to San Diego's 1 miscue. The Colts scored on their first possession, and drove to the Chargers' 22 on their next drive, but Marvin Harrison, playing his first game in 11 weeks after recovering from a knee injury, fumbled at the Chargers' 22 and Marlon McCree recovered. Philip Rivers completed 2 key third-down passes on the ensuing drive, capped by Vincent Jackson's 14-yard touchdown on third-and-8, to tie the game. LaDainian Tomlinson injured his knee on the play prior to Jackson's scoring catch, and did not return. Trailing 10-7, Antonio Cromartie intercepted Peyton Manning's pass on the final play of the half, and weaved his way 89 yards into the end zone, but a holding penalty nullified the return. Undaunted, the Chargers opened the second half with an 83-yard touchdown drive, capped by Rivers' perfect pass to Chris Chambers, between two defenders in the end zone, for a 30-yard touchdown. The Colts drove to the Chargers' 4, but Eric Weddle intercepted Manning's pass to thwart the drive. On their next possession, the Colts took a 17-14 lead on Manning's 9-yard touchdown pass to Reggie Wayne, who clipped the right front pylon while diving for the goal line. On the ensuing possession, faced with third-and-14, Rivers connected on a 22-yard pass to Chambers. Two plays later, on the final play of the third quarter, Rivers dumped a screen pass to Darren Sproles, who broke free down the left sideline for a 56-yard touchdown and 21-17 lead. Rivers injured his knee on the play, and did not return. After an exchange of punts, faced with third-and-9, Manning completed a long 55-yard touchdown pass to Anthony Gonzalez for a 24-21 lead with 10:07 remaining. Billy Volek completed 3 of 4 passes on the next drive, including a 27-yard dump pass to Legedu Naanee, to set up Volek's 1-yard sneak with 4:50 to play. The Colts used Manning's 16-yard pass to Dallas Clark on fourth-and-5 to reach the Chargers' 9 with 2:51 remaining. Joseph Addai gained 2 yards, but then Manning fired three consecutive incomplete passes, the last with 2:01 to play. The Colts' defense forced a punt with 1:30 to play, and Mike Scifres boomed the punt 66 yards. T.J. Rushing's 12-yard return gave Manning the ball at his own 32. After a 5-yard pass to Addai, Manning again threw three straight incompletions, the last over Clark's head with 58 seconds left. Rivers was 14 of 19 for 264 yards and 3 touchdowns, with 1 interception. Volek was 3 of 4 for 48 yards. Manning was 33 of 48 for 402 yards and 3 touchdowns, with 2 interceptions.

San Diego	0	7	14	7	—	28
Indianapolis	7	3	7	7	—	21

Ind— Clark 25 pass from Manning (Vinatieri kick)
SD— Jackson 14 pass from Rivers (Kaeding kick)
Ind— FG Vinatieri 46
SD— Chambers 30 pass from Rivers (Kaeding kick)
Ind— Wayne 9 pass from Manning (Vinatieri kick)
SD— Sproles 56 pass from Rivers (Kaeding kick)
Ind— Gonzalez 55 pass from Manning (Vinatieri kick)
SD— Volek 1 run (Kaeding kick)

Gillette Stadium, Foxborough, Massachusetts
January 12, 2008, Attendance: 68,756
NEW ENGLAND 31, JACKSONVILLE 20—Tom Brady completed a postseason-record 92.9 percent of his passes as the Patriots advanced to the AFC Championship Game for the fifth time in seven seasons. The victory also allowed the Patriots to match the 1972 Dolphins as the only teams to win their first 17 games of a season. The Jaguars began the game with an 80-yard touchdown drive, but New England answered with touchdowns on their first two possessions. The latter was set up by David Garrard's fumble, forced by Ty Warren and recovered by Mike Vrabel at the Jaguars' 29. The Jaguars responded with a 95-yard touchdown drive to tie the game. New England had a chance to score before halftime, but Stephen Gostkowski missed a 35-yard field-goal attempt. Brady completed his first 16 passes until an incompletion to Ben Watson with 10:27 left in the third quarter. However, Brady completed 2 third-down passes on that possession, capped by Wes Welker's 6-yard touchdown to cap an 82-yard drive for a 21-14 lead. The Jaguars answered with a field goal, but Brady then completed all 4 pass attempts on the ensuing 76-yard drive, capped by Watson's 9-yard touchdown catch with 49 seconds left in the third quarter for a 28-17 lead. The Jaguars added Josh Scobee's second field goal of the half to pull within 28-20, but Brady then completed a 53-yard pass to Donte' Stallworth to set up Gostkowski's 35-yard field goal with 6:39 remaining for a 31-20 lead. Rodney Harrison intercepted a pass with 4:08 left, and Brady's final completion, an 8-yard pass to Stallworth on third-and-7, helped run out the clock until just 21 seconds remained. Harrison tied an NFL record with his fourth consecutive postseason game with an interception. Brady was 26 of 28 for 262 yards and 3 touchdowns. Laurence Maroney carried 22 times for 122 yards. Garrard was 22 of 33 for 278 yards and 2 touchdowns, with 1 interception.

Jacksonville	7	7	3	3	—	20
New England	7	7	14	3	—	31

Jax— M. Jones 8 pass from Garrard (Scobee kick)
NE— Watson 3 pass from Brady (Gostkowski kick)
NE— Maroney 1 run (Gostkowski kick)
Jax— Wilford 6 pass from Garrard (Scobee kick)
NE— Welker 6 pass from Brady (Gostkowski kick)
Jax— FG Scobee 39
NE— Watson 9 pass from Brady (Gostkowski kick)
Jax— FG Scobee 25
NE— FG Gostkowski 35

NFC DIVISIONAL PLAYOFFS RESULTS
Includes Second-Round Playoff Games (1982), NFL Conference Championship Games (1967-69), and special playoff games to break ties for NFL Division or Conference Championships (1941, 1943, 1947, 1950, 1952, 1957, 1958, 1965)

Season	Date	Winner (Share)	Loser (Share)	Score	Site	Attendance
2007	Jan. 13	N.Y. Giants ($20,000)	Dallas ($20,000)	21-17	Dallas	63,660
	Jan. 12	Green Bay ($20,000)	Seattle ($20,000)	42-20	Green Bay	72,168
2006	Jan. 14	Chicago ($19,000)	Seattle ($19,000)	27-24*	Chicago	62,184
	Jan. 13	New Orleans ($19,000)	Philadelphia ($19,000)	27-24	New Orleans	70,001
2005	Jan. 15	Carolina ($19,000)	Chicago ($19,000)	29-21	Chicago	62,209
	Jan. 14	Seattle ($19,000)	Washington ($19,000)	20-10	Seattle	67,551
2004	Jan. 16	Philadelphia ($18,000)	Minnesota ($18,000)	27-14	Philadelphia	67,722
	Jan. 15	Atlanta ($18,000)	St. Louis ($18,000)	47-17	Atlanta	70,709
2003	Jan. 11	Philadelphia ($18,000)	Green Bay ($18,000)	20-17*	Philadelphia	67,707
	Jan. 10	Carolina ($18,000)	St. Louis ($18,000)	29-23*	St. Louis	66,165
2002	Jan. 12	Tampa Bay ($17,000)	San Francisco ($17,000)	31-6	Tampa	65,599
	Jan. 11	Philadelphia ($17,000)	Atlanta ($17,000)	20-6	Philadelphia	66,452
2001	Jan. 20	St. Louis ($17,000)	Green Bay ($17,000)	45-17	St. Louis	66,338
	Jan. 19	Philadelphia ($17,000)	Chicago ($17,000)	33-19	Chicago	66,944
2000	Jan. 7	N.Y. Giants ($16,000)	Philadelphia ($16,000)	20-10	East Rutherford	78,765
	Jan. 6	Minnesota ($16,000)	New Orleans ($16,000)	34-16	Minneapolis	63,881
1999	Jan. 16	St. Louis ($16,000)	Minnesota ($16,000)	49-37	St. Louis	66,194
	Jan. 15	Tampa Bay ($16,000)	Washington ($16,000)	14-13	Tampa	65,835
1998	Jan. 10	Minnesota ($15,000)	Arizona ($15,000)	41-21	Minneapolis	63,760
	Jan. 9	Atlanta ($15,000)	San Francisco ($15,000)	20-18	Atlanta	70,262
1997	Jan. 4	Green Bay ($15,000)	Tampa Bay ($15,000)	21-7	Green Bay	60,327
	Jan. 3	San Francisco ($15,000)	Minnesota ($15,000)	38-22	San Francisco	65,018
1996	Jan. 5	Carolina ($14,000)	Dallas ($14,000)	26-17	Charlotte	72,808
	Jan. 4	Green Bay ($14,000)	San Francisco ($14,000)	35-14	Green Bay	60,787

PLAYOFF GAME SUMMARIES

Season	Date	Winner (Share)	Loser (Share)	Score	Site	Attendance
1995	Jan. 7	Dallas ($13,000)	Philadelphia ($13,000)	30-11	Dallas	64,371
	Jan. 6	Green Bay ($13,000)	San Francisco ($13,000)	27-17	San Francisco	69,311
1994	Jan. 8	Dallas ($12,000)	Green Bay ($12,000)	35-9	Dallas	64,745
	Jan. 7	San Francisco ($12,000)	Chicago ($12,000)	44-15	San Francisco	64,644
1993	Jan. 16	Dallas ($12,000)	Green Bay ($12,000)	27-17	Dallas	64,790
	Jan. 15	San Francisco ($12,000)	N.Y. Giants ($12,000)	44-3	San Francisco	67,143
1992	Jan. 10	Dallas ($10,000)	Philadelphia ($10,000)	34-10	Dallas	63,721
	Jan. 9	San Francisco ($10,000)	Washington ($10,000)	20-13	San Francisco	64,991
1991	Jan. 5	Detroit ($10,000)	Dallas ($10,000)	38-6	Detroit	78,290
	Jan. 4	Washington ($10,000)	Atlanta ($10,000)	24-7	Washington	55,181
1990	Jan. 13	N.Y. Giants ($10,000)	Chicago ($10,000)	31-3	East Rutherford	77,025
	Jan. 12	San Francisco ($10,000)	Washington ($10,000)	28-10	San Francisco	65,292
1989	Jan. 7	L.A. Rams ($10,000)	N.Y. Giants ($10,000)	19-13*	East Rutherford	76,526
	Jan. 6	San Francisco ($10,000)	Minnesota ($10,000)	41-13	San Francisco	64,918
1988	Jan. 1	San Francisco ($10,000)	Minnesota ($10,000)	34-9	San Francisco	61,848
	Dec. 31	Chicago ($10,000)	Philadelphia ($10,000)	20-12	Chicago	65,534
1987	Jan. 10	Washington ($10,000)	Chicago ($10,000)	21-17	Chicago	65,268
	Jan. 9	Minnesota ($10,000)	San Francisco ($10,000)	36-24	San Francisco	63,008
1986	Jan. 4	N.Y. Giants ($10,000)	San Francisco ($10,000)	49-3	East Rutherford	75,691
	Jan. 3	Washington ($10,000)	Chicago ($10,000)	27-13	Chicago	65,524
1985	Jan. 5	Chicago ($10,000)	N.Y. Giants ($10,000)	21-0	Chicago	65,670
	Jan. 4	L.A. Rams ($10,000)	Dallas ($10,000)	20-0	Anaheim	66,581
1984	Dec. 30	Chicago ($10,000)	Washington ($10,000)	23-19	Washington	55,431
	Dec. 29	San Francisco ($10,000)	N.Y. Giants ($10,000)	21-10	San Francisco	60,303
1983	Jan. 1	Washington ($10,000)	L.A. Rams ($10,000)	51-7	Washington	54,440
	Dec. 31	San Francisco ($10,000)	Detroit ($10,000)	24-23	San Francisco	59,979
1982	Jan. 16	Dallas ($10,000)	Green Bay ($10,000)	37-26	Dallas	63,972
	Jan. 15	Washington ($10,000)	Minnesota ($10,000)	21-7	Washington	54,593
1981	Jan. 3	San Francisco ($5,000)	N.Y. Giants ($5,000)	38-24	San Francisco	58,360
	Jan. 2	Dallas ($5,000)	Tampa Bay ($5,000)	38-0	Dallas	64,848
1980	Jan. 4	Dallas ($5,000)	Atlanta ($5,000)	30-27	Atlanta	59,793
	Jan. 3	Philadelphia ($5,000)	Minnesota ($5,000)	31-16	Philadelphia	70,178
1979	Dec. 30	Los Angeles ($5,000)	Dallas ($5,000)	21-19	Dallas	64,792
	Dec. 29	Tampa Bay ($5,000)	Philadelphia ($5,000)	24-17	Tampa	71,402
1978	Dec. 31	Los Angeles ($5,000)	Minnesota ($5,000)	34-10	Los Angeles	70,436
	Dec. 30	Dallas ($5,000)	Atlanta ($5,000)	27-20	Dallas	63,406
1977	Dec. 26	Dallas ($5,000)	Chicago ($5,000)	37-7	Dallas	63,260
	Dec. 26	Minnesota ($5,000)	Los Angeles ($5,000)	14-7	Los Angeles	70,203
1976	Dec. 19	Los Angeles [$]	Dallas [$]	14-12	Dallas	63,283
	Dec. 18	Minnesota [$]	Washington [$]	35-20	Minneapolis	47,466
1975	Dec. 28	Dallas [$]	Minnesota [$]	17-14	Minneapolis	48,050
	Dec. 27	Los Angeles [$]	St. Louis [$]	35-23	Los Angeles	73,459
1974	Dec. 22	Los Angeles [$]	Washington [$]	19-10	Los Angeles	77,925
	Dec. 21	Minnesota [$]	St. Louis [$]	30-14	Minneapolis	48,150
1973	Dec. 23	Dallas [$]	Los Angeles [$]	27-16	Dallas	63,272
	Dec. 22	Minnesota [$]	Washington [$]	27-20	Minneapolis	48,040
1972	Dec. 24	Washington [$]	Green Bay [$]	16-3	Washington	52,321
	Dec. 23	Dallas [$]	San Francisco [$]	30-28	San Francisco	59,746
1971	Dec. 26	San Francisco [$]	Washington [$]	24-20	San Francisco	45,327
	Dec. 25	Dallas [$]	Minnesota [$]	20-12	Minneapolis	47,307
1970	Dec. 27	San Francisco [$]	Minnesota [$]	17-14	Minneapolis	45,103
	Dec. 26	Dallas [$]	Detroit [$]	5-0	Dallas	69,613
1969	Dec. 28	Cleveland [$]	Dallas [$]	38-14	Dallas	69,321
	Dec. 27	Minnesota [$]	Los Angeles [$]	23-20	Minneapolis	47,900
1968	Dec. 22	Baltimore [$]	Minnesota [$]	24-14	Baltimore	60,238
	Dec. 21	Cleveland [$]	Dallas [$]	31-20	Cleveland	81,497
1967	Dec. 24	Dallas [$]	Cleveland [$]	52-14	Dallas	70,786
	Dec. 23	Green Bay [$]	Los Angeles [$]	28-7	Milwaukee	49,861
1965	Dec. 26	Green Bay [$]	Baltimore [$]	13-10*	Green Bay	50,484
1958	Dec. 21	N.Y. Giants (#)	Cleveland (#)	10-0	New York	61,274
1957	Dec. 22	Detroit (#)	San Francisco (#)	31-27	San Francisco	60,118
1952	Dec. 21	Detroit (#)	Los Angeles (#)	31-21	Detroit	47,645
1950	Dec. 17	Los Angeles (#)	Chicago Bears (#)	24-14	Los Angeles	83,501
	Dec. 17	Cleveland (#)	N.Y. Giants (#)	8-3	Cleveland	33,054
1947	Dec. 21	Philadelphia (#)	Pittsburgh (#)	21-0	Pittsburgh	35,729
1943	Dec. 19	Washington (¢)	N.Y. Giants (¢)	28-0	New York	42,800
1941	Dec. 14	Chicago Bears (¢)	Green Bay (¢)	33-14	Chicago	43,425

*Sudden death overtime
$ Players received 1/14 of annual salary for playoff appearances.
# Players received 1/12 of annual salary for playoff appearances.
¢ Players received 1/10 of annual salary for playoff appearances.

2007 NFC DIVISIONAL PLAYOFF GAMES
Texas Stadium, Irving, Texas
January 13, 2008, Attendance: 63,660

N.Y. GIANTS 21, DALLAS 17—R.W. McQuarters intercepted a pass in the end zone with nine seconds remaining as the Giants advanced to the NFC Championship Game for the first time in seven seasons. On the game's opening possession, Amani Toomer caught a short pass, spun away from the defense, and raced into the end zone for a 52-yard touchdown. Late in the first quarter, Marion Barber had carries for 36 and 20 yards on a 96-yard touchdown drive to tie the game. The Cowboys' defense then forced a punt, and the offense marched 90 yards in 20 plays, highlighted by 3 third-down completions by Tony Romo, and capped by Barber's 1-yard touchdown run for a 14-7 lead with just 53 seconds left in the half. However, Eli Manning completed passes of 22 and 11 yards to Steve Smith, and a 19-yard pass to Kevin Boss to the Cowboys' 4 with 11 seconds left. Manning completed the drive with a 4-yard touchdown toss to Toomer with seven seconds left in the half to tie the game. The Cowboys opened the second half with a field goal, but late in the quarter McQuarters' 25-yard punt return to the Cowboys' 37, and Manning's 11-yard pass to Smith on third-and-6, led to Brandon Jacobs' 1-yard touchdown run for a 21-17 lead with 13:29 to play. The Giants' defense forced two punts, but the Cowboys got the ball at the Giants' 48 with 1:50 to play. Romo completed three passes to the Giants' 23, but on fourth-and-11 McQuarters intercepted his pass in the end zone with nine seconds remaining. Manning was 12 of 18 for 163 yards and 2 touchdowns. Romo was 18 of 36 for 201 yards and 1 touchdown, with 1 interception. Barber carried 27 times for 129 yards.

N.Y. Giants	7	7	0	7	—	21
Dallas	0	14	3	0	—	17

NYG — Toomer 52 pass from Manning (Tynes kick)
Dall — Owens 5 pass from Romo (Folk kick)
Dall — Barber 1 run (Folk kick)
NYG — Toomer 4 pass from Manning (Tynes kick)
Dall — FG Folk 34
NYG — Jacobs 1 run (Tynes kick)

Lambeau Field, Green Bay, Wisconsin
January 12, 2008, Attendance: 72,168

GREEN BAY 42, SEATTLE 20—Ryan Grant rushed for 201 yards and 3 touchdowns, and Brett Favre added 3 scoring passes, as Green Bay scored the game's final six touchdowns. The Packers outgained the Seahawks 408-200 in total yards. Seattle benefited early as Grant fumbled twice in the first 1:09. Lofa Tatupu recovered the first fumble and returned it 12 yards to the Packers' 1, setting up Shaun Alexander's touchdown 20 seconds into the game. Grant's second fumble was recovered by Jordan Babineaux at the Packers' 49. Matt Hasselbeck's 11-yard touchdown pass to Bobby Engram six plays later gave Seattle a 14-0 lead with 10:59 left in the first quarter. The Packers responded by scoring touchdowns on their next six possessions. Five of the scoring drives covered at least 64 yards, with the exception coming on the first play of the second quarter. With the score tied 14-14, Atari Bigby forced Marcus Pollard to fumble. Aaron Kampman recovered at the Seahawks' 18, and Favre completed a 2-yard touchdown pass to Greg Jennings three plays later for a 21-14 lead. Snow began falling in the second quarter and blanketed the field for the remainder of the game. The Seahawks' defense finally stopped the Packers with 9:11 to play, and the offense drove to the Packers' 41 trailing 42-20, but Hasselbeck threw four consecutive incompletions to end the drive with 8:03 to play. Favre was 18 of 23 for 173 yards and 3 touchdowns. Grant carried 27 times for 201 yards. Hasselbeck was 19 of 33 for 194 yards and 1 touchdown.

Seattle	14	3	3	0	—	20
Green Bay	14	14	7	7	—	42

Sea — Alexander 1 run (J. Brown kick)
Sea — Engram 11 pass from Hasselbeck (J. Brown kick)
GB — Jennings 15 pass from Favre (Crosby kick)
GB — Grant 1 run (Crosby kick)
GB — Jennings 2 pass from Favre (Crosby kick)
Sea — FG J. Brown 29
GB — Grant 3 run (Crosby kick)
GB — B. Jackson 13 pass from Favre (Crosby kick)
Sea — FG J. Brown 27
GB — Grant 1 run (Crosby kick)

AFC WILD CARD PLAYOFF GAMES RESULTS

Season	Date	Winner (Share)	Loser (Share)	Score	Site	Attendance
2007	Jan. 6	San Diego ($20,000)	Tennessee ($18,000)	17-6	San Diego	65,640
	Jan. 5	Jacksonville ($18,000)	Pittsburgh ($20,000)	31-29	Pittsburgh	63,629
2006	Jan. 7	New England ($19,000)	N.Y. Jets ($17,000)	37-16	Foxborough	68,756
	Jan. 6	Indianapolis ($19,000)	Kansas City ($17,000)	23-8	Indianapolis	57,215
2005	Jan. 8	Pittsburgh ($17,000)	Cincinnati ($19,000)	31-17	Cincinnati	65,870
	Jan. 7	New England ($19,000)	Jacksonville ($17,000)	28-3	Foxborough	68,756
2004	Jan. 9	Indianapolis ($18,000)	Denver ($15,000)	49-24	Indianapolis	56,609
	Jan. 8	N.Y. Jets ($15,000)	San Diego ($18,000)	20-17*	San Diego	67,536
2003	Jan. 4	Indianapolis ($18,000)	Denver ($15,000)	41-10	Indianapolis	56,586
	Jan. 3	Tennessee ($15,000)	Baltimore ($18,000)	20-17	Baltimore	69,452
2002	Jan. 5	Pittsburgh ($17,000)	Cleveland ($12,500)	36-33	Pittsburgh	62,595
	Jan. 4	N.Y. Jets ($17,000)	Indianapolis ($12,500)	41-0	East Rutherford	78,524
2001	Jan. 13	Baltimore ($12,500)	Miami ($12,500)	20-3	Miami	72,251
	Jan. 12	Oakland ($17,000)	N.Y. Jets ($12,500)	38-24	Oakland	61,503
2000	Dec. 31	Baltimore (12,500)	Denver ($12,500)	21-3	Baltimore	69,638
	Dec. 30	Miami ($16,000)	Indianapolis ($12,500)	23-17*	Miami	73,193
1999	Jan. 9	Miami ($10,000)	Seattle ($16,000)	20-17	Seattle	66,170
	Jan. 8	Tennessee ($10,000)	Buffalo ($10,000)	22-16	Nashville	66,672
1998	Jan. 3	Jacksonville ($15,000)	New England ($10,000)	25-10	Jacksonville	71,139
	Jan. 2	Miami ($10,000)	Buffalo ($10,000)	24-17	Miami	72,698
1997	Dec. 28	New England ($15,000)	Miami ($10,000)	17-3	Foxborough	60,041
	Dec. 27	Denver ($10,000)	Jacksonville ($10,000)	42-17	Denver	74,481
1996	Dec. 29	Pittsburgh ($14,000)	Indianapolis ($10,000)	42-14	Pittsburgh	58,078
	Dec. 28	Jacksonville ($10,000)	Buffalo ($10,000)	30-27	Buffalo	70,213
1995	Dec. 31	Indianapolis ($7,500)	San Diego ($7,500)	35-20	San Diego	61,182
	Dec. 30	Buffalo ($13,000)	Miami ($7,500)	37-22	Buffalo	73,103

Season	Date	Winner (Share)	Loser (Share)	Score	Site	Attendance
1994	Jan. 1	Cleveland ($7,500)	New England ($7,500)	20-13	Cleveland	77,452
	Dec. 31	Miami ($12,000)	Kansas City ($7,500)	27-17	Miami	67,487
1993	Jan. 9	L.A. Raiders ($7,500)	Denver ($7,500)	42-24	Los Angeles	65,314
	Jan. 8	Kansas City ($12,000)	Pittsburgh ($7,500)	27-24*	Kansas City	74,515
1992	Jan. 3	Buffalo ($6,000)	Houston ($6,000)	41-38*	Buffalo	75,141
	Jan. 2	San Diego ($10,000)	Kansas City ($6,000)	17-0	San Diego	58,278
1991	Dec. 29	Houston ($10,000)	N.Y. Jets ($6,000)	17-10	Houston	61,485
	Dec. 28	Kansas City ($6,000)	L.A. Raiders ($6,000)	10-6	Kansas City	75,827
1990	Jan. 6	Cincinnati ($10,000)	Houston ($6,000)	41-14	Cincinnati	60,012
	Jan. 5	Miami ($6,000)	Kansas City ($6,000)	17-16	Miami	67,276
1989	Dec. 31	Pittsburgh ($6,000)	Houston ($6,000)	26-23*	Houston	59,406
1988	Dec. 26	Houston ($6,000)	Cleveland ($6,000)	24-23	Cleveland	75,896
1987	Jan. 3	Houston ($6,000)	Seattle ($6,000)	23-20*	Houston	50,519
1986	Dec. 28	N.Y. Jets ($6,000)	Kansas City ($6,000)	35-15	East Rutherford	75,210
1985	Dec. 28	New England ($6,000)	N.Y. Jets ($6,000)	26-14	East Rutherford	75,945
1984	Dec. 22	Seattle ($6,000)	L.A. Raiders ($6,000)	13-7	Seattle	62,049
1983	Dec. 24	Seattle ($6,000)	Denver ($6,000)	31-7	Seattle	64,275
1982	Jan. 9	N.Y. Jets ($6,000)	Cincinnati ($6,000)	44-17	Cincinnati	57,560
	Jan. 9	San Diego ($6,000)	Pittsburgh ($6,000)	31-28	Pittsburgh	53,546
	Jan. 8	L.A. Raiders ($6,000)	Cleveland ($6,000)	27-10	Los Angeles	56,555
	Jan. 8	Miami ($6,000)	New England ($6,000)	28-13	Miami	68,842
1981	Dec. 27	Buffalo ($3,000)	N.Y. Jets ($3,000)	31-27	New York	57,050
1980	Dec. 28	Oakland ($3,000)	Houston ($3,000)	27-7	Oakland	53,333
1979	Dec. 23	Houston ($3,000)	Denver ($3,000)	13-7	Houston	48,776
1978	Dec. 24	Houston ($3,000)	Miami ($3,000)	17-9	Miami	72,445

*Sudden death overtime

2007 AFC WILD CARD PLAYOFF GAMES

Qualcomm Stadium, San Diego, California
January 6, 2008, Attendance: 65,640
SAN DIEGO 17, TENNESSEE 6—Philip Rivers passed for 292 yards, and the Chargers' defense allowed just 248 yards, as San Diego won its first playoff game in 13 years. The Titans led 3-0 early in the second quarter and drove to the Chargers' 12, but Shawne Merriman forced Chris Brown to fumble and Shaun Phillips recovered. However, Nate Kaeding missed a 45-yard field-goal attempt and Rob Bironas' second field goal, from 44 yards as the half expired, stretched the Titans' lead to 6-0. The Chargers converted two third downs on their second-half opening 86-yard drive, but had to settle for a field goal. The Chargers' defense then forced a punt, and Rivers began the ensuing 78-yard drive with a 20-yard pass to Vincent Jackson and ended the possession with a 25-yard touchdown pass to Jackson to give the Chargers a 10-6 lead. The Titans drove to the Chargers' 20, but Bironas' 38-yard field-goal attempt was wide left with 14:04 to play. The Chargers then drove 72 yards, highlighted by Chris Chambers' 39-yard catch on third-and-10, and capped by LaDainian Tomlinson's fourth-and-1 leap across the goal line. Tomlinson was met in midair by Stephen Tulloch, and Colin Allred knocked the ball out of his hands once his second effort got him across the goal line. Jeff Fisher challenged the play, but the touchdown call on the field stood and San Diego led 17-6 with 8:45 remaining. Drayton Florence's interception at the Titans' 20 with 3:33 remaining ended Tennessee's final possession. Rivers was 19 of 30 for 292 yards and 1 touchdown, with 1 interception. Chambers had 6 catches for 121 yards, and Jackson added 5 receptions for 114 yards. Vince Young was 16 of 29 for 138 yards, with 1 interception.

Tennessee	3	3	0	0	—	6
San Diego	0	0	10	7	—	17

Tenn — FG Bironas 30
Tenn — FG Bironas 44
SD — FG Kaeding 20
SD — Jackson 25 pass from Rivers (Kaeding kick)
SD — Tomlinson 1 run (Kaeding kick)

Heinz Field, Pittsburgh, Pennsylvania
January 5, 2008, Attendance: 63,629
JACKSONVILLE 31, PITTSBURGH 29—David Garrard's 32-yard fourth-down run set up Josh Scobee's game-winning 25-yard field goal with 37 seconds left as the Jaguars won their first playoff game in eight years. The Steelers outgained the Jaguars 340-239 yards, but Jacksonville's defense forced 4 turnovers and the offense made just enough big plays. The Steelers opened the game with an 80-yard touchdown drive, but Maurice Jones-Drew returned the ensuing kickoff 96 yards to the Steelers' 1. Fred Taylor scored on the next play. In the second quarter, Rashean Mathis returned an interception 63 yards for a touchdown. Moments later, Mathis intercepted another pass that was followed three plays later by Jones-Drew's 43-yard touchdown catch-and-run of a short pass for a 21-7 lead with 8:34 left in the half. The Steelers had a chance to score just before halftime, but Derek Landri intercepted a pass at the Jaguars' 25 to maintain the 14-point lead. Two plays into the second half, James Farrior intercepted a pass to set up Jeff Reed's field goal. The Jaguars answered with an 82-yard touchdown drive. Pittsburgh then drove to the Jaguars' 37. Faced with a fourth-and-12 on the first play of the fourth quarter and trailing 28-10, Pittsburgh went for the first down. Ben Roethlisberger connected on a quick pass to Santonio Holmes that resulted in a 37-yard touchdown. The Steelers' defense then forced a three-and-out, and the offense drove 69 yards, capped by Heath Miller's 14-yard touchdown catch with 10:25 to play. Trailing 28-23, the Steelers converted the 2-point conversion, but a holding penalty wiped out the score. Pittsburgh still went for the 2-point conversion, and Roethlisberger was stopped on a scramble from the 12-yard line. Two plays later, Ike Taylor intercepted a pass and returned it 31 yards to the Jaguars' 16. A defensive pass interference penalty on fourth-and-goal from the Jaguars' 1 kept alive the drive, and Najeh Davenport scored with 6:21 remaining to give Pittsburgh a 29-28 lead. Roethlisberger's 2-point conversion pass for Nate Washington fell incomplete. After an exchange of punts, Dennis Northcutt had a 16-yard return that gave the Jaguars possession at their own 49 with 2:38 remaining. Faced with a fourth-and-2 from the Steelers' 43 with 1:56 to play, Garrard dropped back, and then scrambled right up the middle for 32 yards. Scobee's 25-yard field goal was good with 37 seconds left. Starting from their own 28-yard line, Bobby McCray sacked Roethlisberger on the first play, forced

NFC WILD CARD PLAYOFF GAMES RESULTS

Season	Date	Winner (Share)	Loser (Share)	Score	Site	Attendance
2007	Jan. 6	N.Y. Giants ($18,000)	Tampa Bay ($20,000)	24-14	Tampa	65,621
	Jan. 5	Seattle ($20,000)	Washington ($18,000)	35-14	Seattle	68,297
2006	Jan. 7	Philadelphia ($19,000)	N.Y. Giants ($17,000)	23-20	Philadelphia	69,094
	Jan. 6	Seattle ($19,000)	Dallas ($17,000)	21-20	Seattle	68,058
2005	Jan. 8	Carolina ($17,000)	N.Y. Giants ($19,000)	23-0	East Rutherford	79,378
	Jan. 7	Washington ($17,000)	Tampa Bay ($19,000)	17-10	Tampa	65,514
2004	Jan. 9	Minnesota ($15,000)	Green Bay ($18,000)	31-17	Green Bay	71,075
	Jan. 8	St. Louis ($15,000)	Seattle ($18,000)	27-20	Seattle	65,397
2003	Jan. 4	Green Bay ($18,000)	Seattle ($15,000)	33-27*	Green Bay	71,457
	Jan. 3	Carolina ($18,000)	Dallas ($15,000)	29-10	Charlotte	73,014
2002	Jan. 5	San Francisco ($17,000)	N.Y. Giants ($12,500)	39-38	San Francisco	66,318
	Jan. 4	Atlanta ($12,500)	Green Bay ($17,000)	27-7	Green Bay	65,358
2001	Jan. 13	Green Bay ($12,500)	San Francisco ($12,500)	25-15	Green Bay	59,825
	Jan. 12	Philadelphia ($17,000)	Tampa Bay ($12,500)	31-9	Philadelphia	65,847
2000	Dec. 31	Philadelphia ($12,500)	Tampa Bay ($12,500)	21-3	Philadelphia	65,813
	Dec. 30	New Orleans ($16,000)	St. Louis ($12,500)	31-28	New Orleans	64,900
1999	Jan. 9	Minnesota ($10,000)	Dallas ($10,000)	27-10	Minneapolis	64,056
	Jan. 8	Washington ($16,000)	Detroit ($10,000)	27-13	Washington	79,411
1998	Jan. 3	San Francisco ($10,000)	Green Bay ($10,000)	30-27	San Francisco	66,506
	Jan. 2	Arizona ($10,000)	Dallas ($15,000)	20-7	Dallas	62,969
1997	Dec. 28	Tampa Bay ($10,000)	Detroit ($10,000)	20-10	Tampa	73,361
	Dec. 27	Minnesota ($10,000)	N.Y. Giants ($15,000)	23-22	East Rutherford	77,497
1996	Dec. 29	San Francisco ($10,000)	Philadelphia ($10,000)	14-0	San Francisco	56,460
	Dec. 28	Dallas ($14,000)	Minnesota ($10,000)	40-15	Dallas	64,682
1995	Dec. 31	Green Bay ($13,000)	Atlanta ($7,500)	37-20	Green Bay	60,453
	Dec. 30	Philadelphia ($7,500)	Detroit ($7,500)	58-37	Philadelphia	66,099
1994	Jan. 1	Chicago ($7,500)	Minnesota ($12,000)	35-18	Minnesota	60,347
	Dec. 31	Green Bay ($7,500)	Detroit ($7,500)	16-12	Green Bay	58,125
1993	Jan. 9	N.Y. Giants ($7,500)	Minnesota ($7,500)	17-10	East Rutherford	75,089
	Jan. 8	Green Bay ($7,500)	Detroit ($12,000)	28-24	Detroit	68,479
1992	Jan. 3	Philadelphia ($6,000)	New Orleans ($6,000)	36-20	New Orleans	68,893
	Jan. 2	Washington ($6,000)	Minnesota ($10,000)	24-7	Minnesota	57,353
1991	Dec. 29	Dallas ($6,000)	Chicago ($6,000)	17-13	Chicago	62,594
	Dec. 28	Atlanta ($6,000)	New Orleans ($10,000)	27-20	New Orleans	68,794
1990	Jan. 6	Chicago ($10,000)	New Orleans ($6,000)	16-6	Chicago	60,767
	Jan. 5	Washington ($6,000)	Philadelphia ($6,000)	20-6	Philadelphia	65,287
1989	Dec. 31	L.A. Rams ($6,000)	Philadelphia ($6,000)	21-7	Philadelphia	65,479
1988	Dec. 26	Minnesota ($6,000)	L.A. Rams ($6,000)	28-17	Minnesota	61,204
1987	Jan. 3	Minnesota ($6,000)	New Orleans ($6,000)	44-10	New Orleans	68,546
1986	Dec. 28	Washington ($6,000)	L.A. Rams ($6,000)	19-7	Washington	54,567
1985	Dec. 29	N.Y. Giants ($6,000)	San Francisco ($6,000)	17-3	East Rutherford	75,131
1984	Dec. 23	N.Y. Giants ($6,000)	L.A. Rams ($6,000)	16-13	Anaheim	67,037
1983	Dec. 26	L.A. Rams ($6,000)	Dallas ($6,000)	24-17	Dallas	62,118
1982	Jan. 9	Dallas ($6,000)	Tampa Bay ($6,000)	30-17	Dallas	65,042
	Jan. 9	Minnesota ($6,000)	Atlanta ($6,000)	30-24	Minnesota	60,560
	Jan. 8	Green Bay ($6,000)	St. Louis ($6,000)	41-16	Green Bay	54,282
	Jan. 8	Washington ($6,000)	Detroit ($6,000)	31-7	Washington	55,045
1981	Dec. 27	N.Y. Giants ($3,000)	Philadelphia ($3,000)	27-21	Philadelphia	71,611
1980	Dec. 28	Dallas ($3,000)	Los Angeles ($3,000)	34-13	Dallas	63,052
1979	Dec. 23	Philadelphia ($3,000)	Chicago ($3,000)	27-17	Philadelphia	69,397
1978	Dec. 24	Atlanta ($3,000)	Philadelphia ($3,000)	14-13	Atlanta	59,403

*Sudden death overtime

him to fumble and Landri recovered to clinch the victory. Garrard was 9 of 21 for 140 yards and 1 touchdown, with 2 interceptions. Roethlisberger was 29 of 42 for 337 yards and 2 touchdowns, with 3 interceptions. Hines Ward had 10 receptions for 135 yards.

Jacksonville	7	14	7	3	—	31
Pittsburgh	7	0	3	19	—	29

Pitt	—	Davenport 1 run (Reed kick)
Jax	—	Taylor 1 run (Scobee kick)
Jax	—	Mathis 63 interception return (Scobee kick)
Jax	—	Jones-Drew 43 pass from Garrard (Scobee kick)
Pitt	—	FG Reed 28
Jax	—	Jones-Drew 10 run (Scobee kick)
Pitt	—	Holmes 37 pass from Roethlisberger (Reed kick)
Pitt	—	Miller 14 pass from Roethlisberger (run failed)
Pitt	—	Davenport 1 run (pass failed)
Jax	—	FG Scobee 25

2007 NFC WILD CARD PLAYOFF GAMES

Raymond James Stadium, Tampa, Florida
January 6, 2008, Attendance: 65,621

N.Y. GIANTS 24, TAMPA BAY 14—Eli Manning passed for 2 touchdowns as the Giants, who had won their final seven regular-season road games, again won away from home. Trailing 7-0 early in the second quarter, Manning connected on a 13-yard pass to Amani Toomer on third-and-9 to set up his 5-yard touchdown pass to Brandon Jacobs to tie the game. The Giants' defense then forced a three-and-out. Manning completed another key third-down pass, a 21-yard strike to Steve Smith, that led to Jacobs' 8-yard touchdown for a 14-7 lead. The Giants opened the second half with Corey Webster recovering Micheal Spurlock's fumble to set up a field goal. The Buccaneers then drove to the Giants' 27, but Webster intercepted Jeff Garcia's pass in the end zone for a touchback. The Giants put the game away early in the fourth quarter with a 15-play, 92-yard drive that featured seven carries by Ahmad Bradshaw for 38 yards, and was capped by Manning's 4-yard touchdown pass to Toomer on third-and-goal with 8:03 to play for a 24-7 lead. The Buccaneers answered with an 88-yard touchdown drive, and got the ball back with 2:10 to play, but R.W. McQuarters intercepted Garcia's deep pass with 1:53 remaining to clinch the victory. Manning was 20 of 27 for 185 yards and 2 touchdowns. Garcia was 23 of 39 for 207 yards and 1 touchdown, with 2 interceptions.

| N.Y. Giants | 0 | 14 | 3 | 7 | — | 24 |
| Tampa Bay | 7 | 0 | 0 | 7 | — | 14 |

TB	—	Graham 1 run (Bryant kick)
NYG	—	Jacobs 5 pass from Manning (Tynes kick)
NYG	—	Jacobs 8 run (Tynes kick)
NYG	—	FG Tynes 25
NYG	—	Toomer 4 pass from Manning (Tynes kick)
TB	—	A. Smith 6 pass from Garcia (Bryant kick)

Qwest Field, Seattle, Washington
January 5, 2008, Attendance: 68,297

SEATTLE 35, WASHINGTON 14—Matt Hasselbeck passed for 229 yards and the Seahawks' defense returned 2 fourth-quarter interceptions for touchdowns to lead Seattle to victory. Midway through the first quarter, Fred Smoot recovered a fumble by Shaun Alexander, but replay reversed the call. On the next play, Leonard Weaver ran 17 yards for a touchdown and 7-0 lead. The Redskins punted to end each of their first seven possessions, and on the eighth possession Mike Sellers was stopped for no gain on fourth-and-1 from the Seahawks' 43 with 1:21 left in the half, allowing Seattle to take a 10-0 lead into the locker room. With the score 13-0, the Redskins drove 12 plays in 84 yards, capped by Todd Collins' 7-yard touchdown pass to Antwaan Randle El on third-and-6 on the first play of the fourth quarter. Two plays later, LaRon Landry intercepted Hasselbeck's pass. Three plays after the interception, Collins hit a streaking Santana Moss deep down the left sideline for a 30-yard touchdown and 14-13 Washington lead with 12:38 to play. On the ensuing kickoff, the harsh wind forced the ball to drop suddenly. It fell untouched and was recovered by Anthony Mix at the Seahawks' 14-yard line. However, Shaun Suisham's 30-yard field-goal attempt was wide left with 11:37 remaining. Landry responded with his second interception, at the Redskins' 9, to thwart the drive. But Seattle's defense forced a three-and-out, and Hasselbeck's 15-yard pass to Nate Burleson on third-and-6 set up his 20-yard touchdown pass to D.J. Hackett. Marcus Pollard caught the 2-point conversion pass for a 21-14 lead with 6:06 left. Rock Cartwright returned the ensuing kickoff 55 yards, but on the next play Marcus Trufant intercepted Collins' pass and returned it 78 yards for a touchdown. Washington drove to the Seahawks' 31, but Collins' fourth-down pass fell incomplete with 2:41 remaining. The Redskins' defense forced a final punt, and Jordan Babineaux intercepted Collins' pass and returned it 57 yards for the final touchdown with 27 seconds remaining to complete the scoring. The 2 fourth-quarter interceptions thrown by Collins were his first in 10 years, and the game marked the first time in 18 playoff games that Joe Gibbs had lost when leading in the second half. Gibbs retired two days later. Hasselbeck was 20 of 32 for 229 yards and 1 touchdown, with 2 interceptions. Hackett had 6 catches for 101 yards. Collins was 29 of 50 for 266 yards and 2 touchdowns, with 2 interceptions. Randle El had 10 receptions for 94 yards

| Washington | 0 | 0 | 0 | 14 | — | 24 |
| Seattle | 7 | 3 | 3 | 22 | — | 35 |

Sea	—	Weaver 17 run (J. Brown kick)
Sea	—	FG J. Brown 50
Sea	—	FG J. Brown 33
Wash	—	Randle El 7 pass from Collins (Suisham kick)
Wash	—	S. Moss 30 pass from Collins (Suisham kick)
Sea	—	Hackett 20 pass from Hasselbeck
		(Pollard pass from Hasselbeck)
Sea	—	Trufant 78 interception return (J. Brown kick)
Sea	—	Babineaux 57 interception return (J. Brown kick)

AFC-NFC PRO BOWL RESULTS (1971-2008)
Series tied, 19-19

Year	Date	Winner (Share)	Loser (Share)	Score	Site	Attendance
2008	Feb. 10	NFC ($40,000)	AFC ($20,000)	42-30	Honolulu	50,044
2007	Feb. 10	AFC ($40,000)	NFC ($20,000)	31-28	Honolulu	50,410
2006	Feb. 12	NFC ($40,000)	AFC ($20,000)	23-17	Honolulu	50,190
2005	Feb. 13	AFC ($35,000)	NFC ($17,500)	38-27	Honolulu	50,225
2004	Feb. 8	NFC ($35,000)	AFC ($17,500)	55-52	Honolulu	50,127
2003	Feb. 2	AFC ($30,000)	NFC ($15,000)	45-20	Honolulu	50,125
2002	Feb. 9	AFC ($30,000)	NFC ($15,000)	38-30	Honolulu	50,301
2001	Feb. 4	AFC ($30,000)	NFC ($15,000)	38-17	Honolulu	50,128
2000	Feb. 6	NFC ($25,000)	AFC ($12,500)	51-31	Honolulu	50,112
1999	Feb. 7	AFC ($25,000)	NFC ($12,500)	23-10	Honolulu	50,075
1998	Feb. 1	AFC ($25,000)	NFC ($12,500)	29-24	Honolulu	49,995
1997	Feb. 2	AFC ($20,000)	NFC ($10,000)	26-23 (OT)	Honolulu	50,031
1996	Feb. 4	NFC ($20,000)	AFC ($10,000)	20-13	Honolulu	50,034
1995	Feb. 5	AFC ($20,000)	NFC ($10,000)	41-13	Honolulu	50,529
1994	Feb. 6	NFC ($20,000)	AFC ($10,000)	17-3	Honolulu	50,026
1993	Feb. 7	AFC ($10,000)	NFC ($5,000)	23-20 (OT)	Honolulu	50,007
1992	Feb. 2	NFC ($10,000)	AFC ($5,000)	21-15	Honolulu	50,209
1991	Feb. 3	AFC ($10,000)	NFC ($5,000)	23-21	Honolulu	50,345
1990	Feb. 4	NFC ($10,000)	AFC ($5,000)	27-21	Honolulu	50,445
1989	Jan. 29	NFC ($10,000)	AFC ($5,000)	34-3	Honolulu	50,113
1988	Feb. 7	AFC ($10,000)	NFC ($5,000)	15-6	Honolulu	50,113
1987	Feb. 1	AFC ($10,000)	NFC ($5,000)	10-6	Honolulu	50,101
1986	Feb. 2	NFC ($10,000)	AFC ($5,000)	28-24	Honolulu	50,101
1985	Jan. 27	AFC ($10,000)	NFC ($5,000)	22-14	Honolulu	50,385
1984	Jan. 29	NFC ($10,000)	AFC ($5,000)	45-3	Honolulu	50,445
1983	Feb. 6	NFC ($10,000)	AFC ($5,000)	20-19	Honolulu	49,883
1982	Jan. 31	AFC ($5,000)	NFC ($2,500)	16-13	Honolulu	50,402
1981	Feb. 1	NFC ($5,000)	AFC ($2,500)	21-7	Honolulu	50,360
1980	Jan. 27	NFC ($5,000)	AFC ($2,500)	37-27	Honolulu	49,800
1979	Jan. 29	NFC ($5,000)	AFC ($2,500)	13-7	Los Angeles	46,281
1978	Jan. 23	NFC ($5,000)	AFC ($2,500)	14-13	Tampa	51,337
1977	Jan. 17	AFC ($2,000)	NFC ($1,500)	24-14	Seattle	64,752
1976	Jan. 26	NFC ($2,000)	AFC ($1,500)	23-20	New Orleans	30,546
1975	Jan. 20	NFC ($2,000)	AFC ($1,500)	17-10	Miami	26,484
1974	Jan. 20	AFC ($2,000)	NFC ($1,500)	15-13	Kansas City	66,918
1973	Jan. 21	AFC ($2,000)	NFC ($1,500)	33-28	Dallas	37,091
1972	Jan. 23	AFC ($2,000)	NFC ($1,500)	26-13	Los Angeles	53,647
1971	Jan. 24	NFC ($2,000)	AFC ($1,500)	27-6	Los Angeles	48,222

2008 AFC-NFC PRO BOWL

Aloha Stadium, Honolulu, Hawaii
February 10, 2008, Attendance: 50,044
NFC 42, AFC 30—Adrian Peterson rushed for 129 yards and 2 touchdowns as the NFC rallied to victory. Peterson became only the second rookie to win the Pro Bowl MVP award, joining Marshall Faulk. The NFC outgained the AFC 458-326 in total yards, but Antonio Cromartie helped keep the AFC in the game with 2 interceptions for 77 yards. The AFC scored on its first five possessions, including three touchdowns. The third touchdown was set up by Cromartie's 56-yard interception return and capped by Ben Roethlisberger's 1-yard touchdown pass to T.J. Houshmandzadeh for a 24-7 lead with 12:08 remaining in the second quarter. On the next drive, Tony Romo's 34-yard pass to Terrell Owens on fourth-and-13 seemed to change the momentum, and the pair hooked up for a 6-yard touchdown three plays later to pull within 24-14. Adrian Peterson's 39-yard run set up Matt Hasselbeck's 17-yard touchdown pass to Chris Cooley with 28 seconds left in the half to pull the NFC to within six points at 27-21. On the opening drive of the second half, Hasselbeck completed a 17-yard pass to Torry Holt on fourth-and-2, and Peterson scored on a 17-yard run on the next play for a 28-27 lead. The AFC responded with Rob Bironas' third field goal, but late in the third quarter Owens caught a 27-yard pass from former teammate Jeff Garcia, and the duo connected on a 6-yard touchdown for a 35-30 NFC lead with 12:29 remaining. The AFC drove to the NFC's 27, but Derek Anderson threw four consecutive incomplete passes. Garcia completed a 16-yard pass to Donald Driver on the ensuing 9-play, 73-yard drive, capped by Peterson's 6-yard touchdown run with 2:43 to play for a 42-30 lead. Darren Sharper intercepted Anderson's long pass for a touchback with 20 seconds left to seal the victory. Romo was 9 of 16 for 87 yards and 2 touchdowns, with 1 interception. Hasselbeck was 7 of 9 for 78 yards and 1 touchdown, and Garcia was 8 of 10 for 117 yards and 1 touchdown, with 1 interception. Owens had 8 receptions for 101 yards. Peyton Manning was 11 of 16 for 147 yards and 1 touchdown. Roethlisberger was 5 of 9 for 42 yards, and Anderson was 10 of 26 for 103 yards, with 1 interception.

NFC (42)	Offense	AFC (30)
Terrell Owens (Dallas)	WR	Braylon Edwards (Cleveland)
Flozell Adams (Dallas)	LT	Matt Light (New England)
Steve Hutchinson (Minnesota)	LG	Alan Faneca (Pittsburgh)
Andre Gurode (Dallas)	C	Jeff Saturday (Indianapolis)
Leonard Davis (Dallas)	RG	Logan Mankins (New England)
Chris Samuels (Washington)	RT	Joe Thomas (Cleveland)
Jason Witten (Dallas)	TE	Tony Gonzalez (Kansas City)
Larry Fitzgerald (Arizona)	WR	Reggie Wayne (Indianapolis)
Tony Romo (Dallas)	QB	Peyton Manning (Indianapolis)
Tony Richardson (Minnesota)	FB	Lorenzo Neal (San Diego)
Adrian Peterson (Minnesota)	RB	Joseph Addai (Indianapolis)

Defense

Aaron Kampman (Green Bay)	DE	Jared Allen (Kansas City)	
Kevin Williams (Minnesota)	DT	Albert Haynesworth (Tennessee)	
Pat Williams (Minnesota)	DT	Vince Wilfork (New England)	
Osi Umenyiora (N.Y. Giants)	DE	Kyle Vanden Bosch (Tennessee)	
DeMarcus Ware (Dallas)	OLB	Mike Vrabel (New England)	
Lofa Tatupu (Seattle)	ILB	DeMeco Ryans (Houston)	
Julian Peterson (Seattle)	OLB	James Harrison (Pittsburgh)	
Al Harris (Green Bay)	CB	Asante Samuel (New England)	
Marcus Trufant (Seattle)	CB	Champ Bailey (Denver)	
Ken Hamlin (Dallas)	SS	John Lynch (Denver)	
Darren Sharper (Minnesota)	FS	Ed Reed (Baltimore)	

SUBSTITUTIONS

NFC—Specialists: K—Nick Folk (Dallas). P—Andy Lee (San Francisco). KR—Devin Hester (Chicago). LS—Ethan Albright (Washington). ST—Brendon Ayanbadejo (Chicago). Offense: QB—Brett Favre (Green Bay), Jeff Garcia (Tampa Bay), Matt Hasselbeck (Seattle). RB—Marion Barber (Dallas), Brian Westbrook (Philadelphia). WR—Donald Driver (Green Bay), Torry Holt (St. Louis). TE—Chris Cooley (Washington). G—Shawn Andrews (Philadelphia). T—Chad Clifton (Green Bay). C—Matt Birk (Minnesota). Defense: DL—Darnell Dockett (Arizona). DE—Trent Cole (Philadelphia). LB—Greg Ellis (Dallas), Patrick Willis (San Francisco). CB—Terence Newman (Dallas). S—Roy Williams (Dallas). Not Active: T—Walter Jones (Seattle). DL—Tommie Harris (Chicago). DE—Patrick Kerney (Seattle). LB—Lance Briggs (Chicago). S—Sean Taylor (Washington).

AFC—Specialists: K—Rob Bironas (Tennessee). P—Shane Lechler (Oakland). KR—Josh Cribbs (Cleveland). LS—Ryan Pontbriand (Cleveland). ST—Kassim Osgood (San Diego). Offense: QB—Derek Anderson (Cleveland), Ben Roethlisberger (Pittsburgh). RB—Willis McGahee (Baltimore), Fred Taylor (Jacksonville), LaDainian Tomlinson (San Diego). WR—T.J. Houshmandzadeh (Cincinnati), Chad Johnson (Cincinnati). TE—Kellen Winslow (Cleveland). G—Kris Dielman (San Diego). T—Marcus McNeill (San Diego). C—Dan Koppen (New England). Defense: DL—Casey Hampton (Pittsburgh). DE—Aaron Schobel (Buffalo). LB—Ray Lewis (Baltimore), Shawne Merriman (San Diego). CB—Antonio Cromartie (San Diego). S—Antoine Bethea (Indianapolis), Bob Sanders (Indianapolis). Not Active: QB—Tom Brady (New England). RB—Willie Parker (Pittsburgh). TE—Antonio Gates (San Diego). T—

Jonathan Ogden (Baltimore), Jason Peters (Buffalo). DL—Jamal Williams (San Diego). DE—Jason Taylor (Miami). S—Troy Polamalu (Pittsburgh).

HEAD COACHES

AFC—Norv Turner (San Diego)
NFC—Mike McCarthy (Green Bay)

OFFICIALS

Referee—William Carollo. Umpire—Scott Dawson. Side Judge—Mike Weatherford. Field Judge—Steve Zimmer. Head Linesman—George Hayward. Back Judge—Kirk Dornan. Line Judge—Darryll Lewis.

AFC	17	10	3	0	— 30
NFC	7	14	7	14	— 42

AFC — Neal 1 run (Bironas kick)
NFC — Fitzgerald 6 pass from Romo (Folk kick)
AFC — Houshmandzadeh 16 pass from P. Manning (Bironas kick)
AFC — FG Bironas 33
AFC — Houshmandzadeh 1 pass from Roethlisberger (Bironas kick)
NFC — Owens 6 pass from Romo (Folk kick)
AFC — FG Bironas 48
NFC — Cooley 17 pass from Hasselbeck (Folk kick)
NFC — Peterson 17 run (Folk kick)
AFC — FG Bironas 28
NFC — Owens 6 pass from Garcia (Folk kick)
NFC — Peterson 6 run (Folk kick)

TEAM STATISTICS

	AFC	NFC
Total First Downs	24	28
Rushing	4	9
Passing	15	19
Penalty	5	0
Total Net Yardage	326	458
Total Offensive Plays	63	61
Avg. Gain Per Offensive Play	5.2	7.5
Rushes	10	24
Yards Gained Rushing (Net)	45	169
Avg. Yards per Rush	4.5	7.0
Passes Attempted	51	36
Passes Completed	26	25
Had Intercepted	1	2
Tackled Attempting to Pass	2	1
Yards Lost Attempting to Pass	11	4
Yards Gained Passing (Net)	281	289
Punts	1	0
Avg. Distance	55.0	---
Punt Returns	0	0
Punt Return Yardage	0	0
Kickoff Returns	7	6
Kickoff Return Yardage	169	199
Interception Return Yardage	77	0
Total Return Yardage	246	199
Fumbles	2	2
Fumbles Lost	0	1
Own Fumbles Recovered	2	1
Opponent Fumbles Recovered	1	0
Penalties	2	8
Yards Penalized	10	56
Field Goals	3	0
Field Goals Attempted	3.	0

Third-Down Efficiency	4/12	5/9
Fourth-Down Efficiency	2/3	3/3
Time of Possession	27:44	32:16

INDIVIDUAL STATISTICS

RUSHING: AFC: Roethlisberger 1-18-0, Taylor 3-15-0, McGahee 2-6-0, Addai 1-5-0, Neal 2-1-1, Manning 1-0-0. NFC: Peterson 16-129-2, Barber 6-37-0, Westbrook 1-4-0, Garcia 1-(-1)-0.
PASSING: AFC: Anderson 26-10-103-0-1, Manning 16-11-147-1-0, Roethlisberger 9-54-42-1-0. NFC: Romo 16-9-87-2-1, Garcia 10-8-117-1-1, Hasselbeck 9-7-78-1-0, Lee 1-1-11-0-0.
RECEIVING: AFC: Wayne 5-55-0, Gonzalez 4-79-0, Houshmandzadeh 4-44-2, Addai 3-16-0, Neal 3-8-0, Edwards 2-40-0, Johnson 2-30-0, McGahee 2-9-0, Winslow 1-11-0. NFC: Owens 8-101-2, Cooley 3-41-1, Witten 3-38-0, Fitzgerald 3-25-1, Driver 2-31-0, Holt 2-29-0, Westbrook 2-8-0, Richardson 1-11-0, Peterson 1-9-0.
KICKOFF RETURNS: AFC: Cribbs 6-159-0, Koppen 1-10-0. NFC: Hester 5-165-0, Ware 1-(-1)-0, Witten 0-35-0.
PUNT RETURNS: AFC: none. NFC: none.
PUNTING: AFC: Lechler 1-55-55.0. NFC: none.
INTERCEPTIONS: AFC: Cromartie 2-77-0. NFC: Sharper 1-0-0.
SACKS: AFC: Vanden Bosch 1. NFC: Kampman 1, Umenyiora 1.

2007 AFC-NFC PRO BOWL

Aloha Stadium, Honolulu, Hawaii
February 10, 2007, Attendance: 50,410
AFC 31, NFC 28—The NFC scored two touchdowns within 66 seconds to tie the score with 1:48 remaining, but Nate Kaeding made a 21-yard field goal with no time left as the AFC held off the NFC. With the score 7-7, Adalius Thomas recovered Marc Bulger's fumble and returned it 70 yards for a touchdown to give the AFC a 14-7 lead with 7:42 remaining in the first half. The NFC responded with Frank Gore's 1-yard touchdown run to tie the game. To open the second half, LaDainian Tomlinson ran six times on a nine-play drive, capped by Tomlinson's 3-yard scoring run, to give the AFC a 21-14 lead. Antonio Pierce intercepted a pass at the NFC 6-yard-line to stop a drive late in the third quarter, but on the AFC's next possession Carson Palmer completed a 42-yard touchdown pass to teammate Chad Johnson to give the AFC a 28-14 lead. The NFC drove into the AFC red zone on its next two possessions, but Derrick Burgess' fourth-down sack ended one drive and Romo was stopped for no gain on fourth-and-goal from the 1-yard-line on the second possession with 5:00 left. However, Vince Young fumbled three plays later and Sean Taylor recovered at the AFC 11-yard-line. Four plays later, on fourth-and-3, Steven Jackson scored on a 4-yard run with 2:54 left. A bad snap on

the extra-point attempt, however, forced holder Romo to throw an incomplete pass, leaving the NFC trailing by eight points. The NFC then attempted an onside kick and Ronde Barber recovered. Four plays later, Romo fired a 47-yard touchdown pass to Anquan Boldin, and a 2-point conversion pass to Steve Smith, to tie the game with 1:48 to play. After Palmer converted a fourth-and-1 with a sneak, he attempted a deep pass for Johnson. Defensive pass interference was called when Adrian Wilson, mistakenly thinking the ball had been tipped, hit Johnson before the ball arrived, and the AFC got the ball at the NFC 2-yard-line. Kaeding made the 21-yard field goal as time expired. Palmer, who was selected the game's outstanding player, was 8 of 17 for 190 yards and 2 touchdowns to lead the AFC. Reggie Wayne had 6 receptions for 137 yards. Ed Reed had 2 interceptions. Romo was 11 of 19 for 156 yards and 1 touchdown, with 1 interception, and Bulger was 8 of 15 for 133 yards.

NFC	0	14	0	14	—	28
AFC	0	14	7	10	—	31

NFC— T. Barber 1 run (Gould kick)
AFC— Wayne 72 pass from Palmer (Kaeding kick)
AFC— A. Thomas 70 fumble return (Kaeding kick)
NFC— Gore 1 run (Gould kick)
AFC— Tomlinson 3 run (Kaeding kick)
AFC— C. Johnson 42 pass from Palmer (Kaeding kick)
NFC— S. Jackson 4 run (pass failed)
NFC— Boldin 47 pass from Romo (S. Smith pass from Romo)
AFC— FG Kaeding 21

2006 AFC-NFC PRO BOWL
Aloha Stadium, Honolulu, Hawaii
February 12, 2006, Attendance: 50,190
NFC 23, AFC 17—Derrick Brooks returned an interception 59 yards for a touchdown, and Neil Rackers added 3 field goals, as the NFC held off the AFC. The series is now tied 18-18. The defenses dominated, as the game featured 7 sacks and 10 turnovers. John Lynch's interception and 40-yard return to the NFC 45-yard line set up Peyton Manning's 16-yard touchdown pass to Chris Chambers. With the ball at midfield and holding a 10-3 lead and 48 seconds left in the half, Manning was intercepted for the third time. Roy Williams picked off the pass at the NFC 12, ran 11 yards, handed off to DeAngelo Hall, who raced 57 yards to the AFC 20-yard line. Three plays later, Michael Vick completed a 14-yard touchdown pass to Alge Crumpler to tie the game with two seconds left in the half. In the middle of the third quarter, Brooks intercepted Trent Green's short pass intended for Antonio Gates and returned it 59 yards for a touchdown. Champ Bailey recovered Santana Moss' fumble to spark

a 10-play, 68-yard drive capped by Green's 1-yard run to tie the game 17-17 with 12:47 to play. Matt Hasselbeck engineered a 13-play, 59-yard drive on the ensuing possession to set up Rackers' 22-yard field goal for a 20-17 lead with 6:29 to play. Jeremiah Trotter recovered Steve McNair's fumbled snap at the AFC 18-yard line with 3:42 to play, and Rackers added a 20-yard field goal with 1:10 remaining. The AFC reached the NFC 49-yard line with 29 seconds left, but McNair threw 3 consecutive incompletions and Michael Strahan ended the game with a sack. Brooks was selected the game's outstanding player.

AFC	7	3	0	7	—	17
NFC	0	10	7	6	—	23

AFC — Chambers 16 pass from Manning (Graham kick)
NFC — FG Rackers 32
AFC — FG Graham 31
NFC — Crumpler 14 pass from Vick (Rackers kick)
NFC — D. Brooks 59 interception return (Rackers kick)
AFC — T. Green 1 run (Graham kick)
NFC — FG Rackers 22
NFC — FG Rackers 20

2005 AFC-NFC PRO BOWL
Aloha Stadium, Honolulu, Hawaii
February 13, 2005, Attendance: 50,225
AFC 38, NFC 27—Peyton Manning passed for 130 yards and 3 touchdowns as the AFC won for the fourth time in five years. The NFC outgained the AFC 492-343, but committed 3 turnovers and allowed an onside kick for a touchdown. David Akers missed a 43-yard field goal in the first quarter, and the AFC responded with touchdowns on its next four possessions. Manning completed 3 touchdown passes in the stretch, and Hines Ward registered the first onside kick returned for a touchdown in Pro Bowl history. Manning's final scoring pass, a 12-yard toss to Antonio Gates, was set up by Takeo Spikes' interception near midfield, to take a 28-7 lead with 5:50 left in the half. Michael Vick began the second half for the NFC, and engineered a 73-yard drive, capped by Torry Holt's 27-yard touchdown catch. Lito Sheppard intercepted Tom Brady's pass four plays later, and Vick culminated a 69-yard drive with a 3-yard run to cut the deficit to 28-24 with 3:53 left in the third quarter. An exchange of field goals made the score 31-27 with 9:04 remaining, but Drew Brees connected on a 33-yard pass to Gates on a flea-flicker, and LaDainian Tomlinson scored on third-and-goal from the NFC's 4 with 5:15 to play. Nate Clements' interception of Vick's pass with 2:00 remaining clinched the victory. Manning was 6 of 10 for 130 yards and 3 touchdowns to earn the game's most valuable player award. Brady was 4 of 9 for 48 yards, with 1 interception, and Brees was 2 of 2 for 58

yards. Donovan McNabb was 1 of 8 for 24 yards, with 1 interception. Daunte Culpepper was 9 of 15 for 124 yards, with 1 interception. Vick was 14 of 24 for 205 yards and 1 touchdown, with 1 interception, and became the first player to pass and run for a touchdown in the same Pro Bowl game.

NFC	0	10	14	3	—	27
AFC	14	14	0	10	—	38

AFC — Harrison 62 pass from Manning (Vinatieri kick)
AFC — Ward 41 pass from Manning (Vinatieri kick)
NFC — Westbrook 12 run (Akers kick)
AFC — Ward 39 kickoff return (Vinatieri kick)
AFC — Gates 12 pass from Manning (Vinatieri kick)
NFC — FG Akers 33
NFC — Holt 27 pass from Vick (Akers kick)
NFC — Vick 3 run (Akers kick)
AFC — FG Vinatieri 44
NFC — FG Akers 29
AFC — Tomlinson 4 run (Vinatieri kick)

2004 AFC-NFC PRO BOWL
Aloha Stadium, Honolulu, Hawaii
February 8, 2004, Attendance: 50,127
NFC 55, AFC 52—Marc Bulger passed for a Pro Bowl-record 4 touchdowns as the NFC rallied from a 25-point deficit to win the highest scoring game in Pro Bowl history. The AFC set a record with 626 yards, but committed 6 turnovers which led to 35 points. Steve McNair fired a 90-yard touchdown pass to Chad Johnson on the AFC's first play, and Ed Reed blocked Todd Sauerbrun's punt and returned it 23 yards for a touchdown for a 14-0 lead 3:58 into the game. The AFC led 17-13 in the second quarter when Peyton Manning fired a 50-yard touchdown pass to Marvin Harrison, and his 9-yard scoring pass to Tony Gonzalez on the next possession gave the AFC a 31-13 lead. Jamal Lewis' 22-yard touchdown run gave the AFC a 38-13 lead with 11:08 left in the third quarter. The comeback started when Trent Green fumbled and Leonard Little recovered. Bulger completed a 12-yard touchdown pass to Torry Holt two plays later with 8:08 left in the third quarter. Two plays later, Derrick Mason fumbled and Jerry Azumah returned it 36 yards to the AFC's 7 to set up Bulger's 2-yard touchdown toss to Keenan McCardell. But following an exchange of punts, Green completed a 23-yard touchdown pass to Clinton Portis to give the AFC a 45-27 lead with 13:14 left. The NFC scored 28 points in the next 9:42, set up by Azumah's 60-yard kickoff return, Champ Bailey's interception of a pass by Harrison, and interception returns by Dre' Bly, 32 yards for a touchdown, and Corey Chavous, 39 yards to set up Shaun Alexander's 2-yard touchdown run with

3:32 left, for a 55-45 NFC lead. Manning's 10-yard touchdown pass to Hines Ward with 1:54 left pulled the AFC within three points, and Bulger was intercepted by Brock Marion on fourth-and-10 from the AFC's 28-yard line with 1:15 left. The AFC drove to the NFC 21, but Kris Jenkins sacked Manning for a 12-yard loss, forcing Vanderjagt, who was 37-for-37 on the season but missed from 52 yards just before halftime, to attempt a 51-yard field goal as time expired. But the kick sailed wide right and the NFC prevailed. Bulger was 12 of 21 for 152 yards and 4 touchdowns, with 1 interception, and was selected as the player of the game. Holt had 7 receptions for 128 yards. Manning was 22 of 41 for 342 yards and 3 touchdowns, with 2 interceptions. Mason had 6 catches for 113 yards, and Johnson had 5 receptions for 156 yards.

AFC	17	14	7	14 —	52
NFC	10	3	14	28 —	55

AFC	C. Johnson 90 pass from McNair (Vanderjagt kick)
AFC	Reed 23 return of blocked punt (Vanderjagt kick)
NFC	Alexander 12 run (Wilkins kick)
NFC	FG Wilkins 28
AFC	FG Vanderjagt 27
NFC	FG Wilkins 38
AFC	Harrison 50 pass from Manning (Vanderjagt kick)
AFC	Gonzalez 9 pass from Manning (Vanderjagt kick)
AFC	J. Lewis 22 run (Vanderjagt kick)
NFC	Holt 12 pass from Bulger (Wilkins kick)
NFC	McCardell 2 pass from Bulger (Wilkins kick)
AFC	Portis 23 pass from Green (Vanderjagt kick)
NFC	Crumpler 33 pass from Bulger (Wilkins kick)
NFC	Alexander 5 pass from Bulger (pass failed)
NFC	Bly 32 interception return (Green run)
NFC	Alexander 2 run (Wilkins kick)
AFC	Ward 10 pass from Manning (Vanderjagt kick)

2003 AFC-NFC PRO BOWL
Aloha Stadium, Honolulu, Hawaii
February 2, 2003, Attendance: 50,125
AFC 45, NFC 20—Ricky Williams rushed for a game-high 56 yards, scored 2 touchdowns, and forced a fumble on special teams to earn player of the game honors. The AFC, which led by as many as 39 points, won for the third consecutive time. Jason Taylor's interception three plays into the game set up Williams' first touchdown run, and Rich Gannon's 11-yard touchdown pass to Tony Gonzalez capped a 71-yard drive on the AFC's next possession to take a 14-3 lead. Rod Woodson's interception early in the second quarter

led to Gannon's 13-yard touchdown pass to Travis Henry, and Williams capped another 71-yard drive with a 1-yard run with 47 seconds left in the half to give the AFC a 28-6 lead. Brad Johnson entered the game in the fourth quarter, and Ty Law intercepted a pass and returned it 43 yards for a touchdown on his first possession, and Sam Madison intercepted Johnson during his second drive to set up Peyton Manning's 32-yard touchdown pass to Hines Ward, which gave the AFC a 45-6 lead with 7:31 left. Johnson guided the NFC to touchdowns on its next two possessions, with the help of Julian Peterson's onside kick recovery, for the game's final points. All three AFC quarterbacks passed for at least 100 yards, led by Drew Bledsoe's 9 of 18 for 122-yard performance. Gonzalez had 5 receptions for 98 yards to lead all receivers. The AFC's defense had 6 interceptions, 3 of which were thrown by NFC starter Jeff Garcia.

NFC	3	3	0	14 —	20
AFC	14	14	3	14 —	45

AFC	R. Williams 1 run (Vinatieri kick)
NFC	FG Akers 45
AFC	Gonzalez 11 pass from Gannon (Vinatieri kick)
AFC	Henry 13 pass from Gannon (Vinatieri kick)
NFC	FG Akers 53
AFC	R. Williams 1 run (Vinatieri kick)
AFC	FG Vinatieri 20
AFC	Law 43 interception return (Vinatieri kick)
AFC	Ward 32 pass from Manning (Vinatieri kick)
NFC	Horn 12 pass from B. Johnson (Akers kick)
NFC	Alstott 4 pass from B. Johnson (Akers kick)

2002 AFC-NFC PRO BOWL
Aloha Stadium, Honolulu, Hawaii
February 9, 2002, Attendance: 50,301
AFC 38, NFC 30—Rich Gannon passed for 137 yards and 2 touchdowns to become the first player to earn back-to-back Pro Bowl player of the game honors. The game had an inauspicious beginning for Gannon, who fumbled the game's first snap. Hugh Douglas recovered the fumble and returned the ball to the AFC's 2-yard line to set up Ahman Green's touchdown 27 seconds into the game. After a three-and-out series, Kurt Warner's 23-yard pass to David Boston set up David Akers' 29-yard field goal to give the NFC a 10-0 lead. Gannon responded two plays later with a 55-yard touchdown pass to Marvin Harrison. Deltha O'Neal's 24-yard interception return to the NFC's 6-yard line moments later set up Curtis Martin's 4-yard touchdown run and gave the AFC a 14-10 lead. After the NFC went three-and-out, the AFC needed just five plays, keyed by Gannon's 30-yard pass to Troy Brown, and capped by Priest

Holmes' 39-yard touchdown run to give the AFC its third touchdown in less than six minutes and a 21-10 lead. A 10-play NFC drive led to Akers' second field goal, but Jermaine Lewis' 54-yard kickoff return set up Gannon's 18-yard touchdown pass to Ken Dilger and gave the AFC a 28-10 lead with 12:03 left in the first half. The NFC overcame Shane Lechler's Pro Bowl-record 73-yard punt with Akers' 49-yard field goal just before halftime to cut the deficit to 28-16. Junior Seau's interception at the AFC's 5-yard line early in the fourth quarter thwarted one NFC rally, but Champ Bailey's interception led to Donovan McNabb's 8-yard touchdown pass to Terrell Owens to cut the deficit to 28-23 with 8:12 left. Runs of 29 and 16 yards by Corey Dillon led to Jason Elam's 38-yard field goal and, two plays later, Ty Law intercepted McNabb at the NFC 44-yard line, returned the ball to the NFC 13 before lateralling to Ray Lewis, who dragged three players into the end zone for a 38-23 lead with 2:49 remaining. McNabb's 15-yard touchdown pass to Garrison Hearst with 1:32 left cut the deficit to 38-30, but Rod Woodson recovered the ensuing onside kick to clinch the victory. Gannon was 8 of 10 for 137 yards and 2 touchdowns. McNabb was 12 of 25 for 149 yards and 2 touchdowns, with 2 interceptions, to lead the NFC. Owens had 8 receptions for 122 yards and 1 touchdown.

AFC	21	7	0	10 —	38
NFC	13	3	0	14 —	30

NFC	Green 2 run (Akers kick)
NFC	FG Akers 29
AFC	Harrison 55 pass from Gannon (Elam kick)
AFC	Martin 4 run (Elam kick)
AFC	Holmes 39 run (Elam kick)
NFC	FG Akers 41
AFC	Dilger 18 pass from Gannon (Elam kick)
NFC	FG Akers 49
NFC	Owens 8 pass from McNabb (Akers kick)
AFC	FG Elam 38
AFC	R. Lewis 13 lateral from Law (Elam kick)
NFC	Hearst 15 pass from McNabb (Akers kick)

2001 AFC-NFC PRO BOWL
Aloha Stadium, Honolulu, Hawaii
February 4, 2001, Attendance: 50,128
AFC 38, NFC 17—Rich Gannon completed 12 of 14 passes for 160 yards during the game's first two possessions to win player of the game honors and lead the AFC to victory. Gannon's touchdown passes capped 87- and 90-yard drives and staked the AFC to a 14-0 lead. Gannon, who was still recovering from a separated non-throwing shoulder suffered in the AFC Championship Game, was replaced by Peyton Manning. The Colts' quarterback engineered a scoring drive, capped by Matt Stover's field goal, to give

the AFC a 17-0 lead early in the second quarter. At that point, the AFC had 14 first downs and 231 yards of offense while limiting the NFC to no first downs and 6 yards. Jimmy Smith caught a 2-yard touchdown pass 54 seconds before halftime to give the AFC a 24-3 lead. Third-quarter touchdown passes by Donovan McNabb and Daunte Culpepper trimmed the AFC's lead to 31-17, but Jason Taylor batted down Culpepper's fourth-and-1 pass early in the fourth quarter, and Edgerrin James' 20-yard touchdown run a few plays later iced the game. The NFC attempted a Pro Bowl record 56 pass attempts, and the two teams combined for a Pro Bowl record 98 pass attempts. Tony Gonzalez had 6 receptions for 108 yards, all in the first half, for the AFC. Torry Holt had 7 receptions for 103 yards. Smith's touchdown reception gives him 5 for his career, an AFC-NFC Pro Bowl record.

NFC	0	3	14	0	—	17
AFC	14	10	7	7	—	38

AFC — Gonzalez 8 pass from Gannon (Stover kick)
AFC — Harrison 16 pass from Gannon (Stover kick)
AFC — FG Stover 29
NFC — FG Gramatica 48
AFC — J. Smith 2 pass from Manning (Stover kick)
NFC — Owens 17 pass from McNabb (Gramatica kick)
AFC — Harrison 24 pass from Manning (Stover kick)
NFC — Holt 20 pass from Culpepper (Gramatica kick)
AFC — James 20 run (Stover kick)

2000 AFC-NFC PRO BOWL
Aloha Stadium, Honolulu, Hawaii
February 6, 2000, Attendance: 50,112
NFC 51, AFC 31—Randy Moss earned player of the game honors by setting records with 9 receptions for 212 yards as the NFC defeated the AFC in the highest-scoring Pro Bowl ever. Aeneas Williams intercepted Peyton Manning's pass and raced 62 yards down the left sideline to give the NFC an early 7-0 lead. Kurt Warner's 48-yard pass to Moss on the NFC's first possession set up Jason Hanson's first field goal. Mike Alstott and Jimmy Smith each scored twice in the first half, and Michael Bates' 66-yard kickoff return led to Hanson's Pro Bowl-record tying 51-yard field goal as the half expired to give the NFC a 27-21 lead. Alstott's third touchdown increased the NFC's lead to 37-21, and Derrick Brooks' interception of Mark Brunell and 20-yard return staked the NFC to a 44-24 lead with 11:12 left. The AFC responded with Manning's 52-yard touchdown pass to Smith with 6:30 remaining, but Steve Beuerlein found Moss with a 25-yard scoring pass with 1:05 left to finish the scoring. Warner led the three NFC quarterbacks by completing 8 of 11 passes for 123 yards. Alstott led

all rushers with 13 carries for 67 yards. The NFC forced 6 turnovers. Manning was 17 of 23 for 270 yards and 2 touchdowns, with 2 interceptions. Smith had 8 receptions for 119 yards. The previous record, 64 points, was set in 1980.

AFC	7	14	0	10	—	31
NFC	10	17	10	14	—	51

NFC — A. Williams 62 interception return (Hanson kick)
NFC — FG Hanson 21
AFC — J. Smith 5 pass from Brunell (Mare kick)
NFC — Alstott 1 run (Hanson kick)
AFC — Gonzalez 10 pass from Gannon (Mare kick)
NFC — Alstott 3 run (Hanson kick)
AFC — J. Smith 21 pass from Manning (Mare kick)
NFC — FG Hanson 51
NFC — Alstott 1 run (Hanson kick)
NFC — FG Hanson 23
AFC — FG Mare 33
NFC — Brooks 20 interception return (Hanson kick)
AFC — J. Smith 52 pass from Manning (Mare kick)
NFC — Moss 25 pass from Beuerlein (Hanson kick)

1999 AFC-NFC PRO BOWL
Aloha Stadium, Honolulu, Hawaii
February 7, 1999, Attendance: 50,075
AFC 23, NFC 10—John Elway, appearing in uniform on a football field for the final time, drove the AFC to its initial touchdown and then watched a strong defensive effort as the AFC won the Pro Bowl for the third consecutive season. Elway capped a game-opening 61-yard drive with a touchdown pass to Sam Gash. The AFC led 10-3 late in the first half when Deion Sanders intercepted a Vinny Testaverde pass at the NFC's 10 and raced downfield, only to be caught by Ed McCaffrey at the AFC 3-yard line as the half expired. The NFC drove into AFC territory early in the second half, but Ty Law thwarted the NFC's spirits with a 67-yard interception return for a touchdown to give the AFC a 17-3 lead with 9:42 left in the third quarter. The NFC reached the end zone three minutes later as Emmitt Smith scored, but the AFC responded with a field goal on its ensuing possession. Jason Elam's third field goal with 1:02 remaining finished the scoring. Elway played just one drive and was 4 of 5 for 55 yards and 1 touchdown. Keyshawn Johnson had 7 catches for 87 yards and shared player of the game honors with Law. Chandler completed 9 of 25 passes for 133 yards en route to leading the NFC to its only touchdown. Randy Moss had 7 catches for 108 yards.

NFC	3	0	7	0	—	10
AFC	7	3	10	3	—	23

AFC — Gash 3 pass from Elway (Elam kick)
NFC — FG Anderson 23

AFC — FG Elam 23
AFC — Law 67 interception return (Elam kick)
NFC — E. Smith 3 run (Anderson kick)
AFC — FG Elam 46
AFC — FG Elam 26

1998 AFC-NFC PRO BOWL
Aloha Stadium, Honolulu, Hawaii
February 1, 1998, Attendance: 49,995
AFC 29, NFC 24—Warren Moon guided the AFC to points on all three of his drives, including the winning touchdown from 1 yard with 1:49 left as the AFC scored the game's final 15 points to beat the NFC. Steve Young threw a 22-yard touchdown pass to Herman Moore to cap the game's opening drive and give the NFC a 7-0 lead. Late in the first quarter, Mark Brunell threw a 17-yard touchdown pass to Andre Rison to tie the game. Both touchdown passes came on third-and-8 plays. The NFC responded with a 7-play, 71-yard drive capped by Young's 36-yard touchdown pass to Rob Moore. Trent Dilfer guided the NFC to its third touchdown, keyed by a 21-yard pass to Irving Fryar and 23-yard pass to Mike Alstott, and capped by Dorsey Levens' 12-yard touchdown run with 1:36 left in the half to give the NFC a 21-7 lead. The NFC had a chance to pad its lead on its first possession of the second half, but Jason Hanson missed a 44-yard field goal. The AFC bounced back with a 10-play, 65-yard drive that culminated with Drew Bledsoe's 14-yard touchdown pass to Jimmy Smith late in the third quarter. After Hanson's 35-yard field goal gave the NFC a 24-14 lead with 13:42 left, Moon entered the game and drove the AFC into field-goal range, where Mike Hollis drilled a 48-yard attempt with 8:51 left. Attempting to grind out the clock, Warrick Dunn fumbled, and Darryl Williams recovered at the AFC's 49 with 3:03 remaining. After a holding penalty moved the AFC back 10 yards, Moon fired a 57-yard pass to Tim Brown to set up Eddie George's 4-yard run with 2:31 left. The AFC went for the lead instead of a tie, but Moon's pass to Rison fell incomplete. However, the AFC got the ball back when Chris Chandler fumbled the snap on the NFC's first play, and Michael Sinclair recovered at the NFC's 16 with 2:19 left. Three runs by George set up Moon's winning sneak with 1:49 remaining. Moon's 2-point conversion pass to Brown was incomplete, keeping the AFC's lead at 29-24. The NFC was unable to move beyond its own 31-yard line in the final moments, and the AFC prevailed. Tim Brown had 5 receptions for 129 yards. Moon, who was 4 of 8 for 89 yards, earned player of the game honors.

AFC	7	0	7	15	—	29
NFC	7	14	0	3	—	24

NFC — H. Moore 22 pass from Young (Hanson kick)

AFC — Rison 17 pass from Brunell (Hollis kick)
NFC — R. Moore 36 pass from Young (Hanson kick)
NFC — Levens 12 run (Hanson kick)
AFC — J. Smith 14 pass from Bledsoe (Hollis kick)
NFC — FG Hanson 35
AFC — FG Hollis 48
AFC — George 4 run (pass failed)
AFC — Moon 1 run (pass failed)

1997 AFC-NFC PRO BOWL

Aloha Stadium, Honolulu, Hawaii
February 2, 1997, Attendance: 50,031
AFC 26, NFC 23 (OT)—Cary Blanchard's 37-yard field goal 8:16 into overtime gave the AFC a 26-23 victory. The field goal was an ironic ending to a game that saw Blanchard and NFC kicker John Kasay, who each broke the previous single-season record of 35 field goals, combine to miss 5 of 8 field-goal attempts. The NFC scored on its first two possessions, with Vikings guard Randall McDaniel, who lined up as a fullback, scoring his first professional touchdown to give the NFC a 9-0 lead. However, the follies of the kicking unit began as holder Matt Turk muffed the snap on the extra point attempt. Blanchard booted a 28-yard field goal with 27 seconds left in the half to cut the NFC's lead to 9-3. In the third quarter, Barry Sanders scored from 6 yards out, but Kerry Collins was sacked on the 2-point attempt. A 41-yard pass from Drew Bledsoe to Tony Martin led to Curtis Martin's 3-yard run, and after Ashley Ambrose ran an interception back 54 yards for a touchdown 11 seconds into the fourth quarter, the AFC found itself with a 16-15 lead. The NFC drove for more than six minutes, only to have Kasay miss a 40-yard field goal attempt. After an AFC punt, Cris Carter caught a 47-yard touchdown bomb from Gus Frerotte to put the NFC ahead 23-16. After each team punted, the AFC got the ball on its own 20-yard line with 55 seconds left. Mark Brunell hit Tim Brown with an 80-yard bomb down the right sideline to tie the game with 44 seconds left. Wesley Walls caught a 33-yard pass to give the NFC a chance to win in regulation, but Kasay missed a 39-yard attempt and the game went to overtime. The AFC won the overtime toss, but Blanchard missed a 41-yard field goal attempt. The NFC had to punt after three plays, and Brunell hit Ben Coates with a 43-yard pass on the AFC's first play. After three running plays failed to gain a first down, Blanchard trotted onto the field and made the game-winning kick. The teams combined for a Pro Bowl record 962 total yards. Brunell, who completed 12 of 22 pass attempts for 236 yards, was selected as the player of the game.

AFC	0	3	7	13	3	— 26
NFC	9	0	6	8	0	— 23

NFC — FG Kasay 20

NFC — R. McDaniel 5 pass from Favre (muffed snap)
AFC — FG Blanchard 28
NFC — Sanders 6 run (pass failed)
AFC — Martin 3 run (Blanchard kick)
AFC — Ambrose 54 interception return (pass failed)
NFC — Carter 53 pass from Frerotte (Walls pass from Frerotte)
AFC — T. Brown 80 pass from Brunell (Blanchard kick)
AFC — FG Blanchard 37

1996 AFC-NFC PRO BOWL

Aloha Stadium, Honolulu, Hawaii
February 4, 1996, Attendance: 50,034
NFC 20, AFC 13—Jerry Rice had 6 receptions for 82 yards and 1 touchdown to earn player of the game honors in the NFC's victory. The 49ers' wide receiver, who was named to the Pro Bowl for the tenth consecutive year, caught a 1-yard touchdown pass from Packers quarterback Brett Favre 1:41 into the second quarter to cap an 80-yard drive and give the NFC the lead for good at 10-7. The AFC had taken a 7-0 lead 2:26 into the game when Bengals quarterback Jeff Blake connected with Steelers wide receiver Yancey Thigpen on a Pro Bowl-record 93-yard touchdown pass. The NFC increased its advantage to 20-7 at half-time on Redskins linebacker Ken Harvey's 36-yard interception return for a touchdown and Falcons kicker Morten Andersen's 24-yard field goal. The AFC trimmed its deficit to 20-13 when Colts quarterback Jim Harbaugh teamed with Patriots running back Curtis Martin on a 17-yard touchdown pass in the final minute of the third quarter, but its bid to win or tie was rebuffed twice in the final minutes of the fourth quarter. First, 49ers safety Tim McDonald intercepted Harbaugh's pass in the end zone with 1:50 remaining. Then, after the AFC forced a punt and got the ball back near midfield, Harbaugh drove his team to the NFC's 9-yard line in the closing seconds. But he spiked the ball once to stop the clock and threw 3 consecutive incompletions as time ran out. The AFC outgained the NFC 390 total yards to 287, but its quarterbacks suffered 4 interceptions, including 3 off Harbaugh, the NFL's leading passer during the regular season. The NFC raised its edge to 15-11 in Pro Bowl games since the AFL-NFL merger in 1970.

NFC	3	17	0	0	— 20
AFC	7	0	6	0	— 13

AFC — Thigpen 93 pass from Blake (Elam kick)
NFC — FG Andersen 36
NFC — Rice 1 pass from Favre (Andersen kick)
NFC — Harvey 36 interception return (Andersen kick)
NFC — FG Andersen 24
AFC — Martin 17 pass from Harbaugh (kick failed)

1995 AFC-NFC PRO BOWL

Aloha Stadium, Honolulu, Hawaii
February 5, 1995, Attendance: 50,529
AFC 41, NFC 13—Colts rookie Marshal Faulk rushed for a Pro Bowl-record 180 yards to key the AFC's rout of the NFC. Faulk, who earned the Dan McGuire Trophy as the player of the game, averaged nearly 14 yards on his 13 carries and shattered the previous rushing mark of 112 yards set by O.J. Simpson in the 1973 game. Faulk's 49-yard touchdown run from punt formation in the fourth quarter was the longest in Pro Bowl history. The Seahawks' Chris Warren added 127 yards on 14 carries as the AFC amassed records for rushing yards (400) and total yards (552). Steelers tight end Eric Green caught 2 touchdown passes for the victors. The NFC managed only 196 total yards, a large chunk coming when 49ers quarterback Steve Young and Vikings wide receiver Cris Carter teamed on a 51-yard touchdown pass in the first quarter. That gave the NFC a 10-0 advantage, but the AFC rallied in the second quarter and took the lead for good when the Browns' Leroy Hoard scored on a 4-yard touchdown run 2:07 before halftime.

AFC	0	17	3	21	— 41
NFC	10	0	3	0	— 13

NFC — FG Reveiz 28
NFC — Carter 51 pass from Young (Reveiz kick)
AFC — Green 22 pass from Elway (Carney kick)
AFC — FG Carney 22
AFC — Hoard 4 run (Carney kick)
NFC — FG Reveiz 49
AFC — FG Carney 23
AFC — Warren 11 run (Carney kick)
AFC — Green 16 pass from Hostetler (Carney kick)
AFC — Faulk 49 run (Carney kick)

1994 AFC-NFC PRO BOWL

Aloha Stadium, Honolulu, Hawaii
February 6, 1994, Attendance: 50,026
NFC 17, AFC 3—The NFC converted a blocked punt and a fumble recovery into touchdowns just 2:20 apart in the second half of its victory over the AFC. With the score tied 3-3 late in the third quarter, Saints linebacker Renaldo Turnbull deflected a punt by the Oilers' Greg Montgomery, and the NFC took possession at the AFC's 48-yard line. A 32-yard pass from Bobby Hebert to Falcons teammate Andre Rison positioned Rams running back Jerome Bettis for a 4-yard touchdown run with 1:27 left in the third quarter. Moments later, Rams defensive tackle Sean Gilbert recovered a fumble by Oilers quarterback Warren Moon at the AFC's 19. Hebert then teamed with the Vikings' Cris Carter on a 15-yard touchdown pass 53 seconds into the fourth period. The NFC kept the AFC out of the end zone by maintaining possession for more than 38 minutes and forcing 6 turnovers. Rison

earned the Dan McGuire Trophy as the player of the game by catching 6 passes for 86 yards. The victory was the fourth in the last six years for the NFC, which leads the series 14-10.

NFC	3	0	7	7	—	17
AFC	0	3	0	0	—	3

NFC — FG Johnson 35
AFC — FG Anderson 25
NFC — Bettis 4 run (Johnson kick)
NFC — Carter 15 pass from Hebert (Johnson kick)

1993 AFC-NFC PRO BOWL

Aloha Stadium, Honolulu, Hawaii
February 7, 1993, Attendance: 50,007
AFC 23, NFC 20—Nick Lowery's 33-yard field goal 4:09 into overtime gave the American Conference all-stars an unlikely 23-20 victory over the National Conference. Despite being overwhelmed by the NFC in first downs (30-9), and total yards (471-114), the AFC won because it forced 6 turnovers, blocked a pair of field goals (1 of which was returned for a touchdown), and returned an interception for a score. Special-teams star Steve Tasker of the Bills earned the Dan McGuire Trophy as the player of the game for making 4 tackles, forcing a fumble, and blocking a field goal. The block came with eight minutes left in regulation and the game tied at 13-13. The Raiders' Terry McDaniel picked up the loose ball and ran 28 yards for a touchdown and a 20-13 AFC lead. The NFC rallied behind 49ers quarterback Steve Young, whose fourth-down, 23-yard touchdown pass to Giants running back Rodney Hampton tied the game at 20-20 with 10 seconds left in regulation. Young completed 18 of 32 passes for 196 yards but was intercepted 3 times and lost a fumble when sacked in overtime. Raiders defensive end Howie Long fell on that fumble at the NFC 28-yard line, and five plays later, Lowery converted the winning field goal.

AFC	0	10	3	7	3	— 23
NFC	3	10	0	7	0	— 20

NFC — FG Andersen 27
AFC — Seau 31 interception return (Lowery kick)
NFC — FG Andersen 37
NFC — Irvin 9 pass from Aikman (Andersen kick)
AFC — FG Lowery 42
AFC — FG Lowery 29
AFC — McDaniel 28 blocked field goal return (Lowery kick)
NFC — Hampton 23 pass from Young (Andersen kick)
AFC — FG Lowery 33

1992 AFC-NFC PRO BOWL

Aloha Stadium, Honolulu, Hawaii
February 2, 1992, Attendance: 50,209
NFC 21, AFC 15—Atlanta's Chris Miller threw an 11-yard touchdown pass to San Francisco's Jerry Rice with 4:04 remaining in the game to lift the NFC over the

AFC. It was the NFC's thirteenth win in the 22-game series. The AFC had taken a 15-14 lead when the Raiders' Jeff Jaeger kicked a 27-yard field goal 1:49 into the fourth quarter. But the NFC, aided by a key roughing-the-passer penalty on a third-down incompletion from the AFC 24-yard line, drove 85 yards to the winning score. The Cowboys' Michael Irvin, playing in his first Pro Bowl, caught 8 passes for 125 yards, including a 13-yard touchdown in the first quarter, and was named the player of the game. Rice had 7 catches for 77 yards. Mark Rypien of Washington, the Super Bowl most valuable player one week earlier, completed 11 of 18 passes for 165 yards and 2 touchdowns for the NFC, including a 35-yard pass to Redskins teammate Gary Clark just 26 seconds before halftime. Miller completed 7 of his 10 attempts for 85 yards.

NFC	7	7	0	7	—	21
AFC	7	5	0	3	—	15

AFC — Clayton 4 pass from Kelly (Jaeger kick)
NFC — Irvin 13 pass from Rypien (Lohmiller kick)
AFC — Safety, Townsend tackled Byner in end zone
AFC — FG Jaeger 48
NFC — Clark 35 pass from Rypien (Lohmiller kick)
AFC — FG Jaeger 27
NFC — Rice 11 pass from Miller (Lohmiller kick)

1991 AFC-NFC PRO BOWL

Aloha Stadium, Honolulu, Hawaii
February 3, 1991, Attendance: 50,345
AFC 23, NFC 21—Buffalo's Jim Kelly and Houston's Ernest Givins combined for a 13-yard scoring pass late in the fourth quarter to rally the AFC over the NFC. Phoenix rookie Johnny Johnson scored on runs of 1 and 9 yards to put the NFC ahead 14-3 in the third quarter. Buffalo's Andre Reed, who led all receivers with 4 catches for 80 yards, caught a 20-yard scoring reception from Kelly early in the fourth quarter to move the AFC to within 1 point. Barry Sanders ran 22 yards for a touchdown to increase the NFC's lead to 21-13. Miami's Jeff Cross blocked a 46-yard field-goal attempt by New Orleans' Morten Andersen with seven seconds remaining to preserve the win. Buffalo's Bruce Smith recorded 3 sacks and also had a blocked field goal. Kelly, who completed 13 of 19 passes for 210 yards and 2 touchdowns, was presented the Dan McGuire Award as player of the game. The AFC's victory narrowed the NFC's Pro Bowl series lead to 12-9.

AFC	3	0	3	17	—	23
NFC	0	7	7	7	—	21

AFC — FG Lowery 26
NFC — J. Johnson 1 run (Andersen kick)
AFC — FG Lowery 43

NFC — J. Johnson 9 run (Andersen kick)
AFC — Reed 20 pass from Kelly (Lowery kick)
NFC — Sanders 22 run (Andersen kick)
AFC — FG Lowery 34
AFC — Givins 13 pass from Kelly (Lowery kick)

1990 AFC-NFC PRO BOWL

Aloha Stadium, Honolulu, Hawaii
February 4, 1990, Attendance: 50,445
NFC 27, AFC 21—The NFC captured its second straight Pro Bowl as the defense accounted for a pair of touchdowns and forced 5 turnovers before the eleventh consecutive sellout crowd at Aloha Stadium. The AFC held a 7-6 halftime edge on a 1-yard scoring run by Christian Okoye of the Chiefs. The NFC then rallied with 21 unanswered points in the third quarter. David Meggett of the Giants began the comeback with an 11-yard touchdown reception from Philadelphia's Randall Cunningham. The Rams' Jerry Gray followed with a 51-yard interception return for a score and the Vikings' Keith Millard added an 8-yard fumble return for a touchdown four minutes later to give the NFC a commanding 27-7 lead. Seattle's Dave Krieg rallied the AFC with a 5-yard touchdown pass to Miami's Ferrell Edmunds. Cleveland's Mike Johnson then returned an interception 22 yards for a score to pull the AFC to within 27-21. Gray, who was credited with 7 tackles, was given the Dan McGuire Award as player of the game. Krieg led all quarterbacks by completing 15 of 23 for 148 yards and 1 touchdown. Buffalo's Thurman Thomas topped all receivers with 5 catches for 47 yards, while Indianapolis' Eric Dickerson led all rushers with 46 yards on 15 carries. The win gave the NFC a 12-8 advantage in Pro Bowl games since 1971.

NFC	3	3	21	0	—	27
AFC	0	7	0	14	—	21

NFC — FG Murray 23
NFC — FG Murray 41
AFC — Okoye 1 run (Treadwell kick)
NFC — Meggett 11 pass from Cunningham (Murray kick)
NFC — Gray 51 interception return (Murray kick)
NFC — Millard 8 fumble recovery return (Murray kick)
AFC — Edmunds 5 pass from Krieg (Treadwell kick)
AFC — M. Johnson 22 interception return (Treadwell kick)

1989 AFC-NFC PRO BOWL

Aloha Stadium, Honolulu, Hawaii
January 29, 1989, Attendance: 50,113
NFC 34, AFC 3—The NFC scored 34 unanswered points to snap a two-game losing streak to the AFC before the tenth straight sellout crowd in Honolulu's Aloha

Stadium. Bills kicker Scott Norwood provided the AFC's only points on a 38-yard field goal 6:23 into the game. Touchdown runs by Dallas' Herschel Walker (4 yards) and Atlanta's John Settle (1) brought the NFC a 14-3 halftime lead. Walker added a 7-yard scoring run, the Saints' Morten Andersen kicked field goals of 27 and 51 yards, and Los Angeles Rams' wide receiver Henry Ellard caught an 8-yard scoring pass from Minnesota quarterback Wade Wilson in the second half to complete the scoring. Chicago running back Neal Anderson and Philadelphia quarterback Randall Cunningham, who were both appearing in their first Pro Bowl, also played major roles in the NFC's victory. Anderson rushed 13 times for 85 yards and had 2 receptions for 17. Cunningham, who was voted the game's outstanding player, completed 10 of 14 passes for 63 yards and rushed for 49 yards. The NFC, which had 5 takeaways, outgained the AFC 355 yards to 167 and held a time-of-possession advantage of 35:18 to 24:42. Houston quarterback Warren Moon completed 13 of 20 passes for 134 yards for the AFC. The win gave the NFC an 11-8 advantage in Pro Bowl games.

AFC	3	0	0	0	—	3
NFC	7	7	10	10	—	34

AFC — FG Norwood 38
NFC — Walker 4 run (Andersen kick)
NFC — Settle 1 run (Andersen kick)
NFC — FG Andersen 27
NFC — Walker 7 run (Andersen kick)
NFC — FG Andersen 51
NFC — Ellard 8 pass from Wilson (Andersen kick)

1988 AFC-NFC PRO BOWL
Aloha Stadium, Honolulu, Hawaii
February 7, 1988, Attendance: 50,113
AFC 15, NFC 6—Led by a tenacious pass rush, the AFC defeated the NFC for the second consecutive year before the ninth straight sellout crowd in Honolulu's Aloha Stadium. Buffalo quarterback Jim Kelly scored the game's lone touchdown on a 1-yard run for a 7-6 halftime lead. Colts kicker Dean Biasucci added field goals from 37 and 30 yards to complete the AFC's scoring. Saints kicker Morten Andersen had 25- and 36-yard field goals to account for the NFC's points. AFC defenders held the NFC to 213 yards and recorded 8 sacks. Bills defensive end Bruce Smith, who had 2 sacks among his 5 tackles, was voted the game's outstanding player. Oilers running back Mike Rozier led all rushers with 49 yards on 9 carries. Jets wide receiver Al Toon had 5 receptions for 75 yards. The AFC generated 341 yards total offense and held a time-of-possession advantage of 34:14 to 25:46. By winning, the AFC cut the NFC's lead in the Pro Bowl series to 10-8.

NFC	0	6	0	0	—	6
AFC	0	7	6	2	—	15

NFC — FG Andersen 25

AFC — Kelly 1 run (Biasucci kick)
NFC — FG Andersen 36
AFC — FG Biasucci 37
AFC — FG Biasucci 30
AFC — Safety, Montana forced out of end zone

1987 AFC-NFC PRO BOWL
Aloha Stadium, Honolulu, Hawaii
February 1, 1987, Attendance: 50,101
AFC 10, NFC 6—The AFC defeated the NFC in the lowest-scoring game in AFC-NFC Pro Bowl history. The AFC took a 10-0 halftime lead on Broncos quarterback John Elway's 10-yard touchdown pass to Raiders tight end Todd Christensen and Patriots kicker Tony Franklin's 26-yard field goal. The AFC defense made the lead stand by forcing the NFC to settle for a pair of field goals from 38 and 19 yards by Saints kicker Morten Andersen after the NFC had first downs at the AFC 31-, 7-, 16-, 15-, 5-, and 7-yard lines. Both AFC scores were set up by fumble recoveries by Seahawks linebacker Fredd Young and Dolphins linebacker John Offerdahl, respectively. Eagles defensive end Reggie White, who tied a Pro Bowl record with 4 sacks among his 7 solo tackles, was voted the game's outstanding player. The AFC victory cut the NFC's lead in the Pro Bowl series to 10-7.

AFC	7	3	0	0	—	10
NFC	0	0	3	3	—	6

AFC — Christensen 10 pass from Elway (Franklin kick)
AFC — FG Franklin 26
NFC — FG Andersen 38
NFC — FG Andersen 19

1986 AFC-NFC PRO BOWL
Aloha Stadium, Honolulu, Hawaii
February 2, 1986, Attendance: 50,101
NFC 28, AFC 24—New York Giants quarterback Phil Simms brought the NFC back from a 24-7 halftime deficit to defeat the AFC. Simms, who completed 15 of 27 passes for 212 yards and 3 touchdowns, was named the most valuable player of the game. The AFC had taken its first-half lead behind a 2-yard run by Los Angeles Raiders running back Marcus Allen, who also threw a 51-yard scoring pass to San Diego wide receiver Wes Chandler, an 11-yard touchdown catch by Pittsburgh wide receiver Louis Lipps, and a 34-yard field goal by Steelers kicker Gary Anderson. Minnesota's Joey Browner accounted for the NFC's only score before halftime on a 48-yard interception return. After intermission, the NFC blanked the AFC while scoring 3 touchdowns via a 15-yard catch by Washington wide receiver Art Monk, a 2-yard reception by Dallas tight end Doug Cosbie, and a 15-yard catch by Tampa Bay tight end Jimmie Giles with 2:47 remaining in the game. The victory gave the NFC a 10-6 Pro Bowl record against the AFC.

NFC	0	7	7	14	—	28
AFC	7	17	0	0	—	24

AFC — Allen 2 run (Anderson kick)
NFC — Browner 48 interception return (Andersen kick)
AFC — Chandler 51 pass from Allen (Anderson kick)
AFC — FG Anderson 34
AFC — Lipps 11 pass from O'Brien (Anderson kick)
NFC — Monk 15 pass from Simms (Andersen kick)
NFC — Cosbie 2 pass from Simms (Andersen kick)
NFC — Giles 15 pass from Simms (Andersen kick)

1985 AFC-NFC PRO BOWL
Aloha Stadium, Honolulu, Hawaii
January 27, 1985, Attendance: 50,385
AFC 22, NFC 14—Defensive end Art Still of the Kansas City Chiefs recovered a fumble and returned it 83 yards for a touchdown to clinch the AFC's victory over the NFC. Still's touchdown came in the fourth period with the AFC trailing 14-12 and was one of several outstanding defensive plays in a Pro Bowl dominated by two record-breaking defenses. The teams combined for a Pro Bowl-record 17 sacks, including 4 by New York Jets defensive end Mark Gastineau, who was named the game's outstanding player. The AFC's first score came on a safety when Gastineau tackled running back Eric Dickerson of the Los Angeles Rams in the end zone. The AFC's second score, a 6-yard pass from Miami's Dan Marino to Los Angeles Raiders running back Marcus Allen, was set up by a partial block of a punt by Seahawks linebacker Fredd Young. The NFC leads the series 9-6.

AFC	0	9	0	13	—	22
NFC	0	0	7	7	—	14

AFC — Safety, Gastineau tackled Dickerson in end zone
AFC — Allen 6 pass from Marino (Johnson kick)
NFC — Lofton 13 pass from Montana (Stenerud kick)
NFC — Payton 1 run (Stenerud kick)
AFC — FG Johnson 33
AFC — Still 83 fumble recovery return (Johnson kick)
AFC — FG Johnson 22

1984 AFC-NFC PRO BOWL
Aloha Stadium, Honolulu, Hawaii
January 29, 1984, Attendance: 50,445
NFC 45, AFC 3—The NFC won its sixth Pro Bowl in the last seven seasons by routing the AFC. The NFC was led by the passing of most valuable player Joe Theismann of Washington, who completed 21 of 27 passes for 242 yards and 3 touchdowns. Theismann set Pro Bowl records for completions and touchdown passes. The NFC established Pro Bowl marks for most points scored and fewest points allowed. Running back William

Andrews of Atlanta had 6 carries for 43 yards and caught 4 passes for 49 yards, including scoring receptions of 16 and 2 yards. Los Angeles Rams rookie Eric Dickerson gained 46 yards on 11 carries, including a 14-yard touchdown run, and had 45 yards on 5 catches. Rams safety Nolan Cromwell had a 44-yard interception return for a touchdown early in the third period to give the NFC a commanding 24-3 lead. Green Bay wide receiver James Lofton caught an 8-yard touchdown pass, while tight end teammate Paul Coffman had a 6-yard scoring catch.

NFC	3	14	14	14	—	45
AFC	0	3	0	0	—	3

NFC — FG Haji-Sheikh 23
NFC — Andrews 16 pass from Theismann (Haji-Sheikh kick)
NFC — Andrews 2 pass from Montana (Haji-Sheikh kick)
AFC — FG Anderson 43
NFC — Cromwell 44 interception return (Haji-Sheikh kick)
NFC — Lofton 8 pass from Theismann (Haji-Sheikh kick)
NFC — Coffman 6 pass from Theismann (Haji-Sheikh kick)
NFC — Dickerson 14 run (Haji-Sheikh kick)

1983 AFC-NFC PRO BOWL
Aloha Stadium, Honolulu, Hawaii
February 6, 1983, Attendance: 49,883
NFC 20, AFC 19—Dallas' Danny White threw an 11-yard touchdown pass to the Packers' John Jefferson with 35 seconds remaining to rally the NFC over the AFC. White, who completed 14 of 26 passes for 162 yards, kept the winning 65-yard drive alive with a 14-yard completion to Jefferson on a fourth-and-7 play at the AFC 25. The AFC was ahead 12-10 at halftime and increased the lead to 19-10 in the third period, when Marcus Allen scored on a 1-yard run. San Diego's Dan Fouts, who attempted 30 passes, set Pro Bowl records for most completions (17) and yards (274). Pittsburgh's John Stallworth was the AFC's leading receiver with 7 catches for 67 yards. William Andrews topped the NFC with 5 receptions for 48 yards. Fouts and Jefferson were co-winners of the player of the game award.

AFC	9	3	7	0	—	19
NFC	0	10	0	10	—	20

AFC — Walker 34 pass from Fouts (Benirschke kick)
AFC — Safety, Still tackled Theismann in end zone
NFC — Andrews 3 run (Moseley kick)
NFC — FG Moseley 35
AFC — FG Benirschke 29
AFC — Allen 1 run (Benirschke kick)
NFC — FG Moseley 41
NFC — Jefferson 11 pass from D. White (Moseley kick)

1982 AFC-NFC PRO BOWL
Aloha Stadium, Honolulu, Hawaii
January 31, 1982, Attendance: 50,402
AFC 16, NFC 13—Nick Lowery of Kansas City kicked a 23-yard field goal with three seconds remaining to give the AFC a last-second victory over the NFC. Lowery's kick climaxed a 69-yard drive directed by quarterback Dan Fouts. The NFC gained a 13-13 tie with 2:43 to go when Dallas' Tony Dorsett ran 4 yards for a touchdown. In the drive to the winning field goal, Fouts completed 3 passes, including a 23-yard toss to San Diego teammate Kellen Winslow that put the ball on the NFC's 5-yard line. Two plays later, Lowery kicked the field goal. Winslow, who caught 6 passes for 86 yards, was named co-player of the game along with Tampa Bay defensive end Lee Roy Selmon.

NFC	0	6	0	7	—	13
AFC	0	0	13	3	—	16

NFC — Giles 4 pass from Montana (kick blocked)
AFC — Muncie 2 run (kick failed)
AFC — Campbell 1 run (Lowery kick)
NFC — Dorsett 4 run (Septien kick)
AFC — FG Lowery 23

1981 AFC-NFC PRO BOWL
Aloha Stadium, Honolulu, Hawaii
February 1, 1981, Attendance: 50,360
NFC 21, AFC 7—Eddie Murray kicked 4 field goals and Steve Bartkowski fired a 55-yard scoring pass to Alfred Jenkins to lead the NFC to its fourth straight victory over the AFC and a 7-4 edge in the series. Murray was named the game's most valuable player and missed tying Garo Yepremian's Pro Bowl record of 5 field goals when a 37-yard attempt hit the crossbar with 22 seconds left. The AFC's only score came on a 9-yard pass from Brian Sipe to Stanley Morgan. Bartkowski completed 9 of 21 passes for 173 yards, while Sipe connected on 10 of 15 for 142 yards. Ottis Anderson led all rushers with 70 yards on 10 carries. Earl Campbell, the NFL's leading rusher in 1980, was limited to 24 yards on 8 attempts.

AFC	0	7	0	0	—	7
NFC	3	6	0	12	—	21

NFC — FG Murray 31
AFC — Morgan 9 pass from Sipe (J. Smith kick)
NFC — FG Murray 31
NFC — FG Murray 34
NFC — Jenkins 55 pass from Bartkowski (Murray kick)
NFC — FG Murray 36
NFC — Safety, Shell called for holding in end zone

1980 AFC-NFC PRO BOWL
Aloha Stadium, Honolulu, Hawaii
January 27, 1980, Attendance: 49,800
NFC 37, AFC 27—Chuck Muncie ran for 2 touchdowns and threw a 25-yard option pass for another score to give the NFC its third consecutive victory over the AFC. The Saints' Muncie, who was selected the game's most valuable player, snapped a

3-3 tie on a 1-yard touchdown run at 1:41 of the second quarter, then scored on an 11-yard run in the fourth quarter for the NFC's final touchdown. Two scoring records were set in the game—37 points by the NFC, eclipsing the 33 by the AFC in 1973, and the 64 points by both teams, surpassing the 61 scored in 1973.

NFC	3	20	7	7	—	37
AFC	3	7	10	7	—	27

NFC — FG Moseley 37
AFC — FG Fritsch 19
NFC — Muncie 1 run (Moseley kick)
AFC — Pruitt 1 pass from Bradshaw (Fritsch kick)
NFC — D. Hill 13 pass from Manning (kick failed)
NFC — T. Hill 25 pass from Muncie (Moseley kick)
NFC — Henry 86 punt return (Moseley kick)
AFC — Campbell 2 run (Fritsch kick)
AFC — FG Fritsch 29
NFC — Muncie 11 run (Moseley kick)
AFC — Campbell 1 run (Fritsch kick)

1979 AFC-NFC PRO BOWL
Memorial Coliseum, Los Angeles, CA
January 29, 1979, Attendance: 46,281
NFC 13, AFC 7—Roger Staubach completed 9 of 15 passes for 125 yards, including the winning touchdown on a 19-yard strike to Dallas Cowboys teammate Tony Hill in the third period. The winning drive began at the AFC's 45-yard line after a shanked punt. Staubach hit Ahmad Rashad with passes of 15 and 17 yards to set up Hill's decisive catch. The victory gave the NFC a 5-4 advantage in Pro Bowl games. Rashad, who accounted for 89 yards on 5 receptions, was named the player of the game. The AFC led 7-6 at halftime on Bob Griese's 8-yard scoring toss to Steve Largent late in the second quarter. Largent had 5 receptions for 75 yards. The NFC scored first as Archie Manning marched his team 70 yards in 11 plays, capped by Wilbert Montgomery's 2-yard touchdown run. The AFC's Earl Campbell was the game's leading rusher with 66 yards on 12 carries.

AFC	0	7	0	0	—	7
NFC	0	6	7	0	—	13

NFC — Montgomery 2 run (kick failed)
AFC — Largent 8 pass from Griese (Yepremian kick)
NFC — T. Hill 19 pass from Staubach (Corral kick)

1978 AFC-NFC PRO BOWL
Tampa Stadium, Tampa, Florida
January 23, 1978, Attendance: 51,337
NFC 14, AFC 13—Walter Payton, the NFL's leading rusher in 1977, sparked a second-half comeback to give the NFC the win and tie the series between the two conferences at four victories each. Payton, who was the game's most valuable player, gained 77 yards on 13 carries and

scored the tying touchdown on a 1-yard burst with 7:37 left in the game. Efren Herrera kicked the winning extra point. The AFC dominated the first half of the game, taking a 13-0 lead on field goals of 21 and 39 yards by Toni Linhart and a 10-yard touchdown pass from Ken Stabler to Oakland teammate Cliff Branch. On the NFC's first possession of the second half, Pat Haden put together the first touchdown drive after Eddie Brown returned a punt to the AFC 46-yard line. Haden connected on all 4 of his passes on that drive, finally hitting Terry Metcalf with a 4-yard scoring toss. The NFC continued to rally and, with Jim Hart at quarterback, moved 63 yards in 12 plays to the go-ahead score. During the winning drive, Hart completed 5 of 6 passes for 38 yards and Payton picked up 20 more on the ground.

AFC	3	10	0	0	—	13
NFC	0	0	7	7	—	14

AFC — FG Linhart 21
AFC — Branch 10 pass from Stabler (Linhart kick)
AFC — FG Linhart 39
NFC — Metcalf 4 pass from Haden (Herrera kick)
NFC — Payton 1 run (Herrera kick)

1977 AFC-NFC PRO BOWL
Kingdome, Seattle, Washington
January 17, 1977, Attendance: 64,752
AFC 24, NFC 14—O.J. Simpson's 3-yard touchdown burst at 7:03 of the first quarter gave the AFC a lead it would not surrender, breaking a two-game NFC win streak and giving the AFC stars a 4-3 series lead. The AFC took a 17-7 lead midway through the second period on the first of 2 Ken Anderson touchdown passes, a 12-yard toss to Charlie Joiner. But the NFC mounted a 73-yard drive capped by Lawrence McCutcheon's 1-yard touchdown plunge to pull within 17-14 at the half. Following a scoreless third quarter, player of the game Mel Blount thwarted a possible NFC score when he intercepted Jim Hart's pass in the end zone. Less than three minutes later, Blount again picked off a Hart pass. That set up Anderson's 27-yard touchdown strike to Cliff Branch for the final score.

NFC	0	14	0	0	—	14
AFC	10	7	0	7	—	24

AFC — Simpson 3 run (Linhart kick)
AFC — FG Linhart 31
NFC — Thomas 15 run (Bakken kick)
AFC — Joiner 12 pass from Anderson (Linhart kick)
NFC — McCutcheon 1 run (Bakken kick)
AFC — Branch 27 pass from Anderson (Linhart kick)

1976 AFC-NFC PRO BOWL
Superdome, New Orleans, Louisiana
January 26, 1976, Attendance: 30,546
NFC 23, AFC 20—Mike Boryla, a late substitute who did not enter the game until

5:39 remained, lifted the National Football Conference to the victory over the American Football Conference with 2 touchdown passes in the final minutes. It was the second straight NFC win, squaring the series at 3-3. Until Boryla started firing the ball the AFC was in control, leading 13-0 at the half. Boryla entered the game after Billy Johnson had raced 90 yards with a punt to give the AFC a 20-9 lead. He floated a 14-yard touchdown pass to Terry Metcalf and later fired an 8-yard scoring pass to Mel Gray for the winner.

AFC	0	13	0	7	—	20
NFC	0	0	9	14	—	23

AFC — FG Stenerud 20
AFC — FG Stenerud 35
AFC — Burrough 64 pass from Pastorini (Stenerud kick)
NFC — FG Bakken 42
NFC — Foreman 4 pass from Hart (kick blocked)
AFC — Johnson 90 punt return (Stenerud kick)
NFC — Metcalf 14 pass from Boryla (Bakken kick)
NFC — Gray 8 pass from Boryla (Bakken kick)

1975 AFC-NFC PRO BOWL
Orange Bowl, Miami, Florida
January 20, 1975, Attendance: 26,484
NFC 17, AFC 10—Los Angeles quarterback James Harris, who took over the NFC offense after Jim Hart of St. Louis suffered a laceration above his right eye in the second period, threw 2 touchdown passes early in the fourth period to pace the NFC to its second victory in the five-game Pro Bowl series. The NFC win snapped a three-game AFC victory string. Harris, who was named the player of the game, connected with St. Louis' Mel Gray for an 8-yard touchdown 2:03 into the final period. One minute and 24 seconds later, following a fumble recovery by Washington's Ken Houston, Harris tossed another 8-yard scoring pass to Washington's Charley Taylor for the decisive points.

NFC	0	3	0	14	—	17
AFC	0	0	10	0	—	10

NFC — FG Marcol 33
AFC — Warfield 32 pass from Griese (Gerela kick)
AFC — FG Gerela 33
NFC — Gray 8 pass from J. Harris (Marcol kick)
NFC — Taylor 8 pass from J. Harris (Marcol kick)

1974 AFC-NFC PRO BOWL
Arrowhead Stadium, Kansas City, MO
January 20, 1974, Attendance: 66,918
AFC 15, NFC 13—Miami's Garo Yepremian's fifth field goal—a 42-yard kick with 21 seconds remaining—gave the AFC its third straight victory since the NFC won the inaugural game following the 1970 season. The field goal by Yepremian, who was voted the game's outstanding player,

offset a 21-yard field goal by Atlanta's Nick Mike-Mayer that had given the NFC a 13-12 advantage with 1:41 remaining. The only touchdown in the game was scored by the NFC on a 14-yard pass from Philadelphia's Roman Gabriel to the Rams' Lawrence McCutcheon.

NFC	0	10	0	3	—	13
AFC	3	3	3	6	—	15

AFC — FG Yepremian 16
NFC — FG Mike-Mayer 27
NFC — McCutcheon 14 pass from Gabriel (Mike-Mayer kick)
AFC — FG Yepremian 37
AFC — FG Yepremian 27
AFC — FG Yepremian 41
NFC — FG Mike-Mayer 21
AFC — FG Yepremian 42

1973 AFC-NFC PRO BOWL
Texas Stadium, Irving, Texas
January 21, 1973, Attendance: 37,091
AFC 33, NFC 28—Paced by the rushing and receiving of player of the game O.J. Simpson, the AFC erased a 14-0 first period deficit and built a commanding 33-14 lead midway through the fourth period before the NFC managed 2 touchdowns in the final minute of play. Simpson rushed for 112 yards and caught 3 passes for 58 more to gain unanimous recognition in the balloting for player of the game. Green Bay Packers running back John Brockington scored 3 touchdowns for the NFC.

AFC	0	10	10	13	—	33
NFC	14	0	0	14	—	28

NFC — Brockington 1 run (Marcol kick)
NFC — Brockington 3 pass from Kilmer (Marcol kick)
AFC — Simpson 7 run (Gerela kick)
AFC — FG Gerela 18
AFC — FG Gerela 22
AFC — Hubbard 11 run (Gerela kick)
AFC — O. Taylor 5 pass from Lamonica (kick failed)
AFC — Bell 12 interception return (Gerela kick)
NFC — Brockington 1 run (Marcol kick)
NFC — Kwalick 12 pass from Snead (Marcol kick)

1972 AFC-NFC PRO BOWL
Memorial Coliseum, Los Angeles, CA
January 23, 1972, Attendance: 53,647
AFC 26, NFC 13—Kansas City's Jan Stenerud kicked 4 field goals to lead the AFC from a 6-0 deficit to victory. The AFC defense picked off 3 passes. Stenerud was selected as the outstanding offensive player and his Kansas City teammate, linebacker Willie Lanier, was the game's outstanding defensive player.

AFC	0	3	13	10	—	26
NFC	0	6	0	7	—	13

NFC — Grim 50 pass from Landry (kick failed)
AFC — FG Stenerud 25
AFC — FG Stenerud 23

AFC — FG Stenerud 48
AFC — Morin 5 pass from Dawson
(Stenerud kick)
AFC — FG Stenerud 42
NFC — V. Washington 2 run
(Knight kick)
AFC — F. Little 6 run (Stenerud kick)

1971 AFC-NFC PRO BOWL
Memorial Coliseum, Los Angeles, CA
January 24, 1971, Attendance: 48,222
NFC 27, AFC 6—Mel Renfro of Dallas
broke open the first meeting between the
American Football Conference and National
Football Conference all-star teams as
he returned a pair of punts 82 and 56
yards for touchdowns in the final period to
clinch the NFC victory over the AFC. Renfro
was voted the game's outstanding
back and linebacker Fred Carr of Green
Bay the outstanding lineman.

AFC	0	3	3	0	—	6
NFC	0	3	10	14	—	27

AFC — FG Stenerud 37
NFC — FG Cox 13
NFC — Osborn 23 pass from Brodie
(Cox kick)
NFC — FG Cox 35
AFC — FG Stenerud 16
NFC — Renfro 82 punt return
(Cox kick)
NFC — Renfro 56 punt return
(Cox kick)

Includes AFL All-Star Game played after the 1961-69 seasons.

Date	Result/Honored players	Site (attendance)
Jan. 15, 1939	New York Giants 13, Pro All-Stars 10	Wrigley Field, Los Angeles (20,000)
Jan. 14, 1940	Green Bay 16, NFL All-Stars 7	Gilmore Stadium, Los Angeles (18,000)
Dec. 29, 1940	Chicago Bears 28, NFL All-Stars 14	Gilmore Stadium, Los Angeles (21,624)
Jan. 4, 1942	Chicago Bears 35, NFL All-Stars 24	Polo Grounds, New York (17,725)
Dec. 27, 1942	NFL All-Stars 17, Washington 14	Shibe Park, Philadelphia (18,671)
Jan. 14, 1951	American Conf. 28, National Conf. 27	Los Angeles Memorial Coliseum (53,676)
	Otto Graham, Cleveland, player of the game	
Jan. 12, 1952	National Conf. 30, American Conf. 13	Los Angeles Memorial Coliseum (19,400)
	Dan Towler, Los Angeles, player of the game	
Jan. 10, 1953	National Conf. 27, American Conf. 7	Los Angeles Memorial Coliseum (34,208)
	Don Doll, Detroit, player of the game	
Jan. 17, 1954	East 20, West 9	Los Angeles Memorial Coliseum (44,214)
	Chuck Bednarik, Philadelphia, player of the game	
Jan. 16, 1955	West 26, East 19	Los Angeles Memorial Coliseum (43,972)
	Billy Wilson, San Francisco, player of the game	
Jan. 15, 1956	East 31, West 30	Los Angeles Memorial Coliseum (37,867)
	Ollie Matson, Chi. Cardinals, player of the game	
Jan. 13, 1957	West 19, East 10	Los Angeles Memorial Coliseum (44,177)
	Bert Rechichar, Baltimore, outstanding back	
	Ernie Stautner, Pittsburgh, outstanding lineman	
Jan. 12, 1958	West 26, East 7	Los Angeles Memorial Coliseum (66,634)
	Hugh McElhenny, San Francisco, outstanding back	
	Gene Brito, Washington, outstanding lineman	
Jan. 11, 1959	East 28, West 21	Los Angeles Memorial Coliseum (72,250)
	Frank Gifford, N.Y. Giants, outstanding back	
	Doug Atkins, Chi. Bears, outstanding lineman	
Jan. 17, 1960	West 38, East 21	Los Angeles Memorial Coliseum (56,876)
	Johnny Unitas, Baltimore, outstanding back	
	Gene (Big Daddy) Lipscomb, Baltimore, outstanding lineman	
Jan. 15, 1961	West 35, East 31	Los Angeles Memorial Coliseum (62,971)
	Johnny Unitas, Baltimore, outstanding back	
	Sam Huff, N.Y. Giants, outstanding lineman	
Jan. 7, 1962	AFL West 47, East 27	Balboa Stadium, San Diego (20,973)
	Cotton Davidson, Dallas Texans, player of the game	
Jan. 14, 1962	NFL West 31, East 30	Los Angeles Memorial Coliseum (57,409)
	Jim Brown, Cleveland, outstanding back	
	Henry Jordan, Green Bay, outstanding lineman	
Jan. 13, 1963	AFL West 21, East 14	Balboa Stadium, San Diego (27,641)
	Curtis McClinton, Dallas Texans, outstanding offensive player	
	Earl Faison, San Diego, outstanding defensive player	
Jan. 13, 1963	NFL East 30, West 20	Los Angeles Memorial Coliseum (61,374)
	Jim Brown, Cleveland, outstanding back	
	Gene (Big Daddy) Lipscomb, Pittsburgh, outstanding lineman	
Jan. 12, 1964	NFL West 31, East 17	Los Angeles Memorial Coliseum (67,242)
	Johnny Unitas, Baltimore, player of the game	
	Gino Marchetti, Baltimore, outstanding lineman	
Jan. 19, 1964	AFL West 27, East 24	Balboa Stadium, San Diego (20,016)
	Keith Lincoln, San Diego, outstanding offensive player	
	Archie Matsos, Oakland, outstanding defensive player	
Jan. 10, 1965	NFL West 34, East 14	Los Angeles Memorial Coliseum (60,598)
	Fran Tarkenton, Minnesota, outstanding back	
	Terry Barr, Detroit, outstanding lineman	
Jan. 16, 1965	AFL West 38, East 14	Jeppesen Stadium, Houston (15,446)
	Keith Lincoln, San Diego, outstanding offensive player	
	Willie Brown, Denver, outstanding defensive player	
Jan. 15, 1966	AFL All-Stars 30, Buffalo 19	Rice Stadium, Houston (35,572)
	Joe Namath, N.Y. Jets, most valuable player, offense	
	Frank Buncom, San Diego, most valuable player, defense	
Jan. 15, 1966	NFL East 36, West 7	Los Angeles Memorial Coliseum (60,124)
	Jim Brown, Cleveland, outstanding back	
	Dale Meinert, St. Louis, outstanding lineman	
Jan. 21, 1967	AFL East 30, West 23	Oakland-Alameda County Coliseum (18,876)
	Babe Parilli, Boston, outstanding offensive player	
	Verlon Biggs, N.Y. Jets, outstanding defensive player	
Jan. 22, 1967	NFL East 20, West 10	Los Angeles Memorial Coliseum (15,062)
	Gale Sayers, Chicago, outstanding back	
	Floyd Peters, Philadelphia, outstanding lineman	

Jan. 21, 1968	AFL East 25, West 24	Gator Bowl, Jacksonville, Fla. (40,103)

Joe Namath and Don Maynard, N.Y. Jets, out. off. players
Leslie (Speedy) Duncan, San Diego, out. def. player

Jan. 21, 1968   NFL West 38, East 20 ....Los Angeles Memorial Coliseum (53,289)
     Gale Sayers, Chicago, outstanding back
     Dave Robinson, Green Bay, outstanding lineman

Jan. 19, 1969   AFL West 38, East 25 ....Gator Bowl, Jacksonville, Fla. (41,058)
     Len Dawson, Kansas City, outstanding offensive player
     George Webster, Houston, outstanding defensive player

Jan. 19, 1969   NFL West 10, East 7 ....Los Angeles Memorial Coliseum (32,050)
     Roman Gabriel, Los Angeles, outstanding back
     Merlin Olsen, Los Angeles, outstanding lineman

Jan. 17, 1970   AFL West 26, East 3 ....Astrodome, Houston (30,170)
     John Hadl, San Diego, player of the game

Jan. 18, 1970   NFL West 16, East 13 ....Los Angeles Memorial Coliseum (57,786)
     Gale Sayers, Chicago, outstanding back
     George Andrie, Dallas, outstanding lineman

Jan. 24, 1971   NFC 27, AFC 6 ....Los Angeles Memorial Coliseum (48,222)
     Mel Renfro, Dallas, outstanding back
     Fred Carr, Green Bay, outstanding lineman

Jan. 23, 1972   AFC 26, NFC 13 ....Los Angeles Memorial Coliseum (53,647)
     Jan Stenerud, Kansas City, outstanding offensive player
     Willie Lanier, Kansas City, outstanding defensive player

Jan. 21, 1973   AFC 33, NFC 28 ....Texas Stadium, Irving (37,091)
     O.J. Simpson, Buffalo, player of the game

Jan. 20, 1974   AFC 15, NFC 13 ....Arrowhead Stadium, Kansas City (66,918)
     Garo Yepremian, Miami, player of the game

Jan. 20, 1975   NFC 17, AFC 10 ....Orange Bowl, Miami (26,484)
     James Harris, Los Angeles, player of the game

Jan. 26, 1976   NFC 23, AFC 20 ....Louisiana Superdome, New Orleans (30,546)
     Billy Johnson, Houston, player of the game

Jan. 17, 1977   AFC 24, NFC 14 ....Kingdome, Seattle (64,752)
     Mel Blount, Pittsburgh, player of the game

Jan. 23, 1978   NFC 14, AFC 13 ....Tampa Stadium (51,337)
     Walter Payton, Chicago, player of the game

Jan. 29, 1979   NFC 13, AFC 7 ....Los Angeles Memorial Coliseum (46,281)
     Ahmad Rashad, Minnesota, player of the game

Jan. 27, 1980   NFC 37, AFC 27 ....Aloha Stadium, Honolulu (49,800)
     Chuck Muncie, New Orleans, player of the game

Feb. 1, 1981   NFC 21, AFC 7 ....Aloha Stadium, Honolulu (50,360)
     Eddie Murray, Detroit, player of the game

Jan. 31, 1982   AFC 16, NFC 13 ....Aloha Stadium, Honolulu (50,402)
     Kellen Winslow, San Diego, and Lee Roy Selmon, Tampa Bay, players of the game

Feb. 6, 1983   NFC 20, AFC 19 ....Aloha Stadium, Honolulu (49,883)
     Dan Fouts, San Diego, and John Jefferson, Green Bay, players of the game

Jan. 29, 1984   NFC 45, AFC 3 ....Aloha Stadium, Honolulu (50,445)
     Joe Theismann, Washington, player of the game

Jan. 27, 1985   AFC 22, NFC 14 ....Aloha Stadium, Honolulu (50,385)
     Mark Gastineau, N.Y. Jets, player of the game

Feb. 2, 1986   NFC 28, AFC 24 ....Aloha Stadium, Honolulu (50,101)
     Phil Simms, N.Y. Giants, player of the game

Feb. 1, 1987   AFC 10, NFC 6 ....Aloha Stadium, Honolulu (50,101)
     Reggie White, Philadelphia, player of the game

Feb. 7, 1988   AFC 15, NFC 6 ....Aloha Stadium, Honolulu (50,113)
     Bruce Smith, Buffalo, player of the game

Jan. 29, 1989   NFC 34, AFC 3 ....Aloha Stadium, Honolulu (50,113)
     Randall Cunningham, Philadelphia, player of the game

Feb. 4, 1990   NFC 27, AFC 21 ....Aloha Stadium, Honolulu (50,445)
     Jerry Gray, L.A. Rams, player of the game

Feb. 3, 1991   AFC 23, NFC 21 ....Aloha Stadium, Honolulu (50,345)
     Jim Kelly, Buffalo, player of the game

Feb. 2, 1992   NFC 21, AFC 15 ....Aloha Stadium, Honolulu (50,209)
     Michael Irvin, Dallas, player of the game

Feb. 7, 1993   AFC 23, NFC 20 (OT) ....Aloha Stadium, Honolulu (50,007)
     Steve Tasker, Buffalo, player of the game

Feb. 6, 1994   NFC 17, AFC 3 ....Aloha Stadium, Honolulu (50,026)
     Andre Rison, Atlanta, player of the game

Feb. 5, 1995   AFC 41, NFC 13 ....Aloha Stadium, Honolulu (50,529)
     Marshall Faulk, Indianapolis, player of the game

PRO BOWL ALL-TIME RESULTS

Feb. 4, 1996   NFC 20, AFC 13...Aloha Stadium, Honolulu (50,034)
             Jerry Rice, San Francisco, player of the game

Feb. 2, 1997   AFC 26, NFC 23 (OT)..Aloha Stadium, Honolulu (50,031)
             Mark Brunell, Jacksonville, player of the game

Feb. 1, 1998   AFC 29, NFC 24...Aloha Stadium, Honolulu (49,995)
             Warren Moon, Seattle, player of the game

Feb. 7, 1999   AFC 23, NFC 10...Aloha Stadium, Honolulu (50,075)
             Keyshawn Johnson, N.Y. Jets and Ty Law, New England, co-players of the game

Feb. 6, 2000   NFC 51, AFC 31...Aloha Stadium, Honolulu (50,112)
             Randy Moss, Minnesota, player of the game

Feb. 4, 2001   AFC 38, NFC 17...Aloha Stadium, Honolulu (50,128)
             Rich Gannon, Oakland, player of the game

Feb. 9, 2002   AFC 38, NFC 30...Aloha Stadium, Honolulu (50,301)
             Rich Gannon, Oakland, player of the game

Feb. 2, 2003   AFC 45, NFC 20...Aloha Stadium, Honolulu (50,125)
             Ricky Williams, Miami, player of the game

Feb. 8, 2004   NFC 55, AFC 52...Aloha Stadium, Honolulu (50,127)
             Marc Bulger, St. Louis, player of the game

Feb. 13, 2005   AFC 38, NFC 27...Aloha Stadium, Honolulu (50,225)
             Peyton Manning, Indianapolis, player of the game

Feb. 12, 2006   NFC 23, AFC 17...Aloha Stadium, Honolulu (50,190)
             Derrick Brooks, Tampa Bay, player of the game

Feb. 10, 2007   AFC 31, NFC 28...Aloha Stadium, Honolulu (50,410)
             Carson Palmer, Cincinnati, player of the game

Feb. 10, 2008   NFC 42, AFC 30...Aloha Stadium, Honolulu (50,044)
             Adrian Peterson, Minnesota, most valuable player

SUNDAY NIGHT FOOTBALL, 1978-2007
(Home Team in capitals, games listed in chronological order.)

2007
DALLAS 45, New York Giants 35
NEW ENGLAND 38, San Diego 14
Dallas 34, CHICAGO 10
NEW YORK GIANTS 16, Philadelphia 3
Chicago 27, GREEN BAY 20
New Orleans 28, SEATTLE 17
DENVER 31, Pittsburgh 28
Dallas 38, PHILADELPHIA 17
SAN DIEGO 23, Indianapolis 21
New England 56, BUFFALO 10
NEW ENGLAND 31, Philadelphia 28
PITTSBURGH 24, Cincinnati 10
Indianapolis 44, BALTIMORE 20
Washington 22, NEW YORK GIANTS 10
Washington 32, MINNESOTA 21
Tennessee 16, INDIANAPOLIS 10

2006
Indianapolis 26, NEW YORK GIANTS 21
DALLAS 27, Washington 10
Denver 17, NEW ENGLAND 7
CHICAGO 37, Seattle 6
SAN DIEGO 23, Pittsburgh 13
DENVER 13, Oakland 3
Dallas 35, CAROLINA 14
Indianapolis 27, NEW ENGLAND 20
Chicago 38, NEW YORK GIANTS 20
San Diego 35, DENVER 27
INDIANAPOLIS 45, Philadelphia 21
Seattle 23, DENVER 20
New Orleans 42, DALLAS 17
SAN DIEGO 20, Kansas City 9
Green Bay 26, CHICAGO 7

2005
Indianapolis 24, BALTIMORE 7
Kansas City 23, OAKLAND 17
SAN DIEGO 45, New York Giants 23
ARIZONA 31, San Francisco 14
JACKSONVILLE 23, Cincinnati 20
SEATTLE 42, Houston 10
NEW ENGLAND 21, Buffalo 16
WASHINGTON 17, Philadelphia 10
PITTSBURGH 34, Cleveland 21
Kansas City 45, HOUSTON 17
New Orleans 21, NEW YORK JETS 19
SAN DIEGO 34, Oakland 10
GREEN BAY 16, Detroit 13
CHICAGO 16, Atlanta 3
BALTIMORE 30, Minnesota 23
St. Louis 20, DALLAS 10

2004
DENVER 34, Kansas City 24
CINCINNATI 16, Miami 13
OAKLAND 30, Tampa Bay 20
Pittsburgh 13, MIAMI 3
St. Louis 24, SAN FRANCISCO 14
Baltimore 17, WASHINGTON 10
Minnesota 38, NEW ORLEANS 31
CHICAGO 23, San Francisco 13
BALTIMORE 27, Cleveland 13
NEW ENGLAND 29, Buffalo 6
Green Bay 16, HOUSTON 13
Oakland 25, DENVER 24
Pittsburgh 17, JACKSONVILLE 16
Philadelphia 17, WASHINGTON 14
INDIANAPOLIS 20, Baltimore 10
MIAMI 10, Cleveland 7
NEW YORK GIANTS 28, Dallas 24

2003
TENNESSEE 25, Oakland 20
MINNESOTA 24, Chicago 13
MIAMI 17, Buffalo 7
Indianapolis 55, NEW ORLEANS 21
Cleveland 33, PITTSBURGH 13
SEATTLE 20, San Francisco 19
KANSAS CITY 38, Buffalo 5
Green Bay 30, MINNESOTA 27
ST. LOUIS 33, Baltimore 22
NEW ENGLAND 12, Dallas 0
MIAMI 24, Washington 23
JACKSONVILLE 17, Tampa Bay 10
ATLANTA 20, Carolina 14 (OT)
NEW ORLEANS 45, New York Giants 7
Denver 31, INDIANAPOLIS 17
BALTIMORE 13, Pittsburgh 10 (OT)

2002
HOUSTON 19, Dallas 10
Oakland 30, PITTSBURGH 17
ATLANTA 30, Cincinnati 3
SEATTLE 48, Minnesota 23
Baltimore 26, CLEVELAND 21
Miami 24, DENVER 22
WASHINGTON 26, Indianapolis 21
NEW YORK GIANTS 24, Jacksonville 17
NEW YORK JETS 13, Miami 10
OAKLAND 27, New England 20
Indianapolis 23, DENVER 20 (OT)
NEW ORLEANS 23, Tampa Bay 20
GREEN BAY 26, Minnesota 22
ST. LOUIS 30, Arizona 28
New York Jets 30, NEW ENGLAND 17
Tampa Bay 15, CHICAGO 0

2001
Miami 31, TENNESSEE 23
Denver 38, ARIZONA 17
PHILADELPHIA 40, Dallas 18
SAN FRANCISCO 24, Carolina 14
Oakland 23, INDIANAPOLIS 18
New York Jets 16, NEW ORLEANS 9
SEATTLE 34, Oakland 27
St. Louis 24, NEW ENGLAND 17
Chicago 13, MINNESOTA 6
SAN FRANCISCO 35, Buffalo 0
DENVER 20, Seattle 7
Pittsburgh 26, BALTIMORE 21
New York Jets 29, INDIANAPOLIS 28
Washington 40, NEW ORLEANS 10
Philadelphia 17, TAMPA BAY 13

2000
BUFFALO 16, Tennessee 13
ARIZONA 32, Dallas 31
MIAMI 19, Baltimore 6
Washington 16, NEW YORK GIANTS 6
PHILADELPHIA 38, Atlanta 10
Baltimore 15, JACKSONVILLE 10
Minnesota 28, CHICAGO 16
Oakland 15, SAN DIEGO 13
Carolina 27, ST. LOUIS 24
INDIANAPOLIS 23, New York Jets 15
Jacksonville 34, PITTSBURGH 24
New York Giants 31, ARIZONA 7
Green Bay 28, CHICAGO 6
OAKLAND 31, New York Jets 7
New York Giants 17, DALLAS 13

1999
Pittsburgh 43, CLEVELAND 0
BUFFALO 17, New York Jets 3
NEW ENGLAND 16, New York Giants 14
SEATTLE 22, Oakland 21
GREEN BAY 26, Tampa Bay 23
Washington 24, ARIZONA 10
DETROIT 20, Tampa Bay 3
MIAMI 17, Tennessee 0
SEATTLE 20, Denver 17
JACKSONVILLE 41, New Orleans 23
CAROLINA 34, Atlanta 28
NEW ENGLAND 13, Dallas 6
KANSAS CITY 31, Minnesota 28
Buffalo 31, ARIZONA 21
Washington 26, SAN FRANCISCO 20 (OT)

1998
KANSAS CITY 28, Oakland 8
NEW ENGLAND 29, Indianapolis 6
ARIZONA 17, Philadelphia 3
BALTIMORE 31, Cincinnati 24
KANSAS CITY 17, Seattle 6
Atlanta 34, NEW YORK GIANTS 20
Buffalo 30, CAROLINA 14
Oakland 31, SEATTLE 18
Tennessee 31, TAMPA BAY 22
DETROIT 26, Chicago 3
SAN FRANCISCO 31, New Orleans 20
Denver 31, SAN DIEGO 16
MINNESOTA 48, Chicago 22
New York Jets 21, MIAMI 16
MINNESOTA 50, Jacksonville 10
DALLAS 23, Washington 7

1997
Washington 24, CAROLINA 10
ARIZONA 25, Dallas 22 (OT)
NEW ENGLAND 27, New York Jets 24 (OT)
TAMPA BAY 31, Miami 21
MINNESOTA 28, Philadelphia 19
New Orleans 20, CHICAGO 17
PITTSBURGH 24, Indianapolis 22
CAROLINA 21, Atlanta 12
GREEN BAY 20, Detroit 10
PITTSBURGH 37, Baltimore 0
Oakland 38, SAN DIEGO 13
WASHINGTON 7, New York Giants 7 (OT)
Denver 38, SAN DIEGO 28
MIAMI 33, Detroit 30
Chicago 13, ST. LOUIS 10
SEATTLE 38, San Francisco 9

1996
Buffalo 23, NEW YORK GIANTS 20 (OT)
Miami 38, ARIZONA 10
DENVER 27, Tampa Bay 23
Philadelphia 33, ATLANTA 18
WASHINGTON 31, New York Jets 16
Houston 30, CINCINNATI 27 (OT)
INDIANAPOLIS 26, Baltimore 21
NEW ENGLAND 28, Buffalo 25
San Francisco 24, NEW ORLEANS 17
CAROLINA 27, New York Giants 17
Minnesota 16, OAKLAND 13 (OT)
Green Bay 24, ST. LOUIS 9
New England 45, SAN DIEGO 7
Minnesota 24, DETROIT 22
JACKSONVILLE 20, Seattle 13
SAN DIEGO 16, Denver 10

1995
DENVER 22, Buffalo 7
Philadelphia 31, ARIZONA 19
Dallas 23, MINNESOTA 17 (OT)
Green Bay 24, JACKSONVILLE 14
Oakland 47, NEW YORK JETS 10
Denver 37, NEW ENGLAND 3
New York Giants 24, WASHINGTON 15
Miami 24, SAN DIEGO 14
PHILADELPHIA 31, Denver 13
KANSAS CITY 20, Houston 13
NEW ORLEANS 34, Carolina 26
SAN FRANCISCO 27, Buffalo 17
TAMPA BAY 13, Green Bay 10 (OT)
SEATTLE 44, Oakland 10

1994
San Diego 17, DENVER 34
New York Giants 20, ARIZONA 17
Kansas City 30, ATLANTA 10
Chicago 19, NEW YORK JETS 7
Miami 23, CINCINNATI 7
PHILADELPHIA 21, Washington 17
ARIZONA 20, Pittsburgh 17 (OT)
KANSAS CITY 13, Los Angeles Raiders 3
DETROIT 14, Tampa Bay 9
SAN FRANCISCO 31, Los Angeles Rams 27
New England 12, INDIANAPOLIS 10
Buffalo 42, MIAMI 31
New Orleans 29, ATLANTA 20
Los Angeles Raiders 17, SEATTLE 16
MIAMI 27, Detroit 20

1993
NEW ORLEANS 33, Houston 21
Los Angeles Raiders 17, SEATTLE 13
Dallas 17, PHOENIX 10
NEW YORK JETS 45, New England 7
BUFFALO 17, New York Giants 14
GREEN BAY 30, Denver 27
MIAMI 41, Indianapolis 27
Detroit 30, MINNESOTA 27
WASHINGTON 30, Indianapolis 24
Chicago 16, SAN DIEGO 13
TAMPA BAY 23, Minnesota 10
HOUSTON 23, Pittsburgh 3
SAN FRANCISCO 21, Cincinnati 8
Green Bay 20, SAN DIEGO 13
Philadelphia 20, INDIANAPOLIS 10
MINNESOTA 30, Kansas City 10
HOUSTON 24, New York Jets 0

1992
DENVER 17, Los Angeles Raiders 13
Philadelphia 31, PHOENIX 14
BUFFALO 38, Indianapolis 0
San Francisco 16, NEW ORLEANS 10
NEW YORK JETS 30, New England 21
NEW ORLEANS 13, Los Angeles Rams 10
Pittsburgh 27, KANSAS CITY 3
New York Giants 24, WASHINGTON 7
Cincinnati 31, CHICAGO 28 (OT)
DENVER 27, New York Giants 13
Kansas City 24, SEATTLE 14
SAN DIEGO 27, Los Angeles Raiders 3
Los Angeles Rams 31, TAMPA BAY 27
Green Bay 16, HOUSTON 14
MIAMI 19, New York Jets 17
HOUSTON 27, Buffalo 3

1991
WASHINGTON 45, Detroit 0
Houston 30, CINCINNATI 7
NEW ORLEANS 24, Los Angeles Rams 7
Dallas 17, PHOENIX 9
Denver 13, MINNESOTA 6
Pittsburgh 21, INDIANAPOLIS 3
Los Angeles Raiders 23, SEATTLE 20
Washington 17, NEW YORK GIANTS 13
DENVER 20, Pittsburgh 13
MIAMI 30, New England 20
HOUSTON 28, Cleveland 24
Atlanta 23, NEW ORLEANS 20 (OT)
Los Angeles Raiders 9, SAN DIEGO 7
Minnesota 26, TAMPA BAY 24
Buffalo 35, INDIANAPOLIS 7
SEATTLE 23, Los Angeles Rams 9

1990
NEW YORK GIANTS 27, Philadelphia 20
PITTSBURGH 20, Houston 9
TAMPA BAY 23, Detroit 20
Washington 38, PHOENIX 10
BUFFALO 38, Los Angeles Raiders 24
CHICAGO 38, Los Angeles Rams 9
ATLANTA 38, Cincinnati 17
MINNESOTA 27, Denver 22
San Francisco 24, DALLAS 6
CINCINNATI 27, Pittsburgh 3
Seattle 13, SAN DIEGO 10
MINNESOTA 23, Green Bay 7
MIAMI 23, Philadelphia 20
DETROIT 38, Chicago 21
SEATTLE 17, Denver 12
HOUSTON 34, Pittsburgh 14

1989
Dallas 13, WASHINGTON 3
SAN DIEGO 14, Los Angeles Raiders 12
INDIANAPOLIS 27, New York Jets 10
Los Angeles Rams 20, NEW ORLEANS 17
MINNESOTA 27, Chicago 16
MIAMI 31, New England 10
SEATTLE 23, Los Angeles Raiders 17

1988
HOUSTON 41, Washington 17
Los Angeles Raiders 13, SAN DIEGO 3
Minnesota 43, DALLAS 3
New England 6, MIAMI 3
New York Giants 13, NEW ORLEANS 12
Pittsburgh 37, HOUSTON 34
SEATTLE 42, Denver 14
Los Angeles Rams 38, SAN FRANCISCO 16

1987
NEW YORK GIANTS 17, New England 10
SAN DIEGO 16, Los Angeles Raiders 14
Miami 20, DALLAS 14
SAN FRANCISCO 38, Cleveland 24
Chicago 30, MINNESOTA 24
SEATTLE 28, Denver 21
MIAMI 23, Washington 21
SAN FRANCISCO 48, Los Angeles Rams 0

1986
LOS ANGELES RAMS 29, Dallas 10

1985
Dallas 30, NEW YORK GIANTS 29
SAN DIEGO 54, Pittsburgh 44

1984
Denver 24, CLEVELAND 14
DALLAS 30, New Orleans 27

1983
Los Angeles Raiders 40, DALLAS 38

1982
ATLANTA 17, San Francisco 7

1981
DALLAS 29, Los Angeles 17

1980
DALLAS 42, San Diego 31

1979
DALLAS 30, Los Angeles 6

1978
New England 21, OAKLAND 14
LOS ANGELES 10, Pittsburgh 7
Denver 21, OAKLAND 6

THURSDAY-SATURDAY NIGHT FOOTBALL, 1974-2007

2007
INDIANAPOLIS 41, New Orleans 10 (Thurs.)
Green Bay 37, DETROIT 26 (Thurs.)
DALLAS 34, New York Jets 3 (Thurs.)
Indianapolis 31, ATLANTA 13 (Thurs.)
DALLAS 37, Green Bay 27 (Thurs.)
WASHINGTON 24, Chicago 16 (Thurs.)
HOUSTON 31, Denver 13 (Thurs.)
SAN FRANCISCO 20, Cincinnati 13 (Sat.)
Pittsburgh 41, ST. LOUIS 24 (Thurs.)
Dallas 20, CAROLINA 13 (Sat.)
New England 38, NEW YORK GIANTS 35 (Sat.)

2006
PITTSBURGH 28, Miami 17 (Thurs.)
KANSAS CITY 19, Denver 10 (Thurs.)
CINCINNATI 13, Baltimore 7 (Thurs.)
PITTSBURGH 27, Cleveland 7 (Thurs.)
San Francisco 24, SEATTLE 14 (Thurs.)
Dallas 38, ATLANTA 28 (Sat.)
GREEN BAY 9, Minnesota 7 (Thurs.)
Kansas City 20, OAKLAND 9 (Sat.)
New York Giants 34, WASHINGTON 28 (Sat.)

2005
NEW ENGLAND 30, Oakland 20 (Thurs.)
Kansas City 30, MIAMI 20 (Fri.)
Denver 28, BUFFALO 17 (Sat.)
New York Giants 30, OAKLAND 21 (Sat.)

2004
NEW ENGLAND 27, Indianapolis 24 (Thurs.)
ATLANTA 34, Carolina 31 (OT) (Sat.)
Denver 37, TENNESSEE 16 (Sat.)

2003
WASHINGTON 16, New York Jets 13 (Thurs.)
New England 21, NEW YORK JETS 16 (Sat.)
Philadelphia 31, WASHINGTON 7 (Sat.)

2002
San Francisco 16, NEW YORK GIANTS 13 (Thurs.)
Philadelphia 27, DALLAS 3 (Sat.)

2001
Buffalo 13, JACKSONVILLE 10 (Thurs.)
Indianapolis 35, KANSAS CITY 28 (Thurs.)
Tennessee 13, OAKLAND 10 (Sat.)
TAMPA BAY 22, Baltimore 10 (Sat.)

2000
Detroit 28, TAMPA BAY 14 (Thurs.)
MINNESOTA 24, Detroit 17 (Thurs.)
Buffalo 42, SEATTLE 23 (Sat.)

1999
Kansas City 35, BALTIMORE 8 (Thurs.)
JACKSONVILLE 20, Pittsburgh 6 (Thurs.)
TENNESSEE 21, Oakland 14 (Thurs.)

1998
DETROIT 27, Green Bay 20 (Thurs.)
PHILADELPHIA 17, St. Louis 14 (Thurs.)

1997
KANSAS CITY 31, San Diego 3 (Thurs.)
CINCINNATI 41, Tennessee 14 (Thurs.)

1996
KANSAS CITY 34, Seattle 16 (Thurs.)
INDIANAPOLIS 37, Philadelphia 10 (Thurs.)

1995
ST. LOUIS 21, Atlanta 19 (Thurs.)
Cincinnati 27, PITTSBURGH 9 (Thurs.)
New York Giants 10, ARIZONA 6 (Thurs.)
Indianapolis 10, New England 7 (Sat.)

1994
Cleveland 11, HOUSTON 8 (Thurs.)
MINNESOTA 13, Green Bay 10 (OT) (Thurs.)
MINNESOTA 33, Chicago 27 (OT) (Thurs.)

1993
ATLANTA 30, Los Angeles Rams 24 (Thurs.)

1992
MINNESOTA 31, Detroit 14 (Thurs.)
NEW ORLEANS 22, Atlanta 14 (Thurs.)

1991
Chicago 10, GREEN BAY 0 (Thurs.)

1990
MIAMI 17, New England 10 (Thurs.)
INDIANAPOLIS 35, Washington 28 (Sat.)

1989
Cleveland 24, HOUSTON 20 (Sat.)

1987-88
None

1986
New England 20, NEW YORK JETS 6 (Thurs.)
Cincinnati 30, CLEVELAND 13 (Thurs.)
Los Angeles Raiders 37, SAN DIEGO 31 (OT) (Thurs.)
SAN FRANCISCO 24, Los Angeles Rams 14 (Fri.)

1985
KANSAS CITY 36, Los Angeles Raiders 20 (Thurs.)
Chicago 33, MINNESOTA 24 (Thurs.)
Denver 27, SEATTLE 24 (Fri.)

1984
Pittsburgh 23, NEW YORK JETS 17 (Thurs.)
Washington 31, MINNESOTA 17 (Thurs.)
SAN FRANCISCO 19, Los Angeles Rams 16 (Fri.)

1983
San Francisco 48, MINNESOTA 17 (Thurs.)
CLEVELAND 17, Cincinnati 7 (Thurs.)
Los Angeles Raiders 42, SAN DIEGO 10 (Thurs.)
MIAMI 34, New York Jets 14 (Fri.)

1982
BUFFALO 23, Minnesota 22 (Thurs.)
SAN FRANCISCO 30, Los Angeles Rams 24 (Thurs.)

1981
MIAMI 30, Pittsburgh 10 (Thurs.)
Philadelphia 20, BUFFALO 14 (Thurs.)
HOUSTON 17, Cleveland 13 (Thurs.

1980
TAMPA BAY 10, Los Angeles 9 (Thurs.)
San Diego 27, MIAMI 24 (OT) (Thurs.)
HOUSTON 6, Pittsburgh 0 (Thurs.)

1979
Los Angeles 13, DENVER 9 (Thurs.)
OAKLAND 45, San Diego 22 (Thurs.)
MIAMI 39, New England 24 (Thurs.)

1978
Minnesota 21, DALLAS 10 (Thurs.)

1977
Minnesota 30, DETROIT 21 (Sat.)

1976
Los Angeles 20, DETROIT 17 (Sat.)

1975
LOS ANGELES 10, Pittsburgh 3 (Sat.)

1974
OAKLAND 27, Dallas 23 (Sat.)

Compiled by Elias Sports Bureau
*NFL record.

MONDAY NIGHT RECORDS

SCORING
TOUCHDOWNS
Most Touchdowns, Career
- 36 Jerry Rice, San Francisco, 1985-2000; Oakland, 2001-04; Seattle 2004
- 24 Emmitt Smith, Dallas, 1990-2002; Arizona 2003-04
- 19 Marcus Allen, L.A. Raiders, 1982-1992; Kansas City, 1993-97

Most Touchdowns, Game
- 4 Ron Johnson, N.Y. Giants at Philadelphia, Oct. 2, 1972
   Earl Campbell, Houston vs. Miami, Nov. 20, 1978
   Marcus Allen, L.A. Raiders vs. San Diego, Sept. 24, 1984
   Eric Dickerson, Indianapolis vs. Denver, Oct. 31, 1988
   Emmitt Smith, Dallas at N.Y. Giants, Sept. 4, 1995
   Marshall Faulk, St. Louis at Tampa Bay, Dec. 18, 2000

FIELD GOALS
Most Field Goals, Career
- 51 Gary Anderson, Pittsburgh, 1982-1994; Philadelphia, 1995-96; San Francisco, 1997; Minnesota, 1998-2002; Tennessee, 2003-04
- 48 Jason Elam, Denver, 1993-2007
- 36 Morten Andersen, New Orleans 1982-1994; Atlanta, 1995-2000; N.Y. Giants, 2001; Kansas City, 2002-03; Minnesota, 2004; Atlanta, 2006-07
   Ryan Longwell, Green Bay, 1997-2005; Minnesota, 2006-07

Most Field Goals, Game
- 7 Chris Boniol, Dallas vs. Green Bay, Nov. 18, 1996*
   Billy Cundiff, Dallas at N.Y. Giants, Sept. 15, 2003 (OT)*
- 5 Tim Mazzetti, Atlanta vs. Los Angeles, Oct. 30, 1978
   Roger Ruzek, Dallas at L.A. Rams, Dec. 21, 1987
   Rich Karlis, Minnesota vs. Cincinnati, Dec. 25, 1989
   Nick Lowery, Kansas City vs. Denver, Sept. 20, 1993
   Chris Jacke, Green Bay vs. San Francisco, Oct. 14, 1996 (OT)
   Richie Cunningham, Dallas vs. Philadelphia, Sept. 15, 1997

RUSHING
YARDS GAINED
Most Yards Gained, Career
- 2,434 Emmitt Smith, Dallas, 1990-2002; Arizona, 2003-04
- 1,897 Tony Dorsett, Dallas, 1977-1987; Denver, 1988
- 1,769 Thurman Thomas, Buffalo, 1988-1999; Miami, 2000

Most Yards Gained, Game
- 221 Bo Jackson, L.A. Raiders at Seattle, Nov. 30, 1987
- 216 Ricky Williams, Miami vs. Chicago, Dec. 9, 2002
- 214 Thurman Thomas, Buffalo at N.Y. Jets, Sept. 24, 1990

Longest Run From Scrimage, Game
- 99 Tony Dorsett, Dallas at Minnesota, Jan. 3, 1983 (TD)*
- 91 Bo Jackson, L.A. Raiders at Seattle, Nov. 30, 1987 (TD)
- 83 James Lofton, Green Bay at N.Y. Giants, Sept. 20, 1982 (TD)

TOUCHDOWNS
Most Rushing Touchdowns, Career
- 23 Emmitt Smith, Dallas, 1990-2002; Arizona, 2003-04
- 17 Marcus Allen, L.A. Raiders, 1982-1992; Kansas City, 1993-97

- 14 Eric Dickerson, L.A. Rams, 1983-87; Indianapolis, 1987-1991; L.A. Raiders, 1992; Atlanta, 1993

Most Rushing Touchdowns, Game
- 4 Earl Campbell, Houston vs. Miami, Nov. 20, 1978
   Eric Dickerson, Indianapolis vs. Denver, Oct. 31, 1988
   Emmitt Smith, Dallas at N.Y. Giants, Sept. 4, 1995

PASSING
YARDS GAINED
Most Yards Gained, Career
- 9,654 Dan Marino, Miami, 1983-1999
- 7,878 Brett Favre, Atlanta, 1991; Green Bay, 1992-2007
- 5,148 Joe Montana, San Francisco, 1979-1992; Kansas City, 1993-94

Most Yards Gained, Game
- 458 Joe Montana, San Francisco at L.A. Rams, Dec. 11, 1989
- 448 Marc Bulger, St. Louis at Green Bay, Nov. 29, 2004
- 447 Ken Anderson, Cincinnati vs. Buffalo, Nov. 17, 1975

Longest Pass Play
- 99 Brett Favre to Robert Brooks, Green Bay at Chicago, Sept. 11, 1995 (TD)*
- 97 Bernie Kosar to Webster Slaughter, Cleveland vs. Chicago, Oct. 23, 1989 (TD)
- 95 Joe Montana to John Taylor, San Francisco at L.A. Rams, Dec. 11, 1989 (TD)

TOUCHDOWNS
Most Touchdown Passes, Career
- 74 Dan Marino, Miami, 1983-1999
- 57 Brett Favre, Atlanta, 1991; Green Bay, 1992-2007
- 42 Steve Young, Tampa Bay, 1985-86; San Francisco, 1987-1999

Most Touchdown Passes, Game
- 5 Dave Krieg, Seattle vs. L.A. Raiders, Nov. 28, 1988
   Jim Kelly, Buffalo vs. Cincinnati, Oct. 21, 1991
   Vinny Testaverde, N.Y. Jets vs. Miami, Oct. 23, 2000 (OT)
   Ben Roethlisberger, Pittsburgh vs. Baltimore, Nov. 5, 2007

RECEIVING
PASS RECEPTIONS
Most Pass Receptions, Career
- 254 Jerry Rice, San Francisco, 1985-2000; Oakland, 2001-04; Seattle, 2004
- 124 Andre Reed, Buffalo, 1985-1999; Washington, 2000
- 123 Cris Carter, Philadelphia, 1987-89; Minnesota, 1990-2001; Miami, 2002

Most Pass Receptions, Game
- 14 Herman Moore, Detroit vs. Chicago, Dec. 4, 1995
   Jerry Rice, San Francisco vs. Minnesota, Dec. 18, 1995
- 13 Andre Reed, Buffalo vs. Denver, Sept. 18, 1989
   Terrell Owens, San Francisco vs. Philadelphia, Nov. 25, 2002

YARDS GAINED
Most Yards Gained, Career
- 4,029 Jerry Rice, San Francisco, 1985-2000; Oakland, 2001-04; Seattle, 2004
- 1,783 Andre Reed, Buffalo, 1985-1999; Washington, 2000
- 1,537 Art Monk, Washington, 1980-1993; N.Y. Jets, 1994; Philadelphia, 1995

Most Yards Gained, Game
- 289 Jerry Rice, San Francisco vs. Minnesota, Dec. 18, 1995
- 286 John Taylor, San Francisco at L.A. Rams, Dec. 11, 1989
- 260 Wes Chandler, San Diego vs. Cincinnati, Dec. 20, 1982

TOUCHDOWN

Most Receiving Touchdowns, Career
- 34 Jerry Rice, San Francisco, 1985-2000; Oakland, 2001-04; Seattle, 2004
- 16 Terrell Owens, San Francisco, 1996-2003; Philadelphia, 2004-05; Dallas, 2006-07
- 15 Mark Clayton, Miami, 1983-1992; Green Bay, 1993

Most Receiving Touchdowns, Game
- 3 Ron Johnson, N.Y. Giants at Philadelphia, Oct. 2, 1972
  Wesley Walker, N.Y. Jets at Detroit, Dec. 6, 1982
  Steve Largent, Seattle at San Diego, Oct. 29, 1984
  Mark Clayton, Miami vs. Dallas, Dec. 17, 1984
  Jerry Rice, San Francisco vs. Chicago, Dec. 14, 1987
  Jerry Rice, San Francisco vs. Minnesota, Dec. 18, 1995
  Lamar Thomas, Miami vs. Denver, Dec. 21, 1998
  Ed McCaffrey, Denver vs. Miami, Sept. 13, 1999
  Randy Moss, Minnesota vs. N.Y. Giants, Nov. 19, 2001
  Isaac Bruce, St. Louis at New Orleans, Dec. 17, 2001
  Terrell Owens, Philadelphia at Dallas, Nov. 15, 2004
  Drew Bennett, Tennessee vs. Kansas City, Dec. 13, 2004
  Marvin Harrison, Indianapolis vs. Cincinnati, Dec. 18, 2006

YARDS FROM SCRIMMAGE

Most Scrimmage Yards, Career
- 4,116 Jerry Rice, San Francisco, 1985-2000; Oakland, 2001-04; Seattle, 2004
- 2,836 Emmitt Smith, Dallas, 1990-2002; Arizona, 2003-04
- 2,567 Tony Dorsett, Dallas, 1977-1987; Denver, 1988

INTERCEPTIONS BY

Most Interceptions, Career
- 11 Everson Walls, Dallas, 1981-89; N.Y. Giants, 1990-92; Cleveland, 1992-93
- 9 Merton Hanks, San Francisco, 1991-98; Seattle, 1999
- 8 Emmitt Thomas, Kansas City, 1966-1978

Most Interceptions, Game
- 4 Dick Anderson, Miami vs. Pittsburgh, Dec. 3, 1973*
- 3 Johnny Robinson, Kansas City at Baltimore, Sept. 28, 1970
  Charlie Babb, Miami vs. Oakland, Sept. 22, 1975
  Charles Phillips, Oakland vs. Denver, Dec. 8, 1975
  Mark Murphy, Washington at San Diego, Oct. 31, 1983
  Ken Easley, Seattle at San Diego, Oct. 29, 1984
  Dwayne Harper, San Diego vs. Oakland, Nov. 27, 1995
  Marcus Coleman, N.Y. Jets vs. Miami, Oct. 23, 2000 (OT)
  Keith Bulluck, Tennessee vs. New Orleans, Sept. 24, 2007

Longest Interception Return
- 102 Eddie Anderson, L.A. Raiders at Miami, Dec. 14, 1992 (TD)
- 101 Lito Sheppard, Philadelphia at Dallas, Nov. 15, 2004 (TD)
- 98 Marcus Coleman, N.Y. Jets vs. Miami, Dec. 27, 1999 (TD)
  Rod Woodson, Oakland at Denver, Nov. 11, 2002 (TD)

SACKS

Most Sacks, Career
- 24.5 Bruce Smith, Buffalo, 1985-1999; Washington, 2000-03
- 20.0 Richard Dent, Chicago, 1983-1993, 1995; San Francisco, 1994; Indianapolis, 1996; Philadelphia, 1997
- 18.0 Kevin Greene, L.A. Rams, 1985-1992; Pittsburgh, 1993-95; Carolina, 1996, 1998-99; San Francisco, 1997

PUNTING

Highest Punt Average, Career (Minimum: 25 Punts)
- 46.7 Shane Lechler, Oakland, 2000-07
- 45.1 Hunter Smith, Indianapolis, 1999-2007
- 44.5 Tom Tupa, Phoenix, 1988-1991; Indianapolis, 1992; Cleveland, 1994-95; New England, 1996-98; N.Y. Jets, 1999-2001; Tampa Bay, 2002-03; Washington, 2004

Longest Punt
- 90 Rodney Williams, N.Y. Giants at Denver, Sept. 10, 2001
- 83 Bryan Barker, Jacksonville vs. N.Y. Jets, Oct. 11, 1999
- 74 Craig Colquitt, Pittsburgh vs. Oakland, Dec. 7, 1981

PUNT RETURNS

Longest Punt Return
- 95 John Taylor, San Francisco vs. Washington, Nov. 21, 1988 (TD)
- 94 Dennis McKinnon, Chicago vs. N.Y. Giants, Sept. 14, 1987 (TD)
- 91 JoJo Townsell, N.Y. Jets vs. Seattle, Nov. 9, 1987 (TD)
  Nate Burleson, Minnesota at Indianapolis, Nov. 8, 2004 (TD)

KICKOFF RETURNS

Longest Kickoff Return
- 105 Terry Fair, Detroit vs. Tampa Bay, Sept. 28, 1998 (TD)
- 103 Terrence McGee, Buffalo vs. Dallas, Oct. 8, 2007 (TD)
- 102 Harold Hart, Oakland at Miami, Sept. 22, 1975 (TD)

FUMBLES

Longest Fumble Return
- 99 Don Griffin, San Francisco vs. Chicago, Dec. 23, 1991 (TD)
- 96 Joe Lavender, Philadelphia vs. Dallas, Sept. 23, 1974 (TD)
- 93 Adam Archuleta, St. Louis vs. Tampa Bay, Oct. 18, 2004 (TD)

MONDAY NIGHT FOOTBALL, 1970-2007

(Home Team in capitals, games listed in chronological order.)

2007
CINCINNATI 27, Baltimore 20
SAN FRANCISCO 20, Arizona 17
Washington 20, PHILADELPHIA 12
Tennessee 31, NEW ORLEANS 14
New England 34, CINCINNATI 13
Dallas 25, BUFFALO 24
New York Giants 31, ATLANTA 10
Indianapolis 29, JACKSONVILLE 7
Green Bay 19, DENVER 13 (OT)
PITTSBURGH 38, Baltimore 7
SEATTLE 24, San Francisco 0
DENVER 34, Tennessee 20
PITTSBURGH 3, Miami 0
New England 27, BALTIMORE 24
New Orleans 34, ATLANTA 14
MINNESOTA 13, Chicago 13
SAN DIEGO 23, Denver 3

2006
Minnesota 19, WASHINGTON 16
San Diego 27, OAKLAND 0
JACKSONVILLE 9, Pittsburgh 0
NEW ORLEANS 23, Atlanta 3
PHILADELPHIA 31, Green Bay 9
DENVER 13, Baltimore 3
Chicago 24, ARIZONA 23
New York Giants 36, DALLAS 22
New England 31, MINNESOTA 7
SEATTLE 16, Oakland 0
CAROLINA 24, Tampa Bay 10
JACKSONVILLE 26, New York Giants 10
SEATTLE 34, Green Bay 24
PHILADELPHIA 27, Carolina 24
Chicago 42, ST. LOUIS 27
INDIANAPOLIS 34, Cincinnati 16
New York Jets 13, MIAMI 10

2005
ATLANTA 14, Philadelphia 10
New York Giants 27, NEW ORLEANS 10
Washington 14, DALLAS 13
DENVER 30, Kansas City 10
CAROLINA 32, Green Bay 29
Pittsburgh 24, SAN DIEGO 22
INDIANAPOLIS 45, St. Louis 28
ATLANTA 27, New York Jets 14
PITTSBURGH 20, Baltimore 19
Indianapolis 40, NEW ENGLAND 21
Dallas 21, PHILADELPHIA 20
Minnesota 20, GREEN BAY 17
INDIANAPOLIS 26, Pittsburgh 7
Seattle 42, PHILADELPHIA 0
ATLANTA 36, New Orleans 17
BALTIMORE 48, Green Bay 3
New England 31, NEW YORK JETS 21

2004
Green Bay 24, CAROLINA 14
PHILADELPHIA 27, Minnesota 16
Dallas 21, WASHINGTON 18
Kansas City 27, BALTIMORE 24
Tennessee 48, GREEN BAY 27
ST. LOUIS 28, Tampa Bay 21
CINCINNATI 23, Denver 10
NEW YORK JETS 41, Miami 14
INDIANAPOLIS 31, Minnesota 28
Philadelphia 49, DALLAS 21
New England 27, KANSAS CITY 19
GREEN BAY 45, St. Louis 17
Dallas 43, SEATTLE 39
Kansas City 49, TENNESSEE 38
MIAMI 29, New England 28
ST. LOUIS 20, Philadelphia 7

2003
Tampa Bay 17, Philadelphia 0
Dallas 35, NEW YORK GIANTS 32 (OT)
DENVER 31, Oakland 10
Green Bay 38, CHICAGO 23
Indianapolis 38, TAMPA BAY 35 (OT)
ST. LOUIS 36, Atlanta 0
Kansas City 17, OAKLAND 10
Miami 26, SAN DIEGO 10
New England 30, DENVER 26
Philadelphia 17, GREEN BAY 14
SAN FRANCISCO 30, Pittsburgh 14
TAMPA BAY 19, New York Giants 13
NEW YORK JETS 24, Tennessee 17
St. Louis 26, CLEVELAND 20
Philadelphia 34, MIAMI 27
Green Bay 41, OAKLAND 7

2002
NEW ENGLAND 30, Pittsburgh 14
Philadelphia 37, WASHINGTON 7
TAMPA BAY 26, St. Louis 14
BALTIMORE 34, Denver 23
Green Bay 34, CHICAGO 21
San Francisco 28, SEATTLE 21
PITTSBURGH 28, Indianapolis 10
PHILADELPHIA 17, New York Giants 3
GREEN BAY 24, Miami 10
Oakland 34, DENVER 10
ST. LOUIS 21, Chicago 16
Philadelphia 38, SAN FRANCISCO 17
OAKLAND 26, New York Jets 20
MIAMI 27, Chicago 9
TENNESSEE 24, New England 7
Pittsburgh 17, TAMPA BAY 7
ST. LOUIS 31, San Francisco 20

2001
DENVER 31, New York Giants 20
GREEN BAY 37, Washington 0
San Francisco 19, NEW YORK JETS 17
St. Louis 35, DETROIT 0
DALLAS 9, Washington 7
Philadelphia 10, NEW YORK GIANTS 9
PITTSBURGH 34, Tennessee 7
OAKLAND 38, Denver 28
Baltimore 16, TENNESSEE 10
MINNESOTA 28, New York Giants 16
Tampa Bay 24, ST. LOUIS 17
Green Bay 28, JACKSONVILLE 21
MIAMI 41, Indianapolis 6
St. Louis 34, NEW ORLEANS 21
BALTIMORE 19, Minnesota 3

2000
ST. LOUIS 41, Denver 36
NEW YORK JETS 20, New England 19
Dallas 27, WASHINGTON 21
INDIANAPOLIS 43, Jacksonville 14
KANSAS CITY 24, Seattle 17
MINNESOTA 30, Tampa Bay 23
TENNESSEE 27, Jacksonville 13
NEW YORK JETS 40, Miami 37 (OT)
Tennessee 27, WASHINGTON 21
GREEN BAY 26, Minnesota 20 (OT)
DENVER 27, Oakland 24
Washington 33, ST. LOUIS 20
CAROLINA 31, Green Bay 14
NEW ENGLAND 30, Kansas City 24
INDIANAPOLIS 44, Buffalo 20
TAMPA BAY 38, St. Louis 35
TENNESSEE 31, Dallas 0

1999
Miami 38, DENVER 21
DALLAS 24, Atlanta 7
San Francisco 24, ARIZONA 10
Buffalo 23, MIAMI 18
Jacksonville 16, NEW YORK JETS 6
NEW YORK GIANTS 13, Dallas 10
PITTSBURGH 13, Atlanta 9
Seattle 27, GREEN BAY 7
MINNESOTA 27, Dallas 17
New York Jets 24, NEW ENGLAND 17
DENVER 27, Oakland 21 (OT)
Green Bay 20, SAN FRANCISCO 3
TAMPA BAY 24, Minnesota 17
JACKSONVILLE 27, Denver 24
MINNESOTA 24, Green Bay 20
New York Jets 38, MIAMI 31
ATLANTA 34, San Francisco 29

1998
DENVER 27, New England 21
San Francisco 45, WASHINGTON 10
Dallas 31, NEW YORK GIANTS 7
DETROIT 27, Tampa Bay 6
Minnesota 37, GREEN BAY 24
JACKSONVILLE 28, Miami 21
New York Jets 24, NEW ENGLAND 14
Pittsburgh 20, KANSAS CITY 13
Dallas 34, PHILADELPHIA 0
PITTSBURGH 27, Green Bay 20
Denver 30, KANSAS CITY 7
NEW ENGLAND 26, Miami 23
SAN FRANCISCO 31, New York Giants 7
TAMPA BAY 24, Green Bay 22
SAN FRANCISCO 35, Detroit 13
MIAMI 31, Denver 21
JACKSONVILLE 21, Pittsburgh 3

1997
GREEN BAY 38, Chicago 24
Kansas City 28, OAKLAND 27
DALLAS 21, Philadelphia 20
JACKSONVILLE 30, Pittsburgh 21
San Francisco 34, CAROLINA 21
DENVER 34, New England 13
WASHINGTON 21, Dallas 16
Buffalo 9, INDIANAPOLIS 6
Green Bay 28, NEW ENGLAND 10
Chicago 36, MIAMI 33 (OT)
KANSAS CITY 13, Pittsburgh 10
San Francisco 24, PHILADELPHIA 12
MIAMI 30, Buffalo 13
DENVER 31, Oakland 3
Green Bay 27, MINNESOTA 11
Carolina 23, DALLAS 13
SAN FRANCISCO 34, Denver 17
New England 14, MIAMI 12

1996
CHICAGO 22, Dallas 6
GREEN BAY 39, Philadelphia 13
PITTSBURGH 24, Buffalo 6
INDIANAPOLIS 10, Miami 6
Dallas 23, PHILADELPHIA 19
Pittsburgh 17, KANSAS CITY 7
GREEN BAY 23, San Francisco 20 (OT)
Oakland 13, SAN DIEGO 14
Chicago 15, MINNESOTA 13
Denver 22, OAKLAND 21
SAN DIEGO 27, Detroit 21
DALLAS 21, Green Bay 6
Pittsburgh 24, MIAMI 17
San Francisco 34, ATLANTA 10
OAKLAND 26, Kansas City 7
MIAMI 16, Buffalo 14
SAN FRANCISCO 24, Detroit 14

1995
Dallas 35, NEW YORK GIANTS 0
Green Bay 27, CHICAGO 24
MIAMI 23, Pittsburgh 10
DETROIT 27, San Francisco 24
Buffalo 22, CLEVELAND 19
KANSAS CITY 29, San Diego 23 (OT)
DENVER 27, Oakland 0
NEW ENGLAND 27, Buffalo 14
Chicago 14, MINNESOTA 6
DALLAS 34, Philadelphia 12
PITTSBURGH 20, Cleveland 3
San Francisco 44, MIAMI 20
SAN DIEGO 12, Oakland 6
DETROIT 27, Chicago 7
MIAMI 13, Kansas City 6
SAN FRANCISCO 37, Minnesota 30
Dallas 37, ARIZONA 13

1994
SAN FRANCISCO 44, L.A. Raiders 14
PHILADELPHIA 30, Chicago 22
Detroit 20, DALLAS 17 (OT)
BUFFALO 27, Denver 20
PITTSBURGH 30, Houston 14
Minnesota 27, NEW YORK GIANTS 10
Kansas City 31, DENVER 28
PHILADELPHIA 21, Houston 6
Green Bay 33, CHICAGO 6
DALLAS 38, New York Giants 10
PITTSBURGH 23, Buffalo 10
New York Giants 13, HOUSTON 10
San Francisco 35, NEW ORLEANS 14
L.A. Raiders 24, SAN DIEGO 17
MIAMI 45, Kansas City 28
Dallas 24, NEW ORLEANS 16
MINNESOTA 21, San Francisco 14

1993
WASHINGTON 35, Dallas 16
CLEVELAND 23, San Francisco 13
KANSAS CITY 15, Denver 7
Pittsburgh 45, ATLANTA 17
MIAMI 17, Washington 10
BUFFALO 35, Houston 7
L.A. Raiders 23, DENVER 20
Minnesota 19, CHICAGO 12
BUFFALO 24, Washington 10
KANSAS CITY 23, Green Bay 16
PITTSBURGH 23, Buffalo 0
SAN FRANCISCO 42, New Orleans 7
San Diego 31, INDIANAPOLIS 0
DALLAS 23, Philadelphia 17
Pittsburgh 21, MIAMI 20
New York Giants 24, NEW ORLEANS 14
SAN DIEGO 45, Miami 20
Philadelphia 37, SAN FRANCISCO 34 (OT)

1992
DALLAS 23, Washington 10
Miami 27, CLEVELAND 23
New York Giants 27, CHICAGO 14
KANSAS CITY 27, L.A. Raiders 7
PHILADELPHIA 31, Dallas 7
WASHINGTON 34, Denver 3
PITTSBURGH 20, Cincinnati 0
Buffalo 24, NEW YORK JETS 20
Minnesota 38, CHICAGO 10
San Francisco 41, ATLANTA 3
Buffalo 26, MIAMI 20
NEW ORLEANS 20, Washington 3
SEATTLE 16, Denver 13 (OT)
HOUSTON 24, Chicago 7
MIAMI 20, L.A. Raiders 7
Dallas 41, ATLANTA 17
SAN FRANCISCO 24, Detroit 6

1991
NEW YORK GIANTS 16, San Francisco 14
Washington 33, DALLAS 31
HOUSTON 17, Kansas City 7
CHICAGO 19, New York Jets 13 (OT)
WASHINGTON 23, Philadelphia 0
KANSAS CITY 33, Buffalo 6
New York Giants 23, PITTSBURGH 20
BUFFALO 35, Cincinnati 16
KANSAS CITY 24, L.A. Raiders 21
PHILADELPHIA 30, New York Giants 7
Chicago 34, MINNESOTA 17
Buffalo 41, MIAMI 27
San Francisco 33, L.A. RAMS 10
Philadelphia 13, HOUSTON 6
MIAMI 37, Cincinnati 13
NEW ORLEANS 27, L.A. Raiders 0
SAN FRANCISCO 52, Chicago 14

1990
San Francisco 13, NEW ORLEANS 12
DENVER 24, Kansas City 23
Buffalo 30, NEW YORK JETS 7
SEATTLE 31, Cincinnati 16
Cleveland 30, DENVER 29
PHILADELPHIA 32, Minnesota 24
Cincinnati 34, CLEVELAND 13
PITTSBURGH 41, L.A. Rams 10
New York Giants 24, INDIANAPOLIS 7
PHILADELPHIA 28, Washington 14
L.A. Raiders 13, MIAMI 10
HOUSTON 27, Buffalo 24
SAN FRANCISCO 7, New York Giants 3
L.A. Raiders 38, DETROIT 31
San Francisco 26, L.A. RAMS 10
NEW ORLEANS 20, L.A. Rams 17

1989
New York Giants 27, WASHINGTON 24
Denver 28, BUFFALO 14
CINCINNATI 21, Cleveland 14
CHICAGO 27, Philadelphia 13
L.A. Raiders 14, NEW YORK JETS 7
BUFFALO 23, L.A. Rams 20
CLEVELAND 27, Chicago 7
NEW YORK GIANTS 24, Minnesota 14
SAN FRANCISCO 31, New Orleans 13
HOUSTON 26, Cincinnati 24
Denver 14, WASHINGTON 10
SAN FRANCISCO 34, New York Giants 24
SEATTLE 17, Buffalo 16
San Francisco 30, L.A. RAMS 27
NEW ORLEANS 30, Philadelphia 20
MINNESOTA 29, Cincinnati 21

1988
NEW YORK GIANTS 27, Washington 20
Dallas 17, PHOENIX 14
CLEVELAND 23, Indianapolis 17
L.A. Raiders 30, DENVER 27 (OT)
NEW ORLEANS 20, Dallas 17
PHILADELPHIA 24, New York Giants 13
Buffalo 37, NEW YORK JETS 14
CHICAGO 10, San Francisco 9
INDIANAPOLIS 55, Denver 23
HOUSTON 24, Cleveland 17
Buffalo 31, MIAMI 6
SAN FRANCISCO 37, Washington 21
SEATTLE 35, L.A. Raiders 27
L.A. RAMS 23, Chicago 3
MIAMI 38, Cleveland 31
MINNESOTA 28, Chicago 27

1987
CHICAGO 34, New York Giants 19
NEW YORK JETS 43, New England 24
San Francisco 41, NEW YORK GIANTS 21
DENVER 30, L.A. Raiders 14
Washington 13, DALLAS 7
CLEVELAND 30, L.A. Rams 17
MINNESOTA 34, Denver 27
DALLAS 33, New York Giants 24
NEW YORK JETS 30, Seattle 14
DENVER 31, Chicago 29
L.A. Rams 30, WASHINGTON 26
L.A. Raiders 37, SEATTLE 14
MIAMI 37, New York Jets 28
SAN FRANCISCO 41, Chicago 0
Dallas 29, L.A. RAMS 21
New England 24, MIAMI 10

1986
DALLAS 31, New York Giants 28
Denver 21, PITTSBURGH 10
Chicago 25, GREEN BAY 12
Dallas 31, ST. LOUIS 7
SEATTLE 33, San Diego 7
CINCINNATI 24, Pittsburgh 22
NEW YORK JETS 22, Denver 10
NEW YORK GIANTS 27, Washington 20
L.A. Rams 20, CHICAGO 17
CLEVELAND 26, Miami 16
WASHINGTON 14, San Francisco 6
MIAMI 45, New York Jets 3
New York Giants 21, SAN FRANCISCO 17
SEATTLE 37, L.A. Raiders 0
Chicago 16, DETROIT 13
New England 34, MIAMI 27

1985
DALLAS 44, Washington 14
CLEVELAND 17, Pittsburgh 7
L.A. Rams 35, SEATTLE 24
Cincinnati 37, PITTSBURGH 24
WASHINGTON 27, St. Louis 10
NEW YORK JETS 23, Miami 7
CHICAGO 23, Green Bay 7
L.A. RAIDERS 34, San Diego 21
ST. LOUIS 21, Dallas 10
DENVER 17, San Francisco 16
WASHINGTON 23, New York Giants 21
SAN FRANCISCO 19, Seattle 6
MIAMI 38, Chicago 24
L.A. Rams 27, SAN FRANCISCO 20
MIAMI 30, New England 27
L.A. Raiders 16, L.A. RAMS 6

1984
Dallas 20, L.A. RAMS 13
SAN FRANCISCO 37, Washington 31
Miami 21, BUFFALO 17
L.A. RAIDERS 33, San Diego 30
PITTSBURGH 38, Cincinnati 17
San Francisco 31, NEW YORK GIANTS 10
DENVER 17, Green Bay 14
L.A. Rams 24, ATLANTA 10
Seattle 24, SAN DIEGO 0
WASHINGTON 27, Atlanta 14
SEATTLE 17, L.A. Raiders 14
NEW ORLEANS 27, Pittsburgh 24
MIAMI 28, New York Jets 17
SAN DIEGO 20, Chicago 7
L.A. Raiders 24, DETROIT 3
MIAMI 28, Dallas 21

1983
Dallas 31, WASHINGTON 30
San Diego 17, KANSAS CITY 14
L.A. RAIDERS 27, Miami 14
NEW YORK GIANTS 27, Green Bay 3
New York Jets 34, BUFFALO 10
Pittsburgh 24, CINCINNATI 14
GREEN BAY 48, Washington 47
ST. LOUIS 20, NEW YORK Giants 20 (OT)
Washington 27, SAN DIEGO 24
DETROIT 15, New York Giants 9
L.A. Rams 36, ATLANTA 13
New York Jets 31, NEW ORLEANS 28
MIAMI 38, Cincinnati 14
DETROIT 13, Minnesota 2
Green Bay 12, TAMPA BAY 9 (OT)
SAN FRANCISCO 42, Dallas 17

1982
Pittsburgh 36, DALLAS 28
Green Bay 27, NEW YORK GIANTS 19
L.A. RAIDERS 28, San Diego 24
TAMPA BAY 23, Miami 17
New York Jets 28, DETROIT 13
Dallas 37, HOUSTON 7
SAN DIEGO 50, Cincinnati 34
MIAMI 27, Buffalo 10
MINNESOTA 31, Dallas 27

1981
San Diego 44, CLEVELAND 14
Oakland 36, MINNESOTA 10
Dallas 35, NEW ENGLAND 21
Los Angeles 24, CHICAGO 7
BUFFALO 31, Miami 21
DETROIT 48, Chicago 17
PITTSBURGH 26, Houston 13
DENVER 19, Minnesota 17
DALLAS 29, Buffalo 14
SEATTLE 44, San Diego 23
ATLANTA 31, Minnesota 30
MIAMI 13, Philadelphia 10
OAKLAND 30, Pittsburgh 27
LOS ANGELES 21, Atlanta 16
SAN DIEGO 23, Oakland 10

1980
Dallas 17, WASHINGTON 3
Houston 16, CLEVELAND 7
PHILADELPHIA 35, New York Giants 3
NEW ENGLAND 23, Denver 14
CHICAGO 23, Tampa Bay 0
DENVER 20, Washington 17
Oakland 45, PITTSBURGH 34
NEW YORK JETS 17, Miami 14
CLEVELAND 27, Chicago 21
HOUSTON 38, New England 34
Oakland 19, SEATTLE 17
Los Angeles 27, NEW ORLEANS 7
OAKLAND 9, Denver 3
MIAMI 16, New England 13 (OT)
LOS ANGELES 38, Dallas 14
SAN DIEGO 26, Pittsburgh 17

1979
Pittsburgh 16, NEW ENGLAND 13 (OT)
Atlanta 14, PHILADELPHIA 10
WASHINGTON 27, New York Giants 0
CLEVELAND 26, Dallas 7
GREEN BAY 27, New England 14
OAKLAND 13, Miami 3
NEW YORK JETS 14, Minnesota 7
PITTSBURGH 42, Denver 7
Seattle 31, ATLANTA 28
Houston 9, MIAMI 6
Philadelphia 31, DALLAS 21
LOS ANGELES 20, Atlanta 14
SEATTLE 30, New York Jets 7
Oakland 42, NEW ORLEANS 35
HOUSTON 20, Pittsburgh 17
SAN DIEGO 17, Denver 7

1978
DALLAS 38, Baltimore 0
MINNESOTA 12, Denver 9 (OT)
Baltimore 34, NEW ENGLAND 27
Minnesota 24, CHICAGO 20
WASHINGTON 9, Dallas 5
MIAMI 21, Cincinnati 0
DENVER 16, Chicago 7
Houston 24, PITTSBURGH 17
ATLANTA 15, Los Angeles 7
BALTIMORE 21, Washington 17
Oakland 34, CINCINNATI 21
HOUSTON 35, Miami 30
Pittsburgh 24, SAN FRANCISCO 7
SAN DIEGO 40, Chicago 7
Cincinnati 20, LOS ANGELES 19
MIAMI 23, New England 3

1977
PITTSBURGH 27, San Francisco 0
CLEVELAND 30, New England 27 (OT)
Oakland 37, KANSAS CITY 28
CHICAGO 24, Los Angeles 23
PITTSBURGH 20, Cincinnati 14
LOS ANGELES 35, Minnesota 3
ST. LOUIS 28, New York Giants 0
BALTIMORE 10, Washington 3
St. Louis 24, DALLAS 17
WASHINGTON 10, Green Bay 9
OAKLAND 34, Buffalo 13
MIAMI 17, Baltimore 6
Dallas 42, SAN FRANCISCO 35

1976
Miami 30, BUFFALO 21
Oakland 24, KANSAS CITY 21
Washington 20, PHILADELPHIA 17 (OT)
MINNESOTA 17, Pittsburgh 6
San Francisco 16, LOS ANGELES 0
NEW ENGLAND 41, New York Jets 7
WASHINGTON 20, St. Louis 10
BALTIMORE 38, Houston 14
CINCINNATI 20, Los Angeles 12
DALLAS 17, Buffalo 10
Baltimore 17, MIAMI 16
SAN FRANCISCO 20, Minnesota 16
OAKLAND 35, Cincinnati 20

1975
Oakland 31, MIAMI 21
DENVER 23, Green Bay 13
Dallas 36, DETROIT 10
WASHINGTON 27, St. Louis 17
New York Giants 17, BUFFALO 14
Minnesota 13, CHICAGO 9
Los Angeles 42, PHILADELPHIA 3
Kansas City 34, DALLAS 31
CINCINNATI 33, Buffalo 24
Pittsburgh 32, HOUSTON 9
MIAMI 20, New England 7
OAKLAND 17, Denver 10
SAN DIEGO 24, New York Jets 16

1974
BUFFALO 21, Oakland 20
PHILADELPHIA 13, Dallas 10
WASHINGTON 30, Denver 3
MIAMI 21, New York Jets 17
DETROIT 17, San Francisco 13
CHICAGO 10, Green Bay 9
PITTSBURGH 24, Atlanta 17
Los Angeles 15, SAN FRANCISCO 13
Minnesota 28, ST. LOUIS 24
Kansas City 42, DENVER 34
Pittsburgh 28, NEW ORLEANS 7
MIAMI 24, Cincinnati 3
Washington 23, LOS ANGELES 17

1973
GREEN BAY 23, New York Jets 7
DALLAS 40, New Orleans 3
DETROIT 31, Atlanta 6
WASHINGTON 14, Dallas 7
Miami 17, CLEVELAND 9
DENVER 23, Oakland 23
BUFFALO 23, Kansas City 14
PITTSBURGH 21, Washington 16
KANSAS CITY 19, Chicago 7
ATLANTA 20, Minnesota 14
SAN FRANCISCO 20, Green Bay 6
MIAMI 30, Pittsburgh 26
LOS ANGELES 40, New York Giants 6

1972
Washington 24, MINNESOTA 21
Kansas City 20, NEW ORLEANS 17
New York Giants 27, PHILADELPHIA 12
Oakland 34, HOUSTON 0
Green Bay 24, DETROIT 23
CHICAGO 13, Minnesota 10
DALLAS 28, Detroit 24
Baltimore 24, NEW ENGLAND 17
Cleveland 21, SAN DIEGO 17
WASHINGTON 24, Atlanta 13
MIAMI 31, St. Louis 10
Los Angeles 26, SAN FRANCISCO 16
OAKLAND 24, New York Jets 16

1971
Minnesota 16, DETROIT 13
ST. LOUIS 17, New York Jets 10
Oakland 34, CLEVELAND 20
DALLAS 20, New York Giants 13
KANSAS CITY 38, Pittsburgh 16
MINNESOTA 10, Baltimore 3
GREEN BAY 14, Detroit 14
BALTIMORE 24, Los Angeles 17
SAN DIEGO 20, St. Louis 17
ATLANTA 28, Green Bay 21
MIAMI 34, Chicago 3
Kansas City 26, SAN FRANCISCO 17
Washington 38, LOS ANGELES 24

1970
CLEVELAND 31, New York Jets 21
Kansas City 44, BALTIMORE 24
DETROIT 28, Chicago 14
Green Bay 22, SAN DIEGO 20
OAKLAND 34, Washington 20
MINNESOTA 13, Los Angeles 3
PITTSBURGH 21, Cincinnati 10
Baltimore 13, GREEN BAY 10
St. Louis 38, DALLAS 0
PHILADELPHIA 23, New York Giants 20
Miami 20, ATLANTA 7
Cleveland 21, HOUSTON 10
Detroit 28, LOS ANGELES 23

MONDAY NIGHT WON-LOST RECORDS, 1970-2007
AMERICAN FOOTBALL CONFERENCE

	Balt.	Buff.	Cin.	Cle.	Den.	Hou.	Ind.	Jax.	K.C.	Mia.	N.E.	N.Y.J.	Oak.	Pitt.	S.D.	Tenn.
Total	4-6	17-21	9-18	13-12	25-31-1	0-0	19-10	7-4	20-15	39-34	15-21	17-21	36-23-1	35-22	16-14	17-16
2007	0-3	0-1	1-1		1-2		1-0	0-1		0-1	2-0			2-0	1-0	1-1
2006	0-1		0-1		1-0		1-0	2-0	0-1	0-1	1-0	1-0	0-2	0-1	1-0	
2005	1-1				1-0		3-0			0-1	1-1	0-2		2-1	0-1	
2004	0-1		1-0	0-1			1-0		2-1	1-1	1-1	1-0				1-1
2003			0-1	1-1			1-0		1-0	1-1	1-0	1-0	0-3	0-1	0-1	0-1
2002	1-0			0-2			0-1			1-1	1-1	0-1	2-0	2-1		1-0
2001	2-0			1-1			0-1	0-1		1-0		0-1	1-0	1-0		0-2
2000		0-1		1-1			2-0	0-2	1-1	0-1	1-1	2-0	0-1			3-0
1999		1-0		1-2			2-0			1-2	0-1	2-1		1-0		
1998				2-1			2-0	0-2		1-2	1-2	1-0		2-1		
1997		1-1		2-1		0-1	1-0		2-0	1-2	1-2			0-2	0-2	
1996		0-2		1-0		1-0			0-2	1-2			2-1	3-0	1-1	
1995		1-1	0-2	1-0					1-1	2-1	1-0		0-2	1-1	1-1	
1994		1-1		0-2					1-1	1-0			1-1	2-0	0-1	0-3
1993		2-1		1-0	0-2		0-1		2-0	1-2			1-0	3-0	2-0	0-1
1992	2-0	0-1	0-1	0-2					1-0	2-1		0-1	0-2	1-0		1-0
1991	2-1	0-2							2-1	1-1		0-1	0-2	0-1		1-1
1990	1-1	1-1	1-1	1-1			0-1		0-1	0-1		0-1	2-0	1-0		1-0
1989	1-2	1-2	1-1	2-0								0-1	1-0			1-0
1988	2-0		1-2	0-2		1-1				1-1		0-1	1-1			1-0
1987		1-0		2-1						1-1	1-1	2-1	1-1			
1986		1-0	1-0	1-1						1-2	1-0	1-1	0-1		0-2	0-1
1985		1-0	1-0	1-0						2-1	0-1	1-0	2-0		0-2	0-1
1984	0-1	0-1		1-0						3-0		0-1	2-1	1-1	1-2	
1983	0-1	0-2						0-1	1-1		2-0		1-0	1-0	1-1	
1982	0-1	0-1							1-1		1-0		1-0	1-0	1-1	0-1
1981	1-1		0-1	1-0					1-1		0-1		2-1	1-1	2-1	0-1
1980		1-1		1-2					1-1		1-2	1-0	3-0	0-2	1-0	2-0
1979			1-0	0-2						0-2	0-2	1-1	2-0	2-1	1-0	2-0
1978			1-2				2-1		2-1				1-0	1-1	1-0	
1977		0-1	0-1	1-0			1-1		0-1	1-0	0-1		2-0	2-0		
1976		0-2	1-1				2-0		0-1	1-1	1-0	0-1	2-0	0-1		0-1
1975		0-2	1-0		1-1				1-0	1-1	0-1	0-1	2-0	1-0	1-0	0-1
1974	1-0	0-1			0-2		1-0		2-0		0-1	0-1	2-0			
1973	1-0		0-1	0-0-1			1-1		2-0			0-1	0-0-1	1-1		
1972			1-0				1-0		1-0	1-0	0-1	0-1	2-0		0-1	0-1
1971			0-1				1-1		2-0	1-0		0-1	1-0		0-1	1-0
1970		0-1	2-0				1-1		1-0	1-0		0-1	1-0	1-0	0-1	0-1

MONDAY NIGHT FOOTBALL ALL-TIME STANDINGS
AMERICAN FOOTBALL CONFERENCE

East	W	L	T	Pct.	South	W	L	T	Pct.
Miami	39	34	0	.534	Indianapolis	19	10	0	.655
Buffalo	17	21	0	.447	Jacksonville	7	4	0	.636
New York Jets	17	21	0	.447	Tennessee	17	16	0	.515
New England	15	21	0	.417	Houston	0	0	0	.000

North	W	L	T	Pct.	West	W	L	T	Pct.
Pittsburgh	35	22	0	.614	Oakland	36	23	1	.608
Cleveland	13	12	0	.520	Kansas City	20	15	0	.571
Baltimore	4	6	0	.400	San Diego	16	14	0	.533
Cincinnati	9	18	0	.333	Denver	25	31	1	.447

From 1970-71, tie games were not included in winning percentage.

MONDAY NIGHT WON-LOST RECORDS, 1970-2007
NATIONAL FOOTBALL CONFERENCE

	Ariz.	Atl.	Car.	Chi.	Dall.	Det.	G.B.	Minn.	N.O.	N.Y.G.	Phil.	St.L.	S.F.	Sea.	T.B.	Wash.
Total	5-12-1	9-21	4-3	18-33	40-29	11-13-1	25-25-1	24-23	9-15	18-30-1	24-21	26-27	38-23	16-8	8-8	26-29
2007	0-1	0-2		0-1	1-0		1-0	2-0	1-0		0-1		1-1	1-0		1-0
2006	0-1	0-1	1-1	2-0	0-1		0-2	1-1	1-0	1-1	2-0	0-1		2-0	0-1	0-1
2005		3-0	1-0		1-1		0-3	1-0	0-2	1-0	0-3	0-1		1-0		1-0
2004			0-1	2-1			2-1	0-2			2-1	2-1		0-1	0-1	0-1
2003		0-1	0-1	1-0			2-1		0-2		2-1	2-0	1-0		2-1	
2002			0-3				2-0		0-1		3-0	2-1	1-2	0-1	1-1	0-1
2001				1-0	0-1		2-0	1-1	0-1	0-3	1-0	2-1	1-0		1-0	0-2
2000		1-0		1-1			1-1	1-1				1-2		0-1	1-1	1-2
1999	0-1	1-2		1-2			1-2	2-1	1-0				1-2	1-0	1-0	
1998				2-0	1-1		0-3	1-0	0-2		0-1		3-0		1-1	0-1
1997			1-1	1-1	1-2		3-0	0-1		0-2			3-0			1-0
1996		0-1	2-0	2-1	0-2		2-1	0-1			0-2		2-1			
1995	0-1			1-2	3-0	2-0	1-0	0-2		0-1	0-1		2-1			
1994				0-2	2-1	1-0	1-0	2-0	0-2	1-2	2-0		2-1			
1993		0-1	0-1	1-1			0-1	1-0	0-2	1-0	1-1		1-2			1-2
1992		0-2	0-3	2-1	0-1			1-0	1-0	1-0	1-0		2-0	1-0		1-2
1991			2-1	0-1				0-1	1-0	2-1	2-1	0-1	2-1			2-0
1990						0-1		0-1	1-1	1-1	2-0	0-3	3-0	1-0		0-1
1989			1-1					1-1	1-1	2-1	0-2	0-2	3-0	1-0		0-2
1988	0-1			1-2	1-1			1-0	1-0	1-1	1-0	1-0	1-1	1-0		0-2
1987				1-2	2-1			1-0		0-3		1-2	2-0	0-2		1-1
1986	0-1			2-1	2-0	0-1	0-1				2-1	1-0	2-0			1-1
1985	1-1			1-1	1-1		0-1				0-1	2-1	1-2	0-2		2-1
1984		0-2		0-1	1-1	0-1	0-1		1-0	0-1		1-1	2-0	2-0		1-1
1983	0-0-1	0-1		1-1	2-0		2-1	0-1	0-1	1-1-1		1-0	1-0		0-1	1-2
1982				1-2	0-1	1-0	1-0		0-1					1-0		
1981		1-2		0-2	2-0	1-0		0-3				1-1	2-0	1-0		
1980				1-1	1-1				0-1	0-1	1-0	2-0		0-1	0-1	0-2
1979		1-2			0-2		1-0	0-1	0-1	0-1	1-1	1-0		2-0		1-0
1978		1-0		0-3	1-1			2-0				0-2	0-1			1-1
1977	2-0			1-0	1-1	0-1			0-1			1-1	0-2			1-1
1976	0-1			1-0				1-1			0-1	0-2	2-0			2-0
1975	0-1			0-1	1-1	0-1	0-1	1-0		1-0	0-1	1-0				1-0
1974	0-1	0-1		1-0	0-1	1-0	0-1	1-0	0-1		1-0	1-1	0-2			2-0
1973		1-1		0-1	1-1		1-1	1-1		0-1		1-0	1-0			1-1
1972	0-1	0-1		1-0	1-0	0-2	1-0	0-2	0-1	1-0	0-1	1-0	0-1			2-0
1971	1-1	1-0		0-1	1-0	0-1-1	0-1-1	2-0		0-1		0-2	0-1			1-0
1970	1-0	0-1		0-1	0-1		2-0	1-1	1-0		0-1	1-0	0-2			0-1

MONDAY NIGHT FOOTBALL ALL-TIME STANDINGS
NATIONAL FOOTBALL CONFERENCE

East	W	L	T	Pct.
Dallas	40	29	0	.580
Philadelphia	24	21	0	.533
Washington	26	29	0	.473
New York Giants	18	30	1	.378

North	W	L	T	Pct.
Minnesota	24	23	0	.511
Green Bay	25	25	1	.500
Detroit	11	13	1	.458
Chicago	18	33	0	.353

South	W	L	T	Pct.
Carolina	4	3	0	.571
Tampa Bay	8	8	0	.500
New Orleans	9	15	0	.375
Atlanta	9	21	0	.300

West	W	L	T	Pct.
Seattle	16	8	0	.667
San Francisco	38	23	0	.623
St. Louis	26	27	0	.491
Arizona	5	12	1	.306

From 1970-71, tie games were not included in winning percentage.

THANKSGIVING DAY FOOTBALL, 1920-2007
(Home Team in capitals, games listed in chronological order.)
(AFL)-American Football League, 1960-69.

Nov. 25, 1920
AKRON PROS 7, Canton Bulldogs 0
Decatur Staleys 6, CHICAGO TIGERS 0
ELYRIA (OH) ATHLETICS* 0, Columbus Panhandles 0
DAYTON TRIANGLES 28, Detroit Heralds 0
CHICAGO BOOSTERS* 27, Hammond Pros 0
All-Tonawanda (NY) 14, ROCHESTER JEFFERSONS 3
* Non league team. Games between league teams and non league teams counted in standings in 1920.

Nov. 24, 1921
Canton Bulldogs 14, AKRON PROS 0
Buffalo All-Americans 7, CHICAGO STALEYS 6

Nov. 30, 1922
Buffalo All-Americans 21, ROCHESTER JEFFERSONS 0
CHICAGO CARDINALS 6, Chicago Bears 0
RACINE LEGION 3, Milwaukee Badgers 0
Oorang Indians 18, COLUMBUS PANHANDLES 6
CANTON BULLDOGS 14, Akron Pros 0

Nov. 29, 1923
CANTON BULLDOGS 28, Toledo Maroons 0
CHICAGO BEARS 3, Chicago Cardinals 0
GREEN BAY PACKERS 19, Hammond Pros 0
Milwaukee Badgers 16, RACINE LEGION 0
AKRON PROS 2, Buffalo All-Americans 0

Nov. 27, 1924
AKRON PROS 22, Buffalo Bisons 0
Chicago Bears 21, CHICAGO CARDINALS 0
FRANKFORD YELLOWJACKETS 32, Dayton Triangles 7
CLEVELAND BULLDOGS 53, Milwaukee Badgers 10 (at Canton, Ohio)
Green Bay Packers 17, KANSAS CITY BLUES 6

Nov. 26, 1925
CHICAGO BEARS 0, Chicago Cardinals 0
Kansas City Cowboys 17, CLEVELAND BULLDOGS 0 (at Hartford, Connecticut)
Rock Island Independents 6, DETROIT PANTHERS 3
POTTSVILLE MAROONS 31, Green Bay Packers 0

Nov. 25, 1926
New York Giants 17, BROOKLYN LIONS 0
Los Angeles Buccaneers 9, DETROIT PANTHERS 6
CHICAGO BEARS 0, Chicago Cardinals 0
FRANKFORD YELLOWJACKETS 20, Green Bay Packers 14
POTTSVILLE MAROONS 8, Providence Steam Roller 0
CANTON BULLDOGS 0, Akron Pros 0

Nov. 24, 1927
Chicago Cardinals 3, CHICAGO BEARS 0
POTTSVILLE MAROONS 6, Providence Steam Roller 0
Green Bay Packers 17, FRANKFORD YELLOWJACKETS 9
Cleveland Bulldogs 30, NEW YORK YANKEES 19

Nov. 29, 1928
Providence Steam Roller 7, POTTSVILLE MAROONS 0
DETROIT WOLVERINES 33, Dayton Triangles 0
FRANKFORD YELLOWJACKETS 2, Green Bay Packers 0
CHICAGO BEARS 34, Chicago Cardinals 0

Nov. 28, 1929
New York Giants 21, STATEN ISLAND STAPLETONS 7
FRANKFORD YELLOWJACKETS 0, Green Bay Packers 0
Chicago Cardinals 40, CHICAGO BEARS 6

Nov. 27, 1930
STATEN ISLAND STAPLETONS 7, New York Giants 6
BROOKLYN DODGERS 33, Providence Steam Roller 12
Green Bay Packers 25, FRANKFORD YELLOWJACKETS 7
CHICAGO BEARS 6, Chicago Cardinals 0

Nov. 26, 1931
Green Bay Packers 38, PROVIDENCE STEAM ROLLER 7
STATEN ISLAND STAPLETONS 9, New York Giants 6
CHICAGO BEARS 18, Chicago Cardinals 7

Nov. 24, 1932
CHICAGO BEARS 34, Chicago Cardinals 0
Green Bay Packers 7, BROOKLYN DODGERS 0
STATEN ISLAND STAPLETONS 13, New York Giants 13

Nov. 30, 1933
Chicago Bears 22, CHICAGO CARDINALS 6
New York Giants 10, BROOKLYN DODGERS 0

Nov. 29, 1934	CHICAGO CARDINALS 6, Green Bay Packers 0
	Chicago Bears 19, DETROIT LIONS 16
	New York Giants 27, BROOKLYN DODGERS 0
Nov. 28, 1935	New York Giants 21, BROOKLYN DODGERS 0
	CHICAGO CARDINALS 9, Green Bay Packers 7
	DETROIT LIONS 14, Chicago Bears 2
Nov. 26, 1936	DETROIT LIONS 13, Chicago Bears 7
	New York Giants 14, BROOKLYN DODGERS 0
Nov. 25, 1937	Chicago Bears 13, DETROIT LIONS 0
	BROOKLYN DODGERS 13, New York Giants 13
Nov. 24, 1938	DETROIT LIONS 14, Chicago Bears 7
	BROOKLYN DODGERS 7, New York Giants 7
Nov. 23, 1939#	PHILADELPHIA EAGLES 17, Pittsburgh Steelers 14
Nov. 28, 1940#	Pittsburgh Steelers 7, PHILADELPHIA EAGLES 0

In 1939 and 1940, President Roosevelt moved Thanksgiving one week earlier. Various states celebrated on the date declared by the President, while other states recognized the traditional fourth Thursday of the month. In 1941, Thanksgiving was sanctioned by Congress to be celebrated on the fourth Thursday of November, which it has been ever since.

Nov. 22, 1945	Cleveland Rams 28, DETROIT LIONS 21
Nov. 28, 1946	Boston Yanks 34, DETROIT LIONS 10
Nov. 27, 1947	Chicago Bears 34, DETROIT LIONS 14
Nov. 25, 1948	Chicago Cardinals 28, DETROIT LIONS 14
Nov. 24, 1949	Chicago Bears 28, DETROIT LIONS 7
Nov. 23, 1950	DETROIT LIONS 49, New York Yanks 14
	Pittsburgh Steelers 28, CHICAGO CARDINALS 17
Nov. 22, 1951	DETROIT LIONS 52, Green Bay Packers 35
Nov. 27, 1952	DETROIT LIONS 48, Green Bay Packers 24
	DALLAS TEXANS 27, Chicago Bears 23 (at Akron, Ohio)
Nov. 26, 1953	DETROIT LIONS 34, Green Bay Packers 15
Nov. 25, 1954	DETROIT LIONS 28, Green Bay Packers 24
Nov. 24, 1955	DETROIT LIONS 24, Green Bay Packers 10
Nov. 22, 1956	Green Bay Packers 24, DETROIT LIONS 20
Nov. 28, 1957	DETROIT LIONS 18, Green Bay Packers 6
Nov. 27, 1958	DETROIT LIONS 24, Green Bay Packers 14
Nov. 26, 1959	Green Bay Packers 24, DETROIT LIONS 17
Nov. 24, 1960	DETROIT LIONS 23, Green Bay Packers 10
	(AFL) - NEW YORK TITANS 41, Dallas Texans 35
Nov. 23, 1961	Green Bay Packers 17, DETROIT LIONS 9
	(AFL) - NEW YORK TITANS 21, Buffalo Bills 14
Nov. 22, 1962	DETROIT LIONS 26, Green Bay Packers 14
	(AFL) - New York Titans 46, DENVER BRONCOS 45
Nov. 28, 1963	DETROIT LIONS 13, Green Bay Packers 13
	(AFL) - Oakland Raiders 26, DENVER BRONCOS 10
Nov. 26, 1964	Chicago Bears 27, DETROIT LIONS 24
	(AFL) - Buffalo Bills 27, SAN DIEGO CHARGERS 24
Nov. 25, 1965	DETROIT LIONS 24, Baltimore Colts 24
	(AFL) - SAN DIEGO CHARGERS 20, Buffalo Bills 20
Nov. 24, 1966	San Francisco 49ers 41, DETROIT LIONS 14
	DALLAS COWBOYS 26, Cleveland Browns 14
	(AFL) - Buffalo Bills 31, OAKLAND RAIDERS 10

Nov. 23, 1967	Los Angeles Rams 31, DETROIT LIONS 7 DALLAS COWBOYS 46, St. Louis Cardinals 21 (AFL) - Oakland Raiders 44, KANSAS CITY CHIEFS 22 (AFL) - SAN DIEGO CHARGERS 24, Denver Broncos 20
Nov. 28, 1968	Philadelphia Eagles 12, DETROIT LIONS 0 DALLAS COWBOYS 29, Washington Redskins 20 (AFL) - OAKLAND RAIDERS 13, Buffalo Bills 10 (AFL) - KANSAS CITY CHIEFS 24, Houston Oilers 10
Nov. 27, 1969	Minnesota Vikings 27, DETROIT LIONS 0 DALLAS COWBOYS 24, San Francisco 49ers 24 (AFL) - KANSAS CITY CHIEFS 31, Denver Broncos 17 (AFL) - San Diego Chargers 21, HOUSTON OILERS 17
Nov. 26, 1970	DETROIT LIONS 28, Oakland Raiders 14 DALLAS COWBOYS 16, Green Bay Packers 3
Nov. 25, 1971	DETROIT LIONS 32, Kansas City Chiefs 21 DALLAS COWBOYS 28, Los Angeles Rams 21
Nov. 23, 1972	DETROIT LIONS 37, New York Jets 20 San Francisco 49ers 31, DALLAS COWBOYS 10
Nov. 22, 1973	Washington Redskins 20, DETROIT LIONS 0 Miami Dolphins 14, DALLAS COWBOYS 7
Nov. 28, 1974	Denver Broncos 31, DETROIT LIONS 27 DALLAS COWBOYS 24, Washington Redskins 23
Nov. 27, 1975	Los Angeles Rams 20, DETROIT LIONS 0 Buffalo Bills 32, ST. LOUIS CARDINALS 14
Nov. 25, 1976	DETROIT LIONS 27, Buffalo Bills 14 DALLAS COWBOYS 19, St. Louis Cardinals 14
Nov. 24, 1977	Chicago Bears 31, DETROIT LIONS 14 Miami Dolphins 55, ST. LOUIS CARDINALS 14
Nov. 23, 1978	DETROIT LIONS 17, Denver Broncos 14 DALLAS COWBOYS 37, Washington Redskins 10
Nov. 22, 1979	DETROIT LIONS 20, Chicago Bears 0 Houston Oilers 30, DALLAS COWBOYS 24
Nov. 27, 1980	Chicago Bears 23, DETROIT LIONS 17 (OT) DALLAS COWBOYS 51, Seattle Seahawks 7
Nov. 26, 1981	DETROIT LIONS 27, Kansas City Chiefs 10 DALLAS COWBOYS 10, Chicago Bears 9
Nov. 25, 1982	New York Giants 13, DETROIT LIONS 6 DALLAS COWBOYS 31, Cleveland Browns 14
Nov. 24, 1983	DETROIT LIONS 45, Pittsburgh Steelers 3 DALLAS COWBOYS 35, St. Louis Cardinals 17
Nov. 22, 1984	DETROIT LIONS 31, Green Bay Packers 28 DALLAS COWBOYS 20, New England Patriots 17
Nov. 28, 1985	DETROIT LIONS 31, New York Jets 20 DALLAS COWBOYS 35, St. Louis Cardinals 17
Nov. 27, 1986	Green Bay Packers 44, DETROIT LIONS 40 Seattle Seahawks 31, DALLAS COWBOYS 14
Nov. 26, 1987	Kansas City Chiefs 27, DETROIT LIONS 20 Minnesota Vikings 44, DALLAS COWBOYS 38 (OT)
Nov. 24, 1988	Minnesota Vikings 23, DETROIT LIONS 0 Houston Oilers 25, DALLAS COWBOYS 17
Nov. 23, 1989	DETROIT LIONS 13, Cleveland Browns 10 Philadelphia Eagles 27, DALLAS COWBOYS 0
Nov. 22, 1990	DETROIT LIONS 40, Denver Broncos 27 DALLAS COWBOYS 27, Washington Redskins 17

Nov. 28, 1991	DETROIT LIONS 16, Chicago Bears 6
	DALLAS COWBOYS 20, Pittsburgh Steelers 10
Nov. 26, 1992	Houston Oilers 24, DETROIT LIONS 21
	DALLAS COWBOYS 30, New York Giants 3
Nov. 25, 1993	Chicago Bears 10, DETROIT LIONS 6
	Miami Dolphins 16, DALLAS COWBOYS 14
Nov. 24, 1994	DETROIT LIONS 35, Buffalo Bills 21
	DALLAS COWBOYS 42, Green Bay Packers 31
Nov. 23, 1995	DETROIT LIONS 44, Minnesota Vikings 38
	DALLAS COWBOYS 24, Kansas City Chiefs 12
Nov. 28, 1996	Kansas City Chiefs 28, DETROIT LIONS 24
	DALLAS COWBOYS 21, Washington Redskins 10
Nov. 27, 1997	DETROIT LIONS 55, Chicago Bears 20
	Tennessee Titans 27, DALLAS COWBOYS 14
Nov. 26, 1998	DETROIT LIONS 19, Pittsburgh Steelers 16 (OT)
	Minnesota Vikings 46, DALLAS COWBOYS 36
Nov. 25, 1999	DETROIT LIONS 21, Chicago Bears 17
	DALLAS COWBOYS 20, Miami Dolphins 0
Nov. 23, 2000	DETROIT LIONS 34, New England Patriots 9
	Minnesota Vikings 27, DALLAS COWBOYS 15
Nov. 22, 2001	Green Bay Packers 29, DETROIT LIONS 27
	Denver Broncos 26, DALLAS COWBOYS 24
Nov. 28, 2002	New England Patriots 20, DETROIT LIONS 12
	DALLAS COWBOYS 27, Washington Redskins 20
Nov. 27, 2003	DETROIT LIONS 22, Green Bay Packers 14
	Miami Dolphins 40, DALLAS COWBOYS 21
Nov. 25, 2004	Indianapolis Colts 41, DETROIT LIONS 9
	DALLAS COWBOYS 21, Chicago Bears 7
Nov. 24, 2005	Atlanta Falcons 27, DETROIT LIONS 7
	Denver Broncos 24, DALLAS COWBOYS 21 (OT)
Nov. 23, 2006	Miami Dolphins 27, DETROIT LIONS 10
	DALLAS COWBOYS 38, Tampa Bay Buccaneers 10
	KANSAS CITY CHIEFS 19, Denver Broncos 10
Nov. 22, 2007	Green Bay Packers 37, DETROIT LIONS 26
	DALLAS COWBOYS 34, New York Jets 3
	Indianapolis Colts 31, ATLANTA FALCONS 13

THANKSGIVING DAY RECORDS
*NFL record; stats compiled by Elias Sports Bureau.

SCORING / Most Touchdowns, Game
- 6 Ernie Nevers, Chi. Cardinals vs. Chi. Bears, Nov. 28, 1929*
- 4 Sterling Sharpe, Green Bay at Dallas, Nov. 24, 1994
- 3 By many players

RUSHING / Most Yards Rushing, Game
- 273 O.J. Simpson, Buffalo at Detroit, Nov. 25, 1976
- 198 Bob Hoernschemeyer, Detroit vs. N.Y. Yankees, Nov. 23, 1950
- 195 Earl Campbell, Houston at Dallas, Nov. 22, 1979

PASSING / Most Yards Passing, Game
- 455 Troy Aikman, Dallas vs. Minnesota, Nov. 26, 1998
- 410 Scott Mitchell, Detroit vs. Minnesota, Nov. 23, 1995
- 384 Warren Moon, Minnesota at Detroit, Nov. 23, 1995

PASS RECEIVING
RECEPTIONS / Most Pass Receptions, Game
- 12 Brett Perriman, Detroit vs. Minnesota, Nov. 23, 1995
- Marvin Harrison, Indianapolis at Detroit, Nov. 25, 2004
- 11 Daryl Johnston, Dallas vs. Miami, Nov. 25, 1993
- Michael Irvin, Dallas vs. Kansas City, Nov. 23, 1995

YARDS GAINED / Most Yards on Pass Receptions, Game
- 303 Jim Benton, Cleveland at Detroit, Nov. 22, 1945
- 185 Lance Alworth, San Diego vs. Buffalo, Nov. 26, 1964
- 184 Anthony Carter, Minnesota at Dallas, Nov. 26, 1987 (OT)

NFL INTERNATIONAL GAMES (57)

Date	Site	Teams
August 12, 1950	Ottawa, Canada	N.Y. Giants 27, Ottawa Rough Riders 6
August 11, 1951	Ottawa, Canada	N.Y. Giants 41, Ottawa Rough Riders 18
August 5, 1959	Toronto, Canada	Chi. Cardinals 55, Tor. Argonauts 26
August 3, 1960	Toronto, Canada	Pittsburgh 43, Toronto Argonauts 16
August 15, 1960	Toronto, Canada	Chicago 16, N.Y. Giants 7
August 2, 1961	Toronto, Canada	St. Louis 36, Toronto Argonauts 7
August 5, 1961	Montreal, Canada	Chicago 34, Montreal Allouettes 16
August 8, 1961	Hamilton, Canada	Hamilton Tiger-Cats 38, Buffalo 21
August 25, 1969	Montreal, Canada	Detroit 22, Boston 9
September 11, 1969	Montreal, Canada	Pittsburgh 17, N.Y. Giants 13
August 16, 1976	Tokyo, Japan	St. Louis 20, San Diego 10
August 5, 1978	Mexico City, Mexico	New Orleans 14, Philadelphia 7
August 6, 1983	London, England	Minnesota 28, St. Louis 10
* August 3, 1986	London, England	Chicago 17, Dallas 6
* August 9, 1987	London, England	L.A. Rams 28, Denver 27
* July 31, 1988	London, England	Miami 27, San Francisco 21
August 14, 1988	Goteborg, Sweden	Minnesota 28, Chicago 21
August 18, 1988	Montreal, Canada	N.Y. Jets 11, Cleveland 7
* August 5, 1989	Tokyo, Japan	L.A. Rams 16, San Francisco 13 (OT)
* August 6, 1989	London, England	Philadelphia 17, Cleveland 13
* August 4, 1990	Tokyo, Japan	Denver 10, Seattle 7
* August 5, 1990	London, England	New Orleans 17, L.A. Raiders 10
* August 9, 1990	Montreal, Canada	Pittsburgh 30, New England 14
* August 11, 1990	Berlin, Germany	L.A. Rams 19, Kansas City 3
* July 28, 1991	London, England	Buffalo 17, Philadelphia 13
* August 3, 1991	Berlin, Germany	San Francisco 21, Chicago 7
* August 3, 1991	Tokyo, Japan	Miami 19, L.A. Raiders 17
* August 1, 1992	Tokyo, Japan	Houston 34, Dallas 23
* August 15, 1992	Berlin, Germany	Miami 31, Denver 27
* August 16, 1992	London, England	San Francisco 17, Washington 15
* July 31, 1993	Tokyo, Japan	New Orleans 28, Philadelphia 16
* August 1, 1993	Barcelona, Spain	San Francisco 21, Pittsburgh 14
* August 7, 1993	Berlin, Germany	Minnesota 20, Buffalo 6
* August 8, 1993	London, England	Dallas 13, Detroit 13 (OT)
August 14, 1993	Toronto, Canada	Cleveland 12, New England 9
* July 31, 1994	Barcelona, Spain	L.A. Raiders 25, Denver 22
* August 6, 1994	Tokyo, Japan	Minnesota 17, Kansas City 9
* August 13, 1994	Berlin, Germany	N.Y. Giants 28, San Diego 20
* August 15, 1994	Mexico City, Mexico	Houston 6, Dallas 0
* August 5, 1995	Tokyo, Japan	Denver 24, San Francisco 10
* August 12, 1995	Toronto, Canada	Buffalo 9, Dallas 7
* July 27, 1996	Tokyo, Japan	San Diego 20, Pittsburgh 10
* August 5, 1996	Monterrey, Mexico	Kansas City 32, Dallas 6
* July 27, 1997	Dublin, Ireland	Pittsburgh 30, Chicago 17
* August 4, 1997	Mexico City, Mexico	Miami 38, Denver 19
* August 16, 1997	Toronto, Canada	Green Bay 35, Buffalo 3
* August 1, 1998	Tokyo, Japan	Green Bay 27, Kansas City 24 (OT)
* August 15, 1998	Vancouver, Canada	San Francisco 24, Seattle 21
* August 17, 1998	Mexico City, Mexico	New England 21, Dallas 3
* August 7, 1999	Sydney, Australia	Denver 20, San Diego 17
* August 5, 2000	Tokyo, Japan	Atlanta 20, Dallas 9
* August 19, 2000	Mexico City, Mexico	Indianapolis 24, Pittsburgh 23
* August 27, 2001	Mexico City, Mexico	Dallas 21, Oakland 6
* August 3, 2002	Osaka, Japan	Washington 38, San Francisco 7
* August 2, 2003	Tokyo, Japan	Tampa Bay 30, N.Y. Jets 14
* August 6, 2005	Tokyo, Japan	Atlanta 27, Indianapolis 21
** October 2, 2005	Mexico City, Mexico	Arizona 31, San Francisco 14
** October 28, 2007	London, England	N.Y. Giants 13, Miami 10

* *American Bowl Game*
** *Regular-season Game*

CHICAGO ALL-STAR GAME
Pro teams won 31, lost 9, and tied 2. The game was discontinued after 1976.

Date	Winner	Loser	Attendance
August 31, 1934	Chicago Bears 0	All-Stars 0 (tie)	79,432
August 29, 1935	Chicago Bears 5	All-Stars 0	77,450
September 3, 1936	Detroit Lions 7	All-Stars 7 (tie)	76,000
September 1, 1937	All-Stars 6	Green Bay Packers 0	84,560
August 31, 1938	All-Stars 28	Washington Redskins 16	74,250
August 30, 1939	N.Y. Giants 9	All-Stars 0	81,456
August 29, 1940	Green Bay Packers 45	All-Stars 28	84,567
August 28, 1941	Chicago Bears 37	All-Stars 13	98,203
August 28, 1942	Chicago Bears 21	All-Stars 0	101,100
August 25, 1943	All-Stars 27	Washington Redskins 7	48,471
August 30, 1944	Chicago Bears 24	All-Stars 21	48,769
August 30, 1945	Green Bay Packers 19	All-Stars 7	92,753
August 23, 1946	All-Stars 16	Los Angeles Rams 0	97,380
August 22, 1947	All-Stars 16	Chicago Bears 0	105,840
August 20, 1948	Chicago Cardinals 28	All-Stars 0	101,220
August 12, 1949	Philadelphia Eagles 38	All-Stars 0	93,780
August 11, 1950	All-Stars 17	Philadelphia Eagles 7	88,885
August 17, 1951	Cleveland Browns 33	All-Stars 0	92,180
August 15, 1952	Los Angeles Rams 10	All-Stars 7	88,316
August 14, 1953	Detroit Lions 24	All-Stars 10	93,818
August 13, 1954	Detroit Lions 31	All-Stars 6	93,470
August 12, 1955	All-Stars 30	Cleveland Browns 27	75,000
August 10, 1956	Cleveland Browns 26	All-Stars 0	75,000
August 9, 1957	N.Y. Giants 22	All-Stars 12	75,000
August 15, 1958	All-Stars 35	Detroit Lions 19	70,000
August 14, 1959	Baltimore Colts 29	All-Stars 0	70,000
August 12, 1960	Baltimore Colts 32	All-Stars 7	70,000
August 4, 1961	Philadelphia Eagles 28	All-Stars 14	66,000
August 3, 1962	Green Bay Packers 42	All-Stars 20	65,000
August 2, 1963	All-Stars 20	Green Bay Packers 17	65,000
August 7, 1964	Chicago Bears 28	All-Stars 17	65,000
August 6, 1965	Cleveland Browns 24	All-Stars 16	68,000
August 5, 1966	Green Bay Packers 38	All-Stars 0	72,000
August 4, 1967	Green Bay Packers 27	All-Stars 0	70,934
August 2, 1968	Green Bay Packers 34	All-Stars 17	69,917
August 1, 1969	N.Y. Jets 26	All-Stars 24	74,208
July 31, 1970	Kansas City Chiefs 24	All-Stars 3	69,940
July 30, 1971	Baltimore Colts 24	All-Stars 17	52,289
July 28, 1972	Dallas Cowboys 20	All-Stars 7	54,162
July 27, 1973	Miami Dolphins 14	All-Stars 3	54,103
1974	No game was played		
August 1, 1975	Pittsburgh Steelers 21	All-Stars 14	54,103
July 23, 1976*	Pittsburgh Steelers 24	All-Stars 0	52,895

*Game shortened because of thunderstorms.

NFL PLAYOFF BOWL
Consolation game that matched conference runners-up.
Western Conference won 8, Eastern Conference won 2.
All games played at Miami's Orange Bowl.

January 7, 1961	Detroit Lions 17, Cleveland Browns 16
January 6, 1962	Detroit Lions 38, Philadelphia Eagles 10
January 6, 1963	Detroit Lions 17, Pittsburgh Steelers 10
January 5, 1964	Green Bay Packers 40, Cleveland Browns 23
January 3, 1965	St. Louis Cardinals 24, Green Bay Packers 17
January 9, 1966	Baltimore Colts 35, Dallas Cowboys 3
January 8, 1967	Baltimore Colts 20, Philadelphia Eagles 14
January 7, 1968	Los Angeles Rams 30, Cleveland Browns 6
January 5, 1969	Dallas Cowboys 17, Minnesota Vikings 13
January 3, 1970	Los Angeles Rams 31, Dallas Cowboys 0

AFC VS. NFC (REGULAR SEASON), 1970-2007

	Balt	Buff	Cin	Cle	Den	Hou	Ind	Jax	KC	Mia
1970		0-3	1-2	0-3	2-2		3-0		0-2-1	2-1
1971		0-3	1-2	2-1	1-3		2-1		2-1	3-0
1972		2-0-1	2-1	1-2	1-3		0-3		2-1	3-0
1973		2-1	2-1	1-2	0-3-1		2-1		1-1-1	3-0
1974		2-1	2-1	1-2	2-2		1-2		1-2	2-1
1975		1-2	3-0	1-3	2-1		2-1		2-1	3-0
1976		0-2	2-0	2-0	2-0		0-2		1-1	0-2
1977		1-1	2-1	1-1	1-1		1-1		1-1	2-0
1978		1-1	2-2	4-0	2-2		2-2		0-2	3-1
1979		2-2	2-2	3-1	3-1		1-1		0-2	4-0
1980		3-1	2-2	3-1	3-1		1-1		2-0	4-0
1981		1-3	2-2	3-1	3-1		0-4		2-2	3-1
1982		1-2	1-0	0-2	2-1		0-1-1		0-3	1-1
1983		1-3	3-1	2-2	0-2		2-0		2-2	3-1
1984		1-3	2-2	1-3	3-1		0-4		1-1	4-0
1985		0-2	2-2	1-3	3-1		3-1		2-2	3-1
1986		1-1	3-1	2-2	3-1		1-3		1-1	2-2
1987		1-2	1-2	2-2	2-1-1		1-0		1-2	3-0
1988		2-2	4-0	4-0	3-1		2-2		0-2	3-1
1989		1-3	2-2	3-1	2-2		1-3		2-0	2-0
1990		3-1	1-3	1-3	1-3		2-2		4-0	2-2
1991		3-1	1-3	0-4	2-0		0-4		2-2	3-1
1992		4-0	1-3	2-2	1-3		2-0		2-2	2-2
1993		4-0	2-2	3-1	1-3		0-4		2-2	3-1
1994		1-3	1-3	3-1	1-3		0-2		3-1	2-2
1995		3-1	2-2	1-3	2-2		2-2	0-4	3-1	2-2
1996	2-2	4-0	2-2		3-1		3-1	2-2	4-0	1-3
1997	2-1-1	1-3	2-2		3-1		1-3	2-2	4-0	1-3
1998	1-3	3-1	1-3		3-1		0-4	3-1	3-1	3-1
1999	2-1	3-1	1-2	1-2	2-2		4-0	4-0	2-2	2-2
2000	2-1	2-2	1-2	0-3	3-1		2-2	2-2	2-2	2-2
2001	2-2	1-3	1-2	1-2	3-1		1-3	1-2	1-3	2-2
2002	0-4	3-1	1-3	2-2	4-0	2-2	2-2	2-2	2-2	2-2
2003	3-1	2-2	2-2	2-2	1-3	2-2	3-1	2-2	3-1	3-1
2004	3-1	4-0	4-0	1-3	3-1	1-3	4-0	3-1	1-3	2-2
2005	2-2	0-4	4-0	2-2	3-1	1-3	3-1	3-1	1-3	2-2
2006	3-1	2-2	2-2	1-3	1-3	0-4	3-1	3-1	4-0	3-1
2007	3-1	1-3	1-3	3-1	1-3	3-1	4-0	3-1	1-3	0-4
Total	25-20-1	67-66-1	71-65	60-66	78-62-2	9-15	61-65-1	30-21	67-57-2	90-47

	NE	NYJ	Oak	Pitt	SD	Sea	TB	Tenn	TOTALS
1970	0-3	2-1	1-2	0-3	1-2			0-3	12-27-1
1971	0-3	0-3	1-1-1	1-2	2-1			0-2-1	15-23-2
1972	3-0	1-2	3-0	2-1	0-3			0-3	20-19-1
1973	2-1	0-3	2-1	3-0	1-2			0-3	19-19-2
1974	3-0	2-1	3-0	3-0	1-2			0-3	23-17
1975	1-2	0-3	3-0	2-1	0-3			3-0	23-17
1976	1-1	0-2	3-0	1-1	2-0	1-0	0-1	2-0	16-12
1977	2-0	1-1	1-1	2-0	1-1	3-1		2-0	19-9
1978	2-2	1-3	4-0	3-1	2-2	3-1		2-2	31-21
1979	3-1	3-1	4-0	3-1	3-1	3-1		2-2	36-16
1980	1-3	1-3	2-2	4-0	2-2	1-3		4-0	33-19
1981	0-4	2-0	2-2	3-1	2-2	0-2		1-3	24-28
1982	0-1	4-0	3-0	1-0	1-0	1-0		0-3	15-14-1
1983	2-2	3-1	2-2	2-2	2-2	1-3		1-3	26-26
1984	0-4	0-2	3-1	3-1	4-0	4-0		0-4	26-26
1985	3-1	2-2	3-1	1-3	1-1	2-2		1-3	27-25
1986	3-1	2-2	1-3	2-2	0-4	3-1		2-2	26-26
1987	0-3	0-4	2-2	2-2	2-0	4-0		2-2	23-22-1
1988	2-2	2-0	1-3	1-3	2-2	1-3		3-1	30-22
1989	0-4	1-3	2-2	3-1	2-2	0-4		3-1	24-28
1990	0-4	2-0	3-1	3-1	1-1	2-2		1-3	26-26
1991	1-1	2-2	2-2	0-4	1-3	1-3		1-3	19-33
1992	0-4	0-4	2-2	1-3	2-0	0-4		3-1	22-30
1993	1-1	2-2	3-1	2-2	2-2	0-2		2-2	27-25
1994	4-0	1-3	3-1	2-2	2-2	2-0		0-4	25-27
1995	0-4	0-4	3-1	2-2	3-1	3-1		1-3	27-33
1996	2-2	1-3	1-3	2-2	1-3	2-2		2-2	32-28
1997	1-3	3-1	2-2	2-2	1-3	2-2		4-0	31-28-1
1998	2-2	2-2	3-1	2-2	1-3	3-1		1-3	31-29
1999	3-1	2-2	3-1	3-0	1-3	2-2		3-1	38-22
2000	0-4	3-1	4-0	1-2	0-4	2-2		4-0	30-30
2001	3-1	2-2	3-1	3-0	2-2	1-3		3-1	30-30
2002	3-1	3-1	2-2	2-1-1	2-2			2-2	34-29-1
2003	3-1	0-4	1-3	1-3	2-2			4-0	34-30
2004	4-0	3-1	2-2	4-0	3-1			2-2	44-20
2005	3-1	1-3	2-2	4-0	2-2			1-3	34-30
2006	4-0	3-1	1-3	3-1	4-0			3-1	40-24
2007	4-0	0-4	0-4	3-1	2-2			3-1	32-32
Total	66-68	57-77	86-55-1	82-53-1	63-68	44-44	0-1	68-72-1	1024-922-10

NFC VS. AFC (REGULAR SEASON), 1970-2007

	Ariz	Atl	Car	Chi	Dall	Det	GB	Minn	NO
1970	2-0-1	1-2		1-2	3-0	3-0	2-1	2-1	0-3
1971	2-1	3-0		1-2	3-0	4-0	2-1	2-1	0-1-2
1972	1-2	2-2		1-2	3-0	2-0-1	2-1	1-2	0-3
1973	0-2-1	2-1		2-2	2-1	0-3	1-1-1	2-1	1-2
1974	2-1	0-3		0-3	2-1	1-2	2-1	2-1	0-3
1975	2-1	1-2		0-3	2-1	1-2	0-3	4-0	0-3
1976	1-1	0-2		0-2	2-0	2-0	0-2	2-0	1-2
1977	0-2	0-2		1-1	1-1	2-0	0-3	1-1	0-2
1978	0-4	1-3		0-4	3-1	2-2	2-2	1-3	1-3
1979	1-3	1-3		2-2	1-3	0-4	1-3	1-3	0-4
1980	1-1	2-2		0-4	3-1	0-2	1-3	1-3	1-3
1981	3-1	1-3		4-0	4-0	2-2	1-1	1-3	2-2
1982		1-1		1-1	2-1	0-1	1-1-1	1-3	1-0
1983	3-1	3-1		1-1	2-2	1-3	2-2	4-0	1-3
1984	3-1	1-3		2-2	2-2	0-4	0-4	0-4	3-1
1985	2-2	0-4		3-1	3-1	2-2	0-4	2-0	0-4
1986	1-1	1-3		4-0	1-3	1-3	1-3	1-3	1-3
1987	0-1	0-4		2-2	2-1	0-4	1-2-1	2-1	4-0
1988	1-3	1-3		3-1	0-4	1-1	1-3	2-2	4-0
1989	1-3	2-2		2-2	0-2	1-3	0-2	2-2	4-0
1990	2-2	2-2		2-2	1-1	1-3	1-3	2-2	2-2
1991	1-1	3-1		2-2	3-1	4-0	1-3	0-2	3-1
1992	0-2	2-2		1-3	4-0	2-2	3-1	3-1	3-1
1993	1-1	1-3		2-2	2-2	2-0	3-1	2-2	2-2
1994	3-1	1-3		3-1	3-1	2-2	1-3	2-2	1-3
1995	1-3	2-2	3-1	2-2	4-0	3-1	4-0	3-1	4-0
1996	0-4	0-4	3-1	2-2	2-2	1-3	3-1	1-3	1-3
1997	1-3	2-2	2-2	2-2	2-2	2-2	3-1	3-1	2-2
1998	1-3	3-1	1-3	2-2	1-3	1-3	3-1	4-0	1-3
1999	0-4	0-4	2-2	2-2	1-3	1-3	2-2	2-2	0-4
2000	1-3	1-3	2-2	2-2	1-3	2-2	1-3	3-1	1-3
2001	3-1	1-3	0-4	3-1	0-4	0-4	3-1	1-3	2-2
2002	0-4	2-1-1	3-1	1-3	2-2	0-4	3-1	1-3	2-2
2003	1-3	1-3	2-2	3-1	2-2	1-3	3-1	2-2	1-3
2004	1-3	3-1	1-3	1-3	1-3	1-3	1-3	3-1	2-2
2005	1-3	3-1	3-1	1-3	2-2	2-2	0-4	1-3	2-2
2006	0-4	2-2	2-2	2-2	3-1	1-3	1-3	0-4	1-3
2007	3-1	1-3	0-4	3-1	3-1	3-1	4-0	2-2	1-3
Total	**46-77-2**	**53-87-1**	**24-28**	**66-73**	**78-58**	**54-79-1**	**60-75-3**	**69-69**	**55-83-2**

	NYG	Phil	StL	SF	Sea	TB	Wash	TOTALS
1970	3-0	2-1	2-1	4-0			2-1	27-12-1
1971	1-2	1-2	1-2	2-1			1-2	23-15-2
1972	1-2	2-1	1-2	2-1			1-2	19-20-1
1973	1-2	2-1	3-0	1-2			2-1	19-19-2
1974	1-2	2-1	3-1	0-3			2-1	17-23
1975	2-1	0-3	3-0	1-2			1-2	17-23
1976	0-2	0-2	1-1	1-1	1-0		1-1	12-16
1977	0-2	1-1	2-0	0-2		0-1	1-1	9-19
1978	1-1	3-1	2-2	1-3		2-0	2-2	21-31
1979	1-1	2-2	2-2	0-4		2-0	2-2	16-36
1980	1-3	3-1	2-2	2-2	1-3		1-3	19-33
1981	1-1	3-1	1-3	3-1		0-4	2-2	28-24
1982	1-0	2-1	1-2	1-3		2-1		14-15-1
1983	0-4	1-1	1-3	2-2		1-3	4-0	26-26
1984	2-0	3-1	3-1	3-1		1-1		26-26
1985	2-2	1-1	3-1	3-1		0-4	4-0	25-27
1986	3-1	2-2	2-2	4-0		1-1	3-1	26-26
1987	2-1	3-1	1-2	3-1		0-2		22-23-1
1988	1-1	2-2	2-2	2-2		1-3	1-3	22-30
1989	4-0	3-1	3-1	4-0		0-4	2-2	28-24
1990	3-1	1-3	2-2	4-0		0-2	3-1	26-26
1991	3-1	4-0	1-3	3-1		1-3	4-0	33-19
1992	2-2	3-1	2-2	3-1		0-2	2-2	30-22
1993	2-2	2-2	2-2	2-2		1-3	1-3	25-27
1994	3-1	1-3	2-2	3-1		1-1	1-1	27-25
1995	0-4	1-3	1-3	3-1		2-2	0-4	33-27
1996	2-2	2-2	2-2	4-0		2-2	3-1	28-32
1997	1-3	2-1-1	0-4	2-2		3-1	1-3	28-31-1
1998	3-1	0-4	3-1	2-2		2-2	2-2	29-31
1999	2-2	1-3	3-1	1-3		3-1	2-2	22-38
2000	3-1	3-1	3-1	2-2		3-1	2-2	30-30
2001	2-2	3-1	4-0	4-0		2-2	2-2	30-30
2002	2-2	1-3	2-2	2-2	2-2	3-1	3-1	29-34-1
2003	1-3	3-1	4-0	1-3	2-2	1-3	2-2	30-34
2004	1-3	2-2	1-3	0-4	1-3	1-3	0-4	20-44
2005	3-1	3-1	3-1	1-3	3-1	2-2	0-4	30-34
2006	1-3	1-3	2-2	2-2	2-2	2-2	2-2	24-40
2007	3-1	1-3	0-4	1-3	3-1	1-3	2-2	32-32
Total	**65-63**	**74-62-1**	**76-65**	**79-64**	**13-12**	**41-63**	**69-66**	**922-1024-10**

2007 INTERCONFERENCE GAMES
(Home Team in capital letters)

AFC 32, NFC 32

AFC Victories
INDIANAPOLIS 41, New Orleans 10
SAN DIEGO 14, Chicago 3
Houston 34, CAROLINA 21
JACKSONVILLE 13, Atlanta 7
BALTIMORE 26, Arizona 23
KANSAS CITY 13, Minnesota 10
PITTSBURGH 37, San Francisco 16
Tennessee 31, NEW ORLEANS 14
PITTSBURGH 21, Seattle 0
TENNESSEE 20, Atlanta 13
INDIANAPOLIS 33, Tampa Bay 14
Baltimore 9, SAN FRANCISCO 7
BALTIMORE 22, St. Louis 3
New England 48, DALLAS 27
Indianapolis 31, CAROLINA 7
Cleveland 27, ST. LOUIS 20
Jacksonville 24, TAMPA BAY 23
NEW ENGLAND 52, Washington 7
TENNESSEE 20, Carolina 7
CLEVELAND 33, Seattle 30 (OT)
HOUSTON 23, New Orleans 10
Indianapolis 31, ATLANTA 13
NEW ENGLAND 31, Philadelphia 28
Buffalo 17, WASHINGTON 16
CINCINNATI 19, St. Louis 10
HOUSTON 28, Tampa Bay 14
JACKSONVILLE 37, Carolina 6
SAN DIEGO 51, Detroit 14
Pittsburgh 41, ST. LOUIS 24
New England 38, N.Y. GIANTS 35
CLEVELAND 20, San Francisco 7
DENVER 22, Minnesota 19 (OT)

NFC Victories
WASHINGTON 16, Miami 13 (OT)
Detroit 36, OAKLAND 21
Dallas 37, MIAMI 20
CHICAGO 20, Kansas City 10
GREEN BAY 31, San Diego 24
SEATTLE 24, Cincinnati 21
ATLANTA 26, Houston 16
ARIZONA 21, Pittsburgh 14
N.Y. GIANTS 35, N.Y. Jets 24
Dallas 25, BUFFALO 24
Philadelphia 16, N.Y. JETS 9
TAMPA BAY 13, Tennessee 10
N.Y. Giants 13, MIAMI 10 (London)
Green Bay 19, DENVER 13 (OT)
DETROIT 44, Denver 7
Green Bay 33, KANSAS CITY 22
MINNESOTA 35, San Diego 17
NEW ORLEANS 41, Jacksonville 24
Washington 23, N.Y. JETS 20 (OT)
Chicago 17, OAKLAND 6
Arizona 35, CINCINNATI 27
MINNESOTA 29, Oakland 22
PHILADELPHIA 17, Miami 7
DALLAS 34, N.Y. Jets 3
CHICAGO 37, Denver 34 (OT)
ARIZONA 27, Cleveland 21
GREEN BAY 38, Oakland 7
SAN FRANCISCO 20, Cincinnati 13
N.Y. Giants 38, BUFFALO 21
DETROIT 25, Kansas City 20
SEATTLE 27, Baltimore 6
PHILADELPHIA 17, Buffalo 9

REGULAR SEASON INTERCONFERENCE RECORDS, 1970-2007

AMERICAN FOOTBALL CONFERENCE

East	W	L	T	Pct.
Miami	90	47	0	.657
Buffalo	67	66	1	.504
New England	66	68	0	.493
New York Jets	57	77	0	.425
North	**W**	**L**	**T**	**Pct.**
Pittsburgh	82	53	1	.607
Baltimore	25	20	1	.554
Cincinnati	71	65	0	.522
Cleveland	60	66	0	.476
South	**W**	**L**	**T**	**Pct.**
Jacksonville	30	21	0	.588
Indianapolis	61	65	1	.484
Tennessee	68	72	1	.486
Houston	9	15	0	.375
West	**W**	**L**	**T**	**Pct.**
Oakland	86	55	1	.610
Denver	78	62	2	.556
Kansas City	67	57	2	.540
San Diego	63	68	0	.481

NATIONAL FOOTBALL CONFERENCE

East	W	L	T	Pct.
Dallas	78	58	0	.574
Philadelphia	74	62	1	.544
Washington	69	66	0	.511
New York Giants	65	63	0	.508
North	**W**	**L**	**T**	**Pct.**
Minnesota	69	69	0	.500
Chicago	66	73	0	.475
Green Bay	60	75	3	.446
Detroit	54	79	1	.407
South	**W**	**L**	**T**	**Pct.**
Carolina	24	28	0	.462
New Orleans	55	83	2	.399
Tampa Bay*	41	64	0	.390
Atlanta	53	87	1	.379
West	**W**	**L**	**T**	**Pct.**
San Francisco	79	64	0	.552
St. Louis	76	65	0	.539
Seattle* #	57	56	0	.504
Arizona	46	77	2	.375

* Records include one game played between Seattle and Tampa Bay, won by the Seahawks 13-10, in their inaugural season (1976) when Seattle competed in the NFC and Tampa Bay in the AFC.

\# Seattle was a member of the AFC from 1977-2001.
From 1970-71, tie games were not included in winning percentage.

INTERCONFERENCE VICTORIES, 1970-2007

	REGULAR SEASON				PRESEASON		
	AFC	NFC	Tie		AFC	NFC	Tie
1970	12	27	1	1970	21	28	1
1971	15	23	2	1971	28	28	3
1972	20	19	1	1972	27	25	4
1973	19	19	2	1973	23	35	2
1974	23	17	0	1974	35	25	0
1975	23	17	0	1975	30	26	1
1976	16	12	0	1976	30	31	0
1977	19	9	0	1977	38	25	0
1978	31	21	0	1978	20	19	0
1979	36	16	0	1979	25	18	0
1980	33	19	0	1980	22	20	1
1981	24	28	0	1981	18	19	0
1982	15	14	1	1982	25	16	0
1983	26	26	0	1983	15	24	0
1984	26	26	0	1984	16	19	0
1985	27	25	0	1985	10	22	1
1986	26	26	0	1986	22	17	0
1987	23	22	1	1987	22	22	0
1988	30	22	0	1988	23	16	1
1989	24	28	0	1989	16	27	0
1990	26	26	0	1990	15	29	0
1991	19	33	0	1991	19	27	0
1992	22	30	0	1992	30	22	0
1993	27	25	0	1993	17	22	0
1994	25	27	0	1994	22	16	0
1995	27	33	0	1995	19	26	0
1996	32	28	0	1996	27	19	0
1997	31	28	1	1997	26	17	0
1998	31	29	0	1998	34	16	0
1999	38	22	0	1999	22	25	0
2000	30	30	0	2000	34	17	0
2001	30	30	0	2001	28	23	0
2002	34	29	1	2002	25	24	0
2003	34	30	0	2003	25	21	0
2004	44	20	0	2004	21	18	0
2005	34	30	0	2005	21	29	0
2006	40	24	0	2006	27	24	0
2007	32	32	0	2007	27	24	0
Total	1,024	922	10	Total	905	861	14

WALTER PAYTON NFL MAN OF THE YEAR

The Walter Payton NFL Man of the Year Award is the only NFL award that recognizes a player for his community service activities as well as his excellence on the field. Renamed in 1999 for the legendary Chicago Bears Pro Football Hall of Fame running back, the Walter Payton NFL Man of the Year Award has been given annually since 1970.

YEAR	PLAYER	POS.	TEAM
1970	Johnny Unitas	QB	Baltimore Colts
1971	John Hadl	QB	San Diego Chargers
1972	Willie Lanier	LB	Kansas City Chiefs
1973	Len Dawson	QB	Kansas City Chiefs
1974	George Blanda	QB	Oakland Raiders
1975	Ken Anderson	QB	Cincinnati Bengals
1976	Franco Harris	RB	Pittsburgh Steelers
1977	Walter Payton	RB	Chicago Bears
1978	Roger Staubach	QB	Dallas Cowboys
1979	Joe Greene	DT	Pittsburgh Steelers
1980	Harold Carmichael	WR	Philadelphia Eagles
1981	Lynn Swann	WR	Pittsburgh Steelers
1982	Joe Theismann	QB	Washington Redskins
1983	Rolf Benirschke	K	San Diego Chargers
1984	Marty Lyons	T	New York Jets
1985	Dwight Stephenson	C	Miami Dolphins
1986	Reggie Williams	LB	Cincinnati Bengals
1987	Dave Duerson	S	Chicago Bears
1988	Steve Largent	WR	Seattle Seahawks
1989	Warren Moon	QB	Houston Oilers
1990	Mike Singletary	LB	Chicago Bears
1991	Anthony Muñoz	T	Cincinnati Bengals
1992	John Elway	QB	Denver Broncos
1993	Derrick Thomas	LB	Kansas City Chiefs
1994	Junior Seau	LB	San Diego Chargers
1995	Boomer Esiason	QB	New York Jets
1996	Darrell Green	CB	Washington Redskins
1997	Troy Aikman	QB	Dallas Cowboys
1998	Dan Marino	QB	Miami Dolphins
1999	Cris Carter	WR	Minnesota Vikings
2000*	Derrick Brooks	LB	Tampa Bay Buccaneers
	Jim Flanigan	DT	Chicago Bears
2001	Jerome Bettis	RB	Pittsburgh Steelers
2002	Troy Vincent	CB	Philadelphia Eagles
2003	Will Shields	G	Kansas City Chiefs
2004	Warrick Dunn	RB	Atlanta Falcons
2005	Peyton Manning	QB	Indianapolis Colts
2006*	Drew Brees	QB	New Orleans Saints
	LaDainian Tomlinson	RB	San Diego Chargers
2007	Jason Taylor	DE	Miami Dolphins

* The award was shared in 2000 and 2006.

NUMBER-ONE DRAFT CHOICES

Season	Date	Team	Player	Position	College
2008	April 26-27	Miami	Jake Long	T	Michigan
2007	April 28-29	Oakland	JaMarcus Russell	QB	Louisiana State
2006	April 29-30	Houston	Mario Williams	DE	North Carolina State
2005	April 23-24	San Francisco	Alex Smith	QB	Utah
2004	April 24-25	San Diego	Eli Manning	QB	Mississippi
2003	April 26-27	Cincinnati	Carson Palmer	QB	Southern California
2002	April 20-21	Houston	David Carr	QB	Fresno State
2001	April 21-22	Atlanta	Michael Vick	QB	Virginia Tech
2000	April 15-16	Cleveland	Courtney Brown	DE	Penn State
1999	April 17-18	Cleveland	Tim Couch	QB	Kentucky
1998	April 18-19	Indianapolis	Peyton Manning	QB	Tennessee
1997	April 19-20	St. Louis	Orlando Pace	T	Ohio State
1996	April 20-21	New York Jets	Keyshawn Johnson	WR	Southern California
1995	April 22-23	Cincinnati	Ki-Jana Carter	RB	Penn State
1994	April 24-25	Cincinnati	Dan Wilkinson	DT	Ohio State
1993	April 25-26	New England	Drew Bledsoe	QB	Washington State
1992	April 26-27	Indianapolis	Steve Emtman	DT	Washington
1991	April 21-22	Dallas	Russell Maryland	DT	Miami
1990	April 22-23	Indianapolis	Jeff George	QB	Illinois
1989	April 23-24	Dallas	Troy Aikman	QB	UCLA
1988	April 24-25	Atlanta	Aundray Bruce	LB	Auburn
1987	April 28-29	Tampa Bay	Vinny Testaverde	QB	Miami
1986	April 29-30	Tampa Bay	Bo Jackson	RB	Auburn
1985	April 30-May 1	Buffalo	Bruce Smith	DE	Virginia Tech
1984	May 1-2	New England	Irving Fryar	WR	Nebraska
1983	April 26-27	Baltimore	John Elway	QB	Stanford
1982	April 27-28	New England	Kenneth Sims	DT	Texas
1981	April 28-29	New Orleans	George Rogers	RB	South Carolina
1980	April 29-30	Detroit	Billy Sims	RB	Oklahoma
1979	May 3-4	Buffalo	Tom Cousineau	LB	Ohio State
1978	May 2-3	Houston	Earl Campbell	RB	Texas
1977	May 3-4	Tampa Bay	Ricky Bell	RB	Southern California
1976	April 8-9	Tampa Bay	Lee Roy Selmon	DE	Oklahoma
1975	January 28-29	Atlanta	Steve Bartkowski	QB	California
1974	January 29-30	Dallas	Ed Jones	DE	Tennessee State
1973	January 30-31	Houston	John Matuszak	DE	Tampa
1972	February 1-2	Buffalo	Walt Patulski	DE	Notre Dame
1971	January 28-29	New England	Jim Plunkett	QB	Stanford
1970	January 27-28	Pittsburgh	Terry Bradshaw	QB	Louisiana Tech
1969	January 28-29	Buffalo (AFL)	O.J. Simpson	RB	Southern California
1968	January 30-31	Minnesota	Ron Yary	T	Southern California
1967	March 14	Baltimore	Bubba Smith	DT	Michigan State
1966	November 27, 1965	Atlanta	Tommy Nobis	LB	Texas
	November 28, 1965	Miami (AFL)	Jim Grabowski	RB	Illinois
1965	November 28, 1964	New York Giants	Tucker Frederickson	RB	Auburn
	November 28, 1964	Houston (AFL)	Lawrence Elkins	E	Baylor
1964	December 2, 1963	San Francisco	Dave Parks	E	Texas Tech
	November 30, 1963	Boston (AFL)	Jack Concannon	QB	Boston College
1963	December 3, 1962	Los Angeles	Terry Baker	QB	Oregon State
	December 1, 1962	Kansas City (AFL)	Buck Buchanan	DT	Grambling
1962	December 4, 1961	Washington	Ernie Davis	RB	Syracuse
	December 2, 1961	Oakland (AFL)	Roman Gabriel	QB	North Carolina State
1961	December 27-28, 1960	Minnesota	Tommy Mason	RB	Tulane
	November 23, 1960	Buffalo (AFL)	Ken Rice	G	Auburn
1960	Secret Draft	Los Angeles	Billy Cannon	RB	Louisiana State
	November 22, December 2, 1959	(AFL had no formal first pick)			
1959	December 2, 1958	Green Bay	Randy Duncan	QB	Iowa
1958	December 2, 1957	Chicago Cardinals	King Hill	QB	Rice
1957	November 27, 1956	Green Bay	Paul Hornung	HB	Notre Dame
1956	November 29, 1955	Pittsburgh	Gary Glick	DB	Colorado A&M
1955	January 27-28	Baltimore	George Shaw	QB	Oregon

Season	Date	Team	Player	Position	College
1954	January 28	Cleveland	Bobby Garrett	QB	Stanford
1953	January 22	San Francisco	Harry Babcock	E	Georgia
1952	January 17	Los Angeles	Bill Wade	QB	Vanderbilt
1951	January 18-19	New York Giants	Kyle Rote	HB	Southern Methodist
1950	January 21-22	Detroit	Leon Hart	E	Notre Dame
1949	December 21, 1948	Philadelphia	Chuck Bednarik	C	Pennsylvania
1948	December 19, 1947	Washington	Harry Gilmer	QB	Alabama
1947	December 16, 1946	Chicago Bears	Bob Fenimore	HB	Oklahoma A&M
1946	January 14	Boston	Frank Dancewicz	QB	Notre Dame
1945	April 6	Chicago Cardinals	Charley Trippi	HB	Georgia
1944	April 19	Boston	Angelo Bertelli	QB	Notre Dame
1943	April 8	Detroit	Frank Sinkwich	HB	Georgia
1942	December 22, 1941	Pittsburgh	Bill Dudley	HB	Virginia
1941	December 10, 1940	Chicago Bears	Tom Harmon	HB	Michigan
1940	December 9, 1939	Chicago Cardinals	George Cafego	HB	Tennessee
1939	December 8, 1938	Chicago Cardinals	Ki Aldrich	C	Texas Christian
1938	December 12, 1937	Cleveland	Corbett Davis	FB	Indiana
1937	December 12, 1936	Philadelphia	Sam Francis	FB	Nebraska
1936	February 8	Philadelphia	Jay Berwanger	HB	Chicago

Note: From 1947 through 1958, the first selection in the draft was a Bonus pick, awarded to the winner of a random draw. That club, in turn, forfeited its last-round draft choice. The winner of the Bonus choice was eliminated from future draws. The system was abolished after 1958, by which time all clubs had received a Bonus choice.

NUMBER-ONE DRAFT CHOICES BY POSITION

Quarterbacks:	27
Running Backs:	23
Defensive Linemen:	13
Offensive Linemen:	6
Wide Receivers:	6
Linebackers:	3
Defensive Backs:	1

FIRST-ROUND SELECTIONS

If club had no first-round selection, first player drafted is listed with round in parentheses.

ARIZONA CARDINALS
Year Player, College, Position
1936 Jim Lawrence, Texas Christian, B
1937 Ray Buivid, Marquette, B
1938 Jack Robbins, Arkansas, B
1939 Charles (Ki) Aldrich, TCU, C
1940 George Cafego, Tennessee, B
1941 John Kimbrough, Texas A&M, B
1942 Steve Lach, Duke, B
1943 Glenn Dobbs, Tulsa, B
1944 Pat Harder, Wisconsin, B
1945 Charley Trippi, Georgia, B
1946 Dub Jones, Louisiana State, B
1947 DeWitt (Tex) Coulter, Army, T
1948 Jim Spavital, Oklahoma A&M, B
1949 Bill Fischer, Notre Dame, G
1950 Jack Jennings, Ohio State, T (2)
1951 Jerry Groom, Notre Dame, C
1952 Ollie Matson, San Francisco, B
1953 Johnny Olszewski, California, B
1954 Lamar McHan, Arkansas, B
1955 Max Boydston, Oklahoma, E
1956 Joe Childress, Auburn, B
1957 Jerry Tubbs, Oklahoma, C
1958 King Hill, Rice, B
      John David Crow, Texas A&M, B
1959 Bill Stacy, Mississippi State, B
1960 George Izo, Notre Dame, QB
1961 Ken Rice, Auburn, T
1962 Fate Echols, Northwestern, DT
      Irv Goode, Kentucky, C
1963 Jerry Stovall, Louisiana State, S
      Don Brumm, Purdue, DE
1964 Ken Kortas, Louisville, DT
1965 Joe Namath, Alabama, QB
1966 Carl McAdams, Oklahoma, LB
1967 Dave Williams, Washington, WR
1968 MacArthur Lane, Utah State, RB
1969 Roger Wehrli, Missouri, DB
1970 Larry Stegent, Texas A&M, RB
1971 Norm Thompson, Utah, DB
1972 Bobby Moore, Oregon, RB-WR
1973 Dave Butz, Purdue, DT
1974 J.V. Cain, Colorado, TE
1975 Tim Gray, Texas A&M, DB
1976 Mike Dawson, Arizona, DT
1977 Steve Pisarkiewicz, Missouri, QB
1978 Steve Little, Arkansas, K
      Ken Greene, Washington State, DB
1979 Ottis Anderson, Miami, RB
1980 Curtis Greer, Michigan, DE
1981 E.J. Junior, Alabama, LB
1982 Luis Sharpe, UCLA, T
1983 Leonard Smith, McNeese St., DB
1984 Clyde Duncan, Tennessee, WR
1985 Freddie Joe Nunn, Mississippi, LB
1986 Anthony Bell, Michigan State, LB
1987 Kelly Stouffer, Colorado State, QB
1988 Ken Harvey, California, LB
1989 Eric Hill, Louisiana State, LB
      Joe Wolf, Boston College, G
1990 Anthony Thompson, Indiana, RB (2)
1991 Eric Swann, No College, DE
1992 Tony Sacca, Penn State, QB (2)

1993 Garrison Hearst, Georgia, RB
      Ernest Dye, South Carolina, T
1994 Jamir Miller, UCLA, LB
1995 Frank Sanders, Auburn, WR (2)
1996 Simeon Rice, Illinois, DE
1997 Tom Knight, Iowa, DB
1998 Andre Wadsworth, Florida St., DE
1999 David Boston, Ohio State, WR
      L.J. Shelton, Eastern Michigan, T
2000 Thomas Jones, Virginia, RB
2001 Leonard Davis, Texas, T
2002 Wendell Bryant, Wisconsin, DT
2003 Bryant Johnson, Penn State, WR
      Calvin Pace, Wake Forest, DE
2004 Larry Fitzgerald, Pittsburgh, WR
2005 Antrel Rolle, Miami, DB
2006 Matt Leinart, So. California, QB
2007 Levi Brown, Penn State, T
2008 Dominique Rodgers-Cromartie, Tenn. St., DB

ATLANTA FALCONS
Year Player, College, Position
1966 Tommy Nobis, Texas, LB
      Randy Johnson, Texas A&I, QB
1967 Leo Carroll, San Diego St., DE (2)
1968 Claude Humphrey, Tennessee St., DE
1969 George Kunz, Notre Dame, T
1970 John Small, Citadel, LB
1971 Joe Profit, Northeast Louisiana, RB
1972 Clarence Ellis, Notre Dame, DB
1973 Greg Marx, Notre Dame, DT (2)
1974 Gerald Tinker, Kent State, WR (2)
1975 Steve Bartkowski, California, QB
1976 Bubba Bean, Texas A&M, RB
1977 Warren Bryant, Kentucky, T
      Wilson Faumuina, San Jose St., DT
1978 Mike Kenn, Michigan, T
1979 Don Smith, Miami, DE
1980 Junior Miller, Nebraska, TE
1981 Bobby Butler, Florida State, DB
1982 Gerald Riggs, Arizona State, RB
1983 Mike Pitts, Alabama, DE
1984 Rick Bryan, Oklahoma, DT
1985 Bill Fralic, Pittsburgh, T
1986 Tony Casillas, Oklahoma, NT
      Tim Green, Syracuse, LB
1987 Chris Miller, Oregon, QB
1988 Aundray Bruce, Auburn, LB
1989 Deion Sanders, Florida State, DB
      Shawn Collins, No. Arizona, WR
1990 Steve Broussard, Washington St., RB
1991 Bruce Pickens, Nebraska, DB
      Mike Pritchard, Colorado, WR
1992 Bob Whitfield, Stanford, T
      Tony Smith, So. Mississippi, RB
1993 Lincoln Kennedy, Washington, T
1994 Bert Emanuel, Rice, WR (2)
1995 Devin Bush, Florida State, DB
1996 Shannon Brown, Alabama, DT (3)
1997 Michael Booker, Nebraska, DB
1998 Keith Brooking, Georgia Tech, LB
1999 Patrick Kerney, Virginia, DE
2000 Travis Claridge, So. California, T (2)
2001 Michael Vick, Virginia Tech, QB
2002 T.J. Duckett, Michigan State, RB
2003 Bryan Scott, Penn State, DB (2)
2004 DeAngelo Hall, Virginia Tech, DB
      Michael Jenkins, Ohio State, WR
2005 Roddy White, Ala.-Birmingham, WR
2006 Jimmy Williams, Virginia Tech, DB (2)

2007 Jamaal Anderson, Arkansas, DE
2008 Matt Ryan, Boston College, QB
      Sam Baker, So. California, T

BALTIMORE RAVENS
Year Player, College, Position
1996 Jonathan Ogden, UCLA, T
      Ray Lewis, Miami, LB
1997 Peter Boulware, Florida State, DE
1998 Duane Starks, Miami, DB
1999 Chris McAlister, Arizona, DB
2000 Jamal Lewis, Tennessee, RB
      Travis Taylor, Florida, WR
2001 Todd Heap, Arizona State, TE
2002 Ed Reed, Miami, DB
2003 Terrell Suggs, Arizona State, DE
      Kyle Boller, California, QB
2004 Dwan Edwards, Oregon St., DT (2)
2005 Mark Clayton, Oklahoma, WR
2006 Haloti Ngata, Oregon, DT
2007 Ben Grubbs, Auburn, G
2008 Joe Flacco, Delaware, QB

BUFFALO BILLS
Year Player, College, Position
1960 Richie Lucas, Penn State, QB
1961 Ken Rice, Auburn, T
1962 Ernie Davis, Syracuse, RB
1963 Dave Behrman, Michigan State, C
1964 Carl Eller, Minnesota, DE
1965 Jim Davidson, Ohio State, T
1966 Mike Dennis, Mississippi, RB
1967 John Pitts, Arizona State, S
1968 Haven Moses, San Diego St., WR
1969 O.J. Simpson, So. California, RB
1970 Al Cowlings, So. California, DE
1971 J.D. Hill, Arizona State, WR
1972 Walt Patulski, Notre Dame, DE
1973 Paul Seymour, Michigan, TE
      Joe DeLamielleure, Michigan St., G
1974 Reuben Gant, Oklahoma State, TE
1975 Tom Ruud, Nebraska, LB
1976 Mario Clark, Oregon, DB
1977 Phil Dokes, Oklahoma State, DT
1978 Terry Miller, Oklahoma State, RB
1979 Tom Cousineau, Ohio State, LB
      Jerry Butler, Clemson, WR
1980 Jim Ritcher, North Carolina St., C
1981 Booker Moore, Penn State, RB
1982 Perry Tuttle, Clemson, WR
1983 Tony Hunter, Notre Dame, TE
      Jim Kelly, Miami, QB
1984 Greg Bell, Notre Dame, RB
1985 Bruce Smith, Virginia Tech, DE
      Derrick Burroughs, Memphis St., DB
1986 Ronnie Harmon, Iowa, RB
      Will Wolford, Vanderbilt, T
1987 Shane Conlan, Penn State, LB
1988 Thurman Thomas, Oklahoma St., RB (2)
1989 Don Beebe, Chadron, Neb., WR (3)
1990 James Williams, Fresno State, DB
1991 Henry Jones, Illinois, DB
1992 John Fina, Arizona, T
1993 Thomas Smith, North Carolina, DB
1994 Jeff Burris, Notre Dame, DB
1995 Ruben Brown, Pittsburgh, G
1996 Eric Moulds, Mississippi St., WR
1997 Antowain Smith, Houston, RB
1998 Sam Cowart, Florida State, LB (2)
1999 Antoine Winfield, Ohio State, DB

2000 Erik Flowers, Arizona State, DE	1964 Dick Evey, Tennessee, DT	1978 Ross Browner, Notre Dame, DT
2001 Nate Clements, Ohio State, DB	1965 Dick Butkus, Illinois, LB	Blair Bush, Washington, C
2002 Mike Williams, Texas, T	Gale Sayers, Kansas, RB	1979 Jack Thompson, Washington St., QB
2003 Willis McGahee, Miami, RB	Steve DeLong, Tennessee, T	Charles Alexander, Louisiana St., RB
2004 Lee Evans, Wisconsin, WR	1966 George Rice, Louisiana State, DT	1980 Anthony Muñoz, So. California, T
J.P. Losman, Tulane, QB	1967 Loyd Phillips, Arkansas, DE	1981 David Verser, Kansas, WR
2005 Roscoe Parrish, Miami, WR (2)	1968 Mike Hull, Southern California, RB	1982 Glen Collins, Mississippi State, DE
2006 Donte' Whitner, Ohio State, DB	1969 Rufus Mayes, Ohio State, T	1983 Dave Rimington, Nebraska, C
John McCargo, North Carolina St., DT	1970 George Farmer, UCLA, WR (3)	1984 Ricky Hunley, Arizona, LB
2007 Marshawn Lynch, California, RB	1971 Joe Moore, Missouri, RB	Pete Koch, Maryland, DE
2008 Leodis McKelvin, Troy, DB	1972 Lionel Antoine, Southern Illinois, T	Brian Blados, North Carolina, T
	Craig Clemons, Iowa, DB	1985 Eddie Brown, Miami, WR
CAROLINA PANTHERS	1973 Wally Chambers, Eastern Kentucky, DE	Emanuel King, Alabama, LB
Year Player, College, Position	1974 Waymond Bryant, Tennessee St., LB	1986 Joe Kelly, Washington, LB
1995 Kerry Collins, Penn State, QB	Dave Gallagher, Michigan, DT	Tim McGee, Tennessee, WR
Tyrone Poole, Ft. Valley State, DB	1975 Walter Payton, Jackson State, RB	1987 Jason Buck, Brigham Young, DE
Blake Brockermeyer, Texas, T	1976 Dennis Lick, Wisconsin, T	1988 Rickey Dixon, Oklahoma, DB
1996 Tim Biakabutuka, Michigan, RB	1977 Ted Albrecht, California, T	1989 Eric Ball, UCLA, RB (2)
1997 Rae Carruth, Colorado, WR	1978 Brad Shearer, Texas, DT (3)	1990 James Francis, Baylor, LB
1998 Jason Peter, Nebraska, DT	1979 Dan Hampton, Arkansas, DT	1991 Alfred Williams, Colorado, LB
1999 Chris Terry, Georgia, T (2)	Al Harris, Arizona State, DE	1992 David Klingler, Houston, QB
2000 Rashard Anderson, Jackson St., DB	1980 Otis Wilson, Louisville, LB	Darryl Williams, Miami, DB
2001 Dan Morgan, Miami, LB	1981 Keith Van Horne, So. California, T	1993 John Copeland, Alabama, DE
2002 Julius Peppers, North Carolina, DE	1982 Jim McMahon, Brigham Young, QB	1994 Dan Wilkinson, Ohio State, DT
2003 Jordan Gross, Utah, T	1983 Jim Covert, Pittsburgh, T	1995 Ki-Jana Carter, Penn State, RB
2004 Chris Gamble, Ohio State, DB	Willie Gault, Tennessee, WR	1996 Willie Anderson, Auburn, T
2005 Thomas Davis, Georgia, DB	1984 Wilber Marshall, Florida, LB	1997 Reinard Wilson, Florida State, LB
2006 DeAngelo Williams, Memphis, RB	1985 William Perry, Clemson, DT	1998 Takeo Spikes, Auburn, LB
2007 Jon Beason, Miami, LB	1986 Neal Anderson, Florida, RB	Brian Simmons, North Carolina, LB
2008 Jonathan Stewart, Oregon, RB	1987 Jim Harbaugh, Michigan, QB	1999 Akili Smith, Oregon, QB
Jeff Otah, Pittsburgh, T	1988 Brad Muster, Stanford, RB	2000 Peter Warrick, Florida State, WR
	Wendell Davis, Louisiana St., WR	2001 Justin Smith, Missouri, DE
CHICAGO BEARS	1989 Donnell Woolford, Clemson, DB	2002 Levi Jones, Arizona State, T
Year Player, College, Position	Trace Armstrong, Florida, DE	2003 Carson Palmer, Southern California, QB
1936 Joe Stydahar, West Virginia, T	1990 Mark Carrier, So. California, DB	2004 Chris Perry, Michigan, RB
1937 Les McDonald, Nebraska, E	1991 Stan Thomas, Texas, T	2005 David Pollack, Georgia, LB
1938 Joe Gray, Oregon State, B	1992 Alonzo Spellman, Ohio State, DE	2006 Johnathan Joseph, South Carolina, DB
1939 Sid Luckman, Columbia, QB	1993 Curtis Conway, So. California, WR	2007 Leon Hall, Michigan, DB
Bill Osmanski, Holy Cross, B	1994 John Thierry, Alcorn State, DE	2008 Keith Rivers, So. California, LB
1940 Clyde (Bulldog) Turner, Hardin-Simmons, C	1995 Rashaan Salaam, Colorado, RB	
1941 Tom Harmon, Michigan, B	1996 Walt Harris, Mississippi State, DB	**CLEVELAND BROWNS**
Norm Standlee, Stanford, B	1997 John Allred, So. California, TE (2)	**Year Player, College, Position**
Don Scott, Ohio State, B	1998 Curtis Enis, Penn State, RB	1950 Ken Carpenter, Oregon State, B
1942 Frankie Albert, Stanford, B	1999 Cade McNown, UCLA, QB	1951 Ken Konz, Louisiana State, B
1943 Bob Steber, Missouri, B	2000 Brian Urlacher, New Mexico, LB	1952 Bert Rechichar, Tennessee, DB
1944 Ray Evans, Kansas, B	2001 David Terrell, Michigan, WR	Harry Agganis, Boston U., QB
1945 Don Lund, Michigan, B	2002 Marc Colombo, Boston College, T	1953 Doug Atkins, Tennessee, DE
1946 Johnny Lujack, Notre Dame, QB	2003 Michael Haynes, Penn State, DE	1954 Bobby Garrett, Stanford, QB
1947 Bob Fenimore, Oklahoma State, B	Rex Grossman, Florida, QB	John Bauer, Illinois, G
Don Kindt, Wisconsin, B	2004 Tommie Harris, Oklahoma, DT	1955 Kurt Burris, Oklahoma, C
1948 Bobby Layne, Texas, QB	2005 Cedric Benson, Texas, RB	1956 Preston Carpenter, Arkansas, B
Max Bumgardner, Texas, E	2006 Danieal Manning, Abilene Christian, DB (2)	1957 Jim Brown, Syracuse, RB
1949 Dick Harris, Texas, C	2007 Greg Olsen, Miami, TE	1958 Jim Shofner, Texas Christian, DB
1950 Chuck Hunsinger, Florida, B	2008 Chris Williams, Vanderbilt, T	1959 Rich Kreitling, Illinois, DE
Fred Morrison, Ohio State, B		1960 Jim Houston, Ohio State, DE
1951 Bob Williams, Notre Dame, B	**CINCINNATI BENGALS**	1961 Bobby Crespino, Mississippi, TE
Billy Stone, Bradley, B	**Year Player, College, Position**	1962 Gary Collins, Maryland, WR
Gene Schroeder, Virginia, E	1968 Bob Johnson, Tennessee, C	Leroy Jackson, Western Illinois, RB
1952 Jim Dooley, Miami, B	1969 Greg Cook, Cincinnati, QB	1963 Tom Hutchinson, Kentucky, WR
1953 Billy Anderson, Compton (Calif.) J.C., B	1970 Mike Reid, Penn State, DT	1964 Paul Warfield, Ohio State, WR
1954 Stan Wallace, Illinois, B	1971 Vernon Holland, Tennessee St., T	1965 James Garcia, Purdue, T (2)
1955 Ron Drzewiecki, Marquette, B	1972 Sherman White, California, DE	1966 Milt Morin, Massachusetts, TE
1956 Menan (Tex) Schriewer, Texas, E	1973 Isaac Curtis, San Diego State, WR	1967 Bob Matheson, Duke, LB
1957 Earl Leggett, Louisiana State, T	1974 Bill Kollar, Montana State, DT	1968 Marvin Upshaw, Trinity, Tex., DT-DE
1958 Chuck Howley, West Virginia, G	1975 Glenn Cameron, Florida, LB	1969 Ron Johnson, Michigan, RB
1959 Don Clark, Ohio State, B	1976 Billy Brooks, Oklahoma, WR	1970 Mike Phipps, Purdue, QB
1960 Roger Davis, Syracuse, G	Archie Griffin, Ohio State, RB	Bob McKay, Texas, T
1961 Mike Ditka, Pittsburgh, E	1977 Eddie Edwards, Miami, DT	1971 Clarence Scott, Kansas State, CB
1962 Ronnie Bull, Baylor, RB	Wilson Whitley, Houston, DT	1972 Thom Darden, Michigan, DB
1963 Dave Behrman, Michigan State, C	Mike Cobb, Michigan State, TE	

1973 Steve Holden, Arizona State, WR
Pete Adams, Southern California, T
1974 Billy Corbett, Johnson C. Smith, T (2)
1975 Mack Mitchell, Houston, DE
1976 Mike Pruitt, Purdue, RB
1977 Robert Jackson, Texas A&M, LB
1978 Clay Matthews, So. California, LB
Ozzie Newsome, Alabama, TE
1979 Willis Adams, Houston, WR
1980 Charles White, So. California, RB
1981 Hanford Dixon, So. Mississippi, DB
1982 Chip Banks, So. California, LB
1983 Ron Brown, Arizona State, WR (2)
1984 Don Rogers, UCLA, DB
1985 Greg Allen, Florida State, RB (2)
1986 Webster Slaughter, San Diego St., WR (2)
1987 Mike Junkin, Duke, LB
1988 Clifford Charlton, Florida, LB
1989 Eric Metcalf, Texas, RB
1990 Leroy Hoard, Michigan, RB (2)
1991 Eric Turner, UCLA, DB
1992 Tommy Vardell, Stanford, RB
1993 Steve Everitt, Michigan, C
1994 Antonio Langham, Alabama, DB
Derrick Alexander, Michigan, WR
1995 Craig Powell, Ohio State, LB
1999 Tim Couch, Kentucky, QB
2000 Courtney Brown, Penn State, DE
2001 Gerard Warren, Florida, DT
2002 William Green, Boston College, RB
2003 Jeff Faine, Norte Dame, C
2004 Kellen Winslow, Miami, TE
2005 Braylon Edwards, Michigan, WR
2006 Kamerion Wimbley, Florida St., DE
2007 Joe Thomas, Wisconsin, T
Brady Quinn, Notre Dame, QB
2008 Beau Bell, Nevada-Las Vgas, LB (4)

DALLAS COWBOYS
Year Player, College, Position
1960 None
1961 Bob Lilly, Texas Christian, DT
1962 Sonny Gibbs, TCU, QB (2)
1963 Lee Roy Jordan, Alabama, LB
1964 Scott Appleton, Texas, DT
1965 Craig Morton, California, QB
1966 John Niland, Iowa, G
1967 Phil Clark, Northwestern, DB (3)
1968 Dennis Homan, Alabama, WR
1969 Calvin Hill, Yale, RB
1970 Duane Thomas, West Texas St., RB
1971 Tody Smith, So. California, DE
1972 Bill Thomas, Boston College, RB
1973 Billy Joe DuPree, Michigan St., TE
1974 Ed (Too Tall) Jones, Tennessee St., DE
Charley Young, North Carolina St., RB
1975 Randy White, Maryland, DE
Thomas Henderson, Langston, LB
1976 Aaron Kyle, Wyoming, DB
1977 Tony Dorsett, Pittsburgh, RB
1978 Larry Bethea, Michigan State, DE
1979 Robert Shaw, Tennessee, C
1980 Bill Roe, Colorado, LB (3)
1981 Howard Richards, Missouri, T
1982 Rod Hill, Kentucky State, DB
1983 Jim Jeffcoat, Arizona State, DE
1984 Billy Cannon, Jr., Texas A&M, LB
1985 Kevin Brooks, Michigan, DE
1986 Mike Sherrard, UCLA, WR
1987 Danny Noonan, Nebraska, DT

1988 Michael Irvin, Miami, WR
1989 Troy Aikman, UCLA, QB
1990 Emmitt Smith, Florida, RB
1991 Russell Maryland, Miami, DT
Alvin Harper, Tennessee, WR
Kelvin Pritchett, Mississippi, DT
1992 Kevin Smith, Texas A&M, LB
Robert Jones, East Carolina, LB
1993 Kevin Williams, Miami, WR (2)
1994 Shante Carver, Arizona State, DE
1995 Sherman Williams, Alabama, RB (2)
1996 Kavika Pittman, McNeese St., DE (2)
1997 David LaFleur, Louisiana State, TE
1998 Greg Ellis, North Carolina, DE
1999 Ebenezer Ekuban, North Carolina, DE
2000 Dwayne Goodrich, Tennessee, DB (2)
2001 Quincy Carter, Georgia, QB (2)
2002 Roy Williams, Oklahoma, DB
2003 Terence Newman, Kansas State, DB
2004 Julius Jones, Notre Dame, RB (2)
2005 DeMarcus Ware, Troy, DE
Marcus Spears, Louisiana St., DE
2006 Bobby Carpenter, Ohio State, LB
2007 Anthony Spencer, Purdue, LB
2008 Felix Jones, Arkansas, RB
Mike Jenkins, South Florida, DB

DENVER BRONCOS
Year Player, College, Position
1960 Roger LeClerc, Trinity, Conn., C
1961 Bob Gaiters, New Mexico St., RB
1962 Merlin Olsen, Utah State, DT
1963 Kermit Alexander, UCLA, CB
1964 Bob Brown, Nebraska, T
1965 Dick Butkus, Illinois, LB (2)
1966 Jerry Shay, Purdue, DT
1967 Floyd Little, Syracuse, RB
1968 Curley Culp, Arizona State, DE (2)
1969 Grady Cavness, Texas-El Paso, DB (2)
1970 Bob Anderson, Colorado, RB
1971 Marv Montgomery, So. California, T
1972 Riley Odoms, Houston, TE
1973 Otis Armstrong, Purdue, RB
1974 Randy Gradishar, Ohio State, LB
1975 Louis Wright, San Jose State, DB
1976 Tom Glassic, Virginia, G
1977 Steve Schindler, Boston College, G
1978 Don Latimer, Miami, DT
1979 Kelvin Clark, Nebraska, T
1980 Rulon Jones, Utah State, DE (2)
1981 Dennis Smith, So. California, DB
1982 Gerald Willhite, San Jose St., RB
1983 Chris Hinton, Northwestern, G
1984 Andre Townsend, Mississippi, DE (2)
1985 Steve Sewell, Oklahoma, RB
1986 Jim Juriga, Illinois, T (4)
1987 Ricky Nattiel, Florida, WR
1988 Ted Gregory, Syracuse, NT
1989 Steve Atwater, Arkansas, DB
1990 Alton Montgomery, Houston, DB (2)
1991 Mike Croel, Nebraska, LB
1992 Tommy Maddox, UCLA, QB
1993 Dan Williams, Toledo, DE
1994 Allen Aldridge, Houston, LB (2)
1995 Jamie Brown, Florida A&M, T (4)
1996 John Mobley, Kutztown, LB
1997 Trevor Pryce, Clemson, DT
1998 Marcus Nash, Tennessee, WR
1999 Al Wilson, Tennessee, LB
2000 Deltha O'Neal, California, DB

2001 Willie Middlebrooks, Minnesota, DB
2002 Ashley Lelie, Hawaii, WR
2003 George Foster, Georgia, T
2004 D.J. Williams, Miami, LB
2005 Darrent Williams, Oklahoma St., DB (2)
2006 Jay Cutler, Vanderbilt, QB
2007 Jarvis Moss, Florida, DE
2008 Ryan Clady, Boise State, T

DETROIT LIONS
Year Player, College, Position
1936 Sid Wagner, Michigan State, G
1937 Lloyd Cardwell, Nebraska, B
1938 Alex Wojciechowicz, Fordham, C
1939 John Pingel, Michigan State, B
1940 Doyle Nave, Southern California, B
1941 Jim Thomason, Texas A&M, B
1942 Bob Westfall, Michigan, B
1943 Frank Sinkwich, Georgia, B
1944 Otto Graham, Northwestern, B
1945 Frank Szymanski, Notre Dame, C
1946 Bill Dellastatious, Missouri, B
1947 Glenn Davis, Army, B
1948 Y.A. Tittle, Louisiana State, B
1949 John Rauch, Georgia, B
1950 Leon Hart, Notre Dame, E
Joe Watson, Rice, C
1951 Dick Stanfel, San Francisco, G (2)
1952 Yale Lary, Texas A&M, B (3)
1953 Harley Sewell, Texas, G
1954 Dick Chapman, Rice, T
1955 Dave Middleton, Auburn, B
1956 Hopalong Cassady, Ohio State, B
1957 Bill Glass, Baylor, G
1958 Alex Karras, Iowa, T
1959 Nick Pietrosante, Notre Dame, B
1960 John Robinson, Louisiana State, S
1961 Danny LaRose, Missouri, T (2)
1962 John Hadl, Kansas, QB
1963 Daryl Sanders, Ohio State, T
1964 Pete Beathard, So. California, QB
1965 Tom Nowatzke, Indiana, RB
1966 Nick Eddy, Notre Dame, RB (2)
1967 Mel Farr, UCLA, RB
1968 Greg Landry, Massachusetts, QB
Earl McCullouch, So. California, WR
1969 Altie Taylor, Utah State, RB (2)
1970 Steve Owens, Oklahoma, RB
1971 Bob Bell, Cincinnati, DT
1972 Herb Orvis, Colorado, DE
1973 Ernie Price, Texas A&I, DE
1974 Ed O'Neil, Penn State, LB
1975 Lynn Boden, South Dakota St., G
1976 James Hunter, Grambling, DB
Lawrence Gaines, Wyoming, RB
1977 Walt Williams, New Mexico St., DB (2)
1978 Luther Bradley, Notre Dame, DB
1979 Keith Dorney, Penn State, T
1980 Billy Sims, Oklahoma, RB
1981 Mark Nichols, San Jose State, WR
1982 Jimmy Williams, Nebraska, LB
1983 James Jones, Florida, RB
1984 David Lewis, California, TE
1985 Lomas Brown, Florida, T
1986 Chuck Long, Iowa, QB
1987 Reggie Rogers, Washington, DE
1988 Bennie Blades, Miami, DB
1989 Barry Sanders, Oklahoma St., RB
1990 Andre Ware, Houston, QB
1991 Herman Moore, Virginia, WR

1992 Robert Porcher, South Carolina St., DE	1975 Bill Bain, So. California, G (2)	1968 John Williams, Minnesota, G
1993 Ryan McNeil, Miami, DB (2)	1976 Mark Koncar, Colorado, T	1969 Eddie Hinton, Oklahoma, WR
1994 Johnnie Morton, So. California, WR	1977 Mike Butler, Kansas, DE	1970 Norman Bulaich, Texas Christian, RB
1995 Luther Elliss, Utah, DT	Ezra Johnson, Morris Brown, DE	1971 Don McCauley, North Carolina, RB
1996 Reggie Brown, Texas A&M, LB	1978 James Lofton, Stanford, WR	Leonard Dunlap, North Texas St., DB
Jeff Hartings, Penn State, G	John Anderson, Michigan, LB	1972 Tom Drougas, Oregon, T
1997 Bryant Westbrook, Texas, DB	1979 Eddie Lee Ivery, Georgia Tech, RB	1973 Bert Jones, Louisiana State, QB
1998 Terry Fair, Tennessee, DB	1980 Bruce Clark, Penn State, DE	Joe Ehrmann, Syracuse, DT
1999 Chris Claiborne, So. California, LB	George Cumby, Oklahoma, LB	1974 John Dutton, Nebraska, DE
Aaron Gibson, Wisconsin, T	1981 Rich Campbell, California, QB	Roger Carr, Louisiana Tech, WR
2000 Stockar McDougle, Oklahoma, T	1982 Ron Hallstrom, Iowa, G	1975 Ken Huff, North Carolina, G
2001 Jeff Backus, Michigan, T	1983 Tim Lewis, Pittsburgh, DB	1976 Ken Novak, Purdue, DT
2002 Joey Harrington, Oregon, QB	1984 Alphonso Carreker, Florida St., DE	1977 Randy Burke, Kentucky, WR
2003 Charles Rogers, Michigan State, WR	1985 Ken Ruettgers, So. California, T	1978 Reese McCall, Auburn, TE
2004 Roy Williams, Texas, WR	1986 Kenneth Davis, TCU, RB (2)	1979 Barry Krauss, Alabama, LB
Kevin Jones, Virginia Tech, RB	1987 Brent Fullwood, Auburn, RB	1980 Curtis Dickey, Texas A&M, RB
2005 Mike Wiliams, So. California, WR	1988 Sterling Sharpe, South Carolina, WR	Derrick Hatchett, Texas, DB
2006 Ernie Sims, Florida State, LB	1989 Tony Mandarich, Michigan State, T	1981 Randy McMillan, Pittsburgh, RB
2007 Calvin Johnson, Georgia Tech, WR	1990 Tony Bennett, Mississippi, LB	Donnell Thompson, North Carolina, DT
2008 Gosder Cherilus, Boson College, T	Darrell Thompson, Minnesota, RB	1982 Johnie Cooks, Mississippi St., LB
	1991 Vinnie Clark, Ohio State, DB	Art Schlichter, Ohio State, QB
GREEN BAY PACKERS	1992 Terrell Buckley, Florida State, DB	1983 John Elway, Stanford, QB
Year Player, College, Position	1993 Wayne Simmons, Clemson, LB	1984 Leonard Coleman, Vanderbilt, DB
1936 Russ Letlow, San Francisco, G	George Teague, Alabama, DB	Ron Solt, Maryland, G
1937 Eddie Jankowski, Wisconsin, B	1994 Aaron Taylor, Notre Dame, T	1985 Duane Bickett, So. California, LB
1938 Cecil Isbell, Purdue, B	1995 Craig Newsome, Arizona State, DB	1986 Jon Hand, Alabama, DE
1939 Larry Buhler, Minnesota, B	1996 John Michels, Southern California, T	1987 Cornelius Bennett, Alabama, LB
1940 Harold Van Every, Minnesota, B	1997 Ross Verba, Iowa, T	1988 Chris Chandler, Washington, QB (3)
1941 George Paskvan, Wisconsin, B	1998 Vonnie Holliday, North Carolina, DT	1989 Andre Rison, Michigan State, WR
1942 Urban Odson, Minnesota, T	1999 Antuan Edwards, Clemson, DB	1990 Jeff George, Illinois, QB
1943 Dick Wildung, Minnesota, T	2000 Bubba Franks, Miami, TE	1991 Shane Curry, Miami, DE (2)
1944 Merv Pregulman, Michigan, G	2001 Jamal Reynolds, Florida State, DE	1992 Steve Emtman, Washington, DT
1945 Walt Schlinkman, Texas Tech, B	2002 Javon Walker, Florida State, WR	Quentin Coryatt, Texas A&M, LB
1946 Johnny Strzykalski, Marquette, B	2003 Nick Barnett, Oregon State, LB	1993 Sean Dawkins, California, WR
1947 Ernie Case, UCLA, B	2004 Ahmad Carroll, Arkansas, DB	1994 Marshall Faulk, San Diego St., RB
1948 Earl (Jug) Girard, Wisconsin, B	2005 Aaron Rodgers, California, QB	Trev Alberts, Nebraska, LB
1949 Stan Heath, Nevada, B	2006 A.J. Hawk, Ohio State, LB	1995 Ellis Johnson, Florida, DT
1950 Clayton Tonnemaker, Minnesota, C	2007 Justin Harrell, Tennessee, DT	1996 Marvin Harrison, Syracuse, WR
1951 Bob Gain, Kentucky, T	2008 Jordy Nelson, Kansas State, WR (2)	1997 Tarik Glenn, California, T
1952 Babe Parilli, Kentucky, QB		1998 Peyton Manning, Tennessee, QB
1953 Al Carmichael, So. California, B	**HOUSTON TEXANS**	1999 Edgerrin James, Miami, RB
1954 Art Hunter, Notre Dame, T	**Year Player, College, Position**	2000 Rob Morris, Brigham Young, LB
Veryl Switzer, Kansas State, B	2002 David Carr, Fresno State, QB	2001 Reggie Wayne, Miami, WR
1955 Tom Bettis, Purdue, G	2003 Andre Johnson, Miami, WR	2002 Dwight Freeney, Syracuse, DE
1956 Jack Losch, Miami, B	2004 Dunta Robinson, South Carolina, DB	2003 Dallas Clark, Iowa, TE
1957 Paul Hornung, Notre Dame, B	Jason Babin, Western Michigan, LB	2004 Bob Sanders, Iowa, DB (2)
Ron Kramer, Michigan, E	2005 Travis Johnson, Florida State, DE	2005 Marlin Jackson, Michigan, DB
1958 Dan Currie, Michigan State, C	2006 Mario Williams, North Carolina St., DE	2006 Joseph Addai, Louisiana State, RB
1959 Randy Duncan, Iowa, B	2007 Amobi Okoye, Louisville, DT	2007 Anthony Gonzalez, Ohio State, WR
1960 Tom Moore, Vanderbilt, RB	2008 Duane Brown, Virginia Tech, T	2008 Mike Pollak, Arizona State, G (2)
1961 Herb Adderley, Michigan State, CB		
1962 Earl Gros, Louisiana State, RB	**INDIANAPOLIS COLTS**	**JACKSONVILLE JAGUARS**
1963 Dave Robinson, Penn State, LB	**Year Player, College, Position**	**Year Player, College, Position**
1964 Lloyd Voss, Nebraska, DT	1953 Billy Vessels, Oklahoma, B	1995 Tony Boselli, Southern California, T
1965 Donny Anderson, Texas Tech, RB	1954 Cotton Davidson, Baylor, B	James Stewart, Tennessee, RB
Lawrence Elkins, Baylor, E	1955 George Shaw, Oregon, B	1996 Kevin Hardy, Illinois, LB
1966 Jim Grabowski, Illinois, RB	Alan Ameche, Wisconsin, FB	1997 Renaldo Wynn, Notre Dame, DT
Gale Gillingham, Minnesota, T	1956 Lenny Moore, Penn State, B	1998 Fred Taylor, Florida, RB
1967 Bob Hyland, Boston College, C	1957 Jim Parker, Ohio State, G	Donovin Darius, Syracuse, DB
Don Horn, San Diego State, QB	1958 Lenny Lyles, Louisville, B	1999 Fernando Bryant, Alabama, DB
1968 Fred Carr, Texas-El Paso, LB	1959 Jackie Burkett, Auburn, C	2000 R. Jay Soward, So. California, WR
Bill Lueck, Arizona, G	1960 Ron Mix, Southern California, T	2001 Marcus Stroud, Georgia, DT
1969 Rich Moore, Villanova, DT	1961 Tom Matte, Ohio State, RB	2002 John Henderson, Tennessee, DT
1970 Mike McCoy, Notre Dame, DT	1962 Wendell Harris, Louisiana State, S	2003 Byron Leftwich, Marshall, QB
Rich McGeorge, Elon, TE	1963 Bob Vogel, Ohio State, T	2004 Reggie Williams, Washington, WR
1971 John Brockington, Ohio State, RB	1964 Marv Woodson, Indiana, CB	2005 Matt Jones, Arkansas, WR
1972 Willie Buchanon, San Diego St., DB	1965 Mike Curtis, Duke, LB	2006 Marcedes Lewis, UCLA, TE
Jerry Tagge, Nebraska, QB	1966 Sam Ball, Kentucky, T	2007 Reggie Nelson, Florida, DB
1973 Barry Smith, Florida State, WR	1967 Bubba Smith, Michigan State, DT	2008 Derrick Harvey, Florida, DE
1974 Barty Smith, Richmond, RB	Jim Detwiler, Michigan, RB	

KANSAS CITY CHIEFS

Year	Player, College, Position
1960	Don Meredith, So. Methodist, QB
1961	E.J. Holub, Texas Tech, C
1962	Ronnie Bull, Baylor, RB
1963	Buck Buchanan, Grambling, DT
	Ed Budde, Michigan State, G
1964	Pete Beathard, So. California, QB
1965	Gale Sayers, Kansas, RB
1966	Aaron Brown, Minnesota, DE
1967	Gene Trosch, Miami, DE-DT
1968	Mo Moorman, Texas A&M, G
	George Daney, Texas-El Paso, G
1969	Jim Marsalis, Tennessee State, CB
1970	Sid Smith, Southern California, T
1971	Elmo Wright, Houston, WR
1972	Jeff Kinney, Nebraska, RB
1973	Gary Butler, Rice, TE (2)
1974	Woody Green, Arizona State, RB
1975	Elmore Stephens, Kentucky, TE (2)
1976	Rod Walters, Iowa, G
1977	Gary Green, Baylor, DB
1978	Art Still, Kentucky, DE
1979	Mike Bell, Colorado State, DE
	Steve Fuller, Clemson, QB
1980	Brad Budde, Southern California, G
1981	Willie Scott, South Carolina, TE
1982	Anthony Hancock, Tennessee, WR
1983	Todd Blackledge, Penn State, QB
1984	Bill Maas, Pittsburgh, DT
	John Alt, Iowa, T
1985	Ethan Horton, North Carolina, RB
1986	Brian Jozwiak, West Virginia, T
1987	Paul Palmer, Temple, RB
1988	Neil Smith, Nebraska, DE
1989	Derrick Thomas, Alabama, LB
1990	Percy Snow, Michigan State, LB
1991	Harvey Williams, Louisiana St., RB
1992	Dale Carter, Tennessee, DB
1993	Will Shields, Nebraska, G (3)
1994	Greg Hill, Texas A&M, RB
1995	Trezelle Jenkins, Michigan, T
1996	Jerome Woods, Memphis, DB
1997	Tony Gonzalez, California, TE
1998	Victor Riley, Auburn, T
1999	John Tait, Brigham Young, T
2000	Sylvester Morris, Jackson St., WR
2001	Eric Downing, Syracuse, DT (3)
2002	Ryan Sims, North Carolina, DT
2003	Larry Johnson, Penn State, RB
2004	Junior Siavii, Oregon, DT (2)
2005	Derrick Johnson, Texas, LB
2006	Tamba Hali, Penn State, DE
2007	Dwayne Bowe, Louisiana State, WR
2008	Glenn Dorsey, Louisiana State, DT
	Branden Albert, Virginia, T

MIAMI DOLPHINS

Year	Player, College, Position
1966	Jim Grabowski, Illinois, RB
	Rick Norton, Kentucky, QB
1967	Bob Griese, Purdue, QB
1968	Larry Csonka, Syracuse, RB
	Doug Crusan, Indiana, T
1969	Bill Stanfill, Georgia, DE
1970	Jim Mandich, Michigan, TE (2)
1971	Otto Stowe, Iowa State, WR (2)
1972	Mike Kadish, Notre Dame, DT
1973	Chuck Bradley, Oregon, C (2)
1974	Donald Reese, Jackson State, DE

1975	Darryl Carlton, Tampa, T
1976	Larry Gordon, Arizona State, LB
	Kim Bokamper, San Jose State, LB
1977	A.J. Duhe, Louisiana State, DT
1978	Guy Benjamin, Stanford, QB (2)
1979	Jon Giesler, Michigan, T
1980	Don McNeal, Alabama, DB
1981	David Overstreet, Oklahoma, RB
1982	Roy Foster, Southern California, G
1983	Dan Marino, Pittsburgh, QB
1984	Jackie Shipp, Oklahoma, LB
1985	Lorenzo Hampton, Florida, RB
1986	John Offerdahl, Western Michigan, LB (2)
1987	John Bosa, Boston College, DE
1988	Eric Kumerow, Ohio State, DE
1989	Sammie Smith, Florida State, RB
	Louis Oliver, Florida, DB
1990	Richmond Webb, Texas A&M, T
1991	Randal Hill, Miami, WR
1992	Troy Vincent, Wisconsin, DB
	Marco Coleman, Georgia Tech, LB
1993	O.J. McDuffie, Penn State, WR
1994	Tim Bowens, Mississippi, DT
1995	Billy Milner, Houston, T
1996	Daryl Gardener, Baylor, DT
1997	Yatil Green, Miami, WR
1998	John Avery, Mississippi, RB
1999	J.J. Johnson, Mississippi St., RB (2)
2000	Todd Wade, Mississippi, T (2)
2001	Jamar Fletcher, Wisconsin, DB
2002	Seth McKinney, Texas A&M, C (3)
2003	Eddie Moore, Tennessee, LB (2)
2004	Vernon Carey, Miami, T
2005	Ronnie Brown, Auburn, RB
2006	Jason Allen, Tennessee, DB
2007	Ted Ginn, Ohio State, WR
2008	Jake Long, Michigan, T

MINNESOTA VIKINGS

Year	Player, College, Position
1961	Tommy Mason, Tulane, RB
1962	Bill Miller, Miami, WR (3)
1963	Jim Dunaway, Mississippi, T
1964	Carl Eller, Minnesota, DE
1965	Jack Snow, Notre Dame, WR
1966	Jerry Shay, Purdue, DT
1967	Clint Jones, Michigan State, RB
	Gene Washington, Michigan St., WR
	Alan Page, Notre Dame, DT
1968	Ron Yary, Southern California, T
1969	Ed White, California, G (2)
1970	John Ward, Oklahoma State, DT
1971	Leo Hayden, Ohio State, RB
1972	Jeff Siemon, Stanford, LB
1973	Chuck Foreman, Miami, RB
1974	Fred McNeill, UCLA, LB
	Steve Riley, Southern California, T
1975	Mark Mullaney, Colorado State, DE
1976	James White, Oklahoma State, DT
1977	Tommy Kramer, Rice, QB
1978	Randy Holloway, Pittsburgh, DE
1979	Ted Brown, North Carolina St., RB
1980	Doug Martin, Washington, DT
1981	Mardye McDole, Mississippi St., WR (2)
1982	Darrin Nelson, Stanford, RB
1983	Joey Browner, So. California, DB
1984	Keith Millard, Washington St., DE
1985	Chris Doleman, Pittsburgh, LB
1986	Gerald Robinson, Auburn, DE
1987	D.J. Dozier, Penn State, RB

1988	Randall McDaniel, Arizona State, G
1989	David Braxton, Wake Forest, LB (2)
1990	Mike Jones, Texas A&M, TE (3)
1991	Carlos Jenkins, Michigan St., LB (3)
1992	Robert Harris, Southern Univ., DE (2)
1993	Robert Smith, Ohio State, RB
1994	DeWayne Washington, N. Carolina St., DB
	Todd Steussie, California, T
1995	Derrick Alexander, Florida St., DE
	Korey Stringer, Ohio State, T
1996	Duane Clemons, California, DE
1997	Dwayne Rudd, Alabama, LB
1998	Randy Moss, Marshall, WR
1999	Daunte Culpepper, Central Florida, QB
	Dimitrius Underwood, Michigan St., DE
2000	Chris Hovan, Boston College, DT
2001	Michael Bennett, Wisconsin, RB
2002	Bryant McKinnie, Miami, T
2003	Kevin Williams, Oklahoma State, DT
2004	Kenechi Udeze, Southern California, DE
2005	Troy Williamson, South Carolina, WR
	Erasmus James, Wisconsin, DE
2006	Chad Greenway, Iowa, LB
2007	Adrian Peterson, Oklahoma, RB
2008	Tyrell Johnson, Arkansas State, DB (2)

NEW ENGLAND PATRIOTS

Year	Player, College, Position
1960	Ron Burton, Northwestern, RB
1961	Tommy Mason, Tulane, RB
1962	Gary Collins, Maryland, WR
1963	Art Graham, Boston College, WR
1964	Jack Concannon, Boston College, QB
1965	Jerry Rush, Michigan State, DE
1966	Karl Singer, Purdue, T
1967	John Charles, Purdue, S
1968	Dennis Byrd, North Carolina St., DE
1969	Ron Sellers, Florida State, WR
1970	Phil Olsen, Utah State, DE
1971	Jim Plunkett, Stanford, QB
1972	Tom Reynolds, San Diego St., WR (2)
1973	John Hannah, Alabama, G
	Sam Cunningham, So. California, RB
	Darryl Stingley, Purdue, WR
1974	Steve Corbett, Boston College, G (2)
1975	Russ Francis, Oregon, TE
1976	Mike Haynes, Arizona State, DB
	Pete Brock, Colorado, C
	Tim Fox, Ohio State, DB
1977	Raymond Clayborn, Texas, DB
	Stanley Morgan, Tennessee, WR
1978	Bob Cryder, Alabama, G
1979	Rick Sanford, South Carolina, DB
1980	Roland James, Tennessee, DB
	Vagas Ferguson, Notre Dame, RB
1981	Brian Holloway, Stanford, T
1982	Kenneth Sims, Texas, DT
	Lester Williams, Miami, DT
1983	Tony Eason, Illinois, QB
1984	Irving Fryar, Nebraska, WR
1985	Trevor Matich, Brigham Young, C
1986	Reggie Dupard, So. Methodist, RB
1987	Bruce Armstrong, Louisville, T
1988	John Stephens, Northwestern St., La., RB
1989	Hart Lee Dykes, Oklahoma St., WR
1990	Chris Singleton, Arizona, LB
	Ray Agnew, North Carolina St., DE
1991	Pat Harlow, Southern California, T
	Leonard Russell, Arizona St., RB
1992	Eugene Chung, Virginia Tech, T

1993 Drew Bledsoe, Washington St., QB
1994 Willie McGinest, So. California, DE
1995 Ty Law, Michigan, DB
1996 Terry Glenn, Ohio State, WR
1997 Chris Canty, Kansas State, DB
1998 Robert Edwards, Georgia, RB
     Tebucky Jones, Syracuse, DB
1999 Damien Woody, Boston College, C
     Andy Katzenmoyer, Ohio State, LB
2000 Adrian Klemm, Hawaii, T (2)
2001 Richard Seymour, Georgia, DT
2002 Daniel Graham, Colorado, TE
2003 Ty Warren, Texas A&M, DT
2004 Vince Wilfork, Miami, DT
     Ben Watson, Georgia, TE
2005 Logan Mankins, Fresno State, G
2006 Laurence Maroney, Minnesota, RB
2007 Brandon Meriweather, Miami, DB
2008 Jerod Mayo, Tennessee, LB

NEW ORLEANS SAINTS
Year Player, College, Position
1967 Les Kelley, Alabama, RB
1968 Kevin Hardy, Notre Dame, DE
1969 John Shinners, Xavier, G
1970 Ken Burrough, Texas Southern, WR
1971 Archie Manning, Mississippi, QB
1972 Royce Smith, Georgia, G
1973 Derland Moore, Oklahoma, DE (2)
1974 Rick Middleton, Ohio State, LB
1975 Larry Burton, Purdue, WR
     Kurt Schumacher, Ohio State, T
1976 Chuck Muncie, California, RB
1977 Joe Campbell, Maryland, DE
1978 Wes Chandler, Florida, WR
1979 Russell Erxleben, Texas, P-K
1980 Stan Brock, Colorado, T
1981 George Rogers, South Carolina, RB
1982 Lindsay Scott, Georgia, WR
1983 Steve Korte, Arkansas, G (2)
1984 James Geathers, Wichita State, DE
1985 Alvin Toles, Tennessee, LB
1986 Jim Dombrowski, Virginia, T
1987 Shawn Knight, Brigham Young, DT
1988 Craig Heyward, Pittsburgh, RB
1989 Wayne Martin, Arkansas, DE
1990 Renaldo Turnbull, West Virginia, DE
1991 Wesley Carroll, Miami, WR (2)
1992 Vaughn Dunbar, Indiana, RB
1993 Willie Roaf, Louisiana Tech, T
     Irv Smith, Notre Dame, TE
1994 Joe Johnson, Louisville, DE
1995 Mark Fields, Washington State, LB
1996 Alex Molden, Oregon, DB
1997 Chris Naeole, Colorado, G
1998 Kyle Turley, San Diego State, T
1999 Ricky Williams, Texas, RB
2000 Darren Howard, Kansas St., DE (2)
2001 Deuce McAllister, Mississippi, RB
2002 Donte' Stallworth, Tennessee, WR
     Charles Grant, Georgia, DE
2003 Johnathan Sullivan, Georgia, DT
2004 Will Smith, Ohio State, DE
2005 Jammal Brown, Oklahoma, T
2006 Reggie Bush, So. California, RB
2007 Robert Meachem, Tennessee, WR
2008 Sedrick Ellis, So. California, DT

NEW YORK GIANTS
Year Player, College, Position
1936 Art Lewis, Ohio U., T
1937 Ed Widseth, Minnesota, T
1938 George Karamatic, Gonzaga, B
1939 Walt Neilson, Arizona, B
1940 Grenville Lansdell, So. California, B
1941 George Franck, Minnesota, B
1942 Merle Hapes, Mississippi, B
1943 Steve Filipowicz, Fordham, B
1944 Billy Hillenbrand, Indiana, B
1945 Elmer Barbour, Wake Forest, B
1946 George Connor, Notre Dame, T
1947 Vic Schwall, Northwestern, B
1948 Tony Minisi, Pennsylvania, B
1949 Paul Page, Southern Methodist, B
1950 Travis Tidwell, Auburn, B
1951 Kyle Rote, Southern Methodist, B
     Jim Spavital, Oklahoma A&M, B
1952 Frank Gifford, Southern California, B
1953 Bobby Marlow, Alabama, B
1954 Ken Buck, Pacific, C (2)
1955 Joe Heap, Notre Dame, B
1956 Henry Moore, Arkansas, B (2)
1957 Sam DeLuca, South Carolina, T (2)
1958 Phil King, Vanderbilt, B
1959 Lee Grosscup, Utah, B
1960 Lou Cordileone, Clemson, G
1961 Bruce Tarbox, Syracuse, G (2)
1962 Jerry Hillebrand, Colorado, LB
1963 Frank Lasky, Florida, T (2)
1964 Joe Don Looney, Oklahoma, RB
1965 Tucker Frederickson, Auburn, RB
1966 Francis Peay, Missouri, T
1967 Louis Thompson, Alabama, DT (4)
1968 Dick Buzin, Penn State, T (2)
1969 Fred Dryer, San Diego State, DE
1970 Jim Files, Oklahoma, LB
1971 Rocky Thompson, West Texas St., WR
1972 Eldridge Small, Texas A&I, DB
     Larry Jacobson, Nebraska, DE
1973 Brad Van Pelt, Michigan St., LB (2)
1974 John Hicks, Ohio State, G
1975 Al Simpson, Colorado State, T (2)
1976 Troy Archer, Colorado, DE
1977 Gary Jeter, Southern California, DT
1978 Gordon King, Stanford, T
1979 Phil Simms, Morehead State, QB
1980 Mark Haynes, Colorado, DB
1981 Lawrence Taylor, North Carolina, LB
1982 Butch Woolfolk, Michigan, RB
1983 Terry Kinard, Clemson, DB
1984 Carl Banks, Michigan State, LB
     William Roberts, Ohio State, T
1985 George Adams, Kentucky, RB
1986 Eric Dorsey, Notre Dame, DE
1987 Mark Ingram, Michigan State, WR
1988 Eric Moore, Indiana, T
1989 Brian Williams, Minnesota, C-G
1990 Rodney Hampton, Georgia, RB
1991 Jarrod Bunch, Michigan, RB
1992 Derek Brown, Notre Dame, TE
1993 Michael Strahan, Texas Southern, DE (2)
1994 Thomas Lewis, Indiana, WR
1995 Tyrone Wheatley, Michigan, RB
1996 Cedric Jones, Oklahoma, DE
1997 Ike Hilliard, Florida, WR
1998 Shaun Williams, UCLA, DB
1999 Luke Petitgout, Notre Dame, T
2000 Ron Dayne, Wisconsin, RB

2001 Will Allen, Syracuse, DB
2002 Jeremy Shockey, Miami, TE
2003 William Joseph, Miami, DT
2004 Philip Rivers, North Carolina St., QB
2005 Corey Webster, Louisiana St., DB (2)
2006 Mathias Kiwanuka, Boston College, DE
2007 Aaron Ross, Texas, DB
2008 Kenny Phillips, Miami, DB

NEW YORK JETS
Year Player, College, Position
1960 George Izo, Notre Dame, QB
1961 Tom Brown, Minnesota, G
1962 Sandy Stephens, Minnesota, QB
1963 Jerry Stovall, Louisiana State, S
1964 Matt Snell, Ohio State, RB
1965 Joe Namath, Alabama, QB
     Tom Nowatzke, Indiana, RB
1966 Bill Yearby, Michigan, DT
1967 Paul Seiler, Notre Dame, T
1968 Lee White, Weber State, RB
1969 Dave Foley, Ohio State, T
1970 Steve Tannen, Florida, CB
1971 John Riggins, Kansas, RB
1972 Jerome Barkum, Jackson St., WR
     Mike Taylor, Michigan, LB
1973 Burgess Owens, Miami, DB
1974 Carl Barzilauskas, Indiana, DT
1975 Anthony Davis, So. California, RB (2)
1976 Richard Todd, Alabama, QB
1977 Marvin Powell, So. California, T
1978 Chris Ward, Ohio State, T
1979 Marty Lyons, Alabama, DE
1980 Johnny (Lam) Jones, Texas, WR
1981 Freeman McNeil, UCLA, RB
1982 Bob Crable, Notre Dame, LB
1983 Ken O'Brien, Cal-Davis, QB
1984 Russell Carter, So. Methodist, DB
     Ron Faurot, Arkansas, DE
1985 Al Toon, Wisconsin, WR
1986 Mike Haight, Iowa, T
1987 Roger Vick, Texas A&M, RB
1988 Dave Cadigan, So. California, T
1989 Jeff Lageman, Virginia, LB
1990 Blair Thomas, Penn State, RB
1991 Browning Nagle, Louisville, QB (2)
1992 Johnny Mitchell, Nebraska, TE
1993 Marvin Jones, Florida State, LB
1994 Aaron Glenn, Texas A&M, DB
1995 Kyle Brady, Penn State, TE
     Hugh Douglas, Central St., Ohio, DE
1996 Keyshawn Johnson, So. California, WR
1997 James Farrior, Virginia, LB
1998 Dorian Boose, Washington St., DE (2)
1999 Randy Thomas, Mississippi St., G (2)
2000 Shaun Ellis, Tennessee, DE
     John Abraham, South Carolina, LB
     Chad Pennington, Marshall, QB
     Anthony Becht, West Virginia, TE
2001 Santana Moss, Miami, WR
2002 Bryan Thomas, Ala.-Birmingham, DE
2003 Dewayne Robertson, Kentucky, DT
2004 Jonathan Vilma, Miami, LB
2005 Mike Nugent, Ohio State, K (2)
2006 D'Brickashaw Ferguson, Virginia, T
     Nick Mangold, Ohio State, C
2007 Darrelle Revis, Pittsburgh, DB
2008 Vernon Gholston, Ohio State, LB
     Dustin Keller, Purdue, TE

OAKLAND RAIDERS

Year	Player, College, Position
1960	Dale Hackbart, Wisconsin, CB
1961	Joe Rutgens, Illinois, DT
1962	Roman Gabriel, North Carolina St., QB
1963	George Wilson, Alabama, RB (6)
1964	Tony Lorick, Arizona State, RB
1965	Harry Schuh, Memphis State, T
1966	Rodger Bird, Kentucky, S
1967	Gene Upshaw, Texas A&I, G
1968	Eldridge Dickey, Tennessee St., QB
1969	Art Thoms, Syracuse, DT
1970	Raymond Chester, Morgan St., TE
1971	Jack Tatum, Ohio State, S
1972	Mike Siani, Villanova, WR
1973	Ray Guy, Southern Mississippi, P
1974	Henry Lawrence, Florida A&M, T
1975	Neal Colzie, Ohio State, DB
1976	Charles Philyaw, Texas Southern, DT (2)
1977	Mike Davis, Colorado, DB (2)
1978	Dave Browning, Washington, DE (2)
1979	Willie Jones, Florida State, DE (2)
1980	Marc Wilson, Brigham Young, QB
1981	Ted Watts, Texas Tech, DB
	Curt Marsh, Washington, T
1982	Marcus Allen, So. California, RB
1983	Don Mosebar, So. California, T
1984	Sean Jones, Northeastern, DE (2)
1985	Jessie Hester, Florida State, WR
1986	Bob Buczkowski, Pittsburgh, DE
1987	John Clay, Missouri, T
1988	Tim Brown, Notre Dame, WR
	Terry McDaniel, Tennessee, DB
	Scott Davis, Illinois, DE
1989	Jeff Francis, Tennessee, QB (6)
1990	Anthony Smith, Arizona, DE
1991	Todd Marinovich, So. California, QB
1992	Chester McGlockton, Clemson, DE
1993	Patrick Bates, Texas A&M, DB
1994	Rob Fredrickson, Michigan St., LB
1995	Napoleon Kaufman, Washington, RB
1996	Rickey Dudley, Ohio State, TE
1997	Darrell Russell, Southern California, DT
1998	Charles Woodson, Michigan, DB
	Mo Collins, Florida, T
1999	Matt Stinchcomb, Georgia, T
2000	Sebastian Janikowski, Florida St., K
2001	Derrick Gibson, Florida State, DB
2002	Phillip Buchanon, Miami, DB
	Napoleon Harris, Northwestern, LB
2003	Nnamdi Asomugha, California, DB
	Tyler Brayton, Colorado, DE
2004	Robert Gallery, Iowa, T
2005	Fabian Washington, Nebraska, DB
2006	Michael Huff, Texas, DB
2007	JaMarcus Russell, Louisiana State, QB
2008	Darren McFadden, Arkansas, RB

PHILADELPHIA EAGLES

Year	Player, College, Position
1936	Jay Berwanger, Chicago, B
1937	Sam Francis, Nebraska, B
1938	Jim McDonald, Ohio State, B
1939	Davey O'Brien, Texas Christian, B
1940	George McAfee, Duke, B
1941	Art Jones, Richmond, B (2)
1942	Pete Kmetovic, Stanford, B
1943	Joe Muha, Virginia Military, B
1944	Steve Van Buren, Louisiana St., B
1945	John Yonaker, Notre Dame, E
1946	Leo Riggs, Southern California, B
1947	Neill Armstrong, Oklahoma A&M, E
1948	Clyde (Smackover) Scott, Arkansas, B
1949	Chuck Bednarik, Pennsylvania, C
	Frank Tripucka, Notre Dame, B
1950	Harry (Bud) Grant, Minnesota, E
1951	Ebert Van Buren, Louisiana St., B
	Chet Mutryn, Xavier, B
1952	Johnny Bright, Drake, B
1953	Al Conway, Army, B (2)
1954	Neil Worden, Notre Dame, B
1955	Dick Bielski, Maryland, B
1956	Bob Pellegrini, Maryland, C
1957	Clarence Peaks, Michigan State, B
1958	Walt Kowalczyk, Michigan State, B
1959	J.D. Smith, Rice, T (2)
1960	Ron Burton, Northwestern, RB
1961	Art Baker, Syracuse, RB
1962	Pete Case, Georgia, G (2)
1963	Ed Budde, Michigan State, G
1964	Bob Brown, Nebraska, T
1965	Ray Rissmiller, Georgia, T (2)
1966	Randy Beisler, Indiana, DE
1967	Harry Jones, Arkansas, RB
1968	Tim Rossovich, So. California, DE
1969	Leroy Keyes, Purdue, RB
1970	Steve Zabel, Oklahoma, TE
1971	Richard Harris, Grambling, DE
1972	John Reaves, Florida, QB
1973	Jerry Sisemore, Texas, T
	Charle Young, So. California, TE
1974	Mitch Sutton, Kansas, DT (3)
1975	Bill Capraun, Miami, T (7)
1976	Mike Smith, Florida, DE (4)
1977	Skip Sharp, Kansas, DB (5)
1978	Reggie Wilkes, Georgia Tech, LB (3)
1979	Jerry Robinson, UCLA, LB
1980	Roynell Young, Alcorn State, DB
1981	Leonard Mitchell, Houston, DE
1982	Mike Quick, North Carolina St., WR
1983	Michael Haddix, Mississippi St., RB
1984	Kenny Jackson, Penn State, WR
1985	Kevin Allen, Indiana, T
1986	Keith Byars, Ohio State, RB
1987	Jerome Brown, Miami, DT
1988	Keith Jackson, Oklahoma, TE
1989	Jessie Small, Eastern Kentucky, LB (2)
1990	Ben Smith, Georgia, DB
1991	Antone Davis, Tennessee, T
1992	Siran Stacy, Alabama, RB (2)
1993	Lester Holmes, Jackson State, T
	Leonard Renfro, Colorado, DT
1994	Bernard Williams, Georgia, T
1995	Mike Mamula, Boston College, DE
1996	Jermane Mayberry, Texas A&M-Kingsville, T
1997	Jon Harris, Virginia, DE
1998	Tra Thomas, Florida State, T
1999	Donovan McNabb, Syracuse, QB
2000	Corey Simon, Florida State, DT
2001	Freddie Mitchell, UCLA, WR
2002	Lito Sheppard, Florida, DB
2003	Jerome McDougle, Miami, DE
2004	Shawn Andrews, Arkansas, T
2005	Mike Patterson, So. California, DT
2006	Brodrick Bunkley, Florida State, DT
2007	Kevin Kolb, Houston, QB (2)
2008	Trevor Laws, Notre Dame, DT (2)

PITTSBURGH STEELERS

Year	Player, College, Position
1936	Bill Shakespeare, Notre Dame, B
1937	Mike Basrak, Duquesne, C
1938	Byron (Whizzer) White, Colorado, B
1939	Bill Patterson, Baylor, B (3)
1940	Kay Eakin, Arkansas, B
1941	Chet Gladchuk, Boston College, C (2)
1942	Bill Dudley, Virginia, B
1943	Bill Daley, Minnesota, B
1944	Johnny Podesto, St. Mary's, Calif., B
1945	Paul Duhart, Florida, B
1946	Felix (Doc) Blanchard, Army, B
1947	Hub Bechtol, Texas, E
1948	Dan Edwards, Georgia, E
1949	Bobby Gage, Clemson, B
1950	Lynn Chandnois, Michigan St., B
1951	Butch Avinger, Alabama, B
1952	Ed Modzelewski, Maryland, B
1953	Ted Marchibroda, St. Bonaventure, B
1954	Johnny Lattner, Notre Dame, B
1955	Frank Varrichione, Notre Dame, T
1956	Gary Glick, Colorado A&M, B
	Art Davis, Mississippi State, B
1957	Len Dawson, Purdue, B
1958	Larry Krutko, West Virginia, B (2)
1959	Tom Barnett, Purdue, B (8)
1960	Jack Spikes, Texas Christian, RB
1961	Myron Pottios, Notre Dame, LB (2)
1962	Bob Ferguson, Ohio State, RB
1963	Frank Atkinson, Stanford, T (8)
1964	Paul Martha, Pittsburgh, S
1965	Roy Jefferson, Utah, WR (2)
1966	Dick Leftridge, West Virginia, RB
1967	Don Shy, San Diego State, RB (2)
1968	Mike Taylor, Southern California, T
1969	Joe Greene, North Texas State, DT
1970	Terry Bradshaw, Louisiana Tech, QB
1971	Frank Lewis, Grambling, WR
1972	Franco Harris, Penn State, RB
1973	J.T. Thomas, Florida State, DB
1974	Lynn Swann, So. California, WR
1975	Dave Brown, Michigan, DB
1976	Bennie Cunningham, Clemson, TE
1977	Robin Cole, New Mexico, LB
1978	Ron Johnson, Eastern Michigan, DB
1979	Greg Hawthorne, Baylor, RB
1980	Mark Malone, Arizona State, QB
1981	Keith Gary, Oklahoma, DE
1982	Walter Abercrombie, Baylor, RB
1983	Gabriel Rivera, Texas Tech, DT
1984	Louis Lipps, So. Mississippi, WR
1985	Darryl Sims, Wisconsin, DE
1986	John Rienstra, Temple, G
1987	Rod Woodson, Purdue, DB
1988	Aaron Jones, Eastern Kentucky, DE
1989	Tim Worley, Georgia, RB
	Tom Ricketts, Pittsburgh, T
1990	Eric Green, Liberty, TE
1991	Huey Richardson, Florida, DE
1992	Leon Searcy, Miami, T
1993	Deon Figures, Colorado, DB
1994	Charles Johnson, Colorado, WR
1995	Mark Bruener, Washington, TE
1996	Jamain Stephens, North Carolina A&T, T
1997	Chad Scott, Maryland, DB
1998	Alan Faneca, Louisiana State, G
1999	Troy Edwards, Louisiana Tech, WR
2000	Plaxico Burress, Michigan St., WR
2001	Casey Hampton, Texas, DT

2002 Kendall Simmons, Auburn, G	1982 Barry Redden, Richmond, RB	1988 Anthony Miller, Tennessee, WR
2003 Troy Polamalu, Southern California, DB	1983 Eric Dickerson, So. Methodist, RB	1989 Burt Grossman, Pittsburgh, DE
2004 Ben Roethlisberger, Miami (OH), QB	1984 Hal Stephens, East Carolina, DE (5)	1990 Junior Seau, So. California, LB
2005 Heath Miller, Virginia, TE	1985 Jerry Gray, Texas, DB	1991 Stanley Richard, Texas, DB
2006 Santonio Holmes, Ohio State, WR	1986 Mike Schad, Queen's Univ., Canada, T	1992 Chris Mims, Tennessee, DE
2007 Lawrence Timmons, Florida State, LB	1987 Donald Evans, Winston-Salem, DE (2)	1993 Darrien Gordon, Stanford, DB
2008 Rashard Mendenhall, Illinois, RB	1988 Gaston Green, UCLA, RB	1994 Isaac Davis, Arkansas, G (2)
	Aaron Cox, Arizona State, WR	1995 Terrance Shaw, Stephen F. Austin, DB (2)
ST. LOUIS RAMS	1989 Bill Hawkins, Miami, DE	1996 Bryan Still, Virginia Tech, WR (2)
Year Player, College, Position	Cleveland Gary, Miami, RB	1997 Freddie Jones, North Carolina, TE (2)
1937 Johnny Drake, Purdue, B	1990 Bern Brostek, Washington, C	1998 Ryan Leaf, Washington State, QB
1938 Corbett Davis, Indiana, B	1991 Todd Lyght, Notre Dame, DB	1999 Jermaine Fazande, Oklahoma, RB (2)
1939 Parker Hall, Mississippi, B	1992 Sean Gilbert, Pittsburgh, DE	2000 Rogers Beckett, Marshall, DB (2)
1940 Ollie Cordill, Rice, B	1993 Jerome Bettis, Notre Dame, RB	2001 LaDainian Tomlinson, TCU, RB
1941 Rudy Mucha, Washington, C	1994 Wayne Gandy, Auburn, T	2002 Quentin Jammer, Texas, DB
1942 Jack Wilson, Baylor, B	1995 Kevin Carter, Florida, DE	2003 Sammy Davis, Texas A&M, DB
1943 Mike Holovak, Boston College, B	1996 Lawrence Phillips, Nebraska, RB	2004 Eli Manning, Mississippi, QB
1944 Tony Butkovich, Illinois, B	Eddie Kennison, Louisiana St., WR	2005 Shawne Merriman, Maryland, LB
1945 Elroy (Crazylegs) Hirsch, Wisconsin, B	1997 Orlando Pace, Ohio State, T	Luis Castillo, Northwestern, DT
1946 Emil Sitko, Notre Dame, B	1998 Grant Wistrom, Nebraska, DE	2006 Antonio Cromartie, Florida State, DB
1947 Herman Wedemeyer, St. Mary's, Calif., B	1999 Torry Holt, North Carolina St., WR	2007 Craig Davis, Louisiana State, WR
1948 Tom Keane, West Virginia, B (2)	2000 Trung Canidate, Arizona, RB	2008 Antoine Cason, Arizona, DB
1949 Bobby Thomason, Virginia Military, B	2001 Damione Lewis, Miami, DT	
1950 Ralph Pasquariello, Villanova, B	Adam Archuleta, Arizona State, DB	**SAN FRANCISCO 49ERS**
Stan West, Oklahoma, G	Ryan Pickett, Ohio State, DT	**Year Player, College, Position**
1951 Bud McFadin, Texas, G	2002 Robert Thomas, UCLA, LB	1950 Leo Nomellini, Minnesota, T
1952 Bill Wade, Vanderbilt, QB	2003 Jimmy Kennedy, Penn State, DT	1951 Y.A. Tittle, Louisiana State, B
Bob Carey, Michigan State, E	2004 Steven Jackson, Oregon State, RB	1952 Hugh McElhenny, Washington, B
1953 Donn Moomaw, UCLA, C	2005 Alex Barron, Florida State, T	1953 Harry Babcock, Georgia, E
Ed Barker, Washington State, E	2006 Tye Hill, Clemson, DB	Tom Stolhandske, Texas, E
1954 Ed Beatty, Cincinnati, C	2007 Adam Carriker, Nebraska, DE	1954 Bernie Faloney, Maryland, B
1955 Larry Morris, Georgia Tech, C	2008 Chris Long, Virginia, DE	1955 Dickie Moegle, Rice, B
1956 Joe Marconi, West Virginia, B		1956 Earl Morrall, Michigan State, B
Charles Horton, Vanderbilt, B	**SAN DIEGO CHARGERS**	1957 John Brodie, Stanford, B
1957 Jon Arnett, Southern California, B	**Year Player, College, Position**	1958 Jim Pace, Michigan, B
Del Shofner, Baylor, E	1960 Monty Stickles, Notre Dame, E	Charlie Krueger, Texas A&M, T
1958 Lou Michaels, Kentucky, T	1961 Earl Faison, Indiana, DE	1959 Dave Baker, Oklahoma, B
Jim Phillips, Auburn, E	1962 Bob Ferguson, Ohio State, RB	Dan James, Ohio State, C
1959 Dick Bass, Pacific, B	1963 Walt Sweeney, Syracuse, G	1960 Monty Stickles, Notre Dame, E
Paul Dickson, Baylor, T	1964 Ted Davis, Georgia Tech, LB	1961 Jimmy Johnson, UCLA, CB
1960 Billy Cannon, Louisiana State, RB	1965 Steve DeLong, Tennessee, DE	Bernie Casey, Bowling Green, WR
1961 Marlin McKeever, So. California, E-LB	1966 Don Davis, Cal St.-Los Angeles, DT	Bill Kilmer, UCLA, QB
1962 Roman Gabriel, North Carolina St., QB	1967 Ron Billingsley, Wyoming, DE	1962 Lance Alworth, Arkansas, WR
Merlin Olsen, Utah State, DT	1968 Russ Washington, Missouri, DT	1963 Kermit Alexander, UCLA, CB
1963 Terry Baker, Oregon State, QB	Jimmy Hill, Texas A&I, DT	1964 Dave Parks, Texas Tech, WR
Rufus Guthrie, Georgia Tech, G	1969 Marty Domres, Columbia, QB	1965 Ken Willard, North Carolina, RB
1964 Bill Munson, Utah State, QB	Bob Babich, Miami, Ohio, LB	George Donnelly, Illinois, DB
1965 Clancy Williams, Washington St., CB	1970 Walker Gillette, Richmond, WR	1966 Stan Hindman, Mississippi, DE
1966 Tom Mack, Michigan, G	1971 Leon Burns, Long Beach State, RB	1967 Steve Spurrier, Florida, QB
1967 Willie Ellison, Texas Southern, RB (2)	1972 Pete Lazetich, Stanford, DE (2)	Cas Banaszek, Northwestern, T
1968 Gary Beban, UCLA, QB (2)	1973 Johnny Rodgers, Nebraska, WR	1968 Forrest Blue, Auburn, C
1969 Larry Smith, Florida, RB	1974 Bo Matthews, Colorado, RB	1969 Ted Kwalick, Penn State, TE
Jim Seymour, Notre Dame, WR	Don Goode, Kansas, LB	Gene Washington, Stanford, WR
Bob Klein, Southern California, TE	1975 Gary Johnson, Grambling, DT	1970 Cedrick Hardman, North Texas St., DE
1970 Jack Reynolds, Tennessee, LB	Mike Williams, Louisiana State, DB	Bruce Taylor, Boston U., DB
1971 Isiah Robertson, Southern, LB	1976 Joe Washington, Oklahoma, RB	1971 Tim Anderson, Ohio State, DB
Jack Youngblood, Florida, DE	1977 Bob Rush, Memphis State, C	1972 Terry Beasley, Auburn, WR
1972 Jim Bertelsen, Texas, RB (2)	1978 John Jefferson, Arizona State, WR	1973 Mike Holmes, Texas Southern, DB
1973 Cullen Bryant, Colorado, DB (2)	1979 Kellen Winslow, Missouri, TE	1974 Wilbur Jackson, Alabama, RB
1974 John Cappelletti, Penn State, RB	1980 Ed Luther, San Jose State, QB (4)	Bill Sandifer, UCLA, DT
1975 Mike Fanning, Notre Dame, DT	1981 James Brooks, Auburn, RB	1975 Jimmy Webb, Mississippi St., DT
Dennis Harrah, Miami, T	1982 Hollis Hall, Clemson, DB (7)	1976 Randy Cross, UCLA, C (2)
Doug France, Ohio State, T	1983 Billy Ray Smith, Arkansas, LB	1977 Elmo Boyd, Eastern Kentucky, WR (3)
1976 Kevin McLain, Colorado State, LB	Gary Anderson, Arkansas, WR	1978 Ken MacAfee, Notre Dame, TE
1977 Bob Brudzinski, Ohio State, LB	Gill Byrd, San Jose State, DB	Dan Bunz, Cal St.-Long Beach, LB
1978 Elvis Peacock, Oklahoma, RB	1984 Mossy Cade, Texas, DB	1979 James Owens, UCLA, WR (2)
1979 George Andrews, Nebraska, LB	1985 Jim Lachey, Ohio State, G	1980 Earl Cooper, Rice, RB
Kent Hill, Georgia Tech, T	1986 Leslie O'Neal, Oklahoma State, DE	Jim Stuckey, Clemson, DT
1980 Johnnie Johnson, Texas, DB	James FitzPatrick, So. California, T	1981 Ronnie Lott, So. California, DB
1981 Mel Owens, Michigan, LB	1987 Rod Bernstine, Texas A&M, TE	1982 Bubba Paris, Michigan, T (2)

1983 Roger Craig, Nebraska, RB (2)
1984 Todd Shell, Brigham Young, LB
1985 Jerry Rice, Mississippi Valley St., WR
1986 Larry Roberts, Alabama, DE (2)
1987 Harris Barton, North Carolina, T
      Terrence Flagler, Clemson, RB
1988 Danny Stubbs, Miami, DE (2)
1989 Keith DeLong, Tennessee, LB
1990 Dexter Carter, Florida State, RB
1991 Ted Washington, Louisville, DT
1992 Dana Hall, Washington, DB
1993 Dana Stubblefield, Kansas, DT
      Todd Kelly, Tennessee, DE
1994 Bryant Young, Notre Dame, DT
      William Floyd, Florida State, RB
1995 J.J. Stokes, UCLA, WR
1996 Israel Ifeanyi, So.California, DE (2)
1997 Jim Druckenmiller, Virginia Tech, QB
1998 R.W. McQuarters, Oklahoma St., DB
1999 Reggie McGrew, Florida, DT
2000 Julian Peterson, Michigan St., LB
      Ahmed Plummer, Ohio State, DB
2001 Andre Carter, California, DE
2002 Mike Rumph, Miami, DB
2003 Kwame Harris, Stanford, T
2004 Rashaun Woods, Oklahoma St., WR
2005 Alex Smith, Utah, QB
2006 Vernon Davis, Maryland, TE
      Manny Lawson, North Carolina St., DE
2007 Patrick Willis, Mississippi, LB
      Joe Staley, Central Michigan, T
2008 Kentwan Balmer, North Carolina, DT

SEATTLE SEAHAWKS
Year Player, College, Position
1976 Steve Niehaus, Notre Dame, DT
1977 Steve August, Tulsa, G
1978 Keith Simpson, Memphis St., DB
1979 Manu Tuiasosopo, UCLA, DT
1980 Jacob Green, Texas A&M, DE
1981 Ken Easley, UCLA, DB
1982 Jeff Bryant, Clemson, DE
1983 Curt Warner, Penn State, RB
1984 Terry Taylor, Southern Illinois, DB
1985 Owen Gill, Iowa, RB (2)
1986 John L. Williams, Florida, RB
1987 Tony Woods, Pittsburgh, LB
1988 Brian Blades, Miami, WR (2)
1989 Andy Heck, Notre Dame, T
1990 Cortez Kennedy, Miami, DT
1991 Dan McGwire, San Diego St., QB
1992 Ray Roberts, Virginia, T
1993 Rick Mirer, Notre Dame, QB
1994 Sam Adams, Texas A&M, DT
1995 Joey Galloway, Ohio State, WR
1996 Pete Kendall, Boston College, T
1997 Shawn Springs, Ohio State, DB
      Walter James, Florida State, T
1998 Anthony Simmons, Clemson, LB
1999 Lamar King, Saginaw Valley St., DE
2000 Shaun Alexander, Alabama, RB
      Chris McIntosh, Wisconsin, T
2001 Koren Robinson, North Carolina St., WR
      Steve Hutchinson, Michigan, G
2002 Jerramy Stevens, Washington, TE
2003 Marcus Trufant, Washington State, DB
2004 Marcus Tubbs, Texas, DT
2005 Chris Spencer, Mississippi, C
2006 Kelly Jennings, Miami, DB

2007 Josh Wilson, Maryland, DB (2)
2008 Lawrence Jackson, So. California, DE

TAMPA BAY BUCCANEERS
Year Player, College, Position
1976 Lee Roy Selmon, Oklahoma, DT
1977 Ricky Bell, Southern California, RB
1978 Doug Williams, Grambling, QB
1979 Greg Roberts, Oklahoma, G (2)
1980 Ray Snell, Wisconsin, G
1981 Hugh Green, Pittsburgh, LB
1982 Sean Farrell, Penn State, G
1983 Randy Grimes, Baylor, C (2)
1984 Keith Browner, So. California, LB (2)
1985 Ron Holmes, Washington, DE
1986 Bo Jackson, Auburn, RB
      Roderick Jones, So. Methodist, DB
1987 Vinny Testaverde, Miami, QB
1988 Paul Gruber, Wisconsin, T
1989 Broderick Thomas, Nebraska, LB
1990 Keith McCants, Alabama, LB
1991 Charles McRae, Tennessee, T
1992 Courtney Hawkins, Michigan St., WR (2)
1993 Eric Curry, Alabama, DE
1994 Trent Dilfer, Fresno State, QB
1995 Warren Sapp, Miami, DT
      Derrick Brooks, Florida State, LB
1996 Regan Upshaw, California, DE
      Marcus Jones, North Carolina, DT
1997 Warrick Dunn, Florida State, RB
      Reidel Anthony, Florida, WR
1998 Jacquez Green, Florida, WR (2)
1999 Anthony McFarland, Louisiana St., DT
2000 Cosey Coleman, Tennessee, G (2)
2001 Kenyatta Walker, Florida, T
2002 Marquise Walker, Michigan, WR (3)
2003 Dewayne White, Louisville, DE (2)
2004 Michael Clayton, Louisiana St., WR
2005 Carnell Williams, Auburn, RB
2006 Davin Joseph, Oklahoma, G
2007 Gaines Adams, Clemson, DE
2008 Aqib Talib, Kansas, DB

TENNESSEE TITANS
Year Player, College, Position
1960 Billy Cannon, Louisiana State, RB
1961 Mike Ditka, Pittsburgh, E
1962 Ray Jacobs, Howard Payne, DT
1963 Danny Brabham, Arkansas, LB
1964 Scott Appleton, Texas, DT
1965 Lawrence Elkins, Baylor, WR
1966 Tommy Nobis, Texas, LB
1967 George Webster, Michigan St., LB
      Tom Regner, Notre Dame, G
1968 Mac Haik, Mississippi, WR (2)
1969 Ron Pritchard, Arizona State, LB
1970 Doug Wilkerson, N. Carolina Central, G
1971 Dan Pastorini, Santa Clara, QB
1972 Greg Sampson, Stanford, DE
1973 John Matuszak, Tampa, DE
      George Amundson, Iowa State, RB
1974 Steve Manstedt, Nebraska, LB (2)
1975 Robert Brazile, Jackson State, LB
      Don Hardeman, Texas A&I, RB
1976 Mike Barber, Louisiana Tech, TE (2)
1977 Morris Towns, Missouri, T
1978 Earl Campbell, Texas, RB
1979 Mike Stensrud, Iowa State, DE (2)
1980 Angelo Fields, Michigan St., T (2)
1981 Michael Holston, Morgan St., WR (3)

1982 Mike Munchak, Penn State, G
1983 Bruce Matthews, So. California, T
1984 Dean Steinkuhler, Nebraska, T
1985 Ray Childress, Texas A&M, DE
      Richard Johnson, Wisconsin, DB
1986 Jim Everett, Purdue, QB
1987 Alonzo Highsmith, Miami, RB
      Haywood Jeffires, North Carolina St., WR
1988 Lorenzo White, Michigan State, RB
1989 David Williams, Florida, T
1990 Lamar Lathon, Houston, LB
1991 Mike Dumas, Indiana, DB (2)
1992 Eddie Robinson, Alabama St., LB (2)
1993 Brad Hopkins, Illinois, T
1994 Henry Ford, Arkansas, DE
1995 Steve McNair, Alcorn State, QB
1996 Eddie George, Ohio State, RB
1997 Kenny Holmes, Miami, DE
1998 Kevin Dyson, Utah, WR
1999 Jevon Kearse, Florida, DE
2000 Keith Bulluck, Syracuse, LB
2001 Andre Dyson, Utah, DB (2)
2002 Albert Haynesworth, Tennessee, DT
2003 Andre Woolfolk, Oklahoma, DB
2004 Ben Troupe, Florida, TE (2)
2005 Adam Jones, West Virginia, DB
2006 Vince Young, Texas, QB
2007 Michael Griffin, Texas, DB
2008 Chris Johnson, East Carolina, RB

WASHINGTON REDSKINS
Year Player, College, Position
1936 Riley Smith, Alabama, B
1937 Sammy Baugh, Texas Christian, B
1938 Andy Farkas, Detroit, B
1939 I.B. Hale, Texas Christian, T
1940 Ed Boell, New York U., B
1941 Forest Evashevski, Michigan, B
1942 Orban (Spec) Sanders, Texas, B
1943 Jack Jenkins, Missouri, B
1944 Mike Micka, Colgate, B
1945 Jim Hardy, Southern California, B
1946 Cal Rossi, UCLA, B*
1947 Cal Rossi, UCLA, B
1948 Harry Gilmer, Alabama, B
      Lowell Tew, Alabama, B
1949 Rob Goode, Texas A&M, B
1950 George Thomas, Oklahoma, B
1951 Leon Heath, Oklahoma, B
1952 Larry Isbell, Baylor, B
1953 Jack Scarbath, Maryland, B
1954 Steve Meilinger, Kentucky, E
1955 Ralph Guglielmi, Notre Dame, B
1956 Ed Vereb, Maryland, B
1957 Don Bosseler, Miami, B
1958 Mike Sommer, George
      Washington, B (2)
1959 Don Allard, Boston College, B
1960 Richie Lucas, Penn State, QB
1961 Norman Snead, Wake Forest, QB
      Joe Rutgens, Illinois, DT
1962 Ernie Davis, Syracuse, RB
1963 Pat Richter, Wisconsin, TE
1964 Charley Taylor, Arizona St., RB-WR
1965 Bob Breitenstein, Tulsa, T (2)
1966 Charlie Gogolak, Princeton, K
1967 Ray McDonald, Idaho, RB
1968 Jim Smith, Oregon, DB
1969 Eugene Epps, Texas-El Paso, DB (2)
1970 Bill Bundige, Colorado, DT (2)

1971 Cotton Speyrer, Texas, WR (2)
1972 Moses Denson, Maryland St., RB (8)
1973 Charles Cantrell, Lamar, G (5)
1974 Jon Keyworth, Colorado, TE (6)
1975 Mike Thomas, Nevada-Las Vegas, RB (6)
1976 Mike Hughes, Baylor, G (5)
1977 Duncan McColl, Stanford, DE (4)
1978 Tony Green, Florida, RB (6)
1979 Don Warren, San Diego St., TE (4)
1980 Art Monk, Syracuse, WR
1981 Mark May, Pittsburgh, T
1982 Vernon Dean, San Diego St., DB (2)
1983 Darrell Green, Texas A&I, DB
1984 Bob Slater, Oklahoma, DT (2)
1985 Tory Nixon, San Diego St., DB (2)
1986 Markus Koch, Boise State, DE (2)
1987 Brian Davis, Nebraska, DB (2)
1988 Chip Lohmiller, Minnesota, K (2)
1989 Tracy Rocker, Auburn, DT (3)
1990 Andre Collins, Penn State, LB (2)
1991 Bobby Wilson, Michigan State, DT
1992 Desmond Howard, Michigan, WR
1993 Tom Carter, Notre Dame, DB
1994 Heath Shuler, Tennessee, QB
1995 Michael Westbrook, Colorado, WR
1996 Andre Johnson, Penn State, T
1997 Kenard Lang, Miami, DE
1998 Stephen Alexander, Oklahoma, TE (2)
1999 Champ Bailey, Georgia, DB
2000 LaVar Arrington, Penn State, LB
       Chris Samuels, Alabama, T
2001 Rod Gardner, Clemson, WR
2002 Patrick Ramsey, Tulane, QB
2003 Taylor Jacobs, Florida, WR (2)
2004 Sean Taylor, Miami, DB
2005 Carlos Rogers, Auburn, DB
       Jason Campbell, Auburn, QB
2006 Rocky McIntosh, Miami, LB (2)
2007 LaRon Landry, Louisiana State, DB
2008 Devin Thomas, Michigan State, WR (2)
*Choice lost because of ineligibility

HISTORY OF OVERTIME GAMES
PRESEASON

Aug. 28, 1955	Los Angeles 23, New York Giants 17, at Portland, Oregon
Aug. 24, 1962	Denver 27, Dallas Texans 24, at Fort Worth, Texas
Aug. 10, 1974	San Diego 20, New York Jets 14, at San Diego
Aug. 17, 1974	Pittsburgh 33, Philadelphia 30, at Philadelphia
Aug. 17, 1974	Dallas 19, Houston 13, at Dallas
Aug. 17, 1974	Cincinnati 13, Atlanta 7, at Atlanta
Sept. 6, 1974	Buffalo 23, New York Giants 17, at Buffalo
Aug. 9, 1975	Baltimore 23, Denver 20, at Denver
Aug. 30, 1975	New England 20, Green Bay 17, at Milwaukee
Sept. 13, 1975	Minnesota 14, San Diego 14, at San Diego
Aug. 1, 1976	New England 13, New York Giants 7, at New England
Aug. 2, 1976	Kansas City 9, Houston 3, at Kansas City
Aug. 20, 1976	New Orleans 26, Baltimore 20, at Baltimore
Sept. 4, 1976	Dallas 26, Houston 20, at Dallas
Aug. 13, 1977	Seattle 23, Dallas 17, at Seattle
Aug. 28, 1977	New England 13, Pittsburgh 10, at New England
Aug. 28, 1977	New York Giants 24, Buffalo 21, at East Rutherford, N.J.
Aug. 2, 1979	Seattle 12, Minnesota 9, at Minnesota
Aug. 4, 1979	Los Angeles 20, Oakland 14, at Los Angeles
Aug. 24, 1979	Denver 20, New England 17, at Denver
Aug. 23, 1980	Tampa Bay 20, Cincinnati 14, at Tampa Bay
Aug. 5, 1981	San Francisco 27, Seattle 24, at Seattle
Aug. 29, 1981	New Orleans 20, Detroit 17, at New Orleans
Aug. 28, 1982	Miami 17, Kansas City 17, at Kansas City
Sept. 3, 1982	Miami 16, New York Giants 13, at Miami
Aug. 6, 1983	L.A. Raiders 26, San Francisco 23, at Los Angeles
Aug. 6, 1983	Atlanta 13, Washington 10, at Atlanta
Aug. 13, 1983	St. Louis 27, Chicago 24, at St. Louis
Aug. 18, 1983	New York Jets 20, Cincinnati 17, at Cincinnati
Aug. 27, 1983	Chicago 20, Kansas City 17, at Chicago
Aug. 11, 1984	Pittsburgh 20, Philadelphia 17, at Pittsburgh
Aug. 9, 1985	Buffalo 10, Detroit 10, at Pontiac, Mich.
Aug. 10, 1985	Minnesota 16, Miami 13, at Miami
Aug. 17, 1985	Dallas 27, San Diego 24, at San Diego
Aug. 24, 1985	N.Y. Giants 34, N.Y. Jets 31, at East Rutherford, N.J.
Aug. 15, 1986	Washington 27, Pittsburgh 24, at Washington
Aug. 15, 1986	Detroit 30, Seattle 27, at Detroit
Aug. 23, 1986	Los Angeles Rams 20, San Diego 17, at Anaheim
Aug. 30, 1986	Minnesota 23, Indianapolis 20, at Indianapolis
Aug. 23, 1987	Philadelphia 19, New England 13, at New England
Sept. 5, 1987	Cleveland 30, Green Bay 24, at Milwaukee
Sept. 6, 1987	Kansas City 13, St. Louis 10, at Memphis, Tenn.
Aug. 11, 1988	Seattle 16, Detroit 13, at Detroit
Aug. 19, 1988	Miami 16, Denver 13, at Miami
Aug. 19, 1988	Green Bay 21, Kansas City 21, at Milwaukee
Aug. 20, 1988	Houston 20, Los Angeles Rams 17, at Anaheim
Aug. 21, 1988	Minnesota 19, Phoenix 16, at Phoenix
Aug. 5, 1989	Los Angeles Rams 16, San Francisco 13, at Tokyo, Japan
Aug. 26, 1989	Denver 24, Dallas 21, at Denver
Sept. 1, 1989	N.Y. Jets 15, Kansas City 13, at Kansas City
Aug. 24, 1990	Cincinnati 13, New England 10, at New England
Aug. 16, 1991	Cleveland 24, Washington 21, at Washington
Aug. 17, 1991	Cincinnati 27, Minnesota 24, at Cincinnati
Aug. 23, 1991	Dallas 20, Atlanta 17, at Dallas
Aug. 24, 1991	Cincinnati 19, Green Bay 16, at Green Bay
Aug. 22, 1992	Los Angeles Rams 16, Green Bay 13, at Anaheim
Aug. 8, 1993	Dallas 13, Detroit 13, at London, England
Aug. 12, 1995	Washington 16, Houston 13, at Knoxville, Tenn.
Aug. 19, 1995	Indianapolis 20, Green Bay 17, at Green Bay
Aug. 3, 1996	Minnesota 23, San Diego 20, at Minnesota
Aug. 10, 1996	San Francisco 16, San Diego 13, at San Francisco
Aug. 1, 1998	Green Bay 27, Kansas City 24, at Tokyo, Japan
Aug. 7, 1998	Detroit 13, Arizona 10, at Pontiac, Mich.
Aug. 22, 1998	Minnesota 25, Carolina 22, at Charlotte, N.C.
Aug. 9, 1999	Cleveland 20, Dallas 17, at Canton, Ohio
Aug. 4, 2001	Chicago 16, Cincinnati 13, at Chicago
Aug. 18, 2001	San Diego 23, Miami 20, at Miami
Aug. 18, 2001	Arizona 16, Seattle 13, at Seattle
Aug. 25, 2001	San Diego 13, St. Louis 10, at San Diego
Aug. 10, 2002	Kansas City 17, San Francisco 14, at San Francisco
Aug. 31, 2006	Dallas 10, Minnesota 10, at Dallas

indicates Monday-night game
 # indicates Thursday/Saturday/Sunday-night game
+ indicates Thanksgiving Day game

REGULAR SEASON

Sept. 22, 1974—Pittsburgh 35, Denver 35, at Denver; Steelers win toss. Gilliam's pass intercepted and returned by Rowser to Denver's 42. Turner misses 41-yard field goal. Walden punts and Greer returns to Broncos' 39. Van Heusen punts and Edwards returns to Steelers' 16. Game ends with Steelers on own 26.

Nov. 10, 1974—New York Jets 26, New York Giants 20, at New Haven, Conn.; Giants win toss. Gogolak misses 42-yard field goal. Namath passes to Boozer for five yards and touchdown at 6:53.

Sept. 28, 1975—Dallas 37, St. Louis 31, at Dallas; Cardinals win toss. Hart's pass intercepted and returned by Jordan to Cardinals' 37. Staubach passes to DuPree for three yards and touchdown at 7:53.

Oct. 12, 1975—Los Angeles 13, San Diego 10, at San Diego; Chargers win toss. Partee punts to Rams' 14. Dempsey kicks 22-yard field goal at 9:27.

Nov. 2, 1975—Washington 30, Dallas 24, at Washington; Cowboys win toss. Staubach's pass intercepted and returned by Houston to Cowboys' 35. Kilmer runs one yard for touchdown at 6:34.

Nov. 16, 1975—St. Louis 20, Washington 17, at St. Louis; Cardinals win toss. Bakken kicks 37-yard field goal at 7:00.

Nov. 23, 1975—Kansas City 24, Detroit 21, at Kansas City; Lions win toss. Chiefs take over on downs at own 38. Stenerud kicks 26-yard field goal at 6:44.

Nov. 23, 1975—Oakland 26, Washington 23, at Washington; Redskins win toss. Bragg punts to Raiders' 42. Blanda kicks 27-yard field goal at 7:13.

Nov. 30, 1975—Denver 13, San Diego 10, at Denver; Broncos win toss. Turner kicks 25-yard field goal at 4:13.

Nov. 30, 1975—Oakland 37, Atlanta 34, at Oakland; Falcons win toss. James punts to Raiders' 16. Guy punts and Herron returns to Falcons' 41. Nick Mike-Mayer misses 45-yard field goal. Guy punts to Falcons' end zone. James punts to Raiders' 39. Blanda kicks 36-yard field goal at 15:00.

Dec. 14, 1975—Baltimore 10, Miami 7, at Baltimore; Dolphins win toss. Seiple punts to Colts' 4. Linhart kicks 31-yard field goal at 12:44.

Sept. 19, 1976—Minnesota 10, Los Angeles 10, at Minnesota; Vikings win toss. Tarkenton's pass intercepted by Monte Jackson and returned to Minnesota 16. Allen blocks Dempsey's 30-yard field goal attempt, ball rolls into end zone for touchback. Clabo punts and Scribner returns to Rams' 20. Rusty Jackson punts to Vikings' 35. Tarkenton's pass intercepted by Kay at Rams' 1, no return. Game ends with Rams on own 3.

* **Sept. 27, 1976—Washington 20, Philadelphia 17,** at Philadelphia; Eagles win toss. Jones punts and E. Brown loses one yard on return to Redskins' 40. Bragg punts 51 yards into end zone for touchback. Jones punts and E. Brown returns to Redskins' 42. Bragg punts and Marshall returns to Eagles' 41. Boryla's pass intercepted by Dusek at Redskins' 37, no return. Bragg punts and Bradley returns. Philadelphia holding penalty moves ball back to Eagles' 8. Boryla pass intercepted by E. Brown and returned to Eagles' 22. Moseley kicks 29-yard field goal at 12:49.

Oct. 17, 1976—Kansas City 20, Miami 17, at Miami; Chiefs win toss. Wilson punts into end zone for touchback. Bulaich fumbles into Kansas City end zone, Collier recovers for touchback. Stenerud kicks 34-yard field goal at 14:48.

Oct. 31, 1976—St. Louis 23, San Francisco 20, at St. Louis; Cardinals win toss. Joyce punts and Leonard fumbles on return, Jones recovers at 49ers' 43. Bakken kicks 21-yard field goal at 6:42.

Dec. 5, 1976—San Diego 13, San Francisco 7, at San Diego; Chargers win toss. Morris runs 13 yards for touchdown at 5:12.

Sept. 18, 1977—Dallas 16, Minnesota 10, at Minnesota; Vikings win toss. Dallas starts on Vikings' 47 after a punt early in the overtime period. Staubach scores seven plays later on a four-yard run at 6:14.

* **Sept. 26, 1977—Cleveland 30, New England 27,** at Cleveland; Browns win toss. Sipe throws a 22-yard pass to Logan at Patriots' 19. Cockroft kicks 35-yard field goal at 4:45.

Oct. 16, 1977—Minnesota 22, Chicago 16, at Minnesota;

Bears win toss. Parsons punts 53 yards to Vikings' 18. Minnesota drives to Bears' 11. On a first-and-10, Vikings fake a field goal and holder Krause hits Voigt with a touchdown pass at 6:45.

Oct. 30, 1977—Cincinnati 13, Houston 10, at Cincinnati; Bengals win toss. Bahr kicks a 22-yard field goal at 5:51.

Nov. 13, 1977—San Francisco 10, New Orleans 7, at New Orleans; Saints win toss. Saints fail to move ball and Blanchard punts to 49ers' 41. Wersching kicks a 33-yard field goal at 6:33.

Dec. 18, 1977—Chicago 12, New York Giants 9, at East Rutherford, N.J.; Giants win toss. The ball changes hands eight times before Thomas kicks a 28-yard field goal at 14:51.

Sept. 10, 1978—Cleveland 13, Cincinnati 10, at Cleveland; Browns win toss. Collins returns kickoff 41 yards to Browns' 47. Cockroft kicks 27-yard field goal at 4:30.

* **Sept. 11, 1978—Minnesota 12, Denver 9,** at Minnesota; Vikings win toss. Danmeier kicks 44-yard field goal at 2:56.

Sept. 24, 1978—Pittsburgh 15, Cleveland 9, at Pittsburgh; Steelers win toss. Cunningham scores on a 37-yard "gadget" pass from Bradshaw at 3:43. Steelers start winning drive on their 21.

Sept. 24, 1978—Denver 23, Kansas City 17, at Kansas City; Broncos win toss. Dilts punts to Kansas City. Chiefs advance to Broncos' 40 where Reed fails to make first down on fourth-and-one situation. Broncos march downfield. Preston scores two-yard touchdown at 10:28.

Oct. 1, 1978—Oakland 25, Chicago 19, at Chicago; Bears win toss. Both teams punt on first possession. On Chicago's second offensive series, Colzie intercepts Avellini's pass and returns it to Bears' 3. Three plays later, Whittington runs two yards for a touchdown at 5:19.

Oct. 15, 1978—Dallas 24, St. Louis 21, at St. Louis; Cowboys win toss. Dallas drives from its 23 into field goal range. Septien kicks 27-yard field goal at 3:28.

Oct. 29, 1978—Denver 20, Seattle 17, at Seattle; Broncos win toss. Ball changes hands four times before Turner kicks 18-yard field goal at 12:59.

Nov. 12, 1978—San Diego 29, Kansas City 23, at San Diego; Chiefs win toss. Fouts hits Jefferson for decisive 14-yard touchdown pass on the last play (15:00) of overtime period.

Nov. 12, 1978—Washington 16, New York Giants 13, at Washington; Redskins win toss. Moseley kicks winning 45-yard field goal at 8:32 after missing first down field goal attempt of 35 yards at 4:50.

Nov. 26, 1978—Green Bay 10, Minnesota 10, at Green Bay; Packers win toss. Both teams have possession of the ball four times.

Dec. 9, 1978—Cleveland 37, New York Jets 34, at Cleveland; Browns win toss. Cockroft kicks 22-yard field goal at 3:07.

Sept. 2, 1979—Atlanta 40, New Orleans 34, at New Orleans; Falcons win toss. Bartkowski's pass intercepted by Myers and returned to Falcons' 46. Erxleben punts to Falcons' 4. James punts to Chandler on Saints' 43. Erxleben punts and Ryckman returns to Falcons' 36. James punts and Chandler returns to Saints' 36. Erxleben retrieves punt snap on Saints' 1 and attempts pass. Mayberry intercepts and returns six yards for touchdown at 8:22.

Sept. 2, 1979—Cleveland 25, New York Jets 22, at New York; Jets win toss. Leahy's 43-yard field goal attempt goes wide right at 4:41. Evans's punt blocked by Dykes is recovered by Newton. Ramsey punts into end zone for touchback. Evans punts and Harper returns to Jets' 24. Robinson's pass intercepted by Davis and returned 33 yards to Jets' 31. Cockroft kicks 27-yard field goal at 14:45.

* **Sept. 3, 1979—Pittsburgh 16, New England 13,** at Foxboro; Patriots win toss. Hare runs to Swann at Steelers' 31. Bahr kicks 41-yard field goal at 5:10.

Sept. 9, 1979—Tampa Bay 29, Baltimore 26, at Baltimore; Colts win toss. Landry fumbles, recovered by Kollar at Colts' 14. O'Donoghue kicks 31-yard, first-down field goal at 1:41.

Sept. 16, 1979—Denver 20, Atlanta 17, at Atlanta; Broncos win toss. Broncos march 65 yards to Falcons' 7. Turner kicks 24-yard field goal at 6:15.

Sept. 23, 1979—Houston 30, Cincinnati 27, at Cincinnati; Oilers win toss. Parsley punts and Lusby returns to Bengals' 35. Bahr's 32-yard field goal attempt is wide right at 8:05. Parsley's punt downed on Bengals' 5. McInally punts and Ellender returns to Bengals' 42. Fritsch's third down, 29-yard field goal attempt hits left upright and bounces through at 14:28.

Sept. 23, 1979—Minnesota 27, Green Bay 21, at Minnesota;

Vikings win toss. Kramer throws 50-yard touchdown pass to Rashad at 3:18.

Oct. 28, 1979—Houston 27, New York Jets 24, at Houston; Oilers win toss. Oilers march 58 yards to Jets' 18. Fritsch kicks 35-yard field goal at 5:10.

Nov. 18, 1979—Cleveland 30, Miami 24, at Cleveland; Browns win toss. Sipe passes 39 yards to Rucker for touchdown at 1:59.

Nov. 25, 1979—Pittsburgh 33, Cleveland 30, at Pittsburgh; Browns win toss. Sipe's pass intercepted by Blount on Steelers' 4. Bradshaw pass intercepted by Bolton on Browns' 12. Evans punts and Bell returns to Steelers' 17. Bahr kicks 37-yard field goal at 14:51.

Nov. 25, 1979—Buffalo 16, New England 13, at Foxboro; Patriots win toss. Hare's punt downed on Bills' 38. Jackson punts and Morgan returns to Patriots' 20. Grogan's pass intercepted by Haslett and returned to Bills' 42. Ferguson's 51-yard pass to Butler sets up N. Mike-Mayer's 29-yard field goal at 9:15.

Dec. 2, 1979—Los Angeles 27, Minnesota 21, at Los Angeles; Rams win toss. Clark punts and Miller returns to Vikings' 25. Kramer's pass intercepted by Brown and returned to Rams' 40. Cromwell, holding for 22-yard field goal attempt, runs around left end untouched for winning score at 6:53.

Sept. 7, 1980—Green Bay 12, Chicago 6, at Green Bay; Bears win toss. Parsons punts and Nixon returns 16 yards. Five plays later, Marcol returns own blocked field goal 24 yards for touchdown at 6:00.

Sept. 14, 1980—San Diego 30, Oakland 24, at San Diego; Raiders win toss. Pastorini's first-down pass intercepted by Edwards. Millen intercepts Fouts' first-down pass and returns to San Diego 46. Bahr's 50-yard field goal attempt partially blocked by Williams and recovered on Chargers' 32. Eight plays later, Fouts throws 24-yard touchdown pass to Jefferson at 8:09.

Sept. 14, 1980—San Francisco 24, St. Louis 21, at San Francisco; Cardinals win toss. Swider punts and Robinson returns to 49ers' 32. San Francisco drives 52 yards to St. Louis 16, where Wersching kicks 33-yard field goal at 4:12.

Oct. 12, 1980—Green Bay 14, Tampa Bay 14, at Tampa Bay; Packers win toss. Teams trade punts twice. Lee returns second Tampa Bay punt to Green Bay 42. Dickey completes three passes to Buccaneers' 18, where Birney's 36-yard field goal attempt is wide right as time expires.

Nov. 9, 1980—Atlanta 33, St. Louis 27, at St. Louis; Falcons win toss. Strong runs 21 yards for touchdown at 4:20.

\# **Nov. 20, 1980—San Diego 27, Miami 24,** at Miami; Chargers win toss. Partridge punts into end zone, Dolphins take over on their own 20. Woodley's pass for Nathan intercepted by Lowe and returned 28 yards to Dolphins' 12. Benirschke kicks 28-yard field goal at 7:14.

Nov. 23, 1980—New York Jets 31, Houston 28, at New York; Jets win toss. Leahy kicks 38-yard field goal at 3:58.

\+ **Nov. 27, 1980—Chicago 23, Detroit 17,** at Detroit; Bears win toss. Williams returns kickoff 95 yards for touchdown at 0:21.

Dec. 7, 1980—Buffalo 10, Los Angeles 7, at Buffalo; Rams win toss. Corral punts and Hooks returns to Bills' 34. Ferguson's 30-yard pass to Lewis sets up N. Mike-Mayer's 30-yard field goal at 5:14.

Dec. 7, 1980—San Francisco 38, New Orleans 35, at San Francisco; Saints win toss. Erxleben's punt downed by Hardy on 49ers' 27. Wersching kicks 36-yard field goal at 7:40.

* **Dec. 8, 1980—Miami 16, New England 13,** at Miami; Dolphins win toss. Von Schamann kicks 23-yard field goal at 3:20.

Dec. 14, 1980—Cincinnati 17, Chicago 14, at Chicago; Bengals win toss. Breech kicks 28-yard field goal at 4:23.

Dec. 21, 1980—Los Angeles 20, Atlanta 17, at Los Angeles; Rams win toss. Corral's punt downed at Rams' 34. James punts into end zone for touchback. Corral's punt downed on Falcons' 17. Bartkowski fumbles when hit by Harris, recovered by Delaney. Corral kicks 23-yard field goal on first play of possession at 7:00.

Sept. 27, 1981—Cincinnati 27, Buffalo 24, at Cincinnati; Bills win toss. Cater punts into end zone for touchback. Bengals drive to the Bills' 10 where Breech kicks 28-yard field goal at 9:33.

Sept. 27, 1981—Pittsburgh 27, New England 21, at Pittsburgh; Patriots win toss. Hubach punts and Smith returns five yards to midfield. Four plays later Bradshaw throws 24-yard touchdown pass to Swann at 3:19.

Oct. 4, 1981—Miami 28, New York Jets 28, at Miami; Jets win toss. Teams trade punts twice. Leahy's 48-yard field goal

attempt is wide right as time expires.

Oct. 25, 1981—New York Giants 27, Atlanta 24, at Atlanta; Giants win toss. Jennings' punt goes out of bounds at New York 47. Bright returns Atlanta punt to Giants' 14. Woerner fair catches punt at own 28. Andrews fumbles on first play, recovered by Van Pelt. Danelo kicks 40-yard field goal four plays later at 9:20.

Oct. 25, 1981—Chicago 20, San Diego 17, at Chicago; Bears win toss. Teams trade punts. Bears' second punt returned by Brooks to Chargers' 33. Fouts pass intercepted by Fencik and returned 32 yards to San Diego 27. Roveto kicks 27-yard field goal seven plays later at 9:30.

Nov. 8, 1981—Chicago 16, Kansas City 13, at Kansas City; Bears win toss. Teams trade punts. Kansas City takes over on downs on its own 38. Fuller's fumble recovered by Harris on Chicago 36. Roveto's 37-yard field goal wide, but Chiefs penalized for leverage. Roveto's 22-yard field goal attempt three plays later is good at 13:07.

Nov. 8, 1981—Denver 23, Cleveland 20, at Denver; Browns win toss. D. Smith recovers Hill's fumble at Denver 48. Morton's 33-yard pass to Upchurch and 6-yard run by Preston set up Steinfort's 30-yard field goal at 4:10.

Nov. 8, 1981—Miami 30, New England 27, at New England; Dolphins win toss. Orosz punts and Morgan returns six yards to New England 26. Grogan's pass intercepted by Brudzinski who returns 19 yards to Patriots' 26. Von Schamann kicks 30-yard field goal on first down at 7:09.

Nov. 15, 1981—Washington 30, New York Giants 27, at New York; Giants win toss. Nelms returns Giants' punt 26 yards to New York 47. Five plays later Moseley kicks 48-yard field goal at 3:44.

Dec. 21, 1981—New York Giants 13, Dallas 10, at New York; Cowboys win toss and kick off. Jennings punts to Dallas 40. Taylor recovers Dorsett's fumble on second down. Danelo's 33-yard field goal attempt hits left upright and bounces back. White's pass for Pearson intercepted by Hunt and returned seven yards to Dallas 24. Four plays later Danelo kicks 35-yard field goal at 6:19.

Sept. 12, 1982—Washington 37, Philadelphia 34, at Philadelphia; Redskins win toss. Theismann completes five passes for 63 yards to set up Moseley's 26-yard field goal at 4:47.

Sept. 19, 1982—Pittsburgh 26, Cincinnati 20, at Pittsburgh; Bengals win toss. Anderson's pass intended for Kreider intercepted by Woodruff and returned 30 yards to Cincinnati 2. Bradshaw completes two-yard touchdown pass to Stallworth on first down at 1:08.

Dec. 19, 1982—Baltimore 20, Green Bay 20, at Baltimore; Packers win toss. K. Anderson intercepts Dickey's first-down pass and returns to Packers' 42. Miller's 44-yard field goal attempt blocked by G. Lewis. Teams trade punts before Stenerud's 47-yard field goal attempt is wide right. Teams trade punts again before time expires in Colts possession.

Jan. 2, 1983—Tampa Bay 26, Chicago 23, at Tampa; Bears win toss. Parsons punts to T. Bell at Buccaneers' 40. Capece kicks 33-yard field goal at 3:14.

Sept. 4, 1983—Baltimore 29, New England 23, at New England; Patriots win toss. Cooks runs 52 yards with fumble recovery three plays into overtime at 0:30.

Sept. 4, 1983—Green Bay 41, Houston 38, at Houston; Packers win toss. Stenerud kicks 42-yard field goal at 5:55.

Sept. 11, 1983—New York Giants 16, Atlanta 13, at Atlanta; Giants win toss. Dennis returns kickoff 54 yards to Atlanta 41. Haji-Sheikh kicks 30-yard field goal at 3:38.

Sept. 18, 1983—New Orleans 34, Chicago 31, at New Orleans; Bears win toss. Parsons punts and Groth returns five yards to New Orleans 34. Stabler pass intercepted by Schmidt at Chicago 47. Parsons punt downed by Gentry at New Orleans 2. Stabler gains 36 yards in four passes; Wilson 38 on six carries. Andersen kicks 41-yard field goal at 10:57.

Sept. 18, 1983—Minnesota 19, Tampa Bay 16, at Tampa; Vikings win toss. Coleman punts and Bell returns eight yards to Tampa Bay 27. Capece's 33-yard field goal attempt sails wide at 7:26. Dils and Young combine for 48-yard gain to Tampa Bay 27. Ricardo kicks 42-yard field goal at 9:27.

Sept. 25, 1983—Baltimore 22, Chicago 19, at Baltimore; Colts win toss. Allegre kicks 33-yard field goal nine plays later at 4:51.

Sept. 25, 1983—Cleveland 30, San Diego 24, at San Diego; Browns win toss. Walker returns kickoff 33 yards to Cleveland 37. Sipe completes 48-yard touchdown pass to Holt four plays later at 1:53.

Sept. 25, 1983—New York Jets 27, Los Angeles Rams 24, at New York; Jets win toss. Ramsey punts to Irvin who returns to 25 but penalty puts Rams on own 13. Holmes 30-yard interception return sets up Leahy's 26-yard field goal at 3:22.

Oct. 9, 1983—Buffalo 38, Miami 35, at Miami; Dolphins win toss. Von Schamann's 52-yard field goal attempt goes wide at 12:36. Cater punts to Clayton who loses 11 to own 13. Von Schamann's 43-yard field goal attempt sails wide at 5:15. Danelo kicks 36-yard field goal nine plays later at 13:58.

Oct. 9, 1983—Dallas 27, Tampa Bay 24, at Dallas; Cowboys win toss. Septien's 51-yard field-goal attempt goes wide but Buccaneers penalized for roughing kicker. Septien kicks 42-yard field goal at 4:38.

Oct. 23, 1983—Kansas City 13, Houston 10, at Houston; Chiefs win toss. Lowery kicks 41-yard field goal 13 plays later at 7:41.

Oct. 23, 1983—Minnesota 20, Green Bay 17, at Green Bay; Packers win toss. Scribner's punt downed on Vikings' 42. Ricardo kicks 32-yard field goal eight plays later at 5:05.

* **Oct. 24, 1983—New York Giants 20, St. Louis 20,** at St. Louis; Cardinals win toss. Teams trade punts before O'Donoghue's 44-yard field goal attempt is wide left. Jennings' punt returned by Bird to St. Louis 21. Lomax pass intercepted by Haynes who loses six yards to New York 33. Jennings' punt downed on St. Louis 17. O'Donoghue's 19-yard field goal attempt is wide right. Rutledge's pass intercepted by L. Washington who returns 25 yards to New York 25. O'Donoghue's 42-yard field goal attempt is wide right. Rutledge's pass intercepted by W. Smith at St. Louis 33 to end game.

Oct. 30, 1983—Cleveland 25, Houston 19, at Cleveland; Oilers win toss. Teams trade punts. Nielsen's pass intercepted by Whitwell who returns to Houston 20. Green runs 20 yards for touchdown on first down at 6:34.

Nov. 20, 1983—Detroit 23, Green Bay 20, at Milwaukee; Packers win toss. Scribner punts and Jenkins returns 14 yards to Green Bay 45. Murray's 33-yard field goal attempt is wide left at 9:32. Whitehurst's pass intercepted by Watkins and returned to Green Bay 27. Murray kicks 37-yard field goal four plays later at 8:30.

Nov. 27, 1983—Atlanta 47, Green Bay 41, at Atlanta; Packers win toss. K. Johnson returns interception 31 yards for touchdown at 2:13.

Nov. 27, 1983—Seattle 51, Kansas City 48, at Seattle; Seahawks win toss. Dixon's 47-yard kickoff return sets up N. Johnson's 42-yard field goal at 1:36.

Dec. 11, 1983—New Orleans 20, Philadelphia 17, at Philadelphia; Eagles win toss. Runager punts to Groth who fair catches on New Orleans 32. Stabler completes two passes for 36 yards to Goodlow to set up Andersen's 50-yard field goal at 5:30.

* **Dec. 12, 1983—Green Bay 12, Tampa Bay 9,** at Tampa; Packers win toss. Stenerud kicks 23-yard field goal 11 plays later at 4:07.

Sept. 9, 1984—Detroit 27, Atlanta 24, at Atlanta; Lions win toss. Murray kicks 48-yard field goal nine plays later at 5:06.

Sept. 30, 1984—Tampa Bay 30, Green Bay 27, at Tampa; Packers win toss. Scribner punts 44 yards to Tampa Bay 2. Epps returns Garcia's punt three yards to Green Bay 27. Scribner's punt downed on Buccaneers' 33. Ariri kicks 46-yard field goal 11 plays later at 10:32.

Oct. 14, 1984—Detroit 13, Tampa Bay 7, at Detroit; Buccaneers win toss. Tampa Bay drives to Lions' 39 before Wilder fumbles. Five plays later Danielson hits Thompson with 37-yard touchdown pass at 4:34.

Oct. 21, 1984—Dallas 30, New Orleans 27, at Dallas; Cowboys win toss. Septien kicks 41-yard field goal eight plays later at 3:42.

Oct. 28, 1984—Denver 22, Los Angeles Raiders 19, at Los Angeles; Raiders win toss. Hawkins fumble recovered by Foley at Denver 7. Teams trade punts. Karlis's 42-yard field goal attempt is wide left. Teams trade punts. Wilson pass intercepted by R. Jackson at Los Angeles 45, returned 23 yards to Los Angeles 22. Karlis kicks 35-yard field goal two plays later at 15:00.

Nov. 4, 1984—Philadelphia 23, Detroit 23, at Detroit; Lions win toss. Lions drive to Eagles' 19 in eight plays. Murray's 21-yard field goal attempt hits right upright and bounces back. Jaworski's pass intercepted by Watkins at Detroit 5. Teams trade punts. Cooper returns Black's punt five yards to Eagles' 14. Time expires four plays later with Eagles on own 21.

Nov. 18, 1984—San Diego 34, Miami 28, at San Diego; Chargers win toss. McGee scores eight plays later on a 25-yard run at 3:17.

Dec. 2, 1984—Cincinnati 20, Cleveland 17, at Cleveland; Browns win toss. Simmons returns Cox's punt 30 yards to Cleveland 35. Breech kicks 35-yard field goal seven plays later at 4:34.

Dec. 2, 1984—Houston 23, Pittsburgh 20, at Houston; Oilers win toss. Cooper kicks 30-yard field goal 16 plays later at 5:53.

Sept. 8, 1985—St. Louis 27, Cleveland 24, at Cleveland; Cardinals win toss. O'Donoghue kicks 35-yard field goal nine plays later at 5:27.

Sept. 29, 1985—New York Giants 16, Philadelphia 10, at Philadelphia; Eagles win toss. Jaworski's pass tipped by Quick and intercepted by Patterson who returns 29 yards for touchdown at 0:55.

Oct. 20, 1985—Denver 13, Seattle 10, at Denver; Seahawks win toss. Teams trade punts twice. Krieg's pass intercepted by Hunter and returned to Seahawks' 15. Karlis kicks 24-yard field goal four plays later at 9:19.

Nov. 10, 1985—Philadelphia 23, Atlanta 17, at Philadelphia; Falcons win toss. Donnelly's 62-yard punt goes out of bounds at Eagles' 1. Jaworski completes 99-yard touchdown pass to Quick two plays later at 1:49.

Nov. 10, 1985—San Diego 40, Los Angeles Raiders 34, at San Diego; Chargers win toss. James scores on 17-yard run seven plays later at 3:44.

Nov. 17, 1985—Denver 30, San Diego 24, at Denver; Chargers win toss. Thomas' 40-yard field goal attempt blocked by Smith and returned 60 yards by Wright for touchdown at 4:45.

Nov. 24, 1985—New York Jets 16, New England 13, at New York; Jets win toss. Teams trade punts twice. Patriots' second punt returned 46 yards by Sohn to Patriots' 15. Leahy kicks 32-yard field goal one play later at 10:05.

Nov. 24, 1985—Tampa Bay 19, Detroit 16, at Tampa; Lions win toss. Teams trade punts. Lions' punt downed on Buccaneers' 38. Igwebuike kicks 42-yard field goal 11 plays later at 12:31.

Nov. 24, 1985—Los Angeles Raiders 31, Denver 28, at Los Angeles; Raiders win toss. Bahr kicks 32-yard field goal six plays later at 2:42.

Dec. 8, 1985—Los Angeles Raiders 17, Denver 14, at Denver; Broncos win toss. Teams trade punts twice. Elway's fumble recovered by Townsend at Broncos' 8. Bahr kicks 26-yard field goal one play later at 4:55.

Sept. 14, 1986—Chicago 13, Philadelphia 10, at Chicago; Eagles win toss. Crawford's fumble of kickoff recovered by Jackson at Eagles' 35. Butler kicks 23-yard field goal 10 plays later at 5:56.

Sept. 14, 1986—Cincinnati 36, Buffalo 33, at Cincinnati; Bills win toss. Zander intercepts Kelly's first-down pass and returns it to Bills' 17. Breech kicks 20-yard field goal two plays later at 0:56.

Sept. 21, 1986—New York Jets 51, Miami 45, at New York; Jets win toss. O'Brien completes 43-yard touchdown pass to Walker five plays later at 2:35.

Sept. 28, 1986—Pittsburgh 22, Houston 16, at Houston; Oilers win toss. Johnson's punt returned 41 yards by Woods to Oilers' 15. Abercrombie scores on three-yard run three plays later at 2:35.

Sept. 28, 1986—Atlanta 23, Tampa Bay 20, at Tampa; Falcons win toss. Teams trade punts. Luckhurst kicks 34-yard field goal 10 plays later at 12:35.

Oct. 5, 1986—Los Angeles Rams 26, Tampa Bay 20, at Anaheim; Rams win toss. Dickerson scores four plays later on 42-yard run at 2:16.

Oct. 12, 1986—Minnesota 27, San Francisco 24, at San Francisco; Vikings win toss. C. Nelson kicks 28-yard field goal nine plays later at 4:27.

Oct. 19, 1986—San Francisco 10, Atlanta 10, at Atlanta; Falcons win toss. Teams trade punts twice. Donnelly punts to 49ers' 27. The following play Wilson recovers Rice's fumble at 49ers' 46 as time expires.

Nov. 2, 1986—Washington 44, Minnesota 38, at Washington; Redskins win toss. Schroeder completes 38-yard touchdown pass to Clark four plays later at 1:46.

\#**Nov. 20, 1986—Los Angeles Raiders 37, San Diego 31,** at San Diego; Raiders win toss. Teams trade punts. Allen scores five plays later on 28-yard run at 8:33.

Nov. 23, 1986—Cleveland 37, Pittsburgh 31, at Cleveland; Browns win toss. Teams trade punts. Six plays later Kosar hits

Slaughter with 36-yard touchdown pass at 6:37.

Nov. 30, 1986—Chicago 13, Pittsburgh 10, at Chicago; Bears win toss and kick off. Newsome's punt returned by Barnes to Chicago 49. Butler kicks 42-yard field goal five plays later at 3:55.

Nov. 30, 1986—Philadelphia 33, Los Angeles Raiders 27, at Los Angeles; Eagles win toss. Teams trade punts. Long recovers Cunningham's fumble at Philadelphia 42. Waters returns Allen's fumble 81 yards to Los Angeles 4. Cunningham scores on one-yard run two plays later at 6:53.

Nov. 30, 1986—Cleveland 13, Houston 10, at Cleveland; Oilers win toss and kick off. Gossett punts to Houston 39. Luck's pass intercepted by Minnifield at Cleveland 21. Gossett punts to Houston 34. Luck's pass intercepted by Minnifield at Cleveland 43 who returns 20 yards to Houston 37. Moseley kicks 29-yard field goal nine plays later at 14:44.

Dec. 7, 1986—St. Louis 10, Philadelphia 10, at Philadelphia; Cardinals win toss. White blocks Schubert's 40-yard field goal attempt. Teams trade punts. McFadden's 43-yard field goal attempt is wide left. Schubert's 37-yard field goal attempt is wide right. Cavanaugh's pass intercepted by Carter and returned to Eagles' 48 to end game.

Dec. 14, 1986—Miami 37, Los Angeles Rams 31, at Anaheim; Dolphins win toss. Marino completes 20-yard touchdown pass to Duper six plays later at 3:04.

Sept. 20, 1987—Denver 17, Green Bay 17, at Milwaukee; Packers win toss. Del Greco's 47-yard field goal attempt is short. Teams trade punts. Elway intercepted by Noble who returns 10 yards to Green Bay 34. Davis fumbles on next play and Smith recovers. Two plays later, Karlis's 40-yard field goal attempt is wide left. Time expires two plays later with Packers on own 23.

Oct. 11, 1987—Detroit 19, Green Bay 16, at Green Bay; Lions win toss. Prindle's 42-yard field goal attempt is wide left. Packers punt downed on Detroit 17. Prindle kicks 31-yard field goal 16 plays later at 12:26.

Oct. 18, 1987—New York Jets 37, Miami 31, at New York; Jets win toss. Teams trade punts. Ryan intercepted by Hooper at Jets' 47 who returns 11 yards. Mackey intercepted by Haslett at Jets' 37 who returns 9 yards. Jets punt. Mackey intercepted by Radachowsky who returns 45 yards to Miami 24. Ryan completes eight-yard touchdown pass to Hunter five plays later at 14:26.

Oct. 18, 1987—Green Bay 16, Philadelphia 10, at Green Bay; Packers win toss. Hargrove scores on seven-yard run 10 plays later at 5:04.

Oct. 18, 1987—Buffalo 6, New York Giants 3, at Buffalo; Bills win toss. Schlopy's 28-yard field goal attempt is wide left. Teams trade punts. Rutledge intercepted by Clark who returns 23 yards to Buffalo 40. Schlopy kicks 27-yard field goal nine plays later at 14:41.

Oct. 25, 1987—Buffalo 34, Miami 31, at Miami; Bills win toss. Norwood kicks 27-yard field goal seven plays later at 4:12.

Nov. 1, 1987—San Diego 27, Cleveland 24, at San Diego; Browns win toss. Kosar intercepted by Glenn who returns 20 yards to Browns' 25. Abbott kicks 33-yard field goal three plays later at 2:16.

Nov. 15, 1987—Dallas 23, New England 17, at New England; Cowboys win toss. Walker scores on 60-yard run four plays later at 1:50.

+**Nov. 26, 1987—Minnesota 44, Dallas 38**, at Dallas; Vikings win toss. Coleman's punt downed by Hilton at Cowboys' 37. White intercepted by Studwell who returns 12 yards to Vikings' 37. D. Nelson scores on 24-yard run seven plays later at 7:51.

Nov. 29, 1987—Philadelphia 34, New England 31, at New England; Patriots win toss. Ramsey intercepted by Joyner who returns 29 yards to Eagles' 13. Franklin fair catches Teltschik's punt at Patriots' 13. Franklin's 46-yard field-goal attempt is short. McFadden's 39-yard field goal attempt is wide left. Tatupu fumbles on next play and Cobb recovers. McFadden kicks 38-yard field goal four plays later at 12:16.

Dec. 6, 1987—New York Giants 23, Philadelphia 20, at New York; Giants win toss and kick off. Teams trade punts twice. Teltschik's punt is returned 16 yards by McConkey to Eagles' 33. Three plays later, Allegre's 50-yard field goal attempt is blocked by Kenney and returned 25 yards by Hoage to Eagles' 30. McConkey returns Teltschik's punt four yards to Giants' 44. Allegre kicks 28-yard field goal four plays later at 10:42.

Dec. 6, 1987—Cincinnati 30, Kansas City 27, at Cincinnati; Bengals win toss. Teams trade punts. Breech kicks 32-yard field

goal 16 plays later at 9:44.

Dec. 26, 1987—Washington 27, Minnesota 24, at Minnesota; Redskins win toss. Haji-Sheikh kicks 26-yard field goal six plays later at 2:09.

Sept. 4, 1988—Houston 17, Indianapolis 14, at Indianapolis; Colts win toss. Dickerson fumble recovered by Lyles who returns six yards to Colts' 42. Zendejas kicks 35-yard field goal six plays later at 3:51.

* **Sept. 26, 1988—Los Angeles Raiders 30, Denver 27**, at Denver; Broncos win toss. Teams trade punts twice. Elway intercepted by Lee who returns 20 yards to Broncos' 31. Bahr kicks 35-yard field goal four plays later at 12:35.

Oct. 2, 1988—New York Jets 17, Kansas City 17, at New York; Chiefs win toss. Chiefs punt goes into end zone for touchback. Leahy's 44-yard field goal attempt is wide right. Chiefs punt is returned by Townsell to Jets' 26. Burruss recovers McNeil's fumble at Chiefs' 11. DeBerg intercepted by Humphery at Jets' 49. Three plays later, time expires.

Oct. 9, 1988—Denver 16, San Francisco 13, at San Francisco; Broncos win toss and kick off. Young intercepted by Haynes at Broncos' 32. Denver punt downed at 49ers' 5. Young intercepted by Wilson who returns seven yards to 49ers' 5. Karlis kicks 22-yard field goal two plays later at 8:11.

Oct. 30, 1988—New York Giants 13, Detroit 10, at Detroit; Lions win toss. James's fumble recovered by Taylor at Lions' 22. Three plays later, McFadden kicks 33-yard field goal at 1:13.

Nov. 20, 1988—Buffalo 9, New York Jets 6, at Buffalo; Jets win toss. Vick's fumble recovered by Bennett at Bills' 32. Norwood kicks 30-yard field goal five plays later at 3:47.

Nov. 20, 1988—Philadelphia 23, New York Giants 17, at New York; Eagles win toss. Philadelphia's punt goes into end zone for touchback. Hostetler intercepted by Hoage who returns 11 yards to Giants' 41. Six plays later, Zendejas's 33-yard field-goal attempt is blocked and ball is recovered behind line of scrimmage by Eagles' Simmons, who runs 15 yards for touchdown at 3:09.

Dec. 11, 1988—New England 10, Tampa Bay 7, at New England; Buccaneers win toss and kick off. Staurovsky kicks 27-yard field goal six plays later at 3:08.

Dec. 17, 1988—Cincinnati 20, Washington 17, at Cincinnati; Bengals win toss. Cincinnati's punt returned by Oliphant to Redskins' 16. Grant recovers Williams's fumble at Redskins' 17. Breech kicks 20-yard field goal three plays later at 7:01.

Sept. 24, 1989—Buffalo 47, Houston 41, at Houston; Oilers win toss. Johnson returns Brady's kickoff 17 yards to Oilers' 19. Oilers drive to Buffalo 25, Zendejas's 37-yard field goal blocked, but Bills offsides and Zendejas's second attempt is wide left. Bills' ball and Kelly completes series of passes, including 28-yard game-winner to Andre Reed at 8:42.

Oct. 8, 1989—Miami 13, Cleveland 10, at Miami; Browns win toss. Metcalf returns Stoyanovich's kickoff 20 yards to Browns' 28. Browns drive back 46 yards in eight plays; Bahr wide left on 44-yard field goal attempt. Dolphins ball. Browns called for pass interference on Marino pass to Banks at Cleveland 47. Two plays later, Banks's 20-yard reception at Browns' 23 sets up winning 35-yard field goal by Stoyanovich at 6:23.

Oct. 22, 1989—Denver 24, Seattle 21, at Seattle; Seahawks win toss. Treadwell's 56-yard kickoff returned 18 yards by Jefferson to Seahawks' 27. Seahawks drive to Broncos' 22 in 10 plays, but Johnson's 40-yard field goal attempt wide left. Smith intercepts a Krieg pass and returns it 28 yards to Seahawks' 10. Treadwell kicks winning 27-yard field goal at 7:46.

Oct. 29, 1989—New England 23, Indianapolis 20, at Indianapolis; Patriots win toss. Biasucci kickoff returned 13 yards to Patriots' 23 by Martin. Holding penalty brings ball back to Patriots' 13. After six plays, Feagles punt returned 11 yards by Verdin to Colts' 28. Six plays later, Colts punt to Martin at Patriots' 12. Grogan completes three straight passes to Patriots' 33. Five consecutive runs put New England on Colts' 33. Davis kicks a 51-yard winning field goal for Patriots at 9:46.

Oct. 29, 1989—Green Bay 23, Detroit 20, at Milwaukee; Lions win toss. Sanders touchback on Jacke kickoff. On first play, Murphy intercepts Lions' Peete and returns it three yards to Lions' 26. Fullwood gains five yards on three plays to set up Jacke's 38-yard field goal at 2:14.

Nov. 5, 1989—Minnesota 23, Los Angeles Rams 21, at Minneapolis; Rams win toss. Karlis's kick squibbed 18 yards by Delpino to Rams' 19. Drive stops at Rams' 28. Merriweather blocks Hatcher's punt at 12. Ball rolls out of end zone for safety.

Nov. 19, 1989—Cleveland 10, Kansas City 10, at Cleveland; Browns win toss. Browns punt three times; Chiefs twice; before

Kansas City's Lowery misses 47-yard field goal with 17 seconds remaining in overtime. Kosar's pass intercepted as time expired.

Nov. 26, 1989—Los Angeles Rams 20, New Orleans 17, at New Orleans; Saints win toss. Lansford's kickoff returned 27 yards to Saints' 30. After four plays, Barnhardt punts to Rams' 15. Saints penalized 35 yards for interference to Rams' 43. Three plays later, Everett hits Anderson with 14-yard pass to Saints' 40, then 26-yarder to put Rams in field goal position. Lansford kicks 31-yard field goal at 6:38.

Dec. 3, 1989—Los Angeles Raiders 16, Denver 13, at Los Angeles; Broncos win toss. Bell returns Jaeger kickoff 14 yards to Broncos' 18. Broncos' penalized for illegal block to Broncos' 9. Elway completes three passes for two first downs. On third and eight Elway sacked for 10-yard loss. Horan punts, Adams calls for fair catch at Raiders' 29. Dyal's 26-yard reception moves Raiders to Denver 43. Raiders move ball 34 yards in three plays to set up Jaeger's 24-yard field goal at 7:02.

Dec. 10, 1989—Indianapolis 23, Cleveland 17, at Indianapolis; Browns win toss. Teams trade punts. McNeil returns Colts' punt 42 yards to 42. Seven plays later, Bahr misses 35-yard field goal attempt. Three plays later, Stark punts and McNeil returns ball to 50-yard line. Two plays later, Prior intercepts Kosar's pass at Colts' 42 and returns it 58 yards for touchdown at 10:54.

Dec. 17, 1989—Cleveland 23, Minnesota 17, at Cleveland; Browns win toss. Browns punt to Vikings' 18. Six plays later, Vikings punt to Browns' 22. Nine plays later, Bahr lines up to attempt 31-yard field goal. Holder Pagel takes snap and passes 14 yards to Waiters for touchdown at 9:30.

Sept. 23, 1990—Denver 34, Seattle 31, at Denver; Seahawks win toss. Loville returns kickoff 19 yards to Seahawks' 27. Seahawks drive to Broncos' 26, where Johnson misses 44-yard field goal wide right. Broncos take over and Elway completes series of passes to set up Treadwell's 23-yard field goal at 9:14.

Sept. 30, 1990—Tampa Bay 23, Minnesota 20, at Minnesota; Vikings win toss. Vikings drive to Buccaneers' 31; Igwebuike's 48-yard field goal attempt wide left. Buccaneers drive to Vikings' 43 and punt. Gannon's pass is intercepted at Vikings' 26 by Wayne Haddix. Buccaneers drive to Vikings' 19 to set up Christie's 36-yard field goal at 9:11.

Oct. 7, 1990—Cincinnati 34, Los Angeles Rams 31, at Anaheim; Rams win toss. Berry returns kickoff to Rams' 21. After 3 plays, English punts and Green downs ball at Rams' 47. After 3 plays, Johnson punts and Sutton downs ball at Rams' 29-yard line. After 3 plays, English punts and Price signals fair catch at Bengals' 47. Esiason completes series of passes to 26-yard line to set up Breech's 44-yard field goal at 11:56.

Nov. 4, 1990—Washington 41, Detroit 38, at Detroit; Redskins win toss. Howard downs kickoff on Redskins' 15. After 3 plays, Mojsiejenko punts to Redskins' 45. After 3 plays, Arnold punts to Redskins' 10. Rutledge completes series of passes to set up Lohmiller's 34-yard field goal at 9:10.

Nov. 18, 1990—Chicago 16, Denver 13, at Denver; Broncos win toss. Ezor returns kickoff to Broncos' 12. Both teams have ball twice and have to punt after each possession. Broncos punt after third possession of overtime and Bailey returns 20 yards to Broncos' 34. Harbaugh completes 10-yard pass to Thornton to set up Butler's 44-yard field goal at 13:14.

Nov. 25, 1990—Seattle 13, San Diego 10, at San Diego; Chargers win toss. Lewis returns kickoff to Chargers' 22. After 2 plays, Cox fumbles and ball is recovered by Porter at Chargers' 23. After two plays, Johnson kicks 40-yard field goal at 3:01.

Dec. 2, 1990—Chicago 23, Detroit 17, at Chicago; Lions win toss. Gray returns kickoff to Lions' 35. After 10 plays, Murray misses 35-yard field goal. Bears take possession at Chicago 20. Harbaugh completes 50-yard game-winning pass to Anderson at 10:57.

Dec. 2, 1990—Seattle 13, Houston 10, at Seattle; Seahawks win toss. Warren returns kickoff to Seahawks' 13. After 5 plays, Donnelly punts to Oilers' 23-yard line. Ford's fumble recovered by Wyman. Seahawks take possession at Oilers' 27. After 2 plays, Johnson kicks 42-yard field goal at 4:25.

Dec. 9, 1990—Miami 23, Philadelphia 20, at Miami; Eagles win toss. After 11 plays, Feagles punts to Dolphins' 26. After 6 plays, Roby punts to Eagles' 14 and Harris returns to 25. After 3 plays, Feagles punts to Dolphins' 43. Marino completes series of passes to Eagles' 22. Stoyanovich kicks 39-yard field goal at 12:32.

Dec. 9, 1990—San Francisco 20, Cincinnati 17, at Cincinnati; 49ers win toss. Carter returns kickoff to 49ers' 19. After 10

plays, Cofer kicks 23-yard field goal at 6:12.

* Sept. 23, 1991—Chicago 19, New York Jets 13, at Chicago; Jets win toss. Mathis returns kickoff seven yards to New York's 12. Jets drive to New York 26; Bailey returns punt to Chicago 39. Bears drive to Jets' 44-yard line and punt into the end zone. Jets drive to Bears' 11 where Leahy's 28-yard field goal attempt is wide left. Bears drive from 20 to Jets' 1 where Harbaugh runs for touchdown at 14:42.

Oct. 13, 1991—Los Angeles Raiders 23, Seattle 20, at Seattle; Seahawks win toss. Seahawks begin on 20. After 5 plays, Tuten punts and Brown signals fair catch at Raiders' 24. After 3 plays, Gossett punts and Land downs ball at Seattle 9. After 1 play, Lott intercepts at Seahawks' 19 to set up Jaeger's game-winning 37-yard field goal at 6:37.

Oct. 20, 1991—Cleveland 30, San Diego 24, at San Diego; Chargers win toss. After kickoff, Chargers drive to Browns' 45 and punt to Browns' 6 where Hendrickson downs ball. Browns drive to 38 and punt; Taylor fair catches on Chargers' 14. After 3 plays, Brandon intercepts at Chargers' 30 and scores at 5:58.

Oct. 20, 1991—New England 26, Minnesota 23, at New England; Patriots win toss. Martin returns kickoff 35 yards to New England 22. Patriots drive to Minnesota 19. Staurovsky's 36-yard field goal attempt is wide left. Minnesota drives to the 50 where Newsome punts into end zone. On first play, McMillian intercepts at the 40 for Minnesota. After 2 plays, Marion causes Jordan fumble and Pool recovers at New England 20. New England drives to Minnesota 24 where Staurovsky kicks 42-yard field goal as time expires.

Nov. 3, 1991—New York Jets 19, Green Bay 16, at New York; Packers win toss. Thompson returns kickoff 30 yards to Packers' 39. Green Bay drives to New York 24 where Jacke's 42-yard field-goal attempt is wide right. Jets drive to 50. Aguiar's punt is fumbled by Sikahema and recovered by New York at Packers' 23. After 2 plays, Leahy kicks 37-yard field goal at 9:40.

Nov. 3, 1991—Washington 16, Houston 13, at Washington; Redskins win toss. Mitchell returns kickoff 9 yards to Washington 14. After 4 plays, Goodburn punts and Givins returns to Houston 31. After 1 play, Moon's pass is intercepted by Green at Oilers' 35. After 3 plays, Lohmiller kicks 41-yard field goal at 4:01.

Nov. 10, 1991—Houston 26, Dallas 23, at Houston; Oilers win toss. Pinkett returns kickoff 20 yards to Houston 24. After 6 plays, Montgomery punts and Martin returns to Dallas 24. Cowboys drive to Oilers' 24 where Smith fumbles and McDowell recovers at Oilers' 15. Houston drives to Dallas 5 where Del Greco kicks 23-yard field goal at 14:31.

Nov. 10, 1991—Pittsburgh 33, Cincinnati 27, at Cincinnati; Steelers wins toss. Woodson downs kickoff for touchback. After 3 plays, Stryzinski punts and Barber returns 7 yards to Cincinnati 38. Bengals drive to Pittsburgh 37 where Woods fumbles and Lloyd returns recovery to Cincinnati 44. After 2 plays, O'Donnell passes to Green for 26-yard touchdown at 6:32.

#Nov. 24, 1991—Atlanta 23, New Orleans 20, at New Orleans; Falcons win toss. Falcons begin at 20. After 3 plays, Fulhage punts and Fenerty signals fair catch at New Orleans 43. After 3 plays, Barnhardt punts and Thompson downs ball at Atlanta 23. After 3 plays, Fulhage punts and Fenerty fair catches at New Orleans 25. Saints drive to Atlanta 38 where Andersen misses 55-yard field-goal attempt. After 1 play, Rozier fumbles and Martin recovers on 50. Saints drive to Atlanta 38 where Barnhardt punts to Falcons' 2. Atlanta drives to New Orleans 33 where Johnson kicks 50-yard field goal at 13:03.

Nov. 24, 1991—Miami 16, Chicago 13, at Chicago; Dolphins wins toss. Butler kicks to Miami 20 where Paige returns kickoff 15 yards to 35. Miami drives to Chicago 9 where Stoyanovich kicks 27-yard field goal at 4:11.

Dec. 8, 1991—Buffalo 30, Los Angeles Raiders 27, at Los Angeles; Raiders win toss. Daluiso kicks into end zone for touchback. On third play, Kelso intercepts for Buffalo and returns ball to Bills' 36. Bills drive to Los Angeles 24 where Norwood kicks 42-yard field goal at 2:34.

Dec. 8, 1991—Kansas City 20, San Diego 17, at Kansas City; Chiefs win toss. Carney kicks to Kansas City 10 where Stradford returns 23 yards to 33. After 3 plays, Barker punts to San Diego 4. Chargers drive to 40 where Kidd punts 60 yards into end zone for touchback. Kansas City drives to San Diego 39 where Barker punts 38 yards to 1. After 3 plays, Kidd punts 41 yards to San Diego 42 where Stradford returns 12 yards to 30. Chiefs drive to San Diego 1 where Lowery kicks 18-yard field goal at 11:26.

Dec. 8, 1991—New England 23, Indianapolis 17, at New England; Colts wins toss. Baumann kicks off to Indianapolis 2 where

Martin returns 23 yards to 25. After 3 downs, Stark punts to New England 17 where Henderson returns 8 yards to 25. New England drives to 50 where McCarthy punts and Prior signals fair catch at Indianapolis 15. After 3 plays, Stark punts to New England 40 where Henderson returns 7 yards to 47. After 2 plays, Millen passes to Timpson for 45-yard touchdown at 8:55.

Dec. 22, 1991—Detroit 17, Buffalo 14, at Buffalo; Lions wins toss. Daluiso kicks off to Detroit 20 where Dozier returns 15 yards to Lions 35. Lions drive to Bills' 3 where Murray kicks 21-yard field goal at 4:23.

Dec. 22, 1991—New York Jets 23, Miami 20, at Miami; Jets win toss. Aguiar kicks to Miami's 30 where Logan returns 3 yards to the 33. After 4 downs, Stoyanovich punts to Jets' 15 where Baty returns 8 yards to 23. Jets drive to Miami 12 where Allegre kicks 30-yard field goal at 6:33.

Sept. 6, 1992—Minnesota 23, Green Bay 20, at Green Bay; Vikings win toss. Nelson returns kickoff 14 yards to the Minnesota 23. After 5 plays, Newsome punts 49 yards to Green Bay 21 where Brooks returns 12 yards to the 33. After 2 plays, Glenn intercepts pass at the Vikings' 48. On first play, Allen fumbles and Billups recovers at Green Bay 41. After 3 plays, McJulien punts 33 yards to Vikings' 35. Vikings drive to Minnesota 48; Newsome punts 52 yards for touchdown. After 3 plays, McJulien punts and Parker returns 10 yards to Green Bay 48. Vikings drive to Packers' 9 where Reveiz kicks 26-yard field goal at 10:20.

Sept. 13, 1992—Cincinnati 24, Los Angeles Raiders 21, at Cincinnati; Raiders win toss. Land returns kickoff 13 yards but fumbles at Los Angeles' 20; ball recovered by Bengals' Bennett at Raiders' 21. After 1 play, Breech kicks 34-yard field goal at 1:01.

Sept. 20, 1992—Houston 23, Kansas City 20, at Houston; Chiefs win toss. Carter returns kickoff 25 yards to Kansas City 28. On third play of drive, Birden fumbles at Kansas City 34; ball recovered by Houston's D. Smith at Chiefs' 23. After one play, Del Greco kicks 39-yard field goal at 1:55.

Oct. 11, 1992—Indianapolis 6, New York Jets 3, at Indianapolis; Colts win toss. Verdin returns kickoff 9 yards to Colts' 36. Colts drive to Jets' 30 where Biasucci kicks 47-yard field goal at 3:01.

#Nov. 8, 1992—Cincinnati 31, Chicago 28, at Chicago; Bears win toss. Lewis returns kickoff 22 yards to Chicago's 29. Bears drive to Chicago's 46 where Gardocki punts; fair catch by Wright at the Cincinnati 17. Bengals drive to Bears' 18 where Breech kicks 36-yard field goal at 8:39.

Nov. 15, 1992—New England 37, Indianapolis 34, at Indianapolis; Colts win toss. Verdin returns kickoff 10 yards to Colts' 20; holding penalty brings ball back to Colts' 10. After two plays, Henderson intercepts pass at Colts' 38 and returns it 9 yards to the 29. In three plays, Patriots drive to 1 where Baumann kicks 18-yard field goal at 3:25.

Nov. 29, 1992—Indianapolis 16, Buffalo 13, at Indianapolis; Colts win toss. Verdin returns kickoff 24 yards to Colts' 22. Colts drive to Buffalo 22 where Biasucci kicks 40-yard field goal at 3:51.

* Nov. 30, 1992—Seattle 16, Denver 13, at Seattle; Seahawks win toss. Daluiso kicks through end zone for touchback. After three plays, Tuten punts 53 yards to Denver 18 where Marshall returns for no gain. After three plays, Rodriguez punts 29 yards to Seattle 45 where Warren signals fair catch. Seahawks drive to Denver 15 where Kasay's 33-yard field goal attempt misses. Broncos take over at Denver 20. After three plays, Rodriguez punts 43 yards to Seattle 38 where Warren signals for fair catch. After four plays, Tuten punts 39 yards to Denver 4 where Daniels downs punt. After three plays, Rodriguez punts 46 yards to Denver 48 where Warren returns 10 yards to the 38. Seahawks drive to Denver 14 where Kasay kicks 32-yard field goal at 11:10.

Dec. 13, 1992—Philadelphia 20, Seattle 17, at Seattle; Eagles win toss. Sydner returns kick 12 yards to Eagles' 16; illegal block penalty brings ball back to 8. Eagles drive to Philadelphia 45 where Feagles punts for a touchback. After 6 plays, Tuten punts 45 yards to Philadelphia 22 where Sydner returns 7 yards to 29. After 6 plays, Feagles punts to Seattle 26 where Warren returns 5 yards to 31. After 5 plays, Tuten punts 32 yards to Philadelphia 20 where Sydner signals for fair catch. Eagles drive to Seattle 27 where Ruzek kicks 44-yard field goal with no time remaining.

Dec. 27, 1992—Miami 16, New England 13, at New England; Patriots win toss. Lockwood returns kickoff 15 yards to Patriots' 21. After three plays, McCarthy punts 39 yards to Miami 33 where Miller returns 2 yards to the 35. Miami drives to New Eng-

land 18 where Stoyanovich kicks 35-yard field goal at 8:17.

Sept. 12, 1993—Detroit 19, New England 16, at New England; Patriots win toss. Patriots begin at 20. After 3 plays, Saxon punts 42 yards to Detroit 29 where Gray returns 12 yards to the 41. After 3 plays, Arnold punts 41 yards to New England 12 where Brown returns 16 yards to the 28. Patriots drive to Detroit 44 where Saxon punts into the end zone for a touchback. Detroit drives to New England 20 where Hanson kicks 38-yard field goal at 11:04.

Nov. 7, 1993—Buffalo 13, New England 10, at New England; Patriots win toss. T. Brown returns kickoff 27 yards to Patriots 30. Patriots drive to Buffalo 48 where Bills take over on downs. Bills drive to New England 25 where Metzelaars fumbles, and C. Brown recovers. After 3 plays, Saxon punts 46 yards to Buffalo 24 where Copeland returns 11 yards to the 35. Bills drive to New England 14 where Christie kicks 32-yard field goal at 9:22.

Dec. 19, 1993—Phoenix 30, Seattle 27, at Seattle; Cardinals win toss. Bailey returns kickoff 14 yards to Cardinals 24. Cardinals drive to Seattle 23 where Davis kicks 41-yard field goal at 6:45.

Jan. 2, 1994—Dallas 16, New York Giants 13, at New York; Giants win toss. Meggett returns kickoff 19 yards to Giants 19. After 6 plays, Horan punts 45 yards to Cowboys 25 where Widmer downs punt. Cowboys drive to Giants' 23 where Murray kicks 41-yard field goal at 10:44.

Jan. 2, 1994—New England 33, Miami 27, at New England; Dolphins win toss. McDuffie returns kickoff 21 yards to Miami 27. After 3 plays, Hatcher punts 43 yards to New England 29 where Harris returns 6 yards to the 35. After 2 plays, Brown intercepts pass from Bledsoe and returns 3 yards to Miami 49. After 3 plays, Hatcher punts 37 yards to New England 14 where Harris returns 18 yards to the 32. After 2 plays, Bledsoe passes 36 yards to Timpson for touchdown at 4:44.

Jan. 2, 1994—Los Angeles Raiders 33, Denver 30, at Los Angeles; Broncos win toss. Delpino returns kickoff 12 yards to Denver 25. Broncos drive to Los Angeles 22 where Elam's 40-yard field goal attempt is wide left. Raiders drive to Denver 29 where Jaeger kicks 47-yard field goal at 7:10.

* Jan. 3, 1994—Philadelphia 37, San Francisco 34, at San Francisco; 49ers win toss. Walker returns kickoff, 19 yards to San Francisco 27. 49ers drive to Philadelphia 14 where Cofer misses 32-yard field goal. Eagles start at their 20-yard line, and, after 3 plays, Feagles punts 48 yards to San Francisco 36 where Carter fumbles and 49ers recover. After 7 plays, Willmsmeyer punts 57 yards to Philadelphia 6 where Sikahema returns 16 yards to the 22. Eagles drive to San Francisco 10 where Ruzek kicks 28-yard field goal with no time remaining.

Sept. 4, 1994—Detroit 31, Atlanta 28, at Detroit; Falcons win toss. Falcons start at their own 16 after holding penalty on kickoff. After 3 plays, Alexander punts 41 yards to Detroit 39 where Clay returns 12 yards to Atlanta 49. Detroit drives to Atlanta 20 where Hanson kicks 37-yard field goal at 5:14.

Sept. 11, 1994—New York Jets 25, Denver 22, at New York; Jets win toss. Murrell returns kickoff 24 yards to New York 33. Jets drive to Denver 22 where Lowery kicks 39-yard field goal at 3:57.

* Sept. 19, 1994—Detroit 20, Dallas 17, at Dallas; Lions win toss. Gray returns kickoff 24 yards to Detroit 32. Lions drive to Dallas 34 where Hanson's 51-yard field-goal attempt is blocked by Lett. Cowboys take possession at Dallas 42. Cowboys drive to Detroit 37 where Kennard fumbles and Swilling recovers. Lions take possession at Detroit 45. After 6 plays, Montgomery punts 31 yards to Dallas 16. Cowboys drive to Dallas 49 where Aikman fumbles and Thomas recovers at Dallas 43. Lions drive to Dallas 26 where Hanson kicks 44-yard field goal at 14:33.

Oct. 16, 1994—Arizona 19, Washington 16, at Washington; Redskins win toss. Mitchell returns kickoff 27 yards to Washington 41. Redskins drive to Arizona 34 where Lohmiller's 51-yard field-goal attempt is blocked by Joyner and recovered by Williams who returns it to the Washington 37. After 5 plays, Peterson's 45-yard field-goal attempt is wide right. Redskins take possession at the Washington 36. After 3 plays, Roby punts 36 yards to the Arizona 37 where Robinson returns 3 yards to the 40. After 3 plays, Feagles punts 51 yards for a touchdown. After 1 play, Shuler's pass is intercepted by Hoage who returns it to the Washington 12. Peterson kicks 29-yard field goal at 10:00.

Oct. 16, 1994—Miami 20, Los Angeles Raiders 17, at Miami; Dolphins win toss. McDuffie returns kickoff 19 yards to Miami 23. Dolphins drive to Los Angeles 12 where Stoyanovich kicks 29-yard field goal at 5:46.

Oct. 20, 1994—**Minnesota 13, Green Bay 10,** at Minnesota; Vikings win toss. Ismail returns kickoff 22 yards to Minnesota 29. Vikings drive to Green Bay 9 where Fuad Reveiz kicks 27-yard field goal at 4:26.

Oct. 30, 1994—Detroit 28, New York Giants 25, at New York; Giants win toss. Lewis returns kickoff 16 yards to New York 27. After 3 plays, Horan punts 42 yards to Detroit 24 where Gray calls for fair catch. Detroit drives to New York 6 where Hanson kicks 24-yard field goal at 6:43.

#Oct. 30, 1994—**Arizona 20, Pittsburgh 17,** at Arizona; Steelers win toss. Johnson returns kickoff 24 yards to Pittsburgh 30 where he fumbles and Arizona's Merritt recovers at Pittsburgh 32. After 3 plays, Davis kicks 51-yard field goal at 1:40.

Nov. 6, 1994—Cincinnati 20, Seattle 17, at Seattle; Seahawks win toss. Warren returns kickoff 32 yards to Seattle 33. After 3 plays, Tuten punts 37 yards to Cincinnati 28 where Sawyer calls for fair catch. After 3 plays, Johnson punts 64 yards to Seattle 2 where Truitt downs ball. Seahawks drive to Seattle 38 where Tuten punts 50 yards to Cincinnati 12 and Sawyer returns 5 yards to 17. Blake passes to Scott for 76 yards to Seattle 7. Pelfrey kicks 26-yard field goal at 8:14.

Nov. 6, 1994—Pittsburgh 12, Houston 9, at Houston; Steelers win toss. Stone returns kickoff 15 yards to Pittsburgh 28. After 3 plays, Royals punts 53 yards to Houston 19 where Givins downs ball. After 3 plays, Camarillo punts 57 yards to Pittsburgh 31 where Woodson returns 20 yards to Houston 49. After 3 plays, Royals punts 43 yards to Houston 15 where Coleman returns 3 yards to 18. After 5 plays, Camarillo punts 57 yards to Pittsburgh 12 where Hastings returns 12 yards to 24. Steelers drive to Houston 41 where Royals punts 29 yards to Houston 12, and Coleman calls for fair catch. Brown fumbles on first play and Jones recovers at Houston 22. After 1 play, Anderson kicks 40-yard field goal at 11:24.

Nov. 13, 1994—New England 26, Minnesota 20, at New England; Patriots win toss. Thompson returns kickoff 27 yards to New England 33. Patriots drive to Minnesota 14 where Bledsoe passes 14 yards to Turner for touchdown at 4:10.

Nov. 20, 1994—Pittsburgh 16, Miami 13, at Pittsburgh; Steelers win toss. Stone returns kickoff 15 yards to Pittsburgh 16. Steelers drive to Miami 39 where they lose possession on downs. Dolphins drive to Pittsburgh 47 where Arnold punts 35 yards to Pittsburgh 12 and Oliver downs ball. Steelers drive to Miami 21 where Anderson kicks 39-yard field goal at 10:19.

Nov. 27, 1994—Chicago 19, Arizona 16, at Arizona; Cardinals win toss. Levy returns kickoff 31 yards to Arizona 45. After 5 plays, Feagles punts 38 yards to the end zone for a touchback. Bears drive to Arizona 10 where Butler kicks 27-yard field goal at 8:11.

Nov. 27, 1994—Tampa Bay 20, Minnesota 17, at Minnesota; Buccaneers win toss. Harris returns kickoff 12 yards to Tampa Bay 38. After 6 plays, Stryzinski punts 40 yards to Minnesota 4 where Guliford muffs punt and Buccaneers' Brady recovers. Husted kicks 22-yard field goal at 2:08.

Dec. 1, 1994—**Minnesota 33, Chicago 27,** at Minnesota; Bears win toss. Lewis returns kickoff 23 yards to Chicago 33. Bears drive to Minnesota 22 where Butler's 40-yard field goal attempt is wide left. After 1 play, Moon passes 65 yards to Carter for touchdown at 5:46.

Dec. 4, 1994—Denver 20, Kansas City 17, at Kansas City; Broncos win toss. Milburn returns kickoff 24 yards to Denver 29. After 3 plays, Millen fumbles and Phillips recovers at Denver 35. After 4 plays, Allen fumbles and Smith recovers at Denver 27. After 6 plays, Rouen punts 45 yards to Kansas City 25 where Hughes calls for fair catch. After 3 plays, Aguiar punts 33 yards to Denver 42 where Chiefs down ball. Broncos drive to Kansas City 17 where Elam kicks 34-yard field goal at 12:12.

Sept. 3, 1995—Cincinnati 24, Indianapolis 21, at Indianapolis; Bengals win toss. Dunn returns kickoff 15 yards to Bengals' 17. Cincinnati drives to Indianapolis 29 where Pelfrey kicks 47-yard field goal at 2:36.

Sept. 3, 1995—Atlanta 23, Carolina 20, at Atlanta; Panthers win toss. Baldwin downs kickoff for touchback. Panthers drive to Carolina 42 where Reich fumbles and ball is recovered by Archambeau at Carolina 31. Falcons drive to Panthers' 16 where Andersen kicks 35-yard field goal at 6:17.

Sept. 10, 1995—Indianapolis 27, New York Jets 24, at New York; Jets win toss. Carter downs kickoff for touchback. Jets punt downed at Colts' 37. Colts drive to Jets' 35 where Cofer kicks 52-yard field goal at 4:27.

Sept. 10, 1995—Kansas City 20, New York Giants 17, at Kansas City; Chiefs win toss. Vanover returns kickoff 30 yards

to Chiefs' 28. Aguiar punts to Giants' 3. Horan punts to Chiefs' 49. Chiefs drive to Giants' 6 where Elliott kicks 23-yard field goal at 7:49.

Sept. 17, 1995—Kansas City 23, Oakland 17, at Kansas City; Chiefs win toss. Vanover returns kickoff 28 yards to Chiefs' 41. M. Allen fumbles, ball recovered by Robbins at Raiders' 38. Hasty intercepts pass at Chiefs' 36 and returns it 64 yards for touchdown at 4:27.

Sept. 17, 1995—Atlanta 27, New Orleans 24, at Atlanta; Saints win toss. Hughes returns kickoff 21 yards to Saints' 17. Metcalf returns Wilmsmeyer's punt 18 yards to Saints' 39. Stryzinski punts, fair catch by Hughes at Saints' 14. Wilmsmeyer punt downed at Falcons' 6. Falcons drive to Saints' 3 where Andersen kicks 21-yard field goal at 7:58.

#Sept. 17, 1995—**Dallas 23, Minnesota 17,** at Minnesota; Cowboys win toss. K. Williams returns kickoff 23 yards to Cowboys' 27. E. Smith scores on 31-yard run at 2:26.

Oct. 8, 1995—Indianapolis 27, Miami 24, at Miami; Colts win toss. Warren returns kickoff 25 yards to Colts' 33. Colts drive to Dolphins' 10 where Blanchard kicks 27-yard field goal at 4:58.

Oct. 8, 1995—New York Giants 27, Arizona 21, at New York; Cardinals win toss. Terry returns kickoff 20 yards to Cardinals' 23. Hamilton recovers Krieg's fumble at Cardinals' 36. Lynch recovers Brown's fumble at Cardinals' 38. Armstead intercepts pass at Giants' 42 and returns it 58 yards for touchdown at 4:05.

Oct. 8, 1995—Minnesota 23, Houston 17, at Minnesota; Vikings win toss. Palmer returns kickoff 10 yards to Vikings' 15. Saxon's punt downed at Oilers' 8. Washington intercepts pass at Vikings' 47 and returns it 25 yards to Oilers' 28. R. Smith scores on 20-yard run at 7:10.

Oct. 8, 1995—Philadelphia 37, Washington 34, at Philadelphia; Redskins win toss. Redskins take possession at their 20 after touchback. Turk punt out of bounds at Eagles' 9. Eagles drive to Redskins' 18 where Anderson kicks 35-yard field goal at 10:06.

* Oct. 9, 1995—**Kansas City 29, San Diego 23,** at Kansas City; Chargers win toss. Coleman returns kickoff 24 yards to Chargers' 28. Vanover makes fair catch of Bennett's punt at Chiefs' 15. Coleman makes fair catch of Aguiar's punt at Chargers' 43. Vanover returns Bennett's punt 86 yards for a touchdown at 7:27.

Oct. 15, 1995—Tampa Bay 20, Minnesota 17, at Tampa Bay; Buccaneers win toss. Edmonds returns kickoff 16 yards to Buccaneers' 22. A. Lee returns Roby's punt to Vikings' 48. Vikings drive to Tampa Bays' 35 where Reveiz's 53-yard field-goal attempt is wide right. Buccaneers take over at own 43 and drive to Vikings' 33 where Husted kicks 51-yard field goal at 6:23.

Oct. 22, 1995—Washington 36, Detroit 30, at Washington; Redskins win toss. B. Mitchell returns kickoff 16 yards to Redskins' 27. Turk's punt downed at Lions' 4. D. Green intercepts S. Mitchell's pass and returns it 7 yards for touchdown at 3:41.

Oct. 29, 1995—Carolina 20, New England 17, at New England; Panthers win toss. Baldwin returns kickoff 22 yards to Panthers' 25. Meggett makes fair catch of Barnhardt's punt at Patriots' 9. Guliford returns O'Neill's punt 9 yards to Patriots' 12. Panthers drive to Patriots' 12 where Kasay kicks 29-yard field goal at 7:08.

Oct. 29, 1995—Cleveland 29, Cincinnati 26, at Cincinnati; Browns win toss. Hunter returns kickoff 31 yards to Browns' 31. Bieniemy returns Tupa's punt 9 yards to Bengals' 37. McCardell makes fair catch of Johnson's punt at Browns' 12. Bieniemy returns Tupa's punt 0 yards to Bengals' 38. Hall intercepts Blake's pass and returns it 5 yards to Bengals' 45. Browns drive to Bengals' 11 where Stover kicks 28-yard field goal at 6:30.

Oct. 29, 1995—Arizona 20, Seattle 14, at Arizona; Cardinals win toss. Dowdell returns kickoff 16 yards to Cardinals' 25. Cardinals drive to Seahawks' 10 where G. Davis' 27-yard field goal attempt is blocked. L. Lynch intercepts Friesz's pass at Cardinals' 28 and returns it 72 yards for a touchdown at 11:16.

Nov. 5, 1995—Pittsburgh 37, Chicago 34, at Chicago; Bears win toss. Timpson returns kickoff 23 yards to Bears' 33. Hastings returns Sauerbrun's punt 2 yards to Steelers' 31. Steelers drive to Bears' 6 where N. Johnson kicks 24-yard field goal at 8:19.

Nov. 12, 1995—Minnesota 30, Arizona 24, at Arizona; Vikings win toss. A. Lee returns kickoff 20 yards to Vikings' 25. Moon throws 50-yard touchdown pass to Ismail at 2:16.

Nov. 26, 1995—Arizona 40, Atlanta 37, at Arizona; Falcons win toss. J. Anderson returns kickoff 20 yards to Falcons' 20. Stryzinski fumbles punt snap. Recovered by England at Falcons' 10 where G. Davis kicks 28-yard field goal at 1:43.

#**Dec. 10, 1995—Tampa Bay 13, Green Bay 10**, at Tampa Bay; Buccaneers win toss. Edmonds returns kickoff 24 yards to Buccaneers' 23. Tampa Bay drives to Packers' 29 where Husted kicks 47-yard field goal at 3:46.

#**Sept. 1, 1996—Buffalo 23, New York Giants 20**, at New York; Bills win toss. Daluiso kick is a touchback. Bills drive to Buffalo 46. Toomer returns Mohr's punt to Giants' 16. Dave Brown's fumble recovered by Spielman at Giants' 33. Bills drive to Giants' 16 where Christie kicks 34-yard field goal at 9:08.

Sept. 22, 1996—New England 28, Jacksonville 25, at New England; Patriots win toss. T. Brown returns kickoff 18 yards to Patriots' 29. Patriots drive to Jaguars' 22 where Vinatieri kicks 40-yard field goal at 2:36.

Sept. 29, 1996—Arizona 31, St. Louis 28, at Arizona; Cardinals win toss. Lohmiller kick is a touchback. Cardinals drive to Rams' 7 where G. Davis kicks 24-yard field goal at 1:54.

Oct. 6, 1996—Buffalo 16, Indianapolis 13, at Buffalo; Colts win toss. Christie kick is a touchback. Colts drive to Indianapolis 32. Burris returns Gardocki's punt to Bills' 35. Bills drive to Colts' 48. Mohr punts out of bounds at Colts' 14. Colts drive to Indianapolis 9. Burris returns Gardocki's punt to Colts' 48. Bills drive to Colts' 22 where Christie kicks 39-yard field goal at 9:22.

#**Oct. 6, 1996—Houston 30, Cincinnati 27**, at Cincinnati; Bengals win toss. Dunn returns kickoff 23 yards to Bengals' 34. Bengals drive to Cincinnati 36. Floyd returns L. Johnson's punt to Oilers' 18. Oilers drive to Bengals' 31 where Del Greco kicks 49-yard field goal at 7:07.

* **Oct. 14, 1996—Green Bay 23, San Francisco 20**, at Green Bay; 49ers win toss. D. Carter returns kickoff 23 yards to 49ers' 22. 49ers' drive to San Francisco 25. Howard makes fair catch of Thompson's punt at Packers' 44. Packers drive to 49ers' 35 where Jacke kicks 53-yard field goal at 3:41.

Oct. 27, 1996—Baltimore 37, St. Louis 31, at Baltimore; Rams win toss. J. Thomas returns kickoff 17 yard to Rams' 17. Rams drive to Ravens' 15. F. Miller fumble in field goal formation recovered by S. Moore at Ravens' 17. Ravens drive to Baltimore 49 and turn ball over on downs. Rams drive to Ravens' 40 and turn ball over on downs. Testaverde throws 22-yard scoring pass to M. Jackson at 14:50.

Nov. 10, 1996—Dallas 20, San Francisco 17, at San Francisco; Cowboys win toss. H. Walker returns kickoff 10 yards to Cowboys' 23. Cowboys drive to 49ers' 11 where Boniol kicks 29-yard field goal at 6:17.

Nov. 10, 1996—Arizona 37, Washington 34, at Washington; Cardinals win toss. Blanton's kickoff is a touchback. Cardinals drive to Redskins' 15 where Butler misses 32-yard field goal. Redskins drive to Cardinals' 43 where Turk punts for touchback. L. Johnson fumble returned by Morrison to Cardinals' 27. Redskins drive to Cardinals' 31 where Blanton misses 48-yard field goal. Cardinals drive to Redskins' 15 where Butler kicks 32-yard field goal at 14:27.

Nov. 10, 1996—Tampa Bay 20, Oakland 17, at Tampa Bay; Buccaneers win toss. M. Marshall returns kickoff 15 yards to Bucs' 17. Bucs drive to Tampa Bay 36. T. Brown returns Barnhardt's punt four yards to Raiders' 22. Raiders drive to Oakland 25. M. Marshall returns Gossett's punt nine yards to Bucs' 39. Bucs drive to Raiders' 4 where Husted kicks 23-yard field goal at 11:56.

#**Nov. 17, 1996—Minnesota 16, Oakland 13**, at Oakland; Raiders win toss. Kaufman returns kickoff 32 yards to Raiders' 27. Raiders drive to Oakland 46 where Gossett punts to Vikings' 17. Vikings drive to Raiders' 12 where Sisson kicks 31-yard field goal at 11:53.

Nov. 24, 1996—Jacksonville 28, Baltimore 25, at Baltimore; Jaguars win toss. Jordon returns kickoff 16 yards to Jaguars' 30. Jaguars drive to Jacksonville 37. Barker's punt is downed at Ravens' 6. Ravens drive to Jaguars' 37 where Pritchett recovers Byner's fumble. Jaguars drive to Ravens' 15 where Hollis kicks 34-yard field goal at 9:06.

Nov. 24, 1996—San Francisco 19, Washington 16, at Washington; 49ers win toss. D. Carter returns kickoff 20 yards to 49ers' 32. 49ers drive to Redskins' 20 where Wilkins kicks 38-yard field goal at 3:24.

Dec. 1, 1996—Indianapolis 13, Buffalo 10, at Indianapolis; Bills win toss. Moulds returns kickoff 26 yards to Bills' 25. Bills drive to Colts 49. Stock returns Mohr's punt one yard to Colts' 16. Colts drive to Bills' 32 where Blanchard kicks 49-yard field goal at 10:46.

Aug. 31, 1997—Tennessee 24, Oakland 21, at Tennessee; Oilers win toss. Gray returns kickoff 32 yards to Tennessee 33.

Oilers drive to Tennessee 38. Roby's punt is downed at the Oakland 33. Raiders drive to Oakland 32. Gray returns Araguz punt to Tennessee 35. Oilers drive to Oakland 15 where Del Greco kicks 33-yard field goal at 6:57.

Sept. 7, 1997—Miami 16, Tennessee 13, at Miami; Dolphins win toss. Spikes returns kickoff 48 yards to Tennessee 45. Dolphins drive to Tennessee 11 where Mare kicks 29-yard field goal at 2:15.

#**Sept. 7, 1997—Arizona 25, Dallas 22**, at Arizona; Cowboys win toss. Walker returns kickoff 21 yards to Dallas 25. Cowboys drive to Arizona 43. Gowin punts 43 yards for a touchback. Cardinals drive to Dallas 44. Graham fumbles. Cowboys drive to Arizona 42. Williams fumbles. Cardinals drive to Dallas 3 where Butler kicks 20-yard field goal at 8:30.

Sept. 14, 1997—Washington 19, Arizona 13, at Washington; Cardinals win toss. K. Williams returns kickoff 27 yards to Arizona 34. Cardinals drive to Arizona 40. McElroy fumbles. Redskins drive to Arizona 40. Westbrook catches 40-yard touchdown pass from Frerotte at 1:36.

#**Sept. 14, 1997—New England 27, New York Jets 24**, at New England; Patriots win toss. Hall's kickoff is a touchback. Patriots drive to New England 15. Bledsoe pass intercepted by O. Smith. Jets drive to New York 46. Hansen punts 47 yards. Meggett returns to New England 21. Patriots drive to New York 17 where Vinatieri kicks 34-yard field goal at 8:03.

Sept. 28, 1997—Kansas City 20, Seattle 17, at Kansas City; Seahawks win toss. Broussard returns kickoff 12 yards to Seattle 14. Seahawks drive to Seattle 17. Vanover returns Tuten punt 8 yards to Kansas City 26. Chiefs drive to Seattle 44. Aguiar punt downed at Seattle 11. Seahawks drive to Seattle 26. Moon pass intercepted by Woods and returned 13 yards to 50. Chiefs drive to Seattle 23 where Stoyanovich kicks 41-yard field goal at 13:04.

Oct. 19, 1997—Philadelphia 13, Arizona 10, at Philadelphia; Cardinals win toss. K. Williams returns kickoff 28 yards to Arizona 42. Cardinals drive to Philadelphia 48. Feagles punts 24 yards for touchback. Eagles drive to Arizona 7 where Boniol kicks 24-yard field goal at 4:02.

Oct. 19, 1997—New York Giants 26, Detroit 20, at Detroit; Giants win toss. Pegram returns kickoff 16 yards to New York 18. Giants drive to New York 32. Calloway catches 68-yard touchdown pass from Kanell at 1:40.

Oct. 26, 1997—Denver 23, Buffalo 20, at Buffalo; Broncos win toss and elects to kickoff. Holmes returns kickoff 20 yards to Buffalo 25. Bills drive to Buffalo 23. Mohr punt downed at Denver 40. Broncos drive to Buffalo 48. Rouen punt downed at Buffalo 1. Bills drive to Buffalo 20. Gordon returns Mohr punt to Denver 42. Broncos drive to Buffalo 15 where Elam kicks 33-yard field goal at 13:04.

Oct. 26, 1997—Pittsburgh 23, Jacksonville 17, at Pittsburgh; Steelers win toss. Coleman returns kickoff 23 yards to Pittsburgh 23. Steelers drive to Jacksonville 17. Bettis catches 17-yard touchdown pass from Stewart at 3:47.

* **Oct. 27, 1997—Chicago 36, Miami 33**, at Miami; Dolphins win toss. McPhail returns kickoff 23 yards to Miami 27. Dolphins drive to Miami 36. Kidd punts out of bounds at Chicago 10. Bears drive to the Chicago 39. Sauerbrun punt out of bounds at Miami 27. Reeves recovers Marino fumble at Miami 17. Bears drive to Miami 17 where Jaeger kicks 35-yard field goal at 9:25.

Nov. 2, 1997—New York Jets 19, Baltimore 16, at New York; Jets win toss. Stover's kickoff is a touchback. Jets drive to Baltimore 20 where Hall kicks 37-yard field goal at 4:58.

Nov. 16, 1997—Philadelphia 10, Baltimore 10, at Baltimore; Eagles win toss. Stover's kickoff is a touchback. Eagles drive to Philadelphia 19. Hutton punts 36 yards to Baltimore 45. Ravens drive to Baltimore 36 where Eagles take over on downs. Eagles drive to Baltimore 33 where Ravens take over on downs. Ravens drive to Baltimore 37. Montgomery punts 55 yards, and Solomon returns to Philadelphia 22. Eagles drive to Philadelphia 16. Hutton punts 41 yards, and Roe returns to Baltimore 46. Ravens drive to Philadelphia 35 where Stover's 53-yard field-goal attempt is no good. Eagles drive to Baltimore 22 where Boniol's 40-yard field-goal is no good as time expires.

Nov. 16, 1997—New Orleans 20, Seattle 17, at New Orleans; Seahawks win toss. Brien's kickoff is a touchback. Seahawks start at Seattle 20 where Moon's pass intercepted by Tubbs who returns 15 yards to Seattle 20. Saints Brien kicks 38-yard field goal at 17 seconds.

#**Nov. 23, 1997—New York Giants 7, Washington 7**, at Washington; Redskins win toss. Davis returns kickoff 28 yards to Washington 39. Redskins drive to Washington 36 where Hostetler's pass intercepted by Sehorn who returns minus–2 yards before lateralling to Wooten who returns 5 yards to New York 41. Giants drive to New York 26 where Maynard punts 37 yards to Washington 37. Redskins drive to New York 39 where Hostetler fumble is recovered by Harris at New York 40. Giants drive to New York 43 where Maynard punts 57 yards for a touchback. Washington drives to New York 41. Giants take over on downs at New York 40. Giants drive to Washington 36 where Daluiso's 54-yard field-goal attempt is no good. Redskins drive to Washington 45 where Hostetler's pass intercepted by Sparks at New York 49. Giants drive to Washington 36 where Maynard punts 36 yards for a touchback. Redskins drive to New York 36 where Blanton's 54-yard field-goal attempt is no good. Giants drive to New York 45 where Kanell's pass intercepted by Patton who laterals to Pounds who returns 11 yards to Washington 24 as time expires.

Nov. 30, 1997—Pittsburgh 26, Arizona 20, at Arizona; Cardinals win toss. K. Williams returns kickoff 11 yards to Arizona 23. Cardinals drive to Arizona 18 where Feagles punts 43 yards. Hawkins returns punt 9 yards to Pittsburgh 48. Steelers drive to Arizona 10 where Bettis scores on a 10-yard touchdown run at 5:34.

Dec. 13, 1997—Pittsburgh 24, New England 21, at New England; Steelers win toss. Coleman returns kickoff 19 yards to Pittsburgh 26. Steelers drive to New England 13 where Johnson kicks a 31-yard field goal at 4:43.

Sept. 6, 1998—San Francisco 36, New York Jets 30, at San Francisco; Jets win toss. Richey's kickoff is a touchback. Jets drive to New York 11. Gallery punts 48 yards. McQuarters returns to New York 43. 49ers drive to New York 44. Howard punts 23 yards to New York 21. Johnson calls fair catch. Jets drive to New York 47. Gallery's 49-yard punt downed at San Francisco 4. Hearst runs for a 96-yard touchdown at 4:08.

Sept. 13, 1998—Cincinnati 34, Detroit 28, at Detroit; Lions win toss. Johnson's kickoff is a touchback. Lions drive to Detroit 47 where Mitchell's pass is intercepted by Sawyer and returned for a 58-yard touchdown at 2:06.

Sept. 27, 1998—New Orleans 19, Indianapolis 13, at Indianapolis; Saints win toss. Gardocki's kickoff is returned by Ismail to New Orleans 28. Saints drive to New Orleans 30. Royals punt 64 yards. Poole returns to Indianapolis 12. Colts drive to Indianapolis 20. Gardocki punts 58 yards. Hastings returns to New Orleans 29. Saints drive to New Orleans 32. Royals punts 59 yards. Punt downed at Indianapolis 9. Colts drive to Indianapolis 44 where Manning's pass is intercepted by Drakeford and returned to Indianapolis 36. Saints drive to Indianapolis 33. Wuerffel throws 33-yard touchdown pass to Cleeland at 6:10.

Oct. 25, 1998—Miami 12, New England 9, at Miami; Dolphins win toss. Vinatieri's kickoff is returned by Avery to Miami 15. Dolphins drive to New England 26 where Mare kicks 43-yard field goal at 4:36.

+**Nov. 26, 1998—Detroit 19, Pittsburgh 16**, at Detroit; Lions win toss. Johnson's kickoff is returned by Fair to Detroit 35. Lions drive to Pittsburgh 24 where Hanson kicks 42-yard field goal at 2:52.

Dec. 6, 1998—San Francisco 31, Carolina 28, at Carolina; Panthers win toss. Richey's kickoff is returned by Floyd to Carolina 36. Panthers drive to Carolina 38 where Beuerlein's fumble is recovered by Doleman at Carolina 30. 49ers drive to Carolina 5 where Richey kicks 23-yard field goal at 4:16.

Dec. 13, 1998—Arizona 20, Philadelphia 17, at Philadelphia; Cardinals win toss. Boniol's kickoff is returned by Metcalf to Arizona 28. Cardinals drive to Philadelphia 15 where Jacke kicks 32-yard field goal at 4:30.

Sept. 12, 1999—Dallas 41, Washington 35, at Washington; Redskins win toss. Gowin's kickoff is returned by B. Mitchell to Washington 24. Redskins drive to Washington 47. M. Turk punts 48 yards. Punt downed at Dallas 5. Cowboys drive to Dallas 24. Aikman passes 76-yard touchdown to R. Ismail at 4:09.

Oct. 3, 1999—Baltimore 19, Atlanta 13, at Atlanta; Falcons win toss. Stover's kickoff is returned by Oliver to Atlanta 18. Falcons drive to Atlanta 23. Stryzinski punts 41 yards, out of bounds at Baltimore 36. Baltimore drives to Baltimore 46. Case passes 54-yard touchdown to Armour at 2:29.

Oct. 31, 1999—New York Giants 23, Philadelphia 17, at Philadelphia; Giants win toss. Akers' kickoff is returned by Levingston to New York 27. New York drives to Giants 31. Maynard

punts 43 yards to Philadelphia 26. Rossum returns to Eagles 28. Pederson drives to New York 45. Pederson's pass is intercepted by Strahan at Philadelphia 44. Giants' Peter batted ball up in the air as Pederson backpedaled. Strahan for 44 yards and touchdown at 4:24.

Nov. 14, 1999—Minnesota 27, Chicago 24, at Chicago; Vikings win toss. Boniol kicks to Minnesota 2, Williams touchback. Minnesota starts from own 20. George's pass is intercepted by Harris at Minnesota 29 for -1 yard. Chicago starts at Minnesota 29 and moves to Minnesota 23. Boniol's 41-yard field goal is no good. Minnesota starts from own 31 and drives to Chicago 20. Anderson kicks 38-yard field goal at 9:02.

Nov. 21, 1999—Chicago 23, San Diego 20, at San Diego; Bears win toss. Chicago starts from own 22. Miller completes four consecutive passes and Bears drive to San Diego 22. Enis rushes twice to San Diego 19. Boniol kicks 36-yard field goal at 4:58.

* **Nov. 22, 1999—Denver 27, Oakland 21**, at Denver; Broncos win toss. Denver starts from own 33 and drives to Broncos' 35. Rouen punts 46 yards to Oakland 19. Oakland starts at own 19 and drives to Raiders' 25. Gannon fumbles and Broncos' Pryce recovers at Oakland 25. Denver running back Gary scores on 24-yard run at 2:40.

Nov. 28, 1999—Washington 20, Philadelphia 17, at Washington; Redskins win toss. Akers' kickoff is returned by Thrash for 48 yards to Philadelphia 46. Johnson completes 20-yard pass to Connell to Philadelphia 26. Johnson completes 9-yard pass to Mitchell to Philadelphia 9. Mitchell runs for seven yards to Philadelphia 2. On third down, Washington attempts field goal from Philadelphia 9. Johnson fumbles and recovers at Philadelphia 9. Conway kicks 27-yard field goal at 4:34.

Dec. 19, 1999—Denver 36, Seattle 30, at Denver; Broncos win toss. Peterson kicks to Denver 8. Watson returns kick to Denver 27 for 19 yards. Broncos do not convert a first down. Rouen punts 46 yards, out of bounds at Seattle 25. Kitna passes to Dawkins for 17 yards at Seattle 47. Watters runs for 6 yards to Denver 47. Kitna sacked for 11-yard loss by Crockett. Kitna fumbles, forced by Crockett, recovered by Cadrez at Seattle 37. Cadrez for 37 yards and touchdown at 2:34.

Dec. 26, 1999—Buffalo 13, New England 10, at New England; Patriots win toss. New England's Vinatieri misses 44-yard field goal from Buffalo 26. Buffalo takes over at Bills 34. Flutie passes to Moulds to New England 21 for 17 yards. Moulds fumbles, recovered by Bruschi at Patriots 21. New England drives to own 34. Johnson punts from New England 34 to Buffalo 42. Flutie passes to Price for 7 yards to New England 44. Flutie passes to Moulds for 11 yards to New England 27. Thomas runs for 9 yards to New England 6. Christie kicks 24-yard field goal at 13:12.

#**Dec. 26, 1999—Washington 26, San Francisco 20**, at San Francisco; Redskins win toss. Richey kicks to Washington 9, Thrash returns 13 yards to Washington 22. Johnson passes to Hicks for 25 yards to Washington 47. Centers runs for 12 yards to San Francisco 33. Johnson passes to Centers for 33 yards and touchdown at 2:00.

Jan. 2, 2000—Oakland 41, Kansas City 38, at Kansas City; Raiders win toss. Baker kicks 69 yards from Kansas City 30 to Oakland 1 and out of bounds. Oakland starts at Raiders 40. Gannon passes to Dudley for 21 yards to Kansas City 40. Gannon passes to Brown at Kansas City 16 for 24 yards. Crockett runs to Kansas City 15 for 1 yard. Nedney kicks 33-yard field goal at 3:13.

Sept. 10, 2000—Tennessee 17, Kansas City 14, at Tennessee; Titans win toss. Mason returns kickoff 28 yards to Tennessee 29. Face-mask penalty on Kansas City, 5 yards, enforced at 29. Titans drive to Kansas City 18 where Del Greco kicks 36-yard field goal at 2:58.

Oct. 1, 2000—Dallas 16, Carolina 13, at Carolina; Cowboys win toss. Tucker returns kickoff 20 yards to Dallas 26. Dallas drives to Carolina 6 where Seder kicks 24-yard field goal at 3:52.

Oct. 1, 2000—Washington 20, Tampa Bay 17, at Washington; Redskins win toss. Thrash kickoff 32 yards to Washington 30. Washington gains five yards where Barnhardt punts 52 yards to Tampa Bay 13. Green returns for one yard to Tampa Bay 14. Buccaneers gain one yard to Tampa Bay 15 where Royals punts 50 yards to Washington 35. Sanders returns punt 57 yards to Tampa Bay 8. Davis rushes three times and gets to Tampa Bay 2 where Husted kicks 20-yard field goal at 4:09.

Oct. 8, 2000—Oakland 34, San Francisco 28, at San Francisco; Raiders win toss. Dunn returns kickoff 20 yards to Oakland 19. Raiders drive to San Francisco 17 where Janikowski misses 35-yard field-goal attempt wide right. San Francisco drives to Oakland 11 where Richey's 29-yard field-goal attempt is blocked by Dorsett. Raiders recover at Oakland 16. Oakland drives to San Francisco 31 where Gannon passes to Brown for 31-yard touchdown at 10:15.

Oct. 15, 2000—Buffalo 27, San Diego 24, at Buffalo; Bills win toss. Bills drive to Buffalo 47. Mohr punts 42 yards to San Diego 11. Chargers drive to San Diego 38 where Harbaugh is intercepted at Buffalo 41. Flutie in for injured Johnson. Bills drive to San Diego 28. Christie kicks 46-yard field goal at 8:26.

* **Oct. 23, 2000—New York Jets 40, Miami 37,** at New York; Dolphins win toss. Marion returns kickoff 14 yards to Miami 37. Fielder is intercepted at Miami 46 by Coleman, who returns ball to 39 where he fumbles. Gadsden recovers ball for Dolphins and runs out of bounds at Miami 34. Dolphins drive to New York 43 where Fiedler is intercepted again by Coleman at the Jets 34. Jets drive to Miami 23 where Hall kicks 40-yard field goal at 6:47.

Oct. 29, 2000—Jacksonville 23, Dallas 17, at Dallas; Jaguars win toss. Stith returns kickoff 24 yards to Jacksonville 34. Jaguars drive to Dallas 37 where Brunell passes to Whitted for a 37-yard touchdown at 3:02.

Nov. 5, 2000—Buffalo 16, New England 13, at New England; Patriots win toss. Faulk returns kickoff 38 yards to New England 43. Penalty on New England for offensive holding, 10 yards, enforced at New England 33. Patriots lose one yard on three plays. Johnson punts 43 yards to Buffalo 35. Bills drive to New England 13 where Christie kicks 32-yard field goal at 4:21.

Nov. 5, 2000—Philadelphia 16, Dallas 13, at Philadelphia; Eagles win toss. Mitchell returns kickoff 30 yards to Philadelphia 34. Eagles drive to Dallas 36 where McNabb is intercepted by Wortham at Dallas 30. Wortham returns interception to Dallas 31. Cowboys drive to Dallas 48 where Thomas fumbles. Recovered by Hauck at Dallas 48. Eagles drive to Dallas 13 where Akers kicks 32-yard field goal at 7:52.

* **Nov. 6, 2000—Green Bay 26, Minnesota 20,** at Green Bay; Packers win toss. Rossum returns kickoff 13 yards to Green Bay 18. Packers drive to Minnesota 43 where Favre passes to Freeman for a 43-yard touchdown at 3:27.

Nov. 12, 2000—Philadelphia 26, Pittsburgh 23, at Pittsburgh; Eagles win toss. Mitchell returns kickoff 24 yards to Philadelphia 37. Eagles drive to Pittsburgh 24 where Akers kicks 42-yard field goal at 4:09.

Dec. 17, 2000—New England 13, Buffalo 10, at Buffalo; Bills win toss and elect to defend the South goal. Patriots elect to receive. Jackson returns kickoff 38 yards to New England 48. Patriots drive to Buffalo 31 where they turn the ball over on downs. Bills drive to New England 12 where Christie's 30-yard field goal attempt is blocked by Eaton. Patriots recover at New England 11. Patriots drive to Buffalo 6 where Vinatieri kicks 24-yard field goal at 14:37.

Dec. 24, 2000—Green Bay 17, Tampa Bay 14, at Green Bay; Packers win toss. Rossum returns kickoff 29 yards to Green Bay 38. Packers drive to Tampa Bay 4 where Longwell kicks 22-yard field goal at 6:28.

Sept. 9, 2001—St. Louis 20, Philadelphia 17, at Philadelphia; Eagles win toss. Wilkins' kickoff is a touchback. Eagles drive to Philadelphia 30. Landeta punts 34 yards to St. Louis 36. Rams drive to Philadelphia 8. Wilkins kicks 26-yard field goal at 7:56.

Sept. 9, 2001—San Francisco 16, Atlanta 13, at San Francisco; 49ers win toss. Feely's kickoff is a touchback. 49ers drive to Atlanta 6. Cortez kicks 24-yard field goal at 4:04.

Oct. 14, 2001—New England 29, San Diego 26, at New England; Chargers win toss. Jenkins returns kickoff 39 yards to San Diego 40. Chargers drive to San Diego 45. Bennett punts 32 yards to New England 23. Patriots drive to San Diego 26. Vinatieri kicks 44-yard field goal at 4:00.

Oct. 14, 2001—San Francisco 37, Atlanta 31, at Atlanta; 49ers win toss. Sutherland returns kickoff 24 yards to San Francisco 24. 49ers drive to Atlanta 14. Garcia fumbles, Hall recovers at Atlanta 16. Falcons drive to Atlanta 23. Mohr punts 44 yards to San Francisco 33. Garcia throws 52-yard touchdown to Owens at 8:34.

Oct. 14, 2001—Tennessee 31, Tampa Bay 28, at Tennessee; Buccaneers win toss. D. Smith returns kickoff 17 yards to Tampa Bay 18. Buccaneers forced back to Tampa Bay 9. Royals punts 45 yards to Tennessee 46. Titans drive to Tampa Bay

32. Nedney kicks 49-yard field goal at 1:52.

Oct. 21, 2001—Washington 17, Carolina 14, at Washington; Redskins win toss. Bates returns kickoff 17 yards to Washington 14. Redskins drive to Carolina 5. Conway kicks 23-yard field goal at 1:47.

Oct. 28, 2001—Chicago 37, San Francisco 31, at Chicago; 49ers win toss. Edinger's kickoff is a touchback. M. Brown intercepts Garcia pass and returns it 33 yards for touchdown at 16 seconds.

Nov. 4, 2001—Chicago 27, Cleveland 21, at Chicago; Bears win toss. L. Johnson returns kickoff 31 yards to Chicago 32. Bears drive to Chicago 40. Maynard punts 52 yards to Cleveland 8. M. Brown intercepts Couch pass and returns it 16 yards for touchdown at 2:50.

Nov. 4, 2001—New York Giants 27, Dallas 24, at New York; Cowboys win toss. Swinton returns kickoff 21 yards to Dallas 29. Cowboys drive to New York 48. Knorr punts 33 yards to New York 15. Giants drive to Dallas 24. Andersen kicks 42-yard field goal at 7:12.

Nov. 11, 2001—Pittsburgh 15, Cleveland 12, at Cleveland; Steelers win toss. T. Edwards returns kickoff 21 yards to Pittsburgh 28. Steelers drive to Cleveland 14. Brown kicks 32-yard field goal at 5:22.

Nov. 18, 2001—San Francisco 25, Carolina 22, at Carolina; 49ers win toss. Sutherland returns kickoff 24 yards to San Francisco 26. 49ers drive to Carolina 8. Cortez kicks 26-yard field goal at 4:41.

Dec. 2, 2001—Arizona 34, Oakland 31, at Oakland; Raiders win toss. Gramatica's kickoff is a touchback. Raiders drive to Oakland 40. Lechler punts 37 yards to Arizona 23. Cardinals drive to Arizona 48. Stanley punts 29 yards to Oakland 23. Woods recovers Dunn fumble on Oakland 25. Arizona drives to Oakland 18. Gramatica kicks 36-yard field goal at 7:29.

Dec. 2, 2001—Seattle 13, San Diego 10, at Seattle; Seahawks win toss. Rogers returns kickoff 33 yards to Seattle 30. Seahawks drive to San Diego 6. Lindell kicks 24-yard field goal at 6:23.

Dec. 2, 2001—Tampa Bay 16, Cincinnati 13, at Cincinnati; Buccaneers win toss. F. Murphy returns kickoff 20 yards to Tampa Bay 38. Buccaneers drive to Cincinnati 35. Royals punts 31 yards to Cincinnati 4. Lynch recovers Dillon fumble on Cincinnati 3. Gramatica kicks 21-yard field goal at 5:06.

Dec. 16, 2001—Kansas City 26, Denver 23, at Kansas City; Broncos win toss. Carter returns kickoff 24 yards to Denver 41. Broncos drive to Denver 35. Rouen punts 35 yards to Kansas City 30. Chiefs drive to Denver 23. T. Peterson misses 41-yard field-goal attempt. Broncos drive to Denver 32. Rouen punts 38 yards to Kansas City 30. Chiefs drive to Denver 14. T. Peterson kicks 32-yard field goal at 9:04.

Dec. 16, 2001—New England 12, Buffalo 9, at Buffalo; Bills win toss. Bryson returns kickoff 23 yards to Buffalo 28. Bills drive to Buffalo 48. Moorman punts 52 yards to end zone. Patriots drive to Buffalo 5. Vinatieri kicks 23-yard field goal at 5:45.

Dec. 30, 2001—Cincinnati 26, Pittsburgh 23, at Cincinnati; Steelers win toss. Geason returns kickoff and laterals to Logan who carries ball 9 yards to Pittsburgh 38. Steelers drive to Cincinnati 39. Miller punts 38 yards to Cincinnati 1. Bengals drive to Pittsburgh 13. Rackers kicks 31-yard field goal at 10:52.

Sept. 8, 2002—New York Jets 37, Buffalo 31, at Buffalo; Jets win toss. Morton returns kickoff 96 yards for touchdown at 14 seconds.

Sept. 8, 2002—Green Bay 37, Atlanta 34, at Green Bay; Packers win toss. J. Walker returns kickoff 26 yards to Green Bay 34. Packers drive to Atlanta 39. Bidwell punts 27 yards to Atlanta 12. Falcons drive to Atlanta 14. Mohr punts 46 yards to Green Bay 40. Packers drive to Atlanta 19. Longwell kicks 34-yard field goal at 9:40.

Sept. 8, 2002—New Orleans 26, Tampa Bay 20, at Tampa Bay; Tampa Bay wins toss. Stecker returns kickoff 31 yards to Tampa Bay 42. Buccaneers drive to New Orleans 39. Tupa punts 39 yards into end zone. Saints drive to New Orleans 20. Williams returns Johnson's punt 4 yards to Tampa Bay 46. Buccaneers drive to Tampa Bay 48. Tupa punts 52 yards into end zone. Saints drive to New Orleans 41. Williams returns Johnson's punt -4 yards to Tampa Bay 6. Buccaneers drive to Tampa Bay 5. Tupa pass intercepted by Allen in Tampa Bay end zone at 12:01.

Sept. 15, 2002—Buffalo 45, Minnesota 39, at Minnesota; Buffalo wins toss. Rodgers returns kickoff 22 yards to Buffalo

22. Bills drive to Buffalo 48. Moorman punts 27 yards, downed at Minnesota 25. Vikings drive to Minnesota 32. Richardson punts 45 yards. Downed at Buffalo 23. Bills drive to Minnesota 26. Hollis' 44-yard field-goal attempt is no good. Vikings take over on Minnesota 35. Drive to Minnesota 41. Richardson punts 52 yards. Returned by Rogers 16 yards to Buffalo 24. Bills drive to Minnesota 48. Bledsoe throws 48-yard pass to Price for touchdown at 10:12.

Sept. 22, 2002—Cleveland 31, Tennessee 28, at Tennessee; Cleveland wins toss. White returns kickoff 6 yards to Cleveland 26. Browns drive to Tennessee 15. Dawson kicks 33-yard field goal at 4:09.

Sept. 22, 2002—New England 41, Kansas City 38, at New England; New England wins toss. Branch returns kickoff 30 yards to New England 30. Patriots drive to Kansas City 17. Vinatieri kicks 35-yard field goal at 4:36.

Sept. 29, 2002—Buffalo 33, Chicago 27, at Buffalo; Chicago wins toss. Johnson returns kickoff 19 yards to Chicago 20. Bears drive to Chicago 25. Maynard punts 31 yards to Buffalo 44. Fair catch by Mannelly. Buffalo drives to Chicago 26. Bledsoe throws 26-yard pass to Henry for touchdown at 2:48.

Sept. 29, 2002—Pittsburgh 16, Cleveland 13, at Pittsburgh; Pittsburgh wins toss. Mays returns kickoff 32 yards to Pittsburgh 32. Maddox's pass intercepted by Davis at Pittsburgh 34, returned for no gain. Cleveland drives to Pittsburgh 27. Dawson's 45-yard field-goal attempt no good, tipped at line of scrimmage by Flowers. Steelers take over at Pittsburgh 35. Steelers drive to Cleveland 6, and 24-yard field-goal attempt by Peterson blocked by McKinley, recovered by Peterson, fumbles, recovered by Fiala. Peterson's 31-yard field goal is good at 6:58.

Oct. 20, 2002—Denver 37, Kansas City 34, at Denver; Denver wins toss. Kasper returns kickoff 15 yards to Denver 24. Broncos drive to Denver 33. Rouen punts 43 yards to Kansas City 24. Hall returns punt 13 yards to Kansas City 37. Chiefs drive to Kansas City 43. Stryzinski's punt is blocked and recovered by Burns at Kansas City 32. Denver drives to Kansas City 7. Elam's 25-yard field goal is good at 2:52.

Oct. 20, 2002—Detroit 23, Chicago 20, at Detroit; Detroit wins toss. Edinger's kickoff goes out of bounds at Detroit 2. Lions take over at Detroit 40. Lions drive to Chicago 30. Hanson's 48-yard field goal is good at 4:42.

Oct. 20, 2002—San Diego 27, Oakland 21, at Oakland; San Diego wins toss. Chargers start at San Diego 20 after touchback. Chargers drive to Oakland 19. Tomlinson runs 19 yards for touchdown at 3:33.

Oct. 20, 2002—Arizona 9, Dallas 6, at Arizona; Dallas wins toss. Swinton returns kickoff 26 yards to Dallas 24. Cowboys drive to Dallas 29. Knorr punts 45 yards to Arizona 26. Jackson returns 5 yards to Arizona 31. Cardinals drive to Dallas 38. Player punts 38 yards into end zone. Cowboys take over at Dallas 20. Cowboys drive to Arizona 49. Knorr punts 31 yards to Arizona 18. Fair catch by Jackson. Cardinals drive to Dallas 22. Gramatica's 40-yard field goal is good at 11:45.

Nov. 3, 2002—San Francisco 23, Oakland 20, at Oakland; San Francisco wins toss. Janikowski's kickoff returned to SF 22 by J. Williams. 49ers drive to Oakland 5. Cortez's 23-yard field goal at 8:41.

Nov. 10, 2002—Atlanta 34, Pittsburgh 34, at Pittsburgh; Pittsburgh wins toss. Touchback for kickoff. Pittsburgh starts at own 20, drives to Atlanta 30. Peterson's 48-yard field-goal attempt blocked by Finneran. Atlanta takes over at own 47, drives to Atlanta 33. Mohr punts 47 yards to Randle El, who returns to Pittsburgh 18. Steelers drive to Atlanta 33. Miller punts 22 yards to Atlanta 12, no return. Falcons drive to Atlanta 23. Mohr punts 52 yards. Randle El returns 1 yard to Pittsburgh 26. Steelers drive to Pittsburgh 44. Maddox intercepted by Mathis at Atlanta 43. Mathis returns to Pittsburgh 44. Atlanta drives to Pittsburgh 37. Feely's 56-yard field-goal attempt blocked by Farrior. Pittsburgh takes over on own 49. Maddox pass to Burress downed at Atlanta 1 as time expires.

Nov. 17, 2002—San Diego 20, San Francisco 17, at San Diego; San Diego wins toss. Jenkins returns Cortez kickoff 39 yards to San Diego 38. Chargers drive to San Diego 38. Bennett punts 47 yards to San Francisco 15. Williams returns 9 yards to San Francisco 24. 49ers drive to San Diego 23. Cortez's 41-yard field-goal attempt is no good. San Diego takes over on San Diego 31. Chargers drive to San Francisco 22. Christie's 40-yard field goal is good at 10:49.

Nov. 24, 2002—Chicago 20, Detroit 17, at Chicago; Detroit wins toss. Elects to defend the north goal. Hanson kicks 72 yards. Kick returned 37 yards to Chicago 35. Chicago drives to Detroit 22. Edinger's 40-yard field-goal attempt is good at 6:02.

#Nov. 24, 2002—Indianapolis 23, Denver 20, at Denver; Indianapolis wins toss. Knorr kicks 66 yards. Returned by Walters 28 yards to Indianapolis 32. Colts drive to Denver 33. Vanderjagt's 51-yard field-goal attempt is good at 5:38.

Dec. 1, 2002—Atlanta 30, Minnesota 24, at Minnesota; Minnesota wins toss. Feely kicks 60 yards. Returned by Carter 10 yards to Minnesota 20. Vikings drive to Minnesota 11. Richardson punts 47 yards to Atlanta 42. Returned by Rossum 10 yards to Minnesota 48. Falcons drive to Minnesota 46. Vick runs 46 yards for touchdown at 2:25.

Dec. 1, 2002—Tennessee 32, New York Giants 29, at New York; New York wins toss. Nedney kicks 68 yards. Returned by Joyce 38 yards to New York 40. Giants drive to New York 46. Allen punts 34 yards to Tennessee 20. Fair catch by O'Leary. Titans drive to New York 20. Nedney's 38-yard field goal good at 5:00.

Dec. 1, 2002—San Diego 30, Denver 27, at San Diego; Denver wins toss. Christie kicks 65 yards. Droughns returns 27 yards to Denver 32. Broncos drive to Denver 23. Knorr punts 36 yards to San Diego 41. Fair catch by Dwight. Chargers drive to Denver 19. Christie's 38-yard field-goal attempt blocked. Denver takes over on own 27. Broncos drive to San Diego 32. Elam's 53-yard field-goal attempt is no good. San Diego takes over on own 43. Chargers drive to Denver 9. Christie's field goal is good from 27 yards at 11:59.

Dec. 8, 2002—Arizona 23, Detroit 20, at Arizona; Arizona wins toss. Hanson kicks 64 yards. Kasper returns 19 yards to Arizona 30. Cardinals drive to Detroit 24. Gramatica's 42-yard field-goal attempt is good at 4:12.

Dec. 15, 2002—Seattle 30, Atlanta 24, at Atlanta; Atlanta wins toss. Lindell kicks 69 yards. Returned 17 yards to Atlanta 18 by Rossum. Atlanta drives to Seattle 18. Feely's 36-yard field-goal attempt wide right. Seattle takes over at own 26. Seahawks drive to Atlanta 27. Alexander runs 27 yards for a touchdown at 10:36.

Dec. 29, 2002—New York Giants 10, Philadelphia 7, at N.Y. Giants; Philadelphia wins toss. Bryant kicks 57 yards. Returned by Mitchell 32 yards to Philadelphia 45. Eagles drive to mid-field. Feeley's pass intercepted by Williams at New York 37, returned for no gain. Giants drive to Philadelphia 22. Bryant's 39-yard field-goal attempt is good at 5:10.

Dec. 29, 2002—New England 27, Miami 24, at New England; New England wins toss. Mare kicks 68 yards out of bounds. Patriots begin at own 40. New England drives to Miami 17. Vinatieri's 35-yard field goal is good at 2:03.

Dec. 29, 2002—Seattle 31, San Diego 28, at San Diego; Seattle wins toss. Christie kicks 64 yards. Returned by Williams 26 yards to Seattle 32. Seahawks drive to San Diego 28. Hasselbeck's pass is intercepted by Molden at San Diego 20 and returned 1 yard to the 21. Chargers drive to San Diego 12. Bennett punts 48 yards to Seattle 40. Returned by Engram 8 yards to Seattle 48. Seahawks drive to San Diego 6. Lindell's 24-yard field goal is good at 9:58.

Sept. 14, 2003—St. Louis 27, San Francisco 24, at St. Louis; Rams win toss. Harris returns kick 42 yards to St. Louis 48. Rams drive to San Francisco 10. Wilkins kicks 28-yard field goal at 1:56.

Sept. 14, 2003—Carolina 12, Tampa Bay 9, at Tampa Bay; Panthers win toss. Touchback. Carolina starts at own 20, drives to own 37. Sauerbrun punts 45 yards to Tampa Bay 18. Buccaneers drive to Carolina 42. Tupa punts 34 yards to Carolina 8. Smith returns punt 52 yards to Tampa Bay 40. Panthers drive to Tampa Bay 29. Kasay kicks 47-yard field goal at 11:26.

* Sept. 15, 2003—Dallas 35, New York Giants 32, at New York; Cowboys win toss. Smith returns kickoff 21 yards to Dallas 29. Cowboys drive to Dallas 48. Gowin punts 32 yards to Giants 20. Giants drive to New York 15. Feagles punts 42 yards to Dallas 43. Cowboys drive to New York 6. Cundiff kicks 25-yard field goal at 9:04.

Sept. 21, 2003—New York Giants 24, Washington 21, at Washington; Giants win toss. Begin on New York 6 due to penalty on kickoff return. Giants drive to Washington 11. Bryant kicks 29-yard field goal at 4:15.

Sept. 28, 2003—Oakland 34, San Diego 31, at Oakland; Chargers win toss. Johnson returns kickoff to San Diego 24. Chargers drive to San Diego 36. Bennett punts 46 yards to Oakland 18. Raiders drive to Oakland 8. Lechler punts 49 yards to San Diego 43. Chargers drive to San Diego 39. Bennett punts to Oakland 8. Raiders drive to San Diego 28. Janikowski kicks 46-yard field goal at 9:59.

Oct. 5, 2003—Buffalo 22, Cincinnati 16, at Buffalo; Bengals win toss. Begin drive on Cincinnati 20 after touchback. Bengals drive to Cincinnati 28. Harris punts 29 yards to Buffalo 43. Bills drive to Cincinnati 2. Henry scores on 2-yard touchdown run at 3:53.

* **Oct. 6, 2003—Indianapolis 38, Tampa Bay 35**, at Tampa Bay; Buccaneers win toss. Barlow returns kickoff 30 yards to Tampa Bay 30. Buccaneers drive to Indianapolis 41. Tupa punts to Indianapolis 13. Colts drive to Tampa Bay 11. Vanderjagt kicks 29-yard field goal at 11:13.

Oct. 12, 2003—Carolina 23, Indianapolis 20, at Indianapolis; Panthers win toss. Smart returns kickoff to Carolina 27. Panthers drive to Indianapolis 30. Kasay kicks 47-yard field goal at 5:39.

Oct. 12, 2003—Kansas City 40, Green Bay 34, at Green Bay; Chiefs win toss. Hall returns kick to Kansas City 29. Chiefs drive to Green Bay 30. Andersen misses 48-yard field goal (ball tipped at line). Packers take over possession at Green Bay 39. A. Green fumbles after eight-yard run. Chiefs recover at Kansas City 49. T. Green throws 51-yard touchdown pass to Kennison at 6:18.

Oct. 19, 2003—New England 19, Miami 13, at Miami; Dolphins win toss. Rogers returns kickoff 24 yards to Miami 26. Dolphins drive to New England 17. Mare's 35-yard field-goal attempt no good. Patriots take over on New England 26. Patriots drive to New England 40. Walter punts to Miami 21. Returned by Rogers to Miami 30. Dolphins drive to Miami 45. Fiedler pass intercepted by Poole at New England 18. Brady passes 82 yards to Brown for touchdown at 9:15.

Oct. 26, 2003—Carolina 23, New Orleans 20, at New Orleans; Saints win toss. Lewis returns kickoff 53 yards to Carolina 46. Saints drive to Carolina 37. McAllister fumbles on fourth-and-one. Panthers take over at Carolina 38 and drive to New Orleans 12. Kasay kicks 31-yard field goal at 4:36.

Oct. 26, 2003—Arizona 16, San Francisco 13, at Arizona; Cardinals win toss. 49ers' Pochman kicks out of bounds. Cardinals take possession at Arizona 40 and drive to San Francisco 22. Duncan kicks 39-yard field goal at 4:59.

Nov. 2, 2003—New York Giants 31, New York Jets 28, at New York Jets; Giants win toss. Mitchell returns kick 26 yards to Giants 34. Giants drive to Jets 21. Conway misses 39-yard field-goal attempt. Jets take over on own 30. Drive to Giants 49. Stryzinski's punt returned by Mitchell two yards to Giants 18. Giants drive to own 35. Feagles' punt returned six yards by Moss to Jets 29. Jets drive to Giants 32. Brien's 51-yard field goal attempt is blocked by Allen. Giants take over on own 36, drive to Jets 11. Conway kicks 29-yard field goal at 14:56.

Nov. 9, 2003—New York Jets 27, Oakland 24, at Oakland; Jets win toss. Jordan returns kick 12 yards to New York 25. Jets drive to Oakland 21. Brien kicks 38-yard field goal at 5:56.

Nov. 16, 2003—Miami 9, Baltimore 6, at Miami; Dolphins win toss. Dolphins start at Miami 20 after touchback, drive to Baltimore 45. Turk punts 36 yards to Baltimore 9. Ravens drive to Baltimore 36. Lewis fumbles, recovered by Dolphins' Thomas. Dolphins drive to Baltimore 25. Mare kicks 43-yard field goal at 6:12.

Nov. 16, 2003—New Orleans 23, Atlanta 20, at New Orleans; Saints win toss. Lewis returns kick 39 yards to New Orleans 38. Saints drive to New Orleans 40. McAllister fumbles on Atlanta 2 after 58-yard run. Ball recovered by Falcons' Stewart for touchback. Falcons drive to New Orleans 37. Feely's 54-yard field-goal attempt no good. Saints take over on New Orleans 45. Drive to Atlanta 18. Carney kicks 36-yard field goal at 3:59.

Nov. 23, 2003—New England 23, Houston 20, at Houston; Texans win toss, take over possession at own 13 after penalty on Hollings' return. Patriots intercept Texans at Houston 23. Patriots drive to Houston 19. Vinatieri's 37-yard field-goal attempt blocked. Texans take over at own 27, drive to New England 40. Stanley punts 31 yards to New England 9. Patriots drive to New England 4. Walter punts 31 yards to New England 35. Texans drive to New England 40. Stanley punts 26 yards to New England 14. Patriots drive to Houston 10. Vinatieri kicks 28-yard field goal at 14:19.

Nov. 23, 2003—Baltimore 44, Seattle 41, at Baltimore; Seahawks win toss. Morris returns kick to Seattle 27. Seahawks drive to Seattle 30. Rouen punts 50 yards to Baltimore 20, returned 1 yard by Brightful to Baltimore 21. Ravens drive to Seattle 24. Stover kicks 42-yard field goal at 8:28.

Nov. 23, 2003—St. Louis 30, Arizona 27, at Arizona; Rams win toss. Harris returns kick to St. Louis 14. Rams drive to Arizona 31. Wilkins kicks 49-yard field goal at 3:38.

\# **Dec. 7, 2003—Atlanta 20, Carolina 14**, at Atlanta; Panthers win toss. Smart returns kickoff 19 yards to Carolina 22. Panthers drive to Carolina 29. Delhomme's pass intercepted by Mathis at Carolina 32 and returned for touchdown at 1:19.

Dec. 14, 2003—Denver 23, Cleveland 20, at Cleveland; Browns win toss, start on Cleveland 20 after touchback. Browns drive to Cleveland 17. Gardocki punts 42 yards, returned by O'Neal 6 yards to Denver 47. Broncos drive to Cleveland 7. Elam kicks 25-yard field goal at 5:10.

Dec. 21, 2003—San Francisco 31, Philadelphia 28, at Philadelphia; Eagles win toss, start on Philadelphia 21 after penalty on Thrash's return. McNabb's pass intercepted by 49ers' Parrish and returned 29 yards to Philadelphia 4. On second down, Peterson kicks 22-yard field goal at 1:05.

\# **Dec. 28, 2003—Baltimore 13, Pittsburgh 10**, at Baltimore; Steelers win toss. Mays returns kick to Pittsburgh 20. Steelers drive to Pittsburgh 27. Miller punts 43 yards, returned 6 yards by Brightful to Baltimore 36. Ravens drive to Pittsburgh 29. Stover kicks 47-yard field goal at 3:28.

Sept. 26, 2004—New Orleans 28, St. Louis 25, at St. Louis; Rams win the toss. Furrey returns kick 23 yards to St. Louis 32. Rams drive to own 41. Landeta punts 41 yards to New Orleans 18. Lewis returns punt 15 yards to New Orleans 33. Saints drive to St. Louis 13. Carney kicks 31-yard field goal at 7:04.

Oct. 10, 2004—Minnesota 34, Houston 28, at Houston; Vikings win the toss. Burleson returns kick 29 yards to Minnesota 30. Vikings drive to own 35. Bennett punts 47 yards to Houston 34. Houston drives to own 38. Stanley punts 43 yards to Minnesota 19. Minnesota drives to the 50. Culpepper passes to Robinson for 50-yard touchdown at 7:55.

Oct. 10, 2004—St. Louis 33, Seattle 27, at Seattle; Rams win the toss. Harris returns kick 17 yards to St. Louis 29. Rams drive to own 48. Bulger passes to McDonald for 52-yard touchdown at 3:02.

Oct. 10, 2004—San Francisco 31, Arizona 28, at San Francisco; 49ers win the toss. Jackson returns kick 14 yards to San Francisco 39. 49ers drive to Arizona 14. Peterson kicks 32-yard field goal at 3:23.

Oct. 24, 2004—Philadelphia 34, Cleveland 31, at Cleveland; Eagles win the toss. Reed returns kick 27 yards to Philadelphia 30. Eagles drive to Cleveland 37. Johnson punts 47 yards for touchback. Cleveland drives to own 47. Frost punts 30 yards to Eagles 22. Philadelphia drives to Cleveland 32. Akers kicks 50-yard field goal at 9:58.

Nov. 14, 2004—Jacksonville 23, Detroit 17, at Jacksonville; Jaguars win the toss. Lewis returns kick 17 yards to the Jacksonville 24. Jaguars drive to the Detroit 38. Garrard passes to Smith for 38-yard touchdown at 5:28.

Nov. 14, 2004—Chicago 19, Tennessee 17, at Tennessee; Bears win the toss. Azumah returns kick 22 yards to Chicago 26. Bears drive to own 48. Maynard punts 44 yards to Tennessee. Fair catch by Mason. Volek sacked at Tennessee 0 and fumble is recovered by Miller who is tackled in the end zone for safety at 3:17.

Nov. 14, 2004—Baltimore 20, New York Jets 17, at New York; Jets win the toss. Touchback. Jets drive to own 24. Gowin punts to Baltimore 35. Sams returns punt 9 yards to Baltimore 44. Ravens drive to own 49. Stewart punts 42 yards and ball is downed at the New York 9. Jets drive to own 16. Gowin punts 43 yards to Baltimore 41. Sams returns punt to Baltimore 44. Baltimore drives to New York 24. Stover kicks 42-yard field goal at 7:25.

Dec. 12, 2004—San Francisco 31, Arizona 28, at Arizona; 49ers win the toss. Touchback. 49ers drive to Arizona 37. Lee punts to 34 yards and is downed at Arizona 3. Cardinals drive to own 7. Player punts 51 yards and is returned to Arizona 49. 49ers drive to own 13. Peterson kicks 31-yard field goal at 6:22.

\# **Dec. 18, 2004—Atlanta 34, Carolina 31**, at Atlanta; Panthers win the toss. Broussard returns kick 16 yards to Carolina 19. Delhomme intercepted by Beasley returns pass 30 yards to Carolina 23. Atlanta drives to Carolina 20. Feely kicks 38-yard field goal at 2:25.

Dec. 26, 2004—Indianapolis 34, San Diego 31, at Indianapolis; Colts win the toss. Rhodes returns kick 17 yards to Indianapolis 27. Colts drive to San Diego 17. Vanderjagt kicks 30-yard field goal at 2:47.

Jan. 2, 2005—St. Louis 32, New York Jets 29, at St. Louis; Rams win the toss. Cason returns kick to St. Louis 24. Rams drive to New York 44. Stemke punts into endzone for touchback. Jets drive to own 44. Gowin punts 33 yards. Fair catch at St. Louis 23. Rams drive to own 31. Stemke punts to New York 27 and returned by McCareins two yards. Jets drive to St. Louis 35. Brien misses 53-yard field goal wide right. Rams begin drive from own 43. Rams drive to Jets 13. Wilkins kicks 31-yard field goal at 11:58.

Sept. 25, 2005—Jacksonville 26, New York Jets 20, at New York; Jets win the toss. Miller returns kick for 29 yards to Jets 21. Mathis intercepts Pennington pass and returns to Jets 46. Rhodes intercepts Leftwich pass at Jets 12 for no return. Jets drive ends at own 1. Graham punts 44 yards. Pearman returns punt 11 yards to Jets 34. Leftwich passes to Smith for 36-yard touchdown at 6:05.

Oct. 2, 2005—Washington 20, Seattle 17, at Washington; Redskins win the toss. Betts returns kick for 24 yards to Washington 23. Redskins drive to Seattle 22. Novak kicks a 39-yard field goal at 5:31.

Oct. 16, 2005—Jacksonville 23, Pittsburgh 17, at Pittsburgh; Steelers win the toss. Morgan returns kick for 74 yards to Jacksonville 26. Maddox fumbles and ball is recovered by Jaguars on own 36. Jaguars drive ends on own 16. Hanson punts 48 yards. Randle El returns punt 2 yards to Pittsburgh 35. Mathis intercepts Maddox pass and returned 41 yards for a touchdown at 3:36.

Oct. 16, 2005—Dallas 16, New York Giants 13, at Dallas; Cowboys win the toss. Thompson returns kick 23 yards to Dallas 23. Cowboys drive to Giants 26. Cortez kicks a 45-yard field goal at 3:47.

Oct. 30, 2005—Chicago 19, Detroit 13, at Detroit; Lions win the toss. Drummond returns kick 15 yards to Detroit 22. Lions drive to own 28. Harris punts 45 yards. Wade returns to Chicago 23 for no gain. Bears drive to own 48. Maynard punts 39 yards. Fair catch by Drummond at Detroit 13. Garcia pass intercepted by Tillman and returned 22 yards for a touchdown at 6:17.

Nov. 20, 2005—Baltimore 16, Pittsburgh 13, at Baltimore; Steelers win the toss. Colclough returns kick 16 yards to Pittsburgh 18. Steelers drive ends at own 36. Gardocki punts 27 yards. Ball downed at Baltimore 37. Ravens drive to own 39. Zastudil punts 26 yards. Ball downed at Pittsburgh 35. Steelers drive ends at own 33. Gardocki punts 37 yards. Sams returns punt 14 yards to Baltimore 44. Ravens drive to Pittsburgh 26. Stover kicks 44-yard field goal at 10:51.

+**Nov. 24, 2005—Denver 24, Dallas 21,** at Dallas; Broncos win the toss. Da. Williams returns kick 27 yards to own 32. Broncos drive to Dallas 7. Elam kicks 24-yard field goal at 1:11.

Nov. 27, 2005—St. Louis 33, Houston 27, at Houston; Texans win the toss. Houston drive begins at Houston 20. Texans drive to St. Louis 47. Stanley punts 47 yards. Touchback. Drive begins at St. Louis 20. Fitzpatrick passes to Curtis for 56-yard touchdown at 6:14.

Nov. 27, 2005—San Diego 23, Washington 17, at Washington; Chargers win the toss. Sproles returns kick 22 yards to San Diego 35. Tomlinson runs 41 yards for a touchdown at 34 seconds.

Nov. 27, 2005—Seattle 24, New York Giants 21, at Seattle; Seahawks win the toss. Scobey returns kick 24 yards to Seattle 22. Seahawks drive ends at own 13. Rouen punts 40 yards. Morton returns punt 2 yards to Giants 49. Giants drive to Seattle 36. Feely misses 54-yard field goal. Seahawks drive begins at own 44. Drive ends at Giants 46. Rouen punts 46 yards. Touchback. Drive begins at Giants 20. Seahawks drive to own 27. Feely misses 45-yard field goal. Drive begins at Seattle 35. Seahawks drive to Giants 18. Brown kicks 36-yard field goal at 12:15.

#**Dec. 11, 2005—Green Bay 16, Detroit 13,** at Green Bay; Packers win the toss. Chatman returns kick 33 yards to Green Bay 35. Packers drive to Lions 11. Longwell kicks 28-yard field goal at 5:17.

Dec. 11, 2005—New York Giants 26, Philadelphia 23, at Philadelphia; Eagles win the toss. Hood returns kick 27 yards to Philadelphia 33. Eagles drive ends on own 33. Landeta punts 41 yards. Morton returns punt 7 yards to Giants 33. Manning pass intercepted by Dawkins at Philadelphia 37 and returned for no gain. McMahon fumbles and ball recovered by K. Allen. Fumble returned 2 yards. Giants drive begins on Philadelphia 37. Giants drive to Philadelphia 18. Feely kicks 36-yard field goal at 11:05.

Dec. 24, 2005—Tampa Bay 27, Falcons 24, at Tampa Bay; Buccaneers win the toss. Shepherd returns kick 18 yards and

fumbles. Ball is recovered by Falcons' Heard at Tampa Bay 18. Falcons drive to Tampa Bay 10. Peterson field goal blocked by White. Ball recovered by Kelley and returned 9 yards to Tampa Bay 31. Buccaneers drive to Atlanta 9. Bryant misses 27-yard field goal. Falcons begin drive at own 20. Falcons drive to own 46. Koenen punts 49 yards. Jones returns punt 4 yards to Tampa Bay 9. Buccaneers drive to own 47. Bidwell punts 37 yards out of bounds at Atlanta 16. Falcons drive to Atlanta 24. Koenen punts 53 yards. Jones returns punt 28 yards to Atlanta 49. Buccaneers drive to Atlanta 23. Bryant kicks 41-yard field goal at 14:45.

Jan. 1, 2006—San Francisco 20, Houston 17, at San Francisco; 49ers win the toss. Amey returns kick 15 yards to San Francisco 21. 49ers drive to own 30. Lee punts 39 yards. Ball downed at Houston 31. Texans drive to San Francisco 44. Stanley punts 39 yards. Ball downed at San Francisco 5. 49ers drive to own 49. Lee punts 47 yards. Ball downed at Houston 4. Banks pass intercepted by Adams and laterals to Emanuel. Ball returned 35 yards to Houston 21. 49ers drive to Houston 15. Nedney kicks 31-yard field goal at 11:08.

Sept. 17, 2006—Minnesota 16, Carolina 13, at Minnesota; Panthers win toss. D. Williams returns kick for 19 yards. Drive begins at Panthers 18. Drive ends on Panthers 33. Baker punts 57 yards. M. Moore returns kick 11 yards. Drive begins at Vikings 21. Longwell kicks 19-yard field goal at 7:25.

Sept. 17, 2006—New York Giants 30, Philadelphia 24, at Philadelphia; Giants win toss. Morton returns kick 23 yards. Drive begins at Giants 20. Drive ends at Giants 32. Feagles punts 38 yards. Wynn returns kick 14 yards. Drive begins at Eagles 44. Drive ends at Eagles 36. D. Johnson punts for 49 yards. Morton fair catch. Drive begins at Giants 15. Manning completes 31-yard touchdown pass to Burress at 3:11.

Sept. 17, 2006—Denver 9, Kansas City 6, at Denver; Broncos win toss. Cobbs muffs kick and recovers for no gain. Drive begins at Broncos 16. Elam kicks 39-yard field goal at 9:50.

Oct. 1, 2006—Washington 36, Jacksonville 30, at Washington; Redskins win toss. Cartwright returns kick for 22 yards. Drive begins at Redskins 20. Brunell completes 68-yard touchdown pass to Moss at 13:11.

Oct. 22, 2006—Atlanta 41, Pittsburgh 38, at Atlanta; Falcons win toss. Rossum returns kick for 23 yards. Drive begins at Falcons 21. Andersen kicks 32-yard field goal at 8:04.

Dec. 3, 2006—Cleveland 31, Kansas City 28, at Cleveland; Chiefs win toss. Hall returns kick for 21 yards. Drive begins at Chiefs 20. Drive ends at Chiefs 41. Colquitt punts 42 yards. Northcutt returns punt 5 yards. Drive begins at Browns 22. Dawson kicks 33-yard field goal at 7:25.

Dec. 10, 2006—Tennessee 26, Houston 20, at Houston; Titans win toss. Jones returns kick 36 yards. Drive begins at Texans 43. Young runs for 39-yard touchdown at 11:14.

Dec. 17, 2006—Chicago 34, Tampa Bay 31, at Chicago; Buccaneers win toss. Touchback. Drive begins at Buccaneers 20. Rattay fumbles. Bears recover at Buccaneers 22. Gould misses 37-yard field goal. Drive begins at Buccaneers 27. Bidwell punts 45 yards. Hester returns punt 8 yards and fumbles out of bounds. Drive begins at Bears 29. Maynard punts 47 yards. Drive begins at Buccaneers 2. Bidwell punts 48 yards. Hester returns punt 4 yards. Drive begins at 50-yard line. Gould kicks 25-yard field goal at 3:37.

Dec. 24, 2006—St. Louis 37, Washington 31, at St. Louis; Rams win toss. Ponder returns kickoff 20 yards. Drive begins at Rams 20. Turk punts 44 yards. Drive begins at Redskins 6. Frost punts 57 yards. McDonald returns punt 33 yards. Drive begins at Redskins 39. Jackson runs for 21-yard touchdown at 8:27.

Dec. 31, 2006—Pittsburgh 23, Cincinnati 17, at Cincinnati; Steelers win toss. Holmes returns kickoff 24 yards. Drive begins at Steelers 22. Roethlisberger completes 67-yard touchdown to Holmes at 13:27.

Dec. 31, 2006—San Francisco 26, Denver 23, at Denver; Broncos win toss. Morgan returns kickoff 28 yards. Drive begins at Broncos 27. Ernster punts 46 yards. Leach fair catch. Drive begins at 49ers 12. Lee punts 33 yards. Kircus fair catch. Drive begins at Broncos 11. Ernster punts 54 yards. B. Williams returns punt 12 yards. Drive begins at 49ers 39. Nedney kicks 36-yard field goal at 1:56.

Sept. 9, 2007—Washington 16, Miami 13, at Washington; Redskins win toss. Touchback. Redskins drive to Miami 32. Suisham kicks 39-yard field goal at 9:24.

Sept. 16, 2007—Denver 23, Oakland 20, at Denver; Broncos win toss. Touchback. Drive ends at Denver 28. Sauerbrun punts 51 yards. Higgins returns punt 6 yards to Oakland 27. Janikowski misses 52-yard field goal. Drive begins at Denver 42. Elam kicks 23-yard field goal at 5:48.

Sept. 16, 2007—Detroit 20, Minnesota 17, at Detroit; Vikings win toss. Touchback. Ball recovered by Lions' Rogers at 50. Hanson kicks 37-yard field goal at 8:55.

* **Oct. 29, 2007—Green Bay 19, Denver 13,** at Denver; Packers win toss. Bodiford returns kick 19 yards to Green Bay 18. Favre completes 82-yard touchdown pass to G. Jennings at 14:44.

Nov. 4, 2007—Cleveland 33, Seattle 30, at Cleveland; Seahawks win toss. Burleson returns kick 21 yards to own 30. Drive ends at Cleveland 44 with turnover on downs. Drive begins at Browns 44. Dawson kicks 25-yard field goal at 10:03.

Nov. 4, 2007—Washington 23, New York Jets 20, at New York; Jets win toss. L. Washington returns kick 20 yards to own 29. Offensive holding penalty pushes New York back to own 19 during return. Drive ends on Washington 39. Graham punts 29 yards. Fair catch. Drive begins on Redskins 10. Suisham kicks 46-yard field goal at 7:43.

Nov. 18, 2007—Cleveland 33, Baltimore 30, at Baltimore; Browns win toss. Cribbs returns kick 41 yards to Cleveland 41. Dawson kicks 33-yard field goal at 9:10.

Nov. 18, 2007—New York Jets 19, Pittsburgh 16, at New York; Jets win toss. L. Washington returns kick 12 yards to own 31. Drive ends on New York 38. Graham punts 48 yards. Rossum returns punt 4 yards to own 18. Drive ends on Pittsburgh 20. Sepulveda punts 39 yards. L. Washington returns punt 33 yards to Pittsburgh 26. Nugent kicks 38-yard field goal at 9:57.

Nov. 25, 2007—San Francisco 37, Arizona 31, at Arizona; Cardinals win toss. Breaston returns kick 20 yards to own 21. Drive ends on San Francisco 49. Barr punts 17 yards out of bounds to 49ers' 32. Drive ends on San Francisco 35. Lee punts 49 yards. Illegal block above the waist penalty during Breaston return puts Arizona on own 8. Rackers misses 32-yard field goal. Drive begins on San Francisco 22 and ends at 49ers' 39. Lee punts 59 yards. Illegal block above the waist during Breaston return puts Arizona on own 3. Warner sacked at own 0 and fumbles. Recovered by 49ers' Banta-Cain in end zone for touchdown at 4:56.

Nov. 25, 2007—Chicago 37, Denver 34, at Chicago; Bears win toss. Hester returns kick 4 yards to Chicago 24. Gould kicks 39-yard field goal at 11:19.

Dec. 9, 2007—San Diego 23, Tennessee 17, at Tennessee; Chargers win toss. Touchback. Drive ends on San Diego 47. Scifres punts 51 yards. Downed at Tennessee 2. Drive ends on Titans' 5. Hentrich punts 57 yards. C. Davis returns punt 14 yards to Tennessee 48. Tomlinson scores on 16-yard touchdown run at 7:29.

Dec. 16, 2007—Miami 22, Baltimore 16, at Miami; Ravens win toss. Touchback. Drive ends as Stover misses 44-yard field goal. Drive begins on Dolphins' 34. Camarillo scores on 64-yard touchdown pass from Lemon at 8:14.

Dec. 23, 2007 – Arizona 30, Atlanta 27, at Arizona; Cardinals win toss. Breaston returns kick 25 yards to Arizona 29. Rackers kicks 31-yard field goal at 9:30.

Dec. 30, 2007—New York Jets 13, Kansas City 10, at New York; Jets win toss. L. Washington returns kick 21 yards to New York 30. Nugent kicks 43-yard field goal at 9:47.

Dec. 30, 2007—Denver 22, Minnesota 19, at Denver; Vikings win toss. Touchback. T. Jackson is sacked by McKinley and Winborn, forcing fumble. Ball recovered by Broncos' Dumervil at Minnesota 13. Elam kicks 30-yard field goal at 14:08.

POSTSEASON

Dec. 28, 1958—Baltimore 23, New York Giants 17, at New York in NFL Championship Game; Giants win toss. Maynard returns kickoff to Giants' 20. Chandler punts and Taseff returns one yard to Colts' 20. Ameche scores on 1-yard run at 8:15.

Dec. 23, 1962—Dallas Texans 20, Houston Oilers 17, at Houston in AFL Championship Game; Texans win toss on kickoff. Jancik returns kickoff to Oilers' 33. Norton punts and Jackson makes fair catch on Texans' 22. Wilson punts and Jancik makes fair catch on Oilers' 45. Robinson intercepts Blanda's pass and returns 19 yards to Oilers' 47. Wilson's punt rolls dead at Oilers' 12. Hull intercepts Blanda's pass and returns 23 yards to midfield. Brooker kicks 25-yard field goal at 17:54.

Dec. 26, 1965—Green Bay 13, Baltimore 10, at Green Bay in NFL Divisional Playoff Game; Packers win toss. Moore returns kickoff to Packers' 22. Chandler punts and Haymond returns

nine yards to Colts' 41. Gilburg punts and Wood makes fair catch at Packers' 21. Chandler punts and Haymond returns one yard to Colts' 41. Michaels misses 47-yard field goal. Chandler kicks 25-yard field goal at 13:39.

Dec. 25, 1971—Miami 27, Kansas City 24, at Kansas City in AFC Divisional Playoff Game; Chiefs win toss. Podolak, after a lateral from Buchanan, returns kickoff to Chiefs' 46. Stenerud's 42-yard field goal is blocked. Seiple punts and Podolak makes fair catch at Chiefs' 17. Wilson punts and Scott returns 18 yards to Dolphins' 39. Yepremian misses 62-yard field goal. Scott intercepts Dawson's pass and returns 13 yards to Dolphins' 46. Seiple punts and Podolak loses one yard to Chiefs' 15. Wilson punts and Scott makes fair catch on Dolphins' 30. Yepremian kicks 37-yard field goal at 22:40.

Dec. 24, 1977—Oakland 37, Baltimore 31, at Baltimore in AFC Divisional Playoff Game; Colts win toss. Raiders start on own 42 following a punt late in the first overtime. Oakland works way into field-goal range on Stabler's 19-yard pass to Branch at Colts' 26. Four plays later, on the second play of the second overtime, Stabler hits Casper with a 10-yard touchdown pass at 15:43.

Jan. 2, 1982—San Diego 41, Miami 38, at Miami in AFC Divisional Playoff Game; Chargers win toss. San Diego drives from its 13 to Miami 8. On second-and-goal, Benirschke misses 27-yard field goal attempt wide left at 9:15. Miami has the ball twice and San Diego twice more before the Dolphins get their third possession. Miami drives from the San Diego 46 to Chargers' 17 and on fourth-and-two, on Schamann's 34-yard field goal attempt is blocked by San Diego's Winslow at 11:27. Fouts then completes four of five passes, including a 39-yarder to Joiner that puts the ball on Dolphins' 10. On first down, Benirschke kicks a 29-yard field goal at 13:52.

Jan. 3, 1987—Cleveland 23, New York Jets 20, at Cleveland in AFC Divisional Playoff Game; Jets win toss. Jets' punt downed at Browns' 26. Moseley's 23-yard field goal attempt is wide right. Teams trade punts. Jets' second punt downed at Browns' 31. First overtime period expires eight plays later with Browns in possession at Jets' 42. Moseley kicks 27-yard field goal four plays into second overtime at 17:02.

Jan. 11, 1987—Denver 23, Cleveland 20, at Cleveland in AFC Championship Game; Browns win toss. Broncos hold Browns on four downs. Browns' punt returned four yards to Denver's 25. Elway completes 23- and 28-yard passes to set up Karlis's 33-yard field goal nine plays into drive at 5:38.

Jan. 3, 1988—Houston 23, Seattle 20, at Houston in AFC Wild Card Game; Seahawks win toss. Rodriguez punt to K. Johnson who returns one yard to Houston 15. Zendejas kicks 32-yard field goal 12 plays later at 8:05.

Dec. 31, 1989—Pittsburgh 26, Houston 23, at Houston in AFC Wild Card Playoff Game; Steelers win toss. Steelers punt to Oilers. Oilers' fumble recovered by Woodson and returned three yards. Four plays and 13 yards later, Anderson kicks a 50-yard field goal at 3:26.

Jan. 7, 1990—Los Angeles Rams 19, New York Giants 13, at New York in NFC Divisional Game; Rams win toss. Everett completes two passes to move ball to Giants' 48. White called for pass interference; ball spotted on Giants' 25. Everett hits Anderson with a 30-yard touchdown pass at 1:06.

Jan. 3, 1993—Buffalo 41, Houston 38, at Buffalo in AFC Wild Card Game; Oilers win toss. Oilers begin at 20. After 2 plays, Moon's pass is intercepted by Odomes who returns ball 2 yards to Houston 35. After 2 plays, Christie kicks 32-yard field goal at 3:06.

Jan. 8, 1994—Kansas City 27, Pittsburgh 24, at Kansas City in AFC Wild Card Game; Chiefs win toss. Hughes returns kickoff 20 yards to Kansas City 25. After 3 plays, Barker punts 48 yards to Pittsburgh 18 where Woodson returns 8 yards to the 26. After 6 plays, Royals punts 30 yards to Kansas City 20. Kansas City drives to Pittsburgh 14 where Lowery kicks 32-yard field goal at 11:03.

Jan. 17, 1999—Atlanta 30, Minnesota 27, at Minnesota in NFC Championship Game; Vikings win toss. Palmer returns kickoff 30 yards to Minnesota 29. After four plays, Berger punts 51 yards to Atlanta 7 where Dwight returns 8 yards to Atlanta 15. Falcons drive to Atlanta 36. Stryzinski punts 37 yards to Vikings' 27. Palmer calls fair catch. Vikings drive to Minnesota 39. Berger punts 52 yards to Atlanta 9. Downed by Vikings. Atlanta drives to Minnesota 21 where Andersen kicks 38-yard field goal at 11:52.

Dec. 30, 2000—Miami 23, Indianapolis 17, at Miami in AFC Wild Card Game; Dolphins win toss. Williams returns kickoff

18 yards to Miami 20. Offensive holding penalty on Freeman, 10 yards, ball spotted on Miami 10. Dolphins drive to Miami 29 where Turk punts 53 yards to Indianapolis 18. Colts drive to Miami 31 where Vanderjagt misses 49-yard field-goal attempt wide right. Dolphins drive to Indianapolis 17 where Smith rushes for a 17-yard touchdown at 11:16.

Jan. 19, 2002—New England 16, Oakland 13, at New England in AFC Divisional Playoff Game; Patriots win toss. Pass returns kickoff 24 yards to New England 34. Patriots drive to Oakland 5. Vinatieri kicks 23-yard field goal at 8:29.

Jan. 11, 2003—Tennessee 34, Pittsburgh 31, at Tennessee in AFC Divisional Playoff Game; Tennessee wins toss. Reed kicks 60 yards. Returned by Simon 21 yards to Tennessee 31. Titans drive to Pittsburgh 8. Nedney's 26-yard field goal is good at 2:15.

Jan. 4, 2004—Green Bay 33, Seattle 27, at Green Bay in NFC Wild Card Game; Seahawks win toss. Morris returns kick to Seattle 33. Seahawks drive to Seattle 42. Rouen's 44-yard punt returned by Chatman to Green Bay 26. Packers drive to Green Bay 31. Bidwell punts 35 yards to Seattle 34. Seahawks drive to Seattle 45. Hasselbeck's pass to Bannister intercepted by Packers' Harris and returned 52 yards for touchdown at 4:25.

Jan. 10, 2004—Carolina 29, St. Louis 23, at St. Louis in NFC Divisional Game; Panthers win toss. Smart returns kick to Carolina 32. Panthers drive to St. Louis 27. Kasay's 45-yard field-goal attempt no good. Rams take over at own 35 and drive to Carolina 35. Wilkins' 53-yard field-goal attempt no good. Panthers take over at Carolina 43, drive to Carolina 47. Sauerbrun punts 40 yards to St. Louis 13. Rams drive to Carolina 38. Bulger's pass intercepted by Manning at Carolina 35. Panthers drive to Carolina 31. First overtime ends. On first play of second overtime, Delhomme passes to Smith for 69-yard touchdown at 15:10.

Jan. 11, 2004—Philadelphia 20, Green Bay 17, at Philadelphia in NFC Divisional Game; Eagles win toss. Thrash returns kick to Philadelphia 28. Eagles drive to Philadelphia 24. Johnson punts 49 yards and Packers start at own 32 after holding penalty. Favre's pass intercepted by Dawkins at Philadelphia 31 and returned to Green Bay 34. Eagles drive to Green Bay 13. Akers kicks 31-yard field goal at 4:48.

Jan. 8, 2005—New York Jets 20, San Diego 17, at San Diego in AFC Wild Card Game; Chargers win toss. Dwight returns kick to San Diego 26. Chargers drive to San Diego 35. Scifres punts 39 yards and ball is downed at the New York 26. Jets gain no yards. Gowin punts 41 yards. Parker loses 3 yards on return. San Diego starts on own 30. Chargers drive to New York 22. Kaeding's 40-yard field-goal attempt no good. Jets drive to San Diego 10. Brien kicks 28-yard field goal at 14:55.

Jan. 15, 2005—Pittsburgh 20, New York Jets 17, at Pittsburgh in AFC Divisional Game; Jets win toss. Cotchery returns kick to New York 31. Jets drive to New York 41. Gowin punts 54 yards. Randle El returns 8 yards to Pittsburgh 13. Steelers drive to New York 15. Reed kicks 33-yard field goal at 11:04.

Jan. 14, 2007—Chicago 27, Seattle 24, at Chicago in NFC Divisional Playoff Game; Seahawks win the toss. Burleson returns kickoff 25. Drive begins at Seahawks 30. Plackemeier punts 18 yards. Drive begins at Bears 34. Gould kicks 49-yard field goal at 4:53.

Jan. 20, 2008—New York Giants 23, Green Bay 20, at Green Bay in NFC Championship Game; Packers win toss. K. Robinson returns kick 19 yards to own 26. Favre pass intercepted by Webster and returned 9 yards to Green Bay 34. Tynes kicks 47-yard field goal at 12:34.

NFL POSTSEASON OVERTIME GAMES
(BY LENGTH OF GAME)

Dec. 25, 1971	Miami 27, KANSAS CITY 24	82:40
Dec. 23, 1962	Dallas Texans 20, HOUSTON 17	77:54
Jan. 3 1987	CLEVELAND 23, N.Y. Jets 20	77:02
Dec. 24, 1977	Oakland 37, BALTIMORE 31	75:43
Jan. 10, 2004	Carolina 29, ST. LOUIS 23	75:10
Jan. 8, 2005	N.Y. Jets 20, SAN DIEGO 17	74:55
Jan 2, 1982	San Diego 41, MIAMI 38	73:52
Dec. 26, 1965	GREEN BAY 13, Baltimore 10	73:39
Jan 17, 1999	Atlanta 30, MINNESOTA 27	71:52
Dec. 30, 2000	MIAMI 23, Indianapolis 17	71:16
Jan. 15, 2005	PITTSBURGH 20, N.Y. Jets 17	71:04
Jan 8, 1994	KANSAS CITY 27, Pittsburgh 24	71:03
Jan. 19, 2002	NEW ENGLAND 16, Oakland 13	68:29
Dec. 28, 1958	Baltimore 23, N.Y. GIANTS 17	68:15
Jan. 3, 1988	HOUSTON 23, Seattle 20	68:05

Jan. 11, 1987	Denver 23, CLEVELAND 20	65:38
Jan. 14, 2007	CHICAGO 27, Seattle 24	64:53
Jan. 11, 2004	PHILADELPHIA 20, Green Bay 17	64:48
Jan. 4, 2004	GREEN BAY 33, Seattle 27	64:25
Dec. 31, 1989	Pittsburgh 26, HOUSTON 23	63:26
Jan. 3, 1993	BUFFALO 41, Houston 38	63:06
Jan. 20, 2008	N.Y. Giants 23, GREEN BAY 20	62:26
Jan. 11, 2003	TENNESSEE 34, Pittsburgh 31	61:05
Jan. 7, 1990	L.A. Rams 19, N.Y. GIANTS 13	61:06

Home team in CAPS

There have been 24 overtime postseason games dating back to 1958. In 21 cases, both teams have had at least one possession. Last time: 1/20/08, N.Y. Giants 23, GREEN BAY 20.

OVERTIME GAMES BY YEAR
(REGULAR SEASON)

2007-15	1998-7	1989-11	1980-13
2006-11	1997-17	1988- 9	1979-12
2005-14	1996-14	1987-13	1978-11
2004-12	1995-21	1986-16	1977-6
2003-23	1994-16	1985-10	1976-5
2002-25*	1993-7	1984- 9	1975-9
2001-17	1992-10	1983-19	1974-2
2000-13	1991-15	1982- 4	
1999-11	1990-10	1981-10	

*Record

OVERTIME WON-LOST RECORDS, 1974-2007
(REGULAR SEASON)

Team	Win	Loss	Tie	Pct.
AFC				
Baltimore	6	5	1	.542
Buffalo	17	9	0	.654
Cincinnati	14	10	0	.583
Cleveland	16	13	1	.550
Denver	21	15	2	.579
Houston	0	5	0	.000
Indianapolis	12	9	1	.568
Jacksonville	5	3	0	.625
Kansas City	10	14	2	.423
Miami	12	18	1	.403
New England	16	18	0	.470
N.Y. Jets	14	15	2	.484
Oakland	13	17	0	.433
Pittsburgh	17	11	2	.600
San Diego	12	17	0	.414
Tennessee	12	16	0	.429
NFC				
Arizona	17	14	2	.545
Atlanta	11	17	2	.400
Carolina	4	8	0	.333
Chicago	19	14	0	.576
Dallas	13	11	0	.542
Detroit	12	15	1	.446
Green Bay	11	11	4	.500
Minnesota	17	16	2	.514
New Orleans	7	8	0	.467
N.Y. Giants	15	14	2	.516
Philadelphia	11	16	3	.417
St. Louis	12	8	1	.595
San Francisco	17	13	1	.565
Seattle	8	16	0	.333
Tampa Bay	11	14	1	.442
Washington	19	11	1	.629

OVERTIME GAME SUMMARY—1974-2007

There have been 417 overtime games in regular season play since the rule was adopted in 1974 (15 in 2007 season). Breakdown follows:

RESULTS

222 (9) times the team which won the toss won the game (53.2%)

179 (6) times the team which lost the toss won the game (42.9%)

16 (0) games ended tied (3.8%). Last time: Nov. 10, 2002, Atlanta 34 at Pittsburgh 34.

POSSESSIONS

294 (9) times both teams had at least one possession (70.5%)

123 (6) times the team which won the toss drove for winning score (88 FG, 35 TD) (29.5%)

Of the 417 overtime games, there were 12 miscellaneous situations in which non-standard possessions took place:

8 (0) times the defense or special teams won without registering an official possession (5 interceptions, 1 fumble recovery, 1 blocked punt, 1 blocked field goal) (1.9%)

1 (0) times the special teams forced a fumble on the opening kickoff and drove for the winning score (0.24%)

1 (0) times the punting team recovered a muffed punt and drove for winning score with team muffing punt having no official possessions (0.24%)

2 (0) times the team that won the toss elected to kick and the team receiving the ball drove for winning score (0.48%)

SCORING
289(11) games were decided by a field goal (69.3%)
110 (4) games were decided by a touchdown (26.4%)
2 (0) games were decided by a safety (0.48%)
16 (0) games ended tied (3.8%). Last time: Nov. 10, 2002, Atlanta 34 at Pittsburgh 34.

COIN TOSS
408(15) times the team which won the toss elected to receive (97.8%)
9 (0) times the team which won the toss elected to kick off (4 wins) (2.2%)

Note: The number in parentheses is the 2007 Season Total.

MOST OVERTIME GAMES, SEASON
5	Green Bay Packers, 1983
4	Denver Broncos, 1985, 2007
	Cleveland Browns, 1989
	Minnesota Vikings, 1994
	Arizona Cardinals, 1995
	Minnesota Vikings, 1995
	Arizona Cardinals, 1997
	San Francisco 49ers, 2001
	Atlanta Falcons, 2002
	San Diego Chargers, 2002
	Carolina Panthers, 2003

LONGEST CONSECUTIVE GAME STREAKS WITHOUT OVERTIME (Current)
75 Buffalo Bills (Last OT Game, 10/5/03 vs. Cincinnati Bengals)
(Record: 110, St. Louis/Phoenix Cardinals, 12/7/86-12/19/93)

SHORTEST OVERTIME GAMES
0:14	New York Jets 37, BUFFALO 31; 9/8/02
0:16	CHICAGO 37, San Francisco 31; 10/28/01
0:16	Green Bay 19, DENVER 13; 10/29/07
0:17	NEW ORLEANS 20, Seattle 17; 11/16/97
0:21	Chicago 23, DETROIT 17; 11/27/80
0:30	Baltimore 29, NEW ENGLAND 23; 9/4/83
0:34	San Diego 23, WASHINGTON 17; 11/27/05
0:55	New York Giants 16, PHILADELPHIA 10; 9/29/85

LONGEST OVERTIME GAMES (ALL POSTSEASON GAMES)
22:40	Miami 27, KANSAS CITY 24; 12/25/71
17:54	Dallas Texans 20, HOUSTON 17; 12/23/62
17:02	CLEVELAND 23, New York Jets 20; 1/3/87
15:43	Oakland 37, BALTIMORE 31; 12/24/77
15:10	Carolina 29, ST. LOUIS 23; 1/10/04

Home team in CAPS
There have been 24 overtime postseason games dating back to 1958. In 21 cases, both teams have had at least one possession. Last time: 1/20/08, N.Y. Giants 23, GREEN BAY 20.

OVERTIME SCORING SUMMARY
289	were decided by a field goal
51	were decided by a touchdown pass
30	were decided by a touchdown run
17	were decided by an interception (Atlanta 40, New Orleans 34, 9/2/79; Atlanta 47, Green Bay 41, 11/27/83; New York Giants 16, Philadelphia 10, 9/29/85; Indianapolis 23, Cleveland 17, 12/10/89; Cleveland 30, San Diego 24, 10/20/91; Kansas City 23, Oakland 17, 9/17/95;

New York Giants 27, Arizona 21, 10/8/95; Washington 36, Detroit 30, 10/22/95; Arizona 20, Seattle 14, 10/29/95; Cincinnati 34, Detroit 28, 9/13/98; New York Giants 23, Philadelphia 17, 10/31/99; Chicago 37, San Francisco 31, 10/28/01; Chicago 27, Cleveland 21, 11/4/01; New Orleans 26, Tampa Bay 20, 9/8/02; Atlanta 20, Carolina 14, 12/7/03; Jacksonville 23, Pittsburgh 17, 10/16/05; Chicago 19, Detroit 13, 10/30/05)

3	were decided by a fumble recovery (Baltimore 29, New England 23, 9/4/83; Denver 36, Seattle 30, 12/19/99; San Francisco 37, Arizona 31, 11/24/07)
2	were decided on a fake field goal/touchdown pass (Minnesota 22, Chicago 16, 10/16/77; Cleveland 23, Minnesota 17, 12/17/89)
2	were decided by a kickoff return (Chicago 23, Detroit 17, 11/27/80; New York Jets 37, Buffalo 31, 9/8/02)
2	were decided by a safety (Minnesota 23, Los Angeles Rams 21, 11/5/89; Chicago 19, Tennessee 17, 11/14/04)
1	was decided by a punt return (Kansas City 29, San Diego 23, 10/9/95)
1	was decided on a fake field goal/touchdown run (Los Angeles Rams 27, Minnesota 21, 12/2/79)
1	was decided on a blocked field goal (Denver 30, San Diego 24, 11/17/85)
1	was decided on a blocked field goal/recovery by kicker (Green Bay 12, Chicago 6, 9/7/80)
1	was decided on a blocked field goal/recovery by kicking team (Philadelphia 23, New York Giants 17, 11/20/88)
16	ended tied

OVERTIME RECORDS
Longest Touchdown Pass
99 Yards — Ron Jaworski to Mike Quick, Philadelphia 23, Atlanta 17 (11/10/85)
82 Yards — Tom Brady to Troy Brown, New England 19, Miami 13 (10/19/03); Brett Favre to Greg Jennings, Green Bay 19, Denver 13 (10/29/07)
76 Yards — Troy Aikman to Raghib Ismail, Dallas 41, Washington 35 (9/12/99)

Longest Touchdown Run
96 Yards — Garrison Hearst, San Francisco 36, New York Jets 30 (9/6/98)
60 Yards — Herschel Walker, Dallas 23, New England 17 (11/15/87)
46 Yards — Michael Vick, Atlanta 30, Minnesota 24 (12/1/02)

Longest Field Goal
53 Yards — Chris Jacke, Green Bay 23, San Francisco 20 (10/4/96)
52 Yards — Mike Cofer, Indianapolis 27, New York Jets 24 (9/10/95)
51 Yards — Greg Davis, New England 23, Indianapolis 20 (10/29/89); Greg Davis, Arizona 20, Pittsburgh 17 (10/30/94); Michael Husted, Tampa Bay 20, Minnesota 17 (10/15/95); Mike Vanderjagt, Indianapolis 23, Denver 20 (11/24/02)

Longest Touchdown Plays
99 Yards — (Pass) Ron Jaworski to Mike Quick, Philadelphia 23, Atlanta 17 (11/10/85)
96 Yards — (Run) Garrison Hearst, San Francisco 36, New York Jets 30 (9/6/98)
96 Yards — (Kickoff return) Chad Morton, New York Jets 37, Buffalo 31 (9/8/02)
95 Yards — (Kickoff return) Dave Williams, Chicago 23, Detroit 17 (11/27/80)
86 Yards — (Punt return) Tamarick Vanover, Kansas City 29, San Diego 23 (10/9/95)

NFL'S 10 HIGHEST SCORING WEEKENDS

Point Total	Date	Weekend
788	December 29-30, 2007	17th
788	December 5-6, 2004	13th
788	September 5, 8-9, 2002	1st
762	November 10-11, 1996	11th
761	October 16-17, 1983	7th
753	December 8-9, 2002	14th
752	November 29, December 2-3, 2007	13th
751	September 23-24, 2007	3rd
748	December 18-20, 2004	15th
740	November 29-30, 1998	13th

TOP 10 TELEVISED SPORTS EVENTS OF ALL-TIME
(Based on A.C. Nielsen Figures)

Program	Date	Network	Share	Rating
Super Bowl XVI	1/24/82	CBS	73%	49.1
Super Bowl XVII	1/30/83	NBC	69%	48.6
Winter Olympics	2/23/94	CBS	64%	48.5
Super Bowl XX	1/26/86	NBC	70%	48.3
Super Bowl XII	1/15/78	CBS	67%	47.2
Super Bowl XIII	1/21/79	NBC	74%	47.1
Super Bowl XVIII	1/22/84	CBS	71%	46.4
Super Bowl XIX	1/20/85	ABC	63%	46.4
Super Bowl XIV	1/20/80	CBS	67%	46.3
Super Bowl XXX	1/28/96	NBC	68%	46.0

TEN MOST WATCHED TV PROGRAMS & ESTIMATED TOTAL NUMBER OF VIEWERS
(Based on A.C. Nielsen Figures)

Program	Date	Network	*Total Viewers
Super Bowl XLII	Feb. 3, 2008	FOX	148,300,000
Super Bowl XXXVIII	Feb. 1, 2004	CBS	144,400,000
Super Bowl XL	Feb. 5, 2006	ABC	141,400,000
Super Bowl XLI	Feb. 4, 2007	CBS	139,800,000
Super Bowl XXXVII	Jan. 26, 2003	ABC	138,900,000
Super Bowl XXX	Jan. 28, 1996	NBC	138,488,000
Super Bowl XXVIII	Jan. 30, 1994	NBC	134,800,000
Super Bowl XXXIX	Feb. 6, 2005	FOX	133,700,000
Super Bowl XXXII	Jan. 25, 1998	NBC	133,400,000
Super Bowl XXVII	Jan. 31, 1993	NBC	133,400,000

*Watched some portion of the broadcast

NFL'S TOP FIVE PAID ATTENDANCE TOTALS FOR ALL GAMES

Year	Preseason	Regular Season	Postseason	All Games
2007	4,119,278	17,345,205	792,019	22,256,502
2006	4,083,282	17,340,879	775,551	22,199,712
2005	3,977,388	17,012,453	802,255	21,792,096
2004	3,918,848	17,000,811	788,965	21,708,624
2003	3,919,910	16,913,584	805,546	21,639,040

TEN HIGHEST-RATED *NFL MONDAY NIGHT FOOTBALL* GAMES OF ALL-TIME
(Based on A.C. Nielsen Figures)

Game	Date	Share	Rating
Chicago at Miami	12/2/85	46%	29.6
N.Y. Giants at San Francisco	12/3/90	42%	26.9
Dallas at Washington	10/2/78	43%	26.8
Pittsburgh at San Diego	12/22/80	40%	25.3
Philadelphia at Miami	11/30/81	40%	25.3
Pittsburgh at Houston	12/10/79	40%	25.1
Dallas at Miami	12/17/84	40%	25.1
Pittsburgh at Dallas	9/13/82	42%	24.9
Cincinnati at Oakland	12/6/76	40%	24.7
Dallas at Washington	10/8/73	40%	24.6
Minnesota at Atlanta	11/19/73	40%	24.6

NFL'S 10 BIGGEST SINGLE-GAME ATTENDANCE TOTALS

Date	Site	Game	Teams	Attendance
August 15, 1994	Azteca Stadium	American Bowl (Mexico City)	Cowboys vs. Oilers	112,376
August 17, 1998	Azteca Stadium	American Bowl (Mexico City)	Cowboys vs. Patriots	106,424
August 22, 1947	Soldier Field	College All-Star	Bears vs. All-Stars	105,840
August 4, 1997	Estadio Guillermo Canedo	American Bowl (Mexico City)	Broncos vs. Dolphins	104,629
January 20, 1980	Rose Bowl	Super Bowl XIV	Steelers vs. Rams	103,985
January 30, 1983	Rose Bowl	Super Bowl XVII	Redskins vs. Dolphins	103,667
October 2, 2005	Azteca Stadium	Regular Season	49ers at Cardinals	103,467
January 9, 1977	Rose Bowl	Super Bowl XI	Raiders vs. Vikings	103,438
November 10, 1957	L.A. Coliseum	Regular Season	49ers at Rams	102,368
January 25, 1987	Rose Bowl	Super Bowl XXI	Giants vs. Broncos	101,643

PAID ATTENDANCE

NFL'S TOP 10 PAID ATTENDANCE WEEKENDS

Weekend	Games	Attendance
September 8, 11-12, 2005	16	1,115,018
December 6, 9-10, 2007	16	1,113,376
November 20-21, 2005	16	1,112,555
December 27-28, 2003	16	1,106,818
November 19-20, 2006	16	1,106,739
September 23-24, 2007	16	1,103,570
December 24-26, 2005	16	1,102,701
September 7, 10-11, 2006	16	1,102,102
September 9, 12-13, 2004	16	1,101,332
December 7, 10-11, 2006	16	1,099,794

NFL'S TOP 10 TEAM SINGLE-SEASON HOME PAID ATTENDANCE TOTALS

Year	Club	Games	Attendance
2007	Washington Redskins	8	711,471
2006	Washington Redskins	8	708,952
2004	Washington Redskins	8	707,920
2005	Washington Redskins	8	707,614
2003	Washington Redskins	8	667,033
2002	Washington Redskins	8	663,536
2001	Washington Redskins	8	661,970
2000	Washington Redskins	8	656,599
1980	Detroit Lions	8	634,204
1988	Buffalo Bills	8	631,818

NFL PAID ATTENDANCE

For detailed 2007 attendance, see page 340.

Year	Regular Season		Average	Postseason	Total
2007	17,345,205	(256 games)	#67,755	792,019 (12)	#18,137,224
2006	17,340,879	(256 games)	67,738	775,551 (12)	18,116,430
2005	17,012,453	(256 games)	66,455	802,255 (12)	17,814,708
2004	17,000,811	(256 games)	66,409	788,965 (12)	17,789,776
2003	16,913,584	(255 games***)	66,328	805,546 (12)	17,719,130
2002	16,833,310	(256 games)	65,755	781,944 (12)	17,615,254
2001	16,166,258	(248 games)	65,187	766,905 (12)	16,933,163
2000	16,387,289	(248 games)	66,078	809,132 (12)	17,196,421
1999	16,206,640	(248 games)	65,349	793,759 (12)	17,000,399
1998	15,364,873	(240 games)	64,020	822,885 (12)	16,187,758
1997	14,967,314	(240 games)	62,364	801,879 (12)	15,769,193
1996	14,612,417	(240 games)	60,885	769,310 (12)	15,381,727
1995	15,043,562	(240 games)	62,682	790,906 (12)	15,834,468
1994	14,030,435	(224 games)	62,636	779,738 (12)	14,810,173
1993	13,966,843	(224 games)	62,352	814,607 (12)	14,781,450
1992	13,828,887	(224 games)	61,736	815,910 (12)	14,644,797
1991	13,841,459	(224 games)	61,792	813,247 (12)	14,654,706
1990	13,959,896	(224 games)	62,321	847,543 (12)	14,807,439
1989	13,625,662	(224 games)	60,829	685,771 (10)	14,311,433
1988	13,539,848	(224 games)	60,446	658,317 (10)	14,198,165
1987	11,406,166	(210 games**)	54,315	656,977 (10)	12,063,143
1986	13,588,551	(224 games)	60,663	734,002 (10)	14,322,553
1985	13,345,047	(224 games)	59,567	710,768 (10)	14,055,815
1984	13,398,112	(224 games)	59,813	665,194 (10)	14,063,306
1983	13,277,222	(224 games)	59,273	675,513 (10)	13,952,735
1982	7,367,438	(126 games*)	58,472	#1,033,153 (16)	8,400,591
1981	13,606,990	(224 games)	60,745	637,763 (10)	14,244,753
1980	13,392,230	(224 games)	59,787	624,430 (10)	14,016,660
1979	13,182,039	(224 games)	58,848	630,326 (10)	13,812,365
1978	12,771,800	(224 games)	57,017	624,388 (10)	13,396,188
1977	11,018,632	(196 games)	56,218	534,925 (8)	11,553,557
1976	11,070,543	(196 games)	56,482	492,884 (8)	11,563,427
1975	10,213,193	(182 games)	56,116	475,919 (8)	10,689,112
1974	10,236,322	(182 games)	56,244	438,664 (8)	10,674,986
1973	10,730,933	(182 games)	58,961	525,433 (8)	11,256,366
1972	10,445,827	(182 games)	57,395	483,345 (8)	10,929,172
1971	10,076,035	(182 games)	55,363	483,891 (8)	10,559,926
1970	9,533,333	(182 games)	52,381	458,493 (8)	9,991,826
1969	6,096,127	(112 games) NFL	54,430	162,279 (3)	6,258,406
	2,843,373	(70 games) AFL	40,620	167,088 (3)	3,010,461
1968	5,882,313	(112 games) NFL	52,521	215,902 (3)	6,098,215
	2,635,004	(70 games) AFL	37,643	114,438 (2)	2,749,442
1967	5,938,924	(112 games) NFL	53,026	166,208 (3)	6,105,132
	2,295,697	(63 games) AFL	36,439	53,330 (1)	2,349,027
1966	5,337,044	(105 games) NFL	50,829	74,152 (1)	5,411,196
	2,160,369	(63 games) AFL	34,291	42,080 (1)	2,202,449
1965	4,634,021	(98 games) NFL	47,286	100,304 (2)	4,734,325
	1,782,384	(56 games) AFL	31,828	30,361 (1)	1,812,745
1964	4,563,049	(98 games) NFL	46,562	79,544 (1)	4,642,593
	1,447,875	(56 games) AFL	25,855	40,242 (1)	1,488,117
1963	4,163,643	(98 games) NFL	42,486	45,801 (1)	4,209,444
	1,208,697	(56 games) AFL	21,584	63,171 (2)	1,271,868

Year	Regular Season			Average	Postseason	Total
1962	4,003,421	(98 games)	NFL	40,851	64,892 (1)	4,068,313
	1,147,302	(56 games)	AFL	20,487	37,981 (1)	1,185,283
1961	3,986,159	(98 games)	NFL	40,675	39,029 (1)	4,025,188
	1,002,657	(56 games)	AFL	17,904	29,556 (1)	1,032,213
1960	3,128,296	(78 games)	NFL	40,106	67,325 (1)	3,195,621
	926,156	(56 games)	AFL	16,538	32,183 (1)	958,339
1959	3,140,000	(72 games)		43,617	57,545 (1)	3,197,545
1958	3,006,124	(72 games)		41,752	123,659 (2)	3,129,783
1957	2,836,318	(72 games)		39,393	119,579 (2)	2,955,897
1956	2,551,263	(72 games)		35,434	56,836 (1)	2,608,099
1955	2,521,836	(72 games)		35,026	85,693 (1)	2,607,529
1954	2,190,571	(72 games)		30,425	43,827 (1)	2,234,398
1953	2,164,585	(72 games)		30,064	54,577 (1)	2,219,162
1952	2,052,126	(72 games)		28,502	97,507 (2)	2,149,633
1951	1,913,019	(72 games)		26,570	57,522 (1)	1,970,541
1950	1,977,753	(78 games)		25,356	136,647 (3)	2,114,400
1949	1,391,735	(60 games)		23,196	27,980 (1)	1,419,715
1948	1,525,243	(60 games)		25,421	36,309 (1)	1,561,552
1947	1,837,437	(60 games)		30,624	66,268 (2)	1,903,705
1946	1,732,135	(55 games)		31,493	58,346 (1)	1,790,481
1945	1,270,401	(50 games)		25,408	32,178 (1)	1,302,579
1944	1,019,649	(50 games)		20,393	46,016 (1)	1,065,665
1943	969,128	(40 games)		24,228	71,315 (2)	1,040,443
1942	887,920	(55 games)		16,144	36,006 (1)	923,926
1941	1,108,615	(55 games)		20,157	55,870 (2)	1,164,485
1940	1,063,025	(55 games)		19,328	36,034 (1)	1,099,059
1939	1,071,200	(55 games)		19,476	32,279 (1)	1,103,479
1938	937,197	(55 games)		17,040	48,120 (1)	985,317
1937	963,039	(55 games)		17,510	15,878 (1)	978,917
1936	816,007	(54 games)		15,111	29,545 (1)	845,552
1935	638,178	(53 games)		12,041	15,000 (1)	653,178
1934	492,684	(60 games)		8,211	35,059 (1)	527,743

Record

*Players' 57-day strike reduced 224-game schedule to 126 games.
**Players' 24-day strike reduced 224-game schedule to 210 games.
***The Week 8 Miami at San Diego game is not included. The game was moved to Arizona due to the San Diego wildfires and tickets were distributed at no charge.

ASSOCIATED PRESS NFL MOST VALUABLE PLAYERS

THE FOLLOWING AWARDS WERE NAMED BY *ASSOCIATED PRESS* IN BALLOTING BY A NATIONWIDE PANEL OF MEDIA.

NFL MOST VALUABLE PLAYER AWARD

YEAR	PLAYER	POS.	TEAM	ACCOMPLISHMENTS
1957	Jim Brown	RB	Cleveland Browns	Rushed for league-leading 942 yards and added 9 touchdowns as a rookie.
1958	Gino Marchetti	DE	Baltimore Colts	Leader of defense that permitted league-low 1,291 rushing yards and division-low 203 points.
1959	Charley Conerly	QB	New York Giants	Passed for 14 touchdowns and only 4 interceptions. Led offense to division-leading 284 points.
1960*	Norm Van Brocklin	QB	Philadelphia Eagles	Guided Eagles to first division title since 1949. Passed for 2,471 yards and 24 touchdowns.
	Joe Schmidt	LB	Detroit Lions	After 0-3 start, team went 7-2 when he returned from injury. Scored 2 defensive touchdowns.
1961	Paul Hornung	RB	Green Bay Packers	Led league in scoring for second straight season with 146 points (10 TD, 15 FG, 41 PAT).
1962	Jim Taylor	RB	Green Bay Packers	League rushing champion with 1,474 yards. Scored all-time record 19 touchdowns.
1963	Y.A. Tittle	QB	New York Giants	Set all-time season record with 36 touchdown passes. Guided league's top offense (5,024 yards).
1964	Johnny Unitas	QB	Baltimore Colts	Guided Colts to NFL's best record (12-2) and league's top offensive attack (4,779 yards).
1965	Jim Brown	RB	Cleveland Browns	Leader of NFL's top rushing attack. Led league with 1,544 yards, added 21 total touchdowns.
1966	Bart Starr	QB	Green Bay Packers	Passed for 14 touchdowns and only 3 interceptions. Led Packers to league-best 12-2 record.
1967	Johnny Unitas	QB	Baltimore Colts	Passed for 3,428 yards and 20 touchdowns. Led Colts to 11-1-2 record.
1968	Earl Morrall	QB	Baltimore Colts	Guided Colts to NFL-best 13-1 record. Led league with 26 touchdown passes.
1969	Roman Gabriel	QB	Los Angeles Rams	Led NFL with 24 touchdown passes. Guided Rams to 11-3 record.
1970	John Brodie	QB	San Francisco 49ers	Took 49ers to first division title. Threw NFL-best 24 touchdown passes.
1971	Alan Page	DT	Minnesota Vikings	Led defense that allowed NFL-low 139 points. Vikings won fourth straight NFC Central title.
1972	Larry Brown	RB	Washington Redskins	Led conference with 1,216 rushing yards. Redskins had NFC-best 11-3 record.
1973	O.J. Simpson	RB	Buffalo Bills	Rushed for all-time record 2,003 yards, including three 200-yard performances.
1974	Ken Stabler	QB	Oakland Raiders	Led league with 26 touchdown passes and only 12 interceptions. Raiders had NFL-best 12-2 record.
1975	Fran Tarkenton	QB	Minnesota Vikings	Tied for league-best 12-2 record. Led NFC with 91.7 passer rating.
1976	Bert Jones	QB	Baltimore Colts	Threw 24 touchdowns and only 9 interceptions for 102.5 passer rating.
1977	Walter Payton	RB	Chicago Bears	Rushed for league-leading 1,852 yards and 16 total touchdowns.
1978	Terry Bradshaw	QB	Pittsburgh Steelers	Led Steelers to league-leading 14-2 mark. Set club record with 28 touchdown passes.
1979	Earl Campbell	RB	Houston Oilers	Led league with 1,697 rushing yards and 19 touchdowns.
1980	Brian Sipe	QB	Cleveland Browns	NFL-best 91.4 passer rating. Set Browns' records with 30 touchdown passes and 4,132 yards.
1981	Ken Anderson	QB	Cincinnati Bengals	Led Bengals to first division title since 1973. NFL-high 98.5 passer rating.
1982	Mark Moseley	K	Washington Redskins	Converted 20 of 21 FGs. Set consecutive field-goal record at 23 (including last three in '81).
1983	Joe Theismann	QB	Washington Redskins	Leader of offense that scored NFL record 541 points. Redskins had NFL-best 14-2 record.
1984	Dan Marino	QB	Miami Dolphins	Set NFL records with 5,084 yards and 48 touchdown passes. Led Dolphins to AFC-best 14-2 mark.
1985	Marcus Allen	RB	Los Angeles Raiders	Rushed for league-leading 1,759 yards. Tied for AFC lead with 11 rushing touchdowns.
1986	Lawrence Taylor	LB	New York Giants	Recorded league-high 20.5 sacks, and led Giants' second-ranked defense (297.3).
1987	John Elway	QB	Denver Broncos	In 12 games, passed for 19 touchdowns and 3,198 yards, including four 300-yard games.
1988	Boomer Esiason	QB	Cincinnati Bengals	Led NFL with 97.4 passer rating. Tied for AFC lead with 28 TD passes.
1989	Joe Montana	QB	San Francisco 49ers	Set NFL record with 112.4 passer rating, including 70.2 completion percentage.
1990	Joe Montana	QB	San Francisco 49ers	Led 49ers to league-best 14-2 record. Completed NFC-high 61.7 percent of passes.
1991	Thurman Thomas	RB	Buffalo Bills	Recorded league-high 2,038 yards from scrimmage (1,407 rushing, 631 receiving).

1992	Steve Young	QB	San Francisco 49ers	NFL's top passer with 107.0 rating. Led 49ers to league-best 14-2 record.
1993	Emmitt Smith	RB	Dallas Cowboys	Led league in rushing (1,486 yards) for third straight year despite missing first two games.
1994	Steve Young	QB	San Francisco 49ers	Compiled NFL all-time best 112.8 passer rating. Completed more than 70 percent of his passes.
1995	Brett Favre	QB	Green Bay Packers	Led league with 38 touchdown passes and NFC with 99.5 passer rating.
1996	Brett Favre	QB	Green Bay Packers	Led Packers to top conference record (13-3). Threw NFL-best 39 touchdown passes.
1997*	Brett Favre	QB	Green Bay Packers	Led league with 35 touchdown passes. Led NFC with 3,867 passing yards.
	Barry Sanders	RB	Detroit Lions	Rushed for all-time second-best 2,053 yards, including record 14 straight 100-yard games.
1998	Terrell Davis	RB	Denver Broncos	Rushed for 2,008 yards and scored league-best 23 total touchdowns.
1999	Kurt Warner	QB	St. Louis Rams	Became the second QB in history to have 40 touchdown passes in a season (41).
2000	Marshall Faulk	RB	St. Louis Rams	Set NFL record with 26 touchdowns and led NFC with 2,189 yards from scrimmage.
2001	Kurt Warner	QB	St. Louis Rams	Led NFL with 4,830 passing yards, 36 touchdowns, 68.7 completion percentage, and 101.4 passer rating.
2002	Rich Gannon	QB	Oakland Raiders	Set single-season records with 10 300-yard passing games and 418 completions, and led NFL with 4,689 passing yards.
2003*	Peyton Manning	QB	Indianapolis Colts	Led NFL with 4,267 passing yards, had AFC-best 29 touchdown passes, and posted 99.0 passer rating.
	Steve McNair	QB	Tennessee Titans	Posted NFL-best 100.4 passer rating, passing for 3,215 yards with 24 touchdowns against 7 interceptions.
2004	Peyton Manning	QB	Indianapolis Colts	Set NFL records with 49 touchdown passes and 121.1 passer rating while passing for 4,557 yards.
2005	Shaun Alexander	RB	Seattle Seahawks	Set NFL record with 28 touchdowns and led league with 1,880 rushing yards.
2006	LaDainian Tomlinson	RB	San Diego Chargers	Set NFL record for touchdowns (31) and points scored (186). Rushed for team-record 1,815 yards.
2007	Tom Brady	QB	New England Patriots	Set NFL record with 50 passing touchdowns. Led New England to first 16-0 regular-season record in league history.

Total *Associated Press* **NFL MVPs:** 54
Three-time Winner: Brett Favre
Two-time Winners: Jim Brown, Peyton Manning, Joe Montana, Johnny Unitas, Kurt Warner, Steve Young
* The award was shared in 1960, 1997, and 2003.

ASSOCIATED PRESS MVPs WHO WON SUPER BOWL/NFL CHAMPIONSHIP IN SAME SEASON: 15

1958	Gino Marchetti	Baltimore Colts
1960	Norm Van Brocklin	Philadelphia Eagles
1961	Paul Hornung	Green Bay Packers
1962	Jim Taylor	Green Bay Packers
1966	Bart Starr	Green Bay Packers
1968	Earl Morrall	Baltimore Colts
1978	Terry Bradshaw	Pittsburgh Steelers
1982	Mark Moseley	Washington Redskins
1986	Lawrence Taylor	New York Giants
1989	Joe Montana	San Francisco 49ers
1993	Emmitt Smith	Dallas Cowboys
1994	Steve Young	San Francisco 49ers
1996	Brett Favre	Green Bay Packers
1998	Terrell Davis	Denver Broncos
1999	Kurt Warner	St. Louis Rams

ASSOCIATED PRESS NFL MVP BY POSITION

Quarterback:	33	Defensive End:	1
Running Back:	16	Defensive Tackle:	1
Linebacker:	2	Kicker:	1

ASSOCIATED PRESS MVPs BY TEAM

7	Indianapolis/Baltimore Colts	1	Chicago Bears
			Dallas Cowboys
6	Green Bay Packers		Houston Oilers
			Miami Dolphins
5	San Francisco 49ers		New England Patriots
			Philadelphia Eagles
4	St. Louis/Los Angeles Rams		Pittsburgh Steelers
			San Diego Chargers
3	Cleveland Browns		Seattle Seahawks
	New York Giants		Tennessee Titans
	Oakland/Los Angeles Raiders		
	Washington Redskins		
2	Buffalo Bills		
	Cincinnati Bengals		
	Denver Broncos		
	Detroit Lions		
	Minnesota Vikings		

AP OFFENSIVE PLAYER OF THE YEAR

1973	O.J. Simpson	RB	Buffalo Bills
1974	Ken Stabler	QB	Oakland Raiders
1975	Fran Tarkenton	QB	Minnesota Vikings
1976	Bert Jones	QB	Baltimore Colts
1977	Walter Payton	RB	Chicago Bears
1978	Earl Campbell	RB	Houston Oilers
1979	Earl Campbell	RB	Houston Oilers
1980	Earl Campbell	RB	Houston Oilers
1981	Ken Anderson	QB	Cincinnati Bengals
1982	Dan Fouts	QB	San Diego Chargers
1983	Joe Theismann	QB	Washington Redskins
1984	Dan Marino	QB	Miami Dolphins
1985	Marcus Allen	RB	Los Angeles Raiders
1986	Eric Dickerson	RB	Los Angeles Rams
1987	Jerry Rice	WR	San Francisco 49ers
1988	Roger Craig	RB	San Francisco 49ers
1989	Joe Montana	QB	San Francisco 49ers
1990	Warren Moon	QB	Houston Oilers
1991	Thurman Thomas	RB	Buffalo Bills
1992	Steve Young	QB	San Francisco 49ers
1993	Jerry Rice	WR	San Francisco 49ers
1994	Barry Sanders	RB	Detroit Lions
1995	Brett Favre	QB	Green Bay Packers
1996	Terrell Davis	RB	Denver Broncos
1997	Barry Sanders	RB	Detroit Lions
1998	Terrell Davis	RB	Denver Broncos
1999	Marshall Faulk	RB	St. Louis Rams
2000	Marshall Faulk	RB	St. Louis Rams
2001	Marshall Faulk	RB	St. Louis Rams
2002	Priest Holmes	RB	Kansas City Chiefs
2003	Jamal Lewis	RB	Baltimore Ravens
2004	Peyton Manning	QB	Indianapolis Colts
2005	Shaun Alexander	RB	Seattle Seahawks
2006	LaDainian Tomlinson	RB	San Diego Chargers
2007	Tom Brady	QB	New England Patriots

AP OFFENSIVE ROOKIE OF THE YEAR

1957	Jim Brown	RB	Cleveland Browns
1958	Jimmy Orr	WR	Pittsburgh Steelers
1959	Nick Pietrosante	RB	Detroit Lions
1960	Gail Cogdill	WR	Detroit Lions
1961	Mike Ditka	TE	Chicago Bears
1962	Ron Bull	RB	Chicago Bears
1963	Paul Flatley	WR	Minnesota Vikings
1964	Charley Taylor	WR	Washington Redskins
1965	Gale Sayers	RB	Chicago Bears
1966	Johnny Roland	RB	St. Louis Cardinals
1967	Mel Farr	RB	Detroit Lions
1968	Earl McCullouch	WR	Detroit Lions
1969	Calvin Hill	RB	Dallas Cowboys
1970	Duane Thomas	RB	Dallas Cowboys
1971	John Brockington	RB	Green Bay Packers
1972	Franco Harris	RB	Pittsburgh Steelers
1973	Chuck Foreman	RB	Minnesota Vikings
1974	Don Woods	RB	San Diego Chargers
1975	Mike Thomas	RB	Washington Redskins
1976	Sammy White	WR	Minnesota Vikings
1977	Tony Dorsett	RB	Dallas Cowboys
1978	Earl Campbell	RB	Houston Oilers
1979	Ottis Anderson	RB	St. Louis Cardinals
1980	Billy Sims	RB	Detroit Lions
1981	George Rogers	RB	New Orleans Saints
1982	Marcus Allen	RB	Los Angeles Raiders
1983	Eric Dickerson	RB	Los Angeles Rams
1984	Louis Lipps	WR	Pittsburgh Steelers
1985	Eddie Brown	WR	Cincinnati Bengals
1986	Rueben Mayes	RB	New Orleans Saints
1987	Troy Stradford	RB	Miami Dolphins
1988	John Stephens	RB	New England Patriots
1989	Barry Sanders	RB	Detroit Lions
1990	Emmitt Smith	RB	Dallas Cowboys
1991	Leonard Russell	RB	New England Patriots
1992	Carl Pickens	WR	Cincinnati Bengals
1993	Jerome Bettis	RB	Los Angeles Rams
1994	Marshall Faulk	RB	Indianapolis Colts
1995	Curtis Martin	RB	New England Patriots
1996	Eddie George	RB	Houston Oilers
1997	Warrick Dunn	RB	Tampa Bay Buccaneers
1998	Randy Moss	WR	Minnesota Vikings
1999	Edgerrin James	RB	Indianapolis Colts
2000	Mike Anderson	RB	Denver Broncos
2001	Anthony Thomas	RB	Chicago Bears
2002	Clinton Portis	RB	Denver Broncos
2003	Anquan Boldin	WR	Arizona Cardinals
2004	Ben Roethlisberger	QB	Pittsburgh Steelers
2005	Carnell Williams	RB	Tampa Bay Buccaneers
2006	Vince Young	QB	Tennessee Titans
2007	Adrian Peterson	RB	Minnesota Vikings

AP DEFENSIVE PLAYER OF THE YEAR

1971	Alan Page	DT	Minnesota Vikings
1972	Joe Greene	DT	Pittsburgh Steelers
1973	Dick Anderson	S	Miami Dolphins
1974	Joe Greene	DT	Pittsburgh Steelers
1975	Mel Blount	CB	Pittsburgh Steelers
1976	Jack Lambert	LB	Pittsburgh Steelers
1977	Harvey Martin	DE	Dallas Cowboys
1978	Randy Gradishar	LB	Denver Broncos
1979	Lee Roy Selmon	DE	Tampa Bay Buccaneers
1980	Lester Hayes	CB	Oakland Raiders
1981	Lawrence Taylor	LB	New York Giants
1982	Lawrence Taylor	LB	New York Giants
1983	Doug Betters	DE	Miami Dolphins
1984	Kenny Easley	S	Seattle Seahawks
1985	Mike Singletary	LB	Chicago Bears
1986	Lawrence Taylor	LB	New York Giants
1987	Reggie White	DT	Philadelphia Eagles
1988	Mike Singletary	LB	Chicago Bears
1989	Keith Millard	DT	Minnesota Vikings
1990	Bruce Smith	DE	Buffalo Bills
1991	Pat Swilling	LB	New Orleans Saints
1992	Cortez Kennedy	DT	Seattle Seahawks
1993	Rod Woodson	CB	Pittsburgh Steelers
1994	Deion Sanders	CB	San Francisco 49ers
1995	Bryce Paup	LB	Buffalo Bills
1996	Bruce Smith	DE	Buffalo Bills
1997	Dana Stubblefield	DT	San Francisco 49ers
1998	Reggie White	DE	Green Bay Packers
1999	Warren Sapp	DT	Tampa Bay Buccaneers
2000	Ray Lewis	LB	Baltimore Ravens
2001	Michael Strahan	DE	New York Giants
2002	Derrick Brooks	LB	Tampa Bay Buccaneers
2003	Ray Lewis	LB	Baltimore Ravens
2004	Ed Reed	S	Baltimore Ravens
2005	Brian Urlacher	LB	Chicago Bears
2006	Jason Taylor	DE	Miami Dolphins
2007	Bob Sanders	S	Indianapolis Colts

AP DEFENSIVE ROOKIE OF THE YEAR

1967	Lem Barney	CB	Detroit Lions
1968	Claude Humphrey	DE	Atlanta Falcons
1969	Joe Greene	DT	Pittsburgh Steelers
1970	Bruce Taylor	CB	San Franicsco 49ers
1971	Isiah Robertson	LB	Los Angeles Rams
1972	Willie Buchanon	CB	Green Bay Packers

1973	Wally Chambers	DT	Chicago Bears
1974	Jack Lambert	LB	Pittsburgh Steelers
1975	Robert Brazile	LB	Houston Oilers
1976	Mike Haynes	S	New England Patriots
1977	A.J. Duhe	DT	Miami Dolphins
1978	Al Baker	DE	Detroit Lions
1979	Jim Haslett	LB	Buffalo Bills
1980*	Buddy Curry	LB	Atlanta Falcons
	Al Richardson	LB	Atlanta Falcons
1981	Lawrence Taylor	LB	New York Giants
1982	Chip Banks	LB	Cleveland Browns
1983	Vernon Maxwell	LB	Baltimore Colts
1984	Bill Maas	NT	Kansas City Chiefs
1985	Duane Bickett	LB	Indianapolis Colts
1986	John Offerdahl	LB	Miami Dolphins
1987	Shane Conlan	LB	Buffalo Bills
1988	Erik McMillan	S	New York Jets
1989	Derrick Thomas	LB	Kansas City Chiefs
1990	Mark Carrier	S	Chicago Bears
1991	Mike Croel	LB	Denver Broncos
1992	Dale Carter	CB	Kansas City Chiefs
1993	Dana Stubblefield	DT	San Francisco 49ers
1994	Tim Bowens	DT	Miami Dolphins
1995	Hugh Douglas	DE	New York Jets
1996	Simeon Rice	DE	Arizona Cardinals
1997	Peter Boulware	LB	Baltimore Ravens
1998	Charles Woodson	CB	Oakland Raiders
1999	Jevon Kearse	DE	Tennessee Titans
2000	Brian Urlacher	LB	Chicago Bears
2001	Kendrell Bell	LB	Pittsburgh Steelers
2002	Julius Peppers	DE	Carolina Panthers
2003	Terrell Suggs	LB	Baltimore Ravens
2004	Jonathan Vilma	LB	New York Jets
2005	Shawne Merriman	LB	San Diego Chargers
2006	DeMeco Ryans	LB	Houston Texans
2007	Patrick Willis	LB	San Francisco 49ers

*The award was shared in 1980.

AP COMEBACK PLAYER OF THE YEAR

1998	Doug Flutie	QB	Buffalo Bills
1999	Bryant Young	DT	San Francisco 49ers
2000	Joe Johnson	DE	New Orleans Saints
2001	Garrison Hearst	RB	San Francisco 49ers
2002	Tommy Maddox	QB	Pittsburgh Steelers
2003	Jon Kitna	QB	Cincinnati Bengals
2004	Drew Brees	QB	San Diego Chargers
2005*	Steve Smith	WR	Carolina Panthers
	Tedy Bruschi	LB	New England Patriots
2006	Chad Pennington	QB	New York Jets
2007	Greg Ellis	DE	Dallas Cowboys

*The award was shared in 2005.

AP COACH OF THE YEAR

1957	George Wilson	Detroit Lions
1958	Weeb Ewbank	Baltimore Colts
1959	Vince Lombardi	Green Bay Packers
1960	Buck Shaw	Philadelphia Eagles
1961	Allie Sherman	New York Giants
1962	Allie Sherman	New York Giants
1963	George Halas	Chicago Bears
1964	Don Shula	Baltimore Colts
1965	George Halas	Chicago Bears
1966	Tom Landry	Dallas Cowboys
1967*	George Allen	Los Angeles Rams
	Don Shula	Baltimore Colts
1968	Don Shula	Baltimore Colts
1969	Bud Grant	Minnesota Vikings
1970	Paul Brown	Cincinnati Bengals

1971	George Allen	Washington Redskins
1972	Don Shula	Miami Dolphins
1973	Chuck Knox	Los Angeles Rams
1974	Don Coryell	St. Louis Cardinals
1975	Ted Marchibroda	Baltimore Colts
1976	Forrest Gregg	Cleveland Browns
1977	Red Miller	Denver Broncos
1978	Jack Patera	Seattle Seahawks
1979	Jack Pardee	Washington Redskins
1980	Chuck Knox	Buffalo Bills
1981	Bill Walsh	San Francisco 49ers
1982	Joe Gibbs	Washington Redskins
1983	Joe Gibbs	Washington Redskins
1984	Chuck Knox	Seattle Seahawks
1985	Mike Ditka	Chicago Bears
1986	Bill Parcells	New York Giants
1987	Jim Mora	New Orleans Saints
1988	Mike Ditka	Chicago Bears
1989	Lindy Infante	Green Bay Packers
1990	Jimmy Johnson	Dallas Cowboys
1991	Wayne Fontes	Detroit Lions
1992	Bill Cowher	Pittsburgh Steelers
1993	Dan Reeves	New York Giants
1994	Bill Parcells	New England Patriots
1995	Ray Rhodes	Philadelphia Eagles
1996	Dom Capers	Carolina Panthers
1997	Jim Fassel	New York Giants
1998	Dan Reeves	Atlanta Falcons
1999	Dick Vermeil	St. Louis Rams
2000	Jim Haslett	New Orleans Saints
2001	Dick Jauron	Chicago Bears
2002	Andy Reid	Philadelphia Eagles
2003	Bill Belichick	New England Patriots
2004	Marty Schottenheimer	San Diego Chargers
2005	Lovie Smith	Chicago Bears
2006	Sean Payton	New Orleans Saints
2007	Bill Belichick	New England Patriots

*The award was shared in 1967.

75TH ANNIVERSARY ALL-TIME TEAM
Chosen by a selection committee of media and league personnel in 1994.

Position	Name	Team(s)	Ht.	Wt.	College
OFFENSE					
QB	Sammy Baugh	Washington Redskins (1937-52)	6-2	180	Texas Christian
QB	Otto Graham	Cleveland Browns (1946-55)	6-1	195	Northwestern
QB	Joe Montana	San Francisco 49ers (1979-92), Kansas City Chiefs (1993-94)	6-2	195	Notre Dame
QB	Johnny Unitas	Baltimore Colts (1956-72), San Diego Chargers (1973)	6-1	195	Louisville
RB	Jim Brown	Cleveland Browns (1957-65)	6-2	232	Syracuse
RB	Marion Motley	Cleveland Browns (1946-53), Pittsburgh Steelers (1955)	6-1	238	Nevada-Reno
RB	Bronko Nagurski	Chicago Bears (1930-37, 1943)	6-2	225	Minnesota
RB	Walter Payton	Chicago Bears (1975-87)	5-10	202	Jackson State
RB	Gale Sayers	Chicago Bears (1965-71)	6-0	200	Kansas
RB	O.J. Simpson	Buffalo Bills (1969-77), San Francisco 49ers (1978-79)	6-1	212	Southern California
RB	Steve Van Buren	Philadelphia Eagles (1944-51)	6-1	200	Louisiana State
WR	Lance Alworth	San Diego Chargers (1962-70), Dallas Cowboys (1971-72)	6-0	184	Arkansas
WR	Raymond Berry	Baltimore Colts (1955-67)	6-2	187	Southern Methodist
WR	Don Hutson	Green Bay Packers (1935-45)	6-1	180	Alabama
WR	Jerry Rice	San Francisco 49ers (1985-2000), Oakland Raiders (2001-04), Seattle Seahawks (2004)	6-2	200	Miss. Valley State
TE	Mike Ditka	Chicago Bears (1961-66), Philadelphia Eagles (1967-68), Dallas Cowboys (1969-72)	6-3	225	Pittsburgh
TE	Kellen Winslow	San Diego Chargers (1979-87)	6-5	250	Missouri
T	Roosevelt Brown	New York Giants (1953-65)	6-3	255	Morgan State
T	Forrest Gregg	Green Bay Packers (1956, 1958-70)	6-4	250	Southern Methodist
T	Anthony Muñoz	Cincinnati Bengals (1980-92)	6-6	285	Southern California
G	John Hannah	New England Patriots (1973-85)	6-3	265	Alabama
G	Jim Parker	Baltimore Colts (1957-67)	6-3	273	Ohio State
G	Gene Upshaw	Oakland Raiders (1967-81)	6-5	255	Texas A&I
C	Mel Hein	New York Giants (1931-45)	6-2	225	Washington State
C	Mike Webster	Pittsburgh Steelers (1974-88), Kansas City Chiefs (1989-90)	6-2	250	Wisconsin
DEFENSE					
DE	David (Deacon) Jones	Los Angeles Rams (1961-71), San Diego Chargers (1972-73), Washington Redskins (1974)	6-5	250	Miss. Vocational-South Carolina St.
DE	Gino Marchetti	Dallas Texans (1952), Baltimore Colts (1953-64, 1966)	6-4	245	San Francisco
DE	Reggie White	Philadelphia Eagles (1985-92), Green Bay Packers (1993-1998), Carolina Panthers (2000)	6-5	290	Tennessee
DT	Joe Greene	Pittsburgh Steelers (1969-81)	6-4	260	North Texas State
DT	Bob Lilly	Dallas Cowboys (1961-74)	6-5	260	Texas Christian
DT	Merlin Olsen	Los Angeles Rams (1962-76)	6-5	270	Utah State
LB	Dick Butkus	Chicago Bears (1965-73)	6-3	245	Illinois
LB	Jack Ham	Pittsburgh Steelers (1971-82)	6-1	225	Penn State
LB	Ted Hendricks	Baltimore Colts (1969-73), Green Bay Packers (1974), Oakland/L.A. Raiders (1975-83)	6-7	235	Miami
LB	Jack Lambert	Pittsburgh Steelers (1974-84)	6-4	220	Kent State
LB	Willie Lanier	Kansas City Chiefs (1967-77)	6-1	245	Morgan State
LB	Ray Nitschke	Green Bay Packers (1958-72)	6-3	235	Illinois
LB	Lawrence Taylor	New York Giants (1981-93)	6-3	243	North Carolina
CB	Mel Blount	Pittsburgh Steelers (1970-83)	6-3	205	Southern
CB	Mike Haynes	New England Patriots (1976-82), Los Angeles Raiders (1983-89)	6-2	190	Arizona State
CB	Dick (Night Train) Lane	Los Angeles Rams (1952-53), Chicago Cardinals (1954-59), Detroit Lions (1960-65)	6-2	210	Scottsbluff JC
CB	Rod Woodson	Pittsburgh Steelers (1987-96), San Francisco 49ers (1997), Baltimore Ravens (1998-2001), Oakland Raiders (2002-2003)	6-0	200	Purdue
S	Ken Houston	Houston Oilers (1967-72), Washington Redskins (1973-80)	6-3	198	Prairie View A&M
S	Ronnie Lott	San Francisco 49ers (1981-90), Los Angeles Raiders (1991-92), New York Jets (1993-94)	6-0	200	Southern California
S	Larry Wilson	St. Louis Cardinals (1960-72)	6-0	190	Utah
SPECIAL TEAMS					
P	Ray Guy	Oakland/L.A. Raiders (1973-86)	6-3	190	Southern Mississippi
K	Jan Stenerud	Kansas City Chiefs (1967-79), Green Bay Packers (1980-83), Minnesota Vikings (1984-85)	6-2	190	Montana State
PR	Billy (White Shoes) Johnson	Houston Oilers (1974-80), Atlanta Falcons (1982-87), Washington Redskins (1988)	5-9	170	Widener
KR	Gale Sayers	Chicago Bears (1965-71)	6-0	200	Kansas

75TH ANNIVERSARY ALL-TWO-WAY TEAM
Positions

Quarterback, Defensive Halfback, Punter	Sammy Baugh
Center, Linebacker	Chuck Bednarik
Quarterback, Defensive Halfback, Punter	Earl (Dutch) Clark
Tackle, Defensive Tackle	George Connor
Guard, Defensive Tackle	Danny Fortmann
Center, Defensive Tackle	Mel Hein
Tackle, Defensive Tackle, Punter	Wilbur (Pete) Henry
Back, Defensive Halfback	Bill Hewitt
Fullback, Linebacker, Kicker	Clarke Hinkle
Tackle, Defensive Tackle	Cal Hubbard
End, Defensive Halfback	Don Hutson
Back, Defensive Back	George McAfee
Fullback, Linebacker	Marion Motley
Guard-Tackle, Defensive Tackle	George Musso
Fullback, Linebacker	Bronko Nagurski
Halfback, Defensive Halfback	Ernie Nevers
End, Defensive Back	Pete Pihos
Tackle, Defensive Tackle	Joe Stydahar
Running Back, Defensive Back	Steve Van Buren

50TH ANNIVERSARY TEAM
Chosen by the Hall of Fame Selection Committee in 1969.
Offense

Split End	Don Hutson
Tight End	John Mackey
Tackle	Cal Hubbard
Guard	Jerry Kramer
Center	Chuck Bednarik
Flanker	Elroy Hirsch
Quarterback	Johnny Unitas
Halfback	Jim Thorpe
Halfback	Gale Sayers
Fullback	Jim Brown
Kicker	Lou Groza

Defense

End	Gino Marchetti
Tackle	Leo Nomellini
Linebacker	Ray Nitschke
Cornerback	Dick (Night Train) Lane
Safety	Emlen Tunnell

SUPER BOWL SILVER ANNIVERSARY TEAM
Chosen by the fans in 1990 prior to Super Bowl XXV.

Head Coach	Vince Lombardi

Offense

Quarterback	Joe Montana
Running Back	Franco Harris
Running Back	Larry Csonka
Wide Receiver	Lynn Swann
Wide Receiver	Jerry Rice
Tight End	Dave Casper
Tackle	Art Shell
Tackle	Forrest Gregg
Guard	Gene Upshaw
Guard	Jerry Kramer
Center	Mike Webster

Defense

Defensive End	L.C. Greenwood
Defensive End	Ed (Too Tall) Jones
Defensive Tackle	Joe Greene
Defensive Tackle	Randy White
Inside Linebacker	Jack Lambert
Inside Linebacker	Mike Singletary
Outside Linebacker	Jack Ham
Outside Linebacker	Ted Hendricks
Cornerback	Ronnie Lott
Cornerback	Mel Blount
Safety	Donnie Shell
Safety	Willie Wood

Special Teams

Punter	Ray Guy
Kicker	Jan Stenerud
Kick Returner	John Taylor

All-Decade teams chosen by the Hall of Fame Selection Committee members.

1920s ALL-DECADE TEAM

End	Guy Chamberlin
End	Lavern Dilweg
End	George Halas
Tackle	Ed Healey
Tackle	Wilbur (Pete) Henry
Tackle	Cal Hubbard
Tackle	Steve Owen
Guard	Hunk Anderson
Guard	Walt Kiesling
Guard	Mike Michalske
Center	George Trafton
Quarterback	Jimmy Conzelman
Quarterback	John (Paddy) Driscoll
Halfback	Harold (Red) Grange
Halfback	Joe Guyon
Halfback	Earl (Curly) Lambeau
Halfback	Jim Thorpe
Fullback	Ernie Nevers

1930s ALL-DECADE TEAM

End	Bill Hewitt
End	Don Hutson
End	Wayne Millner
End	Gaynell Tinsley
Tackle	George Christensen
Tackle	Frank Cope
Tackle	Glen (Turk) Edwards
Tackle	Bill Lee
Tackle	Joe Stydahar
Guard	Grover (Ox) Emerson
Guard	Dan Fortmann
Guard	Charles (Buckets) Goldenberg
Guard	Russ Letlow
Center	Mel Hein
Center	George Svendsen
Quarterback	Earl (Dutch) Clark
Quarterback	Arnie Herber
Quarterback	Cecil Isbell
Halfback	Cliff Battles
Halfback	Johnny (Blood) McNally
Halfback	Beattie Feathers
Halfback	Alphonse (Tuffy) Leemans
Halfback	Ken Strong
Fullback	Clarke Hinkle
Fullback	Bronko Nagurski

1940s ALL-DECADE TEAM

End	Jim Benton
End	Jack Ferrante
End	Ken Kavanaugh
End	Dante Lavelli
End	Pete Pihos
End	Mac Speedie
End	Ed Sprinkle
Tackle	Al Blozis
Tackle	George Connor
Tackle	Frank (Bucko) Kilroy
Tackle	Buford (Baby) Ray
Tackle	Vic Sears
Tackle	Al Wistert
Guard	Bruno Banducci
Guard	Bill Edwards
Guard	Garrard (Buster) Ramsey
Guard	Bill Willis
Guard	Len Younce
Center	Charley Brock
Center	Clyde (Bulldog) Turner
Center	Alex Wojciechowicz
Quarterback	Sammy Baugh
Quarterback	Sid Luckman
Quarterback	Bob Waterfield
Halfback	Tony Canadeo
Halfback	Bill Dudley
Halfback	George McAfee
Halfback	Charley Trippi
Halfback	Steve Van Buren
Halfback	Byron (Whizzer) White
Fullback	Pat Harder
Fullback	Marion Motley
Fullback	Bill Osmanski

1950s ALL-DECADE TEAM

Offense

End	Raymond Berry
End	Tom Fears
End	Bobby Walston
Halfback-End	Elroy (Crazylegs) Hirsch
Tackle	Roosevelt Brown
Tackle	Bob St. Clair
Guard	Dick Barwegan
Guard	Jim Parker
Guard	Dick Stanfel
Center	Chuck Bednarik
Quarterback	Otto Graham
Quarterback	Bobby Layne
Quarterback	Norm Van Brocklin
Halfback	Frank Gifford
Halfback	Ollie Matson
Halfback	Hugh McElhenny
Halfback	Lenny Moore
Fullback	Alan Ameche
Fullback	Joe Perry
Kicker	Lou Groza

Defense

End	Len Ford
End	Gino Marchetti
Tackle	Art Donovan
Tackle	Leo Nomellini
Tackle	Ernie Stautner
Linebacker	Joe Fortunato
Linebacker	Bill George
Linebacker	Sam Huff
Linebacker	Joe Schmidt
Halfback	Jack Butler

Halfback	Dick (Night Train) Lane
Safety	Jack Christiansen
Safety	Yale Lary
Safety	Emlen Tunnell

1960s ALL-DECADE TEAM

Offense

Split End	Del Shofner
Split End	Charley Taylor
Flanker	Gary Collins
Flanker	Boyd Dowler
Tight End	John Mackey
Tackle	Bob Brown
Tackle	Forrest Gregg
Tackle	Ralph Neely
Guard	Gene Hickerson
Guard	Jerry Kramer
Guard	Howard Mudd
Center	Jim Ringo
Quarterback	Sonny Jurgensen
Quarterback	Bart Starr
Quarterback	Johnny Unitas
Halfback	John David Crow
Halfback	Paul Hornung
Halfback	Leroy Kelly
Halfback	Gale Sayers
Fullback	Jim Brown
Fullback	Jim Taylor
Kicker	Jim Bakken

Defense

End	Doug Atkins
End	Willie Davis
End	David (Deacon) Jones
Tackle	Alex Karras
Tackle	Bob Lilly
Tackle	Merlin Olsen
Linebacker	Dick Butkus
Linebacker	Larry Morris
Linebacker	Ray Nitschke
Linebacker	Tommy Nobis
Linebacker	Dave Robinson
Cornerback	Herb Adderley
Cornerback	Lem Barney
Cornerback	Bobby Boyd
Safety	Eddie Meador
Safety	Larry Wilson
Safety	Willie Wood
Punter	Don Chandler

1970s ALL-DECADE TEAM

Offense

Wide Receiver	Harold Carmichael
Wide Receiver	Drew Pearson
Wide Receiver	Lynn Swann
Wide Receiver	Paul Warfield
Tight End	Dave Casper
Tight End	Charlie Sanders
Tackle	Dan Dierdorf
Tackle	Art Shell
Tackle	Rayfield Wright
Tackle	Ron Yary
Guard	Joe DeLamielleure
Guard	John Hannah
Guard	Larry Little
Guard	Gene Upshaw
Center	Jim Langer
Center	Mike Webster
Quarterback	Terry Bradshaw
Quarterback	Ken Stabler
Quarterback	Roger Staubach
Running Back	Earl Campbell
Running Back	Franco Harris
Running Back	Walter Payton
Running Back	O.J. Simpson
Kicker	Garo Yepremian

Defense

End	Carl Eller
End	L.C. Greenwood
End	Harvey Martin
End	Jack Youngblood
Tackle	Joe Greene
Tackle	Bob Lilly
Tackle	Merlin Olsen
Tackle	Alan Page
Linebacker	Bobby Bell
Linebacker	Robert Brazile
Linebacker	Dick Butkus
Linebacker	Jack Ham
Linebacker	Ted Hendricks
Linebacker	Jack Lambert
Cornerback	Willie Brown
Cornerback	Jimmy Johnson
Cornerback	Roger Wehrli
Cornerback	Louis Wright
Safety	Dick Anderson
Safety	Cliff Harris
Safety	Ken Houston
Safety	Larry Wilson
Punter	Ray Guy

1980s ALL-DECADE TEAM

Offense

Wide Receiver	Jerry Rice
Wide Receiver	Steve Largent
Wide Receiver	James Lofton
Wide Receiver	Art Monk
Tight End	Kellen Winslow
Tight End	Ozzie Newsome
Tackle	Anthony Munoz
Tackle	Jim Covert
Tackle	Gary Zimmerman
Tackle	Joe Jacoby
Guard	John Hannah
Guard	Russ Grimm
Guard	Bill Fralic
Guard	Mike Munchak
Center	Dwight Stephenson
Center	Mike Webster
Quarterback	Joe Montana
Quarterback	Dan Fouts
Running Back	Walter Payton
Running Back	Eric Dickerson
Running Back	Roger Craig
Running Back	John Riggins

Defense

End	Reggie White
End	Howie Long
End	Lee Roy Selmon
End	Bruce Smith
Tackle	Randy White
Tackle	Dan Hampton
Tackle	Keith Millard
Tackle	Dave Butz
Linebacker	Mike Singletary
Linebacker	Lawrence Taylor
Linebacker	Ted Hendricks
Linebacker	Jack Lambert
Linebacker	Andre Tippett
Linebacker	John Anderson
Linebacker	Carl Banks
Cornerback	Mike Haynes
Cornerback	Mel Blount
Cornerback	Frank Minnifield
Cornerback	Lester Hayes
Safety	Ronnie Lott
Safety	Kenny Easley
Safety	Deron Cherry
Safety	Joey Browner
Safety	Nolan Cromwell

Specialists

Punter	Sean Landeta
Punter	Reggie Roby
Kicker	Morten Andersen
Kicker	Gary Anderson
Kicker	Eddie Murray
Punt Returner	Billy (White Shoes) Johnson
Punt Returner	John Taylor
Kick Returner	Mike Nelms
Kick Returner	Rick Upchurch
Coach	Bill Walsh
Coach	Chuck Noll

1990s ALL-DECADE TEAM

Offense

Wide Receiver	Cris Carter
Wide Receiver	Jerry Rice
Wide Receiver	Tim Brown
Wide Receiver	Michael Irvin
Tight End	Shannon Sharpe
Tight End	Ben Coates
Tackle	William Roaf
Tackle	Gary Zimmerman
Tackle	Tony Boselli
Tackle	Richmond Webb
Guard	Bruce Matthews
Guard	Randall McDaniel
Guard	Larry Allen
Guard	Steve Wisniewski
Center	Dermontti Dawson
Center	Mark Stepnoski
Quarterback	John Elway
Quarterback	Brett Favre
Running Back	Barry Sanders
Running Back	Emmitt Smith
Running Back	Terrell Davis
Running Back	Thurman Thomas

Defense

End	Bruce Smith
End	Reggie White
End	Chris Doleman
End	Neil Smith
Tackle	Cortez Kennedy
Tackle	John Randle
Tackle	Warren Sapp
Tackle	Bryant Young
Linebacker	Kevin Greene
Linebacker	Junior Seau
Linebacker	Derrick Thomas
Linebacker	Cornelius Bennett
Linebacker	Hardy Nickerson
Linebacker	Levon Kirkland
Cornerback	Deion Sanders
Cornerback	Rod Woodson
Cornerback	Darrell Green
Cornerback	Aeneas Williams
Safety	Steve Atwater
Safety	LeRoy Butler
Safety	Carnell Lake
Safety	Ronnie Lott

Specialists

Punter	Darren Bennett
Punter	Sean Landeta
Kicker	Morten Andersen
Kicker	Gary Anderson
Punt Returner	Deion Sanders
Punt Returner	Mel Gray
Kick Returner	Michael Bates
Kick Returner	Mel Gray
Coach	Bill Parcells
Coach	Marv Levy

ALL-TIME AFL TEAM
Chosen by 1969 AFL Hall of Fame Selection Committee members.
Offense

Flanker	Lance Alworth
End	Don Maynard
Tight End	Fred Arbanas
Tackle	Ron Mix
Tackle	Jim Tyrer
Guard	Ed Budde
Guard	Billy Shaw
Center	Jim Otto
Quarterback	Joe Namath
Running Back	Clem Daniels
Running Back	Paul Lowe

Defense

End	Jerry Mays
End	Gerry Philbin
Tackle	Houston Antwine
Tackle	Tom Sestak
Linebacker	Bobby Bell
Linebacker	George Webster
Linebacker	Nick Buoniconti
Cornerback	Willie Brown
Cornerback	Dave Grayson
Safety	Johnny Robinson
Safety	George Saimes

Special Teams

Kicker	George Blanda
Punter	Jerrel Wilson

ALL-TIME NFL TEAM
Chosen by members of the Hall of Fame Selection Committee in 2000 for the book NFL's Greatest.
Offense

Wide Receiver	Don Hutson
Wide Receiver	Jerry Rice
Tight End	John Mackey
Tackle	Roosevelt Brown
Tackle	Anthony Muñoz
Guard	John Hannah
Guard	Jim Parker
Center	Mike Webster
Quarterback	Johnny Unitas
Running Back	Jim Brown
Running Back	Walter Payton

Defense

End	Deacon Jones
End	Reggie White
Tackle	Joe Greene
Tackle	Bob Lilly
Middle Linebacker	Dick Butkus
Outside Linebacker	Jack Ham
Outside Linebacker	Lawrence Taylor
Cornerback	Mel Blount
Cornerback	Dick (Night Train) Lane
Safety	Ronnie Lott
Safety	Larry Wilson

Special Teams

Kicker	Jan Stenerud
Punter	Ray Guy
Kick Returner	Gale Sayers
Punt Returner	Deion Sanders
Special Teams	Steve Tasker

AFL-NFL 1960-1984 ALL-STAR TEAM
Chosen by the Hall of Fame Selection Committee in 1985.
Offense

Quarterback	Johnny Unitas
Running Back	Jim Brown
Running Back	O.J. Simpson
Wide Receiver	Lance Alworth
Wide Receiver	Raymond Berry
Tight End	Kellen Winslow
Tackle	Forrest Gregg
Tackle	Ron Mix
Guard	Jim Parker
Guard	John Hannah
Center	Jim Otto

Defense

End	Gino Marchetti
End	Willie Davis
Tackle	Bob Lilly
Tackle	Merlin Olsen
Linebacker	Dick Butkus
Linebacker	Jack Lambert
Linebacker	Ray Nitschke
Cornerback	Willie Brown
Cornerback	Dick (Night Train) Lane
Safety	Larry Wilson
Safety	Yale Lary

Special Teams

Punter	Ray Guy
Kicker	Jan Stenerud
Kick Returner	Gale Sayers
Kick Returner	Rick Upchurch
Coach	Don Shula
Coach	Vince Lombardi

Records

Compiled by Elias Sports Bureau.
The following records reflect all available official information on the National Football League from its formation in 1920 to date. Also included are all applicable records from the American Football League, 1960-69.

Individuals eligible for Rookie records are players who were in their first season of professional football and had not been on the roster of another professional football team, including teams in other leagues, for any regular-season or postseason games in a previous season. Eligible players, therefore, include those who were under contract to a National Football League club for a previous season but were terminated prior to their club's first regular-season game and not re-signed, or who were placed on Reserve/Injured (or another category of the Reserve List) prior to their club's first regular-season game and were not activated during the rest of the regular season or postseason.

INDIVIDUAL RECORDS

SERVICE
Most Seasons
- 26   George Blanda, Chi. Bears, 1949, 1950-58; Baltimore, 1950; Houston, 1960-66; Oakland, 1967-1975
- 25   Morten Andersen, New Orleans, 1982-1994; Atlanta, 1995-2000; N.Y. Giants, 2001; Kansas City, 2002-03; Minnesota, 2004; Atlanta, 2006-07
- 23   Gary Anderson, Pittsburgh, 1982-1994; Philadelphia, 1995-96; San Francisco, 1997; Minnesota, 1998-2002; Tennessee, 2003-04

Most Seasons, One Club
- 20   Jackie Slater, L.A. Rams, 1976-1994; St. Louis, 1995
-      Darrell Green, Washington, 1983-2002
- 19   Jim Marshall, Minnesota, 1961-1979
-      Bruce Matthews, Houston, 1983-1996; Tennessee, 1997-2001
- 18   Jim Hart, St. Louis, 1966-1983
-      Jeff Van Note, Atlanta, 1969-1986
-      Pat Leahy, N.Y. Jets, 1974-1991

Most Games Played, Career
- 382   Morten Andersen, New Orleans, 1982-1994; Atlanta, 1995-2000; N.Y. Giants, 2001; Kansas City, 2002-03; Minnesota, 2004; Atlanta, 2006-07
- 353   Gary Anderson, Pittsburgh, 1982-1994; Philadelphia, 1995-96; San Francisco, 1997; Minnesota, 1998-2002; Tennessee, 2003-04
- 340   George Blanda, Chi. Bears, 1949, 1950-58; Baltimore, 1950; Houston, 1960-66; Oakland, 1967-1975

Most Consecutive Games Played, Career
- 320   Jeff Feagles, New England, 1988-89; Philadelphia, 1990-93; Arizona, 1994-97; Seattle, 1998-2002; N.Y. Giants, 2003-07 (current)
- 282   Jim Marshall, Cleveland, 1960; Minnesota, 1961-1979
- 255   Brett Favre, Green Bay, 1992-2007 (current)

SCORING
Most Seasons Leading League
- 5   Don Hutson, Green Bay, 1940-44
-    Gino Cappelletti, Boston, 1961, 1963-66
- 3   Earl (Dutch) Clark, Portsmouth, 1932; Detroit, 1935-36
-    Pat Harder, Chi. Cardinals, 1947-49
-    Paul Hornung, Green Bay, 1959-1961
- 2   Jack Manders, Chi. Bears, 1934, 1937
-    Gordy Soltau, San Francisco, 1952-53
-    Doak Walker, Detroit, 1950, 1955
-    Gene Mingo, Denver, 1960, 1962
-    Jim Turner, N.Y. Jets, 1968-69
-    Fred Cox, Minnesota, 1969-1970

Chester Marcol, Green Bay, 1972, 1974
John Smith, New England, 1979-1980
Marshall Faulk, St. Louis, 2000-01

Most Consecutive Seasons Leading League
- 5   Don Hutson, Green Bay, 1940-44
- 4   Gino Cappelletti, Boston, 1963-66
- 3   Pat Harder, Chi. Cardinals, 1947-49
-    Paul Hornung, Green Bay, 1959-1961

POINTS
Most Points, Career
- 2,544   Morten Andersen, New Orleans, 1982-1994; Atlanta, 1995-2000; N.Y. Giants, 2001; Kansas City, 2002-03; Minnesota, 2004; Atlanta, 2006-07 (849-pat, 565-fg)
- 2,434   Gary Anderson, Pittsburgh, 1982-1994; Philadelphia 1995-96; San Francisco, 1997; Minnesota, 1998-2002; Tennessee, 2003-04 (820-pat, 538-fg)
- 2,002   George Blanda, Chi. Bears, 1949, 1950-58; Baltimore, 1950; Houston, 1960-66; Oakland, 1967-1975 (9-td, 943-pat, 335-fg)

Most Points, Season
- 186   LaDainian Tomlinson, San Diego, 2006 (31-td)
- 176   Paul Hornung, Green Bay, 1960 (15-td, 41-pat, 15-fg)
- 168   Shaun Alexander, Seattle, 2005 (28-td)

Most Points, No Touchdowns, Season
- 164   Gary Anderson, Minnesota, 1998 (59-pat, 35-fg)
- 163   Jeff Wilkins, St. Louis, 2003 (46-pat, 39-fg)
- 161   Mark Moseley, Washington, 1983 (62-pat, 33-fg)

Most Seasons, 100 or More Points
- 15   Jason Elam, Denver, 1993-2007
- 14   Gary Anderson, Pittsburgh, 1983-85, 1988, 1991-94; Philadelphia 1996; San Francisco, 1997; Minnesota, 1998-2000; Tennessee, 2003
-    Morten Andersen, New Orleans, 1985-89, 1991-94; Atlanta, 1995, 1997-98; Kansas City, 2002-03
- 12   Adam Vinatieri, New England, 1996-2005; Indianapolis, 2006-07

Most Points, Rookie, Season
- 144   Kevin Butler, Chicago, 1985 (51-pat, 31-fg)
- 141   Mason Crosby, Green Bay, 2007, (48-pat, 31-fg)
- 132   Gale Sayers, Chicago, 1965 (22-td)

Most Points, Game
- 40   Ernie Nevers, Chi. Cardinals vs. Chi. Bears, Nov. 28, 1929 (6-td, 4-pat)
- 36   Dub Jones, Cleveland vs. Chi. Bears, Nov. 25, 1951 (6-td)
-    Gale Sayers, Chicago vs. San Francisco, Dec. 12, 1965 (6-td)
- 33   Paul Hornung, Green Bay vs. Baltimore, Oct. 8, 1961 (4-td, 6-pat, 1-fg)

Most Consecutive Games Scoring
- 360   Morten Andersen, New Orleans, 1983-1994; Atlanta, 1995-2000; N.Y. Giants, 2001; Kansas City, 2002-03; Minnesota, 2004; Atlanta, 2006-07 (current)
- 236   Jason Elam, Denver, 1993-2007 (current)
- 186   Jim Breech, Oakland, 1979; Cincinnati, 1980-1992

TOUCHDOWNS
Most Seasons Leading League
- 8   Don Hutson, Green Bay, 1935-38, 1941-44
- 3   Jim Brown, Cleveland, 1958-59, 1963
-    Lance Alworth, San Diego, 1964-66
-    Emmitt Smith, Dallas, 1992, 1994-95
- 2   By many players

Most Consecutive Seasons Leading League
- 4   Don Hutson, Green Bay, 1935-38, 1941-44
- 3   Lance Alworth, San Diego, 1964-66

2   By many players

Most Touchdowns, Career
208 Jerry Rice, San Francisco, 1985-2000;
     Oakland, 2001-04; Seattle, 2004
     (10-r, 197-p, 1-ret)
175 Emmitt Smith, Dallas, 1990-2002; Arizona, 2003-04
     (164-r, 11-p)
145 Marcus Allen, L.A. Raiders, 1982-1992; Kansas City,
     1993-97 (123-r, 21-p, 1-ret)

Most Touchdowns, Season
31   LaDainian Tomlinson, San Diego, 2006 (28-r, 3-p)
28   Shaun Alexander, Seattle, 2005 (27-r, 1-p)
27   Priest Holmes, Kansas City, 2003 (27-r)

Most Touchdowns, Rookie, Season
22   Gale Sayers, Chicago, 1965 (14-r, 6-p, 2-ret)
20   Eric Dickerson, L.A. Rams, 1983 (18-r, 2-p)
17   Randy Moss, Minnesota, 1998 (17-p)
     Fred Taylor, Jacksonville, 1998 (14-r, 3-p)
     Edgerrin James, Indianapolis, 1999 (13-r, 4-p)
     Clinton Portis, Denver, 2002 (15-r, 2-p)

Most Touchdowns, Game
6   Ernie Nevers, Chi. Cardinals vs. Chi. Bears,
     Nov. 28, 1929 (6-r)
     Dub Jones, Cleveland vs. Chi. Bears, Nov. 25, 1951
     (4-r, 2-p)
     Gale Sayers, Chicago vs. San Francisco, Dec. 12, 1965
     (4-r, 1-p, 1-ret)
5   Jimmy Conzelman, Rhode Island vs. Evansville,
     Oct. 15, 1922 (5-r)
     Bob Shaw, Chi. Cardinals vs. Baltimore, Oct. 2, 1950
     (5-p)
     Jim Brown, Cleveland vs. Baltimore, Nov. 1, 1959 (5-r)
     Abner Haynes, Dall. Texans vs. Oakland,
     Nov. 26, 1961 (4-r, 1-p)
     Billy Cannon, Houston vs. N.Y. Titans, Dec. 10, 1961
     (3-r, 2-p)
     Cookie Gilchrist, Buffalo vs. N.Y. Jets, Dec. 8, 1963 (5-r)
     Paul Hornung, Green Bay vs. Baltimore,
     Dec. 12, 1965 (3-r, 2-p)
     Kellen Winslow, San Diego vs. Oakland,
     Nov. 22, 1981 (5-p)
     Jerry Rice, San Francisco vs. Atlanta, Oct. 14, 1990
     (5-p)
     James Stewart, Jacksonville vs. Philadelphia,
     Oct. 12, 1997 (5-r)
     Shaun Alexander, Seattle vs. Minnesota,
     Sept. 29, 2002 (4-r, 1-p)
     Clinton Portis, Denver vs. Kansas City, Dec. 7, 2003
     (5-r)
4   By many players. Last time:
     Randy Moss, New England vs. Buffalo,
     Nov. 18, 2007 (4-p)
     Terrell Owens, Dallas vs. Washington,
     Nov. 18, 2007 (4-p)

Most Consecutive Games Scoring Touchdowns
18   Lenny Moore, Baltimore, 1963-65
     LaDainian Tomlinson, San Diego, 2004-05
14   O.J. Simpson, Buffalo, 1975
13   John Riggins, Washington, 1982-83
     George Rogers, Washington, 1985-86
     Jerry Rice, San Francisco, 1986-87

POINTS AFTER TOUCHDOWN
Most Seasons Leading League
8   George Blanda, Chi. Bears, 1956; Houston,
     1961-62; Oakland, 1967-69, 1972, 1974
4   Bob Waterfield, Cleveland, 1945; Los Angeles, 1946,
     1950, 1952
3   Earl (Dutch) Clark, Portsmouth, 1932; Detroit,
     1935-36 Jack Manders, Chi. Bears, 1933-35

Don Hutson, Green Bay, 1941-42, 1945

Most (Kicking) Points After Touchdown Attempted, Career
959 George Blanda, Chi. Bears, 1949, 1950-58; Baltimore,
     1950; Houston, 1960-66; Oakland, 1967-1975
859 Morten Andersen, New Orleans, 1982-1994;
     Atlanta, 1995-2000; N.Y. Giants, 2001;
     Kansas City, 2002-03; Minnesota, 2004;
     Atlanta, 2006-07
827 Gary Anderson, Pittsburgh, 1982-1994; Philadelphia
     1995-96; San Francisco, 1997; Minnesota,
     1998-2002; Tennessee, 2003-04

Most (Kicking) Points After Touchdown Attempted, Season
74   Stephen Gostkowski, New England, 2007
70   Uwe von Schamann, Miami, 1984
65   George Blanda, Houston, 1961

Most (Kicking) Points After Touchdown Attempted, Game
10   Charlie Gogolak, Washington vs. N.Y. Giants,
     Nov. 27, 1966
9   Pat Harder, Chi. Cardinals vs. N.Y. Giants,
     Oct. 17, 1948; vs. N.Y. Bulldogs, Nov. 13, 1949
     Bob Waterfield, Los Angeles vs. Baltimore,
     Oct. 22, 1950
     Bob Thomas, Chicago vs. Green Bay, Dec. 7, 1980
8   By many players

Most (One-Point) Points After Touchdown, Career
943 George Blanda, Chi. Bears, 1949, 1950-58; Baltimore,
     1950; Houston, 1960-66; Oakland, 1967-1975
849 Morten Andersen, New Orleans, 1982-1994;
     Atlanta, 1995-2000; N.Y. Giants, 2001;
     Kansas City, 2002-03; Minnesota, 2004,
     Atlanta, 2006-07
820 Gary Anderson, Pittsburgh, 1982-1994; Philadelphia
     1995-96; San Francisco, 1997; Minnesota,
     1998-2002; Tennessee, 2003-04

Most (One-Point) Points After Touchdown, Season
74   Stephen Gostkowski, New England, 2007
66   Uwe von Schamann, Miami, 1984
64   George Blanda, Houston, 1961
     Jeff Wilkins, St. Louis, 1999

Most (One-Point) Points After Touchdown, Game
9   Pat Harder, Chi. Cardinals vs. N.Y. Giants,
     Oct. 17, 1948
     Bob Waterfield, Los Angeles vs. Baltimore,
     Oct. 22, 1950
     Charlie Gogolak, Washington vs. N.Y. Giants,
     Nov. 27, 1966
8   By many players

Most Consecutive (Kicking) Points After Touchdown
371 Jason Elam, Denver, 1993-2002
     Jeff Wilkins, St. Louis, 1999-2007 (current)
348 Matt Stover, Baltimore, 1996-2007 (current)
301 Norm Johnson, Atlanta, 1991-94; Pittsburgh,
     1995-98; Philadelphia, 1999

Highest (Kicking) Points After Touchdown Percentage, Career
(200 points after touchdown)
100.000 Rian Lindell, Seattle, 2000-02; Buffalo, 2003-07
         (248-248)
99.554   Josh Brown, Seatle, 2003-07 (223-224)
99.519   Nate Kaeding, San Diego, 2004-07 (207-208)

Most (Kicking) Points After Touchdown, No Misses, Season
74   Stephen Gostkowski, New England, 2007
64   Jeff Wilkins, St. Louis, 1999
59   Gary Anderson, Minnesota, 1998

Most (Kicking) Points After Touchdown, No Misses, Game
9   Pat Harder, Chi. Cardinals vs. N.Y. Giants,
     Oct. 17, 1948
     Bob Waterfield, Los Angeles vs. Baltimore,
     Oct. 22, 1950
8   By many players

Most Two-Point Conversions, Career
Two-point conversions include AFL (1960-69) and NFL (since 1994).
- 7   Marshall Faulk, Indianapolis, 1994-98; St. Louis, 1999-2005
- 6   Terance Mathis, Atlanta, 1994-2001; Pittsburgh, 2002
- 5   Cris Carter, Minnesota, 1994-2001; Miami, 2002
- Rob Moore, N.Y. Jets, 1994; Arizona, 1995-99
- Willie Jackson, Jacksonville, 1995-97; Cincinnati, 1998-99; New Orleans, 2000-01; Washington, 2002
- Keenan McCardell, Cleveland, 1994-95; Jacksonville, 1996-2001; Tampa Bay, 2002-03; San Diego, 2004-06, Washington, 2007
- Marvin Harrison, Indianapolis, 1996-2007
- Marcus Pollard, Indianapolis, 1995-2004; Detroit, 2005-06, Seattle, 2007
- Todd Heap, Baltimore, 2001-07
- Hines Ward, Pittsburgh, 1998-2007

Most Two-Point Conversions, Season
- 4   Todd Heap, Baltimore, 2003
- 3   Gino Cappelletti, Boston, 1960
- Richie Lucas, Buffalo, 1961
- Ronnie Harmon, San Diego, 1994
- Haywood Jeffires, Houston, 1994
- Tom Tupa, Cleveland, 1994
- Terance Mathis, Atlanta, 1995
- Lamar Smith, Seattle, 1996
- Cris Carter, Minnesota, 1997
- Terrell Davis, Denver, 1997
- James Stewart, Detroit, 2000
- Hines Ward, Pittsburgh, 2002
- Brian Finneran, Atlanta, 2005
- Reggie Bush, New Orleans, 2007
- 2   By many players

Most Two-Point Conversions, Game
- 2   Brett Perriman, Detroit vs. Green Bay, Nov. 6, 1994
- Michael Jackson, Baltimore vs. New England, Oct. 6, 1996
- Terrell Davis, Denver vs. Atlanta, Sept. 28, 1997
- Charles Johnson, Pittsburgh vs. Tennessee, Nov. 1, 1998
- Marshall Faulk, St. Louis vs. Atlanta, Oct. 15, 2000
- Todd Heap, Baltimore vs. Cincinnati, Oct. 19, 2003
- Reggie Bush, New Orleans vs. St. Louis, Nov. 11, 2007
- Tarvaris Jackson, Minnesota vs. Denver, Dec. 30, 2007 (OT)

FIELD GOALS
Most Seasons Leading League
- 5   Lou Groza, Cleveland, 1950, 1952-54, 1957
- 4   Jack Manders, Chi. Bears, 1933-34, 1936-37
- Ward Cuff, N.Y. Giants, 1938-39, 1943; Green Bay, 1947
- Mark Moseley, Washington, 1976-77, 1979, 1982
- 3   Bob Waterfield, Los Angeles, 1947, 1949, 1951
- Gino Cappelletti, Boston, 1961, 1963-64
- Fred Cox, Minnesota, 1965, 1969-1970
- Jan Stenerud, Kansas City, 1967, 1970, 1975

Most Consecutive Seasons Leading League
- 3   Lou Groza, Cleveland, 1952-54
- 2   Jack Manders, Chi. Bears, 1933-34
- Armand Niccolai, Pittsburgh, 1935-36
- Jack Manders, Chi. Bears, 1936-37
- Ward Cuff, N.Y. Giants, 1938-39
- Clark Hinkle, Green Bay, 1940-41
- Cliff Patton, Philadelphia, 1948-49
- Gino Cappelletti, Boston, 1963-64
- Jim Turner, N.Y. Jets, 1968-69
- Fred Cox, Minnesota, 1969-1970

Mark Moseley, Washington, 1976-77
Chip Lohmiller, Washington, 1991-92
Pete Stoyanovich, Miami, 1991-92

Most Field Goals Attempted, Career
- 709   Morten Andersen, New Orleans, 1982-1994; Atlanta, 1995-2000; N.Y. Giants, 2001; Kansas City, 2002-03; Minnesota, 2004; Atlanta, 2006-07
- 672   Gary Anderson, Pittsburgh, 1982-1994; Philadelphia 1995-96; San Francisco, 1997; Minnesota, 1998-2002; Tennessee, 2003-04
- 641   George Blanda, Chi. Bears, 1949, 1950-58; Baltimore, 1950; Houston, 1960-66; Oakland, 1967-1975

Most Field Goals Attempted, Season
- 49   Bruce Gossett, Los Angeles, 1966
- Curt Knight, Washington, 1971
- 48   Chester Marcol, Green Bay, 1972
- 47   Jim Turner, N.Y. Jets, 1969
- David Ray, Los Angeles, 1973
- Mark Moseley, Washington, 1983

Most Field Goals Attempted, Game
- 9   Jim Bakken, St. Louis vs. Pittsburgh, Sept. 24, 1967
- 8   Lou Michaels, Pittsburgh vs. St. Louis, Dec. 2, 1962
- Garo Yepremian, Detroit vs. Minnesota, Nov. 13, 1966
- Jim Turner, N.Y. Jets vs. Buffalo, Nov. 3, 1968
- Billy Cundiff, Dallas vs. N.Y. Giants, Sept. 15, 2003 (OT)
- Rob Bironas, Tennessee vs. Houston, Oct. 21, 2007
- 7   By many players

Most Field Goals, Career
- 565   Morten Andersen, New Orleans, 1982-1994; Atlanta, 1995-2000; N.Y. Giants, 2001; Kansas City, 2002-03; Minnesota, 2004; Atlanta, 2006-07
- 538   Gary Anderson, Pittsburgh, 1982-1994; Philadelphia, 1995-96; San Francisco, 1997; Minnesota, 1998-2002; Tennessee, 2003-04
- 435   Matt Stover, Cleveland, 1991-95; Baltimore, 1996-2007

Most Field Goals, Season
- 40   Neil Rackers, Arizona, 2005
- 39   Olindo Mare, Miami, 1999
- Jeff Wilkins, St. Louis, 2003
- 37   John Kasay, Carolina, 1996
- Mike Vanderjagt, Indianapolis, 2003

Most Field Goals, Rookie, Season
- 35   Ali Haji-Sheikh, N.Y. Giants, 1983
- 34   Richie Cunningham, Dallas, 1997
- 33   Chester Marcol, Green Bay, 1972

Most Field Goals, Game
- 8   Rob Bironas, Tennessee vs. Houston, Oct. 21, 2007
- 7   Jim Bakken, St. Louis vs. Pittsburgh, Sept. 24, 1967
- Rich Karlis, Minnesota vs. L.A. Rams, Nov. 5, 1989 (OT)
- Chris Boniol, Dallas vs. Green Bay, Nov. 18, 1996
- Billy Cundiff, Dallas vs. N.Y. Giants, Sept. 15, 2003 (OT)
- Shayne Graham, Cincinnati vs. Baltimore, Nov. 11, 2007
- 6   By many players

Most Field Goals, One Quarter
- 4   Garo Yepremian, Detroit vs. Minnesota, Nov. 13, 1966 (second quarter)
- Curt Knight, Washington vs. N.Y. Giants, Nov. 15, 1970 (second quarter)
- Roger Ruzek, Dallas vs. N.Y. Giants, Nov. 2, 1987 (fourth quarter)
- Cary Blanchard, Indianapolis vs. Buffalo, Sept. 21 1997 (second quarter)
- Sebastian Janikowski, Oakland vs. Chicago, Oct. 5, 2003 (second quarter)
- Jeff Wilkins, St. Louis vs. Baltimore, Nov. 9, 2003 (fourth quarter)

Lawrence Tynes, Kansas City vs. New England,
  Nov. 27, 2005 (second quarter)
Shayne Graham, Cincinnati vs. Baltimore,
  Nov. 11, 2007 (fourth quarter)
3   By many players

Most Consecutive Games Scoring Field Goals
38   Matt Stover, Baltimore, 1999-2001
31   Fred Cox, Minnesota, 1968-1970
28   Jim Turner, N.Y. Jets, 1970; Denver, 1971-72
     Chip Lohmiller, Washington, 1988-1990

Most Consecutive Field Goals
42   Mike Vanderjagt, Indianapolis, 2002-04
40   Gary Anderson, San Francisco, 1997; Minnesota,
     1998
36   Matt Stover, Baltimore, 2005-06

Longest Field Goal
63   Tom Dempsey, New Orleans vs. Detroit, Nov. 8, 1970
     Jason Elam, Denver vs. Jacksonville, Oct. 25, 1998
62   Matt Bryant, Tampa Bay vs. Philadelphia,
     Oct. 22, 2006
60   Steve Cox, Cleveland vs. Cincinnati, Oct. 21, 1984
     Morten Andersen, New Orleans vs. Chicago,
     Oct. 27, 1991
     Rob Bironas, Tennessee vs. Indianapolis,
     Dec. 3, 2006

Highest Field Goal Percentage, Career (100 field goals)
86.47   Mike Vanderjagt, Indianapolis, 1998-2005;
        Dallas, 2006 (230-266)
85.39   Shayne Graham, Buffalo, 2001; Carolina, 2002;
        Cincinnati, 2003-07 (152-178)
83.82   Matt Stover, Cleveland, 1991-95; Baltimore,
        1996-2007 (435-519)

Highest Field Goal Percentage, Season (Qualifiers)
100.00   Tony Zendejas, L.A. Rams, 1991 (17-17)
         Gary Anderson, Minnesota, 1998 (35-35)
         Jeff Wilkins, St. Louis, 2000 (17-17)
         Mike Vanderjagt, Indianapolis, 2003 (37-37)
96.43   Chris Boniol, Dallas, 1995 (28-27)
96.30   Norm Johnson, Atlanta, 1993 (27-26)
         Pete Stoyanovich, Kansas City, 1997 (27-26)

Most Field Goals, No Misses, Game
8   Rob Bironas, Tennesee vs. Houston, Oct. 21, 2007
7   Rich Karlis, Minnesota vs. L.A. Rams, Nov. 5, 1989
    (OT)
    Chris Boniol, Dallas vs. Green Bay, Nov. 18, 1996
    Shayne Graham, Cincinnati vs. Baltimore,
    Nov. 11, 2007
6   By many players

Most Field Goals, 50 or More Yards, Career
40   Morten Andersen, New Orleans, 1982-1994;
     Atlanta, 1995-2000; N.Y. Giants, 2001;
     Kansas City, 2002-03; Minnesota, 2004;
     Atlanta, 2006-07
37   Jason Elam, Denver, 1993-2007
35   John Kasay, Seattle, 1991-94; Carolina, 1995-2007

Most Field Goals, 50 or More Yards, Season
8   Morten Andersen, Atlanta, 1995
6   Dean Biasucci, Indianapolis, 1988
    Chris Jacke, Green Bay, 1993
    Tony Zendejas, L.A. Rams, 1993
    Mike Vanderjagt, Indianapolis, 1998
    Neil Rackers, Arizona, 2005
    Sebastian Janikowski, Oakland, 2007
5   Fred Steinfort, Denver, 1980
    Norm Johnson, Seattle, 1986
    Kevin Butler, Chicago, 1993
    Jason Elam, Denver, 1995
    Cary Blanchard, Indianapolis, 1996
    Jason Elam, Denver, 1999
    Martin Gramatica, Tampa Bay, 2000, 2002

Paul Edinger, Chicago, 2002
Neil Rackers, Arizona, 2004
Josh Brown, Seattle, 2005
Kris Brown, Houston, 2007

Most Field Goals, 50 or More Yards, Game
3   Morten Andersen, Atlanta vs. New Orleans,
    Dec. 10, 1995
    Neil Rackers, Arizona vs. Seattle, Oct. 24, 2004
    Kris Brown, Houston vs. Miami, Oct. 7, 2007
2   By many players. Last time: Josh Brown,
    Seattle vs. Atlanta, Dec. 30, 2007

SAFETIES
Most Safeties, Career
4   Ted Hendricks, Baltimore, 1969-1973; Green Bay,
    1974; Oakland, 1975-1981; L.A. Raiders, 1982-83
    Doug English, Detroit, 1975-79, 1981-85
3   Bill McPeak, Pittsburgh, 1949-1957
    Charlie Krueger, San Francisco, 1959-1973
    Ernie Stautner, Pittsburgh, 1950-1963
    Jim Katcavage, N.Y. Giants, 1956-1968
    Roger Brown, Detroit, 1960-66; Los Angeles,
    1967-69
    Bruce Maher, Detroit, 1960-67; N.Y. Giants, 1968-69
    Ron McDole, St. Louis, 1961; Houston, 1962;
    Buffalo, 1963-1970; Washington, 1971-78
    Alan Page, Minnesota, 1967-1978; Chicago,
    1979-1981
    Lyle Alzado, Denver, 1971-78; Cleveland,
    1979-1981; L.A. Raiders, 1982-85
    Rulon Jones, Denver, 1980-88
    Steve McMichael, New England, 1980; Chicago,
    1981-1993; Green Bay, 1994
    Kevin Greene, L.A. Rams, 1985-1992; Pittsburgh,
    1993-95; Carolina, 1996, 1998-99;
    San Francisco, 1997
    Burt Grossman, San Diego, 1989-1993;
    Philadelphia, 1994
    Eric Swann, Phoenix, 1991-93; Arizona, 1994-99;
    Carolina, 2000
    Dan Saleaumua, Detroit, 1987-88; Kansas City,
    1989-1996; Seattle, 1997-98
    Derrick Thomas, Kansas City, 1989-1999
    Bryant Young, San Francisco, 1994-2007
2   By many players

Most Safeties, Season
2   Tom Nash, Green Bay, 1932
    Roger Brown, Detroit, 1962
    Ron McDole, Buffalo, 1964
    Alan Page, Minnesota, 1971
    Fred Dryer, Los Angeles, 1973
    Benny Barnes, Dallas, 1973
    James Young, Houston, 1977
    Doug English, Detroit, 1983
    Don Blackmon, New England, 1985
    Tim Harris, Green Bay, 1988
    Brian Jordan, Atlanta, 1991
    Burt Grossman, San Diego, 1992
    Rod Stephens, Seattle, 1993
    Bryant Young, San Francisco, 1996

Most Safeties, Game
2   Fred Dryer, Los Angeles vs. Green Bay,
    Oct. 21, 1973

RUSHING
Most Seasons Leading League
8   Jim Brown, Cleveland, 1957-1961, 1963-65
4   Steve Van Buren, Philadelphia, 1945, 1947-49
    O.J. Simpson, Buffalo, 1972-73, 1975-76

    Eric Dickerson, L.A. Rams, 1983-84, 1986;
      Indianapolis, 1988
    Emmitt Smith, Dallas, 1991-93, 1995
    Barry Sanders, Detroit, 1990, 1994, 1996-97
  3 Earl Campbell, Houston, 1978-1980

Most Consecutive Seasons Leading League
  5 Jim Brown, Cleveland, 1957-1961
  3 Steve Van Buren, Philadelphia, 1947-49
    Jim Brown, Cleveland, 1963-65
    Earl Campbell, Houston, 1978-1980
    Emmitt Smith, Dallas, 1991-93
  2 Bill Paschal, N.Y. Giants, 1943-44
    Joe Perry, San Francisco, 1953-54
    Jim Nance, Boston, 1966-67
    Leroy Kelly, Cleveland, 1967-68
    O.J. Simpson, Buffalo, 1972-73; 1975-76
    Eric Dickerson, L.A. Rams, 1983-84
    Barry Sanders, Detroit, 1996-97
    Edgerrin James, Indianapolis, 1999-2000
    LaDainian Tomlinson, San Diego, 2006-07

ATTEMPTS
Most Seasons Leading League
  6 Jim Brown, Cleveland, 1958-59, 1961, 1963-65
  4 Steve Van Buren, Philadelphia, 1947-1950
    Walter Payton, Chicago, 1976-79
  3 Cookie Gilchrist, Buffalo, 1963-64; Denver, 1965
    Jim Nance, Boston, 1966-67, 1969
    O.J. Simpson, Buffalo, 1973-75
    Eric Dickerson, L.A. Rams, 1983, 1986;
      Indianapolis, 1988
    Emmitt Smith, Dallas, 1991, 1994-95

Most Consecutive Seasons Leading League
  4 Steve Van Buren, Philadelphia, 1947-1950
    Walter Payton, Chicago, 1976-79
  3 Jim Brown, Cleveland, 1963-65
    Cookie Gilchrist, Buffalo, 1963-64; Denver, 1965
    O.J. Simpson, Buffalo, 1973-75
  2 By many players

Most Attempts, Career
  4,409 Emmitt Smith, Dallas, 1990-2002; Arizona, 2003-04
  3,838 Walter Payton, Chicago, 1975-1987
  3,518 Curtis Martin, New England, 1995-97; N.Y. Jets,
      1998-2005

Most Attempts, Season
  416 Larry Johnson, Kansas City, 2006
  410 Jamal Anderson, Atlanta, 1998
  407 James Wilder, Tampa Bay, 1984

Most Attempts, Rookie, Season
  390 Eric Dickerson, L.A. Rams, 1983
  378 George Rogers, New Orleans, 1981
  369 Edgerrin James, Indianapolis, 1999

Most Attempts, Game
  45 Jamie Morris, Washington vs. Cincinnati,
      Dec. 17, 1988 (OT)
  43 Butch Woolfolk, N.Y. Giants vs. Philadelphia,
      Nov. 20, 1983
    James Wilder, Tampa Bay vs. Green Bay,
      Sept. 30, 1984 (OT)
    Rudi Johnson, Cincinnati vs. Houston, Nov. 9, 2003
  42 James Wilder, Tampa Bay vs. Pittsburgh,
      Oct. 30, 1983
    Terrell Davis, Denver vs. Buffalo, Oct. 26, 1997 (OT)
    Ricky Williams, Miami vs. Buffalo, Sept. 21, 2003

YARDS GAINED
Most Yards Gained, Career
  18,355 Emmitt Smith, Dallas, 1990-2002; Arizona, 2003-04
  16,726 Walter Payton, Chicago, 1975-1987
  15,269 Barry Sanders, Detroit, 1989-1998

Most Seasons, 1,000 or More Yards Rushing
  11 Emmitt Smith, Dallas, 1991-2001
  10 Walter Payton, Chicago, 1976-1981, 1983-86
    Barry Sanders, Detroit, 1989-1998
    Curtis Martin, New England, 1995-97; N.Y. Jets,
      1998-2004
  8 Franco Harris, Pittsburgh, 1972, 1974-79, 1983
    Tony Dorsett, Dallas, 1977-1981, 1983-85
    Thurman Thomas, Buffalo, 1989-1996
    Jerome Bettis, L.A. Rams, 1993-94; Pittsburgh,
      1996-2001

Most Consecutive Seasons, 1,000 or More Yards Rushing
  11 Emmitt Smith, Dallas, 1991-2001
  10 Barry Sanders, Detroit, 1989-1998
    Curtis Martin, New England, 1995-97; N.Y. Jets,
      1998-2004
  8 Thurman Thomas, Buffalo, 1989-1996

Most Yards Gained, Season
  2,105 Eric Dickerson, L.A. Rams, 1984
  2,066 Jamal Lewis, Baltimore, 2003
  2,053 Barry Sanders, Detroit, 1997

Most Yards Gained, Rookie, Season
  1,808 Eric Dickerson, L.A. Rams, 1983
  1,674 George Rogers, New Orleans, 1981
  1,605 Ottis Anderson, St. Louis, 1979

Most Yards Gained, Game
  296 Adrian Peterson, Minnesota vs. San Diego,
      Nov. 4, 2007
  295 Jamal Lewis, Baltimore vs. Cleveland, Sept. 14, 2003
  278 Corey Dillon, Cincinnati vs. Denver, Oct. 22, 2000

Most Games, 200 or More Yards Rushing, Career
  6 O.J. Simpson, Buffalo, 1969-1977; San Francisco,
      1978-79
  5 Tiki Barber, N.Y. Giants, 1997-2006
  4 Jim Brown, Cleveland, 1957-1965
    Earl Campbell, Houston, 1978-1984; New Orleans,
      1984-85
    Barry Sanders, Detroit, 1989-1998
    LaDainian Tomlinson, San Diego, 2001-07

Most Games, 200 or More Yards Rushing, Season
  4 Earl Campbell, Houston, 1980
  3 O.J. Simpson, Buffalo, 1973
    Tiki Barber, N.Y. Giants, 2005
  2 Jim Brown, Cleveland, 1963
    O.J. Simpson, Buffalo, 1976
    Walter Payton, Chicago, 1977
    Eric Dickerson, L.A. Rams, 1984
    Greg Bell, L.A. Rams, 1989
    Terrell Davis, Denver, 1997
    Barry Sanders, Detroit, 1997
    Corey Dillon, Cincinnati, 2000
    Marshall Faulk, St. Louis, 2000
    LaDainian Tomlinson, San Diego, 2002
    Ricky Williams, Miami, 2002
    Jamal Lewis, Baltimore, 2003
    LaDainian Tomlinson, San Diego, 2003
    Larry Johnson, Kansas City, 2005
    Willie Parker, Pittsburgh, 2006
    Adrian Peterson, Minnesota, 2007

Most Consecutive Games, 200 or More Yards Rushing
  2 O.J. Simpson, Buffalo, 1973, 1976
    Earl Campbell, Houston, 1980
    Ricky Williams, Miami, 2002

Most Games, 100 or More Yards Rushing, Career
  78 Emmitt Smith, Dallas, 1990-2002; Arizona, 2003-04
  77 Walter Payton, Chicago, 1975-1987
  76 Barry Sanders, Detroit, 1989-1998

Most Games, 100 or More Yards Rushing, Season
  14 Barry Sanders, Detroit, 1997

12 Eric Dickerson, L.A. Rams, 1984
    Barry Foster, Pittsburgh, 1992
    Jamal Anderson, Atlanta, 1998
    Jamal Lewis, Baltimore, 2003
11 O.J. Simpson, Buffalo, 1973
    Earl Campbell, Houston, 1979
    Marcus Allen, L.A. Raiders, 1985
    Eric Dickerson, L.A. Rams, 1986
    Emmitt Smith, Dallas, 1995
    Terrell Davis, Denver, 1998
    Shaun Alexander, Seattle, 2005
    Larry Johnson, Kansas City, 2006

Most Consecutive Games, 100 or More Yards Rushing
14 Barry Sanders, Detroit, 1997
11 Marcus Allen, L.A. Raiders, 1985-86
 9 Walter Payton, Chicago, 1985
    Fred Taylor, Jacksonville, 2000
    Deuce McAllister, New Orleans, 2003
    Larry Johnson, Kansas City, 2005
    LaDainian Tomlinson, San Diego, 2006

Longest Run From Scrimmage
99 Tony Dorsett, Dallas vs. Minnesota, Jan. 3, 1983
    (TD)
98 Ahman Green, Green Bay vs. Denver, Dec. 28, 2003
    (TD)
97 Andy Uram, Green Bay vs. Chi. Cardinals,
    Oct. 8, 1939 (TD)
    Bob Gage, Pittsburgh vs. Chi. Bears, Dec. 4, 1949
    (TD)

AVERAGE GAIN
Highest Average Gain, Career (750 attempts)
6.36 Randall Cunningham, Philadelphia, 1985-1995;
    Minnesota, 1997-99; Dallas, 2000; Baltimore,
    2001 (775-4,928)
5.22 Jim Brown, Cleveland, 1957-1965 (2,359-12,312)
5.14 Eugene (Mercury) Morris, Miami, 1969-1975;
    San Diego, 1976 (804-4,133)

Highest Average Gain, Season (Qualifiers)
8.45 Michael Vick, Atlanta, 2006 (123-1,039)
8.44 Beattie Feathers, Chi. Bears, 1934 (119-1,004)
7.98 Randall Cunningham, Philadelphia, 1990 (118-942)

Highest Average Gain, Game (10 attempts)
17.30 Michael Vick, Atlanta vs. Minnesota, Dec. 1, 2002
    (OT) (10-173)
17.09 Marion Motley, Cleveland vs. Pittsburgh,
    Oct. 29, 1950 (11-188)
16.70 Bill Grimes, Green Bay vs. N.Y. Yanks, Oct. 8, 1950
    (10-167)

TOUCHDOWNS
Most Seasons Leading League
5 Jim Brown, Cleveland, 1957-59, 1963, 1965
4 Steve Van Buren, Philadelphia, 1945, 1947-49
3 Abner Haynes, Dall. Texans, 1960-62
   Cookie Gilchrist, Buffalo, 1962-64
   Paul Lowe, L.A. Chargers, 1960; San Diego, 1961,
   1965
   Leroy Kelly, Cleveland, 1966-68
   Emmitt Smith, Dallas, 1992, 1994-95
   LaDainian Tomlinson, San Diego, 2004, 2006-07

Most Consecutive Seasons Leading League
3 Steve Van Buren, Philadelphia, 1947-49
   Jim Brown, Cleveland, 1957-59
   Abner Haynes, Dall. Texans, 1960-62
   Cookie Gilchrist, Buffalo, 1962-64
   Leroy Kelly, Cleveland, 1966-68

Most Touchdowns, Career
164 Emmitt Smith, Dallas, 1990-2002; Arizona, 2003-04

123 Marcus Allen, L.A. Raiders, 1982-1992; Kansas City,
    1993-97
115 LaDainian Tomlinson, San Diego, 2001-07

Most Touchdowns, Season
28 LaDainian Tomlinson, San Diego, 2006
27 Priest Holmes, Kansas City, 2003
    Shaun Alexander, Seattle, 2005
25 Emmitt Smith, Dallas, 1995

Most Touchdowns, Rookie, Season
18 Eric Dickerson, L.A. Rams, 1983
15 Ickey Woods, Cincinnati, 1988
    Mike Anderson, Denver, 2000
    Clinton Portis, Denver, 2002
14 Gale Sayers, Chicago, 1965
    Barry Sanders, Detroit, 1989
    Curtis Martin, New England, 1995
    Fred Taylor, Jacksonville, 1998

Most Touchdowns, Game
6 Ernie Nevers, Chi. Cardinals vs. Chi. Bears,
   Nov. 28, 1929
5 Jimmy Conzelman, Rhode Island vs. Evansville,
   Oct. 15, 1922
   Jim Brown, Cleveland vs. Baltimore, Nov. 1, 1959
   Cookie Gilchrist, Buffalo vs. N.Y. Jets, Dec. 8, 1963
   James Stewart, Jacksonville vs. Philadelphia,
   Oct. 12, 1997
   Clinton Portis, Denver vs. Kansas City, Dec. 7, 2003
4 By many players

Most Consecutive Games Rushing for Touchdowns
18 LaDainian Tomlinson, San Diego, 2004-05
13 John Riggins, Washington, 1982-83
    George Rogers, Washington, 1985-86
11 Lenny Moore, Baltimore, 1963-64
    Emmitt Smith, Dallas, 1994-95
    Emmitt Smith, Dallas, 1995
    Priest Holmes, Kansas City, 2002

PASSING
Most Seasons Leading League
6 Sammy Baugh, Washington, 1937, 1940, 1943,
   1945, 1947, 1949
   Steve Young San Francisco, 1991-94, 1996-97
4 Len Dawson, Dall. Texans; 1962; Kansas City, 1964,
   1966, 1968
   Roger Staubach, Dallas, 1971, 1973, 1978-79
   Ken Anderson, Cincinnati, 1974-75, 1981-82
3 Arnie Herber, Green Bay, 1932, 1934, 1936
   Norm Van Brocklin, Los Angeles, 1950, 1952, 1954
   Bart Starr, Green Bay, 1962, 1964, 1966
   Peyton Manning, Indianapolis, 2004-06

Most Consecutive Seasons Leading League
4 Steve Young, San Francisco, 1991-94
3 Peyton Manning, Indianapolis, 2004-06
2 Cecil Isbell, Green Bay, 1941-42
   Milt Plum, Cleveland, 1960-61
   Ken Anderson, Cincinnati, 1974-75, 1981-82
   Roger Staubach, Dallas, 1978-79
   Steve Young, San Francisco, 1996-97

PASSER RATING
Highest Passer Rating, Career (1,500 attempts)
96.8 Steve Young, Tampa Bay, 1985-86; San Francisco,
    1987-1999
94.7 Peyton Manning, Indianapolis, 1998-2007
93.2 Kurt Warner, St. Louis, 1998-2003; N.Y. Giants,
    2004; Arizona, 2005-07

Highest Passer Rating, Season (Qualifiers)
121.1 Peyton Manning, Indianapolis, 2004
117.2 Tom Brady, New England, 2007
112.8 Steve Young, San Francisco, 1994

Highest Passer Rating, Rookie, Season (Qualifiers)
- 98.1   Ben Roethlisberger, Pittsburgh, 2004
- 96.0   Dan Marino, Miami, 1983
- 88.2   Greg Cook, Cincinnati, 1969

ATTEMPTS
Most Seasons Leading League
- 5   Dan Marino, Miami, 1984, 1986, 1988, 1992, 1997
- 4   Sammy Baugh, Washington, 1937, 1943, 1947-48
  - Johnny Unitas, Baltimore, 1957, 1959-1961
  - George Blanda, Chi. Bears, 1953; Houston, 1963-65
- 3   Arnie Herber, Green Bay, 1932, 1934, 1936
  - Sonny Jurgensen, Washington, 1966-67, 1969
  - Drew Bledsoe, New England, 1994-96
  - Brett Favre, Green Bay, 1999, 2005-06

Most Consecutive Seasons Leading League
- 3   Johnny Unitas, Baltimore, 1959-1961
  - George Blanda, Houston, 1963-65
  - Drew Bledsoe, New England, 1994-96
- 2   By many players

Most Passes Attempted, Career
- 8,758   Brett Favre, Atlanta, 1991; Green Bay, 1992-2007
- 8,358   Dan Marino, Miami, 1983-1999
- 7,250   John Elway, Denver, 1983-1998

Most Passes Attempted, Season
- 691   Drew Bledsoe, New England, 1994
- 655   Warren Moon, Houston, 1991
- 652   Drew Brees, New Orleans, 2007

Most Passes Attempted, Rookie, Season
- 575   Peyton Manning, Indianapolis, 1998
- 540   Chris Weinke, Carolina, 2001
- 486   Rick Mirer, Seattle, 1993

Most Passes Attempted, Game
- 70   Drew Bledsoe, New England vs. Minnesota, Nov. 13, 1994 (OT)
- 69   Vinny Testaverde, N.Y. Jets vs. Baltimore, Dec. 24, 2000
- 68   George Blanda, Houston vs. Buffalo, Nov. 1, 1964
  - Jon Kitna, Cincinnati vs. Pittsburgh, Dec. 30, 2001 (OT)

COMPLETIONS
Most Seasons Leading League
- 6   Dan Marino, Miami, 1984-86, 1988, 1992, 1997
- 5   Sammy Baugh, Washington, 1937, 1943, 1945, 1947-48
- 4   George Blanda, Chi. Bears, 1953; Houston, 1963-65
  - Sonny Jurgensen, Philadelphia, 1961; Washington, 1966-67, 1969

Most Consecutive Seasons Leading League
- 3   George Blanda, Houston, 1963-65
  - Dan Marino, Miami, 1984-86
- 2   By many players

Most Passes Completed, Career
- 5,377   Brett Favre, Atlanta, 1991; Green Bay, 1992-2007
- 4,967   Dan Marino, Miami, 1983-1999
- 4,123   John Elway, Denver, 1983-1998

Most Passes Completed, Season
- 440   Drew Brees, New Orleans, 2007
- 418   Rich Gannon, Oakland, 2002
- 404   Warren Moon, Houston, 1991

Most Passes Completed, Rookie, Season
- 326   Peyton Manning, Indianapolis, 1998
- 293   Chris Weinke, Carolina, 2001
- 274   Rick Mirer, Seattle, 1993

Most Passes Completed, Game
- 45   Drew Bledsoe, New England vs. Minnesota, Nov. 13, 1994 (OT)
- 43   Rich Gannon, Oakland vs. Pittsburgh, Sept. 15, 2002

- 42   Richard Todd, N.Y. Jets vs. San Francisco, Sept. 21, 1980
  - Vinny Testaverde, N.Y. Jets vs. Seattle, Dec. 6, 1998

Most Consecutive Passes Completed
- 24   Donovan McNabb, Philadelphia vs. N.Y. Giants (10), Nov. 28, 2004; vs. Green Bay (14), Dec. 5, 2004
- 22   Joe Montana, San Francisco vs. Cleveland (5), Nov. 29, 1987; vs. Green Bay (17), Dec. 6, 1987
  - Mark Brunell, Washington vs. Houston, Sept. 24, 2006
  - David Carr, Houston vs. Buffalo, Nov. 19, 2006
- 21   Rich Gannon, Oakland vs. Denver, Nov. 11, 2002

COMPLETION PERCENTAGE
Most Seasons Leading League
- 8   Len Dawson, Dall. Texans, 1962; Kansas City, 1964-69, 1975
- 7   Sammy Baugh, Washington, 1940, 1942-43, 1945, 1947-49
- 5   Joe Montana, San Francisco, 1980-81, 1985, 1987, 1989
  - Steve Young, San Francisco, 1992, 1994-97

Most Consecutive Seasons Leading League
- 6   Len Dawson, Kansas City, 1964-69
- 4   Steve Young, San Francisco, 1994-97
- 3   Sammy Baugh, Washington, 1947-49
  - Otto Graham, Cleveland, 1953-55
  - Milt Plum, Cleveland, 1959-1961
  - Kurt Warner, St. Louis, 1999-2001

Highest Completion Percentage, Career (1,500 attempts)
- 65.61   Chad Pennington, N.Y. Jets, 2000-07 (1,919-1,259)
- 65.09   Kurt Warner, St. Louis, 1998-2003; N.Y. Giants, 2004; Arizona, 2005-07 (2,959-1,926)
- 64.28   Steve Young, Tampa Bay, 1985-86; San Francisco, 1987-1999 (4,149-2,667)

Highest Completion Percentage, Season (Qualifiers)
- 70.55   Ken Anderson, Cincinnati, 1982 (309-218)
- 70.33   Sammy Baugh, Washington, 1945 (182-128)
- 70.28   Steve Young, San Francisco, 1994 (461-324)

Highest Completion Percentage, Rookie, Season (Qualifiers)
- 66.44   Ben Roethlisberger, Pittsburgh, 2004 (295-196)
- 58.45   Dan Marino, Miami, 1983 (296-173)
- 57.18   Byron Leftwich, Jacksonville, 2003 (418-239)

Highest Completion Percentage, Game (20 attempts)
- 91.30   Vinny Testaverde, Cleveland vs. L.A. Rams, Dec. 26, 1993 (23-21)
- 90.91   Ken Anderson, Cincinnati vs. Pittsburgh, Nov. 10, 1974 (22-20)
- 90.48   Lynn Dickey, Green Bay vs. New Orleans, Dec. 13, 1981 (21-19)

YARDS GAINED
Most Seasons Leading League
- 5   Sonny Jurgensen, Philadelphia, 1961-62; Washington, 1966-67, 1969
  - Dan Marino, Miami, 1984-86, 1988, 1992
- 4   Sammy Baugh, Washington, 1937, 1940, 1947-48
  - Johnny Unitas, Baltimore, 1957, 1959-1960, 1963
  - Dan Fouts, San Diego, 1979-1982
- 3   Arnie Herber, Green Bay, 1932, 1934, 1936
  - Sid Luckman, Chi. Bears, 1943, 1945-46
  - John Brodie, San Francisco, 1965, 1968, 1970
  - John Hadl, San Diego, 1965, 1968, 1971
  - Joe Namath, N.Y. Jets, 1966-67, 1972

Most Consecutive Seasons Leading League
- 4   Dan Fouts, San Diego, 1979-1982
- 3   Dan Marino, Miami, 1984-86
- 2   By many players

Most Yards Gained, Career
61,655 Brett Favre, Atlanta, 1991; Green Bay, 1992-2007
61,361 Dan Marino, Miami, 1983-1999
51,475 John Elway, Denver, 1983-1998

Most Seasons, 3,000 or More Yards Passing
16 Brett Favre, Green Bay, 1992-2007
13 Dan Marino, Miami, 1984-1992, 1994-95, 1997-98
12 John Elway, Denver, 1985-1991, 1993-97

Most Yards Gained, Season
5,084 Dan Marino, Miami, 1984
4,830 Kurt Warner, St. Louis, 2001
4,806 Tom Brady, New England, 2007

Most Yards Gained, Rookie, Season
3,739 Peyton Manning, Indianapolis, 1998
2,931 Chris Weinke, Carolina, 2001
2,833 Rick Mirer, Seattle, 1993

Most Yards Gained, Game
554 Norm Van Brocklin, Los Angeles vs. N.Y. Yanks, Sept. 28, 1951
527 Warren Moon, Houston vs. Kansas City, Dec. 16, 1990
522 Boomer Esiason, Arizona vs. Washington, Nov. 10, 1996

Most Games, 400 or More Yards Passing, Career
13 Dan Marino, Miami, 1983-1999
7 Joe Montana, San Francisco, 1979-1990, 1992; Kansas City, 1993-94
   Warren Moon, Houston, 1984-1993; Minnesota, 1994-96; Seattle, 1997-98; Kansas City, 1999-2000
   Peyton Manning, Indianapolis, 1998-2007
6 Dan Fouts, San Diego, 1973-1987
   Drew Bledsoe, New England, 1993-2001; Buffalo, 2002-04; Dallas, 2005-06

Most Games, 400 or More Yards Passing, Season
4 Dan Marino, Miami, 1984
3 Dan Marino, Miami, 1986
2 By many players

Most Consecutive Games, 400 or More Yards Passing
2 Dan Fouts, San Diego, 1982
   Dan Marino, Miami, 1984
   Phil Simms, N.Y. Giants, 1985
   Billy Volek, Tennessee, 2004

Most Games, 300 or More Yards Passing, Career
63 Dan Marino, Miami, 1983-1999
55 Brett Favre, Atlanta, 1991; Green Bay, 1992-2007
51 Dan Fouts, San Diego, 1973-1987

Most Games, 300 or More Yards Passing, Season
10 Rich Gannon, Oakland, 2002
9 Dan Marino, Miami, 1984
   Warren Moon, Houston, 1990
   Kurt Warner, St. Louis, 1999
   Kurt Warner, St. Louis, 2001
8 Dan Fouts, San Diego, 1980
   Kurt Warner, St. Louis, 2000
   Trent Green, Kansas City, 2004
   Marc Bulger, St. Louis, 2006
   Drew Brees, New Orleans, 2006
   Tom Brady, New England, 2007

Most Consecutive Games, 300 or More Yards Passing
6 Steve Young, San Francisco, 1998
   Kurt Warner, St. Louis, 2000
   Rich Gannon, Oakland, 2002
5 Joe Montana, San Francisco, 1982
   Kerry Collins, N.Y. Giants, 2001-02
   Drew Brees, New Orleans, 2006
4 Dan Fouts, San Diego, 1979
   Dan Fouts, San Diego, 1980-81
   Bill Kenney, Kansas City, 1983
   Joe Montana, San Francisco, 1985-86

   Joe Montana, San Francisco, 1990
   Warren Moon, Houston, 1990
   Drew Bledsoe, New England, 1993-94
   Kurt Warner, St. Louis, 1999
   Brian Griese, Denver, 2002
   Daunte Culpepper, Minnesota, 2004
   Trent Green, Kansas City, 2004

Longest Pass Completion (All TDs except as noted)
99 Frank Filchock (to Farkas), Washington vs. Pittsburgh, Oct. 15, 1939
   George Izo (to Mitchell), Washington vs. Cleveland, Sept. 15, 1963
   Karl Sweetan (to Studstill), Detroit vs. Baltimore, Oct. 16, 1966
   Sonny Jurgensen (to Allen), Washington vs. Chicago, Sept. 15, 1968
   Jim Plunkett (to Branch), L.A. Raiders vs. Washington, Oct. 2, 1983
   Ron Jaworski (to Quick), Philadelphia vs. Atlanta, Nov. 10, 1985
   Stan Humphries (to Martin), San Diego vs. Seattle, Sept. 18, 1994
   Brett Favre (to Brooks), Green Bay vs. Chicago, Sept. 11, 1995
   Trent Green (to Boerigter), Kansas City vs. San Diego, Dec. 22, 2002
   Jeff Garcia, (to Davis), Cleveland vs. Cincinnati, Oct. 17, 2004
98 Doug Russell (to Tinsley), Chi. Cardinals vs. Cleveland, Nov. 27, 1938
   Ogden Compton (to Lane), Chi. Cardinals vs. Green Bay, Nov. 13, 1955
   Bill Wade (to Farrington), Chicago Bears vs. Detroit, Oct. 8, 1961
   Jacky Lee (to Dewveall), Houston vs. San Diego, Nov. 25, 1962
   Earl Morrall (to Jones), N.Y. Giants vs. Pittsburgh, Sept. 11, 1966
   Jim Hart (to Moore), St. Louis vs. Los Angeles, Dec. 10, 1972 (no TD)
   Bobby Hebert (to Haynes), Atlanta vs. New Orleans, Sept. 12, 1993
   Charlie Batch (to Morton), Detroit vs. Chicago, Oct. 4, 1998
97 Pat Coffee (to Tinsley), Chi. Cardinals vs. Chi. Bears, Dec. 5, 1937
   Bobby Layne (to Box), Detroit vs. Green Bay, Nov. 26, 1953
   George Shaw (to Tarr), Denver vs. Boston, Sept. 21, 1962
   Bernie Kosar (to Slaughter), Cleveland vs. Chicago, Oct. 23, 1989
   Steve Young (to Taylor), San Francisco vs. Atlanta, Nov. 3, 1991

AVERAGE GAIN
Most Seasons Leading League
7 Sid Luckman, Chi. Bears, 1939-1943, 1946-47
5 Steve Young, San Francisco, 1991-94, 1997
3 Arnie Herber, Green Bay, 1932, 1934, 1936
   Norm Van Brocklin, Los Angeles, 1950, 1952, 1954
   Len Dawson, Dall. Texans, 1962; Kansas City, 1966, 1968
   Bart Starr, Green Bay, 1966-68
   Kurt Warner, St. Louis, 1999-2001

Most Consecutive Seasons Leading League
5 Sid Luckman, Chi. Bears, 1939-1943
4 Steve Young, San Francisco, 1991-94
3 Bart Starr, Green Bay, 1966-68

Kurt Warner, St. Louis, 1999-2001
Highest Average Gain, Career (1,500 attempts)
8.63 Otto Graham, Cleveland, 1950-55 (1,565-13,499)
8.42 Sid Luckman, Chi. Bears, 1939-1950
      (1,744-14,686)
8.16 Norm Van Brocklin, Los Angeles, 1949-1957;
      Philadelphia, 1958-1960
Highest Average Gain, Season (Qualifiers)
11.17 Tommy O'Connell, Cleveland, 1957 (110-1,229)
10.86 Sid Luckman, Chi. Bears, 1943 (202-2,194)
10.55 Otto Graham, Cleveland, 1953 (258-2,722)
Highest Average Gain, Rookie, Season (Qualifiers)
9.411 Greg Cook, Cincinnati, 1969 (197-1,854)
9.409 Bob Waterfield, Cleveland, 1945 (171-1,609)
8.88 Ben Roethlisberger, Pittsburgh, 2004 (295-2,621)
Highest Average Gain, Game (20 attempts)
18.58 Sammy Baugh, Washington vs. Boston,
       Oct. 31, 1948 (24-446)
18.50 Johnny Unitas, Baltimore vs. Atlanta, Nov. 12, 1967
       (20-370)
17.71 Joe Namath, N.Y. Jets vs. Baltimore, Sept. 24, 1972
       (28-496)

TOUCHDOWNS
Most Seasons Leading League
4 Johnny Unitas, Baltimore, 1957-1960
   Len Dawson, Dall. Texans, 1962; Kansas City, 1963,
   1965-66
   Steve Young, San Francisco, 1992-94, 1998
   Brett Favre, Green Bay, 1995-97, 2003
3 Arnie Herber, Green Bay, 1932, 1934, 1936
   Sid Luckman, Chi. Bears, 1943, 1945-46
   Y.A. Tittle, San Francisco, 1955; N.Y. Giants, 1962-63
   Dan Marino, Miami, 1984-86
   Peyton Manning, Indianapolis, 2000, 2004, 2006
2 By many players
Most Consecutive Seasons Leading League
4 Johnny Unitas, Baltimore, 1957-1960
3 Dan Marino, Miami, 1984-86
   Steve Young, San Francisco, 1992-94
   Brett Favre, Green Bay, 1995-97
2 By many players
Most Touchdown Passes, Career
442 Brett Favre, Atlanta, 1991; Green Bay, 1992-2007
420 Dan Marino, Miami, 1983-1999
342 Fran Tarkenton, Minnesota, 1961-66, 1972-78;
     N.Y. Giants, 1967-1971
Most Touchdown Passes, Season
50 Tom Brady, New England, 2007
49 Peyton Manning, Indianapolis, 2004
48 Dan Marino, Miami, 1984
Most Touchdown Passes, Rookie, Season
26 Peyton Manning, Indianapolis, 1998
22 Charlie Conerly, N.Y. Giants, 1948
20 Dan Marino, Miami, 1983
Most Touchdown Passes, Game
7 Sid Luckman, Chi. Bears vs. N.Y. Giants,
   Nov. 14, 1943
   Adrian Burk, Philadelphia vs. Washington,
   Oct. 17, 1954
   George Blanda, Houston vs. N.Y. Titans,
   Nov. 19, 1961
   Y.A. Tittle, N.Y. Giants vs. Washington, Oct. 28, 1962
   Joe Kapp, Minnesota vs. Baltimore, Sept. 28, 1969
6 By many players. Last time:
   Tom Brady, New England vs. Miami, Oct. 21, 2007
Most Games, Four or More Touchdown Passes, Career
21 Dan Marino, Miami, 1983-1999
19 Brett Favre, Atlanta, 1991; Green Bay, 1992-2007

17 Johnny Unitas, Baltimore, 1956-1972;
    San Diego, 1973
    Peyton Manning, Indianapolis, 1998-2007
Most Games, Four or More Touchdown Passes, Season
6 Dan Marino, Miami, 1984
   Peyton Manning, Indianapolis, 2004
5 Dan Marino, Miami, 1986
   Brett Favre, Green Bay, 1996
   Donovan McNabb, Philadelphia, 2004
   Tom Brady, New ENgland, 2007
4 George Blanda, Houston, 1961
   Vince Ferragamo, Los Angeles, 1980
   Steve Young, San Francisco, 1994
   Randall Cunningham, Minnesota, 1998
   Daunte Culpepper, Minnesota, 2004
   Tony Romo, Dallas, 2007
Most Consecutive Games, Four or More Touchdown Passes
5 Peyton Manning, Indianapolis, 2004
4 Dan Marino, Miami, 1984
2 By many players
Most Consecutive Games, Touchdown Passes
47 Johnny Unitas, Baltimore, 1956-1960
36 Brett Favre, Green Bay, 2002-2004
30 Dan Marino, Miami, 1985-87

HAD INTERCEPTED
Most Consecutive Passes Attempted, None Intercepted
308 Bernie Kosar, Cleveland, 1990-91
294 Bart Starr, Green Bay, 1964-65
279 Jeff George, Indianapolis, 1993; Atlanta, 1994
Most Passes Had Intercepted, Career
288 Brett Favre, Atlanta, 1991; Green Bay, 1992-2007
277 George Blanda, Chi. Bears, 1949, 1950-58; Baltimore,
     1950; Houston, 1960-66; Oakland, 1967-1975
268 John Hadl, San Diego, 1962-1972; Los Angeles,
     1973-74; Green Bay, 1974-75; Houston, 1976-77
Most Passes Had Intercepted, Season
42 George Blanda, Houston, 1962
35 Vinny Testaverde, Tampa Bay, 1988
34 Frank Tripucka, Denver, 1960
Most Passes Had Intercepted, Game
8 Jim Hardy, Chi. Cardinals vs. Philadelphia,
   Sept. 24, 1950
7 Parker Hall, Cleveland vs. Green Bay, Nov. 8, 1942
   Frank Sinkwich, Detroit vs. Green Bay, Oct. 24, 1943
   Bob Waterfield, Los Angeles vs. Green Bay,
   Oct. 17, 1948
   Zeke Bratkowski, Chicago vs. Baltimore,
   Oct. 2, 1960
   Tommy Wade, Pittsburgh vs. Philadelphia,
   Dec. 12, 1965
   Ken Stabler, Oakland vs. Denver, Oct. 16, 1977
   Steve DeBerg, Tampa Bay vs. San Francisco,
   Sept. 7, 1986
   Ty Detmer, Detroit vs. Cleveland, Sept. 23, 2001
6 By many players
Most Attempts, No Interceptions, Game
70 Drew Bledsoe, New England vs. Minnesota,
    Nov. 13, 1994 (OT)
63 Rich Gannon, Minnesota vs. New England,
    Oct. 20, 1991 (OT)
60 Davey O'Brien, Philadelphia vs. Washington,
    Dec. 1, 1940

LOWEST PERCENTAGE, PASSES HAD INTERCEPTED
**Most Seasons Leading League, Lowest Percentage, Passes
Had Intercepted**
5 Sammy Baugh, Washington, 1940, 1942, 1944-45,
   1947
3 Charlie Conerly, N.Y. Giants, 1950, 1956, 1959

Bart Starr, Green Bay, 1962, 1964, 1966
Roger Staubach, Dallas, 1971, 1977, 1979
Ken Anderson, Cincinnati, 1972, 1981-82
Ken O'Brien, N.Y. Jets, 1985, 1987-88
2 By many players

Lowest Percentage, Passes Had Intercepted, Career (1,500 attempts)
2.11 Neil O'Donnell, Pittsburgh, 1991-95; N.Y. Jets, 1996-97; Cincinnati, 1998; Tennessee, 1999-2003 (3,229-68)
2.12 Donovan McNabb, Philadelphia, 1999-2007 (3,732-79)
2.31 Mark Brunell, Green Bay, 1994; Jacksonville, 1995-2003; Washington, 2004-06 (4,594-106)

Lowest Percentage, Passes Had Intercepted, Season (Qualifiers)
0.41 Damon Huard, Kansas City, 2006 (244-1)
0.66 Joe Ferguson, Buffalo, 1976 (151-1)
0.90 Steve DeBerg, Kansas City, 1990 (444-4)

Lowest Percentage, Passes Had Intercepted, Rookie, Season (Qualifiers)
1.98 Charlie Batch, Detroit, 1998 (303-6)
2.03 Dan Marino, Miami, 1983 (296-6)
2.10 Gary Wood, N.Y. Giants, 1964 (143-3)

TIMES SACKED
Times Sacked has been compiled since 1963.
Most Times Sacked, Career
516 John Elway, Denver, 1983-1998
494 Dave Krieg, Seattle, 1980-1991; Kansas City, 1992-93; Detroit, 1994; Arizona, 1995; Chicago, 1996; Tennessee, 1997-98
484 Randall Cunningham, Philadelphia, 1985-1995; Minnesota, 1997-99; Dallas, 2000; Baltimore, 2001

Most Times Sacked, Season
76 David Carr, Houston, 2002
72 Randall Cunningham, Philadelphia, 1986
68 David Carr, Houston, 2005

Most Times Sacked, Game
12 Bert Jones, Baltimore vs. St. Louis, Oct. 26, 1980
Warren Moon, Houston vs. Dallas, Sept. 29, 1985
Donovan McNabb, Philadelphia vs. N.Y. Giants, Sept. 30, 2007
11 Charley Johnson, St. Louis vs. N.Y. Giants, Nov. 1, 1964
Bart Starr, Green Bay vs. Detroit, Nov. 7, 1965
Jack Kemp, Buffalo vs. Oakland, Oct. 15, 1967
Bob Berry, Atlanta vs. St. Louis, Nov. 24, 1968
Greg Landry, Detroit vs. Dallas, Oct. 6, 1975
Ron Jaworski, Philadelphia vs. St. Louis, Dec. 18, 1983
Paul McDonald, Cleveland vs. Kansas City, Sept. 30, 1984
Archie Manning, Minnesota vs. Chicago, Oct. 28, 1984
Steve Pelluer, Dallas vs. San Diego, Nov. 16, 1986
Randall Cunningham, Philadelphia vs. L.A. Raiders, Nov. 30, 1986 (OT)
David Norrie, N.Y. Jets vs. Dallas, Oct. 4, 1987
Troy Aikman, Dallas vs. Philadelphia, Sept. 15, 1991
Bernie Kosar, Cleveland vs. Indianapolis, Sept. 6, 1992
10 By many players

RECEIVING
Most Seasons Leading League
8 Don Hutson, Green Bay, 1936-37, 1939, 1941-45
5 Lionel Taylor, Denver, 1960-63, 1965
3 Tom Fears, Los Angeles, 1948-1950

Pete Pihos, Philadelphia, 1953-55
Billy Wilson, San Francisco, 1954, 1956-57
Raymond Berry, Baltimore, 1958-1960
Lance Alworth, San Diego, 1966, 1968-69
Sterling Sharpe, Green Bay, 1989, 1992-93

Most Consecutive Seasons Leading League
5 Don Hutson, Green Bay, 1941-45
4 Lionel Taylor, Denver, 1960-63
3 Tom Fears, Los Angeles, 1948-1950
Pete Pihos, Philadelphia, 1953-55
Raymond Berry, Baltimore, 1958-1960

Most Pass Receptions, Career
1,549 Jerry Rice, San Francisco, 1985-2000; Oakland, 2001-04; Seattle, 2004
1,101 Cris Carter, Philadelphia, 1987-89; Minnesota, 1990-2001; Miami, 2002
1,094 Tim Brown, L.A. Raiders, 1988-1994; Oakland, 1995-2003; Tampa Bay, 2004

Most Seasons, 50 or More Pass Receptions
17 Jerry Rice, San Francisco, 1986-1996, 1998-2000; Oakland, 2001-03
13 Andre Reed, Buffalo, 1986-1994, 1996-99
11 Cris Carter, Minnesota, 1991-2001
Tim Brown, L.A. Raiders, 1993-1994; Oakland, 1995-2003
Shannon Sharpe, Denver 1992-98; Baltimore, 2000-01; Denver, 2002-03
Marvin Harrison, Indianapolis, 1996-2006
Isaac Bruce, St. Louis, 1995-97, 1999-2004, 2006-07

Most Pass Receptions, Season
143 Marvin Harrison, Indianapolis, 2002
123 Herman Moore, Detroit, 1995
122 Cris Carter, Minnesota, 1994
Cris Carter, Minnesota, 1995
Jerry Rice, San Francisco, 1995

Most Pass Receptions, Rookie, Season
101 Anquan Boldin, Arizona, 2003
90 Terry Glenn, New England, 1996
88 Reggie Bush, New Orleans, 2006

Most Pass Receptions, Game
20 Terrell Owens, San Francisco vs. Chicago, Dec. 17, 2000
18 Tom Fears, Los Angeles vs. Green Bay, Dec. 3, 1950
17 Clark Gaines, N.Y. Jets vs. San Francisco, Sept. 21, 1980

Most Consecutive Games, Pass Receptions
274 Jerry Rice, San Francisco, 1985-2000; Oakland, 2001-04
183 Art Monk, Washington, 1983-1993; N.Y. Jets, 1994; Philadelphia, 1995
179 Tim Brown, L.A. Raiders, 1993-94; Oakland, 1995-2003; Tampa Bay, 2004

YARDS GAINED
Most Seasons Leading League
7 Don Hutson, Green Bay, 1936, 1938-39, 1941-44
6 Jerry Rice, San Francisco, 1986, 1989-1990, 1993-95
3 Raymond Berry, Baltimore, 1957, 1959-1960
Lance Alworth, San Diego, 1965-66, 1968

Most Consecutive Seasons Leading League
4 Don Hutson, Green Bay, 1941-44
3 Jerry Rice, San Francisco, 1993-95
2 By many players

Most Yards Gained, Career
22,895 Jerry Rice, San Francisco, 1985-2000; Oakland, 2001-04; Seattle, 2004
14,934 Tim Brown, L.A. Raiders, 1988-1994; Oakland, 1995-2003; Tampa Bay, 2004

14,109   Isaac Bruce, L.A. Rams, 1994; St. Louis, 1995-2007

Most Seasons, 1,000 or More Yards, Pass Receiving
- 14   Jerry Rice, San Francisco, 1986-1996, 1998; Oakland, 2001-02
- 9   Tim Brown, L.A. Raiders, 1993-94; Oakland, 1995-2001
-    Jimmy Smith, Jacksonville, 1996-2002, 2004-05
- 8   Steve Largent, Seattle, 1978-1981, 1983-86
-    Cris Carter, Minnesota, 1993-2000
-    Rod Smith, Denver, 1997-2002, 2004-05
-    Isaac Bruce, St. Louis, 1995-96, 1999-2002, 2004, 2006
-    Marvin Harrison, Indianapolis, 1999-2006
-    Torry Holt, St. Louis, 2000-07
-    Randy Moss, Minnesota, 1998-2003; Oakland, 2005; New England, 2007
-    Terrell Owens, San Francisco, 1998, 2000-03; Philadelphia, 2004; Dallas, 2006-07

Most Yards Gained, Season
- 1,848   Jerry Rice, San Francisco, 1995
- 1,781   Isaac Bruce, St. Louis, 1995
- 1,746   Charley Hennigan, Houston, 1961

Most Yards Gained, Rookie, Season
- 1,473   Bill Groman, Houston, 1960
- 1,377   Anquan Boldin, Arizona, 2003
- 1,313   Randy Moss, Minnesota, 1998

Most Yards Gained, Game
- 336   Willie Anderson, L.A. Rams vs. New Orleans, Nov. 26, 1989 (OT)
- 309   Stephone Paige, Kansas City vs. San Diego, Dec. 22, 1985
- 303   Jim Benton, Cleveland vs. Detroit, Nov. 22, 1945

Most Games, 200 or More Yards Pass Receiving, Career
- 5   Lance Alworth, San Diego, 1962-1970; Dallas, 1971-72
- 4   Don Hutson, Green Bay, 1935-45
-    Charley Hennigan, Houston, 1960-66
-    Jerry Rice, San Francisco, 1985-2000; Oakland, 2001-04; Seattle, 2004
- 3   Don Maynard, N.Y. Giants, 1958; N.Y. Jets, 1960-1972; St. Louis, 1973
-    Wes Chandler, New Orleans, 1978-1981; San Diego, 1981-87; San Francisco, 1988
-    Isaac Bruce, L.A. Rams, 1994; St. Louis, 1995-2007

Most Games, 200 or More Yards Pass Receiving, Season
- 3   Charley Hennigan, Houston, 1961
- 2   Don Hutson, Green Bay, 1942
-    Gene Roberts, N.Y. Giants, 1949
-    Lance Alworth, San Diego, 1963
-    Don Maynard, N.Y. Jets, 1968

Most Games, 100 or More Yards Pass Receiving, Career
- 76   Jerry Rice, San Francisco, 1985-2000; Oakland, 2001-04; Seattle, 2004
- 59   Marvin Harrison, Indianapolis, 1996-2007
- 55   Randy Moss, Minnesota, 1998-2004; Oakland, 2005-06; New England, 2007

Most Games, 100 or More Yards Pass Receiving, Season
- 11   Michael Irvin, Dallas, 1995
- 10   Charley Hennigan, Houston, 1961
-    Herman Moore, Detroit, 1995
-    Marvin Harrison, Indianapolis, 2002
-    Torry Holt, St. Louis, 2003
- 9   Elroy (Crazylegs) Hirsch, Los Angeles, 1951
-    Bill Groman, Houston, 1960
-    Lance Alworth, San Diego, 1965
-    Don Maynard, N.Y. Jets, 1968
-    Stanley Morgan, New England, 1986
-    Mark Carrier, Tampa Bay, 1989
-    Robert Brooks, Green Bay, 1995
-    Isaac Bruce, St. Louis, 1995

-    Jerry Rice, San Francisco, 1995
-    Marvin Harrison, Indianapolis, 1999
-    Jimmy Smith, Jacksonville, 1999
-    David Boston, Arizona, 2001
-    Steve Smith, Carolina, 2005
-    Randy Moss, New England, 2007

Most Consecutive Games, 100 or More Yards Pass Receiving
- 7   Charley Hennigan, Houston, 1961
-    Michael Irvin, Dallas, 1995
- 6   Raymond Berry, Baltimore, 1960
-    Bill Groman, Houston, 1961
-    Pat Studstill, Detroit, 1966
-    Isaac Bruce, St. Louis, 1995
- 5   Elroy (Crazylegs) Hirsch, Los Angeles, 1951
-    Bob Boyd, Los Angeles, 1954
-    Terry Barr, Detroit, 1963
-    Lance Alworth, San Diego, 1966
-    Don Maynard, N.Y. Jets, 1968-69
-    Harold Jackson, Philadelphia, 1971-72
-    Patrick Jeffers, Carolina, 1999
-    Terrell Owens, Philadelphia, 2004
-    Anquan Boldin, Arizona, 2005

Longest Pass Reception (All TDs except as noted)
- 99   Andy Farkas (from Filchock), Washington vs. Pittsburgh, Oct. 15, 1939
-    Bobby Mitchell (from Izo), Washington vs. Cleveland, Sept. 15, 1963
-    Pat Studstill (from Sweetan), Detroit vs. Baltimore, Oct. 16, 1966
-    Gerry Allen (from Jurgensen), Washington vs. Chicago, Sept. 15, 1968
-    Cliff Branch (from Plunkett), L.A. Raiders vs. Washington, Oct. 2, 1983
-    Mike Quick (from Jaworski), Philadelphia vs. Atlanta, Nov. 10, 1985
-    Tony Martin (from Humphries), San Diego vs. Seattle, Sept. 18, 1994
-    Robert Brooks (from Favre), Green Bay vs. Chicago, Sept. 11, 1995
-    Marc Boerigter (from Green), Kansas City vs. San Diego, Dec. 22, 2002
-    Andre Davis (from Garcia), Cleveland vs. Cincinnati, Oct. 17, 2004
- 98   Gaynell Tinsley (from Russell), Chi. Cardinals vs. Cleveland, Nov. 17, 1938
-    Dick (Night Train) Lane (from Compton), Chi. Cardinals vs. Green Bay, Nov. 13, 1955
-    John Farrington (from Wade), Chicago vs. Detroit, Oct. 8, 1961
-    Willard Dewveall (from Lee), Houston vs. San Diego, Nov. 25, 1962
-    Homer Jones (from Morrall), N.Y. Giants vs. Pittsburgh, Sept. 11, 1966
-    Bobby Moore (from Hart), St. Louis vs. Los Angeles, Dec. 10, 1972 (no TD)
-    Michael Haynes (from Hebert), Atlanta vs. New Orleans, Sept. 12, 1993
-    Johnnie Morton (from Batch), Detroit vs. Chicago, Oct. 4, 1998
- 97   Gaynell Tinsley (from Coffee), Chi. Cardinals vs. Chi. Bears, Dec. 5, 1937
-    Cloyce Box (from Layne), Detroit vs. Green Bay, Nov. 26, 1953
-    Jerry Tarr (from Shaw), Denver vs. Boston, Sept. 21, 1962
-    Webster Slaughter (from Kosar), Cleveland vs. Chicago, Oct. 23, 1989
-    John Taylor (from Young), San Francisco vs. Atlanta, Nov. 3, 1991

AVERAGE GAIN

Highest Average Gain, Career (200 receptions)
22.26 Homer Jones, N.Y. Giants, 1964-69; Cleveland, 1970 (224-4,986)
20.83 Buddy Dial, Pittsburgh, 1959-1963; Dallas, 1964-66 (261-5,436)
20.24 Harlon Hill, Chi. Bears, 1954-1961; Pittsburgh, 1962; Detroit, 1962 (233-4,717)

Highest Average Gain, Season (24 receptions)
32.58 Don Currivan, Boston, 1947 (24-782)
31.44 Bucky Pope, Los Angeles, 1964 (25-786)
28.60 Bobby Duckworth, San Diego, 1984 (25-715)

Highest Average Gain, Game (3 receptions)
63.00 Torry Holt, St. Louis vs. Atlanta, Sept. 24, 2000 (3-189)
60.67 Bill Groman, Houston vs. Denver, Nov. 20, 1960 (3-182)
       Homer Jones, N.Y. Giants vs. Washington, Dec. 12, 1965 (3-182)
60.33 Don Currivan, Boston vs. Washington, Nov. 30, 1947 (3-181)

TOUCHDOWNS

Most Seasons Leading League
9 Don Hutson, Green Bay, 1935-38, 1940-44
6 Jerry Rice, San Francisco, 1986-87, 1989-1991, 1993
4 Randy Moss, Minnesota, 1998, 2000, 2003; New England, 2007

Most Consecutive Seasons Leading League
5 Don Hutson, Green Bay, 1940-44
4 Don Hutson, Green Bay, 1935-38
3 Lance Alworth, San Diego, 1964-66
   Jerry Rice, San Francisco, 1989-1991

Most Touchdowns, Career
197 Jerry Rice, San Francisco, 1985-2000; Oakland, 2001-04; Seattle, 2004
130 Cris Carter, Philadelphia, 1987-89; Minnesota, 1990-2001; Miami, 2002
129 Terrell Owens, San Francisco, 1996-2003; Philadelphia, 2004-05; Dallas, 2006-07

Most Touchdowns, Season
23 Randy Moss, New England, 2007
22 Jerry Rice, San Francisco, 1987
18 Mark Clayton, Miami, 1984
    Sterling Sharpe, Green Bay, 1994

Most Touchdowns, Rookie, Season
17 Randy Moss, Minnesota, 1998
13 Bill Howton, Green Bay, 1952
    John Jefferson, San Diego, 1978
12 Harlon Hill, Chi. Bears, 1954
    Bill Groman, Houston, 1960
    Mike Ditka, Chicago, 1961
    Bob Hayes, Dallas, 1965

Most Touchdowns, Game
5 Bob Shaw, Chi. Cardinals vs. Baltimore, Oct. 2, 1950
   Kellen Winslow, San Diego vs. Oakland, Nov. 22, 1981
   Jerry Rice, San Francisco vs. Atlanta, Oct. 14, 1990
4 By many players. Last time:
   Randy Moss, New England vs. Buffalo, Nov. 18, 2007
   Terrell Owens, Dallas vs. Washington, Nov. 18, 2007

Most Consecutive Games, Touchdowns
13 Jerry Rice, San Francisco, 1986-87
11 Elroy (Crazylegs) Hirsch, Los Angeles, 1950-51
    Buddy Dial, Pittsburgh, 1959-1960
10 Carl Pickens, Cincinnati, 1994-95
    Randy Moss, Minnesota, 2003-04

YARDS FROM SCRIMMAGE

Most Scrimmage Yards, Career
23,540 Jerry Rice, San Francisco 1985-2000; Oakland, 2001-04; Seattle, 2004
21,579 Emmitt Smith, Dallas, 1990-2002; Arizona, 2003-04
21,264 Walter Payton, Chicago, 1975-1987

Most Scrimmage Yards, Season
2,429 Marshall Faulk, St. Louis, 1999 (1,381 rush., 1,048 rec.)
2,390 Tiki Barber, N.Y. Giants, 2005 (1,860 rush., 530 rec.)
2,370 LaDainian Tomlinson, San Diego, 2003 (1,645 rush., 725 rec.)

Most Scrimmage Yards, Rookie, Season
2,212 Eric Dickerson, L.A. Rams, 1983 (1,808 rush., 404 rec.)
2,139 Edgerrin James, Indianapolis, 1999 (1,553 rush., 586 rec.)
1,924 Billy Sims, Detroit, 1980 (1,303 rush., 621 rec.)

Most Scrimmage Yards, Game
336 Flipper Anderson, L.A. Rams vs. New Orleans, Nov. 26, 1989 (OT) (336 rec.)
330 Billy Cannon, Houston vs. N.Y. Titans, Dec. 10, 1961 (216 rush., 114 rec.)
315 Adrian Peterson, Minnesota vs. San Diego, Nov. 4, 2007 (296 rush, 19 pass)

INTERCEPTIONS BY

Most Seasons Leading League
3 Everson Walls, Dallas, 1981-82, 1985
2 Dick (Night Train) Lane, Los Angeles, 1952; Chi. Cardinals, 1954
   Jack Christiansen, Detroit, 1953, 1957
   Milt Davis, Baltimore, 1957, 1959
   Dick Lynch, N.Y. Giants, 1961, 1963
   Johnny Robinson, Kansas City, 1966, 1970
   Bill Bradley, Philadelphia, 1971-72
   Emmitt Thomas, Kansas City, 1969, 1974
   Ronnie Lott, San Francisco, 1986; L.A. Raiders, 1991
   Rod Woodson, Baltimore, 1999; Oakland, 2002
   Ty Law, New England, 1998; N.Y. Jets, 2005

Most Interceptions By, Career
81 Paul Krause, Washington, 1964-67; Minnesota, 1968-1979
79 Emlen Tunnell, N.Y. Giants, 1948-1958; Green Bay, 1959-1961
71 Rod Woodson, Pittsburgh, 1987-1996; San Francisco, 1997; Baltimore, 1998-2001; Oakland, 2002-03

Most Interceptions By, Season
14 Dick (Night Train) Lane, Los Angeles, 1952
13 Dan Sandifer, Washington, 1948
    Orban (Spec) Sanders, N.Y. Yanks, 1950
    Lester Hayes, Oakland, 1980
12 By nine players

Most Interceptions By, Rookie, Season
14 Dick (Night Train) Lane, Los Angeles, 1952
13 Dan Sandifer, Washington, 1948
12 Woodley Lewis, Los Angeles, 1950
    Paul Krause, Washington, 1964

Most Interceptions By, Game
4 Sammy Baugh, Washington vs. Detroit, Nov. 14, 1943
   Dan Sandifer, Washington vs. Boston, Oct. 31, 1948
   Don Doll, Detroit vs. Chi. Cardinals, Oct. 23, 1949
   Bob Nussbaumer, Chi. Cardinals vs. N.Y. Bulldogs, Nov. 13, 1949
   Russ Craft, Philadelphia vs. Chi. Cardinals, Sept. 24, 1950
   Bobby Dillon, Green Bay vs. Detroit, Nov. 26, 1953
   Jack Butler, Pittsburgh vs. Washington, Dec. 13, 1953

Austin (Goose) Gonsoulin, Denver vs. Buffalo,
Sept. 18, 1960
Jerry Norton, St. Louis vs. Washington,
Nov. 20, 1960; vs. Pittsburgh, Nov. 26, 1961
Dave Baker, San Francisco vs. L.A. Rams,
Dec. 4, 1960
Bobby Ply, Dall. Texans vs. San Diego, Dec. 16, 1962
Bobby Hunt, Kansas City vs. Houston, Oct. 4, 1964
Willie Brown, Denver vs. N.Y. Jets, Nov. 15, 1964
Dick Anderson, Miami vs. Pittsburgh, Dec. 3, 1973
Willie Buchanon, Green Bay vs. San Diego,
Sept. 24, 1978
Deron Cherry, Kansas City vs. Seattle, Sept. 29, 1985
Kwamie Lassiter, Arizona vs. San Diego,
Dec. 27, 1998
Deltha O'Neal, Denver vs. Kansas City, Oct. 7, 2001

Most Consecutive Games, Passes Intercepted By
8 Tom Morrow, Oakland, 1962-63
7 Tom Landry, N.Y. Giants, 1950-51
Paul Krause, Washington, 1964
Larry Wilson, St. Louis, 1966
Ben Davis, Cleveland, 1968
6 By many players.
Last time: Brian Russell, Minnesota, 2003

YARDS GAINED
Most Seasons Leading League
2 Dick (Night Train) Lane, Los Angeles, 1952;
Chi. Cardinals, 1954
Herb Adderley, Green Bay, 1965, 1969
Dick Anderson, Miami, 1968, 1970
Darren Sharper, Green Bay, 2002; Minnesota, 2005

Most Yards Gained, Career
1,483 Rod Woodson, Pittsburgh, 1987-1996; San Francisco,
1997; Baltimore, 1998-2001; Oakland, 2002-03

1,331 Deion Sanders, Atlanta, 1989-1993; San Francisco,
1994; Dallas, 1995-99; Washington, 2000;
Baltimore, 2004-05
1,282 Emlen Tunnell, N.Y. Giants, 1948-1958; Green Bay,
1959-1961

Most Yards Gained, Season
358 Ed Reed, Baltimore, 2004
349 Charlie McNeil, San Diego, 1961
303 Deion Sanders, San Francisco, 1994

Most Yards Gained, Rookie, Season
301 Don Doll, Detroit, 1949
298 Dick (Night Train) Lane, Los Angeles, 1952
275 Woodley Lewis, Los Angeles, 1950

Most Yards Gained, Game
177 Charlie McNeil, San Diego vs. Houston,
Sept. 24, 1961
170 Louis Oliver, Miami vs. Buffalo, Oct. 4, 1992
167 Dick Jauron, Detroit vs. Chicago, Nov. 18, 1973

Longest Return (All TDs)
106 Ed Reed, Baltimore vs. Cleveland, Nov. 7, 2004
103 Vencie Glenn, San Diego vs. Denver, Nov. 29, 1987
Louis Oliver, Miami vs. Buffalo, Oct. 4, 1992
102 Bob Smith, Detroit vs. Chi. Bears, Nov. 24, 1949
Erich Barnes, N.Y. Giants vs. Dall. Cowboys,
Oct. 15, 1961
Gary Barbaro, Kansas City vs. Seattle, Dec. 11, 1977
Louis Breeden, Cincinnati vs. San Diego, Nov. 8, 1981
Eddie Anderson, L.A. Raiders vs. Miami, Dec. 14, 1992
Donald Frank, San Diego vs. L.A. Raiders,
Oct. 31, 1993
Artrell Hawkins, Cincinnati vs. Houston, Nov. 3, 2002
Marcus Coleman, Houston vs. Kansas City,
Sept. 26, 2004

Lito Sheppard, Philadelphia vs. Dallas, Oct. 8, 2006

TOUCHDOWNS
Most Touchdowns, Career
12 Rod Woodson, Pittsburgh, 1987-1996; San Francisco,
1997; Baltimore, 1998-2001; Oakland, 2002-03
9 Ken Houston, Houston, 1967-1972; Washington,
1973-1980
Aeneas Williams, Phoenix, 1991-93; Arizona,
1994-2000; St. Louis, 2001-04
Deion Sanders, Atlanta, 1989-1993; San Francisco,
1994; Dallas, 1995-99; Washington, 2000;
Baltimore, 2004-05
8 Eric Allen, Philadelphia, 1988-1994; New Orleans,
1995-97; Oakland, 1998-2001
Darren Sharper, Green Bay, 1997-2004;
Minnesota, 2005-07

Most Touchdowns, Season
4 Ken Houston, Houston, 1971
Jim Kearney, Kansas City, 1972
Eric Allen, Philadelphia, 1993
3 Dick Harris, San Diego, 1961
Dick Lynch, N.Y. Giants, 1963
Herb Adderley, Green Bay, 1965
Lem Barney, Detroit, 1967
Miller Farr, Houston, 1967
Monte Jackson, Los Angeles, 1976
Rod Perry, Los Angeles, 1978
Ronnie Lott, San Francisco, 1981
Lloyd Burruss, Kansas City, 1986
Wayne Haddix, Tampa Bay, 1990
Robert Massey, Phoenix, 1992
Ray Buchanan, Indianapolis, 1994
Deion Sanders, San Francisco, 1994
Mark McMillian, Kansas City, 1997
Otis Smith, N.Y. Jets, 1997
Jimmy Hitchcock, Minnesota, 1998
Eric Allen, Oakland, 2000
Derrick Brooks, Tampa Bay, 2002
Antrel Rolle, Arizona, 2007
2 By many players

Most Touchdowns, Rookie, Season
3 Lem Barney, Detroit, 1967
Ronnie Lott, San Francisco, 1981
2 By many players

Most Touchdowns, Game
2 Bill Blackburn, Chi. Cardinals vs. Boston,
Oct. 24, 1948
Dan Sandifer, Washington vs. Boston, Oct. 31, 1948
Bob Franklin, Cleveland vs. Chicago, Dec. 11, 1960
Bill Stacy, St. Louis vs. Dall. Cowboys, Nov. 5, 1961
Jerry Norton, St. Louis vs. Pittsburgh, Nov. 26, 1961
Miller Farr, Houston vs. Buffalo, Dec. 7, 1968
Ken Houston, Houston vs. San Diego, Dec. 19, 1971
Jim Kearney, Kansas City vs. Denver, Oct. 1, 1972
Lemar Parrish, Cincinnati vs. Houston, Dec. 17, 1972
Dick Anderson, Miami vs. Pittsburgh, Dec. 3, 1973
Prentice McCray, New England vs. N.Y. Jets,
Nov. 21, 1976
Kenny Johnson, Atlanta vs. Green Bay,
Nov. 27, 1983 (OT)
Mike Kozlowski, Miami vs. N.Y. Jets, Dec. 16, 1983
Dave Brown, Seattle vs. Kansas City, Nov. 4, 1984
Lloyd Burruss, Kansas City vs. San Diego,
Oct. 19, 1986
Henry Jones, Buffalo vs. Indianapolis, Sept. 20, 1992
Robert Massey, Phoenix vs. Washington, Oct. 4, 1992
Eric Allen, Philadelphia vs. New Orleans,
Dec. 26, 1993

Ken Norton, San Francisco vs. St. Louis,
   Oct. 22, 1995
Otis Smith, N.Y. Jets vs. Tampa Bay, Dec. 14, 1997
Dewayne Washington, Pittsburgh vs. Jacksonville,
   Nov. 22, 1998
Aaron Glenn, Houston vs. Pittsburgh, Dec. 8, 2002
Ronde Barber, Tampa Bay vs. Philadelphia,
   Oct. 22, 2006
Antrel Rolle, Arizona vs. Cincinnati, Nov. 18, 2007

PUNTING
Most Seasons Leading League
   4   Sammy Baugh, Washington, 1940-43
       Jerrel Wilson, Kansas City, 1965, 1968, 1972-73
   3   Yale Lary, Detroit, 1959, 1961, 1963
       Jim Fraser, Denver, 1962-64
       Ray Guy, Oakland, 1974-75, 1977
       Rohn Stark, Baltimore, 1983; Indianapolis, 1985-86
       Shane Lechler, Oakland, 2003-04, 2007
   2   By many players
Most Consecutive Seasons Leading League
   4   Sammy Baugh, Washington, 1940-43
   3   Jim Fraser, Denver, 1962-64
   2   By many players

PUNTS
Most Punts, Career
   1,585   Jeff Feagles, New England, 1988-89; Philadelphia,
           1990-93; Arizona, 1994-97; Seattle, 1998-2002;
           N.Y. Giants, 2003-07
   1,401   Sean Landeta, N.Y. Giants, 1985-1993; L.A. Rams,
           1993-94; St. Louis, 1995-96; Tampa Bay, 1997;
           Green Bay, 1998; Philadelphia, 1999-2002;
           St. Louis, 2003-04; Philadelphia, 2005
   1,226   Lee Johnson, Houston, 1985-87; Cleveland, 1987-
           88; Cincinnati, 1988-1998; New England, 1999-
           2001; Minnesota, 2001; Philadelphia, 2002
Most Punts, Season
   114   Bob Parsons, Chicago, 1981
         Chad Stanley, Houston, 2002
   111   Brad Maynard, N.Y. Giants, 1997
   109   John James, Atlanta, 1978
Most Punts, Rookie, Season
   111   Brad Maynard, N.Y. Giants, 1997
   108   John Teltschik, Philadelphia, 1986
   101   Daniel Pope, Kansas City, 1999
Most Punts, Game
   16   Leo Araguz, Oakland vs. San Diego, Oct. 11, 1998
   15   John Teltschik, Philadelphia vs. N.Y. Giants,
        Dec. 6, 1987 (OT)
   14   Dick Nesbitt, Chi. Cardinals vs. Chi. Bears,
        Nov. 30, 1933
        Keith Molesworth, Chi. Bears vs. Green Bay,
        Dec. 10, 1933
        Sammy Baugh, Washington vs. Philadelphia,
        Nov. 5, 1939
        Carl Kinscherf, N.Y. Giants vs. Detroit, Nov. 7, 1943
        George Taliaferro, N.Y. Yanks vs. Los Angeles,
        Sept. 28, 1951
Longest Punt
   98   Steve O'Neal, N.Y. Jets vs. Denver, Sept. 21, 1969
   94   Joe Lintzenich, Chi. Bears vs. N.Y. Giants, Nov. 16, 1931
   93   Shawn McCarthy, New England vs. Buffalo,
        Nov. 3, 1991

AVERAGE YARDAGE
Highest Average, Punting, Career (250 punts)
   46.47   Shane Lechler, Oakland, 2000-07 (592-27,511)
   45.10   Sammy Baugh, Washington, 1937-1952
           (338-15,245)

44.68   Mat McBriar, Dallas, 2004-07 (275-12,288)
Highest Average, Punting, Season (Qualifiers)
   51.40   Sammy Baugh, Washington, 1940 (35-1,799)
   49.11   Shane Lechler, Oakland, 2007 (73-3,585)
   48.94   Yale Lary, Detroit, 1963 (35-1,713)
Highest Average, Punting, Rookie, Season (Qualifiers)
   45.92   Frank Sinkwich, Detroit, 1943 (12-551)
   45.91   Shane Lechler, Oakland, 2000 (65-2,984)
   45.66   Tommy Davis, San Francisco, 1959 (59-2,694)
Highest Average, Punting, Game (4 punts)
   61.75   Bob Cifers, Detroit vs. Chi. Bears, Nov. 24, 1946
           (4-247)
   61.60   Roy McKay, Green Bay vs. Chi. Cardinals,
           Oct. 28, 1945 (5-308)
   59.50   Darren Bennett, San Diego vs. Pittsburgh,
           Oct. 1, 1995 (4-238)

PUNTS HAD BLOCKED
Most Consecutive Punts, None Blocked
   1,177   Chris Gardocki, Chicago, 1992-94; Indianapolis,
           1995-98; Cleveland, 1999-2003; Pittsburgh,
           2004-06 (current)
     878   Bryan Barker, Kansas City, 1993; Philadelphia, 1994;
           Jacksonville, 1995-2000; Washington, 2001-03
           Green Bay, 2004; St. Louis, 2005
     638   Tom Tupa, New England, 1997-98; N.Y. Jets,
           1999-2001; Tampa Bay, 2002-03;
           Washington, 2004
Most Punts Had Blocked, Career
   14   Herman Weaver, Detroit, 1970-76; Seattle, 1977-1980
        Harry Newsome, Pittsburgh, 1985-89; Minnesota,
        1990-93
   12   Jerrel Wilson, Kansas City, 1963-1977;
        New England, 1978
        Tom Blanchard, N.Y. Giants, 1971-73; New Orleans,
        1974-78; Tampa Bay, 1979-1981
        Jeff Feagles, New England, 1988-89; Philadelphia,
        1990-93; Arizona, 1994-97; Seattle, 1998-2002;
        N.Y. Giants, 2003-07
   11   David Lee, Baltimore, 1966-1978
Most Punts Had Blocked, Season
   6   Harry Newsome, Pittsburgh, 1988
   4   Bryan Wagner, Cleveland, 1990
   3   By many players

PUNTS INSIDE THE 20
Punts Inside the 20 have been compiled since 1976.
Most Punts Inside the 20, Career
   508   Jeff Feagles, New England, 1988-89; Philadelphia,
         1990-93; Arizona, 1994-97; Seattle, 1998-2002;
         N.Y. Giants, 2003-07
   381   Sean Landeta, N.Y. Giants, 1985-1993; L.A. Rams,
         1993-94; St. Louis, 1995-96; Tampa Bay, 1997;
         Green Bay, 1998; Philadelphia, 1999-2002;
         St. Louis, 2003-04; Philadelphia, 2005
   369   Craig Hentrich, Green Bay, 1994-97; Tennessee,
         1998-2007
Most Punts Inside the 20, Season
   42   Andy Lee, San Francisco, 2007
   39   Kyle Richardson, Baltimore, 1999
   36   Brad Maynard, Chicago, 2001
        Chad Stanley, Houston, 2002
        Chad Stanley, Houston, 2003
        Mike Scifres, San Diego, 2007
Most Punts Inside the 20, Game
   8   Mark Royals, Pittsburgh vs. Houston, Nov. 6, 1994
       (OT)
       Bryan Barker, Jacksonville vs. Baltimore,
       Nov. 14, 1999
   7   Josh Miller, Pittsburgh vs. Cincinnati, Dec. 20, 1998

6   By many players

PUNT RETURNS
Most Seasons Leading League
3   Les (Speedy) Duncan, San Diego, 1965-66;
    Washington, 1971
    Rick Upchurch, Denver, 1976, 1978, 1982
2   Dick Christy, N.Y. Titans, 1961-62
    Claude Gibson, Oakland, 1963-64
    Billy (White Shoes) Johnson, Houston, 1975, 1977
    Mel Gray, New Orleans, 1987; Detroit, 1991
    Jermaine Lewis, Baltimore, 1997, 2000

PUNT RETURNS
Most Punt Returns, Career
463   Brian Mitchell, Washington, 1990-99; Philadelphia,
      2000-02; N.Y. Giants, 2003
351   Eric Metcalf, Cleveland, 1989-1994; Atlanta, 1995-
      96; San Diego, 1997; Arizona, 1998; Carolina,
      1999; Washington, 2001; Green Bay, 2002
349   David Meggett, N.Y. Giants, 1989-1994;
      New England, 1995-97; N.Y. Jets, 1998
Most Punt Returns, Season
70   Danny Reece, Tampa Bay, 1979
62   Fulton Walker, Miami-L.A. Raiders, 1985
58   J.T. Smith, Kansas City, 1979
     Greg Pruitt, L.A. Raiders, 1983
     Leo Lewis, Minnesota, 1988
     Desmond Howard, Green Bay, 1996
     Nate Burleson, Seattle, 2007
Most Punt Returns, Rookie, Season
57   Lew Barnes, Chicago, 1986
55   B.J. Sams, Baltimore, 2004
54   James Jones, Dallas, 1980
Most Punt Returns, Game
11   Eddie Brown, Washington vs. Tampa Bay,
     Oct. 9, 1977
10   Theo Bell, Pittsburgh vs. Buffalo, Dec. 16, 1979
     Mike Nelms, Washington vs. New Orleans,
     Dec. 26, 1982
     Ronnie Harris, New England vs. Pittsburgh,
     Dec. 5, 1993
9   Rodger Bird, Oakland vs. Denver, Sept. 10, 1967
     Ralph McGill, San Francisco vs. Atlanta,
     Oct. 29, 1972
     Ed Podolak, Kansas City vs. San Diego,
     Nov. 10, 1974
     Anthony Leonard, San Francisco vs. New Orleans,
     Oct. 17, 1976
     Butch Johnson, Dallas vs. Buffalo, Nov. 15, 1976
     Larry Marshall, Philadelphia vs. Tampa Bay,
     Sept. 18, 1977
     Nesby Glasgow, Baltimore vs. Kansas City,
     Sept. 2, 1979
     Mike Nelms, Washington vs. St. Louis, Dec. 21, 1980
     Leon Bright, N.Y. Giants vs. Philadelphia,
     Dec. 11, 1982
     Pete Shaw, N.Y. Giants vs. Philadelphia,
     Nov. 20, 1983
     Cleotha Montgomery, L.A. Raiders vs. Detroit,
     Dec. 10, 1984
     Phil McConkey, N.Y. Giants vs. Philadelphia,
     Dec. 6, 1987 (OT)
     Andre Hastings, Pittsburgh vs. Cleveland,
     Nov. 13, 1994
     Steve Smith, Carolina vs. Detroit, Sept. 15, 2002
     Reggie Swinton, Arizona vs. Philadelphia,
     Dec. 24, 2005

FAIR CATCHES
Most Fair Catches, Career
231   Brian Mitchell, Washington, 1990-99; Philadelphia,
      2000-02; N.Y. Giants, 2003
162   Tim Brown, L.A. Raiders, 1988-1994; Oakland,
      1995-2003; Tampa Bay, 2004
144   Glyn Milburn, Denver, 1993-95; Detroit, 1996-97;
      Chicago, 1998-2001; San Diego, 2001
Most Fair Catches, Season
33   Brian Mitchell, Philadelphia, 2000
29   Wes Welker, Miami, 2006
27   Leo Lewis, Minnesota, 1989
     Antonio Chatman, Green Bay, 2004
Most Fair Catches, Game
7   Bake Turner, N.Y. Jets vs. Miami, Nov. 20, 1966
    Lem Barney, Detroit vs. Chicago, Nov. 21, 1976
    Bobby Morse, Philadelphia vs. Buffalo, Dec. 27, 1987
6   Jake Scott, Miami vs. Buffalo, Dec. 20, 1970
    Greg Pruitt, L.A. Raiders vs. Seattle, Oct. 7, 1984
    Phil McConkey, San Diego vs. Kansas City,
    Dec. 17, 1989
    Gerald McNeil, Houston vs. Pittsburgh,
    Sept. 16, 1990
    Bobby Engram, Chicago vs. Minnesota,
    Sept. 15, 1996
    Eddie Kennison, New Orleans vs. Baltimore,
    Dec. 19, 1999
    R.W. McQuarters, N.Y. Giants vs. Atlanta,
    Oct. 15, 2007
5   By many players

YARDS GAINED
Most Seasons Leading League
3   Alvin Haymond, Baltimore, 1965-66; Los Angeles,
    1969
2   Bill Dudley, Pittsburgh, 1942, 1946
    Emlen Tunnell, N.Y. Giants, 1951-52
    Dick Christy, N.Y. Titans, 1961-62
    Claude Gibson, Oakland, 1963-64
    Rodger Bird, Oakland, 1966-67
    J.T. Smith, Kansas City, 1979-1980
    Vai Sikahema, St. Louis, 1986-87
    David Meggett, N.Y. Giants, 1989-1990
    Tamarick Vanover, Kansas City, 1995, 1999
Most Yards Gained, Career
4,999   Brian Mitchell, Washington, 1990-99; Philadelphia,
        2000-02; N.Y. Giants, 2003
3,708   David Meggett, N.Y. Giants, 1989-1994;
        New England, 1995-97; N.Y. Jets, 1998
3,601   Darrien Gordon, San Diego, 1993-94, 1996; Denver,
        1997-98; Oakland, 1999-2000; Atlanta, 2001;
        Green Bay, 2002
Most Yards Gained, Season
875   Desmond Howard, Green Bay, 1996
692   Fulton Walker, Miami-L.A. Raiders, 1985
666   Greg Pruitt, L.A. Raiders, 1983
Most Yards Gained, Rookie, Season
656   Louis Lipps, Pittsburgh, 1984
655   Neal Colzie, Oakland, 1975
619   Leon Johnson, N.Y. Jets, 1997
Most Yards Gained, Game
207   LeRoy Irvin, Los Angeles vs. Atlanta, Oct. 11, 1981
205   George Atkinson, Oakland vs. Buffalo, Sept. 15, 1968
199   Eddie Drummond, Detroit vs. Jacksonville,
      Nov. 14, 2004 (OT)
Longest Punt Return (All TDs)
103   Robert Bailey, L.A. Rams vs. New Orleans,
      Oct. 23, 1994
98   Gil LeFebvre, Cincinnati vs. Brooklyn, Dec. 3, 1933
      Charlie West, Minnesota vs. Washington, Nov. 3, 1968

Dennis Morgan, Dallas vs. St. Louis, Oct. 13, 1974
Terance Mathis, N.Y. Jets vs. Dallas, Nov. 4, 1990
97   Greg Pruitt, L.A. Raiders vs. Washington,
     Oct. 2, 1983

AVERAGE YARDAGE
Highest Average, Career (75 returns)
14.06   Devin Hester, Chicago, 2006-07 (89-1,251)
12.78   George McAfee, Chi. Bears, 1940-41, 1945-1950
     (112-1,431)
12.75   Jack Christiansen, Detroit, 1951-58 (85-1,084)
Highest Average, Season (Qualifiers)
23.00   Herb Rich, Baltimore, 1950 (12-276)
21.47   Jack Christiansen, Detroit, 1952 (15-322)
21.28   Dick Christy, N.Y. Titans, 1961 (18-383)
Highest Average, Rookie, Season (Qualifiers)
23.00   Herb Rich, Baltimore, 1950 (12-276)
20.88   Jerry Davis, Chi. Cardinals, 1948 (16-334)
20.73   Frank Sinkwich, Detroit, 1943 (11-228)
Highest Average, Game (3 returns)
51.00   Steve Smith, Carolina vs. Cincinnati, Dec. 8, 2002
     (3-153)
47.67   Chuck Latourette, St. Louis vs. New Orleans,
     Sept. 29, 1968 (3-143)
47.33   Johnny Roland, St. Louis vs. Philadelphia,
     Oct. 2, 1966 (3-142)

TOUCHDOWNS
Most Touchdowns, Career
10   Eric Metcalf, Cleveland, 1989-1994; Atlanta, 1995-
     96; San Diego, 1997; Arizona, 1998; Carolina,
     1999; Washington, 2001; Green Bay, 2002
9   Brian Mitchell, Washington, 1990-99; Philadelphia
     2000-02; N.Y. Giants, 2003
8   Jack Christiansen, Detroit, 1951-58
     Rick Upchurch, Denver, 1975-1983
     Desmond Howard, Washington, 1992-94;
     Jacksonville, 1995; Green Bay, 1996, 1999;
     Oakland, 1997-98; Detroit, 1999-2002
Most Touchdowns, Season
4   Jack Christiansen, Detroit, 1951
     Rick Upchurch, Denver, 1976
     Devin Hester, Chicago, 2007
3   Emlen Tunnell, N.Y. Giants, 1951
     Billy (White Shoes) Johnson, Houston, 1975
     LeRoy Irvin, Los Angeles, 1981
     Desmond Howard, Green Bay, 1996
     Darrien Gordon, Denver, 1997
     Eric Metcalf, San Diego, 1997
     Devin Hester, Chicago, 2006
     Pacman Jones, Tennessee, 2006
2   By many players
Most Touchdowns, Rookie, Season
4   Jack Christiansen, Detroit, 1951
3   Devin Hester, Chicago, 2006
2   By many players
Most Touchdowns, Game
2   Jack Christiansen, Detroit vs. Los Angeles,
     Oct. 14, 1951; vs. Green Bay, Nov. 22, 1951
     Dick Christy, N.Y. Titans vs. Denver, Sept. 24, 1961
     Rick Upchurch, Denver vs. Cleveland, Sept. 26, 1976
     LeRoy Irvin, Los Angeles vs. Atlanta, Oct. 11, 1981
     Vai Sikahema, St. Louis vs. Tampa Bay,
     Dec. 21, 1986
     Todd Kinchen, L.A. Rams vs. Atlanta, Dec. 27, 1992
     Eric Metcalf, Cleveland vs. Pittsburgh, Oct. 24, 1993;
     San Diego vs. Cincinnati, Nov. 2, 1997

Darrien Gordon, Denver vs. Carolina, Nov. 9, 1997
Jermaine Lewis, Baltimore vs. Seattle, Dec. 7, 1997;
     Baltimore vs. N.Y. Jets, Dec. 24, 2000
Steve Smith, Carolina vs. Cincinnati, Dec. 8, 2002
Eddie Drummond, Detroit vs. Jacksonville,
     Nov. 14, 2004 (OT)

KICKOFF RETURNS
Most Seasons Leading League
3   Abe Woodson, San Francisco, 1959, 1962-63
2   Lynn Chandnois, Pittsburgh, 1951-52
     Bobby Jancik, Houston, 1962-63
     Travis Williams, Green Bay, 1967; Los Angeles, 1971
     Mel Gray, Detroit, 1991, 1994
     Michael Bates, Carolina, 1996-97

KICKOFF RETURNS
Most Kickoff Returns, Career
607   Brian Mitchell, Washington, 1990-99; Philadelphia
     2000-02; N.Y. Giants, 2003
459   Allen Rossum, Philadelphia, 1998-99; Green Bay,
     2000-01; Atlanta, 2002-06; Pittsburgh, 2007
421   Mel Gray, New Orleans, 1986-88; Detroit, 1989-
     1994; Houston, 1995-96; Tennessee, 1997;
     Philadelphia, 1997
Most Kickoff Returns, Season
82   MarTay Jenkins, Arizona, 2000
73   Josh Scobey, Arizona, 2003
     Chris Carr, Oakland, 2005
70   Tyrone Hughes, New Orleans, 1996
     Michael Lewis, New Orleans, 2002
Most Kickoff Returns, Rookie, Season
73   Josh Scobey, Arizona, 2003
     Chris Carr, Oakland, 2005
67   Ronney Jenkins, San Diego, 2000
64   Tab Perry, Cincinnati, 2005
Most Kickoff Returns, Game
10   Desmond Howard, Oakland vs. Seattle, Oct. 26, 1997
     Richard Alston, Cleveland vs. Cincinnati,
     Nov. 28, 2004
9   Noland Smith, Kansas City vs. Oakland, Nov. 23, 1967
     Dino Hall, Cleveland vs. Pittsburgh, Oct. 7, 1979
     Paul Palmer, Kansas City vs. Seattle, Sept. 20, 1987
     Eric Metcalf, Atlanta vs. San Francisco,
     Sept. 29, 1996; vs. St. Louis, Nov. 10, 1996
     Michael Bates, Carolina vs. Atlanta, Oct. 4, 1998
     Nate Jacquet, Minnesota vs. Philadelphia,
     Nov. 11, 2001
     Ahmad Merritt, Chicago vs. San Francisco,
     Sept. 7, 2003
     Josh Scobey, Arizona vs. Cleveland, Nov. 16, 2003
     Maurice Hicks, San Francisco vs. San Diego,
     Oct. 15, 2006
     Aveion Cason, Detroit vs. San Diego, Dec. 16, 2007
8   By many players

YARDS GAINED
Most Seasons Leading League
3   Bruce Harper, N.Y. Jets, 1977-79
     Tyrone Hughes, New Orleans, 1994-96
2   Marshall Goldberg, Chi. Cardinals, 1941-42
     Woodley Lewis, Los Angeles, 1953-54
     Al Carmichael, Green Bay, 1956-57
     Timmy Brown, Philadelphia, 1961, 1963
     Bobby Jancik, Houston, 1963, 1966
     Ron Smith, Atlanta, 1966-67
     Chris Carr, Oakland, 2005-06

Most Yards Gained, Career
- 14,014   Brian Mitchell, Washington, 1990-99; Philadelphia, 2000-02; N.Y. Giants, 2003
- 10,520   Allen Rossum, Philadelphia, 1998-99; Green Bay, 2000-01; Atlanta, 2002-06; Pittsburgh, 2007
- 10,250   Mel Gray, New Orleans, 1986-88; Detroit, 1989-1994; Houston, 1995-96; Tennessee, 1997; Philadelphia, 1997

Most Yards Gained, Season
- 2,186   MarTay Jenkins, Arizona, 2000
- 1,809   Josh Cribbs, Cleveland, 2007
- 1,807   Michael Lewis, New Orleans, 2002

Most Yards Gained, Rookie, Season
- 1,752   Chris Carr, Oakland, 2005
- 1,684   Josh Scobey, Arizona, 2003
- 1,577   Justin Miller, N.Y. Jets, 2005

Most Yards Gained, Game
- 304   Tyrone Hughes, New Orleans vs. L.A. Rams, Oct. 23, 1994
- 294   Wally Triplett, Detroit vs. Los Angeles, Oct. 29, 1950
- 278   Chad Morton, N.Y. Jets vs. Buffalo, Sept. 8, 2002 (OT)

Longest Kickoff Return (All TDs)
- 108   Ellis Hobbs, New England, vs. N.Y. Jets, Sept. 9, 2007
- 106   Al Carmichael, Green Bay vs. Chi. Bears, Oct. 7, 1956
-      Noland Smith, Kansas City vs. Denver, Dec. 17, 1967
-      Roy Green, St. Louis vs. Dallas, Oct. 21, 1979
- 105   Frank Seno, Chi. Cardinals vs. N.Y. Giants, Oct. 20, 1946
-      Ollie Matson, Chi. Cardinals vs. Washington, Oct. 14, 1956
-      Abe Woodson, San Francisco vs. Los Angeles, Nov. 8, 1959
-      Timmy Brown, Philadelphia vs. Cleveland, Sept. 17, 1961
-      Jon Arnett, Los Angeles vs. Detroit, Oct. 29, 1961
-      Eugene (Mercury) Morris, Miami vs. Cincinnati, Sept. 14, 1969
-      Travis Williams, Los Angeles vs. New Orleans, Dec. 5, 1971
-      Terry Fair, Detroit vs. Tampa Bay, Sept. 28, 1998

AVERAGE YARDAGE

Highest Average, Career (75 returns)
- 30.56   Gale Sayers, Chicago, 1965-1971 (91-2,781)
- 29.57   Lynn Chandnois, Pittsburgh, 1950-56 (92-2,720)
- 28.69   Abe Woodson, San Francisco, 1958-1964; St. Louis, 1965-66 (193-5,538)

Highest Average, Season (Qualifiers)
- 41.06   Travis Williams, Green Bay, 1967 (18-739)
- 37.69   Gale Sayers, Chicago, 1967 (16-603)
- 35.50   Ollie Matson, Chi. Cardinals, 1958 (14-497)

Highest Average, Rookie, Season (Qualifiers)
- 41.06   Travis Williams, Green Bay, 1967 (18-739)
- 33.08   Tom Moore, Green Bay, 1960 (12-397)
- 32.88   Duriel Harris, Miami, 1976 (17-559)

Highest Average, Game (3 returns)
- 73.50   Wally Triplett, Detroit vs. Los Angeles, Oct. 29, 1950 (4-294)
- 67.33   Lenny Lyles, San Francisco vs. Baltimore, Dec. 18, 1960 (3-202)
- 65.33   Ken Hall, Houston vs. N.Y. Titans, Oct. 23, 1960 (3-196)

TOUCHDOWNS

Most Touchdowns, Career
- 6   Ollie Matson, Chi. Cardinals, 1952, 1954-58; L.A. Rams, 1959-1962; Detroit, 1963; Philadelphia, 1964

     Gale Sayers, Chicago, 1965-1971
-    Travis Williams, Green Bay, 1967-1970; Los Angeles, 1971
-    Mel Gray, New Orleans, 1986-88; Detroit, 1989-1994; Houston, 1995-96; Tennessee, 1997; Philadelphia, 1997
-    Dante Hall, Kansas City, 2000-06; St. Louis, 2007
- 5   Bobby Mitchell, Cleveland, 1958-1961; Washington, 1962-68
-    Abe Woodson, San Francisco, 1958-1964; St. Louis, 1965-66
-    Timmy Brown, Green Bay, 1959; Philadelphia, 1960-67; Baltimore, 1968
-    Michael Bates, Seattle, 1993-94; Cleveland, 1995; Carolina, 1996-2000, 2002; Washington, 2001; N.Y. Jets, 2003; Dallas, 2003
-    Terrence McGee, Buffalo, 2003-07
- 4   Cecil Turner, Chicago, 1968-1973
-    Ron Brown, L.A. Rams, 1984-89, 1991; L.A. Raiders, 1990
-    Jon Vaughn, New England, 1991-92; Seattle, 1993-94; Kansas City, 1994
-    Andre Coleman, San Diego, 1994-96; Seattle, 1997; Pittsburgh, 1997-98
-    Tamarick Vanover, Kansas City, 1995-99, San Diego, 2002
-    Tony Horne, St. Louis, 1998-2000
-    Brian Mitchell, Washington, 1990-99; Philadelphia, 2000-02; N.Y. Giants, 2003
-    Darrick Vaughn, Atlanta, 2000-01; Houston, 2003
-    Josh Cribbs, Cleveland, 2005-07
-    Andre Davis, Cleveland, 2002-04; New England, 2005; Buffalo, 2006; Houston, 2007
-    Devin Hester, Chicago, 2006-07
-    Allen Rossum, Philadelphia, 1998-99; Green Bay, 2000-01; Atlanta, 2002-06; Pittsburgh, 2007

Most Touchdowns, Season
- 4   Travis Williams, Green Bay, 1967
-    Cecil Turner, Chicago, 1970
- 3   Verda (Vitamin T) Smith, Los Angeles, 1950
-    Abe Woodson, San Francisco, 1963
-    Gale Sayers, Chicago, 1967
-    Raymond Clayborn, New England, 1977
-    Ron Brown, L.A. Rams, 1985
-    Mel Gray, Detroit, 1994
-    Darrick Vaughn, Atlanta, 2000
-    Terrence McGee, Buffalo, 2004
-    Andre Davis, Houston, 2007
-    Leon Washington, N.Y. Jets, 2007
- 2   By many players

Most Touchdowns, Rookie, Season
- 4   Travis Williams, Green Bay, 1967
- 3   Raymond Clayborn, New England, 1977
-    Darrick Vaughn, Atlanta, 2000
- 2   By many players

Most Touchdowns, Game
- 2   Timmy Brown, Philadelphia vs. Dallas, Nov. 6, 1966
-    Travis Williams, Green Bay vs. Cleveland, Nov. 12, 1967
-    Ron Brown, L.A. Rams vs. Green Bay, Nov. 24, 1985
-    Tyrone Hughes, New Orleans vs. L.A. Rams, Oct. 23, 1994
-    Chad Morton, N.Y. Jets vs. Buffalo, Sept. 8, 2002 (OT)
-    Devin Hester, Chicago vs. St. Louis, Dec. 11, 2006
-    Andre Davis, Houston vs. Jacksonville, Dec. 30, 2007

COMBINED KICK RETURNS

Most Combined Kick Returns, Career
- 1,070   Brian Mitchell, Washington, 1990-99; Philadelphia, 2000-02; N.Y. Giants, 2003 (p-463, k-607)

739   Allen Rossum, Philadelphia, 1998-99; Green Bay,
     2000-01; Atlanta, 2002-06; Pittsburgh, 2007
     (p-280, k-459)
711   Glyn Milburn, Denver, 1993-95; Detroit, 1996-97;
     Chicago, 1998-2001; San Diego, 2001 (p-304,
     k-407)

Most Combined Kick Returns, Season
114   Michael Lewis, New Orleans, 2002 (p-44, k-70)
     B.J. Sams, Baltimore, 2004 (p-55, k-59)
107   Chris Carr, Oakland, 2005 (p-34, k-73)
     Dante Hall, Kansas City, 2005 (p-42, k-65)
105   Reggie Swinton, Arizona, 2005 (p-42, k-63)

Most Combined Kick Returns, Game
13   Stump Mitchell, St. Louis vs. Atlanta, Oct. 18, 1981
     (p-6, k-7)
     Ronnie Harris, New England vs. Pittsburgh,
     Dec. 5, 1993 (p-10, k-3)
12   Mel Renfro, Dallas vs. Green Bay, Nov. 29, 1964
     (p-4, k-8)
     Larry Jones, Washington vs. Dallas, Dec. 13, 1975
     (p-6, k-6)
     Eddie Brown, Washington vs. Tampa Bay,
     Oct. 9, 1977 (p-11, k-1)
     Nesby Glasgow, Baltimore vs. Denver, Sept. 2, 1979
     (p-9, k-3)
     Tim Dwight, Atlanta vs. Detroit, Nov. 12, 2000
     (p-8, k-4)
     Wes Welker, Miami vs. Buffalo, Dec. 5, 2004
     (p-6, k-6)
     Reggie Swinton, Arizona vs. Philadelphia,
     Dec. 24, 2005 (p-9, k-3)
     Devin Hester, Chicago vs. Detroit, Sept. 30, 2007
     (p-5, k-7)
11   By many players

YARDS GAINED
Most Yards Returned, Career
19,013   Brian Mitchell, Washington, 1990-99; Philadelphia,
     2000-02; N.Y. Giants, 2003 (p-4,999; k-14,014)
13,269   Allen Rossum, Philadelphia, 1998-99; Green Bay,
     2000-01; Atlanta, 2002-06; Pittsburgh, 2007
     (p-2,749, k-10,520)
13,003   Mel Gray, New Orleans, 1986-88; Detroit,
     1989-1994; Houston, 1995-96; Tennessee,
     1997; Philadelphia, 1997 (p-2,753; k-10,250)

Most Yards Returned, Season
2,432   Michael Lewis, New Orleans, 2002 (p-625, k-1,807)
2,214   Josh Cribbs, Cleveland, 2007 (p-405, k-1,809)
2,187   MarTay Jenkins, Arizona, 2000 (p-1, k-2,186)

Most Yards Returned, Game
347   Tyrone Hughes, New Orleans vs. L.A. Rams,
     Oct. 23, 1994 (p-43, k-304)
314   Devin Hester, Chicago vs. Detroit,
     Sept. 30, 2007 (p-95, k-219)
306   Josh Cribbs, Cleveland vs. Baltimore,
     Nov. 18, 2007 (OT) (p-61, k-245)

TOUCHDOWNS
Most Touchdowns, Career
13   Brian Mitchell, Washington, 1990-99; Philadelphia,
     2000-02; N.Y. Giants, 2003 (p-9, k-4)
12   Eric Metcalf, Cleveland, 1989-1994; Atlanta,
     1995-96; San Diego, 1997; Arizona, 1998;
     Carolina, 1999; Washington, 2001; Green Bay,
     2002 (p-10, k-2)
     Dante Hall, Kansas City, 2000-06; St. Louis, 2007
     (p-6, k-6)
11   Devin Hester, Chicago, 2006-07 (p-7, k-4)

Most Touchdowns, Season
6   Devin Hester, Chicago, 2007 (p-4, k-2)

5   Devin Hester, Chicago, 2006 (p-3, k-2)
4   Jack Christiansen, Detroit, 1951 (p-4)
     Emlen Tunnell, N.Y. Giants, 1951 (p-3, k-1)
     Gale Sayers, Chicago, 1967 (p-1, k-3)
     Travis Williams, Green Bay, 1967 (k-4)
     Cecil Turner, Chicago, 1970 (k-4)
     Billy Johnson, Houston, 1975 (p-3, k-1)
     Rick Upchurch, Denver, 1976 (p-4)
     Dante Hall, Kansas City, 2003 (p-2, r-2)
     Eddie Drummond, Detroit, 2004 (p-2, k-2)

Most Touchdowns, Game
2   Jack Christiansen, Detroit vs. Los Angeles,
     Oct. 14, 1951 (p-2); vs. Green Bay,
     Nov. 22, 1951 (p-2)
     Jim Patton, N.Y. Giants vs. Washington,
     Oct. 30, 1955 (p-1, k-1)
     Bobby Mitchell, Cleveland vs. Philadelphia,
     Nov. 23, 1958 (p-1, k-1)
     Dick Christy, N.Y. Titans vs. Denver, Sept. 24, 1961
     (p-2)
     Al Frazier, Denver vs. Boston, Dec. 3, 1961 (p-1, k-1)
     Timmy Brown, Philadelphia vs. Dallas, Nov. 6, 1966
     (k-2)
     Travis Williams, Green Bay vs. Cleveland,
     Nov. 12, 1967 (k-2); vs. Pittsburgh,
     Nov. 2, 1969 (p-1, k-1)
     Gale Sayers, Chicago vs. San Francisco,
     Dec. 3, 1967 (p-1, k-1)
     Rick Upchurch, Denver vs. Cleveland,
     Sept. 26, 1976 (p-2)
     Eddie Payton, Detroit vs. Minnesota, Dec. 17, 1977
     (p-1, k-1)
     LeRoy Irvin, Los Angeles vs. Atlanta, Oct. 11, 1981
     (p-2)
     Ron Brown, L.A. Rams vs. Green Bay,
     Nov. 24, 1985 (k-2)
     Vai Sikahema, St. Louis vs. Tampa Bay,
     Dec. 21, 1986 (p-2)
     Todd Kinchen, L.A. Rams vs. Atlanta, Dec. 27, 1992
     (p-2)
     Eric Metcalf, Cleveland vs. Pittsburgh, Oct. 24, 1993
     (p-2); San Diego vs. Cincinnati, Nov. 2, 1997
     (p-2)
     Tyrone Hughes, New Orleans vs. L.A. Rams,
     Oct. 23, 1994 (k-2)
     Darrien Gordon, Denver vs. Carolina, Nov. 9, 1997
     (p-2)
     Jermaine Lewis, Baltimore vs. Seattle, Dec. 7, 1997
     (p-2); Baltimore vs. N.Y. Jets, Dec. 24, 2000
     (p-2)
     Chad Morton, N.Y. Jets vs. Buffalo, Sept. 8, 2002
     (OT) (k-2)
     Michael Lewis, New Orleans vs. Washington,
     Oct. 13, 2002 (p-1, k-1)
     Dante Hall, Kansas City vs. St. Louis, Dec. 8, 2002
     (p-1, k-1)
     Steve Smith, Carolina vs. Cincinnati, Dec. 8, 2002
     (p-2)
     Eddie Drummond, Detroit vs. Jacksonville,
     Nov. 14, 2004 (OT) (p-2)
     Devin Hester, Chicago vs. St. Louis, Dec. 11, 2006
     (k-2)
     Darren Sproles, San Diego vs. Indianapolis,
     Nov. 11, 2007 (p-1, k-1)
     Devin Hester, Chicago vs. Denver, Nov. 25, 2007
     (p-1, k-1)
     Andre Davis, Houston vs. Jacksonville,
     Dec. 30, 2007 (k-2)

FUMBLES

Most Fumbles, Career
- 161   Warren Moon, Houston, 1984-1993; Minnesota, 1994-96; Seattle, 1997-98; Kansas City, 1999-2000
- 153   Dave Krieg, Seattle, 1980-1991; Kansas City, 1992-93; Detroit, 1994; Arizona, 1995; Chicago, 1996; Tennessee, 1997-98
- 147   Brett Favre, Atlanta, 1991; Green Bay, 1992-2007

Most Fumbles, Season
- 23   Kerry Collins, N.Y. Giants, 2001
  - Daunte Culpepper, Minnesota, 2002
- 21   Tony Banks, St. Louis, 1996
  - David Carr, Houston, 2002
- 18   Dave Krieg, Seattle, 1989
  - Warren Moon, Houston, 1990

Most Fumbles, Game
- 7   Len Dawson, Kansas City vs. San Diego, Nov. 15, 1964
- 6   Sam Etcheverry, St. Louis vs. N.Y. Giants, Sept. 17, 1961
  - Dave Krieg, Seattle vs. Kansas City, Nov. 5, 1989
  - Brett Favre, Green Bay vs. Tampa Bay, Dec. 7, 1998
  - Kurt Warner, St. Louis vs. N.Y. Giants, Sept. 7, 2003
  - Chad Pennington, N.Y. Jets vs. Kansas City, Sept. 11, 2005
- 5   Paul Christman, Chi. Cardinals vs. Green Bay, Nov. 10, 1946
  - Joe Perry, San Francisco vs. Cleveland, Nov. 12, 1950
  - Charlie Conerly, N.Y. Giants vs. San Francisco, Dec. 1, 1957
  - Tom Yewcic, Boston vs. Oakland, Dec. 16, 1962
  - Jack Kemp, Buffalo vs. Houston, Oct. 29, 1967
  - Roman Gabriel, Philadelphia vs. Oakland, Nov. 21, 1976
  - Randall Cunningham, Philadelphia vs. L.A. Raiders, Nov. 30, 1986 (OT)
  - Willie Totten, Buffalo vs. Indianapolis, Oct. 4, 1987
  - Dave Walter, Cincinnati vs. Seattle, Oct. 11, 1987
  - Dave Krieg, Seattle vs. San Diego, Nov. 25, 1990 (OT)
  - Andre Ware, Detroit vs. Green Bay, Dec. 6, 1992
  - Steve Beuerlein, Carolina vs. San Francisco, Nov. 8, 1998
  - Patrick Ramsey, Washington vs. Green Bay, Oct. 20, 2002
  - Eli Manning, N.Y. Giants vs. Buffalo, Dec. 23, 2007

FUMBLES RECOVERED

Most Fumbles Recovered, Career, Own and Opponents'
- 56   Warren Moon, Houston, 1984-1993; Minnesota, 1994-96; Seattle, 1997-98; Kansas City, 1999-2000 (56 own)
- 47   Dave Krieg, Seattle, 1980-1991; Kansas City, 1992-93; Detroit, 1994; Arizona, 1995; Chicago, 1996; Tennessee, 1997-98 (47 own)
- 45   Boomer Esiason, Cincinnati, 1984-1992, 1997; N.Y. Jets, 1993-95; Arizona, 1996 (45 own)

Most Fumbles Recovered, Season, Own and Opponents'
- 12   David Carr, Houston, 2002 (12 own)
- 9   Don Hultz, Minnesota, 1963 (9 opp)
  - Dave Krieg, Seattle, 1989 (9 own)
  - Brian Griese, Denver, 1999 (9 own)
  - Jon Kitna, Seattle, 2000 (9 own)
- 8   Paul Christman, Chi. Cardinals, 1945 (8 own)
  - Joe Schmidt, Detroit, 1955 (8 opp)
  - Bill Butler, Minnesota, 1963 (8 own)
  - Kermit Alexander, San Francisco, 1965 (4 own, 4 opp)

- Jack Lambert, Pittsburgh, 1976 (1 own, 7 opp)
- Danny White, Dallas, 1981 (8 own)
- Dan Marino, Miami, 1988 (7 own, 1 opp)
- Tony Banks, St. Louis, 1998 (8 own)

Most Fumbles Recovered, Game, Own and Opponents'
- 4   Otto Graham, Cleveland vs. N.Y. Giants, Oct. 25, 1953 (4 own)
  - Sam Etcheverry, St. Louis vs. N.Y. Giants, Sept. 17, 1961 (4 own)
  - Roman Gabriel, Los Angeles vs. San Francisco, Oct. 12, 1969 (4 own)
  - Joe Ferguson, Buffalo vs. Miami, Sept. 18, 1977 (4 own)
  - Randall Cunningham, Philadelphia vs. L.A. Raiders, Nov. 30, 1986 (OT) (4 own)
- 3   By many players

OWN FUMBLES RECOVERED

Most Own Fumbles Recovered, Career
- 56   Warren Moon, Houston, 1984-1993; Minnesota, 1994-96; Seattle, 1997-98; Kansas City, 1999-2000
- 47   Dave Krieg, Seattle, 1980-1991; Kansas City, 1992-93; Detroit, 1994; Arizona, 1995; Chicago, 1996; Tennessee, 1997-98
- 45   Boomer Esiason, Cincinnati, 1984-1992, 1997; N.Y. Jets, 1993-95; Arizona, 1996

Most Own Fumbles Recovered, Season
- 12   David Carr, Houston, 2002
- 9   Dave Krieg, Seattle, 1989
  - Brian Griese, Denver, 1999
  - Jon Kitna, Seattle, 2000
- 8   Paul Christman, Chi. Cardinals, 1945
  - Bill Butler, Minnesota, 1963
  - Danny White, Dallas, 1981
  - Tony Banks, St. Louis, 1998

Most Own Fumbles Recovered, Game
- 4   Otto Graham, Cleveland vs. N.Y. Giants, Oct. 25, 1953
  - Sam Etcheverry, St. Louis vs. N.Y. Giants, Sept. 17, 1961
  - Roman Gabriel, Los Angeles vs. San Francisco, Oct. 12, 1969
  - Joe Ferguson, Buffalo vs. Miami, Sept. 18, 1977
  - Randall Cunningham, Philadelphia vs. L.A. Raiders, Nov. 30, 1986 (OT)
- 3   By many players

OPPONENTS' FUMBLES RECOVERED

Most Opponents' Fumbles Recovered, Career
- 29   Jim Marshall, Cleveland, 1960; Minnesota, 1961-1979
- 28   Rickey Jackson, New Orleans, 1981-1993; San Francisco, 1994-95
- 26   Kevin Greene, L.A. Rams, 1985-1992; Pittsburgh, 1993-95; Carolina, 1996, 1998-99; San Francisco, 1997
  - Cornelius Bennett, Buffalo, 1987-1995; Atlanta, 1996-98; Indianapolis, 1999-2000
  - Jason Taylor, Miami, 1997-2007

Most Opponents' Fumbles Recovered, Season
- 9   Don Hultz, Minnesota, 1963
- 8   Joe Schmidt, Detroit, 1955
- 7   Alan Page, Minnesota, 1970
  - Jack Lambert, Pittsburgh, 1976
  - Ray Childress, Houston, 1988
  - Rickey Jackson, New Orleans, 1990

Most Opponents' Fumbles Recovered, Game
- 3   Corwin Clatt, Chi. Cardinals vs. Detroit, Nov. 6, 1949
  - Vic Sears, Philadelphia vs. Green Bay, Nov. 2, 1952
  - Ed Beatty, San Francisco vs. Los Angeles, Oct. 7, 1956

Ron Carroll, Houston vs. Cincinnati, Oct. 27, 1974
Maurice Spencer, New Orleans vs. Atlanta,
   Oct. 10, 1976
Steve Nelson, New England vs. Philadelphia,
   Oct. 8, 1978
Charles Jackson, Kansas City vs. Pittsburgh,
   Sept. 6, 1981
Willie Buchanon, San Diego vs. Denver,
   Sept. 27, 1981
Joey Browner, Minnesota vs. San Francisco,
   Sept. 8, 1985
Ray Childress, Houston vs. Washington, Oct. 30, 1988
John Thierry, Chicago vs. Houston, Oct. 22, 1995
Stephen Boyd, Detroit vs. Chicago, Oct. 4, 1998
Darryl Williams, Seattle vs. Kansas City, Oct. 4, 1998
Rod Woodson, Oakland vs. Pittsburgh, Sept. 15, 2002
Brian Young, St. Louis vs. Baltimore, Nov. 9, 2003
2 By many players

YARDS RETURNING FUMBLES
Longest Fumble Run (All TDs)
104 Jack Tatum, Oakland vs. Green Bay, Sept. 24, 1972
      Aeneas Williams, Arizona vs. Washington,
       Nov. 5, 2000
102 Travis Davis, Pittsburgh vs. Carolina, Dec. 26, 1999
100 Chris Martin, Kansas City vs. Miami, Oct. 13, 1991

TOUCHDOWNS
Most Touchdowns, Career (Total)
5 Jessie Tuggle, Atlanta, 1987-2000
   Jason Taylor, Miami, 1997-2007
4 Bill Thompson, Denver, 1969-1981
   Derrick Thomas, Kansas City, 1989-1999
   Keith Bulluck, Tennessee, 2000-07
   Ronde Barber, Tampa Bay, 1997-2007
3 By many players
Most Touchdowns, Season (Total)
2 Harold McPhail, Boston, 1934
   Harry Ebding, Detroit, 1937
   John Morelli, Boston, 1944
   Frank Maznicki, Boston, 1947
   Fred (Dippy) Evans, Chi. Bears, 1948
   Ralph Heywood, Boston, 1948
   Art Tait, N.Y. Yanks, 1951
   John Dwyer, Los Angeles, 1952
   Leo Sugar, Chi. Cardinals, 1957
   Doug Cline, Houston, 1961
   Jim Bradshaw, Pittsburgh, 1964
   Royce Berry, Cincinnati, 1970
   Ahmad Rashad, Buffalo, 1974
   Tim Gray, Kansas City, 1977
   Charles Phillips, Oakland, 1978
   Kenny Johnson, Atlanta, 1981
   George Martin, N.Y. Giants, 1981
   Del Rodgers, Green Bay, 1982
   Mike Douglass, Green Bay, 1983
   Shelton Robinson, Seattle, 1983
   Erik McMillan, N.Y. Jets, 1989
   Les Miller, San Diego, 1990
   Seth Joyner, Philadelphia, 1991
   Robert Goff, New Orleans, 1992
   Willie Clay, Detroit, 1993
   Tyrone Hughes, New Orleans, 1994
   Chad Brown, Seattle, 1997
   Marcus Robertson, Tennessee, 1997
   Dwayne Rudd, Minnesota, 1998
   Keith McKenzie, Green Bay, 1999
   Ronde Barber, Tampa Bay, 2004
   Leonard Little, St. Louis, 2004
   Antwan Odom, Tennessee, 2005

Adalius Thomas, Baltimore, 2005
Kevin Curtis, Philadelphia, 2007
Most Touchdowns, Career (Own recovered)
2 Ken Kavanaugh, Chi. Bears, 1940-41, 1945-1950
   Mike Ditka, Chicago, 1961-66; Philadelphia,
      1967-68; Dallas, 1969-1972
   Gail Cogdill, Detroit, 1960-68; Baltimore, 1968;
      Atlanta, 1969-1970
   Ahmad Rashad, St. Louis, 1972-73; Buffalo, 1974;
      Minnesota, 1976-1982
   Jim Mitchell, Atlanta, 1969-1979
   Drew Pearson, Dallas, 1973-1983
   Del Rodgers, Green Bay, 1982, 1984; San Francisco,
      1987-88
   Alan Ricard, Baltimore, 2001-05
   Kevin Curtis, St. Louis, 2003-06; Philadelphia, 2007
Most Touchdowns, Season (Own recovered)
2 Ahmad Rashad, Buffalo, 1974
   Del Rodgers, Green Bay, 1982
   Kevin Curtis, Philadelphia, 2007
1 By many players
Most Touchdowns, Career (Opponents' recovered)
5 Jessie Tuggle, Atlanta, 1987-2000
   Jason Taylor, Miami, 1997-2007
4 Derrick Thomas, Kansas City, 1989-1999
   Keith Bulluck, Tennessee, 2000-07
   Ronde Barber, Tampa Bay, 1997-2007
3 By many players
Most Touchdowns, Season (Opponents' recovered)
2 Harold McPhail, Boston, 1934
   Harry Ebding, Detroit, 1937
   John Morelli, Boston, 1944
   Frank Maznicki, Boston, 1947
   Fred (Dippy) Evans, Chi. Bears, 1948
   Ralph Heywood, Boston, 1948
   Art Tait, N.Y. Yanks, 1951
   John Dwyer, Los Angeles, 1952
   Leo Sugar, Chi. Cardinals, 1957
   Doug Cline, Houston, 1961
   Jim Bradshaw, Pittsburgh, 1964
   Royce Berry, Cincinnati, 1970
   Tim Gray, Kansas City, 1977
   Charles Phillips, Oakland, 1978
   Kenny Johnson, Atlanta, 1981
   George Martin, N.Y. Giants, 1981
   Mike Douglass, Green Bay, 1983
   Shelton Robinson, Seattle, 1983
   Erik McMillan, N.Y. Jets, 1989
   Les Miller, San Diego, 1990
   Seth Joyner, Philadelphia, 1991
   Robert Goff, New Orleans, 1992
   Willie Clay, Detroit, 1993
   Tyrone Hughes, New Orleans, 1994
   Chad Brown, Seattle, 1997
   Marcus Robertson, Tennessee, 1997
   Dwayne Rudd, Minnesota, 1998
   Keith McKenzie, Green Bay, 1999
   Ronde Barber, Tampa Bay, 2004
   Leonard Little, St. Louis, 2004
   Antwan Odom, Tennessee, 2005
   Adalius Thomas, Baltimore, 2005
Most Touchdowns, Game (Opponents' recovered)
2 Fred (Dippy) Evans, Chi. Bears vs. Washington,
      Nov. 28, 1948

COMBINED NET YARDS GAINED
Rushing, receiving, interception returns, punt returns, kickoff
returns, and fumble returns
Most Seasons Leading League
5 Jim Brown, Cleveland, 1958-1961, 1964

   4   Brian Mitchell, Washington, 1994-96, 1998
   3   Cliff Battles, Boston, 1932-33; Washington, 1937
        Gale Sayers, Chicago, 1965-67
        Eric Dickerson, L.A. Rams, 1983-84, 1986
        Thurman Thomas, Buffalo, 1989, 1991-92

Most Consecutive Seasons Leading League
   4   Jim Brown, Cleveland, 1958-1961
   3   Gale Sayers, Chicago, 1965-67
        Brian Mitchell, Washington, 1994-96
   2   Cliff Battles, Boston, 1932-33
        Charley Trippi, Chi. Cardinals, 1948-49
        Timmy Brown, Philadelphia, 1962-63
        Floyd Little, Denver, 1967-68
        James Brooks, San Diego, 1981-82
        Eric Dickerson, L.A. Rams, 1983-84
        Thurman Thomas, Buffalo, 1991-92
        Dante Hall, Kansas City, 2003-04

ATTEMPTS
Most Attempts, Career
4,939   Emmitt Smith, Dallas, 1990-2002; Arizona, 2003-04
4,368   Walter Payton, Chicago, 1975-1987
4,016   Curtis Martin, New England, 1995-97; N.Y. Jets, 1998-2005

Most Attempts, Season
  496   James Wilder, Tampa Bay, 1984
  458   Larry Johnson, Kansas City, 2006
  455   Eddie George, Tennessee, 2000

Most Attempts, Rookie, Season
  442   Eric Dickerson, L.A. Rams, 1983
  433   Edgerrin James, Indianapolis, 1999
  401   Curtis Martin, New England, 1995

Most Attempts, Game
   48   James Wilder, Tampa Bay vs. Pittsburgh, Oct. 30, 1983
        LaDainian Tomlinson, San Diego vs. Denver, Dec. 1, 2002 (OT)
   47   James Wilder, Tampa Bay vs. Green Bay, Sept. 30, 1984 (OT)
        Terrell Davis, Denver vs. Buffalo, Oct. 26, 1997 (OT)
   46   Gerald Riggs, Atlanta vs. L.A. Rams, Nov. 17, 1985

YARDS GAINED
Most Yards Gained, Career
23,546 Jerry Rice, San Francisco, 1985-2000; Oakland, 2001-04; Seattle, 2004
23,330 Brian Mitchell, Washington, 1990-99; Philadelphia, 2000-02; N.Y. Giants, 2003
21,803 Walter Payton, Chicago, 1975-1987

Most Yards Gained, Season
2,690   Derrick Mason, Tennessee, 2000
2,647   Michael Lewis, New Orleans, 2002
2,535   Lionel James, San Diego, 1985

Most Yards Gained, Rookie, Season
2,317   Tim Brown, L.A. Raiders, 1988
2,272   Gale Sayers, Chicago, 1965
2,250   Maurice Jones-Drew, Jacksonville, 2006

Most Yards Gained, Game
  404   Glyn Milburn, Denver vs. Seattle, Dec. 10, 1995
  373   Billy Cannon, Houston vs. N.Y. Titans, Dec. 10, 1961
  361   Adrian Peterson, Minnesota vs. Chicago, Oct. 4, 2007

SACKS
Sacks have been compiled since 1982.
Most Seasons Leading League
   2   Mark Gastineau, N.Y. Jets, 1983-84
        Reggie White, Philadelphia, 1987-88
        Kevin Greene, Pittsburgh, 1994; Carolina, 1996
        Michael Strahan, N.Y. Giants, 2001, 2003

Most Sacks, Career
200.0 Bruce Smith, Buffalo, 1985-1999; Washington, 2000-03
198.0 Reggie White, Philadelphia, 1985-1992; Green Bay, 1993-98; Carolina, 2000
160.0 Kevin Greene, L.A. Rams, 1985-1992; Pittsburgh, 1993-95; Carolina, 1996, 1998-99; San Francisco, 1997

Most Sacks, Season
 22.5 Michael Strahan, N.Y. Giants, 2001
 22.0 Mark Gastineau, N.Y. Jets, 1984
 21.0 Reggie White, Philadelphia, 1987
       Chris Doleman, Minnesota, 1989

Most Sacks, Rookie, Season
 14.5 Jevon Kearse, Tennessee, 1999
 13.0 Dwight Freeney, Indianapolis, 2002
 12.5 Leslie O'Neal, San Diego, 1986
       Simeon Rice, Arizona, 1996

Most Sacks, Game
  7.0 Derrick Thomas, Kansas City vs. Seattle, Nov. 11, 1990
  6.0 Fred Dean, San Francisco vs. New Orleans, Nov. 13, 1983
       Derrick Thomas, Kansas City vs. Oakland, Sept. 6, 1998
       Osi Umenyiora, N.Y. Giants vs. Philadelphia, Sept. 30, 2007
  5.5 William Gay, Detroit vs. Tampa Bay, Sept. 4, 1983

Most Seasons, 10 or More Sacks
  13   Bruce Smith, Buffalo, 1986-1990, 1992-98; Washington, 2000
  12   Reggie White, Philadelphia, 1985-1992; Green Bay, 1993, 1995, 1997-98
  10   Kevin Greene, L.A. Rams, 1988-1990, 1992; Pittsburgh, 1993-94; Carolina, 1996, 1998-99; San Francisco, 1997

Most Consecutive Seasons, 10 or More Sacks
   9   Reggie White, Philadelphia, 1985-1992; Green Bay, 1993
   8   John Randle, Minnesota, 1992-99
   7   Lawrence Taylor, N.Y. Giants, 1984-1990
        Bruce Smith, Buffalo, 1992-98

Most Consecutive Games, Sack
  10   Simon Fletcher, Denver, Nov. 15, 1992-Sept. 20, 1993
   9   Bruce Smith, Buffalo, Nov. 16, 1986-Oct. 25, 1987
        Kevin Greene, San Francisco-Carolina, Dec. 7, 1997-Oct. 18, 1998
   8   By many players

MISCELLANEOUS
Longest Return of Missed Field Goal (All TDs)
  109   Antonio Cromartie, San Diego vs. Minnesota, Nov. 4, 2007
  108   Nathan Vasher, Chicago vs. San Francisco, Nov. 13, 2005
        Devin Hester, Chicago vs. N.Y. Giants, Nov. 12, 2006
  107   Chris McAlister, Baltimore vs. Denver, Sept. 30, 2002

TEAM RECORDS

CHAMPIONSHIPS
Most Seasons League Champion
  12   Green Bay, 1929-1931, 1936, 1939, 1944, 1961-62, 1965-67, 1996
   9   Chi. Bears, 1921, 1932-33, 1940-41, 1943, 1946, 1963, 1985
   7   N.Y. Giants, 1927, 1934, 1938, 1956, 1986, 1990, 2007

Most Consecutive Seasons League Champion
   3   Green Bay, 1929-1931

    Green Bay, 1965-67
  2 Canton, 1922-23
    Chi. Bears, 1932-33
    Chi. Bears, 1940-41
    Philadelphia, 1948-49
    Detroit, 1952-53
    Cleveland, 1954-55
    Baltimore, 1958-59
    Houston, 1960-61
    Green Bay, 1961-62
    Buffalo, 1964-65
    Miami, 1972-73
    Pittsburgh, 1974-75
    Pittsburgh, 1978-79
    San Francisco, 1988-89
    Dallas, 1992-93
    Denver, 1997-98
    New England, 2003-04

Most Times Finishing First, Regular Season
  21 N.Y. Giants, 1927, 1933-35, 1938-39, 1941, 1944,
      1946, 1956, 1958-59, 1961-63, 1986,
      1989-1990, 1997, 2000, 2005
    Chi. Bears, 1921, 1932-34, 1937, 1940-43, 1946,
      1956, 1963, 1984-88, 1990, 2001, 2005-06
    Green Bay, 1929-1931, 1936, 1938-39, 1944,
      1960-62, 1965-67, 1972, 1995-97, 2002-04,
      2007
  20 Dallas, 1966-1971, 1973, 1976-79, 1981, 1985,
      1992-96, 1998, 2007
  18 Cleveland Browns, 1950-55, 1957, 1964-65,
      1967-69, 1971, 1980, 1985-87, 1989
    Cle./L.A./St. Louis Rams, 1945, 1949-51, 1955,
      1967, 1969, 1973-79, 1985, 1999, 2001, 2003
    Pittsburgh, 1972, 1974-79, 1983-84, 1992,
      1994-97, 2001-02, 2004, 2007

Most Consecutive Times Finishing First, Regular Season
  7 Los Angeles, 1973-79
  6 Cleveland, 1950-55
    Dallas, 1966-1971
    Minnesota, 1973-78
    Pittsburgh, 1974-79
  5 Oakland, 1972-76
    Chicago, 1984-88
    San Francisco, 1986-1990
    Dallas, 1992-96
    Indianapolis, 2003-07 (current)
    New England, 2003-07 (current)

GAMES WON

Most Consecutive Games Won
  19 New England, 2006-07 (current)
  18 New England, 2003-04
  17 Chi. Bears, 1933-34

Most Consecutive Games Without Defeat
  25 Canton, 1921-23 (won 22, tied 3)
  24 Chi. Bears, 1941-43 (won 23, tied 1)
  23 Green Bay, 1928-1930 (won 21, tied 2)

Most Games Won, Season
  16 New England, 2007
  15 San Francisco, 1984
    Chicago, 1985
    Minnesota, 1998
    Pittsburgh, 2004
  14 By many teams

Most Consecutive Games Won, Season
  16 New England, 2007, entire season
  14 Miami, 1972, entire season
    Pittsburgh, 2004
  13 Chi. Bears, 1934, entire season
    Denver, 1998

    Indianapolis, 2005

Most Consecutive Games Won, Start of Season
  16 New England, 2007, entire season
  14 Miami, 1972, entire season
  13 Chi. Bears, 1934, entire season
    Denver, 1998
    Indianapolis, 2005

Most Consecutive Games Won, End of Season
  16 New England, 2007, entire season
  14 Miami, 1972, entire season
    Pittsburgh, 2004
  13 Chi. Bears, 1934, entire season

Most Consecutive Games Without Defeat, Season
  16 New England, 2007 (won 16), entire season
  14 Miami, 1972 (won 14), entire season
    Pittsburgh, 2004 (won 14)
  13 Chi. Bears, 1926 (won 11, tied 2)
    Green Bay, 1929 (won 12, tied 1)
    Chi. Bears, 1934 (won 13), entire season
    Baltimore, 1967 (won 11, tied 2)
    Denver, 1998 (won 13)
    Indianapolis, 2005 (won 13)

Most Consecutive Games Without Defeat, Start of Season
  16 New England, 2007 (won 16), entire season
  14 Miami, 1972 (won 14), entire season
  13 Chi. Bears, 1926 (won 11, tied 2)
    Green Bay, 1929 (won 12, tied 1), entire season
    Chi. Bears, 1934 (won 13), entire season
    Baltimore, 1967 (won 11, tied 2)
    Denver, 1998 (won 13)
    Indianapolis, 2005 (won 13)

Most Consecutive Games Without Defeat, End of Season
  16 New England, 2007 (won 16), entire season
  14 Miami, 1972 (won 14), entire season
    Pittsburgh, 2004 (won 14)
  13 Green Bay, 1929 (won 12, tied 1), entire season
    Chi. Bears, 1934 (won 13), entire season

Most Consecutive Home Games Won
  27 Miami, 1971-74
  25 Green Bay, 1995-98
  24 Denver, 1996-98

Most Consecutive Home Games Without Defeat
  30 Green Bay, 1928-1933 (won 27, tied 3)
  27 Miami, 1971-74 (won 27)
  25 Chi. Bears, 1923-25 (won 19, tied 6)
    Green Bay, 1995-98 (won 25)

Most Consecutive Road Games Won
  18 San Francisco, 1988-1990
  11 L.A. Chargers/San Diego, 1960-61
    San Francisco, 1987-88
    Pittsburgh, 2004-05
  10 Chi. Bears, 1941-42
    Dallas, 1968-69
    New Orleans, 1987-88
    Dallas, 2006-07
    New England, 2006-07 (current)

Most Consecutive Road Games Without Defeat
  18 San Francisco, 1988-1990 (won 18)
  13 Chi. Bears, 1941-43 (won 12, tied 1)
  12 Green Bay, 1928-1930 (won 10, tied 2)

Most Shutout Games Won or Tied, Season
  10 Pottsville, 1926 (won 9, tied 1)
    N.Y. Giants, 1927 (won 9, tied 1)
  9 Akron, 1921 (won 8, tied 1)
    Canton, 1922 (won 7, tied 2)
    Frankford, 1926 (won 9)
    Frankford, 1929 (won 6, tied 3)
  8 By many teams

Most Consecutive Shutout Games Won or Tied
  13 Akron, 1920-21 (won 10, tied 3)

7 Pottsville, 1926 (won 6, tied 1)
   Detroit, 1934 (won 7)
6 Buffalo, 1920-21 (won 5, tied 1)
   Frankford, 1926 (won 6)
   Detroit, 1926 (won 4, tied 2)
   N.Y. Giants, 1926-27 (won 5, tied 1)

GAMES LOST
Most Consecutive Games Lost
26 Tampa Bay, 1976-1977
19 Chi. Cardinals, 1942-43, 1945
    Oakland, 1961-62
18 Houston, 1972-73
Most Consecutive Games Without Victory
26 Tampa Bay, 1976-77 (lost 26)
23 Rochester, 1922-25 (lost 21, tied 2)
    Washington, 1960-61 (lost 20, tied 3)
19 Dayton, 1927-29 (lost 18, tied 1)
    Chi. Cardinals, 1942-43, 1945 (lost 19)
    Oakland, 1961-62 (lost 19)
Most Games Lost, Season
15 New Orleans, 1980
    Dallas, 1989
    New England, 1990
    Indianapolis, 1991
    N.Y. Jets, 1996
    San Diego, 2000
    Carolina, 2001
    Miami, 2007
14 By many teams
Most Consecutive Games Lost, Season
15 Carolina, 2001
14 Tampa Bay, 1976
    New Orleans, 1980
    Baltimore, 1981
    New England, 1990
13 Oakland, 1962
    Pittsburgh, 1969
    Indianapolis, 1986
    Miami, 2007
Most Consecutive Games Lost, Start of Season
14 Tampa Bay, 1976, entire season
    New Orleans, 1980
13 Oakland, 1962
    Indianapolis, 1986
    Miami, 2007
12 Tampa Bay, 1977
    Detroit, 2001
Most Consecutive Games Lost, End of Season
15 Carolina, 2001
14 Tampa Bay, 1976, entire season
    New England, 1990
13 Pittsburgh, 1969
Most Consecutive Games Without Victory, Season
15 Carolina, 2001 (lost 15)
14 Tampa Bay, 1976 (lost 14), entire season
    New Orleans, 1980 (lost 14)
    Baltimore, 1981 (lost 14)
    New England, 1990 (lost 14)
13 Washington, 1961 (lost 12, tied 1)
    Oakland, 1962 (lost 13)
    Pittsburgh, 1969 (lost 13)
    Indianapolis, 1986 (lost 13)
    Miami, 2007 (lost 13)
Most Consecutive Games Without Victory, Start of Season
14 Tampa Bay, 1976 (lost 14), entire season
    New Orleans, 1980 (lost 14)
13 Washington, 1961 (lost 12, tied 1)
    Oakland, 1962 (lost 13)
    Indianapolis, 1986 (lost 13)

Miami, 2007 (lost 13)
12 Dall. Cowboys, 1960 (lost 11, tied 1), entire season
    Tampa Bay, 1977 (lost 12)
    Detroit, 2001 (lost 12)
Most Consecutive Games Without Victory, End of Season
15 Carolina, 2001
14 Tampa Bay, 1976, (lost 14), entire season
    New England, 1990 (lost 14)
13 Pittsburgh, 1969 (lost 13)
Most Consecutive Home Games Lost
14 Dallas, 1988-89
13 Houston, 1972-73
    Tampa Bay, 1976-77
    N.Y. Jets, 1995-97
11 Oakland, 1961-62
    Los Angeles, 1961-63
    Cincinnati, 1998-99
Most Consecutive Home Games Without Victory
14 Dallas, 1988-89 (lost 14)
13 Houston, 1972-73 (lost 13)
    Tampa Bay, 1976-77 (lost 13)
    N.Y. Jets, 1995-97 (lost 13)
    Philadelphia, 1936-38 (lost 12, tied 1)
Most Consecutive Road Games Lost
24 Detroit, 2001-03
23 Houston, 1981-84
22 Buffalo, 1983-86
Most Consecutive Road Games Without Victory
24 Detroit, 2001-03 (lost 24)
23 Houston, 1981-84 (lost 23)
22 Buffalo, 1983-86 (lost 22)
Most Shutout Games Lost or Tied, Season
8 Frankford, 1927 (lost 6, tied 2)
   Brooklyn, 1931 (lost 8)
7 Dayton, 1925 (lost 6, tied 1)
   Orange, 1929 (lost 4, tied 3)
   Frankford, 1931 (lost 6, tied 1)
6 By many teams
Most Consecutive Shutout Games Lost or Tied
8 Rochester, 1922-24 (lost 8)
7 Hammond, 1922-23 (lost 6, tied 1)
6 Providence, 1926-27 (lost 5, tied 1)
   Brooklyn, 1942-43 (lost 6)

TIE GAMES
Most Tie Games, Season
6 Chi. Bears, 1932
5 Frankford, 1929
4 Chi. Bears, 1924
   Orange, 1929
   Portsmouth, 1932
Most Consecutive Tie Games
3 Chi. Bears, 1932
2 By many teams

SCORING
Most Seasons Leading League
10 Chi. Bears, 1932, 1934-35, 1939, 1941-43,
    1946-47, 1956
9 San Francisco, 1953, 1965, 1970, 1987, 1989,
   1992-95
   L.A./St. Louis Rams, 1950-52, 1957, 1967, 1973,
   1999-2001
7 Green Bay, 1931, 1936-38, 1961-62, 1996
Most Consecutive Seasons Leading League
4 San Francisco, 1992-1995
3 Green Bay, 1936-38
   Chi. Bears, 1941-43
   Los Angeles, 1950-52
   Oakland, 1967-69

St. Louis, 1999-2001
2 By many teams

POINTS
Most Points, Season
589 New England, 2007
556 Minnesota, 1998
541 Washington, 1983
Fewest Points, Season (Since 1932)
37 Cincinnati/St. Louis, 1934
38 Cincinnati, 1933
     Detroit, 1942
51 Pittsburgh, 1934
     Philadelphia, 1936
Most Points, Game
72 Washington vs. N.Y. Giants, Nov. 27, 1966
70 Los Angeles vs. Baltimore, Oct. 22, 1950
66 Rochester vs. *Fort Porter, Oct. 10, 1920
     *Not a member of the American Professional
      Football Association
Most Points, Both Teams, Game
113 Washington (72) vs. N.Y. Giants (41), Nov. 27, 1966
106 Cincinnati (58) vs. Cleveland (48), Nov. 28, 2004
101 Oakland (52) vs. Houston (49), Dec. 22, 1963
Fewest Points, Both Teams, Game
0 In many games. Last time: N.Y. Giants vs. Detroit,
     Nov. 7, 1943
Most Points, Shutout Victory, Game
66 Rochester vs. *Fort Porter, Oct. 10, 1920
     *Not a member of the American Professional
      Football Association
64 Philadelphia vs. Cincinnati, Nov. 6, 1934
62 Akron vs. Oorang, Oct. 29, 1922
Fewest Points, Shutout Victory, Game
2 Akron vs. Buffalo, Nov. 29, 1923
    Kansas City vs. Buffalo, Nov. 21, 1926
    Frankford vs. Green Bay, Nov. 29, 1928
    Green Bay vs. Chi. Bears, Oct. 16, 1932
    Chi. Bears vs. Green Bay, Sept. 18, 1938
Most Points Overcome to Win Game
28 San Francisco vs. New Orleans, Dec. 7, 1980 (OT)
     (trailed 7-35, won 38-35)
26 Buffalo vs. Indianapolis, Sept., 21, 1997
     (trailed 0-26, won 37-35)
25 St. Louis vs. Tampa Bay, Nov. 8, 1987
     (trailed 3-28, won 31-28)
Most Points Overcome to Tie Game
31 Denver vs. Buffalo, Nov. 27, 1960
     (trailed 7-38, tied 38-38)
28 Los Angeles vs. Philadelphia, Oct. 3, 1948
     (trailed 0-28, tied 28-28)
Most Points, Each Half
1st: 49 Green Bay vs. Tampa Bay, Oct. 2, 1983
      48 Buffalo vs. Miami, Sept. 18, 1966
      45 Green Bay vs. Cleveland, Nov. 12, 1967
           Indianapolis vs. Denver, Oct. 31, 1988
           Houston vs. Cleveland, Dec. 9, 1990
           Seattle vs. Minnesota, Sept. 29, 2002
2nd: 49 Chi. Bears vs. Philadelphia, Nov. 30, 1941
      48 Chi. Cardinals vs. Baltimore, Oct. 2, 1950
           N.Y. Giants vs. Baltimore, Nov. 19, 1950
      45 Cincinnati vs. Houston, Dec. 17, 1972
Most Points, Both Teams, Each Half
1st: 70 Houston (35) vs. Oakland (35), Dec. 22, 1963
      63 Philadelphia (42) vs. Detroit (21), Sept. 23, 2007
      62 N.Y. Jets (41) vs. Tampa Bay (21), Nov. 17, 1985
           Indianapolis (35) vs. Cincinnati (27), Nov. 20, 2005
2nd: 66 Cleveland (35) vs. Cincinnati (31), Nov. 28, 2004
      65 Washington (38) vs. N.Y. Giants (27), Nov. 27, 1966

62 L.A. Raiders (31) vs. San Diego (31), Jan. 2, 1983
     Baltimore (38) vs. Seattle (24), Nov. 23, 2003
Most Points, One Quarter
41 Green Bay vs. Detroit, Oct. 7, 1945 (second quarter)
     Los Angeles vs. Detroit, Oct. 29, 1950
     (third quarter)
37 Los Angeles vs. Green Bay, Sept. 21, 1980
     (second quarter)
35 Chi. Cardinals vs. Boston, Oct. 24, 1948
     (third quarter)
     Green Bay vs. Cleveland, Nov. 12, 1967 (first quarter)
     Green Bay vs. Tampa Bay, Oct. 2, 1983
     (second quarter)
Most Points, Both Teams, One Quarter
49 Oakland (28) vs. Houston (21), Dec. 22, 1963
     (second quarter)
48 Green Bay (41) vs. Detroit (7), Oct. 7, 1945
     (second quarter)
     Los Angeles (41) vs. Detroit (7), Oct. 29, 1950
     (third quarter)
     Detroit (34) vs. Chicago (14), Sept. 30, 2007
     (fourth quarter)
47 St. Louis (27) vs. Philadelphia (20), Dec. 13, 1964
     (second quarter)
Most Points, Each Quarter
1st: 35 Green Bay vs. Cleveland, Nov. 12, 1967
      31 Buffalo vs. Kansas City, Sept. 13, 1964
      28 By eight teams
2nd: 41 Green Bay vs. Detroit, Oct. 7, 1945
      37 Los Angeles vs. Green Bay, Sept. 21, 1980
      35 Green Bay vs. Tampa Bay, Oct. 2, 1983
3rd: 41 Los Angeles vs. Detroit, Oct. 29, 1950
      35 Chi. Cardinals vs. Boston, Oct. 24, 1948
      28 By 10 teams
4th: 34 Detroit vs. Chicago, Sept. 30, 2007
      31 Oakland vs. Denver, Dec. 17, 1960
           Oakland vs. San Diego, Dec. 8, 1963
           Atlanta vs. Green Bay, Sept. 13, 1981
      30 N.Y. Jets vs. Miami, Oct. 23, 2000
Most Points, Both Teams, Each Quarter
1st: 42 Green Bay (35) vs. Cleveland (7), Nov. 12, 1967
      41 Tennessee (24) vs. Indianapolis (17), Dec. 5, 2004
      35 Dall. Texans (21) vs. N.Y. Titans (14), Nov. 11, 1962
           Dallas (28) vs. Philadelphia (7), Oct. 19, 1969
           Kansas City (21) vs. Seattle (14), Dec. 11, 1977
           Detroit (21) vs. L.A. Raiders (14), Dec. 10, 1990
           Dallas (21) vs. Atlanta (14), Dec. 22, 1991
           Indianapolis (21) vs. Green Bay (14), Sept 26, 2004
           Miami (21) vs. Buffalo (14), Dec. 5, 2004
           Philadelphia (21) vs. New Orleans (14), Dec. 23, 2007
2nd: 49 Oakland (28) vs. Houston (21), Dec. 22, 1963
      48 Green Bay (41) vs. Detroit (7), Oct. 7, 1945
      47 St. Louis (27) vs. Philadelphia (20), Dec. 13, 1964
3rd: 48 Los Angeles (41) vs. Detroit (7), Oct. 29, 1950
      42 Washington (28) vs. Philadelphia (14), Oct. 1, 1955
      41 Green Bay (21) vs. N.Y. Yanks (20), Oct. 8, 1950
4th: 48 Detroit (34) vs. Chicago (14), Sept. 30, 2007
      42 Chi. Cardinals (28) vs. Philadelphia (14), Dec. 7, 1947
           Green Bay (28) vs. Chi. Bears (14), Nov. 6, 1955
           N.Y. Jets (28) vs. Boston (14), Oct. 27, 1968
           Pittsburgh (21) vs. Cleveland (21), Oct. 18, 1969
           New England (21) vs. Kansas City (21),
             Sept. 22, 2002
      41 Baltimore (27) vs. New England (14), Sept. 18, 1978
           New England (27) vs. Baltimore (14), Nov. 23, 1989
Most Consecutive Games Scoring
420 San Francisco, 1977-2004
274 Cleveland, 1950-1971
260 Minnesota, 1991-2007

TOUCHDOWNS

Most Seasons Leading League, Touchdowns
- 13 Chi. Bears, 1932, 1934-35, 1939, 1941-44, 1946-48, 1956, 1965
- 7 Dallas, 1966, 1968, 1971, 1973, 1977-78, 1980
  San Francisco, 1953, 1970, 1987, 1992-95
  L.A./St. Louis Rams, 1949-1952, 1999-2001
  San Diego, 1963, 1965, 1979, 1981-82, 1985, 2006
- 6 Oakland, 1967-69, 1972, 1974, 1977
  Green Bay, 1932, 1937-38, 1961-62, 1996
  Baltimore/Indianapolis Colts, 1957-59, 1964, 1976, 2004

Most Consecutive Seasons Leading League, Touchdowns
- 4 Chi. Bears, 1941-44
  Los Angeles, 1949-1952
  San Francisco, 1992-95
- 3 Chi. Bears, 1946-48
  Baltimore, 1957-59
  Oakland, 1967-69
  St. Louis, 1999-2001
- 2 By many teams

Most Touchdowns, Season
- 75 New England, 2007
- 70 Miami, 1984
- 67 St. Louis, 2000

Fewest Touchdowns, Season (Since 1932)
- 3 Cincinnati, 1933
- 4 Cincinnati/St. Louis, 1934
- 5 Detroit, 1942

Most Touchdowns, Game
- 10 Rochester vs. *Fort Porter, Oct. 10, 1920
  *Not a member of the American Professional Football Association
  Philadelphia vs. Cincinnati, Nov. 6, 1934
  Los Angeles vs. Baltimore, Oct. 22, 1950
  Washington vs. N.Y. Giants, Nov. 27, 1966
- 9 Rock Island vs. Evansville, Oct. 15, 1922
  Akron vs. Oorang, Oct. 29, 1922
  Racine vs. Louisville, Nov. 5, 1922
  Chi. Cardinals vs. Rochester, Oct. 7, 1923
  Chi. Cardinals vs. Milwaukee, Dec. 10, 1925
  Chi. Cardinals vs. N.Y. Giants, Oct. 17, 1948
  Chi. Cardinals vs. N.Y. Bulldogs, Nov. 13, 1949
  Los Angeles vs. Detroit, Oct. 29, 1950
  Pittsburgh vs. N.Y. Giants, Nov. 30, 1952
  Chicago vs. San Francisco, Dec. 12, 1965
  Chicago vs. Green Bay, Dec. 7, 1980
- 8 By many teams

Most Touchdowns, Both Teams, Game
- 16 Washington (10) vs. N.Y. Giants (6), Nov. 27, 1966
- 14 Chi. Cardinals (9) vs. N.Y. Giants (5), Oct. 17, 1948
  Los Angeles (10) vs. Baltimore (4), Oct. 22, 1950
  Houston (7) vs. Oakland (7), Dec. 22, 1963
- 13 New Orleans (7) vs. St. Louis (6), Nov. 2, 1969
  Kansas City (7) vs. Seattle (6), Nov. 27, 1983 (OT)
  San Diego (8) vs. Pittsburgh (5), Dec. 8, 1985
  N.Y. Jets (7) vs. Miami (6), Sept. 21, 1986 (OT)
  Cincinnati (7) vs. Cleveland (6), Nov. 28, 2004

Most Consecutive Games Scoring Touchdowns
- 166 Cleveland, 1957-1969
- 97 Oakland, 1966-1973
  Minnesota, 1995-2001
- 96 Kansas City, 1963-1970

POINTS AFTER TOUCHDOWN

Most (One-Point) Points After Touchdown, Season
- 74 New England, 2007
- 66 Miami, 1984
- 65 Houston, 1961

Fewest (One-Point) Points After Touchdown, Season
- 2 Chi. Cardinals, 1933
- 3 Cincinnati, 1933
  Pittsburgh, 1934
- 4 Cincinnati/St. Louis, 1934

Most (One-Point) Points After Touchdown, Game
- 10 Los Angeles vs. Baltimore, Oct. 22, 1950
- 9 Chi. Cardinals vs. N.Y. Giants, Oct. 17, 1948
  Pittsburgh vs. N.Y. Giants, Nov. 30, 1952
  Washington vs. N.Y. Giants, Nov. 27, 1966
- 8 By many teams

Most (One-Point) Points After Touchdown, Both Teams, Game
- 14 Chi. Cardinals (9) vs. N.Y. Giants (5), Oct. 17, 1948
  Houston (7) vs. Oakland (7), Dec. 22, 1963
  Washington (9) vs. N.Y. Giants (5), Nov. 27, 1966
- 13 Los Angeles (10) vs. Baltimore (3), Oct. 22, 1950
  Cincinnati (7) vs. Cleveland (6), Nov. 28, 2004
- 12 In many games

Most Two-Point Conversions, Season
- 6 Miami, 1994
  Minnesota, 1997
- 5 Arizona, 1995
  Baltimore, 1996
  Jacksonville, 1996
  Chicago, 1997
  San Francisco, 1998
  Pittsburgh, 2002
- 4 By many teams

Most Two-Point Conversions, Game
- 4 St. Louis vs. Atlanta, Oct. 15, 2000
- 3 Baltimore vs. New England, Oct. 6, 1996
  Pittsburgh vs. Tennessee, Nov. 1, 1998
- 2 By many teams

Most Two-Point Conversions, Both Teams, Game
- 5 Baltimore (3) vs. New England (2), Oct. 6, 1996
  St. Louis (4) vs. Atlanta (1), Oct. 15, 2000
- 3 Seattle (2) vs. Kansas City (1), Oct. 23, 1994
  Minnesota (2) vs. Seattle (1), Nov. 10, 1996
  Pittsburgh (3) vs. Tennessee (0), Nov. 1, 1998
- 2 In many games

FIELD GOALS

Most Seasons Leading League, Field Goals
- 11 Green Bay, 1935-36, 1940-43, 1946-47, 1955, 1972, 1974
- 8 Washington, 1945, 1956, 1971, 1976-77, 1979, 1982, 1992
  L.A./St. Louis Rams, 1949, 1951, 1958, 1966, 1973, 1978, 2003, 2006
- 7 N.Y. Giants, 1933, 1937, 1939, 1941, 1944, 1959, 1983

Most Consecutive Seasons Leading League, Field Goals
- 4 Green Bay, 1940-43
- 3 Cleveland, 1952-54
- 2 By many teams

Most Field Goals Attempted, Season
- 49 Los Angeles, 1966
  Washington, 1971
- 48 Green Bay, 1972
- 47 N.Y. Jets, 1969
  Los Angeles, 1973
  Washington, 1983

Fewest Field Goals Attempted, Season (Since 1938)
- 0 Chi. Bears, 1944
- 2 Cleveland, 1939
  Card-Pitt, 1944
  Boston, 1946
  Chi. Bears, 1947
- 3 Chi. Bears, 1945
  Cleveland, 1945

Most Field Goals Attempted, Game
- 9 St. Louis vs. Pittsburgh, Sept. 24, 1967
- 8 Pittsburgh vs. St. Louis, Dec. 2, 1962
  - Detroit vs. Minnesota, Nov. 13, 1966
  - N.Y. Jets vs. Buffalo, Nov. 3, 1968
  - Dallas vs. N.Y. Giants, Sept. 15, 2003 (OT)
  - Tennessee vs. Houston, Oct. 21, 2007
- 7 By many teams

Most Field Goals Attempted, Both Teams, Game
- 11 St. Louis (6) vs. Pittsburgh (5), Nov. 13, 1966
  - Washington (6) vs. Chicago (5), Nov. 14, 1971
  - Green Bay (6) vs. Detroit (5), Sept. 29, 1974
  - Washington (6) vs. N.Y. Giants (5), Nov. 14, 1976
- 10 In many games

Most Field Goals, Season
- 43 Arizona, 2005
- 39 Miami, 1999
  - St. Louis, 2003
- 37 Carolina, 1996
  - Indianapolis, 2003

Fewest Field Goals, Season (Since 1932)
- 0 Boston, 1932, 1935
  - Chi. Cardinals, 1932, 1945
  - Green Bay, 1932, 1944
  - N.Y. Giants, 1932
  - Brooklyn, 1944
  - Card-Pitt, 1944
  - Chi. Bears, 1944, 1947
  - Boston, 1946
  - Baltimore, 1950
  - Dallas, 1952

Most Field Goals, Game
- 8 Tennessee vs. Houston, Oct. 21, 2007
- 7 St. Louis vs. Pittsburgh, Sept. 24, 1967
  - Minnesota vs. L.A. Rams, Nov. 5, 1989 (OT)
  - Dallas vs. Green Bay, Nov. 18, 1996
  - Dallas vs. N.Y. Giants, Sept. 15, 2003 (OT)
  - Cincinnati vs. Baltimore, Nov. 11, 2007
- 6 By many teams

Most Field Goals, Both Teams, Game
- 9 San Diego (5) vs. Kansas City (4), Sept. 29, 1996
  - Miami (6) vs. New England (3), Oct. 17, 1999
  - Houston (5) vs. Miami (4), Oct. 7, 2007
- 8 Cleveland (4) vs. St. Louis (4), Sept. 20, 1964
  - Chicago (5) vs. Philadelphia (3), Oct. 20, 1968
  - Washington (5) vs. Chicago (3), Nov. 14, 1971
  - Kansas City (5) vs. Buffalo (3), Dec. 19, 1971
  - Detroit (4) vs. Green Bay (4), Sept. 29, 1974
  - Cleveland (5) vs. Denver (3), Oct. 19, 1975
  - New England (4) vs. San Diego (4), Nov. 9, 1975
  - San Francisco (6) vs. New Orleans (2), Oct. 16, 1983
  - Seattle (5) vs. L.A. Raiders (3), Dec. 18, 1988
  - Atlanta (6) vs. New Orleans (2), Nov. 13, 1994
  - Indianapolis (4) vs. San Diego (4), Nov. 3, 1996
  - Dallas (7) vs. N.Y. Giants (1), Sept. 15, 2003 (OT)
  - Oakland (5) vs. Chicago (3), Oct. 5, 2003
  - Buffalo (5) vs. Tennessee (3), Dec. 24, 2006
  - Tennessee (8) vs. Houston (0), Oct. 21, 2007
  - Buffalo (5) vs. Washington (3), Dec. 2, 2007
- 7 In many games

Most Consecutive Games Scoring Field Goals
- 38 Baltimore, 1999-2001
- 31 Minnesota, 1968-1970
- 28 Washington, 1988-1990

SAFETIES
Most Safeties, Season
- 4 Cleveland, 1927
  - Detroit, 1962
  - Seattle, 1993

San Francisco, 1996
Tennessee, 1999
- 3 By many teams

Most Safeties, Game
- 3 L.A. Rams vs. N.Y. Giants, Sept. 30, 1984
- 2 N.Y. Giants vs. Pottsville, Oct. 30, 1927
  - Chi. Bears vs. Pottsville, Nov. 13, 1927
  - Detroit vs. Brooklyn, Dec. 1, 1935
  - N.Y. Giants vs. Pittsburgh, Sept. 17, 1950
  - N.Y. Giants vs. Washington, Nov. 5, 1961
  - Chicago vs. Pittsburgh, Nov. 9, 1969
  - Dallas vs. Philadelphia, Nov. 19, 1972
  - Los Angeles vs. Green Bay, Oct. 21, 1973
  - Oakland vs. San Diego, Oct. 26, 1975
  - Denver vs. Seattle, Jan. 2, 1983
  - New Orleans vs. Cleveland, Sept. 13, 1987
  - Buffalo vs. Denver, Nov. 8, 1987
  - San Francisco vs. St. Louis, Sept. 8, 1996
  - Jacksonville vs. Pittsburgh, Oct. 3, 1999
  - Minnesota vs. Atlanta, Oct. 5, 2003
  - Dallas vs. Arizona, Oct. 5, 2003
  - Buffalo vs. Houston, Nov. 16, 2003

Most Safeties, Both Teams, Game
- 3 L.A. Rams (3) vs. N.Y. Giants (0), Sept. 30, 1984
- 2 Chi. Cardinals (1) vs. Frankford (1), Nov. 19, 1927
  - Chi. Cardinals (1) vs. Cincinnati (1), Nov. 12, 1933
  - Chi. Bears (1) vs. San Francisco (1), Oct. 19, 1952
  - Cincinnati (1) vs. Los Angeles (1), Oct. 22, 1972
  - Chi. Bears (1) vs. San Francisco (1), Sept. 19, 1976
  - Baltimore (1) vs. Miami (1), Oct. 29, 1978
  - Atlanta (1) vs. Detroit (1), Oct. 5, 1980
  - Houston (1) vs. Philadelphia (1), Oct. 2, 1988
  - Cleveland (1) vs. Seattle (1), Nov. 14, 1993
  - Arizona (1) vs. Houston (1), Dec. 4, 1994
  - (Also see previous record)

FIRST DOWNS
Most Seasons Leading League
- 9 Chi. Bears, 1935, 1939, 1941, 1943, 1945, 1947-49, 1955
- 7 San Diego, 1965, 1969, 1980-83, 1985

  L.A./St. Louis Rams, 1946, 1950-51, 1954, 1957, 1973, 2001
- 6 San Francisco, 1965, 1987, 1989, 1993-94, 1998
  - Baltimore/Indianapolis Colts, 1958-59, 1967, 2003, 2005-06

Most Consecutive Seasons Leading League
- 4 San Diego, 1980-83
- 3 Chi. Bears, 1947-49
- 2 By many teams

Most First Downs, Season
- 398 Kansas City, 2004
- 393 New England, 2007
- 387 Miami, 1984

Fewest First Downs, Season
- 51 Cincinnati, 1933
- 64 Pittsburgh, 1935
- 67 Philadelphia, 1937

Most First Downs, Game
- 39 N.Y. Jets vs. Miami, Nov. 27, 1988
  - Washington vs. Detroit, Nov. 4, 1990 (OT)
- 38 Los Angeles vs. N.Y. Giants, Nov. 13, 1966
- 37 Green Bay vs. Philadelphia, Nov. 11, 1962

Fewest First Downs, Game
- 0 N.Y. Giants vs. Green Bay, Oct. 1, 1933
  - Pittsburgh vs. Boston, Oct. 29, 1933
  - Philadelphia vs. Detroit, Sept. 20, 1935
  - N.Y. Giants vs. Washington, Sept. 27, 1942
  - Denver vs. Houston, Sept. 3, 1966

Most First Downs, Both Teams, Game
- 64 Seattle (32) vs. Kansas City (32), Nov. 24, 2002
- 62 San Diego (32) vs. Seattle (30), Sept. 15, 1985
   - Oakland (31) vs. Kansas City (31), Nov. 5, 2000
- 59 Miami (31) vs. Buffalo (28), Oct. 9, 1983 (OT)
   - Seattle (33) vs. Kansas City (26), Nov. 27, 1983 (OT)
   - N.Y. Jets (32) vs. Miami (27), Sept. 21, 1986 (OT)
   - N.Y. Jets (39) vs. Miami (20), Nov. 27, 1988
   - Oakland (31) vs. San Francisco (28), Oct. 8, 2000 (OT)

Fewest First Downs, Both Teams, Game
- 7 Chi. Cardinals (2) vs. Detroit (5), Sept. 15, 1940
- 9 Pittsburgh (1) vs. Boston (8), Oct. 27, 1935
   - Boston (4) vs. Brooklyn (5), Nov. 24, 1935
   - N.Y. Giants (3) vs. Detroit (6), Nov. 7, 1943
   - Pittsburgh (4) vs. Chi. Cardinals (5), Nov. 11, 1945
   - N.Y. Bulldogs (1) vs. Philadelphia (8), Sept. 22, 1949
- 10 Philadelphia (4) vs. Brooklyn (6), Nov. 5, 1944
   - N.Y. Giants (4) vs. Washington (6), Dec. 11, 1960

Most First Downs, Rushing, Season
- 181 New England, 1978
- 177 Los Angeles, 1973
- 176 Chicago, 1985

Fewest First Downs, Rushing, Season
- 36 Cleveland, 1942
   - Boston, 1944
- 39 Brooklyn, 1943
- 40 Philadelphia, 1940
   - Detroit, 1945

Most First Downs, Rushing, Game
- 25 Philadelphia vs. Washington, Dec. 2, 1951
- 23 St. Louis vs. New Orleans, Oct. 5, 1980
- 21 Cleveland vs. Philadelphia, Dec. 13, 1959
   - Green Bay vs. Philadelphia, Nov. 11, 1962
   - Los Angeles vs. New Orleans, Nov. 25, 1973
   - Pittsburgh vs. Kansas City, Nov. 7, 1976
   - New England vs. Denver, Nov. 28, 1976
   - Oakland vs. Green Bay, Sept. 17, 1978
   - Buffalo vs. Washington, Nov. 3, 1996
   - San Francisco vs. Detroit, Dec. 14, 1998
   - Kansas City vs. Atlanta, Oct. 24, 2004

Fewest First Downs, Rushing, Game
- 0 By many teams. Last time:
   - Dallas vs. Washington, Dec. 30, 2007

Most First Downs, Rushing, Both Teams, Game
- 36 Philadelphia (25) vs. Washington (11), Dec. 2, 1951
- 31 Detroit (18) vs. Washington (13), Sept. 30, 1951
- 30 Los Angeles (17) vs. Minnesota (13), Nov. 5, 1961
   - New Orleans (17) vs. Green Bay (13), Sept. 9, 1979
   - New Orleans (16) vs. San Francisco (14), Nov. 11, 1979
   - New England (16) vs. Kansas City (14), Oct. 4, 1981
   - Indianapolis (18) vs. Denver (12), Sept. 30, 2007

Fewest First Downs, Rushing, Both Teams, Game
- 1 Oakland (0) vs. Tennessee (1), Sept. 7, 2003
   - Carolina (0) vs. Detroit (1), Oct. 16, 2005
- 2 Houston (0) vs. Denver (2), Dec. 2, 1962
   - N.Y. Jets, (1) vs. St. Louis (1), Dec. 3, 1995
   - Miami (1) vs. San Diego (1), Dec. 19, 1999
   - New Orleans (0) vs. Baltimore (2), Dec. 19, 1999
   - Baltimore (0) vs. Tennessee (2), Sept. 18, 2005
   - Pittsburgh (1) vs. Baltimore (1), Nov. 5, 2007
- 3 In many games

Most First Downs, Passing, Season
- 259 San Diego, 1985
- 251 Houston, 1990
- 250 Miami, 1986

Fewest First Downs, Passing, Season
- 18 Pittsburgh, 1941
- 23 Brooklyn, 1942
   - N.Y. Giants, 1944
- 24 N.Y. Giants, 1943

Most First Downs, Passing, Game
- 29 N.Y. Giants vs. Cincinnati, Oct. 13, 1985
- 28 Tennessee vs. Oakland, Dec. 19, 2004
- 27 San Diego vs. Seattle, Sept. 15, 1985

Fewest First Downs, Passing, Game
- 0 By many teams. Last time: Cleveland vs.
   - Jacksonville, Dec. 3, 2000

Most First Downs, Passing, Both Teams, Game
- 43 San Diego (23) vs. Cincinnati (20), Dec. 20, 1982
   - Miami (24) vs. N.Y. Jets (19), Sept. 21, 1986 (OT)
   - Tennessee (28) vs. Oakland (15), Dec. 19, 2004
- 42 San Francisco (22) vs. San Diego (20), Dec. 11, 1982
   - Seattle (22) vs. Cleveland (20), Nov. 4, 2007 (OT)
- 41 San Diego (27) vs. Seattle (14), Sept. 15, 1985
   - Miami (26) vs. Cleveland (15), Dec. 12, 1988
   - Kansas City (23) vs. Oakland (18), Nov. 5, 2000

Fewest First Downs, Passing, Both Teams, Game
- 0 Brooklyn vs. Pittsburgh, Nov. 29, 1942
- 1 Green Bay (0) vs. Cleveland (1), Sept. 21, 1941
   - Pittsburgh (0) vs. Brooklyn (1), Oct. 11, 1942
   - N.Y. Giants (0) vs. Detroit (1), Nov. 7, 1943
   - Pittsburgh (0) vs. Chi. Cardinals (1), Nov. 11, 1945
   - N.Y. Bulldogs (0) vs. Philadelphia (1), Sept. 22, 1949
   - Chicago (0) vs. Buffalo (1), Oct. 7, 1979
- 2 In many games

Most First Downs, Penalty, Season
- 47 Buffalo, 2002
   - Indianapolis, 2004
- 44 Dallas, 2005
- 43 Denver, 1994

Fewest First Downs, Penalty, Season
- 2 Brooklyn, 1940
- 4 Chi. Cardinals, 1940
   - N.Y. Giants, 1942, 1944
   - Washington, 1944
   - Cleveland, 1952
   - Kansas City, 1969
- 5 Brooklyn, 1939
   - Chi. Bears, 1939
   - Detroit, 1953
   - Los Angeles, 1953
   - Houston, 1982

Most First Downs, Penalty, Game
- 11 Denver vs. Houston, Oct. 6, 1985
- 9 Chi. Bears vs. Cleveland, Nov. 25, 1951
   - Baltimore vs. Pittsburgh, Oct. 30, 1977
   - N.Y. Jets vs. Houston, Sept. 18, 1988
   - Dallas vs. Detroit, Nov. 20, 2005
- 8 Philadelphia vs. Detroit, Dec. 2, 1979
   - Cincinnati vs. N.Y. Jets, Oct. 6, 1985
   - Buffalo vs. Houston, Sept. 20, 1987
   - Houston vs. Atlanta, Sept. 9, 1990
   - Kansas City vs. L.A. Raiders, Oct. 3, 1993
   - San Francisco vs. New Orleans, Oct. 11, 1998
   - Oakland vs. San Francisco, Oct. 8, 2000 (OT)
   - Philadelphia vs. Chicago, Nov. 3, 2002
   - Detroit vs. Baltimore, Oct. 9, 2005

Most First Downs, Penalty, Both Teams, Game
- 12 Buffalo (7) vs. San Francisco (5), Oct. 4, 1998
   - Detroit (8) vs. Baltimore (4), Oct. 9, 2005
- 11 Chi. Bears (9) vs. Cleveland (2), Nov. 25, 1951
   - Cincinnati (8) vs. N.Y. Jets (3), Oct. 6, 1985
   - Denver (11) vs. Houston (0), Oct. 6, 1985
   - Detroit (6) vs. Dallas (5), Nov. 8, 1987
   - N.Y. Jets (9) vs. Houston (2), Sept. 18, 1988
   - Kansas City (8) vs. L.A. Raiders (3), Oct. 3, 1993
   - Detroit (6) vs. San Diego (5), Nov. 11, 1996
   - Philadelphia (8) vs. Chicago (3), Nov. 3, 2002
   - Arizona (6) vs. St. Louis (5), Dec. 3, 2006
- 10 In many games

NET YARDS GAINED RUSHING AND PASSING

Most Seasons Leading League
- 12   Chi. Bears, 1932, 1934-35, 1939, 1941-44, 1947, 1949, 1955-56
- 9   L.A./St. Louis Rams, 1946, 1950-51, 1954, 1957, 1973, 1999-2001
- 7   San Diego, 1963, 1965, 1980-83, 1985

Most Consecutive Seasons Leading League
- 4   Chi. Bears, 1941-44
-    San Diego, 1980-83
- 3   Baltimore, 1958-1960
-    Houston, 1960-62
-    Oakland, 1968-1970
-    St. Louis, 1999-2001
- 2   By many teams

Most Yards Gained, Season
- 7,075   St. Louis, 2000
- 6,936   Miami, 1984
- 6,800   San Francisco, 1998

Fewest Yards Gained, Season
- 1,150   Cincinnati, 1933
- 1,443   Chi. Cardinals, 1934
- 1,486   Chi. Cardinals, 1933

Most Yards Gained, Game
- 735   Los Angeles vs. N.Y. Yanks, Sept. 28, 1951
- 683   Pittsburgh vs. Chi. Cardinals, Dec. 13, 1958
- 682   Chi. Bears vs. N.Y. Giants, Nov. 14, 1943

Fewest Yards Gained, Game
- −7   Seattle vs. Los Angeles, Nov. 4, 1979
- −5   Denver vs. Oakland, Sept. 10, 1967
- 14   Chi. Cardinals vs. Detroit, Sept. 15, 1940

Most Yards Gained, Both Teams, Game
- 1,133   Los Angeles (636) vs. N.Y. Yanks (497), Nov. 19, 1950
- 1,102   San Diego (661) vs. Cincinnati (441), Dec. 20, 1982
- 1,095   Kansas City (590) vs. Indianapolis (505), Oct. 31, 2004

Fewest Yards Gained, Both Teams, Game
- 30   Chi. Cardinals (14) vs. Detroit (16), Sept. 15, 1940
- 136   Chi. Cardinals (50) vs. Green Bay (86), Nov. 18, 1934
- 154   N.Y. Giants (51) vs. Washington (103), Dec. 11, 1960

Most Consecutive Games, 400 or More Yards Gained
- 11   San Diego, 1982-83
- 9   New England, 2006-07
- 8   St. Louis, 1999-2000

Most Consecutive Games, 300 or More Yards Gained
- 36   Minnesota, 2002-04
- 30   Minnesota, 1999-2000
-    St. Louis, 2000-02
- 29   Los Angeles, 1949-1951

RUSHING

Most Seasons Leading League
- 16   Chi. Bears, 1932, 1934-35, 1939-1942, 1951, 1955-56, 1968, 1977, 1983-86
- 7   Buffalo, 1962, 1964, 1973, 1975, 1982, 1991-92
- 6   Cleveland, 1958-59, 1963, 1965-67
-    San Francisco, 1952-54, 1987, 1998-99

Most Consecutive Seasons Leading League
- 4   Chi. Bears, 1939-1942
-    Chi. Bears, 1983-86
- 3   Detroit, 1936-38
-    San Francisco, 1952-54
-    Cleveland, 1965-67
-    Atlanta, 2004-06
- 2   By many teams

ATTEMPTS

Most Rushing Attempts, Season
- 681   Oakland, 1977

- 674   Chicago, 1984
- 671   New England, 1978

Fewest Rushing Attempts, Season
- 211   Philadelphia, 1982
- 219   San Francisco, 1982
- 225   Houston, 1982

Most Rushing Attempts, Game
- 72   Chi. Bears vs. Brooklyn, Oct. 20, 1935
- 70   Chi. Cardinals vs. Green Bay, Dec. 5, 1948
- 69   Chi. Cardinals vs. Green Bay, Dec. 6, 1936
-    Kansas City vs. Cincinnati, Sept. 3, 1978

Fewest Rushing Attempts, Game
- 6   Chi. Cardinals vs. Boston, Oct. 29, 1933
-    New England vs. Pittsburgh, Oct. 31, 2004
-    Arizona vs. Minnesota, Nov. 26, 2006
- 7   Oakland vs. Buffalo, Oct. 5, 1963
-    Houston vs. N.Y. Giants, Dec. 8, 1985
-    Seattle vs. L.A. Raiders, Nov. 17, 1991
-    Green Bay vs. Miami, Sept. 11, 1994
-    Detroit vs. Minnesota, Dec. 2, 2007
- 8   Denver vs. Oakland, Dec. 17, 1960
-    Buffalo vs. St. Louis, Sept. 9, 1984
-    Detroit vs. San Francisco, Oct. 20, 1991
-    Atlanta vs. Detroit, Sept. 5, 1993
-    St. Louis vs. San Francisco, Nov. 2, 2003
-    N.Y. Jets vs. Denver, Nov. 20, 2005
-    St. Louis vs. Carolina, Nov. 19, 2006
-    Detroit vs. Arizona, Nov. 11, 2007

Most Rushing Attempts, Both Teams, Game
- 108   Chi. Cardinals (70) vs. Green Bay (38), Dec. 5, 1948
- 105   Oakland (62) vs. Atlanta (43), Nov. 30, 1975 (OT)
- 104   Chi. Bears (64) vs. Pittsburgh (40), Oct. 18, 1936

Fewest Rushing Attempts, Both Teams, Game
- 16   Chi. Cardinals (6) vs. Boston (10), Oct. 22, 1933
- 30   Minnesota (15) vs. New England (15), Oct. 30, 2006
- 34   Atlanta (12) vs. Houston (22), Dec. 5, 1993
-    Atlanta (15) vs. San Francisco (19), Dec. 24, 1995
-    Philadelphia (14) vs. San Diego (20), Oct. 23, 2005

YARDS GAINED

Most Yards Gained Rushing, Season
- 3,165   New England, 1978
- 3,088   Buffalo, 1973
- 2,986   Kansas City, 1978

Fewest Yards Gained Rushing, Season
- 298   Philadelphia, 1940
- 467   Detroit, 1946
- 471   Boston, 1944

Most Yards Gained Rushing, Game
- 426   Detroit vs. Pittsburgh, Nov. 4, 1934
- 423   N.Y. Giants vs. Baltimore, Nov. 19, 1950
- 420   Boston vs. N.Y. Giants, Oct. 8, 1933

Fewest Yards Gained Rushing, Game
- −53   Detroit vs. Chi. Cardinals, Oct. 17, 1943
- −36   Philadelphia vs. Chi. Bears, Nov. 19, 1939
- −33   Brooklyn vs. Phil-Pitt, Oct. 2, 1943

Most Yards Gained Rushing, Both Teams, Game
- 595   Los Angeles (371) vs. N.Y. Yanks (224), Nov. 18, 1951
- 574   Chi. Bears (396) vs. Pittsburgh (178), Oct. 10, 1934
- 558   Boston (420) vs. N.Y. Giants (138), Oct. 8, 1933

Fewest Yards Gained Rushing, Both Teams, Game
- −15   Detroit (−53) vs. Chi. Cardinals (38), Oct. 17, 1943
- 4   Detroit (−10) vs. Chi. Cardinals (14), Sept. 15, 1940
- 45   San Diego (21) vs. Philadelphia (24), Oct. 23, 2005

AVERAGE GAIN

Highest Average Gain, Rushing, Season
- 5.74   Cleveland, 1963
- 5.65   San Francisco, 1954

5.56   San Diego, 1963
Lowest Average Gain, Rushing, Season
0.94   Philadelphia, 1940
1.45   Boston, 1944
1.55   Pittsburgh, 1935

TOUCHDOWNS
Most Touchdowns, Rushing, Season
36   Green Bay, 1962
33   Pittsburgh, 1976
32   Kansas City, 2003
     San Diego, 2006
Fewest Touchdowns, Rushing, Season
1   Brooklyn, 1934
2   Chi. Cardinals, 1933
     Cincinnati, 1933
     Pittsburgh, 1934
     Philadelphia, 1935
     Philadelphia, 1936
     Philadelphia, 1937
     Philadelphia, 1938
     Pittsburgh, 1940
     Philadelphia, 1972
     N.Y. Jets, 1995
     Arizona, 2005
3   By many teams
Most Touchdowns, Rushing, Game
9   Rock Island vs. Evansville, Oct. 15, 1922
     Racine vs. Louisville, Nov. 5, 1922
8   Chi. Cardinals vs. Rochester, Oct. 7, 1923
     Kansas City vs. Atlanta, Oct. 24, 2004
7   By many teams
Most Touchdowns, Rushing, Both Teams, Game
9   Rock Island (9) vs. Evansville (0), Oct. 15, 1922
     Racine (9) vs. Louisville (0), Nov. 5, 1922
8   Chi. Cardinals (8) vs. Rochester (0), Oct. 7, 1923
     Canton (7) vs. Cleveland (1), Nov. 25, 1923
     Los Angeles (6) vs. N.Y. Yanks (2), Nov. 18, 1951
     Chi. Bears (5) vs. Green Bay (3), Nov. 6, 1955
     Denver (5) vs. Kansas City (3), Dec. 7, 2003
     Kansas City (8) vs. Atlanta (0), Oct. 24, 2004
7   In many games

PASSING
ATTEMPTS
Most Passes Attempted, Season
709   Minnesota, 1981
699   New England, 1994
686   New England, 1995
Fewest Passes Attempted, Season
102   Cincinnati, 1933
106   Boston, 1933
120   Detroit, 1937
Most Passes Attempted, Game
70   New England vs. Minnesota, Nov. 13, 1994 (OT)
69   N.Y. Jets vs. Baltimore, Dec. 24, 2000
68   Houston vs. Buffalo, Nov 1, 1964
     Cincinnati vs. Pittsburgh, Dec. 30, 2001 (OT)
Fewest Passes Attempted, Game
0   Green Bay vs. Portsmouth, Oct. 8, 1933
     Detroit vs. Cleveland, Sept. 10, 1937
     Pittsburgh vs. Brooklyn, Nov. 16, 1941
     Pittsburgh vs. Los Angeles, Nov. 13, 1949
     Cleveland vs. Philadelphia, Dec. 3, 1950
Most Passes Attempted, Both Teams, Game
112   New England (70) vs. Minnesota (42), Nov. 13, 1994
104   Miami (55) vs. N.Y. Jets (49), Oct. 18, 1987 (OT)
      N.Y. Jets (58) vs. San Francisco (46), Sept. 6, 1998 (OT)
103   Cincinnati (68) vs. Pittsburgh (35), Dec. 30, 2001 (OT)
      Seattle (53) vs. San Diego (50), Dec. 29, 2002 (OT)

Fewest Passes Attempted, Both Teams, Game
4   Chi. Cardinals (1) vs. Detroit (3), Nov. 3, 1935
     Detroit (0) vs. Cleveland (4), Sept. 10, 1937
6   Chi. Cardinals (2) vs. Detroit (4), Sept. 15, 1940
8   Brooklyn (2) vs. Philadelphia (6), Oct. 1, 1939

COMPLETIONS
Most Passes Completed, Season
440   New Orleans, 2007
432   San Francisco, 1995
419   Arizona, 2005
Fewest Passes Completed, Season
25   Cincinnati, 1933
33   Boston, 1933
34   Chi. Cardinals, 1934
Most Passes Completed, Game
45   New England vs. Minnesota, Nov. 13, 1994 (OT)
43   Washington vs. Detroit, Nov. 4, 1990 (OT)
     Oakland vs. Pittsburgh, Sept. 15, 2002
42   N.Y. Jets vs. San Francisco, Sept. 21, 1980
     N.Y. Jets vs. Seattle, Dec. 6, 1998
Fewest Passes Completed, Game
0   By many teams. Last time: Buffalo vs. N.Y. Jets,
     Sept. 29, 1974
Most Passes Completed, Both Teams, Game
71   New England (45) vs. Minnesota (26), Nov. 13, 1994
68   San Francisco (37) vs. Atlanta (31), Oct. 6, 1985
     Denver (34) vs. Oakland (34), Nov. 11, 2002
66   Cincinnati (40) vs. San Diego (26), Dec. 20, 1982
Fewest Passes Completed, Both Teams, Game
1   Chi. Cardinals (0) vs. Philadelphia (1), Nov. 8, 1936
     Detroit (0) vs. Cleveland (1), Sept. 10, 1937
     Chi. Cardinals (0) vs. Detroit (1), Sept. 15, 1940
     Brooklyn (0) vs. Pittsburgh (1), Nov. 29, 1942
2   Chi. Cardinals (0) vs. Detroit (2), Nov. 3, 1935
     Buffalo (0) vs. N.Y. Jets (2), Sept. 29, 1974
     Chi. Cardinals (0) vs. Green Bay (2), Nov. 18, 1934
3   In seven games

YARDS GAINED
Most Seasons Leading League, Passing Yardage
10   San Diego, 1965, 1968, 1971, 1978-1983, 1985
8   Chi. Bears, 1932, 1939, 1941, 1943, 1945, 1949,
     1954, 1964
     Washington, 1938, 1940, 1944, 1947-48, 1967,
     1974, 1989
7   Houston, 1960-61, 1963-64, 1990-92
     L.A./St. Louis Rams, 1946, 1950-51, 1956,
     1999-2001
     Balt./Indianapolis, 1957, 1959, 1960, 1963, 1976,
     2003-04
Most Consecutive Seasons Leading League, Passing Yardage
6   San Diego, 1978-1983
4   Green Bay, 1934-37
3   Miami, 1986-88
     Houston, 1990-92
     St. Louis, 1999-2001
Most Yards Gained, Passing, Season
5,232   St. Louis, 2000
5,018   Miami, 1984
4,870   San Diego, 1985
Fewest Yards Gained, Passing, Season
302   Chi. Cardinals, 1934
357   Cincinnati, 1933
459   Boston, 1934
Most Yards Gained, Passing, Game
554   Los Angeles vs. N.Y. Yanks, Sept. 28, 1951
530   Minnesota vs. Baltimore, Sept. 28, 1969
521   Miami vs. N.Y. Jets, Oct. 23, 1988

Fewest Yards Gained, Passing, Game
-53   Denver vs. Oakland, Sept. 10, 1967
-52   Cincinnati vs. Houston, Oct. 31, 1971
-39   Atlanta vs. San Francisco, Oct. 23, 1976

Most Yards Gained, Passing, Both Teams, Game
884   N.Y. Jets (449) vs. Miami (435), Sept. 21, 1986 (OT)
883   San Diego (486) vs. Cincinnati (397), Dec. 20, 1982
874   Miami (456) vs. New England (418), Sept. 4, 1994

Fewest Yards Gained, Passing, Both Teams, Game
-11   Green Bay (-10) vs. Dallas (-1), Oct. 24, 1965
  1   Chi. Cardinals (0) vs. Philadelphia (1), Nov. 8, 1936
  7   Brooklyn (0) vs. Pittsburgh (7), Nov. 29, 1942

TIMES SACKED

Most Seasons Leading League, Fewest Times Sacked
10   Miami, 1973, 1982-1990
  5   N.Y. Jets, 1965-66, 1968, 1993, 2000
     Indianapolis, 1999-2000, 2004-06
  4   San Diego, 1963-64, 1967-68
     San Francisco, 1964-65, 1970-71

Most Consecutive Seasons Leading League, Fewest Times Sacked
  9   Miami, 1982-1990
  3   St. Louis, 1974-76
     Indianapolis, 2004-06
  2   By many teams

Most Times Sacked, Season
104   Philadelphia, 1986
 78   Arizona, 1997
 76   Houston, 2002

Fewest Times Sacked, Season
  7   Miami, 1988
  8   San Francisco, 1970
     St. Louis, 1975
  9   N.Y. Jets, 1966
     Washington, 1991

Most Times Sacked, Game
12   Pittsburgh vs. Dallas, Nov. 20, 1966
    Baltimore vs. St. Louis, Oct. 26, 1980
    Detroit vs. Chicago, Dec. 16, 1984
    Houston vs. Dallas, Sept. 29, 1985
    Philadelphia vs. N.Y. Giants, Sept. 30, 2007
11   St. Louis vs. N.Y. Giants, Nov. 1, 1964
    Los Angeles vs. Baltimore, Nov. 22, 1964
    Denver vs. Buffalo, Dec. 13, 1964
    Green Bay vs. Detroit, Nov. 7, 1965
    Buffalo vs. Oakland, Oct. 15, 1967
    Denver vs. Oakland, Nov. 5, 1967
    Atlanta vs. St. Louis, Nov. 24, 1968
    Detroit vs. Dallas, Oct. 6, 1975
    Philadelphia vs. St. Louis, Dec. 18, 1983
    Cleveland vs. Kansas City, Sept. 30, 1984
    Minnesota vs. Chicago, Oct. 28, 1984
    Atlanta vs. Cleveland, Nov. 18, 1984
    Dallas vs. San Diego, Nov. 16, 1986
    Philadelphia vs. Detroit, Nov. 16, 1986
    Philadelphia vs. L.A. Raiders, Nov. 30, 1986 (OT)
    L.A. Raiders vs. Seattle, Dec. 8, 1986
    N.Y. Jets vs. Dallas, Oct. 4, 1987
    Philadelphia vs. Chicago, Oct. 4, 1987
    Dallas vs. Philadelphia, Sept. 15, 1991
    Cleveland vs. Indianapolis, Sept. 6, 1992
10   By many teams

Most Times Sacked, Both Teams, Game
18   Green Bay (10) vs. San Diego (8), Sept. 24, 1978
17   Buffalo (10) vs. N.Y. Titans (7), Nov. 23, 1961
    Pittsburgh (12) vs. Dallas (5), Nov. 20, 1966
    Atlanta (9) vs. Philadelphia (8), Dec. 16, 1984
    Philadelphia (11) vs. L.A. Raiders (6), Nov. 30, 1986 (OT)
16   Los Angeles (11) vs. Baltimore (5), Nov. 22, 1964
    Buffalo (11) vs. Oakland (5), Oct. 15, 1967

COMPLETION PERCENTAGE

Most Seasons Leading League, Completion Percentage
14   San Francisco, 1952, 1957-58, 1965, 1981, 1983, 1987, 1989, 1992-97
11   Washington, 1937, 1939-1940, 1942-45, 1947-48, 1969-1970
  8   Green Bay, 1936, 1941, 1961-62, 1964, 1966, 1968, 1998

Most Consecutive Seasons Leading League, Completion Percentage
  6   San Francisco, 1992-97
  4   Washington, 1942-45
     Kansas City, 1966-69
  3   Cleveland, 1953-55
     St. Louis, 1999-2001

Highest Completion Percentage, Season
70.65   Cincinnati, 1982 (310-219)
70.25   San Francisco, 1994 (511-359)
70.19   San Francisco, 1989 (483-339)

Lowest Completion Percentage, Season
22.9   Philadelphia, 1936 (170-39)
24.5   Cincinnati, 1933 (102-25)
25.0   Pittsburgh, 1941 (168-42)

TOUCHDOWNS

Most Touchdowns, Passing, Season
51   Indianapolis, 2004
50   New England, 2007
49   Miami, 1984

Fewest Touchdowns, Passing, Season
0   Cincinnati, 1933
   Pittsburgh, 1945
1   Boston, 1932
   Boston, 1933
   Chi. Cardinals, 1934
   Cincinnati/St. Louis, 1934
   Detroit, 1942
2   Chi. Cardinals, 1932
   Stapleton, 1932
   Chi. Cardinals, 1935
   Brooklyn, 1936
   Pittsburgh, 1942

Most Touchdowns, Passing, Game
7   Chi. Bears vs. N.Y. Giants, Nov. 14, 1943
   Philadelphia vs. Washington, Oct. 17, 1954
   Houston vs. N.Y. Titans, Nov. 19, 1961
   Houston vs. N.Y. Titans, Oct. 14, 1962
   N.Y. Giants vs. Washington, Oct. 28, 1962
   Minnesota vs. Baltimore, Sept. 28, 1969
   San Diego vs. Oakland, Nov. 22, 1981
6   By many teams

Most Touchdowns, Passing, Both Teams, Game
12   New Orleans (6) vs. St. Louis (6), Nov. 2, 1969
11   N.Y. Giants (7) vs. Washington (4), Oct. 28, 1962
    Oakland (6) vs. Houston (5), Dec. 22, 1963
    Cincinnati (6) vs. Cleveland, (5), Sept. 16, 2007
10   San Diego (5) vs. Seattle (5), Sept. 15, 1985
    Miami (6) vs. N.Y. Jets (4), Sept. 21, 1986 (OT)
    San Francisco (6) vs. Atlanta (4), Oct. 14, 1990

PASSES HAD INTERCEPTED

Most Passes Had Intercepted, Season
48   Houston, 1962
45   Denver, 1961
41   Card-Pitt, 1944

Fewest Passes Had Intercepted, Season
5   Cleveland, 1960
   Green Bay, 1966
   Kansas City, 1990

N.Y. Giants, 1990
6 Green Bay, 1964
St. Louis, 1982
Dallas, 1993
Jacksonville, 2005
7 Los Angeles, 1969
Denver, 2005

Most Passes Had Intercepted, Game
9 Detroit vs. Green Bay, Oct. 24, 1943
Pittsburgh vs. Philadelphia, Dec. 12, 1965
8 Green Bay vs. N.Y. Giants, Nov. 21, 1948
Chi. Cardinals vs. Philadelphia, Sept. 24, 1950
N.Y. Yanks vs. N.Y. Giants, Dec. 16, 1951
Denver vs. Houston, Dec. 2, 1962
Chi. Bears vs. Detroit, Sept. 22, 1968
Baltimore vs. N.Y. Jets, Sept. 23, 1973
7 By many teams. Last time: Detroit vs. Cleveland,
Sept. 23, 2001

Most Passes Had Intercepted, Both Teams, Game
13 Denver (8) vs. Houston (5), Dec. 2, 1962
11 Philadelphia (7) vs. Boston (4), Nov. 3, 1935
Boston (6) vs. Pittsburgh (5), Dec. 1, 1935
Cleveland (7) vs. Green Bay (4), Oct. 30, 1938
Green Bay (7) vs. Detroit (4), Oct. 20, 1940
Detroit (7) vs. Chi. Bears (4), Nov. 22, 1942
Detroit (7) vs. Cleveland (4), Nov. 26, 1944
Chi. Cardinals (8) vs. Philadelphia (3), Sept. 24, 1950
Washington (7) vs. N.Y. Giants (4), Dec. 8, 1963
Pittsburgh (9) vs. Philadelphia (2), Dec 12, 1965
10 In many games

PUNTING
Most Seasons Leading League (Average Distance)
7 Denver 1962-64, 1966-67, 1982, 1999
Oakland, 1974-75, 1977-78, 2003-04, 2007
6 Washington, 1940-43, 1945, 1958
Kansas City, 1968, 1971-73, 1979, 1984
5 L.A. Rams, 1946, 1949, 1955-56, 1994

Most Consecutive Seasons Leading League (Average Distance)
4 Washington, 1940-43
3 Cleveland, 1950-52
Denver, 1962-64
Kansas City, 1971-73

Most Punts, Season
116 Houston, 2002
114 Chicago, 1981
113 Boston, 1934
Brooklyn, 1934
Dallas, 2002

Fewest Punts, Season
23 San Diego, 1982
31 Cincinnati, 1982
32 Chi. Bears, 1941

Most Punts, Game
17 Chi. Bears vs. Green Bay, Oct. 22, 1933
Cincinnati vs. Pittsburgh, Oct. 22, 1933
16 Cincinnati vs. Portsmouth, Sept. 17, 1933
Chi. Cardinals vs. Chi. Bears, Nov. 30, 1933
Chi. Cardinals vs. Detroit, Sept. 15, 1940
Oakland vs. San Diego, Oct. 11, 1998
15 Chi. Cardinals vs. Cincinnati, Nov. 12, 1933
N.Y. Giants vs. Chi. Bears, Nov. 17, 1935
Philadelphia vs. N.Y. Giants, Dec. 6, 1987 (OT)

Fewest Punts, Game
0 By many teams. Last time:
Jacksonville vs. Indianapolis, Dec. 2, 2007

Most Punts, Both Teams, Game
31 Chi. Bears (17) vs. Green Bay (14), Oct. 22, 1933
Cincinnati (17), vs. Pittsburgh (14), Oct. 22, 1933

29 Chi. Cardinals (15) vs. Cincinnati (14), Nov. 12, 1933
Chi. Cardinals (16) vs. Chi. Bears (13), Nov. 30, 1933
Chi. Cardinals (16) vs. Detroit (13), Sept. 15, 1940
28 Philadelphia (14) vs. Washington (14), Nov. 5, 1939

Fewest Punts, Both Teams, Game
0 Buffalo vs. San Francisco, Sept. 13, 1992
1 Baltimore (0) vs. Cleveland (1), Nov. 1, 1959
Dall. Cowboys (0) vs. Cleveland (1), Dec. 3, 1961
Chicago (0) vs. Detroit (1), Oct. 1, 1972
San Francisco (0) vs. N.Y. Giants (1), Oct. 15, 1972
Green Bay (0) vs. Buffalo (1), Dec. 5, 1982
Miami (0) vs. Buffalo (1), Oct. 12, 1986
Green Bay (0) vs. Chicago (1), Dec. 17, 1989
Oakland (0) vs. Seattle (1), Dec. 5, 1999
Tampa Bay (0) vs. Minnesota (1), Oct. 29, 2000
New Orleans (0) vs. San Francisco (1), Oct. 20, 2002
2 In many games

AVERAGE YARDAGE
Highest Average Distance, Punting, Season
49.1 Oakland, 2007 (73-3,585)
48.2 Dallas, 2006 (56-2,697)
47.6 Detroit, 1961 (56-2,664)

Lowest Average Distance, Punting, Season
32.7 Card-Pitt, 1944 (60-1,964)
33.8 Cincinnati, 1986 (59-1,996)
33.9 Detroit, 1969 (74-2,510)

PUNT RETURNS
Most Seasons Leading League (Average Return)
9 Detroit, 1943-45, 1951-52, 1962, 1966, 1969, 1991
7 Chi. Cardinals/St. Louis, 1948-49, 1955-56, 1959, 1986-87
6 Green Bay, 1950, 1953-54, 1961, 1972, 1996
Dallas/Kansas City, 1960, 1968, 1970, 1979-1980, 2003

Most Consecutive Seasons Leading League (Average Return)
3 Detroit, 1943-45
2 By many teams

Most Punt Returns, Season
71 Pittsburgh, 1976
Tampa Bay, 1979
L.A. Raiders, 1985
67 Pittsburgh, 1974
Los Angeles, 1978
L.A. Raiders, 1984
65 San Francisco, 1976

Fewest Punt Returns, Season
12 Baltimore, 1981
San Diego, 1982
14 Los Angeles, 1961
Philadelphia, 1962
Baltimore, 1982
15 Houston, 1960
Washington, 1960
Oakland, 1961
N.Y. Giants, 1969
Philadelphia, 1973
Kansas City, 1982

Most Punt Returns, Game
12 Philadelphia vs. Cleveland, Dec. 3, 1950
11 Chi. Bears vs. Chi. Cardinals, Oct. 8, 1950
Washington vs. Tampa Bay, Oct. 9, 1977
10 Philadelphia vs. N.Y. Giants, Nov. 26, 1950
Philadelphia vs. Tampa Bay, Sept. 18, 1977
Pittsburgh vs. Buffalo, Dec. 16, 1979
Washington vs. New Orleans, Dec. 26, 1982
Philadelphia vs. Seattle, Dec. 13, 1992 (OT)
New England vs. Pittsburgh, Dec. 5, 1993

Most Punt Returns, Both Teams, Game
17 Philadelphia (12) vs. Cleveland (5), Dec. 3, 1950
16 N.Y. Giants (9) vs. Philadelphia (7), Dec. 12, 1954
   Washington (11) vs. Tampa Bay (5), Oct. 9, 1977
   Oakland (8) vs. San Diego (8), Oct. 11, 1998
15 Detroit (8) vs. Cleveland (7), Sept. 27, 1942
   Los Angeles (8) vs. Baltimore (7), Nov. 27, 1966
   Pittsburgh (8) vs. Houston (7), Dec. 1, 1974
   Philadelphia (10) vs. Tampa Bay (5), Sept. 18, 1977
   Baltimore (9) vs. Kansas City (6), Sept. 2, 1979
   Washington (10) vs. New Orleans (5), Dec. 26, 1982
   L.A. Raiders (8) vs. Cleveland (7), Nov. 16, 1986

FAIR CATCHES
Most Fair Catches, Season
34 Baltimore, 1971
33 Philadelphia, 2000
32 San Diego, 1969
   Oakland, 2001
Fewest Fair Catches, Season
0 San Diego, 1975
   New England, 1976
   Tampa Bay, 1976
   Pittsburgh, 1977
   Dallas, 1982
1 Cleveland, 1974
   San Francisco, 1975
   Kansas City, 1976
   St. Louis, 1976
   San Diego, 1976
   L.A. Rams, 1982
   St. Louis, 1982
   Tampa Bay, 1982
   Arizona, 2001
2 By many teams
Most Fair Catches, Game
7 Minnesota vs. Dallas, Sept. 25, 1966
   N.Y. Jets vs. Miami, Nov. 20, 1966
   Detroit vs. Chicago, Nov. 21, 1976
   Philadelphia vs. Buffalo, Dec. 27, 1987
6 By many teams

YARDS GAINED
Most Yards, Punt Returns, Season
875 Green Bay, 1996
785 L.A. Raiders, 1985
781 Chi. Bears, 1948
Fewest Yards, Punt Returns, Season
27 St. Louis, 1965
35 N.Y. Giants, 1965
37 New England, 1972
Most Yards, Punt Returns, Game
231 Detroit vs. San Francisco, Oct. 6, 1963
225 Oakland vs. Buffalo, Sept. 15, 1968
219 Los Angeles vs. Atlanta, Oct. 11, 1981
Fewest Yards, Punt Returns, Game
-28 Washington vs. Dallas, Dec. 11, 1966
-23 N.Y. Giants vs. Buffalo, Oct. 20, 1975
   Pittsburgh vs. Houston, Sept. 20, 1970
-20 New Orleans vs. Pittsburgh, Oct. 20, 1968
Most Yards, Punt Returns, Both Teams, Game
282 Los Angeles (219) vs. Atlanta (63), Oct. 11, 1981
245 Detroit (231) vs. San Francisco (14), Oct. 6, 1963
244 Oakland (225) vs. Buffalo (19), Sept. 15, 1968
Fewest Yards, Punt Returns, Both Teams, Game
-18 Buffalo (-18) vs. Pittsburgh (0), Oct. 29, 1972
-14 Miami (-14) vs. Boston (0), Nov. 30, 1969
   Tennessee (-14) vs. New Orleans (0),
      Sept. 21, 2003

-13 N.Y. Giants (-13) vs. Cleveland (0), Nov. 14, 1965

AVERAGE YARDS RETURNING PUNTS
Highest Average, Punt Returns, Season
20.2 Chi. Bears, 1941 (27-546)
19.1 Chi. Cardinals, 1948 (35-669)
18.2 Chi. Cardinals, 1949 (30-546)
Lowest Average, Punt Returns, Season
1.2 St. Louis, 1965 (23-27)
1.5 N.Y. Giants, 1965 (24-35)
1.7 Washington, 1970 (27-45)

TOUCHDOWNS RETURNING PUNTS
Most Touchdowns, Punt Returns, Season
5 Chi. Cardinals, 1959
4 Chi. Cardinals, 1948
   Detroit, 1951
   N.Y. Giants, 1951
   Denver, 1976
   Chicago, 2007
3 Washington, 1941
   Detroit, 1952
   Pittsburgh, 1952
   Houston, 1975
   Los Angeles, 1981
   Cleveland, 1993
   Green Bay, 1996
   Denver, 1997
   San Diego, 1997
   Chicago, 2006
   Tennessee, 2006
Most Touchdowns, Punt Returns, Game
2 Detroit vs. Los Angeles, Oct. 14, 1951
   Detroit vs. Green Bay, Nov. 22, 1951
   Chi. Cardinals vs. Pittsburgh, Nov. 1, 1959
   Chi. Cardinals vs. N.Y. Giants, Nov. 22, 1959
   N.Y. Titans vs. Denver, Sept. 24, 1961
   Denver vs. Cleveland, Sept. 26, 1976
   Los Angeles vs. Atlanta, Oct. 11, 1981
   St. Louis vs. Tampa Bay, Dec. 21, 1986
   L.A. Rams vs. Atlanta, Dec. 27, 1992
   Cleveland vs. Pittsburgh, Oct. 24, 1993
   San Diego vs. Cincinnati, Nov. 2, 1997
   Denver vs. Carolina, Nov. 9, 1997
   Baltimore vs. Seattle, Dec. 7, 1997
   Baltimore vs. N.Y. Jets, Dec. 24, 2000
   Oakland vs. Tennessee, Sept. 29, 2002
   Carolina vs. Cincinnati, Dec. 8, 2002
   Detroit at Jacksonville, Nov. 14, 2004 (OT)
Most Touchdowns, Punt Returns, Both Teams, Game
2 Philadelphia (1) vs. Washington (1), Nov. 9, 1952
   Kansas City (1) vs. Buffalo (1), Sept. 11, 1966
   Baltimore (1) vs. New England (1), Nov. 18, 1979
   L.A. Raiders (1) vs. Philadelphia (1),
      Nov. 30, 1986 (OT)
   Cincinnati (1) vs. Green Bay (1), Sept. 20, 1992
   Oakland (1) vs. Seattle (1), Nov. 15, 1998
   Atlanta (1) vs. Tennessee (1), Nov. 23, 2003
(Also see previous record)

KICKOFF RETURNS
Most Seasons Leading League (Average Return)
8 Washington, 1942, 1947, 1962-63, 1973-74, 1981,
      1995
6 Chicago Bears, 1943, 1948, 1958, 1966, 1972, 1985
   N.Y. Giants, 1944, 1946, 1949, 1951, 1953, 2004
5 Green Bay, 1954, 1964, 1967, 1993, 1998
   New England, 1977, 1980, 1982, 1997, 2006
Most Consecutive Seasons Leading League (Average Return)
3 Denver, 1965-67

2　By many teams

Most Kickoff Returns, Season
- 89　Cleveland, 1999
- 88　New Orleans, 1980
- 87　Atlanta, 1996
- 　　New Orleans, 2001

Fewest Kickoff Returns, Season
- 17　N.Y. Giants, 1944
- 20　N.Y. Giants, 1941, 1943
- 　　Chi. Bears, 1942
- 23　Washington, 1942

Most Kickoff Returns, Game
- 12　N.Y. Giants vs. Washington, Nov. 27, 1966
- 10　By many teams

Most Kickoff Returns, Both Teams, Game
- 19　N.Y. Giants (12) vs. Washington (7), Nov. 27, 1966
- 　　Cleveland (10) vs. Cincinnati (9), Nov. 28, 2004
- 18　Houston (10) vs. Oakland (8), Dec. 22, 1963
- 17　Washington (9) vs. Green Bay (8), Oct. 17, 1983
- 　　San Diego (9) vs. Pittsburgh (8), Dec. 8, 1985
- 　　Detroit (9) vs. Green Bay (8), Nov. 27, 1986
- 　　L.A. Raiders (9) vs. Seattle (8), Dec. 18, 1988
- 　　Oakland (10) vs. Seattle (7), Oct. 26, 1997
- 　　Buffalo (9) vs. Minnesota (8), Sept. 15, 2002 (OT)
- 　　Cincinnati (10) vs. Cleveland (7), Sept. 16, 2007

YARDS GAINED

Most Yards, Kickoff Returns, Season
- 2,296　Arizona, 2000
- 2,173　Houston, 2005
- 2,039　Detroit, 2002

Fewest Yards, Kickoff Returns, Season
- 282　N.Y. Giants, 1940
- 381　Green Bay, 1940
- 424　Chicago, 1963

Most Yards, Kickoff Returns, Game
- 367　Baltimore vs. Minnesota, Dec. 13, 1998
- 362　Detroit vs. Los Angeles, Oct. 29, 1950
- 304　Chi. Bears vs. Green Bay, Nov. 9, 1952
- 　　New Orleans vs. L.A. Rams, Oct. 23, 1994

Most Yards, Kickoff Returns, Both Teams, Game
- 560　Detroit (362) vs. Los Angeles (198), Oct. 29, 1950
- 511　Baltimore (367) vs. Minnesota (144), Dec. 13, 1998
- 501　New Orleans (304) vs. L.A. Rams (197), Oct. 23, 1994

AVERAGE YARDAGE

Highest Average, Kickoff Returns, Season
- 29.4　Chicago, 1972 (52-1,528)
- 28.9　Pittsburgh, 1952 (39-1,128)
- 28.2　Washington, 1962 (61-1,720)

Lowest Average, Kickoff Returns, Season
- 14.7　N.Y. Jets, 1993 (46-675)
- 15.8　N.Y. Giants, 1993 (32-507)
- 15.9　Tampa Bay, 1993 (58-922)

TOUCHDOWNS

Most Touchdowns, Kickoff Returns, Season
- 4　Green Bay, 1967
- 　Chicago, 1970
- 　Detroit, 1994
- 　Houston, 2007
- 3　Los Angeles, 1950
- 　Chi. Cardinals, 1954
- 　San Francisco, 1963
- 　Denver, 1966
- 　Chicago, 1967
- 　New England, 1977
- 　L.A. Rams, 1985
- 　Atlanta, 2000
- 　Buffalo, 2004

N.Y. Jets, 2007

2　By many teams

Most Touchdowns, Kickoff Returns, Game
- 2　Chi. Bears vs. Green Bay, Sept. 22, 1940
- 　Chi. Bears vs. Green Bay, Nov. 9, 1952
- 　Philadelphia vs. Dallas, Nov. 6, 1966
- 　Green Bay vs. Cleveland, Nov. 12, 1967
- 　L.A. Rams vs. Green Bay, Nov. 24, 1985
- 　New Orleans vs. L.A. Rams, Oct. 23, 1994
- 　Baltimore vs. Minnesota, Dec. 13, 1998
- 　N.Y. Jets vs. Buffalo, Sept. 8, 2002 (OT)
- 　Chicago vs. St. Louis, Dec. 11, 2006
- 　Houston vs. Jacksonville, Dec. 30, 2007

Most Touchdowns, Kickoff Returns, Both Teams, Game
- 3　Baltimore (2) vs. Minnesota (1), Dec. 13, 1998
- 2　In many games

FUMBLES

Most Fumbles, Season
- 56　Chi. Bears, 1938
- 　　San Francisco, 1978
- 54　Philadelphia, 1946
- 51　New England, 1973

Fewest Fumbles, Season
- 7　Kansas City, 2002
- 8　Cleveland, 1959
- 10　Indianapolis, 1998
- 　　Minnesota, 1998

Most Fumbles, Game
- 10　Phil-Pitt vs. N.Y. Giants, Oct. 9, 1943
- 　　Detroit vs. Minnesota, Nov. 12, 1967
- 　　Kansas City vs. Houston, Oct. 12, 1969
- 　　San Francisco vs. Detroit, Dec. 17, 1978
- 9　Philadelphia vs. Green Bay, Oct. 13, 1946
- 　Boston at Oakland, Dec. 16, 1962
- 　Kansas City vs. San Diego, Nov. 15, 1964
- 　N.Y. Giants vs. Buffalo, Oct. 20, 1975
- 　St. Louis vs. Washington, Oct. 25, 1976
- 　San Diego vs. Green Bay, Sept. 24, 1978
- 　Pittsburgh vs. Cincinnati, Oct. 14, 1979
- 　Cleveland vs. Seattle, Dec. 20, 1981
- 　Cleveland vs. Pittsburgh, Dec. 23, 1990
- 　Oakland vs. Seattle, Dec. 22, 1996
- 8　By many teams

Most Fumbles, Both Teams, Game
- 14　Chi. Bears (7) vs. Cleveland (7), Nov. 24, 1940
- 　　St. Louis (8) vs. N.Y. Giants (6), Sept. 17, 1961
- 　　Kansas City (10) vs. Houston (4), Oct. 12, 1969
- 13　Washington (8) vs. Pittsburgh (5), Nov. 14, 1937
- 　　Philadelphia (7) vs. Boston (6), Dec. 8, 1946
- 　　N.Y. Giants (7) vs. Washington (6), Nov. 5, 1950
- 　　Kansas City (9) vs. San Diego (4), Nov. 15, 1964
- 　　Buffalo (7) vs. Denver (6), Dec. 13, 1964
- 　　N.Y. Jets (7) vs. Houston (6), Sept. 12, 1965
- 　　Cleveland (7) vs. New Orleans (6), Dec. 12, 1971
- 　　Houston (8) vs. Pittsburgh (5), Dec. 9, 1973
- 　　St. Louis (9) vs. Washington (4), Oct. 25, 1976
- 　　Cleveland (9) vs. Seattle (4), Dec. 20, 1981
- 　　Green Bay (7) vs. Detroit (6), Oct. 6, 1985
- 12　In many games

FUMBLES LOST

Most Fumbles Lost, Season
- 36　Chi. Cardinals, 1959
- 31　Green Bay, 1952
- 29　Chi. Cardinals, 1946
- 　　Pittsburgh, 1950
- 　　Cleveland, 1978

Fewest Fumbles Lost, Season
- 2 Kansas City, 2002
- 3 Philadelphia, 1938
  Minnesota, 1980
- 4 San Francisco, 1960
  Kansas City, 1982
  Minnesota, 1998
  Detroit, 2003

Most Fumbles Lost, Game
- 8 St. Louis vs. Washington, Oct. 25, 1976
  Cleveland vs. Pittsburgh, Dec. 23, 1990
- 7 Cincinnati vs. Buffalo, Nov. 30, 1969
  Pittsburgh vs. Cincinnati, Oct. 14, 1979
  Cleveland vs. Seattle, Dec. 20, 1981
- 6 By many teams

FUMBLES RECOVERED

Most Fumbles Recovered, Season, Own and Opponents'
- 58 Minnesota, 1963 (27 own, 31 opp)
- 51 Chi. Bears, 1938 (37 own, 14 opp)
  San Francisco, 1978 (24 own, 27 opp)
- 50 Philadelphia, 1987 (23 own, 27 opp)

Fewest Fumbles Recovered, Season, Own and Opponents'
- 9 San Francisco, 1982 (5 own, 4 opp)
- 10 Jacksonville, 2006 (6 own, 4 opp)
- 11 Cincinnati, 1982 (5 own, 6 opp)

Most Fumbles Recovered, Game, Own and Opponents'
- 10 Denver vs. Buffalo, Dec. 13, 1964 (5 own, 5 opp)
  Pittsburgh vs. Houston, Dec. 9, 1973 (5 own, 5 opp)
  Washington vs. St. Louis, Oct. 25, 1976
  (2 own, 8 opp)
- 9 St. Louis vs. N.Y. Giants, Sept. 17, 1961
  (6 own, 3 opp)
  Houston vs. Cincinnati, Oct. 27, 1974 (4 own, 5 opp)
  Kansas City vs. Dallas, Nov. 10, 1975 (4 own, 5 opp)
  Green Bay vs. Detroit, Oct. 6, 1985 (5 own, 4 opp)
  Pittsburgh vs. Cleveland, Dec. 23, 1990
  (1 own, 8 opp)
- 8 By many teams

Most Own Fumbles Recovered, Season
- 37 Chi. Bears, 1938
- 28 Pittsburgh, 1987
- 27 Philadelphia, 1946
  Minnesota, 1963

Fewest Own Fumbles Recovered, Season
- 1 Indianapolis, 2006
- 2 Washington, 1958
  Miami, 2000
- 3 Detroit, 1956
  Cleveland, 1959
  Houston, 1982
  New Orleans, 2005

Most Opponents' Fumbles Recovered, Season
- 31 Minnesota, 1963
- 29 Cleveland, 1951
- 28 Green Bay, 1946
  Houston, 1977
  Seattle, 1983

Fewest Opponents' Fumbles Recovered, Season
- 3 Los Angeles, 1974
  Green Bay, 1995
- 4 Philadelphia, 1944
  San Francisco, 1982
  Jacksonville, 2006
- 5 Baltimore, 1982
  Arizona, 1997
  Baltimore, 1998
  Chicago, 2003
  Oakland, 2006

Most Opponents' Fumbles Recovered, Game
- 8 Washington vs. St. Louis, Oct. 25, 1976
  Pittsburgh vs. Cleveland, Dec. 23, 1990
- 7 Buffalo vs. Cincinnati, Nov. 30, 1969
  Cincinnati vs. Pittsburgh, Oct. 14, 1979
  Seattle vs. Cleveland, Dec. 20, 1981
- 6 By many teams

TOUCHDOWNS

Most Touchdowns, Fumbles Recovered, Season, Own and Opponents'
- 5 Chi. Bears, 1942 (1 own, 4 opp)
  Los Angeles, 1952 (1 own, 4 opp)
  San Francisco, 1965 (1 own, 4 opp)
  Oakland, 1978 (2 own, 3 opp)
- 4 Chi. Bears, 1948 (1 own, 3 opp)
  Boston, 1948 (4 opp)
  Denver, 1979 (1 own, 3 opp)
  Atlanta, 1981 (1 own, 3 opp)
  Denver, 1984 (4 opp)
  St. Louis, 1987 (4 opp)
  Minnesota, 1989 (4 opp)
  Atlanta, 1991 (4 opp)
  Philadelphia, 1995 (4 opp)
  Atlanta, 1998 (4 opp)
  New Orleans, 1998 (4 opp)
  Kansas City, 1999 (4 opp)
- 3 By many teams

Most Touchdowns, Own Fumbles Recovered, Season
- 2 Chi. Bears, 1953
  New England, 1973
  Buffalo, 1974
  Denver, 1975
  Oakland, 1978
  Green Bay, 1982
  New Orleans, 1983
  Cleveland, 1986
  Green Bay, 1989
  Miami, 1996
  Buffalo, 2000
  Philadelphia, 2007

Most Touchdowns, Opponents' Fumbles Recovered, Season
- 4 Detroit, 1937
  Chi. Bears, 1942
  Boston, 1948
  Los Angeles, 1952
  San Francisco, 1965
  Denver, 1984
  St. Louis, 1987
  Minnesota, 1989
  Atlanta, 1991
  Philadelphia, 1995
  Atlanta, 1998
  New Orleans, 1998
  Kansas City, 1999
- 3 By many teams

Most Touchdowns, Fumbles Recovered, Game, Own and Opponents'
- 2 By many teams

Most Touchdowns, Fumbles Recovered, Game, Both Teams, Own and Opponents'
- 3 Detroit (2) vs. Minnesota (1), Dec. 9, 1962
  (2 own, 1 opp)
  Green Bay (2) vs. Dallas (1), Nov. 29, 1964 (3 opp)
  Oakland (2) vs. Buffalo (1), Dec. 24, 1967 (3 opp)
  Oakland (2) vs. Philadelphia (1), Sept. 24, 1995
  (3 opp)
  Tennessee (2) vs. Pittsburgh (1), Jan. 2, 2000
  (3 opp)

Most Touchdowns, Own Fumbles Recovered, Game
2 Miami vs. New England, Sept.1, 1996
Most Touchdowns, Opponents' Fumbles Recovered, Game
2 Many times. Last time:
    Chicago vs. Arizona, Oct. 16, 2006
Most Touchdowns, Opponents' Fumbles Recovered, Game, Both Teams
3 Green Bay (2) vs. Dallas (1), Nov. 29, 1964
   Oakland (2) vs. Buffalo (1), Dec. 24, 1967
   Oakland (2) vs. Philadelphia (1), Sept. 24, 1995
   Tennessee (2) vs. Pittsburgh (1), Jan. 2, 2000

TURNOVERS
(Number of times losing the ball on interceptions and fumbles.)
Most Turnovers, Season
65 Denver, 1961
63 San Francisco, 1978
58 Chi. Bears, 1947
    Pittsburgh, 1950
    N.Y. Giants, 1983
Fewest Turnovers, Season
12 Kansas City, 1982
14 N.Y. Giants, 1943
    Cleveland, 1959
    N.Y. Giants, 1990
15 Dallas, 1998
    Jacksonville, 2002
    Kansas City, 2002
    San Diego, 2006
    New England, 2007
Most Turnovers, Game
12 Detroit vs. Chi. Bears, Nov. 22, 1942
    Chi. Cardinals vs. Philadelphia, Sept. 24, 1950
    Pittsburgh vs. Philadelphia, Dec. 12, 1965
11 San Diego vs. Green Bay, Sept. 24, 1978
10 Washington vs. N.Y. Giants, Dec. 4, 1938
    Pittsburgh vs. Green Bay, Nov. 23, 1941
    Detroit vs. Green Bay, Oct. 24, 1943
    Chi. Cardinals vs. Green Bay, Nov. 10, 1946
    Chi. Cardinals vs. N.Y. Giants, Nov. 2, 1952
    Minnesota vs. Detroit, Dec. 9, 1962
    Houston vs. Oakland, Sept. 7, 1963
    Washington vs. N.Y. Giants, Dec. 8, 1963
    Chicago vs. Detroit, Sept. 22, 1968
    St. Louis vs. Washington, Oct. 25, 1976
    N.Y. Jets vs. New England, Nov. 21, 1976
    San Francisco vs. Dallas, Oct. 12, 1980
    Cleveland vs. Seattle, Dec. 20, 1981
    Detroit vs. Denver, Oct. 7, 1984
Most Turnovers, Both Teams, Game
17 Detroit (12) vs. Chi. Bears (5), Nov. 22, 1942
    Boston (9) vs. Philadelphia (8), Dec. 8, 1946
16 Chi. Cardinals (12) vs. Philadelphia (4),
    Sept. 24, 1950
    Chi. Cardinals (8) vs. Chi. Bears (8), Dec. 7, 1958
    Minnesota (10) vs. Detroit (6), Dec. 9, 1962
    Houston (9) vs. Kansas City (7), Oct. 12, 1969
15 Philadelphia (8) vs. Chi. Cardinals (7), Oct. 3, 1954
    Denver (9) vs. Houston (6), Dec. 2, 1962
    Washington (10) vs. N.Y. Giants (5), Dec. 8, 1963
    St. Louis (9) vs. Kansas City (6), Oct. 2, 1983

PENALTIES
Most Seasons Leading League, Fewest Penalties
13 Miami, 1968, 1976-1984, 1986, 1990-91
9   Pittsburgh, 1946-47, 1950-52, 1954, 1963, 1965,
    1968
7   Boston/New England, 1962, 1964-65, 1973, 1987,
    1989, 1993

Most Consecutive Seasons Leading League, Fewest Penalties
9 Miami, 1976-1984
3 Pittsburgh, 1950-52
2 By many teams
Most Seasons Leading League, Most Penalties
16 Chi. Bears, 1941-44, 1946-49, 1951, 1959-1961,
    1963, 1965, 1968, 1976
15 Oakland/L.A. Raiders, 1963, 1966, 1968-69, 1975,
    1982, 1984, 1991, 1993-96, 2003-05
7   L.A./St. Louis Rams, 1950, 1952, 1962, 1969,
    1978, 1980, 1997
Most Consecutive Seasons Leading League, Most Penalties
4 Chi. Bears, 1941-44, 1946-49
   Oakland/L.A. Raiders, 1993-96
3 Chi. Cardinals, 1954-56
   Chi. Bears, 1959-1961
   Oakland, 2003-05
Fewest Penalties, Season
19 Detroit, 1937
21 Boston, 1935
24 Philadelphia, 1936
Most Penalties, Season
158 Kansas City, 1998
156 L.A. Raiders, 1994
     Oakland, 1996
149 Houston, 1989
Fewest Penalties, Game
0 By many teams. Last time:
   Seattle vs. Baltimore, Dec. 23, 2007
Most Penalties, Game
22 Brooklyn vs. Green Bay, Sept. 17, 1944
    Chi. Bears vs. Philadelphia, Nov. 26, 1944
    San Francisco vs. Buffalo, Oct. 4, 1998
21 Cleveland vs. Chi. Bears, Nov. 25, 1951
    Baltimore vs. Detroit, Oct. 9, 2005
20 Tampa Bay vs. Seattle, Oct. 17, 1976
    Oakland vs. Denver, Dec. 15, 1996
Fewest Penalties, Both Teams, Game
0 Brooklyn vs. Pittsburgh, Oct. 28, 1934
   Brooklyn vs. Boston, Sept. 28, 1936
   Cleveland vs. Chi. Bears, Oct. 9, 1938
   Pittsburgh vs. Philadelphia, Nov. 10, 1940
Most Penalties, Both Teams, Game
37 Cleveland (21) vs. Chi. Bears (16), Nov. 25, 1951
35 Tampa Bay (20) vs. Seattle (15), Oct. 17, 1976
34 San Francisco (22) vs. Buffalo (12), Oct. 4, 1998

YARDS PENALIZED
Most Seasons Leading League, Fewest Yards Penalized
13 Miami, 1967-68, 1973, 1977-1984, 1990-91
10 Boston/Washington, 1935, 1953-54, 1956-58,
    1970, 1985, 1995, 1997
7   Pittsburgh, 1946-47, 1950, 1952, 1962, 1965, 1968
    Boston/New England, 1962, 1964-66, 1987, 1989,
    1993
Most Consecutive Seasons Leading League, Fewest Yards Penalized
8 Miami, 1977-1984
3 Washington, 1956-58
   Boston, 1964-66
2 By many teams
Most Seasons Leading League, Most Yards Penalized
15 Chi. Bears, 1935, 1937, 1939-1944, 1946-47,
    1949, 1951, 1961-62, 1968
12 Oakland/L.A. Raiders, 1963-64, 1968-69, 1975,
    1982, 1984, 1991, 1993-94, 1996, 2003
6   Buffalo, 1962, 1967, 1970, 1972, 1981, 1983
    Houston, 1961, 1985-86, 1988-1990

Most Consecutive Seasons Leading League, Most Yards Penalized
- 6 Chi. Bears, 1939-1944
- 3 Houston, 1988-1990
- 2 By many teams

Fewest Yards Penalized, Season
- 139 Detroit, 1937
- 146 Philadelphia, 1937
- 159 Philadelphia, 1936

Most Yards Penalized, Season
- 1,304 Kansas City, 1998
- 1,274 Oakland, 1969
- 1,266 Oakland, 1996

Fewest Yards Penalized, Game
- 0 By many teams. Last time:
    - Seattle vs. Baltimore, Dec. 23, 2007

Most Yards Penalized, Game
- 212 Tennessee vs. Baltimore, Oct. 10, 1999
- 209 Cleveland vs. Chi. Bears, Nov. 25, 1951
- 191 Philadelphia vs. Seattle, Dec. 13, 1992 (OT)

Fewest Yards Penalized, Both Teams, Game
- 0 Brooklyn vs. Pittsburgh, Oct. 28, 1934
    - Brooklyn vs. Boston, Sept. 28, 1936
    - Cleveland vs. Chi. Bears, Oct. 9, 1938
    - Pittsburgh vs. Philadelphia, Nov. 10, 1940

Most Yards Penalized, Both Teams, Game
- 374 Cleveland (209) vs. Chi. Bears (165), Nov. 25, 1951
- 310 Tampa Bay (190) vs. Seattle (120), Oct. 17, 1976
- 309 Green Bay (184) vs. Boston (125), Oct. 21, 1945

DEFENSE

SCORING

Most Seasons Leading League, Fewest Points Allowed
- 11 N.Y. Giants, 1927, 1935, 1938-39, 1941, 1944, 1958-59, 1961, 1990, 1993
    - Chi. Bears, 1932, 1936-37, 1942, 1948, 1963, 1985-86, 1988, 2001, 2005
- 7 Cleveland, 1951, 1953-57, 1994
    - Green Bay, 1929, 1935, 1947, 1962, 1965-66, 1996
- 6 Dallas/Kansas City, 1960, 1962, 1968-69, 1995, 1997

Most Consecutive Seasons Leading League, Fewest Points Allowed
- 5 Cleveland, 1953-57
- 3 Buffalo, 1964-66
    - Minnesota, 1969-1971
- 2 By many teams

Fewest Points Allowed, Season (Since 1932)
- 44 Chi. Bears, 1932
- 54 Brooklyn, 1933
- 59 Detroit, 1934

Most Points Allowed, Season
- 533 Baltimore, 1981
- 501 N.Y. Giants, 1966
- 487 New Orleans, 1980

Fewest Touchdowns Allowed, Season (Since 1932)
- 6 Chi. Bears, 1932
    - Brooklyn, 1933
- 7 Detroit, 1934
- 8 Green Bay, 1932

Most Touchdowns Allowed, Season
- 68 Baltimore, 1981
- 66 N.Y. Giants, 1966
- 63 Baltimore, 1950

FIRST DOWNS

Fewest First Downs Allowed Season
- 77 Detroit, 1935
- 79 Boston, 1935
- 82 Washington, 1937

Most First Downs Allowed, Season
- 406 Baltimore, 1981
- 371 Seattle, 1981
- 368 Cleveland, 1999

Fewest First Downs Allowed, Rushing, Season
- 35 Chi. Bears, 1942
- 40 Green Bay, 1939
- 41 Brooklyn, 1944

Most First Downs Allowed, Rushing, Season
- 179 Detroit, 1985
- 178 New Orleans, 1980
- 175 Seattle, 1981

Fewest First Downs Allowed, Passing, Season
- 33 Chi. Bears, 1943
- 34 Pittsburgh, 1941
    - Washington, 1943
- 35 Detroit, 1940
    - Philadelphia, 1940, 1944

Most First Downs Allowed, Passing, Season
- 230 Atlanta, 1995
- 227 Kansas City, 2002
- 222 Minnesota, 2007

Fewest First Downs Allowed, Penalty, Season
- 1 Boston, 1944
- 3 Philadelphia, 1940
    - Pittsburgh, 1945
    - Washington, 1957
- 4 Cleveland, 1940
    - Green Bay, 1943
    - N.Y. Giants, 1943

Most First Downs Allowed, Penalty, Season
- 56 Kansas City, 1998
- 48 Houston, 1985
- 46 Houston, 1986

NET YARDS ALLOWED RUSHING AND PASSING

Most Seasons Leading League, Fewest Yards Allowed
- 8 Chi. Bears, 1942-43, 1948, 1958, 1963, 1984-86
- 7 Pittsburgh, 1957, 1974, 1976, 1990, 2001, 2004, 2007
- 6 N.Y. Giants, 1938, 1940-41, 1951, 1956, 1959
    - Philadelphia, 1944-45, 1949, 1953, 1981, 1991
    - Minnesota, 1969-1970, 1975, 1988-89, 1993

Most Consecutive Seasons Leading League, Fewest Yards Allowed
- 3 Boston/Washington, 1935-37
    - Chicago, 1984-86
- 2 By many teams

Fewest Yards Allowed, Season
- 1,539 Chi. Cardinals, 1934
- 1,703 Chi. Bears, 1942
- 1,789 Brooklyn, 1933

Most Yards Allowed, Season
- 6,793 Baltimore, 1981
- 6,403 Green Bay, 1983
- 6,391 Seattle, 2000

RUSHING

Most Seasons Leading League, Fewest Yards Allowed
- 10 Chi. Bears, 1937, 1939, 1942, 1946, 1949, 1963, 1984-85, 1987-88
- 7 Detroit, 1938, 1950, 1952, 1962, 1970, 1980-81
    - Philadelphia, 1944-45, 1947-48, 1953, 1990-91
    - Dallas, 1966-69, 1972, 1978, 1992
    - Pittsburgh, 1961, 1976, 1982, 1997, 2001-02, 2004
- 5 N.Y. Giants, 1940, 1951, 1956, 1959, 1986
    - L.A./St. Louis Rams, 1964-65, 1973-74, 1999

Most Consecutive Seasons Leading League, Fewest Yards Allowed
- 4 Dallas, 1966-69

  2 By many teams

Fewest Yards Allowed, Rushing, Season
- 519 Chi. Bears, 1942
- 558 Philadelphia, 1944
- 762 Pittsburgh, 1982

Most Yards Allowed, Rushing, Season
- 3,228 Buffalo, 1978
- 3,106 New Orleans, 1980
- 3,010 Baltimore, 1978

Fewest Touchdowns Allowed, Rushing, Season
- 2 Detroit, 1934
  - N.Y. Giants, 1944
  - Dallas, 1968
  - Minnesota, 1971
- 3 By many teams

Most Touchdowns Allowed, Rushing, Season
- 36 Oakland, 1961
- 31 N.Y. Giants, 1980
  - Tampa Bay, 1986
- 30 Baltimore, 1981

PASSING

Most Seasons Leading League, Fewest Yards Allowed
- 10 Green Bay, 1947-48, 1962, 1964-68, 1996, 2005
- 7 Washington, 1939, 1942, 1945, 1952-53, 1980, 1985
  - Philadelphia 1934, 1936, 1940, 1949, 1981, 1991, 1998
- 6 Chi. Bears, 1938, 1943-44, 1958, 1960, 1963
  - Minnesota, 1969-1970, 1972, 1975-76, 1989
  - Pittsburgh, 1941, 1946, 1951, 1955, 1974, 1990

Most Consecutive Seasons Leading League, Fewest Yards Allowed
- 5 Green Bay, 1964-68
- 2 By many teams

Fewest Yards Allowed, Passing, Season
- 545 Philadelphia, 1934
- 558 Portsmouth, 1933
- 585 Chi. Cardinals, 1934

Most Yards Allowed, Passing, Season
- 4,541 Atlanta, 1995
- 4,427 San Francisco, 2005
- 4,389 N.Y. Jets, 1986

Fewest Touchdowns Allowed, Passing, Season
- 1 Portsmouth, 1932
  - Philadelphia, 1934
- 2 Brooklyn, 1933
  - Chi. Bears, 1934
- 3 Chi. Bears, 1932
  - Green Bay, 1932
  - Green Bay, 1934
  - Chi. Bears, 1936
  - New York, 1939
  - New York, 1944

Most Touchdowns Allowed, Passing, Season
- 40 Denver, 1963
- 38 St. Louis, 1969
- 37 Washington, 1961
  - Baltimore, 1981

SACKS

Most Seasons Leading League
- 5 Oakland/L.A. Raiders, 1966-68, 1982, 1986
- 4 New England/Boston, 1961, 1963, 1977, 1979
  - Dallas, 1966, 1968-69, 1978
  - Dallas/Kansas City, 1960, 1965, 1969, 1990
  - L.A./St. Louis Rams, 1968, 1970, 1988, 1999
  - N.Y. Giants, 1963, 1985, 1998, 2007
- 3 San Francisco, 1967, 1972, 1976
  - N.Y. Giants, 1963, 1985, 1998

New Orleans, 1992, 1997, 2000
Pittsburgh, 1974, 1994, 2001
San Diego, 1962, 1980, 2006

Most Consecutive Seasons Leading League
- 3 Oakland, 1966-68
- 2 Dallas, 1968-69

Most Sacks, Season
- 72 Chicago, 1984
- 71 Minnesota, 1989
- 70 Chicago, 1987

Fewest Sacks, Season
- 11 Baltimore, 1982
- 12 Buffalo, 1982
- 13 Baltimore, 1981

Most Sacks, Game
- 12 Dallas vs. Pittsburgh, Nov. 20, 1966
  - St. Louis vs. Baltimore, Oct. 26, 1980
  - Chicago vs. Detroit, Dec. 16, 1984
  - Dallas vs. Houston, Sept. 29, 1985
  - N.Y. Giants vs. Philadelphia, Sept. 30, 2007
- 11 N.Y. Giants vs. St. Louis, Nov. 1, 1964
  - Baltimore vs. Los Angeles, Nov. 22, 1964
  - Buffalo vs. Denver, Dec. 13, 1964
  - Detroit vs. Green Bay, Nov. 7, 1965
  - Oakland vs. Buffalo, Oct. 15, 1967
  - Oakland vs. Denver, Nov. 5, 1967
  - St. Louis vs. Atlanta, Nov. 24, 1968
  - Dallas vs. Detroit, Oct. 6, 1975
  - St. Louis vs. Philadelphia, Dec. 18, 1983
  - Kansas City vs. Cleveland, Sept. 30, 1984
  - Chicago vs. Minnesota, Oct. 28, 1984
  - Cleveland vs. Atlanta, Nov. 18, 1984
  - Detroit vs. Philadelphia, Nov. 16, 1986
  - San Diego vs. Dallas, Nov. 16, 1986
  - L.A. Raiders vs. Philadelphia, Nov. 30, 1986 (OT)
  - Seattle vs. L.A. Raiders, Dec. 8, 1986
  - Chicago vs. Philadelphia, Oct. 4, 1987
  - Dallas vs. N.Y. Jets, Oct. 4, 1987
  - Philadelphia vs. Dallas, Sept. 15, 1991
  - Indianapolis vs. Cleveland, Sept. 6, 1992
- 10 By many teams

Most Opponents Yards Lost Attempting to Pass, Season
- 666 Oakland, 1967
- 583 Chicago, 1984
- 573 San Francisco, 1976

Fewest Opponents Yards Lost Attempting to Pass, Season
- 72 Jacksonville, 1995
- 75 Green Bay, 1956
- 77 N.Y. Bulldogs, 1949

INTERCEPTIONS BY

Most Seasons Leading League
- 10 N.Y. Giants, 1933, 1937-39, 1944, 1948, 1951, 1954, 1961, 1997
- 8 Green Bay, 1940, 1942-43, 1947, 1955, 1957, 1962, 1965
  - Chi. Bears, 1935-36, 1941-42, 1946, 1963, 1985, 1990
- 6 Kansas City, 1966-1970, 1974

Most Consecutive Seasons Leading League
- 5 Kansas City, 1966-1970
- 3 N.Y. Giants, 1937-39
- 2 By many teams

Most Passes Intercepted By, Season
- 49 San Diego, 1961
- 42 Green Bay, 1943
- 41 N.Y. Giants, 1951

Fewest Passes Intercepted By, Season
- 3 Houston, 1982
- 5 Baltimore, 1982

Oakland, 2005
6 Houston, 1972
St. Louis, 1982
Atlanta, 1996
St. Louis, 2004
Washington, 2006

Most Passes Intercepted By, Game
9 Green Bay vs. Detroit, Oct. 24, 1943
Philadelphia vs. Pittsburgh, Dec. 12, 1965
8 N.Y. Giants vs. Green Bay, Nov. 21, 1948
Philadelphia vs. Chi. Cardinals, Sept. 24, 1950
N.Y. Giants vs. N.Y. Yanks, Dec. 16, 1951
Houston vs. Denver, Dec. 2, 1962
Detroit vs. Chicago, Sept. 22, 1968
N.Y. Jets vs. Baltimore, Sept. 23, 1973
7 By many teams. Last time:
Cleveland vs. Detroit, Sept. 23, 2001

Most Consecutive Games, One or More Interceptions By
46 L.A. Chargers/San Diego, 1960-63
37 Detroit, 1960-63
36 Boston, 1944-47

Most Yards Returning Interceptions, Season
929 San Diego, 1961
712 Los Angeles, 1952
700 Baltimore, 2004

Fewest Yards Returning Interceptions, Season
5 Los Angeles, 1959
25 Washington, 2006
37 Dallas, 1989

Most Yards Returning Interceptions, Game
325 Seattle vs. Kansas City, Nov. 4, 1984
314 Los Angeles vs. San Francisco, Oct. 18, 1964
245 Houston vs. N.Y. Jets, Oct. 15, 1967

Most Yards Returning Interceptions, Both Teams, Game
356 Seattle (325) vs. Kansas City (31), Nov. 4, 1984
338 Los Angeles (314) vs. San Francisco (24),
Oct. 18, 1964
308 Dallas (182) vs. Los Angeles (126), Nov. 2, 1952

Most Touchdowns, Returning Interceptions, Season
9 San Diego, 1961
8 Seattle, 1998
7 Seattle, 1984
St. Louis, 1999

Most Touchdowns Returning Interceptions, Game
4 Seattle vs. Kansas City, Nov. 4, 1984
3 Baltimore vs. Green Bay, Nov. 5, 1950
Cleveland vs. Chicago, Dec. 11, 1960
Philadelphia vs. Pittsburgh, Dec. 12, 1965
Baltimore vs. Pittsburgh, Sept. 29, 1968
Buffalo vs. N.Y. Jets, Sept. 29, 1968
Houston vs. San Diego, Dec. 19, 1971
Cincinnati vs. Houston, Dec. 17, 1972
Tampa Bay vs. New Orleans, Dec. 11, 1977
Minnesota vs. N.Y. Giants, Nov. 25, 2007
2 By many teams

Most Touchdown Returning Interceptions, Both Teams, Game
4 Philadelphia (3) vs. Pittsburgh (1), Dec. 12, 1965
Seattle (4) vs. Kansas City (0), Nov. 4, 1984
3 Los Angeles (2) vs. Detroit (1), Nov. 1, 1954
Cleveland (2) vs. N.Y. Giants (1), Dec. 18, 1960
Pittsburgh (2) vs. Cincinnati (1), Oct. 10, 1983
Kansas City (2) vs. San Diego (1), Oct. 19, 1986
Arizona (2) vs. St. Louis (1), Dec. 30, 2007
(Also see previous record)

PUNT RETURNS
Fewest Opponents Punt Returns, Season
7 Washington, 1962
San Diego, 1982
10 Buffalo, 1982

11 Boston, 1962

Most Opponents Punt Returns, Season
71 Tampa Bay, 1976, 1977
69 N.Y. Giants, 1953
Cleveland, 2000
68 Cleveland, 1974
Cleveland, 1999

Fewest Yards Allowed, Punt Returns, Season
22 Green Bay, 1967
30 Buffalo, 1982
34 Washington, 1962

Most Yards Allowed, Punt Returns, Season
932 Green Bay, 1949
913 Boston, 1947
906 New Orleans, 1974

Lowest Average Allowed, Punt Returns, Season
1.20 Chi. Cardinals, 1954 (46-55)
1.22 Cleveland, 1959 (32-39)
1.55 Chi. Cardinals, 1953 (44-68)

Highest Average Allowed, Punt Returns, Season
18.6 Green Bay, 1949 (50-932)
18.0 Cleveland, 1977 (31-558)
17.9 Boston, 1960 (20-357)

Most Touchdowns Allowed, Punt Returns, Season
4 New York, 1959
Atlanta, 1992
3 Green Bay, 1949
Chi. Cardinals, 1951
L.A. Rams, 1951, 1994
Washington, 1952
Dallas, 1952
Pittsburgh, 1959, 1993
N.Y. Jets, 1968
Cleveland, 1977
Atlanta, 1986
Tampa Bay, 1986
Arizona, 2002
Cincinnati, 2002
Tennessee, 2002
2 By many teams

KICKOFF RETURNS
Fewest Opponents Kickoff Returns, Season
10 Brooklyn, 1943
13 Denver, 1992
15 Detroit, 1942
Brooklyn, 1944

Most Opponents Kickoff Returns, Season
93 Indianapolis, 2003
92 Indianapolis, 2004
New England, 2007
91 Washington, 1983

Fewest Yards Allowed, Kickoff Returns, Season
225 Brooklyn, 1943
254 Denver, 1992
293 Brooklyn, 1944

Most Yards Allowed, Kickoff Returns, Season
2,194 St. Louis, 2001
2,115 St. Louis, 1999
2,053 Kansas City, 2005

Lowest Average Allowed, Kickoff Returns, Season
14.3 Cleveland, 1980 (71-1,018)
14.9 Indianapolis, 1993 (37-551)
15.0 Seattle, 1982 (24-361)

Highest Average Allowed, Kickoff Returns, Season
29.5 N.Y. Jets, 1972 (47-1,386)
29.4 Los Angeles, 1950 (48-1,411)
29.1 New England, 1971 (49-1,427)

Most Touchdowns Allowed, Kickoff Returns, Season
4 Minnesota, 1998

   3   Minnesota, 1963, 1970
       Dallas, 1966
       Detroit, 1980
       Pittsburgh, 1986
       Buffalo, 1997
       Atlanta, 2000
       Arizona, 2005
       Indianapolis, 2007
   2   By many teams

FUMBLES
Fewest Opponents Fumbles, Season
  11   Cleveland, 1956
       Baltimore, 1982
       Tennessee, 1998
  12   Green Bay, 1995
       Cincinnati, 1998
       Jacksonville, 2006
       Baltimore, 2007
  13   Los Angeles, 1956
       Chicago, 1960
       Cleveland, 1963
       Cleveland, 1965
       Detroit, 1967
       San Diego, 1969
       New England, 2005
       Cleveland, 2006
Most Opponents Fumbles, Season
  50   Minnesota, 1963
       San Francisco, 1978
  48   N.Y. Giants, 1980
       N.Y. Jets, 1986
  47   N.Y. Giants, 1977
       Seattle, 1984

TURNOVERS
(Number of times losing the ball on interceptions and fumbles.)
Fewest Opponents Turnovers, Season
  11   Baltimore, 1982
  12   Washington, 2006
  13   San Francisco, 1982
Most Opponents Turnovers, Season
  66   San Diego, 1961
  63   Seattle, 1984
  61   Washington, 1983
Most Opponents Turnovers, Game
  12   Chi. Bears vs. Detroit, Nov. 22, 1942
       Philadelphia vs. Chi. Cardinals, Sept. 24, 1950
       Philadelphia vs. Pittsburgh, Dec. 12, 1965
  11   Green Bay vs. San Diego, Sept. 24, 1978
  10   By 14 teams

ANNUAL SCORING LEADERS

Year	Player, Team	TD	FG	PAT	TP
2007	*Mason Crosby, NFC	0	31	48	141
	Randy Moss, New England, AFC	23	0	0	138
2006	LaDainian Tomlinson, AFC	31	0	0	186
	Robbie Gould, Chicago, NFC	0	32	47	143
2005	Shaun Alexander, Seattle, NFC	28	0	0	168
	Shayne Graham, Cincinnati, AFC	0	28	47	131
2004	Adam Vinatieri, New England, AFC	0	31	48	141
	David Akers, Philadelphia, NFC	0	27	41	122
2003	Jeff Wilkins, St. Louis, NFC	0	39	46	163
	Priest Holmes, Kansas City, AFC	27	0	0	162
2002	Priest Holmes, Kansas City, AFC	24	0	0	144
	Jay Feely, Atlanta, NFC	0	32	42	138
2001	Marshall Faulk, St. Louis, NFC	21	0	0	#128
	Mike Vanderjagt, Indianapolis, AFC	0	28	41	125
2000	Marshall Faulk, St. Louis, NFC	26	0	0	##160
	Matt Stover, Baltimore, AFC	0	35	30	135
1999	Mike Vanderjagt, Indianapolis, AFC	0	34	43	145
	Jeff Wilkins, St. Louis, NFC	0	20	64	124
1998	Gary Anderson, Minnesota, NFC	0	35	59	164
	Steve Christie, Buffalo, AFC	0	33	41	140
1997	Mike Hollis, Jacksonville, AFC	0	31	41	134
	Richie Cunningham, Dallas, NFC	0	34	24	126
1996	John Kasay, Carolina, NFC	0	37	34	145
	Cary Blanchard, Indianapolis, AFC	0	36	27	135
1995	Emmitt Smith, Dallas, NFC	25	0	0	150
	Norm Johnson, Pittsburgh, AFC	0	34	39	141
1994	John Carney, San Diego, AFC	0	34	33	135
	Fuad Reveiz, Minnesota, NFC	0	34	30	132
1993	Jeff Jaeger, L.A. Raiders, AFC	0	35	27	132
	Jason Hanson, Detroit, NFC	0	34	28	130
1992	Pete Stoyanovich, Miami, AFC	0	30	34	124
	Morten Andersen, New Orleans, NFC	0	29	33	120
	Chip Lohmiller, Washington, NFC	0	30	30	120
1991	Chip Lohmiller, Washington, NFC	0	31	56	149
	Pete Stoyanovich, Miami, AFC	0	31	28	121
1990	Nick Lowery, Kansas City, AFC	0	34	37	139
	Chip Lohmiller, Washington, NFC	0	30	41	131
1989	Mike Cofer, San Francisco, NFC	0	29	49	136
	*David Treadwell, Denver, AFC	0	27	39	120
1988	Scott Norwood, Buffalo, AFC	0	32	33	129
	Mike Cofer, San Francisco, NFC	0	27	40	121
1987	Jerry Rice, San Francisco, NFC	23	0	0	138
	Jim Breech, Cincinnati, AFC	0	24	25	97
1986	Tony Franklin, New England, AFC	0	32	44	140
	Kevin Butler, Chicago, NFC	0	28	36	120
1985	*Kevin Butler, Chicago, NFC	0	31	51	144
	Gary Anderson, Pittsburgh, AFC	0	33	40	139
1984	Ray Wersching, San Francisco, NFC	0	25	56	131
	Gary Anderson, Pittsburgh, AFC	0	24	45	117
1983	Mark Moseley, Washington, NFC	0	33	62	161
	Gary Anderson, Pittsburgh, AFC	0	27	38	119
1982	*Marcus Allen, L.A. Raiders, AFC	14	0	0	84
	Wendell Tyler, L.A. Rams, NFC	13	0	0	78
1981	Ed Murray, Detroit, NFC	0	25	46	121
	Rafael Septien, Dallas, NFC	0	27	40	121
	Jim Breech, Cincinnati, AFC	0	22	49	115
	Nick Lowery, Kansas City, AFC	0	26	37	115
1980	John Smith, New England, AFC	0	26	51	129
	*Ed Murray, Detroit, NFC	0	27	35	116
1979	John Smith, New England, AFC	0	23	46	115
	Mark Moseley, Washington, NFC	0	25	39	114
1978	*Frank Corral, Los Angeles, NFC	0	29	31	118
	Pat Leahy, N.Y. Jets, AFC	0	22	41	107
1977	Errol Mann, Oakland, AFC	0	20	39	99
	Walter Payton, Chicago, NFC	16	0	0	96
1976	Toni Linhart, Baltimore, AFC	0	20	49	109
	Mark Moseley, Washington, NFC	0	22	31	97

Year	Player, Team	TD	FG	PAT	TP
1975	O.J. Simpson, Buffalo, AFC	23	0	0	138
	Chuck Foreman, Minnesota, NFC	22	0	0	132
1974	Chester Marcol, Green Bay, NFC	0	25	19	94
	Roy Gerela, Pittsburgh, AFC	0	20	33	93
1973	David Ray, Los Angeles, NFC	0	30	40	130
	Roy Gerela, Pittsburgh, AFC	0	29	36	123
1972	*Chester Marcol, Green Bay, NFC	0	33	29	128
	Bobby Howfield, N.Y. Jets, AFC	0	27	40	121
1971	Garo Yepremian, Miami, AFC	0	28	33	117
	Curt Knight, Washington, NFC	0	29	27	114
1970	Fred Cox, Minnesota, NFC	0	30	35	125
	Jan Stenerud, Kansas City, AFC	0	30	26	116
1969	Jim Turner, N.Y. Jets, AFL	0	32	33	129
	Fred Cox, Minnesota, NFL	0	26	43	121
1968	Jim Turner, N.Y. Jets, AFL	0	34	43	145
	Leroy Kelly, Cleveland, NFL	20	0	0	120
1967	Jim Bakken, St. Louis, NFL	0	27	36	117
	George Blanda, Oakland, AFL	0	20	56	116
1966	Gino Cappelletti, Boston, AFL	6	16	35	119
	Bruce Gossett, Los Angeles, NFL	0	28	29	113
1965	*Gale Sayers, Chicago, NFL	22	0	0	132
	Gino Cappelletti, Boston, AFL	9	17	27	132
1964	Gino Cappelletti, Boston, AFL	7	25	36	#155
	Lenny Moore, Baltimore, NFL	20	0	0	120
1963	Gino Cappelletti, Boston, AFL	2	22	35	113
	Don Chandler, N.Y. Giants, NFL	0	18	52	106
1962	Gene Mingo, Denver, AFL	4	27	32	137
	Jim Taylor, Green Bay, NFL	19	0	0	114
1961	Gino Cappelletti, Boston, AFL	8	17	48	147
	Paul Hornung, Green Bay, NFL	10	15	41	146
1960	Paul Hornung, Green Bay, NFL	15	15	41	176
	*Gene Mingo, Denver, AFL	6	18	33	123
1959	Paul Hornung, Green Bay	7	7	31	94
1958	Jim Brown, Cleveland	18	0	0	108
1957	Sam Baker, Washington	1	14	29	77
	Lou Groza, Cleveland	0	15	32	77
1956	Bobby Layne, Detroit	5	12	33	99
1955	Doak Walker, Detroit	7	9	27	96
1954	Bobby Walston, Philadelphia	11	4	36	114
1953	Gordy Soltau, San Francisco	6	10	48	114
1952	Gordy Soltau, San Francisco	7	6	34	94
1951	Elroy (Crazylegs) Hirsch, Los Angeles	17	0	0	102
1950	*Doak Walker, Detroit	11	8	38	128
1949	Pat Harder, Chi. Cardinals	8	3	45	102
	Gene Roberts, N.Y. Giants	17	0	0	102
1948	Pat Harder, Chi. Cardinals	6	7	53	110
1947	Pat Harder, Chi. Cardinals	7	7	39	102
1946	Ted Fritsch, Green Bay	10	9	13	100
1945	Steve Van Buren, Philadelphia	18	0	2	110
1944	Don Hutson, Green Bay	9	0	31	85
1943	Don Hutson, Green Bay	12	3	36	117
1942	Don Hutson, Green Bay	17	1	33	138
1941	Don Hutson, Green Bay	12	1	20	95
1940	Don Hutson, Green Bay	7	0	15	57
1939	Andy Farkas, Washington	11	0	2	68
1938	Clarke Hinkle, Green Bay	7	3	7	58
1937	Jack Manders, Chi. Bears	5	8	15	69
1936	Earl (Dutch) Clark, Detroit	7	4	19	73
1935	Earl (Dutch) Clark, Detroit	6	1	16	55
1934	Jack Manders, Chi. Bears	3	10	31	79
1933	Ken Strong, N.Y. Giants	6	5	13	64
	Glenn Presnell, Portsmouth	6	6	10	64
1932	Earl (Dutch) Clark, Portsmouth	6	3	10	55

*First season of professional football.
#Cappelletti's total and Faulk's total in 2001 include a two-point conversion.
##Faulk's total in 2000 includes 2 two-point conversions.

ANNUAL TOUCHDOWN LEADERS

Year	Player, Team	TD	Rush	Pass	Ret.
2007	Randy Moss, New England, AFC	23	0	23	0
	Terrell Owens, Dallas, NFC	15	0	15	0
2006	LaDainian Tomlinson, San Diego, AFC	31	28	3	0
	Marion Barber, Dallas, NFC	16	14	2	0
	Steven Jackson, St. Louis, NFC	16	13	3	0
2005	Shaun Alexander, Seattle, NFC	28	27	1	0
	Larry Johnson, Kansas City, AFC	21	20	1	0
2004	Shaun Alexander, Seattle, NFC	20	16	4	0
	LaDainian Tomlinson, San Diego, AFC	18	17	1	0
2003	Priest Holmes, Kansas City, AFC	27	27	0	0
	Ahman Green, Green Bay, NFC	20	15	5	0
2002	Priest Holmes, Kansas City, AFC	24	21	3	0
	Shaun Alexander, Seattle, NFC	18	16	2	0
2001	Marshall Faulk, St. Louis, NFC	21	12	9	0
	Shaun Alexander, Seattle, AFC	16	14	2	0
2000	Marshall Faulk, St. Louis, NFC	26	18	8	0
	Edgerrin James, Indianapolis, AFC	18	13	5	0
1999	Stephen Davis, Washington, NFC	17	17	0	0
	*Edgerrin James, Indianapolis, AFC	17	13	4	0
1998	Terrell Davis, Denver, AFC	23	21	2	0
	*Randy Moss, Minnesota, NFC	17	0	17	0
1997	Karim Abdul-Jabbar, Miami, AFC	16	15	1	0
	Barry Sanders, Detroit, NFC	14	11	3	0
1996	Terry Allen, Washington, NFC	21	21	0	0
	Curtis Martin, New England, AFC	17	14	3	0
1995	Emmitt Smith, Dallas, NFC	25	25	0	0
	Carl Pickens, Cincinnati, AFC	17	0	17	0
1994	Emmitt Smith, Dallas, NFC	22	21	1	0
	*Marshall Faulk, Indianapolis, AFC	12	11	1	0
	Natrone Means, San Diego, AFC	12	12	0	0
1993	Jerry Rice, San Francisco, NFC	16	1	15	0
	Marcus Allen, Kansas City, AFC	15	12	3	0
1992	Emmitt Smith, Dallas, NFC	19	18	1	0
	Thurman Thomas, Buffalo, AFC	12	9	3	0
1991	Barry Sanders, Detroit, NFC	17	16	1	0
	Mark Clayton, Miami, AFC	12	0	12	0
	Thurman Thomas, Buffalo, AFC	12	7	5	0
1990	Barry Sanders, Detroit, NFC	16	13	3	0
	Derrick Fenner, Seattle, AFC	15	14	1	0
1989	Dalton Hilliard, New Orleans, NFC	18	13	5	0
	Christian Okoye, Kansas City, AFC	12	12	0	0
	Thurman Thomas, Buffalo, AFC	12	6	6	0
1988	Greg Bell, L.A. Rams, NFC	18	16	2	0
	Eric Dickerson, Indianapolis, AFC	15	14	1	0
	*Ickey Woods, Cincinnati, AFC	15	15	0	0
1987	Jerry Rice, San Francisco, NFC	23	1	22	0
	Johnny Hector, N.Y. Jets, AFC	11	11	0	0
1986	George Rogers, Washington, NFC	18	18	0	0
	Sammy Winder, Denver, AFC	14	9	5	0
1985	Joe Morris, N.Y. Giants, NFC	21	21	0	0
	Louis Lipps, Pittsburgh, AFC	15	1	12	2
1984	Marcus Allen, L.A. Raiders, AFC	18	13	5	0
	Mark Clayton, Miami, AFC	18	0	18	0
	Eric Dickerson, L.A. Rams, NFC	14	14	0	0
	John Riggins, Washington, NFC	14	14	0	0
1983	John Riggins, Washington, NFC	24	24	0	0
	Pete Johnson, Cincinnati, AFC	14	14	0	0
	*Curt Warner, Seattle, AFC	14	13	1	0
1982	*Marcus Allen, L.A. Raiders, AFC	14	11	3	0
	Wendell Tyler, L.A. Rams, NFC	13	9	4	0
1981	Chuck Muncie, San Diego, AFC	19	19	0	0
	Wendell Tyler, Los Angeles, NFC	17	12	5	0
1980	*Billy Sims, Detroit, NFC	16	13	3	0
	Earl Campbell, Houston, AFC	13	13	0	0
	*Curtis Dickey, Baltimore, AFC	13	11	2	0
	John Jefferson, San Diego, AFC	13	0	13	0
1979	Earl Campbell, Houston, AFC	19	19	0	0
	Walter Payton, Chicago, NFC	16	14	2	0

Year	Player, Team	TD	Rush	Pass	Ret.
1978	David Sims, Seattle, AFC	15	14	1	0
	Terdell Middleton, Green Bay, NFC	12	11	1	0
1977	Walter Payton, Chicago, NFC	16	14	2	0
	Nat Moore, Miami, AFC	13	1	12	0
1976	Chuck Foreman, Minnesota, NFC	14	13	1	0
	Franco Harris, Pittsburgh, AFC	14	14	0	0
1975	O.J. Simpson, Buffalo, AFC	23	16	7	0
	Chuck Foreman, Minnesota, NFC	22	13	9	0
1974	Chuck Foreman, Minnesota, NFC	15	9	6	0
	Cliff Branch, Oakland, AFC	13	0	13	0
1973	Larry Brown, Washington, NFC	14	8	6	0
	Floyd Little, Denver, AFC	13	12	1	0
1972	Emerson Boozer, N.Y. Jets, AFC	14	11	3	0
	Ron Johnson, N.Y. Giants, NFC	14	9	5	0
1971	Duane Thomas, Dallas, NFC	13	11	2	0
	Leroy Kelly, Cleveland, AFC	12	10	2	0
1970	Dick Gordon, Chicago, NFC	13	0	13	0
	MacArthur Lane, St. Louis, NFC	13	11	2	0
	Gary Garrison, San Diego, AFC	12	0	12	0
1969	Warren Wells, Oakland, AFL	14	0	14	0
	Tom Matte, Baltimore, NFL	13	11	2	0
	Lance Rentzel, Dallas, NFL	13	0	12	1
1968	Leroy Kelly, Cleveland, NFL	20	16	4	0
	Warren Wells, Oakland, AFL	12	1	11	0
1967	Homer Jones, N.Y. Giants, NFL	14	1	13	0
	Emerson Boozer, N.Y. Jets, AFL	13	10	3	0
1966	Leroy Kelly, Cleveland, NFL	16	15	1	0
	Dan Reeves, Dallas, NFL	16	8	8	0
	Lance Alworth, San Diego, AFL	13	0	13	0
1965	*Gale Sayers, Chicago, NFL	22	14	6	2
	Lance Alworth, San Diego, AFL	14	0	14	0
	Don Maynard, N.Y. Jets, AFL	14	0	14	0
1964	Lenny Moore, Baltimore, NFL	20	16	3	1
	Lance Alworth, San Diego, AFL	15	2	13	0
1963	Art Powell, Oakland, AFL	16	0	16	0
	Jim Brown, Cleveland, NFL	15	12	3	0
1962	Abner Haynes, Dallas, AFL	19	13	6	0
	Jim Taylor, Green Bay, NFL	19	19	0	0
1961	Bill Groman, Houston, AFL	18	1	17	0
	Jim Taylor, Green Bay, NFL	16	15	1	0
1960	Paul Hornung, Green Bay, NFL	15	13	2	0
	Sonny Randle, St. Louis, NFL	15	0	15	0
	Art Powell, N.Y. Titans, AFL	14	0	14	0
1959	Raymond Berry, Baltimore	14	0	14	0
	Jim Brown, Cleveland	14	14	0	0
1958	Jim Brown, Cleveland	18	17	1	0
1957	Lenny Moore, Baltimore	11	3	7	1
1956	Rick Casares, Chi. Bears	14	12	2	0
1955	*Alan Ameche, Baltimore	9	9	0	0
	Harlon Hill, Chi. Bears	9	0	9	0
1954	*Harlon Hill, Chi. Bears	12	0	12	0
1953	Joseph Perry, San Francisco	13	10	3	0
1952	Cloyce Box, Detroit	15	0	15	0
1951	Elroy (Crazylegs) Hirsch, Los Angeles	17	0	17	0
1950	Bob Shaw, Chi. Cardinals	12	0	12	0
1949	Gene Roberts, N.Y. Giants	17	9	8	0
1948	Mal Kutner, Chi. Cardinals	15	1	14	0
1947	Steve Van Buren, Philadelphia	14	13	0	1
1946	Ted Fritsch, Green Bay	10	9	1	0
1945	Steve Van Buren, Philadelphia	18	15	2	1
1944	Don Hutson, Green Bay	9	0	9	0
	Bill Paschal, N.Y. Giants	9	9	0	0
1943	Don Hutson, Green Bay	12	0	11	1
	*Bill Paschal, N.Y. Giants	12	10	2	0
1942	Don Hutson, Green Bay	17	0	17	0
1941	Don Hutson, Green Bay	12	2	10	0
	George McAfee, Chi. Bears	12	6	3	3
1940	John Drake, Cleveland	9	9	0	0
	Richard Todd, Washington	9	4	4	1

Year	Player, Team	TD	Rush	Pass	Ret.
1939	Andrew Farkas, Washington	11	5	5	1
1938	Don Hutson, Green Bay	9	0	9	0
1937	Cliff Battles, Washington	7	5	1	1
	Clarke Hinkle, Green Bay	7	5	2	0
	Don Hutson, Green Bay	7	0	7	0
1936	Don Hutson, Green Bay	9	0	8	1
1935	*Don Hutson, Green Bay	7	0	6	1
1934	*Beattie Feathers, Chi. Bears	9	8	1	0
1933	*Charlie (Buckets) Goldenberg, Green Bay	7	4	1	2
	John (Shipwreck) Kelly, Brooklyn	7	2	3	2
	*Elvin (Kink) Richards, N.Y. Giants	7	4	3	0
1932	Earl (Dutch) Clark, Portsmouth	6	3	3	0
	Red Grange, Chi. Bears	6	3	3	0

*First season of professional football.

ANNUAL LEADERS—MOST FIELD GOALS MADE

Year	Player, Team	Att.	Made	Pct.
2007	Rob Bironas, Tennessee, AFC	39	35	89.7
	*Mason Crosby, Green Bay, NFC	39	31	79.5
	Robbie Gould, Chicago, NFC	36	31	86.1
2006	Robbie Gould, Chicago, NFC	36	32	88.9
	Jeff Wilkins, St. Louis, NFC	37	32	86.5
	Matt Stover, Baltimore, AFC	30	28	93.3
2005	Neil Rackers, Arizona, NFC	42	40	95.2
	Matt Stover, Baltimore, AFC	34	30	88.2
2004	Adam Vinatieri, New England, AFC	33	31	93.9
	David Akers, Philadelphia, NFC	32	27	84.4
2003	Jeff Wilkins, St. Louis, NFC	42	39	92.9
	Mike Vanderjagt, Indianapolis, AFC	37	37	100.0
2002	Jay Feely, Atlanta, NFC	40	32	80.0
	Martín Gramatica, Tampa Bay, NFC	39	32	82.1
	Adam Vinatieri, New England, AFC	30	27	90.0
2001	Jason Elam, Denver, AFC	36	31	86.1
	*Jay Feely, Atlanta, NFC	37	29	78.4
2000	Matt Stover, Baltimore, AFC	39	35	89.7
	Ryan Longwell, Green Bay, NFC	38	33	86.8
1999	Olindo Mare, Miami, AFC	46	39	84.8
	*Martin Gramatica, Tampa Bay, NFC	32	27	84.4
1998	Al Del Greco, Tennessee, AFC	39	36	92.3
	Gary Anderson, Minnesota, NFC	35	35	100.0
1997	Richie Cunningham, Dallas, NFC	37	34	91.9
	Cary Blanchard, Indianapolis, AFC	41	32	78.1
1996	John Kasay, Carolina, NFC	45	37	82.2
	Cary Blanchard, Indianapolis, AFC	40	36	90.0
1995	Norm Johnson, Pittsburgh, AFC	41	34	82.9
	Morten Andersen, Atlanta, NFC	37	31	83.8
1994	John Carney, San Diego, AFC	38	34	89.5
	Fuad Reveiz, Minnesota, NFC	39	34	87.2
1993	Jeff Jaeger, L.A. Raiders, AFC	44	35	79.5
	Jason Hanson, Detroit, NFC	43	34	79.1
1992	Pete Stoyanovich, Miami, AFC	37	30	81.1
	Chip Lohmiller, Washington, NFC	40	30	75.0
1991	Pete Stoyanovich, Miami, AFC	37	31	83.8
	Chip Lohmiller, Washington, NFC	43	31	72.1
1990	Nick Lowery, Kansas City, AFC	37	34	91.9
	Chip Lohmiller, Washington, NFC	40	30	75.0
1989	Rich Karlis, Minnesota, NFC	39	31	79.5
	*David Treadwell, Denver, AFC	33	27	81.8
1988	Scott Norwood, Buffalo, AFC	37	32	86.5
	Mike Cofer, San Francisco, NFC	38	27	71.1
1987	Morten Andersen, New Orleans, NFC	36	28	77.8
	Dean Biasucci, Indianapolis, AFC	27	24	88.9
	Jim Breech, Cincinnati, AFC	30	24	80.0
1986	Tony Franklin, New England, AFC	41	32	78.0
	Kevin Butler, Chicago, NFC	41	28	68.3
1985	Gary Anderson, Pittsburgh, AFC	42	33	78.6
	Morten Andersen, New Orleans, NFC	35	31	88.6
	*Kevin Butler, Chicago, NFC	37	31	83.8

Year	Player, Team	Att.	Made	Pct.
1984	*Paul McFadden, Philadelphia, NFC	37	30	81.1
	Gary Anderson, Pittsburgh, AFC	32	24	75.0
	Matt Bahr, Cleveland, AFC	32	24	75.0
1983	*Ali-Haji-Sheikh, N.Y. Giants, NFC	42	35	83.3
	*Raul Allegre, Baltimore, AFC	35	30	85.7
1982	Mark Moseley, Washington, NFC	21	20	95.2
	Nick Lowery, Kansas City, AFC	24	19	79.2
1981	Rafael Septien, Dallas, NFC	35	27	77.1
	Nick Lowery, Kansas City, AFC	36	26	72.2
1980	*Ed Murray, Detroit, NFC	42	27	64.3
	John Smith, New England, AFC	34	26	76.5
	Fred Steinfort, Denver, AFC	34	26	76.5
1979	Mark Moseley, Washington, NFC	33	25	75.8
	John Smith, New England, AFC	33	23	69.7
1978	*Frank Corral, Los Angeles, NFC	43	29	67.4
	Pat Leahy, N.Y. Jets, AFC	30	22	73.3
1977	Mark Moseley, Washington, NFC	37	21	56.8
	Errol Mann, Oakland, AFC	28	20	71.4
1976	Mark Moseley, Washington, NFC	34	22	64.7
	Jan Stenerud, Kansas City, AFC	38	21	55.3
1975	Jan Stenerud, Kansas City, AFC	32	22	68.8
	Toni Fritsch, Dallas, NFC	35	22	62.9
1974	Chester Marcol, Green Bay, NFC	39	25	64.1
	Roy Gerela, Pittsburgh, AFC	29	20	69.0
1973	David Ray, Los Angeles, NFC	47	30	63.8
	Roy Gerela, Pittsburgh, AFC	43	29	67.4
1972	*Chester Marcol, Green Bay, NFC	48	33	68.8
	Roy Gerela, Pittsburgh, AFC	41	28	68.3
1971	Curt Knight, Washington, NFC	49	29	59.2
	Garo Yepremian, Miami, AFC	40	28	70.0
1970	Jan Stenerud, Kansas City, AFC	42	30	71.4
	Fred Cox, Minnesota, NFC	46	30	65.2
1969	Jim Turner, N.Y. Jets, AFL	47	32	68.1
	Fred Cox, Minnesota, NFL	37	26	70.3
1968	Jim Turner, N.Y. Jets, AFL	46	34	73.9
	Mac Percival, Chicago, NFL	36	25	69.4
1967	Jim Bakken, St. Louis, NFL	39	27	69.2
	Jan Stenerud, Kansas City, AFL	36	21	58.3
1966	Bruce Gossett, Los Angeles, NFL	49	28	57.1
	Mike Mercer, Oakland-Kansas City, AFL	30	21	70.0
1965	Pete Gogolak, Buffalo, AFL	46	28	60.9
	Fred Cox, Minnesota, NFL	35	23	65.7
1964	Jim Bakken, St. Louis, NFL	38	25	65.8
	Gino Cappelletti, Boston, AFL	39	25	64.1
1963	Jim Martin, Baltimore, NFL	39	24	61.5
	Gino Cappelletti, Boston, AFL	38	22	57.9
1962	Gene Mingo, Denver, AFL	39	27	69.2
	Lou Michaels, Pittsburgh, NFL	42	26	61.9
1961	Steve Myhra, Baltimore, NFL	39	21	53.8
	Gino Cappelletti, Boston, AFL	32	17	53.1
1960	Tommy Davis, San Francisco, NFL	32	19	59.4
	*Gene Mingo, Denver, AFL	28	18	64.3
1959	Pat Summerall, N.Y. Giants	29	20	69.0
1958	Paige Cothren, Los Angeles	25	14	56.0
	*Tom Miner, Pittsburgh	28	14	50.0
1957	Lou Groza, Cleveland	22	15	68.2
1956	Sam Baker, Washington	25	17	68.0
1955	Fred Cone, Green Bay	24	16	66.7
1954	Lou Groza, Cleveland	24	16	66.7
1953	Lou Groza, Cleveland	26	23	88.5
1952	Lou Groza, Cleveland	33	19	57.6
1951	Bob Waterfield, Los Angeles	23	13	56.5
1950	Lou Groza, Cleveland	19	13	68.4
1949	Cliff Patton, Philadelphia	18	9	50.0
	Bob Waterfield, Los Angeles	16	9	56.3
1948	Cliff Patton, Philadelphia	12	8	66.7
1947	Ward Cuff, Green Bay	16	7	43.8
	Pat Harder, Chi. Cardinals	10	7	70.0
	Bob Waterfield, Los Angeles	16	7	43.8

Year	Player, Team	Att.	Made	Pct.
1946	Ted Fritsch, Green Bay	17	9	52.9
1945	Joe Aguirre, Washington	13	7	53.8
1944	Ken Strong, N.Y. Giants	12	6	50.0
1943	Ward Cuff, N.Y. Giants	9	3	33.3
	Don Hutson, Green Bay	5	3	60.0
1942	Bill Daddio, Chi. Cardinals	10	5	50.0
1941	Clarke Hinkle, Green Bay	14	6	42.9
1940	Clarke Hinkle, Green Bay	14	9	64.3
1939	Ward Cuff, N.Y. Giants	16	7	43.8
1938	Ward Cuff, N.Y. Giants	9	5	55.6
	Ralph Kercheval, Brooklyn	13	5	38.5
1937	Jack Manders, Chi. Bears		8	
1936	Jack Manders, Chi. Bears		7	
	Armand Niccolai, Pittsburgh		7	
1935	Armand Niccolai, Pittsburgh		6	
	Bill Smith, Chi. Cardinals		6	
1934	Jack Manders, Chi. Bears		10	
1933	*Jack Manders, Chi. Bears		6	
	Glenn Presnell, Portsmouth		6	
1932	Earl (Dutch) Clark, Portsmouth		3	

*First season of professional football.

ANNUAL RUSHING LEADERS

Year	Player, Team	Att.	Yards	Avg.	TD
2007	LaDainian Tomlinson, San Diego, AFC	315	1,474	4.7	15
	*Adrian Peterson, Minnesota, NFC	238	1,341	5.6	12
2006	LaDainian Tomlinson, San Diego, AFC	348	1,815	5.2	28
	Frank Gore, San Francisco, NFC	312	1,695	5.4	8
2005	Shaun Alexander, Seattle, NFC	370	1,880	5.1	27
	Larry Johnson, Kansas City, AFC	336	1,750	5.2	20
2004	Curtis Martin, N.Y. Jets, AFC	371	1,697	4.6	12
	Shaun Alexander, Seattle, NFC	353	1,696	4.8	16
2003	Jamal Lewis, Baltimore, AFC	387	2,066	5.3	14
	Ahman Green, Green Bay, NFC	355	1,883	5.3	15
2002	Ricky Williams, Miami, AFC	383	1,853	4.8	16
	Deuce McAllister, New Orleans, NFC	325	1,388	4.3	13
2001	Priest Holmes, Kansas City, AFC	327	1,555	4.8	8
	Stephen Davis, Washington, NFC	356	1,432	4.0	5
2000	Edgerrin James, Indianapolis, AFC	387	1,709	4.4	13
	Robert Smith, Minnesota, NFC	295	1,521	5.2	7
1999	*Edgerrin James, Indianapolis, AFC	369	1,553	4.2	13
	Stephen Davis, Washington, NFC	290	1,405	4.8	17
1998	Terrell Davis, Denver, AFC	392	2,008	5.1	21
	Jamal Anderson, Atlanta, NFC	410	1,846	4.5	14
1997	Barry Sanders, Detroit, NFC	335	2,053	6.1	11
	Terrell Davis, Denver, AFC	369	1,750	4.7	15
1996	Barry Sanders, Detroit, NFC	307	1,553	5.1	11
	Terrell Davis, Denver, AFC	345	1,538	4.5	13
1995	Emmitt Smith, Dallas, NFC	377	1,773	4.7	25
	*Curtis Martin, New England, AFC	368	1,487	4.0	14
1994	Barry Sanders, Detroit, NFC	331	1,883	5.7	7
	Chris Warren, Seattle, AFC	333	1,545	4.6	9
1993	Emmitt Smith, Dallas, NFC	283	1,486	5.3	9
	Thurman Thomas, Buffalo, AFC	355	1,315	3.7	6
1992	Emmitt Smith, Dallas, NFC	373	1,713	4.6	18
	Barry Foster, Pittsburgh, AFC	390	1,690	4.3	11
1991	Emmitt Smith, Dallas, NFC	365	1,563	4.3	12
	Thurman Thomas, Buffalo, AFC	288	1,407	4.9	7
1990	Barry Sanders, Detroit, NFC	255	1,304	5.1	13
	Thurman Thomas, Buffalo, AFC	271	1,297	4.8	11
1989	Christian Okoye, Kansas City, AFC	370	1,480	4.0	12
	*Barry Sanders, Detroit, NFC	280	1,470	5.3	14
1988	Eric Dickerson, Indianapolis, AFC	388	1,659	4.3	14
	Herschel Walker, Dallas, NFC	361	1,514	4.2	5
1987	Charles White, L.A. Rams, NFC	324	1,374	4.2	11
	Eric Dickerson, Indianapolis, AFC	223	1,011	4.5	5
1986	Eric Dickerson, L.A. Rams, NFC	404	1,821	4.5	11
	Curt Warner, Seattle, AFC	319	1,481	4.6	13

Year	Player, Team	Att.	Yards	Avg.	TD
1985	Marcus Allen, L.A. Raiders, AFC	380	1,759	4.6	11
	Gerald Riggs, Atlanta, NFC	397	1,719	4.3	10
1984	Eric Dickerson, L.A. Rams, NFC	379	2,105	5.6	14
	Earnest Jackson, San Diego, AFC	296	1,179	4.0	8
1983	*Eric Dickerson, L.A. Rams, NFC	390	1,808	4.6	18
	*Curt Warner, Seattle, AFC	335	1,449	4.3	13
1982	Freeman McNeil, N.Y. Jets, AFC	151	786	5.2	6
	Tony Dorsett, Dallas, NFC	177	745	4.2	5
1981	*George Rogers, New Orleans, NFC	378	1,674	4.4	13
	Earl Campbell, Houston, AFC	361	1,376	3.8	10
1980	Earl Campbell, Houston, AFC	373	1,934	5.2	13
	Walter Payton, Chicago, NFC	317	1,460	4.6	6
1979	Earl Campbell, Houston, AFC	368	1,697	4.6	19
	Walter Payton, Chicago, NFC	369	1,610	4.4	14
1978	*Earl Campbell, Houston, AFC	302	1,450	4.8	13
	Walter Payton, Chicago, NFC	333	1,395	4.2	11
1977	Walter Payton, Chicago, NFC	339	1,852	5.5	14
	Mark van Eeghen, Oakland, AFC	324	1,273	3.9	7
1976	O.J. Simpson, Buffalo, AFC	290	1,503	5.2	8
	Walter Payton, Chicago, NFC	311	1,390	4.5	13
1975	O.J. Simpson, Buffalo, AFC	329	1,817	5.5	16
	Jim Otis, St. Louis, NFC	269	1,076	4.0	5
1974	Otis Armstrong, Denver, AFC	263	1,407	5.3	9
	Lawrence McCutcheon, Los Angeles, NFC	236	1,109	4.7	3
1973	O.J. Simpson, Buffalo, AFC	332	2,003	6.0	12
	John Brockington, Green Bay, NFC	265	1,144	4.3	3
1972	O.J. Simpson, Buffalo, AFC	292	1,251	4.3	6
	Larry Brown, Washington, NFC	285	1,216	4.3	8
1971	Floyd Little, Denver, AFC	284	1,133	4.0	6
	*John Brockington, Green Bay, NFC	216	1,105	5.1	4
1970	Larry Brown, Washington, NFC	237	1,125	4.7	5
	Floyd Little, Denver, AFC	209	901	4.3	3
1969	Gale Sayers, Chicago, NFL	236	1,032	4.4	8
	Dickie Post, San Diego, AFL	182	873	4.8	6
1968	Leroy Kelly, Cleveland, NFL	248	1,239	5.0	16
	*Paul Robinson, Cincinnati, AFL	238	1,023	4.3	8
1967	Jim Nance, Boston, AFL	269	1,216	4.5	7
	Leroy Kelly, Cleveland, NFL	235	1,205	5.1	11
1966	Jim Nance, Boston, AFL	299	1,458	4.9	11
	Gale Sayers, Chicago, NFL	229	1,231	5.4	8
1965	Jim Brown, Cleveland, NFL	289	1,544	5.3	17
	Paul Lowe, San Diego, AFL	222	1,121	5.0	7
1964	Jim Brown, Cleveland, NFL	280	1,446	5.2	7
	Cookie Gilchrist, Buffalo, AFL	230	981	4.3	6
1963	Jim Brown, Cleveland, NFL	291	1,863	6.4	12
	Clem Daniels, Oakland, AFL	215	1,099	5.1	3
1962	Jim Taylor, Green Bay, NFL	272	1,474	5.4	19
	Cookie Gilchrist, Buffalo, AFL	214	1,096	5.1	13
1961	Jim Brown, Cleveland, NFL	305	1,408	4.6	8
	Billy Cannon, Houston, AFL	200	948	4.7	6
1960	Jim Brown, Cleveland, NFL	215	1,257	5.8	9
	*Abner Haynes, Dall. Texans, AFL	156	875	5.6	9
1959	Jim Brown, Cleveland	290	1,329	4.6	14
1958	Jim Brown, Cleveland	257	1,527	5.9	17
1957	*Jim Brown, Cleveland	202	942	4.7	9
1956	Rick Casares, Chi. Bears	234	1,126	4.8	12
1955	*Alan Ameche, Baltimore	213	961	4.5	9
1954	Joe Perry, San Francisco	173	1,049	6.1	8
1953	Joe Perry, San Francisco	192	1,018	5.3	10
1952	Dan Towler, Los Angeles	156	894	5.7	10
1951	Eddie Price, N.Y. Giants	271	971	3.6	7
1950	Marion Motley, Cleveland	140	810	5.8	3
1949	Steve Van Buren, Philadelphia	263	1,146	4.4	11
1948	Steve Van Buren, Philadelphia	201	945	4.7	10
1947	Steve Van Buren, Philadelphia	217	1,008	4.6	13
1946	Bill Dudley, Pittsburgh	146	604	4.1	3
1945	Steve Van Buren, Philadelphia	143	832	5.8	15
1944	Bill Paschal, N.Y. Giants	196	737	3.8	9
1943	*Bill Paschal, N.Y. Giants	147	572	3.9	10

Year	Player, Team	Att.	Yards	Avg.	TD
1942	*Bill Dudley, Pittsburgh	162	696	4.3	5
1941	Clarence (Pug) Manders, Brooklyn	111	486	4.4	5
1940	Byron (Whizzer) White, Detroit	146	514	3.5	5
1939	*Bill Osmanski, Chicago	121	699	5.8	7
1938	*Byron (Whizzer) White, Pittsburgh	152	567	3.7	4
1937	Cliff Battles, Washington	216	874	4.0	5
1936	*Alphonse (Tuffy) Leemans, N.Y. Giants	206	830	4.0	2
1935	Doug Russell, Chi. Cardinals	140	499	3.6	0
1934	*Beattie Feathers, Chi. Bears	119	1,004	8.4	8
1933	Jim Musick, Boston	173	809	4.7	5
1932	*Cliff Battles, Boston	148	576	3.9	3

First season of professional football.

ANNUAL PASSING LEADERS

(Current rating system implemented in 1973)

Year	Player, Team	Att.	Comp.	Yards	TD	Int.	Rating
2007	Tom Brady, New England, AFC	578	398	4,806	50	8	117.2
	Tony Romo, Dallas, NFC	520	335	4,211	36	19	97.4
2006	Peyton Manning, Indianapolis, AFC	557	362	4,397	31	9	101.0
	Drew Brees, New Orleans, NFC	554	356	4,418	26	11	96.2
2005	Peyton Manning, Indianapolis, AFC	453	305	3,747	28	10	104.1
	Matt Hasselbeck, Seattle, NFC	449	294	3,459	24	9	98.2
2004	Peyton Manning, Indianapolis, AFC	497	336	4,557	49	10	121.1
	Daunte Culpepper, Minnesota, NFC	548	379	4,717	39	11	110.9
2003	Steve McNair, Tennessee, AFC	400	250	3,215	24	7	100.4
	Daunte Culpepper, Minnesota, NFC	454	295	3,479	25	11	96.4
2002	Chad Pennington, N.Y. Jets, AFC	399	275	3,120	22	6	104.2
	Brad Johnson, Tampa Bay, NFC	451	281	3,049	22	6	92.9
2001	Kurt Warner, St. Louis, NFC	546	375	4,830	36	22	101.4
	Rich Gannon, Oakland, AFC	549	361	3,828	27	9	95.5
2000	Brian Griese, Denver, AFC	336	216	2,688	19	4	102.9
	Trent Green, St. Louis, NFC	240	145	2,063	16	5	101.8
1999	Kurt Warner, St. Louis, NFC	499	325	4,353	41	13	109.2
	Peyton Manning, Indianapolis, AFC	533	331	4,135	26	15	90.7
1998	Randall Cunningham, Minnesota, NFC	425	259	3,704	34	10	106.0
	Vinny Testaverde, N.Y. Jets, AFC	421	259	3,256	29	7	101.6
1997	Steve Young, San Francisco, NFC	356	241	3,029	19	6	104.7
	Mark Brunell, Jacksonville, AFC	435	264	3,281	18	7	91.2
1996	Steve Young, San Francisco NFC	316	214	2,410	14	6	97.2
	John Elway, Denver, AFC	466	287	3,328	26	14	89.2
1995	Jim Harbaugh, Indianapolis, AFC	314	200	2,575	17	5	100.7
	Brett Favre, Green Bay, NFC	570	359	4,413	38	13	99.5
1994	Steve Young, San Francisco, NFC	461	324	3,969	35	10	112.8
	Dan Marino, Miami, AFC	615	385	4,453	30	17	89.2
1993	Steve Young, San Francisco, NFC	462	314	4,023	29	16	101.5
	John Elway, Denver, AFC	551	348	4,030	25	10	92.8
1992	Steve Young, San Francisco, NFC	402	268	3,465	25	7	107.0
	Warren Moon, Houston, AFC	346	224	2,521	18	12	89.3
1991	Steve Young, San Francisco, NFC	279	180	2,517	17	8	101.8
	Jim Kelly, Buffalo, AFC	474	304	3,844	33	17	97.6
1990	Jim Kelly, Buffalo, AFC	346	219	2,829	24	9	101.2
	Phil Simms, N.Y. Giants, NFC	311	184	2,284	15	4	92.7
1989	Joe Montana, San Francisco, NFC	386	271	3,521	26	8	112.4
	Boomer Esiason, Cincinnati, AFC	455	258	3,525	28	11	92.1
1988	Boomer Esiason, Cincinnati, AFC	388	223	3,572	28	14	97.4
	Wade Wilson, Minnesota, NFC	332	204	2,746	15	9	91.5
1987	Joe Montana, San Francisco, NFC	398	266	3,054	31	13	102.1
	Bernie Kosar, Cleveland, AFC	389	241	3,033	22	9	95.4
1986	Tommy Kramer, Minnesota, NFC	372	208	3,000	24	10	92.6
	Dan Marino, Miami, AFC	623	378	4,746	44	23	92.5
1985	Ken O'Brien, N.Y. Jets, AFC	488	297	3,888	25	8	96.2
	Joe Montana, San Francisco, NFC	494	303	3,653	27	13	91.3
1984	Dan Marino, Miami, AFC	564	362	5,084	48	17	108.9
	Joe Montana, San Francisco, NFC	432	279	3,630	28	10	102.9
1983	Steve Bartkowski, Atlanta, NFC	432	274	3,167	22	5	97.6
	*Dan Marino, Miami, AFC	296	173	2,210	20	6	96.0
1982	Ken Anderson, Cincinnati, AFC	309	218	2,495	12	9	95.3
	Joe Theismann, Washington, NFC	252	161	2,033	13	9	91.3

Year	Player, Team	Att.	Comp.	Yards	TD	Int.	Rating
1981	Ken Anderson, Cincinnati, AFC	479	300	3,754	29	10	98.4
	Joe Montana, San Francisco, NFC	488	311	3,565	19	12	88.4
1980	Brian Sipe, Cleveland, AFC	554	337	4,132	30	14	91.4
	Ron Jaworski, Philadelphia, NFC	451	257	3,529	27	12	91.0
1979	Roger Staubach, Dallas, NFC	461	267	3,586	27	11	92.3
	Dan Fouts, San Diego, AFC	530	332	4,082	24	24	82.6
1978	Roger Staubach, Dallas, NFC	413	231	3,190	25	16	84.9
	Terry Bradshaw, Pittsburgh, AFC	368	207	2,915	28	20	84.7
1977	Bob Griese, Miami, AFC	307	180	2,252	22	13	87.8
	Roger Staubach, Dallas, NFC	361	210	2,620	18	9	87.0
1976	Ken Stabler, Oakland, AFC	291	194	2,737	27	17	103.4
	James Harris, Los Angeles, NFC	158	91	1,460	8	6	89.6
1975	Ken Anderson, Cincinnati, AFC	377	228	3,169	21	11	93.9
	Fran Tarkenton, Minnesota, NFC	425	273	2,994	25	13	91.8
1974	Ken Anderson, Cincinnati, AFC	328	213	2,667	18	10	95.7
	Sonny Jurgensen, Washington, NFC	167	107	1,185	11	5	94.5
1973	Roger Staubach, Dallas, NFC	286	179	2,428	23	15	94.6
	Ken Stabler, Oakland, AFC	260	163	1,997	14	10	88.3
1972	Norm Snead, N.Y. Giants, NFC	325	196	2,307	17	12	
	Earl Morrall, Miami, AFC	150	83	1,360	11	7	
1971	Roger Staubach, Dallas, NFC	211	126	1,882	15	4	
	Bob Griese, Miami, AFC	263	145	2,089	19	9	
1970	John Brodie, San Francisco, NFC	378	223	2,941	24	10	
	Daryle Lamonica, Oakland, AFC	356	179	2,516	22	15	
1969	Sonny Jurgensen, Washington, NFL	442	274	3,102	22	15	
	*Greg Cook, Cincinnati, AFL	197	106	1,854	15	11	
1968	Len Dawson, Kansas City, AFL	224	131	2,109	17	9	
	Earl Morrall, Baltimore, NFL	317	182	2,909	26	17	
1967	Sonny Jurgensen, Washington, NFL	508	288	3,747	31	16	
	Daryle Lamonica, Oakland, AFL	425	220	3,228	30	20	
1966	Bart Starr, Green Bay, NFL	251	156	2,257	14	3	
	Len Dawson, Kansas City, AFL	284	159	2,527	26	10	
1965	Rudy Bukich, Chicago, NFL	312	176	2,641	20	9	
	John Hadl, San Diego, AFL	348	174	2,798	20	21	
1964	Len Dawson, Kansas City, AFL	354	199	2,879	30	18	
	Bart Starr, Green Bay, NFL	272	163	2,144	15	4	
1963	Y.A. Tittle, N.Y. Giants, NFL	367	221	3,145	36	14	
	Tobin Rote, San Diego, AFL	286	170	2,510	20	17	
1962	Len Dawson, Dallas Texans, AFL	310	189	2,759	29	17	
	Bart Starr, Green Bay, NFL	285	178	2,438	12	9	
1961	George Blanda, Houston, AFL	362	187	3,330	36	22	
	Milt Plum, Cleveland, NFL	302	177	2,416	18	10	
1960	Milt Plum, Cleveland, NFL	250	151	2,297	21	5	
	Jack Kemp, L.A. Chargers, AFL	406	211	3,018	20	25	
1959	Charlie Conerly, N.Y. Giants	194	113	1,706	14	4	
1958	Eddie LeBaron, Washington	145	79	1,365	11	10	
1957	Tommy O'Connell, Cleveland	110	63	1,229	9	8	
1956	Ed Brown, Chicago Bears	168	96	1,667	11	12	
1955	Otto Graham, Cleveland	185	98	1,721	15	8	
1954	Norm Van Brocklin, Los Angeles	260	139	2,637	13	21	
1953	Otto Graham, Cleveland	258	167	2,722	11	9	
1952	Norm Van Brocklin, Los Angeles	205	113	1,736	14	17	
1951	Bob Waterfield, Los Angeles	176	88	1,566	13	10	
1950	Norm Van Brocklin, Los Angeles	233	127	2,061	18	14	
1949	Sammy Baugh, Washington	255	145	1,903	18	14	
1948	Tommy Thompson, Philadelphia	246	141	1,965	25	11	
1947	Sammy Baugh, Washington	354	210	2,938	25	15	
1946	Bob Waterfield, Los Angeles	251	127	1,747	18	17	
1945	Sammy Baugh, Washington	182	128	1,669	11	4	
	Sid Luckman, Chicago Bears	217	117	1,725	14	10	
1944	Frank Filchock, Washington	147	84	1,139	13	9	
1943	Sammy Baugh, Washington	239	133	1,754	23	19	
1942	Cecil Isbell, Green Bay	268	146	2,021	24	14	
1941	Cecil Isbell, Green Bay	206	117	1,479	15	11	
1940	Sammy Baugh, Washington	177	111	1,367	12	10	
1939	*Parker Hall, Cleveland	208	106	1,227	9	13	
1938	Ed Danowski, N.Y. Giants	129	70	848	7	8	
1937	*Sammy Baugh, Washington	171	81	1,127	8	14	

Year	Player, Team	Att.	Comp.	Yards	TD	Int.	Rating
1936	Arnie Herber, Green Bay	173	77	1,239	11	13	
1935	Ed Danowski, N.Y. Giants	113	57	794	10	9	
1934	Arnie Herber, Green Bay	115	42	799	8	12	
1933	*Harry Newman, N.Y. Giants	136	53	973	11	17	
1932	Arnie Herber, Green Bay	101	37	639	9	9	

First season of professional football.

ANNUAL PASSING TOUCHDOWN LEADERS

Year	Player, Team	TD
2007	Tom Brady, New England, AFC	50
	Tony Romo, Dallas, NFC	36
2006	Peyton Manning, Indianapolis, AFC	31
	Drew Brees, New Orleans, NFC	26
2005	Carson Palmer, Cincinnati, AFC	32
	Jake Delhomme, Carolina, NFC	24
	Matt Hasselbeck, Seattle, NFC	24
	Eli Manning, N.Y. Giants, NFC	24
2004	Peyton Manning, Indianapolis, AFC	49
	Daunte Culpepper, Minnesota, NFC	39
2003	Brett Favre, Green Bay, NFC	32
	Peyton Manning, Indianapolis, AFC	29
2002	Tom Brady, New England, AFC	28
	Aaron Brooks, New Orleans, NFC	27
	Brett Favre, Green Bay, NFC	27
2001	Kurt Warner, St. Louis, NFC	36
	Rich Gannon, Oakland, AFC	27
2000	Daunte Culpepper, Minnesota, NFC	33
	Peyton Manning, Indianapolis, AFC	33
1999	Kurt Warner, St. Louis, NFC	41
	Peyton Manning, Indianapolis, AFC	26
1998	Steve Young, San Francisco, NFC	36
	Vinny Testaverde, N.Y. Jets, AFC	29
1997	Brett Favre, Green Bay, NFC	35
	Jeff George, Oakland, AFC	29
1996	Brett Favre, Green Bay, NFC	39
	Vinny Testaverde, Baltimore, AFC	33
1995	Brett Favre, Green Bay, NFC	38
	Jeff Blake, Cincinnati, AFC	28
1994	Steve Young, San Francisco, NFC	35
	Dan Marino, Miami, AFC	30
1993	Steve Young, San Francisco, NFC	29
	John Elway, Denver, AFC	25
1992	Steve Young, San Francisco, NFC	25
	Dan Marino, Miami, AFC	24
1991	Jim Kelly, Buffalo, AFC	33
	Mark Rypien, Washington, NFC	28
1990	Warren Moon, Houston, AFC	33
	Randall Cunningham, Philadelphia, NFC	30
1989	Jim Everett, L.A. Rams, NFC	29
	Boomer Esiason, Cincinnati, AFC	28
1988	Jim Everett, L.A. Rams, NFC	31
	Boomer Esiason, Cincinnati, AFC	28
	Dan Marino, Miami, AFC	28
1987	Joe Montana, San Francisco, NFC	31
	Dan Marino, Miami, AFC	26
1986	Dan Marino, Miami, AFC	44
	Tommy Kramer, Minnesota, NFC	24
1985	Dan Marino, Miami, AFC	30
	Joe Montana, San Francisco, NFC	27
1984	Dan Marino, Miami, AFC	48
	Neil Lomax, St. Louis, NFC	28
	Joe Montana, San Francisco, NFC	28
1983	Lynn Dickey, Green Bay, NFC	32
	Joe Ferguson, Buffalo, AFC	26
	Brian Sipe, Cleveland, AFC	26
1982	Terry Bradshaw, Pittsburgh, AFC	17
	Dan Fouts, San Diego, AFC	17
	Joe Montana, San Francisco, NFC	17
1981	Dan Fouts, San Diego, AFC	33
	Steve Bartkowski, Atlanta, NFC	30

Year	Player, Team	TD
1980	Steve Bartkowski, Atlanta, NFC	31
	Dan Fouts, San Diego, AFC	30
	Brian Sipe, Cleveland, AFC	30
1979	Steve Grogan, New England, AFC	28
	Brian Sipe, Cleveland, AFC	28
	Roger Staubach, Dallas, NFC	27
1978	Terry Bradshaw, Pittsburgh, AFC	28
	Roger Staubach, Dallas, NFC	25
	Fran Tarkenton, Minnesota, NFC	25
1977	Bob Griese, Miami, AFC	22
	Ron Jaworski, Philadelphia, NFC	18
	Roger Staubach, Dallas, NFC	18
1976	Ken Stabler, Oakland, AFC	27
	Jim Hart, St. Louis, NFC	18
1975	Joe Ferguson, Buffalo, AFC	25
	Fran Tarkenton, Minnesota, NFC	25
1974	Ken Stabler, Oakland, AFC	26
	Jim Hart, St. Louis, NFC	20
1973	Roman Gabriel, Philadelphia, NFC	23
	Roger Staubach, Dallas, NFC	23
	Charley Johnson, Denver, AFC	20
1972	Billy Kilmer, Washington, NFC	19
	Joe Namath, N.Y. Jets, AFC	19
1971	John Hadl, San Diego, AFC	21
	John Brodie, San Francisco, NFC	18
1970	John Brodie, San Francisco, NFC	24
	John Hadl, San Diego, AFC	22
	Daryle Lamonica, Oakland, AFC	22
1969	Daryle Lamonica, Oakland, AFL	34
	Roman Gabriel, Los Angeles, NFL	24
1968	John Hadl, San Diego, AFL	27
	Earl Morrall, Baltimore, NFL	26
1967	Sonny Jurgensen, Washington, NFL	31
	Daryle Lamonica, Oakland, AFL	30
1966	Frank Ryan, Cleveland, NFL	29
	Len Dawson, Kansas City, AFL	26
1965	John Brodie, San Francisco, NFL	30
	Len Dawson, Kansas City, AFL	21
1964	Babe Parilli, Boston, AFL	31
	Frank Ryan, Cleveland, NFL	25
1963	Y.A. Tittle, N.Y. Giants, NFL	36
	Len Dawson, Kansas City, AFL	26
1962	Y.A. Tittle, N.Y. Giants, NFL	33
	Len Dawson, Dallas, AFL	29
1961	George Blanda, Houston, AFL	36
	Sonny Jurgensen, Philadelphia, NFL	32
1960	Al Dorow, N.Y. Titans, AFL	26
	Johnny Unitas, Baltimore, NFL	25
1959	Johnny Unitas, Baltimore	32
1958	Johnny Unitas, Baltimore	19
1957	Johnny Unitas, Baltimore	24
1956	Tobin Rote, Green Bay	18
1955	Tobin Rote, Green Bay	17
	Y.A. Tittle, San Francisco	17
1954	Adrian Burk, Philadelphia	23
1953	Robert Thomason, Philadelphia	21
1952	Jim Finks, Pittsburgh	20
	Otto Graham, Cleveland	20
1951	Bobby Layne, Detroit	26
1950	George Ratterman, N.Y. Yanks	22
1949	Johnny Lujack, Chi. Bears	23
1948	Tommy Thompson, Philadelphia	25
1947	Sammy Baugh, Washington	25

Year	Player, Team	TD	Year	Player, Team	TD
1946	Sid Luckman, Chi. Bears	17	1939	Frank Filchock, Washington	11
	Bob Waterfield, Los Angeles	17	1938	Bob Monnett, Green Bay	9
1945	Sid Luckman, Chi. Bears	14	1937	Bernie Masterson, Chi. Bears	9
	*Bob Waterfield, Cleveland	14	1936	Arnie Herber, Green Bay	11
1944	Frank Filchock, Washington	13	1935	Ed Danowski, N.Y. Giants	10
1943	Sid Luckman, Chi. Bears	28	1934	Arnie Herber, Green Bay	8
1942	Cecil Isbell, Green Bay	24	1933	*Harry Newman, N.Y. Giants	11
1941	Cecil Isbell, Green Bay	15	1932	Arnie Herber, Green Bay	9
1940	Sammy Baugh, Washington	12	*First season of professional football.		

ANNUAL PASS RECEIVING LEADERS

Year	Player, Team	No.	Yards	Avg.	TD
2007	T.J. Houshmandzadeh, Cincinnati, AFC	112	1,143	10.2	12
	Wes Welker, New England, AFC	112	1,175	10.5	8
	Larry Fitzgerald, Arizona, NFC	100	1,409	14.1	10
2006	Andre Johnson, Houston, AFC	103	1,147	11.1	5
	Mike Furrey, Detroit, NFC	98	1,086	11.1	6
2005	Steve Smith, Carolina, NFC	103	1,563	15.2	12
	Larry Fitzgerald, Arizona, NFC	103	1,409	13.7	10
	Chad Johnson, Cincinnati, AFC	97	1,432	14.8	9
2004	Tony Gonzalez, Kansas City, AFC	102	1,258	12.3	7
	Joe Horn, New Orleans, NFC	94	1,399	14.9	11
	Torry Holt, St. Louis, NFC	94	1,372	14.6	10
2003	Torry Holt, St. Louis, NFC	117	1,696	14.5	12
	LaDainian Tomlinson, San Diego, AFC	100	725	7.3	4
2002	Marvin Harrison, Indianapolis, AFC	143	1,722	12.0	11
	Randy Moss, Minnesota, NFC	106	1,347	12.7	7
2001	Rod Smith, Denver, AFC	113	1,343	11.9	11
	Keyshawn Johnson, Tampa Bay, NFC	106	1,266	11.9	1
2000	Marvin Harrison, Indianapolis, AFC	102	1,413	13.9	14
	Muhsin Muhammad, Carolina, NFC	102	1,183	11.6	6
1999	Jimmy Smith, Jacksonville, AFC	116	1,636	14.1	6
	Muhsin Muhammad, Carolina, NFC	96	1,253	13.1	8
1998	O.J. McDuffie, Miami, AFC	90	1,050	11.7	7
	Frank Sanders, Arizona, NFC	89	1,145	12.9	3
1997	Tim Brown, Oakland, AFC	104	1,408	13.5	5
	Herman Moore, Detroit, NFC	104	1,293	12.4	8
1996	Jerry Rice, San Francisco, NFC	108	1,254	11.6	8
	Carl Pickens, Cincinnati, AFC	100	1,180	11.8	12
1995	Herman Moore, Detroit, NFC	123	1,686	13.7	14
	Carl Pickens, Cincinnati, AFC	99	1,234	12.5	17
1994	Cris Carter, Minnesota, NFC	122	1,256	10.3	7
	Ben Coates, New England, AFC	96	1,174	12.2	7
1993	Sterling Sharpe, Green Bay, NFC	112	1,274	11.4	11
	Reggie Langhorne, Indianapolis, AFC	85	1,038	12.2	3
1992	Sterling Sharpe, Green Bay, NFC	108	1,461	13.5	13
	Haywood Jeffires, Houston, AFC	90	913	10.1	9
1991	Haywood Jeffires, Houston, AFC	100	1,181	11.8	7
	Michael Irvin, Dallas, NFC	93	1,523	16.4	8
1990	Jerry Rice, San Francisco, NFC	100	1,502	15.0	13
	Haywood Jeffires, Houston, AFC	74	1,048	14.2	8
	Drew Hill, Houston, AFC	74	1,019	13.8	5
1989	Sterling Sharpe, Green Bay, NFC	90	1,423	15.8	12
	Andre Reed, Buffalo, AFC	88	1,312	14.9	9
1988	Al Toon, N.Y. Jets, AFC	93	1,067	11.5	5
	Henry Ellard, L.A. Rams, NFC	86	1,414	16.4	10
1987	J.T. Smith, St. Louis, NFC	91	1,117	12.3	8
	Al Toon, N.Y. Jets, AFC	68	976	14.4	5
1986	Todd Christensen, L.A. Raiders, AFC	95	1,153	12.1	8
	Jerry Rice, San Francisco, NFC	86	1,570	18.3	15
1985	Roger Craig, San Francisco, NFC	92	1,016	11.0	6
	Lionel James, San Diego, AFC	86	1,027	11.9	6
1984	Art Monk, Washington, NFC	106	1,372	12.9	7
	Ozzie Newsome, Cleveland, AFC	89	1,001	11.2	5
1983	Todd Christensen, L.A. Raiders, AFC	92	1,247	13.6	12
	Roy Green, St. Louis, NFC	78	1,227	15.7	14
	Charlie Brown, Washington, NFC	78	1,225	15.7	8
	Earnest Gray, N.Y. Giants, NFC	78	1,139	14.6	5

Year	Player, Team	No.	Yards	Avg.	TD
1982	Dwight Clark, San Francisco, NFC	60	913	15.2	5
	Kellen Winslow, San Diego, AFC	54	721	13.4	6
1981	Kellen Winslow, San Diego, AFC	88	1,075	12.2	10
	Dwight Clark, San Francisco, NFC	85	1,105	13.0	4
1980	Kellen Winslow, San Diego, AFC	89	1,290	14.5	9
	*Earl Cooper, San Francisco, NFC	83	567	6.8	4
1979	Joe Washington, Baltimore, AFC	82	750	9.1	3
	Ahmad Rashad, Minnesota, NFC	80	1,156	14.5	9
1978	Rickey Young, Minnesota, NFC	88	704	8.0	5
	Steve Largent, Seattle, AFC	71	1,168	16.5	8
1977	Lydell Mitchell, Baltimore, AFC	71	620	8.7	4
	Ahmad Rashad, Minnesota, NFC	51	681	13.4	2
1976	MacArthur Lane, Kansas City, AFC	66	686	10.4	1
	Drew Pearson, Dallas, NFC	58	806	13.9	6
1975	Chuck Foreman, Minnesota, NFC	73	691	9.5	9
	Reggie Rucker, Cleveland, AFC	60	770	12.8	3
	Lydell Mitchell, Baltimore, AFC	60	544	9.1	4
1974	Lydell Mitchell, Baltimore, AFC	72	544	7.6	2
	Charles Young, Philadelphia, NFC	63	696	11.0	3
1973	Harold Carmichael, Philadelphia, NFC	67	1,116	16.7	9
	Fred Willis, Houston, AFC	57	371	6.5	1
1972	Harold Jackson, Philadelphia, NFC	62	1,048	16.9	4
	Fred Biletnikoff, Oakland, AFC	58	802	13.8	7
1971	Fred Biletnikoff, Oakland, AFC	61	929	15.2	9
	Bob Tucker, N.Y. Giants, NFC	59	791	13.4	4
1970	Dick Gordon, Chicago, NFC	71	1,026	14.5	13
	Marlin Briscoe, Buffalo, AFC	57	1,036	18.2	8
1969	Dan Abramowicz, New Orleans, NFL	73	1,015	13.9	7
	Lance Alworth, San Diego, AFL	64	1,003	15.7	4
1968	Clifton McNeil, San Francisco, NFL	71	994	14.0	7
	Lance Alworth, San Diego, AFL	68	1,312	19.3	10
1967	George Sauer, N.Y. Jets, AFL	75	1,189	15.9	6
	Charley Taylor, Washington, NFL	70	990	14.1	9
1966	Lance Alworth, San Diego, AFL	73	1,383	18.9	13
	Charley Taylor, Washington, NFL	72	1,119	15.5	12
1965	Lionel Taylor, Denver, AFL	85	1,131	13.3	6
	Dave Parks, San Francisco, NFL	80	1,344	16.8	12
1964	Charley Hennigan, Houston, AFL	101	1,546	15.3	8
	Johnny Morris, Chicago, NFL	93	1,200	12.9	10
1963	Lionel Taylor, Denver, AFL	78	1,101	14.1	10
	Bobby Joe Conrad, St. Louis, NFL	73	967	13.2	10
1962	Lionel Taylor, Denver, AFL	77	908	11.8	4
	Bobby Mitchell, Washington, NFL	72	1,384	19.2	11
1961	Lionel Taylor, Denver, AFL	100	1,176	11.8	4
	Jim (Red) Phillips, Los Angeles, NFL	78	1,092	14.0	5
1960	Lionel Taylor, Denver, AFL	92	1,235	13.4	12
	Raymond Berry, Baltimore, NFL	74	1,298	17.5	10
1959	Raymond Berry, Baltimore	66	959	14.5	14
1958	Raymond Berry, Baltimore	56	794	14.2	9
	Pete Retzlaff, Philadelphia	56	766	13.7	2
1957	Billy Wilson, San Francisco	52	757	14.6	6
1956	Billy Wilson, San Francisco	60	889	14.8	5
1955	Pete Pihos, Philadelphia	62	864	13.9	7
1954	Pete Pihos, Philadelphia	60	872	14.5	10
	Billy Wilson, San Francisco	60	830	13.8	5
1953	Pete Pihos, Philadelphia	63	1,049	16.7	10
1952	Mac Speedie, Cleveland	62	911	14.7	5
1951	Elroy (Crazylegs) Hirsch, Los Angeles	66	1,495	22.7	17
1950	Tom Fears, Los Angeles	84	1,116	13.3	7
1949	Tom Fears, Los Angeles	77	1,013	13.2	9
1948	*Tom Fears, Los Angeles	51	698	13.7	4
1947	Jim Keane, Chi. Bears	64	910	14.2	10
1946	Jim Benton, Los Angeles	63	981	15.6	6
1945	Don Hutson, Green Bay	47	834	17.7	9
1944	Don Hutson, Green Bay	58	866	14.9	9
1943	Don Hutson, Green Bay	47	776	16.5	11
1942	Don Hutson, Green Bay	74	1,211	16.4	17
1941	Don Hutson, Green Bay	58	738	12.7	10
1940	*Don Looney, Philadelphia	58	707	12.2	4

Year	Player, Team	No.	Yards	Avg.	TD
1939	Don Hutson, Green Bay	34	846	24.9	6
1938	Gaynell Tinsley, Chi. Cardinals	41	516	12.6	1
1937	Don Hutson, Green Bay	41	552	13.5	7
1936	Don Hutson, Green Bay	34	536	15.8	8
1935	*Tod Goodwin, N.Y. Giants	26	432	16.6	4
1934	Joe Carter, Philadelphia	16	238	14.9	4
	Morris (Red) Badgro, N.Y. Giants	16	206	12.9	1
1933	John (Shipwreck) Kelly, Brooklyn	22	246	11.2	3
1932	Ray Flaherty, N.Y. Giants	21	350	16.7	3

*First season of professional football.

ANNUAL PASS RECEIVING LEADERS (YARDS)

Year	Player, Team	No.	Yards	Avg.	TD
2007	Reggie Wayne, Indianapolis, AFC	104	1,510	14.5	10
	Larry Fitzgerald, Arizona, NFC	100	1,409	14.1	10
2006	Chad Johnson, Cincinnati, AFC	87	1,369	15.7	7
	Roy Williams, Detroit, NFC	82	1,310	16.0	7
2005	Steve Smith, Carolina, NFC	103	1,563	15.2	12
	Chad Johnson, Cincinnati, AFC	97	1,432	14.8	9
2004	Muhsin Muhammad, Carolina, NFC	93	1,405	15.1	16
	Chad Johnson, Cincinnati, AFC	95	1,274	13.4	9
2003	Torry Holt, St. Louis, NFC	117	1,696	14.5	12
	Chad Johnson, Cincinnati, AFC	90	1,355	15.1	10
2002	Marvin Harrison, Indianapolis, AFC	143	1,722	12.0	11
	Randy Moss, Minnesota, NFC	106	1,347	12.7	7
2001	David Boston, Arizona, NFC	98	1,598	16.3	8
	Marvin Harrison, Indianapolis, AFC	109	1,524	14.0	15
2000	Torry Holt, St. Louis, NFC	82	1,635	19.9	6
	Rod Smith, Denver, AFC	100	1,602	16.0	8
1999	Marvin Harrison, Indianapolis, AFC	115	1,663	14.5	12
	Randy Moss, Minnesota, NFC	80	1,413	17.7	11
1998	Antonio Freeman, Green Bay, NFC	84	1,424	17.0	14
	Eric Moulds, Buffalo, AFC	67	1,368	20.4	9
1997	Rob Moore, Arizona, NFC	97	1,584	16.3	8
	Tim Brown, Oakland, AFC	104	1,408	13.5	5
1996	Isaac Bruce, St. Louis, NFC	84	1,338	15.9	7
	Jimmy Smith, Jacksonville, AFC	83	1,244	15.0	7
1995	Jerry Rice, San Francisco, NFC	122	1,848	15.1	15
	Tim Brown, Oakland, AFC	89	1,342	15.1	10
1994	Jerry Rice, San Francisco, NFC	112	1,499	13.4	13
	Tim Brown, L.A. Raiders, AFC	89	1,309	14.7	9
1993	Jerry Rice, San Francisco, NFC	98	1,503	15.3	15
	Tim Brown, L.A. Raiders, AFC	80	1,180	14.8	7
1992	Sterling Sharpe, Green Bay, NFC	108	1,461	13.5	13
	Anthony Miller, San Diego, AFC	72	1,060	14.7	7
1991	Michael Irvin, Dallas, NFC	93	1,523	16.4	8
	Haywood Jeffires, Houston, AFC	100	1,181	11.8	7
1990	Jerry Rice, San Francisco, NFC	100	1,502	15.0	13
	Haywood Jeffires, Houston, AFC	74	1,048	14.2	8
1989	Jerry Rice, San Francisco, NFC	82	1,483	18.1	17
	Andre Reed, Buffalo, AFC	88	1,312	14.9	9
1988	Henry Ellard, L.A. Rams, NFC	86	1,414	16.4	10
	Eddie Brown, Cincinnati, AFC	53	1,273	24.0	9
1987	J.T. Smith, St. Louis, NFC	91	1,117	12.3	8
	Carlos Carson, Kansas City, AFC	55	1,044	19.0	7
1986	Jerry Rice, San Francisco, NFC	86	1,570	18.3	15
	Stanley Morgan, New England, AFC	84	1,491	17.8	10
1985	Steve Largent, Seattle, AFC	79	1,287	16.3	6
	Mike Quick, Philadelphia, NFC	73	1,247	17.1	11
1984	Roy Green, St. Louis, NFC	78	1,555	19.9	12
	John Stallworth, Pittsburgh, AFC	80	1,395	17.4	11
1983	Mike Quick, Philadelphia, NFC	69	1,409	20.4	13
	Carlos Carson, Kansas City, AFC	80	1,351	16.9	7
1982	Wes Chandler, San Diego, AFC	49	1,032	21.1	9
	Dwight Clark, San Francisco, NFC	60	913	15.2	5
1981	Alfred Jenkins, Atlanta, NFC	70	1,358	19.4	13
	Frank Lewis, Buffalo, AFC	70	1,244	17.8	4
	Steve Watson, Denver, AFC	60	1,244	20.7	13

Year	Player, Team	No.	Yards	Avg.	TD
1980	John Jefferson, San Diego, AFC	82	1,340	16.3	13
	James Lofton, Green Bay, NFC	71	1,226	17.3	4
1979	Steve Largent, Seattle, AFC	66	1,237	18.7	9
	Ahmad Rashad, Minnesota, NFC	80	1,156	14.5	9
1978	Wesley Walker, N.Y. Jets, AFC	48	1,169	24.4	8
	Harold Carmichael, Philadelphia, NFC	55	1,072	19.5	8
1977	Drew Pearson, Dallas, NFC	48	870	18.1	2
	Ken Burrough, Houston, AFC	43	816	19.0	8
1976	Roger Carr, Baltimore, AFC	43	1,112	25.9	11
	*Sammy White, Minnesota, NFC	51	906	17.8	10
1975	Ken Burrough, Houston, AFC	53	1,063	20.1	8
	Mel Gray, St. Louis, NFC	48	926	19.3	11
1974	Cliff Branch, Oakland, AFC	60	1,092	18.2	13
	Drew Pearson, Dallas, NFC	62	1,087	17.5	2
1973	Harold Carmichael, Philadelphia, NFC	67	1,116	16.7	9
	*Isaac Curtis, Cincinnati, AFC	45	843	18.7	9
1972	Harold Jackson, Philadelphia, NFC	62	1,048	16.9	4
	Rich Caster, N.Y. Jets, AFC	39	833	21.4	10
1971	Otis Taylor, Kansas City, AFC	57	1,110	19.5	7
	Gene Washington, San Francisco, NFC	46	884	19.2	4
1970	Gene Washington, San Francisco, NFC	53	1,100	20.8	12
	Marlin Briscoe, Buffalo, AFC	57	1,036	18.2	8
1969	Warren Wells, Oakland, AFL	47	1,260	26.8	14
	Harold Jackson, Philadelphia, NFL	65	1,116	17.2	9
1968	Lance Alworth, San Diego, AFL	68	1,312	19.3	10
	Roy Jefferson, Pittsburgh, NFL	58	1,074	18.5	11
1967	Don Maynard, N.Y. Jets, AFL	71	1,434	20.3	10
	Ben Hawkins, Philadelphia, NFL	59	1,265	21.4	10
1966	Lance Alworth, San Diego, AFL	73	1,383	18.9	13
	Pat Studstill, Detroit, NFL	67	1,266	18.9	5
1965	Lance Alworth, San Diego, AFL	69	1,602	23.2	14
	Dave Parks, San Francisco, NFL	80	1,344	16.8	12
1964	Charley Hennigan, Houston, AFL	101	1,546	15.3	8
	Johnny Morris, Chicago, NFL	93	1,200	12.9	10
1963	Bobby Mitchell, Washington, NFL	69	1,436	20.8	7
	Art Powell, Oakland, AFL	73	1,304	17.8	16
1962	Bobby Mitchell, Washington, NFL	72	1,384	19.2	11
	Art Powell, N.Y. Titans, AFL	64	1,130	17.6	8
1961	Charley Hennigan, Houston, AFL	82	1,746	21.3	12
	Tommy McDonald, Philadelphia, NFL	64	1,144	17.9	13
1960	*Bill Groman, Houston, AFL	72	1,473	20.5	12
	Raymond Berry, Baltimore, NFL	74	1,298	17.5	10
1959	Raymond Berry, Baltimore	66	959	14.5	14
1958	Del Shofner, Los Angeles	51	1,097	21.5	8
1957	Raymond Berry, Baltimore	47	800	17.0	6
1956	Billy Howton, Green Bay	55	1,188	21.6	12
1955	Pete Pihos, Philadelphia	62	864	13.9	7
1954	Bob Boyd, Los Angeles	53	1,212	22.9	6
1953	Pete Pihos, Philadelphia	63	1,049	16.7	10
1952	*Billy Howton, Green Bay	53	1,231	23.2	13
1951	Elroy (Crazylegs) Hirsch, Los Angeles	66	1,495	22.7	17
1950	Tom Fears, Los Angeles	84	1,116	13.3	7
1949	Bob Mann, Detroit	66	1,014	15.4	4
1948	Mal Kutner, Chi. Cardinals	41	943	23.0	14
1947	Mal Kutner, Chi. Cardinals	43	944	21.9	7
1946	Jim Benton, Los Angeles	63	981	15.5	6
1945	Jim Benton, Cleveland	45	1,067	23.7	8
1944	Don Hutson, Green Bay	58	866	14.6	9
1943	Don Hutson, Green Bay	47	776	16.5	11
1942	Don Hutson, Green Bay	74	1,211	16.4	17
1941	Don Hutson, Green Bay	58	738	12.7	10
1940	*Don Looney, Philadelphia	58	707	12.2	4
1939	Don Hutson, Green Bay	34	846	24.9	6
1938	Don Hutson, Green Bay	32	548	17.1	9
1937	*Gaynell Tinsley, Chi. Cardinals	36	675	18.8	5
1936	Don Hutson, Green Bay	34	526	15.5	8
1935	Charley Malone, Boston	22	433	19.7	2
1934	Harry Ebding, Detroit	9	257	28.6	2
1933	*Paul Moss, Pittsburgh	18	383	21.3	2

Year	Player, Team	No.	Yards	Avg.	Long	TD
1932	Johnny (Blood) McNally, Green Bay...............................19		326	17.2		3

First season of professional football.

ANNUAL PUNT RETURN LEADERS

Year	Player, Team	No.	Yards	Avg.	Long	TD
2007	Roscoe Parrish, Buffalo, AFC...27		440	16.3	74	1
	Devin Hester, Chicago, NFC...............................42		651	15.5	89	4
2006	Pacman Jones, Tennessee, AFC 34		440	12.9	90	3
	*Devin Hester, Chicago, NFC 47		600	12.8	84	3
2005	Reno Mahe, Philadelphia, NFC...........................21		269	12.8	44	0
	B.J. Sams, Baltimore, AFC...................................33		401	12.2	51	0
2004	Eddie Drummond, Detroit, NFC...........................24		316	13.2	83	2
	Dennis Northcutt, Cleveland, AFC 36		432	12.0	44	0
2003	Dante Hall, Kansas City, AFC 29		472	16.3	93	2
	Brian Westbrook, Philadelphia, NFC 20		306	15.3	84	2
2002	Jimmy Williams, San Francisco, NFC................................20		336	16.8	89	1
	Santana Moss, N.Y. Jets, AFC............................25		413	16.5	63	2
2001	Troy Brown, New England, AFC...........................29		413	14.2	85	2
	Darrien Gordon, Atlanta, NFC.............................31		437	14.1	74	0
2000	Jermaine Lewis, Baltimore, AFC.........................36		578	16.1	89	2
	Az-Zahir Hakim, St. Louis, NFC..........................32		489	15.3	86	1
1999	*Charlie Rogers, Seattle, AFC 22		318	14.5	94	1
	*Mac Cody, Arizona, NFC....................................32		373	11.7	31	0
1998	Deion Sanders, Dallas, NFC 24		375	15.6	69	2
	Reggie Barlow, Jacksonville, AFC 43		555	12.9	85	1
1997	Jermaine Lewis, Baltimore, AFC.........................28		437	15.6	89	2
	David Palmer, Minnesota, NFC............................34		444	13.1	57	0
1996	Desmond Howard, Green Bay, NFC.....................58		875	15.1	92	3
	Darrien Gordon, San Diego, AFC.........................36		537	14.9	81	1
1995	David Palmer, Minnesota, NFC............................26		342	13.2	74	1
	Andre Coleman, San Diego, AFC.........................28		326	11.6	88	1
1994	Brian Mitchell, Washington, NFC.........................32		452	14.1	78	2
	Darrien Gordon, San Diego, AFC.........................36		475	13.2	90	2
1993	*Tyrone Hughes, New Orleans, NFC....................37		503	13.6	83	2
	Eric Metcalf, Cleveland, AFC..............................36		464	12.9	91	2
1992	Johnny Bailey, Phoenix, NFC..............................20		263	13.2	65	0
	Rod Woodson, Pittsburgh, AFC...........................32		364	11.4	80	1
1991	Mel Gray, Detroit, NFC...25		385	15.4	78	1
	Rod Woodson, Pittsburgh, AFC...........................28		320	11.4	40	0
1990	Clarence Verdin, Indianapolis, AFC....................31		396	12.8	36	0
	*Johnny Bailey, Chicago, NFC............................36		399	11.1	95	1
1989	Walter Stanley, Detroit, NFC...............................36		496	13.8	74	0
	Clarence Verdin, Indianapolis, AFC....................23		296	12.9	49	1
1988	John Taylor, San Francisco, NFC.........................44		556	12.6	95	2
	JoJo Townsell, N.Y. Jets, AFC.............................35		409	11.7	59	1
1987	Mel Gray, New Orleans, NFC...............................24		352	14.7	80	0
	Bobby Joe Edmonds, Seattle, AFC.....................20		251	12.6	40	0
1986	*Bobby Joe Edmonds, Seattle, AFC....................34		419	12.3	75	1
	*Vai Sikahema, St. Louis, NFC 43		522	12.1	71	2
1985	Irving Fryar, New England, AFC...........................37		520	14.1	85	2
	Henry Ellard, L.A. Rams, NFC.............................37		501	13.5	80	1
1984	Mike Martin, Cincinnati, AFC...............................24		376	15.7	55	0
	Henry Ellard, L.A. Rams, NFC.............................30		403	13.4	83	2
1983	*Henry Ellard, L.A. Rams, NFC...........................16		217	13.6	72	1
	Kirk Springs, N.Y. Jets, AFC...............................23		287	12.5	76	1
1982	Rick Upchurch, Denver, AFC...............................15		242	16.1	78	2
	Billy Johnson, Atlanta, NFC.................................24		273	11.4	71	0
1981	LeRoy Irvin, Los Angeles, NFC 46		615	13.4	84	3
	*James Brooks, San Diego, AFC 22		290	13.2	42	0
1980	J.T. Smith, Kansas City, AFC...............................40		581	14.5	75	2
	*Kenny Johnson, Atlanta, NFC............................23		281	12.2	56	0
1979	John Sciarra, Philadelphia, NFC 16		182	11.4	38	0
	*Tony Nathan, Miami, AFC 28		306	10.9	86	1
1978	Rick Upchurch, Denver, AFC...............................36		493	13.7	75	1
	Jackie Wallace, Los Angeles, NFC 52		618	11.9	58	0
1977	Billy Johnson, Houston, AFC...............................35		539	15.4	87	2
	Larry Marshall, Philadelphia, NFC 46		489	10.6	48	0
1976	Rick Upchurch, Denver, AFC...............................39		536	13.7	92	4
	Eddie Brown, Washington, NFC 48		646	13.5	71	1

Year	Player, Team	No.	Yards	Avg.	Long	TD
1975	Billy Johnson, Houston, AFC	40	612	15.3	83	3
	Terry Metcalf, St. Louis, NFC	23	285	12.4	69	1
1974	Lemar Parrish, Cincinnati, AFC	18	338	18.8	90	2
	Dick Jauron, Detroit, NFC	17	286	16.8	58	0
1973	Bruce Taylor, San Francisco, NFC	15	207	13.8	61	0
	Ron Smith, San Diego, AFC	27	352	13.0	84	2
1972	Ken Ellis, Green Bay, NFC	14	215	15.4	80	1
	Chris Farasopoulos, N.Y. Jets, AFC	17	179	10.5	65	1
1971	Les (Speedy) Duncan, Washington, NFC	22	233	10.6	33	0
	Leroy Kelly, Cleveland, AFC	30	292	9.7	74	0
1970	Ed Podolak, Kansas City, AFC	23	311	13.5	60	0
	*Bruce Taylor, San Francisco, NFC	43	516	12.0	76	0
1969	Alvin Haymond, Los Angeles, NFL	33	435	13.2	52	0
	*Bill Thompson, Denver, AFL	25	288	11.5	40	0
1968	Bob Hayes, Dallas, NFL	15	312	20.8	90	2
	Noland Smith, Kansas City, AFL	18	270	15.0	80	1
1967	Floyd Little, Denver, AFL	16	270	16.9	72	1
	Ben Davis, Cleveland, NFL	18	229	12.7	52	1
1966	Les (Speedy) Duncan, San Diego, AFL	18	238	13.2	81	1
	Johnny Roland, St. Louis, NFL	20	221	11.1	86	1
1965	Leroy Kelly, Cleveland, NFL	17	265	15.6	67	2
	Les (Speedy) Duncan, San Diego, AFL	30	464	15.5	66	2
1964	Bobby Jancik, Houston, AFL	12	220	18.3	82	1
	Tommy Watkins, Detroit, NFL	16	238	14.9	68	2
1963	Dick James, Washington, NFL	16	214	13.4	39	0
	Claude (Hoot) Gibson, Oakland, AFL	26	307	11.8	85	2
1962	Dick Christy, N.Y. Titans, AFL	15	250	16.7	73	2
	Pat Studstill, Detroit, NFL	29	457	15.8	44	0
1961	Dick Christy, N.Y. Titans, AFL	18	383	21.3	70	2
	Willie Wood, Green Bay, NFL	14	225	16.1	72	2
1960	*Abner Haynes, Dall. Texans, AFL	14	215	15.4	46	0
	Abe Woodson, San Francisco, NFL	13	174	13.4	48	0
1959	Johnny Morris, Chi. Bears	14	171	12.2	78	1
1958	Jon Arnett, Los Angeles	18	223	12.4	58	0
1957	Bert Zagers, Washington	14	217	15.5	76	2
1956	Ken Konz, Cleveland	13	187	14.4	65	1
1955	Ollie Matson, Chi. Cardinals	13	245	18.8	78	2
1954	*Veryl Switzer, Green Bay	24	306	12.8	93	1
1953	Charley Trippi, Chi. Cardinals	21	239	11.4	38	0
1952	Jack Christiansen, Detroit	15	322	21.5	79	2
1951	Claude (Buddy) Young, N.Y. Yanks	12	231	19.3	79	1
1950	*Herb Rich, Baltimore	12	276	23.0	86	1
1949	Verda (Vitamin T) Smith, Los Angeles	27	427	15.8	85	1
1948	George McAfee, Chi. Bears	30	417	13.9	60	1
1947	*Walt Slater, Pittsburgh	28	435	15.5	33	0
1946	Bill Dudley, Pittsburgh	27	385	14.3	52	0
1945	*Dave Ryan, Detroit	15	220	14.7	56	0
1944	*Steve Van Buren, Philadelphia	15	230	15.3	55	1
1943	Andy Farkas, Washington	15	168	11.2	33	0
1942	Merlyn Condit, Brooklyn	21	210	10.0	23	0
1941	Byron (Whizzer) White, Detroit	19	262	13.8	64	0

*First season of professional football.

ANNUAL KICKOFF RETURN LEADERS

Year	Player, Team	No.	Yards	Avg.	Long	TD
2007	Josh Cribbs, Cleveland, AFC	59	1,809	30.7	100	2
	*Aundrae Allison, Minnesota, NFC	20	574	28.7	104	1
2006	Justin Miller, N.Y. Jets, AFC	46	1,304	28.3	103	2
	*Devin Hester, Chicago, NFC	20	528	26.4	96	2
2005	Terrence McGee, Buffalo, AFC	46	1,391	30.2	99	1
	Koren Robinson, Minnesota, NFC	47	1,221	26.0	86	1
2004	Willie Ponder, N.Y. Giants, NFC	36	967	26.9	91	1
	Terrence McGee, Buffalo, AFC	52	1,370	26.3	104	3
2003	Jerry Azumah, Chicago, NFC	41	1,191	29.0	89	2
	*Bethel Johnson, New England, AFC	30	847	28.2	92	1
2002	MarTay Jenkins, Arizona, NFC	20	559	28.0	95	1
	Kevin Faulk, New England, AFC	26	725	27.9	87	1
2001	Ronney Jenkins, San Diego, AFC	58	1,541	26.6	93	2
	*Steve Smith, Carolina, NFC	56	1,431	25.6	99	2

Year	Player, Team	No.	Yards	Avg.	Long	TD
2000	*Darrick Vaughn, Atlanta, NFC	39	1,082	27.7	100	3
	Derrick Mason, Tennessee, AFC	42	1,132	27.0	66	0
1999	Tony Horne, St. Louis, NFC	30	892	29.7	101	2
	Tremain Mack, Cincinnati, AFC	51	1,382	27.1	99	1
1998	*Terry Fair, Detroit, NFC	51	1,428	28.0	105	2
	Corey Harris, Baltimore, AFC	35	965	27.6	95	1
1997	Michael Bates, Carolina, NFC	47	1,281	27.3	56	0
	Aaron Glenn, N.Y. Jets, AFC	28	741	26.5	96	1
1996	Michael Bates, Carolina, NFC	33	998	30.2	93	1
	Tamarick Vanover, Kansas City, AFC	33	854	25.9	97	1
1995	Ron Carpenter, N.Y. Jets, AFC	20	553	27.7	58	0
	Brian Mitchell, Washington, NFC	55	1,408	25.6	59	0
1994	Mel Gray, Detroit, NFC	45	1,276	28.4	102	3
	Randy Baldwin, Cleveland, AFC	28	753	26.9	85	1
1993	Robert Brooks, Green Bay, NFC	23	611	26.6	95	1
	*Raghib Ismail, L.A. Raiders, AFC	25	605	24.2	66	0
1992	Jon Vaughn, New England, AFC	20	564	28.2	100	1
	Deion Sanders, Atlanta, NFC	40	1,067	26.7	99	2
1991	Mel Gray, Detroit, NFC	36	929	25.8	71	0
	Nate Lewis, San Diego, AFC	23	578	25.1	95	1
1990	Kevin Clark, Denver, AFC	20	505	25.3	75	0
	David Meggett, N.Y. Giants, NFC	21	492	23.4	58	0
1989	Rod Woodson, Pittsburgh, AFC	36	982	27.3	84	1
	Mel Gray, Detroit, NFC	24	640	26.7	57	0
1988	*Tim Brown, L.A. Raiders, AFC	41	1,098	26.8	97	1
	Donnie Elder, Tampa Bay, NFC	34	772	22.7	51	0
1987	Sylvester Stamps, Atlanta, NFC	24	660	27.5	97	1
	Paul Palmer, Kansas City, AFC	38	923	24.3	95	2
1986	Dennis Gentry, Chicago, NFC	20	576	28.8	91	1
	Lupe Sanchez, Pittsburgh, AFC	25	591	23.6	64	0
1985	Ron Brown, L.A. Rams, NFC	28	918	32.8	98	3
	Glen Young, Cleveland, AFC	35	898	25.7	63	0
1984	*Bobby Humphery, N.Y. Jets, AFC	22	675	30.7	97	1
	Barry Redden, L.A. Rams, NFC	23	530	23.0	40	0
1983	Fulton Walker, Miami, AFC	36	962	26.7	78	0
	Darrin Nelson, Minnesota, NFC	18	445	24.7	50	0
1982	*Mike Mosley, Buffalo, AFC	18	487	27.1	66	0
	Alvin Hall, Detroit, NFC	16	426	26.6	96	1
1981	Mike Nelms, Washington, NFC	37	1,099	29.7	84	0
	Carl Roaches, Houston, AFC	28	769	27.5	96	1
1980	Horace Ivory, New England, AFC	36	992	27.6	98	1
	Rich Mauti, New Orleans, NFC	31	798	25.7	52	0
1979	Larry Brunson, Oakland, AFC	17	441	25.9	89	0
	Jimmy Edwards, Minnesota, NFC	44	1,103	25.1	83	0
1978	Steve Odom, Green Bay, NFC	25	677	27.1	95	1
	*Keith Wright, Cleveland, AFC	30	789	26.3	86	0
1977	*Raymond Clayborn, New England, AFC	28	869	31.0	101	3
	*Wilbert Montgomery, Philadelphia, NFC	23	619	26.9	99	1
1976	*Duriel Harris, Miami, AFC	17	559	32.9	69	0
	Cullen Bryant, Los Angeles, NFC	16	459	28.7	90	1
1975	*Walter Payton, Chicago, NFC	14	444	31.7	70	0
	Harold Hart, Oakland, AFC	17	518	30.5	102	1
1974	Terry Metcalf, St. Louis, NFC	20	623	31.2	94	1
	Greg Pruitt, Cleveland, AFC	22	606	27.5	88	1
1973	Carl Garrett, Chicago, NFC	16	486	30.4	67	0
	*Wallace Francis, Buffalo, AFC	23	687	29.9	101	2
1972	Ron Smith, Chicago, NFC	30	924	30.8	94	1
	*Bruce Laird, Baltimore, AFC	29	843	29.1	73	0
1971	Travis Williams, Los Angeles, NFC	25	743	29.7	105	1
	Eugene (Mercury) Morris, Miami, AFC	15	423	28.2	94	1
1970	Jim Duncan, Baltimore, AFC	20	707	35.4	99	1
	Cecil Turner, Chicago, NFC	23	752	32.7	96	4
1969	Bobby Williams, Detroit, NFL	17	563	33.1	96	1
	*Bill Thompson, Denver, AFL	18	513	28.5	63	0
1968	Preston Pearson, Baltimore, NFL	15	527	35.1	102	2
	*George Atkinson, Oakland, AFL	32	802	25.1	60	0
1967	*Travis Williams, Green Bay, NFL	18	739	41.1	104	4
	*Zeke Moore, Houston, AFL	14	405	28.9	92	1

Year	Player, Team	No.	Yards	Avg.	Long	TD
1966	Gale Sayers, Chicago, NFL	23	718	31.2	93	2
	*Goldie Sellers, Denver, AFL	19	541	28.5	100	2
1965	Tommy Watkins, Detroit, NFL	17	584	34.4	94	0
	Abner Haynes, Denver, AFL	34	901	26.5	60	0
1964	*Clarence Childs, N.Y. Giants, NFL	34	987	29.0	100	1
	Bo Roberson, Oakland, AFL	36	975	27.1	59	0
1963	Abe Woodson, San Francisco, NFL	29	935	32.2	103	3
	Bobby Jancik, Houston, AFL	45	1,317	29.3	53	0
1962	Abe Woodson, San Francisco, NFL	37	1,157	31.3	79	0
	*Bobby Jancik, Houston, AFL	24	826	30.3	61	0
1961	Dick Bass, Los Angeles, NFL	23	698	30.3	64	0
	*Dave Grayson, Dall. Texans, AFL	16	453	28.3	73	0
1960	*Tom Moore, Green Bay, NFL	12	397	33.1	84	0
	Ken Hall, Houston, AFL	19	594	31.3	104	1
1959	Abe Woodson, San Francisco	13	382	29.4	105	1
1958	Ollie Matson, Chi. Cardinals	14	497	35.5	101	2
1957	*Jon Arnett, Los Angeles	18	504	28.0	98	1
1956	*Tom Wilson, Los Angeles	15	477	31.8	103	1
1955	Al Carmichael, Green Bay	14	418	29.9	100	1
1954	Billy Reynolds, Cleveland	14	413	29.5	51	0
1953	Joe Arenas, San Francisco	16	551	34.4	82	0
1952	Lynn Chandnois, Pittsburgh	17	599	35.2	93	2
1951	Lynn Chandnois, Pittsburgh	12	390	32.5	55	0
1950	Verda (Vitamin T) Smith, Los Angeles	22	742	33.7	97	3
1949	*Don Doll, Detroit	21	536	25.5	56	0
1948	*Joe Scott, N.Y. Giants	20	569	28.5	99	1
1947	Eddie Saenz, Washington	29	797	27.5	94	2
1946	Abe Karnofsky, Boston	21	599	28.5	97	1
1945	Steve Van Buren, Philadelphia	13	373	28.7	98	1
1944	Bob Thurbon, Card.-Pitt.	12	291	24.3	55	0
1943	Ken Heineman, Brooklyn	16	444	27.8	69	0
1942	Marshall Goldberg, Chi. Cardinals	15	393	26.2	95	1
1941	Marshall Goldberg, Chi. Cardinals	12	290	24.2	41	0

*First season of professional football.

ANNUAL INTERCEPTION LEADERS

Year	Player, Team	No.	Yards	TD
2007	Antonio Cromartie, San Diego, AFC	10	144	1
	O.J. Atogwe, St. Louis, NFC	8	125	1
2006	Champ Bailey, Denver, AFC	10	162	1
	Asante Samuel, New England, AFC	10	120	0
	Walt Harris, San Francisco, NFC	8	84	1
	Charles Woodson, Green Bay, NFC	8	61	1
2005	Ty Law, N.Y. Jets, AFC	10	195	1
	Deltha O'Neal, Cincinnati, AFC	10	103	0
	Darren Sharper, Minnesota, NFC	9	276	2
2004	Ed Reed, Baltimore, AFC	9	358	1
	Ken Lucas, Seattle, NFC	6	46	1
	*Chris Gamble, Carolina, NFC	6	15	0
2003	Tony Parrish, San Francisco, NFC	9	202	0
	Brian Russell, Minnesota, NFC	9	185	0
	Ed Reed, Baltimore, AFC	7	132	1
	Marcus Coleman, Houston, AFC	7	95	0
	Patrick Surtain, Miami, AFC	7	59	0
2002	Rod Woodson, Oakland, AFC	8	225	2
	Brian Kelly, Tampa Bay, NFC	8	68	0
2001	*Anthony Henry, Cleveland, AFC	10	177	1
	Ronde Barber, Tampa Bay, NFC	10	86	1
2000	Darren Sharper, Green Bay, NFC	9	109	0
	Samari Rolle, Tennessee, AFC	7	140	1
	Brian Walker, Miami, AFC	7	80	0
1999	Rod Woodson, Baltimore, AFC	7	195	2
	Sam Madison, Miami, AFC	7	164	1
	James Hasty, Kansas City, AFC	7	98	2
	Donnie Abraham, Tampa Bay, NFC	7	115	2
	Troy Vincent, Philadelphia, NFC	7	91	0
1998	Ty Law, New England, AFC	9	133	1
	Kwamie Lassiter, Arizona, NFC	8	80	0

Year	Player, Team	No.	Yards	TD
1997	Ryan McNeil, St. Louis, NFC	9	127	1
	Mark McMillian, Kansas City, AFC	8	274	3
	Darryl Williams, Seattle, AFC	8	172	1
1996	Tyrone Braxton, Denver, AFC	9	128	1
	Keith Lyle, St. Louis, NFC	9	152	0
1995	*Orlando Thomas, Minnesota, NFC	9	108	1
	Willie Williams, Pittsburgh, AFC	7	122	1
1994	Eric Turner, Cleveland, AFC	9	199	1
	Aeneas Williams, Arizona, NFC	9	89	0
1993	Eugene Robinson, Seattle, AFC	9	80	0
	Nate Odomes, Buffalo, AFC	9	65	0
	Deion Sanders, Atlanta, NFC	7	91	0
1992	Henry Jones, Buffalo, AFC	8	263	2
	Audray McMillian, Minnesota, NFC	8	157	2
1991	Ronnie Lott, L.A. Raiders, AFC	8	52	0
	Ray Crockett, Detroit, NFC	6	141	1
	Deion Sanders, Atlanta, NFC	6	119	1
	*Aeneas Williams, Phoenix, NFC	6	60	0
	Tim McKyer, Atlanta, NFC	6	24	0
1990	*Mark Carrier, Chicago, NFC	10	39	0
	Richard Johnson, Houston, AFC	8	100	1
1989	Felix Wright, Cleveland, AFC	9	91	1
	Eric Allen, Philadelphia, NFC	8	38	0
1988	Scott Case, Atlanta, NFC	10	47	0
	Erik McMillan, N.Y. Jets, AFC	8	168	2
1987	Barry Wilburn, Washington, NFC	9	135	1
	Mike Prior, Indianapolis, AFC	6	57	0
	Mark Kelso, Buffalo, AFC	6	25	0
	Keith Bostic, Houston, AFC	6	-14	0
1986	Ronnie Lott, San Francisco, NFC	10	134	1
	Deron Cherry, Kansas City, AFC	9	150	0

Year	Player, Team	No.	Yards	TD
1985	Everson Walls, Dallas, NFC	9	31	0
	Albert Lewis, Kansas City, AFC	8	59	0
	Eugene Daniel, Indianapolis, AFC	8	53	0
1984	Ken Easley, Seattle, AFC	10	126	2
	*Tom Flynn, Green Bay, NFC	9	106	0
1983	Mark Murphy, Washington, NFC	9	127	0
	Ken Riley, Cincinnati, AFC	8	89	2
	Vann McElroy, L.A. Raiders, AFC	8	68	0
1982	Everson Walls, Dallas, NFC	7	61	0
	Ken Riley, Cincinnati, AFC	5	88	1
	Bobby Jackson, N.Y. Jets, AFC	5	84	1
	Dwayne Woodruff, Pittsburgh, AFC	5	53	0
	Donnie Shell, Pittsburgh, AFC	5	27	0
1981	*Everson Walls, Dallas, NFC	11	133	0
	John Harris, Seattle, AFC	10	155	2
1980	Lester Hayes, Oakland, AFC	13	273	1
	Nolan Cromwell, Los Angeles, NFC	8	140	1
1979	Mike Reinfeldt, Houston, AFC	12	205	0
	Lemar Parrish, Washington, NFC	9	65	0
1978	Thom Darden, Cleveland, AFC	10	200	0
	Ken Stone, St. Louis, NFC	9	139	0
	Willie Buchanon, Green Bay, NFC	9	93	1
1977	Lyle Blackwood, Baltimore, AFC	10	163	0
	Rolland Lawrence, Atlanta, NFC	7	138	0
1976	Monte Jackson, Los Angeles, NFC	10	173	3
	Ken Riley, Cincinnati, AFC	9	141	1
1975	Mel Blount, Pittsburgh, AFC	11	121	0
	Paul Krause, Minnesota, NFC	10	201	0
1974	Emmitt Thomas, Kansas City, AFC	12	214	2
	Ray Brown, Atlanta, NFC	8	164	1
1973	Dick Anderson, Miami, AFC	8	163	2
	Mike Wagner, Pittsburgh, AFC	8	134	0
	Bobby Bryant, Minnesota, NFC	7	105	1
1972	Bill Bradley, Philadelphia, NFC	9	73	0
	Mike Sensibaugh, Kansas City, AFC	8	65	0
1971	Bill Bradley, Philadelphia, NFC	11	248	0
	Ken Houston, Houston, AFC	9	220	4
1970	Johnny Robinson, Kansas City, AFC	10	155	0
	Dick LeBeau, Detroit, NFC	9	96	0
1969	Mel Renfro, Dallas, NFL	10	118	0
	Emmitt Thomas, Kansas City, AFL	9	146	1
1968	Dave Grayson, Oakland, AFL	10	195	1
	Willie Williams, N.Y. Giants, NFL	10	103	0
1967	Miller Farr, Houston, AFL	10	264	3
	*Lem Barney, Detroit, NFL	10	232	3
	Tom Janik, Buffalo, AFL	10	222	2
	Dave Whitsell, New Orleans, NFL	10	178	2
	Dick Westmoreland, Miami, AFL	10	127	1
1966	Larry Wilson, St. Louis, NFL	10	180	2
	Johnny Robinson, Kansas City, AFL	10	136	1
	Bobby Hunt, Kansas City, AFL	10	113	0
1965	W.K. Hicks, Houston, AFL	9	156	0
	Bobby Boyd, Baltimore, NFL	9	78	1
1964	Dainard Paulson, N.Y. Jets, AFL	12	157	1
	*Paul Krause, Washington, NFL	12	140	1
1963	Fred Glick, Houston, AFL	12	180	1
	Dick Lynch, N.Y. Giants, NFL	9	251	3
	Roosevelt Taylor, Chicago, NFL	9	172	1
1962	Lee Riley, N.Y. Titans, AFL	11	122	0
	Willie Wood, Green Bay, NFL	9	132	0
1961	Billy Atkins, Buffalo, AFL	10	158	0
	Dick Lynch, N.Y. Giants, NFL	9	60	0
1960	*Austin (Goose) Gonsoulin, Denver, AFL	11	98	0
	Dave Baker, San Francisco, NFL	10	96	0
	Jerry Norton, St. Louis, NFL	10	96	0
1959	Dean Derby, Pittsburgh	7	127	0
	Milt Davis, Baltimore	7	119	1
	Don Shinnick, Baltimore	7	70	0

Year	Player, Team	No.	Avg.	Long
1958	Jim Patton, N.Y. Giants	11	183	0
1957	Milt Davis, Baltimore	10	219	2
	Jack Christiansen, Detroit	10	137	1
	Jack Butler, Pittsburgh	10	85	0
1956	Linden Crow, Chi. Cardinals	11	170	0
1955	Will Sherman, Los Angeles	11	101	0
1954	Dick (Night Train) Lane, Chi. Cardinals	10	181	0
1953	Jack Christiansen, Detroit	12	238	1
1952	*Dick (Night Train) Lane, Los Angeles	14	298	2
1951	Otto Schnellbacher, N.Y. Giants	11	194	2
1950	Orban (Spec) Sanders, N.Y. Yanks	13	199	0
1949	Bob Nussbaumer, Chi. Cardinals	12	157	0
1948	*Dan Sandifer, Washington	13	258	2
1947	Frank Reagan, N.Y. Giants	10	203	0
	Frank Seno, Boston	10	100	0
1946	Bill Dudley, Pittsburgh	10	242	1
1945	Roy Zimmerman, Philadelphia	7	90	0
1944	*Howard Livingston, N.Y. Giants	9	172	1
1943	Sammy Baugh, Washington	11	112	0
1942	Clyde (Bulldog) Turner, Chi. Bears	8	96	1
1941	Marshall Goldberg, Chi. Cardinals	7	54	0
	*Art Jones, Pittsburgh	7	35	0
1940	Clarence (Ace) Parker, Brooklyn	6	146	1
	Kent Ryan, Detroit	6	65	0
	Don Hutson, Green Bay	6	24	0

First season of professional football.

ANNUAL PUNTING LEADERS

Year	Player, Team	No.	Avg.	Long
2007	Shane Lechler, Oakland, AFC	73	49.1	70
	Andy Lee, San Francisco, NFC	105	47.3	74
2006	Mat McBriar, Dallas, NFC	56	48.2	75
	Shane Lechler, Oakland, AFC	77	47.5	67
2005	Brian Moorman, Buffalo, AFC	71	45.7	68
	Josh Bidwell, Tampa Bay, NFC	90	45.6	61
2004	Shane Lechler, Oakland, AFC	73	46.7	67
	Tom Tupa, Washington, NFC	103	44.1	61
2003	Shane Lechler, Oakland, AFC	96	46.9	73
	Todd Sauerbrun, Carolina, NFC	77	44.6	64
2002	Todd Sauerbrun, Carolina, NFC	104	45.5	67
	Chris Hanson, Jacksonville, AFC	81	44.2	64
2001	Todd Sauerbrun, Carolina, NFC	93	47.5	73
	Shane Lechler, Oakland, AFC	73	46.2	65
2000	Darren Bennett, San Diego, AFC	92	46.2	66
	Mitch Berger, Minnesota, NFC	62	44.7	60
1999	Tom Rouen, Denver, AFC	84	46.5	65
	Mitch Berger, Minnesota, NFC	61	45.4	75
1998	Craig Hentrich, Tennessee, AFC	69	47.2	71
	Mark Royals, New Orleans, NFC	88	45.6	64
1997	Mark Royals, New Orleans, NFC	88	45.9	66
	Tom Tupa, New England, AFC	78	45.8	73
1996	John Kidd, Miami, AFC	78	46.3	63
	Matt Turk, Washington, NFC	75	45.1	63
1995	Rick Tuten, Seattle, AFC	83	45.0	73
	Sean Landeta, St. Louis, NFC	83	44.3	63
1994	Sean Landeta, L.A. Rams, NFC	78	44.8	62
	Jeff Gossett, L.A. Raiders, AFC	77	43.9	65
1993	Greg Montgomery, Houston, AFC	54	45.6	77
	Jim Arnold, Detroit, NFC	72	44.5	68
1992	Greg Montgomery, Houston, AFC	53	46.9	66
	Harry Newsome, Minnesota, NFC	72	45.0	84
1991	Reggie Roby, Miami, AFC	54	45.7	64
	Harry Newsome, Minnesota, AFC	68	45.5	65
1990	Mike Horan, Denver, AFC	58	44.4	67
	Sean Landeta, N.Y. Giants, NFC	75	44.1	67
1989	Rich Camarillo, Phoenix, NFC	76	43.4	58
	Greg Montgomery, Houston, AFC	56	43.3	63

Year	Player, Team	No.	Avg.	Long
\1988	Harry Newsome, Pittsburgh, AFC	65	45.4	62
	Jim Arnold, Detroit, NFC	97	42.4	69
1987	Rick Donnelly, Atlanta, NFC	61	44.0	62
	Ralf Mojsiejenko, San Diego, AFC	67	42.9	57
1986	Rohn Stark, Indianapolis, AFC	76	45.2	63
	Sean Landeta, N.Y. Giants, NFC	79	44.8	61
1985	Rohn Stark, Indianapolis, AFC	78	45.9	68
	*Rick Donnelly, Atlanta, NFC	59	43.6	68
1984	Jim Arnold, Kansas City, AFC	98	44.9	63
	*Brian Hansen, New Orleans, NFC	69	43.8	66
1983	Rohn Stark, Baltimore, AFC	91	45.3	68
	Frank Garcia, Tampa Bay, NFC	95	42.2	64
1982	Luke Prestridge, Denver, AFC	45	45.0	65
	Carl Birdsong, St. Louis, NFC	54	43.8	65
1981	Pat McInally, Cincinnati, AFC	72	45.4	62
	Tom Skladany, Detroit, NFC	64	43.5	74
1980	Dave Jennings, N.Y. Giants, NFC	94	44.8	63
	Luke Prestridge, Denver, AFC	70	43.9	57
1979	*Bob Grupp, Kansas City, AFC	89	43.6	74
	Dave Jennings, N.Y. Giants, NFC	104	42.7	72
1978	Pat McInally, Cincinnati, AFC	91	43.1	65
	*Tom Skladany, Detroit, NFC	86	42.5	63
1977	Ray Guy, Oakland, AFC	59	43.3	74
	Tom Blanchard, New Orleans, NFC	82	42.4	66
1976	Marv Bateman, Buffalo, AFC	86	42.8	78
	John James, Atlanta, NFC	101	42.1	67
1975	Ray Guy, Oakland, AFC	68	43.8	64
	Herman Weaver, Detroit, NFC	80	42.0	61
1974	Ray Guy, Oakland, AFC	74	42.2	66
	Tom Blanchard, New Orleans, NFC	88	42.1	71
1973	Jerrel Wilson, Kansas City, AFC	80	45.5	68
	*Tom Wittum, San Francisco, NFC	79	43.7	62
1972	Jerrel Wilson, Kansas City, AFC	66	44.8	69
	Dave Chapple, Los Angeles, NFC	53	44.2	70
1971	Dave Lewis, Cincinnati, AFC	72	44.8	56
	Tom McNeill, Philadelphia, NFC	73	42.0	64
1970	Dave Lewis, Cincinnati, AFC	79	46.2	63
	*Julian Fagan, New Orleans, NFC	77	42.5	64
1969	David Lee, Baltimore, NFL	57	45.3	66
	Dennis Partee, San Diego, AFL	71	44.6	62
1968	Jerrel Wilson, Kansas City, AFL	63	45.1	70
	Billy Lothridge, Atlanta, NFL	75	44.3	70
1967	Bob Scarpitto, Denver, AFL	105	44.9	73
	Billy Lothridge, Atlanta, NFL	87	43.7	62
1966	Bob Scarpitto, Denver, AFL	76	45.8	70
	*David Lee, Baltimore, NFL	49	45.6	64
1965	Gary Collins, Cleveland, NFL	65	46.7	71
	Jerrel Wilson, Kansas City, AFL	69	45.4	64
1964	Bobby Walden, Minnesota, NFL	72	46.4	73
	Jim Fraser, Denver, AFL	73	44.2	67
1963	Yale Lary, Detroit, NFL	35	48.9	73
	Jim Fraser, Denver, AFL	81	44.4	66
1962	Tommy Davis, San Francisco, NFL	48	45.6	82
	Jim Fraser, Denver, AFL	55	43.6	75
1961	Yale Lary, Detroit, NFL	52	48.4	71
	Billy Atkins, Buffalo, AFL	85	44.5	70
1960	Jerry Norton, St. Louis, NFL	39	45.6	62
	*Paul Maguire, L.A. Chargers, AFL	43	40.5	61
1959	Yale Lary, Detroit	45	47.1	67
1958	Sam Baker, Washington	48	45.4	64
1957	Don Chandler, N.Y. Giants	60	44.6	61
1956	Norm Van Brocklin, Los Angeles	48	43.1	72
1955	Norm Van Brocklin, Los Angeles	60	44.6	61
1954	Pat Brady, Pittsburgh	66	43.2	72
1953	Pat Brady, Pittsburgh	80	46.9	64
1952	Horace Gillom, Cleveland	61	45.7	73
1951	Horace Gillom, Cleveland	73	45.5	66
1950	*Fred (Curly) Morrison, Chi. Bears	57	43.3	65

Year	Player, Team	No.	Avg.	Long
1949	*Mike Boyda, N.Y. Bulldogs	56	44.2	61
1948	Joe Muha, Philadelphia	57	47.3	82
1947	Jack Jacobs, Green Bay	57	43.5	74
1946	Roy McKay, Green Bay	64	42.7	64
1945	Roy McKay, Green Bay	44	41.2	73
1944	Frank Sinkwich, Detroit	45	41.0	73
1943	Sammy Baugh, Washington	50	45.9	81
1942	Sammy Baugh, Washington	37	48.2	74
1941	Sammy Baugh, Washington	30	48.7	75
1940	Sammy Baugh, Washington	35	51.4	85
1939	*Parker Hall, Cleveland	58	40.8	80

*First season of professional football.

ANNUAL LEADERS IN SACKS (SINCE 1982)

Year	Player, Team	Sacks
2007	Jared Allen, Kansas City, AFC	15.5
	Patrick Kerney, Seattle, NFC	14.5
2006	Shawne Merriman, San Diego, AFC	17.0
	Aaron Kampman, Green Bay, NFC	15.5
2005	Derrick Burgess, Oakland, AFC	16.0
	Osi Umenyiora, N.Y. Giants, NFC	14.5
2004	Dwight Freeney, Indianapolis, AFC	16.0
	Bertrand Berry, Arizona, NFC	14.5
2003	Michael Strahan, N.Y. Giants, NFC	18.5
	Adewale Ogunleye, Miami, AFC	15.0
2002	Jason Taylor, Miami, AFC	18.5
	Simeon Rice, Tampa Bay, NFC	15.5
2001	Michael Strahan, N.Y. Giants, NFC	22.5
	Peter Boulware, Baltimore, AFC	15.0
2000	La'Roi Glover, New Orleans, NFC	17.0
	Trace Armstrong, Miami, AFC	16.5
1999	Kevin Carter, St. Louis, NFC	17.0
	*Jevon Kearse, Tennessee, AFC	14.5
1998	Michael Sinclair, Seattle, AFC	16.5
	Reggie White, Green Bay, NFC	16.0
1997	John Randle, Minnesota, NFC	15.5
	Bruce Smith, Buffalo, AFC	14.0
1996	Kevin Greene, Carolina, NFC	14.5
	Michael McCrary, Seattle, AFC	13.5
	Bruce Smith, Buffalo, AFC	13.5
1995	Bryce Paup, Buffalo, AFC	17.5
	William Fuller, Philadelphia, NFC	13.0
	Wayne Martin, New Orleans, NFC	13.0
1994	Kevin Greene, Pittsburgh, AFC	14.0
	Ken Harvey, Washington, NFC	13.5
	John Randle, Minnesota, NFC	13.5
1993	Neil Smith, Kansas City, AFC	15.0
	Renaldo Turnbull, New Orleans, NFC	13.0
	Reggie White, Green Bay, NFC	13.0
1992	Clyde Simmons, Philadelphia, NFC	19.0
	Leslie O'Neal, San Diego, AFC	17.0
1991	Pat Swilling, New Orleans, NFC	17.0
	William Fuller, Houston, AFC	15.0
1990	Derrick Thomas, Kansas City, AFC	20.0
	Charles Haley, San Francisco, NFC	16.0
1989	Chris Doleman, Minnesota, NFC	21.0
	Lee Williams, San Diego, AFC	14.0
1988	Reggie White, Philadelphia, NFC	18.0
	Greg Townsend, L.A. Raiders, AFC	11.5
1987	Reggie White, Philadelphia, NFC	21.0
	Andre Tippett, New England, AFC	12.5
1986	Lawrence Taylor, N.Y. Giants, NFC	20.5
	Sean Jones, L.A. Raiders, AFC	15.5
1985	Richard Dent, Chicago, NFC	17.0
	Andre Tippett, New England, AFC	16.5
1984	Mark Gastineau, N.Y. Jets, AFC	22.0
	Richard Dent, Chicago, NFC	17.5

Year	Team	Points
1983	Mark Gastineau, N.Y. Jets, AFC	19.0
	Fred Dean, San Francisco, NFC	17.5
1982	Doug Martin, Minnesota, NFC	11.5
	Jesse Baker, Houston, AFC	7.5

First season of professional football.

POINTS SCORED

Year	Team	Points
2007	New England, AFC	589
	Dallas, NFC	455
2006	San Diego, AFC	492
	Chicago, NFC	427
2005	Seattle, NFC	452
	Indianapolis, AFC	439
2004	Indianapolis, AFC	522
	Green Bay, NFC	424
2003	Kansas City, AFC	484
	St. Louis, NFC	447
2002	Kansas City, AFC	467
	New Orleans, NFC	432
2001	St. Louis, NFC	503
	Indianapolis, AFC	413
2000	St. Louis, NFC	540
	Denver, AFC	485
1999	St. Louis, NFC	526
	Indianapolis, AFC	423
1998	Minnesota, NFC	556
	Denver, AFC	501
1997	Denver, AFC	472
	Green Bay, NFC	422
1996	Green Bay, NFC	456
	New England, AFC	418
1995	San Francisco, NFC	457
	Pittsburgh, AFC	407
1994	San Francisco, NFC	505
	Miami, AFC	389
1993	San Francisco, NFC	473
	Denver, AFC	373
1992	San Francisco, NFC	431
	Buffalo, AFC	381
1991	Washington, NFC	485
	Buffalo, AFC	458
1990	Buffalo, AFC	428
	Philadelphia, NFC	396
1989	San Francisco, NFC	442
	Buffalo, AFC	409
1988	Cincinnati, AFC	448
	L.A. Rams, NFC	407
1987	San Francisco, NFC	459
	Cleveland, AFC	390
1986	Miami, AFC	430
	Minnesota, NFC	398
1985	San Diego, AFC	467
	Chicago, NFC	456
1984	Miami, AFC	513
	San Francisco, NFC	475
1983	Washington, NFC	541
	L.A. Raiders, AFC	442
1982	San Diego, AFC	288
	Dallas, NFC	226
	Green Bay, NFC	226
1981	San Diego, AFC	478
	Atlanta, NFC	426
1980	Dallas, NFC	454
	New England, AFC	441
1979	Pittsburgh, AFC	416
	Dallas, NFC	371
1978	Dallas, NFC	384
	Miami, AFC	372

Year	Team	Points
1977	Oakland, AFC	351
	Dallas, NFC	345
1976	Baltimore, AFC	417
	Los Angeles, NFC	351
1975	Buffalo, AFC	420
	Minnesota, NFC	377
1974	Oakland, AFC	355
	Washington, NFC	320
1973	Los Angeles, NFC	388
	Denver, AFC	354
1972	Miami, AFC	385
	San Francisco, NFC	353
1971	Dallas, NFC	406
	Oakland, AFC	344
1970	San Francisco, NFC	352
	Baltimore, AFC	321
1969	Minnesota, NFL	379
	Oakland, AFL	377
1968	Oakland, AFL	453
	Dallas, NFL	431
1967	Oakland, AFL	468
	Los Angeles, NFL	398
1966	Kansas City, AFL	448
	Dallas, NFL	445
1965	San Francisco, NFL	421
	San Diego, AFL	340
1964	Baltimore, NFL	428
	Buffalo, AFL	400
1963	N.Y. Giants, NFL	448
	San Diego, AFL	399
1962	Green Bay, NFL	415
	Dall. Texans, AFL	389
1961	Houston, AFL	513
	Green Bay, NFL	391
1960	N.Y. Titans, AFL	382
	Cleveland, NFL	362
1959	Baltimore	374
1958	Baltimore	381
1957	Los Angeles	307
1956	Chi. Bears	363
1955	Cleveland	349
1954	Detroit	337
1953	San Francisco	372
1952	Los Angeles	349
1951	Los Angeles	392
1950	Los Angeles	466
1949	Philadelphia	364
1948	Chi. Cardinals	395
1947	Chi. Bears	363
1946	Chi. Bears	289
1945	Philadelphia	272
1944	Philadelphia	267
1943	Chi. Bears	303
1942	Chi. Bears	376
1941	Chi. Bears	396
1940	Washington	245
1939	Chi. Bears	298
1938	Green Bay	223
1937	Green Bay	220
1936	Green Bay	248
1935	Chi. Bears	192
1934	Chi. Bears	286
1933	N.Y. Giants	244
1932	Chi. Bears	160

TOTAL YARDS GAINED

Year	Team	Yards
2007	New England, AFC	6,580
	Green Bay, NFC	5,931

Year	Team	Yards
2006	New Orleans, NFC	6,264
	Indianapolis, AFC	6,070
2005	Kansas City, AFC	6,192
	Seattle, NFC	5,915
2004	Kansas City, AFC	6,695
	Green Bay, NFC	6,357
2003	Minnesota, NFC	6,294
	Kansas City, AFC	5,910
2002	Oakland, AFC	6,237
	Minnesota, NFC	6,192
2001	St. Louis, NFC	6,690
	Indianapolis, AFC	5,955
2000	St. Louis, NFC	7,075
	Denver, AFC	6,554
1999	St. Louis, NFC	6,412
	Indianapolis, AFC	5,726
1998	San Francisco, NFC	6,800
	Denver, AFC	6,092
1997	Denver, AFC	5,872
	Detroit, NFC	5,798
1996	Denver, AFC	5,791
	Philadelphia, NFC	5,627
1995	Detroit, NFC	6,113
	Denver, AFC	6,040
1994	Miami, AFC	6,078
	San Francisco, NFC	6,060
1993	San Francisco, NFC	6,435
	Miami, AFC	5,812
1992	San Francisco, NFC	6,195
	Buffalo, AFC	5,893
1991	Buffalo, AFC	6,252
	San Francisco, NFC	5,858
1990	Houston, AFC	6,222
	San Francisco, NFC	5,895
1989	San Francisco, NFC	6,268
	Cincinnati, AFC	6,101
1988	Cincinnati, AFC	6,057
	San Francisco, NFC	5,900
1987	San Francisco, NFC	5,987
	Denver, AFC	5,624
1986	Cincinnati, AFC	6,490
	San Francisco, NFC	6,082
1985	San Diego, AFC	6,535
	San Francisco, NFC	5,920
1984	Miami, AFC	6,936
	San Francisco, NFC	6,366
1983	San Diego, AFC	6,197
	Green Bay, NFC	6,172
1982	San Diego, AFC	4,048
	San Francisco, NFC	3,242
1981	San Diego, AFC	6,744
	Detroit, NFC	5,933
1980	San Diego, AFC	6,410
	Los Angeles, NFC	6,006
1979	Pittsburgh, AFC	6,258
	Dallas, NFC	5,968
1978	New England, AFC	5,965
	Dallas, NFC	5,959
1977	Dallas, NFC	4,812
	Oakland, AFC	4,736
1976	Baltimore, AFC	5,236
	St. Louis, NFC	5,136
1975	Buffalo, AFC	5,467
	Dallas, NFC	5,025
1974	Dallas, NFC	4,983
	Oakland, AFC	4,718
1973	Los Angeles, NFC	4,906
	Oakland, AFC	4,773

Year	Team	Yards
1972	Miami, AFC	5,036
	N.Y. Giants, NFC	4,483
1971	Dallas, NFC	5,035
	San Diego, AFC	4,738
1970	Oakland, AFC	4,829
	San Francisco, NFC	4,503
1969	Dallas, NFL	5,122
	Oakland, AFL	5,036
1968	Oakland, AFL	5,696
	Dallas, NFL	5,117
1967	N.Y. Jets, AFL	5,152
	Baltimore, NFL	5,008
1966	Dallas, NFL	5,145
	Kansas City, AFL	5,114
1965	San Francisco, NFL	5,270
	San Diego, AFL	5,188
1964	Buffalo, AFL	5,206
	Baltimore, NFL	4,779
1963	San Diego, AFL	5,153
	N.Y. Giants, NFL	5,024
1962	N.Y. Giants, NFL	5,005
	Houston, AFL	4,971
1961	Houston, AFL	6,288
	Philadelphia, NFL	5,112
1960	Houston, AFL	4,936
	Baltimore, NFL	4,245
1959	Baltimore	4,458
1958	Baltimore	4,539
1957	Los Angeles	4,143
1956	Chi. Bears	4,537
1955	Chi. Bears	4,316
1954	Los Angeles	5,187
1953	Philadelphia	4,811
1952	Cleveland	4,352
1951	Los Angeles	5,506
1950	Los Angeles	5,420
1949	Chi. Bears	4,873
1948	Chi. Cardinals	4,705
1947	Chi. Bears	5,053
1946	Los Angeles	3,793
1945	Washington	3,549
1944	Chi. Bears	3,239
1943	Chi. Bears	4,045
1942	Chi. Bears	3,900
1941	Chi. Bears	4,265
1940	Green Bay	3,400
1939	Chi. Bears	3,988
1938	Green Bay	3,037
1937	Green Bay	3,201
1936	Detroit	3,703
1935	Chi. Bears	3,454
1934	Chi. Bears	3,900
1933	N.Y. Giants	2,973
1932	Chi. Bears	2,755

YARDS RUSHING

Year	Team	Yards
2007	Minnesota, NFC	2,634
	Jacksonville, AFC	2,391
2006	Atlanta, NFC	2,939
	San Diego, AFC	2,578
2005	Atlanta, NFC	2,546
	Denver, AFC	2,539
2004	Atlanta, NFC	2,672
	Pittsburgh, AFC	2,464
2003	Baltimore, AFC	2,674
	Green Bay, NFC	2,558
2002	Minnesota, NFC	2,507
	Miami, AFC	2,502

Year	Team	Yards
2001	Pittsburgh, AFC	2,774
	San Francisco, NFC	2,244
2000	Oakland, AFC	2,470
	Minnesota, NFC	2,129
1999	San Francisco, NFC	2,095
	Jacksonville, AFC	2,091
1998	San Francisco, NFC	2,544
	Denver, AFC	2,468
1997	Pittsburgh, AFC	2,479
	Detroit, NFC	2,464
1996	Denver, AFC	2,362
	Washington, NFC	1,910
1995	Kansas City, AFC	2,222
	Dallas, NFC	2,201
1994	Pittsburgh, AFC	2,180
	Detroit, NFC	2,080
1993	N.Y. Giants, NFC	2,210
	Seattle, AFC	2,015
1992	Buffalo, AFC	2,436
	Philadelphia, NFC	2,388
1991	Buffalo, AFC	2,381
	Minnesota, NFC	2,201
1990	Philadelphia, NFC	2,556
	San Diego, AFC	2,257
1989	Cincinnati, AFC	2,483
	Chicago, NFC	2,287
1988	Cincinnati, AFC	2,710
	San Francisco, NFC	2,523
1987	San Francisco, NFC	2,237
	L.A. Raiders, AFC	2,197
1986	Chicago, NFC	2,700
	Cincinnati, AFC	2,533
1985	Chicago, NFC	2,761
	Indianapolis, AFC	2,439
1984	Chicago, NFC	2,974
	N.Y. Jets, AFC	2,189
1983	Chicago, NFC	2,727
	Baltimore, AFC	2,695
1982	Buffalo, AFC	1,371
	Dallas, NFC	1,313
1981	Detroit, NFC	2,795
	Kansas City, AFC	2,633
1980	Los Angeles, NFC	2,799
	Houston, AFC	2,635
1979	N.Y. Jets, AFC	2,646
	St. Louis, NFC	2,582
1978	New England, AFC	3,165
	Dallas, NFC	2,783
1977	Chicago, NFC	2,811
	Oakland, AFC	2,627
1976	Pittsburgh, AFC	2,971
	Los Angeles, NFC	2,528
1975	Buffalo, AFC	2,974
	Dallas, NFC	2,432
1974	Dallas, NFC	2,454
	Pittsburgh, AFC	2,417
1973	Buffalo, AFC	3,088
	Los Angeles, NFC	2,925
1972	Miami, AFC	2,960
	Chicago, NFC	2,360
1971	Miami, AFC	2,429
	Detroit, NFC	2,376
1970	Dallas, NFC	2,300
	Miami, AFC	2,082
1969	Dallas, NFL	2,276
	Kansas City, AFL	2,220
1968	Chicago, NFL	2,377
	Kansas City, AFL	2,227

Year	Team	Yards
1967	Cleveland, NFL	2,139
	Houston, AFL	2,122
1966	Kansas City, AFL	2,274
	Cleveland, NFL	2,166
1965	Cleveland, NFL	2,331
	San Diego, AFL	2,085
1964	Green Bay, NFL	2,276
	Buffalo, AFL	2,040
1963	Cleveland, NFL	2,639
	San Diego, AFL	2,203
1962	Buffalo, AFL	2,480
	Green Bay, NFL	2,460
1961	Green Bay, NFL	2,350
	Dall. Texans, AFL	2,189
1960	St. Louis, NFL	2,356
	Oakland, AFL	2,056
1959	Cleveland	2,149
1958	Cleveland	2,526
1957	Los Angeles	2,142
1956	Chi. Bears	2,468
1955	Chi. Bears	2,388
1954	San Francisco	2,498
1953	San Francisco	2,230
1952	San Francisco	1,905
1951	Chi. Bears	2,408
1950	N.Y. Giants	2,336
1949	Philadelphia	2,607
1948	Chi. Cardinals	2,560
1947	Los Angeles	2,171
1946	Green Bay	1,765
1945	Cleveland	1,714
1944	Philadelphia	1,661
1943	Phil-Pitt	1,730
1942	Chi. Bears	1,881
1941	Chi. Bears	2,263
1940	Chi. Bears	1,818
1939	Chi. Bears	2,043
1938	Detroit	1,893
1937	Detroit	2,074
1936	Detroit	2,885
1935	Chi. Bears	2,096
1934	Chi. Bears	2,847
1933	Boston	2,260
1932	Chi. Bears	1,770

YARDS PASSING

Leadership in this category has been based on net yards since 1952.

Year	Team	Yards
2007	New England, AFC	4,731
	Green Bay, NFC	4,334
2006	New Orleans, NFC	4,503
	Indianapolis, AFC	4,308
2005	Arizona, NFC	4,437
	New England, AFC	4,120
2004	Indianapolis, AFC	4,623
	Minnesota, NFC	4,516
2003	Indianapolis, AFC	4,179
	St. Louis, NFC	3,961
2002	Oakland, AFC	4,475
	St. Louis, NFC	4,154
2001	St. Louis, NFC	4,663
	Indianapolis, AFC	3,989
2000	St. Louis, NFC	5,232
	Indianapolis, AFC	4,282
1999	St. Louis, NFC	4,353
	Indianapolis, AFC	4,066
1998	Minnesota, NFC	4,328
	N.Y. Jets, AFC	3,836

Year	Team	Yards
1997	Seattle, AFC	3,959
	Green Bay, NFC	3,705
1996	Jacksonville, AFC	4,110
	Philadelphia, NFC	3,745
1995	San Francisco, NFC	4,608
	Miami, AFC	4,210
1994	New England, AFC	4,444
	Minnesota, NFC	4,324
1993	Miami, AFC	4,353
	San Francisco, NFC	4,302
1992	Houston, AFC	4,029
	San Francisco, NFC	3,880
1991	Houston, AFC	4,621
	San Francisco, NFC	3,997
1990	Houston, AFC	4,805
	San Francisco, NFC	4,177
1989	Washington, NFC	4,349
	Miami, AFC	4,216
1988	Miami, AFC	4,516
	Washington, NFC	4,136
1987	Miami, AFC	3,876
	San Francisco, NFC	3,750
1986	Miami, AFC	4,779
	San Francisco, NFC	4,096
1985	San Diego, AFC	4,870
	Dallas, NFC	3,861
1984	Miami, AFC	5,018
	St. Louis, NFC	4,257
1983	San Diego, AFC	4,661
	Green Bay, NFC	4,365
1982	San Diego, AFC	2,927
	San Francisco, NFC	2,502
1981	San Diego, AFC	4,739
	Minnesota, NFC	4,333
1980	San Diego, AFC	4,531
	Minnesota, NFC	3,688
1979	San Diego, AFC	3,915
	San Francisco, NFC	3,641
1978	San Diego, AFC	3,375
	Minnesota, NFC	3,243
1977	Buffalo, AFC	2,530
	St. Louis, NFC	2,499
1976	Baltimore, AFC	2,933
	Minnesota, NFC	2,855
1975	Cincinnati, AFC	3,241
	Washington, NFC	2,917
1974	Washington, NFC	2,978
	Cincinnati, AFC	2,804
1973	Philadelphia, NFC	2,998
	Denver, AFC	2,519
1972	N.Y. Jets, AFC	2,777
	San Francisco, NFC	2,735
1971	San Diego, AFC	3,134
	Dallas, NFC	2,786
1970	San Francisco, NFC	2,923
	Oakland, AFC	2,865
1969	Oakland, AFL	3,271
	San Francisco, NFL	3,158
1968	San Diego, AFL	3,623
	Dallas, NFL	3,026
1967	N.Y. Jets, AFL	3,845
	Washington, NFL	3,730
1966	N.Y. Jets, AFL	3,464
	Dallas, NFL	3,023
1965	San Francisco, NFL	3,487
	San Diego, AFL	3,103
1964	Houston, AFL	3,527
	Chicago, NFL	2,841

Year	Team	Points
1963	Baltimore, NFL	3,296
	Houston, AFL	3,222
1962	Denver, AFL	3,404
	Philadelphia, NFL	3,385
1961	Houston, AFL	4,392
	Philadelphia, NFL	3,605
1960	Houston, AFL	3,203
	Baltimore, NFL	2,956
1959	Baltimore	2,753
1958	Pittsburgh	2,752
1957	Baltimore	2,388
1956	Los Angeles	2,419
1955	Philadelphia	2,472
1954	Chi. Bears	3,104
1953	Philadelphia	3,089
1952	Cleveland	2,566
1951	Los Angeles	3,296
1950	Los Angeles	3,709
1949	Chi. Bears	3,055
1948	Washington	2,861
1947	Washington	3,336
1946	Los Angeles	2,080
1945	Chi. Bears	1,857
1944	Washington	2,021
1943	Chi. Bears	2,310
1942	Green Bay	2,407
1941	Chi. Bears	2,002
1940	Washington	1,887
1939	Chi. Bears	1,965
1938	Washington	1,536
1937	Green Bay	1,398
1936	Green Bay	1,629
1935	Green Bay	1,449
1934	Green Bay	1,165
1933	N.Y. Giants	1,348
1932	Chi. Bears	1,013

FEWEST POINTS ALLOWED

Year	Team	Points
2007	Indianapolis, AFC	262
	Tampa Bay, NFC	270
2006	Baltimore, AFC	201
	Chicago, NFC	255
2005	Chicago, NFC	202
	Indianapolis, AFC	247
2004	Pittsburgh, AFC	251
	Philadelphia, NFC	260
2003	New England, AFC	238
	Dallas, NFC	260
2002	Tampa Bay, NFC	196
	Miami, AFC	301
2001	Chicago, NFC	203
	Pittsburgh, AFC	212
2000	Baltimore, AFC	165
	Philadelphia, NFC	245
1999	Jacksonville, AFC	217
	Tampa Bay, NFC	235
1998	Miami, AFC	265
	Dallas, NFC	275
1997	Kansas City, AFC	232
	Tampa Bay, NFC	263
1996	Green Bay, NFC	210
	Pittsburgh, AFC	257
1995	Kansas City, AFC	241
	San Francisco, NFC	258
1994	Cleveland, AFC	204
	Dallas, NFC	248
1993	N.Y. Giants, NFC	205
	Houston, AFC	238

Year	Team	Yards
1992	New Orleans, NFC	202
	Pittsburgh, AFC	225
1991	New Orleans, NFC	211
	Denver, AFC	235
1990	N.Y. Giants, NFC	211
	Pittsburgh, AFC	240
1989	Denver, AFC	226
	N.Y. Giants, NFC	252
1988	Chicago, NFC	215
	Buffalo, AFC	237
1987	Indianapolis, AFC	238
	San Francisco, NFC	253
1986	Chicago, NFC	187
	Seattle, AFC	293
1985	Chicago, NFC	198
	N.Y. Jets, AFC	264
1984	San Francisco, NFC	227
	Denver, AFC	241
1983	Miami, AFC	250
	Detroit, NFC	286
1982	Washington, NFC	128
	Miami, AFC	131
1981	Philadelphia, NFC	221
	Miami, AFC	275
1980	Philadelphia, NFC	222
	Houston, AFC	251
1979	Tampa Bay, NFC	237
	San Diego, AFC	246
1978	Pittsburgh, AFC	195
	Dallas, NFC	208
1977	Atlanta, NFC	129
	Denver, AFC	148
1976	Pittsburgh, AFC	138
	Minnesota, NFC	176
1975	Los Angeles, NFC	135
	Pittsburgh, AFC	162
1974	Los Angeles, NFC	181
	Pittsburgh, AFC	189
1973	Miami, AFC	150
	Minnesota, NFC	168
1972	Miami, AFC	171
	Washington, NFC	218
1971	Minnesota, NFC	139
	Baltimore, AFC	140
1970	Minnesota, NFC	143
	Miami, AFC	228
1969	Minnesota, NFL	133
	Kansas City, AFL	177
1968	Baltimore, NFL	144
	Kansas City, AFL	170
1967	Los Angeles, NFL	196
	Houston, AFL	199
1966	Green Bay, NFL	163
	Buffalo, AFL	255
1965	Green Bay, NFL	224
	Buffalo, AFL	226
1964	Baltimore, NFL	225
	Buffalo, AFL	242
1963	Chicago, NFL	144
	San Diego, AFL	255
1962	Green Bay, NFL	148
	Dall. Texans, AFL	233
1961	San Diego, AFL	219
	N.Y. Giants, NFL	220
1960	San Francisco, NFL	205
	Dall. Texans, AFL	253
1959	N.Y. Giants	170
1958	N.Y. Giants	183
1957	Cleveland	172
1956	Cleveland	177
1955	Cleveland	218
1954	Cleveland	162
1953	Cleveland	162
1952	Detroit	192
1951	Cleveland	152
1950	Philadelphia	141
1949	Philadelphia	134
1948	Chi. Bears	151
1947	Green Bay	210
1946	Pittsburgh	117
1945	Washington	121
1944	N.Y. Giants	75
1943	Washington	137
1942	Chi. Bears	84
1941	N.Y. Giants	114
1940	Brooklyn	120
1939	N.Y. Giants	85
1938	N.Y. Giants	79
1937	Chi. Bears	100
1936	Chi. Bears	94
1935	Green Bay	96
	N.Y. Giants	96
1934	Detroit	59
1933	Brooklyn	54
1932	Chi. Bears	44

FEWEST TOTAL YARDS ALLOWED

Year	Team	Yards
2007	Pittsburgh, AFC	4,262
	Tampa Bay, NFC	4,454
2006	Baltimore, AFC	4,225
	Chicago, NFC	4,706
2005	Tampa Bay, NFC	4,444
	Pittsburgh, AFC	4,544
2004	Pittsburgh, AFC	4,134
	Washington, NFC	4,281
2003	Dallas, NFC	4,056
	Buffalo, AFC	4,313
2002	Tampa Bay, NFC	4,044
	Miami, AFC	4,656
2001	Pittsburgh, AFC	4,137
	St. Louis, NFC	4,471
2000	Tennessee, AFC	3,813
	Washington, NFC	4,474
1999	Buffalo, AFC	4,045
	Tampa Bay, NFC	4,280
1998	San Diego, AFC	4,208
	Tampa Bay, NFC	4,345
1997	San Francisco, NFC	4,013
	Denver, AFC	4,671
1996	Green Bay, NFC	4,156
	Pittsburgh, AFC	4,362
1995	San Francisco, NFC	4,398
	Kansas City, AFC	4,549
1994	Dallas, NFC	4,313
	Pittsburgh, AFC	4,326
1993	Minnesota, NFC	4,406
	Pittsburgh, AFC	4,531
1992	Dallas, NFC	3,931
	Houston, AFC	4,211
1991	Philadelphia, NFC	3,549
	Denver, AFC	4,549
1990	Pittsburgh, AFC	4,115
	N.Y. Giants, NFC	4,206
1989	Minnesota, NFC	4,184
	Kansas City, AFC	4,293
1988	Minnesota, NFC	4,091
	Buffalo, AFC	4,578

Year	Team	Yards	Year	Team	Yards
1987	San Francisco, NFC	4,095	1946	Washington	2,451
	Cleveland, AFC	4,264	1945	Philadelphia	2,073
1986	Chicago, NFC	4,130	1944	Philadelphia	1,943
	L.A. Raiders, AFC	4,804	1943	Chi. Bears	2,262
1985	Chicago, NFC	4,135	1942	Chi. Bears	1,703
	L.A. Raiders, AFC	4,603	1941	N.Y. Giants	2,368
1984	Chicago, NFC	3,863	1940	N.Y. Giants	2,219
	Cleveland, AFC	4,641	1939	Washington	2,116
1983	Cincinnati, AFC	4,327	1938	N.Y. Giants	2,029
	New Orleans, NFC	4,691	1937	Washington	2,123
1982	Miami, AFC	2,312	1936	Boston	2,181
	Tampa Bay, NFC	2,442	1935	Boston	1,996
1981	Philadelphia, NFC	4,447	1934	Chi. Cardinals	1,539
	N.Y. Jets, AFC	4,871	1933	Brooklyn	1,789
1980	Buffalo, AFC	4,101			
	Philadelphia, NFC	4,443			

FEWEST RUSHING YARDS ALLOWED

Year	Team	Yards	Year	Team	Yards
1979	Tampa Bay, NFC	3,949	2007	Minnesota, NFC	1,185
	Pittsburgh, AFC	4,270		Baltimore, AFC	1,268
1978	Los Angeles, NFC	3,893	2006	Minnesota, NFC	985
	Pittsburgh, AFC	4,168		Baltimore, AFC	1,214
1977	Dallas, NFC	3,213	2005	San Diego, AFC	1,349
	New England, AFC	3,638		Carolina, NFC	1,465
1976	Pittsburgh, AFC	3,323	2004	Pittsburgh, AFC	1,299
	San Francisco, NFC	3,562		Washington, NFC	1,304
1975	Minnesota, NFC	3,153	2003	Tennessee, AFC	1,295
	Oakland, AFC	3,629		Dallas, NFC	1,425
1974	Pittsburgh, AFC	3,074	2002	Pittsburgh, AFC	1,375
	Washington, NFC	3,285		Tampa Bay, NFC	1,554
1973	Los Angeles, NFC	2,951	2001	Pittsburgh, AFC	1,195
	Oakland, AFC	3,160		Chicago, NFC	1,313
1972	Miami, AFC	3,297	2000	Baltimore, AFC	970
	Green Bay, NFC	3,474		N.Y. Giants, NFC	1,156
1971	Baltimore, AFC	2,852	1999	St. Louis, NFC	1,189
	Minnesota, NFC	3,406		Baltimore, AFC	1,231
1970	Minnesota, NFC	2,803	1998	San Diego, AFC	1,140
	N.Y. Jets, AFC	3,655		Atlanta, NFC	1,203
1969	Minnesota, NFL	2,720	1997	Pittsburgh, AFC	1,318
	Kansas City, AFL	3,163		San Francisco, NFC	1,366
1968	Los Angeles, NFL	3,118	1996	Denver, AFC	1,331
	N.Y. Jets, AFL	3,363		Green Bay, NFC	1,416
1967	Oakland, AFL	3,294	1995	San Francisco, NFC	1,061
	Green Bay, NFL	3,300		Pittsburgh, AFC	1,321
1966	St. Louis, NFL	3,492	1994	Minnesota, NFC	1,090
	Oakland, AFL	3,910		San Diego, AFC	1,404
1965	San Diego, AFL	3,262	1993	Houston, AFC	1,273
	Detroit, NFL	3,557		Minnesota, NFC	1,536
1964	Green Bay, NFL	3,179	1992	Dallas, NFC	1,244
	Buffalo, AFL	3,878		Buffalo, AFC	1,395
1963	Chicago, NFL	3,176		San Diego, AFC	1,395
	Boston, AFL	3,834	1991	Philadelphia, NFC	1,136
1962	Detroit, NFL	3,217		N.Y. Jets, AFC	1,442
	Dall. Texans, AFL	3,951	1990	Philadelphia, NFC	1,169
1961	San Diego, AFL	3,726		San Diego, AFC	1,515
	Baltimore, NFL	3,782	1989	New Orleans, NFC	1,326
1960	St. Louis, NFL	3,029		Denver, AFC	1,580
	Buffalo, AFL	3,866	1988	Chicago, NFC	1,326
1959	N.Y. Giants	2,843		Houston, AFC	1,592
1958	Chi. Bears	3,066	1987	Chicago, NFC	1,413
1957	Pittsburgh	2,791		Cleveland, AFC	1,433
1956	N.Y. Giants	3,081	1986	N.Y. Giants, NFC	1,284
1955	Cleveland	2,841		Denver, AFC	1,651
1954	Cleveland	2,658	1985	Chicago, NFC	1,319
1953	Philadelphia	2,998		N.Y. Jets, AFC	1,516
1952	Cleveland	3,075	1984	Chicago, NFC	1,377
1951	N.Y. Giants	3,250		Pittsburgh, AFC	1,617
1950	Cleveland	3,154	1983	Washington, NFC	1,289
1949	Philadelphia	2,831		Cincinnati, AFC	1,499
1948	Chi. Bears	2,931			
1947	Green Bay	3,396			

Year	Team	Yards
1982	Pittsburgh, AFC	762
	Detroit, NFC	854
1981	Detroit, NFC	1,623
	Kansas City, AFC	1,747
1980	Detroit, NFC	1,599
	Cincinnati, AFC	1,680
1979	Denver, AFC	1,693
	Tampa Bay, NFC	1,873
1978	Dallas, NFC	1,721
	Pittsburgh, AFC	1,774
1977	Denver, AFC	1,531
	Dallas, NFC	1,651
1976	Pittsburgh, AFC	1,457
	Los Angeles, NFC	1,564
1975	Minnesota, NFC	1,532
	Houston, AFC	1,680
1974	Los Angeles, NFC	1,302
	New England, AFC	1,587
1973	Los Angeles, NFC	1,270
	Oakland, AFC	1,470
1972	Dallas, NFC	1,515
	Miami, AFC	1,548
1971	Baltimore, AFC	1,113
	Dallas, NFC	1,144
1970	Detroit, NFC	1,152
	N.Y. Jets, AFC	1,283
1969	Dallas, NFL	1,050
	Kansas City, AFL	1,091
1968	Dallas, NFL	1,195
	N.Y. Jets, AFL	1,195
1967	Dallas, NFL	1,081
	Oakland, AFL	1,129
1966	Buffalo, AFL	1,051
	Dallas, NFL	1,176
1965	San Diego, AFL	1,094
	Los Angeles, NFL	1,409
1964	Buffalo, AFL	913
	Los Angeles, NFL	1,501
1963	Boston, AFL	1,107
	Chicago, NFL	1,442
1962	Detroit, NFL	1,231
	Dall. Texans, AFL	1,250
1961	Boston, AFL	1,041
	Pittsburgh, NFL	1,463
1960	St. Louis, NFL	1,212
	Dall. Texans, AFL	1,338
1959	N.Y. Giants	1,261
1958	Baltimore	1,291
1957	Baltimore	1,174
1956	N.Y. Giants	1,443
1955	Cleveland	1,189
1954	Cleveland	1,050
1953	Philadelphia	1,117
1952	Detroit	1,145
1951	N.Y. Giants	913
1950	Detroit	1,367
1949	Chi. Bears	1,196
1948	Philadelphia	1,209
1947	Philadelphia	1,329
1946	Chi. Bears	1,060
1945	Philadelphia	817
1944	Philadelphia	558
1943	Phil-Pitt	793
1942	Chi. Bears	519
1941	Washington	1,042
1940	N.Y. Giants	977
1939	Chi. Bears	812
1938	Detroit	1,081
1937	Chi. Bears	933

Year	Team	Yards
1936	Boston	1,148
1935	Boston	998
1934	Chi. Cardinals	954
1933	Brooklyn	964

FEWEST PASSING YARDS ALLOWED

Leadership in this category has been based on net yards since 1952.

Year	Team	Yards
2007	Tampa Bay, NFC	2,728
	Indianapolis, AFC	2,764
2006	Oakland, AFC	2,413
	New Orleans, NFC	2,854
2005	Green Bay, NFC	2,680
	N.Y. Jets, AFC	2,755
2004	Tampa Bay, NFC	2,579
	Miami, AFC	2,592
2003	Dallas, NFC	2,631
	Buffalo, AFC	2,707
2002	Tampa Bay, NFC	2,490
	Indianapolis, AFC	2,917
2001	Miami, AFC	2,829
	Philadelphia, NFC	2,864
2000	Tennessee, AFC	2,423
	Washington, NFC	2,621
1999	Buffalo, AFC	2,675
	Tampa Bay, NFC	2,873
1998	Philadelphia, NFC	2,720
	Oakland, AFC	2,876
1997	Dallas, NFC	2,522
	Indianapolis, AFC	2,820
1996	Green Bay, NFC	2,740
	Pittsburgh, AFC	2,947
1995	N.Y. Jets, AFC	2,740
	Philadelphia, NFC	2,816
1994	Dallas, NFC	2,752
	Houston, AFC	2,795
1993	New Orleans, NFC	2,606
	Cincinnati, AFC	2,798
1992	New Orleans, NFC	2,470
	Kansas City, AFC	2,537
1991	Philadelphia, NFC	2,413
	Denver, AFC	2,755
1990	Pittsburgh, AFC	2,500
	Dallas, NFC	2,639
1989	Minnesota, NFC	2,501
	Kansas City, AFC	2,527
1988	Kansas City, AFC	2,434
	Minnesota, NFC	2,489
1987	San Francisco, NFC	2,484
	L.A. Raiders, AFC	2,727
1986	St. Louis, NFC	2,637
	New England, AFC	2,978
1985	Washington, NFC	2,746
	Pittsburgh, AFC	2,783
1984	New Orleans, NFC	2,453
	Cleveland, AFC	2,696
1983	New Orleans, NFC	2,691
	Cincinnati, AFC	2,828
1982	Miami, AFC	1,027
	Tampa Bay, NFC	1,384
1981	Philadelphia, NFC	2,696
	Buffalo, AFC	2,870
1980	Washington, NFC	2,171
	Buffalo, AFC	2,282
1979	Tampa Bay, NFC	2,076
	Buffalo, AFC	2,530
1978	Buffalo, AFC	1,960
	Los Angeles, NFC	2,048

Year	Team	Yards
1977	Atlanta, NFC	1,384
	San Diego, AFC	1,725
1976	Minnesota, NFC	1,575
	Cincinnati, AFC	1,758
1975	Minnesota, NFC	1,621
	Cincinnati, AFC	1,729
1974	Pittsburgh, AFC	1,466
	Atlanta, NFC	1,572
1973	Miami, AFC	1,290
	Atlanta, NFC	1,430
1972	Minnesota, NFC	1,699
	Cleveland, AFC	1,736
1971	Atlanta, NFC	1,638
	Baltimore, AFC	1,739
1970	Minnesota, NFC	1,438
	Kansas City, AFC	2,010
1969	Minnesota, NFL	1,631
	Kansas City, AFL	2,072
1968	Houston, AFL	1,671
	Green Bay, NFL	1,796
1967	Green Bay, NFL	1,377
	Buffalo, AFL	1,825
1966	Green Bay, NFL	1,959
	Oakland, AFL	2,118
1965	Green Bay, NFL	1,981
	San Diego, AFL	2,168
1964	Green Bay, NFL	1,647
	San Diego, AFL	2,518
1963	Chicago, NFL	1,734
	Oakland, AFL	2,589
1962	Green Bay, NFL	1,746
	Oakland, AFL	2,306
1961	Baltimore, NFL	1,913
	San Diego, AFL	2,363
1960	Chicago, NFL	1,388
	Buffalo, AFL	2,124
1959	N.Y. Giants	1,582
1958	Chi. Bears	1,769
1957	Cleveland	1,300
1956	Cleveland	1,103
1955	Pittsburgh	1,295
1954	Cleveland	1,608
1953	Washington	1,751
1952	Washington	1,580
1951	Pittsburgh	1,687
1950	Cleveland	1,581
1949	Philadelphia	1,607
1948	Green Bay	1,626
1947	Green Bay	1,790
1946	Pittsburgh	939
1945	Washington	1,121
1944	Chi. Bears	1,052
1943	Chi. Bears	980
1942	Washington	1,093
1941	Pittsburgh	1,168
1940	Philadelphia	1,012
1939	Washington	1,116
1938	Chi. Bears	897
1937	Detroit	804
1936	Philadelphia	853
1935	Chi. Cardinals	793
1934	Philadelphia	545
1933	Portsmouth	558

1,000 YARDS RUSHING IN A SEASON

Year	Player, Team	Att.	Yards	Avg.	Long	TD
2007	LaDainian Tomlinson, San Diego[7]	315	1,474	4.68	49	15
	*Adrian Peterson, Minnesota	238	1,341	5.63	73	12
	Brian Westbrook, Philadelphia[2]	278	1,333	4.79	36	7
	Willie Parker, Pittsburgh[3]	321	1,316	4.10	32	2
	Jamal Lewis, Cleveland[6]	298	1,304	4.38	66	9
	Clinton Portis, Washington[5]	325	1,262	3.88	32	11
	Edgerrin James, Arizona[7]	324	1,222	3.77	27	7
	Willis McGahee, Baltimore[3]	294	1,207	4.11	46	7
	Fred Taylor, Jacksonville[7]	223	1,202	5.39	80	5
	Thomas Jones, N.Y. Jets[3]	310	1,119	3.61	36	1
	*Marshawn Lynch, Buffalo	280	1,115	3.98	56	7
	LenDale White, Tennessee	303	1,110	3.66	28	7
	Frank Gore, San Francisco[2]	260	1,102	4.24	43	5
	Joseph Addai, Indianapolis[2]	261	1,072	4.11	23	12
	Justin Fargas, Oakland	222	1,009	4.55	48	4
	Brandon Jacobs, N.Y. Giants	202	1,009	5.00	43	4
	Steven Jackson, St. Louis[3]	237	1,002	4.23	54	5
2006	LaDainian Tomlinson, San Diego[6]	348	1,815	5.22	85	28
	Larry Johnson, Kansas City[2]	416	1,789	4.30	47	17
	Frank Gore, San Francisco	312	1,695	5.43	72	8
	Tiki Barber, N.Y. Giants[6]	327	1,662	5.08	55	5
	Steven Jackson, St. Louis[2]	346	1,528	4.42	59	13
	Willie Parker, Pittsburgh[2]	337	1,494	4.43	76	13
	Rudi Johnson, Cincinnati[3]	341	1,309	3.84	22	12
	Brian Westbrook, Philadelphia	240	1,217	5.07	71	7
	Chester Taylor, Minnesota	303	1,216	4.01	95	6
	Travis Henry, Tennessee[3]	270	1,211	4.49	70	7
	Thomas Jones, Chicago[2]	296	1,210	4.09	30	6
	Edgerrin James, Arizona[6]	337	1,159	3.44	18	6
	Ladell Betts, Washington	245	1,154	4.71	26	4
	Fred Taylor, Jacksonville[6]	231	1,146	4.96	76	5
	Warrick Dunn, Atlanta[5]	286	1,140	3.99	90	4
	Jamal Lewis, Baltimore[5]	314	1,132	3.61	52	9
	Julius Jones, Dallas	267	1,084	4.06	77	4
	*Joseph Addai, Indianapolis	226	1,081	4.78	41	7
	Ahman Green, Green Bay[6]	266	1,059	3.98	70	5
	Deuce McAllister, New Orleans[4]	244	1,057	4.33	57	10
	Michael Vick, Atlanta	123	1,039	8.45	51	2
	Tatum Bell, Denver	233	1,025	4.40	51	2
	Ronnie Brown, Miami	241	1,008	4.18	47	5
2005	Shaun Alexander, Seattle[5]	370	1,880	5.1	88	27
	Tiki Barber, N.Y. Giants[5]	357	1,860	5.2	95	9
	Larry Johnson, Kansas City	336	1,750	5.2	49	20
	Clinton Portis, Washington[4]	352	1,516	4.3	47	11
	Edgerrin James, Indianapolis[5]	360	1,506	4.2	33	13
	LaDainian Tomlinson, San Diego[5]	339	1,462	4.3	62	18
	Rudi Johnson, Cincinnati[2]	337	1,458	4.3	33	12
	Warrick Dunn, Atlanta[4]	280	1,416	5.1	65	3
	Thomas Jones, Chicago	314	1,335	4.3	42	9
	Willis McGahee, Buffalo[2]	325	1,247	3.8	27	5
	Reuben Droughns, Cleveland[2]	309	1,232	4.0	75	2
	Willie Parker, Pittsburgh	255	1,202	4.7	80	4
	*Carnell Williams, Tampa Bay	290	1,178	4.1	71	6
	Steven Jackson, St. Louis	254	1,046	4.1	51	8
	LaMont Jordan, Oakland	272	1,025	3.8	26	9
	Mike Anderson, Denver[2]	239	1,014	4.2	44	12
2004	Curtis Martin, N.Y. Jets[10]	371	1,697	4.6	25	12
	Shaun Alexander, Seattle[4]	353	1,696	4.8	44	16
	Corey Dillon, New England[7]	345	1,635	4.7	44	12
	Edgerrin James, Indianapolis[4]	334	1,548	4.6	40	9
	Tiki Barber, N.Y. Giants[4]	322	1,518	4.7	72	13
	Rudi Johnson, Cincinnati	361	1,454	4.0	52	12
	LaDainian Tomlinson, San Diego[4]	339	1,335	3.9	42	17
	Clinton Portis, Washington[3]	343	1,315	3.8	64	5
	Reuben Droughns, Denver	275	1,240	4.5	51	6
	Fred Taylor, Jacksonville[5]	260	1,224	4.7	46	2
	Domanick Davis, Houston[2]	302	1,188	3.9	44	13
	Ahman Green, Green Bay[5]	259	1,163	4.5	90	7

Year	Player, Team	Att.	Yards	Avg.	Long	TD
	*Kevin Jones, Detroit	241	1,133	4.7	74	5
	Willis McGahee, Buffalo	284	1,128	4.0	41	13
	Warrick Dunn, Atlanta[3]	265	1,106	4.2	60	9
	Deuce McAllister, New Orleans[3]	269	1,074	4.0	71	9
	Chris Brown, Tennessee	220	1,067	4.9	52	6
	Jamal Lewis, Baltimore[4]	235	1,006	4.3	75	7
2003	Jamal Lewis, Baltimore[3]	387	2,066	5.3	82	14
	Ahman Green, Green Bay[4]	355	1,883	5.3	98	15
	LaDainian Tomlinson, San Diego[3]	313	1,645	5.3	73	13
	Deuce McAllister, New Orleans[2]	351	1,641	4.7	76	8
	Clinton Portis, Denver[2]	290	1,591	5.5	65	14
	Fred Taylor, Jacksonville[4]	345	1,572	4.6	62	6
	Stephen Davis, Carolina[4]	318	1,444	4.5	40	8
	Shaun Alexander, Seattle[3]	326	1,435	4.4	55	14
	Priest Holmes, Kansas City[4]	320	1,420	4.4	31	27
	Ricky Williams, Miami[4]	392	1,372	3.5	45	9
	Travis Henry, Buffalo[2]	331	1,356	4.1	64	10
	Curtis Martin, N.Y. Jets[9]	323	1,308	4.1	56	2
	Edgerrin James, Indianapolis[3]	310	1,259	4.1	43	11
	Tiki Barber, N.Y. Giants[3]	278	1,216	4.4	27	2
	*Domanick Davis, Houston	238	1,031	4.3	51	8
	Eddie George, Tennessee[7]	312	1,031	3.3	27	5
	Kevan Barlow, San Francisco	201	1,024	5.1	78	6
	Anthony Thomas, Chicago[2]	244	1,024	4.2	67	6
2002	Ricky Williams, Miami[3]	383	1,853	4.8	63	16
	LaDainian Tomlinson, San Diego[2]	372	1,683	4.5	76	14
	Priest Holmes, Kansas City[3]	313	1,615	5.2	56	21
	*Clinton Portis, Denver	273	1,508	5.5	59	15
	Travis Henry, Buffalo	325	1,438	4.4	34	13
	Deuce McAllister, New Orleans	325	1,388	4.3	62	13
	Tiki Barber, N.Y. Giants[2]	304	1,387	4.6	70	11
	Jamal Lewis, Baltimore[2]	308	1,327	4.3	75	6
	Fred Taylor, Jacksonville[3]	287	1,314	4.6	63	8
	Corey Dillon, Cincinnati[6]	314	1,311	4.2	67	7
	Michael Bennett, Minnesota	255	1,296	5.1	85	5
	Ahman Green, Green Bay[3]	286	1,240	4.3	43	7
	Shaun Alexander, Seattle[2]	295	1,175	4.0	58	16
	Eddie George, Tennessee[6]	343	1,165	3.4	35	12
	Curtis Martin, N.Y. Jets[8]	261	1,094	4.2	35	7
	Duce Staley, Philadelphia[3]	269	1,029	3.8	57	5
	James Stewart, Detroit[2]	231	1,021	4.4	56	4
2001	Priest Holmes, Kansas City[2]	327	1,555	4.8	41	8
	Curtis Martin, N.Y. Jets[7]	333	1,513	4.5	47	10
	Stephen Davis, Washington[3]	356	1,432	4.0	32	5
	Ahman Green, Green Bay[2]	304	1,387	4.6	83	9
	Marshall Faulk, St. Louis[7]	260	1,382	5.3	71	12
	Shaun Alexander, Seattle	309	1,318	4.3	88	14
	Corey Dillon, Cincinnati[5]	340	1,315	3.9	96	10
	Ricky Williams, New Orleans[2]	313	1,245	4.0	46	6
	*LaDainian Tomlinson, San Diego	339	1,236	3.6	54	10
	Garrison Hearst, San Francisco[4]	252	1,206	4.8	43	4
	*Anthony Thomas, Chicago	278	1,183	4.3	46	7
	Antowain Smith, New England[2]	287	1,157	4.0	44	12
	*Dominic Rhodes, Indianapolis	233	1,104	4.7	77	9
	Jerome Bettis, Pittsburgh[8]	225	1,072	4.8	48	4
	Emmitt Smith, Dallas[11]	261	1,021	3.9	44	3
2000	Edgerrin James, Indianapolis[2]	387	1,709	4.4	30	13
	Robert Smith, Minnesota[4]	295	1,521	5.2	72	7
	Eddie George, Tennessee[5]	403	1,509	3.7	35	14
	*Mike Anderson, Denver	297	1,487	5.0	80	15
	Corey Dillon, Cincinnati[4]	315	1,435	4.6	80	7
	Fred Taylor, Jacksonville[2]	292	1,399	4.8	71	12
	*Jamal Lewis, Baltimore	309	1,364	4.4	45	6
	Marshall Faulk, St. Louis[6]	253	1,359	5.4	36	18
	Jerome Bettis, Pittsburgh[7]	355	1,341	3.8	30	8
	Stephen Davis, Washington[2]	332	1,318	4.0	50	11
	Ricky Watters, Seattle[7]	278	1,242	4.5	55	7
	Curtis Martin, N.Y. Jets[6]	316	1,204	3.8	55	9
	Emmitt Smith, Dallas[10]	294	1,203	4.1	52	9

Year	Player, Team	Att.	Yards	Avg.	Long	TD
	James Stewart, Detroit	339	1,184	3.5	34	10
	Ahman Green, Green Bay	263	1,175	4.5	39	10
	Charlie Garner, San Francisco[2]	258	1,142	4.4	42	7
	Lamar Smith, Miami	309	1,139	3.7	68	14
	Warrick Dunn, Tampa Bay[2]	248	1,133	4.6	70	8
	James Allen, Chicago	290	1,120	3.9	29	2
	Tyrone Wheatley, Oakland	232	1,046	4.5	80	9
	Jamal Anderson, Atlanta[4]	282	1,024	3.6	42	6
	Tiki Barber, N.Y. Giants	213	1,006	4.7	78	8
	Ricky Williams, New Orleans	248	1,000	4.0	26	8
1999	*Edgerrin James, Indianapolis	369	1,553	4.2	72	13
	Curtis Martin, N.Y. Jets[5]	367	1,464	4.0	50	5
	Stephen Davis, Washington	290	1,405	4.8	76	17
	Emmitt Smith, Dallas[9]	329	1,397	4.3	63	11
	Marshall Faulk, St. Louis[5]	253	1,381	5.5	58	7
	Eddie George, Tennessee[4]	320	1,304	4.1	40	9
	Duce Staley, Philadelphia[2]	325	1,273	3.9	29	4
	Charlie Garner, San Francisco	241	1,229	5.1	53	4
	Ricky Watters, Seattle[6]	325	1,210	3.7	45	5
	Corey Dillon, Cincinnati[3]	263	1,200	4.6	50	5
	*Olandis Gary, Denver	276	1,159	4.2	71	7
	Jerome Bettis, Pittsburgh[6]	299	1,091	3.7	35	7
	Dorsey Levens, Green Bay[2]	279	1,034	3.7	36	9
	Robert Smith, Minnesota[3]	221	1,015	4.6	70	2
1998	Terrell Davis, Denver[4]	392	2,008	5.1	70	21
	Jamal Anderson, Atlanta[3]	410	1,846	4.5	48	14
	Garrison Hearst, San Francisco[3]	310	1,570	5.1	96	7
	Barry Sanders, Detroit[10]	343	1,491	4.3	73	4
	Emmitt Smith, Dallas[8]	319	1,332	4.2	32	13
	Marshall Faulk, Indianapolis[4]	324	1,319	4.1	68	6
	Eddie George, Tennessee[3]	348	1,294	3.7	37	5
	Curtis Martin, N.Y. Jets[4]	369	1,287	3.5	60	8
	Ricky Watters, Seattle[5]	319	1,239	3.9	39	9
	*Fred Taylor, Jacksonville	264	1,223	4.6	77	14
	Robert Smith, Minnesota[2]	249	1,187	4.8	74	6
	Jerome Bettis, Pittsburgh[5]	316	1,185	3.8	42	3
	Corey Dillon, Cincinnati[2]	262	1,130	4.3	66	4
	Antowain Smith, Buffalo	300	1,124	3.7	30	8
	*Robert Edwards, New England	291	1,115	3.8	53	9
	Duce Staley, Philadelphia	258	1,065	4.1	64	5
	Gary Brown, N.Y. Giants[2]	247	1,063	4.3	45	5
	Adrian Murrell, Arizona[3]	274	1,042	3.8	32	8
	Warrick Dunn, Tampa Bay	245	1,026	4.2	50	2
	Priest Holmes, Baltimore	233	1,008	4.3	56	7
1997	Barry Sanders, Detroit[9]	335	2,053	6.1	82	11
	Terrell Davis, Denver[3]	369	1,750	4.7	50	15
	Jerome Bettis, Pittsburgh[4]	375	1,665	4.4	34	7
	Dorsey Levens, Green Bay	329	1,435	4.4	52	7
	Eddie George, Tennessee[2]	357	1,399	3.9	30	6
	Napoleon Kaufman, Oakland	272	1,294	4.8	83	6
	Robert Smith, Minnesota	232	1,266	5.5	78	6
	Curtis Martin, New England[3]	274	1,160	4.2	70	4
	*Corey Dillon, Cincinnati	233	1,129	4.8	71	10
	Ricky Watters, Philadelphia[4]	285	1,110	3.9	28	7
	Adrian Murrell, N.Y. Jets[2]	300	1,086	3.6	43	7
	Emmitt Smith, Dallas[7]	261	1,074	4.1	44	4
	Marshall Faulk, Indianapolis[3]	264	1,054	4.0	45	7
	Raymont Harris, Chicago	275	1,033	3.8	68	10
	Garrison Hearst, San Francisco[2]	234	1,019	4.4	51	4
	Jamal Anderson, Atlanta[2]	290	1,002	3.5	39	7
1996	Barry Sanders, Detroit[8]	307	1,553	5.1	54	11
	Terrell Davis, Denver[2]	345	1,538	4.5	71	13
	Jerome Bettis, Pittsburgh[3]	320	1,431	4.5	50	11
	Ricky Watters, Philadelphia[3]	353	1,411	4.0	56	13
	*Eddie George, Houston	335	1,368	4.1	76	8
	Terry Allen, Washington[4]	347	1,353	3.9	49	21
	Adrian Murrell, N.Y. Jets	301	1,249	4.1	78	6
	Emmitt Smith, Dallas[6]	327	1,204	3.7	42	12
	Curtis Martin, New England[2]	316	1,152	3.6	57	14

Year	Player, Team	Att.	Yards	Avg.	Long	TD
	Anthony Johnson, Carolina	300	1,120	3.7	29	6
	*Karim Abdul-Jabbar, Miami	307	1,116	3.6	29	11
	Jamal Anderson, Atlanta	232	1,055	4.5	32	5
	Thurman Thomas, Buffalo[8]	281	1,033	3.7	36	8
1995	Emmitt Smith, Dallas[5]	377	1,773	4.7	60	25
	Barry Sanders, Detroit[7]	314	1,500	4.8	75	11
	*Curtis Martin, New England	368	1,487	4.0	49	14
	Chris Warren, Seattle[4]	310	1,346	4.3	52	15
	Terry Allen, Washington[3]	338	1,309	3.9	28	10
	Ricky Watters, Philadelphia[2]	337	1,273	3.8	57	11
	Errict Rhett, Tampa Bay[2]	332	1,207	3.6	21	11
	Rodney Hampton, N.Y. Giants[5]	306	1,182	3.9	32	10
	*Terrell Davis, Denver	237	1,117	4.7	60	7
	Harvey Williams, Oakland	255	1,114	4.4	60	9
	Craig Heyward, Atlanta	236	1,083	4.6	31	6
	Marshall Faulk, Indianapolis[2]	289	1,078	3.7	40	11
	*Rashaan Salaam, Chicago	296	1,074	3.6	42	10
	Garrison Hearst, Arizona	284	1,070	3.8	38	1
	Edgar Bennett, Green Bay	316	1,067	3.4	23	3
	Thurman Thomas, Buffalo[7]	267	1,005	3.8	49	6
1994	Barry Sanders, Detroit[6]	331	1,883	5.7	85	7
	Chris Warren, Seattle[3]	333	1,545	4.6	41	9
	Emmitt Smith, Dallas[4]	368	1,484	4.0	46	21
	Natrone Means, San Diego	343	1,350	3.9	25	12
	*Marshall Faulk, Indianapolis	314	1,282	4.1	52	11
	Thurman Thomas, Buffalo[6]	287	1,093	3.8	29	7
	Rodney Hampton, N.Y. Giants[4]	327	1,075	3.3	27	6
	Terry Allen, Minnesota[2]	255	1,031	4.0	45	8
	Jerome Bettis, L.A. Rams[2]	319	1,025	3.2	19	3
	*Errict Rhett, Tampa Bay	284	1,011	3.6	27	7
1993	Emmitt Smith, Dallas[3]	283	1,486	5.3	62	9
	*Jerome Bettis, L.A. Rams	294	1,429	4.9	71	7
	Thurman Thomas, Buffalo[5]	355	1,315	3.7	27	6
	Eric Pegram, Atlanta	292	1,185	4.1	29	3
	Barry Sanders, Detroit[5]	243	1,115	4.6	42	3
	Leonard Russell, New England	300	1,088	3.6	21	7
	Rodney Hampton, N.Y. Giants[3]	292	1,077	3.7	20	5
	Chris Warren, Seattle[2]	273	1,072	3.9	45	7
	*Reggie Brooks, Washington	223	1,063	4.8	85	3
	*Ron Moore, Phoenix	263	1,018	3.9	20	9
	Gary Brown, Houston	195	1,002	5.1	26	6
1992	Emmitt Smith, Dallas[2]	373	1,713	4.6	68	18
	Barry Foster, Pittsburgh	390	1,690	4.3	69	11
	Thurman Thomas, Buffalo[4]	312	1,487	4.8	44	9
	Barry Sanders, Detroit[4]	312	1,352	4.3	55	9
	Lorenzo White, Houston	265	1,226	4.6	44	7
	Terry Allen, Minnesota	266	1,201	4.5	51	13
	Reggie Cobb, Tampa Bay	310	1,171	3.8	25	9
	Harold Green, Cincinnati	265	1,170	4.4	53	2
	Rodney Hampton, N.Y. Giants[2]	257	1,141	4.4	63	14
	Cleveland Gary, L.A. Rams	279	1,125	4.0	63	7
	Herschel Walker, Philadelphia[2]	267	1,070	4.0	38	8
	Chris Warren, Seattle	223	1,017	4.6	52	3
	Ricky Watters, San Francisco	206	1,013	4.9	43	9
1991	Emmitt Smith, Dallas	365	1,563	4.3	75	12
	Barry Sanders, Detroit[3]	342	1,548	4.5	69	16
	Thurman Thomas, Buffalo[3]	288	1,407	4.9	33	7
	Rodney Hampton, N.Y. Giants	256	1,059	4.1	44	10
	Earnest Byner, Washington[3]	274	1,048	3.8	32	5
	Gaston Green, Denver	261	1,037	4.0	63	4
	Christian Okoye, Kansas City[2]	225	1,031	4.6	48	9
1990	Barry Sanders, Detroit[2]	255	1,304	5.1	45	13
	Thurman Thomas, Buffalo[2]	271	1,297	4.8	80	11
	Marion Butts, San Diego	265	1,225	4.6	52	8
	Earnest Byner, Washington[2]	297	1,219	4.1	22	6
	Bobby Humphrey, Denver[2]	288	1,202	4.2	37	7
	Neal Anderson, Chicago[3]	260	1,078	4.1	52	10
	Barry Word, Kansas City	204	1,015	5.0	53	4
	James Brooks, Cincinnati[3]	195	1,004	5.1	56	5

Year	Player, Team	Att.	Yards	Avg.	Long	TD
1989	Christian Okoye, Kansas City	370	1,480	4.0	59	12
	*Barry Sanders, Detroit	280	1,470	5.3	34	14
	Eric Dickerson, Indianapolis[7]	314	1,311	4.2	21	7
	Neal Anderson, Chicago[2]	274	1,275	4.7	73	11
	Dalton Hilliard, New Orleans	344	1,262	3.7	40	13
	Thurman Thomas, Buffalo	298	1,244	4.2	38	6
	James Brooks, Cincinnati[2]	221	1,239	5.6	65	7
	*Bobby Humphrey, Denver	294	1,151	3.9	40	7
	Greg Bell, L.A. Rams[3]	272	1,137	4.2	47	15
	Roger Craig, San Francisco[3]	271	1,054	3.9	27	6
	Ottis Anderson, N.Y. Giants[6]	325	1,023	3.1	36	14
1988	Eric Dickerson, Indianapolis[6]	388	1,659	4.3	41	14
	Herschel Walker, Dallas	361	1,514	4.2	38	5
	Roger Craig, San Francisco[2]	310	1,502	4.8	46	9
	Greg Bell, L.A. Rams[2]	288	1,212	4.2	44	16
	*John Stephens, New England	297	1,168	3.9	52	4
	Gary Anderson, San Diego	225	1,119	5.0	36	3
	Neal Anderson, Chicago	249	1,106	4.4	80	12
	Joe Morris, N.Y. Giants[3]	307	1,083	3.5	27	5
	*Ickey Woods, Cincinnati	203	1,066	5.3	56	15
	Curt Warner, Seattle[4]	266	1,025	3.9	29	10
	John Settle, Atlanta	232	1,024	4.4	62	7
	Mike Rozier, Houston	251	1,002	4.0	28	10
1987	Charles White, L.A. Rams	324	1,374	4.2	58	11
	Eric Dickerson, L.A. Rams-Indianapolis[5]	283	1,288	4.6	57	6
1986	Eric Dickerson, L.A. Rams[4]	404	1,821	4.5	42	11
	Joe Morris, N.Y. Giants[2]	341	1,516	4.4	54	14
	Curt Warner, Seattle[3]	319	1,481	4.6	60	13
	*Rueben Mayes, New Orleans	286	1,353	4.7	50	8
	Walter Payton, Chicago[10]	321	1,333	4.2	41	8
	Gerald Riggs, Atlanta[3]	343	1,327	3.9	31	9
	George Rogers, Washington[4]	303	1,203	4.0	42	18
	James Brooks, Cincinnati	205	1,087	5.3	56	5
1985	Marcus Allen, L.A. Raiders[3]	390	1,759	4.6	61	11
	Gerald Riggs, Atlanta[2]	397	1,719	4.3	50	10
	Walter Payton, Chicago[9]	324	1,551	4.8	40	9
	Joe Morris, N.Y. Giants	294	1,336	4.5	65	21
	Freeman McNeil, N.Y. Jets[2]	294	1,331	4.5	69	3
	Tony Dorsett, Dallas[8]	305	1,307	4.3	60	7
	James Wilder, Tampa Bay[2]	365	1,300	3.6	28	10
	Eric Dickerson, L.A. Rams[3]	292	1,234	4.2	43	12
	Craig James, New England	263	1,227	4.7	65	5
	Kevin Mack, Cleveland	222	1,104	5.0	61	7
	Curt Warner, Seattle[2]	291	1,094	3.8	38	8
	George Rogers, Washington[3]	231	1,093	4.7	35	7
	Roger Craig, San Francisco	214	1,050	4.9	62	9
	Earnest Jackson, Philadelphia[2]	282	1,028	3.6	59	5
	Stump Mitchell, St. Louis	183	1,006	5.5	64	7
	Earnest Byner, Cleveland	244	1,002	4.1	36	8
1984	Eric Dickerson, L.A. Rams[2]	379	2,105	5.6	66	14
	Walter Payton, Chicago[8]	381	1,684	4.4	72	11
	James Wilder, Tampa Bay	407	1,544	3.8	37	13
	Gerald Riggs, Atlanta	353	1,486	4.2	57	13
	Wendell Tyler, San Francisco[3]	246	1,262	5.1	40	7
	John Riggins, Washington[5]	327	1,239	3.8	24	14
	Tony Dorsett, Dallas[7]	302	1,189	3.9	31	6
	Earnest Jackson, San Diego	296	1,179	4.0	32	8
	Ottis Anderson, St. Louis[5]	289	1,174	4.1	24	6
	Marcus Allen, L.A. Raiders[2]	275	1,168	4.2	52	13
	Sammy Winder, Denver	296	1,153	3.9	24	4
	*Greg Bell, Buffalo	262	1,100	4.2	85	7
	Freeman McNeil, N.Y. Jets	229	1,070	4.7	53	5
1983	*Eric Dickerson, L.A. Rams	390	1,808	4.6	85	18
	William Andrews, Atlanta[4]	331	1,567	4.7	27	7
	*Curt Warner, Seattle	335	1,449	4.3	60	13
	Walter Payton, Chicago[7]	314	1,421	4.5	49	6
	John Riggins, Washington[4]	375	1,347	3.6	44	24
	Tony Dorsett, Dallas[6]	289	1,321	4.6	77	8
	Earl Campbell, Houston[5]	322	1,301	4.0	42	12

Year	Player, Team	Att.	Yards	Avg.	Long	TD
	Ottis Anderson, St. Louis[4]	296	1,270	4.3	43	5
	Mike Pruitt, Cleveland[4]	293	1,184	4.0	27	10
	George Rogers, New Orleans[2]	256	1,144	4.5	76	5
	Joe Cribbs, Buffalo[3]	263	1,131	4.3	45	3
	Curtis Dickey, Baltimore	254	1,122	4.4	56	4
	Tony Collins, New England	219	1,049	4.8	50	10
	Billy Sims, Detroit[3]	220	1,040	4.7	41	7
	Marcus Allen, L.A. Raiders	266	1,014	3.8	19	9
	Franco Harris, Pittsburgh[8]	279	1,007	3.6	19	5
1981	*George Rogers, New Orleans	378	1,674	4.4	79	13
	Tony Dorsett, Dallas[5]	342	1,646	4.8	75	4
	Billy Sims, Detroit[2]	296	1,437	4.9	51	13
	Wilbert Montgomery, Philadelphia[3]	286	1,402	4.9	41	8
	Ottis Anderson, St. Louis[3]	328	1,376	4.2	28	9
	Earl Campbell, Houston[4]	361	1,376	3.8	43	10
	William Andrews, Atlanta[3]	289	1,301	4.5	29	10
	Walter Payton, Chicago[6]	339	1,222	3.6	39	6
	Chuck Muncie, San Diego[2]	251	1,144	4.6	73	19
	*Joe Delaney, Kansas City	234	1,121	4.8	82	3
	Mike Pruitt, Cleveland[3]	247	1,103	4.5	21	7
	Joe Cribbs, Buffalo[2]	257	1,097	4.3	35	3
	Pete Johnson, Cincinnati	274	1,077	3.9	39	12
	Wendell Tyler, Los Angeles[2]	260	1,074	4.1	69	12
	Ted Brown, Minnesota	274	1,063	3.9	34	6
1980	Earl Campbell, Houston[3]	373	1,934	5.2	55	13
	Walter Payton, Chicago[5]	317	1,460	4.6	69	6
	Ottis Anderson, St. Louis[2]	301	1,352	4.5	52	9
	William Andrews, Atlanta[2]	265	1,308	4.9	33	4
	*Billy Sims, Detroit	313	1,303	4.2	52	13
	Tony Dorsett, Dallas[4]	278	1,185	4.3	56	11
	*Joe Cribbs, Buffalo	306	1,185	3.9	48	11
	Mike Pruitt, Cleveland[2]	249	1,034	4.2	56	6
1979	Earl Campbell, Houston[2]	368	1,697	4.6	61	19
	Walter Payton, Chicago[4]	369	1,610	4.4	43	14
	*Ottis Anderson, St. Louis	331	1,605	4.8	76	8
	Wilbert Montgomery, Philadelphia[2]	338	1,512	4.5	62	9
	Mike Pruitt, Cleveland	264	1,294	4.9	77	9
	Ricky Bell, Tampa Bay	283	1,263	4.5	49	7
	Chuck Muncie, New Orleans	238	1,198	5.0	69	11
	Franco Harris, Pittsburgh[7]	267	1,186	4.4	71	11
	John Riggins, Washington[3]	260	1,153	4.4	66	9
	Wendell Tyler, Los Angeles	218	1,109	5.1	63	9
	Tony Dorsett, Dallas[3]	250	1,107	4.4	41	6
	*William Andrews, Atlanta	239	1,023	4.3	23	3
1978	*Earl Campbell, Houston	302	1,450	4.8	81	13
	Walter Payton, Chicago[3]	333	1,395	4.2	76	11
	Tony Dorsett, Dallas[2]	290	1,325	4.6	63	7
	Delvin Williams, Miami[2]	272	1,258	4.6	58	8
	Wilbert Montgomery, Philadelphia	259	1,220	4.7	47	9
	Terdell Middleton, Green Bay	284	1,116	3.9	76	11
	Franco Harris, Pittsburgh[6]	310	1,082	3.5	37	8
	Mark van Eeghen, Oakland[3]	270	1,080	4.0	34	9
	*Terry Miller, Buffalo	238	1,060	4.5	60	7
	Tony Reed, Kansas City	206	1,053	5.1	62	5
	John Riggins, Washington[2]	248	1,014	4.1	31	5
1977	Walter Payton, Chicago[2]	339	1,852	5.5	73	14
	Mark van Eeghen, Oakland[2]	324	1,273	3.9	27	7
	Lawrence McCutcheon, Los Angeles[4]	294	1,238	4.2	48	7
	Franco Harris, Pittsburgh[5]	300	1,162	3.9	61	11
	Lydell Mitchell, Baltimore[3]	301	1,159	3.9	64	3
	Chuck Foreman, Minnesota[3]	270	1,112	4.1	51	6
	Greg Pruitt, Cleveland[3]	236	1,086	4.6	78	3
	Sam Cunningham, New England	270	1,015	3.8	31	4
	*Tony Dorsett, Dallas	208	1,007	4.8	84	12
1976	O.J. Simpson, Buffalo[5]	290	1,503	5.2	75	8
	Walter Payton, Chicago	311	1,390	4.5	60	13
	Delvin Williams, San Francisco	248	1,203	4.9	80	7
	Lydell Mitchell, Baltimore[2]	289	1,200	4.2	43	5
	Lawrence McCutcheon, Los Angeles[3]	291	1,168	4.0	40	9

Year	Player, Team	Att.	Yards	Avg.	Long	TD
	Chuck Foreman, Minnesota[2]	278	1,155	4.2	46	13
	Franco Harris, Pittsburgh[4]	289	1,128	3.9	30	14
	Mike Thomas, Washington	254	1,101	4.3	28	5
	Rocky Bleier, Pittsburgh	220	1,036	4.7	28	5
	Mark van Eeghen, Oakland	233	1,012	4.3	21	3
	Otis Armstrong, Denver[2]	247	1,008	4.1	31	5
	Greg Pruitt, Cleveland[2]	209	1,000	4.8	64	4
1975	O.J. Simpson, Buffalo[4]	329	1,817	5.5	88	16
	Franco Harris, Pittsburgh[3]	262	1,246	4.8	36	10
	Lydell Mitchell, Baltimore	289	1,193	4.1	70	11
	Jim Otis, St. Louis	269	1,076	4.0	30	5
	Chuck Foreman, Minnesota	280	1,070	3.8	31	13
	Greg Pruitt, Cleveland	217	1,067	4.9	50	8
	John Riggins, N.Y. Jets	238	1,005	4.2	42	8
	Dave Hampton, Atlanta	250	1,002	4.0	22	5
1974	Otis Armstrong, Denver	263	1,407	5.3	43	9
	*Don Woods, San Diego	227	1,162	5.1	56	7
	O.J. Simpson, Buffalo[3]	270	1,125	4.2	41	3
	Lawrence McCutcheon, Los Angeles[2]	236	1,109	4.7	23	3
	Franco Harris, Pittsburgh[2]	208	1,006	4.8	54	5
1973	O.J. Simpson, Buffalo[2]	332	2,003	6.0	80	12
	John Brockington, Green Bay[3]	265	1,144	4.3	53	3
	Calvin Hill, Dallas[2]	273	1,142	4.2	21	6
	Lawrence McCutcheon, Los Angeles	210	1,097	5.2	37	2
	Larry Csonka, Miami[3]	219	1,003	4.6	25	5
1972	O.J. Simpson, Buffalo	292	1,251	4.3	94	6
	Larry Brown, Washington[2]	285	1,216	4.3	38	8
	Ron Johnson, N.Y. Giants[2]	298	1,182	4.0	35	9
	Larry Csonka, Miami[2]	213	1,117	5.2	45	6
	Marv Hubbard, Oakland	219	1,100	5.0	39	4
	*Franco Harris, Pittsburgh	188	1,055	5.6	75	10
	Calvin Hill, Dallas	245	1,036	4.2	26	6
	Mike Garrett, San Diego[2]	272	1,031	3.8	41	6
	John Brockington, Green Bay[2]	274	1,027	3.7	30	8
	Eugene (Mercury) Morris, Miami	190	1,000	5.3	33	12
1971	Floyd Little, Denver	284	1,133	4.0	40	6
	*John Brockington, Green Bay	216	1,105	5.1	52	4
	Larry Csonka, Miami	195	1,051	5.4	28	7
	Steve Owens, Detroit	246	1,035	4.2	23	8
	Willie Ellison, Los Angeles	211	1,000	4.7	80	4
1970	Larry Brown, Washington	237	1,125	4.7	75	5
	Ron Johnson, N.Y. Giants	263	1,027	3.9	68	8
1969	Gale Sayers, Chicago[2]	236	1,032	4.4	28	8
1968	Leroy Kelly, Cleveland[3]	248	1,239	5.0	65	16
	*Paul Robinson, Cincinnati	238	1,023	4.3	87	8
1967	Jim Nance, Boston[2]	269	1,216	4.5	53	7
	Leroy Kelly, Cleveland[2]	235	1,205	5.1	42	11
	Hoyle Granger, Houston	236	1,194	5.1	67	6
	Mike Garrett, Kansas City	236	1,087	4.6	58	9
1966	Jim Nance, Boston	299	1,458	4.9	65	11
	Gale Sayers, Chicago	229	1,231	5.4	58	8
	Leroy Kelly, Cleveland	209	1,141	5.5	70	15
	Dick Bass, Los Angeles[2]	248	1,090	4.4	50	8
1965	Jim Brown, Cleveland[7]	289	1,544	5.3	67	17
	Paul Lowe, San Diego[2]	222	1,121	5.0	59	7
1964	Jim Brown, Cleveland[6]	280	1,446	5.2	71	7
	Jim Taylor, Green Bay[5]	235	1,169	5.0	84	12
	John Henry Johnson, Pittsburgh[2]	235	1,048	4.5	45	7
1963	Jim Brown, Cleveland[5]	291	1,863	6.4	80	12
	Clem Daniels, Oakland	215	1,099	5.1	74	3
	Jim Taylor, Green Bay[4]	248	1,018	4.1	40	9
	Paul Lowe, San Diego	177	1,010	5.7	66	8
1962	Jim Taylor, Green Bay[3]	272	1,474	5.4	51	19
	John Henry Johnson, Pittsburgh	251	1,141	4.5	40	7
	Cookie Gilchrist, Buffalo	214	1,096	5.1	44	13
	Abner Haynes, Dall. Texans	221	1,049	4.7	71	13
	Dick Bass, Los Angeles	196	1,033	5.3	57	6
	Charlie Tolar, Houston	244	1,012	4.1	25	7
1961	Jim Brown, Cleveland[4]	305	1,408	4.6	38	8

Year	Player, Team	Att.	Yards	Avg.	Long	TD
	Jim Taylor, Green Bay[2]	243	1,307	5.4	53	15
1960	Jim Brown, Cleveland[3]	215	1,257	5.8	71	9
	Jim Taylor, Green Bay	230	1,101	4.8	32	11
	John David Crow, St. Louis	183	1,071	5.9	57	6
1959	Jim Brown, Cleveland[2]	290	1,329	4.6	70	14
	J.D. Smith, San Francisco	207	1,036	5.0	73	10
1958	Jim Brown, Cleveland	257	1,527	5.9	65	17
1956	Rick Casares, Chi. Bears	234	1,126	4.8	68	12
1954	Joe Perry, San Francisco[2]	173	1,049	6.1	58	8
1953	Joe Perry, San Francisco	192	1,018	5.3	51	10
1949	Steve Van Buren, Philadelphia[2]	263	1,146	4.4	41	11
	Tony Canadeo, Green Bay	208	1,052	5.1	54	4
1947	Steve Van Buren, Philadelphia	217	1,008	4.6	45	13
1934	*Beattie Feathers, Chi. Bears	119	1,004	8.4	82	8

First season of professional football.

200 YARDS RUSHING IN A GAME

Date	Player, Team, Opponent	Att.	Yards	TD
Nov. 4, 2007	Adrian Peterson, Minnesota vs. San Diego	30	296	3
Oct. 14, 2007	Adrian Peterson, Minnesota vs. Chicago	20	224	3
Sept. 16, 2007	Jamal Lewis, Cleveland vs. Cincinnati	27	216	1
Dec. 30, 2006	Tiki Barber, N.Y. Giants vs. Washington	23	234	3
Dec. 7, 2006	Willie Parker, Pittsburgh vs. Cleveland	32	223	1
Nov. 27, 2006	Shaun Alexander, Seattle vs. Green Bay	40	201	0
Nov. 19, 2006	Frank Gore, San Francisco vs. Seattle	24	212	0
Nov. 12, 2006	Willie Parker, Pittsburgh vs. New Orleans	22	213	2
Jan. 1, 2006	Larry Johnson, Kansas City vs. Cincinnati	26	201	3
Dec. 31, 2005	Tiki Barber, N.Y. Giants vs. Oakland	28	203	1
Dec. 17, 2005	Tiki Barber, N.Y. Giants vs. Kansas City	29	220	2
Nov. 20, 2005	Larry Johnson, Kansas City vs. Houston	36	211	2
Oct. 30, 2005	Tiki Barber, N.Y. Giants vs. Washington	24	206	1
Nov. 28, 2004	Rudi Johnson, Cincinnati vs. Cleveland	26	202	2
Nov. 21, 2004	Edgerrin James, Indianapolis vs. Chicago	23	204	1
Dec. 28, 2003	Ahman Green, Green Bay vs. Denver	20	218	2
Dec. 28, 2003	LaDainian Tomlinson, San Diego vs. Oakland	31	243	2
Dec. 21, 2003	Jamal Lewis, Baltimore vs. Cleveland	22	205	2
Dec. 7, 2003	Clinton Portis, Denver vs. Kansas City	22	218	5
Oct. 19, 2003	LaDainian Tomlinson, San Diego vs. Cleveland	26	200	1
Sept. 14, 2003	Jamal Lewis, Baltimore vs. Cleveland	30	295	2
Dec. 29, 2002	*Clinton Portis, Denver vs. Arizona	24	228	2
Dec. 28, 2002	Tiki Barber, N.Y. Giants vs. Philadelphia	32	203	0
Dec. 9, 2002	Ricky Williams, Miami vs. Chicago	31	216	2
Dec. 1, 2002	LaDainian Tomlinson, San Diego vs. Denver	37	220	3
Dec. 1, 2002	Ricky Williams, Miami vs. Buffalo	27	228	2
Sept. 29, 2002	LaDainian Tomlinson, San Diego vs. New England	27	217	2
Dec. 23, 2001	Marshall Faulk, St. Louis vs. Carolina	30	202	2
Nov. 11, 2001	Shaun Alexander, Seattle vs. Oakland	35	266	3
Dec. 24, 2000	Marshall Faulk, St. Louis vs. New Orleans	32	220	2
Dec. 3, 2000	Corey Dillon, Cincinnati vs. Arizona	35	216	1
Dec. 3, 2000	Warrick Dunn, Tampa Bay vs. Dallas	22	210	1
Dec. 3, 2000	*Mike Anderson, Denver vs. New Orleans	37	251	4
Dec. 3, 2000	Curtis Martin, N.Y. Jets vs. Indianapolis	30	203	1
Nov. 19, 2000	Fred Taylor, Jacksonville vs. Pittsburgh	30	234	3
Oct. 22, 2000	Corey Dillon, Cincinnati vs. Denver	22	278	2
Oct. 15, 2000	Marshall Faulk, St. Louis vs. Atlanta	25	208	1
Oct. 15, 2000	Edgerrin James, Indianapolis vs. Seattle	38	219	3
Sept. 24, 2000	Charlie Garner, San Francisco vs. Dallas	36	201	1
Sept. 3, 2000	Duce Staley, Philadelphia vs. Dallas	26	201	1
Nov. 22, 1998	Priest Holmes, Baltimore vs. Cincinnati	36	227	1
Oct. 11, 1998	Terrell Davis, Denver vs. Seattle	30	208	1
Dec. 4, 1997	*Corey Dillon, Cincinnati vs. Tennessee	39	246	4
Nov. 23, 1997	Barry Sanders, Detroit vs. Indianapolis	24	216	2
Oct. 26, 1997	Terrell Davis, Denver vs. Buffalo (OT)	42	207	1
Oct. 19, 1997	Napoleon Kaufman, Oakland vs. Denver	28	227	1
Oct. 12, 1997	Barry Sanders, Detroit vs. Tampa Bay	24	215	2
Sept. 21, 1997	Terrell Davis, Denver vs. Cincinnati	27	215	1
Aug. 31, 1997	Eddie George, Tennessee vs. Oakland (OT)	35	216	1
Sept. 22, 1996	LeShon Johnson, Arizona vs. New Orleans	21	214	2
Nov. 13, 1994	Barry Sanders, Detroit vs. Tampa Bay	26	237	0
Dec. 12, 1993	*Jerome Bettis, L.A. Rams vs. New Orleans	28	212	1

Date	Player, Team, Opponent	Att.	Yards	TD
Oct. 31, 1993	Emmitt Smith, Dallas vs. Philadelphia	30	237	1
Nov. 24, 1991	Barry Sanders, Detroit vs. Minnesota	23	220	4
Dec. 23, 1990	James Brooks, Cincinnati vs. Houston	20	201	1
Oct. 14, 1990	Barry Word, Kansas City vs. Detroit	18	200	2
Sept. 24, 1990	Thurman Thomas, Buffalo vs. N.Y. Jets	18	214	0
Dec. 24, 1989	Greg Bell, L.A. Rams vs. New England	26	210	1
Sept. 24, 1989	Greg Bell, L.A. Rams vs. Green Bay	28	221	2
Sept. 17, 1989	Gerald Riggs, Washington vs. Philadelphia	29	221	1
Dec. 18, 1988	Gary Anderson, San Diego vs. Kansas City	34	217	1
Nov. 30, 1987	*Bo Jackson, L.A. Raiders vs. Seattle	18	221	2
Nov. 15, 1987	Charles White, L.A. Rams vs. St. Louis	34	213	1
Dec. 7, 1986	Rueben Mayes, New Orleans vs. Miami	28	203	2
Oct. 5, 1986	Eric Dickerson, L.A. Rams vs. Tampa Bay (OT)	30	207	2
Dec. 21, 1985	George Rogers, Washington vs. St. Louis	34	206	1
Dec. 21, 1985	Joe Morris, N.Y. Giants vs. Pittsburgh	36	202	3
Dec. 9, 1984	Eric Dickerson, L.A. Rams vs. Houston	27	215	2
Nov. 18, 1984	*Greg Bell, Buffalo vs. Dallas	27	206	1
Nov. 4, 1984	Eric Dickerson, L.A. Rams vs. St. Louis	21	208	0
Sept. 2, 1984	Gerald Riggs, Atlanta vs. New Orleans	35	202	2
Nov. 27, 1983	*Curt Warner, Seattle vs. Kansas City (OT)	32	207	3
Nov. 6, 1983	James Wilder, Tampa Bay vs. Minnesota	31	219	1
Sept. 18, 1983	Tony Collins, New England vs. N.Y. Jets	23	212	3
Sept. 4, 1983	George Rogers, New Orleans vs. St. Louis	24	206	2
Dec. 21, 1980	Earl Campbell, Houston vs. Minnesota	29	203	1
Nov. 16, 1980	Earl Campbell, Houston vs. Chicago	31	206	0
Oct. 26, 1980	Earl Campbell, Houston vs. Cincinnati	27	202	2
Oct. 19, 1980	Earl Campbell, Houston vs. Tampa Bay	33	203	0
Nov. 26, 1978	*Terry Miller, Buffalo vs. N.Y. Giants	21	208	2
Dec. 4, 1977	*Tony Dorsett, Dallas vs. Philadelphia	23	206	2
Nov. 20, 1977	Walter Payton, Chicago vs. Minnesota	40	275	1
Oct. 30, 1977	Walter Payton, Chicago vs. Green Bay	23	205	2
Dec. 5, 1976	O.J. Simpson, Buffalo vs. Miami	24	203	1
Nov. 25, 1976	O.J. Simpson, Buffalo vs. Detroit	29	273	2
Oct. 24, 1976	Chuck Foreman, Minnesota vs. Philadelphia	28	200	2
Dec. 14, 1975	Greg Pruitt, Cleveland vs. Kansas City	26	214	3
Sept. 28, 1975	O.J. Simpson, Buffalo vs. Pittsburgh	28	227	1
Dec. 16, 1973	O.J. Simpson, Buffalo vs. N.Y. Jets	34	200	1
Dec. 9, 1973	O.J. Simpson, Buffalo vs. New England	22	219	1
Sept. 16, 1973	O.J. Simpson, Buffalo vs. New England	29	250	2
Dec. 5, 1971	Willie Ellison, Los Angeles vs. New Orleans	26	247	1
Dec. 20, 1970	John (Frenchy) Fuqua, Pittsburgh vs. Philadelphia	20	218	2
Nov. 3, 1968	Gale Sayers, Chicago vs. Green Bay	24	205	0
Oct. 30, 1966	Jim Nance, Boston vs. Oakland	38	208	2
Oct. 10, 1964	John Henry Johnson, Pittsburgh vs. Cleveland	30	200	3
Dec. 8, 1963	Cookie Gilchrist, Buffalo vs. N.Y. Jets	36	243	5
Nov. 3, 1963	Jim Brown, Cleveland vs. Philadelphia	28	223	1
Oct. 20, 1963	Clem Daniels, Oakland vs. N.Y. Jets	27	200	2
Sept. 22, 1963	Jim Brown, Cleveland vs. Dallas	20	232	2
Dec. 10, 1961	Billy Cannon, Houston vs. N.Y. Titans	25	216	3
Nov. 19, 1961	Jim Brown, Cleveland vs. Philadelphia	34	237	4
Dec. 18, 1960	John David Crow, St. Louis vs. Pittsburgh	24	203	0
Nov. 15, 1959	Bobby Mitchell, Cleveland vs. Washington	14	232	3
Nov. 24, 1957	*Jim Brown, Cleveland vs. Los Angeles	31	237	4
Dec. 16, 1956	*Tom Wilson, Los Angeles vs. Green Bay	23	223	0
Nov. 22, 1953	Dan Towler, Los Angeles vs. Baltimore	14	205	1
Nov. 12, 1950	Gene Roberts, N.Y. Giants vs. Chi. Cardinals	26	218	2
Nov. 27, 1949	Steve Van Buren, Philadelphia vs. Pittsburgh	27	205	0
Oct. 8, 1933	Cliff Battles, Boston vs. N.Y. Giants	16	215	1

First season of professional football.

TIMES 200 OR MORE

110 times by 67 players…Simpson 6; Barber 5; Brown, Campbell, Sanders, Tomlinson 4; Bell, Davis, Dickerson, Dillon, Faulk, Lewis 3; Alexander, James, Johnson, Parker, Payton, Peterson, Portis, Riggs, Rogers, Williams 2.

4,000 YARDS PASSING IN A SEASON

Year	Player, Team	Att.	Comp.	Pct.	Yards	TD	Int.
2007	Tom Brady, New England[2]	578	398	68.9	4,806	50	8
	Drew Brees, New Orleans[2]	652	440	67.5	4,423	28	18
	Tony Romo, Dallas	520	335	64.4	4,211	36	19
	Brett Favre, Green Bay[5]	535	356	66.5	4,155	28	15
	Carson Palmer, Cincinnati[2]	575	373	64.9	4,131	26	20
	Jon Kitna, Detroit[2]	561	355	63.3	4,068	18	20
	Peyton Manning, Indianapolis[8]	515	337	65.4	4,040	31	14
2006	Drew Brees, New Orleans	554	356	64.3	4,418	26	11
	Peyton Manning, Indianapolis[7]	557	362	65.0	4,397	31	9
	Marc Bulger, St. Louis	588	370	62.9	4,301	24	8
	Jon Kitna, Detroit	596	372	62.4	4,208	21	22
	Carson Palmer, Cincinnati	520	324	62.3	4,035	28	13
2005	Tom Brady, New England	530	334	63.0	4,110	26	14
	Trent Green, Kansas City[3]	507	317	62.5	4,014	17	10
2004	Daunte Culpepper, Minnesota	548	379	69.2	4,717	39	11
	Trent Green, Kansas City[2]	556	369	66.4	4,591	27	17
	Peyton Manning, Indianapolis[6]	497	336	67.6	4,557	49	10
	Jake Plummer, Denver	521	303	58.2	4,089	27	20
	Brett Favre, Green Bay[4]	540	346	64.1	4,088	30	17
2003	Peyton Manning, Indianapolis[5]	566	379	67.0	4,267	29	10
	Trent Green, Kansas City	523	330	63.1	4,039	24	12
2002	Rich Gannon, Oakland	618	418	67.6	4,689	26	10
	Drew Bledsoe, Buffalo[3]	610	375	61.5	4,359	24	15
	Peyton Manning, Indianapolis[4]	591	392	66.3	4,200	27	19
	Kerry Collins, N.Y. Giants	545	335	61.5	4,073	19	14
2001	Kurt Warner, St. Louis[2]	546	375	68.7	4,830	36	22
	Peyton Manning, Indianapolis[3]	547	343	62.7	4,131	26	23
2000	Peyton Manning, Indianapolis[2]	571	357	62.5	4,413	33	15
	Jeff Garcia, San Francisco	561	355	63.3	4,278	31	10
	Elvis Grbac, Kansas City	547	326	59.6	4,169	28	14
1999	Steve Beuerlein, Carolina	571	343	60.1	4,436	36	15
	Kurt Warner, St. Louis	499	325	65.1	4,353	41	13
	Peyton Manning, Indianapolis	533	331	62.1	4,135	26	15
	Brett Favre, Green Bay[3]	595	341	57.3	4,091	22	23
	Brad Johnson, Washington	519	316	60.9	4,005	24	13
1998	Brett Favre, Green Bay[2]	551	347	63.0	4,212	31	23
	Steve Young, San Francisco[2]	517	322	62.3	4,170	36	12
1996	Mark Brunell, Jacksonville	557	353	63.4	4,367	19	20
	Vinny Testaverde, Baltimore	549	325	59.2	4,177	33	19
	Drew Bledsoe, New England[2]	623	373	59.9	4,086	27	15
1995	Brett Favre, Green Bay	570	359	63.0	4,413	38	13
	Scott Mitchell, Detroit	583	346	59.3	4,338	32	12
	Warren Moon, Minnesota[4]	606	377	62.2	4,228	33	14
	Jeff George, Atlanta	557	336	60.3	4,143	24	11
1994	Drew Bledsoe, New England	691	400	57.9	4,555	25	27
	Dan Marino, Miami[6]	615	385	62.6	4,453	30	17
	Warren Moon, Minnesota[3]	601	371	61.7	4,264	18	19
1993	John Elway, Denver	551	348	63.2	4,030	25	10
	Steve Young, San Francisco	462	314	68.0	4,023	29	16
1992	Dan Marino, Miami[5]	554	330	59.6	4,116	24	16
1991	Warren Moon, Houston[2]	655	404	61.7	4,690	23	21
1990	Warren Moon, Houston	584	362	62.0	4,689	33	13
1989	Don Majkowski, Green Bay	599	353	58.9	4,318	27	20
	Jim Everett, L.A. Rams	518	304	58.7	4,310	29	17
1988	Dan Marino, Miami[4]	606	354	58.4	4,434	28	23
1986	Dan Marino, Miami[3]	623	378	60.7	4,746	44	23
	Jay Schroeder, Washington	541	276	51.0	4,109	22	22
1985	Dan Marino, Miami[2]	567	336	59.3	4,137	30	21
1984	Dan Marino, Miami	564	362	64.2	5,084	48	17
	Neil Lomax, St. Louis	560	345	61.6	4,614	28	16
	Phil Simms, N.Y. Giants	533	286	53.7	4,044	22	18
1983	Lynn Dickey, Green Bay	484	289	59.7	4,458	32	29
	Bill Kenney, Kansas City	603	346	57.4	4,348	24	18
1981	Dan Fouts, San Diego[3]	609	360	59.1	4,802	33	17
1980	Dan Fouts, San Diego[2]	589	348	59.1	4,715	30	24
	Brian Sipe, Cleveland	554	337	60.8	4,132	30	14
1979	Dan Fouts, San Diego	530	332	62.6	4,082	24	24
1967	Joe Namath, N.Y. Jets	491	258	52.5	4,007	26	28

400 YARDS PASSING IN A GAME

Date	Player, Team, Opponent	Att.	Comp.	Yards	TD
Nov. 25, 2007	Kurt Warner, Arizona vs. San Francisco (OT)	48	34	484	2
Nov. 4, 2007	Drew Brees, New Orleans vs. Jacksonville	49	35	445	3
Sept. 23, 2007	Jon Kitna, Detroit vs. Philadelphia	46	29	446	2
Sept. 16, 2007	Carson Palmer, Cincinnati vs. Cleveland	50	33	401	6
Dec. 10, 2006	Chris Weinke, Carolina vs. N.Y. Giants	61	34	423	1
Nov. 26, 2006	Matt Leinart, Arizona vs. Minnesota	51	31	405	1
Nov. 19, 2006	Drew Brees, New Orleans vs. Cincinnati	52	37	510	2
Nov. 12, 2006	Carson Palmer, Cincinnati vs. San Diego	42	31	440	3
Nov. 5, 2006	Ben Roethlisberger, Pittsburgh vs. Denver	54	38	433	1
Oct. 22, 2006	Joey Harrington, Miami vs. Green Bay	62	33	414	2
Sept. 17, 2006	Peyton Manning, Indianapolis vs. Houston	38	26	400	3
Oct. 2, 2005	Marc Bulger, St. Louis vs. N.Y. Giants	62	40	442	2
Jan. 2, 2005	Marc Bulger, St. Louis vs. N.Y. Jets (OT)	39	29	450	3
Dec. 19, 2004	Daunte Culpepper, Minnesota vs. Detroit	35	25	404	3
Dec. 19, 2004	Billy Volek, Tennessee vs. Oakland	60	40	492	4
Dec. 13, 2004	Billy Volek, Tennessee vs. Kansas City	43	29	426	4
Dec. 6, 2004	Matt Hasselbeck, Seattle vs. Dallas	40	28	414	3
Dec. 5, 2004	Peyton Manning, Indianapolis vs. Tennessee	33	25	425	3
Dec. 5, 2004	Donovan McNabb, Philadelphia vs. Green Bay	43	32	464	5
Nov. 29, 2004	Marc Bulger, St. Louis vs. Green Bay	53	35	448	2
Nov. 28, 2004	Kelly Holcomb, Cleveland vs. Cincinnati	39	30	413	5
Oct. 31, 2004	Peyton Manning, Indianapolis vs. Kansas City	44	25	472	5
Oct. 31, 2004	Jake Plummer, Denver vs. Atlanta	55	31	499	4
Oct. 17, 2004	Daunte Culpepper, Minnesota vs. New Orleans	37	26	425	5
Oct. 10. 2004	Tim Rattay, San Francisco vs. Arizona (OT)	57	38	417	2
Nov. 16, 2003	Peyton Manning, Indianapolis vs. N.Y. Jets	36	27	401	1
Oct. 12, 2003	Trent Green, Kansas City vs. Green Bay (OT)	45	27	400	3
Oct. 12, 2003	Steve McNair, Tennessee vs. Houston	27	18	421	3
Dec. 29, 2002	Matt Hasselbeck, Seattle vs. San Diego (OT)	53	36	449	2
Dec. 1, 2002	Matt Hasselbeck, Seattle vs. San Francisco	55	30	427	3
Nov. 10, 2002	Marc Bulger, St. Louis vs. San Diego	48	36	453	4
Nov. 10, 2002	Tommy Maddox, Pittsburgh vs. Atlanta (OT)	41	28	473	4
Oct. 6, 2002	Drew Bledsoe, Buffalo vs. Oakland	53	32	417	2
Sept. 22, 2002	Tom Brady, New England vs. Kansas City (OT)	54	39	410	4
Sept. 15, 2002	Drew Bledsoe, Buffalo vs. Minnesota (OT)	49	35	463	3
Sept. 15, 2002	Rich Gannon, Oakland vs. Pittsburgh	64	43	403	1
Dec. 30, 2001	Jon Kitna, Cincinnati vs. Pittsburgh	68	35	411	2
Dec. 23, 2001	Chris Chandler, Atlanta vs. Buffalo	40	28	431	2
Nov. 18, 2001	Charlie Batch, Detroit vs. Arizona	62	36	436	3
Nov. 18, 2001	Kurt Warner, St. Louis vs. New England	42	30	401	3
Sept. 23, 2001	Peyton Manning, Indianapolis vs. Buffalo	29	23	421	4
Dec. 24, 2000	Vinny Testaverde, N.Y. Jets vs. Baltimore	69	36	481	2
Dec. 17, 2000	Jeff Garcia, San Francisco vs. Chicago	44	36	402	2
Dec. 3, 2000	Aaron Brooks, New Orleans vs. Denver	48	30	441	2
Nov. 19, 2000	Gus Frerotte, Denver vs. San Diego	58	36	462	5
Nov. 5, 2000	Elvis Grbac, Kansas City vs. Oakland	53	39	504	2
Nov. 5, 2000	Trent Green, St. Louis vs. Carolina	42	29	431	2
Sept. 25, 2000	Peyton Manning, Indianapolis vs. Jacksonville	36	23	440	4
Sept. 4, 2000	Kurt Warner, St. Louis vs. Denver	35	25	441	3
Dec. 26, 1999	Brad Johnson, Washington vs. San Francisco (OT)	47	32	471	2
Dec. 5, 1999	Jeff Garcia, San Francisco vs. Cincinnati	49	33	437	3
Nov. 28, 1999	Jim Harbaugh, San Diego vs. Minnesota	39	25	404	1
Nov. 14, 1999	Jim Miller, Chicago vs. Minnesota (OT)	48	34	422	3
Sept. 26, 1999	Peyton Manning, Indianapolis vs. San Diego	54	29	404	2
Dec. 6, 1998	Vinny Testaverde, N.Y. Jets vs. Seattle	63	42	418	2
Dec. 6, 1998	John Elway, Denver vs. Kansas City	32	22	400	2
Nov. 26, 1998	Troy Aikman, Dallas vs. Minnesota	57	34	455	1
Nov. 23, 1998	Drew Bledsoe, New England vs. Miami	54	28	423	2
Nov. 15, 1998	Jake Plummer, Arizona vs. Dallas	56	31	465	3
Oct. 5, 1998	Randall Cunningham, Minnesota vs. Green Bay	32	20	442	4
Sept. 6, 1998	Glenn Foley, N.Y. Jets vs. San Francisco (OT)	58	30	415	3
Nov. 2, 1997	Tony Banks, St. Louis vs. Atlanta	34	23	401	2
Oct. 26, 1997	Warren Moon, Seattle vs. Oakland	44	28	409	5
Nov. 10, 1996	Boomer Esiason, Arizona vs. Washington (OT)	59	35	522	3
Nov. 3, 1996	Drew Bledsoe, New England vs. Miami	41	30	419	3
Oct. 27, 1996	Vinny Testaverde, Baltimore vs. St. Louis (OT)	51	31	429	3
Oct. 20, 1996	Mark Brunell, Jacksonville vs. St. Louis	52	37	421	0
Sept. 22, 1996	Mark Brunell, Jacksonville vs. New England (OT)	39	23	432	3

Date	Player, Team, Opponent	Att.	Comp.	Yards	TD
Dec. 18, 1995	Steve Young, San Francisco vs. Minnesota	49	30	425	3
Nov. 26, 1995	Dave Krieg, Arizona vs. Atlanta (OT)	43	27	413	4
Nov. 23, 1995	Scott Mitchell, Detroit vs. Minnesota	45	30	410	4
Oct. 1, 1995	Dan Marino, Miami vs. Cincinnati	48	33	450	2
Nov. 20, 1994	Warren Moon, Minnesota vs. N.Y. Jets	50	33	400	2
Nov. 13, 1994	Drew Bledsoe, New England vs. Minnesota (OT)	70	45	426	3
Nov. 6, 1994	Warren Moon, Minnesota vs. New Orleans	57	33	420	3
Sept. 25, 1994	Dan Marino, Miami vs. Minnesota	54	29	431	3
Sept. 4, 1994	Dan Marino, Miami vs. New England (OT)	42	23	473	5
Sept. 4, 1994	Drew Bledsoe, New England vs. Miami (OT)	51	32	421	4
Dec. 19, 1993	Steve Beuerlein, Phoenix vs. Seattle	53	34	431	3
Dec. 5, 1993	Brett Favre, Green Bay vs. Chicago	54	36	402	2
Nov. 28, 1993	Steve Young, San Francisco vs. L.A. Rams	32	26	462	4
Oct. 31, 1993	Jeff Hostetler, L.A. Raiders vs. San Diego	32	20	424	2
Sept. 13, 1992	Steve Young, San Francisco vs. Buffalo	37	26	449	3
Sept. 13, 1992	Jim Kelly, Buffalo vs. San Francisco	33	22	403	3
Nov. 10, 1991	Warren Moon, Houston vs. Dallas (OT)	56	41	432	0
Nov. 10, 1991	Mark Rypien, Washington vs. Atlanta	31	16	442	6
Oct. 13, 1991	Warren Moon, Houston vs. N.Y. Jets	50	35	423	2
Dec. 16, 1990	Warren Moon, Houston vs. Kansas City	45	27	527	3
Nov. 4, 1990	Joe Montana, San Francisco vs. Green Bay	40	25	411	3
Oct. 14, 1990	Joe Montana, San Francisco vs. Atlanta	49	32	476	6
Oct. 7, 1990	Boomer Esiason, Cincinnati vs. L.A. Rams (OT)	45	31	490	3
Dec. 23, 1989	Warren Moon, Houston vs. Cleveland	51	32	414	2
Dec. 11, 1989	Joe Montana, San Francisco vs. L.A. Rams	42	30	458	3
Nov. 26, 1989	Jim Everett, L.A. Rams vs. New Orleans (OT)	51	29	454	1
Nov. 26, 1989	Mark Rypien, Washington vs. Chicago	47	30	401	4
Oct. 2, 1989	Randall Cunningham, Philadelphia vs. Chicago	62	32	401	1
Sept. 24, 1989	Joe Montana, San Francisco vs. Philadelphia	34	25	428	5
Sept. 24, 1989	Dan Marino, Miami vs. N.Y. Jets	55	33	427	3
Sept. 17, 1989	Randall Cunningham, Philadelphia vs. Washington	46	34	447	5
Dec. 18, 1988	Dave Krieg, Seattle vs. L.A. Raiders	32	19	410	4
Dec. 12, 1988	Dan Marino, Miami vs. Cleveland	50	30	404	4
Oct. 23, 1988	Dan Marino, Miami vs. N.Y. Jets	60	35	521	3
Oct. 16, 1988	Vinny Testaverde, Tampa Bay vs. Indianapolis	42	25	469	2
Sept. 11, 1988	Doug Williams, Washington vs. Pittsburgh	52	30	430	2
Nov. 29, 1987	Tom Ramsey, New England vs. Philadelphia	53	34	402	3
Nov. 22, 1987	Boomer Esiason, Cincinnati vs. Pittsburgh	53	30	409	0
Sept. 20, 1987	Neil Lomax, St. Louis vs. San Diego	61	32	457	3
Dec. 21, 1986	Boomer Esiason, Cincinnati vs. N.Y. Jets	30	23	425	5
Dec. 14, 1986	Dan Marino, Miami vs. L.A. Rams (OT)	46	29	403	5
Nov. 23, 1986	Bernie Kosar, Cleveland vs. Pittsburgh (OT)	46	28	414	2
Nov. 17, 1986	Joe Montana, San Francisco vs. Washington	60	33	441	0
Nov. 16, 1986	Dan Marino, Miami vs. Buffalo	54	39	404	4
Nov. 10, 1986	Bernie Kosar, Cleveland vs. Miami	50	32	401	0
Nov. 2, 1986	Tommy Kramer, Minnesota vs. Washington (OT)	35	20	490	4
Nov. 2, 1986	Ken O'Brien, N.Y. Jets vs. Seattle	32	26	431	4
Oct. 27, 1986	Jay Schroeder, Washington vs. N.Y. Giants	40	22	420	1
Oct. 12, 1986	Steve Grogan, New England vs. N.Y. Jets	42	23	401	3
Sept. 21, 1986	Ken O'Brien, N.Y. Jets vs. Miami (OT)	43	29	479	4
Sept. 21, 1986	Dan Marino, Miami vs. N.Y. Jets (OT)	50	30	448	6
Sept. 21, 1986	Tony Eason, New England vs. Seattle	45	26	414	3
Dec. 20, 1985	John Elway, Denver vs. Seattle	42	24	432	1
Nov. 10, 1985	Dan Fouts, San Diego vs. L.A. Raiders (OT)	41	26	436	4
Oct. 13, 1985	Phil Simms, N.Y. Giants vs. Cincinnati	62	40	513	1
Oct. 13, 1985	Dave Krieg, Seattle vs. Atlanta	51	33	405	4
Oct. 6, 1985	Phil Simms, N.Y. Giants vs. Dallas	36	18	432	3
Oct. 6, 1985	Joe Montana, San Francisco vs. Atlanta	57	37	429	5
Sept. 19, 1985	Tommy Kramer, Minnesota vs. Chicago	55	28	436	3
Sept. 15, 1985	Dan Fouts, San Diego vs. Seattle	43	29	440	4
Dec. 16, 1984	Neil Lomax, St. Louis vs. Washington	46	37	468	2
Dec. 9, 1984	Dan Marino, Miami vs. Indianapolis	41	29	404	4
Dec. 2, 1984	Dan Marino, Miami vs. L.A. Raiders	57	35	470	4
Nov. 25, 1984	Dave Krieg, Seattle vs. Denver	44	30	406	3
Nov. 4, 1984	Dan Marino, Miami vs. N.Y. Jets	42	23	422	2
Oct. 21, 1984	Dan Fouts, San Diego vs. L.A. Raiders	45	24	410	4
Sept. 30, 1984	Dan Marino, Miami vs. St. Louis	36	24	429	3
Sept. 2, 1984	Phil Simms, N.Y. Giants vs. Philadelphia	30	23	409	4

Date	Player, Team, Opponent	Att.	Comp.	Yards	TD
Dec. 11, 1983	Bill Kenney, Kansas City vs. San Diego	41	31	411	4
Nov. 20, 1983	Dave Krieg, Seattle vs. Denver	42	31	418	3
Oct. 9, 1983	Joe Ferguson, Buffalo vs. Miami (OT)	55	38	419	5
Oct. 2, 1983	Joe Theismann, Washington vs. L.A. Raiders	39	23	417	3
Sept. 25, 1983	Richard Todd, N.Y. Jets vs. L.A. Rams (OT)	50	37	446	2
Dec. 26, 1982	Vince Ferragamo, L.A. Rams vs. Chicago	46	30	509	3
Dec. 20, 1982	Dan Fouts, San Diego vs. Cincinnati	40	25	435	1
Dec. 20, 1982	Ken Anderson, Cincinnati vs. San Diego	56	40	416	2
Dec. 11, 1982	Dan Fouts, San Diego vs. San Francisco	48	33	444	5
Nov. 21, 1982	Joe Montana, San Francisco vs. St. Louis	39	26	408	3
Nov. 15, 1981	Steve Bartkowski, Atlanta vs. Pittsburgh	50	33	416	2
Oct. 25, 1981	Brian Sipe, Cleveland vs. Baltimore	41	30	444	4
Oct. 25, 1981	David Woodley, Miami vs. Dallas	37	21	408	3
Oct. 11, 1981	Tommy Kramer, Minnesota vs. San Diego	43	27	444	4
Dec. 14, 1980	Tommy Kramer, Minnesota vs. Cleveland	49	38	456	4
Nov. 16, 1980	Doug Williams, Tampa Bay vs. Minnesota	55	30	486	4
Oct. 19, 1980	Dan Fouts, San Diego vs. N.Y. Giants	41	26	444	3
Oct. 12, 1980	Lynn Dickey, Green Bay vs. Tampa Bay (OT)	51	35	418	1
Sept. 21, 1980	Richard Todd, N.Y. Jets vs. San Francisco	60	42	447	3
Oct. 3, 1976	James Harris, Los Angeles vs. Miami	29	17	436	2
Nov. 17, 1975	Ken Anderson, Cincinnati vs. Buffalo	46	30	447	2
Nov. 18, 1974	Charley Johnson, Denver vs. Kansas City	42	28	445	2
Dec. 11, 1972	Joe Namath, N.Y. Jets vs. Oakland	46	25	403	1
Sept. 24, 1972	Joe Namath, N.Y. Jets vs. Baltimore	28	15	496	6
Dec. 21, 1969	Don Horn, Green Bay vs. St. Louis	31	22	410	5
Sept. 28, 1969	Joe Kapp, Minnesota vs. Baltimore	43	28	449	7
Sept. 9, 1968	Pete Beathard, Houston vs. Kansas City	48	23	413	2
Nov. 26, 1967	Sonny Jurgensen, Washington vs. Cleveland	50	32	418	3
Oct. 1, 1967	Joe Namath, N.Y. Jets vs. Miami	39	23	415	3
Sept. 17, 1967	Johnny Unitas, Baltimore vs. Atlanta	32	22	401	2
Nov. 13, 1966	Don Meredith, Dallas vs. Washington	29	21	406	2
Nov. 28, 1965	Sonny Jurgensen, Washington vs. Dallas	43	26	411	3
Oct. 24, 1965	Fran Tarkenton, Minnesota vs. San Francisco	35	21	407	3
Nov. 1, 1964	Len Dawson, Kansas City vs. Denver	38	23	435	6
Oct. 25, 1964	Cotton Davidson, Oakland vs. Denver	36	23	427	5
Oct. 16, 1964	Babe Parilli, Boston vs. Oakland	47	25	422	4
Dec. 22, 1963	Tom Flores, Oakland vs. Houston	29	17	407	6
Nov. 17, 1963	Norm Snead, Washington vs. Pittsburgh	40	23	424	2
Nov. 10, 1963	Don Meredith, Dallas vs. San Francisco	48	30	460	3
Oct. 13, 1963	Charley Johnson, St. Louis vs. Pittsburgh	41	20	428	2
Dec. 16, 1962	Sonny Jurgensen, Philadelphia vs. St. Louis	34	15	419	5
Nov. 18, 1962	Bill Wade, Chicago vs. Dall. Cowboys	46	28	466	2
Oct. 28, 1962	Y.A. Tittle, N.Y. Giants vs. Washington	39	27	505	7
Sept. 15, 1962	Frank Tripucka, Denver vs. Buffalo	56	29	447	2
Dec. 17, 1961	Sonny Jurgensen, Philadelphia vs. Detroit	42	27	403	3
Nov. 19, 1961	George Blanda, Houston vs. N.Y. Titans	32	20	418	7
Oct. 29, 1961	George Blanda, Houston vs. Buffalo	32	18	464	4
Oct. 29, 1961	Sonny Jurgensen, Philadelphia vs. Washington	41	27	436	3
Oct. 13, 1961	Jacky Lee, Houston vs. Boston	41	27	457	2
Dec. 13, 1958	Bobby Layne, Pittsburgh vs. Chi. Cardinals	49	23	409	2
Nov. 8, 1953	Bobby Thomason, Philadelphia vs. N.Y. Giants	44	22	437	4
Oct. 4, 1952	Otto Graham, Cleveland vs. Pittsburgh	49	21	401	3
Sept. 28, 1951	Norm Van Brocklin, Los Angeles vs. N.Y. Yanks	41	27	554	5
Dec. 11, 1949	Johnny Lujack, Chi. Bears vs. Chi. Cardinals	39	24	468	6
Oct. 31, 1948	Sammy Baugh, Washington vs. Boston	24	17	446	4
Oct. 31, 1948	Jim Hardy, Los Angeles vs. Chi. Cardinals	53	28	406	3
Nov. 14, 1943	Sid Luckman, Chi. Bears vs. N.Y. Giants	32	21	433	7

TIMES 400 OR MORE

193 times by 101 players…Marino 13; Manning, Montana, Moon 7; Bledsoe, Fouts 6; Jurgensen, Krieg 5; Bulger, Esiason, Kramer, Testaverde 4; Cunningham, Hasselbeck, Namath, Simms, Warner, Young 3; Anderson, Blanda, Brees, Brunell, Culpepper, Elway, Garcia, Green, Johnson, Kitna, Kosar, Lomax, Meredith, O'Brien, Palmer, Plummer, Rypien, Todd, Volek, Williams 2.

100 PASS RECEPTIONS IN A SEASON

Year	Player, Team	No.	Yards	Avg.	Long	TD
2007	T.J. Houshmandzadeh, Cincinnati	112	1,143	10.2	42	12
	Wes Welker, New England	112	1,175	10.5	42	8
	Reggie Wayne, Indianapolis	104	1,510	14.5	64	10
	Derrick Mason, Baltimore	103	1,087	10.6	79	5
	Brandon Marshall, Denver	102	1,325	13.0	68	7
	Larry Fitzgerald, Arizona[2]	100	1,409	14.1	48	10
2006	Andre Johnson, Houston	103	1,147	11.1	53	5
2005	Larry Fitzgerald, Arizona	103	1,409	13.7	47	10
	Steve Smith, Carolina	103	1,563	15.2	80	12
	Anquan Boldin, Arizona[2]	102	1,402	13.7	54	7
	Torry Holt, St. Louis[2]	102	1,331	13.0	44	9
2004	Tony Gonzalez, Kansas City	102	1,258	12.3	32	7
2003	Torry Holt, St. Louis	117	1,696	14.5	48	12
	Randy Moss, Minnesota[2]	111	1,632	14.7	72	17
	*Anquan Boldin, Arizona	101	1,377	13.6	71	8
	LaDainian Tomlinson, San Diego	100	725	7.3	73	4
2002	Marvin Harrison, Indianapolis[4]	143	1,722	12.0	69	11
	Hines Ward, Pittsburgh	112	1,329	11.9	72	12
	Randy Moss, Minnesota	106	1,347	12.7	60	7
	Eric Moulds, Buffalo	100	1,292	12.9	70	10
	Terrell Owens, San Francisco	100	1,300	13.0	76	13
2001	Rod Smith, Denver[2]	113	1,343	11.9	65	11
	Jimmy Smith, Jacksonville[2]	112	1,373	12.3	35	8
	Marvin Harrison, Indianapolis[3]	109	1,524	14.0	68	15
	Keyshawn Johnson, Tampa Bay	106	1,266	11.9	47	1
	Troy Brown, New England	101	1,199	11.9	60	5
	Marty Booker, Chicago	100	1,071	10.7	66	8
2000	Marvin Harrison, Indianapolis[2]	102	1,413	13.9	78	14
	Muhsin Muhammad, Carolina	102	1,183	11.6	36	6
	Ed McCaffrey, Denver	101	1,317	13.0	61	9
	Rod Smith, Denver	100	1,602	16.0	49	8
1999	Jimmy Smith, Jacksonville	116	1,636	14.1	62	6
	Marvin Harrison, Indianapolis	115	1,663	14.5	57	12
1997	Tim Brown, Oakland	104	1,408	13.5	59	5
	Herman Moore, Detroit[3]	104	1,293	12.4	79	8
1996	Jerry Rice, San Francisco[4]	108	1,254	11.6	39	8
	Herman Moore, Detroit[2]	106	1,296	12.2	50	9
	Carl Pickens, Cincinnati	100	1,180	11.8	61	12
1995	Herman Moore, Detroit	123	1,686	13.7	69	14
	Jerry Rice, San Francisco[3]	122	1,848	15.1	81	15
	Cris Carter, Minnesota[2]	122	1,371	11.2	60	17
	Isaac Bruce, St. Louis	119	1,781	15.0	72	13
	Michael Irvin, Dallas	111	1,603	14.4	50	10
	Brett Perriman, Detroit	108	1,488	13.8	91	9
	Eric Metcalf, Atlanta	104	1,189	11.4	62	8
	Robert Brooks, Green Bay	102	1,497	14.7	99	13
	Larry Centers, Arizona	101	962	9.5	32	2
1994	Cris Carter, Minnesota	122	1,256	10.3	65	7
	Jerry Rice, San Francisco[2]	112	1,499	13.4	69	13
	Terance Mathis, Atlanta	111	1,342	12.1	81	11
1993	Sterling Sharpe, Green Bay[2]	112	1,274	11.4	54	11
1992	Sterling Sharpe, Green Bay	108	1,461	13.5	76	13
1991	Haywood Jeffires, Houston	100	1,181	11.8	44	7
1990	Jerry Rice, San Francisco	100	1,502	15.0	64	13
1984	Art Monk, Washington	106	1,372	12.9	72	7
1964	Charley Hennigan, Houston	101	1,546	15.3	53	8
1961	Lionel Taylor, Denver	100	1,176	11.8	52	4

1,000 YARDS PASS RECEIVING IN A SEASON

Year	Player, Team	No.	Yards	Avg.	Long	TD
2007	Reggie Wayne, Indianapolis[4]	104	1,510	14.5	64	10
	Randy Moss, New England[8]	98	1,493	15.2	65	23
	Chad Johnson, Cincinnati[6]	93	1,440	15.5	70	8
	Larry Fitzgerald, Arizona[2]	100	1,409	14.1	48	10
	Terrell Owens, Dallas[8]	81	1,355	16.7	52	15
	Brandon Marshall, Denver	102	1,325	13.0	68	7
	Braylon Edwards, Cleveland	80	1,289	16.1	78	16
	Marques Colston, New Orleans[2]	98	1,202	12.3	45	11

Year	Player, Team	No.	Yards	Avg.	Long	TD
	Roddy White, Atlanta	83	1,202	14.5	69	6
	Torry Holt, St. Louis[8]	93	1,189	12.8	40	7
	Wes Welker, New England	112	1,175	10.5	42	8
	Tony Gonzalez, Kansas City[3]	99	1,172	11.8	31	5
	Bobby Engram, Seattle	94	1,147	12.2	49	6
	Jason Witten, Dallas	96	1,145	11.9	53	7
	T.J. Houshmandzadeh, Cincinnati[2]	112	1,143	10.2	42	12
	Jerricho Cotchery, N.Y. Jets	82	1,130	13.8	50	2
	Kevin Curtis, Philadelphia	77	1,110	14.4	75	6
	Kellen Winslow, Cleveland	82	1,106	13.5	49	5
	Derrick Mason, Baltimore[6]	103	1,087	10.6	79	5
	Donald Driver, Green Bay[5]	82	1,048	12.8	47	2
	Plaxico Burress, N.Y. Giants[4]	70	1,025	14.6	60	12
	Joey Galloway, Tampa Bay[6]	57	1,014	17.8	69	6
	Steve Smith, Carolina[4]	87	1,002	11.5	74	7
2006	Chad Johnson, Cincinnati[5]	87	1,369	15.7	74	7
	Marvin Harrison, Indianapolis[8]	95	1,366	14.4	68	12
	Reggie Wayne, Indianapolis[3]	86	1,310	15.2	51	9
	Roy Williams, Detroit	82	1,310	16.0	60	7
	Donald Driver, Green Bay[4]	92	1,295	14.1	82	8
	Lee Evans, Buffalo	82	1,292	15.8	83	8
	Anquan Boldin, Arizona[3]	83	1,203	14.5	64	4
	Torry Holt, St. Louis[7]	93	1,188	12.8	67	10
	Terrell Owens, Dallas[7]	85	1,180	13.9	56	13
	Steve Smith, Carolina[3]	83	1,166	14.1	72	8
	Andre Johnson, Houston[2]	103	1,147	11.1	53	5
	Isaac Bruce, St. Louis[8]	74	1,098	14.8	45	3
	Laveranues Coles, N.Y. Jets[2]	91	1,098	12.1	58	6
	Mike Furrey, Detroit	98	1,086	11.1	31	6
	Javon Walker, Denver[2]	69	1,084	15.7	83	8
	T.J. Houshmandzadeh, Cincinnati	90	1,081	12.0	40	9
	Joey Galloway, Tampa Bay[5]	62	1,057	17.1	64	7
	Terry Glenn, Dallas[4]	70	1,047	15.0	54	6
	*Marques Colston, New Orleans	70	1,038	14.8	86	8
2005	Steve Smith, Carolina[2]	103	1,563	15.2	80	12
	Santana Moss, Washington[2]	84	1,483	17.7	78	9
	Chad Johnson, Cincinnati[4]	97	1,432	14.8	70	9
	Larry Fitzgerald, Arizona	103	1,409	13.7	47	10
	Anquan Boldin, Arizona[2]	102	1,402	13.7	54	7
	Torry Holt, St. Louis[6]	102	1,331	13.0	44	9
	Joey Galloway, Tampa Bay[4]	83	1,287	15.5	80	10
	Donald Driver, Green Bay[3]	86	1,221	14.2	59	5
	Plaxico Burress, N.Y. Giants[3]	76	1,214	16.0	78	7
	Marvin Harrison, Indianapolis[7]	82	1,146	14.0	80	12
	Terry Glenn, Dallas[3]	62	1,136	18.3	71	7
	Chris Chambers, Miami	82	1,118	13.6	77	11
	Rod Smith, Denver[6]	85	1,105	13.0	72	6
	Eddie Kennison, Kansas City[2]	68	1,102	16.2	55	5
	Antonio Gates, San Diego	89	1,101	12.4	38	10
	Derrick Mason, Baltimore[5]	86	1,073	12.5	39	3
	Reggie Wayne, Indianapolis[2]	83	1,055	12.7	66	5
	Jimmy Smith, Jacksonville[9]	70	1,023	14.6	45	6
	Antonio Bryant, Cleveland	69	1,009	14.6	54	4
	Randy Moss, Oakland[7]	60	1,005	16.8	79	8
2004	Muhsin Muhammad, Carolina[3]	93	1,405	15.1	51	16
	Joe Horn, New Orleans[4]	94	1,399	14.9	57	11
	Javon Walker, Green Bay	89	1,382	15.5	79	12
	Torry Holt, St. Louis[5]	94	1,372	14.6	75	10
	Isaac Bruce, St. Louis[7]	89	1,292	14.5	56	6
	Chad Johnson, Cincinnati[3]	95	1,274	13.4	53	9
	Tony Gonzalez, Kansas City[2]	102	1,258	12.3	32	7
	Drew Bennett, Tennessee	80	1,247	15.6	48	11
	Reggie Wayne, Indianapolis	77	1,210	15.7	71	12
	Donald Driver, Green Bay[2]	84	1,208	14.4	50	9
	Terrell Owens, Philadelphia[6]	77	1,200	15.6	59	14
	Darrell Jackson, Seattle[3]	87	1,199	13.8	56	7
	*Michael Clayton, Tampa Bay	80	1,193	14.9	75	7
	Jimmy Smith, Jacksonville[8]	74	1,172	15.8	65	6
	Derrick Mason, Tennessee[4]	96	1,168	12.2	37	7

Year	Player, Team	No.	Yards	Avg.	Long	TD
	Rod Smith, Denver[7]	79	1,144	14.5	85	7
	Andre Johnson, Houston	79	1,142	14.5	54	6
	Marvin Harrison, Indianapolis[6]	86	1,113	12.9	59	15
	Eddie Kennison, Kansas City	62	1,086	17.5	70	8
	Ashley Lelie, Denver	54	1,084	20.1	58	7
	Brandon Stokley, Indianapolis	68	1,077	15.8	69	10
	Eric Moulds, Buffalo[4]	88	1,043	11.9	49	5
	Nate Burleson, Minnesota	68	1,006	14.8	68	9
	Hines Ward, Pittsburgh[4]	80	1,004	12.6	58	4
2003	Torry Holt, St. Louis[4]	117	1,696	14.5	48	12
	Randy Moss, Minnesota[6]	111	1,632	14.7	72	17
	*Anquan Boldin, Arizona	101	1,377	13.6	71	8
	Chad Johnson, Cincinnati[2]	90	1,355	15.1	82	10
	Derrick Mason, Tennessee[3]	95	1,303	13.7	50	8
	Marvin Harrison, Indianapolis[5]	94	1,272	13.5	79	10
	Laveranues Coles, Washington[2]	82	1,204	14.7	64	6
	Keenan McCardell, Tampa Bay[5]	84	1,174	14.0	76	8
	Hines Ward, Pittsburgh[3]	95	1,163	12.2	50	10
	Darrell Jackson, Seattle[2]	68	1,137	16.7	80	9
	Steve Smith, Carolina	88	1,110	12.6	67	7
	Santana Moss, N.Y. Jets	74	1,105	14.9	65	10
	Terrell Owens, San Francisco[5]	80	1,102	13.8	75	9
	Amani Toomer, N.Y. Giants[5]	63	1,057	16.8	77	5
2002	Marvin Harrison, Indianapolis[4]	143	1,722	12.0	69	11
	Randy Moss, Minnesota[5]	106	1,347	12.7	60	7
	Amani Toomer, N.Y. Giants[4]	82	1,343	16.4	82	8
	Hines Ward, Pittsburgh[2]	112	1,329	11.9	72	12
	Plaxico Burress, Pittsburgh[2]	78	1,325	17.0	62	7
	Joe Horn, New Orleans[3]	88	1,312	14.9	63	7
	Torry Holt, St. Louis[3]	91	1,302	14.3	58	4
	Terrell Owens, San Francisco[4]	100	1,300	13.0	76	13
	Eric Moulds, Buffalo[3]	100	1,292	12.9	70	10
	Laveranues Coles, N.Y. Jets[2]	89	1,264	14.2	43	5
	Peerless Price, Buffalo	94	1,252	13.3	73	9
	Koren Robinson, Seattle	78	1,240	15.9	83	5
	Jerry Rice, Oakland[14]	92	1,211	13.2	75	7
	Marty Booker, Chicago[2]	97	1,189	12.3	54	6
	Chad Johnson, Cincinnati	69	1,166	16.9	72	5
	Keyshawn Johnson, Tampa Bay[4]	76	1,088	14.3	76	5
	Isaac Bruce, St. Louis[6]	79	1,075	13.6	34	7
	Donald Driver, Green Bay	70	1,064	15.2	85	9
	Jimmy Smith, Jacksonville[7]	80	1,027	12.8	47	7
	Rod Smith, Denver[6]	89	1,027	11.5	46	5
	Derrick Mason, Tennessee[2]	79	1,012	12.8	40	5
	Rod Gardner, Washington	71	1,006	14.2	43	8
2001	David Boston, Arizona[2]	98	1,598	16.3	61	8
	Marvin Harrison, Indianapolis[3]	109	1,524	14.0	68	15
	Terrell Owens, San Francisco[3]	93	1,412	15.2	60	16
	Jimmy Smith, Jacksonville[6]	112	1,373	12.3	35	8
	Torry Holt, St. Louis[2]	81	1,363	16.8	51	7
	Rod Smith, Denver[5]	113	1,343	11.9	65	11
	Keyshawn Johnson, Tampa Bay[3]	106	1,266	11.9	47	1
	Joe Horn, New Orleans[2]	83	1,265	15.2	56	9
	Randy Moss, Minnesota[4]	82	1,233	15.0	73	10
	Troy Brown, New England	101	1,199	11.9	60	5
	Tim Brown, Oakland[9]	91	1,165	12.8	46	9
	Johnnie Morton, Detroit[4]	77	1,154	15.0	76	4
	Jerry Rice, Oakland[13]	83	1,139	13.7	40	9
	Derrick Mason, Tennessee	73	1,128	15.5	71	9
	Curtis Conway, San Diego[3]	71	1,125	15.8	72	6
	Keenan McCardell, Jacksonville[4]	93	1,110	11.9	45	6
	Isaac Bruce, St. Louis[5]	64	1,106	17.3	51	6
	Kevin Johnson, Cleveland	84	1,097	13.1	55	9
	Darrell Jackson, Seattle	70	1,081	15.4	64	8
	Marty Booker, Chicago	100	1,071	10.7	66	8
	Qadry Ismail, Baltimore[2]	74	1,059	14.3	77	7
	Amani Toomer, N.Y. Giants[3]	72	1,054	14.6	60	5
	Willie Jackson, New Orleans	81	1,046	12.9	63	5
	Plaxico Burress, Pittsburgh	66	1,008	15.3	43	6

Year	Player, Team	No.	Yards	Avg.	Long	TD
	Hines Ward, Pittsburgh	94	1,003	10.7	34	4
2000	Torry Holt, St. Louis	82	1,635	19.9	85	6
	Rod Smith, Denver[4]	100	1,602	16.0	49	8
	Isaac Bruce, St. Louis[4]	87	1,471	16.9	78	9
	Terrell Owens, San Francisco[2]	97	1,451	15.0	69	13
	Randy Moss, Minnesota[3]	77	1,437	18.7	78	15
	Marvin Harrison, Indianapolis[2]	102	1,413	13.9	78	14
	Derrick Alexander, Kansas City[3]	78	1,391	17.8	81	10
	Joe Horn, New Orleans	94	1,340	14.3	52	8
	Eric Moulds, Buffalo[2]	94	1,326	14.1	52	5
	Ed McCaffrey, Denver[3]	101	1,317	13.0	61	9
	Cris Carter, Minnesota[8]	96	1,274	13.3	53	9
	Jimmy Smith, Jacksonville[5]	91	1,213	13.3	65	8
	Keenan McCardell, Jacksonville[3]	94	1,207	12.8	67	5
	Tony Gonzalez, Kansas City	93	1,203	12.9	39	9
	Muhsin Muhammad, Carolina[2]	102	1,183	11.6	36	6
	David Boston, Arizona	71	1,156	16.3	70	7
	Tim Brown, Oakland[8]	76	1,128	14.8	45	11
	Amani Toomer, N.Y. Giants[2]	78	1,094	14.0	54	7
1999	Marvin Harrison, Indianapolis	115	1,663	14.5	57	12
	Jimmy Smith, Jacksonville[4]	116	1,636	14.1	62	6
	Randy Moss, Minnesota[2]	80	1,413	17.7	67	11
	Marcus Robinson, Chicago	84	1,400	16.7	80	9
	Tim Brown, Oakland[7]	90	1,344	14.9	47	6
	Germane Crowell, Detroit	81	1,338	16.5	77	7
	Muhsin Muhammad, Carolina	96	1,253	13.1	60	8
	Cris Carter, Minnesota[7]	90	1,241	13.8	68	13
	Michael Westbrook, Washington	65	1,191	18.3	65	9
	Amani Toomer, N.Y. Giants	79	1,183	15.0	80	6
	Keyshawn Johnson, N.Y. Jets[2]	89	1,170	13.2	65	8
	Isaac Bruce, St. Louis[3]	77	1,165	15.1	60	12
	Terry Glenn, New England[2]	69	1,147	16.6	67	4
	Albert Connell, Washington	62	1,132	18.3	62	7
	Johnnie Morton, Detroit[3]	80	1,129	14.1	48	5
	Qadry Ismail, Baltimore	68	1,105	16.3	76	6
	Raghib Ismail, Dallas[2]	80	1,097	13.7	76	6
	Patrick Jeffers, Carolina	63	1,082	17.2	88	12
	Antonio Freeman, Green Bay[3]	74	1,074	14.5	51	6
	Bill Schroeder, Green Bay	74	1,051	14.2	51	5
	Marshall Faulk, St. Louis	87	1,048	12.1	57	5
	Tony Martin, Miami[4]	67	1,037	15.5	69	5
	Darnay Scott, Cincinnati	68	1,022	15.0	76	7
	Rod Smith, Denver[3]	79	1,020	12.9	71	4
	Ed McCaffrey, Denver[2]	71	1,018	14.3	78	7
	Terance Mathis, Atlanta[4]	81	1,016	12.5	52	6
1998	Antonio Freeman, Green Bay[2]	84	1,424	17.0	84	14
	Eric Moulds, Buffalo	67	1,368	20.4	84	9
	*Randy Moss, Minnesota	69	1,313	19.0	61	17
	Rod Smith, Denver[2]	86	1,222	14.2	58	6
	Jimmy Smith, Jacksonville[3]	78	1,182	15.2	72	8
	Tony Martin, Atlanta[3]	66	1,181	17.9	62	6
	Jerry Rice, San Francisco[12]	82	1,157	14.1	75	9
	Frank Sanders, Arizona[2]	89	1,145	12.9	42	3
	Terance Mathis, Atlanta[3]	64	1,136	17.8	78	11
	Keyshawn Johnson, N.Y. Jets	83	1,131	13.6	41	10
	Terrell Owens, San Francisco	67	1,097	16.4	79	14
	Wayne Chrebet, N.Y. Jets	75	1,083	14.4	63	8
	Michael Irvin, Dallas[7]	74	1,057	14.3	51	1
	Ed McCaffrey, Denver	64	1,053	16.5	48	10
	O.J. McDuffie, Miami	90	1,050	11.7	61	7
	Joey Galloway, Seattle[3]	65	1,047	16.1	81	10
	Johnnie Morton, Detroit[2]	69	1,028	14.9	98	2
	Raghib Ismail, Carolina	69	1,024	14.8	62	8
	Carl Pickens, Cincinnati[4]	82	1,023	12.5	67	5
	Tim Brown, Oakland[6]	81	1,012	12.5	49	9
	Cris Carter, Minnesota[6]	78	1,011	13.0	54	12
1997	Rob Moore, Arizona[3]	97	1,584	16.3	47	8
	Tim Brown, Oakland[5]	104	1,408	13.5	59	5
	Yancey Thigpen, Pittsburgh[2]	79	1,398	17.7	69	7

Year	Player, Team	No.	Yards	Avg.	Long	TD
	Jimmy Smith, Jacksonville[2]	82	1,324	16.1	75	4
	Irving Fryar, Philadelphia[5]	86	1,316	15.3	72	6
	Herman Moore, Detroit[4]	104	1,293	12.4	79	8
	Antonio Freeman, Green Bay	81	1,243	15.3	58	12
	Michael Irvin, Dallas[6]	75	1,180	15.7	55	9
	Rod Smith, Denver	70	1,180	16.9	78	12
	Keenan McCardell, Jacksonville[2]	85	1,164	13.7	60	5
	Jake Reed, Minnesota[4]	68	1,138	16.7	56	6
	Shannon Sharpe, Denver[3]	72	1,107	15.4	68	3
	Andre Rison, Kansas City[5]	72	1,092	15.2	45	7
	Cris Carter, Minnesota[5]	89	1,069	12.0	43	13
	Johnnie Morton, Detroit	80	1,057	13.2	73	6
	Joey Galloway, Seattle[2]	72	1,049	14.6	53	12
	Frank Sanders, Arizona	75	1,017	13.6	70	4
	Robert Brooks, Green Bay[2]	60	1,010	16.8	48	7
	Derrick Alexander, Baltimore[2]	65	1,009	15.5	92	9
1996	Isaac Bruce, St. Louis[2]	84	1,338	15.9	70	7
	Jake Reed, Minnesota[3]	72	1,320	18.3	82	7
	Herman Moore, Detroit[3]	106	1,296	12.2	50	9
	Jerry Rice, San Francisco[11]	108	1,254	11.6	39	8
	Jimmy Smith, Jacksonville	83	1,244	15.0	62	7
	Michael Jackson, Baltimore	76	1,201	15.8	86	14
	Irving Fryar, Philadelphia[4]	88	1,195	13.6	42	11
	Carl Pickens, Cincinnati[3]	100	1,180	11.8	61	12
	Tony Martin, San Diego[2]	85	1,171	13.8	55	14
	Cris Carter, Minnesota[4]	96	1,163	12.1	43	10
	*Terry Glenn, New England	90	1,132	12.6	37	6
	Keenan McCardell, Jacksonville	85	1,129	13.3	52	3
	Tim Brown, Oakland[4]	90	1,104	12.3	42	9
	Derrick Alexander, Baltimore	62	1,099	17.7	64	9
	Shannon Sharpe, Denver[2]	80	1,062	13.3	51	10
	Curtis Conway, Chicago[2]	81	1,049	13.0	58	7
	Andre Reed, Buffalo[4]	66	1,036	15.7	67	6
	Brett Perriman, Detroit[2]	94	1,021	10.9	44	5
	Rob Moore, Arizona[2]	58	1,016	17.5	69	4
	Henry Ellard, Washington[7]	52	1,014	19.5	51	2
	Charles Johnson, Pittsburgh	60	1,008	16.8	70	3
1995	Jerry Rice, San Francisco[10]	122	1,848	15.1	81	15
	Isaac Bruce, St. Louis	119	1,781	15.0	72	13
	Herman Moore, Detroit[2]	123	1,686	13.7	69	14
	Michael Irvin, Dallas[5]	111	1,603	14.4	50	10
	Robert Brooks, Green Bay	102	1,497	14.7	99	13
	Brett Perriman, Detroit	108	1,488	13.8	91	9
	Cris Carter, Minnesota[3]	122	1,371	11.2	60	17
	Tim Brown, Oakland[3]	89	1,342	15.1	80	10
	Yancey Thigpen, Pittsburgh	85	1,307	15.4	43	5
	Jeff Graham, Chicago	82	1,301	15.9	51	4
	Carl Pickens, Cincinnati[2]	99	1,234	12.5	68	17
	Tony Martin, San Diego	90	1,224	13.6	51	6
	Eric Metcalf, Atlanta	104	1,189	11.4	62	8
	Jake Reed, Minnesota[2]	72	1,167	16.2	55	9
	Quinn Early, New Orleans	81	1,087	13.4	70	8
	Anthony Miller, Denver[5]	59	1,079	18.3	62	14
	Bert Emanuel, Atlanta	74	1,039	14.0	52	5
	*Joey Galloway, Seattle	67	1,039	15.5	59	7
	Terance Mathis, Atlanta[2]	78	1,039	13.3	54	9
	Curtis Conway, Chicago	62	1,037	16.7	76	12
	Henry Ellard, Washington[6]	56	1,005	17.9	59	5
	Mark Carrier, Carolina[2]	66	1,002	15.2	66	3
	Brian Blades, Seattle[4]	77	1,001	13.0	49	4
1994	Jerry Rice, San Francisco[9]	112	1,499	13.4	69	13
	Henry Ellard, Washington[5]	74	1,397	18.9	73	6
	Terance Mathis, Atlanta	111	1,342	12.1	81	11
	Tim Brown, L.A. Raiders[2]	89	1,309	14.7	77	9
	Andre Reed, Buffalo[2]	90	1,303	14.5	83	8
	Irving Fryar, Miami[3]	73	1,270	17.4	54	7
	Cris Carter, Minnesota[2]	122	1,256	10.3	65	7
	Michael Irvin, Dallas[4]	79	1,241	15.7	65	6
	Jake Reed, Minnesota	85	1,175	13.8	59	4

Year	Player, Team	No.	Yards	Avg.	Long	TD
	Ben Coates, New England	96	1,174	12.2	62	7
	Herman Moore, Detroit	72	1,173	16.3	51	11
	Fred Barnett, Philadelphia[2]	78	1,127	14.4	54	5
	Carl Pickens, Cincinnati	71	1,127	15.9	70	11
	Sterling Sharpe, Green Bay[4]	94	1,119	11.9	49	18
	Anthony Miller, Denver[4]	60	1,107	18.5	76	5
	Andre Rison, Atlanta[3]	81	1,088	13.4	69	8
	Brian Blades, Seattle[3]	81	1,088	13.4	45	4
	Rob Moore, N.Y. Jets	78	1,010	12.9	41	6
	Shannon Sharpe, Denver	87	1,010	11.6	44	4
1993	Jerry Rice, San Francisco[8]	98	1,503	15.3	80	15
	Michael Irvin, Dallas[3]	88	1,330	15.1	61	7
	Sterling Sharpe, Green Bay[4]	112	1,274	11.4	54	11
	Andre Rison, Atlanta[3]	86	1,242	14.4	53	15
	Tim Brown, L.A. Raiders	80	1,180	14.8	71	7
	Anthony Miller, San Diego[3]	84	1,162	13.8	66	7
	Cris Carter, Minnesota	86	1,071	12.5	58	9
	Reggie Langhorne, Indianapolis	85	1,038	12.2	72	3
	Irving Fryar, Miami[2]	64	1,010	15.8	65	5
1992	Sterling Sharpe, Green Bay[3]	108	1,461	13.5	76	13
	Michael Irvin, Dallas[2]	78	1,396	17.9	87	7
	Jerry Rice, San Francisco[7]	84	1,201	14.3	80	10
	Andre Rison, Atlanta[2]	93	1,119	12.0	71	11
	Fred Barnett, Philadelphia	67	1,083	16.2	71	6
	Anthony Miller, San Diego[2]	72	1,060	14.7	67	7
	Eric Martin, New Orleans[3]	68	1,041	15.3	52	5
1991	Michael Irvin, Dallas	93	1,523	16.4	66	8
	Gary Clark, Washington[5]	70	1,340	19.1	82	10
	Jerry Rice, San Francisco[6]	80	1,206	15.1	73	14
	Haywood Jeffires, Houston[2]	100	1,181	11.8	44	7
	Michael Haynes, Atlanta	50	1,122	22.4	80	11
	Andre Reed, Buffalo[2]	81	1,113	13.7	55	10
	Drew Hill, Houston[5]	90	1,109	12.3	61	4
	Mark Duper, Miami[4]	70	1,085	15.5	43	5
	James Lofton, Buffalo[6]	57	1,072	18.8	77	8
	Mark Clayton, Miami[5]	70	1,053	15.0	43	12
	Henry Ellard, L.A. Rams[4]	64	1,052	16.4	38	3
	Art Monk, Washington[5]	71	1,049	14.8	64	8
	Irving Fryar, New England	68	1,014	14.9	56	3
	John Taylor, San Francisco[2]	64	1,011	15.8	97	9
	Brian Blades, Seattle[2]	70	1,003	14.3	52	2
1990	Jerry Rice, San Francisco[5]	100	1,502	15.0	64	13
	Henry Ellard, L.A. Rams[3]	76	1,294	17.0	50	4
	Andre Rison, Atlanta	82	1,208	14.7	75	10
	Gary Clark, Washington[4]	75	1,112	14.8	53	8
	Sterling Sharpe, Green Bay[2]	67	1,105	16.5	76	6
	Willie Anderson, L.A. Rams[2]	51	1,097	21.5	55	4
	Haywood Jeffires, Houston	74	1,048	14.2	87	8
	Stephone Paige, Kansas City	65	1,021	15.7	86	5
	Drew Hill, Houston[4]	74	1,019	13.8	57	5
	Anthony Carter, Minnesota[3]	70	1,008	14.4	56	8
1989	Jerry Rice, San Francisco[4]	82	1,483	18.1	68	17
	Sterling Sharpe, Green Bay	90	1,423	15.8	79	12
	Mark Carrier, Tampa Bay	86	1,422	16.5	78	9
	Henry Ellard, L.A. Rams[2]	70	1,382	19.7	53	8
	Andre Reed, Buffalo	88	1,312	14.9	78	9
	Anthony Miller, San Diego	75	1,252	16.7	69	10
	Webster Slaughter, Cleveland	65	1,236	19.0	97	6
	Gary Clark, Washington[3]	79	1,229	15.6	80	9
	Tim McGee, Cincinnati	65	1,211	18.6	74	8
	Art Monk, Washington[4]	86	1,186	13.8	60	8
	Willie Anderson, L.A. Rams	44	1,146	26.0	78	5
	Ricky Sanders, Washington[2]	80	1,138	14.2	68	4
	Vance Johnson, Denver	76	1,095	14.4	69	7
	Richard Johnson, Detroit	70	1,091	15.6	75	8
	Eric Martin, New Orleans[2]	68	1,090	16.0	53	8
	John Taylor, San Francisco	60	1,077	18.0	95	10
	Mervyn Fernandez, L.A. Raiders	57	1,069	18.8	75	9
	Anthony Carter, Minnesota[2]	65	1,066	16.4	50	4

Year	Player, Team	No.	Yards	Avg.	Long	TD
	Brian Blades, Seattle	77	1,063	13.8	60	5
	Mark Clayton, Miami[4]	64	1,011	15.8	78	9
1988	Henry Ellard, L.A. Rams	86	1,414	16.4	68	10
	Jerry Rice, San Francisco[3]	64	1,306	20.4	96	9
	Eddie Brown, Cincinnati	53	1,273	24.0	86	9
	Anthony Carter, Minnesota	72	1,225	17.0	67	6
	Ricky Sanders, Washington	73	1,148	15.7	55	12
	Drew Hill, Houston[3]	72	1,141	15.8	57	10
	Mark Clayton, Miami[3]	86	1,129	13.1	45	14
	Roy Green, Phoenix[3]	68	1,097	16.1	52	7
	Eric Martin, New Orleans	85	1,083	12.7	40	7
	Al Toon, N.Y. Jets[2]	93	1,067	11.5	42	5
	Bruce Hill, Tampa Bay	58	1,040	17.9	42	9
	Lionel Manuel, N.Y. Giants	65	1,029	15.8	46	4
1987	J.T. Smith, St. Louis[2]	91	1,117	12.3	38	8
	Jerry Rice, San Francisco[2]	65	1,078	16.6	57	22
	Gary Clark, Washington[2]	56	1,066	19.0	84	7
	Carlos Carson, Kansas City[3]	55	1,044	19.0	81	7
1986	Jerry Rice, San Francisco	86	1,570	18.3	66	15
	Stanley Morgan, New England[3]	84	1,491	17.8	44	10
	Mark Duper, Miami[3]	67	1,313	19.6	85	11
	Gary Clark, Washington	74	1,265	17.1	55	7
	Al Toon, N.Y. Jets	85	1,176	13.8	62	8
	Todd Christensen, L.A. Raiders[3]	95	1,153	12.1	35	8
	Mark Clayton, Miami[2]	60	1,150	19.2	68	10
	*Bill Brooks, Indianapolis	65	1,131	17.4	84	8
	Drew Hill, Houston[2]	65	1,112	17.1	81	5
	Steve Largent, Seattle[8]	70	1,070	15.3	38	9
	Art Monk, Washington[3]	73	1,068	14.6	69	4
	*Ernest Givins, Houston	61	1,062	17.4	60	3
	Cris Collinsworth, Cincinnati[4]	62	1,024	16.5	46	10
	Wesley Walker, N.Y. Jets[2]	49	1,016	20.7	83	12
	J.T. Smith, St. Louis	80	1,014	12.7	45	6
	Mark Bavaro, N.Y. Giants	66	1,001	15.2	41	4
1985	Steve Largent, Seattle[7]	79	1,287	16.3	43	6
	Mike Quick, Philadelphia[3]	73	1,247	17.1	99	11
	Art Monk, Washington[2]	91	1,226	13.5	53	2
	Wes Chandler, San Diego[4]	67	1,199	17.9	75	10
	Drew Hill, Houston	64	1,169	18.3	57	9
	James Lofton, Green Bay[5]	69	1,153	16.7	56	4
	Louis Lipps, Pittsburgh	59	1,134	19.2	51	12
	Cris Collinsworth, Cincinnati[3]	65	1,125	17.3	71	5
	Tony Hill, Dallas[3]	74	1,113	15.0	53	7
	Lionel James, San Diego	86	1,027	11.9	67	6
	Roger Craig, San Francisco	92	1,016	11.0	73	6
1984	Roy Green, St. Louis[2]	78	1,555	19.9	83	12
	John Stallworth, Pittsburgh[3]	80	1,395	17.4	51	11
	Mark Clayton, Miami	73	1,389	19.0	65	18
	Art Monk, Washington	106	1,372	12.9	72	7
	James Lofton, Green Bay[4]	62	1,361	22.0	79	7
	Mark Duper, Miami[2]	71	1,306	18.4	80	8
	Steve Watson, Denver[3]	69	1,170	17.0	73	7
	Steve Largent, Seattle[6]	74	1,164	15.7	65	12
	Tim Smith, Houston[2]	69	1,141	16.5	75	4
	Stacey Bailey, Atlanta	67	1,138	17.0	61	6
	Carlos Carson, Kansas City[2]	57	1,078	18.9	57	4
	Mike Quick, Philadelphia[2]	61	1,052	17.2	90	9
	Todd Christensen, L.A. Raiders[2]	80	1,007	12.6	38	7
	Kevin House, Tampa Bay[2]	76	1,005	13.2	55	5
	Ozzie Newsome, Cleveland[2]	89	1,001	11.2	52	5
1983	Mike Quick, Philadelphia	69	1,409	20.4	83	13
	Carlos Carson, Kansas City	80	1,351	16.9	50	7
	James Lofton, Green Bay[3]	58	1,300	22.4	74	8
	Todd Christensen, L.A. Raiders	92	1,247	13.6	45	12
	Roy Green, St. Louis	78	1,227	15.7	71	14
	Charlie Brown, Washington	78	1,225	15.7	75	8
	Tim Smith, Houston	83	1,176	14.2	47	6
	Kellen Winslow, San Diego[3]	88	1,172	13.3	46	8
	Earnest Gray, N.Y. Giants	78	1,139	14.6	62	5

Year	Player, Team	No.	Yards	Avg.	Long	TD
	Steve Watson, Denver[2]	59	1,133	19.2	78	5
	Cris Collinsworth, Cincinnati[2]	66	1,130	17.1	63	5
	Steve Largent, Seattle[5]	72	1,074	14.9	46	11
	Mark Duper, Miami	51	1,003	19.7	85	10
1982	Wes Chandler, San Diego[3]	49	1,032	21.1	66	9
1981	Alfred Jenkins, Atlanta[2]	70	1,358	19.4	67	13
	James Lofton, Green Bay[2]	71	1,294	18.2	75	8
	Steve Watson, Denver	60	1,244	20.7	95	13
	Frank Lewis, Buffalo[2]	70	1,244	17.8	33	4
	Steve Largent, Seattle[4]	75	1,224	16.3	57	9
	Charlie Joiner, San Diego[4]	70	1,188	17.0	57	7
	Kevin House, Tampa Bay	56	1,176	21.0	84	9
	Wes Chandler, N.O.-San Diego[2]	69	1,142	16.6	51	6
	Dwight Clark, San Francisco	85	1,105	13.0	78	4
	John Stallworth, Pittsburgh[2]	63	1,098	17.4	55	5
	Kellen Winslow, San Diego[2]	88	1,075	12.2	67	10
	Pat Tilley, St. Louis	66	1,040	15.8	75	3
	Stanley Morgan, New England[2]	44	1,029	23.4	76	6
	Harold Carmichael, Philadelphia[3]	61	1,028	16.9	85	6
	Freddie Scott, Detroit	53	1,022	19.3	48	5
	*Cris Collinsworth, Cincinnati	67	1,009	15.1	74	8
	Joe Senser, Minnesota	79	1,004	12.7	53	8
	Ozzie Newsome, Cleveland	69	1,002	14.5	62	6
	Sammy White, Minnesota	66	1,001	15.2	53	3
1980	John Jefferson, San Diego[3]	82	1,340	16.3	58	13
	Kellen Winslow, San Diego	89	1,290	14.5	65	9
	James Lofton, Green Bay	71	1,226	17.3	47	4
	Charlie Joiner, San Diego[3]	71	1,132	15.9	51	4
	Ahmad Rashad, Minnesota[2]	69	1,095	15.9	76	5
	Steve Largent, Seattle[3]	66	1,064	16.1	67	6
	Tony Hill, Dallas[2]	60	1,055	17.6	58	8
	Alfred Jenkins, Atlanta	57	1,026	18.0	57	6
1979	Steve Largent, Seattle[2]	66	1,237	18.7	55	8
	John Stallworth, Pittsburgh	70	1,183	16.9	65	8
	Ahmad Rashad, Minnesota	80	1,156	14.5	52	9
	John Jefferson, San Diego[2]	61	1,090	17.9	65	10
	Frank Lewis, Buffalo	54	1,082	20.0	55	2
	Wes Chandler, New Orleans	65	1,069	16.4	85	6
	Tony Hill, Dallas	60	1,062	17.7	75	10
	Drew Pearson, Dallas[2]	55	1,026	18.7	56	8
	Wallace Francis, Atlanta	74	1,013	13.7	42	8
	Harold Jackson, New England[3]	45	1,013	22.5	59	7
	Charlie Joiner, San Diego[2]	72	1,008	14.0	39	4
	Stanley Morgan, New England	44	1,002	22.8	63	12
1978	Wesley Walker, N.Y. Jets	48	1,169	24.4	77	8
	Steve Largent, Seattle	71	1,168	16.5	57	8
	Harold Carmichael, Philadelphia[2]	55	1,072	19.5	56	8
	*John Jefferson, San Diego	56	1,001	17.9	46	13
1976	Roger Carr, Baltimore	43	1,112	25.9	79	11
	Cliff Branch, Oakland[2]	46	1,111	24.2	88	12
	Charlie Joiner, San Diego	50	1,056	21.1	81	7
1975	Ken Burrough, Houston	53	1,063	20.1	77	8
1974	Cliff Branch, Oakland	60	1,092	18.2	67	13
	Drew Pearson, Dallas	62	1,087	17.5	50	2
1973	Harold Carmichael, Philadelphia	67	1,116	16.7	73	9
1972	Harold Jackson, Philadelphia[2]	62	1,048	16.9	77	4
	John Gilliam, Minnesota	47	1,035	22.0	66	7
1971	Otis Taylor, Kansas City[2]	57	1,110	19.5	82	7
1970	Gene Washington, San Francisco	53	1,100	20.8	79	12
	Marlin Briscoe, Buffalo	57	1,036	18.2	48	8
	Dick Gordon, Chicago	71	1,026	14.5	69	13
	Gary Garrison, San Diego[2]	44	1,006	22.9	67	12
1969	Warren Wells, Oakland[2]	47	1,260	26.8	80	14
	Harold Jackson, Philadelphia	65	1,116	17.2	65	9
	Roy Jefferson, Pittsburgh[2]	67	1,079	16.1	63	9
	Dan Abramowicz, New Orleans	73	1,015	13.9	49	7
	Lance Alworth, San Diego[7]	64	1,003	15.7	76	4
1968	Lance Alworth, San Diego[6]	68	1,312	19.3	80	10

Year	Player, Team	No.	Yards	Avg.	Long	TD
	Don Maynard, N.Y. Jets[5]	57	1,297	22.8	87	10
	George Sauer, N.Y. Jets[3]	66	1,141	17.3	43	3
	Warren Wells, Oakland	53	1,137	21.5	94	11
	Gary Garrison, San Diego	52	1,103	21.2	84	10
	Roy Jefferson, Pittsburgh	58	1,074	18.5	62	11
	Paul Warfield, Cleveland	50	1,067	21.3	65	12
	Homer Jones, N.Y. Giants[3]	45	1,057	23.5	84	7
	Fred Biletnikoff, Oakland	61	1,037	17.0	82	6
	Lance Rentzel, Dallas	54	1,009	18.7	65	6
1967	Don Maynard, N.Y. Jets[4]	71	1,434	20.2	75	10
	Ben Hawkins, Philadelphia	59	1,265	21.4	87	10
	Homer Jones, N.Y. Giants[2]	49	1,209	24.7	70	13
	Jackie Smith, St. Louis	56	1,205	21.5	76	9
	George Sauer, N.Y. Jets[2]	75	1,189	15.9	61	6
	Lance Alworth, San Diego[5]	52	1,010	19.4	71	9
1966	Lance Alworth, San Diego[4]	73	1,383	18.9	78	13
	Otis Taylor, Kansas City	58	1,297	22.4	89	8
	Pat Studstill, Detroit	67	1,266	18.9	99	5
	Bob Hayes, Dallas[2]	64	1,232	19.3	95	13
	Charlie Frazier, Houston	57	1,129	19.8	79	12
	Charley Taylor, Washington	72	1,119	15.5	86	12
	George Sauer, N.Y. Jets	63	1,081	17.2	77	5
	Homer Jones, N.Y. Giants	48	1,044	21.8	98	8
	Art Powell, Oakland[5]	53	1,026	19.4	46	11
1965	Lance Alworth, San Diego[3]	69	1,602	23.2	85	14
	Dave Parks, San Francisco	80	1,344	16.8	53	12
	Don Maynard, N.Y. Jets[3]	68	1,218	17.9	56	14
	Pete Retzlaff, Philadelphia	66	1,190	18.0	78	10
	Lionel Taylor, Denver[4]	85	1,131	13.3	63	6
	Tommy McDonald, Los Angeles[3]	67	1,036	15.5	51	9
	*Bob Hayes, Dallas	46	1,003	21.8	82	12
1964	Charley Hennigan, Houston[3]	101	1,546	15.3	53	8
	Art Powell, Oakland[4]	76	1,361	17.9	77	11
	Lance Alworth, San Diego[2]	61	1,235	20.2	82	13
	Johnny Morris, Chicago	93	1,200	12.9	63	10
	Elbert Dubenion, Buffalo	42	1,139	27.1	72	10
	Terry Barr, Detroit[2]	57	1,030	18.1	58	9
1963	Bobby Mitchell, Washington[2]	69	1,436	20.8	99	7
	Art Powell, Oakland[3]	73	1,304	17.9	85	16
	Buddy Dial, Pittsburgh[2]	60	1,295	21.6	83	9
	Lance Alworth, San Diego	61	1,205	19.8	85	11
	Del Shofner, N.Y. Giants[4]	64	1,181	18.5	70	9
	Lionel Taylor, Denver[3]	78	1,101	14.1	72	10
	Terry Barr, Detroit	66	1,086	16.5	75	13
	Charley Hennigan, Houston[2]	61	1,051	17.2	83	10
	Sonny Randle, St. Louis[2]	51	1,014	19.9	68	12
	Bake Turner, N.Y. Jets	71	1,009	14.2	53	6
1962	Bobby Mitchell, Washington	72	1,384	19.2	81	11
	Sonny Randle, St. Louis	63	1,158	18.4	86	7
	Tommy McDonald, Philadelphia[2]	58	1,146	19.8	60	10
	Del Shofner, N.Y. Giants[3]	53	1,133	21.4	69	12
	Art Powell, N.Y. Titans[2]	64	1,130	17.7	80	8
	Frank Clarke, Dall. Cowboys	47	1,043	22.2	66	14
	Don Maynard, N.Y. Titans[2]	56	1,041	18.6	86	8
1961	Charley Hennigan, Houston	82	1,746	21.3	80	12
	Lionel Taylor, Denver[2]	100	1,176	11.8	52	4
	Bill Groman, Houston[2]	50	1,175	23.5	80	17
	Tommy McDonald, Philadelphia	64	1,144	17.9	66	13
	Del Shofner, N.Y. Giants[2]	68	1,125	16.5	46	11
	Jim Phillips, Los Angeles	78	1,092	14.0	69	5
	*Mike Ditka, Chicago	56	1,076	19.2	76	12
	Dave Kocourek, San Diego	55	1,055	19.2	76	4
	Buddy Dial, Pittsburgh	53	1,047	19.8	88	12
	R.C. Owens, San Francisco	55	1,032	18.8	54	5
1960	*Bill Groman, Houston	72	1,473	20.5	92	12
	Raymond Berry, Baltimore	74	1,298	17.5	70	10
	Don Maynard, N.Y. Titans	72	1,265	17.6	65	6
	Lionel Taylor, Denver	92	1,235	13.4	80	12

Year	Player, Team	No.	Yards	Avg.	Long	TD
	Art Powell, N.Y. Titans	69	1,167	16.9	76	14
1958	Del Shofner, Los Angeles	51	1,097	21.5	92	8
1956	Bill Howton, Green Bay[2]	55	1,188	21.6	66	12
	Harlon Hill, Chi. Bears[2]	47	1,128	24.0	79	11
1954	Bob Boyd, Los Angeles	53	1,212	22.9	80	6
	*Harlon Hill, Chi. Bears	45	1,124	25.0	76	12
1953	Pete Pihos, Philadelphia	63	1,049	16.7	59	10
1952	*Bill Howton, Green Bay	53	1,231	23.2	90	13
1951	Elroy (Crazylegs) Hirsch, Los Angeles	66	1,495	22.7	91	17
1950	Tom Fears, Los Angeles[2]	84	1,116	13.3	53	7
	Cloyce Box, Detroit	50	1,009	20.2	82	11
1949	Bob Mann, Detroit	66	1,014	15.4	64	4
	Tom Fears, Los Angeles	77	1,013	13.2	51	9
1945	Jim Benton, Cleveland	45	1,067	23.7	84	8
1942	Don Hutson, Green Bay	74	1,211	16.4	73	17

*First season of professional football.

250 YARDS PASS RECEIVING IN A GAME

Date	Player, Team, Opponent	No.	Yards	TD
Nov. 19, 2006	Lee Evans, Buffalo vs. Houston	11	265	2
Nov. 12, 2006	Chad Johnson, Cincinnati vs. San Diego	11	260	2
Nov. 10, 2002	Plaxico Burress, Pittsburgh vs. Atlanta (OT)	9	253	2
Dec. 17, 2000	Terrell Owens, San Francisco vs. Chicago	20	283	1
Sept. 10, 2000	Jimmy Smith, Jacksonville vs. Baltimore	15	291	3
Dec. 12, 1999	Qadry Ismail, Baltimore vs. Pittsburgh	6	258	3
Dec. 18, 1995	Jerry Rice, San Francisco vs. Minnesota	14	289	3
Dec. 11, 1989	John Taylor, San Francisco vs. L.A. Rams	11	286	2
Nov. 26, 1989	Willie Anderson, L.A. Rams vs. New Orleans (OT)	15	336	1
Oct. 18, 1987	Steve Largent, Seattle vs. Detroit	15	261	3
Oct. 4, 1987	Anthony Allen, Washington vs. St. Louis	7	255	3
Dec. 22, 1985	Stephone Paige, Kansas City vs. San Diego	8	309	2
Dec. 20, 1982	Wes Chandler, San Diego vs. Cincinnati	10	260	2
Sept. 23, 1979	*Jerry Butler, Buffalo vs. N.Y. Jets	10	255	4
Nov. 4, 1962	Sonny Randle, St. Louis vs. N.Y. Giants	16	256	1
Oct. 28, 1962	Del Shofner, N.Y. Giants vs. Washington	11	269	1
Oct. 13, 1961	Charley Hennigan, Houston vs. Boston	13	272	1
Oct. 21, 1956	Billy Howton, Green Bay vs. Los Angeles	7	257	2
Dec. 3, 1950	Cloyce Box, Detroit vs. Baltimore	12	302	4
Nov. 22, 1945	Jim Benton, Cleveland vs. Detroit	10	303	1

*First season of professional football.

2,000 COMBINED NET YARDS GAINED IN A SEASON

Year	Player, Team	Rushing Att.-Yds.	Pass Rec.	Punt Ret.	Kickoff Ret.	Fum. Ret.	Total Yds.
2007	Josh Cribbs, Cleveland	9-61	3-37	30-405	59-1,809	2-0	103-2,312
	Jerious Norwood, Atlanta	103-613	28-277	0-0	52-1,317	0-0	183-2,207
	Brian Westbrook, Philadelphia	278-1,333	90-771	4-79	0-0	0-0	372-2,183
	*Ted Ginn Jr., Miami	4-3	34-420	24-230	63-1,433	2-(-9)	127-2,077
	Leon Washington, N.Y. Jets	71-353	36-213	20-183	47-1,291	1-0	175-2,040
	*Adrian Peterson, Minnesota	238-1,341	19-268	0-0	16-412	3-0	276-2,014
	Maurice Jones-Drew, Jacksonville[3]	167-768	40-407	3-28	31-811	0-0	241-2,014
2006	Steven Jackson, St. Louis	346-1,528	90,806	0-0	0-0	2-0	438-2,334
	LaDainian Tomlinson, San Diego[3]	348-1,815	56-508	0-0	0-0	1-0	405-2,323
	*Maurice Jones-Drew, Jacksonville	166-941	46-436	1-13	31-860	0-0	244-2,250
	Larry Johnson, Kansas City[2]	416-1,789	41-410	0-0	0-0	1-0	458-2,199
	Frank Gore, San Francisco	312-1,695	61-485	0-0	0-0	0-0	373-2,180
	Wes Welker, Miami[2]	0-0	67-687	41-378	48-1,064	1-0	157-2,129
	Tiki Barber, N.Y. Giants[4]	327-1,662	58-465	0-0	0-0	1-0	386-2,127
	Chris Carr, Oakland	0-0	0-0	35-216	69-1,762	1-0	106-2,078
2005	Tiki Barber, N.Y. Giants[3]	357-1,860	54-530	0-0	0-0	1-0	412-2,390
	Dante Hall, Kansas City[4]	7-11	34-436	42-276	65-1,560	2-0	150-2,283
	Wes Welker, Miami	1-5	29-434	43-390	61-1,379	4-0	138-2,208
	Larry Johnson, Kansas City	336-1,750	33-343	0-0	0-0	3-0	372-2,093
2004	Dante Hall, Kansas City[3]	8-56	25-230	23-232	68-1,718	0-0	124-2,236
	Tiki Barber, N.Y. Giants[2]	322-1,518	52-578	0-0	0-0	2-0	376-2,096
	Edgerrin James, Indianapolis[3]	334-1,548	51-483	0-0	0-0	1-0	386-2,031
2003	Dante Hall, Kansas City[2]	16-73	40-423	29-472	57-1,478	0-0	142-2,446
	LaDainian Tomlinson, San Diego[2]	313-1,645	100-725	0-0	0-0	2-0	415-2,370

Year	Player, Team	Rushing Att.-Yds.	Pass Rec.	Punt Ret.	Kickoff Ret.	Fum. Ret.	Total Yds.
	Jamal Lewis, Baltimore	387-2,066	26-205	0-0	0-0	1-0	414-2,271
	Ahman Green, Green Bay	355-1,883	50-367	0-0	0-0	2-0	407-2,250
	Deuce McAllister, New Orleans	351-1,641	69-516	0-0	0-0	3-(-3)	423-2,154
	Priest Holmes, Kansas City[3]	320-1,420	74-690	0-0	0-0	0-0	394-2,110
2002	Michael Lewis, New Orleans	1-15	8-200	44-625	70-1,807	2-0	125-2,647
	Priest Holmes, Kansas City[2]	313-1,615	70-672	0-0	0-0	0-0	383-2,287
	Ricky Williams, Miami	383-1,853	47-363	0-0	0-0	1-0	431-2,216
	LaDainian Tomlinson, San Diego	372-1,683	79-489	0-0	0-0	0-0	451-2,172
	Dante Hall, Kansas City	11-54	20-322	29-390	57-1,354	1-0	118-2,120
2001	Priest Holmes, Kansas City	327-1,555	62-614	0-0	0-0	0-0	389-2,169
	Marshall Faulk, St. Louis[4]	260-1,382	83-765	0-0	0-0	2-0	345-2,147
	Derrick Mason, Tennessee[2]	0-0	73-1,128	20-128	34-748	1-0	128-2,004
2000	Derrick Mason, Tennessee	1-1	63-895	51-662	42-1,132	1-0	158-2,690
	MarTay Jenkins, Arizona	1-(-4)	17-219	1-1	82-2,186	0-0	101-2,402
	Edgerrin James, Indianapolis[2]	387-1,709	63-594	0-0	0-0	0-0	450-2,303
	Marshall Faulk, St. Louis[3]	253-1,359	81-830	0-0	1-18	2-0	337-2,207
	Tiki Barber, N.Y. Giants	213-1,006	70-719	39-332	1-28	5-0	328-2,085
1999	Marshall Faulk, St. Louis[2]	253-1,381	87-1,048	0-0	0-0	0-0	340-2,429
	*Edgerrin James, Indianapolis	369-1,553	62-586	0-0	0-0	2-0	433-2,139
	*Terrence Wilkins, Indianapolis	1-2	42-565	41-388	51-1,134	1-0	136-2,089
	Glyn Milburn, Chicago[2]	16-102	20-151	30-346	61-1,426	2-0	129-2,025
1998	Brian Mitchell, Washington[4]	39-208	44-306	44-506	59-1,337	0-0	186-2,357
	Marshall Faulk, Indianapolis	324-1,319	86-908	0-0	0-0	2-13	412-2,240
	Terrell Davis, Denver[2]	392-2,008	25-217	0-0	0-0	1-0	418-2,225
	Jamal Anderson, Atlanta	410-1,846	27-319	0-0	0-0	1-0	438-2,165
	Garrison Hearst, San Francisco	310-1,570	39-535	0-0	0-0	1-0	350-2,105
1997	Barry Sanders, Detroit[2]	335-2,053	33-305	0-0	0-0	1-0	369-2,358
	Kevin Williams, Arizona	1-(-2)	20-273	40-462	59-1,458	1-0	121-2,191
	Brian Mitchell, Washington[3]	23-107	36-438	38-442	47-1,094	0-0	144-2,081
	Terrell Davis, Denver	369-1,750	42-287	0-0	0-0	2-(-7)	413-2,030
	Jermaine Lewis, Baltimore	3-35	42-648	28-437	41-905	2-0	116-2,025
1995	Brian Mitchell, Washington[2]	46-301	38-324	25-315	55-1,408	0-0	164-2,348
	Emmitt Smith, Dallas[2]	377-1,773	62-375	0-0	0-0	0-0	439-2,148
	Glyn Milburn, Denver	49-266	22-191	31-354	47-1,269	0-0	149-2,080
	Ernie Mills, Pittsburgh	5-39	39-679	0-0	54-1,306	0-0	98-2,024
1994	Brian Mitchell, Washington	78-311	26-236	32-452	58-1,478	0-0	194-2,477
	Barry Sanders, Detroit	331-1,883	44-283	0-0	0-0	0-0	375-2,166
1992	Thurman Thomas, Buffalo[2]	312-1,487	58-626	0-0	0-0	1-0	371-2,113
	Emmitt Smith, Dallas	373-1,713	59-335	0-0	0-0	1-0	433-2,048
	Barry Foster, Pittsburgh	390-1,690	36-344	0-0	0-0	2-(-20)	428-2,014
1991	Thurman Thomas, Buffalo	288-1,407	62-631	0-0	0-0	0-0	350-2,038
1990	Herschel Walker, Minnesota[2]	184-770	35-315	0-0	44-966	4-0	267-2,051
1988	*Tim Brown, L.A. Raiders	14-50	43-725	49-444	41-1,098	7-0	154-2,317
	Roger Craig, San Francisco[2]	310-1,502	76-534	0-0	2-32	2-0	390-2,068
	Eric Dickerson, Indianapolis[4]	388-1,659	36-377	0-0	0-0	1-0	425-2,036
	Herschel Walker, Dallas	361-1,514	53-505	0-0	0-0	3-0	417-2,019
1986	Eric Dickerson, L.A. Rams[3]	404-1,821	26-205	0-0	0-0	2-0	432-2,026
	Gary Anderson, San Diego	127-442	80-871	25-227	24-482	2-0	258-2,022
1985	Lionel James, San Diego	105-516	86-1,027	25-213	36-779	1-0	253-2,535
	Marcus Allen, L.A. Raiders	380-1,759	67-555	0-0	0-0	2-(-6)	449-2,308
	Roger Craig, San Francisco[2]	214-1,050	92-1,016	0-0	0-0	0-0	306-2,066
	Walter Payton, Chicago[4]	324-1,551	49-483	0-0	0-0	1-0	374-2,034
1984	Eric Dickerson, L.A. Rams[2]	379-2,105	21-139	0-0	0-0	4-15	404-2,259
	James Wilder, Tampa Bay	407-1,544	85-685	0-0	0-0	4-0	496-2,229
	Walter Payton, Chicago[3]	381-1,684	45-368	0-0	0-0	1-0	427-2,052
1983	*Eric Dickerson, L.A. Rams	390-1,808	51-404	0-0	0-0	1-0	442-2,212
	William Andrews, Atlanta[2]	331-1,567	59-609	0-0	0-0	2-0	392-2,176
	Walter Payton, Chicago[2]	314-1,421	53-607	0-0	0-0	2-0	369-2,028
1981	*James Brooks, San Diego	109-525	46-329	22-290	40-949	2-0	219-2,093
	William Andrews, Atlanta	289-1,301	81-735	0-0	0-0	0-0	370-2,036
1980	Bruce Harper, N.Y. Jets[2]	45-126	50-634	28-242	49-1,070	3-0	175-2,072
1979	Wilbert Montgomery, Philadelphia	338-1,512	41-494	0-0	1-6	2-0	382-2,012
1978	Bruce Harper, N.Y. Jets	58-303	13-196	30-378	55-1,280	1-0	157-2,157
1977	Walter Payton, Chicago	339-1,852	27-269	0-0	2-95	5-0	373-2,216
	Terry Metcalf, St. Louis[3]	149-739	34-403	14-108	32-772	1-0	230-2,022
1975	Terry Metcalf, St. Louis[2]	165-816	43-378	23-285	35-960	2-23	268-2,462
	O.J. Simpson, Buffalo[2]	329-1,817	28-426	0-0	0-0	1-0	358-2,243
1974	Mack Herron, New England	231-824	38-474	35-517	28-629	3-0	335-2,444

Year	Player, Team	Att.	Rushing Yards	Receptions	Receiving Yards	Scrimm. Yards
	Otis Armstrong, Denver...................263-1,407	38-405	0-0	16-386	1-0	318-2,198
	Terry Metcalf, St. Louis 152-718	50-377	26-340	20-623	7-0	255-2,058
1973	O.J. Simpson, Buffalo 332-2,003	6-70	0-0	0-0	0-0	338-2,073
1966	Gale Sayers, Chicago[2]...................229-1,231	34-447	6-44	23-718	3-0	295-2,440
	Leroy Kelly, Cleveland 209-1,141	32-366	13-104	19-403	0-0	273-2,014
1965	*Gale Sayers, Chicago....................166-867	29-507	16-238	21-660	4-0	236-2,272
1963	Timmy Brown, Philadelphia[2]...........192-841	36-487	16-152	33-945	2-3	279-2,428
	Jim Brown, Cleveland 291-1,863	24-268	0-0	0-0	0-0	315-2,131
1962	Timmy Brown, Philadelphia..............137-545	52-849	6-81	30-831	4-0	229-2,306
	Dick Christy, N.Y. Titans 114-535	62-538	15-250	38-824	2-0	231-2,147
1961	Billy Cannon, Houston.....................200-948	43-586	9-70	18-439	2-0	272-2,043
1960	*Abner Haynes, Dallas Texans 156-875	55-576	14-215	19-434	4-0	248-2,100

First season of professional football.

300 COMBINED NET YARDS GAINED IN A GAME

Date	Player, Team, Opponent	No.	Yards	TD
Nov. 18, 2007	Josh Cribbs, Cleveland vs. Baltimore (OT) 12		309	0
Nov. 4, 2007	*Adrian Peterson, Minnesota vs. San Diego........................31		315	3
Oct. 14, 2007	*Adrian Peterson, Minnesota vs. Chicgo............................25		361	3
Sept. 30, 2007	Devin Hester, Chicago vs. Detroit......................................13		317	1
Dec. 10, 2006	*Maurice Jones-Drew, Jacksonville vs. Indianapolis 19		303	3
Dec. 14, 2003	Derrick Mason, Tennessee vs. Buffalo 21		302	0
Nov. 16, 2003	Jonathan Carter, N.Y. Jets vs. Indianapolis 7		304	2
Dec. 8, 2002	Steve Smith, Carolina vs. Cincinnati.....................................9		313	3
Nov. 24, 2002	Priest Holmes, Kansas City vs. Seattle...............................30		307	3
Oct. 13, 2002	Michael Lewis, New Orleans vs. Washington 8		356	2
Dec. 24, 1999	Jason Tucker, Dallas vs. New Orleans.................................13		331	1
Dec. 7, 1997	Jermaine Lewis, Baltimore vs. Seattle.................................10		308	3
Dec. 25, 1995	Kevin Williams, Dallas vs. Arizona.....................................16		307	2
Dec. 10, 1995	Glyn Milburn, Denver vs. Seattle 33		404	0
Oct. 23, 1994	Tyrone Hughes, New Orleans vs. L.A. Rams 11		347	2
Dec. 11, 1989	John Taylor, San Francisco vs. L.A. Rams 14		321	2
Nov. 26, 1989	Willie Anderson, L.A. Rams vs. New Orleans (OT) 15		336	1
Nov. 28, 1988	*Tim Brown, L.A. Raiders vs. Seattle...................................12		308	1
Dec. 22, 1985	Stephone Paige, Kansas City vs. San Diego..........................8		309	2
Nov. 10, 1985	Lionel James, San Diego vs. L.A. Raiders (OT) 23		345	0
Sept. 22, 1985	Lionel James, San Diego vs. Cincinnati...............................20		316	2
Dec. 21, 1975	*Walter Payton, Chicago vs. New Orleans 32		300	1
Nov. 23, 1975	Greg Pruitt, Cleveland vs. Cincinnati 28		304	2
Nov. 1, 1970	Eugene (Mercury) Morris, Miami vs. Baltimore 17		302	0
Oct. 4, 1970	O.J. Simpson, Buffalo vs. N.Y. Jets 26		303	2
Dec. 6, 1969	Jerry LeVias, Houston vs. N.Y. Jets 18		329	1
Nov. 2, 1969	Travis Williams, Green Bay vs. Pittsburgh 11		314	3
Dec. 18, 1966	Gale Sayers, Chicago vs. Minnesota..................................20		339	2
Dec. 12, 1965	*Gale Sayers, Chicago vs. San Francisco 17		336	6
Nov. 17, 1963	Gary Ballman, Pittsburgh vs. Washington 12		320	2
Dec. 16, 1962	Timmy Brown, Philadelphia vs. St. Louis 19		341	2
Dec. 10, 1961	Billy Cannon, Houston vs. N.Y. Titans 32		373	5
Nov. 19, 1961	Jim Brown, Cleveland vs. Philadelphia 38		313	4
Dec. 3, 1950	Cloyce Box, Detroit vs. Baltimore......................................13		302	4
Oct. 29, 1950	Wally Triplett, Detroit vs. Los Angeles 11		331	1
Nov. 22, 1945	Jim Benton, Cleveland vs. Detroit 10		303	1

First season of professional football.

2,000 SCRIMMAGE YARDS GAINED IN A SEASON

Year	Player, Team	Att.	Rushing Yards	Receptions	Receiving Yards	Scrimm. Yards
2007	Brian Westbrook, Philadelphia 278	1,333	90	771	2,104
2006	Steven Jackson, St. Louis 346	1,528	90	806	2,334
	LaDainian Tomlinson, San Diego[3]....................348	1,815	56	508	2,323
	Larry Johnson, Kansas City[2]............................416	1,789	41	410	2,199
	Frank Gore, San Francisco................................312	1,695	61	485	2,180
	Tiki Barber, N.Y. Giants[3]..................................327	1,662	58	465	2,127
2005	Tiki Barber, N.Y. Giants[2]..................................357	1,860	54	530	2,390
	Larry Johnson, Kansas City 336	1,750	33	343	2,093
2004	Tiki Barber, N.Y. Giants 322	1.518	52	578	2,096
	Edgerrin James, Indianapolis[3]...........................334	1,548	51	483	2,031
2003	LaDainian Tomlinson, San Diego[2]......................313	1,645	100	725	2,370
	Jamal Lewis, Baltimore 387	2,066	26	205	2,271

Year	Player, Team	Att.	Yards	Receptions	Yards	Yards
	Ahman Green, Green Bay	355	1,883	50	367	2,250
	Deuce McAllister, New Orleans	351	1,641	69	516	2,157
	Priest Holmes, Kansas City[3]	320	1,420	74	690	2,110
2002	Priest Holmes, Kansas City[2]	313	1,615	70	672	2,287
	Ricky Williams, Miami	383	1,853	47	363	2,216
	LaDainian Tomlinson, San Diego	372	1,683	79	489	2,172
2001	Priest Holmes, Kansas City	327	1,555	62	614	2,169
	Marshall Faulk, St. Louis[4]	260	1,382	83	765	2,147
2000	Edgerrin James, Indianapolis[2]	387	1,709	63	594	2,303
	Marshall Faulk, St. Louis[3]	253	1,359	81	830	2,189
1999	Marshall Faulk, St. Louis[2]	253	1,381	87	1,048	2,429
	*Edgerrin James, Indianapolis	369	1,553	62	586	2,139
1998	Marshall Faulk, Indianapolis	324	1,319	86	908	2,227
	Terrell Davis, Denver[2]	392	2,008	25	217	2,225
	Jamal Anderson, Atlanta	410	1,846	27	319	2,165
	Garrison Hearst, San Francisco	310	1,570	39	535	2,105
1997	Barry Sanders, Detroit[2]	335	2,053	33	305	2,358
	Terrell Davis, Denver	369	1,750	42	287	2,037
1995	Emmitt Smith, Dallas[2]	377	1,773	62	375	2,148
1994	Barry Sanders, Detroit	331	1,883	44	283	2,166
1992	Thurman Thomas, Buffalo[2]	312	1,487	58	626	2,113
	Emmitt Smith, Dallas	373	1,713	59	335	2,048
	Barry Foster, Pittsburgh	390	1,690	36	344	2,034
1991	Thurman Thomas, Buffalo	288	1,407	62	631	2,038
1988	Roger Craig, San Francisco[2]	310	1,502	76	534	2,036
	Eric Dickerson, Indianapolis[4]	388	1,659	36	377	2,036
	Herschel Walker, Dallas	361	1,514	53	505	2,019
1986	Eric Dickerson, L.A. Rams[3]	404	1,821	26	205	2,026
1985	Marcus Allen, L.A. Raiders	380	1,759	67	555	2,314
	Roger Craig, San Francisco	214	1,050	92	1,016	2,066
	Walter Payton, Chicago[4]	324	1,551	49	483	2,034
1984	Eric Dickerson, L. A. Rams[2]	379	2,105	21	139	2,244
	James Wilder, Tampa Bay	407	1,544	85	685	2,229
	Walter Payton, Chicago[3]	381	1,684	45	368	2,052
1983	*Eric Dickerson, L.A. Rams	390	1,808	51	404	2,212
	William Andrews, Atlanta[2]	331	1,567	59	609	2,176
	Walter Payton, Chicago[2]	314	1,421	53	607	2,028
1981	William Andrews, Atlanta	289	1,301	81	735	2,036
1979	Wilbert Montgomery, Philadelphia	338	1,512	41	494	2,006
1977	Walter Payton, Chicago	339	1,852	27	269	2,121
1975	O.J. Simpson, Buffalo[2]	329	1,817	28	426	2,243
1973	O.J. Simpson, Buffalo	332	2,003	6	70	2,073
1963	Jim Brown, Cleveland	91	1,863	24	268	2,131

*First season of professional football.

300 SCRIMMAGE YARDS GAINED IN A GAME

Date	Player, Team, Opponent	Att.	Yards	TD
Nov. 4, 2007	*Adrian Peterson, Minnesota vs. San Diego	31	315	3
Nov. 24, 2002	Priest Holmes, Kansas City vs. Seattle	30	307	3
Nov. 26, 1989	Flipper Anderson, L.A. Rams vs. New Orleans (OT)	15	336	1
Dec. 22, 1985	Stephone Paige, Kansas City vs. San Diego	8	309	2
Dec. 10, 1961	Billy Cannon, Houston vs. N.Y. Titans	30	330	5
Dec. 3, 1950	Cloyce Box, Detroit vs. Baltimore	12	302	4
Nov. 22, 1945	Jim Benton, Cleveland vs. Detroit	10	303	1

*First season of professional football.

OUTSTANDING PERFORMERS

TOP 20 SCORERS

Player	Years	TD	FG	PAT	TP
Morten Andersen	25	0	565	849	2,544
Gary Anderson	23	0	538	820	2,434
George Blanda	26	9	335	942	2,002
Matt Stover	17	0	435	517	1,822
John Carney	20	0	425	537	1,812
Jason Elam	15	0	395	601	1,786
Norm Johnson	18	0	366	638	1,736
Nick Lowery	18	0	383	562	1,711
Jan Stenerud	19	0	373	580	1,699
Jason Hanson	16	0	385	504	1,659
Eddie Murray	19	0	352	538	1,594
Al Del Greco	17	0	347	543	1,584
John Kasay	16	0	358	430	1,504
Steve Christie	15	0	336	468	1,476
Pat Leahy	18	0	304	558	1,470
Jim Turner	16	1	304	521	1,439
Matt Bahr	17	0	300	522	1,422
Jeff Wilkins	14	0	307	495	1,416
Adam Vinatieri	12	0	311	454	1,389
Mark Moseley	16	0	300	482	1,382

TOP 20 TOUCHDOWN SCORERS

Player	Years	Rush	Rec.	Total Returns	TD
Jerry Rice	20	10	197	1	208
Emmitt Smith	15	164	11	0	175
Marcus Allen	16	123	21	1	145
Marshall Faulk	12	100	36	0	136
Cris Carter	16	0	130	1	131
Terrell Owens	12	2	129	0	131
LaDainian Tomlinson	7	115	14	0	129
Jim Brown	9	106	20	0	126
Randy Moss	10	0	124	1	125
Walter Payton	13	110	15	0	125
Marvin Harrison	12	0	123	0	123
John Riggins	14	104	12	0	116
Lenny Moore	12	63	48	2	113
Shaun Alexander	8	100	12	0	112
Barry Sanders	10	99	10	0	109
Tim Brown	17	1	100	4	105
Don Hutson	11	3	99	3	105
Steve Largent	14	1	100	0	101
Franco Harris	13	91	9	0	100
Curtis Martin	11	90	10	0	100

TOP 20 RUSHERS

Player	Years	Att.	Yards	Avg.	Long	TD
Emmitt Smith	15	4,409	18,355	4.2	75	164
Walter Payton	13	3,838	16,726	4.4	76	110
Barry Sanders	10	3,062	15,269	5.0	85	99
Curtis Martin	11	3,518	14,101	4.0	70	90
Jerome Bettis	13	3,479	13,662	3.9	71	91
Eric Dickerson	11	2,996	13,259	4.4	85	90
Tony Dorsett	12	2,936	12,739	4.3	99	77
Jim Brown	9	2,359	12,312	5.2	80	106
Marshall Faulk	12	2,836	12,279	4.3	71	100
Marcus Allen	16	3,022	12,243	4.1	61	123
Franco Harris	13	2,949	12,120	4.1	75	91
Thurman Thomas	13	2,877	12,074	4.2	80	65
Edgerrin James	9	2,849	11,607	4.1	72	77
John Riggins	14	2,916	11,352	3.9	66	104
Corey Dillon	10	2,618	11,241	4.3	96	82
O.J. Simpson	11	2,404	11,236	4.7	94	61
Fred Taylor	10	2,285	10,715	4.7	80	61
LaDainian Tomlinson	7	2,365	10,650	4.5	85	115
Ricky Watters	10	2,622	10,643	4.1	57	78
Tiki Barber	10	2,217	10,449	4.7	95	55

TOP 20 COMBINED YARDS GAINED

Player	Years	Tot.	Rush.	Rec.	Int. Ret.	Punt Ret.	Kickoff Ret.	Fumble Ret.
Jerry Rice	20	23,546	645	22,895	0	0	6	0
Brian Mitchell	14	23,330	1,967	2,336	0	4,999	14,014	14
Walter Payton	13	21,803	16,726	4,538	0	0	539	0
Emmitt Smith	15	21,564	18,355	3,224	0	0	0	-15
Tim Brown	17	19,682	190	14,934	0	3,320	1,235	3
Marshall Faulk	12	19,190	12,279	6,875	0	0	18	18
Barry Sanders	10	18,308	15,269	2,921	0	0	118	0
Herschel Walker	12	18,168	8,225	4,859	0	0	5,084	0
Marcus Allen	16	17,648	12,243	5,411	0	0	0	-6
Curtis Martin	11	17,421	14,101	3,329	0	0	0	-9
Tiki Barber	10	17,359	10,449	5,183	0	1,181	544	2
Eric Metcalf	13	17,230	2,392	5,572	0	3,453	5,813	0
Thurman Thomas	13	16,532	12,074	4,458	0	0	0	0
Tony Dorsett	12	16,326	12,739	3,554	0	0	0	54
Henry Ellard	16	15,718	50	13,777	0	1,527	364	0
Irving Fryar	17	15,594	242	12,785	0	2,055	505	7
Jim Brown	9	15,459	12,312	2,499	0	0	648	0
Eric Dickerson	11	15,411	13,259	2,137	0	0	0	15
Jerome Bettis	13	15,113	13,662	1,449	0	0	0	2
Glyn Milburn	9	14,911	817	1,322	0	2,984	9,788	0

TOP 20 YARDS FROM SCRIMMAGE

Player	Years	Scrimmage Yards	Rushing Yards	Receiving Yards
Jerry Rice	20	23,540	645	22,895
Emmitt Smith	15	21,579	18,355	3,224
Walter Payton	13	21,264	16,726	4,538
Marshall Faulk	12	19,154	12,279	6,875
Barry Sanders	10	18,190	15,269	2,921
Marcus Allen	16	17,654	12,243	5,411
Curtis Martin	11	17,430	14,101	3,329
Thurman Thomas	13	16,532	12,074	4,458
Tony Dorsett	12	16,293	12,739	3,554
Tiki Barber	10	15,632	10,449	5,183
Eric Dickerson	11	15,396	13,259	2,137
Tim Brown	17	15,124	190	14,934
Jerome Bettis	13	15,111	13,662	1,449
Ricky Watters	10	14,891	10,643	4,248
Edgerrin James	9	14,867	11,607	3,260
Jim Brown	9	14,811	12,312	2,499
Franco Harris	13	14,407	12,120	2,287
Isaac Bruce	14	14,259	150	14,109
James Lofton	16	14,250	246	14,004
Warrick Dunn	11	14,190	10,181	4,009

TOP 20 PASSERS

Player	Years	Att.	Comp.	Pct. Comp.	Yards	Avg. Gain	TD	Pct. TD	Int.	Pct. Int.	Rating
Steve Young	15	4,149	2,667	64.3	33,124	7.98	232	5.6	107	2.6	96.8
Peyton Manning	10	5,405	3,468	64.2	41,626	7.70	306	5.7	153	2.8	94.7
Kurt Warner	10	2,959	1,926	65.1	24,008	8.11	152	5.1	100	3.4	93.2
Tom Brady	8	3,642	2,294	63.0	26,370	7.24	197	5.4	86	2.4	92.9
Joe Montana	15	5,391	3,409	63.2	40,551	7.52	273	5.1	139	2.6	92.3
Carson Palmer	4	2,036	1,305	64.1	14,899	7.32	104	5.1	63	3.1	90.1
Daunte Culpepper	9	2,927	1,867	63.8	22,422	7.66	142	4.9	94	3.2	89.9
Chad Pennington	8	1,919	1,259	65.6	13,738	7.16	82	4.3	55	2.9	88.9
Marc Bulger	6	2,484	1,578	63.5	18,625	7.50	106	4.3	74	3.0	88.1
Drew Brees	7	3,015	1,921	63.7	21,189	7.03	134	4.4	82	2.7	87.9
Jeff Garcia	9	3,300	2,020	61.2	22,825	6.92	149	4.5	77	2.3	87.2
Trent Green	10	3,668	2,228	60.7	27,950	7.62	162	4.4	108	2.9	86.9
Dan Marino	17	8,358	4,967	59.4	61,361	7.34	420	5.0	252	3.0	86.4
Matt Hasselbeck	9	3,138	1,904	60.7	22,333	7.12	142	4.5	84	2.7	86.2
Donovan McNabb	9	3,732	2,189	58.7	25,404	6.81	171	4.6	79	2.1	85.8
Brett Favre	17	8,758	5,377	61.4	61,655	7.04	442	5.0	288	3.3	85.7
Jake Delhomme	7	2,020	1,206	59.7	14,589	7.22	100	5.0	64	3.2	85.2
Rich Gannon	16	4,206	2,533	60.2	28,743	6.83	180	4.3	104	2.5	84.7
Jim Kelly	11	4,779	2,874	60.1	35,467	7.42	237	5.0	175	3.7	84.4
Mark Brunell	14	4,594	2,738	59.6	31,826	6.93	182	4.0	106	2.3	84.2

1,500 or more attempts. The passing ratings are based on performance standards established for completion percentage, interception percentage, touchdown percentage, and average gain. Please consult page 364 for more information.

TOP 20 LEADERS IN PASSES COMPLETED

Brett Favre	5,377
Dan Marino	4,967
John Elway	4,123
Warren Moon	3,988
Drew Bledsoe	3,839
Vinny Testaverde	3,787
Fran Tarkenton	3,686
Peyton Manning	3,468
Joe Montana	3,409
Dan Fouts	3,297
Dave Krieg	3,105
Boomer Esiason	2,969
Kerry Collins	2,918
Troy Aikman	2,898
Steve DeBerg	2,874
Jim Kelly	2,874
Jim Everett	2,841
Johnny Unitas	2,830
Mark Brunell	2,738
Steve McNair	2,733

TOP 20 LEADERS IN PASSING YARDS

Brett Favre	61,655
Dan Marino	61,361
John Elway	51,475
Warren Moon	49,325
Fran Tarkenton	47,003
Vinny Testaverde	46,233
Drew Bledsoe	44,611
Dan Fouts	43,040
Peyton Manning	41,626
Joe Montana	40,551
Johnny Unitas	40,239
Dave Krieg	38,147
Boomer Esiason	37,920
Jim Kelly	35,467
Jim Everett	34,837
Kerry Collins	34,717
Jim Hart	34,665
Steve DeBerg	34,241
John Hadl	33,503
Phil Simms	33,462

TOP 20 LEADERS IN TOUCHDOWN PASSES

Brett Favre	442
Dan Marino	420
Fran Tarkenton	342
Peyton Manning	306
John Elway	300
Warren Moon	291
Johnny Unitas	290
Vinny Testaverde	275
Joe Montana	273
Dave Krieg	261
Sonny Jurgensen	255
Dan Fouts	254
Drew Bledsoe	251
Boomer Esiason	247
John Hadl	244
Len Dawson	239
Jim Kelly	237
George Blanda	236
Steve Young	232
John Brodie	214

TOP 20 LEADERS IN RECEPTION YARDS

Jerry Rice	22,895
Tim Brown	14,934
Isaac Bruce	14,109
James Lofton	14,004
Marvin Harrison	13,944
Cris Carter	13,899
Henry Ellard	13,777
Andre Reed	13,198
Steve Largent	13,089
Terrell Owens	13,070
Irving Fryar	12,785
Art Monk	12,721
Jimmy Smith	12,287
Randy Moss	12,193
Charlie Joiner	12,146
Michael Irvin	11,904
Torry Holt	11,864
Don Maynard	11,834
Rod Smith	11,389
Keenan McCardell	11,373

TOP 20 PASS RECEIVERS

Player	Years	No.	Yards	Avg.	Long	TD
Jerry Rice	20	1,549	22,895	14.8	96	197
Cris Carter	16	1,101	13,899	12.6	80	130
Tim Brown	17	1,094	14,934	13.7	80	100
Marvin Harrison	12	1,042	13,944	13.4	80	123
Andre Reed	16	951	13,198	13.9	83	87
Isaac Bruce	14	942	14,109	15.0	80	84
Art Monk	16	940	12,721	13.5	79	68
Keenan McCardell	16	883	11,373	12.9	76	63
Terrell Owens	12	882	13,070	14.8	91	129
Jimmy Smith	12	862	12,287	14.3	75	67
Irving Fryar	17	851	12,785	15.0	80	84
Rod Smith	12	849	11,389	13.4	85	68
Larry Centers	14	827	6,797	8.2	54	28
Tony Gonzalez	11	820	9,882	12.1	73	66
Steve Largent	14	819	13,089	16.0	74	100
Shannon Sharpe	14	815	10,060	12.3	82	62
Henry Ellard	16	814	13,777	16.9	81	65
Keyshawn Johnson	11	814	10,571	13.0	76	64
Torry Holt	9	805	11,864	14.7	85	71
Randy Moss	10	774	12,193	15.8	82	124

TOP 20 INTERCEPTORS

Player	Years	No.	Yards	Avg.	Long	TD
Paul Krause	16	81	1,185	14.6	81	3
Emlen Tunnell	14	79	1,282	16.2	55	4
Rod Woodson	17	71	1,483	20.9	98	12
Dick (Night Train) Lane	14	68	1,207	17.8	80	5
Ken Riley	15	65	596	9.2	66	5
Ronnie Lott	14	63	730	11.6	83	5
Dave Brown	15	62	698	11.3	90	5
Dick LeBeau	14	62	762	12.3	70	3
Emmitt Thomas	13	58	937	16.2	73	5
Mel Blount	14	57	736	12.9	52	2
Bobby Boyd	9	57	994	17.4	74	4
Eugene Robinson	16	57	762	13.4	49	1
Johnny Robinson	12	57	741	13.0	57	1
Everson Walls	13	57	504	8.8	40	1
Lem Barney	11	56	1,077	19.2	71	7
Pat Fischer	17	56	941	16.8	69	4
Aeneas Williams	14	55	807	14.7	65	9
Eric Allen	14	54	826	15.3	94	8
Willie Brown	16	54	472	8.7	45	2
Darrell Green	20	54	621	11.5	83	6

TOP 20 PUNTERS (MINIMUM 250 PUNTS)

Player	Years	No.	Yards	Avg.	Long	Blk.
Shane Lechler	8	592	27,511	46.5	73	3
Sammy Baugh	16	338	15,245	45.1	85	9
Mat McBriar	4	275	12,288	44.7	75	0
Tommy Davis	11	511	22,833	44.7	82	2
Yale Lary	11	503	22,279	44.3	74	4
Todd Sauerbrun	13	889	39,208	44.1	73	9
Bob Scarpitto	8	283	12,408	43.8	87	4
Horace Gillom	7	385	16,872	43.8	80	5
Donnie Jones	4	277	12,139	43.8	80	2
Mike Scifres	5	290	12,706	43.8	71	1
Andy Lee	4	389	17,030	43.8	81	1
Jerry Norton	11	358	15,671	43.8	78	2
Dave Lewis	4	285	12,447	43.7	63	0
Greg Montgomery	9	524	22,831	43.6	77	8
Don Chandler	12	660	28,678	43.5	90	4
Tom Rouen	12	810	35,189	43.4	76	9
Rick Tuten	11	741	32,190	43.4	73	2
Darren Bennett	11	836	36,316	43.4	66	3
Tom Tupa	17	873	37,862	43.4	73	2
Rohn Stark	16	1,141	49,471	43.4	72	7

TOP 20 KICKOFF RETURNERS (MINIMUM 75 RETURNS)

Player	Years	No.	Yards	Avg.	Long	TD
Gale Sayers	7	91	2,781	30.6	103	6
Lynn Chandnois	7	92	2,720	29.6	93	3
Abe Woodson	9	193	5,538	28.7	105	5
Buddy Young	6	90	2,514	27.9	104	2
Travis Williams	5	102	2,801	27.5	105	6
Joe Arenas	7	139	3,798	27.3	96	1
Justin Miller	3	108	2,929	27.1	103	3
Clarence Davis	8	79	2,140	27.1	76	0
Steve Van Buren	8	76	2,030	26.7	98	3
Lenny Lyles	12	81	2,161	26.7	103	3
Josh Cribbs	3	165	4,397	26.6	100	4
Mercury Morris	8	111	2,947	26.5	105	3
Bobby Jancik	6	158	4,185	26.5	61	0
Mel Renfro	14	85	2,246	26.4	100	2
Terrence McGee	5	203	5,358	26.4	104	5
Bobby Mitchell	14	102	2,690	26.4	98	5
Ollie Matson	14	143	3,746	26.2	105	6
Alvin Haymond	10	170	4,438	26.1	98	2
Noland Smith	3	82	2,137	26.1	106	1
Al Nelson	9	101	2,625	26.0	78	0

TOP 20 PUNT RETURNERS (MINIMUM 75 RETURNS)

Player	Years	No.	Yards	Avg.	Long	TD
Devin Hester	2	89	1,251	14.1	89	7
George McAfee	8	112	1,431	12.8	74	2
Jack Christiansen	8	85	1,084	12.8	89	8
Claude Gibson	5	110	1,381	12.6	85	3
Bill Dudley	9	124	1,515	12.2	96	3
Rick Upchurch	9	248	3,008	12.1	92	8
Desmond Howard	11	244	2,895	11.9	95	8
Billy Johnson	14	282	3,317	11.8	87	6
Mack Herron	3	84	982	11.7	66	0
Billy Thompson	13	157	1,814	11.6	60	0
Santana Moss	7	95	1,092	11.5	63	2
Darrien Gordon	9	314	3,601	11.5	94	6
Henry Ellard	16	135	1,527	11.3	83	4
Rodger Bird	3	94	1,063	11.3	78	0
Bosh Pritchard	6	95	1,072	11.3	81	2
Terry Metcalf	6	84	936	11.1	69	1
Bob Hayes	11	104	1,158	11.1	90	3
Jermaine Lewis	9	295	3,282	11.1	89	6
Floyd Little	9	81	893	11.0	72	2
Louis Lipps	9	112	1,234	11.0	76	3

TOP 20 LEADERS IN SACKS

Player	*Years	No.
Bruce Smith	19	200.0
Reggie White	15	198.0
Kevin Greene	15	160.0
Chris Doleman	15	150.5
Michael Strahan	15	141.5
Richard Dent	15	137.5
John Randle	14	137.5
Leslie O'Neal	13	132.5
Lawrence Taylor	12	132.5
Rickey Jackson	14	128.0
Derrick Thomas	11	126.5
Simeon Rice	12	122.0
Clyde Simmons	15	121.5
Jason Taylor	11	117.0
Sean Jones	13	113.0
Greg Townsend	13	109.5
Pat Swilling	12	107.5
Trace Armstrong	15	106.0
Neil Smith	13	104.5
Jim Jeffcoat	15	102.5

*Years played since 1982 when sacks became an official statistic.

POSTSEASON LEADERS
TOP 10 POSTSEASON RUSHERS

Player	Att.	Yards	Avg.	Long	TD
Emmitt Smith	349	1,586	4.5	65	19
Franco Harris	400	1,556	3.9	50	16
Thurman Thomas	339	1,442	4.3	40	16
Tony Dorsett	302	1,383	4.6	53	9
Marcus Allen	267	1,347	5.0	74	11
Terrell Davis	204	1,140	5.6	62	12
John Riggins	251	996	4.0	43	12
Larry Csonka	225	891	4.0	49	9
Chuck Foreman	229	860	3.8	62	7
Roger Craig	208	841	4.0	80	7

TOP 10 POSTSEASON PASSERS

Player	Att.	Comp.	Pct. Comp.	Yards	Avg. Gain	TD	Pct. TD	Int.	Pct. Int.	Rating
Bart Starr	213	130	61.0	1,753	8.23	15	7.0	3	1.4	104.8
Joe Montana	734	460	62.7	5,772	7.86	45	6.1	21	2.9	95.6
Jake Delhomme	192	113	58.9	1,642	8.55	11	5.7	5	2.6	95.0
Ken Anderson	166	110	66.3	1,321	7.96	9	5.4	6	3.6	93.5
Kurt Warner	268	169	63.1	2,221	8.29	15	5.6	10	3.7	92.3
Joe Theismann	211	128	60.7	1,782	8.45	11	5.2	7	3.3	91.4
Troy Aikman	502	320	63.7	3,849	7.67	23	4.6	17	3.4	88.3
Tom Brady	595	372	62.5	3,954	6.7	26	4.4	12	2.0	88.0
Steve Young	471	292	62.0	3,326	7.06	20	4.2	13	2.8	85.8
Brett Favre	721	438	60.7	5,311	7.4	39	5.4	28	3.9	85.2

TOP 10 POSTSEASON PASS RECEIVERS

Player	No.	Yards	Avg.	Long	TD
Jerry Rice	151	2,245	14.9	72	22
Michael Irvin	87	1,315	15.1	53	8
Andre Reed	85	1,229	14.5	72	9
Thurman Thomas	76	672	8.8	27	5
Cliff Branch	73	1,289	17.7	72	5
Fred Biletnikoff	70	1,167	16.7	57	10
Art Monk	69	1,062	15.4	48	7
Drew Pearson	67	1,105	16.5	83	8
Hines Ward	67	896	13.4	45	8
Tony Nathan	65	649	10.0	39	2

TOP 10 POSTSEASON INTERCEPTION LEADERS

Player	Interceptions
Ronnie Lott	9
Bill Simpson	9
Charlie Waters	9
Lester Hayes	8
Willie Brown	7
Rodney Harrison	7
Dennis Thurman	7
Bobby Bryant	6
Eric Davis	6
Glen Edwards	6
Darrell Green	6
Cliff Harris	6
Ty Law	6
Vernon Perry	6
Aeneas Williams	6

TOP 10 POSTSEASON SACK LEADERS

Player	Sacks
Willie McGinest	16.0
Bruce Smith	14.5
Reggie White	12.0
Charles Haley	11.0
Richard Dent	10.5
Trace Armstrong	10.0
Charles Mann	10.0
Tony Tolbert	10.0
Neil Smith	9.5
Michael Strahan	9.5

Sacks became an official statistic in 1982.

Compiled by Elias Sports Bureau

Super Bowl I, 1/15/67	Super Bowl XXII, 1/31/88
Super Bowl II, 1/14/68	Super Bowl XXIII, 1/22/89
Super Bowl III, 1/12/69	Super Bowl XXIV, 1/28/90
Super Bowl IV, 1/11/70	Super Bowl XXV, 1/27/91
Super Bowl V, 1/17/71	Super Bowl XXVI, 1/26/92
Super Bowl VI, 1/16/72	Super Bowl XXVII, 1/31/93
Super Bowl VII, 1/14/73	Super Bowl XXVIII, 1/30/94
Super Bowl VIII, 1/13/74	Super Bowl XXIX, 1/29/95
Super Bowl IX, 1/12/75	Super Bowl XXX, 1/28/96
Super Bowl X, 1/18/76	Super Bowl XXXI, 1/26/97
Super Bowl XI, 1/9/77	Super Bowl XXXII, 1/25/98
Super Bowl XII, 1/15/78	Super Bowl XXXIII, 1/31/99
Super Bowl XIII, 1/21/79	Super Bowl XXXIV, 1/30/00
Super Bowl XIV, 1/20/80	Super Bowl XXXV, 1/28/01
Super Bowl XV, 1/25/81	Super Bowl XXXVI, 2/3/02
Super Bowl XVI, 1/24/82	Super Bowl XXXVII, 1/26/03
Super Bowl XVII, 1/30/83	Super Bowl XXXVIII, 2/1/04
Super Bowl XVIII, 1/22/84	Super Bowl XXXIX, 2/6/05
Super Bowl XIX, 1/20/85	Super Bowl XL, 2/5/06
Super Bowl XX, 1/26/86	Super Bowl XLI, 2/4/07
Super Bowl XXI, 1/25/87	Super Bowl XLII, 2/3/08

INDIVIDUAL RECORDS

SERVICE
Most Games
- 6 Mike Lodish, Buffalo, XXV-XXVIII; Denver, XXXII-XXXIII
- 5 Marv Fleming, Green Bay, I-II; Miami, VI-VIII
  Larry Cole, Dallas, V-VI, X, XII-XIII
  Cliff Harris, Dallas, V-VI, X, XII-XIII
  Charles Haley, San Francisco, XXIII-XXIV; Dallas, XXVII-XXVIII, XXX
  D.D. Lewis, Dallas, V-VI, X, XII-XIII
  Preston Pearson, Baltimore, III; Pittsburgh, IX; Dallas, X, XII-XIII
  Charlie Waters, Dallas, V-VI, X, XII-XIII
  Rayfield Wright, Dallas, V-VI, X, XII-XIII
  Cornelius Bennett, Buffalo, XXV-XXVIII; Atlanta, XXXIII
  John Elway, Denver, XXI-XXII, XXIV, XXXII-XXXIII
  Glenn Parker, Buffalo, XXV-XXVIII; N.Y. Giants, XXXV
  Bill Romanowski, San Francisco, XXIII-XXIV; Denver, XXXII-XXXIII; Oakland, XXXVII
  Adam Vinatieri, New England, XXXI, XXXVI, XXXVIII, XXXIX; Indianapolis, XLI
  Tedy Bruschi, New England, XXXI, XXXVI, XXXVIII-XXXIX, XLII
- 4 By many players

Most Games, Winning Team
- 5 Charles Haley, San Francisco, XXIII-XXIV; Dallas, XXVII-XXVIII, XXX
- 4 By many players

Most Games, Coach
- 6 Don Shula, Baltimore, III; Miami, VI-VIII, XVII, XIX
- 5 Tom Landry, Dallas, V-VI, X, XII-XIII
- 4 Bud Grant, Minnesota, IV, VIII-IX, XI
  Chuck Noll, Pittsburgh, IX-X, XIII-XIV
  Joe Gibbs, Washington, XVII-XVIII, XXII, XXVI
  Marv Levy, Buffalo, XXV-XXVIII
  Dan Reeves, Denver, XXI-XXII, XXIV; Atlanta, XXXIII
  Bill Belichick, New England, XXXVI, XXXVIII-XXXIX, XLII

Most Games, Winning Team, Coach
- 4 Chuck Noll, Pittsburgh, IX-X, XIII-XIV
- 3 Bill Walsh, San Francisco, XVI, XIX, XXIII
  Joe Gibbs, Washington, XVII, XXII, XXVI
  Bill Belichick, New England, XXXVI, XXXVIII-XXXIX
- 2 Vince Lombardi, Green Bay, I-II
  Tom Landry, Dallas, VI, XII
  Don Shula, Miami, VII-VIII

Tom Flores, Oakland, XV; L.A. Raiders, XVIII
Bill Parcells, N.Y. Giants, XXI, XXV
Jimmy Johnson, Dallas, XXVII-XXVIII
George Seifert, San Francisco, XXIV, XXIX
Mike Shanahan, Denver, XXXII-XXXIII

Most Games, Losing Team, Coach
- 4 Bud Grant, Minnesota, IV, VIII-IX, XI
  Don Shula, Baltimore, III; Miami, VI, XVII, XIX
  Marv Levy, Buffalo, XXV-XXVIII
  Dan Reeves, Denver, XXI-XXII, XXIV; Atlanta, XXXIII
- 3 Tom Landry, Dallas, V, X, XIII

SCORING
POINTS
Most Points, Career
- 48 Jerry Rice, San Francisco-Oakland, 4 games (8-td)
- 34 Adam Vinatieri, New England-Indianapolis, 5 games (7-fg, 13-xp)
- 30 Emmitt Smith, Dallas, 3 games (5-td)

Most Points, Game
- 18 Roger Craig, San Francisco vs. Miami, XIX (3-td)
  Jerry Rice, San Francisco vs. Denver, XXIV (3-td); vs. San Diego, XXIX (3-td)
  Ricky Watters, San Francisco vs. San Diego, XXIX (3-td)
  Terrell Davis, Denver vs. Green Bay, XXXII (3-td)
- 15 Don Chandler, Green Bay vs. Oakland, II (3-pat, 4-fg)
- 14 Ray Wersching, San Francisco vs. Cincinnati, XVI (2-pat, 4-fg)
  Kevin Butler, Chicago vs. New England, XX (5-pat, 3-fg)

TOUCHDOWNS
Most Touchdowns, Career
- 8 Jerry Rice, San Francisco-Oakland, 4 games (8-p)
- 5 Emmitt Smith, Dallas, 3 games (5-r)
- 4 Franco Harris, Pittsburgh, 4 games (4-r)
  Roger Craig, San Francisco, 3 games (2-r, 2-p)
  Thurman Thomas, Buffalo, 4 games (4-r)
  John Elway, Denver, 5 games (4-r)

Most Touchdowns, Game
- 3 Roger Craig, San Francisco vs. Miami, XIX (1-r, 2-p)
  Jerry Rice, San Francisco. vs. Denver, XXIV (3-p); vs. San Diego, XXIX (3-p)
  Ricky Watters, San Francisco vs. San Diego, XXIX (1-r, 2-p)
  Terrell Davis, Denver vs. Green Bay, XXXII (3-r)
- 2 Max McGee, Green Bay vs. Kansas City, I (2-p)
  Elijah Pitts, Green Bay vs. Kansas City, I (2-r)
  Bill Miller, Oakland vs. Green Bay, II (2-p)
  Larry Csonka, Miami vs. Minnesota, VIII (2-r)
  Pete Banaszak, Oakland vs. Minnesota, XI (2-r)
  John Stallworth, Pittsburgh vs. Dallas, XIII (2-p)
  Franco Harris, Pittsburgh vs. Los Angeles, XIV (2-r)
  Cliff Branch, Oakland vs. Philadelphia, XV (2-p)
  Dan Ross, Cincinnati vs. San Francisco, XVI (2-p)
  Marcus Allen, L.A. Raiders vs. Washington, XVIII (2-r)
  Jim McMahon, Chicago vs. New England, XX (2-r)
  Ricky Sanders, Washington vs. Denver, XXII (2-p)
  Timmy Smith, Washington vs. Denver, XXII (2-r)
  Tom Rathman, San Francisco vs. Denver, XXIV (2-r)
  Gerald Riggs, Washington vs. Buffalo, XXVI (2-r)
  Michael Irvin, Dallas vs. Buffalo, XXVII (2-p)
  Emmitt Smith, Dallas vs. Buffalo, XXVIII (2-r)
  Emmitt Smith, Dallas vs. Pittsburgh, XXX (2-r)
  Antonio Freeman, Green Bay vs. Denver, XXXII (2-p)
  Howard Griffith, Denver vs. Atlanta, XXXIII (2-r)
  Eddie George, Tennessee vs. St. Louis, XXXIV (2-r)
  Keenan McCardell, Tampa Bay vs. Oakland, XXXVII (2-r)

Dwight Smith, Tampa Bay vs. Oakland, XXXVII (2-ret)

POINTS AFTER TOUCHDOWN
Most (One-Point) Points After Touchdown, Career
- 13 Adam Vinatieri, New England-Indianapolis, 5 games (13 att)
- 9 Mike Cofer, San Francisco, 2 games (10 att)
- 8 Don Chandler, Green Bay, 2 games (8 att)
  - Roy Gerela, Pittsburgh, 3 games (9 att)
  - Chris Bahr, Oakland-L.A. Raiders, 2 games (8 att)
  - Jason Elam, Denver, 2 games (8 att)

Most (One-Point) Points After Touchdown, Game
- 7 Mike Cofer, San Francisco vs. Denver, XXIV (8 att)
  - Lin Elliott, Dallas vs. Buffalo, XXVII (7 att)
  - Doug Brien, San Francisco vs. San Diego, XXIX (7 att)
- 6 Ali Haji-Sheikh, Washington vs. Denver, XXII (6 att)
  - Martín Gramatica, Tampa Bay vs. Oakland, XXXVII (6 att)
- 5 Don Chandler, Green Bay vs. Kansas City, I (5 att)
  - Roy Gerela, Pittsburgh vs. Dallas, XIII (5 att)
  - Chris Bahr, L.A. Raiders vs. Washington, XVIII (5 att)
  - Ray Wersching, San Francisco vs. Miami, XIX (5 att)
  - Kevin Butler, Chicago vs. New England, XX (5 att)

Most Two-Point Conversions, Game
- 1 Mark Seay, San Diego vs. San Francisco, XXIX
  - Alfred Pupunu, San Diego vs. San Francisco, XXIX
  - Mark Chmura, Green Bay vs. New England, XXXI
  - Kevin Faulk, New England vs. Carolina, XXXVIII

FIELD GOALS
Field Goals Attempted, Career
- 10 Adam Vinatieri, New England-Indianapolis, 5 games
- 6 Jim Turner, N.Y. Jets-Denver, 2 games
  - Roy Gerela, Pittsburgh, 3 games
  - Rich Karlis, Denver, 2 games
  - Jeff Wilkins, St. Louis, 2 games
- 5 Efren Herrera, Dallas, 1 game
  - Ray Wersching, San Francisco, 2 games
  - Jason Elam, Denver, 2 games

Most Field Goals Attempted, Game
- 5 Jim Turner, N.Y. Jets vs. Baltimore, III
  - Efren Herrera, Dallas vs. Denver, XII
- 4 Don Chandler, Green Bay vs. Oakland, II
  - Roy Gerela, Pittsburgh vs. Dallas, X
  - Ray Wersching, San Francisco vs. Cincinnati, XVI
  - Rich Karlis, Denver vs. N.Y. Giants, XXI
  - Mike Cofer, San Francisco vs. Cincinnati, XXIII
  - Jason Elam, Denver vs. Atlanta, XXXIII
  - Jeff Wilkins, St. Louis vs. Tennessee, XXXIV
  - Adam Vinatieri, Indianapolis vs. Chicago, XLI

Most Field Goals, Career
- 7 Adam Vinatieri, New England-Indianapolis, 5 games (10 att)
- 5 Ray Wersching, San Francisco, 2 games (5 att)
- 4 Don Chandler, Green Bay, 2 games (4 att)
  - Jim Turner, N.Y. Jets-Denver, 2 games (6 att)
  - Uwe von Schamann, Miami, 2 games (4 att)
  - Jeff Wilkins, St. Louis, 2 games (6 att)

Most Field Goals, Game
- 4 Don Chandler, Green Bay vs. Oakland, II
  - Ray Wersching, San Francisco vs. Cincinnati, XVI
- 3 Jim Turner, N.Y. Jets vs. Baltimore, III
  - Jan Stenerud, Kansas City vs. Minnesota, IV
  - Uwe von Schamann, Miami vs. San Francisco, XIX
  - Kevin Butler, Chicago vs. New England, XX
  - Jim Breech, Cincinnati vs. San Francisco, XXIII
  - Chip Lohmiller, Washington vs. Buffalo, XXVI
  - Eddie Murray, Dallas vs. Buffalo, XXVIII
  - Jeff Wilkins, St. Louis vs. Tennessee, XXXIV
  - Adam Vinatieri, Indianapolis vs. Chicago, XLI

Longest Field Goal
- 54 Steve Christie, Buffalo vs. Dallas, XXVIII
- 51 Jason Elam, Denver vs. Green Bay, XXXII
- 50 Jeff Wilkins, St. Louis vs. New England, XXXVI
  - John Kasay, Carolina vs. New England, XXXVIII

SAFETIES
Most Safeties, Game
- 1 Dwight White, Pittsburgh vs. Minnesota, IX
  - Reggie Harrison, Pittsburgh vs. Dallas, X
  - Henry Waechter, Chicago vs. New England, XX
  - George Martin, N.Y. Giants vs. Denver, XXI
  - Bruce Smith, Buffalo vs. N.Y. Giants, XXV

RUSHING
ATTEMPTS
Most Attempts, Career
- 101 Franco Harris, Pittsburgh, 4 games
- 70 Emmitt Smith, Dallas, 3 games
- 64 John Riggins, Washington, 2 games

Most Attempts, Game
- 38 John Riggins, Washington vs. Miami, XVII
- 34 Franco Harris, Pittsburgh vs. Minnesota, IX
- 33 Larry Csonka, Miami vs. Minnesota, VIII

YARDS GAINED
Most Yards Gained, Career
- 354 Franco Harris, Pittsburgh, 4 games
- 297 Larry Csonka, Miami, 3 games
- 289 Emmitt Smith, Dallas, 3 games

Most Yards Gained, Game
- 204 Timmy Smith, Washington vs. Denver, XXII
- 191 Marcus Allen, L.A. Raiders vs. Washington, XVIII
- 166 John Riggins, Washington vs. Miami, XVII

Longest Run From Scrimmage
- 75 Willie Parker, Pittsburgh vs. Seattle, XL (TD)
- 74 Marcus Allen, L.A. Raiders vs. Washington, XVIII (TD)
- 58 Tom Matte, Baltimore vs. N.Y. Jets, III
  - Timmy Smith, Washington vs. Denver, XXII (TD)

AVERAGE GAIN
Highest Average Gain, Career (20 attempts)
- 9.6 Marcus Allen, L.A. Raiders, 1 game (20-191)
- 9.3 Timmy Smith, Washington, 1 game (22-204)
- 5.4 Dominic Rhodes, Indianapolis, 1 game (21-113)

Highest Average Gain, Game (10 attempts)
- 10.5 Tom Matte, Baltimore vs. N.Y. Jets, III (11-116)
- 9.6 Marcus Allen, L.A. Raiders vs. Washington, XVIII (20-191)
- 9.3 Willie Parker, Pittsburgh vs. Seattle, XL (10-93)

TOUCHDOWNS
Most Touchdowns, Career
- 5 Emmitt Smith, Dallas, 3 games
- 4 Franco Harris, Pittsburgh, 4 games
  - Thurman Thomas, Buffalo, 4 games
  - John Elway, Denver, 5 games
- 3 Terrell Davis, Denver, 2 games

Most Touchdowns, Game
- 3 Terrell Davis, Denver vs. Green Bay, XXXII
- 2 Elijah Pitts, Green Bay vs. Kansas City, I
  - Larry Csonka, Miami vs. Minnesota, VIII
  - Pete Banaszak, Oakland vs. Minnesota, XI
  - Franco Harris, Pittsburgh vs. Los Angeles, XIV
  - Marcus Allen, L.A. Raiders vs. Washington, XVIII
  - Jim McMahon, Chicago vs. New England, XX
  - Timmy Smith, Washington vs. Denver, XXII
  - Tom Rathman, San Francisco vs. Denver, XXIV
  - Gerald Riggs, Washington vs. Buffalo, XXVI
  - Emmitt Smith, Dallas vs. Buffalo, XXVIII

Emmitt Smith, Dallas vs. Pittsburgh, XXX
Howard Griffith, Denver vs. Atlanta, XXXIII
Eddie George, Tennessee vs. St. Louis, XXXIV

PASSING
PASSER RATING
Highest Passer Rating, Career (40 attempts)
127.8   Joe Montana, San Francisco, 4 games
122.8   Jim Plunkett, Oakland-L.A. Raiders, 2 games
112.8   Terry Bradshaw, Pittsburgh, 4 games

ATTEMPTS
Most Passes Attempted, Career
156   Tom Brady, New England, 4 games
152   John Elway, Denver, 5 games
145   Jim Kelly, Buffalo, 4 games
Most Passes Attempted, Game
58   Jim Kelly, Buffalo vs. Washington, XXVI
51   Donovan McNabb, Philadelphia vs. New England, XXXIX
50   Dan Marino, Miami vs. San Francisco, XIX
Jim Kelly, Buffalo vs. Dallas, XXVIII

COMPLETIONS
Most Passes Completed, Career
100   Tom Brady, New England, 4 games
83   Joe Montana, San Francisco, 4 games
81   Jim Kelly, Buffalo, 4 games
Most Passes Completed, Game
32   Tom Brady, New England vs. Carolina, XXXVIII
31   Jim Kelly, Buffalo vs. Dallas, XXVIII
30   Donovan McNabb, Philadelphia vs. New England, XXXIX
Most Consecutive Completions, Game
13   Joe Montana, San Francisco vs. Denver, XXIV
10   Phil Simms, N.Y. Giants vs. Denver, XXI
Troy Aikman, Dallas vs. Pittsburgh, XXX
9   Jim Kelly, Buffalo vs. Dallas, XXVIII
Neil O'Donnell, Pittsburgh vs. Dallas, XXX
Steve McNair, Tennessee vs. St. Louis, XXXIV
Peyton Manning, Indianapolis vs. Chicago, XLI

COMPLETION PERCENTAGE
Highest Completion Percentage, Career (40 attempts)
70.0   Troy Aikman, Dallas, 3 games, (80-56)
68.0   Joe Montana, San Francisco, 4 games (122-83)
64.1   Tom Brady, New England, 4 games (156-100)
Highest Completion Percentage, Game (20 attempts)
88.0   Phil Simms, N.Y. Giants vs. Denver, XXI (25-22)
75.9   Joe Montana, San Francisco vs. Denver, XXIV (29-22)
73.5   Ken Anderson, Cincinnati vs. San Francisco, XVI (34-25)

YARDS GAINED
Most Yards Gained, Career
1,142   Joe Montana, San Francisco, 4 games
1,128   John Elway, Denver, 5 games
1,001   Tom Brady, New England, 4 games
Most Yards Gained, Game
414   Kurt Warner, St. Louis vs. Tennessee, XXXIV
365   Kurt Warner, St. Louis vs. New England, XXXVI
357   Joe Montana, San Francisco vs. Cincinnati, XXIII
Donovan McNabb, Philadelphia vs. New England, XXXIX
Longest Pass Completion
85   Jake Delhomme (to Muhammad), Carolina vs. New England, XXXVIII (TD)
81   Brett Favre (to Freeman), Green Bay vs. New England, XXXI (TD)

80   Jim Plunkett (to King), Oakland vs. Philadelphia, XV (TD)
Doug Williams (to Sanders), Washington vs. Denver, XXII (TD)
John Elway (to R. Smith), Denver vs. Atlanta, XXXIII (TD)

AVERAGE GAIN
Highest Average Gain, Career (40 attempts)
11.10   Terry Bradshaw, Pittsburgh, 4 games (84-932)
9.62   Bart Starr, Green Bay, 2 games (47-452)
9.41   Jim Plunkett, Oakland-L.A. Raiders, 2 games (46-433)
Highest Average Gain, Game (20 attempts)
14.71   Terry Bradshaw, Pittsburgh vs. Los Angeles, XIV (21-309)
12.80   Jim McMahon, Chicago vs. New England, XX (20-256)
12.43   Jim Plunkett, Oakland vs. Philadelphia, XV (21-261)

TOUCHDOWNS
Most Touchdown Passes, Career
11   Joe Montana, San Francisco, 4 games
9   Terry Bradshaw, Pittsburgh, 4 games
8   Roger Staubach, Dallas, 4 games
Most Touchdown Passes, Game
6   Steve Young, San Francisco vs. San Diego, XXIX
5   Joe Montana, San Francisco vs. Denver, XXIV
4   Terry Bradshaw, Pittsburgh vs. Dallas, XIII
Doug Williams, Washington vs. Denver, XXII
Troy Aikman, Dallas vs. Buffalo, XXVII

HAD INTERCEPTED
Lowest Percentage, Passes Had Intercepted, Career (40 attempts)
0.00   Jim Plunkett, Oakland-L.A. Raiders, 2 games (46-0)
Joe Montana, San Francisco, 4 games (122-0)
0.64   Tom Brady, New England, 4 games (156-1)
1.25   Troy Aikman, Dallas, 3 games (80-1)
Most Attempts, Without Interception, Game
48   Tom Brady, New England vs. N.Y. Giants, XLII
45   Kurt Warner, St. Louis vs. Tennessee, XXXIV
36   Joe Montana, San Francisco vs. Cincinnati, XXIII
Steve Young, San Francisco vs. San Diego, XXIX
Steve McNair, Tennessee vs. St. Louis, XXXIV
Most Passes Had Intercepted, Career
8   John Elway, Denver, 5 games
7   Craig Morton, Dallas-Denver, 2 games
Jim Kelly, Buffalo, 4 games
6   Fran Tarkenton, Minnesota, 3 games
Most Passes Had Intercepted, Game
5   Rich Gannon, Oakland vs. Tampa Bay, XXXVII
4   Craig Morton, Denver vs. Dallas, XII
Jim Kelly, Buffalo vs. Washington, XXVI
Drew Bledsoe, New England vs. Green Bay, XXXI
Kerry Collins, N.Y. Giants vs. Baltimore, XXXV
3   By 11 players

PASS RECEIVING
RECEPTIONS
Most Receptions, Career
33   Jerry Rice, San Francisco-Oakland, 4 games
27   Andre Reed, Buffalo, 4 games
21   Deion Branch, New England, 2 games
Most Receptions, Game
11   Dan Ross, Cincinnati vs. San Francisco, XVI
Jerry Rice, San Francisco vs. Cincinnati, XXIII
Deion Branch, New England vs. Philadelphia, XXXIX
Wes Welker, New England vs. N.Y. Giants, XLII
10   Tony Nathan, Miami vs. San Francisco, XIX
Jerry Rice, San Francisco vs. San Diego, XXIX
Andre Hastings, Pittsburgh vs. Dallas, XXX
Deion Branch, New England vs. Carolina, XXXVIII

Joseph Addai, Indianapolis vs. Chicago, XLI
9   Ricky Sanders, Washington vs. Denver, XXII
    Antonio Freeman, Green Bay vs. Denver, XXXII
    Terrell Owens, Philadelphia vs. New England, XXXIX

YARDS GAINED
Most Yards Gained, Career
589   Jerry Rice, San Francisco-Oakland, 4 games
364   Lynn Swann, Pittsburgh, 4 games
323   Andre Reed, Buffalo, 4 games
Most Yards Gained, Game
215   Jerry Rice, San Francisco vs. Cincinnati, XXIII
193   Ricky Sanders, Washington vs. Denver, XXII
162   Isaac Bruce, St. Louis vs. Tennessee, XXXIV
Longest Reception
85   Muhsin Muhammad (from Delhomme), Carolina vs.
     New England, XXXVIII
81   Antonio Freeman (from Favre), Green Bay vs.
     New England, XXXI (TD)
80   Kenny King (from Plunkett), Oakland vs.
     Philadelphia, XV (TD)
     Ricky Sanders (from Williams), Washington vs.
     Denver, XXII (TD)
     Rod Smith (from Elway), Denver vs. Atlanta, XXXIII

AVERAGE GAIN
Highest Average Gain, Career (8 receptions)
24.4   John Stallworth, Pittsburgh, 4 games (11-268)
23.4   Ricky Sanders, Washington, 2 games (10-234)
22.8   Lynn Swann, Pittsburgh, 4 games (16-364)
Highest Average Gain, Game (3 receptions)
40.33   John Stallworth, Pittsburgh vs. Los Angeles, XIV
        (3-121)
40.25   Lynn Swann, Pittsburgh vs. Dallas, X (4-161)
38.33   John Stallworth, Pittsburgh vs. Dallas, XIII (3-115)

TOUCHDOWNS
Most Touchdowns, Career
8   Jerry Rice, San Francisco-Oakland, 4 games
3   John Stallworth, Pittsburgh, 4 games
    Lynn Swann, Pittsburgh, 4 games
    Cliff Branch, Oakland-L.A. Raiders, 3 games
    Antonio Freeman, Green Bay, 2 games
2   Max McGee, Green Bay, 2 games
    Bill Miller, Oakland, 1 game
    Butch Johnson, Dallas, 2 games
    Dan Ross, Cincinnati, 1 game
    Roger Craig, San Francisco, 3 games
    Ricky Sanders, Washington, 2 games
    John Taylor, San Francisco, 3 games
    Gary Clark, Washington, 2 games
    Don Beebe, Buffalo-Green Bay, 4 games
    Michael Irvin, Dallas, 3 games
    Ricky Watters, San Francisco, 1 game
    Jay Novacek, Dallas, 3 games
    Keenan McCardell, Tampa Bay, 1 game
    Ricky Proehl, St. Louis-Carolina, 3 games
    David Givens, New England, 3 games
    Mike Vrabel, New England, 4 games
    Muhsin Muhammad, Carolina-Chicago, 2 games
Most Touchdowns, Game
3   Jerry Rice, San Francisco vs. Denver, XXIV; vs.
    San Diego, XXIX
2   Max McGee, Green Bay vs. Kansas City, I
    Bill Miller, Oakland vs. Green Bay, II
    John Stallworth, Pittsburgh vs. Dallas, XIII
    Cliff Branch, Oakland vs. Philadelphia, XV
    Dan Ross, Cincinnati vs. San Francisco, XVI
    Roger Craig, San Francisco vs. Miami, XIX
    Ricky Sanders, Washington vs. Denver, XXII

Michael Irvin, Dallas vs. Buffalo, XXVII
Ricky Watters, San Francisco vs. San Diego, XXIX
Antonio Freeman, Green Bay vs. Denver, XXXII
Keenan McCardell, Tampa Bay vs. Oakland, XXXVII

INTERCEPTIONS BY
Most Interceptions By, Career
3   Chuck Howley, Dallas, 2 games
    Rod Martin, Oakland-L.A. Raiders, 2 games
    Larry Brown, Dallas, 3 games
2   Randy Beverly, N.Y. Jets, 1 game
    Jake Scott, Miami, 3 games
    Mike Wagner, Pittsburgh, 3 games
    Mel Blount, Pittsburgh, 4 games
    Eric Wright, San Francisco, 4 games
    Barry Wilburn, Washington, 1 game
    Brad Edwards, Washington, 1 game
    Thomas Everett, Dallas, 2 games
    James Washington, Dallas, 2 games
    Darrien Gordon, San Diego-Denver-Oakland,
    4 games
    Dexter Jackson, Tampa Bay, 1 game
    Dwight Smith, Tampa Bay, 1 game
    Rodney Harrison, San Diego-New England, 4 games
Most Interceptions By, Game
3   Rod Martin, Oakland vs. Philadelphia, XV
2   Randy Beverly, N.Y. Jets vs. Baltimore, III
    Chuck Howley, Dallas vs. Baltimore, V
    Jake Scott, Miami vs. Washington, VII
    Barry Wilburn, Washington vs. Denver, XXII
    Brad Edwards, Washington vs. Buffalo, XXVI
    Thomas Everett, Dallas vs. Buffalo, XXVII
    Larry Brown, Dallas vs. Pittsburgh, XXX
    Darrien Gordon, Denver vs. Atlanta, XXXIII
    Dexter Jackson, Tampa Bay vs. Oakland, XXXVII
    Dwight Smith, Tampa Bay vs. Oakland, XXXVII
    Rodney Harrison, New England vs. Philadelphia,
    XXXIX

YARDS GAINED
Most Yards Gained, Career
108   Darrien Gordon, San Diego-Denver-Oakland,
      4 games
94   Dwight Smith, Tampa Bay, 1 game
77   Larry Brown, Dallas, 3 games
Most Yards Gained, Game
108   Darrien Gordon, Denver vs. Atlanta, XXXIII
94   Dwight Smith, Tampa Bay vs. Oakland, XXXVII
77   Larry Brown, Dallas vs. Pittsburgh, XXX
Longest Return
76   Kelly Herndon, Seattle vs. Pittsburgh, XL
75   Willie Brown, Oakland vs. Minnesota, XI (TD)
60   Herb Adderley, Green Bay vs. Oakland, II (TD)

TOUCHDOWNS
Most Touchdowns, Game
2   Dwight Smith, Tampa Bay vs. Oakland, XXXVII
1   Herb Adderley, Green Bay vs. Oakland, II
    Willie Brown, Oakland vs. Minnesota, XI
    Jack Squirek, L.A. Raiders vs. Washington, XVIII
    Reggie Phillips, Chicago vs. New England, XX
    Duane Starks, Baltimore vs. N.Y. Giants, XXXV
    Ty Law, New England vs. St. Louis, XXXVI
    Derrick Brooks, Tampa Bay vs. Oakland, XXXVII
    Kelvin Hayden, Indianapolis vs. Chicago, XLI

PUNTING
Most Punts, Career
17   Mike Eischeid, Oakland-Minnesota, 3 games
     Mike Horan, Denver-St. Louis, 4 games

16   Brad Maynard, N.Y. Giants-Chicago, 2 games
15   Larry Seiple, Miami, 3 games

Most Punts, Game

11   Brad Maynard, N.Y. Giants vs. Baltimore, XXXV
10   Kyle Richardson, Baltimore vs. N.Y. Giants, XXXV
9   Ron Widby, Dallas vs. Baltimore, V

Longest Punt

63   Lee Johnson, Cincinnati vs. San Francisco, XXIII
62   Rich Camarillo, New England vs. Chicago, XX
61   Jerrel Wilson, Kansas City vs. Green Bay, I

AVERAGE YARDAGE

Highest Average, Punting, Career (10 punts)

46.5   Jerrel Wilson, Kansas City, 2 games (11-511)
43.8   Tom Rouen, Denver-Seattle, 3 games (11-482)
43.0   Kyle Richardson, Baltimore, 1 game (10-430)
      Tom Tupa, New England-Tampa Bay, 2 games
      (12-516)

Highest Average, Punting, Game (4 punts)

50.2   Tom Rouen, Seattle vs. Pittsburgh, XL (6-301)
48.8   Bryan Wagner, San Diego vs. San Francisco, XXIX
      (4-195)
48.7   Chris Gardocki, Pittsburgh vs. Seattle, XL (6-292)

PUNT RETURNS

Most Punt Returns, Career

8   Troy Brown, New England, 3 games
6   Willie Wood, Green Bay, 2 games
   Jake Scott, Miami, 3 games
   Theo Bell, Pittsburgh, 2 games
   Mike Nelms, Washington, 1 game
   John Taylor, San Francisco, 3 games
   Desmond Howard, Green Bay, 1 game
   David Meggett, N.Y. Giants-New England, 2 games
   Darrien Gordon, San Diego-Denver-Oakland,
      4 games
5   Dana McLemore, San Francisco, 1 game

Most Punt Returns, Game

6   Mike Nelms, Washington vs. Miami, XVII
   Desmond Howard, Green Bay vs. New England, XXXI
5   Willie Wood, Green Bay vs. Oakland, II
   Dana McLemore, San Francisco vs. Miami, XIX
4   By nine players

Most Fair Catches, Game

4   Jermaine Lewis, Baltimore vs. N.Y. Giants, XXXV
   Karl Williams, Tampa Bay vs. Oakland, XXXVII
3   Ron Gardin, Baltimore vs. Dallas, V
   Golden Richards, Dallas vs. Pittsburgh, X
   Greg Pruitt, L.A. Raiders vs. Washington, XVIII
   Al Edwards, Buffalo vs. N.Y. Giants, XXV
   David Meggett, N.Y. Giants vs. Buffalo, XXV

YARDS GAINED

Most Yards Gained, Career

94   John Taylor, San Francisco, 3 games
90   Desmond Howard, Green Bay, 1 game
67   David Meggett, N.Y. Giants-New England, 2 games

Most Yards Gained, Game

90   Desmond Howard, Green Bay vs. New England, XXXI
56   John Taylor, San Francisco vs. Cincinnati, XXIII
52   Mike Nelms, Washington vs. Miami, XVII

Longest Return

45   John Taylor, San Francisco vs. Cincinnati, XXIII
34   Darrell Green, Washington vs. L.A. Raiders, XVIII
   Desmond Howard, Green Bay vs. New England, XXXI
   Jermaine Lewis, Baltimore vs. N.Y. Giants, XXXV
32   Desmond Howard, Green Bay vs. New England, XXXI

AVERAGE YARDAGE

Highest Average, Career (4 returns)

15.7   John Taylor, San Francisco, 3 games (6-94)
15.0   Desmond Howard, Green Bay, 1 game (6-90)
11.2   David Meggett, N.Y. Giants-New England, 2 games
      (6-67)

Highest Average, Game (3 returns)

18.7   John Taylor, San Francisco vs. Cincinnati, XXIII (3-56)
15.0   Desmond Howard, Green Bay vs. New England, XXXI
      (6-90)
14.0   Terrence Wilkins, Indianapolis vs. Chicago, XLI
      (3-42)

TOUCHDOWNS

Most Touchdowns, Game

None

KICKOFF RETURNS

Most Kickoff Returns, Career

10   Ken Bell, Denver, 3 games
8   Larry Anderson, Pittsburgh, 2 games
   Fulton Walker, Miami, 2 games
   Andre Coleman, San Diego, 1 game
   Marcus Knight, Oakland, 1 game
7   Preston Pearson, Baltimore-Pittsburgh-Dallas, 5 games
   Stephen Starring, New England, 1 game
   David Meggett, N.Y. Giants-New England, 2 games

Most Kickoff Returns, Game

8   Andre Coleman, San Diego vs. San Francisco, XXIX
   Marcus Knight, Oakland vs. Tampa Bay, XXXVII
7   Stephen Starring, New England vs. Chicago, XX
6   Darren Carrington, Denver vs. San Francisco, XXIV
   Antonio Freeman, Green Bay vs. Denver, XXXII
   Ron Dixon, N.Y. Giants vs. Baltimore, XXXV

YARDS GAINED

Most Yards Gained, Career

283   Fulton Walker, Miami, 2 games
244   Andre Coleman, San Diego, 1 game
210   Tim Dwight, Atlanta, 1 game

Most Yards Gained, Game

244   Andre Coleman, San Diego vs. San Francisco, XXIX
210   Tim Dwight, Atlanta vs. Denver, XXXIII
190   Fulton Walker, Miami vs. Washington, XVII

Longest Return

99   Desmond Howard, Green Bay vs. New England, XXXI
      (TD)
98   Fulton Walker, Miami vs. Washington, XVII (TD)
   Andre Coleman, San Diego vs. San Francisco, XXIX
      (TD)
97   Ron Dixon, N.Y. Giants vs. Baltimore, XXXV (TD)

AVERAGE YARDAGE

Highest Average, Career (4 returns)

42.0   Tim Dwight, Atlanta, 1 game (5-210)
38.5   Desmond Howard, Green Bay, 1 game (4-154)
35.4   Fulton Walker, Miami, 2 games (8-283)

Highest Average, Game (3 returns)

47.5   Fulton Walker, Miami vs. Washington, XVII (4-190)
42.0   Tim Dwight, Atlanta vs. Denver, XXXIII (5-210)
38.5   Desmond Howard, Green Bay vs. New England, XXXI
      (4-154)

TOUCHDOWNS

Most Touchdowns, Game

1   Fulton Walker, Miami vs. Washington, XVII
   Stanford Jennings, Cincinnati vs. San Francisco, XXIII
   Andre Coleman, San Diego vs. San Francisco, XXIX
   Desmond Howard, Green Bay vs. New England, XXXI
   Tim Dwight, Atlanta vs. Denver, XXXIII

Ron Dixon, N.Y. Giants vs. Baltimore, XXXV
Jermaine Lewis, Baltimore vs. N.Y. Giants, XXXV
Devin Hester, Chicago vs. Indianapolis, XLI

FUMBLES
Most Fumbles, Career
5 Roger Staubach, Dallas, 4 games
4 Jim Kelly, Buffalo, 4 games
3 Franco Harris, Pittsburgh, 4 games
  Terry Bradshaw, Pittsburgh, 4 games
  John Elway, Denver, 5 games
  Frank Reich, Buffalo, 4 games
  Thurman Thomas, Buffalo, 4 games
Most Fumbles, Game
3 Roger Staubach, Dallas vs. Pittsburgh, X
  Jim Kelly, Buffalo vs. Washington, XXVI
  Frank Reich, Buffalo vs. Dallas, XXVII
2 Franco Harris, Pittsburgh vs. Minnesota, IX
  Butch Johnson, Dallas vs. Denver, XII
  Terry Bradshaw, Pittsburgh vs. Dallas, XIII
  Joe Montana, San Francisco vs. Cincinnati, XXIII
  John Elway, Denver vs. San Francisco, XXIV
  Thurman Thomas, Buffalo vs. Dallas, XXVIII
  Rex Grossman, Chicago vs. Indianapolis, XLI
  Eli Manning, N.Y. Giants vs. New England, XLII

RECOVERIES
Most Fumbles Recovered, Career
2 Jake Scott, Miami, 3 games (1 own, 1 opp)
  Fran Tarkenton, Minnesota, 3 games (2 own)
  Franco Harris, Pittsburgh, 4 games (2 own)
  Roger Staubach, Dallas, 4 games (2 own)
  Bobby Walden, Pittsburgh, 2 games (2 own)
  John Fitzgerald, Dallas, 4 games (2 own)
  Randy Hughes, Dallas, 3 games (2 opp)
  Butch Johnson, Dallas, 2 games (2 own)
  Mike Singletary, Chicago, 1 game (2 opp)
  John Elway, Denver, 5 games (2 own)
  Jimmie Jones, Dallas, 2 games (2 opp)
  Kenneth Davis, Buffalo, 4 games (2 own)
  Kurt Warner, St. Louis, 2 games (2 own)
Most Fumbles Recovered, Game
2 Jake Scott, Miami vs. Minnesota, VIII (1 own, 1 opp)
  Roger Staubach, Dallas vs. Pittsburgh, X (2 own)
  Randy Hughes, Dallas vs. Denver, XII (2 opp)
  Butch Johnson, Dallas vs. Denver, XII (2 own)
  Mike Singletary, Chicago vs. New England, XX (2 opp)
  Jimmie Jones, Dallas vs. Buffalo, XXVII (2 opp)

YARDS GAINED
Most Yards Gained, Game
64 Leon Lett, Dallas vs. Buffalo, XXVII (opp)
49 Mike Bass, Washington vs. Miami, VII (opp)
46 James Washington, Dallas vs. Buffalo, XXVIII (opp)
Longest Return
64 Leon Lett, Dallas vs. Buffalo, XXVII
49 Mike Bass, Washington vs. Miami, VII (TD)
46 James Washington, Dallas vs. Buffalo, XXVIII (TD)

TOUCHDOWNS
Most Touchdowns, Game
1 Mike Bass, Washington vs. Miami, VII (opp 49 yds)
  Mike Hegman, Dallas vs. Pittsburgh, XIII (opp 37 yds)
  Jimmie Jones, Dallas vs. Buffalo, XXVII (opp 2 yds)
  Ken Norton, Dallas vs. Buffalo, XXVII (opp 9 yds)
  James Washington, Dallas vs. Buffalo, XXVIII
  (opp 46 yds)

COMBINED NET YARDS GAINED
(Rushing, receiving, interception returns, punt returns, kickoff returns, and fumble returns)
ATTEMPTS
Most Attempts, Career
108 Franco Harris, Pittsburgh, 4 games
81 Emmitt Smith, Dallas, 3 games
72 Roger Craig, San Francisco, 3 games
  Thurman Thomas, Buffalo, 4 games
Most Attempts, Game
39 John Riggins, Washington vs. Miami, XVII
35 Franco Harris, Pittsburgh vs. Minnesota, IX
34 Matt Snell, N.Y. Jets vs. Baltimore, III
  Emmitt Smith, Dallas vs. Buffalo, XXVIII

YARDS GAINED
Most Yards Gained, Career
604 Jerry Rice, San Francisco-Oakland, 4 games
468 Franco Harris, Pittsburgh, 4 games
410 Roger Craig, San Francisco, 3 games
Most Yards Gained, Game
244 Andre Coleman, San Diego vs. San Francisco, XXIX
  Desmond Howard, Green Bay vs. New England, XXXI
235 Ricky Sanders, Washington vs. Denver, XXII
230 Antonio Freeman, Green Bay vs. Denver, XXXII

SACKS
Sacks have been compiled since XVII.
Most Sacks, Career
4.5 Charles Haley, San Francisco-Dallas, 5 games
3.0 Danny Stubbs, San Francisco, 2 games
  Leonard Marshall, N.Y. Giants, 2 games
  Jeff Wright, Buffalo, 4 games
  Reggie White, Green Bay, 2 games
  Willie McGinest, New England, 4 games
  Tedy Bruschi, New England, 5 games
  Mike Vrabel, New England, 4 games
2.5 Dexter Manley, Washington, 3 games
  Michael Strahan, N.Y. Giants, 2 games
Most Sacks, Game
3.0 Reggie White, Green Bay vs. New England, XXXI
2.0 Dwaine Board, San Francisco vs. Miami, XIX
  Dennis Owens, New England vs. Chicago, XX
  Otis Wilson, Chicago vs. New England, XX
  Leonard Marshall, N.Y. Giants vs. Denver, XXI
  Alvin Walton, Washington vs. Denver, XXII
  Charles Haley, San Francisco vs. Cincinnati, XXIII
  Danny Stubbs, San Francisco vs. Denver, XXIV
  Jeff Wright, Buffalo vs. Dallas, XXVIII
  Raylee Johnson, San Diego vs. San Francisco, XXIX
  Chad Hennings, Dallas vs. Pittsburgh, XXX
  Tedy Bruschi, New England vs. Green Bay, XXXI
  Michael McCrary, Baltimore vs. N.Y. Giants, XXXV
  Simeon Rice, Tampa Bay vs. Oakland, XXXVII
  Mike Vrabel, New England vs. Carolina, XXXVIII
  Adalius Thomas, New England vs. N.Y. Giants, XLII
  Justin Tuck, N.Y. Giants vs. New England, XLII

TEAM RECORDS

GAMES, VICTORIES, DEFEATS
Most Games
8 Dallas, V-VI, X, XII-XIII, XXVII-XXVIII, XXX
6 Denver, XII, XXI-XXII, XXIV, XXXII-XXXIII
  Pittsburgh, IX-X, XIII-XIV, XXX, XL
  New England, XX, XXXI, XXXVI, XXXVIII-XXXIX, XLII
5 Miami, VI-VIII, XVII, XIX
  Washington, VII, XVII-XVIII, XXII, XXVI
  San Francisco, XVI, XIX, XXIII-XXIV, XXIX

Oakland/L.A. Raiders, II, XI, XV, XVIII, XXXVII

Most Consecutive Games
- 4   Buffalo, XXV-XXVIII
- 3   Miami, VI-VIII
- 2   Green Bay, I-II; XXXI-XXXII
  Dallas, V-VI; XII-XIII; XXVII-XXVIII
  Minnesota, VIII-IX
  Pittsburgh, IX-X; XIII-XIV
  Washington, XVII-XVIII
  Denver, XXI-XXII; XXXII-XXXIII
  San Francisco, XXIII-XXIV
  New England, XXXVIII-XXXIX

Most Games Won
- 5   San Francisco, XVI, XIX, XXIII-XXIV, XXIX
  Dallas, VI, XII, XXVII-XXVIII, XXX
  Pittsburgh, IX-X, XIII-XIV, XL
- 3   Oakland/L.A. Raiders, XI, XV, XVIII
  Washington, XVII, XXII, XXVI
  Green Bay, I-II, XXXI
  New England, XXXVI, XXXVIII-XXXIX
  N.Y. Giants, XXI, XXV, XLII
- 2   Miami, VII-VIII
  Denver, XXXII, XXXIII
  Baltimore/Indianapolis, V, XLI

Most Consecutive Games Won
- 2   Green Bay, I-II
  Miami, VII-VIII
  Pittsburgh, IX-X, XIII-XIV
  San Francisco, XXIII-XXIV
  Dallas, XXVII-XXVIII
  Denver, XXXII-XXXIII
  New England, XXXVIII-XXXIX

Most Games Lost
- 4   Minnesota, IV, VIII-IX, XI
  Denver, XII, XXI-XXII, XXIV
  Buffalo, XXV-XXVIII
- 3   Dallas, V, X, XIII
  Miami, VI, XVII, XIX
  New England, XX, XXXI, XLII
- 2   Washington, VII, XVIII
  Cincinnati, XVI, XXIIL.A./St. Louis Rams, XIV, XXXVI
  Oakland/L.A. Raiders, II, XXXVII
  Philadelphia, XV, XXXIX

Most Consecutive Games Lost
- 4   Buffalo, XXV-XXVIII
- 2   Minnesota, VIII-IX
  Denver, XXI-XXII

SCORING
Most Points, Game
- 55   San Francisco vs. Denver, XXIV
- 52   Dallas vs. Buffalo, XXVII
- 49   San Francisco vs. San Diego, XXIX

Fewest Points, Game
- 3   Miami vs. Dallas, VI
- 6   Minnesota vs. Pittsburgh, IX
- 7   By five teams

Most Points, Both Teams, Game
- 75   San Francisco (49) vs. San Diego (26), XXIX
- 69   Dallas (52) vs. Buffalo (17), XXVII
  Tampa Bay (48) vs. Oakland (21), XXXVII
- 66   Pittsburgh (35) vs. Dallas (31), XIII

Fewest Points, Both Teams, Game
- 21   Washington (7) vs. Miami (14), VII
- 22   Minnesota (6) vs. Pittsburgh (16), IX
- 23   Baltimore (7) vs. N.Y. Jets (16), III

Largest Margin of Victory, Game
- 45   San Francisco vs. Denver, XXIV (55-10)
- 36   Chicago vs. New England, XX (46-10)
- 35   Dallas vs. Buffalo, XXVII (52-17)

Most Points, Each Half
- 1st: 35   Washington vs. Denver, XXII
- 2nd: 30   N.Y. Giants vs. Denver, XXI

Most Points, Each Quarter
- 1st: 14   Miami vs. Minnesota, VIII
  Oakland vs. Philadelphia, XV
  Dallas vs. Buffalo, XXVII
  San Francisco vs. San Diego, XXIX
  New England vs. Green Bay, XXXI
  Chicago vs. Indianapolis, XLI
- 2nd: 35   Washington vs. Denver, XXII
- 3rd: 21   Chicago vs. New England, XX
- 4th: 21   Dallas vs. Buffalo, XXVII

Most Points, Both Teams, Each Half
- 1st: 45   Washington (35) vs. Denver (10), XXII
- 2nd: 46   Tampa Bay (28) vs. Oakland (18), XXXVII

Fewest Points, Both Teams, Each Half
- 1st: 2   Minnesota (0) vs. Pittsburgh (2), IX
- 2nd: 7   Miami (0) vs. Washington (7), VII
  Denver (0) vs. Washington (7), XXII

Most Points, Both Teams, Each Quarter
- 1st: 24   New England (14) vs. Green Bay (10), XXXI
- 2nd: 35   Washington (35) vs. Denver (0), XXII
- 3rd: 24   Washington (14) vs. Buffalo (10), XXVI
- 4th: 37   Carolina (19) vs. New England (18), XXXVIII

TOUCHDOWNS
Most Touchdowns, Game
- 8   San Francisco vs. Denver, XXIV
- 7   Dallas vs. Buffalo, XXVII
  San Francisco vs. San Diego, XXIX
- 6   Washington vs. Denver, XXII
  Tampa Bay vs. Oakland, XXXVII

Fewest Touchdowns, Game
- 0   Miami vs. Dallas, VI
- 1   By 19 teams

Most Touchdowns, Both Teams, Game
- 10   San Francisco (7) vs. San Diego (3), XXIX
- 9   Pittsburgh (5) vs. Dallas (4), XIII
  San Francisco (8) vs. Denver (1), XXIV
  Dallas (7) vs. Buffalo (2), XXVII
  Tampa Bay (6) vs. Oakland (3), XXXVII
- 8   Carolina (4) vs. New England (4), XXXVIII

Fewest Touchdowns, Both Teams, Game
- 2   Baltimore (1) vs. N.Y. Jets (1), III
- 3   In six games

POINTS AFTER TOUCHDOWN
Most (One-Point) Points After Touchdown, Game
- 7   San Francisco vs. Denver, XXIV
  Dallas vs. Buffalo, XXVII
  San Francisco vs. San Diego, XXIX
- 6   Washington vs. Denver, XXII
  Tampa Bay vs. Oakland, XXXVII
- 5   Green Bay vs. Kansas City, I
  Pittsburgh vs. Dallas, XIII
  L.A. Raiders vs. Washington, XVIII
  San Francisco vs. Miami, XIX
  Chicago vs. New England, XX

Most (One-Point) Points After Touchdown, Both Teams, Game
- 9   Pittsburgh (5) vs. Dallas (4), XIII
  Dallas (7) vs. Buffalo (2), XXVII
- 8   San Francisco (7) vs. Denver (1), XXIV
  San Francisco (7) vs. San Diego (1), XXIX
- 7   Washington (6) vs. Denver (1), XXII
  Washington (4) vs. Buffalo (3), XXVI
  Denver (4) vs. Green Bay (3), XXXII

Fewest (One-Point) Points After Touchdown, Both Teams, Game
- 2   Baltimore (1) vs. N.Y. Jets (1), III
  Baltimore (1) vs. Dallas (1), V

Minnesota (0) vs. Pittsburgh (2), IX

Most Two-Point Conversions, Game
  2 San Diego vs. San Francisco, XXIX

Most Two-Point Conversions, Both Teams, Game
  2 San Diego (2) vs. San Francisco (0), XXIX

FIELD GOALS
Most Field Goals Attempted, Game
  5 N.Y. Jets vs. Baltimore, III
     Dallas vs. Denver, XII
  4 Green Bay vs. Oakland, II
     Pittsburgh vs. Dallas, XX
     San Francisco vs. Cincinnati, XVI; XXIII
     Denver vs. N.Y. Giants, XXI
     Denver vs. Atlanta, XXXIII
     St. Louis vs. Tennessee, XXXIV
     Indianapolis vs. Chicago, XLI

Most Field Goals Attempted, Both Teams, Game
  7 N.Y. Jets (5) vs. Baltimore (2), III
     San Francisco (4) vs. Cincinnati (3), XXIII
     St. Louis (4) vs. Tennessee (3), XXXIV
     Denver (4) vs. Atlanta (3), XXXIII
  6 Dallas (5) vs. Denver (1), XII
  5 Green Bay (4) vs. Oakland (1), II
     Pittsburgh (4) vs. Dallas (1), X
     Oakland (3) vs. Philadelphia (2), XV
     Denver (4) vs. N.Y. Giants (1), XXI
     Dallas (3) vs. Buffalo (2), XXVIII
     Indianapolis (4) vs. Chicago (1), XLI

Fewest Field Goals Attempted, Both Teams, Game
  1 Minnesota (0) vs. Miami (1), VIII
     San Francisco (0) vs. Denver (1), XXIV
     Philadelphia (0) vs. New England (1), XXXIXI
     New England (0) vs. N.Y. Giants (1), XLII
  2 Green Bay (0) vs. Kansas City (2), I
     Miami (1) vs. Washington (1), VII
     Minnesota (1) vs. Pittsburgh (1), IX
     Dallas (1) vs. Pittsburgh (1), XIII
     Dallas (1) vs. Buffalo (1), XXVII
     San Diego (1) vs. San Francisco (1), XXIX
     Denver (1) vs. Green Bay (1), XXXII

Most Field Goals, Game
  4 Green Bay vs. Oakland, II
     San Francisco vs. Cincinnati, XVI
  3 N.Y. Jets vs. Baltimore, III
     Kansas City vs. Minnesota, IV
     Miami vs. San Francisco, XIX
     Chicago vs. New England, XX
     Cincinnati vs. San Francisco, XXIII
     Washington vs. Buffalo, XXVI
     Dallas vs. Buffalo, XXVIII
     St. Louis vs. Tennessee, XXXIV
     Indianapolis vs. Chicago, XLI

Most Field Goals, Both Teams, Game
  5 Cincinnati (3) vs. San Francisco (2), XXIII
     Dallas (3) vs. Buffalo (2), XXVIII
  4 Green Bay (4) vs. Oakland (0), II
     San Francisco (4) vs. Cincinnati (0), XVI
     Miami (3) vs. San Francisco (1), XIX
     Chicago (3) vs. New England (1), XX
     Washington (3) vs. Buffalo (1), XXVI
     Atlanta (2) vs. Denver (2), XXXIII
     St. Louis (3) vs. Tennessee (1), XXXIV
     Indianapolis (3) vs. Chicago (1), XLI
  3 In 13 games

Fewest Field Goals, Both Teams, Game
  0 Miami vs. Washington, VII
     Pittsburgh vs. Minnesota, IX
  1 Green Bay (0) vs. Kansas City (1), I
     Minnesota (0) vs. Miami (1), VIII

Pittsburgh (0) vs. Dallas (1), XIII
Washington (0) vs. Denver (1), XXII
San Francisco (0) vs. Denver (1), XXIV
San Francisco (0) vs. San Diego (1), XXIX
Philadelphia (0) vs. New England (1), XXXIX
Pittsburgh (0) vs. Seattle (1), XLI
New England (0) vs. N.Y. Giants (1), XLII

SAFETIES
Most Safeties, Game
  1 Pittsburgh vs. Minnesota, IX; vs. Dallas, X
     Chicago vs. New England, XX
     N.Y. Giants vs. Denver, XXI
     Buffalo vs. N.Y. Giants, XXV

FIRST DOWNS
Most First Downs, Game
  31 San Francisco vs. Miami, XIX
  29 New England vs. Carolina, XXXVIII
  28 San Francisco vs. Denver, XXIV
     San Francisco vs. San Diego, XXIX

Fewest First Downs, Game
  9 Minnesota vs. Pittsburgh, IX
     Miami vs. Washington, XVII
  10 Dallas vs. Baltimore, V
     Miami vs. Dallas, VI
  11 Denver vs. Dallas, XII
     N.Y. Giants vs. Baltimore, XXXV
     Oakland vs. Tampa Bay, XXXVII
     Chicago vs. Indianapolis, XLI

Most First Downs, Both Teams, Game
  50 San Francisco (31) vs. Miami (19), XIX
     Tennessee (27) vs. St. Louis (23), XXXIV
  49 Buffalo (25) vs. Washington (24), XXVI
  48 San Francisco (28) vs. San Diego (20), XXIX

Fewest First Downs, Both Teams, Game
  24 Dallas (10) vs. Baltimore (14), V
     N.Y. Giants (11) vs. Baltimore (13), XXXV
  26 Minnesota (9) vs. Pittsburgh (17), IX
  27 Pittsburgh (13) vs. Dallas (14), X

RUSHING
Most First Downs, Rushing, Game
  16 San Francisco vs. Miami, XIX
  15 Dallas vs. Miami, VI
  14 Washington vs. Miami, XVII
     San Francisco vs. Denver, XXIV
     Denver vs. Green Bay, XXXII

Fewest First Downs, Rushing, Game
  1 New England vs. Chicago, XX
     St. Louis vs. Tennessee, XXXIV
     Oakland vs. Tampa Bay, XXXVII
  2 Minnesota vs. Kansas City, IV; vs. Pittsburgh, IX;
     vs. Oakland, XI
     Pittsburgh vs. Dallas, XIII
     Miami vs. San Francisco, XIX
     N.Y. Giants vs. Baltimore, XXXV
  3 Miami vs. Dallas, VI
     Philadelphia vs. Oakland, XV
     New England vs. Green Bay, XXXI
     Carolina vs. New England, XXXVIII
     Chicago vs. Indianapolis, XLII
     New England vs. N.Y. Giants, XLII

Most First Downs, Rushing, Both Teams, Game
  21 Washington (14) vs. Miami (7), XVII
  19 Washington (13) vs. Denver (6), XXII
     San Francisco (14) vs. Denver (5), XXIV
  18 Dallas (15) vs. Miami (3), VI
     Miami (13) vs. Minnesota (5), VIII
     San Francisco (16) vs. Miami (2), XIX

N.Y. Giants (10) vs. Buffalo (8), XXV
Denver (14) vs. Green Bay (4), XXXII

Fewest First Downs, Rushing, Both Teams, Game
- 7 Oakland (1) vs. Tampa Bay (6), XXXVIII
  New England (3) vs. N.Y. Giants (4), XLII
- 8 Baltimore (4) vs. Dallas (4), V
  Pittsburgh (2) vs. Dallas (6), XIII
  N.Y. Giants (2) vs. Baltimore (6), XXXV
- 9 Philadelphia (3) vs. Oakland (6), XV

PASSING

Most First Downs, Passing, Game
- 19 New England vs. Carolina, XXXVIII
- 18 Buffalo vs. Washington, XXVI
  St. Louis vs. Tennessee, XXXIV
  Philadelphia vs. New England, XXXIX
- 17 Miami vs. San Francisco, XIX
  San Francisco vs. San Diego, XXIXI
  New England vs. N.Y. Giants, XLII

Fewest First Downs, Passing, Game
- 1 Denver vs. Dallas, XII
- 2 Miami vs. Washington, XVII
- 4 Miami vs. Minnesota, VIII

Most First Downs, Passing, Both Teams, Game
- 32 Miami (17) vs. San Francisco (15), XIX
  Philadelphia (18) vs. New England (14), XXXIX
- 31 San Francisco (17) vs. San Diego (14), XXIX
  St. Louis (18) vs. Tennessee (13), XXXIV
  New England (19) vs. Carolina (12), XXXVIII
- 30 Buffalo (18) vs. Washington (12), XXVII
  New England (17) vs. N.Y. Giants (13), XLII

Fewest First Downs, Passing, Both Teams, Game
- 9 Denver (1) vs. Dallas (8), XII
- 10 Minnesota (5) vs. Pittsburgh (5), IX
- 11 Dallas (5) vs. Baltimore (6), V
  Miami (2) vs. Washington (9), XVII

PENALTY

Most First Downs, Penalty, Game
- 4 Baltimore vs. Dallas, V
  Miami vs. Minnesota, VIII
  Cincinnati vs. San Francisco, XVI
  Buffalo vs. Dallas, XXVII
  St. Louis vs. Tennessee, XXXIV
- 3 Kansas City vs. Minnesota, IV
  Minnesota vs. Oakland, XI
  Buffalo vs. Washington, XXVI
  Green Bay vs. Denver, XXXII
  N.Y. Giants vs. Baltimore, XXXV
  St. Louis vs. New England, XXXVI
  Tampa Bay vs. Oakland, XXXVII
  New England vs. Carolina, XXXVIII

Most First Downs, Penalty, Both Teams, Game
- 6 Cincinnati (4) vs. San Francisco (2), XVI
  St. Louis (4) vs. Tennessee (2), XXXIV
- 5 Baltimore (4) vs. Dallas (1), V
  Miami (4) vs. Minnesota (1), VIII
  Buffalo (3) vs. Washington (2), XXVI
  Green Bay (3) vs. Denver (2), XXXII
  New England (3) vs. Carolina (2), XXXVIII
- 4 Kansas City (3) vs. Minnesota (1), IV
  Buffalo (4) vs. Dallas (0), XXVII
  N.Y. Giants (3) vs. Baltimore (1), XXXV
  St. Louis (3) vs. New England (1), XXXVI
  Tampa Bay (3) vs Oakland (1), XXXVII

Fewest First Downs, Penalty, Both Teams, Game
- 0 Dallas vs. Miami, VI
  Miami vs. Washington, VII
  Dallas vs. Pittsburgh, X
  Miami vs. San Francisco, XIX

Pittsburgh vs. Seattle, XL
- 1 Green Bay (0) vs. Kansas City (1), I
  Miami (0) vs. Washington (1), XVII
  Cincinnati (0) vs. San Francisco (1), XXIII
  San Francisco (0) vs. Denver (1), XXIV
  Dallas (0) vs. Buffalo (1), XXVIII
  Dallas (0) vs. Pittsburgh (1), XXX
  Denver (0) vs. Atlanta (1), XXXIII
  Chicago (0) vs. Indianapolis (1), XLI

NET YARDS GAINED RUSHING AND PASSING

Most Yards Gained, Game
- 602 Washington vs. Denver, XXII
- 537 San Francisco vs. Miami, XIX
- 481 New England vs. Carolina, XXXVIII

Fewest Yards Gained, Game
- 119 Minnesota vs. Pittsburgh, IX
- 123 New England vs. Chicago, XX
- 152 N.Y. Giants vs. Baltimore, XXXV

Most Yards Gained, Both Teams, Game
- 929 Washington (602) vs. Denver (327), XXII
- 868 New England (481) vs. Carolina (387), XXXVIII
- 851 San Francisco (537) vs. Miami (314), XIX

Fewest Yards Gained, Both Teams, Game
- 396 N.Y. Giants (152) vs. Baltimore (244), XXXV
- 452 Minnesota (119) vs. Pittsburgh (333), IX
- 481 Washington (228) vs. Miami (253), VII
  Denver (156) vs. Dallas (325), XII

RUSHING
ATTEMPTS

Most Attempts, Game
- 57 Pittsburgh vs. Minnesota, IX
- 53 Miami vs. Minnesota, VIII
- 52 Oakland vs. Minnesota, XI
  Washington vs. Miami, XVII

Fewest Attempts, Game
- 9 Miami vs. San Francisco, XIX
- 11 New England vs. Chicago, XX
  Oakland vs. Tampa Bay, XXXVII
- 13 New England vs. Green Bay, XXXI
  St. Louis vs. Tennessee, XXXIV

Most Attempts, Both Teams, Game
- 81 Washington (52) vs. Miami (29), XVII
- 78 Pittsburgh (57) vs. Minnesota (21), IX
  Oakland (52) vs. Minnesota (26), XI
- 77 Miami (53) vs. Minnesota (24), VIII
  Pittsburgh (46) vs. Dallas (31), X

Fewest Attempts, Both Teams, Game
- 42 New England (16) vs. N.Y. Giants (26), XLII
- 45 Philadelphia (17) vs. New England (28), XXXIX
- 47 St. Louis (22) vs. New England (25), XXXVI

YARDS GAINED

Most Yards Gained, Game
- 280 Washington vs. Denver, XXII
- 276 Washington vs. Miami, XVII
- 266 Oakland vs. Minnesota, XI

Fewest Yards Gained, Game
- 7 New England vs. Chicago, XX
- 17 Minnesota vs. Pittsburgh, IX
- 19 Oakland vs. Tampa Bay, XXXVII

Most Yards Gained, Both Teams, Game
- 377 Washington (280) vs. Denver (97), XXII
- 372 Washington (276) vs. Miami (96), XVII
- 338 N.Y. Giants (172) vs. Buffalo (166), XXV

Fewest Yards Gained, Both Teams, Game
- 136 New England (45) vs. N.Y. Giants (91), XLII
- 157 Philadelphia (45) vs. New England (112), XXXIX
- 158 New England (43) vs. Green Bay (115), XXXI

AVERAGE GAIN

Highest Average Gain, Game
- 7.00 L.A. Raiders vs. Washington, XVIII (33-231)
  - Washington vs. Denver, XXII (40-280)
- 6.64 Buffalo vs. N.Y. Giants, XXV (25-166)
- 6.22 Baltimore vs. N.Y. Jets, III (23-143)

Lowest Average Gain, Game
- 0.64 New England vs. Chicago, XX (11-7)
- 0.81 Minnesota vs. Pittsburgh, IX (21-17)
- 1.73 Oakland vs. Tampa Bay, XXXVII (11-19)

TOUCHDOWNS

Most Touchdowns, Game
- 4 Chicago vs. New England, XX
  - Denver vs. Green Bay, XXXII
- 3 Green Bay vs. Kansas City, I
  - Miami vs. Minnesota, VIII
  - San Francisco vs. Denver, XXIV
  - Denver vs. Atlanta, XXXIII
- 2 Oakland vs. Minnesota, XI
  - Pittsburgh vs. Los Angeles, XIV
  - L.A. Raiders vs. Washington, XVIII
  - San Francisco vs. Miami, XIX
  - N.Y. Giants vs. Denver, XXI
  - Washington vs. Denver, XXII; vs. Buffalo, XXVI
  - Buffalo vs. N.Y. Giants, XXV
  - Dallas vs. Buffalo, XXVIII; vs. Pittsburgh, XXX
  - Tennessee vs. St. Louis, XXXIV
  - Pittsburgh vs. Seattle, XL

Fewest Touchdowns, Game
- 0 By 28 teams

Most Touchdowns, Both Teams, Game
- 4 Miami (3) vs. Minnesota (1), VIII
  - Chicago (4) vs. New England (0), XX
  - San Francisco (3) vs. Denver (1), XXIV
  - Denver (4) vs. Green Bay (0), XXXII
- 3 In nine games

Fewest Touchdowns, Both Teams, Game
- 0 Pittsburgh vs. Dallas, X
  - Oakland vs. Philadelphia, XV
  - Cincinnati vs. San Francisco, XXIII
- 1 In 13 games

PASSING

ATTEMPTS

Most Passes Attempted, Game
- 59 Buffalo vs. Washington, XXVI
- 55 San Diego vs. San Francisco, XXIX
- 51 Philadelphia vs. New England, XXXIX

Fewest Passes Attempted, Game
- 7 Miami vs. Minnesota, VIII
- 11 Miami vs. Washington, VII
- 14 Pittsburgh vs. Minnesota, IX

Most Passes Attempted, Both Teams, Game
- 93 San Diego (55) vs. San Francisco (38), XXIX
- 92 Buffalo (59) vs. Washington (33), XXVI
- 85 Miami (50) vs. San Francisco (35), XIX

Fewest Passes Attempted, Both Teams, Game
- 35 Miami (7) vs. Minnesota (28), VIII
- 39 Miami (11) vs. Washington (28), VII
- 40 Pittsburgh (14) vs. Minnesota (26), IX
  - Miami (17) vs. Washington (23), XVII

COMPLETIONS

Most Passes Completed, Game
- 32 New England vs. Carolina, XXXVIII
- 31 Buffalo vs. Dallas, XXVIII
- 30 Philadelphia vs. New England, XXXIX

Fewest Passes Completed, Game
- 4 Miami vs. Washington, XVII
- 6 Miami vs. Minnesota, VIII
- 8 Miami vs. Washington, VII
  - Denver vs. Dallas, XII

Most Passes Completed, Both Teams, Game
- 53 Miami (29) vs. San Francisco (24), XIX
  - Philadelphia (30) vs. New England (23), XXXIX
- 52 San Diego (27) vs. San Francisco (25), XXIX
- 50 Buffalo (31) vs. Dallas (19), XXVIII

Fewest Passes Completed, Both Teams, Game
- 19 Miami (4) vs. Washington (15), XVII
- 20 Pittsburgh (9) vs. Minnesota (11), IX
- 22 Miami (8) vs. Washington (14), VII

COMPLETION PERCENTAGE

Highest Completion Percentage, Game (20 attempts)
- 88.0 N.Y. Giants vs. Denver, XXI (25-22)
- 75.0 San Francisco vs. Denver, XXIV (32-24)
- 73.5 Cincinnati vs. San Francisco, XVI (34-25)

Lowest Completion Percentage, Game (20 attempts)
- 32.0 Denver vs. Dallas, XII (25-8)
- 37.9 Denver vs. San Francisco, XXIV (29-11)
- 38.5 Denver vs. Washington, XXII (39-15)
  - N.Y. Giants vs. Baltimore, XXXV (39-15)

YARDS GAINED

Most Yards Gained, Game
- 407 St. Louis vs. Tennessee, XXXIV
- 354 New England vs. Carolina, XXXVIII
- 341 San Francisco vs. Cincinnati, XXIII

Fewest Yards Gained, Game
- 35 Denver vs. Dallas, XII
- 63 Miami vs. Minnesota, VIII
- 69 Miami vs. Washington, VII

Most Yards Gained, Both Teams, Game
- 649 New England (354) vs. Carolina (295), XXXVIII
- 615 San Francisco (326) vs. Miami (289), XIX
- 603 St. Louis (407) vs. Tennessee (208), XXXIV
  - San Francisco (316) vs. San Diego (287), XXIX

Fewest Yards Gained, Both Teams, Game
- 156 Miami (69) vs. Washington (87), VII
- 186 Pittsburgh (84) vs. Minnesota (102), IX
- 204 Miami (80) vs. Washington (124), XVII

TIMES SACKED

Most Times Sacked, Game
- 7 Dallas vs. Pittsburgh, X
  - New England vs. Chicago, XX
- 6 Kansas City vs. Green Bay, I
  - Washington vs. L.A. Raiders, XVIII
  - Denver vs. San Francisco, XXIV
- 5 Dallas vs. Denver, XII; vs. Pittsburgh, XIII
  - Cincinnati vs. San Francisco, XVI; XXIII
  - Denver vs. Washington, XXII
  - Buffalo vs. Washington, XXVI
  - Green Bay vs. New England, XXXI
  - New England vs. Green Bay, XXXI
  - Oakland vs. Tampa Bay, XXXVIII
  - New England vs. N.Y. Giants, XLII

Fewest Times Sacked, Game
- 0 Baltimore vs. N.Y. Jets, III; vs. Dallas, V
  - Minnesota vs. Pittsburgh, IX
  - Pittsburgh vs. Los Angeles, XIV
  - Philadelphia vs. Oakland, XV
  - Washington vs. Buffalo, XXVI
  - Denver vs. Green Bay, XXXII; vs. Atlanta, XXXIII
  - Tampa Bay vs. Oakland, XXXVII
  - New England vs. Carolina, XXXVIII
- 1 By 16 teams

Most Times Sacked, Both Teams, Game
- 10 New England (7) vs. Chicago (3), XX
  - Green Bay (5) vs. New England (5), XXXI
- 9 Kansas City (6) vs. Green Bay (3), I
  - Dallas (7) vs. Pittsburgh (2), X
  - Dallas (5) vs. Denver (4), XII
  - Dallas (5) vs. Pittsburgh (4), XIII
  - Cincinnati (5) vs. San Francisco (4), XXIII
- 8 Washington (6) vs. L.A. Raiders (2), XVIII
  - New England (5) vs. N.Y. Giants (3), XLII

Fewest Times Sacked, Both Teams, Game
- 1 Philadelphia (0) vs. Oakland (1), XV
  - Denver (0) vs. Green Bay (1), XXXII
- 2 Baltimore (0) vs. N.Y. Jets (2), III
  - Baltimore (0) vs. Dallas (2), V
  - Minnesota (0) vs. Pittsburgh (2), IX
  - Denver (0) vs. Atlanta (2), XXXIII
  - Chicago (1) vs. Indianapolis (1), XLI
- 3 In five games

TOUCHDOWNS
Most Touchdowns, Game
- 6 San Francisco vs. San Diego, XXIX
- 5 San Francisco vs. Denver, XXIV
- 4 Pittsburgh vs. Dallas, XIII
  - Washington vs. Denver, XXII
  - Dallas vs. Buffalo, XXVII

Fewest Touchdowns, Game
- 0 By 19 teams

Most Touchdowns, Both Teams, Game
- 7 Pittsburgh (4) vs. Dallas (3), XIII
  - San Francisco (6) vs. San Diego (1), XXIX
- 6 Carolina (3) vs. New England (3), XXXVIII
- 5 Washington (4) vs. Denver (1), XXII
  - San Francisco (5) vs. Denver (0), XXIV
  - Dallas (4) vs. Buffalo (1), XXVII
  - Philadelphia (3) vs. New England (2), XXXIX

Fewest Touchdowns, Both Teams, Game
- 0 N.Y. Jets vs. Baltimore, III
  - Miami vs. Minnesota, VIII
  - Buffalo vs. Dallas, XXVIII
- 1 In seven games

INTERCEPTIONS BY
Most Interceptions By, Game
- 5 Tampa Bay vs. Oakland, XXXVII
- 4 N.Y. Jets vs. Baltimore, III
  - Dallas vs. Denver, XII
  - Washington vs. Buffalo, XXVI
  - Dallas vs. Buffalo, XXVII
  - Green Bay vs. New England, XXXI
  - Baltimore vs. N.Y. Giants, XXXV
- 3 By 13 teams

Most Interceptions By, Both Teams, Game
- 6 Baltimore (3) vs. Dallas (3), V
  - Tampa Bay (5) vs. Oakland (1), XXXVII
- 5 Washington (4) vs. Buffalo (1), XXVI
- 4 In 10 games

Fewest Interceptions By, Both Teams, Game
- 0 Buffalo vs. N.Y. Giants, XXV
  - St. Louis vs. Tennessee, XXXIV
- 1 Oakland (0) vs. Green Bay (1), II
  - Miami (0) vs. Dallas (1), VI
  - Minnesota (0) vs. Miami (1), VIII
  - N.Y. Giants (0) vs. Denver (1), XXI
  - Cincinnati (0) vs. San Francisco (1), XXIII
  - New England (0) vs. Carolina (1), XXXVIII
  - N.Y. Giants (0) vs. New England (1), XLII

YARDS GAINED
Most Yards Gained, Game
- 172 Tampa Bay vs. Oakland, XXXVII
- 136 Denver vs. Atlanta, XXXIII
- 95 Miami vs. Washington, VII

Most Yards Gained, Both Teams, Game
- 184 Tampa Bay (172) vs. Oakland (12), XXXVII
- 137 Denver (136) vs. Atlanta (1), XXXIII
- 100 Seattle (76) vs. Pittsburgh (24), XL
  - Indianapolis (94) vs. Chicago (6), XLI

TOUCHDOWNS
Most Touchdowns, Game
- 3 Tampa Bay vs. Oakland, XXXVII
- 1 Green Bay vs. Oakland, II
  - Oakland vs. Minnesota, XI
  - L.A. Raiders vs. Washington, XVIII
  - Chicago vs. New England, XX
  - Baltimore vs. N.Y. Giants, XXXV
  - New England vs. St. Louis, XXXVI
  - Indianapolis vs. Chicago, XLI

PUNTING
Most Punts, Game
- 11 N.Y. Giants vs. Baltimore, XXXV
- 10 Baltimore vs. N.Y. Giants, XXXV
- 9 Dallas vs. Baltimore, V

Fewest Punts, Game
- 1 Atlanta vs. Denver, XXXIII
  - Denver vs. Atlanta, XXXIII
- 2 Pittsburgh vs. Los Angeles, XIV
  - Denver vs. N.Y. Giants, XXI
  - St. Louis vs. Tennessee, XXXIV
- 3 By 11 teams

Most Punts, Both Teams, Game
- 21 N.Y. Giants (11) vs. Baltimore (10), XXXV
- 15 Washington (8) vs. L.A. Raiders (7), XVIII
  - New England (8) vs. Green Bay (7), XXXI
- 13 Dallas (9) vs. Baltimore (4), V
  - Pittsburgh (7) vs. Minnesota (6), IX

Fewest Punts, Both Teams, Game
- 2 Atlanta (1) vs. Denver (1), XXXIII
- 5 Denver (2) vs. N.Y. Giants (3), XXI
  - St. Louis (2) vs. Tennessee (3), XXXIV
- 6 Oakland (3) vs. Philadelphia (3), XV

AVERAGE YARDAGE
Highest Average, Game (4 punts)
- 50.17 Seattle vs. Pittsburgh, XL (6-301)
- 48.75 San Diego vs. San Francisco, XXIX (4-195)
- 48.67 Pittsburgh vs. Seattle, XL (6-292)

Lowest Average, Game (4 punts)
- 31.00 Tampa Bay vs. Oakland, XXXVII (5-155)
- 31.20 Washington vs. Miami, VII (5-156)
- 32.38 Washington vs. L.A. Raiders, XVIII (8-259)

PUNT RETURNS
Most Punt Returns, Game
- 6 Washington vs. Miami, XVII
  - Green Bay vs. New England, XXXI
- 5 By seven teams

Fewest Punt Returns, Game
- 0 Minnesota vs. Miami, VIII
  - Buffalo vs. N.Y. Giants, XXV
  - Washington vs. Buffalo, XXVI
  - Denver vs. Green Bay, XXXII
  - Green Bay vs. Denver, XXXII
  - Atlanta vs. Denver, XXXIII
  - Denver vs. Atlanta, XXXIII

1   By 21 teams

Most Punt Returns, Both Teams, Game
- 10   Green Bay (6) vs. New England (4), XXXI
- 9   Pittsburgh (5) vs. Minnesota (4), IX
- 8   Green Bay (5) vs. Oakland (3), II
       Baltimore (5) vs. Dallas (3), V
       Washington (6) vs. Miami (2), XVII
       N.Y. Giants (5) vs. Baltimore (3), XXXV

Fewest Punt Returns, Both Teams, Game
- 0   Denver vs. Green Bay, XXXII
       Atlanta vs. Denver, XXXIII
- 2   Dallas (1) vs. Miami (1), VI
       Denver (1) vs. N.Y. Giants (1), XXI
       Buffalo (0) vs. N.Y. Giants (2), XXV
       Buffalo (1) vs. Dallas (1), XXVIII
- 3   Kansas City (1) vs. Minnesota (2), IV
       Minnesota (0) vs. Miami (3), VIII
       Washington (1) vs. Denver (2), XXII
       Washington (0) vs. Buffalo (3), XXVI
       Dallas (1) vs. Pittsburgh (2), XXX
       Tennessee (1) vs. St. Louis (2), XXXIV

YARDS GAINED
Most Yards Gained, Game
- 90   Green Bay vs. New England, XXXI
- 56   San Francisco vs. Cincinnati, XXIII
- 52   Washington vs. Miami, XVII

Fewest Yards Gained, Game
- −1   Dallas vs. Miami, VI
       Tennessee vs. St. Louis, XXXIV
- 0   By 12 teams

Most Yards Gained, Both Teams, Game
- 120   Green Bay (90) vs. New England (30), XXXI
- 80   N.Y. Giants (46) vs. Baltimore (34), XXXV
- 74   Washington (52) vs. Miami (22), XVII

Fewest Yards Gained, Both Teams, Game
- 0   Denver vs. Green Bay, XXXII
       Atlanta vs. Denver, XXXIII
- 7   Tennessee (-1) vs. St. Louis (8), XXXIV
- 9   Washington (0) vs. Buffalo (9), XXVI

AVERAGE RETURN
Highest Average, Game (3 returns)
- 18.7   San Francisco vs. Cincinnati, XXIII (3-56)
- 15.0   Green Bay vs. New England, XXXI (6-90)
- 14.0   Indianapolis vs. Chicago, XLI (3-42)

TOUCHDOWNS
Most Touchdowns, Game
- None

KICKOFF RETURNS
Most Kickoff Returns, Game
- 9   Denver vs. San Francisco, XXIV
       Oakland vs. Tampa Bay, XXXVII
- 8   San Diego vs. San Francisco, XXIX
- 7   By eight teams

Fewest Kickoff Returns, Game
- 1   N.Y. Jets vs. Baltimore, III
       L.A. Raiders vs. Washington, XVIII
       Washington vs. Buffalo, XXVI
- 2   By 10 teams

Most Kickoff Returns, Both Teams, Game
- 13   Oakland (9) vs. Tampa Bay (4), XXXVII
- 12   Denver (9) vs. San Francisco (3), XXIV
       San Diego (8) vs. San Francisco (4), XXIX
- 11   Los Angeles (6) vs. Pittsburgh (5), XIV
       Miami (7) vs. San Francisco (4), XIX
       New England (7) vs. Chicago (4), XX
       Green Bay (6) vs. Denver (5), XXXII

Fewest Kickoff Returns, Both Teams, Game
- 5   N.Y. Jets (1) vs. Baltimore (4), III
       Miami (2) vs. Washington (3), VII
       Washington (1) vs. Buffalo (4), XXVI
- 6   In five games

YARDS GAINED
Most Yards Gained, Game
- 244   San Diego vs. San Francisco, XXIX
- 227   Atlanta vs. Denver, XXXIII
- 222   Miami vs. Washington, XVII

Fewest Yards Gained, Game
- 16   Washington vs. Buffalo, XXVI
- 17   L.A. Raiders vs. Washington, XVIII
- 25   N.Y. Jets vs. Baltimore, III

Most Yards Gained, Both Teams, Game
- 292   San Diego (244) vs. San Francisco (48), XXIX
- 289   Green Bay (154) vs. New England (135), XXXI
- 281   N.Y. Giants (170) vs. Baltimore (111), XXXV

Fewest Yards Gained, Both Teams, Game
- 78   Miami (33) vs. Washington (45), VII
- 82   Pittsburgh (32) vs. Minnesota (50), IX
- 92   San Francisco (40) vs. Cincinnati (52), XVI

AVERAGE GAIN
Highest Average, Game (3 returns)
- 44.0   Cincinnati vs. San Francisco, XXIII (3-132)
- 38.5   Green Bay vs. New England, XXXI (4-154)
- 37.0   Miami vs. Washington, XVII (6-222)

TOUCHDOWNS
Most Touchdowns, Game
- 1   Miami vs. Washington, XVII
       Cincinnati vs. San Francisco, XXIII
       San Diego vs. San Francisco, XXIX
       Green Bay vs. New England, XXXI
       Atlanta vs. Denver, XXXIII
       Baltimore vs. N.Y. Giants, XXXV
       N.Y. Giants vs. Baltimore, XXXV
       Chicago vs. Indianapolis, XLI

Most Touchdowns, Both Teams, Game
- 2   Baltimore (1) vs. N.Y. Giants (1), XXXV

PENALTIES
Most Penalties, Game
- 12   Dallas vs. Denver, XII
       Carolina vs. New England, XXXVIII
- 10   Dallas vs. Baltimore, V
- 9   Dallas vs. Pittsburgh, XIII
       Green Bay vs. Denver, XXXII
       Baltimore vs. N.Y. Giants, XXXV

Fewest Penalties, Game
- 0   Miami vs. Dallas, VI
       Pittsburgh vs. Dallas, X
       Denver vs. San Francisco, XXIV
       Atlanta vs. Denver, XXXIII
- 1   Green Bay vs. Oakland, II
       Miami vs. Minnesota, VIII; vs. San Francisco, XIX
       Buffalo vs. Dallas, XXVIII
- 2   By six teams

Most Penalties, Both Teams, Game
- 20   Dallas (12) vs. Denver (8), XII
       Carolina (12) vs. New England (8), XXXVIII
- 16   Cincinnati (8) vs. San Francisco (8), XVI
       Green Bay (9) vs. Denver (7), XXXII
- 15   St. Louis (8) vs. Tennessee (7), XXXIV
       Baltimore (9) vs. N.Y. Giants (6), XXXV

Fewest Penalties, Both Teams, Game
- 2   Pittsburgh (0) vs. Dallas (2), X
- 3   Miami (0) vs. Dallas (3), VI

Miami (1) vs. San Francisco (2), XIX
4 Denver (0) vs. San Francisco (4), XXIV
Atlanta (0) vs. Denver (4), XXXIII

YARDS PENALIZED
Most Yards Penalized, Game
133 Dallas vs. Baltimore, X
122 Pittsburgh vs. Minnesota, IX
94 Dallas vs. Denver, XII
Fewest Yards Penalized, Game
0 Miami vs. Dallas, VI
Pittsburgh vs. Dallas, X
Denver vs. San Francisco, XXIV
Atlanta vs. Denver, XXXIII
4 Miami vs. Minnesota, VIII
10 Miami vs. San Francisco, XIX
San Francisco vs. Miami, XIX
Buffalo vs. Dallas, XXVIII
Most Yards Penalized, Both Teams, Game
164 Dallas (133) vs. Baltimore (31), V
154 Dallas (94) vs. Denver (60), XII
140 Pittsburgh (122) vs. Minnesota (18), IX
Fewest Yards Penalized, Both Teams, Game
15 Miami (0) vs. Dallas (15), VI
20 Pittsburgh (0) vs. Dallas (20), X
Miami (10) vs. San Francisco (10), XIX
38 Denver (0) vs. San Francisco (38), XXIV

FUMBLES
Most Fumbles, Game
8 Buffalo vs. Dallas, XXVII
6 Dallas vs. Denver, XII
Buffalo vs. Washington, XXVI
5 Baltimore vs. Dallas, V
Fewest Fumbles, Game
0 By 19 teams
Most Fumbles, Both Teams, Game
12 Buffalo (8) vs. Dallas (4), XXVII
10 Dallas (6) vs. Denver (4), XII
8 Dallas (4) vs. Pittsburgh (4), X
Fewest Fumbles, Both Teams, Game
0 Los Angeles vs. Pittsburgh, XIV
Green Bay vs. New England, XXXI
Pittsburgh vs. Seattle, XL
1 Oakland (0) vs. Minnesota (1), XI
Oakland (0) vs. Philadelphia (1), XV
Denver (0) vs. Washington (1), XXII
N.Y. Giants (0) vs. Buffalo (1), XXV
Denver (0) vs. Atlanta (1), XXXIII
2 In eight games
Most Fumbles Lost, Game
5 Buffalo vs. Dallas, XXVII
4 Baltimore vs. Dallas, V
Denver vs. Dallas, XII
New England vs. Chicago, XX
3 Chicago vs. Indianapolis, XLI
Most Fumbles Lost, Both Teams, Game
7 Buffalo (5) vs. Dallas (2), XXVII
6 Denver (4) vs. Dallas (2), XII
New England (4) vs. Chicago (2), XX
5 Baltimore (4) vs. Dallas (1), V
Chicago (3) vs. Indianapolis (2), XLI
Fewest Fumbles Lost, Both Teams, Game
0 Green Bay vs. Kansas City, I
Dallas vs. Pittsburgh, X
Los Angeles vs. Pittsburgh, XIV
Denver vs. N.Y. Giants, XXI; vs. Washington, XXII
Buffalo vs. N.Y. Giants, XXV
San Diego vs. San Francisco, XXIX
Dallas vs. Pittsburgh, XXX

Green Bay vs. New England, XXXI
St. Louis vs. Tennessee, XXXIV
Oakland vs. Tampa Bay, XXXVII
Pittsburgh vs. Seattle, XL
Most Fumbles Recovered, Game
8 Dallas vs. Denver, XII (4 own, 4 opp.)
6 Dallas vs. Buffalo, XXVII (1 own, 5 opp.)
5 Chicago vs. New England, XX (1 own, 4 opp.)

TURNOVERS
(Number of times losing the ball on interceptions and fumbles.)
Most Turnovers, Game
9 Buffalo vs. Dallas, XXVII
8 Denver vs. Dallas, XII
7 Baltimore vs. Dallas, V
Fewest Turnovers, Game
0 Green Bay vs. Oakland, II
Miami vs. Minnesota, VIII
Pittsburgh vs. Dallas, X
Oakland vs. Minnesota, XI; vs. Philadelphia, XV
N.Y. Giants vs. Denver, XXI; vs. Buffalo, XXV
San Francisco vs. Denver, XXIV; vs. San Diego, XXIX
Buffalo vs. N.Y. Giants, XXV
Dallas vs. Pittsburgh, XXX
Green Bay vs. New England, XXXI
St. Louis vs. Tennessee, XXXIV
Tennessee vs. St. Louis, XXXIV
Baltimore vs. N.Y. Giants, XXXV
New England vs. St. Louis, XXXVI
1 By many teams
Most Turnovers, Both Teams, Game
11 Baltimore (7) vs. Dallas (4), V
Buffalo (9) vs. Dallas (2), XXVII
10 Denver (8) vs. Dallas (2), XII
8 New England (6) vs. Chicago (2), XX
Chicago (5) vs. Indianapolis (3), XLI
Fewest Turnovers, Both Teams, Game
0 Buffalo vs. N.Y. Giants, XXV
St. Louis vs. Tennessee, XXXIV
1 N.Y. Giants (0) vs. Denver (1), XXI
2 Green Bay (1) vs. Kansas City (1), I
Miami (0) vs. Minnesota (2), VIII
Cincinnati (1) vs. San Francisco (1), XXIII
Carolina (1) vs. New England (1), XXXVIII
New England (1) vs. N.Y. Giants (1), XLII

Compiled by Elias Sports Bureau

Throughout this all-time postseason record section, the following abbreviations are used to indicate various levels of postseason games:

SB — Super Bowl (1966 to date)

AFC — AFC Championship Game (1970 to date) or AFL Championship Game (1960-69)

NFC — NFC Championship Game (1970 to date) or NFL Championship Game (1933-69)

AFC-D — AFC Divisional Playoff Game (1970 to date), AFC Second-Round Playoff Game (1982), AFL Inter-Divisional Playoff Game (1969), or special playoff game to break tie for AFL Division Championship (1963, 1968)

NFC-D — NFC Divisional Playoff Game (1970 to date), NFC Second-Round Playoff Game (1982), NFL Conference Championship Game (1967-69), or special playoff game to break tie for NFL Division or Conference Championship (1941, 1943, 1947, 1950, 1952, 1957, 1958, 1965)

AFC-FR — AFC First-Round Playoff Game (1978 to date)

NFC-FR — NFC First-Round Playoff Game (1978 to date)

Year indicates season in which game took place and does not necessarily reflect calendar year.

POSTSEASON GAME COMPOSITE STANDINGS

	W	L	PCT.	PTS.	OP
Carolina Panthers	6	3	.667	206	170
Green Bay Packers	25	15	.625	950	766
Baltimore Ravens	5	3	.625	148	88
New England Patriots#	21	13	.618	730	666
Pittsburgh Steelers	28	19	.596	1,095	959
San Francisco 49ers	25	17	.595	1,044	853
Oakland Raiders**	25	18	.581	1,028	797
Washington Redskins*	23	17	.575	819	707
Dallas Cowboys	32	24	.571	1,318	1,050
Denver Broncos	17	15	.531	694	794
Miami Dolphins	20	19	.513	780	848
Indianapolis Colts***	17	17	.500	685	695
Philadelphia Eagles	17	17	.500	653	608
Chicago Bears	16	17	.485	702	681
Buffalo Bills	14	15	.483	681	658
New York Giants	20	23	.465	752	810
Jacksonville Jaguars	5	6	.455	262	288
St. Louis Rams††	19	24	.442	770	944
Tennessee Titans†	14	18	.438	569	749
Atlanta Falcons	6	8	.429	298	331
Minnesota Vikings	18	24	.429	824	957
New York Jets	8	11	.421	388	389
Detroit Lions	7	10	.412	365	404
Seattle Seahawks	7	10	.412	356	367
Tampa Bay Buccaneers	6	9	.400	230	279
San Diego Chargers†††	9	14	.391	427	523
Cincinnati Bengals	5	8	.385	263	288
Kansas City Chiefs****	8	13	.381	340	445
Cleveland Browns	11	20	.355	629	728
Arizona Cardinals††††	2	5	.286	122	182
New Orleans Saints	2	6	.250	144	248

* One game played when franchise was in Boston (lost 21-6).

** 12 games played when franchise was in Los Angeles (won 6, lost 6, 268 points scored, 224 points allowed).

*** 15 games played when franchise was in Baltimore (won 8, lost 7, 264 points scored, 262 points allowed).

**** One game played when franchise was Dallas Texans (won 20-17).

\# Two games played when franchise was in Boston (won 26-8, lost 51-10).

† 22 games played when franchise was in Houston and known as the Oilers (won 9, lost 13, 371 points scored, 533 points allowed).

†† One game played when franchise was in Cleveland (won 15-14), 32 games played when franchise was in

Los Angeles (won 12, lost 20, 486 points scored, 683 points allowed).

††† One game played when franchise was in Los Angeles (lost 24-16).

†††† Two games played when franchise was in Chicago (won 28-21, lost 7-0), three games played when franchise was in St. Louis (lost 30-14, lost 35-23, lost 41-16).

INDIVIDUAL RECORDS

SERVICE

Most Games, Career

29 Jerry Rice, San Francisco-Oakland-Seattle (SB 4, NFC 6, AFC 1, NFC-D 2, NFC-FR 4, AFC-FR 1)

27 D.D. Lewis, Dallas (SB 5, NFC 9, NFC-D 12, NFC-FR 1)

26 Larry Cole, Dallas (SB 5, NFC 8, NFC-D 12, NFC-FR 1)
    Bill Romanowski, San Francisco-Philadelphia-Denver-Oakland (SB 5, NFC 5, AFC 3, NFC-D 6, AFC-D 4, NFC-FR 1, AFC-FR 2)

Most Games, Head Coach

36 Tom Landry, Dallas
    Don Shula, Baltimore-Miami

24 Chuck Noll, Pittsburgh
    Mike Holmgren, Green Bay-Seattle

23 Joe Gibbs, Washington

Most Championships Won, Head Coach

6 George Halas, Chicago
   Curly Lambeau, Green Bay

5 Vince Lombardi, Green Bay

4 Guy Chamberlin, Canton Bulldogs-Cleveland Bulldogs-Frankford Yellow Jackets
   Chuck Noll, Pittsburgh

Most Games Won, Head Coach

20 Tom Landry, Dallas

19 Don Shula, Baltimore-Miami

17 Joe Gibbs, Washington

Most Games Lost, Head Coach

17 Don Shula, Baltimore-Miami

16 Tom Landry, Dallas

13 Marty Schottenheimer, Cleveland-Kansas City-San Diego

SCORING

POINTS

Most Points, Career

172 Adam Vinatieri, New England-Indianapolis, 22 games (49-pat, 41-fg)

153 Gary Anderson, Pittsburgh-Philadelphia-San Francisco-Minnesota-Tennessee, 22 games (57-pat, 32-fg)

132 Jerry Rice, San Francisco-Oakland-Seattle, 29 games (22-td)

Most Points, Game

30 Ricky Watters, NFC-D: San Francisco vs. N.Y. Giants, 1993 (5-td)

19 Pat Harder, NFC-D: Detroit vs. Los Angeles, 1952 (2-td, 4-pat, 1-fg)
   Paul Hornung, NFC: Green Bay vs. N.Y. Giants, 1961 (1-td, 4-pat, 3-fg)

18 By many players

Most Consecutive Games Scoring

22 Adam Vinatieri, New England-Indianapolis, 1996-2007 (current)

19 George Blanda, Chi. Bears-Houston-Oakland, 1956-1975

16 Norm Johnson, Seattle-Atlanta-Pittsburgh, 1983-1997

TOUCHDOWNS

Most Touchdowns, Career

22 Jerry Rice, San Francisco-Oakland-Seattle, 29 games (22-p)

21 Thurman Thomas, Buffalo, 21 games (16-r, 5-p)
   Emmitt Smith, Dallas, 17 games (19-r, 2-p)

17 Franco Harris, Pittsburgh, 19 games (16-r, 1-p)

Most Touchdowns, Game

5 Ricky Watters, NFC-D: San Francisco vs. N.Y. Giants, 1993 (5-r)
3 Andy Farkas, NFC-D: Washington vs. N.Y. Giants, 1943 (3-r)
   Tom Fears, NFC-D: Los Angeles vs. Chi. Bears, 1950 (3-p)
   Otto Graham, NFC: Cleveland vs. Detroit, 1954 (3-r)
   Gary Collins, NFC: Cleveland vs. Baltimore, 1964 (3-p)
   Craig Baynham, NFC-D: Dallas vs. Cleveland, 1967 (2-r, 1-p)
   Fred Biletnikoff, AFC-D: Oakland vs. Kansas City, 1968 (3-p)
   Tom Matte, NFC: Baltimore vs. Cleveland, 1968 (3-r)
   Larry Schreiber, NFC-D: San Francisco vs. Dallas, 1972 (3-r)
   Larry Csonka, AFC: Miami vs. Oakland, 1973 (3-r)
   Franco Harris, AFC-D: Pittsburgh vs. Buffalo, 1974 (3-r)
   Preston Pearson, NFC: Dallas vs. Los Angeles, 1975 (3-p)
   Dave Casper, AFC-D: Oakland vs. Baltimore, 1977 (OT) (3-p)
   Alvin Garrett, NFC-FR: Washington vs. Detroit, 1982 (3-r)
   John Riggins, NFC-D: Washington vs. L.A. Rams, 1983 (3-r)
   Roger Craig, SB: San Francisco vs. Miami, 1984 (1-r, 2-p)
   Jerry Rice, NFC-D: San Francisco vs. Minnesota, 1988 (3-p)
   Jerry Rice, SB: San Francisco vs. Denver, 1989 (3-r)
   Kenneth Davis, AFC: Buffalo vs. L.A. Raiders, 1990 (3-r)
   Andre Reed, AFC-FR: Buffalo vs. Houston, 1992 (OT) (3-p)
   Sterling Sharpe, NFC-FR: Green Bay vs. Detroit, 1993 (3-p)
   Napoleon McCallum, AFC-FR: L.A. Raiders vs. Denver, 1993 (3-r)
   Thurman Thomas, AFC: Buffalo vs. Kansas City, 1993 (3-r)
   William Floyd, NFC-D: San Francisco vs. Chicago, 1994 (3-r)
   Ricky Watters, SB: San Francisco vs. San Diego, 1994 (1-r, 2-p)
   Jerry Rice, SB: San Francisco vs. San Diego, 1994 (3-p)
   Emmitt Smith, NFC: Dallas vs. Green Bay, 1995 (3-r)
   Curtis Martin, AFC-D: New England vs. Pittsburgh, 1996 (3-r)
   Terrell Davis, SB: Denver vs. Green Bay, 1997 (3-r)
   Mario Bates, NFC-D: Arizona vs. Minnesota, 1998 (3-r)
   Leroy Hoard, NFC-D: Minnesota vs. Arizona, 1998 (2-r, 1-p)
   Willie Jackson, NFC-FR: New Orleans vs. St. Louis, 2000 (3-p)
   Amani Toomer, NFC-FR: N.Y. Giants vs. San Francisco, 2002 (3-p)
   Shaun Alexander, NFC-FR: Seattle vs. Green Bay, 2003 (OT) (3-r)
   Ryan Grant, NFC-D: Green Bay vs. Seattle, 2007 (3-r)

Most Consecutive Games Scoring Touchdowns

9 Thurman Thomas, Buffalo, 1992-98
8 John Stallworth, Pittsburgh, 1978-1983
   Emmitt Smith, Dallas, 1993-96
7 John Riggins, Washington, 1982-84
   Marcus Allen, L.A. Raiders, 1982-85
   Terrell Davis, Denver, 1996-98
   David Givens, New England, 2003-05 (current)

POINTS AFTER TOUCHDOWN

Most (One-Point) Points After Touchdown, Career

57 Gary Anderson, Pittsburgh-Philadelphia-San Francisco-Minnesota-Tennessee, 22 games (57 att)
49 George Blanda, Chi. Bears-Houston-Oakland, 19 games (49 att)
   Adam Vinatieri, New England-Indianapolis, 22 games (49 att)
42 Mike Cofer, San Francisco, 12 games (44 att)

Most (One-Point) Points After Touchdown, Game

8 Lou Groza, NFC: Cleveland vs. Detroit, 1954 (8 att)
   Jim Martin, NFC: Detroit vs. Cleveland, 1957 (8 att)
   George Blanda, AFC-D: Oakland vs. Houston, 1969 (8 att)
   Mike Hollis, AFC-D: Jacksonville vs. Miami, 1999 (8 att)
7 Danny Villanueva, NFC-D: Dallas vs. Cleveland, 1967 (7 att)
   Raul Allegre, NFC-D: N.Y. Giants vs. San Francisco, 1986 (7 att)
   Mike Cofer, SB: San Francisco vs. Denver, 1989 (8 att)

   Lin Elliott, SB: Dallas vs. Buffalo, 1992 (7 att)
   Doug Brien, SB: San Francisco vs. San Diego, 1994 (7 att)
   Gary Anderson, NFC-FR: Philadelphia vs. Detroit, 1995 (7 att)
   Jeff Wilkins, NFC-D: St. Louis vs. Minnesota, 1999 (7 att)
   Mike Vanderjagt, AFC-FR: Indianapolis vs. Denver, 2004 (7 att)
6 George Blair, AFC: San Diego vs. Boston, 1963 (6 att)
   Mark Moseley, NFC-D: Washington vs. L.A. Rams, 1983 (6 att)
   Uwe von Schamann, AFC: Miami vs. Pittsburgh, 1984 (6 att)
   Ali Haji-Sheikh, SB: Washington vs. Denver, 1987 (6 att)
   Scott Norwood, AFC: Buffalo vs. L.A. Raiders, 1990 (7 att)
   Jeff Jaeger, AFC-FR: L.A. Raiders vs. Denver, 1993 (6 att)
   Jason Elam, AFC-FR: Denver vs. Jacksonville, 1997 (6 att)
   Jeff Wilkins, NFC-D: St. Louis vs. Green Bay, 2001 (6 att)
   Martín Gramatica, SB: Tampa Bay vs. Oakland, 2002 (6 att)
   Jay Feely, NFC-D: Atlanta vs. St. Louis, 2004 (6 att)
   Mason Crosby, NFC-D: Green Bay vs. Seattle, 2007 (6 att)

Most (Kicking) Points After Touchdown, No Misses, Career

57 Gary Anderson, Pittsburgh-Philadelphia-San Francisco-Minnesota-Tennessee, 22 games
49 George Blanda, Chi. Bears-Houston-Oakland, 19 games
   Adam Vinatieri, New England-Indianapolis, 22 games
41 Rafael Septien, Los Angeles-Dallas, 15 games

Most Two-Point Conversions, Career

2 Terrell Owens, San Francisco-Philadelphia-Dallas, 12 games
   Kevin Faulk, New England, 17 games

Most Two-Point Conversions, Game

2 Terrell Owens, NFC-FR: San Francisco vs. N.Y. Giants, 2002

FIELD GOALS

Most Field Goals Attempted, Career

50 Adam Vinatieri, New England-Indianapolis, 22 games
40 Gary Anderson, Pittsburgh-Philadelphia-San Francisco-Minnesota-Tennessee, 22 games
39 George Blanda, Chi. Bears-Houston-Oakland, 19 games

Most Field Goals Attempted, Game

6 George Blanda, AFC: Oakland vs. Houston, 1967
   David Ray, NFC-D: Los Angeles vs. Dallas, 1973
   Mark Moseley, AFC-D: Cleveland vs. N.Y. Jets, 1986 (OT)
   Matt Bahr, NFC: N.Y. Giants vs. San Francisco, 1990
   Steve Christie, AFC: Buffalo vs. Miami, 1992
   Jeff Wilkins, NFC-D: St. Louis vs. Carolina, 2003 (2 OT)
5 By many players

Most Field Goals, Career

41 Adam Vinatieri, New England-Indianapolis, 22 games
32 Gary Anderson, Pittsburgh-Philadelphia-San Francisco-Minnesota-Tennessee, 22 games
22 George Blanda, Chi. Bears-Houston-Oakland, 19 games
   Steve Christie, Buffalo, 12 games

Most Field Goals, Game

5 Chuck Nelson, NFC-D: Minnesota vs. San Francisco, 1987
   Matt Bahr, NFC: N.Y. Giants vs. San Francisco, 1990
   Steve Christie, AFC: Buffalo vs. Miami, 1992
   Brad Daluiso, NFC-FR: N.Y. Giants vs. Minnesota, 1997
   John Kasay, NFC-FR: Carolina vs. Dallas, 2003
   Jeff Wilkins, NFC-D: St. Louis vs. Carolina, 2003 (2 OT)
   Adam Vinatieri, AFC: New England vs. Indianapolis, 2003
   Adam Vinatieri, AFC-D: Indianapolis vs. Baltimore, 2006
4 Gino Cappelletti, AFC-D: Boston vs. Buffalo, 1963
   George Blanda, AFC: Oakland vs. Houston, 1967
   Don Chandler, SB: Green Bay vs. Oakland, 1967
   Curt Knight, NFC: Washington vs. Dallas, 1972
   George Blanda, AFC-D: Oakland vs. Pittsburgh, 1973
   Ray Wersching, SB: San Francisco vs. Cincinnati, 1981
   Tony Franklin, AFC-FR: New England vs. N.Y. Jets, 1986
   Jess Atkinson, NFC-FR: Washington vs. L.A. Rams, 1986
   Luis Zendejas, NFC-D: Philadelphia vs. Chicago, 1988
   Gary Anderson, AFC-FR: Pittsburgh vs. Houston, 1989 (OT)
   Norm Johnson, AFC-D: Pittsburgh vs. Buffalo, 1995
   Chris Boniol, NFC-FR: Dallas vs. Minnesota, 1996

John Kasay, NFC-D: Carolina vs. Dallas, 1996
Mike Hollis, AFC-D: Jacksonville vs. New England, 1998
Al Del Greco, AFC-D: Tennessee vs. Indianapolis, 1999
David Akers, NFC-D: Philadelphia vs. Chicago, 2001
Nate Kaeding, AFC-D: San Diego vs. New England, 2007
3   By many players

Most Consecutive Games Scoring Field Goals
13   Toni Fritsch, Dallas-Houston, 1972-79
12   Adam Vinatieri, New England, 1997-2004
10   David Akers, Philadelphia, 2000-04
      Morten Andersen, New Orleans-Atlanta-Kansas City-
        Minnesota, 1987-2004
      Jason Elam, Denver, 1997-2000, 2003-05 (current)

Most Consecutive Field Goals
16   Gary Anderson, Pittsburgh-Philadelphia, 1989-1995
15   Rafael Septien, Dallas, 1978-1982
14   Mike Hollis, Jacksonville, 1996-99
      John Kasay, Carolina, 1996-2003

Longest Field Goal
58   Pete Stoyanovich, AFC-FR: Miami vs. Kansas City, 1990
55   Jeff Wilkins, NFC-D: St. Louis vs. Atlanta, 2004
54   Ed Murray, NFC-D: Detroit vs. San Francisco, 1983
      Steve Christie, SB: Buffalo vs. Dallas, 1993
      John Carney, AFC-FR: San Diego vs. Indianapolis, 1995

Highest Field Goal Percentage, Career (10 field goals)
92.9   Martín Gramatica, Tampa Bay-Indianapolis-Dallas,
        9 games (14-13)
91.3   John Kasay, Carolina, 9 games (23-21)
90.9   Chuck Nelson, L.A. Rams-Minnesota, 6 games (11-10)

SAFETIES
Most Safeties, Game
1   Bill Willis, NFC-D: Cleveland vs. N.Y. Giants, 1950
    Carl Eller, NFC-D: Minnesota vs. Los Angeles, 1969
    George Andrie, NFC-D: Dallas vs. Detroit, 1970
    Alan Page, NFC-D: Minnesota vs. Dallas, 1971
    Dwight White, SB: Pittsburgh vs. Minnesota, 1974
    Reggie Harrison, SB: Pittsburgh vs. Dallas, 1975
    Jim Jensen, NFC-D: Dallas vs. Los Angeles, 1976
    Ted Washington, AFC: Houston vs. Pittsburgh, 1978
    Randy White, NFC-D: Dallas vs. Los Angeles, 1979
    Henry Waechter, SB: Chicago vs. New England, 1985
    Rulon Jones, AFC-FR: Denver vs. New England, 1986
    George Martin, SB: N.Y. Giants vs. Denver, 1986
    D.D. Hoggard, AFC: Cleveland vs. Denver, 1987
    Bruce Smith, SB: Buffalo vs. N.Y. Giants, 1990
    Reggie White, NFC-FR: Philadelphia vs. New Orleans, 1992
    Willie Clay, NFC-FR: Detroit vs. Green Bay, 1994
    Carnell Lake, AFC-D: Pittsburgh vs. Cleveland, 1994
    Reuben Davis, AFC-D: San Diego vs. Miami, 1994
    Jevon Kearse, AFC-FR: Tennessee vs. Buffalo, 1999
    Brady Smith, NFC-D: Atlanta vs. St. Louis, 2004

RUSHING
ATTEMPTS
Most Attempts, Career
400   Franco Harris, Pittsburgh, 19 games
349   Emmitt Smith, Dallas, 17 games
339   Thurman Thomas, Buffalo, 21 games

Most Attempts, Game
40   Lamar Smith, AFC-FR: Miami vs. Indianapolis, 2000 (OT)
38   Ricky Bell, NFC-D: Tampa Bay vs. Philadelphia, 1979
      John Riggins, SB: Washington vs. Miami, 1982
37   Lawrence McCutcheon, NFC-D: Los Angeles vs. St. Louis,
       1975
      John Riggins, NFC-D: Washington vs. Minnesota, 1982

YARDS GAINED
Most Yards Gained, Career
1,586   Emmitt Smith, Dallas, 17 games
1,556   Franco Harris, Pittsburgh, 19 games
1,442   Thurman Thomas, Buffalo, 21 games

Most Yards Gained, Game
248   Eric Dickerson, NFC-D: L.A. Rams vs. Dallas, 1985
209   Lamar Smith, AFC-FR: Miami vs. Indianapolis, 2000 (OT)
206   Keith Lincoln, AFC: San Diego vs. Boston, 1963

Most Games, 100 or More Yards Rushing, Career
7   Emmitt Smith, Dallas, 17 games
    Terrell Davis, Denver, 8 games
6   John Riggins, Washington, 9 games
    Thurman Thomas, Buffalo, 21 games
5   Franco Harris, Pittsburgh, 19 games
    Marcus Allen, L.A. Raiders-Kansas City, 16 games

Most Consecutive Games, 100 or More Yards Rushing
7   Terrell Davis, Denver, 1997-98
6   John Riggins, Washington, 1982-83
4   Thurman Thomas, Buffalo, 1990-91

Longest Run From Scrimmage
90   Fred Taylor, AFC-D: Jacksonville vs. Miami, 1999 (TD)
80   Roger Craig, NFC-D: San Francisco vs. Minnesota, 1988 (TD)
      Charlie Garner, AFC-FR: Oakland vs. N.Y. Jets, 2001 (TD)
78   Curtis Martin, AFC-D: New England vs. Pittsburgh, 1996 (TD)

AVERAGE GAIN
Highest Average Gain, Career (100 attempts)
5.59   Terrell Davis, Denver, 8 games (204-1,140)
5.04   Marcus Allen, L.A. Raiders-Kansas City, 16 games
       (267-1,347)
4.89   Eric Dickerson, L.A. Rams-Indianapolis, 7 games (148-724)

Highest Average Gain, Game (10 attempts)
15.90   Elmer Angsman, NFC: Chi. Cardinals vs. Philadelphia,
       1947 (10-159)
15.85   Keith Lincoln, AFC: San Diego vs. Boston, 1963 (13-206)
11.31   Zack Crockett, AFC-FR: Indianapolis vs. San Diego, 1995
       (13-147)

TOUCHDOWNS
Most Touchdowns, Career
19   Emmitt Smith, Dallas, 17 games
16   Franco Harris, Pittsburgh, 19 games
    Thurman Thomas, Buffalo, 21 games
12   John Riggins, Washington, 9 games
    Terrell Davis, Denver, 8 games

Most Touchdowns, Game
5   Ricky Watters, NFC-D: San Francisco vs. N.Y. Giants, 1993
3   Andy Farkas, NFC-D: Washington vs. N.Y. Giants, 1943
    Otto Graham, NFC: Cleveland vs. Detroit, 1954
    Tom Matte, NFC: Baltimore vs. Cleveland, 1968
    Larry Schreiber, NFC-D: San Francisco vs. Dallas, 1972
    Larry Csonka, AFC: Miami vs. Oakland, 1973
    Franco Harris, AFC-D: Pittsburgh vs. Buffalo, 1974
    John Riggins, NFC-D: Washington vs. L.A. Rams, 1983
    Kenneth Davis, AFC: Buffalo vs. L.A. Raiders, 1990
    Napoleon McCallum, AFC-FR: L.A. Raiders vs. Denver, 1993
    Thurman Thomas, AFC: Buffalo vs. Kansas City, 1993
    William Floyd, NFC-D: San Francisco vs. Chicago, 1994
    Emmitt Smith, NFC: Dallas vs. Green Bay, 1995
    Curtis Martin, AFC-D: New England vs. Pittsburgh, 1996
    Terrell Davis, SB: Denver vs. Green Bay, 1997
    Mario Bates, NFC-D: Arizona vs. Minnesota, 1998
    Shaun Alexander, NFC-FR: Seattle vs. Green Bay, 2003 (OT)
    Ryan Grant, NFC-D: Green Bay vs. Seattle, 2007

Most Consecutive Games Rushing for Touchdowns
8   Emmitt Smith, Dallas, 1993-96
    Thurman Thomas, Buffalo, 1992-98
7   John Riggins, Washington, 1982-84
    Terrell Davis, Denver, 1996-98
5   Franco Harris, Pittsburgh, 1974-75
    Franco Harris, Pittsburgh, 1977-79
    Curtis Martin, New England-N.Y. Jets, 1996-98
    Jerome Bettis, Pittsburgh, 2004-05

PASSING

PASSER RATING
Highest Passer Rating, Career (150 attempts)
- 104.8   Bart Starr, Green Bay, 10 games
- 95.6   Joe Montana, San Francisco-Kansas City, 23 games
- 95.0   Jake Delhomme, Carolina, 7 games

ATTEMPTS

Most Passes Attempted, Career
- 734   Joe Montana, San Francisco-Kansas City, 23 games
- 721   Brett Favre, Green Bay, 22 games
- 687   Dan Marino, Miami, 18 games

Most Passes Attempted, Game
- 65   Steve Young, NFC-D: San Francisco vs. Green Bay, 1995
- 64   Bernie Kosar, AFC-D: Cleveland vs. N.Y. Jets, 1986 (OT)
-      Dan Marino, AFC-FR: Miami vs. Buffalo, 1995
- 58   Jim Kelly, SB: Buffalo vs. Washington, 1991

COMPLETIONS

Most Passes Completed, Career
- 460   Joe Montana, San Francisco-Kansas City, 23 games
- 438   Brett Favre, Green Bay, 22 games
- 385   Dan Marino, Miami, 18 games

Most Passes Completed, Game
- 36   Warren Moon, AFC-FR: Houston vs. Buffalo, 1992 (OT)
- 33   Dan Fouts, AFC-D: San Diego vs. Miami, 1981 (OT)
-      Bernie Kosar, AFC-D: Cleveland vs. N.Y. Jets, 1986 (OT)
-      Dan Marino, AFC-FR: Miami vs. Buffalo, 1995
-      Peyton Manning, AFC-D: Indianapolis vs. San Diego, 2007
- 32   Neil Lomax, NFC-FR: St. Louis vs. Green Bay, 1982
-      Danny White, NFC-FR: Dallas vs. L.A. Rams, 1983
-      Warren Moon, AFC-D: Houston vs. Kansas City, 1993
-      Neil O'Donnell, AFC: Pittsburgh vs. San Diego, 1994
-      Steve Young, NFC-D: San Francisco vs. Green Bay, 1995
-      Tom Brady, AFC-D: New England vs. Oakland, 2001 (OT)
-      Tom Brady, SB: New England vs. Carolina, 2003

COMPLETION PERCENTAGE

Highest Completion Percentage, Career (150 attempts)
- 66.3   Ken Anderson, Cincinnati, 6 games (166-110)
- 64.3   Warren Moon, Houston-Minnesota, 10 games (403-259)
- 64.2   Rich Gannon, Minnesota-Kansas City-Oakland, 10 games (240-154)

Highest Completion Percentage, Game (15 completions)
- 92.9   Tom Brady, AFC-D: New England vs. Jacksonville, 2007 (28-26)
- 88.0   Phil Simms, SB: N.Y. Giants vs. Denver, 1986 (25-22)
- 86.7   Joe Montana, NFC: San Francisco vs. L.A. Rams, 1989 (30-26)

YARDS GAINED

Most Yards Gained, Career
- 5,772   Joe Montana, San Francisco-Kansas City, 23 games
- 5,311   Brett Favre, Green Bay, 22 games
- 4,964   John Elway, Denver, 22 games

Most Yards Gained, Game
- 489   Bernie Kosar, AFC-D: Cleveland vs. N.Y. Jets, 1986 (OT)
- 458   Peyton Manning, AFC-FR: Indianapolis vs. Denver, 2004
- 433   Dan Fouts, AFC-D: San Diego vs. Miami, 1981 (OT)

Most Games, 300 or More Yards Passing, Career
- 6   Joe Montana, San Francisco-Kansas City, 23 games
- 5   Dan Fouts, San Diego, 7 games
-    Peyton Manning, Indianapolis, 14 games
- 4   Warren Moon, Houston-Minnesota, 10 games
-    Troy Aikman, Dallas, 16 games
-    Dan Marino, Miami, 18 games
-    John Elway, Denver, 22 games
-    Kurt Warner, St. Louis, 7 games

Most Consecutive Games, 300 or More Yards Passing
- 4   Dan Fouts, San Diego, 1979-1981
- 3   Jim Kelly, Buffalo, 1989-1990
-    Warren Moon, Houston, 1991-93

- 2   Daryle Lamonica, Oakland, 1968
-    Ken Anderson, Cincinnati, 1981-82
-    Terry Bradshaw, Pittsburgh, 1979-1982
-    Joe Montana, San Francisco, 1983-84
-    Dan Marino, Miami, 1984
-    Troy Aikman, Dallas, 1994
-    Steve Young, San Francisco, 1994-95
-    Kurt Warner, St. Louis, 1999-2000
-    Peyton Manning, Indianapolis, 2003
-    Marc Bulger, St. Louis, 2003-04
-    Matt Hasselbeck, Seattle, 2003-04

Longest Pass Completion
- 96   Trent Dilfer (to Sharpe), AFC: Baltimore vs. Oakland, 2000 (TD)
- 94   Troy Aikman (to Harper), NFC-D: Dallas vs. Green Bay, 1994 (TD)
- 93   Daryle Lamonica (to Dubenion), AFC-D: Buffalo vs. Boston, 1963 (TD)

AVERAGE GAIN

Highest Average Gain, Career (150 attempts)
- 8.55   Jake Delhomme, Carolina, 7 games (192-1,642)
- 8.45   Joe Theismann, Washington, 10 games (211-1,782)
- 8.43   Jim Plunkett, Oakland/L.A.Raiders, 10 games (272-2,293)

Highest Average Gain, Game (20 attempts)
- 14.71   Terry Bradshaw, SB: Pittsburgh vs. Los Angeles, 1979 (21-309)
- 14.50   Peyton Manning, AFC-FR: Indianapolis vs. Denver, 2003 (26-377)
- 13.88   Peyton Manning, AFC-FR: Indianapolis vs. Denver, 2004 (33-458)

TOUCHDOWNS

Most Touchdown Passes, Career
- 45   Joe Montana, San Francisco-Kansas City, 23 games
- 39   Brett Favre, Green Bay, 22 games
- 32   Dan Marino, Miami, 18 games

Most Touchdown Passes, Game
- 6   Daryle Lamonica, AFC-D: Oakland vs. Houston, 1969
-    Steve Young, SB: San Francisco vs. San Diego, 1994
- 5   Sid Luckman, NFC: Chi. Bears vs. Washington, 1943
-    Daryle Lamonica, AFC-D: Oakland vs. Kansas City, 1968
-    Joe Montana, SB: San Francisco vs. Denver, 1989
-    Kurt Warner, NFC-D: St. Louis vs. Minnesota, 1999
-    Kerry Collins, NFC: N.Y. Giants vs. Minnesota, 2000
-    Peyton Manning, AFC-FR: Indianapolis vs. Denver, 2003
- 4   Otto Graham, NFC: Cleveland vs. Los Angeles, 1950
-    Tobin Rote, NFC: Detroit vs. Cleveland, 1957
-    Bart Starr, NFC: Green Bay vs. Dallas, 1966
-    Ken Stabler, AFC-D: Oakland vs. Miami, 1974
-    Roger Staubach, NFC: Dallas vs. Los Angeles, 1975
-    Terry Bradshaw, SB: Pittsburgh vs. Dallas, 1978
-    Don Strock, AFC-D: Miami vs. San Diego, 1981 (OT)
-    Lynn Dickey, NFC-FR: Green Bay vs. St. Louis, 1982
-    Dan Marino, AFC: Miami vs. Pittsburgh, 1984
-    Phil Simms, NFC-D: N.Y. Giants vs. San Francisco, 1986
-    Doug Williams, SB: Washington vs. Denver, 1987
-    Jim Kelly, AFC-D: Buffalo vs. Cleveland, 1989
-    Joe Montana, NFC-D: San Francisco vs. Minnesota, 1989
-    Warren Moon, AFC-FR: Houston vs. Buffalo, 1992 (OT)
-    Frank Reich, AFC-FR: Buffalo vs. Houston, 1992 (OT)
-    Troy Aikman, SB: Dallas vs. Buffalo, 1992
-    Jeff George, NFC-D: Minnesota vs. St. Louis, 1999
-    Aaron Brooks, NFC-FR: New Orleans vs. St. Louis, 2000
-    Kerry Collins, NFC-FR: N.Y. Giants vs. San Francisco, 2002
-    Peyton Manning, AFC-FR: Indianapolis vs. Denver, 2004
-    Daunte Culpepper, NFC-FR: Minnesota vs. Green Bay, 2004

Most Consecutive Games, Touchdown Passes
- 18   Brett Favre, Green Bay, 1995-2007 (current)
- 13   Dan Marino, Miami, 1983-1995
- 15   Tom Brady, New England, 2001-07 (current)

HAD INTERCEPTED

Lowest Percentage, Passes Had Intercepted, Career (150 attempts)
- 1.41   Bart Starr, Green Bay, 10 games (213-3)
- 2.02   Tom Brady, New England, 17 games (595-12)
- 2.15   Phil Simms, N.Y. Giants, 10 games (279-6)

Most Attempts Without Interception, Game
- 54   Neil O'Donnell, AFC: Pittsburgh vs. San Diego, 1994
- 48   Randall Cunningham, NFC: Minnesota vs. Atlanta, 1998 (OT)
       Tom Brady, SB: New England vs. N.Y. Giants, 2007
- 47   Daryle Lamonica, AFC: Oakland vs. N.Y. Jets, 1968
       Warren Moon, AFC-FR: Houston vs. Pittsburgh, 1989 (OT)

Most Passes Had Intercepted, Career
- 28   Jim Kelly, Buffalo, 17 games
       Brett Favre, Green Bay, 22 games
- 26   Terry Bradshaw, Pittsburgh, 19 games
- 24   Dan Marino, Miami, 18 games

Most Passes Had Intercepted, Game
- 6   Frank Filchock, NFC: N.Y. Giants vs. Chi. Bears, 1946
      Bobby Layne, NFC: Detroit vs. Cleveland, 1954
      Norm Van Brocklin, NFC: Los Angeles vs. Cleveland, 1955
      Brett Favre, NFC-D: Green Bay vs. St. Louis, 2001
- 5   Frank Filchock, NFC: Washington vs. Chi. Bears, 1940
      George Blanda, AFC: Houston vs. San Diego, 1961
      George Blanda, AFC: Houston vs. Dall. Texans, 1962 (OT)
      Y.A. Tittle, NFC: N.Y. Giants vs. Chicago, 1963
      Mike Phipps, AFC-D: Cleveland vs. Miami, 1972
      Dan Pastorini, AFC: Houston vs. Pittsburgh, 1978
      Dan Fouts, AFC-D: San Diego vs. Houston, 1979
      Tommy Kramer, NFC-D: Minnesota vs. Philadelphia, 1980
      Dan Fouts, AFC-D: San Diego vs. Miami, 1982
      Richard Todd, AFC: N.Y. Jets vs Miami, 1982
      Gary Danielson, NFC-D: Detroit vs. San Francisco, 1983
      Jay Schroeder, AFC: L.A. Raiders vs. Buffalo, 1990
      Rich Gannon, SB: Oakland vs. Tampa Bay, 2002
- 4   By many players

PASS RECEIVING

RECEPTIONS

Most Receptions, Career
- 151   Jerry Rice, San Francisco-Oakland-Seattle, 29 games
- 87   Michael Irvin, Dallas, 16 games
- 85   Andre Reed, Buffalo, 21 games

Most Receptions, Game
- 13   Kellen Winslow, AFC-D: San Diego vs. Miami, 1981 (OT)
       Thurman Thomas, AFC-D: Buffalo vs. Cleveland, 1989
       Shannon Sharpe, AFC-FR: Denver vs. L.A. Raiders, 1993
       Chad Morton, NFC-D: New Orleans vs. Minnesota, 2000
- 12   Raymond Berry, NFC: Baltimore vs. N.Y. Giants, 1958
       Michael Irvin, NFC: Dallas vs. San Francisco, 1994
       Darrell Jackson, NFC-FR: Seattle vs. St. Louis, 2004
       Steve Smith, NFC-D: Carolina vs. Chicago, 2005
- 11   Dante Lavelli, NFC: Cleveland vs. Los Angeles, 1950
       Dan Ross, NFC: Cincinnati vs. San Francisco, 1981
       Franco Harris, AFC-FR: Pittsburgh vs. San Diego, 1982
       Steve Watson, AFC-D: Denver vs. Pittsburgh, 1984
       John L. Williams, AFC-D: Seattle vs. Cincinnati, 1988
       Jerry Rice, SB: San Francisco vs. Cincinnati, 1988
       Ernest Givins, AFC-FR: Houston vs. Pittsburgh, 1989 (OT)
       Amp Lee, NFC-D: Minnesota vs. Chicago, 1994
       Jay Novacek, NFC-D: Dallas vs. Green Bay, 1994
       O.J. McDuffie, AFC-FR: Miami vs. Buffalo, 1995
       Jerry Rice, NFC-D: San Francisco vs. Green Bay, 1995
       Hines Ward, AFC-FR: Pittsburgh vs. Cleveland, 2002
       Deion Branch, SB: New England vs. Philadelphia, 2004
       Plaxico Burress, NFC: N.Y. Giants vs.Green Bay, 2007 (OT)
       Wes Welker, SB: New England vs. N.Y. Giants, 2007

Most Consecutive Games, Pass Receptions
- 28   Jerry Rice, San Francisco-Oakland, 1985-2002
- 22   Drew Pearson, Dallas, 1973-1983
- 18   Paul Warfield, Cleveland-Miami, 1964-1974

Cliff Branch, Oakland/L.A. Raiders, 1974-1983
Thurman Thomas, Buffalo, 1989-1998
Shannon Sharpe, Denver-Baltimore-Denver, 1991-2003

YARDS GAINED

Most Yards Gained, Career
- 2,245   Jerry Rice, San Francisco-Oakland-Seattle, 29 games
- 1,315   Michael Irvin, Dallas, 16 games
- 1,289   Cliff Branch, Oakland/L.A. Raiders, 22 games

Most Yards Gained, Game
- 240   Eric Moulds, AFC-FR: Buffalo vs. Miami, 1998
- 227   Anthony Carter, NFC-D: Minnesota vs. San Francisco, 1987
- 221   Reggie Wayne, AFC-FR: Indianapolis vs. Denver, 2004

Most Games, 100 or More Yards Receiving, Career
- 8   Jerry Rice, San Francisco-Oakland-Seattle, 29 games
- 6   Michael Irvin, Dallas, 16 games
- 5   John Stallworth, Pittsburgh, 18 games
      Andre Reed, Buffalo, 21 games
      Hines Ward, Pittsburgh, 11 games

Most Consecutive Games, 100 or More Yards Receiving, Career
- 3   Tom Fears, Los Angeles, 1950-51
      Jerry Rice, San Francisco, 1988-89
      Randy Moss, Minnesota, 1999-2000
- 2   By many players

Longest Reception
- 96   Shannon Sharpe (from Dilfer), AFC: Baltimore vs. Oakland, 2000 (TD)
- 94   Alvin Harper (from Aikman), NFC-D: Dallas vs. Green Bay, 1994 (TD)
- 93   Elbert Dubenion (from Lamonica), AFC-D: Buffalo vs. Boston, 1963 (TD)

AVERAGE GAIN

Highest Average Gain, Career (20 receptions)
- 27.3   Alvin Harper, Dallas, 10 games (24-655)
- 23.7   Willie Gault, Chicago-L.A. Raiders, 12 games (21-497)
- 22.8   Harold Jackson, L.A. Rams-New England-Minnesota-Seattle, 14 games (24-548)

Highest Average Gain, Game (3 receptions)
- 46.3   Harold Jackson, NFC: Los Angeles vs. Minnesota, 1974 (3-139)
- 42.7   Billy Cannon, AFC: Houston vs. L.A. Chargers, 1960 (3-128)
- 42.0   Lenny Moore, NFC: Baltimore vs. N.Y. Giants, 1959 (3-126)

TOUCHDOWNS

Most Touchdowns, Career
- 22   Jerry Rice, San Francisco-Oakland-Seattle, 29 games
- 12   John Stallworth, Pittsburgh, 18 games
- 10   Fred Biletnikoff, Oakland, 19 games
       Antonio Freeman, Green Bay-Philadelphia-Green Bay, 16 games
       Randy Moss, Minnesota-New England, 11 games

Most Touchdowns, Game
- 3   Tom Fears, NFC-D: Los Angeles vs. Chi. Bears, 1950
      Gary Collins, NFC: Cleveland vs. Baltimore, 1964
      Fred Biletnikoff, AFC-D: Oakland vs. Kansas City, 1968
      Preston Pearson, NFC: Dallas vs. Los Angeles, 1975
      Dave Casper, AFC-D: Oakland vs. Baltimore, 1977 (OT)
      Alvin Garrett, NFC-FR: Washington vs. Detroit, 1982
      Jerry Rice, NFC-D: San Francisco vs. Minnesota, 1988
      Jerry Rice, SB: San Francisco vs. Denver, 1989
      Andre Reed, AFC-FR: Buffalo vs. Houston, 1992 (OT)
      Sterling Sharpe, NFC-FR: Green Bay vs. Detroit, 1993
      Jerry Rice, SB: San Francisco vs. San Diego, 1994
      Willie Jackson, NFC-FR: New Orleans vs. St. Louis, 2000
      Amani Toomer, NFC-FR: N.Y. Giants vs. San Francisco, 2002

Most Consecutive Games, Touchdown Passes Caught
- 8   John Stallworth, Pittsburgh, 1978-1983
- 7   David Givens, New England, 2003-05 (current)
- 5   James Lofton, Green Bay-Buffalo, 1982-1990
      Randy Moss, Minnesota, 1998-2000
      Antonio Freeman, Green Bay, 1997-2001
      Hines Ward, Pittsburgh, 2002-05

POSTSEASON RECORDS

INTERCEPTIONS BY
Most Interceptions, Career
- 9 Charlie Waters, Dallas, 25 games
-    Bill Simpson, Los Angeles-Buffalo, 11 games
-    Ronnie Lott, San Francisco-L.A. Raiders, 20 games
- 8 Lester Hayes, Oakland/L.A. Raiders, 13 games
- 7 Willie Brown, Oakland, 17 games
-    Dennis Thurman, Dallas, 14 games
-    Rodney Harrison, San Diego-New England, 13 games

Most Interceptions, Game
- 4 Vernon Perry, AFC-D: Houston vs. San Diego, 1979
- 3 Joe Laws, NFC: Green Bay vs. N.Y. Giants, 1944
-    Charlie Waters, NFC-D: Dallas vs. Chicago, 1977
-    Rod Martin, SB: Oakland vs. Philadelphia, 1980
-    Dennis Thurman, NFC-D: Dallas vs. Green Bay, 1982
-    A.J. Duhe, AFC: Miami vs. N.Y. Jets, 1982
-    Ty Law, AFC: New England vs. Indianapolis, 2003
-    Ricky Manning Jr., NFC: Carolina vs. Philadelphia, 2003
- 2 By many players

Most Consecutive Games, Interceptions
- 4 Aeneas Williams, Arizona-St. Louis, 1998-2001
-    Rodney Harrison, New England, 2004, 2007
- 3 By many players. Last time:
-    R.W. McQuarters, N.Y. Giants, 2007
-    Ike Taylor, Pittsburgh, 2005, 2007 (current)

YARDS GAINED
Most Yards Gained, Career
- 196 Willie Brown, Oakland, 17 games
- 187 Ronnie Lott, San Francisco-L.A.-Raiders, 20 games
- 160 George Teague, Green Bay-Dallas-Miami-Dallas, 12 games

Most Yards Gained, Game
- 108 Darrien Gordon, SB: Denver vs. Atlanta, 1998
- 101 George Teague, NFC-FR: Green Bay vs. Detroit, 1993
- 100 Champ Bailey, AFC-D: Denver vs. New England, 2005

Longest Return
- 101 George Teague, NFC-FR: Green Bay vs. Detroit, 1993 (TD)
- 100 Champ Bailey, AFC-D: Denver vs. New England, 2005
- 98 Darrol Ray, AFC-FR: N.Y. Jets vs. Cincinnati, 1982 (TD)

TOUCHDOWNS
Most Touchdowns, Career
- 3 Willie Brown, Oakland, 17 games
-    Asante Samuel, New England, 14 games
- 2 Lester Hayes, Oakland/L.A. Raiders, 13 games
-    Ronnie Lott, San Francisco-L.A. Raiders, 20 games
-    Darrell Green, Washington, 18 games
-    Melvin Jenkins, Seattle-Detroit, 5 games
-    George Teague, Green Bay-Dallas-Miami-Dallas, 12 games
-    Aeneas Williams, Arizona-St. Louis, 6 games
-    Dwight Smith, Tampa Bay, 4 games

Most Touchdowns, Game
- 2 Aeneas Williams, NFC-D: St. Louis vs. Green Bay, 2001
-    Dwight Smith, SB: Tampa Bay vs. Oakland, 2002
- 1 By many players

PUNTING
Most Punts, Career
- 111 Ray Guy, Oakland/L.A. Raiders, 22 games
- 97 Craig Hentrich, Green Bay-Tennessee, 21 games
- 84 Danny White, Dallas, 18 games
-     Sean Landeta, N.Y. Giants-Tampa Bay-Green Bay-Philadelphia-St. Louis, 18 games

Most Punts, Game
- 14 Dave Jennings, AFC-D: N.Y. Jets vs. Cleveland, 1986 (OT)
- 12 David Lee, AFC-D: Baltimore vs. Oakland, 1977 (OT)
- 11 Ken Strong, NFC: N.Y. Giants vs. Chi. Bears, 1933
-     Jim Norton, AFC: Houston vs. Oakland, 1967
-     Ode Burrell, AFC-D: Houston vs. Oakland, 1969
-     Dale Hatcher, NFC: L.A. Rams vs. Chicago, 1985
-     Brad Maynard, SB: N.Y. Giants vs. Baltimore, 2000

Longest Punt
- 76 Ed Danowski, NFC: N.Y. Giants vs. Detroit, 1935
-     Mike Horan, AFC: Denver vs. Buffalo, 1991
- 72 Charlie Conerly, NFC-D: N.Y. Giants vs. Cleveland, 1950
-     Yale Lary, NFC: Detroit vs. Cleveland, 1953
- 71 Ray Guy, AFC: Oakland vs. San Diego, 1980

AVERAGE YARDAGE
Highest Average, Career (25 punts)
- 44.5 Rich Camarillo, New England, 6 games (35-1,559)
- 44.4 Todd Sauerbrun, Carolina-Denver-New England, 9 games (43-1,911)
- 43.6 Hunter Smith, Indianapolis, 14 games (46-2,007)

Highest Average, Game (4 punts)
- 56.0 Ray Guy, AFC: Oakland vs. San Diego, 1980 (4-224)
- 52.8 Hunter Smith, AFC: Indianapolis vs. New England, 2006 (4-211)
- 52.5 Sammy Baugh, NFC: Washington vs. Chi. Bears, 1942 (6-315)

PUNT RETURNS
Most Punt Returns, Career
- 34 David Meggett, N.Y. Giants-New England-N.Y. Jets, 13 games
-     Brian Mitchell, Washington-Philadelphia, 16 games
- 33 Troy Brown, New England, 20 games
- 25 Theo Bell, Pittsburgh-Tampa Bay, 10 games

Most Punt Returns, Game
- 7 Ron Gardin, AFC-D: Baltimore vs. Cincinnati, 1970
-    Carl Roaches, AFC-FR: Houston vs. Oakland, 1980
-    Gerald McNeil, AFC-D: Cleveland vs. N.Y. Jets, 1986 (OT)
-    Phil McConkey, NFC-D: N.Y. Giants vs. San Francisco, 1986
-    David Meggett, AFC-D: New England vs. Pittsburgh, 1996
-    Reggie Barlow, AFC-FR: Jacksonville vs. New England, 1998
- 6 George McAfee, NFC-D: Chi. Bears vs. Los Angeles, 1950
-    Eddie Brown, NFC-D: Washington vs. Minnesota, 1976
-    Theo Bell, AFC: Pittsburgh vs. Houston, 1978
-    Eddie Brown, NFC: Los Angeles vs. Tampa Bay, 1979
-    John Sciarra, NFC: Philadelphia vs. Dallas, 1980
-    Kurt Sohn, AFC: N.Y. Jets vs. Miami, 1982
-    Mike Nelms, SB: Washington vs. Miami, 1982
-    Anthony Carter, NFC-FR: Minnesota vs. New Orleans, 1987
-    Desmond Howard, SB: Green Bay vs. New England, 1996
-    Nate Jacquet, AFC-FR: Miami vs. Seattle, 1999
-    Derrick Mason, AFC-FR: Tennessee vs. Baltimore, 2003
-    Antonio Chatman, AFC-D: Green Bay vs. Philadelphia, 2003
-    Nate Burleson, NFC-FR: Seattle vs. Washington, 2007
- 5 By many players

YARDS GAINED
Most Yards Gained, Career
- 339 Brian Mitchell, Washington-Philadelphia, 16 games
- 315 Troy Brown, New England, 20 games
- 312 David Meggett, N.Y. Giants-New England-N.Y. Jets, 13 games

Most Yards Gained, Game
- 152 Allen Rossum, NFC-D: Atlanta vs. St. Louis, 2004
- 143 Anthony Carter, NFC-FR: Minnesota vs. New Orleans, 1987
- 141 Bob Hayes, NFC-D: Dallas vs. Cleveland, 1967

Longest Return
- 88 Jermaine Lewis, AFC-D: Baltimore vs. Pittsburgh, 2001 (TD)
- 84 Anthony Carter, NFC-FR: Minnesota vs. New Orleans, 1987 (TD)
- 81 Hugh Gallarneau, NFC-D: Chi. Bears vs. Green Bay, 1941 (TD)

AVERAGE YARDAGE
Highest Average, Career (10 returns)
- 23.9   Allen Rossum, Green Bay-Atlanta, 6 games (10-239)
- 15.3   Robert Brooks, Green Bay, 11 games (14-214)
- 15.2   Anthony Carter, Minnesota-Detroit, 9 games (17-259)

Highest Average Gain, Game (3 returns)
- 50.7   Allen Rossum, NFC-D: Atlanta vs. St. Louis, 2004 (3-152)
- 47.0   Bob Hayes, NFC-D: Dallas vs. Cleveland, 1967 (3-141)
- 33.0   Jermaine Lewis, AFC-D: Baltimore vs. Pittsburgh, 2001 (3-99)

TOUCHDOWNS
Most Touchdowns
- 1   Hugh Gallarneau, NFC-D: Chicago Bears vs. Green Bay, 1941
  Bosh Pritchard, NFC-D: Philadelphia vs. Pittsburgh, 1947
  Charley Trippi, NFC: Chicago Cardinals vs. Philadelphia, 1947
  Verda (Vitamin T) Smith, NFC-D: Los Angeles vs. Detroit, 1952
  George (Butch) Byrd, AFC: Buffalo vs. San Diego, 1965
  Golden Richards, NFC: Dallas vs. Minnesota, 1973
  Wes Chandler, AFC-D: San Diego vs. Miami, 1981 (OT)
  Shaun Gayle, NFC-D: Chicago vs. N.Y. Giants, 1985
  Anthony Carter, NFC-FR: Minnesota vs. New Orleans, 1987
  Darrell Green, NFC-D: Washington vs. Chicago, 1987
  Antonio Freeman, NFC-FR: Green Bay vs. Atlanta, 1995
  Desmond Howard, NFC-D: Green Bay vs. San Francisco, 1996
  Jermaine Lewis, AFC-D: Baltimore vs. Pittsburgh, 2001
  Troy Brown, AFC: New England vs. Pittsburgh, 2001
  Antwaan Randle El, AFC-FR: Pittsburgh vs. Cleveland, 2002
  Santana Moss, AFC-D: N.Y. Jets vs. Pittsburgh, 2004 (OT)
  Allen Rossum, NFC-D: Atlanta vs. St. Louis, 2004
  Steve Smith, NFC: Carolina vs. Seattle, 2005

KICKOFF RETURNS
Most Kickoff Returns, Career
- 36   Brian Mitchell, Washington-Philadelphia, 16 games
- 31   Kevin Williams, Dallas-Buffalo, 12 games
- 29   Fulton Walker, Miami-L.A. Raiders, 10 games

Most Kickoff Returns, Game
- 8   Marc Logan, AFC-D: Miami vs. Buffalo, 1990
  Andre Coleman, SB: San Diego vs. San Francisco, 1994
  Marcus Knight, SB: Oakland vs. Tampa Bay, 2002
- 7   Don Bingham, NFC: Chi. Bears vs. N.Y. Giants, 1956
  Reggie Brown, NFC-FR: Atlanta vs. Minnesota, 1982
  David Verser, AFC-FR: Cincinnati vs. N.Y. Jets, 1982
  Del Rodgers, NFC-D: Green Bay vs. Dallas, 1982
  Henry Ellard, NFC-D: L.A. Rams vs. Washington, 1983
  Stephen Starring, SB: New England vs. Chicago, 1985
  Darick Holmes, AFC-D: Buffalo vs. Pittsburgh, 1995
  Antonio Freeman, NFC: Green Bay vs. Dallas, 1995
  Roell Preston, NFC-FR: Green Bay vs. San Francisco, 1998
  Robert Tate, NFC-D: Minnesota vs. St. Louis, 1999
  Fred McAfee, NFC-D: New Orleans vs. Minnesota, 2000
  Michael Bates, NFC-FR: Dallas vs. Carolina, 2003
  Dante Hall, AFC-D: Kansas City vs. Indianapolis, 2003
  Michael Lewis, NFC: New Orleans vs. Chicago, 2006
- 6   By many players

YARDS GAINED
Most Yards Gained, Career
- 875   Brian Mitchell, Washington-Philadelphia, 16 games
- 677   Fulton Walker, Miami-L.A. Raiders, 10 games
- 632   Kevin Williams, Dallas-Buffalo, 12 games

Most Yards Gained, Game
- 244   Andre Coleman, SB: San Diego vs. San Francisco, 1994

- 220   Ellis Hobbs, AFC: New England vs. Indianapolis, 2006
- 210   Tim Dwight, SB: Atlanta vs. Denver, 1998

Longest Return
- 100   Brian Mitchell, NFC-D: Washington vs. Tampa Bay, 1999 (TD)
- 99   Desmond Howard, SB: Green Bay vs. New England, 1996 (TD)
- 98   Fulton Walker, SB: Miami vs. Washington, 1982 (TD)
  Andre Coleman, SB: San Diego vs. San Francisco, 1994 (TD)

AVERAGE YARDAGE
Highest Average, Career (10 returns)
- 30.1   Carl Garrett, Oakland, 5 games (16-481)
- 30.0   Reggie Barlow, Jacksonville, 8 games (12-360)
- 29.2   Chad Morton, New Orleans-N.Y. Jets-N.Y. Giants, 6 games (14-409)

Highest Average, Game (3 returns)
- 56.7   Les (Speedy) Duncan, NFC-D: Washington vs. San Francisco, 1971 (3-170)
- 51.3   Ed Podolak, AFC-D: Kansas City vs. Miami, 1971 (OT) (3-154)
- 49.0   Les (Speedy) Duncan, AFC: San Diego vs. Buffalo, 1964 (3-147)

TOUCHDOWNS
Most Touchdowns, Career
- 2   Ron Dixon, N.Y. Giants, 4 games
- 1   By many players

Most Touchdowns, Game
- 1   Vic Washington, NFC-D: San Francisco vs. Dallas, 1972
  Nat Moore, AFC-D: Miami vs. Oakland, 1974
  Marshall Johnson, AFC-D: Baltimore vs. Oakland, 1977 (OT)
  Fulton Walker, SB: Miami vs. Washington, 1982
  Stanford Jennings, SB: Cincinnati vs. San Francisco, 1988
  Eric Metcalf, AFC-D: Cleveland vs. Buffalo, 1989
  Andre Coleman, SB: San Diego vs. San Francisco, 1994
  Desmond Howard, SB: Green Bay vs. New England, 1996
  Chuck Levy, NFC: San Francisco vs. Green Bay, 1997
  Tim Dwight, SB: Atlanta vs. Denver, 1998
  Kevin Dyson, AFC-FR: Tennessee vs. Buffalo, 1999
  Charlie Rogers, AFC-FR: Seattle vs. Miami, 1999
  Brian Mitchell, NFC-D: Washington vs. Tampa Bay, 1999
  Tony Horne, NFC-D: St. Louis vs. Minnesota, 1999
  Derrick Mason, AFC: Tennessee vs. Jacksonville, 1999
  Ron Dixon, NFC-D: N.Y. Giants vs. Philadelphia, 2000; SB: N.Y. Giants vs. Baltimore, 2000
  Jermaine Lewis, SB: Baltimore vs. N.Y. Giants, 2000
  Dante Hall, AFC-D: Kansas City vs. Indianapolis, 2003
  Miles Austin, NFC-FR: Dallas vs. Seattle, 2006
  Devin Hester, SB: Chicago vs. Indianapolis, 2006

FUMBLES
Most Fumbles, Career
- 16   Warren Moon, Houston-Minnesota, 10 games
- 14   John Elway, Denver, 22 games
- 13   Tony Dorsett, Dallas, 17 games

Most Fumbles, Game
- 5   Warren Moon, AFC-D: Houston vs. Kansas City, 1993
- 4   Brian Sipe, AFC-D: Cleveland vs. Oakland, 1980
  Randall Cunningham, NFC-FR: Minnesota vs. N.Y. Giants, 1997
- 3   By many players

RECOVERIES
Most Own Fumbles Recovered, Career
- 8   Warren Moon, Houston-Minnesota, 10 games
- 7   John Elway, Denver, 22 games
- 6   Jim Kelly, Buffalo, 17 games

Most Opponents' Fumbles Recovered, Career
- 4   Cliff Harris, Dallas, 21 games

POSTSEASON RECORDS

Harvey Martin, Dallas, 22 games
Ted Hendricks, Baltimore-Oakland/L.A. Raiders, 21 games
Alvin Walton, Washington, 9 games
Monte Coleman, Washington, 21 games
Dave Thomas, Dallas-Jacksonville-N.Y. Giants, 13 games
3 Paul Krause, Minnesota, 19 games
Jack Lambert, Pittsburgh, 18 games
Fred Dryer, Los Angeles, 14 games
Charlie Waters, Dallas, 25 games
Jack Ham, Pittsburgh, 16 games
Mike Hegman, Dallas, 16 games
Tom Jackson, Denver, 10 games
Rich Milot, Washington, 13 games
Mike Singletary, Chicago, 12 games
Darryl Grant, Washington, 16 games
Wes Hopkins, Philadelphia, 3 games
Wilber Marshall, Chicago-Washington, 15 games
Tyrone Braxton, Denver-Miami-Denver, 19 games
Neil Smith, Kansas City-Denver, 16 games
Tony Brackens, Jacksonville, 7 games
Phil Hansen, Buffalo, 14 games
Carnell Lake, Pittsburgh-Jacksonville-Baltimore, 17 games
Jason Gildon, Pittsburgh, 13 games
Tedy Bruschi, New England, 22 games
2 By many players

Most Fumbles Recovered, Game, Own and Opponents'
3 Jack Lambert, AFC: Pittsburgh vs. Oakland, 1975 (3 opp)
Ron Jaworski, NFC-FR: Philadelphia vs. N.Y. Giants, 1981 (3 own)
Devin Hester, NFC-D: Chicago vs. Seattle, 2006 (3-own)
2 By many players

YARDS GAINED
Longest Return
93 Andy Russell, AFC-D: Pittsburgh vs. Baltimore, 1975 (opp, TD)
79 Neil Smith, AFC-D: Denver vs. Miami, 1998 (opp, TD)
64 Leon Lett, SB: Dallas vs. Buffalo, 1992 (opp)

TOUCHDOWNS
Most Touchdowns
1 By many players

COMBINED NET YARDS GAINED
Rushing, receiving, interception returns, punt returns, kickoff returns, and fumble returns.
ATTEMPTS
Most Attempts, Career
454 Franco Harris, Pittsburgh, 19 games
417 Thurman Thomas, Buffalo, 21 games
397 Emmitt Smith, Dallas, 17 games
Most Attempts, Game
43 Lamar Smith, AFC-FR: Miami vs. Indianapolis, 2000 (OT)
42 Curtis Martin, AFC-D: N.Y. Jets vs. Jacksonville, 1998
40 Lawrence McCutcheon, NFC-D: Los Angeles vs. St. Louis, 1975

YARDS GAINED
Most Yards Gained, Career
2,289 Jerry Rice, San Francisco-Oakland-Seattle, 29 games
2,124 Thurman Thomas, Buffalo, 21 games
2,060 Franco Harris, Pittsburgh, 19 games
Most Yards Gained, Game
350 Ed Podolak, AFC-D: Kansas City vs. Miami, 1971 (OT)
329 Keith Lincoln, AFC: San Diego vs. Boston, 1963
285 Bob Hayes, NFC-D: Dallas vs. Cleveland, 1967

SACKS
Sacks have been compiled since 1982.
Most Sacks, Career
16.0 Willie McGinest, New England, 18 games
14.5 Bruce Smith, Buffalo, 20 games
12.0 Reggie White, Philadelphia-Green Bay, 19 games
Most Sacks, Game
4.5 Willie McGinest, AFC-FR: New England vs. Jacksonville, 2005
3.5 Rich Milot, NFC-D: Washington vs. Chicago, 1984
Richard Dent, NFC-D: Chicago vs. N.Y. Giants, 1985
3.0 Richard Dent, NFC-D: Chicago vs. Washington, 1984
Garin Veris, AFC-FR: New England vs. N.Y. Jets, 1985
Gary Jeter, NFC-D: L.A. Rams vs. Dallas, 1985
Carl Hairston, AFC-D: Cleveland vs. N.Y. Jets, 1986 (OT)
Charles Mann, NFC-D: Washington vs. Chicago, 1987
Kevin Greene, NFC-FR: L.A. Rams vs. Minnesota, 1988
Greg Townsend, AFC-D: L.A. Raiders vs. Cincinnati, 1990
Wilber Marshall, NFC: Washington vs. Detroit, 1991
Fred Stokes, NFC-FR: Washington vs. Minnesota, 1992
Pierce Holt, NFC-D: San Francisco vs. Washington, 1992
Tony Casillas, NFC: Dallas vs. San Francisco, 1992
Gerald Williams, AFC-FR: Pittsburgh vs. Kansas City, 1993
Chad Brown, AFC-FR: Pittsburgh vs. Indianapolis, 1996
Reggie White, SB: Green Bay vs. New England, 1996
Warren Sapp, NFC-D: Tampa Bay vs. Green Bay, 1997
Trace Armstrong, AFC-FR: Miami vs. Seattle, 1999
Michael McCrary, AFC-FR: Baltimore vs. Denver, 2000
Willie McGinest, AFC-D: New England vs. Tennessee, 2003

TEAM RECORDS

CHAMPIONSHIPS
Most Seasons League Champion
12 Green Bay, 1929-1931, 1936, 1939, 1944, 1961-62, 1965-67, 1996
9 Chi. Bears, 1921, 1932-33, 1940-41, 1943, 1946, 1963, 1985
7 N.Y. Giants, 1927, 1934, 1938, 1956, 1986, 1990, 2007
Most Consecutive Seasons League Champion
3 Green Bay, 1929-1931
Green Bay, 1965-67

2 Canton, 1922-23
Chi. Bears, 1932-33
Chi. Bears, 1940-41
Philadelphia, 1948-49
Detroit, 1952-53
Cleveland, 1954-55
Baltimore, 1958-59
Houston, 1960-61
Green Bay, 1961-62
Buffalo, 1964-65
Miami, 1972-73
Pittsburgh, 1974-75
Pittsburgh, 1978-79
San Francisco, 1988-89
Dallas, 1992-93
Denver, 1997-98
New England, 2003-04

GAMES, VICTORIES, DEFEATS
Most Seasons Participating in Postseason Games
29 Dallas, 1966-1973, 1975-1983, 1985, 1991-96, 1998-99, 2003, 2006-07
N.Y. Giants, 1933-35, 1938-39, 1941, 1943-44, 1946, 1950, 1956, 1958-59, 1961, 1981, 1984-86, 1989-1990, 1993, 1997, 2000, 2002, 2005-07
27 Cleveland/L.A./St. Louis Rams, 1945, 1949-1952, 1955, 1967, 1969, 1973-1980, 1983-86, 1988-89, 1999-2001, 2003-04
24 Cleveland, 1950-55, 1957-58, 1964-65, 1967-69, 1971-72, 1980, 1982, 1985-89, 1994, 2002
Minnesota, 1968-1971, 1973-78, 1980, 1982, 1987-89, 1992-94, 1996-2000, 2004

Chi. Bears, 1933-34, 1937, 1940-43, 1946, 1950, 1956, 1963, 1977, 1979, 1984-88, 1990-91, 1994, 2001, 2005-06

Green Bay, 1936, 1938-39, 1941, 1944, 1960-62, 1965-67, 1972, 1982, 1993-98, 2001-04, 2007

Pittsburgh, 1947, 1972-79, 1982-84, 1989, 1992-97, 2001-02, 2004-05, 2007

Most Consecutive Seasons Participating in Postseason Games
- 9 Dallas, 1975-1983
- 8 Dallas, 1966-1973
  Pittsburgh, 1972-79
  Los Angeles, 1973-1980
  San Francisco, 1983-1990
- 7 Houston, 1987-1993
  San Francisco, 1992-98

Most Games
- 56 Dallas, 1966-1973, 1975-1983, 1985, 1991-96, 1998-99, 2003, 2006-07
- 47 Pittsburgh, 1947, 1972-79, 1982-84, 1989, 1992-97, 2001-02, 2004-05, 2007
- 43 Oakland/L.A. Raiders, 1967-1970, 1972-77, 1980, 1982-85, 1990-91, 1993, 2000-02
  Cleveland/L.A./St. Louis Rams, 1945, 1949-1952, 1955, 1967, 1969, 1973-1980, 1983-86, 1988-89, 1999-2001, 2003-04
  N.Y. Giants, 1933-35, 1938-39, 1941, 1943-44, 1946, 1950, 1956, 1958-59, 1961-63, 1981, 1984-86, 1989-1990, 1993, 1997, 2000, 2002, 2005-07

Most Games Won
- 32 Dallas, 1967, 1970-73, 1975, 1977-78, 1980-82, 1991-96
- 28 Pittsburgh, 1972, 1974-76, 1978-79, 1984, 1989, 1997, 2001-02, 2004-05
- 25 Oakland/L.A. Raiders, 1967-1970, 1973-77, 1980, 1982-83, 1990, 1993, 2000-02
  San Francisco, 1970-71, 1981, 1983-84, 1988-1990, 1992-94, 1996-98, 2002
  Green Bay, 1936, 1939, 1944, 1961-62, 1965-67, 1982, 1993-97, 2001, 2003, 2007

Most Consecutive Games Won
- 10 New England, 2001, 2003-05
- 9 Green Bay, 1961-62, 1965-67
- 7 Pittsburgh, 1974-76
  San Francisco, 1988-1990
  Dallas, 1992-94
  Denver, 1997-98

Most Games Lost
- 24 Minnesota, 1968-1971, 1973-78, 1980, 1982, 1987-89, 1992-94, 1996-2000, 2004
  L.A./St. Louis Rams, 1949-1950, 1952, 1955, 1967, 1969, 1973-1980, 1983-86, 1988-89, 2000-01, 2003-04
  Dallas, 1966-1970, 1972-73, 1975-76, 1978-1983, 1985, 1991, 1994, 1996, 1998-99, 2003, 2006-07
- 23 N.Y. Giants, 1933, 1935, 1939, 1941, 1943-44, 1946, 1950, 1958-59, 1961-63, 1981, 1984-85, 1989, 1993, 1997, 2000, 2002, 2005-06
- 20 Cleveland, 1951-53, 1957-58, 1965, 1967-69, 1971-72, 1980, 1982, 1985-89, 1994, 2002

Most Consecutive Games Lost
- 6 N.Y. Giants, 1939, 1941, 1943-44, 1946, 1950
  Cleveland, 1969, 1971-72, 1980, 1982, 1985
  Minnesota, 1988-89, 1992-94, 1996
  Detroit, 1991, 1993-95, 1997, 1999 (current)
  Seattle, 1984, 1987-88, 1999, 2003-04
  Kansas City, 1993-95, 1997, 2003, 2006 (current))
  Dallas, 1996, 1998-99, 2003, 2006-07 (current)
- 5 N.Y. Giants, 1958-59, 1961-63
  Los Angeles, 1952, 1955, 1967, 1969, 1973
  Denver, 1977-79, 1983-84
  Baltimore/Indianapolis, 1971, 1975-77, 1987
  Philadelphia, 1980-81, 1988-1990

Indianapolis, 1995-96, 1999-2000, 2002
- 4 Washington, 1972-74, 1976
  Miami, 1974, 1978-79, 1981
  Chi. Cardinals/St. Louis, 1948, 1974-75, 1982
  Boston/New England, 1963, 1976, 1978, 1982
  New Orleans, 1987, 1990-92
  Buffalo, 1995-96, 1998-99 (current)
  N.Y. Giants, 2000, 2002, 2005-06
  San Diego, 1994-95, 2004, 2006

SCORING

Most Points, Game
- 73 NFC: Chi. Bears vs. Washington, 1940
- 62 AFC-D: Jacksonville vs. Miami, 1999
- 59 NFC: Detroit vs. Cleveland, 1957

Most Points, Both Teams, Game
- 95 NFC-FR: Philadelphia (58) vs. Detroit (37), 1995
- 86 NFC-D: St. Louis (49) vs. Minnesota (37), 1999
- 79 AFC-D: San Diego (41) vs. Miami (38), 1981 (OT)
  AFC-FR: Buffalo (41) vs. Houston (38), 1992 (OT)

Fewest Points, Both Teams, Game
- 5 NFC: Detroit (0) vs. Dallas (5), 1970
- 7 NFC: Chi. Cardinals (0) vs. Philadelphia (7), 1948
- 9 NFC: Tampa Bay (0) vs. Los Angeles (9), 1979

Largest Margin of Victory, Game
- 73 NFC: Chi. Bears vs. Washington, 1940 (73-0)
- 55 AFC-D: Jacksonville vs. Miami, 1999 (62-7)
- 49 AFC-D: Oakland vs. Houston, 1969 (56-7)

Most Points, Shutout Victory, Game
- 73 NFC: Chi. Bears vs. Washington, 1940
- 41 NFC: N.Y. Giants vs. Minnesota, 2000
  AFC-FR: N.Y. Jets vs. Indianapolis, 2002
- 38 AFC-D: Dallas vs. Tampa Bay, 1981

Most Points Overcome to Win Game
- 32 AFC-FR: Buffalo vs. Houston, 1992 (trailed 3-35, won 41-38) (OT)
- 24 NFC-FR: San Francisco vs. N.Y. Giants, 2002 (trailed 14-38, won 39-38)
- 20 NFC-D: Detroit vs. San Francisco, 1957 (trailed 7-27, won 31-27)

Most Points, Each Half

1st:	41	AFC: Buffalo vs. L.A. Raiders, 1990
		AFC-D: Jacksonville vs. Miami, 1999
	38	NFC-D: Washington vs. L.A. Rams, 1983
		NFC-FR: Philadelphia vs. Detroit, 1995
	35	NFC: Cleveland vs. Detroit, 1954
		AFC-D: Oakland vs. Houston, 1969
		SB: Washington vs. Denver, 1987
		AFC-FR: Indianapolis vs. Denver, 2004
2nd:	45	NFC: Chi. Bears vs. Washington, 1940
	35	AFC-FR: Buffalo vs. Houston, 1992
		NFC-D: St. Louis vs. Minnesota, 1999
	32	AFC: Indianapolis vs. New England, 2006

Most Points, Each Quarter

1st:	28	AFC-D: Oakland vs. Houston, 1969
	24	AFC-D: San Diego vs. Miami, 1981
		AFC-D: Jacksonville vs. Miami, 1999
	21	NFC: Chi. Bears vs. Washington, 1940
		AFC: San Diego vs. Boston, 1963
		AFC-D: Oakland vs. Kansas City, 1968
		AFC: Oakland vs. San Diego, 1980
		AFC: Buffalo vs. L.A. Raiders, 1990
		NFC: San Francisco vs. Dallas, 1994
2nd:	35	SB: Washington vs. Denver, 1987
	31	NFC-FR: Philadelphia vs. Detroit, 1995
	26	AFC-D: Pittsburgh vs. Buffalo, 1974
3rd:	28	AFC-FR: Buffalo vs. Houston, 1992
	26	NFC: Chi. Bears vs. Washington, 1940
	21	NFC-D: Dallas vs. Cleveland, 1967
		NFC-D: Dallas vs. Tampa Bay, 1981
		AFC-D: L.A. Raiders vs. Pittsburgh, 1983
		SB: Chicago vs. New England, 1985

NFC-D: N.Y. Giants vs. San Francisco, 1986
AFC: Cleveland vs. Denver, 1987
AFC: Cleveland vs. Denver, 1989
NFC-D: St. Louis vs. Minnesota, 1999
4th: 27   NFC: N.Y. Giants vs. Chi. Bears, 1934
      26   NFC-FR: Philadelphia vs. New Orleans, 1992
      24   NFC: Baltimore vs. N.Y. Giants, 1959
OT: 6   NFC: Baltimore vs. N.Y. Giants, 1958
         AFC-D: Oakland vs. Baltimore, 1977
         NFC-D: L.A. Rams vs. N.Y. Giants, 1989
         AFC-FR: Miami vs. Indianapolis, 2000
         NFC-FR: Green Bay vs. Seattle, 2003
         NFC-D: Carolina vs. St. Louis, 2003

TOUCHDOWNS
Most Touchdowns, Game
11   NFC: Chi. Bears vs. Washington, 1940
8   NFC: Cleveland vs. Detroit, 1954
   NFC: Detroit vs. Cleveland, 1957
   AFC-D: Oakland vs. Houston, 1969
   SB: San Francisco vs. Denver, 1989
   AFC-D: Jacksonville vs. Miami, 1999
7   AFC: San Diego vs. Boston, 1963
   NFC-D: Dallas vs. Cleveland, 1967
   NFC-D: N.Y. Giants vs. San Francisco, 1986
   AFC: Buffalo vs. L.A. Raiders, 1990
   SB: Dallas vs. Buffalo, 1992
   SB: San Francisco vs. San Diego, 1994
   NFC-FR: Philadelphia vs. Detroit, 1995
   NFC-D: St. Louis vs. Minnesota, 1999
   AFC-FR: Indianapolis vs. Denver, 2004
Most Touchdowns, Both Teams, Game
12   NFC-FR: Philadelphia (7) vs. Detroit (5), 1995
   NFC-D: St. Louis (7) vs. Minnesota (5), 1999
11   NFC: Chi. Bears (11) vs. Washington (0), 1940
10   NFC: Detroit (8) vs. Cleveland (2), 1957
   AFC-D: Miami (5) vs. San Diego (5), 1981 (OT)
   AFC: Miami (6) vs. Pittsburgh (4), 1984
   AFC-FR: Buffalo (5) vs. Houston (5), 1992 (OT)
   SB: San Francisco (7) vs. San Diego (3), 1994
   NFC-FR: San Francisco (5) vs. N.Y. Giants (5), 2002
   AFC-FR: Indianapolis (7) vs. Denver (3), 2004
Fewest Touchdowns, Both Teams, Game
0   NFC-D: N.Y. Giants vs. Cleveland, 1950
  NFC-D: Dallas vs. Detroit, 1970
  NFC: Los Angeles vs. Tampa Bay, 1979
  AFC-D: Baltimore vs. Indianapolis, 2006
1   NFC: Chi. Cardinals (0) vs. Philadelphia (1), 1948
  NFC-D: Cleveland (0) vs. N.Y. Giants (1), 1958
  AFC: San Diego (0) vs. Houston (1), 1961
  AFC-D: N.Y. Jets (0) vs. Kansas City (1), 1969
  NFC-D: Green Bay (0) vs. Washington (1), 1972
  NFC-FR: New Orleans (0) vs. Chicago (1), 1990
  NFC: N.Y. Giants (0) vs. San Francisco (1), 1990
  AFC-FR: L.A. Raiders (0) vs. Kansas City (1), 1991
  AFC-D: New England (0) vs. Pittsburgh (1), 1997
  NFC: Tampa Bay (0) vs. St. Louis (1), 1999
  AFC: Oakland (0) vs. Baltimore (1), 2000
2   In many games

POINTS AFTER TOUCHDOWN
Most (One-Point) Points After Touchdown, Game
8   NFC: Cleveland vs. Detroit, 1954
  NFC: Detroit vs. Cleveland, 1957
  AFC-D: Oakland vs. Houston, 1969
  AFC-D: Jacksonville vs. Miami, 1999
7   NFC: Chi. Bears vs. Washington, 1940
  NFC-D: Dallas vs. Cleveland, 1967
  NFC-D: N.Y. Giants vs. San Francisco, 1986
  SB: San Francisco vs. Denver, 1989
  SB: Dallas vs. Buffalo, 1992
  SB: San Francisco vs. San Diego, 1994

NFC-FR: Philadelphia vs. Detroit, 1995
NFC-D: St. Louis vs. Minnesota, 1999
AFC-FR: Indianapolis vs. Denver, 2004
6   AFC: San Diego vs. Boston, 1963
  NFC-D: Washington vs. L.A. Rams, 1983
  AFC: Miami vs. Pittsburgh, 1984
  SB: Washington vs. Denver, 1987
  AFC: Buffalo vs. L.A. Raiders, 1990
  AFC-FR: L.A. Raiders vs. Denver, 1993
  AFC-FR: Denver vs. Jacksonville, 1997
  NFC-D: St. Louis vs. Green Bay, 2001
  SB: Tampa Bay vs. Oakland, 2002
  NFC-D: Atlanta vs. St. Louis, 2004)
  NFC-FR: Green Bay vs. Seattle, 2007
Most (One-Point) Points After Touchdown, Both Teams, Game
10   NFC: Detroit (8) vs. Cleveland (2), 1957
  AFC-D: Miami (5) vs. San Diego (5), 1981 (OT)
  AFC: Miami (6) vs. Pittsburgh (4), 1984
  AFC-FR: Buffalo (5) vs. Houston (5), 1992 (OT)
  NFC-FR: Philadelphia (7) vs. Detroit (3), 1995
  AFC-FR: Indianapolis (7) vs. Denver (3), 2004
9   In many games
Fewest (One-Point) Points After Touchdown, Both Teams, Game
0   NFC-D: N.Y. Giants vs. Cleveland, 1950
  NFC-D: Dallas vs. Detroit, 1970
  NFC: Los Angeles vs. Tampa Bay, 1979
  NFC: St. Louis vs. Tampa Bay, 1999
  AFC-D: Baltimore vs. Indianapolis, 2006
Most Two-Point Conversions, Game
2   SB: San Diego vs. San Francisco, 1994
  NFC-FR: Detroit vs. Philadelphia, 1995
  NFC-FR: San Francisco vs.. N.Y. Giants, 2002
1   By many teams

FIELD GOALS
Most Field Goals, Game
5   NFC-D: Minnesota vs. San Francisco, 1987
  NFC: N.Y. Giants vs. San Francisco, 1990
  AFC: Buffalo vs. Miami, 1992
  NFC-FR: N.Y. Giants vs. Minnesota, 1997
  NFC-FR: Carolina vs. Dallas, 2003
  NFC-D: St. Louis vs. Carolina, 2003 (2 OT)
  AFC: New England vs. Indianapolis, 2003
  AFC-D: Indianapolis vs. Baltimore, 2006
4   AFC-D: Boston vs. Buffalo, 1963
  AFC: Oakland vs. Houston, 1967
  SB: Green Bay vs. Oakland, 1967
  NFC: Washington vs. Dallas, 1972
  AFC-D: Oakland vs. Pittsburgh, 1973
  SB: San Francisco vs. Cincinnati, 1981
  AFC-FR: New England vs. N.Y. Jets, 1985
  NFC-FR: Washington vs. L.A. Rams, 1986
  NFC-D: Philadelphia vs. Chicago, 1988
  AFC-FR: Pittsburgh vs. Houston, 1989 (OT)
  AFC-D: Pittsburgh vs. Buffalo, 1995
  NFC-FR: Dallas vs. Minnesota, 1996
  NFC-D: Carolina vs. Dallas, 1996
  AFC-FR: Jacksonville vs. New England, 1998
  AFC-D: Tennessee vs. Indianapolis, 1999
  NFC-D: Philadelphia vs. Chicago, 2001)
  AFC: San Diego vs. New England, 2007
3   By many teams
Most Field Goals, Both Teams, Game
8   NFC-FR: N.Y. Giants (5) vs. Minnesota (3), 1997
  NFC-D: St. Louis (5) vs. Carolina (3), 2003 (2 OT)
7   AFC-FR: Pittsburgh (4) vs. Houston (3), 1989 (OT)
  NFC: N.Y. Giants (5) vs. San Francisco (2), 1990
  NFC-D: Carolina (4) vs. Dallas (3), 1996
  AFC-D: Tennessee (4) vs. Indianapolis (3), 1999
  AFC-D: Indianapolis (5) vs. Baltimore (2), 2006
6   NFC-D: Minnesota (5) vs. San Francisco (1), 1987
  NFC-D: Philadelphia (4) vs. Chicago (2), 1988

AFC: Buffalo (5) vs. Miami (1), 1992
NFC-FR: Carolina (5) vs. Dallas (1), 2003
AFC-FR: New England (3) vs. N.Y. Jets (3), 2006
Most Field Goals Attempted, Game
6   AFC: Oakland vs. Houston, 1967
    NFC-D: Los Angeles vs. Dallas, 1973
    AFC-D: Cleveland vs. N.Y. Jets, 1986 (OT)
    NFC: N.Y. Giants vs. San Francisco, 1990
    AFC: Buffalo vs. Miami, 1992
    NFC-D: St. Louis vs. Carolina, 2003 (2 OT)
5   By many teams
Most Field Goals Attempted, Both Teams, Game
11 NFC-D: St. Louis (6) vs. Carolina (5), 2003 (2 OT)
9   NFC-D: Philadelphia (5) vs. Chicago (4), 1988
    NFC-FR: N.Y. Giants (5) vs. Minnesota (4), 1997
8   NFC-D: Los Angeles (6) vs. Dallas (2), 1973
    NFC-D: Detroit (5) vs. San Francisco (3), 1983
    AFC-D: Cleveland (6) vs. N.Y. Jets (2), 1986 (OT)
    NFC-D: Minnesota (5) vs. San Francisco (3), 1987
    AFC-FR: Houston (4) vs. Pittsburgh (4), 1989 (OT)
    NFC-FR: Chicago (4) vs. New Orleans (4), 1990
    NFC: N.Y. Giants (6) vs. San Francisco (2), 1990

SAFETIES
Most Safeties, Game
1   By many teams
Most Safeties, Both Teams, Game
1   In many games

FIRST DOWNS
Most First Downs, Game
34 AFC-D: San Diego vs. Miami, 1981 (OT)
33 AFC-D: Cleveland vs. N.Y. Jets, 1986 (OT)
32 AFC: Indianapolis vs. New England, 2006
Fewest First Downs, Game
6   NFC: N.Y. Giants vs. Green Bay, 1961
    AFC-D: Baltimore vs. Tennessee, 2000
7   NFC: Green Bay vs. Boston, 1936
    NFC-D: Pittsburgh vs. Philadelphia, 1947
    NFC: Chi. Cardinals vs. Philadelphia, 1948
    NFC: Los Angeles vs. Philadelphia, 1949
    NFC-D: Cleveland vs. N.Y. Giants, 1958
    AFC-D: Cincinnati vs. Baltimore, 1970
    NFC-D: Detroit vs. Dallas, 1970
    NFC: Tampa Bay vs. Los Angeles, 1979
    AFC-D: Baltimore vs. Pittsburgh, 2001
    AFC-FR: Kansas City vs. Indianapolis, 2006
8   By many teams
Most First Downs, Both Teams, Game
59 AFC-D: San Diego (34) vs. Miami (25), 1981 (OT)
55 AFC-FR: San Diego (29) vs. Pittsburgh (26), 1982
54 AFC-FR: Buffalo (28) vs. Miami (26), 1995
Fewest First Downs, Both Teams, Game
15 NFC: Green Bay (7) vs. Boston (8), 1936
19 NFC: N.Y. Giants (9) vs. Green Bay (10), 1939
    NFC: Washington (9) vs. Chi. Bears (10), 1942
20 NFC-D: Cleveland (9) vs. N.Y. Giants (11), 1950

RUSHING
Most First Downs, Rushing, Game
19 NFC-FR: Dallas vs. Los Angeles, 1980
18 AFC-D: Miami vs. Cincinnati, 1973
    AFC: Miami vs. Oakland, 1973
    AFC-D: Pittsburgh vs. Buffalo, 1974
    AFC-FR: Buffalo vs. Miami, 1995
    AFC-FR: Denver vs. Jacksonville, 1997
17 AFC-D: Cincinnati vs. Seattle, 1988
    AFC: Buffalo vs. Kansas City, 1993
Fewest First Downs, Rushing, Game
0   NFC: Los Angeles vs. Philadelphia, 1949
    AFC-D: Buffalo vs. Boston, 1963
    AFC: Oakland vs. Pittsburgh, 1974

NFC-FR: New Orleans vs. Minnesota, 1987
NFC: L.A. Rams vs. San Francisco, 1989
NFC-D: Chicago vs. N.Y. Giants, 1990
AFC-FR: Indianapolis vs. Pittsburgh, 1996
AFC-FR: Seattle vs. Miami, 1999
AFC-D: Miami vs. Jacksonville, 1999
AFC-D: Miami vs. Oakland, 2000
AFC-D: Baltimore vs. Pittsburgh, 2001
AFC-D: Indianapolis vs. New England, 2004
1   By many teams
Most First Downs, Rushing, Both Teams, Game
26 AFC: Buffalo (14) vs. L.A. Raiders (12), 1990
25 NFC-FR: Dallas (19) vs. Los Angeles (6), 1980
23 NFC: Cleveland (15) vs. Detroit (8), 1952
    AFC-D: Miami (18) vs. Cincinnati (5), 1973
    AFC-D: Pittsburgh (18) vs. Buffalo (5), 1974
    AFC-FR: Buffalo (18) vs. Miami (5), 1995
Fewest First Downs, Rushing, Both Teams, Game
2   NFC-FR: New Orleans (1) vs. St. Louis (1), 2000
5   AFC-D: Buffalo (0) vs. Boston (5), 1963
    NFC-D: Washington (1) vs. Tampa Bay (4), 1999
    AFC-FR: Cleveland (2) vs. Pittsburgh (3), 2002
6   NFC: Green Bay (2) vs. Boston (4), 1936
    NFC-D: Baltimore (2) vs. Minnesota (4), 1968
    AFC-D: Houston (1) vs. Oakland (5), 1969
    AFC-FR: N.Y. Jets (1) vs. Houston (5), 1991
    AFC-FR: Denver (1) vs. Baltimore (5), 2000

PASSING
Most First Downs, Passing, Game
24 AFC-FR: Pittsburgh vs. Cleveland, 2002
21 AFC-D: Miami vs. San Diego, 1981 (OT)
    AFC-D: San Diego vs. Miami, 1981 (OT)
    AFC-D: Cleveland vs. N.Y. Jets, 1986 (OT)
    NFC-D: Philadelphia vs. Chicago, (1988)
    AFC-D; Indianapolis vs. San Diego, 2007
20 NFC-FR: Dallas vs. L.A. Rams, 1983
    AFC-D: Buffalo vs. Cleveland, 1989
    AFC-FR: Miami vs. Buffalo, 1995
    NFC-FR: Detroit vs. Philadelphia, 1995
    AFC-FR: San Diego vs. Indianapolis, 1995
    NFC-D: Minnesota vs. St. Louis, 1999
    AFC: Indianapolis vs. New England, 2006
Fewest First Downs, Passing, Game
0   NFC: Philadelphia vs. Chi. Cardinals, 1948
1   NFC-D: N.Y. Giants vs. Washington, 1943
    NFC: Cleveland vs. Detroit, 1953
    SB: Denver vs. Dallas, 1977
2   By many teams
Most First Downs, Passing, Both Teams, Game
42 AFC-D: Miami (21) vs. San Diego (21), 1981 (OT)
    AFC-FR: Pittsburgh (24) vs. Cleveland (18), 2002
38 AFC-FR: Pittsburgh (19) vs. San Diego (19), 1982
    NFC-D: Minnesota (20) vs. St. Louis (18), 1999
36 NFC: Minnesota (19) vs. Atlanta (17), 1998 (OT)
Fewest First Downs, Passing, Both Teams, Game
2   NFC: Philadelphia (0) vs. Chi. Cardinals (2), 1948
4   NFC-D: Cleveland (2) vs. N.Y. Giants (2), 1950
5   NFC: Detroit (2) vs. N.Y. Giants (3), 1935
    NFC: Green Bay (2) vs. N.Y. Giants (3), 1939

PENALTY
Most First Downs, Penalty, Game
7   AFC-D: New England vs. Oakland, 1976
    AFC: Tennessee vs. Oakland, 2002
6   AFC-D: Cleveland vs. N.Y. Jets, 1986 (OT)
    NFC-D: Chicago vs. Carolina, 2005
5   AFC-FR: Cleveland vs. L. A. Raiders, 1982
    NFC-D: San Francisco vs. Minnesota, 1997
    AFC-FR: Miami vs. Buffalo, 1998
    NFC-D: Arizona vs. Minnesota, 1998
    AFC: Pittsburgh vs. New England, 2001

AFC-D: Pittsburgh vs. Tennessee, 2002 (OT)

Most First Downs, Penalty, Both Teams, Game
- 10 AFC: Tennessee (7) vs. Oakland (3), 2002
- 9 AFC-D: New England (7) vs. Oakland (2), 1976
- 8 NFC-FR: Atlanta (4) vs. Minnesota (4), 1982
  - AFC-FR: Miami (5) vs. Buffalo (3), 1998

NET YARDS GAINED RUSHING AND PASSING
Most Yards Gained, Game
- 610 AFC: San Diego vs. Boston, 1963
- 602 SB: Washington vs. Denver, 1987
- 569 AFC: Miami vs. Pittsburgh, 1984

Fewest Yards Gained, Game
- 86 NFC-D: Cleveland vs. N.Y. Giants, 1958
- 99 NFC: Chi. Cardinals vs. Philadelphia, 1948
- 114 NFC-D: N.Y. Giants vs. Washington, 1943
  - NFC: Minnesota vs. N.Y. Giants, 2000

Most Yards Gained, Both Teams, Game
- 1,038 AFC-FR: Buffalo (536) vs. Miami (502), 1995
- 1,036 AFC-D: San Diego (564) vs. Miami (472), 1981 (OT)
- 1,024 AFC: Miami (569) vs. Pittsburgh (455), 1984

Fewest Yards Gained, Both Teams, Game
- 331 NFC: Chi. Cardinals (99) vs. Philadelphia (232), 1948
- 332 NFC-D: N.Y. Giants (150) vs. Cleveland (182), 1950
- 336 NFC: Boston (116) vs. Green Bay (220), 1936

RUSHING
ATTEMPTS
Most Attempts, Game
- 65 NFC: Detroit vs. N.Y. Giants, 1935
- 61 NFC: Philadelphia vs. Los Angeles, 1949
- 59 AFC: New England vs. Miami, 1985

Fewest Attempts, Game
- 8 AFC-D: Miami vs. San Diego, 1994
- 9 SB: Miami vs. San Francisco, 1984
  - NFC: Minnesota vs. N.Y. Giants, 2000
- 10 NFC: L.A. Rams vs. San Francisco, 1989
  - NFC-FR: Atlanta vs. Green Bay, 1995
  - NFC-FR: Detroit vs. Washington, 1999

Most Attempts, Both Teams, Game
- 109 NFC: Detroit (65) vs. N.Y. Giants (44), 1935
- 97 AFC-D: Baltimore (50) vs. Oakland (47), 1977 (OT)
- 91 NFC: Philadelphia (57) vs. Chi. Cardinals (34), 1948

Fewest Attempts, Both Teams, Game
- 32 AFC-D: Houston (14) vs. Kansas City (18), 1993
- 38 NFC-D: Detroit (16) vs. Dallas (22), 1991
- 39 NFC-FR: Atlanta (10) vs. Green Bay (29), 1995

YARDS GAINED
Most Yards Gained, Game
- 382 NFC: Chi. Bears vs. Washington, 1940
- 341 AFC-FR: Buffalo vs. Miami, 1995
- 338 NFC-FR: Dallas vs. Los Angeles, 1980

Fewest Yards Gained, Game
- – 4 NFC-FR: Detroit vs. Green Bay, 1994
- 7 AFC-D: Buffalo vs. Boston, 1963
  - SB: New England vs. Chicago, 1985
- 14 NFC: Miami vs. Denver, 1998
  - AFC: N.Y. Jets vs. Denver, 1998

Most Yards Gained, Both Teams, Game
- 430 NFC: Dallas (338) vs. Los Angeles (92), 1980
- 426 NFC: Cleveland (227) vs. Detroit (199), 1952
- 411 AFC-FR: Buffalo (341) vs. Miami (70), 1995

Fewest Yards Gained, Both Teams, Game
- 77 NFC-FR: Detroit (–4) vs. Green Bay (81), 1994
- 84 NFC-FR: St. Louis (34) vs. New Orleans (50), 2000
- 90 AFC-D: Buffalo (7) vs. Boston (83), 1963
  - NFC-D: Tampa Bay (44) vs. Washington (46), 1999

AVERAGE GAIN
Highest Average Gain, Game
- 9.94 AFC: San Diego vs. Boston, 1963 (32-318)

- 9.29 NFC-D: Green Bay vs. Dallas, 1982 (17-158)
- 8.18 NFC-D: Atlanta vs. St. Louis, 2004 (40-327)

Lowest Average Gain, Game
- – 0.27 NFC-FR: Detroit vs. Green Bay, 1994 (15-(– 4))
- 0.58 AFC-D: Buffalo vs. Boston, 1963 (12-7)
- 0.64 SB: New England vs. Chicago, 1985 (11-7)

TOUCHDOWNS
Most Touchdowns, Game
- 7 NFC: Chi. Bears vs. Washington, 1940
- 6 NFC-D: San Francisco vs. N.Y. Giants, 1993
- 5 NFC: Cleveland vs. Detroit, 1954
  - NFC-D: San Francisco vs. Chicago, 1994
  - AFC-FR: Pittsburgh vs. Indianapolis, 1996
  - AFC-FR: Denver vs. Jacksonville, 1997

Most Touchdowns, Both Teams, Game
- 7 NFC: Chi. Bears (7) vs. Washington (0), 1940
- 6 NFC: Cleveland (5) vs. Detroit (1), 1954
  - NFC-D: San Francisco (6) vs. N.Y. Giants (0), 1993
  - NFC-D: San Francisco (5) vs. Chicago (1), 1994
  - AFC-FR: Denver (5) vs. Jacksonville (1), 1997
- 5 NFC: Chi. Cardinals (3) vs. Philadelphia (2), 1947
  - AFC: San Diego (4) vs. Boston (1), 1963
  - AFC-FR: Cincinnati (3) vs. Buffalo (2), 1981
  - AFC-FR: Pittsburgh (5) vs. Indianapolis (0), 1996
  - NFC-D: Arizona (3) vs. Minnesota (2), 1998
  - NFC-FR: Seattle (3) vs. Green Bay (2), 2003 (OT)

PASSING
ATTEMPTS
Most Attempts, Game
- 66 AFC-FR: Miami vs. Buffalo, 1995
- 65 AFC-D: Cleveland vs. N.Y. Jets, 1986 (OT)
  - NFC-D: San Francisco vs. Green Bay, 1995
- 61 NFC-FR: Minnesota vs. Chicago, 1994

Fewest Attempts, Game
- 5 NFC: Detroit vs. N.Y. Giants, 1935
- 6 AFC: Miami vs. Oakland, 1973
- 7 SB: Miami vs. Minnesota, 1973

Most Attempts, Both Teams, Game
- 102 AFC-D: San Diego (54) vs. Miami (48), 1981 (OT)
- 96 AFC: N.Y. Jets (49) vs. Oakland (47), 1968
- 95 AFC-D: Cleveland (65) vs. N.Y. Jets (30), 1986 (OT)

Fewest Attempts, Both Teams, Game
- 18 NFC: Detroit (5) vs. N.Y. Giants (13), 1935
- 23 NFC: Chi. Cardinals (11) vs. Philadelphia (12), 1948
- 24 NFC-D: Cleveland (9) vs. N.Y. Giants (15), 1950

COMPLETIONS
Most Completions, Game
- 36 AFC-FR: Houston vs. Buffalo, 1992 (OT)
- 34 AFC-D: Cleveland vs. N.Y. Jets, 1986 (OT)
  - AFC-FR: Miami vs. Buffalo, 1995
- 33 AFC-D: San Diego vs. Miami, 1981 (OT)
  - NFC-FR: Minnesota vs. Chicago, 1994)
  - AFC-D: Indianapolis vs. San Diego, 2007

Fewest Completions, Game
- 2 NFC: Detroit vs. N.Y. Giants, 1935
  - NFC: Philadelphia vs. Chi. Cardinals, 1948
- 3 NFC: N.Y. Giants vs. Chi. Bears, 1941
  - NFC: Green Bay vs. N.Y. Giants, 1944
  - NFC: Chi. Cardinals vs. Philadelphia, 1947
  - NFC: Chi. Cardinals vs. Philadelphia, 1948
  - NFC-D: Cleveland vs. N.Y. Giants, 1950
  - NFC-D: N.Y. Giants vs. Cleveland, 1950
  - NFC: Cleveland vs. Detroit, 1953
  - AFC: Miami vs. Oakland, 1973
- 4 NFC: N.Y. Giants vs. Detroit, 1935
  - NFC-D: N.Y. Giants vs. Washington, 1943
  - NFC-FR: Pittsburgh vs. Philadelphia, 1947
  - NFC-D: Dallas vs. Detroit, 1970
  - AFC: Miami vs. Baltimore, 1971

SB: Miami vs. Washington, 1982
AFC-FR: Seattle vs. L.A. Raiders, 1984

Most Completions, Both Teams, Game
64 AFC-D: San Diego (33) vs. Miami (31), 1981 (OT)
57 AFC-FR: Houston (36) vs. Buffalo (21), 1992 (OT)
   NFC-FR: N.Y. Giants (29) vs. San Francisco (28), 2002
56 NFC-D: Dallas (28) vs. Green Bay (28), 1993
   NFC: Minnesota (29) vs. Atlanta (27), 1998 (OT)
   NFC-D: Minnesota (29) vs. St. Louis (27), 1999
   AFC-FR: Pittsburgh (30) vs. Cleveland (26), 2002

Fewest Completions, Both Teams, Game
5 NFC: Philadelphia (2) vs. Chi. Cardinals (3), 1948
6 NFC: Detroit (2) vs. N.Y. Giants (4), 1935
   NFC-D: Cleveland (3) vs. N.Y. Giants (3), 1950
11 NFC: Green Bay (3) vs. N.Y. Giants (8), 1944
   NFC-D: Dallas (4) vs. Detroit (7), 1970

COMPLETION PERCENTAGE
Highest Completion Percentage, Game (20 attempts)
92.9 AFC-D: New England vs. Jacksonville, 2007 (28-26)
88.0 SB: N.Y. Giants vs. Denver, 1986 (25-22)
87.1 NFC: San Francisco vs. L.A. Rams, 1989 (31-27)

Lowest Completion Percentage, Game (20 attempts)
18.5 NFC: Tampa Bay vs. Los Angeles, 1979 (27-5)
20.0 NFC-D: N.Y. Giants vs. Washington, 1943 (20-4)
25.8 NFC: Chi. Bears vs. Washington, 1937 (31-8)

YARDS GAINED
Most Yards Gained, Game
483 AFC-D: Cleveland vs. N.Y. Jets, 1986 (OT)
454 AFC-FR: Indianapolis vs. Denver, 2004
435 AFC: Miami vs. Pittsburgh, 1984

Fewest Yards Gained, Game
3 NFC: Chi. Cardinals vs. Philadelphia, 1948
7 NFC: Philadelphia vs. Chi. Cardinals, 1948
9 NFC-D: N.Y. Giants vs. Cleveland, 1950
   NFC: Cleveland vs. Detroit, 1953

Most Yards Gained, Both Teams, Game
809 AFC-D: San Diego (415) vs. Miami (394), 1981 (OT)
762 NFC-D: Minnesota (388) vs. St. Louis (374), 1999
752 AFC-FR: Cleveland (409) vs. Pittsburgh (343), 2002

Fewest Yards Gained, Both Teams, Game
10 NFC: Chi. Cardinals (3) vs. Philadelphia (7), 1948
38 NFC-D: N.Y. Giants (9) vs. Cleveland (29), 1950
102 NFC-D: Dallas (22) vs. Detroit (80), 1970

TIMES SACKED
Most Times Sacked, Game
9 AFC: Kansas City vs. Buffalo, 1966
   NFC: Chicago vs. San Francisco, 1984
   AFC-D: N.Y. Jets vs. Cleveland, 1986 (OT)
   AFC-D: Houston vs. Kansas City, 1993
8 NFC: Green Bay vs. Dallas, 1967
   NFC: Minnesota vs. Washington, 1987
   NFC-D: Philadelphia vs. Green Bay, 2003 (OT)
7 NFC-D: Dallas vs. Los Angeles, 1973
   SB: Dallas vs. Pittsburgh, 1975
   AFC-FR: Houston vs. Oakland, 1980
   NFC-D: Washington vs. Chicago, 1984
   SB: New England vs. Chicago, 1985
   AFC-FR: Kansas City vs. San Diego, 1992
   AFC-D: Pittsburgh vs. Buffalo, 1992

Most Times Sacked, Both Teams, Game
13 AFC: Kansas City (9) vs. Buffalo (4), 1966
   AFC-D: N.Y. Jets (9) vs. Cleveland (4), 1986 (OT)
12 NFC-D: Dallas (7) vs. Los Angeles (5), 1973
   NFC: Washington (7) vs. Chicago (5), 1984
   NFC: Chicago (9) vs. San Francisco (3), 1984
   AFC-FR: Kansas City (7) vs. San Diego (5), 1992
11 AFC-D: Houston (9) vs. Kansas City (2), 1993

Fewest Times Sacked, Both Teams, Game
0 AFC-D: Buffalo vs. Pittsburgh, 1974

AFC-FR: Pittsburgh vs. San Diego, 1982
AFC: Miami vs. Pittsburgh, 1984
AFC-D: Buffalo vs. Miami, 1990
AFC-D: Denver vs. Houston, 1991
AFC-FR: Buffalo vs. Miami, 1995
AFC-D: Indianapolis vs. Tennessee, 1999)
AFC-D: Indianapolis vs. San Diego, 2007
1 In many games

TOUCHDOWNS
Most Touchdowns, Game
6 AFC-D: Oakland vs. Houston, 1969
   SB: San Francisco vs. San Diego, 1994
5 NFC: Chi. Bears vs. Washington, 1943
   NFC: Detroit vs. Cleveland, 1957
   AFC-D: Oakland vs. Kansas City, 1968
   SB: San Francisco vs. Denver, 1989
   NFC-D: St. Louis vs. Minnesota, 1999
   NFC: N.Y. Giants vs. Minnesota, 2000
   AFC-FR: Indianapolis vs. Denver, 2003
4 By many teams

Most Touchdowns, Both Teams, Game
9 NFC-D: St. Louis (5) vs. Minnesota (4), 1999
8 AFC-FR: Buffalo (4) vs. Houston (4), 1992 (OT)
7 NFC: Chi. Bears (5) vs. Washington (2), 1943
   AFC-D: Oakland (6) vs. Houston (1), 1969
   SB: Pittsburgh (4) vs. Dallas (3), 1978
   AFC-D: Miami (4) vs. San Diego (3), 1981 (OT)
   AFC: Miami (4) vs. Pittsburgh (3), 1984
   AFC-D: Buffalo (4) vs. Cleveland (3), 1989
   SB: San Francisco (6) vs. San Diego (1), 1994
   NFC-FR: Detroit (4) vs. Philadelphia (3), 1995
   NFC-FR: New Orleans (4) vs. St. Louis (3), 2000
   NFC-FR: N.Y. Giants (4) vs. San Francisco (3), 2002

INTERCEPTIONS BY
Most Interceptions By, Game
8 NFC: Chi. Bears vs. Washington, 1940
7 NFC: Cleveland vs. Los Angeles, 1955
6 NFC: Green Bay vs. N.Y. Giants, 1939
   NFC: Chi. Bears vs. N.Y. Giants, 1946
   NFC: Cleveland vs. Detroit, 1954
   AFC: San Diego vs. Houston, 1961
   AFC: Buffalo vs. L.A. Raiders, 1990
   NFC-FR: Philadelphia vs. Detroit, 1995
   NFC-D: St. Louis vs. Green Bay, 2001

Most Interceptions By, Both Teams, Game
10 NFC: Cleveland (7) vs. Los Angeles (3), 1955
   AFC: San Diego (6) vs. Houston (4), 1961
9 NFC: Green Bay (6) vs. N.Y. Giants (3), 1939
8 NFC: Chi. Bears (8) vs. Washington (0), 1940
   NFC: Chi. Bears (6) vs. N.Y. Giants (2), 1946
   NFC: Cleveland (6) vs. Detroit (2), 1954
   AFC-FR: Buffalo (4) vs. N.Y. Jets (4), 1981
   AFC: Miami (5) vs. N.Y. Jets (3), 1982

YARDS GAINED
Most Yards Gained, Game
172 SB: Tampa Bay vs. Oakland, 2002
161 NFC-D: St. Louis vs. Green Bay, 2001
138 AFC-FR: N.Y. Jets vs. Cincinnati, 1982

Most Yards Gained, Both Teams, Game
184 SB: Tampa Bay (172) vs. Oakland (12), 2002
161 NFC-D: St. Louis (161) vs. Green Bay (0), 2001
156 NFC: Green Bay (123) vs. N.Y. Giants (33), 1939

TOUCHDOWNS
Most Touchdowns, Game
3 NFC: Chi. Bears vs. Washington, 1940
   NFC-D: St. Louis vs. Green Bay, 2001
   SB: Tampa Bay vs. Oakland, 2002
2 NFC-D: Los Angeles vs. St. Louis, 1975

NFC-FR: Philadelphia vs. Detroit, 1995)
NFC-FR: Seattle vs. Washington, 2007
1 In many games

Most Touchdowns, Both Teams, Game
3 NFC: Chi. Bears (3) vs. Washington (0), 1940
NFC-D: St. Louis (3) vs. Green Bay (0), 2001
SB: Tampa Bay (3) vs. Oakland (0), 2002
2 NFC-D: Los Angeles (2) vs. St. Louis (0), 1975
NFC-D: Dallas (1) vs. Green Bay (1), 1982
NFC-D: Minnesota (1) vs. San Francisco (1), 1987
NFC-FR: Detroit (1) vs. Green Bay (1), 1993
NFC-FR: Philadelphia (2) vs. Detroit (0), 1995
AFC-FR: Buffalo (1) vs. Jacksonville (1), 1996)
NFC-FR: Seattle (2) vs. Washington (0), 2007
1 In many games

PUNTING
Most Punts, Game
14 AFC-D: N.Y. Jets vs. Cleveland, 1986 (OT)
13 NFC: N.Y. Giants vs. Chi. Bears, 1933
AFC-D: Baltimore vs. Oakland, 1977 (OT)
11 AFC: Houston vs. Oakland, 1967
AFC-D: Houston vs. Oakland, 1969
NFC: L.A. Rams vs. Chicago, 1985
SB: N.Y. Giants vs. Baltimore, 2000
Fewest Punts, Game
0 NFC-FR: St. Louis vs. Green Bay, 1982
AFC-FR: N.Y. Jets vs. Cincinnati, 1982
AFC-FR: Indianapolis vs. Denver, 2003
AFC-D: Kansas City vs. Indianapolis, 2003
AFC-D: Indianapolis vs. Kansas City, 2003
1 By many teams
Most Punts, Both Teams, Game
23 NFC: N.Y. Giants (13) vs. Chi. Bears (10), 1933
22 AFC-D: N.Y. Jets (14) vs. Cleveland (8), 1986 (OT)
21 AFC-D: Baltimore (13) vs. Oakland (8), 1977 (OT)
NFC: L.A. Rams (11) vs. Chicago (10), 1985
SB: N.Y. Giants (11) vs. Baltimore (10), 2000
Fewest Punts, Both Teams, Game
0 AFC-D: Kansas City vs. Indianapolis, 2003
1 NFC-FR: St. Louis (0) vs. Green Bay (1), 1982
2 AFC-FR: N.Y. Jets (0) vs. Cincinnati (2), 1982
SB: Atlanta (1) vs. Denver (1), 1998
AFC-FR: Indianapolis (0) vs. Denver (2), 2003)
AFC-D: New England (1) vs. Jacksonville (1), 2007

AVERAGE YARDAGE
Highest Average, Punting, Game (4 punts)
56.0 AFC: Oakland vs. San Diego, 1980
52.8 AFC: Indianapolis vs. New England, 2006
52.5 NFC: Washington vs. Chi. Bears, 1942
Lowest Average, Punting, Game (4 punts)
24.9 NFC: Washington vs. Chi. Bears, 1937
25.3 AFC-FR: Pittsburgh vs. Houston, 1989
25.5 NFC: Green Bay vs. N.Y. Giants, 1962

PUNT RETURNS
Most Punt Returns, Game
8 NFC: Green Bay vs. N.Y. Giants, 1944
7 By many teams
Most Punt Returns, Both Teams, Game
13 AFC-FR: Houston (7) vs. Oakland (6), 1980
12 AFC-D: New England (7) vs. Pittsburgh (5), 1996
11 NFC: Green Bay (8) vs. N.Y. Giants (3), 1944
NFC-D: Green Bay (6) vs. Baltimore (5), 1965
AFC-FR: Jacksonville (7) vs. New England (4), 1998
Fewest Punt Returns, Both Teams, Game
0 NFC: Chi. Bears vs. N.Y. Giants, 1941
AFC: Boston vs. San Diego, 1963
NFC-FR: Green Bay vs. St. Louis, 1982

AFC-FR: Houston vs. N.Y. Jets, 1991
AFC-D: Denver vs. Houston, 1991
NFC-D: San Francisco vs. Washington, 1992
SB: Denver vs. Green Bay, 1997
SB: Atlanta vs. Denver, 1998
AFC-FR: Oakland vs. N.Y. Jets, 2001
SB: N.Y. Jets vs. Oakland, 2002
AFC-FR: Denver vs. Indianapolis, 2003
NFC-D: Carolina vs. St. Louis, 2003
AFC-D: Indianapolis vs. Kansas City, 2003
1 In many games

YARDS GAINED
Most Yards Gained, Game
155 NFC-D: Dallas vs. Cleveland, 1967
152 NFC-D: Atlanta vs. St. Louis, 2004
150 NFC: Chi. Cardinals vs. Philadelphia, 1947
Fewest Yards Gained, Game
−10 NFC: Green Bay vs. Cleveland, 1965
−9 NFC: Dallas vs. Green Bay, 1966
AFC-D: Kansas City vs. Oakland, 1968
−7 NFC: San Francisco vs. Atlanta, 1998
Most Yards Gained, Both Teams, Game
166 NFC-D: Dallas (155) vs. Cleveland (11), 1967
AFC-D: Baltimore (99) vs. Pittsburgh (67), 2001
160 NFC: Chi. Cardinals (150) vs. Philadelphia (10), 1947
152 NFC-D: Atlanta (152) vs. St. Louis (0), 2004
Fewest Yards Gained, Both Teams, Game
−9 NFC: Dallas (−9) vs. Green Bay (0), 1966
−6 AFC-D: Miami (−5) vs. Oakland (−1), 1970
−3 NFC-D: San Francisco (−5) vs. Dallas (2), 1972

TOUCHDOWNS
Most Touchdowns, Game
1 By 18 teams

KICKOFF RETURNS
Most Kickoff Returns, Game
10 NFC-D: L.A. Rams vs. Washington, 1983
NFC-FR: Detroit vs. Philadelphia, 1995
9 NFC: Chi. Bears vs. N.Y. Giants, 1956
AFC: Boston vs. San Diego, 1963
AFC: Houston vs. Oakland, 1967
SB: Denver vs. San Francisco, 1989
AFC-D: Miami vs. Buffalo, 1990
AFC: L.A. Raiders vs. Buffalo, 1990
AFC: Miami vs. Jacksonville, 1999
SB: Oakland vs. Tampa Bay, 2002
8 By many teams
Most Kickoff Returns, Both Teams, Game
15 AFC-D: Miami (9) vs. Buffalo (6), 1990
14 NFC-FR: Detroit (10) vs. Philadelphia (4), 1995
13 NFC-D: Green Bay (7) vs. Dallas (6), 1982
NFC-FR: Green Bay (7) vs. San Francisco (6), 1998
AFC-FR: N.Y. Jets (8) vs. Oakland (5), 2001
NFC-FR: San Francisco (7) vs. N.Y. Giants (6), 2002
AFC-D: Tennessee (7) vs. Pittsburgh (6), 2002
SB: Oakland (9) vs. Tampa Bay (4), 2002
NFC-FR: Seattle (7) vs. Green Bay (6), 2003 (OT)
AFC-D: Kansas City (7) vs. Indianapolis (6), 2003
AFC: Pittsburgh (8) vs. New England (5), 2004
AFC: New England (8) vs. Indianapolis (5), 2006
Fewest Kickoff Returns, Both Teams, Game
1 NFC: Green Bay (0) vs. Boston (1), 1936
AFC-FR: San Diego (0) vs. Kansas City (1), 1992
2 NFC: Los Angeles (0) vs. Chi. Bears (2), 1950
AFC: Houston (0) vs. San Diego (2), 1961
AFC-D: Oakland (1) vs. Pittsburgh (1), 1972
AFC-D: N.Y. Jets (0) vs. L.A. Raiders (2), 1982
AFC: Miami (1) vs. N.Y. Jets (1), 1982
NFC: N.Y. Giants (0) vs. Washington (2), 1986
3 In many games

YARDS GAINED

Most Yards Gained, Game
- 244 SB: San Diego vs. San Francisco, 1994
- 231 AFC: New England vs. Indianapolis, 2006
- 227 SB: Atlanta vs. Denver, 1998

Most Yards Gained, Both Teams, Game
- 379 AFC-D: Baltimore (193) vs. Oakland (186), 1977 (OT)
- 348 NFC-D: Minnesota (174) vs. St. Louis (174), 1999
- 323 AFC-D: New England (231) vs. Indianapolis (92), 2006

Fewest Yards Gained, Both Teams, Game
- 5 AFC-FR: San Diego (0) vs. Kansas City (5), 1992
- 15 NFC: N.Y. Giants (0) vs. Washington (15), 1986
- 31 NFC-D: Los Angeles (0) vs. Chi. Bears (31), 1950

TOUCHDOWNS

Most Touchdowns, Game
- 1 NFC-D: San Francisco vs. Dallas, 1972
-    AFC-D: Miami vs. Oakland, 1974
-    AFC-D: Baltimore vs. Oakland, 1977 (OT)
-    SB: Miami vs. Washington, 1982
-    SB: Cincinnati vs. San Francisco, 1988
-    AFC-D: Cleveland vs. Buffalo, 1989
-    SB: San Diego vs. San Francisco, 1994
-    SB: Green Bay vs. New England, 1996
-    NFC: San Francisco vs. Green Bay, 1997
-    SB: Atlanta vs. Denver, 1998
-    AFC-FR: Tennessee vs. Buffalo, 1999
-    AFC-FR: Seattle vs. Miami, 1999
-    NFC-D: Washington vs. Tampa Bay, 1999
-    NFC-D: St. Louis vs. Minnesota, 1999
-    AFC: Tennessee vs. Jacksonville, 1999
-    NFC: N.Y. Giants vs. Philadelphia, 2000
-    SB: Baltimore vs. N.Y. Giants, 2000
-    SB: N.Y. Giants vs. Baltimore, 2000
-    AFC-D: Kansas City vs. Indianapolis, 2003
-    NFC-FR: Dallas vs. Seattle, 2006
-    SB: Chicago vs. Indianapolis, 2006

Most Touchdowns, Both Teams, Game
- 2 SB: Baltimore (1) vs. N.Y. Giants (1), 2000

PENALTIES

Most Penalties, Game
- 17 AFC-FR: L.A. Raiders vs. Denver, 1993
- 14 AFC-FR: Oakland vs. Houston, 1980
-     NFC-D: San Francisco vs. N.Y. Giants, 1981
-     AFC: Oakland vs. Tennessee, 2002
- 13 AFC-FR: Houston vs. Cleveland, 1988
-     AFC-D: Houston vs. Denver, 1991
-     NFC-D: Arizona vs. Minnesota, 1998
-     NFC-D: Carolina vs. St. Louis, 2003 (2 OT)

Fewest Penalties, Game
- 0 NFC: Philadelphia vs. Green Bay, 1960
-    NFC-D: Detroit vs. Dallas, 1970
-    AFC-D: Miami vs. Oakland, 1970
-    SB: Miami vs. Dallas, 1971
-    NFC-D: Washington vs. Minnesota, 1973
-    SB: Pittsburgh vs. Dallas, 1975
-    NFC: San Francisco vs. Chicago, 1988
-    SB: Denver vs. San Francisco, 1989
-    AFC-D: L.A. Raiders vs. Cincinnati, 1990
-    AFC-D: Miami vs. San Diego, 1992
-    SB: Atlanta vs. Denver, 1998
-    AFC-FR: N.Y. Jets vs. Oakland, 2001
-    NFC-FR: Carolina vs. Dallas, 2003
- 1 By many teams

Most Penalties, Both Teams, Game
- 27 AFC-FR: L.A. Raiders (17) vs. Denver (10), 1993
- 22 AFC-FR: Oakland (14) vs. Houston (8), 1980
-     NFC-D: San Francisco (14) vs. N.Y. Giants (8), 1981
-     AFC-FR: Houston (13) vs. Cleveland (9), 1988
-     NFC-D: Arizona (13) vs. Minnesota (9), 1998
- 21 AFC-D: Oakland (11) vs. New England (10), 1976

- AFC: Oakland (14) vs. Tennessee (7), 2002

Fewest Penalties, Both Teams, Game
- 1 AFC-D: L.A. Raiders (0) vs. Cincinnati (1), 1990
- 2 NFC: Washington (1) vs. Chi. Bears (1), 1937
-    NFC-D: Washington (0) vs. Minnesota (2), 1973
-    SB: Pittsburgh (0) vs. Dallas (2), 1975
-    NFC-FR: Carolina (0) vs. Dallas (2), 2003
- 3 AFC: Miami (1) vs. Baltimore (2), 1971
-    NFC: San Francisco (1) vs. Dallas (2), 1971
-    SB: Miami (0) vs. Dallas (3), 1971
-    AFC-D: Pittsburgh (1) vs. Oakland (2), 1972
-    AFC-D: Miami (1) vs. Cincinnati (2), 1973
-    SB: Miami (1) vs. San Francisco (2), 1984
-    NFC: San Francisco (0) vs. Chicago (3), 1988
-    AFC: New England (1) vs. Pittsburgh (2), 2004
-    AFC: San Diego (1) vs. New England (2), 2007

YARDS PENALIZED

Most Yards Penalized, Game
- 145 NFC-D: San Francisco vs. N.Y. Giants, 1981
- 133 SB: Dallas vs. Baltimore, 1970
- 130 AFC-FR: L.A. Raiders vs. Denver, 1993

Fewest Yards Penalized, Game
- 0 By many teams

Most Yards Penalized, Both Teams, Game
- 227 AFC-FR: L.A. Raiders (130) vs. Denver (97), 1993
- 206 NFC-D: San Francisco (145) vs. N.Y. Giants (61), 1981
- 201 NFC-FR: Detroit (126) vs. Washington (75), 1999

Fewest Yards Penalized, Both Teams, Game
- 5 AFC-D: L.A. Raiders (0) vs. Cincinnati (5), 1990
- 9 NFC-D: Washington (0) vs. Minnesota (9), 1973
- 11 NFC-FR: Carolina (0) vs. Dallas (11), 2003

FUMBLES

Most Fumbles, Game
- 8 SB: Buffalo vs. Dallas, 1992
- 7 AFC-D: Houston vs. Kansas City, 1993
- 6 By 12 teams

Most Fumbles, Both Teams, Game
- 12 AFC: Houston (6) vs. Pittsburgh (6), 1978
-     SB: Buffalo (8) vs. Dallas (4), 1992
- 10 NFC: Chi. Bears (5) vs. N.Y. Giants (5), 1934
-     SB: Dallas (6) vs. Denver (4), 1977
-     AFC: Jacksonville (5) vs. Tennessee (5), 1999
- 9 NFC-D: San Francisco (6) vs. Detroit (3), 1957
-    NFC-D: San Francisco (5) vs. Dallas (4), 1972
-    NFC: Dallas (5) vs. Philadelphia (4), 1980

Most Fumbles Lost, Game
- 5 SB: Buffalo vs. Dallas, 1992
-    AFC-D: Miami vs. Jacksonville, 1999
- 4 NFC: N.Y. Giants vs. Baltimore, 1958 (OT)
-    AFC: Kansas City vs. Oakland, 1969
-    SB: Baltimore vs. Dallas, 1970
-    AFC: Pittsburgh vs. Oakland, 1975
-    SB: Denver vs. Dallas, 1977
-    AFC: Houston vs. Pittsburgh, 1978
-    AFC: Miami vs. New England, 1985
-    SB: New England vs. Chicago, 1985
-    NFC-FR: L.A. Rams vs. Washington, 1986
-    NFC-FR: Minnesota vs. Dallas, 1996
-    AFC-FR: Buffalo vs. Miami, 1998
-    AFC: N.Y. Jets vs. Denver, 1998
-    AFC: Jacksonville vs. Tennessee, 1999
- 3 By many teams

Fewest Fumbles, Both Teams, Game
- 0 NFC: Green Bay vs. Cleveland, 1965
-    AFC-D: Houston vs. San Diego, 1979
-    NFC-D: Dallas vs. Los Angeles, 1979
-    SB: Los Angeles vs. Pittsburgh, 1979
-    AFC-D: Buffalo vs. Cincinnati, 1981
-    NFC: Minnesota vs. Washington, 1987
-    NFC-D: San Francisco vs. Washington, 1990

NFC: Dallas vs. Green Bay, 1995
AFC-D: New England vs. Pittsburgh, 1996
SB: Green Bay vs. New England, 1996
AFC-FR: Miami vs. Seattle, 1999
AFC-FR: Miami vs. Indianapolis, 2000 (OT)
AFC-D: Baltimore vs. Tennessee, 2000
SB: Pittsburgh vs. Seattle, 2005

1   In many games

RECOVERIES
Most Total Fumbles Recovered, Game

8   SB: Dallas vs. Denver, 1977 (4 own, 4 opp)
7   NFC: Chi. Bears vs. N.Y. Giants, 1934 (5 own, 2 opp)
    NFC-D: San Francisco vs. Detroit, 1957 (4 own, 3 opp)
    NFC-D: San Francisco vs. Dallas, 1972 (4 own, 3 opp)
    AFC: Pittsburgh vs. Houston, 1978 (3 own, 4 opp)
6   AFC: Houston vs. San Diego, 1961 (4 own, 2 opp)
    AFC-D: Cleveland vs. Baltimore, 1971 (4 own, 2 opp)
    AFC-D: Cleveland vs. Oakland, 1980 (5 own, 1 opp)
    NFC: Philadelphia vs. Dallas, 1980 (3 own, 3 opp)
    SB: Dallas vs. Buffalo, 1992 (1 own, 5 opp)
    NFC-D: Green Bay vs. San Francisco, 1996
      (4 own, 2 opp)
    AFC: Denver vs. N.Y. Jets, 1998 (2 own, 4 opp)
    AFC: Tennessee vs. Jacksonville, 1999 (2 own, 4 opp)

Most Own Fumbles Recovered, Game

5   NFC: Chi. Bears vs. N.Y. Giants, 1934
    AFC-D: Cleveland vs. Oakland, 1980
4   By many teams

TOUCHDOWNS
Most Touchdowns, Game

2   SB: Dallas vs. Buffalo, 1992

TURNOVERS
Numbers of times losing the ball on interceptions and fumbles.
Most Turnovers, Game

9   NFC: Washington vs. Chi. Bears, 1940
    NFC: Detroit vs. Cleveland, 1954
    AFC: Houston vs. Pittsburgh, 1978
    SB: Buffalo vs. Dallas, 1992
8   NFC: N.Y. Giants vs. Chi. Bears, 1946
    NFC: Los Angeles vs. Cleveland, 1955
    NFC: Cleveland vs. Detroit, 1957
    SB: Denver vs. Dallas, 1977
    NFC-D: Minnesota vs. Philadelphia, 1980
    NFC-D: Green Bay vs. St. Louis, 2001
7   In many games

Fewest Turnovers, Game

0   By many teams

Most Turnovers, Both Teams, Game

14   AFC: Houston (9) vs. Pittsburgh (5), 1978
13   NFC: Detroit (9) vs. Cleveland (4), 1954
    AFC: Houston (7) vs. San Diego (6), 1961
12   AFC: Pittsburgh (7) vs. Oakland (5), 1975

Fewest Turnovers, Both Teams, Game

0   SB: Buffalo vs. N.Y. Giants, 1990
    AFC-FR: Kansas City vs Pittsburgh, 1993 (OT)
    NFC-FR: Detroit vs. Green Bay, 1994
    AFC-FR: Denver vs. Jacksonville, 1996
    SB: St. Louis vs. Tennessee, 1999
1   AFC-D: Baltimore (0) vs. Cincinnati (1), 1970
    AFC-D: Pittsburgh (0) vs. Buffalo (1), 1974
    AFC: Oakland (0) vs. Pittsburgh (1), 1976
    NFC-D: Minnesota (0) vs. Washington (1), 1982
    NFC-D: Chicago (0) vs. N.Y. Giants (1), 1985
    SB: N.Y. Giants (0) vs. Denver (1), 1986
    NFC: Washington (0) vs. Minnesota (1), 1987
    AFC-D: Cincinnati (0) vs. L.A. Raiders (1), 1990
    NFC: N.Y. Giants (0) vs. San Francisco (1), 1990
    NFC-FR: N.Y. Giants (0) vs. Minnesota (1), 1993
    AFC-FR: L.A. Raiders (0) vs. Denver (1), 1993

NFC: Dallas (0) vs. San Francisco (1), 1993
AFC: Indianapolis (0) vs. Pittsburgh (1), 1995
NFC-D: San Francisco (0) vs. Minnesota (1), 1997
AFC-D: Indianapolis (0) vs. Tennessee (1), 1999
AFC-FR: Baltimore (0) vs. Denver (1), 2000
AFC-D: Baltimore (0) vs. Tennessee (1), 2000
AFC-D: Oakland (0) vs. New England (1), 2001
NFC-FR: Green Bay (0) vs. Seattle (1), 2003 (OT)
AFC-D: Indianapolis (0) vs. Kansas City (1), 2003
AFC-FR: N.Y. Jets (0) vs. San Diego (1), 2004 (OT)
NFC: Philadelphia (0) vs. Atlanta (1), 2003
NFC-FR: Philadelphia (0) vs. N.Y. Giants (1), 2006
NFC-D: Philadelphia (0) vs. New Orleans (1), 2006
NFC-D: N.Y. Giants (0) vs. Dallas (1), 2007

2   In many games

Includes records of AFC-NFC Pro Bowls, 1971-2008
Compiled by Elias Sports Bureau

INDIVIDUAL RECORDS

SERVICE
Most Games
- 12   Randall McDaniel, Minnesota 1990-2000; Tampa Bay 2001
  - Will Shields, Kansas City, 1996-2007
- 11   *Reggie White, Philadelphia, 1987-1993; Green Bay, 1994, 1996-97, 1999
  - Junior Seau, San Diego, 1992-2002
  - Rod Woodson, Pittsburgh, 1990-95, 1997; Baltimore, 2000-02; Oakland, 2003
- 10   Lawrence Taylor, N.Y. Giants, 1982-1991
  - Ronnie Lott, San Francisco, 1982-85, 1987-1991; L.A. Raiders 1992
  - Mike Singletary, Chicago, 1984-1993
  - **Bruce Matthews, Houston, 1989-1995, 1997; Tennessee, 2000, 2002
  - ***Jerry Rice, San Francisco, 1987-88, 1990-94, 1996, 1999; Oakland, 2003

*Also selected, but did not play, in two additional games
**Also selected, but did not play, in four additional games
***Also selected but did not play, in three additional games

SCORING
POINTS
Most Points, Career
- 45   Morten Andersen, New Orleans, 1986-89, 1991, 1993; Atlanta, 1996 (15-pat, 10-fg)
- 30   Jan Stenerud, Kansas City, 1971-72, 1976; Minnesota, 1985 (6-pat, 8-fg)
  - Jimmy Smith, Jacksonville, 1998-2001 (5-td)
  - Marvin Harrison, Indianapolis, 2000-06 (5-td)
- 29   David Akers, Philadelphia, 2002-03, 2005 (8-pat, 7-fg)

Most Points, Game
- 18   John Brockington, Green Bay, 1973 (3-td)
  - Mike Alstott, Tampa Bay, 2000 (3-td)
  - Jimmy Smith, Jacksonville, 2000 (3-td)
  - Shaun Alexander, Seattle, 2004 (3-td)
- 15   Garo Yepremian, Miami, 1974 (5-fg)
  - Jason Hanson, Detroit, 2000 (6-pat, 3-fg)
- 14   Jan Stenerud, Kansas City, 1972 (2-pat, 4-fg)

TOUCHDOWNS
Most Touchdowns, Career
- 5   Jimmy Smith, Jacksonville, 1998-2001 (5-p)
  - Marvin Harrison, Indianapolis, 2000-06 (5-p)
- 4   Mike Alstott, Tampa Bay, 1998-2003 (3-r, 1-p)
  - Tony Gonzalez, Kansas City, 2000-01, 2003-08 (4-p)
  - Hines Ward, Pittsburgh, 2002-05 (3-p, 1-ret)
  - Terrell Owens, San Francisco, 2001-04; Dallas, 2008 (4-p)
- 3   John Brockington, Green Bay, 1972-74 (2-r, 1-p)
  - Earl Campbell, Houston, 1979-1982, 1984 (3-r)
  - Chuck Muncie, New Orleans, 1980; San Diego, 1982-83 (3-r)
  - William Andrews, Atlanta, 1981-84 (1-r, 2-p)
  - Marcus Allen, L.A. Raiders, 1983, 1985-86, 1988; Kansas City, 1994 (2-r, 1-p)
  - Cris Carter, Minnesota, 1994-2001 (3-p)
  - Curtis Martin, New England, 1996-97; N.Y. Jets, 1999, 2002 (2-r, 1-p)
  - Shaun Alexander, Seattle, 2004 (2-r, 1-p)
  - Torry Holt, St. Louis, 2001-02, 2004-06, 2008 (3-p)

Most Touchdowns, Game
- 3   John Brockington, Green Bay, 1973 (2-r, 1-p)
  - Mike Alstott, Tampa Bay, 2000 (3-r)
  - Jimmy Smith, Jacksonville, 2000 (3-p)
  - Shaun Alexander, Seattle, 2004 (2-r, 1-p)
- 2   Mel Renfro, Dallas, 1971 (2-ret)
  - Earl Campbell, Houston, 1980 (2-r)
  - Chuck Muncie, New Orleans, 1980 (2-r)
  - William Andrews, Atlanta, 1984 (2-r)
  - Herschel Walker, Dallas, 1989 (2-r)
  - Johnny Johnson, Phoenix, 1991 (2-r)

Eric Green, Pittsburgh, 1995 (2-p)
Marvin Harrison, Indianapolis, 2001 (2-p)
Ricky Wiilliams, Miami, 2003 (2-r)
Hines Ward, Pittsburgh, 2005 (1-p, 1-ret)
T.J. Houshmandzadeh, Cincinnati, 2008 (2-p)
Terrell Owens, Dallas, 2008 (2-p)
Adrian Peterson, Minnesota, 2008 (2-r)

POINTS AFTER TOUCHDOWN
Most Points After Touchdown, Career
- 15   Morten Andersen, New Orleans, 1986-89, 1991, 1993; Atlanta, 1996 (15 att)
- 11   Adam Vinatieri, New England, 2003, 2005 (11 att)
- 9   Jason Hanson, Detroit, 1998, 2000 (9 att)

Most Points After Touchdown, Game
- 7   Mike Vanderjagt, Indianapolis, 2004 (7 att)
- 6   Ali Haji-Sheikh, N.Y. Giants, 1984 (6 att)
  - Jason Hanson, Detroit, 2000 (6 att)
  - Adam Vinatieri, New England, 2003 (6 att)
  - Nick Folk, Dallas, 2008 (6 att)
- 5   John Carney, San Diego, 1995 (5 att)
  - Matt Stover, Baltimore, 2001 (5 att)
  - Jason Elam, Denver, 2002 (5 att)
  - Jeff Wilkins, St. Louis, 2004 (5 att)
  - Adam Vinatieri, New England, 2005 (5 att)

FIELD GOALS
Most Field Goals Attempted, Career
- 18   Morten Andersen, New Orleans, 1986-89, 1991, 1993; Atlanta, 1996
- 15   Jan Stenerud, Kansas City, 1971-72, 1976; Minnesota, 1985
- 10   Nick Lowery, Kansas City, 1982, 1991, 1993

Most Field Goals Attempted, Game
- 6   Jan Stenerud, Kansas City, 1972
  - Eddie Murray, Detroit, 1981
  - Mark Moseley, Washington, 1983
- 5   Garo Yepremian, Miami, 1974
- 4   Jan Stenerud, Kansas City, 1976
  - Nick Lowery, Kansas City, 1991, 1993
  - Morten Andersen, New Orleans, 1993
  - Cary Blanchard, Indianapolis, 1997
  - John Kasay, Carolina, 1997
  - David Akers, Philadelphia, 2002
  - Jeff Wilkins, St. Louis, 2004

Most Field Goals, Career
- 10   Morten Andersen, New Orleans, 1986-89, 1991, 1993; Atlanta, 1996
- 8   Jan Stenerud, Kansas City, 1971-72, 1976; Minnesota, 1985
- 7   Nick Lowery, Kansas City, 1982, 1991, 1993
  - David Akers, Philadelphia, 2002-03, 2005

Most Field Goals, Game
- 5   Garo Yepremian, Miami, 1974 (5 att)
- 4   Jan Stenerud, Kansas City, 1972 (6 att)
  - Eddie Murray, Detroit, 1981 (6 att)
- 3   Nick Lowery, Kansas City, 1991 (4 att)
  - Nick Lowery, Kansas City, 1993 (4 att)
  - Jason Elam, Denver, 1999 (3 att)
  - Jason Hanson, Detroit, 2000 (3 att)
  - David Akers, Philadelphia, 2002 (4 att)
  - Neil Rackers, Arizona, 2006 (3 att)1995
  - Rob Bironas, Tennessee, 2008 (3 att)

Longest Field Goal
- 53   David Akers, Philadelphia, 2003
- 51   Morten Andersen, New Orleans, 1989
  - Jason Hanson, Detroit, 2000
- 49   Fuad Reveiz, Minnesota, 1995
  - David Akers, Philadelphia, 2002

SAFETIES
Most Safeties, Game
- 1   Art Still, Kansas City, 1983
  - Mark Gastineau, N.Y. Jets, 1985
  - Greg Townsend, L.A. Raiders, 1992

RUSHING

ATTEMPTS

Most Attempts, Career
- 81   Walter Payton, Chicago, 1977-1981, 1984-87
- 68   O.J. Simpson, Buffalo, 1973-77
- 66   Barry Sanders, Detroit, 1990-93, 1995-98

Most Attempts, Game
- 19   O.J. Simpson, Buffalo, 1974
- 17   Marv Hubbard, Oakland, 1974
- 16   O.J. Simpson, Buffalo, 1973
-      Marcus Allen, L.A. Raiders, 1986
-      Adrian Peterson, Minnesota, 2008

YARDS GAINED

Most Yards Gained, Career
- 368   Walter Payton, Chicago, 1977-1981, 1984-87
- 356   O.J. Simpson, Buffalo, 1973-77
- 271   Marshall Faulk, Indianapolis, 1995-96, 1999; St. Louis, 2000, 2002-03

Most Yards Gained, Game
- 180   Marshall Faulk, Indianapolis, 19951995
- 129   Adrian Peterson, Minnesota, 2008
- 127   Chris Warren, Seattle, 1995

Longest Run From Scrimmage
- 49   Marshall Faulk, Indianapolis, 1995 (TD)
- 41   Lawrence McCutcheon, Los Angeles, 1976
-      Natrone Means, San Diego, 1995
-      Marshall Faulk, Indianapolis, 1995
- 39   Chris Warren, Seattle, 1994
-      Priest Holmes, Kansas City, 20021995
-      Adrian Peterson, Minnesota, 2008

AVERAGE GAIN

Highest Average Gain, Career (20 attempts)
- 9.36   Chris Warren, Seattle, 1994-96, (25-234)
- 6.45   Marshall Faulk, Indianapolis, 1995-96, 1999; St. Louis, 2000, 2002-03 (42-271)
- 5.81   Marv Hubbard, Oakland, 1972-74 (36-209)

Highest Average Gain, Game (10 attempts)
- 13.85   Marshall Faulk, Indianapolis, 1995 (13-180)
- 9.07   Chris Warren, Seattle, 1995 (14-127)
- 8.06   Adrian Peterson, Minnesota 2008 (16-129)

TOUCHDOWNS

Most Touchdowns, Career
- 3   Earl Campbell, Houston, 1979-1982, 1984
-    Chuck Muncie, New Orleans, 1980; San Diego, 1982-83
-    Mike Alstott, Tampa Bay, 1998-2003
- 2   John Brockington, Green Bay, 1972-74
-    O.J. Simpson, Buffalo, 1973-77
-    Walter Payton, Chicago, 1977-1981, 1984-87
-    Marcus Allen, L.A. Raiders, 1983, 1985-86, 1988; Kansas City, 1994
-    Herschel Walker, Dallas, 1988-89
-    Johnny Johnson, Phoenix, 1991
-    Barry Sanders, Detroit, 1990-93, 1995-98
-    Curtis Martin, New England, 1996-97; N.Y. Jets, 1999, 2002
-    Ricky Williams, Miami, 2003
-    Shaun Alexander, Seattle, 2004-06
-    LaDainian Tomlinson, San Diego, 2003, 2005-07
-    Adrian Peterson, Minnesota, 2008

Most Touchdowns, Game
- 3   Mike Alstott, Tampa Bay, 2000
- 2   John Brockington, Green Bay, 1973
-    Earl Campbell, Houston, 1980
-    Chuck Muncie, New Orleans, 1980
-    Herschel Walker, Dallas, 1989
-    Johnny Johnson, Phoenix, 1991
-    Ricky Williams, Miami, 2003
-    Shaun Alexander, Seattle, 2004
-    Adrian Peterson, Minnesota, 2008

PASSING

ATTEMPTS

Most Attempts, Career
- 162   Peyton Manning, Indianapolis, 2000-01, 2003-08
- 120   Dan Fouts, San Diego, 1980-84, 1986

- 101   Steve Young, San Francisco, 1993-96, 1998-99

Most Attempts, Game
- 41   Peyton Manning, Indianapolis, 2004
- 32   Bill Kenney, Kansas City, 1984
-      Steve Young, San Francisco, 1993
- 30   Dan Fouts, San Diego, 1983

COMPLETIONS

Most Completions, Career
- 95   Peyton Manning, Indianapolis, 2000-01, 2003-08
- 63   Dan Fouts, San Diego, 1980-84, 1986
- 48   Steve Young, San Francisco, 1993-96, 1998-99

Most Completions, Game
- 22   Peyton Manning, Indianapolis, 2004
- 21   Joe Theismann, Washington, 1984
- 18   Steve Young, San Francisco, 1993

COMPLETION PERCENTAGE

Highest Completion Percentage, Career (40 attempts)
- 68.9   Joe Theismann, Washington, 1983-84 (45-31)
- 67.9   Rich Gannon, Oakland, 2000-03 (53-36)
- 64.4   Jim Kelly, Buffalo, 1988, 1991-92 (45-29)

Highest Completion Percentage, Game (10 attempts)
- 90.0   Archie Manning, New Orleans, 1980 (10-9)
- 85.7   Rich Gannon, Oakland, 2001 (14-12)
- 80.0   Rich Gannon, Oakland, 2002 (10-8)
-      Jeff Garcia, Tampa Bay, 2008 (10-8)

YARDS GAINED

Most Yards Gained, Career
- 1,345   Peyton Manning, Indianapolis, 2000-01, 2003-08
- 890   Dan Fouts, San Diego, 1980-84, 1986
- 614   Steve Young, San Francisco, 1993-96, 1998-99

Most Yards Gained, Game
- 342   Peyton Manning, Indianapolis, 2004
- 274   Dan Fouts, San Diego, 1983
- 270   Peyton Manning, Indianapolis, 2000

Longest Completion
- 93   Jeff Blake, Cincinnati (to Thigpen, Pittsburgh), 1996 (TD)
- 90   Steve McNair, Tennessee (to Johnson, Cincinnati), 2004 (TD)
- 80   Mark Brunell, Jacksonville (to Brown, Oakland), 1997 (TD)

AVERAGE GAIN

Highest Average Gain, Career (40 attempts)
- 8.30   Peyton Manning, Indianapolis, 2000-01, 2003-08 (162-1,345)
- 8.19   Rich Gannon, Oakland, 2000-03 (53-434)
- 8.12   Brett Favre, Green Bay, 1993-94, 1996-97 (57-463)

Highest Average Gain, Game (10 attempts)
- 15.27   Randall Cunningham, Philadelphia, 1991 (11-168)
- 13.70   Rich Gannon, Oakland, 2002 (10-137)
- 13.00   Brett Favre, Green Bay, 1997 (11-143)
-      Peyton Manning, Indianapolis, 2005 (10-130)

TOUCHDOWNS

Most Touchdowns, Career
- 13   Peyton Manning, Indianapolis, 2000-01, 2003-08
- 7   Rich Gannon, Oakland, 2000-03
- 4   Steve Young, San Francisco, 1993-96, 1998-99
-    Marc Bulger, St. Louis, 2004, 2007

Most Touchdowns, Game
- 4   Marc Bulger, St. Louis, 2004
- 3   Joe Theismann, Washington, 1984
-    Phil Simms, N.Y. Giants, 1986
-    Peyton Manning, Indianapolis, 2004
-    Peyton Manning, Indianapolis, 2005
- 2   James Harris, Los Angeles, 1975
-    Mike Boryla, Philadelphia, 1976
-    Ken Anderson, Cincinnati, 1977
-    Jim Kelly, Buffalo, 1991
-    Mark Rypien, Washington, 1992
-    Steve Young, San Francisco, 1998
-    Peyton Manning, Indianapolis, 2000
-    Rich Gannon, Oakland, 2001
-    Peyton Manning, Indianapolis, 2001
-    Rich Gannon, Oakland, 2002

Donovan McNabb, Philadelphia, 2002
Rich Gannon, Oakland, 2003
Brad Johnson, Tampa Bay, 2003
Carson Palmer, Cincinnati, 2007
Tony Romo, Dallas, 2008

HAD INTERCEPTED
Most Passes Had Intercepted, Career
8   Dan Fouts, San Diego, 1980-84, 1986
    Peyton Manning, Indianapolis, 2000-01, 2003-08
6   Jim Hart, St. Louis, 1975-78
5   Ken Stabler, Oakland, 1974-75, 1978
    Donovan McNabb, Philadelphia, 2001-03, 2005
    Jeff Garcia, San Francisco, 2001-03;
      Tampa Bay, 2008
Most Passes Had Intercepted, Game
5   Jim Hart, St. Louis, 1977
4   Ken Stabler, Oakland, 1974
3   Dan Fouts, San Diego, 1986
    Mark Rypien, Washington, 1990
    Steve Young, San Francisco, 1993
    Jim Harbaugh, Indianapolis, 1996
    Vinny Testaverde, N.Y. Jets, 1999
    Jeff Garcia, San Francisco, 2003
    Peyton Manning, Indianapolis, 2006
Most Attempts, Without Interception, Game
27   Joe Theismann, Washington, 1984
    Phil Simms, N.Y. Giants, 1986
26   John Brodie, San Francisco, 1971
    Danny White, Dallas, 1983
23   Dave Krieg, Seattle, 1990

PERCENTAGE, PASSES HAD INTERCEPTED
Lowest Percentage, Passes Had Intercepted, Career
(40 attempts)
0.00   Joe Theismann, Washington, 1983-84 (45-0)
1.89   Rich Gannon, Oakland, 2000-03 (53-1)
2.13   Dave Krieg, Seattle, 1985, 1989-1990 (47-1)

PASS RECEIVING
RECEPTIONS
Most Receptions, Career
37   Jerry Rice, San Francisco, 1987-88, 1990-94, 1996,
      1999; Oakland, 2003
33   Tony Gonzalez, Kansas City, 2000-01, 2003-08
30   Marvin Harrison, Indianapolis, 2000-06
Most Receptions, Game
9   Randy Moss, Minnesota, 2000
8   Steve Largent, Seattle, 1986
    Michael Irvin, Dallas, 1992
    Andre Rison, Atlanta, 1993
    Jimmy Smith, Jacksonville, 2000
    Marvin Harrison, Indianapolis, 2001
    Terrell Owens, San Francisco, 2002
    Steve Smith, Carolina, 2006
    Terrell Owens, Dallas, 2008
7   John Stallworth, Pittsburgh, 1983
    Jerry Rice, San Francisco, 1992
    Isaac Bruce, St. Louis, 1997
    Keyshawn Johnson, N.Y. Jets, 1999
    Randy Moss, Minnesota, 1999
    Warrick Dunn, Tampa Bay, 2001
    Torry Holt, St. Louis, 2001
    Torry Holt, St. Louis, 2004

YARDS GAINED
Most Yards Gained, Career
495   Jerry Rice, San Francisco, 1987-88, 1990-94, 1996,
      1999; Oakland, 2003
492   Tony Gonzalez, Kansas City, 2000-01, 2003-08
462   Marvin Harrison, Indianapolis, 2000-06
Most Yards Gained, Game
212   Randy Moss, Minnesota, 2000
156   Chad Johnson, Cincinnati, 2004
137   Tim Brown, Oakland, 1997
    Reggie Wayne, Indianapolis, 2007
Longest Reception
93   Yancey Thigpen, Pittsburgh (from Blake, Cincinnati),
      1996 (TD)

90   Chad Johnson, Cincinnati (from McNair, Tennessee),
      2004 (TD)
80   Tim Brown, Oakland (from Brunell, Jacksonville),
      1997 (TD)

TOUCHDOWNS
Most Touchdowns, Career
5   Jimmy Smith, Jacksonville, 1998-2001
    Marvin Harrison, Indianapolis, 2000-06
4   Tony Gonzalez, Kansas City, 2000-01, 2003-08
    Terrell Owens, San Francisco, 2001-04; Dallas, 2008
3   Cris Carter, Minnesota, 1994-2001
    Torry Holt, St. Louis, 2001-02, 2004-06, 2008
    Hines Ward, Pittsburgh, 2002-05
Most Touchdowns, Game
3   Jimmy Smith, Jacksonville, 2000
2   William Andrews, Atlanta, 1984
    Eric Green, Pittsburgh, 1995
    Marvin Harrison, Indianapolis, 2001
    T.J. Houshmandzadeh, Cincinnati, 2008
    Terrell Owens, Dallas, 2008

INTERCEPTIONS BY
Most Interceptions By, Career
4   Everson Walls, Dallas, 1982-84, 1986
    Deion Sanders, Atlanta, 1992-94; San Francisco,
      1995; Dallas, 1999
    Champ Bailey, Washington, 2001-04; Denver,
      2005-08
3   Ken Houston, Houston, 1971-73; Washington,
      1974-79
    Jack Lambert, Pittsburgh, 1976-1984
    Ted Hendricks, Baltimore, 1972-74; Green Bay, 1975;
      Oakland, 1981-82; L.A. Raiders, 1983-84
    Mike Haynes, New England, 1978-1981, 1983;
      L.A. Raiders, 1985-87
    Ty Law, New England, 1999, 2002-04;
      N.Y. Jets, 2006
2   By 21 players
Most Interceptions By, Game
2   Mel Blount, Pittsburgh, 1977
    Everson Walls, Dallas, 1982, 1983
    LeRoy Irvin, L.A. Rams, 1986
    David Fulcher, Cincinnati, 1990
    Brian Dawkins, Philadelphia, 2000
    Rod Woodson, Oakland, 2003
    Ed Reed, Baltimore, 2007
    Antonio Cromartie, San Diego, 2008

YARDS GAINED
Most Yards Gained, Career
147   Ty Law, New England, 1999, 2002-04;
      N.Y. Jets, 2006
103   Deion Sanders, Atlanta, 1992-94; San Francisco,
      1995; Dallas, 1999
88   Rod Woodson, Pittsburgh, 1990-95, 1997;
      Baltimore, 2000-02; Oakland, 2003
Most Yards Gained, Game
87   Deion Sanders, Dallas, 1999
77   Antonio Cromartie, San Diego, 2008
73   Rod Woodson, Pittsburgh, 1994
Longest Gain
87   Deion Sanders, Dallas, 1999
73   Rod Woodson, Pittsburgh, 1994 (lateral)
67   Ty Law, New England, 1999 (TD)

TOUCHDOWNS
Most Touchdowns, Career
2   Ty Law, New England, 1999, 2002-04;
      N.Y. Jets, 2006
    Derrick Brooks, Tampa Bay, 1998-2001, 2003,
      2006-07
1   By many
Most Touchdowns, Game
1   Bobby Bell, Kansas City, 1973
    Nolan Cromwell, L.A. Rams, 1984
    Joey Browner, Minnesota, 1986
    Jerry Gray, L.A. Rams, 1990
    Mike Johnson, Cleveland, 1990

Junior Seau, San Diego, 1993
Ken Harvey, Washington, 1996
Ashley Ambrose, Cincinnati, 1997
Ty Law, New England, 1999
Derrick Brooks, Tampa Bay, 2000
Aeneas Williams, Arizona, 2000
Ray Lewis, Baltimore, 2002
Ty Law, New England, 2003
Dre' Bly, Detroit, 2004
Derrick Brooks, Tampa Bay, 2006

PUNTING
Most Punts, Career
33   Ray Guy, Oakland, 1974-79, 1981
23   Rohn Stark, Indianapolis, 1986-87, 1991, 1993
22   Reggie Roby, Miami, 1985, 1990; Washington, 1995
Most Punts, Game
10   Reggie Roby, Miami, 1985
9   Tom Wittum, San Francisco, 1974
Rohn Stark, Indianapolis, 1987
8   Jerrel Wilson, Kansas City, 1971
Tom Skladany, Detroit, 1982
Reggie Roby, Washington, 1995
Longest Punt
73   Shane Lechler, Oakland, 2002
70   Shane Lechler, Oakland, 2002
64   Tom Wittum, San Francisco, 1974
Darren Bennett, San Diego, 1996
Brian Moorman, Buffalo, 2007

AVERAGE YARDAGE
Highest Average, Career (10 punts)
46.73   Reggie Roby, Miami, 1985, 1990; Washington, 1995
(22-1,028)
45.27   Matt Turk, Washington, 1997-99 (15-679)
45.25   Jerrel Wilson, Kansas City, 1971-73 (16-724)
Highest Average, Game (4 punts)
60.75   Shane Lechler, Oakland, 2002 (4-243)
55.50   Darren Bennett, San Diego, 1996 (4-222)
52.00   Matt Turk, Washington, 1999 (4-208)

PUNT RETURNS
Most Punt Returns, Career
13   Rick Upchurch, Denver, 1977, 1979-1980, 1983
11   Vai Sikahema, St. Louis, 1987-88
Eric Metcalf, Cleveland 1994-95; San Diego 1998
10   Mike Nelms, Washington, 1981-83
Most Punt Returns, Game
7   Vai Sikahema, St. Louis, 1987
6   Henry Ellard, L.A. Rams, 1985
Gerald McNeil, Cleveland, 1988
Eric Metcalf, Cleveland, 1995
5   Rick Upchurch, Denver, 1980
Mike Nelms, Washington, 1981
Carl Roaches, Houston, 1982
Johnny Bailey, Phoenix, 1993
Most Fair Catches, Game
2   Jerry Logan, Baltimore, 1971
Dick Anderson, Miami, 1974
Henry Ellard, L.A. Rams, 1985
Isaac Bruce, St. Louis, 1997
Desmond Howard, Detroit, 2001

YARDS GAINED
Most Yards Gained, Career
183   Billy Johnson, Houston, 1976, 1978; Atlanta, 1984
138   Mel Renfro, Dallas, 1971-72, 1974
Rick Upchurch, Denver, 1977, 1979-1980, 1983
135   Eric Metcalf, Cleveland, 1994-95; San Diego 1998
Most Yards Gained, Game
159   Billy Johnson, Houston, 1976
138   Mel Renfro, Dallas, 1971
117   Wally Henry, Philadelphia, 1980
Longest Punt Return
90   Billy Johnson, Houston, 1976 (TD)
86   Wally Henry, Philadelphia, 1980 (TD)
82   Mel Renfro, Dallas, 1971 (TD)

AVERAGE YARDAGE
Highest Average, Career (4 returns)
22.88   Billy Johnson, Houston, 1976, 1978; Atlanta, 1984
(8-183)
21.50   Tony Green, Washington, 1979 (4-86)
15.67   David Meggett, N.Y. Giants, 1990; New England, 1997
Highest Average, Game (3 returns)
39.75   Billy Johnson, Houston, 1976 (4-159)
39.00   Wally Henry, Philadelphia, 1980 (3-117)
21.50   Tony Green, Washington, 1979 (4-86)

TOUCHDOWNS
Most Touchdowns, Game
2   Mel Renfro, Dallas, 1971
1   Billy Johnson, Houston, 1976
Wally Henry, Philadelphia, 1980

KICKOFF RETURNS
Most Kickoff Returns, Career
17   Michael Bates, Carolina, 1997-2001
14   Mel Gray, Detroit, 1991-92, 1995
11   Eric Metcalf, Cleveland, 1994-95; San Diego, 1998
Derrick Mason, Tennessee, 2001, 2004
Most Kickoff Returns, Game
8   Derrick Mason, Tennessee, 2004
7   Mel Gray, Detroit, 1995
Jerry Azumah, Chicago, 2004
6   Greg Pruitt, L.A. Raiders, 1984
David Meggett, New England, 1997
Michael Bates, Carolina, 1998
Steve Smith, Carolina, 2002
Josh Cribbs, Cleveland, 2008

YARDS GAINED
Most Yards Gained, Career
488   Michael Bates, Carolina, 1997-2001
309   Greg Pruitt, Cleveland, 1974-75, 1977-78;
L.A. Raiders, 1984
294   Mel Gray, Detroit, 1991-92, 1995
Most Yards Gained, Game
228   Jerry Azumah, Chicago, 2004
217   Michael Lewis, New Orleans, 2003
192   Greg Pruitt, L.A. Raiders, 1984
Longest Kickoff Return
66   Michael Bates, Carolina, 2000
62   Greg Pruitt, L.A. Raiders, 1984
61   Eugene (Mercury) Morris, Miami, 1972

AVERAGE YARDAGE
Highest Average, Career (4 returns)
43.40   Michael Lewis, New Orleans, 2003 (5-217)
35.00   Les (Speedy) Duncan, Washington, 1972 (5-175)
32.57   Jerry Azumah, Chicago, 2004 (7-228)
Highest Average, Game (3 returns)
43.40   Michael Lewis, New Orleans, 2003 (5-217)
42.00   Michael Bates, Carolina, 2000 (4-168)
35.00   Les (Speedy) Duncan, Washington, 1972 (5-175)

TOUCHDOWNS
Most Touchdowns, Game
1   Hines Ward, Pittsburgh, 2005

FUMBLES
Most Fumbles, Career
6   Dan Fouts, San Diego, 1980-84, 1986
4   Lawrence McCutcheon, Los Angeles, 1974-78
Franco Harris, Pittsburgh, 1973-76, 1978-1981
Jay Schroeder, Washington, 1987
Vai Sikahema, St. Louis, 1987-88
Trent Green, Kansas City, 2004, 2006
3   O.J. Simpson, Buffalo, 1973-77
William Andrews, Atlanta, 1981-84
Joe Montana, San Francisco, 1982, 1984-85, 1988
Walter Payton, Chicago, 1977-1981, 1984-87
Neil Lomax, St. Louis, 1985, 1988
Jim Kelly, Buffalo, 1988, 1991-92
Chris Chandler, Atlanta, 1998-99
Peyton Manning, Indianapolis, 2000-01, 2003-08

Marc Bulger, St. Louis, 2004, 2007

Most Fumbles, Game
- 4 Jay Schroeder, Washington, 1987
  Trent Green, Kansas City, 2004
- 3 Dan Fouts, San Diego, 1982
  Vai Sikahema, St. Louis, 1987
- 2 By 17 players

RECOVERIES
Most Fumbles Recovered, Career
- 3 Harold Jackson, Philadelphia, 1973; Los Angeles, 1974, 1976, 1978 (3-own)
  Dan Fouts, San Diego, 1980-84, 1986 (3-own)
  Randy White, Dallas, 1978, 1980-86 (3-opp)
  Trent Green, Kansas City, 2004, 2006 (3-own)
  Peyton Manning, Indianapolis, 2000-01, 2003-08 (3-own)
- 2 By many players

Most Fumbles Recovered, Game
- 3 Trent Green, Kansas City, 2004 (3-own)
- 2 Dick Anderson, Miami, 1974 (1-own, 1-opp)
  Harold Jackson, Los Angeles, 1974 (2-own)
  Dan Fouts, San Diego, 1982 (2-own)
  Joey Browner, Minnesota, 1990 (2-opp)
  Jessie Armstead, N.Y. Giants, 1999 (1-own, 1-opp)
  Steve Beuerlein, Carolina, 2000 (2-own)

YARDAGE
Longest Fumble Return
- 83 Art Still, Kansas City, 1985 (TD, opp)
- 70 Adalius Thomas, Baltimore, 2007 (TD, opp)
- 51 Phil Villapiano, Oakland, 1974 (opp)

TOUCHDOWNS
Most Touchdowns, Game
- 1 Art Still, Kansas City, 1985
  Keith Millard, Minnesota, 1990
  Adalius Thomas, Baltimore, 2007

SACKS
Sacks have been compiled since 1983.
Most Sacks, Career
- 9.5 Reggie White, Philadelphia, 1987-1993; Green Bay, 1994, 1996-97, 1999
- 9.0 Howie Long, L.A. Raiders, 1984-88, 1990, 1993-1994
- 7.5 Bruce Smith, Buffalo, 1988-1991, 1995-96, 1998-99

Most Sacks, Game
- 4 Mark Gastineau, N.Y. Jets, 1985
  Reggie White, Philadelphia, 1987
- 3 Richard Dent, Chicago, 1985
  Bruce Smith, Buffalo, 1991
- 2.5 Bruce Smith, Buffalo, 1998

TEAM RECORDS

SCORING
Most Points, Game
- 55 NFC, 2004

Fewest Points, Game
- 3 AFC, 1984, 1989, 1994

Most Points, Both Teams, Game
- 107 NFC (55) vs. AFC (52), 2004

Fewest Points, Both Teams, Game
- 16 NFC (6) vs. AFC (10), 1987

TOUCHDOWNS
Most Touchdowns, Game
- 7 AFC, 2004
  NFC, 2004

Fewest Touchdowns, Game
- 0 AFC, 1971, 1974, 1984, 1989, 1994
  NFC, 1987, 1988

Most Touchdowns, Both Teams, Game
- 14 AFC (7) vs. NFC (7), 2004

Fewest Touchdowns, Both Teams, Game
- 1 AFC (0) vs. NFC (1), 1974
  NFC (0) vs. AFC (1), 1987
  NFC (0) vs. AFC (1), 1988

POINTS AFTER TOUCHDOWN
Most Points After Touchdown, Game
- 7 AFC, 2004

Most Points After Touchdown, Both Teams, Game
- 12 AFC (7) vs. NFC (5), 2004

FIELD GOALS
Most Field Goals Attempted, Game
- 6 AFC, 1972
  NFC, 1981, 1983

Most Field Goals Attempted, Both Teams, Game
- 9 NFC (6) vs. AFC (3), 1983

Most Field Goals, Game
- 5 AFC, 1974

Most Field Goals, Both Teams, Game
- 7 AFC (5) vs. NFC (2), 1974

NET YARDS GAINED RUSHING AND PASSING
Most Yards Gained, Game
- 626 AFC, 2004

Fewest Yards Gained, Game
- 114 AFC, 1993

Most Yards Gained, Both Teams, Game
- 1,022 AFC (626) vs. NFC (396), 2004

Fewest Yards Gained, Both Teams, Game
- 424 AFC (202) vs. NFC (222), 1987

RUSHING
ATTEMPTS
Most Attempts, Game
- 50 AFC, 1974

Fewest Attempts, Game
- 9 NFC, 2001

Most Attempts, Both Teams, Game
- 80 AFC (50) vs. NFC (30), 1974

Fewest Attempts, Both Teams, Game
- 32 NFC (9) vs. AFC (23), 2001

YARDS GAINED
Most Yards Gained, Game
- 400 AFC, 1995

Fewest Yards Gained, Game
- 28 NFC, 1992

Most Yards Gained, Both Teams, Game
- 441 AFC (400) vs. NFC (41), 1995

Fewest Yards Gained, Both Teams, Game
- 119 NFC (36) vs. AFC (83), 2001

TOUCHDOWNS
Most Touchdowns, Game
- 3 NFC, 1989, 1991, 2000, 2007
  AFC, 1995

Most Touchdowns, Both Teams, Game
- 4 AFC (2) vs. NFC (2), 1973
  AFC (2) vs. NFC (2), 1980
  NFC (3) vs. AFC (1), 2007

PASSING
ATTEMPTS
Most Attempts, Game
- 58 NFC, 2002

Fewest Attempts, Game
- 17 NFC, 1972

Most Attempts, Both Teams, Game
- 101 NFC (54) vs. AFC (47), 2003

Fewest Attempts, Both Teams, Game
- 42 NFC (17) vs. AFC (25), 1972

COMPLETIONS
Most Completions, Game
- 32 NFC, 1993
  AFC, 2001

Fewest Completions, Game
- 7 NFC, 1972, 1982

Most Completions, Both Teams, Game
- 60 AFC (32) vs. NFC (28), 2001

Fewest Completions, Both Teams, Game
18 NFC (7) vs. AFC (11), 1972

YARDS GAINED
Most Yards Gained, Game
515 AFC, 2004
Fewest Yards Gained, Game
42 NFC, 1982
Most Yards Gained, Both Teams, Game
775 AFC (515) vs. NFC (260), 2004
Fewest Yards Gained, Both Teams, Game
215 NFC (89) vs. AFC (126), 1972

TIMES SACKED
Most Times Sacked, Game
9 NFC, 1985
Fewest Times Sacked, Game
0 AFC, 1998, 1999, 2000, 2003
NFC, 1971, 1997, 2001
Most Times Sacked, Both Teams, Game
17 NFC (9) vs. AFC (8), 1985
Fewest Times Sacked, Both Teams, Game
1 NFC (0) vs. AFC (1), 1997

TOUCHDOWNS
Most Touchdowns, Game
5 AFC, 2004
Most Touchdowns, Both Teams, Game
9 AFC (5) vs. NFC (4), 2004

INTERCEPTIONS BY
Most Interceptions By, Game
6 AFC, 1977, 2003
Most Interceptions By, Both Teams, Game
8 AFC (6) vs. NFC (2), 2003

YARDS GAINED
Most Yards Gained, Game
192 NFC, 2006
Most Yards Gained, Both Teams, Game
265 NFC (192) vs. AFC (73), 2006

TOUCHDOWNS
Most Touchdowns, Game
2 NFC, 2000

PUNTING
Most Punts, Game
10 AFC, 1985
Fewest Punts, Game
0 NFC, 1989, 2008
Most Punts, Both Teams, Game
16 AFC (10) vs. NFC (6), 1985
Fewest Punts, Both Teams, Game
1 NFC (0) vs. AFC (1), 2008

PUNT RETURNS
Most Punt Returns, Game
7 NFC, 1985, 1987
AFC, 1995
Fewest Punt Returns, Game
0 AFC, 1984, 1989, 2008
NFC, 2005, 2008
Most Punt Returns, Both Teams, Game
11 NFC (7) vs. AFC (4), 1985
Fewest Punt Returns, Both Teams, Game
0 NFC (0) vs. AFC (0), 2008

YARDS GAINED
Most Yards Gained, Game
177 AFC, 1976
Fewest Yards Gained, Game
−1 NFC, 1991
Most Yards Gained, Both Teams, Game
263 AFC (177) vs. NFC (86), 1976
Fewest Yards Gained, Both Teams, Game
0 NFC (0) vs. AFC (0), 2008

TOUCHDOWNS
Most Touchdowns, Game
2 NFC, 1971

KICKOFF RETURNS
Most Kickoff Returns, Game
10 AFC, 2004
Fewest Kickoff Returns, Game
1 NFC, 1971, 1984, 1994
AFC, 1988, 1991
Most Kickoff Returns, Both Teams, Game
18 AFC (10) vs. NFC (8), 2004
Fewest Kickoff Returns, Both Teams, Game
5 NFC (2) vs. AFC (3), 1979
AFC (1) vs. NFC (4), 1988
NFC (2) vs. AFC (3), 1992
NFC (1) vs. AFC (4), 1994

YARDS GAINED
Most Yards Gained, Game
247 NFC, 2004
Fewest Yards Gained, Game
6 NFC, 1971
Most Yards Gained, Both Teams, Game
461 NFC (247) vs. AFC (214), 2004
Fewest Yards Gained, Both Teams, Game
99 NFC (48) vs. AFC (51), 1987

TOUCHDOWNS
Most Touchdowns, Game
1 AFC, 2005

FUMBLES
Most Fumbles, Game
10 NFC, 1974
Most Fumbles, Both Teams, Game
15 NFC (10) vs. AFC (5), 1974

RECOVERIES
Most Fumbles Recovered, Game
10 NFC, 1974 (6 own, 4 opp)
Most Fumbles Lost, Game
4 AFC, 1974, 1988
NFC, 1974

YARDS GAINED
Most Yards Gained, Game
87 AFC, 1985

TOUCHDOWNS
Most Touchdowns, Game
1 AFC, 1985, 2007
NFC, 1990

TURNOVERS
(Number of times losing the ball on interceptions and fumbles.)
Most Turnovers, Game
8 AFC, 1974
Fewest Turnovers, Game
0 AFC, 1991, 1997
NFC, 1991, 1995, 1996, 2001
Most Turnovers, Both Teams, Game
12 AFC (8) vs. NFC (4), 1974
Fewest Turnovers, Both Teams, Game
0 AFC vs. NFC, 1991

Rules

2008 NFL ROSTER OF OFFICIALS

Mike Pereira, Vice President of Officiating
Jim Daopoulos, Supervisor of Officials
Ron Baynes, Supervisor of Officials

Neely Dunn, Supervisor of Officials
Johnny Grier, Supervisor of Officials

No.	Name	Position	College
20	Anderson, Barry	Side Judge	North Carolina State
66	Anderson, Walt	Referee	Texas
108	Arthur, Gary	Line Judge	Wright State
26	Baltz, Mark	Head Linesman	Ohio
72	Banks, Michael	Side Judge	Illinois State
55	Barnes, Tom	Line Judge	Minnesota
56	Baynes, Allen	Field Judge	Auburn
32	Bergman, Jeff	Line Judge	Robert Morris
91	Bergman, Jerry	Head Linesman	Robert Morris
34	Blakeman, Clete	Field Judge	Nebraska
23	Boger, Jerome	Referee	Morehouse College
18	Boston, Byron	Line Judge	Austin
74	Bowers, Derick	Head Linesman	East Central
31	Brown, Chad	Umpire	East Texas State
43	Brown, Terry	Field Judge	Tennessee-Knoxville
134	Camp, Ed	Head Linesman	William Paterson
126	Carey, Don	Back Judge	California-Riverside
94	Carey, Mike	Referee	Santa Clara
39	Carlsen, Don	Side Judge	Cal State-Chico
63	Carollo, Bill	Referee	Wisconsin-Milwaukee
11	Carroll, Duke	Field Judge	Ithaca
60	Cavaletto, Gary	Field Judge	Hancock
41	Cheek, Boris	Field Judge	Morgan State
51	Cheffers, Carl	Referee	California-Irvine
95	Coleman, James	Side Judge	Arkansas
65	Coleman, Walt	Referee	Arkansas
99	Corrente, Tony	Referee	Cal State-Fullerton
70	Dawson, Scott	Umpire	Virginia Tech
53	DeFelice, Garth	Umpire	San Diego State
6	Dornan, Kirk	Back Judge	Central Washington
27	Dyer, Lee	Back Judge	Tennessee-Chattanooga
3	Edwards, Scott	Field Judge	Alabama
81	Ellison, Roy	Umpire	Savannah State
61	Ferguson, Keith	Back Judge	San Jose State
64	Ferrell, Dan	Umpire	Cal State-Fullerton
71	Fowler, Ruben	Umpire	Huston-Tillotson
133	Freeman, Steve	Back Judge	Mississippi State
80	Gautreaux, Greg	Field Judge	S.W. Louisiana
19	Green, Scott	Referee	Delaware
49	Hall, Rich	Umpire	Arizona
40	Hannah, Butch	Umpire	Middle Tennessee State
125	Hayes, Laird	Side Judge	Princeton
54	Hayward, George	Head Linesman	Missouri Western
93	Helverson, Scott	Back Judge	Iowa
97	Hill, Tom	Side Judge	Carson Newman
28	Hittner, Mark	Head Linesman	Pittsburg State
85	Hochuli, Ed	Referee	Texas-El Paso
82	Horton, Buddy	Field Judge	Oregon State
37	Howey, Jim	Back Judge	Erskine College
35	Hussey, John	Line Judge	Idaho State
76	Jenkins, Darrell	Umpire	San Jose State
101	Johnson, Carl	Line Judge	Nicholls State
103	Lamberth, Jeff	Side Judge	Texas A&M
73	Larrew, Joe	Side Judge	St. Louis
17	Lawing, Bob	Back Judge	North Carolina State
127	Leavy, Bill	Referee	San Jose State
130	Lewis, Darryll	Line Judge	Dartmouth
106	Mackie, Wayne	Head Linesman	Colgate
92	Madsen, Carl	Umpire	Washington (St. Louis)
107	Marinucci, Ron	Line Judge	Glassboro State
77	McAulay, Terry	Referee	Louisiana State
120	McGrath, John	Head Linesman	Kentucky
8	McKenzie, Dana	Head Linesman	Toledo
110	McKinnely, Phil	Head Linesman	UCLA
48	Mello, Jim	Head Linesman	Northeastern
78	Meyer, Greg	Side Judge	Texas Christian
115	Michalek, Tony	Umpire	Indiana
111	Miles, Terrence	Back Judge	Arizona State
135	Morelli, Pete	Referee	St. Mary's
124	Paganelli, Carl	Umpire	Michigan State
105	Paganelli, Dino	Back Judge	Aquinas College
46	Paganelli, Perry	Back Judge	Hope College
132	Parry, John	Referee	Purdue
15	Patterson, Rick	Side Judge	Wofford
79	Payne, Kent	Head Linesman	Nebraska Wesleyan
9	Perlman, Mark	Line Judge	Salem
10	Phares, Ron	Line Judge	Virginia Tech
47	Podraza, Tim	Line Judge	Nebraska
38	Powers, Eddy	Field Judge	Tennessee
109	Prioleau, Dyrol	Side Judge	Johnson C. Smith
5	Quirk, Jim	Umpire	Delaware
83	Reels, Richard	Back Judge	Chicago State
44	Rice, Jeff	Umpire	Northwestern
57	Riveron, Alberto	Referee	Miami
128	Rose, Larry	Side Judge	Florida
67	Rosenbaum, Doug	Field Judge	Illinois Wesleyan
58	Saracino, Jim	Field Judge	Northern Colorado
21	Schleyer, John	Head Linesman	Millersville
122	Schmitz, Bill	Back Judge	Colorado State
129	Schuster, Bill	Umpire	Alfred
45	Seeman, Jeff	Line Judge	Minnesota
118	Sifferman, Tom	Field Judge	Seattle
30	Slaughter, Gary	Head Linesman	East Texas State
2	Smith, Billy	Back Judge	East Carolina
90	Spanier, Mike	Line Judge	St. Cloud State
24	Stabile, Tom	Head Linesman	Slippery Rock
12	Steed, Greg	Back Judge	Howard
88	Steenson, Scott	Side Judge	North Texas
84	Steinkerchner, Mark	Line Judge	Akron
22	Stelljes, Steve	Head Linesman	Friends
68	Stephan, Tom	Line Judge	Pittsburg State
114	Steratore, Gene	Referee	Kent State
112	Steratore, Tony	Back Judge	California
62	Stewart, Charles	Line Judge	Long Beach State
102	Stritesky, Bruce	Umpire	Embry Riddle
100	Symonette, Tom	Line Judge	Florida
42	Triplette, Jeff	Referee	Wake Forest
75	Vernatchi, Rob	Field Judge	California-Riverside
36	Veteri, Tony	Head Linesman	Manhattan College
25	Waggoner, Bob	Back Judge	Juniata College
96	Wash, Undrey	Umpire	Texas-Arlington
7	Washington, Keith	Side Judge	Virginia Military Institute
116	Weatherford, Mike	Side Judge	Oklahoma State
87	Weidner, Paul	Head Linesman	Cincinnati
50	Weir, Mike	Field Judge	Missouri
119	Wilson, Greg	Side Judge	USC
29	Wilson, Steve	Umpire	Whitworth College
14	Winter, Ron	Referee	Michigan State
4	Wrolstad, Craig	Field Judge	Washington
16	Wyant, David	Side Judge	Virginia
33	Zimmer, Steve	Field Judge	Hofstra

Roster as of May 2008

NUMERICAL ROSTER

No.	Name	Position
2	Billy Smith	BJ
3	Scott Edwards	FJ
4	Craig Wrolstad	FJ
5	Jim Quirk	U
6	Kirk Dornan	BJ
7	Keith Washington	SJ
8	Dana McKenzie	HL
9	Mark Perlman	LJ
10	Ron Phares	LJ
11	Duke Carroll	FJ
12	Greg Steed	BJ
14	Ron Winter	R
15	Rick Patterson	SJ
16	David Wyant	SJ
17	Bob Lawing	BJ
18	Byron Boston	LJ
19	Scott Green	R
20	Barry Anderson	SJ
21	John Schleyer	HL
22	Steve Stelljes	HL
23	Jerome Boger	R
24	Tom Stabile	HL
25	Bob Waggoner	BJ
26	Mark Baltz	HL
27	Lee Dyer	BJ
28	Mark Hittner	HL
29	Steve Wilson	U
30	Gary Slaughter	HL
31	Chad Brown	U
32	Jeff Bergman	LJ
33	Steve Zimmer	FJ
34	Clete Blakeman	FJ
35	John Hussey	LJ
36	Tony Veteri	HL
37	Jim Howey	BJ
38	Eddy Powers	FJ
39	Don Carlsen	SJ
40	Butch Hannah	U
41	Boris Cheek	FJ
42	Jeff Triplette	R
43	Terry Brown	FJ
44	Jeff Rice	U
45	Jeff Seeman	LJ
46	Perry Paganelli	BJ
47	Tim Podraza	LJ
48	Jim Mello	HL
49	Rich Hall	U
50	Mike Weir	FJ
51	Carl Cheffers	R
53	Garth DeFelice	U
54	George Hayward	HL
55	Tom Barnes	LJ
56	Allen Baynes	FJ
57	Alberto Riveron	R
58	Jim Saracino	FJ
60	Gary Cavaletto	FJ
61	Keith Ferguson	BJ
62	Charles Stewart	LJ
63	Bill Carollo	R
64	Dan Ferrell	U
65	Walt Coleman	R
66	Walt Anderson	R
67	Doug Rosenbaum	FJ
68	Tom Stephan	LJ
70	Scott Dawson	U
71	Ruben Fowler	U
72	Michael Banks	SJ
73	Joe Larrew	SJ
74	Derick Bowers	HL
75	Rob Vernatchi	FJ
76	Darrell Jenkins	U
77	Terry McAulay	R
78	Greg Meyer	SJ
79	Kent Payne	HL
80	Greg Gautreaux	FJ
81	Roy Ellison	U
82	Buddy Horton	FJ
83	Richard Reels	BJ
84	Mark Steinkerchner	LJ
85	Ed Hochuli	R
87	Paul Weidner	HL
88	Scott Steenson	SJ
90	Mike Spanier	LJ
91	Jerry Bergman	HL
92	Carl Madsen	U
93	Scott Helverson	BJ
94	Mike Carey	R
95	James Coleman	SJ
96	Undrey Wash	U
97	Tom Hill	SJ
99	Tony Corrente	R
100	Tom Symonette	LJ
101	Carl Johnson	LJ
102	Bruce Stritesky	U
103	Jeff Lamberth	SJ
105	Dino Paganelli	BJ
106	Wayne Mackie	HL
107	Ron Marinucci	LJ
108	Gary Arthur	LJ
109	Dyrol Prioleau	SJ
110	Phil McKinnely	HL
111	Terrence Miles	BJ
112	Tony Steratore	BJ
114	Gene Steratore	R
115	Tony Michalek	U
116	Mike Weatherford	SJ
118	Tom Sifferman	FJ
119	Greg Wilson	SJ
120	John McGrath	HL
122	Bill Schmitz	BJ
124	Carl Paganelli	U
125	Laird Hayes	SJ
126	Don Carey	BJ
127	Bill Leavy	R
128	Larry Rose	SJ
129	Bill Schuster	U
130	Darryll Lewis	LJ
132	John Parry	R
133	Steve Freeman	BJ
134	Ed Camp	HL
135	Pete Morelli	R

Roster as of May 2008

2008 OFFICIALS AT A GLANCE
REFEREES

Walt Anderson, No. **66,** Texas, college officiating coordinator, retired dentist, 13th year.

Jerome Boger, No. **23,** Morehouse College, commercial insurance underwriter, 5th year.

Mike Carey, No. **94,** Santa Clara, owner, skiing accessories, 19th year.

Bill Carollo, No. **63,** Wisconsin-Milwaukee, marketing executive, 20th year.

Carl Cheffers, No. **51,** California-Irvine, sales manager, 9th year.

Walt Coleman, No. **65,** Arkansas, manager dairy processor, 20th year.

Tony Corrente, No. **99,** Cal State-Fullerton, educator, 14th year.

Scott Green, No. **19,** Delaware, president, government support services, 18th year.

Ed Hochuli, No. **85,** Texas-El Paso, attorney, 19th year.

Bill Leavy, No. **127,** San Jose State, retired firefighter, 14th year.

Terry McAulay, No. **77,** Louisiana State, senior computer scientist, 11th year.

Pete Morelli, No. **135,** St. Mary's, high school principal, 12th year.

John Parry, No. **132,** Purdue, financial advisor, 9th year.

Alberto Riveron, No. **57,** Miami, sales, commercial restaurant equipment, 5th year.

Gene Steratore, No. **114,** Kent State, co-owner, supply company, 5th year.

Jeff Triplette, No. **42,** Wake Forest, vice president, world-wide energy company, 13th year.

Ron Winter, No. **14,** Michigan State, university professor, 14th year.

UMPIRES

Chad Brown, No. **31,** East Texas State, executive manager of facilities/student affairs administration, 17th year.

Scott Dawson, No. **70,** Virginia Tech, president/owner, commercial construction company, 14th year.

Garth DeFelice, No. **53,** San Diego State, distribution center manager, beverage company, 11th year.

Roy Ellison, No. **81,** Savannah State, technical staff member, 6th year.

Dan Ferrell, No. **64,** Cal State-Fullerton, director, parts logistics, 6th year.

Ruben Fowler, No. **71,** Huston-Tillotson, retired firefighter, 3rd year.

Rich Hall, No. **49,** Arizona, custom cabinetry, 5th year.

Butch Hannah, No. **40,** Middle Tennessee State, federal probation officer, 10th year.

Darrell Jenkins, No. **76,** San Jose State, retired, 7th year.

Carl Madsen, No. **92,** Washington (St. Louis), MO, partner/owner, office furniture dealership, 12th year.

Tony Michalek, No. **115,** Indiana, eurodollar futures trader, 7th year.

Carl Paganelli, No. **124,** Michigan State, federal probation officer, 8th year.

Jim Quirk, No. **5,** Delaware, consultant, 21st year.

Jeff Rice, No. **44,** Northwestern, attorney, 14th year.

Bill Schuster, No. **129,** Alfred, insurance broker, 9th year.

Bruce Stritesky, No. **102,** Embry Riddle, airline pilot, 3rd year.

Undrey Wash, No. **96,** Texas-Arlington, claims manager, 9th year.

Steve Wilson, No. **29,** Whitworth College, pastor, 10th year.

HEAD LINESMEN

Mark Baltz, No. **26,** Ohio, sales consultant, 20th year.

Jerry Bergman, No. **91,** Robert Morris, sales executive, 7th year.

Derick Bowers, No. **74,** East Central, purchasing supervisor, 6th year.

Ed Camp, No. **134,** William Paterson, physical education teacher, 9th year.

George Hayward, No. **54,** Missouri Western, vice-president and manager, warehouse company, 18th year.

Mark Hittner, No. **28,** Pittsburg State, investment broker, 12th year.

Wayne Mackie, No. **106,** Colgate, director of housing, 2nd year.

John McGrath, No. **120,** Kentucky, senior account executive, 7th year.

Dana McKenzie, No. **8,** Toledo, claims adjuster, 1st year.

Phil McKinnely, No. **110,** UCLA, inventory control, 6th year.

Jim Mello, No. **48,** Northeastern, facilities manager, 5th year.

Kent Payne, No. **79,** Nebraska Wesleyan, teacher, 5th year.

John Schleyer, No. **21,** Millersville, medical sales, 19th year.

Gary Slaughter, No. **30,** East Texas State, general manager, 13th year.

Tom Stabile, No. **24,** Slippery Rock, secondary educational administrator, 14th year.

Steve Stelljes, No. **22,** Friends, business planning manager, 7th year.

Tony Veteri, No. **36,** Manhattan College, physical education teacher, 17th year.

Paul Weidner, No. **87,** Cincinnati, developer, 23rd year.

LINE JUDGES

Gary Arthur, No. **108,** Wright State, president, commercial printing company, 12th year.

Tom Barnes, No. **55,** Minnesota, manufacturing representative, 23rd year.

Jeff Bergman, No. **32,** Robert Morris, president and chief executive officer, medical services, 17th year.

Byron Boston, No. **18,** Austin, tax consultant, 14th year.

John Hussey, No. **35,** Idaho State, sales representative, retail logistics group, 7th year.

Carl Johnson, No. **101,** Nicholls State, district sales manager, 8th year.

Darryll Lewis, No. **130,** Dartmouth, associate professor, 10th year.

Ron Marinucci, No. **107,** Glassboro State, vice president, novelty cone company, 12th year.

Mark Perlman, No. **9,** Salem, teacher, 8th year.

Ron Phares, No. **10,** Virginia Tech, president, construction company, 24th year.

Tim Podraza, No. **47,** Nebraska, banker, 1st year.

Jeff Seeman, No. **45,** Minnesota, brokerage sales, 7th year.

Mike Spanier, No. **90,** St. Cloud State, middle school principal, 10th year.

Mark Steinkerchner, No. **84,** Akron, vice-president, 15th year.

Tom Stephan, No. **68,** Pittsburg State, business broker, 10th year.

Charles Stewart, No. **62,** Long Beach State, retired human services administrator, 17th year.

Tom Symonette, No. **100,** Florida, certified public accountant, 5th year.

Roster as of May 2008

FIELD JUDGES

Allen Baynes, No. **56,** Auburn, realtor, 1st year.
Clete Blakeman, No. **34,** Nebraska, attorney, 1st year.
Terry Brown, No. **43,** Tennessee-Knoxville, probation supervisor, 3rd year.
Duke Carroll, No. **11,** Ithaca, insurance sales, 14th year.
Gary Cavaletto, No. **60,** Hancock, general manager, agricultural operations, 6th year.
Boris Cheek, No. **41,** Morgan State, director of operations and management, 13th year.
Scott Edwards, No. **3,** Alabama, environmental engineer, 10th year.
Greg Gautreaux, No. **80,** S.W. Louisiana, athletic programs manager, 7th year.
Buddy Horton, No. **82,** Oregon State, water service worker, 10th year.
Eddy Powers, No. **38,** Tennessee, sales/design office supply, 7th year.
Doug Rosenbaum, No. **67,** Illinois Wesleyan, financial consultant, 7th year.
Jim Saracino, No. **58,** Northern Colorado, secondary educator, 14th year.
Tom Sifferman, No. **118,** Seattle, manufacturer's representative, 23rd year.
Rob Vernatchi, No. **75,** California-Riverside, enforcement investigator, 5th year.
Mike Weir, No. **50,** Missouri, owner, sporting goods store, 7th year.
Craig Wrolstad, No. **4,** Washington, education, 6th year.
Steve Zimmer, No. **33,** Hofstra, attorney, 12th year.

SIDE JUDGES

Barry Anderson, No. **20,** North Carolina State, builder/developer, 2nd year.
Michael Banks, No. **72,** Illinois State, carpenter foreman, 7th year.
Don Carlsen, No. **39,** Cal State-Chico, retired county school superintendent, 20th year.
James Coleman, No. **95,** Arkansas, electrical engineer, 4th year.
Laird Hayes, No. **125,** Princeton, professor, physical education & athletics, 14th year.
Tom Hill, No. **97,** Carson Newman, teacher, 10th year.
Jeff Lamberth, No. **103,** Texas A&M, attorney, 7th year.
Joe Larrew, No. **73,** St. Louis, attorney, 7th year.
Greg Meyer, No. **78,** Texas Christian, banker, 7th year.
Rick Patterson, No. **15,** Wofford, banker, 13th year.
Dyrol Prioleau, No. **109,** Johnson C. Smith, manager, law firm, 2nd year.
Scott Steenson, No. **88,** North Texas, commercial real estate broker, 18th year.
Larry Rose, No. **128,** Florida, financial planner, 12th year.
Keith Washington, No. **7,** Virginia Military Institute, program financial analyst, 1st year.
Mike Weatherford, No. **116,** Oklahoma State, energy trader, 7th year.
Greg Wilson, No. **119,** USC, law enforcement, 1st year.
David Wyant, No. **16,** Virginia, consulting engineer, 18th year.

BACK JUDGES

Don Carey, No. **126,** California-Riverside, contract manager, 14th year.
Kirk Dornan, No. **6,** Central Washington, purchasing manager, 15th year.
Lee Dyer, No. **27,** Tennessee-Chattanooga, sales manager, 6th year.
Keith Ferguson, No. **61,** San Jose State, sales, 9th year.
Steve Freeman, No. **133,** Mississippi State, custom home builder, 8th year.
Scott Helverson, No. **93,** Iowa, sales, printing and promotions, 6th year.
Jim Howey, No. **37,** Erskine College, director of adult education, 10th year.
Bob Lawing, No. **17,** North Carolina State, certified property management, 12th year.
Terrence Miles, No. **111,** Arizona State, quality control manager, 1st year.
Dino Paganelli, No. **105,** Aquinas College, educator, 3rd year.
Perry Paganelli, No. **46,** Hope College, retired high school administrator, 11th year.
Richard Reels, No. **83,** Chicago State, director of security, court services, 16th year.
Bill Schmitz, No. **122,** Colorado State, general sales manager, 20th year.
Billy Smith, No. **2,** East Carolina, retired federal government, 15th year.
Greg Steed, No. **12,** Howard, computer systems analyst, 6th year.
Tony Steratore, No. **112,** California, PA., co-owner, supply company, 9th year.
Bob Waggoner, No. **25,** Juniata College, probation officer, 12th year.

Roster as of May 2008

1

**TOUCHDOWN, FIELD GOAL,
or SUCCESSFUL TRY**
Both arms extended above head.

2

SAFETY
Palms together above head.

3

FIRST DOWN
Arm pointed toward defensive
team's goal.

4

**DEAD BALL or
NEUTRAL ZONE ESTABLISHED**
One arm above head
with an open hand.
With fist closed: **Fourth Down.**

5

**BALL ILLEGALLY
TOUCHED, KICKED,
or BATTED**
Fingertips tap both shoulders.

6

TIME OUT
Hands crisscrossed above head.
Same signal followed by placing one
hand on top of cap: **Referee's Time Out.**
Same signal followed by arm swung at
side: **Touchback.**

7

**NO TIME OUT or
TIME IN WITH WHISTLE**
Full arm circled to
simulate moving clock.

8

**DELAY OF GAME
or EXCESS TIME OUT**
Folded arms.

9

**FALSE START,
ILLEGAL FORMATION, or
KICKOFF or SAFETY KICK
OUT OF BOUNDS or
KICKING TEAM PLAYER
VOLUNTARILY OUT OF BOUNDS
DURING A PUNT**
Forearms rotated over and over
in front of body.

10

PERSONAL FOUL
One wrist striking the other above head.
Same signal followed by swinging leg:
Roughing the Kicker.
Same signal followed by raised arm
swinging forward:
Roughing the Passer.
Same signal followed by grasping
facemask: **Major Facemask.**

11

HOLDING
Grasping one wrist,
the fist clenched,
in front of chest.

12

**ILLEGAL USE OF HANDS,
ARMS, or BODY**
Grasping one wrist,
the hand open and facing
forward, in front of chest.

13

PENALTY REFUSED, INCOMPLETE PASS, PLAY OVER, or MISSED FIELD GOAL or EXTRA POINT
Hands shifted in horizontal plane.

14

PASS JUGGLED INBOUNDS AND CAUGHT OUT OF BOUNDS
Hands up and down in front of chest (following incomplete pass signal).

15

ILLEGAL FORWARD PASS
One hand waved behind back followed by loss of down signal (23), when appropriate.

16

INTENTIONAL GROUNDING OF PASS
Parallel arms waved in a diagonal plane across body. Followed by loss of down signal (23).

17

INTERFERENCE WITH FORWARD PASS or FAIR CATCH
Hands open and extended forward from shoulders with hands vertical.

18

INVALID FAIR-CATCH SIGNAL
One hand waved above head.

19

**INELIGIBLE RECEIVER
or INELIGIBLE
MEMBER OF KICKING TEAM
DOWNFIELD**
Right hand touching top of cap.

20

ILLEGAL CONTACT
One open hand extended forward.

21

**OFFSIDE, ENCROACHMENT, or
NEUTRAL ZONE INFRACTION**
Hands on hips.

22

ILLEGAL MOTION AT SNAP
Horizontal arc with one hand.

23

LOSS OF DOWN
Both hands held behind head.

24

**INTERLOCKING
INTERFERENCE, PUSHING, or
HELPING RUNNER**
Pushing movement of hands
to front with arms downward.

25

TOUCHING A FORWARD PASS or SCRIMMAGE KICK
Diagonal motion of
one hand across another.

26

UNSPORTSMANLIKE CONDUCT
Arms outstretched,
palms down.

27

ILLEGAL CUT
Hand striking front of thigh.
ILLEGAL BLOCK BELOW THE WAIST
One hand striking front of thigh
preceded by personal-foul signal (10).
CHOP BLOCK
Both hands striking side of thighs
preceded by personal-foul signal (10).
CLIPPING
One hand striking back of calf
preceded by personal-foul signal (10).

28

ILLEGAL CRACKBACK
Strike of an
open right hand
against the right mid-thigh
preceded by personal foul
signal (10).

29

PLAYER DISQUALIFIED
Ejection signal.

30

TRIPPING
Repeated action of right foot
in back of left heel.

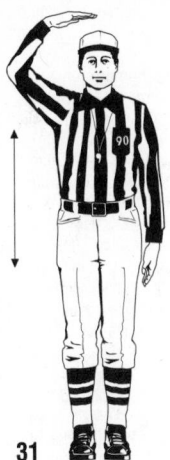

31

**UNCATCHABLE
FORWARD PASS**
Palm of right hand held
parallel to ground above head
and moved back and forth.

32

**TWELVE MEN IN OFFENSIVE HUDDLE
or TOO MANY MEN
ON THE FIELD**
Both hands on top of head.

33

FACEMASK
Grasping facemask with one
hand.

34

ILLEGAL SHIFT
Horizontal arcs with two hands.

35

**RESET PLAY CLOCK–
25 SECONDS**
Pump one arm vertically.

36

**RESET PLAY CLOCK–
40 SECONDS**
Pump two arms vertically.

NFL DIGEST OF RULES

This Digest of Rules of the National Football League has been prepared to aid players, fans, and members of the press, radio, and television media in their understanding of the game.

It is not meant to be a substitute for the official rule book. In any case of conflict between these explanations and the official rules, the rules always have precedence.

In order to make it easier to coordinate the information in this digest, the topics discussed generally follow the order of the rule book.

OFFICIALS' JURISDICTIONS, POSITIONS, AND DUTIES

Referee—General oversight and control of game. Gives signals for all fouls and is final authority for rule interpretations. Takes a position in backfield 10 to 12 yards behind line of scrimmage, favors right side (if quarterback is right-handed passer). Determines legality of snap, observes deep back(s) for legal motion. On running plays, observes quarterback during and after handoff, remains with him until action has cleared away, then proceeds downfield, checking on runner and contact behind him. When runner is downed, Referee determines forward progress from wing official and, if necessary, adjusts final position of ball.

On pass plays, drops back as quarterback begins to fade back, picks up legality of tackle on Head Linesman's side. Changes to complete concentration on quarterback as defenders approach. Primarily responsible to rule on possible roughing action on passer and if ball becomes loose, rules whether ball is free on a fumble or dead on an incomplete pass. Shares responsibility with Umpire, Linesman, and Line Judge on intentional grounding.

During kicking situations, Referee has primary responsibility to rule on kicker's actions and whether or not any subsequent contact by a defender is legal. During punt plays, Referee's position is parallel to kicker and wide. The Referee will announce on the microphone when each period is ended, penalties, a charged team time out, and when the two-minute warning for each half is reached.

Umpire—Primary responsibilities are to rule on players' conduct and actions on scrimmage line, as well as check on their equipment. Lines up approximately four to five yards downfield, varying position from the outside shoulder of one guard to outside shoulder of opposite guard. Looks for possible false start by offensive linemen. Observes legality of contact by both offensive linemen while blocking and by defensive players while they attempt to ward off blockers. Is prepared to call rule infractions if they occur on offense or defense. Moves forward to line of scrimmage when pass play develops in order to insure that interior linemen do not move illegally downfield. If offensive linemen indicate screen pass is to be attempted, Umpire shifts his attention toward screen side, picks up potential receiver in order to insure that he will legally be permitted to run his pattern and continues to rule on action of blockers. Umpire is to assist in ruling on incomplete or trapped passes when ball is thrown overhead or short. On field goal and try-kick attempts, he will become a second umpire with the Side Judge.

Head Linesman—Primarily responsible for ruling on offside, encroachment, and actions pertaining to scrimmage line prior to or at snap. Takes a position straddling the line of scrimmage. Keys on closest setback on his side of the field. On pass plays, Linesman is responsible to clear his receiver approximately seven yards downfield as he moves to a point five yards beyond the line. Linesman's secondary responsibility is to rule on any illegal action taken by defenders on any delay receiver moving downfield. Has full responsibility for ruling on sideline plays on his side, e.g., pass receiver or runner in or out of bounds. Together with Referee, Linesman is responsible for keeping track of number of downs and is in charge of mechanics of his chain crew in connection with its duties.

Linesman must be prepared to assist in determining forward progress by a runner on play directed toward middle or into his side zone. He, in turn, is to signal Referee or Umpire what forward point ball has reached. Linesman is also responsible to rule on legality of action involving any receiver who approaches his side zone. He is to call pass interference when the infraction occurs and is to rule on legality of blockers and defenders on plays involving ball carriers, whether it is entirely a running play, a combination pass and run, or a play involving a kick. Also assists referee with intentional grounding.

Line Judge—Straddles line of scrimmage on side of field opposite Linesman. Keeps time of game as a backup for official clock operator. However, should official clock malfunction or be operated improperly, the time kept by the Line Judge is official. Along with Linesman is responsible for offside, encroachment, and actions pertaining to scrimmage line prior to or at snap. Line Judge keys on closest setback on his side of field. Line Judge is to observe his receiver until he moves at least seven yards downfield. He then moves toward backfield side, being especially alert to rule on any back in motion and on flight of ball when pass is made (he must rule whether forward or backward). Line Judge has primary responsibility to rule whether or not passer is behind or beyond line of scrimmage when pass is made. He also assists in observing actions by blockers and defenders who are on his side of field. After pass is thrown, Line Judge directs attention toward activities that occur in back of Umpire. During punting situations, Line Judge remains at line of scrimmage to be sure that only the end men move downfield until kick has been made. He also rules whether or not the kick crossed line and then observes action by members of the kicking team who are moving downfield to cover the kick. The Line Judge will advise the Referee when time has expired at the end of each period.

Field Judge—Operates on same side of field as Line Judge, 20 yards deep. Keys on widest receiver on his side. Concentrates on path of end or back, observing legality of his potential block(s) or of actions taken against him. Is prepared to rule from deep position on holding or illegal use of hands by end or back or on defensive infractions committed by player guarding him. Has primary responsibility to make decisions involving sideline on his side of field, e.g., pass receiver or runner in or out of bounds.

Field Judge makes decisions involving catching, recovery, or illegal touching of a loose ball beyond line of scrimmage. Rules on plays involving pass receiver, including legality of catch or pass interference. Assists in covering actions of runner, including blocks by teammates and that of defenders. Rules on blocking during punt returns and, together with Back Judge, rules whether or not field goal and try-kick attempts are successful.

Side Judge—Operates on same side of field as Linesman, 20 yards deep. Keys on widest receiver on his side. Concentrates on path of this receiver, observing legality of his potential block(s) or of actions taken against him. Is prepared to rule from deep position on holding or illegal use of hands by the receiver or on defensive infractions committed by player defending him. Has primary responsibility to make decisions involving sideline on his side of field, e.g., pass receiver or runner in or out of bounds.

Side Judge makes decisions involving catching, recovery, or illegal touching of a loose ball beyond line of scrimmage. Rules on plays involving pass receiver, including legality of catch or pass interference. Assists in covering actions of runner, including blocks by teammates and that of defenders and rules on blocking during punt returns. On field goals and try-kick attempts, he becomes a second umpire.

Back Judge—Takes a position 25 yards downfield. In general, favors the tight end's side of field. Usually keys on tight end, concentrates on his path and observes legality of tight end's potential block(s) or of actions taken against him. Is prepared to rule from deep position on holding or illegal use of hands by end or back or on defensive infractions committed by player defending him.

Back Judge times interval between plays on 40/25-second clock plus intermission between two periods of each half. Makes decisions involving catching, recovery, or illegal touching of a loose ball beyond line of scrimmage. Is responsible to rule on plays involving end line. Calls pass interference, fair-catch infractions, and blocking during kick returns and, together with Field Judge, rules whether or not field goal and try-kick attempts are successful.

DEFINITIONS

1. **Chucking:** Warding off an opponent who is in front of a defender by contacting him with a quick extension of arm or arms, followed by the return of arm(s) to a flexed position, thereby breaking the original contact.
2. **Clipping:** Throwing the body across the back of an opponent's leg or hitting him from the back below the waist while moving up from behind unless the opponent is a runner or the contact is above the knee in close line play.
3. **Close Line Play:** The area between the positions normally occupied by the offensive tackles, extending three yards on each side of the line of scrimmage. It is legal to clip above the knee.
4. **Crackback:** Eligible receivers who take or move to a position more than two yards outside the tackle or a player in a backfield position may not block an opponent below the waist toward the ball at the snap and within five yards of the line of scrimmage.
5. **Dead Ball:** Ball not in play.
6. **Double Foul:** A foul by each team during the same down.
7. **Down:** The period of action that starts when the ball is put in play and ends when it is dead.
8. **Encroachment:** When a defensive player enters the neutral zone and makes contact with an opponent before the ball is snapped.
9. **Fair Catch:** An unhindered catch of a kick by a member of the receiving team who must raise one arm a full length above his head and wave his arm from side to side while the kick is in flight.
10. **Foul:** Any violation of a playing rule.
11. **Free Kick:** A kickoff or safety kick. It may be a placekick, dropkick, or punt, except a punt may not be used on a kick-off following a touchdown, successful field goal, or to begin each half or overtime period. A tee cannot be used on a fair-catch or safety kick.
12. **Fumble:** The unintentional loss of player possession of the ball.
13. **Game Clock:** Scoreboard game clock.
14. **Impetus:** The action of a player that gives momentum to the ball and sends it into the end zone.
15. **Live Ball:** A ball legally free-kicked or snapped. It continues in play until the down ends.
16. **Loose Ball:** A live ball not in possession of any player.
17. **Muff:** The touching of a loose ball by a player in an unsuccessful attempt to obtain possession.
18. **Neutral Zone:** The space the length of a ball between the two scrimmage lines. The offensive team and defensive team must remain behind their end of the ball.
    Exception: The offensive player who snaps the ball.
19. **Offside:** A player is offside when any part of his body is beyond his scrimmage or free kick line when the ball is snapped or kicked. Exception: Snapper, holder of placekick or kicker.
20. **Own Goal:** The goal a team is defending.
21. **Play Clock:** 40/25 second clock.
22. **Pocket Area:** Applies from a point two yards outside of either offensive tackle and includes the tight end if he drops off the line of scrimmage to pass protect. Pocket extends longitudinally behind the line back to offensive team's own end line. For purposes of intentional grounding, the pocket is considered tackle to tackle.
23. **Possession of a Pass:** When a player controls the ball throughout the act of clearly touching both feet, or any other part of his body other than his hand(s), to the ground inbounds.
24. **Post-Possession Foul:** A foul by the receiving team that occurs after a ball is legally kicked from scrimmage prior to possession changing. The ball must cross the line of scrimmage and the receiving team must retain the kicked ball unless it is part of a double foul.
25. **Punt:** A kick made when a player drops the ball and kicks it while it is in flight.
26. **Safety:** The situation in which the ball is dead on or behind a team's own goal if the impetus comes from a player on that team. Two points are scored for the opposing team.
27. **Shift:** The movement of two or more offensive players at the same time before the snap.
28. **Striking:** The act of swinging, clubbing, or propelling the arm or forearm in contacting an opponent.
29. **Sudden Death:** The continuation of a tied game into sudden death overtime in which the team scoring first (by safety, field goal, or touchdown) wins.
30. **Touchback:** When a ball is dead on or behind a team's own goal line, provided the impetus came from an opponent and provided it is not a touchdown or a missed field goal attempt when the ball was kicked outside the 20-yard line.
31. **Touchdown:** When any part of the ball, legally in possession of a player inbounds, breaks the plane of the opponent's goal line, provided it is not a touchback.
32. **Unsportsmanlike Conduct:** Any act contrary to the generally understood principles of sportsmanship.

SUMMARY OF PENALTIES

Automatic First Down

1. Awarded to offensive team on all <u>defensive fouls</u> with these exceptions:
   (a) Offside.
   (b) Encroachment.
   (c) Delay of game.
   (d) Illegal substitution.
   (e) Excessive time out(s).
   (f) Neutral zone infraction.
   (g) Running into the kicker.
   (h) More than 11 players on the field at the snap for either team.

Five Yards

1. Defensive holding or illegal use of hands (automatic first down).
2. Delay of game on offense or defense.
3. Delay of kickoff.
4. Encroachment.
5. Excessive time out(s).
6. False start.
7. Illegal formation.
8. Illegal shift.
9. Illegal motion.
10. Illegal substitution.
11. First onside kickoff out of bounds between goal lines and untouched or last touched by kickers.
12. Invalid fair catch signal.
13. More than 11 players on the field at snap for either team.
14. Less than seven men on offensive line at snap.
15. Offside.
16. Failure to pause one second after shift or huddle.
17. Running into kicker.
18. More than one man in motion at snap.
19. Grasping facemask of the ball carrier or quarterback.
20. Player out of bounds at snap.
21. Ineligible member(s) of kicking team going beyond line of scrimmage before ball is kicked.
22. Illegal return.
23. Failure to report change of eligibility.
24. Neutral zone infraction.
25. Ineligible player downfield during passing down.
26. Second forward pass behind the line.

27. Forward pass is first touched by eligible receiver who has gone out of bounds and returned.
28. Forward pass touches or is caught by an ineligible receiver on or behind line.
29. Forward pass thrown from behind line of scrimmage after ball once crossed the line.
30. Kicking team player voluntarily out of bounds during a punt.
31. Twelve (12) men in the huddle.

Ten Yards
1. Offensive pass interference.
2. Holding, illegal use of hands, arms, or body by offense.
3. Tripping by a member of either team.
4. Helping the runner.
5. Deliberately batting or punching a loose ball.
6. Deliberately kicking a loose ball.
7. Illegal block above the waist.

Fifteen Yards
1. Chop block.
2. Clipping below the waist.
3. Fair catch interference.
4. Illegal crackback block by offense.
5. Piling on.
6. Roughing the kicker.
7. Roughing the passer.
8. Twisting, turning, or pulling an opponent by the facemask.
9. Unnecessary roughness.
10. Unsportsmanlike conduct.
11. Delay of game at start of either half.
12. Illegal low block.
13. A tackler using his helmet to butt, spear, or ram an opponent.
14. Any player who uses the top of his helmet unnecessarily.
15. A punter, placekicker, or holder who simulates being roughed by a defensive player.
16. Leaping.
17. Leverage.
18. Any player who removes his helmet after a play while on the field.
19. Taunting.

Five Yards and Loss of Down (Combination Penalty)
1. Forward pass thrown from beyond line of scrimmage.

Ten Yards and Loss of Down (Combination Penalty)
1. Intentional grounding of forward pass (safety if passer is in own end zone). If foul occurs more than 10 yards behind line, play results in loss of down at spot of foul.

Fifteen Yards and Loss of Coin Toss Option
1. Team's late arrival on the field prior to scheduled kickoff.
2. Captains not appearing for coin toss.

Fifteen Yards (and disqualification if flagrant)
1. Striking opponent with fist.
2. Kicking or kneeing opponent.
3. Striking opponent on head or neck with forearm, elbow, or hands whether or not the initial contact is made below the neck area.
4. Roughing kicker.
5. Roughing passer.
6. Malicious unnecessary roughness.
7. Unsportsmanlike conduct.
8. Palpably unfair act. (Distance penalty determined by the Referee after consultation with other officials.)

Fifteen Yards and Automatic Disqualification
1. Using a helmet (not worn) as a weapon.
2. Striking or purposely shoving a game official.

Suspension From Game For One Down
1. Illegal equipment. (Player may return after one down when legally equipped.)

Touchdown Awarded (Palpably Unfair Act)
1. When Referee determines a palpably unfair act deprived a team of a touchdown. (Example: Player comes off bench and tackles runner apparently en route to touchdown.)

FIELD
1. Sidelines and end lines are out of bounds. The goal line is actually in the end zone. A player with the ball in his possession scores a touchdown when the ball is on, above, or over the goal line.
2. The field is rimmed by a white border, six feet wide, along the sidelines. All of this is out of bounds.
3. The hashmarks (inbound lines) are 70 feet, 9 inches from each sideline.
4. Goal posts must be single-standard type, offset from the end line and painted bright gold. The goal posts must be 18 feet, 6 inches wide and the top face of the crossbar must be 10 feet above the ground. Vertical posts extend at least 30 feet above the crossbar. A ribbon 4 inches by 42 inches long is to be attached to the top of each post. The actual goal is the plane extending indefinitely above the crossbar and between the outer edges of the posts.
5. The field is 360 feet long and 160 feet wide. The end zones are 30 feet deep. The line used in try-for-point plays is two yards out from the goal line.
6. Chain crew members and ball boys must be uniformly identifiable.
7. All clubs must use standardized sideline markers. Pylons must be used for goal line and end line markings.
8. End zone markings and club identification at 50 yard line must be approved by the Commissioner to avoid any confusion as to delineation of goal lines, sidelines, and end lines.

BALL
1. The home club shall have 36 balls for outdoor games and 24 for indoor games available for testing with a pressure gauge by the referee two hours prior to the starting time of the game to meet with League requirements. Twelve (12) new footballs, sealed in a special box and shipped by the manufacturer, will be opened in the officials' locker room two hours prior to the starting time of the game. These balls are to be specially marked with the letter "k" and used exclusively for the kicking game.

COIN TOSS
1. The toss of coin will take place within three minutes of kickoff in center of field. The toss will be called by the visiting captain before the coin is flipped. The winner may choose one of three privileges:
   (a) Receive or kick
   (b) Goal his team will defend
   (c) Defer choice to start of second half
2. Immediately prior to the start of the second half, the captains of both teams must inform the officials of their respective choices. The loser of the original coin toss gets first choice, unless the coin toss winner elected to defer.

TIMING
1. The stadium game clock is official. In case it stops or is operating incorrectly, the Line Judge takes over the official timing on the field.
2. Each period is 15 minutes. The intermission between the periods is two minutes. Halftime is 12 minutes, unless otherwise specified.
3. On charged team time outs, the Back Judge starts watch and blows whistle after 1 minute 50 seconds, unless television does not utilize the time for commercial. In this case the length of the time out is reduced to 30 seconds.
4. The Referee will allow necessary time to attend to an injured player, or repair a legal player's equipment.
5. Each team is allowed three time outs each half.
6. Time between plays will be 40 seconds from the end of a given play until the snap of the ball for the next play, or a 25-second interval after certain administrative stoppages and

game delays.

7. Clock will start running when ball is snapped following all changes of team possession.

8. With the exception of the last two minutes of the first half and the last five minutes of the second half, the game clock will be restarted following a player going out of bounds on a play from scrimmage, or after declined penalties when appropriate on the referee's signal.

9. Consecutive team time outs can be taken by opposing teams but the length of the second time out will be reduced to 30 seconds.

10. On kickoff, clock does not start until the ball has been legally touched by player of either team in the field of play.

SUDDEN DEATH

1. The sudden death system of determining the winner shall prevail when score is tied at the end of the regulation playing time of all NFL games. The team scoring first during overtime play shall be the winner and the game automatically ends upon any score (by safety, field goal, or touchdown) or when a score is awarded by Referee for a palpably unfair act.

2. At the end of regulation time the Referee will immediately toss coin at center of field in accordance with rules pertaining to the usual pregame toss. The captain of the visiting team will call the toss prior to the coin being flipped.

3. Following a three-minute intermission after the end of the regulation game, play will be continued in 15-minute periods or until there is a score. There is a two-minute intermission between subsequent periods. The teams change goals at the start of each period. Each team has three time outs per half and all general timing provisions apply as during a regular game. Disqualified players are not allowed to return.
   Exception: In preseason and regular season games there shall be a maximum of 15 minutes of sudden death with two time outs instead of three. General provisions that apply for the fourth quarter will prevail. Try not attempted if touchdown scored.

TIMING IN FINAL TWO MINUTES OF EACH HALF

1. A team cannot buy an excess time out for a penalty. However, a fourth time out is allowed without penalty for an injured player, who must be removed immediately. A fifth time out or more is allowed for an injury and a five-yard penalty is assessed.

2. If the defensive team is behind in the score and commits a foul when it has no time outs left in the final 40 seconds of either half, the offensive team can decline the penalty for the foul and have the time on the clock expire.

3. Fouls that occur in the last five minutes of the fourth quarter as well as the last two minutes of the first half will result in the clock starting on the snap.

TRY

1. After a touchdown, the scoring team is allowed a try during one scrimmage down. The ball may be spotted anywhere between the inbounds lines, two or more yards from the goal line. The successful conversion counts one point by kick; two points for a successful conversion by touchdown; or one point for a safety.

2. The defensive team never can score on a try. As soon as defense gets possession or the kick is blocked or a touchdown is not scored, the try is over.

3. Any distance penalty for fouls committed by the defense that prevent the try from being attempted can be enforced on the succeeding try or succeeding kickoff. Any foul committed on a successful try will result in a distance penalty being assessed on the ensuing kickoff.

4. Only the fumbling player can recover and advance a fumble during a try.

PLAYERS-SUBSTITUTIONS

1. Each team is permitted 11 men on the field at the snap.

2. Unlimited substitution is permitted. However, players may enter the field only when the ball is dead. Players who have been substituted for are not permitted to linger on the field. Such lingering will be interpreted as unsportsmanlike conduct.

3. Players leaving the game must be out of bounds on their own side, clearing the field between the end lines, before a snap or free kick. If player crosses end line leaving field, it is delay of game (five-yard penalty).

4. Offensive substitutes who remain in the game must move onto the field as far as the inside of the field numerals before moving to a wide position.

5. With the exception of the last two minutes of either half, the offensive team, while in the process of substitution or simulated substitution, is prohibited from rushing quickly to the line and snapping the ball with the obvious attempt to cause a defensive foul; i.e., too many men on the field.

6. There never can be 12 or more players in the offensive huddle.

KICKOFF

1. The kickoff shall be from the kicking team's 30-yard line at the start of each half and after a field goal and try. A kickoff is one type of free kick.

2. A one-inch tee may be used (no tee permitted for field goal, safety kick, or try attempt) on a kickoff. The ball is put in play by a placekick.

3. A kickoff may not score a field goal.

4. A kickoff is illegal unless it travels 10 yards OR is touched by the receiving team. Once the ball is touched by the receiving team or has gone 10 yards, it is a free ball. Receivers may recover and advance. Kicking team may recover but NOT advance UNLESS receiver had possession and lost the ball.

5. When a kickoff goes out of bounds between the goal lines without being touched by the receiving team, the ball belongs to the receivers 30 yards from the spot of the kick or at the out-of-bounds spot unless the ball went out-of-bounds the first time an onside kick was attempted. In this case, the kicking team is penalized five yards and the ball must be kicked again.

6. When a kickoff goes out of bounds between the goal lines and is touched last by receiving team, it is receiver's ball at out-of-bounds spot.

7. If the kicking team either illegally kicks off out of bounds or is guilty of a short free kick on two or more consecutive onside kicks, receivers may take possession of the ball at the dead ball spot, out-of-bounds spot, or spot of illegal touch.

SAFETY

1. In addition to a kickoff, the other free kick is a kick after a safety (safety kick). A punt may be used (a punt may not be used on a kickoff).

2. On a safety kick, the team scored upon puts ball in play by a punt, dropkick, or placekick without tee. No score can be made on a free kick following a safety, even if a series of penalties places team in position. (A field goal can be scored only on a play from scrimmage or a free kick after a fair catch.)

FAIR CATCH KICK

1. After a fair catch, the receiving team has the option to put the ball in play by a snap or a fair catch kick (field goal attempt), with fair catch kick lines established ten yards apart. All general rules apply as for a field goal attempt from scrimmage. The clock starts when the ball is kicked. (No tee permitted.)

FIELD GOAL

1. All field goals attempted (kicker) and missed from beyond the 20-yard line will result in the defensive team taking possession of the ball at the spot of the kick. On any field goal attempted and missed where the spot of the kick is on or inside the 20-yard line, ball will revert to defensive team at the 20-yard line.

SAFETY

1. The important factor in a safety is impetus. Two points are scored for the opposing team when the ball is dead on or behind a team's own goal line if the impetus came from a player on that team.

Examples of Safety:

(a) Blocked punt goes out of kicking team's end zone. Impetus was provided by punting team. The block only changes direction of ball, not impetus.

(b) Ball carrier retreats from field of play into his own end zone and is downed. Ball carrier provides impetus.

(c) Offensive team commits a foul and spot of enforcement is behind its own goal line.

(d) Player on receiving team muffs punt and, trying to get ball, forces or illegally kicks (creating new impetus) it into end zone where it goes out of the end zone or is recovered by a member of the receiving team in the end zone.

Examples of Non-Safety:

(a) Player intercepts a pass with both feet inbounds in the field of play and his momentum carries him into his own end zone. Ball is put in play at spot of interception.

(b) Player intercepts a pass in his own end zone and is downed in the end zone, even after recovering in the end zone. Impetus came from passing team, not from defense. (Touchback)

(c) Player passes from behind his own goal line. Opponent bats down ball in end zone. (Incomplete pass)

MEASURING

1. The forward point of the ball is used when measuring.

POSITION OF PLAYERS AT SNAP

1. Offensive team must have at least seven players on line.

2. Offensive players, not on line, must be at least one yard back at snap.
   (Exception: player who takes snap.)

3. No interior lineman may move abruptly after taking or simulating a three-point stance.

4. No player of either team may enter neutral zone before snap.

5. No player of offensive team may charge or move abruptly, after assuming set position, in such manner as to lead defense to believe snap has started. No player of the defensive team within one yard of the line of scrimmage may make an abrupt movement in an attempt to cause the offense to false start.

6. If a player changes his eligibility, the Referee must alert the defensive captain after player has reported to him.

7. All players of offensive team must be stationary at snap, except one back who may be in motion parallel to scrimmage line or backward (not forward).

8. After a shift or huddle all players on offensive team must come to an absolute stop for at least one second with no movement of hands, feet, head, or swaying of body.

9. Quarterbacks can be called for a false start penalty (five yards) if their actions are judged to be an obvious attempt to draw an opponent offside.

10. Offensive linemen are permitted to interlock legs.

USE OF HANDS, ARMS, AND BODY

1. No player on offense may assist a runner except by blocking for him. There shall be no interlocking interference.

2. A runner may ward off opponents with his hands and arms but no other player on offense may use hands or arms to obstruct an opponent by grasping with hands, pushing, or encircling any part of his body during a block. Hands (open or closed) can be thrust forward to initially contact an opponent on or outside the opponent's frame, but the blocker immediately must work to bring his hands on or inside the frame.
   Note: Pass blocking: Hand(s) thrust forward that slip outside the body of the defender will be legal if blocker immediately worked to bring them back inside. Hand(s) or arm(s) that encircle a defender—i.e., hook an opponent—are to be considered illegal and officials are to call a foul for holding. Blocker cannot use his hands or arms to push from behind, hang onto, or encircle an opponent in a manner that restricts his movement as the play develops.

3. Hands cannot be thrust forward above the frame to contact an opponent on the neck, face or head.
   Note: The frame is defined as the part of the opponent's body below the neck that is presented to the blocker.

4. A defensive player may not tackle or hold an opponent other than a runner. Otherwise, he may use his hands, arms, or body only:

   (a) To defend or protect himself against an obstructing opponent.
   Exception: An eligible receiver is considered to be an obstructing opponent ONLY to a point five yards beyond the line of scrimmage unless the player who receives the snap clearly demonstrates no further intention to pass the ball. Within this five-yard zone, a defensive player may chuck an eligible player in front of him. A defensive player is allowed to maintain continuous and unbroken contact within the five-yard zone until a point when the receiver is even with the defender. The defensive player cannot use his hands or arms to push from behind, hang onto, or encircle an eligible receiver in a manner that restricts movement as the play develops. Beyond this five-yard limitation, a defender may use his hands or arms ONLY to defend or protect himself against impending contact caused by a receiver. In such reaction, the defender may not contact a receiver who attempts to take a path to evade him.

   (b) To push or pull opponent out of the way on line of scrimmage.

   (c) In actual attempt to get at or tackle runner.

   (d) To push or pull opponent out of the way in a legal attempt to recover a loose ball.

   (e) During a legal block on an opponent who is not an eligible pass receiver.

   (f) When legally blocking an eligible pass receiver above the waist.
   Exception: Eligible receivers lined up within two yards of the tackle, whether on or immediately behind the line, may be blocked below the waist at or behind the line of scrimmage. NO eligible receiver may be blocked below the waist after he goes beyond the line. (Illegal cut)
   Note: Once the quarterback hands off or pitches the ball to a back, or if the quarterback leaves the pocket area, the restrictions (illegal chuck, illegal cut) on the defensive team relative to the offensive receivers will end, provided the ball is not in the air.

5. A defensive player may not contact an opponent above the shoulders with the palm of his hand except to ward him off on the line. This exception is permitted only if it is not a repeated act against the same opponent during any one contact. In all other cases the palms may be used on head, neck, or face only to ward off or push an opponent in legal attempt to get at the ball.

6. Any offensive player who pretends to possess the ball or to whom a teammate pretends to give the ball may be tackled

provided he is <u>crossing</u> his scrimmage line between the ends of a normal tight offensive line.

7. An offensive player who lines up more than two yards outside his own tackle or a player who, at the snap, is in a backfield position and subsequently takes a position more than two yards outside a tackle may not clip an opponent anywhere nor may he contact an opponent below the waist if the blocker is moving toward the ball and if contact is made within an area five yards on either side of the line. (crackback)

8. A player of either team may block at any time provided it is not pass interference, fair catch interference, or unnecessary roughness.

9. A player may not bat or punch:
   (a) A loose ball (in field of play) <u>toward</u> his opponent's goal line or in any direction in either end zone.
   (b) A ball in player possession.
   Note: If there is any question as to whether a defender is stripping or batting a ball in player possession, the official(s) will rule the action as a legal act (stripping the ball).
   Exception: A forward or backward pass may be batted, tipped, or deflected in any direction at any time by either the offense or the defense.
   Note: A pass in flight that is controlled or caught may only be thrown backward, if it is thrown forward it is considered an illegal bat.

10. No player may deliberately kick any ball except as a punt, dropkick, or placekick.

FORWARD PASS

1. A forward pass may be touched or caught by any eligible receiver. All members of the defensive team are eligible. Eligible receivers on the offensive team are players on either end of line (other than center, guard, or tackle) or players at least one yard behind the line at the snap. A T-formation quarterback is <u>not</u> eligible to receive a forward pass during a play from scrimmage.
   Exception: T-formation quarterback becomes eligible if pass is previously touched by an eligible receiver.

2. An offensive team may make only <u>one</u> forward pass during each play from scrimmage (Loss of 5 yards).

3. The passer must be behind his line of scrimmage (Loss of down and five yards, enforced from the spot of pass).

4. Any eligible offensive player may catch a forward pass. If a pass is touched by one eligible offensive player and touched or caught by a second offensive player, pass completion is legal. Further, all offensive players become eligible once a pass is touched by an eligible receiver or any defensive player.

5. The rules concerning a forward pass and ineligible receivers:
   (a) If ball is touched <u>accidentally</u> by an ineligible receiver on or <u>behind his line</u>: loss of five yards.
   (b) If ineligible receiver is illegally downfield: loss of five yards.
   (c) If touched or caught (intentionally or accidentally) by ineligible receiver <u>beyond</u> the line: loss of 5 yards.

6. The player who first controls and continues to maintain control of a pass will be awarded the ball even though his opponent later establishes joint control of the ball.

7. Any forward pass becomes incomplete and ball is dead if:
   (a) Pass hits the ground or goes out of bounds.
   (b) Pass hits the goal post or the crossbar of either team.

8. A forward pass is complete when a receiver clearly possesses the pass and touches the ground with <u>both feet</u> inbounds while in <u>possession</u> of the ball. If a receiver would have landed inbounds with both feet but is carried or pushed out of bounds while maintaining possession of the ball, pass is complete at the out-of-bounds spot.

9. If a personal foul is committed by the <u>defense prior</u> to the completion of a pass, the penalty is 15 yards from the spot where ball becomes dead.

10. If a personal foul is committed by the <u>offense prior</u> to the completion of a pass, the penalty is 15 yards from the previous line of scrimmage.

INTENTIONAL GROUNDING OF FORWARD PASS

1. Intentional grounding of a forward pass is a foul: loss of down and 10 yards from previous spot if passer is in the field of play or loss of down at the spot of the foul if it occurs more than 10 yards behind the line or safety if passer is in his own end zone when ball is released.

2. Intentional grounding will be called when a passer, facing an imminent loss of yardage due to pressure from the defense, throws a forward pass without a realistic chance of completion.

3. Intentional grounding will not be called when a passer, while out of the pocket and facing an imminent loss of yardage, throws a pass that lands at or beyond the line of scrimmage, even if no offensive player(s) have a realistic chance to catch the ball (including if the ball lands out of bounds over the sideline or end line).

PROTECTION OF PASSER

1. By interpretation, a pass begins when the passer—with possession of ball—starts to bring his hand forward. If ball strikes ground after this action has begun, play is ruled an incomplete pass. If passer loses control of ball prior to his bringing his hand forward, play is ruled a fumble.

2. When a passer is holding the ball to pass it forward, any intentional movement forward of his hand starts a forward pass. If a defensive player contacts the passer or the ball after forward movement begins, and the ball leaves the passer's hand, a forward pass is ruled, regardless of where the ball strikes the ground or a player.

3. No defensive player may run into a passer of a legal forward pass after the ball has left his hand (15 yards). The Referee must determine whether opponent had a <u>reasonable chance to stop his momentum</u> during an attempt to block the pass or tackle the passer while he still had the ball.

4. No defensive player who has an unrestricted path to the quarterback may hit him flagrantly in the area of the knee(s) or below when approaching in any direction.

5. Officials are to blow the play dead as soon as the quarterback is <u>clearly</u> in the grasp and control of any tackler, and his safety is in jeopardy.

6. No defensive player may hit the quarterback in the head, face, or neck.

PASS INTERFERENCE

1. There shall be no interference with a forward pass thrown from behind the line. The restriction for the <u>passing team</u> starts <u>with the snap</u>. The restriction on the <u>defensive team</u> starts <u>when the ball leaves the passer's hand</u>. Both restrictions <u>end when the ball is touched by anyone</u>.

2. The penalty for <u>defensive</u> pass interference is an automatic first down at the spot of the foul. If interference is in the end zone, it is first down for the offense on the defense's 1-yard line. If previous spot was inside the defense's 1-yard line, penalty is half the distance to the goal line.

3. The penalty for <u>offensive</u> pass interference is 10 yards from the previous spot.

4. It is pass interference by either team when any player movement beyond the line of scrimmage significantly hinders the progress of an eligible player of such player's opportunity to catch the ball. Offensive pass interference rules apply from the time the ball is snapped until the ball is touched. Defensive pass interference rules apply from the time the ball is thrown until the ball is touched.
   Actions that constitute defensive pass interference include but are not limited to:

(a) Contact by a defender who is not playing the ball and such contact restricts the receiver's opportunity to make the catch.

(b) Playing through the back of a receiver in an attempt to make a play on the ball.

(c) Grabbing a receiver's arm(s) in such a manner that restricts his opportunity to catch a pass.

(d) Extending an arm across the body of a receiver thus restricting his ability to catch a pass, regardless of whether the defender is playing the ball.

(e) Cutting off the path of a receiver by making contact with him without playing the ball.

(f) Hooking a receiver in an attempt to get to the ball in such a manner that it causes the receiver's body to turn prior to the ball arriving.

Actions that do not constitute pass interference include but are not limited to:

(a) Incidental contact by a defender's hands, arms, or body when both players are competing for the ball, or neither player is looking for the ball. If there is any question whether contact is incidental, the ruling shall be no interference.

(b) Inadvertent tangling of feet when both players are playing the ball or neither player is playing the ball.

(c) Contact that would normally be considered pass interference, but the ball is clearly uncatchable by the involved players.

(d) Laying a hand on a receiver that does not restrict the receiver in an attempt to make a play on the ball.

(e) Contact by a defender who has gained position on a receiver in an attempt to catch the ball.

Actions that constitute offensive pass interference include but are not limited to:

(a) Blocking downfield by an offensive player prior to the ball being touched.

(b) Initiating contact with a defender by shoving or pushing off thus creating a separation in an attempt to catch a pass.

(c) Driving through a defender who has established a position on the field.

Actions that do not constitute offensive pass interference include but are not limited to:

(a) Incidental contact by a receiver's hands, arms, or body when both players are competing for the ball or neither player is looking for the ball.

(b) Inadvertent touching of feet when both players are playing the ball or neither player is playing the ball.

(c) Contact that would normally be considered pass interference, but the ball is clearly uncatchable by involved players.

Note 1: If there is any question whether player contact is incidental, the ruling should be no interference.

Note 2: Defensive players have as much right to the path of the ball as eligible offensive players.

Note 3: Pass interference for both teams ends when the pass is touched.

Note 4: There can be no pass interference at or behind the line of scrimmage, but defensive actions such as tackling a receiver can still result in a 5-yard penalty for defensive holding, if accepted.

Note 5: Whenever a team presents an apparent punting formation, defensive pass interference is not to be called for action on the end man on the line of scrimmage, or an eligible receiver behind the line of scrimmage who is aligned or in motion more than one yard outside the end man on the line. Defensive holding, such as tackling a receiver, still can be called and result in a 5-yard penalty and automatic first down from the previous spot, if accepted. Offensive pass interference rules still apply.

BACKWARD PASS

1. Any pass not forward is regarded as a backward pass. A pass parallel to the line is a backward pass. A runner may pass backward at any time.

2. A backward pass that strikes the ground can be recovered and advanced by either team.

3. A backward pass caught in the air can be advanced by either team.

4. A backward pass in flight may not be batted forward by an offensive player.

FUMBLE

1. The distinction between a fumble and a muff should be kept in mind in considering rules about fumbles. A fumble is the loss of player possession of the ball. A muff is the touching of a loose ball by a player in an unsuccessful attempt to obtain possession.

2. A fumble may be advanced by any player on either team regardless of whether recovered before or after ball hits the ground.

3. A fumble that goes forward and out of bounds will return to the fumbling team at the spot of the fumble unless the ball goes out of bounds in the opponent's end zone. In this case, it is a touchback.

4. On a play from scrimmage, if an offensive player fumbles anywhere on the field during fourth down, only the fumbling player is permitted to recover and/or advance the ball. If any player fumbles after the two-minute warning in a half, only the fumbling player is permitted to recover and/or advance the ball. If recovered by any other offensive player, the ball is dead at the spot of the fumble unless it is recovered behind the spot of the fumble. In that case, the ball is dead at the spot of recovery. Any defensive player may recover and/or advance any fumble at any time.

5. A muffed hand-to-hand snap from center is treated as a fumble.

KICKS FROM SCRIMMAGE

1. Any kick from scrimmage must be made from behind the line to be legal.

2. Any punt or missed field goal that touches a goal post is dead.

3. During a kick from scrimmage, only the end men, as eligible receivers on the line of scrimmage at the time of the snap, are permitted to go beyond the line before the ball is kicked. **Exception:** An eligible receiver who, at the snap, is aligned or in motion behind the line and more than one yard outside the end man on his side of the line, clearly making him the outside receiver, replaces that end man as the player eligible to go downfield after the snap. All other members of the kicking team must remain at the line of scrimmage until the ball has been kicked.

4. Any punt that is blocked and does not cross the line of scrimmage can be recovered and advanced by either team. However, if offensive team recovers it must make the yardage necessary for its first down to retain possession if punt was on fourth down.

5. The kicking team may never advance its own kick even though legal recovery is made beyond the line of scrimmage. Possession only.

6. A member of the receiving team may not run into or rough a kicker who kicks from behind his line unless contact is:

(a) Incidental to and after he had touched ball in flight.

(b) Caused by kicker's own motions.

(c) Occurs during a quick kick, or a kick made after a run behind the line, or after kicker recovers a loose ball on the ground. Ball is loose when kicker muffs snap or snap hits ground.

(d) Defender is blocked into kicker.

The penalty for <u>running</u> into the kicker is 5 yards. For <u>roughing</u> the kicker: 15 yards, an automatic first down and disqualification if flagrant.

7. If a member of the kicking team attempting to down the ball on or inside opponent's 5-yard line carries the ball into the end zone, it is a touchback.

8. Fouls during a punt are enforced from the previous spot (line of scrimmage).
   Exception: Illegal touching, fair-catch interference, invalid fair-catch signal, or personal foul (blocking after a fair-catch signal).

9. While the ball is in the air or rolling on the ground following a punt or field-goal attempt and receiving team commits a foul only before or after gaining possession, receiving team will retain possession and will be penalized for its foul.

10. It will be illegal for a defensive player to jump or stand on any player, or be picked up by a teammate or to use a hand or hands on a teammate to gain additional height in an attempt to block a kick (Penalty: 15 yards, unsportsmanlike conduct).

11. A punted ball remains a kicked ball until it is declared dead or in possession of either team.

12. Any member of the punting team may <u>down</u> the ball anywhere in the field of play. However, it is <u>illegal touching</u> (Official's time out and receiver's ball at spot of illegal touching). This foul does <u>not</u> offset any foul by receivers during the down.

13. Defensive team may advance all kicks from scrimmage (including unsuccessful field goal) whether or not ball crosses defensive team's goal line. Rules pertaining to kicks from scrimmage apply until defensive team gains possession.

14. When a team presents a punt formation, defensive pass interference is not to be called for actions on the widest player eligible to go beyond line. Defensive holding may be called.

FAIR CATCH

1. The member of the receiving team must raise one arm a full length above his head and wave it from side to side while kick is in flight. (Failure to give proper sign: receivers' ball five yards behind spot of signal.) **Note:** It is legal for the receiver to shield his eyes from the sun by raising one hand no higher than the helmet.

2. No opponent may interfere with the fair catcher, the ball, or his path to the ball. Penalty: 15 yards from spot of foul and fair catch is awarded.

3. A player who signals for a fair catch is <u>not</u> required to catch the ball. However, if a player signals for a fair catch, he may not block or initiate contact with any player on the kicking team <u>until the ball touches a player. Penalty: snap 15 yards</u>.

4. If ball is touched by member of kicking team in flight, fair catch signal is off and all rules for a kicked ball apply.

5. Any <u>undue advance</u> by a fair catch receiver is delay of game. No specific distance is specified for undue advance as ball is dead at spot of catch. If player comes to a reasonable stop, no penalty. For penalty, five yards.

6. If time expires while ball is in play and a fair catch is awarded, receiving team may choose to extend the period with one fair catch kick down. However, placekicker may <u>not</u> use tee.

FOUL ON LAST PLAY OF HALF OR GAME

1. On a foul by <u>defense</u> on last play of half or game, the <u>down is replayed</u> if penalty is accepted.

2. On a foul by the offense on last play of half or game, the down is not <u>replayed</u> and the play in which the foul is committed is nullified.
   Exception: Fair catch interference, foul following change of possession, illegal touching. <u>No score by offense counts</u>.

SPOT OF ENFORCEMENT OF FOUL

1. There are four basic spots at which a penalty for a foul is enforced:
   (a) Spot of foul: The spot where the foul is committed.
   (b) Previous spot: The spot where the ball was put in play.
   (c) Spot of snap, backward pass or fumble: The spot where the foul occurred or the spot where the penalty is to be enforced.
   (d) Succeeding spot: The spot where the ball next would be put in play if no distance penalty were to be enforced.
   Exception: If foul occurs after a touchdown and before the whistle for a try, succeeding spot is spot of next kickoff.

2. All fouls committed by <u>offensive</u> team <u>behind</u> the line of scrimmage (except in the end zone) shall be penalized from the <u>previous</u> spot. If the foul is in the end zone, it is a safety.

3. When spot of enforcement for fouls involving defensive holding or illegal use of hands by the defense is behind the line of scrimmage, any penalty yardage to be assessed on that play shall be measured from the line if the foul occurred beyond the line.

DOUBLE FOUL

1. If there is a double foul <u>during</u> a down in which there is a change of possession, the team last gaining possession may keep the ball unless its foul was committed prior to the change of possession.

2. If double foul occurs <u>after</u> a change of possession, the defensive team retains the ball at the spot of its foul or dead ball spot.

3. If one of the fouls of a double foul involves disqualification, that player must be removed, but no penalty yardage is to be assessed.

4. If the kickers foul during a kickoff, punt, safety kick, or field-goal attempt before possession changes, the receivers will have the option of replaying the down at the previous spot (offsetting fouls), or keeping the ball after enforcement for its fouls.

PENALTY ENFORCED ON FOLLOWING KICKOFF

1. When a team scores by touchdown, field goal, extra point, or safety and either team commits a personal foul, unsportsmanlike conduct, or obvious unfair act during the down, the penalty will be assessed on the following kickoff.

EMERGENCIES AND UNFAIR ACTS
Emergencies—Policy

The National Football League requires all League personnel, including game officials, League office employees, players, coaches, and other club employees to use best effort to see that each game—preseason, regular season, and postseason—is played to its conclusion. The League recognizes, however, that emergencies may arise that make a game's completion impossible or inadvisable. Such circumstances may include, but are not limited to, severely inclement weather, natural or manmade disaster, power failure, and spectator interference. Games should be suspended, cancelled, postponed, or terminated when circumstances exist such that comencement or continuation of play would pose a threat to the safety of participants or spectators.

Authority of Commissioner's Office

1. Authority to cancel, postpone, or terminate games is vested only in the Commissioner and the League President (other League office representatives and referees may suspend play temporarily; see point No. 3 under this section and point No. 1 under "Authority of Referee" below). The following definitions apply:
   • **Cancel.** To cancel a game is to nullify it either before or after it begins and to make no provision for rescheduling it or for including its score or other performance statistics in League records.

- **Postpone.** To postpone a game is (a) to defer its starting time to a later date, or (b) to suspend it after play has begun and to make provision to resume it at a later date with all scores and other performance statistics up to the point of postponement added to those achieved in the resumed portion of the game.
- **Terminate.** To terminate a game is to end it short of a full 60 minutes of play, to record it officially as a completed game, and to make no provision to resume it at a later date. The Commissioner or League President may terminate a game in an emergency if, in his opinion, it is reasonable to project that its resumption (a) would not change its ultimate result or (b) would not adversely affect any other interteam competitive issue.
- **Forfeit.** The Commissioner, (except in cases of disciplinary action; see last section on "Removing Team from Field"), League President, and their representatives, including referees, are not authorized unilaterally to declare forfeits. A forfeit occurs only when a game is not played because of the failure or refusal of *one* team to participate. In that event, the other team, if ready and willing to play, is the winner by a score of 2-0.

2. If an emergency arises that may require cancellation, postponement, or termination (see above), the highest ranking representative from the Commissioner's office working the game in a "control" capacity will consult with the Commissioner, League President, or game-day duty officer designated by the League (by telephone, if that person is not in attendance) concerning such decision. If circumstances warrant, the League representative should also attempt to consult with the weather bureau and with appropriate security personnel of the League, club, stadium, and local authorities. If no representative from the Commissioner's office is working the game in a "control" capacity, the referee will be in charge (see "Authority of Referee" below).

3. In circumstances where safety is of immediate concern, the Commissioner's office representative may, after consulting with the referee, authorize a temporary suspension in play and, if warranted, removal of the participants from the playing field. The representative should be mindful of the safety of spectators, players, game officials, nonplayer personnel in the bench areas, and other field-level personnel such as photographers and cheerleaders.

4. If possible, the League-office representative should consult with authorized representatives of the two participating clubs before any decision involving cancellation, postponement, or termination is made by the Commissioner or League President.

5. If the Commissioner or League President decides to cancel, postpone, or terminate a game, his representative at the game or the game-day duty officer will then determine the method(s) for announcing such decision, e.g., by public-address announcement over referee's wireless microphone, by public-address announcement by home club, or by communication to radio, television, and other news media.

Authority of Referee

1. If a referee determines that an emergency warrants immediate removal of participants from the playing field for safety reasons, he may do so on his own authority. If, however, circumstances allow him the time, he must reach the highest ranking full-time League office representative working at the game in a "control" capacity or the game-day duty officer designated by the League (by telephone, if that person is not in attendance) and discuss the actual or potential emergency with such representative or duty officer. That representative or duty officer then will make the final decision on removal of participants from the field or obtain a decision from the Commissioner or League President.

2. If a referee removes participants from the playing field under No. 1 above, he may order them to their respective bench areas or to their locker rooms, whichever is appropriate in the circumstances.

3. After appropriate consultation under No. 1 above, the referee must advise the two participating head coaches of the nature of the emergency and the action contemplated (if the decision has not yet been reached) or of the final decision.

4. The referee must *not*, before a decision is reached, make an announcement on his microphone concerning the possibility of a cancellation, postponement, or termination unless instructed to do so by an appropriate representative of the Commissioner's office.

5. The referee must *not* discuss a forfeit with head coaches or club personnel and must *not* use that term over the referee's microphone (see definition of *forfeit* under No. 1 of "Authority of Commissioner's Office" above).

6. The referee must *not* assess an unsportsmanlike-conduct penalty on the home team for actions of fans that cause or contribute to an emergency.

7. The referee should be mindful of the safety of not only players and officials, but also of the spectators and other nonparticipants.

8. If an emergency involves spectator interference (for example, nonparticipants on the field or thrown objects), the referee immediately should contact the appropriate club or League representative for additional security assistance, including, if applicable, involvement of the League's security representative(s) assigned to the game.

9. The referee may order the resumption of play when he deems conditions safe for all concerned and, if circumstances warrant, after consultation with appropriate representatives of the Commissioner's office.

10. Under no circumstances is the referee authorized to cancel, postpone, terminate, or declare forfeiture of a game unilaterally.

Procedures for Starting and Resuming Games

Subject to the points of authority listed above, League personnel and referees will be guided by the following procedures for starting and resuming games that are affected by emergencies.

1. If, because of an emergency, a regular-season or postseason game is not started at its scheduled time and cannot be played at any later time that same day, the game nevertheless must be played on a subsequent date to be determined by the Commissioner.

2. If an emergency threatens to occur during the playing of a game (for example, an incoming tropical storm), the starting time of the game will not be moved to an earlier time unless there is clearly sufficient time to make an orderly change.

3. All games that are suspended temporarily and resumed on the same day, and all suspended games that are postponed to a later date, will be resumed at the point of suspension. On suspension, the referee will call timeout and make a record of the following: team possessing the ball, direction in which its offense was headed, position of the ball on the field, down, distance, period, time remaining in the period, and any other pertinent information required for an orderly and equitable resumption of play.

4. For regular-season postponements, the Commissioner will make every effort to set the game for no later than two days after its originally scheduled date and at the same site. If unable to schedule at the same site, he will select an appropriate alternative site. If it is impossible to schedule the game within two days after its original date, the Commissioner will attempt to schedule it on the Tuesday of the next calendar week. The Commissioner will keep in mind the potential for competitive inequities if one or both of the involved clubs has already been scheduled for a game close to the Tuesday of that week (for example, a Thursday game).

5. For postseason postponements, the Commissioner will make every effort to set the game as soon as possible after its originally scheduled date and at the same site. If unable to

schedule at the same site, he will select an appropriate alternative site.

6. Whenever postponement is attributable to negligence by a club, the negligent club is responsible for all home club costs and expenses, including, subject to approval by the Commissioner, gate receipts and television-contract income. [See Section 19.11 (C) of the NFL Constitution and Bylaws.]

7. Each home club is strictly responsible for having the playing surface of its stadium well maintained and suitable for NFL play.

UNFAIR ACTS
Commissioner's Authority
The Commissioner has sole authority to investigate and to take appropriate disciplinary or corrective measures if any club action, nonparticipant interference, or emergency occurs in an NFL game which he deems so unfair or outside the accepted tactics encountered in professional football that such action has a major effect on the result of a game.

No Club Protests
The authority and measures provided for in this section (UNFAIR ACTS) do not constitute a protest machinery for NFL clubs to dispute the result of a game. The Commissioner will conduct an investigation under this section only to review an act or occurrence that he deems so unfair that the result of the game in question may be inequitable to one of the participating teams. The Commissioner will not apply his authority under this section when a club registers a complaint concerning judgmental errors or routine errors of omission by game officials. Games involving such complaints will continue to stand as completed.

Penalties for Unfair Acts
The Commissioner's powers under this section (UNFAIR ACTS) include the imposition of monetary fines and draft choice forfeitures, suspension of persons involved, and, if appropriate, the reversal of a game's result or the rescheduling of a game, either from the beginning or from the point at which the extraordinary act occurred. In the event of rescheduling a game, the Commissioner will be guided by the procedures specified above ("Procedures for Starting and Resuming Games" under EMERGENCIES). In all cases, the Commissioner will conduct a full investigation, including the opportunity for hearings, use of game videotape, and any other procedures he deems appropriate.

REMOVING TEAM FROM FIELD
No player, coach, or other person affiliated with a club may remove that club's team from the field during the playing of any game, including preseason, except at the direction of the referee. Any club violating this rule will be subject to disciplinary action by the Commissioner, including possible game forfeiture and sole liability for financial losses suffered by the opposing club and any other affected member clubs of the League. [See Section 9.1 (E) of the NFL Constitution and Bylaws.]

280 Park Avenue, New York, New York 10017 (212) 450-2000

NFL Internet Network: www.NFL.com

Commissioner: Roger Goodell

Executive Vice President/Football Operations: Ray Anderson

Executive Vice President of Media/President and Chief Executive Officer of NFL Network: Steve Bornstein

Executive Vice President of Communications and Public Affairs: Joe Browne

Executive Vice President of NFL Ventures and Business Operations: Eric Grubman

Executive Vice President of Player Programs: Harold Henderson

Executive Vice President of Finance/Chief Financial Officer: Anthony Noto

Executive Vice President of Labor/League Counsel: Jeff Pash